German Dictionary of Chemistry and Chemical Technology

Wörterbuch Chemie und chemische Technik Englisch

Langenscheidt
Routledge
German Dictionary of Chemistry and Chemical Technology
Wörterbuch Chemie und chemische Technik Englisch

Volume/Band 1

GERMAN–ENGLISH
DEUTSCH–ENGLISCH

Edited by Technische Universität Dresden

ROUTLEDGE

London and New York

Founded by Dipl.-Sprachlehrer *Helmut Gross*; compiled in the Study Group for Specialist Lexicography at the Chair for Applied Linguistics and Technical Terminology Research of the Faculty of Linguistics and Literary Studies by Dipl.-Chem. *Joachim Knepper* (main author), Dr. rer. nat. *Wolfgang Borsdorf* and Dipl.-Sprachlehrer *Helmut Gross*; in collaboration with Diplomlehrerin *Aranka Jiranek* and Dipl.-Phys. *Radoměr Wićaz*.

Langenscheidt's Dictionary of Chemistry and Chemical Technology, German–English
5th revised and expanded edition 1997

Printed in Germany by Druckhaus "Thomas Müntzer" GmbH, Bad Langensalza, Thüringen
Printed on acid-free paper

This edition of *Langenscheidt's Dictionary of Chemistry and Chemical Technology, German–English* is published by licence agreement with Langenscheidt Fachverlag GmbH, Berlin

by Routledge
11, New Fetter Lane, London EC4P 4EE

Simultaneously published in the USA and Canada
by Routledge
29 West 35th Street, New York, NY10001

British Library Cataloguing-in-Publication Data
A catalogue record for this book is available from the British Library

Library of Congress Cataloging-in-Publication Data
Applied for

ISBN 0-415-17128-8

Vorwort zur fünften Auflage

Die vorangegangenen Auflagen des Wörterbuchs „Chemie und chemische Technik", Deutsch-Englisch, haben bei Nutzern im In- und Ausland eine gute Aufnahme gefunden. Da die 4. Auflage nun vergriffen ist, entschlossen sich Verlag, Herausgeber und Autoren im Zusammenhang mit der Bearbeitung des gleichnamigen Wörterbuchs Englisch-Deutsch zur Herausgabe einer 5., bearbeiteten und erweiterten Auflage.

Dabei wurden etwa 2000 Neueinträge, vorwiegend aus den Gebieten organische Chemie, Biochemie und physikalische Chemie, eingearbeitet sowie zahlreiche Einträge präzisiert und ergänzt. Neben anderen wurden dafür zahlreiche von der IUPAC (International Union of Pure and Applied Chemistry) herausgegebene Publikationen ausgewertet. Der Herausgeber und die Autoren waren auch bei der vorliegenden Bearbeitung bemüht, den Erwartungen der Nutzer hinsichtlich Genauigkeit und Zuverlässigkeit der Wörterbucheinträge zu entsprechen.

Dem Langenscheidt Fachverlag danken wir für die gute Zusammenarbeit bei der Fertigstellung des Manuskripts. Besonderer Dank gilt der Lektorin Frau Helga Kautz für die fachkundige Begleitung der Arbeiten.

Helfende Kritik und Vorschläge zur Verbesserung des Wörterbuchs nehmen die Autoren gern entgegen und bitten, diese an den Langenscheidt Fachverlag, Crellestraße 28–30, D-10827 Berlin, zu richten.

J. Knepper

Preface to the Fifth Edition

The previous editions of our German-English dictionary *Chemistry and Chemical Technology* have found a very loyal usership in both Germany and abroad. As the fourth edition is now out of print, the publisher, editor and authors decided to produce a revised and expanded 5th edition to accompany the revision of the Englisch-German dictionary of the same name.

Approximately 2000 new entries have been added – primarily from the fields of organic chemistry, biochemistry and physical chemistry – while a great number of existing entries have been expanded upon and made more precise. Many of the publications used by the authors for lexical research came from the International Union of Pure and Applied Chemistry (IUPAC). In carrying out this revision, the publisher and authors once again strove to provide the accuracy and reliability which users of this dictionary have come to expect.

We would like to thank the Langenscheidt Fachverlag for their excellent collaboration in the preparation of the manuscript. Special thanks goes to the reader, Ms. Helga Kautz, for her expert guidance during the course of our work.

The authors welcome any constructive criticism and suggestions aimed at improving this dictionary. Users should send their comments to Langenscheidt Fachverlag, Crellestraße 28–30, D-10827 Berlin.

J. Knepper

Benutzungshinweise • Directions for Use

1. Beispiele für die alphabetische Ordnung • Examples of Alphabetization

1-Brombutan	substituieren
2-Brombutan	substituiert ...... • ~ werden
Bromoaurat(I)	~/einfach
Bromoaurat(III)	~/mehrfach
Bromsäure	1,2-substituiert
N-Bromsuccinimid	*m*-substituiert
Butenpolymer	Substitution
cis-But-2-ensäure	Überzug
trans-But-2-ensäure	ubiquitär
Butin	UDP
BZ	U-Eisen
bz-Phase	Uferfiltrat
B-Zustand	umlagern
Eisen	~/sich
~/pyrophores	Umlagerung
α-Eisen	~ am Aromaten
γ-Eisen	~/entartete
Eisenabstich	~/sigmatrope
Eisen(II)-acetat	1,2-Umlagerung
Eisenbakterien	Umlagerungsreaktion

Zahlen, kursiv gesetzte Stellungs- und Konfigurationssymbole wie *asym-*, *sym-*, *prim-*, *sec-*, *tert-*, *cis-*, *trans-*, *m-*, *o-*, *p-*, *N-*, *d-*, *l-* sowie griechische Buchstaben bleiben bei der alphabetischen Einordnung unberücksichtigt.
Numbers and italicalized symbols denoting position or configuration like *asym-*, *sym-*, *prim-*, *sec-*, *tert-*, *cis-*, *trans-*, *m-*, *o-*, *p-*, *N-*, *d-*, *l-* and Greek letters are disregarded in alphabetization.

2. Bedeutung der Zeichen • Meaning of Signs

/ Elektrode/ionenselektive = ionenselektive Elektrode

( ) gefälltes (präzipitiertes) Calciumsulfat = gefälltes Calciumsulfat *oder* präzipitiertes Calciumsulfat
diffusion (liquid-junction) potential = diffusion potential *or* liquid-junction potential

Diese Bedeutung der runden Klammern gilt nicht für Wertigkeits- und Stellungsangaben in Formeln und chemischen Benennungen.
This meaning of the round brackets does not apply to valency and position indications in formulae and chemical terms.

[ ] Foto[kopier]lack = Fotokopierlack *oder* Fotolack
process[ing] water = processing water *or* process water

( ) Diese Klammern enthalten Erklärungen – These brackets contain explanations

* Kennzeichnet Benennungen nach IUPAC – Marks IUPAC names

• Kennzeichnet Wendungen – Marks phrases

= Abkürzung für – Abbreviation for

Abkürzungen • Abbreviations

agric	agricultural and silvicultural chemistry/land- und forstwirtschaftliche Chemie
Am	American English/amerikanisches Englisch
anal	analytical chemistry/analytische Chemie
bioch	biochemistry/Biochemie
biol	biology/Biologie
biot	biotechnology/Biotechnologie
bot	botany/Botanik
build	chemistry and technology of building materials/Chemie und Technologie der Baustoffe
ceram	ceramics/Keramik
ch	chemistry/Chemie
chromat	chromatography/Chromatographie
coal	coal chemistry/Carbochemie
coat	chemistry and technology of organic coating materials/Chemie und Technologie der Anstrichstoffe
coll	colloid chemistry/Kolloidchemie
cosmet	chemistry and technology of cosmetics and perfumes/Chemie und Technologie der Kosmetika und Riechstoffe
cryst	crystallography and crystal chemistry/Kristallographie und Kristallchemie
distil	distillation apparatus and practice/Destillationstechnik
dye	chemistry and technology of organic dyes/Chemie und Technologie der organischen Farbstoffe
e.g.	(exempli gratia) for example/zum Beispiel
el ch	electrochemistry/Elektrochemie
esp	especially/besonders
f	feminine noun/femininum
ferm	chemistry and technology of fermentation/Gärungschemie und Gärungstechnologie
filtr	filtration equipment and practice/Filtriervorrichtungen und Filtriertechnik
food	food chemistry and technology/Lebensmittelchemie und -technologie
geoch	geochemistry/Geochemie
geol	geology/Geologie
glass	glass technology/Glasherstellung
hyd	hydrochemistry, water and waste-water treatment/Hydrochemie, Wasseraufbereitung und Abwasserbehandlung
lab	laboratory technique and apparatus/Labortechnik und Laborgeräte
m	masculine noun/Maskulinum
med	medicine/Medizin
met	metallurgy and science of metals/Metallurgie und Metallkunde
min	mineralogy and petrography/Mineralogie und Petrographie
min tech	mineral technology/Aufbereitungstechnik
mine	mining/Bergbau
n	neuter noun/Neutrum
nomencl	chemical nomenclature/chemische Nomenklatur
nucl	nuclear science and technology/Kernchemie, Kernphysik und Kerntechnik
org ch	organic chemistry/organische Chemie
pap	pulp and paper chemistry and technology/Zellstoff- und Papierchemie und -technologie
petrol	chemistry and technology of petroleum/Chemie und Technologie des Erdöls

pharm	pharmaceutical chemistry/pharmazeutische Chemie
phot	photographic chemistry/fotografische Chemie
pl	plural/Plural
plast	chemistry and technology of plastics/Chemie und Technologie der Kunststoffe
rubber	rubber technology/Technologie der Gummiherstellung
s.	see/siehe
s.a.	see also/siehe auch
soil	soil chemistry and soil science/Bodenchemie und Bodenkunde
specif	specifically/im engeren Sinne
spectr	spectroscopy/Spektroskopie
sugar	sugar technology/Technologie der Zuckerherstellung
tann	chemistry and technology of leather manufacture/Gerbereichemie und Gerbereitechnologie
tech	technology/Technik und Technologie
text	textile chemistry/Textilchemie
tox	toxicology/Toxikologie
U.K.	in the United Kingdom/in Großbritannien
U.S.	in the United States/in den Vereinigten Staaten von Amerika

A

a 1. = absolut; 2. *s.* antarafacial
A *s.* Anode
Ä. *(= Äther) s.* Ether
AAS *s.* Atomabsorptionsspektralphotometrie
Aasappretur *f (tann)* flesh finish
Aasschmiere *f (tann)* dubbin[g], stuffing mixture
Aasseite *f (tann)* flesh side
ABA *s.* Abwasserbehandlungsanlage
Abart *f* variety, modification
Abbaggern *n (mine)* dredging
Abbau *m* 1. degradation, decomposition, breakdown, fragmentation, *(bioch also)* katabolism, catabolism; 2. mining, working, extracting, winning *(as of coal)* • **~ erleiden** to undergo degradation
~/aerober biologischer aerobic degradation (decomposition, digestion)
~/anaerober biologischer anaerobic degradation (decomposition, digestion)
~/bakterieller bacterial degradation
~/Barbier-Wielandscher Barbier-Wieland degradation *(for eliminating a carbon atom from a side chain)*
~/biochemischer biochemical degradation (decomposition, digestion)
~/biologischer biodegradation, biological digestion *(of organics)*
~/Braunscher Braun degradation *(of tertiary amines)*
~/chemischer chemical degradation
~/Curtiusscher Curtius rearrangement (transformation) *(the decomposition of acid azides to give isocyanates and nitrogen)*
~ durch Licht *s.* ~/photochemischer
~ durch Mikroorganismen *s.* ~/mikrobieller
~ durch Oxidation *s.* ~/oxidativer
~ durch UV-Strahlung ultraviolet degradation
~ durch Wärme *s.* ~/thermischer
~/enzymatischer (fermentativer) enzymatic degradation
~/glykolytischer *(bioch)* glycolytic pathway, Embden-Meyerhof-Parnas scheme [of glycolysis], EMP scheme, homolactic fermentation
~/Hofmannscher Hofmann degradation *(of quaternary ammonium hydroxides)*
~/hydrolytischer hydrolytic degradation
~ im Tiefbau *s.* ~ unter Tage
~/mechanischer *(rubber)* mechanical (mill) breakdown
~/mikrobieller microbial degradation (decomposition)
~ mit Peptisiermitteln *(rubber)* peptization
~ nach Weerman Weerman degradation *(of α-hydroxy amides)*
~/oxidativer oxidative degradation (cleavage)
~/photochemischer photochemical (photolytic, light) degradation, photodegradation, photolysis
~/photooxidativer oxidative photodegradation
~/Ruffscher Ruff degradation *(of sugars)*
~/schrittweiser (stufenweiser) stepwise degradation
~/thermischer thermal degradation, degradation by heat
~/thermooxidativer thermooxidative degradation
~ unter Tage underground (deep) mining
~/von Braunscher *s.* ~/Braunscher
abbaubar 1. *(org ch)* degradable, decomposable; 2. *(mine)* workable
~/biologisch biodegradable
~/biologisch nicht non-biodegradable, resistant to biological degradation, biologically inert
~/nicht non-degradable
Abbaubarkeit *f* 1. *(org ch)* degradability, decomposability; 2. *(mine)* workability
~/biologische biodegradability
abbauen 1. to degrade, to decompose, to disintegrate, to break down, to fragment, *(bioch also)* to catabolize; 2. *(mine)* to mine, to work, to extract, to win
~/biochemisch to degrade biochemically
~/biologisch to digest, to biodegrade *(organics)*
~/mit Peptisiermitteln *(rubber)* to peptize
~/sich to degrade
~/zu Dextrin to dextrinate, to dextrinize
abbauend *(bioch)* catabolic
Abbaufähigkeit *f* degradative ability *(of microorganisms)*
Abbaugeschwindigkeit *f* rate of degradation, decomposition rate
Abbaugrad *m* degree of degradation (decomposition)
Abbaugranulieren *n* granulation
Abbaukurve *f (tox)* degradation curve, decline (disappearance, loss, decay) curve, [residue-]persistence curve
Abbauleistung *f (biot)* efficiency of degradation; *(hyd)* biological efficiency
Abbaumittel *n (rubber)* plasticizing (peptizing) agent, plasticizer, peptizer
Abbauprodukt *n* degradation (decomposition, breakdown) product
Abbaureaktion *f* degradation (degradative) reaction, decomposition (breakdown) reaction
abbauresistent non-degradable, *(hyd specif)* non-biodegradable, resistant to biological degradation, biologically inert
Abbauschritt *m*, **Abbaustufe** *f* step in degradation (decomposition), *(bioch also)* catabolic step
Abbauvorgang *m* degradation (degradative) process, *(bioch also)* catabolic process
Abbauweg *m* degradation (degradative) pathway, *(bioch also)* catabolic pathway (route)
Abbauwirkung *f (rubber)* peptizing effect
Abbauwürdigkeit *f (mine)* workability
abbeizen to strip, to pickle, to remove old paint
Abbeizen *n* [paint] stripping, pickling, removal of old paint

Abbeizmittel *n* paint stripper (remover), organic coating stripper
Abbe-Refraktometer *n* Abbe refractometer
Abbe-Spektrometer *n* Abbe spectrometer
Abbindebeschleuniger *m (build)* [setting, cementing] accelerator
Abbindedauer *f (build)* setting (set-up) time
abbinden *(build)* to set, to harden
Abbinden *n (build)* set[ting], hardening
Abbinderegler *m (build)* quick-setting agent, quick hardener
Abbindeverhalten *n (build)* setting behaviour
Abbindeverzögerer *m (build)* [setting] retarder
Abbindeverzögerung *f (build)* retarding of the set
Abbindezeit *f s.* Abbindedauer
Abblasedruck *m* relieving (blow-off) pressure
abblasen 1. to blow off *(e.g. steam)*; 2. *(pap)* to blow [off] *(a digester)*; 3. *(met)* to blow out *(a blast furnace)*
Abblasen *n* 1. blow[ing]-off *(as of steam)*; 2. *(pap)* [digester] blow, blowing; *(filtr)* blow discharge; 3. *(met)* blowing-out *(of a blast furnace)*
Abblasleitung *f* blow pipe, blowpipe
Abblasprodukt *n (pap)* blow-off
~/gasförmiges blow-pit gas, gaseous blow-off
abblättern to peel [off], to flake [off], to scale [off], to spall [off], to exfoliate
Abblätterungsgrad *m* degree of flaking (scaling)
Abbot-Cox-Färbeverfahren *n* Abbot-Cox process
Abbrand *m (met)* calcine *(product of roasting)*; *(nucl)* burn-up
Abbrandauslauf *m*, **Abbrandaustrag** *m (met)* calcine-discharge outlet
Abbrandkühler *m (met)* calcine cooler
Abbrandmittel *n (agric)* desiccant
Abbrandsammelbehälter *m (met)* calcine-collecting tank
abbrausen *(min tech)* to spray *(classified material)*
Abbrausen *n* **mit Wasser** water spraying
abbrechen to arrest *(a reaction)*; to terminate, to break *(a chain)*; to terminate, to shortstop *(polymerization)*
abbremsen to slow down, to decelerate, to retard; *(nucl)* to moderate
Abbremsung *f* slowing-down, deceleration, retardation; *(nucl)* moderation
abbrennen to burn off *(e.g. old paint)*; *(text)* to singe; to deflagrate *(as of explosives)*
Abbrennen *n* burning-off *(as of old paint)*; *(text)* singeing; deflagration *(as of explosives)*
~/explosionsfreies deflagration
Abbrennlöffel *m* deflagrating (deflagration) spoon
Abbrennmittel *n (agric)* deflagrating agent
abbröckeln to crumble away
Abbruch *m* arrest *(of a reaction)*; termination, breaking *(of a chain)*; termination, shortstopping *(of polymerization)*
Abbruchgröße *f* cut off [size] *(of aerosol particles)*
Abbruchreaktion *f s.* Kettenabbruchreaktion
Abbruchstadium *n* termination stage
abbuffen *(tann)* to buff *(the grain)*
Abdampf *m* exhaust (dead) steam
abdampfen to evaporate [off]; to bleed *(gas chromatography)*
Abdampfen *n* evaporation; bleeding *(gas chromatography)*
Abdampfgefäß *n* evaporating vessel
Abdampfleitung *f* waste-steam line
Abdampfpfanne *f* evaporating pan
Abdampfrückstand *m* residue on evaporation
Abdampfschale *f (lab)* evaporating dish, *(UK also)* basin
Abdampfschalenhalter *m (lab)* dish tongue
abdarren *(ferm)* to kiln-dry
Abdarrtemperatur *f (ferm)* kiln temperature
abdecken 1. to cover [over] *(e.g. a vessel)*; 2. to coat, to cover *(leather)*; 3. *s.* ~/lokal
~/lokal to stop off *(to protect desired areas from chemical action)*
Abdecken *n***/lokales** stopping-off *(protection of desired areas from chemical action)*
~ mit Mutterboden *(hyd)* topsoiling *(of deposited sludge)*
Abdeckpappe *f* carpet felt, felt brown
Abdeckplatte *f* cover [plate]
Abdeckung *f* resist, stop-off [coating] *(electroplating)*
abdekantieren to decant off
abdestillieren to distil off, to strip [off, out], to remove by distillation; to distil off *(of a liquid)*
abdichten to make tight, to seal, to pack, to ca[u]lk; to waterproof; to gasproof
abdiffundieren to diffuse away
Abdiffusion *f* diffusing-away
Abdrift *f (agric)* blow-off, drift *(as of pesticides)*
~ des Sprühmittels spray drift
Abdruck *m* impression, mark, stamp; print; replica *(plastic film produced on surface structures for electron microscopy)*
abdrucken/sich to set off *(of printing ink)*
Abdrucken *n* offset *(of printing ink)*
Abdrücken *n* **von oben** *(plast)* top ejection
abdunsten to evaporate
Abel-Apparat *m s.* Abel-Flammpunkt[s]prüfer
Abel-Flammpunkt[s]prüfer *m* Abel flash-point apparatus, Abel apparatus (tester)
Abel-Pensky-Flammpunkt[s]prüfer *m* Abel-Pensky apparatus (tester)
Abel-Test *m* Abel test *(1. for determining the flash point of an oil; 2. for determining the stability of an explosive)*
Abessinierbrunnen *m (hyd)* driven well
abfahren to scan *(a measuring range)*
~/nochmals to rescan
Abfall *m* 1. waste [material], refuse, scrap; rubbish, *(Am)* garbage; *(plast, glass)* cull; 2. *s.* Abfallen
~/aufgearbeiteter *(plast)* reground material
~/häuslicher *m* domestic (household) waste

~/heißer *(nucl)* hot (high-activity, high-level) waste
~/hochaktiver *s.* ~/heißer
~/radioaktiver nuclear (radioactive) waste
Abfallauge *f* waste (spent) lye, waste (spent) liquor
Abfallbehälter *m (lab)* waste jar
Abfallbehandlung *f s.* Abproduktbehandlung
abfallen to drop, to decrease, to fall [off] *(as of measuring values)*
~/im Farbton to be off-shade
Abfallen *n* drop, decrease, fall *(as of measuring values)*
~ der freien Induktion *(spectr)* free induction decay, FID
~ des Drucks pressure drop
Abfallgummi *m* rubber scrap (waste), scrap (waste) rubber
Abfallholz *n (pap)* waste wood
Abfallkalk *m (agric)* by-product lime
Abfallkübel *m (lab)* waste jar, *(earthenware also)* waste (disposal) crock
Abfallpapier *n* waste (old) paper
Abfallprodukt *n s.* Abprodukt
Abfallsäure *f* waste (residuary) acid
Abfallschlicker *m (ceram)* casting scrap
Abfallstoff *m s.* Abprodukt
Abfallvernichtung *f s.* Abproduktbeseitigung
abfangen to catch, to trap, to intercept, to steal away *(reactive intermediates)*
~/Konzentrationsschwankungen *(hyd)* to smooth out the concentration
Abfangen *n* catching, trapping, interception *(of reactive intermediates)*
Abfangreaktion *f* trapping reaction
abfärben to lose colour, to bleed, to mark off; *(tann)* to colour *(to tan slightly)*
abfehmen *(glass)* to skim
Abfehmer *m (glass)* skimmer
abfeimen *s.* abfehmen
abfiltern *s.* abfiltrieren
abfiltrierbar removable by filtration
abfiltrieren to filter off (out), to remove by filtration
~/in Filterpressen to filter-press
abflammen *(text)* to singe; *(bioch)* to flame *(for killing microorganisms)*
abflecken *(dye)* to stain, to mark off
abfließen to flow [off], to run [off], to drain [off]
~ lassen to drain [off], to run [off], to discharge
Abfließen *n* flowing-off, draining-off, drainage, effluence
Abfluß *m* 1. *s.* Abfließen; 2. discharge [point], outlet, outflow, drain; 3. *s.* Ablauf 3.
Abflußbecken *n (lab)* [bench] sink
Abflußleitung *f* discharge (delivery) line, drain (drainage, runoff, outlet) line; waste line
Abflußmenge *f* outflow, runoff
Abflußmengenmesser *m* effluent recorder
Abflußöffnung *f* discharge opening, discharge outlet (door, aperture, port)
Abflußregler *m* effluent (outlet) weir
Abflußrohr *n* discharge tube (pipe), drainage (delivery) tube, runoff (effluent, outlet) tube; waste tube (pipe)
Abflußschwankung *f (hyd)* effluent flow variation
Abflußstutzen *m* discharge tube (pipe) *(short)*
Abflußventil *n* discharge (outlet) valve
abführen 1. to lead off (away), to carry off, to drain off (away), to draw off, to withdraw *(liquids or gases)*; to exhaust *(gases)*; to dissipate, to eliminate *(heat)*; 2. *(pharm)* to purge
Abführmittel *n (pharm)* cathartic
~/mäßig starkes purgative
~/mildes laxative, mild cathartic
~/starkes drastic, strong purgative
Abfüllabteilung *f* filling plant, *(esp)* bottling plant (department), bottle house, bottlery
Abfüllautomat *m* filling machine, *(esp)* bottling (bottle-filling) machine, bottle filler, bottler
abfüllen/auf Fässer to barrel, to rack
~/auf Flaschen to bottle [in, up], *(Am also)* to can
Abfüllerei *f s.* Abfüllabteilung
Abfüllhahn *m* racking cock
Abfüllmaschine *f s.* Abfüllautomat
Abfüllschlauch *m* racking hose
Abgabe *f* release, liberation, evolution *(as of gases, heat)*; release, donation *(of electrons, ions)*
Abgang *m* 1. loss; 2. waste [material, product]; 3. *s.* Abgänge
Abgänge *mpl (min tech)* [waste] tailings, refuse
Abgangsgruppe *f s.* Austrittsgruppe
Abgangsseite *f* discharge end
Abgas *n* waste (exit) gas, off-gas; exhaust gas *(from combustion engines)*; *(pap)* tail (digester relief) gas
abgasbeständig *(text)* fast to burnt gas fumes, fast to gas fading
Abgasbeständigkeit *f (text)* gas-fume fastness, fastness to burnt gas fumes, fastness to gas fading
abgasecht *s.* abgasbeständig
Abgasempfindlichkeit *f (text)* gas fading
abgasen *(pap)* to relieve *(a digester)*
Abgasen *n (pap)* [digester] relief
~ am Kocherdeckel digester top relief
Abgasfahne *f* [gas] plume
Abgaskanal *m* waste-gas flue
Abgasleitung *f* waste-gas line; *(pap)* relief line
Abgasreiniger *m* collector
Abgasturm *m (pap)* tail-gas tower
Abgasventil *n (pap)* relief (blow-through) valve
Abgasvorwärmer *m* economizer
abgautschen *(pap)* to couch
abgebaut werden to undergo degradation
abgeben to release, to liberate, to give off, to evolve *(e.g. gas, heat)*; to release, to donate, to lose *(electrons, ions)*; to lose *(hydration water)*
Abgeber *m* material (substance) being *or* to be extracted
abgedeckt/mit Metallgewebe (Siebgewebe) *(filtr)* screen-covered

abgehen to leave *(as of vapours)*
~/durch den Schornstein to be lost at the stack
~/über Kopf *(distil)* to leave at the top
abgelagert mature *(wine)*
abgeschlossen/hermetisch hermetically sealed
abgeschnappt sein to be starved of liquid *(of a pump)*
abgestanden flat, stale, insipid *(beverages)*
abgetragen werden to ablate *(by melting, vaporization, or decomposition at high temperatures)*
abgießen to pour off, to drain [off], to run [off]
~/vorsichtig to decant
Abgleichblende *f (spectr)* optical attenuator
Abgleichmethode *f* null[-balance] method, zero method *(of measurement)*
Abgleiten *n* crystal (translation) gliding *(along a crystal plane)*
~ von Ketten chain slipping *(in plastics)*
abgraben to dig off
abgraten *(plast)* to deburr, to deflash
Abgratmaschine *f (plast)* deflashing machine
Abhängigkeitsverbundwirkung *f (tox)* dependent joint action
Abhäsion *f* abhesion *(loss of adhesion)*
abhäsiv abhesive
abhaspeln to reel off, to unreel
abheben/sich to peel [off] *(as of coatings)*; *(ceram)* to peel [off], to shell [off] *(of a glaze)*
Abhebeprüfung *f* peeling test *(for testing the strength of an adhesive-bonded joint)*
abhebern to siphon [off]
Abhilfemaßnahme *f* remedial measure
Abhitze *f* waste heat
Abhitzedampfkessel *m* waste-heat boiler, gas-tube boiler
Abhitzegewinnung *f* [waste-]heat recovery
Abhitzekessel *m s.* Abhitzedampfkessel
Abhitze[koks]ofen *m* waste-heat oven
Abhitzerückgewinnung *f* [waste-]heat recovery
Abietat *n* abietate *(salt or ester of abietic acid)*
Abietinsäure *f* abietic acid *(a resin acid)*
abimpfen *(biot)* to subculture
Abimpfung *f (biot)* subculture
a-Bindung *f* a-bond, axial bond
abkippen/auf Halde to tip, to dispose of
abklappbar retractable
abklappen 1. to retract *(e.g. a lid)*; 2. to dump at sea, to dispose of to sea, to dispose of in the ocean *(waste products)*
Abklappen *n* ocean (sea) dumping, sea burial, waste dumping at sea
abklären to clarify
~/sich to clarify
Abklärflasche *f (lab)* aspirator
Abklärung *f* clarification
abklatschen *(lab)* to spread *(a filter cake)*
abklingen to die (quieten) down, to flatten out *(of a reaction)*; to fade away, to subside *(of vibrations)*
Abklingen *n* **des latenten Bildes** *(phot)* latent-image regression
Abklingkurve *f* fall-off curve *(kinetics)*
abkochen to boil, *(esp pharm)* to decoct; *(text)* to bowk, to buck, to kier-boil
Abkochen *n* boiling, *(esp pharm)* decoction; *(text)* bowking, bucking, kier-boiling, kiering
Abkochung *f (pharm)* decoction
abkratzen to scrape off, to scratch off
abkreiden *(coat)* to chalk, to become chalky
Abkühlbehälter *m (hyd)* quench tank
abkühlen to cool [down], *(if rapidly:)* to chill, *(relating to metal:)* to quench
~ lassen to allow to cool, to let cool
~/sich to cool [down], *(if rapidly:)* to chill
Abkühlung *f* **nach dem Newtonschen Abkühlungsgesetz** Newtonian cooling
Abkühlungsgesetz *n***/Newtonsches** Newton law for cooling (heat loss)
Abkühlungskristallisation *f* freezing-out
Abkühlungskurve *f* cooling curve
Abkühlungsvorrichtung *f (plast)* shrink (cooling) fixture, shrinkage (cooling) jig *(for mouldings)*
Abkühlverfahren *n* **mit Kühltrommeln** dry [drum-]cooling method, chill-roll method *(margarine manufacture)*
Abkühlverlust *m* cooling loss
Abkühlzone *f* cooling zone (compartment, section)
ablagern 1. to sediment, to deposit *(of liquids)*; to dispose of *(waste products)*; 2. *(food)* to age, to mature; to season *(timber)*
~/auf Halde to dispose of to tip, to dispose of by tipping, to deposit on a tip *(waste products)*
~/im Tank to tank *(e.g. pigments)*
~/in Borke *(tann)* to age
~/sich to deposit, to settle [out], *(esp from liquids:)* to sediment, to subside
~/sich wieder to redeposit
Ablagerung *f* 1. deposit, *(esp from liquids:)* sediment, [bottom] settlings, BS, bottoms, dregs, *(esp food, ferm)* lees, foots, *(esp of biological matter:)* fouling; scale *(on the inside of a boiler)*; 2. deposition, sedimentation; disposal [to land] *(of waste products)*; 3. *(food)* ageing, maturing; seasoning *(of timber)*
~ auf Halde disposal to tip
~/dauerhafte (endgültige) final (ultimate) disposal *(of waste products)*
~/saure acid deposition
Ablagerungsgeschwindigkeit *f* rate of deposition (sedimentation), deposition velocity
Ablaß *m* discharge, outlet, drain; vent, relief *(for lessening excessive pressure)*
ablassen to let off (out), to discharge, to exhaust, *(relating to liquid also)* to run [off], to drain [off], to sewer, to tap, *(relating to gas also)* to blow off; to discharge, to drain [down], to exhaust, to tap, to empty *(a vessel)*
Ablaßhahn *m* discharge cock, outlet (delivery, runoff) cock, dispensing spigot
Ablaßkanal *m* drainage channel, *(esp for waste water:)* sewer

Ablaßleitung *f* discharge (delivery) line, drainage (drain, runoff, outlet) line; waste line
Ablaßöffnung *f* discharge opening (outlet, door, aperture, port); vent, relief *(for gases and vapours)*
Ablaßrohr *n* discharge tube (pipe), drainage (delivery) tube, runoff (effluent, outlet) tube; waste tube (pipe)
Ablaßventil *n* discharge valve, drain (outlet) valve
Ablaßvorrichtung *f* discharging device, discharger
Ablation *f* ablation *(wearing away of material by melting, vaporization, or decomposition at high temperatures)*
Ablationsschicht *f* ablative coating
ablativ ablative *(removable by melting, vaporization, or decomposition at high temperatures*
Ablauf *m* 1. *s.* Ablaufen 1.; 2. discharge [point], outlet, outflow, drain; 3. runoff, effluent, efflux *(material)*; *(hyd)* effluent (outgoing) water, outflow, outlet; runoff water *(land treatment of waste water)*; discharge *(from a waste-water treatment plant)*; 4. course *(as of a reaction or process)* • **auf ~ geteilt (graduiert)** calibrated (graduated) to deliver, calibrated for delivery
~ **I** *(sugar)* green syrup
~ **II** *(sugar)* molasses
~ **der Abwasserbehandlungsanlage** *(hyd)* waste treatment effluent, sewage plant effluent
~ **des Absetzbeckens** *(hyd)* clarifier effluent
~ **des Kornkohlefilters** *(hyd)* GAC effluent
~ **eines Betriebs** *(hyd)* plant effluent, waste effluent (discharge), outfall
~/geklärter *(hyd)* underflow *(oil removal)*
~/zeitlicher time course *(of a reaction)*
Ablaufbereich *m (hyd)* outlet section (zone) *(of a sedimentation tank)*
Ablaufbrett *n (lab)* drain[ing] board, drying (apparatus) rack
~/aufhängbares wall-mounting draining board
ablaufen 1. to drain [off], to run [off], to flow [off] *(of liquids)*; to curtain, to sag *(of surface coatings)*; 2. to run, to proceed, to take its course *(of a reaction)*
~ **lassen** to drain [off], to let drain, to run [off], to siphon; *(hyd)* to send to the drain
Ablaufen *n* 1. draining-off, drainage, flowing-off, effluence, outflow *(of liquids)*; curtaining, sagging *(of surface coatings)*; 2. running, proceeding, taking its course *(of a reaction)*
Ablaufende *n* discharge end
Ablaufgüte *f (hyd)* effluent [water] quality
Ablaufkanal *m* effluent (drainage) channel, *(esp for waste water:)* sewer
Ablaufkonzentration *f (hyd)* effluent [waste] concentration
Ablaufleitung *f s.* Abflußleitung
Ablaufqualität *f (hyd)* effluent [water] quality
Ablaufrinne *f s.* Ablaufkanal
Ablaufrohr *n* 1. *(distil)* downpipe, downspout, downtake, downcomer, rundown pipe; 2. *s.* Abflußrohr
Ablaufschurre *f* discharge chute
Ablaufsirup *m (sugar)* centrifugal syrup
Ablaufstutzen *m s.* Abflußstutzen
Ablaufwasser *n (hyd)* effluent water
Ablaufwehr *n* outlet weir (lip), effluent (overflow) weir; *(distil)* exit (overflow) weir
Ablauge *f* waste (spent) lye, waste (spent) liquor; *(pap)* sulphite spent (waste) liquor, spent [pulping] liquor
Ablaugeentfernung *f (pap)* liquor disposal
Ablaugeregeneration *f (pap)* waste-liquor (spent-liquor) recovery
Ablaugetrockensubstanz *f (pap)* waste-liquor (spent-liquor) solids
Ablaugeverbrennung *f (pap)* spent-liquor incineration
abläutern *(ferm)* to lauter; *(plast)* to refine
ablegen to set off *(of printing ink)*
ableitbar derivable
ableiten 1. to lead away (off), to carry off, to drain away (off), to draw off, to withdraw *(liquids or gases)*; to dissipate, to eliminate *(heat)*; 2. to derive *(one chemical compound from another)*
~/in das öffentliche Kanalisationsnetz *(hyd)* to discharge into the municipal sewer system
~/in den Vorfluter *(hyd)* to discharge into a receiving stream
~/in die Kanalisation *(hyd)* to discharge (to drain, to run) to the sewer
Ableitung *f* 1. leading-away, leading-off, carrying-off, drainage, withdrawal *(of liquids or gases)*; dissipation, elimination *(of heat)*; 2. derivation *(of one chemical compound from another)*
Ableitungselektrode *f* reference junction *(pH measurement)*
Ableitungsrohr *n s.* Ablaufrohr
Ableitungsspektrum *n* derivative spectrum
Ablenkblech *n* deflector [plate]
ablenken to deflect, to turn off
Ablenkkammer *f* dust trap *(gas cleaning)*
Ablenkkeil *m (petrol)* whipstock
Ablenkplatte *f* deflector [plate]
Ablenkrinne *f (glass)* deflector
Ablenkrolle *f*, **Ablenktrommel** *f* snub pulley
Ablenkung *f* deflection
Ablenkungssystem *n (anal)* deflection system *(of a mass spectrometer)*
Ablenkwand *f* deflector [plate]
Ablenkwinkel *m* angle of deflection
Ableseblatt *n (lab)* burette [meniscus] reader, antiparallax card, [burette] meniscus holder
Ablesefehler *m (anal)* reading (observational) error
~/parallaktischer parallax error
Ableselupe *f (lab)* reading lens, burette meniscus magnifier
ablesen to read off, to take a reading
Ablesevorrichtung *f (lab)* reading device
Ablesewert *m (lab)* instrument reading
Ablesung *f* reading, readout

ablöschen to quench *(coke, metal)*; to slake *(esp lime)*
~/in (mit) Öl to oil-quench *(metal)*
~/in (mit) Wasser to water-quench *(metal)*
Ablöschmittel *n* quenching medium (agent) *(for metals)*
Ablösearbeit *f (phys ch)* [electronic] work function
Ablösefestigkeit *f (plast)* peel strength
ablösen to strip, to detach, to peel *(e.g. a film)*; to release *(as from a mould)*; to dissolve *(e.g. a soluble substance from a vessel wall)*; to detach *(electrons)*
~/sich to peel [off], to scale [off], to flake [off], to shell [off]
Ablösung *f* **eines Elektrons** electron detachment
Ablösungsebene *f (cryst)* parting plane
Ablösungswirkung *f* release action (effect) *(as of silicone oil in a mould)*
Abluft *f* exhaust (exit) air, outlet (outgoing, leaving) air
Abluftfilter *n* exhaust air filter
Abluftreiniger *m* collector
abmessen to measure [out, off], to meter, to batch *(liquids, bulk material)*
Abmessung *f* size, dimension
abnabeln *(glass)* to shear *(a drop on the feeder)*
Abnahme *f* 1. take-off, withdrawal, discharge *(of liquids or gases)*; *(pap)* pick-up *(of the web from the wire)*; 2. take-off, *(plast also)* take-up, haul-off *(spot or device)*; 3. decrease, loss, drop, fall, reduction *(as of measuring values)*
Abnahmefilz *m (pap)* pick-up (lick-up) felt
~/oberer top felt, overfelt
~/unterer bottom (lower) felt
Abnahmegeschwindigkeit *f (plast)* take-up speed *(of extrudate)*
Abnahmeschaber *m* [roll] doctor
Abnahmevorrichtung *f* take-off equipment
Abnahmewalze *f* take-off roll, discharge roll; *(pap)* pick-up roll
Abnahmezone *f* discharge zone *(of a rotary-drum vacuum filter)*
abnehmen 1. to take off, *(plast also)* to take up, to haul off *(e.g. extrudate)*; to withdraw, to discharge *(liquids or gases)*; *(pap)* to pick up *(the web from the wire)*; 2. to decrease, to drop, to fall, to reduce *(as of measuring values)*
~/die Bahn *(pap)* to take (pick) up the web
~/mittels Schaber to doctor off
~/über Kopf *(distil)* to take overhead
abnorm anomalous, abnormal, irregular
abnutschen to filter by (with, under) suction, *(Am also)* to suction-filter
Abnutschen *n* suction filtration
abnutzen/sich to wear [out]; to abrade *(by friction)*
Abnutzung *f* wear
~ durch Abrieb abrasion, abrasive wear, attrition
abnutzungsbeständig wear-resistant; abrasion-resistant *(to friction)*
Abnutzungsbeständigkeit *f* wear resistance; abrasion resistance *(to friction)*
Abnutzungsfaktor *m* wear factor
Abnutzungsprüfer *m*, **Abnutzungsprüfmaschine** *f* abrasion-testing machine, abrasion tester (machine), abrader
Abnutzungsprüfung *f* wear test; abrasion test *(for friction)*
Abnutzungswiderstand *m* wear resistance; abrasion resistance *(to friction)*
Aböl *n* waste oil
abölen *(tann)* to oil, to stuff
Abperleffekt *m* water repellency (repellent effect)
abpipettieren to pipette off, to withdraw by pipette
abplatzen to exfoliate, to flake [off], to scale [off], to chip [off], to peel [off], to spall
abpressen to press [off], to squeeze [off], to force out, to expel, to express
~/in Filterpressen to filter-press
Abpreßwalze *f* squeezing (squeeze) roll; *(pap)* lump-breaker roll
Abprodukt *n* waste [product]
~/festes solid waste [material], waste solid
~/gewerbliches commercial waste
~/industrielles industrial waste
~/kommunales municipal waste
Abproduktbehandlung *f* waste treatment
Abproduktbeseitigung *f* waste disposal
~ durch Einleitung ins Meer ocean disposal
~ durch Geländeauffüllung landfill disposal [of wastes]
Abproduktnutzung *f*, **Abproduktverwertung** *f* waste utilization
abpuffern to buffer [off]
abpumpen to pump off, to evacuate
abquetschen to squeeze [off]
Abquetschfläche *f (plast)* 1. land [area]; 2. cut-off *(of a press mould)*
Abquetschform *f (plast)* flash mould
Abquetschrand *m (plast)* cut-off *(af a press mould)*
Abquetsch- und Füllform *f (plast)* semipositive mould
Abquetschwalze *f* squeezing (squeeze) roll
Abquetschwerkzeug *n (plast)* flash mould
abrahmen to cream [off], to skim *(milk)*
Abrasion *f* abrasion
Abrasivmittel *n* abrasive
abrauchen to fume off
Abraumhalde *f (mine)* spoil pile
Abraumsalz *n* abraum salt
Abraumsalze *npl*/**Staßfurter** Stassfurt [salt] deposits
abreiben to abrade, to scour
Abreinigung *f* cloth cleaning *(of dust collection filters)*
abreißen to tear off, to pull off; to break *(as of paper webs)*
Abreißen *n* **der Papierbahn** *(pap)* break in the web, sheet break

Abreißmethode *f* detachment method *(for determining surface tensions)*
Abrieb *m* 1. abrasion, abrasive wear, attrition; 2. rubbings, dust
abriebbeständig *s.* abriebfest
abriebfest abrasion-resistant
Abriebfestigkeit *f* abrasion resistance; scuff resistance *(with sliding or rolling friction)*
Abriebprüfmaschine *f* abrasion-testing machine, abrasion tester (machine), abrader
Abriebprüfung *f* abrasion test
~ **in der Trommel nach Cochrane** Cochrane [abrasion] test
Abriebsabnutzung *f s.* Abnutzung durch Abrieb
Abriebverlust *m* abrasion (attrition) loss
Abriebversuch *m* abrasion test
Abriebwiderstand *m* abrasion resistance
Abriebzahl *f* abrasion index
abriegeln to block
Abrin *n* 1. abrine, *N*-methyltryptophan; 2. abrin *(a toxalbuminoid)*
Abriß *m* **der Papierbahn** *(pap)* break in the web, sheet break
abrollen to unreel, to reel off, to unwind
~/sich *(ceram)* to crawl *(of glazing material)*
Abrollgestell *n* reel-off stand, reel (reeling-off, back) stand, unwind[ing] stand
abrösten to roast, to burn *(e.g. ores)*
Abröstung *f***/vollständige** dead roasting
abs. = absolut
ABS 1. *s.* Akrylnitril-Butadien-Styrol; 2. *s.* Abscisinsäure; 3. = Alkylbenzensulfonat
absacken 1. to bag [up] *(bulk material)*; 2. to sag *(of coatings)*
absättigen to saturate *(valencies)*
Absättigung *f* saturation *(of valencies)*
Absatzgestein *n* sedimentary rock
absatzweise batch[wise] *(operation)*
absäuern *(text)* to acidify
Absäuerung *f (text)* acidification; *(pap)* acid souring (stage) *(a bleaching stage)*
absaugen to suck off, to siphon [off], to withdraw, to exhaust; *(filtr)* to filter by (with, under) suction, *(Am also)* to suction-filter
Absaugen *n* suction, siphoning, withdrawal, exhaustion; *(filtr)* suction filtration
Absauger *m s.* Absaugvorrichtung
Absaugkasten *m (plast)* plenum chamber
Absaugvorrichtung *f* exhausting device, exhauster, aspirator; *(text)* suction extractor
Abschabemesser *n* scraper (doctor) knife, scraper (doctor) blade, scraper
abschaben to scrape off, to doctor off
abschälen to peel [off] *(e.g. a foil)*; to skim *(as in the knife-discharge centrifuge)*
~/sich *(ceram)* to peel [off], to shell [off] *(of a glaze)*
Abschaum *m* scum
abschäumen to skim [off], to scum
Abschäumer *m* skimmer
Abschäumlöffel *m* skimmer, skimming ladle
abscheidbar separable, *(from liquids also)* precipitable, settleable, *(from gases also)* settleable, *(esp electrostatically:)* precipitable
Abscheidbarkeit *f* separability, *(from liquids also)* precipitability, settleability, *(from gases also)* settleability, *(esp electrostatically:)* precipitability
Abscheidegrad *m* separation (collection) efficiency *(gas cleaning)*; *(hyd)* solids removal efficiency (performance) *(with vacuum filtration)*; degree of solids recovery, recovery *(with centrifugation)*
Abscheidekammer *f* separating chamber, settling (settlement, fall-out) chamber, expansion (drop-out) box *(gas cleaning)*
abscheiden to separate, to eliminate, to remove, to segregate; to sediment[ate], to precipitate, to throw (lay) down *(bottoms)*; *(min tech)* to discard *(tailings)*; to deposit *(coating material)*; to evolve, to set free, to liberate *(gases)*; to deposit, to sediment *(of a liquid)*
~/elektrochemisch to electrodeposit
~/elektrolytisch *s.* 1. ~/stromlos; 2. ~/elektrochemisch
~/galvanisch *s.* ~/elektrochemisch
~/gemeinsam to co-deposit
~/sich to separate [out], *(of precipitates also)* to settle [down, out], to sediment, to precipitate [out], to deposit, to subside
~/sich baumartig *(cryst)* to tree
~/sich elektrochemisch (elektrolytisch) to plate out
~/sich gemeinsam to co-deposit
~/stromlos to deposit by immersion
Abscheiden *n* separation, elimination, removal, segregation; sedimentation, precipitation *(of bottoms)*; *(min tech)* discard *(of tailings)*; deposition *(of coating material)*; evolution, liberation *(of gases)*; deposition, sedimentation *(of bottoms by a liquid)*
~/akustisches sonic precipitation (agglomeration)
~ **aus der Gasphase/chemisches** chemical vapour deposition, CVD *(via decomposable gaseous intermediates, mostly halides)*
~ **durch Ultraschall** ultrasonic agglomeration
~/elektrisches electrostatic (electrical) precipitation *(gas cleaning)*
~/elektrochemisches electrodeposition *(of coatings)*
~/elektrolytisches *s.* 1. ~/stromloses; 2. ~/elektrochemisches
~/elektrostatisches *s.* ~/elektrisches
~ **fester Schwebstoffe** *(hyd)* suspended solids removal
~ **fester Teilchen** separation of solids (solid particles)
~/galvanisches *s.* ~/elektrochemisches
~/naßmechanisches wet collection (scrubbing)
~/stromloses immersion coating, chemical deposition, *(specif)* immersion coating by chemical reduction, electroless deposition (plating)
~ **von Flüssigkeit** weeping *(as of a gel)*
~ **von Schwermetallen** *(hyd)* heavy metals removal

Abscheider *m* separator, precipitator, catcher, trap; settler, separator (settling) tank *(fluid extraction)*; *(min tech)* collector; *(nucl)* trap
~/belüfteter *(hyd)* air-floatation separator
~/filternder filter-type dust collector, dust[-control] filter, dust collection filter
~ für mitgerissene Flüssigkeit entrainment separator
Abscheideraum *m s.* Abscheidekammer
Abscheidezyklon *m* centrifugal cyclone separator, cyclone
Abscheidung *f* 1. *s.* Abscheiden; 2. deposit, sediment, settling[s], bottom sediments (settlings), B.S., bottoms • **zur ~ gelangen** *s.* abscheiden/ sich
Abscheidungskonstante *f* distribution (partition, segregation) coefficient *(zone melting)*
Abscheidungspotential *n* deposition potential
abscheren to shear [off]
Abscheren *n* shear[ing]
Abscherwirkung *f* shearing action; shearing effect
Abschirmbeton *m* shielding (radiation) concrete, concrete for [atomic] radiation shielding
Abschirmeffekt *m (spectr)* shielding effect
abschirmen to shield, to screen off, to blanket; to protect *(atomic groups in a molecule)*
Abschirmen *n*/**lokales** *s.* Abdecken/lokales
Abschirmkonstante *f (phys ch)* shielding constant; *(nucl)* screening constant
Abschirmung *f*/**diamagnetische** diamagnetic screening
~ durch die Rumpfelektronen (inneren Elektronen) inner-shell shielding
~/magnetische magnetic shielding
Abschirmungszahl *f (nucl)* screening constant
Abschlamm *m* sludge *(coal hydrogenation)*
abschlämmen to elutriate
Abschlämmen *n* elutriation
abschleifen to grind [off], to abrade; to [sand]paper *(to treat with abrasive paper)*
~/auf der Fleischseite *(tann)* to fluff
~/den Narben *(tann)* to buff
abschleudern to centrifuge [off], to spin; *(text)* to hydroextract *(water)*
Abschleudern *n* centrifugation, spinning; *(text)* hydroextraction *(of water)*
abschließen 1. to terminate *(a process)*; 2. to seal *(e.g. a vessel)*
~/wasserdicht to waterproof
abschließend/dicht tight-fitting
Abschluß *m* 1. termination *(of a process)*; 2. seal *(as of a vessel)*; 3. exclusion *(as of air during a reaction)*
~/trockener dry seal
Abschlußdüse *f (plast)* shut-off nozzle
Abschlußwasserschüssel *f* water seal
abschmelzen *(met)* to liquate, to melt down, to smelt; *(glass)* to seal [off]
abschmieren 1. to lubricate; 2. to set off *(of printing ink)*
Abschminkpapier *n* cleansing tissue [paper], facial tissue [paper]
abschmutzen *(dye, coat, tann)* to bleed [off]; to set off *(of printing ink)*
Abschmutzen *n (dye, coat, tann)* bleeding; offset *(of printing ink)*
Abschmutzmakulatur *f s.* Abschmutzpapier
Abschmutzpapier *n* set-off paper, tympan paper
abschneiden to cut off (away), to shear [off]
Abschneider *m s.* Abschneidetisch
Abschneidetisch *m (ceram)* cutting-off table, cutter
Abschnitt *m* 1. region, section *(as in a molecule)*; 2. section, part *(of equipment)*; 3. stage *(of a process)*; 4. period *(of time)*; 5. cutting, chip *(of material)*; 6. *(glass)* cutoff *(of the gather)*
~ abnehmender Trocknungsgeschwindigkeit falling-rate drying period
~ konstanter Trocknungsgeschwindigkeit constant-rate drying period
~/nichthelixartiger *(bioch)* non-helical region (section)
abschöpfen to skim [off]; *(met)* to rabble
Abschrägung *f* 1. bevel, slope, taper *(as on a device)*; 2. bevelling, sloping, tapering
Abschreckalterung *f (met)* quench ag[e]ing
Abschreckbad *n* quenching bath
abschrecken 1. to quench, to cool rapidly, *(met also)* to chill; 2. to deter *(animals)*
~/direkt to direct-quench *(metal)*
~/in Öl to oil-quench *(metal)*
~/in Wasser to water-quench *(metal)*
Abschrecken *n* quenching, rapid cooling, *(met also)* chill[ing]
~/direktes direct quenching *(of metal)*
~ in Öl oil quenching *(of metal)*
~/in Wasser water quenching *(of metal)*
abschreckend repellent *(odour, taste)*
abschreckhärten to quench-harden
Abschreckmittel *n* 1. quenching medium (agent); 2. repellent, deterrent *(against animals)*
~ gegen Blattläuse greenfly repellent
~ gegen Nagetiere rodent repellent
Abschrecköl *n* quench[ing] oil
Abschreckstoff *m s.* Abschreckmittel 2.
Abschreckung *f* 1. repelling, deterring *(of animals)*; 2. *s.* Abschrecken
Abschreckungsmittel *n s.* Abschreckmittel 2.
Abschreckwirkung *f* repellency, deterrent action *(on animals)*
abschuppen/sich to scale [off], to flake [off], to chip
abschwächen 1. to attenuate *(an action)*; *(phot)* to reduce; to tone down *(a colour)*; 2. to weaken, to thin *(e.g. a solution)*
Abschwächer *m (phot)* reducer
~/Farmerscher Farmer's reducer
~/proportionaler (proportional wirkender) proportional reducer
~/subtraktiver (subtraktiv wirkender) subtractive (cutting, subproportianal) reducer

~/superproportionaler (überproportionaler) superproportional reducer
Abschwächung *f* 1. attenuation *(of an action)*; *(phot)* reduction; 2. weakening, thinning *(as of a solution)*
~/örtliche (partielle) *(phot)* local reduction
Abschwächungsmittel *n s.* Abschwächer
abschwemmen to float off, to elutriate
abschwenkbar retractable
Abscisinsäure *f* abscisic acid, ABA *(a plant hormone)*
abseifen to soap
abseigern *(met)* to liquate, to melt down, to smelt
abseihen to strain
absenken to lower *(a level, a temperature)*
Absetzanlage *f* settling unit (plant), sedimentation (precipitation) unit, settler, precipitator, *(hyd also)* clarification unit (plant)
~ mit horizontaler Durchströmung *(hyd)* horizontal-flow clarification unit, horizontal-flow clarifier, horizontal plant
~ mit vertikaler Durchströmung *(hyd)* vertical-flow (up-flow) clarification unit
Absetzapparat *m* settler, precipitator
absetzbar settleable *(e.g. contaminants, floc)*
~/nicht non-settleable
Absetzbarkeit *f* settleability *(as of contaminants, floc)*
Absetzbecken *n* settling tank (basin), sedimentation (precipitation) tank, *(hyd also)* gravity clarifier (settler), quiescent tank (basin)
~/flaches *(hyd)* plain clarifier
~ mit Durchfluß *(hyd)* continuous-flow sedimentation tank
~ mit horizontaler Durchströmung *(hyd)* horizontal-flow [sedimentation] tank
~ mit vertikaler Durchströmung *(hyd)* vertical-flow [sedimentation] tank, continuous vertical tank
~ nach Imhoff *(hyd)* Imhoff tank
~/rechteckiges *(hyd)* rectangular clarifier, rectangular [settling, sedimentation] basin
Absetzbehälter *m* settling (sedimentation) tank, settler; settling (separator) tank, settler *(fluid extraction)*; settling chamber *(in the pebble-heater process)*
Absetzbereich *m s.* Absetzzone
Absetzbottich *m s.* Absetzbehälter
Absetzbütte *f (pap)* draining tank (chest), drainer
Absetzdauer *f (hyd)* settling period (time), clarification time
Absetzeigenschaften *fpl (hyd)* settling properties
absetzen to sediment, to deposit *(of a liquid)*
~/sich to settle [down, out], to sediment, to precipitate, to deposit, to subside
~/sich wieder to redeposit
Absetzen *n* settling, sedimentation, precipitation, deposition, subsiding
~/behindertes *(min tech)* hindered settling
~/freies *(min tech)* free settling
~/gestörtes *s.* ~/behindertes
~/hartes *(coat)* hard settling
~ im Schwerefeld gravitational (gravity) settling (sedimentation)
Absetzer *m* settler, precipitator; coalescer *(for collecting liquid droplets)*
absetzfähig *s.* absetzbar
Absetzfläche *f* settling (sedimentation) area
Absetzgefäß *n s.* Absetzbehälter
Absetzgeschwindigkeit *f* settling (sedimentation) rate, rate of gravity settling, subsidence rate
Absetzglas *n* settling cylinder
~ nach Imhoff *(hyd)* Imhoff [sediment] cone
Absetzgrube *f* settling (sedimentation) pit
Absetzkammer *f* settling (sedimentation) chamber, expansion chamber
Absetzkläranlage *f s.* Absetzanlage
Absetzkonus *m* settling cone
Absetzkurve *f* settling curve
Absetzleistung *f* settling (sedimentation) performance
Absetzplatte *f (glass)* dead plate
Absetzraum *m* settling (sedimentation) chamber
Absetzschlamm *m (hyd)* clarification (clarifier) sludge, sedimentation [tank] sludge
Absetzschleuder *f* sedimentation centrifuge
Absetzstoffänger *m (pap)* sedimentation (gravity) save-all
Absetzstoffe *mpl (hyd)* settleable solids
Absetztank *m s.* Absetzbehälter
Absetzteich *m (hyd)* settling (quiescent) pond
Absetzverhalten *n* settling behaviour
Absetzverhinderungsmittel *n* antisettling (suspending) agent
Absetzversuch *m (hyd)* settling test
Absetzvorgang *m* settling process
Absetzweg *m* settling (sedimentation) path (distance)
Absetzwirkung *f (hyd)* sediment action *(of sludge in activated-sludge process)*
Absetz-Wirkungsgrad *m (hyd)* clarification efficiency
Absetzzeit *f s.* Absetzdauer
Absetzzentrifuge *f* sedimentation[-type] centrifuge, sedimenting (solid-bowl, solid-wall, full-bowl) centrifuge, centrifugal decanter
Absetzzone *f (hyd)* settling zone (region), sedimentation zone *(of a sedimentation tank)*
absieben to screen [out], to sieve [out]; to scalp [out] *(coarser grades)*
absieden to decoct
Absieden *n* decoction
absinken 1. to sediment, to settle [out], to sink, to subside *(of particles)*; 2. to decrease, to drop, to fall *(as of measuring values)*
Absinken *n* 1. sedimentation, settling *(of particles)*; 2. decrease, drop, fall, decline *(as of measuring values)*

Absinkgeschwindigkeit *f* settling (sedimentation) rate (velocity)
Absinth *m s.* Absinthbranntwein
absinthartig absinthine
Absinthbranntwein *m*, **Absinthlikör** *m* absinth[e]
Absitz... *s.* Absetz...
absitzen to settle [down, out], to sediment, to precipitate, to deposit, to subside
~ **lassen** to allow to deposit (settle), to let settle *(from liquids)*
Absitzen *n* settling, sedimentation, precipitation, deposition, subsiding *(for compounds s.* Absetzen*)*
Absitzenlassen *n* sedimentation
Absolu *n* **[de concret]** *(cosmet)* absolute essence (from concrete)
~ **d'enfleurage** *(cosmet)* absolute of enfleurage, enfleurage absolute
Absolutalkohol *m s.* Alkohol/absoluter
Absolutwert *m* absolute value
absondern 1. to separate, to eliminate, to isolate, to segregate; 2. *(biol)* to secrete, to exude *(e.g. resin)*
~**/sich** 1. to separate, to segregate *(from a mixture)*; 2. *(biol)* to exude
Absonderung *f* 1. separation, elimination, isolation, segregation; *(biol)* secretion; 2. *(biol)* secretion, *(relating to useless substances also)* excretum
Absonderungsstoff *m s.* Absonderung 2.
Absorbanz *f (spectr)* absorbance *(preferred term)*, absorbancy, absorbency, extinction, optical density
Absorbat *n* 1. absorbate, absorbed material (substance); 2. *absorbed material together with the absorbent*
Absorbend *m* material to be absorbed
Absorbens *n* absorbent, absorber, absorbing agent (material, substance)
Absorber *m* absorber, absorption apparatus (unit)
~ **mit berieselter Wand** wetted-wall[-column] absorber
absorbierbar absorbable
Absorbierbarkeit *f* absorbability
absorbieren to absorb, to imbibe
~**/wieder** to re-absorb
absorbierend/schwach poorly absorbing
Absorbierkolonne *f s.* Absorptionskolonne
Absorpt *n* absorbate, absorbed material (substance)
Absorptiometer *n* absorptiometer
Absorptiometrie *f* absorptiometry
absorptiometrisch absorptiometric
Absorption *f* absorption
~ **der Röntgenstrahlen (Röntgenstrahlung)** X-ray absorption
~ **in Öl** oil absorption
Absorptionsanalyse *f* absorptiometry
Absorptionsanlage *f* absorption plant (unit, system)
Absorptionsapparat *m s.* Absorber
Absorptionsbande *f* absorption band, spectral absorbance band
Absorptionsbasis *f (pharm)* absorption base
Absorptionsbatterie *f* absorption train *(for gases)*
Absorptionsbereich *m* absorbing region
absorptionsbeschleunigend absorbefacient
Absorptionsbodenkolonne *f* plate-type absorption tower
absorptionsfähig absorptive, absorbent, absorbing
Absorptionsfähigkeit *f* absorbency
Absorptionsflasche *f* absorption bottle
Absorptionsflüssigkeit *f* absorption (absorbing) liquid
absorptionsfördernd absorbefacient
Absorptionsgebiet *n* absorbing region
Absorptionsgefäß *n* absorption vessel; absorption bulb
Absorptionsgeschwindigkeit *f* absorption rate (velocity)
Absorptionsgesetz *n* law of absorption, absorption law
~**/Bouguer-Lambertsches** Bouguer-Lambert law [of absorption], Lambert's absorption law
~**/Henrysches** Henry's law [of absorption]
~**/Lambert-Beersches** Beer-Lambert[-Bouguer] law
~**/Lambertsches** *s.* ~/Bouguer-Lambertsches
Absorptionsgrad *m s.* Absorptionszahl
Absorptionsgrundlage *f (pharm)* absorption base
Absorptionsindex *m* absorption index *(optics)*
Absorptionsintensität *f (spectr)* absorption intensity
Absorptionskälteanlage *f*, **Absorptionskältemaschine** *f* absorption refrigeration system (machine)
Absorptionskante *f (spectr)* absorption edge
Absorptionskoeffizient *m (phys ch, spectr)* absorption coefficient, *(spectr also)* absorptivity
~**/atomarer** *(spectr)* atomic absorption coefficient
~**/Bunsenscher** *(phys ch)* Bunsen [absorption] coefficient
~**/molarer** *(spectr)* molar [decadic] absorption coefficient, molar absorptivity
Absorptionskolben *m* absorption flask
Absorptionskolonne *f* absorption (absorbing) column, *(esp tech)* absorption tower
Absorptionskurve *f* absorption curve
Absorptionsküvette *f (anal)* absorption cell
Absorptionslinie *f* absorption line
Absorptionsmaschine *f* absorption machine
Absorptionsmaximum *n* absorption maximum
Absorptionsmittel *n* absorbing agent (material, substance), absorbent, absorber
Absorptionsöl *n* absorption (absorbent) oil, wash oil
~**/mageres** lean oil
Absorptionspipette *f* absorption [gas] pipette
Absorptionsprozeß *m* absorption process
Absorptionsquerschnitt *m* absorption cross section *(photochemistry)*; *(nucl)* capture cross section

Absorptionsregel *f***/Woodwardsche** *(spectr)* Woodward's rule
Absorptionsrohr *n* absorption tube
Absorptionsröhrchen *n* absorption tube
~/Preglsches *(lab)* Pregl absorption tube
Absorptionsröhre *f* absorption tube
Absorptionssäule *f* absorption (absorbing) column, *(esp tech)* absorption tower
Absorptionssignal *n (spectr)* absorption signal
Absorptionsspektrometer *n* absorption spectrometer
Absorptionsspektroskopie *f* absorption spectroscopy
Absorptionsspektrum *n* absorption spectrum
Absorptionssystem *n* absorption system (unit, plant)
Absorptionsturm *m* absorption (absorbing) tower
Absorptionsverfahren *n* absorption process
Absorptionsvermögen *n* absorbency; *(relating to radiation:)* absorptivity, absorptive power, *(quantitatively also)* absorption coefficient (factor)
Absorptionsvorgang *m* absorption process
Absorptionszahl *f* absorption coefficient (factor) *(for radiation)*, *(specif relating to heat radiation)* absorptivity
absorptiv *s.* absorptionsfähig
Absorptiv *n* material (substance) to be absorbed
abspaltbar capable of being split off, separable
abspalten to split (cleave) off, to eliminate, to abstract *(atoms or atomic groups from molecules)*; to expel *(molecules in elimination reactions)*; to release *(gases)*; to detach *(electrons)*
~/durch Solvolyse *(bioch)* to solvolyze off
~/Schichten to flake
~/sich to split (cleave) off
Abspaltung *f* splitting-off, cleaving-off, elimination *(of atomic groups from molecules)*; expulsion *(of molecules in elimination reactions)*; release *(of gases)*
~ eines Elektrons electron detachment
Abspaltungsreaktion *f* elimination (abstraction) reaction
Abspannen *n (plast)* stripping *(of a mould)*
absperren to shut off; *(coat)* to seal
Absperrhahn *m* stopcock
Absperrmittel *n (coat)* sealer, sealing paint
Absperrschieber *m* gate valve
Absperrstein *m* **des Speisers** *(glass)* feeder gate (plug)
Absperrventil *n* cut-off (shut-off) valve, stop (block) valve
Absperrvorrichtung *f* cut-off (shut-off, stopping) device
absplittern to splinter off, to chip [off]
absprengen *(glass)* to burn off
Absprengen *n (glass)* burn-off, flame cut-off
Absprengkappe *f (glass)* moil
Absprengperlen *fpl* glass filler rings
abspringen to scale [off], to flake [off], to exfoliate, to peel [off], to shell [off]
abspülen to rinse, to swill *(e.g. a vessel)*; to rinse off (down, away), to swill off *(e.g. impurities)*; *(min tech)* to spray
Abstand *m* 1. distance, space, spacing; 2. interval *(period)*
~ zwischen den Energieniveaus *(spectr)* separation of energy levels, energy separation
abstauben *(ceram)* to dust *(a ware before firing)*
Abstaubmaschine *f (ceram)* dusting machine, duster
abstechen to tap [out], to draw off *(liquid metals)*; to dig out *(e.g. a filter cake)*
Abstehzeit *f (rubber)* drop period
abstellen to turn off, to shut off *(water, gas)*; to stop *(a machine)*
Absterbephase *f (biot, hyd)* death (endogenous growth) phase
Abstich *m* 1. tapping *(of liquid metals)*; 2. *s.* Abstichloch
Abstichgaserzeuger *m s.* Abstichgenerator
Abstichgenerator *m* slagging[-ash] producer
~ von Ebelmen Ebelmen producer
Abstichloch *n (met)* taphole, tapping hole
Abstichmaschine *f* tapping device *(calcium carbide manufacture)*
Abstichöffnung *f s.* Abstichloch
Abstichpfanne *f (met)* tapping receiver
Abstichrinne *f (met)* tapping channel, runner
Abstichschirm *m* tapping screen *(of a carbide furnace)*
Abstichschnauze *f s.* Abstichrinne
Abstoff *m s.* Abprodukt
abstoppen to stop [off, up]; *(rubber)* to shortstop *(polymerization)*
Abstoppmittel *n (rubber)* shortstopping agent, shortstop, stopper
Abstoßeffekt *m* repulsive effect
abstoßen 1. to repel *(as by electric charge)*; 2. to discard, to reject *(useless material)*
~/Narben *(tann)* to degrain
abstoßend 1. repellent, repulsive, vile *(esp smell)*; 2. repulsive *(force)*
Abstoßung *f* repulsion
~/Coulombsche Coulomb repulsion
~/elektrostatische electrostatic repulsion
~/interelektronische interelectronic (electron-electron) repulsion
~ zwischen Ionen [gleicher Ladung] ionic repulsion
Abstoßungskraft *f* repulsive force, force of repulsion
~/Coulombsche Coulomb force of repulsion
Abstoßungsmittel *n (text)* repellent
abstrahlen to radiate, to emit
Abstrahlung *f* radiation, emission
Abstrahlungsverlust *m* radiation loss, loss by radiation

abstreichen to skim [off]
Abstreicher *m* skimmer; plough *(on conveyors)*
abstreifen 1. to doctor off *(as from a roll)*; to skim [off] *(scum)*; *(plast)* to eject; 2. *(distil)* to strip [off, out]
Abstreifen *n* **vom Stempel** *(plast)* top ejection
Abstreifer *m* 1. *(distil)* stripper; 2. *s.* Abstreifermesser
Abstreiferkolonne *f (distil)* stripping column (still), stripper
Abstreifermesser *n* scraper (doctor) knife (blade), scraper
Abstreiferöl *n* stripping oil
Abstreiferteil *m*, **Abstreiferzone** *f s.* Abtriebsteil
Abstreifmeißel *m*, **Abstreifmesser** *n s.* Abstreifermesser
Abstreifplatte *f (plast)* stripper plate
Abstreifreaktion *f* stripping reaction
Abstrippzone *f s.* Abtriebsteil
abströmen to flow off (away), to run off *(of liquids)*; to escape *(of gases)*
Abstufung *f (phot)* gradation
abstumpfen 1. *(ch)* to blunt, to neutralize, *(relating to acids also)* to deacidify, *(relating to alkalies also)* to dealkalize; *(tann)* to raise the basicity *(of chrome liquor)*; 2. to blunt *(glassware after cutting)*; 3. *(dye)* to deaden
Absud *m* decoction, decoctum
absüßen to sweeten, to dulcify
Absüßen *n* sweetening, dulcification
Absüßpumpe *f (sugar)* sweet-water pump
Absüßwasser *n (sugar)* sweet water
abtasten to scan *(a measuring range)*
~/nochmals to rescan
abtauchen to dip
Abtauchen *n* dip[ping]
abtauen to defrost *(e.g. a surface)*; to thaw [off] *(ice)*
abtönen to tint, to shade, to tone
Abtöner *m*, **Abtönmittel** *n* tinting agent
Abtönpaste *f* tinting paste
Abtönung *f* 1. tinting, shading; 2. shade; *(phot)* gradation
abtoppen to skim *(petroleum)*
Abtötungskonstante *f* death constant *(sterilization)*
Abtötungskurve *f* death curve *(sterilization)*
Abtötungsrate *f* death rate, rate of death *(sterilization)*
Abtötungstemperatur *f* lethal temperature *(sterilization)*
Abtötungszeit *f* death (sterilization) time
Abtrag *m* [surface] removal, *(esp by corrosion:)* eating away, *(esp by mechanical forces:)* wearing [away], erosion
abtragen to remove, *(esp by corrosion:)* to eat away, *(esp by mechanical forces:)* to wear [away], to erode
Abtragung *f s.* Abtrag
Abtragungsgrad *m (plast)* degree of erosion
Abtränkbrühe *f (tann)* duster
abtreiben to distil off, to strip [off, out]; *(met)* to cupel
Abtreiben *n* simple distillation, stripping; *(met)* cupellation
Abtreiber *m*, **Abtreiberkolonne** *f s.* Abtriebskolonne
Abtreibeteil *n s.* Abtriebsteil
abtrennbar separable
Abtrennbarkeit *f* separability
abtrennen to separate [off], to separate out (away), to isolate *(something from a mixture)*; to abstract, to separate by distillation; to detach *(an electron)*
Abtrennung *f* separation, isolation *(from a mixture)*; abstraction, separation by distillation; detachment *(of an electron)*
~ **des Schlammwassers** *(hyd)* separation of supernatant
~ **eines Elektrons** electron detachment
~ **suspendierter Feststoffteilchen** *(hyd)* suspended solids removal
Abtrennungsarbeit *f* work function [of electrons], electronic work function
Abtrieb *m* simple distillation, stripping
Abtriebsgerade *f (distil)* stripping operating line
Abtriebskolonne *f*, **Abtriebssäule** *f (distil)* stripping column (still), stripper
Abtriebsteil *m* stripping (exhausting) section *(of a fractionating column)*
Abtrift *f* blow-off, drift *(of pesticides)*
abtrocknen to dry [off, up]
Abtropfbrett *n* drying (apparatus) rack, drain[ing] board
~/aufhängbares wall-mounting draining board
abtropfen to drain, to drip (trickle) off
~ **lassen** to drain
Abtropfen *n* drainage
Abtropfenlassen *n* drainage
Abtropfgestell *n* drying (apparatus) rack
Abtropfkanal *m* draining pan *(in flow coating*
abtupfen/mit Fließpapier to blot
abwandern to migrate out *(as of ions)*; *(anal)* to drift *(as of a base-line)*
Abwärme *f* waste heat
Abwärmenutzung *f* waste heat utilization
Abwärmerückgewinnung *f* waste-heat recovery
Abwärts-Dickstoffturm *m (pap)* downflow high-density tower
Abwärtsfilter *n (hyd)* downflow filter
Abwärtsfiltration *f (hyd)* downflow filtration
Abwärtsgasen *n* down-run[ning], down-steaming *(manufacturing of water-gas)*
~ **mit Dampfüberhitzung** back run
Abwärtsstrom *m* downflow, downward flow (current), descending current • **im ~ arbeiten** to operate downflow *(of a filter)* • **im ~ auswaschen** to rinse downflow *(ion exchange)* • **im ~ fahren** to operate downflow *(a filter)*
Abwaschbecken *n* sink
abwaschen to wash [up], to rinse

Abwasser *n* waste (discharge) water, waste, effluent, *(esp of domestic origin:)* sewage; *(pap)* white water
~/abfließendes [gereinigtes] discharge from a waste-water treatment plant, waste treatment effluent, sewage plant effluent
~/abzuleitendes waste discharge, *(from an industrial plant:)* effluent discharge, waste effluent, outfall
~ aus sanitären und sozialen Einrichtungen sanitary waste water *(from industrial plants)*
~/betriebliches plant waste water, plant (factory, works) effluent, plant discharge
~ der chemischen Industrie chemical plant's waste, waste from chemical plants
~ der Erdölverarbeitung waste from refineries (petroleum refining), petroleum refinery waste water, refinery waste
~ der Kokereien coke plant waste, waste from coke plants
~ der Lebensmittelindustrie food industry waste, food plant (processing) waste water, waste from food processing plants
~ der Registerpartie *(pap)* tray water, water from the tray
~ der Zellstoffindustrie pulp mill waste water, pulping waste
~/„dickes" *s.* ~/hochkonzentriertes
~/„dünnes" *s.* ~/gering konzentriertes
~/einfließendes (einströmendes) incoming waste water, entering (influent) waste water, waste-water feed, waste influent
~/einzuleitendes waste discharge; *(from an industrial plant:)* effluent discharge, waste effluent, outfall
~/faser- und füllstoffreiches *(pap)* rich white water
~/frisches fresh waste water
~/geklärtes clarified waste water; *(pap)* filtered water
~/gereinigtes discharge from a waste-water treatment plant, waste treatment effluent, treated effluent, sewage plant effluent
~/gering konzentriertes low-contaminated (low-strength) waste, weak sewage
~/gewerbliches commercial waste
~/häusliches domestic sewage, household (sanitary) sewage, sewage water
~/hochbelastetes *s.* ~/hochkonzentriertes
~/hochkonzentriertes high-contaminated (high-strength) waste, strong sewage
~/industrielles industrial waste water, industrial discharge (effluent), trade effluent (waste)
~/kommunales municipal (community) sewage (waste water)
~/ölhaltiges (ölverschmutztes) oily waste water
~/petrolchemisches *s.* ~ der Erdölverarbeitung
~/phenolhaltiges phenol waste
~/schwach belastetes *s.* ~/gering konzentriertes
~/städtisches town (urban, municipal) sewage
~/starkes (stark verschmutztes) *s.* ~/hochkonzentriertes
~ von Galvanikbetrieben [electro]plating waste, waste from plating shops
~/zufließendes (zulaufendes) *s.* ~/einfließendes
Abwasserabfluß *m s.* Abwasserablauf
Abwasserablauf *m* 1. waste-water effluent (discharge); 2. effluent flow
~ einer Abwasserbehandlungsanlage waste-treatment effluent, sewage-plant effluent, discharge from waste-water treatment plants
~ eines Betriebs plant effluent, waste effluent (discharge), outfall
~ vom Belebungsbecken aeration tank effluent
Abwasserableitung *f* waste discharge
Abwasserableitung *f* **und -beseitigung** *f* sewerage
Abwasserableitungsnetz *n s.* Abwassernetz
Abwasseranfall *m* waste[-water] flow, effluent flow
~/durchschnittlicher average (mean) waste-water flow
~ eines Betriebs flow of plant discharge
~/maximaler peak waste-water flow
~/schwankender variable waste-water flow
Abwasseraufbereitung *f s.* Abwasserbehandlung
Abwasserbakterien *npl* sewage bacteria
Abwasserbehälter *m (pap)* white-water chest
Abwasserbehandlung *f* waste[-water] treatment, effluent treatment, *(esp municipally:)* sewage treatment
~/betriebliche plant waste[-water] treatment
~/biologische biological waste[-water] treatment
~/kommunale municipal sewage treatment
~/landwirtschaftliche land treatment of waste water, land disposal
~ mit Wechseltropfkörpern alternating double filtration
~ nach dem Belebtschlammverfahren activated-sludge waste (sewage) treatment, treatment by activated-sludge technique
~/städtische urban (municipal) sewage treatment
~ über einen Tropfkörper single biological filtration
~/weitergehende third-stage treatment, advanced (tertiary) waste treatment
Abwasserbehandlungsanlage *f* waste-treatment unit, effluent-treatment station *(of an industrial plant)*; [municipal] sewage-treatment plant
~/biologische biological waste-treatment unit
~ mit biologischer Reinigungsstufe secondary sewage-treatment plant
Abwasserbehandlungsverfahren *n* waste[-water] treatment process, *(esp municipally:)* sewage-treatment process
abwasserbelastet sewage-contaminated, polluted *(e.g. river)*
Abwasserbelastung *f* 1. waste-water loading; 2. *s.* Abwasserlast
Abwasser-Belebtschlamm-Gemisch *n* activated-sludge mixture, sludge-sewage mixture, mixed liquor

Abwasserbelüftung *f* waste-water aeration, aeration of sewage
Abwasserbeschaffenheit *f* waste-water quality
Abwasserbeseitigung *f* waste-water disposal, waste disposal (elimination)
Abwasserbodenbehandlung *f s.* Abwasserlandbehandlung
Abwasserdesinfektion *f* waste-water disinfection
Abwasserdickschlamm *m* thickened sludge
Abwassereinleitung *f* waste discharge
Abwassereinleitungsbedingungen *fpl* waste discharge standards, effluent standards (quality requirements, regulations)
Abwassereinleitungsstelle *f* waste-water discharge site, point of waste-water discharge, plant outfall (outlet)
Abwasserentkeimung *f* waste disinfection
Abwasserentsorgung *f s.* Abwasserbeseitigung
Abwasser-Feststoffsuspension *f* water slurry, *(filtr also)* feed sludge, filter feed slurry
Abwasserfiltration *f* waste-water filtration
Abwasserflockung *f* coagulation of wastes
Abwasserganglinie *f* daily flow curve
Abwassergemisch *n* mixture of wastes
Abwassergrenzwerte *mpl* discharge limits
Abwasserinhaltsstoffe *mpl* waste-water components
Abwasserkanal *m* sewer
Abwasserkläreinrichtung *f* waste-water clarifier
Abwasserklärung *f*/**mechanische** waste-water clarification
Abwasserkonzentration *f* waste concentration, strength of sewage
Abwasserlandbehandlung *f* land treatment of waste water, land disposal
Abwasserlast *f* waste-water pollution load, waste-water load[ing], waste load, pollutant (contaminant) load (loading), load of pollution (contamination)
Abwasserleitung *f* sewer (waste) line
Abwassermenge *f* quantity of waste water, waste volume
~/**anfallende** *s.* Abwasseranfall
Abwassermengenschwankung *f* fluctuation (variation) in waste-water flow, influent waste variation
Abwassernetz *n* sewer (sewage) system, sewerage
Abwasserorganismen *mpl* sewage organisms
Abwasserpilz *m* sewage fungus
Abwasserprobe *f* waste-water sample
Abwasserpumpe *f* waste-water pump; *(pap)* backwater (white-water) pump
Abwasserreinigung *f s.* Abwasserbehandlung
Abwasserrohr *n* waste pipe, *(esp municipally:)* sewage (sewer) pipe
Abwasserrohschlamm *m* raw waste-water sludge, fresh [sewage] sludge
Abwasserrückstände *mpl* residues from waste-water treatment *(as sludge, rakings, grit)*
Abwassersammelbehälter *m (pap)* white-water chest
Abwasserschadstoff *m* waste-water pollutant (contaminant)
Abwasserschlamm *m* waste[-treatment] sludge, sludge from waste-water treatment
~/**biochemischer** biological sewage sludge, [waste] biological sludge
~/**eingedickter** *s.* Abwasserdickschlamm
~/**gewerblicher** commercial waste-water sludge
~/**häuslicher** domestic waste-water sludge
~/**industrieller** industrial waste-water sludge
~/**kommunaler** municipal [sewage] sludge
Abwasserschlammbehandlung *f* waste-water sludge treatment
Abwasserschlammsuspension *f* water slurry, *(filtr also)* feed sludge, filter feed slurry
Abwasserschmutzstoff *m* waste-water pollutant (contaminant)
Abwasserstrom *m* waste-water flow, waste[-water] stream
Abwassertechnik *f* waste-water technology
Abwassertechnologie *f* waste-water technology
Abwasserteich *m* [waste-treatment, sewage-treatment] lagoon, waste[-water] pond
~/**aerober (aerob arbeitender)** aerobic lagoon, [aerobic] pond
~/**anaerober (anaerob arbeitender)** anaerobic lagoon (pond)
~/**belüfteter** aerated lagoon (pond)
Abwasserüberwachung *f* waste-water control
Abwasseruntersuchung *f* waste-water examination
Abwasserverbrennung *f* waste-water incineration
Abwasserversenkung *f* deep-well disposal
Abwasserverwertung *f* utilization of waste water, *(esp municipally:)* utilization of sewage
Abwasser-Volumenstrom *m s.* Abwasseranfall
Abwasserwertstoffe *mpl* values in waste water
Abwasserzufluß *m* 1. incoming waste water, entering (influent) waste water, waste-water feed, waste influent; 2. *s.* Abwasseranfall
~ **zum Belebungsbecken** aeration tank influent
Abwasserzulauf *m s.* 1. Abwasserzufluß 1.; 2. Abwasseranfall
Abwehrmittel *n s.* Abschreckmittel 2.
Abwehrprotein *n (med)* immune (antibody) protein
abweichen to deviate, to be different, to differ, to depart *(from a standard or expected value)*
Abweichung *f* deviation, departure
~/**mittlere quadratische** standard deviation, root mean square error, *(in a graph also)* half-peak width *(width at 0.607 h)*
~ **vom Reziprozitätsgesetz** *(phot)* reciprocity [law] failure
~/**zulässige** tolerance, allowance
abweisen to repel
abweisend repellent
~ **gegen klebende (klebrige) Stoffe** antistick

~ **gegen Öl** oil-repellent
~ **gegen Wasser** water-repellent, hydrophobic, hydrophobe
Abweisendausrüstung *f (text)* repellent finish
Abweisungsvermögen *n* repellency
abwelken *(tann)* to sam[my] *(to dry partially)*
Abwelkpresse *f (tann)* samm[y]ing machine
abwerfen to discharge, to dump *(as from a conveyor)*
abwickeln to unwind, to unreel, to reel off
Abwickelvorrichtung *f* pay-off [arrangement], let off [arrangement]
abwiegen to weigh [out, up]
Abwurf *m* 1. discharge, discharging; 2. discharge [point]
Abwurfende *n* discharge end *(as of a conveyor)*
Abwurföffnung *f* discharge opening (outlet, door) *(as of a conveyor)*
Abwurframpe *f (coal)* coke wharf
Abwurfstelle *f* discharge point *(as of a conveyor)*
Abwurfwagen *m* tripper
abzentrifugieren to centrifuge off
Abziehbild *n (ceram)* decalcomania, decal, litho, transfer
Abziehbilderpapier *n* decalcomania (transfer) paper
abziehen 1. to draw off (down), to withdraw, to dispense, to drain off *(liquids)*; *(ferm)* to remove *(the mash)*; to tap *(slag)*; to escape, to issue *(as of vapours)*; 2. to strip *(a dye)*; to peel off *(coatings)*; 3. *(phot)* to print; to transfer *(a design)*; 4. *(plast)* to take up *(extrudate)*
~/auf Fässer to barrel, to rack
~/auf Flaschen to bottle [in, up]
Abziehflotte *f (dye)* stripping bath
Abziehgeschwindigkeit *f (plast)* take-up speed *(of extrudate)*
Abziehhilfsmittel *n (text)* decolorizing (stripping) agent (assistant), decolorizer
Abziehlack *m* decorators' size
Abziehmittel *n s.* Abziehhilfsmittel
Abziehpapier *n s.* Abzugspapier 1.
Abzug *m* 1. *(lab)* [exhaust] hood, fume hood (chamber, closet); 2. discharge [point], outlet, drain; 3. *(phot)* [contact] print; *(pap)* proof [sheet]; 4. *(plast)* take-up *(of extrudate)*
Abzugsende *n* discharge end
Abzugsgeschwindigkeit *f s.* Abziehgeschwindigkeit
Abzugshaube *f* [fume] hood
Abzugskanal *m* discharge duct
Abzugskasten *m (lab)* local exhaust hood, fume closet
Abzugsleitung *f* discharge (drainage, outlet) line; waste line
Abzugspapier *n* proofing paper *(typography)*; *(phot)* printing paper
Abzugspumpe *f* withdrawal pump
Abzugsrohr *n* discharge pipe (tube), drainage (outlet, offtake, effluent) pipe; waste pipe (tube); vent (fume) pipe; *(lab)* vapour tube, fume chamber (duct, exhaust manifold) *(of the Kjeldahl digestion apparatus)*
~/seitliches *(lab)* side tube *(of a fractionating flask)*
Abzugsschleuse *f* sink
Abzugsschrank *m (lab)* fume cupboard (chamber)
Abzugswalze *f (plast)* haul-off roll
Abzweig *m* branch
abzweigen to branch off *(of pipelines)*
Abzweigstück *n* multiway union
Abzweigung *f* 1. branching-off *(of pipelines)*; 2. branch
Acajou *n s.* Acajugummi
Acajugummi *n* cashew (cashawa) gum *(from Anacardium occidentale L.)*
Acen *n (org ch)* acene
Acenaphthen *n (org ch)* acenaphthene
Acetacetat *n (bioch)* acetoacetate
Acetal *n* R–CH(OR')$_2$ acetal, *(specif)* $CH_3CH(OC_2H_5)_2$ acetal, *1,1-diethoxyethane
~/cyclisches cyclic acetal
~/gemischtes mixed acetal
Acetalbildung *f* acetal formation
Acetaldehyd *m* acetaldehyde, *ethanal
~/aktiver active acetaldehyde, 2-hydroxyethyl thiamine pyrophosphate, HETPP
Acetaldehydcyanhydrin *n* acetaldehyde cyanohydrin, lactonitrile, *2-hydroxypropane nitrile
Acetaldol *n* acetaldol, aldol, 3-hydroxybutyraldehyde, *3-hydroxybutanal
Acetalharz *n* acetal resin
acetalisieren to acetalate
Acetalisierung *f* acetalation
Acetamid *n* acetamide
Acetamidin *n (org ch)* acetamidine
p-**Acetamidobenzensulfochlorid** *n p*-acetamidobenzenesulphonyl chloride, *p*-acetylaminobenzenesulphonyl chloride
Acetamidogruppe *f* –$NHCOCH_3$ acetamido (acetylamino) group
Acetanhydrid *n* acetic anhydride
Acetanilid *n* acetanilide, *N*-phenylacetamide
Acetarsol *n* acetarsol, 3-acetylamino-4-hydroxybenzenearsonic acid
Acetat *n* acetate
~/aktiviertes *s.* Acetyl-Coenzym A
Acetatelementarfaden *m* acetate filament
~/verseifter saponified acetate filament
Acetatfaser *f* acetate fibre
Acetatfaserstoff *m* acetate fibre
Acetatokomplex *m* acetate complex
Acetator *m (biot)* acetator, vinegar fermenter
~ **zur submersen Essigsäureherstellung** submerged-culture generator (vinegar fermenter)
Acetatpuffer *m* acetate buffer
Acetatrayon *m(n) s.* Acetatseide
Acetatseide *f* cellulose acetate rayon, acetate filament yarn
~/polyfile acetate multifilament yarn

Acetatstapelfaser *f s.* Acetatfaser
Acetessigester *m s.* Acetessigsäureethylester
Acetessigsäure *f* acetoacetic acid, 3-oxobutyric acid
Acetessigsäurecarboxylase *f* acetoacetic carboxylase
Acetessigsäuredecarboxylase *f* acetoacetic decarboxylase
Acetessigsäureethylester *m* ethyl acetoacetate, acetoacetic ester
Acetimeter *n* acetimeter
Acetoacetylierung *f* acetoacetylation
Acetoethylierung *f* acetoethylation
Acetogenin *n* acetogenin, polyketide, ketide
Acetoin *n* acetoin, dimethylketol, *3-hydroxybutan-2-one
Acetolyse *f* acetolysis
Acetometer *n s.* Acetimeter
Aceton *n* acetone, *propanone, dimethylketone
Aceton-Benzol-Verfahren *n* benzol-acetone process *(for dewaxing petroleum)*
Aceton-Butanol-Gärung *f (biot)* acetone-butanol fermentation
Acetonchloroform *n* acetone chloroform, chloretone,*1,1,1-trichloro-2-hydroxy-2-methylpropane
Acetoncyanhydrin *n* acetone cyanohydrin, ACH, *2-hydroxy-2-methylpropanenitrile
Acetondicarbonsäure *f* acetonedicarboxylic acid, ADA, 3-oxoglutaric acid, *3-oxopentanedioic acid
Acetonharz *n* acetone resin
Acetonierung *f* acetonation
Acetonitril *n* acetonitrile, AN
Acetonkörper *m (bioch)* acetone (ketone) body
acetonlöslich acetone-soluble
Aceton-Natriumhydrogensulfit *n* acetone-sodium hydrogen sulphite, *(dye, phot also)* acetone bisulphite
Acetophenon *n* acetophenone, acetylbenzene, *methyl phenyl ketone
Acetotartrat *n* acetotartrate
Acetotoluid[id] *n s.* Acettoluidid
Acetoxybenzoesäure *f o*-acetoxybenzoic acid, *O*-acetylsalicylic acid
Acetoxygruppe *f* CH_3CO_2– acetoxy (ethanoyloxy) group
Acetoxylierung *f* acetoxylation
Acetoxymercurierung *f* acetoxymercuration
Acetoxymethylierung *f* acetoxymethylation
Acetsäure *f s.* Ethansäure
Acettoluidid *n* acet-toluidide
Acetylaceton *n* acetylacetone, *2,4-pentanedione
Acetylaminoanthrachinon *n* acetylaminoanthraquinone
p-**Acetylaminobenzolsulfonsäurechlorid** *n s.* Acetamidobenzensulfochlorid
Acetylaminogruppe *f* acetylamino group, acetamido group
Acetylbenzen *n* acetylbenzene, *methyl phenyl ketone, acetophenone
Acetylbutyrylcellulose *f* cellulose acetate butyrate, CAB
Acetylcarbonsäure *f s.* Brenztraubensäure
Acetylcellulose *f* acetylated cellulose, cellulose acetate, CA
Acetylchlorid *n* acetyl chloride
Acetylcholin *n* acetylcholine
Acetyl-Coenzym *n* **A** acetyl coenzyme A, acetyl Co A, active acetate
Acetylen *n* 1. acetylene, *ethyne; 2. *s.* Acetylenkohlenwasserstoff
~ **mit endständiger C–C-Dreifachbindung** terminal acetylene
Acetylen-Allen-Umlagerung *f* acetylene-allene rearrangement
Acetylenbrenner *m* oxyacetylene blowpipe (torch)
Acetylencarbonsäure *f* acetylenic acid *(any carboxylic acid having a triple bond)*
Acetylenchemie acetylene chemistry
Acetylendicarbonsäure *f* acetylenedicarboxylic acid, *butynedioic acid
Acetylenentwickler *m* acetylene gas generator
Acetylenid *n s.* Acetylid
acetylenisch acetylenic
Acetylenkohlenwasserstoff *m* acetylenic hydrocarbon, *alkyne
Acetylenruß *m* acetylene black
Acetylen-Sauerstoff-Brennschneiden *n* oxyacetylene (oxygen-acetylene) cutting, autogenous [gas] cutting
Acetylen-Sauerstoff-Schweißen *n* oxyacetylene (oxygen-acetylene) welding, oxywelding, autogenous [gas] welding
Acetylenschwarz *n* acetylene black
Acetylensilber *n* silver acetylide (carbide)
Acetylentetrachlorid *n* *1,1,2,2-tetrachloroethane, acetylene tetrachloride
Acetylenylbenzol *n s.* Ethinylbenzen
Acetylenylcarbinol *n* *prop-2-yn-1-ol, *(deprecated:)* ethynyl carbinol
Acetylenylgruppe *f* $-C \equiv CH$ acetylenyl group (residue), *ethynyl group (residue)
Acetylessigsäure *f s.* Acetessigsäure
Acetylesterase *f* acetyl esterase
Acetylformaldehyd *m s.* Brenztraubensäurealdehyd
Acetylgruppe *f* CH_3CO– acetyl group (residue)
Acetylharnstoff *m* acetylurea, *N*-monoacetylurea
Acetylid *n* $M^{I}_{2}C_2$ acetylide
acetylierbar acetyl[at]able
acetylieren to acetylate, to acetylize
Acetylierung *f* acetyl[iz]ation
Acetylierungskatalysator *m* acetylation catalyst
Acetylierungsmittel *n* acetylation (acetylating) agent
Acetylmethylcarbinol *n s.* Acetoin
N-**Acetylmuraminsäure** *f (bioch)* *N*-acetylmuramic acid
Acetylpapier *n* acetylated paper

N-**Acetyl-***N*-**phenylglycin** *n* *N*-acetylphenylglycine, *N*-phenylaceturic acid
Acetylrest *m s.* Acetylgruppe
Acetylsalicylat *n* acetylsalicylate
Acetylsalicylsäure *f* *O*-acetylsalicylic acid, *o*-acetoxybenzoic acid
N-**Acetyltoluidin** *n s.* Acettoluidid
Acetylureid *n s.* Acetylharnstoff
Acetylzahl *f* acetyl value (number) *(of fats and oils)*
Achat *m (min)* agate
Achatablaufdüse *f s.* Achatausflußrohr
Achatausflußrohr *n* agate tube (jet) *(of a Redwood viscometer)*
Achatmörser *m* agate mortar
Achatplanlager *n* agate plane *(of a balance)*
Achatpolierstein *m* agate burnisher
Achatsteinglätteinrichtung *f (pap)* flint-glazing machine, flint glazer, stone burnisher
Acheson-Graphit *m* Acheson graphite
Acheson-Graphitierungsofen *m*, **Acheson-Ofen** *m* Acheson furnace *(for graphitizing carbon materials)*
Acheson-Verfahren *n* Acheson process *(for producing artificial graphite)*
achiral achiral *(stereochemistry)*
Achiralität *f* achirality *(stereochemistry)*
Achondrit *m (min)* achondrite *(a meteorite)*
Achse *f* axis
~/dreizählige axis of threefold symmetry, three-fold axis of symmetry
~/kristallographische crystal[lographic] axis
~/optische optic[al] axis
~/sechszählige axis of sixfold symmetry, sixfold axis of symmetry
~/vierzählige axis of fourfold symmetry, fourfold axis of symmetry
~/zweizählige axis of twofold symmetry, twofold axis of symmetry
Achsenabschnitt *m (cryst)* intercept, parameter
~/rationaler rational intercept
Achsensymmetrie *f (cryst)* axial symmetry
achsensymmetrisch *(cryst)* axisymmetric
Achsenverhältnis *n* **[/kristallographisches]** [crystallographic] axial ratio, ratio of the intercepts
Achsenwinkel *m (cryst)* axial angle
achtatomig octatomic
Achtergruppe *f* octet
Achterring *m s.* Achtring
Achterschale *f* octet
achtflächig *(cryst)* octahedral, oct.
Achtflächner *m (cryst)* octahedron
Achtring *m* eight-membered ring
achtwertig octavalent
Achtwertigkeit *f* octavalency
acid *s.* azid
Acidoligand *m* anion[ic] ligand
aci-Form *f* aci form *(of nitro compounds)*
Ackerkrume *f* topsoil
Aconitsäure *f* aconitic acid, *propene-1,2,3-tricarboxylic acid
Aconit[um]alkaloid *n* aconitum (aconite) alkaloid
Acoxylierung *f* ac[yl]oxylation
ACP = acyl-carrier protein
Acridan *n* acridan, 9,10-dihydroacridine
Acridin *n (org ch)* acridine
Acridinfarbstoff *m* acridine dye
Acridonfarbstoff *m* acridone dye
Acridonringschluß *m* acridonation
Acriflavin *n* acriflavine, *(pharm also)* flavine
Acrolein *n* acrolein, acraldehyde, *propenal
Acrylaldehyd *m s.* Acrolein
Acrylamid *n* acrylamide, *propenamide
Acrylat *n* acrylate
Acrylatkautschuk *m* acrylate-butadiene rubber, acrylate (acrylic, polyacrylate) rubber
Acryl-Butadien-Kautschuk *m s.* Akrylatkautschuk
Acrylelastomer[e] *n* acrylate (acrylic, polyacrylate) elastomer
Acrylfaser *f* acrylic (polyacrylonitrile) fibre
Acrylfaserstoff *m* acrylic (polyacrylonitrile) fibre
Acrylharz *n* acrylic resin, acrylate (acrylic-acid) resin
Acryllack *m* acrylic lacquer
Acrylnitril *n* acrylonitrile, cyanoethylene, vinyl cyanide, *propene nitrile
Acrylnitril-Butadien-Kautschuk *m* acrylonitrile-butadiene rubber
Acrylnitril-Butadien-Styrol *n* acrylonitrile-butadiene styrene
Acrylnitril-Butadien-Styrol-Copolymer[e] *n* acrylonitrile-butadiene-styrene copolymer
Acrylnitril-Butadien-Styrol-Harz *n* acrylonitrile-butadiene-styrene resin
Acrylnitril-Butadien-Styrol-Kunststoff *m* acrylonitrile-butadiene-styrene plastic
Acrylnitril-Butadien-Styrol-Mischpolymer[e] *n* acrylonitrile-butadiene-styrene copolymer
Acrylnitril-Butadien-Styrol-Polymer[e] *n* acrylonitrile-butadiene-styrene polymer
Acrylonitril *n s.* Acrylnitril
Acryloylchlorid *n* acryloyl chloride
Acrylsäure *f* acrylic acid, *propenoic acid
Acrylsäureamid *n s.* Acrylamid
Acrylsäureester *m* acrylic-acid ester, acrylic ester
Acrylsäuremethylester *m* methyl acrylate
Acrylsäurenitril *n s.* Acrylnitril
ACTH *s.* Hormon/adrenocorticotropes
Actin-Filament *n (bioch)* actin-filament
Actinid[enelement] *n s.* Actinoidenelement
Actinium *n* Ac actinium
Actinium-Emanation *f s.* Radon-219
Actiniumfluorid *n* actinium fluoride
Actiniumhydroxid *n* actinium hydroxide
Actiniumphosphat *n* actinium phosphate
Actiniumreihe *f s.* 1. Actiniumzerfallsreihe; 2. Actinoidenreihe
Actiniumsulfid *n* actinium sulphide
Actiniumzerfallsreihe *f* actinium [decay] series
Actinoid *n s.* Actinoidenelement
Actinoidenelement *n* actinoid [element]

Actinoidengruppe *f s.* Actinoidenreihe
Actinoidenkontraktion *f* actinoid contraction
Actinoidenreihe *f* actinoid group (series)
Actinon *n s.* Radon-219
Actinouran *n* AcU actinouranium *(the uranium isotope of mass 235)*
Actithiazinsäure *f* actithiazic acid, 2-(5-carboxypentyl)-4-thiazolidone
acyclisch acyclic, non-cyclic[al]
Acyl-Alkyl-Diradikal *n* acyl-alkyl biradical
Acyl-Alkyl-Radikalpaar *n* acyl-alkyl radical pair
Acylaminoalkylierung *f* acylaminoalkylation, amidoalkylation
N-**Acylaminocarbonsäure** *f N*-acyl amino carboxylic acid
Acylaminomercurierung *f* acylaminomercuration
Acylanion *n* acyl anion
Acylcarben *n* acyl carbene
Acylglycerin *n*, **Acylglycerol** *n s.* Glycerid
Acylgruppe *f* [carboxylic] acyl group, acyl residue
Acylhalogenid *n* acyl halide *(acid halide of a carboxylic acid)*
acylierbar acylable
acylieren to acylate
Acylierung *f* acylation
Acylierungsmittel *n* acylating agent
Acylium-Ion *n*, **Acylkation** *n* acylium ion, acyl cation
Acyllacton-Umlagerung *f* acyllactone rearrangement
Acyloin *n* acyloin *(a keto alcohol of the general formula R–CO–CH–R'–OH)*
Acyloinaddition *f*, **Acyloinkondensation** *f* acyloin condensation
Acyloinsynthese *f* acyloin synthesis
Acyloinumlagerung *f* acyloin rearrangement
Acyloxylierung *f* ac[yl]oxylation
Acylradikal *n* [free] acyl radical
Acylrest *m s.* Acylgruppe
Acylverschiebung *f*, **Acylwanderung** *f* acyl shift (migration)
Adair-Gleichung *f (bioch)* Adair equation
Adair-Koshland-Némethy-Filmer-Modell *n* induced-fit model, sequential model *(enzyme kinetics)*
Adamantan *n (org ch)* adamantane
adamantoid diamondoid, diamondlike *(ring system)*
Adamin *m (min)* adamite, adamine *(basic zinc arsenate)*
Adamsit *m (min)* adamsite *(a variety of muscovite)*
Adamsit *n* adamsite, 10-chloro-5,10-dihydrophenarsazine
Adams-Katalysator *m* Adams' catalyst *(platinum oxide)*
Adaptorhypothese *f (bioch)* adaptor hypothesis
Addend *m* addend
addieren to add *(an atom or atomic group to a molecule)*
~/sich to add
Addition *f* addition
~/durch Peroxide ausgelöste (initiierte) peroxide-initiated addition, anti-Markovnikov addition
~/elektrophile electrophilic addition
~ im Anti-Markovnikov-Sinn *s.* ~/durch Peroxide ausgelöste
~/ionoide ionic (Markovnikov) addition
~/kationoide *s.* ~/elektrophile
~/oxidative oxidative addition
~/photochemische photoaddition
α-**Addition** *f* α-addition, alpha-addition [reaction]
1,2-Addition *f* 1,2-addition
1,4-Addition *f* 1,4-addition
Additionseffekt *m* additive effect
Additions-Eliminierungs-Mechanismus *m* addition-elimination mechanism
additionsfähig capable of addition
Additionsfähigkeit *f* capability of addition
Additionsmischkristall *m* addition solid solution
Additionsname *n* additive name
Additionspolymer[e] *n* addition polymer
Additionspolymerisation *f* addition polymerization
Additionsprodukt *n* addition product
Additionsreaktion *f* addition reaction
Additionsverbindung *f* addition (additive) compound
Additionsvermögen *n* capability of addition
additiv additive
Additiv *n* additive *(a substance added to another one in small amounts; specif a substance added to mineral-oil products in a quantity from 1 to 10 %)*
~/rostverhinderndes (rostverhütendes) rust-preventing additive
Additivität *f* additivity
Additivitätsprinzip *n* additivity principle *(of the contribution of substituent groups to the properties of the molecule)*
Additivname *m* additive name
Addukt *n* adduct
Adduktkautschuk *m* adduct rubber
Adenin *n* adenine, 6-aminopurine
Adenosindiphosphat *n s.* Adenosindiphosphorsäure
Adenosindiphosphorsäure *f* adenosine diphosphoric acid, adenosine diphosphate, ADP
Adenosinmonophosphat *n s.* Adenosinmonophosphorsäure
Adenosin-5'-monophosphat *n s.* Adenosin-5'-phosphorsäure
Adenosinmonophosphorsäure *f* adenosine monophosphoric acid, adenosine monophosphate, AMP, adenylic acid, AA
Adenosinphosphat *n s.* Adenosinphosphorsäure
Adenosinphosphorsäure *f* adenosinephosphoric acid, adenosine phosphate; *(specif) s.* Adenosinmonophosphorsäure
Adenosin-5'-phosphorsäure *f* adenosine 5'-phosphoric acid, adenosine 5'-monophosphate, AMP, muscle adenylic acid

Adenosinpyrophosphat *n s.* Adenosindiphosphorsäure
Adenosinpyrophosphorsäure *f s.* Adenosindiphosphorsäure
Adenosintriphosphat *n s.* Adenosintriphosphorsäure
Adenosintriphosphatase *f* adenosine triphosphatase
Adenosintriphosphorsäure *f* adenosine triphosphoric acid, adenosine triphosphate, ATP
Adenylat-Cyclase *f (bioch)* adenylate cyclase
Adenylbernsteinsäure *f* adenylosuccinic acid
adenylieren to adenylate
Adenylierung *f* adenylation
Adenylierungsmittel *n* adenylating agent
Adenylosuccinat *n* adenylosuccinate
Adenylpyrophosphat *n s.* Adenosintriphosphorsäure
Adenylpyrophosphorsäure *f s.* Adenosintriphosphorsäure
Adenylsäure *f s.* Adenosinmonophosphorsäure
adenylylieren *(bioch)* to adenylylate
Adenylylierung *f (bioch)* adenylylation
Ader *f (geol)* lode, vein
~/anstehende outcrop
Adermin *n* adermin[e], 3-hydroxy-4,5-di-(hydroxymethyl)-2-methylpyridine *(vitamin B_6)*
ADH *s.* Hormon/antidiuretisches
Adhärend *m* adherend *(a body to be attached to another one by an adhesive)*
Adhärens *n* adhesive [agent, substance], adhesion agent
adhärieren to adhere
adhärierend adherent, adhesive
Adhäsion *f* adhesion, adherence
Adhäsionsarbeit *f* adhesional work, work of adhesion
Adhäsionsbeschleuniger *m* adhesion promoter
Adhäsionsenergie *f* adhesion energy
adhäsionsfähig adherent, adhesive
Adhäsionsfähigkeit *f s.* Adhäsionsvermögen
adhäsionsfeindlich abhesive
Adhäsionsfestigkeit *f* adhesive (adhesion) strength
Adhäsionskraft *f* adhesive force
Adhäsionsprüfer *m* adhesion tester
Adhäsionsspannung *f* adhesive tension (stress)
Adhäsionsvermögen *n* adhesiveness, adhesion (adhesive) power, adherence
adhäsiv adhesive, adherent
Adiabasie *f* adiabaticity
adiabat adiabatic
Adiabate *f* adiabat[ic], adiabatic curve (line)
adiabatisch adiabatic
adiatherman atherm[an]ous
Adion *n* adion *(an ion adsorbed on a surface)*
Adipamid *n* adipamide
Adipat *n* adipate *(salt or ester of adipic acid)*
Adipinsäure *f* adipic acid, *hexanedioic acid
Adipinsäurediamid *n* adipamide
Adipinsäuredinitril *n*, **Adiponitril** *n* adiponitrile
Adjuvans *n (pharm)* adjuvant
Adkins-Katalysator *m* Adkins' catalyst *(containing copper and chromium)*
Admiralitätskohle *f* admiralty steam coal
Admiralitätslegierung *f* admiralty metal (brass) *(a brass containing ~ 1 % Sn)*
Admittanz *f (anal)* admittance
Admittanzmessung *f***/nichtfaradaysche** *(anal)* measurement of non-faradaic admittance
ADP *s.* Adenosindiphosphorsäure
Adrenalin *n* adrenaline, *1-(3,4-dihydroxyphenyl)-2-methylaminoethanol
Adrenocorticotropin *n* adrenocorticotropic hormone, ACTH, corticotropin
Adsorbat *n* adsorbed material (substance), adsorbate; adsorption complex, adsorbent-adsorbate complex (system), adsorbate
Adsorbend *m* material to be adsorbed
Adsorbens *n* adsorbent [material], adsorbing agent (material, substance)
Adsorbensschicht *f* adsorbent bed
Adsorber *m* 1. adsorber *(apparatus)*; 2. *s.* Adsorbens
Adsorberharz *n (hyd)* adsorption resin, resin[ous] adsorbent
adsorbierbar adsorbable
Adsorbierbarkeit *f* adsorbability
adsorbieren to adsorb
~/chemisch to chemisorb
~/physikalisch to adsorb physically
Adsorpt *n* adsorbed material (substance), adsorbate
Adsorption *f* adsorption
~/aktivierte *s.* ~/chemische
~ an Aktivkohle *(hyd)* adsorption on activated carbon, [activated-]carbon adsorption
~/apolare apolar (non-polar) adsorption
~/bevorzugte *s.* ~/selektive
~/biospezifische *(anal)* affinity chromatography
~/chemische chemical (activated) adsorption, chemisorption, chemosorption
~/negative negative adsorption
~/physikalische physical (van der Waals) adsorption, physisorption
~/polare polar adsorption
~/positive positive adsorption
~/reversible reversible adsorption
~/selektive selective (preferential) adsorption
~/van-der-Waalssche *s.* ~/physikalische
Adsorptionsaffinität *f* adsorption affinity
Adsorptionsanalyse *f* adsorption analysis
~/chromatographische *s.* Adsorptionschromatographie
~/radiometrische radiometric adsorption analysis
Adsorptionsapparat *m* adsorber
Adsorptionschromatographie *f* adsorption chromatography, chromatographic adsorption analysis

adsorptionschromatographisch by adsorption chromatography
Adsorptionseigenschaften *fpl* adsorptive (adsorption) properties
Adsorptionsenergie *f* adsorption energy (heat)
Adsorptionserscheinung *f* adsorption phenomenon
adsorptionsfähig adsorbent, adsorptive, adsorbing
Adsorptionsfähigkeit *f* adsorption ability, adsorptive capacity, adsorptiveness
Adsorptionsfilm *m* adsorbed film
Adsorptionsfilter *n* adsorption filter
Adsorptionsfiltration *f* adsorption filtration
Adsorptionsgesetz *n* law of adsorption, adsorption law
~/Gibbssches Gibbs adsorption law
Adsorptionsgleichgewicht *n* adsorption equilibrium
Adsorptionsgleichung *f* adsorption equation
~/Gibbssche Gibbs adsorption equation
Adsorptionsharz *n s.* Adsorberharz
Adsorptionsindikator *m* adsorption indicator
Adsorptionsisostere *f* adsorption isostere
Adsorptionsisotherme *f* adsorption isotherm
~/Freundlichsche Freundlich [adsorption] isotherm
~/Gibbssche Gibbs [adsorption] isotherm
~/Langmuirsche Langmuir [adsorption] isotherm
~ nach Brunauer, Emmett und Teller BET isotherm
Adsorptionsklärmittel *n* sweetener *(for dry cleaning)*
Adsorptionskolonne *f* adsorption (adsorbing, adsorbent) column
Adsorptionskraft *f* force of adsorption, adsorptive force
Adsorptionskurve *f* adsorption curve
Adsorptionsmedium *n* adsorptive (adsorption) medium
Adsorptionsmittel *n* adsorbent [material], adsorbing agent (material, substance); sweetener *(for dry-cleaning)*
Adsorptionsmittelschicht *f* adsorbent bed
Adsorptionspotential *n* adsorption potential
Adsorptionsquellung *f* adsorption swelling
Adsorptionssäule *f* adsorption (adsorbing, adsorbent) column
Adsorptionsschicht *f* adsorbed layer
~/monomolekulare unimolecular [adsorbed] layer, monomolecular layer, monolayer
~/multimolekulare multimolecular [adsorbed] layer, multilayer
Adsorptionsschicht-Gaschromatographie *f* gas-liquid-solid chromatography, GLSC
Adsorptionsstrom *m* adsorption current
Adsorptionstitration *f* **nach Fajans** Fajans [adsorption indicator] method *(argentometry)*
Adsorptionsturm *m* adsorption tower
Adsorptionsverbindung *f* adsorption compound
Adsorptionsverfahren *n* adsorption process
Adsorptionsvermögen *n* adsorption ability, adsorptive capacity, adsorptiveness
Adsorptionsvorgang *m* adsorption process
Adsorptionswaage *f* adsorption balance
Adsorptionswärme *f* heat of adsorption
~/differentiale (differentielle) differential heat of adsorption
~/integrale integral heat of adsorption
Adsorptionszentrum *n* adsorption centre (site)
Adsorptionszone *f* adsorption zone (wave)
adsorptiv *s.* adsorptionsfähig
Adsorptiv *n* adsorptive, material (substance) to be adsorbed
Adsorptivkraft *f* force of adsorption, adsorptive force
Adstringens *n (pharm)* astringent, styptic
adstringent *s.* adstringierend
Adstringenz *f* astringency, stypticity
adstringierend astringent, styptic
ÄDTE *s.* Ethylendiamintetraessigsäure
Adular *m (min)* adular[ia] *(a variety of orthoclase)*
Advektion *f* advection *(horizontal motion of air)*
AeDTE *s.* Ethylendiamintetraessigsäure
aerob *(biol)* aerobic, oxybiotic
Aerobier *m*, **Aerobiont** *m (biol)* aerobe
Aerobiose *f (biol)* aerobiosis, oxybiosis
Aerofall-Mühle *f* Aerofall mill *(an autogenous mill)*
Aerogel *n* aerogel
Aeroklassieren *n* air classifying (sizing), air separation (sweeping, elutriation), pneumatic classification
aerolisieren *s.* aerosolieren
Aeromultizyklon *m* multitube cyclone separator
aerophil air-avid
Aerosol *n* aerosol
Aerosolbombe *f (agric)* aerosol bomb (projector)
Aerosoldose *f s.* Aerosolsprühdose
Aerosolfarbe *f* aerosol paint
aerosolieren to aerosolize, to nebulize
Aerosol[is]ierung *f* aerosolization
Aerosolnebel *m* aerosol mist
Aerosolspray *m* aerosol spray
Aerosolsprühdose *f* aerosol spray can, aerosol dispenser (bomb)
Aerosolsprühgerät *n (agric)* aerosol bomb (projector)
Aerosoltreibmittel *n* aerosol propellant
Aerosolzerstäuber *m s.* 1. Aerosolsprühgerät; 2. Aerosolsprühdose
Aerozyklon *m* cyclone air separator
AES *s.* 1. Auger-Elektronenspektroskopie; 2. Atomemissionsspektroskopie
Aeschynit *m* aeschynite *(a mineral containing cerium, titanium, and thorium)*
Affenschaukel *f (glass)* birdcage, bird swing *(a glass thread spanning the inside of a bottle)*
Affinade *f* affinated (affination) sugar
Affination *f* affination *(treatment of sucrose crystals to free them from residual molasses)*

Affinationssirup *m (sugar)* affination syrup
Affinität *f* affinity
~/chemische chemical affinity
~ zu Schwefel sulphur affinity, affinity for sulphur
~ zu Wasser water affinity
~ zur Faser affinity to the fibre
Affinitätschromatographie *f* affinity chromatography
affinitätschromatographisch by affinity chromatography
Affinitätskonstante *f s.* Dissoziationskonstante
Affinitätskurve *f* affinity curve
Affinitätsmarkierung *f* affinity label[l]ing *(in enzyme reactions)*
AFID = Alkaliflammenionisationsdetektor
AFS *s.* Atomfluoreszenzspektrometrie
Afterkristall *m* pseudomorph
A-Füllmasse *f (sugar)* A massecuite
Agalmatolith *m (min)* agalmatolite *(aluminium dihydroxide tetrasilicate)*
Agar[-Agar] *m(n)* agar[-agar], agar gel, Japan agar (isinglass), Chinese gelatin
Agargel *n s.* Agar
Agargel-Elektrophorese *f (anal)* agar gel electrophoresis
Agarizin *n s.* Agarizinsäure
Agarizinsäure *f* agaric acid
Agarnährboden *m* nutrient agar
Agar[nähr]platte *f* [nutrient] agar plate
Agarröhrchenmethode *f* agar-tube method
Agathendisäure *f* agathene dicarboxylic acid, agathic acid
Agathsäure *f s.* Agathendisäure
Agens *n* agent
~/aktives active agent
~/angreifendes attacking agent
~/chemisches (chemisch wirksames) chemical agent
~/elektrophiles electrophilic agent, electrophile
~/mutagenes (mutationsauslösendes) mutagenic agent, mutagen
~/nitrierendes nitrating agent
~/nitrosierendes nitrosating agent
~/nucleophiles nucleophilic agent, nucleophile
~/sulfonierendes sulphonating agent
~/wirksames active agent
Agglomerat *n* agglomerate
Agglomeration *f* agglomeration
Agglomerationsneigung *f* tendency to agglomerate
agglomerieren to agglomerate
Agglomerierung *f* agglomeration
Agglugen *n s.* Agglutinogen
Agglutinating-Index *m (coal)* agglutinating value
Agglutination *f* agglutination
agglutinieren to agglutinate
agglutinierend agglutinant
Agglutinogen *n* agglutinogen
Aggregat *n* aggregate
~/feines fine[-grained] aggregate
~/grobes coarse aggregate
~/körniges granular aggregate
~/molekulares molecular (molecule) aggregate
~/sekundäres *(coll)* secondary aggregate
Aggregatbildner *m* aggregating agent
Aggregatbildung *f* aggregate formation
Aggregation *f* aggregation
~/molekulare molecular aggregation
Aggregationsgeschwindigkeit *f* rate of aggregation
Aggregationsneigung *f* tendency to aggregate, tendency towards aggregation
Aggregationsvorgang *m* aggregation process
Aggregatstabilität *f* aggregate stability
Aggregatzustand *m* state of aggregation
~/nematischer nematic state *(of liquid crystals)*
~/smektischer smectic state *(of liquid crystals)*
Aggregatzustandsänderung *f* change of state
aggregieren to aggregate
~/sich to aggregate
Aggregierung *f* aggregation
aggressiv aggressive, offensive *(chemicals)*
Aggressivität *f* aggressivity, aggressiveness, offensiveness *(of chemicals)*
Ägirin *m (min)* aegirine *(iron(III) potassium disilicate)*
A-Glas *n* A glass, glass A *(a fibre glass of high alkali content)*
Aglucon *n* aglucon[e] *(non-sugar portion of a glucoside)*
Aglykon *n* aglycon[e] *(non-sugar portion of a glycoside)*
Agon *n* agon, prosthetic (active) group, coenzyme
Agonist *m (pharm)* agonist *(any of a class of remedies which alter cell properties after joining with a receptor)*
Agrarchemie *f* agrochemistry, agricultural chemistry
Agrarchemiker *m* agricultural chemist
Agricolit *m (min)* agricolite, eulytite, eulytine *(bismuth orthosilicate)*
Agrikulturchemie *f s.* Agrarchemie
Agrikulturchemiker *m s.* Agrarchemiker
Agrochemie *f s.* Agrarchemie
Agrochemikalie *f* agricultural chemical, agrochemical
Aguilarit *m (min)* aguilarite *(silver sulphide)*
A-Harz *n* A-stage (one-stage) resin, resol
AHG *s.* Globulin [A]/antihämophiles
Ähnlichkeit *f* similarity; *(phys ch)* similitude *(collectively for geometrical, dynamical and kinematic similarity)*
Ähnlichkeitstheorie *f (tech)* model theory
Ähnlichkeitsverbundwirkung *f (tox)* similar joint action
A-Horizont *m (soil)* A-horizon, eluvial horizon, topsoil
Ahornsirup *m* maple syrup
Ahornsirupkrankheit *f (med)* maple-syrup urine disease *(caused by a lack of enzyme)*

Ahornzucker *m* maple sugar
Ahrens-Verfahren *n* Ahrens process *(gas manufacture)*
AH-Salz *n* 6,6 salt, hexamethylenediamine salt of adipic acid, hexamethylenediamine adipate
AIBN *s.* Azobisisobutyronitril
AICAR = 5(4)-Aminoimidazol-4(5)-carboxamidribotid
Aikinit *m (min)* aikinite *(a complex sulphide of lead, copper, and bismuth)*
Airless-Spritzen *n (coat)* airless spraying
Airlift *m* 1. air lift, mammoth (air-lift) pump; 2. *(petrol)* air lift, air-lift pump, riser *(catalyst-handling system in catalytic cracking)*
Airliftfermenter *m s.* Airliftreaktor
Airliftförderung *f* air lifting
Airliftkracken *n (petrol)* air-lift catalytic cracking, riser cracking
Airliftkrackverfahren *n (petrol)* air-lift process
Airliftreaktor *m (biot)* air-lift bioreactor (fermenter)
Airliftsystem *n* air-lift system
Air-slip-Verfahren *n (plast)* air-slip forming
Aitken-Partikel *n*, **Aitken-Teilchen** *n* Aitken particle *(aerosol particle below 0.1 µm in diameter)*
Ajax-Northrup-Ofen *m* Ajax-Northrup [coreless induction] furnace, Ajax-Northrup high-frequency induction furnace
Ajax-Wyatt-[Niederfrequenz-]Induktionsofen *m s.* Ajax-Wyatt-Ofen
Ajax-Wyatt-Ofen *m* Ajax-Wyatt furnace
Ajmalin *n* ajmaline *(a rauwolfia alkaloid)*
Ajowanöl *n* ajowan oil *(essential oil from Carum copticum (L.) Benth. et Hook.)*
AK *s.* Kieselsäure/aktivierte
Akanthit *m (min)* acanthite *(silver sulphide)*
akarizid acaricidal, miticidal
Akarizid *n* acaricide, miticide
Akaroidgummi *n s.* Akaroidharz
Akaroidharz *n* acaroid resin, [gum] accroides, yacca gum *(from Xanthorrhoea specc.)*
A-Kation *n* class (a) metal ion
Akaziengummi *n* acacia (Arabic) gum, gum arabic *(from Acacia specc., esp from A. senegal (L.) Willd.)*
Akazienrinde *f (tann)* stick (wattle) bark
Akkommodationskoeffizient *m* accommodation coefficient *(chemisorption)*
Akkretion *f* accretion, enlargement *(of aerosols)*
Akku *m s.* Akkumulator
Akkumulation *f* accumulation
Akkumulator *m* accumulator, [storage] battery
~/hydraulischer hydraulic accumulator
Akkumulator[en]säure *f* battery (electrolyte) acid
Akkumulatorzelle *f* storage cell
Akmit *m (min)* acmite *(iron(III) sodium metasilicate)*
AKNF-Modell *n (Adair-Koshland-Némethy-Filmer)* induced-fit model, sequential model *(enzyme kinetics)*
A-Kohle *f* activated carbon *(for compounds s.* Aktivkohle*)*
Akryl... *s.* Acryl...
aktinisch *(phot)* actinic
Aktinolith *m (min)* actinolite *(an inosilicate)*
Aktinometer *n***/chemisches** chemical actinometer *(for determining photons)*
Aktinometrie *f* actinometry *(determination of photons)*
Aktionskonstante *f* frequency factor, [Arrhenius] pre-exponential factor, Arrhenius factor, A factor *(kinetics)*
aktiv active
~/elektrochemisch electroactive
~/lichtelektrisch photoactive
~/nicht *s.* aktivitätsfrei
~/optisch optically active
Aktivanode *f* sacrificial (galvanic, expendable) anode
Aktivator *m* activator, activating agent (substance); promoter, promoting agent *(catalysis)*; *(rubber)* [polymerization] initiator, initiating agent, reaction catalyst; *(met)* energizer *(additive to a carburizer)*
~ für den Beschleuniger *(rubber)* activator of cure (vulcanization), accelerator activator
Aktivatoreffekt *m (tox)* activation
Aktivatorterm *m* activator term (level)
Aktivchlor *n (pap)* available (active) chlorine
Aktivchlorbedarf *m (pap)* available chlorine demand
Aktivchlorgehalt *m (pap)* available chlorine content
Aktiverde *f* active (activated) earth
Aktivgut *n s.* Siebgrobes
aktivierbar activable, capable of being activated
aktivieren to activate; to energize *(molecules)*; *(rubber)* to boost; to radioactivate
Aktivierung *f* activation; energization *(of molecules)*; *(rubber)* boosting; radioactivation
~/photochemische photochemical activation *(of a reaction)*
~/thermische thermal activation *(of a reaction)*
Aktivierungsanalyse *f* activation analysis
~ mit Hilfe geladener Teilchen charged-particle activation analysis, CPAA
~/radiochemische radioactivation analysis
Aktivierungsenergie *f* activation energy
~/Arrheniussche Arrhenius energy of activation, Arrhenius activation energy
Aktivierungsenthalpie *f* activation enthalpy, enthalpy of activation
~/freie Gibbs [free] energy of activation, free energy of activation, activation Gibbs function
Aktivierungsentropie *f* activation entropy
Aktivierungskaskade *f (bioch)* activation cascade *(for phosphorylase)*
Aktivierungsmittel *n* activating agent (substance), activator; *(met)* energizer *(additive to a carburizer)*
Aktivierungsquerschnitt *m* activation cross section

Aktivierungsstadium *n* initiation stage
Aktivierungsvolumen *n* activation volume
Aktivierungswärme *f* heat of activation
Aktivierungszusatz *m (met)* energizer *(additive to a carburizer)*
Aktivität *f* 1. activity *(of a catalyst)*; 2. activity *(corrected mole fraction of a substance in a mixed phase)*; 3. activity, disintegration rate *(of a radioactive substance)*
~ **1** *(phys ch)* unit activity
~/absolute absolute activity
~/biologische biological activity
~/herbizide herbicidal activity
~/katalytische catalytic activity
~/molare molar activity *(enzyme kinetics)*
~/optische optical activity (rotatory power), rotary polarization
~/relative relative activity
~/spezifische specific activity *(enzyme kinetics)*
Aktivitätsanalyse *f s.* Aktivierungsanalyse
Aktivitätsfaktor *m s.* Aktivitätskoeffizient
Aktivitätsförderung *f (bioch)* feed-forward activation (regulation), positive feedback
aktivitätsfrei *(nucl)* cold
Aktivitätskoeffizient *m* activity coefficient (factor)
~/individueller individual activity coefficient
~/kinetischer kinetic activity coefficient
~/mittlerer medium (mean, transfer) activity coefficient
~/praktischer practical activity coefficient
~/rationaler (rationeller) rational activity coefficient
Aktivitätsverhältnis *n* activity ratio
Aktivitätsverlust *m* activity loss, loss in activity, *(if complete:)* loss of activity
Aktivkohle *f* activated carbon
~/gekörnte granulated (granular) activated carbon, GAC, granular carbon, GC
~/pulverförmige powdered activated carbon
Aktivkohleadsorber *m* activated carbon adsorber
Aktivkohleadsorption *f* activated carbon adsorption, adsorption on activated carbon
Aktivkohleanlage *f (petrol)* charcoal plant
Aktivkohle-Behandlung *f* activated-carbon treatment, *(hyd also)* activated-carbon purification
Aktivkohlebett *n (hyd)* activated-carbon bed, carbon [filter] bed
Aktivkohlefilter *n* [activated-]carbon filter
Aktivkohlefiltration *f* [activated-]carbon filtration, CF, filtration with activated carbon
Aktivkohlefüllung *f (hyd)* carbon loading
Aktivkohlepulver *n* powdered activated carbon
Aktivkohleregenerierofen *m* carbon regeneration furnace
Aktivkohletrübe *f (hyd)* water-carbon slurry
Aktivkohleturm *m (biot)* activated-carbon tower
Aktivruß *m* active (reinforcing) black
Aktivsauerstoff *m* active (available) oxygen *(as in bleaching)*
Aktivsauerstoffgehalt *m* active oxygen content *(as of a bleaching agent)*
Aktivschlamm *m s.* Belebtschlamm
Aktivstelle *f* active site (centre)
Aktivstoff *m*, **Aktivsubstanz** *f* active substance (principle, material)
Aktivtonerde *f* activated alumina
Aktivzentrum *n s.* Aktivstelle
Aktor *m* actor *(in induced reactions)*
Akzelerator *m (plast)* accelerator
Akzent *m (nomencl)* prime *(with locants)*
Akzeptor *m* acceptor; electron acceptor
~ **des Elektronenpaares** electron-pair acceptor
Akzeptoreigenschaften *fpl* acceptor properties (ability, power)
Akzeptorniveau *n (phys ch)* acceptor level
Akzeptorort *m (bioch)* acceptor site, A site, entry (recognition, decoding, aminoacyl) site, amino-acyl-tRNA site
Akzeptor-RNA *f*, **Akzeptor-RNS** *f s.* Transfer-Ribonucleinsäure
Akzeptorstelle *f s.* Akzeptorort
Akzeptorterm *m (phys ch)* acceptor level
Akzeptorverbindung *f* acceptor compound
Akzeptorverhalten *n* acceptor behaviour
Akzessibilität *f* accessibility
Akzessorien *npl* accessory minerals (components, constituents)
Akzidenzfarbe *f* job-press ink
AL *s.* Alginatfaserstoff
Alabamin *n s.* Astat
Alabandin *m (min)* alabandite, manganblende *(manganese(II) sulphide)*
Alabaster *m (min)* alabaster *(calcium sulphate 2-water)*
Alabasterglas *n* alabaster glass
Alabasterkarton *m* alabaster [card]board
Alan *n* alane, aluminium hydride
Alanat *n* $M^I[AlH_4]$ tetrahydridoaluminate, alanate *(a complex hydride)*
Alanin *n* alanine, 2-aminopropionic acid
Alantcampher *m* alant camphor, alantolactone, helenin
Alarmgrenze *f* danger point *(waste-water treatment)*
Alarmvorrichtung *f* alarm
ALAT = L-Alanin-2-ketoglutarat-Aminotransferase
Alaun *m* $M^IM^{III}(SO_4)_2 \cdot 12\ H_2O$ alum, *(specif)* $KAl(SO_4)_2 \cdot 12\ H_2O$ potassium (potash) alum; *(pap)* alum *(loosely for aluminium sulphate and several alums proper)*
~/gebrannter dried (burnt, exsiccated) alum
alaungar alum-tanned, alum-dressed, alumed
Alaungerbung *f* alum tannage, tawing
alaunhaltig containing alum, aluminous
Alaunleder *n* alum leather
Alaunlösung *f (pap)* alum liquor *(aluminium sulphate solution)*
Alaunmehl *n* alum flour (meal) *(fine crystalline potash alum)*

Alaunschiefer *m* alum schist (shale, slate)
Alaunspat *m s.* Alunit
Albany-Schlicker *m (ceram)* Albany slip *(prepared from Albany clay)*
Albany-Ton *m (ceram)* Albany clay
Albedo *f* albedo *(reflected fraction of incident sunlight)*
Albert-Effekt *m (phot)* Albert reversal
Albertit *m* albertite *(a bituminous mineral)*
Albit *m (min)* albite *(sodium aluminosilicate)*
Albumin *n* albumin, *(sometimes)* albumen *(one of a class of simple proteins)*
Albuminleim *m* blood glue (adhesive)
Albuminoid *n* albuminoid
Albuminsol *n* albumin sol
Albuminverfahren *n (phot)* albumin process
Albumose *f* albumose *(a protein derivative)*
Albumosesilber *n (pharm)* silver protein
$AlCl_3$-KW-Komplex *m*/**inaktiver** *s.* Aluminiumchlorid-Kohlenwasserstoff-Komplex/inaktiver
Aldarsäure *f (org ch)* aldaric acid
Aldazin *n (org ch)* aldazine
Aldehyd *m* aldehyde
~/aliphatischer aliphatic aldehyde, alkanal
~ C12[L] *dodecanal, aldehyde C-12 [lauric]
Aldehydaminbeschleuniger *m (rubber)* aldehyde-amine accelerator
Aldehydcarbonsäure *f s.* Aldehydsäure
Aldehyddehydrogenase *f* aldehyde dehydrogenase
Aldehyddimerisation *f s.* Aldolkondensation
aldehydfrei aldehyde-free
Aldehydgerbung *f* aldehyde tannage
Aldehydgruppe *f* –CHO aldehyde (aldehydic) group
aldehydig aldehydic
Aldehydigkeit *f s.* Aldehydranzigkeit
Aldehyd-Keton-Umlagerung *f* aldehyde-ketone-rearrangement
Aldehydkondensation *f* aldehyde condensation
Aldehydranzigkeit *f* rancidity with formation of aldehydes
Aldehydreagens *n*/**Feders** Feder solution for aldehydes
Aldehydsäure *f* aldehydic acid
Aldehydsynthese *f*/**Gattermannsche** Gattermann aldehyde synthesis
Aldehydzucker *m* aldehyde sugar
Aldimin *n* aldimine
Aldohexonsäure *f* aldonic (glyconic) acid *(any of several acids derived from an aldose; general formula $HOCH_2(CHOH)_4COOH$)*
Aldohexose *f* aldohexose *(a hexose containing an aldehyde group)*
Aldoketen *n* RCH=C=O aldoketene
Aldol *n* aldol *(any of a class of 3-hydroxyaldehydes), (specif)* $CH_3CH(OH)CH_2CHO$ acetaldol, aldol, 3-hydroxybutyraldehyde
Aldoladdition *f s.* Aldolkondensation
Aldolase *f* aldolase
Aldolisation *f*, **Aldolisierung** *f s.* Aldolkondensation
Aldolkondensation *f* aldol condensation, aldolization
~/gekreuzte crossed aldol condensation
Aldonsäure *f* $HOCH_2(CHOH)_nCOOH$ aldonic acid *(any of a class of acids derived from aldoses)*
Aldose *f* aldose *(any of a class of sugars containing one –CHO group per molecule)*
Aldosteron *n* aldosterone *(a steroid hormone)*
Aldoxim *n* R–CH=NOH aldoxime
Aleuritinsäure *f* aleuritic acid, *9,10,16-trihydroxyhexadecanoic acid
Aleuron *n* aleurone *(reserve protein material)*
Aleuronkörner *npl* aleurone grains
Aleuronschicht *f* aleurone layer
Alexandrit *m (min)* alexandrite *(beryllium aluminate)*
Alfa-Butter *f* Alfa butter *(made by the Alfa process)*
Alfa-Butterung *f s.* Alfa-Verfahren
Alfapapier *n* esparto paper
Alfa-Verfahren *n* Alfa process *(of butter manufacture)*
Alfin-Katalysator *m (rubber)* Alfin catalyst
Alfin-Kautschuk *m* Alfin [catalyzed] polymer
Alfin-Polymerisation *f (rubber)* Alfin [catalyzed] polymerization
Algarotpulver *n (pharm)* algaroth [powder] *(an antimony oxide chloride, essentially $2\ SbOCl \cdot Sb_2O_3$)*
Algenbekämpfungsmittel *n* algaecide, algicide
Algenrohmasse *f*, **Algenrohsubstanz** *f (biot)* algal biomass
Algensäure *f s.* Alginsäure
Algensuspension *f (biot)* algal suspension
Algentrockenmasse *f (biot)* algal dry weight
Algenzucht *f (biot)* cultivation of algae
~ in Freilandkultur (offenen Anlagen) outdoor cultivation of algae
Alginat *n* alginate *(salt or ester of alginic acid)*
Alginatcreme *f (pharm)* alginate cream
Alginatfaden *m (text)* alginate thread
Alginatfaser *f (text)* alginate fibre
Alginatfaserstoff *m (text)* alginate fibre
Alginatseide *f (text)* alginate yarn
Alginit *m* alginite *(a kind of coal)*
Alginsäure *f* alginic acid *(a polymer of D-mannuronic acid)*
Algizid *n* algicide
Alicyclen *pl* alicyclics, alicyclic compounds
alicyclisch alicyclic, cycloaliphatic
alimentär *(bioch, med)* alimentary
Aliphaten *pl* aliphatics, aliphatic compounds
Aliphatenchemie *f* aliphatic chemistry
aliphatisch aliphatic
aliquot *(anal)* aliquot
aliquotieren *(anal)* to aliquot
Alit *m* alite *(a constituent of portland cement clinker)*

alitieren to aluminize *(to make metals oxidation-resistant by heating them with powdered aluminium)*
Alizarin *n* alizarin
Alizarinblau *n* alizarin blue
Alizarinbordeaux *n* alizarin bordeaux *(usually equalling quinalizarin, mordant violet 26)*
Alizarinbrillantgrün *n* alizarin cyanine green, acid green 25
Alizarincyanin *n* alizarin cyanine
Alizarincyaningrün *n* alizarin cyanine green
Alizarinfarbstoff *m* alizarin dye
Alizaringelb *n* alizarin yellow
Alizarinindig[o]blau *n* alizarin indigo blue
Alizarinorange *n* alizarin orange
Alizarinprimverosid *n* alizarin primveroside, ruberythric acid
Alizarinprobe *f (food)* alizarin test
Alizarinrot *n* alizarin red
Alizarinsaphirol *n* **B** alizarin saphirol B, acid blue 45
Alizarinviolett *n* alizarin violet
Alizarolprobe *f (food)* alizarol test *(combined alizarin and alcohol test)*
Alk. *s.* Alkohol
Alkadiin *n (org ch)* alkadiyne
alkal. *s.* alkalisch
Alkali *n* alkali
~/aktives (effektives) *(pap)* active (effective) alkali *($NaOH + Na_2S$, expressed as Na_2O)*
~/eingestelltes (normales, standardisiertes) standard alkali
~/wirksames *s.* ~/aktives
Alkaliacetylid *n* alkali acetylide (carbide)
alkaliähnlich alkali-like
Alkalialkoholat *n* alkali alkoxide (alcoholate)
alkaliarm poor in alkali, low-alkali
Alkaliaufwand *m (pap)* amount of alkali required
Alkalibedarf *m (pap)* amount of alkali required
Alkalibehandlung *f (pap)* alkali [extraction] stage, caustic [extraction] stage, alkaline-washing stage
~ bei hoher Stoffdichte/zweite high-density second caustic extraction
alkalibeständig resistant to alkali[es], alkali-stable, alkali-resistant, alkali-resisting, alkali-proof
~/nicht alkali-unstable, alkali-labile
Alkalibeständigkeit *f* alkali resistance, resistance (stability) to alkali[es]
alkalibildend alkaligenous
Alkalibindemittel *n* alkali-binding agent
Alkaliblau *n* alkali blue, Nicholson blue
Alkaliboden *m* alkali soil, solonetz
Alkalicarbid *n* alkali metal carbide (acetylide)
Alkalicarbonat *n* alkali carbonate
Alkalicellulose *f* alkali cellulose, *(Am)* soda cellulose
~/zerfaserte crumbs
Alkalichelat *n* alkali chelate
Alkalichloridelektrolyse *f* chloralkali electrolysis
Alkalicyanid *n* alkali cyanide
alkaliecht *(dye)* alkali-fast, fast to alkali[es]
alkaliempfindlich alkali-sensitive, sensitive to alkalies
Alkaliempfindlichkeit *f* alkali sensitivity, sensitivity to alkalies
Alkalien *npl* alkalies, alkalis
Alkalien... *s.* Alkali...
Alkaliextraktion *f s.* Alkalibehandlung
Alkalifehler *m* alkali[ne] error *(of a glass electrode)*
Alkalifeldspat *m* alkali feldspar
alkalifest *s.* alkalibeständig
Alkaligehalt *m* alkali content
Alkaligestein *n* alkali rock
Alkaliglas *n* alkali glass
Alkaliglasur *f (ceram)* alkaline glaze
Alkaligranit *m* alkali granite
Alkalihalogenid *n* alkali halide (halogenide)
alkalihaltig alkali-containing
Alkalihydroxid *n* alkali hydroxide
Alkalikalkgestein *n* calc-alkali rock
Alkalikochung *f (pap)* alkaline cook
alkalilabil *s.* alkaliunbeständig
Alkalilauge *f* lye
Alkalilignin *n (pap)* alkali lignin
alkalilöslich alkali-soluble, soluble in alkali[es]
Alkalimenge *f (pap)* quantity of caustic
Alkalimetall *n* alkali[ne] metal
Alkalimetallcarbonat *n* alkali carbonate
Alkalimetallhalogenid *n* alkali halide (halogenide)
Alkalimetallhydroxid *n* alkali hydroxide
Alkalimetalloxid *n* alkali oxide
Alkalimetallpolymer[e] *n*, **Alkalimetallpolymerisat** *n (rubber)* alkali metal polymer
Alkalimetallpolymerisation *f (rubber)* alkali-metal [catalyzed] polymerization
Alkalimeter *n* alkalimeter *(for measuring the proportion of alkali in a solution)*
Alkalimetrie *f* alkalimetry
alkalimetrisch alkalimetric
Alkalinität *f* alkalinity *(referring to hydrogen carbonates dissolved in water)*
Alkaliraffination *f (food)* alkali refining *(of edible oils)*
Alkaliregenerat *n (rubber)* alkali reclaim, alkaline type of reclaim
Alkalireserve *f (med)* alkali reserve
Alkalirückgewinnung *f (pap)* alkali (soda) recovery
Alkalisalz *n* alkali[-metal] salt
alkalisch alkaline, basic • ~ **machen** to alkalify, to alkali[ni]ze, to make alkaline (basic) • ~ **reagieren** to react alkaline • ~ **stellen** *s.* ~ machen • ~ **werden** to alkalify
~ aufgeschlossen (gekocht) *(pap)* alkaline-cooked
~/schwach mildly alkaline, alkalescent, subalkaline
~/stark highly alkaline
Alkalischmachen *n* alkali[ni]zation
Alkalischmelze *f* 1. fusion with alkali, alkali (caustic) fusion; 2. alkali (caustic) fusion, molten alkali [bath]

alkalisieren to alkalify, to alkali[ni]ze, to make alkaline (basic)
Alkalisierung *f* alkali[ni]zation; *(pap)* alkaline purification, alkali refining
Alkalisierungsturm *m (pap)* caustic (alkali extraction) tower *(multistage bleaching)*
Alkalisilicat *n* alkali silicate
Alkalispaltung *f* alkali cleavage
alkalistabil *s.* alkalibeständig
Alkalität *f* alkalinity, basicity, *(quantitatively also)* basic strength
Alkaliturm *m (pap)* 1. reaction tower *(pulping with chlorine)*; 2. *s.* Alkalisierungsturm
alkaliunbeständig alkali-unstable, alkali-labile
alkaliunlöslich alkali-insoluble, insoluble in alkali[es], base-insoluble'
Alkali-Veredelungslauge *f (pap)* alkali refining liquor
Alkaliverfahren *n (rubber)* alkali [reclaiming] process
Alkaliverhältnis *n (pap)* alkali[-to-wood] ratio, chemical[-to-wood] ratio, ratio of chemical to wood
Alkaliverlust *m (pap)* loss of chemical • **den ~ decken** *(pap)* to make up for the loss of chemical
Alkaliwäsche *f* 1. *s.* Alkalibehandlung; 2. *(petrol)* caustic[-soda] wash
Alkalizusatz *m (pap)* alkali make-up, make-up chemical
Alkaloid *n* alkaloid
~ der Peptidgruppe peptide alkaloid
~ mit Chinolinring quinoline-type alkaloid
~ mit Isochinolinring isoquinoline-type alkaloid
~/steroides *s.* Steroidalkaloid
alkaloidartig alkaloid-like
Alkaloidbase *f* alkaloid base
alkaloidisch alkaloidal
Alkaloidvergiftung *f* alkaloid poisoning
Alkalose *f (med)* alcalosis
~/metabolische (nichtrespiratorische) metabolic alkalosis
~/respiratorische respiratory alkalosis
Alkamin *n* alkamine, amino alcohol
Alkan *n* *alkane, paraffin [hydrocarbon], saturated hydrocarbon
~/geradkettiges (unverzweigtes) normal (straight-chain) alkane
~/verzweigtes (verzweigtkettiges) branched-chain alkane
Alkanal *n* alkanal
Alkandiylgruppe *f*, **Alkandiylrest** *n* alkanediyl group, alkylene
Alkanfermentation *f (biot)* alkane fermentation
Alkanhalogenid *n s.* Halogenalkan
Alkanna *f* 1. alkanna, alkanet, Alkanna tinctoria (L.) Tausch.; 2. alkanna, alkanet *(root from 1. containing the colouring matter alkannin)*
Alkannafarbstoff *m*, **Alkannarot** *n s.* Alkannin
Alkannin *n* alkannin *(a red crystalline colouring matter)*
Alkanol *n* alkanol
Alkanolamin *n* alkanolamine
Alkanon *n* alkanone
Alkanphosphonigsäure *f* $RP(OH)_2$ alkylphosphonous (alkylphosphinic) acid, *(Am also)* alkanephosphonous acid
Alkanreihe *f* alkane family
Alkansäure *f* alkanoic acid
Alkaptonurie *f (med)* alkaptonuria, alcaptonuria *(incomplete breakdown of phenylalanine and tyrosine)*
Alkarsin *n* alkarsin, cacodyl oxide
Alkatrien *n (org ch)* alkatriene
Alkatriin *n (org ch)* alkatriyne
Alkazidanlage *f* alkazid plant *(gas purification)*
Alken *n* *alkene, olefin [hydrocarbon]
~/fluoriertes *fluoroalkene, fluoro-olefin
Alkenderivat *n* alkene derivative
Alkenimin *n* alkeneimine
Alkenreihe *f* alkene series (family), olefin series
Alkensäure *f* alkenoic acid *(any of the mono-unsaturated fatty acids)*
Alkenylbenzen *n* alkenylbenzene, aromatic-alkene compound
Alkenylierung *f* alkenylation
Alkenylsulfonat *n* alkenyl sulphonate, *(petrol also)* alpha-olefin sulphonate, AOS
Alkermes *m* grains of kermes *(the dried bodies of various female scales of the genus Kermes)*
Alkiminchelat *n* alkimine chelate
Alkin *n* *alkyne, acetylenic hydrocarbon
Alkinol *n* *alkynol, acetylenic alcohol
Alkinsäure *f* alkynoic acid
Alkinylbenzen *n* alkynylbenzene
Alkohol *m* alcohol, *(specif)* C_2H_5OH ethyl alcohol, *ethanol
~/absoluter absolute (dehydrated, anhydrous) alcohol
~ C 11 *1-undecanol, alcohol C-11
~ C 12 *1-dodecanol, alcohol C-12
~/denaturierter denatured alcohol, methylated spirit
~/dreiwertiger trihydroxylic (trihydric) alcohol
~/einwertiger monohydroxylic (monohydric) alcohol
~/gewöhnlicher fermentation (ethyl) alcohol, *ethanol
~/höherer higher alcohol
~/mehrwertiger polyhydroxylic alcohol, polyhydric (polyhydroxy, polyfunctional) alcohol, polyalcohol, polyol
~/primärer primary alcohol
~/reiner *s.* ~/absoluter
~/sekundärer secondary alcohol
~/technischer commercial (industrial, non-beverage) alcohol, commercial spirit
~/tertiärer tertiary alcohol
~/vergällter *s.* ~/denaturierter
~/vierwertiger tetrahydroxylic (tetrahydric) alcohol
~/wasserfreier *s.* ~/absoluter

~/zweiwertiger dihydroxylic (dihydric) alcohol, dialcohol, diol, *(relating to aliphatic compounds also)* glycol, aliphatic diol
alkoholarm light *(beverage)*
alkoholartig alcohol-like
Alkoholat *n* *alkoxide, alcoholate
Alkoholauszug *m* alcoholic extract
Alkoholdampf *m* alcohol vapour
Alkoholdehydrogenase *f* alcohol dehydrogenase
Alkoholentwöhnungsmittel *n* alcohol deterrent
alkoholfrei alcohol-free, non-alcoholic, soft
Alkoholgärung *f* alcoholic fermentation
Alkoholgehalt *m* alcohol content, alcoholic strength
• **von geringem ~** light *(beverage)*
alkoholhaltig alcoholic, spirituous
alkoholisch alcoholic, spirituous
~/schwach light *(beverage)*
alkoholisch-wäßrig hydroalcoholic
alkoholisieren to alcoholize
Alkoholisierung *f* alcoholization
Alkoholkraftstoff *m* alcohol fuel
alkohollöslich alcohol-soluble, spirit-soluble, soluble in alcohol
Alkoholmesser *m s.* Alkoholometer
Alkohol[o]meter *n* alcohol[o]meter
Alkoholometrie *f* alcoholometry
alkoholometrisch alcoholometric
Alkoholprobe *f* alcohol test
~ zur Milchuntersuchung alcohol coagulation test
Alkoholtest *m* alcohol test
Alkoholthermometer *n* alcohol-in-glass thermometer
alkoholunlöslich insoluble in alcohol
Alkoholyse *f* alcoholysis • **einer ~ unterwerfen** to alcoholyze
Alkosol *n* alcosol *(a colloidal system in which the liquid is alcohol)*
Alkoxyborierung *f* alkoxyboration
Alkoxycarbonylierung *f* alkoxycarbonylation, carbalkoxylation
Alkoxydealkylierung *f* alkoxydealkylation
Alkoxygruppe *f s.* Alkoxylgruppe
Alkoxyhalogenierung *f* alkoxyhalogenation
Alkoxylgruppe *f* $C_nH_{2n+1}O-$ alkoxyl (alkoxy) group, alkoxyl (alkoxy) residue
Alkoxylalkylierung *f* alkoxylalkylation
Alkoxylierung *f* alkoxylation
Alkoxymercurierung *f* alkoxymercuration
Alkyd *n s.* Alkydharz
Alkydharz *n* alkyd [resin]
~/kurzöliges short-oil alkyd
~/langöliges long-oil alkyd
~/mittelöliges medium-oil alkyd
~/styrolisiertes styrenated alkyd
Alkydharzanstrichstoff *m* alkyd paint (coating)
Alkydharzklarlack *m* alkyd varnish
Alkydharzlack *m* 1. alkyd enamel; 2. *s.* Alkydharzanstrichstoff
Alkyl *n* alkyl
Alkylamin *n* alkylamine
Alkylans *n* alkylating agent
Alkylarensulfonat *n* alkylarene sulphonate
Alkylarylsilikon *n s.* Alkylarylsiloxan
Alkylarylsiloxan *n* alkyl aryl siloxane
Alkylarylsulfonat *n s.* Alkylarensulfonat
Alkylat *n* alkylate
Alkylation *f s.* Alkylierung
Alkylbenzen *n* alkylbenzene
Alkylbenzensulfonat *n* alkyl benzene sulphonate, ABS
~/lineares linear alkyl benzene sulphonate, LAS, α-benzenesulphonate
Alkylbenzol *n s.* Alkylbenzen
Alkylbrücke *f* alkyl bridge
1,2-Alkylcarboniumumlagerung *f* 1,2-shift of alkyl, alkyl shift
Alkylcyanid *n* alkyl cyanide
Alkylderivat *n* alkyl derivative
Alkyldihalogenid *n* alkyl dihalide (dihalogenide), *dihaloalkane
Alkylen *n s.* Alken
Alkylgruppe *f* alkyl group (residue)
***n*-Alkylgruppe** *f* normal alkyl group, *n*-alkyl group
Alkylhalogenid *n* alkyl halide (halogenide), *haloalkane
alkylhalogensubstituiert substituted by alkyl halides
Alkylidengruppe *f* alkylidene group
Alkylidenphosphoran *n* phosphonium (phosphorus) ylide, Wittig reagent
Alkylidenrest *m* alkylidene group
alkylieren to alkylate
Alkylierung *f* alkylation, alkanation, alkyl substitution
~/hydrierende hydroalkylation, reductive alkylation
~/katalytische catalytic alkylation
~ mit Fluorwasserstoffsäure (Flußsäure) hydrofluoric-acid alkylation, HF alkylation
~ mit Schwefelsäure sulphuric-acid alkylation
~/reduktive (reduzierende) *s.* ~/hydrierende
~/thermische thermal alkylation
***N*-Alkylierung** *f* *N*-alkylation, nitrogen alkylation
***O*-Alkylierung** *f* *O*-alkylation, oxygen alkylation
Alkylierungsmittel *n* alkylating agent
Alkylierungsverfahren *n* alkylation process
Alkyliodid *n* alkiodide
Alkylmetallverbindung *f* alkylmetal compound
Alkylmonohalogenid *n* alkyl monohalide, *monohaloalkane
Alkylnitrat *n* alkyl nitrate
Alkylperoxid *n* alkyl peroxide
Alkylperoxy-Radikal *n* alkylperoxy radical
Alkylphenolharz *n* alkyl phenol resin
Alkylphenolnovolak *m* alkyl phenol novolak
Alkylphosphonsäure *f* $RP=O(OH)_2$ alkylphosphonic acid
Alkylquecksilberverbindung *f* alkylmercury [compound]

Alkylradikal *n* alkyl radical, *(specif)* free alkyl radical
Alkylrest *m* alkyl residue (group)
Alkylschwefelsäure *f* alkylsulphuric acid
Alkylsilikon *n* *alkyl siloxane, alkyl silicone
~/höheres higher alkyl siloxane
Alkylsulfid *n* alkyl sulphide, thioether
Alkylsulfonat *n* alkyl sulphonate
Alkylsulfonsäure *f* alkylsulphonic acid
Alkylverbindung *f* alkyl compound
Alkylwanderung *f* migration of an alkyl group
Allanit *m (min)* allanite *(a sorosilicate)*
Allantoin *n* allantoin, glyoxylic diureide
Allantoinsäure *f* allantoic acid, diureidoacetic acid
Allelochemikalie *f* allelochemical *(a substance produced by organisms and acting on other organisms)*
Allelopathie *f* allelopathy *(influence of one living plant upon another due to secreted substances)*
Allelopathikum *n (biol)* allelopathic
allelopathisch *(biol)* allelopathic
allelotrop allelotropic
Allelotropie *f* allelotropism *(coexistence of tautomeric forms)*
Allemontit *m* allemontite *(an arsenic antimony mineral)*
Allen *n* allene, *(specif)* $CH_2=C=CH_2$ *propadiene, allene
allenisch *(org ch)* allenic
Allenisomerie *f* allene isomerism
Allen-Kegel *m*, **Allen-Konus** *m (min tech)* Allen cone classifier
Allen-Moore-Zelle *f (el ch)* Allen-Moore cell *(chlor-alkali electrolysis)*
Allergen *n (med)* allergen
Alleskleber *m* all-purpose adhesive
Alles-oder-Nichts-Modell *n* concerted (symmetry) model, all-or-none model *(enzyme kinetics)*
Alles-oder-Nichts-Übergang *m* concerted transition (transfer) *(enzyme kinetics)*
Allesreiniger *m* all-purpose cleaner
Allgegenwart *f* ubiquity
Allgemeinempfindlichkeit *f (phot)* overall sensitivity, emulsion speed
Allgemeinformel *f* general formula
Allgemeinschleier *m (phot)* overall fog
Allgewürz *n* allspice *(from Pimenta dioica (L.) Merr.)*
Allheilmittel *n* panacea, cure-all
Allihn-Kühler *m* Allihn (bulb) condenser
all-*cis*-Isomer[e] *n* all-*cis* isomer
all-*trans*-Isomer[e] *n* all-*trans* isomer
allochthon *(geol)* allochthonous *(not formed in situ)*
Allocrotonsäure *f s.* Isocrotonsäure
Allokatalyse *f* allocatalysis
Allopalladium *n (min)* allopalladium
Allophan *m (min)* allophane *(a phyllosilicate)*
Allophanamid *n* allophanamide, carbamyl urea, biuret
Allophansäureamid *n s.* Allophanamid
Allose *f* allose *(an aldohexose)*
Allosterie *f (bioch)* allosterism
allosterisch allosteric
allothigen *(geol)* allogenic, allothogenic *(formed at an another location)*
allotriomorph *(cryst)* allotriomorphic, anhedral, xenomorphic
allotrop allotropic
Allotrop *n* allotrope, allotropic modification (form) *(of an element)*
Allotropie *f* allotropism, allotropy *(existence of an element in two or more different modifications)*
Allozimtsäure *f* allocinnamic acid, *cis*-cinnamic acid, *cis*-3-phenylacrylic acid
All-sliming-Verfahren *n* all-sliming process *(gold recovery)*
Allylaldehyd *m s.* Acrolein
Allylalkohol *m* allyl alcohol, AA, *prop-2-en-1-ol
Allylanion *n* allyl anion
p-**Allylanisol** *n* *p*-allylanisole, 1-allyl-4-methoxybenzene
Allylbromid *n* allyl bromide, *3-bromopropene
Allylbromierung *f* allylic bromination
Allylchlorid *n* allyl chloride, *3-chloropropene
Allylchlorierung *f* allylic chlorination
Allylen *n s.* Propin
Allylester-Kunststoff *m* allyl plastic
Allylgruppe *f* $CH_2=CH-CH_2-$ allyl (allylic) group (residue)
Allylharz *n* allyl[ic] resin
Allylharz-Kunststoff *m* allyl plastic
Allylierung *f* allylation
allylisch allylic
Allylkation *n* allyl cation
Allylkondensation *f* allylic condensation
Allylradikal *n* [free] allyl radical
Allylrest *m s.* Allylgruppe
Allylsenföl *n* allyl mustard oil
allylständig allylic
Allylsubstitution *f* allylic substitution
Allylumlagerung *f* allylic rearrangement
Allzweckkautschuk *m* general-purpose rubber
Allzwecksynthesekautschuk *m* general-purpose synthetic rubber
Almandin *m (min)* almandine, almandite *(aluminium iron(II) orthosilicate)*
Almén-Nylander-Probe *f* Almén-Nylander test *(for sugar)*
Aloinprobe *f* aloin test *(for detecting blood)*
Alphacellulose *f* alpha (chemical) cellulose, α-cellulose
Alphaspektrum *n* alpha-particle spectrum
Alphastrahlen *mpl* alpha rays
Alphastrahlenquelle *f* alpha-radiation source
Alphastrahler *m* alpha emitter
Alphastrahlung *f* alpha radiation
Alphateilchen *n* alpha particle
Alphazerfall *m* alpha decay (disintegration)

Alphazerfallsenergie *f* alpha disintegration energy
Alphinateilchen *n (nucl)* alphina particle
ALS *s.* Alginatseide
Alstonit *m (min)* alstonite
Altait *m (min)* altaite *(lead telluride)*
altbacken stale • **~ werden** to stale
Altblei *n* scrap lead
Alteisen *n* scrap iron, ferrous scrap
Alterans *n (med)* alterative *(a drug which influences metabolism)*
altern to age *(e.g. a rubber product)*; to undergo ageing, to age, *(of precipitates also)* to digest
Alternativparameter *m* alternative parameter
Alternativverbot *n* mutual exclusion rule *(Raman and infrared spectroscopy)*
Altersbestimmung *f* age determination, *(geol also)* dating
~/absolute *s.* ~/radiometrische
~ durch Radionuklide *s.* ~/radiometrische
~/physikalische (physikalisch-chemische) *s.* ~/radiometrische
~/radiometrische radiometric dating
Alterung *f* ageing, aging, *(of precipitates also)* digestion
~/beschleunigte *s.* ~/künstliche
~ durch Licht light ageing
~ im Geer-Ofen *(rubber)* Geer oven ageing
~ im Wärmeschrank *(rubber)* [air] oven ageing
~ im Zellenofen *(rubber)* test-tube ageing
~ in der Sauerstoffbombe *(rubber)* oxygen-bomb ageing
~/künstliche artificial (accelerated) ageing
~/natürliche natural ageing
~/thermische heat ageing, thermosenescence
alterungsanfällig susceptible to ageing
Alterungsanfälligkeit *f* susceptibility to ageing
alterungsbeständig resistant to ageing, non-ageing
Alterungsbeständigkeit *f* resistance to ageing, ageing resistance
Alterungseigenschaften *fpl* ageing characteristics (properties)
Alterungsgeschwindigkeit *f* rate of ageing
Alterungsprüfung *f* ageing test
~/beschleunigte (künstliche) artificial (accelerated) ageing test
~ nach Geer *(rubber)* Geer oven test
Alterungsschutzmittel *n (rubber, plast)* antioxidant, age-resister
~ gegen Oxidation und Biegerisse *(rubber)* anti-flex-cracking antioxidant
Alterungstest *m* ageing test
Alterungsverhalten *n* ageing performance
Alterungsversuch *m* ageing test
Alterungswiderstand *m s.* Alterungsbeständigkeit
Altgeschmack *m (food)* stale flavour (taste)
Altgummi *m* rubber scrap (waste), scrap (waste) rubber
Altgummibrecher *m* breaking mill for scrap rubber
Altkatalysator *m* used catalyst
Altmaterial *n* waste [material]
Altmetall *n* scrap [metal]
Altöl *n* used oil
Altölemulsion *f (hyd)* oily waste emulsion
Altpapier *n* waste (old) paper
~/aufbereitetes (regeneriertes) recovered (repulped) stock, recovered (repulped) waste paper, old-paper stock
Altpapieraufbereitung *f*, **Altpapierregenerierung** *f* recovery of waste paper
Altpapierstoff *m s.* Altpapier/aufbereitetes
Altpapierstofffärbung *f* waste-paper colouring
Altrohstoff *m* waste material
Altrose *f* altrose *(an aldohexose)*
Altstoff *m s.* Altrohstoff
Alttuberkulin *n (pharm)* old tuberculin
Alu *n s.* Aluminium
alumetieren to alumetize
Aluminat *n* aluminate
Aluminatlauge *f* aluminate liquor (solution), sodium aluminate solution *(Bayer process)*
Aluminatlösung *f s.* Aluminatlauge
Aluminid *n* aluminide
aluminieren to aluminize *(without formation of alloy layers)*
Aluminit *m (min)* aluminite *(hydrous aluminium sulphate)*
Aluminium *n* Al aluminium, *(Am)* aluminum
~/milchsaures *s.* Aluminiumlactat
Aluminiumacetat *n* aluminium acetate
~/basisches aluminium acetate hydroxide
Aluminiumacetylacetonat *n* aluminium acetylacetonate
Aluminiumalkyl *n s.* Trialkylaluminium
Aluminiumarsenat(V) *n* aluminium arsenate(V)
Aluminiumblech *n* sheet aluminium
Aluminiumbromid *n* aluminium bromide
Aluminiumbronze *f* aluminium bronze
Aluminiumcarbid *n* aluminium carbide
Aluminiumchlorat *n* aluminium chlorate
Aluminiumchlorid *n* aluminium chloride
Aluminiumchlorid-Kohlenwasserstoff-Komplex *m/inaktiver* *(petrol)* complex out *(in liquid-phase isomerization)*
Aluminiumerz *n* aluminium ore
Aluminiumflockung *f (hyd)* alum coagulation, coagulation with alum
Aluminiumflockungsmittel *n (hyd)* alum coagulant
Aluminiumfluorid *n* aluminium fluoride
Aluminiumfluorid-Hydrat *n* aluminium fluoride hydrate
Aluminiumfolie *f* aluminium foil
Aluminiumfolien-Kaschierpapier *n* aluminium-foil backing paper
Aluminiumformiat *n* aluminium formate
Aluminium(I)-halogenid *n* aluminium monohalide, aluminium(I) halogenide
Aluminium(III)-halogenid *n* aluminium trihalide, aluminium(III) halogenide

aluminiumhaltig containing aluminium, aluminium-bearing, aluminous, *(esp ores:)* aluminiferous
Aluminiumhexafluorosilicat *n* aluminium hexafluorosilicate
Aluminiumhütte *f* aluminium works
Aluminiumhydroxid *n* aluminium hydroxide
Aluminiumhydroxiddiacetat *n* aluminium diacetate hydroxide
Aluminiumhydroxiddiformiat *n* aluminium diformate hydroxide
Aluminiumhydroxidflocken *fpl (hyd)* alum floc
Aluminiumhydroxidschlamm *m (hyd)* alum (aluminium hydroxide) sludge
Aluminiumiodid *n* aluminium iodide
Aluminiumlack *m* aluminium lake
Aluminiumlactat *n* aluminium lactate
Aluminiumlegierung *f* aluminium alloy
Aluminiummonohalogenid *n s.* Aluminium(I)-halogenid
Aluminiumnaphthenat *n* aluminium naphthenate
Aluminiumnitrat *n* aluminium nitrate
Aluminiumnitrid *n* aluminium nitride
Aluminiumorthohydroxid *n s.* Aluminiumhydroxid
Aluminiumoxid *n* aluminium oxide
Aluminiumoxidhydrat *n* hydrous aluminium oxide
Aluminiumpapier *n* aluminium (silver) paper
Aluminiumpulver *n* aluminium powder
~/gesintertes sintered aluminium powder, S.A.P.
Aluminium-Raffinationselektrolyse *f* **nach Hoopes** Hoopes [electrolytic-refining] process
aluminiumreich rich in aluminium, aluminium-rich
Aluminiumrhodanid *n s.* Aluminiumthiocyanat
Aluminiumseife *f* aluminium soap
Aluminiumsilicatglas *n* aluminosilicate glass
Aluminiumstaub *m* aluminium powder
Aluminiumsulfat *n* aluminium sulphate
~/handelsübliches (technisches) alum
Aluminiumsulfid *n* aluminium sulphide
Aluminiumthiocyanat *n* aluminium thiocyanate
Aluminiumtrialkyl *n s.* Trialkylaluminium
Aluminiumtriäthyl *n s.* Triethylaluminium
Aluminiumtrimethyl *n s.* Trimethylaluminium
Aluminiumwasserstoff *m* aluminium hydride, alane
Aluminogel *n* alumina gel, gelatinous aluminium hydroxide
Aluminon *n* aluminon, ammonium aurinetricarboxylate *(for detecting aluminium)*
Aluminothermie *f* aluminothermics, aluminothermy, Goldschmidt's process
aluminothermisch aluminothermic
Alumogel *m(n) (min)* alumogel, kliachite *(gel of aluminium hydroxide)*
Alumosilicat *n* aluminosilicate
Alunit *m (min)* alunite, alumstone *(hydrous aluminium potassium sulphate)*
Alunitisation *f*, **Alunitisierung** *f* alunitization
Alunogen *m (min)* alunogene, feather alum, hair salt *(aluminium sulphate water(1/18))*
Amadori-Umlagerung *f* Amadori rearrangement *(of glycosylamines into 1-aminoketoses)*
Amagat *n s.* Amagat-Einheit
Amagat-Einheit *f* Amagat unit *(molar volume of a gas at 0 °C and 1 atmosphere)*
Amalgam *m (min)* amalgam *(old collective name for two naturally occurring silver mercury alloys, kongsbergite and moschellandsbergite)*
Amalgam *n* amalgam *(an alloy of mercury)*
Amalgamation *f* amalgamation
~/europäische *(min tech)* barrel amalgamation
Amalgamations... *s.* Amalgamier...
Amalgamator *m s.* Amalgamierapparat
Amalgamelektrode *f* amalgam electrode
Amalgamfaß *n s.* Amalgamierfaß
Amalgamierapparat *m* amalgamation apparatus, amalgamator
amalgamieren to amalgam[ate], to amalgamize
Amalgamieren *n* amalgamation
Amalgamierfaß *n (min tech)* amalgamating barrel
Amalgamierherd *m (min tech)* amalgamating table
Amalgamierpfanne *f (min tech)* amalgamating (amalgamation) pan
Amalgamiertisch *m (min tech)* amalgamating table
Amalgamierung *f* amalgamation
Amalgamierungs... *s.* Amalgamier...
Amalgamverfahren *n* [intermediate] mercury electrode process, mercury-cell process *(electrolysis)*
Amalgamzelle *f* mercury [cathode] cell *(electrolysis)*
Amalgamzersetzer *m* amalgam decomposer *(electrolysis)*
Amanganose *f* grey speck *(of oats on soil deficient in manganese)*
Amarant *n* amaranth, Red No. 2 *(a red acid azo dye)*
Amazonenstein *m*, **Amazonit** *m (min)* amazonite, amazonstone *(potassium aluminosilicate)*
Ambercodon *n (bioch)* amber codon *(an amino-acid sequence which causes the termination of protein biosynthesis)*
Amberglimmer *m* amber (bronze, brown) mica, phlogopite
Amber-Mutante *f (bioch)* amber mutant
ambident *(org ch)* ambident *(possessing two reactive centres)*
ambient ambient, surrounding
ambifunktionell, ambivalent *s.* ambident
Amblygonit *m (min)* amblygonite
Amboinokino *n* East India kino, Malabar kino *(kino gum from Pterocarpus marsupium Roxb.)*
Ambra *f* **[/graue, natürliche]** *(cosmet)* ambergris, ambergrease
Ambrettemoschus *m* musk ambrette, 2,6-dinitro-3-methoxy-4-*tert*-butyltoluene
Ameisenbekämpfungsmittel *n* ant poison
Ameisenfreßlack *m* ant syrup
Ameisenöl *n***/synthetisches** artificial ant oil, furfural

Ameisensäure *f* formic acid, methanoic acid
Ameisensäureamid *n* formamide, *methanamide
Ameisensäureethylester *m* ethyl formate
Ameisensäuremethylester *m* methyl formate
Ameisenvertilgungsmittel *n* ant poison
Americium *n* Am americium
Ames-Test *m* Ames (salmonella) test *(for determining the mutagenicity of chemicals)*
A-Metallion *n* class (a) metal ion
Amethyst *m (min)* amethyst *(a variety of quartz)*
Amianth *m (min)* amiant[h]us *(fine silky asbestos)*
Amid *n* $RCONH_2$ amide, azanide; M^INH_2 [metal] amide
~/polymeres polyamide
~/primäres primary amide
~/sekundäres secondary amide
~/tertiäres tertiary amide
Amidbindung *f* amide linkage
Amidhydrazon *n* amide hydrazone
amidieren to amidate
Amidierung *f* amidation
Amidin *n (org ch)* amidine, *(specif)* $RC(=NH)NH_2$ carboxamidine
Amidinocarbonylgruppe *f s.* Amidinogruppe
***N*-Amidinoglycin** *n* *N*-guanylglycine, guanidinoacetic acid
Amidinogruppe *f* $-C(=NH)NH_2$ amidine group
amidisch amidic
Amidoalkylierung *f* amidoalkylation, acylaminoalkylation
Amidogruppe *f* $-CONH_2$ amido group
Amidokohlensäure *f* carbamic acid
Amidol-Entwickler *m (phot)* amidol developer
Amidophosphorsäure *f* amidophosphoric acid, phosphamic acid
Amidoquecksilber(II)-chlorid *n* amidomercury(II) chloride, infusible white precipitate
Amidoschwefelsäure *f* amidosulphuric acid
Amidosulfat *n* $NH_2SO_3M^I$ amidosulphate
Amidosulfonsäure *f s.* Amidoschwefelsäure
Amidoxim *n* amido oxime
Amidrazon *n* amidrazone
Amidstickstoff *m* amide nitrogen
Amikron *n* amicron, subsubmicron *(a disperse particle invisible under the microscope)*
amikroskopisch amicroscopic, submicroscopic
Amin *n* amine
~/biogenes biogenic amine
~/primäres RNH_2 primary amine
~/sekundäres R_1R_2NH secondary amine
~/tertiäres $R_1R_2R_3N$ tertiary amine
Aminal *n* aminal, geminal diamine
aminartig amine-like
Aminäscher *m (tann)* hair loosening by amines
Aminase *f* aminase
Aminbeschleuniger *m (rubber)* amino accelerator
aminieren to aminate
Aminierung *f* amination
~/reduktive reductive amination
Aminoacetal *n* aminoacetal
Aminoacetanilid *n* aminoacetanilide
Aminoacylierung *f* aminoacylation
Aminoacylort *m s.* Akzeptorort
α-Aminoadipinsäure *f* α-aminoadipic acid
α-Aminoadipinsäure-Weg *m (bioch)* α-aminoadipic-acid pathway
Aminoalkohol *m* amino alcohol, alkamine
α-Aminoalkohol *m* α-amino alcohol, hemiaminal
Aminoanteil *m* amino moiety
Aminoanthrachinon *n* aminoanthraquinone
Aminoäthan *n s.* Ethylamin
2-Aminoäthanol-(1) *n s.* 2-Aminoethan-1-ol
Aminoäthylbenzol *n s.* Aminoethylbenzen
Aminoazidurie *f* aminoaciduria *(excretion of amino acids via the kidneys)*
***p*-Aminoazobenzen** *n* *p*-aminoazobenzene, *(dye also)* aniline yellow
Aminoazobenzensulfonsäure *f* aminoazobenzenesulphonic acid
Aminoazoverbindung *f* aminoazo compound
Aminobenzen *n* aminobenzene, phenylamine, aniline
***p*-Aminobenzensulfonamid** *n* *p*-aminobenzenesulphonamide, sulphanilamide
Aminobenzensulfonsäure *f* aminobenzenesulphonic acid, anilinesulphonic acid
Aminobenzoesäure *f* aminobenzoic acid
***o*-Aminobenzoesäure** *f* *o*-aminobenzoic acid, anthranilic acid
***p*-Aminobenzoesäure** *f* *p*-aminobenzoic acid, PABA
Aminobenzoesäurebutylester *m* butyl aminobenzoate
Aminobenzoesäureethylester *m* ethyl aminobenzoate
Aminobenzol *n s.* Aminobenzen
Aminobenzoyl-I-Säure *f s.* Aminobenzoyl-J-Säure
Aminobenzoyl-J-Säure *f* aminobenzoyl J acid
Aminobenzylierung *f* aminobenzylation
Aminobernsteinsäure *f* aminosuccinic acid, aspartic acid, asparaginic acid, *aminobutanedioic acid
Aminoborierung *f* aminoboration
2-Aminobornan *n* bornylamine, 2-aminobornane
Aminobuttersäure *f (bioch)* aminobutyric acid
γ-Aminobuttersäure *f (bioch)* gamma aminobutyric acid, GABA
2-Aminocamphan *n s.* 2-Aminobornan
Aminocarbonsäure *f s.* Aminosäure
Aminochinolin *n* aminoquinoline, quinolylamine
2-Amino-2-deoxy-α-D-glucopyranose *f* D-glucosamine, 2-amino-2-deoxy-α-D-glucopyranose
Aminodicarbonsäure *f* amino dicarboxylic acid
Aminodimethylbenzen *n*, **Aminodimethylbenzol** *n* aminodimethylbenzene
Aminodinitrophenol *n* aminodinitrophenol
1-Aminododecan *n* *dodecylamine, 1-aminododecane
Aminoessigsäure *f* aminoacetic acid, glycine

1-Aminoethanol *n* 1-aminoethanol
2-Aminoethan-1-ol *n* *2-aminoethan-1-ol, 2-aminoethyl alcohol, monoethanolamine, MEA
Aminoethansäure *f s.* Aminoessigsäure
2-Aminoethansulfonsäure *f* 2-aminoethanesulphonic acid, taurine
1-Aminoethylalkohol *m s.* 1-Aminoethan-1-ol
Aminoethylbenzen *n* aminoethylbenzene
4-Aminofolsäure *f* 4-aminofolic acid, aminopterin
Aminoformiat *n* NH_2COOM^I aminoformate
Aminoglykosid-Antibiotikum *n (biot)* aminoglycoside antibiotic
Aminogruppe *f* NH_2– amino group (residue)
Amino-G-Salz *n* amino G salt
Amino-G-Säure *f* amino-G acid, 2-naphthylamine-6,8-disulphonic acid
Aminokomponente *f* amino moiety
Aminolyse *f* aminolysis
Aminomethan *n* methylamine
aminomethylieren to aminomethylate
Aminomethylierung *f* aminomethylation
Aminonaphthalen *n* naphthylamine
Aminonaphthalendisulfonsäure *f* naphthylaminedisulphonic acid, aminonaphthalenedisulphonic acid
Aminonaphthalensulfonsäure *f* naphthylaminesulphonic acid, aminonaphthalenesulphonic acid
Aminonaphtholdisulfonsäure *f* aminonaphtholdisulphonic acid
Aminonaphtholsulfonsäure *f* aminonaphtholsulphonic acid
Aminooxidase *f* amino oxidase
6-Aminopenicillansäure *f* 6-aminopenicillanic acid, 6-APA
Aminophenetol *n* aminophenetol, phenetidine, aminophenol ethyl ether
Aminophenol *n* aminophenol, hydroxyaniline
Aminophenoläthyläther *m s.* Aminophenetol
p-**Aminophenol-Entwickler** *m (phot) para*-aminophenol developer
p-**Aminophenylarsonsäure** *f p*-aminophenylarsonic acid, arsanilic acid
Aminophenylessigsäure *f* aminophenylacetic acid
p-**Aminophenylsulfonamid** *n s. p*-Aminobenzensulfonamid
Aminoplast *m* aminoplastic
Aminoplastharz *n* amino resin
Aminopolycarbonsäure *f* amino polycarboxylic acid
2-Aminopropionsäure *f* 2-aminopropionic acid, alanine
γ-**Aminopropyltriethoxysilan** *n* γ-aminopropyl triethoxysilane, γ-APT
Amino-R-Salz *n* amino-R salt
Amino-R-Säure *f* amino-R acid, 2-naphthylamine-3,6-disulphonic acid
Aminosalicylsäure *f* aminosalicylic acid, amino-2-hydroxybenzoic acid
Aminosäure *f* amino acid, amino carboxylic acid
~/essentielle *(bioch)* essential amino acid
~/glucogene (glucoplastische) *(bioch)* glucogenic (glycogenic) amino acid
~/ketoplastische *(bioch)* ketogenic amino acid
~ mit basischer und hydrophiler (polarer) Seitenkette amino acid with basic R groups
~ mit neutraler und hydrophiler (polarer) Seitenkette amino acid with polar but neutral R groups
~ mit neutraler und hydrophober (unpolarer) Seitenkette amino acid with non-polar R groups
~ mit saurer und hydrophiler (polarer) Seitenkette amino acid with acidic R groups
~/unentbehrliche *s.* ~/essentielle
α-**Aminosäure** *f* α-amino acid, α-amino carboxylic acid
Amino-ε-Säure *f* epsilon acid, ε-acid, 1-naphthylamine-3,8-disulphonic acid
Aminosäureanalysator *m* amino-acid analyser
Aminosäurearm *m (bioch)* amino-acid arm
Aminosäurechelat *n* amino-acid chelate
Aminosäureeinheit *f* amino-acid unit
Aminosäurefolge *f s.* Aminosäuresequenz
Aminosäuren-Antibiotikum *n (biot)* amino-acid antibiotic
Aminosäureoxidase *f* amino-acid oxidase
Aminosäurepool *m (bioch)* amino-acid pool
Aminosäurereihenfolge *f s.* Aminosäuresequenz
Aminosäurerest *m* amino-acid residue
Aminosäuresequenz *f* amino-acid sequence, sequence of amino-acid residues
Amino-S-Säure *f* amino-S acid, 1-naphthylamine-4,8-disulphonic acid
Aminoteil *m* amino moiety
Aminotoluen *n*, **Aminotoluol** *n* aminotoluene, toluidine
Aminotransferase *f* transaminase
Aminoverbindung *f* amino compound
Aminoxid *n* amine oxide
Aminoxylen *n*, **Aminoxylol** *n* aminoxylene, xylidine, aminodimethylbenzene
Aminozucker *m* amino sugar, glycosamine
Aminsalz *n* amine salt
Aminsynthese *f*/**Gabrielsche** Gabriel phthalimide synthesis, Gabriel synthesis of primary amines
Aminylen *n* aminylene *(free diradical)*
Aminzahl *f* amine value
Amin-Zucker-Bräunung *f (food)* amino-sugar browning, Maillard-type browning, non-enzymatic browning
Ammeter *n s.* Amperemeter
Ammin *n* ammine *(coordination chemistry)*
Amminkomplex *m* ammine complex
Ammonalaun *m s.* Ammoniakalaun
Ammoniak *n* ammonia
~/flüssiges liquid ammonia
~/gasförmiges gaseous ammonia, ammonia gas
~/synthetisches synthetic ammonia
~/verflüssigtes liquefied (liquid) ammonia

~/wasserfreies anhydrous ammonia
~/wäßriges *s.* Ammoniakwasser
Ammoniakabtrieb *m (hyd)* ammonia stripping
Ammoniakabwasser *n* ammonia still waste, spent liquor
Ammoniakalaun *m* ammonia (ammonium) alum
ammoniakalisch ammoniac[al]
Ammoniakanlage *f* ammonia plant
Ammoniakäscher *m (tann)* hair loosening by ammonia
Ammoniakat *n* ammoniate, ammonate
Ammoniakbegasung *f (agric)* ammonia fumigation
Ammoniakbildner *mpl* ammonifiers, ammonifying bacteria
Ammoniak-Chlor-Verfahren *n (hyd)* ammonia-chlorine process
Ammoniakdampf *m* ammonia fume (vapour)
Ammoniakdestillationsapparat *m* ammonia-distillation apparatus
Ammoniakentgiftung *f (bioch)* ammonia detoxication
Ammoniakentwicklung *f* evolution of ammonia
Ammoniakgas *n* ammonia gas, gaseous ammonia
Ammoniakgummi *n* [gum] ammoniac, *(specif)* Persian ammoniac *(from Dorema ammoniacum Don and related specc.)*
~/Afrikanisches African (Moroccan) ammoniac *(from Ferula tingitana L. and F. communis L. var. brevifolia Marcz)*
Ammoniak-Gummiharz *n s.* Ammoniakgummi
ammoniakhaltig ammoniac[al]
Ammoniakhydrat *n* ammonia hydrate
Ammoniakkältemaschine *f* ammonia refrigerating machine
Ammoniakkondensator *m* ammonia condenser
Ammoniak-Lichtpausen *n* ammonia-developed printing
Ammoniaklösung *f* **[/wäßrige]** ammonia [water], aqua ammonia
Ammoniak-Luft-Gemisch *n* ammonia-air mixture
Ammoniakoxidation *f* ammonia oxidation, oxidation of ammonia
Ammoniakseife *f* ammonium soap
Ammoniak-Soda-Verfahren *n* [Solvay's] ammonia soda process, Solvay process
Ammoniakstickstoff *m* ammonia (ammoniacal) nitrogen
Ammoniaksynthese *f* ammonia synthesis
~/Fausersche Fauser [ammonia] process
Ammoniaksyntheseofen *m* synthetic-ammonia apparatus, ammonia-synthesis reactor
Ammoniakverbrennung *f* ammonia oxidation, combustion of ammonia
Ammoniakverdampfer *m* ammonia vaporizer
Ammoniakverdampfung *f* ammonia evaporation (vaporization)
Ammoniakverflüssiger *m* ammonia condenser
Ammoniakwäsche *f* ammonia scrubbing
Ammoniakwäscher *m* ammonia scrubber
Ammoniakwaschturm *m* ammonia scrubber
Ammoniakwasser *n (tech)* ammonia[cal] liquor, crude ammonia liquor, ammonia water, gas liquor
~/konzentriertes (verdichtetes) concentrated ammoniacal liquor
Ammonifikation *f s.* Ammonifizierung
Ammonifizierung *f (agric)* ammonification
Ammonisator *m*, **Ammonisierapparat** *m* ammoniator *(fertilizer technology)*
ammonisieren to ammoniate *(fertilizers)*
Ammonisiergranulator *m* ammoniator-granulator *(fertilizer technology)*
Ammonisier-Granuliertrommel *f* ammoniator-granulator drum, rotary ammoniator-granulator, reaction-granulation drum, rotary-drum ammoniator
Ammonisiertrommel *f* ammoniation drum
Ammonisierung *f* 1. ammoniation *(of fertilizers)*; 2. *s.* Ammonifizierung
Ammonium *n* ammonium
~/schwefelsaures *s.* Ammoniumsulfat
~/stickstoffwasserstoffsaures *s.* Ammoniumazid
Ammoniumacetat *n* ammonium acetate
Ammoniumalaun *m s.* Ammoniakalaun
Ammoniumaluminiumchlorid *n* aluminium ammonium chloride
Ammoniumaluminiumsulfat *n* aluminium ammonium sulphate
Ammoniumamalgam *n* ammonium amalgam
Ammoniumamidocarbonat *n s.* Ammoniumcarbamat
Ammoniumazid *n* ammonium azide
Ammoniumbase *f***/quartäre (quaternäre)** quaternary ammonium base
Ammoniumbenzoat *n* ammonium benzoate
Ammoniumbisulfitkochsäure *f (pap)* ammonia-base [sulphite] acid, ammonia-base [sulphite] liquor
Ammoniumborfluorid *n s.* Ammoniumfluoroborat
Ammoniumbromid *n* ammonium bromide
Ammoniumcalciumarsenat *n* ammonium calcium arsenate
Ammoniumcalciumphosphat *n* ammonium calcium phosphate
Ammoniumcarbamat *n* ammonium carbamate, ammonium aminoformate
Ammoniumcarbaminat *n s.* Ammoniumcarbamat
Ammoniumcarbonat *n* ammonium carbonate
~/handelsübliches commercial ammonium carbonate, salt of hartshorn, sal volatile *(a mixture consisting of ammonium hydrogencarbonate and ammonium carbamate)*
Ammoniumchlorat *n* ammonium chlorate
Ammoniumchlorid *n* ammonium chloride, salmiac
Ammoniumchromalaun *m* chrome ammonium alum, chromium ammonium sulphate *(ammonium chromium sulphate 12-water)*
Ammoniumcyanat *n* ammonium cyanate
Ammoniumcyanid *n* ammonium cyanide
Ammoniumdichromat *n* ammonium dichromate

Ammoniumdihydrogenphosphat *n* ammonium dihydrogenphosphate
Ammoniumdithionat *n* ammonium dithionate
Ammoniumeisenalaun *m* *ammonium iron alum, ferric ammonium alum
Ammoniumeisen(II)-cyanid *n s.* Ammoniumhexacyanoferrat(II)
Ammoniumeisen(III)-oxalat *n* ammonium iron(III) oxalate, ferric ammonium oxalate
Ammoniumfluorid *n* ammonium fluoride
Ammoniumfluoroborat *n* ammonium fluoroborate
Ammoniumformiat *n* ammonium formate
Ammoniumgallium(III)-sulfat *n* ammonium gallium(III) sulphate
Ammoniumgruppe *f* NH_2– ammonium group (residue)
Ammoniumheptamolybdat-4-Wasser *n* ammonium heptamolybdate 4-water
Ammoniumhexachloroplatinat(IV) *n* ammonium hexachloroplatinate(IV)
Ammoniumhexachlorostannat(IV) *n* ammonium hexachlorostannate(IV), pink salt
Ammoniumhexacyanoferrat(II) *n* ammonium hexacyanoferrate(II)
Ammoniumhexafluorosilicat *n* ammonium hexafluorosilicate
Ammoniumhexafluorozirconat *n* ammonium hexafluorozirconate
Ammoniumhydrogencarbonat *n* ammonium hydrogencarbonate
Ammoniumhydrogenfluorid *n* ammonium hydrogenfluoride
Ammoniumhydrogenphosphat *n* ammonium hydrogenphosphate
Ammoniumhydrogensulfat *n* ammonium hydrogensulphate
Ammoniumhydrogensulfid *n* ammonium hydrogensulphide
Ammoniumhydrogensulfit *n* ammonium hydrogensulphite
Ammoniumhydrogentartrat *n* ammonium hydrogentartrate
Ammoniumhydroxid *n* ammonium hydroxide
~/quartäres (quaternäres) quaternary ammonium hydroxide
Ammoniumhypophosphit *n* *ammonium phosphonate, ammonium hypophosphite
Ammoniumiodat *n* ammonium iodate
Ammoniumiodid *n* ammonium iodide
Ammoniumkupfer(II)-sulfat *n* ammonium copper(II) sulphate
Ammoniumlactat *n* ammonium lactate
Ammoniummagnesiumcarbonat *n* ammonium magnesium carbonate
Ammoniummagnesiumphosphat *n* ammonium magnesium phosphate
Ammoniummagnesiumsulfat *n* ammonium magnesium sulphate
Ammoniummanganat(VII) *n s.* Ammoniumpermanganat
Ammoniummangan(II)-phosphat *n* ammonium manganese(II) phosphate
Ammoniummangan(II)-sulfat *n* ammonium manganese(II) sulphate
Ammoniummetaantimonat(V) *n* *ammonium trioxoantimonate(V), ammonium metaantimonate(V)
Ammoniummetaarsenat(III) *n* *ammonium dioxoarsenate(III), ammonium metaarsenite
Ammoniummetaperiodat *n s.* Ammoniumtetroxoiodat
Ammoniummetavanadat *n* *ammonium trioxovanadate(V), ammonium metavanadate
Ammoniummolybdat *n* ammonium molybdate
~/handelsübliches commercial ammonium molybdate, ammonium paramolybdate
~/normales ammonium molybdate
Ammoniumnitrat *n* ammonium nitrate
Ammoniumnitrit *n* ammonium nitrite
Ammoniumorthophosphat *n* ammonium orthophosphate
Ammoniumoxalat *n* ammonium oxalate
Ammoniumparamolybdat *n s.* Ammoniummolybdat/handelsübliches
Ammoniumpentasulfid *n* ammonium pentasulphide
Ammoniumperchlorat *n* ammonium perchlorate
Ammoniumpermanganat *n* ammonium permanganate
Ammoniumperoxochromat *n* ammonium peroxochromate
Ammoniumperoxodisulfat *n* ammonium peroxodisulphate
Ammoniumpersulfat *n s.* Ammoniumperoxodisulfat
Ammoniumphosphat *n* ammonium phosphate, *(specif)* ammonium orthophosphate
Ammoniumpikrat *n* ammonium picrate
Ammoniumpyrrolidindithiocarbamat *n* ammonium pyrrolidine dithiocarbamate, APDC
Ammoniumradikal *n* ammonium [free] radical
Ammoniumrest *m* ammonium residue (group)
Ammoniumrhodanid *n s.* Ammoniumthiocyanat
Ammoniumsalicylat *n* ammonium salicylate
Ammoniumsalz *n* ammonium salt
Ammoniumseife *f* ammonium soap
Ammoniumselenat *n* ammonium selenate
Ammoniumstearat *n* ammonium stearate
Ammoniumstickstoff *m s.* Ammoniakstickstoff
Ammoniumsulfamat *n s.* Ammoniumsulfamidat
Ammoniumsulfamidat *n*, **Ammoniumsulfaminat** *n* ammonium sulphamate, AMS
Ammoniumsulfat *n* ammonium sulphate
Ammoniumsulfid *n* ammonium sulphide
Ammoniumsulfit *n* ammonium sulphite
Ammoniumtartrat *n* ammonium tartrate
Ammoniumtellurat *n* ammonium tellurate

Ammoniumtetrachloroplatinat(II) *n* ammonium tetrachloroplatinate(II)
Ammoniumtetracyanoplatinat(II) *n* ammonium tetracyanoplatinate(II)
Ammoniumtetroxoiodat *n* *ammonium tetraoxoiodate(VII), ammonium metaperiodate
Ammoniumthiocyanat *n* ammonium thiocyanate
Ammoniumthiosulfat *n* ammonium thiosulphate
Ammoniumtrithiocarbonat *n* ammonium trithiocarbonate
Ammoniumvalerat *n* ammonium valerate (valerianate)
Ammoniumverbindung *f* ammonium compound
~/quartäre (quaternäre) quaternary ammonium compound, quat
Ammoniumwolframat *n* *ammonium wolframate, ammonium tungstate
Ammoniumylid *n* ammonium ylide, amine ylide
Ammonolyse *f* ammonolysis
ammonolytisch ammonolytic
Ammonotelie *f* ammonotelism *(excretion of nitrogen as ammonia)*
Ammonotelier *m* ammonotelic animal *(excreting nitrogen as ammonia)*
Ammonoxidation *f* ammoxidation
Ammonpulver *n* ammonium powder *(explosive)*
Ammonsalpetersprengstoff *m* ammonium nitrate explosive
Ammonsalz *n s.* Ammoniumsalz
Ammonsalzküpe *f (text)* ammonia vat
Ammonsulfatsalpeter *m (agric)* ammonium nitrate sulphate
amöbizid amoebicidal
Amöbizid *n* amoebicide
amorph amorphous
Amorphie *f* amorphousness, amorphicity
AMP *s.* Adenosinmonophosphorsäure
Ampere *n* ampere
Amperemeter *n* amperemeter, ammeter
Amperometrie *f* amperometry
amperometrisch amperometric
Amphetamin *n* amphetamine, 1-phenyl-2-propylamine
amphibol *(bioch)* amphibolic
Amphibol *m (min)* amphibole, hornblende *(an inosilicate)*
Amphibolasbest *m (min)* amphibole asbestos
Amphibolfamilie *f*, **Amphibolgruppe** *f (min)* amphibole group
amphibolisch *(bioch)* amphibolic
Amphibolismus *m (bioch)* amphibolism
amphipathisch *(bioch)* amphipathic
amphi-Stellung *f* amphi-position
Ampho-Ion *n* amphion, amphoteric (ampholyte) ion, dipole (dipolar, dual, hybrid) ion, zwitterion, zwitterionic compound, inner (internal, intramolecular) salt
Ampholyt *m* ampholyte, amphoteric electrolyte, amphiprotic substance
Ampholytoid *n* ampholytoid *(an amphoteric soil colloid)*
Amphotensid *n* amphoteric surfactant
amphoter amphoteric, amphiprotic
Amphoterie *f* amphoterism *(phenomenon)*; amphotericity *(of a substance)*
Ampulle *f* ampoule
amu *s.* Masseeinheit/atomare
Amygdalin *n* amygdalin *(a glycoside obtained from bitter almonds)*
Amygdaloid *m (geol)* amygdaloid
Amylacetat *n* amyl acetate
n-**Amylacetylen** *n s.* Hept-1-in
n-**Amylaldehyd** *m s.* Pentanal
Amylalkohol *m* $C_5H_{11}OH$ amyl alcohol, *(specif)* $CH_3(CH_2)_3CH_2OH$ *pentan-1-ol, *(deprecated:)* *n*-amyl alcohol
Amylase *f* amylase
~/dextrinogene dextrinogenic amylase
~/mikrobielle *s.* α-Amylase/bakterielle
α-**Amylase** *f*/**bakterielle** *(biot)* bacterial α-amylase
Amylaseaktivität *f* amylolytic activity
Amylasewirkung *f* amylolytic action
n-**Amyläthin** *n s.* Hept-1-in
Amylcarbinol *n s.* Hexan-1-ol
n-**Amylchlorid** *n* *1-chloropentane, *(deprecated:)* *n*-amyl chloride
n-**Amylen-(1)** *n s.* Pent-1-en
Amylenhydrat *n* *2-methylbutan-2-ol, *(deprecated:)* amylene hydrate
Amylgruppe *f* $CH_3(CH_2)_3CH_2$– amyl group (residue)
Amylnitrit *n* $C_5H_{11}ONO$ amyl nitrite, *(specif)* $(CH_3)_2CHCH_2CH_2ONO$ [ordinary] amyl nitrite, *3-methyl-1-butyl nitrite
Amylodextrin *n* amylodextrin
amyloid amyloid[al]
Amyloid *n* 1. *(pap)* amyloid *(cellulose treated with concentrated sulphuric acid)*; 2. *(med)* amyloid *(antibody globulin abnormally deposited in animal tissues)*
Amylopektin *n* amylopectin *(main component of starch)*
Amyloverfahren *n* amylo fermentation process *(for obtaining alcohol from starchy materials without the use af malt)*
Amylrest *m s.* Amylgruppe
anabol *(bioch)* anabolic
Anabolismus *m (bioch)* anabolism
anabolisch *(bioch)* anabolic
Anacardiumgummi *n* cashew (cashawa) gum *(from Anacardium occidentale L.)*
anaerob anaerobic
Anaerobier *m* anaerobe
~/fakultativer facultative anaerobe
Anaerobiont *m s.* Anaerobier
Anaerobiose *f* anaerobiosis *(life in the absence of oxygen)*
anaerobisch anaerobic

Analcim *m (min)* analcime, analcite *(a tectosilicate)*
Analeptikum *n (pharm)* analeptic, central nervous system stimulant
Analgetikum *n (pharm)* analgesic, pain-reliever, pain-killer
analgetisch analgesic
Analog[e] *n* analogue
Analogiebeziehung *f* analogy equation *(as for expressing the relationship between heat and material transfer)*
Analysator *m s.* Analysengerät
Analyse *f* analysis • **eine ~ durchführen** to perform (run, do) an analysis • **zur ~** *s.* analysenrein
~ **an Ort und Stelle** on-site analysis
~ **atmosphärischer Spurenstoffkomponenten** atmospheric trace component analysis
~ **auf trockenem Wege** dry analysis
~/chemische chemical analysis
~/coulometrische coulometric analysis
~ **der nächsten Nachbarn** *(bioch)* nearest-neighbour base-frequency analysis, nearest-neighbour base sequencing
~/direkte direct analysis
~/diskontinuierliche discontinuous (batch) analysis
~/dynamische on-line analysis
~/elektrochemische electroanalysis
~/erschöpfende exhaustive analysis
~/gravimetrische gravimetric analysis, analysis by weight
~/halbquantitative semiquantitative analysis
~/kolorimetrische colorimetric analysis
~ **mit radioaktiven Reagenzien** radiometric analysis
~/photometrische photometric analysis
~/polarographische polarographic analysis
~/potentiometrische potentiometric analysis
~/praktische commercial analysis
~/qualitative qualitative (compositional) analysis
~/quantitative quantitative analysis
~/radiometrische radiometric analysis
~/röntgenchemische X-ray chemical analysis
~/röntgenspektrochemische X-ray spectrochemical analysis
~/sensorische *(food)* sensory estimation (evaluation, rating) organoleptic estimation
~/technische commercial analysis
~/thermische thermal analysis, thermoanalysis
~/thermogravimetrische thermogravimetric analysis, TGA
~/thermomechanische thermomechanical analysis, TMA
~/thermometrische thermometric analysis
~/trockene dry analysis
~/zerstörungsfreie non-destructive analysis
Analysenbefund *m* analytical result
Analysendurchführung *f* analytical procedure
Analyseneichfunktion *f* calibration function
Analysenergebnis *n* analytical result
Analysenfehler *m* analytical error
Analysenfunktion *f* analytical function
Analysengang *m* scheme (course) of analysis
Analysengerät *n* analyser, analysis apparatus, analytical instrument (unit)
~/diskontinuierlich arbeitendes discontinuous analyser
~/kontinuierlich arbeitendes continuous analyser
Analysenmenge *f* sample quantity
Analysenmethode *f* analytical (analysis) method, method of analysis
Analysenmethodik *f* analytical technique (procedure, operation)
Analysenprobe *f* sample analysed (under analysis)
Analysenprotokoll *n* analysis report
analysenrein reagent-grade, analytical-reagent-quality
Analysenreinheit *f* analytical-reagent quality
Analysensignal *n* analytical signal
Analysensubstanz *f* analysand, substance to be analysed; substance under analysis
Analysensystem *n* analysis system
Analysentrichter *m* fluted funnel, 60° filtration funnel
Analysenverfahren *n s.* Analysenmethodik
Analysenwaage *f* analytical balance
~ **mit Dämpfung** damped balance
Analysenweg *m* analytical approach, scheme of analysis
Analysenwert *m* analytical value
analysierbar analysable
analysieren to analyse
Analysiergerät *n s.* Analysengerät
Analyt *m* analyte
Analytik *f* analytical chemistry
Analytiker *m* analytical chemist (scientist), [chemist-]analyst
analytisch analytic[al]
a-Name *m s.* Aza-Benennung
Anaphorese *f (phys ch)* anaphoresis
Anaphrodisiakum *n (pharm)* anaphrodisiac
anaplerotisch *(bioch)* anaplerotic
anästhesierend anaesthetic
Anästhesierungsmittel *n*, **Anästhetikum** *n* anaesthetic
anästhetisierend *s.* anästhesierend
Anatas *m (min)* anatase *(titanium dioxide)*
Anatoxin *n* anatoxin *(detoxicated toxin)*
Anatto *n(m)* annatto, annotta, arnatto, arnotta *(a colouring matter from Bixa orellana L.)*
Anattofarbstoff *m s.* Anatto
anätzen to etch; *(med)* to cauterize *(by chemicals)*
anbacken to bake on, to stick on
anblasen to blow in *(a blast furnace)*
anbläuen to blue
anbluten *(dye, coat, tann)* to bleed [off, through]
Anbrenn... *s.* Anspring...
anbrennen 1. to ignite, to catch fire; 2. to burn on *(as of moulding sand on a casting)*; 3. *s.* anspringen; 4. *s.* anzünden

Anbrennen *n* 1. burning-on *(as of moulding sand on castings)*; 2. *s.* Anspringen
anbringen to attach, to mount
anbuttern *(food)* to prechurn
Andalusit *m (min)* andalusite, andaluzite *(aluminium oxide silicate)*
Anderthalbfachbindung *f* one-and-a-half bond
Änderung *f* change, alteration
~ der freien Enthalpie Gibbs (standard) free energy change, Gibbs energy change, G
~/physikalische physical change
~/stoffliche change of material, material change
Andesin *m (min)* andesine *(a tectosilicate)*
Andesit *m* andesite *(a volcanic rock)*
Andiffusion *f* arrival *(of diffusing ions or molecules)*, diffusion *(towards a surface)*
Androgen *n* androgen *(any of a class of sex hormones)*
andrucken *(pap)* to proof
andrücken to press, to contact
Andruckpapier *n* proof[ing] paper
Andruckwalze *f* nip roll
aneinanderhaften to stick together
Anelektrolyt *m* non-electrolyte
anellieren *(org ch)* to anellate, to fuse
Anellierung *f (org ch)* anellation, fusion
~/angulare angular anellation
~/lineare linear anellation
Anellierungsname *m* fusion name
Anellierungspräfix *n* fusion prefix
Anellierungsseite *f*, **Anellierungsstelle** *f* side (point, position) of fusion
anerkennen to approve, to schedule, to register *(e.g. a pesticide)*
Anerkennung *f***/amtliche** [government] approval, registration, *(Am also)* label clearance *(as of a pesticide)*
Anerkennungsverfahren *n* approval scheme *(as for pesticides)*
Aneroidbarometer *n* aneroid barometer
Anethol *n* anethole
anfahren to start up *(e.g. a reactor)*
Anfall *m* 1. accumulation; *(hyd)* flow *(of waste water)*; 2. *s.* Anfallmenge
anfällig susceptible
Anfallmenge *f* amount *(as of product or waste)*
Anfang *m* **der Trockenpartie** *(pap)* wet end of the dryer section
Anfangeisen *n (glass)* gathering (punty) iron, gatherer
Anfänger *m (glass)* gatherer *(worker)*
Anfängerpraktikum *n (lab)* elementary course
Anfangsfeuchte[beladung] *f* initial moisture content, IMC
Anfangsgeschwindigkeit *f* initial rate (velocity)
~ der Reaktion initial reaction rate
~ des Färbens *(text)* strike
Anfangsglied *n* initial member; *(nucl)* parent element *(of a decay series)*
Anfangskonzentration *f* initial (starting) concentration
Anfangslöslichkeit *f* initial solubility
Anfangsmenge *f* initial amount
Anfangspunkt *m* initial point
Anfangsretention *f***/maximale** maximum initial retention, MIR *(crop protection)*
Anfangssiedepunkt *m* initial boiling point, I.B.P.
Anfangsspreitungskoeffizient *m* initial spreading coefficient *(as of surfactants)*
Anfangstemperatur *f* initial temperature
Anfangswert *m* initial (starting) value
Anfangszustand *m* initial (original) state
anfärbbar dyeable; *(biol)* stainable
Anfärbbarkeit *f* dyeability, dye receptivity, receptivity to dyestuffs; *(biol)* stainability
anfärben to tint, to tinge, *(with soluble colouring matter:)* to dye, *(chiefly Am)* to color, *(with suspended colouring matter:)* to paint; *(biol)* to stain *(for microscopical investigation)*; *(tann)* to pretan, to colour *(to tan weakly)*
~/direkt *(text)* to dye directly
anfärbend/nicht *(text)* non-dyeing
~/normal *(text)* regular-dyeing
~/stark *(text)* deep-dyeing
Anfärbevermögen *n* dyeing (tinctorial) power
anfeuchten to moisten, to wet, to damp[en], to humidify, *(text also)* to dew; *(tann)* to sammy *(before staking)*
~/in Sägespänen *(tann)* to sawdust
~/vorher *(bioch)* to prewet
~/wieder to rewet
anflanschen to flange
anflecken to stain
Anforderung *f* **an den Reinheitsgrad** purity specification
anfressen to corrode, to eat, to attack
~/punktförmig to pit
angarnieren *(ceram)* to stick up
Angärung *f* pre-fermentation
angeben to denote *(e.g. valence or stoichiometric proportions)*
angefault putrid
angegriffen werden to undergo attack
Angelicasäure *f* angelic acid, 2-methylisocrotonic acid, **cis*-2-methylbut-2-enoic acid
Angeli-Rimini-Reaktion *f* Angeli-Rimini reaction *(for preparing hydroxamic acids)*
angemahlen *(pap)* lightly beaten
angeordnet/regelmäßig regularly ordered
angerben to pretan, to colour
Anger-Mühle *f*, **Anger-Prallmühle** *f* Anger mill
Angle-Methode *f (rubber)* angle method *(for determining the tear propagation strength)*
Angle-Probe *f (rubber)* angle test piece *(for determining the tear propagation strength)*
Anglesit *m (min)* anglesite *(lead sulphate)*
angreifbar attackable, vulnerable *(chemically)*; corrodible *(metal)*; affectable, affectible *(physically as by heat)*

Angreifbarkeit *f* vulnerability, capability of being attacked, liability to attack *(chemically)*; affectability, affectibility *(physically as by heat)*
angreifen to attack *(chemically)*; to corrode, to eat *(metals)*; to affect *(physically as by heat)*
Angriff *m* attack
~ **am benachbarten C-Atom** ortho attack *(on an aromatic ring)*
~ **am gegenüberliegenden C-Atom** para attack *(on an aromatic ring)*
~ **an der** *meta*-**Position** meta attack
~**/bakterieller** bacterial attack
~**/elektrophiler** electrophilic attack
~**/enzymatischer** enzymatic attack
~**/interkristalliner** intergranular attack *(corrosion)*
~**/nucleophiler** nucleophilic attack
~ **von der Rückseite [her]** rear (back-side) attack *(as in Walden inversion)*
Angriffsort *m*, **Angriffsstelle** *f* site (point) of attack
angular angular
Anguß *m (plast)* gate, sprue
~**/direkter** direct gate
~**/ringförmiger** ring gate
Angußausdrückstift *m (plast)* sprue ejector
Angußbuchse *f (plast)* sprue feed bush[ing]
Angußfarbe *f (ceram)* engobe
Angußkegel *m (plast)* gate, sprue
Angußmasse *f (ceram)* engobe
Angußsteg *m (plast)* inlet
Angußverteiler *m (plast)* 1. runner; 2. spreader *(of an injection mould)*
~**/beheizter** hot runner
Angußzieher *m (plast)* sprue puller
anhaften to adhere
Anhaften *n* adherence, adhesion
anhaftend adherent, adhesive
Anhängestäubegerät *n (agric)* traction duster
anharmonisch anharmonic
Anharmonizität *f* anharmonicity
Anharmonizitätskonstante *f* anharmonicity constant
anhäufen to accumulate
~**/sich** to accumulate, to collect
Anhäufung *f* accumulation
anheben to elevate, to raise *(e.g. temperature, boiling point)*; to raise, to energize *(electrons to an excited state)*
Anhebung *f* elevation, raising *(as of temperature, boiling point)*; raising, energization *(of electrons to an excited state)*
Anheftungssequenz *f (bioch)* attachment sequence
anheizen to heat up
Anheizzeit *f* heat-up period
Anhydrid *n* [acid] anhydride
~**/cyclisches** cyclic [acid] anhydride
~**/gemischtes** mixed anhydride
~**/inneres (intramolekulares)** inner (internal, intramolecular) anhydride
~**/symmetrisches** symmetric anhydride
anhydridisieren *s.* anhydrisieren
anhydrisieren to anhydr[id]ize
Anhydrisierung *f* anhydr[id]ization
Anhydrit *m (min)* anhydrite *(anhydrous calcium sulphate)*
Anhydritbinder *m* anhydrite binder
Anhydrobase *f* anhydrobase
Anhydroglucose *f* anhydroglucose
Anhydrozucker *m* anhydrosugar
Anil *n* anil, *N*-phenyl imine
Anilid *n* anilide, *N*-phenyl amide *(an N-acyl derivative of aniline)*; 2. anilide *(a salt of aniline)*
Anilidoessigsäure *f s.* Anilinoessigsäure
Anilin *n* aniline, aminobenzene
~**/salzsaures** *s.* Anilinhydrochlorid
~**/technisches** aniline oil
Anilinblau *n* aniline blue; *(specif) s.* ~/spritlösliches
~**/spritlösliches** *(biol)* aniline blue [2B], spirit blue, acid blue 20 *(triphenylrosaniline hydrochloride)*
Anilinchlorhydrat *n s.* Anilinhydrochlorid
Anilindruck *m* aniline (flexographic) printing, flexography
Anilindruckfarbe *f* aniline (flexographic) ink
Anilinfarbe *f* aniline dye
Anilinfarbstoff *m* aniline dye
Anilinformaldehydharz *n* aniline-formaldehyde resin
Anilingelb *n* aniline yellow, *p*-aminoazobenzene, solvent yellow 1
Anilingummidruck *m s.* Anilindruck
Anilinharz *n* aniline[-formaldehyde] resin
Anilinhydrochlorid *n* aniline hydrochloride, aniline salt
Anilinoderivat *n* anilino derivative
Anilinoessigsäure *f* anilinoacetic acid, *N*-phenylglycine
Anilinogruppe *f* C_6H_5NH- anilino (phenylamino) group
Anilinöl *n* aniline oil *(commercial grade of aniline)*
Anilinpunkt *m* aniline [cloud] point
Anilinpurpur *m* aniline purple, mauveine
Anilinsalz *n s.* Anilinhydrochlorid
Anilinschwarz *n* aniline black, pigment black 1
Anilin-*m*-sulfonsäure *f* aniline-*m*-sulphonic acid, metanilic acid
Anilin-*o*-sulfonsäure *f* aniline-*o*-sulphonic acid, orthanilic acid
Anilin-*p*-sulfonsäure *f* aniline-*p*-sulphonic acid, sulphanilic acid
Anilintrübungspunkt *f* aniline [cloud] point
Anilinvergiftung *f* aniline poisoning
Anilinwasser *n* aniline water
animalisch animal
animalisieren *(text)* to animalize
Animé-Kopal *m* animé copal *(from Hymenaea courbaril L. or Trachylobium hornemannianum Hayne), (specif)* Brazil (Colombia) copal *(from Hymenaea courbaril L.)*

animpfen *(cryst)* to seed; *(biot)* to inoculate, to seed *(a nutrient solution)*
Animpfen *n (cryst)* seeding; *(biot)* inoculation, seeding *(of a nutrient solution)*
Anion *n* anion
~/komplexes complex anion
Anion... *s. a.* Anionen...
Anionbase *f* anion base
Anioncharakter *m* anionic character
Anionelektrode *f* anion electrode
Anionen... *s. a.* Anion...
anionenaktiv anion-active, anionic
Anionenaustausch *m* anion exchange
Anionenaustauscher *m* 1. anion (hydroxyl-form) exchanger, OH-form exchanger, anionite; 2. *(hyd)* anion unit *(of a demineralizing system)*
~ auf Kunstharzbasis anion-exchange resin
~/schwach basischer weak-base (weakly basic) anion exchanger, weak-base deionizer (resin)
~/stark basischer strong-base (strongly basic) anion exchanger, strong-base deionizer (resin)
Anionenaustauschermaterial *n* anion-exchange material
Anionenaustauschfähigkeit *f* anion exchangeability
Anionenaustauschharz *n* anion exchange resin
Anionenbelastung *f (hyd)* anion loading
Anionenelektrode *f* anodized (anodic) electrode
Anionenfehlstelle *f* anion vacancy
Anionenkomplex *m* anion complex
Anionenleerstelle *f*, **Anionenlücke** *f* anion vacancy
Anionenstrom *m* anionic current
Anionenstufe *f (hyd)* anion unit *(of a demineralizing system)*
Anionentrennungsgang *m* anion scheme, scheme of analysis for the anions
anionisch anionic
anionoid anionoid, nucleophilic
anionotrop anionotropic
Anionotropie *f* anionotropy
Anionsäure *f* anion acid
Aniontensid *n* anionic surfactant
Aniscampher *m s.* Anethol
Anisidin *n* anisidine, aminophenol methyl ether
anisodesmisch *(cryst)* anisodesmic
anisodimensional anisodimensional
Anisol *n* anisole, *methoxybenzene, methyl phenyl ether
Anisöl *n* aniseed oil *(from Pimpinella anisum L. and Illicium verum L.)*
anisotrop anisotropic, non-isotropic, aeolotropic
~/optisch optically anisotropic
Anisotropie *f* anisotropy, aeolotropism
Anisotropiefaktor *m* anisotropy (dissymmetry) factor
Anisotropieglied *n* anisotropy term
Anisotropiekegel *m (spectr)* shielding cone, cone of deshielding
Anissäure *f* anisic acid, *p*-methoxybenzoic acid
Ankergruppe *f* active group *(ion exchange)*
Ankerit *m (min)* ankerite *(a variety of dolomite)*
Ankermischer *m*, **Ankerrührer** *m* anchor agitator (mixer), horseshoe mixer
Ankersäule *f* buckstay *(of a furnace)*
ankleben to stick [on]; to paste on; to glue on; to adhere, to stick
anklebend adherent, adhesive
Anklemmrührer *m* portable mixer
Ankochperiode *f (pap)* impregnation (penetration) period
ankohlen to char
ankondensieren to fuse *(a ring to another one)*
ankuppeln *(dye)* to couple
Anlage *f* 1. plant; unit; 2. arrangement *(as of a trial)*; layout *(of a plant)*
~/chemische chemical plant
~/diskontinuierlich arbeitende batch (fill-and-draw) unit
~/im Aufwärtsstrom arbeitende *(hyd, filtr)* upflow unit
~/periodisch arbeitende *s.* ~/diskontinuierlich arbeitende
~ zum Süßen *(petrol)* sweetening plant
~ zur Doktorbehandlung *(petrol)* doctor-treating unit
~ zur Entschwefelung desulphurization plant
~ zur Hydrodesulfurierung *(petrol, coal)* hydrodesulphurization plant
~ zur Lösungsmittelentparaffinierung *(petrol)* solvent-dewaxing plant
~ zur Propanentasphaltierung *(petrol)* propane-deasphalting plant
~ zur Propanentparaffinierung *(petrol)* propane-dewaxing plant
Anlagenleistung *f* plant performance
Anlagentechnik *f* plant technology
anlagern to add *(a chemical compound for preparing an addition compound)*; to attach, to gain *(e.g. a proton or electron – said of an atom or compound)*
~/koordinativ to coordinate *(e.g. molecules)*
~/sich 1. to become attached, to attach oneself, *(esp of atoms or atomic groups:)* to undergo addition, to add; 2. *(physically:)* to adsorb, to undergo adsorption
~/sich koordinativ to coordinate
Anlagerung *f* 1. attachment, *(esp of atoms or atomic groups:)* addition; 2. *(physically:)* adsorption
~/koordinative coordination
Anlagerungskomplex *m* outer complex, high-spin (spin-free) complex
Anlagerungsprodukt *n* addition product
Anlagerungsreaktion *f* addition reaction
Anlagerungsrichtung *f* direction of addition
Anlagerungsverbindung *f* addition compound

anlassen 1. to start [up] *(e.g. a machine)*; 2. to temper *(metals)*
Anlaßfarbe *f* temper colour
Anlaßfilm *m* tarnish [film]
Anlaßöl *n* tempering oil
anlaufen 1. to tarnish, *(esp of lacquers:)* to blush, *(esp of oil varnish:)* to bloom, *(esp of glass:)* to [become] dim; 2. to start [up] *(as of a machine)*; to get under way *(of production)*
Anlauffarbe *f* temper colour
Anlaufperiode *f (phys ch)* induction period
Anlaufschicht *f* tarnish [film]
Anlaufstrecke *f* transition length *(from tube entrance to fully developed flow)*
Anlegegoniometer *n (cryst)* contact goniometer
Anlegeöl *n* gold size *(for attaching gold leaf to surfaces)*
Anlockmittel *n*, **Anlockstoff** *m* attractant *(as for insects)*
Anlösung *f* partial solution
anmachen to temper, to mix *(e.g. mortar, concrete)*
Anmachwasser *n* tempering (mixing) water *(manufacture of concrete)*; *(ceram)* mixing water, water of plasticity
anmaischen to slurry *(coal)*
Anmeldung *f* petition *(for permission of manufacturing esp a pesticide)*
Annabergit *m (min)* annabergite, nickel bloom *(nickel tetraoxoarsenate(V))*
Annäherungseffekt *m* proximity effect *(in enzyme reactions)*
Annahme *f* 1. assumption, hypothesis; 2. acceptance *(as of a theory)*; acquisition *(as of a configuration)*
~/Goudsmit-Uhlenbecksche Goudsmit and Uhlenbeck assumption *(of rotating electrons)*
~/stillschweigende tacit assumption
~/vereinfachende simplifying assumption
annässen to moisten
Annatto *n(m)* *s.* Anatto
annehmen 1. to assume, to suppose, to suggest; 2. to accept *(e.g. a theory)*; 3. to acquire *(a configuration)*; 4. to take on *(a colour)*; 5. *(text)* to take, to accept *(a dye)*
Annihilation *f (phys ch)* annihilation, energy pooling
Annihilationsspektrum *n* annihilation spectrum
Annihilationsstrahlung *f (phys ch)* annihilation radiation
Annulen *n* annulene
[8]**Annulen** *n* [8]annulene, cycloocta-1,3,5,7-tetraene
Anode *f* anode, anelectrode, positive electrode
Anodeneffekt *m* anode effect
Anodenlaufzeit *f* anode life
Anodenpotential *n* anode potential
Anodenraum *m* anode compartment
Anodenreaktion *f* anode reaction
Anodenschlamm *m* anode slime (sludge, mud)
Anodenspannung *f* anode voltage
Anodenstrahl *m* anode ray
Anodenstrom *m* anode current
Anodenstromdichte *f* anodic current density
Anodenverfahren *n (rubber)* anode process
anodisch anodic
~ **wirksam** galvanic *(coating)*
anodisieren *(met)* to anodize
Anodisierung *f (met)* anodizing, anodic oxidation (coating)
Anolyt *m* anolyte *(electrolyte in the anode compartment)*
anomal anomalous, abnormal
Anomalie *f* anomaly
~/optische optical anomaly
α-**Anomalie** *f (rubber)* glass transition, gamma (second-order) transition, vitrification
a-Nomenklatur *f* "a" nomenclature
anomer anomeric *(stereochemistry)*
Anomer[e] *n* anomer *(stereochemistry)*
Anomerisierung *f* anomerization *(stereochemistry)*
anordnen to arrange, to mount, to align *(e.g. parts of an apparatus)*
~/sich to align *(as of chain molecules)*
Anordnung *f* arrangement, array, alignment *(as of chain molecules)*; *(spectr)* mounting *(of a monochromator)*
~ **auf Lücke** *s.* ~/versetzte
~/fluchtende in-line arrangement *(as of tubes)*
~/geometrische *s.* ~/räumliche
~/helikale *(bioch)* helical array
~/lineare linear orientation *(of ligands)*
~/natürliche *s.* ~/periodische
~/octaedrische octahedral orientation *(of ligands)*
~/periodische periodic arrangement *(of the elements)*
~/quadratisch ebene square planar orientation *(of ligands)*
~/quadratisch pyramidale tetragonal pyramidal orientation *(of ligands)*
~/räumliche spatial arrangement (orientation)
~/tetraedrisch verzerrte seesaw orientation *(of ligands)*
~/tetraedrische tetrahedral arrangement (orientation)
~/T-förmige T-shaped orientation *(of ligands)*
~/trigonal bipyramidale trigonal bipyramidal orientation *(of ligands)*
~/trigonal ebene trigonal planar orientation *(of ligands)*
~/trigonal pyramidale trigonal pyramidal orientation *(of ligands)*
~/versetzte staggered arrangement *(as of tubes)*
~/V-förmige angular (bent) orientation *(of ligands)*
Anorganiker *m* inorganic chemist
anorganisch inorganic
anorganisch-chemisch inorganic-chemical
Anorthit *m (min)* anorthite *(calcium aluminium silicate)*

Anorthoklas *m (min)* anorthoclase *(chiefly sodium potassium aluminium silicate)*
Anoxybiose *f* anaerobiosis *(life in the absence of oxygen)*
Anpaßstück *n* adapter, adaptor
Anpassung **f/induzierte** *(bioch)* induced fit
anpasten to make into a paste, to paste
Anpolymerisation *f* grafting
anpolymerisieren to graft
Anprall *m* impact, impingement
anprallen to impact, to impinge
Anpreßdruck *m (pap)* plug pressure *(in perfecting engines)*
anrauhen to roughen
anregbar excitable
Anregbarkeit *f* excitability
Anregekristall *m* seed crystal
anregen to excite *(an atom)*; to activate, to initiate, to start *(a reaction)*; to induce *(crystallization)*
Anregung *f* excitation *(of an atom)*; activation, initiation *(of a reaction)*; induction *(of crystallization)*
~/photochemische photochemical excitation, photoexcitation
~/thermische thermal excitation
~ von Atomen atomic excitation
Anregungsenergie *f* excitation energy
Anregungsfunktion *f* excitation function
Anregungsmittel *n (pharm)* stimulant, stimulus, stimulatory drug
Anregungsniveau *n* excitation (excited) level
Anregungspotential *n* excitation potential
Anregungsquelle *f (spectr)* excitation source
Anregungsspannung *f* excitation voltage
Anregungsspektrum *n* excitation spectrum
Anregungswahrscheinlichkeit *f* excitation probability
Anregungswellenlänge *f (spectr)* excitation wavelength
Anregungszustand *m* excited (energized) state
Anreibbarren *m* pressure bar *(of a roller mill)*
anreiben to grind *(pigments)*; to paste *(e.g. coal for hydrogenation)*
Anreibung *f (coat)* grinding; pasting *(as of coal for hydrogenation)*
Anreicher... *s.* Anreicherungs...
anreichern to enrich; to concentrate, to beneficiate *(ore)*; *(pap)* to fortify *(the cooking acid)*
~/mit Kohlenstoff to carbonize
~/mit Ozon to ozonize, to ozonify
~/mit Sauerstoff to enrich with oxygen, to oxygenate, to oxygenize
~/mit Vitaminen to vitaminize, to enrich (fortify) with vitamins
~/sich to accumulate
Anreicherung *f* 1. enrichment; concentration, beneficiation *(of ore)*; *(pap)* fortification *(of the cooking acid)*; 2. accumulation
~ von Uran-235 uranium[-235] enrichment
Anreicherungsanlage *f (min tech)* concentration plant, concentrator
Anreicherungsfaktor *m (nucl)* enrichment factor
Anreicherungsgerät *n (min tech)* concentrating machine, concentrator
Anreicherungsgrad *m s.* Anreicherungsfaktor
Anreicherungsherd *m (min tech)* concentrating (concentrator, concentrate) table
Anreicherungshorizont *m (soil)* illuvial horizon, B horizon, accumulate layer, zone of illuviation (accumulation), subsoil
Anreicherungsverfahren *n* concentration process (method)
Anreißen *n (text)* first break, *(Am)* first perceptible step *(just perceptible alteration of colour)*
anrühren to temper, to mix *(for preparing a slurry)*; to paste, to make into a paste
ansammeln/sich to accumulate, to collect
Ansammlung *f* accumulation, collection
Ansatz *m* 1. batch, charge, charge (charging) stock, feed material, feed[stock]; *(plast)* formulation; 2. crust *(of undesired solid matter)*; 3. *s.* Ansatzstück
Ansatzrohr *n* attached tube; stem *(of a gas burette)*
Ansatzstück *n* extension limb, lateral
ansäuern to acidify, to make acidic, to acidulate; *(food)* to sour; to leaven *(dough)*
~/erneut to reacidify
Ansäuern *n* acidification, acidulation; *(food)* souring; leavening *(of dough)*
Ansäuerungsmittel *n* acidulant, acidulent
Ansaugdruck *m* suction pressure
ansaugen to draw [in], to suck, to aspirate
Ansaugen *n* drawing, suction, aspiration
Ansaugleistung *f* suction capacity
Ansaugleitung *f* suction line
Ansaugrohr *n* suction pipe (tube)
Ansaugzone *f* cake-forming zone *(vacuum filtration)*
Ansa-Verbindung *f (org ch)* ansa compound
anschärfen *(tann)* to sharpen, to strengthen, to mend *(the lime liquor)*
Anschärf[ungs]mittel *n (tann)* sharpener, sharpening agent
anschließen to attach, to connect
Anschliff *m (geol)* ground (polished) face, ground surface (section) *(for direct-light microscopy)*
Anschlifffläche **f/polierte** *s.* Anschliff
Anschlifftechnik *f (geol)* polished-face technique, polished-surface (polished-specimen) technique
Anschluß *m* 1. attachment, connection *(act)*; 2. *s.* Anschlußstelle; 3. *s.* Anschlußstück
Anschlußleitung *f* connecting pipe
Anschlußrohr *n* connecting tube
Anschlußstelle *f* joint, junction
Anschlußstück *n* connecting piece, connection, joint
anschmutzen to stain; *(text)* to soil
~/künstlich *(text)* to soil artificially

Anschmutzung *f* staining; *(text)* soiling, *(if artificially also)* soiling operation (procedure)
Anschnitt *m (plast)* feed (fill) orifice
~/fächerförmiger *(plast)* fan gate
Anschütz-Aufsatz *m (distil)* Anschütz head
anschwänzen *(ferm)* to sparge
Anschwänzvorrichtung *f (ferm)* sparger
Anschwänzwasser *n (ferm)* sparge water
anschwellen to swell [up]
Anschwemmfilter *n* precoat[ed] filter; *(hyd)* septum filter
Anschwemmfilterschicht *f* filter precoat, precoat filter cake
Anschwemmfiltration *f* precoat filtration; *(hyd)* septum filtration
Anschwemmgut *n*, **Anschwemmittel** *n (filtr)* precoat [material], precoat filtering medium
Anschwemmklärfilter *n* precoat clarifier
Anschwemmschicht *f (filtr)* precoat layer (bed)
• **mit einer ~ versehen** to precoat *(a filter)*
anschwöden *(tann)* to flood, to paint *(the flesh side of hides with lime)*
ansetzen 1. to prepare *(e.g. a reaction mixture)*; 2. to charge *(a furnace)*; 3. to scale, to become encrusted *(with a hard deposit)*; to become covered *(e.g. with rust)*
~/Grünspan to become covered with verdigris
~/Kesselstein to scale, to fur
~/Rost to rust
~/sich to deposit
ANSI = American National Standards Institute
Ansprechdauer *f (anal)* response time
ansprechen to respond *(as to a test or agent)*
Ansprechgeschwindigkeit *f (anal)* speed of response
Ansprechzeit *f s.* Ansprechdauer
Anspringcharakteristik *f (rubber)* scorch characteristic
anspringen *(rubber)* to scorch, to burn, to set (fire, cure) up, to prevulcanize, to precure *(to undergo unintended vulcanization)*
Anspringen *n (rubber)* scorch[ing], burning, set[ting]-up, firing-up, curing-up, prevulcanization, precure, precuring, *(during storage:)* pile (bin) curing
Anspringkurve *f (rubber)* scorch curve
Anspringperiode *f (rubber)* scorch period
Anspringpunkt *m (rubber)* scorch point
Anspringtendenz *f (rubber)* scorch[ing] tendency, scorchiness
Anspringzeit *f (rubber)* scorch time
anspruchsvoll *(agric)* exacting *(with reference to nutrition)*
anstechen to tap *(e.g. a cask or furnace)*
anstehen *(geol)* to crop out, to outcrop
Anstehen *n (geol)* outcrop[ping]
Anstehendes *n (geol)* bedrock
ansteigen to increase, to rise, to grow
Ansteigen *n s.* Anstieg
anstellen 1. to turn on, to start, to set in motion; 2. to carry out, to run *(an experiment)*; 3. *(ferm)* to pitch *(wort)*; to set *(mash)*
~/Versuche to experiment[alize], to run (carry out) experiments
Anstellhefe *f (ferm)* pitching yeast
Anstelltemperatur *f (ferm)* pitching temperature *(for wort)*; set temperature *(for mash)*
Anstellwürze *f (ferm)* original wort
Anstieg *m* increase, rise, growth
Anstiegszeit *f (anal)* rise time *(difference between response time and dead time)*
Anstoß *m* impact, impingement
Anstoßatom *n* knocked-on atom
Anstoßelektron *n* impact electron
anstoßen to impact, to impinge
anstreichbar paintable
Anstreichbarkeit *f* paintability
anstreichen to paint, to brush, to coat
Anstrich *m* paint, coat [of paint]
Anstrichaufbau *m s.* Anstrichsystem
Anstrichbindemittel *n s.* Anstrichstoffbindemittel
Anstrichfarbe *f* paint, pigmented coating *(for compounds s.* Anstrichstoff*)*
Anstrichfehler *m* paint-film defect (fault)
Anstrichfilm *m* paint film
Anstrichfläche *f* abrasive surface *(for safety matches)*
Anstrichmasse *f (ceram)* coating slip
Anstrichmittel *n s.* Anstrichstoff
Anstrichmittelwanne *f* sump *(in the flow-coating process)*
Anstrichschaden *m s.* Anstrichfehler
Anstrichstoff *m* paint, coating [material]
~/anorganischer inorganic paint (coating)
~/chemisch trocknender chemical-reaction paint
~ mit anorganischem Bindemittel *s.* ~/anorganischer
~/ofentrocknender stoving (baking) paint
~/plastischer plastic paint
~/rostschützender antirust paint, rust-protective (rust-resisting) paint
~/seewasserbeständiger marine paint
~/thixotroper thixotropic (gel) paint
~/wäßriger water[-base] paint
Anstrichstoffbindemittel *n* paint (coating) binder
Anstrichstoffindustrie *f* paint and varnish industry
Anstrichstofftechnik *f* paint and varnish technology
Anstrichsystem *n* painting (coating) system
Anstrichtechnik *f* painting technology
Anstrichtrocknung *f* paint drying
ANT *s.* α-Naphthylthioharnstoff
Antagonismus *m* antagonism
Antagonist *m* antagonist; *(bioch)* competitive inhibitor, antimetabolite, metabolic antagonist
antarafacial *(org ch)* antarafacial, a
Antazidum *n (pharm)* [gastric] antacid *(an agent which counteracts superacidity)*

anteigen to make into a paste, to paste, *(rubber also)* to make into a dough
Anteil *m* portion, proportion, constituent [part], component, *(esp if one of two approximately equal portions:)* moiety
~ an suspendierten Feststoffen *(hyd)* suspended solids content (concentration, level)
~/disperser disperse[d] phase
~/elastischer rebound, recovery *(of strain)*
~/hochsiedender (höhersiedender) *(distil)* less volatile component, high-boiling component
~/kristalliner crystalline fraction
~/leichterflüchtiger (leichtersiedender) *(distil)* more volatile component, M.V.C., low-boiling component, light[er] component
~/prozentualer percentage
~/schwererflüchtiger (schwerersiedender) *s.* ~/hochsiedender
~/schwerflüchtiger (schwersiedender) *s.* ~/hochsiedender
~/unverseifbarer unsaponifiable matter (residue)
Anteile *mpl***/fermentierbare** *(biot)* fermentables *(of the substrate)*
Anthanthronfarbstoff *m* anthanthrone dye
Anthelminthikum *n (pharm)* anthelmint[h]ic
anthelminthisch *(pharm)* anthelmint[h]ic
Anthocyan *n* anthocyan[in] *(any of a class of plant pigments)*
Anthocyanidin *n* anthocyanidin *(any of a class of plant pigments)*
Anthocyanin *n s.* Anthocyan
Anthophyllit *m (min)* anthophyllite *(an inosilicate)*
Anthophyllitasbest *m* anthophyllite asbestos
Anthracen *n* anthracene
Anthracenblau *n* anthracene blue
Anthracenöl *n* anthracene (green) oil
Anthracenreihe *f* anthracene series
anthrachinoid anthraquinonoid
Anthrachinolin *n* anthraquinoline
Anthrachinolinchinon *n* anthraquinolinequinone
Anthrachinon *n* anthraquinone
Anthrachinonacridon *n* anthraquinoneacridone
Anthrachinoncarbonsäure *f* anthraquinonecarboxylic acid
Anthrachinonchinolin *n s.* Anthrachinolinchinon
Anthrachinondisulfonsäure *f* anthraquinonedisulphonic acid
Anthrachinonfarbstoff *m* anthraquinone (anthraquinonoid) dye
Anthrachinonklasse *f* anthraquinone class
Anthrachinonküpenfarbstoff *m* anthraquinone vat dye
Anthrachinonreihe *f* anthraquinone series
Anthrachinonsulfonsäure *f* anthraquinonesulphonic acid
Anthranilsäureester *m* anthranilate
Anthraxylon *n (coal)* anthraxylon
Anthrazit *m (coal)* anthracite
Anthrazitgruppe *f (coal)* anthracite group
Anthrimid *n (dye)* anthrimide

Anthron *n* anthrone, 9*H*-anthracen-9-one
anthropogen anthropogenic
Antiabsetzmittel *n* antisettling (suspending) agent
antiadhäsiv abhesive
antiaromatisch *(org ch)* antiaromatic
Antiarthritikum *n (pharm)* antiarthritic
Antibackmittel *n* anticaking agent *(as for protecting granules)*
antibakteriell antibacterial
antibindend antibonding
Antibindung *f* 1. antibond; 2. antibonding
Antibiose *f* antibiosis
Antibiotikabildner *mpl*, **Antibiotikaproduzenten** *mpl* antibiotic-producing microorganisms
antibiotikaresistent resistant to antibiotics, antibiotic-resistant
Antibiotikaresistenz *f* resistance to antibiotics, antibiotic resistance
Antibiotikarückstand *m* antibiotic residue
Antibiotikum *n (pharm)* antibiotic [agent, substance]
~ als Futtermittelzusatz *s.* ~/nutritives
~ gegen Rickettsien antirickettsial antibiotic
~/makrolides macrolide antibiotic
~/nutritives feed-additive antibiotic
~/polyenes polyene antibiotic
antibiotisch *(pharm)* antibiotic
Antichlor *n (text, pap)* antichlor *(for removing chlorine after bleaching)*
Anticodon *n (bioch)* anticodon *(a sequence of three nucleotides)*
Anticodonarm *m (bioch)* anticodon arm
Antidepressivum *n (pharm)* antidepressant
Antidiabetikum *n (pharm)* antidiabetic
antidiabetisch antidiabetic
Antidiarrhoikum *n (pharm)* antidiarrhoeic, styptic
antidiarrhöisch antidiarrhoeal
Antidiazotat *n* antidiazo compound
Antidiuretikum *n (pharm)* antidiuretic
antidiuretisch antidiuretic
Antidot *n (tox)* antidote
Antiemetikum *n (pharm)* antiemetic
Antienzym *n* antienzyme
Antiepileptikum *n (pharm)* antiepileptic
Antifebrilium *n s.* Antipyretikum
Antiferment *n* antienzyme
antiferromagnetisch antiferromagnetic
Antiferromagnetismus *m* antiferromagnetism
Antifertilitätspräparat *n (pharm)* antifertility agent
Antifiebermittel *n s.* Antipyretikum
Antifilzausrüstung *f (text)* antifelting treatment
Antifouling *n*, **Antifoulinganstrichstoff** *m* antifouling [coating], anti-fouling composition (compound)
Antifoulingfarbe *f* anti-fouling [marine] paint, marine anti-fouling paint
antifungal antifungal, fungicidal
Antigen *n (bioch)* antigen
~/agglutinierbares agglutinogen
Antigenität *s.* Antigenwirkung
Antigenwirkung *f (bioch)* antigenicity

Antigorit *m (min)* antigorite *(a variety of serpentine)*
Antihaftmittel *n* antiblock[ing] agent *(for plastics and paper)*
Antihaftvermögen *n* antistick properties
Antihalluzinogen *n (pharm)* neuroleptic [drug], antipsychotic, major tranquilizer
Antihaut[bildungs]mittel *n (coat)* antiskinning agent
Antihidrotikum *n* antihidrotic, antiperspirant, perspiration check
Antihistaminikum *n*, **Antihistaminpräparat** *n (pharm)* antihistamine
Antihormon *n* antihormone
Anti-Hückel-System *n* Möbius system *(a cyclic conjugated hydrocarbon)*
Antihypertonikum *n (pharm)* antihypertensive (hypotensive) drug, blood pressure depressant
antihypertonisch antihypertensive, hypotensive
anti-Isomer[e] *n* anti isomer
Antikatalysator *m* anticatalyst, negative catalyst, inhibitor, retarder
Antikatalyse *f* anticatalysis, negative catalysis, inhibition
antikatalytisch anticatalytic
Antikatode *f* anticathode
Antikglas *n* antique glass
Antiklebvermögen *n* antistick properties
Antiklinalfalle *f (petrol)* anticlinal trap
Antiklopfeffekt *m* antiknock effect
Antiklopfeigenschaften *fpl* antiknock properties
Antiklopfmittel *n* antiknock [agent, additive], knock suppressor, octane improver
Antiklopfwirkung *f* antiknock (antidetonating) action; antiknock effect
Antikoagulans *n*, **Antikoaguliermittel** *n (pharm)* anticoagulant
anti-Konformation *f*, **anti-Konstellation** *f* anti conformation, A *(of macromolecules, torsion angle* $\pm 60°$*)*; *(org ch)* *anticlinal conformation, ac *(torsion angle* $\pm 120°$*)*
Antikonvulsans *n*, **Antikonvulsivum** *n (pharm)* anticonvulsive
antikonzeptionell contraceptive
Antikonzeptivum *n*, **Antikonzipiens** *n (pharm)* contraceptive
Antikörper *m* antibody, immune body
~/monoklonaler *(biot)* monoclonal antibody, MAb
Antikörperbildung *f* antibody production *(in a cell)*
antikorrosiv anticorrosive
antileukozytär antileucocytic
Antimaculepapier *n* tympan (set-off) paper
Antimalariamittel *n (pharm)* antimalarial
Antimalariawirksamkeit *f* antimalarial activity
Anti-Markovnikov-Addition *f* anti-Markovnikov addition, peroxide-initiated addition
Antimaterie *f* antimatter
Antimetabolit *m (bioch)* antimetabolite, metabolite (metabolic) antagonist *(enzyme inhibitor acting mostly in competitive inhibition)*
antimikrobiell antimicrobial
Antimikrobiotikum *n (pharm)* antimicrobial agent
Antimon *n* Sb antimony
~/graues (metallisches) grey (metallic, gamma) antimony
~/schwarzes black (beta) antimony
Antimonat *n* antimonate
Antimonblüte *f (min)* antimony bloom, flowers of antimony, valentinite *(antimony(III) oxide)*
Antimon(III)-bromid *n* antimony(III) bromide, antimony tribromide
Antimonbutter *f* butter of antimony, mineral butter *(antimony(III) chloride)*
Antimon(III)-chlorid *n* antimony(III) chloride, antimony trichloride
Antimon(V)-chlorid *n* antimony(V) chloride, antimony pentachloride
Antimonfahlerz *n (min)* grey copper [ore], copper grey, tetrahedrite *(antimony copper sulphide, often containing iron and silver)*
Antimon(III)-fluorid *n* antimony(III) fluoride, antimony trifluoride
Antimon(V)-fluorid *n* antimony(V) fluoride, antimony pentafluoride
Antimongelb *n* antimony yellow, Naples yellow *(lead antimonate)*
Antimonglanz *m s.* Antimonit
Antimonhalogenid *n* antimony halide (halogenide)
antimonhaltig antimony-containing, *(esp ores:)* antimoniferous, antimony-bearing
Antimonhydrid *n s.* Antimonwasserstoff
Antimonialblei *n s.* Hartblei
Antimonid *n* antimonide
Antimon(III)-iodid *n* antimony(III) iodide, antimony triiodide
Antimon(V)-iodid *n* antimony(V) iodide, antimony pentaiodide
Antimonit *m (min)* antimonite, stibnite, antimony glance, grey antimony *(antimony(III) sulphide)*
Antimonium-Ion *n* stibonium ion
Antimoniumverbindung *f* stibonium compound
Antimonkarmin *n (coat)* antimony cinnabar (vermilion)
Antimonocker *m (min)* antimony ochre *(consisting of oxidation products of antimonite)*
Antimon(III)-oxid *n* antimony(III) oxide, antimony trioxide
Antimon(III,V)-oxid *n* antimony(III,V) oxide, antimony tetraoxide
Antimon(V)-oxid *n* antimony(V) oxide, antimony pentaoxide
Antimon(III)-oxidchlorid *n* antimony(III) chloride oxide
Antimon(V)-oxidchlorid *n* antimony(V) trichloride oxide
Antimon(III)-oxidsulfat *n* antimony(III) oxide sulphate
Antimonpent[a]... *s.* Antimon(V)-...
Antimonregulus *m* regulus of antimony, antimony regulus *(metallic antimony, either virgin or refined)*
Antimonsäure *f* antimonic acid

Antimon(III)-selenid *n* antimony(III) selenide, antimony triselenide
Antimonspeise *f (met)* antimonial speiss
Antimon(III)-sulfat *n* antimony(III) sulphate, antimony trisulphate
Antimon(III)-sulfid *n* antimony(III) sulphide, antimony trisulphide
Antimon(V)-sulfid *n* antimony(V) sulphide, antimony pentasulphide
Antimon(III)-tellurid *n* antimony(III) telluride, antimony tritelluride
Antimontetroxid *n s.* Antimon(III,V)-oxid
Antimontri... *s.* Antimon(III)-...
Antimonwasserstoff *m* antimony hydride, stibane, *(if unsubstituted also)* antimony trihydride, stibine
Antimonweiß *n* antimony white *(antimony(III) oxide)*
Antimonylkaliumtartrat *n s.* Kaliumantimonotartrat
Antimonzinnober *m s.* Antimonkarmin
Antimutagen *n (bioch)* antimutagen *(a substance which lowers the ratio of mutations)*
Antimykotikum *n (pharm)* antifungal agent (drug), fungicide
antimykotisch antifungal, fungicidal • **~ wirken** to have antifungal activity
Antineuralgikum *n (pharm)* antineuralgic
antineuralgisch antineuralgic
Antineutrino *n* antineutrino
Antineutron *n* antineutron
Antinukleon *n* antinucleon
Antioxidans *n*, **Antioxidationsmittel** *n* antioxidant [agent], antioxidizing agent, antioxygen
Antioxygen *n s.* Antioxidans
Antiozonant *m*, **Antiozonisator** *m* antiozonant, antiozidant, sunproofing agent
Antipartikel *n* antiparticle
Antipellagravitamin *n* pellagra-preventive factor, pp factor *(either nicotinic acid or nicotinamide)*
antiperiplanar non-eclipsed, staggered *(stereochemistry)*
Antiperniziosafaktor *m* antipernicious anaemia factor *(a member of the vitamin B_{12} group)*
Antiperspirant *n* antiperspirant, antihidrotic, perspiration check
Antiphasengrenze *f (cryst)* Bloch (domain) wall, boundary of antiphases
Antiphlogistikum *n (pharm)* antiphlogistic [agent]
antiphlogistisch antiphlogistic
Antipode *m* **[/optischer]** antipode, optical antipode (opposite), mirror-image isomer
Antipodenpaar *n* pair of antipodes
~/optisches racemic pair
Antiport *m (bioch)* antiport
antiproteolytisch antiproteolytic
Antiproton *n* antiproton, negative proton
Antipsychotikum *n (pharm)* antipsychotic, neuroleptic [drug], major tranquilizer
Antipyretikum *n (pharm)* antipyretic, febrifuge
antipyretisch antipyretic
Antirachitikum *n (pharm)* antirachitic [agent]
antirachitisch antirachitic
Antireflexbelag *m*, **Antireflexschicht** *f* antireflection (antiflare) coating
Antirheumatikum *n (pharm)* antirheumatic
antirheumatisch antirheumatic
Antirostadditiv *n* rust-inhibiting (rust-preventing) additive
Antischaummittel *n* antifoaming (antifrothing) agent, antifoam [agent, compound]
Antischleiermittel *n (phot)* antifog[ging] agent, antifoggant
Antischweißmittel *n s.* Antitranspirationsmittel
Antiscorcher *m (rubber)* antiscorcher, antiscorching agent, retarder
Antiseptikum *n (pharm)* antiseptic [agent]
~ gegen Schimmel antimildew agent
antiseptisch antiseptic
Antiskabiosum *n (pharm)* scabi[eti]cide
antiskorbutisch antiscorbutic
Antispasmodikum *n (pharm)* antispasmodic
Antispritzmittel *n (food)* antispatterer
Antistatikmittel *n*, **Antistatikum** *n* antistatic [agent, additive], static eliminator
antistatisch antistatic
anti-Stellung *f* anti-position • **in ~ stehen** to be anti
Antisterilitätsvitamin *n* antisterility vitamin
anti-Stokes-Linien *fpl (anal)* anti-Stokes lines, anti-Stokes Raman component
anti-Stokes-Raman-Spektroskopie *f***/kohärente** coherent anti-Stokes Raman spectroscopy, CARS
anti-Stokes-Raman-Streuung *f***/kohärente** coherent anti-Stokes Raman scattering
antisymmetrisch antisymmetric *(orbital)*
anti-syn-Isomerie *f* anti-syn isomerism
Antiteilchen *n* antiparticle
Antitoxin *n* antitoxin
antitoxisch antitoxic
Antitranspirationslotion *f* antiperspirant lotion
Antitranspirationsmittel *n* antiperspirant, antihidrotic, perspiration check
antitumoral antitumour
Antitumormittel *n (pharm)* antitumour agent
Antitussivum *n (pharm)* antitussive
Antivergrauungsmittel *n (text)* antiredeposition agent
antiviral antiviral
Antivitamin *n* antivitamin
Antiweinsäure *f* mesotartaric acid
antreiben to drive
Antrieb *m* drive
Antriebsrolle *f* driving pulley
Antriebstrommel *f* driving pulley
Antriebswelle *f* drive shaft
Antu *s.* α-Naphthylthioharnstoff
Anvulkanisation *f s.* Anspringen
anvulkanisieren *s.* anspringen
anwachsen to increase, to rise
Anwachsen *n* increase, rise

anwärmen to preheat
Anwärmloch *n (glass)* glory hole
Anwärmsektion *f* heating section
Anwärmzeit *f* heating-up period (time)
Anwärmzone *f* preheating zone (compartment)
anweichen *(tann)* to presoak
anwendbar applicable
Anwendbarkeit *f* applicability
anwenden to apply, to use
~/lokal *(pharm)* to use topically (in topical applications)
~/zu reichlich to overuse *(e.g. pesticides)*
Anwendung *f* application, use
Anwendungsbereich *m* range of application (applicability)
Anwendungsgebiet *n* field (area) of application
anwendungsspezifisch application-specified
Anwendungsweise *f* mode (method) of application
Anxiolytikum *n (pharm)* anxiolytic [sedative], tranquillizing drug, [minor] tranquil[l]izer
Anzahl *f* number, quantity
~ der Freiheiten (Freiheitsgrade) *(phys ch)* variance, number of degrees of freedom
~ je Zeiteinheit rate
anzapfen to tap
Anzeige *f* indication, reading *(of a measuring instrument)*
~/diskontinuierliche discontinuous indication
~/fortlaufende continuous indication
Anzeigebereich *m* indicating range, scale span *(of a measuring instrument)*
Anzeigegerät *n*, **Anzeigeinstrument** *n* indicating instrument, indicator
anzeigen to indicate; to register *(measuring values automatically)*
Anzeiger *m s.* Anzeigegerät
anziehen to attract; to draw [in] *(e.g. a liquid)*
~/Feuchtigkeit to gain moisture
Anziehung *f* attraction
~/Coulombsche *s.* ~/elektrische
~ der Elektronen durch den Kern electron-nucleus attraction
~/elektrische (elektrostatische) electrostatic (electrical) attraction, Coulomb (coulombic) attraction
~/intermolekulare [inter]molecular attraction
~/magnetische magnetic attraction
~/van-der-Waalssche van der Waals attraction
~ zwischen Ionen [entgegengesetzter Ladung] ionic attraction
~/zwischenmolekulare [inter]molecular attraction
Anziehungskraft *f* attractive force
~/Coulombsche Coulomb force of attraction
Anziehungskräfte *fpl***/van-der-Waalssche** van der Waals forces [of attraction]
Anzucht *f s.* Kultivierung
anzünden to light *(a burner)*; to ignite, to light, to kindle *(fuels)*; to light, to kindle *(a fire)*
AO *s.* Atomorbital
A-Ort *m s.* Akzeptorort
AOS *s.* Alkenylsulfonat
AP *s.* Anilinpunkt
Apatit *m (min)* apatite *(calcium fluorophosphate)*
aperiodisch aperiodic
Apertur *f* aperture *(measure for the quality of an optical system)*
~/lineare linear aperture
~/numerische numerical aperture
~/relative relative aperture
Apex *m* apex *(of a liquid cyclone)*
Apexdüse *f* apex opening
APF... = Absorptions-Polarisations-Fluoreszenz-...
Apfeläther *m* apple oil *(main constituent isoamyl valerianate)*
Apfelessenz *f* apple essence, apple oil *(esp in alcoholic solution)*
Apfelessig *m* cider vinegar
Apfelmost *m* apple juice (must), *(Am)* [fresh, sweet] cider
Apfelöl *n s.* Apfelessenz
Apfelsaft *m* 1. apple juice *(preserved by heat for sale)*; 2. *s.* Apfelmost
Apfelsäure *f s.* Äpfelsäure
Äpfelsäure *f* malic acid, *hydroxybutanedioic acid
~/natürliche *s.* *L*(–)-Äpfelsäure
l-Äpfelsäure *f s.* *L*(–)-Äpfelsäure
L(–)-**Äpfelsäure** *f* (–)-malic acid, ordinary (common) malic acid
Äpfelsäuredehydr[ogen]ase *f* malic [acid] dehydrogenase
Äpfelsäure-Milchsäure-Gärung *f* malo-lactic fermentation
Apfelsinenschale *f* 1. orange peel *(from Cltrus sinensis (L.) Osbeck)*; 2. *s.* Apfelsinenschaleneffekt
Apfelsinenschaleneffekt *m (coat)* orange peel [effect, appearance] *(a surface defect)*
Apfelsinenschalenhaut *f s.* Apfelsinenschaleneffekt
Apfelsinenschalenöl *n* [sweet] orange-peel oil *(from Citrus sinensis (L.) Osbeck)*
Apfelsüßmost *m s.* Apfelmost
Apfelwein *m* cider, *(Am)* hard (fermented) cider
Aphizid *n (agric)* aphicide
Aphrodisiakum *n* aphrodisiac
API-Abscheider *m (hyd)* API separator
API-Dichte *f (petrol)* API gravity
API-Grad *m (petrol)* degree API
API-Skala *f (petrol)* API scale
AP-Kautschuk *m* EP-rubber, ethylene-propylene rubber, EPR
Aplom *m (min)* aplome *(a garnet)*
Apodisation *f (spectr)* apodization
Apoenzym *n*, **Apoferment** *n* apoenzyme, protector
Apokrensäure *f (soil)* apocrenic acid *(a fulvic acid)*
apolar apolar, non-polar
Apoprotein *n (bioch)* apoprotein
Aporepressor *m (bioch)* aporepressor

Aporphinalkaloid *n* aporphine alkaloid
Apostroph *m (nomencl)* prime *(with locants)*
Apotheker *m* pharmacist, pharmaceutic[al] chemist
Apothekerwaage *f* hand balance
Apo-Umlagerung *f* apo rearrangement
Apparat *m* apparatus
~/Brühlscher *(distil)* Brühl receiver
~ für kontinuierliche Extraktion continuous-extraction apparatus, continuous extractor
~/Kippscher Kipp [gas] generator
~/Marshscher Marsh apparatus *(for detecting arsenic)*
~ nach Schopper-Riegler *(pap)* Schopper-Riegler apparatus
~ zur Kohlendioxidbestimmung carbon dioxide apparatus
Apparatebau *m* apparatus construction
Apparateeinheit *f* unit
Apparategruppe *f* unit
Apparateklemme *f* apparatus clamp
Apparatekonstante *f* apparatus constant
Apparatur *f* apparatus, equipment
appetitanregend stomachic[al]
APPh-... = Absorptions-Polarisations-Phosphoreszenz-...
Applikation *f (agric)* application, placement *(of fertilizers or pesticides)*; *(pharm)* application, administration, dosage *(of a medicine)*
~ aus der Luft aerial (air-to-ground) application
~ unter Abschirmung directed application
~ vom Flugzeug aus aeroplane application
~ vor dem Auspflanzen preplanting application
Applikationsgerät *n (agric)* [mechanical] applicator, application apparatus
Applikationsmethode *f (agric)* placement method
Applikationsweise *f (pharm)* mode of administration
applizieren *(agric)* to apply, to place *(fertilizers or pesticides)*; *(pharm)* to apply, to administer *(a medicine)*
Appret *s.* Appreturmittel
Appreteur *m (text)* finisher
appretieren *(text, tann)* to finish
Appretur *f* 1. *(text, tann)* finishing; 2. *(text, tann)* finish; 3. *s.* Appreturmittel
~/antistatische *(text)* antistatic finish
~/glatttrocknende *(text)* smooth-drying finish
~/griffgebende *(text)* stiffening finish
~/knirschende *(text)* rustling finish
~/schrumpffreie *(text)* unshrinkable (shrink-resist) finish
~/stärkehaltige *(text)* starchy finish
~/wasserabstoßende (wasserabweisende) *(text)* water-repellent finish
~/wasserdichte *(text)* waterproof finish
Appreturmittel *n (text, tann)* finish, finishing agent (compound)
Appreturöl *n* textile oil
aprotid *s.* aprot[on]isch
aprot[on]isch aprotic
APS *s.* Apurinsäure
6-APS *s.* 6-Aminopenicillansäure
APT-Kautschuk *m* ethylene-propylene terpolymer, EPT
Apurinsäure *f (bioch)* apurinic acid
Apyrimidinsäure *(bioch)* apyrimidinic acid
Aquakomplex *m* aquo complex
Aquamarin *m (min)* aquamarine *(a variety of beryl)*
Aquametrie *f* aquametry
Aquarellfarbe *f* water colour
Aquarelltechnik *f* water-colour painting (technique)
Aquarienkitt *m* red-lead putty *(boiled linseed oil plus minium and lead(II) oxide or lead hydroxide carbonate)*
Aquat *n* aquate *(any of various salts containing hydration water esp in non-stoichiometric amounts)*
Aquation *f* aquation, aquatization, aquotization *(coordination chemistry)*
äquatorial equatorial *(stereochemistry)* • **~ stehen** to be equatorial
äquilibrieren to equilibrate
Äquilibrierung *f* equilibration
Äquilibrierungsverfahren *n* equilibration process
äquimolar equimolar
äquimolekular equimolecular
Äquipartitionsprinzip *n*, **Äquipartitionstheorem** *n* equipartition principle (theorem), law of equipartition [of energy]
Äquipotentialfläche *f* equipotential surface, potential energy surface
äquivalent equivalent
Äquivalent *n* equivalent
~/photochemisches photochemical equivalent
Äquivalentgewicht *n s.* Äquivalentmasse
Äquivalentleitfähigkeit *f* equivalent conductance
~ bei unendlicher Verdünnung equivalent conductance at infinite dilution
~ der Ionen equivalent ion[ic] conductance
Äquivalentmasse *f*[**/relative**] equivalent (combining) weight
Äquivalenz *f* equivalence, equivalency
~ von Energie und Masse mass-energy equivalence
Äquivalenzgesetz *n***/photochemisches** Einstein photochemical equivalence law, Einstein law of photochemical equivalence, Einstein-Stark law
~/Stark-Einsteinsches *s.* Äquivalenzgesetz/photochemisches
Äquivalenzleitfähigkeit *f s.* Äquivalentleitfähigkeit
Äquivalenzpunkt *m* equivalence (equivalent) point
Aquoion *n* aquo-ion, aquated ion
Aquokation *n* aquo cation
Aquokomplex *m* aquo complex
Aquopentammincobalt(III)-chlorid *n* aquapentaamminecobalt(III) chloride
Aquotisierung *f s.* Aquation
Aquoverbindung *f* aquo compound
Araban *n* araban *(a pentosan)*

Arabinsäure *f* arabic acid
Arachidonsäure *f* arachidonic acid
Arachinsäure *f* *eicosanoic acid, *(deprecated:)* arachidic acid
Arachisöl *n* arachis (peanut) oil
Aragonit *m (min)* aragonite *(calcium carbonate)*
Araliphat *m* araliphatic compound
araliphatisch araliphatic
Aralkylsilicon *n*, **Aralkylsiloxan** *n s.* Alkylarylsiloxan
Aralkylsulfonat *n s.* Alkylarensulfonat
Aräometer *n* araeometer, hydrometer
~ **mit Thermometer** thermohydrometer
Aräometerskale *f* araeometer (hydrometer) scale
Aräometrie *f* araeometry, hydrometry
aräometrisch araeometric[al], hydrometric[al]
Ararobapulver *n (pharm)* araroba, Goa powder *(from Andira araroba Aguiar)*
Arbeit *f* work *(physics)*
~/äußere external work
~ **der Reaktion/maximale** maximum useful work
~/geleistete work done
~/gesamte total work
~/gewonnene *s.* ~/geleistete
~/maximale (maximal geleistete) maximum work
~/umgesetzte *s.* ~/geleistete
arbeiten/adiabat to operate (run) abiabatically
~/isotherm to operate (run) isothermally
Arbeiten *n* **mit nicht umschaltbarer Elektrode** *(chromat)* single-working electrode mode *(of an electrochemical detector)*
~/pulsierendes dual-working electrode mode *(of an electrochemical detector)*
arbeitend/absatzweise (diskontinuierlich) batch *(apparatus)*
Arbeitsaufwand *m* expenditure of work
arbeitsaufwendig labour-intensive
~/wenig low-labour
Arbeitsbedingungen *fpl* operating conditions
Arbeitsbühne *f* operating floor (platform); drilling floor *(of a rotary-drilling installation)*
Arbeitsbütte *f (pap)* service chest, machine (pulp, supply, stuff) chest
Arbeitsdruck *m* operating (working) pressure
Arbeitselektrode *f* working (measuring) electrode
Arbeitsgang *m* operation
Arbeitsgeschwindigkeit *f* operating speed
Arbeitsherd *m* hearth *(of an air furnace)*
Arbeitshygiene *f* industrial (occupational) hygiene
Arbeitshygieniker *m* industrial (occupational) hygienist
Arbeitsinhalt *m (distil)* operating hold-up
Arbeitsleistung *f* performance
Arbeitslinie *f (distil)* operating (working) line, material-balance line
Arbeitsloch *n s.* Arbeitsöffnung
Arbeitslösung *f* working solution
Arbeitsmethode *f (tech)* procedure, operating method; *(lab)* technique
Arbeitsöffnung *f (glass)* gathering hole (opening)
Arbeitsphase *f s.* Arbeitstakt
Arbeitsplatz *m***/reiner** *(anal)* clean box *(provided with filtered air)*
Arbeitsplatzgrenzwert *m* **für kurzzeitige Belastung** short-time exposure limit, STEL
Arbeitsplatzkonzentration *f***/maximale** maximum allowable concentration, MAC
Arbeitsraum *m* 1. *(tech)* workshop; 2. *s.* Arbeitswanne
Arbeitsrichtung *f (pap)* machine direction, making (long, grain) direction
Arbeitssatz *m (lab)* reagent set
Arbeitsschutz *m* industrial safety
Arbeitsschutzanordnung *f* safety regulation
Arbeitsschutzkleidung *f* safety clothing
Arbeitsschutzsalbe *f* barrier cream
Arbeitsspannung *f* operating (working) voltage
Arbeitsspiel *n s.* Arbeitszyklus
Arbeitsstamm *m (biot)* working strain, producing (production) strain *(of microorganisms)*
Arbeitsstellung *f* operating position
Arbeitsstoff *m* working substance
Arbeitsstrom *m* operating (working) current
Arbeitsstufe *f* operating (working) stage
Arbeitstakt *m* service step (run)
Arbeitstechnik *f* technique
Arbeitstemperatur *f* operating (working) temperature
~/maximale *(chromat)* maximum allowable operating temperature, MAOT
Arbeitstisch *m* laboratory desk (table, bench)
Arbeitsverfahren *n s.* Arbeitstechnik
Arbeitsverlust *m (rubber)* hysteresis
Arbeitsvermögen *n* energy *(of a physical system)*
Arbeitsvolumen *n* working volume, *(biot also)* fermenter (fermentation) volume
Arbeitswanne *f (glass)* working chamber (end), nose
Arbeitsweise *f* 1. [mode of] operation *(of an apparatus)*; 2. *s.* Arbeitsmethode
~/diskontinuierliche batch operation
~ **isokrate (isokratische)** *(anal)* isocratic operation *(using constant composition of eluent)*
~ **mit totalem Rücklauf** total-reflux operation
~/periodische *s.* ~/diskontinuierliche
Arbeitszyklus *m* operating (working, service) cycle, *(ion exchange also)* exhaust-regenerate cycle
Arborizid *n* brushkiller, silvicide
Arcatom-Schweißverfahren *n* atomic hydrogen [arc] welding
Archimedes-Zahl *f* Archimedes number *(fluid mechanics)*
Aren *n* arene, aromatic hydrocarbon
Arenenium-Ion *n* arenium (arenonium) ion
Arenepoxid *n*, **Arenoxid** *n* arene epoxide (oxide)
Arg *s.* Arginin

Argentin *m (min)* argentine *(a pearly variety of calcite)*
Argentit *m (min)* argentite *(silver sulphide)*
Argentometrie *f* argentometry
argentometrisch argentometric
Arge-Synthese *f (coal)* Arge synthesis *(of hydrocarbons from synthesis gas by fixed iron catalysts at medium pressure)*
Arginin *n* 2-amino-5-guanidinovaleric acid
Arginin-Harnstoff-Zyklus *m s.* Harnstoffzyklus
Argininobernsteinsäure *f (bioch)* arginino succinic acid
Argininosuccinat *n (bioch)* arginino succinate
Argon *n* Ar argon
Argonatmosphäre *f* argon atmosphere
Argonclathrat *n* argon clathrate
Argon[ionen]-Laser *m (spectr)* argon [ion] laser
Arin *n* aryne, 1,2-didehydroarene *(any of a class of transient dehydrogenated derivatives of aromatic compounds)*, *(specif)* benzyne
Aristolochiagelb *n s.* Aristolochiasäure
Aristolochiasäure *f* aristolochic acid, aristolochin, aristolochia yellow
Aristolochin *n s.* Aristolochiasäure
Ar^+-Laser *m (spectr)* argon [ion] laser
arm poor *(as in content)*; lean *(gas)*; lean, low-grade *(ores)*; barren, weak *(solution)*; poor, infertile, barren, thin *(soil)*
Armcoeisen *n* Armco iron *(with < 1 % impurities)*
Armerz *n* lean (low-grade) ore
Armgas *n* lean gas
armieren to reinforce
Armierung *f* reinforcement
Armlauge *f* barren liquor (solution) *(in cyaniding)*
Arndt-Eistert-Synthese *f* Arndt-Eistert synthesis *(converting a carboxylic acid to its next higher homologue)*
Arnold-Probe *f* Arnold's test *(for detecting acetoacetic acid in urine)*
Aroma *n* 1. flavour, aroma; 2. *s.* Aromastoff
Aromabakterien *npl* aroma bacteria
Aromabildner *mpl* aroma organisms (producers)
Aromabildung *f* aroma development
Aromafülle *f (food)* ful[l]ness
Aromakomposition *f s.* Aromaträger
Aromastoff *m* aroma (aromatic) substance (body) *(occurring in food)*; congener[ic] *(occurring in distilled beverage spirits)*; aroma ingredient, aromatizing product, flavouring [material, matter, substance] *(for food)*
Aromat *m* aromatic [hydrocarbon, compound]
~/mehrkerniger polynuclear (polycyclic) aromatic hydrocarbon, PAH
Aromatenextraktion *f* aromatics extraction
aromatenfrei free from aromatic hydrocarbons
aromatisch 1. *(org ch)* aromatic; 2. *(food)* aromatic, flavourful
aromatisieren 1. *(org ch)* to aromatize; 2. *(food)* to aromatize, to flavour
Aromatisierung *f* 1. *(org ch)* aromatization; 2. *(food)* aromatization, flavouring
Aromatizität *f* 1. *(org ch)* aromaticity, aromatic character; *(coal)* [carbon] aromaticity *(fraction of carbon in aromatic form)*; 2. *(food)* aromaticity
Aromaträger *m* aroma compound
Aromaverlust *m* aroma loss
Aroylbenzoesäure *f* aroylbenzoic acid
Aroylgruppe *f* aroyl group (residue)
Arrak *m* arra[c]k
arretieren to arrest
Arretierknopf *m* arresting screw
Arretierung *f* 1. arrestment, arresting; 2. *s.* Arretiervorrichtung
Arretiervorrichtung *f* arresting mechanism
Arrhenius-Aktivierungsenergie *f* Arrhenius energy of activation, Arrhenius activation energy
Arrhenius-Diagramm *n* Arrhenius plot
Arrhenius-Gleichung *f* Arrhenius equation
Arrhenius-Parameter *m* Arrhenius parameter
Arsan *n* As_nH_{n+2} arsane, arsenic hydride, *(specif)* AsH_3 arsane, arsine, arsenic(III) hydride, arsenic trihydride
Arsanilsäure *f* arsanilic acid, *p*-aminophenylarsonic acid
Arsen *n* As arsenic
~/gelbes yellow arsenic, α-arsenic
~/graues (metallisches) grey (metallic) arsenic, γ-arsenic
~/schwarzes black arsenic, β-arsenic
Arsenat(III) *n* arsenite
Arsenat(V) *n* arsenate
Arsenblüte *f s.* Arsenolith
Arsen(III)-bromid *n* arsenic(III) bromide, arsenic tribromide
Arsenbutter *f* butter of arsenic *(arsenic(III) chloride)*
Arsen(III)-chlorid *n* arsenic(III) chloride, arsenic trichloride
Arsen(V)-chlorid *n* arsenic(V) chloride, arsenic pentachloride
Arsencobaltsulfid *n* cobalt arsenosulphide
Arsendampf *m* arsenic vapour
Arseneisensinter *m (min)* iron sinter
Arsenerz *n* arsenic ore
Arsenfahlerz *n (min)* tennantite *(a copper arsenide sulphide often containing iron)*
Arsen(III)-fluorid *n* arsenic(III) fluoride, arsenic trifluoride
Arsen(V)-fluorid *n* arsenic(V) fluoride, arsenic pentafluoride
arsenhaltig containing arsenic, arsenical, arsenian, *(esp ores:)* arseniferous, arsenic-bearing
Arsenhydrid *n s.* Arsan
Arsenid *n* arsenide
Arsenik *n* white arsenic, arsenic(III) oxide
~/gelbes yellow arsenic [sulphide], arsenic yellow, king's yellow (gold), royal yellow, orpiment [yellow] *(technically pure arsenic(III) sulphide)*

~/**rotes** *(tann)* red arsenic *(a mixture of arsenic sulphides)*
~/**weißes** *s.* Arsenik
Arsenikalie *f* arsenical
Arsenikblüte *f s.* Arsenolith
Arsenikbrocken *mpl (glass)* glassy (dense) arsenic
Arsenikschwöde *f (tann)* arsenic paint
Arsenikvergiftung *f* arsenic poisoning
Arseninsektizid *n* arsenical insecticide
Arsen(III)-iodid *n* arsenic(III) iodide, arsenic triiodide
Arsen(V)-iodid *n* arsenic(V) iodide, arsenic pentaiodide
Arsenkies *m s.* Arsenopyrit
Arsenkobalt *m (min)* arsenical cobalt *(cobalt arsenide)*
Arsenobenzen *n*, **Arsenobenzol** *n* arsenobenzene
Arsenolith *m (min)* arsenolite *(arsenic(III) oxide)*
Arsenopyrit *m (min)* arsenopyrite, arsenic[al] iron, arsenical pyrite, mispickel *(iron sulpharsenide)*
Arsenosulfid *n* arsenosulphide, sulpharsenide
Arsen(III)-oxid *n* arsenic(III) oxide, arsenic trioxide, white arsenic
Arsen(V)-oxid *n* arsenic(V) oxide, arsenic pentaoxide
Arsen(III)-oxidchlorid *n* arsenic(III) chloride oxide
Arsenpent[a]... *s.* Arsen(V)-...
Arsen(III)-phosphid *n* arsenic(III) phosphide
Arsenprobe *f* arsenic test
~/**Bettendorfsche** Bettendorf's test [for arsenic]
~/**Gutzeitsche** Gutzeit's test [for arsenic]
~/**Marshsche** Marsh's test [for arsenic]
Arsen(III)-säure *f* arsenious acid
Arsen(V)-säure *f* arsenic acid
Arsensäureanhydrid *n s.* Arsen(V)-oxid
Arsen(III)-selenid *n* arsenic(III) selenide, arsenic triselenide
Arsenspeise *f (met)* arsenical speiss
Arsenspiegel *m* arsenic mirror
Arsensulfid *n (tann)* arsenic sulphide *(a mixture mainly consisting of tetraarsenic tetrasulphide and arsenic trisulphide)*
Arsen(III)-sulfid *n* arsenic(III) sulphide, arsenic trisulphide
Arsen(V)-sulfid *n* arsenic(V) sulphide, arsenic pentasulphide
Arsentri... *s. a.* Arsen(III)-...
Arsentrisulfidsol *n* arsenious sulphide sol
Arsenvergiftung *f* arsenic poisoning
~/**chronische (gewerbliche)** arsenicalism
Arsenwasserstoff *m s.* Arsan
Arsin *n* 1. AsR_3 arsine *(any of several organic compounds)*; 2. AsH_3 arsine, arsane, arsenic(III) hydride, arsenic trihydride
~/**primäres** primary arsine
~/**sekundäres** secondary arsine
Arsinoxid *n* arsine oxide
Arsinsäure *f* arsinic acid *(any of several organic acids R_2–As(O)OH)*
Arsoniumgruppe *f* arsonium group (residue)
Arsonium-Ion *n* arsonium ion
Arsoniumrest *m s.* Arsoniumgruppe
Arsoniumverbindung *f* arsonium compound
Arsonsäure *f* arsonic acid *(any of several organic acids R–As(O)$(OH)_2$)*
Arsonylierung *f* arsonation
artspezifisch *(bioch)* species-specific
Arylalkylierung *f* ar[yl]alkylation
Arylalkylsilicon *n s.* Alkylarylsiloxan
Arylazogruppe *f*, **Arylazorest** *m* arylazo group (residue)
Arylen *n* arylene [group], arenediyl group *(any of a class of bivalent radicals derived from an aromatic hydrocarbon)*
Arylengruppe *f*, **Arylenrest** *m s.* Arylen
Arylether *m* aryl (aromatic) ether
Arylgruppe *f* aryl group (residue), Ar
Arylhalogenid *n* aryl halide
arylieren to arylate
Arylierung *f* arylation
Arylkation *n* aryl cation
Arylmethylgruppe *f*, **Arylmethylrest** *m* $ArCH_2$– arylmethyl group
Arylradikal *n* [free] aryl radical
Arylrest *m s.* Arylgruppe
Arylsilicon *n s.* Arylsiloxan
Arylsiloxan *n* aryl siloxane
Arylsulfonsäure *f* arylsulphonic acid
Arylverknüpfung *f* aryl coupling
Aryn *n s.* Arin
Arzneibuch *n* pharmacopoeia • **den Anforderungen des Arzneibuchs entsprechend** pharmacopoeial, *(UK also)* B.P. grade, *(US also)* U.S.P. grade
Arzneidroge *f* drug
Arzneiform *f* [pharmaceutical] dosage form
arzneilich medicinal
Arzneimittel *n* pharmaceutical [preparation], medicinal drug, medicament, remedy, *(if for internal use also)* medicine
~ **auf Sulfonamidbasis** sulphonamide drug, *(if antibacterial:)* sulpha drug
~ **für inneren Gebrauch** medicine
~/**rezeptpflichtiges** prescription pharmaceutical
Arzneimittelchemie *f* pharmaceutical (medicinal) chemistry
Arzneimittelchemiker *m* pharmaceutical (medicinal) chemist
Arzneimittelforschung *f* pharmaceutical (drug) research
Arzneimittelindustrie *f* pharmaceutic[al] industry
Arzneimittelvergiftung *f* drug intoxication
Arzneimittelverordnung *f* medication
Arzneipflanze *f* medicinal (officinal) plant
Arzneistoff *m* medicinal substance
Arzneiverordnung *f s.* Arzneimittelverordnung
Asa foetida *f* asafetida, devil's dung, food of the gods *(a gum resin from Ferula specc.)*

ASAT = Aspartat-Aminotransferase
A-Säure *f* A acid, 6-amino-naphth-1-ol-5-sulphonic acid
Asbest *m* asbestos
Astbestband *n* asbestos tape
Asbestdiaphragma *n* asbestos diaphragm
Asbestdichtung *f* asbestos gasket (packing)
Asbestdrahtnetz *n* asbestos[-covered wire] gauze
Asbestfaser *f* asbestos fibre
Asbestfausthandschuh *m* asbestos mitt[en]
Asbestfilter *n* asbestos filter
Asbestfilz *m* asbestos felt
Asbestfingerling *m* asbestos finger cot
Asbestgarn *n* asbestos yarn
Asbestgewebe *n* asbestos cloth, woven asbestos
Asbesthandschuh *m* asbestos glove
Asbestine *f* *(pap)* asbestine
Asbestkleidung *f* asbestos clothing
Asbestmassescheibe *f* *(filtr)* asbestos-pulp disk
Asbestmembran *f s.* Asbestdiaphragma
Asbestpackung *f* asbestos packing (gasket)
Asbestpapier *n* asbestos paper
Asbestpappe *f* asbestos board
Asbestplatte *f* asbestos board *(composed of asbestos cement)*, asbestos mat *(composed of asbestos fibre)*
Asbestpolster *n* asbestos pad *(as in a Gooch crucible)*
Asbestrohr *n* asbestos pipe
Asbestscheibe *f* asbestos disk
Asbestschicht *f* asbestos pad *(in a Gooch crucible)*
Asbestschiefer *m* asbestos slate
Asbestschnur *f* asbestos cord
Asbeststaub *m* asbestos dust
Asbeststoff *m*, **Asbesttuch** *n s.* Asbestgewebe
Asbestunterlage *f* *(lab)* asbestos mat
Asbestwolle *f* asbestos wool
Asbestzement *m* asbestos cement, cement-asbestos
Asbolan *m* *(min)* asbolan[e], asbolite, black cobalt *(earthy manganese dioxide containing cobalt oxide)*
Asche *f* ash[es]
~/äußere *(coal)* extraneous ash
~/innere *(coal)* inherent ash
~/vulkanische volcanic ash
Asche... *s. a.* Aschen...
Ascheabzug *m* ash removal
~/trockener dry-ash removal
Ascheagglomeration *f* ash agglomeration
aschearm low-ash
Ascheaustrag *m s.* Ascheabzug
Ascheaustragsschleuse *f* ash-discharging vessel
Aschebestimmung *f* ash determination
Ascheentfernung *f s.* Ascheabzug
Ascheerweichungspunkt *m* ash-softening temperature
Aschefall *m* ash pit
aschefrei ash-free, free from ash, *(esp filter paper:)* ashless
Aschefreiheit *f* freedom from ash
Aschegehalt *m* ash content, *(in analysing coal also)* ash yield • **mit hohem ~** high-ash • **mit niedrigem ~** low-ash
Aschegehaltskurve *f* ash curve
Aschegrube *f* ash pit
aschehaltig containing ash
~/schwach low-ash
~/stark high-ash
Aschekasten *m* ash pan
Aschekeller *m* ash pit
Aschen... *s. a.* Asche...
Aschensinter *m* sintered fly ash *(concrete aggregate)*
Aschentuff *m* *(geol)* ash tuff
Äscher *m* 1. *(tann)* lime [liquor]; 2. *s.* Äschergrube; 3. *s.* Äschern
~/angeschärfter sharpened lime *(lime milk treated with sodium sulphide)*
~/fauler rotten (dead) lime
~/frischer fresh (head) lime
~/milder mellow lime
~/toter *s.* ~/fauler
Ascheraum *m* ash pit
Äscherbrühe *f s.* Äscher 1.
aschereich high-ash
Äschergang *m* *(tann)* round of lime
Äschergrube *f* *(tann)* lime pit
äschern *(tann)* to lime
Äschern *n* *(tann)* liming
Ascheschleuse *f* ash-discharging vessel
Ascheschmelzpunkt *m* ash-fusion temperature
Ascheschüssel *f* ash pan
Aschetrichter *m* ash hopper
Aschewaage *f* ash scale
Aschezone *f* ash zone
Aschezusammensetzung *f* ash composition
Ascorbigen *n* ascorbigen *(composed of ascorbic acid and protein)*
Ascorbinsäure *f* ascorbic acid
Ascorbinsäureoxidase *f* ascorbic [acid] oxidase
Asepsis *f* asepsis
aseptisch aseptic
Asp *s.* Asparaginsäure
Asparagin *n* asparagine, *(specif)* $HOOC{-}CH(NH_2)CH_2CONH_2$ β-asparagine
Asparaginsäure *f* aspartic acid, Asp, asparaginic acid, aminosuccinic acid
Aspergillsäure *f* aspergillic acid
Asphalt *m* 1. *(petrol)* petroleum asphalt, [artificial] asphalt; *(build)* asphalt *(asphaltic bitumen mixed with mineral matter)*; 2. *s.* ~/natürlicher
~/natürlicher *(min)* [natural, native] asphalt, mineral (earth) pitch
Asphaltanstrichstoff *m* asphalt (asphaltic) paint (coating)
Asphaltbasis *f* asphalt base *(of crude petroleum)*
Asphaltbasisöl *n* asphalt-base petroleum (crude oil, crude), asphaltic petroleum

Asphaltbeton *m* asphalt concrete
Asphaltbinder *m* asphaltic binder
Asphaltbitumen *n* asphaltic bitumen
Asphalten *n* asphaltene *(high-molecular-weight hydrocarbon)*
Asphaltfotografie *f* asphalt (bitumen) process
Asphaltgestein *n* asphalt rock
asphalthaltig containing asphalt, asphaltic
Asphalthartpappe *f* bitumen board
asphaltisch asphaltic
Asphaltit *m* asphaltite *(natural asphalt)*
Asphaltkalk *m* asphaltic limestone
Asphaltlack *m* asphalt[ic] enamel, asphalt varnish [paint]
Asphaltmakadam *m(n)* asphalt macadam
Asphaltmastix *m* asphalt mastic
Asphaltöl *n s.* Asphaltbasisöl
Asphaltpapier *n* asphalt (tar, pitch) paper, tarred [brown] paper
Asphaltsand *m* asphaltic (tar) sand
Asphaltsee *m* asphalt (pitch) lake
Asphaltverfahren *n s.* Asphaltfotografie
Asphaltzement *m* asphaltic cement
Aspirationspsychrometer *n* aspiration psychrometer
Aspirator *m* aspirator
Asplund-Defibrator-Verfahren *n (pap)* Asplund process
Asp-NH$_2$ *s.* Asparagin
Assamkautschuk *m* Assam (Indian) rubber *(from Ficus elastica Roxb.)*
Assimilat *n* assimilate, photosynthate
Assimilation *f* assimilation
~/magmatische *(geol)* magmatic digestion
Assimilationskraft *f* assimilatory power
assimilierbar assimilable
Assimilierbarkeit *f* assimilability
assimilieren to assimilate
Assoziat *n* supramolecular assembly, complex
Assoziation *f (ch)* [molecular] association; *(min)* association
~ gleichgeladener Ionen self-association
Assoziationsflüssigkeit *f* associated liquid
Assoziationsgrad *m* degree of association
Assoziationskolloid *n* association (micellar) colloid
Assoziationskonstante *f* association constant
Assoziationsreaktion *f* association reaction
Assoziationswärme *f* heat of association
assoziieren to associate
~/sich to associate
Astat *n* At astatine
Astat-Emanation *f s.* Radon-218
astatisch astatic
Astfang *m*, **Astfänger** *m (pap)* knot screen, [jag-] knotter
Asterismus *m (cryst)* asterism
Astknoten *m (pap)* knot *(in wood)*
ASTM = American Society for Testing and Materials
ASTM-Destillation *f* ASTM distillation
ASTM-Spezifikation *f* ASTM specification
ASTM-Standardmethode *f* standard ASTM method
ASTM-Verfahren *n* ASTM method
Aston-Massenspektrograph *m* Aston mass spectrograph
Astra-Druckschneckenkühler *m* Astra pressure cooler *(margarine manufacture)*
Astrakanit *m (min)* astrak[h]anite, blödite *(magnesium sodium sulphate)*
Astrom-Entrindungsmaschine *f (pap)* Astrom chain barker
asymm. *s.* asymmetrisch
Asymmetrie *f* asymmetry, dissymmetry
Asymmetriepotential *n* asymmetry potential
Asymmetriezentrum *n* asymmetric centre, centre of asymmetry
asymmetrisch asymmetric[al], dissymmetric, unsymmetrical, *(nomencl as a prefix:) asym-*
AT *s.* Alttuberkulin
Ataraktikum *n (pharm)* [minor] tranquillizer, tranquillizing drug, anxiolytic [sedative]
Ataxit *m* ataxite *(an iron meteorite)*
at. E. *s.* Einheiten/atomare
Atemgift *n* respiratory poison
Atemnot *f* laboured breathing
Atemschutz *m* respiratory protection
Atemschutzfiltergerät *n* filter respirator
Atemschutzgerät *n* respiratory protective device, breathing apparatus
Atemschutzmaske *f* respirator, breathing mask
Atemschutzvollmaske *f* full facepiece respirator
Atemschwingung *f* [symmetrical] breathing vibration
a-Term *m (nomencl)* "a" term
Äth... *s. a.* Eth...
Äthal *n s.* Hexadecan-1-ol
Äthanalsäure *f s.* Glyoxylsäure
Äthanolal *n s.* Glykolaldehyd
Äthanolsäure *f s.* Glykolsäure
ätherisch essential, volatile, ethereal *(oils)*
atherman atherm[an]ous
Äthinylcarbinol *n s.* Prop-2-in-1-ol
Äthoxylinharz *n s.* Epoxidharz
Äthyläthylen *n s.* But-1-en
Äthylcaprinat *n s.* Decansäureethylester
Äthylcapronat *n s.* Hexansäureethylester
Äthyldimethylmethan *n s.* 2-Methylbutan
Äthylessigsäure *f s.* Buttersäure
Äthylglykol *n s.* 2-Ethoxyethanol
Äthylisopropylcarbinol *n s.* 2-Methylpentan-3-ol
Äthylmercaptan *n s.* Ethanthiol
Äthylmethylcarbinol *n s.* Butan-2-ol
Äthylsulfonsäure *f s.* Ethansulfonsäure
Äthylsulfursäure *f s.* Ethylschwefelsäure
Äthylthioalkohol *m s.* Ethanthiol
A.T. Koch *s.* Alttuberkulin
Atmer *m s.* Aerobier
Atmolyse *f* atmolysis

Atmometer *n* atmometer
atmophil atmophil[e] *(found in the atmosphere)*
Atmosphäre *f* atmosphere
~/indifferente (inerte) inert atmosphere
~/kontrollierte controlled atmosphere *(of a furnace)*
~/metrische *s.* ~/technische
~/mittlere middle atmosphere
~/neue *s.* ~/technische
~/oxidierende oxidizing atmosphere
~/physikalische physical atmosphere, atm *(1 atm = 101325 Pa)*
~/reduzierende reducing atmosphere
~/technische technical atmosphere, at *(1 at = 98066.5 Pa)*
Atmosphärenchemie *f* chemistry of atmosphere, atmospheric chemistry
Atmosphärendruck *m* atmospheric (air) pressure
Atmosphärendruckionisation *f (anal)* atmospheric-pressure ionization, API
atmosphärisch atmospheric[al]
Atmung *f* breathing, respiration
~/anaerobe anaerobic respiration
~/endogene endogenous respiration
~/luftfreie (sauerstofffreie) *s.* ~/anaerobe
Atmungsbahn *f s.* Sequenz/katabolische
Atmungsfähigkeit *f* breathability *(of a coating)*
Atmungsferment *n* respiratory enzyme
~/Warburgsches Warburg's enzyme, *(specif)* cytochrome oxidase
~/Warburgsches gelbes Warburg's yellow enzyme, old yellow enzyme
Atmungsgift *n* respiratory poison
Atmungshemmstoff *m*, **Atmungsinhibitor** *m* respiration inhibitor
Atmungskatalysator *m* respiratory catalyst
Atmungskette *f (bioch)* respiratory (oxidative) chain, electron-transport chain (sequence, system)
Atmungskettenphosphorylierung *f (bioch)* respiratory-chain phosphorylation, oxidative phosphorylation
Atmungskoeffizient *m s.* Atmungsquotient
Atmungskontrolle *f (bioch)* acceptor (respiratory) control *(adenosine triphosphate synthesis)*
Atmungskontrollquotient *m (bioch)* acceptor-control index (ratio)
Atmungsöffnung *f* vent [opening] *(of a tank)*
Atmungspigment *n (bioch)* respiratory pigment
Atmungsquotient *m (bioch)* respiratory quotient (ratio), RQ
Atom *n* atom
~/adsorbiertes adatom, adsorbed atom
~/angeregtes excited (activated) atom
~/angestoßenes knocked-on atom
~ auf Zwischengitterplatz interstitial [atom]
~/endständiges terminal atom
~/heißes (hoch angeregtes) hot atom
~/hochenergiereiches hot atom
~/hochionisiertes stripped atom
~ im Grundzustand normal (ground-state) atom
~/ionisiertes ionized atom
~/isotopes isotopic atom
~/markiertes labelled (tagged) atom, label
~/neutrales neutral atom
~/normales *s.* ~ im Grundzustand
~/sp^2-hybridisiertes *s.* ~/trigonal hybridisiertes
~/tetraedrisches (tetraedrisch koordiniertes) tetrahedral atom
~/trigonal hybridisiertes trigonally hybridized atom
Atom-% *s.* Atomprozent
Atomabsorptionsspektralphotometer *n* atomic absorption spectro[photo]meter
Atomabsorptionsspektralphotometrie *f* atomic absorption spectro[photo]metry, AAS
~ mit elektrothermischer Atomisierung electrothermal atomization atomic absorption spectrophotometry, ETA-AAS, ETAAS
~ mit Mehrelement-Hohlkatodenlampen multi-element atomic absorption spectro[photo]metry
Atomabsorptionsspektrometrie *f s.* Atomabsorptionsspektralphotometrie
Atomabsorptionsspektroskopie *f* atomic absorption spectroscopy
Atomabstand *m s.* Kernabstand
Atomaffinität *f* atomic affinity
Atomaggregat *n* atomic aggregate, aggregate of atoms
Atomanordnung *f s.* Atomkonfiguration
atomar atomic[al]
Atomart *f* atomic species
Atom-Atom-Konformation *f* eclipsed conformation
Atomaufbau *m* atomic structure
Atombau *m* atomic structure
Atombindigkeit *f s.* Atombindungszahl
Atombindung *f* atomic (homopolar) bond, covalent (non-polar) bond, [shared-]electron-pair bond
Atombindungszahl *f* covalency, covalence
Atomdrehung *f* atomic rotation
Atomdurchmesser *m* atomic diameter
Atomelektron *n* atomic electron
Atomemissionsspektrometrie *f* atomic emission spectrometry, AES
~ mit induktiv gekoppeltem Argon-Plasma inductively coupled argon plasma atomic emission spectrometry, ICAP-AES
Atomenergie *f s.* Kernenergie
Atomfaktor *m s.* Atomformfaktor
Atomfluoreszenz *f* atomic fluorescence
Atomfluoreszenzspektrometrie *f* atomic fluorescence spectrometry, AFS
~/laserangeregte laser-excited atomic fluorescence spectrometry, LEAFS
Atomformfaktor *m (cryst)* atomic scattering (form) factor
Atomforschung *f* atomic research
Atomfrequenz *f* atomic frequency
Atomgerüst *n* atomic framework
Atomgewicht *n s.* Atommasse/relative
~/absolutes *s.* Atommasse/absolute
~/relatives *s.* Atommasse/relative

Atomgewichtsbestimmung *f s.* Bestimmung der relativen Atommasse
Atomgitter *n* atom[ic] lattice
Atomgramm *n* gram atom, gram-atomic weight
Atomgröße *f* atomic size
Atomgruppe *f* group of atoms
~/dreiwertige triad
~/einwertige monad
~/fünfwertige pentad
~/mehrwertige polyad
~/vierwertige tetrad
~/zweiwertige diad, dyad
Atomhülle *f* extranuclear (electronic) region
Atomigkeit *f s.* Atomizität
Atomion *n* atomic ion, ionized atom
Atomisator *m* atomizer
Atomiseur *m (agric)* low-volume mist blower, air-blast sprayer, fog generator (appliance), nebulizer
atomisieren to atomize
Atomisierung *f* atomization
atomistisch atomistic
Atomizität *f* atomicity *(number of atoms contained in a molecule)*
Atomkern *m* [atomic] nucleus
Atomkern... *s.* Kern...
Atomkette *f* atomic chain, chain of atoms
Atomkonfiguration *f* [atom, atomic] configuration
Atomkristall *m* covalent crystal
Atomladung *f* atomic charge
Atomlehre *f* atomic theory
Atomlinie *f s.* Spektrallinie
Atom-Lücke-Konformation *f* staggered conformation
Atommasse *f s.* ~/absolute
~/absolute atomic mass, mass of atom
~/relative relative atomic mass, RAM
Atommasseeinheit *f* atomic mass unit
Atommassekonstante *f* atomic mass constant
~/vereinheitlichte unified atomic mass constant
Atommassenskala *f* atomic mass scale
~/vereinheitlichte unified atomic mass scale
Atommassentabelle *f* atomic mass table
Atommassewert *m* atomic mass value
Atommeiler *m s.* Kernreaktor
Atommodell *n* atom[ic] model
~/Bohrsches (Bohr-Rutherfordsches) Bohr atom [model], Bohr-Rutherford atom [model]
~/Bohr-Sommerfeldsches Bohr-Sommerfeld atom [model]
~/Rutherfordsches Rutherford atom [model], nuclear atom [model], nuclear model of the atom
Atommüll *m* radioactive (nuclear) waste
Atommüllbeseitigung *f* radioactive (nuclear) waste disposal
Atomniveau *n* atomic [energy] level
Atomnummer *f* atomic (ordinal) number, A.N., *(symbol)* Z
~/effektive effective atomic number, E.A.N.
~/ungerade odd atomic number
Atomorbital *n* atomic orbital, AO
Atomparachor *m* [gram-]atomic parachor
Atomphysik *f* atomic physics
Atompolarisation *f* atom[ic] polarization
Atomprozent *n* atomic percent[age], atom %
Atomradius *m* atomic radius
~/kovalenter covalent radius [of atoms]
Atomreaktor *m s.* Kernreaktor
Atomrefraktion *f* atomic refraction
Atomrest *m s.* Atomrumpf
Atomrotation *f* atomic rotation
Atomrumpf *m* [atomic] core, [atomic] kernel
Atomschale *f* electron shell
Atomschwingung *f* atomic vibration
Atomspektroskopie *f* atomic spectroscopy
atomspektroskopisch by atomic spectroscopy
Atomspektrum *n* atomic (line) spectrum
Atomspin *m* atomic spin
Atomsprengstoff *m s.* Kernsprengstoff
Atomstrahl *m* atom[ic] beam
Atomstrahlapparat *m* atomic-beam apparatus
Atomstrahlmethode *f* atomic-beam method
Atomstrahlspektroskopie *f* atomic-beam spectroscopy
Atomstruktur *f* atomic structure
Atomsuszeptibilität *f* atomic susceptibility, susceptibility per gram atom
Atomtheorie *f* atomic theory
Atomübertragung *f* atom transfer
Atomübertragungsreaktion *f* atom-transfer reaction
Atomumwandlung *f* atomic transmutation
Atomverband *m* union of atoms
Atomverbindung *f* atomic compound
Atomverhältnis *n (anal)* atomic [combining] ratio, atomic proportion, proportion by atoms
Atomverschiebung *f* atomic shift
Atomvolumen *n* atomic volume
Atomwärme *f* atomic heat
Atomwertigkeit *f s.* Atombindungszahl
Atomzerfall *m* atomic (radioactive) disintegration
Atomzustand *m* atomic state
~/hybridisierter hybrid[ization] atomic state
atoxisch non-toxic, non-poisonous
ATP *s.* Adenosintriphosphorsäure
ATPase *f s.* Adenosintriphosphatase
ATP-Citratlyase *f* ATP-citrate lyase, citrate cleavage enzyme
ATR *s.* Totalreflexion/abgeschwächte
ATR-Einrichtung *f (spectr)* ATR attachment
atro absolutely dry, bone-dry, B.D., *(pap also)* oven-dry, oven-dried, OD
Atrolactinsäure *f* atrolactinic acid, *2-hydroxy-2-phenylpropionic acid
Atropasäure *f* atropic acid, 2-phenylacrylic acid, α-phenylacrylic acid
Atropin *n* atropine, DL-hyoscyamine *(alkaloid)*
Atropisomer[e] *n* atropisomer, atropo-isomer
Atropisomerie *f* atropisomerism, atropo-isomerism

ATR-Technik *f* ATR, attenuated total reflectance
ATR-Zusatzeinrichtung *f (spectr)* ATR attachment
ATS *s.* Ablaugetrockensubstanz
Attapulgit *m* palygorskite, *(deprecated:)* attapulgite *(a phyllosilicate)*
Attenuator *m (bioch)* attenuator *(DNA segment acting as a controlling element)*
Attraktans *n* attractant *(as for insects)*
Attraktion *f* attraction
Attraktionskraft *f* attractive force (power)
Attraktivstoff *m s.* Attraktans
Ätzalkalien *npl* caustic alkalies
Ätzalkalilösung *f* caustic alkaline solution
ätzbar corrodible; *(text)* dischargeable
Ätzbarkeit *f* corrodibility; *(text)* dischargeability
Ätzbaryt *m* caustic baryta *(barium hydroxide)*
Ätzdruck *m (text)* discharge print[ing]
Ätzdruckpaste *f (text)* discharge-printing paste
ätzen to etch; *(text)* to discharge; *(tox)* to cause burns *(on the skin)*, to corrode *(the skin)*; *(med)* to cauterize *(e.g. by chemicals)*
~/makroskopisch to macroetch
Ätzen *n* etching; *(text)* discharge, discharging; *(med)* cauterization *(e.g. by chemicals)*
~/elektrolytisches electrolytic etch[ing]
~ mit Oxidationsmitteln *(text)* oxidation discharge
ätzend caustic; *(med)* cauterant, cauterizing
Ätzfigur *f (cryst)* etch (corrosion) figure
Ätzflüssigkeit *f* etching acid (fluid); engraver's acid *(usually nitric acid)*
Ätzgift *n (tox)* corrosive poison
Ätzkali *n* caustic potash *(potassium hydroxide)*
Ätzkalk *m* 1. caustic (burnt) lime, quicklime *(calcium oxide)*; 2. slaked (hydrated) lime, slacklime *(calcium hydroxide)*
~/freier *(agric, anal)* available lime *(expressed as calcium oxide)*
Ätzlösung *f* etching solution
Ätzmittel *n* etching reagent, etchant; engraver's acid *(usually nitric acid)*; *(text)* discharging agent; *(med)* caustic [agent], cauterant, cautery
~/Frysches Fry reagent *(for etching steel)*
~/Steadsches Stead's reagent *(for detecting phosphorus segregation in steel)*
~ zur Makroätzung macroetching reagent
Ätzmittelemulsion *f (agric)* contact emulsion *(for weed control)*
Ätznatron *n* caustic [soda] *(sodium hydroxide)*
Ätznatronschmelze *f* caustic-soda fusion
Ätzpaste *f s.* Ätzdruckpaste
Ätzreserve *f (text)* discharge resist
Ätzsublimat *n* corrosive mercuric (mercury) chloride, sublimate *(mercury(II) chloride)*
Ätzung *f* 1. chemigraph, chemitype *(an engraving made by chemigraphy)*; 2. *s.* Ätzen
Ätzweiß *n (text)* white discharge
Ätzwirkung *f* causticity
Audibert-Arnu-Dilatometer *n* Audibert-Arnu dilatometer
Audibert-Arnu-Dilatometerverfahren *n* Audibert-Arnu method
aufarbeiten to process *(e.g. ores)*; to work up, to recover, to prepare *(products of value)*; to reprocess, to rework *(used or discarded material)*
~/Topprückstände *(petrol)* to run resid
~/zu Crepe *(rubber)* to crêpe
Aufarbeitung *f* processing *(e.g. of ores)*; working-up, workup, recovery, preparation *(of products of value)*; reprocessing, reworking *(of used or discarded material)*
Aufarbeitungsverlust *m* recovery loss *(as in recovering a product of value)*
Aufbau *m* 1. structure, constitution, build-up, make-up *(of a molecule)*; composition, make-up *(of a chemical compound or mixture)*; set-up, structure, build *(of an apparatus)*; build, construction *(of a plant)*; 2. build-up, formation *(of an electrical field)*; 3. *(bioch)* anabolism; 4. *s.* Aufbauen
~/chemischer chemical structure
~ nach Rezept formulation
~/streifiger *(geol)* banded structure
~/struktureller structural make-up
~/zonaler *(geol)* zonal (zonary) structure, zoning
Aufbaubestandteil *m* building constituent
Aufbauelement *n* structural element (entity, unit); *(coal)* constituent, mazeral
aufbauen to build up, to synthesize *(a chemical compound)*; to set [up], to erect *(an apparatus)*; to make up *(a whole)*
~/ein Mischungsrezept to compound
~/gezielt to make to measure, to tailor[-make] *(e.g. polymers)*
~/nach Maß *s.* ~/gezielt
~/nach Rezept to formulate
~/sich to build up *(of an electrical field)*
Aufbauen *n* building-up, build-up, synthesis *(of a chemical compound)*; setting[-up], erection *(of an apparatus)*
Aufbaugranulieren *n* granulation, pelletizing
Aufbauprinzip *n (phys ch)* aufbau (building-up) principle
Aufbaureaktion *f* build-up reaction; aufbau (chain-extension) reaction *(polymerization)*
Aufbausatz *m* set-up
Aufbauschritt *m (bioch)* anabolic step
Aufbaustoff *m* [detergency, soap] builder
Aufbauvorgang *m* building-up process; *(bioch)* anabolic process
Aufbauweg *m (bioch)* anabolic pathway (route)
aufbereiten to prepare; to treat, to process *(water)*; to condition *(boiler feed water)*; to dress, to beneficiate *(ore)*; *(pap)* to break [in, up] *(rags)*
~/auf nassem Wege *s.* ~/naß
~/auf trockenem Wege *s.* ~/trocken
~/in der Setzmaschine *(min tech)* to jig
~/naß *(min tech)* to wet-clean
~/pneumatisch *s.* ~/trocken
~/trocken *(min tech)* to dry-clean
~/zu Crepe *(rubber)* to crêpe

Aufbereitung *f* preparation; treatment *(of water)*; conditioning *(of boiler feed water)*; dressing, beneficiation *(of ore)*; *(pap)* breaking *(of rags)*, recovery *(of waste paper)*
~ **auf nassem Wege** *s.* ~/nasse
~ **auf trockenem Wege** *s.* ~/trockene
~/bergbauliche mineral dressing, minerals beneficiation
~ **durch Flotation** *s.* ~/flotative
~/flotative floatation beneficiation
~/magnetische magnetic concentration
~/nasse *(min tech)* wet cleaning (washing)
~/pneumatische *s.* ~/trockene
~/trockene *(min tech)* dry (pneumatic) cleaning
~ **zu Crepe** *(rubber)* crêpeing, creping
Aufbereitungsanlage *(hyd)* treatment plant (works); *(hyd)* treatment unit *(of an industrial plant)*; *(min tech)* ore dressing plant
Aufbereitungschemikalie *f (hyd)* treatment (water-treating, processing) chemical
Aufbereitungsherd *m (min tech)* concentrator (concentrating) table
Aufbereitungskonzentrat *n (min tech)* concentrate
Aufbereitungstechnik *f* mineral technology
Aufbereitungsteil *m (glass)* conditioning section (zone) *(of the feeder channel)*
Aufbereitungsstufe *f (hyd)* treatment stage
Aufbereitungstechnologie *f* mineral technology; *(hyd)* treatment technology
aufbewahren to store, to keep
~/im Brutschrank to incubate
~/kühl to store in a cool place
~/lichtgeschützt to keep screened from the light
Aufbewahrung *f* storing, storage, keeping
Aufbewahrungstemperatur *f* storage (holding) temperature
aufblähen to expand, *(rubber, plast also)* to blow
~/sich to intumesce, to swell, to expand
Aufblähung *f* intumescence, swelling *(as of coal with heating)*
Aufblähungsmittel *n s.* Blähmittel
Aufblasekonverter *m* [top-blown] basic oxygen converter, [top-blown] basic oxygen furnace
Aufblas[e]verfahren *n* top-blown oxygen converter process, basic oxygen converter (furnace, steel) process, oxygen process of steelmaking, oxygen lance process
Aufblasverhältnis *n (plast)* blow-up ratio
aufblättern to exfoliate, to delaminate, to cleave *(of laminated material)*
Aufblättern *n* exfoliation, delamination, cleavage *(of laminated material)*
aufbrauchen to use up, to consume *(as in a reaction)*
aufbrausen to effervesce
Aufbrausen *n* effervescence, effervescency
aufbrausend effervescent
aufbrechen to break up *(molecules, bonds)*
Aufbrechen *n* breaking-up, breakup *(of molecules, bonds)*
aufbrennen to fire on *(on-glaze decorations)*
Aufbrenntemperatur *f* firing-on temperature
aufbringen to apply *(coatings)*
~/mit dem Pinsel to brush-apply, to brush on
Aufbringen *n* application *(of coatings)*
~ **von Wasserzeichen** *(pap)* watermarking
Aufdampfen *n* vapour deposition, deposition from vapour, vapour condensation plating
~ **im Vakuum** vacuum deposition, deposition in vacuo
aufdringlich objectionable *(smell)*
aufeinanderfolgend consecutive
Aufenthaltsdauer *f* residence time, holding (hold-up, detention) time, *(hyd also)* hydraulic (fresh-feed) residence time *(in the aeration tank)*
Aufenthaltswahrscheinlichkeit *f* probability of finding *(a particle in a specified location)*
Aufenthaltswahrscheinlichkeitsdichte *f* probability density
Aufenthaltszeit *f s.* Aufenthaltsdauer
Auffangbecken *n (hyd)* catch basin
Auffangbehälter *m* receiving tank, receiver
Auffangelektrode *f* collector (collecting) electrode, collector
auffangen to collect, to catch, to trap, to receive
Auffänger *m* receiver, catcher; electron acceptor; target *(as of an X-ray tube)*; ion collector *(of a mass spectrometer)*
Auffanggefäß *n* collection vessel, receiver, catcher, catch pot, trap; *(lab)* catch container; *(met)* tapping receiver
Auffangrinne *f (glass)* receiver, pickup
Auffangschale *f*, **Auffangwanne** *f (lab)* catch pan
auffärben *(text)* to redye
aufflammen to flash, to burst into flame
Aufflammen *n* flash[ing]
~/verzögertes afterflaming *(fireproofing)*
Aufflußspalt *m (pap)* gate, slot, slice *(of the head box)*
auffrischen *(text)* to revive
auffüllen to fill up *(liquid or bulk material)*, *(esp anal)* to make up to volume; to fill out *(electron shells)*; to replenish *(a store)*
Aufgabe *f* charging, feeding, filling, loading, furnishing
Aufgabeapparat *m* charging (feeding) mechanism, feeder
Aufgabebecherwerk *n* directly fed bucket elevator
Aufgabebehälter *m* feed tank
Aufgabeboden *m (distil)* feed tray (plate)
Aufgabeende *n* feed end
Aufgabegut *n* feed[stock], feed material, charge [stock], batch; feed slurry (pulp) *(as in centrifugation)*; *(filtr)* prefilt [feed, slurry]
Aufgabegutstrom *m* feed stream, input (inlet) stream
Aufgabekasten *m* feed box

Aufgabekohle *f* feed[stock] coal
Aufgabemassestrom *m s.* Aufgabegutstrom
Aufgabeöffnung *f* feed (charging) hole, feed inlet (opening)
Aufgaberinne *f*, **Aufgaberutsche** *f* feed (charging) chute, feed launder
Aufgabeschieber *m* feed gate
Aufgabeschurre *f s.* Aufgaberinne
Aufgabeseite *f* feed end
Aufgabetrichter *m* feed[ing] hopper, charging (loading) hopper, feed[ing] funnel
Aufgabetrog *m* feeding trough
Aufgabevorrichtung *f* feeder, loader
Aufgabewalze *f* feed[ing] roll
aufgasen *(pap)* to fortify *(the cooking acid)*
Aufgasen *n (pap)* fortification *(of the cooking acid)*
aufgeben to feed, *(esp if discontinuously or relating to a definite quantity:)* to charge
Aufgeben *n s.* Aufgabe
Aufgeber *m* feeder, loader
aufgehen to rise *(of yeast, dough)*; *(tann)* to plump *(of pelts)*
~ **lassen** to raise, to leaven *(dough*
aufgeschliffen *(lab)* ground-in
aufgeschlossen/alkalisch *(pap)* alkaline cooked
aufgießen to pour on
Aufglasur *f (ceram)* on-glaze, overglaze
Aufglasurdekoration *f (ceram)* on-glaze decoration, overglaze decoration
Aufglasurfarbe *f (ceram)* on-glaze colour, overglaze (enamel) colour
Aufglasurmalerei *f (ceram)* on-glaze painting, overglaze painting
Aufguß *m* infusion, *(by boiling also)* decoction
Aufgußverfahren *n (ferm)* infusion mashing (method, process)
aufhalden to dispose of to tip, to dispose of by tipping, to deposit on a tip *(waste products)*
Aufhalden *n* disposal to tip *(of waste products)*
aufhärten to add hardness *(to the water)*
Aufhärtung *f* adding of hardness *(to the water)*, hardening
aufhäufen to accumulate
~/sich to accumulate
Aufhäufung *f* accumulation
aufheizen to heat up
Aufheizgeschwindigkeit *f* heating rate
Aufheizsektion *f* heating section
Aufheizung *f* heating[-up]
Aufheizzeit *f* heating-up time (period)
Aufhelleffekt *m s.* Aufhellungseffekt
aufhellen to brighten *(esp by adding optically active agents)*; to bleach, to clear
Aufheller *m* brightener, brightening agent
~/optischer optical bleaching agent, [optical] brightening agent, [optical] whitening agent, optical brightener (bleach), fluorescent brightener (bleach)
Aufhellung *f***/optische** optical brightening (bleaching)
Aufhellungseffekt *m* brightening effect
Aufhellungsmittel *n s.* Aufheller
aufhydrieren to rehydrogenate
Aufhydrierung *f* rehydrogenation
aufkalken *(agric)* to lime *(to a higher pH value)*
Aufkegeln *n* **und Kreuzteilen (Vierteln)** *n (anal)* coning and quartering
aufklappen to dismantle *(e.g. a Sweetland filter)*; to swing open *(as of a Sweetland filter)*
aufklären to elucidate *(e.g. constitution)*
Aufklärung *f* elucidation *(as of constitution)*
aufkleben *(tann)* to paste *(damp hides on boards or metal plates)*
Aufklebepapier *n* pasting (lining) paper
aufklotzen *(text)* to pad
aufkochen to boil up
~ **lassen** to boil up, to bring to the boil
~/wieder to reboil
Aufkochen *n* boiling-up, *(process also)* ebullition
aufkochend ebullient
Aufkocher *m*, **Aufkochofen** *m (petrol)* reboiler [furnace]
Aufkohl... *s.* Aufkohlungs...
aufkohlen *(met)* to carburize
~/im Salzbad to bath-carburize, to liquid-carburize
~/in der Randschicht (Randzone) to case-carburize
~/in festen Kohlungsmitteln to pack-carburize
~/in flüssigen Mitteln *s.* ~/im Salzbad
~/in gasförmigen Mitteln to gas-carburize
Aufkohlen *n (met)* carburizing, carburization
~ **im Salzbad** bath carburizing, liquid (liquid-salt, molten-salt) carburizing
~ **in der Randschicht (Randzone)** case carburizing
~ **in festen Kohlungsmitteln** [solid-]pack carburizing
~ **in flüssigen Mitteln** *s.* ~ im Salzbad
~ **in gasförmigen Mitteln** gas carburizing
Aufkohlungsbad *n (met)* carburizing bath
Aufkohlungsgas *n (met)* carburizing gas
Aufkohlungsgemisch *n (met)* carburizing mixture
Aufkohlungsgeschwindigkeit *f (met)* carburizing rate
Aufkohlungshitze *f (met)* carburizing heat
Aufkohlungsmittel *n (met)* carburizing agent (compound), [case-hardening] carburizer
Aufkohlungsofen *m (met)* carburizing furnace (oven)
Aufkohlungspulver *n (met)* carburizing powder
Aufkohlungssalz *n (met)* carburizing salt
Aufkohlungsschicht *f (met)* [carburized] case
Aufkohlungstiefe *f (met)* carburizing (case) depth
Aufkohlungsverfahren *n (met)* carburizing process
Aufkohlungszone *f (met)* [carburized] case
aufkonzentrieren to concentrate *(an acid)*; *(pap)* to fortify *(the cooking acid)*

Aufkonzentrieren *n* concentration *(of an acid)*; *(pap)* fortification *(of the cooking acid)*
aufkrausen *(tann)* to pommel
Aufladung *f*/**[elektro]statische** electrostatic charging, static electrification
Auflagehumus *m* raw humus, mor
Auflageplatte *f* bed plate
auflaufen/auf das Sieb *(pap)* to enter onto the wire
Auflaufkasten *m (pap)* flow (stuff, breast) box, headbox
Auflaufleder *n (pap)* apron
Auflaufrahmen *m (pap)* deckle
Auflichtelektronenmikroskop *n* direct-light electron microscope
Auflichtmikroskopie *f* direct-light microscopy
auflockern to loosen [up] *(a chemical bond)*; to loosen *(a filter bed)*
auflösbar dissolvable
Auflösbarkeit *f* dissolvability
Auflöseholländer *m (pap)* breaker (broke) beater
auflösen 1. to dissolve; 2. to disintegrate *(into constituent elements)*; to break [in, up], to repulp *(waste paper)*
~/sich 1. to dissolve, to undergo dissolution; 2. to disintegrate *(into constituent elements)*
~/sich wieder to redissolve
Auflösung *f* 1. dissolution; 2. disintegration *(into constituent elements)*; breaking, repulping *(of waste paper)*; 3. *s.* Auflösungsvermögen
~ im Gestein *(geol)* intrastratal solution
~/spezifische *(chromat)* specific resolution
Auflösungsanalyse *f s.* Voltammetrie/inverse
Auflösungsgeschwindigkeit *f* dissolution rate
Auflösungsprozeß *m* dissolving process
Auflösungsvermögen *n (anal, phot)* resolving power, resolution
Aufmachungseinheit *f (text)* package
Aufnahme *f* 1. uptake, take-up *(of substances)*, *(by the human body:)* intake; absorption, take-up, pick-up *(of liquids)*; absorption *(of gases)*; acceptance, acquisition *(of electrons)*; 2. *(phot)* taking; 3. photograph, picture
~/autoradiographische autoradiograph, radioautograph
~/empfohlene tägliche recommended daily allowance, RDA *(of nutrlents)*
~/makrofotografische photomacrograph
~/mikrofotografische photomicrograph
~ von Fremdgerüchen foreign odour pickup
Aufnahmeeisen *n (glass)* gathering iron
aufnahmefähig absorptive, absorbent
Aufnahmefähigkeit *f* [absorbing, absorption] capacity, absorbency
Aufnahmemasse *f* loading *(wood preservation)*
Aufnahmematerial *n (phot)* negative material
Aufnahmespule *f (text)* winding bobbin
Aufnahmetisch *m (glass)* casting table
Aufnahmevermögen *n* capacity *(of containing)*; [absorbing, absorption] capacity, absorbency
aufnehmbar absorbable; *(agric)* available *(nutrients)*
Aufnehmbarkeit *f* absorbability; *(agric)* availability *(of nutrients)*
aufnehmen 1. to take up *(substances)*; *(tox)* to take in; to absorb, to take (pick) up *(liquids)*; to absorb *(gases)*; to gain, to accept, to acquire *(electrons)*; 2. to take a photograph
~/artfremden Geruch to pick up foreign odour
~/Farbe *(text)* to take the dye
~/Glas aus der Schmelze to gather glass
Aufnehmer *m s.* 1. Absorptionsmittel; 2. Extraktionsmittel
Aufoxidation *f* oxidation to higher valency, further oxidation
aufoxidieren to oxidize to higher valency
aufpfropfen to graft *(polymers)*
aufpolymerisieren *s.* aufpfropfen
Aufprall *m* impingement, impact[ion]
aufprallen to impinge, to impact
Aufprallerosion *f* impingement attack
aufpressen *(pap, text, tann)* to emboss
aufquellen to swell [up]
aufrahmen *(rubber, plast, food)* to cream
Aufrahmungsfähigkeit *f* creamability, creaming ability (potential, power)
Aufrahmungsmittel *n* creaming agent
Aufrahmungspotential *n*, **Aufrahmungsvermögen** *n s.* Aufrahmungsfähigkeit
Aufrahmungsvorgang *m* creaming process
aufrauhen to roughen; *(text)* to raise [a nap], to nap
aufrechterhalten to maintain, to keep up
Aufrechterhaltung *f* maintenance, upkeep
~ des Gleichgewichts keeping in equilibrium, equilibration
aufreißen to break up *(surfaces)*
Aufreißen *n* breaking-up, breakup *(of surfaces)*
Aufrollapparat *m (pap)* reeling machine, reel[er], winder
aufrollen *(pap)* to reel [up], to wind [up], to wind (work) up into a reel, to make into a roll; to roll, to fold back *(a rubber stock)*
~/sich *(ceram)* to crawl *(unintendedly during glazing)*
Aufrollen *n (pap)* reeling, winding; rolling, folding *(of a rubber stock)*; *(ceram)* crawling *(a defect during glazing)*
~/dichtes *(pap)* tight winding
~/[klang]hartes *s.* ~/dichtes
Aufrollstange *f (pap)* winder (rewind) shaft
Aufrolltrommel *f (pap)* reel-up drum (cylinder), reeling drum (cylinder)
Aufrollvorrichtung *f* winding (wind-up) arrangement, winding equipment
aufrühren to agitate, to stir up; to repulp, to reslurry
aufsättigen to resaturate, to reconcentrate
Aufsättigung *f* resaturation, reconcentration
aufsaugen to suck (soak) up, to imbibe
Aufsaugen *n*, **Aufsaugung** *f* suction, imbibition

aufschäumbar *(plast)* expandable, foamable
Aufschäumbarkeit *f (plast)* expandability, foamability
aufschäumen to foam, to froth *(a substance)*; *(plast)* to expand, to foam; *(glass)* to reboil; to foam [up], to froth [up], to effervesce *(of a substance)*
aufschäumend effervescent, effervescing
Aufschlag *m* impact, impingement
aufschlagen 1. *(pap)* to refine, to clear, to brush out, to break down, to potch, to poach; 2. *(tann)* to handle, to haul *(hides out of the tanning liquor)*
Aufschläger *m (pap)* refiner, refining (perfecting) engine, refining (perfecting) machine
aufschlämmen to suspend, to slurry
Aufschlämmung *f* suspension, slurry
aufschließbar digestible
Aufschließbarkeit *f* digestibility, digestibleness
aufschließen to digest, to decompose, to open up *(by heat or solvents)*; *(mine)* to develop, to open up; *(biol)* to macerate; *(pap)* to cook, to pulp, to reduce to pulp, to make into pulp; to repulp *(waste paper)*
~/intensiv to cook soft *(cellulose)*
~/mit Säure to acidulate *(calcium phosphate in manufacturing fertilizer phosphates)*
~/unvollständig to cook raw *(cellulose)*
Aufschließgestell *n* digestion stand *(of a Kjeldahl apparatus)*
Aufschließung *f s.* Aufschluß
Aufschluß *m* digestion, decomposition, opening-up *(by heat or solvents)*; *(mine)* development, opening-up; *(biol)* maceration; *(pap)* cooking, pulping
~/alkalischer *(pap)* alkaline pulping
~/chemischer *(pap)* [full] chemical pulping
~ des Holzes/mechanischer *(pap)* mechanical (groundwood) pulping
~/halbchemischer *(pap)* semichemical pulping
~ im Bombenrohr (Einschmelzrohr, Schießrohr) sealed-tube decomposition
~ mit Säure *(pap)* acid pulping; acidulation *(of calcium phosphate for manufacturing fertilizer phosphates)*
~/saurer *(pap)* acid pulping
Aufschlußbohrung *f* 1. exploration drilling; 2. exploration (exploratory) well, wildcat
~/erfolglose unproductive well, dry hole, duster
Aufschlußchemikalie *f s.* Aufschlußmittel
Aufschlußgrad *m* degree of digestion (decomposition); *(pap)* degree of cooking
Aufschlußlauge *f s.* Aufschlußlösung
Aufschlußlösung *f (pap)* pulping (cooking, digestion) liquor; acidulant *(fertilizer industry)*
Aufschlußmittel *n* digesting (decomposing) agent; *(pap)* pulping (cooking) agent (chemical)
Aufschlußmittelgemisch *n* digestion mix
Aufschlußsäure *f* acidulant *(for manufacturing fertilizer phosphates)*
Aufschlußverfahren *n* decomposition process, *(pap)* pulping process
~/alkalisches *(pap)* alkaline process
aufschmelzen to burn on, to weld (flux) on *(e.g. lead to form a coating)*
aufschmieren to smear *(e.g. a lubricant)*
Aufschrumpfen *n* **unter Vakuum** *(plast)* vacuum snap-back forming
aufschwemmen to suspend; *(min tech)* to pulp
Aufschwemmung *f* suspension
aufschwimmen to float, to rise
Aufschwimmen *n* floating, rising, rise • **zum ~ bringen** to float
Aufschwimmgeschwindigkeit *f* rising velocity, *(waste-water floatation also)* rise rate (velocity)
aufspalten 1. to cleave, to crack [up], to split *(chemical compounds)*, *(relating to ring molecules also)* to open; to cleave, to break, to crack [up], to split, to disrupt *(chemical bonds)*; to resolve *(racemic mixtures)*; 2. to split [up], to cleave, to delaminate *(mechanically)*; 3. *s.* ~/sich
~/durch Solvolyse to solvolyze
~/in Fibrillen (Teilfäserchen) to fibrillate *(fibres)*
~/sich 1. to crack, to decompose, to split up *(of chemical compounds)*; to cleave, to crack *(chemical bonds)*; to dissociate *(into ions)*; 2. to split, to cleave, to delaminate *(mechanically)*
Aufspaltung *f* 1. cleavage, cracking, decomposition *(of chemical compounds)*; cleavage, breaking, cracking, splitting, disruption, fission, scission *(of chemical bonds)*; resolution *(of racemic mixtures)*; 2. splitting[-up], cleavage, delamination *(mechanically)*
Aufspaltungsbild *n (phys ch)* splitting pattern
Aufspaltungsfaktor *m* **[/spektroskopischer]** spectroscopic splitting factor, Landé splitting factor g, g factor
aufspeichern to store, to accumulate
~/sich to accumulate
Aufspeicherung *f* storage, accumulation
aufsprengen *(org ch)* to rupture *(a ring)*
Aufsprengung *f (org ch)* rupture *(of a ring)*
aufspritzen to splash on *(e.g. wet material onto a roller dryer)*
aufsprühen to spray on *(e.g. wet material onto a roller dryer)*
aufspüren to prospect *(e.g. ore deposits)*
aufstärken to fortify; *(distil)* to dephlegmate
Aufstärkung *f* fortification; *(distil)* dephlegmation
aufsteigen to rise, to ascend, to pass up[wards]
~/in Blasen to bubble
Aufsteiggeschwindigkeit *f* rising velocity, *(hyd also)* rise rate (velocity)
aufstellen 1. to erect, to set [up], to mount *(e.g. an apparatus)*; 2. to determine, to calculate *(a formula)*; to formulate *(an equation)*
Aufstellung *f* 1. erection, setting[-up], mounting *(as of an apparatus)*; 2 determination, calculation *(of a formula)*; formulation *(of an equation)*
aufsticken *(met)* to nitride

Aufsticken *n (met)* nitride hardening, nitrogen [case-]hardening, nitriding, nitridation
aufstreichen to spread on, to smear; to brush on, to brush-apply
Aufstrich *m (pap)* coat[ing]
Aufstrom *m* ascending (upward) current, upflow, upward flow
aufströmen to entrain *(coal dust in gasification)*
Aufströmen *n* entrainment *(of coal dust in gasification)*
Aufstromklassieren *n* hydraulic classification (separation)
Aufstromklassierer *m* hydraulic (countercurrent) classifier, hydrosizer
auftauen to thaw, to defrost
aufteilen/in gleiche Anteile *(anal)* to aliquot
Auftrag *m* 1. coat[ing]; 2. *s.* Auftragen
auftragen to apply, to coat onto a support *(e.g. coating material)*; *(tann)* to swab *(lime paint)*
~/mit dem Pinsel to brush-apply, to brush on
Auftragen *n* application *(as of coating material)*; *(tann)* swabbing *(of lime paint)*
~/galvanisches electrodeposition
auftragend sein *(pap)* to bulk high
Auftragewerk *n (text)* coating system
Auftragmaschine *f* coating machine, coater
Auftragschweißen *n* hard [sur]facing
Auftragwalze *f* application roll, applicator (feed, feeding) roll
auftreffen to impinge
Auftreffplatte *f* target *(of an X-ray tube)*
auftreiben to ream *(glass piping)*
Auftreiber *m (lab)* reamer
auftreten to occur, to appear
Auftreten *n* occurrence, appearance
~ von Kurzschlußströmungen by-passing, short circuiting *(in a reactor)*
Auftrieb *m* buoyancy
Auftriebskorrektur *f* buoyancy correction *(weighing technique)*
Auftriebskraft *f* buoyancy (buoyant) force
Auftriebsmethode *f* buoyancy method *(for measuring gas density)*
Auftrittsenergie *f s.* Auftrittspotential
Auftrittspotential *n (spectr)* appearance potential
aufwallen to boil [up], to bubble [up]
Aufwallen *n* boiling, bubbling, ebullience, ebullition
aufwallend ebullient
Aufwandmenge *f* amount of application *(as of a pesticide)*
aufwärmen *(glass)* to warm in
Aufwärmloch *n (glass)* glory hole
Aufwärts-Dickstoffturm *m (pap)* upflow high-density tower
Aufwärtsfilter *n (hyd)* upflow (upward-flow) filter
Aufwärtsfiltration *f (hyd)* upflow filtration
Aufwärtsgasen *n* uprun[ning], upsteaming *(manufacturing of water gas)*
Aufwärtskläranlage *f (hyd)* vertical-flow unit, upflow unit
Aufwärtsstrom *m* upflow, upward flow (current), ascending current • **im ~ arbeiten** to operate upflow *(of a filter)* • **im ~ fahren** to operate upflow *(a filter)*
Aufwärtsziehmaschine *f (glass)* updraw machine
Aufwärtsziehverfahren *n (glass)* updraw (Schuller) process
aufweichen to soak; to grow soft, to soften
aufweisen/einen konstanten Wert to show a constant reading
Aufweitung *f* expansion *(of the crystal lattice)*
Aufweitverbindung *f* expanded joint *(of pipes)*
aufwickeln to reel [up], to wind [up]
Aufwickeln *n* reeling[-up], winding[-up], wind-up
~/dichtes *(pap)* tight winding
~/[klang]hartes *s.* ~/dichtes
Aufwickelspule *f (text)* winding bobbin
Aufwickeltrommel *f s.* Aufrolltrommel
Aufwickelvorrichtung *f* winding (wind-up) arrangement, wind-up
aufwirbeln to stir up, to whirl up *(e.g. a suspension by means of a gas stream)*
Aufwirkmaschine *f (food)* dough-forming (dough-moulding) machine
Aufwuchs *m***/biologischer** *s.* Rasen/biologischer
aufzehren to consume *(e.g. a reactant)*
Aufzehrung *f* consumption *(as of a reactant)*
Aufzieheigenschaft *f s.* Aufziehvermögen
aufziehen 1. to attach, to key *(dyes to fibres)*; 2. *(tann)* to handle, to haul *(hides out of the tanning liquor)*
Aufziehen *n* 1. *(dye)* attachment, keying, strike; 2. *(tann)* handling, hauling
~/langsames *(dye)* slow strike
~/mäßiges *(dye)* moderate strike
~/schnelles *(dye)* rapid strike
Aufziehgeschwindigkeit *f (dye)* rate (speed) of absorption
Aufziehkarton *m* mounting board
Aufziehvermögen *n (dye)* absorptive (absorbing) capacity, absorptive (absorbing) power, *(Am)* pile-on property
aufzwirbeln *(bioch)* to unwind, to untwist *(the DNA double strand)*
Aufzwirbelung *f (bioch)* unwinding, untwisting *(of the DNA double strand)*
Augenbrauenstift *m* eyebrow pencil
Augenfarbstoff *m*, **Augenpigment** *n* eye (visual) pigment, photopigment
augenreizend lachrymatory, irritating the eye
Augenreizstoff *m* lachrymator, eye irritant
Augenreizung *f* eye irritation
Augensalbe *f* eye ointment
Augenschatten *m*, **Augenschattenschminke** *f s.* Lidschatten
Augenschutz *m* eye protection
Augentropfen *mpl* eye drops
Augenwasser *n* eyewash
Auger-Ausbeute *f (phys ch)* Auger yield

Auger-Effekt *m (phys ch)* Auger effect
Auger-Elektron *n* Auger electron
Auger-Elektronen-Ausbeute *f* Auger yield
Auger-Elektronenspektroskopie *f* Auger [electron] spectroscopy, AES
~ **mit Röntgenstrahlanregung** X-ray-induced Auger electron spectroscopy, XAES
Augustinsson-Auftragung *f (bioch)* Augustinsson plot
Aurat *n* aurate *(a salt of auric acid)*
Aureolin *n* aureolin, cobalt (Indian) yellow *(potassium hexanitrocobaltate)*
Aurin *n* aurin[e] dyestuff, *(specif)* $(HOC_6H_4)_2=C_6H_4=O$ aurin[e]
Auripigment *n (min)* auripigment *(arsenic(III) sulphide)*; orpiment [yellow], yellow arsenic [sulphide], arsenic yellow, king's yellow (gold), royal yellow *(arsenic(III) sulphide)*
Auron *n* aurone *(any of several flavonoids)*
ausäthern *s.* ausethern
ausbalancieren to equilibrate, to counterbalance
Ausbalancieren *n* equilibration
ausbauen to fill out *(electron shells)*
Ausbesserungslack *m* touch-up paint
Ausbeute *f* yield, recovery, gain ratio • **mit hoher** ~ high-yield
~**/brauchbare** fair yield
~**/spezifische** *(biot)* specific yield *(mg product/mg cell dry weight)*
~**/theoretische** theoretical yield
Ausbeuteerhöhung *f* increase in yield, yield increase
Ausbeutefaktor *m* efficiency factor, initiator efficiency *(radical polymerization)*
Ausbeutekoeffizient *m (biot)* 1. process yield coefficient *(fermentation process)*; 2. *s.* Ertragskoeffizient
ausbeuten to exploit *(mineral resources)*
Ausbeuteverlust *m* yield loss
Ausbeutung *f* exploitation *(of mineral resources)*
~**/sekundäre** *(petrol)* secondary recovery
ausbilden/sich to form
Ausbildung *f* formation
~ **von Bindungen** bond formation
~ **von Kurzschlußströmungen** by-passing, short-circuiting *(in a reactor)*
Ausbiß *m (mine)* outcrop; *(petrol)* [surface] seepage
Ausblasbehälter *m* blow pit (tank, vat), receiving (wash) tank
ausblasen to blow out; *(pap)* to blow [off] *(a digester)*
Ausblasen *n (pap)* blowing, blow *(of the digester)*
~ **mit Druckluft** air blowing
Ausblasgas *n (pap)* blow-pit gas, gaseous blow-off
Ausblasleitung *f* blow[-out] line
Ausblasrohr *n* blowpipe
Ausblasschieber *m*, **Ausblasventil** *n* blow[-off] valve, blow-off
ausbleichen to bleach out *(something)*; to fade
Ausbleichen *n* **in Abgasatmosphäre** *(text)* gas fading
ausbleichend fading
~**/nicht** fadeless
ausbleien to lead-line, to lead-clad
Ausbleiung *f* lead lining (cladding)
ausblenden to mask out, to stop out (down) *(a region of the spectrum)*
ausblühen to bloom [out], to effloresce *(of crystals)*
Ausblühen *n* blooming, efflorescence *(of crystals)*
~ **von Schwefel** *(rubber)* sulphur blooming, sulphuring-up
ausblühend/nicht *(rubber)* non-blooming
Ausblühung *f (cryst, min)* bloom, efflorescence; *(ceram)* scumming
ausbluten *(dye, coat, tann)* to bleed [off, through], to mark off; *(chromat)* to bleed
Ausbluten *n* **der Säule** *(chromat)* column bleed
Ausbrand *m* burn-out
ausbreiten to spread [out], to diffuse, to propagate
~**/sich** to spread [out], to diffuse, to propagate
Ausbreitung *f* spreading, diffusion, propagation
Ausbreitungsfaktor *m (bioch)* spreading factor, hyaluronidase *(a family of enzymes)*
Ausbreitungsgeschwindigkeit *f* speed of propagation
Ausbreitungskoeffizient *m* spreading coefficient, SC
Ausbrennartikel *m (text)* burnt-out fabric
ausbrennen *(text)* to burn out; *(coal, petrol)* to burn out (off); to deflagrate *(of explosives)*
Ausbrenner *m (text)* burnt-out fabric
ausbringen 1. to discharge; 2. *(agric)* to apply, to place *(fertilizers or pesticides)*; 3. to yield, to produce
~**/breitwürfig (flächenhaft)** *(agric)* to apply (place) broadcast
Ausbringen *n* 1. discharge, discharging; 2. *(agric)* application, placement, placing *(of fertilizers or pesticides)*; 3. yield, recovery
~ **aus der Luft** air-to-ground application
~**/breitwürfiges (flächenhaftes)** bulk spreading, overall application
~**/ganzflächiges** overall application, *(in the presence of crops also)* overhead application
~ **in flüssiger Form** spraying
~ **unter Abschirmung** directed application
~ **vom Flugzeug aus** aeroplane application
~ **vor dem Auspflanzen** preplanting application
Ausbringungsgerät *n (agric)* [mechanical] applicator, application apparatus
Ausbringungsmethode *f*, **Ausbringungsweise** *f* *(agric)* application method, distribution (placement) method
Ausbringungszeit *f (agric)* time of application
Ausbruch *m (petrol)* blow-out
Ausbruchgestein *n* effusive rock, extrusive (volcanic) rock

Ausbruchpreventer *m (petrol)* blow-out preventer
ausdampfen to evaporate
Ausdampfen *n* evaporation
ausdämpfen to steam; *(distil)* to strip [off, out]
Ausdämpfer *m (distil)* [side] stripper
Ausdämpf[er]kolonne *f (distil)* stripper [column], stripping column (still), steam-stripping still
Ausdämpfsektion *f* stripping section *(of a fractionating column)*
Ausdämpfungsteil *m s.* Ausdämpfsektion
ausdehnbar expansible, expandable, extensible, extendible
Ausdehnbarkeit *f* expansibility, expandability, extensibility, extendibility
ausdehnen to expand, to extend
~/sich to expand, to increase in volume *(as with heat)*; to spread *(over an area)*
Ausdehnung *f* 1. expansion, extension *(act or process)*; 2. extension *(range)*
~/adiabatische adiabatic expansion
~/isenthalpische isenthalpic expansion
~/isotherme isothermal expansion
~/kubische *s.* ~/räumliche
~/lineare linear expansion
~/prozentuale expansion percentage
~/räumliche cubic[al] expansion
~/thermische thermal expansion
ausdehnungsfähig 1. expansive, expansile *(e.g. gas)*; 2. *s.* ausdehnbar
Audehnungsfähigkeit *f* 1. expansiveness *(as of gases)*; 2. *s.* Ausdehnbarkeit
Ausdehnungskoeffizient *m* coefficient of expansion, expansion coefficient, isobaric coefficient of thermal expansion, isobaric thermal expansivity
~/kubischer coefficient of cubic[al] expansion, coefficient of volume expansion
~/linearer coefficient of linear expansion
~/räumlicher *s.* ~/kubischer
~/thermischer coefficient of thermal expansion
Ausdehnungskondenswasserableiter *m* expansion trap
Ausdehnungsmesser *m* extensometer
Ausdehnungsthermometer *n* expansion thermometer
Ausdehnungsvermögen *n* expansiveness *(as of gases)*
Ausdehnungszahl *f s.* Ausdehnungskoeffizient
ausdestillieren to distil out
Ausdrückbolzenfeder *f (plast)* return spring
ausdrücken 1. to press out, to squeeze [out], to express; 2. to push out, to blow out, to discharge *(solid material)*; *(plast)* to eject
Ausdrücken *n* 1. squeeze, expression; 2. discharge *(of solid material)*; *(plast)* ejection
~/automatisches *(plast)* automatic ejection
~ von Hand *(plast)* hand ejection
~ von unten *(plast)* bottom ejection
Ausdrücker *m (plast)* ejector, knockout
Ausdrückhilfsvorrichtung *f (plast)* extractor
Ausdrückkolben *m (plast)* ejection ram
Ausdrückleitung *f (pap)* blow[-out] line
Ausdrückmaschine *f (coal)* pusher machine
Ausdrückplatte *f (plast)* ejector (ejection, knock-out) plate
Ausdrückrahmen *m (plast)* ejector frame
Ausdrückstange *f (plast)* ejector (knockout) bar, pull rod
Ausdrückstempel *m (plast)* ejection pad
Ausdrückstift *m (plast)* ejector (knockout) pin
~/mit Federkraft betätigter spring ejector
Ausdrücktraverse *f (plast)* ejection connecting bar
ausethern to extract (shake out) with ether, *(broadly)* to extract, to shake out
Ausethern *n* ether extraction, *(broadly)* extraction, shaking-out
ausfahren *(ceram)* to draw *(the kiln)*; *(filtr)* to slide out *(e.g. a Kelly filter)*
Ausfall *m* 1. loss *(of material)*; 2. failure, breakdown, outage *(of an apparatus)*; 3. discharge [point]
~ durch Ermüdung fatigue failure
ausfällbar precipitable
Ausfällbarkeit *f* precipitability
ausfallen 1. to precipitate [out], to settle [out], to come down, to separate out, to sediment, to deposit, to subside *(from a solution)*; 2. to fail, to break down *(of an apparatus)*
ausfällen to precipitate, to throw down; to cement *(a metal by a more active one)*
ausfällend precipitative
Ausfallklappe *f* discharge door
Ausfallkonus *m* discharge cone
Ausfallöffnung *f* discharge opening (outlet, door, aperture, port)
Ausfallseite *f* discharge end
Ausfällung *f* precipitation, cementation *(of a metal by a more active one)*
Ausfällungsanlage *f* precipitation plant, precipitator
Ausfällungsmittel *n* precipitant, precipitating agent, precipitator
ausfaulen *(hyd)* to digest *(of sludge)*
Ausfaulen *n*, **Ausfaulung** *f (hyd)* digestion *(of sludge)*
Ausfingern *n (chromat)* fingering [effect]
~/viskoses viscous fingering
ausflammen *(glass)* to sting out
Ausflammverlust *m (glass)* sting-out loss
ausfließen to flow out, to discharge, to effuse
Ausfließen *n* outflow, discharge, effusion, effluence
~/freies *(petrol)* natural flow
ausfließend effluent
ausflocken to flocculate, to coagulate, to clot, to curd[le], *(coll also)* to pectize
Ausflockung *f* flocculation, coagulation, clotting, curdling, *(coll also)* pectization • **zur ~ bringen** to flocculate, to coagulate
~/gegenseitige *(coll)* mutual coagulation (precipitation)

Ausflockungsmittel *n* flocculating (coagulating) agent, flocculant, coagulant, coagulator
Ausfluß *m* 1. effluent, efflux, outflow *(material)*; 2. effluence, efflux, outflow *(process)*; 3. drain, outlet *(site)*
Ausflußdauer *f* efflux time, time of outflow
Ausflußdüse *f (pap)* slice nozzle
Ausflußgeschwindigkeit *f (el ch)* outflow velocity
Ausflußöffnung *f* discharge opening (outlet, door, aperture, port)
Ausflußplastometer *n* **nach Marzetti** Marzetti plastometer
Ausflußrohr *n* effluent (discharge) tube (pipe)
Ausflußschlitz *m*, **Ausflußspalt** *m (pap)* gate, slice, slot *(of the headbox)*
Ausflußzeit *f s.* Ausflußdauer
ausformen to shape out, to perfect
Ausformen *n* **des Reifens** *(rubber)* tyre shaping
ausfressen *(met)* to scour *(the furnace lining)*
Ausfressung *f (met)* scouring *(in the furnace lining)*
Ausfressungen *fpl (rubber)* backrinding *(of mould-parting lines)*
ausfrieren to freeze out; to demarg[ar]inate, to destearinate, to destearinize, to winterize *(oils)*
Ausfrieren *n* freeze-out, freezing-out; demargarination, destearinization, winterization *(of oils)*; *(hyd)* freezing *(for desalinizing sea water)*
Ausfriertasche *f* cold trap
Ausfrierverfahren *n* 1. freeze-thaw process *(for concentrating aqueous solutions or suspensions)*; 2. *(hyd)* freezing [desalination] process
ausführen/einen Versuch to run (carry out) an experiment
Ausfüllungszone *f s.* Anreicherungshorizont
ausfüttern *(met)* to line
Ausgang *m (bioch)* donor (condensing) site, peptidyl-tRNA site, P site
Ausgangselement *n* parent element *(of a radioactive series)*
Ausgangsfeststoffgehalt *m* **des Schlamms** *(hyd)* initial concentration of solids in sludge, solids content of the initial sludge, dry solids in the initial sludge
Ausgangsflüssigkeit *f (distil)* feed liquor
Ausgangsgestein *n* parent (mother, source) rock
Ausgangsgut *n* starting material
Ausgangskonzentration *f* initial concentration
~ **der Beimengung (Verunreinigung)** initial solute concentration *(in zone-melting theory)*
Ausgangslinie *f* **im Massenspektrum** parent [mass] peak
Ausgangslösung *f* initial (parent) solution
Ausgangsmaterial *n* starting (parent, raw) material, parent substance, stock, source
~ **für Krackverfahren** cracking feed (feedstock, stock)
Ausgangsöl *n* charge oil
Ausgangsprobe *f (anal)* gross sample
Ausgangsprodukt *n* starting product
Ausgangspunkt *m* 1. starting point; *(bioch)* initiation site; 2. zero [point] *(of a scale)*
Ausgangsquerschnitt *m* original cross section
Ausgangsspalt *m* exit slit
Ausgangsstamm *m (biot)* original strain *(of microorganisms)*
Ausgangsstellung *f* original position
Ausgangsstoff *m*, **Ausgangssubstanz** *f s.* 1. Ausgangsmaterial; 2. Ausgangselement
Ausgangssubstrat *n (biot)* basal (main growth) medium
Ausgangsverbindung *f* parent compound
Ausgangszustand *m* original (initial) state
Ausgastechnik *f (chromat)* gas-phase stripping technique
Ausgasung *f* **in geschlossenem Kreislauf** *(chromat)* closed-loop stripping
ausgebildet/gut *(cryst)* well-developed
ausgebraucht spent *(solution)*
ausgehärtet/nicht *(plast)* undercured
ausgeheizt *(rubber)* fully cured
ausgehen *(geol)* to outcrop, to crop out
Ausgehendes *n (geol)* outcrop
ausgekleidet/basisch *(met)* basic-lined
~/mit Glas glass-lined
~/sauer *(met)* acid-lined
ausgemauert/feuerfest firebrick-lined
ausgereift mature
ausgerüstet/flammfest (flammsicher) flameproofed
~/knitterarm (knitterecht) anticreased, creaseproofed
ausgetauscht werden/in nucleophiler Substitution to undergo nucleophilic displacement
Ausgiebigkeitsfaktor *m*, **Ausgiebigkeitswert** *m (coat)* yield value
ausgießen to pour out
Ausgießverfahren *n (plast)* slush moulding *(for hollow bodies consisting of PVC paste)*
Ausgleich *m* compensation; counterbalance *(esp of a force)*; make-up *(esp for material lost or used up)*; equilibration, levelling *(esp of weights)*; smoothing-out, balancing-out *(esp of concentrations)*
Ausgleich... *s. a.* Ausgleichs...
Ausgleichbecken *n (hyd)* balancing (equalization) basin (tank), equalizer *(for smoothing-out concentrations)*
Ausgleichbehälter *m* balancing tank
Ausgleichbunker *m* surge hopper
ausgleichen to compensate; to [counter]balance *(esp a force)*; to make up *(esp losses of material)*; to equilibrate, to level [out] *(esp weights)*; to smooth (balance) out *(esp concentrations)*
Ausgleicher *m* expansion joint
Ausgleichgefäß *n (tech)* expansion tank (vessel); *(lab)* levelling bottle
ausgleichglühen *(met)* to soak
Ausgleichinstrument *n* null-balance instrument

Ausgleichkolben *m* levelling bulb
Ausgleichmeßinstrument *n* null-balance instrument
Ausgleichs... *s. a.* Ausgleich...
Ausgleichsdüngung *f* compensation fertilization
Ausgleichsentwickler *m (phot)* compensating developer
ausglühen to glow [thoroughly], to heat [thoroughly]; *(met)* to anneal
Ausglühen *n***/vollständiges** *(met)* true (full) annealing
Ausguß *m* drain, sink; [pour-out] lip, spout *(as of a beaker)*; *(petrol)* mud outlet *(of a rotary-drilling installation)*
Ausgußbecken *n* [bench] sink
Ausgußleitung *f* waste line
Aushängen *n* **an der Luft** *(text)* exposure to the air
aushärten 1. *(met)* to precipitation-harden *(relating to steel)*; to age[-harden] *(relating to light metal)*; 2. *(coat, plast)* to cure, to harden; 3. to harden *(relating to fats)*; 4. to set *(of concrete)*
Aushärtung *f* 1. *(met)* precipitation hardening *(of steel)*; ageing, age-hardening *(of light metal)*; 2. *(coat, plast)* curing, cure; 3. hardening *(of fats)*; 4. setting, set *(of concrete)*
~/photochemische photocuring *(as of polymers in the form of a film)*
~/vorzeitige *(plast)* premature curing *(moulding defect)*
Aushärtungsgeschwindigkeit *f (coat, plast)* speed of cure
Aushärtungszeit *f (coat, plast)* cure (curing) time
Aushauchung *f* exhalation *(as from volcanoes)*
aushebern to siphon [off]
Ausheizung *f (rubber)* full (complete) cure (vulcanization)
Aushöhlung *f* cavity
~/formgebende *(plast)* mould cavity
auskalken to lime out *(in manufacturing organic intermediates)*
auskippen to dump
ausklauben *(min tech)* to remove, to pick [off]
~/von Hand to remove by hand, to pick [off] by hand, to [hand-]pick
auskleiden to line
~/mit Blei to lead-line
~/mit einem Gitterwerk to honeycomb
~/mit Filz to felt
~/mit Graphit to line with graphite, to graphitize, *(Am also)* to graphite
Auskleidung *f* lining *(act or material)*
~ aus feuerfesten Steinen firebrick lining
~ aus Nickelstahl nickel-steel lining
~/basische *(met)* basic lining
~/feuerfeste refractory lining
~ mit Blei lead lining
~/saure *(met)* acid lining
Auskleidungswerkstoff *m* lining material
auskochen 1. to boil out *(a vessel)*; to decoct *(material)*; *(text)* to boil off (out) *(as for removing gum, wax, or dye)*; 2. to deflagrate *(of explosives)*
Auskochen *n* 1. boiling-out *(of vessels)*; decoction *(of material)*; *(text)* boiling-off, boiling-out; 2. deflagration *(of explosives)*
auskohlen to carbonize *(wool)*
Auskohlen *n* carbonization, carbonizing *(of wool)*
Auskopierpapier *n (phot)* print[ing]-out paper, P.O. P.
auskratzen to scratch out, to scrape out, to rake [out]
auskreiden *(coat)* to chalk, to become chalky
auskristallisieren to crystallize [out]
~/wieder to recrystallize
Auslaß *m* 1. discharge *(act)*; 2. discharge [point], outlet, exit, drain, outflow, runoff
auslassen *(food)* to render, to try [out] *(fat)*
Auslaßrohr *n* discharge (outlet) tube (pipe)
Auslaßschleuse *f* outlet sluice
Auslaßventil *n* outlet valve, delivery (discharge) valve
Auslauf *m* discharge [point], outlet, exit, drain, outflow, runoff • **auf ~ geteilt (graduiert)** calibrated (graduated) to deliver, calibrated for delivery
Auslaufbecher *m* flow (viscosity) cup
Auslaufdauer *f* delivery time *(of a burette or pipette)*; flow time *(for determining the viscosity)*
Auslaufdüse *f (pap)* slice nozzle
auslaufen 1. to run out, to flow out, *(unintentionally)* to leak out *(of liquids)*; 2. to discharge, *(unintentionally:)* to leak *(of vessels)*; 3. to spread, to feather, to run *(of paint, of writing ink on paper)*
Auslaufende *n* discharge end
Auslaufgeschwindigkeit *f* discharge velocity; *(pap)* spouting (stock) velocity, speed of the stock; *(hyd)* overflow velocity
Auslauföffnung *f* discharge opening (outlet, door, aperture, port)
Auslaufrohr *n* discharge (outlet) tube (pipe)
Auslaufrutsche *f*, **Auslaufschurre** *f* discharge chute
Auslaufspitze *f* outlet tip *(of a burette or pipette)*
Auslaufventil *n* tap
~/gekrümmtes bib tap
Auslaufverlust *m* exit loss
auslaugbar leachable, extractable, extractible
Auslaugbarkeit *f* leachability, extractability
Auslaugbehälter *m*, **Auslaugbottich** *m* leaching tank (vat, vessel), leach
auslaugen to leach [out], to lixiviate, to extract; to imbibe *(sugar cane)*; *(soil)* to eluviate, to dilute *(nutrients from the eluvial horizon)*
Auslaugung *f* leach[ing], lixiviation, extraction; imbibition *(of sugar cane)*; *(soil)* eluviation, chemical denudation
Auslaugungshorizont *m s.* Auswaschungshorizont
Auslaugungsverfahren *n (ferm)* infusion mashing (process)

Auslaugungszone *f s.* Auswaschungshorizont
Auslegen *n* sizing *(of a plant)*
auslenken to deflect
Auslenkung *f* deflection
Auslenk[ungs]winkel *m* angle of deflection
Auslese *f* selection
auslesen to select, to pick out, *(min tech)* to remove, to pick [off]
~/von Hand to remove by hand, to pick [off] by hand, to [hand-]pick
Auslesen *n* selection; *(min tech)* removal, picking
~ von Hand hand picking (cleaning, sorting), *(min tech)* hand picking
Auslöscheffekt *m (phys ch)* quenching effect
auslöschen to extinguish, to quench *(optically)*; to quench *(an electric arc)*; to extinguish *(a flame)*
Auslöschung *f* extinction *(polarimetry, X-ray diffraction)*
auslösen 1. to initiate, to bring about *(a reaction)*; to trigger *(a chain reaction)*; 2. to dissolve out *(substances by solvents)*
Auslösezähler *m*, **Auslösezählrohr** *n (nucl)* self-quenched (self-quenching) counter
Auslösung *f* 1. initiation *(of a reaction)*; triggering *(of a chain reaction)*; 2. dissolving-out *(of substances by solvents)*
Auslösungsgeschwindigkeit *f* **des Lignins** *(pap)* rate of delignification
ausmachen to make up *(e.g. the main constituent)*
ausmahlen to grind [thoroughly]
Ausmahlung *f* grinding
~/feine fine grinding
~/grobe coarse grinding
Ausmahlungsgrad *m* degree of fineness
ausmauern to brick-line
Ausmauerung *f* brick lining *(act or material)*
ausmustern *(text)* to cast
ausnutzen to utilize
~/vollständig to exhaust
Ausnutzung *f* utilization
~/vollständige exhaustion
Ausnutzungsgrad *m* efficiency, *(agric)* recovery *(of fertilizer by a crop)*
ausphotometrieren *(chromat)* to determine photometrically
Ausphotometrieren *n (chromat)* photometric determination
auspressen 1. to press out, to express, to force out, to squeeze [out]; 2. *(plast)* to extrude
Auspressen *n* 1. pressing, expression, squeeze; 2. *(plast)* extrusion, extruding
Auspuffgas *n* exhaust gas
auspumpen to evacuate, to exhaust, to pump out
Auspumpen *n* evacuation, exhaustion
ausquetschen to squeeze [out], to press out, to express, to force out
Ausquetschen *n* squeeze, pressing, expression
ausräuchern to fumigate, to smoke [out]
Ausräuchern *n* fumigation, smoking
ausräumen to discharge *(e.g. a reactor)*; *(hyd)* to unload *(a sludge-drying bed)*
Ausräumung *f* discharge *(as of a reactor)*; *(hyd)* unloading *(of a sludge-drying bed)*
ausrecken *(tann)* to strike (set) out
Ausregnen *n* rain out, in-cloud scavenging *(of pollutants by raindrops)*
ausreifen to ripen, to mature
Ausreifung *f* ripening, maturation
Ausreißer *m (anal)* outlier, maverick; escape peak
ausrichten to align
~/sich to align, to orient
Ausrichtung *f* alignment, directional distribution, orientation
ausrühren/mit Mononitrotoluen to detoluate *(to remove nitro compounds in TNT manufacture)*
Ausrühren *n* **mit Mononitrotoluen** detoluation *(removal of nitro compounds in TNT manufacture)*
ausrüsten 1. to equip; 2. *(pap, text)* to finish
~/knirschend *(text)* to scroop
Ausrüster *m (text)* finisher
Ausrüstung *f* 1. equipment; 2. *(pap, text)* finish[ing]
~/antistatische antistatic finish
~/chemische chemical proofing
~/glatttrocknende smooth-drying finish
~/hydrophobe water-repellent finish
~/knitterarme (knitterechte) crease-resistant finish (treatment), anticrease (non-crease) finish, *(Am)* crush proofing
~/schmutzabstoßende (schmutzabweisende) dirt-repellent treatment
~/schrumpffreie unshrinkable (shrink-resist) finish
Ausrüstungsabteilung *f (pap)* finishing department (plant)
Ausrüstungsgegenstände *mpl* equipment
Ausrüstungsmittel *n***/verrottungshemmendes** *(text)* anti-mildew agent
Ausrüstungssaal *m (pap)* finishing room
Aussalzchromatographie *f* salting-out chromatography, hydrophobic interaction chromatography, HIC
Aussalzeffekt *m* salting-out effect
aussalzen to salt out, *(esp soap:)* to grain, to cut
Aussalzung *f* salting out, *(esp of soap:)* graining, cutting
Aussalzwirkung *f* salting-out action
aussaugen to suck out, to exhaust
ausschaufeln to scoop [out], to shovel out
Ausschaufeln *n* **von Hand** hand scooping
ausscheiden to separate, to eliminate; *(min tech)* to screen out; to discard *(tailings)*; to deposit, to sediment *(of a liquid)*; to evolve, to set free, to liberate *(gases)*; *(biol)* to excrete, *(esp resins:)* to exude
~/sich to separate [out], *(of precipitates also)* to settle [out], to sediment, to deposit, to precipitate [out], to subside; *(biol)* to exude *(esp of resins)*

Ausscheiden *n* separation, elimination; *(min tech)* discard *(of tailings)*; deposition, sedimentation *(of bottoms by a liquid)*; evolution, liberation *(of gases)*; *(biol)* excretion, *(esp of resins:)* exudation
Ausscheidung *f* 1. *s.* Ausscheiden; 2. sediment, settling[s], bottom sediment (settlings), B.S., bottoms, deposit; *(ferm)* lees, dregs; *(biol)* excretion product, excretum, *(esp of resins:)* exudate • **zur ~ gelangen** *s.* sich ausscheiden
ausscheidungshärten to age-harden
Ausscheidungshärten *n* age (precipitation) hardening
Ausscheidungsprodukt *n s.* Ausscheidung 2.
Ausscheidungsverfahren *n***[/Steffensches]** Steffen process *(for desugarizing molasses)*
ausschlacken to slag
Ausschlag *m* deflection *(of a pointer)*
ausschlagen to deflect
Ausschlagen *n* deflection *(of a pointer)*
Ausschlag[meß]instrument *n* deflection instrument
ausschlämmen to elutriate
Ausschlämmen *n* elutriation
ausschleppen to drag out
Ausschleppverluste *mpl* drag-out losses
ausschleudern 1. to eject, to jet; *(nucl)* to emit, to eject, to expel *(particles)*; 2. to centrifuge
Ausschließungsprinzip *n***/ Paulisches** [Pauli] exclusion principle
Ausschluß *m* exclusion
~ von Luft exclusion of air
Ausschlußchromatographie *f* size-exclusion chromatography, SEC, gel filtration
ausschlußchromatographisch by exclusion chromatography, by gel filtration
Ausschlußkonzept *n (chromat)* size-exclusion model
Ausschlußvolumen *n* excluded volume *(of a coiled macromolecule)*
ausschmelzen *(met)* to fuse, to smelt; *(food)* to render, to try out *(fat)*
Ausschmelzmodell *n* investment (fusible alloy) pattern *(foundry)*
ausschneiden *(plast)* to blank
ausschöpfen *(glass)* to ladle
Ausschuß *m* 1. reject, waste [material]; *(plast)* cull; 2. *s.* Ausschußpapier
Ausschußpapier *n* mill (machine) broke, broken paper (material), brokes, waste paper (stuff)
ausschütteln to shake out, to extract by shaking
~/mit Ether to extract (shake out) with ether
Ausschütteln *n* shake, shaking[-out], extraction by shaking, solvent partition
ausschütten to dump [out], to pour out; *(bioch)* to spill out *(hormones)*
ausschwefeln to sulphur *(e.g. a vat)*; *(rubber)* to sulphur up
Ausschwefeln *n* sulphuration *(as of vats)*; *(rubber)* sulphur blooming, sulphuring-up
ausschwefelnd/nicht *(rubber)* non-blooming
ausschwimmen *(coat)* to flood *(to segregate horizontally)*
ausschwitzen *(bot, text)* to exude *(e.g. resin or lubricant)*; *(petrol)* to sweat
Ausschwitzen *n* **des Schmälzmittels** *(text)* lubricant exudation
Ausschwitzungsprodukt *n* exudate, exudation
Aussehen *n* appearance, look
~/blumenkohlähnliches cauliflower appearance *(of a coke button)*
~/glänzendes gloss
~/mattes dullness
Außenanstrichfarbe *f* exterior paint
Außenbahnbindung *f* outer-orbital bond *(chemical-bond theory)*
Außenbahnkomplex *m* outer-orbital complex *(chemical-bond theory)*
außenbeheizt externally heated
Außenbeheizung *f* external heating
Außenbeständigkeit *f* outdoor (exterior) durability
Außenbewitterung *f* outdoor weathering
aussenden to emit, to radiate *(light)*; to emanate, to emit, to issue *(e.g. radioactive particles)*
Außendruck *m* external pressure
Aussendung *f* emission, radiation *(of light)*; emanation, emission *(as of radioactive particles)*
Außenelektron *n* outer (outside, external) electron, valence[-shell] electron
Außenfläche *f* external (outer) surface
Außenlack *m* exterior paint, *(if transparent:)* exterior varnish
Außenluft *f* external air, outdoor (outside) air
Außenluftqualität *f* outdoor (ambient) air quality
Außenoberfläche *f s.* Außenfläche
Außenorbital... *s.* Außenbahn...
Außenrohr *n* outside pipe
Außenrohrschlange *f* external coil
Außenrüttler *m* external vibrator
Außenschale *f* external shell, outer[most] shell
Außenschleifen *n (ceram)* external grinding
außenseitig external
Außensphärenkomplex *m* outer-sphere complex *(coordination chemistry)*
Außenzahnradpumpe *f* external-gear pump
Außerbetriebsetzung *f* shut[down]
außermittig off-centre
aussetzen 1. to expose *(as to radiation or air)*; 2. to fail *(of an engine)*
Aussetzen *n* 1. exposure *(as to radiation or air)*; 2. failure *(of an engine)*
aussieben to screen [out]
aussommern *(ceram)* to weather
aussondern to separate [out], to eliminate; *(min tech)* to discard *(tailings)*
Aussondern *n* separation, elimination; *(min tech)* discard
aussortieren to cull, to eliminate; *(min tech)* to discard *(tailings)*

Aussortieren *n* culling, elimination; *(min tech)* discard
Ausspritzer *m (ceram)* spit-out *(a defect)*
ausspülen to rinse [out], to scour, to flush [out], to swill out
ausstanzen *(plast)* to blank
Ausstattung *f* equipment
Ausstattungspapier *n* fancy (letter, note) paper, *(Am)* correspondence (decorated) paper
aussteinen to brick-line
Ausstellungs-Schauglas *n* museum jar
Ausstoß *m* 1. [production] output, make; 2. discharge *(of solid material)*; 3. *(plast)* ejection; lift, set of mouldings *(produced in one pressing operation)*; 4. emission *(of pollutants)*
~/automatischer *(plast)* automatic ejection
ausstoßen 1. to eject, to expel *(e.g. radioactive particles)*; 2. to expel *(molecules in elimination reactions)*; 3. to push out, to discharge *(solid material)*; *(rubber)* to dump; *(plast)* to eject; 4. *(tann)* to set out, to strike out *(hides)*; to emit *(pollutants)*
Ausstoßen *n* 1. ejection, expulsion *(as of radioactive particles)*; 2. expulsion *(of molecules in elimination reactions)*; 3. pushing out, discharge *(of solid material)*; *(rubber)* dumping; *(plast)* ejection; 4. *(tann)* setting-out, striking-out
~ des Säuleninhalts *(chromat)* column extrusion
Ausstoßer *m (plast)* ejector
Ausstoßmaschine *f (coal)* pusher machine
Ausstoßrate *f* output rate
Ausstoßtemperatur *f (rubber)* dump temperature
Ausstoßzone *f (plast)* metering zone (section) *(af an extruder)*
ausstrahlen to radiate, to emit *(light)*; to emit, to emanate, to issue *(e.g. radioactive particles)*
~/wieder to reradiate, to re-emit
Ausstrahlung *f* radiation, emission *(of light)*; emission, emanation *(as of radioactive particles)*
~/spezifische emittance, radiant excitance
Ausstrahlungsverlust *m* radiation loss
ausstreichen 1. to spread out *(on a surface)*; 2. *(geol)* to outcrop, to crop out
Ausstreichen *n (geol)* outcrop[ping]
ausströmen 1. to flow out, to discharge, to effuse, *(unintentionally:)* to leak out *(of liquids)*, to escape *(of gases, steam)*; 2. to emanate, to emit *(heat)*
~ lassen to discharge, to run
Ausströmen *n* 1. outflow, discharge, effluence, effusion, *(unintentionally:)* leak[age] *(of liquids)*, escape *(of gases, steam)*; 2. emanation, emission *(of heat)*
Ausströmgeschwindigkeit *f s.* Ausströmungsgeschwindigkeit
Ausströmöffnung *f* discharge opening (outlet, door, aperture, port)
Ausströmungsgeschwindigkeit *f* discharge velocity; outflow velocity *(polarography)*; *(pap)* spouting (stock) velocity, speed of the stock
Ausströmverlust *m* exit loss
aussüßen *(pap)* to [re]causticize *(to convert soda or potash into NaOH or KOH)*
austarieren to tare, to [counter]balance
Austausch *m* exchange *(of ions, heat)*; substitution, placement *(of groups of atoms)*; substitution *(of material)*
~/wechselseitiger interchange
Austauschabteilung f/regenerative regeneration section *(of a plate pasteurizer)*
Austauschadsorption *f* exchange adsorption
austauschaktiv capable of substituting, substitutable *(atomic group)*
Austauschaktivität *f* substitutability
Austauschazidität *f (soil)* exchange acidity
austauschbar exchangeable *(ions)*; substitutable, replaceable *(groups of atoms)*; substitutable *(material)*
~/wechselseitig interchangeable
Austauschbarkeit *f* exchangeability *(of ions)*; substitutability, replaceability *(of groups of atoms)*; substitutability *(of material)*
~/wechselseitige interchangeability
Austauschbehälter *m* resin tank *(ion exchange)*
Austauschboden *m (distil)* plate, tray
~/gelochter perforated plate (tray), sieve plate (tray)
Austauschchromatographie *f* [ion-]exchange chromatography
Austauschdüngung *f* exchange fertilization
austauschen to exchange *(ions)*; to substitute, to replace *(groups of atoms)*; to substitute *(material)*
~/wechselseitig to interchange
Austauschenergie *f* exchange [binding] energy
Austauschentartung *f (phys ch)* exchange degeneracy
Austauscher *m* exchanger *(apparatus or material)*
Austauscherbett *n* ion-exchange bed
Austauscherharz *n* ion-exchange resin
~/chelatbildendes chelate [ion-exchange] resin
~ mit Gelstruktur gel-type resin, isoporous resin
~ mit Kanalstruktur macroporous (macroreticular) resin, MRR
~ zur Entkarbonisierung [ion-exchange] dealkalizer resin
Austauscherharzvolumen *n* resin (bed) volume
Austauscherkolonne *f* exchange column
Austauscherkorn *n* ion-exchange bead
Austauscherkügelchen *n s.* Austauscherkorn
Austauschermasse *f* [ion-]exchange medium
Austauschermaterial *n* ion-exchange material (medium)
Austauschersäule *f* ion-exchange column
Austauschervolumen *n s.* Austauscherharzvolumen
austauschfähig *s.* 1. austauschaktiv; 2. austauschbar
Austauschfähigkeit *f s.* 1. Austauschaktivität; 2. Austauschbarkeit; 3. Austauschkapazität
Austauschfeuchtemenge *f***/ spezifische** drying rate

Austauschfläche *f* exchange surface *(mass transfer)*
Austauschgerbstoff *m***/synthetischer** exchange (replacement) syntan
Austauschgeschwindigkeit *f* exchange rate
Austauschglied *n s.* Austauschintegral
Austauschglocke *f (distil)* bubble cap, dome
Austauschgrad *m* **für O_2** *s.* Austauschwirkungsgrad für O_2
Austauschharz *n s.* Austauscherharz
Austauschintegral *n* exchange integral (term) *(quantum chemistry)*
Austauschkalk *m (soil)* exchangeable calcium
Austauschkapazität *f* [ion-]exchange capacity
Austauschkoeffizient *m* transfer coefficient *(mass transfer)*
Austauschkolonne *f* rectifying (rectification) column
Austauschkomplex *m*, **Austauschkörper** *m (soil)* exchange complex, ion-exchange compound
Austauschkraft *f* exchange force
Austauschname *m (nomencl)* replacement name
Austauschplatz *m* [ion-]exchange site *(of an ion exchanger)*
Austauschrate *f* transfer rate *(mass transfer)*
~ **für O_2** *(hyd)* oxygen transfer rate, rate of oxygen transfer *(in g $O_2/m^3 \cdot h$)*
Austauschreaktion *f* substitution (replacement) reaction, *(esp relating to ions:)* exchange reaction
Austauschsäule *f s.* Austauschkolonne
Austauschstoff *m* substitute
Austauschstrom *m (el ch)* exchange current
Austauschstromdichte *f (el ch)* exchange current density
Austauschtransport *m (bioch)* antiport
Austauschvermögen *n s.* Austauschkapazität
Austauschwechselwirkung *f (spectr)* exchange interaction
Austauschwirkungsgrad *m* **für O_2** *(hyd)* oxygen transfer efficiency
Austauschzyklus *m* service (loading) cycle, service (operating) run, exhaustion cycle *(ion exchange)*
Austenit *m (met)* austenite *(a solid solution of carbon in gamma iron)*
Austenitformhärten *n (met)* ausforming
austenitisch *(met)* austenitic
austenitisieren *(met)* to austen[it]ize
Austenitisierung *f (met)* austenitization
Austenitisierungstemperatur *f (met)* austenitizing temperature
Austrag *m* 1. *s.* Austragen; 2. discharge [point], outlet, exit; 3. *(el ch)* drag-out
Austragapparat *m* discharge apparatus (device), discharger
Austragdüse *f* discharge nozzle; skimming nozzle *(of a centrifuge)*; apex valve *(of a hydrocyclone)*
Austrageinrichtung *f s.* Austragapparat
austragen to discharge; *(min tech)* to discard *(tailings)*
Austragen *n* discharge; *(min tech)* discard
Austragende *n* discharge (outlet) end
Austraggutstrom *m* output (outlet) stream
Austragklappe *f* discharge door
Austragkonus *m* discharge cone
Austragmassestrom *m* output (outlet) stream
Austragmesser *n* discharge knife
Austragöffnung *f* discharge opening (outlet, door, aperture, port)
Austragpflug *m* plough *(of a conveyor)*
Austragrinne *f* discharge chute
Austragrohr *n* discharge (outlet) tube (pipe)
Austragrost *m* discharge grate (grating)
Austragrutsche *f* discharge chute
Austrags... *s.* Austrag...
Austragschieber *m* discharge gate
Austragschleuse *f* outlet sluice, exit lock
Austragschlitzschieber *m* discharge gate
Austragschnecke *f* discharge scroll
Austragschurre *f* discharge chute
Austragseite *f* discharge (outlet) end
Austragstelle *f* discharge [point], outlet, exit
Austragventil *n* discharge (outlet) valve
Austragvorrichtung *f* discharging apparatus (device), discharger
Austragwalze *f* discharge roll
Austragzone *f (plast)* metering zone (section) *(of an extruder)*
Austreibekolonne *f (distil)* stripper [column], stripping column (still), side stripper, strip action still
austreiben to expel, to dispel, to drive off (out), to sweep out *(gases from liquids)*; *(distil)* to strip [off, out], to distil off
Austreiben *n* expulsion *(of gases from liquids)*; stripping, desorption *(of sorbed gases from sorbent material)*; *(distil)* stripping
~ **mit Luft** air stripping
Austreiber *m* generator *(of an absorption refrigeration system)*
austreten to escape, to leave, to pass out, to issue *(of gases, liquids)*; to exude *(esp of resins)*; to leave *(of electrons, groups of atoms)*
Austreten *n* escape *(of gases, liquids)*; exudation *(esp of resins)*
Austrieb *m (plast)* fin, flash; *(rubber)* excess stock *(rubber)*, overflow, spew, spue
Austriebnut *f (plast)* groove spew
Austritt *m* 1. *(phys ch)* emission *(as of heat, light, or electrons)*; 2. *s.* Austreten; 3. discharge [point] exit, outlet; outflow
~ **an der Oberfläche** *(petrol)* surface seepage
Austrittsarbeit *f* work function *(of electrons or ions)*
Austrittsende *n* discharge end
Austrittsfähigkeit *f* leaving ability *(of electrons)*
Austrittsgeschwindigkeit *f* discharge velocity
Austrittsgruppe *f (org ch)* leaving group
Austrittsöffnung *f* discharge opening (outlet, door, aperture, port)
Austrittsrohr *n* discharge (outlet) pipe (tube), offtake [pipe]; outflow (effluent) pipe

Austrittsspalt *m* exit slit *(of a spectroscope)*; *(pap)* slice, slot, gate *(of the headbox)*
~ **des Extruderkopfes** *(plast)* die lips
Austrittsstelle *f* discharge [point], exit, outlet; outflow
Austrittsstrom *m* exit (effluent) stream
Austrittsverlust *m* exit loss
austrocknen to dry [out, up], to exsiccate
Austrockner *m (tann)* drying oven
Austrocknung *f* drying, exsiccation
Ausvulkanisation *f* full cure (vulcanization), complete cure
Ausvulkanisationszeit *f* vulcanization (vulcanizing) time
ausvulkanisiert *(rubber)* fully cured
Auswahl *f* selection
auswählen to select
Auswahlregel *f (phys ch)* selection principle (rule)
auswalzen to roll into a plate, to laminate; to mill *(soap chips)*; *(plast)* to calender
~/**zu einem Fell** *s.* ~/zu Platten
~/**zu Platten** *(rubber)* to sheet [out]
auswandern to migrate out *(as of ions)*
Auswaschapparat *m (food)* rinser
auswaschen to wash [out], to rinse [out], to flush [out], to scour *(e.g. a vessel)*, to scrub *(gases)*; to wash *(a filter cake)*; to leach [out], to wash out *(soluble substances)*; *(chromat)* to elute; *(soil)* to eluviate, to leach [out] *(nutrients from the eluvial horizon)*
Auswaschen *n* wash out, below-cloud scavenging *(of pollutants by atmospheric precipitation)*
~ **mit Säure** acid wash[ing]
~ **mit Waschöl** oil wash[ing]
~ **mit Wasser** water wash[ing]
Auswaschgeschwindigkeit *f (hyd)* rinse flow rate *(ion exchange)*
Auswaschkolonne *f (petrol)* scrubber column
Auswaschung *f (soil)* eluviation, leach[ing] *(of nutrients from the eluvial horizon)*
Auswaschungshorizont *m (soil)* eluvial horizon, A-horizon
Auswaschungsverlust *m* washing-out loss; *(soil)* leaching loss
Auswaschvorgang *m (hyd)* rinse cycle, rinsing operation *(ion exchange)*
Auswässerungsgrad *m (phot)* washing rate
auswechselbar exchangeable, substitutable, replaceable
Auswechselbarkeit *f* exchangeability, substitutability, replaceability
auswechseln to exchange, to substitute, to replace
Ausweitung *f* **der Außenelektronenschale** expansion of the valence shell
auswerfen to push out, to discharge *(solid material)*; *(rubber)* to dump; *(plast)* to eject
Auswerfen *n* pushing-out, discharge *(of solid material)*; *(rubber)* dumping; *(plast)* ejection
Auswerfer *m (plast)* ejector, knockout
Auswerferstift *m (plast)* ejector (knockout) pin
Auswerfstempel *m (plast)* ejection pad
Auswintern *n (ceram)* wintering, weathering
Auswurfvorrichtung *f (plast)* ejector, knockout
auszementieren to cement *(a metal by a more active one)*
Auszementierung *f* cementation *(of a metal by a more active one)*
ausziehbar extractable, extractible
ausziehen 1. to extract, to leach, to lixiviate *(material containing valuable components)*; to extract, to leach out *(soluble substances)*; to exhaust *(e.g. a dye liquor)*; 2. to pull out, to attenuate *(glass into a capillary)*
~/**zu Fellen (Platten)** *(rubber)* to sheet [out] *(on the calender)*
Ausziehen *n* 1. extraction, leach[ing], lixiviation *(of material containing valuable components)*; extraction, leaching-out *(of soluble substances)*; exhaustion *(as of a dye liquor)*; 2. pulling-out, attenuation *(of glass into a capillary)*
~ **des Heizschlauchs** *(rubber)* de-bagging [operation]
~ **zu Fellen (Platten)** *(rubber)* sheet calendering, sheeting[-out]
Ausziehtusche *f* India ink
Auszug *m* extract, essence; leachate
~/**alkoholischer** alcoholic extract
~/**wäßriger** water leachate
authigen *(geol)* authigenic, authigenous *(formed in place)*
autochthon *(geol)* autochthonous *(lying in place)*
Autogenbrennschneiden *n s.* Autogenschneiden
Autogenmühle *f* autogenous mill
Autogenschmelzen *n* autogenous smelting
Autogenschneiden *n* autogenous [gas] cutting, oxyacetylene (oxygen-acetylene) cutting
Autogenschweißen *n* autogenous [gas] welding, oxyacetylene (oxygen-acetylene) welding, oxywelding
Autohäsion *f* autohesion *(adhesion caused by self-diffusion)*
Autohydratation *f (geol)* autohydration
Autoionisation *f* autoionization, preionization
Autokatalysator *m* autocatalytic agent
Autokatalyse *f* autocatalysis, self-catalysis
autokatalytisch autocatalytic
Autoklav *m* 1. autoclave, [large-]pressure cooker; 2. *s.* Autoklavheizpresse • **im Autoklaven behandeln (kochen)** to autoclave
~/**stehender (vertikaler)** vertical autoclave
Autoklavenbehandlung *f* autoclaving
Autoklavenpresse *f s.* Autoklavheizpresse
Autoklavheizpresse *f (rubber)* autoclave press, vulcanizer autoclave, pot heater [vulcanizer]
autoklavieren to autoclave
Autokollimationsspektrograph *m* autocollimating spectrograph
Autolack *m* automobile lacquer, automotive coating (finish)

Autolith *m (geol)* autolith, cognate inclusion
Autolysat *n (biol)* autolysate
Autolyse *f (biol)* autolysis, autolytic decomposition
• **~ auslösen** to autolyze, to induce autolysis
• **der ~ unterliegen, ~ erleiden** to autolyze, to undergo autolysis
autolytisch *(biol)* autolytic
Autometamorphose *f (geol)* autometamorphism
Autometasomatose *f (geol)* autometasomatism
automorph *(min)* automorphic, idiomorphic, idiomorphous, euhedral
Autophagie *f (bioch)* autophagy
Autoprotolyse *f* autoprotolysis, self-ionization
Autoprotolysegleichgewicht *n* autoprotolysis equilibrium
Autoprotolysekonstante *f* autoprotolysis (self-ionization) constant
Autoprotolysereaktion *f* autoprotolysis (self-ionization) reaction
Autoracemisation *f*, **Autoracemisierung** *f* autoracemization
Autoradiogramm *n* autoradiograph, radioautograph
Autoradiographie *f* autoradiography, radioautography
autoradiographisch autoradiographic, radioautographic
autotroph *(biol)* autotrophic
Autotrophie *f (biol)* autotrophy
Autotypie[druck]papier *n* autotype (half-tone) paper
Autovakzine *f* autovaccine, autogenous vaccine
Autoxidation *f* autoxidation, autooxidation, *(specif)* spontaneous oxidation
~/durch Kautschukgifte beschleunigte *(rubber)* metallic poisoning
Autoxidationsreaktion *f* autoxidation reaction
Autoxidator *m* autoxidator
Auxin *n* auxin *(a growth regulator in plants)*
auxochrom auxochromic
Auxochrom *n* auxochrome, auxochromic group
~/negatives negative (acidic) auxochromic group
~/positives positive (basic) auxochromic group
auxotroph *(biol)* auxotrophic
Aventurinfeldspat *m (min)* aventurine feldspar
Aventuringlas *n* aventurine glass
Aventuringlasur *f (ceram)* aventurine glaze
Aventurinquarz *m (min)* aventurine quartz *(silicon(IV) oxide)*
Avitaminose *f* avitaminosis, vitamin-deficiency disease
Avivage *f (text)* reviving
avivieren *(text)* to revive
Aviviermittel *n (text)* reviving agent
Avocadofett *n*, **Avocadoöl** *n (cosmet)* avocado oil *(from Persea specc.)*
Avogadro-Konstante *f* Avogadro constant, N_A *(number of particles in 1 mol of a substance)*
Avogadro-Zahl *f* Avogadro number, N_0 *(dimensionless Avogadro constant)*
Avrami-Gleichung *f* Avrami equation *(of crystallization)*
Awapfefferwurzel *f (pharm)* kava, cava *(from Piper methysticum G. Forst.)*
axial axial
Axialkompressor *m* axial[-flow] compressor
Axiallüfter *m* propeller (axial-flow) fan
~ mit Leiträdern vaneaxial fan
Axialpumpe *f* propeller (axial-flow) pump
axialsymmetrisch axially symmetric[al], axisymmetric
Axialventilator *m s.* Axiallüfter
Axialverdichter *m* axial[-flow] compressor
Axialvermischung *f* axial (longitudinal) mixing
Axonometrie *f (cryst)* axonometry
AZ 1. *(= Azetatfaserstoff) s.* Acetatfaserstoff; 2. *s.* Acetylzahl
Aza-Benennung *f s.* Aza-Name
Azan *n* N_nH_{n+2} azane
Aza-Name *m (nomencl)* "a"[-term] name
Aza-Nomenklatur *f* "a" nomenclature
Azelainaldehyd *m* azelaic aldehyde
Azelainsäure *f* azelaic acid, *nonanedioic acid
Azelat *n* azelate *(salt or ester of azelaic acid)*
Azen *n* :NR nitrene, azene, imene, imidogen
azeotrop azeotropic
Azeotrop *n* azeotrope, azeotropic mixture
~/binäres binary azeotrope
~ mit Maximumsiedepunkt maximum-boiling azeotrope, high-boiling azeotrope
~ mit Minimumsiedepunkt minimum-boiling azeotrope, low-boiling azeotrope
~/ternäres ternary azeotrope
Azeotropbildner *m (distil)* azeotroping (entraining) agent, azeotrope-former, entrainer
Azeotropbildung *f* azeotrope formation
Azeotropdestillation *f* azeotropic (entrainment) distillation
Azeotropie *f* azeotropy
azeotropisch azeotropic
Azeotropmischung *f* azeotrope, azeotropic mixture
Azeotroppunkt *m* azeotropic point
Azeotropzusammensetzung *f* azeotropic composition; *(plast)* azeotropic copolymerization composition
Azet... *s. a.* Acet...
Azetimeter *n*, **Azetometer** *n* acetometer, acetimeter *(for testing vinegar)*
azid acidic *(having the character of an acid)*
Azid *n* M^IN_3 azide, hydrazoate; *(org ch)* RN_3 azide
azidifizieren to acidify *(an H atom)*
Azidifizierung *f* acidification *(of an H atom)*
Azidimeter *n* acidimeter, acidometer
Azidimetrie *f* acidimetry
azidimetrisch acidimetric
Azidität *f* acidity, acid strength
~/aktuelle active acidity
~/hydrolytische hydrolytic acidity
~/potentielle potential (total, reserve) acidity

Aziditätsbestimmung *f* determination of acidity
Aziditätsfunktion *f* acidity function
~/Hammettsche Hammett acidity function
Aziditätsgrad *m* degree of acidity
Aziditätskonstante *f* acidity constant
Azidivinylphosphinoxid *n* azidivinylphosphine oxide
Azidogruppe *f* $-N_3$ azido group
Azidoid *n (soil)* acidoid
Azidokomplex *m* acido complex
Azidolyse *f* acidolysis
azidolytisch acidolytic
azidophil acidophilic, acidophilous, oxyphil[e], oxyphilic, oxyphilous
Azidose *f (med)* acidosis
~/diabetische diabetic acidosis *(accumulation of ketone bodies in the blood)*
Azimethylen *n* azimethylene, diazomethane
Aziminobenzol *n* aziminobenzene, 1,2,3-benzotriazole
Azimut[al]quantenzahl *f* azimuthal (subsidiary) quantum number, orbital [angular momentum] quantum number
Azin *n* azine *(any of two classes af organic compounds containing two or more N atoms)*
Azinfarbstoff *m* azine (phenazine-based) dye
Azlacton *n* azlactone, oxazolone
Azlacton-Kondensation *f***/Erlenmeyer-Plöchlsche** Erlenmeyer-Plöchl azlactone synthesis *(to yield a-amino acids)*
A-Z-Lösung *f (biol)* Hoagland solution *(a nutrient solution containing microelements)*
Azoapparatur *f (text)* azo[-dye] unit
Azobenzen *n* azobenzene, diphenyldiimide, diphenyldiazene
Azobindung *f* azo link
Azobisisobutyronitril *n* azobisisobutyronitrile, AIBN
Azobrücke *f* azo link
Azodicarbonamid *n* azodicarbonamide, azoformamide
Azodispersionsfarbstoff *m* disperse azo dye
Azofarbstoff *m* azo dye
~/auf der Faser erzeugter *s.* ~/unlöslicher
~/unlöslicher azoic [dye], insoluble azo dye, *(Am also)* ice color
Azogelb *n* azo yellow
Azogruppe *f* $-N=N-$ azo group
Azoimid *n* azoimide, hydrazoic acid
Azokomponente *f* azo component
Azokörper *m* $R-N=N-R'$ azo compound
Azokupplung *f* azocoupling, diazocoupling
Azol *n* azole *(any of a class of heterocyclic compounds containing N)*
Azomethan *n* azomethane
Azomethin *n* $R_2C=NR'$ azomethine, *(if RHC=NR' also)* Schiff base, Schiff's base
Azomethinfarbstoff *m* azomethine dye
Azomethinverbindung *f s.* Azomethin
Azophenylen *n* azophenylene, phenazine
Azoreihe *f* azo series
Azotometer *n* azotometer, nitrometer
Azoverbindung *f* $R-N=N-R'$ azo compound
Azoxybenzen *n* azoxybenzene
Azoxygruppe *f* azoxy group
Azoxyverbindung *f* azoxy compound
Azulen *n* azulene *(bicyclic hydrocarbon possessing 10 p-electrons)*
A-Zustand *m (plast)* A stage
azyklisch *s.* acyclisch

B

Babassufett *n*, **Babassuöl** *n* babassu (babussu) oil *(palm oil from Orbignya speciosa Berk.)*
Babbit *n*, **Babit[t]-Metall** *n* Babbit metal *(any of a class of alloys containing tin, lead, and antimony)*
Babcock-Kugelringmühle *f* Babcock & Wilcox pulverizer (ball-and-ring mill), Babcock mill
Babo-Blech *n*, **Babo-Siedeblech** *n s.* Babo-Trichter
Babo-Trichter *m (lab)* Babo funnel
Babypresse *f (pap)* baby (pony) press
Bachbildung *f* channel formation, channelling *(as in column packings or reactors)*
Backe *f* jaw *(as of a clamp or breaker)*
~/feste anvil jaw *(of a jaw breaker)*
Backeigenschaft *f* 1. *(food)* baking property (quality, value, characteristics); 2. *(coal)* caking property
backen 1. *(food)* to bake; 2. *(ch)* to bake *(amines for the purpose of sulphonation)*; *(coal)* to cake
Backenbrecher *m* jaw breaker (crusher)
Backenwerkzeug *n (plast)* bar mould
Bäckerhefe *f* baker's yeast
Bäckermargarine *f s.* Backmargarine
Backerrohr *n* tubular heater
Backfähigkeit *f* 1. *(coal)* caking power; 2. *s.* Backeigenschaft
Backfähigkeitsverlust *m (coal)* loss of caking power
Backfähigkeitsverminderung *f (coal)* reduction of caking power
Backfähigkeitszahl *f (coal)* index of caking power, caking index
~ nach Campredon Campredon index
~ nach Roga Roga index
Backfett *n* shortening, pastry fat
Backgroundkonzentration *f* background concentration (background) level, baseline concentration
Backhefe *f s.* Bäckerhefe
Backkohle *f* caking coal
Backmargarine *f* bakery margarine, confectionery (cake, pastry) margarine
Backpulver *n* baking powder
~/phosphathaltiges phosphate powder
Backqualität *f s.* Backeigenschaft 1.

Backverfahren *n* baking process *(for sulphonating amines)*
Backverhalten *n (coal)* caking properties
Backvermögen *n s.* Backfähigkeit 1.
Backzahl *f s.* Backfähigkeitszahl
Bacon-Hochdruckzelle *f* Bacon high-pressure hydrogen cell
Bad *n* bath, *(tech also)* dip, steep; *(text)* bath, liquor
~/altes *(text)* standing bath
~/galvanisches *s.* Galvanisierelektrolyt
~/stehendes *(text)* standing bath
badaufkohlen *(met)* to liquid-carburize, to bath-carburize
Badaufkohlen *n (met)* liquid (bath) carburizing, liquid-salt (molten-salt) carburizing
badeinsetzen *s.* badaufkohlen
Bademittel *n (agric)* [animal] dip *(as for controlling vermin)*
Badeöl *n* bath oil
Badepräparat *n* bath preparation
~/brausendes (sprudelndes) bubble bath
Badepulver *n* bath powder
Badesalz *n* bath salt
Badezusatz *m* bath preparation
Badflüssigkeit *f* bath fluid
Badthermostat *m* thermostatic bath
badzementieren *s.* badaufkohlen
Baekeland-Verfahren *n* Baekeland process *(condensation of phenols and formaldehyde to yield resins)*
Baeyer-Phenol-Aldehyd-Kondensation *f* Baeyer phenol-aldehyde condensation
Baeyer-Probe *f* Baeyer test, permanganate test *(for detecting alkenes)*
Baeyer-Spannung *f (org ch)* [Baeyer's] angle strain
Baeyer-Villiger-Oxidation *f*, **Baeyer-Villiger-Reaktion** *f* Baeyer-Villiger oxidation (reaction) *(of ketones into esters)*
Bagasse *f* [sugar cane] bagasse, begass[e], megass[e] *(remains of sugar cane)*
Bagassefeuerung *f* 1. bagasse firing; 2. bagasse furnace
Bahn *f* 1. orbit *(of electrons surrounding a nucleus)*; path *(of particles leaving an atom)*; 2. *(bioch)* route, pathway; 3. *(pap, plast, text)* web
~/anabolische *(bioch)* anabolic route (pathway)
~/Bohrsche Bohr orbit
~/endlose *(plast)* web
~/katabolische *(bioch)* catabolic route (pathway)
~/stabile (stationäre) stable orbit *(of an electron)*
Bahnabnahme *f* **[mit Oberfilz]** *(pap)* lick-up
Bahnabriß *m s.* Bahnriß
Bahnbewegung *f* orbital motion *(of electrons)*
Bahndrehimpuls *m* orbital [angular] momentum
Bahndrehimpulsquantenzahl *f* azimuthal (subsidiary) quantum number, orbital [angular momentum] quantum number
~/magnetische magnetic quantum number
Bahnelektron *n* orbital electron
Bahnentrockner *m* 1. *(pap, text)* sheeting (web) dryer; 2. *s.* Bandtrockner
Bahnmetall *n a lead alloy consisting of 98 % Pb, 0.7 % Ca, 0.6 % Na, 0.04 % Li, 0.02 % Si, 0.02 % Al*
Bahnmoment *n***/magnetisches** orbital magnetic moment
Bahnriß *m (pap)* break in the web, sheet break
~ in der Naßpartie wet[-end] break
~ in der Rollenschneidmaschine slitter break
~ in der Trockenpartie dry break
Bainit *m (met)* bainite
~/oberer upper bainite
~/unterer lower bainite
Bainitumwandlung *f (phys ch)* bainite transition
Baisalz *n* bay (solar) salt
Bajonettkupplung *f* bayonet coupling (joint)
Baker-Nathan-Effekt *m s.* Hyperkonjugation
Baker-Venkataraman-Umlagerung *f* Baker-Venkataraman rearrangement *(of 2-acyloxy acetophenones into 1,3-diketones)*
bakteriell bacterial
Bakterien *npl***/aerobe** aerobic bacteria
~/anaerobe anaerobic bacteria
~/aromabildende aroma bacteria
~/denitrifizierende denitrifying bacteria, denitrifiers
~/desulfurierende sulphate-reducing (sulphur-reducing) bacteria, sulphate reducers
~/methanogene methanogenic (methane-forming) bacteria, methanogens
~/methanoxidierende methane-oxidizing bacteria
~/methylotrophe methylotrophic bacteria, methylotrophs
~/nitrifizierende nitrifying bacteria, nitrobacteria *(collectively for nitrite and nitrate bacteria)*
~/nitrogene *s.* ~/stickstoffbindende
~/säurebildende acid-forming (acid-producing) bacteria, acid-formers, acid-producers
~/sporenbildende spore-forming (spore-producing) bacteria, spore formers
~/stäbchenförmige rod-shaped bacteria
~/stickstoffbindende nitrogen-fixing bacteria
~/thermophile (wärmeliebende) thermophilic bacteria
Bakterien-α-Amylase *f s.* α-Amylase/bakterielle
bakteriendicht bacteria-tight
Bakteriendichte *f (biot)* bacterial cell density
Bakterieneinwirkung *f* bacterial attack
Bakterieneiweiß *n s.* Protein/bakterielles
Bakterienenzym *n* bacterial enzyme
Bakterienfarbstoff *m* bacterial pigment
Bakterienfärbung *f* bacteria staining
Bakterienfermentation *f* bacterial fermentation
Bakterienfilter *n* bacteriological filter, bacteria-retaining filter
Bakterienflocken *fpl (biot)* bacterial floc
Bakterieninfektion *f (biot)* contamination with bacteria
Bakterienkultur *f* bacterial culture

Bakterienmischkultur *f (biot)* mixed bacterial culture
Bakterienpräparat *n* bacteria preparation
Bakterienprotease *f* bacterial protease
Bakterienrasen *m s.* Rasen/biologischer
Bakterienstamm *m* bacterial strain
Bakterientätigkeit *f* bacterial activity
bakterientötend bacteri[o]cidal
Bakterientrockenmasse *f (biot)* bacterial dry weight, dry weight bacterial cells
Bakterienwachstum *n* bacterial growth
bakterienwachstumshemmend bacteriostatic
Bakterienzahl *f (hyd)* bacterial (bacteriological) count, bacterial number
Bakterienzelle *f* bacterial cell
Bakteriochlorophyll *n (bioch)* bacteriochlorophyll
Bakteriolysin *n* bacteriolysin
Bakteriophag[e] *m* [bacterio]phage
Bakteriostase *f* bacteriostasis
Bakteriostatikum *n* bacteriostat[ic]
bakteriostatisch bacteriostatic
bakterizid bacteri[o]cidal
Bakterizid *n* bactericide
Balasrubin *m (min)* balas ruby
Balata *f* balata *(rubber-like raw material from Mimusops balata Crueger)*
Baldrianöl *n* valerian oil *(from Valeriana officinalis L.)*
Baldriansäure *f* valeric acid, *pentanoic acid
Baldriansäureethylester *m* ethyl valerate
Balg *m (rubber)* diaphragm, bladder
Balkenrührer *m* straight-arm paddle agitator
Balkenwaage *f* beam balance
~/gleicharmige equal-arm balance
~/ungleicharmige unequal-arm balance
Ballast[stoff] *m* impurity, diluent *(as of fuel)*; *(food)* bulk
Ballastventilboden *m* ballast tray
ballen to ball [up]
~/sich to ball [up]
Ballen *m (rubber, text)* bale
Ballenlisseuse *f (text)* bale backwashing unit
Ballenspalter *m*, **Ballenspaltmaschine** *f (rubber)* bale cutter (splitting machine, splitter)
Ballenzerteiler *m* agglomerate breaker, lump-breaker *(as in mixers)*
Ballformpresse *f (rubber)* ball moulding press
ballig bearbeiten to crown, to camber *(e.g. rolls, profiles)*
Balligkeit *f* crown *(of rolls and profiles)*
Balling-Grad *m (sugar)* [degree] Balling
Ballon *m* balloon flask; demijohn; *(esp for acids:)* carboy; *(rubber)* bulb
Ballonausgießer *m* carboy pourer
Ballonentleerer *m* carboy emptier
Ballonkipper *m* carboy tipper
Balmer-Formel *f* Balmer formula
Balmer-Serie *f* Balmer series *(of the hydrogen spectrum)*
Balmer-Terme *mpl (phys ch)* Balmer terms
Balsam *m* balsam, balm
~/Indischer *s.* ~/Peruanischer
~/Peruanischer Peru (black) balsam *(from Myroxylon balsamum (L.) Harms var. pereirae)*
~/Schwarzer *s.* ~/Peruanischer
Balsamharz *n*, **Balsamkolophonium** *n* gum (common) rosin
Baly-Gefäß *n*, **Baly-Rohr** *n* Baly cell (tube) *(for measuring absorption)*
Bamford-Stevens-Reaktion *f* Bamford-Stevens reaction *(for preparing diazoalkanes)*
Bananenbindung *f* banana (bent) bond, banana-like (banana-shaped) bond
Banbury-Innenmischer *m* Banbury [mixer], intensive mixer
Banbury-Kneter *m s.* Banbury-Innenmischer
Banbury-Lancaster-Verfahren *n (rubber)* hot Banbury process, thermodynamic process *(a reclaiming process)*
Banbury-Mischer *m s.* Banbury-Innenmischer
Band *n* 1. band, tape; apron, belt, band, strand *(of a conveyor)*; strip chart *(of a recorder)*; 2. *(phys ch)* band
~/erlaubtes *(phys ch)* allowed band
~/verbotenes *(phys ch)* forbidden band, energy gap
Bandabwurfwagen *m* tripper
bandagieren *(rubber)* to wrap
Bandantrieb *m* chart drive *(of a strip-chart recorder)*
Banddurchhang *m* belt sag
Banddüngung *f (agric)* side-dressing
Bande *f* [spectral] band; *(chromat)* band
~ des Obertons *(spectr)* overtone band
~/heiße *(spectr)* hot band *(an energy-releasing combination band)*
Bandeindruck *m* chain mark *(a defect in glass)*
Bandenaufspaltung *f (spectr)* band splitting
Bandenbreite *f (spectr, chromat)* bandwidth
Bandenfolge *f (spectr)* band sequence
Bandenform *f (spectr)* band shape (contour)
Bandengruppe *f (spectr)* band group
Bandenhöhe *f (spectr, chromat)* band height
Bandenintensität *f (spectr)* band intensity
Bandenkante *f (spectr)* band edge (head)
Bandenkontur *f s.* Bandenform
Bandenkopf *m s.* Bandenkante
Bandenlage *f (spectr, chromat)* band position
Bandenmitte *f s.* Bandenzentrum
Bandenparameter *m (spectr)* band parameter
Bandenreihe *f s.* Bandenfolge
Bandenschulter *f (spectr)* shoulder
Bandenspektrum *n* band[ed] spectrum, molecular spectrum
Bandensystem *n* band system
Bandenverbreiterung *f (spectr, chromat)* band broadening, *(chromat also)* column band broadening, zone spreading
Bandenzentrum *n (spectr)* band origin (centre), zero line (gap)

Bändertheorie *f* **der Festkörper** band theory of solids
Bänderung *f (geol)* banding
Bandfilter *n* belt (band) filter
Bandfilterpresse *f (hyd)* belt [filter] press, belt pressure filter
Bandförderer *m* belt (band) conveyor
Bandheizkörper *m* band (strip) heater, heater band
Bandheizung *f* band (strip) heating
Bandklassierer *m* drag classifier
Bandmesser *n* band knife
Bandmischer *m* ribbon mixer (blender)
Bandpaßfilter *m*, **Band-pass-Filter** *m (spectr)* bandpass filter
Bandrührer *m* ribbon-blade agitator
Bandsaugfilter *n* [rotary-drum] belt-type vacuum filter
Bandschleifenwagen *m* tripper
Bandschnecke *f* ribbon flight *(a screw conveyor)*
Bandschneckenmischer *m* ribbon mixer (blender)
Bandschreiber *m* strip-chart recorder
Bandsieb *n* travelling-belt screen
Bandspannung *f* belt tension
Bandtheorie *f* **der Festkörper** band theory of solids
Bandtrockner *m* belt [tunnel, trough] dryer, conveyor dryer, moving-band dryer
Bandwaage *f* conveyor scale, [feed-]belt weigher, weigh[ing] belt
Bandzellenfilter *n* travelling-pan filter, TP filter
Bank *f* 1. *(geol)* bed, stratum; 2. *(glass)* bench, siege *(of a pot furnace)*
Bankbürette *f* microburet[te]
Bankpostpapier *n* bank paper (post), bond [paper]
Baratte *f (text)* baratte, xanthator, [xanthating] churn
Barbados-Aloe *f (pharm)* Barbados (Curaçao) aloe *(from Aloe vera L.)*
Barbier-Wieland-Abbau *m*, **Barbier-Wieland-Reaktion** *f* Barbier-Wieland degradation (reaction) *(of carboxylic acids)*
Barbitalnatrium *n* barbital sodium
Barbiturat *n (org ch)* barbiturate
Barbitursäure *f* barbituric acid, pyrimidinetrione
Barcol-Härte *f (plast)* Barcol hardness
Bari-Sol-Verfahren *n* Barisol (Bari-sol) process *(for deparaffinizing oil)*
Baritflint[glas] *n* barium flint [glass]
Baritkron[glas] *n* barium crown [glass]
Barium *n* Ba barium
Bariumacetat *n* barium acetate
Bariumacetylid *n s.* Bariumcarbid
Bariumazid *n* barium azide, barium hexanitride
Bariumcarbid *n* barium carbide
Bariumchlorat *n* barium chlorate
Bariumchlorid *n* barium chloride
Bariumdichromat *n* barium dichromate
Bariumdiphosphat *n* barium diphosphate
Bariumdivanadat(V) *n* barium divanadate(V)
Bariumflintglas *n s.* Baritflint
Bariumformiat *n* barium formate
Bariumgetter *m* barium getter
bariumhaltig barium-containing, containing barium
Bariumhexachloroplatinat(IV) *n* barium hexachloroplatinate(IV), barium chloroplatinate(IV)
Bariumhexacyanoferrat(II) *n* barium hexacyanoferrate(II), barium cyanoferrate(II)
Bariumhexafluorosilicat *n* barium hexafluorosilicate, barium fluorosilicate
Bariumhydrid *n* barium hydride
Bariumhydrogenphosphat *n* barium hydrogenphosphate
Bariumhydrogensulfid *n* barium hydrogensulphide
Bariumhydroxid *n* barium hydroxide
Bariumhypochlorit *n* barium hypochlorite
Bariumiodat *n* barium iodate
Bariumiodid *n* barium iodide
Bariumkronglas *n s.* Baritkron
Bariumlack *m* barium lake
Bariummanganat(VII) *n s.* Bariumpermanganat
Bariummetasilicat *n* barium metasilicate, barium trioxosilicate
Bariumorthosilicat *n* barium orthosilicate, barium tetraoxosilicate
Bariumoxid *n* barium oxide
Bariumperchlorat *n* barium perchlorate
Bariumpermanganat *n* barium permanganate
Bariumperoxid *n* barium peroxide
Bariumperoxodisulfat *n* barium peroxodisulphate
Bariumpyrophosphat *n s.* Bariumdiphosphat
Bariumpyrovanadat(V) *n s.* Bariumdivanadat(V)
Bariumrhodanid *n s.* Bariumthiocyanat
Bariumsaccharatverfahren *n* barium [saccharate] process, barytation method *(for desugaring molasses)*
Bariumsilicofluorid *n s.* Bariumhexafluorosilicat
Bariumsulfat *n* barium sulphate
~/gefälltes precipitated barium sulphate
Bariumsulfid *n* barium sulphide, barium monosulphide
Bariumsulfit *n* barium sulphite
Bariumtetracyanoplatinat(II) *n* barium tetracyanoplatinate(II), barium cyanoplatinate(II)
Bariumtetroxosilicat *n s.* Bariumorthosilicat
Bariumthiocyanat *n* barium thiocyanate, barium rhodanide
Bariumtrioxosilicat *n s.* Bariummetasilicat
Bariumwolframat *n* barium wolframate, barium tungstate
Barker-Turm *m (pap)* Barker tower *(milk-of-lime system)*
Barkometer *n (tann)* barkometer, barktrometer
Barkometerwert *m (tann)* Bk figure *(indicating the density of a solution)*
Barn *n (nucl)* barn *(a unit of area for measuring cross section)*
Barometerdruck *m* barometric pressure
Barometerformel *f* barometer formula

Barometerrohr *n* barometer tube
Barometrie *f* barometry
barometrisch barometric
Baroscampher *m* Baros (Borneo, Sumatra) camphor *(from Dryobalanops aromatica Gaertn. f.)*
Barren *m* [pressure] bar *(of a roller mill)*; *(met)* ingot, billet
Barrenguß *m* ingot casting
Barriere *f* barrier
Bart *m* 1. *(tech)* burr *(as on castings)*; 2. *(chromat)* beard
Bartbildung *f* fronting, leading, bearding *(in a chromatogram)*
Bartgrasöl *n* citronella oil *(from Cymbopogon nardus (L.) Rendle and C. winterianus Jowitt)*
Bartlett-Kraft *f (nucl)* Bartlett force
Barton-Reaktion *f* Barton reaction *(photolysis of a nitrite)*
Bart-Reaktion *f* Bart reaction *(for preparing arenearsonic acids)*
Barvoys-Verfahren *n* Barvoys process *(for cleaning coal)*
Barylith *m (min)* barylite *(barium beryllium disilicate)*
Baryon *n (nucl)* baryon
Barysphäre *f (geol)* barysphere, centrosphere, earth's core (nucleus)
Baryt *m (min)* barite, baryte[s], heavy spar *(barium sulphate)*
Barytageschicht *f s.* Barytschicht
Barytbeton *m* baryte concrete
Baryterde *f s.* Bariumoxid
Barytflint *n s.* Baritflint
Barytgelb *n* baryta yellow, ultramarine (Steinbühl) yellow, yellow ultramarine, lemon chrome, gelbin *(barium chromate)*
Barytkron *n s.* Baritkron
Barytpapier *n (phot)* baryta paper
Barytsalpeter *m (min)* nitrobarite *(barium nitrate)*
Barytschicht *f (phot)* baryta coating (layer)
Barytverfahren *n s.* Bariumsaccharatverfahren
Barytwasser *n (anal)* baryta water *(aqueous solution of barium hydroxide)*
Barytweiß *n* fixed (permanent) white, blanc fixe *(precipitated barium sulphate)*
Barytzinkweiß *n* zinc baryta white, Orr's white
Basalt *m* basalt
basalthaltig containing basalt, basaltic
basaltisch basaltic
Basaltware *f (ceram)* basalt ware
Base *f* base
~/Fischersche Fischer base, 1,3,3-trimethyl-2-methyleneindoline
~ für Sulfitkochsäure *(pap)* bisulphite liquor base
~/harte hard base *(according to Pearson's classification)*
~/komplementäre *(bioch)* complementary base
~/korrespondierende conjugate base
~/Millonsche Millon's base *(a mercurammine compound)*
~/organische organic base
~/Schiffsche R'N=CHR Schiff (Schiff's) base, azomethine [compound]
~/schwache weak base
~/seltene *(bioch)* rare (minor) base *(purine or pyrimidine derivative)*
~/starke strong base
~/stickstoffhaltige nitrogenous base
~/Trögersche Tröger's base *(a doubly tertiary amine)*
~/weiche soft base *(according to Pearson's classification)*
Basekatalyse *f* base (basic, hydroxide-ion) catalysis
~/allgemeine general base catalysis
~/spezifische specific base catalysis
basekatalysiert base-catalyzed
~/allgemein general-base-catalyzed
Basenanhydrid *n* basic anhydride
Basenäquivalenz *f (bioch)* base equivalence *(within DNA)*
Basenaufstockungskräfte *fpl s.* Bindung/hydrophobe
Basenaustausch *m* base exchange
Basenaustauscher *m* **zur Wasserenthärtung** base-exchange water softener
Basenaustauscherenthärtung *f (hyd)* base-exchange [water] softening
Basenaustauschfähigkeit *f* base-exchange capacity, cation exchangeability
Basenaustauschkapazität *f* base-exchange capacity *(quantitatively)*
Basenbindungsvermögen *n* base-binding capacity (power)
Basen-Excisionsreparatur *f (bioch)* base excision repair
Basengehalt *m* basicity *(of a solution)*; *(soil)* alkalinity
basengesättigt *(soil)* base-saturated
Basenkatalyse *f s.* Basekatalyse
Basenkomplementarität *f* complementarity of bases *(in DNA)*
Basenkupplung *f s.* Basenpaarung
Basenmineralindex *m* base-mineral index
Basenpaar *n (bioch)* base pair
Basenpaarung *f (bioch)* base pairing
Basensättigung *f (soil)* base saturation
Basensättigungsgrad *m (soil)* degree of base saturation, base status, base-saturation percentage
Basensequenz *f (bioch)* base (nucleotide) sequence
Basensequenzanalyse *f* **der nächsten Nachbarn** *(bioch)* nearest-neighbour base-frequency analysis, nearest-neighbour base sequencing
Basenstapelung *f (bioch)* base stacking
Basenstärke *f* base (basic) strength
Basentriplett *n (bioch)* codon, coding (nucleotide) triplet

Basenumtausch *m (soil)* base exchange
basenungesättigt *(soil)* base-unsaturated
Baseose *f (med)* alcalosis
BASF-Flesch-Demag-Verfahren *n (coal)* BASF Flesch-Demag process *(gasification of small-sized coal in downstream operation)*
Basilikumöl *n* basil oil *(from Ocimum basilicum L.)*
basiphil *(bot)* basophilous *(growing preferably in alkaline soil)*
Basis *f* base, basis; *(phys ch)* base region
~/asphaltische *(petrol)* asphalt base
~/gemischte *(petrol)* mixed (intermediate) base
~/naphthenische *(petrol)* naphthene base
~/paraffinische *(petrol)* paraffin base
basisch basic, alkaline; *(met)* basic • **~ ausgekleidet** *(met)* basic-lined • **~ stellen** *(dye)* to basify, to make alkaline, to alkal[in]ize
~/schwach weakly (feebly) basic, low-alkalinity
~/stark strongly basic, high-alkalinity
~ zugestellt *s.* ~ ausgekleidet
Basischstellen *n* basification
Basiseinheit *f* base (fundamental) unit *(of a system of units)*
Basisfunktion *f (anal)* basis function
Basisgewicht *n s.* Masse je Flächeneinheit
Basislinie *f (anal)* base-line
Basislinienänderung *f s.* Basisliniendrift
Basisliniendrift *f (anal)* base-line drift
Basislinientrennung *f (chromat)* 6 σ separation
Basispeak *m (anal)* base-line signal
Basistechnik *f (biot)* basic technique
Basisvektor *m (anal)* basis vector
Basit *m* basite, basic (subsilicic) rock
Basizität *f* 1. alkalinity, basicity *(of a solution)*; 2. basicity, basic capacity *(of an acid)*; 3. basicity *(of atoms, ions, or molecules)* • **die ~ schwächend** base-weakening
~/aktuelle active alkalinity
~/Freiberger *(tann)* Freiberg value for basicity *(of chrome liquors)*
~ nach Schorlemmer *(tann)* Schorlemmer basicity *(of chrome liquors)*
Basizitätsbestimmung *f (tann)* precipitation figure test *(applied to chrome liquors)*
basizitätsvermindernd base-weakening
Basoid *n (soil)* basoid *(colloidal substance saturated with OH ions)*
basophil basophile, basophilic, basophilous *(having an affinity for basic dyes)*; 2. *(bot)* basophilous *(growing preferably in alkaline soils)*
Basophile[r] *m (med)* basophil[e]
Bassin *n* basin, tank
Bassoragummi *n* gum bassora *(any of various low-grade kinds of gum tragacanth or other similar gums)*
Bassorin *n* bassorin *(a pectin-like substance obtained from certain gums)*
bastardisieren to hybridize *(chemical-bond theory)*
Bastardisierung *f* hybridization *(chemical-bond theory)*
~/tetraedrische tetrahedral hybridization
~/trigonale trigonal hybridization, sp^2 hybridization
sp^2-Bastardisierung *f s.* Bastardisierung/trigonale
Bastardorbital *n* hybrid [bond] orbital
Bastardstruktur *f* hybrid structure
Bastseide *f* raw (gum) silk, grege, greige
Batch *m (rubber)* batch
Batch-Fermentation *f (biot)* batch[-process] fermentation, batch-fed fermentation
Batch-Fermenter *m (biot)* batch fermenter
Batch-Kultur *f (biot)* batch culture
Batch-off-Vorrichtung *f (rubber)* batch-off equipment
Batch-Sterilisation *f (biot)* batch sterilization
Bathmetall *n* bath metal *(a copper-zinc alloy)*
bathochrom bathochromic
Bathochromie *f* bathochromic shift (displacement)
Batholith *m (geol)* batholith, bathylith
Batikfärberei *f* batik dyeing
Batikpapier *n* batik paper
Batsch[ing]öl *n* batching oil *(for steeping jute fibres)*
Batterie *f* battery *(a group of uniform devices)*; bench *(a group of retorts in a coke oven)*; *(el ch)* battery
~/galvanische voltaic battery
batteriegespeist battery-operated
Batteriekohle *f* battery carbon
Batteuse *f (cosmet)* batteuse *(agitator kettle for extractions)*
Batylalkohol *m* batyl alcohol, glycerol 1-octadecyl ether
Batzen *m* [large] lump; *(ceram)* blank, clot; *(pap)* knot
Bau *m* 1. structure, constitution *(of a molecule)*; set-up, structure, build *(of an apparatus)*; 2. building, build[ing]-up, construction, structure, setting
Bauart *f* build, make, design
Baubestandteil *m* building constituent
Bauchstäuber *m* chest-type hand duster *(for pesticides)*
Baueinheit *f* building unit
~/strukturelle structural building unit
Bauelement *n* structural element (entity, unit)
Bauer-Mühle *f* Bauer double-disk refiner
Baufehler *m (cryst)* structural defect
Bauformel *f* constitutional formula *(of molecules)*
Bauglas *n* structural glass
Baukalk *m* building (mason's) lime *(chiefly calcium hydroxide)*
Baukastenprinzip *n* modular (building-brick) principle
Baukeramik *f* building (structural) ceramics
Baumé-Grad *m* degree Baumé
Baumé-Skale *f* Baumé scale
Baumfärbeapparat *m (text)* beam dyeing machine
Baumfärbeautoklav *m (text)* beam autoclave
Baumfärberei *f (text)* beam dyeing
Baumkristall *m* dendrite

Baumwachs *n (agric)* grafting wax
Baumwollaffinität *f (dye)* affinity for cotton
Baumwollblau *n* cotton blue
Baumwolldichtung *f* cotton packing
Baumwolle *f* cotton
~/cyanethylierte cyanoethylated cotton
~/egrenierte cotton lint
~/tote (unreife) dead cotton
Baumwollegreniermaschine *f* cotton gin
Baumwollentkörnungsmaschine *f* cotton gin
Baumwollfaden *m* cotton thread
Baumwollfarbstoff *m* cotton dye, *(Am also)* cotton color
Baumwollfaser *f* cotton fibre
Baumwollfaserdichtung *f* cotton fibre gasket
Baumwollfilz *m (pap)* cotton felt
~ mit Asbestzusatz asbestos felt
Baumwollgewebe *n* cotton fabric (cloth)
Baumwollhadern *pl (pap)* cotton rags
Baumwollhalbstoff *m (pap)* cotton [rag] pulp
Baumwollinters *pl* [cotton] linters
Baumwollkalanderwalze *f (pap)* cotton bowl (roll) *(of a calender)*
Baumwollkernöl *n* cotton[seed] oil
Baumwollkord *m (rubber)* cotton cord
Baumwollkurzhaar *n* cotton fuzz
Baumwollpackung *f* cotton packing
Baumwollpapier *n* cotton paper
Baumwollsaathartfett *n* hydrogenated cotton[-seed] oil
Baumwollsaatlecithin *n* cottonseed lecithin
Baumwollsaatöl *n*, **Baumwollsamenöl** *n* cotton-seed oil
Baumwolltrockenfilz *m (pap)* cotton dry[er] felt
Baumwollumpen *mpl (pap)* cotton rags
Baumwollwachs *n* cotton wax
Baumwollwalze *f (pap)* cotton bowl (roll) *(of a calender)*
Baumwollwaschmittel *n* cotton-washing detergent
Baupappe *f* building [paper] board
Bauplatte *f* building (structural) board
Bauprinzip *n* building principle
Baur-Moschus *m* Baur musk *(synthetic musk)*
Bausand *m* builder's sand
bauschig *(text, pap)* bulky • **~ sein** to bulk high
Bauschigkeit *f (text, pap)* bulkiness
Baustein *m* building block (brick, unit), structural element (entity, unit) *(as of a chemical compound)*; *(lab)* module
~/elementarer elementary building block
~/fundamentaler (grundlegender) fundamental (basic) building block
Baustoff *m* building (construction) material
~/keramischer ceramic building material
Bauterrakotta *f (ceram)* architectural terra-cotta
Bauxit *m* bauxite, beauxite
bauxitisch bauxitic
Bauzement *m* building cement
Bauziegel *m* building brick

Bayberrytalg *m* myrtle tallow (wax), bayberry (myrica) tallow (wax) *(from Myrica specc.)*
Bayer-Verfahren *n* Bayer process *(digestion of bauxite in sodium hydroxide solution)*
Bayöl *n* bay (myrcia) oil *(from Pimenta racemosa (Mill.) I. W. Moore)*
Bdellium *n***/Indisches** Indian bdellium *(balsamic resin from Commiphora mukul Engl.)*
beanspruchen 1. to stress; 2. to expose *(as to aggressive agents)*
Beanspruchung *f* 1. stressing, stress application; 2. stress *(force acting across a unit area)*; *3.* exposure *(as to aggressive agents)*
~/chemische chemical exposure
~/dynamische dynamic stress
~/schwingende vibrating stress
~/sinusförmig schwingende waved stress
~/statische static stress
Beanspruchungs-Dehnungs-Diagramm *n* stress-strain diagram
Beanspruchungs-Dehnungs-Linie *f* stress-strain curve
Beanspruchungsgeschwindigkeit *f***/mittlere** mean rate of stressing
bearbeitbar workable
Bearbeitbarkeit *f* workability
bearbeiten to work, to treat, to process, to machine
~/ballig to crown, to camber *(e.g. rolls, profiles)*
~/im Knetwerk to pug *(plastic materials)*
Bearbeitung *f* working, treatment, processing, machining
Bearbeitungsspannung *f* fabrication stress
Bearbeitungstechnik *f* processing technique
Beattie-Bridgeman-Zustandsgleichung *f (phys ch)* Beattie-Bridgeman equation [of state]
Bebeerin *n*, **Bebirin** *n* curine, bebeerine *(alkaloid)*
bebrausen *(min tech)* to spray *(classified material)*
Bebrausen *n* **mit Wasser** water spraying
Bebrausungsdüse *f* spray nozzle
bebrüten *(biot)* to incubate *(the fermentation broth)*
Bebrütung *f (biot)* incubation *(of the fermentation broth)*
Béchamp-Reaktion *f*, **Béchamp-Reduktion** *f* Béchamp reaction (reduction) *(of aromatic nitro compounds)*
~-Verfahren *n* Béchamp process *(for producing primary aromatic amines)*
Becher *m* cup; *(lab)* beaker; *(tech)* bucket, scoop *(as of an elevator)*
~/rotierender rotary (rotating) cup
~/schnellrotierender spinning cup
Becheraufzug *m*, **Becherelevator** *m s.* Becherwerk
Becherfließzahl *f (plast)* moulding index, cup flow figure
Becherglas *n* beaker
~/hohes tall-form beaker
~ mit Ausguß lipped beaker
~ ohne Ausguß lipless beaker

Becherglaszange *f* beaker tongs
Becherschließzeit *f s.* Becherfließzahl
Becherteilung *f* pitch of buckets
Becherversprüher *m* spinning-cup atomizer (sprayer), rotary-cup atomizer (sprayer)
Becherwerk *n* bucket elevator
~ mit Becherstrang continuous-bucket elevator
~ mit Einzelbechern spaced-bucket elevator
Becherwerkextrakteur *m* basket band extractor
~/kombinierter rectangular basket extractor
~/stehender vertical basket extractor
Becherwerkextraktor *m s.* Becherwerkextrakteur
Becherzeit *f s.* Becherfließzahl
Becherzerstäuber *m s.* Becherversprüher
Becken *n* 1. basin, tank; 2. *s.* Ausgußbecken
~/Dortmunder *(hyd)* Dortmund [vertical flow sedimentation] tank
Beckenablauf *m (hyd)* clarifier effluent
Beckenzulauf *m (hyd)* clarifier influent
Becker-Ofen *m* Becker oven
Beckmann-Thermometer *n* Beckmann thermometer
Beckmann-Umlagerung *f* Beckmann [oxime-amide] rearrangement
Bedarf *m* requirements, demands • **den ~ decken an** to meet the requirements (demands) of
Bedeckung *f***/monomolekulare** *(phys ch)* monolayer coverage
Bedeckungsgrad *m (phys ch)* degree of coverage
bedienbar operable
~/leicht easy-to-operate
Bedienbarkeit *f* operability
~/leichte *s.* Bedienungskomfort
bedienen to operate, to run, to handle *(e.g. an apparatus)*
Bedienkomfort *m s.* Bedienungskomfort
Bedienung *f* operation, running, handling *(as of an apparatus)*
Bedienungsbühne *f* operating floor (platform), bench
~/koksseitige coke-side bench *(of a coke oven)*
~/maschinenseitige pusher-side bench *(of a coke oven)*
Bedienungskomfort *m* operational convenience, ease (simplicity) of servicing, ease of serviceability
Bedingungen *fpl***/milde (schonende)** mild conditions
Bedingungsgefüge *n* set of conditions
bedruckbar printable
Bedruckbarkeit *f* printability, printing properties
bedrucken to print
Bedrucken *n***/beidseitiges** *(text)* double-face printing
bedüsen to nozzle *(with a liquid)*
beeinflussen to influence, to affect, *(esp negatively)* to interfere with
~/störend to interfere with
Beeinflussung *f* affection, *(esp negatively:)* interference
~/allosterische *(bioch)* allosteric regulation
beeinträchtigen to interfere with
beenden to finish, to complete; to terminate, to break *(the growth of a chain molecule)*
Beendigung *f* finishing, completion; termination *(of chain growth)*
beeteln *(text)* to beetle *(to flatten and compact)*
Beetle-Maschine *f (text)* beetling machine, beetler
befestigen to attach, to mount
befeuchten to moisten, to wet, to damp[en], to humidify, to water, to dew; *(pap)* to wet out (up)
Befeuchter *m* moistener, humidifier *(specif for gummed surfaces)*; *(pap)* wetting machine
Befeuchtung *f* moistening, wetting, damp[en]ing, humidification, watering, dewing; *(pap)* wetting-up, wetting-out
Befeuchtungsapparat *m* humidifier
Befeuchtungsdüse *f* humidifying nozzle
Befeuchtungsmaschine *f (text)* damping machine
befeuern to fire, to heat
~/direkt to direct-fire
beflecken to stain
beflocken *(plast)* to flock
Beflocken *n (plast)* flocking, flock spraying
befreien to liberate *(from contaminants)*
~/von flüchtigen Bestandteilen to devolatilize
~/von Kationen to decationize
~/von Kesselstein to [de]scale
~/von Lignin to delignify *(wood)*
~/von Lösungsmittel to desolventize
Befreiung *f* liberation *(from contaminants)*
Befund *m* result
~/nichtssagender (nicht aussagekräftiger) *(anal)* empty result
~/röntgenographischer X-ray result
begasen 1. *(agric, food)* to fumigate, to gas; 2. *(hyd, biot)* to aerate
Begaser *m (hyd, biot)* aerator
Begasse *f s.* Bagasse
Begasung *f* 1. *(agric, food)* fumigation, gassing, exposure to gas; 2. *(hyd, biot)* aeration
Begasungsapparat *m s.* Begaser
Begasungsfilter *n* air stone, fritted gas bubbler; gas dispersion (distribution) tube
Begasungsmittel *n (agric, food)* fumigant
Begasungsrohr *n* gas dispersion (distribution) tube, sparger
Begegnung *f* encounter *(of molecules in solutions)*
begichten to burden, to charge *(a blast furnace)*
Begichtungsöffnung *f (met)* throat
begießen to water, to irrigate; *(ceram)* to engobe
Beginn-Kochpunkt *m*, **Beginn-Siedepunkt** *m* initial boiling point, I.B.P.
Begleitalkaloid *n* companion alkaloid
Begleiter *m s.* Begleitstoff
Begleitreaktion *f* concurrent reaction
Begleitstoff *m*, **Begleitsubstanz** *f* companion [substance], accompanying substance, admixture; *(hyd)* minor constituent

begünstigt/energetisch energetically favoured (favourable)
Beguß *m*, **Begußmasse** *f* *(ceram)* engobe
Begußton *m* *(ceram)* slip clay
Behälter *m* vessel, receptacle, container, *(for liquids esp if large:)* tank, *(esp if circular and open:)* basin; *(for gases:)* holder; *(if funnel-shaped, for bulk material:)* hopper
~/unterirdischer underground reservoir (storage tank)
Behälterglas *n* container glass
Behälterpappe *f* container board
behandeln to treat, to process
~/anodisch *(met)* to anodize
~/chemisch to treat with chemicals, to chemicalize
~/im Autoklaven to autoclave
~/im Faß *(tann)* to drum
~/in der Küpe *(dye)* to vat
~/in Kleienbeize (Schrotbeize) *(tann)* to drench
~/mit Arsen to arsenicate
~/mit Bleicherde to clay
~/mit Brom to brominate
~/mit Bromat to bromate, to treat with a bromate
~/mit Chlor to chlorinate, to chlorinize
~/mit Chlorid to chloridize
~/mit Chlorwasserstoff to hydrochlorinate
~/mit Dampf to steam
~/mit Formaldehyd to treat with formaldehyde, *(esp pharm)* to formalinize, to formolize
~/mit Gips to plaster *(wine)*; to burtonize, to gypsum *(brewing water)*
~/mit Glycerol to glycerolize, to glycerolate
~/mit Hitze to heat-treat
~/mit Kalk to lime out *(as in manufacturing organic intermediates)*
~/mit Kopfdünger *(agric)* to top-dress
~/mit Lake *(food, tann)* to brine
~/mit Ozon to ozonize, to ozonify
~/mit Salzlake (Salzlösung) *(food, tann)* to brine
~/mit Säure to treat with acid; *(tann)* to drench
~/mit Schwefel to sulphur
~/mit schwefliger Säure *(sugar)* to sulphite
~/mit Siliconen to silicone-treat, to siliconize
~/mit Wasserdampf to steam
~/nochmals to re-treat
~/übermäßig to overtreat
Behandlung *f* treatment, processing
~/anodische *(met)* anodizing, anodization, anodic treatment (oxidation, coating)
~/chemische treatment with chemicals, chemicalization
~/drucklose non-pressure treatment *(wood preservation)*
~/enzymatische (fermentative) enzyme treatment
~ im Faß *(tann)* drumming
~ in Abwasserteichen *(hyd)* pond treatment, ponding, lagooning
~ industrieller Abwässer industrial waste-water treatment, trade effluent treatment
~ industrieller und häuslicher Abwässer/gemeinsame combined municipal/industrial waste-water treatment
~ mit Bleicherde clay treatment
~ mit Chlorwasserstoff hydrochlorination
~ mit Doktorlauge (Doktorlösung) *(petrol)* doctor treatment (sweetening)
~ mit Lake *s.* ~ mit Salzlake
~ mit Promotor/thermische *(rubber)* promoted heat treatment
~ mit Salzlake (Salzlösung) *(food, tann)* brining
~ mit Säure acid treatment
~ mit schwefliger Säure *(sugar)* sulphitation
~ mittels Umkehrosmose *(hyd)* reverse-osmosis treatment
~ nach dem Anstreichverfahren brush treatment *(wood preservation)*
~ nach dem Furnos-Verfahren Furnos treatment *(wood preservation)*
~ nach dem Sprühverfahren spray treatment *(wood preservation)*
~/nochmalige re-treatment
~ ohne Druckanwendung *s.* ~/drucklose
~/schmutzabstoßende (schmutzabweisende) *(text)* dirt-repellent treatment
~/thermische heat treatment
~/thermomechanische *(met)* thermomechanical treatment
~ vor dem Auspflanzen preplanting treatment *(of a soil with pesticides)*
~ während der Winterruhe dormant treatment *(of plants with pesticides)*
~/wiederholte re-treatment
Behandlungsabschnitt *m* processing section
Behandlungsanlage *f* treatment plant; treatment unit *(of an industrial plant)*
Behandlungsbedingungen *fpl* treatment conditions
Behandlungschemikalie *f* treatment (processing) chemical, *(hyd also)* water-treating chemical
Behandlungsfolge *f* treatment sequence
Behandlungsgefäß *n* treater
Behandlungsgut *n* material being *or* to be treated
Behandlungskammer *f* *(plast)* plenum chamber
Behandlungsschema *n* treatment scheme
Behandlungsstufe *f* treatment stage
Behandlungstechnologie *f* treatment technology
Behandlungsverfahren *n* treating process
Behandlungsziel *n* treatment goal
Beharrungsvermögen *n* inertia
Beharrungszustand *m* steady (stationary) state
beharzen *(plast)* to resin
beheizbar heatable
beheizen to heat, to fire, to warm [up]
beheizt/direkt direct-fired
~/indirekt indirect-fired
~/mit Dampf steam-heated
~/mit Öl oil-fired, oil-heated
Beheizung *f* heating, firing

~/dielektrische dielectric heating
~/direkte direct heating
~ durch Bogenentladung electrical-discharge heating
~ durch Elektronenbeschuß electron-bombardment heating
~/elektrische electric heating
~/indirekte indirect (external) heating
~/induktive induction heating
~ mit Gas gas-fired heating
~ mit Kohle coal-fired heating
~ mit Öl oil-fired heating
Beheizungsapparat *m* heater
Beheizungsgas *n* fuel (heating) gas
Behen-Öl *n* ben (behen) oil, oil of ben *(from Moringa aptera Gaertn., less frequently from M. oleifera Lam.)*
Behenolsäure *f* behenolic acid, *docos-13-ynoic acid
Behensäure *f* *docosanoic acid, *(deprecated:)* behenic acid
Behenylalkohol *m* behenyl alcohol, docosyl alcohol, *docosan-1-ol
behindern to hinder, to inhibit, to embarrass
Behinderung *f* hindrance, inhibition, embarrassment
~ der freien Drehbarkeit einer Bindung bond hindrance (inhibition) *(chemical-bond theory)*
Behinderungsisomerie *f* atropo-isomerism
beidseitigglatt *(pap)* glazed on both sides
Beigeschmack *m* foreign flavour (taste)
Beilstein-Probe *f* Beilstein's test *(for detecting halogens in organic compounds)*
beimengen to admix
Beimengung *f* 1. admixture *(act)*; 2. admixture, impurity; solute *(zone melting)*
beimischen to admix
Beimischung *f* 1. admixture *(act)*; 2. admixture, impurity • **mit Beimischungen** impure
beimpfen *(biot)* to seed, to inoculate
Beimpfung *f (biot)* seeding, inoculation
Beinschwarz *n* bone (animal) black
Beiprodukt *n s.* Nebenprodukt
beißend acrid, pungent *(taste, smell)*
Beistoff *m* inert ingredient; corrective *(in building up active-substance mixtures)*
Beiwert *m*, **Beizahl** *f* index; factor; coefficient
Beizbad *n (met)* scouring bath
Beizbehandlung *f* **mit Säure** *(tann)* drenching
Beize *f* 1. mordant *(for treating textiles or microscopic preparations)*; stain *(for treating rubber, glass, or wood)*; *(tann)* bate; *(agric)* pickle; *(met)* scouring agent, pickle; 2. *s.* Beizen
~/basische *(text)* metallic mordant
beizen to mordant *(textiles or microscopic preparations)*; to stain *(rubber, glass, or wood)*; *(tann)* to bate; *(agric)* to pickle; *(met)* to pickle, to scour *(for removing scale)*
~/mit Schwefelsäure *(met)* to vitriol
Beizenfärberei *f (text)* mordant dyeing
Beizenfarbstoff *m (text)* mordant dye[stuff], adjective dye
Beizenverfahren *n (text)* chromate process, chromate [dyeing] method
Beizfarbe *f s.* Beizenfarbstoff
Beizmittel *n*, **Beizstoff** *m s.* Beize 1.
Beizung *f s.* Beizen
bekämpfen to control
Bekämpfung *f* control
~/biologische biological control
~ von Wirbellosen control of invertebrates
Bekämpfungsmaßnahme *f (agric)* control measure
bekleben *(pap)* to line, to laminate, to paste, to paper
Beklebepapier *n* liners, lining paper, pasting [paper]
beklebt/einseitig *(pap)* single-lined
~/zweiseitig double-lined
beklopfen to rap
Beladung *f* 1. charging, feeding, loading; *(hyd)* loading *(ion exchange)*; 2. load; *(of liquids:)* concentration
beladen to charge, to feed, to load
beladen/mit Kohlenstoff carbon-fouled *(catalyst)*
~/mit Koks coke-contaminated *(catalyst)*
Beladeöffnung *f* charging (feed) hole (door), feed inlet
Beladung *f* **und Regenerierung** *f (hyd)* exhaust-regenerate cycle *(ion exchange)*
Beladungskolonne *f (hyd)* resin tank *(ion exchange)*
Beladungsvorgang *m (hyd)* service (loading) cycle (step), service (operating) run, exhaustion cycle (reaction) *(ion exchange)*
Belag *m* coat[ing], cover[ing], layer, *(if thin:)* film; scale, encrustation *(esp of alien substance)*; overlay *(for wood)*; *(food)* bloom
~/deckender coverage *(as of insecticides)*
~/reflexmindernder antiflare (antireflection) coating
~/sekundärer secondary deposit *(of pesticides)*
Belastbarkeit *f (tech)* loadability, load-bearing capacity; *(distil)* loading capacity; *(anal)* loadability, maximum possible loading
belasten 1. to load, to weight; *(text, pap)* to weight *(with fillers or sizing material)* ; 2. to stress; 3. *(distil, hyd)* to load
belastet/mit Schmutzstoffen polluted, contaminated *(water, air)*
~/organisch *(hyd)* organic-laden, organic-containing
Belastung *f (distil, hyd)* loading, *(hyd quantitatively:)* load, loading [rate]; *(tox)* exposure
~/anthropogene anthropogenic discharge
~ durch Abwasser *s.* Abwasserlast
~ durch organische Stoffe *(hyd)* organic contamination
~ durch Schwermetalle *(hyd)* heavy-metal contamination

~/hydraulische *(hyd)* hydraulic load (loading, loading rate), liquid loading [rate]

~ mit Abwasserinhaltsstoffen *s.* Abwasserlast

~ mit organischen Inhaltsstoffen *(hyd)* organic load[ing]

~/produktionsbedingte *(hyd)* process contamination

~/statische static loading

~/zeitgewichtete durchschnittliche *(tox)* time-weighted average, TWA

Belastungsbereich *m (hyd)* loading range, range of loading rates

Belastungsgrenzwert *m***/kurzzeitiger** *(tox)* short-time exposure limit, STEL

Belastungsschaumzahl *f (text)* lather value in presence of dirt

Belastungsschwankung *f (hyd)* load fluctuation, variation in loadings

Belastungsverhalten *n* loading behaviour

beleben to activate *(e.g. floatation)*

Beleber *m* activator *(e.g. floatation)*

Belebtschlamm *m (hyd)* activated sludge, active (biological) sludge

Belebtschlammanlage *f s.* Belebungsanlage

Belebtschlammbecken *n s.* Belebungsbecken

Belebtschlammflocken *fpl (hyd)* activated-sludge floc, aerated-sludge floc, microbial floc

Belebtschlammgehalt *m (hyd)* mixed-liquor suspended solids [concentration, level], MLSS, solids in aeration (incubation) basin, activated biomass concentration

Belebtschlammkonzentration *f s.* Belebtschlammgehalt

Belebtschlammreaktivierung *f*, **Belebtschlammregenerierung** *f (hyd)* contact stabilization of activated sludge

Belebtschlammregenerierungsbecken *n (hyd)* contact tank

Belebtschlammrückführung *f*, **Belebtschlammrücklauf** *m (hyd)* sludge recycle (return), solids recycle

Belebtschlammtrockensubstanz *f (hyd)* dry weight of MLSS

Belebtschlammverfahren *n s.* Belebungsverfahren

Belebungs... *s. a.* Belebtschlamm...

Belebungsanlage *f (hyd)* activated-sludge [waste treatment] plant, activated-sludge unit

~ mit Schlammstabilisierung extended aeration plant

Belebungsbecken *n (hyd)* aeration tank, aeration (aerated) basin, activated-sludge tank

Belebungsverfahren *n (hyd)* activated-sludge process (method)

~/hochbelastetes high-rate activated-sludge process

~/klassisches conventional activated-sludge process

~ mit abgestufter O_2-Zuführung tapered-aeration activated-sludge process

~ mit Reinsauerstoff pure-oxygen activated-sludge process

~ mit Schlammregenerierung contact-stabilization activated-sludge process

~ mit verteilter Abwasserzuführung step-aeration activated-sludge process

belegen to cover, to coat; *(rubber)* to skim[coat] *(frictioned tissue)*

~/beidseitig (zweiseitig) to double-coat

Belegen *n* covering, coating; *(rubber)* skim coating

Belegung *f***/monomolekulare** *(phys ch)* monolayer coverage

Beleuchtungsmittel *n* illuminant

Beleuchtungsstärke *f* illuminance

belichten to expose to light; *(phot)* to expose

Belichtung *f* exposure to light; *(phot)* exposure
• **bei ~** on exposure to light

~/lange *(phot)* prolonged exposure

Belichtungsbereich *m (phot)* range of exposure

Belichtungsbreite *f (phot)* exposure latitude (range)

Belichtungsdauer *f (phot)* duration of exposure, exposure time

Belichtungsschleier *m (phot)* optical fog

Belichtungsspielraum *m*, **Belichtungsumfang** *m s.* Belichtungsbreite

Belichtungszeit *f s.* Belichtungsdauer

Belit *m* belite *(a crystal type in portland cement clinker)*

Belladonnaalkaloid *n* belladonna alkaloid

Belleek-Porzellan *n* Belleek china

Bell-Verfahren *n (met)* Bell process *(removal of P and Si by iron oxide)*

Belousov-Zabotinskij-Reaktion *f* Belousov-Zhabotinskii reaction, BZ reaction *(an oscillating reaction)*

Belt-Filter *n s.* Bandsaugfilter

belüften to aerate

Belüfter *m (hyd)* aerator

Belüfterring *m (hyd)* diffuser (sparge) ring

Belüftung *f* aeration

~/mechanische *(hyd)* mechanical aeration

Belüftungsbecken *n s.* Belebungsbecken

Belüftungseinrichtung *f (hyd)* aeration device, aerator

Belüftungselement *n* [differential] aeration cell, oxygen [concentration] cell *(corrosion)*

Belüftungshahn *m* aeration cock

Belüftungskapazität *f (hyd)* aeration capacity

~/projektierte aeration design capacity

Belüftungskolben *m* aeration flask

Belüftungskreisel *m (hyd)* propeller aerator

Belüftungsleitung *f* aeration line

Belüftungsmittel *n (build)* air-entraining additive (admixture, compound, agent)

Belüftungsrate *f (biot)* aeration rate

Belüftungssystem *n* aeration (ventilation) system; *(hyd)* aeration (air-diffusion) system

Belüftungstank *m s.* Belebungsbecken

Belüftungsturbine *f (hyd)* turbine aerator
Belüftungszeit *f (hyd)* aeration time, detention time in the aeration tank
Belüftungszelle *f s.* Belüftungselement
bemessen to size *(a treatment unit)*
bemessert *(pap)* equipped (fitted) with bars (knives)
Bemesserung *f (pap)* filling, tackle *(of a Hollander beater)*; set of bars *(of a refiner)*
Bemessung *f* sizing *(of a treatment unit)*
benachbart adjacent, neighbouring, vicinal, juxtaposed *(substituents)*
Bence-Jones-Eiweißkörper *m*, **Bence-Jones-Protein** *n* Bence-Jones protein
Bender-Prozeß *m (petrol)* Bender (lead-sulphide) process *(for sweetening distillates)*
Benedict-Metall *n* Benedict metal *(a copper-nickel alloy)*
Benedict-Nickel *n* Benedict nickel *(an alloy consisting of Zn, Ni, Pb, and Sn)*
benennen *(nomencl)* to name, to denominate
Benennung *f (nomencl)* 1. naming, denomination; 2. name, term
~/funktionelle functional name
~/nach den IUPAC-Regeln gebildete IUPAC name
~ nach den Regeln von Stock Stock naming
~/nach der Genfer Nomenklatur gebildete Geneva name
~/systematische systematic name
~/unsystematische unsystematic name
Benennungssystem *n (nomencl)* naming system
benetzbar wettable, hydrophilic, hydrophile
~/leicht easily wetted
~/nicht non-wettable, hydrophobic, hydrophobe
Benetzbarkeit *f* wettability, ability of being wetted
benetzen to perfuse, *(with water also)* to wet, to moisten, to humidify, to dew, to water, to damp[en]; to suffuse *(of a liquid)*
Benetzung *f* perfusion, *(with water also)* wetting, moistening, humidification, dewing, watering, damp[en]ing
~/vollkommene complete wetting
Benetzungsfähigkeit *f* wetting power (ability)
Benetzungskoeffizient *m* spreading coefficient, SC
Benetzungsmittel *n* wetting agent (aid), wetter
Benetzungsspannung *f* wetting tension
Benetzungsverfahren *n (agric)* steeping method *(for seed protection)*
Benetzungsvermögen *n* wetting power (ability)
Benetzungswärme *f* heat of wetting
Benetzungswinkel *m* wetting (contact) angle
Bengalkino *n* Bengal (butea) gum *(from Butea superba Roxb.)*
Bengough-Stuart-Verfahren *n* Bengough-Stuart process, chromic-acid [anodizing] process
Ben-Öl *n* oil of ben *(from Moringa aptera Gaertn., less frequently from M. oleifera Lam.)*
Bentonit[ton] *m* bentonite [clay]
Benutzungsnachlauf *m* after-drainage *(of a burette or pipette)*
Benzalaceton *n* benzalacetone, *4-phenyl-but-3-en-2-one
Benzalacetophenon *n s.* Benzylidenacetophenon
Benzalchlorid *n* benzal chloride, α,α dichlorotoluene, benzylidene chloride
Benzaldehyd *m* benzaldehyde
Benzalgrün *n* malachite (benzal) green
Benzamid *n* benzamide
Benzaminsäure *f m*-aminobenzoic acid
2,3-Benzanthracen *n* 2,3-benzanthracene, naphthacene
Benzanthron *n* benzanthrone
Benzanthronchinolin *n* benzanthronequinoline
Benzanthronfarbstoff *m* benzanthrone dye
Benzanthronreihe *f* benzanthrone series
Benzen *n* benzene, *(commercial product:)* benzole, benzol
~/anorganisches inorganic benzene, borazole, triborine triamine
Benzen... *s. a.* Benzol... *for commercial and technological terms*
Benzenabkömmling *m* benzene derivative
Benzenazimid *n* benzeneazimide, benzotriazole, aziminobenzene
Benzenboronsäure *f* benzeneboronic acid
Benzencarbonsäure *f* benzene carboxylic acid, *(specif)* C_6H_5COOH benzoic acid
Benzendampf *m* benzene vapour
Benzenderivat *n* benzene derivative
Benzendiazoanilid *n* benzenediazoanilide, diazoaminobenzene, 1,3-diphenyltriazen
Benzendiazoniumchlorid *n* benzenediazonium chloride
Benzendicarbonsäure *f* benzenedicarboxylic acid
Benzendruckextraktion *f* benzene-pressure extraction
Benzenenium-Ion *n s.* Benzenium-Ion
Benzenhexacarbonsäure *f* benzene-hexacarboxylic acid, mellitic acid
Benzenhexachlorid *n* benzene hexachloride, BHC, hexachlorocyclohexane
Benzenium-Ion *n* $C_6H_7^+$ benzenium (benzenonium, phenonium) ion, benzene carbonium ion
Benzenkern *m* benzene ring (nucleus)
Benzenkohlenwasserstoffe *mpl* benzene (aromatic) hydrocarbons, aromatics
benzenlöslich benzene-soluble, soluble in benzene
Benzenmonosulfonsäure *f* benzenesulphonic acid
Benzenreihe *f* benzene series
Benzenring *m* benzene ring (nucleus)
Benzensulfinsäure *f* benzenesulphinic acid
Benzensulfonamid *n* benzene sulphonamide
Benzensulfonsäure *f* benzenesulphonic acid
Benzensulfonsäureamid *n s.* Benzensulfonamid
Benzentetracarbonsäure *f* benzenetetracarboxylic acid

Benzentricarbonsäure *f* benzenetricarboxylic acid
benzenunlöslich benzene-insoluble, insoluble in benzene
Benzidin *n* benzidine, 4,4'-diaminobiphenyl
Benzidinbase *f* benzidine base
Benzidinprobe *f* benzidine test *(for detecting blood)*
Benzidinumlagerung *f* benzidine rearrangement (transformation, conversion)
~/halbe (halbseitige) semidine rearrangement (transformation)
Benzil *n* benzil, bibenzoyl, diphenyl diketone
Benzil-2,2'-dicarbonsäure *f* benzil-2,2'-dicarboxylic acid
Benzilsäure *f* benzilic acid
Benzilsäureumlagerung *f* benzilic-acid rearrangement
Bis-**Benzimidazolaufheller** *m bis*-benzimidazole brightener
Benz-in *n* benzyne, 1,2-didehydrobenzene
Benzin *n (ch)* benzin[e]; gasoline, petrol, [motor] spirit *(as a motor fuel)*; [petroleum] naphtha *(esp for technical purposes or as a reformer feedstock)*
~/bleifreies unleaded (lead-free) gasoline
~/butanfreies debutanized gasoline
~/direkt herausdestilliertes straight-run gasoline, distillate gasoline, straight-run benzine, S.R.B.
~/gebleites *s.* ~/verbleites
~/gesüßtes sweet gasoline
~/hochklopffestes high-octane gasoline
~/hochoctaniges (hochoctanzahliges) high-octane gasoline
~/instabiles unstabilized (unstable) gasoline, *(Am also)* wild gasoline
~/klopffestes antiknock gasoline
~/leichtes gasoline *(boiling range 30 to 100 °C)*, light gasoline (benzine, spirit, naphtha)
~/mit Tetraethylblei versetztes *s.* ~/verbleites
~/reformiertes reformed gasoline
~/saures sour gasoline
~/schweres heavy gasoline *(boiling range 150 to 210 °C)*
~/stabiles (stabilisiertes) stabilized (stable) gasoline
~/süßes sweet gasoline
~/unstabiles (unstabilisiertes) *s.* ~/instabiles
~/verbleites leaded (ethyl) gasoline
~/wildes *s.* ~/instabiles
Benzinadditiv *n* gasoline additive
Benzinbereich *m* gasoline range
Benzindampf *m* gasoline vapour
Benzingewinnungsanlage *f* gasoline plant
Benzinraffination *f* gasoline refining
Benzinwäscher *m (petrol)* naphtha wash tower
Benzinrückgewinnung *f (petrol)* naphtha recovery
Benzinsiedebereich *m* gasoline range
Benzoat *n* benzoate
Benzo[b]chinolin *n* benzo[*b*]quinoline, acridine
Benzo[c]chinolin *n* benzo[*c*]quinoline, phenanthridine
5,6-Benzochinolin *n* benzo[*f*]quinoline, 5,6-benzoquinoline
7,8-Benzochinolin *n* benzo[*h*]quinoline, 7,8-benzoquinoline
o-**Benzochinon** *n o*-benzoquinone, orthoquinone
p-**Benzochinon** *n p*-benzoquinone, quinone *(proper)*, *cyclohexadiene-1,4-dione
Benzodiazin *n* benzodiazine
Benzoe *f*, **Benzoeharz** *n* benzoin, benzoin (Benjamin) gum (resin) *(from Styrax specc.)*
Benzoesäure *f* benzoic acid, benzenecarboxylic acid
Benzoesäureanhydrid *n* benzoic anhydride
Benzoesäurebenzylester *m* benzyl benzoate
Benzoesäureethylester *m* ethyl benzoate
Benzoesäuremethylester *m* methyl benzoate
Benzoesäurephenylester *m* phenyl benzoate
o-**Benzoesäuresulfimid** *n o*-sulphobenzoic imide, saccharin
Benzofuran *n* benzofuran, coumarone, cumarone
benzoid benzenoid
Benzoin *n* benzoin, α-hydroxybenzyl phenyl ketone
Benzoinkondensation *f* benzoin condensation
Benzol *n* 1. benzole, benzol *(commercial product)*; 2. *s.* Benzen • **mit ~ anreichern (beladen, sättigen)** to benzolize
~/technisches commercial benzole
/vordestilliertes once-run benzole
90er Benzol *n* 90's benzole
Benzol... *s. a.* Benzen... *for chemical compounds*
Benzolabscheider *m* benzole separator
Benzolabtreiber *m* benzole still
Benzolanlage *f* benzole plant
Benzoldestillieranlage *f* benzole still
benzolgesättigt benzolized
Benzolgewinnung *f* benzole recovery
Benzolkondensator *m* benzole condenser
Benzolphosphonsäure *f s.* Phenylphosphorsäure
Benzolpumpe *f* benzole pump
Benzol-Schwefeldioxid-Verfahren *n* sulphur dioxide-benzole process *(for dewaxing petroleum)*
Benzolthermometer *n* benzole thermometer
Benzolvorlauf *m* benzole forerunnings (fronts)
Benzolvorprodukt *n* once-run benzole
Benzolwäscher *m* benzole scrubber (washer)
Benzolwaschöl *n* benzole wash (absorbing) oil
Benzolnitril *n* benzonitrile, cyanobenzene
Benzoorange *n* **R** benzoorange R, direct orange 8
Benzopersäure *f* perbenzoic acid
Benzophenanthren *n* benzophenanthrene
Benzophenon *n* benzophenone, *benzoyl benzene, *diphenyl ketone
Benzopyrazin *n* benzpyrazine, quinoxaline, 1,4-benzodiazine
Benzopyren *n* benzopyrene
2,3-Benzopyridin *n* 2,3-benzpyridine, benzo[*b*]pyridine, quinoline, 1-benzazine

3,4-Benzopyridin *n* 3,4-benzpyridine, benzo[*c*]-pyridine, isoquinoline, 2-benzazine
Benzopyrimidin *n* benzpyrimidine
Benzopyron *n* benzopyrone
1,2-Benzopyron *n* 1,2-benzopyrone, coumarin, 2 H-chromen-2-one, α-chromone
2,3-Benzopyrrol *n* 2,3-benzpyrrole, indole
Benzotriazol *n* benzotriazole
Benzotrichlorid *n* benzotrichloride, α,α,α-trichlorotoluene
Benzoylameisensäure *f* benzoylformic acid, phenylglyoxylic acid
Benzoylaminoessigsäure *f s.* Benzoylglycin
Benzoylbenzol *n s.* Benzophenon
Benzoylglycin *n*, **Benzoylglykokoll** *n* benzoylglycine, benzoylaminoacetic acid, hippuric acid
Benzoylgrün *n s.* Benzalgrün
Benzoylgruppe *f* C_6H_5CO- benzoyl group (residue)
Benzoylhydroperoxid *n s.* Benzopersäure
benzoylieren to benzoylate
Benzoylierung *f* benzoylation
~/zweifache dibenzoylation
Benzoyl-I-Säure *f*, **Benzoyl-J-Säure** *f* benzoyl J acid
Benzoyloxylierung *f* benzoyloxylation
Benzoylperoxid *n* benzoyl peroxide, dibenzoyl peroxide
Benzoylphenylcarbinol *n s.* Benzoin
Benzoylrest *m s.* Benzoylgruppe
Benzphenanthren *n* benzophenanthrene
Benzpyren *n* benzopyrene
Benzylacetat *n* benzyl acetate
Benzylalkohol *m* benzyl alcohol
Benzylbenzen *n* benzylbenzene, diphenylmethane
Benzylbenzoat *n* benzyl benzoate
Benzylbutyrat *n* benzyl butyrate
Benzylcarbinol *n s.* 2-Phenylethanol
Benzylcellulose *f* benzyl cellulose
Benzylchlorid *n* benzyl chloride, α-chlorotoluene
Benzylcinnamat *n* benzyl cinnamate, cinnamein
Benzylcyanid *n* benzyl cyanide, ω-cyanotoluene, phenylacetonitrile
Benzylessigsäure *f* benzylacetic acid, hydrocinnamic acid, *3-phenylpropionic acid
Benzylglyoxylsäure *f s.* Phenylbrenztraubensäure
Benzylgruppe *f* $C_6H_5CR_2-$ benzylic group (residue), *(specif)* $C_6H_5CH_2-$ benzyl group (residue)
Benzylidenacetophenon *n* benzylideneacetophenone, benzalacetophenone, chalcone, *1,3-diphenylpropenone
Benzylidenchlorid *n* benzylidene chloride, α,α-dichlorotoluene, benzal chloride
Benzylierung *f* benzylation
Benzylisochinolin *n* benzylisoquinoline
Benzylpenaldinsäure *f* benzylpenaldic acid, penaldic-G acid
Benzylpenicillin *n* benzylpenicillin
Benzylpenicilloinsäure *f* benzylpenicilloic acid, penicilloic-G acid
Benzylpenillosäure *f* benzylpenilloic acid, penilloic-G acid
Benzylpenillsäure *f* benzylpenillic acid, penillic-G acid
Benzylphenylcarbinol *n s.* 1,2-Diphenylethanol
Benzylpropionat *n* benzyl propionate
Benzylradikal *n* benzyl radical, *(specif)* free benzyl radical
Benzylrest *m s.* Benzylgruppe
Benzylsalicylat *n* benzyl salicylate
Benzyn *n* benzyne, 1,2-didehydrobenzene
beobachtbar observable *(as of processes)*
Beobachtbarkeit *f* observability *(as of processes)*
beobachten to observe, to watch, to study
Beobachtung *f* observation • **sich der ~ entziehen** to escape observation
Beobachtungsfehler *m* observational error
beräumen *(hyd)* to unload *(a sludge-drying bed)*
Beräumung *f (hyd)* unloading *(of a sludge-drying bed)*
Berechnung *f* **von Trennstufe zu Trennstufe** *(distil)* tray-to-tray calculation (procedure)
Beregnungsdüngung *f* dressing by spray irrigation
Beregnungsprüfung *f*, **Beregnungsversuch** *m* *(text)* rain test
Bereich *m* 1. region, range *(as of measurement or of state)*; 2. area, region *(locally)*; region, section *(as of a molecule)*; 3. sphere *(as of a science)*
~/dynamischer dynamic range *(of an analyser)*
~/femtomolarer femtomolar range *(from* 10^{-12} *to* 10^{-15}*)*
~/kristalliner crystalline region
~/nichthelikaler *(bioch)* non-helical region (section)
~/plastischer plastic range
~/sichtbarer *(spectr)* visible range (region)
~/steriler *(biot)* sterile area
bereiten to prepare, to make [ready]
bereitet/frisch freshly prepared
Bereitung *f* preparation, making
Berg *m (anal)* peak *(for compounds s. under* Peak*)*
Bergabdiffusion *f* nucleation and growth *(in an alloy)*
Bergabwärtsreaktion *f* downhill reaction
Bergamottöl *n* bergamot oil *(from Citrus aurantium L. ssp. bergamia)*
Bergaufdiffusion *f* spinodal decomposition *(in a supersaturated alloy)*
Bergbau *m* mining
~/untertägiger underground (deep) mining
Bergbauabwasser *n* mine drainage [water]
Bergbaurückstände *mpl* mine wastes
Bergbausprengstoff *m* mining explosive (powder)
Bergblau *n* verditer blue *(a basic copper carbonate)*
Berge *pl (min tech)* tailings, tails, waste tailing, refuse
Bergeaustrag *m (min tech)* tailings (refuse) discharge (extraction)
Bergeaustragsöffnung *f (min tech)* tailings-discharge (refuse-discharge) port

Bergemittel *n* gangue [mineral], matrix
Berggrün *n* malachite green *(ground malachite or similar pigment made synthetically)*
Bergius-Hochdruckverfahren *n*, **Bergius-Hydrierverfahren** *n* Bergius [hydrogenation] process
Bergkork *m (min)* mountain cork *(an asbestos)*
Bergkristall *m (min)* rock crystal *(a variety of quartz)*
Bergkupfer *n* native copper
Bergleder *n (min)* mountain leather *(an asbestos)*
Bergmann-Serie *f (spectr)* Bergmann series
Bergmilch *f (min)* rock milk, agaric mineral *(calcium carbonate)*
Bergtalg *m s.* Bergwachs
Bergung *f (bioch)* salvage
Bergwachs *n (min)* ozokerite, earth (ader) wax, native paraffin
berieseln to sprinkle, to spray; to scrub *(gases)*
Berieselung *f* sprinkling, spraying; scrubbing *(of gases)*
~ zur Staubbindung *(coal)* dust proofing
Berieselungskondensator *m* atmospheric condenser
Berieselungskühler *m* spray cooler
Berieselungsverflüssiger *m* atmospheric condenser
Berkefeld-Filter *n* Berkefeld filter
Berkelium *n* Bk berkelium
Berl-Sattel[körper] *m* Berl saddle *(a filling body)*
Bernoulli-Gleichung *f* **idealer Flüssigkeiten** Bernoulli equation without friction
Bernstein *m* amber, succinite
Bernsteinlack *m* amber varnish
Bernsteinöl *n* amber oil
Bernsteinsäure *f* succinic acid, *butanedioic acid
Bernsteinsäuredialdehyd *m* succindialdehyde, *butane-1,4-dial
Bernsteinsäuredibenzylester *m* dibenzyl succinate
Bernsteinsäuredichlorid *n* succinyl chloride
Bernsteinsäurediethylester *m* diethyl succinate
Bernsteinsäureimid *n* succinimide, 2,5-dioxopyrrolidine
Bernsteinsäuremonoamid *n* succinic acid monoamide, succinamic acid
Berstdruckfestigkeit *f* bursting strength
bersten to crack, to break, *(esp of surfaces)* to burst
Berstfestigkeit *f* bursting strength
Berstscheibe *f* rupture (bursting) disk *(in pressure relief devices)*
Berstwiderstand *m (plast, pap)* bursting strength
Berthelot-Bombe *f (phys ch)* Berthelot bomb
Berthelot-Gleichung *f (phys ch)* Berthelot equation
Berthelot-Kalorimeter *n* Berthelot calorimeter
Berthelot-Mahler-Bombenkalorimeter *n* Berthelot-Mahler bomb calorimeter
Berthelot-Mahler-Kröcker-Bombe *f (phys ch)* Mahler (Kröcker) bomb
Berthelot-Prinzip *n (phys ch)* Thomsen-Berthelot principle
Berthollide *npl* berthollid[e]s, berthollide (non-Daltonian, non-daltonide, non-stoichiometric) compounds
Berthollidverbindungen *fpl s.* Berthollide
Berufskrankheit *f* occupational disease
beruhigen to kill *(a smelt)*; to deoxidize *(steel)*
Beruhigungsbecken *n (hyd)* quiescent basin; equalization tank (basin), equalizing basin *(for floating scum)*
Beruhigungsbehälter *m s.* Beruhigungsbecken
Beruhigungskammer *f* settling chamber *(in the pebble-heater process)*
Beruhigungsmittel *n (pharm)* sedative; *(met)* killing agent
berühren to contact
~/sich to contact
Berührungsfläche *f* surface of contact, *(quantitatively:)* area of contact
Berührungsgift *n* [direct] contact poison, contact toxicant
Berührungsgrenze *f* contact boundary
Berührungskorrosion *f* galvanic (contact) corrosion, bimetallic (two-metal) corrosion
Berührungslinie *f* **der Walzen** roll nip *(e.g. between calender rolls)*
Berührungsmetamorphose *f (geoch)* contact metamorphism (metamorphosis)
Berührungstrocknen *n* contact (conduction, indirect) drying
Berührungswinkel *m* contact angle *(in testing surface-active substances)*
Berührungszeit *f* time of contact
Berührungszone *f* area (surface) of contact
Beryll *m (min)* beryl *(beryllium aluminium silicate)*
Beryllat *n* beryllate
Beryllerde *f s.* Berylliumoxid
Beryllid *n* beryllide
Berylliose *f s.* Berylliumkrankheit
Beryllium *n* Be beryllium
Berylliumcarbid *n* beryllium carbide
Berylliumcarbonat *n* beryllium carbonate
Berylliumchlorid *n* beryllium chloride
Berylliumhalogenid *n* beryllium halide (halogenide)
Berylliumhydrid *n* beryllium hydride
Berylliumhydroxid *n* beryllium hydroxide
Berylliumiodid *n* beryllium iodide
Berylliumkrankheit *f (med)* beryllium disease, beryll[i]osis *(lung damage caused by inhalation of beryllium dust)*
Berylliumorthosilicat *n* beryllium orthosilicate, beryllium tetraoxosilicate
Berylliumoxid *n* beryllium oxide
Berylliumsulfat *n* beryllium sulphate
Berylliumsulfid *n* beryllium sulphide
Berylliumtarget *n* beryllium target
Berylliumtetroxosilicat *n s.* Berylliumorthosilicat
Beryllose *f s.* Berylliumkrankheit

besanden *(ceram)* to sand *(a mould)*
Besandung *f (ceram)* sanding *(of a mould)*
Besatz *m (ceram)* setting
Besatzfläche *f (ceram)* setting space
Besatzhöhe *f (ceram)* setting height
Besatzraum *m (ceram)* setting space
besäumen *(plast)* to trim
Besäummaschine *f (plast)* trimming machine, trimmer
Beschaffenheit *f* quality, constitution, nature, *(of man-made products also)* make
~/grießartige grittiness
~/klumpige lumpiness
~/körnige graininess, grain
~/mehlige mealiness
~/stückige lumpiness
beschallen to sonicate
Beschallung *f* sonication
beschichten to coat, *(esp with metal:)* to plate; to laminate *(as with a plastic film)*; to overlay *(as with veneer)*
~/durch Tauchen to dip-coat
~/mit Blei to lead-coat
~/mit Gips to plaster
~/mit Graphit to coat with graphite, to graphitize, *(Am also)* to graphite
~/mit Platin to platinize, to platinate
~/mit Rhodium to rhodanize
~/mit Thorium to thoriate
Beschichten *n* coating, *(esp with metal:)* plating; laminating *(as with a plastic film)*; overlaying *(as with veneer)*
~ aus Lösungen solution coating
~ durch Streichen spread coating
~ durch Tauchen dip coating
~/einseitiges *(pap)* one-sided (single-sided) coating
~ endloser Bahnen web coating
~ mit Rakel knife coating
~ mittels Extruders extrusion coating
~ über Schneckenpresse extrusion coating
~/zweiseitiges *(pap)* double coating
beschichtet/mit Gummi rubber-coated, rubber-covered
~/mit Schaumstoff foam-backed
Beschichtung *f s.* 1. Beschichten; 2. Schicht
Beschichtungsstoff *m* coating [material]
~/anorganischer inorganic coating [material]
~ für Metalle metal coating [material]
~/organischer organic coating [material]
Beschichtungstechnik *f (lab)* coating technique
beschicken to feed, to charge, to fill, to load, to furnish; *(nucl)* to fuel *(a reactor)*; *(met)* to burden
~/zwangsläufig to force-feed
Beschicker *m* stoker *(a mechanical device for feeding solid fuel)*
Beschickertrog *m* feeding trough
Beschickung *f* 1. feeding, charging, filling, loading, furnishing; *(nucl)* fuelling; *(met)* burdening; 2. *s.* Beschickungsmaterial
~/ruhende static charge *(of an intermittent gas-making retort)*
~/selbsttätige automatic feed
Beschickungsautomat *m* automatic feeder
Beschickungsbehälter *m* feed tank
Beschickungsbühne *f* feeding (charging) platform
Beschickungsbunker *m* feeding (charging) bin
Beschickungseinrichtung *f s.* Beschickungsvorrichtung
Beschickungshöhe *f (met)* stock level
Beschickungsmaterial *n* feed[stock], feed material, *(with discontinuous operation also)* charge [stock], load, batch; *(met)* burden
Beschickungsmulde *f* charging box *(for an open-hearth furnace)*
Beschickungsoberfläche *f (met)* stock line
Beschickungsoberkante *f s.* Beschickungsoberfläche
Beschickungsöffnung *f* feed inlet (opening, hole), charging hole
Beschickungsrinne *f* feed (charging) chute
Beschickungsrohr *n* feed pipe (tube)
Beschickungsrutsche *f* feed (charging) chute
Beschickungssäule *f (met)* stock column
Beschickungsschleuse *f* entry lock, inlet sluice, *(if conical:)* lock hopper
Beschickungsschurre *f* feed (charging) chute
Beschickungsseite *f* feed end
Beschickungstrichter *m* feed[ing] hopper, feed[-ing] funnel, charging (loading) hopper (funnel)
Beschickungstür *f* feed[ing] door, charging (filling) door
Beschickungsvorrichtung *f* feeder, loader, *(for solid fuel also)* stoker
Beschickungszone *f (plast)* feed zone (section)
beschießen *(nucl)* to bombard
Beschießen *n (nucl)* bombardment
Beschlag *m* bloom; *(glass)* tarnish *(defect)*
beschlagen to bloom
beschleunigen to accelerate, to promote, to speed [up]
Beschleuniger *m* 1. accelerator, promoter, accelerating (promoting) agent; 2. *(nucl)* [particle] accelerator • **ohne ~** *(rubber)* unaccelerated, non-accelerated
~/anorganischer *(rubber)* inorganic accelerator
~/basischer *(rubber)* basic accelerator
~/langsamer *(rubber)* slow[-acting] accelerator
~/linearer *(nucl)* linear accelerator
~ mit verzögertem Vulkanisationseinsatz delayed-action accelerator
~/mittelschneller (mittelstarker) *(rubber)* moderate accelerator, medium[-speed] accelerator
~/organischer *(rubber)* organic accelerator
~/saurer *(rubber)* acidic accelerator
~/schneller (schnellwirkender) *(rubber)* fast[-curing] accelerator, rapid accelerator
~/schwacher (schwachwirkender) *s.* ~/langsamer
~/starker (starkwirkender) *s.* ~/schneller

Beschleunigeraktivator *m (rubber)* accelerator activator, activator of cure (vulcanization)

Beschleunigerbatch *m (rubber)* accelerator masterbatch

Beschleunigerdosierung *f (rubber)* accelerator level

beschleunigerfrei *(rubber)* unaccelerated, non-accelerated

beschleunigerhaltig *(rubber)* accelerated

Beschleunigersystem *n (rubber)* accelerating system

Beschleunigervormischung *f (rubber)* accelerator masterbatch

Beschleunigerwirkung *f (rubber)* accelerating activity

beschleunigt accelerated

~/nicht unaccelerated, non-accelerated

Beschleunigung *f* acceleration, promotion

~/anchimere anchimeric assistance *(of the reaction rate by neighbouring groups)*

~/negative deceleration

~/sterische steric acceleration, B strain effect

Beschleunigungsdruckhöhe *f* acceleration head *(in a pump)*

Beschleunigungseffekt *m* accelerating effect

Beschleunigungshöhe *f* acceleration head *(in a pump)*

Beschleunigungskammer *f (nucl)* accelerating chamber

Beschleunigungsspannung *f* accelerating potential

Beschleunigungsverhältnis *n* relative centrifugal force *(centrifuging)*

Beschleunigungsvermögen *n* accelerating ability

Beschleunigungszone *f* accelerating zone

beschmieren to smear

beschmutzen to soil, to pollute, to stain *(esp with greasy matter:)* to smear

beschneiden to cut, to trim

Beschuß *m (nucl)* bombardment

~ mit Elektronen electron bombardment

beschweren *(pap, text)* to weight, to load *(with fillers or sizing material)*

Beschwerungsmaterial *n* weighting (loading) material (agent), load[ing]

Beschwerungsstoff *m* high-gravity solid *(in dense-medium separations)*

beseitigen to eliminate, to remove; to dispose of *(waste products)*

~/durch Geländeauffüllung to dispose of by landfill

Beseitigung *f* elimination, removal; disposal *(of waste products)*

~ des radioaktiven Abfalls radioactive-waste (nuclear-waste) disposal

~ durch Abklappen disposal to (at) sea, ocean (marine) disposal

~ durch Einleitung in die Kanalisation disposal to sewers

~ durch Einleitung ins Meer disposal to (at) sea, ocean (marine) disposal

~ durch Geländeauffüllung landfill disposal

~ durch Verkippen ins Meer *s.* ~ durch Abklappen

~ fester Abprodukte solid-waste disposal

~ von Geschmack taste removal, removal of taste

besetzen to populate, to occupy, to fill *(an energy level)*; to occupy *(a lattice vacancy)*; to charge *(e.g. a furnace)*; to fit *(as with knives)*

Besetzung *f* population, occupation, filling *(of an energy level)*; occupation *(of a lattice vacancy)*; charging *(as of a furnace)*; fitting *(as with knives)*

~ des Orbitals orbital population

~/inverse inverted population

Besetzungsgrad *m* degree of population *(of an energy level)*

Besetzungsinversion *f* population inversion *(of an energy level)*

Besetzungsschema *n* population (filling) diagram *(of molecular orbitals)*

Besetzungsunterschied *m* population difference *(of energy levels)*

Besetzungszahl *f* occupation number *(number of electrons in a shell)*

Besetzungszahldifferenz *f s.* Besetzungsunterschied

Besichtigungsöffnung *f* inspection hatch

besprengen to sprinkle, to water

bespritzen to spray, to sprinkle

besprühen to spray, to dew

Besprühen *n* **aus der Luft** *(agric)* aerial spraying

~/elektrostatisches electrostatic spraying

~ mit Wasser water spraying

~ vom Flugzeug aus *(agric)* aeroplane spraying

~ zur Staubbindung dust proofing *(as of coal)*

Bessemer-Birne *f (met)* Bessemer converter

Bessemer-Kleinbirne *f*, **Bessemer-Kleinkonverter** *m (met)* baby Bessemer converter

Bessemer-Konverter *m (met)* Bessemer converter

Bessemer-Konverterstahl *m* Bessemer steel

Bessemer-Konverterverfahren *n s.* Bessemer-Verfahren

bessemern *(met)* to bessemerize, to convert

Bessemer-Roheisen *n* Bessemer pig (iron)

Bessemer-Schlacke *f* Bessemer (acid) slag

Bessemer-Stahl *m* Bessemer (acid) steel

Bessemer-Verfahren *n (met)* Bessemer (converter) process, *(specif)* acid [Bessemer] process

~/basisches basic Bessemer (converter) process, basic process, Thomas[-Gilchrist] process

~/saures acid Bessemer (converter) process, acid process

beständig resistant, resisting, stable *(to an agent)*, *(esp dye, text)* fast, proof; persistent *(biocide)*; durable, stable *(material)* • **gut ~ sein** to last well

~/an der Luft stable in air

~/chemisch chemically resistant (stable), resistant (stable) to chemical attack

~ gegen Alkalien resistant to alkali[es], alkali-resistant, alkali-stable

~ **gegen oxidative Einflüsse** resistant (stable) to oxidation, oxidatively stable
~ **gegen Säuren** resistant to acid[s], acid-resistant, acid-stable
~ **gegen Wasser** resistant (stable) to water, water-resistant
~**/thermisch** heat-resistant, thermally stable *(e.g. plastics)*
Beständigkeit *f* resistance, stability *(to an agent)*, *(esp dye, text)* fastness, proofness; persistence *(of a biocide)*; durability, stability *(of a material)*
~**/chemische** chemical resistance (stability), resistance (stability) to chemical attack
~ **der Flocken** *(hyd)* floc strength
~ **des Schaums** *(coll)* stability (lifetime) of the foam; *(ferm)* head retention, firmness of the head
~ **gegen Abblättern (Abplatzen)** spalling resistance
~ **gegen Abrieb** resistance to abrasion (wear)
~ **gegen Alkalien** resistance (stability) to alkali[es], alkali resistance
~ **gegen Chemikalien** resistance to chemicals
~ **gegen chemische Einwirkungen** *s.* ~/chemische
~ **gegen den Koronaeffekt** resistance to corona [discharge], corona resistance
~ **gegen Gase** resistance to gases
~ **gegen hartes Wasser** resistance to hard water
~ **gegen hohe Temperaturen** resistance to high temperature[s], high-temperature resistance (stability)
~ **gegen Lösungsmittel** resistance to solvents, solvent resistance
~ **gegen oxidative Einflüsse** resistance to oxidation, oxidation (oxidative) resistance
~ **gegen Säuren** resistance (stability) to acid[s], acid resistance
~**/thermische** heat resistance, thermal stability *(as of plastics)*
Beständigmachen *n* proofing
Bestandteil *m* constituent, component, ingredient
~**/acetonlöslicher** *(plast)* acetone-soluble matter
~**/aktiver** *s.* ~/wirksamer
~**/dispergierender** dispersion (dispersive) medium
~**/disperser** disperse[d] phase, internal phase
~**/färbender** colouring principle
~**/flüchtiger** volatile (fugitive) constituent
~**/gasförmiger** *s.* ~/flüchtiger
~**/giftiger** toxic principle
~**/integranter (integrierender)** integral constituent
~**/leichtflüchtiger** *s.* ~/flüchtiger
~**/makropetrographischer** macrocomponent, macroconstituent
~**/mikropetrographischer** microcomponent, microconstituent
~**/nichtzuckerartiger** non-sugar, *(esp)* aglycon *(of a glycoside)*
~**/wesentlicher** integral (essential) constituent
~**/wirksamer** active ingredient (principle)
~**/zuckerfreier (zuckerfremder)** *s.* ~/nichtzuckerartiger
Bestandteile *mpl***/flüchtige** volatile matter, v.m., VM, volatiles
~**/nichtflüchtige** non-volatile matter
α**-Bestandteile** *mpl (coal)* α fraction
β**-Bestandteile** *mpl (coal)* β fraction
γ**-Bestandteile** *mpl (coal)* γ fraction
bestäuben to dust, to powder
~**/mit Talkum** *(rubber)* to soapstone
bestehen aus to be made up of, to consist of
bestimmbar determinable, *(qualitatively also)* identifiable
Bestimmbarkeit *f* determinability, *(qualitatively also)* identifiability
bestimmen to determine
~**/qualitativ** to determine qualitatively, to identify
~**/quantitativ** to determine quantitatively, to quantitate, to estimate
Bestimmung *f* determination
~ **an Ort und Stelle** in-situ determination
~**/Barfoedsche** Barfoed's test *(for monosaccharides)*
~**/blinde** *s.* Blindbestimmung
~ **der Methoxylgruppen nach Zeisel** Zeisel methoxyl determination
~ **der Nachbarschaftshäufigkeit** *(bioch)* nearest-neighbour base sequencing, nearest-neighbour base-frequency analysis
~ **der relativen Atommasse** atomic-weight determination
~ **der relativen Molekülmasse** molecular-weight determination
~ **der relativen Molekülmasse nach [der Mikromethode von] Rast** Rast's molecular-weight determination, Rast microprocedure, micro Rast
~ **der Wirksamkeit** test for potency
~ **des organisch gebundenen Kohlenstoffs** *(hyd)* TOC determination
~**/kolorimetrische** colorimetric determination
~ **nach Mohr** Mohr titration (method) *(argentometry)*
~ **nach Volhard** Volhard titration (method) *(argentometry)*
~**/nochmalige** redetermination
~**/photometrische** photometric determination
~**/qualitative** qualitative determination, identification
~**/quantitative** quantitative determination, quantitation, estimation
~ **vor Ort** in-situ determination
Bestimmungsoperation *f s.* Bestimmungsverfahren
Bestimmungsportion *f* determination quantity
Bestimmungsverfahren *n* determination procedure
bestrahlen to [ir]radiate; *(nucl)* to bombard
~**/mit Röntgenstrahlen** to X-ray
Bestrahlung *f* [ir]radiation; *(nucl)* bombardment
~ **mit energiereicher (harter) Strahlung** high-energy irradiation

Bestrahlungsstärke *f (spectr)* irradiance
Betacellulose *f* beta cellulose
Betadickenmesser *m* beta[-absorption] gauge
BET-Adsorptionsisotherme *f* BET isotherm
Beta-Fraktion *f* beta fraction *(in the pyridine extraction of hard coal)*
Betain *n* betaine *(any of a class of zwitterionic compounds)*, *(specif)* betaine, *NNN*-trimethylammonioacetate, oxyneurine, lycine
Beta-Lactam-Antibiotikum *m (biot)* β-lactam antibiotic
Betarückstreuung *f* beta backscatter[ing]
Betaspektrum *n* beta-ray spectrum
Betastrahlen *mpl* beta rays
Betastrahlen-Dickenmesser *m* beta[-absorption] gauge
Betastrahlenquelle *f* beta-radiation source
Betastrahler *m* beta emitter
Betastrahlung *f* beta radiation
~/negative K [electron] capture
Betastruktur *f* sheet structure *(of proteins)*
Betateilchen *n* beta particle
betätigt/durch Elektromotor motor-operated
~/elektromechanisch electromechanically operated
~/hydraulisch hydraulic operated
~/manuell manually operated
Betätigungsorgan *n* actuator
betatop *(nucl)* betatopic
Betatron *n* betatron
betäubend anaesthetic
Betaumwandlung *f s.* Betazerfall
Betazerfall *m* beta decay (disintegration), beta-ray decay (disintegration)
Betazerfallsenergie *f* beta decay (disintegration) energy
BET-Gleichung *f (phys ch)* BET equation, Brunauer-Emmett-Teller relationship
Bethellisieren *n* Bethell treatment *(wood preservation)*
BET-Isotherme *f* BET isotherm
Beton *m* concrete
~/armierter reinforced concrete
~/belüfteter air-entrained (air-entraining) concrete
~/bewehrter reinforced concrete
~/entfeinter no-fines concrete
~/erdfeuchter earth-moist concrete
~/fetter rich (good) concrete
~/feuerfester refractory concrete
~/grüner (junger) green concrete
~/magerer lean[-mixed] concrete, poor concrete
~ mit Haufwerksporosität single-sized concrete
~/plastischer plastic concrete
~/steifer earth-moist concrete
~/vorgefertigter precast concrete
~/vorgepackter prepacked (grouted) concrete
~/vorgespannter prestressed concrete
~/weicher plastic concrete
Betonbelüfter *m* air-entraining additive (admixture, agent, compound)
Betonblock *m* concrete block
Betonfestigkeit *f* concrete strength
Betonmasse *f* concrete mass
Betonmauerstein *m* concrete brick
Betonpumpe *f* concrete pump
Betonstein *m* concrete brick
Betonturm *m (pap)* concrete acid tower
Betonverdichtung *f* compaction of concrete
Betonzerfall *m* concrete disintegration
Betonzuschlag[stoff] *m* concrete aggregate
Betrag *m* amount, quantum, value
betreiben to operate, to drive, to run
~/adiabat to operate (run) adiabatically
~/isotherm to operate (run) isothermally
Betrieb *m* 1. plant, works, factory; 2. operation
• **außer ~ [befindlich]** out of operation, idle
• **außer ~ setzen** to shut [down], to close down *(a factory)*; to cut out of service, to put out of operation, to stop *(a machine)* • **in ~ [befindlich]** in operation, at (in) work, working, on-stream
• **in ~ nehmen** *s.* in ~ setzen • **in ~ sein** to be in operation, to run, to be running (working, operating) *(of a machine)* • **in ~ setzen** to put (set) in operation, to set in action, to start [up], to prime *(a machine)*
~/chargenweiser *s.* ~/diskontinuierlicher
~/chemischer chemical plant (works)
~/diskontinuierlicher batch operation
~/ganzjähriger year-round operation
~ im Abwärtsstrom *(hyd, filtr)* downflow operation
~ im Aufwärtsstrom *(hyd, filtr)* upflow operation
~/kontinuierlicher continuous operation
~ mit flüssigem Schlackenabzug slagging operation, operation under slagging conditions
~/wartungsfreier unattended operation
betrieben/diskontinuierlich discontinuous, *(Am also)* batch
~/hydraulisch hydraulic-operated
~/kontinuierlich continuous
~/mit Atomkraft atomic-powered
~/mit Gas gas fuel[l]ed
~/mit Kernenergie atomic-powered
~/mit Luft air-driven
~/stetig (ununterbrochen) continuous
Betriebsabwasser *n (hyd)* plant waste water, plant (factory, works) effluent, plant discharge
Betriebsabwasseranfall *m (hyd)* plant effluent flow
Betriebsanlage *f* plant, works
Betriebsbedingungen *fpl* operating conditions
betriebsbereit operable, serviceable, ready for operation (use)
Betriebsbereitschaft *f* operability, serviceability, operating condition
Betriebschemiker *m* industrial (works) chemist
Betriebsdampf *m* operating steam
Betriebsdaten *pl* operating parameters (characteristics)
Betriebsdauer *f* operating (working) life
Betriebsdestillation *f* works distillation

Betriebsdrehzahl *f* operating speed
Betriebsdruck *m* operating (working) pressure
Betriebshöhe *f (biot)* working (fermenter) level
Betriebsinhalt *m (tech)* hold-up, *(distil also)* column hold-up
Betriebskanalisation *f (hyd)* plant sewer
Betriebskosten *pl* operating cost (charge)
Betriebslinie *f (distil)* operating (material-balance) line
Betriebsparameter *mpl s.* Betriebsdaten
Betriebsreaktor *m* commercial[-scale] reactor
Betriebssäurewecker *m (food)* bulk starter
Betriebssicherheit *f* safety of operation
Betriebsstillegung *f* plant shut-down
Betriebsstoffwechsel *m (bioch)* energy (respiratory) metabolism *(historical term)*
Betriebsstörung *f* upset, stoppage, breakdown
Betriebstemperatur *f* operating (working) temperature
Betriebsunterbrechung *f* downtime, down period
Betriebsverhalten *n* performance
Betriebsvolumen *n (biot)* working (fermenter, fermentation) volume
Betriebswasser *n s.* Brauchwasser
Betriebsweise *f* mode of operation
Betriebszustand *m* operating state
~/stationärer operating steady state
Bett *n (tech, geol)* bed
~/ruhendes (statisches) *(tech)* fixed (static) bed
~/wallendes *(tech)* ebullating (ebullated) bed *(special form of a fluidized bed)*
Betthöhe *f*, **Bettiefe** *f (tech)* bed depth (height, level), *(hyd also)* media depth
Bettstreckung *f (hyd)* bed expansion
Betts-Verfahren *n* Betts process *(for refining lead)*
Bettvolumen *n* bed volume
Betulin *n* betulin, betula (birch) camphor *(a triterpenoid alcohol)*
Betweenanen *n* betweenanene *(any of a class of bicyclic alkenes)*
Beuche *f (text)* 1. kier-boiling, kiering, bowking, bucking; 2. *s.* Beuchflotte
Beuchechtheit *f (text)* fastness to kier-boiling
beuchen *(text)* to kier-boil, to bowk, to buck
Beuchfaß *n (text)* kier, bowking (bucking) tub
Beuchflotte *f (text)* kier liquor (lye), bowking (bucking) liquor (lye)
Beuchhilfsmittel *n (text)* kier[-boiling] assistant
Beuchkessel *m (text)* [bowking] kier
Beugung *f* diffraction
~ am Kristall[gitter] crystal diffraction
~ der Röntgenstrahlen X-ray diffraction
~ hochenergetischer Elektronen *s.* ~ schneller Elektronen
~ langsamer (niederenergetischer) Elektronen low-energy electron diffraction, LEED
~ schneller Elektronen high-energy electron diffraction, HEED
Beugungsbild *n* diffraction pattern
Beugungserscheinung *f* diffraction phenomenon
Beugungsgitter *n* diffraction grating
Beugungsring *m* diffraction ring
Beugungsspektrum *n* diffraction (normal) spectrum
Be- und Entlüftung *f* venting *(of tanks)*
Be- und Entlüftungseinrichtung *f* venting device *(for tanks)*
Beurteilung *f***/visuelle** visual examination
Beutel *m* bag
Beutelfilter *n* bag filter
beuteln to bolt, to sift *(e.g. flour)*
Beutelpapier *n* bag paper
Beutelschließmaschine *f*, **Beutelschweißmaschine** *f* bag sealing machine
bevorzugt/energetisch energetically favourable (favoured)
bewässern to water, to irrigate
Bewässerung *f* watering, irrigation
bewegen to move; to agitate *(e.g. a reaction mixture)*; *(rapidly up and down or to and fro:)* to jig
beweglich mobile, movable
Beweglichkeit *f* mobility
~ der Nährstoffe *(biol)* nutrient mobility
~/elektrophoretische electrophoretic mobility
Bewegtbett *n* moving bed
Bewegtbettadsorber *m* moving-bed adsorber
Bewegtbettadsorption *f* moving-bed adsorption
Bewegtbettreaktor *m* moving-bed reactor
Bewegtbettverfahren *n* moving-bed process
Bewegung *f* motion; agitation *(as of a reaction mixture)*
~/Brownsche Brownian motion (movement)
~/drehende rotary (rotational) motion
~/fortschreitende translational motion
~/pulsierende pulsation
~/rotierende rotary (rotational) motion
Bewegungsenergie *f* kinetic energy
Bewegungsgesetze *npl***/Newtonsche** Newton laws of motion
Bewegungsgröße *f* momentum
Bewegungsrichtung *f* direction of motion
bewehren to reinforce
Bewehrung *f* reinforcement
Beweis *m* proof
beweisen to proof
bewerten to evaluate, to rate *(properties)*
Bewertung *f* evaluation, rating *(of properties)*
~/organoleptische (sinnesphysiologische) *(food)* organoleptic (sensory) evaluation
bewettern 1. *(mine)* to ventilate; 2. *s.* bewittern
Bewetterung *f* 1. *(mine)* ventilation; 2. *s.* Bewitterung
bewirken to cause, to effect, to bring about, to produce, to give rise to
bewittern to weather
Bewitterung *f* 1. weathering; 2. *s.* Bewitterungsbeanspruchung
Bewitterungsbeanspruchung *f* outdoor weathering (exposure), atmospheric exposure

Bewitterungsechtheit *f* weathering fastness
Bewitterungsgerät *n* weathering device, *(text also)* weatherometer
Bewitterungsprüfung *f* weathering (exposure) testing
Bewitterungsversuch *m* weathering test, *(esp)* outdoor weathering (exposure) test
Bewoid-Leim *m (pap)* Bewoid size
Bewoid-Verfahren *n (pap)* Bewoid process
Bewuchs *m* fouling, marine growth
~/biologischer *s.* Rasen/biologischer
bezeichnen *(nomencl)* 1. to notate, to designate; 2. *s.* benennen
~/mit Buchstaben to letter
Bezeichnung *f (nomencl)* 1. notation, designation; 2. *s.* Benennung
Bezeichnungssystem *n (nomencl)* system of notation, notation system
Bezeichnungsweise *f (nomencl)* notation, manner (method) of notation
~/Ewens-Bassettsche Ewens-Bassett system *(of indicating valencies)*
~/Stocksche Stock notation (scheme), Stock's system *(of indicating valencies)*
Beziehung *f* relation[ship]
~/Debyesche *(phys ch)* Debye relation
~ der freien Enthalpie/lineare linear free-energy relation[ship], LFE relationship, linear Gibbs energy relation
~/Duprésche *(phys ch)* Dupré equation
~/gegenseitige correlation
~/isokinetische isokinetic relationship
~/Maxwellsche *(phys ch)* Maxwell relation
~/van Vlecksche *(spectr)* van Vleck equation
Beziehungen *fpl***/räumliche (sterische)** space relations
beziffern to number, to index, to indicate, to label
Bezifferung *f* numbering, indexing, indication, labelling
~/im Uhrzeigersinn clockwise numbering
Bezifferungssystem *n* numbering system
Bezirk *m* region, range *(as of measurement or state)*; *(cryst)* domain *(in ferromagnetic substances)*
~/kristalliner crystalline region
~/Weißscher *(cryst)* Weiss [molecular magnetic] field, ferromagnetic domain
Bezugsbasis *f* basis
~ Masse der handelsüblich trockenen Substanz commercial dry [weight] basis, CDW
~ Masse des feuchten Stoffs wet[-weight] basis, WWB
~ Trockenmasse bone-dry-weight basis, BDWB, dry[-weight] basis
~ Trockenstoffmasse (Trockensubstanzmasse) *s.* ~ Trockenmasse
Bezugselektrode *f* reference (comparison) electrode
Bezugskraftstoff *m* reference fuel
Bezugslinie *f (spectr)* standard (comparison) line
Bezugssignal *n (anal)* reference peak
Bezugsspannung *f* reference voltage
Bezugsstandard *m* reference standard
Bezugssubstanz *f* reference (standard) substance (compound)
Bezugssystem *n* reference system
Bezugstreibstoff *m* reference fuel
Bezugszustand *m (phys ch)* reference state
B-Füllmasse *f (sugar)* B (second-grade) massecuite, intermediate fillmass
BHA *s.* Butylhydroxyanisol
B-Harz *n* B-stage resin, resitol
B-Horizont *m (soil)* B-horizon, illuvial horizon
Biacetyl *n* biacetyl, *butanedione
Biallyl *n s.* Hexa-1,5-dien
Biaryl *n (org ch)* biaryl
biaxial *(cryst)* biaxial
Bibeldruckpapier *n* bible paper, [Oxford] India paper
Bibenzoyl *n s.* Benzil
Bibenzyl *n* bibenzyl, *sym*-diphenylethane
Bibergeil *n (pharm, cosmet)* castor
Bicheroux-Verfahren *n* Bicheroux process *(flat-glass manufacture)*
bicyclisch bicyclic, dicyclic
Bicyclus *m* bicyclic compound
Biegeeigenschaft *f* flexural property
Biegeermüdung *f s.* Biegerißbildung
Biegefestigkeit *f* bending strength, transverse (flexural) strength
Biegemodul *m* flexural modulus
biegen to bend, to flex
Biegeofen *m (glass)* bending furnace
Biegeprobe *f*, **Biegeprüfung** *f s.* Biegeversuch
Biegerißbildung *f* flex cracking
Biegerißfestigkeit *f*, **Biegerißwiderstand** *m* flex[-cracking] resistance, resistance to flex cracking
Biegeschwingung *f (spectr)* bending vibration
Biegesteifigkeit *f* flexural rigidity, stiffness in bend (flexure)
Biegeversuch *m* bend[ing] test, flexural-strength test
~ in der Kälte cold-bend test
Biegewalze *f (glass)* bending roll *(Colburn sheet process)*
biegsam flexible, pliable, pliant
Biegsamkeit *f* flexibility, pliability
~ bei niedriger Temperatur cold flex
Biegung *f* bend, flexure
Biegungs... *s.* Biege...
Bienengift *n* bee venom
Bienenharz *n* bee glue, propolis, balm
Bienenkorbkoks *m* beehive[-oven] coke
Bienenkorbofen *m* beehive oven, beehive coke (coking) oven
Bienenkorbofenkoks *m* beehive[-oven] coke
Bienenvorwachs *n s.* Bienenharz
Bienenwachs *n* beeswax
~/gebleichtes bleached beeswax, white wax

Bier *n* beer, *(collectively also)* malt beverages; *(if top-fermented and strongly hopped:)* ale
~/dunkles dark beer
~/helles pale (light) beer
~/leichtes mild beer
~/obergäriges top-fermented (top-fermentation) beer
~/schwach gehopftes mildly hopped beer
~/stark gehopftes strongly hopped beer
~/untergäriges bottom-fermented (bottom-fermentation) beer
bierartig beery *(taste, smell)*
Bierbrauen *n* brewing
Bierbrauer *m* brewer
Bierbrauerei *f* brewery
Bierdeckelpappe *f* coaster board
Bierer-Davis-Bombe *f (phys ch)* Bierer-Davis oxygen bomb
Bieressig *m* beer vinegar
Bierhefe *f* beer yeast, brewing (brewer's, brewery) yeast
Bierstein *m* beer stone (scale) *(on the inside surfaces of brewing apparatus)*
Biertreber *pl* brewer's grains
Bierwürze *f* brewer's wort
Bifaser *f s.* Bikomponentenfaser
bifunktionell bifunctional, difunctional
Bi-Gas-Verfahren *n (coal)* Bi-gas process *(two-stage gasification of coal with oxygen and steam)*
Biguanid *n* biguanide, diguanide
Biharnstoff *m* biurea, dicarbamylhydrazine
Bihexyl *n s.* Dodecan
Bikoloreffekt *m (text)* bicolour effect
Bikomponentenfaser *f (text)* bicomponent (conjugate) fibre
Bilanz *f* balance
Bilanzgleichung *f* balanced equation
bilanzieren to balance *(a reaction equation)*
Bilanzraum *m* control volume *(energy balance)*
Bild *n (phot)* image
~/äußeres latentes surface latent image
~/latentes latent image
~/negatives negative image
~/oberflächiges latentes *s.* ~/äußeres latentes
~/positives positive image
bilden to form *(e.g. crystals or a precipitate)*; to make up *(e.g. the main component)*
~/Blasen to bubble *(of gas or water)*; to blister *(of metal or paint)*; to vesicate, to blister *(of the skin)*
~/Chelate to chelate
~/ein Gel to gel[ate]
~/ein Sol to solate
~/eine Kruste to encrust, to incrust
~/einen Bleibaum *(el ch)* to tree
~/einen Bodenkörper (Bodensatz) *s.* ~/einen Niederschlag
~/einen Komplex to complex
~/einen Niederschlag to [form a] precipitate, to sediment, to settle [down, out], to deposit, to subside; to sediment, to deposit *(of a solution)*
~/Kanäle to rat-hole *(as of bulk material in fluidizing)*
~/Klumpen to clot, to clog
~/Kristalle to crystallize [out]; to form crystals
~/Luppen *(met)* to ball [up]
~/Mizellen to micellize
~/Runzeln *(coat)* to wrinkle
~/Schlacke to slag; *(coal)* to clinker
~/sich to form, *(esp of crusts or layers also)* to build up
bildsam plastic, *(esp relating to metal:)* ductile
~/wenig *(ceram)* short *(of a clay body)*
Bildsamkeit *f* plasticity, *(esp relating to metal:)* ductility
Bildstein *m (min)* pencil stone, agalmatolite *(a variety of pyrophyllite)*
Bildung *f* formation *(as of crystals or a precipitate)*, *(esp of crusts or layers also)* build-up
~ eines Bodenkörpers (Niederschlags) sedimentation, deposition
~/erneute reformation
~ in der Atmosphäre atmospheric formation
~ von Calciumcarbonatstein *(hyd)* calcium-carbonate scaling
~ von Einschlußverbindungen clathrate formation
~ von Härteabscheidungen (Inkrustationen) *(hyd)* formation of hardness scale
~ von Kurzschlußströmungen short-circuiting *(rheology)*
~ von Myzelpellets *(biot)* fungal pelleting
Bildungsenergie *f* energy of formation
Bildungsenthalpie *f* enthalpy of formation, heat of formation at constant pressure
Bildungsfunktion *f* formation function *(coordination chemistry)*
Bildungsgeschwindigkeit *f* rate of formation (generation), rate of appearance
Bildungskonstante *f* formation constant
Bildungsmechanismus *m* mechanism of formation
Bildungsort *m (geol)* place of formation • **am ~ liegend** autochthonous
Bildungspotential *n* formation potential
~ für Trihalomethane *(hyd)* trihalomethane formation potential, THMFP
Bildungsprodukt *n (biot)* fermentation (conversion) product
Bildungsrate *f* rate of formation
~/spezifische *(biot)* specific production efficiency (rate), specific rate of product formation *(mg product/mg cell dry weight · h)*
Bildungsreaktion *f* formation reaction
Bildungswärme *f* heat of formation
~/atomare atomic heat of formation
~/molare heat of formation per mole
Bildungsweg *m (bioch)* anabolic route
Bildungsweise *f* mode of formation
Bilirubin *n (bioch)* bilirubin
Biliverdin *n (bioch)* biliverdin
Billiter-Zelle *f* Billiter cell *(electrolysis)*
Bimetall *n* bimetal
bimetallisch bimetallic

Bimetallthermometer *n* bimetallic thermometer
bimodular *(anal)* bimodal
bimolekular bimolecular
Bimsbeton *m* pumice concrete
Bimsen *n (tann)* buffing
Bimskiesbeton *m s.* Bimsbeton
Bimsmaschine *f (tann)* buffing machine
Bimsseife *f* pumice soap
Bimsstaub *m* pumice powder
Bimsstein *m* pumice [stone]
bimssteinartig pumiceous
Bimssteinpulver *n* pounce
Bimssteinseife *f s.* Bimsseife
Bimssteintuff *m* pumice tuff
binär binary
Binde... *s. a.* Bindungs...
Bindebaustoff *m s.* Binder
Bindeglied *n (org ch)* binding link *(between molecules)*; *(tech)* link
Bindekörper *m (coat)* binder
Bindemittel *n* binding (bonding) agent (material), binder; adhesive agent (substance), adhesive; *(pharm)* excipient *(as for pills)*; *(geol)* cement, cementing agent, agglutinant
Bindemittellösung *f* [coating, paint] vehicle, carrier, medium
binden 1. to bond, to link, to bind *(atoms)*; 2. to adsorb *(dust particles)*; to absorb *(gases)*; *(bot, soil)* to fix *(atmospheric nitrogen)*; 3. *(esp geol)* to cement, to agglutinate *(particles)*; 4. *s.* abbinden
~/komplex to complex
~/koordinativ to coordinate *(atoms or molecules)*
~/sich to bind *(to a molecule)*
Binder *m (build)* binder, binding agent (material)
~/hydraulischer hydraulic binder
Binderkoks *m* binder coke
Bindestrich *m s.* Bindungsstrich
Bindeton *m* bond[ing] clay
bindig *(soil)* tenacious
Bindigkeit *f* 1. covalence *(chemical-bond theory)*; 2. *(soil)* tenacity
~/maximale maximum covalence
Bindung *f* 1. bonding, linkage, binding *(of atoms)*; adsorption *(of dust particles)*; absorption *(of gases)*; *(bot, soil)* fixation *(of atmospheric nitrogen)*; 2. bond *(between atoms)* • **eine ~ eingehen** to bond • **eine ~ herstellen** to make a bond
~ an einen Ionenaustauscher *(biot)* ionic bonding (binding) to a carrier *(enzyme immobilization)*
~/anderthalbfache one-and-a-half bond, three-halves bond
~/äquatoriale equatorial bond, e-bond
~/axiale axial bond, a-bond
~/chemische 1. chemical bonding; 2. chemical bond
~/dative [koordinative] *s.* ~/koordinative 2.
~/delokalisierte delocalized bond
~/doppelte double [covalent] bond
~/dreifache triple [covalent] bond
~/einpolare *s.* ~/homöopolare
~/elektrostatische (elektrovalente) *s.* ~/heteropolare
~/energiereiche high-energy bond
~/gebogene bent (banana) bond, banana-like (banana-shaped) bond
~/glykosidische glycosidic bond
~/halbpolare *s.* ~/koordinative 2.
~/heteropolare [hetero]polar bond, ionic (electrostatic, electrovalent) bond, electrovalence
~/homöopolare homopolar (atomic) bond, covalent (non-polar) bond, [shared-]electron-pair bond
~/hydrophobe *(bioch)* hydrophobic interaction, *(deprecated:)* hydrophobic bond
~/intermolekulare intermolecular bond
~/ionare (ionogene) *s.* ~/heteropolare
~/koordinative 1. coordination; 2. dipolar (coordinate, dative) bond, donor-acceptor bond
~/kovalente *s.* ~/homöopolare
~/lokalisierte localized bond
~/mehrfache multiple bond
~/metallische metal[lic] bond
~/nichtkovalente non-covalent bond
~/nichtlokalisierte *s.* ~/delokalisierte
~/peptidartige peptide bond
~/polare *s.* 1. ~/heteropolare; 2. ~/polare kovalente
~/polare kovalente polar [covalent] bond
~/schwache weak bond
~/semicyclische semicyclic bond
~/semipolare *s.* ~/koordinative
~/silicatische silicate bond
~/symbio[n]tische *(bot, soil)* symbiotic fixation *(of atmospheric nitrogen)*
~/unitarische *s.* ~/homöopolare
~/unpolare [kovalente] *s.* ~/homöopolare
~/van-der-Waalssche van der Waals bond
~ zwischen zwei H-Ketten heavy-heavy interchain bond *(protein chemistry)*
~/zwischenmolekulare intermolecular bond
δ-Bindung *f* δ bond, delta bond
π-Bindung *f* π bond, pi bond
σ-Bindung *f* σ bond, sigma bond
Bindungsabstand *m s.* Bindungslänge
Bindungsachse *f* bond[ing] axis
Bindungsart *f* bond type
Bindungsbildung *f* bond formation
Bindungsbruch *m* bond breakage (breaking)
Bindungscharakter *m* bond character
Bindungsdehnung *f* bond stretching
Bindungsdipol *m* bond dipole
Bindungsdipolmoment *n* bond dipole moment
Bindungsdissoziationsenergie *f* bond-dissociation energy
Bindungsdissoziationsenthalpie *f* bond dissociation enthalpy
Bindungsdublett *n s.* Bindungselektronenpaar
Bindungselektron *n* bonding electron, valency (outermost, optical) electron
Bindungselektronenpaar *n* bonding (sharing) electron pair, bonding pair of electrons, shared pair of electrons

Bindungsenergie *f***[/mittlere]** [mean] bond energy, bonding energy
bindungsfähig bondable
Bindungsfähigkeit *f* bondability, bonding (combining) power
Bindungsfestigkeit *f* bond[ing] strength
Bindungsfolge *f* bond succession
Bindungsgrad *m* bond number (order)
Bindungskompression *f* bond shortening
Bindungskraft *f* 1. bond[ing] force, combining force; 2. *s.* Bindungsfähigkeit
Bindungslänge *f* bond length (distance)
Bindungslockerung *f* antibonding
bindungslos non-bonded
Bindungsmoment *n* bond moment
Bindungsorbital *n* bond orbital
Bindungsordnung *f s.* Bindungsgrad
Bindungsort *m* binding site
Bindungsparachor *m* structural parachor *(chemical-bond theory)*
Bindungspolarität *f* bond polarity
Bindungsprotein *n (bioch)* binding protein
~/periplasmatisches periplasmic binding protein
Bindungsrefraktion *f* bond refraction
Bindungsregion *f s.* Bindungsort
Bindungsrichtung *f* bond direction (orientation)
Bindungsschwingung *f* bond vibration
Bindungsspaltung *f* bond cleavage (fission, scission, dissociation)
~/heterolytische heterolysis, heterolytic [bond] cleavage, heterolytic [bond] fission
~/homolytische homolysis, homolytic [bond] cleavage, homolytic [bond] fission, bond dissociation
Bindungsspaltungsenergie *f* bond dissociation energy
Bindungsspannung *f* binding strain
Bindungsspezifität *f* bond (relative group) specificity *(of an enzyme)*
Bindungssphäre *f* boundary (bounding) surface *(chemical-bond theory)*
Bindungsstärke *f* bond[ing] strength
Bindungsstauchung *f* bond compression
Bindungsstelle *f s.* Bindungsort
Bindungsstrich *m* bonding dash *(in structural formulae)*
Bindungssystem *n* bond system
~/farbbestimmendes chromophore *(in a larger sense)*
Bindungstheorie *f* chemical-bond theory
~ der Elektronenpaarbindungen (Valenzstrukturen) electron-pair (valence-bond) theory, VB theory, Heitler-London-Slater-Pauling theory, HLSP theory
Bindungstyp *m s.* Bindungsart
Bindungsumgruppierung *f* bond rearrangement
Bindungsvektor *m* bond vector
Bindungsvermögen *n s.* Bindungsfähigkeit
Bindungsverschiebung *f* bond shift[ing], bond migration
Bindungswechsel *m* bonding change
Bindungsweise *f* mode of linkage
Bindungswertigkeit *f s.* Bindigkeit
Bindungswinkel *m* bond (valence) angle, interbonding angle
Bindungszahl *f* bond number
Bingham-Körper *m* Bingham body (plastic)
Bingham-plastisch Bingham-plastic
Bingham-Zahl *f* Bingham number
Binnendruck *m* cohesion (internal, intrinsic) pressure
Binodal-Kurve *f (phys ch)* binodal curve, conodal (coexistence) curve
bioabbaubar biodegradable
Bioaffinitätschromatographie *f* affinity chromatography
Bioaktivität *f* biological activity
~ der Mikroorganismen microbial activity
Bioautographie *f (chromat)* bioautography *(detection of antibiotics on nutrient media by studying the growth inhibition of inoculated microorganisms)*
Biobergbau *m (biot)* microbial leaching, microbiological (bacterial) leaching
Biochemie *f* biochemistry, biological chemistry
Biochemikalie *f* biochemical [product]
Biochemiker *m* biochemist
biochemisch biochemical
Biochip *m (biot)* biochip, biologically based microchip
Bioelektronik *f* bioelectronics
Biofilter *n* biofilter, biological filter
Bioflavonoid *n* bioflavonoid
Bioflockulant *m (biot)* bioflocculant
Biogas *n* biogas, *(hyd also)* digester (sludge) gas, sewage (sewer) gas
Biogasanlage *f* biogas plant
Biogasreaktor *m* biogas (anaerobic) digester
biogen biogenic, biogenous
Bio-Hochreaktor *m (hyd)* biotower
Bioingenieurtechnik *f*, **Bioingenieurwesen** *n s.* Bioverfahrenstechnik
Bioinsektizid *n (biot)* bioinsecticide, microbial insecticide
Biokatalysator *m* biocatalyst, biochemical catalyst, ergone
Biokatalyse *f* biocatalysis
biokatalytisch biocatalytic
Biokonversion *f (biot)* bioconversion, biochemical (microbial) conversion, biotransformation, biochemical (microbial) transformation
Biokristall *m* biocrystal
Bioleaching *n s.* Biobergbau
Biolith *m* biolith, biogenic (organic) rock
biolumineszent bioluminescent
Biolumineszenz *f* bioluminescence
Biomakromolekül *n s.* Biopolymer
Biomasse *f* biomass
~/mikrobielle microbial mass
~/pflanzliche plant biomass

Biomassebildung *f* biomass formation
Biomassegewinnung *f* biomass production
Biomassekonzentration *f* biomass concentration; microbial concentration, concentration of microorganisms (suspended biomass)
~ **im Ablauf** effluent biomass concentration
~ **im biologischen Rasen** fixed-film biomass concentration *(trickling filter process)*
Biomasseproduktion *f* biomass production
Biomasseträger *mpl* biomass support particles
Biooxidation *f* bio-oxidation, biological oxidation
Biopolymer[e] *n* biopolymer, biological polymer, biomacromolecule
~**/informatives** informational macromolecule
Bioprozeßtechnik *f* bioprocess technology
Bioreaktor *m (biot)* bioreactor, biological (biochemical microbiological) reactor
~**/gerührter** stirred (mixed, agitated) bioreactor
~**/unbegaster (unbelüfteter)** unaerated bioreactor
Bios *n* **I** *(org ch)* inositol
~ **II** *(org ch)* biotin
Biosäule *f (biot)* column reactor
Bioschlamm *m (hyd)* biological sludge, activated (active) sludge
Biose *f* biose *(monosaccharide containing two carbon atoms)*
Biosensor *m (biot)* biosensor, biologically based sensor
~ **mit Mehrfachfunktion** multifunction biosensor, multisensor
Biosid *n* bioside
Biosorption *f* biosorption
Biosphäre *f* biosphere
Biosuspension *f (biot)* microbial suspension
Biosynthese *f* biosynthesis
~**/gesteuerte (gelenkte)** *(biot)* controlled biosynthesis
~**/gerichtete** *(biot)* directed biosynthesis
Biosynthesekette *f* biosynthetic chain
Biosyntheseleistung *f (biot)* efficiency of biosynthesis
Biosyntheseweg *m* biosynthetic (biosynthesis) pathway (route)
~**/unverzweigter** unbranched biosynthetic pathway
~**/verzweigter** branched biosynthetic pathway
Biotank *m s.* Bioreaktor
Biotechnik *f* biotechnology
biotechnisch biotechnological
Biotechnologie *f* biotechnology
biotechnologisch biotechnological
Biotest *m (tox)* bioassay [test], biological assay (test)
biotisch biotic
Biotransformation *f s.* Biokonversion
Biotreibstoff *m (biot)* power alcohol, fuel ethanol
Biotrockenmasse *f (biot)* dry weight of biomass
Bioverfahrenstechnik *f* bioengineering
Bioverfügbarkeit *f (pharm)* bioavailability
biozid biocidal *(killing organisms)*
Biozid *n* biocide *(chemical which kills organisms), (in a narrower sense)* pesticide, [pest] control agent
Biphenyl *n* biphenyl, phenylbenzene
Biphenyldicarbonsäure *f* biphenyl-2,2'-dicarboxylic acid, diphenic acid
Biphenyle *npl***/polychlorierte** polychlorinated biphenyls, PCB's
Biphthalidensäure *f s.* Benzil-2,2'-dicarbonsäure
Bipolarzelle *f* bipolar cell *(electrolysis)*
~ **von Dow** Dow cell
Biquarz *m* biquartz
Biradikal *n* biradical, diradical
Birch-Hückel-Reaktion *f* Birch reduction *(of organic compounds by metallic sodium dissolved in liquid ammonia)*
Birge-Sponer-Extrapolation *f (phys ch)* Birge-Sponer extrapolation
Birkeland-Eyde-Verfahren *n* Birkeland-Eyde process *(for manufacturing nitric acid)*
Birkencampher *m* birch (betula) camphor, betulinol *(a triterpenoid alcohol)*
Birkenöl *n* [sweet-]birch oil
Birkenrindenöl *n* birch bark oil
Birkenteer *m* birch tar
Birkenteeröl *n* birch tar oil
Birnenäther *m* pear essence *(alcoholic solution of amyl acetate)*
Birnenöl *n* pear (banana) oil *(amyl acetate)*
Bisabolen *n* bisabolene *(a monocyclic sesquiterpene)*
bis-axial bis-axial
Bischler-Napieralski-Reaktion *f* Bischler-Napieralski reaction *(for synthesizing isoquinoline)*
Bis-β-chloräthyläther *m s.* 2,2'-Dichlordiethylether
Bis-harnstoff *m s.* Biharnstoff
Biskuitbrand *m (ceram)* biscuit firing, biscuitting
Biskuitbrandware *f s.* Biskuitware
Biskuitporzellan *n (ceram)* biscuit [porcelain], bisque
Biskuitware *f (ceram)* biscuit, bisque, bisquitted (biscuit-fired) ware
Bismarckbraun *n* Bismarck (vesuvine) brown, vesuvin
Bismut *n* Bi bismuth
Bismutan *n* Bi_nH_{n+2} bismutane, bismuth hydride, *(specif)* BiH_3 bismuthane, bismuthine, bismuth hydride
Bismutat *n* bismuthate
Bismut(III)-chlorid *n* bismuth(III) chloride, bismuth trichloride
Bismutdioxid *n* bismuth dioxide
Bismuterz *n* bismuth ore
bismuthaltig bismuth-containing, *(esp relating to ores:)* bismuthiferous, bismuth-bearing
Bismuthydrid *n s.* Bismutan
Bismut(III)-hydroxid *n* bismuth(III) hydroxide, bismuth trihydroxide

Bismutin *n* 1. BiR_3 bismuthine *(any of several organic compounds)*; 2. BiH_3 bismuthane, bismuthine, bismuth hydride
Bismut(III)-iodat *n* bismuth(III) iodate
Bismut(III)-iodid *n* bismuth(III) iodide, bismuth triiodide
Bismutit *m (min)* bismutite *(bismuth carbonate oxide)*
Bismutmonosulfid *n s.* Bismut(II)-sulfid
Bismut(III)-oxid *n* bismuth(III) oxide, bismuth trioxide
Bismut(V)-oxid *n* bismuth(V) oxide, bismuth pentaoxide
Bismutoxidcarbonat *n* bismuth carbonate oxide
Bismutoxidchlorid *n* bismuth chloride oxide
Bismutoxidiodid *n* bismuth iodide oxide
Bismutpentoxid *n s.* Bismut(V)-oxid
Bismutsäure *f* bismuthic acid
Bismut(III)-sulfat *n* bismuth(III) sulphate
Bismut(II)-sulfid bismuth(II) sulphide, bismuth monosulphide
Bismut(III)-sulfid bismuth(III) sulphide, bismuth trisulphide
Bismuttri... *s.* Bismut(III)-...
Bismutwasserstoff *m s.* Bismutan
Bisphenol *n* bisphenol, methylenediphenol
bistabil bistable *(reacting system)*
Bistabilität *f* bistability *(of a reacting system)*
Bister *m(n)* manganese brown
Bisulfit *n s.* Hydrogensulfit
Bisulfit-Additionsverbindung *f*, **Bisulfitaddukt** *n* bisulphite addition compound
Bisulfitzellstoff *m (pap)* sulphite pulp
bitter bitter • **~ machen** to embitter, to imbitter *(e.g. beer)*
Bittererde *f s.* Magnesiumoxid
Bitterkleesalz *n s.* Kleesalz
Bittermandelessenz *f s.* Bittermandelöl/künstliches
Bittermandelöl *n* bitter almond oil, amygdala amara oil
~/künstliches 1. artificial (synthetic) essential oil of almonds *(chemically benzaldehyde)*; 2. *s.* ~/unechtes
~/unechtes *(cosmet)* mirbane (myrbane) oil, essence of mirbane *(chemically nitrobenzene)*
Bittermandelölcampher *m* bitter almond oil camphor, benzoin, α-hydroxybenzyl phenyl ketone
Bittermandelölgrün *n* malachite green, basic green 4, green verditer *(a triphenylmethane dye)*
Bittersalz *n* bitter salt, Epsom salt[s], *(min)* epsomite *(magnesium sulphate 7-water)*
Bittersalzquelle *f (pharm)* bitter spring
Bittersäure *f* bitter acid
Bitterspat *m (min)* magnesite, bitter spar *(magnesium carbonate)*
Bitterstoff *m* bitter principle (substance), *(ferm also)* bittern
~/nichtglykosidischer amaroid
Bitterstoffwert *m (ferm)* bitterness value *(of hops)*
Bitterwasser *n* bitter water
Bitterwert *m s.* Bitterstoffwert
Bitterwurzel *f* gentian [root]
Bitumen *n* bitumen, *(specif)* asphaltic bitumen
~/geblasenes *s.* Blasbitumen
Bitumenanstrich *m* bituminous coating
Bitumenanstrichstoff *m* bituminous paint (coating)
Bitumendachpappe *f* asphaltic felt
Bitumenemulsion *f* bituminous emulsion, emulsified bitumen
Bitumenfarbe *f s.* Bitumenanstrichstoff
bitumenhaltig bituminous
Bitumenlack *m* bituminous varnish
Bitumenpapier *n* asphalt (tar, pitch) paper, tarred [brown] paper
Bitumenpappe *f* bitumen board
Bitumenpreßmasse *f* bituminous plastic, bituminous moulding composition
Bitumensand *m* bituminous sand
Bitumenschiefer *m* bituminous (oil) shale
Bitumenschutzschicht *f* bituminous coating
bituminös, bitumisch bituminous
Biuret *n* biuret, ureidoformamide
Biuretprobe *f* biuret test *(for proteins)*
Biuret-Reagens *n* biuret reagent *(alkaline copper sulphate solution)*
Biuretreaktion *f* biuret reaction *(for determining proteins)*
bivalent bivalent, divalent
Bivalenz *f* bivalence, divalence
bivariant bivariant, divariant
Bivinyl *n* *buta-1,3-diene, *(deprecated:)* bivinyl
Bixin *n (food)* bixin *(dye from Bixa orellana L.)*
bizyklisch *s.* bicyclisch
Bizyklus *m s.* Bicyclus
B-Kation *n* class (b) metal ion
Bladder *m (rubber)* bladder
Blähen *n* intumescence, swelling *(of coal)*
Blähgrad *m s.* Blähungsgrad
Blähgraphit *m* exfoliated graphite
Blähindex *m s.* Blähungsgrad
Blähmittel *n* expanding agent, *(rubber, plast also)* blowing agent
Blähprobe *f (coal)* swelling test
Blähschiefer *m* expanded shale
Blähschlamm *m* bulking sludge
Blähschlammbildung *f* sludge bulking
Blähton *m* expanded (foamed) clay, lightweight expanded clay [aggregate], foamclay
Blähungsgrad *m (coal)* swelling index (number)
~/freier free swelling index
~ ohne Belastung der Kohle *s.* ~/freier
Blähvermögen *n (coal)* swelling power
Blähzahl *f s.* Blähungsgrad
Blanc fixe *n* blanc fixe, permanent white *(precipitated barium sulphate)*
Blanchierapparat *m (food)* blancher
blanchieren *(food)* to blanch
Blankfilter *n* polishing (clarifying) filter

Blankfiltration *f* polishing [filtration], clarification
blankfiltrieren to polish
Blankfix *n s.* Blanc fixe
blankglühen to bright-anneal
Blankglühen *n* bright anneal[ing]
Blankglühofen *m* bright-annealing furnace
Blankkochen *n (sugar)* blank boiling
blankstoßen *(tann)* to glaze
Blasanlage *f (plast)* blow moulder, blow-moulding machine
Blasbitumen *n* blown bitumen, [air-]blown asphalt, mineral rubber
Blas-Blas-Verfahren *n (glass)* blow-and-blow process
Bläschen *n* bubble
Bläschenbeton *m* air-entrained (air-entraining) concrete
Bläschenbildung *f* bubbling
Blasdruck *m* blowing pressure
Blase *f* 1. bubble; blister *(a defect in material), (met also)* blow-hole, gas cavity, *(plast also)* void, *(glass also)* cat eye; *(pap)* bell; vesication, blister *(on the skin)*; 2. distillation boiler, still pot, *(with rectifying apparatus:)* reboiler • **Blasen bilden** to bubble *(of gas or water)*; to blister *(of metal or paint)*; to vesicate, to blister *(of the skin)* • **in Blasen aufsteigen** to bubble [up] • **in Blasen aufsteigen lassen** to bubble
~/äußere *(met)* subcutaneous blow-hole
~/offene *(plast)* open bubble *(a moulding defect)*
Blasebalg *m* bellows
Blasegas *n* blow (blast) gas *(in manufacturing producer gas)*
blasen to blow
~/mit Druckluft to air-blow
Blasen *n* blow[ing]
~ mit Bodenwind bottom blowing
~ mit Luft air blowing
~/seitliches *(met)* side blowing
Blasenbildung *f* 1. bubbling, formation of bubbles; *(tech)* blistering, blister formation; 2. *(med)* vesication, blistering • **zur ~ reizen** *(med)* to vesicate, to blister
Blasenbildungsgrad *m (techn)* degree of blistering
Blasendestillationsanlage *f***/kontinuierliche** continuous shell still
Blasendestillierapparat *m* pot still
Blasendruckmethode *f (phys ch)* maximum bubble pressure method
Blasenflüssigkeit *f (destil)* reboiler liquid
blasenfrei bubble-free *(liquid)*; *(plast)* free from voids; *(met)* free from blow-holes
Blasengalle *f (med)* [gall]bladder bile
Blasengröße *f* bubble size
Blasenkammer *f (nucl)* bubble chamber
Blasenkupfer *n* blister copper
Blasenlassen *n (glass)* blocking
Blasenmethode *f s.* Blasendruckmethode
Blasenoberfläche *f* bubble surface
Blasenrückstand *m* still residue
Blasensäule *f* bubble column
Blasensäulenfermenter *m (biot)* bubble column (tower) fermenter
Blasensäulenreaktor *m* bubble column
Blasenverdampfung *f* nucleate boiling
Blasenzähler *m* bubble counter
Blasenziehen *n* blistering, blister formation
blasenziehend *(med)* vesicant, vesicatory, blistering
Blaseperiode *f* blow period
Blasfolie *f (plast)* blown film
Blasform *f (met)* [air-blast] tuyère, twyer
Blasformebene *f (met)* tuyère level
Blasformen *n (plast)* blow moulding
~ von Folienhalbzeug sheet blow moulding
Blasformteil *n (plast)* blow moulding
Blashochofen *m (met)* blast furnace
Blaskopf *m* blow head
Blaslanze *f (met)* [oxygen] lance
Blasluft *f* blow air; *(glass)* puff
Blasmaschine *f* blow moulder, blow-moulding machine
Blasöl *n* blown oil
Blasrohr *n* blow-pipe
Blasstahl *m* basic oxygen [furnace] steel
Blasstahlkonverter *m* [top-blown] basic oxygen converter, [top-blown] basic oxygen furnace
Blasstahlverfahren *n* basic oxygen [converter] process, basic oxygen furnace (steel) process, top-blown oxygen converter process, oxygen process of steelmaking, oxygen-lance process
Blasstahlwerk *n* [basic-]oxygen steel plant
Blastank *m (pap)* blow (wash, receiving) tank, blow pit (vat)
Blasverfahren *n* blowing process, *(met also)* pneumatic process
Blaswerkzeug *n (plast)* blow[ing] mould
Blatt *n* 1. *(tech)* leaf *(of a filter or of metal)*; paddle, blade, shovel *(as of an agitator)*; 2. *(pap)* sheet; *(cryst)* folium; *(ceram)* bat *(for producing flat ware)*
Blattapplikation *f (agric)* foliage application *(as of pesticides)*
blattbildend *(pap)* sheet-forming
Blattbildung *f (pap)* sheet formation
Blättchen *n (cryst)* leaflet
blättchenförmig foliate, leaf-like
Blattdüngung *f (agric)* leaf dressing
Blatter *f (glass)* blister *(a defect)*
Blätter *npl* shavings *(in soap manufacture)*
Blättererz *n (min)* nagyagite
Blättergelatine *f s.* Blattgelatine
blätterig *s.* blättrig
Blätterkohle *f* cannel (candle, jet) coal
Blätterserpentin *m (min)* antigorite *(a variety of serpentine)*
Blättertellur *n s.* Blättererz
Blattfarbstoff *m* leaf pigment

Blattfilter *n* leaf filter
Blattformermaschine *f (ceram)* bat-making (batting-out) machine
blattförmig foliate, leaf-like
Blattgelatine *f* sheet gelatin
Blattgold *n* gold leaf
Blattgrün *n* leaf green, chlorophyll
Blattlänge *f (pap)* length of the sheet
Blattlausbekämpfungsmittel *n* aphicide
blättrig lamellar, foliated; *(min)* spathic, spathose
Blattrührer *m* vane stirrer, paddle (leaf) agitator
Blattscheibe *f s.* Blattformermaschine
Blattsilicat *n (min)* phyllosilicate
Blattverbrennungen *fpl (agric)* foliage burn *(as by pesticides)*
Blattzinn *n* tin foil
Blau *n* blue *(sensation or substance)*
~/Berliner *(ch)* Prussian (Berlin) blue, *(commercially)* iron (cyanide) blue *(a complex iron cyanide)*
~/Braunschweiger *s.* ~/Bremer
~/Bremer Bremen blue, blue verditer, copper blue *(a basic copper carbonate)*
~/Meldolas Meldola's blue *(an oxazine dye)*
~/Neuwieder *s.* ~/Bremer
~/Pariser *s.* ~/Berliner
~/Preußisch *s.* ~/Berliner
~/Thénards Thénard blue, cobalt blue (ultramarine), king's blue *(cobalt aluminate)*
~/Turnbulls *s.* ~/Berliner
Blaualgen *fpl* blue-green algae
Blauanlaufen *n* blueing *(of tools)*; blooming *(of oil varnishes)*
Blaudruck *m* 1. blue-printing *(in a narrower sense, using ferroprussiates)*; 2. blueprint
Blaudruckverfahren *n* ferroprussiate process
blauempfindlich *s.* blausensibilisiert
bläuen to blue
Blaufarbenglas *n* smalt, powder blue *(cobalt(II) potassium silicate)*
Blaugas *n s.* Kokswassergas
Blau-Gas *n* Blau gas *(an oil gas)*
Blauholz *n* Campeachy (Campechy) wood, logwood *(from Haematoxylum campechianum L.)*
Blaumasse *f (text)* cuprammonium cellulose
Blaupackpapier *n* mill wrapper (wrapping)
Blaupause *f* blueprint, cyanotype • **eine ~ herstellen** to blueprint
Blaupauspapier *n* blue-print paper, cyano paper
Blausäure *f* hydrogen cyanide, hydrocyanic acid
Blausäureglykosid *n* cyanogenetic (cyanophoric) glycoside
Blausäureoxid *n* formonitrile oxide, fulminic acid
Blauschönung *f (ferm)* blue fining
blausensibilisiert blue-sensitive, blue-sensitized
Blaustich *m (text)* blue cast
blaustichig bluish
Blauton *m* blue shade
Bläuung *f* blueing
Bläuungsmittel *n* blueing [agent] *(for improving the degree of whiteness)*
Blauverschiebung *f* blue-shift, hypsochromic effect
Blauwassergas *n s.* Kokswassergas
Blaw-Knox-Mühle *f* Blaw-Knox mill *(a jet mill)*
Blaze-Gitter *n (spectr)* blazed grating
Blaze-Wellenlänge *f (spectr)* blaze wavelength
Blaze-Winkel *m (spectr)* blaze angle
Blech *n (met)* sheet, plate
~/gelochtes perforated plate
Blei *n* Pb lead • **mit ~ auskleiden** to lead-line, to lead-clad • **mit ~ überziehen** to lead-coat
~/raffiniertes refined lead
Bleiabfälle *mpl* scrap lead
Blei(II)-acetat *n* lead(II) acetate, lead diacetate
Blei(IV)-acetat *n* lead(IV) acetate, lead tetraacetate
Bleiacetatpapier *n* lead[-acetate] paper
Bleiakkumulator *m* lead (lead-acid) accumulator (battery), lead storage battery
Bleialkalisilicatglas *n* lead-alkali silicate glass
Bleialkyle *npl*/**gemischte** mixed lead alkyls, MLA *(an antiknock agent)*
Bleiantimonat *n* lead antimonate
Blei(II)-arsenat(V) *n* lead(II) tetraoxoarsenate(V)
bleiausgekleidet lead-lined
Bleiauskleidung *f* lead lining, internal lead cladding
Bleiazid *n* lead azide, lead azoimide
Bleibaum *m (el ch)* lead tree • **einen ~ bilden** to tree
Bleibenzin *n* leaded (ethyl) gasoline
Bleibenzoat *n* lead benzoate
Bleiblock *m* lead block
~ nach Trauzl Trauzl lead block *(for testing explosives)*
Bleiblockausbauchung *f* lead-block expansion *(in testing explosives)*
Bleiblockprobe *f* lead-block expansion test *(for evaluating explosives)*
~ nach Trauzl Trauzl [lead-block] test
Bleibromat *n* lead bromate
Blei(II)-bromid *n* lead(II) bromide, lead dibromide
Bleibronze *f* leaded bronze
Bleicaprinat *n* *lead decanoate, *(deprecated:)* lead caprate
Bleicapronat *n* *lead hexanoate, *(deprecated:)* lead caproate
Bleicaprylat *n* *lead octanoate, *(deprecated:)* lead caprylate
Bleicarbonat *n* lead carbonate
Bleichanlage *f* bleach[ing] plant, bleachery
Bleichapparat *m* bleaching apparatus; bleacher
Bleichbad *n s.* Bleichflotte
bleichbar bleachable
Bleichbarkeit *f* bleachability
Bleichbedarf *m s.* Bleichmittelbedarf
Bleichbottich *m* bleaching vat (chest)
Bleichchlor *n*/**aktives (wirksames)** *(pap)* available chlorine
Bleichdauer *f* bleaching period
Bleiche *f* bleach[ing]
~/kalte *(pap)* cold bleach[ing]

~/natürliche *(text)* natural bleach[ing], grass bleach[ing], grassing
~/optische optical bleach[ing]
~/warme *(pap)* warm bleach[ing]
Bleichecht fast to bleach[ing], resistant to bleaching
Bleichechtheit *f* fastness to bleach[ing], resistance to bleaching, bleach-fastness
Bleicheffekt *m* bleaching efficiency
bleichen 1. *(of human agent:)* to bleach, to whiten, to brighten, to decolorize; 2. *(of substances:)* to bleach, to fade
~ auf eine höhere Weiße *(pap)* to whiten, to brighten
~/elektrolytisch *(pap)* to bleach electrolytically
~/mit Schwefeldioxid *(text)* to stove
~/unvollständig *(pap)* to underbleach
Bleichen *n* bleach[ing]
Bleichende *n* end of the bleaching period
Bleicher *m* 1. *s.* Bleichapparat; 2. bleacher *(profession)*
Bleicherde *f* 1. bleaching (decolorizing) earth (clay), active earth; 2. *s.* Bleicherdeboden
~/aktivierte (künstlich aktive) *(petrol)* activated clay
~/naturaktive (natürliche) *(petrol)* naturally occurring clay, natural (non-activated) clay, fuller's earth
~/säureaktivierte *(petrol)* acid clay
Bleicherdebehandlung *f* clay treating (treatment) *(of oils)*
~ nach dem Kontaktverfahren *(petrol)* clay contacting
Bleicherdeboden *m* podzol[ic] soil, podzol
Bleicherdekontakt *m* clay catalyst (contact)
Bleicherderaffination *f s.* Bleicherdebehandlung
Bleicherei[anlage] *f s.* Bleichanlage
bleichfähig *s.* bleichbar
Bleichflotte *f*, **Bleichflüssigkeit** *f (text, pap)* bleaching liquor (lye, solution)
Bleichgrad *m* degree of bleaching
Bleichhilfsmittel *n* bleaching assistant
Bleichholländer *m (pap)* [bleaching] potcher, bleaching (potching, poaching) engine, poacher
Bleichkalk *m* chlorinated lime, chloride of lime, bleaching powder
Bleichkammer *f* bleaching chamber
Bleichkessel *m* bleaching vat (chest)
Bleichkufe *f* bleaching vat (chest)
Bleichlauge *f* bleaching liquor (solution)
~/Javellesche Javel[le] water *(aqueous solution of potassium hypochlorite)*
Bleichlorat *n* lead chlorate
Blei(II)-chlorid *n* lead(II) chloride, lead dichloride
Blei(IV)-chlorid *n* lead(IV) chloride, lead tetrachloride
Bleichlorit *n* lead chlorite
Bleichlösung *f s.* Bleichlauge
Bleichmittel *n* bleaching agent (material), bleach; decolorizing agent, decolorizer, decolorant
~/optisches optical bleaching (brightening) agent, optical (fluorescent) brightener (bleach)
~/oxidierend wirkendes oxidizing bleach (bleaching agent)
~/reduzierend wirkendes reducing bleach (bleaching agent)
Bleichmittelaufwand *m s.* Bleichmittelbedarf
Bleichmittelbedarf *m* bleach requirements (demand)
Bleichmittelverbrauch *m* bleach consumption
Bleichpulver *n s.* Bleichkalk
Blei(II)-chromat *n* lead(II) chromate
Bleichsand *m* bleached sand
Bleichschlamm *m (pap)* bleach sludge
Bleichsoda *f* bleaching soda *(a mixture of sodium carbonate and sodium or potassium silicate)*
Bleichstiefel *m (text)* J box
Bleichstufe *f* bleaching stage
Bleichton *m* bleaching clay
Bleichtrommel *f (pap)* tumbler
Bleichturm *m (pap)* bleaching tower, bleacher
Bleichverfahren *n* bleaching process; *(phot)* bleach-out process
Bleichverhältnis *n (pap)* bleach ratio
Bleichwirkung *f* bleaching action; bleaching effect
Bleicyanat *n* lead cyanate
Bleicyanid *n* lead cyanide
Bleidi... *s. a.* Blei(II)-...
Bleidiarsenat(V) *n* lead diarsenate(V)
Bleidichtung *f* lead packing, lead gasket *(for parts without relative motion)*
Bleidioxid *n s.* Blei(IV)-oxid
Blei(II)-dioxoarsenat(III) *n* lead dioxoarsenate(III)
Bleidiphosphat *n* lead diphosphate, lead pyrophosphate
Bleidithionat *n* lead dithionate
Bleidraht *m* lead wire
Bleielektrode *f* lead electrode
Bleiempfindlichkeit *f* lead susceptibility *(of fuels)*
bleien to lead *(fuels)*
Bleiessig *m*, **Bleiextrakt** *m* vinegar of lead, Goulard's extract *(aqueous solution of basic lead acetates)*
Bleifarbe *f* lead paint
Bleiferrat(III) *n* lead ferrite(III)
Blei(II)-fluorid *n* lead(II) fluoride, lead difluoride
Blei(II)-formiat *n* lead(II) formate
bleifrei lead-free, leadless
Bleifritte *f (ceram)* lead frit
Bleigehalt *m* lead content • **mit hohem ~** rich in lead; high-leaded *(fuel)*
Bleiglanz *m (min)* lead glance, galena, galenite *(lead(II) sulphide)*
Bleiglas *n* lead glass
bleiglasiert *(ceram)* lead-glazed
Bleiglasur *f (ceram)* lead glaze
Bleiglätte *f* litharge, yellow lead oxide *(lead(II) oxide)*
bleihaltig lead-containing, *(esp ores:)* plumbiferous
Blei(II)-hexacyanoferrat(II) *n* lead(II) hexacyanoferrate(II)

Blei(II)-hexacyanoferrat(III) *n* lead(II) hexacyanoferrate(III)
Blei(II)-hexafluorosilicat *n* lead(II) hexafluorosilicate, lead fluorosilicate
Blei(II)-hydrogenarsenat(V) *n* lead(II) hydrogenarsenate(V)
Bleihydroxid *n* lead hydroxide
Bleiiodat *n* lead iodate
Blei(II)-iodid *n* lead(II) iodide, lead diiodide
Bleikammer *f* lead chamber
Bleikammerkristalle *mpl* chamber crystals *(nitrosylsulphuric acid)*
Bleikammerverfahren *n* [lead-]chamber process *(for producing sulphuric acid)*
Bleikontamination *f (tox)* lead contamination
Bleikrankheit *f s.* Bleivergiftung
Bleikristallglas *n* lead crystal glass
Bleilässigkeit *f (ceram)* lead solubility
Bleilegierung *f* lead alloy
Bleilöslichkeit *f (ceram)* lead solubility
Bleimantelverfahren *n (rubber)* lead press technique
Bleimantelvulkanisation *f* lead press cure
Bleimennige *f* red lead [oxide], minium *(lead(II) tetraoxoplumbate(IV))*
Bleimetaarsenat(III) *n* lead dioxoarsenate(III), *(deprecated:)* lead metaarsenite
Bleimetaarsenat(V) *n* lead trioxoarsenate(V), *(deprecated:)* lead metaarsenate
Bleimetaborat *n* lead metaborate
Bleimetaphosphat *n* lead metaphosphate
Bleimetasilicat *n* lead metasilicate
Bleimetatitanat *n* lead metatitanate
Bleimetavanadat(V) *n* lead metavanadate
Bleimolybdat(VI) *n* lead molybdate(VI)
Bleimonoxid *n s.* Blei(II)-oxid
Blei(II)-nitrat *n* lead(II) nitrate
Blei(II)-nitrit *n* lead(II) nitrite
Bleiofen *m* lead blast furnace
Blei(II)-orthoarsenat(V) *n* lead(II) tetraoxoarsenate(V), lead(II) arsenate, *(deprecated:)* lead(II) orthoarsenate
Blei(II)-orthophosphat *n* lead(II) orthophosphate, lead(II) phosphate
Blei(II)-oxalat *n* lead(II) oxalate
Bleioxid *n***/rotes** *s.* Bleimennige
Blei(II)-oxid *n* lead(II) oxide, lead monooxide
Blei(VI)-oxid *n* lead(IV) oxide, lead dioxide
Blei(II,IV)-oxid *n* 1. trilead tetraoxide, lead(II) tetraoxoplumbate(IV); 2. dilead trioxide, lead(II) trioxoplumbate(IV)
Blei(II)-oxidacetat *n* lead(II) acetate oxide
Bleioxidrot *n s.* Bleimennige
Bleipackung *f* lead packing
Bleipapier *n* lead[-acetate] paper
Blei(II)-perchlorat *n* lead(II) perchlorate
Blei(II)-peroxodisulfat *n* lead(II) peroxodisulphate
Bleipfanne *f* lead pan
Blei(II)-phosphat *n* lead(II) phosphate; *(specif) s.* Blei(II)-orthophosphat
Bleiphosphit *n* lead phosphonate, lead phosphite
Bleipikrat *n* lead picrate
Bleiplatte *f* lead plate
Bleipyro... *s.* Bleidi...
Bleiraffination *f* lead refining
Bleiregulus *m (anal)* lead regulus
Blei(II)-rhodanid *n s.* Blei(II)-thiocyanat
Bleirohr *n* lead pipe
Bleirohrleitung *f* lead pipe line
Bleirohrschlange *f* lead coil
Bleisammler *m s.* Bleiakkumulator
Bleischachtofen *m* lead blast furnace
Bleischlamm *m* lead sludge
Bleischmelzofen *m* lead blast furnace
Bleischutzschicht *f* lead coating
Bleiseife *f* lead soap
Blei(II)-selenat *n* lead(II) selenate
Blei(II)-selenid *n* lead(II) selenide
Bleisuboxid *n* lead suboxide *(a mixture of lead and lead(II) oxide)*
Blei(II)-sulfat *n* lead(II) sulphate
Blei(II)-sulfid *n* lead(II) sulphide
Bleisulfidbehandlung *f s.* Bleisulfidsüßen
Bleisulfidsüßen *n (petrol)* lead-sulphide sweetening (treating), Bender sweetening
Bleisulfidverfahren *n (petrol)* Bender [lead-sulphide] process
Blei(II)-sulfit *n* lead(II) sulphite
Blei(II)-tellurid *n* lead(II) telluride
Bleitetraacetat *n s.* Blei(IV)-acetat
Bleitetraäthyl *n s.* Tetraethylblei
Bleitetrachlorid *n s.* Blei(IV)-chlorid
Bleitetramethyl *n s.* Tetramethylblei
Blei(II)-thiocyanat *n* lead(II) thiocyanate
Bleithiosulfat *n* lead thiosulphate
Bleiüberzug *m s.* Bleischutzschicht
Bleiventilator *m* lead fan
Bleivergiftung *f* lead poisoning, saturnism, plumbism
Bleivitriol *n s.* Blei(II)-sulfat
Bleiwasserstoff *m* lead hydride, plumbane
Bleiweiß *n* white lead, ceruse *(lead carbonate hydroxide)*
~/feines flake white
Blei(II)-wolframat *n* lead(II) wolframate, lead(II) tungstate
Blei-Zinn-Antimon-Lagermetall *n* babbit[t] metal
Blei-Zinn-Lot *n* lead-tin solder
Bleizucker *m* sugar of lead, salt of Saturn *(lead(II) acetate)*
Bleizylinderprobe *f s.* Bleiblockprobe
Blende *f* 1. shield, screen; orifice *(of a flowmeter)*; *(spectr)* attenuator; diaphragm, lens stop *(of a camera)*; 2. *(min)* blende *(any of several sulphidic minerals)*; 3. *s.* Zinkblende
blenden *(petrol)* to blend
Blendendurchflußmesser *m* orifice [flow]meter
Blenden[einlauf]kante *f* orifice edge *(of a flowmeter)*

Blendenmischer *m* orifice mixer
Blendenströmungsmesser *m* orifice [flow]meter
Bleu *n* **de Lyon** Lyons blue, bleu de Lyon *(chlorine salt of triphenylrosaniline)*
blind dull, tarnished *(surface)* • ~ **werden** to tarnish
Blindanalyse *f* blank analysis
Blindbestimmung *f* blank determination
Blindboden *m* false bottom
Blindflansch *m* blind flange, blank
Blindlösung *f* blank solution
Blindprobe *f s.* Blindversuch
Blindrohr *n* dummy tube
Blindscheibe *f* blind
Blindtitration *f* blank titration
Blindversuch *m* blank [test], negative control • **einen ~ anstellen (durchführen)** to run a blank, to perform a blank test
~/doppelter *(pharm)* double blank test
Blindwerden *n* tarnish[ing] *(of surfaces)*
Blindwert *m* blank reading (value, measure); *(tox)* predosage level
Blindwertprobe *f s.* Blindbestimmung
Blindwertstreuung *f* blank scatter, scatter of blank measures
Blisterkupfer *n* blister copper
Blitzdämpfen *n (text)* flash ageing
Blitzdämpfer *m (text)* flash ager
Blitzlampe *f* flash lamp
Blitzlicht *n* flashlight
Blitzlichtphotolyse *f* flash photolysis
Blitzlichtphotolyseapparatur *f* flash photolysis apparatus
Blitzlichtpulver *n* flashlight powder
Blitzlichtspektroskopie *f* flash photolysis
Blitzpasteurisierapparat *m (food)* flash pasteurizer
Blitzpulver *n* lycopodium powder *(from club mosses)*
Blitzröstofen *m (met)* flash roaster (burner)
~ nach Nichols-Freeman Nichols-Freeman flash roaster
Blitzröstung *f (met)* flash (shower) roasting
Blitzverdampfung *f* instantaneous vaporization
Bloch-Wand *f (cryst)* Bloch wall, domain wall
Block *m* 1. block *(e.g. a piece of material)*; *(met)* ingot *(of iron)*; pig *(of non-ferrous metal)*; 2. block *(comprising equal or similar elements)*; 3. *(bioch)* block *(site, state, or process)*
~/genetischer *(bioch)* genetic block
Blockbild *n* block diagram
Blockcopolymer[e] *n*, **Blockcopolymerisat** *n* block [co]polymer
Blockcopolymerisation *f* block [co]polymerization
Blockeis *n* can (cake) ice
Blocken *n (plast)* blocking *(undesired adhesion between two sheets)*
Blocker *m (bioch)* blocking agent
Blockform *f* ingot mould
Blockgießen *n*, **Blockguß** *m* ingot casting
blockieren to block, to mask *(reactive groups or sites)*; to block *(reactions)*
Blockierung *f* blocking, masking *(of reactive groups or sites)*; blocking *(of reactions)*
blockig blocky
Blockkokille *f* ingot mould
Blocklehm *m* boulder clay
Blockmischpolymerisat *n s.* Blockcopolymer
Blockmutante *f (biot)* blocked mutant
Blockpolymer[e] *n s.* Blockcopolymer
Blockpolymerisation *f s.* 1. Blockcopolymerisation; 2. Substanzpolymerisation
Blockpresse *f* block press
Blockschälchen *n (lab)* clearing (staining) well *(as for microscopy)*
Blockschaltbild *n* block diagram
Blockung *f s.* Blockierung
Blockzahl *f* run number *(of polymers)*
Blockzelle *f (spectr)* cavity cell
Blöße *f (tann)* pelt
Blubber *m (food)* whale blubber
Blume *f* 1. bouquet, aroma, flavour *(as of wine)*; head *(on beer)*; 2. *(tann)* exudation, bloom
Blumendünger *m* flower fertilizer
Blumenkohlende *n*, **Blumenkohlkopf** *m* cauliflower end *(of a piece of oven coke)*
Blumenkohlstruktur *f* cauliflower appearance *(of a coke button)*
Blumenseidenpapier *n* flower tissue
Blutalbumin *n s.* Blutserumalbumin
Blutalbuminleim *m* blood glue (adhesive)
blutdrucksenkend hypotensive, antihypertensive
blutdrucksteigernd raising blood pressure, pressor
Blutduftstoff *m* blood scent
bluten *(dye, coat, tann)* to bleed [off, through]
Blütenöl *n (cosmet)* flower oil
~/absolutes absolute flower oil, flower absolute
~/konkretes floral concrete
Blutfarbstoff *m* blood pigment
Blutfleck *m* blood stain
blutgefäßerweiternd vasodilating
blutgefäßverenge[r]nd vasoconstrictive
Blutgerinnung *f* blood coagulation (clotting)
blutgerinnungshemmend inhibiting blood coagulation
Blutgift *n* blood poison, *(as war gas also)* systemic poison
Blutholz *n s.* Blauholz
Blutkohle *f* blood char[coal]
Blutlack *m* button lac
Blutlaugensalz *n***/gelbes** yellow prussiate of potash, yellow potassium prussiate, potassium hexacyanoferrate(II)
~/rotes red prussiate of potash, red potassium prussiate, potassium hexacyanoferrate(III)
Blutmehl *n* blood meal, dried blood *(a fertilzer)*
Blutplasma *n* blood plasma
Blutplasmaersatz *m* blood plasma extender
Blutprobe *f (anal)* blood sample

Blutprotein *n* blood protein
Blutserum *n* blood serum
Blutserumalbumin *n* blood [serum] albumin, serum albumin, seralbumin
Blutstein *m (min)* blood stone, red iron ore, reddle *(iron(III) oxide)*
blutstillend styptic
Blutstillstift *m* styptic pencil
Blutstillungsmittel *n* styptic
Blutwasseralbumin *n s.* Blutserumalbumin
Blutzucker *m* blood sugar (glucose)
B-Metallion *n* class (b) metal ion
Bobine *f (text)* bobbin
Bock *m (tann)* horse
Boden *m* 1. *(tech)* bottom, base *(as of a vessel)*; *(distil)* plate, tray; deck *(as of flat screens)*; 2. soil
• **mit halbkugeligem (rundem) ~** round-bottomed
~/idealer *s.* ~/theoretischer
~/neutraler *(agric)* sweet soil
~/praktischer *(distil)* actual (practice) plate
~/saurer acidic soil
~/theoretischer *(distil)* theoretical (perfect) plate
~/versetzter *(glass)* offset punt (base) *(a defect)*
~ zur Neuverteilung redistributor *(in packed columns)*
Bodenabblaß *m* bottom discharge
Bodenaggregat *n* soil aggregate
Bodenaggregation *f* soil aggregation
Bodenanalyse *f* soil analysis
Bodenatmung *f* soil respiration
Bodenazidität *f* soil acidity
Bodenbegasung *f* soil fumigation
Bodenbegasungsmittel *n* soil fumigant
Bodenbegiftung *f* soil poisoning
Bodenbegiftungsmittel *n* soil poison
Bodenbildung *f (soil)* pedogenesis
Bodenblasen *n (met)* bottom blowing
Bodenbohrer *m* soil-sample auger
Bodenchemie *f* soil chemistry
Bodendesinfektion *f* soil sterilization, *(specif)* soil fumigation
Bodendesinfektionsmittel *n* soil sterilant, *(specif)* soil fumigant
Bodendispergierung *f (agric)* autodisintegration *(with sodium ions in excess)*
bodeneigen *(geol)* autochthonous
Bodenentleerung *f* bottom discharge
Bodenentseuchung *f s.* Bodendesinfektion
Bodenerhärtungsmittel *n s.* Bodenstabilisator
Bodenfeuchte *f*, **Bodenfeuchtigkeit** *f* soil moisture
Bodenfliese *f* floor tile
Bodenflüssigkeit *f s.* Bodenwasser
Bodenfraktion *f (distil)* bottom fraction
bodenfremd *(geol)* allochthonous
Bodenfruchtbarkeit *f* soil fertility
Bodenfungizid *n* soil fungicide
Bodengare *f* tilth
Bodengefüge *n* soil structure
Bodenhöhe *f (anal, distil)* plate height
Bodenhorizont *m* soil horizon
Bodeninversion *f* ground level inversion
Bodenkolloid *n* soil colloid
Bodenkolonne *f (distil)* plate (tray) column
Bodenkomplex *m***/adsorbierender** *(soil)* base-exchange complex
Bodenkonus *m* conical (pyramidal) base *(of a flash roaster)*
Bodenkörper *m* 1. excess solute, solid (undissolved) solute, excess (undissolved) solid *(in equilibrium with its solution)*; 2. *s.* Bodenprodukt
Bodenkörpermenge *f* amount (quantity) of excess solute
Bodenkörperregel *f (coll)* disperse-phase rule
Bodenkorrosion *f* soil corrosion
Bodenkunde *f* soil science, pedology
Bodenkundler *m* soil scientist, pedologist
bodenkundlich pedologic[al]
Bodenlanze *f* soil injector
Bodenlösung *f* soil solution
Bodenluft *f* soil air
Bodenmelioration *f s.* Bodenverbesserung
Bodenmessung *f* ground-based measurement
Bodenmikrobiologie *f* soil microbiology
Bodenmikroorganismen *mpl* soil microorganisms
Bodenmüdigkeit *f* soil exhaustion (sickness)
Bodennähe *f* ground level *(as of air pollutants)*
Bodennährstoff *m* soil nutrient
Bodenpassage *f (hyd)* ground passage
Boden-pH-Wert *m* soil pH
Bodenplatte *f* 1. bottom plate; 2. *s.* Bodenfliese
Bodenprobe *f* sample of soil
Bodenprodukt *n (distil)* bottom product, bottoms
Bodenprofil *n* soil profile
Bodenreaktion *f* soil reaction
Bodensatz *m* sediment, subsidence, [bottom] settlings, B.S., dregs, bottoms, *(esp food, ferm)* lees, foots
Bodensatzwäscher *m (pap)* dregs washer
Bodensäule *f s.* Bodenkolonne
Bodenschicht *f* bottom layer
Bodenschlamm *m (hyd)* bottom sludge
Bodenschlange *f* tank-bottom coil
Bodenstabilisator *m* soil stabilizer (stabilizing agent)
bodenständig *s.* bodeneigen
Bodenstein *m* bed (base) stone, bedder *(of an edge-runner mill)*
Bodensteine *mpl* bottom brickwork
Bodenstein-Prinzip *n* Bodenstein [steady-state] approximation, steady-state [approximation] method, stationary-state method
Bodenstruktur *f* soil structure
Bodenstrukturverbesserung *f s.* Bodenverbesserung
Bodentyp *m* soil type
Bodenventil *n* bottom valve

Bodenverbesserung *f* soil conditioning (improvement, amendment)

Bodenverbesserungsmittel *n* soil conditioner (ameliorant), [soil] amendment

Bodenverdichtung *f* soil compaction

Bodenveredelung *f s.* Bodenverbesserung

Bodenversauerung *f* 1. soil souring (acidification); 2. soil sourness

Bodenverschmutzung *f* soil contamination

Bodenwasser *n* soil water (solution)

Bodenwirkungsgrad *m (distil)* plate efficiency [factor], tray efficiency [factor]

~ nach Murphree Murphree [plate] efficiency

Bodenzahl *f (distil, chromat)* number of plates, plate number, *(chromat also)* plate count

~/effektive height equivalent to an effective theoretical plate, HEETP

~/praktische (tatsächliche) number of actual plates (trays)

~/theoretische theoretical plate number, number of theoretical plates (trays)

~/wirkliche *s.* ~/praktische

Bogen *m* 1. sheet *(of paper or pulp)*; 2. [electric] arc

Bogen... *s. a.* Lichtbogen...

Bogen-Anregung *f* arc excitation

Bogenentladung *f* arc discharge

bogengeglättet *(pap)* sheet-calendered

Bogengewicht *n s.* Masse je Bogen

Bogenhalbstoff *m (pap)* lap[ped] pulp, laps (sheets) of pulp, [solid] pulp board

Bogenkalander *m (pap)* sheet calender

Bogenlänge *f (pap)* length of sheet

Bogenpapier *n* sheet (ream) paper, sheeted paper, paper in sheets

Bogensatinage *f (pap)* sheet calendering

bogensatiniert *(pap)* sheet-calendered

Bogenschneiden *n (pap)* sheeting

Bogensieb *n* sieve-bend screen, DSM screen

Bogensortierung *f (pap)* sheet sorting

Bogenspektrum *n* arc spectrum

Bogenstreichmaschine *f (pap)* sheet coater

Bogenzähler *m*, **Bogenzählgerät** *n (pap)* sheet counter, sheet counting device

Boghead-Kännel-Kohle *f* boghead cannel [coal]

Bogheadkohle *f* boghead [coal], bitumenite

Böhmit *m (min)* boehmite *(a crystalline form of aluminium oxide and hydroxide)*

Bohnerwachs *n* floor wax (polish)

Bohnerz *n* pea ore

Bohn-Schmidt-Reaktion *f* Bohn-Schmidt reaction *(for preparing polyhydroxyanthraquinones)*

Bohranlage *f* drilling rig

bohrbar drillable

Bohrbarkeit *f* drillability

Bohrbrunnen *m (hyd)* drilled well

Bohrdruckmesser *m* drillometer

Bohr-Effekt *m (bioch)* Bohr effect *(with haemoglobin)*

bohren/nach Erdöl to bore (drill, prospect) for oil

Bohren *n (petrol)* drilling

~ auf Neuland exploration drilling

~/gerichtetes directional drilling

Bohrer *m (petrol)* drill; auger *(as for sampling soil)*

Bohrflüssigkeit *f* drilling fluid

~/schlammartige *s.* Bohrschlamm

Bohrgarnitur *f* drilling string

Bohrgerät *n* drilling rig

Bohrgestänge *n* drill pipe

Bohrgut *n* drill cuttings

Bohrium *n* Bh bohrium *(element 107)*

Bohrkern *m (geol)* core

Bohrklein *n* drill cuttings

Bohrloch *n* borehole, *(petrol also)* [oil] well

Bohrlochabsperrvorrichtung *f (petrol)* blow-out preventer

Bohrlochkopf *m* well head

Bohrlochkopfgas *n* casing-head gas

Bohrlochverfahren *n* borehole producer method *(in underground gasification)*

Bohrlochwand[ung] *f* borehole wall

Bohrmast *m* drilling mast

Bohrmeißel *m* drilling bit

Bohrplattform *f* drilling platform

Bohrrohr *n* drill (casing) pipe

Bohrseil *n* drilling cable

Bohrschlamm *m* drilling mud

Bohrschmand *m* drill cuttings

Bohrspülung *f* drilling fluid

Bohrstrang *m* drilling string

Bohrturm *m* [drilling] derrick

~/stationärer fixed derrick

Bohrung *f* 1. boring, bore, [bore]hole; perforation, orifice *(of a screen)*; 2. *(petrol)* [oil] well; 3. *s.* Bohren

~ auf Neuland 1. *(petrol)* exploration (exploratory) well, wildcat; 2. *s.* Bohren auf Neuland

~/freifließende *(petrol)* flowing well

~/fündige *(petrol)* discovery well

~/trockene *(petrol)* unproductive well, dry hole, duster

Bohrwerkzeug *n* drilling tool

Bol *m s.* Bolus

Bollmann-Extrakteur *m* Bollmann extractor

Bolometer *n* bolometer *(a resistance thermometer)*

bolometrisch bolometric

Boltzmann-Faktor *m* Boltzmann factor

Boltzmann-Konstante *f* Boltzmann constant

Boltzmann-Statistik *f* [Maxwell-]Boltzmann statistics

Boltzmann-Theorem *n* Boltzmann distribution law

Boltzmann-Verteilung *f (phys ch)* Boltzmann distribution

Bolus *m (min)* bole *(any of various hydrous aluminium silicates)*

~ alba *s.* ~/weißer

~/roter red bole

~/weißer white bole, bolus alba, china (porcelain) clay, kaolin[e]

Bombage *f* 1. crown[ing], camber *(of rolls or profiles)*; 2. *(food)* blowing of cans
bombardieren *(nucl)* to bombard
Bombardierung *f (nucl)* bombardment
Bombay-Katechu *n* Pegu catechu (cutch), black (dark) catechu (cutch) *(from Acacia catechu Willd.)*
Bombay-Macis *m* Bombay mace *(from Myristica malabarica Lam.)*
Bombe *f* bomb; [pressure] cylinder *(for liquefied gas)*
~/Berthelotsche *s.* ~ nach Berthelot/kalorimetrische
~/kalorimetrische calorimeter (calorimetric, explosion) bomb, [oxygen] bomb calorimeter
~ nach Berthelot/kalorimetrische Berthelot (Kröcker, Mahler) bomb
~/Reidsche Reid apparatus
~/vulkanische *(geol)* bomb
Bombenkalorimeter *n s.* Bombe/kalorimetrische
Bombenmethode *f* bomb method *(for determining sulphur)*
Bombenofen *m (lab)* Carius (bomb) furnace
Bombenrohr *n* **[nach Carius]** *(lab)* Carius (bomb) tube
Bombensauerstoff *m* cylinder oxygen
bombieren to crown, to camber *(rolls or profiles)*
Bombierung *f s.* Bombage
Boms *m (ceram)* case *(a piece of kiln furniture)*
Bonbonsirup *m* starch syrup
Bongkreksäure *f* bongkrekic acid *(antibiotic, respiration inhibitor)*
Boot *n (lab)* boat
Bootform *f* boat (tub) form *(stereochemistry)*
Bootkonformation *f* boat (tub) conformation
Bor *n* B boron
Boracit *m (min)* boracite *(a tectoborate)*
Boran *n* borane, boron hydride, *(specif)* BH_3 borane(3)
Boranat *n* hydridoborate, *tetrahydridoborate
Borat *n* borate, *(specif)* $M^I_3BO_3$ orthoborate, trioxoborate
Boratglas *n* borate glass
Boräthan *n s.* Diboran(6)
Boräthyl *n s.* Triethylboran
Boratperoxyhydrat *n* peroxyborate *(an addition compound)*
Boratphosphor *m* borate phosphor
Boratpuffer *m* borate buffer
Borax *m* borax, sodium tetraborate 10-water, *(min also)* tincal
~/gebrannter (kalzinierter) calcined borax, burnt (anhydrous, dehydrated) borax, borax usta, sodium tetraborate
~/octaedrischer octahedral borax, jeweller's borax, sodium tetraborate 5-water
~ usta *s.* ~/gebrannter
Boraxglas *n* borax glass
Boraxperle *f* borax bead
Boraxsee *m* borax lake
Borazin *n* borazine, *(specif)* $B_3N_3H_6$ borazine, borazole
Borazol *n s.* Borazin
Bor(III)-bromid *n* boron(III) bromide, boron tribromide
Borbutan *n s.* Tetraboran
Borcarbid *n* boron carbide
Borcarbonylhydrid *n s.* Borincarbonyl
Bor(III)-chlorid *n* boron(III) chloride, boron trichloride
Bordeauxbrühe *f* Bordeaux mixture *(a fungicide)*
Bordeaux-Terpentin *n(m)* Bordeaux (French oil) turpentine *(from Pinus pinaster Ait.)*
Bördelflansch *m* lap-joint flange
Bördelverbindung *f* flared-fitting joint *(of tubing)*
Bordüngemittel *n* boron fertilizer
Borfaden *m* boron filament
Bor(III)-fluorid *n* boron(III) fluoride, boron trifluoride
Borfluorwasserstoffsäure *f s.* Tetrafluoroborsäure
Borhydrid *n* boron hydride, borane
Borid *n* boride
Borin *n* borine *(any of a class of compounds B_nH_{n+2})*, *(specif)* BH_3 borane(3)
Borincarbonyl *n* borane carbonyl
Bor(III)-iodid *n* boron(III) iodide, boron triiodide
Borkezustand *m (tann)* crust condition *(of leather)*
Bormangel *m* boron deficiency
Bornan *n (org ch)* bornane
Borneocampher *m* Borneo camphor, Baros (Sumatra, Malayan) camphor *(from Dryobalanops aromatica Gaertn. f.)*
Borneol *n* borneol, bornyl alcohol, 2-hydroxybornane
Borneolacetat *n s.* Bornylacetat
Bornesit *m*, **Bornesitol** *n* bornesitol *(1-O-methylether of myoinositol)*
Born-Haber-Kreisprozeß *m* Born-Haber [thermochemical] cycle
Bornitrid *n* boron nitride
Born-Oppenheimer-Näherung *f* Born-Oppenheimer approximation *(for estimating electronic transitions)*
Bornylacetat *n* bornyl acetate, borneol acetate
Bornylalkohol *m s.* Borneol
Bornylamin *n* bornylamine, 2-aminobornane
Bornylan *n s.* Bornan
Bornylchlorid *n* 2-chlorobornane, bornyl chloride
Bornylen *n* bornylene, 2-bornene
Borobutan *n s.* Tetraboran
Boroscampher *m s.* Borneocampher
Borosilicat *n* borosilicate
Borosilikatglas *n* borosilicate (hard) glass
Borosilikatkronglas *n* borosilicate crown [glass]
Borowolframat *n s.* Wolframatoborat
Bor(III)-oxid *n* boron(III) oxide, boron trioxide, boric oxide
Borphosphat *n s.* Borphosphoroxid
Borphosphid *n* boron phosphide
Borphosphoroxid *n* boron phosphorus oxide *(a double oxide of B_2O_3 and P_2O_5)*
Borsäure *f* boric acid, *(specif)* $B(OH)_3$ orthoboric acid, trioxoboric acid

Borsäureanhydrid *n s.* Bor(III)-oxid
Borsäureester *m* boric-acid ester, borate ester
Borstahl *m* boron steel
Bort *m* boort, boart, bort *(a diamond of inferior quality)*
Bort *n* boort, boart, bort *(abrasive diamond powder)*
Borte *f* bulb edge *(of window glass)*
Bortri... *s. a.* Bor(III)-...
Bortriäthyl *n s.* Triethylboran
Borverbindung *f* boron compound • **mit Borverbindungen versetzen** to boronate *(fertilizers)*
Borwasserstoff *m* boron hydride, borane
Böschungswinkel *m* angle of repose (rest) *(of bulk material)*
Bose-Einstein-Gas *n* Bose-Einstein gas
Bose-Einstein-Statistik *f* Bose-Einstein statistics
Boson *n* boson
bossieren *(ceram)* to emboss
Boswellinsäure *f* boswellic acid *(a mixture of two isomeric hydroxytriterpene acids)*
Botany-Bay-Harz *n* Botany Bay gum *(from Xanthorrhoea hastilis R.Br.)*
Botany-Bay-Kino *n* Botany Bay kino *(from Eucalyptus resinifera Sm.)*
Boten-Ribonucleinsäure *f*, **Boten-RNA** *f* messenger ribonucleic acid, messenger RNA
Bottich *m* tub, vat
Boucherie-Verfahren *n* Boucherie process *(wood preservation)*
Boudouard-Gleichgewicht *n* producer-gas equilibrium
Boudouard-Reaktion *f* air-carbon reaction
Bouillon *f (pharm)* broth
Bouillonkultur *f (pharm)* broth culture
Bouillonverdünnungsmethode *f (pharm)* broth dilution method
Bourbonal *n* bourbonal, 3-ethoxy-4-hydroxybenzaldehyde
Bourdon-Röhre *f* Bourdon [pressure] gauge
Bourgeois-Verfahren Acetomatic *n (biot)* Bourgeois process *(submerged manufacture of acetic acid)*
Bouveault-Blanc-Reduktion *f* Bouveault-Blanc reduction *(of esters to alcohols)*
Boyle-Kurve *f* Boyle curve
Boyle-Punkt *m*, **Boyle-Temperatur** *f* Boyle point (temperature)
BP *s.* Brennpunkt
Brackelsberg-Ofen *m (met)* Brackelsberg furnace
Brackett-Serie *f (spectr)* Brackett series *(of the hydrogen atom)*
brackig brackish
Brackwasser *n* brackish water
Bradford-Bestimmung *f* Bradford assay *(protein chemistry)*
Bradley-Mühle *f* Bradley mill *(a pendulum roller mill)*
~ mit drei Pendeln (Pendelrollen) Bradley three-roll[er] mill
Bragg-Methode *f* Bragg method [of crystal analysis], Bragg rotating crystal method
Bragg-Spektrometer *n* Bragg spectrometer
Bramme *f (met)* slab
Brand *m* 1. burning; *(ceram)* firing, burning, baking; 2. fire; 3. *(ceram)* burn *(batch of ceramic ware)*
Brandbekämpfung *f* fire fighting
Brandfleck *m* scorch, burn, burned spot
Brandgefahr *f* fire hazard
Brandgel *n* incendiary gel
Brandprobe *f (met)* fire assay
Brandriß *m (glass, ceram)* fire (firing) crack
Brandschiefer *m* carbonaceous shale
Brandschutz *m* fire protection (prevention)
brandsicher fireproof • **~ machen** to fireproof
Brandsichermachen *n* fireproofing
Branntkalk *m* burnt (burned) lime, caustic lime, quicklime *(calcium oxide)*
~/gemahlener *(agric)* ground burnt lime
Branntwein *m* [distilled] spirit[s], *(loosely:)* alcohol
~/denaturierter (vergällter) denatured alcohol
Branntweinbrennerei *f* distillery
Branntweinhefe *f* distillery (distillers') yeast
Brasilnuß *f* Brazil (para, cream) nut *(seeds from Bertholletia excelsa Humb. et Bonpl.)*
Brasilsäure *f* brazilic (brasilic) acid
Brassidinsäure *f*, **Brassinsäure** *f* brassidic acid, **trans*-docos-13-enoic acid
Brassylsäure *f* brassylic acid, *tridecanedioic acid
Brauchbarkeit *f* practicality *(of a method)*
Brauchwasser *n* plant (industrial) water, mill (commercial) water
Brauchwasseraufbereitung *f* plant (industrial) water treatment
Brauchwasserbedarf *m* water requirements in manufacturing, industrial water demand
Brauchwasserversorgung *f* plant (industrial) water supply
brauen to brew
Brauer *m* brewer
Brauerei *f* 1. brewery, brewhouse; 2. brewing
Brauereichemie *f* brewing chemistry
Brauereiindustrie *f* brewing industry
Brauereimalz *n s.* Braumalz
Brauereitechnologie *f* brewing technology
Brauereiwasser *n* brew[ing] water, brewing liquor
Braugerste *f* brewing (brewer's, malting) barley
Brauhaus *n s.* Brauerei 1.
Brauhopfen *m* hop for brewing
Brauindustrie *f s.* Brauereiindustrie
Braukessel *m s.* Braupfanne
Braumalz *n* brewer's malt, malt for brewing
Braun *n* brown *(sensation or substance)*
~/Florentiner Florence brown, Vandyke red *(copper(II) hexacyanoferrate(II))*
~/Kasseler Cassel brown (earth), ulmin brown *(bituminous earthy brown coal)*
Braunbleierz *n (min)* brown (green) lead ore, pyromorphite *(lead chloride phosphate)*

Brauneisenerz *n (min)* brown iron ore (stone), limonite *(a variety of goethite)*
Braunerde *f* brown soil
Braunfärbung *f* brown coloration
Braunglas *n* amber glass
Braunglasur *f (ceram)* brown glaze
Braunholzpappe *f s.* Braunschliffpappe
Braunhuminsäure *f (soil)* brown humic acid
Braunit *(min)* braunite *(a manganese silicate)*
Braunkohle *f* lignite, *(esp if low-quality:)* brown coal, *(according to the ASTM coal classification:)* lignitic coal
~/bituminöse bituminous lignite, lignitous (subbituminous) coal
~/braune brown lignite
~/erdige earthy brown coal (lignite)
~/erhärtete *s.* ~/verfestigte
~/faserige fibre brown coal
~/holzartige (lignitische) *s.* ~/xylitische
~/lockere (nicht erhärtete, nichtverfestigte) *s.* ~/unverfestigte
~/schieferige foliaceous brown coal
~/schwarze black lignite
~/steinkohlenähnliche *s.* ~/bituminöse
~/unverfestigte brown coal *(proper)*
~/verfestigte lignite *(according to the ASTM coal classification)*
~/xylitische xylite, woody lignite (brown coal)
Braunkohlenbrennstaub *m s.* Braunkohlenstaub
Braunkohlenbrikett *n* brown-coal briquette
Braunkohlenbrikettierung *f* brown-coal briquetting
Braunkohlengaserzeuger *m* brown-coal generator
Braunkohlenholz *n s.* Braunkohlenxylit
Braunkohlenhydrierung *f* hydrogenation of brown coal
Braunkohlenkoks *m* lignitic (brown-coal) coke
Braunkohlenlignit *m s.* Braunkohlenxylit
Braunkohlenschwelbrikett *n* carbonized brown-coal briquette
Braunkohlenschwelkoks *m* brown-coal char
Braunkohlenstadium *n* lignite stage
Braunkohlenstaub *m* pulverized (powdered) brown coal
Braunkohlenteer *m* lignite (brown-coal) tar
Braunkohlenxylit *m(n)* xylite, woody lignite (brown coal)
Braunlehm *m* brown loam
Braunschliff *m (pap)* brown mechanical pulp
Braunschliffpappe *f* brown mechanical pulp board; leather board
Braunstein *m* manganese dioxide
Braunton *m* brown shade
Brauntonung *f (phot)* sepia toning
Bräunung *f (food)* browning
~/enzymatische enzymatic browning
~/nichtenzymatische non-enzymatic browning, Maillard-type (amino-sugar) browning
~ vom Maillard-Typus *s.* ~/nichtenzymatische
Bräunungsgrad *m (food)* degree of browning
Bräunungsmittel *n (food)* browning aid (ingredient, material)
Bräunungsreaktion *f (food)* browning reaction
~/nichtenzymatische non-enzymatic browning reaction, Maillard (carbonyl-amine) reaction
Bräunungszusatz *m s.* Bräunungsmittel
Braunwerden *n (food)* browning; darkening *(of wine)*
Braupfanne *f* brew (wort) kettle, [wort] copper
Brauqualität *f* brewing quality (value) *(as of barley)*
Braureis *m* brewer's rice
Brause *f* 1. spray[er], sprinkler; 2. *s.* Brauselimonade
Brauselimonade *f* carbonated beverage, soda water, *(Am also)* [soda] pop
brausen to spray, to sprinkle; to effervesce
Brausen *n* spraying, sprinkling; effervescence, effervescency
brausend effervescent, effervescing
Brausepulver *n* effervescent powder (salt)
Brauwasser *n* brewing water (liquor)
Brauwert *m s.* Brauqualität
Brauzucker *m* brewing (brewer's) sugar
Bravais-Gitter *n (cryst)* Bravais lattice
Bravaisit *m (min)* bravaisite *(aluminium dihydrogen-tetrasilicate)*
Breakermischung *f (rubber)* breaker stock (compound)
Breathing-Schwingung *f* [symmetrical] breathing vibration
Brechbacke *f* crusher jaw
~/feststehende fixed jaw
~/schwingende moving jaw, swing[ing] jaw
Brecheisen *n (rubber)* [mould] breaker, mould-breaking (mould-clearing) jack, mould cracker
brechen 1. to break; to mill, to crush *(rock, ore)*; to chop *(bark)*; to roll *(flax)*; to break, to crack *(of emulsions)*; 2. to refract, to break *(light)*
~/eine Emulsion to break (crack) an emulsion, to demulsify, to de-emulsify
Brechen *n* 1. breaking, breakage; milling, crush[-ing] *(of rock, ore)*; chopping *(of bark)*; rolling *(of flax)*; 2. refraction, breaking *(of light)*
~ einer Emulsion breaking (cracking) of an emulsion, demulsification, de-emulsification; emulsion breakdown (breaking) *(process)*
Brecher *m* crusher
Brecherrahmen *m* fixed seat *(of a jaw crusher)*
Brecherwalzwerk *n* breaker, breaking (breakdown) mill; *(rubber)* cracker (cracking) mill
Brechgut *n* material being *or* to be crushed
Brechkegel *m* crushing cone (head)
Brechkoks *m* broken coke
Brechmaul *n*, **Brechmaulöffnung** *f* feed opening *(of a crusher)*
Brechmittel *n (pharm)* emetic
Brechnußpulver *n (pharm)* powdered strychnos seed *(from Strychnos nux-vomica L.)*
Brechplatte *f* crushing (breaker) plate
Brechpunkt *m (petrol)* breaking point; *(hyd)* break-point
~ nach Fraass *(petrol)* Fraass breaking point

Brechpunktchlorung *f (hyd)* breakpoint (free-residual) chlorination
Brechpunktkurve *f (hyd)* breakpoint curve, chlorine dose-residual curve
Brechschwinge *f s.* Breckbacke/schwingende
Brechung *f (phys ch)* refraction
Brechungsdispersion *f* refractive dispersion
Brechungsindex *m*, **Brechungskoeffizient** *m s.* Brechzahl
Brechungsvermögen *n* refractivity
Brechungswinkel *m* angle of refraction
Brechungszahl *f s.* Brechzahl
Brechwalze *f* crushing (crusher) roll
Brechwalzwerk *n* crushing (crusher) rolls
Brechweinstein *m* tartar emetic, potassium antimonotartrate
Brechzahl *f* refraction (refractive) index
Bredt-Regel *f (org ch)* Bredt's rule *(relating to bonds in bridged-ring systems)*
Brei *m* pulp, paste
~/dünner slurry
brei[art]ig pulpy
Breitbandantibiotikum *n* broad-spectrum antibiotic
Breitbandentkopplung *f* broad-band (wide-band) decoupling
Breitbandspektrum *n* broad-band spectrum
Breitbleiche *f (text)* open-width bleaching
Breitbrenner *m (lab)* flat-flame (fish-tail) burner
Breitbrenneraufsatz *m* burner wing top (tip), flat burner head, [burner] flame spreader
Breitenwirksamkeit *f* broad-spectrum effectiveness *(as of pesticides)*
Breitfärbemaschine *f (text)* padding machine (mangle), pad[der]
Breitlinienkernresonanz *f* broad-line (wide-line) NMR
Breitlinien[kernresonanz]spektroskopie *f* broad-line (wide-line) NMR spectroscopy
Breitschlitzdüse *f (plast)* slot die *(for sheet forming)*
Breitspektrumantibiotikum *n s.* Breitbandantibiotikum
Breitstrahldüse *f* slot (flat-spray) nozzle
Breitwaschmaschine *f (text)* open-width washing machine
breitwürfig *(agric)* broadcast *(application of chemicals)*
Brekzie *f* breccia *(fragmental rock)*
brekzienartig brecciated
Brekzienbildung *f* brecciation
bremsen to slow down, to decelerate, to retard; to inhibit *(a reaction)*; *(nucl)* to moderate
Bremsen *n* slowing down, deceleration, retardation, retarding; inhibition *(of a reaction)*; *(nucl)* moderation
Bremsmittel *n* retarding agent (material), retarder
Bremsstrahlung *f (nucl)* bremsstrahlung
Bremssubstanz *f (nucl)* moderator, slowing-down agent
Bremsung *f (nucl)* moderation
Bremsvermögen *n (nucl)* stopping power
Bremsvorrichtung *f* **der Zentrifuge** centrifuge brake kit
Bremswirkung *f* drag effect *(Debye-Hückel theory of strong electrolytes)*
Brennapparat *m s.* Brenngerät
brennbar combustible, burnable, *(esp relating to liquids:)* [in]flammable
~/nicht incombustible, non-combustible, *(esp relating to liquids:)* non-flammable
Brennbares *n* combustible[s]
Brennbarkeit *f* combustibility, *(esp relating to liquids:)* [in]flammability
Brennbereich *m (ceram)* firing range
Brenndauer *f* burning time; *(ceram)* firing time
Brenneigenschaften *fpl (ceram)* firing properties
Brennelement *n s.* Brennstoffelement 1
brennen 1. to burn; *(ceram)* to fire, to burn, to bake; to calcine *(e.g. limestone)*; to bake *(shaped green carbon bodies)*; 2. to distil *(alcohol)*; 3. *(text)* to crab
~/weiß *(ceram)* to fire to a white colour
~/zu Porzellan to porcelainize
Brennen *n* 1. burning; *(ceram)* firing, burning, baking; calcining, calcination *(as of limestone)*; baking *(of shaped green carbon bodies)*; 2. distillation *(of alcohol)*; 3. *(text)* crabbing
Brenner *m* 1. *(lab, tech)* burner; [welding] gun, torch; 2. distiller *(profession)*
~ für flüssigen Brennstoff liquid-fuel burner
~ mit Vormischung premix burner
~ ohne Vormischung direct (nozzle-mix) burner
~ zum Anheizen (Anlassen) starting burner *(of a furnace)*
Brennerei *f (ferm)* distillery
Brennereibetrieb *m* 1. *s.* Brennerei; 2. distilling (distillery) operation
Brennereihefe *f* distillery (distillers') yeast
Brennereiindustrie *f* distilling industry
Brennereimaische *f* distillery mash
Brennereischlempe *f* stillage, [distillery] slop, vinasse, spent wash
Brennerflamme *f* burner flame
Brennerhals *m (glass)* port neck
Brennerhaus *n* burner (hot) house *(for manufacturing carbon black)*
Brennermaul *n (glass)* port mouth (opening)
Brennermund *m* burner throat
Brennermundstück *n* burner tip
Brennermündung *f s.* Brennermaul
Brennerrinne *f* burner channel
Brennerrohr *n* burner tube, barrel *(as of a Bunsen burner)*
Brennerstein *m* burner tile
Brennerzunge *f (glass)* tongue [tile], midfeather, mid-wall
Brennfarbe *f (ceram)* fired colour
Brennfehler *m (ceram)* firing defect (fault)
Brenngas *n* fuel (combustible) gas

Brenngemisch *n* combustion mixture
Brenngerät *n* distillation apparatus *(in alcohol distillation)*
Brenngeschwindigkeit *f* rate of combustion; *(ceram)* burning rate, rate of burning
brennhärten *(met)* to flame-harden
Brennhilfsmittel *n (ceram)* piece (item) of kiln furniture
Brennintervall *n (ceram)* firing range
Brennkammer *f* combustion chamber (space); *(ceram)* firebox, firing box (chamber)
Brennkanal *m* 1. *(ceram)* firing channel; 2. *s.* Brennschacht
Brennkapsel *f (ceram)* fireclay box, saggar, sagger
Brennkegel *m (ceram)* pyrometric cone
~ **nach Orton** Orton cone
~ **nach Seger** Seger cone
Brennkurve *f (ceram)* firing curve
Brennmalz *n* distillers' (distillery) malt
Brennmaterial *n* fuel
Brennofen *m (ceram)* kiln
~/intermittierender periodic kiln
~ **mit direktem (offenem) Feuer** open-flame kiln
~/periodischer (periodisch arbeitender) periodic kiln
Brennöl *n* burning oil
Brennplatte *f (ceram)* bat
Brennprobe *f s.* Brennversuch
Brennpunkt *m* 1. burning (fire) point *(of liquid fuel)*; 2. focus *(optics)*
Brennraum *m* furnace chamber, combustion chamber (space)
Brennreife *f (ceram)* maturity
Brennriß *m (glass, ceram)* fire (firing) crack
Brennrohr *n s.* Brennerrohr
Brennschacht *m (met)* combustion chamber *(of a hot-blast stove)*
Brennschneiden *n*/**autogenes** oxyacetylene (oxygen-acetylene) cutting
Brennschwindung *f (ceram)* fire (firing) shrinkage, firing contraction
Brennspiritus *m* mineralized methylated spirit
Brennstab *m s.* Brennstoffstab
Brennstaub *m* pulverized (powdered) fuel
brennstaubgefeuert pulverized-fuel-fired
Brennstoff *m* [combustion] fuel; [nuclear] fuel
~/fester solid fuel
~/flüssiger liquid fuel
~/fossiler fossil fuel
~/gasförmiger gaseous fuel
~/künstlicher prepared fuel
~/mineralischer *s.* ~/fossiler
~/rauchfreier (rauchloser) smokeless fuel
~/rußfreier *s.* ~/rauchfreier
~/synthetischer prepared fuel
~/umweltfreundlicher clean fuel
~/veredelter prepared fuel
Brennstoffasche *f* fuel ash
Brennstoffbett *n* fuel bed
~/festes fixed fuel bed
~/fluidisiertes (kochendes) s. ~/wirbelndes
~/ruhendes *s.* ~/festes
~/wirbelndes fluidized fuel bed
Brennstoffchemie *f* fuel chemistry
Brennstoffchemiker *m* fuel chemist
Brennstoffeinsparung *f* economy in fuel
Brennstoffelement *n* 1. *(nucl)* fuel element; 2. *(el ch)* fuel cell
Brennstoffofen *m* fuel-heated furnace
Brennstofforschung *f* fuel research
Brennstoffschicht *f*, **Brennstoffschüttung** *f s.* Brennstoffbett
Brennstoffstab *m*, **Brennstoffstange** *f (nucl)* fuel rod
Brennstoffstaub *m s.* Brennstaub
Brennstofftechnologie *f* fuel technology
Brennstoffverwertung *f* fuel utilization
Brennstoffwiederaufarbeitung *f*, **Brennstoffwiederaufbereitung** *f* [nuclear] fuel reprocessing, reactor fuel reprocessing
Brennstoffwiederaufbereitungsanlage *f (nucl)* fuel-reprocessing plant
Brennstoffzelle *f (el ch)* fuel cell
Brennstütze *f (ceram)* post, upright, prop
Brenntemperatur *f (ceram)* firing temperature
~/maximale peak firing temperature
Brennunterlage *f (ceram)* bat
Brennverhalten *n (ceram)* firing behaviour
Brennversuch *m (text)* burning test
Brennwert *m* calorific value
~/molarer *s.* ~/stoffmengenbezogener
~/spezifischer gross heat of combustion, *(deprecated terms:)* gross calorific value, higher heating value
~/stoffmengenbezogener heat of combustion per mole
Brennzeit *f s.* Brenndauer
Brennzone *f* combustion zone *(of a blast furnace)*; calcining zone (compartment) *(of a lime furnace)*
Brenzcatechin *n* catechol, pyrocatechol, **o*-dihydroxybenzene
Brenzcatechindimethylether *m* catechol dimethyl ether, veratrol, *1,2-dimethoxybenzene
Brenzcatechinmonoethylether *m* catechol monoethyl ether, *o*-ethoxyphenol, guaethol
Brenzcatechinmonomethylether *m* catechol methyl ether, *o*-methoxyphenol, guaiacol
brenzlig empyreumatic *(smell)*
Brenzschleimsäure *f* pyromucic acid, furan-2-carboxylic acid
Brenztraubensäure *f* pyruvic acid, *2-oxopropionic acid
Brenztraubensäurealdehyd *m* pyruvic aldehyde, methylglyoxal, *2-oxopropionaldehyde
Brenzweinsäure *f* pyrotartaric acid, methylsuccinic acid, *2-methylbutane-1,4-dioic acid
Brevifolincarbonsäure *f (tann)* brevifolincarboxylic acid

Brevilagin *m (tann)* brevilagin
Brewster-Winkel *m* Brewster angle
Briefpapier *n* letter (note) paper, *(Am)* correspondence paper
Briefumschlag-Konformation *f* envelope conformation
Briefumschlagpapier *n* envelope paper
Brightstock *m*, **Brightstock-Öl** *n (petrol)* bright stock
Brikett *n* briquet[te]
~/pechgebundenes pitch-bound briquette
Brikettfabrik *f* briquetting (briquette) plant
Brikettfestigkeit *f* briquette strength
Brikettieranlage *f* briquetting (briquette) plant (installation)
brikettierbar briquettable
Brikettierbarkeit *f* briquettability, briquetting properties (qualities)
Brikettierdruck *m s.* Brikettierpreßdruck
Brikettiereigenschaften *fpl s.* Brikettierbarkeit
brikettieren to briquette
brikettierfähig *s.* brikettierbar
Brikettierkohle *f* briquetting (briquette) coal
Brikettiermaschine *f* briquetting (briquette) machine
Brikettierpech *n* briquetting pitch
Brikettierpreßdruck *m* briquetting pressure
Brikettierpresse *f* briquetting (briquette) press
Brikettiersteinkohle *f* briquetting (briquette) coal
Brikettierungs... *s.* Brikettier...
Brikettierverfahren *n* briquetting method (technique)
Brikettierwalzen *fpl* briquetting rolls
Brikettierwerk *n s.* 1. Brikettfabrik; 2. Brikettiermaschine
Brikettkohle *f* briquetting (briquette) coal
Brikettkoks *m* briquette coke
Brikettpech *n* briquetting pitch
Brikettpresse *f s.* Brikettierpresse
Brikettwalzenpresse *f* roll-type briquetting (briquette) machine, Belgium roll machine
brillant brilliant
Brillantalizarinblau *n* brilliant alizarin blue
Brillantfarbstoff *m* brilliant dye
Brillantgelb *n* brilliant yellow
Brillantgrün *n* brilliant (emerald) green *(a basic triphenylmethane dye)*; emerald green, chrome green, Mittler's green, Guignet's green *(hydrated chromium oxide)*
Brillantine *f* brilliantine
Brillantrosa *n* brilliant pink
Brillanz *f* brilliance, brilliancy
Brillouin-Polyeder *n (cryst)* Brillouin polyhedron
Brillouin-Zone *f (cryst)* Brillouin zone
Brinellhärte *f* Brinell hardness
Brinellprobe *f* Brinell test *(for determining the hardness of metals)*
Brinellzahl *f* Brinell number *(for characterizing the hardness of metals)*
bringen:
~/auf Typ *(dye)* to bring to standard strength
~/in Kontakt to contact
~/in Lösung to bring (put) into solution
~/ins Gleichgewicht to bring into equilibrium, to equilibrate
~/zum Erlöschen to extinguish
~/zum Kochen to bring (raise) to the boil
~/zum Schäumen to foam, to froth
~/zum Stehen to arrest *(a reaction)*
~/zur Ausflockung to coagulate, to curdle
~/zur Detonation to detonate
~/zur Explosion to explode
~/zur Kristallisation to crystallize out
~/zur Reaktion to react
Brisanz *f* brisance, shattering power
Brisanzwert *m* brisance value
Bristolkarton *m* Bristol board
Britanniametall *n* Britannia metal *(a tin alloy containing antimony, copper, and some bismuth)*
Brochantit *m (min)* brochantite *(a basic copper sulphate)*
Brocken *m* lump *(as of coal, sugar)*; bat *(as of clay or plaster)*
Brockenfüllung *f (hyd)* stone bed, rock fill, filter stones *(of a trickling filter)*
bröcklig friable, crumbly
Bröckligkeit *f* friability, crumbliness
Brom *n* Br bromine
Bromacetaldehyd *m* bromoacetaldehyde, *bromoethanal
Bromacetol *n* bromacetol, *2,2-dibromopropane
Bromaceton *n* bromoacetone, *1-bromopropanone
Bromacetoxylierung *f* bromoacetoxylation
Bromacetylierung *f* bromoacetylation
Bromacylierung *f* bromoacylation
Bromal *n* bromal, tribromoacetaldehyde, *tribromoethanal
Bromalid *n (org ch)* bromalide
Bromalkan *n* bromoalkane
Bromalkylierung *f* bromoalkylation
Bromallylalkohol *m* bromoallyl alcohol
Bromaminsäure *f* bromamine acid, 1-amino-4-bromoanthraquinone-2-sulphonic acid
Bromanil *n* bromanil, tetrabromo-*p*-benzoquinone
Bromanilsäure *f* bromanilic acid, 3,6-dibromo-2,5-dihydroxy-*p*-benzoquinone
Bromat *n* $M^{I}BrO_3$ bromate • **mit ~ behandeln** to bromate
Bromäthan *n*, **Bromäthyl** *n s.* Bromethan
Bromäthylen *n s.* Bromethen
Bromatometrie *f* bromatometry
bromatometrisch bromatometric
Brombenzen *n* bromobenzene
Brombenzoesäure *f* bromobenzoic acid
Brombenzol *n s.* Brombenzen
***N*-Brombernsteinsäureimid** *n N*-bromosuccinimide, NBS
1-Brombutan *n* 1-bromobutane
2-Brombutan *n* 2-bromobutane
Brombutansäure *f s.* Brombuttersäure

Brombuttersäure *f* bromobutyric acid, *bromobutanoic acid
Brombutylkautschuk *m* bromobutyl (brominated butyl) rubber
Bromcampher *m* bromocamphor, bromated (brominated, monobrominated) camphor
Bromchlorargyrit *m (min)* bromchlorargyrite, embolite *(silver bromide chloride)*
Bromcresol *n* bromocresol
Bromcresolgrün *m* bromocresol green *(a pH indicator)*
Bromcresolpurpur *m* bromocresol purple *(a pH indicator)*
Bromcyan *n*, **Bromcyanid** *n* bromine cyanide, cyanogen bromide
Bromdampf *m* bromine vapour
Bromdecahydrat *n s.* Brom-10-Wasser
Bromdesoxyuridin *n* bromodeoxyuridine, BrdUrd
Bromdesulfonierung *f* bromodesulphonation
Bromessigsäure *f* bromoacetic acid, *bromoethanoic acid
Bromethan *n* bromoethane
Bromethanal *n* *bromoethanal, bromoacetaldehyde
2-Bromethanol *n* *2-bromoethanol, 2-bromoethyl alcohol
Bromethansäure *f s.* Bromessigsäure
Bromethen *n* bromoethylene, *bromoethene, vinyl bromide
2-Bromethylalkohol *m s.* 2-Bromethanol
Brometon *n* brometone, *1,1,1-tribromo-2-methylpropan-2-ol
Brom(III)-fluorid *n* bromine(III) fluoride, bromine trifluoride
Brom(V)-fluorid *n* bromine(V) fluoride, bromine pentafluoride
Bromgelatineplatte *f (phot)* gelatin bromide plate
Bromgoldsäure *f s.* Tetrabromogold(III)-Säure
Bromgraphit *m* bromine graphite
bromhaltig containing bromine, bromine-containing
Bromhydrin *n* bromohydrin
Bromid *n* $M^{I}Br$ bromide
Bromidpapier *n (phot)* bromide (bromic-silver) paper
bromieren to brominate
~/zweifach to dibrominate
Bromierung *f* bromination
~/zweifache dibromination
Bromierungsmittel *n* brominating agent
Bromierungsreaktion *f* bromination reaction
Bromismus *m (tox)* bromism
2-Bromisobuttersäure *f* 2-bromoisobutyric acid, *2-bromo-2-methylpropanoic acid
Bromitentschlichtung *f (text)* sodium-bromite desizing
Bromkresol *n s.* Bromcresol
Bromlactonisierung *f* bromolactonization
Brommethan *n* bromomethane
Brommethyl *n s.* Brommethan
Brommethylierung *f* bromomethylation
2-Brom-2-methylpropan *n* 2-bromo-2-methylpropane
Brommonofluorid *n* bromine monofluoride
Brommonosilan *n* bromomonosilane, bromosilane
Bromoantimonat *n* bromoantimonate
Bromoaurat(I) *n* $M^{I}[AuBr_2]$ bromoaurate(I), dibromoaurate(I)
Bromoaurat(III) *n* $M^{I}[AuBr_4]$ bromoaurate(III), tetrabromoaurate(III)
Bromoform *n* bromoform, *tribromomethane
Bromoiodat(I) *n* $M^{I}[IBr_2]$ bromoiodate(I)
Bromolyse *f* brominolysis
Bromometrie *f* bromometry
bromometrisch bromometric
Bromonium-Ion *n* bromonium ion
Bromoniumverbindung *f* bromonium compound
Bromoplatin(II)-säure *f* bromoplatinic(II) acid, tetrabromoplatinic(II) acid
Bromoplatin(IV)-säure *f* bromoplatinic(IV) acid, hexabromoplatinic(IV) acid
Bromostannat *n* bromostannate
Bromozinkat *n* bromozincate
Brompentafluorid *n* bromine pentafluoride
Bromphenol *n* bromophenol
Bromphenolblau *n* bromophenol blue, tetrabromophenolsulphonephthalein *(a pH indicator)*
Bromphosgen *n* bromophosgene, carbonyl bromide, *carbon dibromide oxide
Brompropansäure *f s.* Brompropionsäure
1-Brompropen *n* 1-bromopropene
3-Brompropen *n* *3-bromopropene, allyl bromide
Brompropionsäure *f* bromopropionic acid
Bromsäure *f* bromic acid
Bromsilan *n* bromosilane, *(specif)* SiH_3Br bromomonosilane, bromosilane
Bromsilber *n (phot)* silver bromide
Bromsilberdruck *m* bromide print
Bromsilberpapier *n s.* Bromidpapier
***N*-Bromsuccinimid** *n* *N*-bromosuccinimide
Bromthymol *n* bromothymol, 4-bromo-2-isopropyl-5-methylphenol
Bromthymolblau *n* bromothymol blue, dibromothymolsulphonephthalein *(a pH indicator)*
Bromtoluen *n* bromotoluene
Bromtoluol *n s.* Bromtoluen
Bromtrichlorsilan *n* bromotrichlorosilane
Bromtrifluorid *n* bromine trifluoride
Bromwasser *n* bromine water
Brom-10-Wasser *n* bromine 10-water, bromine decahydrate
Bromwasserstoff *m* hydrogen bromide
Bromwasserstoffabspaltung *f* dehydrobromination
bromwasserstoffsauer bromohydric
Bromwasserstoffsäure *f* hydrobromic acid
α-Bromxylen *n*, **α-Bromxylol** *n* α-bromoxylene
Bromzahl *f (anal)* bromine number *(for characterizing the degree of unsaturation of fatty oils)*

Brönner-Säure *f (dye)* Brönner's acid *(naphth-2-ylamine-6-sulphonic acid)*
Brönsted-Base *f* Brønsted[-Lowry] base
Brönsted-Beziehung *f* Brønsted relation (correlation)
Brönsted-Diagramm *n* Brønsted plot
Brönsted-Katalysegesetz *n* [Brønsted] catalysis law
Brönsted-Konzept *n* Brønsted[-Lowry] theory *(of acids and bases)*
Brönsted-Säure *f* Brønsted[-Lowry] acid, proton[ic] acid, hydrogen acid
Bronze *f* bronze, *(specif)* tin bronze
Bronzefleck *m* bronze speck *(a defect in paper)*
Bronzelack *m* bronzing lacquer
Bronzepapier *n* bronze paper
Bronzepulver *n* bronze powder
Bronzetinktur *f* bronzing liquid (fluid)
bronzieren to bronze
Brookit *m (min)* brookite *(titanium dioxide)*
Brotmehl *n* bread flour
Brotteig *m* bread dough
Bruch *m* 1. breaking, breakage, fracture *(process)*; *(min)* cleavage *(the manner in which a mineral may be cleft or split)*; 2. break[age], fracture *(result)*; *(min)* fracture *(texture of a broken surface)*; 3. scrap *(discarded metal collected for melting down)*; *(ceram, glass)* breakage *(broken ware)*; cullet *(broken glass for remelting)*; curd *(the coagulated part of milk used for cheese-making)*; 4. casse *(a disorder in wine)*
~ der C–C-Bindung C–C bond breakage
~/glasiger vitreous fracture
~/hakiger hackly fracture
~/interkristalliner intercrystalline fracture
~/intrakristalliner *s.* ~/transkristalliner
~/transkristalliner transcrystalline (transgranular) fracture
~/würfelförmiger *(glass)* dice
~/zeitabhängiger fatigue failure (fracture)
Bruchbearbeitung *f (food)* curd treatment
Bruchbildung *f (food)* curd formation
Bruchdehnung *f* strain after fracture, strain at break; *(pap)* tensile stretch
Bruchebene *f* fracture plane
Bruchfestigkeit *f* 1. fracture strength; 2. *(food)* curd firmness (strength); 3. *s.* Rohbruchfestigkeit
Bruchfläche *f* fracture facet (surface)
Bruchglas *n* cullet
Bruchgramm *n* fractional weight
brüchig brittle • **~ machen** to make brittle, to embrittle • **~ werden** to become brittle, to embrittle
Brüchigkeit *f* brittleness
Bruchkorn *n (food)* curd grain (particle)
Bruchlast *f (pap)* breaking strain
Bruchmesser *n (food)* curd knife
Bruchmodul *m (ceram)* modulus of rupture
Bruchpapier *n* waste stuff
Bruchpunkt *m (rubber)* breaking point
bruchsicher shatterproof
Bruchstelle *f (bioch)* nick *(in DNA)*
Bruchstück *n* fragment; *(nucl)* fission fragment
Bruchstückion *n* fragment ion
Bruchzeit *f (rubber)* flex-life time
Brucinpapier *n* brucine paper *(for detecting nitrous acid)*
Brücke *f* bridge *(chemical-bond theory)*; *(plast, rubber)* cross-link[age]; *(glass)* bridge [wall]
Brückenatom *n* bridge atom
brückenbildend bridging
Brückenbildung *f* bridging; *(pap)* arching *(of chips in the silo)*
Brückenbindung *f* bridge-type bond
~/polysulfidische polysulphidic bridge (cross-link, link)
Brückenglied *n* binding link *(between molecules)*; *(plast, rubber)* bridge-type cross-link
Brücken-Ion *n* bridged ion
Brücken-Kohlenwasserstoff *m* bridged hydrocarbon
Brückenkopf *m* bridgehead *(in bridge-ring systems)*
Brückenkopfatom *n* bridgehead atom
Brückenname *m*, **Brückenpräfix** *n (nomencl)* bridge name
Brückenring *m* bridge[d] ring
Brückenringsystem *n* bridge-ring system
Brückenringverbindung *f* bridged-ring compound
Brückensauerstoff *m* bridging oxygen
Brückenschaltung *f* bridge [circuit]
~/Wheatstonesche Wheatstone bridge circuit
Brückenverbindung *f s.* Brückenringverbindung
Brückenwand *f (glass)* bridge [wall]
Brückenwannenofen *m (glass)* bridge-type furnace
Brüden *m* exhaust (dead) steam, vapour
Brüdenabscheider *m* vapour condenser, demister
Brüdenaustritt *m* vapour outlet
Brüdendampf *m s.* Brüden
Brüdenhaube *f* vapour hood, air dome
Brüdenkondensat *n* vapour condensate
Brüdenkondensator *m s.* Brüdenabscheider
Brüdenraum *m* vapour head (chamber, space), flash chamber, body *(of an evaporator)*
Brüdenschlottrockner *m* cascade (tower) dryer
Brüdenverdichter *m* vapour compressor
Brüdenverdichtung *f* vapour compression
Brühe *f* broth *(a culture medium)*; *(tann)* liquor; *(agric)* wash *(pest control)*
~/Bordelaiser Bordeaux mixture *(fungicide)*
~/Burgunder Burgundy mixture, soda bordeaux *(fungicide)*
~/maskierte *(tann)* masked liquor (solution)
~/unmaskierte *(tann)* straight liquor (solution)
Brühebehälter *m (agric)* spray tank
brühen *(text)* to bowk, to kier-boil
Brühen *n (text)* bowking, bocking, kier boiling
Brühenmesser *m (tann)* bark[tr]ometer
Brunauer-Emmett-Teller-Adsorptionsisotherme *f* Brunauer Emmett-Teller isotherm, BET isotherm

brünieren to brown *(metal surfaces)*
Brunnen *m* 1. well, *(hyd also)* water well; *(natural fountain:)* spring, *(specif)* mineral spring; *(petrol)* [oil] well; 2. mineral waters
~/fließender *(petrol)* flowing well
Brunnenkopf *m (hyd)* well head
Brunnenwasser *n* well water
Brunnenwasserversorgung *f* well-water supply
Brustkalander *m (rubber)* inverted L type of calender
Brustwalze *f (pap)* breast roll
brütbar *(nucl)* fertile
Brütbarkeit *f (nucl)* fertility
Brüten *n (nucl)* breeding, fertilization
Brüter *m s.* Brutreaktor
brutfähig *s.* brütbar
Brutluft *f (biot)* fermentation air
Brutmaterial *n (nucl)* fertile material
Brutreaktor *m (nucl)* breeder reactor
~/schneller fast breeder reactor
Brutschrank *m* incubator • **im ~ aufbewahren** to incubate
~ mit natürlicher Luftumwälzung gravity convection incubator
Brutstoff *m s.* Brutmaterial
Bruttoformel *f* empirical [molecular] formula
~/einfachste simplest [possible] formula, stoichiometric formula
~/wahre true (empirical molecular) formula
Bruttogleichung *f* overall equation *(of a reaction)*
Brutto-Komplexbildungskonstante *f*, **Brutto-Komplexstabilitätskonstante** *f* overal formation constant
Bruttoprobe *f (anal)* gross sample
Bruttoreaktion *f* overall reaction
Bruttovorgang *m* gross process
Bruttozusammensetzung *f* gross composition
Brutvorgang *m (nucl)* breeding [process], fertilization
Bruun-Kolonne *f (distil)* Bruun column
BSB *m (biochemischer Sauerstoffbedarf)* BOD, biochemical oxygen demand
~ des Abwasserzuflusses *(hyd)* influent BOD [level, concentration], BOD of incoming waste water
BSB-Abbau *m (hyd)* BOD removal
BSB-Abbauleistung *f (hyd)* efficiency of BOD removal
BSB-Ablaufkonzentration *f (hyd)* outlet BOD, effluent BOD level
BSB-Abnahme *f (hyd)* BOD reduction
BSB-Belastung *f (hyd)* BOD loading
BSB-Bestimmung *f (hyd)* BOD determination (test)
BSB-Endwert *m (hyd)* final (residual) BOD
BSB-Entfernung *f (hyd)* BOD removal
BSB-Gehalt *m (hyd)* BOD content (level)
BSB-Konzentration *f (hyd)* BOD concentration
~ im Ablauf *s.* BSB-Ablaufkonzentration
~/im Ablauf verbleibende *s.* BSB-Restkonzentration im Ablauf
~ im Zulauf *s.* BSB-Zulaufkonzentration
BSB-Last *f (hyd)* BOD loading
BSB-Minderung *f (hyd)* BOD reduction
BSB-Restkonzentration *f* **im Ablauf** *(hyd)* residual (final) BOD
BSB-Rückgang *m (hyd)* BOD reduction
BSB-Senkung *f (hyd)* BOD reduction
BSB-Test *m (hyd)* BOD test (determination)
BSB-Verminderung *f (hyd)* BOD reduction
BSB-Wert *m (hyd)* BOD level
BSB_5-Wert *m* five-day BOD, five-days biochemical oxygen demand, BOD_5
BSB-Zulaufkonzentration *f (hyd)* influent BOD [level, concentration], BOD of incoming waste water
B-strain-Effekt *m s.* Beschleunigung/sterische
BTÄ *(Bleitetraäthyl) s.* Tetraethylblei
BTM *s.* Biotrockenmasse
BTX-Aromaten *mpl* benzene-toluene-xylenes, BTX
Buccocampher *m* buchucamphor, buccocamphor, diosphenol, *2-hydroxy-6-isopropyl-3-methylcyclohex-2-en-1-one
Buchbinderpappe *f* [book]binder's board
Buchdruckfarbe *f* letterpress ink
Buchdruckpapier *n* book[-printing] paper, *(Am)* text paper
Bucheckernöl *n* beechnut oil
Buchenholzspäne *mpl (biot)* beechwood shavings *(manufacture of acetic acid)*
Buchenholzteerkreosot *n* beechwood creosote
Buchenspäne *mpl s.* Buchenholzspäne
Bucherer-[Lepetit-]Reaktion *f* Bucherer reaction *(conversion of a naphthylamine to a naphthol or vice versa)*
Bücherpappe *f* [book]binder's board
Büchner-Nutsche *f*, **Büchner-Trichter** *m* Büchner filter (funnel)
Büchse *f* can; *(food)* tin can, preserve can (tin)
Büchsenmilch *f* canned milk
Buchstabenbuna *m* lettered buna rubber, letter grade of buna
Budde-Effekt *m (phot)* Budde effect
buffieren *f (tann)* to buff
Bügelarmausrüstung *f s.* Bügelfreiausrüstung
bügelecht fast to ironing
Bügelechtheit *f* fastness to ironing
Bügelfreiausrüstung *f (text)* no-iron finish
Bügelmethode *f* detachment method *(for determining surface tensions)*
Bühne *f s.* Bedienungsbühne
Bukett *n* bouquet *(as of wine)*
Bukkokampfer *m s.* Buccocampher
Bullers-Ring *m (ceram)* Bullers ring *(for measuring temperatures in a kiln)*
Bülwern *n (glass)* blocking
Buna *m(n) s.* Bunakautschuk
Bunakautschuk *m* buna [rubber]
Bunakrümel *mpl* crumbs of buna [rubber]
Bunalatex *m* buna latex

bündeln to concentrate *(rays)*
Bündelrohraustauscher *m s.* Rohrbündelwärmeübertrager
Bündelung *f* concentration *(of rays)*
Bunker *m* bunker, bin, silo, [storage] tank, *(if funnel-shaped:)* [storage] hopper
Bunker-C-Öl *n s.* Bunkeröl C
Bunkerkohle *f* bunker coal
Bunkeröl *n* bunker fuel [oil]
~ **C** bunker C fuel [oil]
Bunsenbrenner *m* Bunsen burner
Bunsenflamme *f* Bunsen flame
Bunsentrichter *m* Bunsen (long-stemmed) funnel
Bunsenventil *n* Bunsen valve
Buntätzen *n (text)* coloured discharge
Bunte-Bürette *f* Bunte [gas] burette
Bunte-Salz *n* Bunte salt *(salts, usually sodium salts, of S-alkylthiosulphuric acid)*
Buntglas *n* coloured glass
Buntglaspapier *n* diaphanic paper
Buntkupferkies *m (min)* peacock ore, horse-flesh ore, purple copper ore, bornite *(copper(II) iron(II) sulphide)*
Buntpapier *n* coloured paper
Buntpappe *f* tinted cardboard
Bürette *f* burette
~/automatische automatic burette
~/Buntesche Bunte [gas] burette
~ **mit automatischer Nullpunkteinstellung** automatic zero burette
~ **mit Schellbach-Streifen** Schellbach burette
~ **nach Squibb** Squibb burette
Bürettenbürste *f* burette brush
Bürettenhahn *m* burette stopcock (valve)
Bürettenhalter *m s.* Bürettenklemme
Bürettenklemme *f* burette clamp (holder)
~/zweiarmige double-beam burette holder
Bürettenquetschhahn *m* burette pinchcock
Bürettensperrhahn *m s.* Bürettenhahn
Bürettenspitze *f* burette jet (tip, outlet tube) *(a replacement part)*
Bürettentrichter *m* burette filler (funnel)
Burgers-Vektor *m (cryst)* Burgers vector
Burgers-Versetzung *f (cryst)* screw (Burgers) dislocation
Burgunderharz *n*, **Burgunderpech** *n* Burgundy pitch
Bürste *f* brush
bürsten to brush
Bürstenauftrag *m* brush application
Bürstenbelüfter *m (hyd)* brush aerator
Bürstenbelüftungswalze *f (hyd)* brush aerator
Bürstenentstauber *m* brush sifter
Bürstenfeuchter *m (pap)* brush damper
Bürstenglättung *f (pap)* brush polishing
Bürstenphase *f (chromat)* brushed phase
Bürstenphasenchromatographie *f* brushed-phase chromatography *(using organically modified carriers)*
Bürstenschaber *m (pap)* brush doctor
Bürstenstreichmaschine *f* brush coater (spreader, spreading machine)
Bürstenstrich *m* brush coating
Bürstenfärberei *f*, **Bürstfärbung** *f* brush dyeing
Bürstmaschine *f* brush[ing] machine
Burt-Filter *n* Burt filter *(a leaf filter with rotating filter drum)*
Burton-Clark-Spaltverfahren *n (petrol)* Burton-Clark [cracking] process
burtonisieren to burtonize, to gypsum *(brewing water)*
Burton-Spaltverfahren *n (petrol)* Burton [cracking] process
Butadien *n* butadiene, *(specif)* buta-1,3-diene
Buta-1,3-dien *n*, **Butadien-(1,3)** *n* buta-1,3-diene
Butadien-Acrylnitril-Copolymerisat *n* butadiene-acrylonitrile copolymer
Butadien-Acrylnitril-Kautschuk *m* butadiene-acrylonitrile rubber, nitrile[-butadiene] rubber, NBR
Butadienanlage *f* butadiene plant
Butadiencopolymerisat *n* butadiene copolymer
Butadienkautschuk *m* butadiene rubber, BR
Butadienpolymer[e] *n*, **Butadienpolymerisat** *n* butadiene polymer
Butadien-Styren-Copolymerisat *n* butadiene-styrene copolymer
Butadien-Styren-Kautschuk *m* butadiene-styrene rubber, styrene-butadiene rubber, SBR
~/ölgestreckter oil-extended styrene-butadiene rubber, OE-SBR, oil-extended (oil-master-batched) polymer, OEP
~/ölhaltiger (ölplastizierter) *s.* ~/ölgestreckter
Butadien-Styren-Latex *m* butadiene-styrene latex
Butadien-Vinylpyridin-Copolymerisat *n* butadiene-vinylpyridine copolymer
Butadiin *n* butadiyne
Butan *n* butane
i-**Butan** *n* *2-methylpropane, *(deprecated:)* isobutane
n-**Butan** *n* butane *(proper)*
Butanal *n* *butanal, butyric aldehyde
Butan-1,4-dial *n*, **Butandial-(1,4)** *n* *butane-1,4-dial, succindialdehyde
Butan-1,4-dicarbonsäure *f*, **Butandicarbonsäure-(1,4)** *f* *butane-1,4-dicarboxylic acid, *hexanedioic acid, adipic acid
Butan-2,3-diol *n*, **Butandiol-(2,3)** *n* *butane-2,3-diol, 2,3-dihydroxybutane
Butan-2,3-dion *n*, **Butandion-(2,3)** *n* butane-2,3-dione
Butandisäure *f* *butanedioic acid, *ethane-1,2-dicarboxylic acid, succinic acid
butanfrei butane-free
butanhaltig butane-containing
Butan-1-ol, Butanol-(1) *n* butan-1-ol
Butan-2-ol *n*, **Butanol-(2)** *n* butan-2-ol
sec-**Butanol** *n s.* Butan-2-ol
tert-**Butanol** *n* *2-methylpropan-2-ol, *tert*-butyl alcohol

Butanol-Aceton-Gärung *f s.* Aceton-Butanol-Gärung
Butanol-(3)-al-(1) *n s.* 3-Hydroxybutanal
Butan-2-on *n*, **Butanon-(2)** *n* *butan-2-one, 2-oxobutane
Butansäure *f s.* Buttersäure
Butantetrol *n* butanetetrol
Butantrennkolonne *f* debutanizer
Buteakino *n* butea gum, gum butea, Bengal kino *(from Butea superba Roxb.)*
Butein *n* butein *(a chalcone derivative)*
But-1-en, Buten-(1) *n* but-1-ene
But-2-en *n*, **Buten-(2)** *n* but-2-ene
But-2-enal *n*, **Buten-(2)-al-(1)** *n* *but-2-enal, crotonic aldehyde
Butendisäure *f* butenedioic acid, ethylene-1,2-dicarboxylic acid
cis-**Butendisäureanhydrid** *n* **cis*-butenedioic anhydride, maleic anhydride, furan-2,5-dione
Butenpolymer[e] *n* butylene polymer
cis-**But-2-ensäure** *f*, *cis*-**Buten-(2)-säure** *f* **cis*-but-2-enoic acid, isocrotonic acid
trans-**But-2-ensäure** *f*, *trans*-**Buten-(2)-säure** *f* **trans*-but-2-enoic acid, crotonic acid
Butin *n* 1. butin, 7,3',4'-trihydroxyflavanone; 2. butyne *(either of two isomeric alkynes)*
But-1-in *n*, **Butin-(1)** *n* but-1-yne
But-2-in *n*, **Butin-(2)** *n* but-2-yne
Butindisäure *f* butynedioic acid
Butler-Volmer-Gleichung *f (el ch)* Butler-Volmer equation
Bütte *f* vat, tub
Büttenersatzpapier *n* imitation hand-made paper
Büttenpapier *n* vat (hand-made, genuine) paper
~ **mit imitiertem Büttenrand** *s.* ~/imitiertes
~**/imitiertes** imitation hand-made paper
Büttenpapierfabrik *f* vat mill, hand-made paper mill
Büttenrand *m (pap)* deckle edge • **mit** ~ deckled • **mit zweiseitigem** ~ double-deckled
~**/echter** deckle edge
~**/zweiseitiger** double deckle
Butter *f*/**wiederaufgefrischte** processed (renovated) butter
Butteraroma *n* butter aroma, buttery flavour
butterartig buttery
Butterbereitung *f s.* Butterherstellung
Butterbrotpapier *n* greaseproof (grease-resistant) paper
Butterei *f* butter factory, butter-making plant
Buttererzeugung *f* 1. butter production *(economically)*; 2. *s.* Butterherstellung
Butterfarbe *f* butter dye, *(Am also)* butter color
Butterfaß *n* [butter] churn
Butterfehler *m* butter defect
Butterfertiger *m* [butter] churn
Butterfett *n* butter fat
Butterformmaschine *f* butter-moulding machine
Buttergelb *n* butter yellow, *p*-dimethylaminoazobenzene
Butterherstellung *f* churning, manufacture of butter, butter-making
Butterkorn *n* butter grain (granule)
Buttermilch *f* buttermilk
Buttermischmaschine *f* butter-blending machine
buttern to churn [to butter]
Buttern *n* churning, butter-making
Butterpapier *n* butter [parchment] paper
Butterrefraktometer *n* butyro-refractometer
Buttersäure *f* butyric acid, *butanoic acid
i-**Buttersäure** *f* isobutyric acid, *2-methylpropanoic acid
Buttersäureethylester *m* ethyl butyrate
Buttersäurebakterien *npl* butyric acid bacteria
Buttersäurebenzylester *m* benzyl butyrate
Buttersäuregärung *f* butyric[-acid] fermentation
Butterschmalz *n* butter grease, rendered butter
Butterserum *n* butter serum
Butterungsanlage *f s.* Butterungsmaschine
butterungsfähig churnable
Butterungsfähigkeit *f* churnability
Butterungsmaschine *f* [butter] churn, butter-making machine
Büttgeselle *m (pap)* dipper
Butylacetat *n*, *n*-**Butylacetat** *n* butyl acetate
Butylacetylen *n s.* Hex-1-in
n-**Butylalkohol** *m s.* Butan-1-ol
sec-**Butylalkohol** *m s.* Butan-2-ol
tert-**Butylalkohol** *m s.* *tert*-Butanol
Butylaminobenzoat *n* butyl aminobenzoate
Butylbromid *n*, *prim*-*n*-**Butylbromid** *n* *1-bromobutane, butyl bromide
sec-**Butylbromid** *n* *2-bromobutane, *sec*-butyl bromide
tert-**Butylbromid** *n* *2-bromo-2-methylpropane, *tert*-butyl bromide
Butylcarbinol *n s.* Pentan-1-ol
Butylchlorid *n* butyl chloride, *chlorobutane, *(specif)* 1-chlorobutane
1-Butylen *n s.* But-1-en
2,3-Butylenglykol *n* 2,3-butylene glycol, *butane-2,3-diol
Butylenpolymer[e] *n* butylene polymer
Butylgruppe *f* C_4H_9- butyl group (residue)
Butylhalogenid *n* butyl halide
Butylhydroxyanisol *n (food)* butylated hydroxyanisole, BHA *(antioxidant)*
Butylierung *f* butylation
n-**Butylierung** *f* *n*-butylation
Butylkautschuk *m* butyl rubber, BR
Butylkautschukmischung *f* butyl [rubber] compound
Butylkautschukvulkanisat *n* butyl [rubber] vulcanizate
Butyllatex *m* butyl latex
Butyllösung *f (rubber)* butyl cement
Butylmischung *f s.* Butylkautschukmischung
Butylperbenzoat *n* butyl perbenzoate
Butylradikal *n* 1. [free] butyl radical; 2. *s.* Butylgruppe

Butylregenerat *n (rubber)* butyl reclaim
Butylreifen *m* butyl tyre
Butylrest *m s.* Butylgruppe
Butylschlauch *m* butyl [inner] tube
Butylstearat *n* butyl stearate
Butyraldehyd *m* butyric aldehyde, butanal
Butyrat *n* butyrate
Butyrometer *n* butyrometer
Butyron *n* *heptan-4-one, butyrone
Bypass-Probengeber *m (chromat)* bypass injector
BZ *s.* Backfähigkeitszahl
bz-Phase *f (coll)* smectic phase
B-Zustand *m (plast)* B stage

C

C *s.* Chemiefaserstoff
CA 1. *s.* Celluloseacetat; 2. = anorganische Chemiefaserstoffe
CAB 1. *s.* Celluloseacetatbutyrat; 2. *(**c**ritical **a**ir **b**last) s.* Luftmenge/kritische
Cabalglas *n* cabal glass
Cabanholz *n s.* Camholz
CAB-Test *m (coal)* critical air blast test
CAB-Wert *m (coal)* critical air blast value
Cadaverin *n* cadaverine, *pentano 1,5-diamine, pentamethylenediamine
Cadinen *n* cadinene *(a bicyclic sesquiterpene)*
Cadmium *n* Cd cadmium
Cadmiumacetat *n* cadmium acetate
Cadmiumchlorat *n* cadmium chlorate
Cadmiumdiphosphat *n* cadmium diphosphate, cadmium pyrophosphate
Cadmiumdithionat *n* cadmium dithionate
Cadmiumelektrode *f* cadmium electrode
Cadmiumgelb *n* cadmium yellow, aurora (orient) yellow *(cadmium sulphide)*
cadmiumhaltig cadmium-bearing
Cadmiumhexacyanoferrat(II) *n* cadmium hexacyanoferrate(II)
Cadmiumhydroxid *n* cadmium hydroxide
Cadmium-Nickel-Sammler *m* cadmium-nickel storage cell, nickel-cadmium accumulator (cell)
Cadmium(II)-oxid *n* cadmium oxide
Cadmiumpyrophosphat *n s.* Cadmiumdiphosphat
Cadmiumrot *n* cadmium red
Cadmiumselenat *n* cadmium selenate
Cadmiumselenid *n* cadmium selenide
Cadmiumsulfat *n* cadmium sulphate
Cadmiumsulfid *n* cadmium sulphide
Cadmiumsulfit *n* cadmium sulphite
Cadmiumtellurid *n* cadmium telluride
Cadmiumvergiftung *f* cadmium poisoning
Cadmiumwolframat *n* cadmium wolframate, cadmium tungstate
Caesium *n* Cs caesium
Caesiumalaun *m* caesium alum
Caesiumaluminiumsulfat *n* aluminium caesium sulphate
Caesiumacetat *n* caesium acetate
Caesiumbromid *n* caesium bromide
Caesiumchlorid *n* caesium chloride
Caesiumdisulfid *n* caesium disulphide
Caesiumhexasulfid *n* caesium hexasulphide
Caesiumhydrid *n* caesium hydride
Caesiumhydroxid *n* caesium hydroxide
Caesiumiodid *n* caesium iodide
Caesiummetaperiodat *n* caesium tetraoxoiodate(VII), *(deprecated:)* caesium metaperiodate
Caesiumnitrat *n* caesium nitrate
Caesiumoxid *n* caesium oxide
Caesiumpentaiodid *n* caesium pentaiodide
Caesiumsulfat *n* caesium sulphate
Caesiumsulfid *n* caesium sulphide
Caesiumtetrasulfid *n* caesium tetrasulphide
Caesiumtetroxoiodat(VII) *n* caesium tetraoxoio date(VII)
Cahn-Ingold-Prelog-System *n* Cahn-Ingold-Prelog system, CIP system *(for designating absolute configuration)*
Cairngormstone *m (min)* cairngorm [stone], smoky quartz
Ca-KH *s.* Kalziumkarbonathärte
Calcit *m (min)* calcite, calc-spar, lime spar *(calcium carbonate)*
Calcium *n* Ca calcium
Calciumacetat *n* calcium acetate
~/rohes (technisches) crude calcium acetate, grey acetate, grey lime
Calciumacetylid *n s.* Calciumcarbid
Calciumalginatfaser *f* calcium alginate fibre
Calciumalginatfaserstoff *m* calcium alginate fibre
Calciumaluminat *n* calcium aluminate
Calciumarsenat *n* calcium arsenate, *(specif)* $Ca_3(AsO_4)_2$ tricalcium arsenate(V), calcium arsenate(V)
Calciumarsenid *n* calcium arsenide
Calciumbisulfit *n s.* Calciumhydrogensulfit
Calciumbisulfitkochsäure *f (pap)* calcium bisulphite cooking liquor, calcium-base acid (liquor)
Calciumcarbid *n* calcium carbide, calcium acetylide, carbide *(proper)*
Calciumcarbonat *n* calcium carbonate
~/gefälltes (präzipitiertes) precipitated calcium carbonate
Calciumcarbonathärte *f (hyd)* calcium carbonate hardness
Calciumcarbonatstein *m (hyd)* calcium carbonate scale
Calciumchelat *n* calcium chelate
Calciumchlorat *n* calcium chlorate
Calciumchlorid *n* calcium chloride
Calciumchloridrohr *n (lab)* calcium chloride tube
Calciumchromat *n* calcium chromate
Calciumcitrat *n (pharm)* lime citrate
Calciumcyanamid *n* calcium cyanamide
Calciumcyanid *n* calcium cyanide
Calciumdichromat *n* calcium dichromate

Calciumdihydrogenphosphat *n* calcium dihydrogenphosphate
Calciumdiphosphat *n* calcium diphosphate, calcium pyrophosphate
Calciumdithionat *n* calcium dithionate
Calciumfluorid *n* calcium fluoride
Calciumgluconat *n* calcium gluconate
calciumhart *(hyd)* calcium-hard
Calciumhärte *f (hyd)* calcium hardness
Calciumhexafluorosilicat *n* calcium hexafluorosilicate
Calciumhexacyanoferrat *n* calcium hexacyanoferrate
Calciumhydrid *n* calcium hydride
Calciumhydrogencarbonat *n* calcium hydrogencarbonate
Calciumhydrogenphosphat *n* calcium hydrogenphosphate
Calciumhydrogensulfid *n* calcium hydrogensulphide
Calciumhydrogensulfit *n* calcium hydrogensulphite
Calciumhydroxid *n* calcium hydroxide
Calciumhypochlorit *n* calcium hypochlorite
Calciumhypochlorit-Bleichlauge *f* [calcium hypochlorite] bleach liquor
Calciumhypophosphat *n* calcium hypophosphate
Calciumhypophosphit *n* calcium hypophosphite, calcium phosphinate
Calciumiodat *n* calcium iodate
Calciumiodid *n* calcium iodide
Calciumlack *m* calcium lake
Calciumligninsulfonat *n*, **Calciumlignosulfonat** *n* calcium lignosulphonate
Calciummanganat(VII) *n s.* Calciumpermanganat
Calciummangel *m (agric)* calcium deficiency
Calciummetaborat *n* calcium metaborate
Calciummetaplumbat(IV) *n s.* Calciumtrioxoplumbat(IV)
Calciummetasilicat *n* calcium metasilicate, calcium trioxosilicate
Calciummolybdat *n* calcium molybdate
Calciumnichtcarbonathärte *f (hyd)* calcium noncarbonate hardness
Calciumnitrat *n* calcium nitrate
Calciumnitrid *n* calcium nitride
Calciumnitrit *n* calcium nitrite
Calciumorthoarsenat *n* tricalcium arsenate(V), calcium arsenate(V)
Calciumorthophosphat *n* calcium orthophosphate
Calciumorthoplumbat(IV) *n s.* Calciumtetroxoplumbat(IV)
Calciumorthosilicat *n* calcium orthosilicate, dicalcium tetraoxosilicate
Calciumoxid *n* calcium oxide
Calciumoxiderzeugnis *n (ceram)* lime refractory
Calciumpektat *n* calcium pectate
Calciumpermanganat *n* calcium permanganate
Calciumperoxid *n* calcium peroxide
Calciumphosphat *n* calcium phosphate, *(specif)* $Ca_3(PO_4)_2$ calcium orthophosphate
Calciumphosphid *n* calcium phosphide
Calciumplumbat(II) *n* calcium plumbate(II)
Calciumpyrophosphat *n s.* Calciumdiphosphat
Calciumrhodanid *n s.* Calciumthiocyanat
Calciumsaccharat *n* calcium saccharate
Calciumseife *f* calcium soap
Calciumselenat *n* calcium selenate
Calciumsilicatschlacke *f* phosphate slag *(in manufacturing phosphorus in electric furnaces)*
Calciumspiegel *m* calcium level *(of blood)*
Calciumstearat *n* calcium stearate
Calciumsulfat *n* calcium sulphate
~/gefälltes (präzipitiertes) precipitated calcium sulphate, precipitated gypsum
Calciumsulfhydrat *n s.* Calciumhydrogensulfid
Calciumsulfid *n* calcium sulphide
Calciumsulfit *n* calcium sulphite
Calciumtetroxoplumbat(IV) *n* dicalcium tetraoxoplumbate(IV), calcium plumbate(IV)
Calciumtetroxosilicat *n s.* Calciumorthosilicat
Calciumthiocyanat *n* calcium thiocyanate
Calciumthiosulfat *n* calcium thiosulphate
Calciumtrioxoplumbat(IV) *n* calcium trioxoplumbate(IV)
Calciumtrioxosilicat *n s.* Calciummetasilicat
Calciumwolframat *n* calcium wolframate, calcium tungstate
Calebassenalkaloid *n s.* Calebassencurare-Alkaloid
Calebassencurare *n* calabash (gourd) curare *(from Strychnos specc.)*
Calebassencurare-Alkaloid *n* calabash[-curare] alkaloid, C-alkaloid
Caliche *m* caliche, natural Chilean saltpetre
Californium *n* Cf californium
Calixaren *n (org ch)* calixarene
C-Alkaloid *n n s.* Calebassencurare-Alkaloid
C-Alkylierung *f* C-alkylation
Calvin-Bassham-Zyklus *m s.* Calvin-Zyklus
Calvin-Pflanze *f s.* C_3-Pflanze
Calvin-Zyklus *m* Calvin[-Bassham] cycle, Calvin pathway, C_3 pentose phosphate cycle, C_3 pathway, ribulose diphosphate cycle *(of CO_2 assimilation)*
Camba[l]holz *n s.* Camholz
Camholz *n (dye)* camwood *(from Baphia nitida Afz.)*
Campecheholz *n (dye)* Campeachy (Campechy) wood, logwood *(from Haematoxylum campechianum L.)*
Camphan *n s.* Bornan
Camphan-2-on *n s.* Campher
Camphen *n* camphene *(a bicyclic terpene hydrocarbon)*
Camphenumlagerung *f (org ch)* camphene rearrangement
Campher *m* camphor, camphan-2-one *(a bicyclic terpene ketone)*

~/künstlicher artificial (synthetic) camphor, 2-chlorobornane
~/natürlicher natural camphor *(from Cinnamomum camphora (L.) Sieb.)*
D-**Campher** *m* (+)-camphor, Japan camphor
L-**Campher** *m* (–)-camphor, Matricaria camphor
campherartig camphoraceous
Campherblume *f*, **Campherblüte** *f* flowers of camphor
Campherliniment *n* camphorated oil, camphor liniment
Camphermethode *f* camphor method *(for determining molecular weights)*
~ nach Rast Rast camphor method, Rast [molecular weight] method, Rast micromethod
Campheröl *n* camphor oil *(from Cinnamomum camphora (L.) Sieb.)*
~/leichtes light camphor oil
~/weißes white camphor oil
Camphersäure *f* camphoric acid, 1,2,2-trimethylcyclopentane-1,3-dicarboxylic acid
Camphersäureanhydrid *n* camphoric anhydride, 1,2,2-trimethylcyclopentane-1,3-dicarboxylic anhydride
Camphersäure-3-monoamid *n* camphoric acid α-monoamide, camphoramic acid, 3-carbamoyl-1,2,2-trimethyl-cyclopentanecarboxylic acid
Campherweißöl *n* white camphor oil
Campholsäure *f* campholic acid, 1,2,2,3-tetramethylcyclopentane-1-carboxylic acid
Camphonansäure *f* camphonanic acid, 1,2,2-trimethylcyclopentane-1-carboxylic acid
α-**Camphoramsäure** *f* α-camphoramic acid, 3-carbamoyl-1,2,2-trimethylcyclopentanecarboxylic acid
Camphoronsäure *f* camphoronic acid, 2,3-dimethylbutane-1,2,3-tricarboxylic acid
Camps-Reaktion *f* Camps reaction *(formation of hydroxyquinolines by ring closure)*
Canalgre *n (tann)* canalgre *(roots of Rumex hymenosepalus Torr.)*
Candelkohle *f s.* Cannelkohle
Ca-NKH *s.* Kalzium-Nichtkarbonathärte
Cannel-Braunkohle *f* brown-coal cannel
Cannelkohle *f* cannel (candle, jet) coal
Canneloidkohle *f* canneloid coal
Cannizzaro-Reaktion *f* Cannizzaro reaction *(aldehyde dismutation)*
CAP *s.* Celluloseacetatpropionat
Caprinaldehyd *m* *decanal, *(deprecated:)* capric aldehyde
Caprinamid *n* *decanamide, *(deprecated:)* capric amide
Caprinat *n* *decanoate *(salt or ester of decanoic acid), (deprecated:)* caprate
n-**Caprinsäure** *f* *decanoic acid, *(deprecated:)* capric acid
Caprinsäureanhydrid *n* *decanoic anhydride, *(deprecated:)* capric anhydride
Caprinsäureethylester *m* *ethyl decanoate, *(deprecated:)* ethyl caprate
Caprolactam *n* caprolactam
n-**Capronaldehyd** *m* *hexanal, *(deprecated:)* caproic aldehyde
Capronat *n* *hexanoate *(a salt or ester of hexanoic acid), (deprecated:)* capronate, caproate
Capronitril *n* *hexane nitrile, *(deprecated:)* capronitrile
n-**Capronsäure** *f* *hexanoic acid, *(deprecated:)* caproic acid
Capronsäureanhydrid *n* *hexanoic anhydride, *(deprecated:)* caproic anhydride
Capronsäureethylester *m* *ethyl hexanoate, *(deprecated:)* ethyl caproate
n-**Caprylaldehyd** *m* *octanal, *(deprecated:)* caprylic aldehyde
n-**Caprylalkohol** *m* *1-octanol, *(deprecated:)* caprylic alcohol
Caprylat *n* *octanoate *(a salt or ester of octanoic acid), (deprecated:)* caprylate
Capryliden *n s.* Oct-1-in
Caprylonitril *n* *octane nitrile, *(deprecated:)* caprylonitrile
n-**Caprylsäure** *f* *octanoic acid, *(deprecated:)* *n*-caprylic acid
Capsomer *n (bioch)* capsomere
Caran *n* carane, 3,7,7-trimethylbicyclo[4,1,0]heptane
Carbachol *n* carbachol, carbamylcholine chloride
Carbalkoxylierung *f* alkoxycarbonylation, carbalkoxylation
Carbamat *n* NH_2COOR carbamate, aminoformate *(salt or ester of carbamic acid)*
Carbamid *n* carbamide, urea
Carbamidharz *n* urea resin
Carbamidkunststoff *m* urea plastic
Carbamidsäure *f* carbamic acid, aminoformic acid
Carbamidsäureethylester *m* ethyl carbamate, ethyl aminoformate
Carbaminat *n* carbamate
Carbaminsäure *f s.* Carbamidsäure
Carbamoylcarbonsäure *f* carbamoyl carboxylic acid, amic acid
2-Carbamoylessigsäure *f* 2-carbamoylacetic acid
Carbamoylethylierung *f* carbam[o]ylethylation
N-**Carbamoylglycin** *n* carbamoylglycine, hydantoic acid
Carbamoylierung *f* carbam[o]ylation, carboxamidation
5-Carbamoylnicotinsäure *f* 5-carbamoylnicotinic acid
Carbamylierung *f s.* Carbamoylierung
Carbanilsäure *f* carbanilic acid, phenylcarbamic acid
Carbanion *n* carbanion
Carbarson *n* carbarsone, *N*-carbamoylarsanilic acid
Carbazol *n* carbazole, dibenzopyrrole
Carbazolfarbstoff *m* carbazole dye

Carbazolindophenol *n* carbazole indophenol
Carbazolring *m* carbazole ring
Carbazolsynthese *f*/**Graebe-Ullmannsche** Graebe-Ullmann synthesis of carbazoles
Carbazon *n* carbazone, *(specif)* $H_2NNHCON{=}NH$ carbazone
Carben *n* $R_1{-}C{-}R_2$ carbene, *(specif)* $:CH_2$ carbene, methylene
Carbeniat-Anion *n*, **Carbeniat-Ion** *n s.* Carbanion
Carbeniatstruktur *f* carbeniate structure
Carbeninsertion *f* carbene insertion
Carbeniumion *n*, **Carbeniumkation** *n* carbenium ion, carbocation *(having three-coordinate carbon)*
Carbeniumsalz *n* carbenium salt
Carbeniumstruktur *f* carbenium structure
Carbenoid *n* carbenoid
Carbethoxylierung *f* carb[o]ethoxylation, ethoxycarbonylation
Carbethoxymethylierung *f* carbethoxymethylation, ethoxycarbonylmethylation
Carbid *n* carbide, *(specif)* CaC_2 calcium carbide, calcium acetylide
~/**gesintertes** sintered [hard, metal] carbide
~/**hartes** hard [metal] carbide
~/**interstitielles** interstitial carbide
Carbidacetylen *n* carbide acetylene
Carbidausscheidung *f (met)* carbide precipitation
Carbideinfallentwickler *m* carbide-to-water [acetylene] generator
Carbidgerüst *n* carbide skeleton
Carbidhartmetall *n* cemented [hard] carbide, cemented hard metal
carbidisch carbidic
Carbidkalk *m* carbide (acetylene) lime *(impure calcium hydroxide)*
Carbidofen *m* carbide furnace
~/**offener** open carbide furnace
~/**rotierender** rotating-hearth carbide furnace
Carbidschmelzofen *m s.* Carbidofen
Carbidskelett *n* carbide skeleton
Carbinol *n* 1. carbinol *(any of the branched-chain derivatives of methanol, deprecated term)*; 2. *s.* Methanol
Carboanhydr[at]ase *f s.* Carbonatanhydratase
Carbobenzoxylierung *f* carbobenzoxylation
Carbobromierung *f* bromoformylation, bromocarbonylation
Carbochemie *f* coal chemistry
Carbocyanin *n (dye)* carbocyanine
carbocyclisch carbocyclic, homocyclic, isocyclic
Carbocyclus *m* carbocyclic compound, homocyclic (isocyclic) compound
Carbodicarbonyl *n s.* Trikohlenstoffdioxid
Carbodiimid *n* carbodiimide
Carbodithiosäure *f* dithiocarboxylic acid
carbofunktionell carbon-functional, organofunctional
Carbohalogenierung *f* carbohalogenation, haloformylation, halocarbonylation
Carbokation *n* carbocation *(positively charged carbon atom)*
Carbolöl *n* carbolic oil
Carbolsäure *f* carbolic acid, phenol, hydroxybenzene
~/**rohe** cresylic acid *(a crude mixture of phenols, cresols, and xylenols)*
Carbolschwefelsäure *f s.* Phenolsulfonsäure
Carbomethoxylierung *f* carbomethoxylation, methoxycarbonylation
Carbon *n* C carbon *(for compounds s.* Kohlenstoff*)*
Carbonado *m* carbonado, black (carbon) diamond
Carbon-Alkohol-Extrakt *m (hyd)* carbon-alcohol extract, CAE
Carbonat *n* $M^I_2CO_3$ carbonate
Carbonatalkalität *f (hyd)* carbonate alkalinity, CA
Carbonatanhydratase *f* carbonic anhydrase
Carbonatbleiweiß *n* white lead, ceruse *(lead carbonate hydroxide)*
Carbonatgestein *n* carbonate rock
Carbonathärte *f (hyd)* carbonate hardness (alkalinity), temporary hardness
Carbonathärtebildner *mpl (hyd)* carbonate-hardness constituents
Carbonatisation *f*, **Carbonatisierung** *f (geoch)* carbonatization
Carbonatochelat *n* carbonato chelate
Carbonatokomplex *m* carbonato complex
Carbonatsediment *n* carbonate sediment
Carbonatstein *m (hyd)* carbonate scale
Carbon-Chloroform-Extrakt *m (hyd)* carbon-chloroform extract, CCE
Carbonisation *f* 1. *(food)* carbonation, aeration, impregnation with carbon dioxide; 2. carbonation *(sodium carbonate manufacture)*
Carbonisator *m s.* Carbonisierungskolonne
carbonisieren 1. *(food)* to carbonate, to aerate, to impregnate with carbon dioxide; 2. to carbonate *(in sodium-carbonate manufacture)*
Carbonisierungskolonne *f* carbonating tower *(in sodium-carbonate manufacture)*
carbonitrieren to carbonitride *(steel)*
Carbonitrierung *f* carbonitriding, ni-carbing *(of steel)*
Carbonitril *n* carbonitrile
Carboniumion *n* 1. carbonium ion *(having five-coordinate carbon)*; 2. *s.* Carbeniumion
Carboniumsalz *n* 1. carbonium salt; 2. *s.* Carbeniumsalz
Carbonohydrazid *n* carbonohydrazide, carbazide, *(specif)* $H_2NNHCONHNH_2$ carbonohydrazide, carbazide
Carbonsäure *f* carboxylic acid
~/**einbasige** monocarboxylic acid
~/**dreibasige** tricarboxylic acid
~/**mehrbasige** polycarboxylic acid
~/**zweibasige** dicarboxylic acid
Carbonsäureabbau *m*/**Barbier-Wielandscher** Barbier-Wieland degradation (reaction)

Carbonsäureamid *n* carboxylic acid amide, carboxamide, carboxazylic acid
Carbonsäureaufbau *m*/**Arndt-Eistertscher** Arndt-Eistert synthesis
Carbonsäure-Reduktion *f*/**McFadyen-Stevenssche** McFadyen-Stevens reduction
Carbon-Test *m (petrol)* carbon-residue test
Carbon-Wert *m (petrol)* carbon-residue value
Carbonyl *n* carbonyl [compound], metal carbonyl
Carbonylaktivität *f* carbonyl activity
Carbonylaminoreaktion *f (food)* carbonyl-amine reaction, Maillard reaction, non-enzymatic browning reaction
Carbonylbromid *n* carbonyl bromide, bromophosgene
Carbonylchlorid *n* carbonyl chloride, phosgene
Carbonyleisen *n* carbonyl iron
Carbonylgruppe *f* $>C=O$ carbonyl group
~/ketonartig gebundene ketonic (ketone) carbonyl group, ketonic (ketone, keto) group
carbonylieren to carbonylate
Carbonylierung *f* carbonylation
Carbonylkohlenstoff *m* carbonyl carbon
Carbonyloxid *n* carbonyl oxide
Carbonylsauerstoff *m* carbonyl oxygen
Carbonylsulfid *n* carbonyl sulphide
Carbonylverbindung *f* carbonyl compound
~/vinyloge vinylogous carbonyl compound
Carbonylverfahren *n (met)* carbonyl process
Carboran *n* carborane, *carbaborane
Carbothiosäure *f* monothiocarboxylic acid
Carboxamid *n* carboxamide, carboxylic acid amide
Carboxamidin *n* $RC(=NH)NH_2$ carboxamidine, amidine
Carboxyalkylierung *f* carboxyalkylation
Carboxyethylierung *f* carboxyethylation
Carboxylase *f* carboxylase
Carboxylat *n* carboxylate *(a salt or ester of a carboxylic acid)*
Carboxylat-Ion *n* carboxylate ion
Carboxylatkautschuk *m* carboxylic (acid) rubber
Carboxylatkomplex *m* carboxylate complex
Carboxylende *n* C-terminal group (residue) *(in proteins)*
Carboxylgruppe *f* $-COOH$ carboxyl group
carboxylieren to carboxylate
Carboxylierung *f* carboxylation
Carboxylkautschuk *m s.* Carboxylatkautschuk
Carboxymethoxyessigsäure *f* diglycolic (diglycollic) acid
Carboxymethylcellulose *f* carboxymethylcellulose, CM cellulose, CMC
Carboxymethylierung *f* carboxymethylation
Carboxymethyl-trimethylammonium *n* betaine, *NNN*-trimethylammonioacetate, oxyneurine, lycine
Carbylamin *n* $R-N=C$ isocyanide, *(deprecated:)* carbylamine
Carbylaminreaktion *f* isocyanide reaction, carbylamine test *(for detecting primary amines)*

Carius-Aufschluß *m* Carius method *(for determining halogens, sulphur, and phosphorus in organic compounds)*
Carius-Rohr *n (lab)* Carius (bomb) tube
Carminativum *n (pharm)* carminative
Carminsäure *f* carminic acid
Carneol *m (min)* carnelian, cornelian *(a chalcedony)*
Carnot-Prozeß *m (phys ch)* Carnot cycle
Caroten *n* carotene
Carotenoid *n (org ch)* carotenoid
Carotin *n s.* Caroten
Carpamsäure *f* carpamic acid
Carrageen *n* carrag[h]een, chondrus *(from marine algae Chondrus crispus and Gigartina mamillosa)*
Carrageenan *n* carrageenan *(a polysaccharide mixture obtained from several red algae)*
Carrier *m*/**mobiler** *(bioch)* mobile carrier
Carthagenakautschuk *m* tuno gum *(from Castilloa elastica Cerv.)*
Carthamusöl *n* carthamus (safflower) oil *(from the seeds of Carthamus tinctorius L.)*
Carvacrol *n* carvacrol, 2-hydroxy-4-isopropyl-1-methylbenzene
Carvon *n* carvone *(a monocyclic terpenoid ketone)*
Casale-Verfahren *n* Casale process *(ammonia synthesis)*
Casein *n* casein
~/mizellares micellar casein
Caseinat *n* caseinate
Caseindeckfarbe *f (tann)* casein coating colour
Caseinfarbe *f* casein paint
Caseinfaser *f* casein fibre (staple)
Caseinfaserstoff *m* casein fibre
Caseinleim *m* casein glue
Caseinmizelle *f* casein micelle
Caseinnatrium *n (pharm)* casein-sodium
Caseinogen *n* caseinogen
Caseinsäure *f* caseinic acid *(a diaminotrihydroxydodecanoic acid)*
Caseinspinnlösung *f (text)* casein dope
Casinghead-Benzin *n* casing-head gasoline
Casinghead-Gas *n* casing-head gas
Cassiopeium *n s.* Lutetium
Cassiterit *m (min)* cassiterite, tin stone *(tin(IV) oxide)*
Castner-Zelle *f (el ch)* Castner cell
Cat-Benzin *n* cat-cracked gasoline
Catcracken *n* cat cracking, catalytic (catalyst) cracking
Catcracker *m* cat cracker, catalytic (catalyst) cracker
Catcrack-Verfahren *n* catalytic-cracking process
Catechin *n* catechin, catechol, *(specif)* 3,3',4',5,7-pentahydroxyflavan, catechin
Catecholamin *n* catecholamine
Catenan *n (org ch)* catenane
Catena-Schwefel *m* μ-sulphur *(a modification of plastic sulphur)*

Catena-Verbindung *f (org ch)* catena (catenation) compound
Catformen *n (petrol)* catforming
Catforming-Verfahren *n (petrol)* catforming process
Cavitand *m (org ch)* cavitand
Cay-Cay-Butter *f* cay-cay fat *(from Irvingia oliveri Pierre)*
CaZ *s.* Cetanzahl
C_2-Bruchstück *n (bioch)* two-carbon fragment
C–C-Abstand *m s.* C–C-Bindungslänge
C–C-Bindung *f*[/einfache] *s.* C–C-Einfachbindung
C=C-Bindung *f s.* C–C-Doppelbindung
C≡C-Bindung *f s.* C–C-Dreifachbindung
C–C-Bindungslänge *f* C–C bond length
C–C-Doppelbindung *f* carbon[-carbon] double bond, C=C bond, olefinic linkage
C–C-Dreifachbindung *f* carbon[-carbon] triple bond, C≡C bond, acetylenic linkage
C–C-Einfachbindung *f* carbon[-carbon] single bond, carbon-carbon bond, C–C bond
C–C-Kernabstand *m s.* C–C-Bindungslänge
CCP = Carboxyl-Carrier-Protein
CC-Ruß *m* conducting (conductive) channel black
CCSC-Verfahren *n (pap)* cold [caustic] soda process, cold caustic semichemical process
CCT *s.* Conradson-Carbon-Test
C/C-Verbundwerkstoff *m* carbon-carbon composite, carbon fibre-reinforced carbon, CFC
C–C-Verknüpfung *f s.* C–C-Vernetzung
C–C-Vernetzung *f* carbon-carbon cross-linking
C–C-Vernetzungsstelle *f* carbon-[to-]carbon cross-link, C-C cross-link
CDAA *s.* 2-Chlor-*N,N*-diallylacetamid
CDEC = 2-Chlor-allyl-*N,N*-diethyldithiocarbamat
C_4-Dicarbonsäureweg *m (bioch)* C_4 cycle (pathway), C_4 dicarboxylic acid cycle, Hatch-Slack [CO_2 incorporation] pathway
cDNS *s.* DNA/komplementäre
CdR-Protein *n (bioch)* calcium-dependent regulatory protein
CE *s.* Eiweißchemiefaserstoff
Ceara-Kautschuk *m* Ceara rubber *(from Manihot glaziovii Muell. Arg.)*
CED *(**c**ohesive **e**nergy **d**ensity) s.* Energiedichte/kohäsive
Cedren *n* cedrene *(a tricyclic sesquiterpene)*
Cedrol *n* cedrol, cedar (cedarwood) camphor *(a sesquiterpenoid alcohol)*
C_2-Einheit *f (bioch)* two-carbon fragment
Celluloid *n* celluloid
Cellulose *f* cellulose
~/native (natürliche) natural cellulose
~/oxidierte oxycellulose
~/regenerierte regenerated cellulose
α-Cellulose *f* alpha (chemical) cellulose, α-cellulose
β-Cellulose *f* beta cellulose, β-cellulose
γ-Cellulose *f* gamma cellulose, γ-cellulose
Celluloseabbau *m* cellulose decomposition
Celluloseabfälle *mpl (biot)* cellulosic waste material *(as a substrate)*
Celluloseabkömmling *m* cellulose derivative, cellulosic
Celluloseacetat *n* cellulose acetate, CA, acetylated cellulose
Celluloseacetatbutyrat *n* cellulose acetate butyrate
Celluloseacetatfaser *f* cellulose acetate fibre
Celluloseacetatfaserstoff *m* cellulose acetate fibre
Celluloseacetatmembran *f (hyd)* cellulose acetate membrane *(reverse osmosis)*
Celluloseacetatpropionat *n* cellulose acetate propionate
Celluloseacetatseide *f* cellulose acetate rayon, acetate filament yarn
Celluloseacetatspinnlösung *f* cellulose acetate dope
Cellulosechemiefaser *f* cellulosic fibre
Cellulosechemiefaserstoff *m* cellulosic fibre
Cellulosederivat *n* cellulose derivative, cellulosic
Cellulosediacetat *n* cellulose diacetate, *(text also)* secondary [cellulose] acetate
Cellulosedichtung *f* cellulose gasket
Celluloseerzeugnis *n* cellulosic
Celluloseester *m* cellulose ester
Celluloseether *m* cellulose ether
Celluloseethylether *m* ethylcellulose
Cellulosefaser *f* cellulose fibre
Cellulosefaserstoff *m* cellulose fibre
Cellulosefibrille *f* cellulose fibril
Celluloseflocken *fpl* cotton flock
Celluloseformiat *n* cellulose formate
Celluloseglykolsäure *f* carboxymethylcellulose, CMC
Cellulosehydrat *n* cellulose hydrate
Cellulosekohle *f* cellulose coal
Celluloselack *m* cellulose lacquer
Cellulosenitrat *n* cellulose nitrate
Cellulosenitratlack *m* cellulose nitrate lacquer
Cellulosepropionat *n* cellulose propionate
Celluloseregeneratfaser *f* regenerated cellulose fibre
Celluloseregeneratfaserstoff *m*, **Celluloseregeneratseide** *f* regenerated cellulose fibre
Cellulosesalpetersäureester *m* cellulose nitrate
Cellulosetriacetat *n* cellulose triacetate, *(text also)* primary [cellulose] acetate
Cellulosetrinitrat *n* cellulose trinitrate
Cellulose-Verzuckerung *f* saccharification of cellulose
Cellulosexanthat *n s.* Cellulosexanthogenat
Cellulosexanthogenat *n* cellulose xanthate
Cellulosexanthogensäure *f* cellulose xanthic acid
Cellulosezersetzer *mpl (agric)* cellulose decomposers *(bacteria)*
cellulosisch cellulosic
Celsius-Skala *f*, **Celsius-Temperaturskala** *f* centigrade (Celsius) scale

Celsius-Thermometerskala *f s.* Celsius-Skala

C-endständig C-terminal *(amino acids in proteins)*

Centromer *n (bioch)* centromer

Cephalin *n (bioch)* cephalin, kephalin *(any of various glycerophospholipids), (specif)* 3-phosphatidyl ethanolamine *or* 3-phosphatidyl serine

Cephalosporansäure *f* cephalosporanic acid *(parent compound of an antibiotic)*

Cephalosporin *n* cephalosporin *(antibiotic)*

Cer *n* Ce cerium

Ceramid *n (bioch)* ceramide, *N*-acylsphingosine

Cerasinsäure *f s.* Lignocerinsäure

Cer(III)-bromid *n* cerium(III) bromide, cerium tribromide

Cercarbid *n* cerium carbide

Cer(III)-carbonat *n* cerium(III) carbonate

Cer(III)-chlorid *n* cerium(III) chloride, cerium trichloride

Cerdioxid *n s.* Cerium(IV)-oxid

Cerealieneiweiß *n* cereal protein

Cerebronsäure *f (bioch)* cerebronic acid

Cerebrosid *n* cerebroside *(a lipoid)*

Čerenkov-Strahlung *f (nucl)* Cherenkov radiation

Cererde *f s.* Cer(IV)-oxid

Ceresin *n* ceresin [wax], ceresine

Cerevitinov-Bestimmung *f* Zerewitinoff determination *(of active H atoms)*

Cer(III)-fluorid *n* cerium(III) fluoride, cerium trifluoride

Cer(IV)-fluorid *n* cerium(IV) fluoride, cerium tetrafluoride

Cer(III)-hydroxid *n* cerium(III) hydroxide, cerium trihydroxide

Cer(IV)-hydroxid *n* cerium(IV) hydroxide, cerium tetrahydroxide

Cer(IV)-hydroxidnitrat *n* cerium(IV) hydroxide nitrate

Cerimetrie *f* ceri[o]metry, cerate oxidimetry

Cerini-Dialysator *m* Cerini dialyzer

Cerit *m* cerite *(a siliceous cerium mineral)*

Ceriterde *f* cerite earth *(any of one group of rare-earth metal oxides)*

Cermet *n* cer[a]met, ceramal, ceramel

Cer-Mischmetall *n* misch metal

Cer(III)-nitrat *n* cerium(III) nitrate, cerium trinitrate

Cer(IV)-nitrat *n* cerium(IV) nitrate, cerium tetranitrate

Cer(III)-orthophosphat *n* cerium(III) orthophosphate

Cerotinsäure *f* hexacosanoic acid, *(deprecated:)* cerotic acid

Cer(III)-oxid *n* cerium(III) oxide, cerium trioxide

Cer(IV)-oxid *n* cerium(IV) oxide, cerium dioxide

Cer(III)-oxidchlorid *n* cerium(III) oxide chloride

Cersilicid *n* ceric silicide

Cer(III)-sulfat *n* cerium(III) sulphate

Cer(IV)-sulfat *n* cerium(IV) sulphate

Cer(III)-sulfid *n* cerium(III) sulphide, cerium trisulphide

Certetrafluorid *n s.* Cer(IV)-fluorid

Cerussit *m (min)* cerussite *(lead carbonate)*

Cerylalkohol *m* ceryl alcohol, *hexacosan-1-ol

Cetan *n* *hexadecane, *(deprecated:)* cetane

Cetanol *n s.* Cetylalkohol

Cetanzahl *f*, **Cetanziffer** *f* cetane number (rating)

Cetoleinsäure *f* cetoleic acid, *docos-11-enoic acid

Cetylalkohol *m* *hexadecan-1-ol, *(deprecated:)* cetyl alcohol

Cetylessigsäure *f* stearic acid, *octadecanoic acid, *(deprecated:)* cetylacetic acid

Cetylmercaptan *n s.* Hexadecan-1-thiol

Cetylpalmitat *n* hexadecyl palmitate, cetin, *(deprecated:)* cetyl palmitate

Cetylsäure *f* palmitic acid, *hexadecanoic acid, *(deprecated:)* cetylic acid

Ceylon-Kardamom *m(n)* Ceylon cardamom *(from Elettaria major Sm.)*

Ceylon-Zimt *m* Ceylon cinnamon *(from Cinnamomum zeylanicum Bl.)*

CFAR-Atomisator *m (spectr)* carbon-filament atom reservoir atomizer

CFC-Verbundwerkstoff *m* carbon-carbon composite, carbon fibre-reinforced carbon, CFC

CFR-Motormethode *f* CFR motor method *(for measuring the antiknock qualities of fuels)*

CFR-Prüfmotor *m* CFR [test] engine, Cooperative Fuel Research engine *(for measuring the antiknock qualities of fuels)*

C-Füllmasse *f (sugar)* C massecuite, final (third-grade) massecuite

C-Futter *n* carbon lining *(of a blast furnace)*

Chabasit *m (min)* chabasite, chabazite *(a tectosilicate)*

Chagrinleder *n* shagreen

Chalcedon *m (min)* chalcedony *(a variety of quartz)*

Chalkanthit *m (min)* chalcanthite, blue (copper) vitriol *(copper(II) sulphate 5-water)*

Chalkogen *n* chalcogen *(any of the elements oxygen, sulphur, selenium, tellurium)*

Chalkogenid *n* chalcogenide *(a binary compound of a chalcogen)*

Chalkon *n* chalcone, chalkone, *(specif)* $C_6H_5COCH=CHC_6H_5$ chalcone, chalkone, 1,3-diphenylpropenone, benzylideneacetophenone, benzalacetophenone

Chalkophanit *m (min)* chalcophanite *(hydrous manganese and zinc oxide)*

Chalkopyrit *m (min)* chalcopyrite, chalkopyrite, copper pyrites *(copper(I) iron(III) sulphide)*

Chalkosin *m (min)* chalcosine *(copper(I) sulphide), (specif)* low-chalcosine *(the variety stable below 105 °C)*

Chalkosin(-H) *m (min)* high-chalcosine *(the variety of copper(I) sulphide stable above 105 °C)*

Chalon *n* chalone *(any of a class of compounds which inhibit cell division)*

Chamaenol *n* chamenol, 1-methoxy-2-hydroxy-4-isopropylbenzene
Chamäleon *n***/mineralisches** chameleon mineral *(potassium manganate)*
Chaminsäure *f* chaminic acid *(a monoterpene derivative)*
Chamoispapier *n (phot)* cream paper
Champacablütenöl *n (cosmet)* Champaca oil *(from Michelia longifolia Blume and M. champaca L.)*
Chamsäure *f* chamic acid *(a monoterpene derivative)*
Chance-Kegel *m (min tech)* Chance cone
Chance-Sandflotationsverfahren *n*, **Chance-Sandschwimmverfahren** *n* Chance [sand-floatation] process
Channel-[Black-]Anlage *f* channel black plant
Channel-Black-Verfahren *n* channel process
Channel-Ruß *m* channel (impingement) black *(a gas black)*
chaotrop *(bioch)* chaotropic
Charakter *m* 1. *(ch)* character; 2. base *(of crude petroleum)*
~/abweisender repellency
~/amphoterer amphotericity
~/aromatischer aromatic character, aromaticity
~/asphaltischer asphalt base *(of crude petroleum)*
~/edler *(el ch)* noble character (nature), nobility
~/kovalenter covalent character *(of a bond)*
~/ölabweisender oil repellency
~/ungesättigter unsaturation
~/wasserabweisender water repellency
Charakterisierung *f* characterization *(as of chemical compounds)*
~ durch eine Formel formulation
Charakteristik *f* characteristics; characteristic curve
Chardonnet-Seide *f* chardonnet silk
Charge *f* charge [stock], batch, feed material, feed [stock], load; batch *(product)*
Chargenbetrieb *m* batch operation
Chargendestillation *f* batch distillation
Chargenmasse *f* batch weight
Chargenmischer *m* batch mixer
Chargennitrierung *f* batch nitration
Chargennummer *f* maker's serial number
Chargenprozeß *m s.* Chargenverfahren
Chargentrockner *m* batch dryer
Chargenverfahren *n* batch process
Chargenwaage *f* batch scale
chargenweise batchwise
Charge-transfer-Komplex *m* charge-transfer complex, electron-donor-acceptor complex
chargieren 1. to charge, to load, to feed, to fill; 2. *(text)* to weight *(to add sizing material)*
Chargiertür *f* charging (filling) door, feed[ing] door
Charpy-Prüfung *f* Charpy test *(for measuring the breaking strength of materials under impact)*
C-Harz *n* C-stage resin, resite
Chassis *n***/absolutes** *(cosmet)* absolute chassis
Chaulmoograöl *n (pharm)* chaulmoogra (hydnocarpus, Gynocardia) oil *(from Hydnocarpus specc.)*
Chaulmoograsäure *f* chaulmoogric acid, 13-cyclopent-2-enyltridecanoic acid
Chaulmugraöl *n s.* Chaulmoograöl
Chavikolmethylether *m* chavicol methyl ether, esdragol, 1-allyl-4-methoxybenzene
C-H-Bindung *f* carbon-hydrogen bond
Chebulagsäure *f* chebulagic acid *(an ellagitannin)*
Chebulinsäure *f* chebulinic acid *(a gallotannin)*
Chebulsäure *f* chebulic acid *(a gallotannin)*
Chedakristall *m (geoch)* chadacryst, xenocryst
Chelat *n s.* Chelatverbindung
chelatartig chelate-like
Chelataustauscher *m s.* Chelatharz
chelatbildend chelate-forming, chelating
Chelatbildner *m* chelating agent
Chelatbildung *f* chelation, chelate formation
Chelatbildungskonstante *f* chelate formation constant
Chelatbindung *f* chelate linkage
Chelatdonatorgruppe *f* chelate donor group
Chelateffekt *m* effect of chelation, chelate effect
Chelatfarbstoff *m* chelate pigment
chelatgebunden chelated
Chelatgruppe *f* chelating group
Chelatharz *n* chelate [ion-exchange] resin, chelating [ion exchange] resin
Chelation *f s.* Chelatbildung
chelatisieren to chelate
Chelatkatalyse *f* chelate catalysis
Chelatkomplex *m s.* Chelatverbindung
Chelatligand *m* chelating ligand
Chelatometrie *f* chelatometry, chelatometric titration
chelatometrisch chel[at]ometric
Chelator *m s.* Chelatbildner
Chelatring *m* chelate ring
Chelatstabilität *f* chelate stability
Chelatstabilitätskonstante *f* chelate stability constant
Chelatstruktur *f* chelate structure
Chelatverbindung *f* chelate [compound, complex], crab's-claw complex
Chelidonsäure *f* chelidonic acid, γ-pyrone-2,6-dicarboxylic acid
Chemie *f* chemistry
~/aliphatische aliphatic chemistry
~/allgemeine general chemistry
~/analytische analytical chemistry
~/angewandte applied chemistry
~/anorganische inorganic chemistry
~/beschreibende descriptive chemistry
~/biologische biological chemistry, biochemistry
~ der Atmosphäre chemistry of atmosphere, atmospheric chemistry
~ der Heterocyclen (heterocyclischen Verbindungen) heterocyclic chemistry
~ der Hochpolymeren polymer (high polymeric) chemistry
~ der Kohlenstoffverbindungen chemistry of the carbon compounds

~ **der Koordinationsverbindungen** chemistry of coordination compounds, coordination chemistry
~ **der Milch [und Milchprodukte]** dairy chemistry
~ **der siliciumorganischen Verbindungen** organo-silicon chemistry
~ **des Farbensehens** colour vision chemistry
~ **des Wassers** water (aquatic) chemistry, hydrochemistry
~**/deskriptive** descriptive chemistry
~ **exotischer Atome** chemistry of exotic atoms
~**/experimentelle** experimental chemistry
~**/forensische** forensic (legal) chemistry
~**/forstwirtschaftliche** silvicultural chemistry
~**/fotografische** photographic chemistry, chemistry of photography
~**/geologische** geological chemistry, geochemistry
~**/gerichtliche** *s.* ~/forensische
~**/heiße** *s.* ~ heißer Atome
~ **heißer Atome** hot-atom chemistry, recoil chemistry
~ **hoher Energien** high-energy chemistry
~**/industrielle** industrial chemistry
~**/klinische** clinical chemistry
~**/kosmetische** cosmetic chemistry
~**/landwirtschaftliche** agricultural chemistry, agrochemistry
~**/makromolekulare** polymer (high-polymeric) chemistry
~**/medizinische** medical chemistry
~**/metallurgische** metallurgical chemistry
~**/mineralogische** mineral[ogical] chemistry
~ **neuer Atome** chemistry of exotic atoms
~**/ökologische** environmental chemistry
~**/organische** organic chemistry
~**/pharmazeutische** pharmaceutic[al] chemistry, medicinal chemistry
~**/physikalische** physical chemistry
~**/physiologische** physiologic[al] chemistry
~**/präparative** preparative chemistry
~**/reine** pure chemistry
~**/siliciumorganische** organosilicon chemistry
~**/synthetische** synthetic chemistry
~**/synthetische organische** synthetic organic chemistry
~**/technische** technological chemistry
~**/theoretische** theoretical chemistry
~**/toxikologische** toxicological chemistry
Chemieabwasser *n (hyd)* waste [water] from chemical plants, chemical plant's waste
Chemieanlage *f* chemical plant
Chemieanlagenbau *m* chemical-plant construction
Chemieausrüstung *f* chemical equipment
Chemiebetrieb *m* chemical works (plant)
Chemiefaser *f (text)* man-made fibre, staple [fibre] *(a fibre of relatively short length cut from continuous filaments)*
Chemiefaserindustrie *f* man-made-fibre industry
Chemiefaserstoff *m (text)* man-made fibre
~ **aus natürlichen Polymeren** natural polymer fibre
~ **aus synthetischen Polymeren** synthetic [polymer] fibre
Chemiefeindlichkeit *f* chemophobia
Chemiegrundstoff *m* basic chemical [material]
Chemieholz *n (pap)* pulpwood
Chemieindustrie *f* chemical [processing] industry
Chemieingenieur *m* chemical engineer
Chemieingenieurtechnik *f* chemical engineering technology
Chemieingenieurwesen *n* chemical engineering
Chemieingenieurwissenschaft *f* chemical engineering science
Chemielabor *n* chemistry laboratory
Chemielaborant *m* laboratory assistant
Chemiemüll *m* chemical waste[s]
Chemiepumpe *f* chemical (process) pump
Chemierohstoff *m* chemical raw material
Chemieschliff *m (pap)* chemigroundwood
Chemieseide *f* man-made continuous filament yarn
Chemietechnik *f* chemical technology
chemietechnisch chemical-technological, chemico-technological
Chemietechnologe *m* chemical technologist
Chemiewerk *n* chemical works (plant)
Chemiezellstoff *m* dissolving (rayon) pulp
Chemikalie *f* chemical
~**/fotografische** photographic chemical
~**/industrielle** industrial chemical
Chemikalien *fpl*/ **dosierte (zugesetzte)** chemical feed
Chemikalienbedarf *m* chemical requirements
chemikalienbeständig resistant to chemicals, chemical-resistant
Chemikalienbeständigkeit *f* resistance to chemicals
Chemikaliendosierpumpe *f* chemical feed pump
Chemikaliendosierung *f* chemical feeding
Chemikaliendosis *f* chemical dosage
Chemikalieneinsatz *m* chemical application (utilization)
chemikalienfest *s.* chemikalienbeständig
Chemikaliengehalt *m* chemical content
Chemikalienkosten *pl* chemical costs
chemikalienresistent *s.* chemikalienbeständig
Chemikalienrückführung *f* chemical recovery, recovery (conservation) of chemicals
Chemikalienüberschuß *m* excess chemical
Chemikalienverbrauch *m* chemical consumption
Chemikalienverhältnis *n (pap)* chemical[-to-wood] ratio
Chemikalienverlust *m* loss of chemicals, chemical loss
Chemikalienzugabe *f* chemical addition (feeding, introduction)
Chemikalienzulauf *m* 1. chemical feed; 2. chemical feed inlet
Chemikalienzusatz *m* 1. *s.* Chemikalienzugabe; 2. *(quantitatively:)* chemical feed
Chemikalienzuteileinrichtung *f* chemical feed equipment, chemical feeder

Chemiker *m* chemist
~/forschender research chemist
~/industrieller industrial chemist
~/organischer *s.* Organochemiker
~/technischer technical (technological) chemist
~/verantwortlicher chemist in charge
~/wissenschaftlich tätiger research chemist
Chemikerin *f* woman chemist
Chemilumineszenz *f* chemiluminescence
Chemilumineszenz-Analysator *m*, **Chemilumineszenz-Meßgerät** *n* chemiluminescence analyser
Chemilumineszenz-Methode *f (anal)* chemiluminescent method
chemilumineszierend chemiluminescent
chemisch chemical • **auf chemischem Wege** by a chemical route, by chemical means, chemically
Chemischreiniger *m (text)* dry cleaner
Chemischreinigung *f (text)* dry cleaning
chemisch-technisch chemical-technological, chemico-technological
chemisch-technologisch chemical-technological, chemico-technological
Chemisierung *f* chemicalization *(as of agriculture)*
Chemismus *m* chemism *(of a reaction)*
chemisorbieren to chemisorb, to chemosorb
Chemisorption *f* chemisorption, chemosorption, chemical (activated) adsorption
Chemolumineszenz *f s.* Chemilumineszenz
Chemophobie *f* chemophobia
chemoselektiv chemoselective *(reagent)*
Chemoselektivität *f* chemoselectivity *(of a reagent)*
chemosorbieren *s.* chemisorbieren
Chemostat *m (biot)* chemostat
Chemosteril[is]ans *n*, **Chemosterilisierungsmittel** *n* chemosterilant
Chemosynthese *f* chemosynthesis *(microbiology)*
chemosynthetisch chemosynthetic *(microbiology)*
chemotaktisch *(biol)* chemotactic *(moving in relation to chemical agents)*
Chemotaxis *f (biol)* chemotaxis, chemotaxy *(movement in relation to chemical agents)*
Chemotaxonomie *f (biol)* chemotaxonomy, chemical taxonomy, biochemical systematics
Chemotechniker *m* chemical technician
Chemotherapeutikum *n* chemotherapeutant, chemotherapeutic agent
chemotherapeutisch chemotherapeutic[al]
Chemotherapie *f* chemotherapy, chemotherapeutics
chemotropisch *(biol)* chemotropic
Chemotropismus *m (biol)* chemotropism *(orientation in relation to chemicals)*
chemotroph chemo[auto]trophic
Chemotrophie *f (biol)* chemoautotrophy *(gain of assimilation energy from oxidation processes)*
Chemurgie *f* chemurgy *(industrial utilization of organic raw materials)*
Chenodesoxycholsäure *f (bioch)* chenodeoxycholic acid
Chenopodiumöl *n (pharm)* chenopodium oil *(from Chenopodium ambrosioides L. var. anthelminthicum Gray)*
Cheshunt-Mischung *f* Cheshunt compound *(a pesticide consisting of $CuSO_4$ and $(NH_4)_2CO_3$)*
Chiastolith *m* chiastolite *(a variety of andalusite)*
Chibouharz *n* tacamahaca [gum], West Indian elemi *(from Bursera gummifera L.)*
Chicagoblau *n* Chicago blue *(any of several direct dyes)*
Chicagosäure *f* Chicago acid, 2 S acid, 1-amino-8-hydroxynaphthalene-2,4-disulphonic acid
Chicle *m* chicle (zapota) gum *(from Achras sapota L.)*
chiffrieren *(nomencl)* to cipher
Chiffriersystem *n (nomencl)* ciphering system
Chiffrierung *f (nomencl)* ciphering, cipher notation
Chilesalpeter *m* Chile saltpetre (nitre, nitrate), Chilean (Chilian) nitrate, soda nitre *(sodium nitrate)*
~/roher caliche, natural Chilean saltpetre
Chimylalkohol *m* chimyl alcohol, *2,3-dihydroxypropyl hexadecylether
Chinaalkaloid *n s.* Chinarindenalkaloid
Chinagelb *n* yellow arsenic [sulphide], arsenic (king's) yellow (gold), royal yellow, orpiment [yellow] *(technically pure arsenic(III) sulphide)*
Chinagrün *n* Chinese green, locao, locaonic acid *(natural dye from Rhamnus specc.)*
Chinaholzöl *n* tung (China wood) oil *(from the seeds of Aleurites fordii Hemsl.)*
Chinaldin *n* quinaldine, 2-methylquinoline
Chinaldinalkyliodid *n* quinaldine alkiodide
Chinaldinchelat *n* quinaldine chelate
Chinaldinsäure *f* quinaldic acid, quinoline-2-carboxylic acid
Chinalizarin *n* quinalizarin, 1,2,5,8-tetrahydroxyanthraquinone
Chinametall *n* Chinese bronze *(a Cu-Ag-Pb-Au alloy)*
Chinapapier *n* China (Chinese, Indian) paper, India [proof] paper
Chinarindenalkaloid *n* cinchona (quinoline-type) alkaloid
Chinasäure *f* quinic acid, *1,3,4,5-tetrahydroxycyclohexane-1-carboxylic acid
Chinasilber *n* China (Chinese) silver *(a Cu-Ni-Sn-Ag alloy)*
Chinatalg *m* Chinese vegetable tallow *(from Sapium sebiferum (L.) Roxb.)*
Chinäthylin *n s.* Dihydrochinin
Chinawachs Chinese [tree] wax, insect wax, vegetable spermaceti *(secreted by scales)*
Chinaweiß *n* Chinese white *(zinc oxide)*
Chinazolin *n* quinazoline, 5,6-benzpyrimidine
Chinesischweiß *n s.* Chinaweiß
Chinhydron *n (org ch)* quinhydrone
Chinhydronelektrode *f* quinhydrone electrode
Chinidin *n* quinidine *(a cinchona alkaloid)*
Chinidinsulfat *n* quinidine sulphate

Chinin *n* quinine *(a cinchona alkaloid)*
Chininhydrochlorid *n* quinine hydrochloride
Chininsulfat *n* quinine sulphate
Chiniofon *n* chiniofon, 8-hydroxy-7-iodoquinoline-5-sulphonic acid
Chinizarin *n* quinizarin, 1,4-dihydroxyanthraquinone
Chinizarinkondensation *f* quinizarin condensation
chinoid quin[on]oid
Chinolat *n* quinolate *(salt or ester of quinolinic acid)*
Chinolin *n* quinoline, chinoline, 2,3-benzpyridine
Chinolinalkaloid *n* quinoline alkaloid
Chinolinblau *n* cyanine blue, pigment blue 15
Chinolin-4-carbonsäure *f* quinoline-4-carboxylic acid, cinchoninic acid
Chinolinethyliodid *n* quinoline ethiodide
Chinolinfarbstoff *m* quinoline dye
Chinolinsäure *f* quinolinic acid, pyridine-2,3-dicarboxylic acid
Chinolinsynthese *f* quinoline synthesis
~/Combessche Combes quinoline synthesis
~/Friedländersche Friedländer quinoline synthesis
~/Skraupsche Skraup quinoline synthesis
Chinolizidin *n* quinolizidine
Chinolizidinalkaloid *n* quinolizidine (lupin) alkaloid
Chinolizidinring *m* quinolizidine ring
Chinolylamin *n* quinolylamine, aminoquinoline
Chinon *n* quinone, *(specif)* *p*-benzoquinone, cyclohexadiene-1,4-dione
***o*-Chinon** *n* *o*-benzoquinone, orthoquinone
***p*-Chinon** *n* *p*-benzoquinone, *cyclohexadiene-1,4-dione
Chinondiimin *n* quinonediimine
Chinondioximvernetzung *f*, **Chinondioximvulkanisation** *f* *(rubber)* quin[on]oid cure
Chinonfarbstoff *m* quin[on]oid dye
Chinonimin *n* quinonimine, quinone imine
Chinoniminfarbstoff *m* quinone imine dye
Chinonmethid *n* quinone methide
Chinonmonoxim *n* quinone monoxime
Chinonoxim *n* quinonoxime
Chinonring *m* quinone ring
Chinoxalin *n* quinoxaline, benzo-1,4-diazine
Chinuclidin *n* quinuclidine, 1,4-ethylenepiperidine
chiral chiral *(stereochemistry)*
Chiralität *f* chirality *(stereochemistry)*
Chiralitätszentrum *n* chiral centre *(stereochemistry)*
Chitin *n* chitin *(a polysaccharide)*
chitinig, chitinös chitinous
Chitosamin *n* chitosamine, D-glucosamine, GlcN, 2-amino-2-deoxy-D-glucopyranose
Chlathrat *n s.* Clathrat
Chlor *n* Cl chlorine • **mit ~ behandeln** to chlorinate, to chlorinize
~/aktives *s.* ~/wirksames
~/freies [wirksames] *(hyd)* free [available] chlorine
~/gebundenes *(hyd)* combined chlorine
~/gebundenes wirksames *(hyd)* combined available chlorine
~/gelöstes organisches (organisch gebundenes) *(hyd)* dissolved organic chlorine, DOCl
~/überschüssiges *(hyd)* excess chlorine
~/wirksames active (available) chlorine
Chloracetal *n* chloroacetal, diethyl chloroacetal
Chloracetaldehyd *m* chloroacetaldehyde, *chloroethanal
Chloraceton *n* chloroacetone, *chloropropanone
Chloracetophenon *n* chloroacetophenone, *(specif)* α-chloroacetophenone
Chloracetylierung *f* chloroacetylation
Chlorakne *f* *(med)* chloracne
Chloral *n* chloral, trichloroacetaldehyde
Chloralhydrat *n* chloral hydrate, trichloroacetaldehyde hydrate
Chloralkali *n* alkali-chlorine
Chloralkalielektrolyse *f* chlor-alkali electrolysis (operation)
Chloralkali-Elektrolyseanlage *f* chlor-alkali (alkali-chlorine) factory
Chloralkali-Elektrolysezelle *f* chlor-alkali (alkali-chlorine) cell
Chlorameisensäure *f* chloroformic acid
Chlorameisensäureester *m* chloroformic acid ester, chloroformate, chlorocarbonate
Chlorameisensäuretrichlormethylester *m* trichloromethyl chloroformate, diphosgene
Chloramin *n*, ***N*-Chloramin** *n* chloramine, *N*-chloroamine, *(specif)* NH_2Cl chloramine
Chloraminierung *f* chloroamination
Chloraminverfahren *n* *(hyd)* chloramine process, chloramination, ammonia-chlorine process, combined residual chlorination
Chlor-Ammoniak-Verfahren *n s.* Chloraminverfahren
Chloranil *n* chloranil, tetrachlor-*p*-benzoquinone
Chloranilin *n* chloroaniline
Chloranlage *f* *(hyd)* chlorinator
Chloranthrachinon *n* chloroanthraquinone
Chlorarylierung *f* chloroarylation
Chlorat *n* M^IClO_3 chlorate
Chloräthan *n*, **Chloräthyl** *n s.* Chlorethan
2-Chloräthylalkohol *m s.* 2-Chlorethanol
Chloräthylen *n s.* Chlorethen
Chlorator *m s.* Chlorierungskessel
Chloratsprengstoff *m* chlorate explosive
Chloraufschluß *m* *(pap)* pulping with chlorine
~ nach Pomilio-Celdecor Celdecor-Pomilio process
Chlorbedarf *m* *(hyd)* chlorine demand
Chlorbenzen *n* chlorobenzene
Chlorbenzilat *n* chlorobenzilate, ethyl-4,4'-dichlorobenzilate
Chlorbenzoesäure *f* chlorobenzoic acid
Chlorbenzol *n s.* Chlorbenzen
Chlorbenzolcarbonsäure *f s.* Chlorbenzoesäure
Chlorbernsteinsäure *f* chlorosuccinic acid
Chlorbleiche *f* chlorine bleaching; *(text)* chemic[k]
Chlorbromsilberpapier *n* *(phot)* chlorobromide paper

1-Chlorbutan *n* 1-chlorobutane
Chlorbutylkautschuk *m* chlorobutyl rubber, chlorinated butyl rubber
Chlorcalciumröhrchen *n (lab)* calcium chloride tube
Chlorcalciumzylinder *m* [gas] drying jar
Chlorcresol *n* chlorocresol
Chlorcyan *n* cyanogen chloride, chlorine cyanide
Chlorcyanhydrin *n* chlorocyanohydrin
Chlordehydroxylierung *f* chlorodehydroxylation
2-Chlor-*N,N*-diallylacetamid *n* 2-chloro-*N,N*-diallylacetamide, CDAA *(a herbicide)*
Chlordimethylarsin *n* chlorodimethylarsine, cacodyl chloride
Chlordinitrobenzen *n*, **Chlordinitrobenzol** *n* chlorodinitrobenzene
Chlordioxid *n* chlorine dioxide
Chlordioxidbleiche *f (pap)* chlorine dioxide bleaching
Chlordioxid-Bleichlauge *f (pap)* chlorine dioxide bleaching liquor
Chlordioxid-Bleichstufe *f (pap)* chlorine dioxide bleaching stage
Chlordosis *f (hyd)* chlorine dosage
chlorecht fast to chlorine
Chlorechtheit *f* chlorine fastness, fastness to chlorine
Chloreinwirkungsbecken *n (hyd)* chlorine contact basin
Chlorelektrode *f* chlorine electrode
Chlorellagsäure *f* chlorellagic acid
chloren to chlorinate; *(text)* to chemick *(to treat with calcium hypochlorite)*
~/erneut *(hyd)* to rechlorinate
Chloressigsäure *f* chloroacetic acid
Chlorethan *n* chloroethane
2-Chlorethanol *n* 2-chloroethanol, 2-chloroethyl alcohol
Chlorethansäure *f* chloroethanoic acid, chloroacetic acid
Chlorethen *n* *chloroethene, vinyl chloride
Chlorethylgruppe *f* $ClCH_2CH_2$– chloroethyl group
Chlorethylierung *f* chloroethylation
Chloreton *n* chloretone, acetone chloroform, 1,1,1-trichloro-2-hydroxy-2-methylpropane
Chlorfluorierung *f* chlorofluorination
chlorfrei chlorine-free
Chlorgas *n* chlorine gas
Chlorgasanlage *f (hyd)* chlorinator
Chlorgeruch *m (hyd)* chlorine odour
Chlorgeschmack *m (hyd)* chlorinous taste
chlorhaltig chlorine-containing
Chlorheptoxid *n s.* Chlor(VII)-oxid
1-Chlorhexan *n* 1-chlorohexane
Chlorhydrin *n* chlorohydrin
Chlorhydrochinon *n* chlorohydroquinone, chloroquinol
Chlorid *n* M^ICl chloride
chloridfrei free from chloride
chloridhaltig chloride-containing
Chloridhärte *f (hyd)* chloride hardness
Chloridpapier *n (phot)* [silver-]chloride paper
Chloridschmelze *f* chloride melt
Chloridsole *f* chloride brine
chlorieren to chlorinate; *(min tech)* to chloridize, to chloridate *(to treat with chlorine or with a chloride)*
Chlorierer *m s.* Chlorierungskessel
Chlorierung *f* chlorination; *(min tech)* chloridization, chloridation *(treatment with chlorine or with a chloride)*
~ bei niedriger Stoffdichte *(pap)* low-density chlorination
~ in der Seitenkette *(org ch)* side-chain chlorination
~ in saurem Medium *(pap)* acidic chlorination
~/photochemische *(org ch)* photochemical chlorination
Chlorierungsbehälter *m*, **Chlorierungsgefäß** *n s.* Chlorierungskessel
Chlorierungskessel *m* chlorinating vessel, chlorinator
Chlorierungsmittel *n* chlorinating agent
Chlorierungsprodukt *n* chlorinated product, chlorinate
Chlorierungsstufe *f* chlorination (chlorine) stage
Chlorierungsturm *m* chlorination tower, chlorinator; *(pap)* reaction tower *(pulp bleaching)*
Chlorierungsverfahren *n* method of chlorination
Chlorinität *f* chlorinity, Cl%
Chloriodierung *f* chloroiodination, iodochlorination
Chlor-IPC *n* chloro-IPC, C-IPC, chloroisopropyl-*N*-phenylcarbamate *(a herbicide)*
Chlorit *m (min)* chlorite *(any of a series of phyllosilicates)*
Chlorit *n* M^IClO_2 chlorite
Chloritbleiche *f (text)* chlorite bleaching
Chloritbleichechtheit *f (text)* chlorite bleaching fastness
Chloritisation *f*, **Chloritisierung** *f (geoch)* chloritization
Chloritoid *m (min)* chloritoid *(a neso-subsilicate)*
Chloritschiefer *m (geol)* chlorite schist
Chlorkalk *m* chlorinated lime, chloride of lime
Chlorkautschuk *m* chlorinated rubber
Chlorkautschuk[anstrich]farbe *f* chlorinated-rubber paint
Chlorkautschuklack *m* chlorinated-rubber lacquer
Chlorknallgas *n* chlorine detonating gas *(mixture of chlorine and hydrogen)*
Chlorknallgaskette *f* hydrogen-hydrochloric acid cell
Chlorkohlensäure *f s.* Chlorameisensäure
Chlorkohlenwasserstoff *m* chlorinated hydrocarbon
Chlorlignin *n (pap)* chlorolignin, chlorinated lignin
Chlorlösung *f***/hochkonzentrierte** *(hyd)* full-strength chlorine solution
~/wäßrige chlorine solution
Chlormenge *f (hyd)* chlorine dosage

Chlormercurierung *f* chloromercuration
Chlormethan *n* *chloromethane, methyl chloride
Chlormethin *n* chlormethine, mustine, *N*-di-(2-chloroethyl)methylamine hydrochloride
Chlormethoxylierung *f* chloromethoxylation
Chlormethyl *n s.* Chlormethan
o-**Chlormethylbenzen** *n*, *o*-**Chlormethylbenzol** *n* 2-chloro-1-methylbenzene, *o*-chlorotoluene
Chlormethylierung *f* chloromethylation
Chlormonosilan *n* chloromonosilane, chlorosilane
Chlormonoxid *n s.* Chlor(I)-oxid
Chlornaphthalen *n* chloronaphthalene
Chlornitrobenzen *n*, **Chlornitrobenzol** *n* chloronitrobenzene
Chlornitroparaffin *n* chloronitroparaffin
Chloroantimonat *n* chloroantimonate
Chloroargentat *n* chloroargentate
Chloroaurat(I) *n* $M^I[AuCl_2]$ chloroaurate(I), dichloroaurate(I)
Chloroaurat(III) *n* $M^I[AuCl_4]$ chloroaurate(III), tetrachloroaurate(III)
Chlorobromat *n* chlorobromate
Chlorocadmat *n* chlorocadmate
Chlorochromat *n* $M^I[CrO_3Cl]$ chlorochromate
Chloroctahydrat *n s.* Chlor-8-Wasser
Chlorocuprat *n* chlorocuprate
Chloroform *n* chloroform, trichloromethane
chloroformlöslich soluble in chloroform
Chloroformlöslichkeit *f* solubility in chloroform
Chlorogensäure *f* chlorogenic acid, 3-[3,4-dihydroxycinnamoyl]quinic acid
Chlorogold(III)-säure *f* chloroauric(III) acid, tetrachloroauric(III) acid
Chloroguanid *n* chloroguanide, 1-(*p*-chlorophenyl)-5-isopropylbiguanide
Chloroiodat *n* chloroiodate
Chloroiridat(III) *n* $M^I_3[IrCl_6]$ chloroiridate(III), hexachloroiridate(III)
Chlorokomplex *m* chlorocomplex
Chlorolyse *f* chlorinolysis
Chloromanganat *n* chloromanganate
Chloromercurat *n* chloromercurate
Chloromolybdat *n* chloromolybdate
Chloroniobat *n* chloroniobate
Chloronium-Ion *n* chloronium ion
Chloroniumverbindung *f* chloronium compound
Chloroosmat(III) *n* $M^I_3[OsCl_6]$ chloroosmate(III), hexachloroosmate(III)
Chloropalladat(II) *n* $M^I_2[PdCl_4]$ chloropalladate(II), tetrachloropalladate(II)
Chloropentammincobalt(III)-chlorid *n* chloropentaamminecobalt(III) chloride
Chloropentamminplatin(IV)-chlorid *n* chloropentaammineplatinum(IV) chloride
Chlorophosphat *n* chlorophosphate
Chlorophyll *n (bioch)* chlorophyll, leaf green
Chlorophyllid *n (bioch)* chlorophyllide
Chlorophyllkorn *n*, **Chloroplast** *m (biol)* chloroplast
Chloroplatinat(II) *n* $M^I_2[PtCl_4]$ chloroplatinate(II), tetrachloroplatinate(II)
Chloroplatinat(IV) *n* $M^I_2[PtCl_6]$ chloroplatinate(IV), hexachloroplatinate(IV)
Chloroplatin(IV)-säure *f* chloroplatinic(IV) acid, hexachloroplatinic(IV) acid
Chloroplumbat(IV) *n* $M^I_2[PbCl_6]$ chloroplumbate
Chloropren *n* chloroprene, *2-chlorobuta-1,3-diene
Chloroprenkautschuk *m* chloroprene rubber, CR
Chlororhenat *n* chlororhenate
Chlororhodat(III) *n* $M^I_3[RhCl_6]$ chlororhodate(III), hexachlororhodate(III)
Chlororuthenat(IV) *n* $M^I_2[RuCl_6]$ chlororuthenate(IV)
Chlorosäure *f* chloro acid *(coordination chemistry)*
Chloroschwefelsäure *f* chlorosulphuric acid
Chlorose *f* 1. *(bot)* chlorosis *(yellowing of green parts as due to mineral deficiencies)*; 2. *(med)* chlorosis *(an iron-deficiency anaemia)*
Chlorostannat *n* chlorostannate
Chlorosulfat *n* chlorosulphate
chlorosulfonieren *s.* chlorsulfonieren
Chlorotellurat(IV) *n* $M^I_2[TeCl_6]$ chlorotellurate(IV), hexachlorotellurate(IV)
Chlorotitanat(IV) *n* $M^I_2[TiCl_6]$ chlorotitanate(IV), hexachlorotitanate(IV)
Chlorowolframat *n* *chlorowolframate, chlorotungstate
Chlor(I)-oxid *n* chlorine(I) oxide, dichlorine monooxide
Chlor(IV)-oxid *n* chlorine(IV) oxide, chlorine dioxide
Chlor(VII)-oxid *n* chlorine(VII) oxide, dichlorine heptaoxide
Chloroxybenzol *n s.* Chlorphenol
Chlorozinkat *n* chlorozincate
Chlorozirconat(IV) *n* chlorozirconate(IV), hexachlorozirconate(IV)
Chlorparaffin *n* chlorinated paraffin
1-Chlorpentan *n* 1-chloropentane
Chlorphenol *n* chlorophenol, chlorinated phenol
Chlorphenylendiamin *n* chlorophenylenediamine
Chlorphenylierung *f* chlorophenylation
o-m-p-**Chlorphenylierung** *f o,m,p*-chlorophenylation
Chlorphosphonierung *f*, **Chlorphosphonylierung** *f* chlorophosphonation, chlorophosphonylation
Chlorpikrin *n* chloropicrin, trichloronitromethane
1-Chlorpropan *n* 1-chloropropane
2-Chlorpropan *n* 2-chloropropane
3-Chlorpropan-1,2-diol *n* *3-chloropropane-1,2-diol, [glycerol] α-monochlorohydrin
Chlorpropanon *n* *chloropropanone, chloroacetone
3-Chlorprop-1-en *n*, **3-Chlorpropen-(1)** *n* 3-chloroprop-1-ene
Chlorpropham *n s.* Chlor-IPC
2-Chlorpropionsäure *f* 2-chloropropionic acid
3-Chlorpropionsäure *f* 3-chloropropionic acid

Chlorpropyl *n s.* 1-Chlorpropan
3-Chlorpropylen *n s.* 3-Chlorprop-1-en
3-Chlorpropylenoxid *n* 3-chloropropylene oxide, *chloromethyloxiran, α-epichlorhydrin
Chlorretention *f*, **Chlorrückhaltevermögen** *n* chlorine retention
Chlorsäure *f* chloric acid
Chlorschiefer *m (geol)* chlorite schist
Chlorschwefel *m s.* Dischwefeldichlorid
Chlorsilan *n* chlorosilane, *(specif)* SiH_3Cl chloromonosilane
~/organisches organochlorosilane
Chlorsilber *n (phot)* silver chloride
Chlorsilberpapier *n (phot)* [silver-]chloride paper
chlorsulfonieren to chlorosulphonate
Chlorsulfonierung *f* chlorosulphonation
Chlorsulfonsäure *f s.* Chloroschwefelsäure
Chlortetracyclin *n* chlorotetracycline, CTC, aureomycin *(an antibiotic)*
Chlortetroxid *n* chlorine tetraoxide
o-**Chlortoluen** *n*, *o*-**Chlortoluol** *n o*-chlorotoluene
α-**Chlortoluen** *n*, α-**Chlortoluol** *n* α-chlorotoluene
Chlortrifluorethylen *n* chlorotrifluoroethylene, CFE
Chlortrocknung *f* chlorine drying
Chlorturm *m s.* Chlorierungsturm
Chlorüberschuß *m (hyd)* [free] residual chlorine, [amount of] chlorine residual, free [available] chlorine residual, excess [of] chlorine
~/gebundener combined residual chlorine
Chlorung *f (hyd)* chlorination
~/alkalische chlorination (oxidation) under alkaline conditions
~/erneute rechlorination
~ über den Durchbruchspunkt hinaus breakpoint chlorination
Chlorungsmittel *n (hyd)* chlorinating agent, chlorination chemical
Chlorungsverfahren *n (hyd)* method of chlorination
Chlorverbindung *f*/**organische** organochlorine compound
Chlorverbindungen *fpl*/**extrahierbare organische** *(hyd)* extractable organic chlorine compounds, EOCl
Chlorverbrauch *m* chlorine consumption
Chlorverbrauchszahl *f (pap)* chlorine number
Chlorverflüssigung *f* chlorine liquefaction
Chlorwasser *n* chlorine water, *(esp hyd)* chlorine solution
Chlor-8-Wasser *n* chlorine-8-water, chlorine octahydrate
Chlor-Wasser-Lösung *f (hyd)* chlorine solution
~/hochkonzentrierte full-strength chlorine solution
Chlorwasserstoff *m* hydrogen chloride
~/flüssiger liquid hydrogen chloride
~/gasförmiger *s.* Chlorwasserstoffgas
~/trockener anhydrous hydrogen chloride
~/verflüssigter liquid hydrogen chloride
~/wasserfreier *s.* ~/trockener
~/wasserhaltiger (wäßriger) aqueous hydrogen chloride
Chlorwasserstoffanlagerung *f* addition of hydrogen chloride
Chlorwasserstoffgas *n* hydrogen chloride gas, gaseous hydrogen chloride
Chlorwasserstofflösung *f* hydrogen chloride solution
chlorwasserstoffsauer chlorohydric
Chlorwasserstoffsäure *f* hydrochloric acid
α-**Chlorxylen** *n*, α-**Chlorxylol** *n* α-chloroxylene
Chlorzahl *f (pap)* chlorine number
Chlorzelle *f* chlorine cell *(electrolysis)*
Chlorzinklauge *f (tech)* zinc-chloride solution
Chlorzugabe *f (hyd)* addition of chlorine
Chlorzurückhaltung *f s.* Chlorretention
Chlorzusatz *m s.* Chlorzugabe
Cholesterin *n s.* Cholesterol
cholesterinisch *s.* cholesterisch
cholesterisch cholesteric
Cholesterol *n (bioch)* cholesterol
Cholesterolspiegel *m (med)* cholesterol level
Cholsäure *f* cholic acid, 3,7,12-trihydroxy-5β-cholan-24-oic acid
Chondrit *m* chondrite *(a meteoric stone)*
Choriongonadotropin *n* chorionic gonadotropin
Chorismasäure *f (bioch)* chorismic acid
Chorismat *n (bioch)* chorismate
Chorisminsäure *f s.* Chorismasäure
C-Horizont *m (soil)* C-horizon
Christbaum *m (petrol)* Christmas tree *(at the well head for controlling oil or gas production)*
Christmas-Faktor *m (bioch)* Christmas factor
Chrom *n* Cr Chrom *n*
Chrom(II)-acetat *n* chromium(II) acetate, chromous acetate
Chrom(III)-acetat *n* chromium(III) acetate, chromic acetate
Chromalaun *m* chrome alum, *(specif)* $KCr(SO_4)_2 \cdot 12H_2O$ potassium (potash) chrome alum, chrome potash alum
Chromammin *n* chromammine, chromium ammine
Chromat *n* $M^I_2CrO_4$ chromate
Chromatgelatine *f* chrome (chromatic) gelatin
chromat[is]ieren to chromate, to chromatize
Chromatobarverfahren *n (anal)* chromatobar technique
Chromatogramm *n* chromatogram
~/absteigendes descending chromatogram
~/äußeres external (liquid) chromatogram
~/differentielles differential chromatogram
~/fließendes *s.* ~/äußeres
~/inneres internal chromatogram
Chromatographie *f* chromatography
~/absteigende descending chromatography
~/flußprogrammierte flow-programmed chromatography
~/hydrophobe hydrophobic [interaction] chromatography
~/mehrdimensionale multidimensional chromatography, MDC

~ **mit normaler Substanzmenge** full-scale chromatography
~ **mit umgekehrten (vertauschten) Phasen** reversed-phase (rear-phase) chromatography
~**/temperaturprogrammierte** programmed-temperature [gas] chromatography
~**/zweidimensionale** two-dimensional chromatography
Chromatographiegefäß *n* chromatography tank
~ **für die aufsteigende Methode** ascending chromatography tank
Chromatographiekammer *f* chromatographic (chromatography) chamber, chromatographic cabinet
Chromatographiepapier *n* chromatographic paper
chromatographierbar capable of being chromatographed
chromatographieren to chromatograph
Chromatographierkammer *f s.* Chromatographiekammer
Chromatographierohr *n* chromatographic tube
Chromatographiesäule *f* chromatographic column
chromatographisch chromatographic
Chromatometrie *f* chromatometry, dichromate titration
chromatometrisch chromatometric
Chromatopackverfahren *n (chromat)* chromatopack method (technique)
Chromatophor *n (biol)* chromatophore
Chromatopileverfahren *n* chromatopile method (technique) *(variant of paper chromatography)*
Chromatothermographie *f* chromatothermography
Chromatverfahren *n (text)* chromate [dyeing] method
Chromaventurin *m (glass)* chrome (green) aventurine *(a defect)*
Chrombeize *f (text)* chrome (chromium) mordant
Chrombeizverfahren *n (text)* chrome mordant process
Chrom(II)-bromid *n* chromium(II) bromide, chromium dibromide
Chrom(III)-bromid *n* chromium(III) bromide, chromium tribromide
Chrombrühe *f (tann)* chrome liquor
Chrom(II)-carbonat *n* chromium(II) carbonate
Chromcarbonyl *n* chromium carbonyl, chromium hexacarbonyl
Chrom(II)-chlorid *n* chromium(II) chloride, chromium dichloride
Chrom(III)-chlorid *n* chromium(III) chloride, chromium trichloride
Chromdi... *s. a.* Chrom(II)-...
chromdiffundieren to chromize
Chromdioxid *n s.* Chrom(IV)-oxid
Chromeisenerz *n s.* Chromit
2*H*-Chromen-2-on *n s.* α-Chromon
Chromentwicklungsfarbstoff *m* afterchrome (chrome-developed) dye
Chromerz *n* chromium ore
Chromfarbstoff *m s.* Chromierungsfarbstoff
chromfeucht *(tann)* blue wet
Chrom(II)-fluorid *n* chromium(II) fluoride, chromium difluoride
Chrom(III)-fluorid *n* chromium(III) fluoride, chromium trifluoride
Chromformiat *n* chromium formate
chromgar, chromgegerbt chrome tanned
Chromgelb *n* chrome yellow, lemon chrome *(mixture or mixed crystals of lead chromate and lead sulphate)*
Chromgerbbrühe *f (tann)* chrome liquor
chromgerben to chrome
Chromgerbung *f* chrome (chromium) tannage, chroming
Chromglimmer *m (min)* chrome mica
Chromgrubengerbung *f* chrome pit tannage
Chrom(II)-hydroxid *n* chromium(II) hydroxide
Chrom(III)-hydroxid *n* chromium(III) hydroxide
chromieren *(dye)* to chrome; to chromize *(metals)*
Chromierfarbstoff *m s.* Chromierungsfarbstoff
Chromierung *f (dye)* chroming; chromizing *(of metals)*
~ **aus der flüssigen Phase** salt-bath chromizing *(of metals)*
~ **aus der Gasphase** gas chromizing *(of metals)*
Chromierungsfarbstoff *m* chrome [mordant] dye
Chrom(II)-iodid *n* chromium(II) iodide, chromium diiodide
Chromit *m (min)* chromite, chrome iron ore, chromic iron *(iron(II) chromium(III) oxide)*
Chromknoten *m s.* Chromaventurin
Chromkomplex *m* chromium complex
Chromleder *n* chrome leather
~**/frisch gegerbtes** blue chrome leather
Chromleim *m* chrome glue
Chrommolybdänstahl *m* chrome molybdenum steel
Chrommonosulfid *n s.* Chrom(II)-sulfid
Chrommonoxid *n s.* Chrom(II)-oxid
Chrom-Muskovit *m (min)* fuchsite *(a phyllosilicate)*
Chromnickelstahl *m* chrome nickel steel
Chrom(III)-nitrat *n* chromium(III) nitrate
Chromnitrid *n* chromium nitride
Chromocker *m (min)* chrome ochre *(a phyllosilicate)*
Chromodruck *m* [multi]colour printing
Chromoersatzkarton *m* imitation chromo board
Chromogen *n* chromogen *(a compound containing a chromophore)*
Chromoisomer[e] *n* chromoisomer
Chromoisomerie *f* chromoisomerism
Chromomer *n (bioch)* chromomer
Chromon *n* chromone, benzopyrone
α-**Chromon** *n* α-chromone, 1,2-benzopyrone, coumarin, 2*H*-chromen-2-one
chromophor chromophoric
Chromophor *m* chromophore, *(specif)* chromophoric (colour-bearing) group
Chromoproteid *n*, **Chromoprotein** *n* chromoprotein

Chromorange *n* chrome orange *(a basic lead chromate)*
Chromorohpapier *n* chromo base (body) paper
Chrom(III)-orthophosphat *n* chromium(III) orthophosphate, chromium(III) phosphate
Chromosmiumessigsäurelösung *f*/**Flemmings** *(biol)* Flemming solution *(a fixative)*
Chromosphäre *f* [solar] chromosphere
Chromotropsäure *f* chromotropic acid, 4,5-dihydroxynaphthalene-2,7-disulphonic acid
Chrom(II)-oxalat *n* chromium(II) oxalate, chromous oxalate
Chrom(II)-oxid *n* chromium(II) oxide, chromium monooxide
Chrom(III)-oxid *n* chromium(III) oxide, dichromium trioxide
Chrom(IV)-oxid *n* chromium(IV) oxide, chromium dioxide
Chrom(VI)-oxid *n* chromium(VI) oxide, chromium trioxide
Chrom(VI)-oxidchlorid *n s.* Chromylchlorid
Chromoxidgrün *n* chrome [oxide] green, green cinnabar, oil green *(chromium(III) oxide)*
~ **feurig** *s.* Chromoxidhydratgrün
Chromoxidhydratgrün *n* chrome (emerald) green, Mittler's (Guignet's) green, transparent chromium oxide *(hydrated chromium oxide)*
Chrompapier *n* chromo paper
Chromphosphid *n* chromium phosphide
Chromrot *n* chromate (chrome, Persian) red, American vermilion *(a basic lead chromate)*
Chromsäure *f* chromic acid
Chromsäureoxidation *f* chromic-acid oxidation
Chromsäureverfahren *n* chromic-acid process, Bengough-Stuart process *(anodic oxidation)*
Chromschwefelsäure *f (lab)* [chromic acid] cleaning mixture
Chromstahl *m* chromium (chrome) steel
Chrom(II)-sulfat *n* chromium(II) sulphate
Chrom(III)-sulfat *n* chromium(III) sulphate
Chrom(II)-sulfid *n* chromium(II) sulphide, chromium monosulphide
Chrom(II,III)-sulfid *n* chromium(II,III) sulphide, trichromium tetrasulphide
Chrom(III)-sulfid *n* chromium(III) sulphide, dichromium trisulphide
Chromtetrasulfid *n s.* Chrom(II,III)-sulfid
Chromtri... *s. a.* Chrom(III)-...
Chromtrioxid *n s.* Chrom(VI)-oxid
Chromverstärker *m (phot)* chromium intensifier
Chromylchlorid *n* chromyl chloride, chromium(VI) dichloride dioxide
Chromzinnober *m s.* Chromrot
Chronoamperometrie *f (anal)* chronoamperometry
~ **mit anodischer Auflösung durch linearen Potentialanstieg** anodic stripping chronoamperometry with linear potential sweep
Chronocoulometrie *f (anal)* chronocoulometry
Chronopotentiometrie *f (anal)* chronopotentiometry
~/**derivative** derivative chronopotentiometry
Chrysamin *n* chrysamine *(a coal-tar dye)*
Chrysanthemum[monocarbon]säure *f* chrysanthemumic acid, chrysanthemummonocarboxylic acid *(a cyclopropane derivative)*
Chrysatropasäure *f* chrysatropic acid, scopoletin, 7-hydroxy-6-methoxycoumarin
Chrysen *n* chrysene, 1,2-benzophenanthrene
Chrysergonsäure *f* chrysergonic acid *(a fungal pigment from Claviceps purpurea (Fr.) Tul.)*
Chrysin *n* chrysin, 5,7-dihydroxyflavone
Chrysoberyll *m (min)* chrysoberyl, gold beryl *(beryllium aluminate)*
Chrysoidin *n* chrysoidine, 2,4-diamonoazobenzene
Chrysokoll *m (min)* chrysocolla *(copper(II) metasilicate)*
Chrysophanol *n s.* Chrysophansäure
Chrysophansäure *f* chrysophanic acid, chrysophanol, 1,8-dihydroxy-3-methylanthraquinone
Chrysopras *m (min)* chrysoprase *(a variety of quartz)*
Chrysotil *m (min)* chrysotile, Canadian asbestos
Chrysotilasbest *m (min)* serpentine asbestos
C/H-Verhältnis *n* C/H ratio
Chymase *f*, **Chymosin** *n* chymosin, chymase, rennin
Chylomikron *n* chylomicron *(microscopically visible lipid particle in blood plasma or lymph)*
CI = Colour Index
Čičibabin-Kohlenwasserstoff *m* Chichibabin hydrocarbon
CIDEP *s.* Elektronenpolarisation/chemisch induzierte dynamische
CI-Massenspektrometer *n* chemical ionization mass spectrometer
Cinchonaalkaloid *n s.* Chinarindenalkaloid
Cinchonidin *n* cinchonidine *(alkaloid)*
Cinchoninsäure *f* cinchoninic acid, quinoline-4-carboxylic acid
cine-Substitution *f (org ch)* cine-substitution
Cinnabarit *m (min)* cinnabar, liver ore *(mercury(II) sulphide)*
Cinnamal *n*, **Cinnamaldehyd** *m s.* Zimtaldehyd
Cinnamat *n* cinnamate *(salt or ester of cinnamic acid)*
Cinnamein *n* cinnamein, benzyl cinnamate
Cinnamsäure *f s.* Zimtsäure
Cinnamylaldehyd *m s.* Zimtaldehyd
Cinnamylalkohol *m s.* Zimtalkohol
Cinnolin *n* cinnoline, 1,2-benzodiazine
CI-Nummer *f s.* Colour-Index-Nummer
CIPC *s.* Chlor-IPC
CIP-System *n s.* Cahn-Ingold-Prelog-System
cis-Addition *f* cis addition
cis-cis-Isomer[e] *n* cis-cis isomer
cis-Form *f* cis form
cis-Isomer[e] *n* cis isomer
cis-Konformation *f* cis conformation, C *(torsion angle* $\pm$ *180°)*

cis-Lage *f* cis position
cis-Leiter-Konformation *f (bioch)* ladder conformation *(of deoxyribonucleic acid)*
cisoid cisoid
cis-orientiert cis-oriented
cis-Säure *f* cis acid
cis-ständig cis • ~ **[angeordnet] sein** to be cis
cis-Stellung *f* cis position
cis-taktisch *(plast)* cistactic
cis-Taktizität *f (plast)* cistacticity
cis-trans-Gemisch *n* mixture of cis and trans isomers
cis-trans-Isomer[e] *n* cis-trans isomer, geometric isomer
cis-trans-Isomerie *f* cis-trans isomerism, geometric isomerism
cis-trans-Umwandlung *f* cis-trans conversion
Cistron *n (bioch)* [DNA] cistron
Citraconsäure *f* citraconic acid, *cis-methyl-butenedioic acid
Citral *n* **A** citral a, geranial, **trans*-3,7-dimethyl-octa-2,6-dienal
~ **B** citral b, neral, **cis*-3,7-dimethylocta-2,6-dienal
***cis*-Citral** *n s.* Citral B
***trans*-Citral** *n s.* Citral A
Citrat *n* citrate *(salt or ester of citric acid)*
citratlöslich *(soil)* citrate-soluble
Citratlöslichkeit *f (soil)* citrate solubility
Citrat(*si*)-Synthase *f (bioch)* condensing enzyme
Citratzyklus *m (bioch)* citric-acid (tricarboxylic-acid) cycle, TCA cycle, Krebs cycle
Citrazinsäure *f* citrazinic acid, *2,6-dihydroxypyridine-4-carboxylic acid
Citrin *m (mln)* citrine, false topaz *(a variety of quartz)*
Citronellal *n*, **Citronellaldehyd** *m* citronellal, *3,7-dimethyl-oct-6-enal
Citronellöl *n* citronella oil *(from Cymbopogon specc.)*
Citronensäure *f* citric acid, *2-hydroxypropane-1,2,3-tricarboxylic acid
Citronensäuregärung *f* citric-acid fermentation
Citronensäuretriethylester *m* triethyl citrate
Citronensäurezyklus *m s.* Citratzyklus
Citronin *n* **A** *(dye)* sulphur yellow S
Citrovorumfaktor *m* citrovorum factor, leucovorin, N^5-formyltetrahydrofolic acid, folinic acid
Citrusöl *n* citrus oil
C-Kette *f* carbon chain
C_3-Kette *f* three-carbon chain
C_6-Kette *f* six-carbon chain
C_1-Körper *m (bioch)* one-carbon compound
C_3-Körper *m (bioch)* three-carbon compound
C_4-Körper *m (bioch)* four-carbon compound
Claisen-Kolben *m* Claisen [distilling] flask
Claisen-Kondensation *f* Claisen condensation *(between esters or between esters and ketones)*
Claisen-Schmidt-Kondensation *f* Claisen-Schmidt condensation *(for preparing unsaturated aldehydes or ketones)*
Claisen-Umlagerung *f* Claisen rearrangement *(O-allyl C-allyl ortho rearrangement)*
Clarain *m* clarain *(constituent of bright coal)*
Clarkes *npl*, **Clarke-Zahlen** *fpl (geoch)* Clarke numbers, clarkes
Clathrat *n* clathrate [inclusion compound], cage compound
Clathratbildner *m* clathrate former
Clathratbildung *f*, **Clathration** *f* clathrate formation
Clathratverbindung *f s.* Clathrat
Claude-Verfahren *n* Claude process *(synthesis of ammonia from nitrogen and hydrogen)*
Claus-Anlage *f* Claus [sulphur] plant
Clausius-Mosotti-Formel *f*, **Clausius-Mosotti-Gleichung** *f (phys ch)* Clausius-Mosotti equation
Claus-Ofen *m* Claus reactor *(for converting hydrogen sulphide to sulphur)*
Cl-Austauscher *m (hyd)* chloride-form (Cl-form) exchanger *(ion exchange)*
Claus-Verfahren *n* Claus process *(for converting hydrogen sulphide to sulphur)*
Clavicepsalkaloid *n* ergot alkaloid
Clavin[alkaloid] *n* clavine [alkaloid]
Clayden-Effekt *m (phot)* Clayden effect
Clayton-Gas *n* Clayton gas *(mixture of SO_2 and N_2)*
Clemmensen-Reduktion *f* Clemmensen reduction *(of aldehydes or ketones to hydrocarbons)*
Clerici-Lösung *f* Clerici's solution *(of thallium malonate and thallium formate)*
Cleveland-Flammpunkt[s]prüfer *m*, **Cleveland-Gerät** *n* Cleveland open tester (cup), Cleveland apparatus
Cleve-Säure *f* Cleve's acid *(naphth-1-ol-5-sulphonic acid or any of several naphth-1-ylamine sulphonic acids)*
Cleve-Säure-1,6 *f* Cleve's acid-1,6, Cleve's 1,6 acid, Cleve's β acid, naphth-1-ylamine-6-sulphonic acid
Cleve-Säure-1,7 *f* Cleve's acid-1,7, Cleve's 1,7 acid, naphth-1-ylamine-7-sulphonic acid
Cleve-Säure-6 *f s.* Cleve-Säure-1,6
Clupanodonsäure *f* clupanodonic acid *(any of several polyunsaturated carboxylic acids, specif docosa-4,7,11-trien-18-ynoic acid)*
Clupein *n* clupeine *(a protamine)*
Clusius-Dickel-Verfahren *n* Clusius-Dickel method, thermal-diffusion method *(for separating isotopes)*
Clusius-Trennrohr *n* Clusius column *(for separating isotopes)*
Cluster-ion *n* cluster ion
CM-Cellulose *f* CM cellulose, carboxymethylcellulose, CMC
CMP = kapazitiv gekoppeltes Mikrowellenplasma
CN *s.* Chemiefaserstoff aus natürlichen Polymeren
C/N-Verhältnis *n (soil, biot)* C/N ratio, carbon-to-nitrogen ratio
CoA *s.* Coenzym A
CO_2-Akzeptor-Verfahren *n (coal)* CO_2 acceptor process *(coal gasification with heat carriers)*

Cobalamin *n (bioch)* cobalamine, corrinoid, corrin, corphyrin, vitamin B12 compound
Cobalt *n* Co cobalt
~/radioaktives radioactive cobalt, radiocobalt, *(specif)* ^{60}Co cobalt-60
Cobalt-60 *n* ^{60}Co cobalt-60
Cobalt... *s. a.* Kobalt... *for technical terms*
Cobalt(II)-acetat *n* cobalt(II) acetate
Cobalt(III)-acetat *n* cobalt(III) acetate
Cobaltammin *n* cobalt ammine
Cobalt(II)-arsenat *n* cobalt(II) arsenate, *(specif)* $Co_3(AsO_4)_2$ cobalt(II) orthoarsenate
Cobaltat *n* cobaltate
Cobalt(II)-bromat *n* cobalt(II) bromate
Cobalt(II)-bromid *n* cobalt(II) bromide, cobalt dibromide
Cobalt(II)-carbonat *n* cobalt(II) carbonate
Cobaltchelat *n* cobalt chelate
Cobalt(II)-chlorat *n* cobalt(II) chlorate
Cobalt(II)-chlorid *n* cobalt(II) chloride, cobalt dichloride
Cobaltchloridpapier *n* cobalt chloride test paper
Cobalt(II)-chromat *n* cobalt(II) chromate
Cobalt(II)-cyanid *n* cobalt(II) cyanide
Cobaltdi... *s. a.* Cobalt(II)-...
Cobaltdisulfid *n* cobalt disulphide
Cobalt(II)-fluorid *n* cobalt(II) fluoride, cobalt difluoride
Cobalt(III)-fluorid *n* cobalt(III) fluoride, cobalt trifluoride
Cobalt(II)-hexacyanoferrat(II) *n* cobalt(II) hexacyanoferrate(II)
Cobalt(II)-hexacyanoferrat(III) *n* cobalt(II) hexacyanoferrate(III)
Cobalt(II)-hexafluorosilicat *n* cobalt(II) hexafluorosilicate, cobalt fluorosilicate
Cobalt(II)-hydroxid *n* cobalt(II) hydroxide
Cobalt(III)-hydroxid *n* cobalt(III) hydroxide
Cobaltiak *n* cobalt(III) ammine
Cobalt(II)-iodat *n* cobalt(II) iodate
Cobalt(II)-iodid *n* cobalt(II) iodide, cobalt diiodide
Cobaltin *m (min)* cobaltine, cobalt glance *(cobalt sulpharsenide)*
Cobaltkatalysator *m*, **Cobaltkontakt** *m* cobalt catalyst
Cobaltmonoselenid *n s.* Cobalt(II)-selenid
Cobaltmonosulfid *n s.* Cobalt(II)-sulfid
Cobaltmonoxid *n s.* Cobalt(II)-oxid
Cobalt(II)-nitrat *n* cobalt(II) nitrate
Cobalt(II)-orthoarsenat(V) *n* cobalt(II) orthoarsenate, cobalt(II) arsenate
Cobalt(II)-orthophosphat *n* cobalt(II) orthophosphate, cobalt(II) phosphate
Cobalt(II)-orthosilicat *n* cobalt(II) orthosilicate
Cobalt(II)-orthotitanat *n* cobalt(II) orthotitanate
Cobaltoxid *n* cobalt oxide, *(specif)* CoO cobalt(II) oxide
Cobalt(II)-oxid *n* cobalt(II) oxide, cobalt monooxide
Cobalt(II,III)-oxid *n* cobalt(II,III) oxide, tricobalt tetraoxide
Cobalt(III)-oxid *n* cobalt(III) oxide, dicobalt trioxide
Cobalt(II)-perchlorat *n* cobalt(II) perchlorate
Cobalt(II)-perrhenat *n* cobalt(II) perrhenate, cobalt(II) tetraoxorhenate(VII)
Cobalt(II)-phosphat *n* cobalt(II) phosphate, *(specif)* $Co_3(PO_4)_2$ cobalt(II) orthophosphate
Cobalt(II)-phosphit *n* *cobalt phosphonate, cobalt(II) phosphite
Cobaltphthalocyanin *n* cobalt phthalocyanine
Cobalt(II)-rhodanid *n s.* Cobalt(II)-thiocyanat
Cobaltseife *f* cobalt soap
Cobalt(II)-selenat *n* cobalt(II) selenate
Cobalt(II)-selenid *n* cobalt(II) selenide
Cobalt(II)-sulfat *n* cobalt(II) sulphate
Cobalt(III)-sulfat *n* cobalt(III) sulphate
Cobalt(II)-sulfid *n* cobalt(II) sulphide
Cobalt(II)-sulfit *n* cobalt(II) sulphite
Cobalttetracarbonyl *n* cobalt tetracarbonyl
Cobalttetroxid *n s.* Cobalt(II,III)-oxid
Cobalt(II)-tetroxorhenat(VII) *n s.* Cobalt(II)-perrhenat
Cobalt(II)-tetroxosilicat *n s.* Cobalt(II)-orthosilicat
Cobalt(II)-thiocyanat *n* cobalt(II) thiocyanate, cobalt(II) rhodanide
Cobalttricarbonyl *n* cobalt tricarbonyl
Cobalttrifluorid *n s.* Cobalt(III)-fluorid
Cobalttrioxid *n s.* Cobalt(III)-oxid
Cobaltwolframat *n* *cobalt wolframate, cobalt tungstate
Cobamid *n (bioch)* cobamide
Cochenillesäure *f* cochenillic acid, 5-hydroxytoluene-2,3,4-tricarboxylic acid
Cochrane-Trommelprüfung *f* Cochrane [abrasion] test
Code *m***/genetischer** *(bioch)* genetic code
Codeeinheit *f s.* Codon
Codehydr[ogen]ase *f* **I** *s.* Nicotinamid-adenin-dinucleotid
~ **II** *s.* Nicotinamid-adenin-dinucleotidphosphat
Codeinon *n (org ch)* codeinone
Codenummer *f* **der Gruppe** *(coal)* group number
~ **der Klasse** class number
~ **der Untergruppe** subgroup number
Codestillation *f* codistillation
Codetriplett *n s.* Codon
Codewort *n (bioch)* code word
Codeziffer *f (coal)* subgroup number
~/Dritte subgroup number
~/Erste class number
~/Zweite group number
codieren *(bioch)* to code *(the sequence of amino acids)*
Codon *n (bioch)* codon, coding (nucleotide) triplet
Codon-Synonym *n (bioch)* codon synonym
C-O-Doppelbindung *f* carbonyl double bond
COED-Verfahren *n (coal)* COED process *(fluidized-bed coal pyrolysis)*

Coelestin *m (min)* coelestine *(strontium sulphate)*
CO_2-Entfernung *f* carbon-dioxide removal
CO_2-Entgaser *m (hyd)* decarbonator, carbonating tower, degasifier for CO_2 removal
CO_2-Entsorgung *f (biot)* CO_2 removal
CO_2-Entwickler *m*, **CO_2-Entwicklungsapparat** *m* carbon dioxide generator
Coenzym *n* coenzyme, prosthetic (active) group
~ **I** *s.* Nicotinamid-adenin-dinucleotid
~ **II** *s.* Nicotinamid-adenin-dinucleotidphosphat
~ **A** coenzyme A, HSCoA
coenzymatisch *(bioch)* coenzymatic
CO_2-Erstarrungsverfahren *n (met)* CO_2 process *(a mouldmaking process)*
Cofaktor *m (biot)* cofactor *(enzyme technology)*
Coferment *n s.* Coenzym
Coffein *n* caffeine, 1,3,7-trimethylxanthine
coffeinarm low-caffeine
coffeinfrei caffeine-free, decaffeinated
coffeinhaltig caffeinic, containing caffeine
Coffein-Natriumbenzoat *n (pharm)* caffeine and sodium benzoate
Coffein-Natriumsalicylat *n (pharm)* caffeine and sodium salicylate
CO_2-Fixierung *f* CO_2 fixation
COGAS-Verfahren *n (coal)* COGAS process *(pyrolysis and gasification of coal)*
C=O-Gruppe *f* $>C=O$ group, carbonyl group
CO-Hämoglobin *n* carboxyhaemoglobin, carbon monoxy haemoglobin
Cohuneöl *n* cohune (corozo-nut) oil *(seed oil from Orbignya cohune (Mart.) Dahlgr.)*
Coin-Technik *f (text)* coin technique
Coion *n (phys ch)* co-ion
Cokatalysator *m* co-catalyst
Cokatalyse *f* co-catalysis
Co-Kontakt *m* cobalt catalyst
Cokondensation *f (plast)* co-condensation
CO-Konvertierung *f (coal)* carbon monoxide conversion (shift), CO conversion, water-gas shift, shift conversion
Colaminkephalin *n* 3-phosphatidyl ethanolamine
CO_2-Laser *m* CO_2 laser
Colburn-Verfahren *n (glass)* Colburn [sheet] process, Libbey-Owens process, LOF-Colburn process
Coldcreme *f* cold cream
Coldrubber *m* cold [polymerized] rubber, low-temperature polymer (rubber), LTP
Colemanit *m (min)* colemanite *(a hydrous calcium borate)*
Collin-Ofen *m* Collin oven *(a coke oven)*
CO_2-Löscher *m* carbon dioxide fire extinguisher
Colour-Index-Nummer *f* Colour Index number, CI No.
Columbium *n s.* Niob
Comonomer[e] *n* comonomer
compoundieren to compound *(oils)*
Compoundöl *n* compounded oil *(a lubricant)*
Compreg *n* compreg, compressed resin-impregnated wood
Compton-Effekt *m* Compton effect, Compton scattering
Compton-Elektron *n* Compton [recoil] electron
Compton-Rückstoßteilchen *n* Compton recoil particle
Compton-Streuung *f s.* Compton-Effekt
Compton-Verschiebung *f* Compton shift
Compton-Wellenlänge *f* Compton wavelength *(of an electron)*
computergestützt computer-aided, computer-assisted
Conchinin *n* quinidine, conquinine, conchinine *(a cinchona alkaloid)*
Conducting-Channel-Ruß *m* conducting (conductive) channel black
Coniferylalkohol *m* coniferyl alcohol, 4-γ-hydroxypropenyl-2-methoxyphenol
Coniin *n* coniine, 2-propylpiperidine *(alkaloid)*
Conradson-Carbon *n* Conradson coke (carbon) residue
Conradson-Carbon-Test *m* Conradson [carbon] test
Conradson-Carbon-Wert *m s.* Conradson-Verkokungswert
Conradson-Methode *f* Conradson [coking] method, Conradson carbon residue method
Conradson-Test *m s.* Conradson-Carbon-Test
Conradson-Verkokungswert *m*, **Conradson-Verkokungszahl** *f* Conradson coke number (value), Conradson value
Containerpappe *f* container board
Convolvulinolsäure *f* convolvulinolic acid, 11-hydroxytetradecanoic acid
Convolvulinsäure *f* convolvulinic acid *(a glucoside)*
COOH-Gruppe *f* –COOH carboxyl group
Copalin *m (min)* copalite, copaline, highgate resin *(an amber-like fossil resin)*
Cope-Eliminierung *f* Cope elimination *(pyrolysis of amine oxides)*
Cope-Umlagerung *f (org ch)* Cope rearrangement
Copigment *n (bioch)* copigment
Copolyaddition *f* copolyaddition
Copolykondensation *f* copolycondensation
Copolymer[e] *n* copolymer
~/alternierendes alternating copolymer
~ **mit hohem Styrolgehalt** high-styrene copolymer
~/statistisches random copolymer
Copolymerisat *n s.* Copolymer
Copolymerisatfaser *f* copolymer fibre
Copolymerisatfaserstoff *m* copolymer fibre
Copolymerisation *f* copolymerization
~/alternierende alternating copolymerization
~/azeotrope azeotropic copolymerization
~/ionische ionic copolymerization
~ **mit Vernetzung** copolymerization with cross-linking
~/radikalische radical copolymerization
~/statistische random copolymerization

Copolymerisationsgleichung *f* copolymer equation
Copolymerisationsparameter *m* [copolymerization, monomer] reactivity ratio
Copolymerisationsdiagramm *n* copolymer composition plot
Copolymerisationsverhalten *n* copolymerization behaviour
copolymerisieren to copolymerize
Copolymerkette *f* copolymer chain
Copolymerzusammensetzung *f* copolymer composition
Coppée-Flammofen *m* Coppée oven *(a coke oven)*
Coprogen *n* coprogen *(a sideramine)*
Cordierit *m (min)* cordierite *(a silicate of aluminium, iron, and magnesium)*
Cordieritkeramik *f* cordierite ceramics
Cordieritporzellan *n* cordierite porcelain
Cordieritweißware *f* cordierite whiteware
Cordit *m* cordite *(an explosive)*
Corepressor *m* corepressor *(enzyme kinetics)*
Corilagin *n* corilagin *(an ellagitannin)*
Corium *n (tann)* corium
Cori-Zyklus *m (bioch)* Cori cycle
Corning-Band-Maschine *f (glass)* Corning ribbon machine
Corning-Glas *n* Corning glass *(for electrodes)*
Cornu-Prisma *n (spectr)* Cornu prism
Coronand *m* coronand *(monocyclic crown compound)*
Coronat *n* coronate *(chelate complex of a coronand)*
Corpus-luteum-Hormon *n* progestational hormone, progesterone
Corpus-luteum-Präparat *n (pharm)* luteoid
Corrin *n*, **Corrinoid** *n (bioch)* corrin, corrinoid, cobalamine, corphyrin, vitamin B12 compound
Corrinringsystem *n (bioch)* corrin ring system
Corticoid *n (bioch)* corticoid
Corticosteroid *n (bioch)* corticosteroid
Corticosteron *n* corticosterone *(an adrenocortical hormone)*
Corticotropin *n* corticotropin, adrenocorticotropic hormone, ACTH
Cortin *n* cortin *(collectively for a group of adrenocortical hormones)*
Cortisol *n* cortisol *(an adrenocortical hormone)*
Cortison *n* cortison *(an adrenocortical hormone)*
Co-Stufenpolymerisation *f* step-growth (step-reaction) copolymerization
Cosubstrat *n (bioch)* cosubstrate
Cosynthese *f (biot)* cosynthesis
Cotoin *n* cotoin, *(specif)* $C_6H_2(OH)_2(OCH_3)COC_6H_5$ cotoin, 2,6-dihydroxy-4-methoxy-benzophenone
Co-Transport *m (bioch)* symport *(one form of carrier transport)*
Cotton-Effekt *m (phys ch)* Cotton effect *(anomalous optical rotation near absorption bands)*
Cottonhartfett *n* hydrogenated cotton[seed] oil
Cottonöl *n* cotton[seed] oil
Cottrell-Abscheider *m* Cottrell precipitator
Cottrell-Entstaubungsverfahren *n* Cottrell [electric precipitation] process
Cottrell-Filter *n*, **Cottrell-Staubfilter** *n s.* Cottrell-Abscheider
Couepinsäure *f* couepic acid, licanic acid *(either of two isomeric oxoalkenoic acids)*
Couette-Apparat *m s.* Couette-Viskosimeter
Couette-Strömung *f* Couette flow *(rheology)*
Couette-Viskosimeter *n* Couette viscometer, rotating-cylinder viscometer of Couette
Coulomb-Energie *f* coulombic energy
Coulomb-Feld *n* Coulomb field
Coulomb-Gesetz *n* Coulomb law
Coulomb-Glied *n*, **Coulomb-Integral** *n* Coulomb integral
Coulomb-Potential *n* Coulomb potential
Coulomb-Wechselwirkung *f* coulombic interaction
Coulometer *n* coulo[mb]meter, voltameter
~/coulometrisches coulometric coulometer
~/kolorimetrisches colorimetric coulometer
Coulometrie *f* coulometry
~/amperostatische amperostatic (galvanostatic) coulometry, coulometry at constant current
~ bei konstantem Potential *s.* ~/potentialkontrollierte
~ bei konstanter Stromstärke *s.* ~/amperostatische
~/galvanostatische *s.* ~/amperostatische
~ mit anodischer Auflösung/potentialkontrollierte anodic-stripping controlled-potential coulometry
~ mit kontinuierlich geändertem Potential potential-scanning coulometry
~/potentialkontrollierte (potentiostatische) potentiostatic (controlled-potential) coulometry
coulometrisch coulometric
Coulteria-Rotholz *n (dye)* Lima wood *(from Caesalpinia tinctoria (H.B.K.) Benth.)*
Coupage *f (food)* blending
Covellin *m (min)* covellite, covelline, indigo copper, blue copper *(copper(II) sulphide)*
CO_2-Verfahren *n (met)* CO_2 process *(a mould-making process)*
Covolumen *n (phys ch)* covolume
Cowrikopal *m s.* Kaurikopal
Cozymase *f s.* Nicotinamid-adenin-dinucleotid
CP *s.* Cellulosepropionat
CP-^{13}C-NMR-Verfahren *n s.* Kreuzpolarisations-^{13}C-NMR-Technik
C-Peptid *n (bioch)* connecting peptide
C_3-Pflanze *f* C_3 plant *(producing three-carbon compounds as first intermediates of photosynthesis)*
C_4-Pflanze *f* C_4 plant *(producing four-carbon compounds as first intermediates of photosynthesis)*
C-Quelle *f (biot)* carbon source
CRA-Atomisator *m (spectr)* carbon rod atomizer
Crabtree-Effekt *m (bioch)* Crabtree effect

Craig-Verteilung *f* countercurrent distribution
Craqueléeglas *n s.* Krakeleeglas
Craqueléeglasur *f s.* Krackglasur
Crazing-Effekt *m (rubber)* crazing
Creep-Test *m (rubber)* creep test
Creme *f* cream
~/enthaarende depilatory cream
~/fettfreie *s.* ~/nichtfettende
~/hautnährende nourishing cream, skin food
~/nichtfettende greaseless cream
cremeartig, cremig creamy
Crêpe *m s.* Crepekautschuk
Crepekautschuk *m* crêpe rubber, crêpe, crepe
~/weißer pale crêpe
Crepeninsäure *f* crepenynic acid, **cis*-octadec-9-en-12-ynoic acid
Crescent-Methode *f (rubber)* crescent tear test, crescent method *(for determining tearing strength)*
Crescent-Probe *f (rubber)* crescent test-piece
Cresol *n* cresol, hydroxytoluene, methylphenol
Cresolharz *n* cresol (cresylic) resin
Cresolphthalein *n* cresolphthalein
m-**Cresolpurpur** *m* cresol purple, *m*-cresolsulphonephthalein
Cresolrot *n* cresol red, *o*-cresolsulphonephthalein
Cresolsulfophthalein *n* cresolsulphonephthalein
Cresotinsäure *f* cresotic (cresotinic) acid, hydroxytoluic acid
Cresylsäure *f* coal-tar-derived cresylic acid *(a mixture of o-, m-, and p-cresol)*
Criegee-Reaktion *f* Criegee reaction *(for splitting glycol compounds)*
Crinis veneris *(min)* cupid's darts, flèche d'amour, love arrows *(a fibrous variety of rutile)*
Crismer-Test *m (food)* Crismer test *(for characterizing fats)*
Croceinsäure *f* crocein acid, naphth-2-ol-8-sulphonic acid
Croning-Formmaske *f* shell mould *(foundry)*
Croning-Formmaskenverfahren *n* Croning process, C process, shell-moulding process *(foundry)*
Crookes-Glas *n* Crookes glass *(absorbing ultraviolet light)*
Cross-Cellulose *f* Cross cellulose
Cross-over-Punkt *m (bioch)* cross-over point *(of the respiratory chain)*
Cross-Verfahren *n (petrol)* Cross process
Crotonaldehyd *m* crotonaldehyde, *but-2-enal
Crotonisierung *f* crotonization
Crotonöl *n* croton (tiglium) oil *(from Croton tiglium L.)*
Crotonsäure *f* crotonic acid, *but-2-enoic acid, *(specif) trans*-but-2-enoic acid
α-**Crotonsäure** *f* crotonic acid *(proper)*, α-crotonic acid, **trans*-but-2-enoic acid
β-**Crotonsäure** *f* isocrotonic acid, β-crotonic acid, **cis*-but-2-enoic acid
Crotonsäureethylester *m* ethyl crotonate
Crotonylen *n* crotonylene, *but-2-yne
Croupon *m (tann)* butt
crouponieren *(tann)* to butt
Crude *n s.* 1. Crudeasbest; 2. Roherdöl
Crudeasbest *m* crude asbestos
Cryptand *m* cryptand *(spherical crown compound)*
Cryptat *n* cryptate *(chelate complex of a cryptand)*
CS *s.* 1. Synthesefaserstoff; 2. Citronensäure
C-Säure *f* C acid, naphth-2-ylamine-4,8-disulphonic acid
C_4-Säurenzyklus *m (bioch)* C_4 cycle (pathway), C_4 dicarboxylic acid cycle, Hatch-Slack [CO_2 incorporation] pathway
CSF-Verfahren *n (coal)* CSF process *(extraction and hydrogenation of coal)*
C-Stahl *m* carbon steel
C_1-Stoffwechsel *m* one-carbon metabolism
CSV *s.* Sauerstoffverbrauch/chemischer
ct *s.* cis-taktisch
CT-Bande *f (spectr)* charge transfer band
C-terminal C-terminal *(of amino acids in proteins)*
CT-Komplex *m* charge-transfer complex, electron-donor-acceptor complex
CTP = Cytidin-5'-triphosphat
CT-Spektrum *n* charge transfer spectrum
c_0t-Wert *n (bioch)* c_0t value *(measure of the rate of renaturation of DNA)*
$CuCl_2$-Verfahren *n (petrol)* copper chloride [sweetening] process
Cudbear *m* cudbear, persio, persis *(dried paste of archil, a lichen dye)*
Cuen *n s.* Kupferethylendiamin
Čugaev-Reaktion *f* Chugaev reaction *(for obtaining alkenes)*
Cuite *f* cuit, bright silk *(completely degummed silk)*
Cumalinsäure *f* coumalic acid, coumalinic acid, 2-oxo-2H-pyran-5-carboxylic acid
Cumarilsäure *f* coumarilic acid, benzofuran-2-carboxylic acid
Cumarin *n* coumarin, cumarin, 1,2-benzopyrone, 2*H*-chromen-2-one, α-chromone
Cumarinsäure *f* coumarinic acid, *cis-o*-coumaric acid
Cumarinsäurelacton *n* coumarinic lactone
Cumarinsynthese *f*/**Pechmannsche** Pechmann condensation (coumarin synthesis)
Cumaron *n* benzofuran, *(deprecated:)* coumarone, cumarone
Cumaron-2-carbonsäure *f s.* Cumarilsäure
Cumaronharz *n*, **Cumaron-Inden-Harz** *n* coumaron[-indene] resin
Cumarsäure *f* coumaric (cumaric) acid, hydroxycinnamic acid, *(specif) o*-coumaric acid, *trans-o*-hydroxycinnamic acid
Cumarylchinasäure *f* coumaroylquinic acid *(a depside)*
Cumen *n* cumene, 2-phenylpropane, isopropylbenzene

Cumenhydroperoxid *n* cumene hydroperoxide, CHP
Cumol *n s.* Cumen
C-Umsatz *m (coal)* carbon conversion
Cuparen *n* cuparene, *p*-(1',2',2'-trimethylcyclopentyl-)toluene
Cuparensäure *f* cuparenic acid, *p*-(1',2',2'-trimethylcyclopentyl-)benzoic acid
Cuprat *n* cuprate
Cuprit *m (min)* cuprite, red (ruby) copper ore *(copper(I) oxide)*
Cuprouranit *n (min)* cupro uranite
Curaçao-Aloe *f (pharm)* Curaçao (Barbados) aloe *(from Aloe vera L.)*
Curare *n* curare, curara *(an arrow poison from several menispermaceae and loganiaceae)*
Curarealkaloid *n* curare alkaloid
Curcumin curcumin, turmeric yellow *(colouring principle of turmeric)*
Curie-Punkt *m*, **Curie-Temperatur** *f* Curie point (temperature) *(marking the transition between ferromagnetism and paramagnetism)*
Curium *n* Cm curium
curlatieren *(pap)* to curlate
Curlatieren *n (pap)* curlation
Curlator *m (pap)* curlator
Curometer *n (rubber)* curometer *(for determining vulcanizatian curves)*
Curtin-Hammett-Prinzip *n (org ch)* Curtin-Hammett principle
Curtius-Abbau *m*, **Curtius-Reaktion** *f* Curtius degradation, Curtius reaction (rearrangement, transformation) *(of acid azides to give primary amines)*
Cuskhygrin *n* cuskhygrine *(alkaloid)*
Cutback-Bitumen *n* cutback [bitumen], bitumen cutback
CuZ *s.* Kupferzahl
CV-Anlage *f (rubber)* CV unit
CVD-Beschichtungstechnik *f*, **CVD-Verfahren** *n* chemical vapour deposition, CVD *(via decomposable gaseous intermediates, mostly halides)*
C_1-Verbindung *f (bioch)* one-carbon compound
C_3-Verbindung *f (bioch)* three-carbon compound
C_4-Verbindung *f (bioch)* four-carbon compound
CW-Technik *f (anal)* continuous-wave technique
Cyan *n* cyanogen, oxalonitrile
Cyan... *s. a.* Zyan... *for technical terms*
Cyanalkylierung *f* cyanoalkylation
Cyanamid *n* cyanamide, carbodiimide
Cyanamidverfahren *n* cyanamide process *(for producing ammonia)*
Cyanat *n* ROC≡N cyanate *(salt or ester of cyanic acid)*
Cyanbad *n s.* Cyanidbad
Cyanbadhärten *n s.* Cyanieren
Cyanbenzen *n*, **Cyanbenzol** *n* cyanobenzene, benzonitrile
Cyanchlorid *n* chlorine cyanide, cyanogen chloride
Cyanethylierung *f* cyanoethylation
Cyangruppe *f* CN– cyano group
Cyanhydrin *n* cyanohydrin *(any of a class of compounds R'–C(OH)(CN)–R")*
Cyanid *n* RCN cyanide *(salt or derivative of hydrogen cyanide)*
Cyanidbad *n* cyanide [salt] bath *(for hardening steel)*
Cyanidlaugerei *f*, **Cyanidlaugung** *f (met)* cyanidation, cyaniding
Cyanidsalzbad *n s.* Cyanidbad
cyanieren to cyanide *(steel)*
Cyanieren *n* cyaniding, cyanide [case-]hardening *(of steel)*
Cyanierung *f (org ch)* cyanation, cyanogenation, cyanylation
~/oxidative oxycyanation, oxidative cyanation
Cyanin *n* 1. cyanin *(an anthocyanin)*; 2. *s.* Cyaninfarbstoff
Cyaninfarbstoff *m* cyanine dye
Cyaniodid *n* iodine cyanide, cyanogen iodide
Cyanit *m (min)* cyanite, kyanite, disthene *(aluminium oxide orthosilicate)*
Cyankali *n s.* Kaliumcyanid
Cyanmethylierung *f* cyanomethylation
Cyanoargentat *n* cyanoargentate
Cyanoaurat(I) *n* $M^I[Au(CN)_2]$ cyanoaurate(I), dicyanoaurate(I)
Cyanoaurat(III) *n* $M^I[Au(CN)_4]$ cyanoaurate(III), tetracyanoaurate(II)
Cyanochromat(II) *n* $M^I_4[Cr(CN)_6]$ cyanochromate(II), hexacyanochromate(II)
Cyanochromat(III) *n* $M^I_3[Cr(CN)_6]$ cyanochromate(III), hexacyanochromate(III)
Cyanocobaltat(II) *n* $M^I_4[Co(CN)_6]$ cyanocobaltate(II), hexacyanocobaltate(II)
Cyanocobaltat(III) *n* $M^I_3[Co(CN)_6]$ cyanocobaltate(III), hexacyanocobaltate(III)
Cyanoferrat(II) *n* $M^I_4[Fe(CN)_6]$ cyanoferrate(II), hexacyanoferrate(II)
Cyanoferrat(III) *n* $M^I_3[Fe(CN)_6]$ cyanoferrate(III), hexacyanoferrate(III)
Cyanoferrat(III)-komplex *m* cyanoferrate(III) complex, hexacyanoferrate(III) complex
Cyanomanganat(II) *n* $M^I_4[Mn(CN)_6]$ cyanomanganate(II), hexacyanomanganate(II)
Cyanomanganat(III) *n* $M^I_3[Mn(CN)_6]$ cyanomanganate(III), hexacyanomanganate(III)
Cyanomolybdat *n* cyanomolybdate
Cyanoniccolat *n* cyanoniccolate, cyanonickelate
Cyanoosmat(II) *n* $M^I_4[Os(CN)_6]$ cyanoosmate(II), hexacyanoosmate(II)
Cyanoplatinat(II) *n* $M^I_2[Pt(CN)_4]$ cyanoplatinate(II), tetracyanoplatinate(II)
Cyanoplatinat(IV) *n* $M^I_4[Pt(CN)_6]$ cyanoplatinate(IV), hexacyanoplatinate(IV)
Cyanovanadat *n* cyanovanadate
Cyanowolframat(IV) *n* $M^I_4[W(CN)_8]$ cyanotungstate(IV), *octacyanowolframate(IV)

Cyanradikal *n* [free] cyano radical
Cyanrest *m s.* Cyangruppe
Cyansalzbad *n*, **Cyansalzschmelze** *f s.* Cyanidbad
Cyansäure *f* cyanic acid
Cyansäureester *m* ROC≡N cyanate
Cyanurchlorid *n* cyanuric chloride
Cyanursäure *f* cyanuric acid
Cyanursäureamid *n* cyanuramide, triaminotriazine, melamine
Cyanursäurechlorid *n s.* Cyanurchlorid
Cyanwasserstoff *m*, **Cyanwasserstoffsäure** *f* hydrogen cyanide
cyclisch cyclic
cyclisieren *(org ch)* to cyclize; *(rubber)* to cyclize *(under the influence of oxygen)*
Cyclisierung *f (org ch)* cyclization; *(rubber)* cyclization, oxygen vulcanization
Cyclisierungsreaktion *f* cyclization reaction
Cyclit *m*, **Cyclitol** *n* cyclitol *(an isocyclic polyalcohol)*
Cycloaddition *f (org ch)* cycloaddition
~/1,3-dipolare 1,3-dipolar cycloaddition
~/photochemische photocycloaddition
cycloaliphatisch cycloaliphatic, alicyclic
Cycloalkadien *n* cycloalkadiene
Cycloalkan *n* *cycloalkane, cyclane, naphthene
Cycloalkatrien *n* cycloalkatriene
Cycloalken *n* cycloalkene, cyclic olefin
Cycloalkenylierung *f* cycloalkenylation
Cycloalkin *n* cycloalkyne
Cycloalkylgruppe *f* cycloalkyl group
Cycloalkylierung *f* cycloalkylation
Cycloalkylrest *m* cycloalkyl group
Cyclobutan *n* cyclobutane
Cyclodecan *n* cyclodecane
Cyclodehydratisierung *f* cyclodehydration
cyclodehydrieren to cyclodehydrogenate, to dehydrocyclize
Cyclodehydrierung *f* cyclodehydrogenation, dehydrocyclization
Cyclodextrin *n* cyclodextrin, Schardinger dextrin
α-Cyclodextrin *n* α-cyclodextrin, cyclomaltohexaose
β-Cyclodextrin *n* β-cyclodextrin
Cyclodimerisierung *f* cyclodimerization
Cycloeliminierung *f* cycloelimination, cycloreversion, retroaddition, retrocycloaddition
Cycloheptan *n* cycloheptane
Cycloheptanol *n* *cycloheptanol, suberyl alcohol
Cyclohepta-1,3,5-trien *n* cyclohepta-1,3,5-triene, tropilidene
Cyclohepta-2,4,6-trienon *n* cyclohepta-2,4,6-trienone, tropone
Cycloheptatrienylium-Ion *n* cycloheptatrienylium ion, tropylium ion
Cyclohexadien *n* *cyclohexadiene, dihydrobenzene
Cyclohexadien-1,4-dion *n*, **Cyclohexadiendion-(1,4)** *n* *cyclohexadiene-1,4-dione, *p*-benzoquinone
Cyclohexan *n* *cyclohexane, hexahydrobenzene
Cyclohexanring *m* cyclohexane ring
Cyclohexan-1,2-dicarbonsäure *f* *cyclohexane-1,2-dicarboxylic acid, hexahydrophthalic acid
Cyclohexanol *n* *cyclohexanol, hexahydrophenol
Cyclohexen *n* cyclohexene, tetrahydrobenzene
Cycloheximid *n* cycloheximide, actidione *(antibiotic)*
Cyclohexylierung *f* cyclohexylation
Cyclokautschuk *m* cyclorubber, cyclized rubber
Cyclokautschuklatex *m* cyclized latex
Cyclokohlenwasserstoff *m* cyclic hydrocarbon
Cyclokondensation *f* cyclocondensation
Cyclononan *n* cyclononane
Cyclooctadien *n* cyclooctadiene
Cyclooctan *n* cyclooctane
Cyclooctatetraen *n* cyclooctatetraene
Cycloocta-1,3,5,7-tetraen *n* cycloocta-1,3,5,7-tetraene, [8]annulene
Cycloolefin *n s.* Cycloalken
Cyclooligomerisation *f* cyclooligomerization
Cycloparaffin *n s.* Cycloalkan
Cyclopentadien *n* cyclopentadiene
Cyclopentadienyl-Anion *n* cyclopentadienyl anion
Cyclopentan *n* cyclopentane
Cyclopentylierung *f* cyclopentylation
Cyclopeptid *n* cyclic peptide
Cyclophan *n*, **Cyclo-phenylalkan** *n* cyclophane *(bridged aromatic system)*
Cyclopropan *n* cyclopropane
Cyclopropandicarbonsäure *f* cyclopropanedicarboxylic acid
Cyclopropanring *m* cyclopropane ring
Cyclopropenylkation *f* cyclopropenyl cation
Cyclosilicat *n (min)* cyclosilicate, ring silicate
Cyclosiloxan *n* cyclosiloxane, cyclic siloxane
Cyclotriborazan *n* borazene, borazole
Cyclotrimerisation *f* cyclotrimerization
Cycloversion-Verfahren *n* cycloversion process *(of catalytic reforming)*
Cymen *n*, **Cymol** *n* cymene, isopropyltoluene, isopropylmethylbenzene
Cymophenol *n* cymophenol, carvacrol, 2-hydroxy-4-isopropyl-1-methylbenzene
Cystathionurie *f (med)* cystathionuria
Cystein *n* cysteine, *2-amino-3-mercaptopropionic acid
Cysteinsäure *f* cysteic acid, *2-amino-3-sulphopropionic acid
Cystin *n* cystine, dicysteine, *3,3'-dithio-bis[2-aminopropanoic acid]
Cystin-Bindeglied *n*, **Cystin-Brücke** *f* cystine link
Cystinurie *f (med)* cystinuria
Cytidylsäure *f (bioch)* cytidylic acid
Cytochemie *f* cytochemistry
Cytochrom *n* cytochrome
Cytochromoxidase *f* cytochrome (indophenol) oxidase, Warburg's respiratory enzyme
Cytochromreductase *f* cytochrome reductase

Cytokinin *n* cytokinin *(any of various plant growth factors)*
Cytoplasma *n (biol)* cytoplasm
Cytosol *n (bioch)* cytosol
Cytotoxin *n* cytotoxin
cytotoxisch cytotoxic
CZ *s.* Cellulosechemiefaserstoff
Czako-Hahn *m (lab)* T-shape 120° bore stopcock
Czapek-Dox-Medium *n*, **Czapek-Dox-Nährboden** *m* Czapek-Dox medium
Czerny-Turner-Aufstellung *f (spectr)* Czerny-Turner arrangement
C-Zustand *m (plast)* C stage
C_3-Zyklus *m (bioch)* C_3 cycle (pathway), C_3 pentose phosphate cycle, Calvin[-Bassham] cycle, Calvin pathway, ribulose diphosphate cycle *(of CO_2 assimilation)*
C_4-Zyklus *m (bioch)* C_4 cycle (pathway), C_4 dicarboxylic acid cycle, Hatch-Slack [CO_2 incorporation] pathway

D

d- = dextrogyr
D *s.* Dichte
2,4-D *s.* 2,4-Dichlorphenoxyessigsäure
DABS = 4-Dimethylaminoazobenzen-4'-sulfochlorid
Dakin-Reaktion *f* Dakin reaction *(oxidation of phenolic aldehydes to polyphenols)*
Dalapon *n* dalapon, sodium 2,2-dichloropropionate *(a herbicide)*
Daltonide *npl* daltonides, daltonian (daltonide) compounds
Dammar[harz] *n* dammar [resin], gum dammar *(esp from several species of the family Dipterocarpaceae)*
~/Schwarzes black dammar resin *(from Canarium specc.)*
Dämmbeton *m* insulation concrete
dAMP *s.* Desoxyadenosin-5'-phosphat
Dampf *m* vapour, *(specif)* water vapour, steam; fume *(visible volatile chemicals)* • **in ~ überführen** to vaporize • **mit ~ behandeln** to treat with steam, to steam • **mit ~ beheizt** steam-heated
~/direkter live steam, prime (direct, open) steam
~/gesättigter saturated vapour; saturated steam
~/gespannter *s.* ~/direkter
~/indirekter exhaust steam
~ konstanten Drucks constant-pressure steam
~/perlender sparge steam
~/trockengesättigter dry saturated steam
~/über Kopf abgehender overhead vapour
~/überhitzter superheated steam
Dampfabstreifer *m*, **Dampfabstreiferkolonne** *f (distil)* stripping column, stripper
Dampfanschluß *m* steam joint
Dampfantrieb *m* steam drive
Dampfaufbereitung *f (ceram)* hot preparation, steam tempering
Dampfautoklav *m* steam autoclave
Dampfbad *n* steam bath
Dampfbedarf *m* steam requirements (demand)
dampfbehandelt steam-treated, steamed; steam-cured *(concrete)*
Dampfbehandlung *f* steam treatment, steaming; steam curing *(of concrete)*
dampfbeheizt steam-heated
Dampfbeheizung *f* steam heating
Dampfblanchieren *n (food)* steam blanching
Dampfblase *f* vapour bubble; steam bubble
Dampfdestillation *f* steam distillation
dampfdicht 1. vapour-tight, *(relating to water vapour:)* steam-tight *(e.g. joint)*; 2. *s.* dampfundurchlässig
Dampfdichte *f* vapour density, v.d.
Dampfdichtebestimmung *f*, **Dampfdichtemessung** *f* vapour-density determination (measurement)
Dampfdruck *m* vapour pressure (tension), v.p., VP
~/nach Reid Reid vapour pressure, R.V.P.
Dampfdruckdiagramm *n* vapour-pressure diagram
Dampfdruckerniedrigung *f* vapour-pressure lowering (depression)
~/relative relative lowering of vapour pressure
Dampfdruckgefälle *n* vapour-pressure gradient
Dampfdruckkurve *f* vapour-pressure curve
Dampfdruckosmometer *n* vapour-pressure osmometer
Dampf-Druckstrahlpumpe *f s.* Dampfstrahlpumpe
Dampfdruckthermometer *n* vapour-pressure thermometer
Dampfdurchdringtiefe *f (distil)* [static] submergence
Dampfdurchflußmesser *m s.* Dampfmengenmesser
dampfdurchlässig permeable to vapour
Dampfdurchlässigkeit *f* vapour permeability
Dampfdurchtrittsschlitz *m (distil)* slot
Dampfdüsenblasverfahren *n (glass)* steam-blowing process
Dampfeinlaß *m* steam inlet (entrance)
Dampfeinlaßkopf *m (pap)* steamfit, steam joint *(of a dryer cylinder)*
Dampfeintritt *m s.* Dampfeinlaß
Dampf-Eisen-Verfahren *n* steam-iron process *(for producing hydrogen)*
dampfen to steam
dämpfen 1. to steam, *(text also)* to age *(to fix dyeings and prints)*; *(pap)* to presteam *(chips before cooking)*; *(food)* to deodorize with steam; 2. to damp[en] *(e.g. a motion)*; to damp[en], to attenuate *(e.g. the violence of a reaction)*
Dämpfen *n* 1. steaming, *(text also)* ageing *(fixing of dyeings and prints)*; *(pap)* presteaming *(of chips before cooking)*; *(food)* steam deodorization *(of fats)*; 2. damp[en]ing *(as of a motion)*; damp[en]ing, attenuation *(as of a violent reaction)*

Dampfentfettung *f* vapour degreasing
Dampfentwickler *m* steam generator, boiler
Dämpfer *m* steamer, *(text also)* [steam] ager; *(food)* deodorizer *(for fats)*
dampferhärtet steam-cured *(concrete)*
Dampferhärtung *f* steam curing *(of concrete)*
Dämpferpassage *f (text)* steaming, ageing *(for fixing dyeings and prints)*
Dampferzeuger *m* steam generator, boiler
Dampferzeugerinhaltswasser *n* boiler water
Dampferzeugerspeisewasser *n* boiler feed[ing] water
Dampferzeugung *f* steam generation (raising)
Dampferzeugungsanlage *f* steam generating (raising) plant, boiler plant
Dämpfestutzen *m s.* Dampfhals
Dampffeuerlöschanlage *f* steam-snuffing line
dampfflüchtig steam-volatile
Dampf-Flüssigkeits-Gemisch *n* vapour-liquid mixture
dampfförmig vaporous
Dampffüllapparat *m (pap)* steam chip distributor
Dampfgefäß *n* steam autoclave
Dampfgeschwindigkeit *f* vapour rate (velocity)
dampfgetrieben steam-driven
dampfgetrocknet steam-dried
Dampfgummi *n s.* Dextrin
Dampfhals *m (distil)* riser [tube, pipe], chimney *(of a tray)*
Dampfhärten *n* steam curing *(of concrete)*
Dampfheizschlange *f* steam coil
Dampfheizung *f* steam heating
Dampfheizungsrohr *n* steam pipe (tube)
Dampfkalorimeter *n* steam calorimeter
Dampfkamin *m s.* Dampfhals
Dampfkammer *f* steam chamber (chest)
Dampfkanal *m (plast)* steam channel
Dampfkanne *f (lab)* steam can
Dampfkessel *m* [steam] boiler
Dampfkesselkohle *f* steam[-raising] coal
Dampfknetwerk *n* pug
Dampfkohle *f* steam[-raising] coal
Dampfkondensat *n* steam condensate
Dampfkopf *m s.* Dampfeinlaßkopf
Dampfleitung *f* steam line, *(if large:)* steam main
Dampfleitungsrohr *n* steam pipe (tube)
Dampf-Luft-Gemisch *n* vapour-air mixture
Dampfmachen *n (tann)* tempering
Dampfmantel *m* steam jacket • **mit** ~ steam-jacketed
Dampfmengenmesser *m* steam [flow-]meter
Dampfphase *f* vapour phase
Dampfphasekracken *n (petrol)* vapour-phase cracking
Dampfphasenchromatographie *f s.* Gaschromatographie
Dampfphaseninhibitor *m* vapour-phase inhibitor, V.P.I.
Dampfphasenisomerisierung *f* vapour-phase isomerization
Dampfphasennitrierung *f* vapour-phase nitration
Dampfphasenoxidation *f* vapour-phase oxidation
Dampfphaseverfahren *n* vapour-phase process
Dampfpumpe *f* steam pump
Dampfpunkt *m* steam point, boiling point of water
Dampfraum *m* 1. vapour head (chamber, space), flash chamber, body *(of an evaporator)*; 2. headspace *(vapour phase above liquid phase in a closed vessel)*
Dampfraumanalysator *m (chromat)* headspace analyser
Dampfregister *n* steam battery
Dampfrohr *n* steam pipe (tube)
Dampfsammler *m* steam collector (accumulator)
Dampf-Sauerstoff-Vergasung *f (coal)* steam-oxygen gasification
Dampfschlange *f* steam coil
Dampfschmalz *n (food)* steam lard, *(Am also)* prime steam lard
Dampfspannung *f s.* Dampfdruck
Dampfspeicher *m* steam collector (accumulator)
Dampfstauer *m* expansion trap
Dampfstoßverfahren *n (plast)* steam-moulding process
Dampfstrahl *m* steam jet
Dampfstrahlapparat *m* steam-jet apparatus
Dampfstrahlejektor *m* steam-jet ejector, steam-motivated (steam-operated) ejector
Dampfstrahlinjektor *m s.* Dampfstrahlpumpe
Dampfstrahlkühlung *f* steam-jet refrigeration
Dampfstrahlpumpe *f* steam injector
Dampfstrahlsauger *m s.* Dampfstrahlejector
Dampfstrom *m* vapour stream
Dampftrichter *m* steam-heated funnel
Dampftrockenapparat *m s.* Dampftrockner
Dampftrockenschrank *m* steam drying oven
Dampftrockner *m* steam dryer; vapour dryer *(using a vaporizable liquid drying agent)*
Dampfturbinenöl *n* steam-turbine oil
Dampfturbogebläse *n* steam-driven turboblower
Dampfüberhitzer *m* steam superheater
dampfundurchlässig impervious to water vapour
Dampfung *f* steaming *(in manufacturing water gas)*
Dämpfung *f* 1. steaming; *(pap)* presteaming *(of chips before cooking)*; 2. damp[en]ing *(as of a motion)*; *(rubber)* hysteresis; damp[en]ing, attenuation *(as of a violent reaction)*
Dämpfungseinrichtung *f* damping device *(as of analytical balances)*
Dämpfungsfaktor *m* damping factor (coefficient)
Dämpfungsflüssigkeit *f* damping fluid
Dämpfungsgerät *n* **nach Roelig** *(rubber)* Roelig hysteresis apparatus
Dämpfungsmittel *n* damping medium
Dämpfungsschleife *f (rubber)* tensile hysteresis loop
Dämpfungsverhalten *n* damping properties

Dämpfungswaage *f* damped balance
Dämpfungszylinder *m* dash pot
Dampfventil *n* steam valve
Dampfverbrauch *m* steam consumption
Dampfversprühung *f* steam atomization
Dampfvulkanisation *f (rubber)* steam curing (cure, vulcanization)
Dampfzersetzung *f* steam decomposition
Dampfzersetzungsgrad *m* [degree of] steam decomposition
Dampfzerstäubung *f* steam atomization
Dampfzufuhr *f* steam supply
Dampfzustand *m* vapour state
Dampfzylinder *m* steam cylinder
Dampfzylinderöl *n* steam-cylinder [lubricating] oil, steam-cylinder stock
Daniell-Element *n*, **Daniell-Kette** *f* Daniell cell
Danner-Verfahren *n* Danner process *(for manufacturing glass tubing)*
Dansylierung *f (org ch)* dansylation
DAP *s.* Diallylphthalatharz
Darmfett *n* gut fat
Darmöl *n (pharm)* intestinal lubricant
Darmsaft *m* intestinal juice
Darre *f* 1. drying kiln, kiln dryer; *(ferm)* malt [drying] kiln, oast; 2. *s.* Darrhaus
darren to kiln-dry, to kiln *(e.g. malt)*
Darren *n* kiln-drying, kilning *(as of malt)*
Darrgewicht *n s.* Darrmasse
Darrhaus *n* oast-house
Darrhorde *f* kiln floor
Darrmalz *n* kilned (kiln-dried) malt
Darrmasse *f (pap)* dry wood weight, moisture-free weight
Darrofen *m* drying kiln, kiln dryer
darstellbar/rein isolable *(natural product)*
darstellen to prepare, to make; to isolate *(natural products)*
~/in reinem Zustand *s.* ~/rein
~/räumlich to represent spatially
~/rein to prepare in pure form, to prepare in a pure condition (state), to isolate *(natural products)*
Darstellung *f* 1. preparation, making; isolation *(of natural products)*; 2. representation *(as of measuring values)*
~/formelmäßige formulation
~/graphische graphical (diagrammatic) representation, graph, chart, diagram
~ im Labor laboratory preparation
~/präparative laboratory preparation
~/räumliche spatial representation
Darstellungsbedingung *f* condition of preparation
Darstellungsmethode *f* method of preparation, preparative method
Darstellungsweise *f* mode of preparation
Darzens-Erlenmeyer-Claisen-Kondensation *f s.* Darzens-Reaktion
Darzens-Reaktion *f* Darzens [glycidic ester] condensation
Dasymeter *n* dasymeter *(for determining the density of a gas)*
Daten *pl***/kritische** *(phys ch)* critical constants (data)
~/röntgenographische X-ray data
Dauer *f* **eines Arbeitszyklus** cycle time *(of a treatment unit)*; drum cycle time *(of a rotary vacuum filter)*
Dauerbeanspruchung *f* repeated stress
Dauerbehandlung *f* long-term treatment
Dauerbetrieb *m* continuous operation (working)
Dauerbiegebeanspruchung *f* repeated flexural stress
Dauerbiegefestigkeit *f* repeated flexural strength, flex[ing] life; *(tann)* bending endurance
Dauerbiegespannung *f* repeated flexural stress
Dauerbruch *m* fatigue failure (fracture)
Dauerelektrode *f* [Söderberg] continuous electrode, self-baking electrode
Dauererhitzung *f s.* Dauerpasteurisation
Dauerfestigkeit *f* endurance (fatigue) limit
Dauerfixierung *f (text)* permanent set
Dauerform *f* permanent mould *(foundry)*
~/metallische permanent metal mould, gravity die
Dauerformgießverfahren *n s.* Dauerformgußverfahren
Dauerformguß *m* permanent-mould casting, gravity die-casting
Dauerformgußstück *n* [gravity] die-casting
Dauerformgußverfahren *n* permanent-mould casting process, gravity die-casting process
Dauergießform *f s.* Dauerform
dauerhaft durable, permanent, stable
Dauerhumus *m* stable humus
Dauerknickversuch *m* flex-cracking test
Dauerkultur *f* continuous culture *(of microorganisms)*
Dauermilch *f* preserved milk
Dauermilchwaren *fpl* milk preserves
Dauerpasteurisation *f (food)* vat (holding, holder) pasteurization
Dauerschwingfestigkeit *f* endurance (fatigue) limit
Dauerschwingkorrosion *f* corrosion fatigue
Dauerstandfestigkeit *f s.* Zeitstandfestigkeit
Dauerstrichbetrieb *m (spectr)* continuous-wave technique
Dauerwanne *f (glass)* continuous tank
Dauerwärmebeständigkeit *f* continuous heat resistance
Dauerwellenlösung *f*, **Dauerwellflüssigkeit** *f (cosmet)* permanent-wave lotion (solution), [hair-] waving lotion
Dauerwellpräparat *n (cosmet)* permanent-wave preparation
Daumenbrecher *m* sawtooth crusher
Daunendruckpapier *n* featherweight paper, *(Am)* bulking paper
2,4-DB *s.* 4(2',4'-Dichlorphenoxy)buttersäure
DBPC *s.* 2,6-Di-*tert*-butyl-*p*-cresol
DC *s.* Dünnschichtchromatographie

dCMP *s.* Desoxycytidin-5'-phosphat
DDNP *s.* Diazodinitrophenol
DDT *s.* Dichlordiphenyltrichlorethan
DE *s.* 1. Defometerelastizität; 2. Dextroseäquivalent
Dead-end-Inhibitor *m (bioch)* dead-end complex (inhibitor) *(inactive enzyme-inhibitor complex)*
Dead-stop-Methode *f (anal)* dead-stop method (technique)
Dead-stop-Titration *f* dead-stop titration
Dead-stop-Titrationskurve *f* dead-stop titration curve
Dead-stop-Verfahren *n s.* Dead-stop-Methode
DEAE-Cellulose *f (anal)* DEAE cellulose
dealkylieren *s.* desalkylieren
de-Broglie-Beziehung *f* de Broglie relation[ship]
de-Broglie-Gleichung *f* de Broglie equation
de-Broglie-Welle *f* de Broglie wave, matter wave
de-Broglie-Wellenlänge *f* de Broglie wavelength
debromieren to debrominate
Debromierung *f* debromination
Debutanisator *m* debutanizer
Debutanisierung *f* debutanization
Debutanisierungskolonne *f* debutanizer
Debutylierung *f* debutylation
De-*tert*-butylierung *f* de-*tert*-butylation
Debye *n s.* Debye-Einheit
Debye-Einheit *f* Debye [unit], D *(non-SI unit of dipole moment of molecules)*
Debye-Falkenhagen-Effekt *m* Debye-Falkenhagen effect *(dispersion of conductance)*
Debye-Funktion *f* Debye function
Debye-Grenzfrequenz *f* Debye frequency
Debey-Hückel-Beziehung *f s.* Debey-Hückel-Gleichung
Debye-Hückel-Gleichung *f (phys ch)* Debey-Hückel equation
~/erweiterte extended Debye-Hückel equation, EDHE
Debye-Hückel-Theorie *f (phys ch)* Debye-Hückel theory
Debye-Länge *f* Debye length
Debyeogramm *n s.* Debye-Scherrer Diagramm
Debye-Scherrer-Aufnahme *f*, **Debye-Scherrer-Diagramm** *n (cryst)* Debye-Scherrer diagram (pattern, photograph)
Debye-Scherrer-Methode *f (cryst)* Debye-Scherrer[-Hull] method
Debye-Temperatur *f* [Debye] characteristic temperature
Debye-Waller-Faktor *m* Debye-Waller factor *(X-ray scattering)*
Decaboran *n* decaborane
Deca-2,4-diensäure *f* deca-2,4-dienoic acid
Decahydrat *n* decahydrate
Decahydronaphthalen *n* decahydronaphthalene
Decan *n* decane
Decanal *n* decanal
Decanamid *n* decanamide
Decan-1,10-dicarbonsäure *f* decane-1,10-dicarboxylic acid, dodecanedioic acid
Decandisäure *f* *decanedioic acid, sebacic acid
Decansäure *f* decanoic acid
Decansäureanhydrid *n* decanoic anhydride
Decansäureethylester *m* ethyl decanoate
Decansäuremethylester *m* methyl decanoate
Decapeptid *n* decapeptide
~/cyclisches cyclodecapeptide
Decarbalkoxylierung *f* decarbalkoxylation
Decarbethoxylierung *f* decarbethoxylation
Decarbobenzoxylierung *f* decarbobenzoxylation
Decarbo-*tert*-butoxylierung *f* decarbo-*tert*-butoxylation
Decarbomethoxylierung *f* decarbomethoxylation
decarbonylieren to decarbonylate
Decarbonylierung *f* decarbonylation
decarboxylieren to decarboxylate
~/oxidativ to decarboxylate oxidatively
decarboxylierend decarboxylative
Decarboxylierung *f* decarboxylation
~/bromierende bromodecarboxylation
~/chlorierende chlorodecarboxylation
~/halogenierende halodecarboxylation
~/oxidative oxidative decarboxylation
Dec-1-en *n* dec-1-ene
Decensäure *f* decenoic acid
Dechiffrierung *f (bioch)* cracking *(of the genetic code)*
dechlorieren to dechlorinate
Dechlorierung *f* dechlorination
Dec-1-in *n* dec-1-yne
Deck *n* deck *(of a concentrating table)*
Deckablauf *m (sugar)* wash syrup
Deckanstrich *m (coat)* 1. finish[ing] *(act)*; 2. finish[-ing] coat, finish, top coat[ing], topcoat, cover coat[ing]
Deckappretur *f*, **Deckauftrag** *m (tann)* coating finish
Deckdruck *m (text)* blotch printing
Decke *f* 1. cover; 2. *s.* Deckgebirge
Deckel *m* lid, cap, top, cover, hood • **mit einem ~ verschlossen (versehen)** lidded
~ der Petrischale Petri dish top
Deckelrahmen *m (pap)* deckle frame
Deckelriemen *m (pap)* deckle (boundary) strap
~/oberer upper run of the deckle strap
~/unterer lower run of the deckle strap
decken to cover, to top *(with a finish or another dye)*; to cover *(as of a pigment)*
~/die Chemikalienverluste *(pap)* to make up for the loss of chemical
~/einander (sich) to coincide *(stereochemistry)*
deckend/einander coincident *(stereochemistry)*
Deckerdruck *m (text)* blotch printing
Deckfähigkeit *f s.* Deckvermögen
Deckfarbe *f* topcoat paint, finish[ing] paint
Deckgebirge *n (mine)* overburden, roof rock, rock cover
Deckglas *n* cover glass, *(microscopy also)* slide cover glass

Deckgrün *n* chrome green *(a mixture of iron blue and chrome yellow)*
Deckgummi *m* rubber cover *(of a conveyor)*
Deckkraft *f s.* Deckvermögen
Decklack *m* topcoat (finishing) enamel
Decklauge *f* covering lye *(in refining potassium chloride)*
Deckmittel *n* covering agent (material, medium)
Deckplatte *f* cover[plate]
Deckschicht *f* 1. top (final, cover) coating *(as of a protective coating system)*; coating *(spontaneously formed)*, *(if thin:)* film *(as of oxides)*; 2. *s.* Deckgebirge
~/oxidische oxide coating *(on metals)*
Deckung *f* 1. coincidence *(in space or time)*; *(cryst)* self-coincidence; 2. *(phot)* extinction, optical density • **zur ~ bringen** to make [to] coincide
~ der Chemikalienverluste *(pap)* make-up of chemical loss
deckungsgleich superimposable
~/nicht non-superimposable
Deckvermögen *n* covering power, coverage, *(of paints also)* hiding (obliterating, opacifying) power
Decodierungsort *m s.* Akzeptorort
Decyanethylierung *f* decyanoethylation
Decyanierung *f* decyanation
Decyclisierung *f* decyclization, ring cleavage (opening)
n-**Decylalkohol** *m* *decan-1-ol, *(deprecated:)* *n*-decyl alcohol
n-**Decylen** *n s.* Dec-1-en
n-**Decylsäure** *f s.* Decansäure
Dedimerisierung *f* dedimerization
Dedolomitisierung *f (geol)* dedolomitization
Dees *pl s.* Duanten
Deethanisator *m* de-ethanizer
deethanisieren to de-ethanize
Deethanisierung *f* de-ethanization
Defäkation *f (sugar)* defecation, liming
defekt defective, faulty
Defekt *m* defect, fault, *(in material also)* flaw; *(cryst)* defect, imperfection
~/eindimensionaler (linienhafter) *(cryst)* line[ar] defect
Defektelektron *n* defect electron, [electron] hole
Defektelektronenleitung *f s.* Defektleitung
Defektelektronenzentrum *n* V-centre *(a colour centre in spectroscopy)*
Defektgitter *n* defect lattice
Defekthalbleiter *m s.* Defektleiter
Defektleiter *m (phys ch)* defect [semi]conductor, p-type [semi]conductor
Defektleitung *f (phys ch)* hole conduction
Defektmutante *f (biot)* auxotrophic mutant
Defibrator *m (pap)* pulpwood grinder
defibrieren *(pap)* to defibre, to defibrate, to reduce to fibres, *(Am also)* to [de]fiberize
Defibrierung *f (pap)* defib[e]ring, defibration, *(Am also)* [de]fiberization
defibrillieren *(pap)* to fibrillate
Defibrillierung *f (pap)* fibrillation
defibrinieren to defibrinate *(blood)*
Defibrinierung *f* defibrination *(of blood)*
definiert/gut well-defined *(e.g. compound)*
~/mangelhaft (schlecht) ill-defined, poorly defined
~/ungenau (unscharf) vaguely (faintly) defined
Deflagration *f* deflagration
deflagrieren to deflagrate
Defo... *s. a.* Defometer...
Defoliationsmittel *n (agric)* defoliant
Defomeßgerät *n*, **Defometer** *n (rubber)* Defo plastometer
Defometerelastizität *f (rubber)* Defo elasticity
Defometerhärte *f (rubber)* Defo hardness
Defometerwert *m (rubber)* Defo value
Defometerzahl *f (rubber)* Defo number
Deformation *f* deformation
~/bleibende residual (plastic, permanent) deformation, residual set
~/elastische elastic deformation
~/irreversible (plastische) *s.* ~/bleibende
~/postkristalline *(geol)* postcrystalline deformation
~/präkristalline *(geol)* precrystalline deformation
Deformationsschwingung *f* deformation (scissor) vibration, deformation mode *(of molecules)*
Deformationsverhalten *n* deformation response
deformieren to deform
Deformylierung *f* deformylation
degenerieren *(phys ch)* to degenerate
degeneriert *(phys ch, bioch)* degenerate
~/dreifach triply (three-fold) degenerate *(energy level)*
~/fünffach quintuply degenerate *(energy level)*
~/vierfach quadruply (four-fold) degenerate *(energy level)*
~/zweifach doubly (two-fold) degenerate *(energy level)*
Degeneriertheit *f (bioch)* degeneracy *(of the genetic code)*
Degermanylierung *f* degermanylation
Degradation *f* 1. *(soil)* degradation; 2. *s.* Abbau
degradieren *(soil)* to degrade
Degras *m(n) (tann)* degras, sod oil, moellon
degummieren *(text)* to boil off (out), to degum
Degummieren *n (text)* boil[ing]-off, degumming
dehalogenieren to dehalogenate
Dehalogenierung *f* dehalogenation
dehnbar extensible, expansible, expandable, expandible, *(esp of metal:)* ductile
Dehnbarkeit *f* extensibility, expansibility, expandability, *(esp of metal:)* ductility
dehnen to extend, to expand, to stretch
Dehnfuge *f* expansion joint
Dehngrenze *f* tensile stress at a given elongation, yield strength, proof stress, *(deprecated:)* [tensile] modulus
0,2 %-Dehngrenze *f* 0.2 % offset yield strength (stress), 0.2 % proof stress, yield strength 0.2 % offset

Dehnung *f* extension, expansion, stretch, *(esp relating to materials testing:)* strain
~/bleibende plastic (permanent) strain, offset
~/elastische elastic strain, *(text also)* stretch
~/irreversible *s.* ~/bleibende
~/reversible *s.* ~/elastische
Dehnungsausgleicher *m* expansion joint
dehnungsfähig *s.* dehnbar
Dehnungsfuge *f* expansion joint
Dehnungsmesser *m*, **Dehnungsmeßgerät** *n* extensometer
Dehnungsrest *m (rubber)* tensile set
Dehnungs-Spannungs-Kurve *f s.* Spannungs-Dehnungs-Linie
Dehydracetsäure *f* dehydracetic (dehydroacetic) acid, DHA, 3-acetyl-2-hydroxy-6-methylpyran-4-one
Dehydrase *f s.* Dehydrogenase
Dehydratase *f* dehydrase
Dehydratation *f s.* Dehydratisierung 1. *und* 2.
Dehydration *f s.* Dehydrierung
dehydratisieren 1. to dehydrate *(to remove H and OH as water from compounds)*; 2. to dehydrate *(e.g. hydrates)*; 3. *(food)* to dehydrate, to desiccate, to dry
Dehydratisierung *f* 1. dehydration *(removal of H and OH as water from compounds)*; 2. dehydration *(as of hydrates)*; 3. *(food)* dehydration, desiccation, drying
Dehydratisierungsmittel *n* dehydrating agent, dehydrator
Dehydrier... *s.* Dehydrierungs...
dehydrieren to dehydrogenate, to dehydrogenize
dehydrierend dehydrogenative
Dehydrierung *f* dehydrogenation
Dehydrierungskatalysator *m* dehydrogenation (dehydrogenating) catalyst
Dehydrierungsmittel *n* dehydrogenating agent
Dehydroacetsäure *f s.* Dehydracetsäure
Dehydroaromat *m* dehydroarene
1,2-Dehydroaromat *n* aryne, 1,2-didehydroarene
Dehydroaromatisierung *f* dehydroaromatization
Dehydrobase *f* dehydro base
Dehydrobenzen *n*, **Dehydrobenzol** *n* dehydrobenzene
1,2-Dehydrobenzen *n* benzyne, 1,2-didehydrobenzene
Dehydroborierung *f* dehydroboration
dehydrobromieren to dehydrobrominate
Dehydrobromierung *f* dehydrobromination
Dehydrochinasäure *f* dehydroquinic acid, *1,3,4-trihydroxy-5-oxocyclohexanecarboxylic acid
dehydrochlorieren to dehydrochlorinate
Dehydrochlorierung *f* dehydrochlorination
Dehydrocyanierung *f* dehydrocyanation
Dehydrocyclisierung *f* dehydrocyclization
Dehydrocyclodimerisierung *f* dehydrocyclodimerization
Dehydrodimerisierung *f* dehydrodimerization, oxidative dimerization
Dehydroessigsäure *f s.* Dehydracetsäure
Dehydrofluorierung *f* dehydrofluorination
Dehydrogenase *f* dehydrogenase
Dehydrogeraniumsäure *f* dehydrogeranic acid *(an alkenoic acid)*
dehydrohalogenieren to dehydrohalogenate
Dehydrohalogenierung *f* dehydrohalogenation
Dehydroiodierung *f* dehydroiodination
Dehydroisomerisierung *f* dehydroisomerization
Dehydroxyalkylierung *f* dehydroxyalkylation
Dehydroxylierung *f* dehydroxylation
Dehydroxymercurierung *f* dehydroxymercuration
Dehydroxymethylierung *f* dehydroxymethylation
DE-Inhaltswasser *n s.* Dampferzeugerinhaltswasser
D-Einheit *f* difunctional (bifunctional) unit, D unit *(structural element of macromolecules)*
deinken to deink *(waste paper)*
Deinking-Anlage *f (pap)* deinking plant
Deinterkalation *f* deintercalation, disintercalation
Deiodierung *f* deiodination
Deionat *n (hyd)* deionized (demineralized) water *(ion exchange)*
Deionatgüte *f (hyd)* effluent [water] quality *(ion exchange)*
Deionisation *f* deionization, DI
deionisieren to deionize
Deionisierung *f* deionization, DI
Deisobutanisator *m* deisobutanizer
deisobutanisieren to deisobutanize
Deisobutanisierung *f* deisobutanization
Deka... *s. a.* Deca... *for chemical compounds*
Dekalzifikation *f (bioch)* decalcification
dekalzifizieren *(bioch)* to decalcify
Dekalzifizierung *f (bioch)* decalcification
Dekameter *n* dielectrometer, dielectric constant meter
Dekametrie *f* dielectrometry, dielectric constant measurement
Dekantation *f* decantation, decanting, pouring-off
Dekanter *m*, **Dekanteur** *m s.* Dekantiergefäß
dekantieren to decant, to pour off
Dekantiergefäß *n*, **Dekantiertopf** *m* decanter, decanting jar
Dekantierung *f s.* Dekantation
Dekantierzentrifuge *f* centrifugal decanter, sedimentation (sedimenting) centrifuge, solid-bowl (solid-wall, full-bowl) centrifuge
dekarbonisieren *(petrol)* to decarbonize, to decoke
Dekarbonisierung *f (petrol)* decarbonization, decoking
Dekatierechtheit *f (text)* fastness to decatizing
dekatieren *(text)* to decatize, to decate, to hot-press
Dekatieren *n s.* Dekatur
Dekatur *f (text)* decatizing, decating, hot-pressing
Dekaturechtheit *f (text)* fastness to decatizing
Dekokt *n* decoctum, decoction
Dekoktionsverfahren *n (ferm)* decoction process
Dekontaminationsindex *m (nucl)* decontamination index

dekontaminieren *(nucl)* to decontaminate
Dekontaminierung *f (nucl)* decontamination
Dekontaminierungsmittel *n (nucl)* decontaminating agent (chemical, substance)
Dekorationsfolie *f s.* Dekorfolie
Dekorationspapier *n* decorating paper
Dekorationsschichtstoff *m* decorative laminate
Dekorationsseidenpapier *n* decorating tissue paper, decoration tissue
Dekorbrand *m (ceram)* decoration (enamel) firing
Dekorfolie *f* decorative sheet (foil), [decorative] overlay *(as for particle board)*
Dekorpapier *n* decorating paper
Dekorschicht *f* decorative coating
Dekrepitation *f (cryst)* decrepitation
dekrepitieren *(cryst)* to decrepitate
Dekulator *m (pap)* deculator, stock deaerator
Del-Faktor *m (biot)* design criterion *(measure for evaluating sterilization)*
Delftware *f (ceram)* delftware, delf[t], delph[ware]
delignifizieren *(pap)* to delignify
Delignifizierung *f (pap)* delignification
Delignifizierungsmittel *n (pap)* delignifying agent
Delikateßmargarine *f* high-class table margarine
delokalisieren *(phys ch)* to delocalize
Delokalisierung *f (phys ch)* delocalization
Delokalisierungseffekt *m* delocalization effect
Delokalisierungsenergie *f* delocalization (resonance, mesomeric) energy
Delphinsäure *f s.* Isovaleriansäure
Delphintran *m* dolphin oil
Deltaelektron *n* delta electron
Deltastrahl *m* delta ray
Delves-cup-Technik *f (spectr)* Delves-cup technique
demargarinieren to demargarinate, to destearinate, to destearinize, to winterize *(oils)*
Demargarinieren *n*, **Demargarinisation** *f* demargarination, destearinization, winterization *(of oils)*
demaskieren to demask *(coordination chemistry)*
Demaskierung *f* demasking *(coordination chemistry)*
de-Mattia-Biegeprüfmaschine *f*, **de-Mattia-Knickermüdungsprüfer** *m* De Mattia [flexing] machine
Demercurierung *f* demercuration
Demesylierung *f* demesylation
Demetallierung *f* demetalation
Demethanisator *m* demethanizer
demethanisieren to demethanize
Demethanisierung *f* demethanization
Demethoxylierung *f* demethoxylation
demethylieren to demethylate
Demethylierung *f* demethylation
Demineralisation *f* demineralization
demineralisieren to demineralize
Demjanov-Umlagerung *f* Demjanov rearrangement *(of primary cycloaliphatic amines)*
Demodulationspolarographie *f (anal)* demodulation polarography
Demulgator *m* demulsifier, emulsion breaker
demulgieren to demulsify, to de-emulsify, to break, to crack
Demulgieren *n*, **Demulgierung** *f* demulsification, de-emulsification, breaking, cracking
Denaturation *f s.* Denaturierung
denaturierbar *(bioch)* denaturable
Denaturierbarkeit *f (bioch)* denaturability
denaturieren 1. *(food)* to denature, to denaturize, *(ethanol also)* to methylate; 2. *(bioch)* to denature
Denaturierung *f* 1. *(food)* denaturation, *(of ethanol also)* methylation; 2. *(bioch)* denaturation
~/reversible *(bioch)* reversible denaturation
Denaturierungsmittel *n (food)* denaturant, denaturing agent
Dendrit *m (cryst)* dendrite
dendritisch *(cryst)* dendritic[al]
Denitration *f* denitration
Denitrator *m s.* 1. Denitrierapparat; 2. Denitrierturm
Denitrierapparat *m* denitrator
denitrieren to denitrate
Denitrierturm *m* denitration tower, denitrator [tower]
Denitrierung *f* denitration
Denitrierungs... *s.* Denitrier...
Denitrifikanten *mpl*, **Denitrifikationsbakterien** *npl* denitrifying bacteria, denitrifiers
Denitrifikation *f* denitrification *(reduction of nitrates brought about by denitrifying bacteria)*
Denitrifikatoren *mpl s.* Denitrifikanten
denitrifizieren to denitrify
Denitrifizierung *f s.* Denitrifikation
Denitrosierung *f* denitrosation
de-Nora-Zelle *f* de Nora [mercury] cell *(chlor-alkali electrolysis)*
Densimeter *n* densimeter, densitometer, *(for liquids also)* hydrometer; *(phot)* densitometer
Densimetrie *f* densimetry
Densitometer *n (phot)* densitometer
Densitometrie *f (phot)* densitometry
Densograph *m s.* Densitometer
Densometer *n s.* Densitometer
Dentalgold *n*, **Dentalgoldlegierung** *f* dental gold [alloy]
Dentallegierung *f* dental alloy
Dentalporzellan *n* dental porcelain
Dentin *n* dentin[e]
Depentanisator *m* depentanizer
depentanisieren to depentanize
Depentanisierung *f* depentanization
Dephlegmation *f s.* Dephlegmierung
Dephlegmator *m (distil)* dephlegmator, [counter-current] partial condenser, partial-condensation head
dephlegmieren *(distil)* to dephlegmate
Dephlegmierung *f (distil)* dephlegmation, partial condensation
dephosphorylieren to dephosphorylate
Dephosphorylierung *f* dephosphorylation
Depilation *f* depilation

Depilatorium *n* depilatory, hair remover
Depiliercreme *f* depilatory cream
depilieren to depilate, to remove hair from
Depilierung *f* depilation
Depolarisation *f* depolarization
Depolarisationsfaktor *m* depolarization factor
Depolarisationsgrad *m* degree of depolarization
Depolarisator *m* depolarizer
depolarisieren to depolarize
depolymerisieren to depolymerize
Depolymerisierung *f* depolymerization
Depolymerisation *f* depolymerization
~ **über eine Reaktionskette** chain-reaction depolymerization
Deponie *f* 1. disposal [to land] *(of waste products)*; 2. [waste] disposal site, *(in hollows)* landfill
~/geordnete sanitary landfill
~/untertägige underground burial, deep burial on land *(of waste products)*
deponieren to dispose of *(waste products)*, *(if underground also)* to bury
Deposition f/nasse wet deposition *(of pollutants from the atmosphere)*
~/saure acid deposition
~/trockene dry deposition
Depositionsgeschwindigkeit *f* deposition velocity
Depot *n* 1. storehouse, storage, store; 2. *(geol)* deposit
Depotfett *n (bioch)* depot fat
Depotprotein *n (bioch)* depot protein
Depression *f* depression
Depropanisator *m* depropanizer
depropanisieren to depropanize
Depropanisierung *f* depropanization
Depropanisierungskolonne *f* depropanizer
deproteinisieren to deproteinize
Deproteinisierung *f* deproteinization
Deprotonierung *f* deprotonation
Deprotonierungs-Protonierungs-Reaktion *f* deprotonation-protonation reaction
Depsid *n* depside *(ester consisting of two or more phenolic benzoic acids)*
Depsidon *n (org ch)* depsidone
Depsipeptid *n (bioch)* depsipeptide
Depsipeptid-Antibiotikum *n (biot)* depsipeptide antibiotic
Derbyrot *n s.* Chromrot
Derepression *f (biot)* derepression
Derivat *n* derivative • **in ein ~ überführen** *(anal)* to derivatize
~/organisches organoderivative
Derivatbildung *f* 1. formation of derivatives; 2. *s.* Derivatisierung
Derivatisierung *f (anal)* derivatization
~ **nach der Trennsäule** *(chromat)* post-column derivatization
~ **vor der Trennsäule** *(chromat)* pre-column derivatization
derivativ derivative
Derivativpolarographie *f (anal)* derivative polarography
Derivativspektroskopie *f* derivative spectroscopy
Derivativspektrum *n* derivative spectrum
DES *s.* Diethylstilböstrol
Desacetoxylierung *f* deacetoxylation
desacylieren to deacylate
Desacylierung *f* deacylation
Desadenylylierung *f (bioch)* deadenylylation
desaktivieren to deactivate, to inactivate *(catalysts)*; to deactivate, to de-energize *(molecules)*
Desaktivierung *f* deactivation, inactivation *(of catalysts)*; deactivation, de-energization *(of molecules)*
~/strahlende radiative deactivation
~/strahlungslose radiationless deactivation
Desaldolierung *f* dealdolization
Desalkoxylierung *f* dealkoxylation
desalkylieren to dealkylate
Desalkylierung *f* dealkylation
~**reduktive (reduzierende)** hydrodealkylation, reductive dealkylation
desamidieren to deamidate
Desamidierung *f* deamidation
Desaminase *f* deaminase
desaminieren to deaminate
~/oxidativ to deaminate oxidatively
Desaminierung *f* deamination
~/oxidative oxidative deamination
Desaromatisierung *f* dearomatization
Desarylierung *f* dearylation
Desensibilisator *m (phot)* desensitizer
desensibilisieren *(phot, bioch)* to desensitize
Desensibilisierung *f (phot, bioch)* desensitization
Deserpidin *n* deserpidine, 11-demethoxyreserpine *(a rauwolfia alkaloid)*
Desethoxylierung *f* deethoxylation
Desethylierung *f* deethylation
deshalogenieren *s.* dehalogenieren
Design n/molekulares *(bioch)* molecular modelling
desilifizieren *(geoch)* to desilicate
Desilifizierung *f (geoch)* desilication
Desilylierung *f* desilylation
Desinfektion *f* disinfection
~ **des Wassers** *(hyd)* water disinfection
Desinfektionslösung *f* disinfectant solution
Desinfektionsmittel *n*, **Desinfiziens** *n* disinfectant
~ **mit Reinigungswirkung** detergent-sanitizer
desinfizieren to disinfect
desinfizierend disinfectant
Desinfizierung *f* disinfection
Desintegration *f* disintegration
Desintegrationstheorie *f* theory of radioactive disintegration
Desintegrator *m s.* 1. Desintegratorgaswäscher; 2. Desintegratormühle
Desintegratorgaswäscher *m* disintegrator [gas] washer, disintegrator
~ **nach Theisen** Theisen disintegrator
~ **nach Zschocke** Zschocke disintegrator

Desintegratormühle *f* disintegrator, *(specif)* cage (squirrel-cage) disintegrator (mill), bar mill; *(pap)* chip crusher, chipbreaker, rechipper
Desintegratorwäscher *m s.* Desintegratorgaswäscher
desintegrieren to disintegrate
Desmin *m (min)* desmine, stilbite *(a tectosilicate)*
Desmoenzym *n*, **Desmoferment** *n* desmo-enzyme *(any of a group of extracellular enzymes)*
Desmolyse *f* desmolysis
desmotrop desmotropic
Desmotropie *f* desmotropy, desmotropism, dynamic isomerism
Desodorans *n* deodorant, deodorizer
Desodorant-Lotion *f* deodorant lotion
Desodoration *f* deodorization
Desodoreur *m* deodorizer *(an apparatus for deodorizing fats and oils)*
desodorieren to deodorize
desodorierend deodorant
Desodorierer *m s.* Desodoreur
Desodorierung *f* deodorization
Desodorierungsmittel *n* deodorant, deodorizer
desodorisieren *s.* desodorieren
desorbierbar desorbable
Desorbierbarkeit *f* desorbability
desorbieren to desorb, to strip [off, out]
~/mit Wasserdampf to steam
Desorption *f* desorption, stripping
Desorptionskurve *f* desorption curve
Desosamin *n* desosamine *(a xylohexose derivative)*
Desoxidation *f* deoxid[iz]ation, deoxygenation
Desoxidationsmittel *n* deoxidant, deoxidizer, deoxidizing agent, *(met also)* scavenger
desoxidieren to deoxidize, to deoxidate, to deoxygenate, *(met also)* to scavenge
Desoxyadenosin-5'-phosphat *n (bioch)* deoxyadenylic acid
Desoxycholsäure *f* deoxycholic acid *(a bile acid)*
Desoxycorticosteron *n (bioch)* deoxycorticosterone
Desoxycytidin-5'-phosphat *n (bioch)* deoxycytidylic acid
Desoxyguanosin-5'-phosphat *n (bioch)* deoxyguanylic acid
Desoxypentose *f* deoxypentose *(a monosaccharide)*
Desoxypentosenucleinsäure *f (bioch)* deoxypentose nucleic acid
Desoxyribonuclease *f (bioch)* deoxyribonuclease, DNase
Desoxyribonucleinsäure *f (bioch)* deoxyribonucleic acid, DNA *(for compounds s. under* DNA*)*
Desoxyribonucleoprotein *n (bioch)* deoxyribonucleoprotein
Desoxyribose *f* deoxyribose *(a monosaccharide)*
Desoxythymidin-5'-phosphat *n (bioch)* deoxythymidine 5'-phosphate
Desoxyzucker *m (bioch)* deoxy sugar
desozon[is]ieren to deozonize
Dessertwein *m* dessert wine
destabilisieren to destabilize, to make unstable
Destannylierung *f* destannylation
Destillans *n* material being distilled
Destillat *n* distillate
~/leichtes light distillate
~/mittleres middle distillate
Destillatabnahme *f* product take-off, distillate drain
Destillatbenzin *n* straight-run gasoline, distillate gasoline, straight-run benzine, S.R.B.
Destillateur *m* distiller
Destillatfangrinne *f* distillate [collection] gutter
Destillatfraktion *f* distillate fraction
Destillatheizöl *n* distillate fuel oil
Destillation *f* distillation
~/abbauende *s.* ~/trockene
~/absteigende downward distillation
~/azeotrope azeotropic (entrainment) distillation
~/destruktive *s.* ~/trockene
~/differentielle differential distillation
~/direkte straight[-run] distillation, simple distillation
~/diskontinuierliche batch distillation
~/durch Sonnenbestrahlung *(hyd)* solar evaporation (distillation)
~ eines Mehrkomponentensystems (Mehrstoffgemischs) multicomponent distillation
~ eines Zweikomponentensystems (Zweistoffgemischs) binary distillation
~/einfache *s.* ~/direkte
~/einfache kontinuierliche simple continuous distillation
~/erneute redistillation, rerun[ning]
~/erste primary distillation
~/extrahierende (extraktive) extractive distillation
~/fraktionierende (fraktionierte) fractional distillation, fractionation
~/geschlossene equilibrium distillation
~/gewöhnliche simple (straight) distillation
~/halbkontinuierliche semicontinuous distillation
~ im Vakuum vacuum distillation, distillation under vacuum (reduced pressure)
~/integrale equilibrium distillation
~/isobare isobaric distillation, distillation at constant pressure
~/isotherme isothermal distillation, distillation at constant temperature
~/katalytische catalytic distillation
~/kontinuierliche continuous distillation
~/mehrmalige einfache simple batch distillation
~ mit fallendem Film falling-film distillation
~ mit Zusatzstoff[en] codistillation
~ nach ASTM ASTM distillation
~/nochmalige redistillation, rerun[ning]
~/offene differential distillation
~/primäre primary distillation
~/schonende gentle distillation
~/stetige continuous distillation
~/trockene dry (destructive) distillation

~ **unter vermindertem Druck** *s.* ~/im Vakuum
~ **von Zweistoffgemischen/kontinuierliche (stetige)** continuous binary distillation
Destillations... *s. a.* Destillier...
Destillationsanlage *f (tech)* distillation (distilling) plant, distillery, still; *(lab)* distillation unit, still
~/diskontinuierlich arbeitende batch-distillation plant (unit)
~/kontinuierlich arbeitende continuous-distillation plant (unit)
Destillationsapparat *m* distillation apparatus, still
~ **für Benzolvorprodukt** once-run[ning] still
~ **mit fallendem Film** falling-film still
~ **mit rotierender Verdampferfläche** rotary still
~ **mit Verteilerbürsten** wiped-film still
~ **nach Savalle** Savalle's still
Destillationsapparatur *f* distillation assembly
Destillationsbenzin *n s.* Destillatbenzin
Destillationsbereich *m* distillation range
Destillationsdruck *m* distillation pressure
Destillationseinheit *f* distillation (distilling) unit
Destillationserzeugnis *n* distillation product, running
Destillationsfraktion *f* distillate fraction
Destillationsgas *n* distillation gas
Destillationsgeschwindigkeit *f* distillation rate
Destillationsgut *n* distilland, material to be distilled; material being distilled
Destillationskurve *f*, **Destillationslinie** *f* distillation curve
Destillationsmaterial *n s.* Destillationsgut
Destillationsprodukt *n* distillation product
Destillationsretorte *f* distillation (distilling) retort
Destillationsrückstand *m* distillation (still) residue
~/kurzer short residue (residuum)
~/langer long residue (residuum)
Destillationsstufe *f* distillation stage
Destillationsturm *m* distillation tower
Destillationsverlust *m* distillation loss
Destillationsvorgang *m* distillation process
Destillationswasser *n* distillation water
destillativ by [means of] distillation
Destillatkraftstoff *m* distillate fuel
Destillatkühler *m* distillate cooler
Destillatöl *n* distillate oil
Destillatsammelrinne *f* distillate [collection] gutter
Destillatsammler *m s.* Destilliervorlage
Destillatschmieröl *n* distillate lubricating oil
Destillatstock *m (petrol)* distillate stock
Destillatvorlage *f s.* Destilliervorlage
Destillatzusammensetzung *f* distillate composition
Destillier... *s. a.* Destillations...
Destillierarbeit *f* distillation (distilling) operation
Destillieraufsatz *m* distillation head, stillhead, distillation connecting tube
~ **nach Claisen** Claisen stillhead
destillierbar distillable
~/mit Dampf (Trägerdampf, Wasserdampf) steam-distillable
Destillierbarkeit *f* distillability
Destillierbetrieb *m* 1. distillation (distilling) plant, distillery; 2. distillation (distilling) operation
Destillierblase *f* distillation boiler, still pot, *(with rectifying apparatus:)* reboiler
~ **mit direkter Beheizung** direct-fired reboiler
Destilliereinrichtung *f* distillation equipment
destillieren to distil
~/erneut to redistil, to rerun
~/fraktioniert to fractionate
~/mit Dampf (Trägerdampf, Wasserdampf) to steam-distil
~/nochmals *s.* ~/erneut
~/stufenweise to fractionate
~/wiederholt *s.* ~/erneut
Destilliergefäß *n s.* Destillierblase
Destillierhaus *n* still house
Destillierkolben *m* distillation flask
Destillierkolonne *f* distillation column
~ **mit Glockenböden** bubble-cap (bubble-tray) column
Destillierkopf *m s.* Destillieraufsatz
Destillierofen *m* distillation furnace, retort furnace (oven)
Destillierrohr *n* distillation tube
Destilliersäule *f* distillation column
destilliert/doppelt twice-distilled
~/dreifach triple-distilled
~/unter Vakuum vacuum-distilled, distilled in vacuo
~/zweifach twice-distilled
Destilliervorlage *f* [distillate, distillation] receiver
Destilliervorstoß *m* adapter
Destruktion *f* destruction
destruktiv destructive
Desulfatierung *f* desulphation
Desulfinierung *f* desulfination
desulfonieren to desulphonate
Desulfonierung *f* desulphonation
desulfurieren to desulphurize, to desulphur
Desulfurierung *f* desulphurization, desulphuration
~/reduktive (reduzierende) reductive desulphurization
Desulfurikanten *mpl* sulphate reducers, sulphate-reducing bacteria, sulphur-reducing bacteria
Desuridylderivat *n (bioch)* deuridylic derivative
Desylchlorid *n* desyl chloride, α-chloro-α-phenylacetophenone
Detachiermittel *n (text)* stain (spot) remover, spotting agent
Detachur *f (text)* stain removal
Detailzeichenpapier *n* detail paper
detektierbar *s.* nachweisbar
Detektion *f*/**amperometrische** *(anal)* amperometric detection
~/coulometrische coulometric detection
~/potentiometrische *(anal)* potentiometric detection
Detektionsmethode *f* detection method, method of detection
~/elektrochemische electrochemical method of detection

Detektor *m (anal)* detector
~/elektrochemischer electrochemical detector
~/flammenphotometrischer flame photometric detector
~/massenspektrometrischer mass-spectrometric detector
~/phasenempfindlicher phase-sensitive detector
~/pulsierend arbeitender elektrochemischer dual-working electrode electrochemical detector
~/thermoionischer thermal ionization detector, TID
Detektoranzeige *f* detector output
Detektorempfindlichkeit *f* detector sensitivity, detectivity
Detektorküvette *f* detector [flow] cell
Detektorsignal *n* detector signal
Detektorzelle *f s.* Detektorküvette
Detergens *n* [synthetic] detergent, syndet, soapless soap
Detergent *m* 1. detergent *(for holding in suspension insoluble matter)*; 2. *s.* Detergens
Detergentzusatz *m* detergent additive
Detonation *f* detonation
Detonationsgeschwindigkeit *f* detonation rate
Detonationsübertragung *f* transmission of detonation
detonieren to detonate
detosylieren to detosylate
Detosylierung *f* detosylation
Detritierung *f* detritiation
Detritus *m (geol)* detritus, detrital material; *(hyd)* detritus, tripton *(suspended non-living debris)*
Detritylierung *f* detritylation
Detroit-Lichtbogenschaukelofen *m* Detroit rocking [arc] furnace
Deuterid *n* deuteride
deuterieren to deuterate, to deuterize
Deuterierung *f* deuteration
Deuterierungsgrad *m* degree of deuteration
Deuteriogruppe *f* deuterio group
Deuterium *n* $^{2}_{1}H$, D deuterium, heavy hydrogen
~/schweres $^{3}_{1}H$, T tritium
Deuteriumlampe *f (spectr)* deuterium arc (gas-discharge) lamp
deuteriummarkiert deuterated, deuterized
Deuteriumoxid *n* deuterium oxide, heavy water
Deuteriumuntergrundkompensation *f (spectr)* deuterium arc background correction
Deuteron *n (nucl)* deuteron
Devitrit *m (glass)* devitrite *(a product of devitrification)*
Devulkanisation *f* devulcanization
devulkanisieren to devulcanize
Dewar-Gefäß *n* Dewar [flask, vessel] *(for holding liquid gases)*
DE-Wert *m s.* Dextroseäquivalent
Dextran *n (bioch)* dextran[e]
~/klinisches *(biot)* clinical dextran
~/natives native dextran
Dextrin *n* dextrin[e], British (starch) gum
Dextrinbildung *f* dextrinization
dextrinieren to dextrinize
Dextrinierung *f* dextrinization
Dextrinleim *m* dextrin adhesive (glue)
Dextrinogenamylase *f* dextrinogenic amylase
Dextrinstärke *f* soluble starch
dextrogyr *s.* rechtsdrehend
Dextronsäure *f s.* D-Gluconsäure
Dextropimarsäure *f* (+)-pimaric acid, dextropimaric acid
Dextrose *f* dextrose, D-glucose *(a monosaccharide)*
Dextroseäquivalent *n (food)* dextrose equivalent [value], DE *(content of reducing sugars)*
Dezigrammbereich *m (anal)* decigram range *(0.1 to 1 g)*
Dezimalwaage *f* decimal balance
Dezimol *n* decimol
DFB *s.* Druckfeuerbeständigkeit
dGMP *s.* Desoxyguanosin-5'-phosphat
DH *s.* Defometerhärte
D.I. *s.* Diesel-Index
diablastisch *(cryst)* diablastic
Diacetonalkohol *m* diacetone alcohol, 4-hydroxy-4-methyl-pentan-2-one
Diacetyl *n s.* Biacetyl
Diacetylen *n s.* Butadiin
Diacetylierung *f* diacetylation
Diacetylmorphin *n* diacetylmorphine, diamorphine, heroin *(a narcotic)*
Diacylamin *n* diacylamine
Diacylperoxid *n* diacyl peroxide
Diagenese *f (geol)* diagenesis *(post-depositional alteration of sediments)*
diagenetisch *(geol)* diagenetic *(post-depositionally altered)*
Diagnostikum *n* diagnostic reagent
Diagonalbeziehung *f* diagonal relationship *(in the periodic system)*
Diagramm *n* graph, diagram, chart, graphical (diagrammatic) representation
~/doppeltlogarithmisches log-log plot, Ellingham diagram
Diagrammband *n s.* Diagrammstreifen
Diagrammpapier *n* plotting (graph) paper, recorder chart
Diagrammpapierantrieb *m* chart drive *(of a strip-chart recorder)*
Diagrammstreifen *m* strip chart *(of a recorder)*
Dialdehyd *m* dialdehyde
Dialkylalkoxyphosphin *n* $R_2P(OR)$ alkyl dialkylphosphinite
Dialkylbenzen *n*, **Dialkylbenzol** *n* dialkylbenzene
Dialkylboran *n* dialkylborane
Dialkylchlorphosphin *n* R_2PCl dialkylchlorophosphine, dialkylphosphinous chloride
Dialkyl-dialkylamino-phosphin *n* $R_2P(NR_2)$ dialkyl-dialkylamino-phosphine, *N,N*-dialkyl-dialkylphosphinous amide

Dialkylether *m* dialkyl ether
Dialkylhydroxyphosphin *n* $R_2P(OH)$ dialkylphosphinous acid
dialkylieren to dialkylate
Dialkylierung *f* dialkylation
Dialkylmalon[säure]ester *m* dialkylmalonic ester
Dialkylphosphorigsäurechlorid *n* $(RO)_2PCl$ dialkoxychlorophosphine, dialkylphosphorochloridite
Dialkylsulfid *n* alkyl sulphide, thioether, thiaalkane
Dialkylzink *n* dialkylzinc
Diallyl *n s.* Hexa-1,5-dien
Diallylphthalat *n* diallyl phthalate, DAP
Diallylphthalatharz *n* diallyl phthalate resin
Dialursäure *f* dialuric acid, 5-hydroxybarbituric acid
Dialysat *n* dialysate
Dialysator *m* dialyser
Dialyse *f* dialysis
Dialysenpresse *f* filter-press dialyser
Dialysierapparat *m* dialyser
dialysierbar dialysable
dialysieren to dialyse
Dialysierfläche *f* dialysing area
Dialysiergut *n* material to be dialysed; material being dialysed
Dialysierhülse *f* dialysis tubing
Dialysiermembran *f* dialysing membrane
Dialysierzelle *f* dialysis (dialytic) cell
Diamagnetikum *n* diamagnet, diamagnetic [substance]
diamagnetisch diamagnetic
Diamagnetismus *m* diamagnetism
Diamant *m* diamond
~/schwarzer carbonado, black (carbon) diamond
diamantartig diamond-like
diamanten adamantine
Diamantfarbstoff *m* diamond dye
Diamantgitter *n (cryst)* diamond lattice
Diamantglanz *m* brilliant lustre
Diamantgrün *n* emerald (brilliant) green *(a basic triphenylmethane dye)*
diamanthart adamantine
Diamantmörser *m* diamond (crushing, percussion) mortar
diamantoid diamondoid, diamond-like *(ring system)*
Diamantpackung *f (cryst)* diamond packing
Diamantschneider *m* diamond cutter
Diamantschwarz *n* diamond black
Diamantstruktur *f (cryst)* diamond structure
Diamanttinte *f* diamond ink *(for etching glassware)*
Diamid *n* diamide, hydrazine
Diamin *n* diamine
Diaminchelat *n* diamine chelate
Diaminoanthrachinon *n* diaminoanthraquinone
2,4-Diaminoazobenzen *n* 2,4-diaminoazobenzene, chrysoidine
Diaminobenzen *n* diaminobenzene, phenylenediamine
4,4'-Diaminobiphenyl *n* 4,4'-diaminobiphenyl, benzidine
1,6-Diaminohexan *n* 1,6-diaminohexane, hexamethylene diamine
2,6-Diaminohexansäure *f* 2,6-diaminohexanoic acid, lysine
1,2-Diaminopropan *n s.* Propan-1,2-diamin
Diaminostilben *n* diaminostilbene, stilbenediamine, 1,2-diphenylethylenediamine
Diaminotoluen *n* diaminotoluene, toluylenediamine
diaminvernetzt *(rubber)* diamine-cross-linked
Diamminquecksilber(II)-chlorid *n* diamminemercury(II) chloride, diammine mercuric chloride, fusible white precipitate
Diammoniumhydrogenphosphat *n* ammonium hydrogenphosphate
Diamorphin *n* diamorphine, diacetylmorphine, heroin *(a narcotic)*
Diamylphthalat *n* diamyl phthalate
Dian *n* bisphenol A, *2,2-di-*p*-hydroxyphenylpropane
Dianion *n* dianion
Dianisidin *n* dianisidine, diaminodimethoxybiphenyl
Dianthrachinonindigo *m* dianthraquinoneindigo
Dianthrachinonylamin *n*, **Dianthrimid** *n* dianthrimide, dianthraquinonylamine
Diantimonat(V) *n* diantimonate(V)
Diantimonpentoxid *n* diantimony pentaoxide, antimony(V) oxide
Diantimon(V)-säure *f* diantimonic(V) acid
Diaphaniepapier *n* diaphanic paper
Diaphoretikum *n (pharm)* diaphoretic, sudorific
diaphoretisch diaphoretic, sudorific
Diaphragma *n* diaphragm, membrane
Diaphragmaelektrolyse *f* diaphragm cell electrolysis (process)
Diaphragmalauge *f* diaphragm caustic *(electrolysis)*
Diaphragmasack *m* membrane bag *(in dialysis)*
Diaphragmaverfahren *n s.* Diaphragmaelektrolyse
Diaphragmazelle *f* diaphragm cell *(electrolysis)*
~ mit leerem Katodenraum unsubmerged diaphragm cell
~ mit vollem Katodenraum submerged diaphragm cell
diäquatorial, diäquatorisch diequatorial *(stereochemistry)*
Diarsenat(III) *n* diarsenite
Diarsenat(V) *n* diarsenate
Diarsendisulfid *n s.* Tetrarsentetrasulfid
Diarsenpentasulfid *n* diarsenic pentasulphide, arsenic(V) sulphide
Diarsenpentoxid *n* diarsenic pentaoxide, arsenic(V) oxide
Diarsen(V)-säure *f* diarsenic acid
Diarsentrioxid *n* diarsenic trioxide, arsenic(III) oxide, arsenic
Diarsentrisulfid *n* diarsenic trisulphide, arsenic(III) sulphide
1,2-Diarylhydrazin *n* 1,2-diarylhydrazine, hydrazoarene, 1,2-diaryldiazane
Diaspor *m (min)* diaspore *(α-aluminium hydroxide oxide)*

Diasporton *m* diaspore clay
Diastase *f s.* Amylase
diastereomer diastereo[iso]meric
Diastereomer[e] *n* diastereo[iso]mer
Diäth... *s. a.* Dieth...
Diäthen *n s.* Buta-1,3-dien
diatherm[an] diathermanous, diathermic
Diathermansie *f* diatherma[n]cy
Diäthin *n s.* Butadiin
Diäthylacetylen *n s.* Hex-3-in
Diäthylen *n s.* Buta-1,3-dien
Diäthylenoxid *n s.* Tetrahydrofuran
Diäthylformal *n s.* Diethoxymethan
Diatomeenerde *f* diatomaceous (infusorial) earth, kieselguhr
Diatomeenschlamm *m* diatom ooze
Diauxie *f* diauxy *(diphasic or polyphasic course of growth with microorganisms)*
diauxisch diauxic *(said of the growth of microorganisms which shows a diphasic or polyphasic course)*
diaxial diaxial
Diazacyanin *n (dye)* diazacyanine
1,4-Diazanaphthalen *n* 1,4-diazanaphthalene, 1,4-benzodiazine, quinoxaline
Diazen *n* diazene, diimide
1,2-Diazin *n* 1,2-diazine, pyridazine
1,3-Diazin *n* 1,3-diazine, pyrimidine
1,4-Diazin *n* 1,4-diazine, pyrazine
Diazoamidobenzol *n s.* Diazoaminobenzen
Diazoaminobenzen *n* diazoaminobenzene, 1,3-diphenyltriazene
Diazoaminoverbindung *f* R–N=N–NHR diazoamino compound
Diazoanhydrid *n* diazo anhydride
Diazocyclohexadienon *n s.* Diazooxid
Diazodinitrophenol *n* diazodinitrophenol, DDNP
Diazofarbstoff *m* diazo dye
Diazogruppe *f* –N=N– diazo group
Diazohydroxid *n* diazohydroxide
Diazokomponente *f* diazo (diazonium) component
Diazokupplung *f* diazo (azo) coupling
1,2-Diazol *n* 1,2-diazole, pyrazole
Diazolösung *f* diazo solution
Diazomethan *n* diazomethane
Diazomethanreaktion *f* diazomethane reaction
Diazoniumgruppe *f* $[Ar{-}N{\equiv}N]^+$ diazonium group
Diazonium-Ion *n* diazonium ion
Diazoniumsalz *n* diazonium salt
Diazooxid *n* diazooxide, diazophenol, diazocyclohexadienone
Diazopapier *n* diazotype paper
Diazophenol *n s.* Diazooxid
Diazoreaktion *f* diazo reaction
~/Paulysche Pauly [protein] reaction
Diazorest *m* –N=N– diazo group
Diazotat *n* R–N=N–OM diazoate, diazotate
diazotierbar diazotizable
diazotieren to diazotize
Diazotierung *f* diazotization
Diazotierungskomponente *f* diazo (diazonium) component, *(dye also)* primary component
Diazotypie *f* 1. diazo copy; 2. *s.* Diazotypieverfahren
Diazotypieverfahren *n* diazo print[ing], diazotype, diazotypy, dyeline print, whiteprint, diazotype (dyeline) process *(a blue-printing process)*
Diazotypiepapier *n* diazotype paper
Diazoverbindung *f* diazo compound
Diazoxid *n* diazo oxide
Dibasizität *f* dibasicity
Dibenzanthrachinon *n* dibenzanthraquinone
Dibenzoanthracen *n* dibenzanthracene
Dibenzo-1,4-dioxin *n*, **Dibenzo-*p*-dioxin** *n* dibenzo-1,4-dioxin, dibenzo-*p*-dioxin, dioxin
~/polychloriertes polychlorinated dibenzo-1,4-dioxin, PCDD
Dibenzofuran *n* dibenzofuran
~/polychloriertes polychlorinated dibenzofuran, PCDF
Dibenzopyran *n* dibenzopyran, dibenzo[a,e]pyran, xanthene
Dibenzopyrenchinon *n* dibenzopyrenequinone
Dibenzo[b,e]pyridin *n* dibenzo[b,e]pyridine, benzo[b]quinoline, acridine
Dibenzo-γ-pyron *n* dibenzopyrone, xanthone
Dibenzopyrrol *n* dibenzopyrrole, carbazole
Dibenzothiazin *n* dibenzothiazine
Dibenzoyl *n s.* Benzil
dibenzoylieren to dibenzoylate
Dibenzoylierung *f* dibenzoylation
Dibenzoylperoxid *n* dibenzoyl peroxide, benzoyl peroxide
Dibenzyl *n s.* Bibenzyl
Dibenzylether *m* dibenzyl ether
Dibenzylierung *f* dibenzylation
Dibenzylsuccinat *n* dibenzyl succinate
Dibismuttriselenid *n* dibismuth triselenide, bismuth(III) selenide
Diboran *n* diborane
Diboran(4) *n* B_2H_4 diborane(4)
Diboran(6) *n* B_2H_6 diborane(6), diborane *(proper)*
Diboranid *n* diboranide
Dibortetrachlorid *n* diboron tetrachloride
Dibromanthrachinon *n* dibromoanthraquinone
Dibrombenzen *n*, **Dibrombenzol** *n* dibromobenzene
Dibromdichlorsilan *n* dibromodichlorosilane
1,2-Dibromethan *n* 1,2-dibromoethane
Dibromid *n* dibromide
dibromieren to dibrominate
Dibromierung *f* dibromination
Dibromindigo *m(n)* dibromoindigo
Dibrommethan *n* dibromomethane
Dibrompropan *n* dibromopropane
Dibromthymolsulfophthalein *n* dibromothymolsulphonephthalein, bromothymol blue *(a pH indicator)*
Dibromverbindung *f* dibromo compound
2,6-Di-*tert*-butyl-*p*-cresol *n* 2,6-di-*tert*-butyl-*p*-cresol, 4-methyl-2,6-di-*tert*-butylphenol *(an antioxidant)*

Dibutylphthalat *n* dibutyl phthalate, DBP

Dibutylsebacat *n* dibutyl sebacate

Dibutyryl-cAMP *n (bioch)* dibutyryl cyclic AMP

Dicalciumdiphosphat *n* dicalcium diphosphate, calcium pyrophosphate

Dicarbonsäure *f* dicarboxylic acid

Dicarboxylat-Carrier *m (bioch)* dicarboxylate carrier

Dichlon *n* dichlone, 2,3-dichloro-1,4-naphthoquinone *(a herbicide)*

2,2-Dichloracetamid *n* 2,2-dichloroacetamide

Dichloracetylierung *f* dichloroacetylation

Dichloranilin *n* dichloroaniline

Dichloranthrachinon *n* dichloroanthraquinone

Dichlorbenzen *n*, **Dichlorbenzol** *n* dichlorobenzene

Dichlorderivat *n* dichloro derivative

1,2-Dichlordiethylether *m* 1,2-dichloroethyl ethyl ether, 1,2-dichlorodiethyl ether

2,2'-Dichlordiethylether *m* di-2-chloroethyl ether, 2,2'-dichlorodiethyl ether

Dichlordiethylsulfid *n* dichlorodiethyl sulphide, di-2-chloroethyl sulphide

Dichlordifluormethan *n* dichlorodifluoromethane

Dichlordiphenyltrichlorethan *n* dichlorodiphenyltrichloroethane, DDT *(a contact insecticide)*

Dichloressigsäure *f* dichloroacetic acid, dichloroethanoic acid

Dichlorethan *n* dichloroethane

Dichlorethansäure *f* dichloroethanoic acid, dichloroacetic acid

Dichlorether *m s.* 1,2-Dichlordiethylether

1,1-Dichlorethylen *n* 1,1-dichloroethylene, vinylidene chloride

Dichlorfluormethan *n* dichloromonofluoromethane

Dichlorheptoxid *n* dichlorine heptaoxide, chlorine(VII) oxide

Dichlorid *n* dichloride

Dichlorierung *f* dichlorination

Dichlormethan *n* dichloromethane

Dichlornaphthalen *n* dichloronaphthalene

Dichlorotetramminplatin(IV)-chlorid *n* dichlorotetraammineplatinum(IV) chloride

Dichloroxid *n* dichlorine monooxide, chlorine(I) oxide

tris-**(2,4-Dichlorphenoxyethyl)phosphit** *n tris*-(2,4-dichlorophenoxyethyl)phosphite, 2,4-DEP *(a herbicide)*

4-(2',4'-Dichlorphenoxy)buttersäure *f* 4,(2',4'-dichlorophenoxy)butyric acid, 2,4-DB *(a herbicide)*

2,4-Dichlorphenoxyessigsäure *f* 2,4-dichlorophenoxyacetic acid, 2,4-D *(a herbicide)*

Dichlorphosphin *n* dichlorophosphine, phosphonous dichloride

Dichlorprop *n* dichlorprop, 2,4-DP, 2-(2',4'-dichlorophenoxy)propionic acid *(a herbicide)*

Dichlorpropan *n* dichloropropane

Dichlortriazin *n* dichlorotriazine

Dichroismus *m (cryst, coll)* dichroism

dichroitisch *(cryst, coll)* dichroic

Dichromat *n* $M^I_2Cr_2O_7$ dichromate

dichromatisch dichromatic, dichroic

Dichromatschwefelsäure *f s.* Chromschwefelsäure

Dichromtrioxid *n* dichromium trioxide, chromium(III) oxide

dicht tight, proof, impermeable, impenetrable, impervious; leaktight, leakproof; dense, close-grained, fine-grained, compact *(structure)*

Dicht... *s. a.* Dichtungs...

dichtbrennend *(ceram)* dense-burning

Dichte *f* 1. density, *(specif)* mass density, D *(mass of a substance per unit volume)*; strength *(of a solution)*; 2. *s.* ~/optische

~ **in API-Graden** *(petrol)* API gravity

~ **nach dem Brand** *(ceram)* fired density

~/optische optical density

Dickablauge *f (pap)* concentrated black liquor

~/relative relative density *(ratio of the density of a material to the density of some standard material)*

~/scheinbare apparent density

~/wahre (wirkliche) true density

Dichteanreicherung *f* gravity concentration

Dichtebestimmung *f* densimetry

~ **von Flüssigkeiten** hydrometry

Dichtegradient *m* density gradient

Dichtegradientenzentrifugation *f (anal)* density-gradient centrifugation

Dichtekurve *f (phot)* characteristic curve, H and D curve

Dichtemesser *m* densimeter

Dichtemessung *f* densimetry

dichten to make tight, to seal, to pack, to ca[u]lk

Dichtesortierung *f* density separation (cut), gravity concentration

Dichteverhältnis *n* relative density *(ratio of the density of a material to the density of some standard material at the same state of matter)*

Dichtewaage *f* density balance

Dichtezahl *f s.* Dichte/relative

Dichtfläche *f s.* Dichtungsfläche

dichtgepackt *(cryst)* close-packed

Dichtheit *f*, **Dichtigkeit** *f* tightness, proofness; leak tightness, leakproofness

Dichtkonus *m (chromat)* ferrule

Dichtmaterial *n*, **Dichtmittel** *n* sealant

dichtpolen to pole down *(copper for eliminating sulphur)*

Dichtpolen *n* poling-down *(of copper for eliminating sulphur)*

Dichtring *m* packing (sealing) ring

Dichtschnur *f* packing (sealing) strip

dichtschweißen to seal-weld

Dichtstoff *m s.* Dichtmaterial

Dichtung *f* packing, seal, *(for parts without relative motion also)* static seal, gasket, *(for moving parts also)* dynamic seal

~/druckausgeglichene (druckentlastete) balanced seal

~/eingefaßte envelope gasket
~/halbmetallische semimetallic packing
~/umhüllte envelope gasket
Dichtungsdruck *m* sealing pressure
Dichtungsfläche *f* seal face, sealing [sur]face, gasketing area
Dichtungsflüssigkeit *f* sealing liquid (fluid)
Dichtungsmanschette *f* gasket
Dichtungsmasse *f* lute, luting, ca[u]lking compound
Dichtungsmaterial *n* packing (sealing, gasketing) material
~ für Rohrgewindeverbindungen pipe dope
Dichtungsring *m* packing (sealing) ring
Dichtungssatz *m* packing set
Dichtungsschnur *f* packing (sealing) strip
Dichtungswerkstoff *m s.* Dichtungsmaterial
Dickablauge *f (pap)* concentrated black liquor, evaporated (thick) black liquor
Dickdruckpapier *n* featherweight paper, *(Am)* bulking paper
Dicke *f* thickness; *(text)* size *(of fibrous material)*; *(glass)* substance, strength *(of flat glass)*; *(pap)* caliper
~ des biologischen Rasens *(hyd)* biological film thickness *(trickling-filter process)*
Dickenmesser *m* thickness gauge (tester), caliper
dickflüssig viscous, viscose, thick, syrupy, ropy
• **~ werden** to thicken, to inspissate
Dickflüssigkeit *f* viscosity, thickness, ropiness
Dickglas *n* thick [sheet] glass
dickgriffig sein *(pap)* to bulk high
Dicklauge *f* concentrated (strong) liquor; *(pap)* concentrated (evaporated, thick) black liquor
Dicklaugenaustritt *m* concentrated liquor outlet
Dicklegung *f* souring *(of milk)*
Dickmilch *f* fermented (cultured, set) milk
Dicksaft *m (sugar)* thick juice
Dickschlamm *m* thickened (concentrated) sludge, *(as discharge of a thickener also)* thickened liquor, thick slime, thickener pulp
Dickschlammaustrag *m* thickened-liquor outlet, thick-slime discharge
Dickschlammzone *f* sludge zone
Dickstoff *m (pap)* slush (high-density) pulp, slush (thick) stock
Dickstoff-Abwärts[bleich]turm *m (pap)* downflow high-density tower
Dickstoff-Aufwärts[bleich]turm *m (pap)* upflow high-density tower
Dickstoffbehälter *m (pap)* slush pulp storage
Dickstoffbleiche *f (pap)* high-density bleaching, bleaching at high consistency
Dickstoffbleichstufe *f (pap)* high-density [bleaching] stage
Dickstoffbleichturm *m (pap)* high-density bleacher
Dickstoffendbleiche *f (pap)* final bleaching at high consistency
Dickstoffmahlung *f (pap)* high-consistency refining, HCR
Dickstoffpumpe *f* sludge (thick-liquor) pump; *(pap)* thick-stock pump
Dickstoffvorratsbehälter *m (pap)* slush pulp storage
dicktaflig *(cryst)* thick-tabular
Dickungsmittel *n* thickening agent, thickener, viscosifier
dickwandig thick-wall[ed], heavy-wall[ed]
Dickwerden *n* thickening *(as of milk)*
Dicobalttrioxid *n* dicobalt trioxide, cobalt(III) oxide
Dicobalttrisulfid *n* dicobalt trisulphide, cobalt(III) sulphide
Dicrotalinsäure *f s.* Dicrotalsäure
Dicrotalsäure *f* dicrotalic acid, 3-hydroxy-3-methylglutaric acid
Dicrotolsäure *f s.* Dicrotalsäure
Dicyan *n* $N{\equiv}C{-}C{\equiv}N$ dicyanogen, cyanogen [gas], oxalonitrile
1,1-Dicyanethen *n* 1,1-dicyanoethylene
Dicyandiamid *n* dicyandiamide
Dicyanoaurat(I) *n* $M^I[Au(CN)_2]$ dicyanoaurate(I), cyanoaurate(I)
Dicystein *n* cystine, dicysteine, *3,3'-dithio-*bis*(2-aminopropanoic acid)
Didepsid *n* didepside *(ester consisting of two phenolic benzoic acids)*
Diderivat *n* diderivative
Didier-Bubiag-Verfahren *n* Didier-Bubiag process *(of coal gasification)*
Didym *n* 1. didymium *(a mixture containing neodymium and praseodymium)*; 2. *s.* Didymmetall
Didymerde *f s.* Didymoxid
Didymmetall *n* didymium *(an alloy consisting of neodymium and praseodymium)*
Didymoxid *n historically for a mixture of praseodymium oxide and neodymium oxide*
Dieckmann-Reaktion *f* Dieckmann reaction *(intramolecular condensation of esters)*
Diederwinkel *m* torsion (rotational) angle, angle of rotation *(stereochemistry)*
Dieisentrioxid *n* diiron trioxide, iron(III) oxide, ferric oxide
Dieisentrisulfid *n* diiron trisulphide, iron(III) sulphide, ferric sulphide
Dielektrikum *n* dielectric [material], non-conductor
dielektrisch dielectric, non-conducting
Dielektrizitätskonstante *f***[/absolute]** [absolute] permittivity
~/relative *s.* Dielektrizitätszahl
Dielektrizitätskonstante-Messer *m* dielectrometer, dielectric constant meter
Dielektrizitätszahl *f* relative dielectric constant, relative permittivity, specific inductive capacity, SIC
Dielektro[be]heizung *f* dielectric heating
Dielektrometrie *f* dielectrometry, dielectric constant measurement
Dielkometrie *f s.* Dielektrometrie
Diels-Alder-Reaktion *f*, **Diels-Alder-Synthese** *f* Diels-Alder reaction (addition, condensation), diene reaction (synthesis)

Dien *n* diene *(a compound with two esp conjugated C-C double bonds)*
Dienkautschuk *m* diene rubber
Dienol-Benzol-Umlagerung *f* dienol-benzene rearrangement
Dienon-Phenol-Umlagerung *f* dienone-phenol rearrangement
dienophil dienophilic
Dienophil *n* dienophile
Dienpolymer[e] *n*, **Dienpolymerisat** n diene[-based] polymer
Diensynthese *f* diene synthesis
~/Diels-Aldersche *s.* Diels-Alder-Reaktion
Diesel-Index *m* diesel index
Dieselklopfen *n* diesel knock
Dieselkraftstoff *m* diesel fuel (oil)
Dieselöl *n s.* Dieselkraftstoff
Dieselschmieröl *n* diesel engine oil
Dieseltreibstoff *m s.* Dieselkraftstoff
Diester *m* diester
Dieterici-Zustandsgleichung *f (phys ch)* Dieterici equation [of state]
Diethanolamin *n* *2,2'-iminodiethanol, diethanolamine, DEA
Dietherat *n* dietherate
1,1-Diethoxyethan *n* *1,1-diethoxyethane, acetal
Diethoxymethan *n* *diethoxymethane, diethylformal, formaldehyde diethyl acetal
Diethylamin *n* diethylamine
Diethylaminoethylcellulose *f* diethyl aminoethyl cellulose, DEAE cellulose
Diethyldisulfid *n* diethyl disulphide
Diethyldithiocarbamidsäure *f* diethyldithiocarbamic acid
Diethylendiamin *n* diethylenediamine, piperazine
Diethylenglykol *n* diethylene glycol, DEG, *di(-2-hydroxyethyl) ether
Diethylenglykoldimethylether *n* diethylene glycol dimethyl ether, diglyme
***N,N*-Diethylenharnstoff** *m* bisethyleneurea
Diethylentriaminpentaessigsäure *f* diethylenetriamine pentaacetic acid, DTPA
Diethylether *m* diethyl ether
Diethylmagnesium *n* diethylmagnesium
Diethylmalonat *n* diethyl malonate, malonic ester
Diethylrhodamin *n* diethylrhodamine
Diethylsebacat *n* diethyl sebacate
Diethylstilböstrol *n* diethylstilboestrol
Diethylsuccinat *n* diethyl succinate
Diethylsulfat *n* diethyl sulphate
Diethylsulfid *n* diethyl sulphide, ethylthioethane
Diethylzink *n* diethylzinc
Differentialchromatogramm *n* differential chromatogram
Differentialdestillation *f* differential distillation
Differentialdetektor *m* differential detector *(gas chromatography)*
Differentialdialyse *f (anal)* differential dialysis
Differentialenthalpiemeter *n s.* Differentialkalorimeter
Differentialflotation *f* differential (selective) floatation
Differentialkalorimeter *n* differential [scanning] calorimeter
Differentialmanometer *n* differential manometer
Differentialmethode *f* differential method *(for obtaining kinetic data)*
Differentialphotometrie *f* differential photometry
Differentialpolarographie *f s.* Differenzpolarographie
Differential-Puls-Polarographie *f s.* Differenz-Pulspolarographie
Differentialreaktor *m* differential reactor
Differentialrefraktometer *n* differential refractometer
Differential-Thermoanalysator *m* differential thermal analyser, DTA
Differential-Thermoanalyse *f* differential thermal analysis, DTA
differentialthermoanalytisch by differential thermal analysis
Differential-Thermogravimetrie *f* derivative (differential) thermogravimetry
Differentialtitration *f* differential titration
Differentialzentrifugation *f (bioch)* differential centrifugation
Differentiation *f*/**gravitative** *(geoch)* gravitative differentiation
Differenzbande *f (spectr)* difference band
Differenzdruck *m* differential pressure
Differenzdruckhöhe *f* differential head
Differenzdruckmesser *m*, **Differenzmanometer** *n* differential-pressure meter, differential manometer
Differenzpolarographie *f (anal)* differential polarography
Differenzpotentiometrie *f (anal)* differential potentiometry
Differenz-Pulspolarographie *f (anal)* differential pulse polarography
Differenzspektrum *n* difference spectrum
Differenzverzinnen *n* differential tin coating
Differenzvoltammetrie *f (anal)* differential voltammetry
Diffraktion *f* diffraction
Diffraktionserscheinung *f* diffraction phenomenon
Diffraktometrie *f (anal)* diffraction analysis
diffundieren to diffuse
Diffusat *n* diffusate
Diffusatzelle *f* diffusate cell, *(with water also)* water cell
Diffuseur *m* diffuser, diffusor, diffusing tank, diffusion cell
Diffusion *f* diffusion
~/äußere external diffusion
~/axiale axial (longitudinal) diffusion
~/behinderte restricted diffusion
~/erleichterte *(bioch)* facilitated diffusion
~ in Längsrichtung *s.* ~/axiale
~/innere internal (pore) diffusion

~/molekulare molecular diffusion
~/radiale radial diffusion
~ von Festkörpern solid[-state] diffusion
Diffusionsabscheider *m* denuder system *(for separating gases and aerosol particles)*
Diffusionsapparat *m s.* Diffuseur
Diffusionsbatterie *f* diffusion battery
diffusionsbedingt, diffusionsbestimmt *s.* diffusionsgesteuert
diffusionschromieren to chromize
diffusionsfähig diffusible
Diffusionsfähigkeit *f* diffusibility
Diffusionsgalvanispannung *f s.* Diffusionspotential
Diffusionsgeschwindigkeit *f* diffusion rate
Diffusionsgesetz *n***/Ficksches** Fick's law [of diffusion]
~/erstes (1.) Ficksches Fick's first law of diffusion
~/zweites (2.) Ficksches Fick's second law of diffusion
diffusionsgesteuert diffusion-controlled, under diffusion control, diffusion-limited
diffusionsglühen to homogenize *(alloys)*
Diffusionsglühen *n* homogenization, homogenizing *(of alloys)*
Diffusionsgrenzstrom *m (phys ch)* limiting (maximum) diffusion current
Diffusionskoeffizient *m*, **Diffusionskonstante** *f* diffusion coefficient, diffusivity
Diffusionskontrolle *f s.* Diffusionssteuerung
diffusionskontrolliert *s.* diffusionsgesteuert
Diffusionskonzept *n* differential diffusion model *(gel chromatography)*
Diffusionsmethode *f* diffusion method
Diffusionsmischen *n* diffusive mixing
Diffusionsnebelkammer *f* diffusion cloud chamber
Diffusionspotential *n* diffusion (liquid-junction) potential
Diffusionspumpe *f* [vapour] diffusion pump
~ mit Quecksilberfüllung mercury-vapour pump
Diffusionspumpenöl *n* diffusion-pump oil
Diffusionsrohsaft *m (sugar)* diffusion (raw) juice
Diffusionsschicht *f* diffusion layer
~/Nernstsche Nernst [diffusion] layer
Diffusionsschnitzel *npl (sugar)* wet pulp
Diffusionsspannung *f* diffusion (liquid-junction) potential
Diffusionssteuerung *f (phys ch)* diffusion control
Diffusionsstrom *m (phys ch)* 1. diffusion[-controlled] current; 2. diffusive flux
~/maximaler maximum (limiting) diffusion current
Diffusionsstromkonstante *f* diffusion-current constant
Diffusionsüberspannung *f* diffusion overpotential
diffusionsverchromen to chromize
Diffusionsverchromen *n* chromizing, chromium impregnation
Diffusionsverfahren *n* gaseous diffusion process *(for separating isotopes)*
Diffusionsverlust *m (sugar)* diffusion loss
Diffusionsvermischen *n* diffusive mixing
Diffusionsvermögen *n* diffusibility
Diffusionswiderstand *m* diffusion[al] resistance, resistance to diffusion
Diffusionszahl *f* diffusion coefficient
diffusorisch diffusional
Difluoraminierung *f* difluoroamination
Difluordichlormethan *n s.* Dichlordifluormethan
Difluorid *n* difluoride
Difluorierung *f* difluorination
Difluormethylierung *f* difluoromethylation
Diformiat *n* diformate
difunktionell difunctional, D, bifunctional
Digalliumtrioxid *n* digallium trioxide, gallium(III) oxide
m-**Digallussäure** *f* digallic acid, *m*-digallic acid, gallic acid 3-monogallate, 5,6-dihydroxy-3-carboxyphenyl ester of gallic acid
digerieren to digest *(by heat or solvents)*
Digerieren *n* digestion *(by heat or solvents)*
Digerierkolben *m* digestion flask, digester
Digerman *n* digermane, germanium hexahydride
Digermanat *n* $M^I_2Ge_2O_5$ digermanate
Digestion *f (bioch, pharm)* digestion
Digestionskolben *m s.* Digerierkolben
Digestivum *n (pharm)* digestive, digester
Digestor *m s.* Digerierkolben
Digestorium *n (lab)* [fume] hood, fume chamber (cupboard, closet)
Digitoninfällung *f* digitonin precipitation *(for detecting vegetable fat)*
Diglycerid *n* diglyceride
Diglykolsäure *f* diglycolic (diglycollic) acid, *2,2'-oxydiethanoic acid
Dihalogenalkan *n* alkyl dihalide
Dihalogenid *n* dihalogenide, dihalide
Dihalogenierung *f* dihalogenation
Diharnstoff *m s. p*-Urazin
Diheptadecylketon *n* diheptadecyl ketone, stearone, pentatriacontan-18-one
Dihexyl *n s.* Dodecan
Dihexylphthalat *n* dihexyl phthalate, DHP
Dihydrat *n* dihydrate
Dihydrobenzol *n s.* Cyclohexadien
Dihydrochinin *n* dihydroquinine, hydroquinine, quinethyline
Dihydrogenarsenat(V) *n* $M^IH_2AsO_4$ dihydrogenarsenate
Dihydrogendodecawolframat(VI) *n* $M^I_6[H_2W_{12}O_{40}]$ *dihydrogendodecawolframate(VI), dihydrogendodecatungstate(VI)
Dihydrogendodecawolframsäure *f* *dihydrogendodecawolframic acid, dihydrogendodecatungstic acid
Dihydrogenmonophosphat *n s.* Dihydrogenphosphat
Dihydrogenphosphat *n* $M^IH_2PO_4$ dihydrogen phosphate

Dihydrogensalz *n* dihydrogen salt *(of a tribasic acid)*
Dihydroliponsäure *f (bioch)* dihydrolipoic acid
Dihydroorotsäure *f (bioch)* dihydroorotic acid
Dihydrostufe *f* dihydric stage
2,5-Dihydroxybenzoesäure *f* 2,5-dihydroxybenzoic acid, gentisic acid
Dihydroxybernsteinsäure *f* dihydroxysuccinic acid, tartaric acid, *2,3-dihydroxybutanedioic acid
1,5-Dihydroxynaphthalen-3,7-disulfonsäure *f* 1,5-dihydroxynaphthalene-3,7-disulphonic acid, red acid
Dihydroxyphenylalanin *n* dihydroxyphenylalanine, dopa, DOPA
2,3-Dihydroxypropanal *n* *2,3-dihydroxypropanal, glyceraldehyde
2,3-Dihydroxypropansäure *f* *2,3-dihydroxypropanoic acid, glyceric acid
Dihydroxyverbindung *f* dihydroxy compound
Dihydroxyxylen *n*, **Dihydroxyxylol** *n* dihydroxyxylene, xylorcinol
3,4-Dihydroxyzimtsäure *f* 3,4-dihydroxycinnamic acid, caffeic acid
Diimid *n* diimide, diazene
Diioddisulfid *n* diiodine disulphide
Diiodid *n* diiodide
Diiodmethan *n* diiodomethane
Diiodtetroxid *n* diiodine tetraoxide
3,5-Diiodtyrosin *n* 3,5-diiodotyrosine, iodogorgoic acid
Diisocyanat *n* diisocyanate *(a compound having two –N=C=O groups)*
Diisodecylphthalat *n (plast)* diisodecyl phthalate, DIDP
Diisononylphthalat *n (plast)* diisononyl phthalate, DINP
Diisooctylphthalat *n (plast)* diisooctyl phthalate, DIOP
Diisopropylether *m* diisopropyl ether
Diisopropylmethan *n* diisopropylmethane, *2,4-dimethylpentane
Dikabutter *f*, **Dikafett** *n* Di[k]ka butter *(from Irvingia gabonensis Baill.)*
Dikaliumdisulfat *n* dipotassium disulphate, potassium disulphate
Dikaliumhydrogenphosphat *n* dipotassium hydrogenphosphate
Diketoester *m* diketo ester
Diketon *n* diketone
dilatant *(coll)* dilatant
Dilatanz *f (coll)* dilatancy, shear thickening, inverse plasticity
Dilatation *f* dilatation
Dilatometer *n* dilatometer
Dilatometertest *m* dilatometer test
~ **nach Audibert-Arnu** Audibert-Arnu dilatometer test
Dilatometrie *f* dilatometry
dilatometrisch dilatometric
Dilitursäure *f* dilituric acid, nitromalonylurea, 5-nitrobarbituric acid
Dillöl *n* dill (anethum) oil *(from Anethum graveolens L.)*
Dimangansilicid *n* dimanganese silicide, manganese(II) silicide
Dimangantrioxid *n* dimanganese trioxide, manganese(III) oxide
Dimedon *n (anal)* dimedon, 5,5-dimethylcyclohexane-1,3-dione
dimensionieren to size
Dimensionierung *f* sizing
Dimensionsanalyse *f (tech)* dimensional analysis
dimensionsstabil dimensionally stable
Dimensionsstabilisierung *f* dimensional stabilization
Dimensionsstabilität *f* dimensional stability
Dimensionstheorie *f (tech)* dimensional analysis
dimer dimeric
Dimer[e] *n* dimer
dimerisieren to dimerize, *(process also)* to undergo dimerization
Dimerisierung *f* dimerization
~/oxidative oxidative dimerization, dehydrodimerization
~/reduktive (reduzierende) reductive dimerization, hydrodimerization
Di-π-methan-Umlagerung *f* di-π-methane rearrangement *(photochemistry)*
1,2-Dimethoxybenzen *n*, **1,2-Dimethoxybenzol** n 1,2-dimethoxybenzene
Dimethoxymethan *n* *dimethoxymethane, methylal, formaldehyde dimethyl acetal
Dimethoxymethylgruppe *f* $-CH(OCH_3)_2$ dimethoxymethyl group
Dimethylacetylen *n s.* But-2-in
Dimethylamin *n* dimethylamine
Dimethylanilin *n* dimethylaniline, aminoxylene, aminodimethylbenzene
Dimethylarsinchlorid *n s.* Dimethylchlorarsin
Dimethylarsinsäure *f* dimethylarsinic acid, cacodylic acid
bis-**Dimethylarsyl** *n s.* Kakodyl
asym-**Dimethyläthylen** *n s.* 2-Methylpropen
sym-**Dimethyläthylen** *n s.* But-2-en
Dimethyläthylcarbinol *n s.* 2-Methylbutan-2-ol
Dimethylbenzen *n* dimethylbenzene, xylene
2,5-Dimethylbenzoesäure *f* 2,5-dimethylbenzoic acid, *p*-xylylic acid
Dimethylbenzol *n s.* Dimethylbenzen
α,α-**Dimethylbenzylalkohol** *m* 2-phenyl-2-propanol, dimethylphenyl carbinol, DMPC
Dimethylcarbinol *n s.* Propan-2-ol
Dimethylchinon *n* dimethylbenzoquinone, xyloquinone
Dimethylchlorarsin *n* chlorodimethylarsine, cacodyl chloride
5,5-Dimethylcyclohexan-1,3-dion *n s.* Dimedon
Dimethyldichlorsilan *n* dimethyldichlorosilane

Dimethylenimin *n* dimethyleneimine, aziridine
Dimethylether *m* dimethyl ether
Dimethylformal *n* formaldehyde dimethyl acetal, *dimethoxymethane, methylal
Dimethylformamid *n* dimethyl formamide, DMF
Dimethylglyoxal *n* dimethylglyoxal, biacetyl, *butane-2,3-dione
Dimethylketol *n* dimethylketol, acetoin, *3-hydroxybutan-2-one
Dimethylketon *n* dimethyl ketone, acetone, *propanone
***N,N*-Dimethylmethansulfon[säure]amid** *n N,N*-dimethylmethane sulfonamide
Dimethylolharnstoff *m* dimethylolurea, 1,3-bis-hydroxymethylurea
Dimethylphenol *n* dimethylphenol, xylenol
Dimethylphenylcarbinol *n* 2-phenyl-2-propanol, dimethylphenyl carbinol, DMPC
Dimethylphthalat *n* dimethyl phthalate, DMP
2,2-Dimethylpropansäure *f*, **2,2-Dimethylpropionsäure** *f* 2,2-dimethylpropionic acid, *2,2-dimethylpropanoic acid, pivalic acid
Dimethylsulfat *n* dimethyl sulphate
Dimethylsulfoxid *n* dimethyl sulphoxide, DMSO
Dimethylterephthalat *n* dimethyl terephthalate, DMT
Dimethylzink *n* dimethyl zinc
dimolekular bimolecular
Dimolybdäntrioxid *n* dimolybdenum trioxide, molybdenum(III) oxide
dimorph dimorphic, dimorphous
Dimroth-Kühler *m (lab)* Dimroth condenser
Dinatriumhydrogenarsenat(III) *n* sodium hydrogenarsenite
Dinatriumhydrogenarsenat(V) *n* sodium hydrogenarsenate
Dinatriumhydrogenphosphat *n* disodium hydrogenphosphate
Dinatriummethylarsonat *n* disodium methyl arsonate, DMA
Dinatriumpentacyanonitrosylferrat(II) *n* disodium pentacyanonitrosylferrate(II), sodium nitroprusside, sodium nitroprussiate
Dinatriumsalz *n* disodium salt
Dinickeltrioxid *n* dinickel trioxide, nickel(III) oxide
Dinitranilin *n s.* Dinitroanilin
Dinitrid *n* dinitride
dinitrieren to dinitrate
Dinitrierung *f* dinitration
Dinitril *n* dinitrile
Dinitrilfaser *f* dinitrile fibre
Dinitrilfaserstoff *m* dinitrile fibre
Dinitroaminophenol *n s.* Aminodinitrophenol
Dinitroanilin *n* dinitroaniline
Dinitroanthrachinon *n* dinitroanthraquinone
Dinitrobenzoesäure *f* dinitrobenzoic acid
Dinitrobiphenyl *n* dinitrobiphenyl
Dinitrobiphenyldicarbonsäure *f s.* Dinitrodiphensäure
Dinitrochlorbenzen *n*, **Dinitrochlorbenzol** *n s.* Chlordinitrobenzen
Dinitrocresol *n* dinitrocresol
4,6-Dinitro-*o*-cresol *n* 4,6-dinitro-*o*-cresol, DNOC, DNC *(a pesticide)*
2,4-Dinitro-6-cyclohexylphenol *n* 2,4-dinitro-6-cyclohexylphenol, DNOCHP
Dinitrodiphensäure *f* dinitrodiphenic acid, dinitrobiphenyl-dicarboxylic acid
Dinitrodiphenyl *n s.* Dinitrobiphenyl
2,4-Dinitrofluorbenzen *n*, **2,4-Dinitrofluorbenzol** n *s.* Fluor-2,4-dinitrobenzen
Dinitrokörper *m* dinitrobody
Dinitromischsäure *f* dinitro mixed acid
Dinitrophenol *n* dinitrophenol
Dinitrophenolat *n* dinitrophenate
Dinitrophenylderivat *n* dinitrophenyl derivative, DNP derivative
Dinitroresorcinol *n* dinitroresorcinol
Dinitrotoluen *n*, **Dinitrotoluol** *n* dinitrotoluene
Dinitrotoluylsäure *f* dinitrotoluic acid
Dinitroverbindung *f* dinitro compound
Dinoseb *n* Dinoseb, DNBP, 2-*sec*-butyl-4,6-dinitrophenol *(a pesticide)*
Dioctylketon *n* dioctyl ketone, *heptadecan-9-one, nonylone
Dioctylphthalat *n (plast)* dioctyl phthalate, DOP, *di(2-ethylhexyl) phthalate
Diodenlaser *m* diode (semiconductor) laser
Diol *n* diol, dialcohol, dihydroxylic (dihydric) alcohol
~/geminales geminal diol
~/vicinales vicinal diol
1,2-Diol *n* vicinal diol
Diolefin *n* diolefin *(a hydrocarbon with two double bonds)*
diolefinisch diolefinic
Diopsid *m (min)* diopside *(calcium magnesium silicate)*
Dioptas *m (min)* dioptase, emerald copper (malachite) *(a copper silicate)*
Diorsellinsäure *f s.* Lecanorsäure
Diosphenol *n* diosphenol, buchucamphor, buccocamphor, *2-hydroxy-6-isopropyl-1-methyl-cyclohex-2-en-1-one
Dioxan *n* dioxan
Dioxid *n* dioxide
Dioxin *n* dibenzo-1,4-dioxin, dibenzo-*p*-dioxin, dioxin, *(specif)* 2,3,7,8-tetrachlorodibenzo-1,4-dioxin, 2,3,7,8-tetrachlorodibenzo-*p*-dioxin, 2,3,7,8-TCDD, TCDD, dioxin
Dioxindol *n* dioxindole, 2,3-dihydro-3-hydroxy-2-oxoindole
Dioxoborat *n* M^IBO_2 dioxoborate, metaborate
Dioxoborsäure *f* dioxoboric acid, metaboric acid
Dioxodisiloxan *n* dioxodisiloxane
Dioxolan *n* dioxolane
1,3-Dioxophthalan *n s.* Phthalsäureanhydrid
Dipeptid *n* dipeptide
Diperiodat *n* $M^I_4I_2O_9$ dimesoperiodate, enneaoxodiiodate(VII)
Diphensäure *f* diphenic acid, *biphenyl-2,2-dicarboxylic acid

Diphenyl *n s.* 1. Biphenyl; 2. Diphyl
Diphenylacetylen *n s.* Diphenylethin
Diphenylamin *n* diphenylamine, DPA, phenylaniline
Diphenylaminblau *n* diphenylamine blue, *tris*-(4-anilinophenyl)methanol
Diphenylaminorange *n s.* Orange IV
Diphenylbenzen *n*, **Diphenylbenzol** *n* diphenylbenzene, *terphenyl
Diphenyldicarbonsäure-(2,2') *f s.* Diphensäure
Diphenyldiimid *n* diphenyldiimide, diphenyldiazene, *azobenzene
Diphenyldiketon *n* *diphenyl diketone, diphenylglyoxal, benzil, bibenzoyl
Diphenyldisulfid *n* diphenyl disulphide
Diphenylenimid *n s.* Diphenylenimin
Diphenylenimin *n* diphenyleneimine, carbazole, dibenzopyrrole
Diphenylessigsäure *f* diphenylacetic acid
1,2-Diphenylethan *n* 1,2-diphenylethane, bibenzyl
1,2-Diphenylethanol *n* 1,2-diphenylethanol
Diphenylethen *n* diphenylethylene, stilbene
Diphenylether *m* diphenyl ether, phenoxybenzene
Diphenylethin *n* diphenylethyne, tolane
Diphenylfarbstoff *m* diphenyl dye
Diphenylglykolsäure *f* diphenylglycollic acid, benzilic acid
Diphenylglyoxal *n s.* Diphenyldiketon
Diphenylimid *n s.* Diphenylenimin
Diphenylin *n* diphenyline, 2,4'-diaminobiphenyl
Diphenylketon *n* *diphenyl ketone, benzophenone, benzoyl benzene
Diphenylmethanfarbstoff *m* diphenylmethane dye
Diphenyloxid *n s.* Diphenylether
Diphenylphenylen *n s.* Diphenylbenzen
***N,N'*-Diphenyl-*p*-phenylendiamin** *n N,N'*-diphenyl-*p*-phenylenediamine, DPPD
1,3-Diphenylpropenon *n* 1,3-diphenylpropenone, chalcone, benzylideneacetophenone
Diphenylthiocarbazon *n* diphenylthiocarbazone, dithizone
1,3-Diphenyltriazen *n* diazoaminobenzene, 1,3-diphenyltriazene
Diphosgen *n* diphosgene, trichloromethyl chloroformate
Diphosphan *n* diphosphane
Diphosphat *n* $M^{I}_{4}P_2O_7$ diphosphate, pyrophosphate
Diphosphen *n* phosphene
Diphosphin *n* phosphyne
Diphosphit *n* $M^{I}_{2}P_2H_2O_5$ diphosphonate, *(deprecated:)* diphosphite
Diphosphoglycerinsäure *f* diphosphoglyceric acid
Diphosphopyridinnucleotid *n s.* Nicotinsäureamid-adenin-dinucleotid
Diphosphorsäure *f* diphosphoric acid, pyrophosphoric acid
Diphosphortetraiodid *n* diphosphorus tetraiodide
Diphosphortriselenid *n* diphosphorus triselenide
Diphosphortrisulfid *n* diphosphorus trisulphide, phosphorus(III) sulphide, phosphorous sulphide
Diphthalyl *n* *biphthalyl, *(deprecated:)* diphthalyl
Diphthalylsäure *f* diphthalylic acid, benzil-2,2'-dicarboxylic acid
Diphyl *n a mixture of biphenyl and diphenyl ether*
Dipicolinsäure *f* dipicolinic acid, pyridine-2,6-dicarboxylic acid
Dipikrylamin *n* dipicrylamine, di-2,4,6-trinitrophenylamine, hexite
Dipol *m* dipole
1,3-Dipol *m* 1,3-dipolar compound
Dipolachse *f* dipole axis
dipolar dipolar
1,3-dipolar 1,3-dipolar
Dipolassoziation *f* dipole association
Dipol-Dipol-Anziehung *f* dipole-dipole attraction
Dipol-Dipol-Kraft *f* [permanent] dipole-dipole force
Dipol-Dipol-Wechselwirkung *f* dipolar (dipole-dipole) interaction, dipolar (spin-spin) coupling
dipolfrei non-dipolar
Dipolglied *n* dipole term
Dipolkopplung *f s.* Dipol-Dipol-Wechselwirkung
Dipolkraft *f* dipole force
Dipol-Ladungs-Wechselwirkung *f* charge-dipole interaction
dipollos non-dipolar
Dipolmessung *f* dipole measurement
Dipolmolekül *n* dipolar (dipole) molecule
Dipolmoment *n* dipole moment
~/elektrisches electric [dipole] moment
~/induziertes induced dipole moment
~/magnetisches magnetic [dipole] moment
Dipolmomentoperator *m* dipole-moment operator
Dipolstrahlung *f* dipole radiation
Dipolübergangsmoment *n***[/elektrisches]** *(spectr)* transition [dipole] moment
diprimär *(org ch)* diprimary
Dipropylacetylen *n* *oct-4-yne, *(deprecated:)* dipropylacetylene
Dipropylketon *n* *heptan-4-one, di-*n*-propyl ketone
Dip-Verfahren *n (rubber)* dip [reclaiming] process
Dipyr *m (min)* dipyre *(a variety of scapolite)*
Dipyrrolylmethen *n*, **Dipyrromethen** *n* dipyrromethene, pyrromethene, dipyrrin
Diradikal *n* *biradical, diradical
Direktabschreckung *f* direct quenching *(of metals)*
Direktapplikation *f***/dosierte** *(tox)* topical application *(for testing the efficiency of an insecticide)*
Direktdampf *m* live (open) steam, prime (direct) steam
Direktdruck *m* direct printing
Direktexpansionskühler *m* direct-expansion chiller
Direktfarbstoff *m* direct (substantive) dye (dyestuff), *(Am also)* direct color
Direktmethode *f (tox)* direct-feeding test *(for detecting pesticide residues by contacting animals with the substance to be checked)*
Direkt-Positiv-Prozeß *m (phot)* reversal process

Direktpotentiometrie *f* direct potentiometry
Direktreduktion *f (met)* direct [ore] reduction
Direktreduktionsverfahren *n (met)* direct reduction process *(for producing iron)*
Direktspinnverfahren *n (text)* direct spinning system
Direktsynthese *f* direct synthesis *(as for obtaining chlorosilanes)*
Direktverfahren *n (dye)* flushing process
Direkt-Zerstäuber-Brenner-Kombination *f (spectr)* direct-injection burner
direktziehend *(dye)* direct, substantive
Dirheniumheptoxid *n* dirhenium heptaoxide, rhenium(VII) oxide
Dirheniumtrioxid *n* dirhenium trioxide, rhenium(III) oxide
Dirhodan *n* $(SCN)_2$ thiocyanogen
Dirhodiumtrioxid *n* dirhodium trioxide, rhodium(III) oxide
dirigieren to direct *(a substituent into a position)*
dirigierend/nach der *meta*-**Stellung** meta-directing
~/nach der *ortho*-**Stellung** ortho-directing
~/nach der *ortho*- **und** *para*-**Stellung** ortho-para-directing
Disaccharid *n* disaccharide
Disauerstoff *m* dioxygen
Disazofarbstoff *m* bisazo (disazo) dye
Dischwefeldichlorid *n* disulphur dichloride
Dischwefelheptoxid *n* disulphur heptaoxide
Dischwefelpentoxiddichlorid *n s.* Disulfurylchlorid
Dischwefelsäure *f* disulphuric acid
Dischwefeltrioxid *n* disulphur trioxide, sulphur(III) oxide
Dischwefelwasserstoff *m* hydrogen disulphide, disulphane
Disco-Schwelverfahren *n (coal)* Disco process
disekundär disecondary
Diselendichlorid *n* diselenium dichloride
Disilan *n* disilane
Disilberfluorid *n* disilver fluoride, silver subfluoride
Disilberhydrogenphosphat *n* disilver hydrogenphosphate
Disilberpentacyanonitrosylferrat(II) *n* disilver pentacyanonitrosylferrate(II), silver nitroprusside, silver nitroprussiate
Disilicat *n* disilicate
Disilicid *n* disilicide
Disiliciumhexachlorid *n* *hexachlorodisilane, disilicon hexachloride
Disilikan *n s.* Disilan
Disilikoäthan *n s.* Disilan
Disiloxan *n* disiloxane
Disinterkalation *f* deintercalation, disintercalation
Disk-Elektrophorese *f (anal)* disc electrophoresis *(having a discontinuous gel system)*
diskelektrophoretisch *(anal)* by disc electrophoresis
diskontinuierlich discontinuous, batch[wise], intermittent *(operation)*
diskotisch diskotic, disk-like *(liquid crystals)*
Diskriminierung *f (anal)* discrimination
Dislokation *f (cryst)* dislocation
Dismembrator *m* pin[ned]-disk disintegrator, pin mill
dismulgieren to demulsify, to de-emulsify, to break, to crack *(an emulsion)*
Dismulgieren *n* demulsification, de-emulsification, emulsion breakdown (breaking), breaking (cracking) of emulsions
Dismulgierzentrifuge *f* liquid/liquid-phase separator
Dismutation *f* dismutation
dismutativ dismutative
dismutieren to dismutate
Dismutierung *f s.* Dismutation
Dispensation *f (pharm)* dispensation
Dispensatorium *n (pharm)* dispensatory
dispensieren *(pharm)* to dispense
Dispergens *n s.* Dispersionsmittel 1.
dispergierbar dispersible
Dispergierbarkeit *f* dispersibility
dispergieren to disperse; to peptize, to deflocculate *(colloids)*
dispergierend dispersive
Dispergier[hilfs]mittel *n s.* Dispersionsmittel 1.
Dispergierung *f* dispersion, dispersal; peptization, deflocculation *(of colloids)*
~/elektrische electrical dispersion, electrodispersion *(of metals)*
Dispergierungs... *s.* Dispergier...
Dispergierwirkung *f* dispersing action
Dispergiervermögen *n* dispersing power (property)
dispers dispersed, *(esp Am also)* disperse
Dispersant *m s.* Dispersionsmittel 1.
Dispersantadditiv *n s.* Dispersionszusatz
Dispersantwirkung *f* dispersing effect
Dispersion *f* 1. dispersion, dispersal *(of particles)*; 2. dispersion, disperse system; 3. dispersion *(of waves)*, *(quantitatively also)* dispersivity, differential refractivity
~/axiale axial dispersion *(in a tubular reactor)*
~/grobe coarse dispersion
~/kolloide colloidal dispersion
~/spezifische specific dispersivity *(of waves)*
Dispersionsanalyse *f* dispersion analysis
Dispersionsazofarbstoff *m* disperse azo dye
Dispersionseffekt *m* dispersion effect
~ der Leitfähigkeit *(el ch)* dispersion of conductance, Debye-Falkenhagen effect
Dispersionsfarbstoff *m* disperse[d] dye, *(Am also)* dispersed color
Dispersionsformel *f* dispersion formula
Dispersionsfunktion *f (chromat)* dispersion function
Dispersionsgrad *m* degree of dispersion; *(coll)* dispersity
Dispersionskoeffizient *m* eddy diffusivity
Dispersionskolloid *n* dispersion colloid, dispersoid
Dispersionskonstante *f* dispersive constant
Dispersionskraft *f* 1. dispersion force, London (transient polarization) force *(acting between molecules)*; 2. *s.* Dispersionsvermögen

Dispersionskurve *f* dispersion curve
Dispersionsmedium *n s.* Dispersionsphase
Dispersionsmittel *n* 1. dispersing (deflocculating) agent, dispersant, deflocculant, deflocculator; 2. *s.* Dispersionsphase
Dispersionsmodell *n* axial dispersion model *(of mixing in a reactor)*
Dispersionsmühle *f* dispersing mill
Dispersionsphase *f* continuous (external) phase, disperse (dispersive, dispersion) medium *(of a disperse system)*
Dispersionsspektrum *n* dispersive spectrum
Dispersionsverfahren *n* dispersion method *(for obtaining disperse systems)*
Dispersionsvermögen *n* dispersive (dispersing) power (property)
Dispersionszusatz *m* dispersing (dispersant) additive
Dispersität *f* dispersity
Dispersitätsgrad *m s.* Dispersionsgrad
dispersiv dispersive
Dispersoid *n* dispersoid
Dispersoidanalyse *f* dispersoid analysis
Dispersoidologie *f* dispersoidology, *(seldom used for)* colloid chemistry
Dispersum *n* internal (discontinuous) phase, disperse[d] phase *(of a disperse system)*
Dispiro-Verbindung *f* dispiro compound (hydrocarbon)
disproportionieren to disproportionate
Disproportionierung *f* disproportionation, self-oxidation-reduction, auto-oxidation-reduction
~ **von Radikalen** radical disproportionation
Disproportionierungsabbruch *m* termination by disproportionation *(of a chain reaction)*
Disproportionierungsreaktion *f* disproportionation reaction
disrotatorisch *(org ch)* disrotatory
Dissimilation *f (bioch)* dissimilation, catabolism
dissimilatorisch *(bioch)* dissimilative, catabolic
Dissipation *f* [energy] dissipation
dissipativ dissipative
dissoziabel dissociable, *(esp if into ions)* ionizable
Dissoziation *f* dissociation, splitting-up, *(esp if into ions)* ionization
~/durch Oberflächen induzierte surface-induced dissociation, SID
~/elektrolytische electrolytic ionization (dissociation)
~/stoßinduzierte collision-induced dissociation, CID
~/thermische thermal dissociation
Dissoziationsdruck *m* dissociation pressure
Dissoziationsenergie *f* [bond-]dissociation energy
Dissoziationsenthalphie *f* enthalpy of dissociation
Dissoziationsgeschwindigkeit *f* velocity of dissociation
Dissoziationsgleichgewicht *n* dissociation equilibrium
Dissoziationsgrad *m* degree of dissociation
~/thermischer degree of thermal dissociation
Dissoziationsgrenze *f* dissociation limit
Dissoziationskonstante *f* dissociation constant, *(with acids and bases also)* affinity constant; instability constant *(of complex ions)*
Dissoziationskontinuum *n* dissociation continuum
Dissoziationsreaktion *f* dissociation reaction
Dissoziationsstufe *f* dissociation step
Dissoziationswärme *f* heat of dissociation
dissoziieren to dissociate, to split up, *(esp if into ions)* to ionize
Distanzstück *n* spacer
Distex-Verfahren *n* Distex process, extractive distillation
Disthen *m (min)* disthene, cyanite, kyanite *(aluminium oxide orthosilicate)*
Distickstoffmonoxid *n* dinitrogen monooxide, nitrogen(I) oxide
Distickstoffpentasulfid *n* dinitrogen pentasulphide, nitrogen(V) sulphide
Distickstoffpentoxid *n* dinitrogen pentaoxide, nitrogen(V) oxide
Distickstofftetroxid *n* dinitrogen tetraoxide
Distickstofftrioxid *n* dinitrogen trioxide, nitrogen(III) oxide
Distributionsverhältnis *n* distribution ratio
disubstituiert disubstituted, bis-substituted
Disubstitution *f* disubstitution
Disubstitutionsprodukt *n* disubstitution product
Disulfan *n* disulphane, hydrogen disulphide
Disulfat *n* $M^I_2S_2O_7$ disulphate
Disulfid *n* disulphide
Disulfidbindung *f s.* Disulfidbrücke
Disulfidbrücke *f* disulphide bridge (bond, cross-link), –S–S-linkage, *(bioch also)* interchain disulphide bond, cystine link
Disulfidspange *f (bioch)* intrachain disulphide bond, intrastrand linkage
Disulfiram *n* disulphiram, tetraethylthiuram disulphide
Disulfit *n* $M^I_2S_2O_5$ disulphite
Disulfitomercurat(II) *n* $M^I_2[Hg(SO_3)_2]$ disulphitomercurate(II), sulphitomercurate(II)
Disulfonat *n* disulphonate
disulfonieren to disulphonate
Disulfonierung *f* disulphonation
Disulfonsäure *f*, **Disulfosäure** *f* disulphonic acid
Disulfurylchlorid *n* disulphuryl chloride
Ditantalat *n* $M^I_4Ta_2O_7$ ditantalate
Ditellurat *n* $M^I_2Te_2O_7$ ditellurate
Diterpen *n* diterpene
Diterpenalkaloid *n* diterpenoid alkaloid
Diterpenoid *n* diterpenoid
ditertiär ditertiary
Dithalliummonoxid *n* dithallium monooxide, thallium(I) oxide
Dithiazin *n* dithiazine, 3,3'-diethylthiadicarbocyanine
Dithiazolanthrachinonfarbstoff *m* dithiazolanthraquinone dye

Dithioacetal *n* dithioacetal, mercaptal
Dithioarsenat(II) *n* dithioarsenite
3,3'-Dithiobis(2-aminopropionsäure) *f* *3,3'-dithio*bis*(2-aminopropanoic acid), cystine, dicysteine
Dithiocarbamat *n* NH_2CSSM^I dithiocarbamate
Dithiocarbamatbeschleuniger *m (rubber)* dithiocarbamate accelerator
Dithiocarbamidsäure *f* dithiocarbamic acid
Dithiocarbaminsäure *f s.* Dithiocarbamidsäure
Dithiocarboxylierung *f* dithiocarboxylation
Dithioketal *n* dithioketal, mercaptole
Dithiokohlensäure *f* dithiocarbonic acid
Dithiokohlensäure-*O*-ethylester *m* dithiocarbonic *O*-ethyl ester, xanthogenic acid, ethylxanthogenic acid
Dithiolkohlensäure *f* dithiocarbonic acid
Dithionat *n* dithionate
Dithionit *n* $M^I_2S_2O_4$ dithionite; *(dye)* $Na_2S_2O_4$ [sodium] dithionite, [sodium] hydrosulphite
Dithionitbleiche *f (pap)* sodium hydrosulphite bleaching
Dithionit-Natronlauge *f (dye)* caustic hydrosulphite solution
Dithionsäure *f* dithionic acid
Dithiooxalsäure *f* dithio-oxalic acid
Dithiooxalsäurediamid *n s.* Dithiooxamid
Dithiooxamid *n* dithiooxamide, rubeanic acid
Dithiophosphat *n* $M^I_3PS_2O_2$ dithiophosphate
Dithiophosphorsäure *f* dithiophosphoric acid
Dithiosalicylsäure *f* dithiosalicylic acid, 2-hydroxybenzenethionothiolic acid
Dithiosäure *f* $C_nH_{2n+1}CSSH$ dithio acid
Dithioverbindung *f* dithio compound
Dithizon *n* dithizone, diphenylthiocarbazone
Dititantrioxid *n* dititanium trioxide, titanium(III) oxide
Dititantrisulfid *n* dititanium trisulphide, titanium(III) sulphide
ditrigonal-skalenoedrisch *(cryst)* ditrigonal-scalenohedral
Diuranat *n* $M^I_2U_2O_7$ diuranate
Diurantrisulfid *n* diuranium trisulphide, uranium(III) sulphide
Diuretikum *n (pharm)* diuretic
diuretisch diuretic
Divanadat *n* $M^I_4V_2O_7$ divanadate
Divanadiumpentoxid *n* divanadium pentaoxide, vanadium(V) oxide
Divanadiumtrioxid *n* divanadium trioxide, vanadium(III) oxide
Divanadiumtrisulfid *n* divanadium trisulphide, vanadium(III) sulphide
divariant bivariant, divariant
Divaricatsäure *f* divaricatic acid *(a depside of divaric acid)*
Divarsäure *f* divaric acid, *2,4-dihydroxy-6-propylbenzoic acid
Dividierer *m* ratio-recording spectrometer
Dividivi *pl (tann)* divi-divi, libi-dibi *(husks of Caesalpinia coriaria (Jacq.) Willd.)*
Divinyl *n s.* Buta-1,3-dien
Divinylensulfid *n s.* Thiophen
Divinylether *m* divinyl ether
Diwasserstoff *m* H_2 dihydrogen
Diwolframat *n* diwolframate, ditungstate
Dixon-Ring *m* Dixon packing *(made from wire gauze)*
Djelutung *m*, **Djelutungharz** *n* jelutong *(a copal from Dyera specc. and Parthenium argentatum A. Gray)*
Djenkolsäure *f* djenkolic acid
DK *s.* 1. Dielektrizitätskonstante; 2. Dieselkraftstoff
DK-Meter *n s.* Dekameter
D-Konfiguration *f* D configuration
DMF *s.* Dimethylformamid
DMSO *s.* Dimethylsulfoxid
DNA *f* DNA, deoxyribonucleic acid
~/denaturierte denatured DNA
~/doppelsträngige double-strand[ed] DNA
~/einzelsträngige single-strand[ed] DNA
~/komplementäre complementary DNA, cDNA
~/mitochondriale mitochondrial DNA
~/neukombinierte (rekombinierte) recombinant DNA, rDNA
DNA-Kopie *f* copy DNA, cDNA
DNA-Ligase *f* DNA ligase
DNA-Neukombination *f s.* DNA-Rekombination
DNA-Polymerase *f* DNA polymerase
~/RNA-abhängige RNA-directed DNA polymerase, reverse transcriptase
DNA-Rekombination *f* DNA recombination
DNA-Rekombinationstechnik *f (biot)* recombinant DNA technology; recombinant DNA technique
DNA-Replikation *f* DNA replication
DNase *s.* Desoxyribonuclease
DNA-Sequenz *f* DNA sequence
DNA-Strang *m* DNA strand
DNBP *s.* Dinoseb
DNC, DNOC *s.* 4,6-Dinitro-*o*-cresol
DNOCHP *s.* 2,4-Dinitro-6-cyclohexylphenol
DNOK *s.* 4,6-Dinitro-*o*-cresol
DNP *s.* Dinitrophenol
DNP-Derivat *n s.* Dinitrophenylderivat
DNS *(Desoxyribonucleinsäure) s.* DNA
Döbereiner-Triaden *fpl* triads of Döbereiner
Dobson-Einheit *f* Dobson unit *(ozone content of air)*
Docht *m* wick
~ für Spirituslampen burner wick
Dochtlampe *f* wick[-fed] lamp
Docke *f* skein *(looped yarn esp of definite weight and consisting of several hanks)*
Docosahexaensäure *f* docosahexaenoic acid
Docosan *n* docosane
Docosan-1-ol *n* docosan-1-ol
Docosansäure *f* docosanoic acid
Docosensäure *f* docosenoic acid

Docos-11-ensäure *f* docos-11-enoic acid, cetoleic acid
Docos-13-insäure *f* docos-13-ynoic acid
prim-n-**Docosylalkohol** *m s.* Docosan-1-ol
Dodecahydrat *n* dodecahydrate
Dodecamolybdatophosphat *n* $M^I_3[PMo_{12}O_{40}]$ dodecamolybdophosphate
Dodecan *n* dodecane
Dodecanal *n* *dodecanal, dodecylaldehyde
Dodecan-1-carbonsäure *f* *tridecanoic acid, dodecane-1-carboxylic acid
Dodecandisäure *f* dodecanedioic acid
Dodecan-1-ol *n* *dodecan-1-ol, alcohol C-12
Dodecansäure *f* *dodecanoic acid, lauric acid
Dodecansäureethylester *m* dodecanoic acid ethyl ester, ethyl laurate
Dodecan-1-thiol *n* dodecanethiol
Dodecawolframatophosphat *n* $M^I_3(PW_{12}O_{40}]$ dodecawolframophosphate, dodecatungstophosphate
Dodec-1-en *n* dodec-1-ene
Dodecensäure *f* dodecenoic acid
Dodec-2-endisäure *f* dodec-2-enedioic acid, traumatic acid
Dodec-2-in *n* dodec-2-yne
Dodecylaldehyd *m s.* Dodecanal
n-**Dodecylalkohol** *m s.* Dodecan-1-ol
Dodecylamin *n* dodecylamine
α-**Dodecylen** *n s.* Dodec-1-en
Dodecylgruppe *f* dodecyl group
n-**Dodecylmercaptan** *n s.* Dodecan-1-thiol
Dodeka... *s. a.* Dodeca...
Dodekaeder *n (cryst)* dodecahedron
Dodez... *s.* Dodec...
Dodge-Backenbrecher *m* Dodge [jaw] crusher
Doebner-Miller-Reaktion *f* Doebner Miller reaction (synthesis) *(for obtaining quinoline and its derivatives)*
Doebner-Reaktion *f*, **Doebner-Synthese** *f* Doebner reaction (synthesis) *(for obtaining substituted cinchoninic acids)*
Dokos... *s.* Docos...
Doktorbehandlung *f (petrol)* doctor treatment (sweetening)
Doktorlauge *f*, **Doktorlösung** *f (petrol)* doctor solution
doktor-negativ *(petrol)* sweet[ened], doctor-sweet
doktor-positiv *(petrol)* sour
Doktorsüßen *n s.* Doktorbehandlung
Doktorsüßungsverfahren *n (petrol)* doctor process
Doktortest *m (petrol)* doctor test
Doktorverfahren *n s.* Doktorsüßungsverfahren
Dokumentenpapier *n* document paper, *(Am)* deed paper
Dolichol *n (bioch)* dolichol
dollieren *(tann)* to buff
Dolomit *m (min)* dolomite, magnesian limestone *(calcium magnesium carbonate)*
Dolomitgestein *n* dolomite [rock]
dolomitisch dolomitic
dolomitisieren *(geoch)* to dolomitize
Dolomitisierung *f (geoch)* dolomitization
Dolomitkalk *m* dolomitic (dolomite) lime *(calcium magnesium oxide)*
Dolomitkalkstein *m* dolomitic limestone
Dolomitknolle *f* coal ball *(a petrifaction in coal)*
Dolomitstein *m* dolomite brick
Dom *m (distil)* stillhead
Domäne *f (cryst)* domain
~/ferromagnetische ferromagnetic domain, Weiss [molecular magnetic] field
Domänenwand *f (cryst)* domain (Bloch) wall
Donator *m* donor, donator
Donator-Akzeptor-Bindung *f* donor-acceptor bond, dipolar (coordinate) bond, coordination [bond]
Donator-Akzeptor-Komplex *m* donor-acceptor complex, charge transfer complex
Donator-Akzeptor-Wechselwirkung *f* donor-acceptor interaction
Donatoratom *n* donor (ligating) atom *(coordination chemistry)*
Donatoreigenschaften *fpl* donor properties
Donatorgruppe *f* donor group
Donatormolekül *n* donor molecule
Donatorniveau *n* donor level
Donatorort *m (bioch)* donor (condensing) site, peptidyl-tRNA site, P site
Donatorsolvens *n* donor solvent
Donatorstärke *f* donor power
Donatorsubstanz *f* donor reagent
Donatorterm *m s.* Donatorniveau
Donatorverbindung *f* donor compound
Donnan-Effekt *m* Donnan effect
Donnan-Gleichgewicht *n* Donnan [membrane] equilibrium
Donnan-Potential *n* Donnan potential
Donnelly-Krackverfahren *n (petrol)* Donnelly process
Donor *m s.* Donator
Dopa *n s.* Dihydroxyphenylalanin
Dopachinon *n (bioch)* DOPA quinone
Dope *m(n)*, **Dope-Mittel** *n* dope *(a substance added to mineral-oil products in quantities below 1 %)*
dopen to dope *(to treat mineral-oil products with a dope)*
Dope-Stoff *m s.* Dope
Dopingmittel *n (pharm)* dope
Doppelanion *n* dianion
Doppelarmkneter *m* double-arm mixer
Doppelbandpolieren *n (glass)* twin polishing
Doppelbandschleifen *n (glass)* twin grinding
Doppelbild *n (phot)* ghost image
Doppelbindung *f* double [covalent] bond
~/gehäufte *s.* ~/kumulierte
~/gekreuzte crossed double bond
~/halbpolare *s.* ~/semipolare

~/isolierte isolated double bond
~/konjugierte conjugated double bond
~/kumulierte cumulated double bond
~/mesomeriefähige resonating double bond
~/nichtkonjugierte non-conjugated double bond
~/olefinische olefinic double bond
~/semicyclische semicyclic [double] bond
~/semipolare semipolar bond, dative (coordinate) bond, dative covalence
Doppelbindungscharakter *m* double-bond character
doppelbrechend doubly refracting (refractive), birefringent
Doppelbrechung *f* double refraction, birefringence
~/elektrische electrical double refraction
~/optische optical birefringence
~/positive positive double refraction
Doppeleinzelheizer *m (rubber)* twin curing unit, double (twin) press, twin heater
doppelfarbig *(cryst, coll)* dichroic
Doppelfarbigkeit *f (cryst, coll)* dichroism
Doppelflügelwäscher *m (min tech)* logwasher
Doppelfokussierung *f* double focusing
Doppelgaserzeuger *m*, **Doppelgasgenerator** *m (coal)* predistillation [gas] producer, carbonizing (double gas, two-stage) generator, two-zone gasifier
Doppelgebläse *n* double bulb blower
Doppelheizer *m s.* Doppeleinzelheizer
doppelhelikal *(bioch)* double-helical
Doppelhelix *f (bioch)* double (duplex) helix, double-strand[ed] helix
Doppelkegelbindung *f* sandwich bond *(coordination chemistry)*
Doppelkegelmischer *m* double-cone mixer
Doppelkegelstruktur *f* sandwich structure *(coordination chemistry)*
Doppelkegel-Trommelmischer *m s.* Doppelkonusmischer
Doppelkolbenpresse *f* double-ram press
Doppelkolonne *f* double column
Doppelkonusmischer *m* double-cone blender (mixer)
Doppelkrümmer *m* return bend
Doppellactatverfahren *n (soil)* double-lactate method
Doppelleerstelle *f* divacancy *(a crystal defect)*
Doppellinie *f (spectr)* doublet
Doppelmembran *f (bioch)* bilayer membrane
Doppelmolekül *n* double[d] molecule
Doppelmonochromator *m (spectr)* double monochromator
Doppelmuffe *f (lab)* clamp holder, bosshead
Doppeloxid *n* double oxide
Doppelpaddelmischer *m* double-arm mixer
Doppelpechpapier *n* tarred [brown] paper, tar (pitch, asphalt) paper
Doppelpfeil *m* double[-headed] arrow, reversible arrows *(with equilibrium reactions)*
Doppelpistole *f s.* Doppelspritzpistole
Doppelpresse *f* dual press
Doppelquarz *m* biquartz
Doppel-Reifeneinzelheizer *m (rubber)* double (twin) tyre press
Doppelresonanzmethode *f (spectr)* double-resonance method (technique)
Doppelrohr *n* double tube
Doppelrohraustauscher *m s.* Doppelrohrwärmeaustauscher
Doppelrohrkondensator *m* double-pipe condenser
Doppelrohrkristallisator *m* double-pipe crystallizer
Doppelrohrprobenstecher *m* concentric-tube thief
Doppelrohrverflüssiger *m s.* Doppelrohrkondensator
Doppelrohrwärmeaustauscher *m*, **Doppelrohrwärmeübertrager** *m* double-pipe heat exchanger, concentric-tube heat exchanger
Doppelrührwerk *n* double agitator
Doppelsalz *n* double salt
~/sulfatisches double sulphate
Doppelsäule *f* double column
Doppelscharlach *m (dye)* Biebrich (scarlet) red
Doppelscheibenmühle *f (pap)* double-disk refiner
~ System Bauer Bauer double-disk refiner
Doppelscheibenrefiner *m s.* Doppelscheibenmühle
Doppelschicht *f (phys ch)* double layer; *(bioch)* bilayer
~/diffuse diffuse double layer
~/elektrische (elektrochemische) electric[al] double layer, EDL, double-charge layer
~/Gouy-Chapmansche Gouy layer
Doppelschichtfilm *m (phot)* double-coated film
Doppelschnecke *f* twin screw (worm)
Doppelschneckenextruder *m* twin-screw extruder
Doppelsitzventil *n* double-seat[ed] valve
Doppelspalt *m* double slit
Doppelspat *m*/**Isländischer** Iceland spar *(a transparent variety of calc-spar)*
Doppelspritzpistole *f (coat)* two-nozzle [spray] gun
Doppelstrahlgerät *n*, **Doppelstrahlspektrometer** *n* double-beam spectro[photo]meter
Doppelstrang *m (bioch)* double strand, duplex *(of DNA)*
Doppelstrangbruch *m (bioch)* double-strand break
Doppelstrang-DNA *f (bioch)* double-strand DNA
doppelsträngig *(bioch)* double-strand[ed], double-helical, bihelical; *(tech)* two-stranded *(e.g. conveyor)*
Doppelsulfat *n* double sulphate
Doppelsuperphosphat *n* double superphosphate, concentrated (triple) superphosphate *(a fertilizer)*
Doppeltonpolarographie *f (anal)* double tone polarography
doppeltwirkend double-acting
Doppelwalzenpresse *f* double-roll press
Doppelwalzentrockner *m* twin-drum dryer
doppelwandig double-walled

Doppelweg-Anordnung *f (spectr)* double-pass arrangement
Doppelwellendampfmischer *m (pap)* double-shaft pulp (steam) mixer
Doppelwellenmischer *m* double-shaft[ed] mixer
Doppelwellenmuldenmischer *m* twin-rotor mixer
Doppler-Breite *f (spectr)* Doppler [half-]width
Doppler-Effekt *m (spectr)* Doppler effect, Doppler [frequency] shift
Doppler-Verbreiterung *f (spectr)* Doppler broadening
Doppler-Verschiebung *f s.* Doppler-Effekt
Dorn *m* 1. *(tech)* pin; 2. [extruder] core, mandrel *(extrusion moulding)*
Dorr-Eindicker *m* Dorr thickener (agitator), Dorr settling tank
dörren 1. to dry, to desiccate, to dehydrate *(fruit)*; to dry-cure *(meat)*; 2. *s.* darren
Dörren *n* 1. drying, desiccation, dehydration *(of fruit)*; dry curing *(of meat)*; 2. *s.* Darren
Dörrfleckenkrankheit *f* grey speck *(of oats on soil deficient in manganese)*
Dörrgemüse *n* dried vegetables
Dorr-Klassierer *m* Dorr [rake] classifier
~ mit Schüssel Dorr bowl classifier
Dorr-Rechenklassierer *m s.* Dorr-Klassierer
Dorschleberöl *n*, **Dorschlebertran** *m* cod-liver oil
Dortmundbrunnen *m (hyd)* Dortmund [vertical flow sedimentation] tank
Dosenkonserven *fpl* canned food
Dosenmilch *f* canned milk
Dosieranlage *f* dosing plant
Dosierapparat *m* dosing apparatus, metering (proportioning) apparatus
Dosierbandwaage *f* weighing (balanced-weigh) belt
Dosiereinrichtung *f* dosing mechanism, metering (proportioning) mechanism, feeder
~ für Chemikalien chemical feeder
~ für Flüssigkeiten liquid feeder
dosieren to dose, to meter, to proportion, to batch
Dosiergerät *n s.* Dosierapparat
Dosiergeschwindigkeit *f* chemical feed rate
Dosierhahn *m s.* Dosierventil
Dosierlöffel *m (lab)* measuring spoon
Dosierpumpe *f* dosing pump, metering (proportioning, controlled-volume, feed) pump; *(plast)* spinning pump
Dosierschleife *f (chromat)* bypass injector
Dosierschraube *f* proportioning screw
Dosierspritze *f* hypodermic syringe *(gas chromatography)*
Dosiersystem *n* sample injection system *(gas chromatography)*
Dosierung *f* dosage, dosing, metering, proportioning; *(chromat)* sampling, injection
~ mit Gasstromteilung *(chromat)* split sampling (injection)
~ ohne Gasstromteilung *(chromat)* splitless sampling (injection)
Dosierungs... *s.* Dosier...
Dosierventil *n* loop valve *(gas chromatography)*
Dosiervorrichtung *f s.* Dosiereinrichtung
Dosimeter *n* dosimeter, dosemeter, dosage meter
Dosimetrie *f* dosimetry, dosage measurement
Dosis *f* dose, dosage
~/giftig wirkende *s.* ~/toxische
~/kleinste wirksame minimum effective dose
~/letale lethal (fatal) dose
~/mittlere effektive median effective dose
~/mittlere letale median lethal dose, lethal dose 50
~/subletale sublethal dose
~/therapeutische therapeutic dose
~/tödliche *s.* ~/letale
~/toxische toxic dose
Dosisbereich *m* dose range
Dosiseffekt *m s.* Dosiswirkung
Dosisleistung *f* dose rate
Dosisleistungsmesser *m* dose rate meter
Dosismesser *m*, **Dosismeßgerät** *n s.* Dosimeter
Dosismessung *f s.* Dosimetrie
Dosisrate *f s.* Dosisleistung
Dosiswirkung *f* dosage response
Dosis-Wirkungs-Kurve *f* dosage-response curve
Dotter *m(n)* [egg] yolk, vitellus
Dotteröl *n* cameline (dodder) oil *(from the seeds of Camelina sativa Crantz)*
Doublettspektrum *n* doublet spectrum
Doublettstruktur *f* doublet structure
Down-Syndrom *n (med)* Down's syndrome, trisomy 21, mongolism
d.P. *s.* Packung/dichteste
2,4-DP *s.* Dichlorprop
DPE *s.* Diethylentriaminpentaessigsäure
2,3-DPG = 2,3-Diphosphoglycerat
DPN *(Diphosphopyridinnucleotid) s.* Nicotinsäureamid-adenin-dinucleotid
DPP *s.* Differenz-Pulspolarographie
DPPD *s. N,N'*-Diphenyl-*p*-phenylendiamin
Drachenblutharz *n* dragon's blood [resin], dracorubin *(from Daemonorops draco Blume or from Dracaena specc.)*
Dragée *n* dragée
Dragierkessel *m* coating pan, mushroom mixer
Draht *m* 1. wire; 2. *(text)* twist
~/falscher *(text)* false twist
Drahtbarren *m* wire bar
Drahtemail *n*, **Drahtemaillack** *m* wire enamel
Drahterteilung *f*, **Drahtgebung** *f (text)* twist
Drahtgestrick *n* knitted wire mesh *(packing material)*
Drahtgewebe *n* wire cloth (gauze), metal fabric
Drahtglas *n* wire[d] glass
Drahtkorb *m* **für Exsikkatoren** desiccator cage (guard)
Drahtnetz *n* wire gauze (net)
Drahtnetzfüllkörper *m* wire-gauze packing

Drahtnetzspirale *f* gauze plug *(in a combustion tube)*
Drahtrohrmodell *n* wire model *(as of a pipe system)*
Drahtsieb *n* wire screen (sieve), metal screen
Drahtspiralenfilter *n* coil[-type vacuum] filter
drahtumwickelt wire-wound
Draht- und Schnurfang *m (pap)* string catcher
Drainage *f s.* Dränung
Drakorubin[harz] *n s.* Drachenblutharz
Drall *m* 1. spin, angular momentum, moment of momentum; 2. *(text)* twist
Dralldüse *f* swirl[-plate] nozzle, hollow-cone nozzle
Drän *m s.* Dränstrang
Dränage *f s.* Dränung
Dränagerohr *n s.* Dränrohr
dränieren to drain
Dränkammer *f* draining pan *(in flow coating)*
Dränrohr *n*, **Dränröhre** *f* field-drain pipe, drainage pipe (tube), *(hyd also)* underdrain, *(Am)* drain tile
Drän[rohr]strang *m* drain
Dränsystem *n* drain system
Dräntunnel *m s.* Dränkammer
Dränung *f* drainage
~/künstliche *(soil)* artificial drainage
Drastikum *n (pharm)* drastic, strong purgative
Drechsel-Waschflasche *f (lab)* Drechsel bottle
Drehachse *f* axis of rotation; *(cryst)* axis of symmetry
~/dreizählige *(cryst)* threefold (triad) axis of symmetry
~/sechszählige *(cryst)* sixfold (hexad) axis of symmetry
~/vierzählige *(cryst)* fourfold (tetrad) axis of symmetry
~/zweizählige *(cryst)* twofold (diad) axis of symmetry
Drehbandkolonne *f (distil)* spinning band column, rotating-strip column
drehbar rotatable
Drehbarkeit *f* rotatability
~/freie free rotation
Drehbohren *n (petrol)* rotary drilling
Drehbrenner *m s.* Drehölbrenner
Drehdiagramm *n s.* Drehkristallaufnahme
Drehdurchführung *f* rotary joint *(as for fluids in piping)*
d-**drehend** *s.* (+)-drehend
l-**drehend** *s.* (–)-drehend
(+)-drehend dextrorotatory, dextrogyrate
(–)-drehend laevorotatory, laevogyrate
Drehetagenofen *m (hyd)* multiple-hearth incinerator *(sludge incineration)*
Drehfilter *n* rotary (rotating) filter, drum filter
Drehfiltration *f* rotary filtration
Drehhalter *m s.* Drehkreuz
Drehimpuls *m* angular momentum, moment of momentum, spin
~/innerer intrinsic angular momentum *(of elementary particles)*
Drehimpulsoperator *m* angular momentum operator
Drehimpulsquantenzahl *f* azimuthal (subsidiary) quantum number, orbital [angular momentum] quantum number
Drehimpulsvektor *m (spectr)* rotating vector
Drehknotenfänger *m (pap)* rotary (rotating, revolving) strainer, [revolving] drum strainer
Drehkocher *m (pap)* rotary (revolving) boiler (digester)
Drehkolbenpumpe *f* lobe pump
Drehkreuz *n* spider
Drehkristall *m* rotating (rotation) crystal
Drehkristallaufnahme *f*, **Drehkristalldiagramm** *n* rotating-crystal photograph (diagram), X-ray rotation photograph
Drehkristallkamera *f* rotating-crystal camera
Drehkristallmethode *f*, **Drehkristallverfahren** *n* rotating-crystal method *(of crystal analysis)*
~ von Bragg Bragg method [of crystal analysis], Bragg treatment
Drehkülbelform *f (glass)* paste mould
Drehmaschine *f (ceram)* jiggering machine, jigger
Drehmoment *n* torque
Drehofen *m* rotary kiln, *(esp met)* rotary furnace
Drehofenmantel *m* rotary-kiln shell
Drehölbrenner *m* rotary-cup [oil] burner, rotary (spinning-cup) burner
Drehrichtung *f* direction of rotation
Drehrohr *n* revolving tube, rotating cylinder
Drehrohrofen *m* rotary kiln
Drehrost *m* rotating (revolving) grate
Drehscheibe *f* 1. rotary (rotating) disk *(as of an extractor)*; 2. *(ceram)* potter's wheel
Drehscheibenextrakteur *m*, **Drehscheibenextraktor** *m* rotary-disk contactor (extractor, tower)
Drehscheibenfilter *n* disk-type rotary vacuum filter, rotary disk filter
Drehscheibenkolonne *f s.* Drehscheibenextrakteur
Drehschieberölpumpe *f* rotary slide-valve oil pump
Drehschieberverdichter *m* [sliding-]vane compressor
Drehschwingung *f (spectr)* twisting vibration
Drehsieb *n* rotary screen
Drehsinn *m* sense of rotation
Drehspäne *mpl* turnings
Drehsprenger *m (hyd)* rotary distributor *(of a trickling-filter plant)*
Drehspulgalvanometer *n* moving-coil galvanometer
~ von D'Arsonval D'Arsonval galvanometer
Drehtank *m (glass)* revolving pot
Drehtisch *m* 1. *(lab)* turntable; 2. *(petrol)* rotary table (machine)
Drehtischantrieb *m (petrol)* rotary-machine drive
Drehtrommel *f* rotary (rotating) drum (cylinder), tumbler, tumbling barrel
Drehtrommeltrockner *m* rotary [drum] dryer, rotatory dryer

Drehung *f* 1. rotation; 2. *(text)* twist[ing] • **ohne ~** *(text)* twistless
~ der Polarisationsebene *s.* ~/optische
~ [der Polarisationsebene]/magnetische magnetic rotation, Faraday effect
~/molare molar rotation
~/molekulare molecular rotation
~/optische optical rotation
~/spezifische specific rotation
drehungsfixiert *(text)* twist-set
drehungsfrei *(text)* twistless
Drehungssinn *m* sense of rotation
Drehungsvermögen *n* rotatory power
~/magnetisches magnetic rotatory power
~/molares molar rotatory power
~/optisches optical activity (rotatory power)
~/spezifisches specific rotatory power
Drehungswinkel *m***/optischer** *s.* Drehwert
Drehvermögen *n s.* Drehungsvermögen
Drehverteiler *m* rotating (revolving) distributor
Drehwaage *f* torsion balance
Drehwanne *f (glass)* revolving pot
Drehwert *m* amount (angle) of rotation
Drehwertanteil *m* rotatory contribution
Drehwinkel *m***[/optischer]** *s.* Drehwert
Drehzahl *f* number of revolutions, rate of rotation, speed
~/kritische critical speed
~/spezifische specific speed
Drehzerstäuber *m* rotary[-cup] atomizer, spinning-cup atomizer *(of an oil burner)*
Drehzerstäuberbrenner *m s.* Drehölbrenner
Dreiäschersystem *n s.* Dreigrubenäschersystem
dreiatomig triatomic
Dreibandenspektrum *n* three-banded spectrum
dreibasig tribasic, triprotic *(acid)*; tribasic, triacid *(base)*
dreibindig trivalent, tervalent *(relating to homopolar bonds)*
Dreiblattrührer *m* three-bladed agitator
Dreibuchstabensymbol *n (bioch)* three-letter word *(of the genetic code)*
Dreidecker *m*, **Dreidecker-Siebmaschine** *f* triple-decked screen
Dreieck *n***/Pascalsches** Pascal's triangle
Dreieckskoordinatensystem *n* triangular diagram
Dreieckwellenpolarographie *f (anal)* triangular-wave polarography
~/zyklische cyclic triangular wave polarography
Dreieckwellenvoltammetrie *f (anal)* triangular wave voltammetry
Drei[er]elektronenbindung *f* three-electron bond
Dreierkombination *f (bioch)* triplet [codon] *(in the genetic code)*
Dreierreaktion *f* termolecular reaction
Dreierring *m s.* Dreiring
Dreierstoß *m* ternary collision, triple (three-body) collision
Dreifachaufsatz *m* triple-neck adapter, three-neck[ed] adapter
Dreifachbindung *f* triple [covalent] bond
dreifachnegativ [geladen] trinegative
dreifachpositiv [geladen] tripositive
Dreifarbigkeit *f (cryst)* trichroism
Dreifingerklemme *f (lab)* burette clamp
dreifunktionell trifunctional
Dreifuß *m* 1. *(lab)* tripod; 2. *(ceram)* [wedge] stilt *(a piece of kiln furniture)*
Dreifußstativ *n (lab)* tripod retort stand
dreiglied[e]rig three-membered
Dreigrubenäschersystem *n (tann)* three-pit [liming] system
Dreigutapparat *m s.* Dreiproduktapparat
Dreigutscheider *m s.* Dreiproduktscheider
dreihalsig three-neck[ed]
Dreihalskolben *m* three-neck[ed] flask
Dreihalsrundkolben *m* round-bottom three-neck[ed] flask
Dreikant *m (ceram)* saddle *(a piece of kiln furniture)*
Dreikohlenstoffkörper *m* three-carbon compound
Drei-Kohlenstoff-Tautomerie *f* three-carbon tautomerism
Dreikolbendruckpumpe *f* three-piston pump
Dreikomponentensystem *n* ternary (tertiary three-component) system
Dreikörperverdampfer *m* triple-effect evaporator (evaporating unit)
Dreimaischverfahren *n (ferm)* three-mash method
Dreipressenschleifer *m (pap)* three-pocket grinder
Dreiprodukt[en]apparat *m* three-product unit
Dreiprodukt[en]scheider *m* three-product separator
dreiprotonig triprotic, tribasic *(acid)*
Dreiring *m* three-membered [carbon] ring
dreisäurig triacid, tribasic *(base)*
dreischauflig three-bladed *(agitator)*
Dreischichtmineral *n (soil)* 2:1 type clay
Dreischichtplatte *f* three-layer board
Dreischichttonmineral *n (soil)* 2:1 type clay
Dreistoffgemisch *n* ternary (three-component) mixture
Dreistofflegierung *f* ternary (three-component) alloy
Dreistoffsystem *n* ternary (three-component) system
Dreistufenbleiche *f (pap)* three-stage bleaching
Dreistufen-Gegenstromwäsche *f* three-stage countercurrent washing
Dreistufenreaktion *f* three-step reaction
Dreistufenverdampfer *m s.* Dreikörperverdampfer
Dreistufenwäsche *f* three-stage washing
Dreiwalzenkalander *m* three-bowl (three-roll) calender
Dreiwalzenmühle *f*, **Dreiwalzenstuhl** *m* three-roll mill
Dreiweg[e]hahn *m* 1. *(lab)* three-way stopcock (tap); 2. *s.* Dreiwegventil
~ mit Bohrung senkrecht zur Achse T-bore stopcock
~ nach Czako T-shape 120° bore stopcock

Dreiwegventil *n* three-way valve
dreiwertig trivalent, tervalent *(element)*; tribasic, triprotic *(acid)*; tribasic, triacid *(base)*; trihydric *(alcohol)*
Dreiwertigkeit *f* trivalency, tervalency *(of an element)*; tribasicity *(of an acid or base)*
dreizählig 1. *(cryst)* triad, threefold; 2. *s.* dreizähnig
dreizähnig tridentate, terdentate *(ligand)*
Dreizellenapparat *m (el ch)* three-compartment electrodialysing device, three-chamber cell
Dreizentrenbindung *f* three-centre bond
Dreizentrenorbital *n* three-centre orbital
Dressler-Muffel *f (ceram)* Dressler muffle
Dressler-Ofen *m (ceram)* Dressler kiln
Drewboy-Scheider *m (min tech)* Drewboy separator
Drift *f (anal)* drift *(as of a base line)*
driften *(anal)* to drift *(as of a base line)*
Driftrohr *n*, **Driftröhre** *f* drift tube, DT
drillen *(agric)* to drill *(e.g. fertilizers)*
drillfähig *(agric)* drillable *(as of fertilizers)*
Drillfähigkeit *f (agric)* drillability *(as of fertilizers*
Drillingspumpe *f* triplex pump
Drillometer *n (petrol)* drillometer
Dritte-Partner-Effekt *m (phys ch)* matrix [interference] effect
Drittluft *f* tertiary air
Droge *f* drug
~/pflanzliche vegetable drug
~/tierische animal drug
Drogenkunde *f* pharmacognosy, pharmacogn[os]ia
Drogenkundler *m* pharmacognosist
drogenkundlich pharmacognostic
Droseron *n* droserone, 3,5-dihydroxy-2-methyl-1,4-naphthoquinone
Drosselgerät *n* variable-head meter *(a flowmeter)*
Drosselklappe *f*, **Drosselklappenventil** *n* butterfly valve
drosseln to slow down, to choke, to throttle
Drosselpfropfen *m* porous plug
Drosselscheibe *f* orifice plate *(flow measurement)*
Drosselstelle *f* constriction, restriction, throttle
Drosselventil *n* butterfly valve
DRP-Modell *n* dense random packing model
Druck *m* 1. pressure; 2. printing *(process)*; 3. print *(printed material)* • **unter ~ setzen** to pressurize
~ am Umfang peripheral pressure
~/atmosphärischer atmospheric (air) pressure
~ auf Kammzug *(text)* top printing
~/barometrischer barometric pressure
~ der expandierenden Gaskappe *(petrol)* gas cap drive
~/hydrostatischer hydrostatic head
~/innerer internal pressure; intrinsic (cohesion) pressure
~/kritischer critical pressure
~/lithographischer lithographic printing, lithography
~/osmotischer osmotic pressure, OP
~/reduzierter *(phys ch)* 1. reduced pressure *(ratio of pressure to critical pressure)*; 2. *s.* ~/verminderter
~/statischer static pressure *(of a fluid)*
~/verminderter reduced pressure
Druckabfall *m* pressure drop (loss)
~ infolge Reibung pressure drop due to friction, pressure loss from friction, friction drop
druckabhängig pressure-dependent
Druckabhängigkeit *f* pressure dependence
Druck-Aktivkohlefilter *n (hyd)* pressure carbon contactor
Druckanschluß *m* pressure port
Druckanstieg *m* pressure increase, increase in pressure
Druckaufnahmefläche *f (plast)* pressure pad
Druckausgleich *m* pressure compensation
Druckausgleichsgefäß *n* pressure-compensating vessel
Druckball *m* pressure bulb
Druckbegrenzungsventil *n* pressure relief valve
Druckbehälter *m* 1. pressure vessel (tank); 2. *(pap)* pressure container (accumulator)
Druckbelüfter *m s.* Druckluftbelüfter
Druckbirne *f s.* Druckfaß
Druckbombe *f* bomb
Druckdecke *f s.* Drucktuch
Druckdeckenwäscher *m s.* Drucktuchwäscher
Druckdestillat *n* pressure distillate, P.D.
Druckdestillation *f* pressure distillation
Druckdestillationsanlage *f* vapour compression evaporator, VC evaporator *(desalination of sea water)*
druckdicht pressure-tight
Druckdifferential *n* pressure differential
Druckdifferenz *f* pressure difference
Druckdurchtränkung *f (pap)* pressure impregnation, penetration under pressure, forced penetration
Druckdüse *f* pressure nozzle
Druckeigenschaften *fpl (pap)* printing properties
Druckeintritt *m* pressure port
drücken to press, to push *(e.g. a lever or button)*; to push out, to discharge *(e.g. coke from a coke oven)*; to blow *(a liquid into a reservoir)*; to squeeze, to extract under pressure; *(min tech)* to depress *(to cause to sink)*
Druckenergie *f* pressure energy
Druckentnahmestelle *f* pressure tap
Drücker *m (min tech)* depressant
Druckereihilfsmittel *n* printing additive
Druckerhöhung *f* pressure increase, increase in pressure
Druckerschwärze *f* printing (printer's) ink
Druckextraktion *f* pressure extraction
~ mit Benzen (Benzol) benzene pressure extraction
Druckfarbe *f* printing ink
~ für Flachdruck planographic [printing] ink

~ **für Heliogravüre** photogravure ink
~ **für Hochdruck** typographic [printing] ink
~ **für Offsetdruck** offset [printing] ink
~ **für Rotationstiefdruck** rotogravure ink
~ **für Siebdruck** screen-process ink
~ **für Silk-Screen-Druck** silk-screen ink
~ **für Steindruck** lithographic [printing] ink, litho ink
~ **kurze** short ink
~ **lange** long ink
Druckfärben *n* pressure dyeing
Druckfarbenaufnahmevermögen *n (pap)* ink receptivity
Druckfarbenbindemittel *n (pap)* ink binder
Druckfaß *n* blowcase, acid egg
Druckfestigkeit *f* compressive (compression) strength
Druckfeuerbeständigkeit *f* refractoriness under load
Druckfilter 1. pressure filter, pressure-filtration funnel; 2. *(hyd)* rapid pressure filter, pressure rapid filter
~ **S** Sweetland filter
Druckfilternutsche *f* pressure nutsche
Druckfilterpresse *f s.* Druckfilter 2.
Druckfiltration *f*, **Druckfiltrieren** *n* pressure filtration
Druckflasche *f* pressure cylinder
Druckflotation *f (hyd)* [pressurized-]air floatation, dissolved-air pressure floatation, dissolved-air floatation without recycle, DAF
Druckflotationsanlage *f (hyd)* air floatation clarifier (unit)
Druckflotation-Teilstromverfahren *n (hyd)* dissolved air-floatation with recycle
Druckflüssigkeitsspeicher *m* hydraulic accumulator
Druckgaserzeuger *m (coal)* pressurized-gas producer, pressure gasifier
Druckgasflasche *f s.* Druckflasche
Druckgasgenerator *m s.* Druckgaserzeuger
Druckgefälle *n* pressure difference
Druckgefäß *n* pressure vessel (tank)
druckgießen to [pressure-]diecast
Druckgießen *n* [pressure] diecasting, pressure casting
Druckgießform *f* diecasting (pressure-casting) die
Druckgießmaschine *f* [pressure-]diecasting machine
~ **für Kaltkammerverfahren** cold-chamber [diecasting] machine
~ **für Warmkammerverfahren** hot-chamber [diecasting] machine
Druckgießverfahren *n* diecasting process
Druckgradient-Korrekturfaktor *m (chromat)* pressure gradient correction factor
Druckgrün *n* chrome green *(a mixture of iron blue and chrome yellow)*
Druckgrund *m* stock *(for printing)*
Druckguß *m* [pressure] diecasting, pressure casting • **im ~ herstellen** *s.* druckgießen
Druckguß... *s. a.* Druckgieß...
Druckgußlegierung *f* diecasting alloy
Druckgußstück *n*, **Druckgußteil** *n* [pressure] diecasting
Druckhärte *f* indentation hardness
Druckhöhe *f s.* ~/statische
~/dynamische velocity head
~/statische [pressure, static] head
Druckhub *m* delivery (discharge) stroke *(of a pump)*
Druckhydrierung *f* hydrogenation under pressure, pressure hydrogenation
~/spaltende *(petrol)* hydrocracking
Druckimprägnierung *f (pap)* pressure impregnation, penetration under pressure, forced penetration
Druckkammer *f* pressure chamber
Druckkessel *m* 1. pressure vessel (tank); 2. pressure pot *(paint spraying technique)*
Druckknopf *m* push button
Druckknopfschalter *m* push-button switch
Druckkochen *n* pressure boil[ing], boiling under pressure
Druckkörper *m (filtr)* pressure case (cylinder)
Druckkristallisation *f* piezocrystallization
Druckkühler *m* pressure cooler
Drucklaugung *f (min tech)* pressure leaching
Druckleiste *f (plast)* pressure pad
Druckleitung *f* pressure line; delivery line *(of a pump)*
drucklos without [the use of] pressure, pressureless
Druckluft *f* compression (compressed) air
Druckluftanlage *f s.* Druckluftbelüftungsanlage
Druckluftbelüfter *m (hyd)* diffused aerator, submerged (sparger) aerator, air diffuser
~ **mit Rührwerk (Turbinenrührer)** combination aerator
Druckluftbelüftung *f (hyd)* diffused aeration, submerged (bubble) aeration
Druckluftbelüftungsanlage *f (hyd)* diffuser (diffused-air) unit
Druckluftbelüftungssystem *n (hyd)* diffuser (diffused-air) system
druckluftbetätigt air-operated, air-driven
Druckluftdüse *f* air-atomizing (gas-atomizing, two-fluid) nozzle
Drucklufteintritt *m* blow port *(for blowing off the filter cake)*
Druckluftflotation *f s.* Druckflotation
Druckluftförderung *f* air lifting
Druckluftförderverfahren *n* air-lift process
Druckluftformen *n* **mit Vorstreckung** *(plast)* plug-assist pressure forming
Druckluftgießmaschine *f* air-operated diecasting machine
Drucklufttheber *m* air lift, mammoth (air-lift) pump
Drucklufthebersystem *n* air-lift system

Druckluftleitung *f* compressed-air line
Druckluftpistole *f* blow gun
Drucklufttrüttler *m* pneumatic (air-driven) vibrator
Druckluft-Schwefelverbrennungsofen *m (pap)* spray-type sulphur burner
Druckluftspritzen *n (coat)* compressed-air spraying
Druckluftventil *n* pneumatic (air) valve
Druckluftvernebler *m (agric)* power[-operated] sprayer
Druckluftversprüher *m* pneumatic (auxiliary-fluid) atomizer; *(pap)* spray[ing] gun *(for producing sulphur dioxide)*
Druckluftversprühung *f* pneumatic [nozzle] atomization, auxiliary-fluid atomization
Druckluftvibrator *m* pneumatic (air-driven) vibrator
Druckluftzerstäuber *m* 1. pneumatic atomizer *(for solids)*; 2. *s.* Druckluftversprüher
Druckluftzerstäubung *f* 1. pneumatic atomization *(of solids)*; 2. *s.* Druckluftversprühung
Druckmesser *m* pressure gauge, manometer
~/piezoelektrischer piezometer
Druckminderer *m s.* Druckminder[ungs]ventil
Druckminderung *f* pressure reduction (decrease)
Druckminder[ungs]ventil *n* [pressure-]reducing valve
Druckmischer *m* bubbler
Drucknutsche *f* pressure nutsche
Druckpapier *n* print[ing] paper
Druckpaste *f* print[ing] paste
Druckreibungshöhe *f* discharge friction head
Druckrohr *n* pressure pipe (tube); delivery pipe *(of a pump)*
Drucksack *m (plast)* pressure bag
Drucksackmethode *f (plast)* pressure-bag moulding
Drucksandfilter *n (hyd)* pressure sand filter
Drucksäurebehälter *m (pap)* pressure container (accumulator)
Druckscheibe *f (plast)* pressure pad
Druckschlauch *m* 1. pressure hose; 2. *s.* Druckschlauchmaterial
Druckschlauchmaterial *n* pressure tubing
Druckschwingungsdämpfer *m* pulsation damper, [pulsation] snubber
Druckseite *f* delivery side *(of a pump)*
Druckseparator *m (pap)* selectifier [screen]
Drucksintern *n* sintering under pressure, hot pressing
Druckspannung *f* compressive stress
Druckspeicher *m* pressure tank
~/hydraulischer hydraulic accumulator
Drucksprung *m* pressure jump
druckspülen to jet
Druckstange *f* coke pusher ram *(for discharging coke)*
Drucksteigerung *f* pressure increase, increase in pressure
Drucksterilisator *m*, **Drucksterilisierapparat** *m* autoclave sterilizer
Druckstoß *m* pressure surge; water hammer, hydraulic shock *(as in an evaporator)*
Druckstrahlpumpe *f* injector
Druckströmung *f* pressure flow; pressure backflow *(in an extruder)*
Drucktaste *f* push button
Druckträger *m* stock *(for printing)*
Drucktuch *n (text)* blanket
Drucktuchwäscher *m (text)* blanket washer
Druckturm *m* pressure tower
Druckumlauffermenter *m (biot)* pressure cycle reactor
druckunabhängig pressure-independent
Druckventil *n* pressure [control] valve; delivery valve *(of a pump)*
Druckverbreiterung *f* pressure (collision) broadening *(of spectral lines)*
Druckverdampfer *m* pressure evaporator
Druckverdickungsmittel *n (text)* print[ing] thickener
Druckverfahren *n* 1. pressure process; 2. printing process
Druckverformung *f* 1. [permanent] compression set *(physics)*; 2. *(plast, rubber)* compression moulding
~/bleibende *s.* Druckverformung 1.
Druckverformungsrest *m s.* Druckverformung 1.
Druckvergaser *m (coal)* pressure gasifier, pressurized gas producer
~ mit flüssigem Schlackenabzug slagging pressure gasifier
Druckvergasung *f (coal)* [elevated-]pressure gasification
Druckverhältnis *n* compression ratio
Druckverlust *m* 1. pressure loss; *(hyd)* loss of hydraulic head, head loss; 2. pressure drop
~ eines Kolonnenbodens/trockener *(distil)* dry-plate pressure drop
~/trockener *(distil)* dry pressure drop
Druckversprüher *m* pressure atomizer
Druckversprühung *f* pressure atomization
Druckwalze *f* 1. pressure (compression) roll; *(tann)* grip roll; 2. printing roll
Druckwasserreaktor *m* pressurized-water reactor, PWR
Druckwasserstoffraffination *f (petrol)* hydrorefining
Druckwasserwäsche *f* water scrubbing
Druckwelle *f* blast
Druckzerstäuber *m s.* Druckversprüher
Druckzylinder *m (plast)* pressure cylinder
Drummond-Kalklicht *n* Drummond's limelight
Druse *f (min)* druse
Dry-blend-Strangpressen *n (plast)* dry-blend extrusion
D's *s.* Duanten
DS *s.* Diethylstilböstrol
dTA = derivative Thermoanalyse
DTA *s.* Differential-Thermoanalyse
DTG *s.* Differential-Thermogravimetrie

dTMP *s.* Desoxythymidin-5'-phosphat
Dualzerfall *m* branched (multiple) disintegration (decay), branching
Duanten *mpl (nucl)* dees *(D-shaped electrodes in a cyclotron)*
Dubbs-Krackverfahren *n (petrol)* Dubbs cracking process
Dublett *n* 1. *(spectr)* doublet; 2. duplet, doublet *(the structure in which two atoms share a pair of electrons)*
Dublettabstand *m (spectr)* doublet separation
Dublettaufspaltung *f (spectr)* doublet splitting
Dublettspektrum *n* doublet spectrum
Dublettstruktur *f* doublet structure
Dublettsystem *n (spectr)* doublet system
Dublett-Term *m (spectr)* doublet term
Dublettzustand *m* doublet state
Dubnium *n* Db dubnium *(element 104)*
Duff-Reaktion *f* Duff reaction *(formylation of phenol)*
Dufour-Effekt *m (phys ch)* Dufour effect
Duft *m* pleasant smell, perfume
~/starker fragrance, aroma
~/würziger aroma
~/zarter scent
duftend sweet-smelling, scented
~/stark fragrant, aromatic
~/würzig aromatic
~/zart [sweet-]scented
Duftlockstoff *m (biol)* scent attractant
Duftträger *m (cosmet)* perfume carrier
Dühring-Dampfdruckgerade *f* Dühring line
Dühring-Regel *f* Dühring's rule *(for vapour pressures of related liquids)*
Dükerzulauf *m* siphon feed *(of a clarifier)*
duktil ductile
Duktilität *f* ductility
Dulcit *m*, **Dulcitol** *n* dulcitol *(a sugar alcohol)*
Dulong-Petit-Regel *f (phys ch)* Dulong and Petit's law
Düngelanze *f* soil injector
Düngemaschine *f* fertilizing machine
Düngemischkalk *m* compound lime fertilizer
Düngemittel *n* fertilizer
~/anorganisches mineral fertilizer
~/langsam wirkendes *s.* ~/nachhaltig wirkendes
~/mineralisches mineral fertilizer
~/nachhaltig wirkendes sustained-release fertilizer
Düngemittelbedarf *m* fertilizer needs (requirements)
Düngemittelindustrie *f* fertilizer industry
Düngemitteltechnologie *f* fertilizer technology
Düngemittelverbrauch *m* fertilizer consumption
düngen to fertilize, to dress
~/mit Kalk to lime, to fertilize with lime
Dünger *m* fertilizer, *(esp of animal excreta also)* [farm] manure
Düngermühle *f* fertilizer mill
Düngernährstoff *m* fertilizer nutrient
Düngerphosphor *m* fertilizer phosphorus
Düngerstickstoff *m* fertilizer nitrogen
Düngerwalze *f* fertilizer roll
Düngerwert *m s.* Düngewert
Düngesalz *n* fertilizing (manure) salt
Düngewert *m* fertilizer (manurial) value
Düngung *f* fertilization, [fertilizer] dressing • **auf ~ ansprechen (reagieren)** to respond to fertilizing
~/aviotechnische *s.* ~ durch Flugzeuge
~ durch Flugzeuge aeroplane fertilization
Düngungsempfehlung *f* fertilization recommendation
Düngungspflug *m* fertilizing plough
Dunkelfärbung *f* darkening
Dunkelfeldbeleuchtung *f* dark-field (dark-ground) illumination
Dunkelfeldmikroskop *n* dark-field microscope
Dunkelkammer *f* dark-room
Dunkelkammerbeleuchtung *f* dark-room illumination
Dunkelmalz *n* dark malt
Dunkelöl *n* black oil
Dunkelperiode *f*, **Dunkelphase** *f* dark phase *(of photosynthesis)*
Dunkelraum *m* dark space
~/Astonscher Aston dark space
~/Crookesscher (Hittorfscher) Crookes (Hittorf, cathode) dark space
~/innerer *s.* ~/Crookesscher
Dunkelreaktion *f* dark[ness] reaction *(photochemistry)*
Dunkelrotglut *f* dull redness (red heat)
Dunkelstrom *m (spectr)* dark current
Dunkelwerden *n* darkening
Dunlop-Pendel *n (rubber)* Dunlop pendulum
Dunlop-Tripsometer *n (rubber)* Dunlop tripsometer
Dunlop-Verfahren *n (rubber)* Dunlop process
Dünnablauge *f (pap)* dilute (weak) black liquor
Dunnachie-Ofen *m (ceram)* Dunnachie kiln
Dünndruckpapier *n* bible paper, [Oxford] India paper
dünnflüssig thin, highly liquid (fluid), low-viscosity
Dünnflüssigkeit *f* thinness, low viscosity
Dünnglas *n* thin [sheet] glass; micro-glass *(for use in microscopy)*
dünngriffig sein *(pap)* to bulk low
Dünnlauge *f* weak (dilute) liquor
Dünnlaugeneintritt *m* feed liquor inlet *(as on an evaporator)*
Dünnmaische *f (ferm)* thin (lauter) mash
Dünnsaft *m (sugar)* thin juice
Dünnschicht *f* thin layer, [thin] film
Dünnschichtabsorber *m* wetted-wall[-column] absorber
Dünnschichtchromatogramm *n* thin-layer chromatogram
Dünnschichtchromatographie *f* thin-layer chromatography, TLC
~/zweidimensionale two-dimensional TLC (thin-layer chromatography)

dünnschichtchromatographisch by thin-layer chromatography
Dünnschichtdestillation *f* film distillation
Dünnschichtdestillator *m* film still
Dünnschichtelektrophorese *f* thin-layer electrophoresis
Dünnschichtfilm *m (phot)* thin emulsion film
Dünnschicht-Kapillarsäule *f* wall-coated open tubular capillary column, WCOT column *(gas chromatography)*
Dünnschichtteilchen *n (chromat)* porous layer bead, PLB, pellicular packing (support), solid core support
Dünnschichttrockner *m* film dryer
Dünnschichtverdampfer *m* film evaporator
~ mit rotierenden Wischern agitated-film evaporator
Dünnschlamm *m (hyd)* dilute sludge
Dünnschliff *m (min)* thin section
~/polierter polished thin section
Dünnschlifftechnik *f* thin-section technique
Dünnschliffverfahren *n* thin-section method
Dünnschnitt *m* thin section *(microscopy)*
Dünnsole *f* weak brine
Dünnstoffbleiche *f (pap)* low-density bleaching
Dünnstoff-Turmbleiche *f (pap)* low-density tower bleaching
dünntaflig *(cryst)* thin-tabular
dünnwandig thin-walled
Dünnwasser *n (hyd)* low-concentrated (low-strength) waste, weak sewage; permeate *(reverse osmosis)*
Dunst *m* 1. damp, haze *(consisting of droplets)*; fume, smoke *(consisting of solid particles)*; 2. bad smell
Dunsthaube *f* hood, air dome
Dunsthorizont *m* haze horizon
Duosolanlage *f* Duo-sol solvent extraction plant
Duosolextraktion *f* Duo-sol extraction
Duosolverfahren *n* Duo-sol [solvent extraction] process, two-solvent process
Duplexdruck *m (text)* double-face printing
Duplexkarton *m* duplex cardboard
Duplexmischer *m* duplex blender
Duplexpapier *n* duplex paper
Duplexpappe *f* duplex board
Duplexpumpe *f* duplex (two-throw) pump
Duplexschmelzverfahren *n* duplex process *(for steelmaking)*
Duplexstahl *m* duplex steel
Duplexverfahren *n s.* Duplexschmelzverfahren
Du-Pont-Biegeprüfmaschine *f*, **Du-Pont-Ermüdungsmaschine** *f (rubber)* Du Pont machine
Du-Pont-Grasselli-Abriebmaschine *f (rubber)* Du Pont-Grasselli-Williams machine
Du-Pont-Kettenermüdungsmaschine *f s.* Du-Pont-Biegeprüfmaschine
Du-Pont-Verfahren *n* Du Pont process *(ammonia oxidation)*
Durain *m* durain *(a constituent of coal)*
durcharbeiten 1. to work (knead) thoroughly *(e.g. a dough)*; 2. to homogenize *(an emulsion)*; 3. *(el ch)* to work [in], to deal with, to dummy *(a plating bath)*; 4. *(text)* to pole; 5. *(tann)* to pummel *(hides)*
~/im Faß *(tann)* to drum
durchbeißen to penetrate *(of a tan)*
Durchbelüftung *f* through [air] circulation
durchbiegen/sich to sag
Durchbiegung *f* sag[ging]
durchblasen to blow through
durchbluten *(dye, coat, tann)* to bleed [through], to strike through
Durchbluten *n (dye, coat, tann)* bleeding, strike-through
durchbohren to bore [through]
Durchbohrung *f* boring
durchbrechen to break through *(ion exchange, filtration)*
Durchbruch *m* breakthrough, leakage *(ion exchange, filtration)*
~ bei geringer Konzentration low-level breakthrough
Durchbruchkurve *f* breakthrough (leakage) curve
Durchbruchpunkt *m* break[through] point, point of breakthrough
Durchbruchverhalten *n* breakthrough behaviour
Durchbruchzeit *f* **[des Inertpeaks]** *s.* Durchflußzeit
durchdringbar penetrable, permeable
Durchdringbarkeit *f* penetrability, permeability
durchdringen to penetrate, to permeate
~/sich to interpenetrate
~/vollständig to impenetrate
durchdringend penetrating *(e.g. odour)*
Durchdringung *f* penetration, permeation
Durchdringungsfähigkeit *f s.* Durchdringungsvermögen
Durchdringungskomplex *m* penetration complex, inner (low-spin, inner-orbital, spin-paired) complex
Durchdringungskraft *f s.* Durchdringungsvermögen
Durchdringungsmittel *n (text)* penetrating agent
Durchdringungsnetzwerk *n (plast)* interpenetrating network, IPN
Durchdringungstheorie *f* penetration theory *(gas absorption)*
Durchdringungsvermögen *n* penetrating power, permeativity
Durchdringungszwillinge *mpl (cryst)* penetration twins
Durchdringungswahrscheinlichkeit *f (nucl)* penetration probability
durchdrücken to force through
durchfahren *(anal)* to scan *(a measuring range)*
~/nochmals to rescan
Durchfahren *n (anal)* scan *(of a measuring range)*
Durchfalloch *n*, **Durchfallöffnung** *f* drop hole
Durchfärbbarkeit *f (text)* penetrability
Durchfärbemittel *n (text)* penetrating agent

durchfärben 1. *(of human agent:)* to dye thoroughly (completely); 2. *(of a dyestuff:)* to penetrate
durchfeuchten to moisten thoroughly
durchfließen to flow (pass, run) through
Durchfluß *m* 1. flow, flowing-through, passage; 2. *(glass)* throat, flow hole; 3. *s.* Durchflußstrom
Durchflußbeiwert *m s.* Durchflußkoeffizient
Durchflußdetektor *m (anal)* flow-sensitive detector
Durchflußfermenter *m (biot)* continuous fermenter
Durchflußgeschwindigkeit *f* flow rate
Durchflußkoeffizient *m* flow (discharge) coefficient
Durchflußkühlung *f* once-through cooling
Durchflußkühlwasser *n* once-through cooling water
Durchflußkurve *f* flow curve
Durchflußmengenmesser *m* flowmeter, rato (fluid) meter, rate-of-flow volume meter
~/elektromagnetischer magnetic meter
~ für Flüssigkeiten liquid (stream) meter
Durchflußmengenmessung *f* flow measurement
Durchflußmesser *m* 1. *(chromat)* syphon counter; 2. *s.* Durchflußmengenmesser
Durchflußmischreaktor *m* tank-type flow reactor, continuous-flow stirred-tank reactor
Durchflußpasteurisation *f (food)* continuous pasteurization
Durchflußreaktor *m* [continuous-]flow reactor, continuous reactor
Durchflußrefraktometer *n (chromat)* differential refractometer [detector], RI (refractive index) detector
Durchflußrührfermenter *m (biot)* continuous stirred-tank fermenter
Durchflußrührkessel *m* continuous stirred tank
Durchflußrührkesselfermenter *m s.* Durchflußrührfermenter
Durchflußstrom *m* flow rate
Durchflußstrom-Stellglied *n* flow controller
Durchflußwiderstand *m (filtr)* resistance to flow
Durchflußzahl *f* flow (discharge) coefficient
Durchflußzeit *f (chromat)* [gas] hold-up time, time of passage *(period between injection and detection)*
durchfressen to eat through, to corrode
durchführbar/technisch practicable, feasible
Durchführbarkeit *f* practicality
durchführen to carry out, to run, to perform, to conduct
Durchgang *m* passage
Durchgangsofen *m (food)* continuous bake oven
Durchgangszeit *f s.* Durchlaufzeit
durchgasen *(agric, food)* to fumigate
Durchgasung *f (agric, food)* fumigation
Durchgasungsmittel *n (agric, food)* fumigant, fumigator
durchgerben to tan thoroughly
Durchgerbung *f (tann)* leathering
Durchgerbungszahl *f* tanning index
Durchhang *m* 1. sag[ging]; 2. *(phot)* region of underexposure, toe, foot *(of the characteristic curve)*
durchhängen to sag
Durchhängen *n* sag[ging]
durchkneten to knead [thoroughly]
durchkochen to cook thoroughly
Durchlaß *m* 1. passage; 2. *(glass)* throat, flow hole
~/bodengleicher (normaler) *(glass)* straight throat
~/tiefer (tiefliegender) *(glass)* sump throat, drop (submarine, submerged) throat
~/versenkter *s.* ~/tiefer
Durchlaß-Abdeckstein *m (glass)* throat cover
Durchlaßgrad *m (phot, anal)* transmission ratio, transmittance, transmittancy
durchlässig permeable
~/einseitig semipermeable
~ für Wärmestrahlen diathermanous, diathermic
Durchlässigkeit *f* 1. permeability *(relating to particles)*; 2. transmittance *(relating to radiation)*
~/einseitige semipermeability
~ für Wärmestrahlen diathermancy
~/innere internal transmittance
~/optische transmittance
~/wahre internal transmittance
Durchlässigkeitsfaktor *m* transmission coefficient *(kinetics)*
Durchlässigkeitsgrenze *f (spectr)* transmission limit
Durchlaßprofil *n (spectr)* band pass, spectral bandpass
Durchlaßquerschnitt *m* flow area
Durchlaß-Seitenstein *m (glass)* throat check, dice (sleeper) block
Durchlaßzahl *f* transmissivity *(radiation of heat)*
Durchlauf *m* passage
durchlaufen 1. to run (pass) through *(e.g. stages)*; 2. *s.* hindurchlaufen; 3. *s.* durchströmen
Durchlaufentwicklung *f* overrun development *(paper chromatography)*; continuous development *(thin-layer chromatography)*
Durchlaufgeschwindigkeit *f* flow rate
Durchlaufglühofen *m (met)* continuous-annealing furnace
Durchlaufglühung *f (met)* continuous annealing
Durchlaufkühlofen *m (glass)* continuous-annealing lehr
Durchlaufkühlung *f* once-through cooling; *(glass)* continuous annealing
Durchlaufmahlung *f* open-circuit grinding
Durchlaufofen *m (met)* continuous furnace; *(ceram)* continuous kiln
Durchlauftechnik *f s.* Durchlaufentwicklung
Durchlaufverdampfer *m* once-through evaporator, single-pass (one-pass) evaporator
Durchlaufverfahren *n* continuous process
Durchlaufzeit *f* retention time, detention (transit, hold-up) time, holding time (period)
durchleiten to pass [through]
Durchlicht *n* transmitted light
Durchlichtmethode *f* transmitted-light technique *(microscopy)*
durchlüften to aerate

Durchlüftung *f* aeration; through [air] circulation *(in a dryer)*
Durchmessereffekt *m (phot)* Eberhard effect
durchmischen to intermix, to mix (blend) together; to mix thoroughly
Durchmischung *f* intermixture; thorough mixing
~/ideale perfect mixing
~/vollständige complete mixing
Durchmischungskoeffizient *m* eddy diffusivity
durchmustern *(pharm, biot)* to screen *(for valuable compounds)*
Durchmusterungsprogramm *n (pharm, biot)* screening programme
durchnumerieren *(nomencl)* to number
Durchnumerierungssystem *n (nomencl)* numbering system
durchpressen to squeeze through
durchräuchern 1. *(food)* to smoke thoroughly; 2. to fumigate *(a chamber)*
Durchreißen *n (pap)* further tearing
Durchreißfestigkeit *f s.* Durchreißwiderstand
Durchreißprüfer *m* **nach Elmendorf** *(pap)* Elmendorf tester
Durchreißwiderstand *m (pap)* tear[ing] resistance, tear[ing] strength
Durchreißwiderstandsprüfung *f (pap)* tear[ing] test
durchrühren to stir, to agitate
Durchrühren *n* stirring, agitation
durchsacken to sag
Durchsacken *n* sag[ging]
Durchsatz *m* throughput, *(relating to a liquid also)* flow rate
Durchsatzstrom *m s.* Durchsatz
Durchscheinbarkeit *f (ceram)* translucence, translucency
durchscheinen to shine through; to show through *(of printing ink)*
Durchscheinen *n* shining-through; show-through *(of printing ink)*
durchscheinend translucent, translucid
~/nicht opaque
Durchschlag *m* breakdown *(of a dielectric)*
durchschlagen 1. *(dye, coat, tann)* to bleed [through], to strike through; 2. to puncture *(a dielectric)*
Durchschlagen *n* 1. *(dye, coat, tann)* bleeding, strike-through; 2. puncture *(of a dielectric)*
Durchschlagfestigkeit *f***/dielektrische (elektrische)** dielectric strength, breakdown (puncture) strength, electric strength
Durchschlagpapier *n* carbon copy[ing] paper, copy[ing] paper, copyings, *(Am)* manifold paper
Durchschlag[s]spannung *f* breakdown voltage
durchschlämmen *(soil)* to percolate
Durchschlämmung *f (soil)* percolation
Durchschnittsausbeute *f* average yield
Durchschnittsbetrag *m* average amount
Durchschnittsfettgehalt *m* average fat content
Durchschnittsprobe *f* average sample
Durchschnittswert *m* average (mean) value, mean
Durchschreib[e]papier *n* carbon paper, carbonic (carbonized) paper
Durchschubofen *m (ceram)* sliding-bat (pushed-bat) kiln
durchschütteln to shake
Durchschütteln *n* shake, shaking
durchseihen to strain, to percolate
Durchseihen *n* straining, [per]colation
durchsetzen to put through, to batch, to handle *(a definite quantity of material)*
Durchsicht *f* 1. examination, inspection; 2. *(pap)* look-through
durchsichtig transparent
Durchsichtigkeit *f* transparency
durchsickern 1. *(filtr)* to trickle through, to seep through, to percolate, to strain; 2. to leak
~ lassen to pass [through], to percolate, to strain *(a liquid)*
Durchsickern *n* 1. percolation, seepage; 2. leak
durchsieben to screen *(e.g. coal, gravel)*; to sieve, to sift *(e.g. flour)*
durchspülen to wash thoroughly (through)
Durchspülung *f* thorough (through) washing
durchstrahlen/mit Röntgenstrahlen to X-ray
Durchstrahlungsdiagramm *n (cryst)* front reflection pattern
durchströmen to flow [through], to pass, *(gas chromatography also)* to be swept through
Durchströmquerschnitt *m* flow area
durchtränken to soak, to impregnate, to imbibe, to penetrate, to saturate
Durchtränkung *f* soaking, impregnation, imbibition, penetration, saturation
Durchtränkungsgeschwindigkeit *f (pap)* rate of penetration *(of the chips)*
Durchtränkungsgrad *m (pap)* extent of penetration *(of the chips)*
Durchtritt *m* passage
Durchtrittsfaktor *m (el ch)* transfer coefficient, symmetry factor
Durchwachsung *f (cryst)* intergrowth
Durchwachsungszwillinge *mpl (cryst)* penetration twins
durchwärmen to warm thoroughly; *(glass)* to reheat *(the parison)*
Durchwärmen *n* thorough warming; *(glass)* reheat *(of the parison)*
durchwaschen to wash through (thoroughly)
Durchwaschen *n* thorough (through) washing
durchweichen to soak, to wet [through]
Durchweichzone *f (met)* soaking zone *(of an annealing furnace)*
Durchzeichenpapier *n* tracing paper
Durchzeichnung *f* **der Schatten** *(phot)* shadow detail
Durit *m* durain *(a constituent of coal)*

Durol *n* 1,2,4,5-tetramethylbenzene, *(deprecated:)* durene
Duromer[e] *n* duromer
Durometer *n* durometer, hardness tester (meter)
Durometerhärte *f* durometer (Shore) hardness
Duroplast *m* thermosetting plastic (resin), thermoset [resin]
Durville-Gießverfahren *n* Durville casting process *(foundry)*
Durylsäure *f* durylic acid, 2,4,5-trimethylbenzoic acid
Duschrinne *f* runoff gutter for wet cooling *(in margarine making)*
Duschverfahren *n* ice-water (wet-cooling) method *(in margarine making)*
Düse *f* 1. nozzle; *(plast)* die; *(met)* tuyere; 2. orifice *(in a steam trap)*
~/rotierende rotating (rotary, spinning) nozzle
~ zum Strangpressen von Folien *(plast)* flat die
Düsenbeiwert *m* nozzle coefficient
Düsenblasverfahren *n (glass)* jet process, *(specif)* air-blowing process *or* steam-blowing process
Düsenboden *m s.* Düsenlochboden
Düsenbohrung *f (text)* spinneret hole
Düsenebene *f (met)* tuyère level
Düsenentgaser *m (hyd)* atomizing deaerator (stripper), spray-type degasifier
Düsenfärbemaschine *f (text)* jet dyeing machine
Düsenfärbung *f (text)* dope (spin) dyeing
düsengefärbt *(text)* dope-dyed, spin-dyed, spun-dyed, mass-dyed, solution-dyed
Düsenhals *m* nozzle throat
Düsenhalter *m (plast)* die adapter
Düsenkeller *m* underjet cellar *(of an underjet coke oven)*
Düsenkondens[at]ableiter *m* orifice trap
Düsenkörper *m (plast)* die body, *(Am)* die base
Düsenkraftstoff *m s.* Düsentreibstoff
Düsenleitungen *fpl* underjet piping *(of an underjet coke oven)*
Düsenlochboden *m* base of the bushing *(glass-fibre manufacture)*
Düsenmischer *m* nozzle mixer
Düsenöffnung *f (met)* tuyère opening
Düsenpaßstück *n (plast)* die adapter
Düsensicherheitsventil *n* nozzle-type relief valve
Düsenstock *m (met)* tuyère stock
düsentexturiert *(text)* air-bulked
Düsentreibstoff *m* fuel for jet planes, [turbo]jet fuel
Düsentrockner *m* jet dryer
Düsentrocknung *f* jet drying
Düsenverengung *f* nozzle throat
Düsenversprüher *m* nozzle atomizer
Düsenversprühung *f* nozzle atomization
Düsenzerstäuber *m* nozzle atomizer
Düsenzerstäubung *f* nozzle atomization
Düsenzone *f (met)* tuyère zone
Dutch-Flüssigkeit *f* Dutch liquid *(1,2-dichloroethane)*
Dwight-Lloyd-Sintermaschine *f* Dwight-Lloyd sintering machine
Dynamik *f* dynamics
~/chemische chemical dynamics
~ der Fluide fluid dynamics
Dynamit *n* dynamite
Dypnon *n* dypnone, a-methylchalcone, *1,3-diphenylbut-2-en-1-one
Dyson-Notationssystem *n (nomencl)* Dyson [notation] system
Dysprosium *n* Dy dysprosium
Dysprosiumcarbonat *n* dysprosium carbonate
Dysprosiumchlorid *n* dysprosium chloride
Dysprosiumnitrat *n* dysprosium nitrate
Dysprosiumorthophosphat *n* dysprosium orthophosphate, dysprosium phosphate
Dysprosiumoxid *n* dysprosium oxide
Dysprosiumsulfat *n* dysprosium sulphate
Dysprotid *n* proton don[at]or, protonic acid, Brønsted-Lowry acid
dystroph *(soil)* dystrophic

E

EAD = Elektronenanlagerungsdetektor
Eadie-Hofstee-Auftragung *f* Eadie-Hofstee plot *(of kinetic data)*
Eadie-Hofstee-Gleichung *f (bioch)* Eadie-Hofstee equation
Eadie-Hofstee-Methode *f* Eadie-Hofstee method *(for treating kinetic data)*
Eagle-Mühle *f* Eagle mill *(a fluid-energy mill)*
EA-MS *s.* Elektronenanlagerungs-Massenspektroskopie
Easy-care-Ausrüstung *f (text)* easy-care finish
Easy-Processing-Channel-Ruß *m* easy-processing channel black, EPC black
Eau de Cologne *n(f)* cologne [water], eau de cologne
Eau de javelle *n(f)* eau de javel[le], javel[le] water *(aqueous solution of sodium or potassium hypochlorite)*
Eau de Labarraque *n(f)* eau de Labarraque *(aqueous solution of sodium hypochlorite)*
Eberhard-Effekt *m (phot)* Eberhard effect
e-Bindung *f* e-bond, equatorial bond
Ebullioskop *n* ebullioscope, ebulliometer
Ebullioskopie *f* ebullioscopy
ebullioskopisch ebullioscopic
EC *s.* Ethylcellulose
Echelettegitter *n (spectr)* echelette (blazed) grating
Echelongitter *n (spectr)* echelon grating
Echimidinsäure *f* echimidinic acid *(a C_7 trihydroxy acid)*
Echinochrom *n* **A** echinochrome A, *2-ethyl-3,5,6,7,8-pentahydroxynaphtho-1,4-quinone
echt 1. fast *(dye)*; 2. genuine *(noble metal, leather, gem)*; real, pure *(silk)*

~/äußerst *(dye)* exceedingly fast
~/mäßig *(dye)* moderately fast
Echtbase *f s.* Echtfarbbase
Echt-Bütten[papier] *n* genuine handmade paper, vat paper
Echt-Büttenpapier-Herstellung *f* papermaking by hand, handmade paper making
Echtdrahtverfahren *n (text)* conventional twisting
Echtfarbbase *f*, **Echtfärbebase** *f* fast base, *(Am also)* fast color base
Echtfärben *n*, **Echtfärberei** *f* fast dyeing
Echtfärbesalz *n* fast salt, *(Am also)* fast color salt
echtfarbig fast-dyed
Echtfarbstoff *m* fast dye
echtgefärbt fast-dyed
Echtheit *f* fastness *(of dyes)*; genuineness *(of noble metals or gems)*
Echtheitsprüfung *f (dye)* fastness test
Echtlichtgelb *n* hydrazine yellow, tartrazine *(a pyrazole derivative)*
Echtneublau *n* **3 R** fast blue 3 R, Meldola blue, basic blue 6
Echtorange *n* fast orange
Echtorangebase *f* fast orange base
Echtpergamentpapier *n* parchment paper, vegetable parchment
Echtrosa *n* fast pink
Echtrot *n* fast red
Echtrotbase *f* fast red base
Echtrot-GL-Base *f* fast red GL base
Echtsalz *n s.* Echtfärbesalz
Echtscharlach *m* fast scarlet
Echtscharlachbase *f* fast scarlet base
Echtscharlach-G-Base *f* fast scarlet G base
Echtwollgelb *n s.* Echtlichtgelb
Ecken *fpl***/tote** dead spaces, dead (stagnant) zones
Eckenfeuerung *f* tangential firing
Eckventil *n* angle valve
Ecruseide *f* ecru silk *(a partially degummed silk)*
E-Cu *s.* E-Kupfer
ED_{50} *s.* Dosis/mittlere effektive
EDA-Komplex *m s.* Elektronen-Donor-Akzeptor-Komplex
edel noble, unreactive, non-reactive
Edeleanu-Extrakt *m* Edeleanu extract *(obtained by solvent extraction)*
Edeleanu-Verfahren *n* Edeleanu process *(solvent extraction using liquid sulphur dioxide)*
Edelerde *f* activated (active) earth
Edelgas *n* noble (inert, rare) gas
Edelgaschemie *f* noble-gas chemistry
Edelgasclathrat *n* noble-gas (inert-gas) clathrate
Edelgaseinschlußverbindung *f s.* Edelgasclathrat
Edelgaskonfiguration *f* noble-gas [electronic] configuration, inert-gas [electronic] structure, octet structure
Edelgasoktett *n* noble-gas (inert-gas) octet
Edelgasrumpf *m* noble-gas [electronic] core, inert-gas core
Edelgasschale *f* noble-gas [electron] shell, inert-gas shell
Edelmetall *n* noble (precious) metal
Edelrost *m* patina
Edelsalz *n* abraum salt
Edelstein *m* precious stone, gemstone
Edelzellstoff *m (pap)* [high] alpha pulp, processed (purified wood) pulp
Edison-Akkumulator *m (el ch)* Edison accumulator (cell)
Edman-Abbau *m (bioch)* Edman degradation *(of proteins)*
Edwards-Ofen *m (met)* Edwards roaster
ED-Weg *m (bioch)* Entner-Doudoroff pathway
E-Effekt *m s.* Effekt/elektromerer
E-Eisen *n* electrolytic iron
EEVA = Elektronen-Energie-Verlust-Analyse
Effekt *m***/allosterischer** *(bioch)* allosteric (second-site) effect
~/bathochromer *(dye)* bathochromic effect
~/dielektrischer dielectric effect
~/elektromerer *s.* ~/mesomerer
~/elektrophoretischer electrophoretic effect
~/elektroviskoser electroviscous effect
~/heterotroper *(bioch)* heterotropic effect
~/homotroper *(bioch)* homotropic effect
~/hyperchromer *(bioch, spectr)* hyperchromic effect
~/hypochromer *(spectr)* hypochromic effect
~/hypsochromer *(dye)* hypsochromic effect
~/induktiver *(phys ch)* inductive (induction) effect, I effect
~/katalytischer catalytic effect
~/kataphoretischer *s.* ~/elektrophoretischer
~/klopfhemmender (klopfhindernder) antiknock effect
~/lichtelektrischer *s.* ~/photoelektrischer
~/longitudinaler *s.* ~/elektrophoretischer
~/magnetokalorischer magnetocaloric effect
~/mechanokalorischer mechanocaloric effect
~/mesomerer mesomeric (electromeric, resonance) effect
~/nivellierender *(phys ch)* levelling effect
~/photoakustischer photoacoustic effect
~/photoelektrischer photoelectric effect
~/piezoelektrischer piezo[electric] effect
~/polarer *(org ch)* polar effect
~/sterischer steric effect
~/synergistischer synergistic effect, synergism
~/thermoelektrischer thermoelectric effect
~/thermomagnetischer thermomagnetic effect
α-Effekt *m (org ch)* α-effect, alpha-effect *(enhancement of nucleophilicity)*
effektiv efficient, effective
Effektivhöhe *f* **des Schornsteins** effective chimney (stack) height
Effektivität *f* efficiency, effectiveness
~/katalytische catalytic efficiency
Effektor *m (bioch)* effector

~/allosterischer allosteric effector, modifier, determinant *(enzyme kinetics)*
~/heterotroper heterotropic effector
~/homotroper homotropic effector
Effloreszenz *f (min)* efflorescence
effloreszieren *(min)* to effloresce
Effusion *f* effusion
Effusionsmethode *f* effusion method *(for measuring vapour pressures)*
effusiv *(geol)* effusive
Effusivgestein *n s.* Ergußgestein
EFG, EF-G *(bioch)* elongation factor EF-G
EFT, EF-T *(bioch)* elongation factor EF-T
egal *(dye)* level
egalfärben *(text)* to level, to dye level
Egalfärben *n (text)* levelling, level dyeing
egalisieren *s.* egalfärben
Egalisierer *m*, **Egalisier[hilfs]mittel** *n (text)* levelling agent, level dyeing assistant
Egalisierung *f s.* 1. Egalfärben; 2. Egalität
Egalität *f (dye)* levelness
E-Glas *n* E glass, glass E *(a fibre glass of low alkali content)*
Egoutteur *m (pap)* watermarking dandy [roll], dandy [roll]
Egoutteur[wasser]zeichen *n (pap)* dandy roll watermark
Egrenieren *n (text)* ginning
Egreniermaschine *f (text)* [cotton] gin
EGW *s.* Einwohnergleichwert
eiabtötend ovicidal
Eialbumin *n* egg albumin
eichen to calibrate *(e.g. measuring apparatus)*; to adjust *(balance weights or measures)*; to gauge *(vessels)*
Eichfunktion *f* calibration function
Eichkraftstoff *m* reference fuel
Eichkurve *f* calibration curve (graph)
Eichlösung *f* calibrating solution
Eichmarke *f* calibration mark
Eichmatrix *f* calibration matrix
Eichspannung *f* reference voltage
Eichstandard *m* calibration standard
Eichstrich *m* calibration mark
Eichtreibstoff *m* reference fuel
Eichung *f* calibration *(as of measuring apparatus)*; adjustment *(of balance weights or measures)*; standard calibration, gauging *(of vessels)*
Eichwiderstand *m* shunt
Eicosan *n* eicosane
Eicosansäure *f* *eicosanoic acid, arachidic acid
Eicosatetraensäure *f* *eicosatetraenoic acid, eicosane-tetraenoic acid
Eicos-9-ensäure *f* *eicos-9-enoic acid, gadoleic acid
Eieralbumin *n* egg albumin
Eierbrikett *n* ovoid
Eiergift *n* ovicide *(a kind of pesticide)*
Eieröl *n* egg-yolk oil
Eierschalenporzellan *n (ceram)* egg-shell porcelain
Eierschaligkeit *f (ceram)* egg-shelling *(of the glaze)*
Eigelb *n* [egg] yolk, vitellus
~/flüssiges liquid egg yolk
Eigelbnachgare *f (tann)* egging
Eigelböl *n* egg-yolk oil
Eigenabsorption *f* self-absorption
Eigenadsorption *f* self-adsorption
Eigenassoziation *f* self-association
Eigendiffusion *f* self-diffusion
Eigendissoziation *f* self-dissociation, self-ionization, autoprotolysis
Eigendrehimpuls *m* intrinsic angular momentum, spin *(of elementary particles)*
Eigenenzym *n* inherent enzyme
Eigenfarbe *f* self-colour
Eigenfrequenz *f* natural frequency *(of vibration)*
Eigenfunktion *f (phys ch)* eigenfunction
~/orthogonale orthogonal eigenfunction
Eigengewicht *n* own weight
Eigenhalbleiter *m* intrinsic semiconductor
eigenhärtend *(plast)* self-curing
Eigenindikation *f (anal)* self-diagnostics
Eigenion *n* common ion
Eigenionisation *f* autoionization
Eigenkeim *m* crystal nucleus, nucleus of crystallization, nucleation centre
Eigenkonvektion *f* natural convection
Eigenmasse *f* own mass
Eigenparität *f (nucl)* intrinsic parity
Eigenpolymerisation *f* homopolymerization
Eigenpotential *n* self-potential
Eigenpotentialkurve *f* self-potential curve
Eigenschaft *f* property
~/abhäsive abhesiveness
~/abweisende repellency
~/additive additive property
~/extensive extensive property
~/innere intrinsic property
~/intensive intensive property
~/kolligative colligative property *(depending only on the number of particles)*
~/konstitutive constitutive property
~/ölabweisende oil repellency
~/periodische periodic property *(of the elements)*
~/physikalische physical property
~/thermische thermal property
~/wasserabweisende water repellency
Eigenschaften *fpl*/**backtechnische** *(food)* baking properties (characteristics)
~/filtertechnische filtration properties
Eigenschwingung *f* normal (fundamental) vibration, normal mode of vibration *(of molecules)*
Eigenwasseraufbereitung *f*/**häusliche** *(hyd)* home water treatment
Eigenwasserversorgung *f (hyd)* individual water supply
Eigenwert *m* eigenvalue
Eigenzustand *m* eigenstate

Eiglobulin *n* egg globulin
Eignung *f* suitability
Eiklar *n* [egg] albumen, egg white, glair[e]
Eimer *m* bucket *(as of an elevator)*
einachsig [/optisch] [optically] uniaxial
einarbeiten 1. to work in, to intermingle *(constituents of a mix)*; 2. to work [in], to deal with, to dummy *(a plating bath)*
einatomar *s.* einatomig
einatomig monoatomic
Einatomigkeit *f* monoatomicity
Ein-Aus-Regelung *f* automatic-start-and-stop control
Einbadchrombrühe *f (tann)* one-bath chrome liquor
Einbadchromgerbung *f* one-bath [chrome] tannage
Einbadchrom[ier]verfahren *n (text)* one-bath chroming method
Einbadgerbung *f s.* Einbadchromgerbung
Einbadverfahren *n (text)* one-bath (single-bath) method
Einbandtrockner *m* single-conveyor dryer
einbasig monobasic, monoprotic *(acid)*; monobasic, monoacid *(base)*
Einbau *m* 1. insertion *(as of atoms into a lattice)*; incorporation *(as of nutrients into organic substance)*; 2. *s.* Einbauten
~ **von Deuterium (schwerem Wasserstoff)** deuteration
einbauen to insert *(e.g. atoms into a lattice)*; to incorporate *(e.g. nutrients into organic substance)*
Einbaugenerator *m* built-in producer
Einbauteil *n* fill member *(as of a cooling tower)*
Einbauten *mpl* internals, *(in a cooling tower also)* pack, fill, *(in a rotary dryer also)* [internal] flights; baffles *(for directing a fluid stream)*
einbetonieren to incorporate into concrete *(radioactive waste)*
einbetten to embed, to imbed; *(met)* to pack *(as with a carburizing powder)*; to embed *(completely in a medium)*; to encapsulate *(by dip coating)*; to pot *(in a container)*
Einbettentsalzung *f (hyd)* monobed deionization
Einbettungsmasse *f (ceram)* ground-mass, matrix; *(met)* packing material
Einbettungsmittel *n (met)* packing material; embedding medium *(microscopy)*
Einbettungswerkstoff *m* embedding material; *(met)* packing material
einbindig monovalent, univalent *(relating to homopolar bonds)*
einblasen to blow in
Einblasen *n***/seitliches** *(met)* side blowing
Einbrand *m (ceram)* 1. firing-on, maturing; 2. *s.* Einmalbrand
Einbrennemaillack *m*, **Einbrennemaille** *f* stoving (baking) enamel
einbrennen to burn in *(e.g. pigments)*, *(esp ceram)* to fire on, to mature, *(esp coat)* to stove, to bake; *(spectr)* to burn in
Einbrennen *n* burning-in *(as of pigments)*, *(esp ceram)* firing-on, maturing, *(esp coat)* stoving, baking; *(spectr)* burn-in
Einbrennfarbe *f* stoving (baking) paint
Einbrennlack *m* stoving (baking) varnish; *(if pigmented:)* stoving (baking) lacquer
Einbrennlackierung *f* 1. stove enamelling; 2. stoving (baking) finish
Einbrennofen *m (coat)* stoving (baking) oven, stove
Einbrennverfahren *n (coat)* stoving process; *(ceram)* firing-on process
einbringen to introduce, to place; *(pap)* to pack *(the chips)*
~**/Beton** to pour (place) concrete
Einbringen *n* introduction, placing
~ **der Hackschnitzel** *(pap)* chip packing (filling)
~**/nesterweises** *(agric)* spot application
Einbringtiefe *f (agric)* depth of application
Eindampfapparat *m* evaporator
eindampfen to evaporate, to concentrate by evaporation, to boil down, to inspissate
~**/zur Trockne** to evaporate to dryness
Eindampfen *n* evaporation, concentration by evaporation, boildown, boiling-down, inspissation
Eindampfer *m* evaporator
Eindampfpfanne *f* evaporation (evaporating) pan
Eindecker *m*, **Eindeckersiebmaschine** *f* single-deck[ed] screen
Eindickapparat *m s.* Eindicker 1.
Eindickbecken *n (hyd)* thickening tank
Eindickbütte *f (pap)* draining tank (chest), drainer
eindicken to thicken, to concentrate, *(esp by evaporation:)* to boil down, to inspissate, *(esp food)* to condense; *(pap)* to decker; *(coat)* to body
~ **durch Erhitzen (Hitzebehandlung)** *s.* ~/thermisch
~**/thermisch** to heat-thicken; *(coat)* to heat-body; to durmolize, to calorize *(e.g. linseed oil)*
Eindicker *m* 1. thickener, concentrator; *(pap)* decker; 2. *s.* Eindickmittel
~ **mit Mittelsäule** centre-column[-supported] thickener
~ **mit Randantrieb** traction thickener
Eindickfilter *n* filter thickener
Eindickmaschine *f (pap)* decker
Eindickmittel *n* thickening agent, thickener, viscosifier
Eindickung *f* thickening, concentration, *(esp by evaporation)* boildown, inspissation, *(esp food)* condensation; *(pap)* deckering; *(coat)* bodying
~ **durch Flotation** *(hyd)* floatation thickening
~**/vorherige** initial thickening
Eindickungsgrad *m* degree of thickening
Eindickungsrate *f (hyd)* sludge dewatering rate
Eindickungsverhinderungsmittel *n (coat)* antilivering agent
Eindick[ungs]zone *f* thickening region (section, zone), *(hyd also)* sludge zone
eindiffundieren to diffuse in[wards]

eindimensional one-dimensional, unidimensional
eindosen *(food)* to can, to tin
eindrehen *(ceram)* to jolley
eindringen to penetrate, to permeate, *(of liquids or gases also)* to diffuse; *(geol)* to intrude
Eindringen *n* penetrating, penetration, permeation, *(of liquids or gases also)* diffusion; *(geol)* intrusion
Eindringfähigkeit *f s.* Eindringvermögen
Eindringhärte *f s.* Eindruckhärte
Eindringtheorie *f* penetration theory *(of mass transfer)*
Eindringtiefe *f* [depth of] penetration; depth of indentation *(hardness testing)*
Eindringungsmittel *n (text)* penetrating agent
Eindringvermögen *n* penetrating ability, penetrativity, permeativity
eindrücken 1. to indent; 2. to blow in *(e.g. a gas into a vessel)*
Eindruckhärte *f* indentation hardness *(materials testing)*
eindunsten to evaporate down
Eindunstung *f* evaporation, evaporating-down
~/solare solar evaporation
einebnen to level
Einebnungsstange *f* coal leveller bar, levelling bar
Einebnungsvorrichtung *f* levelling device
ein-ein-wertig uniunivalent
Einelektronbindung *f s.* Einelektronenbindung
Einelektronenatom *n* one-electron atom
Einelektronenaustauschreaktion *f* one-electron transfer process *(in radical reactions)*
Einelektronenbindung *f* one-electron (single-electron) bond, singlet link[age]
Einelektronenoperator *m* one-electron operator
Einelektronenorbital *n* one-electron orbital
Einelektronenreduktion *f* one-electron reduction
einengen to evaporate to low (small) bulk, to concentrate to small volume
Einetagenpresse *f* single-daylight (one-daylight) press
Einfachbindung *f* single [covalent] bond
Einfachbindungsorbital *n* single-bond orbital
Einfachfilter *n* single-medium filter
Einfachform *f s.* Einfachwerkzeug
Einfachgarn *n* single yarn
einfachnegativ [geladen] uninegative
einfachpositiv [geladen] unipositive
Einfachsalz *n* simple (single) salt
Einfachstreuung *f (phys ch)* single scattering
Einfachsubstitution *f* monosubstitution
Einfachwalzwerk *n* single-roll mill
Einfachwerkzeug *n (plast)* single-impression mould, single-cavity mould (tool)
einfachwirkend single-acting *(e.g. pump)*
Einfachzucker *m* simple sugar, monosaccharide
Einfahrhub *m* return stroke
einfallend incident *(rays)*
Einfallstelle *f (plast)* sink mark, sunk spot *(a moulding defect)*
Einfall[s]winkel *m* angle of incidence
Einfang *m (nucl)* capture
einfangen *(nucl)* to capture
Einfangquerschnitt *m (nucl)* capture cross section
einfarbig *(phat)* monochromatic, monochrome
einfetten to grease
einfließen to flow in
~ lassen to infuse, to run in
Einfließen *n* inflow
Einfluß *m* influence
~/dirigierender directive influence
Einflüsse *mpl***/äußere** outside influences
Einformen *n***/maschinelles** *(ceram)* machine moulding
einfrieren 1. *(food)* to freeze; 2. to freeze *(chemical reactions)*; 3. *(glass, plast, rubber)* to exhibit transition
Einfrieren *n* 1. *(food)* freezing; 2. freezing *(of chemical reactions)*; 3. *(glass, plast, rubber)* transition
Einfriergebiet *n (plast)* transition interval
Einfrierpunkt *m s.* Einfriertemperatur
Einfriertemperatur *f (glass, plast, rubber)* glass [transition] temperature, transition temperature, Tg point, Tg
einfügen to insert *(e.g. atoms into interstitial lattice sites)*
Einfügen *n* insertion *(as of atoms into interstitial lattice sites)*
einführen to introduce
Einführung *f* introduction
Einführungsseil *n (pap)* leading-through tape, rope carrier
einfüllen to fill [in], to feed [in], to charge, to load
Einfülltrichter *m (lab)* chemical funnel; *(tech)* [feed, charge] hopper, loading (charging) hopper
Eingabe *f* food[ing]
Eingang *m (bioch)* entry site, acceptor (recognition, decoding, aminoacyl-tRNA) site
Eingangstemperatur *f* inlet temperature
eingebaut built-in
eingeben to feed, to charge
eingehen 1. to go *(into a product)*; 2. *(text)* to shrink, to contract
~/eine Bindung to bond
~/eine chemische Reaktion to enter into [chemical] reaction
~/eine [chemische] Verbindung to enter into chemical combination (union), to combine
eingelagert intercalated, intercalary *(molecules, ions)*
Ein-Gen-ein-Enzym-Hypothese *f (bioch)* one gene-one enzyme hypothesis
Ein-Gen-ein-Messenger-Theorie *f (bioch)* one gene-one polypeptide chain concept
eingeschliffen ground-in
eingesprengt *(geol)* disseminated
eingetauscht *(soil)* echange-adsorbed
Eingrabtest *m (text)* soil burial test

Eingrubenäschersystem *n (tann)* one-pit liming system
eingruppieren to classify
Eingruppierung *f* classification
Einhängegestell *n (el ch)* plating rack
Einhängekühler *m* finger-type condenser, acorn (cold finger) condenser, cold finger
Einheit *f* 1. unit *(as of measuring values)*; 2. *(tech)* unit, set
~/chemische chemical unit
~ der Röntgendosis X-ray unit
~ der Stromstärke unit of current
~/difunktionelle difunctional (bifunctional) unit, D unit *(a structural element of macromolecules)*
~/elementare elementary unit
~/internationale international unit, I.U. *(of biochemically active substances)*
~/molekulare molecular unit
~/monofunktionelle monofunctional unit, M unit *(of macromolecules)*
~/monomere monomer unit
~/morphologische morphological unit
~/sich wiederholende repeat[ing] unit
~/ständig wiederkehrende repeat[ing] unit
~/strukturelle structural unit
~/tetrafunktionelle tetrafunctional unit, Q unit *(of macromolecules)*
~/trifunktionelle trifunctional unit, T unit *(of macromolecules)*
~/wiederkehrende repeat[ing] unit
Einheiten *fpl* **/atomare** atomic units [Hartree], Hartree units *(based on mass and charge of the electron and Planck's constant divided by 2π)*
einheitlich uniform, *(relating to composition also)* homogeneous
~/chemisch chemically uniform
~/vollkommen uniform throughout
Einheitlichkeit *f* uniformity, *(relating to composition also)* homogeneity
~/chemische chemical uniformity
Einheitsfläche *f* unit area
Einheitszelle *f s.* Elementarzelle
Einhordendarre *f* single-floor (single-deck) kiln
Einhorn-Reaktion *f (org ch)* Einhorn (haloform) reaction
einhüllen to envelop, to enwrap; *(hyd)* to enmesh *(e.g. dirt particles)*; to encapsulate *(liquid drops)*
Einkammereindicker *m* single-compartment thickener, unit thickener
einkapseln to encapsulate; *(biot)* to microencapsulate, to prill *(an enzyme)*
einkerben to notch, to indent
einkernig mononuclear
einkochen 1. *(food)* to bottle, *(Am)* to can; 2. *s.* ~ lassen
~ lassen *(lab)* to boil down
Einkochen *n* 1. *(lab)* boildown, boiling-down; 2. *(food)* bottling, *(Am)* canning
Einkochglas *n (food)* preserving bottle, vacuum jar
Einkohlenstoffverbindung *f* one-carbon compound
Einkomponentensystem *n (phys ch)* unary (one-component) system; *(plast, coat)* one-component system, one-pack[age] system, single-pack[age] system
Einkornbeton *m* single-sized concrete
Einkornschüttung *f (hyd, filtr)* single-medium filter bed
Einkörperverdampfer *m* single-effect evaporator
Einkörperverdampfung *f* single-effect evaporation
Einkristall *m* single crystal, monocrystal
Einkristallaufnahme *f* crystallogram
Einkristallfaden *m* single-crystal filament
Einkristallfaser *f* single-crystal fibre, [crystal] whisker
Einkristallmonochromator *m* crystal monochromator
einlaben *(food)* to rennet
einladig *s.* einwertig
Einlage *f (pap)* filler [board], middle, centre, core *(of triplex board)*; *(plast)* insert
einlagern 1. to store; 2. *(cryst)* to insert, to include; to intercalate *(guest molecules between layers*
~/schichtförmig to interleave
~/zwischen Schichten to interleave
Einlagerung *f* 1. storing, storage; 2. *(cryst)* insertion, inclusion; intercalation *(of guest molecules between layers)*
Einlagerungsatom *n* interstitial [atom]
Einlagerungscarbid *n* interstitial carbide
Einlagerungsfremdatom *n* impurity interstitial, interstitial impurity atom
Einlagerungshydrid *n* interstitial hydride
Einlagerungslegierung *f* interstitial alloy
Einlagerungsmischkristall *m* interstitial [solid] solution
Einlagerungsphase *f* interstitial phase
Einlagerungsschicht *f* intercalated layer
Einlagerungsstruktur *f* interstitial structure
Einlagerungsverbindung *f* interstitial compound; intercalation compound
~/schichtförmig ausgebildete lamellar compound
~ 1. Stufe first-stage intercalation compound, stage 1 intercalation compound
~ 2. Stufe second-stage intercalation compound, stage 2 intercalation compound
~ 3. Stufe third-stage intercalation compound, stage 3 intercalation compound
Einlaß *m* inlet, intake
Einlaßkanal *m* inlet duct
Einlaßrohr *n* inlet (feed) pipe (tube)
Einlaßventil *n* inlet valve
Einlauf *m* 1. inlet, point of entry; 2. influent *(material)*
Einlaufbereich *m* inlet section (zone) *(as of a sedimentation tank)*
einlaufen 1. to flow in; 2. *(text)* to shrink, to contract
~ lassen to run in, to infuse

Einlaufen *n* 1. inflow; 2. *(text)* shrinkage, shrinking, contraction
einlaufend/nicht *(text)* non-shrinking, unshrinkable
Einlauföffnung *f* inlet port
Einlaufrohr *n* feed (influent) pipe (tube)
Einlaufstelle *f* point of entry, inlet
Einlaufverlust *m* entrance (entry) loss
Einlaufverteilerkasten *m* feed-splitter box
Einlegemaschine *f (glass)* batch charger (feeder)
Einlegevorbau *m (glass)* doghouse
Einlegevorrichtung *f s.* Einlegemaschine
Einlegewand *f (glass)* end (back, gable) wall
einleiten 1. to introduce, to pass in *(material)*; *(hyd)* to discharge, to run, to drain *(as into a sewer system)*; 2. to initiate, to start *(a reaction)*
~/ins Meer to dispose of to sea, to dispose of in the ocean *(waste products)*
~/Luft to introduce air, *(hyd also)* to entrain air
Einleitung *f* 1. introduction, passing-in *(of material)*; 2. initiation, start *(of a reaction)*
~ von Luft introduction of air, *(hyd also)* air entrainment (input)
Einleitungsbedingungen *fpl (hyd)* discharge standards (regulations), effluent limitations (restrictions)
Einleitungsrohr *n* inlet (feed) pipe (tube)
Einleitungsstelle *f* 1. *s.* Einlaufstelle; 2. *(hyd)* discharge point, point of waste-water discharge
~ eines Betriebs *(hyd)* plant (mill) outfall
Einling *m s.* Einkristall
Ein-Lösungsmittel-Verfahren *n (petrol)* single-solvent process
Einmachglas *n s.* Einkochglas
einmaischen *(ferm)* to mash
Einmaischverfahren *n (ferm)* single-mash process
Einmalbrand *m (ceram)* single fire (firing)
einmischen *(rubber)* to incorporate
Einmischung *f (rubber)* incorporation
einmitten to centre
Einmitten *n* centr[e]ing
Einmuldenunterschubrost *m* single-retort [underfeed] stoker
Einnährstoffdüngemittel *n* single-nutrient fertilizer
einnehmen 1. *(pharm)* to take; 2. to occupy *(e.g. the interstices in a lattice)*; to cover *(an area)*; to occupy *(a volume)*
einölen to oil; *(tann)* to anoint
einpacken to wrap, to pack[age]; *(met)* to pack *(with a carburizing powder)*
Einpackmittel *n (met)* packing material
Einpackpapier *n* wrapping (packing) paper, *(Am)* package (packaging) paper
einpegeln/sich to level off *(as of pH values)*
Einpendelmühle *f* single-roll mill
Einphasensystem *n* one-phase system, homogeneous system
Einphasenumesterung *f* random interesterification *(of fats)*
einpipettieren to pipette *(a liquid into a vessel)*
einpökeln to cure
Einpökeln *n* curing, cure
einpolar non-polar, homopolar, covalent *(bond)*
einprägen to indent; *(pap, text, tann)* to emboss, to goffer
einpressen to inject *(e.g. gas)*; *(pap, text, tann)* to emboss, to goffer; *(plast)* to mould in
Einpressen *n* injection *(as of gas)*; *(pap, text, tann)* embossing, goffering; *(plast)* moulding-in
~ von Wasser *(petrol)* water flooding
Einpreßteil *n (plast)* insert
einprotonig monoprotic, monobasic *(acid)*
einpudern to powder, to dust
Einrad-Karrenstäuber *m (agric)* wheelbarrow-type duster
einregeln to adjust
einreißen to tear
Einreißfestigkeit *f*, **Einreißwiderstand** *m* tear initiation strength
Einrichtung *f* installation, facility; arrangement; equipment
~/abwassertechnische *(hyd)* waste-water treatment installation (facility)
Einriß *m* tear
einrühren to stir in
Einsaatkultur *f (biot)* seed culture
Einsackstelle *f s.* Einfallstelle
einsalben *(pharm)* to rub with ointment, to smear
Einsalzeffekt *m* salting-in effect, diverse-ion effect
einsalzen 1. *(food)* to salt away (down), to rouse; 2. to salt in *(to improve the solubility of a substance by adding an electrolyte)*
~/trocken to dry-salt, to dry-cure
Einsatz *m* 1. application *(as of a chemical)*; 2. *(tech)* charging, feeding, batching; 3. *(met)* [carburized] case; 4. tray *(as of a desiccator or column)*; 5. *s.* Einsatzgut
Einsatzbad *n (met)* carburizing bath
Einsatzbecken *n (lab)* bench sink
Einsatzbehälter *m (ceram)* setter *(a piece of kiln furniture)*
Einsatzgas *n* feed gas
Einsatzgebiet *n* area (field) of application
Einsatzgemisch *n (met)* carburizing mixture
Einsatzgut *n* feed[stock], feed material, charge [stock], charging stock
~ für Krackverfahren cracking feed (stock, feedstock)
Einsatzhärtbarkeit *f (met)* case hardenability
Einsatzhärte *f (met)* case hardness
Einsatzhärtebad *n (met)* case-hardening bath
Einsatzhärtekasten *m (met)* case-hardening box
einsatzhärten *(met)* to case-harden
Einsatzhärten *n (met)* case-hardening
Einsatzhärteofen *m (met)* case-hardening furnace
Einsatzhärtungstiefe *f (met)* case depth
Einsatzheizkörper *m* cartridge heater
Einsatzkasten *m s.* Einsatzhärtekasten
Einsatzkohle *f* feed[-stock] coal

Einsatzmaterial *n s.* Einsatzgut
Einsatzmenge *f* amount (quantity) required, dose, dosage, input
Einsatzmittel *n (met)* case-hardening material (compound)
Einsatzofen *m (petrol)* charge heater
Einsatzöl *n (petrol)* charge oil
Einsatzplatte *f (chromat)* chamber plate
Einsatzpulver *n (met)* carburizing (cementing) powder
Einsatzrichtlinie *f* specification
Einsatzschicht *f***/gehärtete** *(met)* [hardened] case
Einsatzschichtdicke *f (met)* case thickness
Einsatzstahl *m* case-hardening steel; case-hardened steel
~/legierter alloy case-hardening steel
Einsatzstoff *m s.* Einsatzgut
Einsatztiefe *f (met)* case depth
Einsatztopf *m (met)* case-hardening pot
Einsatztulpe *f (lab)* crucible adapter
Einsatzverchromen *n* chromizing, chromium cementation
Einsatzverzögerung *f (rubber)* delayed action
einsaugen to suck [in, up], to imbibe, to absorb
Einsaugen *n* suction, imbibition, absorption
einsäurig monoacid, monobasic *(base)*
Einschachtgenerator *m (coal)* single-shaft gasifier
Einschalenanalysenwaage *f* single-pan analytical balance
einschalten to switch on, to turn on
Einscheibenrefiner *m (pap)* single-disk refiner
Einscheibensicherheitsglas *n* tempered safety glass
Einschichtenfilter *n* single-medium filter
Einschichtenfilterbett *n* single-medium bed (layer)
Einschichtensicherheitsglas *n s.* Einscheibensicherheitsglas
einschieben to insert *(atoms or groups)*
~/sich to insert *(of atoms or groups*
Einschiebung *f s.* Einschub
Einschlagpapier *n* wrapping (packing) paper, wrapper
Einschlagseidenpapier *n* tissue wrapper (wrapping paper), wrapping (packing, commercial) tissue
Einschlämmtechnik *f (chromat)* slurrying (slurry-packing) technique, high-pressure wet packing technique
einschleifen to grind in
einschleusen *(bioch)* to funnel
einschließen to enclose, to [en]trap, to include, to occlude; to enmesh *(particles as in a network)*
~/in Mikrokapseln *(biot)* to microencapsulate, to prill *(an enzyme)*
Einschluß *m* enclosure, entrapment, inclusion, occlusion; enmeshment *(of particles as in a network)*
~/enallogener *s.* ~/exogener
~/endogener *(geol)* cognate inclusion, autolith
~/exogener *(geol)* exogenous enclosure, xenolith
~/fremder *s.* ~/exogener
~/homöogener *s.* ~/endogener
~ in Gelmatrix *(biot)* gel enclosure, incorporation into a gel
~ in Mikrokapseln *(biot)* [micro]encapsulation, prilling *(of an enzyme)*
Einschlußflockung *f (hyd)* sweep-floc mechanism
Einschlußmittel *n* embedding medium *(microscopy)*
Einschlußverbindung *f* inclusion compound (complex), enclosure compound
einschmelzen 1. to fuse (seal) in *(e.g. in a glass tube)*; 2. *(met)* to melt [down]
Einschmelzen *n* 1. fusing-in, sealing-in *(e.g. in a glass tube)*; 2. *(met)* melting[-down], meltdown
Einschmelzrohr *n* sealing (sealed) tube
~ nach Carius Carius (bomb) tube
Einschmelzung *f* 1. magmatic digestion; 2. *s.* Einschmelzen
einschmieren to smear; *(tann)* to dub
Einschneckenextruder *m* single-screw extruder (extruding machine)
Einschnürung[sstelle] *f* constriction, waist, throat *(as of a tube)*, *(esp in flow measurement:)* vena contracta
Einschrittreaktion *f* one-step reaction
einschrumpfen to shrink, to contract
Einschrumpfung *f* shrinkage, contraction
Einschub *m* insertion *(of atoms or groups)*; *(bioch)* intercalation *(of planar ring systems between the stacked bases of nucleic acids)*
~ des Monomeren monomer insertion
Einschubheizkörper *m* cartridge heater
Einschubreaktion *f* insertion reaction
einschütten to fill in; *(tech)* to charge, to load, to feed [in]
Einschütttrichter *m* [feed, charge] hopper, loading (charging) hopper
Einschwemmungshorizont *m (soil)* illuvial horizon
einseitig one-sided
einseitigglatt *(pap)* glazed on one side, machine-glazed
einsetzbar applicable
Einsetzbarkeit *f* applicability
einsetzen 1. to apply *(e.g. a certain chemical)*; 2. to charge, to feed, to batch *(a certain quantity)*; 3. to insert, to place in *(mechanically)*; *(ceram)* to set; 4. *(met)* to carburize; 5. to start *(of a reaction)*
~/im Salzbad *s.* ~/in flüssigen Mitteln
~/in festen Mitteln *(met)* to pack-carburize
~/in flüssigen Mitteln *(met)* to liquid-carburize, to bath-carburize
~/in gasförmigen Mitteln *(met)* to gas-carburize
~/in Zementationskästen *(met)* to box-carburize
Einsetzen *n* 1. application *(as of a certain chemical)*; charging, feeding, batching *(of a certain quantity)*; 2. insertion *(mechanically)*; *(ceram)* setting; 3. *(met)* carburizing, carburization; 4. start, onset *(of a reaction)*

~ **im Salzbad** *s.* ~ in flüssigen Mitteln
~ **in festen Mitteln** *(met)* solid[-pack] carburizing, pack carburizing
~ **in flüssigen Mitteln** *(met)* liquid[-salt] carburizing, bath carburizing
~ **in gasförmigen Mitteln** *(met)* gas carburizing
~ **in Zementationskästen** *(met)* box carburizing
Einsetzmulde *f* charging box
einsickern to seep in, to trickle in, to soak in, to infiltrate
Einsickern *n* seepage, trickling, soaking, infiltration
einsinken to sink in
Einsitzventil *n* single-seat[ed] valve
einspänen *(tann)* to sawdust
einspannen to clamp, to fix, to attach
Einspannrahmen *m (plast)* clamping frame
einspeisen to charge, to feed [in]
Einspeisevorrichtung *f* feeder
Einspeisung *f* 1. charging, feeding; 2. charge, charging stock, feed[stock]
einspielen/sich to level off *(as of pH value)*
Einsprengling *m (geol)* inset, phenocryst
Einsprengung *f (geol)* dissemination
Einspritzblock *m* [sample] injection port, injection block *(gas chromatography)*
Einspritzdruck *m* injection pressure
einspritzen to inject, *(plast also)* to mould in
Einspritzkondensator *m* jet (wet) condenser
Einspritzstelle *f (chromat)* injection site, [sample] injection port
Einspritzsystem *n (chromat)* autoinjector
Einspritzteil *n (plast)* insert
Einspritzung *f* injection
Einspritzventil *n (chromat)* injection valve
Einspritzvorrichtung *f (chromat)* injector
einstäuben to dust, to powder
Einsteigluke *f*, **Einsteigöffnung** *f* manhole, manway
Einsteigschacht *m (hyd)* manhole
Einstein *n* Einstein, E *(1 mole of photons)*
Einstein-Gleichung *f* Einstein equation
Einsteinium *n* Es einsteinium
einstellen to adjust *(e.g. instruments)*; to standardize *(chemicals)*
~**/auf den Nullpunkt** to zero
~**/eine Lösung auf N** to set a solution to N
~**/sauer** to acidify
~**/sich** to establish *(as of equilibrium)*
Einstellthermometer *n* adjustable-zero thermometer
Einstelltränkung *f* butt treatment *(wood preservation)*
Einstellung *f* adjustment *(as of instruments)*; standardization *(of chemicals)*; establishment *(of chemical equilibrium)*
~ **des pH-Werts** pH adjustment
Einstoffkraftstoff *m* monofuel
Einstoffmasse *f*, **Einstoffscherben** *m (ceram)* single-component (single-material) body
Einstoffsystem *n* unary (one-component) system
Einstofftreibstoff *m* monofuel
Einstoffversprühung *f* single-fluid atomization
Einstoffzerstäubung *f s.* Einstoffversprühung
Einstrahlgerät *n (spectr)* single-beam instrument
Einstrang-DNA *f s.* Einzelstrang-DNA
einsträngig single-strand[ed]
Einstrangkette *f* single-strand chain *(conveying)*
einströmen to flow in
Einströmen *n* inflow
Einströmgeschwindigkeit *f* rate of inflow
Einströmrohr *n* influent pipe
Einstufen[holländer]bleiche *f (pap)* single-stage bleaching
Einstufenhomogenisierung *f* single-stage homogenization
Einstufenreaktion *f* single-step (one-step) reaction
Einstufenverdampfer *m* single-effect evaporator
Einstufenverdampfung *f* single-effect evaporation
Einstufenverfahren *n* one-stage (one-step) process; *(plast)* one-shot process
einstufig single-stage, single-step, one-stage, one-step
Ein-Substrat-Enzym *n* enzyme catalyzing one-substrate reactions
Ein-Substrat-Mechanismus *m (bioch)* one-substrate mechanism
Ein-Substrat-Reaktion *f (bioch)* one-substrate reaction
einsumpfen *(ceram)* to soak, to wet
eintauchen to dip, to plunge, to immerse, to immerge
Eintauchen *n* dip[ping], plunging, immersion
Eintauchkolorimeter *n* immersion (dipping) colorimeter
Eintauchnutsche *f* immersion filter tube
Eintauchrefraktometer *n* immersion (dipping) refractometer
Eintauchrohr *n* immersion pipe (tube)
Eintauchtiefe *f* [depth of] submergence; *(distil)* static submergence
Eintauchverhältnis *n* submergence ratio
Eintauchwalze *f* immersion roll
Eintauchwalzentrockner *m* dip-feed drum dryer
Eintauschstärke *f (soil)* replacing power
einteigen to dough [in]
einteilen to classify; to divide *(e.g. a scale)*
~**/in Abstände** to space
~**/in Grade** to graduate
~**/nach Korn[größen]klassen** to size
Einteilung *f* classification; division *(as of a scale)*
• **mit [genauer] ~ versehen** to graduate, to scale
~ **nach dem Inkohlungsgrad** rank classification *(of coals)*
Einteilungssystem *n* classification system
Eintrag *m* 1. charge, charging stock, feed[stock], feed material, load; *(pap)* furnish; 2. charging, feeding, loading, introduction *(of material into a reactor)*, *(esp lab)* placing *(in a vessel)*; *(hyd)* transfer *(of oxygen into water)*; *(pap)* furnishing; input *(of matter or energy into a system)*
~**/anthropogener** anthropogenic input *(into the environment)*

eintragen 1. to charge, to feed [in], to load, to introduce *(material into a reactor)*, *(esp lab)* to place *(in a vessel)*; *(hyd)* to transfer *(oxygen into water)*; *(pap)* to furnish; 2. to plot *(in a coordinate system)*; to register *(a trademark)*
Eintragkasten *m* feed box
Eintragmenge *f* **in der Zeiteinheit** rate of feeding, feed rate
Eintragöffnung *f* charging door (hole), feed inlet (hole)
Eintragrohr *n* feed pipe (tube)
Eintragseite *f* feed end
Eintragverteilerkasten *m* feed-splitter box
Eintragvorrichtung *f* feeding device, feeder
Eintragzelle *f* entry lock, inlet sluice
eintreten 1. to enter *(of material being charged)*; 2. to occur *(of an event)*
Eintritt *m* 1. entry, entrance *(of material)*; 2. *s.* Eintrittsstelle; 3. occurrence *(of an event)*
Eintrittsfenster *n (spectr)* entrance aperture (port)
Eintrittsöffnung *f* inlet [port], intake
Eintrittsspalt *m* entrance slit *(of a prism spectrograph)*
Eintrittsstelle *f* point of entry, inlet, intake
Eintrittsstrom *m* inlet stream
Eintrittstemperatur *f* inlet temperature
Eintrittsverlust *m* entry (entrance) loss
eintrocknen to dry [up]
Einwaage *f* weighed portion
einwägen to weigh in
Einwalzenbrecher *m* single-roll crusher
Einwalzenmühle *f*, **Einwalzenstuhl** *m* single-roll mill; *(coat)* uniroll mill
Einwalzentrockner *m* single-drum dryer
einwandern to migrate in *(as of ions)*
einwässern to steep, to soak
Einwässern *n* steeping, steep[age], soaking
einwecken *s.* einkochen
Einwegbehälter *m* non-returnable container, single-trip (one-trip) container
Einwegflasche *f* single-trip (one-trip) bottle
Einweghahn *m* single-bore stopcock
einweichen to steep, to soak
Einweichen *n* steeping, steep[age], soaking
~/übermäßiges oversteeping *(of malt)*
Einweichflüssigkeit *f* steeping liquor, *(text also)* steep
Einweichkufe *f (text)* steeping pan
Einweichsektion *f (petrol)* soaking section *(of a pipe furnace)*
Einweichtrog *m (text)* steeping pan
Einweichwasser *n (ferm)* steeping water
einwerfen *(tech)* to load, to charge, to feed
einwertig monovalent, univalent *(element)*; monobasic, monoprotic *(acid)*; monobasic, monoacid *(base)*; monohydric *(alcohol)*
Einwertigkeit *f* monovalence, monovalency, univalence, univalency *(of an element)*; monobasicity *(of an acid or base)*
einwickeln to wrap
Einwickelpapier *n s.* Einschlagpapier
einwiegen *s.* einwägen
einwirken to act
~ auf/störend to interfere with, to affect
~ lassen/aufeinander to react
Einwirkung *f* action
Einwirkungsdauer *f* exposure (contact) time, duration of exposure
Einwirkungsstelle *f* emission sink, receptor area *(for pollutants)*
Einwirkungszeit *f s.* Einwirkungsdauer
Einwohnergleichwert *m (hyd)* population equivalent
Einwurföffnung *f* charging hole (door), feed hole (inlet)
einzählig *s.* einzähnig
einzähnig monodentate, unidentate *(coordination chemistry)*
Einzeldosis *f (pharm)* single dose
Einzeldünger *m* straight (single) fertilizer
Einzeldüngung *f* straight fertilization
Einzelelektrode *f* single electrode, half-cell, half-element
Einzelenzym *n (bioch)* individual enzyme
Einzelfaden *m (glass)* basic fibre
Einzelfaser *f* single (individual) fibre • **in Einzelfasern zerlegen** to defibre, to defibrate, to reduce to fibres, to shred, *(Am also)* to [de]fiberize
Einzelfermentation *f (biot)* single-stage fermentation
Einzelglied *n* member
Einzelheizer *m (rubber)* unit vulcanizer (press), watch-case curing press, individual curing unit (press)
Einzelhelix *f (bioch)* single-strand[ed] helix
Einzelion *n* single ion
Einzelionenaktivität *f* single-ion activity
Einzelkolonie *f (biot)* single colony
Einzelkorngefüge *n (soil)* single-grained structure
Einzelkornsedimentation *f* settling of discrete particles
Einzelkornstruktur *f s.* Einzelkorngefüge
Einzelkristall *m s.* Einkristall
Einzellerprotein *n (biot)* single-cell protein, SCP
~/texturiertes texture microbial protein, TMP
Einzellinie *f (spectr)* single line
Einzelnährstoffdüngemittel *n s.* Einzeldünger
Einzelofen *m (ceram)* individual kiln
Einzelpeaktrennung *f (chromat)* peak splitting *(undesired)*
Einzelpotential *n* single[-electrode] potential
Einzelprobe *f* single sample, sampling (sample) unit
Einzelring *m (nomencl)* single (individual) ring
Einzelschritt *m* single step
Einzelstrang *m* single strand
Einzelstrangbruch *m (biot)* single-strand break
Einzelstrang-DNA *f* single-strand[ed] DNA

einzelsträngig single-strand[ed]
Einzelwasserversorgung *f (hyd)* individual water supply
Einzelzelle *f (biot)* single (individual) cell
einziehen *(pap)* to put on *(a wire screen)*
~/in sich to absorb *(a fluid)*
Einzugsgebiet *n (hyd)* catchment [area, basin]
Einzugswinkel *m* angle of nip *(of a roll crusher)*
Einzugszone *f* feed zone *(of an extruder)*
einzwängen to squeeze *(e.g. atoms into interstices)*
ein-zwei-wertig unibivalent
Einzylinderpumpe *f* single-cylinder pump
Einzylinderschermaschine *f (plast)* single-shearing machine
Eirich-Mischer *m (ceram)* Eirich mixer *(a wet pan)*
Eis *n* ice; *(food)* ice cream
~/gestoßenes (zerkleinertes) chopped (crushed) ice
Eisbad *n* ice bath
Eisblock *m* ice cake
Eisblumenbildung *f (coat)* frosting, *(caused by gas fumes also)* gas checking; *(plast)* frosting *(a defect)*
Eisblumenglas *n* frosted glass
Eisbordeaux *n (dye)* ice bordeaux
Eisen *n* Fe iron
~/dreiwertiges trivalent (ferric) iron
~/nichthämgebundenes non-haem iron
~/pyrophores (reduziertes) pyrophoric iron *(prepared by hydrogen reduction)*
~/zweiwertiges bivalent (divalent, ferrous) iron
α-**Eisen** *n* alpha iron
β-**Eisen** *n* beta iron
γ-**Eisen** *n* gamma iron
δ-**Eisen** *n* delta iron
Eisenablauf *m* iron runoff
Eisenabscheider *m* tramp-iron magnet (magnetic separator)
Eisenabstich *m* 1. iron tapping; 2. *s.* Eisenabstichloch
Eisenabstichloch *n* iron taphole (tapping hole, notch)
Eisenabstichrinne *f* iron runner
Eisen(II)-acetat *n* iron(II) acetate, ferrous acetate
Eisenalaun *m* iron alum *(any of several salts $Me^{I}Fe(SO_4)_2 \cdot 12\ H_2O$)*
Eisenammoniakalaun *m s.* Ammoniumeisenalaun
Eisen(III)-ammoniumcitrat *n***/braunes** *(pharm)* iron-ammonium citrate brown
Eisen(III)-ammoniumoxalat *s.* Ammoniumeisen(III)-oxalat
eisenarm poor in iron, low-iron
Eisenarsenid *n* iron arsenide
Eisenauslauf *m s.* Eisenablauf
Eisenausscheider *m s.* Eisenabscheider
Eisenbahnkesselwagen *m*, **Eisenbahntankwagen** *m* rail tank [car], tank car (wagon)
Eisenbakterien *npl* iron[-oxidizing] bacteria, iron-depositing bacteria, iron oxidizers (depositors) *(Leptothrix, Crenothrix, and Gallionelia specc.)*
Eisenbasis/auf iron-base
Eisenbeize *f (dye)* iron [acetate] liquor, black liquor (mordant)
Eisenblaudruck *m* cyanotype, blueprint *(proper)*
~/negativer [negative] cyanotype
~/positiver positive cyanotype
Eisenblech *n* sheet iron, iron plate
~/verzinntes tin-plate, tinplate
Eisenbohrspäne *mpl* iron borings
Eisenborid *n* iron boride
Eisen(II)-bromid *n* iron(II) bromide, iron dibromide, ferrous bromide
Eisen(III)-bromid *n* iron(III) bromide, iron tribromide, ferric bromide
Eisencarbid *n* iron carbide; *(met)* Fe_3C cementite, cemented carbide, iron carbide
Eisen(II)-carbonat *n* iron(II) carbonate, ferrous carbonate
Eisen(II)-chelat *n* iron(II) chelate, ferrous chelate
Eisen(III)-chelat *n* iron(III) chelate, ferric chelate
Eisen(II)-chlorid *n* iron(II) chloride, iron dichloride, ferrous chloride
Eisen(II,III)-chlorid *n* iron(II,III) chloride, ferrosoferric chloride
Eisen(III)-chlorid *n* iron(III) chloride, iron trichloride, ferric chloride
Eisenchlorose *f* iron chlorosis *(a plant disease caused by iron deficiency)*
Eisen(III)-chromat *n* iron(III) chromate, ferric chromate
Eisen(III)-cyanid *n* iron(III) cyanide, iron tricyanide, ferric cyanide
Eisen-*bis*-cyclopentadienyl *n* dicyclopentadienyliron, ferrocene
Eisendi... *s. a.* Eisen(II)-...
Eisen(III)-dichromat *n* iron(III) dichromate, ferric dichromate
Eisen(III)-diphosphat *n* iron(III) diphosphate, ferric pyrophosphate
Eisen(II)-disulfid *n* iron(II) disulphide
Eisenerz *n* iron ore
~/phosphorarmes Bessemer ore *(containing less than 0.09 % phosphorus)*
Eisenfeilspäne *mpl* iron filings
Eisenfleck *m* iron speck *(a paper defect)*; iron stain *(in wood)*
Eisen(III)-Flockung *f (hyd)* ferric iron coagulation
Eisen(II)-fluorid *n* iron(II) fluoride, iron difluoride, ferrous fluoride
Eisen(III)-fluorid *n* iron(III) fluoride, iron trifluoride, ferric fluoride
Eisen(II)-formiat *n* iron(II) formate, ferrous formate
Eisen(III)-formiat *n* iron(III) formate, ferric formate
eisenfrei iron-free, non-ferrous
eisenführend *s.* eisenhaltig
Eisengehalt *m* iron content (level) • **mit hohem** ~ high-iron
Eisenglanz *m (min)* specular iron (ore), specularite *(a variety of haematite)*

Eisenglimmer *m* micaceous iron ore
Eisengruppe *f* iron group
eisenhaltig iron-containing, *(esp ores:)* iron-bearing
eisen(II)-haltig ferroan
eisen(III)-haltig ferrian
Eisen(III)-hämochromogen *n* ferrihaemochromogen, ferrihaemochrome
Eisen(II)-hämoglobin *n* ferrohaemoglobin
Eisen(III)-hämoglobin *n* ferrihaemoglobin
Eisen(II)-hexachloroplatinat(IV) *n* iron(II) hexachloroplatinate(IV), iron(II) chloroplatinate(IV)
Eisen(II)-hexacyanoferrat(II) *n* iron(II) hexacyanoferrate(II), iron(II) cyanoferrate(II)
Eisen(II)-hexacyanoferrat(III) *n* iron(II) hexacyanoferrate(III), iron(II) cyanoferrate(III)
Eisen(II,III)-hexacyanoferrat(III) *n* iron(II,III) hexacyanoferrate(III)
Eisen(III)-hexacyanoferrat(II) *n* iron(III) hexacyanoferrate(II), iron(III) cyanoferrate(II)
Eisenhochofen *m* iron blast furnace
Eisenhüttenwesen *n s.* Eisenmetallurgie
Eisen(II)-hydroxid *n* iron(II) hydroxide, ferrous hydroxide
Eisen(III)-hydroxid *n* iron(III) hydroxide, ferric hydroxide
Eisenhydroxidflocken *fpl (hyd)* iron [hydroxide] floc
Eisenhydroxidschlamm *m (hyd)* iron [hydroxide] sludge
Eisen(III)-hydroxidsol *n* iron(III) hydroxide sol, ferric hydroxide sol
Eisen(III)-hypophosphit *n* iron(III) hypophosphite, ferric hypophosphite, *iron(III) phosphinate
Eisen(II)-iodid *n* iron(II) iodide, iron diiodide, ferrous iodide
Eisenkatalysator *m* iron catalyst
Eisenkegel *m* cone *(of a blast furnace)*
Eisenkies *m (min)* pyrite, iron pyrite[s], mundic *(iron(II) disulphide)*
Eisenkitt *m* iron (rust, iron-rust) cement
Eisenklinker *m* blue brick
Eisenkontakt *m s.* Eisenkatalysator
Eisen(II)-lactat *n* iron(II) lactate, ferrous lactate
Eisenlegierung *f* iron alloy
Eisenmennige *f* stone red, red ochre (rudd)
Eisenmetall *n* ferrous metal
Eisenmetallurgie *f* ferrous (iron) metallurgy
Eisenmeteorit *m* iron meteorite, meteoric iron, [holo]siderite
Eisenmonosulfid *n s.* Eisen(II)-sulfid
Eisenmonoxid *n s.* Eisen(II)-oxid
Eisen-Nickel-Kern *m s.* Nickeleisenkern
Eisennickelkies *m (min)* pentlandite *(an iron nickel sulphide)*
Eisen(II)-nitrat *n* iron(II) nitrate, ferrous nitrate
Eisen(III)-nitrat *n* iron(III) nitrate, ferric nitrate
Eisennitrid *n* iron nitride
Eisen(II)-orthoarsenat(V) *n* *iron(II) tetraoxoarsenate(V), ferrous arsenate
Eisen(III)-orthoarsenat(V) *n* *iron(III) tetraoxoarsenate(V), ferric arsenate
Eisen(II)-orthophosphat *n* iron(II) orthophosphate, ferrous orthophosphate, ferrous phosphate
Eisen(III)-orthophosphat *n* iron(III) orthophosphate, ferric orthophosphate, ferric phosphate
Eisen(II)-oxalat *n* iron(II) oxalate, ferrous oxalate
Eisenoxid *n* iron oxide, *(specif)* iron(II) oxide
Eisen(II)-oxid *n* iron(II) oxide, iron monooxide, ferrous oxide
Eisen(II,III)-oxid *n* iron(II,III) oxide, triiron tetraoxide, ferrosoferric oxide
Eisen(III)-oxid *n* iron(III) oxide, diiron trioxide, ferric oxide, ferric trioxide
Eisen(III)-oxidhydrat *n* hydrated iron(III) oxide, hydrated ferric oxide
Eisenoxidrot *n* iron oxide red, red oxide, chemical red
Eisenoxidschwarz *n* black rouge *(iron(II,III) oxide)*
Eisenoxygenase *f s.* Cytochromoxidase
Eisenpentacarbonyl *n* iron pentacarbonyl
Eisen(II)-perchlorat *n* iron(II) perchlorate, ferrous perchlorate
Eisenphosphattrübung *f* ferric phosphate haze *(of beer)*
Eisenphospid *n* iron phosphide
Eisen(II)-phthalocyanin *n* iron(II) phthalocyanine, ferrous phthalocyanine
Eisenporphyrin *n (bioch)* iron porphyrin
Eisenporphyrinenzym *n (bioch)* haem (iron porphyrin) enzyme
Eisenprotein *n (bioch)* iron protein
Eisenpulver *n* iron powder, powdered iron
Eisen(III)-pyrophosphat *n s.* Eisen(III)-diphosphat
Eisenquelle *f (pharm)* chalybeate spring
eisenreich rich in iron, high-iron
Eisen(III)-resinat *n* iron(III) resinate, ferric resinate
Eisen(II)-rhodanid *n s.* Eisen(II)-thiocyanat
Eisenrost *m* [iron] rust
Eisenrot *n* red bole *(iron(III) oxide)*
Eisen(II)-salz *n* iron(II) salt, ferrous salt
Eisen(III)-salz *n* iron(III) salt, ferric salt
Eisenschlamm *m* iron sludge
Eisenschmelzklinker *n* blue brick
Eisenschrott *m* scrap iron, ferrous scrap
Eisenschwamm *m* iron sponge, sponge iron
Eisenschwarz *n s.* Eisenoxidschwarz
Eisen-Schwefel-Protein *n* iron-sulphur protein
Eisen-Schwefel-Zentrum *n (bioch)* iron-sulphur centre
Eisen-Silber-Verfahren *n* silver-iron process, Vandyke (sepia negative) process, brownprint *(reprography)*
Eisen(II)-silicat *n* iron(II) silicate, ferrous silicate
Eisensilicid *n* iron silicide
Eisensinter *m (min)* iron sinter *(iron(III) orthoarsenate)*
Eisenspäne *mpl* iron chips

Eisenspat *m (min)* spathic iron [ore], siderite *(iron(II) carbonate)*
Eisenstein *m* ironstone *(a sedimentary rock rich in iron)*
Eisenstich *m s.* Eisenabstich
Eisen(II)-sulfat *n* iron(II) sulphate, ferrous sulphate
Eisen(III)-sulfat *n* iron(III) sulphate, ferric sulphate
Eisen(II)-sulfid *n* iron(II) sulphide, ferrous sulphide
Eisen(III)-sulfid *n* iron(III) sulphide, ferric sulphide
Eisen(II)-sulfit *n* iron(II) sulphite, ferrous sulphite
Eisentetracarbonyl *n* iron tetracarbonyl
Eisen(II)-thiocyanat *n* iron(II) thiocyanate, ferrous thiocyanate
Eisen(III)-thiocyanat *n* iron(III) thiocyanate, ferric thiocyanate
Eisen(II)-thiosulfat *n* iron(II) thiosulphate, ferrous thiosulphate
Eisentiegel *m* iron crucible
Eisentri... *s.* Eisen(III)-...
Eisen(II)-Verbindung *f* iron(II) compound, ferrous compound
Eisen(III)-Verbindung *f* iron(III) compound, ferric compound
Eisenvitriol *m (min)* iron vitriol, copperas, melanterite *(iron(II) sulphate 7-water)*
Eisenvitriol *n* iron vitriol, [green] copperas, green vitriol, iron(II) sulphate 7-water
Eisenwasser *n (pharm)* chalybeate water
Eisessig *m* glacial acetic acid
Eisfabrik *f* ice plant
Eisfarbe *f*, **Eisfarbstoff** *m* azoic dye, insoluble azo dye, *(Am also)* ice color
eisgekühlt ice-cooled
Eisglas *n* frosted glass
Eishydrat *n* gas hydrate, gas clathrate compound
Eiskalorimeter *n* ice calorimeter
~ nach Bunsen Bunsen ice calorimeter
eiskalt ice-cold
Eiskrem *f* ice cream
Eiskristall *m* ice crystal
Eiskühlung *f* ice cooling (refrigeration)
Eismaschine *f (food)* ice-cream freezer
Eismühle *f* ice crusher
Eispapier *n* ice paper
Eistein *m (min)* oolite *(chiefly calcium carbonate)*
Eiswasser *n* ice water
Eiweiß *n* 1. *(bioch)* protein *(for compounds s. under* Protein*)*; 2. *(food)* egg white, albumen, glair
Eiweiß... *s. a.* Protein...
Eiweißappretur *f (tann)* albumen finish
Eiweißchemiefaser *f (text)* protein man-made fibre
Eiweißchemiefaserstoff *m (text)* protein man-made fibre
Eiweißentzug *m (med)* protein deprivation
Eiweißfaktor *m***/tierischer** *(bioch)* extrinsic factor, vitamin B_{12}, *(historically:)* animal protein factor
Eiweißharnen *n (bioch)* proteinuria
Eiweißkörper *m (bioch)* protein
~/regenerierter natürlicher *(text)* regenerated naturally occurring protein
Eiweißleim *m* protein adhesive, glair
Eiweißmangel *m* protein deficiency
Eiweißrast *f (ferm)* protein rest
eiweißreich protein-rich
Eiweißspalter *m (text)* digester *(for protein stain removal)*
Eiweißstickstoff *m* protein nitrogen
Eiweißstoff *m s.* Protein
Eiweißtrübung *f* protein haze *(as of beer)*
Eiweißzucker *m* glycoprotein, glycoproteid
Ejektor *m* ejector, eductor
ekliptisch eclipsed, opposed *(stereochemistry)*
Eklogit *m* eclogite *(a metamorphic rock)*
Eklogithülle *f*, **Eklogitschale** *f (geoch)* eclogite shell
Eko *m s.* Ekonomiser
Ekonomiser *m* economizer, boiler feed preheater
Ektoenzym *n* ectoenzyme *(localized on the outer surface of the cell)*
Ektohormon *n* ectohormone, pheromone
Ektotoxin *n* exotoxin
Ektylharnstoff *m* ectylurea, 2-ethyl-*cis*-crotonylurea
E-Kupfer *n* electrolytic copper
Elaidin[is]ierung *f* elaidinization *(conversion of oleic acid into its trans isomer)*
Elaidinprobe *f (food)* elaidin test *(for detecting oleic acid)*
Elaidinsäure *f* elaidic acid, **trans*-octadec-9-enoic acid
Elain *n* olein, commercial oleic acid
Elainsäure *f* oleic acid, **cis*-octadec-9-enoic acid
Eläostearinsäure *f* elaeostearic acid, *octadeca-9,11,13-trienoic acid
Elast *m s.* Elastomer
Elastikator *m* elasticator *(a plasticizing agent)*
Elastin *n* elastin *(a scleroprotein)*
elastisch elastic
Elastizität *f* elasticity; *(tann)* run
Elastizitätsgrenze *f* elastic limit
~/technische yield strength
Elastizitätsmodul *m* modulus of elasticity, Young's modulus [of elasticity], elastic modulus
Elastizitätsprüfung *f* elasticity test
elastomer elastomeric
Elastomer[e] *n* elastomer
Elastomerfaser *f* elastomeric fibre, *(Am)* snap-back fiber
Elastomerfaserstoff *m* elastomeric fibre, *(Am)* snap-back fiber
Elbs-Reaktion *f* Elbs reaction *(formation of anthracene derivatives)*
Elefantenhautbildung *f (rubber)* crazing
elektrisch electric[al]
~ neutral uncharged
Elektrizität *f* electricity
Elektrizitätsleiter *m* conductor of electricity, electric conductor

Elektrizitätsmenge *f* quantity of electricity
Elektroabscheider *m s.* Elektrofilter
Elektroabscheidung *f s.* Elektrofiltration
Elektroaffinität *f* electron affinity
elektroaktiv electroactive
Elektroanalyse *f* electroanalysis
elektroanalytisch electroanalytical
Elektroätzen *n* electrolytic etch[ing]
Elektrobeheizung *f* electric heating
Elektrobrenner *m* electric burner
Elektrochemie *f* electrochemistry
~/technische industrial electrochemistry
Elektrochemiker *m* electrochemist
elektrochemisch electrochemical • **auf elektrochemischem Wege** by an electrochemical route
Elektrochromatographie *f* electrochromatography, electropherography
Elektrode *f* electrode
~/grüne green electrode *(before baking)*
~/ionenselektive (ionensensitive) ion-selective (ion-sensitive) electrode
~/mehrfache multiple electrode
~ **nach Söderberg** *s.* ~/selbst[ein]brennende
~/reversible reversible electrode
~/ringförmige annular electrode
~/selbstbackende *s.* ~/selbst[ein]brennende
~/selbst[ein]brennende Soderberg [continuous] electrode, [Soderberg] self-baking electrode
~/umkehrbare *s.* ~/reversible
~/vorgebackene (vorgebrannte) prebaked electrode
Elektrodekantation *f* electrodecantation
elektrodekantiert electrodecanted
Elektrodekantierung *f* electrodecantation
Elektrodenabstand *m* interelectrode distance
Elektrodenkammer *f* electrode chamber (compartment) *(of an electrodialyser)*
Elektrodenkohle *f* electrode carbon
elektrodenlos electrodeless
Elektrodenmasse *f* electrode paste
~ **für Söderberg-Elektroden** Soderberg paste
~/grüne (rohe) green paste
Elektrodenmaterial *n* electrode material
Elektrodenpech *n* electrode pitch
Elektrodenpotential *n* electrode potential
~/formales formal electrode potential
Elektrodenreaktion *f* electrode reaction
Elektrodenspannung *f* electrode voltage
Elektrodenstampfmasse *f s.* Elektrodenmasse
Elektrodenwerkstoff *m s.* Elektrodenmaterial
Elektrodenzerstäubung *f s.* Elektrodispersion
Elektrodialysator *m* electrodialyser
~ **nach Pauli** Pauli electrodialyser
Elektrodialyse *f* electrodialysis, ED
Elektrodialyseanlage *f* electrodialysis unit
Elektrodialysezelle *f* electrodialysis cell
Elektrodispersion *f (coll)* electrodispersing, electrodispersion, electrical dispersion *(of metals)*
Elektroendosmose *f* electro[end]osmosis
Elektroenergiebedarf *m* energy (power) requirements (needs)
Elektroentstauber *m s.* Elektrofilter
Elektroentstaubung *f* electrical (electrostatic) precipitation
Elektrofilter *n* electrical (electrostatic) precipitator
~ **in Einzonenanordnung** single-stage electrical precipitator
~ **in Zweizonenanordnung** two-stage electrical precipitator
Elektrofilterschlot *m* vertical-flow electrical precipitator
Elektrofiltration *f* electrical (electrostatic) precipitation, electrofiltration
Elektrofokussierung *f (anal)* electrofocussing, isoelectric focussing
Elektrographie *f (anal)* electrographic analysis, electrography, electrosolution technique
elektrographisch *(anal)* electrographic
Elektrographit *m* electrographite
Elektrogravimetrie *f* electrogravimetric (electrodeposition) analysis, electrolytic [deposition] analysis, analytical electrodeposition
elektrogravimetrisch electrogravimetric
Elektroheizung *f* electric heating
elektroinaktiv electroinactive, non-electroactive
Elektroisolieröl *n* electrical insulating oil
Elektrokapillarität *f* electrocapillarity
Elektrokapillarkurve *f* electrocapillary curve
Elektrokatalysator *m* fuel-cell catalyst
Elektrokeramik *f* electroceramics
elektrokinetisch electrokinetic
elektrokratisch *(coll)* electrocratic *(stabilized by electric charge)*
Elektrolichtbogenofen *m* electric-arc furnace
Elektrolumineszenz *f* electroluminescence, electrogenerated chemiluminescence, electrochemiluminescence, ECL
Elektrolyse *f* electrolysis
~ **bei kontrolliertem Potential** controlled-potential electrolysis
~/innere internal electrolysis *(working without external current source)*
~ **mit Quecksilberkatode** mercury-cathode electrolysis
Elektrolyseapparatur *f*, **Elektrolysegerät** *n (lab)* electrolyzer
Elektrolysezelle *f* electrolysis (electrolytic) cell
~ **mit Söderberg-Elektrode** Soderberg cell
elektrolysieren to electrolyse
Elektrolysierzelle *f s.* Elektrolysezelle
Elektrolyt *m* electrolyte; electroplating solution (bath)
~/amphoterer amphoteric electrolyte, ampholyte
~/ein-ein-wertiger uniunivalent electrolyte, 1:1 electrolyte
~/ein-zwei-wertiger unibivalent electrolyte
~/fester solid electrolyte
~/indifferenter indifferent (base) electrolyte, support[ing] electrolyte *(polarography)*

~/kolloider colloidal electrolyte
~/schwacher weak electrolyte
~/starker strong electrolyte
~/1-1-wertiger *s.* ~/ein-ein-wertiger
Elektrolytbehälter *m* electroplating tank (bath)
Elektrolytbleiche *f (pap)* electrolytic bleach
Elektrolytbrücke *f* salt bridge
Elektrolyteisen *n* electrolytic iron
Elektrolytfällung *f* precipitation by electrolytes
Elektrolytflüssigkeit *f* electroplating solution (bath)
Elektrolytgleichgewicht *n* ionic equilibrium
Elektrolytgleichrichter *m* electrolytic rectifier
elektrolytisch electrolytic
Elektrolytkoagulation *f (coll)* flocculation by electrolytes
Elektrolytkondensator *m* electrolytic capacitor
Elektrolytkupfer *n* electrolytic copper
Elektrolytlösung *f* electrolytic (ionic) solution, solution of electrolytes; electroplating solution (bath)
Elektrolytnickel *n* electrolytic (cathode) nickel
Elektrolytpulver *n* electrolytic powder
Elektrolytschlüssel *m s.* Elektrolytbrücke
Elektrolytsilber *n* electrolytic silver
Elektrolyttheorie *f* theory of electrolytes
Elektrolytverfahren *n* electrolytic method (process, technique)
Elektrolytvorlaufverfahren *n (chromat)* ion-exclusion process
Elektrolytwasserstoff *m* electrolytic hydrogen
Elektrolytzink *n* electrolytic zinc
Elektromagnetrolle *f* electromagnetic pulley *(in belt conveyors)*
elektromer electromeric
Elektron *n* electron *(s. a. under* Elektronen*)*
~/anteiliges *s.* ~/gemeinsames
~/antibindendes antibonding electron
~/aufgeteiltes *s.* ~/gemeinsames
~/äußeres outer (outside, external) electron
~ der inneren Schalen *s.* ~/inneres
~/einsames unshared (non-bonding) electron
~/freies (frei bewegliches) free electron
~/gemeinsames shared electron
~/gepaartes paired electron
~/gestreutes scattered electron
~/hydratisiertes hydrated electron
~/inneres inner[-shell] electron
~/lockerndes antibonding electron
~/nichtbindendes *s.* ~/einsames
~/niederenergetisches low-energy electron
~/optisches optical (valence, outermost) electron
~/positives positive electron, posit[r]on, antielectron
~/primäres primary (initiating) electron
~/schnelles high-speed electron
~/sekundäres secondary electron
~/supraleitendes superconducting electron
~/ungepaartes *s.* ~/einsames
π-Elektron *n* π electron, pi electron, unsaturation electron
σ-Elektron *n* σ electron, sigma electron
Elektron-Defektelektron-Paar *n* electron-hole (hole-electron) pair
elektronegativ electronegative
Elektronegativität *f* electronegativity
~ nach Pauling Pauling electronegativity
Elektronegativitätsskala *f* scale of electronegativity
Elektronen *npl*:
• **~ abgeben** to release (lose) electrons • **~ aufnehmen** to accept electrons, to gain (acquire) electrons • **~ [ent]ziehen** to withdraw electrons
~ mit antiparallelen Spinmomenten spin-paired electrons
~ mit parallelen Spinmomenten spin-non-paired electrons
Elektronenabgabe *f* electron release (donation)
Elektronenabgabevermögen *n* electron-releasing potency
elektronenabgebend electron-releasing, electron-donating, electron-providing
Elektronenabgeber *m* electron donor
Elektronenablösung *f* electron detachment
elektronenabstoßend electron-repelling
Elektronenabstoßung *f* electron-electron repulsion, interelectronic repulsion
elektronenaffin electron-attracting
Elektronenaffinität *f* electron affinity
Elektronenakzeptor *m* electron acceptor
Elektronenakzeptorstärke *f* electron acceptor strength
Elektronenanlagerung *f* electron attachment
Elektronenanlagerungs-Massenspektroskopie *f* electron-attachment mass spectroscopy, EA-MS
Elektronenanordnung *f s.* Elektronenkonfiguration
Elektronenanregung *f* electron excitation
Elektronenanregungsenergie *f* electronic excitation energy
Elektronenanregungsspektroskopie *f* electronic spectroscopy
Elektronenanregungsspektrum *n* electronic spectrum
elektronenanziehend electron-attracting
Elektronenäquivalent *n* electron (reducing) equivalent
elektronenarm electron-deficient
Elektronenaufbau *m s.* Elektronenstruktur
Elektronenaufnahme *f* electron acceptance, gain of electrons
elektronenaufnehmend electron-accepting
Elektronenaufnehmer *m* electron acceptor
Elektronenauslösung *f s.* Elektronenabgabe
Elektronenaustausch *m* electron exchange
Elektronenaustauscher *m* electron exchanger
Elektronenaustauscherharz *n* electron-exchange resin
Elektronenaustrittsarbeit *f* electronic work function
Elektronenbahn *f* electron[ic] orbit
Elektronenbande *f* electronic band

Elektronenbelegung *f* electron population
Elektronenbeschleunigung *f* electron acceleration
Elektronenbeschuß *m* electron bombardment
Elektronenbesetzung *f* electron population
Elektronenbeugung *f* electron diffraction
Elektronenbeugungsanalyse *f* electron diffraction analysis
Elektronenbeugungsbild *n*, **Elektronenbeugungsdiagramm** *n* electron diffraction pattern
Elektronenbeugungsversuch *m* electron diffraction experiment
Elektronendichte *f* electron (electronic charge) density; electron probability density
Elektronendichtediagramm *n* electron[-density] map
Elektronendichteverteilung *f* electronic charge distribution
Elektronendon[at]or *m* electron donor
Elektronen-Donor-Akzeptor-Komplex *m* charge transfer complex, electron-donor-acceptor complex
Elektronendoppelresonanz *f (anal)* electron double resonance, ELDOR
Elektronendublett *n* doublet, duplet
Elektroneneinfang *m* electron capture
Elektroneneinfangdetektor *m* electron capture detector
Elektronenemission *f* electron[ic] emission
~/induzierte induced electron emission, IEE
~/thermische thermionic emission
Elektronenenergie *f* electron[ic] energy
Elektronenentzug *m* electron removal
Elektronenfalle *f*, **Elektronenfänger** *m* electron trap
Elektronenfluß *m* electron flow
Elektronenformel *f* electron-dot formula (structure), electronic (dot) formula, Lewis formula (structure)
Elektronengas *n* electron gas
Elektronengeber *m* electron donor
elektronengekoppelt electron-coupled
Elektronengitter *n* electron lattice
Elektronengrundzustand *m* electronic ground state, ground (zeroth) electronic state
Elektronengruppe *f* electron group
Elektronenhaftstelle *f* electron trap
Elektronenhalbleiter *m* electronic semiconductor
Elektronenhülle *f* electronic (extranuclear) region
Elektronenkonfiguration *f* electron[ic] configuration, electron[ic] arrangement, orbital electron arrangement
~ der äußeren Schale valence-shell [electronic] configuration
~ im Grundzustand ground-state [electronic] configuration
Elektronenkonzentration *f* electron density
Elektronenkorrelation *f* electron correlation
Elektronenkreisbahn *f* electron[ic] orbit
Elektronenladung *f* electron[ic] charge
Elektronenladungswolke *f* electron[ic] charge cloud
Elektronenlawine *f* [electron] avalanche, Townsend avalanche
Elektronenleiter *m* electronic conductor
Elektronenleitfähigkeit *f* electronic conductivity
Elektronenleitung *f* electronic conduction
elektronenliefernd *s.* elektronenspendend
Elektronenloch *n* electron hole
Elektronenloslösung *f s.* Elektronenabgabe
Elektronenlücke *f* electron gap
Elektronenmangel *m* electron deficiency, shortage of electrons
Elektronenmangelhydrid *n* electron-deficient hydride
Elektronenmangelverbindung *f* electron-deficient compound
Elektronenmasse *f* electron [rest] mass
Elektronenmikroskop *n* electron microscope
Elektronenmikroskopie *f* electron microscopy
Elektronenmikrosonde *f* electron microprobe, EMP
Elektronennehmer *m* electron acceptor
Elektronenniveau *n* electronic [energy] level, term
Elektronenoktett *n* electron octet
~ in der Valenzschale valence-shell octet of electrons
Elektronenoktett-Anordnung *f* octet structure, eight-electron configuration, noble-gas [electronic] configuration
Elektronenorbital *n* electron[ic] orbital
Elektronenpaar *n* electron pair
~/bindendes bonding pair of electrons
~/einsames (freies) lone [electron] pair, lone (unshared) pair of electrons
~/gemeinsames shared pair [of electrons], sharing electron pair
Elektronenpaarabstoßung *f* electron-pair repulsion, interpair repulsion
Elektronenpaarakzeptor *m* electron-pair acceptor
Elektronenpaaranordnung *f* electron-pair orientation
Elektronenpaarbindung *f* 1. [shared-]electron-pair bond, covalent (non-polar) bond, homopolar (atomic) bond *(state)*; 2. covalent bonding *(process)*
π-Elektronenpaarbindung *f* π bond, pi bond
σ-Elektronenpaarbindung *f* σ bond, sigma bond
Elektronenpaardonator *m* electron-pair donor
Elektronenpaarmethode *f s.* Valenzbindungsmethode
Elektronenpolarisation *f* electron polarization
~/chemisch induzierte dynamische chemically induced dynamic electron polarization
Elektronenpulsradiolyse *f* electron-pulse radiolysis
Elektronenquelle *f* electron source
Elektronenreichweite *f* range of electrons
Elektronenresonanz *f s.* Elektronenspinresonanz
Elektronenruh[e]masse *f* electron [rest] mass
Elektronenschale *f* electron shell
Elektronenschlucker *m* electron acceptor
Elektronensextett *n* electron sextet

π-Elextronensextett *n* aromatic sextet
elektronenspendend electron-donating, electron-releasing, electron-providing
Elektronenspender *m* electron donor
Elektronenspektroskopie *f* electron spectroscopy
~ **für die chemische Analyse** X-ray-induced photoelectron spectroscopy, electron spectroscopy for chemical analysis
Elektronenspektrum *n* 1. electron spectrum; 2. *s.* Elektronenanregungsspektrum
Elektronenspin *m* electron spin
Elektronenspinquantenzahl *f* electron spin quantum number
Elektronenspinresonanz *f* electron paramagnetic (spin) resonance, EPR, ESR, paramagnetic [electronic] resonance, PMR
Elektronenspinresonanzspektroskopie *f* electron paramagnetic (spin) resonance spectroscopy, EPR spectroscopy, ESR spectroscopy
Elektronensprung *m* electron jump
Elektronensprungspektrum *n s.* Elektronenanregungsspektrum
Elektronenstoß *m* electron impact
Elektronenstoßionisation *f* electron impact ionization
Elektronenstoßmassenspektrum *n* electron-impact mass spectrum
Elektronenstoßmethode *f (anal)* electron impact method, EI method
Elektronenstrahl *m* electron beam *(if bundled)*; electron ray *(if single)*
Elektronenstrahllaser *m* free-electron laser, FEL
Elektronenstrahlmikroanalysator *m* electron-probe microanalyser
Elektronenstrahlmikroanalyse *f* electron-probe microanalysis, EPMA
Elektronenstrahlmikrosonde *f* electron [micro]probe, EMP
Elektronenstrahlschmelzen *n* electron-beam melting
Elektronenstrom *m* electron flow
Elektronenstruktur *f* electron[ic] structure
2π-Elektronensystem *n* two-pi-electron system
6π-Elektronensystem *n* six-pi-electron system
Elektronenterm *m (phys ch)* electronic term value
Elektronentheorie *f* electronic theory
~ **der Metalle** free-electron theory of metals
~ **der Valenz** electronic theory of valency
Elektronenträger *m* electron carrier
Elektronentransport *m* electron transport
Elektronentransportkette *f (bioch)* electron-transport chain (sequence, system), ETS, respiratory chain
Elektronentransportpartikel *npl (bioch)* electron transport particles, ETP
Elektronen-Tunnel-Spektrometrie *f*/**unelastische** inelastic electron tunnel spectrometry
Elektronenübergang *m* electronic transition
~/**spinerlaubter** spin-allowed electronic transition
Elektronenüberschuß *m* excess (surplus) of electrons
Elektronenüberschußhalbleiter *m* n-type semiconductor
elektronenübertragend electron-transferring, electron-carrying
Elektronenüberträger *m* electron carrier
Elektronenüberträgerprotein *n* electron-transferring (electron-carrier) protein
Elektronenübertragung *f* electron transfer
~ **nach dem Außensphärenmechanismus** outer-sphere electron transfer
~ **nach dem Brückenmechanismus (Innensphärenmechanismus)** inner-sphere electron transfer
Elektronenübertragungsreaktion *f* electron-transfer reaction
Elektronenunterschuß *m* electron deficiency, shortage of electrons
elektronenverbrauchend electron-accepting
Elektronenverbraucher *m* electron acceptor
Elektronenverschiebung *f* electron shift (displacement)
Elektronenverteilung *f* electron distribution
Elektronenvolt *n* electron-volt, eV, E.V.
Elektronenwanderung *f* electron migration
Elektronenwelle *f* electron wave
Elektronenwolke *f* electron[ic] cloud
Elektronenzentrum *n* F-centre *(a colour centre in spectroscopy)*
elektronenziehend electron-attracting, electron-pulling, electron-withdrawing, electrophilic
Elektronenzug *m* electron attraction
Elektronenzusammenstoß *m* electron collision
Elektronenzustand *m* electron[ic] state
Elektronenzyklotronresonanz *f* electron cyclotron resonance, ECR
elektroneutral electrically neutral
Elektroneutralität *f* electroneutrality
elektronisch electronic
Elektron-Kern-Doppelresonanz *f (anal)* electron nuclear double resonance, ENDOR
Elektron-Positron-Paar *n* electron-positron pair
Elektroofen *m* electric furnace
Elektroosmose *f* electro[end]osmosis
Elektropherogramm *n* electropherogram
Elektropherographie *f* electropherography, electrochromatography
elektrophil electrophilic, electron-attracting, electron-withdrawing
Elektrophil *n* electrophile, electrophilic reagent
Elektrophilie *f* electrophilicity, *(quantitatively also)* electrophilic power
Elektrophorese *f* electrophoresis
~ **auf Trägern** electropherography, electrochromatography
~/**freie (trägerfreie)** free (moving-boundary) electrophoresis, Tiselius method
Elektrophoreseapparatur *f*, **Elektrophoresegerät** *n* electrophoresis (electrophoretic) apparatus, electrophoretor

Elektrophoresekammer *f* electrophoresis cabinet, migration chamber
Elektrophoresetrog *m* electrophoresis tank
elektrophoretisch electrophoretic
elektroplattieren to electroplate, *(specif)* to coat (plate) continuously *(steel strip)*
Elektroplattieren *n* electroplating, *(specif)* continuous strip coating *(of steel strip)*
elektropolieren to electropolish, to electrobrighten
Elektropolieren *n* electrolytic polishing, electropolishing, electrobrightening
Elektroporzellan *n* electrical porcelain
elektropositiv electropositive
Elektroraffination *f* electrorefining, electrolytic refining
Elektroreinigen *n* electrical (electrostatic) precipitation, electrofiltration
Elektrorüttler *m* electrically driven vibrator
Elektroscheiden *n* electrostatic separation
~ **mit Korona-Walzenscheider** high-tension separation
Elektroschmelze *f* electrofusion
Elektroschmelzverfahren *n (met)* electric[-furnace] process
Elektrosortieren *n s.* Elektroscheiden
Elektrostahl *m* electrosteel, electric[-furnace] steel
Elektrostahlverfahren *n* electric[-furnace] process
Elektrostatikspritzen *n (coat)* electrostatic spraying
elektrostatisch electrostatic
Elektrostriktion *f* electrostriction
Elektrosynthese *f* electrosynthesis
~/organische organic electrosynthesis
Elektro-Teerfilter *n*, **Elektro-Teerscheider** *m* electrostatic tar filter
elektrothermisch electrothermal, electrothermic
Elektrothermoanalyse *f* electrothermal analysis, ETA
Elektrotunnelofen *m* electric tunnel kiln
Elektro-Ultrafiltration *f* electroultrafiltration
elektrovalent electrovalent
Elektrovalenz *f* 1. electrovalence *(of an atom in an ionic bond)*; 2. *s.* Ionenbeziehung
Elektrovibrator *m s.* Elektrorüttler
Elektrowalzenscheider *m* rotor separator
Elektrum *m (min)* electrum *(a natural alloy of gold and silver)*
Elektuarium *n (pharm)* electuary
Element *n s.* 1. ~/chemisches; 2. ~/elektrochemisches; 3. Grundbestandteil
~/atmophiles atmophile element *(an element comparatively concentrated in the atmosphere)*
~/biophiles biophile element
~/chalkophiles chalcophile element
~/chemisches [chemical] element
~ **der Actiniumreihe** actinoid [element]
~ **der Lanthanreihe** lanthanoid [element]
~/dreiwertiges trivalent element
~ **einer Hauptgruppe** main group element
~/einwertiges monovalent (univalent) element
~/elektrochemisches electrochemical cell, galvanic (voltaic) cell (element)
~/essentielles *(bioch)* essential element
~/fünfwertiges pentavalent element
~/galvanisches *s.* ~/elektrochemisches
~/lithophiles *(geoch)* lithophile element
~/markiertes tagged element
~/mehrwertiges polyvalent (multivalent) element
~/monoisotopes monoisotopic element
~/radioaktives radioactive element, radioelement
~/reversibles *(el ch)* reversible cell (element)
~/siderophiles *(geoch, met)* siderophile element *(having little affinity to oxygen and sulphur)*
~/superschweres superheavy element, SHE
~/umkehrbares *s.* ~/reversibles
~/vierwertiges tetravalent (quadrivalent) element
~/zweiwertiges divalent (bivalent) element
elementar *(ch)* elemental
Elementaranalyse *f* ultimate (elemental, elementary) analysis
Elementaranalysenapparat *m* combustion train
Elementarbaustein *m* elementary building block
Elementarbestandteil *m* elementary constituent
Elementareinheit *f* elementary unit
Elementarfaden *m (text)* filament, continuous fibre (filament) *(a natural or man-made fibre of great or indefinite length)*
~/schmelzgesponnener melt-spun filament
Elementarfadenbildung *f (text)* filament forming
Elementarfadenbündel *n (text)* strand
Elementarfadenkabel *n (text)* tow
Elementargebilde *n* elementary entity
Elementarkörper *m s.* Elementarzelle
Elementarladung *f* elementary (unit) charge
Elementarmembran *f (bioch)* unit membrane
Elementarobjekt *n* elementary entity
Elementarquantum *n***/elektrisches** *s.* Elementarladung
Elementarreaktion *f* elementary reaction
~/chemische elementary chemical reaction
Elementarschritt *m* elementary [reaction] step, simple step
Elementarschwefel *m* elemental sulphur
Elementarteilchen *n* elementary (fundamental) particle
Elementarvorgang *m* elementary process
~/chemischer elementary chemical process
Elementarwürfel *m (cryst)* cube
~/flächenzentrierter face-centred cube
Elementarzelle *f (cryst)* unit (structure) cell
Elementsymbol *n* chemical sign (symbol)
Elementumwandlung *f* transmutation
Elemi[harz] *n* elemi *(from several specc. of Burseraceae, Rutaceae, and Humiriaceae)*
Elemiöl *n* elemi oil *(from Canarium luzonicum Miquel)*
Elevator *m* elevator, *(of a rotary-drilling installation also)* drill pipe elevator
Elfenbeinkarton *m* ivory cardboard

Elimination *f s.* Eliminierung
eliminierbar eliminable
Eliminierbarkeit *f* eliminability
eliminieren to eliminate, *(hyd also)* to remove *(water constituents)*
Eliminierung *f* elimination, *(hyd also)* removal *(of water constituents)*
~ **feiner suspendierter Partikel** *(hyd)* fine-particulate removal
~/**ionische** ionic elimination
~ **suspendierter Partikel** *(hyd)* particulate removal
α-Eliminierung *f (org ch)* α-elimination, alpha-elimination
Eliminierungs-Additions-Mechanismus *m* elimination-addition mechanism
Eliminierungsleistung *f (hyd)* removal efficiency (performance)
Eliminierungsreaktion *f* elimination reaction
Elixier *n* elixir
Ellagengerbstoff *m* ellagitannin
Ellagsäure *f* ellagic acid *(a phenolic dilactone)*
Elmendorf-Prüfgerät *n (pap)* Elmendorf tester
Elmo-Pumpe *f* [Nash] Hytor pump
Elongation *f (bioch)* elongation *(of polypeptide chains)*
Elongationsfaktor *m (bioch)* elongation (propagation, transfer) factor
~ **EF-Ts** Ts elongation factor
~ **EF-Tu** Tu elongation factor
Elongationszyklus *m (bioch)* elongation cycle
Elsholtziaöl *n (cosmet)* Elsholtzia oil *(from Elsholtzia ciliata (Thunb.) Hyl.)*
Elterndoppelstrang *m (bioch)* parent double strand *(of DNA)*
Elternstamm *m (biot)* parent strain *(of microorganisms)*
Eluat *n* eluate *(liquid obtained by washing out adsorbed substances)*
Eluent *m* eluent, eluant, elutant, eluting agent (solvent)
Eluentenstrom *m* eluent stream
eluieren to elute
Elution *f* elution
~/**affine** affinity elution
~/**stufenweise** stepwise elution
Elutionsanalyse *f* elution analysis
Elutionsbande *f* elution band
Elutionschromatogramm *n* elution chromatogram
Elutionschromatographie *f* elution chromatography
elutionschromatographisch by elution chromatography
Elutionsentwicklung *f* elution development
Elutionsgeschwindigkeit *f* rate of elution
Elutionsgipfel *m* eluting peak
Elutionsgradientchromatographie *f* gradient elution (liquid) chromatography
Elutionskraft *f (chromat)* solvent strength parameter
Elutionskurve *f* elution curve, concentration profile
Elutionsmittel *n s.* Eluent
Elutionstechnik *f* elution technique
Elutriator *m* elutriator *(used for separating fine catalyst particles in moving-bed cracking)*
Eluvialhorizont *m (soil)* eluvial horizon, A-horizon
Email *n* [vitreous] enamel, *(Am)* porcelain enamel
Emailfarbe *f (ceram)* enamel (overglaze, vitrifiable) colour
Emaillack *m s.* Emaillackfarbe
Emaillackfarbe *f* enamel (hard-gloss) paint, *(loosely:)* enamel
~/**ofentrocknende** stoving enamel
~/**physikalisch trocknende** lacquer enamel
Emaille *f s.* Email
emaillieren to enamel
Emaillierofen *m* enamelling kiln
Emailwaren *fpl* enamel ware
Emanation *f (nucl)* [radioactive] emanation
emanieren to emanate
Emballage *f* packing (packaging) material, packing, package
Embden-Meyerhof-Parnas-Abbauweg *m*, **Embden-Meyerhof-Parnas-Weg** *m (bioch)* Embden-Meyerhof-Parnas pathway (scheme), EMP pathway (scheme), glycolytic pathway, homolactic fermentation
Emde-Abbau *m* Emde degradation *(of quaternary ammonium salts)*
Emeraldgrün *n* emerald green *(Guignet green or a mixture of Schweinfurth green and coal-tar colours)*
Emerson-Effekt *m* Emerson (enhancement) effect *(photosynthesis)*
Emersverfahren *n (biot)* surface[-culture] process
Emetikum *n (pharm)* emetic
Emission *f* emission, issue, *(nucl also)* ejection, expulsion
~ **in die Umwelt** environmental emission
~/**kalte** field emission
~/**lichtelektrische** photoemission
~/**spontane** spontaneous emission
~/**stimulierte** stimulated emission
~/**thermische** thermionic emission
Emissionsdetektor *m (anal)* emission detector
Emissionselektrode *f* emitter electrode
Emissionsgrad *m* [thermal] emissivity *(of bodies radiating heat)*
Emissionsgrenzwert *m* **für Luftverunreinigungen** maximum emission concentration, air emission standard
Emissionskataster *m* emission inventory
Emissionskoeffizient *m (spectr)* emissivity, emission coefficient
Emissionslinie *f* emission line
Emissionsminderung *f* emission control
Emissionsquelle *f* emission source
~/**mobile** mobile source [of emission] *(of air pollutants)*

Emissionssenke *f* emission sink, receptor area *(for pollutants)*
Emissionsspektralanalyse *f* emission spectroscopy
emissionsspektralanalytisch by emission spectroscopy
Emissionsspektrometer *n* emission spectrometer
Emissionsspektroskopie *f* emission spectroscopy
~/optische optical emission spectroscopy, OES
Emissionsspektrum *n* emission spectrum
Emissionsstrom *m* emission flux
Emissionsvermögen *n* 1. emissive power; 2. *s.* Emissionskoeffizient
Emissionszahl *f s.* Emissionsgrad
Emitter *m* emitter
emittieren to emit, to radiate *(light)*; to emit, to issue, to emanate *(e.g. radioactive particles)*
emittierend emissive
EMK electromototive force, e.m.f., EMF
EMK-Normal *n* standard of e.m.f.
Emmenagogum *n (pharm)* emmenagogue
E-Modul *m* elastic modulus, Young's modulus [of elasticity], modulus of elasticity
Empfänger *m (bioch)* target
empfängnisverhütend contraceptive
empfindlich susceptible, sensitive *(material)*; labile, sensitive *(chemicals)*; sensitive, delicate *(instrument, test)*
~ gegen Schwefel *(agric)* sulphur-shy
~/höchst exceedingly sensitive *(test)*
Empfindlichkeit *f* susceptibility, sensitivity, sensitiveness *(of material)*, *(phot also)* speed; lability, sensitivity *(of chemicals)*; sensitivity *(of instruments, tests)*
~ gegen Oxidation susceptibility to oxidation
~ gegen Reibung sensitivity to friction
~/spektrale spectral responsivity (response, sensitivity)
Empfindlichkeitsbereich *m (phot)* range of sensitivity
Empfindlichkeitsmesser *m (phot)* sensitometer
Empfindlichmachen *n (phot)* sensitization, sensitizing
Empfindungsschwelle *f***/individuelle** individual perception threshold, IPT *(odour testing)*
empirisch empirical, through trial and error
emporheben 1. to lift; to buoy up *(in a liquid)*; 2. to energize, to raise *(electrons into an excited state)*
emporkriechen to creep up *(the sides of a vessel)*
emporsteigen to rise, to ascend, to pass up[wards]
emporziehen *(glass)* to pull upward[s]
Emprotid *n* proton acceptor, Brønstedt-Lowry base
EMP-Weg *m s.* Embden-Meyerhof-Parnas-Weg
empyreumatisch empyreumatic *(smell)*
Emscherbrunnen *m* Imhoff tank *(water purification)*
Emulgator *m* 1. emulsification machine, emulsifier; 2. emulsifier, emulsifying agent
~/nichtionogener non-ionic emulsifier
Emulgens *n s.* Emulgator 2.
emulgierbar emulsifiable, emulsible
Emulgierbarkeit *f* emulsifiability, emulsibility
emulgieren to emulsify
Emulgiermaschine *f s.* Emulgator 1.
Emulgiermittel *n s.* Emulgator 2.
Emulgierung *f* emulsification
Emulgiervermögen *n* emulsifying power
Emulsion *f* emulsion
~/beständige tight emulsion
~/feinkörnige *(phot)* fine-grain[ed] emulsion
~/feste solid emulsion, lisoloid *(a colloidal system consisting of a liquid surrounded by a solid phase)*
~/fotografische photographic (sensitive) emulsion
~/gehärtete *(phot)* hardened emulsion
~/geringempfindliche *(phot)* slow emulsion
~/grobkörnige *(phot)* coarse-grain[ed] emulsion
~/hart arbeitende *s.* ~/kontrastreich arbeitende
~/hochempfindliche *(phot)* fast (high-speed) emulsion
~/kontrastarm arbeitende *(phot)* low-contrast emulsion
~/kontrastreich arbeitende *(phot)* high-contrast emulsion
~/lichtempfindliche *s.* ~/fotografische
~ niedriger Empfindlichkeit *s.* ~/geringempfindliche
~/panchromatische *(phot)* panchromatic emulsion
~/pharmazeutische pharmaceutic[al] emulsion
~/schnellbrechende quick-breaking emulsion
~/wäßrige aqueous emulsion
emulsionieren to emulsify
emulsionsartig emulsive
Emulsionsbeständigkeit *f* emulsion stability
Emulsionsbildner *m* emulsifying agent, emulsifier
Emulsionsbildung *f* emulsification
Emulsionsbrecher *m s.* Emulsionsspalter
Emulsionscopolymerisation *f* emulsion copolymerization
Emulsionsentmischer *m s.* Emulsionsspalter
Emulsionsentmischung *f s.* Emulsionsspaltung
Emulsionskolloid *n s.* Emulsoid
Emulsionsöl *n* emulsion oil
Emulsionspolymer[e] *n*, **Emulsionspolymerisat** *n* emulsion polymer
Emulsionspolymerisation *f* emulsion polymerization
Emulsions-Polyvinylchlorid *n* emulsion polyvinylchloride
Emulsionsschicht *f (phot)* emulsion layer
Emulsionsschleier *m (phot)* emulsion fog
Emulsionsspalter *m* emulsion breaker, demulsifier
Emulsionsspaltung *f* breaking (cracking) of emulsions, de-emulsification, demulsification *(act)*; emulsion breakdown (breaking) *(process)*
Emulsionsspinnverfahren *n (text)* emulsion spinning
Emulsionsspülung *f (petrol)* emulsion-type mud
Emulsionsstabilisator *m* emulsion stabilizer
Emulsionsstabilität *f* emulsion stability

Emulsionsträger *m (phot)* emulsion support
Emulsionstyp *m* emulsion type
Emulsionsunterlage *f s.* Emulsionsträger
Emulsionsverdichtung *f*, **Emulsionsverdickung** *f* emulsion thickening, creaming
Emulsionsvermittler *m* emulsifying agent, emulsifier
Emulsionswäsche *f (text)* emulsion scouring
Emulsoid *n* emulsoid [colloid]
Emulsor *m s.* Emulgator 1.
Enamin *n (org ch)* enamine
enantiomer enantiomeric, enantiomorphic, enantiomorphous
Enantiomer[e] *n* enantiomer, enantiomorph, enantiomorphous (mirror-image) isomer, optical isomer (antipode), antimer
Enantiomerie *f* enantiomerism, enantiomorphism, optical (mirror-image) isomerism
enantiomorph *s.* enantiomer
enantioselektiv *(org ch)* enantioselective
Enantioselektivität *f (org ch)* enantioselectivity
enantiotrop enantiotropic
Enantiotropie *f* enantiotropy
Enargit *m (min)* enargite *(arsenic(III) copper(I,II) sulphide)*
Endablauf *m (hyd)* final effluent (discharge), waste treatment effluent, sewage plant effluent
Endatom *n* terminal atom
Endbleiche *f* final bleaching
Endbleichstufe *f (pap)* whitening stage *(in which the pulp reaches its maximum whiteness)*
Enddruck *m* final pressure, *(vacuum technology also)* ultimate (maximum) vacuum
Ende *n* end *(as of a reaction, process, or chain molecule)*
~/glattes *(bioch)* blunt end
~/klebriges (kohäsives) *(bioch)* sticky end
~/verengtes constricted end *(of a pipe)*
endergon[isch] endergonic, energy-demanding
Enderzeugnis *n s.* Endprodukt 1.
Endfestigkeit *f* final strength
Endfeuchte[beladung] *f* final moisture content, FMC
Endfläche *f* base *(of a crystal)*
Endgeschwindigkeit *f* terminal velocity *(of particles in a fluid)*
~ des Absetzens terminal settling velocity
Endglied *n (nucl)* final member *(of a disintegration series)*
Endgruppe *f* terminal (end) group *(of a molecule)*
~/C-terminale C-terminal group (residue) *(in proteins)*
Endgruppenanalyse *f*, **Endgruppenbestimmung** *f* end group analysis
Endhypochloritbleiche *f (pap)* last hypochlorite treatment, final hypochlorite stage
Endiol *n (org ch)* enediol
Endkochpunkt *m* final boiling point, F.B.P.
Endkomponente *f* final (end) component
Endkonzentration *f* final concentration (strength)
Endlagerung *f* final (ultimate) disposal *(of waste products)*
Endlauge *f* final lye *(as in fertilizer manufacture)*
Endlosfaser *f s.* Elementarfaden
Endlosgarn *n (text)* continuous-filament yarn
Endlöslichkeit *f* final solubility
Endlossieb *n (pap)* endless wire
Endmelasse *f (sugar)* blackstrap [molasses], final (end, discard) molasses
Endoamylase *f (bioch)* alpha (dextrogenic, liquefying) amylase
endocyclisch endocyclic *(e.g. double bond)*
Endoenzym *n* 1. *s.* Enzym/intrazelluläres; 2. *enzyme acting on the inner part of a chain molecule*
endogen endogenous
endokrin endocrine
Endomethylenbrücke *f* endomethylene bridge
• **mit ~** endomethylene-bridged
Endomorphose *f (geol)* endomorphism
Endopeptidase *f* endopeptidase
endo-Produkt *n* endo product
Endosmose *f* endosmosis
endosmotisch endosmotic
endotherm endothermic
Endotoxin *n* endotoxin
Endpotential *n* end-point potential
Endprobe *f* test sample *(product of sample reduction)*
Endprodukt *n (phys ch)* end product, final [reaction] product; *(tech)* final product, finished (consumer) product
Endprodukthemmung *f (bioch)* end-product inhibition
~/konzertierte (multivalente) concerted inhibition
Endproduktrepression *f (biot)* end product repression, coordinate repression
Endpunkt *m* end point *(as of a titration)*
Endpunktabstand *m* end-to-end distance, chain-end distance
Endpunktsbestimmung *f* end point determination
~ nach Mohr Mohr method
~ nach Volhard Volhard method
Endpunktserkennung *f* end-point detection
Endreinigung *f (hyd)* final [effluent] treatment
Endschneide *f* end (terminal) knife edge *(of a balance)*
Endsiedepunkt *m* final boiling point, F.B.P.
Endspreitungskoeffizient *m (coll)* final spreading coefficient
endständig terminal • **mit endständiger Hydroxylgruppe** hydroxyl-terminated
Endstellung *f* terminal position
Endstoff *m* end product, final [reaction] product
Endtemperatur *f* final (end) temperature
Endtrocknung *f* final drying
Endumsatz *m* final conversion
Endung *f (nomencl)* ending, termination
Endvakuum *n* ultimate (maximum) vacuum

Endvergärung *f* final fermentation
Endwäsche *f* final washing
Endweiße *f (pap)* final brightness
End-zu-End-Anlagerung *f* end-to-end polymerization
Endzustand *m* final state
energetisch begünstigt (bevorzugt) energetically favourable (favoured)
Energie *f (phys ch)* energy; *(tech)* power, *(esp relating to electricity:)* energy • **von geringer ~** low-energy, poor in energy
~/Coulombsche coulombic energy
~ der Grenzfläche/freie interfacial free energy
~/freie free energy, *(specif)* Helmholtz free energy, maximum work function
~/innere intrinsic (internal) energy
~/kinetische kinetic energy
~/molare freie molar free energy
~/nukleare nuclear energy
~/potentielle potential energy
~/thermische thermal energy
Energieabgabe *f* energy output, release of energy
energieabgebend *s.* energieliefernd
energieabhängig energy-dependent, energy-linked
Energieabhängigkeit *f* energy dependence
Energieabnahme *f* decrease in energy
Energieänderung *f* energy change, *(quantitatively also)* change in energy [content]
energiearm low-energy, poor in energy
Energieaufwand *m* expenditure of energy
energieaufwendig high-energy-requiring
Energieaustausch *m* energy exchange, interchange of energy
Energieband *n s.* Energiebereich
Energiebarriere *f s.* Energieschwelle
Energiebedarf *m (phys ch)* energy demand; *(tech)* power demand (requirements, needs), *(esp relating to electricity:)* energy demand (needs)
Energiebeitrag *m* energy contribution
Energiebereich *m* energy range (band), band
~/erlaubter allowed band
~/leerer empty band
~/nicht besetzter empty band
~/nicht zugelassener *s.* ~/verbotener
~/unbesetzter empty band
~/verbotener forbidden band, energy gap
~/zugelassener allowed band
Energieberg *m s.* Energieschwelle
energiebereitstellend *s.* energieliefernd
Energiebetrag *m* amount of energy
Energiebilanz *f* energy balance
Energiebilanzgleichung *f* total-energy equation
Energiebrutreaktor *m (nucl)* power breeder
Energiedegradation *f* degradation of energy
Energiediagramm *n s.* Energieniveaudiagramm
Energiedichte *f* energy density
~/kohäsive cohesive energy density, C.E.D.
Energiedifferenz *f* energy difference
energiedispersiv energy-dispersive, energy-dispersion
Energiedissipation *f* dissipation of energy
Energieeinheit *f* energy unit
Energieeintrag *m* energy input
energieerhaltend energy-conserving
Energieerhaltung *f* energy conservation
Energieerhaltungssatz *m* energy principle, law of conservation of energy
Energiefläche *f* energy surface
energiefreigebend *s.* energieliefernd
Energiegebirge *n s.* Energieschwelle
Energiegewinn *m* gain in energy
Energieinhalt *m* energy content
Energiekette *f* energy chain
Energieladung *f (bioch)* energy charge
Energielieferant *m* source of energy
energieliefernd energy-releasing, energy-yielding, exoergic, *(esp bioch)* exergonic
Energielücke *f* energy gap, forbidden band
Energieniveau *n* energy level, term
~ des Atoms atomic [energy] level
Energieniveaudiagramm *n*, **Energieniveauschema** *n* energy[-level] diagram, level scheme, state diagram
Energieprinzip *n* energy principle, law of conservation of energy
Energieprofil *n* [potential-]energy profile
Energiequant *n* energy quantum
Energiequantelung *f* quantization of energy
Energiequantum *n* energy quantum
Energiequelle *f* source of energy
Energiereaktor *m* power reactor
energiereich high-energy, rich in energy, energy-rich
Energie-Reichweite-Beziehung *f* range-energy relation
Energiesammler *m (bioch)* energy trap (sink), trapping centre
Energieschranke *f s.* Energieschwelle
Energieschwelle *f* energy barrier (hump)
Energiespender *m* source of energy
Energiestoffwechsel *m* energy metabolism
Energiestufe *f*, **Energieterm** *m* energy level, term
Energietransfer *m s.* Energieüberführung
Energieüberführung *f* energy transfer[ence]
Energieübergang *m* energy transfer
Energieüberschuß *m* excess energy
Energieübertragung *f* energy transfer[ence]
~/lineare linear energy transfer, LET
Energieumformung *f s.* Energieumwandlung 2.
Energieumsatz *m (bioch)* energy turnover
Energieumsetzung *f s.* Energieumwandlung
Energieumwandlung *f* 1. energy change; 2. *(intentionally:)* transformation of energy, energy conversion
Energieumwandlungstechnik *f* energy conversion technology
Energieunterschied *m* energy difference

Energieverbrauch *m* energy consumption, *(tech also)* power consumption
energieverbrauchend energy-requiring, energy-demanding, endoergic, *(esp bioch)* endergonic
Energieverlust *m* loss of energy
Energieverlust-Spektroskopie *f* energy-loss spectroscopy, ELS
Energieverteilung *f* energy distribution
Energieverteilungsgesetz *n***/Boltzmannsches** Boltzmann distribution law
Energiewall *m s.* Energieschwelle
Energiewandlung *f s.* Energieumwandlung
Energiezufuhr *f* energy input
Energiezustand *m* energy state
~ **des Atoms** atomic state
energisch vigorous, drastic *(treatment)*
Enfleurage *f (cosmet)* enfleurage *(method for obtaining odoriferous substances by absorption with fats)*
Enfleurageöl *n (cosmet)* absolute of enfleurage, enfleurage absolute
Engel-Verfahren *n (plast)* Engel process *(a powder sintering process)*
Enghalsflasche *f* narrow-mouth[ed] bottle
Enghalskolben *m* narrow-mouth[ed] flask, narrow-neck[ed] flask
engklassiert closely graded
Engler-Kolben *n* Engler flask
Englischrot *n* polishing rouge *(iron(III) oxide)*
Engobe *f (ceram)* engobe
Engobeton *m (ceram)* slip clay
engobieren *(ceram)* to engobe
engporig fine-pore[d], finely pored, small-pore[-size]
engsiedend *(distil)* close-boiling
Engspektrumantibiotikum *n (biot)* narrow-spectrum antibiotic
E-Nickel *n* electrolytic (cathode) nickel
En-Komponente *f (org ch)* ene
Enneoxodiiodat(VII) *n* $M^I_4I_2O_9$ enneaoxodiiodate(VII)
Enol *n (org ch)* enol
Enolase *f* enolase
Enolat *n (org ch)* enolate
Enolatmesomerie *f*, **Enolatresonanz** *f* enolate mesomerism (resonance)
Enolform *f* enol[ic] form
enolisch enolic
enolisierbar enolizable
enolisieren to enolize
Enolisierung *f* enolization
Enolkonstante *f* keto-enol constant
Enophil *n (org ch)* enophile
En-Reaktion *f (org ch)* ene reaction
Enstatit *m (min)* enstatite *(magnesium metasilicate)*
entacetylieren to deacetylate
Entacetylierung *f* deacetylation
entaktivieren to deactivate; *(nucl)* to decontaminate
Entaktivierung *f* deactivation; *(nucl)* decontamination
entalkylieren to dealkylate
Entalkylierung *f* dealkylation
entamidieren to deamidate
Entamidierung *f* deamidation
entarretieren to unlock; to release *(the beam of a balance)*
Entarretierung *f* unlocking; beam release *(weighing)*
entarten to deteriorate; *(phys ch)* to degenerate
entartet/dreifach *(phys ch)* triply (three-fold) degenerate
~/fünffach quintuply (five-fold) degenerate
~/vierfach quadruply (four-fold) degenerate
~/zweifach doubly (two-fold) degenerate
Entartung *f* deterioration; *(phys ch)* degeneracy
~/zufällige *(phys ch)* accidental degeneracy
Entartungsgrad *m (phys ch)* degree of degeneracy
Entartungstemperatur *f (phys ch)* degeneracy temperature
Entarylierung *f* dearylation
entaschen to deash
Entaschung *f* deashing
entasphaltieren to deasphalt
Entasphaltierung *f* deasphalting, deasphaltation
~ **mit Propan** propane deasphalting
entäthanisieren *s.* entethanisieren
entbasen *(soil)* to dealkalize
entbasten to decorticate *(vegetable fibres)*; to degum, to scour, to boil off (out) *(silk)*
Entbasten *n* decortication *(of vegetable fibres)*; degumming, scouring, boil[ing]-off *(of silk)*
Entbastungsbad *n (text)* degumming liquor (bath), scouring (boiling-off) liquor
~/gebrochenes broken degumming liquor
Entbastungsflotte *f s.* Entbastungsbad
Entbastungsmittel *n (text)* degumming (scouring) agent
Entbasung *f (soil)* dealkalization
entbehrlich *(bioch)* non-essential
entbenzol[ier]en to debenzolize
Entbenzol[ier]ung *f* debenzolization
entbinden *s.* freisetzen
entbittern to debitter[ize]
Entblätterungsmittel *n (agric)* defoliant
entbromen to debrominate
Entbromung *f* debromination
Entbrühungssieb *n* drain (rinse) screen
Entbutaner *m (petrol)* debutanizer
entbutanisieren to debutanize
Entbutanisierkolonne *f* debutanizer
Entbutanisierung *f* debutanization
entchloren to dechlorinate
Entchlorung *f* dechlorination
Entchlorungsanlage *f (hyd)* dechlorinator
Entchlorungsmittel *n* dechlorinating agent
Entdeckungsbohrung *f (petrol)* discovery well
entdrillen *s.* entspiralisieren

enteisen to de-ice, to defrost
enteisenen to deferrize *(e.g. water)*
Enteisener *m (hyd)* iron-removal plant
Enteisenung *f* deferrization *(as of water)*
~ **mittels Enteisenungsfilters** *(hyd)* iron filtration, IF
Enteisenungsanlage *f* iron-removal plant
Enteisenungsfilter *n (hyd)* iron [removal] filter
Enteisenungsfiltration *f (hyd)* iron filtration, IF
Enteisung *f* de-icing, defrosting
Enteisungsanlage *f* de-icer, defroster
enteiweißen to deproteinize
Enteiweißung *f* deproteinization
Entemaillieren *n* de-enamelling
entemulsionieren to demulsify, to de-emulsify, to break, to crack *(an emulsion)*
Entemulsionieren *n* demulsification, de-emulsification, emulsion breakdown (breaking), cracking of emulsions
Entethaner *m* de-ethanizer
entethanisieren to de-ethanize
Entethanisierung *f* de-ethanization
Entfaltung *f* unfolding *(as of macromolecules)*; *(bioch)* denaturation *(of proteins)*
entfärben to decolour, to decolorize, to discolour, to bleach; *(pap)* to whiten, to brighten; to deink *(waste paper)*
~/sich to decolour, to decolorize, to discolour, to bleach out
entfärbend decolorant
Entfärber *m s.* Entfärbungsmittel
Entfärbung *f* decolorization, discoloration, bleaching; *(pap)* whitening, brightening; deinking *(of waste paper)*
~ **in Abgasatmosphäre** *(text)* gas fading
Entfärbungserde *f (petrol)* decolorizing (bleaching) earth, decolorizing clay
Entfärbungshilfsmittel *n s.* Entfärbungsmittel
Entfärbungskohle *f* decolorizing carbon (charcoal), char
Entfärbungsmittel *n* decolorizing (stripping) agent (assistant), decolorizer, decolorant
entfernbar removable
entfernen to eliminate, to remove, to discharge, to abstract
~/durch Filtration to remove by filtration, to filter out
~/durch Spülen *(hyd, filtr)* to flush to waste
Entfernen *n* elimination, removal, discharge, abstraction
~ **der organischen Restverschmutzung** *(hyd)* residual organic removal
~ **des Schwimmschlamms** *(hyd)* sludge skimming
~ **durch Aktivkohle** *(hyd)* activated carbon removal
~ **grobdisperser Inhaltsstoffe** *(hyd)* suspended solids removal
~ **organischer Inhaltsstoffe** *(hyd)* organic[s] removal
~ **von Geruchsbeeinträchtigungen** *(hyd)* odour removal
~ **von Geschmacksbeeinträchtigungen** *(hyd)* taste removal
Entferner *m* remover
Entfernung *f s.* Entfernen
entfetten to degrease, to defat; to scour *(wool)*
Entfettung *f* degreasing, defatting; scouring *(of wool)*
~/elektrolytische electrolytic degreasing
Entfettungsmittel *n* degreasing agent, degreaser
entfeuchten to dehumidify, to dehydrate, to desiccate, to dry
Entfeuchtung *f* dehumidification, dehydration, desiccation, drying
Entfeuchtungsmittel *n* desiccating (drying) agent, desiccant
entflammbar [in]flammable
~/nicht uninflammable, non-[in]flammable, flameproof
Entflammbarkeit *f* [in]flammability
Entflammbarkeitsbereich *m* flammable limits
entflammen to flash, to inflame, to burst into flame; to inflame *(something)*
Entflammung *f* inflammation
Entflammungstemperatur *f* ignition (kindling) point (temperature)
entflocken *(coll)* to deflocculate
~/sich to deflocculate
Entflockung *f* deflocculation
entfluorieren to defluorinate
Entfluorierung *f* defluorination
Entformungsmittel *n* [mould-]release agent, [mould-]release medium, mould lubricant
entfrosten to defrost, to thaw
entgasen to degas, to degasify, to outgas; *(coal)* to coke, to carbonize; to carbonize *(wood)*; *(plast)* to vent, to breathe *(the mould)*
Entgaser *m* degasser, degasifier
Entgasung *f* degassing, degasification, outgassing; *(coal)* coking, carbonization; dry distillation, carbonization *(of wood)*; *(plast)* venting, breathing *(of the mould)*
Entgasungsanlage *f* degasser, degasifier, degasification unit
Entgasungsgas *n (coal)* carbonization gas
Entgasungsgerät *n* degasser, degasifier
Entgasungsraum *m (hyd)* degasification chamber
Entgasungsschacht *m* carbonization chamber *(of a predistillation gas producer)*
Entgasungsverfahren *n (coal)* carbonization process
entgegenwirken to counteract
entgehen/der Aufmerksamkeit to escape notice (observation)
entgerben to de-tan
entgiften to detoxicate, to detoxify; *(nucl)* to decontaminate
Entgiftung *f* detoxication, detoxification; *(nucl)* decontamination
entglasen to devitrify

Entglasung *f* devitrification
entgraten to trim, to fettle, *(plast also)* to deburr, to deflash
Enthaareisen *n (tann)* unhairing knife
enthaaren to depilate, to epilate, *(tann also)* to dehair, to unhair
enthaarend depilatory
Enthaarung *f* depilation, epilation, *(tann also)* dehairing, unhairing
Enthaarungscreme *f (cosmet)* depilatory cream
Enthaarungsmaschine *f (tann)* unhairing machine
Enthaarungsmittel *n (cosmet, tann)* depilatory [agent], depilitant, epilator, hair remover
Enthaarungspulver *n (cosmet)* depilatory powder
Enthaarungswachs *n (cosmet)* epilating wax
Enthalpie *f* enthalpy, heat content
~/[Gibbssche] freie free enthalpy, Gibbs [free] energy, Gibbs function, free energy G
~/partielle molare freie partial molar Gibbs function
Enthalpieänderung *f* enthalpy change
Enthalpie-Entropie-Diagramm *n* enthalpy-entropy chart (diagram), Mollier chart
Enthalpiemetrie *f* enthalpimetric analysis
enthalpiemetrisch enthalpimetric
enthärten *(hyd)* to soften, to remove hardness from *(water)*
~/durch Kalkfällung to lime-soften, to lime-treat
Enthärter *m* 1. softener, softening agent (chemical); 2. *s.* Enthärtungsanlage
Enthärtung *f (hyd)* softening
~ durch Fällverfahren precipitation softening, softening by precipitation
~ durch Kalkfällung lime softening, softening by lime treatment
~ im Teilstromverfahren split-stream softening
~ mit Phosphat phosphate treatment
~ mittels Ionenaustauschs ion-exchange softening
~ mittels Neutralaustauschs sodium cycle softening
Enthärtungsanlage *f (hyd)* softening unit (plant), [water] softener
~ für das Kalk-Soda-Verfahren lime-soda softener
~ mit Fällverfahren precipitation softener
~ mit Kalkfällung lime softening precipitation unit, lime softener
Enthärtungschemikalie *f. s.* Enthärtungsmittel
Enthärtungsmittel *n (hyd)* softener, softening agent (chemical); alkali builder *(in soaps)*
Enthärtungsperiode *f (hyd)* softening run
entholzen *(text)* to decorticate
Entholzen *n (text)* decortication
Entionisation *f* deionization
entionisieren to deionize
Entionisierung *f* deionization
Entisobutaner *m (petrol)* deisobutanizer
entisobutanisieren to deisobutanize
Entisobutanisierkolonne *f* deisobutanizer
Entisobutanisierung *f* deisobutanization
Entisol *m (soil)* entisol, recent sol *(according to US Soil Taxonomy)*
entkalken *(bioch, soil)* to decalcify
entkälken *(tann)* to delime
Entkalkung *f (bioch, soil)* decalcification
Entkälkung *f (tann)* deliming
Entkälkungsmittel *n (tann)* deliming agent
entkarbonisieren *(hyd)* to decarbonate, to decarbonize, *(by ion exchange also)* to dealkalize
Entkarbonisierung *f (hyd)* decarbon[iz]ation, *(by ion exchange also)* dealkalization, dealkalizing
~ im Teilstromverfahren split-stream dealkalization
~ mittels Kalks [partial] lime softening
Entkarbonisierungsanlage *f* decarbonator
entkeimen to sterilize, *(relating to pathogenic organisms:)* to disinfect
Entkeimen *n* **des Malzes** *(ferm)* malt cleaning
entkeimend germicidal
Entkeimung *f* sterilization, *(relating to pathogenic organisms:)* disinfection
Entkeimungsapparat *m* sterilizer
Entkeimungsfiltration *f* sterile filtration
Entkeimungsmittel *n* germicide, *(esp soil)* sterilant, *(for killing pathogenic organisms:)* disinfectant
Entkeimungswirkung *f* germicidal effect
entkernen *(text)* to gin *(cotton fibre)*
entkieseln *(hyd)* to desilicify
Entkieselung *f (hyd)* desilicification
entknäueln/sich to uncoil *(of molecules)*
Entknäuelung *f* uncoiling *(of molecules)*
entkohlen 1. *(petrol)* to decarbonize, to decoke; 2. *(met)* to decarburize; 3. *(text)* to carbonize *(raw wool)*
Entkohlung *f* 1. *(petrol)* decarbonization, decoking; 2. *(met)* decarburization; 3. *(text)* carbonization *(removal of burs from raw wool)*
entkoppeln *(bioch)* to uncouple, to decouple; *(spectr)* to decouple
Entkoppler *m (bioch)* uncoupler, uncoupling agent
Entkopplung *f (bioch)* uncoupling, decoupling; *(spectr)* decoupling
~/heteronukleare *(spectr)* heteronuclear spin-decoupling
~/homonukleare *(spectr)* homonuclear spin-decoupling
entkrusten to [de]scale
entkupfern to decopperize
Entladeklappe *f* discharge door
entladen 1. *(tech)* to discharge, to unload; 2. to discharge *(physics)*
Entladeöffnung *f* discharge opening
Entladevorrichtung *f* discharging apparatus (device), discharger
Entladung *f* 1. *(tech)* discharge, unloading; 2. discharge *(physics)*
Entladungselektrode *f* discharge electrode
Entladungserscheinung *f* discharge phenomenon
Entladungslampe *f***/ elektrodenlose** *(spectr)* electrodeless discharge lamp, EDL

Entladungspotential *n* discharge potential
Entladungsröhre *f* [gas] discharge tube
Entlastungsventil *n* relief (unloading) valve
Entlaubungsmittel *n* defoliant
entleeren to discharge, to empty, to drain [down], to evacuate *(a vessel)*; to siphon, to drain *(a liquid)*; to dump *(bulk material)*
Entleerung *f* discharge, emptying, drainage, evacuation *(of a vessel)*; siphoning, drainage *(of a liquid)*; dumping *(of bulk material)*
Entleerungsklappe *f* discharge door
Entleerungsschieber *m* discharge gate
Entleerungsstutzen *m* discharge (runoff) pipe
Entleerungsvorrichtung *f* discharging device, discharger
entlüften to deaerate, to degas, to bleed *(e.g. a vessel)*; *(ceram)* to de-air *(the clay)*; *(plast) to* breathe, to vent, to degas *(the mould)*; *(pap)* to relieve *(a digester)*
Entlüfter *m* deaerator
Entlüftung *f* 1. deaeration, degassing, bleeding *(as of a vessel)*; *(ceram)* de-airing *(of clay)*; *(plast)* breathing, venting, degassing *(of the mould)*; *(pap)* relief *(of a digester)*; 2. *s.* Entlüftungseinrichtung
Entlüftungsapparat *m s.* Entlüftungseinrichtung 2.
Entlüftungseinrichtung *f* 1. air relief (vent); 2. deaerator *(as of a steam generator)*
Entlüftungskammer *f (ceram)* de-airing chamber *(of a vacuum extrusion press)*
Entlüftungskanal *m* vent channel; *(plast)* mould vent
Entlüftungsleitung *f* vent line
Entlüftungsöffnung *f* air vent (relief)
Entlüftungspause *f (plast)* dwell *(on moulding)*
Entlüftungsrohr *n* vent (blow) pipe
Entlüftungsventil *n* vent valve
entmagnetisieren to demagnetize
Entmagnetisierung *f* demagnetization
~/adiabatische adiabatic demagnetization
entmanganen to demanganize
Entmanganung *f* demanganization
Entmanganungsfilter *n (hyd)* manganese filter
Entmethaner *m* demethanizer
entmethanisieren to demethanize
Entmethanisierung *f* demethanization
entmethylieren to demethylate
Entmethylierung *f* demethylation
entmineralisieren to demineralize
Entmineralisierung *f* demineralization
entmischen/sich to unmix, to separate, to segregate; to break, to crack, to deteriorate *(of emulsions)*; to disintegrate *(of fertilizers)*
Entmischung *f* unmixing, separation, segregation; disintegration *(of fertilizers)*
~ einer Emulsion emulsion breaking (breakdown), breaking (cracking) of emulsions
~/liquide *(geol)* liquation [differentiation] *(of fused rock)*
~/spinodale spinodal decomposition *(of a supersaturated liquid or solid solution)*
Entmischungschemikalie *f* emulsion breaking chemical, chemical emulsion breaker
Entnahme *f* 1. take-off, offtake, withdrawal, discharge; *(glass)* take-out; 2. *s.* Entnahmestelle; 3. *s.* Entnahmevorrichtung
~/doppelphasige double withdrawal *(on extracting)*
~/einphasige single withdrawal *(on extracting)*
~/vollständige diamond separation, completion of square *(on extracting)*
~/wechselphasige alternate withdrawal *(on extracting)*
Entnahmebauwerk *n (hyd)* intake
Entnahmeende *n* discharge end
Entnahmeflasche *f (hyd)* sample bottle
Entnahmegerät *n* sampler
Entnahmegreifer *m (glass)* take-out tongs (jaw)
Entnahmeloch *n (glass)* gathering hole (opening)
Entnahmemenge *f (hyd)* water withdrawal
Entnahmeöffnung *f* discharge opening (aperture)
Entnahmestelle *f* discharge point; *(glass)* gathering hole (opening); *(hyd)* sampling point (site), point of sampling; *(hyd)* intake location (site)
Entnahmeteil *n (glass)* working chamber (end)
Entnahmeverhältnis *n (distil)* rate of withdrawal
Entnahmevorrichtung *f* discharging device, discharger, discharge, take-off, offtake; *(glass)* take-out [mechanism]
entnaphthal[is]ieren to denaphthalize
Entnaphthal[is]ierung *f* denaphthalization
entnehmen to take off, to withdraw, to discharge; *(glass)* to take out
~/eine Probe to sample, to take (draw, withdraw) a sample
Entner-Doudoroff-Abbauweg *m*, **Entner-Doudoroff-Weg** *m (bioch)* Entner-Doudoroff pathway
entolen *(tann)* to deolate
entölen to deoil
Entolung *f (tann)* deolation
Entölung *f* deoiling
entomopathogen entomopathogenic *(causing illness of insects)*
entorientieren to disorient
entozonisieren to deozonize
Entozonisierung *f* deozonation
Entozonung *f s.* Entozonisierung
entparaffinieren to deparaffin[ize], to dewax
Entparaffinierung *f* deparaffinization, dewaxing
~ mit Lösungsmitteln solvent dewaxing
~ mit Propan propane dewaxing
Entparaffinierungsanlage *f* dewaxing plant
Entpentaner *m* depentanizer
entpentanisieren to depentanize
Entpentanisierung *f* depentanization
entphenol[ier]en to dephenolize, to dephenolate
Entphenolierung *f* dephenol[iz]ation
Entphenolierungsanlage *f* dephenolizing plant
Entphenolung *f s.* Entphenolierung
entphosphoren to dephosphorize
Entphosphorung *f* dephosphorization
entpickeln *(tann)* to depickle

Entpolarisierungsgrad *m* degree of depolarization
entpolymerisieren to depolymerize
Entpolymerisierung *f* depolymerization
Entpropaner *m* depropanizer
entpropanisieren to depropanize
Entpropanisierkolonne *f* depropanizer
Entpropanisierung *f* depropanization
entquellen *(tann)* to deplete
entrahmen to cream [off], to skim *(milk)*
Entrahmung *f* creaming, skimming *(of milk)*
Entrahmungsschärfe *f (food)* creaming (skimming) efficiency
Entrahmungszentrifuge *f* milk (cream) separator, milk centrifuge
entrinden *(pap)* to [de]bark, to peel, *(Am also)* to ross
Entrinder *m (pap)* barking machine, barker
~/hydraulischer hydraulic (stream) barker
entrindet *(pap)* bark-free
Entrindung *f (pap)* [de]barking, peeling, *(Am also)* rossing
~/chemische chemical [de]barking
~/hydraulische hydraulic [de]barking
~/mechanische mechanical [de]barking
Entrindungsanlage *f (pap)* barking plant
Entrindungsmaschine *f (pap)* barking machine, barker
Entrindungstrommel *f (pap)* barking drum, tumbler
Entropie *f* entropy
~/absolute molare third-law entropy
~ der Nullpunktskonfiguration zero-point configurational entropy
~/molare molar entropy
~/partielle molare partial molar entropy
Entropieabnahme *f* entropy decrease
Entropieänderung *f* entropy change
Entropieanteil *m* entropy contribution
Entropieeffekt *m* entropy effect
Entropieelastizität *f* rubber (long-range) elasticity
Entropieerzeugung *f* entropy production (generation)
Entropiefaktor *m* frequency factor, [Arrhenius] pre-exponential factor, Arrhenius factor, A factor *(kinetics)*
Entropiesatz *m* law of entropy
Entropieverlust *m* loss of entropy
Entropiewert *m* entropy value
Entropiezunahme *f*, **Entropiezuwachs** *m* entropy increase, positive entropy change, gain of entropy
Entrostungsmittel *n* rust-removing agent, rust remover
entrußen to desoot
entsaften *(food)* to juice
entsalzen to free from salt; to desalinate, to desalt *(sea water)*; to deionize, to demineralize *(fresh water)*; *(petrol)* to desalt
Entsalzer *m s.* Entsalzungsaggregat
Entsalzung *f* desalin[iz]ation, desalting *(of sea water)*; deionization, demineralization *(of fresh water)*; *(petrol)* desalting
Entsalzungsaggregat *n* desalinating (desalination, desalting) unit, desalinator *(for sea-water treatment)*; deionizing unit, deionizer, demineralizer *(for fresh-water treatment)*; *(petrol)* desalter
Entsalzungsanlage *f* desalinating (desalination, desalting) plant *(for sea-water treatment)*; deionization plant *(for fresh-water treatment)*
Entsalzungswasser *n (petrol)* desalter waste water
entsanden *(hyd)* to degrit
entsäuern to deacidify, to neutralize
Entsäuerung *f* deacidification, neutralization
~/kontinuierliche continuous neutralization *(on making margarine)*
entschälen *(text)* to boil off (out), to degum; to scour *(silk)*
Entschälen *n (text)* boiling-off, degumming; scouring *(of silk)*
entschäumen to defoam, *(mechanically:)* to skim [off]
Entschäumer *m* 1. *(biot)* foam separator; 2. *s.* Entschäumungsmittel
Entschäumung *f* defoaming, *(mechanically:)* skimming[-off]
Entschäumungsmittel *n* defoaming agent, defoamer, foam breaker (killer)
entschlacken to slag, to free from slag
Entschlackung *f* slagging, *(coal also)* clinker discharge
entschlammen to desludge, *(relating to very fine particles:)* to deslime
entschleimen to deslime; to degum *(oil)*
entschlichten *(text)* to desize, to free from size; *(glass)* to clean
Entschlichten *n***/enzymatisches (fermentatives)** *(text)* enzyme desizing
~/thermisches *(glass)* heat cleaning
Entschlichtungsbad *n (text)* desizing bath
Entschlichtungsmittel *n (text)* desizing agent
Entschlüsselung *f* deciphering, cracking *(of the genetic code)*
entschwefeln to desulphur[ize]
Entschwefelung *f* desulphur[iz]ation
~/hydrierende hydrodesulphurization, HDS
~/physikalische physical desulphurization
~/trockene dry desulphurization
Entschweißbad *n (text)* scouring bath *(for wool)*
entschweißen *(text)* to scour, to degrease *(wool)*
Entschweißen *n (text)* scouring, degreasing, desuinting *(of wool)*
Entschweißungsmittel *n (text)* scouring (degreasing) agent, degreaser
entseuchen 1. *(med)* to disinfect; 2. *(nucl)* to decontaminate
Entseuchung *f* 1. *(med)* disinfection; 2. *(nucl)* decontamination
Entseuchungsfaktor *m*, **Entseuchungsgrad** *m (nucl)* decontamination factor
Entseuchungsindex *m (nucl)* decontamination index
Entseuchungsmittel *n (nucl)* decontaminating agent (chemical)

entsilbern to desilver[ize]
Entsilberung *f* desilverization, desilvering
entsorgen to dispose
Entsorgung disposal
Entsorgungsstandort *m* disposal site
entspannen to expand, to release; *(pap)* to relieve *(a digester)*
Entspanner *m* expansion valve
Entspannung *f* expansion, release, stress relief; *(pap)* relief *(of a digester)*
Entspannungsdestillation *f* **[/kontinuierliche]** flash distillation, continuous equilibrium vaporization
Entspannungsflotation *f (hyd)* dissolved air floatation, DAF
Entspannungsglühen *n (met)* stress relief annealing, stress-relieving anneal
Entspannungskammer *f* flash chamber (vessel, trap) *(of a flash evaporator)*
Entspannungskühler *m* flash cooler
Entspannungsmaschine *f* expansion engine, expander [machine]
Entspannungsofen *m (met)* stress-relieving furnace
Entspannungsventil *n* expansion valve
Entspannungsverdampfer *m* flash evaporator, flasher
Entspannungsverdampfung *f* flash (instantaneous) vaporization, flash evaporation
Entspannungsversuch *m (plast)* [stress-]relaxation experiment
Entspannungszone *f (hyd)* air release zone *(of a floatation thickener)*
entspiralisieren *(bioch)* to untwist, to unwind *(the DNA double strand)*
Entspiralisierung *f (bioch)* untwisting, unwinding *(of the DNA double strand)*
entstabilisieren to destabilize
Entstabilisierung *f* destabilization
Entstabilisierungsphase *f (hyd)* destabilization stage *(coagulation)*
entstanden/an Ort und Stelle *(geol)* autochthonous
entstauben to [de]dust
entstäuben *s.* entstauben
Entstauber *m* dust catcher (collector, separator, settler); elutriator *(moving-bed cracking)*
Entstaubung *f* dedusting
~/elektrische (elektrostatische) electrical (electrostatic) precipitation
Entstäubungsapparat *m (pap)* dusting machine, duster *(for rags)*
Entstaubungsgrad *m* collection efficiency
~/logarithmischer decontamination factor, DF
entstearin[is]ieren to destearinate, to destearinize, to demarg[ar]inate, to winterize *(oils)*
Entstearin[is]ierung *f* destearin[iz]ation, demarg[ar]ination, winterization *(of oils)*
entstehen to originate, to be formed, to form
Entstehung *f* origination, formation, generation, nascency; *(geoch)* genesis *(as of coal or petroleum)*
Entstehungsort *m (geol)* site of formation
entstrahlen *(nucl)* to decontaminate
Entstrahlung *f (nucl)* decontamination
entteeren to detar
Entteerer *m* tar separator (extractor)
Entteerung *f* detarring, tar separation
enttoluolen to detoluate
Enttoluolen *n* detoluation
entwachsen to dewax
Entwachsen *n* **mit Lösungsmitteln** solvent dewaxing
entwässerbar dewaterable
Entwässerbarkeit *f* dewaterability
Entwässerer *m* dehydrator
entwässern to dehydrate, to dewater, to desiccate, to dry; *(pap)* to drain *(the web in the wet part)*; to decker *(to pass pulp over a wet machine)*
Entwässerung *f* dehydration, dewatering, desiccation, drying; *(pap)* drainage *(of the web)*; deckering *(of pulp)*
~/mechanische mechanical dewatering
~ mittels Bandfilterpresse *(hyd)* belt pressing
Entwässerungsanlage *f* dehydration plant, concentrator
Entwässerungsgerät *n* dehydrator
Entwässerungsgeschwindigkeit *f (hyd)* rate of dewatering, dewatering speed; *(pap)* rate of drainage
Entwässerungsgrad *m (hyd)* degree (level) of dewatering; *(pap)* freeness [value]
Entwässerungsgradprüfer *m (pap)* freeness tester
Entwässerungsgradprüfung *f (pap)* freeness test
Entwässerungskolonne *f* dehydration column
Entwässerungsleistung *f (hyd)* dewatering performance
Entwässerungsleitung *f* drain line; *(hyd)* sewer line
Entwässerungsmaschine *f (pap)* decker, thickener, concentrator, wet machine
Entwässerungsmittel *n* dehydrating agent, dehydrator
Entwässerungsnetz *n* sewer (sewage) system, sewerage [system] • **mit einem ~ versehen** to sewer
~ eines Betriebs plant sewer
~/getrenntes separate sanitary sewer system
~/städtisches municipal sewer system
Entwässerungsperiode *f (pap)* drainage period
Entwässerungssieb *n* drain (rinse) screen
Entwässerungssystem *n s.* Entwässerungsnetz
Entwässerungswiderstand *m (pap)* drainage resistance
Entwässerungszeit *f (pap)* drainage period
Entwässerungszone *f (hyd)* [cake] drying zone, liquid extraction zone, dewatering part *(of a vacuum filter)*

entweichen to escape, to leak [out], to issue, to leave
Entweichen *n* escape, leak
~ **von Dämpfen** outbreathing
entwesen to disinfest
Entwesung *f* disinfestation
entwickeln 1. to evolve, to generate, to liberate, to release *(e.g. gas or heat)*; 2. to develop, to evolve *(e.g. a method)*; 3. to develop *(a photograph or chromatogram)*
~/sich to evolve, to be evolved, to form, to be formed
~/zur Betriebsreife to bring to the commercial stage
Entwickler *m (phot)* developing agent, developer; *(dye)* developing agent, developer, coupling component
~/erschöpfter *(phot)* exhausted developer
~/fotografischer photographic developer
~ **für Papiere** *(phot)* print developer
~/gerbender *(phot)* tanning developer
~/hart (kontrastreich) arbeitender *(phot)* high-contrast developer
~/verbrauchter *(phot)* exhausted developer
~/weich arbeitender *(phot)* low contrast (soft-working) developer
Entwicklerbad *n (phot)* developing bath
Entwicklerflecken *mpl (phot)* developer stains
Entwicklerformel *f* developer formula
Entwicklerlösung *f (phot)* developer (developing) solution
Entwicklerschale *f (phot, lab)* developing dish
Entwicklersubstanz *f (phot)* developing agent
Entwicklertank *m (phot)* developing tank
Entwicklervorschrift *f* developer formula
Entwicklerzusatz *m (phot)* developer improver
Entwicklung *f* 1. evolution, generation, liberation, release *(as of gas or heat)*; development, evolution *(as of a method)*; 2. development *(of a photograph or a chromatogram)*
~/absteigende *(chromat)* descending development
~/aufsteigende *(chromat)* ascending development
~/ausgedehnte *(phot)* prolonged development
~/horizontale *(chromat)* horizontal development
~/kontrollierte *(phot)* see-saw development
~ **nach Sicht** *(phot)* development by inspection
~ **nach Zeit** *(phot)* development by time
~/verlängerte *(phot)* prolonged development
~ **von Sauerstoff bei Belichtung** *(bioch)* photoevolution of oxyen
Entwicklungsbad *n (phot)* developing bath
Entwicklungsdauer *f (phot)* development time
Entwicklungsdose *f (phot)* developing tank
Entwicklungsfaktor *m (phot)* development factor, gamma value
~/Watkinsscher Watkins [development] factor
Entwicklungsfarbstoff *m* developed (ingrain) dye
Entwicklungsgerät *n***/chromatographisches** chromatography apparatus
Entwicklungsgeschwindigkeit *f (phot)* development rate
Entwicklungskammer *f* developing (chromatography) chamber
~ **für die aufsteigende Methode** ascending chromatography tank
Entwicklungskoeffizient *m***/arithmetischer** *(phot)* Watkins [development] factor
Entwicklungslösung *f (phot)* developer (developing) solution
Entwicklungspapier *n (phot)* development (developing) paper
Entwicklungsschleier *m (phot)* development (chemical) fog
Entwicklungsstadium *n* development stage
Entwicklungssubstanz *f (phot)* developing agent
Entwicklungstechnik *f* development technique
Entwicklungsverfahren *n* development technique
Entwicklungszyklus *m (biot)* developmental cycle
Entwindungszahl *f* deconvolution count *(mercerization of cotton)*
entwismuten to debismuth[ize]
Entwulsten *n (rubber)* debeading, bead removal
Entwulster *m (rubber)* debeader, debeading machine, bead cutter
entziehen to abstract, to extract, to withdraw
~/sich der Beobachtung to escape notice
Entziehung *f s.* Entzug
entzinken to dezinc[ify]
Entzinkung *f* dezincification
entzinnen to detin
Entzinnung *f* detinning
entzuckern to desugar[ize]
Entzuckerung *f* desugarization
Entzug *m* abstraction, extraction, removal, withdrawal
entzündbar [in]flammable, ignitable, ignitible
~/leicht readily flammable (ignitible), easy to ignite
~/nicht non-flammable
Entzündbarkeit *f* [in]flammability, ignitability, ignitibility
entzünden to ignite, to kindle, to light, to inflame
~/sich to ignite, to kindle, to light, to inflame
entzundern *(met)* to [de]scale, to scour
entzündlich *s.* entzündbar
entzündungshemmend *(pharm)* antiphlogistic, anti-inflammatory
Entzündungspunkt *m s.* Zündpunkt
entzwirnen *s.* entspiralisieren
Enzianviolett *n* gentian violet
Enzym *n* enzyme • **mit Enzymen anreichern** to enzymize
~/acylübertragendes acyl[-carrier] enzyme
~/adaptives adaptive enzyme
~/adsorbiertes (adsorptiv gebundenes) adsorbed enzyme
~/allosterisches allosteric enzyme, oligomeric (regulatory) enzyme
~/analytisches analytical enzyme
~/citratkondensierendes [citrate-]condensing enzyme, citrate synthase, citrogenase

~/citratspaltendes citrate cleavage enzyme, ATP-citrate lyase
~/doppelköpfiges double-headed enzyme
~/eingekapseltes *s.* ~/gekapseltes
~/eingeschlossenes *(biot)* entrapped enzyme
~/eiweißabbauendes (eiweißspaltendes) proteolytic (protein-digesting) enzyme, protease
~/extrazelluläres extracellular (exocellular) enzyme, exoenzyme
~/fettspaltendes lipolytic enzyme
~/fixiertes *s.* ~/immobilisiertes
~ für die Analytik analytical enzyme
~/gekapseltes *(biot)* microencapsulated (MEC) enzyme
~/gelbes flavoprotein, yellow enzyme
~/immobilisiertes bound enzyme; *(biot)* immobilized enzyme
~/in Fasern eingeschlossenes *(biot)* fibre-entrapped enzyme
~/in Gel eingeschlossenes *(biot)* gel-entrapped enzyme
~ in Mikrokapseln *s.* ~/gekapseltes
~/industrielles *(biot)* industrial enzyme, enzyme of industrial importance
~/induzierbares inducible enzyme
~/induziertes induced enzyme
~/intrazelluläres intracellular (endocellular) enzyme, endoenzyme
~/katabol[isch]es catabolic enzyme
~/konstitutives constitutive enzyme
~/kooperatives oligomeres *s.* ~/allosterisches
~/kovalent gebundenes *(biot)* covalently bonded (bound) enzyme, CVB enzyme
~/matrixgebundenes *s.* ~/trägergebundenes
~/mikrobielles microbial enzyme
~/mikroenkapsuliertes *s.* ~/gekapseltes
~/natives native enzyme
~/originäres natural enzyme
~/pektinabbauendes (pektinspaltendes) pectolytic (pectic) enzyme, pectinase
~/pektisches (pektolytisches) *s.* ~/pektinabbauendes
~/proteinspaltendes (proteolytisches) *s.* ~/eiweißabbauendes
~/quervernetztes *(biot)* cross-linked enzyme
~/sessiles *s.* ~/intrazelluläres
~/stärkeabbauendes (stärkespaltendes) starch-splitting enzyme, starch-reducing (starch-converting, amylolytic) enzyme, amylase
~/technisches *s.* ~/industrielles
~/trägerfixiertes (trägergebundenes) *(biot)* [carrier-]bound enzyme
~/urikolytisches uricolytic enzyme
~/verzweigend wirkendes branching (branch-point) enzyme, Q enzyme
~/zitratkondensierendes *s.* ~/citratkondensierendes
~/zweiköpfiges double-headed enzyme
Enzymabbau *m* enzyme degradation
Enzymaktivität *f* enzyme (enzymatic) activity
~/spezifische specific enzyme activity
Enzymäscher *m (tann)* enzyme unhairing
enzymatisch enzym[at]ic
Enzymaufarbeitung *f* enzyme preparation (recovery)
Enzymausbeute *f (biot)* enzyme yield
Enzymbehandlung *f* enzyme treatment
Enzymbeladung *f (biot)* enzyme loading *(per unit reactor volume)*
Enzymbildner *mpl (biot)* enzyme-producing microorganisms
Enzymbildung *f* enzyme formation (production) *(by microorganisms)*
Enzymbindung *f*/**adsorptive** *(biot)* enzyme bonding through adsorption
~/kovalente covalent bonding (attachment) to a carrier
Enzymbiosynthese *f* enzyme biosynthesis
Enzymchemie *f* enzyme chemistry
Enzymdonator *m* enzyme donor
Enzymeinheit *f* enzyme unit
Enzymeinschluß *m (biot)* enzyme inclusion (incorporation), entrapment of enzymes
Enzymeiweiß *n s.* Enzymprotein
Enzymelektrode *f* enzyme electrode
Enzymerkennungsregion *f* enzyme recognition site *(of transfer ribonucleic acid)*
Enzymextrakt *m* enzyme extract
Enzymfixierung *f (biot)* enzyme fixation
Enzymforscher *m* enzymologist
enzymgebunden enzyme-bound
Enzymgruppe *f* subclass *(classification of enzymes)*
Enzymherstellung *f (biot)* enzyme production
Enzymimmobilisierung *f (biot)* enzyme immobilization
Enzyminaktivierung *f* enzyme inactivation
Enzyminduktion *f (biot)* enzyme induction
Enzyminhibitor *m* enzyme inhibitor
Enzymkatalyse *f* enzyme (enzymatic) catalysis
enzymkatalysiert enzyme-catalyzed
Enzymkinetik *f* enzyme kinetics
Enzymkomplex *m* enzyme complex
Enzymkomplexierung *f* enzyme complexation
Enzymkonzentrat *n (biot)* enzyme concentrate
Enzymmechanismus *m* mechanism of enzyme action, enzymatic machinery
Enzymmembranreaktor *m (biot)* enzyme-membrane reactor
Enzymologe *m* enzymologist
Enzymologie *f* enzymology
Enzympräparat *n*, **Enzympräparation** *f* enzyme preparation
Enzym-Produkt-Komplex *m* enzyme-product complex
Enzymproduzenten *mpl (biot)* enzyme-producing microorganisms
Enzymprotein *n* enzyme protein, apoenzyme, colloid carrier

Enzymreaktion *f* enzyme (enzymatic) reaction
Enzymreaktor *m (biot)* enzyme reactor
Enzymrepression *f* enzyme repression
enzymresistent enzyme-resistant
Enzymrückgewinnung *f (biot)* enzyme recovery
Enzymschritt *m* enzymatic step
Enzymspezifität *f* enzyme specificity
Enzymstabilisierung *f (biot)* enzyme stabilization
Enzymstabilität *f* enzyme stability
Enzym-Substrat-Komplex *m* enzyme-substrate complex, ES complex, Michaelis[-Menten] complex
~/intermediärer enzyme-substrate intermediate
Enzymsynthese *f* enzyme synthesis
Enzymsystem *n* enzyme system
Enzymtechnik *f* enzyme technology
Enzymtechnologie *f* enzyme technology
Enzymträger *m (biot)* enzyme carrier, binding support
Enzymtröpfchen *n (biot)* enzyme droplet
Enzymumwandlung *f* enzym[at]ic conversion
Enzymverlust *m (biot)* loss of enzyme, enzyme loss
Enzymwirkung *f* enzyme action
E-Ofen *m s.* Elektroofen
Eosin *n* eosin, tetrabromofluorescein
Eosinfarbstoffsäure *f s.* Eosinsäure
eosinophil *(biol)* eosinophil[e], eosinophilic *(staining readily with eosin)*
Eosinsäure *f (dye)* bromo acid *(acid form of tetrabromofluorescein)*
EP *s.* 1. Epoxidharz; 2. Erstarrungspunkt
EPC-Ruß *m* EPC black, easy processing channel black
Ephedrin *n* ephedrine, α-hydroxy-β-methylaminopropylbenzene
Ephedrinhydrochlorid *n* ephedrine hydrochloride
Epichlorhydrin *n* epichlorohydrin, α-epichlorohydrin, chloropropylene oxide, chloromethyloxiran
Epidot *m (min)* epidote *(an aluminium calcium silicate)*
Epigenese *f*/**molekulare** *(bioch)* molecular epigenesis, self-assembly
epigenetisch *(bioch)* epigenetic *(originating from simpler precursors)*
Epihalogenhydrin *n* epihalohydrin
Epilation *f* epilation
Epilatorium *n s.* Epiliermittel
epilieren to epilate
Epiliermittel *n* epilator
Epilierwachs *n* epilating wax
Epilimnion *n* epilimnion *(surface layer of lakes)*
epimer epimeric
Epimer[e] *n* epimer[ide]
Epimerie *f* epimerism
epimerisieren to epimerize
Epimerisierung *f* epimerization
epitaktisch *(cryst)* epitaxial *(growing in oriented manner on a different crystalline substrate)*
Epitaxie *f (cryst)* epitaxy *(oriented growth on a different crystalline substrate)*
Epithelschutzvitamin *n* antiinfective (antixerophthalmic) vitamin, vitamin A
Epoxid *n* epoxide, oxirane
Epoxidgruppe *f s.* Epoxidring
Epoxidharz *n* epoxide (epoxy, ethoxylene) resin
Epoxidharzklebstoff *m* epoxy (epoxide resin) adhesive
Epoxidharzvernetzung *f* epoxy cure
Epoxidkleber *m s.* Epoxidharzklebstoff
Epoxidring *m* epoxide (epoxy) ring
Epoxidweichmacher *m* epoxide plasticizer
Epoxidation *f* epoxidation
epoxidieren to epoxidize
Epoxidierung *f s.* Epoxidation
Epoxyethan *n* *epoxyethane, oxiran, ethylene oxide, EO
Epoxygruppe *f s.* Epoxidring
Epoxyharz *n s.* Epoxidharz
1,2-Epoxypropan *n* 1,2-epoxypropane, 2-methyloxirane, propylene oxide
EP-Schmiermittel *n* EP (extreme-pressure) lubricant
Epsilonsäure *f* 1. $C_{10}H_5(OH)(SO_3H)_2$ epsilon acid, ε-acid, naphth-1-ol-3,6-disulphonic acid; 2. *s.* Amino-ε-säure
EPTC *s.* Ethyldipropylthiocarbamat
E-PVC *s.* Emulsions-Polyvinylchlorid
ER *s.* Retikulum/endoplasmatisches
Erbinerde *f s.* Erbiumoxid
Erbium *n* Er erbium
Erbiumchlorid *n* erbium chloride
Erbiumnitrat *n* erbium nitrate
Erbiumoxid *n* erbium oxide
Erbiumsulfat *n* erbium sulphate
erbsengroß pea-size
Erbsenstein *m (min)* pisolite *(calcium carbonate)*
Erdalkali *n* alkaline earth
Erdalkalicarbonat *n* alkaline-earth carbonate
Erdalkalichelat *n* alkaline-earth chelate
Erdalkalien *npl* alkaline earths
Erdalkalihydrogencarbonat *n* alkaline-earth hydrogencarbonate
Erdalkalihydrogencarbonatfällung *f* **mittels Kalkmilch** *(hyd)* [partial] lime softening
Erdalkaliionen *npl (hyd)* hardness[-producing] ions
Erdalkalimetall *n* alkaline-earth metal
Erdalkaliphosphat *n* alkaline-earth phosphate
Erdalkaliphosphor *m* alkaline-earth phosphor *(luminophore)*
Erdalkalisalz *n* alkaline-earth salt, *(hyd also)* hardness[-forming] salt, hardness[-causing] mineral, hard-water mineral
erdartig earthy
Erdbecken *n (hyd)* earthen basin
~/durchflossenes lagoon
Erdbodenkorrosion *f* soil corrosion
Erdbraun *n* umber *(a naturally occurring brown earth)*
Erdbraunkohle *f* earthy brown coal

Erde *f (ch)* earth; *(agric)* soil, earth
~/aktivierte activated (active) earth *(for bleaching)*
~/Kasseler Cassel earth (brown), ulmin brown *(a natural pigment)*
~/naturaktive natural earth *(for bleaching)*
erden to earth
Erden *pl***/seltene** rare earths
Erdfarbe *f s.* Erdpigment
Erdfaulversuch *m (text)* soil burial test
erdfeucht earth-moist
Erdgas *n* natural gas
~/feuchtes (nasses) wet [natural] gas
~/saures sour gas *(containing hydrogen sulphide and thiols)*
~/synthetisches synthetic (substitute) natural gas, SNG
~/trockenes dry [natural] gas
~/verflüssigtes liquefied natural gas, LNG
Erdgasabtrennung *f (petrol)* gas separation
Erdgasaustauschgas *n s.* Erdgas/synthetisches
Erdgasbenzin *n* natural gasoline
Erdgasersatzgas *n s.* Erdgas/synthetisches
Erdgaslagerstätte *f* deposit of natural gas
Erdgaspipeline *f* natural gas pipeline
Erdgasquelle *f* gas well
Erdgasrohrleitung *f* natural gas pipeline
erdig earthy
Erdkern *m* earth's core (nucleus), barysphere, centrosphere
Erdkruste *f* earth's crust
Erdleitung *f* underground line, buried duct
Erdnuß *f* peanut, groundnut *(from Arachis hypogaea L.)*
Erdnußbutter *f* peanut butter
Erdnußeiweiß *n* peanut protein
Erdnußeiweißfaser *f (text)* peanut protein [staple] fibre
Erdnußfaser *f (text)* peanut fibre
Erdnußfaserstoff *m (text)* peanut fibre
Erdnußhartfett *n* hydrogenated peanut oil
Erdnußkuchen *m* peanut cake
Erdnußlecithin *n* peanut lecithin
Erdnußöl *n* peanut oil
~/gehärtetes *s.* Erdnußhartfett
Erdnußsäure *f* arachidic acid, *eicosanoic acid
Erdöl *n* petroleum, rock oil
~/asphaltbasisches (asphaltisches) asphalt-base petroleum (crude oil, crude), asphaltic petroleum
~ auf Asphaltbasis *s.* ~/asphaltbasisches
~ auf gemischter Basis *s.* ~/gemischtbasisches
~ auf Naphthenbasis *s.* ~/naphthenbasisches
~ auf Paraffinbasis *s.* ~/paraffinbasisches
~/gemischtbasisch-asphaltisches intermediate asphaltic petroleum
~/gemischtbasisch-paraffinisches intermediate paraffinic petroleum
~/gemischtbasisches mixed-base petroleum (crude oil, crude)
~/naphthenbasisches naphthene-base petroleum (crude oil, crude), naphthenic petroleum
~/naphthenisch-aromatisches naphthenic-aromatic petroleum
~/naphthenisches *s.* ~/naphthenbasisches
~/nichtasphaltisches non-asphaltic petroleum
~/paraffinbasisches (paraffinisches) paraffin-base petroleum (crude oil, crude), paraffinic petroleum
~/paraffinisch-naphthenisches paraffinic-naphthenic petroleum
~/rohes crude petroleum (oil), crude
Erdölabwasser *n s.* Erdölraffinerieabwasser
Erdölasphalt *m* petroleum (artificial) asphalt, asphaltic residue
Erdölbasis *f* base of crude petroleum
Erdölbildung *f* petroleum (oil) genesis
Erdölbitumen *n s.* Erdölasphalt
Erdölbohrloch *n* petroleum (oil) well
Erdölbohrung *f* 1. oil-well drilling; 2. *s.* Erdölbohrloch
Erdölceresin *n* petroleum ceresin
Erdölchemie *f* petroleum chemistry, petrochemistry
Erdölchemikalie *f* petrochemical
Erdöldestillat *n* petroleum distillate
~/gesüßtes sweet oil
~/saures sour oil
~/süßes sweet oil
Erdöldestillation *f* petroleum distillation
Erdöldestillationsrückstand *m* petroleum distillation residue
Erdölentstehung *f* petroleum (oil) genesis
Erdölfalle *f* oil trap
Erdölfeld *n* oil field (pool, reservoir)
~ mit Gaskappe gas cap-drive field
~ mit Gastrieb gas-drive field
~ mit Wassertrieb water-drive field
~ unter Gaskappendruck gas cap-drive field
Erdölfolgeprodukt *n* petroleum product
Erdölförderung *f* petroleum production [from wells]
Erdölfraktion *f* petroleum fraction
erdölführend petroliferous, petroleum-bearing, oil-bearing
Erdölgas *n* petroleum gas
~/verflüssigtes liquefied petroleum gas, L.P. gas, L.P.G.
Erdölgenesis *f* petroleum (oil) genesis
erdölhaltig *s.* erdölführend
Erdölharz *n* petroleum resin
Erdölindikation *f* oil indication (show)
Erdölindustrie *f* petroleum (oil) industry
Erdölkohlenwasserstoff *m* petroleum hydrocarbon
Erdölkoks *m* petroleum (still) coke
Erdöllagerstätte *f* oil deposit, oil-field
Erdölmuttergestein *n* oil[-source] rock, mother rock
Erdölparaffin *n* petroleum wax
Erdölpech *n* petroleum pitch
Erdölprodukt *n* petroleum product

Erdölquelle *f* petroleum (oil) well
Erdölraffination *f* petroleum refining
Erdölraffinerie *f* petroleum (oil) refinery
Erdölraffinerieabwasser *n (hyd)* waste from petrochemical (petroleum refining) plants, petroleum refinery waste water, refinery waste
Erdölresiduum *n* petroleum residue
Erdölrückstand *m* petroleum residue
Erdölschwerbenzin *n* petroleum naphtha
Erdölspeichergestein *n* reservoir rock
erdölstämmig petroleum-based
Erdöltechnologie *f* petroleum technology
Erdölteer *m* petroleum tar
Erdölverarbeitung *f* petroleum refining
Erdölvorkommen *n* oil occurrence; oil deposit
Erdölwachs *n* petroleum wax
Erdpech *n* 1. mineral pitch, asphalt[e]; 2. *(min)* elastic bitumen, mineral caoutchouc, elaterite
Erdpigment *n* earth (mineral, natural) pigment, earth colour
Erdrinde *f* earth's crust
Erdschellack *m (dye)* Botany Bay gum *(from Xanthorrhoea hastilis R.Br.)*
Erdschwarz *n* slate black, black chalk *(a natural pigment)*
erdverlegt buried
Erdverrottungstest *m (text)* soil burial test
Erdwachs *n (min)* earth (ader) wax, native paraffin, ozokerite
~/gereinigtes ceresin [wax], ceresine
Ereignisfolge *f* sequence of events
Erethismus *m* erethism *(abnormal irritability as caused by mercury poisoning)*
erfassen to detect, to identify *(as in analyses)*
Erfassungsgrenze *f (anal)* detection (identification) limit
~/absolute absolute detection limit
~/relative relative detection limit
~/untere lower (minimum) detection limit
Erfolgsbohrung *f (petrol)* discovery well
Erfolgsorgan *n (bioch)* target
erforschen to investigate, to examine, to elucidate
Ergänzungsstoff *m (food)* minor nutrient
ergeben to yield
Ergebnis *n*/**experimentelles** experimental result
ergiebig high-yield
ergießen/sich to flush, to pour, to spill
Ergin *n* biocatalyst, biochemical catalyst, ergone
Ergobolismus *m (bioch)* ergobolism, energy metabolism *(obsolete term)*
Ergolinalkaloid *n s.* Ergotalkaloid
Ergosterin *n s.* Ergosterol
Ergosterol *n* ergosterol
Ergotalkaloid *n* ergot alkaloid
Ergotamin *n* ergotamine *(an ergot alkaloid)*
Ergotismus *m (tox)* ergotism
Ergußgestein *n* effusive (extrusive, volcanic) rock
Erhalt *m* obtaining *(as by synthesis)*
erhalten 1. to obtain *(as by synthesis)*; 2. to retain *(e.g. flavour)*
~/rein to obtain pure (in pure form), to obtain in a pure condition (state)
erhältlich/im Handel commercially available (obtainable)
Erhaltung *f* conservation *(as of mass or energy)*
Erhaltungsdüngung *f (agric)* maintenance dressing
Erhaltungskultur *f (biot)* maintenance culture
Erhaltungssatz *m* conservation law
~ der Energie *s.* Energieerhaltungssatz
~ der Masse (Materie) *s.* Massenerhaltungssatz
Erhaltungsstoffwechsel *m (bioch)* maintenance metabolism *(obsolete term)*
erhärten to harden, to set; *(if too rapidly or unintentionally:)* to set up
Erhärtung *f* 1. hardening, set[ting]; *(if too rapidly or unintentionally:)* set-up; 2. *(geol)* lithification, induration
erhitzen to heat
~/auf (bis zur) Rotglut to heat to redness, to make red-hot
~/auf (bis zur) Weißglut to incandesce
~/gelinde to heat gently (moderately, slightly)
~/in der Retorte to retort
~/mit fächelnder Flamme to brush with the free flame
~/sich to heat
~/unter Rückfluß *(distil)* to reflux
~/zum Sieden to heat to boiling
Erhitzer *m* heater
Erhitzung *f* heating
~/dielektrische dielectric heating
~/rote *(tann)* red heat discoloration *(of hides due to bacteria)*
Erhitzungsbehandlung *f (food)* heat processing
erhitzungsbeständig resistant to heat
Erhitzungsbeständigkeit *f* heat resistance (stability), thermal stability, resistance to heat
erhöhen to increase *(e.g. number, quantity)*; to raise, to elevate *(e.g. temperature, boiling point)*
~/den Weißgehalt *(pap)* to whiten
~/sich to rise *(as of temperature, boiling point)*; to increase *(of number, quantity)*
Erhöhung *f (act:)* raising, raise, elevation; *(process:)* rise, elevation *(as of temperature, boiling point)*; increase *(of number or quantity)*
erholen/sich *(tech)* to recover
Erholung *f (tech)* recovery
~/elastische *(rubber)* elastic recovery, rebound
~/zeitabhängige *(text)* recovery
erkalten to cool [down], to chill
~ lassen to allow to chill, to chill
Erkennbarkeit *f* perceptibility, recognizability, detectability
Erkennungsmittel *n* detector substance; *(food)* indicator ingredient (substance)
Erkennungsregion *f (bioch)* recognition site (sequence), acceptor (entry, aminoacyl tRNA, decoding) site, A site
Erkensator *m (pap)* erkensator

erkochen *(pap)* to cook
erkocht/alkalisch *(pap)* alkaline-cooked
Erkochung *f (pap)* cooking
Erlenmeyer-Kolben *m* Erlenmeyer flask
~/weithalsiger wide-mouthed Erlenmeyer flask, beaker flask
erlöschen 1. to go out, *(gradually:)* to die out (down) *(of a flame)*; 2. to die down, to subside *(of a reaction)*
Erlöschen *n* 1. going-out, *(gradually:)* dying-out, dying-down *(of a flame)*; 2. dying-down, subsidence *(of a reaction)*
ermitteln to elucidate, to establish, to determine, to find out
Ermittlung *f* elucidation, establishment, determination
~ der Klopffestigkeit [anti]knock rating
ermüden *(tech)* to fatigue
Ermüdung *f (tech)* fatigue
Ermüdungsbeständigkeit *f* fatigue resistance (strength), resistance to fatigue
Ermüdungsbruch *m* fatigue failure (fracture)
Ermüdungserscheinung *f (tech)* fatigue
Ermüdungsfestigkeit *f s.* Ermüdungsbeständigkeit
Ermüdungsgrenze *f* fatigue limit
Ermüdungsprüfung *f* fatigue test; *(rubber)* flex-cracking test
Ermüdungsschutzmittel *n (rubber)* anti-flex-cracking antioxidant
Ermüdungswiderstand *m* fatigue resistance
Ernährung *f* nourishment, *(esp biol, med)* nutrition
~/fehlerhafte malnutrition
~/heterotrophe heterotrophy
~/mineralische mineral nutrition
Ernährungsansprüche *mpl s.* Nährstoffbedarf
ernährungsbedingt *(med)* alimentary
Ernährungsforscher *m* nutritionist
Ernährungsforschung *f* nutritional investigation
Ernährungsphase *f (biot)* trophophase *(growth of microorganisms)*
Ernährungswissenschaft *f* nutrition science
Ernährungswissenschaftler *m* nutrition scientist, nutritionist
erniedrigen *s.* herabsetzen
~/sich to decrease *(as of boiling point)*
Erniedrigung *f (act:)* depression, lowering; *(process:)* decrease *(as of boiling point)*
Ernte *f (biot)* harvest *(of the fermentation product)*
ernten *(biot)* to harvest *(the fermentation product)*
Erosionskorrosion *f* erosion corrosion
erproben to test
Erprobung *f* testing
~ im Feldversuch field testing
~ in einer Pilotanlage pilot planting
erregbar excitable
Erregbarkeit *f* excitability
erregen to excite, to activate
Erregerlinie *f (anal)* exciting line
Erregerstrahlung *f* exciting radiation
Erregung *f* excitation, activation
Erregungsenergie *f* excitation energy
Ersatz *m* 1. replacement, substitution; 2. substitute
~/isomorpher *(bioch)* isomorphous replacement
Ersatzerdgas *n* substitute (synthetic) natural gas, SNG
Ersatzdüngung *f* compensation fertilization
Ersatzname *m s.* Ersetzungsname
Ersatzstoff *m* substitute
Erscheinung *f* phenomenon
Erscheinungspotential *n s.* Auftrittspotential
erschließen 1. to elucidate; 2. *(min, hyd)* to develop
Erschließung *f* 1. elucidation; 2. *(min, hyd)* development
erschmelzen to smelt *(metals)*
erschöpfen/sich to squeeze *(of resources)*
erschöpfend exhaustive
Erschöpfung *f* exhaustion *(as of a dye bath)*; exhaustion, squeeze *(of natural resources)*
Erschöpfungspunkt *m (hyd)* exhaustion point *(ion exchange)*
erschütterungsfrei vibration-free, vibrationless
Erschütterungsvorrichtung *f* rapper *(for cleaning electrodes)*
erschweren *(text)* to weight
Erschwerungsmittel *n (text)* weighting agent, weighter
ersetzbar replaceable, displaceable, substitutable
ersetzen to replace, to displace, to substitute
Ersetzen *n* replacement, displacement, substitution
Ersetzungsname *m* replacement name
erspinnen to spin *(chemical fibres)*
Erspinnen *n* spinning *(of chemical fibres)*
~ aus der Schmelze melt spinning, [melt] extrusion
~ aus Lösungen solution (solvent) spinning
Erspinnfärbung *f* spin (dope) dyeing
erspinngefärbt spin-dyed, spun-dyed, dope-dyed, *(in a melt also)* mass-dyed, *(in solution also)* solution-dyed
Erspinnlösung *f* spinning solution, [spinning] dope
erstarren to solidify, to harden, to set, to freeze, to congeal, *(esp coll)* to gel[ate]
~ lassen to solidify, to congeal, to set
~/wieder to refreeze; to regelate *(of ice)*
~/zu Gelee to jelly, to jellify, to gel[ate], to gelatinate, to gelatinize
Erstarren *n*, **Erstarrung** *f* solidification, hardening, set[ting], freezing, congealing, congelation, *(esp coll)* gelation
Erstarrungsgestein *n s.* Eruptivgestein
Erstarrungsintervall *n* solidification range
Erstarrungskurve *f* freezing[-point] curve, solidus curve *(of a melt)*
Erstarrungspunkt *m*, **Erstarrungstemperatur** *f* solidification (setting) point, s.p., freezing (congealing) point (temperature)
Erstarrungswärme *f* heat of solidification
Erstbelichtung *f (phot)* first (initial) exposure
Erstdestillation *f* primary distillation

ersticken to blanket, to choke *(fire)*
Erstkomponente *f (dye)* primary component, diazo (diazonium) component
Erstluft *f* primary air
Erstproduktzucker *m* first raw (product) sugar
Erstsubstituent *m* first substituent
Ertrag *m (agric)* yield; *(biot)* growth yield *(of microorganisms)*
Ertragsfähigkeit *f (agric)* productive capacity, crop-producing power *(of a soil)*
Ertragsgesetz *n (agric)* law of yields
Ertragskoeffizient *m (biot)* growth yield coefficient *(of microorganisms)*
Ertragswirkung *f (agric)* effect on yield *(of fertilizers)*
Erucasäure *f* erucic acid, **cis*-docos-13-enoic acid
Erucylalkohol *m* erucyl alcohol, *docos-13-en-1-ol
eruptieren *(petrol)* to blow out
Eruption *f (petrol)* blow-out
Eruptionskopf *m s.* Eruptionskreuz
Eruptionskreuz *n (petrol)* Christmas tree *(at the well head for controlling oil or gas production)*
eruptiv *(geol)* eruptive, igneous
Eruptivgestein *n* eruptive (igneous) rock
Eruptivkreuz *n s.* Eruptionskreuz
Eruptivstock *m (geol)* boss
erwärmen to heat, *(specif)* to heat gently (moderately, slightly), to warm
~/erneut to reheat
~/gelinde (mäßig) to warm gently (moderately, slightly)
~/sich to heat, to warm [up]
~/vorsichtig *s.* ~/gelinde
Erwärmung *f* heating, *(specif)* gentle heating, moderate (slight) heating, warming
~/dielektrische dielectric heating
~/erneute reheating
~/induktive induction heating
Erwärmungsgeschwindigkeit *f* heating rate
Erwartungswert *m* 1. expected value, expectation *(statistics)*; 2. *s.* ~/quantenmechanischer
~/quantenmechanischer expectation value
erweichen to soften
~/mit Peptisiermitteln *(rubber)* to peptize
~/thermisch to heat-soften
Erweichung *f* softening
~ mit Peptisiermitteln *(rubber)* peptization
~/thermische thermal (heat) softening
Erweichungsbereich *m*, **Erweichungsintervall** *n* softening range
Erweichungsmittel *n* softening agent, softener, emollient
Erweichungspunkt *m* softening point (temperature), *(glass specif)* Littleton [softening] point, seven-point-six temperature, 7.6 temperature *(at which the viscosity is $10^{7.6}$ poise)*
~ KS *s.* ~ nach Krämer-Sarnow
~ nach Krämer-Sarnow Kraemer and Sarnow softening point (temperature) *(e.g. on investigating fats, pitch)*
~ nach Vicat *(plast)* Vicat softening point (temperature), V.S.P., Vicat needle point
~ „Ring und Kugel" ring-and-ball softening point *(e.g. in investigating fats, pitch)*
~ RuK *s.* ~ „Ring und Kugel"
Erweichungstemperatur *f s.* Erweichungspunkt
Erweichungszone *f s.* Erweichungsbereich
Erweichungszustand *m* softening stage
erweitern to expand
~/sich to expand
Erweiterung *f* **der Außenelektronenschale** expansion of the valence shell
Erweiterungsbohrung *f (petrol)* appraisal well
Erythorbinsäure *f* erythorbic acid, isoascorbic acid
Erythren *n* erythrene, *buta-1,3-diene
Erythrin *m (min)* erythrine, erythrite, cobalt bloom *(cobalt(II) tetraoxoarsenate(V))*
Erythrinaalkaloid *n* erythrina alkaloid
Erythrit *m s.* Erythritol
Erythritol *n* erythritol, *1,2,3,4,-tetrahydroxybutane
Erythrodextrin *n* erythrodextrin[e]
Erythroform *f* erythro form *(stereochemistry)*
Erythrogensäure *f* erythrogenic acid, isanic acid, *octadec-17-ene-9,11-diynoic acid
Erythrosin *n* erythrosine *(disodium salt of tetraiodofluorescein)*
Erz *n* ore
~/abbauwürdiges pay ore
~/armes lean (low-grade) ore
~/bauwürdiges pay ore
~/feines fine ore
~/gemengtes complex ore
~/geringhaltiges (geringwertiges) lean (low-grade) ore
~/hochwertiges high-grade ore
~/komplexes complex ore
~/oxidisches oxidized ore
~/polymetallisches complex ore
~/primäres (protogenes) primary (protogenic) ore
~/reiches (reichhaltiges) high-grade ore
~/sulfidisches sulphide ore
~/zusammengesetztes complex ore
Erzanreicherung *f* concentration (enrichment) of ores
Erzaufbereitung *f* ore dressing (beneficiation)
~/mikrobielle *(biot)* microbial leaching, microbiological (bacterial) leaching
Erzaufbereitungsanlage *f* ore-dressing (ore-beneficiation) plant
Erzaufbereitungsverfahren *n* ore-dressing (ore-beneficiation) process
Erzbett *n* ore bed
erzbildend metallogen[et]ic
Erzbrecher *m* ore crusher (breaker)
Erzbrocken *m* lump of ore
Erzbrücke *f* ore bridge
Erzbunker *m* ore bunker
erzeugen to manufacture, to make, to produce *(e.g. chemicals)*; to generate *(e.g. steam)*

Erzeugnis *n* product, *(esp if relating to its origin)* make; *(distil)* liquid product
~/feuerfestes refractory [product]
~/grobkeramisches heavy clay product (ware)
~/hochtonerdehaltiges feuerfestes high-alumina refractory [product]
~/keramisches ceramic article (product), ceramic
~/pflegeleichtes *(text)* wash and wear product, w & w product
~/schmelzgeformtes fusion-cast refractory
Erzeugnispalette *f* production pattern, product slate
Erzeugnisse *npl***/feinkeramische** fine ceramics (ceramic ware)
~/oxidkeramische oxide-ceramic products, oxide ceramics
~/pyrotechnische pyrotechnics
Erzeugung *f* manufacture, making, make, *(esp over a specified period)* production; generation *(as of steam)*
Erzeugungsprogramm *n* production pattern
Erzfall *m* ore shoot
erzführend ore-bearing, metalliferous
Erzgangart *f* ore gangue
erzhaltig ore-bearing, metalliferous
Erzlager *n*, **Erzlagerstätte** *f* ore deposit, orebody
Erzmineral *n* ore mineral
Erzmöller *m* ore burden
Erzprobe *f (met)* 1. ore assay; 2. ore sample
erzreich rich in ore
Erzteilchen *n* ore particle
Erztrübe *f* ore pulp
~/wäßrige aqueous pulp of ground ore
Erzverteilung *f***/zonale (zonare)** *(geol)* zonal distribution of minerals, mineral zoning
Erzvorbereitung *f* ore preparation
Erzvorbereitungsanlage *f* ore-preparation plant
Erzvorkommen *n* ore deposit, orebody
Erzwäsche *f* 1. ore washing (cleaning); 2. ore washery
ES *s.* Emissionsspektroskopie
Eschka-Methode *f* Eschka method *(for determining total sulphur content)*
ESG *s.* Einscheibensicherheitsglas
E-Silber *n* electrolytic silver
ESMA *s.* 1. Elektronenstrahlmikroanalyse; 2. Elektronenstrahlmikroanalysator
Espartopapier *n* esparto paper
Espartowachs *n (pap)* esparto wax
Espartozellstoff *m* esparto pulp
Espartozellstoffabrik *f* esparto mill
ESR *s.* Elektronenspinresonanz
ESR-Spektroskopie *f* ESR (EPR) spectroscopy
eßbar edible, esculent, comestible
Eßbarkeit *f* edibility, edibleness
Esse *f* chimney, [smoke]stack
Essence absolue [de concrète] *f (cosmet)* absolute from concrete
Essence absolue d'enfleurage *f (cosmet)* enfleurage absolute
Essence concrète *f (cosmet)* concrete [oil]
essentiell essential
Essenz *f* essence
Essig *m* vinegar
Essigbakterien *npl s.* Essigsäurebakterien
Essigbildner *m s.* Essiggenerator
Essigester *m s.* Essigsäureethylester
Essigfabrik *f* vinegar factory
Essiggärung *f* vinegar fermentation, acetic[-acid] fermentation
Essiggeist *m s.* Dimethylketon
Essiggenerator *m (biot)* vinegar (trickling) generator
Essiggeruch *m* acetous odour
Essigherstellung *f* manufacture of vinegar, acetification
Essigmesser *m* acetometer, acetimeter
Essigmutter *f* mother of vinegar *(a slimy substance consisting of microorganisms)*
Essigprüfer *m s.* Essigmesser
Essigsäure *f* acetic acid, *ethanoic acid
~/aktive *s.* ~/aktivierte
~/aktivierte active acetate, acetyl coenzyme A, acetyl CoA
Essigsäurealdehyd *m s.* Acetaldehyd
Essigsäureamid *n* acetamide
Essigsäureamylester *m* amyl acetate
Essigsäureanhydrid *n* acetic anhydride, *ethanoic anhydride
Essigsäurebakterien *npl* acetic-acid bacteria, vinegar bacteria
Essigsäurebenzylester *m* benzyl acetate
Essigsäurebildung *f* formation of acetic acid
Essigsäurebornylester *m* bornyl acetate
Essigsäurebutylester *m* butyl acetate
Essigsäurechlorid *n* acetyl chloride
Essigsäureethylester *m* ethyl acetate, acetic ester
Essigsäuregärung *f* acetic[-acid] fermentation, vinegar fermentation
Essigsäuregenerator *m s.* Essiggenerator
Essigsäureherstellung *f***/submerse** *(biot)* submerged production of vinegar
Essigsäuremethylester *m* methyl acetate
Essigsäurephenylester *m* phenyl acetate
Essigsäurepropylester *m* propyl acetate
Essigsäuretoluidid *n* acetotoluidide
Essigsäureureid *n* acetylurea, *N*-monoacetylurea
E-Stahl *m s.* Elektrostahl
Ester *m* ester
~/aktivierter activated ester
~/cyclischer cyclic ester
~/innerer intra-ester, inter-ester
Esterase *f* esterase
Esteraustausch *m* ester exchange
Esterbildung *f* ester formation
Esterbindung *f* ester bond
Esterenolat *n* ester enolate
Esterharz *n* ester gum
Esterhydrolyse *f* ester hydrolysis

esterifizieren *s.* verestern
Esterkondensation *f* ester condensation
~/Claisensche Claisen condensation
~/Dieckmannsche [intramolekulare] Dieckmann condensation (reaction)
Esteröl *n* [organic] ester oil, [organic] ester lubricant
Ester-Pool *m (bioch)* ester pool *(a group of phosphoric-acid esters possessing a sugar component)*
Esterspaltung *f* ester cleavage
~ nach Hunsdiecker Hunsdiecker cleavage (reaction)
Esterumlagerung *f* rearrangement of esters
Esterverseifung *f* ester saponification
Esterzahl *f* ester number (value)
Estragol *n* estragole, chavicol methyl ether, *1-allyl-4-methoxybenzene
Estragonöl *n* tarragon oil *(from Artemisia dracunculus L.)*
Etagenhöhe *f* daylight *(of a multiplaten press)*
Etagennutsche *f* multiplate (horizontal plate) filter
Etagenpresse *f* multidaylight press, [multiple-] daylight press, [multi]platen press
Etagenvulkanisierpresse *f (rubber)* daylight curing press
Etagenwalzwerk *n* multiplex-roll plant
Ethan *n* ethane
Ethanal *n* *ethanal, acetaldehyde
Ethanamid *n* acetamide, ethanamide
Ethandial *n* *ethanedial, oxaldehyde, glyoxal
Ethandiamid *n* oxamide, oxalic acid diamide
1,2-Ethandiamin *n s.* Ethylendiamin
Ethan-1,2-dicarbonsäure *f* *ethane-1,2-dicarboxylic acid, *butanedioic acid, succinic acid
Ethan-1,2-diol *n* *ethane-1,2-diol, ethylene glycol, EG
Ethandisäure *f* *ethanedioic acid, oxalic acid
Ethanol *n* *ethanol, ethyl alcohol
Ethanolamin *n* ethanolamine, *(specif)* *2-aminoethane-1-ol, colamine
Ethanolfermentation *f s.* Ethanolgärung
Ethanolgärung *f* ethanol[ic] fermentation
~/schnelle *(biot)* rapid ethanol fermentation
Ethanolgehalt *m* ethanol content (strength)
ethanolisch ethanolic
Ethanolkephalin *n* 3-phosphatidyl ethanolamine
ethanollöslich ethanol-soluble, soluble in ethanol
ethanolunlöslich ethanol-insoluble, insoluble in ethanol
Ethanolyse *f* ethanolysis
Ethansäure *f* *ethanoic acid, acetic acid
Ethansäureanhydrid *n* *ethanoic anhydride, acetic anhydride
Ethansulfonsäure *f* ethanesulphonic acid
Ethanthiol *n* *ethanethiol, ethyl hydrosulphide
Ethen *n* *ethene, ethylene
Ethencarbonsäure *f* ethylenecarboxylic acid, *propenoic acid, acrylic acid
Ethenkohlenwasserstoff *m s.* Ethylenkohlenwasserstoff
Ethenol *n* *ethenol, vinyl alcohol
Ethenylgruppe *f s.* Vinylgruppe
Ether *m* R–O–R' ether, *(specif)* $C_2H_5OC_2H_5$ diethyl ether, ordinary ether
~/absoluter *s.* ~/wasserfreier
~/aromatischer aromatic (aryl) ether
~/cyclischer cyclic ether
~/einfacher R–O–R symmetrical ether
~/gemischter R'–O–R" mixed (unsymmetrical) ether
~/symmetrischer *s.* ~/einfacher
~/unsymmetrischer *s.* ~/gemischter
~/wasserfreier absolute ether
Etherat *n* etherate
Etherbildung *f* ether formation
Etherbindung *f* ether bond
Etherextraktion *f* ether extraction
etherisch ethereal, etherial
etherlöslich ether-soluble, soluble in ether
Etherspaltung *f* ether cleavage
etherunlöslich ether-insoluble, insoluble in ether
Ethidiumbromid *n (bioch)* ethidium bromide
Ethin *n* acetylene, *ethyne
Ethindicarbonsäure *f* acetylenedicarboxylic acid, *butynedioic acid
Ethinkohlenwasserstoff *m* acetylenic (acetylene) hydrocarbon, *alkyne
Ethinylbenzen *n* ethynylbenzene
Ethinylgruppe *f* –C≡CH ethynyl group
ethinylieren to ethynylate
Ethinylierung *f* ethynylation
Ethinylrest *m s.* Ethinylgruppe
Ethisteron *n* ethisterone, 17α-hydroxy-4-pregnen-20-yn-3-one
Ethoxalylierung *f* ethoxalylation
Ethoxyanilin *n* ethoxyaniline, phenetidine, aminophenol ethyl ether
Ethoxybenzen *n* ethoxybenzene, ethyl phenyl ether, phenetole
Ethoxybenzoesäure *f* ethoxybenzoic acid
Ethoxyethan *n* *ethoxyethane, diethyl ether
2-Ethoxyethanol *n* *2-ethoxyethanol, 2-ethoxyethyl alcohol
2-Ethoxyethylalkohol *m s.* 2-Ethoxyethanol
m-**Ethoxyphenol** *n* **m*-ethoxyphenol, resorcinol monoethyl ether
o-**Ethoxyphenol** *n* **o*-ethoxyphenol, catechol monoethyl ether, guaethol
p-**Ethoxyphenol** *n* **p*-ethoxyphenol, quinol monoethyl ether
p-**Ethoxyphenylharnstoff** *m* *p*-ethoxyphenylurea, dulcin
Ethylacetat *n* ethyl acetate, acetic ester
Ethylacetoacetat *n* ethyl acetoacetate
Ethylacetylen *n* *but-1-yne, ethyl acetylene
Ethylal *n* ethylal, *diethoxymethane, formaldehyde diethyl acetal

Ethylalkohol *m* ethyl alcohol, *ethanol
~/wasserfreier absolute [ethyl] alcohol
Ethylaluminium *n* triethylaluminium
Ethylamin *n* ethylamine
Ethylaminobenzoat *n* ethyl aminobenzoate
Ethylat *n* $C_2H_5OM^I$ ethylate, ethoxide
Ethylbenzen *n* ethylbenzene
Ethylbenzin *n* ethyl gasoline
Ethylbenzoat *n* ethyl benzoate
Ethylbromid *n* *bromoethane, ethyl bromide
Ethylbutyrat *n* ethyl butyrate, *ethyl butanoate
Ethylcarbamat *n* ethyl aminoformate, ethyl carbamate
Ethylcellulose *f* ethylcellulose
Ethylchlorid *n* *chloroethane, ethyl chloride
Ethylcinnamat *n* ethyl cinnamate
Ethylcrotonat *n* ethyl crotonate
2-Ethyl-*cis*-crotonylharnstoff *m* 2-ethyl-*cis*-crotonylurea, ectylurea
Ethylcyanid *n* ethyl cyanide, propionitrile
Ethylcyclohexan *n* ethylcyclohexane
Ethyldipropylthiocarbamat *n* ethyl-*N,N*-dipropylthiocarbamate, EPTC *(a herbicide)*
Ethyldisulfid *n*, **Ethyldithioethan** *n s.* Diethyldisulfid
Ethylen *n* 1. ethylene, *ethene; 2. *s.* Ethylenkohlenwasserstoff
Ethylenbromhydrin *n* *2-bromoethanol, ethylene bromohydrin
Ethylenbromid *n s.* Ethylendibromid
Ethylenbrücke *f* ethylene bridge
Ethylenchlorhydrin *n* *2-chloroethanol, ethylene chlorohydrin
Ethylenchlorid *n s.* Ethylendichlorid
Ethylencyanhydrin *n* ethylene cyanohydrin, 3-hydroxypropanenitrile
Ethylendiamin *n* ethylenediamine, 1,2-ethanediamine
Ethylendiamintetraacetat *n* ethylenediamine tetraacetate
Ethylendiamintetraessigsäure *f* ethylenediamine tetraacetic acid, EDTA
Ethylendibromid *n* *1,2-dibromoethane, ethylene dibromide, EDB
Ethylen-1,2-dicarbonsäure *f* ethylene-1,2-dicarboxylic acid, butenedioic acid
Ethylendichlorid *n* *1,2-dichloroethane, ethylene dichloride, EDC
Ethylen-Ethylacrylat-Copolymerisat *n* ethylene ethyl acrylate copolymer, EEA
Ethylenglykol *n* ethylene glycol, EG, *ethane-1,2-diol
Ethylenglykolmonoethylether *m* ethylene glycol ethyl ether, *2-ethoxyethanol
Ethylengruppe *f* $-CH_2CH_2$ ethylene group
Ethylenharnstoff *m* imidazolidin-2-one, ethylene urea
Ethylenimin *n* ethyleneimine, aziridine
Ethylenisomerie *f* ethylene isomerism
Ethylenkohlenwasserstoff *m* ethylenic hydrocarbon, *alkene, olefin[e]
Ethylenmilchsäure *f* ethylenelactic acid, *3-hydroxypropionic acid
Ethylenoxid *n* ethylene oxide, EO, oxiran, *epoxyethane
Ethylen-Propylen-Copolymerisat *n* ethylene-propylene copolymer
Ethylen-Propylen-Kautschuk *m* ethylene-propylene rubber, EP-rubber, EPR
Ethylen-Propylen-Terpolymerisat *n* ethylene-propylene terpolymer, EPT
Ethylenreihe *f* ethylene series
Ethylen-Vinylacetat-Copolymerisat *n* ethylene-vinylacetate copolymer, EVA
Ethylester *m* ethyl ester
Ethylethen *n* ethylethylene
Ethylether *m s.* Diethylether
Ethylethylen *n s.* Ethylethen
Ethylfluid *n* ethyl fluid *(an antiknock additive, mainly consisting of tetraethyl lead)*
Ethylformiat *n* ethyl formate
Ethylgruppe *f* C_2H_5- ethyl group (residue)
Ethylhalogenid *n* ethyl halide (halogenide)
Ethylhexanoat *n* ethyl hexanoate
Ethylhydrogensulfat *n* ethyl hydrogensulphate, ethylsulphuric acid
Ethylhydrosulfid *n* ethyl hydrosulphide, *ethanethiol
Ethylidenchlorid *n* ethylidene chloride, *1,1-dichloroethane
Ethylidenmilchsäure *f* lactic acid, ethylidenelactic acid, *2-hydroxypropionic acid
ethylieren to ethylate
Ethylierung *f* ethylation
Ethylierungsmittel *n* ethylating reagent
Ethyliodid *n* *iodoethane, ethyl iodide
Ethyliodidverbindung *f* ethiodide
Ethyllactat *n* ethyl lactate
Ethyllaurat *n* ethyl laurate
Ethylmethylacetylen *n* *pent-2-yne, *(deprecated:)* ethyl methyl acetylene
Ethylmethylsulfid *n* ethyl methyl sulphide
Ethylnitrat *n* ethyl nitrate
Ethylnitrit *n* ethyl nitrite
Ethylphenylacetat *n* ethyl phenyl acetate
Ethylphenylether *m* ethyl phenyl ether, ethoxybenzene, phenetole
Ethylphenylketon *n* ethyl phenyl ketone, propiophenone
Ethylphthalat *n* diethyl phthalate
Ethylpolysiloxan *n* *polyethylsiloxane, ethyl silicone
Ethylpropionat *n* ethyl propionate
Ethylradikal *n* [free] ethyl radical
Ethylrest *m s.* Ethylgruppe
Ethylrot *n* ethyl red *(a quinoline dye)*
Ethylschwefelsäure *f* ethyl sulphuric acid, ethyl hydrogensulphate

Ethylsilicat-Gießverfahren *n (ceram)* ethyl silicate casting process
Ethylsilicon *n s.* Ethylpolysiloxan
Ethylstearat *n* ethyl stearate
Ethylsulfat *n s.* Diethylsulfat
Ethylsulfid *n s.* Diethylsulfid
Ethylthioethan *n* ethylthioethane, diethyl sulphide
Ethylurethan *n* ethyl aminoformate, ethyl carbamate
Ethylvalerat *n* ethyl valerate
Ethylvalerianat *n s.* Ethylvalerat
Ethylxanthogensäure *f* ethylxanthogenic acid, xanthogenic acid, dithiocarbonic acid *O*-ethyl ester
Etikett *n* label; tag
etikettieren to label; to tag
Etruria-Mergel *m (ceram)* etruria marl
Ettringit *m (min)* ettringite *(aluminium calcium hydroxide sulphate)*
Eudalin *n* eudalene, 7-isopropyl-1-methylnaphthalene
Eudialyt *m (min)* eudialyte *(a cyclosilicate containing zirconium)*
Eudiometer *n* eudiometer *(for measuring volume changes of gases during combustion)*
Eugenol *n* eugenol, 1-allyl-4-hydroxy-3-methoxybenzene
Euglobulin *n (bioch)* euglobulin
Eukalyptol *n* eucalyptol, cineole, cineole-1,8
Eukalyptuskino *n* ribbon gum kino *(from Eucalyptus specc.)*
Euklas *m (min)* euclase *(aluminium beryllium hydroxide orthosilicate)*
Eukolloid *n* eucolloid
Eulytin *m (min)* eulytine, eulytite *(bismuth(III) orthosilicate)*
Europium *n* Eu europium
Europium(II)-chlorid *n* europium(II) chloride, europium dichloride
Europium(III)-chlorid *n* europium(III) chloride, europium trichloride
Europiumdichlorid *n s.* Europium(II)-chlorid
Europiumoxid *n* europium oxide
Europiumsulfat *n* europium sulphate
Europiumtrichlorid *n s.* Europium(III)-chlorid
Eutektikum *n* eutectic [mixture]
eutektisch eutectic
eutektoid eutectoid
Eutektoid *n* eutectoid
Eutervorlage *f*, **Eutervorstoß** *m (distil)* udder[-type receiver changer]
eutroph *(hyd)* eutrophic *(rich in dissolved plant nutrients)*
Eutrophierung *f (hyd)* eutrophication
Euxenit *m* euxenite *(a rare-earth mineral)*
evakuieren to evacuate, to exhaust
Evakuierung *f* evacuation, exhaustion
Evans-Element *n*, **Evans-Korrosionselement** *n* [differential] aeration cell, oxygen [concentration] cell
Evaporation *f* evaporation; *(hyd quantitatively:)* evaporation loss
evaporieren to evaporate
Evaporimeter *n* evaporimeter, evaporometer
Evaporisation *f* evaporation
Evelyn-Röhrchen *n* Evelyn tube *(turbidimetry)*
Ewens-Bassett-Zahl *f (nomencl)* Ewens-Bassett number, charge number *(of ionic charge)*
E_T-Wert *m* E_T-value *(for characterizing the polarity of solvents)*
Exaltation *f*/**optische** [optical] exaltation *(in molar refraction)*
Excimer *n (spectr)* excimer, excited dimer *(consisting of an excited and a non-excited molecule of the same kind)*
Excimerlaser *m* excimer laser
Exciplex *m* exciplex, excited complex *(consisting of an excited molecule A and a non-excited molecule B)*
Excisionsreparatur *f* excision repair *(of deoxyribonucleic acid)*
Excitonentransfer *m (bioch)* exciton transfer
Exergie *f (phys ch)* exergy
exergon[isch] exoergic, energy-releasing, energy-yielding, *(esp bioch)* exergonic
Exhalation *f* exhalation, outgassing *(as from volcanoes)*
Exhalographie *f (anal)* vacuum hot extraction analysis
Exhaustor *m* exhauster
Exinit *m (coal)* exinite
exinitisch *(coal)* exinitic
existenzfähig capable of existence
Exkret *n (biol)* excretum
Exkretion *f (biol)* excretion
exkretorisch *(biol)* excretory
exocyclisch exocyclic
Exoelektron *n* exoelectron
Exoenzym *n* 1. *s.* Enzym/extrazelluläres; 2. *enzyme acting on the terminal parts of a chain molecule*
exoergonisch *s.* exergon
exokrin exocrine
Exopolysaccharid *n* exopolysaccharide
Exosmose *f* exosmosis
exosmotisch exosmotic
exotherm[isch] exothermic, heat-liberating
~/schwach mildly exothermic
Exotoxin *n* exotoxin
expandieren to expand, to dilate
expansibel expansible
Expansion *f* expansion, dilatation
~/adiabatische adiabatic expansion
~/is[o]enthalpische isenthalpic expansion
~/isotherme isothermal expansion
Expansionsmaschine *f* expansion engine, expander [machine]
Expansionsnebelkammer *f (nucl)* expansion [cloud] chamber, cloud chamber

Expansionsturbine *f* turboexpander
Expansionsventil *n* expansion valve
Expansivzement *m* expanding (expansive) cement
Expektorans *n*, **Expektorantium** *n* *(pharm)* expectorant
Experiment *n* experiment *(for compounds s. under* Versuch*)*
Experimentalchemie *f* experimental chemistry
Experimentalvorlesung *f* demonstration lecture
Experimentator *m* experimentalist, experimen[ta]tor
experimentell experimental
Experimentelles *n* experimental *(in treatises)*
experimentieren to experiment[alize]
Experimentieren *n* experimentation
Experimentierkunst *f s.* Experimentiertechnik
Experimentiertechnik *f* experimental technique
explodierbar *s.* explosiv
explodieren to explode
~ **lassen** to explode, to blow up
Exploration *f* exploration
Explorationsbohrloch *n (petrol)* exploration (exploratory) well, wildcat
Explorationsbohrung *f* 1. *(petrol)* exploration drilling; 2. *s.* Explorationsbohrloch
explosibel *s.* explosiv
Explosion *f* explosion, blast, shot • **zur ~ bringen** to set off
explosionsartig explosive
Explosionsbereich *m* explosive range (limits)
Explosionsdruck *m* explosion pressure
Explosionsfähigkeit *f s.* Explosivität
Explosionsgefahr *f* explosion hazard, danger of explosion
explosionsgefährlich explosive, explosible
explosionsgeschützt explosion-proof
Explosionsgeschwindigkeit *f* explosion velocity
Explosionsgrenze *f* explosive (explosion, explosivity) limit
~**/obere** upper explosive limit, UEL
~**/untere** lower explosive limit, LEL
Explosionsmethode *f* explosion method *(for determining molar heat)*
Explosionspipette *f* explosion pipette
Explosionsprodukt *n* explosion product
Explosionspunkt *m (petrol)* shot point
explosionssicher explosion-proof
Explosionsverfahren *n (pap)* explosion (Masonite) process *(chemigroundwood process)*
Explosionswärme *f* heat of explosion
Explosionswirkung *f* explosive action; explosive effect
explosiv explosive, explosible
~**/nicht** non-explosive
Explosivität *f* explosiveness, explosivity, explosibility
Explosivstoff *m* explosive
~**/brisanter** high explosive, H.E.
Explosivstoffchemie *f* chemistry of explosives
Exponent *m* exponent, superscript numeral, numeric superscript
~**/Bornscher** *(phys ch)* Born exponent
Exponentialpapier *n* semilog[arithmic] paper
exponieren to expose *(as to radiation or air)*; *(phot)* to expose [to light]
Exposition *f* exposure *(as to radiation or air)*; *(phot)* exposure [to light]
Expositionsdauer *f*, **Expositionszeit** *f (tox)* exposure duration (time), length of exposure *(as of animals to pesticides)*
Expressionsvektor *m (bioch)* expression vector
Exsikkator *m (lab)* desiccator
~ **mit Einsatz** filled desiccator
~ **nach Scheibler** Scheibler desiccator
Exsikkatordeckel *m* desiccator lid
Exsikkatorplatte *f* desiccator plate (disk)
Exsudat *n* exudate, exudation
Exsudation *f* exudation
Extender *m* extender, extending filler
Extenderweichmacheröl *n (rubber)* extending oil
Extinktion *f (spectr)* absorbance, absorbancy, extinction, optical density
Extinktionskoeffizient *m (spectr)* absorbance (extinction) coefficient
~**/molarer [dekadischer]** molar [decadic] absorption coefficient, molar absorptivity
~**/spezieller (spezifischer)** absorbency index, absorptivity *(proper)*
Extinktionskonstante *f s.* Extinktionskoeffizient
Extinktionskurve *f* extinction curve
extrahierbar extractable, extractible
Extrahierbarkeit *f* extractability, extractibility
extrahieren to extract, to leach, to lixiviate *(material containing valuable components)*; to extract, to leach out *(soluble substances)*
~**/erschöpfend** to exhaust
~**/gemeinsam** to coextract
Extrahieren *n* extraction, leach[ing], lixiviation *(of material containing valuable components)*; extraction, leaching-out *(of soluble substances)*
extrahierend extractive
Extrakolonneneffekt *m (chromat)* extracolumn effect
Extrakt *m* extract, essence
~**/alkoholischer** alcoholic extract
~**/Goulards** Goulard's extract, vinegar of lead *(aqueous solution of basic lead acetates)*
~**/trockener** dry extract
Extraktabnahme *f (ferm)* attenuation *(diminution of density of wort resulting from its fermentation)*
Extraktausbeute *f* extract yield
Extraktbrühe *f* extract liquor
Extraktende *n (petrol)* extract end
Extrakteur *m* extractor, extraction apparatus; contactor *(for solvent extraction)*
~ **mit Förderschnecken** screw-conveyor extractor
~ **mit waagerechten Siebplattenförderern** travelling-belt extractor

~/kontinuierlich arbeitender continuous extractor, continuous-extraction apparatus
~/liegender horizontal extractor
~/stehender vertical extractor
Extraktherstellung *f* extract manufacture
Extrakthydrierung *f* extract hydrogenation
Extraktion *f* extraction, leach[ing], lixiviation *(of material containing valuable components)*; extraction, leaching-out *(of soluble substances)*
~/diskontinuierliche discontinuous extraction
~ **fest-flüssig** solid-liquid extraction, leaching
~ **flüssig-flüssig** liquid[-liquid] extraction, solvent extraction
~ **in flüssigen Systemen** *s.* ~ flüssig-flüssig
~/kontinuierliche continuous extraction
~ **mit flüssigem** CO_2 *(biot)* liquid carbon dioxide extraction
~ **mit Gas im superkritischen Zustand** *s.* ~ mit überkritischen Gasen
~ **mit überkritischen Gasen** *(coal)* supercritical gas extraction
~/übermäßige overextraction
~ **von Feststoffen** *s.* ~ fest-flüssig
Extraktionsanalyse *f* extraction analysis
Extraktionsanlage *f* extraction plant
Extraktionsapparat *m* extraction apparatus, extractor; contactor *(for solvent extraction)*
~ **nach Bollmann** Bollmann extractor
~ **nach Soxhlet** Soxhlet [extractor]
Extraktionsaufsatz *m* extraction head; extractor jacket *(of an extraction apparatus)*
Extraktionsbatterie *f* extraction battery
Extraktionsbenzin *n* extraction naphtha
Extraktionsbrühe *f (tann)* leach liquor
Extraktionschromatographie *f* extraction chromatography
Extraktionsgefäß *n* extraction (extracting) vessel, *(esp with water also)* leaching tank (trough, vat, vessel), leach
Extraktionsgrad *m* degree of extraction
Extraktionsgut *n* material being *or* to be extracted
Extraktionsharz *n* wood rosin
Extraktionshülse *f* extraction thimble
~ **nach Soxhlet** Soxhlet thimble
Extraktionskolben *m* extraction flask
Extraktionskolonne *f* extraction column; contactor *(for solvent extraction)*
Extraktionskolophonium *n* wood rosin
Extraktionsmaschine *f* contactor *(for solvent extraction)*
Extraktionsmittel *n* extracting agent (solvent), extractant, *(esp for extracting soluble principles from drugs:)* menstruum
Extraktionspresse *f* filtration extractor
Extraktionsrückstand *m* extraction residue, *(pharm, food also)* marc, mark
Extraktionssäule *f* extraction column
Extraktionsstoff *m (distil)* separating agent
Extraktionssystem *n* extraction system
Extraktionsturm *m* extraction tower
Extraktionswäsche *f (text)* solvent scouring
Extraktionszeit *f* **je Charge** extraction cycle
extraktiv extractive
Extraktivdestillation *f* extractive distillation
Extraktivstoff *m s.* Extraktstoff
Extraktor *m s.* Extrakteur
Extraktphase *f* extract phase
Extraktseite *f (petrol)* extract end
Extraktstoff *m* extractive material (matter, substance), extractive
Extraktstripper *m* extract stripper extraction
Extraktverdampfer *m* extract evaporator
extramitochondrial *(bioch)* extramitochondrial *(occurring or existing outside of mitochondria)*
extranuklear extranuclear extraction
Extreme-pressure-Schmiermittel *n* extreme-pressure lubricant, EP lubricant
Extremum *n s.* Extremwert
Extremwert *m* extreme [value], extremum
Extrinsic-Faktor *m (bioch)* extrinsic factor
Extrudat *n* extrudate
Extruder *m* extruder, extruding machine, extrusion press
~/schneckenloser screwless extruder
Extruderfolie *f* extruded film
Extruderkopf *m* extruder (extrusion) head, *(plast also)* die head
Extrudermundstück *n* extruder (extrusion) die
extrudern *s.* extrudieren
Extrudersiegeln *n (plast)* extruded bead sealing
Extruderzylinder *m* extruder barrel
extrudieren *(plast)* to extrude
Extrudieren *n (plast)* extruding, extrusion
~ **mit Kühlwalzen** chill-roll extrusion
~ **von Trockenmischung** dry-blend extrusion
Extrudiererzeugnis *n* extrudate, extruded article
Extrudiermasse *f* extrusion compound
Extrusion *f (geol)* extrusion
Extrusionsblasen *n*, **Extrusionsblasformen** *n* extrusion blowing
Extrusionsgeschwindigkeit *f* extrusion speed
Extrusivgestein *n s.* Ergußgestein
Exzenterantrieb *m* eccentric drive
Exzenterpresse *f* eccentric press
Exzenterschwingsiebmaschine *f* eccentrically driven vibrating screen
exzentrisch eccentric[al], off-centre
Exzeßfunktion *f (phys ch)* excess function
Exzisionsreparatur *f (bioch)* excision repair
Exziton *n (phys ch)* exciton
EZ *s.* Esterzahl
E-Zink *n* electrolytic zinc

F

FA = Fluoreszenzanregung
FAAS = flammenlose Atomabsorptionsspektroskopie
Fabric-Presse *f (pap)* fabric press

Fabrik *f***/chemische** chemical works (plant)
Fabrikabwasser *n s.* Fabrikationsabwasser
Fabrikat *n* product, article; make *(as of a specific plant or country)*
Fabrikation *f* manufacture, make, making, *(esp over a specified period:)* production
Fabrikationsabfälle *mpl* industrial waste[s]
~/unvulkanisierte rubber scrap (waste), scrap (waste) rubber
Fabrikationsabwasser *n* process waste water
Fabrikationsgang *m* manufacturing process
Fabrikationsprogramm *n* production pattern (slate)
Fabrikationssicherheit *f* processing safety
Fabrikationswasser *n* process[ing] water, water for manufacturing use
Fabrikmarke *f* trademark, make
Fabrikwasser *n s.* 1. Fabrikationswasser; 2. Fabrikationsabwasser
Fabry-Perot-Interferometer *n (spectr)* Fabry-Perot interferometer
Fabry-Perot-Platte *f (spectr)* Fabry-Perot plate
Fabry-Syndrom *n (med)* Fabry's disease *(accumulation of ceramide trihexoside caused by galactosidase deficiency)*
fächeln to fan; to waft *(for testing odours)*
Fächerdüse *f* fan nozzle
F-Actin *n* F actin *(a fibrillar muscle protein)*
FAD *s.* Flavin-adenin-dinucleotid
fad[e] stale, insipid, flat, tasteless, dead • **~ werden** to stale
Faden *m* filament *(as of carbon or metal)*; thread *(as of glass, plastic, rubber)*; *(text)* yarn *(for knitting or weaving fabrics)*; thread *(for sewing)*; *(glass)* string *(a defect)*; *(nucl)* pinch *(of the ion current)*
~/einfacher *(text)* single yarn
~/metallisierter *(text)* metallized yarn
Fadenbildung *f s.* Fadenziehen
Fadenchromatographie *f* filament chromatography
Fadenendenabstand *m* end-to-end distance, chain-end distance *(of macromolecules)*
fadenförmig threadlike
Fadengalvanometer *n* string galvanometer
Fadenkorrektur *f* [emergent] stem correction, exposed thread correction *(with liquid thermometers)*
Fadenmolekül *n* thread[like] molecule, filamentary (linear) molecule
Fadenprobe *f (sugar)* string-proof test
Fadenstruktur *f* threadlike structure
Fadenthermometer *n* thread thermometer
~ nach Mahlke Mahlke thread thermometer
Fadenziehen *n* 1. *(coat)* cobwebbing, stringing *(a defect)*; 2. *(text)* fibre drawing
fadenziehend ropy, stringy
Fadeometer *n (text)* fadiometer
Fadheit *f* staleness, insipidness, flatness
Fagergren-Zelle *f* Fagergren floatation machine
fahl flat *(shade)*
Fahlerz *n (min)* fahlerz, fahlore *(collectively for tennantite and tetrahedrite)*
~/dunkles tetrahedrite *(a copper antimony sulphide often containing zinc)*
~/lichtes tennantite *(a copper arsenic sulphide often containing iron)*
Fahrbenzin *n***[/normales]** motor (regular) spirit (gasoline)
Fahrdieselkraftstoff *m* automotive diesel fuel (oil)
Fahrdieselöl *n s.* Fahrdieselkraftstoff
fahren to operate, to run *(e.g. an apparatus)*
~/diskontinuierlich to operate intermittently (batchwise)
Fahrweise *f (ch)* [mode of] operation
~/adiabat[isch]e adiabatic operation
~/diskontinuierliche batch operation
~ im Abwärtsstrom *(hyd, filtr)* downflow operation
~ im Aufwärtsstrom *(hyd, filtr)* upflow operation
~ im Gleichstrom *(hyd, filtr)* co-current operation
~/isotherme isothermal operation
~ mit flüssigem Schlackenabzug slagging operation, operation under slagging conditions
~ mit totalem Rücklauf *(distil)* total-reflux operation
~ ohne Destillatabnahme *(distil)* total-reflux operation
~/periodische batch operation
~/zirkulierende recycling
Fahrzeuglack *m* automotive coating (finish)
Fäkalabwasser *n (hyd)* human waste
Fäkalien *pl* faecal matter, faeces
Fäkalwasser *n s.* Fäkalabwasser
Faktis *m (rubber)* factice, rubber substitute
~/brauner brown (dark) factice, brown substitute
~/weißer white factice (substitute)
Faktor *m* factor, coefficient; volumetric (titrimetric) factor *(titrimetry)*; gravimetric (analytical) factor *(gravimetry)*
~ VIII *(bioch)* antihaemophilic factor, AHF
~ IX *(bioch)* Christmas factor
~/Boltzmannscher *(phys ch)* Boltzmann factor
~/elektronischer *(phys ch)* electronic factor
~/geometrischer *(phys ch)* geometric factor
~/gyromagnetischer gyromagnetic factor, g-factor
~/innerer *(bioch)* intrinsic factor *(a substance produced by stomach and intestinal mucosa)*
~/Oligomycinempfindlichkeit übertragender *(bioch)* oligomycin-sensitivity-conferring factor (protein)
~/präexponentieller *(phys ch)* [Arrhenius] pre-exponential factor, Arrhenius (A) factor, frequency factor
~/sterischer *(phys ch)* steric (probability) factor
~/stöchiometrischer stoichiometric factor (coefficient)
~/van't-Hoffscher *(phys ch)* van't Hoff factor
~/vorexponentieller *s.* ~/präexponentieller
*g-***Faktor** *m* g-factor, gyromagnetic factor
~/Landéscher Landé g-factor, [Landé] splitting factor g *(gyromagnetic ratio of electrons)*
Faktorengefüge *n*, **Faktorenkonstellation** *f* *(bioch)* set of conditions

Fällanlage *f* precipitator
Fällbad *n (text)* spinning bath, coagulating (coagulation) bath, precipitating (precipitation) bath
fällbar precipitable
Fällbarkeit *f* precipitability
Falle *f* trap
~/antiklinale *(petrol)* anticlinal trap
~/chemotropische chemotropic trap *(for pest control)*
~/stratigraphische *(petrol)* stratigraphic trap
~/strukturelle (strukturgebundene) *(petrol)* structural trap
~/tektonische *(petrol)* structural trap
fallen 1. to fall, to drop *(as of bulk material)*; 2. to decrease, to fall, to drop *(as of measuring values)*
fällen to precipitate, to throw down
~/elektrochemisch (elektrolytisch) to electrodeposit
Fallen *n* drop *(as of bulk material)*; decrease, fall, drop *(as of measuring values)*; fall *(as of a liquid level)*
Fällen *n s.* Fällung 1.
fällend precipitative
Fallengift *n (agric)* poison for traps
Fallfilmabsorber *m* falling-film absorber
Fallfilmkolonne *f (distil)* falling-film still
Fallfilmkonzentrierer *m* falling-film concentrator *(as for sulphuric acid)*
Fallfilmverdampfer *m* falling-film evaporator, downflow evaporator
Fällflüssigkeit *f* precipitating liquid
Fallgeschwindigkeit *f* velocity (rate) of fall
Fallhärteprüfer *m* scleroscope
Fällkasten *m* precipitation box (tank), precipitator
Fällkolonne *f* precipitation column; carbonating tower *(manufacture of sodium carbonate)*
Fallkörperviskosimeter *n* falling-body viscometer
Fallkugel *f* drop weight
Fällkupfer *n* cement copper
Fallmischer *m* tumbler (tumbling) mixer, tumbler
Fällmittel *n s.* Fällungsmittel
Falloch *n* drop hole
Fallout *m* fallout *(particles which settle from the atmosphere), (specif) s.* ~/radioactiver
~/radioaktiver radioactive (atomic) fallout
Fallout *n* fallout *(the settling of particles from the atmosphere)*
Fallprobe *f s.* Fallprüfung
Fallprüfung *f* [drop] shatter test *(for coke)*
Fallraum *m* gravity chamber *(gas cleaning)*
Fallrohr *n (distil)* downpipe, downspout, downtake, downcomer, delivery pipe
Fallrohrkondensator *m* barometric condenser
Fällschlamm *m s.* Fällungsschlamm
Fallstromabsorber *m* wetted-wall[-column] absorber
Fallstromverdampfer *m* falling-film evaporator, downflow evaporator
Fällturm *m* precipitation column; carbonating tower *(manufacture of sodium carbonate)*
Fällung *f* 1. precipitation; 2. precipitate
~ aus homogenen Lösungen (Systemen) precipitation from homogeneous solution, PFHS
~/chemische chemical precipitation
~/fraktionierte (gebrochene) fractional precipitation
~/gemeinsame *(rubber)* coflocculation
~/isoelektrische *(coll)* isoelectric precipitation
~/rhythmische rhythmic precipitation
~/stufenweise fractional precipitation
~/unvollständige incomplete precipitation
~/vollständige complete precipitation
Fällungsagens *n s.* Fällungsmittel
Fällungsanalyse *f* [volumetric] precipitation analysis, precipitation titration
Fällungsanlage *f* precipitating plant, precipitator
Fällungschemikalie *f (hyd)* softening chemical
Fällungschromatographie *f* precipitation chromatography
Fällungsform *f* precipitated form *(in gravimetric analysis)*
Fällungskatalysator *m* precipitated (precipitation) catalyst
Fällungsmaßanalyse *f s.* Fällungsanalyse
Fällungsmittel *n* precipitating agent, precipitant, *(hyd also)* softening agent
Fällungsreagens *n s.* Fällungsmittel
Fällungsreaktion *f* precipitation reaction
Fällungsschlamm *m (hyd)* softening (precipitated) sludge, *(specif)* lime softening sludge
Fällungstitration *f s.* Fällungsanalyse
Fällungsvermögen *n* precipitating power
Fällungsvorgang *m* precipitation process
Fällungswirkung *f* precipitating action
Faltblatt *n (bioch)* [β-]pleated sheet *(of a polypeptide chain)*
Faltblattstruktur *f (bioch)* [pleated-]sheet structure, pleated-sheet conformation *(of polypeptide chains)*
~/antiparallele antiparallel pleated-sheet structure
~/parallele parallel pleated-sheet structure
Falte *f (glass)* fold, lap *(a surface defect)*; *(text)* wrinkle, crease
Falten *fpl (glass)* washboard, ladder *(a surface defect)*
~/senkrechte scrub (brush) marks *(a surface defect)*
Faltenbalg *m* corrugated bellows
Faltenfilter *n* pleated (folded, fluted) filter
Faltschachtelkarton *m* [folding] boxboard, carton
Faltungsdicke *f*, **Faltungshöhe** *f s.* Faltungslänge
Faltungsintegral-Voltammetrie *f* **mit linearem Spannungsanstieg** *(anal)* convolution-integral linear-sweep voltammetry
Faltungslänge *f* fold period (height) *(of macromolecules)*
falzen *(pap)* to fold; *(tann)* to shave
~/im Kalkzustand *(tann)* to green-shave
Falzfestigkeit *f s.* Falzwiderstand

Falzmaschine *f (tann)* shaving machine
Falzwiderstand *m* folding endurance (resistance, strength)
Falzwiderstandsprüfgerät *n (pap)* fold-testing machine, folding tester
Falzwiderstandsprüfung *f (pap)* folding-endurance test
Falzzahl *f (pap)* number of folds
Familie *f* family *(as in the periodic system)*
~/radioaktive radioactive (decay) family (chain), radioactive [decay] series, decay series
Fang *m s.* Fänger
Fangarbeit *f (petrol)* fishing
Fangdorn *m (petrol)* fishing tap
Fangelektrode *f* collecting electrode, collector [electrode]
Fangen *n (petrol)* fishing
Fänger *m* 1. *(tech)* catcher, trap; 2. *s.* Fängersubstanz
Fängersubstanz *f* scavenger *(e.g. for radicals, electrons)*
Fangglocke *f (petrol)* overshot
Fangmagnet *m (petrol)* fishing magnet
Fangmuffe *f (petrol)* overshot
Fangstelle *f (nucl)* trap
Fangstoff *m* 1. *(pap)* recovered stock (material); 2. getter *(vacuum technology)*
Fangstoffanlage *f (pap)* stuff catcher, pulp saver, save-all [tray]
Fangstück *n (glass)* bait
Fangtaschenelektrode *f* pocket (tulip, hollow) electrode
Fantasiepapier *n* fancy paper, *(Am)* decorated paper
Faraday *n s.* Faraday-Konstante
Faraday-Effekt *m* Faraday effect, magnetic rotation
Faraday-Konstante *f* Faraday constant, faraday, F *(equivalent to 96486 coulomb)*
Faraday-Strom *m* faradaic current
Farbabbeizmittel *n* paint remover
Farbänderung *f* change in colour, colour change
~/negative hypsochromic shift
~/positive bathochromic shift
Farbanstrich *m* paint coat[ing]
Farbaufhellung *f* lightening of the colour; hypsochromic shift *(dye theory)*
Farbaufnahmevermögen *n* dye receptivity
Farbbad *n* dye bath (liquor)
färbbar dyeable
Färbbarkeit *f* dyeability
Farbbase *f* dye (colour) base
Farbbeize *f* stain *(for glass, wood)*
farbbeständig colour-fast, non-discolouring, fadeless
Farbbeständigkeit *f* colour fastness (stability)
Farbbestandteil *m* colouring principle
Farbbildner *m* colour former
Farbbindemittel *n* paint binder (vehicle)
Farbbrillanz *f* brilliance, brilliancy
Farbe *f* 1. colour *(sensation)*; 2. colouring matter, *(Am also)* color; *(in or for suspension:)* paint, pigment; *(for walls and ceilings:)* distemper; *(for artists:)* paint, colour; *(in or for solution:)* dye; *(for typography:)* [printing] ink; *(for glass:)* stain • **~ annehmen** to colour • **die ~ verlieren** to discolour, to fade
~/anwuchsverhindernde *s.* ~/bewuchsverhindernde
~/ausgezehrte *(tann)* tailing[s], tails
~/bewuchsverhindernde antifouling [marine] paint
~/deckende body colour
~/fluoreszierende fluorescent paint
~ für Anilingummidruck (Flexodruck, Flexographie) aniline (flexographic) ink
~ für Lichtdruck photogelatin ink
~/gebrauchsfertige ready-mixed paint, do-it-yourself paint
~/glänzende gloss [printing] ink *(typography)*
~/graphische [printing] ink
~/keramische ceramic colour
~/lösungsmittelverdünnbare solvent-thinned paint
~/nachleuchtende phosphorescent paint
~/phosphoreszierende phosphorescent paint
~/plastische plastic paint
~/streichfertige ready-to-brush paint
~/wasserverdünnbare water-thinned paint
Färbeapparat *m* dyeing apparatus
Färbebad *n* dye bath (liquor)
Färbebase *f* dye (colour) base
Färbebeschleuniger *m (text)* dyeing accelerant, carrier
Färbebottich *m s.* Färbekufe
farbecht colour-fast, non-discolouring, fadeless
Farbechtheit *f* colour fastness (stability)
Farbechtheitsmesser *m*, **Farbechtheitsprüfer** *m (text)* fadiometer
Färbeeigenschaft *f* dyeing property
Färbefähigkeit *f s.* Färbekraft
Färbeflotte *f (text)* dye bath (liquor)
Färbeflottenbehälter *m s.* Färbekufe
Färbegeschwindigkeit *f* rate of dyeing
Färbegestell *n* slide staining rack (tray) *(microscopy)*
Färbehilfsmittel *n* dyeing assistant (aid)
Färbehülse *f (text)* dyeing cone
Färbeindex *m (bioch)* colour index *(measure of the haemoglobin content per erythrocyte)*
Färbekasten *m* staining dish (trough) *(microscopy)*
~ nach Coplin Coplin jar
Färbekessel *m s.* Färbekufe
Färbekraft *f* colouring (tinctorial) power; *(text)* dyeing power
Färbekufe *f (text)* dye back, dye[ing] vessel, dye[ing] vat
Färbeküvette *f* staining dish (trough) *(microscopy)*
Färbelack *m*[**/roter**] lac (Indian) lake, lac lac, lake lac
Färbemaschine *f* dyeing machine

Färbemittel *n* colouring matter (agent)
~ für die Mikroskopie microscopic stain
farbempfindlich *(phot)* colour-sensitive
Farbempfindlichkeit *f (phot)* colour sensitivity
färben to colour, *(using suspensions:)* to paint, *(using solutions:)* to dye, *(slightly:)* to tint, to tinge, *(using dry colouring matter:)* to pigment; to stain *(esp wood, glass, or tissues for microscopy)*; *(food)* to add colorants, to colour
~/direkt *(text)* to dye directly
~/im Faß *(tann)* to drum-dye
~/im Garn *(text)* to yarn-dye
~/im Tauchverfahren to dip-dye, to colour by dipping
~/in der Trommel *(text)* to drum-dye
~/nach Farbvorlage (Muster) *(text)* to match
~/sich to colour, to stain *(locally)*
~/sich dunkel (dunkler) to darken
~/unmittelbar *s.* ~/direkt
Färben *n* colouring, *(using suspensions:)* painting, *(using solutions:)* dyeing, *(slight:)* tinting, tinging, *(using dry colouring matter:)* pigmenting; staining *(esp of wood, glass, or of tissues for microscopy)*; *(food)* colouring
~ auf stehendem Bad *(text)* standing-bath dyeing
~ im Garn *(text)* yarn dyeing
~ im Holländer *(pap)* beater dyeing (colouring)
~ im Metallbad *(text)* molten-metal dyeing
~ im Packsystem *(text)* pack[age] dyeing
~ im Stoff *s.* ~ in der Masse
~ im Strang *(text)* rope (hank) dyeing
~ im Stück *(text)* piece dyeing
~ im Tauchverfahren dip dyeing, colouring by dipping
~ in der Flocke *(text)* [loose] stock dyeing
~ in der Masse *(pap)* beater dyeing (colouring), dyeing (colouring) in the pulp; *(plast)* mass dyeing
~ in der Wolle *(text)* stock dyeing
~ in Gegenwart von Lösungsmitteln *(text)* solvent dyeing
~/kontinuierliches *(text)* continuous dyeing
~ nach Farbvorlage (Muster) *(text)* matching
~/ungleiches (ungleichmäßiges) *(text)* ending
~ unter Druck pressure dyeing
~ unter HT-Bedingungen *(text)* high-temperature dyeing
~ von Faserstoffmischungen *(text)* union dyeing
~ von Kammzug *(text)* top dyeing
~ von Kreuzspulen *(text)* cheese dyeing
Farbenabweichung *f* chromatic aberration
Farbenatlas *m* colour atlas
Farbenbindemittel *n* paint binder (vehicle)
Farbenchemie *f s.* 1. Farbstoffchemie; 2. Lack-und Farbenchemie
Farbendruck *m* 1. [multi]colour printing; 2. colour print
Farbenfehler *m* chromatic aberration
Farbengang *m (tann)* suspender set, round of handlers, *(Am)* rocker yard
Farbenschönheit *f* brilliance, brilliancy
Farbensehen *n* colour vision
Farbensensibilisierung *f (phot)* optical (dye) sensitization (sensitizing)
Farbentfernung *f (hyd)* colour removal
Farbentwickler *m (phot)* colour developer
Farbentwicklung *f (phot)* colour development
Farbenzwischenstoff *m s.* Farbstoffzwischenprodukt
Färber *m* dyer
Färberei *f* 1. dyeing; 2. dye-house, dye-works
Färbereihilfsmittel *n* dyeing assistant (aid)
farberhöhend hypsochromic
Farberhöhung *f* hypsochromic shift
Färbestern *m (text)* star frame
Färbeverhalten *n* dyeing properties
Färbevermögen *n* colouring (tinctorial) power
Färbezeit *f (text)* dyeing time (cycle); staining time *(microscopy)*
Farbfehler *m* 1. colour defect, off-colour; 2. chromatic aberration *(optics)*
Farbfilm *m (phot)* colour film
Farbfilter *n* colour filter
Farbfleck *m* colour spot *(a defect in paper)*
Farbflotte *f (text)* dye bath (liquor)
Farbfotografie *f* colour photography
farbfrei *s.* farblos
farbgebend 1. colour-causing *(e.g. water constituents)*; 2. chromophoric *(atomic group)*
Farbglas *n* stained (coloured) glass
Farbgrube *f (tann)* [suspender] pit
Farbholz *n* dyewood
Farbindikator *m* colour indicator
Farbintensität *f* colour intensity, colouring strength
Farbkomparator *m* colour comparator
Farbkraft *f* colouring (tinctorial) power; *(text)* dyeing power
farbkräftig of strong colouring (tinctorial) power; highly (intensely) coloured, brilliant
Farblack *m (text, anal)* lake, *(Am also)* color lake
farblos colourless, free from colour
Farblosigkeit *f* colourlessness, freedom from colour
Farblösung *f s.* Farbstofflösung
Farbmalz *n* coloured (roasted, black) malt
Farbmittel *n* colouring matter (substance, agent), colorant
Farbnuance *f* shade, tint, tinge, tone, hue, *(text also)* cast
Farbpigment *n* coloured (paint) pigment
Farbprinzip *f* colouring principle
Farbreaktion *f* colour reaction
Farbreinigung *f (hyd)* colour removal
Farbsalz *n* dye salt
Farbschattierung *f s.* Farbnuance
Farbschönheit *f* brilliance, brilliancy
farbschwach weakly (feebly) coloured
Farbskala *f* colour range (scale, chart)
Farbspritzen *n* spray painting, paint spraying
~/elektrostatisches electrostatic paint spraying

Farbspritzpistole *f* paint spray[ing] gun, paint sprayer
~/elektrostatische electrostatic spray gun
Farbspritztechnik *f* paint spraying technique
farbstark intensely (highly) coloured, brilliant
Farbstärke *f* colouring (tinctorial) strength
Farbstoff *m* colouring matter (substance), colorant; dye[stuff] *(soluble organic compound)*; pigment *(insoluble matter of organic or inorganic origin)*; stain *(for wood, glass, microscopical investigation)*; *(biol)* pigment
~/adjektiver adjective (mordant) dye
~/anthrachinoider anthraquinone (anthraquinonoid) dye
~/basischer basic dye; basic stain *(for microscopy)*
~/beizenfärbender *s.* ~/adjektiver
~/blauer blue; *(for improving the degree of whiteness:)* blueing
~/direktziehender direct (substantive) dye
~/dispergierter disperse[d] dye
~/echter fast dye
~ für Holländerfärbung *(pap)* beater dye
~ für Kalanderfärbung *(pap)* calender dye
~ für Massefärbung *(pap)* beater dye
~/gemischter mixed dye
~/indigoider indigoid dye
~/kationischer cationoid dye
~/kombinierbarer compatible dye
~/natürlicher natural dye (colouring matter), biochrome
~/pflanzlicher plant pigment, *(for use:)* plant colouring matter, vegetable dye
~/saurer acid[ic] dye
~/sensibilisierender sensitizing dye
~/substantiver substantive (direct) dye
~/unechter fugitive dye
farbstoffaffin dye-affinitive
Farbstoffaffinität *f* dye affinity • **mit erhöhter ~** deep-dyeing
Farbstoffaufnahme *f* dye uptake (absorption, acceptance)
Farbstoffaufnahmevermögen *n* dye receptivity, receptivity to dyestuffs
Farbstoffbase *f* dye (colour) base
Farbstoffchemie *f* dye[stuff] chemistry
Farbstoffchemiker *m* dye chemist
Farbstoffechtheit *f* dye fastness
Farbstoffixiermittel *n* dye-fixing agent, dye fixative
Farbstoffixierungsgeschwindigkeit *f* rate of dye fixation
Farbstoffklasse *f* class of dyestuffs
Farbstofflaser *m (spectr)* dye laser
Farbstofflösung *f* dye solution
~ für Kalanderfärbung *(pap)* calender solution
Farbstoffreagens *n (bioch)* colour[-producing] reagent
Farbstoffschutzschicht *f (phot)* dye layer, backing [layer]
Farbstoffsortiment *n* range (assortment) of dyes
Farbstoffsuspension *f* pigment suspension
Farbstoffträger *m (biol)* chromatophore
Farbstoffzusatz *m (food)* 1. colouring matter, colorant; 2. addition (admixture) of colouring matter
Farbstoffzwischenprodukt *n* dye intermediate
Farbtafel *f* colour chart *(as for universal indicators)*
Farbtiefe *f* depth of colour
Farbton *m* shade, tint, tone, hue, *(text also)* cast • **einen ~ treffen** to match a shade • **im ~ abfallen** to be off-shade
Farbtonänderung *f* change in shade, alteration of shade
Farbtonbeständigkeit *f*, **Farbtonechtheit** *f* colour fastness (stability)
Farbtonumschlag *m s.* Farbtonänderung
Farbtönung *f s.* Farbton
Farbtonverschiebung *f* shift (displacement) of shade
~/bathochrome bathochromic shift (displacement), red-shift
~/hypsochrome hypsochromic shift (displacement), blue-shift
farbtragend chromophoric
Farbträger *m* chromophore, chromophoric group; *(coat)* substrate
Farbumschlag *m* change in colour, [sharp] colour change, *(titrimetry also)* indicator transition
Färbung *f* 1. *s.* Färben; 2. coloration, colour *(phenomenon, s. a.* Farbton*)*; *(biol)* pigmentation; 3. *(result of treatment with suspensions:)* paint, *(with solutions:)* dye; *(of wood, glass, tissues for microscopy:)* stain • **eine ~ erteilen** to impart a colour *(as to a flame)*
~/blaue blueness
~/Gramsche Gram staining *(for bacteria)*
~/leere (matte) dead dyeing
~/stippenfreie *(text)* speck-free dyeing
~/stumpfe (tote) dead dyeing
Färbungsbremsmittel *n* dye retardant
Farbunterschied *m* difference in colour
Farbveränderung *f s.* Farbänderung
Farbvergleicher *m* colour comparator
Farbvergleichszylinder *m* colour-comparator tube
Farbverschiebung *f s.* Farbtonverschiebung
farbverstärkend auxochromic
farbvertiefend bathochromic
Farbvertiefung *f* bathochromic shift
Farbwanderung *f* swealing *(during the drying of textiles)*
Farbwechsel *m* change in colour, colour change
Farbzahl *f (min)* colour index
Farbzentrum *n (spectr)* colour centre
Fardon-Verfahren *n (biot)* Fardon process *(submerged production of vinegar)*
Farin[zucker] *m* brown sugar, muscovado
Faser *f (biol)* fibre; *(text)* [staple] fibre *(a natural or man-made fibre of comparatively short length)*
~/anorganische inorganic fibre
~/gemahlene milled fibre

~/gesponnene spun fibre
~/keramische ceramic fibre
~/mineralische mineral fibre
~/native (natürliche) natural fibre
~/organische organic fibre
~/pflanzliche vegetable fibre
~/polynosische polynosic fibre
~/synthetische [completely, fully] synthetic fibre, synthetic polymer fibre, synthetic
~/tierische animal fibre
Faserabbau *m* fibre disintegration
Faseraffinität *f (dye)* affinity for the fibre
faserartig fibrous
Faserband *n (text)* sliver
faserbildend fibre-forming
Faserbildung *f* fibre formation
Faserbraunkohle *f* fibre brown coal
Faserbrei *m (pap)* fibrous pulp (mass), pulp slurry (stock), slush [of] stock
Faserbreipreßteil *n (plast)* pulp moulding
Faserbruchstücke *npl (pap)* fragments of fibres
Faserbündel *n (pap)* fibre bundle; *(text)* strand
Fäserchen *n* fibril[la]
Faserdiagramm *n* fibre diagram (photograph)
Faserfilter *n* felt[-fabric] filter
Faserfilz *m (pap)* web of fibre[s], [paper] web, mat
Faserflug *m (text)* linters
Fasergefüge *n* fibrous structure
Fasergewebe *n* fabric [cloth]
Fasergewirre *n s.* Faservlies
Fasergut *n***/loses** *(text)* loose stock
Faserhalbstoff *m (pap)* half-stuff, half-stock
~/eingetragener pulp (fibrous) furnish, beater charge
Faserhaut *f (text)* sheath, shell, skin
Faserholz *n (pap)* pulpwood
faserig fibrous
Faserinkrustierung *f* fibre incrustation
Faserkalk *m* fibrous (vein) chalk
Faserkohle *f* fibrous coal
Faserkristall *m* [crystal] whisker
Faserlänge *f* fibre length (staple), staple [length]
Fasermantel *m (text)* sheath, shell, skin
Fasermasse *f s.* Faserbrei
Fasermaterial *n (pap)* fibrous material
Fasermischung *f* fibre blend
Faserplatte *f* fibre board
Faserprotein *n* fibrous protein, structural (skeletal) protein, scleroprotein
Faserrohstoff *m* fibrous raw material, crude fibre material, raw papermaking material, raw (paper) stock
Faserrückgewinnung *f (pap)* fibre recovery
Faserrückgewinnungsanlage *f (pap)* stuff catcher, pulp saver, save-all [tray]
Faserschädigung *f* damage to fibres
Faserschichtfilter *n* felt-fabric filter
Faserschutzmittel *m* fibre-protective agent
Faserserpentin *m (min)* chrysotile, Canadian asbestos
Faserstoff *m (text)* fibre, fibrous material
~/anorganischer inorganic fibre
~/keramischer ceramic fibre
~/metallischer metallic [fibre]
~/natürlicher natural fibre
~/organischer organic fibre
~/pflanzlicher vegetable fibre
~/polynosischer polynosic fibre
~/synthetischer [completely, fully] synthetic fibre, synthetic polymer fibre, synthetic
faserstoffbildend fibre-forming
Faserstoffbildung *f* fibre formation
Faserstoffbrei *m s.* Faserbrei
Faserstoffchemie *f* chemistry of fibres
Faserstoffknoten *m (pap)* knot
Faserstoffschutzmittel *n* fibre-protective agent
Faserstoffstruktur *f (text)* fibre structure
Faserstoffsuspension *f (pap)* pulp suspension (slurry)
Faserstruktur *f (text)* fibre structure; *(min)* fibrous structure
Fasersuspension *f* 1. fibre suspension; 2. *s.* Farbstoffsuspension
Fasertorf *m* moss peat
Faserverfilzung *f (pap)* felting (matting) of the fibres
Faserverkettung *f (pap)* bonding of the fibres, interfibre bonding
Faserverlust *m (pap)* fibre (stock) loss
Faservlies *n (text)* non-woven fabric
Faservliesfilter *n* felt[-fabric] filter
Faserwiedergewinnung *f (pap)* fibre recovery
fasrig fibrous
Faß *n* drum, vat, *(if wooden:)* barrel, cask, *(if small:)* keg, *(if very large:)* tun • **im ~ behandeln (durcharbeiten)** *(tann)* to drum
Faßabfüller *m*, **Faßabfüllmaschine** *f* [cask-]racking machine, [cask] racker
Faßabfüllung *f* barrel[l]ing, racking
Faßamalgamation *f* barrel amalgamation
Faßäscher *m*, **Faßäscherung** *f (tann)* drum liming
Faßbier *n* keg beer
fassen to hold *(a certain quantity)*; to take *(a load)*
Fässeramalgamation *f* barrel amalgamation
Faßfärbung *f (tann)* drum dyeing
Faßfettung *f (tann)* drum stuffing
Faßfüller *m s.* Faßabfüller
Faßgeläger *n (food)* bottoms
Faßgerbung *f* drum tannage
Faßgut *n (met)* hutch product
Faßschmiere *f (tann)* drum stuffing
Fassungsvermögen *n* capacity
Fassungswinkel *m* angle of nip *(on roll crushers)*
Fast-Extrusion-Furnace-Ruß *m (rubber)* fast-extrusion furnace black, FEF black
Fastie-Ebert-Anordnung *f*, **Fastie-Ebert-Aufstellung** *f (spectr)* Fastie-Ebert mounting

Fastkristall *m* liquid crystal, paracrystal
Faugeron-Ofen *m (ceram)* Faugeron kiln *(a tunnel kiln)*
Fauläscher *m (tann)* dead (rotten) lime
Faulbecken *n***[/offenes]** *(hyd)* digestion basin
Faulbehälter *m (hyd)* digestion tank, [anaerobic] digester
~/geschlossener closed digester
~/zweiter secondary digestion tank
faulen 1. *(biol)* to putrefy; *(hyd)* to digest; 2. *(ceram)* to sour, to age, to mature
Faulen *n* 1. *(biol)* putrefaction; *(hyd)* digestion; 2. *(ceram)* souring, ageing
faulend putrescent
faulfähig putrefiable, putrescible; *(hyd)* digestible
~/nicht unputrefiable, imputrescible; *(hyd)* indigestible
Faulfähigkeit *f* putrescibility; *(hyd)* digestibility
Faulgas *n (hyd)* digester (sludge) gas, sewage (sewer) gas
Faulgrube *f s.* Faulbecken
faulig putrid
Fäulnis *f* putrefaction
Fäulnisbakterien *npl* putrefactive bacteria
fäulnisbeständig rotproof, rot-resistant
Fäulnisbeständigkeit *f* rotproofness, rot resistance
fäulnisbewohnend *(biol)* saprophytic
Fäulnisbewohner *m* saprophyte, saprophytic organism
fäulniserregend putrefactive, putrefacient, saprogenic, saprogenous
fäulnisfähig *s.* faulfähig
fäulnisfest *s.* fäulnisbeständig
Fäulnisgärung *f* putrefactive fermentation
fäulnisverhindernd, fäulnisverhütend rotproofing
Fäulnisverhütungsmittel *n* rotproofing agent
fäulniswidrig *s.* fäulnisverhindernd
Faulraum *m (hyd)* digester chamber (compartment)
Faulschlamm *m (hyd)* digesting sludge, [anaerobic] digested sludge; sapropel *(hydrobiology)*
Faulschlammgestein *n* sapropelite
Faulschlammkohle *f* sapropelic coal
Faulung *f (hyd)* [anaerobic] digestion, anaerobic decomposition *(of sludge)*
~/zweistufige two-stage digestion
faulungsunfähig *(hyd)* indigestible
Faulwasser *n (hyd)* anaerobic digester supernatant
Faulzeit *f (hyd)* digestion period
Faulzone *f (hyd)* septic zone
Fauser-Verfahren *n* Fauser [ammonia] process
Faustregel *f* rule of thumb
Faustzahl *f* round figure
Favorskij-Umlagerung *f* Favorskii rearrangement *(of α-haloketones to acids or esters)*
Fayalit *m (min)* fayalite *(iron(II) orthosilicate)*
Fayence *f (ceram)* faience
~/Delfter delft[ware], delph[ware]
Fayenceware *f* faience ware
Fäzes *pl* faecal matter, faeces
Fazies *f (geol)* facies
FCC-Anlage *f (petrol)* FCC unit, fluid catalytic cracking unit (plant), FCCU
FCC-Verfahren *n (petrol)* fluid catalytic [cracking] process
FCKW *s.* Fluorchlorkohlenwasserstoff
FDP-Weg *m s.* Embden-Meyerhof-Parnas-Weg
Fed-Batch-Kultur *f (biot)* fed-batch culture
Fed-Batch-Verfahren *n (biot)* fed-batch fermentation
Feder *f (tech)* spring
federbelastet spring-loaded
Federbildung *f (ceram)* feathering *(a glaze fault)*
Federkraftwälzmühle *f* **nach Loesche** Loesche mill
Federleichtpapier *n* featherweight paper, *(Am)* bulking paper
Federsicherheitsventil *n* spring safety valve, spring-actuated relief valve
Federwaage *f* spring balance
Feedback *n***/negatives** *(bioch)* feedback inhibition
~/positives positive feedback, feed-forward activation
Feedback-Hemmung *f*, **Feedback-Inhibition** *f (bioch)* feedback inhibition
Feedback-Mechanismus *m (bioch)* feedback mechanism
Feedback-Regulation *f (bioch)* feedback control (regulation)
feedback-unempfindlich *(biot)* feedback-insensitive
Feedermaschine *f (glass)* gob-fed machine
Feederverfahren *n (glass)* feeder (gob) process
Feedforward-Mechanismus *m (bioch)* feed-forward mechanism
Feeding-Fermentation *f (biot)* fed-batch fermentation
FEF-Ruß *m (rubber)* FEF black, fast extrusion furnace black
Fehlbenennung *f* misnomer
Fehlbohrung *f (petrol)* unproductive well, dry hole, duster
Fehler *m* 1. defect, flaw, fault *(in material)*; *(cryst)* defect, imperfection; 2. error *(statistics)*
~/methodischer error of method
~/mittlerer quadratischer root mean square error, standard deviation, *(in a graph also)* half-peak width *(width at 0.607 h)*
~/parallaktischer parallax error
~/persönlicher *s.* ~/subjektiver
~/prozentualer percentage error
~/subjektiver personal error
~/systematischer systematic (constant) error, *bias [error]
~/wahrer error of measurement, error in measuring
~/zufälliger accidental (random, indeterminate) error
Fehlerausgleich *m* compensation of errors
fehlerfrei *(cryst)* defect-free

Fehlerfunktion *f* error function, erfc
Fehlergrenze *f* limit of error
fehlerhaft defective, faulty, imperfect
Fehlerintegral *n* error function, erfc
Fehlerkompensation *f* compensation of errors
Fehlernährung *f* malnutrition
Fehlerquelle *f* source of error
Fehlersuche *f* fault finding
Fehlersuche *f* **und -beseitigung** *f* trouble shooting
Fehlerursache *f* source of error
Fehlfärbung *f* faulty dyeing
Fehlgärung *f* faulty fermentation
fehlgeordnet *(cryst)* disordered
Fehlgeruch *m (food)* off-odour
Fehlgeschmack *m (food)* off-taste
Fehlgitter *n s.* Fehlstellengitter
Fehlordnung *f (cryst)* disorder
~/Frenkelsche Frenkel disorder
Fehlordnungskonzentration *f (cryst)* defect concentration
Fehlstelle *f (cryst)* [lattice] defect; holiday, void *(in a coating)*
~/Frenkelsche Frenkel defect
~/punktförmige point defect
Fehlstellengitter *n* defect lattice
Fehlstellenhalbleiter *m* extrinsic semiconductor
Fehlstellenkonzentration *f (cryst)* defect concentration
Fehlstellenpaar *n***/Frenkelsches** *(cryst)* Frenkel pair, vacancy-interstitial (interstitial-vacancy) pair
Fehlstellenwanderung *f (cryst)* defect motion
Feilspäne *mpl* filings
Feinanteile *mpl s.* Feingut
Feinaufspaltung *f (spectr)* fine splitting
feinausgemahlen finely ground
Feinausmahlung *f* fine grinding
Feinboden *m* fine soil *(particle size < 2 mm)*
Feinbrechen *n* fine crushing
Feinbrecher *m* fine crusher
Feinbürette *f* microburette
Feinchemikalie *f* fine chemical
Feindestillation *f* precision distillation
feindispers finely dispersed
Feineinstellung *f* fine adjustment *(of a measuring instrument)*
feinen *(met)* to refine
Feinerde *f s.* Feinboden
Feinerz *n* fine ore
Feines *n s.* Feingut
Feinfilter *n* polishing (clarifying) filter
Feinfiltration *f* polishing [filtration], clarification
Feinfolie *f (plast)* film *(thickness < 0.01 inch)*
Feinfoliengießmaschine *f* film casting machine
Feingefüge *f s.* Mikrostruktur
Feingehalt *m* fineness *(of a gold or silver alloy in parts per thousand)*
feingepulvert finely powdered
Feinguß *m* precision casting
Feingut *n* 1. *(min tech)* fine material, fines, slime; 2. *s.* Feinkorn 1.
Feingutüberlauf *m (min tech)* slime overflow
Feinheit *f* fineness *(as of particles or fibres)*
Feinheitsgrad *m* degree of fineness
Feinheitsmodul *m* fineness modulus
Feinkeramik *f* fine ceramics (ceramic ware)
Feinklassierung *f* fine-size fractionation (separation)
Feinkohle *f* fine coal, [coal] fines
Feinkontrolle *f s.* Feinregelung
Feinkorn *n* 1. undersize [material, product], fines, minus material *(classifying)*, *(screening also)* screen undersize (fines); 2. *(geol)* grain; 3. *(phot)* fine grain
Feinkornbild *n (phot)* fine-grain image
Feinkornemulsion *f (phot)* fine-grain emulsion
Feinkornentwickler *m (phot)* fine-grain developer
Feinkornentwicklung *f (phot)* fine-grain development
feinkörnig fine-grain[ed], fine; *(min)* close-grained *(texture)*
Feinkörnigkeit *f* fine graininess
feinkristallin[isch] finely crystalline, fine-grained
Feinkühlen *n (glass)* fine annealing
feinmahlen to grind finely; *(pap)* to refine, to clear, to brush out
Feinmahlung *f* fine grinding; *(pap)* refining, clearing, brushing-out
Feinmanipulator *m* micromanipulator *(microscopical technique)*
Feinmühle *f* fine-grinding mill, fine grinder, pulverizing mill, pulverizer
Feinpapier *n* fine paper, F.p.
Feinpapierfabrik *f* fine mill
Feinpappe *f* fine board
feinporig fine-pore[d]
Feinpostpapier *n* bank paper (post), bond [paper]
Feinpulver *n* fine powder
feinpulverig finely powdered
Feinpulvriges *n (plast)* fines *(as of moulding material)*
Feinrechen *m (hyd)* fine-screen unit
Feinregelung *f* fine control (adjustment), *(bioch also)* metabolic fine control
Feinregulierung *f s.* Feinregelung
Feinreinigung *f* ultrapurification
Feinsand *m* fine sand *(grain size 0.2 to 0.02 mm)*
Feinschicht-Walzentrockner *m* drum film dryer
Feinschleifen *n* fine grinding
Feinschliff *m* fine grinding
Feinseife *f* toilet soap
Feinsieb *n* fine sieve
Feinsortierer *m* fine (secondary, second) screen
Feinsortierung *f* fine (secondary) screening
Feinstaub *m* fine dust
Feinsteinzeug *n (ceram)* fine stoneware
Feinstmahlung *f* pulverizing
Feinstmühle *f* pulverizing mill, pulverizer

Feinstoff *m (pap)* accepted (screened) stock, accepts
Feinstoffe *mpl (plast)* fines *(as of moulding material)*
feinstreifig fine-banded, finely banded
Feinstreinigung *f***/ionogene** *(hyd)* polishing *(ion exchange)*
Feinstruktur *f* fine structure *(of atomic spectra)*
Feinstrukturanalyse *f s.* Kristallstrukturanalyse
Feinstrukturkonstante *f (spectr)* fine-structure constant
~/Sommerfeldsche Sommerfeld fine-structure constant
feinstückig small-sized
Feintrub *m (ferm)* fine (cold) trub, cold sludge (break)
feinvermahlen to grind finely
Feinvermahlen *n* fine grinding
feinverteilt finely dispersed (divided)
Feinwägung *f* high-precision weighing, fine weigh
Feinwäsche *f* fine-fabric laundering
Feinwaschmittel *n* fine-fabric detergent, light-duty detergent
feinzerkleinern to comminute
Feinzerkleinerung *f* comminution
Feinzerteilung *f* dispersion, dispersal
Feinzuschlag *m (build)* fine aggregate
FEL *s.* Freielektronenlaser
Feld *n (phys ch)* field • **nach tieferen Feldern verschoben** *(spectr)* downfield
~/atomares atomic field
~/elektrostatisches electrostatic field
~/entmagnetisierendes demagnetizing field
~/magnetisches magnetic field
~/selbstkonsistentes self-consistent field, SCF
Feldbrennofen *m (ceram)* clamp
Felddesorption *f* field desorption, FD
Felddüngungsversuch *m* field fertilization test
Feldeffekt *m (phys ch)* field (direct) effect
Feldeffekttransistor *m***/chemisch sensitiver** chemically sensitive field effect transistor, CHEMFET, ChemFET
~/ionensensitiver ion-sensitive field effect transistor, ISFET
Feldelektronenemission *f* field emission
Feldelektronenmikroskop *n* field emission microscope
Feldemission *f* field emission
Feldemissions[elektronen]mikroskop *n* field emission microscope
Feld-Fluß-Fraktionierung *f (chromat)* field flow fractionation
Feldhomogenität *f (spectr)* field homogeneity
Feldionisation *f* field ionization, FI
Feldionisations-Massenspektrometrie *f* field-ionization mass spectrometry, FIMS
Feldleistung *f* field performance (efficiency) *(of pesticides)*
Feldofen *m (ceram)* clamp
Feldrichtung *f (phys ch)* field direction
Feldspat *m (min)* fel[d]spar, feldspath
~/als Massebestandteil verwendeter *(ceram)* body spar
~/erdiger clay-stone
~/zur Glasherstellung verwendeter glass spar
feldspathaltig *(min)* fel[d]spathic
Feldspatoid *m*, **Feldspatvertreter** *m (min)* feldspathoid
Feldspritzrohr *n (agric)* boom sprayer, spray boom
Feldstärke *f* field strength
Feldstärkeeffekt *m* Wien effect
Feldsweep *m (spectr)* field sweep
Feldtest *m s.* Feldversuch
Feldvalenzverbindung *f* field valency compound
Feldversuch *m* field experiment (test, trial)
Feldwirksamkeit *f* field performance (efficiency) *(of pesticides)*
Felgenband *n (rubber)* flap
Felgenbandheizer *m (rubber)* flap mould (vulcanizer)
Felit *m* felite *(a crystalline constituent of portland cement clinker)*
Fell *n (rubber)* sheet, band
Fellgett-Vorteil *m (spectr)* Fellgett (multiplex) advantage
Femtogrammbereich *m (anal)* femtogram range *(10^{-15} to 10^{-12} g)*
Fenac *n* fenac, 2,3,6-trichlorophenylacetic acid *(a herbicide)*
Fenchelöl *n* fennel[-seed] oil *(from Foeniculum vulgare Mill.)*
Fenchol *n s.* Fenchylalkohol
Fenchylalkohol *m* fenchyl alcohol, fenchol, 1,3,3-trimethylbicyclo [1,2,2]-heptan-2-ol
Fensterglas *n* window glass
~ doppelter Dicke double-strength glass
~ einfacher Dicke single-strength glass
Fensterglaszylinder *m (glass)* roller
Fensterkitt *m* [glazier's, painter's] putty
Fensterpapier *n* diaphanic paper
Fensterputzmittel *n* window cleaner
Fenuron *n* fenuron, 1,1-dimethyl-3-phenylurea *(a herbicide)*
Ferment *n* enzyme, ferment *(for compounds s. a. under* Enzym*)*
~/geformtes organized ferment *(historically, enzymatically active cells)*
~/gelbes *s.* Flavinenzym
~/organisiertes *s.* ~/geformtes
~/ungeformtes (unorganisiertes) enzyme, *(historically:)* unorganized ferment
Ferment... *s.* Enzym...
Fermentation *f* fermentation *(for compounds s.* Gärung*)*
Fermentationsabwasser *n* effluent from fermentation plants
Fermentationsanlage *f* fermentation plant
Fermentationsausbeute *f* fermentation yield
Fermentationsbedingungen *fpl* fermentation (incubation) conditions

Fermentationsbrühe *f* fermentation broth (liquor, slurry, solution), fermenter broth
~/enzymhaltige enzyme broth
~/verbrauchte spent fermentation broth
Fermentationsdauer *f* length of fermentation, fermentation (incubation) period
Fermentationsflüssigkeit *f s.* Fermentationsbrühe
Fermentationsgefäß *n* fermentation vessel
Fermentationskinetik *f* fermentation kinetics
Fermentationskontrolle *f* fermentation (bioprocess) control
Fermentationslösung *f s.* Fermentationsbrühe
Fermentationsluft *f* fermentation air
Fermentationsmedium *n* fermentation medium
Fermentationsrate *f* fermentation (conversion) rate, rate of product formation
~/spezifische specific production efficiency (rate), specific rate of product formation *(mg product/mg cell dry weight · h)*
~/volumetrische volumetric production efficiency (rate), volumetric rate of reaction *(mg product/l · h)*
Fermentationsreaktor *m s.* Fermenter
Fermentationsrohstoffe *mpl* industrial fermentation medium, fermentation raw material, feedstock
Fermentationsrückstand *m* fermentation residue
Fermentationssteuerung *f* fermentation (bioprocess) control
Fermentationsstufe *f* fermentation stage
Fermentationssubstrat *n* fermentation substrate
Fermentationstank *m* fermentation vessel
Fermentationstechnik *f* fermentation [bio]technology
Fermentationsweg *m* fermentation (fermentative) pathway, fermentation route
Fermentationszeit *f s.* Fermentationsdauer
Fermentationszyklus *m* fermentation (bioprocess) run
fermentativ enzym[at]ic, ferment[at]ive
Fermentator *m s.* Fermenter
Fermenter *m***[/biotechnologischer]** fermenter, [bio]reactor
~ für diskontinuierliches Verfahren batch fermenter
~ für kontinuierliches Verfahren continuous fermenter, through-flow bioreactor
~/vollständig gemischter completely mixed fermenter, homogeneously mixed bioreactor, well mixed [flow] reactor
Fermenterbrühe *f s.* Fermentationsbrühe
Fermenterdurchsatz *m* fermenter throughput
Fermenterflüssigkeit *f s.* Fermentationsbrühe
Fermenterinhalt *m* fermenter contents
Fermenterkapazität *f s.* Fermentervolumen
Fermenterleistung *f* fermenter performance
Fermentervolumen *n* fermenter volume, fermentation (working) volume
Fermenter-Vorkultur *f* fermenter preculture
fermentierbar fermentable
Fermentierbarkeit *f* fermentability
fermentieren to ferment
Fermentiergefäß *n s.* Fermentationsgefäß
Fermentierung *f s.* Fermentation
Fermentor *m s.* Fermenter/biotechnologischer
Fermi-Alter *n* Fermi age *(of neutrons)*
Fermi-Alterstheorie *f* Fermi age theory (model) *(of neutrons)*
Fermi-Dirac-Statistik *f* Fermi[-Dirac] statistics
Fermi-Dirac-Verteilungsfunktion *f* Fermi-Dirac distribution function
Fermi-Energie *f* Fermi energy
Fermi-Fläche *f* Fermi surface
Fermi-Gas *n* Fermi[-Dirac] gas
Fermi-Kante *f s.* Fermi-Niveau
Fermi-Konstante *f* Fermi constant
Fermi-Niveau *n* Fermi [characteristic energy] level
Fermion *n (nucl)* fermion
Fermi-Resonanz *f* Fermi resonance
Fermi-Statistik *f s.* Fermi-Dirac-Statistik
Fermi-Temperatur *f* Fermi temperature
Fermi-Theorie *f* **[des β-Zerfalls]** Fermi [beta decay] theory
Fermium *n* Fm fermium
Fermi-Verteilung *f* Fermi distribution
Fernambukholz *n*, **Fernambuko** *n (dye)* brazilwood *(wood of Caesalpinia specc.)*
Fernanzeige *f* remote indication
Fernbachkolben *m* Fernbach flask *(for propagating microorganisms)*
Fernbedienung *f*, **Fernbetätigung** *f* remote operation
Fernerkundung *f* remote sensing
Ferngas *n* pipeline [quality] gas
Fernkopplung *f (phys ch)* long-range coupling (interaction)
Fernleitung *f* [long-distance] pipeline
Fernordnung *f (cryst)* long-range [crystalline] order
Fernordnungsgrad *m (cryst)* long-range order
Fernsteuerung *f* remote control
Fernthermometer *n* telethermometer, distance (recording) thermometer
Ferrat(III) *n* $M^{I}FeO_2$ ferrate(III)
Ferrichrom *n* ferrichrome
Ferriform *f* ferric form, *iron(III) form
ferrimagnetisch ferrimagnetic
Ferrimagnetismus *m* ferrimagnetism
Ferrisalz *n* ferric salt, *iron(III) salt
Ferrit *m* 1. *(met)* ferrite *(a solid solution of carbon in alpha or delta iron)*; 2. ferrite *(a magnetic material of the formula* $M^{II}Fe_2O_4$*)*
ferritisch ferritic
Ferrobor *n* ferroboron
Ferrocen *n* ferrocene, dicyclopentadienyl iron
Ferrocenpolymer[e] *n* ferrocene polymer
Ferrochrom *n* ferrochromium
Ferrocyankupfermembran *f (biol)* copper ferrocyanide membrane, *(better:)* copper(II) hexacyanoferrate(II) membrane *(for demonstrating osmosis)*
Ferroelektrikum *n* ferroelectric [material, substance]

ferroelektrisch ferroelectric
Ferroform *f* ferrous form, *iron(II) form
Ferroin *n* ferroin *(any of a class of complexes of tertiary heterocyclic amines)*
Ferrolegierung *f* ferro-alloy
Ferromagnetikum *n* ferromagnetic [material, substance]
ferromagnetisch ferromagnetic
Ferromagnetismus *m* ferromagnetism
Ferromangan *n* ferromanganese
Ferromolybdän *n* ferromolybdenum
Ferronickel *n* ferronickel
Ferrophosphor *m* ferrophosphorus
Ferrosalz *n* ferrous salt, *iron(II) salt
Ferrosilicium *n* ferrosilicon
Ferrospinell *m (min)* hercynite *(iron(II) aluminate)*
Ferrotantal *n* ferrotantalum
Ferrotitan *n* ferrotitanium
Ferrovanadium *n* ferrovanadium
Ferrowolfram *n* ferrotungsten
Ferroxylindikator *m* ferroxyl indicator
Ferrozirconium *n* ferrozirconium
Fertigbearbeitung *f* finish[ing]
Fertigbeton *m* ready-mixed concrete
Fertigblasen *n (glass)* final blow[ing]
Fertigbleiche *f (pap)* final bleaching
Fertigbrand *m***/eierschaliger** *(ceram)* egg-shell finish
fertigen to produce, to manufacture, to make *(technical articles)*
Fertigerzeugnis *n s.* Fertigprodukt
Fertigform *f (glass)* blow[ing] mould
Fertigformboden *m (glass)* [blow mould] bottom plate
fertiggeformt finally shaped
Fertigkochperiode *f (pap)* pulping period
fertigmahlen *(pap)* to refine, to clear, to brush out
Fertigmehl *n (food)* ready-mixed flour
Fertigplatte *f (chromat)* chromatoplate
Fertigpräparat *n (pharm)* preparation
Fertigprodukt *n* final (finished) product (stock)
Fertigsintern *n* full (final) sintering
Fertigstellung *f* **in Bogen** *(pap)* sheeting
Fertigung *f* production, manufacture, fabrication *(of technical articles)*
Fertigungsspannung *f* fabrication stress
fertil fertile
Fertilität *f* fertility
Fertilitätsvitamin *n* antisterility vitamin
Ferulasäure *f* ferulic acid, 4-hydroxy-3-methoxycinnamic acid
Feruloylchinasäure *f* feruloylquinic acid *(a depside)*
Fe-S-Cluster *m s.* Eisen-Schwefel-Zentrum
fest 1. solid *(as opposed to liquid)*; strong, firm, rigid *(gel)*; 2. strong, stable *(chemical bond)*; strong *(material or joint)*; resistant, stable *(to destructive influences)* • **~ werden** to solidify, to harden, to set, to congeal, *(esp coll)* to gel[ate] • **~ werden lassen** to solidify, to set, to congeal
festbacken to cake
Festbestandteil *m* solid
Festbett *n* fixed bed, static (dense) bed
Festbettadsorber *m* fixed-bed adsorber
Festbettaustauscher *m s.* Festbettionenaustauscher
Festbettgenerator *m* fixed-bed gasifier (generator)
Festbettionenaustauscher *m* fixed-bed [ion] exchanger
~ zur Enthärtung *(hyd)* fixed-bed water softener
Festbettkatalysator *m* fixed-bed catalyst, static catalyst
Festbettkolonne *f* fixed-bed column
Festbettkontakt *m s.* Festbettkatalysator
Festbett-Porenvolumen *n* fixed-bed voidage
Festbettreaktor *m* fixed-bed reactor, *(biot also)* fixed-bed (packed-bed) bioreactor (fermenter)
~/katalytischer catalytic fixed-bed reactor, fixed-bed catalytic reactor
Festbettsynthese *f* fixed-bed synthesis
Festbettverfahren *n* fixed-bed process
Festbitumen *n* solid bitumen
festblasen *(glass)* to blow down
Festblasen *n (glass)* settle blow
Festbrennen *n (ceram)* firing-on, stoving *(of onglaze decorations)*
Festbrennstoff *m* solid fuel
festdrücken *(lab)* to press down *(a precipitate in a funnel)*
Festelektrolyt *m* solid electrolyte
Fest-fest-Grenzfläche *f* solid-solid interface
Fest-flüssig-Extraktion *f* solid[-liquid] extraction, leaching
Fest-flüssig-Grenzfläche *f* solid-liquid interface
festfressen/sich to seize, to freeze *(as of joints)*
Festfressen *n* seizing, seizure, freezing *(as of joints)*
Festgehalt *m s.* Feststoffgehalt
festhaftend tenacious, adherent
festheften to affix
Festiger *m* solidifying agent
Festigkeit *f* 1. strength, stability *(of a chemical bond)*; strength, firmness, rigidity *(of a gel)*; strength *(of a material or joint)*; resistance, strength, stability *(to destructive influences)*
~/chemische chemical resistance (stability), resistance (stability) to chemical attack
~/dielektrische dielectric strength, breakdown (puncture) strength
~/thermische thermal stability (resistance), heat stability, thermostability
Festigkeit-Masse-Verhältnis *n* strength-to-weight ratio
Festigkeitseinbuße *f s.* Festigkeitsverlust
Festigkeitsfaktor *m* stability factor
Festigkeitsprüfer *m*, **Festigkeitsprüfmaschine** *f* strength tester (testing machine); *(rubber)* tensile[-strength] tester, tensile[-strength] testing machine

Festigkeitsrückgang *m* loss in strength
Festigkeitsverlust *m* loss in strength *(if partially)*; loss of strength *(if totally)*
Festkautschuk *m* solid (dry) rubber
festklemmen to clamp
~/sich to seize
Festkörper *m* solid
~/aktiver *(chromat)* active solid
~/ionischer ionic solid
~/modifizierter aktiver *(chromat)* modified active solid
~/quasieindimensionaler quasi one-dimensional solid
Festkörperdiffusion *f* solid[-state] diffusion
Festkörperlaser *m* solid-state laser
Festkörperlöslichkeit *f* solid solubility
Festkörperphysik *f* solid-state physics
Festkörperreaktion *f* solid-state reaction
Festkörperzustand *m* solid state
Festkraftstoff *m* solid fuel
festlegen to fix *(nutrients in a soil)*
~/biologisch to immobilize *(nutrients by the action of soil microorganisms)*
Festlegung *f* fixation *(of nutrients in a soil)*
~/biologische immobilization *(of nutrients by the action of soil microorganisms)*
Festlinie *f (distil)* solidus curve (line)
Festoondämpfer *m (text)* festoon ager
Festparaffin *n* solid paraffin, paraffin wax
Festphasen-Peptidsynthese *f*, **Festphasen-Verfahren** *n* Merrifield [peptide] synthesis, solid-phase protein synthesis
Festpunkt *m* fixed point
Festschichtkügelchen *n (chromat)* porous layer bead
feststampfen to ram, to tamp
feststellbar 1. determinable, detectable, detectible; 2. fastenable
feststellen 1. *(anal)* to determine, to identify, to detect; to establish *(e.g. the structure of molecules)*; 2. to arrest, to fasten, to fix *(mechanically)*
Feststellung *f (anal)* determination, identification, detection; establishment *(as of the structure of molecules)*
Feststoff *m* solid [matter, substance]
Feststoffabscheidung *f* solids separation (capture, recovery), separation of solid particles
Feststoffanfall *m***[/laufender]** solids flux
Feststoffanteil *m s.* Feststoffgehalt
Feststoffaufnahmevermögen *n* solids-holding capacity
Feststoffausbeute *f s.* Feststoffleistung
Feststoffbelastung *f* solids load[ing]
Feststoffbett *n* solid bed
~/bewegtes moving bed
~/ruhendes (statisches) fixed (static) bed
Feststoffdichte *f* true density *(as of coke)*; particle density *(sedimentation)*
Feststoffdifferenz *f* **zwischen Ein- und Auslauf** solids budget *(sedimentation)*
Feststoffdurchsatz *m* solids throughput
Feststoffdurchsatzleistung *f* solids-handling capacity
Feststoffe *mpl* **flockiger Struktur** flocculent solids
~/suspendierte *(hyd)* suspended solids, SS, suspended solid matter *($> 5 \cdot 10^{-4}$ mm)*
Feststoffentfernung *f* solids removal
Feststoffentwässerung *f (hyd)* sludge dewatering
Feststoffextraktion *f* [liquid-]solid extraction, solid-phase extraction, leaching
Feststoff-Feststoff-Reaktion *f* solid-solid reaction
Feststofffluß *m* solids flux
Feststoff-Gegenstromextraktion *f* countercurrent extraction of solids, countercurrent leaching
Feststoffgehalt *m* solids [content], solids concentration (level)
~ der Schwarzlauge *(pap)* black liquor solids
~ im Ablauf *(hyd)* effluent solids concentration
~ im Abwasserzulauf *(hyd)* suspended solids of incoming waste water
~ im Einlauf *s.* ~ im Zulauf
~ im Naßschlamm (Rohschlamm) *(hyd)* feed solids [concentration] *(centrifugation)*
~ im Rücklaufschlamm *(hyd)* recycle solids (sludge) concentration
~ im Schwimmschlamm *(hyd)* float solids concentration
~ im Überlaufwasser (Zentrifugat) *(hyd)* centrifugate solids concentration [out]
~ im Zulauf *(hyd)* influent (feed) solids concentration
Feststoffgemisch *n* solids mixture, bulk blend
feststoffhaltig solids-bearing
Feststoffkatalysator *m* heterogeneous catalyst, solid (contact) catalyst
Feststoffkonzentration *f s.* Feststoffgehalt
Feststoffleistung *f* capture (recovery) performance *(centrifugation and vacuum filtration)*
Feststoffoberfläche *f* solid surface
Feststofformulierung *f (agric)* dust formulation
Feststoffphase *f* solid phase
Feststoffreaktion *f* solid-solid reaction
Feststoffsorbens *n*, **Feststoffsorptionsmittel** *n* solid sorbent (sorption agent), sorbent solid
Feststoffteilchen *n* solids particle
Feststoffteilchen *npl***/suspendierte** particulates, suspended particles, *(esp hyd)* suspended solids, SS, suspended solid matter *($> 5 \cdot 10^{-4}$ mm)*
Feststoffverweilzeit *f* solids residence time
Festsubstanz *f s.* Feststoff
Festteilchen *n s.* Feststoffteilchen
Festtreibstoff *m* solid [rocket] fuel, solid [rocket] propellant
Festwerden *n* solidification, hardening, set[ting], freezing, congelation, congealing, *(esp coll)* gelation
Fe-S-Zentrum *n s.* Eisen-Schwefel-Zentrum
fett *(ch)* fatty *(e.g. oil)*
Fett *n (ch, food)* fat; *(tech)* grease
~/ausgelassenes rendered fat

~/ausgelassenes tierisches grease
~/festes solid fat
~/gebleichtes bleached fat
~/gehärtetes hardened (hydrogenated) fat
~/hydriertes *s.* ~/gehärtetes
~/natürliches natural fat
~/pflanzliches vegetable (plant) fat
~/technisches commercial grease, inedible fat
~/tierisches animal fat
Fettabbau *m* fat breakdown
Fettabscheider *m (hyd)* grease remover (separator), fat-collecting device
Fettabscheidung *f (hyd)* grease removal
Fettabweisungsvermögen *n* grease (fat) repellency
fettähnlich fatlike
Fettaldehyd *m* alkanal
Fettalkohol *m* fatty alcohol
~/höherer long-chain fatty alcohol
Fettalkoholsulfat *n s.* Fettalkylsulfat
Fettalkylsulfat *n* fatty alkyl sulphate
Fettamin *n* fatty amine *(any of a series of aliphatic amines derived from fats)*
Fettansatz *m* fat blend *(as for margarine making)*
fettartig fatlike
Fettausschlag *m (tann)* fatty [acid] spew
fettbeständig resistant to grease, grease-resistant
Fettbeständigkeit *f* resistance to grease, grease resistance
Fettbestimmung *f* fat determination
Fettbrühe *f (tann)* fat liquor
Fettchemie *f* fat chemistry
fettdicht greaseproof
Fettdichtigkeit *f* greaseproofness
Fettemulsion *f* fat emulsion
fetten *(tech)* to grease, to lubricate; *(tann)* to oil, to stuff; to compound *(oils)*
Fetten *n (tech)* greasing, lubrication; *(tann)* oiling, stuffing
~ im Faß *(tann)* drum oiling (stuffing)
Fettfang *m*, **Fettfänger** *m s.* Fettabscheider
Fettfleck *m* grease spot, smear
Fettflecke[n] *mpl (tann)* fat spue *(a defect in leather)*
Fettfleckphotometer *n* grease-spot photometer
fettfrei non-fat[ty], fat-free
fettfreundlich lipophilic, fat-liking
fettgar *(tann)* chamois, oil-tanned
Fettgehalt *m* fat content
~ der Butter butter-fat content
Fettgehaltsbestimmung *f* test for fat content
Fettgerbung *f* chamois (oil) tannage
Fettgewebe *n (biol)* adipose tissue
Fettglanz *m (min)* greasy lustre
fetthaltig fat-containing, fatty, adipose
Fetthärtung *f*, **Fetthydrierung** *f* fat hardening (hydrogenation)
Fetthydrolyse *f* fat hydrolysis, saponification of fat
fettig fatty, oily, greasy, unctuous *(consistency or substance)*
Fettigkeit *f* fattiness, oiliness, greasiness, unctuousness
Fett-in-Wasser-Emulsion *f* fat-in-water emulsion
Fettkalk *m* fat (rich) lime
Fettkäse *m* fat cheese
Fettkohle *f* fat coal
~/kurzflammige fat short-flame coal
~/langflammige fat long-flame coal
Fettkomposition *f s.* Fettmischung
Fettkreide *f*/**lithographische** lithographic crayon
Fettkristall *m* fat crystal
Fettkügelchen *n* fat globule
Fettkügelchenmembran *f* fat globule membrane
Fettkügelchenprotein *n* fat globule protein
Fettlicker *m (tann)* fat liquor
fettlickern *(tann)* to fat-liquor
Fettlöser *m* grease (fat) solvent
Fettlöserseife *f* fat-dissolving soap
fettlöslich fat-soluble, soluble in fat, liposoluble
Fettlöslichkeit *f* fat solubility, solubility in fat, liposolubility
Fettlösungsmittel *n* grease (fat) solvent
Fettmischung *f* fat blend *(as for margarine making)*
Fettöl *n (ch)* fat[ty] oil, fixed oil *(as opposed to volatile oil)*
Fettoxidation *f* fat oxidation
Fettpech *n* fatty acid pitch
Fettphase *f* fatty phase
Fettprobe *f* fat sample
fettreich high-fat, rich in fat
Fettreif *m* fat bloom *(deposit of crystals of cocoa butter on chocolates)*
Fettreihe *f (org ch)* fatty (aliphatic) series
Fettsäure *f* fatty acid
~/einfach ungesättigte monounsaturated (monoethenoid) fatty acid
~/essentielle essential fatty acid, EFA
~/freie free fatty acid, FFA
~/geradzahlige even-numbered fatty acid
~/gesättigte saturated fatty acid
~/höhere long-chain fatty acid, fat acid *(containing 12 to 24 carbon atoms)*
~/mehrfach ungesättigte polyunsaturated (polyethenoid) fatty acid
~ mit drei C-Atomen three-carbon acid
~ mit einer Doppelbindung *s.* ~/einfach ungesättigte
~ mit zwei C-Atomen two-carbon acid
~/mittlere medium-chain fatty acid
~/niedere lower fatty acid
~/ungeradzahlige odd-numbered fatty acid
~/ungesättigte unsaturated fatty acid
Fettsäureamid *n* fatty [acid] amide
Fettsäureester *m* fatty acid ester
Fettsäureranzidität *f*, **Fettsäureranzigkeit** *f* hydrolytic rancidity
Fettsäurerest *m* fatty acid radical
Fettschmiere *f (tann)* dubbin[g], stuffing mixture, fat liquor

fettspaltend lipolytic, fat-splitting
Fettspaltung *f* lipolysis, fat splitting, cleavage of fats
Fettstift *m* marking (wax) pencil
Fettstoff *m* fatty matter (substance)
Fettstoffwechsel *m* fat (triglyceride) metabolism
Fettsubstanz *f* fatty matter (substance)
Fettsynthese *f* fat synthesis
Fetttröpfchen *n* fat globule
fettundurchlässig greaseproof
Fettundurchlässigkeit *f* greaseproofness
Fettung *f (tann)* stuffing
Fettusche *f* tusche
~/lithographische lithographic tusche
Fettverderb *m* fat deterioration
Fettverlust *m* fat loss
Fettverseifung *f* saponification of fat, fat hydrolysis
feucht moist, damp, wet, *(relating to air also)* humid • **~ werden** to become moist (wet), to moisten
Feuchtapparat *m (pap)* wetting machine, damper
Feuchte *f* moisture, dampness, wetness, *(relating to air also)* humidity
~/absolute absolute humidity *(of air)*
~ der lufttrockenen Probe *s.* ~/hygroskopische
~/gebundene bound moisture
~/hygroskopische air-dried moisture
~/kritische critical humidity *(of air)*; critical moisture content *(of solids)*
~/relative relative humidity, R.H., percentage humidity (saturation) *(of air)*
Feuchteanteil *m* moisture content wet weight basis
Feuchteaufnahme *f* moisture absorption (pickup)
Feuchteaufnahmevermögen *n* moisture-carrying capacity *(of air)*
Feuchteausdehnung *f* moisture expansion
Feuchtebeladung *f* humidity *(of a gas)*; moisture content *(of a solid)*
~/kritische critical humidity *(of a gas)*; critical moisture content *(of a solid)*
feuchtebeständig moisture-resistant, moistureproof
Feuchtebeständigkeit *f* moisture resistance
Feuchtebestimmung *f* estimation of moisture
Feuchtediagramm *n* humidity (psychrometric) chart
feuchtefest moisture-resistant, moistureproof
Feuchtefestigkeit *f* moisture resistance
Feuchtegefälle *n* moisture gradient
Feuchtegehalt *m* moisture content, *(specif)* moisture content dry weight basis
~/absoluter *s.* Feuchtesatz
~ bezogen auf Feuchtmasse *s.* Feuchteanteil
~ bezogen auf Trockenmasse *s.* Feuchtesatz
~/relativer *s.* Feuchteanteil
Feuchtegrad *m s.* Feuchtesatz
Feuchteinrichtung *f s.* Feuchter
Feuchtemesser *m* hygrometer; moisture meter (tester) *(for determining the percentage of moisture in a material)*
feuchten *(pap)* to wet out (up)
Feuchter *m (pap)* wetting machine, damp[en]er
Feuchtesatz *m* moisture content dry weight basis
Feuchteverlust *m* moisture loss
Feuchtglätte *f*, **Feuchtglättwerk** *n (pap)* nip rolls, intermediate rolls (calender)
Feuchtgut *n* wet (damp) product (feed) *(on drying)*
Feuchthaltemittel *n* moisturizer, humectant
Feuchtigkeit *f s.* Feuchte
Feuchtigkeits... *s. a.* Feuchte...
feuchtigkeitsabweisend moisture-repellent
Feuchtigkeitsanalyse *f* moisture analysis
Feuchtigkeitsfilm *m* moisture film
Feuchtigkeitsmeßgerät *n s.* Feuchtemesser
Feuchtigkeitstafel *f s.* Feuchtediagramm
Feuchtkugeltemperatur *f* wet bulb (wet-surface) temperature
Feuchtlagerbeständigkeit *f* resistance to damp storing
Feuchtluft *f* humified (moisture-laden) air
Feuchtlufttrockner *m (ceram)* humidity dryer
Feuchtlufttrocknung *f (ceram)* humidity drying
Feuchtmaschine *f s.* Feuchter
Feuchtthermometer *n* wet-bulb thermometer
Feuchttrockner *m (ceram)* humidity dryer
Feuchttrocknung *f (ceram)* humidity drying
Feuchtung *f* damp[en]ing; *(pap)* wetting-out, wetting-up
Feuchtwalze *f (pap)* damping roll
feuchtwarm damp warm
Feuer *n* fire
~/hartes (hohes) *(ceram)* hard fire
Feueraluminieren *n* hot-dip aluminizing
feuerbeständig fire-resistant, *(esp ceram)* refractory; *(by treatment:)* fireproof • **~ machen** to fireproof
Feuerbeständigkeit *f* fire resistance, *(esp ceram)* refractoriness; *(by treatment:)* fireproofness
Feuerbeton *m s.* Feuerfestbeton
Feuerbrücke *f* fire bridge *(of a reverberatory furnace)*
feuerfest *s.* feuerbeständig
Feuerfestbeton *m* refractory concrete
Feuerfestkeramik *f* refractory ceramics
Feuerfestmaterial *n* refractory [material]
Feuerfestton *m* fireclay, refractory clay
Feuerfortschritt *m (ceram)* fire travel *(in the kiln)*
feuerhemmend fire-retardant, fire-retarding
Feuerkammer *f s.* Feuerraum
Feuerlöschbrause *f* drench (safety, emergency) shower
Feuerlöschdecke *f* fire blanket
Feuerlöscher *m*, **Feuerlöschgerät** *n* [fire] extinguisher
Feuerlöschmittel *n* fire-extinguishing agent
Feuerlöschpumpe *f* fire pump
Feuerlösch-Schaummittel *n* fire-fighting foam
Feuerlöschwasser *n* water for fire protection
feuern to fire, to fuel

Feueröffnung *f* fire mouth
Feueropal *m (min)* fire opal
feuerpolieren *(glass)* to fire-polish, to fire-finish, to fire-glaze
Feuerpolitur *f (glass)* fire polish[ing], fire finishing (glazing)
Feuerraffination *f* fire refining
feuerraffinieren to fire-refine
Feuerraum *m* combustion chamber (space), furnace chamber, firebox *(of an industrial furnace)*
Feuerschutzfarbe *f* flameproofing paint
Feuerschutzmittel *n* flameproofing (fireproofing) agent, fire retardant
feuersicher *s.* feuerbeständig
Feuerstein *m (min)* firestone, flint [stone]
Feuerstrecke *f* fire zone *(as in underground gasification)*
Feuerton *m s.* Feuerfestton
Feuerung *f* 1. firing; 2. *s.* Feuerraum; 3. *s.* Feuerungsmaterial
Feuerungsmaterial *n* fuel
Feuerverbleien *n* hot-dip lead coating
Feuervergolden *n* fire (amalgam) gilding
Feuerverzinken *n* [hot-dip] galvanizing, zinc dipping
Feuerverzinnen *n* hot-dip tinning
Feuerwerk *n* 1. fireworks, firework display, pyrotechnics; 2. *s.* Feuerwerkskörper
Feuerwerker *m* pyrotechnist, pyrotechnician
Feuerwerkerei *f* pyrotechnics, pyrotechny
Feuerwerkskörper *m* firework
Feuerwerkstechnik *f* pyrotechnics
feuerwiderstandsfähig *s.* feuerbeständig
Feuerzeug *n* lighter
~/Döbereinersches Döbereiner's lamp
Feuerzone *f* fire zone *(as in underground gasification)*
Feuerzug *m* flue
ff. = feuerfest
FF-Ruß *m (rubber)* fine furnace black, FF black
FGAR = *N*-Formylglycinamidribotid
FIA *s.* Fließinjektionsanalyse
Fibrillärprotein *n* fibrillar (fibrous) protein
Fibrille *f (biol, text)* fibril[la]
Fibrillenbildung *f* fibrillation
fibrillieren to fibrillate
Fibrillierung *f* fibrillation
Fibrin *n (bioch)* fibrin
Fibrinogen *n (bioch)* fibrinogen
fibrinolytisch fibrinolytic
Fibroin *n* fibroin *(the insoluble protein of silk)*
fibrös fibrous
Fichtennadelöl *n* pine-needle oil *(from pine and fir needles)*
Fichtenöl *n* spruce turpentine, *(pap also)* sulphite turpentine
Fichtensulfitablauge *f (pap)* spent spruce sulphite liquor
Fiebermittel *n* antipyretic, febrifuge
fiebersenkend antipyretic, febrifuge, antifebrile
Figuren *fpl*/**Widmannstättensche** Widmannstätten patterns *(metallography)*
Filament *n (text)* filament, continuous fibre (filament) *(a natural or man-made fibre of great or indefinite length)*
Filicinsäure *f* filicinic acid, 1,1-dimethylcyclohexane-2,4,6-trione
Filixsäure *f* filixic (filicic) acid *(a mixture of homologous phloroglucine derivatives)*
Film *m* film
~/biologischer *s.* Rasen/biologischer
~/dünnschichtiger *(phot)* thin emulsion film
~/fallender *(distil)* falling film
~/flüssig-expandierter *(phys ch)* liquid expanded film
~/fotografischer photographic film
~/monomolekularer monomolecular (unimolecular) film (layer), monolayer
~/panchromatischer *(phot)* panchromatic film, pan-film
~/selbsttragender (trägerloser) *(plast)* self-supporting film
Filmabfall *m (phot)* waste film
Filmband *n (phot)* film strip
Filmbearbeitung *f (phot)* film processing
filmbildend film-forming, filmogenic
Filmbildner *m* film former, film-forming component (material, substance), filmogen
Filmbildung *f* film formation
Filmdeckung *f* film coverage *(of wetting agents)*
Filmdicke *f* film thickness
Filmdiffusion *f* film diffusion
Filmfermenter *m (biot)* [biological, microbial] film fermenter
~/vollständig gemischter completely mixed microbial film fermenter, CMMFF
Filmgießmaschine *f (plast)* film casting machine
Filmgrundlage *f s.* Filmschichtträger
Filmkondensation *f* film[-type] condensation
Film-Penetrationstheorie *f* film-penetration theory *(of mass transfer)*
Filmreaktor *m s.* Filmfermenter
Filmschichtträger *m (phot)* film base, support
Filmstreifen *m (phot)* film strip
Filmträger *m*, **Filmunterlage** *f s.* Filmschichtträger
Filmverarbeitung *f (phot)* [film] processing
Filmverdampfung *f* film boiling
~/partielle transition boiling
Filter *n(m)* filter, *(if working without pressure also)* strainer
~/aschefreies ashless (ash-free) filter
~/bakteriendichtes bacteriological (bacteria-retaining) filter
~/biologisch arbeitendes *(hyd)* biological filter, biofilter
~/druckloses *s.* ~/hydrostatisches
~ für katalytische Oxidation *(hyd)* catalytic oxidizing filter *(for removing iron)*
~/glattes *(lab)* plain filter
~/hydrostatisches gravity (hydrostatic head) filter

~/loses bed filter
~ mit automatischer Rückspülung *(hyd)* automatic backwash filter, ABW filter
~ mit körnigem Filtermaterial granular [medium] filter
~ mit loser Schicht bed filter
~ mit Obenaufgabe top-feeding filter
~ mit Untenaufgabe bottom-feeding filter
~/offenes open filter
~/pulvermetallurgisches metal-powder filter
~/zellenloses non-cellular filter
Filterablauf *m* filter effluent, filtrate, *(hyd also)* filtered (effluent) water
Filteranlage *f* filtration plant (unit), filter unit
Filterapparatur *f* filtration assembly
Filterbett *n* filter (filtration) bed
~ mit Filtermaterial gleichen Korndurchmessers unisize grain bed
Filterbetterschöpfung *f* bed exhaustion
Filterbetthöhe *f* filter bed height
Filterbettiefe *f* filter bed height
Filterbeutel *m* filter bag
Filterblatt *n* filter leaf
Filterboden *m* 1. filter floor (bottom); 2. filter[ing] plate
Filterbottich *m* filter tank (vat)
Filterdurchflußgeschwindigkeit *f* flow rate through the filter, filter [flow] rate
Filtereindicker *m* filter thickener
Filtereinsatz *m* 1. catch pot *(as in a pipe)*; 2. *s.* Filterelement
Filterelement *n* filter[ing] element
filterfähig *s.* filtrierbar
Filterfilz *m (pap)* filter felt *(for recovering fibres)*
Filterfläche *f* filter surface [area], filtering surface, filter [bed] area, area of filtration
Filtergeschwindigkeit *f s.* Filterdurchflußgeschwindigkeit
Filtergewebe *n* filter (filtration) cloth (fabric)
Filtergleichung *f* filtration equation
Filtergut *n* prefilt [slurry, feed], material being *or* to be filtered
Filterhaut *f (hyd)* schmutzdecke, deck of turbidity, mat
Filterhilfe *f s.* Filterhilfsmittel
Filterhilfsmittel *n* filter aid, filtration accelerator
~ zur Schlammkonditionierung *(hyd)* sludge conditioning chemical, chemical conditioning aid
Filterhilfsschicht *f* filter precoat, precoat filter cake
Filterhilfsstoff *m s.* Filterhilfsmittel
Filterkammer *f* filter chamber
Filterkapazität *f* filter capacity, filtering (filtration) capacity
Filterkasten *m* filter tank (vat)
Filterkerze *f* filter candle (cartridge)
Filterkies *m* filter gravel
Filterkuchen *m* filter cake, [filter]cake
~/feuchter wet cake
~ mit hohem Feststoffgehalt high-solids cake
Filterkuchenabfall *m* [filter-]cake release
Filterkuchenabnahme *f* [filter-]cake removal
Filterkuchenbildung *f* [filter-]cake formation
Filterkuchenfeststoffgehalt *m* filter-cake solids, solids content (concentration) of the filter cake
Filterkuchenfeuchtegehalt *m* filter-cake moisture content
Filterkuchenleistung *f* [filter-]cake capacity
Filterkuchenwäsche *f* [filter-]cake washing
Filterlaufzeit *f* length of a filter run, filter run [length], filter run[ning] time; service life of a filter, operating (useful) life of a filter
Filterleistung *f* filter performance, *(in vacuum filtration also)* filter yield *(in kg/m^2 · h)*
Filtermasse *f* filter mass
~ aus faserigen Stoffen filtermasse
Filtermaterial *n s.* Filtermedium
Filtermatte *f* filter mat
Filtermedium *n* filter medium (material), filtering (filtration) medium
~/angeschwemmtes precoat filtering medium, precoat[ing] material
~/faseriges loses filtermasse medium
Filtermittel *n s.* Filtermedium
Filtermittelschicht *f* filter[ing] pad *(of fibrous material)*
Filtermittelwiderstand *m s.* Filterwiderstand des Filtermittels
filtern to filter *(esp gases) (for compounds s.* filtrieren*)*
Filtern *n* filtration *(esp of gases)*
Filternutsche *f* nutsch[e], nutsch filter
~ nach Büchner Büchner funnel (filter)
Filterpaketchromatographie *f* chromatopack method (technique)
Filterpapier *n* filter paper
~ für qualitative Analysen qualitative filter paper
~ für quantitative Analysen quantitative filter paper
Filterpapiereinheit *f (biot)* filter-paper unit
Filterpapierscheibe *f* filter-paper disk, circle (circular piece) of filter paper
Filterpapierstreifen *m* strip of filter paper
Filterpatrone *f* filter cartridge (candle)
Filterphotometer *n* filter photometer
Filterplatte *f* filter[ing] plate; *(plast)* screen pack
Filterpresse *f* filter press
Filterpreßmasse *f* filter pad
Filterrahmen *m* filter frame
Filterröhrchen *n (lab)* filter tube
~ nach Barber pressure filter tube
Filterröhre *f* filter tube
Filterrückstand *m* filtration residue
Filtersack *m* filter bag
Filterscheibe *f* filter disk
~ nach Witt *(lab)* Witt [filter] plate
Filterschicht *f* 1. layer of filtering material *(of a multilayer filter)*; 2. *s.* Filtermittelschicht; 3. *s.* Filterschüttschicht
~/obere top layer of the filter bed, top of the filter
~/untere bottom layer of the filter bed

Filterschlauch *m* filter bag
Filterschüttschicht *f* filter (filtration) bed
~ **aus einer einzigen Kornfraktion** single-medium filter bed
Filterschüttung *f s.* Filterschüttschicht
Filtersieb *n* filter screen
Filterspülabwasser *n (hyd)* backwash waste
Filterspülwasser *n* filter backwash water
Filterstab *m*, **Filterstäbchen** *n (lab)* filter stick
Filterstein *m* filter[ing] stone, *(for diffusing gases also)* gas [diffuser] stone, air stone, sintered (fritted gas) bubbler
Filterstoff *m s.* Filtertuch
Filterstoffänger *m (pap)* filter save-all
Filtertiegel *m* filtering crucible
~ **nach Gooch** Gooch crucible (filter)
Filtertrichter *m* filtering (fritted-disk) funnel
Filtertrog *m* filter tank (vat); *(hyd)* sludge trough (vat)
Filtertrommel *f* filter drum
Filtertrommeleintauchtiefe *f* [filter-]drum submergence
Filtertuch *n* filter (filtration) cloth (fabric)
Filtertuchwiderstand *m* cloth resistance
Filterung *f* filtration *(of gases)*
Filterungs... *s.* Filter... *and* Filtrations...
Filterverfahren *n (coal)* percolation method *(in underground gasification)*
Filterverstopfung *f* filter blinding
Filterwanne *f* filter tank (vat)
Filterwäsche *f* filter cleaning
Filterwasser *n (pap)* filtered water
Filterwiderstand *m* resistance to filtration, flow resistance
~ **des Filtermittels** filter-medium resistance, flow resistance in the filter bed
~ **des Filtertuchs** cloth resistance
Filterwirkung *f* filtering action; filtering effect
Filterwirkungsgrad *m* filter efficiency
Filterzelle *f* filter cell (unit)
Filterzentrifuge *f s.* Filtrierzentrifuge
Filterzulauf *m* filter influent
Filtrat *n* filtrate, filter effluent, *(hyd also)* filtered (effluent) water
Filtratablauf *m* filtrate outlet (exit), *(hyd also)* filtered water outlet
Filtratauslauf *m*, **Filtrataustritt** *m s.* Filtratablauf
Filtratfeststoffgehalt *m* filtrate solids [concentration]
Filtratgüte *f* filtrate quality, *(hyd also)* effluent [water] quality
Filtration *f* filtration, *(without pressure also)* straining • **durch ~ entfernen** to remove by filtration, to filter out • **durch ~ keimfrei machen** *(biot)* to filter aseptically, to sterilize by filtration
~**/adsorptive** *(chromat)* frontal analysis
~**/biologische** *(hyd)* biological filtration
~ **im Abwärtsstrom** downflow filtration
~ **im Aufwärtsstrom** upflow filtration
~ **in Filterpressen** filter pressing
~ **mit Drehfiltern** rotary filtration
~ **mit konstanter Filtriergeschwindigkeit** constant-rate filtration
~ **mittels Anschwemmfilters** septum filtration
~ **ohne Bildung eines Filterkuchens** non-cake-forming filtration
~ **über A-Kohle (Aktivkohle)** *(hyd)* activated-carbon filtration, filtration with activated carbon, carbon filtration, CF
~ **über gekörnte Aktivkohle** *(hyd)* granular-activated-carbon filtration, GAC filtration
~ **über körniges Filtermaterial** granular-medium filtration, [granular] bed filtration
~ **über Sand** sand filtration
~ **unter Ausnutzung der Schwerkraft** gravity (natural) filtration
~ **unter konstantem Filtrationsdruck** constant-pressure filtration
~ **unter vermindertem Druck** filtration under reduced pressure
Filtrations... *s. a.* Filtrier...
Filtrationsabscheidung *f s.* Filtrationsentstaubung
Filtrationsanreicherung *f (biot)* filtration enrichment
Filtrationsdauer *f* filtration (filtering, filter) time
Filtrationsdruck *m* filtering (filtration) pressure
Filtrationseigenschaften *fpl* filtration properties
Filtrationsentstauber *m* filter-type dust collector, dust[-control] filter, dust collection filter
Filtrationsentstaubung *f* dust[-control] filtration
Filtrationsgeschwindigkeit *f* filtering (filtration) rate
Filtrationshilfe *f* filter aid
Filtrationskonstante *f* filtration constant
Filtrationskurve *f* filtration curve
Filtrationsleistung *f s.* Filterleistung
Filtrationsperiode *f* filter run, filtration phase *(as opposed to backwash period)*
Filtrationszentrifuge *f s.* Filtrierzentrifuge
Filtrationszeit *f s.* Filtrationsdauer
Filtrationszyklus *m* filtration cycle
Filtratqualität *f s.* Filtratgüte
Filtratsammelleitung *f* discharge manifold
Filtrex-Abscheider *m* louver separator
Filtrier... *s. a.* Filtrations... *and* Filter...
Filtrieranordnung *f* filtration assembly
filtrierbar filt[e]rable
~**/leicht** freely filt[e]rable, free-filtering
~**/nicht** unfilt[e]rable
~**/schwer** poorly (difficultly) filterable
Filtrierbarkeit *f* filterability, filtering ability
filtrieren to filter, to filtrate, *(without pressure also)* to strain
~**/durch Ultrafilter** to ultrafilter
~**/erneut** to refilter
~**/in Filterpressen** to filter-press
~**/klar** to polish, to clarify
~ **lassen/sich** to filter *(well or poorly)*
~**/nochmals** to refilter
~**/unter Druck** to filter with pressure, to force through the filter

Filtrieren *n s.* Filtration
Filtrierstativ *n (lab)* filter (funnel) rack (stand)
Filtrierstutzen *m* filtrate jar
Filtriervorrichtung *f* filter assembly
Filtrierzentrifuge *f* filtering centrifuge (centrifugal), centrifugal [filter], screen (perforate bowl) centrifuge
Filz *m* felt • **mit ~ auskleiden** to line with felt, to felt • **mit ~ überziehen** to cover with felt, to felt
~/endloser *(pap)* endless felt
~/gerippter *(pap)* ribbed felt
Filzärmel *m (tann)* felt sleeve *(of a sammying machine)*
filzartig felt-like
Filzbildung *f* felting
Filzdichtung *f* felt packing (seal, gasket)
Filzeigenschaft *f* felting property
filzen *(text)* to felt; *(pap)* to felt together
Filzfähigkeit *f* felting power
Filzfreiausrüstung *f (text)* antifelting treatment
Filzinstandhalter *m (pap)* felt conditioner
Filzinstandhaltung *f (pap)* felt conditioning
Filzkalander *m* felt calender
Filzlauf *m (pap)* felt travel
Filzleitwalze *f (pap)* felt-leading roll
filzlos *(pap)* feltless
Filzmarke *f*, **Filzmarkierung** *f* felt mark *(a defect in paper)*
Filzpackung *f* felt packing (seal, gasket)
Filzpappe *f* felt board
Filzreinigung *f (pap)* felt cleaning
Filzsauger *m (pap)* felt suction box
Filzschleife *f (pap)* endless felt
Filzschrumpfung *f (text)* felting shrinkage
Filzseite *f* felt (top) side *(of paper)*
Filzspannwalze *f (pap)* felt stretching (tightener) roll, hitch roll
Filzstrang *m (pap)* felt run
Filztrockenzylinder *m*, **Filztrockner** *m (pap)* felt dryer (drying cylinder)
Filztrum *m(n) (pap)* felt run
~/rücklaufender return felt run
~/vorlaufender felt run
Filztuch *n (pap)* felt [blanket]
~/endloses endless felt
Filzvermögen *n* felting power *(of fibres)*
Filzwalze *f (pap)* felt-covered couch roll
Filzwäsche *f (pap)* 1. felt cleaning; 2. *s.* Filzwäscher
Filzwascheinrichtung *f s.* Filzwäscher
Filzwäscher *m (pap)* felt cleaner (washer)
FIMS, FI-Massenspektroskopie *f* field-ionization mass spectrometry, FIMS
finalisieren to formulate
Finalisierung *f* formulation
Finalprodukt *n* final (finished, consumer) product
Fine-Furnace-Ruß *m (rubber)* fine furnace black, FF black
Fine-Thermal-Ruß *m (rubber)* fine thermal black, FT black *(gas black of small particle size)*
Finger *m*/**kalter** *(lab)* cold finger [condenser, trap], finger-type condenser, acorn condenser
Fingerabdruckbereich *m (spectr)* finger-print region
Fingerabdruckmethode *f s.* Fingerprinttechnik
Fingerhut *m (ceram)* thimble *(a piece of kiln furniture)*
Fingerling *m* fingerstall, finger cot *(protective equipment)*
Fingerprintgebiet *n (spectr)* finger-print region
Fingerprinttechnik *f (bioch)* technique of fingerprinting
Fingerrührer *m* finger agitator
Finkelstein-Austausch *m*, **Finkelstein-Reaktion** *f (org ch)* Finkelstein exchange (reaction)
FIR *s.* Infrarotgebiet/fernes
Firestone-Flexometer *n (rubber)* Firestone flexometer
Firestone-Plastometer *n (rubber)* Firestone[-Dillon] plastometer
Firnis *m* boiled oil
~/japanischer Japanese (Chinese) lacquer *(from Rhus verniciflua Stokes)*
~/lithographischer litho[graphic] varnish
~ von Martaban Burmese lacquer *(from Melanorrhoea usitata Wall.)*
fischartig fishy *(smell, taste)*
Fischauge *n* fish eye *(a defect in plastics)*
Fischbekämpfungsmittel *n* piscicide
Fischer-Analyse *f* Fischer assay *(for determining the tar yield of coal)*
Fischer-Base *f* Fischer base, 1,3,3-trimethyl-2-methyleneindoline
Fischer-Hepp-Umlagerung *f* Fischer-Hepp rearrangement *(of aromatic nitrosamines to p-nitrosoarylamines in the presence of acids)*
Fischer-Projektion *f* Fischer projection *(for displaying molecules)*
~/gedrehte rotated Fischer projection
Fischer-Tropsch-Anlage *f* Fischer-Tropsch plant
Fischer-Tropsch-Benzin *n* Fischer-Tropsch naphtha
Fischer-Tropsch-Synthese *f* Fischer-Tropsch synthesis *(of hydrocarbons)*
Fischgeschmack *m* reversion flavour, fishy taste *(of spoiled fats)*
Fischgift *n* 1. *(med)* ichthyotoxin; 2. *(agric)* fish poison *(e.g. several pesticides)*
fischig fishy *(smell, taste)* • **~ werden** to revert *(of fats)*
Fischigkeit *f* fishiness *(of spoiled fats)*
Fischigwerden *n* reversion *(of fats)*
Fischleberöl *n*, **Fischlebertran** *m* fish liver oil
Fischleim *m* isinglass, ichthyocol[l], fish gelatin (glue)
Fischmehl *n* fish meal, *(if finely ground:)* fish flour; fish tankage *(fertilizer)*
Fischöl *n* fish oil
Fischschuppen *fpl* fish scale *(a defect in enamel)*
Fischschuppenessenz *f (cosmet)* fish scale essence

Fischschwanzbrenner *m (lab)* fish-tail (bats-wing) burner
Fischschwanzmeißel *m (petrol)* fish-tail bit
Fischsilber *n (coat, cosmet)* pearl essence
Fischsterben *n (tox)* fish kill
Fischtran *m* fish oil (fat)
Fischvergiftung *f* poisoning from fish, ichthyism[us], ichthyotoxism
Fiset[te]holz *n (dye)* fustet, young fustic *(from Cotinus coggygria Scop.)*
Fixage *f (phot)* fixing, fixation
Fixateur *m (cosmet)* fixative *(added to a perfume)*
Fixativ *n (dye)* fixative, fixing agent
Fixierbad *n (phot)* fixing (hypo) bath, fixer
~/härtendes hardening fixing bath
~/saures acid fixing bath
fixieren to fix
Fixiergeschwindigkeit *f (phot)* rate of fixing, fixing speed
Fixierlösung *f* fixing solution
Fixiermittel *n* 1. *(phot)* fixing agent, fixer; *(text)* fixing agent; 2. *s.* Fixativ
Fixiernatron *n (phot)* hyposulphite, hypo *(sodium thiosulphate)*
Fixiernatronzerstörer *m (phot)* hypo eliminator
Fixiernatronzerstörung *f (phot)* hypo elimination
Fixiersalz *n (phot)* fixing salt, fixer; *(specif) s.* Fixiernatron
~/saures acid fixer
Fixierung *f* fixation
~/nichtsymbiotische *(agric)* non-symbiotic fixation, free fixation, azofication *(of atmospheric nitrogen)*
~/symbiotische *(agric)* symbiotic fixation *(of atmospheric nitrogen)*
Fixierungsflüssigkeit *f* fixing solution
~/Bendasche *(biol)* Benda solution *(consisting of osmic acid, chromic acid, and glacial acetic acid)*
Fixierungsmittel *n* fixative, fixing agent *(for fixing living tissue)*
Fixiervorgang *m* fixing process
Fixpunkt *m* fixed point
F-Kalander *m (rubber)* inverted L calender
Flachband *n* flat belt
Flachbecken *n (hyd)* plain clarifier
Flachbrunnen *m (hyd)* shallow well
Flachdichtung *f* flat gasket
Flachdruckfarbe *f* planographic [printing] ink
Fläche *f* 1. surface; *(cryst)* face; 2. [surface] area *(as of an industrial plant)*
~/offene open area *(as of a sieve)*
Flächenabscheider *m* envelope (screen) filter *(gas-solid separation)*
Flächenbedarf *m* land (space) requirements *(of an industrial plant)*
Flächenbehandlung *f (agric)* blanket application, broadcast treatment *(as with herbicides)*
Flächenbelastung *f (hyd)* surface loading [rate], loading rate per unit area *(drying beds: kg/m^2 · a; sedimentation tanks, trickling filters: m^3/m^2 · h)*
~/hydraulische hydraulic loading per unit area
Flächenbeschickung *f s.* Flächenbelastung
Flächendüngung *f (agric)* bulk spreading [of fertilizers]
Flächeneinheit *f* unit area
Flächenfixierung *f (text)* flat setting
Flächenfraß *m* general corrosion
Flächengebilde *n*/**textiles** textile fabric
Flächengewicht *n s.* Masse je Flächeneinheit
Flächengröße *f* [surface] area
Flächenkorrosion *f* general corrosion
Flächenpotential *n* surface potential
Flächenwinkel *m (cryst)* interfacial angle
flächenzentriert *(cryst)* face-centred
~/einseitig one-face centred
~/kubisch face-centred cubic
Flachglas *n* flat glass
Flachglasofen *m* flat-glass furnace
Flachglockenboden *m (distil)* low-riser plate (tray)
Flachgurt *m* flat belt
Flachkegelbrecher *m* short-head cone crusher
Flachriemen *m* flat belt
Flachsdichtung *f*, **Flachspackung** *f* flax packing
Flachsröste *f* 1. retting; 2. ret[tery] *(plant)*
Flachsrösterei *f* ret[tery]
Flachsrotte *f s.* Flachsröste
Flachstrahldüse *f* slot (flat-spray) nozzle
Flachtrog *m (coal)* shallow bath
Flachware *f (glass, ceram)* flat ware
Flachwurfsieb *n* oscillating screen
flammbeständig flame-resistant, uninflammable, non-[in]flammable, flameproof
Flammbeständigkeit *f* flame resistance (resistivity), uninflammability, non-flammability
Flamme *f* flame • **mit fächelnder ~ erhitzen (erwärmen)** to brush with the free flame
~/freibrennende free (naked) flame
~/kleine small flame
~/leuchtende luminous (surface) flame
~/nichtleuchtende non-luminous flame, volume flame
~/offene free (naked) flame
~/rauschende roaring flame
~/rußende smoky flame
Flammen-AAS *f*, **Flammenatomabsorptionsspektr[alphot]ometrie** *f* flame AAS, flame atomic absorption spectrometry
Flammenaufprall *m* flame impingement
Flammenblasverfahren *n (glass)* flame-blowing process
Flammenbogen *n* flame (flaming) arc
Flammenfärbung *f* flame coloration
Flammenfortpflanzung *f* flame propagation
Flammenfortpflanzungsgeschwindigkeit *f s.* Flammengeschwindigkeit
Flammenfront *f* flame front
Flammenführung *f* firing *(of an industrial furnace)*
~/aufsteigende up-draught firing
~/horizontale horizontal-draught firing
~/überschlagende down-draught firing

Flammengeschwindigkeit *f* flame velocity (speed), velocity of flame propagation
flammenhärten to flame-harden
Flammenhärtung *f* flame hardening
flammenhemmend flame-retardant
Flammenionisation *f* flame ionization
Flammenionisationsdetektor *m* flame ionization detector, FID
Flammenofen *m s.* Flammofen
Flammenphotometer *n* flame photometer
Flammenphotometerdetektor *m (anal)* flame photometric detector
Flammenphotometrie *f* flame photometry
flammenphotometrisch flame-photometric
Flammenrückschlag *m* flareback, flashback
Flammenschutz... *s.* Flammschutz...
Flammenspektrometrie *f* flame spectrometry
Flammenspektroskopie *f* flame spectroscopy
Flammenspektrum *n* flame spectrum
Flammenspritzen *n* flame spraying (spray coating)
Flammentemperatur *f* flame temperature
Flammenverzögerungsmittel *n* flame retardant (retarder)
Flammenverzögerungsvermögen *n* flame retardancy
Flammenwächter *m* flame failure safeguard
flammfest flameproof
Flammfestausrüstung *f (text)* flameproof finish (impregnation), fireproof (flame-resistant) finish (impregnation)
Flammfestigkeit *f* flameproofness
Flammfestimprägnierung *f s.* Flammfestausrüstung
Flammfestmachen *n* flameproofing
Flammfront *f* flame front
flammhärten to flame-harden
Flammhärtung *f* flame hardening
Flammkaschierung *f* flame lamination
Flammkohle *f* flame coal
Flammofen *m* reverberatory (air) furnace; *(ceram)* reverberatory kiln
Flammofenfrischverfahren *n (met)* puddling process
Flammpunkt *m* flash point
~ im geschlossenen Tiegel closed[-cup] flash point
~ im offenen Tiegel open[-cup] flash point
Flammpunktapparat *m*, **Flammpunktgerät** *n s.* Flammpunktprüfer
Flammpunktprüfer *m* flash-point apparatus (tester), flash tester
~/geschlossener closed[-cup] flash tester
~ nach Abel-Pensky Abel-Pensky [flash-point] tester
~ nach Pensky-Martens Pensky-Martens [flash-point] tester
~ nach Pensky-Martens/geschlossener Pensky-Martens closed tester
~ nach Tagliabue/geschlossener Tagliabue (Tag) closed tester
~/offener open[-cup] flash tester
Flammpunktprüfgerät *n s.* Flammpunktprüfer
Flammpunktstiegel *m* flash cup
Flammrohr *n* fire tube, flue
Flammrohrkessel *m* fire-tube boiler
Flammruß *m (rubber)* lampblack
Flammschutzausrüstung *f*, **Flammschutzimprägnierung** *f s.* Flammfestausrüstung
Flammschutzmittel *n* flameproofing (fireproofing) agent
flammsicher flameproof
Flammsicherheit *f* flameproofness
Flammsichermachen *n* flameproofing
Flammstrahlen *n* flame cleaning (descaling) *(of metal surfaces)*
flammwidrig *s.* flammbeständig
Flansch *m* flange, socket
~/loser lap-joint (slip-on) flange
Flanschbolzen *m* flange bolt
Flanschdichtung *f* flange gasket (seal)
Flanschenrohr *n* flanged[-end] pipe
Flanschfitting *m(n)* flanged fitting
Flanschfläche *f* flange face
Flanschformstück *n* flanged fitting
Flanschschraube *f* flange bolt
Flanschstirnfläche *f* flange face
Flanschstück *n* flanged fitting
Flanschverbindung *f* flanged joint
Flasche *f* bottle, flask
~/Florentiner *(distil)* Florentine flask (receiver)
~/Mariottesche *(lab)* Mariotte bottle (flask), aspirator
~/Woulfesche *(lab)* Woulfe bottle
Flaschenabfüllerei *f* bottling plant, bottle house, bottlery
Flaschenabfüllmaschine *f* bottling machine, bottler
Flaschenabfüllung *f* bottling
Flaschenabgabe *f (glass)* bottle delivery
Flaschenabzug *m* bottling
Flaschenbier *n* bottle[d] beer
Flaschenbürste *f* bottle brush
Flaschenfüllerei *f s.* Flaschenabfüllerei
Flaschengärung *f* bottle fermentation
Flaschengas *n* cylinder gas, *(propane or butane or mixture of both:)* bottle[d] gas
Flaschengestell *n (lab)* reagent rack
Flaschenglas *n* bottle glass
Flaschenkappe *f* bottle cap
Flaschenmilch *f* bottled milk
Flaschenofen *m (ceram)* bottle kiln (oven)
Flaschenschleuder *f* bottle centrifuge
Flaschenspule *f (text)* bottle bobbin
Flaschenstopfen *m* bottle stopper
Flaschenverschluß *m* bottle cap
Flaschenwein *m* bottled wine
Flaschenzentrifuge *f* bottle centrifuge
Flash-Destillat *n (petrol)* flash distillate
~/primäres primary flash distillate, P.F.D.

Flash-Kammer *f (distil)* flash chamber (vessel, trap)
Flash-Kurve *f (distil)* [single-]flash curve
Flash-Raum *m s.* Flash-Kammer
Flash-Röster *m (met)* flash roaster (burner)
Flash-Verdampfung *f* flash (instantaneous) evaporation
~/mehrstufige multiflash evaporation, MSF (multistage flash) evaporation
Flaum *m (food)* bloom *(as on certain fruits or cocoa products)*
Flavan *n (org ch)* flavan
Flavanoid *n (org ch)* flavanoid
Flavanon *n (org ch)* flavanone
Flavanthron *n (org ch)* flavanthrone
Flaviansäure *f* flavianic acid, 2,4-dinitronaphth-1-ol-7-sulphonic acid
Flavin *n* flavin[e], *(specif)* isoalloxazine
~/elektronenübertragendes electron-transfer flavin, ETF
Flavin-adenin-dinucleotid *n* flavin[e] adenine dinucleotide, FAD
Flavinenzym *n*, **Flavinferment** *n* flavin[e] enzyme, flavoenzyme, flavoprotein, yellow enzyme
Flavinmononucleotid *n* flavin[e] mononucleotide, FMN, riboflavin-5'-phosphate
Flavon *n (org ch)* flavone
Flavonfarbstoff *m* flavone pigment
Flavoproteid *n*, **Flavoprotein** *n s.* Flavinenzym
Flavyliumsalz *n* flavylium salt, 2-phenylchromenylium salt
Flechtenfarbstoff *m* lichen dye
Flechtensäure *f* lichen acid
Flechtströmung *f s.* Strömung/turbulente
Fleck *m* spot, *(if undesirable also)* speck, blotch, stain; *(chromat)* spot
~/magischer *(bioch)* magic spot *(consisting of guanosine phosphates in the synthesis of ribosomal RNA)*
Fleckenbenzin *n* cleaner's naphtha (solvent)
Fleckenbildung *f* spotting, specking
~ durch hartes Wasser hard-water spotting
~ durch weiches Wasser soft-water spotting
Fleckenentferner *m* stain (spot) remover
Fleckenentfernung *f* stain (spot) removal
Fleckenentfernungsmittel *n* stain (spot) remover
fleckenfrei spot-free *(surface)*
Fleckenseife *f* scouring soap
Fleckentfernung *f s.* Fleckenentfernung
Fleckenunempfindlichkeit *f (plast)* stain resistance
Fleischaroma *n* meat flavour
Fleischbrühe *f* broth
Fleischdüngemehl *n* garbage tankage
Fleischeiweiß *n* meat protein
Fleischextrakt *m* meat extract
Fleischfuttermehl *n* digester tankage, meat meal
Fleischguano *m s.* Fleischdüngemehl
Fleischmehl *n (agric)* [animal] tankage, *(as feed also)* digester tankage, meat meal, *(as fertilizer also)* garbage tankage
Fleischmilchsäure *f* sarcolactic acid, L*(+)*-lactic acid, dextrorotatory lactic acid
Fleischmürbesalz *n (food)* meat tenderizer
Fleischprotein *n* meat protein
Fleischseite *f (tann)* flesh side
Fleischspalt *m (tann)* flesh split
Fleischzartmachung *f*[**/künstliche**] *(food)* meat tenderization
Fleming-Methode *f* Fleming method *(for determining penicillin)*
Flesch-Winkler-Verfahren *n* Flesch-Winkler process *(gasification of small-sized coal in downstream operation)*
Fletcher-Bleichturm *m (pap)* Fletcher bleacher
Fletton-Ziegel *m* fletton
Fletton-Ziegelton *m* Fletton brick clay
flexibel flexible
flexibilisieren *(plast)* to flexibilize
Flexibilität *f* flexibility
Flexodruck *m*, **Flexographie** *f* flexographic (aniline) printing, flexography
Flexometer *n (rubber)* flexometer
Fl. g. T. *s.* Flammpunkt im geschlossenen Tiegel
Fliegenbekämpfungsmittel *n* antifly preparation, fly poison
Fliegenfängerpapier *n* fly paper
Fliegengift *n* fly poison
Fliegenpapier *n* fly paper
Fliegenstein *m (min)* native arsenic
Fliegermethode *f* F3 method *(for octane rating)*
Fliehkraft *f* centrifugal force
Fliehkraftabscheider *m* centrifugal separator (collector)
Fliehkraftabscheidung *f* centrifugal separation
Fliehkraftklassierer *m* centrifugal classifier
Fliehkraftmaschine *f* **nach Roelig** Roelig hysteresis apparatus
Fliehkraftmühle *f* centrifugal mill
Fliehkraftpendelmühle *f* pendulum roller mill
Fliehkraftreiniger *m* centrifugal cleaner, *(Am)* centrifiner
Fliehkraftscheibe *f* centrifugal disk
Fliehkraftscheider *m s.* Fliehkraftabscheider
Fliehkraftsichter *m* centrifugal classifier
Fliehkraftversprüher *m* centrifugal atomizer, spinning disk [atomizer]
Fliehkraftversprühung *f* centrifugal atomization
Fliehkraftwalzenmühle *f s.* Fliehkraftpendelmühle
Fliehkraftzerstäuber *m s.* Fliehkraftversprüher
Fliese *f* tile, slab
~ für Sonderzwecke special-purpose tile
~/trockengepreßte dust-pressed tile
fließbar *s.* fließfähig
Fließbeständigkeit *f* resistance to flow
Fließbetrieb *m* continuous operation (working)
Fließbett *n* fluid[ized] bed, boiling bed *(for compounds s.* Wirbelschicht*)*
Fließbett... *s. a.* Wirbelschicht...
Fließbetthöhe *f* fluidized-bed depth

Fließbettkatalysator *m* fluidized catalyst, fluid[-bed] catalyst
Fließbettporenvolumen *n***/minimales** minimum porosity for fluidization
Fließbettvulkanisation *f* fluid-bed vulcanization
Fließbild *n s.* Fließdiagramm
Fließdehnung *f* yield strain
Fließdiagramm *n* flow diagram (chart, sheet)
Fließdialyse *f* continuous dialysis
Fließeigenschaften *fpl s.* Fließverhalten
fließen 1. to flow, to run; *(coat)* to flow; 2. to yield *(materials science)*
~ **lassen** to run *(a liquid)*
Fließen *n* 1. flow, flux; plastic flow *(one kind of deformation)*; 2. yield *(materials science)*
~/Binghamsches Bingham[-plastic] flow
~/gleichmäßiges smooth fluidization *(fluidized-bed technique)*
~/kaltes cold flow *(of thermoplastics)*
~/Newtonsches Newtonian flow
~/nicht-Newtonsches non-Newtonian flow
~/plastisches plastic flow
~/pseudoplastisches pseudoplastic flow
~/schlechtes *(plast)* low flow
~/strukturviskoses pseudoplastic flow
~/viskoses viscous flow
Fließerscheinung *f* yield phenomenon *(as in metals under tension)*
Fließexponent *m (plast)* flow index
fließfähig flowable; fusible *(melt)*
Fließfähigkeit *f* flowability, fluidity; fusibility *(of a melt)*
Fließfestigkeit *f* resistance to flow
Fließformen *n (rubber)* transfer moulding'
Fließgeschwindigkeit *f* flow rate (velocity), liquid flow velocity
~ **des Schlamms** *(hyd)* sludge flow rate
~ **des Wassers** *(hyd)* water [flow] rate, water velocity, rate of water flow
Fließgewässer *n***/als Vorfluter dienendes** *(hyd)* receiving stream
Fließgleichgewicht *n* dynamic equilibrium (steady state), steady (stationary) state
Fließgleichgewichtszustand *m s.* Fließgleichgewicht
Fließgrenze *f* 1. yield point *(materials testing)*; *(coat)* yield value; *(met)* flow point; 2. *s.* ~/Binghamsche
~/Binghamsche yield stress *(rheology)*
~/praktische yield strength *(materials testing)*
~/untere yield value *(materials testing)*
Fließinjektionsanalyse *f* flow-injection analysis, FIA
Fließkunde *f* rheology, science of flow
Fließkurve *f* flow curve
Fließmittel *n (chromat)* [mobile] solvent
Fließmittelfront *f (chromat)* solvent front
Fließmitteltrog *m (chromat)* solvent trough
Fließmittelwanderungsstrecke *f (chromat)* solvent migration distance

Fließpapier *n* absorbent paper
Fließpapier-Filterpresse *f* blotter press
Fließpunkt *m* melting point, m.p.; pour point *(of oils)*; *(met)* flow point
Fließpunkterniedriger *m* pour-point depressant *(for oils)*
Fließpunktprüfung *f* pour-point test *(applied to oils)*
Fließrichtung *f* flow direction
Fließschema *n s.* Fließdiagramm
Fließschicht *f s.* Fließbett
Fließschlamm *m (hyd)* liquid sludge
Fließschmelzpunkt *m* slip point
Fließspannung *f* yield stress
Fließspeiser *m (glass)* flow feeder
Fließspeisung *f* gravity feed *(of an apparatus with liquids)*
Fließstaubkontakt *m* fluidized catalyst, fluid[-bed] catalyst
Fließtemperatur *f* flow temperature; *(met)* flow point
Fließverfahren *n s.* Wirbelschichtverfahren
Fließverfestigung *f* shear thickening
Fließverhalten *n* flow (rheological) behaviour, flow[ing] properties
Fließvermögen *n* flowability, fluidity; fusibility *(of a melt)*
Fließweg *m* flow path
Fließwert *m (coat)* yield value
Fließzone *f* fluidized zone *(of a fluidized-bed reactor)*
Flint *m (min)* flint, firestone *(a variety of opal)*
Flintglas *n* flint glass
Flintstein *m* flint pebble
Flintsteinmahlkörper *m* flint pebble
Flip-flop-Enzym *n* flip-flop enzyme
Flitter *m (min)* spangle; *(glass)* glass frost, frost glass, tinsel
Flöckchen *n* floccule
Flockdruck *m (text)* flock print
Flocke *f* flake, *(esp in suspensions:)* floc; *(text)* flock
flockegefärbt *(text)* stock-dyed
flocken to flocculate, to coagulate, to clot, to curdle, *(coll also)* to peptize; *(hyd)* to coagulate, to flocculate
Flocken *fpl (hyd)* floc[s] • ~ **bilden** to agglomerate into floc[s]
~/absetzfähige settleable floc
~/biologische biological floc
Flockenabsetzgeschwindigkeit *f (hyd)* floc settling rate
flockenartig flake-like, flocculent
Flockenbast *m (text)* cottonin, cottonized bast fibre
flockenbildend *(hyd)* floc-building
Flockenbildung *f* flocculation, coagulation, clotting; *(hyd)* floc formation (building)
Flockenbildungsphase *f (hyd)* flocculation (floc-building) stage
Flockendichte *f (hyd)* floc density

Flockenfestigkeit *f (hyd)* floc strength
flockengefärbt *(text)* stock-dyed
Flockengröße *f (hyd)* size of floc [particles]
Flockenschlamm *m (hyd)* flocculated sludge, floc solids
Flockensedimentation *f (hyd)* floc settling
Flockensinkgeschwindigkeit *f (hyd)* floc settling rate
Flockenstabilität *f (hyd)* floc strength
Flockenvolumen *n (hyd)* floc volume
Flockenvolumenkonzentration *f (hyd)* floc volume concentration
Flockenwachstum *n (hyd)* floc growth
Flockenwirbelschicht *f s.* Flockenwirbelzone
Flockenwirbelzone *f (hyd)* blanket of sludge, sludge (fluidized) blanket
Flockenzone *f s.* Flockenwirbelzone
Flocker *m s.* Flockungsmittel
flockig flocculent
Flockseide *f* flock silk *(from cocoon waste)*
Flockulant *m (hyd)* polymer flocculant
Flockulantendosis *f (hyd)* flocculant dosage
Flockulantenzugabe *f (hyd)* flocculant addition
Flockulation *f s.* Flokkulation
Flockung *f* flocculation, coagulation, clotting, curdling, *(coll also)* pectization; *(hyd)* coagulation *(esp using metal coagulants)*, flocculation *(esp using polymer flocculants)*
~ **mit Aluminiumsalzen** *(hyd)* alum coagulation
~ **mit Eisen(III)-Salzen** *(hyd)* ferric-iron coagulation
~ **und Sedimentation** *f (hyd)* clarification-flocculation, flocculation with sedimentation
Flockungsanlage *f (hyd)* coagulation (flocculation) unit
Flockungsbecken *n (hyd)* coagulation basin, flocculation (flocculating) basin, flocculator
Flockungsbehandlung *f (hyd)* coagulation (coagulant) treatment *(esp using metal coagulants)*, flocculation (flocculant) treatment *(esp using polymer flocculants)*
Flockungsbeschleuniger *m s.* Flockungshilfsmittel
Flockungschemikalie *f s.* Flockungsmittel
Flockungseigenschaften *fpl (hyd)* coagulating (flocculating) properties
Flockungseinrichtung *f (hyd)* flocculator
Flockungsfähigkeit *f s.* Flockungsvermögen
Flockungsfiltration *f (hyd)* coagulation-filtration
Flockungshilfsmittel *n (hyd)* coagulation (flocculation) aid *(as ground clay or activated silica)*
Flockungskammer *f (hyd)* flocculation chamber
Flockungsklärapparat *m***[/kombinierter]** *s.* Flokkungsreaktor
Flockungskraft *f s.* Flockungsvermögen
Flockungsmittel *n (hyd)* coagulant *(esp metal salts)*, flocculant *(esp polymers)*
~/„klassisches" [metal] coagulant *(Al or Fe salt)*
~/polymeres [polymer] flocculant
Flockungsmittelbeimischung *f (hyd)* coagulant *or* flocculant addition
Flockungsmitteldosis *f (hyd)* coagulant *or* flocculant dosage
Flockungsmitteleinsatz *m (hyd)* coagulant *or* flocculant application
Flockungsmittelmenge *f (hyd)* quantity of coagulant *or* flocculant
Flockungsmittelzugabe *f (hyd)* coagulant *or* flocculant addition
Flockungsraum *m (hyd)* flocculation chamber
Flockungsreaktor *m (hyd)* reactor-clarifier, flocculator, flocculation tank
Flockungsschlamm *m (hyd)* coagulant sludge, coagulated chemical sludge, sludge produced by coagulation
Flockungsverfahren *n (hyd)* coagulation (flocculation) process
Flockungsverlauf *m* flocculation process
Flockungsvorgang *m* flocculation process, *(hyd also)* coagulation-flocculation process
Flockungsvermögen *n* flocculating ability (power)
Flockungswert *m* flocculation value *(of an electrolyte)*
Flokkulator *m s.* Flockungsreaktor
Flokkulation *f* flocculation *(using polymer flocculants)*
Floretteseide *f* floret[te] silk, floss silk
Florey-Einheit *f* Florey [Oxford] unit *(an international unit of penicillin no longer used)*
Florideenstärke *f* floridean starch *(from several red algae)*
Florpostpapier *n* onion skin
Flory-Temperatur *f* Flory theta temperature
Fl. o. T. *s.* Flammpunkt im offenen Tiegel
Flotation *f* flo[a]tation
~/differentielle differential (selective) floatation
~ **durch mechanischen Lufteintrag** air floatation [clarification]
~/kollektive collective (bulk) floatation
~ **mit dispergierter Luft** dispersed-air floatation
~ **mit gelöstem Gas** dissolved-gas floatation
~ **mit gelöster Luft** dissolved-air floatation, DAF
~/selektive (sortenweise) *s.* ~/differentielle
Flotationsabgänge *mpl* floatation tailings
Flotationsanlage *f* floatation plant; *(hyd)* floatation thickener *(sludge thickening)*
Flotationsberge *pl* floatation tailings
Flotationschemikalie *f* floatation aid
Flotationsgerät *n*, **Flotationsmaschine** *f* floatation machine (apparatus, separator)
Flotationsmittel *n* floatation [re]agent
~/drückend wirkendes depressant
Flotationsöl *n* floatation oil
Flotationsprobe *f* floatation assay
Flotationsraum *m* floatation tank
Flotationsreagens *n* floatation [re]agent
Flotationsschwefel *m* floatation sulphur, gas sulphur
Flotationsstoffänger *m (pap)* floatation save-all
Flotationsverfahren *n* floatation process

Flotationszelle *f* floatation cell (unit)
Flotationszone *f* floatation zone
flotierbar floatable
Flotierbarkeit *f* floatability
flotieren to float *(e.g. ore)*
Flotieren *n* flo[a]tation
Flotte *f* liquor
Flottenaufnahme *f (text)* pick-up [of liquor]
Flottenkreislauf *m (text)* liquor circulation
Flottenlauf *m (text)* liquor flow
Flottenmenge *f (text)* amount of liquor
Flottenverhältnis *n (text)* liquor (bath) ratio, bath length; *(pap)* liquor[-to-wood] ratio, liquid-to-solid ratio
Flottenzirkulation *f (text)* liquor circulation
Flottenzulauf *m (text)* liquor flow
Flöz *n (mine)* stratum, layer, *(if thin also)* seam
Flözvergasung *f* underground gasification
flüchtig volatile, fugitive
~/leicht highly (readily) volatile, high-volatile
~/mit Dampf (Trägerdampf, Wasserdampf) steam-distillable
~/schwer difficultly volatile, slow-evaporating, heavy
~/schwerer less volatile
Flüchtige *n* volatile matter, v.m.
Flüchtigkeit *f* volatility
~/relative relative volatility
Flugasche *f* fly ash
Flugaschenabscheider *m* fly-ash precipitator (collector)
Flugaschenabscheidung *f* fly-ash precipitation (collection)
Flugbahn *f (nucl)* path
Flugbenzin *n* aviation gasoline (spirit)
Flügel *m* blade, shovel, vane, paddle *(as of an agitator)*
Flügelmischer *m s.* Flügelrührer
Flügelpigment *n* wing pigment *(as of butterflies)*
Flügelpumpe *f* vane pump
Flügelradanemometer *n* vane anemometer
Flügelradlüfter *m* propeller fan
Flügelradzähler *m* rotating (current, velocity) meter *(flow measurement)*
Flügelrührer *m* blade (paddle) agitator (mixer)
Flügelzellenpumpe *f* vane pump
Flugkraftstoff *m* aviation fuel
Flugmotorenbenzin *n* aviation gasoline (spirit)
Flugmotorenöl *n* aviation oil
Flugstaub *m* entrained dust *(in fluidized-bed processes)*
Flugstaubverfahren *n* entrained catalyst system *(a variety of the Fischer-Tropsch hydrocarbon synthesis)*
Flugstaubverlust *m* stack loss
Flugstaubwolke *f* entrained dust cloud *(in entrained-bed processes)*
Flugstaubwolkenreaktor *m s.* Flugstromreaktor
Flugstromreaktor *m* transport (entrained-bed) reactor
Flugstromverfahren *n* entrained-bed process, fully entrained process *(as for gasifying coal)*
Flugstromvergaser *m (coal)* entrained-bed gasifier, suspension (fully entrained) gasifier
Flugstromvergasung *f (coal)* entrained-bed gasification, suspension (dilute-phase) gasification, entrainment (pulverized-coal) gasification
Flugwolke *f s.* Flugstaubwolke
Flugwolkeverfahren *n s.* Flugstromverfahren
Flugzeit-Massenspektrometer *n* TOF (time-of-flight) mass spectrometer
Flugzeitspektrometer *n* TOF (time-of-flight) spectrometer
Flugzeugausbringung *f* aeroplane application *(as of pesticides)*
Flugzeug-Düngerstreuen *n* aeroplane fertilization
fluid fluid
Fluid *n* fluid
~/ideales ideal fluid, perfect (non-viscous) fluid
~/Pascalsches *s.* ~/ideales
~/reales actual fluid
~/reibungsfreies *s.* ~/ideales
~/strömendes flowing fluid
Fluidbewegung *f* fluid motion (movement, travel)
Fluid-coking-Verfahren *n (petrol)* fluid coking [process]
Fluiddichte *f* fluid density
Fluidextrakt *m (pharm)* fluid (liquid) extract
Fluid-Feststoff-Reaktion *f* fluid-solid [heterogeneous] reaction
~/katalytische fluid-solid catalytic reaction
~/nichtkatalytische fluid-solid non-catalytic reaction
Fluid-Feststoff-Reaktor *m* fluid-solid reactor
Fluid-Hydroformen *n (petrol)* fluid hydroforming
Fluidisation *f* fluidization
fluidisieren to fluidize
Fluidisieren *n* **zur Flugstaubwolke mit pneumatischer Förderung** disperse-phase fluidization with pneumatic transport
Fluidität *f (phys ch)* fluidity *(reciprocal of viscosity)*
Fluidkoks *m (petrol)* fluid coke
Fluidkrackverfahren *n (petrol)* fluid catalytic [cracking] process
Fluid-Mosaic-Membranmodell *n (bioch)* fluid mosaic model
Fluidsystem *n* fluid[ized] system
Fluidtechnik *f* fluid-bed technique, fluidization (fluidized-bed, boiling-bed) technique
Fluidverfahren *n* fluid-bed process, fluid[ized] process
Fluo... *(for chemical compounds) s.* Fluoro...
Fluor *n* F fluorine
Fluoralkan *n* fluoroalkane, fluorinated alkane, aliphatic fluorocarbon
Fluoralken *n* *fluoroalkene, fluoro-olefin
Fluoralkenylierung *f* fluoroalkenylation
Fluoralkylierung *f* fluoroalkylation
Fluoraminierung *f* fluoroamination

Fluoranthen *n (org ch)* fluoranthene
Fluorbenzen *n*, **Fluorbenzol** *n* fluorobenzene
Fluorcarbonfaser *f* fluorocarbon fibre
Fluorcarbonfaserstoff *m* fluorocarbon fibre
Fluorcarbonkautschuk *m* fluorocarbon rubber
Fluorcarbonkunststoff *m* fluoroplastic
Fluorchlorkohlenwasserstoff *m* chlorofluorocarbon, CFC, freon
Fluor-2,4-dinitrobenzen *n* fluoro-2,4-dinitrobenzene, DNFB
Fluorelastomer[e] *n* fluorocarbon elastomer, fluoroelastomer
Fluoren *n* fluorene, 2,3-benzindene, diphenylenmethane
Fluorescein *n* fluoresc[e]in
Fluoresceinnatrium *n* sodium fluorescein uranine
Fluoressigsäure *f* fluoroacetic acid
Fluoreszenz *f* fluorescence
~/langsame slow (delayed) fluorescence
~/laserinduzierte laser-induced fluorescence, LIF
~/sensibilisierte sensitized fluorescence
~/verzögerte delayed fluorescence
Fluoreszenzanalyse *f* fluorescence analysis
Fluoreszenzausbeute *f* fluorescence quantum yield
Fluoreszenzbande *f* fluorescence band
Fluoreszenzdetektor *m* fluorescence detector
Fluoreszenzfarbe *f* fluorescent paint
Fluoreszenzfarbstoff *m* fluorescent dye
Fluoreszenzindikator *m* fluorescent indicator
Fluoreszenzindikatoranalyse *f* fluorescence indicator analysis, FIA
Fluoreszenzlicht *n* fluorescent light
Fluoreszenzlöschung *f* fluorescence quenching
Fluoreszenzmessung *f s.* Fluorometrie
Fluoreszenzmikroskopie *f* fluorescence microscopy
Fluoreszenzpolarisation *f* fluorescence polarization
Fluoreszenzschirm *m* fluorescent screen
Fluoreszenzspektrometer *n* fluorescence spectrometer
Fluoreszenzspektroskopie *f* fluorescence spectroscopy
Fluoreszenzspektrum *n* fluorescence spectrum
Fluoreszenzstoff *m* fluorescent agent (substance)
Fluoreszenzstrahlung *f* fluorescence radiation
fluoreszieren to fluoresce
fluoreszierend fluorescent
fluorhaltig fluorine-containing
Fluorid *n* $M^{I}F$ fluoride
Fluoridglas *n* fluoride glass
fluoridieren to fluoridize, to fluoridate *(drinking water)*
Fluoridierung *f* fluoridation *(of drinking water)*
fluorieren to fluorinate
Fluorierung *f* fluorination
Fluorierungsmittel *n* fluorinating agent
Fluorimetrie *f s.* Fluorometrie
fluorisieren *s.* fluoridieren
Fluorit *m (min)* fluorite, fluor-spar *(calcium fluoride)*
Fluoritstruktur *f (cryst)* fluorite structure
Fluorkautschuk *m* fluorinated (fluorine) rubber
Fluorkohlenwasserstoff *m* fluorocarbon
Fluorkronglas *n* fluor crown glass, fluorcrown
Fluoroaluminat *n* fluoroaluminate
Fluoroantimonat *n* fluoroantimonate
Fluoroarsenat *n* fluoroarsenate
Fluoroberyllat *n* fluoroberyllate
Fluoroborat *n* fluoroborate, tetrafluoroborate
Fluoroborsäure *f* fluoroboric acid, tetrafluoroboric acid
Fluoroferrat *n* fluoroferrate
Fluoroform *n* fluoroform, trifluoromethane
Fluorohafnat *n* fluorohafnate
Fluoroiodat *n* fluoroiodate
Fluorokieselsäure *f* fluorosilicic acid, hexafluorosilicic acid, sand acid
Fluorolefin *n* *fluoroalkene, fluoro-olefin
Fluorometer *n* fluorometer, fluorimeter, fluophotometer *(for measuring fluorescence)*
Fluorometrie *f* fluorometry, fluorimetry
fluorometrisch fluorometric, fluorimetric
Fluoronium-Ion *n* fluoronium ion
Fluoroniumverbindung *f* fluoronium compound
Fluorophor *m* fluorophore, fluorogen *(a radical which causes fluorescence)*
Fluorophosphat *n* fluorophosphate
Fluorophotometer *n s.* Fluorometer
Fluoroschwefelsäure *f* fluorosulphuric acid
Fluorosilicat *n* fluorosilicate
Fluorostannat *n* fluorostannate
Fluorotantalat *n* fluorotantalate
Fluorowolframat *n* *fluorowolframate, fluorotungstate
Fluoroxid *n s.* Sauerstoffdifluorid
Fluorsiliconkautschuk *m* fluorosilicone rubber
Fluorsulfonsäure *f s.* Fluoroschwefelsäure
Fluorüberträger *m* fluorinating agent
Fluorwasserstoff *m* hydrogen fluoride
Fluorwasserstoffalkylierung *f* hydrofluoric-acid alkylation, HF alkylation
Fluorwasserstofflaser *m* hydrogen fluoride laser, HF laser
fluorwasserstoffsauer hydrofluoric
Fluorwasserstoffsäure *f* hydrofluoric acid
Fluorwasserstoff[säure]verfahren *n (petrol)* hydrofluoric-acid process, HF process
FluoSolids-Verfahren FluoSolids process *(of roasting sulphides)*
Flur *m (ceram)* corridor *(of a dryer)*
flushen *(coat)* to flush
Flushkneter *m (coat)* flusher *(kneading machine for preparing pigment paste)*
Flushpaste *f (coat)* flushed colour
Flushverfahren *n (coat)* flushing process
Fluß *m* 1. flow, flux; 2. *s.* Flußmittel
~/gestoppter stopped flow *(for measuring reaction velocities)*
~/kalter *(plast)* cold flow

Flüssebilanz *f***/vertikale** net vertical flux
Flußgeschwindigkeit *f***/nominelle lineare** *(chromat)* nominal linear flow
flüssig liquid, fluid • **~ werden** to liquefy, to melt, to fuse, to flux
Flüssig-Adsorptionschromatographie *f* liquid-solid chromatography
Flüssigchromatographie *f s.* Flüssigkeitschromatographie
Flüssigdünger *m* liquid fertilizer
Flüssigextraktion *f s.* Flüssig-flüssig-Extraktion
Flüssig-fest-Chromatogramm *n* liquid-solid chromatogram
Flüssig-fest-Chromatographie *f* liquid-solid chromatography, LSC
Flüssig-fest-Grenzfläche *f* liquid-solid interface
Flüssig-fest-Reaktion *f* liquid-solid[-phase heterogeneous] reaction
Flüssigfilmtheorie *f* two-film theory *(gas absorption)*
Flüssig-flüssig-Chromatographie *f* liquid-liquid chromatography, LLC
Flüssig-flüssig-Extraktion *f* liquid[-liquid] extraction, solvent extraction
Flüssig-flüssig-Verteilung *f* liquid-liquid partition
Flüssig-flüssig-Verteilungschromatographie *f* liquid-liquid partition chromatography
Flüssiggas *n* liquefied [petroleum] gas, L.P. gas, L.P.G., liquid gas *(liquefied hydrocarbons)*
Flüssig-Gas-Chromatographie *f* liquid-gas chromatography, LGC
Flüssig-Gel-Chromatographie *f* liquid-gel chromatography
Flüssigkeit *f* 1. liquid *(as opposed to solid or gas)*; *(tech, food, biol)* liquor; 2. liquidity, fluidity *(state)*
~/anisotrope anisotropic (crystalline) liquid
~/assoziierte associated liquid
~/Bendasche *(biol)* Benda solution *(a mixture of osmic, chromic, and glacial acetic acid)*
~/dekantierte decantate
~/Diverssche Divers' liquid *(concentrated solution of NH_4NO_3 in liquid ammonia)*
~/geförderte liquid being pumped
~/geklärte clarified liquid (liquor)
~/kristalline (mesomorphe) *s.* ~/anisotrope
~/mitgerissene entrained liquid (liquor)
~/Muthmannsche Muthmann's liquid *(1,1,2,2-tetrabromoethane)*
~/Newtonsche Newtonian fluid
~/nicht-Newtonsche non-Newtonian fluid
~/normale normal (non-polar, non-associated) liquid
~/polare polar liquid
~/pseudoplastische pseudoplastic fluid
~/rheoinstabile *s.* ~/zeitabhängige [nicht-Newtonsche]
~/rheopexe rheopectic fluid
~/rheostabile *s.* ~/zeitunabhängige [nicht-Newtonsche]
~/schwere *(min tech)* dense (heavy) medium
~/strukturviskose pseudoplastic fluid
~/thixotrope thixotropic fluid
~/überstehende supernatant liquid (liquor)
~/versprühte spray liquid
~/Wackenrodersche Wackenroder's solution *(a mixture of polythionic acids)*
~/zeitabhängige [nicht-Newtonsche] time-dependent [non-newtonian] fluid
~/zeitunabhängige [nicht-Newtonsche] time-independent [non-newtonian] fluid
~/zu versprühende spray liquid
Flüssigkeit-Dampf-Gemisch *n* vapour-liquid mixture
Flüssigkeit-Dampf-Grenzfläche *f* liquid-vapour interface
Flüssigkeit-Flüssigkeit-Grenzfläche *f* liquid-liquid interface, liquid junction, dineric interface
Flüssigkeitsabgabe *f* release of liquid, *(of gels also)* weeping
Flüssigkeitsabscheider *m* coalescer *(for collecting liquid droplets)*
Flüssigkeitsaufnahme *f* uptake of liquid, imbibition, *(text also)* pick-up
Flüssigkeitsbadvulkanisation *f* liquid curing
Flüssigkeitsbarren *m* bar of solvent *(in zone melting)*
Flüssigkeitsbereich *m* liquid range
Flüssigkeitsbewegung *f* liquid motion (movement, travel)
Flüssigkeitscharakter *m (phys ch)* fluidity *(reciprocal of viscosity)*
Flüssigkeitschromatograph *m* liquid chromatograph
Flüssigkeitschromatographie *f* liquid chromatography, LC
~/schnelle high-pressure liquid chromatography, HPLC
~/überkritische supercritical fluid chromatography
flüssigkeitschromatographisch by liquid chromatography
Flüssigkeitsdichte *f* fluid density
Flüssigkeitsdiffusionspotential *n* liquid-junction potential, diffusion potential
Flüssigkeitsdruckdüse *f* pressure nozzle
Flüssigkeitsdurchsatz *m* liquid throughput
Flüssigkeitseinlaß *m***/direkter** *(chromat)* direct liquid introduction, DLI
Flüssigkeitseinsatz *m* batch of liquid
Flüssigkeitsfassungsvermögen *n* liquid holding volume
Flüssigkeitsfilm *m* liquid film
Flüssigkeitsfiltration *f* liquid filtration
flüssigkeitsfrei liquid-free
Flüssigkeitsgemisch *n* liquid mixture
Flüssigkeits-Glasthermometer *n* liquid-in-glass thermometer
Flüssigkeitsinhalt *m (distil)* liquid hold-up
Flüssigkeitskalorimeter *n* water calorimeter

Flüssigkeitskatode *f* pool cathode
Flüssigkeitskomponente *f*/**leichtere** light phase *(centrifuging)*
Flüssigkeitskörper *m* fluid (liquid) body
Flüssigkeitslaser *m (anal)* liquid laser
Flüssigkeitsmasse *f* fluid (liquid) body
Flüssigkeitsmischer *m* liquid mixer
~/kontinuierlicher flow (line) mixer
Flüssigkeitsniveau *n* liquid level
Flüssigkeitsphase *f* liquid phase
Flüssigkeitspotential *n* diffusion (liquid, junction) potential
Flüssigkeitsreibung *f* viscous force, internal friction
Flüssigkeitsringgebläse *n* liquid-piston rotary blower
Flüssigkeitsringverdichter *m* liquid-piston rotary compressor
Flüssigkeitssäule *f* column of liquid
Flüssigkeitsschicht *f* liquid layer
Flüssigkeitsspiegel *m* liquid (surface) level
Flüssigkeitsstand *m* liquid level
Flüssigkeitsstand[s]anzeiger *m* liquid-level meter; gauge glass
Flüssigkeitsstand[s]messung *f* liquid-level measurement
Flüssigkeitsstrahl *m* jet of liquid
Flüssigkeitsstrom *m* liquid flow; *(tech)* liquor flow
Flüssigkeitsströmung *f* liquid flow; *(tech)* liquor flow
Flüssigkeitsthermometer *n* liquid expansion thermometer
Flüssigkeitsüberstand *m* supernatant liquid (liquor)
Flüssigkeitsverlust *m* loss of liquid
Flüssigkeitsverschluß *m* liquid seal *(as for stirrers)*
Flüssigkeitsversprüher *m* liquid atomizer
Flüssigkeitsversprühung *f* liquid atomization
Flüssigkeitsverteiler *m* liquid distributor
Flüssigkeitsvolumen *n* liquid body
Flüssigkeitsvorlage *f (lab)* [liquid-]receiver
Flüssigkeitszerstäuber *m s.* Flüssigkeitsversprüher
Flüssigkeitszylinder *m* stream tube *(rheology)*
Flüssigköder *m* wet bait *(pest control)*
Flüssigkristall *m* liquid crystal, mesophase
~/cholester[in]ischer cholesteric liquid crystal
~/lyotroper lyotropic liquid crystal
~/nematischer nematic liquid crystal
~/smektischer smectic liquid crystal
~/thermotroper thermotropic liquid crystal
Flüssigkultur *f (biot)* liquid culture
Flüssiglinie *f (distil)* liquidus curve (line)
Flüssigluftsprengstoff *m* oxyliquit
Flüssigmetallbrennstoff *m (nucl)* liquid-metal reactor fuel
Flüssigphase *f* liquid phase
Flüssigphaseisomerisierung *f* liquid-phase isomerization
Flüssigphasekatalysator *m* liquid-phase catalyst
Flüssigphasekracken *n* liquid-phase cracking
Flüssigphaseoxidation *f* liquid-phase oxidation
Flüssigphasepolymerisation *f* liquid-phase polymerization
Flüssigphasereaktion *f* liquid-phase reaction, liquid-liquid reaction
Flüssigphaseverfahren *n* liquid-phase process
Flüssigsauerstoff *m* liquid oxygen
Flüssigstäuber *m* liquiduster *(an apparatus for the joint spraying of pesticides in liquid and powder form)*
Flüssigstickstoff *m* liquid nitrogen
Flüssigstickstoffwäsche *f* nitrogen wash process *(for scrubbing synthesis gas)*
Flüssigszintillation *f* liquid scintillation
Flüssigszintillationszählung *f (bioch)* liquid scintillation counting
Flüssigtreibstoff *m* liquid fuel *(propellant)*
Flüssig-Verteilungschromatographie *f* liquid-liquid [partition] chromatography, liquid partition chromatography
Flüssigwerden *n* liquefaction, melting, fusing, fluxing
Flüssigzucker *m* liquid sugar
Flußkies *m* river gravel
Flußmesser *m* flow (rate) meter, fluid meter
Flußmittel *n* flux[ing agent], *(lab also)* fusion reagent; soldering flux; brazing flux
flußmittelfrei flux-free
Flußsäure *f* hydrofluoric acid
Flußsäurealkylierung *f* hydrofluoric-acid alkylation, HF alkylation
Flußsäureverfahren *n (petrol)* hydrofluoric-acid process, HF process
Flußspat *m (min)* fluor-spar, fluorite *(calcium fluoride)*
Flußstahl *m* ingot iron (steel)
Flußtechnik *f* flow technique *(for measuring reaction velocities)*
Flußverschmutzung *f*, **Flußverunreinigung** *f* river (stream) pollution
Flußwasser *n* river (stream) water
Flußwasserentnahme *f (hyd)* stream withdrawal
Flußwasserentnahmebauwerk *n (hyd)* river-water intake, intake for stream withdrawal
Flußwassergüte *f (hyd)* stream-water quality, quality of river water
fluten 1. *(distil)* to flood *(e.g. a packed column)*; 2. *(petrol)* to flood *(oil sand)*
Fluten *n* 1. *(distil)* flooding *(as of a packed column)*; 2. *(petrol)* [water] flooding *(of oil sand)*; 3. *(coat)* flow coating
Flutkammer *f (coat)* flow-coating chamber
Flutlackieren *n* flow coating
Flutpunkt *m (distil)* flooding point
Fluttunnel *m (coat)* flow-coating chamber
Flutung *f (distil)* flooding
Flutzone *f (coat)* flow-coating section

fluxen *(met, petrol)* to flux, *(petrol also)* to cut back
Fluxöl *n (petrol)* flux [oil]
fl. z. *s.* flächenzentriert
3-F-Mechanismus *m s.* Feld-Fluß-Fraktionierung
F-1-Methode *f* F 1 (research) method *(for octane rating)*
F-2-Methode *f* F 2 (motor) method *(for octane rating)*
FMN *s.* Flavinmononucleotid
FM-Zyklotron *n* frequency-modulated cyclotron, synchrocyclotron
Foid *m (min)* feldspathoid
fokussieren to focus
Fokussiersystem *n* focussing system *(of a mass spectrometer)*
Fokussierung *f*/**isoelektrische** *(anal)* isoelectric focussing, electrofocussing
Folat *n* folate, pteroylglutamate *(salt or ester of folic acid)*
Folgereaktion *f* consecutive reaction, subsequent (successive, stepwise) reaction
Folgestrang *m (bioch)* following strand *(of DNA)*
Folie *f (plast)* film, *(if thickness > 0.01 inch:)* sheeting *(as a web)*, sheet *(as a piece)*, *(esp relating to metal:)* foil
~/biaxial gereckte (verstreckte) biaxially oriented film
~/extrudierte extruded film *or* sheet
~/gegossene cast film *or* sheet
~/gepreßte pressed sheet
~/geschälte sliced film *or* sheet
~/geschäumte expanded sheet
~/gespritzte *s.* ~/extrudierte
~/kalandrierte calendered film *or* sheet
~/stranggepreßte *s.* ~/extrudierte
Foliefaser *f* split fibre
Folienblaskopf *m (plast)* blow head
Folienblasmaschine *f (plast)* film blowing machine
Foliendämmung *f* multiple-layer insulation *(cryogenics)*
Folienformung *f (plast)* film formation (forming), *(relating to products with thickness > 0.01 inch:)* sheet formation (forming)
Foliengießmaschine *f (plast)* casting machine for film formation, solution-casting machine
Folienisolierung *f s.* Foliendämmung
Folienpapier *n* foil paper
Folienschneidmaschine *f (plast)* slicing machine
Folienstrangpressen *n (plast)* film extrusion, *(relating to products with thickness > 0.01 inch:)* sheet extrusion
Folin-Ciocaltean-Reagens *n (bioch)* Folin-Ciocaltean reagent *(molybdophosphate-tungstophosphate mixture)*
Folin-Denis-Reagens *n (food)* Folin-Denis reagent *(for detecting phenol)*
Folinsäure *f* folinic acid, N^5-formyltetrahydrofolic acid, leucovorin, citrovorum factor
Folliberin *n* follicle-stimulating hormone releasing hormone, FSH-RH
Follikelhormon *n* follicular (oestrus-producing) hormone, oestrogen
Follikelreifungshormon *n*, **Follikelstimulierungshormon** *n* follicle-stimulating hormone, FSH
Folsäure *f* folic acid, pteroylglutamic acid, PGA
Fond *m (nucl)* background
Fondcreme *f (cosmet)* foundation cream, make-up base
Förderanlage *f* conveyor
Förderband *n* 1. conveyor (conveying) belt, apron; 2. *s.* Gurtbandförderer
Förderbandtrockner *m* conveyor dryer, belt [tunnel] dryer, moving-band dryer
Förderbandwaage *f* weighing belt
Förderbehälter *m (petrol)* lift tank
Förderbohrung *f (petrol)* development (exploitation) well
Förderbraunkohle *f* raw lignite
Förderdruck *m* discharge (delivery) pressure
Fördereigenschaften *fpl* conveying characteristics
Fördereinrichtung *f* conveyor; *(for vertical transportation:)* lift
Förderer *m* conveyor
~/pneumatischer air conveyor
Fördererz *n* run-of-mine ore, raw (as-mined) ore
Förderflüssigkeit *f* liquid being *or* to be pumped
Fördergefäß *n* skip [car]
Fördergerät *n* conveyor
Fördergeschwindigkeit *f* delivery rate *(as of a pump)*
Fördergurt *m* conveyor (conveying) belt
Fördergut *n* material being *or* to be conveyed
Förderhöhe *f* discharge (delivery) head *(as of a pump)*
Förderhub *m* discharge (delivery) stroke *(as of a pump)*
Förderkohle *f* run-of-mine coal, raw coal
Förderkübel *m* skip [car]
Förderlänge *f* conveyor length
Förderleistung *f* delivery [volume], discharge, *(of pumps also)* displacement
Förderleitung *f* delivery line
Förderluft *f* conveying air, *(directed upwards also)* lift air
Fördermedium *n* carrier vehicle *(hydraulic transportation)*
Fördermenge *f s.* Förderleistung
fördern 1. to mine, to extract, to win *(e.g. coal)*; 2. to convey *(bulk material)*; to deliver, to discharge *(of pumps, compressors)*; 3. to promote *(e.g. a reaction)*; to stimulate *(e.g. growth)*
Förderrohr *n* delivery pipe
Förderrutsche *f* oscillating conveyor
Förderschnecke *f* 1. conveying (conveyor) screw (worm); 2. *s.* Schneckenförderer
Förderseil *n* hoisting rope
Förderseite *f* delivery side *(as of a pump)*

Förderstrecke *f* conveyed length, length of travel
Förderstrom *m* rate of delivery (discharge, flow), delivery
Förderung *f* 1. mining, extracting, winning *(as of coal)*; 2. conveying *(of bulk material)*; delivery, discharge *(of pumps, compressors)*; 3. promotion *(as of reaction)*; stimulation *(as of growth)*
~ **im Tagebau** surface (open-cut, open-cast) mining, open pit method, *(esp relating to ores:)* [surface] quarrying
~ **im Tiefbau (Untertagebau)** deep mining, underground mining (working)
~ **mittels Airlifts** air lifting, air-lift transport
~ **mittels Druckgases** gas lifting
~ **mittels Druckluft** *s.* ~ mittels Airlifts
~ **mittels Gaslifts** gas lifting
~**/pneumatische** air conveying
~**/übermäßige** over-stimulation *(as of growth)*
Fördervolumen *n s.* Förderleistung
Fördervorrichtung *f* conveyor; *(for vertical transportation:)* lift
Förderwagen *m* trolley
Förderwasser *n* carriage (transport) water, water carrier vehicle *(for suspended particles)*
Förderweg *m* conveyed length, length of travel
Form *f* 1. form, shape; *(isomerism:)* form; 2. *(tech)* mould • **in gebundener** ~ in combined form
~**/blanke** *(glass)* uncoated mould
~**/chinoide** quino[no]id form
~**/einteilige** *(glass)* block mould
~**/enantiomorphe** enantiomorph, enantiomer, enantiomorphous form (isomer), optical antipode (isomer), antimer
~**/flexible** boat form (conformation) *(stereochemistry)*
~**/furanoide** furanose form *(of sugars)*
~**/gestaffelte** staggered form (conformation) *(stereochemistry)*
~**/gestreckte** extended (open-chain) form (conformation) *(stereochemistry)*
~**/geteilte** *(glass)* split mould
~**/getrocknete** dry-sand mould *(foundry)*
~**/grüne** green-sand mould *(foundry)*
~**/hohe** tall form *(of laboratory vessels)*
~**/intermediäre** intermediate form *(1. of stereoisomers; 2. of products)*
~**/linksdrehende** laevo[rotatory] form, (–) form *(of an optically active compound)*
~**/mehrteilige** *(glass)* split mould
~**/metallische** [permanent] metal mould *(foundry)*
~ **mit Heizkanälen** *(plast)* cored mould
~**/nasse** green-sand mould *(foundry)*
~**/niedrige** low form *(of laboratory vessels)*
~**/polymorphe** polymorphic form, polymorph
~**/pyranoide** pyranose form *(of sugars)*
~**/rechtsdrehende** dextro[rotatory] form, (+) form *(of an optically active compound)*
~**/replikative** *(bioch)* replicative form
~**/schiefe** gauche (skew) form (conformation) *(stereochemistry)*
~**/starre** chair form (conformation) *(stereochemistry)*
~**/synclinale** *s.* ~/schiefe
~**/tautomere** tautomeric form, dynamic isomer
~**/trockene** dry-sand mould *(foundry)*
~**/ungetrocknete** green-sand mould *(foundry)*
~**/verdeckte** eclipsed form (conformation) *(stereochemistry)*
~**/windschiefe** *s.* ~/schiefe
~**/zweiteilige** *(glass)* split mould
aci-**Form** *f* aci form *(of a nitro compound)*
d-**Form** *f*, **(+)-Form** *f s.* Form/rechtsdrehende
l-**Form** *f*, **(–)-Form** *f s.* Form/linksdrehende
Formal *n* formal, formaldehyde acetal *(any acetal derived from formaldehyde and an alcohol)*
Formaldehyd *m* formaldehyde, *methanal
Formaldehydacetal *n s.* Formal
Formaldehyddiethylacetal *n* formaldehyde diethyl acetal, *diethoxymethane
Formaldehyddimethylacetal *n* formaldehyde dimethyl acetal, methylal, *dimethoxymethane
Formaldehydgerbung *f* formaldehyde tanning
Formaldehydnatriumsulfoxylat *n* sodium formaldehydesulphoxylate, SFS, sodium sulphoxylate formaldehyde
Formaldehydoxim *n s.* Formaldoxim
Formaldehydsulfoxylat *n* formaldehydesulphoxylate
Formaldehydsulfoxylsäure *f* formaldehydesulphoxylic acid
Formaldoxim *n* formaldoxime, formaldehyde oxime
Formalladung *f (phys ch)* formal charge
Formalpotential *n (phys ch)* formal potential
Formamid *n (org ch)* formamide
Formamidin *n (org ch)* formamidine
Formänderung *f* deformation, strain
Formänderungsrest *m* residual (permanent) deformation (set)
~ **bei Dehnungsbeanspruchung** residual (permanent) deformation at elongation
~ **bei Druckbeanspruchung** [permanent] compression set
Formänderungs-Spannungs-Linie *f s.* Beanspruchungs-Dehnungs-Linie
Formanilid *n* formanilide, formylaniline
Formart *f* state of aggregation (matter)
Formartikel *m* moulded article (part, product), moulding
Format *n* size
Formation *f (geol)* formation
~**/ölführende** producing formation
Formatpapier *n* sheeted (sheet, ream) paper, paper in sheets
Formatwalze *f (pap)* press roll *(of a cylinder board machine)*
Formatzylinder *m s.* Formatwalze
Formazan *n (org ch)* formazan
formbar formable, shap[e]able, ductile; mouldable
Formbarkeit *f* formability, shap[e]ability, ductility; mouldability

Formbeständigkeit *f (plast, text)* dimensional stability
~ **in der Wärme** *(plast)* heat deflection (distortion) point (temperature)
~ **in der Wärme nach Vicat** *(plast)* Vicat softening point (temperature), V.S.P., Vicat needle point
Formboden *m (glass)* bottom plate
Formdichtung *f* moulded seal
Formeinstreichmittel *n s.* Formentrennmittel
Formel *f* formula
~/allgemeine general formula
~/angenäherte approximate formula
~/Balmersche Balmer formula
~/einfachste (empirische) *s.* ~/stöchiometrische
~/geradkettige straight-chain formula
~/perspektivische perspective formula
~/Ritzsche Ritz formula
~/stöchiometrische stoichiometric (empirical) formula, simplest [possible] formula
~/wahre true formula
Formelbild *n* graphic formula
Formeleinheit *f* formula unit
Formelgewicht *n*, **Formelmasse** *f* formula weight
Formelregister *n* formula index
Formelsprache *f* chemical shorthand
Formelumsatz *m* formula conversion
formen to form, to shape; to mould
~/zu Krümeln *(rubber)* to pelletize
~/zu Kügelchen (Pellets) to pellet[ize], to pill
Formen *n* **in Grünsand** green-sand moulding *(foundry)*
~ **in Lehm** loam moulding *(foundry)*
~ **in Trocken[guß]sand** dry[-sand] moulding *(foundry)*
~ **mit Ausschmelzmodellen** investment moulding *(foundry)*
~ **mit Wachs[ausschmelz]modellen** lost-wax moulding *(foundry)*
~/nachträgliches *(plast)* postforming
Formenbau *m* mould making
formpressen *(plast)* to mould
Formenbrecher *m (rubber)* mould breaker (cracker), mould-breaking (mould-clearing) jack
Formeneinstreichmittel *n s.* Formentrennmittel
Formeneis *n* can ice
Formengips *m* moulding plaster
Formennaht *f* parting (joint) line, match (mould) mark (seam) *(a defect in glass)*
Formenöffner *m s.* Formenbrecher
Formenrahmen *m (rubber)* dipping rack
Formenschluß *m* mould closing
Formenschmiere *f*, **Formenschmiermittel** *n* *(glass)* mould lubricant, dope
Formenschwindmaß *n* mould shrinkage
Formentrennmittel *n* [mould-]release agent, mould release (lubricant)
Formentrennung *f* mould release
Formfaktor *m (nucl)* form factor; *(rubber)* shape factor
Formgebung *f* forming, shaping, profiling
Formgebungsmaschine *f (ceram)* shaping machine; glass-forming machine
Formgrat *m (plast)* fin
Formgußstück *n* casting
Formheizung *f (rubber)* mould cure (curing, vulcanization)
Formherstellung *f* mould making
Formhöhlung *f (plast)* mould cavity
Formhydroxamsäure *f*, **Formhydroximsäure** *f* formhydroxamic acid, formhydroximic acid
Formiat *n* $HCOOM^{I}$ *formate, formiate
Formimidierung *f* formimidation
N-**Formiminoglutamat** *n (bioch)* *N*-formiminoglutamate
N-**Formiminoglutaminsäure** *f (bioch)* *N*-formiminoglutamic acid
Formkammer *f* moulding chamber
Formkanal *m* briquetting channel *(of a briquetting press)*
Formkoks *m* formed (shaped) coke
Formkoksverfahren *n* formed-coke process *(for carbonizing low-rank coals)*
Formkörper *m***/grüner** shaped green body
Formling *m***/grüner** shaped green body
Formmaschine *f* moulding machine, moulder
Formmaske *f* shell mould *(foundry)*
Formmaskenverfahren *n* **[nach Croning]** shell-moulding process, Croning process, C process *(foundry)*
Formmasse *f (plast)* moulding material (compound)
~/hitzehärtbare *s.* ~/wärmehärtbare
~/kittartige dough moulding material
~ **mit Faserstoffüllung (Faserstoffverstärkung)** fibre-filled moulding material
~/wärmehärtbare thermosetting moulding material
Formnest *n (plast)* mould cavity
Formöffnung *f* mould (tuyère) opening *(foundry)*
Formolyse *f* formolysis
Formonitriloxid *n* formonitrile oxide, fulminic acid
Formose *f* formose *(a mixture of aldoses and ketoses)*
Formplatte *f (plast)* platen; pattern plate *(foundry)*
~/bewegliche *(plast)* movable (moving) platen
~/feststehende *(plast)* stationary platen
Formpresse *f (plast)* moulding (compression) press
Formpressen *n (plast)* [compression] moulding
~ **mit Hochfrequenzheizung (Hochfrequenzvorwärmung)** high-frequency (radio-frequency) moulding
Formpreßstoff *m (plast)* compression-moulding material
Formsand *m* moulding sand
~/grüner green [moulding] sand
~/gut gasdurchlässiger open (free-venting) sand
~/nasser *s.* ~/grüner
~/natürlicher natural [moulding] sand, naturally bonded sand
~/synthetischer synthetic [moulding] sand
~/wenig gasdurchlässiger poor-venting sand

Formschließeinheit *f (plast)* mould clamp
Formschließkraft *f (plast)* mould-clamping force
Formschließzeit *f (plast)* mould-closing time
Formstanze *f (plast)* punch press
Formstanzen *n (plast)* pressure forming
Formstoff *m* moulded material
Formstück *n* fitting *(for pipes and hoses)*
Formtechnik *f* moulding technique
Formteil *n* moulding, blank, shape
~/gegossenes cast moulding
~/nachgeformtes postformed moulding
~/nichtausgeformtes (unvollständiges) short moulding
Formteile *npl* moulded articles (goods, parts, products)
~/spritzgegossene injection-moulded articles
Formtrennmittel *n s.* Formentrennmittel
formulieren to formulate
Formulierung *f* formulation *(1. expressing with a formula; 2. compounding in accordance with a recipe)*
Formungsdruck *m (plast)* forming pressure
Formungstemperatur *f (plast)* forming temperature
Formunterteil *n (plast)* force
Formveränderung *f* deformation, strain
Formvulkanisation *f* press (mould) cure
Formwiderstand *m* form drag *(fluid mechanics)*
Formylaceton *n* formylacetone, acetoacetaldehyde
Formylbenzen *n*, **Formylbenzol** *n s.* Benzaldehyd
Formylessigsäure *f* formylacetic acid
Formylgruppe *f* –C(=O)H formyl group (residue)
Formylhydroperoxid *n* formyl hydroperoxide, performic acid
formylieren to formylate
Formylierung *f* formylation
Formylierungsreagens *n* formylating reagent
Formylradikal *n* [free] formyl radical
Formylrest *m s.* Formylgruppe
Formyltribromid *n s.* Bromoform
Formyltrichlorid *n s.* Chloroform
Formyltriiodid *n s.* Iodoform
Formzeit *f (plast)* moulding time
Forschungschemiker *m* research chemist
Forschungslabor[atorium] *n* research laboratory
Forschungsreaktor *m* research (discovery) reactor
Forsterit *m (min)* forsterite *(magnesium orthosilicate)*
Forsteriterzeugnis *n***/feuerfestes** forsterite refractory
Forsteritporzellan *n* forsterite porcelain
Forsteritstein *m***/feuerfester** forsterite refractory brick
Forsteritweißware *f* forsterite whiteware
fortpflanzen to propagate *(e.g. a reaction chain)*
~/sich to propagate *(as of a reaction)*
Fortpflanzung *f* propagation
Fortpflanzungsgeschwindigkeit *f* propagation velocity
Fortpflanzungsreaktion *f* propagation reaction
Fortpflanzungsrichtung *f* direction of propagation
Fortpflanzungsstadium *n* propagation stage
Fortpflanzungszyklus *m* propagation sequence *(of a chain reaction)*
Fortrat-Diagramm *n (spectr)* Fortrat parabola
Fortreißfestigkeit *f s.* Weiterreißwiderstand
fortschreiten to proceed, to advance, to progress
fortschwemmen to float off
fortspülen to wash away, to rinse (flush) away
fortwandern to migrate out *(as of ions)*
fossil *(geol)* fossil
Fossilbrennstoff *m* fossil fuel
fossilisieren to fossilize
F_0-Teil *n (bioch)* F_0 factor *(of the ATP synthetase)*
Foto... *s. a.* Photo...
Fotochemikalie *f* photographic chemical
Fotoemulsion *f* photographic (sensitive) emulsion
Fotokopie *f* [silver halide] photocopy
Fotokopieren *n* [silver halide] photocopying
Foto[kopier]lack *m* [photo]resist *(photolithography)*
Fotoldruckverfahren *n* fotol (ferrogelatin) process *(reprography)*
Fotomaterial *n* sensitive (sensitized) material
Fotopapier *n* photo[graphic] paper
Fotoplatte *f* photo[graphic] plate
Fotorohpapier *n* photographic base paper
Fotoschale *f* developing dish
Foulard *m (text)* padding machine (mangle), padder, pad
Foulardbehandlung *f (text)* slop-padding
Foulardfärbung *f (text)* pad[ded] dyeing
foulardieren *(text)* to [slop-]pad
Foulardierlösung *f (text)* pad (padding) bath (liquor)
Foulard-Jigger-Verfahren *n (text)* pad-jig process
Fourcault-Verfahren *n (glass)* Fourcault [sheet-drawing] process
Fourier-Spektroskopie *f s.* Fourier [transform] spectroscopy
fourierspektroskopisch by Fourier transform spectroscopy
Fourier-Transformation *f (anal)* Fourier transform[ation], FT
Fourier-Transformations-... *s.* Fourier-Transform-...
Fourier-Transform-IR-Spektrometer *n* Fourier transform infrared spectrometer, FT-IR spectrometer
Fourier-Transform-IR-Spektrometrie *f* Fourier transform infrared spectrometry, FT-IR spectrometry
Fourier-Transform-Massenspektrometrie *f* Fourier transform mass spectrometry, FTMS
Fourier-Transform-NMR-Spektroskopie *f* Fourier transform NMR spectroscopy, FT-NMR spectroscopy, FTNMR
Fourier-Transform-Spektrometer *n* Fourier transform spectrometer

Fourier-Transform-Spektrometrie *f* Fourier transform spectrometry
Fourier-Transform-Spektroskopie *f* Fourier [transform] spectroscopy
FP. *s.* Flammpunkt
FPD *s.* Flammenphotometerdetektor
fragmentieren to fragment *(e.g. molecules)*
Fragmentierung *f* fragmentation *(as of molecules)*
Fragmentierungsmuster *n* fragmentation (cracking) pattern *(the characteristic mass spectrum of a compound)*
Fragment-Ion *n* fragment ion
Fragmentpeak *m (spectr)* fragment peak
Fraktion *f* 1. *(distil)* fraction, cut; 2. size fraction *(in classifying)*
~/hochsiedende (höhersiedende) high-boiling (higher-boiling) fraction, heavy fraction
~/leichte *s.* ~/niedrigsiedende
~/mittlere middle fraction
~/niedrigsiedende low-boiling fraction, light fraction
~/schwere (schwerer flüchtige) *s.* ~/hochsiedende
~/schwer[er]siedende *s.* ~/hochsiedende
~/tiefsiedende *s.* ~/niedrigsiedende
α-Fraktion *f* alpha fraction *(in the pyridine extraction of hard coal)*
β-Fraktion *f* beta fraction *(in the pyridine extraction of hard coal)*
γ-Fraktion *f* gamma fraction *(in the pyridine extraction of hard coal)*
Fraktionator *m s.* Fraktionierkolonne
Fraktionierapparat *m* fractionating apparatus
Fraktionierbürste *f (distil)* wiper
fraktionieren to fractionate, to fraction
Fraktioniergerät *n* fractionating apparatus
Fraktionierkolben *m* fractionating flask
Fraktionierkolonne *f*, **Fraktioniersäule** *f* fractionating column, fractionator
fraktioniert fractional
Fraktionierturm *m* fractionating tower
Fraktionierung *f* fractionation, *(distil also)* fractional distillation
~ von Polymeren polymer fractionation
Fraktionsabscheidegrad *m*, **Fraktionsentstaubungsgrad** *m* fractional[-weight collection] efficiency *(classifying)*
Fraktionskolben *m* fractionating flask
Fraktionssammler *m* fraction collector
Fraktogramm *n* chromatographic spectrum (profile)
Frameshift-Mutation *f (biot)* frameshift mutation
Francium *n* Fr francium
Franck-Condon-Prinzip *n (phys ch)* Franck-Condon principle
Frangulaemodin *n* frangula-emodin, 1,3,8-trihydroxy-6-methylanthraquinone
Franklinit *m (min)* franklinite *(zinc ferrite)*
Fransenmizelle *f* fringed micelle
Frasch-Verfahren *n* Frasch process *(of mining sulphur by superheated water)*
Fraßgift *n* stomach poison
~ für Insekten stomach insecticide
Frauenmilch *f* human (breast) milk
Fraunhofer-Linien *fpl* Fraunhofer lines
frei free; vacant *(orbitals)*
~/praktisch substantially free
~ von Feststoffen solids-free
Freialdehydigkeit *f (food)* rancidity with formation of aldehydes
Freibewitterung *f s.* Freiluftbewitterung
freibrennend free-burning
Freidampfheizung *f*, **Freidampfvulkanisation** *f* open-steam cure (curing)
Freie-Enthalpie-Beziehung *f*/**lineare** linear free energy relation[ship], LFE relationship, linear Gibbs energy relation
Freielektronenlaser *m* free-electron laser, FEL
Freifallklassierer *m* non-mechanical classifier
Freifallmischer *m* tumbling mixer, tumbler
Freifallscheider *m* plate separator *(for electrostatic separation)*
Freiflußventil *n* inclined-seat valve
Freigold *n* free gold
Freihandblasen *n* off-hand glassworking
Freiharz *n (pap)* free rosin (resin)
Freiharzgehalt *m (pap)* content of free rosin
Freiharzleim *m (pap)* free-rosin size, acid size
~/stabilisierter protected rosin size, high free protected size
Freiheit *f (phys ch)* variance, degree of freedom • **in ~ setzen** to liberate, to release • **ohne ~** non-variant, invariant
Freiheitsgrad *m (phys ch)* degree of freedom, variance
Freiheizung *f (rubber)* open cure (vulcanization)
Freilandversuch *m* field experiment (test, trial)
Freiluftbewitterung *f* outdoor weathering, natural exposure
Freiluftbewitterungsversuch *m* outdoor weathering test
Freiluftbrenner *m* air-atomizing burner
Freilufttrocknung *f* air drying, *(ceram also)* hack drying
Freiname *m* non-proprietary name, generic name (term)
Freischwefel *m (rubber)* [true] free sulphur
freisetzen to release, to liberate, to set free
Freisetzung *f* release, liberation
Freisetzungshormon *n* releasing hormone
~ für ACTH corticotropin-releasing factor, CRF, *corticoliberin
Freivulkanisation *f* open cure (vulcanization)
Freiwerden *n* liberation
freiwillig spontaneous
Fremdasche *f (coal)* extraneous ash
Fremdatom *n* foreign (impurity) atom
Fremdbestandteil *m s.* Fremdstoff
Fremd-DNA *f (biot)* foreign DNA
Fremdeisen *n* tramp iron

Fremdelektrolyt *m* foreign electrolyte
Fremdelement *n* foreign element
Fremdenzym *n* external enzyme
Fremdgas *n* foreign gas
Fremdgeruch *m* foreign odour
Fremdgeschmack *m* foreign flavour (taste)
fremdgestaltig *(cryst)* xenomorphic, allotriomorphic, anhedral
Fremdgut *n* tramp material
Fremdhalbleiter *m* impurity semiconductor
Fremdion *n* foreign ion, *(cryst also)* non-lattice ion
fremdionig foreign-ion
Fremdkeim *m* crystal nucleus, nucleus of crystallization *(consisting of foreign material)*
Fremdkörper *m (anal)* foreign body
Fremdkraftringmühle *f*, **Fremdkraftrollmühle** *f*, **Fremdkraftwälzmühle** *f* ring[-roll] mill, centrifugal attrition mill, centrifugal grinder
Fremdleiter *m s.* Fremdstoffhalbleiter
Fremdling *m (geol)* xenocryst
Fremdmolekül *n* foreign molecule
Fremdpeak *m* spurious (ghost) peak
Fremdprotein *n (biot)* foreign protein
Fremdstoff *m* admixture, impurity, foreign (extraneous) matter (material, substance)
~ **in Futtermitteln** feed additive
~ **in Lebensmitteln** food additive
Fremdstoffhalbleiter *m* impurity (extrinsic) semiconductor
Fremdstoffkonzentration *f* solute concentration *(in zone melting)*
Fremdstromkorrosion *f* electrocorrosion
Fremdsubstanz *f s.* Fremdstoff
Frenkel-Defekt *m*, **Frenkel-Fehlordnung** *f (cryst)* Frenkel defect (disorder) *(lattice vacancy plus interstitial atom)*
Frenkel-Paar *n (cryst)* Frenkel (vacancy-interstitial) pair
Frequenz *f* frequency, *(specif)* linear frequency, ν *(Hz* sec^{-1}*)* *or* angular frequency, ω *(rad* sec^{-1}*)*
~**/charakteristische** characteristic frequency, proper (natural) frequency
~ **der Seriengrenze** *(spectr)* convergence frequency
Frequenzband *n* frequency band
Frequenzbedingung *f***/Bohrsche** Bohr frequency condition
Frequenzbereich *m* frequency range (region)
Frequenzdifferenz *f* frequency difference
Frequenzdomäne *f (spectr)* frequency domain
Frequenzfaktor *m* frequency factor, [Arrhenius] pre-exponential factor, Arrhenius factor, A factor *(kinetics)*
Frequenzgang *m* frequency function
Frequenzgebiet *n s.* Frequenzbereich
Frequenzmethode *f***/variable** *(spectr)* continuous-wave technique, CW technique
Frequenzschärfe *f (spectr)* frequency selectivity
Frequenzspektrum *n* frequency domain spectrum
Frequenzverdopplung *f* frequency doubling
Frequenzverschiebung *f* frequency shift
Frequenzverteilung *f* frequency distribution
fressen to corrode
Freundlich-Isotherme *f* Freundlich [adsorption] isotherm
Freund-Reaktion *f* Freund reaction (synthesis) *(for preparing alicyclic compounds from dihalides)*
FRH *(=Follikel-stimulierendes Hormon Releasing-hormon) s.* Folliberin
Friedel-Crafts-Acylierung *f* Friedel-Crafts acylation
Friedel-Crafts-Alkylierung *f* Friedel-Crafts alkylation
Friedel-Crafts-Katalysator *m* Friedel-Crafts catalyst (agent)
Friedel-Crafts-Kondensation *f* Friedel-Crafts condensation
Friedel-Crafts-Reaktion *f* Friedel-Crafts reaction (synthesis) *(for preparing hydrocarbons or ketones)*
Friedländer-Synthese *f* Friedländer synthesis *(for preparing quinoline derivatives)*
Fries-Reaktion *f* Fries reaction (rearrangement, migration) *(conversion of phenolic esters into hydroxyketones)*
Friktion *f* friction
friktionieren *(rubber)* to friction
Friktionierkalander *m s.* Friktionskalander
Friktionseffekt *m* frictional effect
~**/differentieller** directional frictional effect
Friktionskalander *m* friction (frictioning) calender
Friktionsmischung *f (rubber)* friction compound
Friktionsstreifen *m (rubber)* chafer [strip]
Friktionsverhältnis *n* friction ratio
Frings-Generator *m (biot)* Frings acetator
Frings-Verfahren *n (biot)* Frings process *(for manufacturing vinegar)*
frischbereitet freshly prepared
Frischbeton *m* ready-mixed concrete, fresh (green) concrete
Frischdampf *m* live steam, direct (prime, open) steam
frischen *(met)* to blow
Frischgas *n* make-up gas
frischgefällt freshly precipitated
Frischhaltepapier *n* avenized paper
Frischkatalysator *m* fresh catalyst
Frischkautschuk *m* new rubber
Frischlauge *f (pap)* white (fresh cooking) liquor
Frischluft *f* fresh air
Frischmilch *f* fresh (freshly drawn) milk
Frischperiode *f (met)* boil period
Frischsäure *f* fresh acid
Frischschlamm *m (hyd)* fresh [sewage] sludge, raw waste-water sludge
Frischwasser *n* fresh water
Frischwassereintritt *m (hyd)* hard-water inlet *(ion exchange)*

Frisiercreme *f* hair cream
Fritte *f* 1. *(ceram)* frit, agglomerate; 2. *(tech)* diffuser (air) stone *(for dissolving gas in a liquid)*; 3. *(agric)* frit *(containing micronutrients)*; 4. *s.* Glasfritte
Fritteglasur *f (ceram)* fritted glaze
fritten 1. *(ceram)* to frit, to sinter, to agglomerate *(by heat)*; to sinter, to agglomerate *(under the influence of heat)*; 2. *(glass)* to drag-ladle, to dragade, *(Am)* to shrend *(cullet)*
Frittenporzellan *n* fritted porcelain
Frittenwaschflasche *f (lab)* sintered-plate washbottle
Fritteofen *m (ceram)* frit kiln
Fritz-Verfahren *n* Fritz method *(a churning process)*
Front *f (chromat)* front, boundary *(of the mobile solvent)*
Frontalanalyse *f (chromat)* frontal analysis
Frontalchromatographie *f* frontal chromatography
Frontanalyse *f s.* Frontalanalyse
frostbeständig frost-resistant, frostproof
Frostbeständigkeit *f* frost resistance, resistance to frost (freezing)
frosten *(food)* to deep freeze
Frosten *n (food)* deep freezing, freezing preservation
Frostpunkt *m* frost (freezing) point
Frostschutzmittel *n* antifreeze [agent]
frostsicher *s.* frostbeständig
Froude-Zahl *f* Froude number *(fluid mechanics)*
Fruchtaroma *n* fruit essence
Fruchtäther *m* fruit essence
fruchtbar fertile *(soil)*
Fruchtbarkeit *f* fertility *(of soil)*
Fruchtbrei *m* pomace, squash
Fruchtessenz *f* fruit essence
Fruchtessig *m* fruit vinegar
Fruchtreifungshormon *n* ethylene, *ethene
Fruchtsaft *m* [fruit] juice
Fruchtsäure *f* fruit acid
Fruchtschale *f (pharm)* cortex
Fruchtseidenpapier *n* fruit paper (tissue)
Fruchtzucker *m s.* Fructose
Fructosan *n* fructosan *(a polysaccharide)*
Fructose *f* fructose, fruit sugar, Fru
Fructosestoffwechsel *m (bioch)* metabolism of fructose
Fructosid *n* fructoside *(a glycoside)*
Frue-Vanner *m (min tech)* Frue vanner *(a concentrating table)*
frühhochfest fast-setting *(concrete)*
Frühzündung *f* preignition
Fry-Ätzmittel *n*, **Fry-Reagens** *n* Fry reagent *($CuCl_2$ in HCl, for etching steel)*
F-Säure *f* F acid *(1. $C_{10}H_6(OH)SO_3H$ naphth-2-ol-7-sulphonic acid; 2. $C_{10}H_6(NH_2)SO_3H$ naphth-2-ylamine-7-sulphonic acid)*
f-Serie *f (spectr)* fundamental series
FSH *s.* Follikelstimulierungshormon
F-strain-Effekt *m s.* Verzögerung/sterische
FT-IR-Spektrometrie *f s.* Fourier-Transform-IR-Spektrometrie
FT-Ruß *m (rubber)* FT black, fine thermal black
Fuchs *m (met)* skimmer *(for separating the slag flowing with the molten iron)*
Fuchsin *n* fuchsin[e], magenta, rosaniline
Fuchsinfarbstoff *m* fuchsine (rosaniline) dye
Fuchsonimin *n (dye)* fuchsonimine
Fugat *n* centrifugate
Fugazität *f (phys ch)* fugacity
~ 1 unit fugacity
Fugazitätskoeffizient *m (phys ch)* fugacity coefficient
Fühler *m* sensing device, sensor, detector
führen 1. to conduct *(a process)*; to run *(a factory)*; 2. to lead, to conduct, to pipe *(e.g. vapour in piping)*
~/im Kreislauf to recycle, to [re]circulate
~/in Rohrleitungen to pipe
Führungsgröße *f* reference variable (input) *(control engineering)*
Führungslager *n* guide [bearing], bearing assembly *(as of an agitator)*
Führungsrolle *f* guide roll
Führungsseil *n (pap)* leading-through tape, rope carrier
Führungstrichter *m (glass)* guide funnel
Führungswalze *f* guide roll
Füllbeton *m* poor concrete, lean[-mixed] concrete
Füllbunker *m* charging bin
Fülldichte *f (pap)* chip capacity
füllen 1. to fill; *(tech)* to feed, to charge, to load, to furnish *(e.g. a furnace or reactor)*; *(distil)* to pack *(a column with packing material)*; *(lab)* to prime *(a burner with fuel)*; 2. to load, to fill *(a product with fillers)*, *(pap also)* to weight, *(rubber also)* to pigment; *(tann)* to feed, to fill *(incompletely tanned leather with additional tanning material)*
~/auf (in) Flaschen to bottle [in, up]
~/mit Füllkörpern *(distil)* to pack
~/wieder to refill
Füller *m s.* 1. Füllstoff; 2. Füllmaschine
Fulleren *n (org ch)* fullerene
Fullererde *f* fuller's earth
Fuller-Lehigh-Mühle *f* Fuller-Lehigh mill
Fuller-Mühle *f* Fuller mill *(a ball-and-ring mill)*
Füllfaktor *m (plast)* bulk factor
Füllfaser *f* staple for filling
Füllform *f* positive mould
Füllgas *n* filling gas
Füllgerbung *f* plumping tannage
Füllgut *n* 1. *s.* Füllmaterial 1.; 2. *(plast)* mould charge
Füllhöhe *f* filling level, fill height
Füllhöhenmessung *f* level measurement
Füllklappe *f* charging (filling) door

Füllkörper *m* 1. filler [material], filling [agent, material]; 2. *(esp distil)* packing body, piece of packing
Füllkörper *mpl* packing *(of or for a column or tower)*
~ **aus Glas** glass packing
~ **aus Porzellan** porcelain packing
~**/geschüttete** dumped packing
~**/schalenporöse** *(chromat)* porous layer beads, pellicular packing (support), solid core support
~**/schüttbare** dump (random tower) packing
Füllkörperabsorber *m* packed absorber
Füllkörperabsorptionskolonne *f* packed absorption column
Füllkörperabsorptionsturm *m* packed absorption tower
Füllkörperentgaser *m (hyd)* packed column degasifier, packed stripping tower
Füllkörperhöhe *f* packed height
~**/äquivalente** height equivalent to a theoretical plate (stage), HETP, HETS
Füllkörperkolonne *f*, **Füllkörpersäule** *f* packed column
Füllkörperschichthöhe *f* height of packing
Füllkörperturm *m* packed tower
Füllmaschine *f* filling machine, filler
~ **für Flüssigkeiten** liquid filler (filling machine)
Füllmasse *f* 1. *s.* Füllstoff 1.; 2. *(sugar)* massecuite, magma, fillmass
Füllmaterial *n* 1. load, batch, feed[stock], feed material, charge, charging stock *(as for a reactor)*; packing [material] *(as for a column or tower)*; packing medium *(of a trickling filter)*; 2. *s.* Füllstoff 1.
Füllmittel *n s.* Füllstoff 1.
Fülloch *n*, **Füllöffnung** *f* charging (filling) door, feed inlet (hole)
Füllraum *m (plast)* loading chamber, pot
Füllraumform *f*, **Füllraumwerkzeug** *n* positive mould
Füllrohr *n* charging pipe
Füllrumpf *m s.* Fülltrichter
Füllschlitten *m (ceram)* sliding carriage
Füllstand *m* filling level, fill height
Füllstandsmessung *f* level measurement
Füllstation *f* filling plant (room), *(esp)* bottling plant (room), bottle house, bottlery
Füllstoff *m* 1. filler, filling (loading) material, load[-er], *(rubber also)* pigment; 2. *s.* Füllmaterial 1.
~**/aktiver** *(rubber)* active (reinforcing) filler (pigment)
~**/heller** *(rubber)* white (non-black) filler (pigment), light-coloured filler
~**/heller aktiver** *(rubber)* white (non-black) reinforcing filler (pigment)
~**/inaktiver (inerter)** *(rubber)* inert (inactive) filler, non-reinforcing filler, cheapener
~**/mineralischer** mineral filler
~**/passiver** *s.* ~/inaktiver
~**/verstärkender** *s.* ~/aktiver
Füllstoffdispergierung *f* filler dispersion
Füllstoffdosierung *f* dosage of filler, filler loading, *(rubber also)* pigment loading, pigmentation
füllstofffrei unfilled, unloaded, filler-free, *(rubber also)* non-pigmented
füllstoffhaltig filled, loaded, *(rubber also)* pigmented
Füllstoffkaolin *m(n) (pap)* filler clay
Füllstoffnester *npl (rubber)* filler specks
Füllstoffverteilung *f* filler dispersion
Füllstutzen *m* charging (filling, feeding) pipe
Fülltablett *n (plast)* charging (loading) tray *(for compression moulds)*
Fülltrichter *m* 1. [charge, feed] hopper, feed[ing] funnel; 2. cup *(of a blast furnace)*
Fülltrichter-Auslaufstutzen *m* feed throat
Füllturm *m* packed tower *(as for absorption)*
Füllung *f* 1. filling; *(tech)* feeding, charging, loading, furnishing *(as of a furnace or reactor)*; 2. filling, loading *(of a product for conditioning)*, *(rubber also)* pigmentation; 3. *s.* Füllmaterial 1.; 4. *s.* Füllstoff 1.
~ **mit Kalkstein** *(pap)* stone charging
~ **mit Ruß** *(rubber)* [carbon] black loading
Füllungsgrad *m* degree of filling
Füllvolumen *n* filling volume; *(tech)* feeding (charging, loading) volume; *(biot)* working (fermenter, fermentation) volume
Füllvorrichtung *f* **für Preßwerkzeuge** *s.* Fülltablett
Füllzylinder *m (plast)* pot
Fulminat *n* $CNOM^I$ fulminate
Fulminsäure *f* fulminic acid, carbyloxime
Fulvalen *n (org ch)* fulvalen
Fulven *n* fulvene *(5-methylene-cyclopenta-1,3-diene or any of its derivatives)*
Fulvenkohlenwasserstoff *m* fulvene *(any of the derivatives of 5-methylene-cyclopenta-1,3-diene)*
Fulvosäure *f* fulvic acid *(any of several water-soluble humic acids)*
Fumarat *n* fumarate *(salt or ester of fumaric acid)*
Fumarole *f (geol)* fumarole
Fumarsäure *f* fumaric acid, **trans*-butenedioic acid
Fumigazin *n* fumigacin, helvolic acid *(antibiotic)*
Fundamentalbaustein *m* fundamental (basic) building block
Fundamentaleinheit *f* fundamental (basic) unit
Fundamentalgebilde *n* fundamental entity
Fundamentalgleichung *f (phys ch)* fundamental equation
Fundamentalprozeß *m* basic process
Fundamentalpunkt *m* fixed point
Fundamentalserie *f (spectr)* fundamental series
Fundamentalteilchen *n* fundamental particle
Fundamentplatte *f* base plate
Fundbohrung *f (petrol)* discovery well
fünfbasig pentabasic, pentaprotic *(acid)*; pentabasic, pentaacid *(base)*
Fünfeck *n* pentagon *(as of a cyclic compound)*
Fünferring *m s.* Fünfring

fünfgliedrig five-membered
Fünfkörperverdampfer *m* quintuple-effect evaporator
Fünfring *m* five-membered ring
fünfsäurig pentaacid *(base)*
Fünfstufenbleiche *f (pap)* five-stage bleaching
Fünfstufenverdampfer *m s.* Fünfkörperverdampfer
Fünfwalzenmühle *f*, **Fünfwalzenstuhl** *m* five-roll mill
fünfwertig pentavalent, quinquevalent *(element)*; pentabasic, pentaprotic *(acid)*; pentabasic, pentaacid *(base)*; pentahydric *(alcohol)*
Fünfwertigkeit *f* pentavalence, pentavalency, quinquevalence *(of elements)*
fünfzählig *s.* fünfzähnig
fünfzähnig pentadentate *(ligand)*
Fungistatikum *n* fungistat
fungistatisch fungistatic
fungitoxisch fungitoxic
fungizid fungicidal, antifungal
Fungizid *n* fungicide, *(pharm also)* antifungal drug
~/direktes direct (eradicant) fungicide
~/kupferhaltiges copper fungicide
~ mit kurativer Wirkung *s.* ~/direktes
~/nichtsystemisches non-systemic fungicide
~/quecksilberhaltiges mercurial fungicide
~/systemisches systemic fungicide
~ zur Schorfbekämpfung apple-scab fungicide
fungizidresistent fungicide-resistant
Funkelrauschen *n (anal)* flicker noise
Funkenanregung *f (spectr)* spark excitation
Funkenentladung *f* spark discharge
Funkenkammer *f (nucl)* spark chamber
Funken-Massenspektrometrie *f* spark source mass spectrometry, SSMS
Funkenspektrum *n* spark (flash) spectrum
Funkenstrecke *f* spark gap, *(quantitatively also)* gap width
Funksonde *f* radiosonde
Funktion *f* function
~/Debyesche Debye function
~/Gibbssche free energy G
~/periodische periodic function
~/thermodynamische thermodynamic function
Funktionalität *f* functionality
Funktionsprüfung *f* bench test (check)
Furacrylsäure *f s.* Furylacrylsäure
Fural *n*, **2-Furaldehyd** *m s.* Furfural
Furalessigsäure *f s.* Furylacrylsäure
Furan *n (org ch)* furan
Furanaldehyd *m s.* Furfural
2-Furancarbinol *n s.* Furfurylalkohol
2-Furancarbonal *n s.* Furfural
Furancarbonsäure *f* furancarboxylic acid
Furandion *n* furandione
Furanharz *n* furan resin
Furanoseform *f* furanose form *(of sugars)*
Furanosid *n* furanoside
Furazan *n (org ch)* furazan
Furche *f*/**große** *(bioch)* deep groove *(of the DNA model)*
~/kleine shallow groove *(of the DNA model)*
Furchendüngung *f* furrow fertilization
Furchenrieselung *f* ridge-and-furrow system *(waste-water treatment)*
Furfural *n* furfural, 2-furylaldehyde
Furfuralanlage *f* furfural extraction plant
2-Furfuraldehyd *m s.* Furfural
Furfuralextraktion *f* furfural extraction
Furfuralextraktionsanlage *f* furfural extraction plant
Furfuralharz *n* furfural resin
Furfuralkohol *m s.* Furfurylalkohol
Furfuralraffination *f (petrol)* furfural refining
Furfuralstripper *m (petrol)* furfural stripper
Furfuralverfahren *n (petrol)* furfural process, furfural extraction (refining, solvent) process
Furfuralwaschturm *m (petrol)* furfural treating tower
Furfuran *n s.* Furan
Furfurol *n s.* Furfural
2-Furfurylaldehyd *m s.* Furfural
Furfurylalkohol *m*, **α-Furfurylalkohol** *m* furfuryl alcohol, 2-hydroxymethylfuran
Furil *n* furil, αα-furil, di-2-furylglyoxal, di-α-furyl diketone
Furnace-Ruß *m* furnace [combustion] black
Furnace-Verfahren *n (rubber)* furnace [combustion] process, continuous-furnace method *(for producing soot)*
Furocumarin *n (org ch)* furocoumarin
Furoin *n* furoin, αα-furoin, 1,2-difuryl-2-oxoethanol
Furol *n s.* Furfural
Furoylgruppe *f* furoyl group
Furylacrylsäure *f* furylacrylic acid, 3-α-furylacrylic acid, furfuralacetic acid
2-Furylaldehyd *m s.* Furfural
2-Furylcarbinol *n s.* Furfurylalkohol
Fusain *m* fusain *(a charcoal-like microscopic constituent of coal)*
Fusarinsäure *f* fusaric acid, 5-butylpyridine-2-carboxylic acid
Fusarsäure *f s.* Fusarinsäure
Fuselöl *n* fusel oil, fousel (potato, grain) oil
Fusidinsäure *f* fusidic acid *(antibiotic)*
Fusinit *m s.* Fusit
Fusion *f (nucl)* fusion
Fusionsname *m (nomencl)* fusion name
Fusit *m* fusi[ni]te *(a microscopic structure found in fusain)*
Fußbodenbelag *m* floor covering, flooring
Fußbodenreiniger *m* floor cleaner
Fußventil *n* foot (suction) valve
Fustet *m s.* Fustik
Fustik *m (dye)* fustic, fustet
~/Alter (Echter) old fustic *(from Chlorophora tinctoria Gaudich.)*
~/Junger young fustic *(from Cotinus coggygria Scop.)*

Fustikholz *n s.* Fustik
Futter *n* 1. *(met)* lining, refractory; 2. *(agric)* feed[-stuff], feeding stuff; *(biot)* feed
~/basisches *(met)* basic lining (refractory)
~/saures *(met)* acid lining (refractory)
Futterkonservierung *f* feed preservation
Futtermittel *n (agric)* feed[stuff], feeding stuff, animal food (feeding material)
Futtermittelzusatz[stoff] *m* feed additive (supplement), nutritional supplement
füttern 1. *(met)* to line; 2. *(biot)* to feed *(microorganisms)*
Futterrohre *npl (petrol)* casing
Futterrohreinbau *m (petrol)* casing, introduction of casing
Futterseidenpapier *n* envelope lining [tissue]
Futtersupplement *n s.* Futtermittelzusatz
Fütterungsantibiotikum *n (biot)* feed-additive antibiotic, antibiotic used in animal feed
Futterwert *m* feed value
Futterzusatz *m s.* Futtermittelzusatz
FUV = ferner Ultraviolettbereich
F-Zentrum *n (spectr)* F-centre *(a colour centre)*

G

Gabanholz *n (dye)* camwood *(from Baphia nitida Afz.)*
Gabbro *m* gabbro *(an igneous rock)*
Gabbroschale *f (geoch)* intermediate layer, sima
Gabe *f (pharm)* dose
~/größte maximum dose
Gabriel-Synthese *f* Gabriel phthalimide synthesis [of primary amines], Gabriel synthesis
G-Actin *n* G actin *(a globular muscle protein)*
Gadoleinsäure *f* gadoleic acid, eicos-9-enoic acid
Gadolinium *n* Gd gadolinium
Gadoliniumacetat *n* gadolinium acetate
Gadoliniumchlorid *n* gadolinium chloride
Gadoliniumfluorid *n* gadolinium fluoride
Gadoliniumnitrat *n* gadolinium nitrate
Gadoliniumoxid *n* gadolinium oxide
Gadoliniumsulfat *n* gadolinium sulphate
Gagat *m* gagate, jet *(a mineral of the nature of coal)*
Gaillard-Kammer *f* Gaillard tower *(for concentrating sulphuric acid)*
Gaillard-Turbozerstäuber *m* Gaillard disperser
α-**Gal** = α-Galactosidase
Galactan *n (bioch)* galactan
Galactarsäure *f* galactosaccharic acid, mucic acid *(a tetrahydroxydicarboxylic acid)*
Galactonsäure *f* galactonic acid *(a sugar acid)*
Galactozuckersäure *f s.* Galactarsäure
Galacturonsäure *f* galacturonic acid *(a pentahydroxycarboxylic acid)*
Galaktagogum *n (pharm)* galactagogue *(milk-ejecting agent)*
Galaktometer *n* [ga]lactometer
Galaktosämie *f (med)* galactosaemia
Galambutter *f* Galam (Bambuk, shea) butter *(from Butyrospermum parkii (Don) Kotschy)*
Galbanum *n* galbanum *(a gum resin from Ferula specc.)*
Galenikum *n (pharm)* galenical
Galenit *m (min)* galena, galenite *(lead(II) sulphide)*
Galgant *m*, **Galgantwurzel** *f* galanga[l] *(from Alpinia specc.)*
Gallamid *n (org ch)* gallamide
Gallanilid *n (org ch)* gallanilide
Gallat *n* 1. gallate(III) *(gallium compound)*; 2. 3,4,5-trihydroxybenzoate, gallate *(salt or ester af gallic acid)*
Galle *f* 1. *(med)* bile, gall; 2. *(glass)* gall, salt water; 3. *(tann, bot)* gall
Gallein *n* gallein *(a quinonoid dye)*
Gallenfarbstoff *m (med)* bile pigment
Gallenflüssigkeit *f (med)* bile, gall
Gallensäure *f* bile acid
Gallenstein *m (med)* gallstone, biliary calculus
gallentreibend *(pharm)* cholagogic
Gallert *n* gelatin[e], jelly, gelatinous mass (substance)
gallertartig gelatinous, gelatiniform, jelly-like
Gallertbildung *f* jellification
Gallerte *f s.* Gallert
gallertig *s.* gallertartig
Gallium *n* Ga gallium
Gallium(III)-bromid *n* gallium(III) bromide, gallium tribromide
Gallium(II)-chlorid *n* gallium(II) chloride, gallium dichloride
Gallium(III)-chlorid *n* gallium(III) chloride, gallium trichloride
Galliumdichlorid *n s.* Gallium(II)-chlorid
Gallium(III)-fluorid *n* gallium(III) fluoride, gallium trifluoride
Galliumhexacyanoferrat(II) *n* gallium hexacyanoferrate(II), gallium cyanoferrate(II)
Gallium(III)-hydroxid *n* gallium(III) hydroxide
Gallium(III)-iodid *n* gallium(III) iodide, gallium triiodide
Galliummonoxid *n s.* Gallium(II)-oxid
Gallium(III)-nitrat *n* gallium(III) nitrate
Gallium(I)-oxid *n* gallium(I) oxide, digallium oxide
Gallium(II)-oxid *n* gallium(II) oxide, gallium monooxide
Gallium(III)-oxid *n* gallium(III) oxide, digallium trioxide
Gallium(III)-sulfat *n* gallium(III) sulphate
Gallium(III)-sulfid *n* gallium(III) sulphide, digallium trisulphide
Galliumtri... *s.* Gallium(III)-...
Gallotannin *n s.* Gallusgerbsäure
Gallusgerbsäure *f* gallotannic acid, gallotannin, tannic acid *(proper) (glucose esterified with gallic acid or depsides of it)*

gallussauer gallic
Gallussäure *f* gallic acid, 3,4,5-trihydroxybenzoic acid
Gallussäureamid *n s.* Gallamid
Gallussäureanilid *n s.* Gallanilid
Gallussäure-3-monogallat *n s. m*-Digallussäure
Galmei *m* 1. *(min)* calamine, galmei, galmey; 2. *(pharm)* calamine *(zinc oxide with a small amount of ferric oxide)*
~/edler *(min)* smithsonite *(zinc carbonate)*
Galmeistein *m s.* Galmei 2.
Galvanikabwasser *n (hyd)* [electro]plating waste, waste from plating shops
Galvani-Potential *n (el ch)* Galvani (inner) potential
galvanisch 1. galvanic *(cell, current, anode)*; 2. electroplated, electrodeposited *(coating)*
Galvanisierbad *n s.* 1. Galvanisierelektrolyt; 2. Galvanisierbehälter
Galvanisierbehälter *m* [electro]plating tank
Galvanisierbetrieb *m* electroplating plant
Galvanisierelektrolyt *m* electroplating solution
galvanisieren to electroplate, to plate
Galvanisiergehänge *n* plating rack
Galvano *n* electrotype *(typography)*
Galvanoformung *f* electroforming, galvanoplastics, galvanoplasty
Galvanolumineszenz *f* galvanoluminescence
Galvanometer *n* galvanometer
~/astatisches astatic galvanometer
~/ballistisches ballistic galvanometer
~/schreibendes galvanometer recorder
Galvanometerschreiber *m* galvanometer recorder
Galvanoplastik *f* electroforming, galvanoplastics, galvanoplasty; electrotyping *(typography)*
galvanoplastisch galvanoplastic
Galvanoskop *n* galvanoscope
Galvanostegie *f* electroplating
Galvanotechnik *f* electroplating and electroforming [technology]
Gambir *n* gambi[e]r, pale catechu, white cutch *(from Uncaria gambir Roxb.)*
Gamma *n s.* Gammawert
~ unendlich *s.* Gammagrenzwert
Gammagrenzwert *m (phot)* gamma infinity
Gammasäure *f* gamma acid, γ-acid, 1-hydroxy-naphth-7-ylamin-3-sulphonic acid
Gammastrahlen *mpl* gamma rays
Gammastrahlendetektor *m* gamma-ray detector
Gammastrahlenquelle *f* gamma-ray source
Gammastrahlung *f* gamma radiation
Gammaumwandlung *f (rubber)* glass transition, gamma (second-order) transition, vitrification
Gammawert *m (phot)* gamma value, development factor
Gamma-Zeit-Kurve *f (phot)* time-gamma curve
Gang *m* 1. *(geol)* vein, dike, *(of metal ore also)* lode; 2. *(ch)* course *(of a reaction)*; 3. *(tech)* flight *(as of a worm shaft)* • **in ~ halten** to keep in progress *(a reaction)* • **in ~ setzen** to initiate, to start up *(a reaction)*
Gangart *f (mine)* gangue, gang, waste rock, matrix
Gangerz *n* vein ore
Ganggestein *n* 1. *(geol)* dike rock, dykite; 2. *s.* Gangart
Ganghöhe *f (tech, bioch)* pitch *(of a screw or an alpha helix)*
Gängigkeit *f (bioch)* helix sense
Ganglienblocker *m*, **Ganglioplegikum** *n (pharm)* ganglion blocking agent, ganglionic blockader
Gangsteigungswinkel *m* helix angle *(as of an extruder screw)*
Gangtrockner *m (ceram)* corridor dryer
Gänsekötigerz *n* goose dung ore, ganomatite *(an iron arsenate containing silver and cobalt)*
Ganzflächenapplikation *f (agric)* overall application, *(when crops are growing also)* overhead application *(of pesticides)*
Ganzflächenbehandlung *f (agric)* overall (non-selective) treatment
Ganzflächenbesprühung *f (agric)* overall spraying
Ganzreifenregenerat *n (rubber)* whole-tyre reclaim
Ganzstoff *m (pap)* whole (finished) stuff, paper[-making] stock
Ganzstoffaufbereitung *f (pap)* stock preparation
Ganzstoffmahlmaschine *f (pap)* perfecting (refining) engine (machine), refiner
Ganzstoffmahlung *f (pap)* beating of stock
Ganzstoffreinigung *f (pap)* stock cleaning (clean-up)
Ganzstoffsortierer *m (pap)* stock screen
Ganzzeug *n s.* Ganzstoff
Ganzzeugbereitung *f s.* Ganzstoffaufbereitung
Ganzzeugholländer *m (pap)* Hollander [beater, beating engine], pulp engine (grinder), stuff engine
gar unctuous *(soil)*
Gär... *s. a.* Gärungs...
Gärablauge *f* effluent from fermentation plants
Gärbild *n* fermentation picture
Gärbottich *m* fermentation vat (vessel), fermenter
Garbrand *m (ceram)* maturing, soaking, final firing
Garbrandbereich *m (ceram)* maturing range
garbrennen *(ceram)* to mature, to soak
Gärbstahl *m* shear steel, refined steel (iron, bar), merchant bar
Gärdauer *f* fermentation period, length of fermentation
Gardine *f (coat)* curtain *(a film fault)*
Gardinenbildung *f* curtaining, sagging *(of surface coatings)*
Gardschanbalsam *m* gurjun balsam *(from Dipterocarpus alatus Roxb.)*
Gare *f* unctuousness, [good] tilth *(of soil)*
gären to ferment, to yeast
Gärer *mpl s.* Anaerobier
gärfähig fermentable
Gärfähigkeit *f* fermentability
Gärflüssigkeit *f* fermenting liquor, wash
Gärführung *f* fermentation method
Gargarisma *n (pharm)* gargarism, gargle

Gargoylismus *m (med)* gargoylism, Hurler's disease *(accumulation of mucopolysaccharides caused by inherited enzyme deficiency)*
Gärkammer *f (biot)* fermentation (incubation) chamber
Gärkeller *m* fermenting (fermentation) cellar
Gärkelleranlage *f* fermentation plant
Gärkolben *m* fermentation flask
Gärkraft *f* fermentative (fermenting) power
Garkupfer *n* refined (casting, tough-pitch) copper
Garlauge *f (fert)* refining lye
Gärlösung *f s.* Gärflüssigkeit
Garn *n (text)* spun[-staple] yarn, yarn
~ **aus Rohseidenabfällen** spun silk
~**/einfädiges** single yarn
~**/hochvoluminöses** high-bulk yarn
Garnfärbeapparat *m* yarn-dyeing machine
Garnfärben *n* yarn dyeing
Gärniederschlag *m* lees, bottoms
Garnierit *m (min)* garnierite *(nickel silicate)*
Garnierschlicker *m (ceram)* joining slip
Garnkörper *m (text)* bobbin, package
Garnnummer *f* count (number) of yarn, yarn size
Gärprüfung *f* fermentation test
Garpunkt *m (ceram)* maturing point
Gärraum *m* fermenting (fermentation) room
Gärreductaseprobe *f* fermentation reductase test
Gärröhrchen *n* fermentation tube
~ **nach Durham** Durham tube
Gärröhre *f s.* Gärröhrchen
Garschaum[graphit] *m* keesh, kish
Gärtank *m* fermentation (fermenting) tank, fermenter
Gartemperatur *f (ceram)* maturing (soaking) temperature
Gärtemperatur *f* fermentation temperature, fermenter set temperature
Gärung *f* fermentation
~**/aerobe** aerobic (oxidative) fermentation
~**/alkalische** *(hyd)* methane fermentation
~**/alkoholische** alcohol[ic] fermentation
~**/anaerobe** anaerobic fermentation
~**/bakterielle** bacterial fermentation
~**/belüftete** aerated fermentation
~**/direkte** direct fermentation
~**/diskontinuierliche** batch[-process] fermentation, batch-fed fermentation
~**/eigentliche** *s.* ~/anaerobe
~**/einstufige** single-stage fermentation
~**/halbkontinuierliche** semicontinuous fermentation
~**/heterofermentative** heterolactic (mixed) fermentation
~ **im Haufen** heap fermentation *(as of cocoa beans)*
~**/industrielle** industrial fermentation
~**/kontinuierliche** continuous fermentation
~**/mikrobielle** microbial fermentation
~**/milchsaure** lactic[-acid] fermentation
~ **mit Vakuumsystem** vacuum fermentation, vacuferm
~**/offene** open fermentation
~**/oxidative** oxidative (aerobic) fermentation
~**/saure** acid fermentation
~**/schleimige** ropy fermentation
~**/schnelle** rapid [ethanol] fermentation
~**/semikontinuierliche** semicontinuous fermentation
~**/statische** *s.* ~/diskontinuierliche
~**/vollkontinuierliche** continuous fermentation
~**/zellfreie** cell-free fermentation
Gärungs... *s. a.* Gär...
Gärungsablauf *m* fermentation pathway (route), course of fermentation
~**/zeitlicher** time course of fermentation
Gärungsabschnitt *m* fermentation step
Gärungsalkohol *m* fermentation alcohol
Gärungsamylalkohol *m* fermentation amyl alcohol
Gärungschemie *f* fermentation chemistry, zymurgy
Gärungsenzym *n* fermentation enzyme
~**/oxidierendes** triosephosphate dehydrogenase
gärungserregend fermentative, zymogenic, zymogenous
Gärungsessig *m* fermentation vinegar
Gärungsethanol *n* fermentation ethanol
Gärungsferment *n s.* Gärungsenzym
Gärungsgewerbe *n* fermentation industry
Gärungsgleichung *f***/Harden-Youngsche** Harden-Young fermentation equation
gärungshemmend antifermentative
Gärungsindustrie *f* fermentation industry
Gärungsmechanismus *m* mechanism of fermentation
Gärungsmilchsäure *f* lactic acid of fermentation, DL-lactic acid, ordinary lactic acid, i-lactic acid *(optically inactive)*
Gärungsorganismus *m* organized ferment
Gärungsprodukt *n* fermentation product
Gärungsrückstand *m* fermentation residue
Gärungsschaum *m* bloom
Gärungstechnik *f* zymotechnics, fermentation technology
gärungstechnisch zymotechnic[al]
Gärungstechnologie *f* fermentation technology
gärungsverhindernd antifermentative
Gärungsverlauf *m s.* Gärungsablauf
Gärungsvorgang *m* fermentation process
Garungszeit *f (coal)* coking time
Gärverfahren *n* fermentation method (process), bioprocess
Gärverlust *m* fermentation loss
Gärvermögen *n* fermentative (fermenting) power
Gärwirkung *f* fermentative action
Gas *n* gas
~**/aufkohlendes** *(met)* carburizing gas
~**/ausgetriebenes** stripped gas
~**/brennbares** combustible gas
~**/heizkräftiges (heizwertreiches)** *s.* ~ mit hohem Heizwert
~**/ideales** ideal (perfect) gas

~/inaktives (indifferentes) *s.* ~/inertes
~/inertes inert (inactive, indifferent) gas
~/kohlenwasserstoffhaltiges hydrocarbon (HC) gas
~/künstlich hergestelltes manufactured gas
~ mit geringem Heizwert low-heating-value gas, low-Btu gas
~ mit hohem Heizwert high-heating-value gas, high-Btu gas
~ mit mittlerem Heizwert medium-Btu gas
~/permanentes permanent gas
~/reaktionsträges *s.* ~/inertes
~/reales imperfect (real, actual) gas
~/reiches rich gas *(gross calorific value 7500 to 8500 kcal/m^3, equalling 31401 to 35588 kJ/m^3)*
~/saures 1. sour gas *(containing acid components as hydrogen sulphide, carbon dioxide, and hydrogen cyanide)*; 2. acid gas *(carbon dioxide, hydrogen sulphide)*
~/staubhaltiges dust-laden gas
~/technisches industrial gas, *(esp if combustible:)* manufactured gas
~/träges *s.* ~/inertes
~/überschüssiges excess (surplus) gas
~/verflüssigtes liquefied gas
Gasabführung *f* gas offtake
Gasabgang *m* gas outlet
Gasabgangsrohr *n* gas outlet pipe
Gasableitungsrohr *n* gas offtake pipe
Gasabscheider *m* gas separator
Gasabscheidung *f* 1. gas separation; 2. *s.* Gasentwicklung
Gasabsorptionschromatographie *f s.* Gas-flüssig-Chromatographie
Gasabtrennung *f* gas separation
Gasabzug *m* gas offtake
Gasabzug[s]rohr *n* gas offtake pipe; fume pipe
~/fallendes downcomer
~/steigendes gas uptake
Gasadsorptionschromatographie *f s.* Gas-fest-Chromatographie
Gasanalyse *f* gas analysis
~/volumetrische volumetric gas analysis
Gasanalysenapparat *m* gas analysis apparatus
~ nach Orsat Orsat [gas analysis] apparatus, Orsat analyser
gasanalytisch gas-analytical
Gasanreicherung *f* gas enrichment
Gasanstalt *f s.* Gaswerk
Gasanzünder *m* burner lighter
gasartig gaseous
Gasatmosphäre *f***/indifferente (inerte)** inert-gas atmosphere
Gasaufbereitung *f* gas processing (treating, treatment)
gasaufkohlen to gas-carburize *(steel)*
Gasaufkohlung *f* gas carburizing *(of steel)*
Gasaufnahme *f* gas absorption (uptake)
Gasausbeute *f*, **Gasausbringung** *f* gas output
Gasaushauchung *f* outgassing *(of a volcano)*
Gasaustausch *m (hyd)* gas transfer
Gasaustauschgeschwindigkeit *f (hyd)* rate of gas transfer
Gasaustauschkoeffizient *m (hyd)* gas transfer coefficient
Gasaustritt *m* 1. escape of gas; 2. gas outlet
Gasaustrittsöffnung *f* gas outlet
Gasaustrittstemperatur *f* exit gas temperature
Gasbedarf *m* gas requirements
Gasbehälter *m* gas tank (container), *(esp for town gas:)* gasholder, gasometer
gasbeheizt gas-heated
Gasbeheizung *f* gas[-fired] heating
gasbeständig resistant to gases
Gasbeständigkeit *f* resistance to gases
Gasbeton *m* gas (gassy) concrete
gasbildend gas-forming
Gasbildung *f* formation of gas
Gasbläschen *n* gas bubble
Gasblase *f* 1. gas bubble; 2. *s.* Gaseinschluß
Gasbleiche *f (pap)* gas bleaching
Gasbohrung *f (petrol)* gas well
Gasbrenner *m* gas burner
Gasbrunnen *m* gas well
Gasbürette *f* gas[-measuring] burette
~/Buntesche Bunte [gas] burette
~/Hempelsche Hempel [gas] burette
gascarbonitrieren to gas-cyanide, to carbonitride, to dry-cyanide, to dry-nitride *(steel)*
Gaschromatogramm *n* gas chromatogram
Gaschromatograph *m* gas chromatograph
Gaschromatographie *f* gas chromatography, GC
~/inverse inverse gas chromatography, IGC
~ mit Temperaturprogramm programmed temperature gas chromatography
~/präparative preparative gas chromatography
Gaschromatographie-Massenspektrometrie-Kopplung *f* gas chromatography-mass spectrometry coupling, GC-MS
gaschromatographisch by gas chromatography; gas-chromatographic *(technique, system)*
Gascoulometer *n* gas coulometer
gascyanieren *s.* gascarbonitrieren
gasdicht gastight, gasproof
Gasdichte *f* gas density
Gasdichtemessung *f* measurement of gas density
Gasdichtewaage *f* gas [density] balance
Gasdichtigkeit *f* gastightness
Gasdichtung *f* gas seal
Gasdiffusion *f* gaseous diffusion
Gasdiffusionstrennsäule *f* gaseous diffusion separator
Gasdiffusionsverfahren *n* gaseous diffusion process *(for separating isotopes)*
Gasdispersion *f* gas dispersion
Gasdruck *m* gas pressure (drive)
Gasdurchflußmesser *m* gas flowmeter
Gasdurchflußzählrohr *n (nucl)* gas-flow counter tube, gas-flow radiation counter, flow counter

Gasdurchgang *m* gas passage
gasdurchlässig permeable to gas, gas-permeable
Gasdurchlässigkeit *f* permeability to gas, gas permeability
Gasdurchlässigkeitszahl *f (met)* permeability number *(of moulding sand)*
Gase *npl*/**nitrose** nitrous gases
Gäse *f* seed *(a defect in glass)*
gasecht *(text)* fast to burnt gas fumes, fast to gas fading
Gasechtheit *f (text)* gas-fume fastness, fastness to burnt gas fumes, fastness to gas fading
Gaseinleitungsrohr *n* gas-entry tube
Gaseinpressen *n* gas injection
Gaseinschluß *m* blister *(a flaw in material; foundry also)* gas cavity, blow hole
gaseinsetzen *(met)* to gas-carburize
Gaseinsetzen *n (met)* gas carburizing
Gaseintritt *m* gas inlet
Gaseintrittstemperatur *f* inlet gas temperature
Gaselektrode *f* gas electrode
Gaselement *n (el ch)* gas cell
gasen 1. to gas; 2. to steam *(in producing water gas)*
~/abwärts to steam downwards
~/aufwärts to steam upwards
~/von oben *s.* ~/abwärts
~/von unten *s.* ~/aufwärts
Gasen *n* 1. gassing; 2. steaming, make, run *(in producing water gas)*
~ **in absteigender Richtung** down-steaming, down-run[ning]
~ **in aufsteigender Richtung** up-steaming, up-run[ning]
Gasentartung *f (phys ch)* gas degeneracy *(near absolute zero)*
Gasentladungsröhre *f* [gas] discharge tube
Gasentlösungsdruck *m (petrol)* dissolved-gas drive, solution gas drive
Gasentlösungslagerstätte *f (petrol)* solution gas-drive reservoir, depletion-type reservoir
Gasentnahme *f* gas offtake
Gasentschwefelung *f* gas desulphurization
Gasentwickler *m s.* Gasentwicklungsapparat
Gasentwicklung *f* generation (evolution) of gas, gassing
Gasentwicklungsapparat *m* gas generator
~/Kippscher Kipp [gas] generator, Kipp's apparatus
Gasentwicklungsflasche *f (lab)* generating bottle
Gasentwicklungsgefäß *n* gas generator, evolution vessel
Gaserhitzer *m* gas heater, *(if working batchwise:)* regenerator, *(if working continuously:)* recuperator
Gaserzeuger *m (tech)* gas producer (generator)
~ **mit Treppenrost** step-grate producer
Gaserzeugung *f* gas manufacture (making, production)
Gaserzeugungsanlage *f* gas[-making] plant
Gaserzeugungsverfahren *n* gas-making process
~ **nach Didier-Bubiag** Didier-Bublag process
~ **von Ahrens** Ahrens process
Gas-fest-Chromatographie *f* gas-solid chromatography, GSC, gas adsorption chromatography
Gas-Feststoff-Chromatographie *f s.* Gas-fest-Chromatographie
Gas-Feststoff-Reaktion *f* gas-solid [heterogeneous] reaction
~/katalytische gas-solid catalytic reaction
~/nichtkatalytische gas-solid non-catalytic reaction
Gasfeuerung *f* gas-fuel firing
Gasfilter *n* 1. gas filter, *(lab also)* gas filtering (filtration) tube; 2. chemical filtering element *(respiratory protection)*
Gasfiltration *f* gas filtration
Gasflamme *f* gas flame
Gasflammkohle *f* gas flame coal
Gasflasche *f* gas cylinder
Gas-flüssig-Chromatographie *f* gas-liquid [partition] chromatography, GLC
Gas-flüssig-fest-Chromatographie *f* gas-liquid-solid chromatography, GLSC
Gas-Flüssigkeits-Chromatographie *f s.* Gas-flüssig-Chromatographie
Gas-flüssig-Reaktion *f* gas-liquid reaction
Gas-flüssig-Reaktor *m* gas-liquid reactor
Gasförderung *f s.* Gasliftförderung
gasförmig gaseous
gasführend gas-bearing
Gasfüllung *f* gas fill
Gas-Furnace-Verfahren *n (rubber)* gas furnace process
gasgefeuert gas-fired
Gasgehalt *m* gas content
Gasgemisch *n* gas mixture
Gasgenerator *m* gas producer (generator)
Gasgesetz *n* gas law
~/ideales *s.* Zustandsgleichung idealer Gase
Gasgewinnung *f* **aus Mülldeponien** landfill gas extraction
Gasgleichgewicht *n* gas equilibrium
Gasgleichung *f* gas equation
~/ideale *s.* Zustandsgleichung idealer Gase
Gasglühkörper *m*, **Gasglühlichtstrumpf** *m* gas mantle
Gasgrenzschicht *f* gaseous boundary layer
Gashahn *m* gas [stop]cock
Gasheber *m* gas lift
Gasheizkranz *m* ring burner
Gasheizung *f* gas[-fired] heating, gas-fuel firing
Gasherstellung *f s.* Gaserzeugung
Gashydrat *m* gas hydrate *(any of a group of clathrate compounds)*
Gashydratbildung *f* formation of gas hydrates
gasieren *(text)* to gas
Gasieren *n (text)* gassing, gas singeing
Gasinchromieren *n* gas chromizing

Gasindustrie *f* gas industry
Gasinjektion *f* gas injection
Gas-Ion *n* gaseous ion
Gaskalk *m (agric)* gas lime
Gaskalorimeter *n* gas calorimeter
Gaskammerofen *m (ceram)* gas chamber kiln
Gaskappe *f (petrol)* gas cap
Gaskappendruck *m (petrol)* gas cap drive
Gaskappenlagerstätte *f (petrol)* gas cap-drive field (reservoir)
Gaskette *f (el ch)* gas cell
Gaskohle *f* gas[-making] coal
Gaskohlung *f* gas carburizing *(of steel)*
Gaskohlungsofen *m* gas-carburizing furnace
Gaskoks *m* gas[-house] coke
Gaskomponente *f* gaseous component
Gaskompressor *m* gas compressor
Gaskonstante *f* gas[-law] constant
~/allgemeine [general] gas constant
~/molare molar gas constant
~/universelle *s.* ~/allgemeine
Gaskonzentration *f* gas concentration (strength)
Gaskopf *m (petrol)* gas cap
Gaskühler *m* gas cooler
Gaskühlung *f* gas cooling
Gasküvette *f (spectr)* gas cell
Gaslagerstätte *f* gas field (reservoir)
Gaslaser *m* gas laser
Gasleitung *f* gas main
Gaslift *m* gas lift
Gasliften *n s.* Gasliftförderung
Gasliftförderung *f* gas lift[ing], gas-lift transport
Gasliftventil *n* gas-lift valve
Gasliftverfahren *n* gas-lift method
Gas-Liquidus-Chromatographie *f s.* Gas-flüssig-Chromatographie
Gaslöslichkeit *f* gas solubility
Gaslöslichkeitskonstante *f* Henry's law constant
Gasmaske *f* gas mask
Gasmaus *f s.* Gassammelröhre
Gasmenge *f*/**übergehende (übertragene)** *(hyd)* quantity of gas transferred
Gasmesser *m* gas meter
~/nasser wet gas meter
~/trockener dry gas meter
Gasmuffelofen *m (ceram)* gas muffle kiln
Gasnitrieren *n* gas nitriding *(of steel)*
Gasöl *n (petrol)* gas oil
~/bei Normaldruck gewonnenes atmospheric gas oil, AGO
~/leichtes light gas oil, LGO
~/schweres heavy gas oil, HGO
Gasöldestillat *n* gas-oil distillate
Gasöl-Fermentation *f (biot)* gas-oil fermentation (process)
Gas-Öl-Separator *m (petrol)* oil/gas separator, gas[-oil] separator
~/mehrstufiger multistage [oil/gas] separator
Gas-Öl-Trennung *f (petrol)* gas separation
Gas-Öl-Trennvorrichtung *f s.* Gas-Öl-Separator
Gasöl-Verfahren *n s.* Gasöl-Fermentation
Gas-Öl-Verhältnis *n* gas/oil ratio
Gasometer *m* 1. *(lab)* gasometer; 2. *s.* Gasbehälter
gaspermeabel gas-permeable
Gasphase *f* gas phase; vapour phase *(in high-pressure hydrogenation)*
Gasphasechlorierung *f* gas-phase chlorination
Gasphasehydrierofen *m* vapour-phase converter
Gasphasehydrierung *f* vapour-phase hydrogenation
Gasphasekatalysator *m* vapour-phase catalyst
Gasphasekracken *n* vapour-phase cracking
Gasphaseninhibitor *m* vapour-phase inhibitor, V.P.I.
Gasphasenisomerisierung *f* vapour-phase isomerization
Gasphasenitrierung *f* vapour-phase nitration
Gasphasenoxidation *f* vapour-phase oxidation
Gasphaseofen *m* vapour-phase converter
Gasphasepolymerisation *f* vapour-phase polymerization, gaseous (gas-phase) polymerization
Gasphasereaktion *f* gas-phase reaction
~/homogene homogeneous gas-phase reaction
Gasphaseverfahren *n* vapour-phase process
Gaspipette *f* gas pipette
~/Hempelsche Hempel gas pipette
Gasquelle *f* gas well
Gasraum *m* gas space; *(pap)* top *(of a digester)*
Gasreaktion *f* gas[eous] reaction
Gasreduktion *f (met)* gaseous reduction
Gasreiniger *m* gas cleaner *(esp for removing solid and liquid components)*; gas purifier *(esp for removing gaseous components)*
Gasreinigung *f* gas cleaning (clarification) *(esp removing solid and liquid components)*; gas purification *(esp removing gaseous components)*
Gasreinigungsmasse *f* gas-purifying material
Gasretorte *f* gas retort
Gasretortenkoks *m* gas-retort coke
Gasretortenteer *m* gas-retort tar
Gasruß *m* gas black (soot)
Gassammelleitung *f* gas collecting main *(of a coke-oven battery)*
Gassammelröhre *f* gas collection (collecting) tube, gas sampling tube (pipette), sample tube
Gassäule *f* gas column
Gasscheider *m s.* Gas-Öl-Separator
Gasschieber *m* gas valve
Gasschiefer *m* cannel (candle, jet) coal
Gasschmelzschweißen *n* gas (autogenous) welding
Gasschutzgerät *n* chemical cartridge respirator
~ ohne Maske mouthpiece type of cartridge respirator
Gasschweißen *n s.* Gasschmelzschweißen
Gasschwund *m (text)* gas fading
Gassengen *n (text)* gas singeing, gassing
Gassengmaschine *f (text)* gas-singeing machine

Gasseparator *m s.* Gas-Öl-Separator
Gas-Solidus-Chromatographie *f s.* Gas-fest-Chromatographie
Gasspüler *m* bubbler
Gasspürgerät *n* gas detector
~ **für Halogenide** halide leak detector
Gasstrippen *n (hyd)* gas stripping
Gasstrom *m* gas stream (flow)
~**/[ungleich] geteilter** *(chromat)* split flow
Gasstromteiler *m (chromat)* [sample] splitter
Gasströmung *f* gas flow
Gast *m* guest *(within a host molecular entity)*
Gastatom *n* guest atom
Gastechnik *f* gas technology
Gasteer *m* gas[works] tar
Gastelement *n* guest element
Gastheorie *f***/kinetische** kinetic theory of gases
Gasthermometer *n* gas thermometer
~ **konstanten Drucks** constant-pressure gas thermometer
~ **konstanten Volumens** constant-volume gas thermometer
~ **konstanter Dichte** *s.* ~ konstanten Volumens
Gastkomponente *f* guest component
Gastkristall *m (geol)* chadacryst, xenocryst
Gastmolekül *n* guest (enclosed) molecule
Gastrennanlage *f s.* Gas-Öl-Separator
Gastrennung *f* gas separation
Gastrieb *m (petrol)* gas drive
Gastrieblagerstätte *f* gas-drive field (reservoir)
Gasübergangskoeffizient *m (hyd)* gas transfer coefficient
~ **für Sauerstoff** oxygen transfer coefficient
gasundurchlässig impervious (impermeable) to gas, gastight, gasproof
Gasung *f s.* Gasen 2.
Gasuntersuchungsapparat *m* gas analysis apparatus
Gasventil *n* gas valve
Gasventilator *m* gas fan
Gasverdichter *m* gas compressor
Gasverflüssigung *f* gas liquefaction
Gasverflüssigungsanlage *f* **nach Linde** Linde refrigerator
Gasvergiftung *f* gas poisoning, gassing
Gasverteilleitung *f* distribution gas main
Gasverteilungschromatographie *f s.* Gas-flüssig-Chromatographie
Gasverteilungsfritte *f* gas diffuser stone, air stone, fritted gas bubbler, sintered bubbler
Gasvorlage *f* gas collecting main *(of a coke-oven battery)*
Gaswaage *f* gas [density] balance, dasymeter
Gaswäsche *f* 1. gas washing (scrubbing), wet gas cleaning; 2. gas-washing system
~ **im Turmwäscher (Waschturm)** gas scrubbing
Gaswaschen *n s.* Gaswäsche 1.
Gaswäscher *m* gas washer, scrubber
Gaswaschflasche *f (lab)* gas-washing bottle
~**/Drechselsche** Drechsel bottle
Gaswaschsystem *n* gas-washing system
Gaswaschturm *m* gas-washing tower, scrubbing tower, tower scrubber
Gaswasser *n* ammonia water (liquor), ammoniacal (gas) liquor
Gaswechselquotient *m* gas exchange quotient
Gaswegumschaltung *f (chromat)* backflush
Gaswerk *n* gasworks, gas[-making] plant
Gaswerkskoks *m* gas[-house] coke
Gaswerksretorte *f* gas[-making] retort
Gaswerksteer *m* gas[works] tar
Gaszähler *m* gas meter
~**/nasser** wet gas meter
~**/trockener** dry gas meter
Gaszelle *f (el ch)* gas cell
gaszementieren to gas-carburize *(steel)*
Gaszentrifuge *f* gas centrifuge
Gaszentrifugenverfahren *n* gas centrifuge process *(for separating isotopes)*
Gaszentrifugieren *n* gas centrifugation
Gaszuführung *f* 1. gas supply (inlet) *(process)*; 2. gas inlet *(junction)*
Gaszuführungsrohr *n* gas feed pipe (tube), gas inlet pipe, gas conductor
Gaszuleitung *f s.* Gaszuführung
Gaszustand *m* gaseous state
Gatsch *m* [paraffin] slack wax
Gattermann-Koch-Synthese *f* Gattermann-Koch reaction *(for preparing phenolic aldehydes)*
Gattermann-Reaktion *f* Gattermann reaction *(for preparing halogen-substituted aromatic compounds)*
Gatterrührer *m* gate agitator (mixer), *(with horizontal paddles between stationary fingers also)* shear-bar agitator (mixer)
Gattungsname *m* generic name (term)
gauche-Konformation *f* gauche conformation, G *(torsion angle ± 120°)*
Gaucher-Krankheit *f*, **Gaucher-Syndrom** *n (med)* Gaucher's disease *(deficiency of glucocerebrosidase)*
gaußförmig *(anal)* Gaussian
Gauß-Orbital *n* Gaussian-type orbital, GTO
Gauß-Profil *n (spectr)* Gaussian band shape
Gautschbrett *n (pap)* couch
Gautschbruchbütte *f (pap)* couch box (pit)
Gautsche *f (pap)* couch press
gautschen *(pap)* to couch, to line, to laminate
Gautscher *m (pap)* couchman, coucher
Gautschpresse *f (pap)* couch press
Gautschwalze *f (pap)* couch[-press] roll, couching roll
~**/obere** top couch-press roll
~**/untere** bottom couch-press roll
GAW *s.* Gesamtanionenwert
Gay-Lussac-Gesetz *n* Gay-Lussac law
Gay-Lussac-Turm *m* Gay-Lussac tower
Gaze *f* gauze
GDP *s.* Guanosindiphosphat

geäschert/in der Grube *(tann)* pit-limed
gebändert *(geol)* banded
Gebiet *n* region, range *(as of a diagram or scale)*
~ **der Normalbelichtung** *(phot)* region of correct (normal) exposure, straight[-line] portion, straight line *(of the characteristic curve)*
~ **der Röntgenstrahlen** X-ray region (range)
~ **der Überbelichtung** *(phot)* region of overexposure, shoulder, knee *(of the characteristic curve)*
~ **der Unterbelichtung** *(phot)* region of underexposure, toe, foot *(of the characteristic curve)*
~/**geradliniges** *s.* ~ der Normalbelichtung
~/**plastisches** plastic range
Gebilde *n* entity
~/**disperses** dispersed entity
~/**elementares** elementary entity
~/**individuelles** individual entity
~/**kolloid[al]es** colloidal entity
~/**komplexes** complex entity
~/**mehrkerniges** polynuclear entity
~/**molekulares** molecular entity
~/**natürliches** natural entity
~/**physikalisches** physical entity
~/**strukturelles** structural entity
Gebirge *n (mine)* ground
Gebläse *n* fan, [air] blower, air blast system
Gebläsebrenner *m* blowlamp, blowtorch, bench blowpipe, blast (nozzle-mix) burner, blast (glass blower's) lamp
Gebläseentstauber *m* dust collecting fan, fan-impeller collector
Gebläselampe *f s.* Gebläsebrenner
Gebläseluft *f s.* Gebläsewind
Gebläsemischen *n* air (gas) agitation
Gebläsemischer *m* air-agitated mixer
geblasen/vor der Lampe *(glass)* lamp-blown, lampworked
Gebläse[schacht]ofen *m* blast furnace *(for obtaining iron)*
~ **für NE-Metalle** non-ferrous blast furnace
Gebläsewind *m* [air] blast
Gebräu *n* brew
gebrauchen/übermäßig to overuse *(e.g. pesticides)*
Gebrauchsanweisung *f* direction[s] for use
Gebrauchsdauer *f* [liquid] pot life *(of reaction coatings)*
Gebrauchseigenschaft *f (text)* wearing quality
Gebrauchsfähigkeitsdauer *f* shelf (storage) life
gebrauchsfertig ready for use, ready-to-use
Gebrauchsleistung *f* performance
Gebrauchstemperatur *f* service temperature
Gebrauchswasser *n s.* Brauchwasser
Gebrauchswertdauer *f* working (operating, useful, service) life
gebraucht spent *(e.g. solution)*
gebunden combined; bonded, bound, linked, connected *(chemical-bond theory)* • **in gebundener Form** in combined form, in the combined state
~/**chemisch** chemically bonded
~/**doppelt** doubly bonded
~/**dreifach** triply bonded
~/**einfach** singly bonded
~/**einpolar (homöopolar)** *s.* ~/kovalent
~/**keramisch** ceramic-bonded
~/**koordinativ** coordinate, complexed
~/**kovalent** covalently bonded
~/**organisch** organically bonded
~/**unpolar** *s.* ~/kovalent
~/**vierfach** quadruply bonded
~/**vierfach koordinativ** four-coordinate[d]
~/**zweifach** doubly bonded
Gedächtniseffekt *m (nucl)* memory effect
gedeckt/einseitig *(pap)* single-lined
~/**zweiseitig** double-lined
gediegen *(min, met)* virgin, elemental, native, massive
gedoktert *(petrol)* doctor-sweet
geeicht/auf Ablauf (Auslauf) calibrated to deliver, calibrated for delivery *(by an authority)*
~/**auf Einguß** calibrated to contain, calibrated for content *(by an authority)*
Geer-Alterung *f (rubber)* Geer oven ageing
Geer-Alterungsprüfung *f (rubber)* Geer oven test
Geer-Ofen *m (rubber)* Geer oven
Geer-Ofenalterung *f (rubber)* Geer oven ageing
Gefahrenklasse *f* danger class
gefährlich dangerous, harmful
Gefährlichkeit *f* dangerousness, harmfulness
Gefälle *n* drop, slope; *(quantitatively)* gradient • **mit** ~ slanted *(e.g. pipe)*
Gefällezuführung *f* gravity feed
gefärbt coloured *(naturally)*; *(by human agent:)* dyed, *(Am also)* colored
~/**deutlich** appreciably coloured
~/**dunkel** dark-coloured
~/**im Holländer (Stoff)** *(pap)* dyed in the beater (stuff), *(Am also)* pulp-colored
~/**in der Flocke** *(text)* stock-dyed
~/**in der Masse** *s.* ~/im Holländer
~/**in der Wolle** *(text)* stock-dyed
~/**schwach** feebly (weakly) coloured
Gefäß *n* vessel, receptacle, container, *(made of glass or earthenware also)* jar, *(if spherical also)* bulb, *(if large also)* vat
~/**Geißlersches (Mohrsches)** Geissler-Mohr absorption (potash) bulb
~/**Weinhold-Dewarsches** Dewar [flask, vessel] *(for holding liquid gases)*
gefäßerweiternd vasodilating
Gefäßerweiterungsmittel *n (pharm)* vasodilator, vasodepressor
gefäßkontrahierend *s.* gefäßverengend
Gefäßofen *m (met)* vessel (closed-vessel) furnace
gefäßverengend vasoconstrictive
Gefäßverengungsmittel *n (pharm)* vasoconstrictor
Gefäßversuch *m (agric)* pot experiment (study, test)
Gefluder *n*, **Gefluter** *n (min tech)* sluice
geformt/von Hand *(ceram)* hand-moulded

Gefrierapparat *m* freezing apparatus, freezer
Gefrier-Brandzeichen *n (tann)* freeze brand
gefrieren to freeze, to congeal
~ **lassen** to freeze, to congeal
~/schnell to quick-freeze
Gefrieren *n* freezing, congealing, congelation
~ **in bewegter Luft** [air-]blast freezing
~/langsames slow freezing
~/schnelles quick (fast, sharp) freezing
Gefrierentwässerung *f* 1. *(hyd)* freeze-thaw process *(sludge treatment)*; 2. *s.* Gefriertrocknung
Gefriergeschwindigkeit *f* freezing rate (velocity)
Gefrierkonservierung *f* freezing of foods, frozen-pack
Gefrierkurve *f* freezing[-point] curve
Gefrierlagerung *f* freezing (frozen) storage
Gefrierpunkt *m* freezing point (temperature), frost point
Gefrierpunktmesser *m* cryoscope
Gefrierpunktsdepression *f s.* Gefrierpunktserniedrigung
Gefrierpunktserniedrigung *f* freezing-point depression (lowering)
~/molale (molare, molekulare) molal freezing-point[-depression] constant, molal (molar, molecular) depression constant, cryoscopic constant
Gefrierschutzmittel *n* antifreeze [agent]
Gefrierschutzprotein *n (bioch)* antifreeze protein
gefriertrocknen to freeze-dry, to lyophilize, *(food also)* to dehydrofreeze
Gefriertrockner *m* freeze dryer (drying apparatus)
Gefriertrocknung *f* freeze drying, lyophilization, *(food also)* dehydrofreezing
Gefriertrocknungsanlage *f s.* Gefriertrockner
Gefrierverfahren *n (hyd)* freezing [desalination] process
Gefüge *n (met)* [grain] structure, grain; *(geol)* rock fabric, *(relating to the larger features:)* structure, *(relating to the smaller features:)* texture
~/bainitisches *s.* ~ der Zwischenstufe
~ **der oberen Zwischenstufe** *(met)* upper bainite
~ **der unteren Zwischenstufe** *(met)* lower bainite
~ **der Zwischenstufe** *(met)* bainite [structure], bainitic structure
~/schiefriges *(geol)* schistose structure
Gefügebestandteil *m* structural consituent, *(coal also)* maceral
Gefügekunde *f (geol)* petrofabrics
gefügelos *(met, geol)* structureless, devoid of structure, *(relating to the smaller features:)* textureless, devoid of texture
gefüllt/mit Füllstoffen *(pap, tann)* filled, loaded; *(rubber)* loaded, pigmented
gegenblasen *(glass)* to blow back *(in the blow-and-blow process)*
Gegenblasen *n (glass)* counter blow *(in the blow-and-blow process)*
Gegendruck *m* counterpressure, back pressure
Gegendruckabfüllapparat *m*, **Gegendruckfüller** *m* counterpressure (isobarometric) filler (racker)
gegeneinanderlaufend contrarotating *(rolls)*
Gegenelektrode *f* counterelectrode
Gegen-EMK *f* counter (back) electromotive force, counter (back) e.m.f.
Gegenfluß *m s.* Gegenstrom
Gegengewicht *n s.* Gegenmasse
Gegengift *n s.* Gegenmittel
Gegenion *n* counterion, gegenion
Gegenladung *f* counter charge
gegenläufig counterrotating, contrarotating
Gegenmasse *f* counterweight, counterpoise
Gegenmaßnahme *f* remedial measure
Gegenmittel *n (tox)* antidote
Gegenmonomer[e] *n* comonomer
Gegenreaktion *f* opposing reaction, opposed (oppositely directed) reaction
Gegensinn-RNA *f (bioch)* antisense RNA
Gegenstrom *m* countercurrent [flow], counterflow
• **im** ~ countercurrent[ly], in countercurrent, in counterflow
Gegenstromapparat *m s.* 1. Gegenstromklassierer; 2. Gegenstromextraktionsapparat
Gegenstromauswaschung *f* countercurrent washing
Gegenstromchromatographie *f* countercurrent chromatography
Gegenstromdekantation *f* countercurrent decantation
Gegenstromdestillation *f* rectification
~/diskontinuierliche batch rectification
~/kontinuierliche (stetige) continuous rectification
~/unstetige batch rectification
Gegenströmer *m s.* Gegenstromwärmeaustauscher
Gegenstromextraktion *f* countercurrent extraction (separation)
Gegenstromextraktionsapparat *m* countercurrent contactor
~ **nach Podbielniak** Podbielniak [centrifugal] extractor, Podbielniak [centrifugal] contactor
Gegenstromfahrweise *f* countercurrent operation
Gegenstromführung *f* backward-feed operation *(as of multiple-effect evaporators)*
Gegenstromhydrolyse *f* countercurrent hydrolysis
Gegenstromklassieren *n* countercurrent (hydraulic) classification
Gegenstromklassierer *m* countercurrent (hydraulic) classifier, hydrosizer
Gegenstromkühler *m (tech)* countercurrent cooler; *(distil)* countercurrent condenser
Gegenstromkühlturm *m* countercurrent cooling tower
Gegenstromprinzip *n* countercurrent principle
• **nach dem** ~ countercurrent[ly], in countercurrent, in counterflow
Gegenstromregenerierung *f* countercurrent regeneration
Gegenstromsystem *n* countercurrent system

Gegenstromtrockner *m* countercurrent dryer
Gegenstromverdichter *m s.* Gegenstromkühler
Gegenstromverteilung *f* countercurrent distribution
Gegenstromwärmeaustauscher *m* countercurrent heat exchanger
Gegenstromwäsche *f* countercurrent washing
Gegentausch *m (bioch)* antiport *(one form of transport by a carrier)*
Gegenuhrzeigersinn/im anticlockwise
Gegenurspannung *f* counter (back) electromotive force, counter (back) e.m.f.
Gehalt *m* content, concentration; load[ing] *(of a fluid with undesired matter)* • **auf ~ prüfen** *(pharm, met)* to assay
~ an aktivem Bleichchlor (Chlor) *(pap)* available chlorine content
~ an Flüchtigem (flüchtigen Bestandteilen) volatile[-matter] content
~ an freien Fettsäuren free-fatty-acid content
~ an gelöstem Sauerstoff *(hyd)* dissolved oxygen content (level)
~ an gelösten Stoffen (Wasserinhaltsstoffen) *(hyd)* total dissolved solids [level], TDS, dissolved solids [concentration, content, level], dissolved-solute load
~ an Gesamttrockenmasse total-solids content
~ an organisch gebundenem Kohlenstoff *(hyd)* TOC (total organic carbon) content
~ an organischen Inhaltsstoffen *(hyd)* organic content
~ an suspendierten Feststoffen *(hyd)* suspended solids content (concentration, level)
~ an Trockenmasse (Trockensubstanz) solid[s] content
~ an Wasserinhaltsstoffen *(hyd)* impurity level
~ an wirksamem Bleichchlor (Chlor) *(pap)* available chlorine content
~/organischer *s.* ~ an organischen Inhaltsstoffen
~/prozentualer percentage
α-Gehalt *m (pap)* alpha cellulose content
gehärtet/selektiv selectively hydrogenated *(fat)*
~/teilweise partially hydrogenated, part-hydrogenated *(fat)*
~/ungenügend *(plast)* undercured
Gehäuse *n* casing, case, *(esp of pumps, motors, bearings)* housing, *(if rectangular also)* box, *(if domed, hemispherical or spherical also)* shell
Gehäusemesser *npl (pap)* shell bars, bars in the shell, bars on the casing *(of a perfecting engine)*
Geheimtinte *f* sympathetic (secret) ink
gehen:
~/in Lösung to go into solution, to dissolve
~ lassen to raise, to leaven *(dough)*
~/zugrunde *(nucl)* to decay, to die
gehindert/sterisch sterically hindered
Gehirnlipid *n* brain lipid
Gehman-Test *m (rubber)* Gehman torsion test
Gehölzvernichtung *f (agric)* brush control
Gehölzvernichtungsmittel *n* brushkiller, silvicide
Geigenharz *n* pine resin, rosin, colophony *(from Pinus specc.)*
Geiger-Müller-Zählrohr *n (nucl)* Geiger[-Müller] counter, Geiger[-Müller] tube, G-M counter (tube)
Geiger-Nuttall-Beziehung *f (nucl)* Geiger-Nuttall rule
Geiger-Zähler *m s.* Geiger-Müller-Zählrohr
Geißler-Röhre *f* Geissler tube
Geister *mpl (anal)* ghosts
Geisterbild *n (phot)* ghost image
Geisterpeak *m (anal)* ghost (spurious) peak
Geistersalz *n s.* Hirschhornsalz
gekocht/alkalisch *(pap)* alkaline-cooked
gekörnt granular, granulate[d], grained, grainy
Gekrätz *n (met)* sweepings, sweeps
Gekrösestein *m (min)* tripestone *(calcium sulphate)*
gekrümmt bent *(e.g. tube)*; curved *(line, surface)*
Gel *n (coll)* gel
~/resolubles (reversibles) reversible gel
~/thixotropes thixotrope
~/unelastisches rigid gel
~/wiederauflösbares reversible gel
geladen/dreifach triply charged
~/dreifach negativ trinegative
~/dreifach positiv tripositive
~/einfach singly charged
~/einfach negativ uninegative
~/einfach positiv unipositive
~/entgegengesetzt oppositely charged
~/fünffach quintuply charged
~/fünffach negativ pentanegative, quinque-negative
~/fünffach positiv pentapositive, quinque-positive
~/gleichsinnig identically charged
~/negativ negatively charged, negative
~/positiv positively charged, positive
~/vierfach quadruply charged
~/vierfach negativ tetranegative
~/vierfach positiv tetrapositive
~/zweifach doubly charged
~/zweifach negativ dinegative
~/zweifach positiv dipositive
Geländeauffüllung *f* landfill *(waste or sludge disposal)*
Geländebedarf *m* land (space) requirements *(of an industrial plant)*
Geländekampfstoff *m* persistent chemical agent
gelartig *(coll)* gel-like, gelatinous
Gelatine *f* gelatin[e]
gelatineartig gelatinous, gelatiniform
Gelatineeffekt *m (phot)* gelatin effect
Gelatineemulsion *f (phot)* gelatin emulsion
gelatinegeleimt *(pap)* gelatin-sized, glue-sized, animal-sized, animal tub-sized
gelatinehaltig gelatinous
Gelatinekultur *f* gelatin culture

Gelatineleimung *f (pap)* gelatin (glue) sizing, animal [tub-]sizing
Gelatineschicht *f (phot)* gelatin layer
Gelatineschutzschicht *f (phot)* gelatin protective layer
Gelatinesol *n* gelatin sol
gelatinieren *(food)* to gelatinize, to gelatinate, to jellify, to jelly
Gelatiniermittel *n* gelatinizing (gelling) agent, gelatinizer
Gelatinierung *f* gelatin[iz]ation, gelatification, gelation, jellification
Gelatinierungstemperatur *f* gel point, gelation temperature
gelatinös gelatinous, gelatiniform
Gel-Ausschluß-Chromatographie *f s.* Gelpermeationschromatographie
Gelb *n* yellow *(sensation or substance)*
~/Kasseler Cassel yellow, Turner's (Verona, mineral) yellow *(a basic lead chloride)*
~/Steinbühler Steinbühl (barxta) yellow, yellow ultramarine, lemon chrome, gelbin *(barium chromate)*
~/Turners *s.* -/Kasseler
Gelbätze *f s.* Gelbbeize
Gelbbeere *f***/Französische** *(dye)* Avignon berry (grain) *(from Rhamnus infectoria L.)*
Gelbbeize *f (glass)* yellow (silver) stain
Gelbbleierz *n (min)* yellow lead ore, wulfenite *(lead molybdate)*
Gelbglas *n* yellow arsenic [sulphide], king's yellow (gold), arsenic (royal) yellow, orpiment [yellow] *(technically pure arsenic(III) sulphide)*
Gelbglut *f* yellow heat
Gelbguß *m* yellow brass
Gelbharz *n* Botany Bay gum *(from Xanthorrhoea hastilis R.Br.)*
Gelbholz *n (dye)* fustic
~/Echtes old fustic *(from Chlorophora tinctoria Gaud.)*
~/Kubanisches Cuba wood *(a sort of old fustic)*
~/Ungarisches fustet, young fustic *(from Cotinus coggygria Scop.)*
Gelbholzextrakt *m* fustic extract
Gelbildung *f* gel formation, gelling, gelation, jellification
Gelbin *n* gelbin *(calcium chromate)*
Gelbkörperreifungshormon *n* luteinizing hormone, LH, interstitial-cell-stimulating hormone, ICSH, prolan B
Gelbmessing *n high-zinc brass containing 20 to 45 % of zinc*
Gelbstich *m*, **Gelbstichigkeit** *f* yellow cast, yellowish tinge
Gelbstoff *m* fulvic acid *(any of several water-soluble humic acids)*
Gelbstroh *n (pap)* straw
Gelbstrohstoff *m (pap)* coarse straw pulp, [yellow mechanical] straw pulp
Gelbton *m* yellow shade
Gelbware *f (ceram)* yellow (cane) ware
Gelbwerden *n (pap)* yellowing
Gelbwurz[el] *f* turmeric, curcuma, Indian saffron, Curcuma longa L.
Gelchromatographie *f* gel [permeation] chromatography, GPC
Gelee *n* jelly • **zu ~ erstarren** to gelatinize, to gelatinate, *(Am also)* to jellify
Gelée royale *f (pharm)* royal jelly, queen-bee's nutrient jelly
Geleffekt *m (plast)* gel effect, Trommsdorff effect
geleimt *(pap)* sized
~/doppelt double-sized
~/mit Gelatine gelatin-sized, glue-sized, animal-sized, animal tub-sized
~/mit Natronwasserglas silicate-sized
~/mit Tierleim *s.* ~/mit Gelatine
1/2geleimt half-sized, 1/2 sized
1/4geleimt quarter-sized, 1/4 sized
Geleinschluß *m (biot)* incorporation into a gel, gel enclosure *(of enzymes)*
Gelelektrophorese *f (anal)* gel electrophoresis
Gelenkregion *f (bioch)* hinge region *(of the heavy chain of immunoglobulin)*
Gelfiltration *f* gel filtration, molecular exclusion (sieve) chromatography
Gelharz *n (hyd)* gel-type resin, isoporous resin
Geliereinheit *f* **des Pektins** pectin grade
gelieren *(coll, food)* to gel[ate], to jelly
Gelierkraft *f* gelling quality
Geliermittel *n*, **Gelierstoff** *m* gelatinizing (gelling) agent, gelatinizer
Gelierung *f (coll, food)* gelation, jellification
Gelierungstemperatur *f* gel point, gelation temperature
gelinde gentle, slight *(e.g. heating)*
Gelmatrix *f (bioch)* gel matrix
Gelose *f* gelose, *(broadly)* agar [gel], agar-agar, Japan agar (isinglass), Chinese gelatin
Gelöste *n (anal)* dissolved solids, DS, solute [material]
Gelöst-O_2-... *s.* Gelöstsauerstoff...
Gelöstsauerstoff *m* dissolved oxygen, DO
Gelöstsauerstoffgehalt *m (hyd)* dissolved oxygen content (level)
Gelöstsauerstoffkonzentration *f (hyd)* dissolved oxygen concentration
Gelpermeationschromatographie *f* gel [permeation] chromatography, GPC
Gelpunkt *m* gel point *(polycondensation)*
Gelsäure *f* gel column, *(anal also)* molecular-exclusion column
Gelseminsäure *f* gelseminic acid, scopoletin, 7-hydroxy-6-methoxycoumarin
Gel-Sol-Gel-Umwandlung *f* gel-sol-gel transformation
Gel-Sol-Übergang *m* gel-sol transition
Gel-Sol-Umwandlung *f* gel-sol transformation, peptization, solation

Gelstruktur *f* gel-type structure *(of an ion-exchange resin)*
Gelteilchen *n* gel particle
Gelteilchengehalt *m (plast)* gel content
Gelteilchenzählung *f (plast)* gel count
Gelzeit *f* gel[ling] time
Gelzustand *m (coll)* gel state (condition) • **in den ~ übergehen** to gel
gem- *s.* geminal
Gemeinschaftskläranlage *f (hyd)* municipal-industrial waste treatment plant
Gemenge *n* solids mixture, bulk blend; *(glass)* batch
~/scherbenfreies *(glass)* raw batch
Gemengehaus *n (glass)* batch house
Gemengemischer *m (glass)* batch mixer
Gemengesatz *m (glass)* batch formula
Gemengespeicher *m (glass)* batch charger (feeder)
Gemengestein *m (glass)* batch stone *(a defect)*
Gemengteil *m (min)* constituent, component; ingredient *(of a bulk blend)*
~/akzessorischer accessory constituent (component)
geminal geminal, gem- *(two identical substituents on the same carbon atom)*
Gemisch *n* mixture, mix
~/azeotropes azeotropic mixture, azeotrope, constant-boiling-point mixture
~/binäres binary mixture
~/dystektisches dystectic mixture *(a mixture having a maximum melting point)*
~/eutektisches eutectic [mixture]
~/inniges intimate mixture, blend
~/Johnsons Johnson's mixture *(a pesticide)*
~/optisch-inaktives optically inactive compound
~/racemisches racemic mixture
~/reduzierendes reduction mixture
~/tonfreies *(ceram)* non-clay body
Gemischtphase *f (petrol)* mixed phase
Gemischtphasekracken *n (petrol)* mixed-phase cracking
gemittelt average
Gen *n* gene, [DNA] cistron
~/springendes *s.* Transposon
Genaktivierung *f (bioch)* gene activation
Genamplifikation *f (biot)* gene amplification
Genauguß *m* precision casting
Genauigkeit *f* accuracy, *(esp anal)* precision
Genauigkeitsgrad *m* degree of accuracy
Generator *m* producer, generator *(for manufacturing gas or steam)*
Generatorbrennstoff *m* generator fuel
Generatorgas *n* producer gas
Generatorgasgleichgewicht *n* producer-gas equilibrium
Generatorgaserzeugung *f* producer gas generation
Generatorkohle *f* producer coal
Generatorschacht *m* generator *(proper, the chamber for holding the fuel)*
Generatorverfahren *n***[/englisches]** *(biot)* trickling generator process, generator method *(of acetification)*
generieren to generate *(e.g. reactive species)*
Generierung *f* generation *(as of reactive species)*
Genese *f*, **Genesis** *f* genesis *(as of coal or petroleum)*
Genexpression *f* gene expression
genießbar edible, esculent, comestible
Genießbarkeit *f* edibility
Genin *n* genin *(non-carbohydrate portion of glycosides related to sterols)*
Genklonierung *f (biot)* gene cloning
Genmanipulation *f (biot)* gene (genetic) manipulation
Gentechnik *f (biot)* genetic technique
Gentechnologie *f (biot)* gene (genetic) technology, genetic engineering
Gentianaviolett *n* gentian violet *(a mixture of pararosaniline derivatives)*
Gentisinsäure *f* gentisic acid, 2,5-dihydroxybenzoic acid
Gentransfer *m*, **Genübertragung** *f (biot)* gene transfer
Genußfett *n s.* Speisefett
Genußsäure *f* culinary (food) acid, edible [organic] acid
Genverpflanzung *f (biot)* gene transfer
Genvervielfachung *f (biot)* gene amplification
Geochemie *f* geochemistry
Geochemiker *m* geochemist
geochemisch geochemical
Geode *f (geol)* amygdule, amygdale, geode
geordnet/sterisch stereoregular
Geosphäre *f* geosphere
gepackt/dicht *(cryst)* close-packed
~/hexagonal dicht hexagonal close-packed, hcp
~/kubisch dicht cubic close-packed, ccp
gepastet *(tann)* paste-dried
gepreßt/trocken *(ceram)* dry-pressed
geprüft und anerkannt/amtlich scheduled *(e.g. pesticides)*
gequantelt quantized
geradkettig straight-chain, unbranched-chain
Geradsichtspektroskop *n* direct-vision spectroscope
geradzahlig even-number[ed] *(e.g. fatty acid)*
Geranial *n* geranial, citral a, *trans*-3,7-dimethylocta-2,6-dienal
Geraniol *n* geraniol *(either of two dimethyloctadienol isomers)*
Geranium[gras]öl *n***/Ostindisches** Indian geranium (grass) oil, rusa oil *(from Cymbopogon martini (Roxb.) Stapf)*
Geraniumsäure *f* geranic acid *(either of two dimethylheptadienecarboxylic acid isomers)*
Gerät *n* 1. *(ch)* apparatus, *(if no specific term otherwise implicit:)* device; instrument *(esp for measuring)*; 2. *(collectively:)* apparatus[es], *(esp Am)* equipment

~ **für den Verkokungstest** apparatus for determining carbon residue
~/**registrierendes (selbstschreibendes)** [self-]recording instrument, recorder
~ **zur Kohlensäurebestimmung** carbon dioxide apparatus
Geräte *npl* apparatus[es], *(esp Am)* equipment
~/**wissenschaftliche** scientific apparatus, research equipment
Gerätefehler *m* instrumental error
Gerätekonstante *f* apparatus constant
Gerätepark *m*, **Gerätschaften** *pl s.* Geräte
Gerbanlage *f* tanning plant, tanyard, tannery
Gerbbrühe *f* tanning (tan, tanner's) liquor, ooze
~/**süße** mellow tan liquor
Gerbeffekt *m* tanning effect
gerben to tan
~/**mit Chromsalzen** to chrome
Gerber *m* tanner
Gerberbaum *m* beam *(for mechanical treatment of hides)*
Gerberbock *m* horse
Gerberei *f* 1. tannage, tannery, tanning; 2. tanning plant, tanyard, tannery
~/**eigentliche** tanning proper
Gerbereiabwasser *n (hyd)* tannery waste
Gerbereichemie *f* chemistry of tanning (leather manufacture)
Gerbereichemiker *m* leather chemist
Gerberlohe *f* tan bark
~/**ausgelaugte** spent tan
Gerberrot *n* tanner's red, phlobaphene
Gerberwolle *f (text)* slipe wool
Gerbextrakt *m* tanning (tannin) extract
Gerbfaß *n* tanning drum
Gerinnen *n* coagulation, congelation, curdling
Gerbgrube *f* tanning (tan, suspender) pit, tannin vat
Gerbholz *n* tanwood
Gerblösung *f* tanning (tannin) solution
Gerbmaterial *n s.* Gerbmittel
Gerbmethode *f* tanning method
Gerbmittel *n* tanning material, tan
~/**pflanzliches** vegetable tan
Gerbmittelauszug *m* tanning (tannin) extract
Gerbmittelvorrat *m* tannery stock
Gerböl *n* tanning oil
Gerbrinde *f* tan (tanner's, tanning) bark
Gerbsäure *f* tannic acid, *(specif)* gallotannic acid
gerbsäurehaltig tanniferous
Gerbsäuremesser *m* barkometer, barktrometer, tannometer
Gerbstoff *m* 1. tanning agent, *(if of vegetable origin also)* tannin; 2. *s.* Gerbmittel
~/**gebundener** fixed tannin
~/**kondensierter** condensed (non-hydrolyzable) tannin
~/**künstlicher** *s.* ~/synthetischer
~/**pflanzlicher** [vegetable] tannin
~/**synthetischer** syntan, synthetic tannin (tanning agent)
Gerbstoffauszug *m* tanning (tannin) extract
~/**unsulfitierter** ordinary tanning extract
Gerbstoffbrühe *f s.* Gerbbrühe
Gerbstoffextrakt *m* tanning (tannin) extract
Gerbstoffgehalt *m* tannin content
gerbstoffhaltig tanniferous
Gerbstoffixierung *f* tannin fixation
Gerbstofflösung *f* tannin solution
Gerbstoffpflanze *f* tanniferous (tanning) plant
Gerbstoffrot *n* tanner's red, phlobaphene
Gerbtrommel *f* tanning drum
Gerbung *f* 1. tannage, tanning, tannery; 2. *(phot)* tanning
~/**beschleunigte** accelerated tannage
~/**eigentliche** tanning proper
~/**pflanzliche** vegetable tannage
~/**synthetische** syntan tannage
~/**vegetabilische** vegetable tannage
Gerbverfahren *n* tanning method (process)
Gerbvermögen *n* tanning power
Gerbvorgang *m* tanning process
Gerbwert *m* tanning value
Gerbwirkung *f* tanning action; tanning effect
Gerichtschemie *f* forensic (legal) chemistry
Gerichtschemiker *m* forensic (legal) chemist
geriffelt, gerillt ribbed, grooved
geringinkohlt *(coal)* low-rank
geringwertig low-grade, poor
gerinnbar coagulable, congealable
Gerinnbarkeit *f* coagulability
Gerinne *n (min tech)* sluice, trough, launder
gerinnen to coagulate, to congeal, to curd[le], to clot, *(relating to milk also)* to sour
~ **lassen** to coagulate, to congeal, to curd[le]
Gerinnen *n* coagulation, congelation, curdling, clotting, *(relating to milk also)* souring
Gerinnsel *n* clot, curd
Gerinnung *f s.* Gerinnen
Gerinnungseigenschaften *fpl* curd characteristics *(of milk)*
Gerinnungsfaktor *m* clotting factor *(any of a group of compounds involved in blood clotting)*
gerinnungshemmend anticoagulant
Gerinnungspunkt *m* coagulation (curdling) point, *(milk also)* setting point
gerippt ribbed
German *n* germane, *(specif)* GeH_4 monogermane, germane, germanium tetrahydride
Germanat *n* germanate *(salt or ester of germanic acid)*
Germanium *n* Ge germanium
Germanium(II)-bromid *n* germanium(II) bromide, germanium dibromide, germanous bromide
Germanium(IV)-bromid *n* germanium(IV) bromide, germanium tetrabromide, germanic bromide
Germaniumbromoform *n* germanium bromoform, *tribromogermane
Germanium(II)-chlorid *n* germanium(II) chloride, germanium dichloride, germanous chloride

Germanium(IV)-chlorid *n* germanium(IV) chloride, germanium tetrachloride, germanic chloride
Germaniumchloroform *n* germanium chloroform, *trichlorogermane
Germaniumdi... *s. a.* Germanium(II)-...
Germaniumdioxid *n s.* Germanium(IV)-oxid
Germaniumdisulfid *n s.* Germanium(IV)-sulfid
Germanium(II)-fluorid *n* germanium(II) fluoride, germanium difluoride, germanous fluoride
Germanium(IV)-fluorid *n* germanium(IV) fluoride, germanium tetrafluoride, germanic fluoride
Germaniumhexahydrid *n* germanium hexahydride, digermane
Germaniumimid *n* germanium imide
Germanium(II)-iodid *n* germanium(II) iodide, germanium diiodide, germanous iodide
Germanium(IV)-iodid *n* germanium(IV) iodide, germanium tetraiodide, germanic iodide
Germaniummonosulfid *n s.* Germanium(II)-sulfid
Germaniummonoxid *n s.* Germanium(II)-oxid
Germanium(II)-nitrid *n* germanium(II) nitride, trigermanium dinitride
Germanium(IV)-nitrid *n* germanium(IV) nitride, trigermanium tetranitride
Germaniumoctahydrid *n* germanium octahydride, trigermane
Germanium(II)-oxid *n* germanium(II) oxide, germanium monooxide, germanous oxide
Germanium(IV)-oxid germanium(IV) oxide, germanium dioxide, germanic oxide
Germaniumoxidchlorid *n* germanium dichloride oxide
Germanium(IV)-oxidhydrat *n* soluble germanium dioxide
Germaniumsäure *f* germanic acid
Germanium(II)-sulfid *n* germanium(II) sulphide, germanium monosulphide, germanous sulphide
Germanium(IV)-sulfid *n* germanium(IV) sulphide, germanium disulphide, germanic sulphide
Germaniumtetra... *s. a.* Germanium(IV)...
Germaniumtetrahydrid *n* germanium tetrahydride, monogermane, germane
Germizid *n* germicide
Germylierung *f* germylation
Gerstenberg-Komplektor *m* Gerstenberg complector plant *(for manufacturing margarine)*
Gerstenmalz *n* barley malt, malted barley
Gerstenmehl *n* barley flour, *(if coarsely ground:)* barley meal
Gerstenstärke *f* barley starch
Gerstenzucker *m* barley sugar
Geruch *m* smell, *(esp if unpleasant:)* odour, *(if pleasant:)* scent, *(Am)* perfume, *(if pleasant but penetrating:)* aroma
~/angenehmer scent, pleasant smell
~/artfremder foreign odour
~/beißender pungent smell
~/durchdringender penetrating odour
~/frucht[art]iger fruity odour (fragrance)
~ nach faulen Eiern rotten-egg odour
~/obstartiger *s.* ~/frucht[art]iger
~/penetranter penetrating odour
~/ranziger rancid odour
~/stechender pungent smell
~/übler bad smell, stench, stink
~/unangenehmer [unpleasant] odour
geruchlos inodorous, odourless, odour-free
• **~ machen** to deodorize
Geruchlosigkeit *f* inodorousness
geruchsaktiv odour-bearing, odorous
Geruchsbekämpfung *f* odour control
Geruchsbelästigung *f* nasal nuisance
geruchsbeseitigend deodorant
Geruchsbeseitigung *f*, **Geruchsentfernung** *f* deodorization; *(hyd)* odour removal
geruchsbildend odour causing, odour-producing
Geruchsbildner *m* odour-causing (odour-producing) substance
geruchsfrei *s.* geruchlos
Geruchsprüfung *f* test for odour
Geruchsschwelle *f s.* Geruchsschwellenkonzentration
Geruchsschwellenkonzentration *f* threshold-odour concentration, threshold of odour, odour (nuisance) threshold
~/individuelle individual perception threshold, IPT *(odour testing)*
Geruchsschwellenwert *m (hyd)* threshold odour number, T.O.
Geruchsstoff *m* odorous substance, odour-causing, (odour-producing, odour-bearing) substance; *(food)* flavouring matter; *(cosmet)* perfume
Geruchsverbesserer *m* odour improver
Geruchsverbesserung *f* odour improvement
Geruchsverschluß *m* water seal, [siphon] trap
geruchsverursachend odour-causing, odour-producing
Gerüst *n* 1. skeleton *(as of a molecule)*; 2. *(tech)* framework
Gerüsteiweiß *n*, **Gerüsteiweißstoff** *m* structural (skeletal, fibrous) protein, scleroprotein
Gerüstkonformation *f*/**ungeordnete** *(bioch)* random coil [conformation]
Gerüstpolysaccharid *n* skeletal polysaccharide
Gerüstschwingung *f* skeletal vibration
Gerüstsilicat *n (min)* tectosilicate
Gerüststoff *m*, **Gerüstsubstanz** *f* 1. *(bioch)* skeletal substance; 2. [detergency, soap] builder *(a substance added to synthetic detergents)*
Gerüstumlagerung *f* skeletal rearrangement
Gesamtablauf *m* 1. overall course *(of a reaction)*; 2. *(hyd)* total plant discharge (effluent) *(of a sewage-treatment plant)*
Gesamtabwasseranfall *m* **eines Betriebs** flow of total plant discharge
Gesamtabwasserlast *f* **eines Betriebes** total plant discharge (effluent)

Gesamtalkali *n*, **Gesamtalkaligehalt** *m (anal)* total alkali *(calculated as potassium hydroxide)*; *(pap)* total chemical, total alkalinity *(active alkali and sodium carbonate)*
Gesamtalkalität *f (hyd)* total alkalinity
Gesamtalkaloide *npl* total alkaloids
Gesamtanionen *npl s.* Gesamtanionenwert
Gesamtanionenwert *m (hyd)* total anion content, total anion[s]
Gesamtarbeit *f (phys ch)* total work
Gesamtausbeute *f* total (overall) yield
Gesamt-Austauschkapazität *f (soil)* total exchangeable bases
Gesamtbahn[dreh]impuls *m* total orbital angular momentum
Gesamtbakterienzahl *f (hyd)* total bacterial level
Gesamtbasizität *f (tann)* overall basicity
Gesamtbelastung *f* total load *(of a balance)*
Gesamtbindungsenergie *f* total binding energy
Gesamt-BSB-Belastung *f (hyd)* total BOD (biochemical oxygen damand)
Gesamtdrehimpuls *m* total angular momentum
Gesamtdrehimpulsquantenzahl *f* total angular momentum quantum number, inner quantum number
Gesamtdruck *m* total pressure
Gesamtdurchsatz *m* total throughput
Gesamtechtheit *f (text)* all-round fastness
Gesamteigendrehimpuls *m* total electron spin angular momentum
Gesamtemissionsvermögen *n* total emissivity (emissive power)
Gesamtenergie *f* total energy
Gesamtentropie *f* total entropy
Gesamtentstaubungsgrad *m* overall collection efficiency
Gesamtfeststoffgehalt *m*, **Gesamtfeststoffmenge** *f (hyd)* total solids, T.S.
Gesamtfestsubstanz *f (rubber)* total solids, T.S., solid material
Gesamtfläche *f* 1. total area; 2. *s.* Gesamtoberfläche
Gesamtflüchtigkeit *f* overall volatility
Gesamtgehalt *m* **an organisch gebundenem Kohlenstoff** *(hyd)* total organic carbon, TOC
~ **an organischen Inhaltsstoffen** *(hyd)* overall organic substances
~ **an Organohalogenverbindungen** *(hydl* total organic halides, TOX
~ **an** SO_2 *(pap)* total sulphur dioxide
~ **an suspendierten Feststoffen** *(hyd)* total suspended solids, total solids in suspension
~ **an Trihalo[gen]methanen** *(hyd)* total trihalomethanes, TTHM level, TTHMs
Gesamtgeschwindigkeit *f* overall rate (velocity)
Gesamthärte *f (hyd)* total [water] hardness
Gesamtheizzeit *f (rubber)* curing (total vulcanizing) time
Gesamtionengehalt *m (hyd)* total ionic content
Gesamtkapazität *f (hyd)* total capacity *(of an ion exchanger)*
Gesamtkationen *npl s.* Gesamtkationenwert
Gesamtkationenwert *m (hyd)* total cation content, total cation[s]
Gesamtkohlensäure *f (hyd)* total carbon dioxide
Gesamtkohlenstoff *m (hyd)* total carbon, TC
Gesamtkontrast *m (phot)* overall contrast
Gesamtkonzentration *f* total concentration
Gesamtladung *f (el ch)* total charge
Gesamtlänge *f* contour (extended) length *(of a molecular chain)*
Gesamtlängenverhältnis *n (text)* stretch ratio
Gesamtleitfähigkeit *f*, **Gesamtleitvermögen** *n* total (resultant) conductance
Gesamtlösung *f* bulk solution
Gesamtmasse *f* total mass
Gesamtmenge *f (anal)* entire (parent) lot, entire mass
~ **an gelösten Stoffen (Wasserinhaltsstoffen)** *s.* Gehalt an gelösten Stoffen
~ **des anfallenden Betriebsabwassers** *(hyd)* total plant discharge (effluent)
Gesamtmolarität *f* total molarity
Gesamtmolzahl *f* total number of moles
Gesamtnährstoffbedarf *m* nutrient requirements
Gesamtoberfläche *f* total surface
Gesamtorbitaldrehimpuls *m* resultant orbital angular momentum
Gesamt-P *m*, **Gesamtphosphat** *n s.* Gesamtphosphor
Gesamtphosphor *m (hyd)* total [amount of] phosphorus
Gesamtpolarisation *f* total polarization
Gesamtquellung *f* total swelling
Gesamtreaktion *f* overall (total) reaction
Gesamtreaktionsgeschwindigkeit *f* overall (total) rate of reaction
Gesamtreaktionsordnung *f* overall (total) order of reaction
Gesamtrestchlorgehalt *m (hyd)* total residual chlorine
Gesamtretentionsvolumen *n (chromat)* total retention volume
Gesamtretentionszeit *f (chromat)* total retention time
Gesamtsalzgehalt *m (hyd)* total mineral level, total salts
Gesamtsauerstoffbedarf *m (hyd)* total oxygen demand, TOD
Gesamtschwebstoffe *mpl*, **Gesamtschwebstoffgehalt** *m (hyd)* total suspended solids [level], total solids in suspension
Gesamtschwefel *m (rubber)* total sulphur
Gesamtschwindung *f (ceram)* total shrinkage
Gesamt-SO_2**-Gehalt** *m (pap)* total sulphur dioxide
Gesamtspindrehimpuls *m* total electron spin angular momentum, resultant spin angular momentum

Gesamtstickstoff *m*, **Gesamtstickstoffgehalt** *m* *(anal)* total nitrogen, overall nitrogen content
Gesamtstrahlungspyrometer *n* total-radiation pyrometer
Gesamtstrom *m* total current
Gesamtteilchenzahl *f (hyd)* total particle count
Gesamttrockenmasse *f*, **Gesamttrockensubstanz** *f (hyd)* total dry solids; *(food)* total solids, T.S.
Gesamtübergangswahrscheinlichkeit *f (phys ch)* total transition probability
Gesamtumsatz *m* overall conversion
Gesamtvolumen *n* total volume
Gesamtwasserbedarf *m* total water requirements, overall water demand
Gesamtwasserentnahme *f* total water withdrawal
Gesamtwasserverbrauch *m (hyd)* total water use[d]
Gesamtwirkung *f* overall effect
Gesamtwirkungsgrad *m* overall efficiency *(as of a pump)*
~/thermischer overall thermal efficiency
Gesamtzusatzmenge *f (pap)* total make-up
Gesäß *n (glass)* siege, bench *(of a pot furnace)*
gesättigt saturated *(solution or compound)*
geschichtet lamellar
geschiefert *(geol)* schistose, schistous
Geschirr *n (tann)* vat
~/Deutsches *(pap)* stamping (hammer) mill, stamper, stamps, stocks
Geschirreinigungsmittel *n*, **Geschirrspülmittel** *n* dishwashing detergent, rinse aid for dishwashing
Geschlechtshormon *n* sex hormone
geschlossenkettig closed-chain
geschlossenzellig closed-cell *(foamed plastic)*
Geschmack *m* taste, *(if pleasant:)* flavour • **von angenehmem** ~ tasteful • **von unangenehmem** ~ distasteful
~/altöliger oiliness *(as of spoiled fats)*
~/fischiger fishy taste, fishiness
~/ranziger rancid taste
~/saurer acid taste
~/seifiger soapy taste
~/talgiger tallowy taste
geschmacklos *(ch)* tasteless, free from taste; *(food)* tasteless, insipid
Geschmacklosigkeit *f (ch)* tastelessness, freedom from taste; *(food)* tastelessness, insipidness, insipidity
Geschmacksabweichung *f* off-taste, off-flavour
Geschmacksabwertung *f s.* Geschmacksbeeinträchtigung
geschmacksaktiv taste-bearing
geschmacksbeeinträchtigend impairing the flavour (taste)
Geschmacksbeeinträchtigung *f* impairment of the flavour (taste), flavour deterioration (reversion)
Geschmacksfehler *m* flavour defect, off-flavour
geschmacksfrei tasteless, free from taste
Geschmacksfreiheit *f* tastelessness, freedom from taste
Geschmackskorrigens *n (pharm)* taste improver
Geschmacksprüfung *f* test for taste
Geschmacksschwelle[nkonzentration] *f (hyd)* taste threshold, threshold of taste
Geschmacksschwellenwert *m (hyd)* threshold taste number
Geschmacksstoff *m (food)* flavouring matter (substance); *(hyd)* taste-causing (taste-bearing) substance
geschmacksverändernd taste-modifying
Geschmacksveränderung *f* modification of taste, *(food also)* flavour change
Geschmacksverbesserer *m* taste improver
geschmacksverbessernd taste-improving
Geschmacksverbesserung *f* improvement in taste
Geschmacksverstärker *m (food)* flavour enhancer
geschmacksverursachend taste-causing, taste-producing
geschützt/gesetzlich proprietary
~/vor Licht protected from light
Geschwindigkeit *f* velocity, speed *(as of particles)*; rate *(as of reactions)*
~ **der Elementarreaktion** elementary reaction rate
~ **der Glykolyse** *(bioch)* glycolytic flux
~ **der Hinreaktion** forward reaction rate, forward rate [of reaction]
~ **der Moleküle** molecular velocity (speed)
~ **der Rückreaktion** reverse reaction rate, reverse rate [of reaction], back rate
~ **der Zonenwanderung** zone-travel rate, zone (zoning) speed *(in zone melting)*
~ **des Aufstroms** upward velocity
~/durchschnittliche *s.* ~/mittlere
~ **im Hohlraumbereich** *(chromat)* interstitial velocity
~/kritische critical velocity (speed) *(of fluid flow)*
~/mittlere mean velocity, average speed
~/mittlere quadratische root-mean-square speed (velocity), RMS speed
~/wahrscheinlichste most probable velocity (speed) *(of molecules)*
geschwindigkeitsabhängig velocity-dependent
geschwindigkeitsbestimmend rate-limiting, rate-controlling, rate-determining
Geschwindigkeitsdifferenz *f* difference of velocity
Geschwindigkeitsfeld *n* velocity field *(fluid mechanics)*
Geschwindigkeitsfokussierung *f* velocity focus[s]ing
Geschwindigkeitsgefälle *n* velocity gradient
Geschwindigkeitsgesetz *n s.* Geschwindigkeitsgleichung
Geschwindigkeitsgleichung *f* rate[-of-reaction] equation, empirical differential rate equation, rate law
~ **erster Ordnung** first-order rate equation (law)
~ **gebrochener Ordnung** fractional-order rate equation (law)

~ **pseudo-erster Ordnung** pseudo-first-order rate equation (law)
~ **zweiter Ordnung** second-order rate equation (law)
Geschwindigkeitsgradient *m* velocity gradient
Geschwindigkeitsgrenzschicht *f* hydrodynamic boundary layer
Geschwindigkeitshöhe *f* velocity head *(fluid mechanics)*
Geschwindigkeitskoeffizient *m* velocity coefficient
Geschwindigkeitskomponente *f* velocity component
Geschwindigkeitskonstante *f* rate coefficient, *(relating to elementary reactions:)* [reaction-]rate constant, unitary rate constant
~ **der bimolekularen Reaktion** bimolecular rate constant
~ **der Hinreaktion** forward rate constant
~ **der Löschreaktion/bimolekulare** quenching constant
~ **der Rückreaktion** reverse rate constant
~ **erster Ordnung** first-order rate constant
~ **pseudo-erster Ordnung** pseudo-first-order rate constant
~ **zweiter Ordnung** second-order rate constant
Geschwindigkeitsprofil *n* velocity[-distribution] profile *(in a reactor)*
geschwindigkeitsunabhängig velocity-independent
Geschwindigkeitsverteilung *f* distribution of velocities (speeds), velocity distribution
Geschwindigkeitsverteilungsgesetz *n* velocity-distribution law
~/asymptotisches *s.* ~/universelles
~/Maxwellsches Maxwell-Boltzmann velocity-distribution law
~/universelles universal velocity-distribution law
Geschwindigkeitswert *m* velocity coefficient
geschwulsterregend oncogenic, oncogenous
Gesenk *n (plast)* female form (mould), force; *(met)* die
Gesenkblock *m (plast)* cavity block
Gesenkplatte *f (plast)* [cavity] retainer plate, *(Am)* retainer
Gesetz *n* law, principle • **ein ~ befolgen, einem ~ folgen (gehorchen)** to obey a law
~/Amagatsches Amagat (Leduc) law *(of combining volumes of a gas mixture)*
~/Avogadrosches Avogadro law (hypothesis) *(of the number of molecules in gases)*
~/Beersches Beer law *(of light absorption)*
~/Bouguer-Lambert-Beersches *s.* ~/Lambert-Beersches
~/Bouguer-Lambertsches Bouguer-Lambert law [of absorption], Lambert's absorption law
~/Boyle-Mariottesches law of Boyle-Mariotte, Boyle (Mariotte) law *(of gas pressure and volume)*
~/Bunsen-Roscoesches *(phot)* Bunsen-Roscoe [reciprocity] law
~/Curie-Weisssches Curie-Weiss law *(relating to the temperature dependence of the magnetic susceptibility)*
~/Daltonsches Dalton law *(of partial pressures)*
~ **der äquivalenten Proportionen** law of equivalent proportions
~ **der Gleichverteilung der Energie** law of equipartition of energy, equipartition principle
~ **der konstanten Proportionen** law of constant (definite) proportions, Prout law
~ **der konstanten Wärmesummen** *s.* ~/Hesssches
~ **der multiplen Proportionen** law of multiple proportions
~ **der Periodizität** periodic law
~ **der rationalen Indizes (Parameterverhältnisse)** *s.* ~/Haüysches
~ **der Transfusionsgeschwindigkeiten/Grahamsches** Graham law of diffusion
~ **der unabhängigen Ionenwanderung** law of independent migration of ions
~/Drapersches Draper law *(of chemically effective radiation)*
~/Faradaysches Faraday law *(electrolysis)*
~/Ficksches Fick law [of diffusion]
~/Gay-Lussacsches Gay-Lussac law *(of gas volume and temperature)*
~/Grotthus[s]-Drapersches Grotthus[s]-Draper law *(photochemistry)*
~/Haüysches *(cryst)* Haüy law, rational index law
~/Hesssches Hess's law [of heat summation], law of constant heat summation
~/Kirchhoffsches Kirchhoff's law *(of the temperature dependence of reaction enthalpies)*
~/Kohlrauschsches Kohlrausch law *(of independent migration of ions)*
~/Lambert-Beersches Beer-Lambert[-Bouguer] law, [Bouguer-]Lambert-Beer law *(of light absorption)*
~/Lambertsches *s.* ~/Bouguer-Lambertsches
~/Moseleysches Moseley law *(of the wave numbers in X-ray spectra)*
~/Panethsches Paneth rule *(radiochemistry)*
~ **von der Erhaltung der Energie** law of conservation of energy, energy principle
~ **von der Erhaltung der Masse** law of conservation of mass (matter)
~ **von der Rationalität der Achsenabschnitte** *(cryst)* law of rational intercepts, law of rationality of intercepts
~ **von der Wiederkehr der gleichen Massenverhältnisse** law of reciprocal proportions *(by I.B. Richter)*
gesichert/statistisch statistically valid
Gesichtsmaske *f* 1. face mask; 2. *(cosmet)* face pack
Gesichtspackung *f (cosmet)* face pack
Gesichtspuder *m (cosmet)* face powder
Gesichtsschutz *m* face protector
Gesichtswasser *n (cosmet)* face lotion

gespalten werden to undergo cleavage (scission)
~ **werden/leicht** to be readily cleaved
Gespinst *n (text)* spun[-staple] yarn
gestaffelt staggered, non-eclipsed *(stereochemistry)*
Gestagen *n* progestational hormone
Gestalt *f* shape, form; *(cryst)* morphology
Gestalteinheit *f (cryst)* morphological unit
gestalten to shape, to form
gestaltlos amorphous
Gestaltresonanz *f (phys ch)* shape resonance
Gestaltsänderung *f* deformation, strain
~/bleibende permanent deformation (set), residual deformation (set), set
Gestänge *n (petrol)* drill pipe
Gestängeanheber *m (petrol)* [drill pipe] elevator
Gestängeverbinder *m (petrol)* tool joint *(of a rotary-drilling installation)*
Gestank *m* bad smell, stench, stink
Gestein *n* rock, *(mine also)* ground
~/anstehendes bedrock
~/autoklastisches autoclastic rock, autoclast
~/basisches basic (subsilicic) rock, basite
~/biogenes biogenic (organic) rock, biolith
~/bioklastisches bioclastic rock, bioclast
~/chorismatisches chorismite
~ **der Alkalireihe** alkali rock
~ **der Orthoreihe** ortho rock
~/endogenes endogenetic rock
~/exogenes exogenetic rock
~/geschiefertes schistose rock
~/holokristallines holocrystalline rock
~/hybrides hybrid rock
~/hydroklastisches hydroclastic rock
~/intermediäres *s.* ~/neutrales
~/magmatisches magmatic (igneous) rock
~/metamorphes metamorphic (metamorphosed) rock, metamorphite
~/neutrales neutral (intermediate) rock
~/organogenes *s.* ~/biogenes
~/plutonisches plutonic rock, irruptive (hypogene) rock, plutonite
~/polymetamorphes polymetamorphic rock
~/pyroklastisches pyroclastic rock
~/saures acid (silicic) rock
~/taubes waste rock, gangue, matrix
~/vulkanisches volcanic rock
Gesteinschemie *f* petrochemistry
gesteinschemisch petrochemical
Gesteinsgang *m* vein, dike
Gesteinsglas *n* natural glass
Gesteinsgrus *m* rock waste
Gesteinshülle *f*, **Gesteinskruste** *f* lithosphere
Gesteinskunde *f* petrography
Gesteinsmantel *m* lithosphere
Gesteinsmehl *n (agric)* crushed rocks
Gesteinsschutt *m* detritus, detrital material, rock waste
Gesteinssprengstoff *m* rock explosive
Gesteinswolle *f* rock wool
Gestell *n* 1. rack; 2. *(met)* hearth, crucible *(of a blast furnace)*
gesteuert/selbsttätig self-controlled
gestrecktkettig extended-chain
gestrichen *(pap)* coated
~/einseitig coated on one side
~/in der Maschine machine-coated
~/zweiseitig double-coated, coated on both sides
gesundheitsgefährdend hazardous to health
Gesundheitsgefährdung *f* health hazard
gesundheitsschädlich dangerous (injurious) to health, harmful, deleterious
gesüßt *(petrol)* sweet[ened]
geteilt/auf Ablauf (Auslauf) graduated (calibrated) to deliver, graduated for delivery
~/auf Einguß graduated (calibrated) to contain, graduated for content
~/bis zur Spitze graduated (calibrated) to jet *(pipette)*
Getränk *n* beverage, drink, potable
~/alkoholfreies alcohol-free (non-alcoholic) beverage, soft drink
~/alkoholisches alcoholic (spirituous) beverage, spirit
~/berauschendes intoxicating liquor, intoxicant
~/carbonisiertes carbonated beverage
~/geistiges *s.* ~/alkoholisches
~/hochprozentiges alkoholisches strong drink, *(Am)* hard drink
~/mit CO_2 imprägniertes carbonated beverage
getränkt/mit Öl oil-impregnated
Getreidebegasungsmittel *n* grain fumigant
Getreidebranntwein *m* grain alcohol
Getreideessig *m* grain vinegar
Getreidekeimöl *n* cereal seed oil
Getreidemaische *f* grain mash
Getreidemehl *n* flour, *(if coarsely ground:)* [corn] meal
Getreideschlempe *f* distillers' [spent] grains
Getreidestärke *f* cereal starch
Getrenntfluß *m* segregated flow
Getriebehebewerk *n (petrol)* drawworks
Getriebeöl *n* gear oil
getrocknet/auf dem Dachboden (Trockenboden) *(pap)* loft-dried
~/auf der Maschine *(pap)* cylinder-dried, machine-dried, steam-dried
~/im Sprühverfahren spray-dried
~/im Trockenschrank oven-dried, oven-dry, OD
~/im Zerstäubungsverfahren spray-dried
getrübt *(food)* hazy, cloudy, feculent
Getter *m*, **Gettermetall** *n* getter *(vacuum technology)*
gettern to getter *(vacuum technology)*
Getterstoff *m* getter *(vacuum technology)*
Gewässeraufsichtsorgan *n* water pollution control authority
Gewässerbelastung *f* water pollution

Gewässerreinhaltung *f*, **Gewässerschutz** *m* water pollution control, water protection
Gewässerverschmutzung *f*, **Gewässerverunreinigung** *f* water pollution
Gewebe *n* 1. fabric [cloth], cloth, web, *(text also)* textile [fabric]; 2. [biological] tissue
~/baumwollenes cotton fabric
~/beschichtetes coated fabric
~/biologisches biological tissue
~/gekrepptes crêpe, crepe
~/gestrichenes coated fabric
~/gummiertes rubberized fabric, rubbered (rubber-coated, proofed) fabric, proofing
~/kaschiertes coated (combined) fabric
~/pflanzliches plant tissue
~/selbstglättendes self-smoothing fabric
~/tierisches animal tissue
Gewebeabscheider *m* fabric dust collector
Gewebedruck *m* textile printing
Gewebeeinlage *f (rubber)* textile insert (insertion, casing)
Gewebeextrakt *m* tissue extract
Gewebefilter *n* fabric filter, woven[-fabric] filter
gewebefrei fabric-free *(e.g. rubber product)*
Gewebehormon *n* tissue hormone
Gewebekrumpfmaschine *f (text)* shrinking machine
Gewebekultur *f (biot)* tissue culture
~/pflanzliche plant tissue culture
Gewebekulturmedium *n (biot)* tissue-culture medium
Gewebelage *f (rubber)* carcass (casing) ply
Gewebepapier *n* reinforced paper, papyrolin *(cloth-faced or cloth-centred paper)*
Gewebeschlauch *m* woven hose
Gewebeschnitzel *npl (plast)* macerated fabric
Gewebeschnitzelpreßmasse *f (plast)* fabric-filled moulding compound (material)
Gewebs... *s.* Gewebe...
Gewerbemüll *m* commercial solid waste[s]
~/hausmüllähnlicher commercial refuse
Gewerbeschutzsalbe *f* barrier cream
Gewicht *n* 1. weight *(the force by which the mass of a substance is attracted by gravity; unit: N)*; 2. *s.* Gewichtstück; 3. *s.* Wägestück
~/spezifisches *s.* Wichte
~/statistisches *(phys ch)* statistical weight
Gewichtsabweichung *f* off-weight
Gewichtsanalyse *f* gravimetric analysis, analysis by weight
Gewichtsänderung *f* weight change
Gewichtsanteile *mpl s.* Gewichtsprozent
Gewichtskonstanz *f* constancy of weight, constant weight • **bis zur ~ glühen** to ignite to constant weight
Gewichtsmittel *n* weight average
Gewichtsmolarität *f s.* Molalität
Gewichtsprozent *n* percentage (per cent) by weight, w/w per cent
Gewichtssatz *m s.* Wägesatz
Gewichtsteil *m* part by weight
Gewichtstitration *f***/potentiometrische** potentiometric weight titration
Gewichtsstück *n* weight *(a heavy object of indefinite mass for counterbalancing)*
Gewichtsveränderung *f* variation in weight
Gewichtsverlust *m* loss in weight, weight loss
Gewichtszunahme *f* gain in weight, weight increase
Gewindefitting *n(m) s.* Gewinderohrverbindung
Gewindeformstück *n* screwed fitting
Gewinderohr *n* threaded pipe
Gewinde[rohr]verbindung *f* screwed fitting, threaded joint
gewinnen 1. to obtain, to recover *(a reaction product)*; to isolate *(from natural products)*; 2. *(mine)* to mine, to extract, to win
~/in reinem Zustand to obtain pure (in pure form), to obtain in a pure condition (state)
Gewinnung *f* 1. recovery *(of a reaction product)*; isolation *(from natural products)*; 2. *(mine)* mining, extraction, winning
~ durch Flotation floatation recovery
Gewölbe *n* crown *(of a melting furnace)*
gewölbt domed, convex; dished, concave
Gewürz *n* seasoning, *(of vegetable origin:)* spice, *(esp salt and pepper:)* condiment
Gewürznelke *f* clove *(from Syzygium aromaticum (L.) Merr. et L. M. Perry)*
Gewürznelkenöl *n* clove (caryophyllus) oil
g-Faktor *m* g-factor, gyromagnetic factor
~/Landéscher Lande g-factor, [Landé] splitting factor g *(gyromagnetic ratio of electrons)*
GFK *s.* Kunststoff/glasfaserverstärkter
GFS *s.* Glasfaserschichtstoff
GGG *s.* Grauguß/globularer
GH *s.* Gesamthärte
Ghatti *n* gum ghatti, India gum *(from Anogeissus latifolia Wall.)*
Gibberellin *n (bioch)* gibberellin
Gibberellinsäure *f (bioch)* gibberellic acid
Gibbs-Helmholtz-Gleichung *f* Gibbs-Helmholtz equation
Gibbs-Zelle *f* Gibbs cell *(electrolysis)*
Gicht *f (met)* 1. throat, top *(part of a blast furnace)*; 2. stock, burden, charge[stock], feed
Gichtbrücke *f (met)* hoist bridge
Gichtbühne *f (met)* charge floor
Gichtgas *n* furnace (blast-furnace) gas
Gichtglocke *f (met)* bell
Gichthöhe *f (met)* stock level
Gichtsonde *f (met)* stock level (line) indicator
Gichtstaub *m (met)* blast-furnace dust
Gichtverteiler *m (met)* distributor
~/drehbarer revolving (rotating) distributor
Gieseler-Plastometer *n* Gieseler plastometer
Gieß... *s. a.* Guß...
gießbar 1. capable of being poured, pourable; 2. castable *(molten material)*

Gießbarkeit *f* 1. pourability; 2. castability *(of molten material)*
Gießbett *n* pig bed *(foundry)*
gießen 1. to pour; 2. to cast *(molten material into moulds)*; to teem *(molten ferrous metal into ingot moulds)*
~/in Kokille to diecast
~/statisch fallend to teem downhill
~/statisch steigend to teem uphill
~/unter Druck to pressure-diecast
Gießen *n* 1. pouring; 2. casting *(of molten material into moulds)*; teeming *(of molten ferrous metal into ingot moulds)*
~ in getrocknete Sandformen dry-sand casting
~ in grüne (ungetrocknete) Sandformen green-sand casting
~/kontinuierliches continuous casting
~ mit verlorener Gußform [precision] investment casting
~/statisch fallendes downhill teeming
~/statisch steigendes uphill teeming
~ unter Druck pressure diecasting
~ von Hohlkörpern in Hohlformen flow casting
Gießer *m* founder, foundryman, caster
Gießerei *f* foundry
Gießereieisen *n* foundry [pig] iron
Gießerei[kern]harz *n* foundry resin
Gießereikoks *m* foundry coke
Gießereikupolofen *m* foundry cupola
Gießereiroheisen *n* foundry [pig] iron
Gießereischmelzkoks *m* foundry coke
Gießfähigkeit *f s.* Gießbarkeit
Gießfilm *m s.* Gießfolie
Gießfläche *f (plast)* casting area
Gießfleck *m (ceram)* casting spot (stain), flashing *(a defect)*
Gießfolie *f (plast)* cast film, *(if thickness > 0.01 inch:)* cast sheet
Gießform *f* [casting] mould
Gießharz *n* cast[ing] resin
Gießhaut *f (ceram)* casting skin
Gießkern *m (ceram, met)* core
Gießlackierung *f* curtain coating
Gießling *m* casting
Gießloch *n* casting hole
Gießlöffel *m* ladle
Gießmaschine *f* casting machine
Gießmasse *f (ceram)* casting (liquid) slip
Gießmittel *n (agric)* gravity-fed spray
Gießnaht *f* casting seam (line)
Gießpfanne *f* tilting hopper *(foundry)*
Gießrinne *f* gutter *(foundry)*
Gießschlicker *m (ceram)* casting (liquid) slip
~/tonfreier non-clay casting slip
Gießtisch *m (glass)* casting table
Gießverfahren *n* casting process
Gift *n* poison, toxicant, toxic [substance]
~/ökonomisches *s.* Pflanzenschutzmittel
~/pflanzliches plant poison
~/protektives (protektiv wirkendes) *(agric)* protective toxicant
~/systemisches *(agric)* systemic poison
~/tierisches venom
~/vorbeugend wirkendes *s.* ~/protektives
Gifteinwirkung *f* toxic action
Giftgas *n* poison[ous] gas
Giftgetreide *n* poisoned grain
gifthaltig containing poison
Giftheber *m* siphon for poisons
giftig poisonous, toxic[al] • **giftig sein für** to be toxic to
~/äußerst extremely poisonous (toxic)
~ für Pflanzen toxic to plants
~/schwach mildly poisonous (toxic)
~/stark highly (very, quite) poisonous (toxic), dangerously poisonous
Giftigkeit *f* toxicity, poisonousness
~/akute acute toxicity
~/chronische chronic toxicity
~ für Pflanzen phytotoxicity
~ für Säugetiere mammalian toxicity
Giftkies *m s.* Arsenopyrit
Giftköder *m* poison (toxic) bait
~ gegen Nagetiere rodent bait
Giftkunde *f* toxicology
Giftkundiger *m* toxicologist
Giftmehl *n (met)* white arsenic
Giftmüll *m* toxic (hazardous) waste[s]
Giftpapier *n* insecticide paper
Giftsachverständiger *m* toxicologist
Giftstoff *m* toxicant, toxic [substance]
Giftwert *m* toxic limit *(of wood preservatives)*
Giftwirkung *f* poisoning (poisonous, toxic) action; poisoning effect
gilben to [go] yellow, *(pap also)* to discolour, to age
Gingergrasöl *n* ginger-grass oil *(chiefly from Cymbopogon martini (Roxb.) Stapf var. sofia)*
Gipfel *m (anal)* mode *(of a distribution)*
Gipfelpunkt *m* peak *(of a curve)*
Gips *m (min)* gypsum *(calcium sulphate-2-water)* • **mit ~ behandeln** to plaster *(wine)*; to burtonize, to gypsum *(brewing water)*
~/gebrannter calcined (anhydrous) gypsum, gypsum cement, plaster of Paris *(essentially calcium sulphate 0.5-water)*
~/kristalliner *s.* Gips
~/totgebrannter dead-burned gypsum
gipsen to plaster *(wine)*; to burtonize, to gypsum *(brewing water)*; *(agric)* to gypsum
Gipsform *f* plaster mould
gipsführend *(geoch)* gypsiferous, gypsum-bearing
gipshaltig gypsiferous, gypseous
Gipshärte *f (hyd)* sulphate hardness
Gipsmörtel *m* gypsum mortar, plaster [mortar]
gipsreich gypseous *(brewing water)*
Gipsstein *m (hyd)* calcium sulphate scale
Gipssteinbildung *f (hyd)* calcium sulphate scaling
Girbotol-Verfahren *n* Girbotol [amine] process *(for removing acid constituents from gases)*

Girlandenrolle *f* suspended-cable idler *(conveying)*
Gisbe *f s.* Gispe
Gismondin *m (min)* gismondine, gismondite *(a hydrous calcium aluminium silicate)*
Gispe *f* seed *(a defect in glass)*
Gitter *n* 1. *(cryst)* lattice; 2. grating *(optics)*; 3. *(tech)* grating, grid; checker chamber *(Am)* chequer chamber *(of a blast-furnace stove)*
~/flächenzentriertes face-centred lattice
~/flächenzentriertes [ortho]rhombisches face-centred orthorhombic lattice
~/geblaztes *(spectr)* blazed grating *(grooves shaped in a sawtooth pattern)*
~/hexagonales hexagonal lattice
~/ideales perfect lattice
~/innenzentriertes body-centred lattice
~/kubisches cubic lattice
~/kubisch-flächenzentriertes face-centred cubic lattice
~/kubisch-innenzentriertes body-centred cubic lattice
~/metallisches metallic lattice
~/molekulares molecular lattice
~/raumzentriertes *s.* ~/innenzentriertes
~/tetragonal raumzentriertes body-centred tetragonal lattice
Gitterabstand *m (cryst)* lattice distance (spacing), spacing of the planes
Gitteraufbau *m (cryst)* lattice structure
Gitteraufweitung *f (cryst)* lattice expansion
Gitterbau *m (cryst)* lattice structure
Gitterbaufehler *m (cryst)* lattice defect
Gitterboden *m (distil)* [turbo]grid tray
Gitterdefekt *m (cryst)* lattice defect
Gitterebene *f (cryst)* lattice (atomic, net) plane
Gittereinschlußverbindung *f* lattice inclusion compound
Gitterenergie *f (cryst)* lattice energy
Gitterenthalpie *f* lattice enthalpy
Gitterexpansion *f (cryst)* lattice expansion
Gitterfehler *m (cryst)* lattice defect (imperfection, irregularity)
~/eindimensionaler line[ar] defect
~/flächenhafter surface defect
~/linienhafter line[ar] defect
~/punktförmiger point defect
Gitterfehlordnung *f (cryst)* lattice misalignment
Gitterfehlstelle *f s.* Gitterleerstelle
Gitterfläche *f (cryst)* lattice face
Gitterfurche *f (spectr)* grating groove
Gitterhohlraum *m s.* Zwischengitterplatz
Gitterion *n (cryst)* lattice ion
Gitterkonstante *f (cryst)* lattice constant
Gitterkräfte *fpl (cryst)* lattice forces
Gitterleerstelle *f (cryst)* lattice vacancy, hole [position], vacant site, vacant lattice site (position)
Gitterloch *n*, **Gitterlücke** *f s.* Gitterleerstelle
Gittermauerwerk *n* chequerwork, chequer brickwork, *(Am)* checkerwork, checker
Gitterorientierung *f (cryst)* lattice orientation
Gitterperiode *f s.* Gitterabstand
Gitterplatz *m (cryst)* lattice site (position)
~/unbesetzter *s.* Gitterleerstelle
Gitterpunkt *m (cryst)* lattice point
Gitterraum *m* chequer chamber, *(Am)* checker chamber *(of a blast-furnace stove)*
Gitterrostboden *m (distil)* [turbo]grid tray
Gitterrührer *m s.* Gatterrührer
Gitterschwingung *f* lattice vibration, *(spectr also)* lattice mode
Gitterspektralapparat *m (anal)* grating instrument
Gitterspektrograph *m* [diffraction] grating spectrograph
Gitterspektrophotometer *n* grating spectrophotometer
Gitterspektroskop *n* grating spectroscope
Gitterspektrum *n* grating (diffraction, normal) spectrum
Gitterstein *m s.* Gitterwerksstein
Gitterstelle *f (cryst)* lattice site (position)
Gitterstörstelle *f (cryst)* imperfection site
Gitterstörung *f s.* Gitterfehler
Gitterstrichfurche *f (spectr)* grating groove
Gitterstruktur *f* lattice structure
Gitterverband *m* lattice structure
Gitterverbindung *f* lattice compound
Gitterverzerrung *f (cryst)* lattice distortion
Gitterwerk *n s.* Gittermauerwerk
Gitterwerksstein *m* chequer brick, *(Am)* checker brick
GKE *s.* Kalomelelektrode/gesättigte
GKW *s.* Gesamtkationenwert
GL *s.* Glasfaserstoff
Glabratsäure *f s.* Lecanorsäure
Glacépapier *n* enamel[led] paper
~/gebürstetes brush enamel paper
Glanz *m* lustre, gloss, brightness
~/matter sheen *(as of powder or silk)*
~/metallischer metallic lustre
Glanzabzug *m (phot)* glossy print
Glanzappretur *f* 1. *(text)* glazed finish; 2. *s.* Glanzauftrag
Glanzauftrag *m (tann)* lustre (glossy) finish, season
Glanzausrüstung *f (text)* 1. glossing; 2. glazed finish
Glanzausrüstungsmittel *n (text)* lustring agent
Glanzbeständigkeit *f (coat)* gloss retention
Glanzbildner *m* brightener, brightening agent *(electroplating)*
Glanzbraunkohle *f* bright brown coal, black (bituminous) lignite, pitch coal
Glanzeffekt *m* gloss, lustre, shiny effect
glänzen to shine, to glitter, to glisten; to glaze, to season, to satine *(the leather)*
~/elektrochemisch (elektrolytisch) to electrobrighten, to electropolish
Glänzen *n*/**elektrochemisches (elektrolytisches)** electrobrightening, electropolishing, anodic brightening

glänzend lustrous, glossy, bright
Glanzerhaltung *f* gloss retention
Glanzfarbe *f* glazing varnish; gloss [printing] ink *(typography)*
Glanzfaser *f (text)* glaze fibre
Glanzfirnis *m* gloss varnish *(typography)*
Glanzglasur *f (ceram)* bright glaze
Glanzgold *n* bright gold, *(ceram also)* liquid gold
Glanzhaltung *f* gloss retention
Glanzkohle *f* bright coal; *(specif) s.* Glanzbraunkohle
Glanzlack *m* gloss varnish
glanzlos lustreless, dull, mat[t], non-bright, *(of colours also)* dead
Glanzlosigkeit *f* lustrelessness, dullness, mattness
Glanzmesser *m (pap)* gloss meter, glossimeter, glarimeter
Glanzmetall *n* speculum metal *(an alloy chiefly consisting of Cu and Sn)*
Glanzpalladium *n* bright palladium
Glanzpapier *n* flint[-glazed] paper
Glanzpappe *f* glazed board
Glanzplatin *n* bright platinum
Glanzsilber *n* bright silver
Glanzstoff *m (text)* copper rayon
glanzstoßen *(tann)* to glaze, to enamel
Glanzstoßmaschine *f (tann)* glazing machine
Glanzstoßzurichtung *f (tann)* glazed finish
Glanzweiß *n* satin white (spar) *(a pigment)*
Glanzwinkel *m (cryst)* glancing (Bragg) angle
Glas *n* 1. glass *(material)*, *(broadly also)* glassy material; 2. glassware *(equipment)* • **mit ~ ausgekleidet** glass-lined
~/alkaliarmes low-alkali glass
~/alkalihaltiges alkali glass
~/braunes amber glass
~/chemisch verfestigtes chemically strengthened glass
~/chemisch widerstandsfähiges chemically resistant glass
~/farbiges coloured glass
~/feuerfestes heat-resisting glass
~/freihandgeblasenes off-hand (free-blown) glass
~/geblasenes blown glass
~/gehärtetes *s.* 1. ~/thermisch gehärtetes; 2. ~/verfestigtes
~/geriffeltes (geripptes) fluted (ribbed) glass
~/geschliffenes cut glass
~/gezogenes drawn glass
~/gispiges seedy glass
~/hitzebeständiges heat-resisting glass
~/im Hafen geschmolzenes pot[-melted] glass
~/in der Wanne geschmolzenes tank glass
~/in Formen geblasenes mould-blown glass
~/kohlegelbes amber glass
~/kugelfestes (kugelsicheres) bullet-proof (bullet-resistant) glass
~/kurzes short glass
~/langes long glass
~/leicht schmelzbares soft [sealing] glass
~/leicht verarbeitbares sweet glass
~ mit hohem Brechungsindex/optisches dense glass
~ mit Luftblasendekor bubble glass
~/mundgeblasenes handblown (hand-made) glass
~/opakes opaque (opal) glass
~/optisches optical glass
~/organisches organic glass
~/photochrom[atisch]es photochromic glass
~/photosensibles (photosensitives) photosensitive glass
~/phototropes *s.* ~/photochromes
~/reflexfreies non-reflecting glass
~/schlieriges cordy glass
~/schußfestes *s.* ~/kugelfestes
~/thermisch gehärtetes (verfestigtes) heat-strengthened (heat-toughened, heat-treated) glass
~/verfestigtes strengthened (toughened) glass
~/vorgespanntes prestressed glass
~/vulkanisches *(geol)* volcanic glass
~/wärmeabsorbierendes heat-absorbing glass
~/weiches soft glass
glasähnlich glassy, glass-like, vitreous
Glasampulle *f* glass ampoule
glasarmiert glass[-fibre] reinforced
glasartig glassy, glass-like, vitreous; *(ceram)* vitrified, vitreous
Glasartikel *mpl* glassware
Glasätzung *f* glass etching
Glasauskleidung *f* glass lining • **mit ~** glass-lined
Glasballon *m* glass balloon flask, *(if cushioned:)* glass carboy, *(if enclosed in wickerwork with wicker handle:)* demijohn
Glasband *n* ribbon of glass
Glasbaustein *m* glass brick (block)
Glasbearbeitung *f* glass working (manipulation)
Glasbecher *m* glass beaker
glasbildend glass-forming
Glasbildner *m* glass-forming substance, glass former
Glasbildungstemperatur *f* glass-transition temperature *(at which the viscositiy of the glass is 10^{13} dPa s)*
Glasblasen *n* glass blowing
Glasbläser *m* glass-blower
Glasbläserlampe *f* glass-blower's lamp
Glasbläserpfeife *f* blow pipe, blow[ing] iron
Glas-Büchner-Trichter *m (lab)* slit sieve funnel
Glasbürste *f* glass brush
Glasdeckel *m* glass lid
~ mit Schliff ground-glass lid
Glaselektrode *f* glass [membrane] electrode
Glasemaille *f* glass enamel *(glass coating of enamel-like composition)*
glasemailliert glassed
Gläserbürste *f (lab)* beaker (jar) brush
Glaserdiamant *m* cutting diamond

Glaserit *m (min)* aphthitalite, glaserite *(potassium sodium sulphate)*
Glaserkitt *m* [glazier's] putty, painter's (whiting) putty
gläsern vitreous, glassy
Glasfabrik *f* glassworks, glass factory (house)
Glasfabrikation *f s.* Glasherstellung
Glasfaden *m* glass filament
Glasfarbe *f* glass colorant, *(Am also)* glass color
Glasfaser *f* 1. glass fibre; 2. *s.* Glasfasermaterial
Glasfasererzeugnis *n* glass-fibre (fibre-glass) product
Glasfaserfilter *n* glass-fibre filter
Glasfasergarn *n* glass-fibre yarn, staple-fibre glass yarn
Glasfasergewebe *n* glass[-fibre] fabric, woven-glass-fibre cloth, glass cloth
Glasfaserlaminat *n* glass-fibre laminate
Glasfasermaterial *n* fibre (fibrous, spun) glass
~/vorimprägniertes prepreg
Glasfaserpapier *n* glass-fibre paper
Glasfaserprodukt *n s.* Glasfasererzeugnis
Glasfaserschichtstoff *m* glass-fibre laminate
Glasfaserstoff *m* fibre (fibrous, spun) glass
glasfaserverstärkt glass[-fibre] reinforced
Glasfaserverstärkung *f* glass[-fibre] reinforcement
Glasfaservlies *n* glass-fibre veil, chopped (chopper) strand mat
Glasfehler *m* glass defect
Glasfilter *n* glass filter; sintered-glass (fritted-glass) filter
Glasfiltergerät *n* sintered-glass filtering device
Glasfilternutsche *f* [all-]glass suction filter
Glasfilterplatte *f* sintered-glass (fritted-glass) plate
~/runde sintered-glass (fritted-glass) disc
Glasfiltertiegel *m* sintered-glass [filtering] crucible, glass filtering crucible
Glasfiltertrichter *m* sintered glass [filtering] funnel, glass suction filter [funnel]
Glasfläschchen *n* [glass] vial
Glasfluß *m* glass flow
Glasformgebung *f* glass forming
Glasformstück *n* glass fitting
Glasformung *f* glass forming
Glasfritte *f* sintered-glass (fritted-glass) filter
Glasgalle *f (glass)* [glass] gall, salt water
Glasgefäß *n* glass vessel
Glasgemenge *n* glass batch
Glasgeräte *npl* glassware
Glasgespinst *m s.* Glasfaserstoff
Glasglanz *m (min)* vitreous (glassy) lustre
Glasglocke *f* glass bell, bell-jar
Glashafen *m* glass[-melting] pot
Glashafenofen *m* glass pot furnace
Glashahn *m* glass stopcock (tap)
Glashäkchen *n (lab)* glass hook
glashart glass-hard
Glashärte *f* glass hardness
Glashaut *f (plast)* cellulose film
Glashersteller *m* glass manufacturer (maker)
Glasherstellung *f* glass manufacture (making)
Glashütte *f* glassworks, glass factory (house)
glasieren *(ceram)* to glaze
Glasiermaschine *f (ceram)* glazing machine
glasig vitreous, glassy, glass-like; *(geol)* vitrophyric, vitreous
Glaskapillaren-Gaschromatographie *f* glass-capillary gas chromatography, GL-GC
Glaskappe *f* glass cap
~ mit Schliffhülse external ground-glass cap, ground-on cap
Glaskeramik *f* glass ceramic[s], vitroceramic, devitrified (neo-ceramic) glass
glasklar glass-clear
Glasklebstoff *m* glass adhesive
Glaskohlenstoff *m* glass-like carbon, glassy (vitreous) carbon
Glaskolben *m* glass flask (bulb)
Glaskopf *m*/**brauner** *(min)* brown iron ore (stone), limonite *(hydrous iron(III) oxide)*
~/roter reddle, red iron ore *(earthy iron(III) oxide)*
Glaskugel *f* glass bulb *(e.g. used as an absorption vessel)*; [glass] marble *(glass-fibre manufacture)*
Glaskugelbürette *f* bulb burette
Glasküvette *f* glass cuvette, cell
Glasmacher *m* glass-maker, [glass] blower
Glasmacherpfeife *f* blow pipe, blow[ing] iron
Glasmacherseife *f* glass[makers'] soap *(manganese dioxide)*
Glasmasse *f* glass mass
Glasmembran *f* glass membrane *(as of a glass electrode)*
Glasmesser *n* glass-cutting knife
Glas-Metall-Verschmelzung *f*, **Glas-Metall-Verschweißung** *f* glass-[to-]metal seal
Glasnadelinjektor *m* moving-needle (falling-needle) injector *(gas chromatography)*
Glasnutsche *f s.* Glasfilternutsche
Glasofen *m* glass[-melting] furnace
Glaspapier *n* glass paper *(1. an abrasive paper; 2. an insulating material)*
Glasperle *f* glass bead
Glasphase *f* vitreous (glassy) phase (state)
Glasplatte *f* glass plate, *(if thin)* sheet of glass
Glasposten *m* [glass] gob, gather of glass
Glasprismenspektrograph *m* glass spectrograph
Glaspulver *n* glass powder
Glasrohr *n* glass pipe (tube); *(collectively:)* glass piping (tubing)
Glasröhre *f* glass pipe (tube)
Glasrohrleitung *f* glass pipeline
Glasrohrmaterial *n* glass piping (tubing)
Glasrührer *m* glass stirrer
Glassatz *m (glass)* batch
Glasschale *f* glass dish
Glasscheibe *f* 1. pane [of glass] *(of a window)*; 2. *s.* Glasplatte
Glasschleifen *n*, **Glasschliff** *m* glass grinding

Glasschmelze *f* glass melt
Glasschmelzofen *m* glass[-melting] furnace
Glasschmelzwanne *f* [glass-]melting tank
Glasschneiden *n* glass cutting
Glasschneider *m* glass cutter *(tool or worker)*
Glasseide *f* glass silk
Glasseidenmatte *f* chopped (chopper) strand mat, continuous glass strand mat
Glasseidenpapier *n* transparent tissue paper, glass tissue
Glasseidenroving *m s.* Glasseidenstrang
Glasseidenspinnfaden *m* continuous glass filament
Glasseidenstrang *m* [glass-fibre] roving, glass-fibre strand
~/geschnittener chopped strand
Glasseife *f* glass[makers'] soap
Glassinterplatte *f s.* Glasfilterplatte
Glasspektrograph *m* glass spectrograph
Glasspiralkolonne *f* **nach Widmer** Widmer spiral column
Glasstab *m* glass rod, cane
Glasstapelfasergarn *n* staple-fibre glass yarn, glass-fibre yarn
Glasstopfen *m* glass stopper • **mit ~** glass-stoppered
~/eingeschliffener ground[-glass] stopper
Glasstopfenflasche *f* glass-stoppered bottle
Glasstruktur *f* glass structure
Glastechnik *f* glass technology
Glastechnologie *f* glass technology
Glastemperatur *f s.* Glasumwandlungspunkt
Glasträne *f* glass tear (drop)
Glastrichter *m* glass funnel
Glastropfen *f* glass drop (tear); [glass] gob *(on a glass-blower's pipe)*
Glastuff *m (geol)* vitric tuff
Glasübergang *m s.* Glasumwandlung
Glasübergangsbereich *m* glass transition region
Glasumwandlung *f* glass transition, *(rubber also)* gamma (second-order) transition, vitrification
Glasumwandlungspunkt *m*, **Glasumwandlungstemperatur** *f* glass[-transition] temperature, Tg [point], *(rubber also)* second-order transition temperature (point)
Glasur *f (ceram)* glaze
~/ausgeschmolzene matured glaze
~/deckende opaque glaze
~/gebrannte fired glaze
~/gefrittete fritted glaze
~/gesprenkelte mottled glaze
~/kratzfeste scratch-resisting glaze
~/opake (trübe) opaque glaze
Glasuraufnahme *f (ceram)* pick-up of glaze
Glasurbrand *m (ceram)* glost firing, glaze baking
Glasurbrandofen *m (ceram)* glost kiln
Glasurfehler *m (ceram)* glaze fault
Glasurlehm *m (ceram)* slip clay
Glasurofen *m (ceram)* glost kiln
Glasurschicht *f (ceram)* glaze coating
Glasurschlicker *m (ceram)* glaze slip
Glasurschmelze *f (ceram)* glaze batch
Glasursitz *m (ceram)* glaze fit
Glasurspat *m (ceram)* glaze spar
Glasurton *m (ceram)* slip clay
Glasurüberzug *m s.* Glasurschicht
Glaswanne *f (lab)* glass trough; *(glass)* glass tank
Glaswannenofen *m* glass tank furnace
Glaswaren *fpl* glassware
Glaswerk *n* glassworks, glass factory (house)
Glaswolle *f* glass wool
Glaswollefilter *n* glass-wool filter
~ zur Luftsterilisation *(biot)* glass-wool air filter
Glaszement *m* glass cement
Glasziegel *m* glass block (brick)
Glaszustand *m* vitreous (glassy, glass-like) state
Glaszylinder *m* jar
glatt 1. smooth *(surface)*; 2. plain *(shape)*; 3. smooth *(e.g. course of reaction)*
~/hydraulisch hydraulically smooth *(piping)*
Glattbrand *m (ceram)* glost firing
Glattbrandofen *m (ceram)* glost kiln
glattbrennen *(ceram)* to glost-fire
Glätte *f* smoothness *(of a surface)*; *(pap)* glaze
glätten to smooth, to polish; *(glass)* to flatten; *(pap)* to glaze, to smooth, to enamel, to plate, to [super]calender; *(tann)* to scud
Glätten *n* **auf der Bürstmaschine** *(pap)* brush polishing
~ mit Achatstein flint glazing, flinting
~ von Bogenpapieren sheet calendering
~ von Rollenpapieren web calendering
Glätteprüfer *m*, **Glätteprüfgerät** *n (pap)* smoothness tester
Glättezahl *f (pap)* smoothness number
Glättfilz *m (pap)* glazing felt
Glättmaschine *f* calender [machine] *(for compounds s.* Kalander*)*
Glattofen *m (ceram)* glost kiln
Glattrohr *n* bare tube
Glättschaberstreichmaschine *f (pap)* trailing blade coater
Glattscherben *mpl (ceram)* [glost] pitchers
glattschleifen to grind smooth
glattschmelzen *(lab)* to fire-polish, to fire-finish, to fire-glaze
Glattstreicher *m* leveller
Glattwalze *f* smooth[-surfaced] roll
Glättwalze *f* spreader *(of a cylinder dryer)*; *(pap)* smoothing roll
Glattwalzenbrecher *m* smooth-roll crusher
Glätt[walzen]werk *n* calender [machine] *(for compounds s.* Kalander*)*
Glättwerkspartie *f (pap)* surfacing end
Glauberit *m (min)* glauberite *(calcium sodium sulphate)*
Glaubersalz *n* Glauber salt, *(min also)* mirabilite *(sodium sulphate 10-water)*

Glaukodot *m (min)* glaucodot[e] *(cobalt iron sulpharsenide)*
Glaukophan *m (min)* glaucophane *(an inosilicate)*
GLC *(Gas-Liquidus-Chromatographie) s.* Gasflüssig-Chromatographie
Gleiboden *m s.* Gleyboden
gleichartig of the same kind, homogeneous
Gleichartigkeit *f* homogeneity, homogeneousness
gleichgestaltig *(cryst)* isomorphic, isomorphous
Gleichgestaltigkeit *f (cryst)* isomorphism
Gleichgewicht *n* equilibrium, balance • **das ~ wiederherstellen** to re-establish equilibrium • **dem ~ zustreben** to go toward equilibrium • **~ herstellen** to establish equilibrium • **im ~ halten** to keep in equilibrium, to equilibrate • **im ~ sein** to be at (in) equilibrium • **ins ~ bringen (setzen)** to equilibrate, to bring into equilibrium
~/annäherndes near-equilibrium
~/bewegliches mobile equilibrium
~/Boudouardsches producer-gas equilibrium
~/Donnansches Donnan [membrane] equilibrium
~/dynamisches dynamic equilibrium, steady state
~/eingefrorenes retarded equilibrium
~/heterogenes heterogeneous equilibrium
~/homogenes homogeneous equilibrium
~/indifferentes neutral equilibrium
~/metastabiles metastable equilibrium
~/photochemisches (photostationäres) photochemical equilibrium (stationary state), photoequilibrium, photostationary state
~/radioaktives radioactive equilibrium
~/thermisches thermal equilibrium
~/thermodynamisches thermodynamic equilibrium
~/vorgelagertes pre-equilibrium, prior equilibrium
Gleichgewichtsabstand *m* equilibrium [interatomic] distance, equilibrium internuclear separation
Gleichgewichtsapparatur *f (distil)* equilibrium still
Gleichgewichtsbedingungen *fpl* equilibrium conditions
Gleichgewichtsbeziehungen *fpl* equilibrium relationships
Gleichgewichtsdampfdruck *m* equilibrium vapour pressure
Gleichgewichtsdestillation *f* equilibrium distillation
Gleichgewichtsdialyse *f (bioch)* equilibrium dialysis
Gleichgewichtsdruck *m* equilibrium pressure
Gleichgewichtseinstellung *f* establishment of equilibrium
Gleichgewichtsfeuchte[beladung] *f* equilibrium moisture content
Gleichgewichtsgalvanispannung *f s.* Gleichgewichtspotential
Gleichgewichtskasten *m* equilibrium box *(theory of gas reactions)*
~ nach van't Hoff van't Hoff equilibrium (reaction) box
Gleichgewichtskernabstand *m s.* Gleichgewichtsabstand
Gleichgewichtskonstante *f* equilibrium constant
~/thermodynamische thermodynamic equilibrium constant
Gleichgewichtskonzentration *f* equilibrium concentration; *(bioch)* steady-state concentration
Gleichgewichtslage *f* position of equilibrium
Gleichgewichtslinie *f* tie line, conode *(in the equilibrium diagram)*
Gleichgewichtsmethode *f* equilibrium method *(ion exchange)*
Gleichgewichtspotential *n* equilibrium (steady-state) potential
Gleichgewichtsprozeß *m* equilibrium process
Gleichgewichtsquellung *f (rubber)* equilibrium swelling
Gleichgewichtsreaktion *f* balanced reaction
Gleichgewichtssiedekurve *f* [single-]flash curve
Gleichgewichts-Sinkgeschwindigkeit *f* terminal falling velocity; *(if bottoms are being formed:)* terminal settling velocity *(of settling particles)*
Gleichgewichtstemperatur *f* equilibrium temperature
Gleichgewichtsumsatz *m* equilibrium conversion
Gleichgewichtsverdampfung *f* equilibrium [flash] vaporization
Gleichgewichtsverhältnis *n* equilibrium ratio
Gleichgewichtsverteilung *f* equilibrium distribution, steady-state distribution, SSD
Gleichgewichtsverteilungskoeffizient *m* equilibrium distribution (partition) coefficient, *(zone melting also)* equilibrium segregation coefficient
Gleichgewichtswasser *n* equilibrium water
Gleichgewichtswassergehalt *m* equilibrium moisture content
Gleichgewichtswert *m* equilibrium value
Gleichgewichtszustand *m* equilibrium state
Gleichlauf *m* synchronism • **mit ~** synchronized, even-speed *(e.g. rolls)*
gleichmäßig uniform, even *(also of a process)*; smooth *(e.g. course of a reaction)*; *(dye)* level
Gleichmäßigkeit *f* uniformness, evenness *(also of a process)*; smoothness *(as of a reaction)*; *(dye)* levelness
Gleichrichtung *f***/Faradaysche** *(anal)* faradaic rectification
Gleichstrom *m* 1. cocurrent (concurrent, parallel) flow *(of two fluids)*; 2. direct current, d.c., D.C. *(of electricity)* • **im ~ [geführt]** cocurrent *(fluids)*
Gleichstrombogen *m s.* Gleichstromlichtbogen
Gleichstromdestillation *f s.* ~/einfache
~/diskontinuierliche simple batch distillation
~/einfache simple (direct) distillation
~/kontinuierliche simple continuous distillation
Gleichstromfahrweise *f* cocurrent operation
Gleichstromlichtbogen *m* d.c. arc
Gleichstrompolarogramm *n* d.c. polarogram
Gleichstrompolarograph *m* d.c. polarograph
Gleichstrompolarographie *f* d.c. polarography
gleichstrompolarographisch by d.c. polarography

Gleichstromregenerierung *f* cocurrent regeneration
Gleichstromverfahren *n* **nach Didier-Bubiag** Didier-Bubiag process *(of coal gasification)*
Gleichung *f* equation
~/Arrheniussche Arrhenius equation
~/Berthelotsche Berthelot equation
~/bilanzierte balanced equation
~/Boltzmannsche Boltzmann [transport] equation
~/Braggsche Bragg equation
~/chemische chemical[-reaction] equation, reaction equation
~/Clausius-Clapeyronsche Clapeyron-Clausius equation
~/Debyesche Debye equation
~/empirische empirical equation
~/Gibbs-Duhemsche Gibbs-Duhem equation
~/Langmuirsche Langmuir isotherm equation
~/Maxwellsche Maxwell relation, Maxwell [thermodynamic] relationship
~/stöchiometrische stoichiometric (balanced) equation
~/van-der-Waalssche van der Waals equation [of state]
~/van't-Hoffsche van't Hoff equation
~/van Vlecksche van Vleck equation
~ von Brunauer, Emmett und Teller Brunauer-Emmett-Teller equation (relationship), BET equation
~ von Grunwald und Winterstein Grunwald-Winterstein equation *(a linear Gibbs energy relation)*
Gleichverteilung *f* equipartition, equidistribution
Gleichverteilungssatz *m* **[der Energie]** equipartition principle (theorem), law of equipartition [of energy]
gleichwertig equivalent
Gleichwertigkeit *f* equivalence
gleichzeitig simultaneous, coincident
Gleichzeitigkeit *f* simultaneity, simultaneousness, coincidence
Gleitausgleicher *m s.* Gleitdehnungsausgleicher
Gleitblechsystem *n (chromat)* baffle system
Gleitdehnungsausgleicher *m* slip-type expansion joint
Gleitebene *f (cryst)* slip[ping] plane, glide (gliding) plane
gleiten to slide, to slip
Gleiten *n* slide, slip
Gleitfähigkeit *f* slip
Gleitmittel *n* lubricant, lubricating agent, lube, slip additive (agent); *(pharm)* intestinal lubricant; *(plast)* external lubricant; mould lubricant *(foundry)*
Gleitmodul *m* shear modulus [of elasticity], modulus of rigidity (elasticity in shear)
Gleitrichtung *f (cryst)* glide direction
Gleitung *f* crystal (translation) gliding *(along a crystal plane)*
Gleitwinkel *m* angle of slide *(of bulk material)*
Glessit *m* glessite *(a fossil resin resembling amber)*
Gley[boden] *m* gley [soil]
Glied *n* **einer Zerfallsreihe** *(nucl)* member of a disintegration series
~/vorletztes penultimate unit *(of a polymer chain)*
Gliederbandförderer *m* apron conveyor
Gliederwalze *f* section roller
glimmen to glow [feebly]; to smoulder, to burn faintly
Glimmen *n* [feeble] glow; smouldering
Glimmentladung *f* glow discharge
Glimmer *m* mica
glimmerähnlich mica-like
glimmerartig micaceous
Glimmermineral *n* mica
Glimmersandstein *m* micaceous sandstone
Glimmerschiefer *m* mica schist
Glimmschicht *f***/negative** *(spectr)* cathode[-glow] layer
glitschig slippery
Globar *m (spectr)* Globar *(silicon carbide rod as light source)*
Globarlampe *f (spectr)* Globar lamp
Globosid *n (bioch)* globoside
globulär globular
Globulärprotein *n* globular protein
Globulin *n* globulin *(any of a class of simple proteins)*
~ [A]/antihämophiles antihaemophilic factor, AHF
γ-Globulin *n* gamma globulin, GG
Glocke *f (distil)* [bubble] cap, bubbler; crown *(of a melting furnace)*; bell, cone *(of a blast furnace)*; *(lab)* bell jar *(for protecting objects esp under vacuum)*
~/Brühlsche *(distil)* Brühl receiver
~/große large bell *(of a blast furnace)*
~/kleine small bell *(of a blast furnace)*
~ mit Dampfkamin *(distil)* cap-and-riser assembly
~ mit gezacktem Rand *(distil)* serrated bubbler
Glockenboden *m (distil)* bubble[-cap] tray, bubble[-cap] plate
Glockenbodenkolonne *f (distil)* bubble-cap column, bubble-tray (bubble-plate) column
Glockenbronze *f* bell bronze
Glockengasbehälter *m* liquid-seal gasholder
Glockenkappe *f (distil)* [bubble] cap, bubbler
Glockenkolonne *f s.* Glockenbodenkolonne
Glockenmessing *n* bell brass
Glockenmetall *n* bell metal
Glockenmühle *f* cone mill, conical grinder, rotary crusher
Glockenstange *f* bell beam *(of a blast furnace)*
Glockentrichter *m (lab)* thistle funnel (tube)
~ mit Schleife und Kugel thistle funnel with safety bulb
Glocken- und Trichter[gicht]verschluß *m* bell and hopper, cup and cone *(of a blast furnace)*
Glover *m s.* Glover-Turm
Glover-Säure *f* Glover [tower] acid, brown oil of vitriol, B.O.V. *(chamber process)*
~/technisch reine best brown oil of vitriol, b.b.o.v., B.B.O.V.

Glover-Turm *m* Glover tower *(chamber process)*
Glover-Turmsäure *f s.* Glover-Säure
Glover-West-Ofensystem *n* Glover-West system
Glover-West-Retorte *f* Glover-West coking (continuous vertical) retort
Glu *s.* Glutaminsäure
Glucagon *n* glucagon *(a protein produced by the pancreas)*
Glucan *n (org ch)* glucan
Glucinerde *f s.* Berylliumoxid
Glucinium *n s.* Beryllium
D-**Glucitol** *n* D-glucitol, D-sorbitol, D-sorbite, sorbol
Glucocorticoid *n* glucocorticoid *(an adrenal cortex hormone)*
Glucomannan *n* glucomannan
Gluconeogenese *f (bioch)* gluconeogenesis *(formation of sugars from non-carbohydrate precursors)*
D-**Gluconsäure** *f* D-gluconic acid
Gluconsäurelacton *n* gluconolactone
D-**Glucosamin** *n* D-glucosamine, GlcN, chitosamine, 2-amino-2-deoxy-*D*-glucopyranose
Glucosazon *n* glucosazone
Glucose *f* glucose, *(specif) D*-glucose, dextrose
~/aktive uridine-diphosphate glucose, UDP-glucose, UDPG, UDPGlc
d-**Glucose** *f s. D*-Glucose
D-**Glucose** *f* D-glucose, dextrose
Glucosephosphat *n* glucose phosphate
Glucoserest *m* glucose residue
Glucosesirup *m* glucose syrup
Glucosetoleranz *f (med)* glucose tolerance
Glucosid *n* glucoside *(a glucoside that yields glucose on hydrolysis)*
glucosidisch glucosidic, glucosidal
Glucozuckersäure *f* glucosaccharic acid, saccharic acid, glucaric acid *(one form of 2,3,4,5-tetrahydroxyhexanedioic acid)*
D-**Glucuronat**-*L*-**Gulonat-Weg** *m s.* Glucuronatweg
Glucuronatweg *m (bioch)* glucuronate pathway
Glucuronat-Xylulose-Zyklus *m s.* Glucuronatweg
Glucuronid *n* glucuronide, glucuronoside
Glucuronsäure *f* glucuronic (glycuronic) acid
Glucuronsäurelacton *n* glucuronolactone
Glühaufschluß *m* calcination
Glühbrand *m (ceram)* biscuit firing, biscuitting
glühelektrisch thermionic
glühen to ignite, *(esp limestone, ores:)* to calcine; *(ceram)* to bake; *(met)* to anneal; to glow *(of a hot substance)*
~/bis zur Gewichtskonstanz (Massekonstanz) to ignite to constant weight
~/nochmals to re-ignite
Glühen *n* ignition, *(esp of limestone, ores:)* calcination; *(ceram)* baking; *(met)* anneal[ing]; glow *(of a hot substance)*
~/entspannendes *(met)* stress-relieving anneal, stress relief [anneal]
~/graphitisierendes *(met)* graphitizing
~/homogenisierendes *(met)* homogenizing
~ in Schutzgas *(met)* bright annealing
~/isothermes *(met)* isothermal annealing
~/normalisierendes *(met)* normalizing
~/rekristallisierendes *(met)* recrystallization annealing
~/stabilisierendes *(met)* stabilizing
glühend glowing; red-hot *(metal)*; incandescent *(hot body)*; *(geol)* igneous *(magma)*
Glühfaden *m* incandescent filament
Glühfadenpyrometer *n* disappearing-filament (hot-filament) pyrometer
Glühkasten *m*, **Glühkiste** *f (met)* annealing box
Glühkörper *m* incandescent mantle
Glühlampe *f* incandescent [lamp]
Glühofen *m (ceram)* heating furnace; kiln; *(met)* annealing furnace
Glühphosphat *n* thermal phosphate, fused (calcined) phosphate *(a fertilizer)*
Glühröhrchen *n* ignition [test] tube
Glührohrprobe *f* ignition tube test
Glührückstand *m* residue on ignition
Glühschale *f (lab)* ignition dish
~/rechteckige combustion barge
Glühschiffchen *n* combustion boat
Glühstrumpf *m* incandescent mantle
Glühtopf *m (met)* annealing pot (can)
Glühverlust *m* loss on ignition, LOI, ignition loss
Glühzone *f* incandescent zone
Glu-NH$_2$ *s.* Glutamin
Glutamat *n* glutamate *(salt or ester of glutamic acid)*
Glutamin *n* glutamine
Glutamincysteinglykokoll *n s.* Glutathion
Glutamindehydrogenase *f s.* Glutaminsäuredehydrogenase
Glutaminsäure *f* glutamic acid, 1-aminopropane-1,3-dicarboxylic acid
Glutaminsäuredehydrase *f s.* Glutaminsäuredehydrogenase
Glutaminsäuredehydrogenase *f* glutamic acid dehydrogenase
Glutaminsäuresemialdehyd *m* glutamic acid semialdehyde
γ-**Glutaminsäurezyklus** *m (bioch)* γ-glutamyl cycle
Glutaraldehyd *m* glutaraldehyde, glutaric dialdehyde, 1,3-pentanedial
Glutardialdehyd *m s.* Glutaraldehyd
Glutarsäure *f* glutaric acid, propane-1,3-dicarboxylic acid
Glutarsäuredialdehyd *m s.* Glutaraldehyd
Glutathion *n* glutathione, glutamylcysteinylglycine
Glutbeständigkeit *f* resistance to glow heat
Glutbeständigkeitsprüfung *f (plast)* glow bar test, glowing hot-body test
Gluten *n (bioch)* gluten
Glutfestigkeit *f s.* Glutbeständigkeit
Glutflußgestein *n s.* Eruptivgestein
Glv. *s.* Glühverlust

Gly *s.* Glykokoll
Glyceraldehyd *m* glyceraldehyde, *2,3-dihydroxypropanal
Glycerat *n* glycerate *(salt or ester of glyceric acid)*
Glycerid *n* glyceride, acylglycerol *(ester of glycerol with fatty acids)*
~/einfaches simple glyceride
~/gemischtes (gemischtsäuriges) mixed (component) glyceride
~/reines *s.* ~/einfaches
~/unvollständig verestertes partial glyceride
Glycerin *n s.* Glycerol
Glycerinaldehyd *m s.* Glyceraldehyd
glycerinieren *s.* glycerolieren
Glycerinsäure *f s.* Glycersäure
Glycerol *n* glycerol, *propane-1,2,3-triol • **mit ~ behandeln** to glycerolize, to glycerolate
Glycerol-α-chlorhydrin *n* glycerol α-chlorohydrin, *3-chloropropane-1,2-diol
Glyceroldiacetat *n* glycerol diacetate, diacetylglycerol, diacetin
Glycerolgärung *f* glycerol fermentation
glycerolieren to glycerolize, to glycerolate
Glycerolkomponente *f (bioch)* glycerol moiety
Glycerolmonoacetat *n* glycerol monoacetate, monoacetin
Glycerolmonostearat *n* glycerol monostearate, GMS, monostearin
Glycerolphosphat *n* glycerophosphate
Glycerolphosphat-Shuttle *m (bioch)* glycerol phosphate shuttle
Glycerolphosphorsäure *f* glycerophosphoric acid
Glycerol-Phthalsäure-Harz *n s.* Glyptalharz
Glyceroltrinitrat *n* glycerol trinitrate, glyceryl trinitrate
Glyceroltripalmitat *n s.* Glyceroltripalmitinsäureester
Glyceroltripalmitinsäureester *m* glycerol tripalmitate, tripalmitin
Glyceroltristearat *n s.* Glyceroltristearinsäureester
Glyceroltristearinsäureester *m* glycerol tristearate, tristearin
Glyceroltrioleat *n s.* Glyceroltrioleinsäureester
Glyceroltrioleinsäureester *m* glycerol trioleate, triolein, olein
Glycerophospholipid *n (bioch)* glycerophospholipid, phosphoglyceride, phosphatide
Glycersäure *f* glyceric acid, *2,3-dihydroxypropanoic acid
Glycerylmonostearat *n s.* Glycerolmonostearat
Glycidylether *m* glycidyl ether
Glycin *n* glycine, aminoacetic acid
Glycinerde *f s.* Berylliumoxid
Glykan *n* glycan, polysaccharide
Glykocholsäure *f* glycocholic acid *(a bile acid)*
Glykocyamin *n* glycocyamine, guanidinoacetic acid
Glykogen *n* glycogen, animal (liver) starch
Glykogenabbau *m (bioch)* glycogenolysis
Glykogenese *f (bioch)* glycogenesis
Glykogenolyse *f (bioch)* glycogenolysis
Glykogensäure *f s. D*-Gluconsäure
Glykogenspeicherkrankheit *f* glycogen storage disease, glycogenosis
Glykogenverzweigungsenzym *n* branching (branch-point) enzyme, Q enzyme
Glykokoll *n* glycine, glycocoll, aminoacetic acid
Glykokollkupfer *n* glycine copper, copper glycine
Glykol *n* $C_nH_{2n}(OH)_2$ glycol, [aliphatic] diol, dihydric alcohol, *(specif)* ethane-1,2-diol
1,2-Glykol *n* ethylene glycol, *1,2-ethane-1,2-diol
Glykolaldehyd *m* glycol[l]aldehyde, hydroxyacetaldehyde
Glykolbad *n (lab)* glycol bath
Glykolchlorhydrin *n* *2-chloroethanol, glycol chlorohydrin
Glykoldibromid *n s.* 1,2-Dibromethan
Glykolharnstoff *m* glycollylurea, hydantoin, imidazolidine-2,4-dione
Glykolipid *n (bioch)* glycolipid[e]
Glykolmonoethylether *m s.* Ethylenglykolmonoethylether
Glykolsäure *f* glycolic (glycollic) acid, hydroxyacetic acid
glykolspaltend glycol-splitting
Glykolyse *f (bioch)* glycolysis, homolactic fermentation, Embden-Meyerhof-Parnas scheme (pathway)
~/aerobe aerobic glycolysis
***d*-Glykonsäure** *f s. D*-Gluconsäure
Glykoproteid *n*, **Glykoprotein** *n* glycoprotein, glycopeptide
Glykose *f s.* Glucose
Glykosid *n* glycoside, oside
~/herzaktives cardiac glycoside
Glykosidbindung *f* glycosidic bond
Glykosidierung *f* glycosylation
glykosidisch glycosidic
Glykosphingolipid *n (bioch)* glycosphingolipid
Glykosurie *f* glycosuria *(excretion of sugars in urine)*
Glykosylamin *n* glycosylamine, *N*-glycoside
Glykosylierung *f* glycosylation
Glyoxal *n* glyoxal, oxalaldehyde, *ethanedial
Glyoxalin *n s.* Imidazol
Glyoxalsäure *f s.* Glyoxylsäure
Glyoxylatzyklus *m (bioch)* glyoxylate cycle
Glyoxylsäure *f* glyoxylic acid
Glyoxylsäurezyklus *m s.* Glyoxylatzyklus
Glyptal[harz] *n* glyptal [resin], glycerol phthalic resin, phthalic glyceride resin
GMP Guanosin-5'-monophosphat
Gneist *m (tann)* scud *(fat and lime soap remaining on hides or skins)*
GnRH *(**Go**nadotropin-**R**eleasing-**H**ormon) s.* Gonadoliberin
Goapulver *n (pharm)* Goa powder, araroba *(from Andira araroba Aguiar)*
Goethit *m (min)* goethite, göthite, *(iron hydroxide oxide)*
Golay-Detektor *m (spectr)* detector Golay, Golay cell

Golay-Gleichung *f* Golay equation
Golay-Zelle *f s.* Golay-Detektor
Gold *n* Au gold
Goldamalgam *m (min)* gold amalgam
Goldaventurin *m* gold aventurine
Goldbromsäure *f s.* Tetrabromogold(III)-säure
Goldbromwasserstoff *m s.* Tetrabromogold(III)-säure
Goldbronze *f* gold bronze
Gold(I)-chlorid *n* gold(I) chloride, gold monochloride, aurous chloride
Gold(III)-chlorid *n* gold(III) chloride, gold trichloride, auric chloride
Gold(I,III)-chlorid *n* gold(I,III) chloride, digold tetrachloride, auroso-auric chloride
Goldchlorwasserstoffsäure *f s.* Tetrachlorogold(III)-säure
Gold(I)-cyanid *n* gold(I) cyanide, gold monocyanide, aurous cyanide
Gold(III)-cyanid *n* gold(III) cyanide, gold tricyanide, auric cyanide
Golddekor *n (ceram)* gold decoration
Goldfolie *f* gold foil
goldführend auriferous, gold-bearing
Goldgehalt *m* gold content
goldhaltig gold-bearing, *(geoch also)* auriferous
Gold(III)-hydrogenbromid *n s.* Tetrabromogold(III)-säure
Goldhydrosol *n* gold hydrosol
Gold(I)-hydroxid *n* gold(I) hydroxide, aurous hydroxide
Gold(III)-hydroxid *n* gold(III) hydroxide, auric hydroxide, auric acid
Goldmono... *s. a.* Gold(I)-...
Goldmonoxid *n s.* Gold(I)-oxid
Goldorange *n* methyl (gold) orange
Gold(I)-oxid *n* gold(I) oxide, digold monooxide, aurous oxide
Gold(III)-oxid *n* gold(III) oxide, digold trioxide, auric oxide
Goldpräparat *n* gold preparation
Goldpurpur *m***/Cassiusscher** Cassius (gold-tin) purple *(colloidal tin oxide with adsorbed colloidal gold)*
Goldquarz *m* auriferous quartz
Goldrubinglas *n* gold ruby [glass]
Goldsalz *n* sodium tetrachloroaurate
Goldsand *m* auriferous sand (gravel), wash
Goldsäure *f s.* Gold(III)-hydroxid
Goldschmidt-Radius *m* Goldschmidt radius *(of ions)*
Goldschmidt-Verfahren *n* Goldschmidt process, aluminothermics, aluminothermy
Goldschwefel *m* golden antimony sulphide, antimonial saffron, antimony red *(antimony(V) sulphide)*
Goldseife *f (geol)* gold-placer
Goldsol *n* gold sol
Goldsolreaktion *f (med)* gold sol test
Goldstaub *m* gold dust
Gold(I)-sulfid *n* gold(I) sulphide, digold sulphide, aurous sulphide
Gold(III)-sulfid *n* gold(III) sulphide, digold trisulphide, auric sulphide
Gold(I,III)-sulfid *n* gold(I,III) sulphide, digold disulphide, auroso-auric sulphide
Goldtönung *f (phot)* gold toning
Goldtri... *s.* Gold(III)-...
Goldwäsche[rei] *f* gold washing
Goldzahl *f (coll)* gold number
Gomartharz *n* tacamahac[a] gum, West Indian elemi *(from Bursera gummifera L.)*
Gomberg-Bachmann-Reaktion *f* Gomberg-Bachmann[-Hey] reaction *(for synthesizing biaryls)*
Gomberg-Reaktion *f* Gomberg reaction *(for obtaining free radicals)*
Gonadoliberin *n* gonadoliberin, GnRH
Goniometer *n (cryst)* goniometer
goniometrisch *(cryst)* goniometric
Goochtiegel *m* Gooch crucible (filter)
Goochtiegelhalter *m* crucible adapter
Goodrich-Flexometer *n (rubber)* Goodrich flexometer
Goodyear-Winkelmaschine *f (rubber)* Goodyear angle machine
Gordon-Plastikator *m (rubber)* Gordon plasticator
Goslarit *m (min)* goslarite, zinc vitriol *(hydrous zinc sulphate)*
GOT = Glutamat-Oxalacetat-Transaminase
Gottignies-Ofen *m (ceram)* Gottignies kiln *(an electric multipassage kiln)*
Gould-Jacobs-Reaktion *f* Gould-Jacobs reaction *(formation of 4-hydroxyquinolines)*
Gouy-Chapman-Schicht *f (hyd)* diffused layer *(coagulation)*
GÖV *s.* Gas-Öl-Verhältnis
G-6-P = Glucose-6-Phosphat
G6PDH = Glucose-6-phosphatdehydrogenase
GPF-Ruß *m (rubber)* general-purpose furnace black, GPF black
GPT = Glutamat-Pyruvat-Transaminase
Grad *m* degree; grade *(of purity of chemicals)* • **in Grade [ein]teilen** to graduate
~ **API** *(petrol)* degree API
~ **Baumé** degree Baumé, °Bé
~ **Celsius** degree centigrade (Celsius), deg C, °C
~ **der Unordnung** *(phys ch)* degree of disorder
~ **deutscher Härte** *(hyd)* German degree of hardness, degree German *(1 °dH = 10.0 mg CaO/l H_2O)*
~ **englischer Härte** *(hyd)* English degree of hardness, degree Clark (English, British) *(1 °eH = 8.0 mg CaO/l H_2O)*
~ **Fahrenheit** degree Fahrenheit, deg F, °F
~ **französischer Härte** *(hyd)* French degree of hardness, degree French *(1 °fH = 5.6 mg CaO/l H_2O)*
~ **Kelvin** *s.* Kelvin
~ **Twaddell** *m* degree Twaddell, °Tw
Gradation *f (phot)* gradation, development factor, gamma value

Gradationskurve *f s.* Schwärzungskurve
Gradeinteilung *f* graduation, division
Gradient *m* gradient
Gradientchromatographie *f* gradient elution chromatography
Gradient-Dünnschichtchromatographie *f* gradient thin-layer chromatography
Gradient[en]elution *f* gradient elution
Gradientpackung *f (chromat)* gradient packing
Gradientschicht *f* gradient layer
Gradientschichttechnik *f* gradient layer technique
gradieren to graduate *(solutions by evaporation)*
Gradieren *n* graduation *(of solutions by evaporation)*
graduieren to graduate, to calibrate
graduiert/auf Ablauf (Auslauf) graduated (calibrated) to deliver, graduated for delivery
~/auf Einguß graduated (calibrated) to contain, graduated for content
Graduierung *f* graduation, calibration
gradweise gradual
Graebe-Ullmann-Synthese *f* Graebe-Ullmann synthesis *(of carbazoles)*
Graftpolymer[e] *n* graft [polymer]
Graham-Salz *n* Graham's salt *(a sodium metaphosphate glass)*
grainieren *(pap)* to grain, to press
Gram-Farbstoff *m* Gram stain *(bacteriology)*
Gram-Färbung *f* Gram staining *(bacteriology)*
Grammäquivalent *n (phys ch)* gram equivalent, eq
Grammatitstrahlstein *m (min)* tremolite *(an inosilicate)*
Grammatom *n* gram atom, gram-atomic weight
Grammbereich *m (anal)* gram range *(1 to 10 g)*
Grammion *n* gram ion
Grammol[ekül] *n* gram molecule (mole), gram-molecular weight, mole
Grammsuszeptibilität *f* susceptibility per gram, specific (mass) susceptibility
Grammval *n s.* Grammäquivalent
gramnegativ Gram-negative *(bacteriology)*
grampositiv Gram-positive *(bacteriology)*
Granalie *f* granule, pellet, agglomerate
Granat *m (min)* garnet
Granat[schel]lack *m* garnet lac
Granitschale *f (geoch)* granitic layer, sial
Granitwalze *f (pap)* granite roll
Granulat *n* granulate, granular material, *(molten droplets which have solidified:)* shot
Granulatformen *n* agglomerating, agglomeration *(of powder by means of a liquid)*
Granulatformer *m s.* Granulator
Granulation *f* granulation, granulating, graining, *(solidification of molten droplets also)* shotting, *(of powder by means of a liquid also)* agglomeration
Granulatkorn *n* pellet, granule, *(formed from powder also)* agglomerate
Granulator *m* granulator, pelletizer, granulating (pelletizing) machine
Granulieranlage *f* granulation plant
Granulierapparat *m s.* Granulator
granulieren to granulate, to grain
granuliert granulate[d], grained
Granulierteller *m* pan granulator
Granuliertrommel *f* rotary-drum granulator, [rotary] granulation drum
Granulierung *f s.* Granulation
Granulierverfahren *n (ceram)* granule method
granulometrisch granulometric *(classifying)*
granulös granular, grainy, granulate
Granulum *n* granule
Graphit *m* graphite • **mit ~ auskleiden** to line with graphite, to graphitize, *(Am also)* to graphite • **mit ~ beschichten** to coat with graphite, to graphitize, *(Am also)* to graphite
~/expandierter exfoliated graphite
~/künstlicher synthetic (artificial) graphite
~/primärer kish, keesh *(foundry)*
~/pyrolytischer pyrolytic graphite
graphitähnlich graphite-like
Graphitanode *f* graphite anode
graphitartig graphite-like
Graphitboot *n* graphite boat *(in zone melting)*
Graphitbrenner *m* graphite burner
Graphit-Einlagerungsverbindung *f* graphite intercalation compound, GIC
Graphitelektrode *f* graphite electrode
Graphitfaden *m* graphite filament
Graphitfaser *f* graphite fibre
Graphitfluorid *n* graphite fluoride
Graphitfolie *f* graphite foil
graphitgebremst *(nucl)* graphite-moderated
Graphitgitter *n* graphite lattice
Graphitglühen *n* graphitizing
graphithaltig graphitic, containing graphite
Graphithydrogensulfat *n* graphite hydrogensulphate
graphitierbar graphitizable
Graphitierbarkeit *f* graphitizability
graphitieren to graphitize, *(Am also)* to graphite
Graphitierofen *m* graphitizing furnace
Graphitierung *f* graphitization
~/katalytische catalytic graphitization
~/thermische graphitization heat treatment
Graphitierungsgrad *m* degree of graphitization
Graphit-Interkalationsverbindung *f* graphite intercalation compound, GIC
graphitisch graphitic
graphitisieren *s.* graphitieren
Graphitmaterial *n* graphite material
graphitmoderiert *(nucl)* graphite-moderated
Graphitofen *m s.* Graphitrohrküvette
Graphitoxid *n* graphite oxide, graphitic acid
Graphitpapier *n* graphite paper
Graphitpulver *n* graphite powder
Graphitreaktor *m (nucl)* graphite-moderated reactor
~/natriumgekühlter sodium graphite reactor

Graphitrohr *n (spectr)* graphite tube
Graphitrohrküvette *f*, **Graphitrohrofen** *m (spectr)* graphite [resistance] furnace
Graphitrohrtechnik *f (spectr)* graphite-furnace AAS, furnace technique
Graphitsalz *n* graphite (graphitic) salt
Graphitsäure *f s.* Graphitoxid
Graphitschicht *f* graphite layer
Graphitschiffchen *n* graphite boat *(in zone melting)*
Graphitstab *m* graphite rod
Graphittiegel *m* graphite (plumbago) crucible
Graphitverbindung *f* graphitic compound
Graphit-Wärmeaustauscher *m*, **Graphit-Wärmeübertrager** *m* graphite heat exchanger
Graphitwerkstoff *m* graphite material
Graphitwhisker *m* graphite whisker
Grappierzement *m* grappier cement
Grasbaumharz *n* acaroid gum (resin), accroides (grass-tree, black-boy) gum *(from Xanthorrhoea specc.)*
Gräserbekämpfungsmittel *n* grass killer
Grashof-Zahl *f* Grashof number, free-convection number
Grasöl *n*/**Indisches** *(cosmet)* lemon-grass oil, East Indian verbena oil *(from Cymbopogon specc.)*
Grat *m* burr *(produced in cutting metal)*; flash, fin *(on castings)*; *(plast)* burr, flash; *(rubber)* flash, rind
Gratlinie *f*, **Gratnaht** *f (plast)* joint (spew, flash) line
Gratus-Strophantin *n* G-strophantin *(a glucoside)*
Grauguß *m* grey [cast] iron; *(from a mould:)* grey-iron casting
~/**globularer (sphärolithischer)** nodular (spheroidal graphite) iron, ductile iron
Grauhuminsäure *f (soil)* grey humic acid
Graukalk *m* 1. grey lime (acetate), vinegar salt *(crude calcium acetate)*; 2. *(agric)* dolomitic lime *(calcium magnesium oxide)*
Graukarton *m* grey cardboard
Graukörper *m* grey body
Graupappe *f* grey (news) board
Grauschwefel *m* winnowed (wind-blown) sulphur
Grauspießglanz *m (min)* grey antimony, antimony glance, antimonite, stibnite *(antimony(III) sulphide)*
Grauwacke *f (geol)* greywacke
Gravimetrie *f* gravimetry
gravimetrisch gravimetric[al]
Gravitationsdifferentiation *f (geol)* gravitative differentiation
Gravitationsfeld *n* gravitational field
Gravitationskraft *f* force of gravitation (gravity), gravitational force (pull)
Gravitationswasser *n (hyd)* seep water
Gray-Dampfphase-Prozeß *m s.* Gray-Prozeß
Gray-King-Kokstypus *m* Gray-King [assay] coke type
Gray-King-Test *m*, **Gray-King-Verkokungstest** *m* Gray-King assay [test]
Gray-Prozeß *m* Gray process *(for treating gasoline with bleaching earth)*
Great-Northern-Schleifer *m (pap)* Great Northern grinder
Greaves-Etchells-Ofen *m* Greaves-Etchells furnace *(an arc-heated furnace)*
Greenawalt-Pfanne *f*, **Greenawalt-Sinterpfanne** *f (met)* Greenawalt sintering machine
Grège[seide] *f* grege, greige, gum silk
Greifer *m* scoop
Greisen *m (geol)* greisen
Greisenbildung *f (geol)* greisening, greisenization
Grenzdextrin *n* limit (residual) dextrin
Grenze *f* 1. limit; 2. boundary *(as of an atom or phase)*
0,2 %-Grenze *f* 0.2 % offset yield strength (stress), 0.2 % proof stress, yield strength 0.2 % offset *(materials testing)*
Grenzenergie *f*/**Fermische** Fermi [characteristic energy] level
Grenzfläche *f* boundary (bounding) surface, interface, junction
~ **fest-fest** solid-solid interface
~ **fest-flüssig** solid-liquid interface
~ **flüssig-flüssig** liquid-liquid interface, liquid junction, dineric interface
~ **flüssig-gasförmig** liquid-vapour interface
~ **Luft gegen Flüssigkeit** air-liquid interface
~ **Öl gegen Wasser** oil-water interface
~/**wandernde** moving boundary
grenzflächenaktiv interface-active, interfacially active, surface-active, surface-tension-lowering
Grenzflächenaktivität *f* interfacial (surface) activity
Grenzflächenenergie *f* interfacial energy
Grenzflächenerscheinung *f* interfacial phenomenon
Grenzflächenfilm *m* interfacial film *(in emulsions)*
Grenzflächen[poly]kondensation *f* interfacial polycondensation
Grenzflächenpolymerisation *f* interfacial polymerization
Grenzflächenpotential *n* junction potential
Grenzflächenreibungsarbeit *f* interfacial work
Grenzflächenspannung *f* interfacial tension
Grenzflächenturbulenz *f* interfacial turbulence
Grenzflächenwinkel *m* interfacial angle
Grenzformel *f*/**mesomere** resonance formula
Grenzfrequenz *f* limiting frequency
Grenzgeschwindigkeit *f* terminal settling velocity *(sedimentation)*
Grenzgesetz *n* limiting law
~/**Debye-Hückelsches** Debye-Hückel limiting law, DHLL
Grenzkohlenwasserstoff *m s.* Alkan
Grenzkonformation *f* full conformation *(stereochemistry)*
Grenzkonzentration *f* limiting concentration; *(tox)* maximum permissible (admissible) concentration
~ **von Wasserinhaltsstoffen** *(hyd)* maximum contaminant level, MCL
Grenzkorngröße *f*/**obere** upper size
~/**untere** lower size

Grenzlastspielzahl *f* fatigue life *(materials testing)*
Grenzleitfähigkeit *f* equivalent conductance at infinite dilution
Grenzlinie *f* interface line *(between two components)*
Grenzorbital *n* frontier orbital
Grenzschicht *f* boundary layer
~/laminare laminar boundary layer
~/turbulente turbulent (Prandtl) boundary layer
Grenzschwingspielzahl *f* fatigue life *(materials testing)*
Grenzsieblinie *f* grading limit
Grenzstrom *m* limiting current
Grenzstromdichte *f* limiting current density
Grenzstromtitration *f* amperometric titration
Grenzstruktur *f* limiting structure
~/mesomere contributing structure, resonance (resonating) structure
Grenzverhältnis *n* limiting ratio
Grenzviskosität *f*, **Grenzviskositätszahl** *f* intrinsic viscosity, limiting viscosity number
Grenzwert *m* limiting value, limit, *(relating to toxic materials also)* boundary (tolerance) limit
Grenzzustand *m* limiting state
Grieß *m* oversize [material, product] *(air classifying)*
grießartig gritty
Grießprobe *f (glass)* powder test
Griff *m* 1. handle *(of an apparatus)*; 2. *(pap, text, tann)* feel, handle, *(pap also)* bulk, *(text also)* hand *(property of material)*
~/weicher *(text)* soft handle
Griffappretur *f (text)* stiffening
griffig of good feel (handle), *(pap also)* bulky
• **~ sein** to have a good feel (handle), *(pap also)* to bulk
Griffigkeit *f (pap, text, tann)* feel, handle, *(pap also)* bulk, *(text also)* hand
Griffin-Mühle *f* Griffin [ring-roll] mill
Grignardierung *f (org ch)* grignardization
Grignard-Reagens *n (org ch)* Grignard reagent *(solution of an organometallic halide)*
Grignard-Reaktion *f (org ch)* Grignard reaction *(for obtaining organometallic halides)*
Grignard-Späne *mpl (org ch)* magnesium chips *(for Grignard syntheses)*
Grignard-Synthese *f (org ch)* Grignard synthesis *(using a Grignard reagent)*
Grignard-Verbindung *f (org ch)* Grignard compound
Grignard-Verfahren *n (org ch)* Grignard method (process)
GRK-Technik *f s.* Graphitrohrtechnik
grob 1. coarse *(screen)*; 2. coarse, rough *(e.g. bulk material)*; 3. rough *(method)*
Grobabscheider *m* precleaner *(gas cleaning)*
grobätzen to macroetch
Grobausmahlung *f* coarse grinding
Grobbrechen *n* coarse crushing
Grobbrecher *m* coarse crusher
grobdispers coarsely dispersed
Grobeinstellung *f* coarse adjustment
grobfaserig coarse-fibred
Grobfilter *n* coarse (roughing) filter
Grobgefüge *n s.* Makrogefüge
Grobgut *n* 1. coarse material, *(hyd also)* coarse solids; *(pap)* oversize chips; 2. *s.* Grobkorn
Grobgutaustrag *m* sand discharge *(of a classifier)*
Grobkeramik *f* 1. heavy ceramics *(branch)*; 2. heavy clay product (ware)
Grobkeramikindustrie *f* heavy clay industry
Grobklassieren *n* coarse sizing
Grobkorn *n* oversize [material, product], tailings, tails, plus material *(classifying)*, *(screening also)* screen oversize, plus mesh
grobkörnig coarse-grained
Grobkörnigkeit *f* coarseness
grobkristallin coarse-crystalline, coarsely crystalline
grobmahlen to crush, to grind coarsely
Grobmahlung *f* crushing, coarse grinding
grobmaschig coarse-mesh[ed]
grobnarbig *(tann)* coarse-grained
Grobrechen *m (hyd)* coarse rack
Grobsand *m* coarse sand, grit
Grobsiebung *f* coarse (rough) screening
Grobsortierer *m* coarse screen
Grobsortierung *f* coarse [material] screening
Grobspäne *mpl (pap)* oversize chips
Grobstaub *m* grit *(in the atmosphere)*
Grobstoff *m (pap)* groundwood (screen) rejects, rejected stock, junk, screenings, screens, tailings, tails
Grobstoffe *mpl (hyd)* coarse solids
Grobstoffentfernung *f (hyd)* coarse solids removal, removal of rakings
Grobstoffrückhalt *m s.* Grobstoffentfernung
grobteilig coarse
Grobton *m* coarse clay
Grobtrub *m (ferm)* hot sludge
Grobvakuum *n* low vacuum
Grobwägung *f* coarse weigh, low-precision weighing
Grobwaschmittel *n* heavy-duty [fabric, laundry] detergent
grobzerkleinern to crush, to grind coarsely
Grobzerkleinerung *f* crushing, coarse grinding
Grobzuschlag *m* coarse aggregate
Großanlage *f* large-scale unit
Großbetrieb *m* large-scale plant; *(as opposed to pilot plant:)* full-scale plant
Großchemie *f* large-scale chemistry
Größe *f (phys ch)* quantity
~/additive (extensive) extensive quantity
~/intensive intensive quantity
~/kritische critical constant
~/partielle molare partial molar (molal) quantity
~/reduzierte reduced variable (property)
Größenbestimmung *f* size determination *(classifying)*

Größenordnung *f* order of magnitude
Größenverteilung *f* size distribution *(classifying)*
Großerzeuger *m* large producer
Großfermenter *m (biot)* large[-scale] fermenter, large-volume fermenter
großindustriell large-scale
großionig large-ion
Großkoks *m* large coke
großoberflächig high-area *(e.g. catalyst)*
großporig large-pored
Großproduktion *f* large-scale production (manufacture, fabrication); *(as opposed to pilot-plant production:)* full-scale factory production
Großproduzent *m* large producer
Großprozeß *m* large-scale process
Großraumgärverfahren *n* charmat process *(for producing sparkling wine)*
Großraumzentrifuge *f* high-capacity centrifuge
Großreaktor *n* large[-scale] reactor
Großring *m* large ring, macrocycle
Großringverbindung *f* macrocyclic compound, macroring (large-ring) compound
großstückig blocky, lumpy
großtechnisch large-scale; *(as opposed to pilot-scale:)* full-scale
Grossular *m (min)* grossular[ite] *(a garnet)*
Großversuch *m* large-scale test
Grotrian-Diagramm *n (spectr)* Grotrian diagram
Grübchen *n (plast)* pit *(a moulding defect)*
Grübchenbildung *f (plast)* pitting
Grube *f* 1. pit; 2. mine **in der ~ geäschert** *(tann)* pit-limed
Grubenabwasser *n* mine drainage [water]
Grubenäscher *m (tann)* 1. pit liming *(process)*; 2. pit lime *(substance)*
Grubengas *n* mine gas, filty, fire-damp
Grubengerbung *f* pit tannage
Grubenkohle *f* run-of-mine coal
Grubenwasser *n* mine water
Grudekoks *m char made by low-temperature carbonization of raw lignite*
Grün *n* green *(sensation or substance)*
~/Böttgers *s.* ~/Kasseler
~/Chinesisches Chinese green, locao *(a natural dye from Rhamnus specc.)*
~/Kasseler Cassel (manganese) green *(barium manganate)*
~/Mittlers Mittler's (chrome) green *(hydrated chromium oxide)*
~/Pariser *s.* ~/Schweinfurter
~/Rinmans Rinman's (cobalt) green *(consisting essentially of cobalt and zinc oxides)*
~/Rosenstiehls *s.* ~/Kasseler
~/Scheeles Scheele's green *(copper arsenite)*
~/Schweinfurter Paris (Schweinfurth) green *(copper acetate arsenite)*
~/Spanisches *s.* Grünspan
~/Wiener *s.* ~/Schweinfurter
Grünablauf *m (sugar)* green syrup
Grünbleierz *n (min)* green (brown) lead ore, pyromorphite *(lead chloride phosphate)*
Grund *m (tann)* scud *(remaining fat and lime soap on hides or skins)*
Grundanstrich *m* 1. priming *(act)*; 2. primer [coat], priming (prime) coat, primary (ground) coat
Grundanstrichfarbe *f* priming (prime) paint
Grundanstrichmittel *n*, **Grundanstrichstoff** *m* primer [coating], priming coat material
Grundausstattung *f* typical (small-scale) equipment, typical inventory
Grundbaueinheit *f* basic (fundamental) building unit
Grundbaustein *m* basic (fundamental) building block; base unit, [basic] repeating unit *(of polymers)*
~ D difunctional (bifunctional) unit, D unit *(for building up polymers)*
~ M monofunctional unit, M unit *(for building up polymers)*
~ T trifunctional unit, T unit *(for building up polymers)*
Grundbestandteil *m* main (principal, chief) component, main constituent (ingredient), base, basis
Grundchemikalie *f* basic (key) chemical
Grunddüngung *f* basal dressing
Grundeinheit *f* 1. basic (fundamental) unit, *(esp of polymers)* base unit, [basic] repeating unit; 2. base (fundamental) unit *(of a system of units)*
~/strukturelle [basic] structural unit, structural element (entity)
Gründeldruck *m (text)* blotch printing
Grundelektrolyt *m* support[ing] electrolyte, base (indifferent) electrolyte *(polarography)*
Grundfarbe *f* 1. primary colour *(theory of colours)*; 2. *s.* Grundanstrichfarbe
Grundfläche *f* basis, base
Grundformel *f* fundamental formula
~/stöchiometrische stoichiometric (simplest) formula
Grundfraktion *f (petrol)* primary fraction
Grundgas *n* complementary gas *(eines Gasgemischs)*
Grundgebilde *n* fundamental entity
Grundgerüst *n* parent structure, basic framework *(of a molecule)*; backbone, skeleton *(of a chain molecule)*
~/cyclisches parent ring system
Grundgesamtheit *f* 1. universe, population *(statistics)*; 2. *(anal)* entire (parent) lot, entire mass
Grundgestein *n* bedrock
Grundieranstrich *m s.* Grundanstrich
grundieren *(coat)* to prime; *(tann, dye)* to bottom
Grundierfarbe *f* 1. *(dye)* bottoming dye[stuff]; 2. *s.* Grundanstrichfarbe
Grundiermittel *n* primer
Grundierung *f* 1. *s.* Grundanstrich; 2. *s.* Grundanstrichmittel; 3. *(tann, dye)* bottoming
Grundkohlenwasserstoff *m* parent hydrocarbon
Grundkomponente *f s.* Grundbestandteil

Grundkörper *m* parent (mother) substance
Grundlack *m (coat)* primer [coating]; *(tann)* bottom lacquer
Grundlage *f*/**Parrsche** Parr's basis *(in Seyler's coal chart)*
~/**verfahrenstechnische** engineering basis
Grundlagenchemie *f* fundamental chemistry
Grundlagencreme *f (cosmet)* make-up base, foundation cream
~/**flüssige** foundation lotion
Grundlagenforschung *f* basic [science] research, pure research
Grundlagenwissenschaft *f* basic science
Grundlinie *f (anal)* base line
Grundlinien *fpl (spectr)* persistent (ultimate) lines
Grundliniendrift *f (anal)* base-line drift
Grundlinienstabilität *f (anal)* base-line stability
Grundlösung *f* basis solution
Grundluft *f* soil air
Grundmann-Synthese *f* Grundmann synthesis *(for obtaining aldehydes)*
Grundmasse *f (geol, ceram, met)* matrix, groundmass
Grundmetall *n* principal (base) metal *(of an alloy)*
Grundmischung *f (rubber)* masterbatch, base stock (compound, mix), mother (blank) stock
Grundmolekül *n* basic (fundamental) molecule *(esp of polymers:)* base molecule, monomer
~/**bifunktionelles** bifunctional monomer
Grundmonomereinheit *f* monomer[ic] unit
Grundnährstoff *m (food)* major nutrient
Grundniveau *n s.* Grundzustand
Grundobjekt *n* fundamental entity
Grundoperation *f* 1. basic (fundamental) operation; 2. *s.* ~/physikalische
~ **der chemischen Verfahrenstechnik** chemical engineering unit operation
~/**physikalische** basic physical operation, *(esp chemical engineering:)* unit operation
Grundplatte *f* base (bottom) plate, bed [plate]
Grundprozeß *m* fundamental (basic) process
~/**stofflicher (verfahrenstechnischer)** unit process
Grundreaktion *f* basic (fundamental) reaction
Grundschlamm *m (hyd)* bottom sludge
Grundschwingung *f* fundamental (normal) vibration, normal mode of vibration
Grundschwingungsbande *f (spectr)* fundamental band
Grundschwingungsfrequenz *f (spectr)* fundamental [vibration] frequency
Grundskelett *n s.* Grundgerüst
Grundstoff *m* basic (fundamental) substance
~/**chemischer** basic chemical [material], key chemical
~/**unentbehrlicher** *(agric)* essential element
Grundstoffwechsel *m (bioch)* primary metabolism
Grundstrom *m (phys ch)* residual current
Grundstruktur *f* basic structure
Grundsubstanz *f* parent (mother) substance *(of chemical compounds)*; *(bioch)* ground substance *(as of tissues)*
Grundsubstrat *n (biot)* basal (main growth) medium
Grundterm *m s.* Grundzustand
Grundumsatz *m (bioch)* basal metabolism, basal metabolic rate
Grundverfahren *n* basic (fundamental) method (process)
Grundviskosität *f* intrinsic viscosity
Grundvorgang *m* basic (fundamental) process
Grundwasser *n* ground water
~/**uferfiltriertes** riverbank filtrate
Grundwasseranreicherung *f* replenishment of ground water, ground-water recharge, ground level replenishing
Grundwasserbeschaffenheit *f s.* Grundwassergüte
Grundwasserentnahme *f* ground-water withdrawal
Grundwassererschließung *f* ground-water development
Grundwassergüte *f* ground-water quality
Grundwasserhorizont *m* zone of saturation
Grundwasserleiter *m* [ground-]water aquifer, underground aquifer
Grundwasseroberfläche *f* [ground-]water table, [ground-]water level
Grundwasserspeicher *m s.* Grundwasserleiter
Grundwasserspiegel *m* 1. *(hyd)* ground-water level, level of the water table *(as in a well)*; 2. *s.* Grundwasseroberfläche
Grundwasserstauer *m* aquiclude
Grundwasserträger *m s.* Grundwasserleiter
Grundwasserverschmutzung *f*, **Grundwasserverunreinigung** *f* ground-water pollution (contamination)
Grundwasservorkommen *n* ground-water source
Grundwasservorrat *m* ground-water supply
Grundwasserzone *f* zone of saturation
Grundwerk *n (pap)* bedplate, dead (beater) plate *(of a hollander beater)*
Grundwerksfassung *f*, **Grundwerkskasten** *m (pap)* bedplate box
Grundwerksmesser *npl (pap)* bedplate bars (knives) *(of a beater)*
Grundwein *m (ferm)* base wine
Grundzustand *m (phys ch)* ground state (term), atomic ground (unexcited) state, normal state
~/**elektronischer** electronic ground state, ground (zeroth) electronic state
Grünerde *f* green earth *(any of various siliceous pigments used by artists)*
Grünfestigkeit *f* green strength *(1. of moulding sand; 2. of ceramic ware)*
Grünform *f* green-sand mould *(foundry)*
Grünformsand *m* green [moulding] sand *(foundry)*
Grünglas *n* green glass
Grüngußsand *m s.* Grünformsand
Grünlauge *f (pap)* green liquor

Grünlaugenbehälter *m (pap)* green liquor storage [tank]
Grünlaugenklärer *m*, **Grünlaugenklärtank** *m (pap)* green liquor clarifier
Grünlaugenklärung *f (pap)* green liquor clarification
Grünlaugenvorratstank *m (pap)* green liquor storage [tank]
Grünling *m* green compact *(in powder metallurgy)*
Grünmalz *n (ferm)* green malt
Grünmasse *f (tann)* green weight *(of hides and skins)*
Grünöl *n* green (anthracene) oil
Grünpellet *n* green (moist) pellet
Grünsand *m* green [moulding] sand *(foundry)*
Grünsandform *f* green-sand mould *(foundry)*
Grünsandformen *n* green-sand moulding *(foundry)*
Grünsäure *(petrol)* green [sulphonic] acid *(mixture of water-soluble sulphonic acids)*
Grünschlick *m* green mud
Grünschwefel *m* green sulphur *(in gas purification)*
Grünsirup *m (sugar)* green syrup
Grünspan *m* verdigris, aerugo *(a mixture of basic copper(II) acetates)*
~/gereinigter (kristallisierter) neutral verdigris *(copper(II) acetate hydrate)*
Grünstärke *f* raw starch
Grünstein *m (geol)* greenstone
Gruppe *f* group *(of atoms)*; family, group *(in the periodic system)*; subclass *(of the enzyme classifying system)*; set, battery, bank *(of equipment)*
~/aktive 1. active (prosthetic) group, coenzyme, agon *(enzymology)*; 2. *s.* ~/austauschaktive
~/aktivierende activating group
~/analytische analytical group
~/austauschaktive active group *(ion exchange)*
~/austretende leaving group
~/auxochrome *(dye)* auxochromic group, auxochrome
~/bathochrome *(dye)* bathochromic group, bathochrome, bathychrome
~/brückenbildende bridging group
~/chromophore *(dye)* chromophoric (colour-bearing) group, chromophore
~ der Eisenmetalle iron group
~/die Substitution desaktivierende substitution-deactivating group
~/eintretende entering group
~/elektrofuge electrofuge
~/endständige terminal group
~/erste *(anal)* insoluble chloride group
~/farberhöhende hypsochromic group
~/farbgebende (farbtragende) *s.* ~/chromophore
~/farbvermehrende (farbverstärkende) *s.* ~/auxochrome
~/farbvertiefende *s.* ~/bathochrome
~/funktionelle functional group
~/geschützte protected group
~/haptophore haptophoric group, haptophore *(portion of a toxin molecule which binds it to a body cell)*
~/hypsochrome *(dye)* hypsochromic group, hypsochrome
~/inaktivierende deactivating group
~/löslichmachende solubilizing group
~/meta-dirigierende meta-directing group, meta director
~/nichtpolare funktionelle non-polar functional group
~/nucleofuge nucleofuge
~/nucleophile nucleophilic (electron-releasing) group
~/nullte zero group *(in the periodic system)*
~/ortho-para-dirigierende ortho-para-directing group, ortho-para director
~/osmophore osmophore
~/polare funktionelle polar functional group
~/prosthetische prosthetic (conjugate) group *(protein chemistry)*, *(relating to enzymes also)* active group, coenzyme
~/reaktionsfähige (reaktive) reactive group
~/terminale terminal group
~/toxophore toxophoric group, toxophore
~/zweite *(anal)* insoluble sulphide group
~/zybotaktische *(phys ch)* cybotactic group *(of molecules which exhibit crystal-like arrangement in certain liquids)*
Gruppenanalyse *f* group analysis
Gruppeneinteilung *f (anal)* group separation, separation into groups
Gruppenfrequenz *f (spectr)* group frequency
Gruppengeschwindigkeit *f* group velocity *(of waves)*
Gruppennummer *f* group number *(coal classification)*
Gruppenparameter *m* group parameter *(coal classification)*
Gruppenreagens *n* group reagent
Gruppensilicat *n (min)* sorosilicate
gruppenspezifisch group-specific *(enzyme)*
Gruppenspezifität *f* [absolute] group specificity *(of enzymes)*
Gruppentranslokation *f (bioch)* group translocation
Gruppenüberträger *m (bioch)* group transfer agent
Gruppenübertragung *f (bioch)* group transfer
Gruppenübertragungsreaktion *f (bioch)* group transfer reaction
Gruppenversuch *m* group experiment
Gruppenziffer *f s.* Gruppennummer
gruppieren to group
Gruppierung *f* grouping
Grus *m (soil)* grit; *(coal)* breeze
GS *s.* Geschmacksschwellenwert
G-Salz *n* G salt, 2-naphthol-6,8-disulphonic acid dipotassium salt
G-Säure *f* G acid, 2-naphthol-6,8-disulphonic acid
GSC *(**G**as-**S**olidus-**C**hromatographie) s.* Gas-fest-Chromatographie
GSK *s.* Geschmacksschwellenkonzentration

g-Strophantin *n* G-strophantin *(a glycoside)*
g.T. *s.* Tiegel/geschlossener
GTP *s.* Guanosintriphosphat
GU *s.* Gummifaserstoff
Guajacol *n* guaiacol, *o*-methoxyphenol
Guajakharz *n* guaiac [resin], gum guaiac *(from Guajacum officinale L. and G. sanctum L.)*
Guajen *n* 1. $C_{15}H_{24}$ guaiene *(a sesquiterpene)*; 2. $C_{10}H_6(CH_3)_2$ 2,3-dimethylnaphthalene, guaiene
Guajol *n* guaiol *(a sesquiterpene alcohol)*
Guanidin *n* guanidine, iminourea
Guanidinbeschleuniger *m* guanidine accelerator
Guanidinoessigsäure *f* guanidinoacetic acid
Guanin *n* guanine, 6-hydroxy-2-aminopurine
Guano *m* guano *(a fertilizer esp from partly decomposed bird excrements)*
Guanosin *n* guanosine, guanine riboside *(a nucleoside)*
Guanosindiphosphat *n (bioch)* guanosine diphosphate
Guanosintriphosphat *n (bioch)* guanosine triphosphate
Guanylsäure *(bioch)* guanylic acid
Guaran *n* guar gum *(a mucilage from Cyamopsis tetragonoloba (L.) Taub.)*
Guarana *n*, **Guaranapaste** *f* guarana *(a paste from the seeds of Paullinia cupana Kunth containing caffeine)*
Guaruma-Wachs *n* guaruma wax *(from Calathea lutea G.F.W. Mey.)*
Guäthol *n* guaethol, catechol monoethyl ether
Guayana-Elemi *n* elemi of Guiana *(from Icica viridiflora Lam.)*
Guayule *f*, **Guayule-Kautschuk** *m* guayule rubber *(from Parthenium argentatum A. Gray)*
Guggenheim-Verfahren *n* Guggenheim process *(for obtaining pure sodium nitrate from Chile saltpetre)*
Gugul *n* Indian bdellium *(balsamic resin from Commiphora mukul Engl.)*
Guignetgrün *n* Guignet's green, chrome (Mittler's) green *(hydrated chromic oxide)*
Guineakörner *npl* grains of paradise *(from Aframomum melegueta Schum.)*
Gulf-HDS-Verfahren *n (petrol)* Gulf HDS process *(for hydrogenating desulphurization)*
Gültigkeit *f*/**universelle** *(bioch)* universality *(of the genetic code)*
Gültigkeitsbereich *m* range of obedience *(of a scientific law)*
Gum *m (petrol)* gum
~/aktueller existent (preformed) gum
~/möglicher (potentieller) potential (ultimate) gum
~/vorgebildeter (vorhandener) *s.* ~/aktueller
gumbildend *(petrol)* gum-forming
Gumbildung *f (petrol)* gum formation, gumming
Gumbildungstest *m (petrol)* gum test
Gumgehalt *m (petrol)* gum content
Gummi *m* rubber • **mit ~ ausgekleidet** rubber-lined • **mit ~ beschichtet** rubber-coated
~/halbharter semihard rubber, semiebonite
~/mikroporöser microporous rubber
~/poröser porous rubber
Gummi *n* gum
~/arabisches gum arabic, acacia (Arabic) gum *(from Acacia specc., esp from A. senegal (L.) Willd.)*
Gummi Ghatti *n* gum ghatti, India gum *(from Anogeissus latifolia Wall.)*
Gummiabfälle *mpl* rubber scrap (waste), scrap (waste) rubber
Gummiarabikum *n s.* Gummi/arabisches
gummiartig rubber-like, rubbery
Gummiartikel *m* rubber article (product)
Gummiauskleidung *f* rubber lining
Gummiband *n* rubber band
~/endloses rubber belt
Gummibelag *m* rubber covering
Gummichemie *f* rubber chemistry
Gummichemiker *m* rubber chemist
Gummideckplatte *f* rubber cover
Gummidichtung *f* rubber packing (seal) *(on moving parts)*; rubber gasket *(with static application)*
Gummielastizität *f* rubber (long-range) elasticity
Gummielementarfaden *m* rubber filament
gummieren to rubber[ize]
Gummierung *f* 1. rubberizing, proofing; 2. rubber coat[ing]; *(inner surfaces:)* rubber lining
Gummifaden *m* rubber thread
Gummifaser *f* rubber fibre
Gummifaserstoff *m* rubber fibre
Gummifinger *m (lab)* rubber fingerstall (finger cot)
Gummigurtförderer *m* rubber belt conveyor
Gummigutt *n* [gum] gamboge, camboge, cambogia *(from Garcinia specc.)*
Gummihaar *n* rubberized hair
Gummihandschuhe *mpl* rubber gloves
Gummiharz *n* gum resin
Gummiindustrie *f* rubber [manufacturing] industry
gummiisoliert rubber-insulated
Gummilack *m* gum lac *(crude shellac)*
Gummilösung *f* rubber solution; rubber cement
Gummilösungsmittel *n* rubber solvent
Gummimanschette *f* rubber sleeve *(as for filtering crucibles)*
Gummi-Metall-Verbindung *f* 1. rubber-to-metal bonding *(act)*; 2. rubber-to-metal bond *(result)*
Gummipackung *f s.* Gummidichtung
Gummiquetscher *m* squeegee
Gummiriemen *m* rubber belt
Gummiring *m* rubber ring (annulus)
Gummirohr *n* rubber tube
Gummisack *m (plast)* rubber bag
Gummisack-Formverfahren *n s.* Gummisack-Preßverfahren
Gummisack-Preßverfahren *n (plast)* [pressure] bag moulding
Gummisackverfahren *n*/**abgewandeltes** *(plast)* autoclave moulding

Gummischeibe *f* rubber washer
Gummischlauch *m* rubber hose (tubing)
Gummischlauchmaterial *n* rubber tubing
Gummischnittfaden *m* cut rubber thread
Gummistempel *m (ceram)* rubber stamp
Gummistopfen *m* rubber stopper (bung)
~/doppelt durchbohrter two-hole rubber stopper
~/durchbohrter bored rubber stopper
Gummistöpsel *m s.* Gummistopfen
Gummitaschenventil *n* pinch valve
Gummitechnologe *m* rubber technologist
Gummitechnologie *f* rubber technology
Gummitreibriemen *m* rubber belt
Gummiwalze *f* rubber-covered roll
Gummiwaren *fpl* rubber goods (products, articles)
~/technische mechanical rubber goods
Gummiwerk *n* rubber factory, rubber[-manufacturing] plant
Gummiwischer *m (lab)* rubber-tipped glass rod, [rubber] policeman, bobby
Gummizucker *m* pectin sugar, arabinose, pectinose
Gumtest *m (petrol)* gum test
Gur-Dynamit *n* guhr dynamite
Gurgelmittel *n (pharm)* gargarism, gargle
Gurjunbalsam *m* gurjun balsam, gurjan (gardjan, gargan) balsam *(from Dipterocarpus alatus Roxb.)*
Gurjunbalsamöl *n* gurjun balsam oil, Indian wood oil
Gurt *m* belt
~/gemuldeter troughed belt
Gurtbandförderer *m* belt (band) conveyor
~/gemuldeter troughed-belt conveyor
~ mit Gummigurt rubber belt conveyor
Gurtbecherwerk *n* belt[-and-bucket] elevator
Gurtdurchhang *m* belt sag
Gurtförderer *m s.* Gurtbandförderer
Gurtreiniger *m* belt cleaner *(of a belt conveyor)*
Gurtspannung *f* belt tension
Gurtwerkstoff *m* belting
Guß *m* 1. casting *(product)*; 2. *s.* Gießen
Guß... *s. a.* Gieß...
Gußblase *f* blow hole, blister *(a material fault)*
Gußblock *m* ingot
Gußeisen *n* cast iron
~ mit Kugelgraphit[/graues] *s.* Grauguß/globularer
~/siliziumlegiertes silicon cast iron
~/weißes white cast iron
Gußeisenarmierung *f* cast-iron armouring
Gußeisenretorte *f* cast-iron retort
gußeisern cast-iron
Gußfehler *m* casting defect, *(on the surface also)* scar
Gußglas *n* rolled glass
Gußhaut *f* skin *(foundry)*
Gußlegierung *f* cast[ing] alloy
Gußrohr *n* cast pipe
Gußstahl *m* cast steel
Gußstahlfilterpresse *f* cast-steel filter press
Gußstahl-Hochdruckautoklav *m* cast-steel high-pressure autoclave
Gußstück *n*, **Gußteil** *n* casting
Gußwalze *f* forming roll *(in manufacturing sheet glass)*
Gut *n* material, stuff *(if already treated also)* product
~/abgeröstetes *(met)* calcine
~/aufschwimmendes *(min tech)* floating material (fraction), floats
~/getrocknetes dry product
~/magnetisches magnetic material, magnetics
~/magnetisierbares magnetizable material, magnetics
~/nichtmagnetisches non-magnetic material, non-magnetics
~/nichtmagnetisierbares non-magnetizable material, non-magnetics
~/trocknendes material being dried
~/zu behandelndes material to be treated
~/zu handhabendes material to be handled
~/zu trocknendes material to be dried
Gutabscheider *m* product collector (separator)
Gutaufgabe *f s.* Guteintrag
Gutaustrag *m*, **Gutaustritt** *m* 1. discharge *(act or process)*; 2. discharge [point]
Gutbrandbereich *m (ceram)* maturing range
Gutbrandtemperatur *f (ceram)* maturing temperature
Gutbrennen *n (ceram)* maturing
Güte *f* quality, *(food also)* goodness
Güteanforderungen *fpl s.* Gütebedingungen
Gütebedingungen *fpl* quality standards
~ für Trinkwasser potable (drinking) water standards (regulations)
Gütegrad *m* grade
Guteintrag *m* 1. charging *(act or process)*; 2. charging point
Güteklasse *f* grade
Gütekontrolle *f* quality control
Gütekriterien *npl s.* Gütemerkmale
Gütemerkmale *npl* quality criteria
~ des Abwassers waste-water characteristics
Gutentnahme *f s.* Gutaustrag
Güteparameter *mpl s.* Gütemerkmale
Gütesicherung *f (anal)* quality assurance
Gutfeuchte *f* product moisture
Gutstoff *m (pap)* accepted (screened) stock, accepts
Guttapercha *f(n)* gutta-percha *(from Payena and Palaquium specc.)*
Gutverlust *m* product loss
Gutverweilzeit *f* residence time
Guyard-Reaktion *f* Guyard reaction *(oxidation of Mn^{++} by MnO_4^-)*
GV *s.* Glühverlust
GW *s.* Wasser/gebundenes
Gynocardsäure *f* gynocardic acid *(a mixture of acids found in chaulmoogra oil)*, *(specif)* chaulmoogric acid, 13-(cyclopent-2-enyl)tridecanoic acid
Gyro-Dampfphase[krack]verfahren *n*, **Gyro-Spaltverfahren** *n* Gyro [vapour-phase] process

H

H *s.* Heizwert
H_o *(oberer Heizwert) s.* Brennwert/spezifischer
H_u *(unterer Heizwert) s.* Heizwert/spezifischer
Haar *n* hair, *(text collectively)* hair fibre
Haarbehandlungsmittel *n (cosmet)* hair [treatment] preparation
Haarbleichmittel *n* hair bleach (bleaching agent)
Haarcreme *f* hair cream
haarentfernend depilatory
Haarentfernung *f* depilation, epilation
Haarentfernungscreme *f* depilatory cream
Haarentfernungsmittel *n (cosmet, tann)* depilatory [agent], depilitant, epilator, hair remover
Haarfarbe *s.* Haarfärbemittel
Haarfärbemittel *n* hair dye
~/chemisch wirkendes permanent hair dye
Haarfestiger *m* setting lotion, waveset [product]
Haarfixiercreme *f* hair cream
Haarkosmetikum *n* hair cosmetic
Haarkristall *m* [crystal] whisker
Haarlack *m* hair lacquer
haarlockernd depilatory
Haarlockerung *f* depilation, epilation, *(tann also)* unhairing, dehairing
~/enzymatische (fermentative) *(tann)* enzyme unhairing
Haarlockerungsmittel *n s.* Haarentfernungsmittel
Haarlotion *f* hair lotion
Haarnadelrohr *n* hairpin tube
Haarnadelrohrbündel *n* hairpin coil
Haarnadelwärmeaustauscher *m*, **Haarnadelwärmeübertrager** *m* heat exchanger with hairpin tubes
Haarpflegemittel *n* hair [treatment] preparation
Haarreinigungsmittel *n* hair wash
Haarriß *m* hair crack, craze *(surface defect)*
Haarrißbildung *f* hair-[line] cracking, [micro]crazing *(on surfaces)*; *(glass)* crizzling *(a defect)*
Haarrisse *mpl (ceram)* crazing *(a defect in glazes)*; *(glass)* crizzle *(a defect)*; *(ceram, glass)* crackle *(for decorative purposes)*
Haarrißglasur *f (ceram)* crackle glaze
Haarröhrchen *n* capillary [tube]
Haarröhrchenwirkung *f* capillarity, capillary action
Haartöner *m*, **Haartönungsmittel** *n* hair tint
Haarwäsche *f*, **Haarwaschmittel** *n* hair wash (shampoo)
Haarwasser *n* hair tonic
Haarwellotion *f* wavesetting lotion
Haber-Bosch-Verfahren *n* Haber[-Bosch] process *(for synthesizing ammonia from H_2 and N_2)*
Habitus *m* habit *(as of crystals)*
H-Abspaltungsreaktion *f* hydrogen abstraction reaction
Hacke *f s.* Hackmaschine
hacken *(pap)* to chip, to chop
Hacker *m s.* Hackmaschine
Hackmaschine *f (pap)* chipper, chopper, chipping (chopping) machine
Hackmesser *n (pap)* chipper knife
Hackschnitzel *npl (pap)* [wood] chips
Hackschnitzelbehälter *m s.* Hackschnitzelsilo
Hackschnitzelfüllung *f (pap)* chip filling (packing), filling with chips
Hackschnitzellagerung *f (pap)* chip storage
Hackschnitzelsilo *n (pap)* chip silo, chip [storage] bin
Hackschnitzelsortiermaschine *f (pap)* chip screen
Hackschnitzelspeicher *m (pap)* chip loft
Häckselmaschine *f (pap)* chopping machine, chopper, cutter *(for straw)*
häckseln *(pap)* to chop, to cut *(straw)*
Hackspan *m (pap)* [wood] chip
Hackspanlänge *f (pap)* chip length
Hadern *pl (pap)* rags
Hadernaufbereitung *f (pap)* pulping of rags
Hadernaufbereitungsanlage *f (pap)* rag mill
Hadernaufschluß *m (pap)* pulping of rags
Hadernbleiche *f (pap)* bleaching of rag pulp (stock)
Haderndrescher *m (pap)* rag willow (thrasher), devil
Hadernfaser *f (pap)* rag fibre
Haderngehalt *n (pap)* rag content
Hadernhalbstoff *m (pap)* all-rag furnish, rag pulp (stuff, stock), non-woody pulp
Hadernhalbstoffbleiche *f (pap)* bleaching of rag pulp (stock)
Hadernhalbstoffpapier *n* [all-]rag paper
Hadernhalbzeug *n s.* Hadernhalbstoff
Hadernkocher *m (pap)* rag (bleach) boiler
Hadernkochung *f (pap)* cooking of rags
Hadernpapier *n* [all-]rag paper
Hadernpapierfabrik *f* rag mill
Hadernpapierherstellung *f* rag paper making
Hadernpappe *f* rag board
Hadernschneider *m (pap)* rag cutter (chopper)
Hadernstäuber *m (pap)* rag duster
Hadernstoff *m s.* Hadernhalbstoff
Hadron *n (nucl)* hadron
Hadsel-Mühle *f*, **Hadsel-Prallmühle** *f* Hadsel mill
Haematit *m s.* Hämatit
Hafen *m (glass, ceram)* pot
~/eingeglaster *(glass)* glazed pot
~/gedeckter *s.* ~/geschlossener
~/geschlossener *(glass)* hooded (covered) pot; *(ceram)* closed pot
~/glasierter *(glass)* glazed pot
~/offener *(glass, ceram)* open pot
~/verdeckter *s.* ~/geschlossener
Hafenbank *f (glass)* siege, bench *(of a pot furnace)*
Hafenglas *n* pot-[melted] glass
Hafenofen *m (glass)* pot furnace
Hafenschmelze *f (glass)* pot melting
Hafentemperofen *m (glass)* pot arch
Haferstärke *f* oat starch
Hafnat *n* $M^I_2HfO_3$ hafnate

Hafnium *n* Hf hafnium
Hafniumcarbid *n* hafnium carbide
Hafniumdioxid *n s.* Hafnium(IV)-oxid
Hafnium(IV)-oxid *n* hafnium(IV) oxide, hafnium dioxide
Hafniumoxidchlorid *n* hafnium dichloride oxide
Hafniumsulfat *n* hafnium sulphate
Hafniumtetrachlorid *n* hafnium tetrachloride
HAF-Ruß *m (rubber)* high abrasion furnace black, HAF black
Haftarbeit *f (phys ch)* adhesional work, work of adhesion
haften to adhere, to stick
Haften *n* adhesion, adherence, sticking
~ **am Werkzeug** *(plast)* mould sticking
haftend, haftfähig adhesive, adherent
Haftfähigkeit *f* adhesiveness, adherence, adhesive power (capacity), sticking power (capacity)
~/anfängliche initial retention *(of pesticides)*
Haftfestigkeit *f* tenacity, adhesive strength
Haftinhalt *m (distil)* [liquid] hold-up
Haftkleber *m* contact[-bonding] adhesive, pressure-sensitive adhesive
Haftmittel *n* adhesive, sticking agent; *(rubber)* bonding agent; *(text)* coupling agent *(for laminates)*; *(agric)* deposit builder *(in pesticide formulations)*
~/metallkeramisches ceramic-metal adhesive
Haftspannung *f* adhesive stress (tension)
Haftstelle *f (phys ch)* trap *(as for recombination of electrons and defect electrons)*
Haftstoff *m s.* Haftmittel
Haftung *f s.* Haften
Haftvermittler *m* adhesion promoter, *(plast also)* coupling (anchoring) agent
Haftvermögen *n s.* Haftfähigkeit
Hagen-Poiseulle-Gesetz *n s.* Hagen-Poiseulle-Strömungsgesetz
Hagen-Poiseulle-Gleichung *f* Poiseulle's equation (formula) *(of laminar flow in pipes)*
Hagen-Poiseulle-Strömung *f* Poiseulle flow
Hagen-Poiseulle-Strömungsgesetz *n* Poiseulle's law, Hagen-Poiseulle law *(of laminar flow in pipes)*
Hägglund-Verfahren *n* Hägglund process *(saccharification of wood)*
Hahn *m* cock, tap, plug valve (cock, bib)
~/Karlsruher T-shape 120° bore cock
~ **mit hebelgelüftetem Küken** lever-sealed plug cock
~ **mit schräger Bohrung** oblique cock
~ **mit senkrechter Bohrung** straight cock
Hahn-Aufsatz *m (distil)* Hahn head
Hahnenfuß *m (ceram)* [cock-]spur *(an item of kiln furniture)*
Hahnfett *n* tap (stopcock) grease
Hahnhülse *f* socket, cock shell (barrel)
Hahnium *n* Hn hahnium *(element 108)*
Hahnkapillare *f (distil)* capillary stopcock (tap)
Hahnkegel *m s.* Hahnküken
Hahnküken *n* [cock] plug, *(Am also)* stopper
Hahnrohr *n* **des Orsat-Apparates** Orsat gas manifold
Hahnschmiermittel *n* tap (stopcock) lubricant
Hahnsicherung *f* locking device
Hahnsystem *n* **des Orsat-Apparates** Orsat gas manifold
Hahnventil *n* plug valve (cock, bib) *(for compounds s.* Hahn*)*
Halbacetal *n* hemiacetal
halbacetalartig, halbacetalisch hemiacetal-like
Halbaminal *n* hemiaminal, α-amino alcohol
Halbanthrazit *m* semianthracite, lean (dry steam) coal
Halbantigen *n (bioch)* hapten, haptene
halbautomatisch semiautomatic
halbchemisch semichemical
Halbchinon *n* semiquinone
halbdirekt semidirect
halbdurchlässig semipermeable
Halbedelstein *m* semiprecious stone
Halbelement *n (phys ch)* half-element, half-cell
Halbentbasten *n (text)* soupling
Halbester *m* semi-ester, half-ester
Halbfärbezeit *f* time of half-dyeing
halbfest semisolid
halbfeuerfest semirefractory
halbflächig *(cryst)* hemihedral
halbflüssig semiliquid, semifluid
Halbformal *n* hemiformal *(any of the hemiacetals of formaldehyde)*
Halbfusinit *m* semifusinite *(a maceral of coal)*
halbgebleicht *(pap)* half-bleached, semibleached
halbgeleimt *(pap)* half-sized, 1/2 sized
halbgeordnet *(phys ch)* semi-ordered
halbglasartig *(ceram)* semivitreous, semivitrified
halbhart half-hard *(cold-rolled metal)*; medium-hard *(pitch)*; semihard *(rubber)*; semirigid *(plastic)*
Halbhartgummi *m* semiebonite, semihard rubber
Halbhöhenbreite *f (anal)* [peak] width at half height, [peak] half width
Halbhydrat *n* hemihydrate
Halbkarton *m* cardboard
Halbkoks *m* coal char
Halbkolloid *n* semicolloid
Halbkonserve *f* partly preserved food
halbkontinuierlich semicontinuous, semibatch
Halbkristallglas *n* half-crystal
halbkristallin[isch] semicrystalline, hemicrystalline, hypocrystalline
Halblebenszeit *f (biot)* half life *(of enzyme activity)*
halbleitend semiconducting, semiconductive
Halbleiter *m* semiconductor
~/elektronischer electronic semiconductor
~/gemischter compensated semiconductor
~ **mit Eigenleitfähigkeit** intrinsic semiconductor
Halbleiterlaser *m* semiconductor (diode) laser
Halbleitermaterial *n* semiconducting material
Halb-Leiterpolymer[e] *n* semiladder polymer

Halbleiterschicht *f* semiconducting layer
Halbleitersperrschicht *f* semiconductor junction
Halbleiterteilchenzähler *m* semiconductor particle counter
Halbleiterübergang *m* semiconductor junction
Halbleiterverbindung *f* semiconducting compound
Halbleitung *f* semiconductivity
Halblösung *f (pap)* weak acid
Halbmaske *f* half-mask facepiece *(respiratory protection)*
halbmatt semi-mat[t], *(Am also)* semimatte, *(phot also)* half-mat[t], semigloss[y]; *(text)* semidull
Halbmattglasur *f (ceram)* semi-mat glaze
Halbmetall *n* semimetal, crossroads element
Halbmetallglanz *m (min)* submetallic lustre
halbmetallisch semimetallic
Halbmikroanalyse *f* semimicro (centigram) analysis
Halbmikroanalysenwaage *f* semimicro balance
Halbmikroansatz *m* semimicro batch
Halbmikroarbeitstechnik *f*, **Halbmikroarbeitsweise** *f s.* Halbmikromethode
Halbmikrobestimmung *f* semimicro determination
Halbmikroextraktion *f* semimicro extraction
Halbmikromaßstab/im semimicro-scale
Halbmikromethode *f* semimicro method, centigram procedure
~ **nach Kjeldahl** semimicro Kjeldahl method *(for determining the nitrogen content)*
~ **nach Rast** semimicro Rast method *(for determining molecular weights)*
Halbmikropräparation *f* semimicro preparation
Halbmikroprobe *f* *meso sample, semimicro sample *(0.1 to 0.01 g)*
Halbmikrotechnik *f s.* Halbmikromethode
Halbmikro-Torsionswaage *f* semimicro torsion balance
Halbmikroverfahren *n s.* Halbmikromethode
Halbmikrowaage *f* semimicro balance
Halbmuffelofen *m* semimuffle kiln
halbnaß semidry
Halbneutralisationspunkt *m* half neutralization point
halbpolar semipolar
Halbporzellan *n* semiporcelain, vitreous china
halbquantitativ semiquantitative
Halbsandwichverbindung *f* half-sandwich compound
Halbsäure *f (pap)* weak acid
Halbschatten *m* 1. half-shade; 2. *s.* Halbschattenwinkel
Halbschattennicol *m* half-shade Nicol *(polarimetry)*
Halbschattenpolarimeter *n*, **Halbschattenpolarisator** *m* half-shade polarimeter
Halbschattenwinkel *m* half-shade angle *(polarimetry)*
Halbsesselform *f* half-chair form *(stereochemistry)*
halbstarr semirigid
Halbstoff *m (pap)* half-stuff, half-stock • **zu ~ aufschließen** *(pap)* to make into [a] pulp, to reduce to pulp, to pulp
~ **in Bogenform (Pappenform)** half-stuff board, [solid] pulp board, sheets (laps) of pulp, lap[ped] pulp
~/textiler non-woody pulp
~/trockener *s.* ~ in Bogenform
Halbstoffholländer *m (pap)* half-stuff beater, breaking[-in] engine, breaker [engine], rag engine (breaker), Hollander washer
Halbstoffholländerwalze *f (pap)* breaker roll (drum)
Halbstoffsortierer *m (pap)* pulp screen
Halbstufenpotential *n* half-wave potential
Halbstundenlack *m* half-hour synthetic *(a nitrocellulose lacquer)*
halbsynthetisch semisynthetical
halbtechnisch pilot-[plant-]scale
Halbtrivialname *m* semitrivial (semisystematic) name
halbtrocken semidry
Halbtrockenpressen *n (ceram)* semidry pressing
halbtrocknend semidrying
Halbultrabeschleuniger *m (rubber)* semiultra accelerator
halbverglast *(ceram)* semivitreous, semivitrified
Halbverkokung *f* semicoking, semicarbonization
Halbwachs *n* propolis, bee glue, balm
Halbwassergas *n* semi water gas
Halbweißöl *n* half-white oil
Halbwelle *f* half wave
Halbwellenpotential *n* half-wave potential
Halbwert[s]breite *f (anal)* half-width [at half maximum], HWHM, half-intensity width *(of a signal)*
Halbwerts[schicht]dicke *f (phys ch)* half-thickness, half-value thickness (layer)
Halbwertszeit *f* 1. half-life [period], half-time, half-value period, time (period) of half-change *(of reactants)*; *(nucl)* [radioactive] half life; *(biot)* half life *(of enzyme activity)*; 2. *s.* ~ der Reaktion; 3. *s.* Rückstands-Halbwertszeit
~ **der Reaktion** [reaction] half-life, [reaction] half-time, half reaction time
Halbwertszeitmethode *f* method of half-times *(for determining the reaction order)*
Halbwollfärben *n* union dyeing
Halbwollfarbstoff *m* union dye
Halbzelle *f (phys ch)* half-cell, half-element
Halbzellenpotential *n* half-cell potential
Halbzellstoff *m* semichemical pulp
Halbzellstoffanlage *f s.* Halbzellstoffwerk
Halbzellstoffaufschluß *m* semichemical pulping
Halbzellstoffwerk *n* semichemical plant, semichemical-pulp mill
Halbzeug *n s.* Halbstoff
Haldane-Beziehung *f*, **Haldane-Gleichung** *f* Haldane relationship *(enzyme kinetics)*
Halde *f (min tech)* tip, [waste] dump
Haldenlaugung *f*, **Haldenleaching** *n (min tech)* [waste-]dump leaching, slope leaching
Hall-Effekt *m* Hall effect *(a galvanomagnetic effect)*
halluzinogen *(tox)* hallucinogenic, psycho[to]mimetic

Halluzinogen *n (tox)* hallucinogen, psychodysleptic, psychotomimetic [drug], psychedelic drug
Hall-Verfahren *n* Hall process *(1. for obtaining aluminium; 2. for gasification of oil)*
Halmyrolyse *f* halmyrolysis *(chemical destruction or rearrangement of a sediment on the sea floor)*
Halo *m (phot, spectr, chromat)* halo
Halochromie *f* halochromism *(phenomenon)*; halochromy *(property)*
Halochromieerscheinung *f* halochromic effect, halochromism
Haloform-Reaktion *f (org ch)* haloform (Einhorn) reaction
Halogen *n* halogen
Halogenabkömmling *m* halo[gen] derivative
Halogenacylierung *f* haloacylation
Halogenaddition *f* halogen addition
Halogenalkan *n* haloalkane, alkyl halide
Halogenalkylierung *f* haloalkylation
Halogenaminierung *f* haloamination
Halogenanilin *n* haloaniline, halogenated aniline
Halogenanthrachinon *n* haloanthraquinone
Halogenarylierung *f* haloarylation
Halogenbenzen *n*, **Halogenbenzol** *n* halobenzene
Halogenborierung *f* haloboration
Halogenbrücke *f* halogen bridge
Halogencarbonsäure *f* haloacid
α-Halogencarbonsäure *f* α-halogenated acid, α-haloacid
Halogendemetallierung *f* halodemetalation
Halogenderivat *n* halo[gen] derivative
Halogenelektrode *f* halogen electrode
Halogenentzug *m* removal of halogen
Halogenethan *n* haloethane, ethyl halide
Halogenfettsäure *f s.* Halogencarbonsäure
Halogenglühlampe *f* halogen lamp
halogenhaltig halogen-containing
Halogenhydrin *n* halohydrin *(any of a class of glycerol derivatives)*
Halogenid *n* halide, halogenide
~/siliciumorganisches *s.* Halogensilan/organisches
Halogenidphosphor *m* halide phosphor *(a halide exhibiting phosphorescence)*
halogenieren to halogenate
α-halogeniert α-halogenated, alpha-halogenated
halogeniert/mehrfach polyhalogenated
Halogenierung *f* halogenation
~ in der Seitenkette side-chain halogenation
α-Halogenierung *f* alpha-halogenation
Halogenierungsgrad *m* degree of halogenation
halogenisieren *s.* halogenieren
Halogenketon *n* haloketone
Halogenkohlenwasserstoff *m* halogenated hydrocarbon, halocarbon
Halogenlactonisierung *f* halolactonization
Halogenlampe *f* halogen [filament] lamp, tungsten-halogen lamp, halide lamp
Halogenmethan *n* halomethane, methyl halide
Halogenmethyl *n s.* Halogenmethan
Halogennachweis *m* detection of halogens • **zum ~** for detecting halogens
Halogenoform *n* haloform *(any of the triholomethanes)*
Halogenolyse *f* halogenolysis
Halogensilan *n* halogenosilane, halosilane
~/organisches organohalogenosilane, organohalosilane, organosilicon halide
Halogensilber *n (phot)* silver halide
Halogensilberemulsion *f (phot)* silver-halide emulsion
halogensubstituiert halogen-substituted
Halogenüberträger *m* halogen carrier
Halogenverbindung *f* halo[gen] compound
Halogenverbindungen *fpl***/organische** haloorganic (halogenated organic) compounds, HOC, haloorganics, organic halides, organohalides
Halogenwasserstoff *m* hydrogen halide (halogenide), hydrohalogen
Halogenwasserstoffabspaltung *f* removal of hydrogen halide
Halogenwasserstoffentzug *m* removal of hydrogen halide
Halogenwasserstoffsäure *f* hydrohalic acid
Halometer *n* sali[ni]meter *(a hydrometer for salt solutions)*
Halonium-Ion *n* halonium ion
Haloniumsalz *n* halonium salt
Halophyt *m (bot)* halophyte
Halotrichit *m (min)* halotrichite, iron alum *(aluminium iron(II) sulphate 22-water)*
Hals *m* neck *(as of a bottle or shaft)*
Halsbildung *f* necking *(in drawing fibres)*
haltbar durable, stable • **~ machen** to preserve, to conserve • **unbegrenzt ~ sein** to keep indefinitely • **~ verpackt** packed for prolonged storage
Haltbarkeit *f* durability, stability; *(food)* storage (keeping) quality
Haltbarkeitsdauer *f* life[time], service (length of) life; *(food)* keeping time
Haltbarkeitsprüfung *f* durability test
Haltbarkeitszeit *f s.* Haltbarkeitsdauer
Haltbarmachung *f* preservation, conservation
~/chemische *(food)* chemical preservation
~ für beschränkte Zeit temporary preservation
~ von Lebensmitteln food preservation
Haltedruck *m* net positive suction head, NPSH *(of a pump)*
Halteklemme *f s.* Halteschelle
halten to support *(mechanically)*; to keep, to maintain *(e.g. a definite temperature)*
~/am Kochen (Sieden) to keep at the boil
~/im Gleichgewicht to equilibrate, to keep in equilibrium
~/in der Schwebe to keep (maintain) in suspension
~/in Lösung to keep in solution
~/in Suspension to keep in suspension
~/instand to maintain
~/konstant to maintain constant
~/nahe am Sieden to keep near the boil

Haltepunkt *m***[/eutektischer]** [eutectic] halt
Halter *m s.* Halterung
Halterollen *fpl***/seitliche** edge rolls *(sheet-glass manufacture)*
Halterung *f* holder, clamp, clip, gripping mechanism
Halteschelle *f* joint clamp, adapter *(for ground-glass joints)*
~ **für Kegelschliffverbindungen** cone-and-socket joint clamp, socket-to-cone adapter
~ **für Kugelschliffverbindungen** ball-and-socket joint clamp, socket-to-ball adapter
Haltevorrichtung *f s.* Halterung
Haltewalze *f* nip roller
Haltezeit *f* residence time, retention (hold-up, holding, detention) time
Häm *n (bioch)* haem, protohaem, *(esp Am)* heme
Hamamelitannin *n (tann)* hamamelitannin
Hämatin *n* haematin *(oxidized form of haem)*
Hämatit *m (min)* [red] haematite *(iron(III) oxide)*
Hämatit[roh]eisen *n* haematite [pig] iron
Hämeisen *n* haem iron
Hämenzym *n* haem (iron porphyrine) enzyme
Hämiglobin *n* haemiglobin, methaemoglobin
Hamilton-Operator *m (phys ch)* Hamiltonian [operator], energy operator
Hämin *n* haemin, ferrihaem
Häminchlorid *n* haemin chloride, protohaemin
Hammelfett *n*, **Hammeltalg** *m* mutton fat (tallow)
Hammer *m* beater *(of the hammer mill)*
Hammerbrecher *m* hammer crusher
Hammermühle *f* hammer mill (disintegrator)
Hammerschlag *m* hammer scale *(iron(II,III) oxide)*
Hammerwalke *f (text)* fulling stocks
Hammett-Beziehung *f (phys ch)* Hammett relation (correlation), rho-sigma correlation, $\varrho\sigma$-correlation
Hammett-Diagramm *n (phys ch)* Hammett plot
Hammett-Funktion *f (phys ch)* Hammett acidity function
Hammett-Gleichung *f* Hammett equation, [Hammett] $\varrho\sigma$ equation, rho-sigma equation
Hammett-Korrelation *f s.* Hammett-Beziehung
Hammond-Postulat *n*, **Hammond-Prinzip** *n* Hammond postulate (principle) *(kinetics)*
Hämochrom[ogen] *n* haemochromogen, haemochrome
Hämocyanin *n* haemocyanin *(a respiratory pigment of numerous invertebrate animals)*
Hämogen *n (bioch)* extrinsic factor, vitamin B_{12}
Hämogenase *f (bioch)* intrinsic factor
Hämoglobin *n* haemoglobin, Hb
~**/desoxygeniertes (reduziertes)** *s.* ~/sauerstoffarmes
~ **S** haemoglobin S, sickle-cell haemoglobin
~**/sauerstoffarmes** deoxygenated haemoglobin
Hämolymphe *f* haemolymph
hämolysieren to haemolyze
Hämolysin *n* haemolysin *(toxic substance produced by certain bacteria)*
Hämoprotein *n* haemoprotein, haem (iron porphyrine) protein
Hämostatikum *n s.* Hämostyptikum
Hämostyptikum *n (pharm)* haemostatic, styptic
hämostyptisch haemostatic, styptic
Handauflegeverfahren *n (plast)* hand (wet) lay-up technique, contact (impression) moulding
Handaustrag *m* hand scooping
Handbeschickung *f* hand charging
handbetätigt manually operated, hand-operated
Handbetrieb *m* manual (hand) operation
handbetrieben manually operated, hand-operated
Handbütten *n* vat paper, [genuine] hand-made paper
Handbüttenrand *m (pap)* deckle [edge]
Handcreme *f* hand cream
Handdruck *m* block printing
Handelsbenzol *n* commercial benzole
~**/90er** 90's benzole
Handelsbezeichnung *f s.* Handelsname
Handelscarbid *n* commercial carbide
Handelschemiker *m* commercial chemist
Handelsdünger *m* commercial fertilizer
Handelskohle *f* commercial coal
Handelsmuster *n* trade sample
Handelsname *m* trade name (term), commercial name
Handelsprodukt *n* commercial product
~**/formuliertes** formulation
Handelsqualität *f* commercial (market) grade
Handelssorte *f* market type (grade)
Handelstannin *n* tannic acid of commerce *(a product consisting of gallic acid glucose esters with penta-m-digalloyl-β-glucose as chief constituent)*
handelsüblich commercial, commercially available
Handentwicklung *f (phot)* see-saw development
Handfeuerlöscher *m* fire extinguisher, portable [fire] extinguisher
Handform *f (plast)* hand mould
Handformen *n*, **Handformgebung** *f (ceram)* hand modelling (moulding)
Handgebläse *n* hand-power air blower *(made of rubber bulbs)*
handgeformt *(ceram)* hand-modelled, hand-moulded
Handgriff *m* handle
Handhabbarkeit *f***/leichte** ease of use, ease (simplicity) of servicing
handhaben to handle
~ **lassen/sich** to handle
Handhabung *f* handling
Handklaubung *f (coal)* hand picking (cleaning, sorting)
Handleimung *f (pap)* hand sizing
Handloch *n* hand hole
Handlotion *f* hand lotion
Handmuster *n (pap)* hand (pulp, test) sheet
Handpapier *n s.* Handbütten
Handpappe *f* cylinder board
Handpflegemittel *n* hand preparation
Handpresse *f (plast)* hand press
Handrad *n* handwheel

Handregelung *f* manual control
Handscheidung *f s.* Handklaubung
Handschuhbox *f (nucl)* glove box
Handsieben *n* hand sieving
handsortiert hand-sorted
Handsortierung *f* sorting by hand, hand sorting
Handspritze *f*, **Handspritzgerät** *n (agric)* hand[-held] sprayer
Handspritzpistole *f* hand [spray] gun
Handsprühgerät *n (agric)* hand[-held] sprayer
Handstäubegerät *n*, **Handstäuber** *m (agric)* hand[-operated] duster; *(if pneumatically operated:)* hand [dust] gun
Handsteuerung *f* manual control
Handtuchpapier *n* towelling paper
Handverstäuber *m s.* Handstäubegerät
Handvorrat *m* **an Chemikalien** *(lab)* side-shelf reagents
Handwerkzeug *n (plast)* hand mould
Handzentrifuge *f* hand[-driven] centrifuge
Handzerstäuber *m s.* Handsprühgerät
Hanf *m*/**Indischer** *(pharm)* Indian hemp *(dried summits of Cannabis indica Lam.)*
Hanffaser *f* hemp fibre *(from Cannabis sativa L.)*
Hanföl *n* hemp[seed] oil *(from Cannabis sativa L.)*
Hanfpapier *n* hemp paper
Hanfsamenöl *n s.* Hanföl
Hängeäscher *m (tann)* rocker
Hängebandtrockner *m* festoon (loop) dryer
Hängedämpfer *m (text)* festoon ager
hängen to hang; to be attached *(as of atoms)*
hängenbleiben to stick, to hang up
Hängetrockner *m* festoon (loop) dryer
Hängezentrifuge *f* [top-]suspended centrifuge, overdriven centrifuge
Hanglaugung *f*, **Hangleaching** *n (min tech)* heap leaching
Hansagelb *n* Hansa yellow *(any of various azo dyes)*
Hantelmodell *n* dumb-bell model *(of a molecule)*
Hantelprüfkörper *m (rubber)* dumb-bell test piece, dumb-bell strip, dumb bell
Hapten *n (bioch)* hapten, haptene
Harden-Young-Ester *m* Harden-Young ester, 1,6-fructofuranose diphosphate
Hardgrove-Maschine *f*, **Hardgrove-Mühle** *f* Hardgrove machine (mill) *(for determining grindability)*
Hardinge-Kaskadenmühle *f* Hardinge cascade mill
Hardinge-Mühle *f* Hardinge conical [ball] mill, Hardinge mill
Hard-Processing-Channel-Ruß *m* hard processing channel black, HPC black
Harfe *f (lab)* assembly
Hargreaves-Bird-Zelle *f (el ch)* Hargreaves-Bird cell
Hargreaves-Verfahren *n* Hargreaves process *(for obtaining HCl and Na_2SO_4 or K_2SO_4)*
Harmalaalkaloid *n* harmal[a] alkaloid
harmlos harmless, innocuous, benign
Harmlosigkeit *f* harmlessness, innocuousness, benignity
Harmotom *m (min)* harmotome *(a tectosilicate)*
Harn *m* urine
Harnanalyse *f* urinalysis, uranalysis, urine analysis
Harnantiseptikum *n* urinary antiseptic
Harngrieß *m (med)* gravel
Harnsäure *f* uric acid, 2,6,8-trihydroxypurine
harnsäureausscheidend *(bioch)* uricotelic
Harnsäureausscheider *m (bioch)* uricotelic animal
Harnsäurederivat *n* uric-acid derivative
Harnsäurereagens *n* **nach Folin-Denis** Folin-Denis reagent for uric acid
Harnsäurestein *m (med)* uric-acid calculus
Harnstein *m (med)* urinary calculus
Harnstoff *m* urea, carbamide
Harnstoffaddukt *n* urea adduct
Harnstoff-Aldehyd-Harz *n s.* Harnstoff-Formaldehyd-Harz
Harnstoffanlage *f (tech)* urea plant
harnstoffausscheidend *(bioch)* ureotelic
Harnstoffausscheider *m (bioch)* ureotelic animal
Harnstoff-Bisulfit-Löslichkeit *f (text)* urea-bisulphite solubility
Harnstoff-Calciumnitrat *n* calcium-nitrate-urea
Harnstoffdenaturierung *f (bioch)* urea denaturation
Harnstoffderivat *n*/**herbizides** urea herbicide
Harnstoffeinschlußverbindung *f* urea clathrate (inclusion compound)
Harnstoffentparaffinierung *f* urea dewaxing *(of lubricating-oil stocks)*
Harnstoff-Formaldehyd-Harz *n* urea[-formaldehyde] resin, polyurea
Harnstoff-Formaldehyd-Kondensat[ionsprodukt] *n* urea-formaldehyde condensation product, urea formaldehyde
Harnstoff-Formaldehyd-Leim *m* urea-formaldehyde glue
Harnstoffgitter *n* urea lattice
Harnstoffharz *n s.* Harnstoff-Formaldehyd-Harz
Harnstoffherbizid *n* urea herbicide
Harnstoffkalksalpeter *m s.* Harnstoff-Calciumnitrat
Harnstoffkomplex *m*, **Harnstoffkomplexverbindung** *f* urea complex
Harnstoffkondensat *n* urea condensate
Harnstoffmolekülverbindung *f* urea molecular compound
Harnstofformaldehyd *m s.* Harnstoff-Formaldehyd-Kondensat
harnstoffspaltend ureolytic
Harnstoffstickstoff *m (med)* urea nitrogen
Harnstofftrennung *f s.* Harnstoffentparaffinierung
Harnstoffzyklus *m (bioch)* urea (ornithine) cycle, Krebs-Henseleit cycle
harntreibend diuretic
Harris-Verfahren *n* Harris process *(for softening lead)*

Harrop-Ofen *m* Harrop kiln *(a tunnel kiln)*
hart hard *(as of metals, water, radiation)*; *(text)* crisp • ~ **werden** to harden, to solidify, to chill, to set
Hartanodisation *f*, **Hartanodisieren** *n* hard anodizing
Hartasphalt *m* hard asphalt
härtbar hardenable
Härtbarkeit *f* hardenability
Hartblei *n* hard[ened] lead, antimonial lead, regulus metal *(a lead alloy containing up to 15 % antimony)*
Hartbrandstein *m (ceram)* hard-burned (hard-fired) brick
Hartbraunkohle *f* hard brown coal
Hartcarbid *n* hard [metal] carbide
Härte *f* hardness *(as of metals, water, radiation)*
~/bleibende *(hyd)* permanent (non-carbonate) hardness
~ der [gehärteten] Randschicht *(met)* case hardness
~/durch Calcium verursachte *(hyd)* calcium hardness
~/permanente *s.* ~/bleibende
~/schwindende *s.* ~/temporäre
~/temporäre *(hyd)* temporary (carbonate) hardness carbonate alkalinity
~/vorübergehende *s.* ~/temporäre
Härteabscheidungen *fpl (hyd)* hardness (mineral) scale, hard-water depositions (residue)
Härtebad *n* hardening (hardener) bath
Härtebestimmung *f* determination of hardness, hardness testing
härtebildend *(hyd)* hardness-forming, hardness-causing, hardness-producing
Härtebildner *m (hyd)* hardness constituent, hardness-producing substance
Härtedurchbruch *m (hyd)* hardness leakage (bleed), hard-water bleed
Härtefaktor *m* hardness factor
Härtefixierbad *n (phot)* hardening fixer (fixing bath)
härtefrei *(hyd)* hardness-free, zero-hardness
Härtegehalt *m (hyd)* hardness level
Härtegrad *m* degree of hardness *(for compounds s. under* Grad*)*
Härtekasten *m (met)* case-hardening box
Härtekatalysator *m (plast)* curing catalyst
Härtelösung *f (phot)* hardening solution
Härtemesser *m s.* Härteprüfer
Härtemittel *n* hardening agent, hardener
härten *(met)* to harden; *(plast, coat)* to cure; *(glass)* to temper, to strengthen; to hydrogenize, to hydrogenate, to harden *(fats and oils)*
~/durch Nitrierung to nitride *(steel)*
~/im Cyan[salz]bad to cyanide *(steel)*
~/im Einsatz[verfahren] to case-harden *(steel)*
~/im Ofen *(plast, coat)* to stove, *(Am)* to bake
~/in Luft to air-harden *(steel)*
~/in Öl to oil-harden *(steel)*
~/in Wasser to water-harden *(steel)*
~/oberflächlich to surface-harden
Härten *n (met)* hardening; *(plast, coat)* curing, cure; *(glass)* tempering, strengthening; hydrogenation, hardening *(of fats and oils)*
~ im Ofen *(plast, coat)* stoving, *(Am)* baking
~/photochemisches *(plast, coat)* photocuring
~/selektives *(food)* selective hydrogenation
~/vorzeitiges *(plast)* premature curing *(a moulding defect)*
Härteöl *n* hardening oil
Härteprüfer *m* hardness tester (meter); *(using a drill:)* durometer; *(using the rebound of a ball:)* scleroscope; *(using a stylus:)* sclerometer
Härteprüfung *f* hardness test[ing]
~ nach Knoop Knoop hardness test
Härtepulver *n (met)* case-hardening powder
Härter *m (plast, coat)* curing (hardening) agent, hardener
Härteschicht *f (met)* [hardened] case
Härteskala *f* scale of hardness
~ nach Mohs Mohs' scale [of hardness]
Härtestufe *f* degree of hardness
Härtetiefe *f* depth of hardening
Härtezahl *f (rubber)* coefficient of hardness
Härtezeit *f (met)* hardening time; *(plast, coat)* curing (cure) time; *(plast)* stoving time *(of cast resins)*
Härtezyklus *m (plast)* curing cycle
Hartfaser *f* hard fibre
Hartfaserplatte *f* hard-board
Hartferrit *m (ceram)* hard ferrite
Hartfett *n* solid (hard) fat; hydrogenated (hardened) fat
Hartgewebe *n* laminated fabric, synthetic-resin-bonded fabric sheet
Hartgips *m* hard plaster
Hartglas *n* resistance (hard) glass
Hartglasgefäß *n* resistance-glass bottle
Hartglaskolben *m* resistance-glass flask
Hartgummi *m* hard rubber, ebonite, vulcanite
~/zelliger cellular ebonite
Hartgummimischung *f* hard-rubber mix
Hartgummiplatte *f* hard-rubber sheet
Hartgummiwalze *f* hard-rubber-covered roll
Hartguß *m* chilled (white) cast iron, chill-cast iron
Hartharz *n* hard resin
Hartkautschuk *m s.* Hartgummi
hartkochen to undercook, to cook raw *(cellulose)*
Hartkochung *f* undercooking *(of cellulose)*
Hartkoks *m* hard coke
Hartlegierung *f* hard alloy
Hartlot *n* brazing (hard) solder, brazing alloy (metal)
hartlöten to braze, to hard-solder
~/im Lötbad to dip-braze
Hartmasse *f (ceram)* hard paste, pâte dure
Hartmetall *n* hard metal *(composite consisting of hard materials and metals)*, *(specif) s.* ~/gesintertes
~/gesintertes cemented [hard] carbide, sintered carbide, cemented hard metal

Hartmetallegierung *f* hard metal alloy *(consisting of carbides and usually cobalt as a binder)*
Hartmetallwerkstoff *m* cemented carbide material
Hartoxidation *f* hard anodizing *(of metals)*
Hartpapier *n* hard (bakelite, laminated) paper, synthetic-resin-bonded paper sheet
Hartpappe *f* hard-board, panel board
Hartparaffin *n* hard (solid) paraffin, ceresin [wax]
Hartpech *n* hard pitch
Hartpetrolat[um] *n* dry petrolatum
Hartporzellan *n* hard[-paste] porcelain
Hart-PVC *n* unplasticized (rigid) PVC
Hartree-Einheiten *fpl* atomic units Hartree, Hartree units *(based on mass and charge of the electron and Planck's constant divided by 2π)*
Hartree-Fock-Methode *f* Hartree-Fock method *(molecular theory)*
Hartsalz *n* hard salt *(crude potash salt containing $MgSO_4$)*
Hartschaum[stoff] *m (plast)* rigid foam
Hartseide *f* hard (ecru) silk
Hartseife *f* hard soap
Hartspiritus *m* solid alcohol
Hartstoff *m* hard material
Härtung *f s.* Härten
Härtungsautoklav *m* hardening vessel *(for fats)*
Härtungsgeruch *m* hydrogenation (hardening) flavour
Härtungsgeschmack *m* hydrogenation (hardening) flavour
Härtungskatalysator *m (plast)* curing catalyst
Härtungsmittel *n* 1. hardening agent, hardener; 2. *s.* Härter
Härtungsperiode *f (plast)* curing cycle
Härtungstiefe *f* depth of hardening
Härtungszeit *f s.* Härtezeit
Hartverchromen *n* hard chrome-plating
Hartwachs *n* hard wax
Hartwasser *n* hard water
Hartwasserbeständigkeit *f* resistance to hard water
Hartwerden *n* hardening, set[ting]
Hartzerkleinerung *f* crushing (size reduction) of hard material
Harz *n* resin; *(petrol)* gum; *(pap)* rosin *(colophony)*; *(as a deleterious component in paper pulp:)* pitch
~/aktuelles *s.* ~/vorgebildetes
~ aus Rohterpentin pine resin (rosin), [common] rosin, colophony
~/fossiles fossil resin
~/freies *(pap)* free rosin
~ für Kontaktpreßverfahren (Niederdruckpreßverfahren) *(plast)* contact pressure resin
~/gehärtetes cured resin
~ im A-Zustand A-stage resin
~ im B-Zustand B-stage resin
~ im C-Zustand C-stage resin
~/lösliches soluble resin
~/mögliches *(petrol)* ultimate (potential) gum
~/natürliches natural resin
~/ölmodifiziertes oil-modified resin
~/ölreaktives oil-reactive resin
~/potentielles *s.* ~/mögliches
~/schädliches *(pap)* pitch
~/vorgebildetes (vorhandenes) *(petrol)* existent (preformed) gum
harzähnlich resin-like
Harzappretur *f (tann)* resin finish
harzartig resinous, resinoid, resiny
Harzbett *n* resin bed, bed of ion-exchange resin
Harzbettstreckung *f* bed expansion *(ion exchange)*
harzbildend *(bot)* resin-forming; *(petrol)* gum-forming
Harzbildnertest *m (petrol)* gum test
Harzbildung *f (bot)* resin formation; *(petrol)* gum formation, gumming
Harzeinschluß *m (plast)* resin pocket *(a moulding defect)*
Harzemulsion *f (pap)* rosin (size) milk, rosin size, size emulsion
~/stabilisierte protected rosin size, high free protected size
Harzessenz *f* resin (rosin) spirit, pinolin[e], pinolene
Harzgang *m (bot)* resin duct (canal)
Harzgehalt *m* resin content; *(petrol)* gum content
Harzgeist *m s.* Harzessenz
harzgeleimt *(pap)* sized with rosin size
Harzgerbung *f* resin tannage
harzhaltig resiniferous, resinous; *(pap)* pitchy *(pulp)*
Harzhöhe *f* depth of resin bed, resin-bed depth *(ion exchange)*
harzig resinous, resiny
Harzkanal *m s.* Harzgang
Harzkomponente *f* resin constituent
Harzkorn *n* resin bead *(ion exchange)*
Harzkörper *m (coal)* resinous body
Harzkügelchen *n s.* Harzkorn
Harzlack *m* resinous varnish
Harzleim *m (pap)* rosin size
Harzleimpulver *n (pap)* dry rosin size
Harzleimung *f (pap)* rosin sizing
Harzlösung *f (coat)* resin solution; *(pap)* rosin (size) milk, size emulsion
Harzmasse *f* resinous matter (substance)
Harzmilch *f s.* Harzemulsion
Harznest *n (plast)* resin pocket *(a moulding defect)*
Harzneubildung *f (petrol)* ultimate (potential) gum
Harzöl *n* resin oil, liquid resin
Harz-Öl-Farbe *f* oleoresinous paint
Harz-Öl-Lack *m* oleoresinous varnish
Harz-Öl-Verhältnis *n* resin-to-oil ratio, resin/oil ratio
Harz-Paraffin-Emulsion *f (pap)* rosin-wax emulsion
Harz-Paraffin-Leim *m (pap)* rosin-wax size
Harzpaste *f* paste resin
Harzpech *n* resin pitch
harzreich rich in resin, resinous
Harzsäure *f* oleoresin (resin, rosin) acid
Harzschwierigkeiten *fpl (pap)* pitch trouble[s]

Harzseife *f* resin soap *(salt of a resin acid)*
Harzsprit *m s.* Harzessenz
Harzstoff *m* resinous matter (substance)
Harztasche *f (plast)* resin pocket *(a moulding defect)*
Harzträger *m (plast)* resin[ous] binder; *(rubber)* active filler
Harzvernetzung *f (rubber)* resin cure
Harzverschmutzung *f* resin contamination *(ion exchange)*
Harzvulkanisation *f (rubber)* resin cure
Haschisch *n(m)* hashish, hasheesh, haschisch, marihuana, marijuana *(from Cannabis indica Lam.)*
Haspeläscher *m (tann)* paddle liming
Haspelfärbeapparat *m (text)* winch dyeing machine
Haspelgeschirr *n (tann)* paddle
Haspelkufe *f (text)* dye (winch) back
haspeln *(tann)* to paddle; *(text)* to reel [up]
Haspelseide *f* grege, greige, gum silk
Hatchettin *m (min)* hatchettine, hatchettite, mineral tallow *(a naturally occurring paraffin mixture)*
Hatch-Slack-Kortschak-Zyklus *m (bioch)* Hatch-Slack [CO_2 incorporation] pathway, C_4 [dicarboxylic acid] cycle, C_4 pathway
Haube *f (tech)* hood, head, cap, *(esp of a furnace)* dome, crown
Haubenofen *m (ceram)* top-hat kiln
Hauch *m (food)* bloom *(as on fruits or cocoa products)*
Hauchbildung *f* blooming *(esp of oil varnishes)*
• ~ **zeigen** to bloom
Haufen *m* heap, pile
Haufenlaugung *f*, **Haufenleaching** *n (min tech)* heap leaching
Haufenspeicher *m* pile
Häufigkeit *f* frequency; abundance *(as of an element or isotope)*
Häufigkeitsfaktor *m* frequency factor, [Arrhenius] pre-exponential factor, Arrhenius factor, A factor *(kinetics)*
Häufigkeitsverteilung *f* frequency distribution
Häufigkeitsverteilungskurve *f* frequency-distribution curve
Haufwerk *n* bed *(as of a filter)*
Haufwerkfilter *n* bed filter
Hauptachse *f* principal axis
Hauptalkaloid *n* main alkaloid, major (principal, chief) alkaloid
Hauptbande *f (spectr)* centre band
Hauptbestandteil *m* main (principal, chief) component, main constituent (ingredient), base, basis; *major constituent *(100 to 1 %)*; major element *(of an alloy)*
Hauptbrücke *f (nomencl)* main bridge
Hauptdampfleitung *f* main steam pipe
Hauptfarbstoff *m* principal colouring material
Hauptfermentation *f (biot)* production (trade) fermentation
Hauptfermenter *m (biot)* main (production) fermenter
Hauptfluß *m (plast)* drag flow *(in an extruder)*
Hauptfraktion *f* main fraction
Hauptgärung *f* main fermentation
Hauptglucosid *n* main (chief) glucoside
Hauptgruppe *f* 1. main group *(of the periodic system)*; 2. *(nomencl)* principal function; 3. major class *(of the enzyme classifying system)*
Haupt-Histokompatibilitätskomplex *m (bioch)* major histocompatibility complex, MHC
Hauptinhaltsstoff *m (hyd)* major constituent
Hauptkalkung *f s.* Hauptscheidung
Hauptkanal *m s.* Hauptsammler
Hauptkette *f* main chain, parent (fundamental) chain, backbone [chain], skeleton *(of a branched molecule)*
Hauptklasse *f s.* Hauptgruppe 3.
Hauptkolonne *f (distil)* main column
Hauptkomponente *f s.* Hauptbestandteil
Hauptkristallisation *f* primary cystallization
Hauptkultur *f (biot)* main (production) culture
Hauptkulturmedium *n (biot)* basal (main growth) medium
Hauptlauf *m (distil)* main fraction
Hauptleitung *f* main
Hauptmaische *f (ferm)* main mash
Hauptmasse *f*, **Hauptmenge** *f* bulk
Hauptnährstoff *m (agric)* macroelement, macronutrient, major element
Hauptname *m (pharm)* heading
Hauptperiode *f* reaction period *(of calorimetric measurements)*
Hauptprodukt *n* main product, major (principal, chief) product
Hauptquantenzahl *f* principal (total) quantum number
Hauptreaktion *f* main (major, principal) reaction
Hauptreinigung *f (hyd)* main treatment
Hauptring *m (nomencl)* main ring
Hauptrohr *n* main
Hauptsammler *m (hyd)* main sewer (collection channel)
Hauptsatz *m* **der Thermodynamik** law of thermodynamics
~ **der Thermodynamik/nullter** zeroth law of thermodynamics
Hauptsäule *f (chromat)* analytical column *(as opposed to the precolumn)*
Hauptschale *f* main shell *(of an atom)*
Hauptscheidung *f (sugar)* main defecation (liming)
~/kalte cold main defecation
Hauptschneide *f* principal (central, centre) knife edge *(of a balance)*
Hauptserie *f (spectr)* principal series
Hauptsteinkohlenformation *f* coal measures
Hauptstoffwechsel *m (bioch)* primary metabolism
Hauptstoffwechselweg *m (bioch)* amphibolic pathway
Hauptstrang *m* main *(as of a pipe system)*
Hauptstreifenart *f* lithotype *(of hard coal)*

Hauptsymmetrieebene *f (cryst)* unit (standard) plane
Hauptträgheitsachse *f (spectr)* principal axis of inertia
Hauptvalenz *f* primary (principal) valency
Hauptvalenzbindung *f* primary (major) valency bond
Hauptwürze *f (ferm)* original (first) wort
Hausbrand *m s.* Hausbrandmaterial
Hausbrandkohle *f* domestic (household) coal
Hausbrandkoks *m* domestic coke
Hausbrandmaterial *n* domestic fuel
Hausenblasenleim *m* isinglass, ichthyocoll[a], fish glue (gelatine)
Haushaltabfall *m* domestic (household) waste
Haushaltabwasser *n* domestic sewage
Haushaltbrennstoff *m* domestic fuel
Haushaltchemie *f* domestic chemistry
Haushaltessig *m* household vinegar
Haushaltmargarine *f* household margarine
Haushaltmüll *m* domestic (household) refuse, domestic (private) rubbish
Haushaltporzellan *n* domestic porcelain, household china
Haushaltwaschmittel *n* household [laundry] detergent, household laundering formulation, consumer detergent
Hausmüll *m s.* Haushaltmüll
H-Austausch *m s.* Wasserstoffaustausch
Haut *f* 1. *(coat, met)* skin; 2. *(tann)* hide
~/ungegerbte rawhide
Hautbildung *f (coat, met)* skin formation
Hautbräunungsmittel *n* suntan preparation (make-up)
Häutchen *n* film, membrane
Hautdesinfektionsmittel *n* skin disinfectant
Hauterkrankung *f* skin condition
Hauterweichungsmittel *n* skin softener
Hautleim *m* skin (hide, leather) glue
Hautlotion *f* skin lotion
Hautnährcreme *f* nourishing (lubricating) cream, skin food
Hautpergament *n* animal parchment, skin (natural, writing) parchment
Hautpulver *n (tann)* hide powder
Hautreinigungscreme *f* cleansing cream
hautreizend skin-irritant
Hautreizstoff *m* skin irritant
Hauttonikum *n* skin tonic
Häutungshormon *n (biol)* skin-shedding hormone
Hautverhinderer *m*, **Hautverhinderungsmittel** *n s.* Hautverhütungsmittel
Hautverhütungsmittel *n (coat)* antiskinning agent, skinning inhibitor
Haüyn *m (min)* hauyne *(a tectosilicate)*
Havarie *f* upset
Haworth-Formel *f* Haworth [projection] formula *(for sugars)*
HB *s.* Brinellhärte
Hb *s.* Hämoglobin
Hb-CO *s.* Kohlenmonoxidhämoglobin
H-Bindung *f* 1. hydrogen bonding (linkage); 2. hydrogen bridge bond
HBL *s.* Harnstoff-Bisulfit-Löslichkeit
HbS *s.* Sichelzellenhämoglobin
HBT *s.* Harzbildnertest
HCH *s.* Hexachlorcyclohexan
HCl-Gas *n* hydrochloric-acid gas
HCR-Mahlung *f (pap)* high-consistency refining, HCR
HD-Öl *n* HD oil, heavy-duty oil
HD-Protein *n s.* Protein/helixdestabilisierendes
HDS-Verfahren *n* HDS (hydrodesulphurization) process
Heater-Verfahren *n* heater process *(for regenerating rubber)*
Heavy-Duty-Öl *n s.* HD-Öl
Hebel *m* lever
Hebeleiste *f* lifting (lifter) bar *(as of a rotary dryer)*
Hebelgesetz *n* **für Phasendiagramme** *(phys ch)* lever rule
heben to lift, to elevate; to promote, to energize *(electrons into an excited state)*
Heber *m (lab)* siphon, syphon; *(tech)* lift
~/elektrolytischer salt bridge
Heberleitung *f* lift line (pipe) *(for lifting the catalyst in catcracking)*
hebern to siphon, to syphon
Hebestange *f* lever
Hebevorrichtung *f* lift[ing device], elevator
Hebewerk *n* drawworks
Hebezeug *n (petrol)* hoisting gear
He-Cd$^+$-Laser *m* helium-cadmium laser, cadmium-helium laser
Heckrolle *f*, **Hecktrommel** *f* tall pulley
Hefe *f* yeast
~/industriell genutzte industrial yeast
~/obergärige top[-fermentation] yeast
~/osmophile osmophilic yeast
~/reinrassige pure-culture yeast
~/untergärige bottom[-fermentation] yeast, low (lager) yeast
~/wilde wild yeast
Hefeadenylsäure *f* yeast adenylic acid *(a mixture of adenosine 2'-phosphate and adenosine 3'-phosphate)*
hefeartig yeast-like
Hefeautolysat *n* yeast autolysate
Hefebottich *m*, **Hefebütte** *m (ferm)* yeast tub
Hefeeiweiß *n* yeast protein
Hefeextrakt *m* yeast extract
Hefefermentation *f*, **Hefegärung** *f* yeast fermentation
hefegetrieben yeast-leavened, yeast-raised
Hefekultur *f* yeast culture
Hefekulturapparat *m* yeast propagator
Hefengut *n*, **Hefenmaische** *f (ferm)* yeast mash
Hefenucleinsäure *f* yeast nucleic acid

Hefepilz *m* yeast [plant]
Hefe-RNA *f* yeast RNA
Hefeschleuder *f*, **Hefeseparator** *m (ferm)* yeast separator
Hefestamm *m (biot)* yeast strain
hefig yeast-like
Hefteisen *n (glass)* punty [iron]
heftig vigorous *(e.g. reaction)*
Heftpflaster *n* adhesive plaster (tape)
Hehner-Zahl *f (food)* Hehner value *(percentage of water-insoluble fatty acids in fat)*
Heidemoorkrankheit *f (agric)* reclamation disease *(caused by copper shortage)*
Heilbuttleberöl *n*, **Heilbuttlebertran** *m* halibut liver oil, haliver oil
Heildosis *f* therapeutic dose
Heilmittel *n* therapeutic agent, curative drug
~/antibiotisches antibiotic [agent]
Heilquelle *f* medicinal (mineral) spring (well)
Heilwässer *npl* medicinal waters
Heilwirkung *f* curative action; curative effect
Heisenberg-Darstellung *f* Heisenberg representation *(quantum mechanics)*
heiß 1. hot; 2. *(nucl)* highly [radio]active, hot
• ~ **werden** to become hot, to heat
Heißalkalisierung *f (pap)* hot [alkali] refining
Heißaluminieren *n* hot-dip aluminizing
Heißatomchemie *f* hot-atom chemistry, recoil chemistry
Heißatomreaktion *f* hot-state reaction
Heißaufbereitung *f (ceram)* steam tempering, hot preparation
Heißblasen *n* blow[ing] *(in producing water gas)*
Heißblaseperiode *f* blow period *(in producing water gas)*
Heißchlorierung *f* hot chlorination
Heißchromatographie *f* hot chromatography
Heißdampf *m* superheated steam
Heißdampfregenerat *n (rubber)* steam reclaim
Heißdampfverfahren *n (rubber)* steam (thermal) process *(a reclaiming method)*
Heißfärben *n (text)* high-temperature dyeing
Heißfiltration *f* hot filtration
heißfixieren *(plast, text)* to heat-set
Heißgas *n* hot gas
Heißgaseintritt *m* hot-gas inlet
Heißgaserzeuger *m* hot-gas producer
Heißgasschweißen *n* hot-gas welding
Heißgassiegeln *n* hot-gas sealing *(of sheets)*
heißgereckt *(text)* hot-stretched, hot-drawn
Heiß-Kalt-Behandlung *f*, **Heiß-Kalt-Tränkung** *f* hot-and-cold open tank treatment *(wood preservation)*
Heiß-Kalt-Verfahren *n (nucl)* dual temperature [exchange] process *(for producing deuterium)*
Heiß-Kalt-Wasserstoffisotopen-Austauschverfahren *n s.* Heiß-Kalt-Verfahren
Heißkanal-Spritzgießen *n (plast)* hot-runner moulding
Heißkanal-Spritzgießwerkzeug *n (plast)* hot-runner mould
Heißkanal-Spritzguß *m (plast)* hot-runner moulding
heißkleben *(plast)* to heat-seal
Heißkleber *m* hot-setting adhesive
Heißklebrigkeit *f* hot tack
Heißkonditionierung *f* **von Abwasserschlamm** *(hyd)* sludge conditioning by heat treatment, pressure cooking treatment of sludge
Heißlauge *f* hot brine *(potash industry)*
Heißluft *f* hot (heated) air
Heißluftalterung *f* **[im Geer-Ofen]** *(rubber)* hot-air ageing, Geer (air) oven ageing
Heißluftheizung *f s.* Heißluftvulkanisation
Heißluftkammer *f*, **Heißluftraum** *m* hot-air chamber
Heißluftschrank *m* hot-air oven, air-circulating oven
Heißluftsterilisation *f* hot-air sterilization
Heißluftsterilisator *m*, **Heißluftsterilisierschrank** *m* hot-air sterilizer
Heißluftstrom *m* hot-air stream (current)
Heißlufttrockenkammer *f* hot-air chamber
Heißlufttrockenmaschine *f (text)* hot flue
Heißlufttrocknung *f* hot-air drying; *(hyd)* heat drying *(of sludge)*
Heißluftvulkanisation *f* air cure (vulcanization), hot-air (dry-air, dry-heat) cure, hot-air vulcanization, HAV
~/kontinuierliche continuous [hot-]air cure
Heißluftvulkanisierschrank *m* air vulcanizer
Heißmastikation *f*, **Heißmastizierung** *f* hot mastication
Heißmischen *n* hot mixing
Heißnebel *m (agric)* thermal aerosol
Heißnetzer *m*, **Heißnetzmittel** *n* hot wetting agent
Heißölfärben *n (text)* hot-oil dyeing
Heiß-Pottasche-Verfahren *n*, **Heiß-Pottasche-Wäsche** *f* hot potassium carbonate scrubbing *(for removing acid constituents from gases)*
Heißpresse *f (pap)* hot press
heißpressen to hot-press, *(relating to powders also)* to sinter under pressure
Heißräuchern *n* hot smoking *(at 80 to 100 °C)*
Heißsäureverfahren *n* hot-acid process *(catalytic polymerization)*
Heißschleifen *n (pap)* hot grinding
Heißschliff *m (pap)* hot-ground pulp
heißsiegelbar *(plast)* heat sealable
Heißsiegelbarkeit *f (plast)* heat sealability
heißsiegeln *(plast)* to heat-seal
heißsintern to hot-press, to sinter under pressure
heißspritzen *(coat)* to hot-spray
Heißspritzlack *m* hot-spray lacquer
heißtauchen *(coat)* to hot-dip *(for applying organic coatings for temporary protection)*; *(plast)* to dip-mould *(using external moulds for producing gloves etc.)*

Heißtauchmasse *f (coat)* hot-melt (hot-dip) coating
Heißtauchschutzschicht *f (coat)* hot-melt (hot-dip) coating
Heißtrockenfarbe *f* heat-set ink
Heißtrub *m (ferm)* hot sludge
heißveredeln *(pap)* to refine by the hot [alkali] process
Heißveredelung *f (pap)* hot [alkali] refining
Heißverlösen *n (fert)* hot dissolution
Heißverschweißen *n (plast)* heat welding, *(esp relating to films:)* thermal (heat) sealing
heißverstreckt *(text)* hot-stretched, hot-drawn
Heißverstreckung *f (text)* hot stretching (drawing)
Heißverzinken *n* [hot-dip] galvanizing
Heißvulkanisation *f* hot cure (vulcanization)
heißvulkanisierbar heat-curable
heißvulkanisierend heat-curing, hot-vulcanizing
heißvulkanisiert heat-cured, hot-cured, hot-vulcanized
Heißwasser *n* hot water
Heißwasserbehälter *m* hot-water tank (accumulator)
Heißwasserblanchieren *n (food)* [hot-]water blanching
Heißwasserdekatur *f (text)* roll boiling
Heißwasserfixierung *f (text)* hydrosetting
Heißwasserpumpe *f* hot-water pump
Heißwasserrohr *n* hot-water pipe
Heißwasserspülung *f* hot-water wash
Heißwassertrichter *m (lab)* hot-water funnel, heating funnel, funnel heater
Heißwind *m (met)* hot[-air] blast, heated air
Heißwindleitung *f* hot-[air-]blast main, hot-blast line
Heißwindring *m*, **Heißwindringleitung** *f (met)* bustle pipe
Heitler-London-Methode *f* Heitler-London method, HL method *(quantum chemistry)*
Heitler-London-Slater-Pauling-Methode *f* Heitler-London-Slater-Pauling method, HLSP method, electron-pair (valence-bond) method, VB method *(quantum chemistry)*
Heitler-London-Slater-Pauling-Theorie *f* Heitler-London-Slater-Pauling theory, HLSP theory, electron-pair (valence-bond) theory, VB theory *(quantum chemistry)*
Heitler-London-Theorie *f* Heitler-London theory, HL theory *(quantum chemistry)*
Heizaggregat *n* heater assembly
Heizapparat *m* heater; *(rubber)* vulcanizer, vulcanizing apparatus
Heizbad *n* heating bath
Heizbalg *m (rubber)* diaphragm, bladder
Heizband *n* heating tape (band), strip (band) heater
Heizbank *f*/**Koflersche** *(lab)* Kofler [hot] bench
heizbar heatable
Heizbinde *f s.* Heizband
Heizblock *m* heating block
Heizbrennstoff *m* fuel
Heizdampf *m* heating steam
Heizdampfeintritt *m* heating steam inlet
Heizeffekt *m* heating (calorific) effect
Heizeinsatzstück *n (plast)* adapter heater
Heizelement *n* heating element (unit), heater
Heizelementschweißen *n (plast)* heated-tool welding
heizen to heat, to fire, to fuel; *(rubber)* to cure, to vulcanize
Heizen *n*/**direktes** direct heating
~/**indirektes** indirect heating
heizend/langsam *(rubber)* slow-curing
~/**rasch (schnell)** *(rubber)* fast-curing, quick-curing
Heizer *m* heater *(apparatus)*; *(rubber)* vulcanizer, vulcanizing apparatus
Heizfläche *f* heating surface; *(quantitatively:)* area of heating surface
Heizflächenbelastung *f* heat flux
~/**maximale** peak (maximum) flux
Heizflächenofen *m* externally heated oven
Heizflamme *f* volume (non-luminous) flame *(of a Bunsen burner)*
Heizflansch *m* flange-type heater
Heizflüssigkeit *f* thermal liquid, heat transfer fluid, heat carrier
Heizgas *n* fuel (heating) gas
Heizgeflecht *n* heating blanket
Heizgerät *n* heater
Heizgeschwindigkeit *f (rubber)* cure (vulcanization) rate
Heizgruppe *f (pap)* dryer group (section)
Heizgut *n* heating load
Heizkammer *f* heating chamber; calandria *(of an evaporator)*
Heizkeil *m (plast)* heated wedge
Heizkeilschweißen *n* heated-wedge (heated-tool) welding
Heizkörper *m* heating unit (element), heater
Heizkraft *f* calorific power
heizkräftig of high calorific value
Heizleiter *m* heating resistor
Heizmantel *m* heating jacket (blanket, mantle)
~/**ölgespeister** oil jacket
Heizoberflächentemperatur *f (pap)* dryer surface temperature
Heizöl *n* fuel (heating) oil
~ **auf Erdölbasis** petroleum fuel oil
~/**destilliertes** distillate fuel oil
Heizpatrone *f* cartridge heater
Heizplatte *f* heating (hot) plate (platen)
Heizplattentrockner *m* jacketed shelf dryer
Heizpresse *f* hot press
Heizraum *m* heating chamber; calandria *(of an evaporator)*
Heizrohr *n* fire (heating) tube
Heizrohrkessel *m* fire-tube boiler
Heizschlange *f* heating coil
Heizschlauch *m (rubber)* curing bag (tube), air bag
Heizschlauchmischung *f (rubber)* air-bag stock

Heizschnur *f* heating cord
Heizspirale *f* heating coil
Heizstrahler *m* radiant heater
Heiztellertrockner *m* rotary jacketed-shelf dryer
Heiztemperatur *f (rubber)* curing (cure) temperature, vulcanizing (vulcanization) temperature
Heiztisch *m (lab)* hot stage
Heiztischmikroskop *n* hot-stage microscope
Heizung *f* heating; *(rubber)* cure, vulcanization
~/dielektrische dielectric heating
~/elektrische electric heating
~ in Formen *(rubber)* mould cure (vulcanization)
~ mit elektrischer Heizdecke *(plast)* electric blanket heating
Heizvorrichtung *f* heating device, heater
Heizwand *f* heating wall
Heizwert *m* 1. *(phys ch)* calorific value *(per unit weight or unit volume), (specif)* net calorific value; 2. *(broadly:)* fuel value
~/molarer *s.* ~/stoffmengenbezogener
~/oberer *s.* Brennwert/spezifischer
~/spezifischer net calorific value, lower heating value
~/stoffmengenbezogener heat of combustion, heat[ing] value
~/unterer *s.* ~/spezifischer
heizwertarm of low calorific value
heizwertreich of high calorific value
Heizwertverlust *m* loss of calorific value
Heizwiderstand *m* heating resistor
Heizzeit *f (rubber)* curing (vulcanizing) time
Heizzone *f* heat[ing] zone
~/hintere *(plast)* rear heat zone
~/mittlere *(plast)* centre heat zone
~/vordere *(plast)* front heat zone
Heizzug *m* [heating] flue
Heizzyklus *m* heating cycle
Heizzylinder *m* heating (heated) cylinder
Hektographenmasse *f s.* Hektographentinktur
Hektographentinktur *f*, **Hektographentinte** *f* copying ink *(for spirit duplicating and gelatin printing)*
Hektographie *f* 1. gelatin (hectographic) printing; 2. *s.* Spiritusumdruckverfahren
Helianthin *n* 1. helianthin[e], *p*-(*p*-dimethylaminophenylazo) benzenesulphonic acid; 2. *(sometimes:)* methyl orange, helianthin[e] *(sodium salt of 1.)*
Helicen *n (org ch)* helicene
helikal *(bioch)* helical
Helioechtrot *n* Helio fast red, Harrison red *(a derivative of m-nitro-p-toluidine)*
Heliographie *f*, **Heliogravüre** *f* photogravure, asphalt (bitumen) process
Heliotrop *m (min)* heliotrope, bloodstone *(a subvariety of chalcedony)*
Helium *n* He helium
Helium-Cadmium-Laser *m* helium-cadmium laser, cadmium-helium laser
Heliumdetektor *m*, **Heliumionisationsdetektor** *m* *(anal)* helium ionization detector
Heliumkern *m* helium nucleus, α-particle
Heliumverflüssigung *f* helium liquefaction
Helix *f (bioch)* helix
~/doppelsträngige double-strand[ed] helix, double helix
~/dreisträngige superhelix, triple[-stranded] helix
~/einsträngige single-strand[ed] helix
~/linksdrehende (linksgängige) left-handed helix
~/rechtsdrehende (rechtsgängige) right-handed helix
α-Helix *f (bioch)* alpha helix
γ-Helix *f (bioch)* gamma helix
helixförmig *(bioch)* helical
Helix-Knäuel-Übergang *m*, **Helix-Knäuel-Umwandlung** *f (bioch)* helix-coil transition
Helixkonformation *f* helical conformation
Helixstruktur *f* helix (helical, helicoidal) structure *(of protein molecules)*
Helizität *f* helicity *(1. quantum mechanics; 2. bonding theory)*
Helizitätszustand *m* helicity state *(quantum mechanics)*
Helles *n s.* Bier/helles
Hellicht-Entwicklung *f (phot)* desensitization
Helligkeit *f* brightness, luminosity, *(esp quantitatively)* luminous intensity, intensity of light
Helligkeitsumfang *m (phot)* brightness range
Hellperiode *f*, **Hellphase** *f* light phase *(photochemistry)*
Hellreaktion *f* light reaction *(photochemistry)*
Hell-Volhard-Zelinsky-Reaktion *f* Hell-Volhard-Zelinsky reaction *(α-halogenation of aliphatic carboxylic acids)*
Helm *m (tech)* head; *(distil)* stillhead, still dome, [distillation] head
Helmholtz-Fläche *f (el ch)* Helmholtz plane
~/äußere outer Helmholtz plane
~/innere inner Helmholtz plane
Helmholtz-Schicht *f s.* Helmholtz-Fläche
Helminthagogum *n (pharm)* helminthagogue, vermifuge
Helvin *m (min)* helvin[e], helvite *(a tectosilicate)*
Helvolinsäure *f* helvolic acid, fumigacin *(antibiotic)*
Hemellithol *n* hemellitene, hemimellitene, 1,2,3-trimethylbenzene
Hemellithsäure *f* hemellitic acid, 2,3-dimethylbenzoic acid
Hemiacetal *n (org ch)* hemiacetal
Hemialdol *n (org ch)* hemialdol
Hemicellulose *f* hemicellulose, pseudocellulose
hemiedrisch *(cryst)* hemihedral
Hemiketal *n* hemiketal *(hemiacetal of a ketone)*
Hemikolloid *n* hemicolloid
Hemimellithsäure *f* hemimellitic acid, benzene-1,2,3-tricarboxylic acid
Hemimellitol *n s.* Hemellithol
Hemimellitsäure *f s.* Hemimellithsäure

Hemipinsäure *f* hemipic (hemipinic) acid, 3,4-dimethoxyphthalic acid
Hemiterpen *n (org ch)* hemiterpene
hemmen to inhibit, to retard
hemmend inhibitory, inhibitive, retardant
Hemmstoff *m* inhibiting (retarding) substance (agent), inhibitor, retarder, anticatalyst, negative catalyst; *(biol)* growth inhibitor
~/kompetitiver *(bioch)* competitive inhibitor
Hemmung *f* inhibition, retardation, anticatalysis, negative catalysis
~/kompetitive competitive inhibition *(enzyme kinetics)*
~/konzertierte *(bioch)* concerted inhibition
~/multivalente *s.* ~/konzertierte
~/nichtkompetitive non-competitive inhibition *(enzyme kinetics)*
~/unkompetitive uncompetitive (anticompetitive) inhibition *(enzyme kinetics)*
~ zweiter Art *s.* ~/nichtkompetitive
Hemmungshof *m s.* Hemmungszone
Hemmungskurve *f* inhibition curve
Hemmungszone *f* zone of inhibition *(sterile zone in a penicillium culture)*
Hemmwirkung *f (bioch)* inhibitory action; inhibitory effect
Hempel-Bürette *f* Hempel [gas] burette
Hempel-Pipette *f* Hempel gas pipette
Hendec... *s.* Undec...
Henderson-Hasselbalch-Gleichung *f* Henderson-Hasselbalch equation *(for buffer systems)*
Heneicosan *n* heneicosane
Heneicosandisäure *f* heneicosanedioic acid, Japanic acid
Henry-Konstante *f (phys ch)* Henry's law constant
Hentriacontan *n* hentriacontane
Hepar sulfuris *n* hepar sulphuris *(technical potassium sulphide)*
Heparprobe *f* hepar test *(for detecting sulphur)*
hepatotoxisch *(med)* hepatotoxic
Heptachlor *n* heptachlor *(an insecticide)*
Heptadecan-9-on *n*, **Heptadecanon-(9)** *n* *heptadecan-9-one, dioctyl ketone
Heptadecansäure *f* heptadecanoic acid
Heptafluorid *n* heptafluoride
Heptaldehyd *m s.* Heptanal
Heptamethylen *n s.* Cycloheptan
Heptamolybdat *n* $M^I_6[Mo_7O_{24}]$ heptamolybdate
Heptan *n* heptane
n-**Heptan** *n* heptane *(proper)*
Heptanal *n* heptanal
Heptan-1-carbonsäure *f* heptane-1-carboxylic acid, octanoic acid
Heptan-1,7-dicarbonsäure *f* *heptane-1,7-dicarboxylic acid, *nonanedioic acid, azelaic acid
Heptandisäure *f* *heptanedioic acid, *pentane-1,5-dicarboxylic acid, pimelic acid
Heptan-4-on *n*, **Heptanon-(4)** *n* *heptan-4-one, butyrone
Heptansäure *f* heptanoic acid
Heptasulfid *n* heptasulphide
heptavalent heptavalent, septivalent
Heptavalenz *f* heptavalence, septivalence
Hept-1-in *n*, **Heptin-(1)** *n* hept-1-yne
Heptose *f* heptose *(monosaccharide containing 7 carbon atoms per molecule)*
Heptoxid *n* heptaoxide
Heptoxotetraborat *n* $M^I_2B_4O_7$ heptaoxotetraborate, tetraborate
Heptoxotetraborsäure *f* heptaoxotetraboric acid, tetraboric acid
n-**Heptylacetylen** *n s.* Non-1-in
n-**Heptylaldehyd** *m s.* Heptanal
n-**Heptylalkohol** *m* heptan-1-ol
Heptylcarbinol *n s.* Octan-1-ol
Heptylpenaldinsäure *f* heptylpenaldic acid, penaldic-K acid
Heptylpenicilloinsäure *f* heptylpenicilloic acid, penicilloic-K acid
Heptylpenillosäure *f* heptylpenilloic acid, penilloic-K acid
Heptylpenillsäure *f* heptylpenillic acid, penillic-K acid
n-**Heptylsäure** *f s.* Heptansäure
herabmindern *s.* herabsetzen
herabrieseln to trickle down
herabrinnen to trickle down
herabsetzen to lower, to reduce, to decrease; to slow down *(the velocity)*; to relieve [down] *(the pressure)*
Herabsetzung *f* lowering, reduction, decrease; slowing-down *(of velocity)*; relief *(of pressure)*
herabspülen *s.* hinabspülen
herabtröpfeln to trickle down
herausdestillieren to distil out, to top
herausdiffundieren to diffuse out
herausdrücken to push (blow) out *(as from a reactor)*; to squirt [out] *(as from a nozzle)*
herausheben to lift out *(e.g. a filter)*
herauskochen to boil off
herauslösen to dissolve out, to lixiviate, to leach [out], *(esp relating to adsorbed substances:)* to eluate, to elute
herausnehmen to take out; to release *(from a mould)*
herauspressen to press (squeeze) out, to expel *(e.g. oil)*
herausschleppen *(distil)* to entrain out
herausschleudern *(nucl)* to eject
herausspalten *(org ch)* to cleave out
Herausspalten *n* **aus einem Komplex** decomplexing *(as of metal ions)*
herausspülen to rinse out; to eluate, to elute *(adsorbed substances from a solid adsorbent)*
herausstoßen to push out, to discharge *(e.g. coke from a coke oven)*
heraustreiben to expel, to drive out (off) *(e.g. gases)*

herb harsh, hard, sour; rough, dry *(wine)*
Herbar[ium]papier *n* herbarium paper
Herbe *f*, **Herbheit** *f (food)* harshness, hardness, tartness, sourness; roughness, dryness *(of wine)*
herbizid herbicidal[ly active]
Herbizid *n* herbicide, weed-killer, weed control agent
~ gegen Gräser grass killer
~/nichtselektives non-selective herbicide
~/selektives (selektiv wirkendes) selective herbicide
~/staubförmiges herbicidal dust
~/systemisches systemic (translocated) herbicide, translocation weed-killer
~/total wirkendes *s.* ~/nichtselektives
~/translokales (translokal wirkendes) *s.* ~/systemisches
Herbizidwirkung *f* herbicidal action; herbicidal effect
Herd *m (min tech)* [concentrating] table, concentrate (concentrator) table; *(met)* hearth
Herdarbeit *f*, **Herdaufbereitung** *f s.* Herdsortieren
Herdflotation *f* table floatation
Herdfrischstahl *m* open hearth steel
Herdfrischverfahren *n* open-hearth process
~/basisches basic open-hearth process
~/saures acid open-hearth process
Herdglas *n (glass)* slag
Herdofen *m* hearth furnace
Herdplatte *f* deck, table *(of a concentrating table)*
Herdsortieren *n (min tech)* tabling
~/nasses wet tabling
~/trockenes dry tabling
Herdtafel *f s.* Herdplatte
Herdwagenofen *m (ceram)* bogie kiln, truck [chamber] kiln, trolley hearth kiln, car-bottom kiln
hergestellt/großtechnisch produced on the large scale
Heringsöl *n*, **Heringstran** *m* herring oil
Herkunft *f* origin, source • **pflanzlicher** ~ of vegetable (plant) origin, plant-derived • **tierischer** ~ of animal origin
Herleitung *f* derivation
hermetisch [abgeschlossen, dicht, verschlossen] hermetic[al]
Hermite-Operator *m (anal)* Hermitian operator
Heroin *n* heroin, diacetylmorphine *(a narcotic)*
Héroult-Lichtbogenofen *m* Héroult furnace
Herreshoff-Ofen *m* Herreshoff furnace (burner)
Herschel-Effekt *m (phot)* Herschel effect
Hershberg-Rührer *m* Hershberg stirrer
herstellen 1. *(tech)* to manufacture, to make, to produce; *(lab)* to prepare; 2. to establish *(e.g. equilibrium or contact)*
~/gezielt to make to measure, to tailor[-make] *(e.g. polymers)*
~/großtechnisch to produce on the large scale
~/im Druckguß to [pressure-]diecast *(foundry)*
~/im Sandguß to sand-cast *(foundry)*
~/Masterbatches *(rubber)* to masterbatch, to mix into a masterbatch
~/nach Maß *s.* ~/gezielt
~/Vormischungen *s.* ~/Masterbatches
Hersteller[betrieb] *m*, **Herstellerfirma** *f* manufacturer, maker, producer
Herstellung *f* 1. *(esp relating to know-how:)* manufacture, make, *(esp relating to economical aspects:)* production; *(lab)* preparation; 2. establishment *(as of equilibrium or contact)*
~/großtechnische large-scale production; *(as opposed to pilot-plant production:)* full-scale factory production
~ in halbtechnischem Maßstab pilot[-plant-scale] production
~/mikrobielle (mikrobiologische) *(biot)* microbial (microbiological) production
~ von Formartikeln (Formteilen) moulding
~ von Gießkernen core making *(foundry)*
~ von kleinen Mengen small-scale production
~ von Latexmischungen latex compounding
~ von Vormischungen *(rubber)* masterbatching
~ von Vormischungen auf nassem Wege *(rubber)* wet masterbatching
~ von Wasserzeichen *(pap)* watermarking
Herstellungsdatum *n* date of manufacture
Herstellungsmethode *f* manufacturing method, method of production, *(esp lab)* method of preparation, preparative method
Herstellungsprogramm *n* production pattern, product slate
Herstellungsverfahren *n* manufacturing process
herunterkochen/weit to cook soft *(cellulose)*
herunterkühlen to cool down
herunterrieseln to trickle down
hervorrufen to bring about, to produce, to evolve
herzaktiv *s.* herzwirksam
Herzgift *n* heart poison
Herzglykosid *n* cardiac glycoside
Herz- und Trockenfäule *f* crown rot *(of sugar beets on soil deficient in boron)*
Herz-Verbindung *f (dye)* [intermediate] Herz compound *(a benzodithiazole)*
herzwirksam cardioactive, cardiac-active
HE-Schweißen *n s.* Heizelementschweißen
Hesperetinsäure *f* hesperetic acid, 3-hydroxy-4-methoxycinnamic acid
HET-Anhydrid *n* HET anhydride, chlorendic anhydride
Hetaren *n s.* Heteroaren
Hetarylgruppe *f s.* Heteroarylgruppe
Heteroalken *n* heteroalkene
Heteroallen *n* heteroallene
heteroanalog hetero-analogous
Heteroaren *n*, **Heteroaromat** *m* heteroarene, hetarene
Heteroarylgruppe *f*, **Heteroarylrest** *m* heteroaryl (hetaryl) group
Heteroatom *n* heteroatom

Heteroauxin *n (bioch)* heteroauxin, 3-indolylacetic acid
heterocyclisch *(org ch)* heterocyclic
Heterocyclus *m (org ch)* heterocycle, heterocyclic [compound]
Heterocyclylgruppe *f*, **Heterocyclylrest** *m* heterocyclyl group
Heterodien *n* heterodiene
Heteroentkopplung *f s.* Entkopplung/heteronukleare
heterofermentativ *(bioch)* heterofermentative
heterogen heterogeneous
Heterogenität *f* heterogeneity
Heterogenkatalyse *f* heterogeneous catalysis
Heterogenreaktor *m (nucl)* heterogeneous reactor
Heterokopplung *f s.* Kopplung/heteronukleare
Heterokumulen *n* heterocumulene
Heterolyse *f* heterolysis, heterolytic cleavage (fission, bond fission)
heterolytisch heterolytic
Heterometrie *f* heterometry *(a method of titration)*
heteronuklear heteronuclear
heteropolar heteropolar
heteropolymer heteropolymeric
Heteropolymer[e] *n*, **Heteropolymerisat** *n* heteropolymer, heterogeneous polymer
Heteropolymerisation *f* heteropolymerization
Heteropolysaccharid *n* heteropolysaccharide
Heteropolysäure *f* heteropoly acid
Heteroring *m* heterocyclic ring
Heterosid *n (org ch)* heteroside
Heterosphäre *f* heterosphere *(upper part of the atmosphere)*
heterotaktisch *(plast)* heterotactic
Heterotaktizität *f (plast)* heterotacticity
heterotroph *(biol)* heterotrophic
Heterotrophie *f (biol)* heterotrophy
HETPP *(2-**H**ydroxy**e**thyl**t**hiamin**p**yro**p**hosphat) s.* Acetaldehyd/aktiver
HETP-Wert *m (distil)* height equivalent to a theoretical plate, HETP, plate height
HET-Säure *f*, **Hetsäure** *f* chlorendic acid, hexachloroendomethylenetetrahydrophthalic acid
Heuschreckenabwehrmittel *n* grasshopper repellent
Hevea-Kautschuk *m* hevea rubber *(from Hevea brasiliensis (H.B.K.) Muell. Arg.)*
Hevea-Latex *m* hevea latex
Hexaboran *n* hexaborane
Hexaborid *n* hexaboride
Hexabromdisilan *n* hexabromodisilane
Hexabromid *n* hexabromide
Hexabromoplatinat(IV) *n* $M^I_2[PtBr_6]$ hexabromoplatinate(IV), bromoplatinate(IV)
Hexabromoplatin(IV)-säure *f* hexabromoplatinic(IV) acid, bromoplatinic(IV) acid
Hexacarbonyl *n* hexacarbonyl
Hexachlorbenzen *n*, **Hexachlorbenzol** *n* hexachlorobenzene, HCB, perchlorobenzene
Hexachlorcyclohexan *n* hexachlorocyclohexane
Hexachlordisilan *n* hexachlorodisilane
Hexachlorethan *n* hexachloroethane, perchloroethane
Hexachlorid *n* hexachloride
Hexachloroiridat(III) *n* $M^I_3[IrCl_6]$ hexachloroiridate(III), chloroiridate(III)
Hexachloroosmat(III) *n* $M^I_3[OsCl_6]$ hexachloroosmate(III)
Hexachloroosmat(IV) *n* $M^I_2[OsCl_6]$ hexachloroosmate(IV)
Hexachloropalladat(IV) *n* $M^I_2[PdCl_6]$ hexachloropalladate(IV)
Hexachlorophen *n* hexachlorophene, *3,3',5,5',6,6'-hexachloro-2,2'-dihydroxydiphenylmethane
Hexachloroplatinat(IV) *n* $M^I_2[PtCl_6]$ hexachloroplatinate(IV), chloroplatinate(IV)
Hexachloroplatin(IV)-säure *f* hexachloroplatinic(IV) acid, chloroplatinic(IV) acid
Hexachlororhodat(III) *n* $M^I_3[RhCl_6]$ hexachlororhodate(III), chlororhodate(III)
Hexachlororuthenat(IV) *n* $M^I_2[RuCl_6]$ hexachlororuthenate(IV)
Hexachlorotellurat(IV) *n* $M^I_2[TeCl_6]$ hexachlorotellurate(IV), chlorotellurate(IV)
Hexachlorotitanat(IV) *n* $M^I_2[TiCl_6]$ hexachlorotitanate(IV), chlorotitanate(IV)
Hexachlorozinn(IV)-säure *f* hexachlorostannic acid
Hexachlorozirconat(IV) *n* $M^I_2[ZrCl_6]$ hexachlorozirconate(IV), chlorozirconate(IV)
Hexacosan-1-ol *n*, **1-Hexacosanol** *n* *hexacosan-1-ol, ceryl alcohol
Hexacosansäure *f* *hexacosanoic acid, cerotic acid, cerinic acid
Hexacyanochromat(II) *n* $M^I_4[Cr(CN)_6]$ hexacyanochromate(II), cyanochromate(II)
Hexacyanochromat(III) *n* $M^I_3[Cr(CN)_6]$ hexacyanochromate(III), cyanochromate(III)
Hexacyanocobaltat(III) *n* $M^I_3[Co(CN)_6]$ hexacyanocobaltate(III), cyanocobaltate(III)
Hexacyanoeisen(II)-säure *f* hexacyanoferric(II) acid
Hexacyanoeisen(III)-säure *f* hexacyanoferric(III) acid
Hexacyanoferrat(II) *n* $M^I_4[Fe(CN)_6]$ hexacyanoferrate(II), cyanoferrate(II)
Hexacyanoferrat(III) *n* $M^I_3[Fe(CN)_6]$ hexacyanoferrate(III), cyanoferrate(III)
Hexacyanoferrat(III)-komplex *m* hexacyanoferrate(III) complex, cyanoferrate(III) complex
Hexacyanomanganat(II) *n* $M^I_4[Mn(CN)_6]$ hexacyanomanganate(II)
Hexacyanomanganat(III) *n* $M^I_3[Mn(CN)_6]$ hexacyanomanganate(III)
Hexacyanomangan(II)-säure *f* $H_4[Mn(CN)_6]$ hexacyanomanganic(II) acid
Hexacyanoosmat(II) *n* $M^I_4[Os(CN)_6]$ hexacyanoosmate(II)

Hexacyanoplatinat(IV) *n* $M^I_4[Pt(CN)_6]$ hexacyanoplatinate(IV)
Hexadecan *n* hexadecane
Hexadecan-1-ol *n*, **Hexadecanol-(1)** *n* hexadecan-1-ol
Hexadecansäure *f* hexadecanoic acid
Hexadecan-1-thiol *n* hexadecane-1-thiol
n-**Hexadecylalkohol** *m s.* Hexadecan-1-ol
n-**Hexadecylmercaptan** *n s.* Hexadecan-1-thiol
n-**Hexadecylsäure** *f s.* Hexadecansäure
Hexa-1,5-dien *n*, **Hexadien-(1,5)** hexa-1,5-diene
Hexa-2,4-diendisäure *f*, **Hexadien-(2,4)-disäure** *f* *hexa-2,4-dienedioic acid, muconic acid
Hexa-2,4-diensäure *f*, **Hexadien-(2,4)-säure** *f* *hexa-2,4-dienoic acid, sorbic acid
Hexaedrit *m* hexahedrite *(nickel-containing meteoric iron)*
Hexaethyltetraphosphat *n* hexaethyltetraphosphate, HETP
Hexafluorid *n* hexafluoride
Hexafluoroferrat(III) *n* $M^I_3[FeF_6]$ hexafluoroferrate(III)
Hexafluorokieselsäure *f* hexafluorosilicic acid, fluorosilicic acid
Hexafluoromanganat(IV) *n* $M^I_2[MnF_6]$ hexafluoromanganate(IV), fluoromanganate(IV)
Hexafluorophosphat *n* $M^I[PF_6]$ hexafluorophosphate
Hexafluorophosphorsäure *f* hexafluorophosphoric acid
Hexafluorosilicat *n* $M^I_2[SiF_6]$ hexafluorosilicate, fluorosilicate
Hexafluorostannat(IV) *n* $M^I_2[SnF_6]$ hexafluorostannate(IV), fluorostannate(IV)
hexagonal *(cryst)* hexagonal
Hexahelicen *n (org ch)* hexahelicene
Hexahydrat *n* hexahydrate
Hexahydrid *n* hexahydride
Hexahydrobenzen *n*, **Hexahydrobenzol** *n* hexahydrobenzene, *cyclohexane
Hexahydrocymen *n*, **Hexahydrocymol** *n* hexahydrocymene, menthane, *1-isopropyl-methylcyclohexane
Hexahydrophenol *n* hexahydrophenol, cyclohexanol
Hexahydrophthalsäure *f* hexahydrophthalic acid, *cyclohexane-1,2-dicarboxylic acid
Hexahydrotoluen *n*, **Hexahydrotoluol** *n* hexahydrotoluene, *methylcyclohexane
Hexahydroxoantimonat *n* $M^I[Sb(OH)_6]$ hexahydroxoantimonate, hydroxoantimonate
Hexahydroxoantimonsäure *f* hexahydroxoantimonic acid, hydroxoantimonic acid
Hexahydroxostannat(IV) *n* $M^I_2[Sn(OH)_6]$ hexahydroxostannate(IV)
Hexahydroxybenzen *n*, **Hexahydroxybenzol** *n* hexahydroxybenzene
Hexahydroxycyclohexan *n* *hexahydroxycyclohexane, inositol
Hexaiodid *n* hexaiodide
Hexaiodoplatin(IV)-säure *f* hexaiodoplatinic(IV) acid, iodoplatinic(IV) acid
Hexamethylen *n s.* Cyclohexan
Hexamethylendiamin *n* hexamethylene diamine, HMDA
Hexamethylendiaminadipat *n* hexamethylene diamine adipate, 6,6 salt, nylon salt
Hexamethylendiammoniumadipat *n s.* Hexamethylendiaminadipat
Hexamethylentetramin *n* hexamethylenetetramine, hexamine, metheneamine
Hexamin *n* 1. hexamine, methenamine, hexamethylenetetramine; 2. di-2,4,6-trinitrophenylamine, hexanitrodiphenylamine, hexite
Hexammincobalt(III)-chlorid *n* hexaamminecobalt(III) chloride
Hexammingallium(III)-chlorid *n* hexaamminegallium(III) chloride
Hexamminnickel(II)-bromid *n* hexaamminenickel(II) bromide
Hexamminnickel(II)-chlorid *n* hexaamminenickel(II) chloride
Hexamminnickel(II)-iodid *n* hexaamminenickel(II) iodide
Hexamminplatin(IV)-chlorid *n* hexaammineplatinum(IV) chloride
Hexan *n* hexane
Hexanal *n* hexanal
Hexan-1,6-dicarbonsäure *f*, **Hexandicarbonsäure-(1,6)** *f* hexane-1,6-dicarboxylic acid, octanedioic acid
Hexandisäure *f* *hexanedioic acid, adipic acid
Hexanitrid *n* hexanitride
Hexanitrocobaltat(II) *n* $M^I_4[Co(NO_2)_6]$ hexanitrocobaltate(II), nitrocobaltate(II)
Hexanitrocobaltat(III) *n* $M^I_3[Co(NO_2)_6]$ hexanitrocobaltate(III), nitrocobaltate(III)
Hexanitroiridat(III) *n* hexanitroiridate(III), nitroiridate(III)
Hexanitroniccolat(II) *n* $M^I_4[Ni(NO_2)_6]$ hexanitroniccolate(II), hexanitronickelate(II)
Hexanitrorhodat(III) *n* $M^I_3[Rh(NO_2)_6]$ hexanitrorhodate(III)
Hexan-1-ol *n*, **Hexanol-(1)** *n* hexan-1-ol
n-**Hexanol** *n s.* Hexan-1-ol
Hexansäure *f* hexanoic acid
Hexansäureethylester *m* ethyl hexanoate
1,4,7,10,13,16-Hexaoxacyclooctadecan *n* 1,4,7,10,13,16-hexaoxacyclooctadecane, 18-crown 6
Hexaquo... hexaaqua..., hexaaquo...
Hexasilan *n* hexasilane
Hexasilicat *n* hexasilicate
hexasubstituiert hexasubstituted
Hexasulfid *n* hexasulphide
Hexatantalat *n* $M^I_8Ta_6O_{19}$ hexatantalate
Hexathionat *n* $M^I_2[S_6O_6]$ hexathionate
hexavalent hexavalent

Hexavalenz *f* hexavalence
Hexawolframat *n* *hexawolframate, hexatungstate
Hexen *n* hexene
Hex-1-en *n*, **Hexen-(1)** *n* hex-1-ene
Hexenmehl *n* lycopodium powder
Hex-1-in *n*, **Hexin-(1)** *n* hex-1-yne
Hex-2-in *n*, **Hexin-(2)** *n* hex-2-yne
Hex-3-in *n*, **Hexin-(3)** *n* hex-3-yne
Hexit *m*, **Hexitol** *n* hexitol *(any of the hexahydroxy alcohols* $HOCH_2[CHOH]_4CH_2OH$*)*
Hexonbase *f* hexone base
Hexose *f* hexose *(monosaccharide containing 6 oxygen atoms per molecule)*
Hexosemonophosphat-Weg *m (bioch)* hexose monophosphate shunt, pentose phosphate pathway, pentose cycle, phosphogluconate pathway
Hexoxoiodat(VII) *n* $M^{I}_5O_6$ hexaoxoiodate(VII), orthoperiodate
Hexoxoiod(VII)-säure *f* hexaoxoiodic(VII) acid, orthoperiodic acid
Hexoxotellursäure *f* hexaoxotelluric acid, orthotelluric acid, telluric acid
n-**Hexylacetylen** *n s.* Oct-1-in
n-**Hexylaldehyd** *m s.* Hexanal
n-**Hexylalkohol** *m s.* Hexan-1-ol
n-**Hexylchlorid** *n s.* 1-Chlorhexan
Hexylessigsäure *f s.* Octansäure
Hexylsäure *f s.* Hexansäure
HF-... *s.* 1. Hochfrequenz...; 2. Fluorwasserstoff...
HFS *s.* Hyperfeinstruktur
Hg-Destillationsapparat *m* mercury still
Hg-Fungizid *n* mercurial fungicide
H^+**-Gradient** *m* proton electrochemical gradient
Hg-Sammelpipette *f* mercury pipette
Hgw *s.* Hartgewebe
HID *s.* Heliumionisationsdetektor
High-Abrasion-Furnace-Ruß *m (rubber)* high-abrasion furnace black, HAF black
High-Modulus-Furnace-Ruß *m (rubber)* high-modulus furnace black, HMF black
High-Structure-Ruß *m (rubber)* high-structure [carbon] black
High-Yield-Stoff *m (pap)* high-yield pulp
Hildebrandt-Extrakteur *m* Hildebrandt (U-tube) extractor
Hilfsausrüstung *f* ancillary equipment
Hilfselektrode *f* auxiliary electrode
~ **zum Öffnen des Abstichlochs** tapping electrode
Hilfsgas *n* reactant gas *(mass spectrometry)*
Hilfsgasion *n* reactant ion *(mass spectrometry)*
Hilfsgerbstoff *m*/**synthetischer** auxiliary (neutral) syntan
Hilfsknotenfänger *m (pap)* auxiliary strainer, back knotter
Hilfskolben *m (plast)* auxiliary ram
Hilfskolonne *f (distil)* stripping column (still), stripper
Hilfskomplexbildner *m* auxiliary complexing agent
Hilfslöser *m*, **Hilfslösungsmittel** *n* cosolvent, indirect (latent) solvent; *(distil)* solvent
Hilfsmittel *n* 1. auxiliary contrivance (device); 2. *s.* Hilfsstoff
Hilfsoperation *f* ancillary operation
Hilfsstandard *m* subsidiary standard
Hilfssteuerleitung *f* pilot supply line
Hilfssteuerung *f* pilot control • **mit** ~ pilot-controlled, pilot-operated
Hilfssteuerventil *n* pilot valve
Hilfsstoff *m* auxiliary (supplementary) agent, aid, *(esp pharm)* adjuvant; corrective *(in building-up active-substance mixtures)*; *(distil)* separating agent
Hilfsthermometer *n* auxiliary thermometer
Hilfsvorrichtung *f* auxiliary contrivance (device)
~ **zum Ausdrücken** *(plast)* extractor
Hill-Akzeptor *m s.* Hill-Reagens
Hill-Gleichung *f (bioch)* Hill equation
Hill-Koeffizient *m (bioch)* Hill coefficient
Hill-Reagens *n (bioch)* Hill reagent *(any of a number of chemical compounds inducing the Hill reaction)*
Hill-Reaktion *f (bioch)* Hill reaction
Himmelblau *n* celestial (ethereal) blue *(any of several iron blue pigments)*
hinabspülen to rinse (wash) down
hinaufheben to lift
hinausdrücken to push out, to blow out *(as of a reactor)*; to squirt [out] *(as through a nozzle)*
hinauswandern to migrate out *(as of ions)*
Hinderung *f* hindrance
~/**biologische** biological hindrance
~ **der freien Drehbarkeit** hindered rotation
~/**kinetische** kinetic hindrance
~/**sterische** steric hindrance (inhibition, limitation)
hindurchdiffundieren to diffuse through
hindurchdrücken to press (force) through
hindurchlaufen to pass [through], to percolate *(as through a medium)*, *(filtr also)* to strain, to filter; to pass [through] *(as through a sieve)*
~ **lassen** to pass [through], to percolate *(e.g. through a medium)*, *(filtr also)* to strain, to filter
Hindurchlaufen *n* passage, percolation *(as through a medium)*, *(filtr also)* straining, filtering; passage *(as through a sieve)*
hindurchleiten to pass
hindurchperlen to bubble *(of a gas passing a liquid)*
~ **lassen** to bubble *(a gas through a liquid)*
hindurchpressen to force through
hindurchsickern to percolate
hindurchtransportieren to sweep through *(gas chromatography)*
Hindurchwandern *n* **der Schmelzzone (Zone)** zone travel[ling] *(in zone melting)*
hineinfressen/sich to eat *(as of an acid into metal)*
hineinwandern to migrate in *(as of ions)*
Hinokiflavon *n* hinokiflavone *(a biflavonyl)*
Hinokisäure *f* hinokiic acid *(a sesquiterpene derivative)*
Hinreaktion *f* direct (forward) reaction

Hinsberg-Probe *f* Hinsberg [amine] test
Hinsberg-Reaktion *f* Hinsberg reaction *(for separating primary, secondary, and tertiary amines)*
Hintergrund *m (nucl, anal)* background
Hintergrundkonzentration *f* background (baseline) concentration, background level
Hintergrundstrahlung *f (anal)* background emission
Hintermauerung *f* backing[-up] *(as of a furnace)*
hin- und herbewegen to reciprocate; *(tann)* to rock *(pelts in a rocker frame)*
~/sich to reciprocate
hin- und hergehen to reciprocate
hinzufügen, hinzugeben to add
hinzuwandern to migrate in *(as of ions)*
H-Ion *n* hydrogen ion, H ion
H-Ionen... *s.* Wasserstoffionen...
H^+-Ionen-Gradient *m* proton electrochemical gradient
Hippursäure *f* hippuric acid, benzoylaminoacetic acid
Hiragonsäure *f* hiragonic acid, *hexadeca-6,10,14-trienoic acid
Hirschhornsalz *n* [salt of] hartshorn, commercial ammonium carbonate, sal volatile *(a mixture consisting of ammonium hydrogencarbonate and ammonium carbamate)*
Hirsch-Trichter *m* Hirsch funnel
His *s.* Histidin
Histamin *n* histamine, 4-(ω-aminoethyl)-glyoxaline
Histaminphosphat *n* histamine phosphate
Histidin *n* histidine, 2-amino-3-imidazolylpropionic acid
Histochemie *f* histochemistry
Histosol *m (soil)* histosol
Hitzdrahtanemometer *n* hot-wire anemometer
Hitze *f* heat
Hitze... *s. a.* Wärme...
Hitzebad *n* heating bath
hitzebeständig heat-resistant, thermoduric *(microorganisms)*; heat-resistant *(steel, more than 600 °C)*
Hitzebeständigkeit *f* heat resistance *(1. of microorganisms; 2. of steel, more than 600 °C)*
hitzedenaturierbar heat-denaturable
Hitzedenaturierbarkeit *f* heat denaturability
hitzedenaturiert heat-denatured
Hitzedenaturierung *f* heat denaturation
hitzefest *s.* hitzebeständig
Hitzeflockung *f* heat flocculation
Hitzeinaktivierung *f* heat inactivation
Hitzekoagulation *f* heat coagulation
Hitzelabilität *f* heat lability
Hitzemauer *f* heat barrier
hitzeresistent heat-resistant, thermoduric *(microorganisms)*
Hitzeresistenz *f* heat resistance *(of microorganisms)*
Hitzeschädigung *f* heat damage
Hitzespaltung *f* thermal decomposition, decomposition by heat
hitzestabil thermostable, heat-stable *(enzymes, vitamins)*
Hitzestabilität *f* thermostability, heat stability *(of enzymes, vitamins)*
Hitzesterilisation *f* heat sterilization
hitzesterilisiert heat-sterilized
H-Kette *f s.* Kette/schwere
HKL *s.* Hohlkatodenlampe
HLB-Wert *m (text)* hydrophilic-lipophilic balance, HLB
HLSP-Theorie *f s.* Heitler-London-Slater-Pauling-Theorie
HM *s.* Hartmetall
HM-... *s.* Halbmikro...
HMF-Ruß *m (rubber)* HMF black, high-modulus furnace black
HMP-Weg *m s.* Hexosemonophosphat-Weg
hnRNA heterogeneous nuclear RNA
H_o *(oberer Heizwert) s.* Brennwert/spezifischer
hochaggregiert highly aggregated
hochaktiv highly active, *(nucl also)* high-level active, highly radioactive; *(rubber)* fully reinforcing
hochalkalisch highly alkaline, superalkaline
hocharomatisch highly aromatic
hochaschehaltig high-ash
hochauflösend *(anal)* high-resolution
Hochauflösung *f (anal)* high resolution
Hochausbeutestoff *m (pap)* high-yield pulp
Hochausbeute-Sulfitzellstoff *m (pap)* high-yield sulphite pulp
Hochausbeutezellstoff *m (pap)* high-yield pulp
hochausraffiniert highly refined
hochbasisch highly basic
Hochbauschgarn *n* high-bulk yarn
hochbeansprucht highly stressed
Hochbehälter *m* overhead (elevated) tank
hochbelastet highly (heavily) loaded
hochbleihaltig high-leaded *(e.g. alloy)*
Hochbunker *m* overhead hopper
hochchloren, hochchlorieren to superchlorinate *(water)*
Hochchlorung *f (hyd)* superchlorination
hochdispers highly disperse
Hochdosistoleranz *f* high dose tolerance *(immunology)*
Hochdruck *m* 1. high pressure; 2. typographic (relief) printing
Hochdruckbehälter *m* high-pressure vessel
~/gewickelter wrapped interlocking-bands vessel
Hochdruckchemie *f* high-pressure chemistry
Hochdruckchromatographie *f* high-pressure chromatography
hochdruckchromatographisch by high-pressure chromatography
Hochdruckdampf *m* high-pressure steam, HP steam
Hochdruckdampferhärtung *f (build)* high-pressure steam curing
Hochdruckdampfverfahren *n (rubber)* high-pressure process, Palmer process *(a reclaiming process)*

Hochdruckdichtung *f* high-pressure packing
Hochdruckdüngelanze *f (agric)* high-pressure soil injector
Hochdruckfarbe *f* typographic [printing] ink
Hochdruckfiltration *f* high-pressure filtration
Hochdruck-Flüssigkeitschromatographie *f* high-performance (high-pressure) liquid chromatography, HPLC
~ **mit umgekehrten Phasen** reversed-phase HPLC
Hochdruck-flüssigkeitschromatographisch by high-pressure liquid chromatography
Hochdruckgefäß *n s.* Hochdruckbehälter
Hochdruckhomogenisator *m* high-pressure homogenizer
Hochdruckhydrierung *f* high-pressure hydrogenation
~ **in flüssiger Phase** high-pressure liquid-phase hydrogenation
Hochdruckhydrier[ungs]verfahren *n* **nach Bergius** Bergius process, berginization
Hochdruckjigger *m (text)* high-pressure jig
Hochdruckkessel *m* high-pressure boiler
Hochdruckkochkessel *m (text)* high-pressure boiling kier
Hochdruckkompressor *m* high-pressure compressor
Hochdrucklaminieren *n* high-pressure laminating
Hochdruckleitung *f* high-pressure line
Hochdruckpackung *f* high-pressure packing
Hochdruckpolyethylen *n* high-pressure (low-density, L.D.) polyethylene, LDPE, branched polyethylene
Hochdruckpressen *n (plast)* high-pressure moulding
Hochdruckpumpe *f* high-pressure (high-head) pump
Hochdruckschicht[preß]stoff *m* high-pressure laminate
Hochdrucksprühgerät *n* high-pressure sprayer
Hochdruckstoffauflauf *m (pap)* high-pressure headbox, pressurized headbox
Hochdrucksynthese *f* high-pressure synthesis
Hochdrucktechnik *f* high-pressure technology
Hochdruckverdichter *m* high-pressure compressor
Hochdruckverfahren *n* 1. high-pressure process; 2. typographic (relief) process
Hochdruckvergasung *f (coal)* high-pressure gasification
Hochdruck-Wasserstoff-Sauerstoff-Brennstoffelement *n* high-pressure hydrogen cell
Hochdruckwasserstrahl *m* high-pressure water jet
Hochdruckzelle *f* **von Bacon** Bacon high-pressure hydrogen cell
hocheisenhaltig high-iron
hochempfindlich highly sensitive
Hochenergiechemie *f* high-energy chemistry
Hocherhitzer *m (food)* flash pasteurizer
Hocherhitzung *f (food)* flash pasteurization, flashing
hochevakuiert highly evacuated
hochexplosiv highly explosive, violently (dangerously) explosive
Hochfest-Kohlenstoffaser *f* carbon fibre type HT *(Young's modulus between 150 and 300 GPa)*
Hochfeuer *n (ceram)* full fire
hochfeuerfest highly refractory, superrefractory
hochflüchtig highly volatile
hochfördern to pass up[wards], to elevate
Hochfrequenzbeheizung *f s.* Hochfrequenzerhitzung
Hochfrequenzerhitzung *f*, **Hochfrequenzerwärmung** *f* high-frequency (radio-frequency) heating, electronic heating
Hochfrequenzheizung *f* 1. *(rubber)* high-frequency curing; 2. *s.* Hochfrequenzerhitzung
Hochfrequenzinduktionsofen *m* high-frequency induction furnace, coreless induction furnace
Hochfrequenzkonduktometrie *f (anal)* high-frequency conductometry
Hochfrequenzpolarographie *f (anal)* radio-frequency polarography
Hochfrequenzschweißen *n (plast)* high-frequency welding (bar sealing)
Hochfrequenzschweißgerät *n*, **Hochfrequenzsiegelgerät** *n (plast)* high-frequency sealing machine, bar sealer
Hochfrequenzsiegeln *n s.* Hochfrequenzschweißen
Hochfrequenzsirene *f* ultrasonic agglomerator *(dust collection)*
Hochfrequenztitration *f* high-frequency titration, impedimetric titration
Hochfrequenztitrator *m*, **Hochfrequenztitrimeter** *n* high-frequency titrator
Hochfrequenztrockner *m* high-frequency dryer
Hochfrequenztrocknung *f* high-frequency drying
Hochfrequenzverleimung *f* high-frequency gluing
Hochfrequenzvorwärmung *f* high-frequency preheating
hochgebrannt *(ceram)* hard-fired, high-fired, hard-burned
hochgefüllt *(rubber, pap)* highly (heavily) loaded (filled)
Hochgehen *n* lifting *(of a coating by the action of a solvent)*
hochgekohlt high-carbon *(e.g. steel)*
hochgemahlen *(pap)* highly beaten
hochgereinigt highly purified
hochgeschwefelt high-sulphur
hochgespannt highly strained *(e.g. ring system)*
hochgiftig highly (very) poisonous (toxic), quite poisonous (toxic), dangerously poisonous
Hochglanz *m* high gloss
hochglänzend high-gloss, high-lustrous, highly lustrous
Hochglanzpapier *n* bright enamel paper
hochgliedrig many-membered, multimembered
hochheizen to heat up
hochhitzebeständig resistant to high temperature[s]

Hochhitzebeständigkeit *f* resistance to high temperature[s]
hochinkohlt high-rank
hochkapazitiv high-capacity, large-capacity
hochklopffest highly knockproof, high-octane *(carburetting fuel)*
hochkohlenstoffhaltig high-carbon *(e.g. steel)*
hochkolloidal highly colloidal
hochkomprimiert highly compressed
hochkonzentriert highly concentrated, high-concentration
Hochkräusen *pl (ferm)* rocky krausen, *(Am)* high curls
hochkriechen to creep up *(the sides of a vessel)*
Hochkupferglanz *m (min)* high-chalcocite *(copper(I) sulphide)*
Hochkurzerhitzung *f*, **Hochkurzpasteurisation** *f (food)* short-time heat processing, high-temperature short-time pasteurization (heat treatment), HTST pasteurization
Hochlasttropfkörper *m s.* Tropfkörper/hochbelasteter
hochlegiert highly alloyed
Hochleistungs-Dünnschichtchromatographie *f* high-performance thin-layer chromatography, HPTLC
Hochleistungselement *n (agric)* microelement, micronutrient, minor [nutrient] element
Hochleistungsextruder *m* heavy-duty extruder
hochleistungsfähig high-capacity, large-capacity
Hochleistungsflüssigchromatographie *f* high-performance (high-pressure) liquid chromatography, HPLC
Hochleistungs-Flüssigkeits-Affinitätschromatographie *f* high-performance liquid affinity chromatography, HPLAC
Hochleistungsgerät *n (lab)* high-performance instrument
Hochleistungskalander *m (pap)* supercalender
Hochleistungskessel *m* high-duty boiler
Hochleistungsmutante *f (biot)* high-performance mutant, high-producing (high-yield) mutant
Hochleistungsöl *n* heavy-duty oil, HD oil
Hochleistungssäule *f (chromat)* high-capacity column
Hochleistungsstamm *m (biot)* high-producing (high-yield) strain *(of microorganisms)*
Hochleistungstrockner *m* high-duty dryer
Hochleistungszentrifuge *f* high-speed (high-capacity) centrifuge
Hochmahlverfahren *n s.* Hochmüllerei
Hochmodul-Kohlenstoffaser *f* carbon fibre type HM (high modulus) *(Young's modulus larger than 300 GPa)*
hochmolekular high-molecular
Hochmoortorf *m* moor peat
Hochmüllerei *f (food)* high (reduction) milling, high (open) grinding
Hochnaßmodulfaser *f* high-wet-modulus fibre, HWM
Hochnaßmodulfaserstoff *m* high-wet-modulus fibre, HWM
Hochoctanbenzin *n* high-octane gasoline (petrol)
hochoctanig high-octane
Hochoctankraftstoff *m* high-octane fuel
hochoctanzahlig high-octane
Hochofen *m* blast furnace
Hochofenanlage *f* blast-furnace plant
Hochofenfutter *n* blast-furnace lining
Hochofengas *n* blast-furnace gas
Hochofengestell *n* blast-furnace hearth
Hochofengicht *f* 1. throat, top *(of a furnace)*; 2. *s.* Hochofenmöller
Hochofengichtgas *n* blast-furnace gas
Hochofenkoks *m* [blast-]furnace coke
Hochofenmöller *m* charge [stock], burden, stock, feed
Hochofenschlacke *f* blast-furnace slag
Hochofenverfahren *n* blast-furnace process
Hochofenwerk *n* blast-furnace plant
Hochofenwind *m* furnace blast
Hochofenwinderhitzer *m* blast-furnace stove, air-blast (hot-blast) stove
Hochofenwürfel *m* blast-furnace cube
Hochofenzement *m* portland blast-furnace cement, blast-furnace [slag] cement *(containing up to 80 % blast-furnace slag)*
Hochoffsetdruck *m* dry offset printing
hochohmig high-resistance
hochorientiert highly oriented *(bond)*
hochphosphorhaltig high-phosphorus
hochplastisch highly plastic
hochpolarisierbar highly polarizable
hochpolymer high-polymeric, highly polymerized
Hochpolymer[e] *n* high polymer
hochporös highly porous
hochprozentig high-percent, high-percentage, high-analysis; *(relating to spirits:)* strong, *(Am also)* hard
hochraffiniert highly refined
hochreaktionsfähig, hochreaktiv highly reactive
hochrein highly pure (purified), high-purity
Hochreinigung *f* ultrapurification *(zone melting)*
hochsauerstoffhaltig high-oxygen
hochschmelzend high-melting[-point], high-fusion
hochschrumpfend *(text)* high-shrinking
hochschwefelhaltig high-sulphur, rich in sulphur
Hochseeverklappung *f* offshore disposal *(of waste)*
hochselektiv highly selective
hochsiedend high-boiling, heavy
Hochsieder *m* high boiler *(e.g. a solvent)*
Hochsintern *n*, **Hochsinterung** *f* full (final) sintering *(of metals)*
Hochspannungselektrophorese *f* high-voltage electrophoresis
Hochspannungs[elektro]porzellan *n* high-voltage (high-tension) porcelain

höchstauflösend *(spectr)* very-high-resolution
Höchstdruckkessel *m* very-high-pressure boiler
Höchstdruckschmierstoff *m* extreme-pressure lubricant, EP lubricant
Höchstdruckspritzen *n***[/druckluftloses]** *(coat)* airless spraying
hochstellen *(met)* to tip for blowing *(a converter)*
Höchstkonzentration *f***/zulässige** *(tox)* maximum permissible (admissible, allowable) concentration, MAC
Höchstmenge *f***/duldbare (zulässige)** *(tox)* [maximum] tolerance
höchstrein ultrapure
Hochstruktur-Ruß *m (rubber)* high-structure [carbon] black
Hochtemperaturbehandlung *f* high-temperature treatment
hochtemperaturbeständig resistant to high temperature[s], stable at high temperature[s]
Hochtemperaturbeständigkeit *f* high-temperature resistance (stability, durability)
Hochtemperaturchemie *f* high-temperature chemistry
Hochtemperaturdestillation *f* high-temperature distillation
Hochtemperatureigenschaften *fpl* high-temperature properties
Hochtemperaturentgasung *f s.* Hochtemperaturverkokung
Hochtemperaturfärbemaschine *f (text)* high-temperature dyeing machine
Hochtemperaturfärben *n (text)* high-temperature dyeing
Hochtemperaturgasgenerator *m (coal)* high-temperature [gas] generator, high-temperature gasifier
Hochtemperaturkochung *f (pap)* high-temperature digestion
Hochtemperaturkoks *m* high-temperature coke
Hochtemperaturkorrosion *f* high-temperature corrosion, dry (hot) corrosion
Hochtemperaturlegierung *f* high-temperature alloy
Hochtemperaturofen *m* high-temperature furnace; *(ceram)* high-temperature kiln
Hochtemperaturpolymer[e] *n*, **Hochtemperaturpolymerisat** *n* high-temperature polymer, hot polymer
Hochtemperaturpolymerisation *f* high-temperature polymerization, hot polymerization
Hochtemperaturpyrolyse *f* high-temperature pyrolysis, HTP
Hochtemperaturreaktor *m* high-temperature reactor
Hochtemperaturschmierfett *n* high-temperature grease
Hochtemperaturteer *m* high-temperature tar
Hochtemperaturtunnelofen *m (ceram)* high-temperature tunnel kiln
Hochtemperatur-Überdruckfärben *n (text)* high-temperature pressure dyeing
Hochtemperaturvergaser *m s.* Hochtemperaturgasgenerator
Hochtemperaturverhalten *n* high-temperature behaviour
Hochtemperaturverkokung *f* high-temperature carbonization (coking)
Hochtemperaturvulkanisation *f* high-temperature cure (vulcanization)
Hochtemperaturwerkstoff *m* high-temperature material
Hochtemperatur-Winkler-Gasgenerator *m* high-temperature Winkler gasifier
hochtourig high-speed
hochtoxisch *s.* hochgiftig
hochungesättigt highly unsaturated
Hochvakuum *n* high vacuum
Hochvakuumdestillation *f* high-vacuum distillation
Hochvakuumtechnik *f* high-vacuum technique
hochveredelt highly refined, high-added-value *(product)*; highly finished *(surface)*
hochverstärkend *(rubber)* fully reinforcing
hochviskos highly viscous, high-viscosity
hochweiß extra white
hochwertig of high quality, high-quality, *(esp of raw materials:)* high-grade
hochwirksam highly active, potent
hochzähflüssig *s.* hochviskos
Hochzahl *f (nomencl)* numeric superscript, superscript numeral
Hochziehen *n (coat)* lifting *(by the action of solvents)*
hochzinnhaltig tin-rich
Hof *m (phot, spectr, chromat)* halo
Hoffmann-Ofen *m (ceram)* Hoffmann kiln
Hofmann-Abbau *m* Hofmann degradation *(of amides)*
Hofmann-Eliminierung *f* Hofmann elimination *(of quaternary ammonium hydroxides)*
Hofmann-Martius-Umlagerung *f* Hofmann-Martius rearrangement *(of hydrohalides of N-alkylanilines into alkylanilines)*
Hofmann-Orientierung *f (org ch)* Hofmann orientation
Hogness-Box *f (bioch)* Hogness box *(certain sequence of thymine and adenine in the DNA)*
Höhe *f* **des Schornsteins/effektive** effective chimney (stack) height
~einer theoretischen Trennstufe height equivalent to a theoretical stage (plate), HETS, HETP
~ einer Übertragungseinheit *(distil)* height of one transfer unit, HTU
~/geodätische potential head
Höhenformel *f***/barometrische** barometric formula
Höhenliniendiagramm *n* contour map
~ der Potentialfläche potential-energy contour map
Höhenstrahlen *mpl* cosmic rays
Höhenstrahlung *f* cosmic radiation
höhergliedrig higher-membered
höherhalogeniert polyhalogenated
höherprozentig higher-percentage, higher-analysis

höherschmelzend higher-melting
höhersiedend higher-boiling, heavier
höherwertig of higher valence, higher-valent, higher-valency *(chemical-bond theory)*; polyhydric *(alcohol)*; higher-analysis *(as of a commercial product)*
Hohlblock *m (ceram)* hollow block
Höhlenleaching *n***[/reines]** *s.* In-situ-Laugung
Hohlfaser *f* hollow fibre
Hohlfasermembran *f (hyd)* hollow fibre membrane *(reverse osmosis)*
Hohlform *f (plast)* die
Hohlglas *n* hollow [glass]ware
Hohlguß *m (ceram)* drain (hollow) casting
Hohlkatode *f* hollow cathode
Hohlkatodenlampe *f* hollow-cathode lamp
Hohlkegeldüse *f* hollow-cone nozzle
Hohlkörper *m (plast)* hollow article (body, part)
Hohlkörperblasen *n (plast)* blow moulding
Hohlleiter *m (spectr)* wave guide
Hohlprofil *n* hollow profile
Hohlraum *m* cavity, hollow (void) space; *(plast)* void *(a defect)*; *(chromat)* interstice
~/lufterfüllter soil air space
Hohlraumanteil *m (chromat)* interstitial fraction
Hohlraumbildung *f* formation of cavities; cavitation *(in moving liquids)*
Hohlraumfilter *n* granular-bed separator *(gas cleaning)*
hohlraumfrei free from cavities; *(plast)* free from voids
Hohlraumresonator *m (spectr)* cavity resonator
Hohlraumstrahler *m* black-body radiator
Hohlraumstrahlung *f* black-body radiation
Hohlraumvolumen *n* void (pore) volume *(of a catalyst)*; *(chromat)* interstitial volume; *(soil)* volume of pore space
Hohlsog *m* cavitation *(in moving liquids)*
Hohlsprühkegel *m* hollow spray cone
Hohlsprühkegeldüse *f* hollow-cone nozzle
Hohlstein *m* hollow brick; hollow tile
Hohlware *f (ceram)* hollow ware
Hohlwelle *f* hollow shaft
Hohlzapfen *m* hollow journal
Hohlzapfenaustrag *m* trunnion discharge *(as of a mill)*
Hohlziegel *m* hollow brick; hollow tile
Holarrhenaalkaloid *n* holarrhena alkaloid
Holdcroft-Stäbe *mpl (ceram)* Holdcroft bars
Holländer *m (pap)* Hollander, Hollander beater (beating engine), pulp (stuff) engine, pulp grinder
~ mit mehreren Grundwerken multiplate beater
Holländereintrag *m (pap)* furnish[ing]
Holländerfärbung *f (pap)* beater dyeing (colouring)
Holländerfüllung *f (pap)* furnish[ing]
Holländermesser *npl (pap)* knives, teeth, bars
Höllenstein *m* caustic silver, lunar caustic *(silver nitrate)*
Holmes-Manley-Verfahren *n (petrol)* Holmes-Manley process
Holmium *n* Ho holmium
Holmiumchlorid *n* holmium chloride
Holmiumhydroxid *n* holmium hydroxide
Holmiumoxid *n* holmium oxide
Holmiumsulfat *n* holmium sulphate
Holocellulose *f* holocellulose
holoedrisch *(cryst)* holohedral
Holoenzym *n* holoenzyme
Holographie *f* holography
holographisch holographic
holokristallin holocrystalline
Holosid *n (org ch)* holoside
Holosiderit *m* holosiderite *(meteoric iron)*
Holst-Verfahren *n (pap)* Holst process *(for making chlorine-dioxide bleaching liquor)*
Holz *n***/gerbstoffhaltiges** tanwood
Holzasche *f* wood ash[es]
Holzäther *m s.* Dimethylether
Holzaufbereitung *f (pap)* wood preparation
Holzaufschluß *m (pap)* pulping of wood
~ mit Salpetersäure nitric-acid pulping
Holzbeize *f* stain
Holzbottich *m*, **Holzbütte** *f* wooden tub (vat)
Holzcellulose *f* wood cellulose
Holzchemie *f* wood chemistry
Holzdestillation *f* wood distillation
Holzdurchtränkung *f (pap)* penetration of wood (chips) *(with cooking liquor)*
Holzessig *m* wood vinegar, pyroligneous acid *(crude acetic acid obtained by wood distillation)*
Holzfaser *f* wood fibre
Holzfilter *n* wooden filter
holzfrei *(pap)* wood-free
Holzfülldichte *f (pap)* chip capacity
Holzfüllung *f (pap)* chip filling (packing)
~ ohne Füllapparat gravity filling
Holzgas *n* wood[-distillation] gas; wood producer gas
Holzgefüge *n (coal)* woody structure
Holzgeist *m***[/roher]** wood (pyroligneous) spirit, natural methanol
Holzgewicht *n (pap)* wood weight
Holzgummi *n* xylan *(a pentosan)*
holzhaltig *(pap)* wood-containing, woody
Holzhydrolyse *f* wood hydrolysis
holzig woody
Holzkalk *m (dye)* pyrolignite of lime *(crude calcium acetate)*
Holzkarton *m* wood-pulp cardboard *(from mechanical pulp)*
Holzkochung *f (pap)* cooking of wood
Holzkohle *f* [wood] charcoal
~/aktive (aktivierte) active (activated) charcoal
~/fossile (mineralische) fossil (mineral) charcoal, mother of coal
Holzkohleneisen *n* charcoal pig iron
~/schwedisches Swedish iron
Holzkohlen[hoch]ofen *m* charcoal-fired [blast] furnace

Holzkohlenroheisen *n s.* Holzkohleneisen
Holzkonservierung *f* wood preservation; *(build)* timber proofing
Holzleim *m* wood[working] glue, wood[-bonding] adhesive
Holzmasse *f* 1. *s.* Holzschliff; 2. *(pap)* wood weight
Holzmehl *n*/**feines** wood flour
~/**grobes** wood meal
Holzöl *n*[/**Chinesisches**] tung oil, China (Chinese) wood oil *(chiefly from the seeds of Aleurites fordii Hemsl.)*
Holzöl-Eisblumenbildung *f s.* Holzölerscheinung
Holzölerscheinung *f*, **Holzölkrankheit** *f (coat)* gas checking *(a defect)*
Holzopal *m (min)* wood opal
Holzpech *n* Stockholm pitch
Holzputzerei *f (pap)* wood room
Holzsäure *f* wood acid *(formed when wood is heated to 120 °C)*
Holzschacht *m (pap)* magazine *(of a grinder)*
Holzschleifer *m (pap)* [pulpwood] grinder
Holzschleiferei *f (pap)* [mechanical-]pulp mill, groundwood mill, grinder house (room)
Holzschleifmaschine *f (pap)* [pulpwood] grinder
Holzschliff *m (pap)* wood pulp, *(specif)* mechanical pulp • **zu ~ verschleifen** to reduce to pulp, to make into [a] pulp, to pulp
~/**brauner** brown mechanical pulp
~/**chemischer** chemigroundwood
~ **in Bogenform (Pappenform)** *s.* Holzschliffpappe
~/**mechanischer** mechanical pulp (wood pulp), MWP, groundwood [pulp]
Holzschliffaser *f (pap)* groundwood fibre
Holzschliffblätter *npl s.* Holzschliffpappe
Holzschliffbleiche *f (pap)* groundwood bleaching
Holzschliffentwässerungsmaschine *f (pap)* pulp[-drying] machine, half-stuff machine, wet [press] machine, press-pâte
Holzschlifferzeugung *f (pap)* manufacture of mechanical wood pulp, mechanical (groundwood) pulping
holzschliffhaltig *(pap)* wood-containing, woody
Holzschliffpapier *n* groundwood (wood-containing, woody) paper
Holzschliffpappe *f (pap)* wood-pulp board, board (sheets, laps) of mechanical wood pulp
Holzschliffverfahren *n (pap)* groundwood process
Holzschnitzel *npl (pap)* [wood] chips, chippings
Holzschutz *m* wood preservation; *(build)* timber proofing
Holzschutzmittel *n* wood preservative
~/**kombiniertes** fire-retardant preservative
~/**wasserlösliches** water-borne-type preservative, WB-type preservative
Holzspäne *mpl s.* Holzschnitzel
Holzspiritus *m alcohol derived from destructive distillation or saccharification of wood*
Holzsplitter *m* wood speck *(a defect in paper)*
Holzstoff *m* 1. lignin; 2. *s.* Holzschliff
Holzstruktur *f (coal)* woody structure
Holzsubstanz *f* ligneous substance
Holzteer *m* wood tar
Holzteerkreosot *n* wood[-tar] creosote
Holzverkohlung *f* wood carbonization, charcoal burning
Holzverleimung *f* wood bonding
Holzverzuckerung *f* saccharification of wood
Holzvorbereitung *f (pap)* wood preparation
Holzvorschub *m (pap)* advance of wood *(in a grinder)*
Holzzellstoff *m* 1. *(pap)* [chemical] wood pulp, CWP; 2. *s.* Holzcellulose
Holzzucker *m* wood sugar, xylose
HOMO *s.* Molekülorbital/höchstes besetztes
homoaromatisch *(org ch)* homoaromatic
Homoaromatizität *f (org ch)* homoaromaticity
homocyclisch *(org ch)* homocyclic, isocyclic, carbocyclic
Homocyclus *m (org ch)* homocycle, homocyclic [compound]
Homocysteinurie *f (med)* homocysteinuria
homodispers monodisperse
Homoentkopplung *f s.* Entkopplung/homonukleare
homofermentativ *(bioch)* homofermentative
homogen homogeneous
~/**vollkommen (vollständig)** perfectly homogeneous, homogeneous throughout
Homogenisator *m*, **Homogenisierapparat** *m* homogenizer
homogenisieren 1. to homogenize; 2. *(ceram)* to wedge
Homogenisierkopf *m* homogenizer (homogenizing) head (valve)
Homogenisiermaschine *f* homogenizer
Homogenisierung *f* 1. homogenization, homogenizing *(as of emulsions)*; 2. *(ceram)* wedging
Homogenisierungsglühen *n* homogenization, homogenizing *(of alloys)*
Homogenität *f* homogeneity
Homogenkatalyse *f* homogeneous catalysis
Homogenkinetik *f* homogeneous kinetics
Homogenreaktion *f* homogeneous reaction
Homogenreaktor *m (nucl)* homogeneous reactor
Homogentisinsäure *f* homogentisic acid, quinolacetic acid
Homoisocitronensäure *f (bioch)* homoisocitric acid
Homokonjugation *f (org ch)* homoconjugation
homolog homologous
Homolog[e] *n* homologue, homolog
Homologisierung *f* homologization
Homolyse *f* homolysis, homolytic [bond] cleavage, homolytic [bond] fission, bond dissociation
homolytisch homolytic
homonuklear homonuclear
homöopolar covalent, homopolar, non-polar *(chemical-bond theory)*
homopolymer homopolymeric

Homopolymer[e] *n*, **Homopolymerisat** *n* homopolymer
Homopolymerisation *f* homopolymerization
homopolysaccharid *n* homopolysaccharide
Homosphäre *f* homosphere *(lower part of the atmosphere)*
4-Homosulfanilamid *n* 4-homosulphanilamide, α-aminotoluene-4-sulphonamide
Homotropyliumkation *n* homotropylium cation
Honig *m* honey
Honigpflanze *f* honey (nectariferous) plant
Honigstein *m (min)* mellite *(a hydrous aluminium mellitate)*
Honigsteinsäure *f* mellitic acid, benzene-hexacarboxylic acid
Honigwein *m* mead
Hooker-Diaphragmazelle *f*, **Hooker-Zelle** *f* Hooker [diaphragm] cell *(for electrolyzing brine)*
Hoopes-Verfahren *n* Hoopes [electrolytic-refining] process
hopfen to hop *(the wort)*
Hopfenanbau *m* hop growing
Hopfenbittere *f* bitterness of hops
Hopfenbittersäure *f* hop bitter acid
α-Hopfenbittersäure *f* α-lupulinic acid, α-bitter acid, humulone
β-Hopfenbittersäure *f* β-lupulinic acid, β-bitter acid, lupulone
Hopfendarre *f* hop dryer (kiln)
Hopfenextrakt *m* hop extract[ive]
Hopfenharz *n* hop resin
Hopfenmehl *n* lupulin, hop flour
Hopfenöl *n* hop oil
Hopfenpektin *n* hop pectin
Höppler-Kugelfallviskosimeter *n*, **Höppler-Viskosimeter** *n* Höppler [falling-ball] viscometer
HO_2-Radikal *n* HO_2-radical, hydroperoxyl radical
Horde *f* [kiln] floor, tray *(as of a dryer)*
Hordein *n* hordein *(a prolamine)*
Hordenschranktrockner *m* cabinet shelf dryer
Hordenschwingtrockner *m* vibrating tray dryer
Hordentrockner *m* tray dryer
Hordenwagen *m* tray truck
Horizont *m (soil)* layer, horizon, level
~/organischer dark humus layer
Horizontalbeziehung *f* horizontal relationship *(in the periodic system)*
Horizontalchromatographie *f* horizontal chromatography
Horizontalentwicklung *f (chromat)* horizontal development
Horizontalkammer *f* horizontal chamber
Horizontalkammerofen *m* horizontal oven
~ mit senkrechten Heizzügen vertical-flue oven
Horizontalkanal *m* horizontal flue *(as for off-gas)*
Horizontalklärer *m* horizontal clarifyer *(waste-water treatment)*
Horizontalkolonne *f (distil)* horizontal still
Horizontalofen *m s.* Horizontalkammerofen
Horizontalretorte *f* horizontal retort
Horizontalrohrverdampfer *m* horizontal[-tube] evaporator
Horizontaltechnik *f (chromat)* horizontal technique
Horizontalzelle *f* horizontal [diaphragm] cell *(electrolysis)*
Horizontalzentrifuge *f* horizontal centrifuge
Horizontalziehverfahren *n (glass)* horizontal sheet drawing process
Horizontalzug *m* horizontal flue *(as for off-gas)*
Hormon *n* hormone
~/adrenocorticotropes adrenocorticotropic hormone, corticotropin
~/antidiuretisches antidiuretic hormone, ADH, vasopressin
~/follikelstimulierendes follicle-stimulating hormone, FSH
~/interstitielle Zellen stimulierendes *s.* ~/luteinisierendes
~/lactotropes *s.* Prolactin
~/luteinisierendes luteinizing hormone, LH, interstitial-cell-stimulating hormone, ICSH, prolan B
~/luteotrop[h]es *s.* Prolactin
~/Melanotropin-release-inhibierendes *melanostatin, melanotropin inhibitory hormone
~/melanozytenstimulierendes melanocyte-stimulating hormone, *melanotropin
~/neurohypophysäres neurohypophyseal (posterior-lobe) hormone
~/östrogenes oestrus-producing hormone
~/somatotropes somatotropic hormone, somatropin, STH
~/thyreotropes thyrotrop[h]ic (thyroid-stimulating) hormone, TH, thyrotrop[h]in
~/zwischenzellenstimulierendes *s.* ~/luteinisierendes
hormonal hormonal • **~ gesteuert** under hormonal control
hormonell *s.* hormonal
Hormonrezeptor *m (bioch)* hormone receptor
hornähnlich horn-like
Hornblende *f (min)* hornblende, amphibole *(an inosilicate)*
~/Gemeine common hornblende
Hornblendeasbest *m (min)* amphibole asbestos
Hornmehl *n (agric)* horn meal
Hornquecksilber *n (min)* horn mercury, calomel *(mercury(I) chloride)*
Hornsilber *n (min)* horn silver, chlorargyrite, cerargyrite *(silver chloride)*
Hornspatel *m* horn spatula
Hornstein *m (min)* hornstone, chert *(a mineral related to chalcedony)*
Hornsubstanz *f* keratin
Hosenmischer *m* twin-shell (vee-type) mixer (blender)
Hosenrohr *n* wye
Hot-pit-Gerbung *f* hot pitting
Hottenroth-Zahl *f (text)* Hottenroth number

Houben-Hoesch-Synthese *f* Houben-Hoesch synthesis *(of ketones)*
Houdresid-Verfahren *n* Houdresid process *(a catalytic cracking or reforming process)*
Houdriflow-Kracken *n (petrol)* Houdriflow catalytic cracking
Houdriformen *n*, **Houdriformierung** *f* houdriforming *(a variety of catalytic reforming)*
Houdriforming-Anlage *f (petrol)* houdriformer
Houdry-Einstufendehydrierungsverfahren *n* **für Butan** Houdry butane dehydrogenation process
Houdry-Festbettkracken *n (petrol)* Houdry fixed-bed catalytic cracking
Houdry-Festbettverfahren *n (petrol)* Houdry fixed-bed process
Houdry-Krackverfahren *n*/**katalytisches** *(petrol)* Houdry catalytic cracking process
Howard-Kristallisator *m* Howard crystallizer
HOZ *s.* Hochofenzement
Hp *s.* Hartpapier
HPC-Ruß *m (rubber)* hard processing channel black, HPC black
HP-Verfahren *n s.* Heiß-Pottasche-Verfahren
HR *s.* Rockwellhärte
HSAB-Konzept *n* HSAB principle *(acid-base theory)*
H-Säure *f* H acid, 1-aminonaphth-8-ol-3,6-disulphonic acid
HSK-Zyklus *m s.* Hatch-Slack-Kortschak-Zyklus
HT-... *s.* Hochtemperatur...
5-HT *s.* 5-Hydroxytryptamin
HTST-Erhitzung *f s.* Hochkurzerhitzung
HTU *s.* Höhe einer Übertragungseinheit
HTW-Gasgenerator *m* high-temperature Winkler gasifier
H_u *(unterer Heizwert) s.* Heizwert/spezifischer
Huanaco-Koka *f* Huanuca coca *(from Erythroxylum coca Cam.)*
Huang-Minlon-Reaktion *f*, **Huang-Minlon-Reduktion** *f* Huang-Minlon reaction (reduction) *(of aldehydes and ketones)*
Hub *m* stroke [length] *(of a pump)*; vibration amplitude, stroke *(screening)*
Hubblech *n* lifting plate *(as of a rotary dryer)*
Hubel *m (ceram)* clot, blank
Hubkolbenpumpe *f* reciprocating pump
Hublänge *f s.* Hub
Hubleiste *f* lifting (lifter) bar *(as of a rotary dryer)*
Hübnerit *m (min)* huebnerite, hübnerite *(manganese(II) tungstate)*
Hubrückschlagventil *n* lift check valve
Hubschaufel *f* lifting (radial) flight *(of a rotary dryer)*
Hubschaufeleinbau *m* lifting (radial) flights *(of a rotary dryer)*
~ **mit abgewinkelten Schaufeln** lip flights
~ **mit ebenen Schaufeln** flat flights
Hubseil *n* hoisting rope
Hubtür *f* tweel, tuille
Hubventil *n* globe valve
Hubvorrichtung *f* lifting device
Hubzahl *f* number of strokes
Hückel-Molekülorbital *n* Hückel molecular orbital
Hückel-Regel *f (org ch)* Hückel (4n + 2) rule, Hückel rule *(relating to conjugated hydrocarbons having 4n + 2π-electrons)*
Hückel-System *n* Hückel system *(a cyclic conjugated hydrocarbon having 4n + 2π-electrons)*
Hühneraugenmittel *n (pharm)* corn remover
Hülle *f* 1. shell, envelope, sheath *(of an atom)*; 2. *(tech)* jacket, sheath[ing], cover, shell
Hüllenelektron *n* extranuclear electron
Hüllpapier *n* wrapping (packing) paper, wrapper *(of high quality)*
Hüllprotein *n* coat (capsid) protein
Hülse *f* 1. *(tech)* socket, jacket; socket *(of a ground joint)*; 2. *(pap)* core, centre; 3. *(lab)* thimble *(for extracting)*
~/keglige *(text)* cone
Hülsenlosfärben *n (text)* muff dyeing
Humanserumalbumin *n (pharm, bioch)* human serum albumin, HSA
Humantoxizität *f* human toxicity
Humat *n (soil)* humate
Humboldtin *m (min)* humboldtine *(iron oxalate)*
Hume-Rothery-Phase *f (cryst)* Hume-Rothery phase
Humifizierung *f (soil)* humification
Huminkohle *f* humic coal
Huminsäure *f* humic acid
Huminstoff *m*, **Huminsubstanz** *f* humic substance (matter)
Humit *m* 1. *(min)* humite *(a fluorine-containing magnesium silicate)*; 2. humic coal
Humulon *n* humulone, α-lupulinic acid
Humus *m* humus
Humusanreicherung *f* accumulation of humus
Humusboden *m* humus soil
Humusbraunkohle *f* humic brown coal
Humuscarbonatboden *m* rendzina
Humuskohle *f s.* Humusbraunkohle
Humusortstein *m (soil)* humic ortstein
Humussäure *f* humic acid
Humusstoff *m s.* Huminstoff
Humusstoffhorizont *m (soil)* H-layer
Humussubstanz *f s.* Huminstoff
Hund-Mulliken-Lennard-Jones-Hückel-Theorie Hund-Mulliken-Lennard-Jones-Hückel theory, molecular-orbital theory
Hunsdiecker-Reaktion *f* 1. Hunsdiecker reaction *(decarboxylation of the silver salt of an organic acid)*; 2. *s.* Hunsdiecker-Spaltung
Hunsdiecker-Spaltung *f* Hunsdiecker cleavage *(of esters)*
Hunter-Syndrom *n (med)* Hunter's disease *(accumulation of glycosaminoglycans caused by inherited enzyme deficiency)*
Huntington-Pendel[rollen]mühle *f* Huntington [ring-roll] mill

Hustenmittel *n* antitussive
Hut *m (geol)* cap
~/Eiserner iron hat, gossan, gozzan
Hutmanschette *f (tech)* flange seal
Hütte *f (met)* refinery, smelting plant
Hüttenbims *m* foamed slag
Hüttenblei *n one kind of pure lead containing 99.75 to 99.95 % Pb*
Hüttenchemie *f* metallurgical chemistry
Hüttenchemiker *m* metallurgical chemist
Hütteningenieur *m* metallurgical engineer
Hüttenkoks *m* metallurgical (blast-furnace) coke
Hüttenkunde *f* metallurgy
hüttenmännisch metallurgical
Hüttenrauch *m* flue dust
Hüttenstaub *m* flue dust
Hüttentechnik *f* metallurgical technology
Hütten-Weichblei *n* soft (chemical) lead *(of more than 99.9 % purity)*
Hüttenwerk *n s.* Hütte
Hüttenwesen *n* metallurgy
Hüttenzement *m* blast-furnace [slag] cement, slag cement
HV *s.* Vickers-Härte
H-Versprödung *f* hydrogen embrittlement
HWM-Faser *f* high-wet-modulus fibre, HWM
HWM-Faserstoff *m* high-wet-modulus fibre, HWM
Hyalbiuronsäure *f (bioch)* hyalbiuronic acid
hyalin hyaline
Hyalophan *m (min)* hyalophane *(a tectosilicate)*
Hyaluronsäure *f* hyaluronic acid *(a mucopolysaccharide)*
Hyazinth *m (min)* hyacinth *(zirconium orthosilicate)*
hybrid hybrid
Hybrid *n* hybrid
~/digonales *s. sp*-Hybrid
sp-**Hybrid** *n sp*-hybrid, digonal hybrid
Hybridfunktion *f* hybrid function *(bonding theory)*
hybridisieren to hybridize
Hybridisierung *f* hybridization
~/digonale *s. sp*-Hybridisierung
~/intraspezifische *(biot)* intraspecific hybridization
~/tetraedrische *s.* sp^3-Hybridisierung
~/trigonale *s.* sp^2-Hybridisierung
sp-**Hybridisierung** *f sp* hybridization, digonal hybridization
sp^2-**Hybridisierung** *f* sp^2-hybridization, trigonal hybridization
sp^3-**Hybridisierung** *f* sp^3 hybridization, tetrahedral hybridization
Hybridom *n (biot)* hybridoma [cell]
Hybridomtechnik *f (biot)* monoclonal antibody technology
Hybridorbital *n* hybrid [bond] orbital
sp-**Hybridorbital** *n* hybrid *sp* orbital
Hybridstruktur *f* hybrid structure
Hybridzelle *f (biot)* hybrid cell
~/antikörperproduzierende *(biot)* hybridoma [cell]
Hybridzustand *m* hybrid state

Hydantoinsäure *f* hydantoic acid, ureidoacetic acid
Hydnocarpussäure *f* hydnocarpic acid, *11-(2-cyclopentenyl) undecanoic acid
Hydracrylsäure *f* hydracrylic acid, *3-hydroxypropionic acid
Hydrane-Verfahren *n (coal)* hydrane process *(for gasifying coal with hydrogen in two stages)*
Hydrangeasäure *f* hydrangeic acid, 3,4'-dihydroxystilbene-2-carboxylic acid
Hydrat *n* hydrate
Hydratation *f* hydration, aqua[tiza]tion
~ der Ionen ionic hydration
Hydratationsenergie *f* hydration energy
Hydratationsgrad *m* degree of hydration
Hydratationssphäre *f* hydration sphere
Hydratationswärme *f* heat of hydration
Hydratationszahl *f* hydration number
Hydratbildung *f* hydrate formation
Hydratcellulose *f* hydrocellulose, hydrated cellulose, cellulose hydrate
Hydrathülle *f* hydration sheath, water envelope
Hydration *f s.* Hydratation
hydratisieren to hydrate, to aquate
Hydratisierung *f* hydration, aqua[tiza]tion
Hydratisierungs... *s.* Hydratations...
Hydrator *m* hydrator
Hydratwasser *n* water of hydration
Hydraulikakkumulator *m* hydraulic accumulator
Hydraulikflüssigkeit *f* hydraulic fluid (medium)
Hydraulikkolben *m* hydraulic ram
Hydraulikspeicher *m* hydraulic accumulator
Hydrazid *n* hydrazide
Hydrazidimid *n* hydrazide imide
Hydrazin *n* hydrazine
~/wasserfreies anhydrous hydrazine
Hydrazingelb *n* **O** hydrazine yellow, tartrazine *(a pyrazole derivative)*
Hydrazinhydrat *n* hydrazine hydrate
Hydrazinolyse *f*, **Hydrazinspaltung** *f* hydrazinolysis
Hydrazinthiocarbonsäureamid *n* aminothiourea, thiosemicarbazide
Hydrazoaren *n* hydrazoarene, 1,2-diarylhydrazine, 1,2-diaryldiazane
Hydrazobenzen *n*, **Hydrazobenzol** *n* hydrazobenzene
Hydrazon *n* hydrazone
Hydrazoverbindung *f* hydrazo compound
Hydrid *n* hydride
~/interstitielles interstitial hydride
~/komplexes complex hydride
~/metallartiges (metallisches) transition-metal binary hydride
~/salzartiges saline hydride
Hydridbildner *m* hydride-forming element
Hydrid-Ion *n* hydride ion
Hydridkomplex *m* complex hydride
Hydridoborat *n* $M^I[BH_4]$ hydridoborate, tetrahydridoborate

Hydridverfahren *n* hydride process *(for making metal powder)*
Hydridverschiebung *f* hydride shift
Hydridverschiebungssatz *m* hydride displacement law
Hydrierapparat *m* hydrogenator
Hydrierautoklav *m* hardening vessel *(fat hardening)*
hydrierbar hydrogenable
Hydrierbenzin *n* hydrogenation gasoline (spirit)
hydrieren to hydrogenate, to hydrogenize
~/katalytisch to hydrogenate catalytically
Hydrieren *n* hydrogenation
Hydriergas *n* hydrogenating gas
Hydrierkatalysator *m* hydrogenating (hydrogenation) catalyst
Hydrierofen *m* converter
Hydrierreaktion *f* hydrogenating reaction
hydriert/selektiv selectively hydrogenated
~/teilweise partially hydrogenated, part-hydrogenated
Hydrierung *f* hydrogenation
~/abbauende (destruktive) destructive hydrogenation
~ in flüssiger Phase *s.* ~ in Sumpfphase
~ in Gasphase vapour-phase hydrogenation
~ in Sumpfphase sump-phase (liquid-phase) hydrogenation
~/katalytische catalytic hydrogenation
~/selektive selective hydrogenation
~/spaltende *s.* ~/abbauende
Hydrierungs... *s.* Hydrier...
Hydrierverfahren *n* hydrogenation process, *(food also)* hardening process
Hydriervergaser *m (coal)* hydrogasifier, hydrogasification reactor
Hydrierwärme *f* heat of hydrogenation
Hydrinden *n* hydrindene, indane
Hydrindon *n* hydrindone, indanone
Hydroaluminierung *f* hydroalumination
Hydroaromaten *pl* hydroaromatic compounds
hydroaromatisch hydroaromatic
Hydroborierung *f* hydroboration *(addition of diborane to alkenes)*
Hydrobromid *n* hydrobromide
Hydrobromierung *f* hydrobromination
Hydrocarbalkoxylierung *f* hydrocarbalkoxylation
Hydrocarbomethoxylierung *f* hydrocarbomethoxylation, hydromethoxycarbonylation
Hydrocarbonylierung *f*, **Hydrocarboxylierung** *f* hydrocarboxylation, hydrocarbonylation
Hydrocellulose *f* hydrocellulose
Hydrocelluloseacetat *n (text)* secondary [cellulose] acetate, cellulose diacetate
Hydrochemie *f* hydrochemistry, water (aquatic) chemistry
Hydrochinin *n s.* Dihydrochinin
Hydrochinon *n* quinol, hydroquinone, *p*-dihydroxybenzene
Hydrochinonclathrat *n* quinol clathrate
Hydrochinonentwickler *m (phot)* hydroquinone developer
Hydrochinonessigsäure *f* quinolacetic acid, homogentisic acid
Hydrochlorid *n* hydrochloride
Hydrochlorierung *f* hydrochlorination
Hydrochlorkautschuk *m* rubber hydrochloride
Hydrocol-Verfahren *n* Hydrocol process *(for producing high-octane gasoline from natural gas)*
Hydrocumarsäure *f* hydrocoumaric acid, 3-hydroxyphenylpropionic acid
Hydrocyanierung *f* hydrocyanation
Hydrodemethylierung *f* hydrodemethylation
Hydrodesalkylierung *f* hydrodealkylation, reductive dealkylation
Hydrodesulfurierung *f* hydrodesulphurization, HDS
Hydrofixierung *f (text)* hydrosetting
Hydrofluorid *n* hydrofluoride
Hydrofluorierung *f* hydrofluorination
Hydrofluorkautschuk *m* rubber hydrofluoride
Hydroformat *n (petrol)* hydroformate
Hydroformer *m (petrol)* hydroformer
hydroformieren *(petrol)* to hydroform *(to reform by catalytic dehydrogenation and cyclization)*
Hydroforming-Produkt *n (petrol)* hydroformate
Hydroformylierung *f* hydroformylation, oxo synthesis
Hydrogel *n* hydrogel
Hydrogen *n* H hydrogen
Hydrogenarsenat *n* $M^I_2HAsO_4$ hydrogenarsenate
Hydrogenase *f* hydrogenase
Hydrogencarbonat *n* M^IHCO_3 hydrogencarbonate
Hydrogencarbonatalkalität *f (hyd)* bicarbonate alkalinity
Hydrogencyanid *n* hydrogen cyanide, hydrocyanic acid
Hydrogenfluorid *n* M^IHF_2 hydrogen difluoride
Hydrogenolyse *f* hydrogenolysis
Hydrogenorthophosphat *n s.* Hydrogenphosphat
Hydrogenoxalat *n* $M^IOOC-COOH$ hydrogenoxalate
Hydrogenperoxid *n* hydrogen peroxide, dioxidane
hydrogenperoxidecht fast to hydrogen peroxide
Hydrogenphosphat *n* $M^I_2HPO_3$ hydrogenphosphate
Hydrogensalz *n* acid salt
Hydrogensulfat *n* M^IHSO_4 hydrogensulphate
Hydrogensulfid *n* M^IHS hydrogensulphide
Hydrogensulfit *n* M^IHSO_3 hydrogensulphite
Hydrogermylierung *f* hydrogermylation
Hydroglimmer *m (min)* hydromica, hydrous mica
Hydroguttapercha *f(n)* hydro-gutta-percha
Hydroiodierung *f* hydroiodination
Hydroisomerisierung *f* hydroisomerization, reductive isomerization
Hydrokautschuk *m* hydrogenated rubber, hydrorubber

Hydroklassieren *n* wet classification
Hydrokondensation *f* hydrocondensation, reductive condensation
Hydrokrackanlage *f (petrol)* hydrocracker
Hydrokracken *n (petrol)* hydrocracking, hydrogenation cracking, HC
Hydrokracker *m s.* Hydrokrackanlage
Hydrokrackkatalysator *m (petrol)* hydrocracking catalyst, hydrocracker
Hydrokrackprodukt *n (petrol)* hydrocrackate
Hydrokultur *f s.* Hydroponik
Hydrol *n*/**Michlers** Michler's hydrol, di-(*p*-dimethylaminophenyl)methanol
Hydrolase *f* hydrolase, hydrolytic enzyme
Hydrolysat *n* hydrolyzate
~/enzymatisches enzymatic hydrolyzate
Hydrolyse *f* hydrolysis • **~ erleiden** to undergo hydrolysis, to hydrolyze
~/alkalische alkaline (base) hydrolysis
~/enzymatische enzymatic hydrolysis
~/partielle partial (restricted) hydrolysis
~/saure acid hydrolysis
~/vorhergehende *(pap)* preimpregnation, preliminary impregnation (penetration) *(of the chips)*
hydrolysebeständig resistant to hydrolysis
Hydrolysebeständigkeit *f* resistance to hydrolysis, hydrolytic stability
Hydrolysegrad *m* degree of hydrolysis
Hydrolysenkonstante *f* hydrolysis constant
Hydrolyseprodukt *n* product of hydrolysis
Hydrolyseresistenz *f*, **Hydrolysestabilität** *f s.* Hydrolysebeständigkeit
hydrolysierbar hydrolyzable
hydrolysieren to hydrolyze; to undergo hydrolysis, to hydrolyze
hydrolytisch hydrolytic
Hydrometallurgie *f* hydrometallurgy, wet metallurgy
hydrometallurgisch hydrometallurgical
Hydrometeor *m* hydrometeor
Hydron *n* hydron *(any of the cations of a hydrogen isotope)*
Hydronaphthalen *n* hydronaphthalene
Hydroniumion *n* hydronium (oxonium) ion, H_3O^+ ion
Hydroniumionenaktivität *f* hydronium-ion activity
Hydroniumionenkonzentration *f* hydronium-ion concentration • **mit gleicher ~** isohydric
Hydroperoxid *n* hydroperoxide
Hydroperoxidumlagerung *f* hydroperoxide rearrangement
Hydroperoxyradikal *n* hydroperoxyl radical, HO_2-radical
Hydrophan *m (min)* hydrophane *(a variety of opal)*
hydrophil hydrophilic, hydrophile
Hydrophilie *f* hydrophilicity
hydrophob hydrophobic, hydrophobe, water-repellent
Hydrophobchromatographie *f* hydrophobic [interaction] chromatography
Hydrophobie *f* hydrophobicity
Hydrophobiermittel *n* hydrophobing agent, water repellent
Hydrophobierung *f* hydrophobing
Hydrophobierungsmittel *n s.* Hydrophobiermittel
Hydroplumbierung *f* hydroplumbation
Hydropolymerisation *f* hydropolymerization
Hydroponik *f (agric)* hydroponic culture, hydroponics
Hydrosilylierung *f* hydrosilylation
Hydrosol *n* hydrosol, aquasol
Hydrospaltanlage *f (petrol)* hydrocracking unit
Hydrosphäre *f* hydrosphere
Hydrostannylierung *f* hydrostannation
hydrostatisch hydrostatic
Hydrosulfit *n s.* Dithionit
Hydrosulfitbleiche *f (pap)* sodium-hydrosulphite bleaching
hydrothermal hydrothermal
Hydrothermalsynthese *f (geoch, min)* hydrothermal synthesis
Hydrotorf *m* hydro peat
Hydrotropie *f* hydrotropy
Hydroxamsäure *f (org ch)* hydroxamic acid
Hydroxid *n* hydroxide
Hydroxidflocken *fpl (hyd)* [metal] hydroxide floc
Hydroxidion *n* hydroxide ion, OH^- ion
Hydroxidionenaktivität *f* hydroxide ion activity
Hydroxidsalz *n* hydroxide salt
Hydroxidschlamm *m (hyd)* [metal] hydroxide sludge
Hydroxoaluminat *n* hydroxoaluminate
Hydroxoantimonat *n s.* Hexahydroxoantimonat
Hydroxokomplex *m* hydroxo complex
Hydroxoniumion *n s.* Hydroniumion
Hydroxosalz *n* hydroxo salt
Hydroxostannat *n* hydroxostannate
Hydroxotrifluoroborat *n* $M^I[B(OH)F_3]$ trifluorohydroxoborate
Hydroxozinkat *n* hydroxozincate
Hydroxyacetaldehyd *m* hydroxyacetaldehyde, glycollaldehyde
Hydroxyaldehyd *m* hydroxyaldehyde
Hydroxyalkylierung *f* hydroxyalkylation
Hydroxybenzen *n* hydroxybenzene, phenol
Hydroxybenzoesäure *f* hydroxybenzoic acid, phenolic benzoic acid, phenolic acid
o-**Hydroxybenzoesäure** *f o*-hydroxybenzoic acid, salicylic acid
Hydroxybenzol *n* hydroxybenzene, phenol
o-**Hydroxybenzylalkohol** *m o*-hydroxybenzyl alcohol, α,2-dihydroxytoluene, salicyl alcohol, saligenin
Hydroxybernsteinsäure *f* hydroxysuccinic acid, malic acid, *hydroxybutanedioic acid
Hydroxybrücke/mit hydroxy-bridged
3-Hydroxybutanal *n* *3-hydroxybutanal, 3-hydroxybutyraldehyde, acetaldol, aldol
Hydroxybutandisäure *f s.* Hydroxybernsteinsäure
3-Hydroxybutan-2-on *n* *3-hydroxybutan-2-one, dimethylketol, acetoin

Hydroxybutylierung *f* hydroxybutylation
3-Hydroxybutyraldehyd *m s.* 3-Hydroxybutanal
Hydroxycarbonsäure *f* hydroxycarboxylic acid, hydroxy acid
3-Hydroxycarbonsäure *f* 3-hydroxycarboxylic acid, β-hydroxycarboxylic acid, β-hydroxy acid
Hydroxychinolin *n* hydroxyquinoline
Hydroxydinitrobenzen *n (bioch)* dinitrophenol
22-Hydroxydocosansäure *f* *22-hydroxydocosanoic acid, phellonic acid
Hydroxyessigsäure *f* hydroxyacetic acid, glycollic acid, *hydroxyethanoic acid
Hydroxyethansäure *f s.* Hydroxyessigsäure
Hydroxyethylcellulose *f* hydroxyethylcellulose
Hydroxyethylierung *f* hydroxyethylation
Hydroxyfettsäure *f* hydroxy-fatty acid
Hydroxygruppe *f s.* Hydroxylgruppe
Hydroxyketon *n* hydroxy ketone, keto alcohol
Hydroxylamin *n* hydroxylamine
Hydroxylammoniumchlorid *n* hydroxylammonium chloride
Hydroxylammoniumnitrat *n* hydroxylammonium nitrate
Hydroxylammoniumsulfat *n* hydroxylammonium sulphate
Hydroxylaustausch *m (hyd)* hydroxyl-cycle anion exchange
Hydroxylderivat *n* hydroxy derivative
Hydroxylgruppe *f* hydroxyl (hydroxy) group, OH group • **mit einer** ~ monohydric *(alcohol, phenol)* • **mit endständiger** ~ hydroxyl-terminated • **mit mehreren** ~ polyhydric *(alcohol, phenol)*
~/phenolische phenolic hydroxyl group
hydroxyl[gruppen]haltig containing hydroxyl [groups], hydroxy
hydroxylieren to hydroxylate
Hydroxylierung *f* hydroxylation
Hydroxylradikal *n* OH radical, HO radical, hydroxyl radical
Hydroxylsauerstoff *m* hydroxylic oxygen
Hydroxylzahl *f* hydroxyl value (number) *(of fats and fatty oils)*
Hydroxymalonsäure *f* hydroxymalonic acid, tartronic acid, *hydroxymethanedicarboxylic acid
Hydroxymercurierung *f* hydroxymercuration
Hydroxymethylgruppe *f* $-CH_2OH$ hydroxymethyl group
Hydroxymethylharnstoff *m* hydroxymethylurea, methylolurea
Hydroxymethylierung *f* hydroxymethylation
1-Hydroxymethyl-4-isopropenyl-cyclohexen *n* 1-hydroxymethyl-4-isopropenyl cyclohexene, perilla alcohol, perillyl alcohol
2-Hydroxy-2-methylpropionitril *n* 2-hydroxy-2-methylpropane nitrile, acetone cyanohydrin
Hydroxynaphthalen *n* *naphthol, hydroxynaphthalene
Hydroxynaphthalencarbonsäure *f s.* Hydroxynaphthoesäure
Hydroxynaphtoesäure *f* hydroxynaphthoic acid
3-Hydroxy-2-naphthoesäure *f* 3-hydroxy-2-naphthoic acid, *(dye also)* beta-oxynaphthoic acid, BON
Hydroxynitrierung *f* oxynitration, oxidative nitration
α-Hydroxynitril *n* alpha-hydroxy nitrile, cyanohydrin, cyanhydrin
Hydroxyölsäure *f s.* Ricinolsäure
2-Hydroxyphenylessigsäure *f* phenylhydroxyacetic acid
2-Hydroxypropannitril *n* 2-hydroxypropane nitrile, lactonitrile, acetaldehyde cyanohydrin
3-Hydroxypropannitril *n* 3-hydroxypropane nitrile, ethylene cyanohydrin
2-Hydroxypropansäure *f s.* 2-Hydroxypropionsäure
2-Hydroxypropionsäure *f* *2-hydroxypropionic acid, lactic acid
3-Hydroxypropionsäure *f* *3-hydroxypropionic acid, ethylenelactic acid
Hydroxy-Rest *m s.* Hydroxylgruppe
Hydroxysäure *f* hydroxycarboxylic acid, hydroxy acid
2-Hydroxysäure *f*, **α-Hydroxysäure** *f* 2-hydroxycarboxylic acid, α-hydroxy acid
3-Hydroxysäure *f*, **β-Hydroxysäure** *f* 3-hydroxycarboxylic acid, β-hydroxy acid
Hydroxysäureester *m* hydroxy ester
hydroxysubstituiert hydroxy-substituted
Hydroxythallierung *f* oxythallation
Hydroxytoluen *n* hydroxytoluene, methylphenol, cresol
5-Hydroxytryptamin *n* 5-hydroxytryptamine, *serotonin, 3-(2-aminoethyl)-5-hydroxyindole
Hydroxyxylen *n*, **Hydroxyxylol** *n* hydroxyxylene, xylenol, dimethylphenol
Hydroxyzimtsäure *f* hydroxycinnamic acid, coumaric acid, *hydroxyphenylpropenoic acid
2-Hydroxyzimtsäurelacton *n* coumarin, 2H-chromen-2-one, α-chromone, 1,2-benzopyrone
Hydrozimtaldehyd *m* hydrocinnamic aldehyde, hydrocinnamaldehyde, *3-phenylpropanal
Hydrozimtalkohol *m* hydrocinnamyl alcohol, 3-phenylpropan-1-ol
Hydrozimtsäure *f* hydrocinnamic acid, 3-phenylpropionic acid
Hydrozinkit *m (min)* hydrozincite *(a basic zinc carbonate)*
Hydrozyklon *m* hydroclone, hydrocyclone, liquid cyclone [separator], hydraulic cyclone separator, wet cyclone classifier
Hygas-Verfahren *n* Hygas process *(for gasifying coal with hydrogen)*
Hygas-Vergaser *m (coal)* Hygas gasifier
Hygienisierung *f* sanitization
hygr. *s.* hygroskopisch
Hygrinsäure *f* hygrinic acid, 1-methylpyrrolidine-2-carboxylic acid

Hygrometer *n* hygrometer
~/elektrolytisches electrolytic hygrometer
~/kapazitives capacitance hygrometer
~/mechanisches mechanical hygrometer
Hygrometrie *f* hygrometry
hygroskopisch hygroscopic[al], water-absorbing, water-attracting
Hygroskopizität *f* hygroscopicity
Hylit *m(n)* xylite, [woody] lignite, woody brown coal
Hymatomelansäure *f (soil)* hymatomelanic acid
DL-**Hyoscyamin** *n* DL-hyoscyamine, atropine *(alkaloid)*
Hypazidität *f s.* Hypoazidität
Hyperammonämie *f (med)* hyperammonaemia
Hyperazidität *f* hyperacidity, superacidity *(of gastric juice)*
Hypercholesterolämie *f (med)* hypercholesterolaemia, hypercholesteraemia
hyperchrom hyperchromic *(exhibiting enlarged extinction)*
Hyperchromie *f* 1. hyperchromism *(enlarged extinction)*; 2. *(bioch)* hyperchromicity *(of the DNA with thermal denaturation)*
Hyperchromie-Effekt *m* hyperchromic effect *(with thermal denaturation of DNA)*
Hyperfeinaufspaltung *f s.* Hyperfeinstrukturaufspaltung
Hyperfeinspektrum *n* hyperfine spectrum
Hyperfeinstruktur *f* hyperfine structure
Hyperfeinstrukturaufspaltung *f* hyperfine splitting
Hyperfeinstrukturkopplung *f* hyperfine coupling
Hyperfeinwechselwirkung *f (spectr)* hyperfine interaction
Hyperfiltration *f* hyperfiltration *(a branch of reverse osmosis)*
Hyperformierung *f (petrol)* hyperforming
Hyperglykämie *f (med)* hyperglycaemia
hyperglykämisch *(med)* hyperglycaemic
Hypergol *m* hypergol, hypergolic fuel (rocket propellant)
Hyperkern *m* hypernucleus
Hyperkonjugation *f* hyperconjugation, no-bond resonance
Hyperladung *f (nucl)* hypercharge
Hyperlipämie *f (med)* hyperlipaemia *(enlarged fat content in blood)*
Hyperlipidämie *f (med)* hyperlipaemia *(in a larger sense; enlarged fat and lipoid content in blood)*
Hyperlipoidämie *f s.* Hyperlipidämie
Hyperon *n* hyperon *(a superheavy elementary particle)*
Hyper-Raman-Effekt *m* hyper-Raman effect, HRE
Hypersensibilisierung *f* hypersensitization
Hypersensibilität *f* hypersensitivity
Hypersorption *f* hypersorption
Hypersthen *m (min)* hypersthene *(an inosilicate)*
Hyperthyreoidismus *m*, **Hyperthyreose** *f (med)* hyperthyroidism, Graves' disease, exophthalmic goiter

Hypervitaminose *f* hypervitaminosis
hypidiomorph *(min)* hypidiomorphic, subhedral
Hypnotikum *n* hypnotic, soporific, somnifacient, somnificant, sleeping drug
Hypo *n* hypo *(sodium thiosulphate)*
Hypoazidität *f* subacidity, hypoacidity *(of gastric juice)*
Hypoborat *n* hypoborate
Hypobromit *n* M^IOBr hypobromite
Hypochlorit *n* M^IOCl hypochlorite
Hypochloritanlage *f (hyd)* hypochlorinator, hypochlorinating unit
Hypochloritbehandlung *f* 1. *(petrol)* hypochlorite treatment (sweetening); 2. *s.* Hypochloritbleiche
Hypochloritbleiche *f (pap, text)* hypochlorite bleaching (treatment)
~ bei hoher Stoffdichte *(pap)* high-density hypochlorite bleaching
Hypochloritbleichechtheit *f* fastness to hypochlorite bleaching
Hypochloritbleichlauge *f* hypochlorite bleach [liquor]
Hypochloritbleichstufe *f (pap)* hypochlorite bleaching stage
Hypochloritendbleiche *f (pap)* last (final) hypochlorite bleaching
Hypochloritsüßen *n (petrol)* hypochlorite sweetening (treatment)
Hypochloritverfahren *n (hyd)* hypochlorination
Hypocholesterolämie *f (med)* hypocholesterolaemia
hypochrom hypochromic *(exhibiting reduced extinction)*
Hypochromie *f* hypochromism *(reduced extinction)*; hypochromicity *(of nucleic acids)*
Hypoglykämie *f (med)* hypoglycaemia
hypoglykämisch *(med)* hypoglycaemic
Hypohalogenierung *f* hypohalogenation
Hypohalogenit *n* hypohalite
Hypoidöl *n* hypoid lubricant
Hypoiodit *n* M^IOI hypoiodite
hypokristallin hypocrystalline
Hypolimnion *n* hypolimnion *(lower stratum in a lake)*
Hypomagma *n* hypomagma
Hyponitrit *n* $M^I_2N_2O_2$ hyponitrite
Hypophosphat *n* $M^I_4P_2O_6$ hypophosphate
Hypophosphit *n* $M^IH_2PO_2$ *phosphinate, hypophosphite
Hypophosphorsäure *f* hypophosphoric acid
Hypophysenhinterlappenextrakt *m* posterior-pituitary extract
Hypophysenhinterlappenhormon *n* neurohypophyseal (posterior-lobe) hormone
Hypophysenhinterlappenpulver *n* posterior-pituitary powder, posterior pituitary
Hypophysenhormon *n* hypophyseal hormone
Hypophysenvorderlappenhormon *n* adenohypophyseal (anterior-pituitary) hormone

Hypotensivum *n* antihypertensive drug, blood-pressure depressant
Hypothese *f*/**Avogadrosche** Avogadro hypothesis (law)
~/**chemiosmotische (chemisch-osmotische)** *(bioch)* chemiosmotic hypothesis *(of phosphorylation)*
~/**chemische** *(bioch)* chemical-coupling hypothesis *(of phosphorylation)*
~ **der Energiequanten/Plancksche** Planck's hypothesis *(of quantized energy)*
~ **der induzierten Anpassung** induced-fit hypothesis (theory), sequential hypothesis *(enzyme kinetics)*
~/**Goudsmit-Uhlenbecksche** Goudsmit and Uhlenbeck assumption *(of rotating electrons)*
~/**Proutsche** Prout hypothesis *(of atomic structure)*
hypothetisch hypothetical
Hypothyreoidismus *m*, **Hypothyreose** *f (med)* hypothyroidism
Hypovitaminose *f* hypovitaminosis
Hypoxanthin *n* hypoxanthine, 6-hydroxypurine
hypsochrom hypsochromic
Hypsochromie *f* hypsochromic shift
Hysterese *f* hysteresis
~/**ferromagnetische** ferromagnetic hysteresis
Hysteresekurve *f*, **Hystereseschleife** *f* hysteresis loop
Hystereseverlust *m* hysteresis loss
Hysteresis *f s.* Hysterese

I

I.A. *s.* Ionenaustauscher
Iatrochemie *f* iatrochemistry
Iatrochemiker *m* iatrochemist
Ibogaalkaloid *n* iboga alkaloid
ICDH = Isocitratdehydrogenase
iC$_4$-Kreislauf *m s.* Isobutankreislauf
ICP *s.* Plasma/induktiv gekoppeltes
ICS *s.* Isocitronensäure
ICSH *(**i**nterstitial-**c**ell-**s**timulating **h**ormone) s.* Hormon/luteinisierendes
iC$_4$-Umlauf *m s.* Isobutankreislauf
ideal ideal, perfect, *(cryst also)* defect-free • **sich ~ verhalten** to behave perfectly
Idealgitter *n (cryst)* ideal (perfect) lattice
Idealität *f* ideality
Idealkristall *m* ideal (perfect) crystal
Idealverhalten *n* ideal behaviour
Idealzustand *m* ideality
identifizierbar identifiable
identifizieren to identify
Identifizierung *f* identification
Identität *f* identity
Identitätsperiode *f* identity period *(of a macromolecule)*; *(bioch)* pitch *(of a helix)*
idiochromatisch idiochromatic
idiomorph *(min)* idiomorphic, idiomorphous, euhedral, automorphic *(having the proper crystal form)*
Idiophase *f (biot)* idiophase, production (product formation) phase
Idose *f* idose *(a monosaccharide)*
Idrialin *m (min)* idrialine, idrialite *(a naturally occurring hydrocarbon)*
Iduronsäure *f* iduronic acid
I.E. *s.* Einheit/internationale
I-Effekt *m s.* Induktionseffekt
IES *s.* Indolyl-3-essigsäure
I-Kalander *m* four-bowl stack type of calender
Ile *s.* Isoleucin
Ilhurinbalsam *m* Illorin gum *(from Daniella thurifera Bennett)*
Ilkovič-Gleichung *f (phys ch, anal)* Ilkovič equation
Illingworth-Verfahren *n (coal)* Illingworth process *(a low-temperature carbonization process)*
Illinium *n s.* Promethium
Illit-Gruppe *f* illite series *(general term for micaceous clay minerals)*
Illustrationsdruckpapier *n* half-tone paper
Illuvialhorizont *m (soil)* illuvial horizon, B-horizon, zone of illuviation (accumulation), subsoil
Ilmenit *m (min)* ilmenite *(iron(II) metatitanate)*
Imbecillität *f*/**Föllingsche** *(med)* phenylketonuria
imbibieren to imbibe
Imbibition *f* imbibition
Imen *n* nitrene, *(deprecated:)* imene
Imhoff-Brunnen *m (hyd)* Imhoff tank
Imhoff-Trichter *m (hyd)* Imhoff [sediment] cone
Imid *n* imide
Imidazol *n* imidazole, 1,3-diazole
Imidazolalkaloid *n* imidazole alkaloid
Imidoester *m* imido ester, imino ether
Imidogen *n* nitrene, *(deprecated:)* imidogen
Imidogruppe *f* imido group (residue)
Imidoharnstoff *m s.* Iminoharnstoff
Imidol *n s.* Pyrrol
Imidosalpetersäure *f* imide of nitric acid, nitramide
Imidsäure *f* imidic acid
Imin *n* 1. $R^1R^2C=NR^3$ imine; 2. *aminylene *(free diradical)*, *(deprecated:)* imine
Iminiumverbindung *f* iminium compound
Iminoäther *m s.* Imidoester
Iminogruppe *f* –NH– imino group (residue), aminediyl group
Iminoharnstoff *m* iminourea, carbamidine, guanidine
Iminosäure *f* imino acid
Iminoverbindung *f* imino compound, imine
Immediumfilter *n (hyd)* Immedium filter
Immergan-Gerbung *f* Immergan process *(tanning with paraffin sulphochlorides)*
Immersion *f* immersion
Immersionsflüssigkeit *f* immersion liquid (fluid)
Immersionsöl *n* immersion oil
Immission *f* air-borne pollution, pollutant input, immission

Immissionsdosis *f* immission dose
Immissionsrate *f* immission rate
Immissionsstrom *m* immission flux
immobilisieren to immobilize *(e.g. enzymes or nutrients)*
Immobilisierung *f* immobilization *(as of enzymes or nutrients)*
Immobilisierungsmittel *n (biot)* immobilizing agent, immobilization chemical
Immunantwort *f (bioch)* immune response
Immunbiologie *f* immunobiology
immunchemisch *s.* immunochemisch
Immunelektrophorese *f (anal)* immunoelectrophoresis
Immunglobulin *n* immunoglobulin, Ig, immune [serum] globulin, antibody globulin
immunisieren to immunize
Immunisierung *f* immunization
Immunität *f* immunity
Immunkörper *m* antibody, immune body
Immunmodulator *m* immunomodulator *(agent which enhances or suppresses certain immune reactions)*
Immunochemie *f* immunochemistry
immunochemisch immunochemical
Immunologie *f* immunology
Immunserum *n* immune serum
Immunstimulans *n* immunostimulant *(agent which enhances certain immune reactions)*
Immunsuppressor *m* immunosuppressor, immunosuppressant *(agent which suppresses certain immune reactions)*
IMP *s.* Inosin-5'-monophosphat
Impaktion *f* impaction *(as of particles with gas cleaning)*
Impaktor *m* impactor *(for measuring dust in air)*
Impedanz *f (anal)* impedance
Impellerrührer *m* impeller agitator
impermeabel impermeable, impenetrable, impervious
Impermeabilität *f* impermeability, impenetrability, imperviousness
impfen *(cryst, biot)* to seed, to inoculate
Impffermenter *m (biot)* inoculum (culture) fermenter (tank), seed [culture] fermenter, seed tank
Impfgut *n (biot)* inoculum
Impfgutanzucht *f (biot)* inoculum cultivation (build-up), cultivation of inoculum
Impfgutkonservierung *f (biot)* inoculum preservation
Impfhefe *f (biot)* yeast inoculum
Impfkessel *m s.* Impffermenter
Impfkristall *m* seed crystal
Impfkultur *f (biot)* seed culture
~ **für Fermenter** fermentation culture
Impfling *m s.* Impfkristall
Impflösung *f (biot)* inoculation (inoculum) medium
Impfschlitzverfahren *n* gun injection *(wood preservation)*
Impftank *m s.* Impffermenter
Impfung *f (cryst, biot)* seeding, inoculation
Impinger *m* impinger *(for sampling particulate matter, vapours, and gases in air)*
Imprägniereffizienz *f (chromat)* coating efficiency, CE
imprägnieren to impregnate, to imbibe; *(text)* to [water]proof, to impregnate; *(pap)* to penetrate, to impregnate *(chips)*
~/flammfest (flammsicher) to flameproof
~/mit CO_2 to carbonate, to aerate, to impregnate *(beverages)*
~/mit Schwefel to sulphurize
~/wasserabstoßend (wasserabweisend) to make water-repellent
~/wasserdicht to waterproof
Imprägniergeschwindigkeit *f (pap)* rate of penetration *(of the chips with liquor)*
Imprägnierharz *n* impregnating resin
Imprägnierlösung *f* impregnating solution; *(rubber)* dope
Imprägniermittel *n* impregnant, impregnation [material], impregnating material, proofing
Imprägnierung *f* 1. impregnation, imbibition *(act)*; *(text)* [water]proofing impregnation; *(pap)* penetration, impregnation *(of the chips)*; 2. impregnation, finish *(state)*
~/flammfeste (flammsichere) flameproof finish
~/wasserabstoßende (wasserabweisende) water-repellent finish
~/wasserdichte waterproof finish
Imprägnierungsperiode *f (pap)* penetration period (time)
Impulsbilanz *f* momentum balance
Impulsbilanzgleichung *f* momentum balance equation
Impulsmoment *n* moment of momentum, angular momentum
Impulsraum *m* momentum space
Impulssiegeln *n* impulse sealing *(as of films)*
Impulsstrom *m* momentum flux *(of liquids per unit time and unit volume)*
Impulstransport *m* momentum transport
Impulsübertragung *f* momentum transfer
Impulsverteilungsgesetz *n*/**Maxwell-Boltzmannsches** Maxwell-Boltzmann distribution law
inaktiv inactive, inert, passive, *(rubber also)* non-reinforcing
~/elektrochemisch electroinactive, non-electroactive
~/optisch optically inactive
inaktivieren to inactivate, to deactivate, to block, *(reactive groups or sites also)* to mask
Inaktivierung *f* inactivation, deactivation, blocking, *(of reactive groups or sites also)* masking
~/thermische thermal (heat) inactivation
Inaktivierungsfaktor *m (biot)* inactivation factor
Inaktivität *f* inactivity
Inaktivruß *m* inactive (inert, non-reinforcing) black

Inbetriebnahme *f* start-up, starting[-up]
inchromieren to chromize
Inchromierstahl *m* chromized steel
Inchromierung *f* chromizing
~ **aus der Gasphase** gas chromizing
Indan *n* indane, hydrindene
Indanon *n* indanone, hydrindone
Indanthron *n* indanthrone
Indanthron-Küpenfarbstoff *m* indanthrone vat dye
Inden *n* indene
Inden-Cumaron-Harz *n* coumarone[-indene] resin
Index *m* index, value, script
~/chemotherapeutischer therapeutic index
~/hochgestellter (oberer) *(nomencl)* upper index, superscript
~/rechts oben angebrachter (befindlicher) *(nomencl)* right[-hand] superscript
~/tiefgestellter (unterer) *(nomencl)* lower index, subscript
Indican *n (bioch)* indican
Indicanreaktion *f* indican reaction *(for detecting glucosidase)*
indifferent inert, indifferent, inactive, passive
Indifferenz *f* inertness, indifference
~/chemische chemical inertness
Indigblau *n s.* Indigoblau
Indigo *m(n)* indigo [blue]
~/natürlicher natural indigo
Indigoblau *n* indigo [blue]
Indigofarbstoff *m* indigoid [dye]
Indigopapier *n* indigo paper
Indigosol *n* indigosol *(any of several sulphuric-acid esters of leuco vat dyes)*
Indigotin *n* indigotin, indigo [blue]
Indikator *m (chem)* indicator, *(relating to isotopes preferably:)* tracer; *(food)* indicator ingredient (substance)
~/basischer basic indicator
~/einfarbiger one-colour indicator
~/externer external (outside) indicator
~/interner internal indicator
~/isotoper isotopic tracer (indicator)
~/radioaktiver radioactive tracer (indicator), radiotracer
~/saurer acid indicator
~/zweifarbiger two-colour indicator
Indikatoratom *n* tracer atom
Indikatorbakterien *npl (hyd)* indicator bacteria
Indikatorbase *f* basic indicator
Indikatordiagramm *n* indicator diagram
Indikatorelektrode *f* indicator electrode
Indikatorelement *n* tracer element
Indikatorenzym *n (bioch)* marker enzyme
Indikatorfarbstoff *m* indicator dye
Indikatorgemisch *n* mixed indicator
Indikatorisotop *n* [isotopic] tracer
Indikatorkonstante *f* indicator constant
Indikatorlösung *f* indicator solution
Indikatormethode *f* tracer method
Indikatororganismen *mpl (hyd)* indicator organisms
Indikatorpapier *n* [colour-]indicator paper, test paper, *(Am)* reaction paper
Indikatorsäure *f* acid indicator
Indikatorsubstanz *f* indicator, *(relating to isotopes preferably:)* tracer
Indikatorumschlag *m* indicator change
Indischgelb *n* 1. Indian (cobalt) yellow, aureolin *(potassium hexanitrocobaltate)*; 2. *s.* ~/echtes
~/echtes Indian yellow, piuri *(from Mangifera indica L.)*
Indium *n* In indium
Indium(I)-chlorid *n* indium(I) chloride, indium monochloride
Indium(II)-chlorid *n* indium(II) chloride, indium dichloride
Indium(III)-chlorid *n* indium(III) chloride, indium trichloride
Indium(III)-cyanid *n* indium(III) cyanide, indium tricyanide
Indiumdi... *s.* Indium(II)-...
Indium(III)-hydroxid *n* indium(III) hydroxide
Indium(III)-iodat *n* indium(III) iodate
Indiummono... *s.* Indium(I)-...
Indiummonoxid *n s.* Indium(II)-oxid
Indium(II)-oxid *n* indium(II) oxide, indium monooxide
Indium(III)-oxid *n* indium(III) oxide, diindium trioxide
Indium(III)-sulfat *n* indium(III) sulphate, diindium trisulphate
Indium(II)-sulfid *n* indium(II) sulphide, indium monosulphide
Indium(III)-sulfid *n* indium(III) sulphide, diindium trisulphide
Indiumtri... *s.* Indium(III)-...
Individualität *f***/chemische** chemical individuality
Individuum *n* individual, individual entity (substance)
~/chemisches chemical individual, individual chemical entity (substance), chemically individual substance
Indizes *mpl***/Bravaissche** *(cryst)* Bravais-Miller indices
~/Millersche Miller [crystal] indices
indizieren *(nomencl)* to index, to label, to indicate
Indizierung *f (nomencl)* indexing, labelling, indication
Indol *n* indole, 2,3-benzpyrrole
Indolalkaloid *n* indole alkaloid
Indolbrenztraubensäure *f s.* Indolylbrenztraubensäure
Indolbuttersäure *f s.* Indolylbuttersäure
Indolnachweis *m* indole test
Indolsynthese *f***/Fischersche** Fischer indole synthesis
Indolylbrenztraubensäure *f* indolylpyruvic acid
Indolylbuttersäure *f* indolylbutyric acid
Indolyl-3-essigsäure *f* 3-indolylacetic acid

Indopheninreaktion f/Baeyers Baeyer's indophenin[e] reaction
Indophenol *n* indophenol
Indoxyl *n* indoxyl, 3-hydroxyindole
Indoxylcarbonsäure *f* indoxylcarboxylic acid
Induktion *f* induction
~/asymmetrische *(org ch)* asymmetric induction
~/sequentielle *(biot)* sequential induction
Induktionseffekt *m* induction (inductive) effect, I effect, field effect
Induktionserwärmung *f* induction heating
Induktionsfaktor *m* induction factor
induktionshärten to induction-harden
Induktionshärtung *f* induction hardening
Induktionsheizgerät *n* induction heater
Induktionsheizung *f* induction heating
Induktionskraft *f* induction (Debye) force, induced dipole force
Induktionsoberflächenhärtung *f* induction surface hardening
Induktionsofen *m* induction (inductance, induction-heated) furnace
~/kernloser coreless (high-frequency) induction furnace
Induktionsperiode *f* induction period
Induktionszeit *f s.* Induktionsperiode
Induktionszerfall *m***/freier** *(spectr)* free induction decay
Induktiv[be]heizung *f* induction heating
Induktor *m* inductor *(in chemical reactions)*, *(bioch also)* inducer
Industrie f/biotechnologische bioprocess industry
~/chemische chemical industry
~/feinkeramische fine ceramic industry
~/grobkeramische heavy-clay industry
~/keramische ceramic industry
~/organisch-chemische organic-chemical industry
~/petrolchemische petrochemicals industry
~/pharmazeutische pharmaceutic[al] industry
~/[weiter]verarbeitende processing industry
Industrieabfälle *mpl* industrial (trade) waste
Industrieabgas *n* industrial off-gas
Industrieabwasser *n* industrial waste water, industrial discharge (effluent), trade effluent (waste)
Industrieabwasserbehandlung *f* industrial waste-water treatment, trade effluent treatment
Industrieabwasserreinigung *f s.* Industrieabwasserbehandlung
Industriealkohol *m* commercial (industrial) alcohol (spirit), non-beverage alcohol
Industrieanlage *f* industrial plant
Industriebrennstoff *m* industrial fuel
Industriechemie *f* industrial chemistry
Industriechemikalie *f* industrial chemical
Industriechemiker *m* industrial chemist
Industrie-Enzym *n (biot)* industrial enzyme, enzyme of industrial importance
Industriefermenter *m (biot)* commercial[-scale] fermenter
Industriefilter *n* plant filter
Industriegas *n* industrial gas
Industriegasbrenner *m* industrial gas burner
Industriekohle *f* industrial coal
Industriemüll *m* industrial solid waste[s]
Industriemüllbeseitigung *f* industrial solid waste disposal
Industrieofen *m* industrial furnace, *(esp ceram)* industrial kiln
Industrieschlamm *m* industrial sludge
Industriestaub *m* industrial dust
Industriewasser *n* industrial water, water for industrial purpose (use)
Industriewasserbedarf *m* industrial water demand, water requirements in manufacturing
Industriewasserversorgung *f* industrial water supply
ineinandergewunden interwound, twisted *(macromolecules)*
inert inert, inactive, passive, indifferent
Inertgas *n* inert gas, indifferent (inactive) gas
Inertgasatmosphäre *f* inert-gas atmosphere
Inertgase *npl* inerts
Inertia *f (phot)* inertia
inertieren *(coal)* to render inert
Inertinit *m* inertinite *(general term for some macerals of hard coal)*
inertisieren *s.* inertieren
Inertstoff *m*, **Inertsubstanz** *f* inert substance
Infektion *f (biot)* contamination *(with foreign microorganisms)*
Infektionsgefahr *f (biot)* risk of contamination
infektionsgefährdet sein *(biot)* to have a high risk of contamination
Infektionsmikroorganismen *mpl (biot)* contaminant (contaminating) microorganisms, contaminants
Infiltration *f* infiltration
inflammabel inflammable, infl.
~/nicht non-[in]flammable
infrarot infrared, ultrared
Infrarot *n* 1. infrared [radiation]; 2. *s.* Infrarotgebiet
Infrarotabsorption *f* infrared absorption
Infrarotabsorptionsspektroskopie *f* infrared absorption spectroscopy
Infrarotabsorptionsspektrum *n* infrared absorption spectrum
infrarot-aktiv infrared-active
Infrarotanalyse *f* infrared analysis
Infrarotbeheizung *f* infrared heating
Infrarotbereich *m s.* Infrarotgebiet
Infrarotdetektor *m (chromat)* infrared detector
Infrarotdunkelstrahler *m* far-infrared radiation element
infrarotdurchlässig infrared-transmitting, infrared-transparent
Infrarotdurchlässigkeit *f* infrared transmittance (transmission)
Infrarotfotografie *f* infrared photography
Infrarotfrequenz *f* infrared frequency

Infrarotgasanalysator *n* infrared gas analyser
Infrarotgebiet *n* infrared [spectral] region
~/fernes far infrared [spectral region], FIR
~/mittleres mid infrared [spectral region]
~/nahes near infrared [spectral region], NIR
Infrarotheizgerät *n* infrared heater
Infrarotheizung *f* infrared heating
Infrarothellstrahler *m* near-infrared radiation element
infrarot-inaktiv infrared-inactive
Infrarotlampe *f* infrared lamp (radiator)
Infrarotlicht *n* infrared light
Infrarotmikroskop *n* infrared microscope
Infrarotphotometer *n* infrared photometer
Infrarotreaktivierung *f* **von Kornkohle** *(hyd)* infrared granular carbon reactivation
Infrarotspektralphotometer *n*, **Infrarotspektrometer** *n* infrared spectro[photo]meter
Infrarotspektroskopie *f* infrared spectroscopy
Infrarotspektrum *n* infrared spectrum
Infrarotstrahler *m* infrared radiator (lamp)
Infrarotstrahlung *f* infrared radiation
Infrarottrockenofen *m* infrared drying oven
Infrarottrockner *m* infrared dryer
Infrarottrocknung *f* infrared drying
Infrarotuntersuchung *f* infrared study
Infrarotvorwärmung *f* infrared preheating
Infus *n (pharm)* infusion *(solution obtained by steeping vegetable matter in a hot solvent)*
Infusion *f* infusion
Infusionslösung *f (pharm)* infusion
Infusionsverfahren *n (ferm)* infusion mashing (process)
Infusorienerde *f* diatom[aceous] earth, infusorial earth, kieselguhr
Infusum *n s.* Infus
Ingangsetzen *n* start-up, starting[-up]
Ingenieurchemie *f* engineering chemistry
Ingenieurtechnik *f***/chemische** chemical engineering technology
Ingenieurwesen *n***/chemisches** chemical engineering
Inglasurdekor *n (ceram)* in-glaze (inter-glaze) decoration
Ingot *m (met)* ingot
Ingrain-Farbe *f* ingrain dye
Ingrediens *n*, **Ingredienz** *f* ingredient
Ingwergrasöl *n* ginger-gras oil *(chiefly from Cymbopogon martini (Roxb.) Stapf var. sofia)*
Ingweröl *n* ginger oil
INH *s.* Isonicotinsäurehydrazid
Inhalt *m* content *(relating to energy, heat)*; contents *(something contained in a vessel)*; content[s], capacity, volume *(of a vessel)*
Inhaltsstoff *m* ingredient, constituent
Inhaltsstoffe *mpl (hyd)* [water] constituents • **frei von organischen Inhaltsstoffen** organic-free
~/abbauresistente organische refractory (non-biodegradable) organics, biologically inert refractory matter
~/biologisch stabile (nicht abbaubare) organische *s.* ~/abbauresistente organische
~/gelöste dissolved constituents
~/persistente (resistente) organische *s.* ~/abbauresistente organische
Inhaltswasser *n* **für Dampferzeuger** boiler water
inhibieren to inhibit, *(polymerization also)* to shortstop
inhibierend inhibitive, inhibitory, inhibiting
Inhibition *f* inhibition
Inhibitor *m* inhibitor, inhibiting substance, retarder, retarding agent, *(relating to polymerization also)* stopper, shortstop, shortstopping agent
~/anodischer anodic inhibitor
~/katodischer cathodic inhibitor
~/kompetitiver *(bioch)* competitive inhibitor, antimetabolite, metabolic antagonist
Inhibitor-Polypeptid *n (bioch)* inhibitory polypeptide
~/gastrisches gastric inhibitory polypeptide, GIP
Inhibitorwirkung *f* inhibitory (inhibiting) effect
inhomogen inhomogeneous, non-homogeneous
Inhomogenität *f* inhomogeneity, non-homogeneity
Initialsprengstoff *m* initiator, initiating (primary) explosive, primer, detonator, initial detonating agent
Initialzündung *f (bioch)* sparking *(of fatty-acid oxidation)*
Initiationscodon *n (bioch)* [chain] initiation codon, initiator codon
Initiationsfaktor *m (bioch)* initiation factor, IF
Initiationskomplex *m (bioch)* initiation complex
Initiator *m* initiator, initiating agent
Initiatorcodon *n*, **Initiatortriplett** *n s.* Initiationscodon
Initiierbarkeit *f* sensitiveness to initiation *(of an explosive)*
initiieren to initiate, to start
Initiierung *f* initiation
Initiierungskomplex *m s.* Initiationskomplex
Initiierungsstadium *n* initiation stage
Injektion *f* injection
Injektionsmetamorphose *f (geol)* injection metamorphism
Injektionsnadel *f* hypodermic needle *(gas chromatography)*
Injektionspflugschar *n (agric)* injection ploughshare *(for liquid fertilizers)*
Injektionsspritze *f* hypodermic syringe, injection (sample-charging) syringe *(gas chromatography)*
~ **für Septuminjektion** septum injection device *(gas chromatography)*
Injektionsventil *n (anal)* injection valve
Injektionszerstäuber *m* gas-atomizing (two-fluid) nozzle
Injektor *m (agric)* [soil] injector, injector gun *(for soil fumigation)*
~ **mit Temperaturprogramm** *(chromat)* programmed-temperature vaporizer, PTV

Injektormischer *m* injector mixer

Inklusion *f* inclusion

Inklusionsverbindung *f* inclusion compound

inkohärent incoherent *(radiation)*

Inkohärenz *f* incoherence *(of radiation)*

inkohlen to coalify

Inkohlung *f* coalification, carbonification

Inkohlungsband *n* coalification band

Inkohlungsgrad *m* degree of coalification, rank • **von hohem ~** high-rank • **von mittlerem ~** medium-rank • **von niedrigem ~** low-rank

Inkohlungsmaßstab *m* rank parameter

Inkohlungsreihe *f* coalification series

Inkohlungsstadium *n* stage of coalification

Inkohlungsstreifen *m* coalification band

Inkohlungsstufe *f* stage of coalification

Inkohlungsvorgang *m* coalification process

inkompatibel incompatible *(as of pesticides or pharmaceuticals)*

Inkompatibilität *f* incompatibility *(as af pesticides or pharmaceuticals)*

Inkorporation *f (bioch)* incorporation

Inkorporieren *(bioch)* to incorporate

Inkrustation *f* incrustation, encrustation

Inkrustationen *fpl* **durch Härtebildner** *(hyd)* hardness (mineral) scale, hard-water depositions (residue)

Inkrusten *pl* incrustants, encrustants, incrusting material (matter, substance)

inkrustieren to incrust, to encrust

Inkrustierung *f s.* Inkrustation

Inkrustsubstanzen *fpl s.* Inkrusten

Inkubation *f (biot)* incubation

Inkubationsprobe *f (dye)* incubation test

Inkubationszeit *f (biot)* incubation period

inkubieren *(biot)* to incubate

Inkulturnahme *f s.* Kultivierung

Inlösunggehen *n* dissolution

Innenanstrich *m* interior (indoor) finish

Innenanstrichfarbe *f* interior (indoor) paint

innenbürtig *(geol)* endogenous

Innendruck *m* internal pressure

Innenfilter *n* inside drum filter, internal [rotary-]drum filter

Innenfläche *f* inner surface

Innengummi *m* innerliner *(of a tyre)*

Innenkühlung *f* internal cooling

Innenlack *m* interior varnish *(chemically drying)*; interior lacquer *(physically drying)*

Innenlösung *f* internal reference solution *(of a glass electrode)*

Innenmischer *m* closed mixer

Innenoberfläche *f* internal surface [area], inner surface [area]

Innenorbitalkomplex *m* inner orbital complex

Innenpuffer *m s.* Innenlösung

Innenrohr *n* inside pipe

Innenrohrschlange *f* tank coil

Innenrüttler *m (build)* immersion (poker, needle) vibrator

Innenschale *f* inner shell *(of an atom)*

Innensphärenkomplex *m* inner-sphere complex

Innenstruktur *f* internal structure

Innenthermometer *n* internal thermometer

Innentrommelfilter *n s.* Innenfilter

Innenvibrator *m s.* Innenrüttler

Innenwand *f* inside wall

Innenwasser *n* inherent moisture

Innenzellen[trommel]filter *n s.* Innenfilter

innenzentriert *(cryst)* space-centred, body-centred

innerbetrieblich in-plant, intraplant

Innere *n* **der flüssigen Phase** bulk liquid, bulk of the liquid phase

innerkomplex inner-complex

Innerkomplex *m* inner[-orbital] complex, penetration (low-spin, spin-paired) complex

Innerkomplex-Anion *n* inner-complex anion

Innerkomplex-Kation *n* inner-complex cation

Innerkomplexsalz *n* inner-complex salt

innerlich *(pharm)* internal

innermolekular intramolecular

innersekretorisch endocrine

Innertherapeutikum *n* systemic [chemical] *(pest control)*

innertherapeutisch systemic *(pest control)*

innig intimate *(e.g. contact or mixture)*

Ino *s.* Inosin

Inosilicat *n (min)* inosilicate, chain silicate *(any of a class of polymeric silicates)*

Inosin *n* inosine *(a riboside)*

Inosin-5'-monophosphat *n*, **Inosinsäure** *f* inosine-5'-monophosphate, IMP, inosinic acid *(a nucleotide)*

Inositol *m* inositol, hexahydroxycyclohexane

Insektenabwehrmittel *n* insect repellent, insectifuge

Insektenanlockmittel *n* insect attractant

Insektenbekämpfungsmittel *n s.* Insektizid

Insektenfarbstoff *m* insect pigment

Insektenlockstoff *m* insect attractant

insektenpathogen entomopathogenic

Insektenpuder *m*, **Insektenpulver** *n* insect powder

insektenschonend *s.* insektenverträglich

Insektenschutzmittel *n s.* Insektenabwehrmittel

insektentötend insecticidal

Insektentötungsmittel *n s.* Insektizid

Insektenvertilgungspapier *n* insecticide paper

insektenverträglich non-insecticidal *(e.g. fungicides)*

Insektenwachs *n* insect (Chinese tree) wax, vegetable spermaceti *(secreted by scales)*

insektizid insecticidal

Insektizid *n* insecticide

~/endolytisches [systemisches] endolytic insecticide

~/endometatoxisches [systemisches] endometatoxic insecticide

~/mikrobielles microbial insecticide, bioinsecticide

~/pflanzliches insecticide of plant origin, botanical

~/protektives (protektiv wirkendes) protective insecticide
~/selektives (selektiv wirkendes) selective insecticide
~/systemisches systemic insecticide
Insektizidaktivität *f* insecticidal power
Insektizidität *f* insecticidal efficiency
Insektizidnebel *m* insecticidal fog
Insektizidrauch *m* insecticidal smoke
Insektizidresistenz *f* insecticide resistance *(of animals)*
Insektizidsprühdose *f* insecticide bomb
Inselsilicat *n (min)* nesosilicate
Insertion *f* insertion *(of atoms or groups into bonds)*
~ des Monomeren monomer insertion
Insertionspolymerisation *f* insertion polymerization
insilizieren to siliconize *(metals for protection)*
Insilizierung *f* siliconization *(of metals for protection)*
in situ in place, in situ
In-situ-Analyse *f* in situ analysis
In-situ-Laugung *f*, **In-situ-Leaching** *n (min tech)* in situ leaching, leaching in place, underground leaching
In-situ-Polymerisation *f* in-situ polymerization
instabil unstable, instable, labile, transient, *(relating to isotopes also)* evanescent
~/thermisch thermolabile, heat-labile
Instabilität *f* instability, lability, transience
Instabilitätskonstante *f* instability constant *(as of complex ions)*
Instandhaltung *f* maintenance, upkeep
Instandhaltungsaufwand *m* maintenance requirements
Instantkaffee *m* instant (soluble) coffee
Instrument *n***/registrierendes (selbstschreibendes)** recorder, recording instrument, grapher
Instrumentalanalyse *f*, **Instrumentenanalyse** *f* instrumental analysis
Instrumentenfehler *m* instrumental error
Insulin-Rezeptor *m (bioch)* insulin receptor
Integralchromatogramm *n* integral chromatogram
Integraldetektor *m* integral detector *(gas chromatography)*
Integralreaktor *m* integral [tubular-flow] reactor
Integrations-Wirtsfaktor *m (bioch)* integration host factor, IHF
Intensität *f* intensity
Intensitätsgröße *f* intensive quantity *(being independent of the mass of the system concerned)*
Intensitätsmessung *f (anal)* intensity measurement
Intensitätsregeln *fpl (phys ch)* intensity rules
intensitätsschwach low-intensity
intensitätsstark high-intensity
Intensitätsverhältnis *n (spectr)* intensity ratio; transmittancy *(colorimetry)*
Intensitätsverteilung *f (spectr)* intensity distribution
Intensivbelüftung *f (hyd)* high-rate aeration
Intensivbiologie *f s.* Belebungsverfahren/hochbelastetes
intensivieren to intensify
Intensivierung *f* intensification
Intensivkühler *m* jacketed coil condenser
interatomar interatomic
intercistronisch *(bioch)* intercistronic *(situated between two genes on the RNA chain)*
Interferenz *f* interference *(physics)*
Interferenzbild *n* interference figure (pattern)
Interferenzerscheinung *f* interference phenomenon
Interferenzfarbe *f* interference colour
Interferenzfigur *f s.* Interferenzbild
Interferenzfilter *n* interference filter
Interferenzmikroskop *n* interference microscope
Interferenzring *m* interference ring
Interferenzspektralapparat *m*, **Interferenzspektroskop** *n* interferometer
Interferenzstreifen *m* interference fringe
interferieren to interfere
Interferogramm *n (spectr)* interferogram
Interferometer *n (anal)* interferometer
Interferometrie *f (anal)* interferometry
~ aufgrund der Brechzahländerung refractively scanned interferometry
Interferon *n (biot)* interferon, Ifn, IFN
Interhalogen *n*, **Interhalogenverbindung** *f* interhalogen [compound]
interionisch interionic
Interkalat *n* intercalate
Interkalation *f* intercalation *(1. introduction of guest molecules between layers; 2. insertion of planar ring systems between the stacked bases of nucleic acids)*
Interkalationsschicht *f* intercalated layer
Interkalationsverbindung *f* intercalation compound
~ 1. Stufe first-stage intercalation compound, stage 1 intercalation compound
~ 2. Stufe second-stage intercalation compound, stage 2 intercalation compound
~ 3. Stufe third-stage intercalation compound, stage 3 intercalation compound
Interkalatschicht *f* intercalated layer
interkalieren to intercalate *(to introduce guest molecules between layers)*
interkaliert intercalated *(molecules, ions)*
Interkombination *f (spectr)* intercombination
Interkombinationsverbot *n (spectr)* prohibition of intercombination
Interkonversion *f* interconversion [reaction]
interkonvertierbar interconvertible
Interkonvertierbarkeit *f* interconvertibility
interkristallin intercrystalline
intermediär intermediate
Intermediärmetabolismus *m (bioch)* intermediary metabolism
Intermediärprodukt *n* intermediate product (substance), [reaction] intermediate

Intermediärstoffwechsel *m (bioch)* intermediary metabolism
Intermediärverbindung *f* intermediate [compound]
Intermediat *n s.* Zwischenprodukt
intermolekular intermolecular
Internationale Union *f* **für reine und angewandte Chemie** International Union of Pure and Applied Chemistry, IUPAC *(for compounds s. under* IUPAC*)*
intern *(pharm)* internal
Interstitiallösung *f s.* Interstitialmischkristall
Interstitialmischkristall *m* interstitial [solid] solution
interstitiell interstitial
Intersystem-Crossing *n*, **Intersystemübergang** *m* intersystem cross[ing], ISC *(between terms of different multiplicity)*
Intervall *n* interval, space
Interzellularpigment *n* intercellular pigment *(in animals)*
Intoxikation *f* poisoning, *(med also)* intoxication
intramolekular intramolecular
intrazellulär intracellular, endocellular
Intron *n*, **Intron-Sequenz** *f (bioch)* intervening sequence, IVS
intrudieren *(geol, plast)* to intrude
Intrusion *f (geol, plast)* intrusion
Intrusionsgestein *n*, **Intrusivgestein** *n* intrusive (irruptive) rock
Intussuszeption *f (biol)* intussusception *(interposition of new substances into growing cell membranes)*
Inulacampher *m* alantolactone, helenin[e]
invariabel invariable
invariant invariant, non-variant
Invariante *f*/**adiabatische** adiabatic invariant
Inversion *f* inversion
~ **der Konfiguration** *s.* ~/Waldensche
~/**Waldensche** Walden inversion, inversion of configuration
Inversionsdrehachse *f (cryst)* inversion axis
Inversionshöhe *f* inversion height *(in the atmosphere)*
Inversionspunkt *m (distil)* phase-inversion point
Inversionsschicht *f* inversion layer
Inversionstemperatur *f* inversion temperature
Inversionszentrum *n* inversion centre *(of a molecule)*
Inverspolarographie *f s.* Inversvoltammetrie
Inversvoltammetrie *f* **[an der Anode]** *(anal)* anodic stripping analysis (voltammetry), ASV
inversvoltammetrisch by anodic stripping analysis
Invertemulsion *f* invert emulsion *(as of pesticide formulations)*
invertieren to invert *(the configuration of a molecule)*
Invertierung *f* inversion *(of the configuration of a molecule)*
Invertseife *f* invert (cationic) soap
Invertzucker *m* invert[ed] sugar
~/**durch Hydrolyse mit Säuren gewonnener** acid-inverted sugar
Investmentguß *m* [precision] investment casting *(foundry)*
In-vitro-Rekombination *f (biot)* in vitro recombination
Iod *n* I iodine
~/**radioaktives** radioactive iodine, radioiodine, *(specif)* ^{131}I iodine-131
Iodanlage *f* **zur Trinkwasserentkeimung** *(hyd)* iodine disinfection unit, iodination unit, iodinator
Iodat *n* $M^{I}IO_3$ iodate
Iodatmethode *f* iodate method *(for determining sodium dithionite)*
Iodazid *n* iodine azide
Iodbenzen *n*, **Iodbenzol** *n* iodobenzene
Iod(I)-bromid *n* iodine(I) bromide, iodine monobromide
Iod(III)-bromid *n* iodine(III) bromide, iodine tribromide
Iodchinolin *n* iodoquinoline
Iod(I)-chlorid *n* iodine(I) chloride, iodine monochloride
Iod(III)-chlorid *n* iodine(III) chloride, iodine trichloride
Iodchlorierung *f* iodochlorination, chloroiodination
Iodcyanid *n* iodine cyanide, cyanogen iodine
Ioddampf *m* iodine vapour
Ioddioxid *n* iodine dioxide
Iodethan *n* iodoethane
Iodethanverbindung *f* ethiodide
Iod(V)-fluorid *n* iodine(V) fluoride, iodine pentafluoride
Iod(VII)-fluorid *n* iodine(VII) fluoride, iodine heptafluoride
Iodgorgosäure *f (org ch)* iodogorgoic acid
iodhaltig iodine-containing
Iodheptafluorid *n s.* Iod(VII)-fluorid
Iodhydrin *n* iodohydrin
Iod(I)-hydroxid *n* iodine hydroxide
Iodid *n* $M^{I}I$ iodide
Iodidstärkepapier *n* starch iodide paper
iodieren to iodize, to iodinate
Iodierung *f* iodization, iodination
Iodkaliumstärkepapier *n* potassium-iodide starch paper
Iodkohle *f* iodized active carbon
Iodlactonisierung *f* iodolactonization
Iodlösung *f* iodine solution
~/**Lugolsche** Lugol's solution
Iodmethan *n* *iodomethane, methyl iodide
Iodmono... *s.* Iod(I)-...
Iodoaurat(III) *n* $M^{I}[AuI_4]$ iodoaurate(III), tetraiodoaurate(III)
Iodoform *n* iodoform, tri-iodomethane
Iodoformprobe *f* iodoform test *(for investigating alcohols)*
Iodolyse *f* iodolysis
Iodomercurat(II) *n* $M^{I}_2[HgI_4]$ iodomercurate(II), tetraiodomercurate(II)
Iodometrie *f* iodometry, iodimetry

iodometrisch iodometric, iodimetric
Iodonium-Ion *n* iodonium ion
Iodoniumverbindung *f* iodonium compound
Iodoplatinsäure *f* iodoplatinic acid, hexaiodoplatinic(IV) acid
Iod(V)-oxid *n* iodine(V) oxide, diiodine pentaoxide
Iodpentafluorid *n s.* Iod(V)-fluorid
Iodpentoxid *n s.* Iod(V)-oxid
Iodsäure *f* iodic acid
Iodspeisesalz *n* iodized [table] salt
Iodstärke *f* iodide of starch, starch-iodine complex
Iodstärkepapier *n* starch iodide paper
Iodstärkereaktion *f (bioch, anal)* iodine colour reaction
Iodtinktur *f* tincture [of] iodine
Iodtri... *s.* Iod(III)...
Iodüberschuß *m* excess [of] iodine, *(hyd also)* iodine residual
Iodwasserstoffgleichgewicht *n* hydrogen-iodide equilibrium
Iodwasserstoffsäure *f* hydroiodic acid
Iodzahl *f* iodine [absorption] value, I.V., iodine (Huebl) number *(characterizing the unsaturation of a compound or mixture)*
~ **nach Hanus** Hanus iodine value
~**/rhodanometrische** thiocyanogen number (value)
Iodzahlbestimmung *f (food)* iodine test
Iodzahlkolben *m (food)* iodine flask
Ion *n* ion
~ **auf Zwischengitterplatz** interstitial ion
~**/einfach geladenes** mono-ion
~**/eintauschendes** *(soil)* competitor ion
~**/einwertiges** mono-ion
~**/geminales** geminal (geminate) ion
~**/gittereigenes** lattice ion
~**/hydratisiertes** hydrated ion, aquo-ion
~**/komplexes** complex ion
~**/metastabiles** *(spectr)* metastable ion
~**/negatives** negative ion, anion
~**/positives** positive ion, cation
~**/potentialbestimmendes** potential-determining ion
~**/primär rekombinierendes** *s.* ~/geminales
~**/schnelles** high-speed ion
ional ionic
Ionen *npl* **bei chemischer Ionisation/negative** *(anal)* negative ions with chemical ionization, NCI
~ **bei Elektronenstoßionisation/negative** *(anal)* negative ions with electron impact ionization, NEI
Ionenadsorption *f* adsorption of ions
Ionenadsorptionsvermögen *n* ion-adsorbing capacity
Ionenaggregat *n* aggregate of ions
Ionenaktivität *f* ion[ic] activity
Ionenaktivitätskoeffizient *m* ion[ic] activity coefficient
Ionenaktivitätsprodukt *n* ion activity product, IAP
Ionenantagonismus *m (bioch)* ion antagonism
Ionenäquivalentleitfähigkeit *f* ionic equivalent conductance, equivalent ion[ic] conductance
Ionenart *f* ionic species
Ionenassoziation *f* ion association
Ionenatmosphäre *f (phys ch)* ion[ic] atmosphere, ion cloud
Ionenaufnahme *f* ion absorption
Ionenausschluß *m* ion exclusion
Ionenausschlußchromatographie *f* ion exclusion chromatography
Ionenaustausch *m* ion[ic] exchange
~ **mit H-Austauscher** hydrogen cycle [cation] exchange, H-form exchange, hydrogen-cation exchange, ion exchange in (on) the hydrogen cycle
~ **mit Natriumaustauscher** sodium-cycle exchange, Na-form exchange, ion exchange in (on) the sodium cycle
~ **mit Neutralaustauscher** *s.* ~ mit Natriumaustauscher
Ionenaustauschbehälter *m* resin tank
Ionenaustauschchromatographie *f* ion-exchange chromatography
Ionenaustauscher *m* ion exchanger, ion-exchange material
~ **auf Kunstharzbasis** *s.* Ionenaustauscherharz
~**/erschöpfter** exhausted ion exchanger
~ **in der Cl-Form** chloride-form (Cl-form) exchanger
~ **in der H-Form (H_2-Form)** hydrogen[-form] exchanger, H-form exchanger, hydrogen-cation exchanger
~ **in der Na-Form (Natriumform)** sodium (Na-form) exchanger
~ **in der OH-Form** hydroxyl-form (OH-form) exchanger
~**/in der Wasseraufbereitung eingesetzter** water-treatment ion exchanger
Ionenaustauscheranlage *f* ion-exchange unit (system)
~ **in Teilstromschaltung** split-stream ion-exchange unit
~**/kontinuierlich arbeitende** continuous ion-exchange unit
~ **zur Enthärtung** ion-exchange softener
~ **zur Entkarbonisierung** ion-exchange dealkalizer
~ **zur Neutralisation** ion-exchange neutralizer
Ionenaustauscherbett *n* ion-exchange bed
Ionenaustauscherharz *n* ion-exchange resin *(for compounds s.* Austauscherharz*)*
Ionenaustauschermaterial *n* ion-exchange material (medium)
Ionenaustauschermembran *f* ion-exchange membrane
Ionenaustauschersäule *f* ion-exchange column
Ionenaustauschgleichgewicht *n* ion-exchange equilibrium
Ionenaustauschharz *n s.* Ionenaustauscherharz
Ionenaustauschreaktion *f* ion-exchange reaction

Ionenaustauschtechnik *f* ion-exchange technology
Ionenaustauschtrennung *f* ion-exchange separation
Ionenaustauschvollentsalzungsanlage *f* ion-exchange demineralizer
Ionenbelastung *f (hyd)* ion[ic] load
Ionenbeschuß *m* ion[ic] bombardment
Ionenbestandteil *m* ion constituent *(according to McInnes)*
Ionenbeweglichkeit *f* ion[ic] mobility
Ionenbewegung *f* ion[ic] movement, ion[ic] motion
Ionenbeziehung *f* ionic bond, heteropolar (polar, electrostatic, electrovalent) bond, electrovalence
Ionenbildung *f* formation of ions, ionization
Ionenbindung *f* 1. electrovalent linkage, ionic (polar, heteropolar, electrostatic) linkage *(process)*; 2. *s.* Ionenbeziehung
Ionenbombardement *n s.* Ionenbeschuß
Ionencarrier *m s.* Ionophor
Ionencharakter *m* ionic character
Ionenchromatographie *f* ion chromatography
ionenchromatographisch ion-chromatographic, by ion chromatography
Ionendetektor *m* ion detector
Ionendichte *f* ion density
Ionendipolkomplex *m* ion-dipole complex
Ionendipolkräfte *fpl* ion-dipole forces
Ionendurchbruch *m* ion leakage *(ion exchange)*
Ionenenergie-Spektroskopie *f* **zum Nachweis metastabiler Zerfälle** direct analysis of daughter ions, DADI, mass-analysed ion kinetics spectrometry, ion kinetic energy spectroscopy, IKES
ionenerzeugend ionogenic
Ionenfarbe *f* ion colour
Ionenformel *f* ionic formula
Ionengehalt *m* ionic content
Ionengeschwindigkeit *f* ionic speed (velocity)
Ionengetterpumpe *f* getter-ion (sputter-ion) pump
Ionengitter *n (cryst)* ionic [crystal] lattice
Ionengleichgewicht *n* ionic equilibrium (balance)
Ionengleichung *f* ionic equation
Ionengröße *f* ion[ic] size
Ionenhydrat *n* ion hydrate
Ionenhydratation *f* ionic hydration
Ionenhydration *f s.* Ionenhydratation
ioneninaktiv non-ionic, non-ionizing, non-ionogenic
Ionenkonzentration *f* ionic concentration
Ionenkräfte *fpl* ionic forces
Ionenkristall *m* ionic crystal
Ionenladung *f* ionic charge
Ionenladungszahl *f* ionic charge number
Ionenlawine *f* avalanche of ions
Ionenleiter *m* ionic (electrolytic) conductor
Ionenleitfähigkeit *f* ion[ic] conductivity
~/spezifische ion[ic] conductance
Ionenleitung *f* ionic conduction
Ionenmasse *f* ionic mass
Ionenmikrosonde *f* ion [micro]probe
Ionenmolekel *f*, **Ionenmolekül** *n* ionic molecule
Ionen-Molekül-Reaktion *f* ion-molecule reaction
Ionenpaar *n* ion pair
~/äußeres loose ion pair, *(esp if separated by only a single solvent molecule:)* solvent-shared ion pair, *(esp if separated by more than one solvent molecule:)* solvent-separated ion pair
~/inneres tight ion pair, intimate (contact) ion pair
~/solvensgetrenntes *s.* ~/äußeres
Ionenpaarbildung *f* ion-pair formation, ion pairing
Ionenpaarchromatographie *f* ion-pair chromatography
~ mit Umkehrphasen reversed-phase ion-pair chromatography
Ionenpolymerisation *f* ionic polymerization
Ionenprodukt *n* ion[ic] product
Ionenquelle *f* ion source
Ionenradius *m* ionic radius
~/Goldschmidtscher Goldschmidt radius
Ionenreaktion *f* ion[ic] reaction, ion-ion reaction
Ionenreihe *f***/Hofmeistersche** lyotropic order (series)
Ionenrekombination *f* ion[-ion] recombination
Ionenresonanz-Hochfrequenzspektrometer *n* ion-resonant spectrometer
Ionenretardierung *f (chromat)* ion retardation
Ionenrichtgitter *n* ion focus grid *(in a spectrometer)*
Ionenschlupf *m* ion slippage *(ion exchange)*
ionenselektiv ion-selective
Ionenselektivität *f* ion selectivity
ionensensitiv ion-sensitive, *(relating to electrodes also:)* ion-selective
Ionensorte *f* ionic species
ionenspezifisch ion-specific
Ionenstärke *f* ionic strength
~ Null zero ionic strength
Ionenstrahl *m* ion beam
Ionenstrahl-Mikroanalyse *f* ion-probe microanalysis, IMA
Ionenstrahl-Spektralanalyse *f* ion-beam spectrochemical analysis, IBSCA
Ionenstreuungsspektroskopie *f* ion-scattering spectroscopy, ISS
Ionenstrom *m* ionic current
Ionenstruktur *f* ionic structure
Ionensuszeptibilität *f* ionic susceptibility *(susceptibility per gram ion)*
Ionentrennung *f* ion separation
Ionenumtausch *m* ion exchange
Ionenverbindung *f* ionic (polar, heteropolar) compound
Ionenverteilung *f* distribution of ions
Ionenverzögerung *f (chromat)* ion retardation
Ionenwanderung *f* ion[ic] migration, migration of ions
~/unabhängige independent migration of ions
Ionenwanderungsgeschwindigkeit *f* ionic speed (velocity)
Ionenwechselwirkung *f* ionic (ion-ion) interaction, interionic action

Ionenwertigkeit *f* ionic valence
Ionenwind *m* ionic (electric) wind
Ionenwolke *f (phys ch)* ion cloud, ion[ic] atmosphere
Ionenzustand *m* ionic state
Ionenzyklotron-Resonanz *f* ion-cyclotron resonance, ICR
Ion-Ion-Rekombination *f* ion[-ion] recombination
Ion-Ion-Wechselwirkung *f s.* Ionenwechselwirkung
Ionisation *f* ionization
~ **bei Atmosphärendruck** atmospheric-pressure ionization, API
~/chemische chemical ionization
~/differentielle *s.* ~/spezifische
~/direkte chemische direct chemical ionization, DCI
~ **durch Laser** laser-enhanced ionization, LEI
~/lawinenartige cumulative ionization
~/schonende soft ionization
~/spezifische specific ionization
~/thermische thermal ionization
Ionisationsarbeit *f s.* Ionisationsenergie
Ionisationsdetektor *m* ionization detector
Ionisationsenergie *f* ionization energy
~/erste first ionization energy
~/zweite second ionization energy
Ionisationsfähigkeit *f* ionizing power
Ionisationsgrad *m* degree of ionization
Ionisationsisomerie *f* ionization isomerism
Ionisationskammer *f* ionization chamber
Ionisationspotential *n* ionization (ionizing) potential
~/erstes first ionization potential
Ionisationsreaktion *f* ionization reaction
Ionisationsspannung *f s.* Ionisationspotential
Ionisationsspektrometer *n* ionization spectrometer
Ionisationsstärke *f* specific ionization
Ionisationsvakuummeter *n* ionization [vacuum] gauge
~ **mit heißer Katode** thermionic (hot-filament) ionization gauge
Ionisationsvermögen *n* ionizing power
Ionisationswärme *f* heat of ionization
Ionisationszustand *m* state of ionization
ionisch ionic
ionisierbar ionizable, capable of ionization
ionisieren to ionize
ionisiert ionized, ionic
~/einfach singly ionized
~/zweifach doubly ionized
Ionisierung *f s.* Ionisation
Ionisierungs... *s. a.* Ionisations...
Ionisierungsbereich *m (spectr)* ionizing region
Ionisierungsquerschnittdetektor *m (chromat)* cross-section detector
ionogen ionogenic
ionoid *(org ch)* ionic *(addition)*
Ionomer[e] *n* ionomer
ionometrisch ionometric
ionophil ionophilic
ionophor *(bioch)* ionophoric
Ionophor *n (bioch)* ionophore, ionophoric agent, ion carrier
Ionophorese *f* ionophoresis
ionotrop ionotropic
Ionotropie *f* ionotropy
I.P. *s.* Punkt/isoelektrischer
IPC *s.* Isopropyl-*N*-phenylcarbamat
Ipecacuanhaalkaloid *n* ipecacuanha alkaloid
ipso-Angriff *m*, **ipso-Substitution** *f (org ch)* ipso-attack
IP-Standardmethode *f (petrol)* standard IP method
IQD *s.* Ionisierungsquerschnittdetektor
IR *s.* Infrarot
IR-Abfall *m*, **iR-Abfall** *m s.* Spannungsabfall/ohmscher
Irdengut *n*, **Irdenware** *f* earthenware
Iridium *n* Ir iridium
Iridosmium *n (min)* iridosmine, iridium-osmine
irisieren to be iridescent, to iridesce
Irisieren *n* iridescence
irisierend iridescent
Irispapier *n* iridescent paper, mother-of-pearl paper
irreversibel irreversible, non-reversible
IR-Spektralbereich *m s.* Infrarotgebiet
I-Säure *f s.* J-Säure
i-s-Diagramm *n* enthalpy-entropy chart (diagram), Mollier chart
isenthalpisch *(phys ch)* isenthalpic *(e.g. expansion)*
isentrop *(phys ch)* is[o]entropic *(e.g. series of reactions)*
Isentrope *f (phys ch)* isentrope *(the representation of an isentropic process in a thermodynamic diagram)*
isentropisch *s.* isentrop
Islandspat *m (min)* Iceland spar *(calcium carbonate)*
Isoalkan *n* isoalkane
Isoalloxazin *n* isoalloxazine, flavin[e]
Isoamylaldehyd *m* isoamyl aldehyde, *3-methylbutanal
Isoamylalkohol *m* isoamyl alcohol, *3-methylbutan-1-ol
Isoamylnitrat *n* isoamyl nitrate, *3-methylbutyl nitrate
Isoamylvalerianat *n* isoamyl valerate, *3-methylbutyl valerate
Isoascorbinsäure *f D*-araboascorbic acid, isoascorbic acid, erythorbic acid
Isobaldriansäure *f s.* Isovaleriansäure
isobar isobaric
Isobar *n* [nuclear] isobar[e]
Isobare *f (phys ch)* isobar
Isobernsteinsäure *f* isosuccinic acid, methylmalonic acid, ethane-1,1-dicarboxylic acid
Isobutan *n* isobutane, *2-methylpropane
Isobutankreislauf *m (petrol)* isobutane recycle

Isobutanol *n s.* Isobutylalkohol
Isobutanumlauf *m (petrol)* isobutane recycle
Isobuten *n s.* 2-Methylpropen
Isobuttersäure *f* isobutyric acid, *2-methylpropionic acid
Isobutylalkohol *m* isobutyl alcohol, *2-methylpropan-1-ol
Isobutylcarbinol *n s.* Isoamylalkohol
Isobutylen *n s.* 2-Methylpropen
Isobutylen-Isopren-Kautschuk *m* isobutylene-isoprene rubber, IIR
Isobutylessigsäure *f* *4-methylpentanoic acid, 4-methylvaleric acid, *(deprecated:)* isobutyl acetic acid
Isobutylierung *f* isobutylation
Isobutylmercaptan *n s.* 2-Methylpropan-1-thiol
Isocapronsäure *f s.* 4-Methylpentansäure
Isochinolin *n* isoquinoline, benzo[*c*]pyridine, 2-benzazine
Isochinolinalkaloid *n* isoquinoline alkaloid
Isochore *f (phys ch)* isochore
Isocitratdehydrogenase *f* isocitric acid dehydrogenase
Isocitronensäure *f* isocitric acid, *1-hydroxypropane-1,2,3-tricarboxylic acid
Isocrat *s.* Isokrat
Isocrotonsäure *f* isocrotonic acid, **cis*-but-2-enoic acid
Isocyanat *n* R–N=C=O isocyanate
Isocyanatkleber *m* isocyanate adhesive
Isocyanatkunststoff *m* isocyanate resin
Isocyanid *n* R–N≡C isocyanide, isonitrile, carbylamine
Isocyanursäure *f* isocyanuric acid, fulminuric acid
isocyclisch isocyclic, homocyclic, carbocyclic
Isocyclus *m* isocyclic (homocyclic, carbocyclic) compound
Isodecanol *n (plast, text, pap)* isodecanol, isodecyl alcohol *(mixture of isomers of C_{10} alcohols)*
isodiametrisch isodiametric
Isodiazotat *n* antidiazo compound
isodimensional isodimensional
isodispers isodisperse, monodisperse
Isodurol *n* isodurene, *1,2,3,5-tetramethylbenzene
Isodurylsäure *f* isodurylic acid, trimethylbenzoic acid
isodynam isodynamic
isoelektrisch isoelectric
isoelektronisch isoelectronic, isosteric
isoenthalpisch isenthalpic
Isoenzym *n* isoenzyme, isozyme
Isoeugenol *n* isoeugenol, 2-methoxy-4-propenylphenol
Isoferulasäure *f s.* Hesperetinsäure
Isoflavon *n* isoflavone
Isogel *n (coll)* isogel
Isohemipinsäure *f* isohemipinic acid, 4,5-dimethoxyisophthalic acid
Isokale *f* isocal, isocalorific line
Iso-Kautschuk *m* isorubber
isokrat isocratic *(maintaining constant composition as of an eluant)*
Isolation *f* 1. insulation [material]; insulation; resist, stop-off [coating] *(electroplating)*; 2. insulation *(against something)*
Isolations... *s. a.* Isolier...
Isolationswiderstand *m* insulation resistance
Isoleucin *n* isoleucine, ileu *(an amino acid)*
isolierbar isolable
Isolierbeton *m s.* Dämmbeton
isolieren 1. *(ch)* to isolate, to separate, to segregate; 2. to insulate *(against something)*
Isolierlack *m* insulating varnish
Isoliermasse *f* insulation compound
Isoliermaterial *n* insulation [material]
Isoliermischung *f (rubber)* insulating compound (stock)
Isoliermittel *n* insulating medium
Isolieröl *n* [electrical] insulating oil
Isolierpapier *n* [electrical] insulating paper
Isolierpappe *f* insulating (fuller) board
Isolierschlauch *m* insulation tubing
Isolierstein *m* insulating brick
Isolierstoff *m* insulation [material]
Isolierstreifen *m* insulation strip
Isolierung *f* 1. *(ch)* isolation, separation, segregation; 2. insulation *(against something)*
Isologe *n* isologue
isomer isomeric
~/optisch enantiomeric
Isomer *n* isomer, isomeric compound
~/geometrisches geometric[al] isomer, cis-trans isomer
~/optisches optical isomer (antipode), enantiomer, antimer, mirror-image isomer
m-**Isomer** *n m*-isomer, meta isomer
o-**Isomer** *n o*-isomer, ortho isomer
p-**Isomer** *n p*-isomer, para isomer
isomerenfrei free from isomers
Isomerengemisch *n* mixture of isomers
Isomerenpaar *n*/**optisch aktives** pair of optical isomers
Isomere *n s.* Isomer
Isomerie *f* isomerism
~/geometrische geometrical (cis-trans) isomerism
~/optische optical isomerism, enantiomerism, mirror-image isomerism
~/räumliche (stereochemische) stereoisomerism, space isomerism
anti-syn-**Isomerie** *f* anti-syn isomerism
Isomerisation *f s.* Isomerisierung
isomerisieren to isomerize
~/sich to isomerize, to undergo isomerization
Isomerisierung *f* isomerization, molecular rearrangement
~/entartete degenerate isomerization
~ in der Dampfphase vapour-phase isomerization
~ in der Flüssigphase liquid-phase isomerization

~ in der Gasphase gas-phase isomerization
~/photochemische photoisomerization
~/reduktive (reduzierende) reductive isomerization, hydroisomerization
~/spontane spontaneous isomerization
Isomerisierungsreaktion *f* isomerization reaction
Isomerisierungsverfahren *n* isomerization process
isomorph *(cryst)* isomorphous
Isomorphie *f (cryst)* isomorphism
Isomorphieregel *f*/**Mitscherlichsche** *(cryst)* Mitscherlich's law of isomorphism
Isomorphismus *m (cryst)* isomorphism
Isoniazid *n s.* Isonicotinsäurehydrazid
Isonicotinsäure *f* isonicotinic acid, pyridine-4-carboxylic acid
Isonicotinsäurehydrazid *n* isonicotinic acid hydrazide, isoniazid, INAH
Isonitril *n* isonitrile, isocyanide, carbylamine
Isonitrosoverbindung *f* oxime, isonitroso compound
Isooctan *n* isooctane, *(specif)* $(CH_3)_2CHCH_2C(CH_3)_3$ 2,2,4-trimethylpentane
Isooctanol *n s.* Isooctylalkohol
Isooctylalkohol *m* *6-methylheptanol, isooctyl alcohol
Isopentan *n* *2-methylbutane, isopentane
Isopersulfocyansäure *f* isoperthiocyanic acid
Isophthalsäure *f* isophthalic acid, *m*-phthalic acid, benzene-*m*-dicarboxylic acid
Isoplethe *f* isopleth
Isopolymorphie *f* isopolymorphism
Isopolysäure *f* isopoly acid
Isopren *n* isoprene, *2-methylbuta-1,3-diene
Isoprenkautschuk *m* isoprene rubber, IR
Isoprenoid *n* isoprenoid *(general term for terpenes and steroids)*
Isoprenregel *f (org ch)* isoprene rule
Isopropylalkohol *m* propan-2-ol
Isopropylamin *n* isopropylamine, 2-aminopropane, *1-methylethylamine
Isopropylbenzen *n* isopropylbenzene, cumene, 2-phenylpropane
Isopropylcarbinol *n s.* 2-Methylpropan-1-ol
Isopropylchlorid *n* *2-chloropropane, isopropyl chloride
Isopropylessigsäure *f s.* Isovaleriansäure
Isopropylether *m s.* Diisopropylether
Isopropylgruppe *f* $(CH_3)_2CH-$ isopropyl group (residue)
Isopropylidenaceton *n s.* Mesityloxid
Isopropylierung *f* isopropylation
Isopropyl-*N*-phenylcarbamat *n* isopropyl-*N*-phenylcarbamate, IPC *(a herbicide)*
isosmotisch is[o]osmotic, isotonic
isoster isosteric, isoelectronic
Isostere *f (phys ch)* isostere
Isosterie *f* isosterism
isosterisch *s.* isoster
Isosynthese *f* isosynthesis
Isotache *f* isotach, isokinetic line, isovel
Isotachophorese *f (anal)* isotachophoresis *(special type of electrophoresis)*
isotaktisch isotactic
Isotaktizität *f* isotacticity
Isoteniskop *n* isoteniscope *(a device for determining the saturation vapour pressure of liquids)*
isotherm isothermal
Isotherme *f* isotherm
~/van-der-Waalssche van der Waals isotherm
isothermisch isothermal
Isothiocyanat *n*, **Isothiocyansäureester** *m* isothiocyanate, mustard oil
Isoton *n (nucl)* isotone
isotonisch isotonic, is[o]osmotic
isotop isotopic
Isotop *n* isotope
~/instabiles *s.* ~/radioaktives
~/künstlich erzeugtes artificial isotope
~/langlebiges long-lived isotope
~/nichtradioaktives *s.* ~/stabiles
~/radioaktives radioactive (unstable) isotope, radioisotope
~/schweres heavy isotope
~/stabiles stable (non-radioactive) isotope
Isotopenanalyse *f* isotopic analysis
Isotopenaustausch *m* isotope (isotopic) exchange
Isotopeneffekt *m s.* Isotopieeffekt
Isotopengemisch *n* mixture of isotopes, isotopic mixture
Isotopengewicht *n s.* Massewert
Isotopenhäufigkeit *f* isotopic abundance
~/natürliche natural abundance
Isotopenindikator *m* isotopic tracer (indicator)
isotopenmarkiert [isotopically] labelled
Isotopenmasse *f* isotopic (isotope) mass
Isotopenmethode *f* tracer (atom tagging) method
isotopenrein isotopically pure
Isotopenreinheit *f* isotopic purity
Isotopensubstitution *f* isotopic substitution
Isotopentechnik *f* tracer technique, *(bioch also)* isotope incorporation technique
Isotopentracer *m s.* Isotopenindikator
Isotopentrennung *f* isotope (isotopic) separation
Isotopenverbindung *f* isotopic compound
Isotopenverdünnung *f* isotopic dilution
Isotopenverdünnungsanalyse *f* isotopic dilution analysis
Isotopenverdünnungsmethode *f* isotope dilution procedure
Isotopenverhältnis *n* abundance (isotopic) ratio
Isotopenzusammensetzung *f* isotopic composition
Isotopie *f* isotopism, isotopy
Isotopieeffekt *m* isotope effect
~/kinetischer kinetic isotope effect
~/primärer kinetischer primary kinetic isotope effect
~/sekundärer kinetischer secondary kinetic isotope effect

isotrop *(cryst)* isotropic

~/optisch optically isotropic

Isotropie *f (cryst)* isotropism, isotropy

isotyp *(cryst)* isotypic

Isotypie *f (cryst)* isotypy

Isovaleraldehyd *m* isovaleraldehyde, *3-methylbutanal

Isovaleriansäure *f*, **Isovalersäure** *f* isovaleric acid, *3-methylbutanoic acid

Isovole *f* isovol *(line of equal volatile matter)*

Isoxylylsäure *f* isoxylylic acid, *p*-xylylic acid, *2,5-dimethylbenzoic acid

Isozym *n s.* Isoenzym

Istaufnahme *f* net absorption *(wood preservation)*

Itaconsäure *f* itaconic acid, *prop-2-ene-1,2-dicarboxylic acid

IT-Diagramm *n* IT diagram, heat-content/temperature diagram

It-Stoff *m* asbestos-rubber material *(for sealing)*

IUC-Regel *f (nomencl)* IUC rule

I-U-Kennlinie *f*, **I-U-Kurve** *f s.* Strom-Spannungs-Kurve

IUPAC IUPAC, International Union of Pure and Applied Chemistry

IUPAC-Dyson-Notation *f (nomencl)* IUPAC-Dyson notation

IUPAC-Dyson-System *n (nomencl)* IUPAC-Dyson [notation] system

IUPAC-Regel *f (nomencl)* IUPAC rule

IUPAC-System *n (nomencl)* IUPAC system

Ivanov-Reaktion *f* Ivanov reaction *(synthesis of hydroxy acids)*

Izod-Prüfung *f (plast)* Izod impact test

IZSH *s.* Hormon/luteinisierendes

J

Jablonski-Diagramm *n*, **Jablonski-Termschema** *n (phys ch)* Jablonski diagram

Jaborandiöl *n* Jaborandi oil *(from the leaves of Pilocarpus pennatifolius Lem.)*

Jackson-Meisenheimer-Komplex *m (org ch)* Meisenheimer complex (compound, adduct)

Jacquinot-Vorteil *m (spectr)* Jacquinot advantage

Jade *m (min)* jade *(a gemstone derived from jadeite or nephrite)*

Jahn-Teller-Phasenübergang *m* Jahn-Teller transition

Jahrestonnen *fpl s.* Tonnen je Jahr

Jalousiedrosselklappe *f* louvre

Jalousietrockner *m* louvre dryer

Jantzen-Verteilung *f* countercurrent extraction (separation)

Janusgrün *n* Janus green *(redox indicator; stain for microscopy)*

Japancampher *m* Japan camphor *(from Cinnamomum camphora (L.) Sieb.)*

Japanlack *m* japan, Japan lacquer, *(specif)* Japanese (Chinese) lacquer *(from Rhus verniciflua Stokes)*

Japanpapier *n* Japan[ese] paper

Japansäure *f* Japanic acid, *heneicosane-1,21-dioic acid

Japanseidenpapier *n* Japanese tissue paper

Japantalg *m* Japan tallow (wax) *(from Rhus succedanea L. and R. verniciflua Stokes)*

Japanwachs *n s.* Japantalg

Jargon *m (min)* jargo[o]n *(zirconium orthosilicate)*

Jaspis *m (min)* jasper *(a variety of quartz)*

Jaspisware *f (ceram)* jasper ware

Jaspopal *m (min)* jaspopal, Jasper opal

jato, Jato *(**Ja**hres**to**nnen) s.* Tonnen je Jahr

Jatrochemie *f s.* Iatrochemie

Javakunstpapier *n* batik paper

Jensen-Turm *m (pap)* Jensen tower

Jequié-Kautschuk *m* Jequie rubber, mule gum *(from Manihot dichotoma Ule)*

Jervasäure *f* jervasic acid, chelidonic acid, γ-pyrone-2,6-dicarboxylic acid

Jet[t] *m(n)* jet, gagate *(a variety of lignite)*

J-Gefäß *n (text)* J box

Jigger *m (text)* jig[ger]

jj-Kopplung *f (phys ch)* jj coupling

Jod *n s.* Iod

Jodäthyl *n s.* Iodethan

Jodmethyl *n s.* Iodmethan

Jodsilber *n (phot)* silver iodide

Johannisbrotgummi *n* carob[-seed] gum, caroban, locust-bean gum *(from Ceratonia siliqua L.)*

Johnson-Rauschen *n (anal)* Johnson (thermal) noise

Joliotium *n* Jl joliotium *(element 105)*

Jordan-Kegel[stoff]mühle *f*, **Jordan-Mühle** *f (pap)* Jordan engine (mill, refiner), jordan, refining (perfecting) engine

José-Papier *n* lens paper (tissue) *(for wiping optical lenses)*

Joule *n* joule, J *(SI unit of work, energy, and heat)*

Joule-Thomson-Effekt *m* Joule-Thomson effect

~/differentieller differential Joule-Thomson effect

Joule-Thomson-Koeffizient *m* Joule-Thomson coefficient

J-Peptid *n (bioch)* joining peptide

J-Säure *f* J acid, 2-aminonaphth-5-ol-7-sulphonic acid

J-Säure-Harnstoff *m* J acid urea

Juchtenleder *n* Russian leather

Juchtenöl *n (tann)* birch bark oil

Judäakaroben *fpl (dye)* carob (turpentine) galls *(from Pistacia terebinthus L.)*

Juglon *n* juglone, 5-hydroxy-1,4-naphthoquinone

Jungfernkautschuk *m* [caucho] virgin rubber *(from Sapium thomsoni God.)*

Jungfernöl *n* virgin [olive] oil *(obtained from the first light pressing in the cold)*

Jungfernquecksilber *n* native mercury

Jungfustik *m (dye)* young fustic, fustet *(from Cotinus coggygria Scop.)*
Junghopfen *m* green hop
Jungkräusen *pl (ferm)* low krausen
Juniperinsäure *f* juniperic acid, *16-hydroxyhexadecanoic acid
Justage *f s.* Justierung
justieren to adjust, to rectify *(instruments)*
Justierschraube *f* adjusting screw *(as of a balance)*
justiert/auf Auslauf calibrated (graduated) to deliver, calibrated for delivery
~/auf Einguß calibrated to contain, calibrated for content
Justierung *f* adjustment, rectification *(of an instrument)*
Jutedichtung *f*, **Jutepackung** *f* jute packing
Juvabion *n (bioch)* paper factor *(a plant constituent which acts as juvenile hormone)*
Juvenilhormon *n* juvenile hormone *(of insects)*
Juwelierborax *m* jeweller's borax, octahedral borax *(sodium tetraborate 5-water)*
JZ *(Jodzahl) s.* Iodzahl

K

KA 1. *(= Kaseinfaserstoff) s.* Caseinfaserstoff; 2. *s.* Kläranlage
Kabelbohranlage *f (petrol)* cable-tool installation (rig)
Kabelbohren *n (petrol)* cable-tool drilling
Kabelbohrgerät *n s.* Kabelbohranlage
Kabelbohrverfahren *n (petrol)* cable-tool method
Kabelisolieröl *n* cable oil
Kabelisolierpapier *n* cable paper
Kabelmantel *m* cable coating
Kabelöl *n* cable oil
Kabelpapier *n* cable paper
Kachel *f (ceram)* tile
Kachelpresse *f* pot press *(as for expression of oilseeds)*
Kadavermehl *n* animal (garbage) tankage
Kaffee *m*/**löslicher** soluble (instant) coffee
Kaffeebohne *f* coffee bean (nib)
Kaffee-Ersatz[stoff] *m* coffee substitute
Kaffee[-Extrakt]pulver *n* instant (soluble) coffee
Kaffeesäure *f* caffeic acid, 3,4-dihydroxycinnamic acid
Kaffeesäureester *m* **der Chinasäure** caffeoylquinic acid, chlorogenic acid
Kaffeesäure-3-methylether *m* caffeic acid 4-methyl ether, 3-hydroxy-3-methoxycinnamic acid, ferulic acid
Kaffeesäure-4-methylether *m* caffeic acid 4-methyl ether, hesperetic acid
Kaffein *n* caffeine, 1,3,7-trimethylxanthine
Kaffeinsäure *f s.* Kaffeesäure
Käfig *m* cage *(consisting of molecules in liquids and solids)*
Käfigeffekt *m* [solvent] cage effect
Käfig[einschluß]verbindung *f* cage (clathrate) compound, clathrate [inclusion compound]
Käfigwand *f (cryst)* cage wall
Kahlappretur *f (text)* pileless finish
Kahm *m*, **Kahmhaut** *f* pellicle *(of bacteria or moulds on liquids)*
Kainit *m* 1. *(min)* kainit[e] *(magnesium potassium chloride sulphate)*; 2. kainit[e] *(mixture of potash salts containing 19 to 24 % KCl)*
Kaisergrün *n s.* Grün/Schweinfurter
Kajeputöl *n (pharm)* cajeput oil *(from Melaleuca leucadendron L.)*
KAK *s.* Kationenaustauschkapazität
Kakao *m* cocoa, chocolate *(powder or drink)*
Kakaobohne *f* cacao (cocoa) bean *(from Theobroma cacao L..)*
Kakaobutter *f*, **Kakaofett** *n*, **Kakaoöl** *n* cocoa butter (oil, fat), cacao butter
Kakaopulver *n* cocoa [powder]
Kakodyl *n* cacodyl, tetramethyldiarsine
Kakodylchlorid *n* cacodyl chloride, chlorodimethylarsine
Kakodyloxid *n* cacodyl oxide
Kakodylsäure *f* cacodylic acid, dimethylarsinic acid
Kakothelin *n* cacotheline *(a nitro derivative of brucine)*
Kakoxen *m (min)* cacoxene, cacoxenite *(iron(III) trihydroxide orthophosphate)*
Kalander *m* calender [machine]
~ in Tandemanordnung *(rubber)* tandem calender
~ mit Walzenschränkung *(rubber)* swivel-roll (crossed-axes) machine
~ zum Belegen von Geweben *(rubber)* [skim-] coating calender, skimming calender
~ zum Ziehen von Platten *(rubber)* sheeting calender
Kalandereffekt *m (rubber)* calender grain
Kalanderfärbung *f (pap)* calender staining (colouring), padding, stuffing
Kalanderfolie *f (plast)* calendered film
Kalanderführer *m* calender operator
Kalanderleimung *f (pap)* calender sizing
kalandern to calender
Kalanderplatte *f (rubber)* calendered sheet
Kalandersaal *m* calender department
Kalandersatz *m* calender stack
Kalanderschrumpfung *f (rubber)* calender shrinkage
Kalanderständer *m* calender frame
Kalanderwalze *f* calender roll (bowl)
Kalanderwalzenpapier *n* calender roll (bowl) paper, woollen paper
Kalanderwalzensatz *m* calender stack
kalandrieren *s.* kalandern
Kälberlab *n*, **Kälberrennin** *n* calf rennet (rennin)
Kaldo-Verfahren *n s.* Kalling-Domnarvet-Verfahren
Kalebassencurare *n s.* Calebassencurare
Kaledonischbraun *n* umber *(a naturally occurring brown pigment)*

Kali *n s.* 1. Kalisalz; 2. Kalidüngemittel; 3. Reinkali; 4. Kalium
~/schwefelsaures sulphate of potash *(a fertilizer chiefly consisting of K_2SO_4)*
Kalialaun *m (min)* potash alum, kalinite *(aluminium potassium sulphate 12-water)*
Kaliapparat *m (lab)* potash bulb, alkalimeter *(for determining carbon dioxide)*
~ nach Geißler (Mohr) Geissler-Mohr absorption (potash) bulb
kalibrieren to calibrate *(measuring apparatus)*; to size *(e.g. tubing)*
Kalibriermischung *f* calibration mixture
Kalibrierung *f* calibration *(of measuring apparatus)*; sizing *(as of tubing)*
Kalidüngemittel *n*, **Kalidünger** *m* potash (potassic) fertilizer
Kalifeldspat *m (min)* potash feldspar
Kaliglas *n* potash glass
Kaliglimmer *m (min)* potash (potassium) mica, muscovite *(a phyllosilicate)*
kalihaltig potassiferous, *(esp of ores)* potash-bearing
Kaliindustrie *f* potash industry
Kalilager *n* potash deposit
Kalilauge *f* potash lye, caustic potash solution, potassium hydroxide solution
~/alkoholische alcoholic [caustic] potash
Kalimagnesia *f* [single sulphate of] potash magnesia *(a fertilizer consisting of schoenite or leonite)*
Kalimangel *m (agric)* potassium shortage (deficiency)
kalireich high-potash
Kalirohsalz *n (fert)* potash ore, mine-run salt
Kalisalpeter *m* saltpetre, nitre, nitrate of potash *(potassium nitrate)*
Kalisalz *n* potash [salt], potassiferous salt
Kalisalzlager *n*, **Kalisalzlagerstätte** *f* potash deposit
Kalischmelze *f* potash fusion
Kaliseife *f* potassium soap, potash [soft] soap
Kalium *n* K potassium
Kaliumacetat *n* potassium acetate
Kaliumalaun *m* potassium (potash) alum, aluminium potassium sulphate 12-water
Kaliumaluminat *n* potassium aluminate
Kaliumaluminiumalaun *m s.* Kaliumalaun
Kaliumaluminiumsulfat *n* aluminium potassium sulphate
Kaliumalumosilicat *n* potassium aluminosilicate
Kaliumamalgam *n* potassium amalgam
Kaliumamid *n* potassium amide
Kaliumammoniumtartrat *n* ammonium potassium tartrate
Kaliumantimonotartrat *n* potassium antimonotartrate
Kaliumantimonyltartrat *n s.* Kaliumantimonotartrat
Kaliumarsenat(III) *n* potassium arsenite
Kaliumaurat *n* potassium aurate
Kaliumazid *n* potassium azide
Kaliumborotartrat *n* potassium borotartrate
Kaliumbromat *n* potassium bromate
Kaliumbromid *n* potassium bromide
Kaliumcalciumsulfat *n* calcium potassium sulphate
Kaliumcarbonat *n* potassium carbonate
Kaliumcarbonyl *n* potassium carbonyl
Kaliumchlorat *n* potassium chlorate
Kaliumchlorid *n* potassium chloride
Kaliumchlorit *n* potassium chlorite
Kaliumchromalaun *m* chrome [potash] alum, potassium chrome alum, common chrome alum
Kaliumchromat *n* potassium chromate
Kaliumcitrat *n* potassium citrate
Kaliumcobalt(II)-sulfat *n* cobalt(II) potassium sulphate
Kaliumcyanat *n* potassium cyanate
Kaliumcyanid *n* potassium cyanide
Kaliumdichromat *n* potassium dichromate
Kaliumdicyanoargentat *n* potassium dicyanoargentate
Kaliumdicyanoaurat(I) *n* potassium dicyanoaurate (I)
Kaliumdihydrogenarsenat *n* potassium dihydrogenarsenate
Kaliumdihydrogenphosphat *n* potassium dihydrogenphosphate
Kaliumdiphosphat *n* *potassium diphosphate, potassium pyrophosphate
Kaliumdisulfat *n* potassium disulphate
Kaliumdisulfit *n* potassium disulphite
Kaliumdodecawolframatosilicat *n* potassium dodecawolframosilicate, potassium dodecatungstosilicate
Kaliumeisen(III)-chlorid *n* iron(III) potassium chloride, ferric potassium chloride
Kaliumeisen(III)-oxalat *n* iron(III) potassium oxalate, ferric potassium oxalate
Kaliumeisen(III)-sulfat-12-Wasser *n* iron(III) potassium sulphate 12-water, ferric potassium sulphate 12-water, iron potassium alum
Kaliumethylxanthogenat *n* potassium ethyl xanthate
Kaliumfluorid *n* potassium fluoride
Kaliumfluoroberyllat *n* potassium fluoroberyllate
Kaliumformiat *n* potassium formate
Kaliumgallium(III)-sulfat *n* gallium potassium sulphate
Kaliumgraphit *m* potassium graphite
kaliumhaltig potassium-containing, potassic
Kaliumhexabromoplatinat(IV) *n* potassium hexabromoplatinate(IV)
Kaliumhexachloroiridat(IV) *n* potassium hexachloroiridate(IV)
Kaliumhexachloroosmat(III) *n* potassium hexachloroosmate(III)
Kaliumhexachloroosmat(IV) *n* potassium hexachloroosmate(IV)
Kaliumhexachloropalladat(IV) *n* potassium hexachloropalladate(IV)

Kaliumhexachloroplatinat(IV) *n* potassium hexachloroplatinate(IV)
Kaliumhexacyanocobaltat(II) *n* potassium hexacyanocobaltate(II)
Kaliumhexacyanoferrat(II) *n* potassium hexacyanoferrate(II), yellow prussiate of potash, yellow potassium prussiate
Kaliumhexacyanoferrat(III) *n* potassium hexacyanoferrate(III), red prussiate of potash, red potassium prussiate
Kaliumhexafluorosilicat *n* potassium hexafluorosilicate
Kaliumhexafluorotitanat(IV) *n* potassium hexafluorotitanate(IV)
Kaliumhexafluorozirconat(IV) *n* potassium hexafluorozirconate(IV)
Kaliumhexaiodoplatinat(IV) *n* potassium hexaiodoplatinate(IV)
Kaliumhexanitrocobaltat(III) *n* potassium hexanitrocobaltate(III)
Kaliumhexylxanthogenat *n* potassium hexyl xanthate
Kaliumhydrid *n* potassium hydride
Kaliumhydrogenarsenat(V) *n* potassium hydrogenarsenate
Kaliumhydrogencarbonat *n* potassium hydrogencarbonate
Kaliumhydrogenfluorid *n* potassium hydrogenfluoride
Kaliumhydrogenoxalat *n* potassium hydrogenoxalate
Kaliumhydrogenphosphat *n* potassium hydrogenphosphate
Kaliumhydrogenphthalat *n* potassium hydrogenphthalate
Kaliumhydrogensulfat *n* potassium hydrogensulphate
Kaliumhydrogensulfid *n* potassium hydrogensulphide
Kaliumhydrogensulfit *n* potassium hydrogensulphite
Kaliumhydrogentartrat *n* potassium hydrogentartrate
Kaliumhydroxid *n* potassium hydroxide
Kaliumhydroxidschmelze *f* 1. potassium hydroxide fusion, molten potassium hydroxide; 2. potassium hydroxide fusion *(act)*
~/alkoholische fusion with alcoholic potassium hydroxide
Kaliumhyperoxid *n* potassium hyperoxide
Kaliumhypochlorit *n* potassium hypochlorite
Kaliumiodat *n* potassium iodate
Kaliumiodatstärkepapier *n* potassium-iodate starch paper
Kaliumiodid *n* potassium iodide
Kaliumiodidstärkeindikator *m* potassium-iodide-starch indicator
Kaliumiodidstärkepapier *n* potassium-iodide starch paper
Kaliumlactat *n* potassium lactate
Kaliumlinie *f (spectr)* potassium line
Kaliummagnesiumsulfat *n* magnesium potassium sulphate
Kaliummanganat *n* potassium manganate
Kaliummanganat(VII) *n s.* Kaliumpermanganat
Kaliummetaborat *n* potassium metaborate
Kaliummetaperiodat *n* potassium metaperiodate, potassium periodate, potassium tetraoxoiodate(VII)
Kaliummetaphosphat *n* potassium metaphosphate
Kaliummetasilicat *n* potassium metasilicate, potassium silicate, potassium trioxosilicate
Kaliummethoxid *n s.* Kaliummethylat
Kaliummethylat *n* potassium methylate
Kaliummonosulfid *n* potassium monosulphide, potassium sulphide
Kaliumnatriumcarbonat *n* potassium sodium carbonate
Kaliumnatriumhexanitrocobaltat(III) *n* potassium sodium hexanitrocobaltate(III)
Kaliumnatriumtartrat *n* potassium sodium tartrate
Kaliumnitrat *n* potassium nitrate
Kaliumnitrid *n* potassium nitride
Kaliumnitrit *n* potassium nitrite
Kaliumnitroprussiat *n s.* Kaliumnitroprussid
Kaliumnitroprussid *n* potassium nitroprusside, dipotassium pentacyanonitrosylferrate(II)
Kaliumoleat *n* potassium oleate, *(specif)* octadec-9-enoate
Kaliumorthoarsenat(III) *n s.* Kaliumarsenat(III)
Kaliumorthophosphat *n* potassium orthophosphate
Kaliumosmat(VI) *n* potassium osmate(VI)
Kaliumoxalat *n* potassium oxalate
Kaliumoxid *n* potassium oxide
Kaliumpalmitat *n* potassium palmitate
Kaliumparawolframat *n* potassium parawolframate, potassium paratungstate
Kaliumpentachloroamminplatinat(IV) *n* potassium amminepentachloroplatinate(IV)
Kaliumpentasulfid *n* potassium pentasulphide
Kaliumpentathionat *n* potassium pentathionate
Kaliumperchlorat *n* potassium perchlorate
Kaliumpermanganat *n* potassium permanganate
Kaliumpermanganatverbrauch *m (hyd)* permanganate consumption (value), PV
Kaliumperoxid *n* potassium peroxide
Kaliumperoxoborat *n* potassium peroxoborate
Kaliumperoxocarbonat *n s.* Kaliumperoxodicarbonat
Kaliumperoxochromat *n* potassium peroxochromate
Kaliumperoxodicarbonat *n* potassium peroxodicarbonate
Kaliumperoxodisulfat *n* potassium peroxodisulphate, potassium peroxosulphate
Kaliumperrhenat *n* potassium perrhenate
Kaliumphenolat *n* potassium phenate, potassium phenoxide

Kaliumphosphat *n* potassium phosphate, *(specif)* potassium orthophosphate
Kaliumpyrophosphat *n s.* Kaliumdiphosphat
Kaliumpyrosulfit *n s.* Kaliumdisulfit
Kaliumquecksilberiodid *n* mercury potassium iodide
Kaliumrhodanid *n s.* Kaliumthiocyanat
Kaliumseife *f s.* Kaliseife
Kaliumselenat *n* potassium selenate
Kaliumselenid *n* potassium selenide
Kaliumselenit *n* potassium selenite
Kaliumselenocyanat *n* potassium selenocyanate
Kaliumsilbernitrat *n* potassium silver nitrate
Kaliumstearat *n* potassium stearate
Kaliumsulfat *n* potassium sulphate
Kaliumsulfid *n* potassium sulphide, *(specif)* potassium monosulphide
Kaliumsulfit *n* potassium sulphite
Kaliumtartrat *n* potassium tartrate
Kaliumtetraborat *n* potassium tetraborate
Kaliumtetrabromoaurat(III) *n* potassium tetrabromoaurate(III)
Kaliumtetrabromoplatinat(II) *n* potassium tetrabromoplatinate(II)
Kaliumtetrachloroaurat(III) *n* potassium tetrachloroaurate(III)
Kaliumtetrachloropalladat(II) *n* potassium tetrachloropalladate(II)
Kaliumtetrachloroplatinat(II) *n* potassium tetrachloroplatinate(II)
Kaliumtetracyanoaurat(III) *n* potassium tetracyanoaurate(III)
Kaliumtetracyanomercurat(II) *n* potassium tetracyanomercurate(II)
Kaliumtetracyanoniccolat(II) *n* potassium tetracyanoniccolate(II)
Kaliumtetracyanoplatinat(II) *n* potassium tetracyanoplatinate(II)
Kaliumtetracyanozincat *n* potassium tetracyanozincate
Kaliumtetrafluoroborat *n* potassium tetrafluoroborate
Kaliumtetraoxalat *n* potassium tetraoxalate
Kaliumtetrasilicat *n* potassium tetrasilicate
Kaliumtetrasulfid *n* potassium tetrasulphide
Kaliumtetrathionat *n* potassium tetrathionate
Kaliumtetroxoiodat *n s.* Kaliummetaperiodat
Kaliumtetroxorhenat(VII) *n s.* Kaliumperrhenat
Kaliumthioarsenat(III) *n* potassium thioarsenite
Kaliumthioarsenat(V) *n* potassium thioarsenate
Kaliumthiocarbonat *n* potassium thiocarbonate, potassium trithiocarbonate
Kaliumthiocyanat *n* potassium thiocyanate, potassium rhodanide
Kaliumthiocyanatpapier *n* potassium thiocyanate paper
Kaliumthiosulfat *n* potassium thiosulphate
Kaliumtrioxosilicat *n s.* Kaliummetasilicat
Kaliumtrioxostannat(IV) *n* potassium trioxostannate(IV)
Kaliumwolframat *n* potassium wolframate, potassium tungstate
Kaliumxanthogenat *n* potassium xanthate, *(specif)* C_2H_5OCSSK potassium ethylxanthate
Kaliwasserglas *n* potassium (potash) water glass, soluble water (potash) glass
Kalk *m* lime • **aus dem ~ falzen** *(tann)* to greenshave • **mit ~ behandeln** to lime out *(manufacture of organic intermediates)* • **mit ~ düngen** to lime
~/an der Luft erhärtender non-hydraulic lime
~/durch feuchte Luft gelöschter air-slaked lime
~/essigsaurer vinegar salt
~/gebrannter burnt (burned, caustic) lime, quicklime *(calcium oxide)*
~/gelöschter hydrated (slaked, water-slaked) lime, lime hydrate *(calcium hydroxide)*, *(agric also)* agricultural hydrate
~/hochhydraulischer Roman cement (lime), Parker's cement
~/hydraulischer hydraulic (water) lime *(a lime which will harden under water)*
~/ungelöschter unslaked lime, quicklime *(calcium oxide)*
~/Wiener Vienna lime *(pulverized dolomite)*
Kalkalkaligestein *n* calc-alkali[c] rock
Kalkammoniak *n* kalkammon *(a fertilizer)*
Kalkammonsalpeter *m* nitrochalk
Kalkanreicherungshorizont *m (soil)* lime accumulation horizon, lime pan
kalkarm *(soil)* deficient in lime, sour
kalkartig limy, calcareous
Kalkäscher *m* 1. *(tann)* liming; lime pit; lime liquor; 2. *(text)* liming, lime boil
~/reiner *(tann)* straight lime liquor
Kalkäscherwolle *f (text)* slipe wool
Kalkbad *n* lime bath
Kalkbedarf *m* lime requirements
Kalkbeton *m* lime concrete
Kalkbeuche *f (text)* lime boil, liming
Kalkbilanz *f (agric)* lime balance
Kalkblau *n* copper blue, blue verditer, Bremen blue *(copper(II) hydroxide)*
Kalkboden *m* limy (calcareous) soil
Kalkbrei *m (tann)* lime cream (paint); *(build)* lime slurry
Kalkbrennen *n* lime burning
Kalkbrennofen *m* lime kiln
Kalkbrühe *f (agric)* lime wash, whitewash
Kalkchlorose *f (agric)* lime-induced chlorosis
Kalkchromgelb *n* gelbin *(calcium chromate)*
Kalkchromgranat *m (min)* lime-chrome garnet, calcium-chromium garnet
Kalkdosis *f (hyd)* lime dosage
Kalkdüngemittel *n*, **Kalkdünger** *m* lime [fertilizer], *(specif)* agricultural limestone, agstone
kalkecht *(dye, coat)* fast to lime

Kalkechtheit *f (dye, coat)* fastness to lime
kalken 1. *(sugar)* to lime, to defecate; *(agric)* to lime; *(hyd)* to soften with lime; 2. to lime out *(manufacture of organic intermediates)*; 3. to whitewash *(e.g. walls)*
Kalkentzuckerungsverfahren *n* Steffen process *(for desugarizing molasses)*
Kalkfällung *f (hyd)* lime precipitation
Kalkfällungsschlamm *m (hyd)* lime [softening] sludge
kalkfalzen *(tann)* to green-shave
kalkfeindlich *s.* kalkfliehend
Kalkfeldspat *m (min)* lime feldspar
Kalkflecken *mpl* 1. *(tann)* lime blasts (specks), blasting *(a result of incorrect liming)*; 2. *(phot)* drying marks
kalkfliehend calcifuginous, calciphobic, lime-intolerant *(plant)*
Kalkgestein *n* calcareous rock
Kalkglas *n* lime glass
kalkhaltig limy, calcareous
Kalkhärte *f (hyd)* calcium hardness
kalkhold *s.* kalkliebend
Kalkhydrat *n s.* Kalk/gelöschter
kalkig limy, calcareous
Kalk-Kohlensäure-Gleichgewicht *n (hyd)* carbonate-bicarbonate equilibrium
Kalk-Kohlensäure-Verfahren *n (sugar)* lime-carbon-dioxide process, alternate liming and carbonation procedure
Kalkkruste *f (geol)* calcareous crust, caliche
Kalklicht *n*/**Drummondsches** Drummond's limelight
kalkliebend calcicolous, calciphilic *(plant)*
Kalklöschen *n* lime slaking (hydration)
Kalklöschturm *m* slaking tower
Kalkmergel *m* lime marl
Kalkmilch *f* milk (slurry) of lime, lime milk; *(tann)* cream of lime; *(agric)* lime wash, whitewash *(a suspension of calcium hydroxide or hydrated lime in water)*
Kalkmilchscheidung *f (sugar)* defecation with milk of lime, wet liming
Kalkmilchsystem *n (pap)* milk-of-lime system
Kalkmörtel *m* lime mortar
Kalkmudde *f (geol)* calcareous mud
Kalknatronglas *n* soda-lime glass
Kalk-Nichtkarbonathärte *f (hyd)* calcium non-carbonate hardness
Kalkofen *m* lime kiln
Kalkoolith *m (min)* calcareous oolite, *(as rock also)* oolitic limestone
Kalkpflanze *f* calcicole, calciphile
Kalkputz *f* lime plaster
kalkreich rich in lime, high-lime
Kalkringofen *m* lime ring furnace *(for lime burning)*
Kalk-Rost-Schicht *f*, **Kalk-Rost-Schutzschicht** *f* chalky-rust film *(as in water supply lines)*
Kalksaccharat *n* lime saccharate
Kalksaccharatverfahren *n* **nach Steffen** Steffen process *(for desugarizing molasses)*
Kalksalpeter *m* nitrate of lime, lime saltpetre, calcium nitrate; *(min)* lime saltpetre, kalksaltpetre, nitrocalcite
Kalksandstein *m* sandy (psammitic) limestone
Kalkschachtofen *m* lime tunnel furnace
Kalkschatten *mpl (tann)* lime blasts (specks), blasting *(a result of incorrect liming)*
Kalkscheidung *f (sugar)* lime defecation
Kalkschlamm *m* lime mud (sludge); *(pap)* carbonate sludge, paper-mill sludge
Kalkschlammwäscher *m* lime mud washer
Kalkschwefelleber *f* liver of lime, sulphurated lime *(a mixture of calcium sulphides and calcium sulphate)*
Kalkschwefelnatriumäscher *m (tann)* sharpened lime *(cream of lime treated with sodium sulphide)*
Kalkseife *f* lime soap
Kalksilt *m (geol)* calcareous mud
Kalksinter *m (geol)* calcareous sinter
Kalk-Soda-Verfahren *n* 1. lime-soda caustic process *(for producing sodium hydroxide)*; 2. *(hyd)* lime-soda [softening] process, cold lime process
Kalkspat *m (min)* calc-spar, calcite *(calcium carbonate)*
Kalkstein *m* limestone
~/dolomitischer dolomitic (high-magnesium) limestone
Kalksteineinlauf *m (pap)* limestone charging
Kalksteinfüllung *f (pap)* limestone packing
Kalkstickstoff *m* nitrolime, lime nitrogen *(calcium cyanamide)*
Kalkstickstoffverfahren *n* cyanamide process *(for producing ammonia)*
Kalkteig *m (build)* lime putty *(calcium hydroxide containing free water)*
Kalktrichterofen *m* lime funnel furnace
Kalktuff *m* calcareous tufa, tufaceous limestone, tufa
Kalktünche *f* limewash
Kalktunnelofen *m* lime tunnel kiln
Kalküberschuß *m (hyd)* excess of lime
Kalküberschußverfahren *n (hyd)* excess-lime process
Kalkung *f* 1. *(sugar)* liming, defecation; *(agric)* liming; *(hyd)* [partial] lime softening; 2. liming-out *(manufacture of organic intermediates)*; 3. whitewashing *(as of walls)*
Kalkverfahren *n (hyd)* [partial] lime softening process
Kalkversorgungsgrad *m (agric)* lime status
Kalkwasser *n* lime water *(an alkaline aqueous solution of calcium hydroxide)*
Kalkwasserpumpe *f (hyd)* lime feeder
Kalk-Zeolith-Verfahren *n (hyd)* lime-zeolite [softening] process
Kallait *m (min)* kallaite, turquois[e] *(a hydrous basic aluminium copper phosphate)*

Kallidin *n* kallidin *(a decapeptide)*
Kallikrein *n* kallikrein *(a pancreatic enzyme)*
Kalling-Domnarvet-Verfahren *n (met)* Kaldo process *(oxygen process of steelmaking)*
Kallitypieverfahren *n* kallitype *(reprography)*
Kalomel *m (min)* calomel, horn mercury *(mercury(I) chloride)*
Kalomel *n s.* Quecksilber(I)-chlorid
Kalomelelektrode *f* calomel electrode
~/gesättigte saturated calomel electrode, S.C.E.
Kalomelnormalelektrode *f* normal calomel electrode
Kalorie *f* calorie *(non-SI unit of heat energy; 1 cal = 4.1868 J)*
~/thermochemische thermochemical calorie *(non-SI unit of heat energy; 1 cal_{th} = 4.184 J)*
Kaloriengehalt *m* calorie content
Kalorimeter *n* calorimeter
~/adiabatisches adiabatic calorimeter
~ für Gase gas calorimeter
~/isothermes isothermal calorimeter
~ von Nernst Nernst calorimeter
Kalorimeterbombe *f* calorimeter (calorimetric, explosion) bomb, [oxygen] bomb calorimeter
Kalorimeterflüssigkeit *f* calorimetric liquid (fluid)
Kalorimetergefäß *n* calorimeter (calorimetric) vessel
Kalorimeterschälchen *n* calorimeter fusion cup
Kalorimetrie *f* calorimetry
kalorimetrisch calorimetric[al]
kalorisch caloric
kalorisieren to calorize *(steel or cast iron)*
Kalottenmodell *n* space-filling model *(of molecules)*
Kalotypie *f (phot)* calotype process
kaltabbindend cold-curing, cold-setting
Kaltalkalisierung *f (pap)* cold [alkali] refining
Kaltansatzlack *m* cold-cut varnish
kaltblasen to steam *(in producing water gas)*
Kaltblasen *n* steaming, run *(in producing water gas)*
Kaltbleiche *f (pap)* cold bleach[ing]
kaltbrüchig *(met)* cold-short
Kaltbrüchigkeit *f (met)* cold shortness
Kaltdampftechnik *f (spectr)* cold-vapour technique
Kaltdampfverdichteranlage *f* vapour-compression system
Kälte *f* cold[ness]
Kälteanlage *f* refrigerating (cooling) plant
Kältebad *n* cold bath
kältebeständig cold-resistant, resistant to cold
Kältebeständigkeit *f* resistance to cold, cold (low-temperature) resistance
Kältebeständigkeitsprüfung *f* cold (low-temperature) test
Kältebiegeprüfung *f* cold-bend test
Kältebruchtemperatur *f* brittle-point temperature, brittleness (brittle) temperature
kälteerzeugend frigorific, refrigerant
Kälteerzeugung *f* cold production
Kälteerzeugungsanlage *f* refrigerating (cooling) plant
Kältefestigkeit *f s.* 1. Kältebeständigkeit; 2. Kältesprödigkeitspunkt
Kälteflexibilität *f* low-temperature flexibility
Kälteisolierung *f* low-temperature insulation
Kälteleistung *f* refrigeration performance
Kälteleistungszahl *f* performance coefficient
Kältemaschine *f* refrigerating (cooling) machine, refrigerator
Kältemaschinenanlage *f* refrigerating (cooling) plant
Kältemischung *f* freezing mixture
Kältemittel *n* refrigerant
Kältemitteldampf *m* refrigerant vapour
Kälteprüfung *f* low-temperature test, cold test
Kältesole *f* refrigerating brine, cooling (cold) brine
Kältesprödigkeit *f* low-temperature brittleness
Kältesprödigkeitspunkt *m (rubber)* brittle point
Kältestabilisierung *f* chill-proofing *(of beer)*
Kältetechnik *f* low-temperature engineering (technology)
Kälteträger *m* secondary refrigerant, *(esp)* refrigerating brine, cooling (cold) brine
Kältetrub *m (ferm)* cold sludge
Kältetrübung *f (ferm)* chill haze
Kälteverhalten *n* low-temperature behaviour (characteristics, properties)
kaltfärbend cold-dyeing
Kaltfetten *n (tann)* dubbing, hand stuffing
Kaltfiltration *f* cold filtration
Kaltformteil *n (plast)* cold moulding
Kaltgärhefe *f* cold-tolerant yeast
Kaltgas *n* cold gas
Kaltgasanlage *f* gas-cycle refrigeration system
kalthärten *(plast)* to cure cold; *(met)* to work-harden
kalthärtend 1. *(plast)* cold-curing, cold-setting; 2. *s.* kaltvulkanisierend
Kalthärtung *f (plast)* cold curing; *(met)* work hardening
Kaltkammerdruckgießen *n*, **Kaltkammerdruckguß** *m* cold-chamber die-casting (pressure casting) *(foundry)*
Kaltkatoden-Ionisationsvakuummeter *n* cold-cathode ionization gauge, Penning (Philips) gauge
Kaltkautschuk *m* cold [polymerized] rubber, low-temperature polymer (rubber), LTP
Kaltkleber *m* cold adhesive
Kaltlack *m* cold-cut varnish
Kaltlagerung *f* cold storage
Kaltlatex *m* cold rubber latex
Kaltlauge *f* cool brine *(potash industry)*
Kaltleim *m* cold glue
Kaltlötmittel *n* cold-soldering flux
Kaltluft *f* cold air
Kaltmahlen *n* cold milling
Kaltmalerei *f (glass)* cold painting
Kaltmastikation *f*, **Kaltmastizierung** *f (rubber)* cold mastication
Kaltnatron-Halbzellstoff *m* cold soda pulp
Kaltnatronverfahren *n s.* Kaltsodaverfahren

Kaltnetzer *m* cold wetting agent
Kaltpolymerisation *f* cold polymerization
kaltpressen 1. *(met)* to cold-press; *(plast)* to cold-mould; 2. to cold-press, to cold-draw *(oils)*
Kaltpreßmasse *f (plast)* cold-moulding compound (material)
kaltpreßschweißen to cold-weld
Kalträucherei *f (food)* cold smoking
kalträuchern *(food)* to cold-smoke
kaltrecken *(plast)* to cold-draw
Kaltrecken *n (plast)* cold drawing (stretching, orientation)
Kaltsäureverfahren *n* cold acid process *(catalytic polymerization)*
kaltschlagen *s.* kaltpressen 2.
Kaltschleifen *n (pap)* cold grinding
Kaltschliff *m (pap)* cold-ground pulp
Kaltschmieren *n s.* Kaltfetten
Kaltsodastoff *m (pap)* cold soda pulp
Kaltsodaverfahren *n (pap)* cold [caustic] soda process, cold caustic semichemical process
Kaltsterilisation *f* cold sterilization
Kaltstich *m* cold pass *(in powder rolling)*
Kaltstrecken *n s.* Kaltrecken
Kaltumformen *n* cold forming (working)
kaltverarbeiten to cold-work
kaltveredeln *(pap)* to refine by the cold [alkali] process
Kaltveredelung *f (pap)* cold [alkali] refining
kaltverfestigen to work-harden *(metals)*
Kaltverformung *f s.* Kaltumformen
kaltverpressen *(plast)* to cold-mould
Kaltverstrecken *n s.* Kaltrecken
Kaltverweil-Färbeverfahren *n (text)* pad-batch process
Kaltvulkanisat *n* cold vulcanizate
Kaltvulkanisation *f* cold curing (cure, vulcanization)
~ **nach dem Dunstverfahren** vapour curing
kaltvulkanisieren to cure (vulcanize) at room temperature
kaltvulkanisierend room-temperature-curing, room-temperature-vulcanizing, RTV
Kaltwalzen *n* cold rolling
Kaltwalzstich *m s.* Kaltstich
Kaltwaschechtheit *f* fastness to cold washing
Kaltwasserextrakt *m* cold-water extract
Kaltwellbehandlung *f (cosmet)* cold[-permanent] waving
Kaltwelle *f (cosmet)* cold wave
Kaltwellösung *f* cold-[permanent-]waving lotion, cold-permanent-wave lotion
Kaltwellpräparat *n* cold-permanent-waving preparation, cold-permanent-wave preparation
Kaltwerden *n* cooling[-down]
Kaltwind *m (met)* cold[-air] blast
kaltziehen to cold-draw *(metals)*
Kalzimeter *n (soil)* calcimeter
Kalzination *f s.* Kalzinierung
kalzinieren to calcine, to burn
Kalzinierofen *m* calcining furnace, calciner
Kalzinierung *f* calcination, calcining, burning
Kalzinierungsprodukt *n* calcine, calx
Kalzinierzone *f* calcining zone (compartment)
Kalzium *n s.* Calcium
Kalzium... *s. a.* Calcium...
Kalziumkarbonathärte *f (hyd)* calcium carbonate hardness
Kalzium-Nichtkarbonathärte *f (hyd)* calcium noncarbonate hardness
Kamazit *m (min)* kamacite *(a nickel-iron alloy occurring in meteoric iron)*
Kamin *m* [smoke]stack, chimney; *(distil)* riser [pipe, tube], chimney *(of a cap)*
Kamineffekt *m* chimney effect
Kaminklappe *f* stack valve
Kaminkühlturm *m* atmospheric (natural-draught) cooling tower
Kaminstummel *m (distil)* riser [pipe, tube], chimney
Kaminwirkung *f* chimney effect
Kaminzug *m* draught, *(Am)* draft
Kammblende *f (spectr)* comb-shaped shutter, comb attenuator
Kammer *f* chamber, cabinet, box, *(if one of several:)* compartment
~/feuchte humidity chamber; *(lab)* moist-chamber culture dish
~/ringförmige annular chamber
Kammerabscheider *m* [gravity] settling chamber, expansion (fall-out) chamber, drop-out box *(gas cleaning)*
Kammerbegasung *f* chamber fumigation *(pest control)*
Kammerfilterpresse *f* chamber [filter] press, recessed-plate [filter] press
Kammerjäger *m* exterminator
Kammerofen *m (met)* chamber furnace; *(ceram)* chamber (box) kiln
Kammerofenkoks *m* oven coke
Kammerpresse *f s.* Kammerfilterpresse
Kammerraum *m* chamber space *(in manufacturing sulphuric acid)*
Kammerreaktion *f* chamber reaction *(in manufacturing sulphuric acid)*
Kammerringofen *m* annular chamber kiln
Kammersättigung *f (chromat)* chamber saturation
Kammersäure *f* chamber [sulphuric] acid
Kammerscheider *m***[/elektrostatischer]** plate separator
Kammertrockner *m* cabinet[-type air] dryer *(with only one chamber)*; compartment dryer *(with multiple chambers)*; *(ceram)* chamber dryer
~ **mit Hordenwagen** [tray-]truck dryer
Kammerverfahren *n* chamber process *(for manufacturing sulphuric acid)*
Kammervergasung *f* chamber fumigation *(pest control)*

Kammerwärmeaustauscher *m*, **Kammerwärmeübertrager** *m* plate heat exchanger
Kammerzentrifuge *f* multichamber centrifuge
Kammzug *m (text)* slubbing, top
Kammzugdruck *m (text)* vigoureux printing
Kammzugfärbeapparat *m (text)* top-dyeing machine
Kammzugfärben *n (text)* top dyeing
Kampescheholz *n* Campe[a]chy wood, logwood *(from Haematoxylum campechianum L.)*
Kampfer *m s.* Campher
Kämpferol *n* kaempferol, 3,4',5,7-tetrahydroxyflavone
Kampfmittel *n*/**biologisches** biological warfare agent
Kampfstoff *m* warfare agent
~/**biologischer** *s.* Kampfmittel/biologisches
~/**blasenziehender** blister agent, vesicant
~/**chemischer** chemical weapon (warfare agent), war gas
~/**erstickender** choking gas
~/**flüchtiger** non-persistent chemical agent
~/**hautschädigender** blister gas (agent), vesicant
~/**kurzwirkender** *s.* ~/flüchtiger
~/**lakrimogener** *s.* ~/tränenreizender
~/**langwirkender** *s.* ~/seßhafter
~/**lungenschädigender** lung irritant (injurant)
~/**psychotoxischer** psychochemical
~/**seßhafter** persistent chemical agent
~/**tränenreizender** lachrymator, lacrimator
Kamyr-Bleichturm *m (pap)* Kamyr bleacher
Kamyr-Schleifer *m (pap)* Kamyr grinder
Kanadabalsam *m s.* Kanadaterpentin
Kanadaterpentin *n(m)* Canada turpentine, balsam of fir *(from Abies balsamea (L.) Mill.)*
Kanadol *n* canadol *(a light ligroin)*
Kanal *m* 1. *(tech)* canal, *(esp if tubular:)* channel, duct; 2. channel *(of an inclusion compound)*
Kanalbildung *f* channel formation, channelling *(as in column packings or reactors)*
Kanaldispersion *f* eddy (turbulent) dispersion (diffusion)
Kanaleinschlußverbindung *f* channel inclusion compound
Kanalisation *f*, **Kanalisationsnetz** *n s.* Kanalisationssystem
Kanalisationssystem *n (hyd)* sewer (sewage) system, sewerage [system]
~/**städtisches** municipal sewer system
Kanalisierung *f* channel[l]ing *(with ion diffraction)*
Kanalnetz *n s.* Kanalisationssystem
Kanalruß *m (rubber)* channel (impingement) black
~/**mittelverarbeitbarer** medium processing channel black, MPC black
Kanalrußverfahren *n (rubber)* channel method (process)
Kanalschwarz *n s.* Kanalruß
Kanalstrahl *m* canal (positive) ray
Kanalstruktur *f* macroporous structure *(of an ion-exchange resin)*
Kanaltrockner *m* tunnel dryer, drying tunnel
Kanangaöl *n* cananga oil *(from Cananga odorata (Lam.) Hook. f. et Thoms.)*
Kandelillawachs *n* candelilla wax *(from Pedilanthus pavonis (Klotzsch et Gcke.) Boiss.)*
Kandelit *m*, **Kandelkohle** *f s.* Kännelkohle
Kandelzucker *m s.* Kandis[zucker]
Kandis[zucker] *n* candy [sugar], sugar (rock) candy
Kaneel *m*/**Echter** Ceylon cinnamon *(from Cinamomum zeylanicum Bl.)*
Kanister *m* can
Kanne *f (text)* can
Kännelkohle *f* cannel (candle, jet) coal
Kante *f* edge
Kanteneffekt *m (phot)* edge effect
Kantenfilter *n (spectr)* cut-off filter
Kantenschärfe *f (phot)* acutance
Kantenschliff *m (glass)* edging
Kantenversetzung *f (cryst)* edge dislocation
Kantenwinkel *m (cryst)* interfacial angle
kantig angular
Kanutillawachs *n s.* Kandelillawachs
Kanyabutter *f* kanya (Sierra Leone, lamy) butter *(from Pentadesma butyraceum Sabine)*
kanzerogen carcinogenic, cancerigenic, cancer-producing, cancer-causing
~/**nicht** non-carcinogenic
Kanzerogen *n* carcinogen
Kaolin *m* kaolin[e], china (porcelain) clay, white bole, bolus alba
~ **für kautschuktechnische Zwecke** rubber clay
~/**geschlämmter** washed kaolin, water-washed clay
~/**harter** hard [rubber] clay
~/**kolloidaler** colloidal kaolin
~/**trockenaufbereiteter** *(pap)* air-floated clay
~/**weicher** soft [rubber] clay
~/**Zettlitzer** Zettlitz kaolin
Kaolinbrei *m (pap)* clay[-water] slurry
Kaolindispersion *f (pap)* clay milk
Kaolinfüllstoff *m (pap)* clay filler
kaolingefüllt *(pap)* clay-filled
kaolingestrichen *(pap)* clay-coated
Kaolinisation *f* kaolinization
kaolinisieren to kaolinize
Kaolinisierung *f* kaolinization
Kaolinit *m (min)* kaolinite *(aluminium hydroxide silicate)*
kaolinitisch kaolinitic
Kaolinlager *n*, **Kaolinlagerstätte** *f* kaolin deposit
Kaolinmilch *f*, **Kaolintrübe** *f (pap)* clay milk
Kaolinvorkommen *n* kaolin deposit
Kaon *n (nucl)* kaon [particle], K meson
Kap-Aloe *f (pharm)* cape aloe *(from Aloe ferox Mill.)*
Kapazitätsfaktor *m s.* Massenverteilungsverhältnis
Kapazitätsstrom *m* capacity current, charging (double-layer) current *(polarography)*
Kapbeerenwachs *n s.* Myrikatalg
Kapelle *f* 1. *(met)* cupel; 2. *s.* Abzugsschrank

Kapgummi *n* cape gum *(from Acacia specc.)*
kapillar capillary
kapillaraktiv capillary-active, surface-active
Kapillaraktivität *f* capillary (surface) activity
Kapillaranalyse *f* capillary analysis
Kapillaraszension *f* capillary rise
Kapillarattraktion *f s.* Kapillarität
Kapillarbruch *m (text)* capillary breaking
Kapillarchemie *f* capillary chemistry
Kapillarchromatographie *f s.* 1. Kapillarrohrchromatographie; 2. Kapillar-Gaschromatographie
Kapillardepression *f* capillary depression
Kapillardruck *m* capillary pressure
Kapillare *f* capillary [tube]
~/gewendelte *(chromat)* coiled open tube
~/Lugginsche *(phys ch)* Luggin capillary, capillary salt bridge
Kapillarelektrometer *n* capillary electrometer
Kapillaren *fpl***/gestrickte** *(chromat)* knitted capillaries (tubes)
Kapillar-Gaschromatographie *f (anal)* capillary gas chromatography
~ **mit Mikrosäulen** microbore chromatography
Kapillarhahn *m* capillary stopcock
kapillarinaktiv capillary-inactive
Kapillarität *f* capillarity
Kapillaritätskonstante *f* capillary constant
Kapillaritätstheorie *f* **der Gastrennung** capillary theory of separation
Kapillarkondensation *f* capillary condensation (sorption)
Kapillarkonstante *f* capillary constant
Kapillarmethode *f* capillary rise (tube) method *(for determining surface tension)*
Kapillarpipette *f* capillary pipette
Kapillarrohr *n*, **Kapillarröhrchen** *n* capillary [tube]
Kapillarrohrchromatographie *f* capillary [column] chromatography
Kapillarrohre *npl* capillary tubing
Kapillarsäule *f (chromat)* capillary column, *(specif)* open tubular [capillary] column
~/enge narrow-bore open tubular column, small-bore column
~/gefüllte packed capillary column
~/weite wide-bore [open tubular] column
Kapillärsirup *m* starch syrup
Kapillarsperrhahn *m* capillary stopcock
Kapillarviskosimeter *n* capillary viscometer, viscosity pipette
~ **nach Ostwald** Ostwald [capillary] viscometer, Ostwald viscosity pipette
~ **nach Ubbelohde** Ubbelohde viscometer
Kapillarwasser *n (soil)* capillary water
Kapillarwirkung *f* capillary action (attraction)
Kapok *m (text)* kapok, capoc *(fruit fibres esp from Ceiba pentandra Gaertn.)*
Kapoköl *n* kapok oil *(seed oil from Ceiba pentandra Gaertn.)*
Kappe *f* cap; crown, cap *(of a furnace or kiln)*; *(glass)* moil
Kapsel *f* capsule; *(ceram)* saggar, sagger
Kapselgebläse *n* positive displacement (rotary) blower
kapseln to can, to encase, to enclose *(e.g. a pump or motor)*; to waterproof
Kapselpumpe *f* lobe pump
Kapselton *m (ceram)* saggar clay
Kapsenberg-Schmiere *f (lab)* Kapsenberg lubricant
Kapsid *n (bioch)* capsid protein, [viral] coat protein
Karamel *m* caramel, caramelized sugar
Karamelbier *n* malt beer
Karamelgeruch *m* caramel[ized] flavour
Karamelgeschmack *m* caramel[ized] flavour
Karamelisationsbräunung *f* caramelization browning
karamelisieren to caramelize
Karamelisierung *f* caramelization
Karamelmalz *n* caramel (crystal) malt
Karayagummi *n* karaya (sterculia) gum, [gum] karaya, Indian tragacanth *(chiefly from Sterculia urens Roxb.)*
Karayaschleim *m* karaya mucilage *(from Sterculia specc.)*
Karbid *n s.* Carbid
Karbo... *s. a.* Carbo...
Karbonifikation *f (geoch)* coalification, carbonification
Karbonisation *f* 1. *(text)* carbonizing, carbonization *(removal of burrs from raw wool)*; 2. *(food)* carbonation, impregnation [with carbon dioxide], aeration; 3. carbonation *(sodium carbonate manufacture)*
~/nasse *(text)* wet carbonizing
~/trockene *(text)* dry carbonizing
karbonisieren 1. *(text)* to carbonize *(wool)*; 2. *(food)* to carbonate, to impregnate [with carbon dioxide], to aerate; 3. to carbonate *(in sodium-carbonate manufacture)*
Karbonisierhilfsmittel *n*, **Karbonisiernetzmittel** *n* *(text)* carbonizing assistant
Karbonkohle *f* carboniferous coal
Karbonpapier *n* carbon paper, carbonic (carbonized) paper
karbothermisch *(met)* carbothermic, carbothermal
Karburator *m* carburet[t]or *(for carburetting gases)*
karburieren to carburet *(gases)*
Kardamomöl *n* cardamom (cardamon) oil *(from Elettaria cardamomum (L.) White et Maton)*
Kardiotonikum *n (pharm)* cardiotonic, cardiac tonic
Karenzfrist *f* preharvest interval *(after application of pesticides)*
Karitebutter *f* shea (Bambuk, Galam) butter *(from Butyrospermum parkii (Don) Kotschy)*
Karkasse *f (rubber)* carcass, carcase, casing, case *(of a tyre)*
Karkasseneinlage *f s.* Karkaßlage
Karkassengummi *m* carcass (casing) rubber
Karkaßlage *f (rubber)* carcass (casing) ply

Karkaßmischung *f (rubber)* carcass stock (compound), casing (body) stock
Karl-Fischer-Reagens *n* Karl Fischer reagent *(for determining the amount of water in various substances)*
Karl-Fischer-Titration *f* Karl Fischer titration
Karl-Fischer-Wasserbestimmung *f* Karl Fischer titration
Karnaubawachs *n* carnauba (Brazil) wax *(from Copernicia prunifera (Muell.) H.E. Moore)*
Karpatenbalsam *m* Carpathian (Hungarian) turpentine *(from Pinus cembra L.)*
Karrag[h]een *n (pharm)* carrag[h]een, chondrus *(from marine algae Chondrus crispus (L.) Stackh. and Gigartina mamillosa (Gooden. et Woodw.) J. Agardh)*
Karragheenmoos *n s.* Karrag[h]een
Karrenspritze *f*, **Karrenspritzgerät** *n (agric)* hand-propelled sprayer
Karrensprühgerät *n*, **Karrenzerstäuber** *m s.* Karrenspritze
Karte *f***/ topographische** biochemical map *(as of RNA)*
Karteikarton *m* index board
Kartenpapier *n* map (chart, plan) paper, *(Am)* geography paper
Kartoffelmaische *f* potato mash
Kartoffelmehl *n s.* Kartoffelstärke
Kartoffelschlempe *f* potato slump
Kartoffelspiritus *m*, **Kartoffelsprit** *m* potato alcohol (spirits)
Kartoffelstärke *f* potato starch (flour), farina
Kartoffelwalzmehl *n* potato meal
Karton *m* cardboard, [paper]board
~/gegautschter duplex cardboard
~/geklebter pasteboard, pasted board
~/gestrichener coated [card]board
Kartonagenpappe *f* [folding] boxboard, carton
Kartonfabrik *f* paperboard mill
Kartonmaschine *f* paperboard (vat) machine, board [making] machine
Kartonpapier *n* cardboard
Kartothekkarton *m* index board
Karusselltrockner *m (ceram)* dobbin *(a type of dryer)*
~ mit Luftstromtrocknung jet drying dobbin
Karyolymphe *f (bioch)* karyolymph, nuclear sap
karzinogen carcinogenic, carcinogenous, cancer-causing
~/nicht non-carcinogenic
Karzinogen *n* carcinogen
kaschieren *(pap)* to laminate, to line, to paste, to paper; *(plast)* to laminate, to coat, *(esp using metal:)* to clad
Kaschieren *n* **mit stranggepreßter Folie** *(plast)* extrusion coating
Kaschierpapier *n* lining (pasting) paper, liners
kaschiert/mit Kupfer copper-clad
Kaschunuß *f* cashew nut *(from Anacardium occidentale L.)*
Käse *m* cheese
~/gereifter ripened cheese
~/grüner (ungereifter) green cheese
käseartig curd[l]y
Käsebruch *m* [cheese] curd
Käsefarbe *f* cheese colouring
Käseherstellung *f* cheese making
Kasein *n s.* Casein
Käsemolke *f* cheese whey
Käserei *f* 1. cheese making; 2. cheese factory
Käsereifung *f* cheese ripening
Käsereimilch *f* cheese milk
Käsereimolke *f* cheese whey
Käsewachs *n* cheese wax
Kasha-Regel *f* Kasha['s] rule *(relating to the fluorescence of polyatomic aromatic compounds)*
käsig curd[l]y
Kaskade *f (tech)* cascade *(kind of multistage systems)*
Kaskadenbelüfter *m (hyd)* cascading (gravity) aerator
Kaskadenboden *m* cascade tray *(rectification)*
Kaskadenbodenkolonne *f* baffle[-plate] column, baffle tower [extractor], baffle extraction tower
Kaskadenimpaktor *m* cascade impactor *(for sampling solid and liquid suspensoids in gases)*
Kaskadenmethode *f* cascade method *(gas liquefaction)*
Kaskadenmühle *f* cascade mill
Kaskadenofen *m* cascade burner
Kaskadenreaktor *m* series of stirred-tank reactors, series of perfect mixers, stirred-tank reactors in series
Kaskadenschaltung *f* cascade system
Kaskadentrockner *m* cascade dryer
Kaskadenverdampfer *m* cascade (multiple-effect) evaporator
Kasserollenzange *f* casserole tongs
Kassiaöl *n* cassia (Chinese) oil *(from Cinnamomum aromaticum Nees)*
Kassiazimt *m* Chinese cinnamon *(from Cinnamomum aromaticum Nees)*
Kastanien-Braunerde *f* chestnut soil
kastenaufkohlen to box-carburize *(steel)*
Kastenbandfilter *n* travelling-pan filter, TP filter
Kastenbeschicker *m* box feeder
kasteneinsetzen to box-carburize *(steel)*
kastenglühen to box-anneal *(castings)*
Kastenglühofen *m* box-annealing furnace
Kastenkristallisator *m* tank crystallizer
Kastenmälzerei *f* box malting
kastenzementieren to box-carburize *(steel)*
Kastor *m s.* Kastorzucker
Kastoröl *n* castor oil *(from Ricinus communis L.)*
Kastorzucker *m* castor sugar
Käswasser *n* lactoserum, whey, milk serum
katabol[isch] *(bioch)* catabolic
katabolisieren to catabolize
Katabolismus *m (bioch)* katabolism, catabolism

Katabolit *m (bioch)* catabolite
Katabolitrepression *f (bioch)* catabolite (catabolic) repression *(one form of enzyme repression)*
Kataklase *f (geol)* cataclasis
Katal *n (bioch)* katal, enzyme unit *(of enzyme activity)*
Katalaseaktivität *f* catalase activity
Katalasekomplex *m* catalase complex
Katalaseprobe *f* catalase test
Katalasewirkung *f* catalase action
Katalysator *m* [reaction] catalyst, catalyzer, cat
~/beweglicher (bewegter) moving catalyst
~/bifunktioneller bifunctional (dual-function) catalyst *(having e.g. a cracking and a hydrogenating component)*
~ der homogenen Katalyse homogeneous catalyst
~/enzymatischer *(bioch)* enzyme catalyst
~/fest angeordneter *s.* ~/ruhender
~/fester 1. solid catalyst; 2. *s.* ~/ruhender
~/festliegender *s.* ~/ruhender
~/gepulverter powdered catalyst
~/heterogener heterogeneous (contact) catalyst
~ in Pillenform pelletized catalyst
~/komplexkoordinativer coordination (complexing) catalyst
~/monofunktioneller single-function catalyst
~/negativer negative catalyst, anticatalyst, retarder, inhibitor
~ ohne Stützmaterial (Träger) unsupported catalyst
~/oxidischer oxide catalyst
~/perlförmiger bead catalyst
~/pillenförmiger pelletized catalyst
~/platinhaltiger platinum catalyst
~/positiver positive catalyst
~/pulverisierter (pulvriger) powdered catalyst
~/ruhender static (fixed-bed) catalyst
~/sich bewegender moving catalyst
~/stereospezifischer stereospecific catalyst
~/technischer commercial catalyst
~/vorreduzierter prereduced catalyst
Katalysatorabfall *m (petrol)* complex out *(in liquid-phase isomerization)*
Katalysatoraktivität *f* catalyst activity
Katalysatorauswaschkolonne *f* catalyst scrubber column
Katalysatorbett *n* catalyst bed
~/bewegtes moving catalyst bed
~/festes (festliegendes) *s.* ~/ruhendes
~/ruhendes (stationäres) static bed of catalyst, fixed catalyst bed
Katalysatordesaktivierung *f* catalyst deactivation
Katalysatorgemisch *n* catalyst mixture
Katalysatorgift *n* catalyst (catalytic) poison, paralyzer
Katalysatorkammer *f* catalyst chamber
Katalysatorkation *n* catalyst cation
Katalysatorkomplex *m* catalyst-reactant complex
Katalysatorkorn *n* catalyst particle
Katalysatorkreislauf *m* catalyst circulation (cycle, recycle)
Katalysatorleistung *f* catalyst performance
Katalysatoroberfläche *f* catalyst surface
Katalysator-Öl-Verhältnis *n* catalyst/oil ratio, catalyst-to-oil ratio
Katalysatorpellet *n*, **Katalysatorpille** *f* catalyst pellet
Katalysatorpulver *n s.* Katalysatorstaub
Katalysatorregenerator *m* regenerator, kiln *(catalytic cracking)*
Katalysatorregenerierung *f* catalyst regeneration
Katalysatorschicht *f* catalyst bed
~/festliegende static bed of catalyst
Katalysatorschlamm *m* catalyst slurry
Katalysatorselektivität *f* catalyst selectivity
Katalysatorstaub *m* catalyst dust, powdered catalyst
Katalysatorstripper *m* catalyst removal column
Katalysatorsystem *n* catalyst system
Katalysatorträger *m* catalyst support (carrier)
Katalysatorumlauf *m s.* Katalysatorkreislauf
Katalysatorvergiftung *f* catalyst poisoning
Katalysatorwirksamkeit *f* catalyst activity
Katalysatorwirkung *f* catalyst action
Katalyse *f* catalysis
~/bifunktionelle bifunctional catalysis
~/elektrophile electrophilic catalysis *(by Lewis acids)*
~/heterogene heterogeneous catalysis, contact (surface) catalysis
~/homogene homogeneous catalysis
~/kovalente covalent catalysis
~/mizellare micellar catalysis
~/negative inhibition, *(deprecated:)* negative catalysis
~/nukleophile nucleophilic catalysis
~/positive positive catalysis
~/spezifische specific catalysis
~/stereospezifische stereospecific catalysis
Katalysegesetz *n*/**Brönstedsches** [Brønsted] catalysis law
Katalysekonstante *f* catalytic coefficient
Katalysemechanismus *m* catalytic mechanism
~/enzymatischer *(bioch)* enzyme mechanism
Katalyseofen *m* catalytic reactor
Katalysewirkung *f* catalytic action; catalytic effect
katalysieren to catalyse
katalysiert/basisch base-catalysed
~/sauer acid-catalysed
katalytisch catalytic
Kataphorese *f* cataphoresis
kataphoretisch cataphoretic
Katechin *n s.* Catechin
Katechingerbstoff *m* catechol tan
Katechu *n (tann, dye, pharm)* catechu, cutch, *(pharm specif)* black (dark) catechu *(from Acacia catechu Willd.)*
~/Braunes [black, dark] catechu, Pegu catechu (cutch) *(from Acacia catechu Willd.)*
~/Gelbes pale catechu, white cutch, gambi[e]r, catechu [gum] *(from Uncaria gambir Roxb.)*

Kathämoglobin *n (bioch)* kathaemoglobin
Katharometer *n* katharometer, hot-wire reference and detector cell *(a thermal-conductivity cell)*
Kathartikum *n (pharm)* cathartic
Kathedralglas *n* cathedral glass
Kathode *f s.* Katode
Kation *n* cation • **von Kationen befreien** to decationize
~/komplexes complex cation
kationaktiv *s.* kationenaktiv
kationenaktiv cation-active, cationic
Kationen-Anionen-Austauscher *m (hyd)* two-bed cation-anion exchanger
Kationenaustausch *m* cation exchange
Kationenaustauschadsorption *f* cation-exchange adsorption
Kationenaustauschbett *n* cation-exchange bed
Kationenaustauscher *m* cation[ic] exchanger, *(as part of a demineralizing system:)* cation unit
~/schwach saurer *(hyd)* weak-acid cation exchanger, weakly acidic cation exchanger, carboxylic exchanger
~/stark saurer *(hyd)* strong-acid cation exchanger, strongly acidic cation exchanger, sulphonic exchanger
Kationenaustauscher... *s.* Kationenaustausch...
Kationenaustauschfähigkeit *f* cation exchange ability
Kationenaustauschharz *n* cation-exchange resin
Kationenaustauschkapazität *f* cation-exchange capacity, CEC, total exchangeable bases
Kationenaustauschmaterial *n* cation-exchange material
Kationenaustauschsäule *f* cation-exchange column
Kationenaustauschverfahren *n* cation-exchange method
Kationenbelastung *f (hyd)* cation loading
Kationenelektrode *f* cathodized (cathodic) electrode
Kationenfehlstelle *f*, **Kationenleerstelle** *f* cation vacancy, vacant cation site
Kationen-Neutralaustausch-Verfahren *n (hyd)* sodium cation exchanger process, sodium cycle exchange
Kationenschwarm *m (coll)* cation swarm
Kationenstufe *f (hyd)* cation unit *(of a demineralizing system)*
Kationentrennungsgang *m* scheme of analysis for the cations, cation scheme
Kationenüberführungszahl *f* cation transference number
Kationenumtausch *m* cation exchange
kationisch cationic
Kationit *m* cation exchanger
kationkapillaraktiv cation-active
kationoid cationoid, electrophilic, electron-attracting, electron-withdrawing
kationotrop cationotropic
Kationotropie *f* cationotropy
Kationsäure *f (phys ch)* cation[ic] acid
Kationseife *f* cationic (invert) soap
Kationtensid *n* cationic [surfactant]
Katkracken *n (petrol)* cat (catalyst, catalytic) cracking
~ im Orthoflow-Verfahren Orthoflow catalytic cracking
Katode *f* cathode, negative electrode
~/flüssige pool cathode
Katodenabfall *m s.* Katodenspannungsabfall
Katodenblock *m* cathode assembly *(electrolysis)*
Katodendunkelraum *m* cathode (Crookes) dark space
Katodenglimmschicht *f* cathode-glow layer
Katodenkupfer *n* cathode (electrolytic) copper
Katodenlumineszenz *f* cathode luminescence, cathodoluminescence
Katodennickel *n* cathode (electrolytic) nickel
Katodenpotential *n* cathode potential
Katodenraum *m* cathode compartment
Katodenreaktion *f* cathode reaction
Katodenspannungsabfall *m* cathode drop *(drop of emf near the cathode)*
Katodenstrahl *m* cathode ray
Katodenstrahlpolarograph *m (anal)* single-sweep polarograph
Katodenstrahlpolarographie *f (anal)* single-sweep polarography
Katodenstrahlröhre *f* cathode-ray tube
Katodenstrom *m* cathode current
Katodenzerstäubung *f* cathode sputtering
katodisch cathodic
Katodolumineszenz *f s.* Katodenlumineszenz
Katolyt *m* catholyte *(electrolyte surrounding a cathode)*
Katzenauge *n (min)* cat's eye *(a variety of either quartz or chrysoberyl)*
Katzengold *n (min)* cat gold *(a partly weathered biotite)*
Katzensilber *n (min)* cat silver, potassium mica, muscovite *(a phyllosilicate)*
Kauren *n* kaurene *(a terpene)*
Kauri-Butanol-Wert *m*, **Kauri-Butanol-Zahl** *f (coat)* kauri-butanol number (value)
Kaurigum *m*, **Kauriharz** *n s.* Kaurikopal
Kaurikopal *m* kauri copal (gum, resin), cowrie *(from Agathis australis Salisb.)*
Kauriöl *n* kauri oil *(from Agathis australis Salisb.)*
Kaurireduktionsprüfung *f* kauri-reduction test
Kaustifizieranlage *f (pap)* causticizing department (plant, room)
Kaustifizierbehälter *m*, **Kaustifizierbottich** *m (pap)* causticizing tank, causticizer
kaustifizieren *(pap)* to [re]causticize
Kaustifizierung *f (pap)* causticization, [re]causticizing
Kaustikum *n (med)* caustic agent
kaustisch caustic
kaustizieren *s.* kaustifizieren

Kauterisation *f (med)* cauterization, cautery *(burning of tissue with a caustic or heat)*
Kautschuk *m(n)* rubber, caoutchouc
~/anorganischer phosphorus dichloride nitride
~/cyclisierter cyclized rubber, cyclorubber
~/eiweißarmer (enteiweißter) deproteinized rubber
~/gefrorener frozen rubber
~/kalt polymerisierter cold [polymerized] rubber, low-termperature polymer (rubber), LTP
~/künstlicher *s.* ~/synthetischer
~ mit geringem Spannungswert low-modulus rubber
~ mit hohem Spannungswert high-modulus rubber
~ mit mittlerem Spannungswert medium-modulus rubber
~ mit niederem Spannungswert low-modulus rubber
~/ölgestreckter (ölhaltiger, ölplastizierter) oil-extended rubber
~/regenerierter reclaimed rubber, reclaim, shoddy
~/synthetischer synthetic rubber, artificial (man-made, chemical) rubber
~/technisch klassifizierter technically classified rubber, T.C. rubber
~/totgewalzter (totmastizierter) dead-rolled (dead-milled) rubber, dead rubber
~/übermastizierter *s.* ~/totgewalzter
~/universeller general-purpose rubber
~/vulkanisierter vulcanized (cured) rubber
kautschukähnlich, kautschukartig rubber-like
Kautschukballen *m* bale of rubber
Kautschukbaum *m* rubber tree
Kautschukchemie *f* rubber chemistry
Kautschukchemiker *m* rubber chemist
Kautschukderivat *n* rubber derivative
Kautschukdibromid *n* rubber dibromide
Kautschukelastizität *f* rubber (long-range) elasticity
Kautschukfell *n* rubber sheet
Kautschuk-Füllstoff-Gel-Komplex *m* rubber-filler gel
Kautschuk-Füllstoff-Mischung *f* rubber-filler (rubber-pigment) mixture (stock)
Kautschukgehalt *m* rubber-hydrocarbon content, RHC
Kautschukgift *n* rubber poison
Kautschukhydrochlorid *n* rubber hydrochloride
Kautschukhydrofluorid *n* rubber hydrofluoride
Kautschukindustrie *f* rubber[-manufacturing] industry
Kautschuk-Klebestoff *m* rubber-base adhesive
Kautschukkohlenwasserstoff *m* rubber hydrocarbon
Kautschukkuchen *m (rubber)* slab
Kautschuk-KW *m s.* Kautschukkohlenwasserstoff
Kautschuklatex *m* rubber latex
~/synthetischer synthetic[-rubber] latex
kautschuklöslich rubber-soluble
Kautschuklösung *f* rubber solution (cement)
Kautschuklösungsmittel *n* rubber solvent
Kautschukmilch *f*, **Kautschukmilchsaft** *m* rubber latex (milk)
Kautschukmischung *f* rubber stock (mixture, compound)
Kautschukpflanze *f* rubber[-yielding] plant, rubber-producing (rubber-bearing) plant
Kautschukplantage *f* rubber plantation
Kautschukplatte *f (rubber)* slab
Kautschukpulver *n* rubber powder
Kautschukqualität *f* grade of rubber
Kautschuk-Schwefel-Mischung *f* rubber-sulphur blend (compound, mixture, stock)
Kautschukspalter *m (rubber)* bale cutter (splitting machine), splitter
Kautschuktechnologe *m* rubber technologist
Kautschuktechnologie *f* rubber technology
Kautschukträger *m s.* Kautschukpflanze
Kautschuktrockengehalt *m* dry rubber content, DRC
Kautschuktrockensubstanz *f (rubber)* solid material, total solids, T.S.
Kautschukverarbeitung *f*/**trockene** dry rubber manufacture
Kautschukvulkanisat *n* rubber vulcanizate, vulcanized (cured) rubber
Kavitation *f* cavitation
Kawaharz *n* kava resin *(from Piper methysticum G. Forst.)*
Kawain *n* kawain, 5,6-dihydro-4-methoxy-6-styrylpyran-2-one
Kawasäure *f* kawaic (kavaic) acid, *3-methoxy-7-phenyl-2,4,6-heptatrienoic acid
Kaysam-Prozeß *m (rubber)* Kaysam process
KBr-Pille *f*, **KBr-Scheibe** *f s.* KBr-Tablette
KBr-Tablette *f (spectr)* potassium bromide pellet
KD-Effekt *m* knockdown effect *(of certain pesticides)*
KDPG-Weg *m* Entner-Doudoroff pathway *(of glucose degradation via 2-keto-3-deoxy-6-phosphogluconate)*
Kefir *m (food)* kefir, kephir
Kefirkörner *npl (food)* kefir grains (seeds)
Kegel *m* 1. *(met)* cone *(of a blast furnace)*; 2. *s.* Kegelrotor
~/pyrometrischer *(ceram)* pyrometric (fusion) cone
~/standardisierter *(ceram)* standard cone
Kegelbrecher *m* cone (conical, gyratory) crusher
Kegeldichtring *m* V-ring, V-seal
Kegel-Filtrierzentrifuge *f* conical-screen centrifuge
Kegelgranulator *m* short-head cone crusher
Kegelmesser *npl (pap)* core bars, bars on the rotor, bars in the plug *(of a perfecting engine)*
Kegelmischer *m* conical mixer
Kegelmühle *f* 1. conical grinder, cone mill, rotary crusher; 2. *s.* Kegelstoffmühle
Kegelrefiner *m (pap)* conical refiner
Kegelring *m*, **Kegelringdichtung** *f* V-ring, V-seal

Kegelrotor *m (pap)* rotor, core, cone, plug *(of a perfecting engine)*
~ der Kegelstoffmühle jordan plug (rotor)
Kegelschliffverbindung *f* conical [ground-glass] joint, tapered joint
Kegelstoffmühle *f (pap)* perfecting engine, jordan, refining machine (engine), refiner
Kegelstrahldüse *f* swirl[-plate] nozzle, hollow-cone nozzle
Kegeltrommel *f* conical bowl *(as of a centrifuge)*
Keilschieber *m* wedge gate valve
Keilspaltsieb *n* wedge-wire screen
Keilstreifen *m* **[nach Matthias]** *(chromat)* tapered strip
Keim *m* 1. *(cryst)* nucleus; 2. *(med, food, hyd)* germ, microbe
~/krankheitserregender (pathogener) *(food, hyd)* pathogen
Keimabtötung *f s.* Keimtötung
Keimbildner *m (cryst)* nucleation (nucleating) agent, nucleator
Keimbildung *f (cryst)* nucleation, nucleus formation, formation of nuclei
~/athermische *s.* ~/heterogene
~/heterogene heterogeneous (induced) nucleation
~/homogene homogeneous (spontaneous) nucleation
~/primäre primary nucleation
~/sekundäre secondary (surface) nucleation
~/simultane *s.* ~/heterogene
~/spontane (sporadische) *s.* ~/homogene
~/thermische *s.* ~/homogene
~ und Keimwachstum *n* nucleation and growth
Keimbildungsarbeit *f* nucleation energy
Keimbildungsgeschwindigkeit *f* nucleation rate, rate of nucleation
Keimbildungstheorie *f (cryst)* nucleation hypothesis
keimfrei *(med)* sterile, aseptic • **~ machen** to sterilize, to degerm
Keimfreiheit *f (med)* sterility, asepsis
Keimfreimachung *f (med)* sterilization, degermation
Keimkristall *m* seed crystal
Keimöl *n (food)* germ oil
keimtötend sterilizing, germicidal, disinfectant
Keimtötung *f* kill[ing] of germs, kill[ing] of microbes
Keimungsmedium *n (biot)* germination (spore-germinating) medium
Keimzahl *f* 1. *(cryst)* number of nuclei; 2. *(med, food, hyd)* bacterial count, number of bacteria *(per unit amount of sample)*
K-Einfang *m* K[-electron] capture
Kekulé-Formel *f (org ch)* Kekulé formula
Kekulé-Grenzstrukturen *fpl*, **Kekulé-Strukturen** *fpl* Kekulé[-like] structures
K-Elektron *n* K electron
K-Elektroneneinfang *m s.* K-Einfang
Kelle *f (glass)* ladle
Kellerbehandlung *f (ferm)* cellar treatment
Kellog-Flugstaubverfahren *n (coal)* Kellog fluidized synthesis *(of hydrocarbons)*
Kellogg-Synthese *f s.* Kellog-Flugstaubverfahren
Kellog-Verfahren *n* 1. *(coal)* Kellog [coal] gasification process, Kellog molten salt process; 2. *s.* Kellog-Flugstaubverfahren
Kelly-Filter *n*, **Kelly-Presse** *f* Kelly filter
Kelly-Stange *f (petrol)* kelly
Kelp *n* kelp *(the ashes of seaweed)*
Kelter *f (ferm)* [grape, wine] press
keltern to press *(grapes)*
Kelvin-Skale *f* Kelvin [temperature] scale
Kelvin-Temperatur *f* thermodynamic (absolute) temperature
Kennelkohle *f s.* Kännelkohle
Kennlinie *f* characteristic curve
Kennwert *m* characteristic [value]
~/verarbeitungstechnischer processing characteristic
Kennzahl *f* characteristic, coefficient, number, value, index
~/Froudesche Froude['s] number *(fluid mechanics)*
Kennziffer *f s.* Kennzahl
Kerametall *n* cermet, ceramal
Keramik *f* ceramics *(art, process, or products)*
~ für chemische Zwecke chemical ceramics
~/technische technical ceramics
Keramikchemiker *m* ceramic chemist
Keramiker *m* ceramist
Keramikfaser *f* ceramic fibre (staple)
Keramikfilter *n* ceramic filter
Keramikschüttung *f* ceramic packing
keramisch ceramic
Kerargyrit *m (min)* cerargyrite, chlorargyrite, horn silver *(silver chloride)*
Kerasin *n* kerasin *(a cerebroside)*
Keratansulfat *n (bioch)* kerato sulphate
Keratin *n* keratin *(a scleroprotein)*
Keratinisation *f (biol)* keratinization
Kerbeinflußzahl *f s.* Kerbwirkungszahl
kerbempfindlich notch-sensitive
Kerbempfindlichkeit *f* notch sensitivity
kerben to notch
Kerbschlagzähigkeit *f* notch impact resistance (strength)
~ nach Izod *(plast)* Izod impact strength
Kerbwirkungsfaktor *m*, **Kerbwirkungszahl** *f* notch factor *(materials science)*
Kermes *m* 1. *(dye)* kermes [grains], kermes berries, grains of kermes, scarlet corns *(the dried bodies of the females of various scales, genus Kermes)*; 2. kermes scarlet, kermes [dye]; 3. kermes [mineral] *(a double compound of antimony trisulphide and antimony trioxide)*
~/mineralischer *s.* Kermes 3.
Kermesfarbstoff *m s.* Kermes 2.
Kermesit *m (min)* kermesite, red antimony *(antimony(III) oxide sulphide)*

Kermeskörner *npl s.* Kermes 1.
Kermessäure *f* kermesic acid *(an anthraquinone derivative)*
Kermesscharlach *m s.* Kermes 2.
Kern *m* nucleus *(of an atom, of a cell, of crystallization)*; *(pap)* plug, rotor, core, cone *(of a perfecting machine); (lab)* cone *(of a ground-glass joint)*; *(tann)* butt; *(rubber)* carcass; *(bot)* heartwood
~/anellierter *s.* ~/kondensierter
~/aromatischer *(org ch)* aromatic (benzene) nucleus
~ der Kegelstoffmühle *(pap)* jordan plug (rotor)
~/dunkler *(pap)* burnt centre *(in a chip)*
~/kondensierter *(org ch)* condensed (fused) nucleus
~/schwarzer *(ceram)* black core (heart)
Kernabstand *m* internuclear (interatomic) distance, bond length
Kernänderung *f* nuclear change
Kernanregung *f* nuclear excitation
Kernaufbau *m* nuclear structure
Kernbaustein *m* nuclear constituent (particle), nucleon
Kernbildung *f* nucleation, nucleus formation, formation of nuclei *(crystallization, condensation)*
Kernbindemittel *n*, **Kernbinder** *m* core binder (binding agent) *(foundry)*
Kernbohren *n (petrol)* coring
Kernbohrer *m (petrol)* core drill
Kernbrennstoff *m* nuclear (fission) fuel
Kernbruchstück *n* nuclear fragment
Kernchemie *f* nuclear chemistry
Kerndiagramm *n***/elektrisches** *(petrol)* electric log *(in electrical coring)*
Kerndichte *f* nuclear density
Kerndrall *m s.* Kernspin
Kerndrehimpuls *m* nuclear spin (angular momentum)
Kerneigenschaft *f* nuclear property
Kerneinfang *m* nuclear capture
Kerneisen *n* core iron *(reinforcement for heavy cores in foundry)*
Kernemulsion *f (nucl)* nuclear [track] emulsion
Kernemulsionstechnik *f (nucl)* nuclear emulsion technique
Kernen *n (geol)* coring, *(for measuring purposes also)* logging
~/elektrisches electrical coring
Kernenergie *f* nuclear (atomic) energy
Kernenergieniveau *n* nuclear energy level
Kernenergieniveaudichte *f* nuclear energy level density
Kernenzym *n (bioch)* core enzyme
Kernfaden *m (text)* core thread
Kernfeld *n* nuclear field
Kernfeldkräfte *fpl* nuclear forces
Kernfestigkeit *f* core strength *(foundry)*
Kernforschung *f* nuclear research
Kernfusion *f* nuclear fusion
Kern-g-Faktor *m (phys ch)* nuclear g factor
Kerngrundsubstanz *f (bioch)* nuclear sap, karyolymph, enchylema
Kernguß *m (ceram)* solid casting
kernhalogeniert ring-halogenated
Kernhalogenierung *f* ring halogenation
Kernherstellung *f* core making *(foundry)*
Kernholz *n* heartwood
Kerninduktion *f* nuclear induction
Kernisobar *n* nuclear isobar
Kernisomere *n* nuclear isomer
Kernisomerie *f* nuclear isomerism
Kernit *m (min)* kernite *(a hydrous basic sodium borate)*
Kern-Kern-Achse *f s.* Kernverbindungsachse
Kern-Kern-Doppelresonanz *f (anal)* internuclear double resonance, INDOR
Kern-Kern-Verbindungsachse *f s.* Kernverbindungsachse
Kernkettenreaktion *f* nuclear chain reaction
Kernkräfte *fpl* nuclear forces
Kernladung *f* nuclear charge
~/effektive effective charge
Kernladungszahl *f* atomic (ordinal) number, A.N., *(symbol)* Z
~/effektive effective atomic number, E.A.N.
~/ungerade odd atomic number
Kernmagnetismus *m* nuclear magnetism
Kernmagneton *n* nuclear magneton
Kernmantelstruktur *f (text)* skin-core structure
Kernmasse *f* nuclear mass
Kernmassezahl *f* [nuclear] mass number, nuclear number
Kernmaterie *f* nuclear matter
Kernmembran *f (bioch)* nuclear membrane
Kernmodell *n* nuclear model
Kernmoment *n***/magnetisches** nuclear magnetic moment
Kernnährstoff *m (agric)* primary nutrient (element)
Kernniveau *n* nuclear energy level
Kernniveaudichte *f* nuclear energy level density
Kernöl *n* 1. *(food)* kernel oil; 2. core oil *(foundry)*
Kern-Overhauser-Effekt *m* nuclear Overhauser effect, NOE
Kernparamagnetismus *m* nuclear paramagnetism
Kernphotoeffekt *m* nuclear photoeffect (photoelectric effect)
Kernphysik *f* nuclear physics
Kernpolarisation *f* nuclear polarization
~/chemisch induzierte dynamische chemically induced dynamic nuclear polarization, CIDNP
Kernpotential *n* nuclear potential
Kernquadrupolmoment *n* nuclear quadrupole moment
Kernquadrupolresonanz *f* nuclear quadrupole resonance, NQR
Kernquadrupolresonanzspektroskopie *f* nuclear quadrupole resonance spectroscopy
Kernquadrupol-Wechselwirkung *f* nuclear quadrupole coupling
Kernradius *m* nuclear radius

Kernreaktion *f* nuclear reaction
Kernreaktionsformel *f*, **Kernreaktionsgleichung** *f* nuclear reaction equation (formula), nuclear equation
Kernreaktor *m* [nuclear] reactor
~/thermischer thermonuclear reactor
Kernresonanz *f* nuclear resonance
~/hochauflösende magnetische high-resolution nmr (nuclear magnetic resonance)
~/magnetische nuclear magnetic resonance, nmr
Kernresonanzabsorption *f* nuclear resonance absorption
Kernresonanzspektrometer *n* nuclear magnetic resonance spectrometer, nmr spectrometer
Kernresonanzspektroskopie *f***[/magnetische]** nuclear magnetic resonance spectroscopy, nmr spectroscopy *(for compounds s.* NMR-Spektroskopie*)*
Kernresonanzspektrum *n***[/magnetisches]** nuclear magnetic resonance spectrum, nmr spectrum
Kern-Ribonucleinsäure *f* nuclear ribonucleic acid, nRNA
Kernrohr *n* inner pipe
Kernsaft *m (bioch)* nuclear sap, karyolymph, enchylema
Kernsand *m* core sand *(foundry)*
Kernsandbindemittel *n*, **Kernsandbinder** *m* core binder (binding agent) *(foundry)*
Kernseife *f* curd soap
Kernspaltung *f***[/gesteuerte]** nuclear fission (disintegration)
Kernspaltungsenergie *f* fission energy
Kernspaltungsspektrum *n* nuclear fission spectrum
Kernspektroskopie *f* nuclear spectroscopy
Kernspin *m* nuclear spin (angular momentum)
Kernspinmoment *n* nuclear spin moment
Kernspin-Operator *m (spectr)* nuclear spin operator
Kernspinquantenzahl *f* nuclear spin quantum number
Kernspinresonanz *f* nuclear magnetic resonance, nmr
Kernsprengstoff *m* nuclear explosive
Kernspur *f* nuclear track
Kernspuremulsion *f* nuclear [track] emulsion
Kernspuremulsionstechnik *f* nuclear emulsion technique
Kernstabilität *f* nuclear stability
Kernstatistik *f* nuclear statistics
Kernstoß *m* nuclear collision
Kernstrahlung *f* nuclear radiation
Kernströmung *f* turbulent core *(as opposed to the laminar boundary layer in pipes)*
Kernstruktur *f* nuclear structure
kernsubstituiert substituted in the ring
Kernsubstitution *f* substitution in the ring
Kernsynthese *f (org ch)* nuclear synthesis; *(nucl)* [nuclear] fusion
Kerntechnik *f* nucleonics
Kernteilchen *n* nuclear particle (constituent), nucleon
Kerntemperatur *f* nuclear temperature
Kernterm *m* nuclear energy level
Kerntheorie *f* nuclear theory
Kernübergang *m* nuclear transition
Kernumwandlung *f* transmutation, nuclear transformation
~/künstliche artificial transmutation (transformation)
Kernveränderung *f* nuclear change
Kernverbindungsachse *f*, **Kernverbindungslinie** *f* internuclear axis (line)
Kernverdampfung *f* nuclear evaporation
Kernverschmelzung *f* [nuclear] fusion
Kernwicklung *f (pap)* centre rewind method
Kernzerfall *m* nuclear decay (disintegration)
Kernzersplitterung *f*, **Kernzertrümmerung** *f (nucl)* spallation
Kernzone *f* core *(foundry)*
Kernzusammenstoß *m* nuclear collision
Kerosin *n* kerosine, paraffin [oil]
Kerosinschiefer *m* kerosine shale
Kerr-Effekt *m* Kerr effect
~/elektrooptischer electrooptical Kerr effect
~/magnetooptischer magnetooptical Kerr effect
~/ramaninduzierter Raman-induced Kerr effect, RIKE
Kerr-Konstante *f* Kerr constant
Kerr-Zelle *f (spectr)* Kerr cell
Kerze *f* candle; *(filtr)* tube, candle
Kerzenfilter *n* tube (tubular) filter, cartridge (candle) filter
Kessel *m* boiler; bowl shell *(of a laboratory centrifuge)*; *(rubber)* tank, pan
Kesselanlage *f* boiler plant
Kesselblech *n* boiler plate
Kesselbrunnen *m (hyd)* dug well
Kesseldampf *m* boiler steam
Kesseldruckimprägnierung *f*, **Kesseldrucktränkung** *f* pressure process *(wood preservation)*
Kesselkohle *f* steam[-raising] coal
~/kokende coking steam coal
Kesselschlacke *f* boiler ash[es]
Kesselspeisepumpe *f* boiler feed pump
Kesselspeisewasser *n* boiler feed[ing] water
Kesselstein *m* [boiler] scale, hardness (mineral) scale, fur • **~ ansetzen** to scale, to fur • **~ entfernen** to [de]scale
Kesselsteinablagerung *f* scale deposit
Kesselsteinbekämpfung *f* scale control
Kesselsteinbekämpfungsmittel *n* scale control chemical
kesselsteinbildend scale-forming
Kesselsteinbildner *m* scale former, scale-forming material (substance)
Kesselsteinbildung *f* scale formation (build-up), scaling
Kesselsteinentfernung *f* boiler scale removal, [de]scaling
Kesselsteingegenmittel *n*, **Kesselsteinlösemittel** *n* descaling agent, descaler

Kesselsteinverhütungsmittel *n* scale inhibitor, antinucleating agent
Kesselwagen *m* tank car (wagon) *(railway)*; tank truck *(road)*
Kesselwasser *n s.* Kesselspeisewasser
Kessylalkohol *m* kessyl alcohol
Kessylketon *n* kessyl ketone
Kesting-Verfahren *n (pap)* Kesting electrolytic process *(for producing chlorine-dioxide bleaching liquor)*
Kestner-Verdampfer *m* Kestner long-tube evaporator, long-tube vertical-film evaporator, LTV evaporator
Kestose *f* kestose *(a trisaccharide)*
Ketal *n s.* Ketonacetal
Ketalisierung *f* ketalization
Ketazin *n* ketazine *(an azine formed from a ketone)*
Keten *n (org ch)* keten[e]
Ketenbase *f* keten[e] base
Ketimid *n*, **Ketimin** *n* $R_1R_2C=NH$ ketimine, ketonimine
Ketimin-Enamin-Tautomerie *f* ketimine-enamine tautomerism
Ketin *n* ketine, 2,5-dimethylpyrazine
Ketipinsäure *f* ketipic acid, 3,4-dioxoadipic acid, *3,4-dioxohexanedioic acid
Keto... *s. a.* Keton... *and* Oxo...
Ketoamin *n* ketoamine
Ketoanaloges *n* keto analog[ue]
Ketobernsteinsäure *f* oxosuccinic acid, oxalacetic acid
3-Ketobuttersäure *f* 3-oxobutyric acid, acetoacetic acid
Ketocarben *n* keto carbene
Ketocarbonsäure *f* keto carboxylic acid, keto acid
Ketocarbonsäureester *m* keto ester
Keto-Enol-Tautomerie *f* keto-enol tautomerism
Ketoester *m* keto[nic] ester, ketocarboxylic (keto-acid) ester
Ketofettsäure *f s.* Ketosäure
Ketoform *f* keto form
Ketofunktion *f* ketonic function
ketogen *(bioch)* ketogenic
Ketogenese *f (bioch, med)* ketogenesis, ketone-body formation
Ketoglutarsäure *f* oxoglutaric acid, ketoglutaric acid, *(specif)* 2-oxoglutaric acid, *2-oxopentanedioic acid
3-Ketoglutarsäure *f* 3-oxoglutaric acid, acetonedicarboxylic acid, ADA
Ketogruppe *f* keto group, ketonic [carbonyl] group, ketone [carbonyl] group
Ketoheptose *f* ketoheptose
Ketohexose *f* ketohexose
Ketoindan *n s.* Hydrindon
Ketoketen *n* $R^1R^2C=C=O$ ketoketene
Ketol *n* ketol, keto alcohol, hydroxy ketone, *(specif)* monohydroxy ketone
Ketolactam *n* keto lactam
Ketolyse *f* ketolysis
ketolytisch ketolytic
Ketomalonsäure *f* oxomalonic acid, mesoxalic acid, *oxo-propanedioic acid
Keton *n (org ch)* ketone
~/cyclisches cyclic ketone
~/gemischtes R^1-CO-R^2 mixed ketone
~/makrocyclisches macrocyclic ketone, macroring (large-ring) ketone
~/Michlers Michler's ketone, di-*p*-dimethylaminophenyl ketone
Keton... *s. a.* Keto...
Ketonacetal *n* ketone acetal, ketal
Ketonaldehyd *m* keto aldehyde
Ketonalkohol *m* keto alcohol, ketol, hydroxy ketone
Ketonämie *f (med)* ketonaemia
Keton-Benzol-Verfahren *n (petrol)* benzole-ketone process *(dewaxing)*
Ketonbildung *f* ketone formation
Ketoncarbonyl *n*, **Ketongruppe** *f s.* Ketogruppe
ketonhaltig ketonic
Ketonharz *n* ketone resin
ketonig ketonic • ~ **werden** to ketonize *(esp of fats)*
Ketonimid *n*, **Ketonimin** *n s.* Ketimid
ketonisieren to ketonize
Ketonisierung *f* ketonization
Ketonkörper *m (bioch)* ketone (acetone) body
Ketonkörperbildung *f*, **Ketonkörperentstehung** *f (bioch, med)* ketogenesis, ketone-body formation
Ketonmoschus *m (cosmet)* ketone musk, musk ketone, musk C *(a xylene derivative)*
Ketonperoxid *n* ketone peroxide
Ketonranzigkeit *f* ketonic rancidity
Ketonspaltung *f* ketonic cleavage (fission)
Ketonstruktur *f* keto (ketonic) structure
Ketonsynthese *f*/**Friedel-Craftssche** Friedel-Crafts ketone synthesis
Ketonurie *f* ketonuria *(abnormal excretion of ketones via the urine)*
Ketopentose *f* ketopentose *(a ketonic sugar)*
Ketosäure *f* keto acid
Ketosäureester *m s.* Ketocarbonsäureester
Ketose *f* 1. ketose, ketonic sugar; 2. *s.* Ketosis
Ketosid *n* ketoside *(a glycoside which yields a ketose on hydrolysis)*
ketosidisch ketosidic
Ketosis *f (med)* ketosis, ketoacidosis *(an abnormal increase of ketones in the body)*
Ketosteroid *n (org ch)* ketosteroid
4-Ketovaleriansäure *f s.* Lävulinsäure
Ketoverbindung *f* keto (ketonic) compound
Ketovinylierung *f* ketovinylation
Ketoxim *n* ketoxime
Ketozucker *m* ketose, ketonic sugar
Kette *f* chain; *(el ch)* cell, element; *(text)* warp • **mit geschlossener** ~ *(org ch)* closed-chain • **mit offener** ~ *(org ch)* open-chain • **mit verzweigter** ~ *(org ch)* branched-chain
~/anticlinal enantiomorphe anticlined enantiomorphous chain *(of a polymer)*

~/anticlinal isomorphe anticlined isomorphous chain *(of a polymer)*
~/anticlinale anticlined chain *(of a polymer)*
~/cyclische *(org ch)* closed chain
~/einsträngige single-strand chain *(conveying)*
~/elektrochemische *s.* ~/galvanische
~/enantiomorphe enantiomorphous chain *(of a polymer)*
~/galvanische galvanic cell (couple), voltaic cell
~/gerade *s.* ~/unverzweigte
~/geschlossene *(org ch)* closed chain
~/gestreckte extended chain *(of a polymer)*
~/isoclinal isomorphe isoclined isomorphous chain *(of a polymer)*
~/isoclinale isoclined chain *(of a polymer)*
~/isomorphe isomorphous chain *(of a polymer)*
~/leichte light chain, L *(of an immunoglobulin)*
~/normale *s.* ~/gerade
~/offene *(org ch)* open chain
~/ringförmige *(org ch)* closed chain
~/schwere heavy chain, H *(of an immunoglobulin)*
~/sekundäre *(el ch)* secondary cell
~/unverzweigte *(org ch)* straight (unbranched) chain
~/verzweigte *(org ch)* branched chain
~/zweisträngige double-strand chain *(conveying)*
Kettenabbrecher *m* chain stopper, free-radical chain terminator
Kettenabbruch *m* chain termination (breakage)
~ durch Disproportionierung [chain] termination by disproportionation
~ durch Kombination (Rekombination) [chain] termination by coupling, coupling termination
Kettenabbruchmittel *n s.* Kettenabbrecher
Kettenabbruchreaktion *f* chain-termination reaction, chain-terminating (chain-breaking, chain-stopping) reaction
Kettenabbruchstelle *f* chain-terminating site
Kettenachse *f* chain axis
kettenartig chain-like
Kettenbecherwerk *n* chain [and bucket] elevator
Kettenbeweglichkeit *f (org ch)* chain mobility (flexibility)
Kettenbruchstück *n* chain segment
Kettenende *n (org ch)* chain end
Kettenendenabstand *m* end-to-end distance, chain-end distance
Kettenentrinder *m (pap)* chain barker
Kettenfaltung *f (org ch)* chain folding
Kettenförderer *m* chain conveyor; chain elevator
Kettenform *f (org ch)* chain form
~/offene open-chain form
Kettenfortpflanzung *f* chain propagation
Kettenfortpflanzungsreaktion *f* chain-propagating reaction
Kettenglied *n* 1. link *(of a polymer or conveyor)*; 2. propagation sequence *(of a chain reaction)*
Kettenisomer[e] *n* chain (skeletal) isomer
Kettenisomerie *f* chain (skeletal) isomerism
Kettenklemme *f (lab)* chain clamp
Kettenkonformation *f* chain conformation *(of a polymer)*
Kettenlänge *f* chain length
~/kinetische *(plast)* kinetic chain length
Kettenlinie *f (phys ch)* sag curve
kettenlos chainless
Kettenmechanismus *m* chain[-reaction] mechanism
~/verzweigter branched-chain mechanism
Kettenmerzerisiermaschine *f (text)* chain mercerizer
Kettenmolekül *n* chain molecule
~/lineares linear chain molecule
~/starres rigid chain molecule
Kettenpolymerisation *f* chain[-growth] polymerization
~/kationische cationic chain polymerization
~/radikalische [free-]radical polymerization
~/ringöffnende ring-opening chain polymerization
Kettenräumer *m (hyd)* chain scraper
Kettenreaktion *f* chain reaction
~/nukleare nuclear chain reaction
~/radikalische free-radical chain reaction
Kettenreaktionsmechanismus *m s.* Kettenmechanismus
Kettenreduktion *f* chain reduction
Kettenregler *m* chain transfer agent *(polymerization)*
Kettenrost *m* chain (travelling) grate
Kettenrostfeuerung *f* chain-grate stoker
Kettenschleifer *m (pap)* chain grinder
Kettensegment *n* chain segment
Kettensegmentbeweglichkeit *f* chain-segment mobility, segmental mobility
Kettensegmentbewegung *f* segmental motion
Kettensilicat *n* inosilicate, chain silicate
Kettenspaltung *f* chain scission (splitting)
Kettenstart *m* chain initiation
Kettenstrang *m* strand of chain *(conveying)*
Kettenstruktur *f* chain structure
kettentragend chain-carrying, chain-propagating
Kettenträger *m* chain carrier (initiator)
Kettenüberträger *m* chain-transfer agent
Kettenübertragung *f* chain transfer
Kettenübertragungsreaktion *f* chain-transfer reaction
Kettenverbindung *f* chain compound
Kettenverlängerung *f* chain extension (lengthening); *(bioch)* elongation *(of polypeptide chains)*
Kettenverzweigung *f* chain branching
Kettenverzweigungsmechanismus *m* branched-chain mechanism
Kettenwachstum *n* chain growth (propagation)
Kettenwachstumspolymerisation *f s.* Kettenpolymerisation
Kettschlichte *f (text)* warp size
Kettschlichten *n (text)* warp sizing
Ketyl *n* ketyl
Keupermergel *m* keuper marl
kg-Molarität *f s.* Kilogramm-Molarität

KH *s.* Karbonathärte
Kharisalz *n (tann)* Khari salt *(a natural salt mixture containing chiefly sodium sulphate)*
Khellin *n* khellin *(a furanochromone derivative)*
Kiefernharz *n* pine resin
Kiefernholz *n* Scotch fir, pinewood *(from Pinus sylvestris L.)*
Kiefernholzteer *m* pine tar
Kiefernnadelöl *n* pine-needle oil, Scotch fir oil *(from Pinus sylvestris L.)*
Kiefernöl *n* tall oil, tallol, talloel, liquid resin (rosin)
Kiefernteer *m* pine tar
Kienöl *n* pine oil *(from Pinus specc.)*
Kies *m* gravel; *(mine, met)* pyrites
Kiesabbrand *m (met)* roasted pyrites
Kiesabröstung *f* roasting (burning) of pyrites
Kiesel *m* pebble
Kieselerde *f s.* Siliciumdioxid
Kieselfluorwasserstoffsäure *f s.* Fluorokieselsäure
Kieselgalmei *m s.* Kieselzinkerz
Kieselgel *n* silica gel, gelatinous silica
~/getrocknetes dried silica gel, silica xerogel
Kieselgestein *n* siliceous (silica) rock
Kieselglas *n* vitreous silica, silica glass
~/durchscheinendes fused (translucent vitreous) silica
~/durchsichtiges transparent [vitreous] silica, fused quartz, quartz glass
~/klares *s.* ~/durchsichtiges
~/undurchsichtiges non-transparent vitreous silica
Kieselgur *f* kieselguhr, infusorial earth, diatomaceous earth
Kieselgurfilter *n (hyd)* diatomaceous-earth filter, DE filter, diatomite filter
Kieselpflanze *f* calcifuge
Kieselsäure *f* silicic acid, *(specif)* H_4SiO_4 orthosilicic acid, tetraoxosilicic acid
~/aktivierte *(hyd)* activated silica
Kieselsäureester *m* silicic-acid ester, silicon ester
Kieselsäuregel *n s.* Kieselgel
kieselsäurehaltig containing silica, siliceous
Kieselsäuresol *n s.* Kieselsol
Kieselsinter *m (min)* siliceous sinter, geyserite
Kieselsol *n* silica sol
Kieselstein *m* pebble
Kieselxerogel *n s.* Kieselgel/getrocknetes
Kieselzinkerz *n (min)* hemimorphite *(zinc dihydroxide disilicate)*
Kieserit *m (min)* kieserite *(magnesium sulphate 1-water)*
Kiesfilter *n* gravel (sand) filter
kiesig gravelly
Kiliani-[Fischer-]Reaktion *f* **Kiliani-[Fischer]-Synthese** *f* Kiliani[-Fischer] reaction, Kiliani[-Fischer] synthesis *(of higher sugars via cyanohydrins)*
Kiln *m* kiln, regenerator *(in catalytic cracking)*
Kilogramm-Molarität *f* molality, molal concentration
Kimberlit *m* kimberlite *(an agglomerate biotite-peridotite)*
Kinderpuder *m* baby powder
Kinetik *f* kinetics
~/chemische chemical (reaction) kinetics
Kinetiker *m* kineticist
Kinetin *n* kinetin, 6-furfurylaminopurine
kinetisch kinetic
Kinin *n (bioch)* kinin
Kino *n* kino [gum]
~/Bengalisches Bengal kino, butea gum *(from Butea superba Roxb.)*
~/Indisches East India kino, Malabar kino *(from Pierocarpus marsupium Roxb.)*
~/Westindisches Jamaica kino *(from the bark of Coccoloba uvifera L.)*
Kinogerbsäure *f* kinotannic acid
Kinogummi *n,* **Kinoharz** *n s.* Kino
Kipp *m s.* Gasentwicklungsapparat/Kippscher
Kippaufzug *m* skip hoist
kippen to tilt, to dump
Kipphorde *f (ferm)* dumping floor
Kipphordenumlauftrockner *m* tilting (reversing) pan dryer
Kippkübel *m* skip [car]
Kipptrommelmischer *m* tilting-drum mixer
Kippvorrichtung *f* tilting device, tilter
Kirnapparat *m s.* Kirne
Kirndauer *f* churning period *(margarine manufacture)*
Kirne *f* [emulsion] churn *(margarine manufacture)*
kirnen to churn *(margarine)*
Kirnmaschine *f s.* Kirne
Kirnung *f* churning *(margarine manufacture)*
Kirschgummi *n* cherry gum
Kirschner-Zahl *f* Kirschner value
Kirschrotglut *f* cherry-red heat
kistenglühen to box-anneal *(metals)*
Kistenglühofen *m* box-annealing furnace
Kistenpappe *f* container board
Kitt *m* cement, *(esp for sealing:)* lute; *(for glass:)* putty
~/hüpfender bouncing putty
kitten to cement; to putty *(glass)*
Kitten *n* cementation; puttying *(of glass)*
Kittharz *n (biol)* propolis, bee glue, balm
Kittsubstanz *f (bioch)* cement substance
Ki-Z *s.* Kirschner-Zahl
Kjeldahl-Apparat *m* Kjeldahl digestion apparatus
Kjeldahl-Bestimmung *f* Kjeldahl determination
Kjeldahl-Kolben *m* Kjeldahl flask
Kjeldahl-Methode *f* Kjeldahl [nitrogen] method, Kjeldahl nitrogen procedure
Kjellin-Ofen *m* Kjellin furnace *(an induction furnace)*
KK *s.* Kohlenstoff/kohlenstoffaserverstärkter
Klammer *f* 1. *(lab)* clamp, clip; 2. *(nomencl)* bracket
~/eckige *(nomencl)* square bracket
~/runde *(nomencl)* parenthesis, round bracket
Klammersicherung *f (lab)* joint clamp

Klang *m (pap)* rattle, snappiness, *(Am)* crackle
Klappe *f* lid, door; disk *(of a valve)*
Klappenboden *m* valve tray
Klappenrückschlagventil *n* swing check valve
Klapprost *m* dumping grate
klar clear *(e.g. liquid)* • **~ werden** to clarify, to [become] clear
Kläranlage *f* waste (sewage, effluent) treatment plant
~/kommunale [municipal] sewage treatment plant, sewage plant (works)
~/städtische city sewage treatment plant
Kläranlagenablauf *m* waste treatment effluent, sewage plant effluent, discharge from a waste-water treatment plant
Klärapparat *m* clarifying apparatus, clarifier, settler
Klärbad *n (text)* clearing bath
Klärbassin *n*, **Klärbecken** *n s.* Absetzbecken
Klärbehälter *m s.* Klärgefäß
Klärbrunnen *m (hyd)* clearwell
Kläre *f (sugar)* liquor
Kläreffekt *m* clarification effect
Kläreindicker *m (hyd)* clarifier-thickener, thickener-clarifier
Klareis *n* clear (crystal) ice
klären to clarify, to clear, to purify; *(sugar)* to defecate; *(ferm)* to fine
~/sich to clarify, to [become] clear
Klärfilter *n* clarifying (polishing) filter
Klarfiltrat *n* clear filtrate
Klarfiltration *f*, **Klärfiltration** *f* clarification, polishing [filtration]
Klärfläche *f (hyd)* clarification area, surface area for clarification
~/äquivalente Σ value *(of a centrifuge)*
~/durchsatzbezogene unit area *(per metric ton of dry solids per day with thickeners)*
Klärflockulator *m (hyd)* clariflocculator
Klarflüssigkeit *f* clarified liquid (liquor); overflow product *(wet classification)*
Klärgefäß *n* clarifying tank, settling (precipitation, sedimentation) tank, clarifier, settler, precipitator
Klärgeschwindigkeit *f (hyd)* clarification rate
Klarglasur *f (ceram)* clear glaze
Klärgrube *f* settling pit, settler
Klarheit *f* clarity, clearness *(as of a filtrate or crystal)*
Klärhilfsmittel *n* clarifying agent, clarifier, clarificant
Klarifikation *f* clarification
Klarifikator *m* clarifier
Klarit *m (coal)* clarain
Klarlack *m* varnish
Klärleistung *f* clarifying capacity
Klärmittel *n* clarifying agent, clarifier, clarificant; *(ferm)* fining agent
Klarodurit *m* clarodurite *(a banded variety of hard coal)*
Klarpunkt *m* clear point *(precipitation analysis)*
Klärrückstand *m* sewage sludge *(waste-water treatment)*
Klärschlamm *m (hyd)* clarification (clarifier) sludge, sedimentation [tank] sludge; *(agric)* sludge fertilizer
Klarsichtmittel *n* antifog[ging] agent, antifoggant
Klärspitze *f*[**/konische**] cone classifier
Klärtank *m s.* Klärgefäß
Klärung *f* clarification, purification; *(sugar)* defecation; *(ferm)* fining
~/mechanische sedimentation
~ über Knochenkohle *(sugar)* bone-black filtration
Klärvorrichtung *f* clarifier
Klärwanne *f* settling pit, settler
Klarwaschbad *n* clearing bath
Klarwasser *n* 1. *s.* Reinwasser; 2. *(hyd)* underflow *(oil removal)*
Klarwassergüte *f*, **Klarwasserqualität** *f s.* Reinwassergüte
Klärwerk *n s.* Kläranlage
Klärwirkung *f (hyd)* clarification effect
Klärwirkungsgrad *m (hyd)* clarification efficiency
Klärzentrifuge *f* clarifying centrifuge, centrifugal clarifier
Klärzone *f* clarification zone, clear-solution (free-settling) zone *(as in a thickener)*
Klasse *f* class *(as of compounds or substances)*
Klassenbenennung *f (nomencl)* class name
Klassenkennzeichen *n (coal)* class parameter
Klassenname *m (nomencl)* class name
Klassennummer *f (coal)* class number
Klassenparameter *m (coal)* class parameter
Klassenziffer *f (coal)* class number
Klassierapparat *m s.* Klassierer
Klassierbecken *n* classifying pool
klassieren to classify, to class, to size, to grade [into size]
~/wieder *(hyd)* to regrade *(filtering material by backwashing)*
Klassierer *m* classifier
~/hydraulischer water classifier
~/mechanischer mechanical classifier
Klassiergerät *n s.* Klassierer
Klassiergut *n* material being *or* to be classified (sized)
Klassierkegel *m* cone classifier
Klassiersieb *n* sizing screen
Klassiertrog *m* classifier trough
Klassierung *f* sizing, [size] classification, [size] grading
~/hydraulische water classification
~ nach dem Prinzip des freien Absetzens free-settling classification
~ nach dem Prinzip des gestörten Absetzens hindered-settling classification
Klassierzyklon *m* cyclone classifier
Klassifikation *f (nomencl)* classification
Klassifikationssystem *n (nomencl)* system of classification
Klassifikator *m s.* Klassierer
klassifizieren *(nomencl)* to classify
Klassifizierung *f (nomencl)* classification

klastisch *(geol)* clastic
Klathrat *n* clathrate [inclusion compound], clathrate (cage) compound
Klathratbildung *f* clathrate formation
Klathratverbindung *f s.* Klathrat
Klaubeband *n (min tech)* inspection belt
klauben *(min tech)* to pick, to sort
~/von Hand to hand-pick
Klauenöl *n* neatsfoot oil
Klebe... *s. a.* Kleb...
Klebeband *n* [cellulose] adhesive tape
Klebekarton *m* pasteboard
Klebelack *m* decorators' size
Klebelösung *f (rubber)* cement
~ auf Nitrilkautschukbasis nitrile cement
Klebemittel *n s.* Klebstoff
kleben to bond, to stick, to glue, to cement, to paste; to adhere, to stick
Kleben *n* [adhesive] bonding, sticking, gluing, cementation, pasting; adherence, adhesion
~ durch Anlösen (Anquellen) *(plast)* solvent welding
klebend sticky, adhesive, adherent
Kleber *m s.* 1. Klebereiweiß; 2. Klebstoff
Klebereiweiß *n (food, bioch)* gluten
Klebestelle *f (glass)* tear *(defect)*
Klebetrockenverfahren *n (tann)* pasting process
Klebetrocknung *f (tann)* paste drying, pasting
Klebezement *m (rubber)* cement
klebfähig adhesive, adherent
Klebfähigkeit *f s.* Klebvermögen
Klebfilm *m* adhesive film
Klebfläche *f* bonded area
Klebfolie *f* adhesive film
klebfrei tack-free
klebfreudig *(rubber)* tacky
Klebfuge *f* glue line
Klebharz *n* adhesive resin
Klebkraft *f* adhesive capacity (power), adhesiveness, adherence
Klebpapier *n* adhesive (gummed) paper
klebrig sticky, tacky, tenaceous • **~ machen** to tackify
Klebrigkeit *f* stickiness, tackiness, tenacity
Klebrigmacher *m (rubber)* tackifying (tack-producing) agent, tackifier
Klebstoff *m* adhesive [agent, substance], cementing material, cement, paste
~ auf Eiweißgrundlage glair[e]
~/flüssiger solvent-based adhesive, solvent cement
~/härtender curing adhesive
~/heißabbindender (heißhärtender) thermosetting (hot-setting) adhesive, hot glue
~/hitzehärtbarer *s.* ~/heißabbindender
~/kalthärtender cold-setting (cold-cure) adhesive
~/thermoplastischer thermoplastic adhesive
~/wärmehärtbarer *s.* ~/heißabbindender
Klebstoffgrundstoff *m* adhesive base
Klebstoffilm *m* adhesive film
Klebstoffpulver *n* powder adhesive
Klebstoffschicht *f* adhesive layer
Klebstreifen *m* [cellulose] adhesive tape
Klebtechnik *f (plast)* cementing technique
Klebverbindung *f* adhesive bond
Klebvermögen *n* adhesive capacity (power), adhesiveness, adherence
Kleeblattform *f*, **Kleeblattstruktur** *f* cloverleaf arrangement (conformation), four-leaf clover-type structure *(of transfer RNA)*
Kleesalz *n* salt[s] of sorrel (lemon), sorrel salt, sal acetosella *(potassium tetraoxalate pure or mixed with potassium hydrogenoxalate)*
Kleesäure *f* oxalic acid, *ethanedioic acid
Kleiderimprägnierung *f* clothing impregnation
Kleie *f* bran
Kleieköder *m* poison bran bait *(insect control)*
Kleiekulturmethode *f (biot)* bran culture method
Kleiemehl *n* beeswing
Kleienbeize *f (tann)* bran drench[ing]
Kleieverfahren *n s.* Kleiekulturmethode
Klein-Bessemer-Birne *f*, **Klein-Bessemer-Konverter** *m* baby Bessemer converter
Kleinfermenter *m (biot)* small fermenter
Kleingaserzeuger *m* small-scale gasifier
Kleingefüge *n s.* Mikrostruktur
Kleinkläranlage *f (hyd)* small waste-water treatment plant
Kleinkohle *f* small (small-sized) coal
Kleinkonverter *m* baby converter
kleinkristallin finely crystalline
kleinlückig fine-pored
Kleinreihe *f (tech)* short run
Kleinringverbindung *f (org ch)* small-ring compound
Kleinschreiber *m* miniature recorder
Kleinschüttelgerät *n*, **Kleinschüttler** *m (lab)* minishaker
Kleinserie *f (tech)* short run
kleinstückig small-sized
Kleinvernebler *m (agric)* hand fogger
Kleinverstäuber *m (agric)* hand[-operated] duster
Kleinversuch *m* small-scale experiment
Kleinwinkelstreuung *f (phys ch)* small-angle scattering
Kleister *m* paste
Klemme *f* clamp, clip
~/große *(lab)* condenser clamp
Klemmring *m* locking ring
Klemmverbindung *f*, **Klemmverschraubung** *f* compression-type fitting
Kletterfilmverdampfer *m* rising-film (climbing-film) evaporator, upward-flow evaporator
Klimaanlage *f* air-conditioning plant (system)
Klimagerät *n* air-conditioning apparatus, [air] conditioner
Klimakammer *f* climatic chamber
Klimaregelung *f* [air] conditioning
klimatisieren to [air-]condition

Klimatisierung *f* [air] conditioning
Klimatisierungsanlage *f s.* Klimaanlage
klingeln to pink, to knock *(of a carburettor engine)*
Klingeln *n* pinking, ping, knock[ing] *(of a carburettor engine)*
Klinker[stein] *m* clinker [brick], engineering brick
Klinkerverfahren *n* clinker process
Klinkerziegel *m s.* Klinker
Klinochlor *m (min)* clinochlore, clinochlorite *(a phyllosilicate)*
Klinoklas *m (min)* clinoclase, clinoclasite *(a basic copper arsenate)*
Klonauswahltheorie *f* clonal theory *(of antibody formation)*
Klonierung *f (biot)* cloning
Klopfbremse *f* antiknock [agent, additive], knock suppressor, octane improver
Klopfbremswirkung *f* antiknock (antidetonating) action; antiknock effect
Klopfeigenschaft *f* knocking property
klopfempfindlich prone to knocking, knock-prone
Klopfempfindlichkeit *f s.* Klopfneigung
klopfen to knock, to pink *(of a carburetting fuel)*
Klopfen *n* knock[ing], pinking, ping *(of a carburetting fuel)*
Klopfer *m* rapper *(gas cleaning)*
klopffest knockproof *(carburetting fuel)*
Klopffestigkeit *f* 1. antiknock quality, knock resistance; 2. *s.* Klopfwert
klopffrei 1. knock-free, knockless, non-knocking *(ignition of carburetting fuel)*; 2. *s.* klopffest
klopffreudig prone to knocking, knock-prone
Klopffreudigkeit *f*, **Klopfneigung** *f* knock proneness, knocking propensity
Klopfprüfmotor *m* knock-rating engine
Klopfprüfung *f* [anti]knock rating
klopfstark prone to knocking, knock-prone
Klopfstärke *f* knock intensity
Klopfvorrichtung *f (filtr)* knocker; rapper *(gas cleaning)*
Klopfwerk *n (filtr)* knocker
Klopfwert *m* antiknock (knock) value (rating) *(of carburetting fuel)*
Klopfwertbestimmung *f*, **Klopfwertprüfung** *f* [anti]knock rating
Klotz *m*, **Klotzbad** *n s.* Klotzflotte
Klotzchassis *n (text)* pad box
Klotz-Dämpf-Färbeverfahren *(text)* pad-steam process
klotzen *(text)* to pad
Klotzen *n*, **Klotzfärben** *n (text)* pad dyeing, [slop-]padding
Klotzfärbeverfahren *n (text)* pad dyeing process
Klotzfärbung *f (text)* pad dyeing
Klotz-Fixier-Verfahren *n (text)* pad-fix process
Klotzflotte *f (text)* [slop] pad liquor, pad[ding] bath
Klotzhilfsmittel *n (text)* padding auxiliary
Klotzmaschine *f (text)* padding machine (mangle), pad[der]
Klotz-Roll-Verfahren *n (text)* pad-roll method
Klotz-Trocken-Kondensierverfahren *n (text)* pad-dry process
Klotztrog *m (text)* pad box
Klotz-Verweil-Verfahren *n (text)* pad-store process
klumpen to agglomerate, to clog, to clot
Klumpen *m* lump, clot, bat
Klumpenbildung *f* agglomeration, clogging, clotting
klumpig lumpy • ~ **werden** *s.* klumpen
Klumpigkeit *f* lumpiness
Klystron *n (anal)* klystron [valve]
KM *s.* Kernmagneton
K-Meson *n* K meson
KMK *s.* Mizellkonzentration/kritische
KMR = kernmagnetische Resonanz
KMR-... *s.* NMR-...
Knab-Ofen *m* sole-flue oven
Knallgas *n* detonating gas, *(specif)* oxyhydrogen gas
Knallgascoulometer *n* oxygen-hydrogen coulometer
Knallgaselement *n* hydrogen-oxygen fuel cell
Knallgasflamme *f* oxyhydrogen flame
Knallgasgebläse *n* oxyhydrogen blowpipe (burner, torch)
Knallgasreaktion *f* hydrogen-oxygen reaction
Knallgaszelle *f* hydrogen-oxygen fuel cell
Knallquecksilber *n* fulminating mercury, mercury (mercuric) fulminate
Knallsäure *f* fulminic acid, formonitrile oxide
Knallsilber *n* 1. *(originally:)* fulminating silver *(a mixture of Ag_3N and Ag_2NH)*; 2. AgCNO silver fulminate
Knallzündschnur *f* detonating fuse
Knäuel *n(m)* coil *(as of a macromolecule)*
~/statistisches random (statistical) coil
Knäuelmolekül *n* coiled molecule
Knäuelung *f* coiling *(as of a macromolecule)*
Knetarm *m* mixing arm (blade)
~/Z-förmiger sigma blade
kneten to knead
~/zu Teig to dough [in]
Kneter *m s.* Knetwerk
Knetgut *n* material being *or* to be kneaded (mixed)
Knetlegierung *f* wrought alloy
Knetmaschine *f s.* Knetwerk
Knetmischer *m* kneader mixer
Knetorgan *n* kneading (mixing) element
Knetschaufel *f* mixing blade; *(rubber)* rotor *(of a closed mixer)*
Knetschnecke *f* mixing screw
Knetteller *m* [rotary] kneading table
Knettrog *m (rubber)* mixing chamber *(of a closed mixer)*
Knetwalze *f* kneading roll
Knetwerk *n* kneading machine, kneader, [dough] mixer, pug mill
KNF-Modell *n (bioch)* KNF model *(of the bonding of ligands to proteins according to Koshland, Nemety, and Filmer)*
Knickbeständigkeit *f s.* Knickfestigkeit
Knickfestigkeit *f (tann)* burst[ing] strength

Knickpunkt *m* (break) *(as of a curve)*; critical moisture point *(in drying processes)*; *(hyd)* breakpoint
Knickpunktchlorung *f (hyd)* breakpoint (free-residual) chlorination
Knickpunktfeuchte *f*, **Knickpunkt-Feuchtebeladung** *f* critical humidity (moisture content) *(theory of drying)*
Knickpunktkurve *f (hyd)* breakpoint curve, chlorine dose-residual curve
Knickschwingung *f (spectr)* bending vibration
Knie *n* elbow [fitting], ell
Kniehebelbackenbrecher *m* [double] toggle crusher, Blake jaw crusher
Kniehebelpresse *f* toggle [lever] press
Kniestück *n* elbow [fitting], ell
Knirschgriffappretur *f (text)* rustling finish
Knistersalz *n* decripitating salt
knitterbeständig, knitterecht *s.* knitterfest
Knittererholungsvermögen *n (text)* crease recovery
Knittererholungswinkel *m (text)* angle of crease recovery, crease angle
knitterfest *(text)* crease-resistant, crease-proof, non-creasing, *(Am)* non-crushable, crush-proof, crush-resistant
Knitterfestappretur *f*, **Knitterfestausrüstung** *f (text)* crease-resistant finish, anticrease (non-crease) finish (treatment), *(Am)* crush proofing
Knitterfestigkeit *f (text)* crease (creasing, wrinkle) resistance
Knitterfreiheit *f s.* Knitterfestigkeit
knittern *(text)* to crease, to wrinkle, *(Am)* to crush
Knitterpapier *n* creased paper
Knitterung *f (text)* creasing, wrinkling, crushing
Knitterwiderstand *m s.* Knitterfestigkeit
Knitterwinkel *m s.* Knittererholungswinkel
Knoblauchöl *n* garlic oil *(from Allium sativum L.)*
Knochenasche *f* bone ash
Knochenfett *n* bone fat
Knochengelatine *f* bone gelatin
Knochenkohle *f* animal char[coal], bone char[coal], spodium
Knochenleim *m* bone glue
Knochenöl *n* bone oil
Knochenporzellan *n* bone china
Knochenschwarz *n* animal (bone) black
Knochenteer *m* bone tar
knochentrocken *(ceram)* bone-dry, B.D., white-hard
Knockdown-Mittel *n* knockdown agent (poison) *(any of a class of immediately acting insecticides)*
Knockdown-Wirkung *f* knockdown effect *(of certain insecticides)*
Knock-out-Punkt *m* knock-out point *(in testing insecticides)*
Knoevenagel-Kondensation *f (org ch)* Knoevenagel condensation *(of aldehydes and ketones with compounds having an activated methylene group)*
Knöllchenbakterien *npl* nodule-forming bacteria, root-nodule bacteria *(Rhizobium specc.)*
knollig *(min)* nodular
Knopflack *m* button lac
Knopfprobe *f*, **Knopfprüfung** *f (ceram)* [flow] button test, fusion flow test *(for testing the fusibility of an enamel frit)*
Knopfschellack *m* button lac
Knoten *m (pap, glass)* knot *(a defect)*
Knotenebene *f* nodal plane *(wave mechanics)*
Knotenfänger *m (pap)* knot screen (strainer), [jag-] knotter
~/rotierender rotary (rotating) strainer, revolving [drum] strainer
Knotenfängerschlitz *m (pap)* screen slot
Knotenfläche *f* nodal plane *(wave mechanics)*
Knotenpunkt *m* branch point *(of metabolism)*
Knudsen-Diffusion *f* Knudsen diffusion
Knudsen-Diffusionskoeffizient *m* Knudsen diffusivity
Knüppel *m (met)* billet
Koagel *n* coagel
Koagulans *n s.* Koagulationsmittel
Koagulans-Verfahren *n (rubber)* coagulant dipping process
Koagulant *m s.* Koagulationsmittel
Koagulat *n* coagulate, coagulum
Koagulation *f* coagulation, clotting, curdling, *(coll also)* pectization
~/rasche *(coll)* fast coagulation
~/thixogene *(coll)* rheopexy
Koagulationsbad *n (text)* coagulating (coagulation) bath
Koagulationsdauer *f* coagulation period
Koagulationsfiltration *f (hyd)* coagulation-filtration
Koagulationsmittel *n* coagulant, coagulator, coagulating agent
Koagulationstauchverfahren *n (rubber)* coagulant dipping process
Koagulationsvermögen *n* coagulating power
Koagulationsvitamin *n* antihaemorrhagic vitamin, phylloquinone
Koagulationswert *m (coll)* coagulation value
Koagulator *m s.* Koagulationsmittel
Koagulatplatte *f (rubber)* slab of coagulum
koagulierbar coagulable
Koagulierbarkeit *f* coagulability
koagulieren to coagulate, to curd[le], to clot, *(coll also)* to pectize
Koagulum *n s.* Koagulat
Koaleszenz *f* coalescence
koaleszieren, koal[is]ieren to coalesce
Koaxialzylinderviskosimeter *n* coaxial cylinder viscometer
Koazervat *n* coacervate
Koazervation *f*, **Koazervierung** *f* coacervation
Kobalt *s.* Cobalt
Kobalt... *s. a.* Cobalt... *for chemical terms*
Kobaltblau *n* cobalt (ultramarine, king's) blue *(cobalt aluminate)*

Kobaltblüte *f (min)* cobalt bloom, erythrine, erythrite *(cobalt(II) orthoarsenate)*
Kobaltgelb *n* cobalt yellow, Indian yellow, aureolin *(potassium hexanitrocobaltate)*
Kobaltglanz *m (min)* cobaltine, cobalt glance *(cobalt sulpharsenite)*
Kobaltglas *n* cobalt glass
Kobaltgrün *n* cobalt (Rinman's) green
Kobaltkies *m (min)* linnaeite, cobalt pyrites *(cobalt(II,III) sulphide)*
Kobaltsikkativ *n*, **Kobalttrockner** *m (coat)* cobalt drier
Kobaltultramarin *n s.* Kobaltblau
Kobaltvitriol *m (min)* cobalt vitriol, bieberite *(cobalt(II) sulphate 7-water)*
Kochbedingungen *fpl (pap)* cooking conditions
kochbeständig resistant (fast) to boiling
Kochbeständigkeit *f* resistance (fastness) to boiling
Kochchemikalie *f (pap)* cooking agent (reagent, chemical)
Kochdauer *f* period of boiling; *(food, pap)* period of cooking, cooking time, *(pap also)* digestion time
kochecht *s.* kochbeständig
kochen to boil; *(food, pap)* to cook, *(pap also)* to digest, to boil; to be wild *(of rimming steel)*
~/auf Korn *(sugar)* to boil to grain, *(Am also)* to sugar off *(esp maple sap)*
~/im Autoklaven to autoclave
~/nochmals to reboil
~/unter Rückfluß *(distil)* to reflux
~/unvollständig *(pap)* to undercook
Kochen *n* boil[ing]; *(food, pap)* cooking, *(pap also)* digestion, boil; *(met)* boil *(of a blown smelt)* • **am ~ halten** to keep at the boil • **zum ~ bringen** to raise (bring) to the boil
~ auf Korn *(sugar)* boiling to grain, crystal boiling, evaporative crystallization
~/nochmaliges reboiling; *(food, pap)* recooking
~ unter Druck boiling under pressure
Kocher *m (food)* cooker; *(pap)* cooker, digester, kier
~/liegender *(pap)* horizontal digester
~/rotierender *(pap)* revolving (rotary) digester
~/stehender *(pap)* vertical (upright) digester
Kocherabgas *n (pap)* digester relief gas, release
Kocherausblasen *n (pap)* digester blow
Kocherdeckel *m (pap)* digester cover
Kocherdruck *m (pap)* digester pressure
Kocherei *f (pap)* digester house; *(sugar)* boiling house
Kochereintrag *m s.* Kocherinhalt
Kocherführer *m s.* Kochermeister
Kocherfüllapparat *m (pap)* chip distributor (packer)
Kocherfüllung *f s.* Kocherinhalt
Kochergrube *f (pap)* blow pit (tank), wash (receiving) tank
Kocherinhalt *m (pap)* digester charge (contents), furnish, cook
~/ausgeblasener blow
Kocherleerung *f (pap)* digester blow
Kochermeister *m (pap)* cook[er], boilerman
Kocherraum *m s.* Kochervolumen
Kocherturnus *m*, **Kocherumtrieb** *m (pap)* digester cycle
Kochervolumen *n (pap)* digester capacity (space)
kochfest *s.* kochbeständig
Kochfett *n* cooking fat
Kochflasche *f s.* Kochkolben
Kochflüssigkeit *f s.* Kochlauge
Kochgeschmack *m* cooked flavour (taste)
Kochgut *n (pap)* digester charge, furnish, cook
Koch-Haaf-Reaktion *f* Koch-Haaf reaction *(for obtaining carboxylic acids)*
Kochkäse *m* cook[ed] cheese
Kochkessel *m* cooking kettle (vat)
Kochkolben *m* boiling (Florence) flask, round-bottom [boiling] flask
Kochlauge *f (pap)* cooking liquor, digestion (pulping) liquor
Kochlaugenanlage *f (pap)* liquor-making plant
Kochlaugenbehälter *m (pap)* liquor tank
Kochlaugenherstellung *f (pap)* cooking-liquor manufacture (preparation)
Kochlaugenleitung *f (pap)* liquor-circulating line
Kochlaugenvorratstank *m (pap)* liquor tank
Kochlösung *f s.* Kochlauge
Kochmaische *f* decoction mash
Kochperiode *f (met)* boil period
Kochprobe *f s.* Kochprüfung
Kochprüfung *f (food, tann)* boiling test
Kochpunkt *m s.* Siedepunkt
Kochraum *m s.* Kochervolumen
Kochsalz *n* common salt
Kochsalzlösung *f* solution of common salt, sodium chloride solution
~/physiologische *(pharm)* physiological saline (salt solution), saline, isotonic sodium chloride solution, *(Am also)* normal saline (salt solution)
~ zum Regenerieren *s.* Kochsalzsole zum Regenerieren
Kochsalzmenge *f* salt dosage, amount of salt [for regeneration] *(ion exchange)*
Kochsalzsole *f* sodium chloride brine
~ zum Regenerieren regenerant brine, brine regenerant, water-softener [regeneration] brine *(ion exchange)*
Koch-Säure *f* Koch acid, naphth-1-ylamine-3,6,8-trisulphonic acid
Kochsäure *f (pap)* cooking acid (liquor), digestion liquor
~/hochkonzentrierte (hochprozentige) *(pap)* high-strength (full-strength) cooking acid, strong acid
Kochsäureanlage *f (pap)* acid[-making] plant
Kochsäuredruckspeicher *m (pap)* pressure container (accumulator)
Kochsäureherstellung *f (pap)* cooking-acid manufacture (preparation)

Kochsäureleitung *f (pap)* acid-circulating line
Kochsäureumlauf *m*, **Kochsäurezirkulation** *f (pap)* cooking-acid circulation
Kochschnitzel *npl (pap)* [wood] chips, chippings
Kochstation *f (pap)* digester house; *(sugar)* boiling house
Kochstoff *m (pap)* digester charge, furnish, cook
Kochtrub *m (ferm)* hot sludge
Kochung *f (pap)* cook[ing], digestion, boil
~/alkalische alkaline cook
~/direkte direct (quick) cook
~/indirekte indirect (slow) cook
~ nach Mitscherlich/indirekte Mitscherlich cook process
~ nach Ritter-Kellner/direkte Ritter-Kellner cook process
~/unvollständige undercooking
Kochverfahren *n (ferm)* decoction process
Kochvorgang *m (pap)* cooking process
Kochwasser *n* cooking water, water for cooking
Kochzeit *f s.* Kochdauer
Kochzyklus *m (pap)* cooking cycle
Köder *m* bait, baiting agent
Ködergift *n* poison for baits
Ködermittel *n s.* Köder
Kodestillation *f* codistillation
Koeffizient *m*/**kritischer** *(phys ch)* critical compression factor
~/ökonomischer *(biot)* growth yield coefficient *(growth of microorganisms)*
~/osmotischer osmotic coefficient
~/respiratorischer respiratory quotient (ratio)
~/stöchiometrischer stoichiometric coefficient (factor)
Koexistenz *f* coexistence *(as of two phases)*
koexistieren to coexist
Koferment *n s.* Coenzym
Kogag-Ofen *m* Kogag oven *(for coking coal)*
Kogasinverfahren *n (coal)* Kogasin (Fischer-Tropsch) process (synthesis)
kohärent coherent
Kohärenz *f* coherence
kohärieren to cohere
Köhäsion *f* cohesion
Kohäsionsarbeit *f* work of cohesion
Kohäsionsdruck *m* cohesion pressure, internal (intrinsic) pressure
Kohäsionsenergiedichte *f* cohesive energy density
Kohäsionsfestigkeit *f* cohesive strength
Kohäsionskraft *f* cohesive (cohesion) force
kohäsiv cohesive
Kohle *f* 1. coal; 2. *(el ch)* carbon [electrode]
~/anthrazitische anthracitic coal
~/aufgegebene *(tech)* feed[-stock] coal
~/backende caking coal
~/bituminöse bituminous (soft) coal
~/brikettierte briquetted coal
~ der Kalksteingruppe limestone coal
~/eingesetzte *(tech)* feed[-stock] coal
~/fossile fossil (mineral, natural) coal
~/gasreiche bituminöse high-volatile bituminous coal
~/geringbituminöse low-volatile bituminous [steam] coal
~/glänzende bright coal
~/grubenfeuchte pit-moist coal
~/gut backende strongly caking coal, high-caking coal
~/gut kokende (verkokbare) strongly coking coal
~/harzreiche resinous coal
~/hochflüchtige [bituminöse] high-volatile [bituminous] coal
~/humitische humic coal
~/karbonische carboniferous coal
~/kohlenstoffreiche carbonaceous coal
~/künstliche artificial coal; *(if made from wood, blood, or bones:)* char[coal]
~/kurzflammige short-flame coal
~/langflammige long-flame coal
~/lignitische lignite
~/magere lean coal
~/mäßig backende medium-caking coal
~/mäßig kokende (verkokbare) medium-coking coal
~/matte dull coal
~/metabituminöse metabituminous coal
~/mineralische *s.* ~/fossile
~ mit erhöhtem Wasserstoffgehalt perhydrous coal
~ mit geringem Backvermögen weakly caking coal
~/mittelbackende medium-caking coal
~/mittelflüchtige [bituminöse] medium-volatile [bituminous] coal
~/natürliche *s.* ~/fossile
~/nichtbackende non-caking coal
~/nichtkokende (nicht verkokbare) non-coking coal
~/niedrigflüchtige [bituminöse] low-volatile bituminous [steam] coal
~/orthobituminöse orthobituminous coal
~/parabituminöse parabituminous coal
~/perbituminöse perbituminous coal
~/perhydrierte perhydrous coal
~/pulverisierte powdered (pulverized) coal
~/pyrogene heat-altered coal *(having lost its caking power by the action of hot rock)*
~/reine pure coal material (substance); *(min tech)* pure (clean) coal *(with minimum ash content)*
~/sapropelitische sapropelic coal
~/schlecht kokende (verkokbare) weakly coking coal
~/schwachbackende weakly caking coal
~/schwachkokende weakly coking coal
~/selbstbackende *(el ch)* self-baking electrode
~/semibituminöse semibituminous coal
~/starkbackende high-caking coal, strongly caking coal

~/streifige banded coal
~/subbituminöse subbituminous (lignitous) coal, bituminous (black) lignite
~/subhydrierte subhydrous coal
~/synthetische artificial coal
~/unverkokbare *s.* ~/nichtkokende
~/vorgebrannte *(el ch)* prebaked electrode
~/wasserstoffarme subhydrous coal
~/wasserstoffreiche perhydrous coal
kohleähnlich coal-like
Kohleanmaischung *f* coal slurrying
Kohleart *f* type (species) of coal
kohleartig coal-like
Kohleaufbereitung *f* coal preparation (dressing)
Kohleaufbereitungsanlage *f* coal-preparation plant
Kohleaufgabe *f* coal feed[ing], coal charging
Kohleaufgabeschleuse *f* coal-charging vessel *(as of a pressure gasifier)*
kohlebeheizt coal-heated
Kohlebeheizung *f* coal[-fired] heating
Kohlebeschickung *f* coal feed[ing], coal charging
Kohlebeschickungsmaschine *f* coal-charging machine
Kohlebestandteil *m* coal constituent (component)
kohlebildend coal-forming
Kohlebildung *f* coal formation (genesis)
Kohlebildungsvorgang *m* coal-forming process
Kohlebogen *m* carbon arc
Kohlebohrer *m (lab)* charcoal borer
Kohlebraun *n* Cassel brown (earth), ulmin brown *(a naturally occurring pigment)*
Kohlebrei *m* coal slurry (paste)
Kohlebunker *m* coal bunker; coal [storage] hopper *(for bottom discharge)*
Kohlechemie *f* coal chemistry
Kohledestillation *f* distillation of coal
Kohledurchsatz *m* coal throughput
Kohleeinspeisung *f* coal feeding
Kohleeinteilung *f* coal classification
Kohleelektrode *f* carbon [electrode]
Kohleentgasung *f* coal carbonization
Kohleentschwefelung *f* coal desulphurization
Kohle-Erz-Brikett *n* coal-ore briquette
Kohle-Erz-Gemisch *n* coal-ore mixture
Kohleextrakt *m* coal extract
Kohleextraktion *f* coal extraction
Kohlefaden-Atomisator *m (spectr)* carbon-filament atom reservoir atomizer
Kohlefadenlampe *f* carbon filament lamp
Kohlefeuerung *f* coal firing
Kohlefilter *n* carbon (char) filter
Kohlefleck *m* carbon spot *(a defect in paper)*
Kohlefolgeprodukt *n* coal product
Kohleforschung *f* coal research
kohleführend coal-bearing
Kohlefüllmasse *f*, **Kohlefüllung** *f* coal charge *(as in an oven)*; *(hyd)* carbon loading
Kohlefüllwagen *m* coal-charging car, oven-charging car
kohlegefeuert coal-fired
Kohlegefügebestandteil *m* coal maceral
kohlegeheizt coal-heated
Kohlegelbglas *n* amber glass
Kohlegemisch *n* coal blend (mixture)
Kohlegenesis *f* coal formation (genesis)
Kohlehydrat *n s.* Kohlenhydrat
Kohlehydrierung *f* coal hydrogenation
Kohle-Kalk-Verhältnis *n* lime-to-coke ratio *(carbide manufacture)*
Kohlekammer *f* coal stall *(in coal hydrogenation)*
Kohleklasse *f* coal class
Kohleklassifikation *f* coal classification
~ nach dem Inkohlungsgrad rank classification of coals
Kohleklassifizierung *f s.* Kohleklassifikation
Kohleklassifizierungsschaubild *n* coal chart
~/Seylers Seyler's [coal] chart
Kohleklein *n* small[-sized] coal
Kohlekomponente *f* coal component (constituent)
Kohlelager *n* 1. *(geol)* coal deposit; 2. *(tech)* coal store
Kohlelichtbogen *m* carbon arc
Kohlemahlung *f* coal milling (grinding, pulverization)
Kohlemaische *f* coal slurry
Kohlemischung *f* coal blend (mixture)
Kohlemodell *n* coal model
Kohlemolekül *n* coal molecule
Kohlemühle *f* coal pulverizer (mill), coal-pulverizing (coal-grinding, coal-dust) mill
kohlen 1. to carburize *(steel)*; 2. to char *(of wood)*
Kohlen *n* 1. carburization, carburizing *(of steel)*; 2. charring *(of wood)*
Kohlen... *s. a.* Kohle...
Kohlenasche *f* coal ash
Kohlenband *n* coal band
Kohlenbrikett *n* coal briquette
Kohlencharge *f* coal charge
Kohlendioxid *n* carbon dioxide
~/aggressives *(hyd)* aggressive carbon dioxide
~/festes solid carbon dioxide, dry ice
~/überschüssiges *s.* ~/aggressives
Kohlendioxid... *s. a.* CO_2-...
Kohlendioxid-Akzeptor-Verfahren *n (coal)* CO_2 acceptor process *(coal gasification with heat carriers)*
Kohlendioxidassimilation *f* carbon dioxide assimilation
Kohlendioxidentfernung *f* carbon-dioxide removal
Kohlendioxidlaser *m* CO_2 laser
Kohlendioxidlöscher *m* carbon dioxide fire extinguisher
Kohlendioxidschnee *m* carbon dioxide ice (snow)
Kohlendioxidüberträger *m* carbon dioxide carrier
Kohlendisulfid *n* carbon disulphide
Kohlenentstehung *f* coal formation (genesis)
Kohlenfeld *n* panel of coal *(in underground gasification)*
Kohlenfüllhahn *m* coal inlet valve *(of a gasifier)*

Kohlengas *n* coal gas
Kohlengattung *f* species of coal
Kohlengestein *n* carbonaceous rock
Kohlengesteinskunde *f* coal petrology
Kohlengrus *m* coal breeze
Kohlenhydrat *n* carbohydrate, saccharide
Kohlenhydratanteil *m* carbohydrate moiety *(as of glycoproteins)*
Kohlenhydrat-Antibiotikum *n (biot)* carbohydrate-containing antibiotic
Kohlenhydratauslösung *f (pap)* dissolution of carbohydrates
Kohlenhydratchemie *f* carbohydrate chemistry
Kohlenhydratentzug *m (med)* carbohydrate deprivation
Kohlenhydratquelle *f (biot)* carbohydrate source
Kohlenhydratstoffwechsel *m* carbohydrate metabolism
Kohlenhydratzufuhr f/verminderte *(med)* carbohydrate restriction
Kohlenlademaschine *f* coal-load instrument
Kohlenladung *f* coal charge
Kohlenmazeral *n* coal maceral
Kohlenmeiler *m* coal heap
Kohlenmonosulfid *n* carhon monosulphide
Kohlenmonoxid *n* carbon monooxide
Kohlenmonoxidboran *n* borine carbonyl
Kohlenmonoxidhämoglobin *n* carbon monooxyhaemoglobin, carboxyhaemoglobin, carbonylhaemoglobin
Kohlenmonoxidhydrierung *f* carbon monoxide hydrogenation
Kohlenmonoxidkonversion *f* carbon monoxide conversion (shift), CO conversion, water-gas shift, shift conversion
Kohlenoxid *n s.* Kohlenmonoxid
Kohlenoxidbromid *n* carbon dibromide oxide, carbonyl bromide, bromophosgene
Kohlenoxidchlorid *n* carbon dichloride oxide, carbonyl chloride, phosgene
Kohlenoxidhämoglobin *n s.* Kohlenmonoxidhämoglobin
Kohlenoxidsulfid *n* carbon oxide sulphide, carbonyl sulphide
Kohlenpetrographie *f* coal petrography
Kohlenpetrologie *f* coal petrology
Kohlenpreßling *m* coal briquette
Kohlenrang *m*, **Kohlenrangstufe** *f* coal rank
Kohlensäule *f* column of coal *(as for determining its plasticity)*
Kohlensäure *f* carbonic acid; *(tech)* carbon dioxide
~/angreifende *(hyd)* aggressive carbon dioxide
~/festgebundene *(hyd)* bound carbon dioxide
~/freie *(hyd)* free carbon dioxide
~/[ganz] gebundene *(hyd)* bound carbon dioxide
~/halbgebundene *(hyd)* half-bound carbon dioxide
~/überschüssige freie *(hyd)* excess carbon dioxide
Kohlensäureanhydr[at]ase *f* carbonic anhydrase
Kohlensäurediamid *n s.* Carbamid
Kohlensäuredichlorid *n s.* Kohlenoxidchlorid
Kohlensäureerstarrungsverfahren *n* CO_2 process *(foundry)*
Kohlensäurelöscher *m s.* Kohlendioxidlöscher
Kohlensäuremonamid *n s.* Carbamidsäure
Kohlensäurepatrone *f* sparklet bulb
Kohlensäureschnee *m* carbon dioxide ice (snow), dry ice
Kohlensäureschneelöscher *m s.* Kohlendioxidlöscher
Kohlensäureschreiber *m* CO_2 recorder
Kohlenschwelung *f* coal carbonization
Kohlensetzmaschine *f* coal jig
Kohlenstaub *m* coal dust, breeze; pulverized (powdered) coal
Kohlenstaubbrenner *m* pulverized-coal burner
Kohlenstaubfeuerung *f* pulverized-coal firing, PC firing, suspension firing of coal
Kohlenstaubmahlung *f* coal milling (grinding, pulverization)
Kohlenstaubmühle *f s.* Kohlemühle
Kohlenstaub-Wasser-Trübe *f* coal/water slurry *(in elevated-pressure gasification)*
Kohlenstoff *m* C carbon • **mit ~ beladen** carbon-fouled *(catalyst)*
~/aktiver (aktivierter) active (activated) carbon
~/anorganischer (anorganisch gebundener) *(hyd)* total inorganic carbon, TIC
~/fester (fixer) fixed carbon, FC
~/freier free carbon
~/gelöster organischer (organisch gebundener) *(hyd)* dissolved organic carbon, DOC
~/gelöster und ungelöster organisch gebundener *s.* ~/organisch gebundener
~/glasartiger glass-like carbon, glassy (vitreous) carbon
~/graphitierbarer graphitizable carbon
~/graphitischer graphitic carbon
~/kohlenstoffaserverstärkter carbon-carbon composite, carbon fibre-reinforced carbon, CFC
~/nichtflüchtiger organisch gebundener *(hyd)* non-volatile total organic carbon
~/nichtgraphitischer non-graphitic carbon
~/organisch gebundener *(hyd)* total organic carbon, TOC
~/radioaktiver *s.* Kohlenstoff-14
~/totaler organischer *s.* ~/organisch gebundener
α-Kohlenstoff *m* alpha-carbon, α-carbon
Kohlenstoff-14 *m* ^{14}C carbon-14, radioactive carbon, radiocarbon
Kohlenstoffablagerung *f* carbon deposit
Kohlenstoffaden *m* carbon filament
Kohlenstoffalter *n*, **Kohlenstoff-14-Alter** *n* radiocarbon age
kohlenstoffarm poor in carbon, low-carbon *(e.g. steel)*
Kohlenstoffaser *f* carbon fibre
Kohlenstoffaserfilz *m* carbon felt
Kohlenstoffasergewebe *n* carbon fibre fabric

Kohlenstoffaser-Kohlenstoff-Verbundwerkstoff *m* carbon fibre-reinforced carbon, CFC, carbon-carbon composite
Kohlenstoffassimilation *f* carbon assimilation
Kohlenstoffatom *n***/asymmetrisches** asymmetric carbon atom
~/primäres primary carbon atom
~/sekundäres secondary carbon atom
~/tertiäres tertiary carbon atom
Kohlenstoffbilanz *f (agric)* carbon balance
Kohlenstoffbindung *f***/doppelte** *s.* Kohlenstoff-Doppelbindung
~/dreifache *s.* Kohlenstoff-Dreifachbindung
~/einfache *s.* Kohlenstoff-Einfachbindung
Kohlenstoffblock *m (met)* carbon block
Kohlenstoffchemie *f* chemistry of the carbon compounds
Kohlenstoffdioxid *n s.* Kohlendioxid
Kohlenstoffdisulfid *n* carbon disulphide
Kohlenstoff-Doppelbindung *f* carbon[-carbon] double bond, carbon-to-carbon double bond, C=C bond
Kohlenstoff-Dreifachbindung *f* carbon[-carbon] triple bond, carbon-to-carbon triple bond, C≡C bond
Kohlenstoffdreiring *m* three-membered carbon ring
Kohlenstoff-Einfachbindung *f* carbon[-carbon] single bond, carbon-to-carbon single bond, C–C bond
Kohlenstoffeinsatzstahl *m* carbon-carburizing steel, carbon case-hardening steel
Kohlenstofffaser *f s.* Kohlenstoffaser
kohlenstofffrei free from carbon
Kohlenstoff-Fünfring *m* five-membered carbon ring
Kohlenstoffgarn *n* carbon yarn
Kohlenstoffgehalt *m* carbon content • **mit hohem** ~ high-carbon • **mit mittlerem** ~ medium-carbon • **mit niedrigem** ~ low-carbon
Kohlenstoffgerüst *n* carbon skeleton
Kohlenstoffgewebe *n* carbon fibre fabric
Kohlenstoff-Halogen-Bindung *f* carbon-halogen bond
kohlenstoffhaltig containing carbon, carbonaceous
Kohlenstoffilz *m* carbon felt
Kohlenstoffkette *f* carbon chain
~/geschlossene closed carbon chain
Kohlenstoff-Kohlenstoff-Bindung *f* carbon-carbon bond, C–C bond
Kohlenstoffkörper *m* carbon body
Kohlenstoffmaterial *n* carbon material
Kohlenstoff-14-Methode *f* ^{14}C method, radiocarbon method
Kohlenstoffmonosulfid *n* carbon monosulphide
Kohlenstoffnachweis *m* detection of carbon
Kohlenstoffpotential *n* carburizing level *(of steel)*
Kohlenstoffquelle *f (biot)* carbon source
Kohlenstoffradikal *n* carbon-centred radical
kohlenstoffreich rich in carbon, high-carbon
Kohlenstoffring *m* carbon ring
~/sechsgliedriger six-membered carbon ring, six-carbon[-atom] ring
~/siebengliedriger seven-membered carbon ring, seven-carbon[-atom] ring
Kohlenstoffrückstand *m* carbon residue
~ nach Conradson *(petrol)* Conradson coke (carbon) residue
Kohlenstoffschicht *f* carbon layer, *(relating to graphite also)* carbon sheet
Kohlenstoffselenidsulfid *n* carbon selenide sulphide
Kohlenstoff-Silicium-Bindung *f* carbon-silicon bond
Kohlenstoff-12-Skala *f* carbon-12 scale *(of atomic weights)*
Kohlenstoffstahl *m* carbon steel
~/reiner plain (straight) carbon steel
Kohlenstoffstein *m* carbon brick
Kohlenstoff-Stickstoff-Gerüst *n* carbon-nitrogen skeleton
Kohlenstoff-Stickstoff-Verhältnis *n (soil, biot)* carbon-to-nitrogen ratio, C/N ratio
Kohlenstofftelluridsulfid *n* carbon telluride sulphide
Kohlenstofftetrabromid *n* carbon tetrabromide, *tetrabromomethane, perbromomethane
Kohlenstofftetrachlorid *n* carbon tetrachloride, *tetrachloromethane, perchloromethane
Kohlenstoffumsatz *m (coal)* carbon conversion
Kohlenstoffumsetzungsgrad *m*, **Kohlenstoffumwandlungsgrad** *m (coal)* carbon conversion ratio
Kohlenstoffverbindung *f* carbon compound
~/ringförmige carbocyclic compound
Kohlenstoffverlust *m* carbon loss
Kohlenstoff-Wasserstoff-Bindung *f* carbon-hydrogen bond
Kohlenstoff-Wasserstoff-Verhältnis *n* C/H ratio
Kohlenstoff-Whisker *m* carbon whisker
Kohlenstoffzustellung *f* carbon lining *(of a blast furnace)*
Kohlensuboxid *n s.* Trikohlenstoffdioxid
Kohlensubsulfid *n s.* Trikohlenstoffdisulfid
Kohlenteer *m* coal tar
Kohlenteerdestillat *n* coal-tar distillate
Kohlenteeröl *n* coal-tar oil
Kohlenteerpech *n* coal-tar pitch
Kohlenteer-Solventnaphtha *n(f)* coal-tar naphtha
Kohlentrichter *m* coal hopper
Kohlenverwertung *f* coal utilization
Kohlenvorratsbunker *m* coal bunker; coal storage hopper *(for bottom discharge)*
Kohlenwäsche *f* 1. coal cleaning (washing); 2. coal-cleaning plant
Kohlenwassergas *n* coal water gas
Kohlenwasserstoff *m* hydrocarbon
~/acyclischer acyclic (aliphatic) hydrocarbon

~/alicyclischer alicyclic (cycloaliphatic) hydrocarbon
~/aliphatischer aliphatic hydrocarbon
~/aromatischer aromatic (benzene) hydrocarbon
~/chlorierter chlorinated hydrocarbon
~/cyclischer cyclic hydrocarbon
~/cycloaliphatischer *s.* ~/alicyclischer
~/fluorierter fluorinated hydrocarbon, fluorocarbon
~/geradkettiger straight-chain hydrocarbon
~/gesättigter saturated (paraffin) hydrocarbon, alkane
~/höherer higher hydrocarbon
~/kettenförmiger open-chain hydrocarbon, aliphatic hydrocarbon
~ mit gerader Kette straight-chain hydrocarbon
~ mit verzweigter Kette branched-chain hydrocarbon
~/offenkettiger *s.* ~/kettenförmiger
~/paraffinischer *s.* ~/gesättigter
~/polycyclischer polycyclic hydrocarbon, polycyclohydrocarbon
~/polycyclischer aromatischer polycyclic (polynuclear) aromatic hydrocarbon, PAH
~/polymerer hydrocarbon polymer, polyhydrocarbon
~/ringförmiger cyclic hydrocarbon
~/verzweigtkettiger branched-chain hydrocarbon
Kohlenwasserstoffarm *m* spacer *(of a gel in affinity chromatography)*
Kohlenwasserstoffcracken *n* hydrocarbon cracking
Kohlenwasserstoffende *n* hydrocarbon tail *(as of a fatty acid)*
Kohlenwasserstoff-Fermentation *f (biot)* hydrocarbon fermentation
Kohlenwasserstoffgas *n* hydrocarbon gas, HC gas
Kohlenwasserstoffgemisch *n* hydrocarbon mixture
Kohlenwasserstoffgruppe *f* hydrocarbon group (residue)
Kohlenwasserstoffharz *n* hydrocarbon resin
Kohlenwasserstoffkette *f* hydrocarbon chain
kohlenwasserstofflöslich hydrocarbon-soluble
Kohlenwasserstofföl *n* hydrocarbon oil
Kohlenwasserstoffradikal *n* free hydrocarbon radical
Kohlenwasserstoffreihe *f* family of hydrocarbons
Kohlenwasserstoffrest *m s.* Kohlenwasserstoffgruppe
Kohlenwasserstoffrestgehalt *m (hyd)* residual content of hydrocarbons
Kohlenwasserstoffspaltung *f* hydrocarbon cracking
Kohlenwasserstoffsynthese *f*/**Kolbesche** Kolbe electrolysis (electrochemical) reaction
Kohlenwasserstoffwachs *n* hydrocarbon wax
Kohlepapier *n* carbon paper
Kohlepartikel *n* coal particle
Kohlepaste *f* coal paste
Kohlepechbrikett *n* pitch-bound briquette
Kohleprobe *f*, **Kohleprobekörper** *m* coal sample
Kohlepulver *n* pulverized (powdered) coal
Kohlepyrolyse *f* coal pyrolysis
Kohleraffinerie *f* coal refinery
Kohlerohrofen *m s.* Graphitrohrküvette
Kohleschiffchen *n* carbon boat
Kohleschlamm *m* coal slurry
Kohleschleuse *f* coal lock, coal-charging vessel *(as of a pressure gasifier)*
Kohleschönung *f (food)* carbon treatment
Kohleschüttung *f* coal charge
Kohleschwarz *n* carbon black
kohlestämmig coal-derived
Kohlestreifen *m* coal band
Kohlestreifenart *f* type of band, microlithotype
Kohlestruktur *f* coal structure
Kohlesubstanz *f* coal material (substance)
Kohleteilchen *n* coal particle
Kohletiegel *m* carbon crucible
Kohletrockner *m* coal dryer
Kohletyp *m* type of coal
Kohleumwandlung *f* coal conversion
Kohlevarietät *f* variety of coal
Kohleverbrauch *m* coal consumption; *(hyd)* carbon utilization rate
Kohleveredlung *f* coal conversion
Kohleveredlungsanlage *f* coal-conversion plant
Kohleveredlungsverfahren *n* coal-conversion process
Kohleverflüssigung *f* coal liquefaction, hydroliquefaction of coal
Kohleverflüssigungsanlage *f* coal liquefaction plant
Kohlevergasung *f* coal gasification
Kohleverkokung *f* coal carbonization
Kohlevermahlung *f* coal milling (grinding, pulverization)
Kohleverschwelung *f* coal carbonization
Kohleverteiler *m* coal distributor *(as of a pressure gasifier)*
Kohlevorkommen *n* coal deposit
Kohlewandlung *f* coal conversion
Kohle-Wasser-Suspension *f* coal-water slurry
Kohlewertstoff *m* coal chemical, coal-derived chemical product
Kohlewertstoffgewinnung *f* coal-chemical recovery
Kohlezerstäuber *m* coal atomizer
Kohlezufuhr *f* coal feed
Kohlezwischenbunker *m* auxiliary coal hopper
kohlig carbonaceous
Kohlrausch-Brücke *f (phys ch)* Kohlrausch bridge
Kohlsaatöl *n* rape[-seed] oil, colza oil
Kohlung *f (met)* carburization
Kohlungsbad *n (met)* carburizing bath
Kohlungsgas *n (met)* carburizing gas
Kohlungsmittel *n (met)* carburizing agent, [case-hardening] carburizer

Kohlungsofen *m (met)* carburizing furnace (oven)
Kohlungspegel *m (met)* carburizing level
Kohlungspulver *n (met)* carburizing powder
Kohlungssalz *n (met)* carburizing salt
Kohlungstiefe *f (met)* carburizing (carburization) depth, case depth
Kohobation *f (distil)* cohobation
kohobieren *(distil)* to cohobate
KOH-Zahl *f (rubber)* KOH number
koinzident coincident
Koinzidenz *f* coincidence
Koinzidenzanordnung *f (nucl)* coincidence arrangement
Koinzidenzmethode *f (spectr)* coincidence method
Koinzidenzzähler *m (nucl)* coincidence counter
Koinzidenzzählung *f (nucl)* coincidence counting
koinzidieren to coincide
Kojisäure *f* kojic acid, 5-hydroxy-2-hydroxymethyl-γ-pyrone
Kokaalkaloid *n* coca alkaloid
Kokain *n* cocaine
Kokainhydrochlorid *n* cocaine hydrochloride
Kokatalysator *m* co-catalyst
Kokatalyse *f* co-catalysis
koken to coke
Kokerei *f* carbonizing plant, coking (coke) plant
~ mit bewegter Beschickung (Ladung) continuous carbonizing plant
~ mit ruhender Beschickung (Ladung) static carbonizing plant
Kokereiabwasser *n (hyd)* coke plant waste, waste from coke plants
Kokereianlage *f s.* Kokerei
Kokereibenzol *n* coke-oven benzole
Kokereigas *n* coke-oven gas
Kokereiindustrie *f* coke (carbonizing) industry
Kokereiofen *m* coke (coking) oven
Kokereiteer *m* coke-oven tar
Kokille *f* ingot mould *(for steel)*; [permanent] metal mould, gravity die *(for castings)*
Kokillengießmaschine *f* diecasting machine
Kokillenguß *m* ingot casting *(of steel)*; permanent-mould casting, gravity diecasting
Kokillengußstück *n*, **Kokillengußteil** *n* gravity die casting
Kokkolith *m (min)* coccolite *(a granular variety of pyroxene)*
Kokon *m* cocoon
Kokondensation *f (plast)* co-condensation
Kokonseide *f* florette (floss) silk
Kokosbutter *f s.* Kokosfett
Kokosfett *n* coconut butter (oil), copra oil
Kokoshartfett *n* hydrogenated coconut oil
Kokoskuchen *m* coconut (copra) cake
Kokoskuchenmehl *n* coconut (copra) meal
Kokosmilch *f* coconut milk (water)
Kokosöl *n s.* Kokosfett
Kokospreßkuchen *m s.* Kokoskuchen
Koks *m* coke
~/hüttenfähiger metallurgical coke
~/kalzinierter calcined coke
~/metallurgischer metallurgical coke
~ zur Wassergaserzeugung water-gas coke
Koksabwurframpe *f* coke wharf
Kok-Saghys-Kautschuk *m* kok-saghyz rubber *(from Taraxacum bicorne Dahlst.)*
Koksaschenbeton *m* breeze concrete
Koksausdrücken *n* coke discharge
Koksausdrückmaschine *f* coke-discharging machine, coke discharger (pusher)
Koksausdrückstange *f* coke pusher ram
Koksausstoß *m* coke discharge
Koksausstoßmaschine *f s.* Koksausdrückmaschine
Koksausstoßseite *f* coke[-discharge] side *(of a coke oven)*
Koksaustrag *m* coke discharge
Koksaustragevorrichtung *f* coke discharger
Koksaustragewalze *f* coke extractor
Koksband *n* coke belt conveyor
Koksbatterie *f s.* Koksofenbatterie
koksbeladen coke-contaminated *(catalyst)*
Koksbildung *f* coke formation
Koksbildungsvermögen *n* coking power
Koksbrecher *m* coke breaker
Koksbrikett *n* coke briquette
Koksbunker *m* coke bunker
Koksdrückmaschine *f s.* Koksausdrückmaschine
Kokseigenschaften *fpl* coke properties
Koksextraktor *m* coke extractor *(a discharging device)*
Koksfestigkeit *f* strength of coke
Koksführungsschild *m* coke guide
Koksführungswagen *m* coke guide
~ mit Türabhebemaschine coke guide and door machine
Koksgas *n* coke-oven gas
koksgefeuert coke-fired
Koksgenerator *m* coke producer
Koksgrus *m* coke breeze
Kokskammer *f* coke (coking) chamber *(of a coking plant or in cracking petrol)*
Kokskohle *f* coking (carbonization) coal
Kokskuchen *m* coke button
Kokskuchenführungswagen *m s.* Koksführungswagen
Kokskühlrampe *f* coke wharf
Kokskühlung *f* coke cooling
Kokskühlzone *f* coke cooling zone
Kokslöschbeton *m* breeze concrete
Kokslöschturm *m* coke quenching tower
Kokslöschung *f* coke quenching
~/nasse wet quenching
~/trockene dry quenching
Kokslöschwagen *m* [coke-]quenching car
Kokslöschwasser *n* quenching water
Koksofen *m* coke (coking) oven
~ mit Nebenproduktengewinnung by-product (chemical-recovery) coke oven
~ mit Unterbrennern underjet coke oven

Koksofenanlage *f s.* Kokereianlage
Koksofenbatterie *f* coke-oven battery, retort battery, carbonizing bench
Koksofenfüllwagen *m* coal-charging car
Koksofengas *n* coke-oven gas
Koksofenkammer *f* coking (coke) chamber
Koksofenteer *m* coke-oven tar
Koksrampe *f* coke wharf
Koksrückstand *m* **nach Conradson** *(petrol)* Conradson coke (carbon) residue
~ **nach Ramsbottom** Ramsbottom coke (carbon) residue
Koksschleuse *f* coke extractor *(a discharging device)*
Koksseite *f* coke[-discharge] side *(of a coke oven)*
Koksstaub *m* coke dust
Kokstransportband *n* coke belt conveyor
Kokstyp[us] *m* coke type
~ **nach Gray-King** Gray-King [assay] coke type
Koksvergasung *f* coke gasification
Kokswagen *m* coke car, [coke-]quenching car
Kokswassergas *n* blue [water] gas
Kokumbutter *f* kokum (Goa) butter *(from Garcinia indica Choisy)*
Kokungsdestillationsanlage *f* coking still
Kokungsofen *m s.* Koksofen
Kokungsvermögen *n* coking power
Kolatur *f* colature *(liquid which has been strained)*
Kölbel *n (glass)* parison
Kolben *m* 1. *(lab)* flask, bulb; 2. *(tech)* piston, plunger, ram
Kolbenbürette *f* syringe burette *(potentiometry)*
Kolbendruckgießmaschine *f* piston-type diecasting machine
Kolbenfläche *f* piston area
Kolbenkompressor *m* reciprocating compressor
Kolbenpumpe *f* piston pump
~ **mit hin- und hergehendem Kolben** reciprocating pump
~ **mit rotierendem Kolben** rotary pump
Kolbenraum *m* plunger compartment
Kolbensetzmaschine *f (min tech)* plunger-type fixed-sieve jig
~**/Harzer** Harz [fixed-sieve] jig
Kolbenspritzgußmaschine *f (plast)* plunger-type injection machine
Kolbenstange *f* piston rod
Kolbenstangendichtung *f*, **Kolbenstangenpackung** *f* piston-rod packing
Kolbenstrangpresse *f (plast)* ram extruder
Kolbenstrangpressen *n (plast)* ram extrusion
Kolbenträger *m (lab)* flask holder (support)
Kolbenverbrennung *f (anal)* [oxygen] flask combustion
Kolbenverdichter *m* reciprocating compressor
Kolbenvorplastizierung *f (plast)* ram-type preplastication
Kolbe-Schmitt-Synthese *f* Kolbe-Schmitt synthesis *(of aromatic hydroxy acids)*
Kolbe-Synthese *f* **von Kohlenwasserstoffen** Kolbe hydrocarbon synthesis, Kolbe electrolysis (electrochemical) reaction
kolieren to strain
Kolieren *n* colation, straining
Kollagen *n* collagen *(a scleroprotein)*
Kollektivflotation *f* collective (bulk) floatation
Kollektor *m (min tech)* collector, promoter, collecting (promoting) agent
Kollergang *m* edge (pan, Chilean) mill, edge runner, kollergang, pan crusher
~ **mit perforierter Mahlbahn** perforated edge mill
Kollergangstein *m* runner [stone]
Kollermühle *f s.* Kollergang
kollern to disintegrate (grind) in an edge mill
Kollerstein *m* runner [stone]
Kollerstoff *m (pap)* [machine, mill] broke, brokes, broken [material, paper]
kollidieren to collide
α-Kollidin *n* α-collidine, 4-ethyl-2-methylpyridine
β-Kollidin *n* β-collidine, 3-ethyl-4-methylpyridine
γ-Kollidin *n* γ-collidine, 2,4,6-trimethylpyridine
sym-**Kollidin** *n s.* γ-Kollidin
Kollimatorlinse *f (spectr)* collimating lens
Kollimatorspiegel *m (spectr)* collimating mirror
Kollinit *m (coal)* collinite
Kollision *f* collision
Kollisionsfrequenz *f* frequency of [particle] collisions
Kollodium *n* collodion
Kollodiummembran *f* collodion membrane
Kollodium-Ultrafilter *n* collodion ultrafilter
Kollodiumverfahren *n***/nasses** *(phot)* wet collodion process
Kollodiumwolle *f* collodion cotton (wool), soluble nitrocellulose (guncotton, cotton), pyroxylin[e], pyrocellulose *(a lower-nitrated cellulose)*
kolloid colloid[al]
Kolloid *n* colloid
~**/festes** solid colloid
~**/globuläres** globular colloid
~**/heteropolares** heteropolar colloid
~**/hydrophiles** hydrophilic colloid
~**/irresolubles (irreversibles)** irresoluble (irreversible) colloid
~**/lyophiles** lyophile colloid
~**/lyophobes** lyophobe colloid
~**/resolubles (reversibles)** resoluble (reversible) colloid
kolloidal colloid[al]
Kolloidchemie *f* colloid chemistry, collochemistry
Kolloidchemiker *m* colloid chemist
kolloidchemisch colloid-chemical, colloidochemical
kolloiddispers colloid-disperse, colloidally dispersed
Kolloidelektrolyt *m* colloidal electrolyte
Kolloidgebilde *n* colloidal entity
kolloidgelöst colloidally dissolved

Kolloidik *f* colloid science
Kolloidkaolin *n* colloidal kaolin
Kolloidkunde *f*, **Kolloidlehre** *f* colloid science
Kolloidlösung *f* colloidal solution
Kolloidmühle *f* colloid mill
~/Oderberger Oderberg [colloid] mill
~/Plausonsche Plauson [colloid] mill
Kolloidpartikel *n* colloidal particle
Kolloidschwefel *m* colloidal sulphur
Kolloidsystem *n* colloidal system
Kolloidteilchen *n* colloidal particle
Kolloidzustand *m* colloidal state
Kolloxylin *n s.* Kollodiumwolle
Kölnischwasser *n* cologne [water]
Kolonne *f* column, *(esp tech also)* tower
~/atmosphärische atmospheric column
~ für Zweistoffgemische binary column
~/leere wetted-wall column
~ mit rotierendem Zylinder rotating-core column
~ mit rotierenden Scheiben rotary-disk tower (contactor, extractor)
~ mit schwingenden Siebböden reciprocating-plate column
~/pulsierte pulse column, pulsed tower
~/quasi-unendliche *(chromat)* infinite-diameter column
~ zur Azeotropdestillation azeotropic column
Kolonnendestillation *f* column distillation
Kolonnendurchmesser *m* column diameter
Kolonnenfüllung *f* column packing
~/geordnete stacked packing
~/geschüttete dumped packing
Kolonnenhöhe *f* column height
Kolonneninhalt *m***/dynamischer** *(distil)* operating hold-up
Kolonnenkopf *m* still head, top of the column
Kolonnenwirkungsgrad *m* column efficiency
Kolophonium *n* colophony, pine resin, rosin *(from Pinus specc.)*
kolorieren *(phot)* to colour
Kolorimeter *n* colorimeter
~/lichtelektrisches (objektives) photoelectric colorimeter
~/visuelles visual colorimeter
Kolorimeterrohr *n* colorimeter tube
~ nach Hehner Hehner cylinder
~ nach Neßler Nessler cylinder
Kolorimeterröhre *f*, **Kolorimeterzylinder** *m s.* Kolorimeterrohr
Kolorimetrie *f* colorimetry
~/lichtelektrische (objektive) photocolorimetry
~/visuelle visual colorimetry
kolorimetrisch colorimetric
Kolorist *m (text)* colourist
Kolzaöl *n* colza oil, rape[-seed] oil
Kombination *f***/lineare** linear combination *(as of atomic orbitals)*
~ von Radikalen radical combination
Kombinationsabbruch *m* coupling termination, [chain] termination by coupling
Kombinationsdünger *m* compound fertilizer, multi-nutrient (mixed) fertilizer
Kombinationsfilter *n* combination mechanical-chemical filter
Kombinationsgerbung *f* combination tannage
Kombinationsprinzip *n***/Ritz-Rydbergsches** *(phys ch)* Ritz-Rydberg combination principle, Ritz [combination] principle
Kombinationsreaktion *f* combination reaction
Kombinationsschwingung *f* combination vibration
Kombinationsschwingungsbande *f (spectr)* combination band
Kombinationstrockner *m (coat)* combination dryer
Kombinationsweise *f* mode of combination
kombinieren to combine; *(dye)* to couple
kommafrei *(bioch)* commaless *(code)*
Kommunalabwasser *n* municipal (community) sewage (waste water)
Kommunalabwasserreinigung *f s.* Abwasserbehandlung/kommunale
kompakt compact, solid
Kompakt *m s.* Kompaktpuder
Kompaktanlage *f (hyd)* compact plant
kompaktieren to compact
Kompaktiermaschine *f* compactor [mill], compacting mill
Kompaktierung *f* compaction
Kompaktpuder *m (cosmet)* compact powder
Komparator *m* comparator *(colorimetry)*
~/visueller visual comparator
Kompartiment *n (bioch)* compartment
kompartimentiert *(bioch)* compartmentalized
Kompartimentierung *f (bioch)* compartment[aliz]ation
~ des Stoffwechsels metabolic compartmentation
kompatibel compatible
Kompatibilität *f* compatibility
Kompensation *f* compensation
Kompensationsmethode *f* compensation method, [null-]balance method, null (zero) method
~/Poggendorffsche Poggendorff compensation method
Kompensations-*p*H-Meter *n* compensation *p*H-meter
Kompensationsschaltung *f s.* Kompensationsmethode
Kompensationsschreiber *m* self-balancing recorder
Kompensationswägung *f* direct weighing
Kompensator *m* 1. compensator; 2. expansion joint *(of piping)*; 3. bias control *(as of a polarograph)*
kompensieren to compensate, to counterbalance; *(dye)* to offset
Komplementärfarbe *f* complementary colour
Komplementarität *f* complementarity, complementariness

Komplementation *f*, **Komplementierung** *f* complementation *(gene research)*
Komplex *m* complex • **im ~ binden** to complex
~/aktivierter activated complex, transition state *(kinetics)*
~ aus Repressor und Corepressor *(bioch)* repressor-corepressor complex
~/koordinierter coordination complex
~/mehrkerniger polynuclear complex
~/organomineralischer *(soil)* organo-clay (clay-humus) complex
~/polynuklearer polynuclear complex
~/schwach gebundener hypoligated complex
~/stark gebundener hyperligated complex
~/ternärer ternary (central) complex *(enzyme kinetics)*
~/verbrauchter *(petrol)* complex out *(in liquid-phase isomerization)*
~/Wernerscher Werner complex *(chemical-bond theory)*
1:1-Komplex *m* 1:1 complex
2:1-Komplex *m* 2:1 complex
π-Komplex *m (org ch)* pi-adduct, π-adduct
σ-Komplex *m (org ch)* sigma-adduct, σ-adduct
komplexaktiv *s.* komplexbildend
komplexbildend complex-forming, complexing
~/nicht non-complexing
Komplexbildner *m* complexing (sequestering) agent, complexer, sequestrant, coordinator
Komplexbildung *f* complex formation, complexation, sequestration
Komplexbildungsgleichgewicht *n* complex-formation equilibrium
Komplexbildungskonstante *f s.* Komplexstabilitätskonstante
Komplexbildungsreaktion *f* complex-formation reaction
Komplexbildungstitration *f* complexation titration
Komplexchemie *f* coordination chemistry, chemistry of coordination compounds
Komplexdissoziationskonstante *f* instability constant
Komplexerz *n* complex ore
Komplexgebilde *n* complex entity
komplexgebunden coordinate
komplexieren to complex
Komplexierung *f* complexation
Komplex-Ion *n* complex ion
Komplexität *f (nomencl)* complexity
Komplexkatalysator *m* coordination (complexing) catalyst
Komplexkatalyse *f* coordination catalysis
Komplexkoazervation *f* complex coacervation
Komplexometrie *f* complexometry, complexation analysis
komplexometrisch complexometric, compleximetric
Komplexsalz *n* complex salt
~/inneres inner complex salt
Komplexstabilitätskonstante *f* formation (stability) constant
~/individuelle *s.* ~/konsekutive
~/konditionelle conditional formation constant
~/konsekutive stepwise (successive) formation constant
~/stufenweise *s.* ~/konsekutive
Komplexverbindung *f* coordination (complex) compound
~/innere inner complex compound
Kompliziertheit *f (nomencl)* complexity
Komponente *f* component, constituent, moiety
~/aktive *(dye)* diazo component, diazonium (primary) component
~/dienophile dienophile
~/endständige *(nomencl)* end component
~/hochsiedende (höhersiedende) *(distil)* less-volatile component, high-boiling component
~/leichterflüchtige (leichtersiedende) *s.* ~/niedrigsiedende
~/leichtest siedende lighter-than-light component
~/leichtsiedende *s.* ~/niedrigsiedende
~/niedrigsiedende *(distil)* more volatile component, M.V.C., low-boiling component, light[er] component, low boiler
~/passive *(dye)* coupling (secondary) component
~/saure acid component
~/schwererflüchtige (schwerersiedende) *s.* ~/hochsiedende
~/schwerflüchtige (schwersiedende) *s.* ~/hochsiedende
~/tiefsiedende *s.* ~/niedrigsiedende
Kompound *n*, **Kompoundmasse** *f (plast)* compound *(mechanical polymer blend)*
kompressibel compressible
Kompressibilität *f* compressibility
~/adiabate (adiabatische) adiabatic compressibility
Kompressibilitätsfaktor *m* compressibility (compression) factor
Kompressibilitätskoeffizient *m*[**/kubischer**] compressibility coefficient, isothermal compressibility
Kompression *f* compression
Kompressionsanlage *f* compressor plant
Kompressionsarbeit *f* work of compression
Kompressionsbereich *m (hyd)* compression region *(sedimentation)*
Kompressionsdampfkälteanlage *f s.* Kompressionskälteanlage
Kompressionshahn *m* pet cock
Kompressionskälteanlage *f* compression refrigerating system, vapour-compression system
Kompressionskältemaschine *f* compression refrigerating machine, vapour-compression machine
Kompressionsmanometer *n* **nach McLeod** McLeod gauge
Kompressionsmodul *m* compressive (bulk) modulus
Kompressionspunkt *m (hyd)* compression point *(sedimentation)*

Kompressionsschrumpf *m (text)* compressive (compression) shrinkage
Kompressions-Verdrängungsverfahren *n (rubber, plast)* compression moulding
Kompressionsverhältnis *n* compression ratio
~/höchstes nutzbares highest useful compression ratio, H.U.C.R.
Kompressionswärme *f* heat of compression
Kompressionszone *f* compression zone (region)
Kompressor *m* compressor
~/einstufiger single-stage compressor
~/mehrstufiger multistage compressor
komprimierbar compressible
Komprimierbarkeit *f* compressibility
komprimieren to compress, *(relating to solids also)* to compact
Komproportionierung *f* comproportionation *(kind of redox reaction)*
Konche *f (food)* [longitudinal] conche
konchieren *(food)* to conche, to mill
Kondensat *n* condensate, condensation product
Kondensatabführung *f*, **Kondensatableitung** *f* condensate removal
Kondensation *f* 1. condensation *(of gas or vapour)*; 2. *(org ch)* condensation *(as of esters)*; fusion, anellation, annulization, condensation *(of cyclic compounds)*
~/Claisensche Claisen condensation *(of esters)*
~/extramolekulare self-condensation
~/kapillare capillary condensation
~/partielle partial condensation, *(distil also)* dephlegmation
~/reduktive (reduzierende) reductive condensation, hydrocondensation
~/retrograde retrograde condensation
Kondensationsanlage *f* condensing system
Kondensationsdruck *m* condensation (condensing) pressure
Kondensationsenthalpie *f* enthalpy of condensation
Kondensationsfläche *f* condensing surface
Kondensationsharz *n* condensation resin
Kondensationshygrometer *n* dew-point hygrometer
Kondensationskalorimeter *n* steam calorimeter
Kondensationskammer *f* condensing chamber
Kondensationskeim *m*, **Kondensationskern** *m* condensation nucleus (centre)
Kondensationskurve *f*, **Kondensationslinie** *f* *(distil)* condensation (dew-point) curve
Kondensationsmethode *f* condensation method
Kondensationsmittel *n* condensing agent
Kondensationspolymer[e] *n* condensation polymer
Kondensationspolymerisation *f* condensation polymerization
Kondensationsprodukt *n* condensation product, condensate
Kondensationsreaktion *f* condensation reaction
Kondensationsrohr *n* condensing tube
Kondensationsschritt *m* condensation step
Kondensationsstelle *f* point (position, side) of fusion, common face *(of rings)*
Kondensationsturm *m* condensing tower
Kondensationswärme *f* heat of condensation
Kondensationszentrum *n* condensation (nucleation) centre (site) *(vapour-liquid phase transition)*
Kondensationszwischenprodukt *n* half-condensation product
Kondensatlagerstätte *f (petrol)* condensate reservoir
Kondensator *m* 1. condenser; 2. *(el ch)* capacitor
~/barometrischer barometric condenser
~/elektrolytischer electrolytic capacitor
~ mit Kühlschlange worm-type condenser
Kondensatorkühler *m* condenser
Kondensator[seiden]papier *n* condenser paper, condenser tissue [paper]
Kondensatrückleiter *m* lift steam trap, boiler return trap
kondensierbar condensable
~/nicht non-condensable
Kondensierbarkeit *f* condensability
kondensieren 1. to condense, to precipitate *(gas or vapour)*; 2. *(org ch)* to condense *(e.g. esters)*; to fuse, to anellate, to annulize, to condense *(cyclic compounds)*; 3. *(food)* to condense, to inspissate; 4. *s.* ~/sich
~/miteinander *(org ch)* to fuse together, to condense [together]
~/sich to condense, to precipitate
~/sich wieder to recondense
~/wieder to recondense
Kondensieren *n***/festes** *s.* Solidensieren
Kondensmagermilch *f* condensed skim milk
Kondensmilch *f* condensed milk, concentrated (evaporated) milk
~/gezuckerte sweetened condensed milk
Kondensmilchfabrik *f* milk condensery (condensing plant)
Kondensstelle *f s.* Kondensationsstelle
Kondenstopf *m* steam trap
Kondensvollmilch *f* condensed whole milk
Kondenswasser *n* condensed (condensate) water
Kondenswasserableiter *m* steam trap
Kondenswasserhahn *m* pet cock
Konditionieranlage *f* conditioning plant (unit)
Konditionierapparat *m* conditioning apparatus, conditioner
konditionieren to condition; *(relating to humidity:)* to [air-]condition
Konditionierung *f* conditioning; *(relating to humidity:)* air conditioning
~/thermische *s.* Heißkonditionierung von Abwasserschlamm
Konduktanz *f (phys ch)* conductance
Konduktometrie *f* conductometry, conductimetry
konduktometrisch conductometric, conductimetric
Konfektion *f s.* Konfektionierung 2.

konfektionieren 1. to formulate; 2. *(rubber)* to assemble, to build
Konfektionierlaboratorium *n* regulatory laboratory *(for preparing pesticides)*
Konfektionierlösung *f (rubber)* assembling solution, cement
Konfektioniermaschine *f (rubber)* tyre-building machine (drum), lay-up machine
Konfektionierraum *m s.* Konfektionsabteilung
Konfektioniertisch *m (rubber)* assembling table
Konfektionierung *f* 1. formulation; 2. *(rubber)* assembly, building
Konfektionsabteilung *f (rubber)* assembling (assembly) department
Konfektionsklebrigkeit *f (rubber)* building tack
Konfektionslösung *f (rubber)* assembling solution
Konfiguration *f* [spatial] configuration, molecular configuration
~/absolute absolute configuration
~/erzwungene forced configuration
~/relative relative configuration
Konfigurationsbeweis *m* proof of configuration
Konfigurationserhalt *m*, **Konfigurationserhaltung** *f* retention of configuration, configuration retention
Konfigurationsformel *f* configurational (space) formula
Konfigurationsisomer[e] *n* configurational isomer
Konfigurationsisomerie *f* configurational isomerism
konfigurationsstabil configurationally stable
Konfigurationssymbol *n* configurational symbol
Konfigurationsumkehr *f*, **Konfigurationswechsel** *m* inversion of configuration, Walden inversion
Konfigurationswechselwirkung *f* configuration interaction, CI
konfigurativ configurational
Konformation *f* conformation, conformational structure *(1. stereochemistry; 2. collectively for the tertiary and quaternary structure of proteins)*
~/anticlinale anticlinal conformation, ac *(torsion angle ±120°)*
~/antiperiplanare antiperiplanar conformation, ap *(torsion angle ±180°)*
~/äquatoriale equatorial conformation
~/axiale axial conformation
~/ekliptische *s.* ~/synperiplanare
~/gestaffelte *s.* ~/antiperiplanare
~/gewinkelte puckered conformation
~/native *(bioch)* native conformation
~/polare *s.* ~/axiale
~/synclinale synclinal conformation, sc *(torsion angle ±60°)*
~/synperiplanare synperiplanar conformation, sp *(torsion angle 0°)*
~/teilweise verdeckte *s.* ~/anticlinale
~/verdeckte *s.* ~/synperiplanare
~/windschiefe *s.* ~/synclinale
anti-**Konformation** *f* 1. anti conformation, A *(with macromolecules, torsion angle ±60°)*; 2. *s.* Konformation/antiperiplanare
cis-**Konformation** *f* cis conformation, C *(with macromolecules, torsion angle ±180°)*
gauche-**Konformation** *f* gauche conformation, G *(with macromolecules, torsion angle ±120°)*
trans-**Konformation** *f* trans conformation, T *(with macromolecules, torsion angle 0°)*
Konformationsanalyse *f* conformational analysis
Konformationsänderung *f* conformational change
Konformationsformel *f* conformational formula
Konformationsisomer[e] *n* conformational isomer, conformer
Konformationsisomerie *f* conformational (rotational) isomerism
konformationsstabil conformationally stable
Konformationswinkel *m* torsion (rotational) angle, angle of rotation
konformer conformational
Konformer[e] *n s.* Konformationsisomer[e]
Konglomerat *n* conglomerate
Kongofarbstoff *m* Congo dye *(any of a group of azo dyes)*
Kongokopal *m* Congo copal (gum) *(a semifossil resin from Copaifera specc.)*
Kongokorinth *n (dye)* Congo corinth
Kongopapier *n* Congo paper
Kongorot *n* Congo red, direct red 28 *(an azo dye)*
Kongorubin *n* Congo rubin[e], direct red 17 *(an azo dye)*
Kongreßverfahren *n (ferm)* congress method
Kongreßwürze *f (ferm)* congress wort
Königinnensubstanz *f* queen-bee's substance *(biologically active substance of the queen-bee's salivary glands)*
Königsgelb *n* king's yellow (gold), royal yellow, yellow arsenic [sulphide], arsenic yellow, orpiment [yellow] *(arsenic(III) sulphide)*
Königswasser *n* aqua regia, aq. reg., chloronitrous (chloroazotic, nitrohydrochloric) acid
konisch conical, cone-shaped • **~ zulaufen** to taper
~ zulaufend taper[ing], tapered
Konizität *f* conicity; taper *(of piping)*
Konjugatbildung *f (bioch)* conjugate formation
Konjugation *f* conjugation
~/gekreuzte cross conjugation
Konjugationsenergie *f s.* Delokalisierungsenergie
konjugieren to conjugate
konjugiert conjugate[d]
Konkavgitter *n (spectr)* concave grating
Konkavgitterspektrograph *m* concave-grating spectrograph
konkret *(cosmet)* concrete *(e.g. oil)*
Konkret *n (cosmet)* concrete [oil]
Konkretion *f (geol)* concretion
Konkurrenzhemmung *f* competitive inhibition *(enzyme kinetics)*
Konkurrenzmethode *f* competition method *(for investigating fast reactions)*
Konkurrenzreaktion *f* competitive reaction, competing (concurrent) reaction

Ko[n]node *f (phys ch)* conode, tie line *(in the equilibrium diagram)*
konrotatorisch *(org ch)* conrotatory
Konserve *f (food)* preserve
Konservendose *f* tin [can], can
Konservenfabrik *f* canning (preserving) plant, cannery, *(Am)* packing house
Konservenfabrikation *f* canning
Konservenglas *n* preserving bottle, vacuum jar
Konservenherstellung *f* canning
Konservenindustrie *f* canning (canned foods) industry
konservieren *(tech)* to conserve, to preserve; *(food)* to preserve, *(esp by drying, salting, or smoking:)* to cure; *(tann)* to cure
~/durch Kälte to deep-freeze
~/in Dosen to can, to tin
konservierend preservative
konserviert/mit Ammoniak *(rubber)* ammonia-preserved
Konservierung *f (tech)* conservation, preservation; *(food)* preservation, *(esp by drying, salting, or smoking:)* cure, curing; *(tann)* cure, curing
~/chemische *(food)* chemical preservation
~ durch Salzlakenbehandlung *(tann)* brine cure (curing)
~ in Dosen *(food)* canning, tinning
Konservierungsmittel *n (tech, food)* preservative [agent], preserving agent; *(food, tann)* curing agent
~/chemisches chemical preservative
Konservierungssalz *n* curing salt
Konservierungsstoff *m s.* Konservierungsmittel
konsistent consistent
Konsistenz *f* consistency, consistence; *(coat)* body
~/pastöse (teigige) doughiness
Konsistenzregler *m* consistency regulator
Konsistometer *n* consistometer
konstant constant • **~ halten** to maintain (keep) constant
Konstantdruckpumpe *f* constant-pressure pump
Konstante *f* constant [quantity]
~/Boltzmannsche Boltzmann constant *(thermodynamics)*
~ der inneren Reibung viscosity coefficient
~/ebullioskopische ebullioscopic constant, molal boiling-point[-elevation] constant
~/Faradaysche Faraday constant, faraday, F *(equivalent to 96486 coulomb)*
~/gyromagnetische gyromagnetic factor, g-factor, spectroscopic splitting factor
~/katalytische catalytic coefficient
~/kryoskopische cryoscopic constant, molal freezing-point[-depression] constant
~/Madelungsche Madelung constant
~/Plancksche Planck (action) constant, [Planck] quantum of action
~/Poissonsche Poisson's ratio
~/Rydbergsche Rydberg constant (number)
~/van-der-Waalssche van der Waals constant
Konstanten *fpl*/**kritische** critical constants (data)
Konstanthaltung *f* **eines Stamms** *(biot)* strain maintenance
Konstantpumpe *f* constant-displacement pump
konstantsiedend constant-boiling
Konstellation *f s.* Konformation
konstituierend constituent
Konstitution *f* constitution • **die ~ aufklären (bestimmen, ermitteln)** to elucidate (establish, determine) the structure
Konstitutionsaufklärung *f*, **Konstitutionsbestimmung** *f* structure elucidation, establishment (determination) of constitution
Konstitutionsbeweis *m* proof (evidence) of structure
Konstitutionserforschung *f*, **Konstitutionsermittlung** *f s.* Konstitutionsaufklärung
Konstitutionsformel *f* constitutional formula, structure (line, graphic) formula, [valence] structural formula
Konstitutionswasser *n* constitutional water, water of constitution
konstitutiv constitutive
Konstruktionsmerkmal *n* design feature
Konstruktionswerkstoff *m* material of construction
Kontakt *m* 1. contact; 2. heterogeneous catalyst, solid (contact) catalyst *(s. a. under* Katalysator*)* • **in ~ bringen** to [bring into] contact • **miteinander in ~ kommen** to [enter into] contact
~/beweglicher (bewegter) moving catalyst
~/fester (festliegender) *s.* ~/ruhender
~/perlförmiger bead catalyst
~/ruhender static (fixed-bed) catalyst
Kontakt... *s. a.* Katalysator...
Kontaktabzug *m (phot)* contact print
Kontaktautoklav *m* contactor
Kontaktbacke *f* contact shoe *(for electrodes)*
Kontaktbahnentrockner *m* roller dryer *(for drying webs)*
Kontaktbaustoff *m* electrical contact material
Kontaktbett *n* catalyst bed
~/festes (festliegendes) *s.* ~/ruhendes
~/ruhendes (stationäres) static bed of catalyst
Kontaktdauer *f* time of contact
Kontaktdüngung *f* contact fertilization
Kontaktfiltration *f* contact filtration
Kontaktfläche *f* surface (area) of contact
Kontaktgefrieren *n* contact freezing
Kontaktgetterung *f* contact gettering *(vacuum technology)*
Kontaktgift *n* 1. catalyst (catalytic) poison, paralyzer; 2. *(agric)* [direct] contact poison, contact toxicant
Kontakthemmung *f (bioch)* contact (density) inhibition *(of cellular growth)*
Kontaktherbizid *n* contact herbicide (weed-killer)
Kontakthof *m (geol)* [contact] aureole, contact (exomorphic) zone, metamorphic aureole

Kontaktinsektizid *n* contact insecticide
~ **mit Dauerwirkung** residual contact insecticide
~/**protektives** protective contact insecticide
Kontaktionenpaar *n* contact ion pair, tight (intimate) ion pair
Kontaktkammer *f* catalyst chamber
Kontaktkatalysator *m s.* Kontakt 2.
Kontaktkatalyse *f* contact catalysis, heterogeneous (surface) catalysis
kontaktkatalytisch contact-catalytic
Kontaktkleber *m*, **Kontaktklebstoff** *m* contact[-bonding] adhesive
Kontaktkopie *f (phot)* contact print
Kontaktkopieren *n (phot)* contact printing
Kontaktkopiergerät *n (phot)* contact printer
Kontaktkorrosion *f* galvanic (contact) corrosion, bimetallic (two-metal) corrosion
Kontaktmetamorphose *f (geoch)* contact metamorphism (metamorphosis)
Kontaktmineral *n* contact mineral
Kontaktmittelemulsion *f* contact emulsion *(for weed control)*
Kontaktofen *m* catalytic reactor, converter
Kontakt-Öl-Verhältnis *n* catalyst-to-oil ratio, catalyst/oil ratio
Kontaktor *m* contactor *(1. an autoclave; 2. a solvent extractor)*
Kontaktpapier *n (phot)* contact [printing] paper, silver-chloride paper
Kontaktpille *f* catalyst pellet
Kontaktpotentialdifferenz *f* difference of potential on direct contact
Kontaktpressen *n (plast)* contact (impression) moulding, hand lay-up (technique)
Kontaktraffination *f (petrol)* contact treatment
Kontaktraum *m* contact space
Kontaktrohr *n* catalyst tube
Kontaktrührphase *f (hyd)* slow mix period, slow mixing step *(flocculation)*
Kontaktsäure *f* contact [sulphuric] acid
Kontaktschicht *f* catalyst bed
Kontaktschwefelsäure *f* contact [sulphuric] acid
Kontaktschwefelsäureverfahren *n* contact process (method)
Kontaktstaub *m* catalyst dust, powdered catalyst
Kontaktstoff *m s.* Kontakt 2.
Kontaktthermometer *n* contact thermometer
Kontaktträger *m* catalyst carrier (support)
Kontakttrocknung *f* contact drying, conduction (indirect) drying, drying by contact
Kontaktumlauf *m* catalyst circulation (cycle, recycle)
Kontaktverfahren *n* 1. contact process; 2. *(pap)* cast coating; 3. *(phot)* contact printing
Kontaktverschiebung *f (spectr)* contact shift
Kontakt-Wechselwirkung *f (phys ch)* contact interaction
Kontaktwerkstoff *m* electrical contact material
Kontaktwinkel *m* contact angle
Kontaktwirkung *f* contact action
~/**endomorphe** *(geol)* endomorphism
~/**exomorphe** *(geol)* exomorphism
Kontaktzeit *f* contact time
~ **im leeren Filterbett** *(hyd)* empty-bed contact (retention) time, EBCT *(activated-carbon filtration)*
Kontaminanten *mpl* contaminants, *(specif)* food contaminants, incidental food additives; *(biot)* contaminants, contaminant (contaminating) microorganisms
Kontamination *f* contamination, *(esp)* radioactive contamination, contamination with radioactivity
Kontaminationsgefahr *f* risk of contamination
kontaminationsgefährdet susceptible to contamination
kontaminieren to contaminate, *(esp)* to contaminate with radioactivity
Kontinuebetrieb *m (text)* continuous operation (working, processing) • **im** ~ by a continuous process
Kontinuebleiche *f (text)* continuous bleaching
Kontinue-Breitbleichanlage *f (text)* continuous open-width bleaching machine
Kontinuedämpfer *m (text)* continuous steamer
Kontinuefärbemaschine *f (text)* continuous-dyeing machine
Kontinuefärben *n (text)* continuous dyeing
Kontinuespinnverfahren *n (text)* continuous spinning
Kontinueverfahren *n (text)* continuous process
kontinuierlich continuous
~ **arbeitend** continuous
Kontinuitätsgleichung *f* continuity (mass-balance) equation
Kontinuum *n* continuum
Kontinuumlampe *f*, **Kontinuumlichtquelle** *f. s.* Kontinuumstrahler
Kontinuumstrahler *m (anal)* continuum source
kontrahieren to contract
Kontraktion *f* contraction
Kontraktionsberührungswinkel *m* receding contact angle *(testing of tension depressors)*
Kontraktionskoeffizient *m* coefficient of contraction
Kontraktionsstelle *f* vena contracta *(flow measurement)*
Kontrast *m (phot)* contrast
~/**weicher** soft contrast
kontrastarm *(phot)* low-contrast, thin
Kontrastarmut *f (phot)* flatness
Kontrastentwickler *m (phot)* high-contrast developer
Kontrastfaktor *m (phot)* development factor, gamma value
Kontrastfärbung *f (text)* differential dyeing
Kontrastmittel *n (med)* contrast medium
kontrastreich *m (phot)* high-contrast, contrasty
Kontrastumfang *m (phot)* contrast (brightness) range

Kontrastverminderung *f (phot)* decrease in contrast, reduction in image contrast
Kontrollanalyse *f* check analysis
Kontrolle *f* check[ing], inspection; control *(of a reaction)* • **außer ~ geraten** to get out of control (hand), to run wild
~/kinetische kinetic control
~/thermodynamische thermodynamic (equilibrium) control
Kontrollenzym *n (bioch)* regulatory enzyme
Kontrollfläche *f (agric)* check plot
Kontrollhahn *m*, **Kontrollhahnventil** *n* test cock
Kontrollharz *n* mock resin *(affinity chromatography)*
kontrollieren to check, to inspect; to control *(a reaction)*
Kontrollinie *f (spectr)* standard line
Kontrollmechanismus *m (bioch)* control mechanism
Kontrollstab *m (nucl)* control rod
Konturendiagramm *n* contour map
~ der Energie energy contour map
Konturenschärfe *f (phot)* acutance; *(text)* sharpness in print outline
Konturlänge *f* contour (extended) length *(of a molecular chain)*
Konturliniendiagramm *n s.* Konturendiagramm
Konus *m* cone; *(pap)* plug, rotor, cone, core *(of a perfecting engine)*
~ der Kegelstoffmühle *(pap)* jordan plug
konusartig cone-shaped, conical
Konusfärbeapparat *m* cone dyeing apparatus
Konusmischer *m* conical mixer
Konusmühle *f* cone mill, conical [ball] mill
Konus-Platte-Viskosimeter *n* cone-and-plate viscometer
Konussiebtrommel *f* conical screen
Konvektion *f* convection, convective flow of heat
~/erzwungene forced convection
~/freie natural convection
Konvektionsheizung *f* convection heating
Konvektionsmischen *n* convective mixing
Konvektionsstrom *m s.* Konvektionsströmung
Konvektionsströmung *f* convection current
Konvektionstrockner *m* convection dryer
Konvektionstrocknung *f* convection (direct) drying
Konvektionsvermischen *n* convective mixing
Konvektionswärme *f* convection (convected) heat
konvektiv convective
Konvergenz *f* convergence, convergency
Konvergenzgrenze *f (phys ch)* convergence limit
Konversion *f* 1. *(food)* conversion *(of starch)*; 2. *s.* Konvertierung
~/enzymatische enzymatic (enzyme) conversion
~ mit Säure acid conversion
Konversionsreaktor *m (nucl)* conversion reactor, converter
Konversionssalpeter *m* conversion (converted) saltpetre
Konversions[schutz]schicht *f* [surface-]conversion coating
~/anorganische inorganic conversion coating
~/chemische chemical conversion coating
Konverter *m* 1. *(met, text)* converter; *(coal)* shift converter; 2. *s.* Konversionsreaktor • **im ~ verblasen** *(met)* to convert, to bessemerize
~/bodenblasender *(met)* bottom-blown converter
~/drehbarer *(met)* rotating converter
~/normal blasender *(met)* bottom-blown converter
~/rotierender *(met)* rotating converter
~/seitlich blasender *(met)* side-blown converter
Konverterauskleidung *f (met)* converter lining
Konverterfrischverfahren *n (met)* converter (converting, Bessemer) process
Konverterfutter *n (met)* converter lining
Konvertermittelstück *n* body *(the cylindrical part of a steel converter)*
Konverterprozeß *m s.* Konverterfrischverfahren
Konverterreaktor *m s.* Konversionsreaktor
Konverterstahl *m* converter (Bessemer) steel
~/sauerstoffgefrischter basic oxygen [furnace] steel
Konverterverfahren *n* 1. *s.* Konverterfrischverfahren; 2. *(text)* tow-to-top process
Konverterzustellung *f (met)* converter lining
konvertieren to convert; to shift *(synthesis gas)*
Konvertierung *f* conversion; shift *(of synthesis gas)*
Konvertierungsgrad *m* degree of conversion
Konvertierungsofen *m* shift converter
Konvertierungsreaktion *f* conversion reaction
~ des Kohlenmonoxids carbon-monoxide-shift reaction, water-gas-shift reaction
Konvertierungsverfahren *n* conversion process (method)
konz. *s.* konzentriert
Konzentrat *n* concentrate
~/emulgierbares emulsifiable concentrate *(pest control)*
Konzentrataustrag *m* concentrate discharge
Konzentration *f* concentration, *(relating to solutions preferably:)* strength • **zur ursprünglichen ~ lösen** to reconstitute
~ an gelöstem Sauerstoff dissolved-oxygen concentration
~/bodennahe ground level concentration *(of chemical species in the air)*
~ der organischen Inhaltsstoffe organic concentration
~ der suspendierten Feststoffe suspended solids concentration
~ Eins unit concentration
~/gesamte ionale total ionic concentration
~/höchstzulässige *(tox)* maximum permissible (allowable, admissible) concentration, MAC
~ in Prozent per cent concentration
~/molale molal concentration, molality
~/molare molar concentration, [concentration in] molarity

~ **Null** zero concentration
~/**prozentuale** per cent concentration, concentration in per cent
~/**quasistationäre** steady-state concentration
konzentrationsabhängig concentration-dependent
Konzentrationsabhängigkeit *f* concentration dependence
Konzentrationsänderung *f* concentration change, change of concentration
Konzentrationsanlage *f* concentration plant
Konzentrationsausgleich *m* smoothing-out of concentration
Konzentrationsbereich *m* concentration range
Konzentrationseinheit *f* concentration unit
Konzentrationselement *n (el ch)* concentration cell
~ **mit Überführung** concentration cell with transference
~ **ohne Überführung** concentration cell without transference
Konzentrationsgefälle *n*, **Konzentrationsgradient** *m* concentration gradient
Konzentrationsgrenzwert *m* **von Wasserinhaltsstoffen** *(hyd)* maximum contaminant level, MCL
Konzentrationskette *f (el ch)* concentration cell
Konzentrationsmaßeinheit *f* concentration unit
Konzentrationspolarisation *f* concentration polarization
Konzentrationsprofil *n* concentration profile, *(chromat also)* elution curve
Konzentrationsschwankung *f* variation (fluctuation) in concentration • **Konzentrationsschwankungen abfangen** *(hyd)* to smooth out the concentration
Konzentrationsüberspannung *f* concentration (polarization) overvoltage (overpotential)
Konzentrationsverhältnis *n* ratio of concentrations
Konzentrationsverteilungsverhältnis *n (chromat)* concentration distribution ratio
Konzentrationswert *m* concentration level
Konzentrationszelle *f (el ch)* concentration cell
Konzentratschaum *m (min tech)* concentrate-laden froth
konzentrieren to concentrate
~/**durch Abdunsten** to graduate
Konzentrieren *n* concentration *(of a solution)*
~ **durch Abdunsten** graduation
konzentriert concentrated, conc.
~/**doppelt** double-strength
Konzentrierungsanlage *f* concentration plant
Konzept *n* **der Diffusionsbehinderung** differential diffusion model *(gel chromatography)*
konzertiert *(bioch)* concerted
kooperativ *(bioch)* cooperative
Kooperativität *f (bioch)* cooperativity
~/**negative** negative cooperativity
~/**positive** positive cooperativity
Kooperativitätsmodell *n (bioch)* model of cooperativity (cooperative behaviour)
Kooperativitätsverhalten *n (bioch)* cooperative behaviour
Koordinaten *fpl* **der Atomschwerpunkte im Gitter** *(cryst)* atomic parameters
Koordination *f* coordination *(chemical-bond theory)*
~ **im Sinne von Werner** Werner-type coordination
Koordinationsbestreben *n* coordination tendency, tendency to coordinate
Koordinationsbindung *f* coordinate bond, dipolar (dative, donor-acceptor) bond, coordination [bond]
Koordinationschemie *f* coordination chemistry, chemistry of coordination compounds
Koordinationseinheit *f* coordination unit
Koordinationsgebilde *n* coordination entity
Koordinationsgeometrie *f* coordination geometry
Koordinationsgitter *n* coordination lattice
Koordinationsgruppe *f* coordination (coordinated) group
Koordinationskatalyse *f* coordination catalysis
Koordinationskomplex *m* coordination complex
Koordinationskörper *m* coordination entity
Koordinationslehre *f* coordination theory
~/**Wernersche** Werner [coordination] theory
Koordinationspolyeder *n* coordination polyhedron
Koordinationspolymerisation *f* coordination polymerization
Koordinationsschale *f* coordination shell
Koordinationssphäre *f* coordination sphere
Koordinationsstelle *f* coordination site
Koordinationstheorie *f* coordination theory
Koordinationsverbindung *f* coordination compound
Koordinationszahl *f* coordination (covalency) number, ligancy
koordinativ coordinate
koordiniert/dreifach three-coordinate
~/**fünffach** pentacoordinate, five-coordinate
~/**sechsfach** hexacoordinate, six-coordinate
~/**vierfach** tetracoordinate, four-coordinate
Kopaivabalsam *m s.* Kopaivaterpentin
Kopaivaöl *n* copaiba oil *(from Copaifera specc.)*
Kopaivaterpentin *n(m)* copaiba resin, Jesuit's balsam *(from Copaifera specc.)*
Kopal *m* copal [resin], gum copal *(collectively for high-melting resins esp of fossil origin)*
~/**Amerikanischer** Colombia (Brazil) copal *(from Hymenaea courbaril L.)*
Kopf *m (tech)* head; *(met)* top • **über ~ abgehen** *(distil)* to leave at the top
~/**schwimmender** floating head *(of a heat exchanger)*
Kopfdünger *m* top-dressing, direct-application fertilizer • **mit ~ behandeln** to top-dress
Kopfdüngung *f* top-dressing
Kopfform *f (glass)* ring (finish) mould, neckring
Kopffraktion *f (distil)* top fraction
Kopfkalkung *f (agric)* top liming
Kopf-Kopf-Addition *f*, **Kopf-Kopf-Anlagerung** *f* head-to-head addition

Kopf-Kopf-Anordnung *f* head-to-head arrangement
Kopf-Kopf-Polymerisation *f* head-to-head polymerization
Kopf-Kopf-Struktur *f* head-to-head structure
Kopf-Kopf-Verkettung *f*, **Kopf-Kopf-Verknüpfung** *f* head-to-head linkage
Kopfprodukt *n (distil)* overhead [product], overheads, top product
Kopfraum *m* headspace *(vapour phase above liquid phase in closed vessels)*
Kopfraumanalyse *f (chromat)* headspace [gas] analysis
Kopfrolle *f* head pulley *(of a conveyor)*
Kopf-Schwanz-Addition *f*, **Kopf-Schwanz-Anlagerung** *f* head-to-tail addition
Kopf-Schwanz-Anordnung *f* head-to-tail arrangement
Kopf-Schwanz-Kondensation *f* head-to-tail condensation
Kopf-Schwanz-Polymerisation *f* head-to-tail polymerization
Kopf-Schwanz-Struktur *f* head-to-tail structure
Kopf-Schwanz-Verkettung *f*, **Kopf-Schwanz-Verknüpfung** *f* head-to-tail linkage
Kopftemperatur *f (distil)* overhead temperature
Kopf- und Bodenschmelzen *n (met)* top-and-bottom smelting
Kopfwalze *f (pap)* bottom couch-press roll
Kopfwaschmittel *n (cosmet)* hair shampoo (wash)
Kopie *f (phot)* print; copy *(reprography)*
~/positive positive print
Kopiedruckfarbe *f* copying ink
kopieren *(phot)* to print; to copy *(reprography)*
Kopiergerät *n (phot)* contact printer; copier *(reprography)*
Kopierlack *m* resist *(photolithography)*
Kopierpapier *n (phot)* print[ing] paper; copy[ing] paper *(reprography)*
Kopierseidenpapier *n* copying tissue paper
Kopierstift *m* copying (indelible) pencil
Kopiertinte *f* copying ink
koplanar coplanar *(bond system)*
Koplanarität *f* coplanarity *(of a bond system)*
Koppers-Becker-Ofen *m s.* Koppers-Becker-Verbundkoksofen
Koppers-Becker-Verbundkoksofen *m* Koppers-Becker [combination coke] oven
~ mit Unterbrennern Koppers-Becker [combination] underjet coke oven
Koppers-Ofen *m (coal)* Koppers oven
Koppers-Totzek-Generator *m (coal)* Koppers-Totzek gasifier
Koppers-Totzek-Verfahren *n* Koppers-Totzek [gasification] process, K-T [gasification] process *(for gasifying pulverized coal)*
Koppers-Verfahren *n* Koppers process *(for gas cleaning)*
Kopplung *f (dye, phys ch)* coupling
~/chemiosmotische (chemisch-osmotische) chemiosmotic coupling *(with respiratory-chain phosphorylation)*
~/chemische chemical coupling *(with respiratory-chain phosphorylation)*
~/feste *(bioch)* tight coupling *(of mitochondria)*
~/heteronukleare *(spectr)* heteronuclear coupling
~/lockere (lose) *(bioch)* loose coupling
~/Russel-Saunderssche Russell-Saunders coupling, LS coupling *(of spins and moments of momentum)*
Kopplungsfaktor *m (bioch)* coupling factor
Kopplungskonstante *f (spectr)* coupling constant
Kopra *f* copra *(dried coconut meat)*
Kops *m (text)* cop
Kopsfärbeapparat *m (text)* cop dyeing machine
Korallenkalk *m* coral lime
Korallenschlick *m* coral mud
Korarima-Malagetta *m (food)* Madagascar cardamom *(from Aframomum angustifolium Schum.)*
Korbflasche *f* basket bottle, *(holding from 1 to 10 gallons:)* demijohn, *(esp for acids:)* carboy
Korbpresse *f* basket (curb) press
Kord[faden] *m (rubber)* cord
Kordgewebe *n (rubber)* cordage, cord fabric
Kordherd *m (min tech)* corduroy blanket table
Kordlage *f (rubber)* carcass (casing) ply
Koriander *m* coriander [seed] *(from Coriandrum sativum L.)*
Kork *m* 1. [natural] cork *(material)*; 2. *(bot)* [bark] cork, phellem; 3. *s.* Korken • **aus ~** subereous
korkähnlich, korkartig cork-like, corky, suberose, suberous
Korkbohrer *m (lab)* cork borer
Korkbohrerschärfer *m (lab)* cork-borer sharpener
Korkdichtung *f* cork gasket
Korken *m* cork *(stopper)*
Korkgewebe *n (bot)* cork, phellem
Korkmehl *n* cork powder
Kork[mehl]papier *n* cork paper
Korkpresse *f (lab)* cork press (softener, squeezer)
Korkrinde *f s.* Kork 1.
Korkring *m* cork ring
Korksäure *f* suberic acid, octanedioic acid
Korkstopfen *m* cork
Korkwachs *n* cork wax
Korn *n* grain, particle; *(phot, cryst)* grain; *(rubber)* pellet; bead *(ion exchange)* • **auf ~ [ver]kochen** *(sugar)* to boil to grain, *(Am also)* to sugar off *(esp maple sap)*
~/grobes *(phot)* coarse grain
Kornbildung *f (sugar)* graining
Kornbranntwein *m* grain alcohol
Körnchen *n* granule, [small] grain; *(rubber)* pellet
Körnchenbildung *f* granulation
Korndichte *f* grain (granule) density, apparent density *(of bulk material)*
Korndurchmesser *m* grain (granule) size
~/wirksamer effective grain size

körnen to grain, to granulate; *(rubber)* to pellet[ize] *(soot)*
Körnerhaufwerk *n* granular bed, bed of granular solids
Körnerlack *m* grained (seed) lac
Körnerschüttung *f s.* Körnerhaufwerk
Körnerzinn *n* grain tin
Kornfilter *n* granular [medium] filter
Kornform *f* grain (particle) shape
Kornfraktion *f* size fraction *(classifying)*
~/feine fine sizes, fines
Kornfuß *m (sugar)* footing *(crystals added for more rapid crystallization)*
Korngestalt *f s.* Kornform
Korngrenze *f (cryst)* grain boundary
Korngrenzenangriff *m* intergranular (grain-boundary) attack *(with corrosion)*
Korngrenzendiffusion *f* grain-boundary diffusion
Korngrenzenkorrosion *f (cryst)* intergranular (grain-boundary) corrosion
Korngröße *f* particle (grain) size, *(in screening also)* grade, screen size
~/mittlere average particle size
Korngrößenbereich *m* [particle-]size range, range of particle size[s]
Korngrößenbestimmung *f* particle-size determination
Korngrößenklasse *f* size fraction
Korngrößenmessung *f* particle-size measurement
Korngrößenverteilung *f* particle-size distribution
Korngruppe *f* size fraction
körnig granular, granulate[d], grainy, grained
• **~ machen** to granulate, to grain
~/gleichmäßig equigranular
Körnigkeit *f* granularity, graininess; *(phot)* graininess
Körnigmachen *n* granulation, graining
Kornkennlinie *f* particle-size distribution curve
Kornklasse *f* [size] fraction
Kornkochen *n (sugar)* boiling to grain, crystal boiling
Kornkohle *f* granular (granulated) activated carbon, GAC, granular carbon, GC
Kornkohlebehandlung *f (hyd)* GAC (granular carbon) treatment
Kornkohlefeinanteile *mpl (hyd)* GAC (granular carbon) fines
Kornkohlefilter *n* GAC (granular carbon) filter
Kornkohlefilteranlage *f* GAC (granular carbon) plant
Kornkohlefiltersäule *f* GAC (granular carbon) column
~/im Abwärtsstrom arbeitende downflow GAC column
~/im Aufwärtsstrom arbeitende upflow GAC column
Kornkohlefiltration *f* GAC (granular carbon) filtration
Kornkohlefüllung *f* GAC (granular carbon) loading
Kornkohlereaktivierung *f* GAC (granular carbon) reactivation
~ im Fließbett fluid-bed GAC reactivation
~ im Mehretagenofen multiple hearth GAC reactivation
~ im Wirbelbett *s.* ~ im Fließbett
kornlos grain-free
Kornmittel *n* average particle size
Kornoberfläche *f* grain surface
Kornpolymerisation *f* bead (suspension) polymerization
Kornscheide *f* size (mesh) of separation, cut size (point), critical diameter *(classifying)*
Kornspanne *f. s.* Korngrößenbereich
Körnung *f* grain size, *(screening also:)* screen size; *(phot)* granularity
Körnungsanalyse *f* size[-frequency] analysis
Körnungsbereich *m s.* Korngrößenbereich
Körnungsgesetz *n* law of size distribution
Körnungslinie *f* particle-size distribution curve
Körnungsmodul *n* fineness modulus
Kornvergröberung *f s.* Kornwachstum
Kornverteilung *f* particle-size distribution
Kornverteilungsgesetz *n* law of size distribution
~/Rosin-Rammlersches Rosin-Rammler exponential law
Kornverteilungskurve *f* particle-size distribution curve
Kornwachstum *n* grain growth, secondary recrystallisation
Kornzwischenraumvolumen *n* intergranular (void) volume
Koronabeständigkeit *f* corona resistance, resistance to corona [discharge]
Koronaentladung *f* corona [discharge]
Korona-Walzenscheider *m* high-tension separator
koronisieren to coronize *(glass cloth for rendering it crease-resistant)*
Körper *m (tech)* body; effect *(of an evaporator)*
• **~ geben** *(coat)* to body
~/Binghamscher [plastischer] Bingham plastic (body)
~ des Weins wine body
~/diamagnetischer diamagnetic material (substance)
~/fester solid [matter]
~/grauer *(phys ch)* grey body
~/Hookescher Hookean solid *(an ideal solid)*
~/ideal-elastischer *s.* ~/Hookescher
~/keramischer ceramic body
~/paramagnetischer paramagnetic [material, substance]
~/schwarzer black body
Körperfarbe *f* pigment
Körperfett *n* body fat
Körperflüssigkeit *f* body fluid
körpergebend *(coat)* bodying
Körpergehalt *m***/scheinbarer** *(plast)* false body
Körperpflegemittel *n* cosmetic

Körperpuder *m* body powder
Korpuskel *n (nucl)* corpusc[u]le, particle
Korpuskularstrahlung *f* corpuscular (particle) radiation
Korrektionsgröße *f* correction term
Korrekturfaktor *f* 1. correction factor; 2. normality (titrimetric, volumetric) factor *(the numerical value of the normality of a solution)*
~/substanzspezifischer relative response factor *(gas chromatography)*
Korrekturglied *n* correction term
Korrekturkoeffizient *m* correction factor
Korrekturlesen *n (bioch)* proofreading *(DNA polymerase)*
Korrelation *f* correlation
Korrelationskoeffizient *m (anal)* correlation coefficient
Korrelationstabelle *f (anal)* correlation table
korrespondierend conjugate *(acid, base)*
Korrigens *n (pharm)* corrigent, corrective
korrodieren to corrode, to eat; to undergo corrosion, to corrode
Korrosimeter *n* corrosion meter, corrosimeter *(based on electrical-conductivity measurements)*
Korrosion *f* corrosion • **der ~ unterliegen** to undergo corrosion, to corrode
~/ebenmäßige uniform corrosion
~/flächenhafte general corrosion
~/galvanische galvanic (contact) corrosion
~/interkristalline intergranular (intercrystalline) corrosion
~/örtliche local[ized] corrosion
~/selektive selective (preferential) corrosion
korrosionsanfällig susceptible to corrosion, corrodible
Korrosionsanfälligkeit *f* susceptibility to corrosion, corrodibility
korrosionsbeständig corrosion-resistant, resistant to corrosion, non-corroding
Korrosionsbeständigkeit *f* corrosion resistance, resistance to corrosion
Korrosionsbestreben *n s.* Korrosionsneigung
Korrosionselement *n (el ch)* corrosion cell
korrosionsempfindlich *s.* korrosionsanfällig
Korrosionsermüdung *f* corrosion fatigue [cracking]
korrosionsfest *s.* korrosionsbeständig
Korrosionsgeschwindigkeit *f* corrosion rate (velocity), rate of [corrosive] attack
Korrosionshemmer *m*, **Korrosionshemmstoff** *m s.* Korrosionsinhibitor
korrosionsinaktiv non-corrosive
Korrosionsinhibitor *m* corrosion inhibitor, anticorrosive agent
Korrosionsmedium *n*, **Korrosionsmittel** *n* corrosive [agent, medium], corrodent
Korrosionsneigung *f* corrosion tendency (propensity), tendency to corrode
Korrosionsprodukt *n* corrosion product
Korrosionsprüfgerät *n* corrosion test apparatus
Korrosionsprüfung *f* corrosion testing
Korrosionsrate *f* corrosion rate
Korrosionsschutz *m* corrosion control (protection), protection from corrosion
~/aktiver *collectively for measures influencing the state of a corroding system, as proper design, inhibition, cathodic and anodic protection, conditioning of corrosive media*
~/anodischer anodic protection
~/katodischer cathodic protection
~/passiver corrosion protection by coatings
~/temporärer (zeitweiliger) temporary corrosion protection
korrosionsschützend corrosion-protective, anticorrosive, corrosion-preven[ta]tive
Korrosionsschutzmittel *n* corrosion-protective agent, anti-corrosive agent, corrosion protective (preventative)
Korrosionsschutzpapier *n* corrosion-protective paper, anti-corrosion (anti-tarnish) paper
korrosionssicher *s.* korrosionsbeständig
Korrosionsstrom *m* corrosion current
Korrosionssystem *n* corrosion system
Korrosionstest *m* corrosion test
korrosionsverhütend corrosion-preven[ta]tive, corrosion-preventing
Korrosionsverhütung *f* corrosion prevention
Korrosionsversuch *m* corrosion test
Korrosionsverzögerer *m s.* Korrosionsinhibitor
Korrosionswiderstand *m* corrosion resistance *(quantitatively)*
korrosionswirksam corrosive
korrosiv corrosive
Korrosivität *f* corrosiveness, corrosivity
Korund *m (min)* corundum *(α-aluminium oxide)*
Koschenille *f (dye)* cochineal
Koseiseide *f* Kosey silk *(from regenerated fibroin)*
Koshland-Modell *n* induced-fit model (hypothesis), sequential model *(enzyme kinetics)*
Kosmetikchemiker *m* cosmetic chemist
Kosmetikpräparat *n* cosmetic preparation
Kosmetikum *n* cosmetic
Kosmetologie *f* cosmetology
Kosmochemie *f* cosmochemistry
kosten to taste *(a substance)*
Kostinky-Effekt *m (phot)* Kostinky effect
Kot *m* faecal matter, faeces
kotonisieren to cottonize *(flax or hemp)*
Kötzer *m (text)* cop
kovalent covalent, homopolar
~ gebunden covalently bonded
Kovalenz *f* 1. covalence, covalency; 2. *s.* Kovalenzbindung
Kovalenzbindung *f* covalent [chemical, electron-pair] bond, homopolar (atomic) bond, non-polar [covalent] bond, [shared-]electron-pair bond, shared-pair [chemical] bond
Kovalenzbindungswinkel *m* covalent bond angle
Kováts-Index *m (chromat)* Kovats (retention) index

Kp. *(= Kochpunkt) s.* Siedepunkt
krabben *(text)* to crab
Krabbmaschine *f (text)* crab
krachen *(text)* to rustle
Krachen *n (text)* rustle, scroop
krachend *(text)* scroopy *(feel)*
Krackanlage *f* cracking plant, cracker
~/katalytische catalytic cracking plant, cat[alytic] cracker
Krackbedingungen *fpl* cracking conditions
~/milde mild cracking conditions
~/scharfe severe cracking conditions
Krackbehandlung *f* cracking treatment
Krackbenzin *n* cracked gasoline
~/katalytisches cat-cracked gasoline
Krackdestillat *n* cracked distillate
Krackeinsatz *m s.* Krackgut
kracken to crack
~/katalytisch to cat-crack
~/mild to give a mild cracking treatment
~/scharf to give a severe cracking treatment
Kracken *n* cracking
~ am Katalysator *s.* -/katalytisches
~ auf flüssigen Rückstand residue cracking, flashing
~ auf Koks[rückstand] non-residue cracking, coking
~/fluidkatalytisches fluid catalytic cracking
~/hydrierendes hydrogenation cracking, hydrocracking, HC
~ im Orthoflow-Verfahren/katalytisches Orthoflow catalytic cracking
~ in der Dampfphase (Gasphase) vapour-phase cracking
~ in Flüssigphase (flüssiger Phase) liquid-phase cracking
~ in gemischt flüssiger und dampfförmiger Phase mixed-phase cracking
~ in Wirbelschicht/katalytisches fluid catalytic cracking, FCC
~ in Wirbelschicht mit Fließbettkatalysator *s.* ~ in Wirbelschicht/katalytisches
~/ionisches *s.* ~/katalytisches
~/katalytisches cat[alytic] cracking
~ mit Katalysatorbett bed cracking
~ mit Kokungsarbeitsweise *s.* ~ auf Koks
~ mit Rückstandsarbeitsweise *s.* ~ auf flüssigen Rückstand
~ mit suspendiertem Katalysator suspensoid [catalytic] cracking
~ nach dem Airliftverfahren riser cracking
~ nach der Entspannungsfahrweise *s.* ~ auf flüssigen Rückstand
~ nach der Verkokungsfahrweise *s.* ~ auf Koks
~/rückstandsloses *s.* ~ auf Koks
~/selektives selective cracking
~/thermisches thermal cracking
~/thermisch-katalytisches (thermokatalytisches) thermal-catalytic cracking
~ über Ionen *s.* ~/katalytisches
Krackfraktion *f* cracked fraction
Krackgas *n* cracker (cracking) gas
Krackglasur *f (ceram)* crackle glaze
Krackgut *n* cracking feedstock (stock, feed)
Krackmittelöl *n* cycle stock
Krackofen *m* cracking furnace
Krackraum *m* cracking chamber
Krackreaktion *f* cracking reaction
Krackreaktor *m* cracking reactor
Krackröhrenerhitzer *m*, **Krackröhrenofen** *m* tubular cracking furnace
Krackrohstoff *m s.* Krackgut
Krackung *f s.* Kracken
Krackverfahren *n* cracking process
~ nach Cross Cross process
~ nach Holmes und Manley Holmes-Manley process
~ nach Winkler und Koch Winkler-Koch process
Krackvorgang *m* cracking process
Krackzone *f* cracking zone
Kraft *f (phys ch)* force; power
~/abstoßende repulsive force
~/abweisende repellency *(as of a surface for water)*
~/bewegende *(tech)* momentum
~/Coulombsche Coulomb (coulombic) force, electrostatic force
~/elektromotorische electromotive force, e.m.f., EMF
~/elektrostatische *s.* ~/Coulombsche
~/flockende flocculating (flocculation) power
~/gegenelektromotorische counter-electromotive force, counter e.m.f., back electromotive force, back e.m.f.
~/magnetomotorische magnetomotive force, m.m.f.
~/molekulare [inter]molecular force
~/nachschaffende *(agric)* supplying power *(of a soil)*
~/nucleophile nucleophilicity, nucleophilic power
~/ölabweisende oil repellency
~/rücktreibende restoring force *(in oscillating molecules)*
~/treibende moving force, agency
~/wasserabweisende water repellency
~/zwischenmolekulare [inter]molecular force
Kraftaufwand *m*, **Kraftbedarf** *m* power requirements (needs)
Kräfte *fpl*/**van-der-Waalssche** van der Waals forces [of attraction]
Kräftefeld *n* **des Atoms** atomic field
kraftentfaltend *(bioch)* force-generating *(myosin)*
Kraftfeld *n* force field
Kraftgas *n s.* Generatorgas
kräftig vigorous *(shaking, agitation)*
kräftigend *(pharm)* tonic; roborant
Kräftigungsmittel *n (pharm)* tonic, roborant
Kraftkonstante *f* force constant
Kraft-Längenänderungs-Diagramm *n* load-elongation (load-extension) diagram
Kraftlinie *f* line of force

Kraft[pack]papier *n* kraft (strong) paper, kraft wrapping paper, kraft
~/imitiertes imitation kraft paper
Kraftpapiermaschine *f* kraft paper machine
Kraftschaufel *f* power shovel *(conveying)*
Kraftspiritus *m s.* Kraftsprit
Kraftsprit *m* power (fuel) alcohol
Kraftstoff *m* automotive (transportation) fuel, [power] fuel
~/bleifreier unleaded (non-leaded) fuel
~/fester solid fuel
~ für Fahrdieselmotoren automotive diesel fuel, diesel fuel (oil) for road vehicles
~/gebleiter leaded (lead-base) fuel, ethylized fuel
~/hochklopffester *s.* ~/hochoctaniger
~/hochoctaniger (hochoctanzahliger) high-octane fuel
~/klopffester knockless (antiknock) fuel
~/verbleiter *s.* ~/gebleiter
Kraftstoffadditiv[e] *n* fuel additive
Kraftstoffbehälter *m* fuel tank
Kraftstoffempfindlichkeit *f* sensitivity *(difference between octane numbers obtained by F1 method and F2 method)*
Kraftstoffklopfen *n* fuel knock
Kraftstofftank *m s.* Kraftstoffbehälter
Kraft-Verlängerungs-Kurve *f* load-elongation curve, load-extension curve
Kraft-Verlängerungs-Schaubild *n s.* Kraft-Längenänderungs-Diagramm
Kraftwirkung *f* force effect
Kraftzellstoff *m (pap)* kraft pulp
Kraftzellstoffkocher *m (pap)* kraft digester
Kraftzellstoffverfahren *n (pap)* kraft process
Krählarm *m* raking arm, agitator (rake) arm *(of a thickener)*; rabble [arm], rabbler *(of a multiple-hearth furnace)*
Krählblech *n* raking blade *(of a thickener)*; rabble [blade] *(of a multiple-hearth furnace)*
krählen to rake *(material in a thickener)*; to rabble *(material in a multiple-hearth furnace)*
Krähler *m s.* 1. Krählarm; 2. Krählblech
Krählwerk *n* raking mechanism, rake [mechanism] *(of a thickener)*
Krählwerksantrieb *m* rake arm drive *(of a thickener)*; rabble arm drive *(of a multiple-hearth furnace)*
Krakeleeglas *n* crackled glass
Krakeleeglasur *f (ceram)* crackle glaze
Krämer-Mühle *f* Krämer mill *(a beater mill)*
Krampfgift *n* tetanic poison
krampflindernd anticonvulsant
krampflösend spasmolytic
Krankheit f/Gauchersche *(med)* Gaucher's disease *(deficiency of glucocerebrosidase)*
krankheitserregend pathogenic
Krankheitserreger *m* pathogen
krappen *(text)* to crab
Krappfarbstoff *m* madder *(from Rubia tinctorum L.)*
Krapplack *m* madder lake
Krapprot *n* turkey (alizarine) red, madder
Krappwurzel *f* madder [root] *(from Rubia tinctorum L.)*
Krater *m* 1. *(plast)* crater; 2. [charge] crucible *(of bulk material in a reactor)*
Kratzband *n* 1. drag classifier; 2. *s.* Kratzerförderer
Krätzblei *n* slag lead
Kratze *f s.* Krählarm
Krätze *f (met)* blue dust (powder) *(by-product of zinc reduction)*
kratzen to scrape, to scratch
Kratzenband *n s.* Kratzerförderer
Kratzer *m* 1. scratch; *(glass)* cat scratch *(a defect)*; 2. *s.* Kratzerförderer; 3. *s.* Krählarm
Kratzerförderer *m* flight[ed] conveyor
~/einsträngiger single-strand flight conveyor
~/zweisträngiger double-strand flight conveyor
Kratzerkette *f* scraper chain
kratzfest scratch-proof, scratch-resistant
Kratzfestigkeit *f* scratch proofness (resistance); *(ceram)* scratch hardness
Kratzprobe *f* scratch test
Kratz-Rohrkristallisator *m* scraped-pipe crystallizer
Kräuselfaden *m s.* Kräuselgarn
Kräuselfestigkeit *f s.* Kräuselungsbeständigkeit
Kräuselgarn *n* crimped (crinkled) yarn
Kräusellack *m* wrinkle varnish (finish)
kräuseln *(text)* to crimp, to crinkle, to crêpe; *(pap)* to curlate; *(coat)* to wrinkle
~/sich *(text)* to crimp, to crinkle; *(coat)* to wrinkle; *(phot)* to frill
Kräuseln *n (ceram)* curling *(a defect)*; *(pap)* curlation; *(text)* crimping, crinkling, crêp[e]ing
Kräuselung *f* 1. *(text)* crimping, crinkling, crêp[e]ing; *(coat)* wrinkling; 2. *(text)* crimp
~/latente *(text)* latent crimp
Kräuselungsbeständigkeit *f (text)* crimp rigidity
Kräusen *pl (ferm)* krausen, kräusen, bloom, *(Am)* curls
~/hohe rocky krausen, *(Am)* high curls
~/weiße low krausen, *(Am)* low curls
Kräusenstadium *n (ferm)* krausen (cauliflower) stage
Kreatin *n (bioch)* creatine
Kreatinin *n (bioch)* creatinine
krebsauslösend *s.* krebserregend
krebserregend carcinogenic, carcinogenous, cancer-causing, cancer-producing
~/nicht non-carcinogenic
Krebs-Henseleit-Zyklus *m (bioch)* Krebs-Henseleit cycle, urea (ornithine) cycle
Krebs-Kornberg-Zyklus *m s.* Glyoxylatzyklus
Krebs-Martius-Zyklus *m s.* Krebs-Zyklus
Krebszement *m* grappier cement
Krebs-Zyklus *m* Krebs cycle, TCA (tricarboxylic-acid) cycle, citric acid cycle
Kreide *f* chalk
~/gefällte precipitated chalk (whiting)

~/gemahlene whiting
~/geschlämmte und gemahlene *s.* ~/präparierte
~/lithographische lithographic crayon
~/präparierte prepared chalk
~/präzipitierte *s.* ~/gefällte
kreideartig chalky
kreiden *(coat)* to become chalky, to chalk
Kreidepapier *n* chalk paper; *s.* Kreidereliefpapier
Kreidepulver *n* whitening dust (powder)
Kreidereliefpapier *n*, **Kreidezurichtepapier** *n* chalk overlay paper
kreidig chalky
Kreidigkeit *f* chalkiness
Kreidungsgrad *m (coat)* degree of chalking
Kreisbahn *f* [circular] orbit
Kreisblattschreiber *m* circular-chart recorder
Kreisel *m*/**asymmetrischer** asymmetric-top molecule
~/rotierender spinning top *(as for oil burners)*
~/symmetrischer symmetric-top molecule
Kreiselbelüfter *m (hyd)* propeller aerator
Kreiselbrecher *m* gyratory crusher
Kreiselerhitzer *m (food)* cylindrical batch pasteurizer
Kreiselgebläse *n* centrifugal (turbine) blower, turboblower
Kreiselkompressor *m* centrifugal compressor
Kreiselkraftdüse *f* swirl[-plate] nozzle
Kreiselmolekül *n*/**asymmetrisches** asymmetric-top molecule
~/symmetrisches symmetric-top molecule
Kreiselpumpe *f* centrifugal pump
Kreiselpumpenmischapparat *m* centrifugal pump mixer
Kreiselradkompressor *m* centrifugal compressor
Kreiselradlüfter *m* centrifugal fan
Kreiselradverdichter *m* centrifugal compressor
Kreiselsichter *m* whizzer classifier
Kreiselversprüher *m*, **Kreiselzerstäuber** *m* spinning-top atomizer (sprayer)
kreisen to rotate, to revolve, *(if rapidly:)* to spin; to circulate *(in a closed cycle)*
Kreisfrequenz *f* angular frequency
Kreislauf *m* 1. cycle, circuit *(scheme)*; 2. circulation *(of liquid or gas)* • **im ~ führen** to recycle, to [re]circulate • **in den ~ zurückführen** to return to the circuit, to recycle, to recirculate
~ der Elemente/geochemischer geochemical cycling of elements
~ des Wassers water recycle (cycle, circuit), circulation of water
~ des Wassers/natürlicher *s.* ~/hydrologischer
~/enterohepatischer *(bioch)* enterohepatic circulation *(of bile acids)*
~/geschlossener closed circuit, complete cycle
~/hydrologischer hydrological cycle
Kreislaufchlorwasserstoff *m (petrol)* recycle hydrogen chloride
Kreislauffahren *n*, **Kreislauffahrweise** *f s.* Kreislaufführung
Kreislaufführung *f* [re]cycling, recirculation
Kreislaufgas *n* recycle gas
Kreislaufnutzung *f* **des Wassers** *s.* Kreislaufwasserführung
Kreislauföl *n* recycle oil
Kreislaufpumpe *f* circulating pump, circulator
Kreislaufreaktor *m* recycle (loop) reactor
Kreislaufrückwasser *n (pap)* white water
Kreislaufsystem *n* circulation system
Kreislauftechnik *f (chromat)* recycle technique
Kreislaufverfahren *n* recycling procedure *(in extracting)*
Kreislaufwasser *n* recycled water, recirculated (recycling, circuit) water
Kreislaufwasserführung *f* recycling (recirculation) of water, water recirculation
Kreislaufwasserstoff *m (petrol)* recycle hydrogen
Kreismesser *n (pap)* disk (circular slitting) knife, slitter
Kreisprozeß *m* cycle, cyclic process
~/Born-Haberscher Born-Haber [thermochemical] cycle
~/Carnotscher Carnot cycle
~/Szent-Györgyi-Krebsscher *s.* Krebs-Zyklus
~/thermodynamischer thermodynamic cycle
Kreis-Reaktion *f* Kreis test *(for peroxide rancidity)*
Kreisschwingsieb *n* circle-thrown screen
Krem *f* cream *(for compounds s.* Creme*)*
Krensäure *f (soil)* crenic acid *(a fulvic acid)*
Kreosot *n* creosote, *(specif)* wood[-tar] creosote
Kreosotal *n s.* Kreosotcarbonat
Kreosotcarbonat *n* creosote carbonate
kreosotieren to creosote
Kreosotöl *n* creosote oil, *(specif)* coal-tar creosote oil
Kreponierbad *n (text)* crêp[e]ing bath (liquor)
kreponieren *(text)* to crêpe, to crimp, to crinkle
Krepp *m* 1. *(text)* crêpe; 2. *s.* Kreppkautschuk
Kreppapier *n* crêpe paper
Kreppbad *n s.* Kreponierbad
kreppen *(pap, text)* to crêpe, *(text also)* to crimp, to crinkle
Kreppkautschuk *m* crêpe [rubber]
~/weißer pale crêpe
Krepp-Pack[papier] *n* crêpe wrapping paper
Kreppseidenpapier *n* crêpe tissue paper
Kreppstoff *m (text)* crêpe
Kreuzbalkenrührer *m* cross-arm paddle mixer
Kreuzband[magnet]scheider *m* cross-belt [magnetic] separator
Kreuzeinbau *m* cross flights *(of a rotary dryer)*
Kreuzgegenströmer *m s.* Kreuzgegenstrom-Wärmeübertrager
Kreuzgegenstrom-Wärmeübertrager *m* spiral-tube heat exchanger
Kreuzkopfbohrer *m (lab)* charcoal borer
Kreuzpolarisation *f* cross polarization, CP
~ mit Rotation um den magischen Winkel cross-polarization magic angle spinning, CP-MAS

Kreuzpolarisations-^{13}C-NMR-Technik *f (spectr)* cross-polarization ^{13}C-NMR technique
Kreuzreaktion *f* cross reaction
Kreuzresistenz *f (tox)* cross resistance
Kreuzschichtstoff *m (plast)* cross-laminate
Kreuzspule *f (text)* cheese
~/konische cone
Kreuzspulfärbeapparat *m (text)* cheese dyeing machine
Kreuzstrom *m* cross flow; cross current
Kreuzstromboden *m (distil)* cross-flow tray
Kreuzstromkühlturm *m* cross-flow cooling tower
Kreuzströmung *f* cross flow
Kreuzstück *n* cross
Kreuzteilen *n (anal)* quartering
kriechen to creep; *(ceram)* to crawl *(of glaze)*
Kriechen *n* creep, *(ceram)* crawling *(a defect during glazing)*
~/stationäres secondary (steady-state) creep
Kriechfestigkeit *f* creep resistance (strength)
Kriechgeschwindigkeit *f* creep rate
Kriechkurve *f* creep curve
Kriechpunkt *m* creep point
Kriechstromfestigkeit *f* track[ing] resistance
Kriechversuch *m* creep test (experiment) *(materials testing)*
Kriechwegbildung *f* tracking
Kriechwiderstand *m* creep resistance (strength)
Krinkelgarn *n* crimped (crinkled) yarn
Krispelmaschine *f (tann)* boarding machine
krispeln *(tann)* to board, to grain, to pommel
Kristall *m* crystal
~/cholester[in]ischer flüssiger cholesteric liquid crystal
~/flüssiger liquid crystal, crystalline liquid, mesophase
~/gestörter imperfect crystal
~/homöopolarer *s.* ~/kovalenter
~/kovalenter covalent (valence) crystal
~/lyotroper flüssiger lyotropic liquid crystal
~/nematischer flüssiger nematic liquid crystal
~/optisch positiver positive crystal
~/piezoelektrischer piezoelectric crystal
~/pseudomorpher pseudomorph
~/realer imperfect crystal
~/rotierender rotating (rotation) crystal
~/smektischer flüssiger smectic liquid crystal
~/thermotroper flüssiger thermotropic liquid crystal
~/xenomorpher xenomorphic (allotriomorphic) crystal, anhedron
Kristallabscheider *m*, **Kristallabscheideraum** *m* crystallizing chamber
Kristallachse *f* crystal (crystallographic) axis
Kristallaggregat *n* crystal[line] aggregate
~/van-der-Waalssches van der Waals crystal aggregate
kristallartig crystal-like, crystalline
Kristallaustrag *m* crystal discharge
Kristallbau *m* crystal structure
Kristallbaufehler *m* crystal defect, lattice defect (imperfection)
Kristallbett *n* crystal bed
Kristallchemie *f* crystal chemistry
kristallchemisch crystallochemical
Kriställchen *n* small crystal
Kristalldruse *f (geoch)* [crystal] druse, geode
Kristallebene *f* crystal (crystallographic) plane
Kristalleigenschaft *f* crystal property
Kristalleis *n* crystal (clear) ice
Kristaller *m s.* Kristallisator 1.
Kristallfehler *m s.* Kristallbaufehler
Kristallfeld *n* crystal[line] field
Kristallfeldaufspaltung *f* crystal-field (zero-field) splitting
Kristallfeldtheorie *f* crystal field theory
Kristallfläche *f* crystal face
Kristallform *f* crystal form (shape) • **in ~** in crystalline form
Kristallgitter *n* crystal lattice
Kristallgitterspektrograph *m* crystal grating spectrograph
Kristallgitterspektrometer *n* crystal [diffraction] spectrometer
Kristallgittertyp *m (cryst)* lattice type
Kristallglas *n* crystal glass, *(Am)* rock crystal
Kristallglasur *f (ceram)* crystal[line] glaze
Kristallgummi *n s.* Dextrin
Kristallhabitus *m* crystal habit
Kristallhaufwerk *n* crystal[line] aggregate
Kristallierer *m* crystallizer
kristallin crystalline
~/nicht non-crystalline, amorphous
kristallinisch *s.* kristallin
Kristallinität *f* crystallinity
Kristallinitätsgrad *m* degree of crystallinity
Kristallisat *n* crystallizate, crop [of crystals], crystalline crop (product); solid *(in zone melting)*
Kristallisation *f* crystallization • **die ~ anregen (auslösen)** to induce crystallization • **zur ~ bringen** to crystallize out
~ durch Animpfen (Impfen) seeded crystallization
~/extraktive extractive crystallization
~/fraktionierte fractional crystallization
~/primäre primary cystallization
~/sekundäre secondary crystallization
~/spontane spontaneous (unseeded) crystallization
~/ungeleitete uncontrolled crystallization
Kristallisations... *s. a.* Kristallisier...
Kristallisationsbedingung *f* condition of crystallization
Kristallisationsdifferentiation *f (geol)* crystallization differentiation, fractional crystallization
kristallisationsfähig crystallizable
~/nicht non-crystallizable
Kristallisationsfähigkeit *f* crystallizability
Kristallisationsgefäß *n* crystallizing vessel
Kristallisationsgeschwindigkeit *f* rate of crystallization

Kristallisationskeim *m* crystal nucleus, nucleus of crystallization • **als ~ wirken** to nucleate
Kristallisationskeimbildung *f* nucleation, formation of nuclei
Kristallisationskeimzahl *f* number of nuclei
Kristallisationskern *m* crystal nucleus, nucleus of crystallization *(consisting of foreign material)*
Kristallisationskinetik *f* crystallization kinetics
Kristallisationslösung *f* crystallizing solution
Kristallisationsneigung *f* tendency to crystallize
Kristallisationspapier *n* ice paper
Kristallisationsprodukt *n* crystalline product (crop), crop [of crystals], crystallizate
Kristallisationsraum *m* crystallizing chamber
Kristallisationstendenz *f* tendency to crystallize
Kristallisationsvermögen *n* crystallizability
Kristallisationswagen *m* crystallization truck [for wet cooling], crystallization wag[g]on *(margarine making)*
Kristallisationswärme *f* heat of crystallization
Kristallisationswiderstand *m* resistance to crystallization
Kristallisationszentrum *n* crystallization (nucleation) centre, nucleation site
Kristallisator *m* 1. crystallizer *(apparatus)*; 2. *(ceram)* mineralizer
~/klassierender classifying crystallizer
~/offener feststehender tank crystallizer, crystallizing tank
Kristallisier... *s. a.* Kristallisations...
Kristallisierapparat *m* crystallizer
kristallisierbar crystallizable
~/nicht non-crystallizable
Kristallisierbarkeit *f* crystallizability
Kristallisierbecken *n* crystallizing pond *(as in a saltern)*
Kristallisierbehälter *m* crystallizing tank, tank crystallizer
kristallisieren to crystallize [out]
Kristallisiermulde *f*, **Kristallisierpfanne** *f s.* Kristallisierbehälter
Kristallisierschale *f* crystallization (crystallizing) dish
Kristallisierwiege *f* **[/Wulff-Bocksche]** Wulff-Bock crystallizer
Kristallit *m* crystallite
Kristallittheorie *f (glass)* crystallite (microheterogeneity) theory
Kristallkeim *m s.* Kristallisationskeim
Kristallkern *m s.* Kristallisationskern
Kristallklasse *f* crystal (symmetry) class, class of crystal symmetry, symmetry (point) group
Kristallkörnchen *n (sugar)* grain
Kristallmonochromator *m (spectr)* crystal monochromator
Kristalloberfläche *f* crystal surface
Kristallographie *f* crystallography
~/chemische chemical crystallography
kristallographisch crystallographic
Kristalloid *n* crystalloid
Kristallolumineszenz *f* crystalloluminescence
Kristallose *f* sodium (soluble) saccharin, sodium benzosulphimide
Kristallphase *f* crystalline phase
Kristallphosphor *m* crystalline phosphor
Kristallphosphoreszenz *f* crystal phosphorescence
Kristallpolster *n* crystal bed
Kristallpulver *n* crystal (crystalline) powder
Kristallsaccharin *n s.* Kristallose
Kristall[schütt]schicht *f*, **Kristallschüttung** *f* crystal bed
Kristallsoda *f* salt of soda, soda [crystals], washing soda *(sodium carbonate 10-water)*
Kristallspektrograph *m* crystal grating spectrograph
Kristallspektrometer *n* crystal [diffraction] spectrometer
Kristallstörung *f* crystal imperfection
Kristallstruktur *f* crystal structure
~/geordnete organized crystal structure
Kristallstrukturanalyse *f* crystal[-structure] analysis
~/röntgenographische X-ray crystal[-structure] analysis, X-ray crystallographic analysis
Kristallstrukturbestimmung *f* crystal-structure determination, crystallographic structure determination
Kristallsymmetrie *f* crystal symmetry
Kristallsystem *n* crystal (crystallographic) system
~/hexagonales hexagonal [crystal] system
~/kubisches cubic [crystal] system, regular system
~/monoklines monoclinic [crystal] system
~/orthorhombisches [ortho]rhombic [crystal] system
~/reguläres *s.* ~/kubisches
~/rhombisches *s.* ~/orthorhombisches
~/rhomboedrisches rhombohedral [crystal] system, trigonal system
~/tetragonales tetragonal [crystal] system
~/trigonales *s.* ~/rhomboedrisches
~/triklines triclinic [crystal] system
Kristalltuff *m (geol)* crystal tuff
Kristallversetzung *f* crystal dislocation
Kristallviolett *n* crystal violet, hexamethyl-*p*-rosaniline hydrochloride
Kristallwachstum *n* crystal growth
Kristallwasser *n* water of crystallization
kristallwasserfrei free from water of crystallization, anhydrous
Kristallwinkel *m* crystal angle
Kristallzüchtung *f* crystal growing (growth)
Kristallzucker *m* crystallized (granulated) sugar
Kristallzwilling *m* crystal twin, twin [crystal]
Krokodilklemme *f* alligator clip
Krokydolith *m* crocidolite, cape (blue) asbestos, cape blue *(a mineral of the amphibole group)*
Kroll-Verfahren *n (met)* Kroll process *(a reduction process)*
18-Krone-6 *f* 18-crown 6, *1,4,7,10,13,16-hexaoxacyclooctadecane

Kron-Effekt *m (phot)* Kron effect
Kronenblock *m* crown block *(of a rotary-drilling installation)*
Kronenether *m* crown ether *(a cyclic polyether)*
Kronenverbindung *f (org ch)* crown compound
Kronenverschließmaschine *f (food)* crowner
Kronenverschluß *m (food)* crown cap (cork)
Kronflintglas *n* crown flint glass, lead crown glass
Kronglas *n* crown [optical] glass, crown
K-Röntgenstrahlung *f* K radiation
Kropf *m (pap)* backfall, descent plate, weir *(of a beater)*
Kropfkrone *f (pap)* backfall crest (crown) *(of a beater)*
Krötengift *n* toad venom (poison)
Krume *f (soil, agric)* topsoil
Krümel *m(n) (soil)* crumb; *(rubber)* pellet, *(sometimes also)* crumb
Krümelbuna *m(n)* crumbs of buna synthetic rubber
Krümelgefüge *n (agric)* crumb structure
krümelig crumbly, friable
krümeln to crumble; *(using a liquid:)* to agglomerate
Krümelstruktur *f (agric)* crumb structure
Krümelung *f* crumbling; *(using a liquid:)* agglomeration
Krümmer *m (tech)* elbow [fitting]; *(lab)* bent-tube connection, bent tube, angle connector, elbow
~ mit rechtwinkliger Ablenkung right-angle elbow, ell
Krümmer-Durchfluß[mengen]messer *m* elbow meter *(flow measurement)*
Krümmung *f* bend, curvature, camber
Krümmungsfaktor *m* tortuosity factor *(diffusion theory)*
krumpfbeständig *s.* krumpffest
krumpfen *(text)* to shrink
krumpffest *(text)* shrink-resistant, shrinkproof, unshrinkable
Krumpffestausrüstung *f (text)* shrink-resist finish, unshrinkable finish
Krumpffestigkeit *f (text)* shrink resistance, unshrinkability
Krumpffestmachen *n (text)* shrinkproofing
krumpffrei *(text)* non-shrinking
Krumpfmaschine *f (text)* shrinking machine
Krumpfung *f (text)* shrinkage, shrinking
~/erzwungene (kompressive) compressive (compression) shrinkage
Krupon *m (tann)* butt
kruponieren *(tann)* to butt
Krupp-Lurgi-Schwelverfahren *n (coal)* Krupp-Lurgi process
Krupp-Renn-Verfahren *n (met)* Krupp Renn process
Kruste *f* crust, incrustation, encrustation *(as on heated surfaces of dryers)*; crust *(of the earth)*; *(food)* rind; • **eine ~ bilden** to form a crust, to encrust, to incrust
Kryogenik *f* cryogenics
Kryohydrat *n* cryohydrate
kryohydratisch cryohydric
Kryolith *m (min)* cryolite, ice stone, Greenland spar *(sodium fluoroaluminate)*
Kryoskop *n* cryoscope
Kryoskopie *f* cryoscopy
Kryotechnik *f* cryogenic (low-temperature) engineering, cryogenics
Kryptand *m (org ch)* cryptand *(spherical crown compound)*
Kryptobase *f* cryptobase
kryptobimolekular pseudo-first-order
Kryptocyanin *n* kryptocyanine, 1,1'-diethyl-4,4'-carbocyanine iodide
Kryptoion *n* crypto-ion
Kryptoionenreaktion *f* crypto-ionic reaction
kryptoionisch crypto-ionic
kryptokristallin cryptocrystalline
Kryptomeren *n* cryptomerene *(a diterpene derivative)*
Krypton *n* Kr krypton
Krypton[ionen]-Laser *m* krypton[-ion] laser
K-Säure *f* K acid, 1-aminonaphth-8-ol-4,6-disulphonic acid
K-Schale *f* K-shell *(of an atom)*
KU *s.* Kuoxamfaserstoff
Kuba[gelb]holz *n* Cuba wood *(a sort of the dyewood from Chlorophora tinctoria Gaud.)*
Kubeben *fpl (pharm)* cubebs *(from Piper cubeba L.f.)*
Kübel *m* tub, vat; bucket *(esp in conveying)*
Kübelaufzug *m* skip hoist
Kubierschky-Nitrierapparat *m* Kubierschky nitrator
Kubierschky-Turm *m* Kubierschky tower *(for recovering bromine from brines)*
kubisch cubic
kubisch-flächenzentriert *(cryst)* face-centred cubic
kubisch-innenzentriert *s.* kubisch-raumzentriert
kubisch-raumzentriert *(cryst)* body-centred cubic
Kuchen *m (ch, tech)* cake; *(glass)* shear cake
Kuchenabnahme *f* cake discharge
Kuchenaustrag *m* cake discharge
Kuchendicke *f* cake thickness
Kuchendickefühler *m* cake thickness detector (sensing device)
Kuchendurchsatz *m* cake throughput
Kuchenentfeuchtung *f* cake dewatering
Kuchenfeststoffgehalt *m* cake solids [content, concentration], dry-cake solids
Kuchenfeuchte *f* cake moisture (dryness)
Kuchenfeuchtegehalt *m* cake moisture content
Kuchenfeuchtigkeit *f s.* Kuchenfeuchte
Kuchenfiltration *f* cake filtration
Kuchenführungswagen *m (coal)* coke guide
Kuchenhöhe *f s.* Kuchendicke
Kuchenleistung *f* cake yield
Kuchenrestfeuchte *f* residual cake moisture

Kuchenstärke *f s.* Kuchendicke
Kuchenwiderstand *m* cake resistance, resistance of filter cake
Kufe *f* vat, tub, back, beck
Kugel *f* sphere, globe; *(tech)* ball *(as in bearings or mills)*; *(met)* pellet; *(lab)* bulb
Kügelchen *n* spherule, globule; *(met)* pellet; *(plast)* bead
Kugeldruckhärte *f* ball-puncture resistance
Kugeldruckprüfung *f*, **Kugeldrucktest** *m* ball test
Kugelfallmethode *f* falling-ball (falling-sphere) method *(for determining viscosities)*
Kugelfallprüfung *f* falling-ball [impact] test
Kugelfallviskosimeter *n* falling-ball (falling-sphere) viscometer, ball viscometer
Kugelfallwerk *n* drop-weight device
Kugelform *f* spherical (globular) form
kugelförmig spherical, globular
Kugelförmigkeit *f* sphericity
Kugelfüllung *f* ball charge *(as of a tumbling mill)*
Kugelgraphit *m* nodular (spheroidal) graphite
Kugelgraphit[grau]guß *m* nodular (spheroidal graphite) iron, ductile iron
Kugelhaufenreaktor *m (nucl)* pebble [bed] reactor, PBR
kugelig *s.* kugelförmig
Kugelkocher *m (pap)* spherical boiler (cooker, digester)
Kugelkreisel *m* spherical-top molecule
Kugelkühler *m* ball (bulb) condenser
~ **nach Allihn** Allihn condenser
kugelmahlen to ball-mill
Kugelmühle *f* ball mill (grinder), *(specif)* pebble mill *(filled with flint pebbles or porcelain balls)* • **in der ~ mahlen** to ball-mill
~/konische conical ball mill
~/schwingende vibrating (oscillating) ball mill, vibratory (vibration, oscillatory) ball mill
~/zylindrisch-konische *s.* ~/konische
Kugelmühlenmethode *f* ball-mill method *(for determining the grindability of coal)*
Kugelpackung *f (cryst)* packing of spheres
~/dichteste close[st] packing [of spheres], close-packed arrangement (array, structure)
~/hexagonal dichteste hexagonal close[st] packing [of spheres], hcp
~/kubisch dichteste cubic close[st] packing [of spheres], ccp
Kugelprotein *n* globular protein
Kugelpulver *n* ball powder *(a propellant powder in the form of spherules)*
Kugelringmühle *f* ball-and-ring (ball-and-race) mill, ball roller mill
~ **für Kohlenstaubmahlung** ball-and-ring coal pulverizer
Kugelrückschlagventil *n* ball-check valve, ball check
Kugelschale *f* spherical shell
Kugelschliffverbindung *f* spherical [ground-glass] joint, ball-and-cup (ball-and-socket) joint
Kugelschreiberfarbmasse *f* ball-point pen ink
kugelsintern to pelletize, to nodulize *(ore)*
Kugel-Stäbchen-Modell *n* ball-and-stick model *(of molecules)*
Kugelsymmetrie *f* spherical symmetry
kugelsymmetrisch spherically symmetrical
Kugelventil *n* ball valve
Kugelverschlußdüse *f* ball-check nozzle
Kuhbutterfett *n* cow milk fat
Kuheuter *n s.* Eutervorlage
Kühlanlage *f* refrigerating (cooling) plant
Kühlapparat *m* cooling apparatus, cooler; *(for temperatures below 0 °C:)* chiller
Kühlauto *n* refrigerator truck
Kühlbad *n* cooling (refrigerated) bath
Kühlbereich *m (glass)* annealing range
Kühlcreme *f (cosmet)* cold cream
kühlen to cool, *(esp food)* to refrigerate; *(quickly by immersion:)* to chill, to quench
~/mit Wasser to water-cool
Kühlen/unter with cooling
Kühler *m* 1. *(lab)* [vapour, steam] condenser; sheet cooler *(for sheet glass)*; 2. *s.* Kühlvorrichtung
~/Allihnscher Allihn condenser
~/Liebigscher Liebig condenser
~ **nach Friedrichs** Friedrichs [reflux] condenser
~ **nach West** West condenser
Kühlerklemme *f (lab)* condenser clamp
Kühlermantel *m (lab)* condenser jacket
Kühlerschweinchen *n (lab)* condenser jacket
Kühlerwascher *m* washer-cooler
Kühlfalle *f* cold (cryogenic) trap
Kühlfalte *f (glass)* chill (settle) mark *(a surface defect)*
Kühlfeld *n (text)* cooling zone
Kühlfinger *m (lab)* cold finger, cold-finger (finger-type) condenser, cold-finger trap, acorn condenser
Kühlfläche *f* cooling surface; *(quantitatively:)* area of cooling surface
Kühlflüssigkeit *f* cooling liquid
Kühlgeschwindigkeit *f* cooling rate
Kühlgrenztemperatur *f* wet-bulb (wet-surface) temperature
Kühlhalle *f*, **Kühlhaus** *n* cold store
Kühlhausaufbewahrung *f* cold storage
Kühlkammer *f* cooling chamber
Kühlkanal *m* cooling channel; *(glass)* lehr
Kühllagerung *f* cold storage
Kühlluft *f* cooling air (wind)
Kühlmantel *m* cooling jacket
Kühlmedium *n*, **Kühlmittel** *n* cooling agent (medium) coolant
Kühloberfläche *f s.* Kühlfläche
Kühlofen *m (glass)* [annealing] lehr, annealing oven, leer
~/kontinuierlich arbeitender continuous annealing lehr

Kühlofenbeschicker *m (glass)* lehr loader, stacker
Kühlöl *n* cooling oil
Kühlplatte *f (lab)* cool plate
Kühlpunkt *m***/oberer** *s.* Kühltemperatur/obere
~/unterer *s.* Kühltemperatur/untere
Kühlraum *m* cold-storage room
Kühlraumaufbewahrung *f*, **Kühlraumlagerung** *f* cold storage
Kühlrippe *f* cooling fin
Kühlriß *m (ceram)* dunt, cooling crack
Kühlrißbildung *f (ceram)* dunting
Kühlrohr *n* cooling (chilling) tube, *(for solidifying margarine also:)* cooling (chilling) cylinder; *(distil)* condensing tube
Kühlschacht *m (glass)* vertical lehr
Kühlschiff *n (ferm)* coolship, cooler
Kühlschlange *f* cooling coil, *(distil also)* worm
Kühlschrank *m* refrigerator
Kühlsole *f* [refrigerating] brine, secondary refrigerant
Kühlsystem *n* cooling (refrigeration) system
~ mit einer gekühlten Walze single-drum system *(margarine making)*
~ mit Walzenpaar double-drum system *(margarine making)*
Kühltank *m* cooling tank
Kühltankwagen *m* refrigerated trailer (tank truck); *(railway:)* refrigerated car
Kühlteich *m* cooling pond
Kühltemperatur *f***/obere** *(glass)* annealing temperature (point), A.P., 13.0 temperature *(at which the viscosity is 10^{13} poises)*
~/untere *(glass)* strain temperature (point), St.P.
Kühltrommel *f* cooling drum
Kühltrommelverfahren *n* dry [drum-]cooling process *(margarine making)*
Kühltrub *m (ferm)* cold sludge (trub, break), fine trub
Kühlturm *m* cooling tower; chilling tower *(petroleum dewaxing)*
~ mit natürlichem Zug natural-draught cooling tower, atmospheric cooling tower
~/selbstbelüfteter *s.* ~ mit natürlichem Zug
Kühlturmkamin *m* cooling-tower casing
Kühlturmzusatzwasser *n* cooling-tower make-up
Kühlung *f* cooling, *(esp food)* refrigeration; *(quickly by immersion:)* chilling, quench[ing]
~ mit Wasser water cooling
Kühlungskristallisator *m* cooling (cooler) crystallizer
Kühlvorrichtung *f* cooling facility, cooler
Kühlwagen *m*, **Kühlwaggon** *m* refrigerator (refrigeration) car
Kühlwalze *f* cooling roll
Kühlwanne *f* cooling vat
Kühlwascher *m* washer-cooler
Kühlwasser *n* cooling water
~ für Durchflußkühlung once-through cooling water
Kühlwasseraufbereitung *f* cooling-water treatment
Kühlwasseraustritt *m* cooling-water outlet
Kühlwasserkreislauf *m* cooling-water circuit (loop), cooling loop
Kühlwirkung *f* cooling action; cooling effect
Kühlzentrifuge *f* refrigerated centrifuge
Kühlzone *f* cooling zone (compartment, section)
Kühlzylinder *m* cooling cylinder (roll); *(pap)* sweat cylinder (roll)
Kuhmilch *f* cow milk
Kuhn-Roth-Bestimmung *f* Kuhn-Roth determination *(of terminal methyl groups)*
Kuhpockenlymphe *f* vaccine
KUK *(**K**ationen**u**mtausch**k**apazität) s.* Kationenaustauschkapazität
Küken *n (lab)* stopper, plug
~/massives solid stopper
Külbel *n (glass)* parison
Kulör *f* sugar colouring (dye)
kultivieren *(biot)* to cultivate
kultiviert/in Nährlösung *(biot)* solution-grown
Kultivierung *f (biot)* cultivation
~ von Mikroorganismen microbe cultivation, cultivation of microorganisms
Kultur *f* 1. *(biot)* culture; 2. *s.* Kultivierung
~ auf halbfestem Substrat semisolid culture
~/diskontinuierliche batch culture
~/frisch eingesäte seed culture
~/gefriergetrocknete lyophilized culture
~ im hängenden Tropfen [hanging-]drop culture
~ in statischem Zustand steady-state culture
~/kontinuierliche continuous culture
~/statische steady-state culture
~/submerse submerged culture
~/wachstumsaktive actively (rapidly) growing culture
Kulturbedingungen *fpl (biot)* culture (cultural) conditions
Kulturbrühe *f s.* Kulturflüssigkeit
Kulturfiltrat *n* culture filtrate
Kulturflüssigkeit *f (biot)* culture solution (broth, liquid, fluid), nutrient broth
~/überstehende culture supernatant
Kulturgefäß *n (agric)* pot
Kulturhefe *f (biot)* culture[d] yeast, industrial yeast, barm
Kulturkolben *m (biot)* culture (propagating) flask, culture bottle
~ nach Fernbach Fernbach flask
~ nach Roux Roux culture bottle
Kulturlösung *f s.* Kulturflüssigkeit
Kulturmedium *n (biot)* culture medium
Kulturplatte *f (biot)* culture plate
Kultursammlung *f (biot)* collection [of cultures] of microorganisms, culture collection
Kulturstamm *m (biot)* strain
Kümmelöl *n* caraway oil *(from Carum carvi L.)*
kumulativ cumulative

Kumulen *n* cumulene *(any of a class of compounds having three or more cumulated double bonds)*
Kunstasphalt *m* [artificial] asphalt, petroleum asphalt
Kunstdruckpapier *n* art paper
Kunstdünger *m s.* Handelsdünger
Kunsteis *n* artificial (manufactured) ice
Kunstfaser *f s.* Chemiefaser
Kunstfaserstoff *m s.* Chemiefaserstoff
Kunstfaserzellstoff *m s.* Chemiezellstoff
Kunstfett *n* synthetic fat
Kunsthaar *n* artificial hair
Kunstharz *n* synthetic resin
~ **zur Naßfestleimung** *(pap)* wet-strength resin
Kunstharzappretur *f s.* Kunstharzausrüstung
Kunstharzausrüstung *f (text)* [synthetic-]resin finish
~ **mit verzögerter Formfixierung** deferred-curing finish
Kunstharzaustauscher *m s.* Kunstharzionenaustauscher
Kunstharzbehandlung *f (text)* resin treatment
Kunstharzdispersion *f* synthetic resin dispersion, latex
Kunstharzionenaustauscher *m* ion-exchange resin, resinous exchanger
Kunstharzkitt *m* synthetic-resin cement
Kunstharzkleber *m*, **Kunstharzklebstoff** *m* synthetic-resin adhesive
Kunstharzlack *m* synthetic-resin varnish
Kunstharzpulver *n* synthetic-resin powder
Kunstharzsperrholz *n* resin-bonded plywood
Kunsthonig *m* artificial honey
Kunsthorn *n* artificial horn, casein plastic
Kunstkautschuk *m* synthetic rubber, artificial (man-made, chemical) rubber
Kunstkautschukklebstoff *m* synthetic-rubber adhesive
Kunstkautschuklatex *m* synthetic[-rubber] latex
Kunstkautschukmischung *f* synthetic-rubber mix (stock, compound)
Kunstkohle *f* artificial coal
Kunstkohlenstoff *m* artificial carbon
Kunstkohlenstoff-Formkörper *m* carbon artifact, artificial carbon article (body)
Kunstleder *n* artificial (imitation) leather
Künstlerfarbe *f* artists' colour
künstlich artificial, non-natural, *(relating to products also)* synthetic, man-made, manufactured
Kunstlicht *n* artificial light
Kunstmist *m* artificial manure
Kunstrahm *m* artificial cream
Kunstseide *f s.* 1. Chemieseide; 2. Viskoseseide
Kunststoff *m* plastic [material], engineering plastic
~ **aus Harnstoff-Formaldehyd-Harz** urea-formaldehyde plastic
~/duroplastischer thermosetting plastic (resin), thermoset [resin]
~/faserverstärkter fibre-reinforced plastic, FRP
~/glasfaserverstärkter glass-fibre reinforced plastic, GRP
~/halbharter semirigid plastic
~/harter rigid plastic
~/hitzehärtbarer *s.* ~/wärmehärtbarer
~/thermoplastischer thermoplastic [material]
~/verstärkter reinforced plastic
~/wärmehärtbarer thermosetting plastic (resin), thermoset [resin]
~/weicher (weichgestellter) flexible (non-rigid) plastic
Kunststoffansatz *m* plastic composition
Kunststoffbeutel *m* plastic bag
Kunststofferzeugnis *n* plastic product
Kunststoffolie *s.* Kunststoffolie
Kunststoffmischung *f* plastic composition
Kunststoffolie *f* plastic film (foil) *(if thickness < 0.01 inch)*; sheeting, *(if pieces:)* sheet *(if thickness > 0.01 inch)*
Kunststoffrohr *n* plastic pipe
Kunststoffrohrmaterial *n* plastic piping
Kunststoffsack *n* plastic bag
Kunststoffschmelze *f* plastic melt
Kunststoffschutzschicht *f* plastic coating
Kunststoffschweißen *n* welding of plastics
Kunststoffüberzug *m* 1. plastic covering (sheathing) *(prefabricated)*; 2. *s.* Kunststoffschutzschicht
Kunststoffverarbeiter *m* plastics processor
Kunststoffverarbeitung *f* plastics (polymer) processing
Kunststoffwerkstoff *m* engineering plastic, plastic [material]
Kunstumblattpapier *n* cigar wrapping paper
Kuoxam *n* ammoniacal copper oxide solution, cuprammonium [hydroxide] solution, cuprammonia
Kuoxamcellulose *f* cuprammonium cellulose
Kuoxamfaser *f* cuprammonium rayon staple fibre, cuprammonium (cupro) staple
Kuoxamfaserstoff *m* cuprammonium rayon
Kuoxamseide *f* continuous-filament cuprammonium
Kuoxam-Spinnverfahren *n* cuprammonia process
Küpe *f (dye)* vat • **in der ~ behandeln** to vat
~/ammoniakalische ammonia vat
~/blinde blank vat
Kupellation *f (met)* cupellation
kupellieren *(met)* to cupel
küpen *(dye)* to vat
Küpenfärberei *f* vat dyeing
Küpenfarbstoff *m* vat dye[stuff], *(Am also)* vat color
Küpenflüssigkeit *f (dye)* vat liquor
Küpensäure *f (dye)* vat acid
Küpensäureverfahren *n (dye)* vat-acid process
Kupfer *n* Cu copper
~/aktives activated copper
~/elementares elemental copper
~/gediegen[es] native copper

~/hammergares tough-pitch copper
~ hoher Leitfähigkeit high-conductivity copper, H.C. copper
~/sauerstofffreies oxygen-free copper, O.F. copper
~/stranggepreßtes coalesced copper
~/zähgepoltes tough-pitch copper
Kupfer(II)-acetat *n* copper(II) acetate, cupric acetate
Kupferacetatarsenit *n s.* Kupferarsenitacetat
Kupfer(I)-acetylid *n* copper(I) acetylide, copper(I) carbide, cuprous acetylide
Kupferamalgamelektrode *f* copper amalgam electrode
Kupferammin *n* copper ammine
Kupfer(I)-antimonid *n* copper(I) antimonide, cuprous antimonide
kupferarm poor in copper, low-copper, copper-lean
Kupfer(II)-arsenat(III) *n* copper(II) arsenite, cupric arsenite
Kupfer(II)-arsenat(V) *n* copper(II) arsenate, cupric arsenate
Kupfer(I)-arsenid *n* copper(I) arsenide, cuprous arsenide
Kupferarsenitacetat *n* copper acetoarsenite *(approximately $Cu(CH_3COO)_2 \cdot 3\ Cu(AsO_2)_2$)*
Kupferätze *f (glass)* copper stain
Kupferaventurin *m* gold aventurine
Kupferbad *n s.* Kupferelektrolyt
Kupferbeize *f (glass)* copper stain
Kupfer(II)-benzoat *n* copper(II) benzoate, cupric benzoate
Kupferblau *n* verditer blue *(a basic copper carbonate)*
Kupferblech *n* 1. sheet copper *(material)*; 2. copper sheet, *(if thick)* copper plate
Kupfer(II)-borid *n* copper(II) boride
Kupfer(II)-bromat *n* copper(II) bromate, cupric bromate
Kupfer(II)-bromid *n* copper(II) bromide, copper dibromide, cupric bromide
Kupferbruch *m* copper casse *(a disorder in wine)*
Kupferbrühe *f (agric)* copper spray
Kupfer(II)-butyrat *n* copper(II) butyrate, cupric butyrate
Kupfercarbid *n* copper(I) carbide, copper(I) acetylide, cuprous acetylide
Kupfer(II)-chelat *n* copper(II) chelate, cupric chelate
Kupfer(I)-chlorid *n* copper(I) chloride, copper monochloride, cuprous chloride
Kupfer(II)-chlorid *n* copper(II) chloride, copper dichloride, cupric chloride
Kupferchloridverfahren *n (petrol)* copper chloride [sweetening] process
Kupfer(II)-citrat *n* copper(II) citrate, cupric citrate
Kupfercoulometer *n* copper coulometer (voltameter)
Kupfer(I)-cyanid *n* copper(I) cyanide, copper monocyanide, cuprous cyanide
Kupfer(II)-cyanid *n* copper(II) cyanide, copper dicyanide, cupric cyanide
Kupferdampflaser *m* copper-vapour laser
Kupferdi... *s. a.* Kupfer(II)-...
Kupferdichromat *n* copper dichromate
Kupferdichtung *f* copper gasket
Kupferdrehspäne *mpl* copper turnings
Kupferdruckfarbe *f* copperplate ink
Kupferdruckpapier *n* [soft] plate paper, etching paper
Kupferelektrode *f* copper electrode
Kupferelektrolyt *m* copper plating bath (solution)
Kupfererz *n* copper ore
Kupferethylendiamin *n (text)* cupriethylenediamine
Kupferfaser *f* 1. copper fibre; 2. *s.* Kuoxamfaser
Kupferfaserstoff *m* 1. copper fibre; 2. *s.* Kuoxamfaserstoff
Kupferfeilspäne *mpl* copper filings
Kupfer(II)-fluorid *n* copper(II) fluoride, copper difluoride, cupric fluoride
Kupferfolie *f* copper foil
Kupfer(II)-formiat *n* copper(II) formate, cupric formate
Kupferfungizid *n* copper fungicide
Kupfergehalt *m* copper content • **mit hohem ~** high-copper
Kupferglanz *m* copper glance *(a mineral group)*
Kupfergraphit *m* copper graphite
kupferhaltig copper-containing, *(esp relating to ores:)* copper-bearing, cupriferous
Kupfer(I)-hexacyanoferrat(II) *n* copper(I) hexacyanoferrate(II)
Kupfer(I)-hexacyanoferrat(III) *n* copper(I) hexacyanoferrate(III)
Kupfer(II)-hexacyanoferrat(II) *n* copper(II) hexacyanoferrate(II)
Kupfer(II)-hexacyanoferrat(III) *n* copper(II) hexacyanoferrate(III)
Kupfer(I)-hexafluorosilicat *n* copper(I) hexafluorosilicate, cuprous fluorosilicate
Kupfer(II)-hexafluorosilicat *n* copper(II) hexafluorosilicate, cupric fluorosilicate
Kupfer(I)-hydrid *n* copper(I) hydride
Kupfer(II)-hydrogenarsenat(III) *n* copper(II) hydrogenarsenite, cupric hydrogenarsenite
Kupfer(II)-hydroxid *n* copper(II) hydroxide, cupric hydroxide
Kupferhydroxidlösung *f*/**ammoniakalische** *s.* Kupferoxidammoniak
Kupferindig[o] *m (min)* indigo copper, blue copper, covellite, covelline *(copper(II) sulphide)*
Kupfer(II)-iodat *n* copper(II) iodate, cupric iodate
Kupfer(I)-ion *n* copper(I) ion, cuprous ion
Kupfer(II)-ion *n* copper(II) ion, cupric ion
Kupfer(I)-ionen-Verfahren *n (text)* cuprous-ion method
Kupferkalkbrühe *f* Bordeaux mixture *(a fungicide)*
Kupfer(I)-katalysator *m* cuprous catalyst

Kupferkies *m (min)* chalcopyrite, chalkopyrite, copper pyrites *(copper(II) iron(II) sulphide)*
Kupferkomplex *m* copper complex
Kupferkonverter *m* copper converter
Kupferkopf *m* copper head *(a defect in enamel)*
Kupferkunstseide *f s.* Kuoxamseide
Kupfer(II)-lactat *n* copper(II) lactate, cupric lactate
Kupferlasur *m (min)* blue copper ore, azurite
Kupfer-Leaching *n (min tech, biot)* copper leaching
Kupferlegierung *f* copper alloy
Kupfermangel *m* copper deficiency
Kupfer(II)-metaborat *n* copper(II) metaborate
Kupfermineral *n* copper mineral
Kupfermonoxid *n s.* Kupfer(II)-oxid
kupfern *(dye, text)* to copperize
Kupfernachbehandlung *f* copper aftertreatment
Kupfernaphthenat *n* copper naphthenate
Kupfer-Nickel-Legierung *f* cupronickel alloy
Kupfer-Nickel-Rohstein *m (met)* nickel matte
Kupfer(II)-nitrat *n* copper(II) nitrate, cupric nitrate
Kupfernitrid *n* copper nitride
Kupfer(II)-nitroprussiat *n*, **Kupfer(II)-nitroprussid** *n s.* Kupfer[II]-pentacyanonitrosylferrat
Kupfer(II)-oleat *n* copper(II) oleate, cupric oleate
Kupfer(II)-orthophosphat *n* copper(II) orthophosphate, copper(II) phosphate, cupric phosphate
Kupfer(II)-oxalat *n* copper(II) oxalate, cupric oxalate
Kupferoxid *n* copper oxide, *(specif)* copper(II) oxide, copper monooxide, cupric oxide
Kupfer(I)-oxid *n* copper(I) oxide, cuprous oxide, red copper oxide
Kupfer(II)-oxid *n* copper(II) oxide, copper monooxide, cupric oxide
Kupferoxidammoniak *n* ammoniacal copper oxide solution, cuprammonium [hydroxide] solution, cuprammonia
Kupferoxidammoniakcellulose *f* cuprammonium cellulose
Kupferoxidammoniak-Spinnverfahren *n* cuprammonia process
Kupfer(II)-oxidchlorid *n* copper(II) chloride oxide, cupric chloride oxide
Kupfer(II)-pentacyanonitrosylferrat *n* copper(II) pentacyanonitrosylferrate, cupric nitroprusside, cupric nitroprussiate
Kupferperoxid *n* copper peroxide
Kupfer(I)-phosphid *n* copper(I) phosphide, tricopper monophosphide, cuprous phosphide
Kupfer(II)-phosphid *n* copper(II) phosphide, tricopper diphosphide, cupric phosphide
Kupfer(II)-phosphit *n* *copper(II) phosphonate, copper(II) phosphite, cupric phosphite
Kupferphthalocyanin *n* copper phthalocyanine
Kupferpulver *n* copper powder
kupferreich high-copper, rich in copper
Kupfer(I)-rhodanid *n s.* Kupfer(I)-thiocyanat
Kupfer(II)-rhodanid *n s.* Kupfer(II)-thiocyanat
Kupferron *n* cupferron, ammonium *N*-nitrosophenylhydroxylamine
Kupferrubinglas *n* copper ruby glass
Kupfer(II)-salicylat *n* copper(II) salicylate, cupric salicylate
Kupfersalzlösungswäsche *f* copper-liquor scrubbing *(for removing carbon monooxide from gases)*
Kupferschachtofen *m* copper blast furnace
Kupferschaum *m (min)* copper froth, froth copper, tyrolite
Kupferschmelzofen *m* copper blast furnace
Kupferseide *f s.* Kuoxamseide
Kupferseife *f* copper soap
Kupfer(II)-selenat *n* copper(II) selenate, cupric selenate
Kupfer(I)-silicid *n* copper(I) silicide, cuprous silicide
Kupfersodabrühe *f* soda bordeaux, Burgundy mixture *(a fungicide)*
Kupferstaub *m* copper dust *(a fungicide)*
Kuper(II)-stearat *n* copper(II) stearate, cupric stearate
Kupferstein *m*/**armer** *(met)* copper matte
~/reicher copper bottom
Kupfersteinkonverter *m* copper converter
Kupfersteinverblasen *n* copper converting
Kupferstreifenkochprobe *f* copper strip test *(for determining active sulphur)*
Kupfer(I)-sulfat *n* copper(I) sulphate, cuprous sulphate
Kupfer(II)-sulfat *n* copper(II) sulphate, cupric sulphate
Kupfer(II)-sulfid *n* copper(II) sulphide, cupric sulphide
Kupfer(I)-sulfit *n* copper(I) sulphite, cuprous sulphite
Kupfersüßen *n (petrol)* copper sweetening
Kupfer(II)-tartrat *n* copper(II) tartrate, cupric tartrate
Kupfer(II)-tetramminhydroxid *n* tetraamminecopper hydroxide, ammoniacal copper hydroxide
Kupfer(I)-thiocyanat *n* copper(I) thiocyanate, cuprous thiocyanate
Kupfer(II)-thiocyanat *n* copper(II) thiocyanate, cupric thiocyanate
Kupfertrübung *f s.* Kupferbruch
Kupferung *f (dye)* copperization, treatment with copper
~/oxidative oxidative copperization
Kupferverfahren *n (petrol)* copper sweetening process
Kupfervitriol *m (min)* copper (blue) vitriol, chalcanthite *(copper(II) sulphate 5-water)*
Kupferwasser *n s.* Eisenvitriol
Kupferwasserstoff *m* copper hydride
Kupfer(II)-wolframat *n* *copper(II) wolframate, cupric wolframate, cupric tungstate
Kupferzahl *f (sugar)* copper reducing power, K value; *(pap, text)* copper number (index, value)
Kupfer-Zinn-Legierung *f* copper-tin alloy
kupieren *(food)* to blend
Kupolofen *m* cupola [furnace]

Kupolofenausmauerung *f*, **Kupolofenfutter** *n* cupola lining
Kupolofenstein *m* cupola brick
Kuppel *f* crown *(of a glass furnace)*
kuppeln *(dye)* to couple
~/alkalisch to couple in alkaline solution
~/sauer to couple in acid solution
Kuppelofen *m s.* Kupolofen
Kupplung *f (dye)* coupling
~/oxidative oxidative coupling
~/reduktive (reduzierende) reductive coupling
Kupplungsbottich *m*, **Kupplungsbütte** *f (dye)* coupling vat
Kupplungsgeschwindigkeit *f (dye)* coupling rate
Kupplungskomponente *f (dye)* coupling (secondary) component
Kupplungskufe *f (dye)* coupling vat
Kupplungsreaktion *f (dye)* coupling reaction
Kurbelpresse *f* crank press
Kurbelwinkel *m* crank angle *(a measure for ignition delay)*
Kürbiskernöl *n* pumpkin [seed] oil *(from Cucurbita pepo L.)*
Kurchialkaloid *n* holarrhena alkaloid
Kurchirinde *f (pharm)* kurchee (kurchi) bark *(from Holarrhena antidysenterica Wall.)*
Kurkumapapier *n* turmeric paper *(an indicator paper)*
Kurkumaprobe *f* turmeric test
Kurrunjeöl *n* Pongam (Hongay) oil *(from Pongamia pinnata (L.)Merr.)*
Kurtschatovium *n* Db dubnium *(element 104)*, *(deprecated:)* kurchatovium
Kurve *f* curve, graph *(of plotted data)*, *(if recorded automatically also)* trace
~/binodale binodal curve, conodal (coexistence) curve
~/charakteristische *(phot)* characteristic curve, Hurter and Driffield curve, H and D curve
~ gleichen Gehalts an flüchtiger Substanz line of equal volatile matter, isovol
~ gleichen Heizwerts isocalorific line, isocal
~ gleichen Kohlenstoffgehalts isocarbon line
~/polarographische polarographic curve, polarogram
~/sensitometrische *s.* ~/charakteristische
~/voltammetrische *(el ch)* voltammogram
Kurvenanpassung *f (anal)* curve fitting
Kurvendurchhang *m (phot)* foot, toe, region of underexposure *(of the characteristic curve)*
Kurvenschreiber *m* function plotter, X-Y recorder
kurz *(ceram)* short *(clay body)*
Kurzalterung *f* accelerated (artificial) ageing *(materials testing)*
Kurzbezeichnung *f***/chemische** abbreviated chemical name
Kurzhalskolben *m* short-neck[ed] flask
Kurzhalsrundkolben *m* short-neck round-bottom flask, bolt-head flask
Kurzhalsstehkolben *m* short-neck flat-bottom flask
Kurzkettenverzweigung *f* short-chain branching
kurzkettig short-chain
kurzlebig short-lived *(chemical element, radical, compound)*
Kurzname *m***/chemischer** abbreviated chemical name
Kurznaßbeize *f (agric)* instant dip
Kurznotation *f***[/Clelandsche]** *(bioch)* shorthand notation *(of reaction mechanisms)*
Kurzperiode *f* short period *(in the periodic table)*
Kurzperiodensystem *n* short periodic table
kurzprismatisch *(cryst)* short-prismatic
Kurzprüfung *f s.* Kurzzeitprüfung
Kurzrohrverdampfer *m* short-tube evaporator
Kurzschleifentrockner *m (text)* short-loop dryer, roller dryer
Kurzschluß *m s.* Kurzschlußströmung
Kurzschlußelektrolyse *f* internal electrolysis
Kurzschlußströmung *f* bypass *(in a reactor)*
• **Ausbildung** *f* **(Auftreten** *n***) von Kurzschlußströmungen** bypassing, short-circuiting *(in a reactor)*
Kurztest *m s.* Kurzzeitversuch
Kurzventuridüse *f* short-tube venturi
Kurzversuch *m s.* Kurzzeitversuch
Kurzwegdestillation *f* short-path [high-vacuum] distillation
Kurzwegdestillierapparat *m* short-path still
Kurzzeiterhitzer *m (food)* high-temperature short-time pasteurizer
Kurzzeiterhitzung *f (food)* short-time heat processing, high-temperature short-time pasteurization (heat treatment), HTST pasteurization
Kurzzeitfermentation *f (biot)* short-term fermentation
Kurzzeitpasteurisation *f s.* Kurzzeiterhitzung
Kurzzeitprobenahme *f* instantaneous sampling, spot (grab) sampling
Kurzzeitprüfung *f* accelerated (short-time, short-term) testing
Kurzzeittest *m s.* Kurzzeitversuch
Kurzzeittrockner *m* short-retention-time dryer
Kurzzeitversuch *m* accelerated (short-time, short-term) test
Kurzzeitwecker *m (lab)* interval timer
Kuteragummi *n* kuteera (kateera, kateira) gum, gum kuteera *(from Sterculia, Cochlospermum, or Astragalus specc.)*
Kutinit *m (coal)* cutinite
Kuvert-Konformation *f* envelope-form conformation
Küvette *f (anal)* cell, cuvet[te]
~ nach Tiselius/U-förmige Tiselius cell *(for electrophoresis)*
Küvettenhalter *m (anal)* cell holder
Küvettenwechsler *m (anal)* cell changer
Kw. *s.* Königswasser
K-Wert *m (plast)* K value, K factor
~ nach Fikentscher Fikentscher K-value *(characterizing the molecular weight of high polymers)*

KW-Stoff *m s.* Kohlenwasserstoff
kyanisieren to kyanize *(to protect wood by saturating it with aqueous mercuric chloride)*
Kynurenin *n* kynurenine, 3-anthraniloyl-L-alanine
Kynurensäure *f* kynurenic acid, 4-hydroxyquinoline-2-carboxylic acid
Kynurin *n* kynurine, 4-hydroxyquinoline
Kynursäure *f* kynuric acid, *o*-carboxyoxanilic acid

L

L. *s.* löslich
l- = lävogyr
L *s.* 1. Löslichkeitsprodukt; 2. Leuchtdichte
Lab *n* rennet • **mit ~ versetzen** to rennet *(milk)*
labbehandelt rennet-treated *(e.g. casein)*
Labbruch *m* rennet curd
Labcasein *n* rennet[-precipitated] casein
Labdan[um]... *s.* Ladanum...
laben to rennet *(milk)*
Labenzym *n s.* Labferment
Labessenz *f*, **Labextrakt** *m* rennet extract
Labfähigkeit *f* rennetability, renneting ability, rennet coagulability
Labferment *n* rennin, chymosin
~/mikrobielles microbial rennet
Labgärprobe *f* rennet[-fermentation] test
Labgärung *f* rennet fermentation
Labgerinnung *f* rennet clotting (coagulation)
Labgerinnungsfähigkeit *f s.* Labfähigkeit
Labgerinnungszeit *f* rennet-clotting time, renneting time
labil labile, unstable, instable
~/thermisch thermolabile, heat-labile
Labilität *f* lability, unstableness, instability
Labkäse *m* rennet cheese
Labkäsebruch *m* rennetcurd
Labkoagulation *f* rennet clotting (coagulation)
Labor *n s.* Laboratorium
Laborabriebversuch *m* laboratory abrasion test
Laborant *m* laboratory assistant
Laborantin *f* [female] laboratory assistant
Laborapparat *m* laboratory apparatus (instrument)
Laborarbeit *f* laboratory work
Laboratorium *n* laboratory, lab
~/chemisches chemical (chemistry) laboratory
~/heißes *(nucl)* hot laboratory
~/wissenschaftlich-technisches science-technology-type laboratory
Laboratoriums... *s.* Labor...
Laborausrüstung *f*, **Laborausstattung** *f* laboratory (research) equipment
Laborbecken *n* laboratory sink
Laborbedingungen *fpl* laboratory conditions
Laborbestimmung *f* laboratory determination
Laborchemikalie *f* laboratory chemical
Laboreinrichtung *f* laboratory equipment
Laborfermenter *m (biot)* laboratory[-scale] fermenter
Laborgerät *n* laboratory apparatus
Laborgeräte *npl* laboratory apparatus (equipment), labware
~ aus Glas laboratory glassware
Laborglas *n* chemically resistant glass
Laborgrundoperation *f* laboratory unit operation, LUO
Laborkolonne *f* laboratory column
Laborkugelmühle *f* laboratory jar mill
labormäßig *s.* Labormaßstab/im
Labormaßstab/im on a (the) laboratory scale, lab[oratory]-scale
Labormethode *f* laboratory method
Laborofen *m* laboratory furnace
Labor-*p*H-Meter *n* laboratory *p*H meter
Laborporzellan *n* laboratory [chemical] porcelain
Laborpraktikum *n* laboratory course (period)
Laborprobe *f* laboratory sample
Laborprüfung *f* laboratory testing
Laborreaktor *m* laboratory (bench-scale) reactor
Laborrührer *m* laboratory agitator (stirrer)
Laborrührwerk *n* laboratory agitator (stirrer)
Laborstamm *m (biot)* laboratory strain *(of microorganisms)*
Labortagebuch *n* laboratory manual
Labortechnik *f* laboratory technique
labortechnisch 1. laboratory *(e.g. equipment)*; 2. *s.* Labormaßstab/im
Labortisch *m* laboratory table (bench, desk)
Laboruntersuchung *f* laboratory investigation (examination), bench-scale study
Laborverfahren *n* laboratory process (procedure, operation)
Laborversuch *m* laboratory test
Labpulver *n* rennet powder
Labquark *m* rennet curd
Labstärke *f* rennet strength
labträge slow-renneting *(milk)*
Labung *f* renneting *(of milk)*
Labungsfähigkeit *f s.* Labfähigkeit
Labyrinthdichtung *f* labyrinth seal
Labyrinthfaktor *m* tortuosity factor *(diffusion theory)*
Labyrinthkondenswasserableiter *m* labyrinth trap
Labyrinthspaltdichtung *f* labyrinth seal
Labzeit *f* rennet-clotting time, renneting time
Laccainsäure *f* laccainic acid
Lachgas *n* laughing gas *(nitrogen(I) oxide)*
Lachsfett *n*, **Lachsöl** *n* salmon oil
Lack *m* 1. [clear] varnish *(chemically drying)*; [clear] lacquer *(physically drying)*; paint, pigmented coating *(in a larger sense)*; lac[k] *(of animal or vegetable origin)*; lake *(organic compounds on a carrier, esp alumina)*; 2. *s.* Lackfarbe 1.
~/fetter long-oil varnish
~ für Außenanstriche exterior varnish
~ für Innenanstriche interior varnish
~/halbfetter medium-oil varnish
~/kalthärtender cold-hardening varnish
~/magerer short-oil varnish

~/mittelfetter medium-oil varnish
~/ofentrocknender stoving (baking) varnish
~/pigmentierter *s.* Lackfarbe 1.
~/überfetteter extra long-oil varnish
Lackbenzin *n* varnish-makers' [and painters'] naphtha, V.M.P. naphtha, painter's naphtha
Lackbildung *f* varnishing *(of pesticide components on plants)*
Lackentferner *m* paint (lacquer, varnish) remover
Lackfarbe *f* 1. topcoat (finish, finishing) paint; enamel [paint]; topcoat enamel *(very hard and glossy drying)*; lacquer *(physically drying)*; 2. *s.* Lackfarbstoff
~ für Außenanstriche exterior enamel
~ für Innenanstriche interior enamel
~/ofentrocknende stoving (baking) enamel
Lackfarbstoff *m* lacquer dye; *(if adsorbed on a carrier as on alumina:)* lake dye, *(Am also)* lake color
~/roter lac dye *(obtained from stick lac)*
Lackgewebe *n* varnished fabric
Lackgießen *n* curtain coating
Lackharz *n* varnish (coating) resin
lackieren 1. to lacquer *(using products drying by evaporation)*, *(in a larger sense:)* to paint; to varnish *(using transparent products)*; to enamel *(using products yielding very hard coatings)*; 2. *(cosmet)* to enamel *(e.g. nails)*
Lackiererei *f* paint shop
Lackiertrommel *f* paint barrel, barrel coater
Lack-Lack *m* lac (Indian) lake, lac (lake) lac *(a product prepared from lac dye)*
Lackleder *n* patent leather, enamelled (japanned, Japan) leather
Lacklösungsmittel *n* lacquer solvent
Lackmoid *n* lacmoid, lackmoid
Lackmus *n(m)* litmus, lacmus, lakmus, lichen blue *(a lichen dye)*
Lackmuspapier *n* litmus [test] paper
Lackmustinktur *f* litmus solution
Lacköl *n* varnish oil
Lackpapier *n* varnished (varnishing) paper
Lack- und Farbenchemie *f* paint chemistry
Lack- und Farbenchemiker *m* paint chemist
Lack- und Farbenindustrie *f* paint and varnish industry
Lack- und Farbentechnik *f* paint and varnish technology
Lackvorhang *m* curtain
Lackvorratsbehälter *m* sump *(in flow-coating)*
Lactagogum *n s.* Galaktagogum
Lactalbumin *n* lactalbumin, milk albumin
Lactam *n* lactam
β-Lactam-Antibiotikum *n (biot)* β-lactam antibiotic
Lactamform *f (org ch)* lactam form
β-Lactamring *m* β-lactam ring
Lactarinsäure *f* lactarinic acid, 6-oxo-octadecanoic acid
Lactarsäure *f s.* Stearinsäure
Lactat *n* lactate
Lactatdehydrase *f s.* Lactatdehydrogenase
Lactatdehydrogenase *f* lactic dehydrogenase
Lactatgärung *f (bioch)* lactate fermentation
Lactatmethode *f (soil)* double-lactate method
Lacticodehydrase *f s.* Lactatdehydrogenase
Lactid *n* lactide *(any of a group of dilactones)*
Lactim *n* lactim
Lactimform *f (org ch)* lactim form
Lactinsäure *f s.* Milchsäure
Lactobionsäure *f* lactobionic acid
lactogen *(bioch, med)* lactogenic
Lactoglobulin *n* lactoglobulin, milk globulin
Lacton *n* lactone
Lactonbildung *f* lactonization, lactone formation
Lactonbindung *f* lactonic bond
lactonisieren to lactonize
Lactonisierung *f* lactonization
Lactonitril *n* lactonitrile, *2-hydroxypropane nitrile
Lactonregel *f* **[/Hudsonsche]** [Hudson] lactone rule *(of optical rotation)*
Lactonring *m* lactone ring
Lactonsäure *f* 1. lactone acid, lactonic acid *(any of several acids with a lactone ring bearing the carboxyl group)*; 2. *s.* Galactonsäure
Lactosurie *f (med)* lactosuria
Lactotropin *n s.* Laktationshormon
Lactoylgruppe *f* $CH_3CH(OH)CO-$ lactoyl group (residue)
Lactylharnstoff *m* lactylurea
Lactylmilchsäure *f* lactyllactic acid
Ladangummi *n*, **Ladanharz** *n s.* Ladanum
Ladanum[harz] *n* ladanum, labdanum [resin] *(an oleoresin from Cistus specc.)*
Ladanumöl *n* la[b]danum oil *(from Cistus specc.)*
laden 1. to load, to charge *(bulk material)*; 2. *(phys ch)* to charge
Ladestrom *m* charging current, capacity (double-layer) current *(polarography)*
Ladung *f* 1. load, charge, batch *(of bulk material)* 2. *(phys ch)* charge • **[mit] entgegengesetzter ~** unlike-charged • **[mit] gleicher ~** like-charged
~/elektrische electric charge
~/elektrostatische electrostatic charge
~/entgegengesetzte opposite charge
~/formale formal charge
~/gleichnamige like charge
~ Null zero charge
~/partielle partial (fractional) charge
~/ruhende static charge *(of an intermittent gas-making retort)*
~/ungleichnamige unlike charge
Ladungsaustausch *m* charge exchange, CE
Ladungsdichte *f* 1. *(phys ch)* charge density; 2. loading density *(of explosives)*
~ der Elektronen electronic charge density
Ladungsdichteverteilung *f (phys ch)* charge distribution
~ der Elektronen electronic charge distribution

Ladungsdifferenz *f s.* Ladungsunterschied
Ladungsdoppelschicht *f* electric double layer
Ladungsinkrementpolarographie *f (anal)* incremental charge polarography
Ladungskonzentration *f* loading density *(of explosives)*
ladungslos uncharged
Ladungsmenge *f* charge quantity, amount of charge
Ladungsneutralisation *f (hyd)* charge neutralization *(coagulation)*
Ladungsschwerpunkt *m* charge centre, centre of charge
ladungstragend charge-carrying
Ladungsträger *m (phys ch)* charge carrier
Ladungstrennung *f* separation of charge
Ladungsüberführungsbande *f (spectr)* charge transfer band
Ladungsüberschuß *m* excess of charge
Ladungsübertragung *f* charge transfer
~/dissoziative dissociative charge transfer
Ladungsübertragungsbande *f* charge-transfer band
Ladungsübertragungskomplex *m* charge-transfer complex, electron-donor-acceptor complex
Ladungsübertragungsspektrum *n* charge-transfer spectrum
Ladungsunterschied *m (phys ch)* difference in charge
Ladungsverschiebungschromatographie *f* charge-transfer chromatography
Ladungsverteilung *f s.* Ladungsdichteverteilung
Ladungsvorzeichen *n* charge sign
Ladungswolke *f (phys ch)* [electron, electronic] charge cloud
~ einer π-Bindung π cloud
Ladungszahl *f (nomencl)* charge (Ewens-Bassett) number *(of ionic charge)*
Lage *f* 1. position; 2. layer; ply *(as of laminated material)*; 3. *(geol)* stratum • **in natürlicher ~** *(geol)* autochthonous, in place, in situ
Lageenergie *f* potential energy
Lagehöhe *f* potential head *(fluid mechanics)*
Lagenlösung *f (rubber)* ply separation
Lagentextur *f (geol)* banded structure
Lager *n* 1. store, storage; 2. *(tech)* bearing *(as of shafts)*; 3. *s.* Lagerstätte
-/ölfreies (ölloses) oilless bearing
lagerbar storable
Lagerbarkeit *f* storability
Lagerbehälter *m* storage tank (vessel)
lagerbeständig stable in storage, resistant in storage
Lagerbeständigkeit *f* stability in storage, resistance to storage, storage stability (resistance, quality)
Lagerbier *n* stock beer, *(esp)* lager [beer]
Lagerdauer *f (food)* storage period (life), shelf life
lagerfähig *s.* lagerbar
Lagergefäß *n s.* Lagerbehälter
Lagerhalle *f* store[house], storage
Lagerhaltbarkeit *f s.* Lagerbeständigkeit
Lagerhaus *n s.* Lagerhalle
Lagerkeller *m* storage cellar
Lagermetall *n* bearing metal
lagern 1. to store, *(bulk material also)* to stockpile; 2. *(ceram)* to age, to sour *(moistened clay)*
~/im Tank to tank
~/in Borke *(tann)* to age
~/kühl to store in a cool place
~/trocken to store in a dry place
Lagerraum *m* storage room, storeroom
Lagerstabilität *f s.* Lagerbeständigkeit
Lagerstätte *f (geol)* layer, bed, deposit, lode, seam; *(petrol)* field, reservoir
~ mit Gasentlösungsdruck *(petrol)* depletion-type field (reservoir), solution gas-drive field (reservoir)
~ mit Gaskappe *(petrol)* gas cap-drive field (reservoir)
~ mit Wassertrieb *(petrol)* water-drive field (reservoir)
~/unter Gasdruck (Gastrieb) stehende *(petrol)* gas-drive field (reservoir)
~/unter Schwerkraft entölende *(petrol)* gravity drainage reservoir
Lagerstättenvergasung *f (coal)* underground gasification
Lagertank *m* storage tank (vessel)
Lagertemperatur *f* storage temperature
Lager- und Verarbeitbarkeitsdauer *f* shelf (storage) life
Lagerung *f* 1. storage, *(of bulk material also)* stockpiling; 2. *(ferm)* secondary fermentation; 3. *(tech)* bearing
~ unter Wasser *(pap)* water storage
~/unterirdische underground storage
Lagerungsdauer *f* storage period
Lagerungstemperatur *f s.* Lagertemperatur
Lagerungsvorschrift *f* storage regulation
Lagervorrat *m* stock
Lagerweißmetall *n* white metal
Lag-Phase *f* lag phase (time)
Lainer-Effekt *m (phot)* Lainer effect
Lake *f* [salt] brine • **mit ~ behandeln** to brine
Lakenbehandlung *f* brining
lakenkonserviert *(tann)* brine-cured
Lakenkonservierung *f (tann)* brine curing (cure)
Lakmoid *n s.* Lackmoid
lakrimogen lachrymatory
Lakritze *f* liquorice, licorice *(from Glycyrrhiza glabra L.)*
Lakt... *s. a.* Lact... *for chemical compounds*
Laktationshormon *n* lactogenic (luteotrophic) hormone, *prolactin
Laktobutyrometer *n* lactobutyrometer
Laktodensimeter *n* lactodensimeter
Laktogen *n s.* Laktationshormon
Laktometer *n* galactometer, lactometer

lakustrisch *(geoch)* lacustrine
lamellar lamellar
Lamelle *f* lamella
Lamellenmethode *f* detachment method *(for determining surface tensions)*
laminar laminar
Laminarbox *f* laminar flow hood *(microbiology)*
Laminarströmung *f* laminar (streamline) flow
Laminat *n* laminate, laminated material (plastic)
laminieren to laminate
Laminierharz *n* laminating resin
laminiert/mit Schaumstoff foam-backed
Laminierung *f* lamination
Lampe *f (glass)* [glass blower's] lamp, blowtorch, bench blowpipe • **vor der ~ geblasen** lamp-blown, lampworked
Lampenarbeit *f (glass)* lampworking
Lampenbläser *m (glass)* lampworker
Lampenbläserei *f (glass)* lampworking
lampengeblasen *(glass)* lamp-blown, lamp-worked
Lampenmethode *f (petrol)* lamp method *(for determining sulphur content)*
Lampenpetroleum *n* lamp (illuminating) oil
Lampenruß *m*, **Lampenschwarz** *n* lampblack
Lana *f* **philosophica** *s.* Zinkblumen
Lanatosid *n* lanatoside *(a glycoside)*
Lancashire-Kessel *m* Lancashire boiler *(an internally fired boiler having two flues)*
Landé-Faktor *m* **g** Landé g-factor, [Landé] splitting factor g *(chemical-bond theory)*
Landkartenpapier *n* map (chart, plan) paper, *(Am)* geography paper
Landwirtschaftschemie *f* agricultural chemistry, agrochemistry
Lang[absetz]becken *n (hyd)* rectangular clarifier, rectangular [settling, sedimentation] basin
Langarmzentrifuge *f* long-arm centrifuge
längen to stretch
Längenänderung *f* change in length, *(increase:)* elongation
~/bleibende plastic elongation, offset
Längenzunahme *f* elongation, extension
längerkettig *(org ch)* longer-chain
langfas[e]rig long-fibre
Langfilz *m (pap)* long felt *(in cylinder board machines)*
Langhalskolben *m* long-neck flask
Langhalsrundkolben *m* round-bottom long-neck flask
Langhalsstehkolben *m* flat-bottom long-neck flask, Florence (boiling) flask
Langholz *n (pap)* log
Langkettenverzweigung *f* long-chain branching
langkettig long-chain
langlebig long-lived *(isotope, pollutant)*
langlebigst longest-lived *(isotope, pollutant)*
Langlochziegel[stein] *m* horizontally perforated brick
Langmuir-Isotherme *f* Langmuir adsorption isotherm
Langperiode *f* long period *(in the periodic table)*
Langperiodensystem *n* long periodic table
langprismatisch *(cryst)* long-prismatic, elongate-prismatic
Langrohrverdampfer *m* long-tube evaporator
Langrohr-Vertikalverdampfer *m* long-tube vertical-film evaporator, LTV evaporator
Langrohr-Vertikalverdampfung *f* long-tube vertical evaporation, LTV evaporation
Längsabscheider *m*, **Längsabsetzbecken** *n s.* Langabsetzbecken
Längsachse *f* long axis
Langsamfilter *n (hyd)* slow [sand] filter, English (low-rate) filter
Langsamfiltration *f (hyd)* slow [sand] filtration
langsamflüchtig slow-evaporating
Langsamkochung *f (pap)* slow cook
Langsammischen *n*, **Langsamrühren** *n (tech)* slow mix[ing], *(lab)* slow stirring
Langsamrührphase *f (hyd)* slow mix period, slow mixing step
langsamwirkend slow-acting
langsamziehend *(dye)* slow-striking
Längsbecken *n s.* Langabsetzbecken
Längsdiffusion *f* longitudinal (axial) diffusion
Langsieb *n* **der Papiermaschine** Fourdrinier wire
Langsieb[papier]maschine *f* Fourdrinier [paper machine]
Langsiebpartie *f (pap)* Fourdrinier part (section)
Längsreibe[maschine] *f (food)* [longitudinal] conche
Längsrippenrohr *n* long-fin tube
Längsschneidemaschine *f*, **Längsschneider** *m (pap)* reel-slitting (roll-slitting) machine, rereeling (rewinding, slitting) machine, slitter, rewinder
Längsspritzkopf *m (plast)* horizontal (axial extruder) head
Längsvermischung *f* longitudinal (axial) mixing
Langweggaszelle *f*, **Langwegküvette** *f (spectr)* long-path gas cell, long-pathlength cell
Langzeitbelüftung *f (hyd)* extended aeration
Langzeitbelüftungsanlage *f (hyd)* extended aeration plant
Langzeitbeobachtung *f* long-term observation
Langzeitbrennöl *n* long-time burning oil, signal oil
Langzeitfermentation *f (biot)* long-term fermentation
Langzeittrend *m* long-term trend
Langzeittrockner *m* long-retention-time dryer
Langzeitversuch *m* long-term experiment (test)
Lanocerinsäure *f* lanoceric acid *(higher fatty acid)*
Lanolin *n* lanolin[e] *(refined wool grease)*
Lanopalminsäure *f* lanopalminic acid, *2-hydroxyhexadecanoic acid
Lanthan *n* La lanthanum
Lanthanacetylid *n s.* Lanthancarbid
Lanthanbromid *n* lanthanum bromide

Lanthancarbid *n* lanthanum carbide
Lanthancarbonat *n* lanthanum carbonate
Lanthanchlorid *n* lanthanum chloride
Lanthanerde *f s.* Lanthan(III)-oxid
Lanthanfluorid *n* lanthanum fluoride
Lanthanhydroxid *n* lanthanum hydroxide
Lanthanid *n s.* Lanthanoid
Lanthaniden... *s.* Lanthanoiden...
Lanthaniodat *n* lanthanum iodate
Lanthannitrat *n* lanthanum nitrate
Lanthanoid *n*, **Lanthanoidenelement** *n* lanthanoid [element]
Lanthanoidengruppe *f s.* Lanthanoidenreihe
Lanthanoidenkontraktion *f* lanthanoid contraction
Lanthanoidenmetall *n* lanthanoid metal
Lanthanoidenreihe *f* lanthanoid series (group)
Lanthan(III)-oxid *n* lanthanum(III) oxide, lanthanum trioxide
Lanthanreihe *f s.* Lanthanoidenreihe
Lanthansalz *n* lanthanum salt
Lanthansulfat *n* lanthanum sulphate
Lanthantrioxid *n s.* Lanthan(III)-oxid
Lanzettnadel *f (lab)* lancet-point dissecting needle
Lapachoholz *n (dye)* lapacho *(from Tabebuia and Tecoma specc.)*
Lapachol *n* lapachol *(a naphthoquinone derivative)*
Lapachosäure *f s.* Lapachol
Lapislazuli *m (min)* lapis [lazuli], lazurite *(a tectosilicate)*
Lard *n (food)* lard, pig fat
Lardöl *n* lard (grease) oil
Lariatether *m* lariat ether *(a crown ether)*
Larixinsäure *f* larixinic acid, maltol
Larmor-Frequenz *f (spectr)* Larmor frequency
Larmor-Präzession *f (spectr)* Larmor precession
Larvalhormon *n* juvenile hormone *(of insects)*
Larvengift *n*, **Larvizid** *n* larvicide, larvacide
LAS *s.* Alkylbenzensulfonat/lineares
Laser *m*/**abstimmbarer** *(spectr)* tunable laser
~/**chemischer** chemical laser
~/**durchstimmbarer** *(spectr)* tunable laser
~/**gepulster** pulsed laser
~/**kontinuierlicher** continuous-wave laser, CW laser
~/**modengekoppelter** mode-locked laser
~/**phasengekoppelter** mode-locked laser
Laser-Anregung *f (spectr)* laser excitation
Laserchemie *f* laser chemistry
Laser-Desorptions-Massenspektrometrie *f* laser desorption mass spectrometry, LD
Laserlicht *n* laser light
Laserlicht-Kleinwinkelstreuung *f* low-angle laser light scattering, LALLS
Laserlichtquelle *f* laser source
Laser-Massenspektrometrie *f* laser mass spectrometry, LAMS
Laser-Mikrospektralanalyse *f* laser microprobe mass analysis, LAMMA
Laseroszillator *m* laser
Laserstrahl *m* laser beam
Lassaigne-Probe *f* Lassaigne test *(for detecting nitrogen)*
Lassoether *m* lariat ether *(a crown ether)*
Last *f* load
~/**biologische** *s.* BSB-Last
Last-Durchbiegungskurve *f (plast)* load deflection curve
Lastschale *f* left-hand pan *(of a balance)*
Lastschwankung *f (hyd)* load fluctuation, variation in loadings
Lasttrum *m(n)* carrying side, top strand, *(relating to belt conveyors also)* drive belt
Lasurit *m s.* Lapislazuli
Latensifikation *f (phot)* latensification
Latenzzeit *f* period of latency (induction)
Lateritboden *m* lateritic soil
Lateritisierung *f* lateritization *(of rocks)*
Latex *m* latex
~/**aufgerahmter** creamed latex
~/**eingedampfter (eingedickter)** evaporated latex
~/**frisch gezapfter** field latex
~/**konzentrierter** concentrated latex
~/**künstlicher** synthetic[-rubber] latex
~ **mit niedrigem Ammoniakgehalt** low-ammonia latex
~/**normaler** normal latex
~/**zentrifugierter** centrifuged latex
Latexanstrichfarbe *f s.* Latexfarbe
Latexbecher *m (rubber)* collection (tapping) cup
Latex-Chlorkautschuk *m* latex-chlorinated rubber
Latexfaden *m* latex thread
Latexfarbe *f* latex[-based water] paint
latexführend latex-bearing, laticiferous
Latexgummifaden *m* latex thread
Latexkonzentrat *n* latex concentrate
Latexmischung *f* latex compound
Latexschaum[gummi] *m* latex foam [rubber], foamed latex rubber
Latexschwamm *m* latex foam sponge
Latextechnologie *m* latex technology
Latschenkiefernöl *n* dwarf pine-needle oil *(from Pinus mugo Turra)*
Lattentrommel *f (tann)* slatted drum • **in der ~ behandeln (durcharbeiten)** to drum
Lattenzaun-Porphyrin *n (org ch)* fenced porphyrin
Latwerge *f (pharm)* electuary
Laubgrün *n* chrome [oxide] green, green cinnabar *(chromium(III) oxide)*
Laubholz *n* hardwood
Laubholzschliff *m* hardwood groundwood
Laubholzzellstoff *m* hardwood pulp
Laudanum *n (pharm)* laudanum *(a tincture of opium)*
Laue-Aufnahme *f s.* Laue-Diagramm
Laue-Aufnahmetechnik *f s.* Laue-Verfahren
Laue-Diagramm *n (cryst)* Laue pattern
Laue-Gleichungen *fpl* Laue equations
Laue-Verfahren *n (cryst)* Laue [X-ray] method

Laue-Versuch *m* Laue experiment
Lauf *m* 1. travel *(as of a reactant)*; course *(of a reaction)*; 2. run *(of a machine)*
Laufbandtrockner *m* festoon (loop) dryer
Laufdauer *f* wear life
Laufeigenschaften *fpl* runnability *(of paper)*
laufen 1. to run, to flow *(of a liquid)*; to sag, to curtain *(of surface coatings)*; 2. to run *(of an experiment or a reaction)*; 3. to run *(of a machine)*; to travel *(of the paper machine wire)*
~ **lassen** to draw down *(into a vessel)*
laufend/gleichschnell synchronous, even-speed *(e.g. rolls)*
Läufer *m* 1. *(coat)* curtain *(faulty film)*; 2. *s.* Laufstein
Läuferbildung *f* sagging, curtaining *(of surface coatings)*
Lauffläche *f (rubber)* tread, wearing surface
Laufflächenabnutzung *f*, **Laufflächenabrieb** *m (rubber)* tread wear
Laufflächengummi *m* tread rubber
Laufflächenmischung *f (rubber)* [tyre-]tread stock, tread compound (mix)
Laufflächenspritzkopf *m (rubber)* tread head
Laufflächenspritzmaschine *f (rubber)* tread extruder
Laufgeschwindigkeit *f* travel rate
Laufmittel *n (chromat)* mobile solvent
Laufmittelfront *f (chromat)* solvent front
Laufmittelgemisch *n (chromat)* solvent system
Laufrad *n* impeller
~/geschlossenes enclosed (closed, shrouded) impeller *(of a centrifugal pump)*
~/halboffenes semienclosed (semiopen) impeller *(of a centrifugal pump)*
Laufrichtung *f* 1. *(pap)* running direction, making (machine, grain, long) direction, direction of travel; 2. *(chromat)* flow direction
Laufrolle *f* idler
Laufschaufel *f* impeller blade (vane)
Laufsteg *m (tech)* walkway
Laufstein *m* runner [stone], mill runner, muller [wheel]
Laufstreifen *m***/roher** *(rubber)* camelback *(for retreading tyres)*
Laufstreifenspritzmaschine *f (rubber)* tread extruder
Laufterm *m* variable (current) term
Laufzeit *f* 1. [wear] life, service (operating, useful) life; 2. running time *(of a chromatogram)*
~ **zwischen zwei Regenerierungen** *(hyd)* exhaust-regenerate cycle *(ion exchange)*
Lauge *f* 1. lye *(alkaline solution)*; 2. *(tech)* liquor; leach[ate] *(solution obtained by leaching)*; *(text)* buck *(for washing or bleaching)*
~/eingestellte standard base
~/Javellesche eau de Javel[le], Javelle water *(a bleaching agent)*
~/metallhaltige *(min tech)* leach liquor (solution)
~/standardisierte standard base
Lauge-Maßlösung *f (anal)* standard base
Laugemittel *n* leaching agent
laugen *(min tech)* to leach [out], to lixiviate; *(text)* to buck, to mercerize
~/mikrobiell *(min tech, biot)* to leach with microorganisms
Laugen *n* 1. *(text)* mercerizing, mercerization; 2. *s.* Laugung
~/spannungsloses mercerization without tension
~ **unter Spannung** mercerization with tension
Laugenaustritt *m* liquor outlet *(as on an evaporator)*
Laugenbehandlung *f* 1. lye treating; 2. *(petrol)* caustic[-soda] wash, alkali wash
laugenbeständig resistant to alkali[es], alkali-resistant, lye-proof, caustic-proof
Laugenbeständigkeit *f* resistance to alkali[es], alkali resistance
Laugenbrüchigkeit *f s.* Laugensprödigkeit
Laugeneintritt *m* liquor inlet *(as on an evaporator)*
laugenfest *s.* laugenbeständig
Laugengehalt *m* alkali content
Laugenregeneration *f* caustic regeneration *(ion exchange)*; *(pap)* liquor (waste-liquor, spent-liquor) recovery
Laugensalz *n s.* Hirschhornsalz
Laugensprödigkeit *f* caustic cracking (embrittlement) *(of metals)*
Laugenstation *f (pap)* liquor-making plant
Laugenturm *m (pap)* reaction tower *(in pulping with chlorine)*
Laugenumlauf *m (pap)* circulation of liquor
Laugenverhältnis *n (pap)* liquor[-to-wood] ratio
Laugenwäsche *f (petrol)* caustic[-soda] wash, alkali wash
Laugenzirkulation *f s.* Laugenumlauf
laugieren *(text)* to buck, to mercerize
Laugung *f* 1. *(min tech)* leach[ing], lixiviation; 2. *(petrol)* caustic[-soda] wash, alkali wash
~/bakteriell begünstigte *(min tech, biot)* bacterially supported leaching
~/biologische *s.* ~/mikrobielle
~/direkte bakterielle *(min tech, biot)* direct bacterial leaching
~ **in der Grube** *(min tech, biot)* underground (in situ) leaching, leaching in place
~ **in situ** *s.* ~ in der Grube
~/indirekte bakterielle *s.* ~/bakteriell begünstigte
~/mikrobielle *(min tech, biot)* microbial leaching, bacterial (microbiological) leaching
Laugungsflüssigkeit *f* leaching fluid (solution)
Laugungsmittel *n* leaching agent
Lauraldehyd *m* lauraldehyde, lauric aldehyde, aldehyde C-12, *dodecanal
Laurat *n* laurate *(salt or ester of lauric acid)*
Laurent-Säure *f* Laurent's acid, 1-naphthylamine-5-sulphonic acid
Laurinaldehyd *m s.* Lauraldehyd
Laurinsäure *f* lauric acid, *dodecanoic acid

Laurinsäureethylester *m* ethyl laurate
Lauroleinsäure *f* lauroleic acid, *dodec-9-enoic acid
Laurylalkohol *m* lauryl alcohol, alcohol C-12, *dodecan-1-ol
Laurylamin *n* laurylamine, *dodecylamine
Laurylmercaptan *n s.* Dodecan-1-thiol
Läuse[bekämpfungs]mittel *n* lousicide, *(med also)* pediculicide
Läusepulver *n* louse powder
Lautamasse *f s.* Lux-Masse
Läuterboden *m* false bottom; *(ferm)* strainer [bottom]
Läuterbottich *m (ferm)* lauter tub (tun)
Lautermaische *f*, **Läutermaische** *f (ferm)* lauter mash
Läutermittel *n (glass)* [re]fining agent
läutern *(filtr)* to clarify, to purify; *(min tech)* to wash, to scavenge; *(ferm)* to lauter; *s.* lauterschmelzen
lauterschmelzen *(glass)* to [re]fine, to plain, to found *(to free from bubbles)*
Läuterungsmittel *n s.* Läutermittel
Läuterwanne *f (glass)* plaining (refining) chamber (end), refiner, nose
Läuterzone *f (glass)* refining zone
Lava *f* lava
Lavandinöl *n* lavandin oil *(from a hybrid Lavandula angustifolia Mill. x L. latifolia (L. fil.) Medik.)*
Lavendelöl *n* lavender [flower] oil *(from Lavandula specc.)*
Lavendelwasser *n (cosmet)* lavender water
Laves-Phase *f* Laves phase *(an intermetallic structure)*
lävogyr *s.* linksdrehend
Lävopimarsäure *f* (–)-pimaric acid, laevopimaric acid, (–)-sapietic acid
Lävulinsäure *f* laevulinic acid, 4-oxovaleric acid, *4-oxopentanoic acid
Lävulose *f* laevulose, fructose *(a monosaccharide)*
Lawine *f (phys ch)* avalanche
Lawrentium *n* Lr lawrencium
Lawson *n* lawsone, 2-hydroxy-1,4-naphthoquinone
Laxans *n*, **Laxativum** *n (pharm)* laxative, mild cathartic
L-Band *n s.* Leitungsband
LCAO-Methode *f* linear-combination-of-atomic-orbitals method, LCAO method
~ **der Molekülorbitale** LCAO molecular-orbital method, LCAO MO method
~/selbstkonsistente LCAO self-consistent method
LCAO-Molekülorbital *n* LCAO molecular orbital, LCAO MO
LCAO-MO-Methode *f* LCAO molecular-orbital method, LCAO MO method
LCAO-Näherung *f* LCAO approximation, linear-combination-of-atomic-orbitals approximation
LCM-Vulkanisation *f* liquid curing
LD *s.* 1. Laser-Desorptions-Massenspektrometrie; 2. Dosis/letale
LD 50, LD_{50} *s.* Dosis/mittlere letale
LD-Aufblaseverfahren *n*, **LD-Blasstahlverfahren** *n* Linz-Donawitz process, L-D process
LDH *s.* Lactatdehydrogenase
LD-Verfahren *n s.* LD-Aufblaseverfahren
leachen *s.* laugen/mikrobiell
Leaching-Anlage *f (min tech, biot)* leaching plant
Leaching-Flüssigkeit *f*, **Leaching-Lösung** *f s.* Laugungsflüssigkeit
Leaching-Verfahren *n (min tech, biot)* leaching process
Leachlösung *f s.* Laugungsflüssigkeit
Lea-Zahl *f* Lea [peroxide] value *(for characterizing oils and fats)*
Lebedev-Verfahren *n* Lebedev process *(for obtaining butadiene)*
Lebensdauer *f* lifetime, life [period], durability, useful (operating, working) life
~ **eines Austauscherharzes** resin life
~/erwartbare *s.* Lebenserwartung
~/mittlere *(phys ch)* average (mean) life (lifetime)
Lebenserwartung *f* service life expectancy
Lebensgefahr *f* life hazard, danger of life
Lebensgift *n* biocide *(chemical which kills organisms)*
Lebensmittel *npl* food, edibles, comestibles
~/diätetische dietary food
~/eiweißreiche *s.* ~/proteinreiche
~/gefrorene frozen food
~/halbfeuchte intermediate moisture food *(containing 15 to 35 % of water)*
~/proteinreiche [high-]protein food
~/tiefgefrorene frozen food
Lebensmittelabfälle *mpl* food wastes
Lebensmittelanreicherung *f* food fortification *(e.g. with vitamins)*
Lebensmittelbestandteil *m* food component
Lebensmittelbestrahlung *f* food irradiation
Lebensmittelchemie *f* food chemistry
Lebensmittelchemiker *m* food chemist
Lebensmittelfarbe *f s.* Lebensmittelfarbstoff
Lebensmittelfarbstoff *m* food dye (colorant)
Lebensmittelgesetz *n* food law
Lebensmittelindustrie *f* food[stuff] industry, food-processing (provisions) industry
Lebensmittelkonservierung *f* food preservation
Lebensmittelmikrobiologie *f* food microbiology
Lebensmitteltechnologe *m* food technologist
Lebensmitteltechnologie *f* food technology
Lebensmittelüberwachung *f* food control
Lebensmittelverarbeitung *f* food processing
Lebensmittelverderb *m* food deterioration (spoilage)
Lebensmittelzusatz[stoff] *m* [intentional, human] food additive
lebensnotwendig *(biol)* essential
Leberöl *n* liver oil
leberschädigend hepatotoxic
Leberstärke *f* animal starch, glycogen

Lebertran *m* liver oil, *(specif)* cod-liver oil
Lebertranemulsion *f* cod-liver oil emulsion
lebhaft vigorous, brisk *(reaction)*; bright, vivid *(colour)*
Lebhaftigkeit *f* vigorousness, briskness *(of a reaction)*; brightness, vividness *(of colour)*
Leblanc-Soda *f* Leblanc soda
Leblanc-Verfahren *n* Leblanc process *(for obtaining soda)*
Lecanorsäure *f* lecanoric acid *(a lichen acid)*
Lecithin *n* lecithin *(any of a class of phospholipids)*
Lecithinnaßschlamm *m* wet lecithin sludge
leck leaking • ~ **sein** to leak, to run
Leck *n* leak
Leckage *f* leakage
lecken to leak, to run
Lecken *n* leakage
Leckflüssigkeit *f* leakage
leckfrei leakproof, leaktight
Leckgas *n* escaping *or* entering gas, leakage
Leckluft *f* escaping *or* entering air, leakage, *(vacuum technology also)* inleakage
Lecksaft *m (pharm)* linctus
lecksicher leakproof, leaktight
Leckströmung *f* leakage flow
Lecksuche *f* leak testing
Lecksucher *m*, **Lecksuchgerät** *n* leak detector
Leckverlust *m* leakage, slippage loss, slip
Leckwässer *npl (hyd)* leaks
Leckweg *m* leakage path
Leclanché-Element *n* Leclanché cell
Leder *n* leather
~/leeres empty leather *(result of incorrect tanning)*
~/pflanzlich gegerbtes bark leather
~/synthetisches artificial leather, imitation (man-made) leather
~/weißgares white leather
lederähnlich, lederartig leather-like, resembling leather, leathery
Lederausschlag *m (tann)* bloom, exudation
Lederaustauschstoff *m s.* Leder/synthetisches
Lederfett *n* leather grease
lederhart *(ceram)* leather-hard
Lederhaut *f (tann)* corium
Lederindustriechemiker *m* leather chemist
Lederkitt *m* leather cement
Lederkohle *f* leather charcoal
Lederleim *m* leather (skin, hide) glue
Lederpappe *f*[**/braune**] leather board
~/imitierte imitation leather board
Lederpflegemittel *n* leather-dressing agent
Lederschmiere *f (tann)* stuffing [mixture]
Lederwalze *f (tann)* bend (butt) roller
Lederzurichter *m (tann)* currier
leer 1. empty; evacuated; 2. *(cryst)* empty, vacant; 3. vacant *(orbital)*
leerblasen *(pap)* to blow [off] *(a digester)*
Leerblasen *n* **des Zellstoffkochers** *(pap)* digester blow
leeren to empty
Leerlauf *m (bioch)* idling (resting) state *(of the respiratory chain)*
leerlaufen to drain
~ **lassen** to drain [down] *(e.g. a tank)*
Leerlaufen *n* drainage
Leerlaufregulierung *f* inlet-valve control unloading *(of a compressor)*
Leerlaufspannung *f* self-stress *(in the wall of a centrifuge)*
Leermedikament *n (pharm)* placebo
Leerplatz *m s.* Leerstelle
Leerstelle *f (cryst)* lattice vacancy, hole [position], vacant lattice position (site)
Leerstellensenke *f (cryst)* vacancy sink
Leerstellenpaar *n* vacancy pair
Leertrum *m(n)* slack side, return strand (side), *(relating to belt conveyors also)* return belt
Leerventil *n* outlet (discharge) valve
Leerversuch *m* blank experiment (trial, test), blank
Leerwert *m* blank reading (value); *(nucl)* background
legieren to alloy
Legierung *f* alloy
~/Arndsche Arnd's alloy *(a reductant consisting of Cu and Mn)*
~/binäre binary alloy
~/Devardasche Devarda's alloy *(a reductant consisting of Cu, Al, and Zn)*
~/eutektische eutectic alloy
~/leichtschmelzende low-melting alloy, fusible alloy
~/Lipowitzsche Lipowitz's metal (alloy) *(a fusible Bi-Cd-Pb-Sn alloy)*
~ **nach Rose** Rose's metal (alloy) *(a fusible Bi-Pb-Sn alloy)*
~/niedrigschmelzende *s.* ~/leichtschmelzende
~/pyrophore pyrophoric alloy
~/quaternäre quaternary alloy
~/ternäre ternary alloy
~/Woodsche Wood's metal (alloy) *(a fusible Bi-Cd-Pb-Sn alloy)*
Legierungsbestandteil *m*, **Legierungselement** *n* alloying element (agent, constituent, ingredient)
legierungsfreudig easily (readily) alloying (amalgamating)
Legierungskomponente *f s.* Legierungsbestandteil
Legierungsskelettkatalysator *m* [alloy] skeleton catalyst, Raney catalyst
Lehm *m* loam, clay
lehmartig loamy, clayey, clayish
Lehmform *f* loam mould *(foundry)*
Lehmformen *n* loam moulding *(foundry)*
Lehmglasur *f (ceram)* slip glaze
lehmhaltig loamy, clayey, clayish
lehmig loamy, clayey, clayish
Leichengift *n* ptomaine
Leichtbauplatte *f* building board
Leichtbenzin *n* light gasoline (naphtha, spirit)
Leichtbeton *m* lightweight concrete
~ **mit Koksaschenzusatz** breeze concrete

Leichterflüchtige *n s.* Leichtersiedende
leichtersiedend lower-boiling, light
Leichtersiedende *n* more volatile component, M.V.C., lighter (low-boiling) component, light phase
Leichtflintglas *n* light flint glass
leichtflüchtig highly (readily) volatile
Leichtflüchtigkeit *f* high volatility
Leichtgut *n* light material; light fraction
leichtlöslich readily (freely) soluble • ~ **sein** to dissolve readily
Leichtmetall *n* light metal
Leichtmineral *n* light mineral
Leichtöl *n* light oil
Leichtparaffin *n* light liquid paraffin
leichtschmelzbar, leichtschmelzend low-melting[-point], low-fusion
leichtsiedend low-boiling, light
Leichtsiedende *n s.* Leichtersiedende
Leichtstein *m* lightweight brick
Leichtstoffabscheider *m (hyd)* light-solids remover
leichtviskos low-viscosity
Leichtwaschmittel *n* light-duty detergent, fine-fabric detergent
Leichtwasserreaktor *m* light-water reactor
leichtzersetzlich readily (easily) decomposing
Leichtzuschlagstoff *m* lightweight aggregate
Leim *m* glue; *(pap)* sizing material (agent), size • **mit ~ bestreichen** to glue
~/freiharzreicher (hochfreiharzhaltiger) *(pap)* high free rosin size
~/pflanzlicher vegetable glue
~/tierischer animal [protein] glue, animal gelatine (adhesive); *(pap)* animal size
Leimaufnahme *f (pap)* pickup of size
Leimbad *n (pap)* size bath
leimbar *(pap)* sizable
Leimbarkeit *f (pap)* sizability
Leimbrühe *f s.* Leimlösung
Leimbütte *f s.* Leimtrog
leimen to glue; *(pap)* to size
Leimfarbe *f* calcimine, *(if suspended:)* distemper
Leimfleck *m (pap)* size speck (spot)
Leimgürtel *m (agric)* greaseband
Leimkocher *m (pap)* size cooker
Leimleder *n (tann)* hide scrapings (shavings)
Leimlösung *f (pap)* size (sizing) solution
Leimmilch *f (pap)* size emulsion *(milk)*
Leimmittel *n s.* Leim
Leimpresse *f (pap)* [surface] sizing press
Leimpressenwalze *f (pap)* sizing press roll
Leimring *m (agric)* greaseband
Leimstoff *m s.* Leim
Leimsüß *n s.* Glykokoll
Leimtrog *m (pap)* size (sizing) vat (tub)
Leimüberschuß *m (pap)* excess size
Leimung *f (pap)* sizing • **mit mittlerer ~** half-sized, ½ sized • **mit schwacher ~** soft-sized, slack-sized, S.S. • **mit starker ~** hard-sized, H.S., strongly sized
~ im Stoff engine sizing, E.S., beater (pulp) sizing, sizing in the engine (stuff)
~ in der Masse *s.* ~ im Stoff
~ mit Gelatine animal tub sizing, A.T.S., gelatin sizing
~ mit Natronwasserglas silicate sizing
~ mit Tierleim *s.* ~ mit Gelatine
Leimungsgrad *m (pap)* degree of sizing
Leimwalze *f (pap)* sizing press roll
Leimwanne *f s.* Leimtrog
Leimzucker *m s.* Glykokoll
Leindotteröl *n* cameline (dodder) oil *(from the seeds of Camelina sativa Crantz)*
Leinen[gewebe] *n* linen [fabric]
Leinenhadern *mpl*, **Leinenlumpen** *mpl (pap)* linen rags
Leinenpapier *n* 1. linen paper *(made of linen rags)*; 2. linen (reinforced) paper cloth-mounted paper; 3. linen[-embossed] paper, linen-finished paper
Leinenprägekalander *m (pap)* linenizing calender
Leinenprägen *n (pap)* linenizing
Leinenprägepresse *f (pap)* linenizing calender
Leinenprägung *f (pap)* linen finish, *(Am)* cloth (Damask) finish
Leinenstoff *m* linen [fabric]
Leinkuchen *m* linseed cake
Leinöl *n* linseed oil
Leinölfirnis *m* boiled linseed oil
Leinöllack *m* linseed-oil varnish
Leinölsäure *f s.* Linolsäure
Leinöl-Standöl *n* calorized linseed oil
Leinsamenschleim *m* linseed mucilage
Leinwandgewebe *n***/geteertes** tarpaulin
Leiste *f***/dreieckige** *(ceram)* saddle *(a piece of kiln furniture)*
Leistung *f* 1. power *(in strictly physical sense)*; 2. *s.* ~/erbrachte; 3. *s.* Leistungsverhalten; 4. *s.* Leistungsvermögen
~/erbrachte output *(as of a plant)*
~/katalytische catalytic performance
Leistungsaufnahme *f* power consumption
Leistungsbeiwert *m* power number *(on agitating)*
Leistungsbrutreaktor *m (nucl)* power breeder reactor
leistungsfähig *(tech)* efficient
Leistungsfähigkeit *f (tech)* efficiency, capacity
~/katalytische catalytic efficiency
Leistungsfaktor *m* power factor
Leistungskennlinie *f*, **Leistungskurve** *f* performance curve
Leistungsreaktor *m (nucl)* power reactor
Leistungsstamm *m (biot)* production strain, producing (working) strain *(of microorganisms)*
Leistungsverhalten *n (tech)* performance
Leistungsvermögen *n* capacity
Leistungszahl *f* 1. performance coefficient (number); 2. *s.* Leistungsbeiwert
Leitatom *n (nomencl)* pilot atom

Leitblech *n* deflector [plate], baffle [plate] • **mit Leitblechen [versehen]** baffled • **ohne Leitbleche** unbaffled
Leitelektrolyt *m* support[ing] electrolyte, base (indifferent) electrolyte
leiten 1. to lead, to pipe; to direct *(a liquid or gas stream towards something)*; 2. to control *(a reaction)*; 3. to conduct *(electricity, heat)*
~/in Rohrleitungen to pipe
leitend conducting, conductive
~/schlecht poorly conducting
***n*-leitend** n-type [semi]conducting, excess [semi-] conducting
***p*-leitend** p-type [semi]conducting, defect [semi-] conducting
Leitenzym *n* marker enzyme
Leiter *m* conductor
~/elektrischer conductor of electricity, electrical conductor
~/elektrolytischer electrolytic (ionic) conductor
~ erster Klasse (Ordnung) electronic conductor
~/schlechter poor conductor
~ zweiter Klasse (Ordnung) *s.* ~/elektrolytischer
Leiterpolymer[e] *n* ladder (double-chained) polymer
leitfähig conductive
Leitfähigkeit *f* conductance, conducting power, conductivity *(in a larger sense)*
~/elektrische electric[al] conductivity
~/elektrolytische electrolytic conductance (conductivity)
~/elektronische electronic conductivity
~ in Schichtrichtung/elektrische in-plane electrical conductivity
~/lichtelektrische photoconductivity
~/molare molar conductance
~/photoelektrische photoconductivity
~/spezifische specific conductance, conductivity *(proper)*
~/thermische thermal conductivity
Leitfähigkeitsband *n s.* Leitungsband
Leitfähigkeitselektron *n s.* Leitungselektron
Leitfähigkeitserhöhung *f* increase in conductance (conductivity)
Leitfähigkeitskoeffizient *m* conductance ratio
Leitfähigkeits-Konzentrations-Kurve *f* conductivity-concentration curve
Leitfähigkeitskurve *f* conductance curve
Leitfähigkeitsmeßbrücke *f* conductance bridge
Leitfähigkeitsmeßgerät *n* conductometer, conductimeter, conductance meter, conductivity apparatus
Leitfähigkeitsmessung *f* conductance (conductivity) measurement
Leitfähigkeitsmeßzelle *f* conductance (conductivity) cell
Leitfähigkeitsmethode *f (anal)* conductometric (conductance) method
Leitfähigkeitsstrom *m* conduction current
Leitfähigkeitstitration *f* conductometric (conductance) titration
Leitfähigkeitswasser *n* conductivity (conductance) water
Leitfähigkeitszelle *f s.* Leitfähigkeitsmeßzelle
Leitisotop *n* [isotopic] tracer
Leitisotopenmethode *f*, **Leitisotopentechnik** *f* tracer technique (method), atom tagging method, *(bioch also)* isotope incorporation technique
Leitrad *n*, **Leitring** *m* diffusion ring *(as of a pump)*
Leitrohr *n* shroud ring, draught tube *(of an agitator)*
Leitrolle *f* guide roll, snub pulley
Leitsalz *n s.* Leitelektrolyt
Leitschaufel *f* guide vane *(as of a turbine)*
Leitung *f* 1. line, duct, pipe[line]; 2. cable, wire *(in an electric circuit)*; 3. conduction *(of electricity or heat)*
~/elektrolytische electrolytic conduction
~/erdverlegte underground line, buried duct
~ für den Schlammaustrag sludge-discharge line
~/unterirdische *s.* ~/erdverlegte
Leitungsband *n* conductivity (conduction) band
~/leeres (unbesetztes) empty band
Leitungselektron *n* conduction electron
Leitungsnetz *n (hyd)* water distribution system
Leitungsrohr *n* duct, line, pipe[line]
Leitungsvermögen *n s.* Leitfähigkeit
Leitungswasser *n* tap (municipal) water
Leitvermögen *n s.* Leitfähigkeit
Leitwalze *f* lead[ing] roll, guide roll; *(pap)* dipping (size) roll *(in vat sizing)*; *(pap)* wire[-guide] roll
Leitwert *m***/elektrischer** electrical conductance
Lektin *n (bioch)* lectin *(any of a class of glycoproteins)*
Lektinologie *f (bioch)* lectinology
Lemongrasöl *n (cosmet)* lemon-grass oil, East Indian verbena oil *(from Cymbopogon flexuosus Stapf and C. citratus (DC.) Stapf)*
Lenkblech *n s.* Leitblech
lenken to control *(a process)*; to direct *(a substituent)*
Lenkung *f* control *(of a process)*; direction *(of a substituent)*
Lennard-Jones-Potential *n* Lennard-Jones potential
Lenzpumpe *f* sump pump
Lepidomelan *m (min)* lepidomelane *(a phyllosilicate)*
Lepton *n* lepton *(any of a family of light elementary particles)*
Lesch-Nyhan-Syndrom *n* Lesch-Nyhan syndrome *(genetically induced lack in guanine phosphoribosyl transferase)*
Leseband *n (min tech)* picking (inspection) belt
lesen *(min tech)* to pick, to sort
Lessing-Ring *m* Lessing ring *(a variety of a Raschig ring)*
letal *(tox)* lethal, deadly poisonous
Letalität *f (tox)* lethality
Letternmetall *n* type metal

Leuchtbakterien *npl* luminescent (luminous) bacteria
Leuchtdichte *f* luminance, brightness
Leuchtdichtepyrometer *n* [partial-]radiation pyrometer
Leuchtelektron *n* optical electron, valency (outermost) electron
leuchten to give [off] light, to radiate [light], to glow, to luminesce
Leuchten *n* radiation [of light], glow, luminosity
~/kaltes luminescence
leuchtend luminous, luminiferous; brilliant, bright *(colour)*
~/schwach faintly luminous
~/stark highly luminous
Leuchterscheinung *f* luminous effect
Leuchtfaden *m* incandescent filament
Leuchtfarbe *f* luminous (luminescent) paint
~/fluoreszierende fluorescent paint
~/nachleuchtende (phosphoreszierende) phosphorescent paint
Leuchtflammenbrenner *m* direct (nozzle-mix) burner
Leuchtfleck *m (phot)* light spot
Leuchtgas *n* 1. illuminating gas; 2. *s.* Stadtgas
Leuchtkraft *f* luminosity; brilliance, brightness *(of colours)*
Leuchtmittel *n* illuminant
Leuchtöl *n* illuminating (lamp) oil, *(broadly)* kerosine
Leuchtpetroleum *n* illuminating (lamp) oil
Leuchtstärke *f* luminosity
Leuchtstoff *m* illuminant; luminophore, luminescent substance
~/aufhellender *(text)* fluorescent brightener (brightening agent, whitening agent, white dye)
Leuchtwirkung *f* luminous effect
Leucin *n* leucine, 2-amino-4-methylvaleric acid
Leucit *m (min)* leucite *(potassium aluminodisilicate)*
Leuckart-Reaktion *f* Leuckart reaction *(alkylation of amines)*
Leukindigo *m* leucoindigo
Leukoalizarin *n* leucoalizarin
Leukoanthocyan *n* leucoanthocyanin, anthocyanogen
Leukobase *f* leuco base
Leukochinizarin *n* leucoquinizarine
Leukoester *m* leuco ester
Leukoform *f* leuco form
Leukogen *n* leucogen *(a solution of sodium hydrogensulphite in water)*
Leukoindigo *m* leucoindigo
Leukomalachitgrün *n* leucomalachite green
Leukopararosanilin *n* leucopararosaniline
Leukophan *m (min)* leucophanite, leucophane *(a sorosilicate)*
Leukosalz *n* leuco salt
Leukoschwefelsäureester *m* leucosulphuric acid ester
Leukotetraschwefelsäureester *m* leucotetrasulphuric acid ester
Leukotrien *n (org ch)* leukotriene
Leukoverbindung *f* leuco compound
Leukovorin *n* leucovorin, citrovorum factor, N^5-formyltetrahydrofolic acid, folinic acid SF
Leukozyt *m*/**basophiler** *(med)* basophil[e]
Leuna-Abstichgenerator *m (coal)* Leuna slagging gasifier, Leuna low-pressure slagging fixed-bed gasifier
Leuna-Verfahren *n (coal)* Bergius process, berginization
Levyn *m (min)* levyne, levynite *(calcium dialuminotrisilicate)*
Lewis-Addukt *n* Lewis adduct
Lewis-Azidität *f* Lewis acidity
Lewis-Base *f* Lewis base
Lewis-Basizität *f* Lewis basicity
Lewis-Säure *f* Lewis acid
LFE-Beziehung *f s.* Beziehung der freien Enthalpie/lineare
LFSE *s.* Ligandenfeldstabilisierungsenergie
LFT *s.* Ligandenfeldtheorie
LH *s.* Luteinisierungshormon
LHP-Chlorophyll *n (bioch)* light-harvesting-protein chlorophyll
Libbey-Owens-Verfahren *n* Libbey-Owens[-Ford Colburn] process, LOF-Colburn process, Colburn process *(for manufacturing sheet glass)*
Libidibi *pl (tann)* divi-divi *(from Caesalpinia coriaria (Jacq.) Willd.)*
Licaniasäure *f*, **Licansäure** *f* licanic acid, couepic acid
Lichenin *n* moss starch
licht light *(colour)*
Licht *n* light • **am (im)** ~ under illumination, on exposure to light • **vor** ~ **geschützt** protected from light
~/auffallendes incident light
~/diffuses diffused (scattered) light
~/durchfallendes transmitted light
~/einfallendes incident light
~/gestreutes scattered light
~/kaltes cold light
~/künstliches artificial light
Lichtabbau *m* photodegradation, photochemical (photolytic, light) degradation, degradation by light
lichtabsorbierend light-absorbing
Lichtabsorption *f* light absorption
Lichtalterung *f* light ageing
Lichtarbeit *f* luminous energy, quantity of light
Lichtatmung *f (bot, bioch)* photorespiration
lichtbeständig insensitive (resistant) to light, nonfading, *(Am also)* lightfast
Lichtbeständigkeit *f* resistance to light, light resistance, *(Am also)* lightfastness
Lichtbeugung *f* diffraction of light
Lichtblitz *m* flash of light, photoflash
Lichtbogen *m*[**/elektrischer**] [electric] arc
lichtbogenbeständig arc-resistant, arc-proof
Lichtbogenbeständigkeit *f* arc resistance

Lichtbogenelektroofen *m s.* Lichtbogenofen
Lichtbogenentladung *f* arc discharge
lichtbogenfest *s.* lichtbogenbeständig
Lichtbogenheizung *f* arc heating
Lichtbogenkohle *f* arc carbon
Lichtbogenlampe *f* arc lamp
Lichtbogenofen *m* electric-arc furnace, arc[-heated] furnace
~/direkter *s.* ~ mit direkter Beheizung
~/indirekter *s.* ~ mit indirekter Beheizung
~ mit direkter Beheizung direct arc[-heated] furnace
~ mit indirekter Beheizung indirect arc[-heated] furnace
~ mit reiner Strahlungsbeheizung *s.* ~ mit indirekter Beheizung
Lichtbogenschweißen *n* arc welding
~/atomares atomic hydrogen [arc] welding
Lichtbogenstrahlungsofen *m* indirect arc[-heated] furnace
Lichtbogenverfahren *n* 1. arc process *(for uniting atmospheric nitrogen and oxygen)*; 2. electric arc process *(for producing acetylene from hydrocarbons)*
Lichtbogenwiderstandsofen *m* arc resistance furnace
lichtbrechend refractive
Lichtbrechung *f* refraction of light
Lichtbündel *n* beam of light
Lichtchlorierung *f* photochemical chlorination
lichtdicht lightproof, lighttight
Lichtdichtheit *f* lightproofness, lighttightness
Lichtdruck *m* photomechanical printing
Lichtdruckfarbe *f* photogelatin ink
Lichtdruckgelatine *f* photogelatin
Lichtdruckverfahren *n* photogelatin process
lichtdurchlässig transparent, translucent
Lichtdurchlässigkeit *f (qualitatively:)* transparency, light transmission, clarity; *(quantitatively:)* light transmittance
lichtecht *s.* lichtbeständig
Lichtechtheitsmesser *m (text)* fadiometer
Lichtechtheitsprüfung *f (text)* light test
Lichteinfluß/unter on exposure to light, under illumination
lichtelektrisch photoelectric
lichtempfindlich sensitive to light, light-sensitive, photosensitive • **~ machen** *(phot)* to sensitize
Lichtempfindlichkeit *f* sensitivity to light, light sensitivity, photosensitivity
Lichtempfindlichmachen *n (phot)* sensitization
Lichtenergie *f* light energy
Lichterscheinung *f* luminous phenomenon (effect)
lichterzeugend luminiferous, photogenic
Lichtfilter *n* light filter
Lichtfleck *m (phot)* light spot
lichtgeschützt protected from light
Lichtgeschwindigkeit *f* velocity of light
Lichthof *m* halo
Lichthofschutzschicht *f (phot)* antihalation (anti-halo) backing (coating), anti-halo layer • **ohne ~** unbacked
Lichtintensität *f* intensity of light
lichtkatalysiert light-catalyzed, photocatalyzed
Lichtmenge *f* quantity of light, luminous energy
Lichtmessung *f (anal)* photometry
Lichtmikroskop *n* light microscope
Lichtpausautomat *m* blueprinter
Lichtpause *f* blueprint, blue print, *(if based on diazo compounds also)* diazo copy, *(if based on ferricyanide also)* blue negative print
lichtpausen to make (take) a blue print, to blueprint
Lichtpausen *n* blueprinting, blueprint *(in a larger sense)*, *(if based on diazo compounds also)* diazo print[ing], ammonia-developed printing
Lichtpausgewebe *n* translucent tracing cloth
Lichtpauspapier *n* blueprint paper, *(if based on diazo compounds also)* diazo paper
Lichtphase *f* light phase *(of photosynthesis)*
Lichtpolarisation *f* polarization of light
Lichtquant *n* photon, light quant[um]
Lichtquelle *f* light (luminous) source
Lichtreaktion *f* photochemical (light) reaction, photoreaction
lichtschluckend light absorbing
Lichtschutz *m* protection from light
Lichtstabilisator *m* light stabilizer
Lichtstärke *f* luminosity, light (luminous) intensity
Lichtstärkemessung *f* photometric analysis, photometry
Lichtstrahl *m* light ray, *(if bundled:)* beam of light
Lichtstreuung *f* light scattering
Lichtstreuungsmessung *f* light-scattering measurement
Lichtstreuungsmethode *f* light scattering method *(for determining molecular weights)*
Lichtstrom *m* luminous flux
Lichtstromdichte *f* luminous-flux density
lichtundurchlässig opaque, lightproof, lighttight • **~ machen** to lightproof
Lichtundurchlässigkeit *f* opacity, lighttightness
Lichtwelle *f* light wave
Lichtwiderstand *m* photoresistor, photoconductive cell
Lichtwirkung *f* effect of light, luminous effect
Licker *m (tann)* fat liquor
Lick-up-Bahnabnahme *f (pap)* lick-up
Lick-up-Filz *m (pap)* lick-up overfelt (wet felt, felt)
Lidar *n* LIDAR *(**L**ight **D**etection **A**nd **R**anging)*
Liderung *f* packing *(of a pump)*
Lidschatten *m (cosmet)* eye-shadow
Liebermann-Storch-Test *m* Liebermann-Storch test *(for detecting rosin)*
Liebig-Kühler *m* Liebig condenser
Liebstöckelöl *n* lovage (levisticum) oil *(from Levisticum officinale W.D.J. Koch)*
Lieferbeton *m* ready-mixed concrete
Lieferdruck *m* discharge (delivery) pressure

Lieferer *m* supplier
Liefergeschwindigkeit *f* delivery speed (rate)
liefern to deliver, to generate, to yield *(as in a reaction)*; to donate, to furnish, to contribute *(electrons)*
Lieferseite *f* delivery side *(as of a pump)*
Lieferstrom *m* delivery
liegen/zutage *(geol)* to crop out, to outcrop
liegend/am Bildungsort (Entstehungsort) *(geol)* autochthonous
Liegepresse *f (pap)* straight-through press
Liesegang-Ringe *mpl (coll)* Liesegang rings
Liftbehälter *m* lift tank
liften to lift *(catalysts)*
Liften *n* lifting *(as of catalysts)*
~ **mit Druckluft** air lifting
Liftleitung *f* lift line (pipe) *(for lifting catalysts)*
Lifttopf *m* lift pot
Ligand *m* ligand
~/allgemeiner *(chromat)* general ligand
~/ambidenter (ambivalenter) ambidentate ligand
~/anionischer anion[ic] ligand
~/gruppenspezifischer *s.* ~/allgemeiner
~/mehrzähliger (mehrzähniger) polydentate (multidentate) ligand
~/neutraler neutral ligand
Ligandenaustausch *m* ligand exchange
Liganden[austausch]chromatographie *f* ligand exchange chromatography
Ligandenfeld *n* ligand field
Ligandenfeldaufspaltung *f* ligand field splitting
Ligandenfeldstabilisierungsenergie *f* ligand-field stabilization energy
Ligandenfeldtheorie *f* ligand field theory
Ligandenkonzentration *f* ligand concentration
Ligation *f s.* Ligierung
Ligatoratom *n* ligating (donor) atom *(coordination chemistry)*
Ligatur *f* joint clamp *(for ground-glass joints)*
~ **für Kugelschliffe** ball-and-socket joint clamp
ligieren *(bioch)* to ligate *(to join complementary ends of DNA)*
Ligierung *f (bioch)* ligation *(joining complementary ends of DNA)*
Lignan *n* lignan
lignifizieren to lignify
Lignifizierung *f* lignification
Lignin *n* lignin
~/chloriertes *(pap)* chlorinated lignin, chlorolignin
~/restliches *(pap)* residual lignin, lignin residues
Ligninabbau *m* lignin degradation
Ligninauslösung *f*, **Ligninentfernung** *f (pap)* dissolution (removal) of lignin
Ligningehalt *m* lignin content
Ligninherauslösung *f s.* Ligninauslösung
Ligninkohle *f* lignin coal
Ligninpech *n (pap)* lignin pitch *(concentrated sulphite waste liquor)*
ligninreich rich in lignin
Ligninreste *mpl (pap)* lignin residues, residual lignin
Ligninsulfonsäure *f* lignosulphonic acid
~/nach Hägglund bestimmte feste Hägglund's solid lignosulphonic acid
~/nach Kullgren bestimmte wasserlösliche Kullgren lignosulphonic acid
Lignit *m s.* Xylit
Lignocellulose *f* lignocellulose *(cellulose associated with lignin)*
Lignocerinsäure *f* *tetracosanoic acid, *(deprecated:)* lignoceric acid
Lignosulfonsäure *f s.* Ligninsulfonsäure
Ligroin *n* ligroin[e] *(with boiling range from 90 °C to 120 °C)*
limnisch *(geoch)* limnic, lacustrine
Limonen *n* limonene, *(+)-4-isopropenyl-1-methylcyclohexene
Limonit *m (min)* limonite, brown iron ore (stone)
Linde-Anlage *f* Linde refrigerator *(for liquefying gases)*
Lindemann-Glas *n* Lindemann glass *(transparent to X-rays)*
Linderungsmittel *n (pharm)* palliative
Linde-Verfahren *n* Linde process *(for air liquefaction)*
linear linear, *(relating to chain molecules also)* unbranched • ~ **polarisiert** linearly polarized, plane-polarized
Linearbereich *m (anal)* linear range
Linearbeschleuniger *m (nucl)* linear accelerator
Lineardispersion *f (spectr)* linear dispersion
~/reziproke reciprocal linear dispersion
Linearkolloid *n* linear (fibrous) colloid
Linearkombination *f* linear combination
~ **von Atomorbitalen** linear combination of atomic orbitals, LCAO
Linearpolyethylen *n* linear (low-pressure) polyethylene
Linearpolymer[e] *n* linear polymer
Linearprotein *n* fibrous protein
Lineweaver-Burk-Auftragung *f s.* Lineweaver-Burk-Diagramm
Lineweaver-Burk-Diagramm *n* Lineweaver-Burk plot, double-reciprocal plot *(of kinetic data)*
Lineweaver-Burk-Gleichung *f* Lineweaver-Burk equation *(kinetics)*
Lineweaver-Burk-Methode *f* Lineweaver-Burk method *(for treating kinetic data)*
Linie *f***/Anti-Stokessche** anti-Stokes line *(in Raman spectra)*
~ **gleichen Gehalts an flüchtiger Substanz** isovol, line of equal volatile matter
~ **gleichen Heizwertes** isocal, isocalorific line
~ **gleichen Kohlenstoffgehalts** isocarbon line
~/Stokessche Stokes line *(in Raman spectra)*
~/verbotene *(spectr)* forbidden line
Linien *fpl***/beständige** *s.* Grundlinien
~/Fraunhofersche *(spectr)* Fraunhofer lines
~/letzte *s.* Grundlinien
~/Neumannsche *(cryst)* Neumann lines

Linienbreite *f (spectr)* line width
~/natürliche natural line width
Liniendefekt *m*, **Linienfehler** *m (cryst)* line[ar] defect
Linienform *f (spectr)* line shape
Liniengitter *n (spectr)* line (ruled) grating
Linienintensität *f (spectr)* line intensity
Linienkoinzidenz *f s.* Linienüberlagerung
Linienkontur *f (spectr)* line contour
Linienschreiber *m* continuous-line recorder
Linienspektrum *n* line (discrete) spectrum
Linienüberlagerung *f* line (spectral) overlap
Linienverbreiterung *f* broadening of spectral lines
Liniment *n (pharm)* liniment
Linksdraht *m (text)* S twist
linksdrehend laevorota[to]ry, laevo, *(esp cryst)* left-handed
Linksdrehung *f* laevorotation, *(esp cryst)* left-handed rotation
Linksform *f* laevo[rotatory] form, (–)-form *(of an optically active compound)*
Linksgängigkeit *f* left-handed sense *(of a helix)*
Linkskristall *m* left-handed crystal
Linksmilchsäure *f* D(–)-lactic acid, laevolactic acid
Linksquarz *m* left-handed quartz
Linkssäure *f* laevo[rotatory] acid
Linksweinsäure *f s. D*(–)-Weinsäure
linkszirkular polarisiert left-circularly polarized, left-hand circularly polarized
Linoleat *n* linoleate, linolate *(salt or ester of linoleic acid)*
Linolensäure *f* linolenic acid, *(spefic)* α-linolenic acid, *octadeca-9-*cis*,12-*cis*,15-*cis*-trienoic acid
Linolsäure *f* linoleic acid, *octadeca-9,12-dienoic acid
Linoxyn *n* linoxyn, linoxylin *(a substance obtained by oxidation and polymerization of linseed oil)*
Linse *f***/thermische** *(spectr)* thermal lens
Linsenapertur *f* lens aperture
Linsenerz *n* liroconite *(aluminium copper(II) trihydroxide arsenate(V))*
linsenförmig lenticular
Linsenglas *m* optical glass
Linsenöffnung *f* lens aperture
Lint *m*, **Lintbaumwolle** *f* lint cotton
Lintershalbstoff *m (pap)* linters pulp
Lintwolle *f* lint cotton
Linz-Donawitz-Verfahren *n* Linz-Donawitz process, L-D process *(for steelmaking)*
Lipid *n (bioch)* lipid[e]
~/amphiphiles amphiphilic (amphipathic) lipid
~/einfaches simple lipid
~/komplexes (polares) *s.* Lipoid
Lipidantioxidans *n* lipid antioxidant
Lipidautoxidation *f* lipid autooxidation
lipidlöslich lipid-soluble
Lipidoxidation *f* lipid oxidation
Lipidspeicherkrankheit *f (med)* lysosomal (lipid-storage) disease, lipidosis
Lipidstoffwechsel *m* lipid metabolism
Lipoid *n (bioch)* lipoid, complex (compound, conjugated, polar) lipid
Lipolyse *f* lipolysis, fat splitting
lipolytisch lipolytic, fat-splitting
α-Liponsäure *f* α-lipoic acid, 3-(4-carboxybutyl)-1,2-dithiolane
lipophil lipophilic, lipophile
Lipopolysaccharid *n* lipopolysaccharide
Lipoproteid *n s.* Lipoprotein
Lipoprotein *n* lipoprotein, lipoproteid[e]
~ **geringer Dichte** low-density lipoprotein, LDL
~ **hoher Dichte** high-density lipoprotein, HDL
~ **sehr geringer Dichte** very-low-density lipoprotein, VLDL
~ **sehr hoher Dichte** very-high-density lipoprotein, VHDL
Liposomen *npl (bioch)* liposomal artifacts
Lippenglanz *m (cosmet)* lip-gloss
Lippenpomade *f (cosmet)* lipsalve
Lippenstift *m (cosmet)* lipstick
Lippentupfpapier *n (cosmet)* facial (cleansing) tissue
Liquation *f (geol)* liquation [differentiation] *(process of separating of magmatic fusions)*
Liquid-Polymer[e] *n (rubber)* [polysulphide] liquid polymer
Liquiduskurve *f*, **Liquiduslinie** *f* liquidus [curve, line] *(of a melting diagram)*
Liquidus-Liquidus-Chromatographie *f* liquid-liquid chromatography, L.L.C.
Liquidus-Solidus-Chromatographie *f* liquid-solid chromatography, L.S.C.
Liquidustemperatur *f* liquidus (limiting crystallization) temperature, *(glass also)* limiting devitrification temperature
Lisseuse *f (text)* backwashing machine
Lissieren *n (text)* backwashing
Liter *n***/Mohrsches** Mohr litre *(gas volumetry)*
Literaturspektrum *n* library [reference] spectrum
Liter-Molarität *f* molarity, molar concentration
Lithifikation *f (geol)* lithification, induration
Lithium *n* Li lithium
Lithiumacetylid *n s.* Lithiumcarbid
Lithiumalanat *n s.* Lithiumaluminiumhydrid
Lithiumalkyl *n* alkyl lithium
Lithiumaluminat *n* lithium aluminate
Lithiumaluminiumhydrid *n* lithium aluminium hydride, lithium tetrahydridoaluminate
Lithiumamid *n* lithium amide
Lithiumaryl *n* aryl lithium
Lithiumbromid *n* lithium bromide
Lithiumcarbid *n* lithium carbide, *dilithium acetylide
Lithiumcarbonat *n* lithium carbonate
Lithiumchlorat *n* lithium chlorate
Lithiumchlorid *n* lithium chloride
Lithiumdihydrogenphosphat *n* lithium dihydrogenphosphate
Lithiumhydrid *n* lithium hydride

Lithiumhydroxid *n* lithium hydroxide
Lithiumiodat *n* lithium iodate
Lithiummethyl *n* methyllithium
Lithiumnitrat *n* lithium nitrate
Lithiumnitrid *n* lithium nitride
Lithiumnitrit *n* lithium nitrite
Lithiumorthoarsenat(V) *n* lithium orthoarsenate, *lithium tetraoxoarsenate(V)
Lithiumorthosilicat *n* lithium orthosilicate, *lithium tetraoxosilicate
Lithiumoxid *n* lithium oxide
Lithiumperoxid *n* lithium peroxide
Lithiumphosphat *n* lithium phosphate, *(specif)* Li_3PO_4 lithium orthophosphate
Lithiumrhodanid *n s.* Lithiumthiocyanat
Lithiumselenid *n* lithium selenide
Lithiumsilicid *n* lithium silicide
Lithiumsulfat *n* lithium sulphate
Lithiumsulfid *n* lithium sulphide
Lithiumsulfit *n* lithium sulphite
Lithiumthiocyanat *n* lithium thiocyanate
Lithiumwolframat *n* lithium wolframate (tungstate)
Lithocholsäure *f* lithocholic acid
Lithographenfirnis *m* lithographic (litho) varnish
Lithographenkalk *m*, **Lithographenschiefer** *m* lithographic limestone
Lithographie *f* lithography, lithographic printing
Lithographiefarbe *f* lithographic [printing] ink, litho ink
Lithographiekreide *f* lithographic crayon
Lithographiepapier *n* lithographic [printing] paper, litho
Lithographiestein *m* lithographic limestone
Litholrot *n* lithol red
Lithometeor *m* lithometeor
Lithopon *n*, **Lithopone** *f* lithopone, zinc baryta white, Orr's white *(consisting of ZnS and $BaSO_4$)*
Lithosphäre *f (geol)* lithosphere
Lithotype *f (coal)* lithotype, rock type
Littleton-Punkt *m (glass)* Littleton [softening] point, seven-point-six temperature, 7.6 temperature *(at which the viscosity is $10^{7.6}$ poises)*
Littrow-Anordnung *f*, **Littrow-Aufstellung** *f (spectr)* Littrow mounting
Littrow-Spektrograph *m* Littrow spectrograph
Littrow-Spiegel *m (spectr)* Littrow mirror
Ljungström-Regenerator *m*, **Ljungström-Vorwärmer** *m* Ljungstrom heater (regenerator)
L-Kalander *m* L type of calender
L-Kette *f s.* Kette/leichte
L-Konfiguration *f* L configuration
ll *s.* leichtlöslich
LLC *s.* Liquidus-Liquidus-Chromatographie
Lobarsäure *f* lobaric acid *(a lichen acid)*
Lobeliaalkaloid *n* lobelia alkaloid
Lobry-de-Bruyn-van-Ekenstein-Umlagerung *f* Lobry de Bruyn-van Ekenstein transformation *(of α-hydroxy aldehydes into α-hydroxy ketones and vice versa)*
Loch *n* 1. hole; 2. *(phys ch)* [electron] hole, hole position, defect electron; *(cryst)* [lattice] vacancy, vacant lattice position (site), hole; 3. *(plast)* pinhole, pit *(a moulding defect)*
Lochblech *n* perforated (punched) plate
Lochblechsieb *n* perforated-metal (punched-plate) screen
Lochbrennen *n (spectr)* hole burning
~/photochemisches photochemical hole burning, PHB
Lochdüngung *f (agric)* hole dressing
Loch-Elektron-Paar *n* hole-electron pair
Löcherleitung *f* hole conduction, defect (p-type) conduction
Lochfraß *m* pitting
Lochfraßkorrosion *f* pitting corrosion
Lochleitung *f s.* Löcherleitung
Lochmaß *n*[**/lichtes**] clear space [between the wires], [size of] aperture *(screening)*
Lochplatte *f* perforated plate; *(filtr)* strainer
Lochpresse *f* punch press
Lochscheibe *f (plast)* breaker plate
Lochstanze *f* punch press
Lochstein *m* perforated brick
Lochtrommel *f* perforated basket *(of a centrifuge)*
Lochwalze *f* perforated (holey) roll
Lochweite *f s.* Lochmaß
Lochwerte *mpl* perforation *(of a screen)*
Lochziegel[stein] *m* perforated (hollow) brick; hollow tile
locker fluffy *(bulk material, precipitate)*
lockern 1. to loosen [up] *(a chemical bond)*; 2. *(food)* to leaven *(dough)*
lockernd antibonding *(chemical-bond theory)*
Lockerstelle *f (cryst)* loose position, flaw
Lockerung *f* 1. antibond[ing], loosening *(chemical-bond theory)*; 2. *(food)* leavening *(of dough)*
Lockerungsgas *n (food)* leavening gas
Lock-in-Verstärker *m (spectr)* lock-in amplifier
Lockmittel *n* attractant
Lockspeise *f* food lure *(insect control)*
Lockstoff *m* attractant
~ zur Eiablage oviposition lure *(insect control)*
Lockstoffeigenschaften *fpl* attractive properties
Lockwirkung *f* attractant (attractive) action
Loesche-Kohlen[staub]mühle *f* Loesche coal mill
Löffel *m* 1. *(glass)* ladle; 2. bucket *(of an elevator)*; 3. *(lab)* spoon
Logarithmenpapier *n* logarithmic paper
log-Phase *f s.* Wachstumsphase/logarithmische
Lohbrühe *f (tann)* bark liquor
~/ausgezehrte (verbrauchte) spent bark liquor
Lohe *f (tann)* bark [of tan]
Lohgerbung *f* bark tannage (tanning)
Lohgrube *f (tann)* tan[ning] pit, handler
Lohmühle *f (tann)* bark mill
Lokalanalgetikum *n* local analgesic
Lokalanästhetikum *n* local (topical) anaesthetic

Lokalelement *n* local (microgalvanic) cell, local galvanic element (couple)
Lokalisation *f* localization [of position], location
lokalisieren to localize, to locate
Lokalkorrosion *f* localized corrosion
Lokao *n* locao, Chinese green *(natural dye from Rhamnus specc.)*
London-[van der Waals-]Kraft *f* London (dispersion) force, transient polarization force
Longifolen *n* longifolene *(a tricyclic sesquiterpene)*
Longitudinaldiffusion *f* longitudinal (axial) diffusion
Lorbeerbutter *f*, **Lorbeeröl** *n* laurel oil, [sweet] bay oil, bay fat *(from Laurus nobilis L.)*
Lorbeerwachs *n s.* Myrikatalg
Lorentz-Profil *n (spectr)* Lorentzian profile, Lorentzian line (band) shape
Lorentz-Verbreiterung *f* pressure (collision) broadening *(of spectral lines)*
Loröl *n s.* Lorbeerbutter
Los-Angeles-Smog *m* photochemical smog
lösbar 1. breakable *(chemical bond)*; 2. detachable *(from a surface)*; 3. resolvable *(problem)*; 4. capable of being disconnected, dissoluble *(joint)*; 5. *s.* löslich
~/leicht easy to disconnect *(e.g. ground-glass joints)*
Lösbarkeit *f* 1. detachability *(esp from a surface)*, 2. resolvability *(of a problem)*; 3. capability of being disconnected, dissolubility; 4. *s.* Löslichkeit
Löschanlage *f* quenching station *(for coke)*
Löschbrause *f* emergency (safety, drench) shower
Lösche *f* breeze
löschen 1. to extinguish *(fire)*; to quench *(coke)*; 2. to slake, to hydrate *(lime)*; 3. to quench *(an electric arc)*; 4. to quench *(a reaction)*
Löscher *m* 1. hydrator, slaker *(for lime)*; 2. quencher, quenching agent *(kinetics, photochemistry)*
Löschgas *n* quench[ing] gas
Löschkalk *m* slaked (water-slaked, hydrated) lime, slacklime, lime hydrate, *(agric also)* agricultural lime (hydrate) *(calcium hydroxide)*
Löschkarton *m* absorbent (blotting) board
Löschmaschine *f* hydrator, slaker *(for lime)*
Loschmidt-Konstante *f*, **Loschmidt-Zahl** *f s.* Avogadro-Konstante
Löschpapier *n* blotting paper
Löschpapierprüfgerät *n* blotting paper tester
Löschstation *f* quenching station *(for coke)*
Löschturm *m* quenching tower *(for coke)*
Löschung *f*/**dynamische** dynamic quenching *(of fluorescence)*
~/statische static quenching *(of fluorescence)*
Löschwagen *m* quenching car *(for coke)*
Löschwasser *n* water for fire protection
lose [in] bulk
Löse... *s. a.* Lösungs...
Lösebehälter *m* 1. *(hyd)* dissolving chamber; 2. *s.* Lösetank
Lösefähigkeit *f s.* Lösevermögen
Lösegeschwindigkeit *f* rate of dissolution
Lösegut *n* material being *or* to be dissolved, material being *or* to be extracted
Lösekraft *f s.* Lösevermögen
lösen 1. to dissolve *(in a solvent)*; 2. to break, to crack, to disrupt *(a chemical bond)*; 3. to detach *(matter from a surface, an electron from a shell)*; 4. to resolve *(a problem)*; 5. to disconnect, to undo *(a joint)*
~/sich to dissolve, to go into solution
~/wieder to redissolve
~/zur ursprünglichen Konzentration to reconstitute
lösend dissolving, solvent
Löser *m* 1. *(hyd)* dissolving chamber; 2. *s.* Lösungsmittel
Lösetank *m (pap)* [smelt] dissolving tank, dissolving chest, dissolver
Lösevermögen *n* solvent (solubilizing) power, solvency
~/latentes (mittelbares) latent solvency
lösl. *s.* löslich
löslich soluble • **~ machen** to solubilize
~/einigermaßen *s.* ~/mäßig
~/gegenseitig mutually soluble
~/größtenteils substantially soluble
~/gut *s.* ~/leicht
~/ineinander mutually soluble
~/leicht readily (freely) soluble
~/mäßig moderately (reasonably) soluble
~/nicht insoluble, non-soluble
~/schwach *s.* ~/schwer
~/schwer poorly soluble, slightly (sparingly, difficultly) soluble
~/sehr leicht very soluble, v.s., highly soluble
~/sehr schwer (wenig) very slightly soluble, v.s.s., extremely insoluble (slightly soluble)
~/teilweise partially soluble
~/unbegrenzt soluble in all proportions
~/wechselseitig *s.* ~/gegenseitig
~/wenig *s.* ~/schwer
Löslichkeit *f* solubility
~/gegenseitige mutual solubility, intersolubility
~ in festem Zustand solid solubility *(of metals)*
~ in Wasser aqueous (water) solubility
~/wechselseitige *s.* ~/gegenseitige
Löslichkeitsdiagramm *n* solubility chart
Löslichkeitseigenschaften *fpl* solubility properties
Löslichkeitserniedrigung *f* decrease in solubility
Löslichkeitsgleichgewicht *n* solubility equilibrium
Löslichkeitskoeffizient *m*, **Löslichkeitskonstante** *f* solubility coefficient
Löslichkeitskurve *f* solubility [product] curve, liquidus curve
Löslichkeitsparameter *m* solubility parameter
Löslichkeitsprodukt *n* solubility product
~/konditionelles conditional solubility product
Löslichkeitsunterschied *m* difference in solubility

Löslichkeitsverbesserer *m s.* Löslichkeitsvermittler
Löslichkeitsverhalten *n* solubility behaviour
Löslichkeitsverminderung *f* decrease in solubility; common ion effect *(in the presence of a second electrolyte with a common ion)*
Löslichkeitsvermittler *m* solutizer, solubilizer, solubility promoter, solutizing agent
Löslichkeitsverringerung *f s.* Löslichkeitsverminderung
Löß *m* loess
Lößboden *m* loess soil
Lossen-Abbau *m* Lossen rearrangement *(of aromatic hydroxamic acids or their derivatives into isocyanates)*
Lößkindel *n (geol)* loess kindchen *(calcium carbonate)*
Lößlehm *m* loess loam
Lößpuppe *f s.* Lößkindel
Lost *n s.* Dichlordiethylsulfid
Losttherapie *f* mustard therapy
Lösung *f* 1. solution; 2. dissolution *(act or process)* • **in ~ bringen** to bring (put) into solution • **in ~ gehen** to go into solution, to dissolve • **in ~ halten** to keep in solution
~/alkalische alkaline solution
~/alkoholische alcoholic solution
~/äquimolare equimolar solution
~/Benedictsche Benedict solution, Benedict's reagent *(for detecting reducing sugars)*
~/Bialsche Bial reagent *(for detecting pentoses)*
~/Cramersche Cramer solution *(for detecting reducing sugars)*
~/echte true solution
~/eingestellte standard solution
~/Fehlingsche Fehling's solution (reagent), Fehling's
~/feste solid solution *(amorphous or crystalline)*
~/Flemmingsche *(biol)* Flemming solution *(a fixative)*
~/Flicksche Flick solution *(of HCl and H_2F_2 for etching aluminium)*
~/flüssige liquid solution *(as opposed to a solid solution)*
~/Fowlersche *(pharm)* Fowler solution *(a 1 % solution of potassium arsenite)*
~/geimpfte seeded solution
~/gepufferte buffered solution
~/gesättigte saturated solution
~/gewichtsmolare molal solution
~/Hainesche Haine reagent *(for detecting glucose)*
~/heiß gesättigte hot-saturated solution
~/hydrotrope hydrotropic solution
~/hypertonische hypertonic solution
~/hypotonische hypotonic solution
~/ideal verdünnte dilute ideal solution
~/ideale perfect (ideal) solution
~/interstitielle feste interstitial [solid] solution
~/irreguläre irregular solution
~/isosmotische (isotonische) isosmotic (isotonic) solution
~/Knappsche Knapp solution *(of $Hg(CN)_2$ and NaOH for determining glucose)*
~/Knopsche *(agric)* Knop's solution
~/kolloidale *s.* ~/kolloide
~/kolloide colloidal solution
~/Lugolsche Lugol's solution *(aqueous solution of potassium iodide and iodine)*
~/molale molal solution
~/molare molar solution
~/nichtwäßrige non-aqueous solution
~/normale standard solution, *(specif)* normal solution, N solution
~/Ostsche Ost's solution *(of $CuSO_4$, Na_2CO_3, and $NaHCO_3$, for detecting glucose)*
~/Pavysche Pavy solution *(for detecting glucose)*
~/pseudoideale pseudoideal solution
~/reale real solution
~/Ringersche *(med)* Ringer solution (fluid), Ringer artificial serum
~/Sachssesche Sachsse solution *(for determining glucose)*
~/salpetersaure nitric-acid solution
~/salzsaure hydrochloric-acid solution
~/saure acid solution
~/schwefelsaure sulphuric-acid solution
~/selbstvulkanisierende *(rubber)* self-curing (self-vulcanizing) cement
~/standardisierte standard solution
~/übersättigte supersaturated solution
~/ungeimpfte unseeded solution
~/ungesättigte unsaturated solution
~/verdünnte dilute solution, dilution
~/volumenmolare molar solution
~/wäßrige aqueous (water) solution
~/Wijssche Wijs [iodine monochloride] solution *(for determining the iodine number)*
m-**Lösung** *f* molar solution
1m-**Lösung** *f* 1.0 molar solution
0,1m-**Lösung** *f*, *m/10*-**Lösung** *f* decimolar (tenth molar) solution
0,01m-**Lösung** *f*, *m/100*-**Lösung** *f* centimolar solution
0,001m-**Lösung** *f*, *m/1000*-**Lösung** *f* millimolar solution
n-**Lösung** *f* normal solution
1n-**Lösung** *f* N solution
0,1n-**Lösung** *f*, *n/10*-**Lösung** *f* decinormal (tenth normal) solution
0,01n-**Lösung** *f*, *n/100*-**Lösung** *f* centinormal solution
0,001n-**Lösung** *f*, *n/1000*-**Lösung** *f* millinormal solution
Lösungen *fpl* **gleichen Dampfdrucks** isopiestic solutions
Lösungs... *s. a.* Löse...
Lösungsaustritt *m* liquor outlet *(as on an evaporator)*

Lösungsbehälter *m (rubber)* dip[ping] tank
Lösungsbenzin *n* mineral (petroleum) spirit[s]
Lösungsbeschleuniger *m s.* Lösungsvermittler
Lösungschromatographie *f* solubilization chromatography
Lösungsdruck *m* solution pressure
~/elektrolytischer electrolytic solution pressure
Lösungseintritt *m* liquor inlet *(as on an evaporator)*
Lösungsenthalpie *f* enthalpy of solution
Lösungsfigur *f (cryst)* corrosion (etch) figure
Lösungsgleichgewicht *n* solution equilibrium
Lösungsglühen *n (met)* solution [heat] treatment
Lösungshilfsmittel *n* solvent assistant
Lösungskasten *m (rubber)* dip[ping] tank
Lösungskondensation *f* solution polycondensation
Lösungskonzentration *f* solution strength
Lösungsmittel *n* solvent, dissolver, dissolvent, *(esp for extracting soluble principles from drugs:)* menstruum
~/aktives active (true) solvent
~/aprot[on]isches aprotic solvent
~/differenzierendes differentiating solvent
~/dipolares aprot[on]isches dipolar-aprotic solvent
~/echtes *s.* ~/aktives
~ für Chemischreinigung dry-cleaning solvent (fluid)
~/gemischtes mixed solvent
~/glasartig erstarrendes *(spectr)* rigid solvent
~/hochsiedendes high-boiling solvent, high boiler
~/latentes latent (indirect) solvent, cosolvent
~/leichtflüchtiges fast solvent
~/mittelbares *s.* ~/latentes
~/mittelsiedendes medium-boiling solvent, medium boiler
~/nichtwäßriges non-aqueous solvent
~/niedrigsiedendes low-boiling solvent, low boiler
~/nivellierendes levelling solvent
~/organisches organic solvent
~/polares polar solvent
~/polares aprot[on]isches polar-aprotic solvent
~/prot[on]isches protic solvent
~/schlechtes poor solvent
~/schnellflüchtiges fast solvent
~/selektives selective solvent
~/wasserstoffabgebendes (wasserstoffübertragendes) donor solvent *(for extracting coal)*
lösungsmittelabhängig solvent-dependent
Lösungsmittelabhängigkeit *f* solvent dependence
lösungsmittelabstoßend lyophobe, lyophobic
lösungsmittelanziehend lyophile, lyophilic
Lösungsmittelbehandlung *f* solvent treatment
lösungsmittelbeständig fast to solvents, solvent-resisting
Lösungsmittelbeständigkeit *f* fastness to solvents, solvent resistance
Lösungsmitteldampf *m* solvent vapour
Lösungsmitteleffekt *m* solvent effect
Lösungsmittelentparaffinierung *f (petrol)* solvent dewaxing
Lösungsmittelextraktion *f* liquid extraction
lösungsmittelfest *s.* lösungsmittelbeständig
lösungsmittelfrei solventless
Lösungsmittelfront *f (chromat)* solvent front
Lösungsmittelgemisch *n* solvent mixture, mixed solvent
Lösungsmittelgerbung *f* solvent tannage
Lösungsmittelgleichgewicht *n* solvent balance
Lösungsmittel-Isotopieeffekt *m* solvent isotope effect
Lösungsmittelkäfig *m* solvent cage
Lösungsmittelkleber *m*, **Lösungsmittelklebstoff** *m* solvent-type (solvent-based) adhesive, solvent cement
Lösungsmittelmolekül *n* solvent molecule
Lösungsmittelphase *f* solvent phase
Lösungsmittelraffination *f* solvent refining
lösungsmittelraffiniert solvent-refined
Lösungsmittelretention *f* solvent retention
Lösungsmittelrückgewinnung *f* solvent recovery
Lösungsmittelrückgewinnungsanlage *f* solvent-recovery plant (unit)
Lösungsmittelschale *f* solvent dish
Lösungsmittelschweißen *n* solvent welding
Lösungsmittelspektrum *n* solvent spectrum
Lösungsmittelstabilisierung *f (biot)* solvent stabilization
Lösungsmittelsystem *n* solvent system
Lösungsmitteltrog *m (chromat)* solvent trough, developer feed tank
Lösungsmittelverfahren *n (text)* solvent process
Lösungsmittelverschiebung *f (spectr)* solvent shift
Lösungsmittelwäsche *f (text)* solvent scouring
Lösungsmittelwiedergewinnung *f* solvent recovery
Lösungspolymerisation *f* solvent (solution) polymerization
Lösungspunkt *m***/kritischer** critical solution point, indifferent (consolute) point
Lösungsraffination *f* solvent refining
Lösungsreaktion *f* reaction in solution, solution reaction
Lösungsregenerierverfahren *n* solution reclaiming process
Lösungsschweißen *n* solvent welding
Lösungsspektrum *n* solution spectrum
Lösungsspinnen *n (text)* solution (solvent) spinning
Lösungstemperatur *f* solution temperature
~/kritische consolute (critical solution) temperature
~/obere kritische upper consolute (critical solution) temperature
~/untere kritische lower consolute (critical solution) temperature
Lösungstension *f* solution pressure
Lösungstrog *m (rubber)* dip[ping] tank
Lösungsverbesserer *m s.* Lösungsvermittler
Lösungsverhalten *n* solution behaviour

Lösungsvermittler *m* solutizer, solubilizer, solubility promoter, solutizing agent, solution assistant
Lösungsverwitterung *f (soil)* disintegration by solution
Lösungsvorgang *m* dissolving process
Lösungswärme *f* heat of solution
~/differentiale (differentielle) *s.* ~/partielle
~/integrale integral (total) heat of solution
~/partielle partial (differential) heat of solution
Lot *n* solder
lötbar solderable
löten to solder
lötfähig *s.* lötbar
Lötfett *n* paste flux
Lötglas *n* solder [sealing] glass, sealing glass
Löthilfsmittel *n* soldering agent, flux
Lotion *f (cosmet)* lotion, wash; *(pharm)* lotion
~/desodorierende deodorant lotion
~/transpirationsverringernde antiperspirant lotion
Lötlampe *f* [blow]torch, blowlamp
Lotlegierung *f* solder alloy
Lötmetall *n* solder
Lötmittel *n s.* 1. Lötmetall; 2. Löthilfsmittel
Lötpaste *f* paste solder *(containing all components for soldering)*
Lötrohr *n* [mouth] blowpipe
Lötrohranalyse *f* blowpipe analysis
Lötrohrkohle *f* blowpipe charcoal
Lötrohrmundstück *n* blowpipe mouthpiece
Lötrohrprobe *f* blowpipe test (assay, proof)
Lötrohrprobierkunde *f s.* Lötrohranalyse
Lötsäure *f* soldering acid
Lötstelle *f* soldered joint, soldering
Lötverbindung *f* soldered joint, soldering
Lötwasser *n* soldering fluid (liquid)
Lötzinn *n* soldering tin, plumber's solder
Lowry-Bestimmung *f* Lowry assay *(protein chemistry)*
Lowry-Methode *f* Lowry method [for protein determination]
Low-structure-Ruß *m (rubber)* low-structure [carbon] black
LP-Beton *m* air-entrained (air-entraining) concrete
LP-Bildner *m (build)* air-entraining additive (admixture, agent, compound)
LPS *s.* Lipopolysaccharid
I-RNA *s.* RNA/lösliche
LSC *s.* Liquidus-Solidus-Chromatographie
L-Schale *f* L-shell *(of an atom)*
LSD *s.* Lysergsäurediethylamid
Lsgm. *s.* Lösungsmittel
LS-Kopplung *f (spectr)* LS coupling, Russell-Saunders coupling, electron spin-orbit coupling (interaction)
LTH *s.* Hormon/lactotropes
Lücke *f (cryst)* [lattice] vacancy, vacant lattice position (site), hole [position]; gap, interstice *(between the regular lattice sites)*
Lückentechnik *f (anal)* vacancy permeation chromatography
Lückenvolumen *n* intergranular (void) volume
Luft *f* air • **an der** ~ on exposure to air
~/atmosphärische atmospheric air
~/flüssige liquid air
~/mit Feuchtigkeit beladene moisture-laden air
~/überschüssige excess air
Luftablaß *m* air relief
Luftabschluß *m* exclusion of air • **unter** ~ out of contact with air, with air excluded, in the absence of air, sealed from the air, *(biol also)* under anaerobic conditions
Luftabschreckung *f (glass)* air quenching
luftangetrieben air-driven
Luftanreicherung *f (hyd)* aeration
~ **des gesamten Abwasserstroms** total (direct) aeration
~ **des Kreislaufwassers** aeration of [effluent] recycle
~ **eines Abwasserteilstroms** partial aeration
Luftanwesenheit *f* presence of air
Luftaufbereitung *f (min tech)* dry (pneumatic) cleaning
Luftauftrieb *m* buoyancy of the air
Luftausschluß *m s.* Luftabschluß
Luftbad *n* air bath (jacket)
Luftbedarf *m* air requirements
Luftbefeuchter *m* air humidifier
Luftbefeuchtung *f* air humidifying (moistening)
Luftbegasung *f (hyd, biot)* aeration
luftbeständig stable in air
luftbewegt air-operated
Luftblase *f* air bubble, *(on the surface:)* blister; *(phot, glass)* air bell; *(pap)* foam mark, air bell
Luftbombenalterung *f (rubber)* air bomb ageing (test), air pressure [heat] test
Luftbürste *f (pap, plast)* air brush (knife)
Luftbürstenstreichmaschine *f (pap)* air brush coater
Luftdämpfungseinrichtung *f* air damping device *(on precision balances)*
luftdicht 1. airtight *(e.g. container)*; 2. *s.* luftundurchlässig
Luftdichtigkeit *f* 1. airtightness *(as of a container)*; 2. *s.* Luftundurchlässigkeit
Luftdruck *m* air pressure
Luft-Druckalterung *f s.* Luftbombenalterung
Luftdruckmesser *m* barometer
Luftdruckmessung *f* barometry
Luftdruckregler *m* air pressure regulator
Luftdruckschreiber *m* barograph
luftdurchlässig air-permeable, permeable to air
Luftdurchlässigkeit *f* air permeability, permeability to air
Luftdurchlässigkeitsprüfer *m* densimeter, densometer
~ **nach Schopper** *(pap)* Schopper densimeter
Luftdüsenblasverfahren *n (glass)* air-blowing process
Lufteingang *m* air intake, blast inlet *(in underground gasification)*

Lufteinschluß *m* 1. inclusion of air *(process)*; 2. inclusion of air, [en]trapped air, *(if material fault also)* air pocket, [air] blister, air void
Lufteintrag *m*, **Lufteintragung** *f (hyd)* air entrainment (input), introduction of air
Lufteinwirkung/unter on exposure to air
Luftelektrizität *f* atmospheric electricity
luftempfindlich air-sensitive
Lüften *n (plast)* venting, breathing, degassing *(of the mould)*
Lüfter *m* fan, blower
~ mit geraden Schaufeln straight-blade fan
~ mit rückwärtsgekrümmten Schaufeln backward-curved-blade fan
~ mit vorwärtsgekrümmten Schaufeln forward-curved-blade fan
Lufterhitzer *m* air heater, *(if working batchwise:)* regenerator, *(if working continuously:)* recuperator
Luftfeuchte *f* air humidity, atmospheric moisture
Luftfeuchtemesser *m* hygrometer
Luftfeuchtemessung *f* hygrometry
Luftfeuchtigkeit *f s.* Luftfeuchte
Luftfilter *n* air filter
Luftförderer *m* air conveyor
luftfrei air-free
Luftfreiheit *f* freedom from air
Luftführung *f* **im Kreislauf (Umluftbetrieb)** air recirculation
Luftgas *n s.* Generatorgas
Luftgebläse *n* forced-draught fan (blower), air blower
Luftgefrierapparat *m* [air-]blast freezer
Luftgegenwart *f* presence of air
luftgekühlt air-cooled
luftgesättigt air-saturated
Luftgeschwindigkeit *f* air velocity
luftgesteuert air-operated
luftgetrieben air-driven
luftgetrocknet air-dried; *(tann)* air-conditioned
Luft-Glas-Fläche *f (phot)* glass-air interface
Luftgüteindex *m* air pollution (quality) index
Lufthahn *m* air cock
lufthärten to air-harden
Lufthärter *m*, **Lufthärtestahl** *m* air-hardening steel
Lufthärtung *f* air hardening
Luftheber *m* air lift, mammoth (air-lift) pump
Luftherd *m (min tech)* air (dry) table
Luftherdsortieren *n (min tech)* dry tabling
Lufthülle *f* atmosphere
Luftkalk *m* non-hydraulic lime
Luftkammer *f (min tech)* air chamber; *(glass)* air regenerator chamber; plenum chamber *(for gas cleaning)*
Luftkampfstoff *m* non-persistent chemical agent
Luftkanal *m* air duct
Luftklappe *f* air register
Luftkolben *m* air slug *(of an air-lift pump)*
Luftkonditionieranlage *f* air-conditioning plant
Luftkonditionierung *f* air conditioning
Luftkühler *m (lab)* air condenser; *(tech)* air-cooled heat exchanger
Luftkühlung *f* air cooling
luftleer evacuated, exhausted • **~ machen** to evacuate, to exhaust
Luftleitung *f* air line; airblast main *(of a producer)*
Luftmantel *m* air jacket
Luftmasse *f* air mass
Luftmenge *f***/kritische** *(coal)* critical air blast, C.A.B.
Luftmesser *n (pap)* air knife
Luftmesserstreichmaschine *f (pap)* air-knife coater
Luftmesserstreichverfahren *n (pap)* air-knife coating
Luftmeßstellennetz *n* air-sampling network
Luftmörtel *m* non-hydraulic mortar
Luftmotor *m (lab)* air motor
Luftoxidation *f* air oxidation, atmospheric (aerial) oxidation, oxidation by air (atmospheric oxygen)
Luftpeak *m (anal)* air peak
Luftpore *f* air void
Luftporenbeton *m* air-entrained concrete
Luftporenbildner *m (build)* air-entraining additive (admixture, agent, compound)
Luftporenbildung *f* air entrainment
Luftporenzement *m* air-entraining cement
Luftpostpapier *n* air-mall paper
Luftprobe *f* air sample
Luftqualitätsindex *m*, **Luftqualitätskennziffer** *f s.* Luftgüteindex
Luftqualitätsmerkmal *f* air-quality characteristic
Luftqualitätsüberblick *m* air-pollution survey
Luftqualitätsüberwachungsstation *f* air-monitoring station
Luftrakelauftragmaschine *f* air-blade coater
Luftregenerativkammer *f (glass)* air regenerator chamber
Luftreifen *m (rubber)* pneumatic [tyre]
Luftreinhalteplan *m* air resource management
Luftreinigung *f* cleaning of air
Luftrückführung *f* air recirculation
Luftsack *m (glass)* bubble *(in a parison)*
Luftsauerstoff *m* atmospheric oxygen
Luftschadstoff *m* atmospheric contaminant
Luftschieber *m* air register
Luftschlauch *m (rubber)* inner (air) tube
Luftschlauchmischung *f (rubber)* inner-tube compound
Luftschlauchregenerat *n (rubber)* inner-tube reclaim
Luftschleier *m* aerial fog
Luftsetzapparat *m (min tech)* dry cleaner
Luftspalt *m* air gap
Luftspülung *f (hyd)* air cleaning (scour) *(of a filter)*
Luftsterilisation *f (biot)* air sterilization, sterilization of fermentation air
Luftstickstoff *m* atmospheric nitrogen

Luftstrahlgebläse *n*, **Luftstrahlpumpe** *f* compressed-air ejector
Luftstrippen *n (hyd)* air stripping *(of ammonia)*
Luftstrom *m* draught (blast, current) of air, air flow (stream)
Luftstrommühle *f* air-swept mill
Luftstromsichter *m* air-swept classifier
Luftstromsichtung *f* air-flow classification
Luftstromtexturieren *n (text)* air-jet crimping (texturing)
Luftstromtrockner *m* [air-]jet dryer
Luftstromtrocknung *f* [air-]jet drying
Lufttaupunkt *m* air dew point
Lufttrennung *f* air separation
lufttrocken air-dry
~ **und mineral[stoff]frei** dry and mineral-matter-free, d.m.m.f., D.M.F.
Lufttrockner *m* air (atmospheric) dryer; *(lab)* balance desiccator
Lufttrocknung *f* air drying
Luftüberschuß *m* excess of air
Luftüberwachung *f* air monitoring, air pollution control
Luftüberwachungsanlage *f* dust monitor; *(nucl)* radiation monitor
Luftüberwachungsgebiet *n* air pollution control district
luftundurchlässig air-impermeable, airtight
Luftundurchlässigkeit *f* air impermeability, airtightness
Lüftung *f* aeration
Lüftungsbecken *n s.* Belebungsbecken
Lüftungsöffnung *f* air vent (relief), vent
Lüftungszeit *f s.* Belüftungszeit
Luftventilator *m* air blower
Luftverbesserungsmittel *n* room (space) deodorant, air refresher, *(with disinfecting properties also)* air sanitizer
Luftverflüssigung *f* air liquefaction
Luftverschmutzung *f* air pollution
Luftverteiler *m (hyd, biot)* air diffuser, [air] sparger
Luftverunreinigung *f* air pollution
Luftvorwärmer *m* air preheater
Luftvorwärmung *f* air preheat[ing]
Luftwäsche *f (min tech)* dry (pneumatic) cleaning
Luft-Wasser-Spülung *f (hyd)* air-and-water backwashing *(of a filter)*
Luftzerlegung *f* air separation
Luftzirkulation *f* air circulation
Luftzufuhr *f* air supply; *(hyd)* air entrainment (input), introduction of air
Luftzuführung *f* 1. *s.* Luftzufuhr; 2. air inlet (supply) *(site)*
Luftzutritt *m* access of air • **unter** ~ in the presence of air, *(biol also)* under aerobic conditions
Lukas-Test *m* Lukas test *(for detecting alcohol)*
lumineszent luminescent
Lumineszenz *f* luminescence
~**/verzögerte** delayed luminescence
Lumineszenzanalyse *f* luminescent analysis
Lumineszenzfarbe *f* luminescent (luminous) paint
Lumineszenzindikator *m* luminescent indicator
Lumineszenzspektroskopie *f* luminescence spectroscopy
Lumineszenzspektrum *n* luminescence spectrum
Lumineszenzstrahler *m s.* Luminophor
lumineszieren to luminesce
lumineszierend luminescent
Luminophor *m* luminophore, luminescent substance
Luminosität *f* luminosity
Lummer-Gehrcke-Platte *f (spectr)* Lummer-Gehrcke plate
LUMO *s.* Molekülorbital/niedrigstes unbesetztes
Lumpen *mpl (pap)* rags
Lumpenhalbstoff *m (pap)* rag pulp (stuff, stock), all-rag furnish
Lumpenpapier *n* [all-]rag paper
Lumpenschneider *m (pap)* rag cutter
Lungengift *n* lung injurant
Lunker *m* pipe *(foundry)*; *(plast)* bubble
~**/primärer** primary pipe
~**/sekundärer** secondary pipe
Lunkerbildung *f*, **Lunkern** *n*, **Lunkerung** *f* piping *(foundry)*
Lunte *f* 1. *(glass)* sliver; 2. fuse *(for setting off explosives)*
Lupinenalkaloid *n* lupin[e] alkaloid
Lüpke-Pendel *n (rubber)* Lüpke pendulum (resiliometer) *(a testing instrument)*
Luppe *f (met)* 1. ball, *(esp having a cross section of > 225 cm^2:)* bloom; 2. hollow billet *(tube manufacture)* • **Luppen bilden** to ball [up]
Luppenbildung *f (met)* balling
α-**Lupulinsäure** *f* α-lupulinic acid, humulone
β-**Lupulinsäure** *f*, **Lupulon** *n* β-lupulinic acid, lupulone
Lurgi-Druckgaserzeuger *m*, **Lurgi-Druckgasgenerator** *m s.* Lurgi-Druckvergaser
Lurgi-Druckgasverfahren *n* Lurgi pressure-gasification (high-pressure) process
Lurgi-Druckvergaser *m* Lurgi [pressure] gasifier, Lurgi [pressure] generator
Lurgi-Druckvergasungsanlage *f* Lurgi gasification plant
Lurgi-Druckvergasungsverfahren *n s.* Lurgi-Druckgasverfahren
Lurgi-Spülgas-Schwelanlage *f* Lurgi Spülgas carbonization plant
Lurgi-Spülgas[schwel]verfahren *n* Lurgi Spülgas low-temperature carbonization process
Lüsterfarbe *f (ceram)* lustre colour
Lüsterglasur *f (ceram)* lustre glaze
Lustgas *n s.* Lachgas
Lüstriermittel *n (text)* lustring agent
luteinisieren *(bioch)* to luteinize
Luteinisierungshormon *n* luteinizing hormone, LH, interstitial-cell-stimulating hormone, ICSH

Luteotrophin *n s.* Luteotropin
Luteotropin *n* *prolactin *n,* PRL, luteotropic hormone, LTH
Lutetium *n* Lu lutetium
Lutetiumchlorid *n* lutetium chloride
Lutetiumerde *f s.* Lutetiumoxid
Lutetiumoxid *n* lutetium oxide
Lutetiumsulfat *n* lutetium sulphate
Lutidin *n* lutidine, dimethylpyridine
Lutoide *npl (rubber)* lutoids
lutro *s.* lufttrocken
Luvo *m s.* Luftvorwärmer
Lux-Masse *f* luxmasse *(essentially iron(III) oxide hydrate, for absorbing hydrogen sulphide and hydrogen cyanide)*
Luxusaufnahme *f,* **Luxuskonsum** *m* luxury consumption *(uptake of unnecessary amounts of nutrients by plants)*
L-Walzenkalander *m* L type of calender
Lyat-Ion *n* lyate ion
Lycin *n* lycine, betaine, *NNN*-trimethylammonioacetate, oxyneurine
Lycopen *n* lycopene *(a natural dye)*
Lydit *m (min)* lydite, lydian stone, touchstone
Lyman-Serie *f (spectr)* Lyman series
Lyoenzym *n,* **Lyoferment** *n* lyo-enzyme
Lyogel *n* lyogel
Lyolysis *f s.* Solvolyse
Lyonium-Ion *n* lyonium ion
lyophil lyophile, lyophilic
Lyophilisat *n (biot)* lyophilized culture
Lyophilisation *f s.* Lyophilisierung
lyophilisieren to lyophilize, to freeze-dry
Lyophilisierung *f* lyophilization, freeze drying (dehydration)
lyophob lyophobe, lyophobic
Lyse *f (biot)* cell lysis
Lysergsäure *f* lysergic acid
Lysergsäure-Alkaloid *n* lysergic acid alkaloid
Lysergsäurediethylamid *n* lysergic acid diethylamide, LSD
Lysin *n* 1. *(bioch)* lysine, *2,6-diaminohexanoic acid; 2. *(med)* lysin *(a substance capable of disintegrating bacteria or cells)*
Lysogenisierung *f (bioch)* lysogenation
Lysogenisierungsfrequenz *f (bioch)* frequency of lysogenation
Lysozym *n* lysozyme *(a bacteriolytic enzyme)*
Lysozymaktivität *f (bioch)* lytic activity of lysozyme
LZ *s.* Leistungszahl

M

M *s.* Massenzahl
Macassar-Öl *n* Macassar (kussum) oil *(from Schleichera specc.)*
MacDougall-Ofen *m* MacDougall furnace *(a multi-hearth furnace)*

machen:
~/alkalisch to make alkaline (basic), to alkalify, to alkali[ni]ze, to basify
~/brandsicher to fireproof
~/durch Filtration keimfrei *(biot)* to filter aseptically, to sterilize by filtration
~/durch Gefriertrocknung haltbar *(food)* to dehydrofreeze
~/einen Blindversuch to run a blank
~/feuerbeständig to fireproof
~/geruchlos to deodorize
~/haltbar to preserve, to prepare, to cure, *(food also)* to can
~/keimfrei *(med)* to sterilize
~/körnig to granulate, to grain
~/lichtempfindlich *(phot)* to sensitize
~/löslich to solubilize
~/luftleer to evacuate, to exhaust
~/mottenecht *(text)* to mothproof
~/radioaktiv to radioactivate
~/sichtbar to visualize
~/spannungsfrei *(met, glass, ceram)* to anneal
~/spröde to embrittle, to make brittle
~/stückig to agglomerate
~/unempfindlich *(phot)* to desensitize
~/unlöslich to insolubilize
~/unwirksam to inactivate, to block, to mask *(reactive groups or sites)*; to block *(reactions)*
~/verfallen *(tann)* to bring down, to deplete, to fall *(pelts)*
~/wasserdicht (wasserundurchlässig) *(text)* to waterproof
~/weich to soften *(e.g. water, plastics)*
~/zähflüssig to thicken
Mach-Kennzahl *f s.* Machzahl
mächtig *(mine)* thick
Mächtigkeit *f (mine)* thickness
Machzahl *f* Mach number *(fluid mechanics)*
Mackie-Linie *f (phot)* Mackie line
Madelung-Konstante *f (cryst)* Madelung constant *(of lattice energy)*
Madelung-Synthese *f* Madelung reaction *(for obtaining indoles)*
Madiöl *n* madia oil *(from Madia sativa Mol.)*
Magazin *n* 1. storehouse, storage, store; 2. *(pap)* magazine
Magazinschleifer *m (pap)* magazine grinder
~/hydraulischer hydraulic magazine grinder
Magengift *n* stomach poison
Magensaft *m* gastric juice
Magensäure *f* gastric acid
Magenta *n* magenta, fuchsin[e], rosaniline
mager 1. lean *(e.g. ore, concrete, coal)*; 2. *(food)* fatless; 3. *(soil)* poor, infertile, thin
Magerbeton *m* lean[-mixed] concrete, poor concrete
Magererz *n* lean (low-grade) ore
Magerkalk *m* poor lime
Magerkäse *m* skim-milk cheese

Magerkohle *f* lean (dry steam) coal, semianthracite
Magermilch *f* skim[med] milk, separated milk
~/eingedickte (kondensierte) condensed skim milk
Magermilchpulver *n* skim-milk powder, non-fat dry milk, dry skim milk
magern *(ceram)* to shorten, *(esp using crushed firebricks:)* to grog
Mageröl *n* lean oil *(as for an absorption column)*
Magerton *m* lean clay
Magerungsmittel *n* leaning material; *(ceram)* shortening (non-plastic) material, *(esp crushed firebricks:)* grog
Magma *n* magma
Magmagestein *n* magmatic (igneous) rock
magmatisch magmatic, igneous
Magmatit *m s.* Magmagestein
Magnesia *f* magnesium oxide, magnesia
~/calcinierte (gebrannte) calcined magnesium oxide
Magnesiabinder *m (build)* magnesia cement, Sorel (magnesium oxychloride) cement
Magnesiaeisenglimmer *m (min)* black (dark) mica, biotite
magnesiahaltig containing magnesia, magnesian, magnesial
Magnesiahärte *f (hyd)* magnesium (Mg) hardness
Magnesiamilch *f* milk of magnesia, magnesia magma
Magnesiamixtur *f* magnesia mixture *(aqueous solution of NH_4Cl, NH_4OH and $MgCl$)*
Magnesiasalpeter *m (min)* nitromagnesite *(magnesium nitrate)*
Magnesiazement *m s.* Magnesiabinder
Magnesiospinell *m (min)* spinel *(magnesium aluminate)*
Magnesitbinder *m s.* Magnesiabinder
Magnesitstein *m***[/feuerfester]** magnesite brick
Magnesium *n* Mg magnesium
Magnesiumacetat *n* magnesium acetate
Magnesiumband *n* magnesium ribbon
Magnesiumbasis/auf magnesium-base
Magnesiumbisulfitkochsäure *f (pap)* magnesium-base acid (liquor, sulphite liquor)
Magnesiumbranntkalk *m* dolomitic (dolomite) lime *(calcium magnesium oxide)*
Magnesiumbromid *n* magnesium bromide
Magnesiumcarbonat *n* magnesium carbonate
Magnesiumchlorid *n* magnesium chloride
Magnesiumdiäthyl *n s.* Diethylmagnesium
Magnesiumdihydrogenphosphat *n* magnesium dihydrogenphosphate
Magnesiumdiphosphat *n* magnesium diphosphate, magnesium pyrophosphate
Magnesiumdrehspäne *mpl* magnesium turnings
Magnesiumfluorid *n* magnesium fluoride
Magnesiumgrundlage/auf magnesium-base
magnesiumhaltig containing magnesium, *(esp relating to ores:)* magnesium-bearing
Magnesiumhexachlorostannat(IV) *n* magnesium hexachlorostannate(IV)
Magnesiumhydrid *n* magnesium hydride
Magnesiumhydrogenarsenat(V) *n* magnesium hydrogenarsenate(V)
Magnesiumhydrogencarbonat *n* magnesium hydrogencarbonate
Magnesiumhydrogenphosphat *n* magnesium hydrogenphosphate
Magnesiumhydroxid *n* magnesium hydroxide
Magnesiumhypophosphit *n* magnesium hypophosphite, *magnesium phosphinate
Magnesiumiodid *n* magnesium iodide
Magnesiumkarbonathärte *f (hyd)* magnesium carbonate hardness
Magnesiummanganat(VII) *n s.* Magnesiumpermanganat
Magnesiummangel *m (agric)* magnesium shortage
Magnesium-Nichtkarbonathärte *f (hyd)* magnesium non-carbonate hardness
Magnesiumnitrat *n* magnesium nitrate
Magnesiumorthoarsenat(III) *n* magnesium orthoarsenite, *magnesium trioxoarsenate(III)
Magnesiumoxid *n* magnesium oxide
Magnesiumperchlorat *n* magnesium perchlorate
Magnesiumpermanganat *n* magnesium permanganate
Magnesiumperoxid *n* magnesium peroxide
Magnesiumphosphit *n* magnesium phosphite, *magnesium phosphonate
Magnesiumphthalocyanin *n* magnesium phthalocyanine
Magnesiumpulver *n* magnesium powder (dust)
Magnesiumpyrophosphat *n s.* Magnesiumdiphosphat
Magnesiumsulfat *n* magnesium sulphate
Magnesiumsulfathärte *f (hyd)* magnesium sulphate hardness
Magnesiumsulfid *n* magnesium sulphide
Magnesiumsulfit *n* magnesium sulphite
Magnetanker *m* magnetic (stirring) bar *(of a magnetic stirrer)*
Magnetband *n* magnetic tape
Magnetbandrolle *f* magnetic pulley *(in belt conveyors)*
Magneteisenerz *n*, **Magneteisenstein** *m s.* Magnetit
Magnetfeld *n* magnetic field
Magnetfilter *n* magnetic filter
magnetisch magnetic
magnetisierbar magnetizable
magnetisieren to magnetize
Magnetisierung *f* magnetization
Magnetisierungskurve *f* magnetization curve
Magnetit *m (min)* magnetite, magnetic iron [ore] *(iron(II,III) oxide)*
Magnetkies *m (min)* magnetic pyrites, pyrrhotite, pyrrhotine *(iron(II) sulphide)*
Magnetochemie *f* magnetochemistry

Magneton *n* magneton *(a unit of the magnetic moment)*
~/Bohrsches Bohr magneton
Magnetorotation *f* magnetic rotation, Faraday effect
Magnetquantenzahl *f* magnetic quantum number
Magnetrolle *f s.* Magnetbandrolle
Magnetrührer *m* magnetic stirrer
Magnetscheiden *n* magnetic separation
Magnetscheider *m* magnetic separator
Magnetsortieren *n* magnetic separation
Magnettrommel *f* magnetic drum
Magnettrommelscheider *m* magnetic drum [separator], induced-roll [magnetic] separator, rotor separator
Magnetvibrator *m* electromagnetic vibrator
Mahlbahn *f* grinding surface
mahlbar grindable
Mahlbarkeit *f* grindability
Mahlbarkeitsindex *m* **nach Hardgrove** Hardgrove grindability index
Mahlbarkeitsprüfung *f*, **Mahlbarkeitstest** *m* grindability test
Mahlbarkeitszahl *f* grindability index (value)
Mahldruck *m (pap)* beating pressure *(in a Hollander beater)*; *(pap)* plug pressure *(in perfecting engines)*
Mahleffekt *m (pap)* effect of beating
mahlen to grind, to mill; *(pap)* to beat *(in a Hollander beater)*; *(pap)* to refine, to clear, to brush out *(in a refiner)*
~/auf Staubfeinheit to pulverize
~/in der Kugelmühle to ball-mill
~/wieder *(plast)* to regrind
Mahlfeinheit *f*, **Mahlfeinheitsgrad** *m* fineness of grind[ing]
Mahlfläche *f s.* Mahlbahn
Mahlgang *m s.* Mahlscheibenmühle
Mahlgeschirr *n s.* Stoffmühle
Mahlgrad *m* 1. *(pap)* freeness [value], degree of beating; 2. *s.* Mahlfeinheit
Mahlgradbestimmung *f (pap)* freeness test
Mahlgradprüfer *m (pap)* freeness (beaten stuff) tester
~ nach Schopper-Riegler Schopper-Riegler apparatus
Mahlgradprüfung *f (pap)* freeness test
Mahlgut *n* 1. material being *or* to be ground; 2. *(pap)* [fibrous, pulp] furnish, *(for a Hollander beater also)* beating material, beater charge
Mahlhilfe *f* grinding aid
Mahlhilfsmittel *n (pap)* beater additive
Mahlhilfsstoff *m* grinding aid
Mahlholländer *m (pap)* Hollander [beater, beating engine], pulp engine (grinder), stuff engine
Mahlkammer *f* grinding (pulverizing) chamber
Mahlkörper *m* grinding medium
Mahlkugel *f* grinding ball
Mahlmaschine *f* grinding machine; *(pap)* beating engine, beater
Mahlmüllerei *f (food)* [flour] milling
Mahlorgan *n* grinding element
Mahlraum *m s.* Mahlkammer
Mahlring *m* grinding (pulverizing, bull) ring *(in a roller mill)*
Mahlscheibe *f* grinding disk *(of a disk mill)*
Mahlscheibenmühle *f* disk (attrition) mill, disk grinder
Mahlschüssel *f* grinding pan, bowl
Mahlstein *m* grindstone, millstone
Mahlstoff *m s.* Mahlgut 2.
Mahlteller *m (ceram)* grinding pan
Mahltrocknung *f* mill drying
Mahltrocknungsanlage *f* dryer-pulverizer
Mahlung *f* grinding, milling; *(pap)* beating *(in a Hollander beater)*; *(pap)* refining, clearing, brushing-out *(in a refiner)*
~/autogene autogenous grinding
~/feine fine grinding
~/grobe coarse grinding
~ im geschlossenen Kreislauf closed-circuit grinding
~ in der Kugelmühle ball milling, *(plast also)* mill mixing
~/rösche *(pap)* free beating
~/schmierige *(pap)* wet (slow) beating
Mahlwalze *f* grinding roll, *(in edge-runner mills:)* muller [wheel]; *(pap)* beater (beating) roll, Hollander (knife) roll
Mahlwerkzeug *n (pap)* set of bars
Mahlwiderstand *m* grinding resistance
Mahlwirkung *f (pap)* beating action
Mahlzeug *n (pap)* beating material *(active portion of the beating apparatus)*
Maillard-Reaktion *f (food)* Maillard reaction, carbonylamine reaction, non-enzymatic browning [reaction]
Maischapparat *m* masher
Maischbottich *m* mash tub
Maische *f (ferm)* mash *(in producing beer)*; must *(in producing wine)* • ~ abziehen to remove the mash
~/gesäuerte sour[ed] mash
~/süße sweet mash
Maischebottich *m s.* Maischbottich
Maischefilter *n* mash filter
Maische[koch]kessel *m s.* Maischepfanne
maischen to mash, to dough [in]
Maischepfanne *f* mash tun (copper, kettle)
Maischverfahren *n* mashing process
Maiseinweichwasser *n s.* Maisquellwasser
Maiskeimöl *n* maize [germ] oil, *(Am)* corn oil
Maismehl *n* maize flour, *(if coarse:)* maize meal, *(Am)* corn flour *or* meal
Maisöl *n s.* Maiskeimöl
Maisprotein *n* maize protein
Maisquellwasser *n (biot)* maize steep liquor, *(Am)* corn steep liquor

Maisstärke *f* maize starch, *(Am)* corn starch
Maisstärkemaische *f (biot)* maize mash, *(Am)* corn mash
Malszucker *m* maize sugar, *(Am)* corn sugar
Majolika *f (ceram)* majolica, maiolica
Majoranöl *n* majoram oil *(from Majorana hortensis Moench)*
Majoritäts[ladungs]träger *m* majority carrier
MAk *s.* Antikörper/monoklonaler
MAK *s.* Arbeitsplatzkonzentration/maximale
Makajabutter *f* macaja (micauba) oil *(a palm kernel oil from Acrocomia sclerocarpa Mart.)*
Make-up-Creme *f (cosmet)* cream make-up
Makroanalyse *f* macroanalysis
makroanalytisch macroanalytical
Makroansatz *m (lab)* macro batch
makroätzen *(met)* to macroetch
Makroätzung *f (met)* macroetching
Makroraufnahme *f* photomacrograph
Makrobestandteil *m* macroconstituent, macrocomponent
Makrochemie *f* macrochemistry
makrochemisch macrochemical
makrocyclisch macrocyclic
Makrocyclus *m s.* Verbindung/makrocyclische
makrofibrillär macrofibrillar
Makrofibrille *f* macrofibrill
Makroflocken *fpl (hyd)* macrofloc
Makrofoto *n* photomacrograph
Makrofotografie *f* 1. photomacrography; 2. photomacrograph
Makrogefüge *n* macrostructure
Makro-Ion *n* macroion
Makrokomponente *f s.* Makrobestandteil
makrokristallin macrocrystalline
Makrolid *n (org ch)* macrolide
Makrolid-Antibiotikum *n* macrolide antibiotic
~/polyenes polyene macrolide antibiotic
Makromethode *f* macromethod
Makromolekül *n* macromolecule, giant (large) molecule
~/fadenförmiges thread[-like] molecule, filamentary (linear) molecule
~/informatives *(bioch)* informational macromolecule
~/lineares *s.* ~/fadenförmiges
makromolekular macromolecular
Makronährstoff *m (agric)* macronutrient, macroelement, major element
Makropore *f* macropore *(as in activated carbon)*
Makroprobe *f* macro sample *(> 0.1 g)*
Makroradikal *n* macroradical
makroretikulär macroreticular
Makroring *m* macroring, large ring *(consisting of 13 or more members)*
makroskopisch macroscopic
Makrostruktur *f* macrostructure
Makrotetrolid *n (org ch)* macrotetrolide
MAK-Wert *m s.* Arbeitsplatzkonzentration/maximale
Malabarkino *n* Malabar (East India) kino *(kino gum from Pterocarpus marsupium Roxb.)*
Malabartalg *m* piney tallow, Dhupa fat *(seed fat from Vateria indica L.)*
Malachit *m (min)* malachite *(copper(II) carbonate dihydroxide)*
Malachitgrün *n* malachite green, Victoria (benzal, benzaldehyde) green, basic green 4 *(a triphenylmethane dye)*
Malagetta *m***/Abessinischer (Madagassischer)** Madagascar cardamom *(from Aframomum angustifolium Schum.)*
Malagettapfeffer *m* grains of paradise *(from Aframomum melegueta (Rosc.) Schum.)*
Malakon *m (min)* malacon *(a nesosilicate containing zirconium)*
Malaprade-Reaktion *f* Malaprade reaction *(oxidative cleavage of glycols and α-amino alcohols)*
Malaria[bekämpfungs]mittel *n* antimalarial [drug]
Malariawirksamkeit *f (pharm)* antimalarial activity
Malat *n* malate *(salt or ester of malic acid)*
Malat-Aspartat-[Glutamat-]Shuttle *m (bioch)* malate-aspartate shuttle
Malatdehydrogenase *f* malic [acid] dehydrogenase
Malatenzym *n* malic enzyme
Maleat *n*, **Maleinat** *n* maleate, maleinate *(salt or ester of maleic acid)*
Maleinsäure *f* maleic acid, **cis*-butenedioic acid, **cis*-ethylene-1,2-dicarboxylic acid
Maleinsäureanhydrid *n* maleic anhydride, **cis*-butenedioic anhydride, 2,5-furandione
Maleinsäurehydrazid *n s.* Maleinylhydrazin
Maleinylhydrazin *n* maleic hydrazide, MH
Malergold *n* mosaic gold, ormolu *(tin(IV) sulphide)*
Malett[o]rinde *f (tann)* mallet bark *(from Eucalyptus specc., esp E. occidentalis Endl.)*
Malinsäure *f s.* Äpfelsäure
Malonat *n* malonate *(salt or ester of malonic acid)*
Malonestersynthese *f* malonic ester synthesis
Malonsäure *f* malonic acid, methane-dicarboxylic acid
Malonsäurediethylester *m* diethyl malonate, malonic ester
Malonsäuredinitril *n* malonitrile
Malonsäureester *m s.* Malonsäurediethylester
Malonyl-Coenzym *n* **A** malonyl coenzyme A
N,N'-**Malonylharnstoff** *m N,N'*-malonylurea, barbituric acid
Malonylierung *f* malonylation
Maltodextrin *n* maltodextrin
Maltol *n* maltol, larixinic acid
Maltonsäure *f s. D*-Gluconsäure
Maltose *f* maltose, malt sugar
Maltosedextrin *n* maltodextrin
Maltosesirup *m* malt extract
Malz *n* malt
~/dunkles dark malt
~/geröstetes roasted malt
~/geschrotetes ground (crushed) malt, malt meal, grist

~/helles white (ordinary) malt
~/Pilsner Pilsen malt
Malzamylase *f* malt amylase
malzartig malty
Malzbereitung *f* malting
Malzbier *n* malt beer
Malzdarre *f* malt [drying] kiln
malzen, mälzen to malt
Malzentkeimungsmaschine *f* malt cleaner
Malzenzym *n* malt enzyme
Mälzer *m* maltster
Mälzerei *f* 1. malting; 2. *s.* Malzfabrik
Malzessig *m* malt vinegar
Malzextrakt *m* malt extract
Malzfabrik *f* malt-house, malting plant
Malzgerste *f* malting barley
Malzkeim *m* malt rootlet
Malzmeister *m* maltster
Malzmilch *f* malt slurry
Malzputze *f s.* Malzputzmaschine
Malzputzen *n* malt cleaning
Malzputzmaschine *f* malt cleaner
Malzquetsche *f*, **Malzquetscher** *m* malt mill (crusher)
Malzrumpf *m* malt hopper
Malzstärke *f* malt starch
Malztenne *f* malt[ing] floor
Malztrichter *m* malt hopper
Mälzung *f* malting
Mälzungsschwund *m* malting loss
Malzzerkleinerungsapparat *m s.* Malzquetsche
Malzzucker *m* malt sugar, maltose
Mammutpumpe *f* air lift, mammoth (air-lift) pump
Mammutrührwerk *n* air-lift mixer
Manchesterbraun *n* Manchester brown
Manchestergelb *n* Manchester (Martius) yellow
Manchester-Ofen *m (ceram)* Manchester kiln
Mandel *f* 1. *(food)* almond *(from Prunus amygdalus Batsch)*; 2. *(geol)* amygdale, amygdule, geode
Mandelat *n* mandelate *(salt or ester of mandelic acid)*
Mandelöl *n* almond oil
Mandelsäure *f* mandelic acid, 2-hydroxy-2-phenylacetic acid
para-**Mandelsäure** *f* DL-mandelic acid
Mandelsäurebenzylester *m* benzyl mandelate
Mandelsäuretropylester *m* mandelyltropine, homatropine, phenylglycollyltropine
Mangabeirakautschuk *m* Mangabeira rubber *(from Hancornia speciosa Gomez)*
Mangan *n* Mn manganese
Mangan(II)-acetat *n* manganese(II) acetate
manganarm poor in manganese, low-manganese
Manganat *n* manganate
Manganat(IV) *n* manganate(IV), manganite
Manganat(VII) *n* permanganate
Manganbister *m(n)* manganese brown
Manganblende *f (min)* manganblende, alabandite *(manganese(II) sulphide)*
Manganborat *n* manganese borate
Manganbraun *n* manganese brown *(manganese(III) hydroxide)*
Mangan(II)-bromid *n* manganese(II) bromide, manganese dibromide
Manganbronze *f* manganese bronze
Mangancarbid *n* manganese carbide
Mangan(II)-carbonat *n* manganese(II) carbonate
Mangan(II)-chlorid *n* manganese(II) chloride, manganese dichloride
Mangan(IV)-chlorid *n* manganese(IV) chloride, manganese tetrachloride
Mangan(II)-cyanwasserstoffsäure *f s.* Hexacyanomangan(II)-säure
Mangandi... *s. a.* Mangan(II)-...
Mangan(II)-dihydrogenphosphat *n* manganese(II) dihydrogenphosphate
Mangandioxid *n s.* Mangan(IV)-oxid
Mangan(II)-diphosphat *n* manganese(II) diphosphate, manganese(II) pyrophosphate
Mangandisilicid *n* manganese disilicide
Mangandisulfid *n s.* Mangan(IV)-sulfid
Mangan-Epidot *m (min)* manganepidote
Manganerz *n* manganese ore
Mangan(II)-fluorid *n* manganese(II) fluoride, manganese difluoride
Mangan(III)-fluorid *n* manganese(III) fluoride, manganese trifluoride
Mangangrün *n* manganese (Rosenstiehl's, Cassel) green *(barium manganate)*
manganhaltig containing manganese, manganiferous
Manganhartstahl *m* manganese steel
Manganheptoxid *n s.* Mangan(VII)-oxid
Mangan(II)-hexacyanoferrat(II) *n* manganese(II) hexacyanoferrate(II)
Mangan(II)-hexafluorosilicat *n* manganese(II) hexafluorosilicate
Mangan(II)-hydrogenphosphat *n* manganese(II) hydrogenphosphate
Mangan(II)-hydroxid *n* manganese(II) hydroxide
Mangan(II)-hypophosphit *n* manganese(II) hypophosphite, *manganese(II) phosphinate
Mangan(II)-iodid *n* manganese(II) iodide
Manganit *m (min)* manganite *(manganese(III) hydroxide oxide)*
Manganit *n s.* Manganat(IV)
Mangankiesel *m* 1. *s.* Rhodonit; 2. *a mixture of quartz and rhodochrosite*
Manganknolle *f (geol)* manganese (ferromanganese) nodule
Mangan(II)-metasilicat *n* manganese(II) metasilicate, manganese trioxosilicate
Manganmonosulfid *n s.* Mangan(II)-sulfid
Manganmonoxid *n s.* Mangan(II)-oxid
Mangan(II)-nitrat *n* manganese(II) nitrate
Manganometrie *f* permanganometry
Mangan(II)-orthophosphat *n* manganese(II) orthophosphate, manganese(II) phosphate

Mangan(II)-orthosilicat *n* manganese(II) orthosilicate, dimanganese tetraoxosilicate
Manganoxid *n***/rotes** *s.* Mangan(II,IV)-oxid
Mangan(II)-oxid *n* manganese(II) oxide, manganese monooxide
Mangan(II,IV)-oxid *n* manganese(II,IV) oxide, trimanganese tetraoxide, red manganese oxide
Mangan(III)oxid *n* manganese(III) oxide, dimanganese trioxide
Mangan(IV)-oxid *n* manganese(IV) oxide, manganese dioxide
Mangan(VI)-oxid *n* manganese(VI) oxide, manganese trioxide
Mangan(VII)-oxid *n* manganese(VII) oxide, dimanganese heptaoxide
Mangan(III)-oxidhydrat *n* hydrated manganese(III) oxide
Manganphosphid *n* manganese phosphide
Mangan(II)-phosphit *n* manganese(II) phosphite, *manganese(II) phosphonate
Mangan(II)-pyrophosphat *n s.* Mangan(II)-diphosphat
manganreich rich in manganese, high-manganese
Manganresinat *n* manganese resinate
Mangan(II)-rhodanid *n s.* Mangan(II)-thiocyanat
Mangansäure *f* manganic acid
Mangan(VII)-säure *f s.* Permangansäure
Manganschwarz *n* manganese black *(manganese(IV) oxide)*
Manganseife *f* manganese soap
Mangan(II)-silicid *n* manganese(II) silicide, dimanganese silicide
Mangansiliciumstahl *m* silicon-manganese steel, silicomanganese steel
Manganspat *m (min)* dialogite, rhodochrosite *(manganese(II) carbonate)*
Manganstahl *m* manganese steel
Mangan(II)-sulfat *n* manganese(II) sulphate
Mangan(III)-sulfat *n* manganese(III) sulphate
Mangan(II)-sulfid *n* manganese(II) sulphide, manganese monosulphide
Mangan(IV)-sulfid *n* manganese(IV) sulphide, manganese disulphide
Mangantetrachlorid *n s.* Mangan(IV)-chlorid
Mangan(II)-thiocyanat *n* manganese(II) thiocyanate
Mangantitration *f* **nach Volhard** Volhard manganese titration *(permanganometry)*
Mangantrifluorid *n s.* Mangan(III)-fluorid
Mangantrioxid *n s.* Mangan(VI)-oxid
Manganvitriol *m (min)* mallardite *(manganese(II) sulphate 7-water)*
Mangel *m* 1. deficiency, *(agric also)* starvation; 2. *(tech)* fault, defect
Mangelelektron *n (phys ch)* defect electron, electron hole
Mangelerscheinung *f (agric)* deficiency symptom; *(bioch)* deficiency manifestation
Mangelkrankheit *f (agric, med)* deficiency disease
Mangelleiter *m (phys ch)* p-type conductor, hole conductor
Mangelleitung *f (phys ch)* p-type conduction, defect (hole) conduction
Mangelmutante *f (biot)* auxotrophic mutant
Mangelsymptom *n (agric)* deficiency symptom
Mangeltrockner *m (ceram)* mangle [dryer]
Mangroverindenextrakt *m(n) (tann)* mangrove cutch, kutch
Manicoba-Kautschuk *m* manicoba (Ceará) rubber *(from Manihot specc.)*
Manilakopal *m* Manila copal *(from Agathis specc.)*
~/halbfossiler pontianac, pontianak [gum], gum pontianak *(a copal from Agathis alba (Lam.) Foxw.)*
Manilakraftpapier *n*, **Manila[pack]papier** *n* Manila (Manilla) paper
Manipulation *f***/genetische (gentechnologische)** *(biot)* genetic (gene) manipulation
Manipulator *m (lab)* manipulator *(in automatic analysers)*
Mankettinußöl *n* Manketti nut oil *(from Ricinodendron rautaneni Schinz)*
Manna *n(f)* manna *(from Fraxinus ornus L.)*
Mannan *n* mannan *(a polysaccharide)*
Mannazucker *m s.* Mannit
Mannich-Base *f* Mannich base
Mannich-Reaktion *f* Mannich reaction *(aminomethylation and variations of it)*
Mannit *m*, **Mannitol** *n* mannitol *(a sugar alcohol)*
Mannloch *n* manhole, manway
Mannlochdeckel *m* manhole cover
Mannogalactan *n* mannogalactan, galactomannan
Manometer *n* manometer, pressure gauge
~/kapazitives capacitance [pressure] gauge
manometrisch manometric
Manool *n* manool *(a bicyclic diterpene)*
Manschette *f (tech)* collar, sleeve
~/drehbare movable collar *(of a Bunsen burner)*
Manschettendichtung *f* oil seal ring
Mantel *m (tech)* casing, sheath[ing], *(esp for heating or cooling:)* jacket, mantle; shell *(of a boiler)*; *(rubber)* sheath[ing], cover *(of cables)*; cover *(of a tyre)*; *(text)* skin, sheath *(of core-spun yarn)*
Mantelbehälter *m*, **Mantelgefäß** *n* jacketed vessel
Mantelkessel *m* shell-type boiler
Mantelkühler *m* jacket cooler
Mantelmesser *npl (pap)* shell bars, bars in the shell, bars on the casing *(of a perfecting engine)*
Mantelmischung *f (rubber)* sheath[ing] compound *(as for cables)*
Mantelraum *m* shell side *(as of a heat exchanger)*
Mantelraummedium *n* shell-side medium (liquid) *(of a heat exchanger)*
Mantelrohr *n* jacketed pipe (tube)
MAO = Monoaminooxidase
Marakaibobalsam *m* Maracaibo resin *(from Copaifera specc.)*
Marantastärke *f* arrowroot *(from Maranta arundinacea L. and related specc.)*
Marbel *f (glass)* marver [plate]

marbeln *(glass)* to marver *(a gather on a flat plate)*
Marbelplatte *f (glass)* marver [plate]
Marcy-Mühle *f* Marcy [ball] mill *(having a lateral grating discharge)*
Margarine *f* margarine
~/aus Pflanzenfetten hergestellte vegetable margarine
~/aus Tierfetten hergestellte animal fat margarine
~/mit Molke hergestellte whey margarine
~/zum Tränen neigende weeping (leaking) margarine
Margarineanlage *f* margarine[-making] plant
Margarinearoma *n* margarine flavour
Margarineemulsion *f* margarine emulsion
Margarinefabrik *f* margarine factory (works)
Margarinefarbe *f* margarine colouring *(substance)*
Margarinefärbung *f* margarine colouring
Margarinefett *n* margarine fat
Margarineherstellung *f* margarine making (manufacture)
Margarineindustrie *f* margarine industry
Margarinekonservierungsmittel *n* margarine preservative
Margarineschmalz *n* margarine fat
Margarinestrang *m* strand (bar) of margarine
Margarinsäure *f* margaric acid, *heptadecanoic acid
Marihuana *n* marihuana, marijuana, hasheesh, hashish *(from Cannabis indica Lam.)*
Marinade *f (food)* pickle, souse
Marineblau *n* navy blue
Marinekohle *f* navigation coal
Marineleim *m* marine glue
Marineöl *n* marine [animal] oil
marinieren *(food)* to pickle, to souse
Mark *n* 1. *(food)* pulp; 2. *(bot)* pith
Marke *f* mark *(as of calibration)*; brand
Markenbezeichnung *f*, **Markenname** *m* brand name
Markenspitze *f* levelling wire *(of a Redwood viscometer)*
Marker-Enzym *n (bioch)* marker enzyme
Marker-Protein *n (bioch)* marker protein
Markersubstanz *f (chromat)* marker
markieren to mark; *(anal)* to label, to tag
~/mit Deuterium to deuterate
Markieren *n*/**affines** *(chromat)* affinity label[l]ing
Markierfilz *m (pap)* marking (ribbed, ribbing) felt
markiert/radioaktiv radioactively labelled, radiolabelled
Markierung *f* 1 marking; *(anal)* label[l]ing, tagging; 2. mark
~ der Siebnaht seam mark *(a defect in paper)*
~ durch die Heizplatte *(plast)* platen mark *(a defect)*
~ durch überfließendes Material skid *(a defect in injection-moulded plastics)*
~/isotope *(anal)* atom tagging
~/spritzerförmige splash *(a defect in injection-moulded plastics)*
Markierungselement *n (anal)* tracer element
Markierungssubstanz *f (anal)* tracer, *(esp chromat)* marker
Markovnikov-Addition *f* Markovnikov addition *(of hydrogen halides to aliphatic double bonds)*
Markovnikov-Regel *f (org ch)* Markovnikov's rule *(of the direction of addition to aliphatic double bonds)*
Markpapier *n*/**Chinesisches** rice paper *(from the pith of Tetrapanax papyriferum (Hook.) K. Koch)*
Marmor *m* marble
Marmorlösungsversuch *m (hyd)* marble test
Marmorpapier *n* marble[d] paper
Marsgestein *n* Martian rock
Martensit *m (met)* martensite *(the hard constituent of which quenched steel is chiefly composed)*
Martensitaushärtung *f (met)* maraging
martensitisch *(met)* martensitic
Martiusgelb *n* Martius (Manchester) yellow, acid yellow 24
Marzetti-Plastometer *n (rubber)* Marzetti plastometer
Mascara *m* mascara *(a cosmetic for colouring the eyebrows)*
Masche *f* mesh *(screening)* • **mit steigender ~** coarsened at top *(screen decks)*
Maschendrahtfüllkörper *mpl* mesh packings
Maschenweite *f* mesh size, screen aperture, clear opening
Maschenzahl *f* mesh *(number of openings per linear inch)*
Maschinenausfallzeit *f* downtime, down period
Maschinenbreite *f (pap)* width of the machine
Maschinenbütte *f (pap)* machine chest, service (pulp, supply, stuff) chest
Maschinenbüttenpapier *n* machine-made (cylinder-made) deckle-edge paper, mouldmade paper
Maschinenformen *n* machine moulding
Maschinengeschwindigkeit *f (pap)* machine speed
maschinengestrichen *(pap)* machine-coated
maschinengetrocknet *(pap)* machine-dried, cylinder-dried, steam-dried
maschinenglatt *(pap)* machine-finished, MF
Maschinenglätte *f (pap)* machine finish, MF
Maschinenglättwerk *n* calender [machine]
Maschinengraupappe *f* chip board
Maschinenkalander *m s.* Maschinenglättwerk
Maschinenöl *n* machine (machinery) oil
Maschinenpapier *n* machine[-made] paper
Maschinenpappe *f* mill board
Maschinenrichtung *f (pap)* machine direction (way), making (grain, long) direction
Maschinenrolle *f (pap)* machine (mill, jumbo) roll
Maschinenschmieröl *n s.* Maschinenöl
Maschinensieb *n (pap)* Fourdrinier wire
Maschinenstrich *m* [paper] machine coating, on-machine coating
Maschinentorf *m* machine[-cut] peat

maschinentrocken *s.* maschinengetrocknet
Maskenform *f* shell mould *(foundry)*
Maskenformen *n* shell moulding *(foundry)*
Maskenformverfahren *n* shell-moulding process, Croning process, C process *(foundry)*
maskieren *(ch, tann)* to mask, to sequester *(ions)*; *(ceram)* to mask
Maskierung *f (ch, tann)* masking, sequestration *(of ions)*; *(ceram)* masking
~ mit Formiaten *(tann)* formate masking *(of chrome liquors)*
Maskierungsmittel *n*, **Maskierungsreagens** *n* masking (sequestering) agent (reagent), sequestrant
Maskierungsvermögen *n (ch, tann)* masking (sequestering) power, masking ability; *(ceram)* masking power (ability) *(of a glaze)*
Masonite-Verfahren *n (pap)* Masonite (explosion) process *(chemigroundwood process)*
Maß *n* measure • **nach ~ aufbauen** to tailor[-make], to make to measure *(e.g. polymers)*
Massagecreme *f* massage (lubricating) cream
Maßanalyse *f* volumetric (titrimetric) analysis *(for compounds s.* Titration*)*
maßanalytisch volumetric, titrimetric
Maßbeständigkeit *f* dimensional stability
Masse *f* 1. mass, *(if loose also)* bulk; *(ceram)* body, paste; 2. *(quantitatively:)* mass, *(ch, tech esp in word compounds often loosely:)* weight
~/aktive *(phys ch)* active mass
~/atomare atomic mass
~/bildsame *(ceram)* plastic body
~/biologische *s.* Biomasse
~ des feuchten Stoffs wet weight
~/gebrannte *(ceram)* fired body
~/halbplastische *(ceram)* stiff-plastic body
~/harzige resinous matter (substance)
~ je Bogen *(pap)* weight of a sheet of paper
~ je Flächeneinheit *(pap)* substance, substance weight (number), basis (basic) weight
~ je Ries *(pap)* weight per ream
~/keramische ceramic body (paste, mix)
~ mit hohem Aluminiumoxidgehalt *(ceram)* high-alumina body
~ mit hohem Berylliumoxidgehalt *(ceram)* high-beryllia body
~ mit hohem Magnesiumoxidgehalt *(ceram)* high-magnesia body
~ mit hohem Titanoxidgehalt *(ceram)* high-titania body
~ mit hohem Tonerdegehalt *(ceram)* high-alumina body
~ mit hohem Zirconiumoxidgehalt *(ceram)* high-zirconia body
~ mit niedrigem Verlustfaktor *(ceram)* low-loss body
~/molare molar mass
~/molekulare molecular mass
~/nicht schwindende *(ceram)* non-shrinking body
~/plastische plastic material; *(ceram)* plastic body
~/reduzierte *(phys ch)* reduced mass
~/tonfreie *(ceram)* non-clay body
~/ungebrannte *(ceram)* raw body
~/weichplastische *(ceram)* soft-plastic body
Masse% *s.* Masseprozent
Masse... *s. a.* Massen...
Masseabfall *m (ceram)* body scrap
Masseänderung *f* mass change, change in mass
Masseäquivalent *n* mass equivalent
Masseaufbereitung *f (ceram)* body preparation
Masseausbeute *f (biot)* growth yield *(growth of microorganisms)*
Massedefekt *m (nucl)* mass defect
Massedosiervorrichtung *f (plast)* weight feeder (feeding device)
Masseeinheit *f* mass unit
~/atomare atomic mass unit, amu
~/vereinheitlichte atomare unified atomic mass unit
Masse-Energie-Äquivalenzprinzip *n* mass-energy equivalence principle
Masse-Energie-Beziehung *f*, **Masse-Energie-Gleichung** *f* mass-energy relation
Massefärbung *f (pap)* beater dyeing (colouring), dyeing (colouring) in the pulp
massegeleimt *(pap)* beater-sized, pulp-sized, engine-sized, E.S., sized in the engine (stuff)
Maßeinteilung *f* scale *(of a measuring instrument)*
Massekammer *f (plast)* plenum chamber
Massekeller *m (ceram)* maturing cellar
Massekonstanz *f* constant weight • **bis zur ~ glühen** to ignite to constant weight
Massekuchen *m s.* Masseplatte
Massel *f (met)* pig
Masselbeet *n*, **Masselbett** *n (met)* pig bed
Masseleimung *f (pap)* beater (pulp) sizing, engine sizing, E.S., sizing in the engine (stuff)
Masseleisen *n* pig iron, ferrocarbon
Masselgießmaschine *f (met)* pig-casting machine
Massen... *s. a.* Masse...
Massenabsorptionskoeffizient *m* mass-absorption coefficient
Massenanalyse *f* routine analysis
Massenäquivalent *n* mass equivalent
Massenbereich *m* mass range *(in mass spectrometry)*
Massenbeton *m* mass concrete
Massenbilanz *f* mass balance
Massenbilanzgleichung *f* mass-balance equation, continuity equation
Massenchromatographie *f* mass chromatography, MC
Massendefekt *m* mass defect
Massendichte *f* mass density
Masseneffekt *m* mass effect
Massenerhaltung *f* conservation of mass (matter)
Massenerhaltungssatz *m* law of conservation of mass (matter)

Massenfluß *m* flux
Massenfragmentographie *f (anal)* mass fragmentography, MF, selected ion monitoring, SIM
Massenkonzentration *f* mass per unit volume
Massenkultivierung *f (biot)* large-scale cultivation
Massenmischungsverhältnis *n* mass mixing ratio
Massenpeak *m* **im Massenspektrum** parent [mass] peak
Massenschwund *m s.* Massedefekt
Massenskala *f* mass scale
Massenspektrogramm *n* mass spectrogram
Massenspektrograph *m* mass spectrograph
~/Astonscher Aston mass spectrograph
~/doppeltfokussierender double-focus[s]ing mass spectrograph
Massenspektrographie *f* mass spectrography
Massenspektrometer *n* mass spectrometer
Massenspektrometrie *f* mass spectrometry, MS
massenspektrometrisch mass-spectrometric, by mass spectrometry
Massenspektroskopie *f* mass spectroscopy
massenspektroskopisch mass-spectroscopic, by mass spectroscopy
Massenspektrum *n* mass spectrum
Massenstrom *m* mass flux
Massenstromdichte *f* mass current density
Massenstück *n s.* Wägestück
Massensuszeptibilität *f* mass (specific) susceptibility, susceptibility per gram *(in magnetization)*
Massentransport-Term *m (chromat)* mass-transfer term
Massenverhältnis *n* mass ratio
~ flüssig zu fest mass ratio of liquid to solid
Massenverteilungsverhältnis *n (chromat)* mass distribution ratio, capacity factor
Massenwert *m s.* Massewert
Massenwirkungsgesetz *n* law (principle) of mass action, mass-action expression (law), Guldberg and Waage law
Massenwirkungskonstante *f* equilibrium constant
Massenzahl *f s.* Massezahl
Massenzucht *f (biot)* large-scale cultivation
Masseplatte *f (filtr)* pulp disk, filter pad *(consisting of filter aid)*
Massepolymerisation *f* mass (bulk) polymerization
Masseprozent *n* percentage by mass, mass percentage
Massequirl *m (ceram)* [mixing] blunger *(a vat with stirrers for mixing clay)*
massereich *(nucl)* massive
Massescherben *mpl (ceram)* pitchers
Masseschlagmaschine *f (ceram)* kneading machine (table), kneader
Masseschlicker *m (ceram)* body slip
Massestrang *m (ceram)* clay column
Massestück *n s.* Wägestück
Masseteil *n* part by weight
Masseübergangszone *f* adsorption zone (wave)
Masseveränderung *f s.* Masseänderung
Masseversatz *m (ceram)* batch
Massewert *m* mass value
Massey-Papier *n* Massey [process-coated] paper
Massezahl *f* [nuclear] mass number, nuclear number
Massezusammensetzung *f (ceram)* body composition
Massezylinder *m (plast)* injection (shooting, plasticating) cylinder
Massicot *m* massicot, lead ochre *(a yellow powder consisting of lead(II) oxide)*
mäßig gentle, slight *(heating)*
massiv massive, solid
Massivguß *m (ceram)* solid casting
Massivreifen *m* solid[-rubber] tyre, *(Am)* band tire
Maßkolben *m (lab)* measuring flask, volumetric (graduated) flask
Maßlöffel *m (lab)* measuring spoon
Maßlösung *f* standard solution
~ einer Lauge standard base
~ einer Säure standard acid
maßschneidern *s.* aufbauen/gezielt
Maßstab *m* scale • **in großem (großtechnischem)** ~ on a large scale • **in halbtechnischem** ~ on a pilot-plant scale, on a semicommercial scale • **in präparativem** ~ on a preparative scale
Maßstab[s]vergrößerung *f (tech)* scale-up, scaling-up
Maßzylinder *m* measuring (graduated) cylinder
Masterbatch *m (rubber)* masterbatch, mother stock • **Masterbatches herstellen** to mix into a masterbatch, to masterbatch • **mit Masterbatches mischen** to masterbatch
Mastikation *f (rubber)* mastication
~ auf Walzwerken open-mill mastication
~/heiße hot mastication
~/kalte cold mastication
Mastikator *m (rubber)* masticator
Mastix *m* mastic [gum], mastix, gum (Chios) mastic, pistachia galls *(from Pistacia lentiscus L.)*
~/Amerikanischer American mastic *(from Schinus molle L.)*
Mastixharz *n s.* Mastix
mastizieren *(rubber)* to masticate
Mastiziermaschine *f (rubber)* masticator
Mastkultur *f s.* Hauptkultur
Masurium *n s.* Technetium
Masut *m* maz[o]ut, masut
Material *n* material, substance, matter
~/abgeröstetes *(met)* calcine
~/aus der Schmelze kristallisiertes bulk-crystallized material
~/basisches feuerfestes basic refractory [material]
~/ferroelektrisches ferroelectric [material, substance]
~/ferromagnetisches ferromagnetic [material, substance]
~/feuerfestes refractory [material]
~/filmbildendes film-forming material (substance), film former, filmogen
~/halbleitendes semiconducting material

~/lichtempfindliches *(phot)* sensitive (sensitized) material
~/mineralisches mineral matter (substance)
~/neutrales feuerfestes neutral refractory [material]
~/saures feuerfestes acid refractory [material]
~/schmelzkristallisiertes bulk-crystallized material
~/spaltbares *(nucl)* fissionable material
~/thermoadhäsives thermoadhesive [material]
~/zu reformierendes *(petrol)* reformer feedstock
~/zu verarbeitendes [feed]stock
Materialänderung *f s.* Materialveränderung
Materialbilanz *f* material balance
Materialfehler *m* fault, defect, flaw
Materialfeuchte *f* moisture content wet weight basis
Materialfluß *m* flux of material
Materialveränderung *f* material change, change of material
Materialzerstörung *f* **durch Mikroorganismen** biodeterioration of materials
Materie *f* matter
~/feste solid [matter]
materiell material
Materieteilchen *n* particle of matter, material particle
Materiewelle *f* matter (de Broglie) wave
Materiewellenlänge *f* de Broglie wavelength
Mathieson-Quecksilberzelle *f*, **Mathieson-Zelle** *f* Mathieson [mercury] cell *(electrolysis)*
Matrix *f* matrix, *(geol, ceram also)* groundmass
Matrixanpassung *f (biot)* matrix designing
Matrixbestandteil *m* matrix element
Matrixeffekt *m (phys ch)* matrix [interference] effect
Matrize *f* [mould] cavity *(of a compression mould)*; *(bioch)* template
Matrizenmechanik *f* matrix (quantum) mechanics
Matrizenname *m (nomencl)* replacement name
Matrizen-Ribonucleinsäure *f s.* Messenger-Ribonucleinsäure
Matrizentheorie *f* template theory *(of antibody formation)*
matt mat[t], dull, lustreless *(esp surfaces)*; flat, dead *(esp colours)* • **~ werden** to dull
Mattätze *f (glass)* frosting
mattätzen *(glass)* to frost
Mattbraunkohle *f* dull brown coal
Mattglanz *m* low lustre (gloss); matt (dull) finish, *(tann also)* dead finish
Mattglasur *f (ceram)* matt glaze
Mattheit *f* mattness, dullness *(esp of surfaces)*; flatness, deadness *(esp of colours)*
Matthias-Streifen *m (chromat)* tapered strip
mattieren to mat, to dull *(esp surfaces)*; to flat, to deaden *(esp colours)*; *(glass)* to frost; *(text)* to delustre
~/mit Sandstrahl *(glass)* to sandblast
Mattierungsmittel *n (coat)* flatting agent; *(text)* delustrant, delustring (dulling) agent
Mattkohle *f* dull coal
Mattlack *m* flat varnish
Mattsalz *n (glass)* frosting agent
Mauerwerk *n* brickwork
Mauerziegel *m* [building] brick
mauken *(ceram)* to mature, to age, to sour
Maukkeller *m (ceram)* maturing cellar
Maul *n* inlet *(of a jaw breaker)*
Maulpresse *f* jaw-type press, gap type press, open-side (open-gap, C-frame) press
Maulwurfpumpe *f* close-coupled pump
Mauvein *n***[/Perkins]** mauvein[e], Perkin's mauve (purple, violet) *(a quinone dye)*
Maximadämpfer *m* maximum suppressor *(polarography)*
Maximaldosis *f* maximal dose
Maximalladung *f* saturation (limiting) charge *(as of dust particles with electrostatic precipitation)*
Maximalschwärzung *f (phot)* maximum density
Maximalvalenz *f* maximum valency
~/negative maximum negative valency
~/positive maximum positive valency
Maximum *n* maximum, peak
~/verdecktes *(cryst)* hidden maximum
Maximumazeotrop *n* maximum-boiling azeotrope, high-boiling azeotrope
Maximum-Siedepunkt *m* maximum boiling point
Maxwell-Boltzmann-Statistik *f* Maxwell-Boltzmann statistics
Maxwell-Boltzmann-Verteilung *f* Maxwell-Boltzmann distribution *(of particle velocities)*
Mazeral *n (coal)* maceral, constituent
Mazeralgruppe *f (coal)* maceral group
Mazeration *f* maceration
Mazerator *m* macerator, blendor
mazerieren to macerate
Mazis *m* mace *(from Myristica fragrans Houtt.)*
McCabe-Thiele-Verfahren *n (distil)* McCabe-Thiele method (construction) *(for estimating the number of plates)*
MCD = Magnetocirculardichroismus
McDougall-Ofen *m* McDougall furnace (roaster) *(a multihearth roaster)*
McLafferty-Umlagerung *f* McLafferty rearrangement *(with fragmentation in mass spectrometry)*
McLeod-Manometer *n*, **McLeod-Vakuummeter** *n* McLeod gauge
MCPA *s.* 2-Methyl-4-chlorphenoxyessigsäure
McQuaid-Ehn-Probe *f* McQuaid-Ehn test *(for determining particle sizes)*
Mechanik *f* **der Fluide** fluid mechanics
Mechanismus *m* mechanism, machinery *(of a reaction)*
~/elektronischer electronic mechanism *(of catalysis)*
~/geordneter ordered mechanism
~/katalytischer catalytic mechanism
~/nichtsequentieller *(bioch)* ping-pong mechanism
~/radikalischer free-radical mechanism

~/sequentieller *(bioch)* sequential (single-displacement) mechanism
~/ungeordneter random mechanism
Mechanochemie *f* mechanochemistry
mechanochemisch mechanochemical
Mechlorethamin *n* chlormethine, mechlorethamine, mustine, **N*-di-(2-chloroethyl) methylamine hydrochloride
MED = mikrowellenemissionsspektralphotometrischer Detektor
Median[wert] *m (anal)* median [value] *(of measurements)*
Mediator *m (bioch)* mediator *(substance acting as a messenger)*
Medikament *n s.* Arzneimittel
Medium *n* 1. medium *(for compounds s. a.* Substrat*)*; 2. *s.* Nährmedium
~/aggressives (angreifendes) aggressive medium
~/strömendes flowing fluid; fluid medium *(fluid-bed technology)*
~/umgebendes circumambient medium
Medium-Processing-Channel-Ruß *m (rubber)* medium processing channel black, MPC black
Medium-Thermal-Ruß *m* medium thermal black, MT black
Medizinalöl *n* medicinal oil
Meeresablagerung *f (geol)* marine sediment
Meeresgrund *m (geol)* ocean floor
Meereswasser *n s.* Meerwasser
Meerrettichperoxidase *f* horse-radish peroxidase
Meersalz *n* sea (marine) salt, *(if obtained by solar evaporation also)* solar (bay) salt
Meerschaum *m (min)* sea foam, meerschaum, sepiolite *(a phyllosilicate)*
Meerwasser *n* sea (ocean) water
meerwasserbeständig resistant to sea water
Meerwasserbeständigkeit *f* resistance to sea water
Meerwasserentsalzung *f* desalination of sea water
meerwasserresistent *s.* meerwasserbeständig
Meerwasserverdampfung *f* sea-water evaporation
Meerwasserverschmutzung *f*, **Meerwasserverunreinigung** *f* marine pollution, pollution of ocean water
Meerwein-Ponndorf-Verley-Carbonylreduktion *f* Meerwein-Ponndorf-Verley reduction
Meerwein-Schuster-Reaktion *f* Meerwein-Schuster reaction *(for arylating alkenes)*
M-Effekt *m s.* Mesomerieeffekt
Mehl *n (food)* flour, *(if coarsely ground:)* meal; *(tech, ch)* flour, dust, *(if coarser:)* meal, powder
~/angereichertes *s.* ~/vitaminiertes
~/vitaminiertes *(food)* enriched flour
mehlartig *s.* mehlig
Mehlbleichmittel *n* flour-bleaching agent
Mehlbleichung *f* flour bleaching
Mehleiweiß *n s.* Mehlprotein
mehlig floury, mealy, farinaceous
Mehligkeit *f* mealiness
Mehlprotein *n* flour (cereal) protein
Mehlstoff *m (pap)* flour
Mehlverbesserungsmittel *n* flour improver *(for increasing the baking qualities)*
mehratomig polyatomic
Mehrbahnofen *m (ceram)* multipassage kiln
Mehrbandtrockner *m* multistage belt dryer, multiple-belt [tunnel] dryer, multiconveyor [tunnel] dryer
mehrbasig polybasic, multibasic *(acid)*
Mehrbasigkeit *f* polybasicity
Mehrbereichsöl *n* multigrade oil
Mehrdeckersiebmaschine *f* multideck (multiple-deck) screen
Mehrelektronenatom *n* many-electron atom
Mehrenzymsystem *n (biot)* multienzyme complex (system)
Mehretagenofen *m* multihearth (multiple-hearth) furnace
Mehretagenpresse *f* multidaylight (multiple-daylight) press, multiplaten press
Mehretagenröstofen *m* multihearth (multiple-hearth) roaster (roasting furnace)
~ nach Herreshoff Herreshoff roaster (furnace)
~ nach McDougall McDougall roaster (furnace)
~ nach Nichols Nichols roaster (furnace)
~ nach Wedge Wedge roaster (furnace)
Mehrfachapparat *m (tech)* multiplo [unit]
Mehrfachbindung *f* multiple bond
Mehrfachdurchgang *m* double passing *(of radiation in spectrometers)*
Mehrfachelektrode *f* multiple electrode
Mehrfachentwicklung *f (chromat)* multiple development
Mehrfachform *f s.* Mehrfachwerkzeug
Mehrfachhalogenierung *f* polyhalogenation
Mehrfachion *n* polyion
Mehrfachkeilstreifen *m (chromat) multiple tapered strip with paper cut like saw-teeth*
Mehrfachpunktschreiber *m* multipoint recorder
Mehrfachreflexion *f* multiple reflection
Mehrfachresistenz *f (biot)* multiple resistance
Mehrfachsäulensystem *n (chromat)* multiple column
Mehrfachschicht *f* multilayer, multimolecular [adsorbed] layer
Mehrfachstreuung *f (phys ch)* multiple (plural) scattering
Mehrfachsubstitution *f* polysubstitution
Mehrfachverdampfer *m* multiple-effect evaporator
Mehrfachwerkzeug *n (plast)* multi-impression mould, *(Am)* multi-cavity mold; *(plast)* composite mould *(containing dissimilar impressions within a common bolster)*
~ mit getrennten Füllräumen separate-pot mould
Mehrfachzerfall *m (nucl)* multiple (branched) disintegration (decay), branching
Mehrfachzyklon *m* multiple[-unit] cyclone
Mehrfarbendruck *m* [multi]colour printing

Mehrfarbeneffekt *m* multicolour[ed] effect
mehrfarbig multicolour[ed], polychromatic; *(cryst)* pleochroic, polychroic
Mehrfarbigkeit *f* polychromatism; *(cryst)* pleochro[-mat]ism, polychroism
mehrfunktionell polyfunctional
mehrgängig multipass *(e.g. heat exchanger)*
Mehrgutapparat *m* multiproduct unit
Mehrhalskolben *m (lab)* multinecked flask
Mehrkammereindicker *m* tray thickener
~ **mit parallelgeschalteten Kammern** balanced tray thickener
Mehrkammermühle *f* [multi]compartment mill, compound mill
Mehrkammerofen *m* multichamber kiln
Mehrkammerrohrmühle *f s.* Mehrkammermühle
Mehrkammerzentrifuge *f* multichamber centrifuge
Mehrkanalanalysator *m (spectr)* multi-channel analyser
~**/optischer** optical multi-channel analyser, OMA
Mehrkanaldurchschubofen *m (ceram)* multipassage kiln
Mehrkerngebilde *n* polynuclear entity
mehrkernig polynuclear
Mehrkernkomplex *m* polynuclear complex
Mehrkolbenpumpe *f* multipiston pump
Mehrkomponentenanalyse *f* multicomponent analysis
Mehrkomponentengemisch *n* multicomponent mixture
Mehrkomponentensystem *n* multicomponent system
Mehrkörperextraktionsanlage *f* pot plant *(liquid-solid extraction)*
Mehrkörperkräfte *fpl (phys ch)* many-body forces
Mehrkörperproblem *n (phys ch)* many-body problem
Mehrkörperverdampfung *f s.* Mehrstufenverdampfung
mehrladig *s.* mehrwertig
mehrlagig multi-ply
Mehrmulden-Unterschubrost *m* multiple-retort [underfeed] stoker
Mehrnährstoffdünger *m* mixed (multinutrient, compound) fertilizer
Mehrpendelmühle *f* multiroll mill
Mehrphasensystem *n* multiphase system
mehrphasig multiphase
Mehrplatten[schnell]gefrierapparat *m* multiplate freezer
Mehrpressenschleifer *m (pap)* pocket grinder
Mehrproduktenapparat *m* multiproduct unit
mehrprotonig polybasic *(acid or base)*
Mehrrundsiebmaschine *f (pap)* multicylinder (multivat) machine
mehrsäurig polyacid, multiacidic *(base)*
Mehrscheiben[sicherheits]glas *n* laminated safety [sheet] glass, laminated glass
Mehrscheibenversprüher *m* multiple-disk atomizer
Mehrscheibenzerstäuber *m* multiple-disk atomizer
Mehrschichtenadsorption *f* multilayer (multimolecular-layer) adsorption
Mehrschichtenfilter *n* multilayer filter, multimedia (mixed-media, graded-density) filter
Mehrschichtenfilterbett *n* multimedia (graded) bed
Mehrschichtenfiltration *f* mixed-media filtration
Mehrschichten[sicherheits]glas *n s.* Mehrscheibensicherheitsglas
mehrschichtig multi-ply
Mehrschneckenextruder *m (plast)* multiscrew extruder
Mehrstoffgemisch *n* multicomponent mixture
Mehrstoffkatalysator *m* mixed catalyst
Mehrstoffsystem *n* multicomponent system
mehrsträngig multistranded *(e.g. macromolecular chains)*
Mehrstromwärmeübertrager *m* multipass exchanger
Mehrstufenbleiche *f (pap)* multistage bleaching
Mehrstufeneindampfung *f s.* Mehrstufenverdampfung
Mehrstufenkompressor *m* multistage compressor
Mehrstufenpolarogramm *n* multiple polarogram
Mehrstufenschubzentrifuge *f* multistage reciprocating-pusher centrifuge
Mehrstufenseparator *m (petrol)* multistage separator
Mehrstufensynthese *f* many-step synthesis
Mehrstufenverdampfer *m* multieffect evaporator, multistage (multiple-effect, cascade) evaporator
Mehrstufenverdampfung *f* multieffect evaporation, multistage (multiple-effect) evaporation
Mehrstufenverdichter *m* multistage compressor
Mehrstufenwäscher *m* multistage washer
mehrstufig multistage, multiple-stage, multistep
Mehrwalzenbrecher *m* multiroll crusher
Mehrwalzenmühle *f* multiroll mill
Mehrwalzenstuhl *m* multiroll mill
Mehrweg[e]hahn *m* multiport plug valve
mehrwertig multivalent, polyvalent, polyad; polybasic *(acid or base)*; polyhydric *(alcohol, phenol)*
Mehrwertigkeit *f* multivalence, polyvalence; polybasicity *(of an acid or base)*
mehrzählig *s.* mehrzahnig
mehrzahnig, mehrzähnig multidentate, polydentate *(coordination chemistry)*
Mehrzellenelektrodialysator *m* multimembrane electrodialyser
Mehrzellenflotationsgerät *n*, **Mehrzellenflotationsmaschine** *f* multicell floatation machine
Mehrzentrenbindung *f* multicentre bond
Mehrzentrenreaktion *f* multicentre reaction
Mehrzweckreinigungsmittel *n* all-purpose cleaner
Meiler[haufen] *m* pile, heap *(for producing charcoal)*
M-Einheit *f (plast)* monofunctional unit, M unit *(for building up polymers)*
Meisenheimer-Komplex *m (org ch)* Meisenheimer complex (compound, adduct)

Meißel *m* **für hartes Gebirge (Gestein)** *(petrol)* hard-formation bit, rock bit
~ für lockeres Gebirge (Gestein) soft-formation bit
Meitnerium *n* Mt meitnerium *(element 109)*
MEK methyl ethyl ketone, MEK, ethyl methyl ketone, butan-2-one
MEK-Benzol-Entparaffinierungsanlage *f (petrol)* MEK-benzene dewaxing plant
MEK-Benzol-Verfahren *n (petrol)* MEK-benzene [dewaxing] process
MEK-Entparaffinierung *f (petrol)* MEK dewaxing
Méker-Brenner *m (lab)* Meker burner
Mekkabalsam *m* Mecca balsam, balm of Gilead *(from Commiphora opobalsamum (L.) Engl.)*
Mekonsäure *f* meconic acid, 3-hydroxy-4-pyrone-2,6-dicarboxylic acid
MEK-Verfahren *n (petrol)* MEK [dewaxing] process
Melamin *n* melamine, triaminotriazine
Melamin-Formaldehydharz *n*, **Melaminharz** *n* melamine[-formaldehyde] resin
Melamin-Phenolharz *n* melamine-phenolic resin
Melampyrin *n*, **Melampyrit** *m s.* Dulcitol
Melangedruck *m (text)* vigoureux printing
Melangegarn *n* mixture yarn *(made from fibres of different colour)*
Melanoidin *n* melanoidin[e] *(colouring matter and aromatic ingredient of malt)*
melanokrat *(geol)* melanocratic *(containing dark minerals)*
Melanoliberin *n (bioch)* *melanoliberin, melanotropin-releasing hormone
Melasse *f (sugar)* [sugar house] molasses, treacle
melassebildend *(sugar)* molasses-forming, melassigenic
Melasseentzuckerung *f* desugarizing of molasses
Melasseschnitzel *npl (sugar)* molasses-dried-beet pulp
Melassesirup *m s.* Melasse
Meldeeinrichtung *f*, **Melder** *m* alarm
Meldolablau *n* Meldola's blue, new blue R, basic blue 6
Melibiose *f* melibiose *(a disaccharide)*
Melierung *f (pap)* mottling
Melilotsäure *f* melilotic acid, *o*-hydrocoumaric acid, 3-*o*-hydroxyphenylpropionic acid
Melinophan *m (min)* melinophane *(a sorosilicate)*
Melioration *f (agric)* amelioration, melioration, amendment
meliorieren *(agric)* to ameliorate, to meliorate
Melissenöl *n* melissa oil, [lemon] balm oil *(from Melissa officinalis L.)*
Melissinsäure *f* *triacontanoic acid, *(deprecated:)* melissic acid
Melissylalkohol *m* melissyl alcohol, myricyl alcohol *(loosely for triacontan-1-ol or hentriacontan-1-ol)*
Melkfett *n* milking grease
Mellithsäure *f* mellitic acid, benzenehexacarboxylic acid
Membran *f* membrane, diaphragm, partition [wall]
~ für Umkehrosmose reverse osmosis membrane (barrier)
~/halbdurchlässige *s.* ~/semipermeable
~/ionenaustauschende ion-exchange membrane
~/selektiv-permeable permselective membrane
~/semipermeable semipermeable membrane
Membranelektrode *f* membrane electrode
Membranfilter *n* membrane filter
Membranfiltration *f* membrane filtration
Membranfluß *m (bioch)* membrane flow
membrangebunden *(bioch)* membrane-bound
Membrangleichgewicht *n* membrane equilibrium
~/Donnansches Donnan [membrane] equilibrium
Membranhydrolyse *f* membrane hydrolysis
Membrankolbensetzmaschine *f (min tech)* diaphragm-actuated jig
Membrankompressor *m* diaphragm compressor
Membranlipid *n (bioch)* membrane lipid
Membranosmometer *n* membrane osmometer
Membranpotential *n* membrane potential
Membranpumpe *f* diaphragm pump
Membranreaktor *m (biot)* ultrafiltration reactor
Membransortierer *m* diaphragm screen
Membrantransport *m (bioch)* membrane transport
Membranventil *n* diaphragm valve
Membranverdichter *m* diaphragm compressor
Membranwiderstand *m* flow resistance of the membrane *(reverse osmosis)*
Memory-Effekt *m (nucl)* memory effect
Mendeleev-System *n*, **Mendelejew-System** *n* Mendeléeff [periodic] system, Mendeleev [periodic] table
Mendelevium *n* Md mendelevium
Mendheim-Ofen *m (ceram)* Mendheim kiln *(a gas-fired chamber kiln)*
Menge *f* quantity, quantum, amount, *(of an agent to be applied also)* dose
~/adsorbierte amount adsorbed
~/äquivalente equivalent
~/aufgenommene intake
~/heilende *(pharm)* therapeutic dose
~/schädigende *(pharm)* toxic dose
~/theoretische (theoretisch nötige) theoretical quantity
mengen to mix, to mingle, to blend
Mengenbestimmung *f* quantitation
Mengenmesser *m* quantity meter
Mengenstrom *m* mass flux
Mengenstrommesser *m* flow (rate, fluid) meter, flowmeter
~ für Flüssigkeiten liquid meter
Mengenstrommessung *f* flow measurement
Mengenverhältnis *n* proportion, ratio
Meni-Öl *n* Meni oil *(from Lophira alata Banks)*
Meniskus *m* meniscus
Meniskusvisierblende *f* meniscus reader *(titration)*
Mennige *f* minium, red lead [oxide] *(lead(II) tetraoxoplumbate(IV))*
Mennigepaste *f* red-lead paste

Menopausengonadotropin *n (bioch)* human menopausal gonadotropin, hMG
Menschenserumalbumin *n s.* Humanserumalbumin
Menschutkin-Reaktion *f* Menschutkin reaction *(of amines with haloalkanes)*
Mensur *f* measuring (graduated) cylinder, graduate
Menthadien *n (org ch)* menthadiene
p-**Menthan** *n p*-menthane, 1-isopropyl-4-methylcyclohexane
Menthen *n* menthene, *(specif)* 1-isopropyl-4-methylcyclohexene
Menthon *n* menthone, 2-isopropyl-5-methylcyclohexanone
Mercapsol-Verfahren *n* Mercapsol process *(for desulphurizing petroleum distillates)*
Mercaptal *n* dithioacetal, *(old term:)* mercaptal *(any of a class of condensation products of thiols with aldehydes)*
Mercaptan *n* thiol, *(org ch deprecated, petrol still often:)* mercaptan
mercaptanarm *(petrol)* poor in thiols (mercaptans), low-thiol
Mercaptanentfernung *f (petrol)* thiol (mercaptan) removal
Mercaptanextraktion *f (petrol)* thiol (mercaptan) extraction
mercaptanreich *(petrol)* rich in thiols (mercaptans), high-thiol, mercaptan-rich
Mercaptanumwandlung *f (petrol)* thiol (mercaptan) conversion
Mercaptid *n* thiolate, *(old term:)* mercaptide *(a metallic derivative of a thiol)*
Mercaptobenzoesäure *f* mercaptobenzoic acid
Mercaptoessigsäure *f* mercaptoacetic acid, thioglycollic acid
Mercaptoethansäure *f s.* Mercaptoessigsäure
Mercaptoethylierung *f* mercaptoethylation
Mercaptogruppe *f* –SH thiol group, mercapto (sulphanyl, sulphydryl) group
Mercaptol *n* dithioketal, *(old term:)* mercaptol[e] *(any of a class of condensation products of thiols with ketones)*
2-Mercaptopropionsäure *f* 2-mercaptopropionic acid, thiolactic acid
Mercaptorest *m s.* Mercaptogruppe
Mercapto-Schwefel *m* mercaptan sulphur
mercurierbar capable of being mercurized *(organic compounds)*
mercurieren to mercurize, to mercurate *(organic compounds)*
Mercurierung *f* mercur[iz]ation *(of organic compounds)*
Mercurimetrie *f* mercurimetry *(titration with a mercury(II) nitrate solution)*
mercurimetrisch mercurimetric
Mercurodesilylierung *f* mercurodesilylation
Mercurometrie *f* mercurometry *(titration with a mercury(I) nitrate solution)*
mercurometrisch mercurometric
Mergel *m* marl
mergelig marly
Mergelton *m* marl clay
Merichinon *n (org ch)* semiquinone
Meroxen *m (min)* meroxene *(the most common variety of biotite)*
Merrifield-Synthese *f* Merrifield [peptide] synthesis, solid-phase protein synthesis
Mersol *n* alkane sulphochloride
Merzerisation *f (text)* mercerization
~/spannungslose mercerization without tension, slack mercerization
~ unter Spannung mercerization with tension
Merzerisierechtheit *f (text)* fastness to mercerization
merzerisieren *(text)* to mercerize
Merzerisierhilfsmittel *n (text)* mercerizing assistant
Merzerisierlauge *f (text)* mercerizing bath
Merzerisiermaschine *f (text)* mercerizing machine
~/kettenlose chainless mercerizing machine
Mescalin *n* mescaline, *β-[3,4,5-trimethoxyphenyl]-ethylamine
Mesitinspat *m*, **Mesitit** *m (min)* mesitine [spar], mesitite *(ferroan magnesite)*
Mesitylen *n* mesitylene, *1,3,5-trimethylbenzene
Mesitylen-2-carbonsäure *f* mesitoic acid, *2,4,6-trimethylbenzoic acid
Mesityloxid *n* mesityl oxide, *4-methylpent-3-en-2-one
Mesoatom *n s.* Mesonenatom
Meso-Form *f (org ch)* meso form
mesoionisch mesoionic
Mesokolloid *n* mesocolloid
mesomer mesomeric
Mesomerie *f* mesomerism, resonance
~ zwischen Ionenbindung und kovalenter Bindung ionic-covalent resonance
Mesomeriebegriff *m* concept of mesomerism (resonance)
Mesomerieeffekt *m* mesomeric (electromeric) effect, resonance effect
Mesomerieenergie *f* mesomeric (resonance) energy
mesomeriefrei free from mesomerism, resonance-free
Mesomeriepfeil *m* double-headed arrow
mesomeriestabilisiert resonance-stabilized
Mesomeriestabilisierung *f* resonance stabilization
Mesomerievorstellung *f s.* Mesomeriebegriff
mesomorph mesomorphic, mesomorphous
Meson *n (nucl)* meson *(an elementary particle)*
~/neutrales neutral meson, neutretto
μ-Meson *n* μ-meson, mu meson, muon
π-Meson *n* π-meson, pi meson, pion
Meson[en]atom *n* mesonic atom
Mesonenfeld *n* meson field
Mesonentheorie *f* meson theory

mesonisch mesonic
Mesopause *f* mesopause
Mesoperiodat *n* mesoperiodate, pentaoxoiodate(VII)
Mesophase *f* mesophase, liquid crystal
Mesoprobe *f* *meso sample, semimicro sample *(0.1 to 0.01 g)*
Mesosphäre *f* mesosphere
Meso-Spuren-Analyse *f* *meso-trace analysis *(sample weight 0.1 to 0.01 g)*
Mesotartarsäure *f s.* Mesoweinsäure
Mesothorium *n* mesothorium
Mesotron *n s.* Meson
Mesoverbindung *f (org ch)* meso compound
Mesoweinsäure *f* mesotartaric acid
Mesoxalsäure *f* mesoxalic acid, oxomalonic acid, *oxo-propanedioic acid
meßbar measurable
Meßbarkeit *f* measurability
Meßbehälter *m* measuring vessel
Meßbereich *m* measuring (measurable) range, range of measurement
Meßblende *f* orifice meter (flowmeter, plate)
Meßbrücke *f* bridge [circuit]
Meßdüse *f* flow nozzle *(flow measurement)*
Meßeinrichtung *f* measuring device
Meßelektrode *f* measuring electrode, indicating (indicator) electrode
messen to measure
~/nochmals to remeasure
Messenger *m***/sekundärer (zweiter)** *(bioch)* second messenger
Messenger-Ribonucleinsäure *f*, **Messenger-RNA** *f (bioch)* messenger ribonucleic acid, messenger RNA, mRNA
Messer *m s.* Meßgerät
Messer *n* knife, *(pap also)* bar
~ der Kegelstoffmühle *(pap)* jordan bar
~/feststehendes *(pap)* dead knife
Messerabstand *m (pap)* spacing between bars
Messerblock *m (pap)* beater (dead) plate, bed-plate *(of a Hollander beater)*
Messerentrinder *m (pap)* knife (disk) barker (barking machine)
Messergarnierung *f (pap)* filling, tackle *(of a Hollander beater)*; set of bars *(of a refiner)*
Messerholländer *m (pap)* Hollander, Hollander beater (beating engine), stuff (pulp) engine, pulp grinder
Messernarbe *f (glass)* shear mark *(a defect)*
Messerscheibenentrinder *m s.* Messerentrinder
Messerstreichmaschine *f (plast)* knife coater
Messerwalze *f (pap)* Hollander roll, beater (beating, knife) roll
Messerwellenquerschneider *m (pap)* revolving-knife cutting machine, rotary [knife] cutter
Messerwerk *n s.* Messerblock
Meßfehler *m* measurement error
Meßfühler *m* sensor, sensing element
Meßgefäß *n* measuring vessel, graduate
Meßgenauigkeit *f* measuring (measurement) accuracy, accuracy in (of) measurement, precision of measurement
Meßgerät *n* measuring device (instrument), meter, *(esp for measuring pressure, volume:)* gauge
~/anzeigendes indicating instrument
~/naßchemisches wet test meter
~/registrierendes recording instrument, recorder
Meßgerinne *n* flume *(flow measurement)*
Meßglas *n* measuring glass
Meßglied *n* measurement element
Meßgröße *f* quantity being *or* to be measured
Messing *n* brass
~ mit hohem Zinkgehalt high[-zinc] brass
~ mit niedrigem Zinkgehalt low[-zinc] brass
α-Messing *n* alpha brass
β-Messing *n* beta brass
Messingblüte *f (min)* aurichalcite *(a basic copper zinc carbonate)*
Messingdichtung *f* brass gasket
Messinggewicht *n s.* Messingwägestück
Messingwägestück *n* brass weight
Meßinstrument *n s.* Meßgerät
Meßkammer *f* measuring chamber
Meßkapillare *f*, **Meßkapillarrohr** *n* stem *(of a thermometer)*
Meßkelch *m (lab)* measuring cup
Meßkolben *m (lab)* measuring (volumetric) flask
~/auf Auslauf geeichter delivery flask
~ mit [einer] Marke one-mark volumetric flask
Meßlatte *f* gauge stick
Meßlöffel *m (lab)* measuring spoon
Meßmethode *f* method of measurement, measurement technique
Meßpipette *f* measuring (graduated) pipette
~ nach Mohr Mohr measuring pipette
Meßreihe *f* series of measurements
Meßstab *m* dip stick *(for measuring liquid level)*
Meßstelle *f* measuring point; measuring junction *(of a thermocouple)*
Messung *f* measurement
~ des Dipolmoments dipole measurement
~ des Formänderungsrestes *(rubber)* permanent-set test *(in tension or compression)*
~/diskontinuierliche discontinuous measuring
~/elektrometrische electrometric measurement
~/kontinuierliche continuous measuring
~ nach einer Skale scaling
~/potentiometrische potentiometric measurement
~/röntgenographische X-ray measurement
~/turbidimetrische turbidimetric (turbidity) measurement
Meßungenauigkeit *f* measuring (measurement) accuracy, accuracy in (of) measurement, precision of measurement
Meßvorrichtung *f s.* Meßeinrichtung
Meßwagen *m (petrol)* measuring van
Meßwalze *f (pap)* metering roll

Meßwert *m* measured value
Meßwertbündelung *f (anal)* bunching
Meßzelle *f* measuring cell
Meßzylinder *m* measuring (graduated) cylinder
~ **nach Crow** Crow receiver *(a receiver with a conical base)*
Mesylat *n* mesylate, methane sulphonate
Mesylchlorid *n* methanesulphonyl chloride
Mesylester *m s.* Mesylat
Mesylierung *f* mesylation
Metaaluminat *n* M^IAlO_2 metaaluminate
Meta-Anthrazit *m* meta-anthracite
Metaarsenat(III) *n* M^IAsO_2 metaarsenite
Metaarsenat(V) *n* M^IAsO_3 metaarsenate
Metaarsen(V)-säure *f* metaarsenic acid
Metaaurat(III) *n* M^IAuO_2 metaaurate(III)
metabolisierbar *(bioch)* metabolizable
metabolisieren *(bioch)* to metabolize
Metabolismus *m (bioch)* metabolism
Metabolit *m (bioch)* metabolite, product of metabolism
~**/primärer** primary metabolite, primary product of metabolism
~**/sekundärer** secondary metabolite, secondary product of metabolism
Metabolitenkompartimentierung *f (bioch)* metabolic compartmentation
Metabolitkonzentration *f (biot)* product concentration
Metaborat *n* M^IBO_2 metaborate, dioxoborate
Metaborsäure *f* metaboric acid, dioxoboric acid
Metachromverfahren *n (text)* metachrome [dyeing] method, chromate [dyeing] method, chromate process
Metacinnabarit *m (min)* metacinnabar[ite] *(mercury(II) sulphide)*
meta-dirigierend meta-directing
Meta-Isomer[e] *n* meta isomer, *m*-isomer
Metakaolin *m* metakaolin
Metakieselsäure *f* metasilicic acid, trioxosilicic acid
Metaldehyd *m* metaldehyde
Metall *n* metal
~**/edles** noble metal
~**/gediegenes** native [metal]
~**/gelochtes** perforated metal
~**/gepulvertes** powder[ed] metal, metal powder
~**/passives** passive metal
~**/Rosesches** Rose's metal (alloy)
~**/schmelzflüssiges** molten metal
~**/unedles** base metal
~**/Woodsches** Wood's metal
Metallabscheidung *f* metal deposition
~**/katodische** cathodic deposition of metals
Metallaggregat *n* metallic aggregate
metallaktiviert metal-activated
Metallalkyl *n s.* Alkylmetallverbindung
Metallamid *n* M^INH_2 [metal] amide, azanide
Metallatom *n* metal[lic] atom
Metallauftrag *m* 1. metal application; 2. metallic coating
Metallbad *n* [molten-]metal bath
Metallbadfärbeverfahren *n (text)* molten-metal [dyeing] process, Standfast molten-metal process
Metallbadfärbung *f (text)* molten-metal dyeing
Metallbadverfahren *n s.* Metallbadfärbeverfahren
Metallbeize *f* metallic mordant
Metallbindung *f* metal[lic] bond, metal-metal bond
Metallborhydrid *n*, **Metallborwasserstoff** *m* $M^I[BH_4]$ tetrahydridoborate, hydridoborate
Metallcarbid *n* metal carbide
Metallcarbonyl *n* metal carbonyl, carbonyl [compound]
Metallchelat *n s.* Metallchelatkomplex
Metallchelatbindung *f* metal-chelate bond
Metallchelatchromatographie *f* metal-chelate affinity chromatography
Metallchelatkomplex *m*, **Metallchelatverbindung** *f* metal-chelate complex (compound), metal chelate
Metallchemie *f* metal chemistry
Metalldampflaser *m* metal vapour laser
Metallderivat *n* metal derivative
Metalldesaktivator *m* metal deactivator
Metall-Dewar-Gefäß *n* Dewar [vessel] *(for holding liquid gases)*
Metalldichtung *f* metal[lic] packing, metal seal *(for moving parts)*; metal gasket *(for parts without relative motion)*
Metall-Donatorbindung *f* metal-donor bond
metallen metallic
Metallenzym *n* metalloenzyme
Metallextraktion *f* metal extraction
Metallfarbe *f* metallic ink *(printing)*
Metallfärbung *f* metal colouring
Metallfaser *f* metallic fibre
Metallfaserstoff *m* metallic [fibre]
Metallfilter *n* porous-metal filter
Metallflansch *m* metal flange
Metallfolie *f* metal foil
Metallform *f* [permanent] metal mould, gravity die *(foundry)*
metallfrei metal-free
metallführend metalliferous
Metallgarn *n* metallic yarn
Metallgehalt *m* metal content, *(relating to an ore also)* tenor
Metallgewebe *n* metal fabric (gauze), wire cloth (gauze) • **mit ~ abgedeckt** *(filtr)* screen-covered
Metallgewinnung *f* metal extraction
Metallgitter *n* metallic lattice
Metallglanz *m* metallic lustre
metallhaltig metal-containing, *(esp ores:)* metalliferous
Metallhüttenwesen *n* non-ferrous metallurgy
Metallhydrid *n* metal hydride
Metallierung *f (org ch)* metalation
Metall-Ion *n* metal[lic] ion
metallisch metallic
metallisieren to metallize

Metallisierung *f* metallization
Metall-Isolator-Übergang *m* metal-insulator transition, metal-nonmetal transition
Metallizität *f* metallicity
Metallkalorimeter *n*/**Nernstsches** Nernst calorimeter
Metallkatalysator *m* metal[lic] catalyst, metallo catalyst
metallkatalysiert metal-catalyzed
Metallkeramik *f s.* Pulvermetallurgie
Metallketyl *n* ketyl
Metallkleben *n* adhesive bonding of metals
Metallkleber *m*, **Metallklebstoff** *m* metal-bonding adhesive
Metallkomplex *m* metal complex
Metallkomplex-Säurefarbstoff *m* metal mordant dye
Metallkönig *m s.* Regulus
Metallkontakt *m s.* Metallkatalysator
Metallkonzentration *f*/**biologisch verfügbare** bioavailable metal level
~/toxische toxic metal level
Metallkunde *f* metallography *(in a larger sense)*, physical metallurgy
Metallkundler *m* physical metallurgist
Metall-Metall-Austausch *m* metal-metal exchange
Metallocen *n* metallocene *(organometallic coordination compound)*
Metalloenzym *n* metalloenzyme
Metalloge *m s.* Metallkundler
metallogen *(geoch)* metallogen[et]ic
Metallogie *f s.* Metallkunde
Metallograph *m* metallographer
Metallographie *f* metallography
metallographisch metallographic
Metalloid *n s.* Nichtmetall
Metalloporphyrin *n* metalloporphyrin
metallorganisch organometallic, metallo-organic, metalorganic
Metallorganyl *n s.* Verbindung/metallorganische
Metallothionein *n* metallothionein *(protein with high affinity to heavy metals)*
Metallotropie *f* metallotropy
Metalloxid *n* metal[lic] oxide
Metalloxidvernetzung *f (rubber)* metallic-oxide cure
Metallpackung *f* metal[lic] packing
Metallpapier *n* metal paper
Metallphthalocyanin *n* metal phthalocyanine
Metallpigment *n* metal[lic] pigment
Metallprotein *n* metalloprotein
Metallpuffer *m* metal buffer
Metallpulver *n* metal powder, powder[ed] metal
Metallpulverfilter *n* metal-powder filter
Metallpulverpreßling *m* powder-metal compact *(in powder metallurgy)*
Metallputzmittel *n* metal cleaner
Metallreiniger *m* metal cleaner
Metallsalzbeize *f* metallic mordant
Metallsalzdosis *f (hyd)* metal coagulant dose (dosage)
Metallsalzflockung *f (hyd)* coagulation with metal salts
Metallsalzflockungsmittel *n (hyd)* metal coagulant *(Al or Fe salt)*
Metallsalz[zugabe]menge *f s.* Metallsalzdosis
Metallschaum *m* dross
Metallschicht *f* metal[lic] coating
Metallschlauch *m* [flexible] metal hose
Metallschmelze *f* molten (fused) metal; [molten] metal bath
Metallseife *f* metallic soap
Metallsieb *n* metal (wire) screen
Metallsol *n* metal sol
Metallspatel *m (lab)* metal spatula
Metallspritzbeschichten *n s.* Metallspritzen
Metallspritzen *n* metal spraying, [spray] metallizing
Metallstearat *n* metal stearate
Metallsulfid *n* metal sulphide
Metallüberzug *m* 1. metal cladding; 2. *s.* Schutzschicht/metallische
Metallurg[e] *m* metallurgist
Metallurgie *f* metallurgy
/erzeugende production (product) metallurgy, extraction (extractive) metallurgy
~/physikalische physical metallurgy
~/verarbeitende adaptive metallurgy
metallurgisch metallurgical
Metallverbindung *f* 1. metal[lic] compound; 2. bonding (joining) of metals; *(rubber)* bonding to metals; 3. metal joint (seal) *(result of 2.)*
Metallverklebung *f s.* Metallkleben
Metall-Wasserstoff-Austausch *m* metal-hydrogen exchange
Metall-Weichstoffdichtung *f* semimetallic packing
Metallzustand *m* metallic state
metamer metameric
Metamer[e] *n* metamer
Metamerie *f* metamerism *(one form of structural isomerism)*
Metametall *n* metametal
metamorph *(geol)* metamorphic
Metamorphit *m* metamorphite, metamorphic (metamorphosed) rock
Metamorphose *f (geol)* metamorphism, metamorphosis, transition
~/kinetische (mechanische) dynamometamorphism, dynamic metamorphism
Metanilsäure *f* metanilic acid, aniline-*m*-sulphonic acid
Metaperiodat *n* $M^{I}IO_4$ metaperiodate, periodate, tetraoxoiodate(VII)
Metaperiodsäure *f* metaperiodic acid, periodic acid, tetraoxoiodic(VII) acid
Metaphosphat *n* $(M^{I}PO_3)_n$ metaphosphate
Metaphosphit *n* $M^{I}PO_2$ metaphosphite
Metaphosphorsäure *f* metaphosphoric acid
Metaplumbat(IV) *n* $M^{I}_2PbO_3$ metaplumbate(IV), trioxoplumbate(IV)

Metasilicat *n* $M^I_2SiO_3$ metasilicate, trioxosilicate
metastabil metastable
Metastabilität *f* metastability
meta-ständig meta, in meta position • **~ sein** to be [located, situated] meta
meta-Stellung *f* meta position • **in ~** in meta position, meta • **nach der ~ dirigierend** meta-directing
meta-Substituent *m* meta substituent
meta-substituiert meta-substituted, *m*-substituted
meta-Substitution *f* meta substitution
Metatellurat(VI) *n* $M^I_2TeO_4$ metatellurate(VI), tetraoxotellurate(VI)
Metathese *f* metathesis, double (mutual) decomposition
Metathesereaktion *f* metathesis (metathetical) reaction, double-decomposition reaction
metathetisch metathetic[al]
Metathioarsenat(III) *n* M^IAsS_2 metathioarsenite, dithioarsenate(III)
Metathioarsenat(V) *n* M^IAsS_3 metathioarsenate, trithioarsenate(V)
Metathiostannat(IV) *n* $M^I_2SnS_3$ metathiostannate(IV), trithiostannate(IV)
Metatitanat(IV) *n* $M^I_2TiO_3$ metatitanate(IV), trioxotitanate(IV)
Metauransäure *f s.* Uranylhydroxid
Metavanadat *n* M^IVO_3 metavanadate, trioxovanadate(V)
meta-Verbindung *f* meta compound
Metawolframat *n s.* Dihydrogendodecawolframat(VI)
Metawolframsäure *f s.* Dihydrogendodecawolframsäure
Metazinnsäure *f* metastannic acid
Metazirconat(IV) *n* $M^I_2ZrO_3$ metazirconate(IV), trioxozirconate(IV)
Meteoreisen *n* meteoric iron, iron meteorite, [holo-]siderite
Meteorit *m* meteorite
Meteringschnecke *f (plast)* metering screw *(of an extruder)*
Meteringzone *f (plast)* metering zone (section) *(of an extruder)*
Methacrolein *n*, **Methacrylaldehyd** *m* methacrolein, methacrylaldehyde
Methacrylat *n* methacrylate
2-Methacrylsäure *f* 2-methylacrylic acid, MAA, 2-methylpropenoic acid
Methacrylsäuremethylester *m* methyl methacrylate, methyl 2-methylacrylate
Methallylchlorid *n* methallyl chloride
Methämoglobin *n* methaemoglobin, haemiglobin
Methan *n* methane
Methanal *n* methanal, formaldehyde
Methanamid *n* formamide
Methanbakterien *npl* methane[-forming] bacteria
Methanbildungsreaktion *f* methane-forming reaction
Methandicarbonsäure *f* *methanedicarboxylic acid, *propanedioic acid, malonic acid
Methanfermentation *f (biot)* methane fermentation *(production of biomass with methane as carbon source)*
Methangärung *f* **[/alkalische]** *(biot, hyd)* methane fermentation *(production of methane from waste products)*
Methangewinnung *f* methane recovery
Methanisator *m s.* Methanisierungsreaktor
methanisieren to methanize *(e.g. synthesis gas)*
Methanisierung *f* methanation *(as of synthesis gas)*
~/katalytische catalytic methanation
Methanisierungsreaktor *m* methanation reactor, methanator
Methanisierungsstufe *f* methanation step
Methanol *n* *methanol, methyl alcohol
Methanolfermentation *f (biot)* methanol fermentation
methanolisch methanolic
Methanolyse *f* methanolysis
Methanoxidierer *mpl (biot)* methane-oxidizing bacteria
methanreich rich in methane, high-methane
Methansäure *f* *methanoic acid, formic acid
Methansulfonat *n*, **Methansulfonsäureester** *m* methane sulphonate, mesylate
Methansulfonylchlorid *n* methanesulphonyl chloride
Met-Hb *s.* Methämoglobin
Methenamin *n* metheneamine, hexamethylenetetramine
Methid *n (org ch)* methide
Methin *n (dye)* methine
Methinbrücke *f* =CH– methine bridge
Methinfarbstoff *m* methine dye
Methingruppe *f* =CH– methine group
Methinwasserstoffatom *n* methine hydrogen
Methionin *n* methionine, 4-methylmercapto-2-aminobutyric acid
Methode *f* method, procedure, technique
~/absteigende *(chromat)* descending technique
~/aufsteigende *(chromat)* ascending technique
~/Beckmannsche Beckmann method *(for determining molecular weights)*
~/bewährte well-tested method
~/Curtiussche Curtius method *(of decomposing acid azides for preparing primary amines)*
~ der Chemical Abstracts *(nomencl)* Chemical Abstracts method
~ der Dampfdichtebestimmung vapour-density method *(for estimating molecular weights)*
~ der freischwebenden Zone floating-zone method *(zone melting)*
~ der Gefrierpunktserniedrigung freezing-point method *(for determining molecular weights)*
~ der geneigten Platte *(phys ch)* tilting plate method *(for measuring the contact angle)*
~ der kritischen Luftmenge *(coal)* critical air blast method

~ **der linearen Kombination von Atomorbitalen** linear-combination-of-atomic-orbitals method, LCAO method
~ **der Molekularstrahlen** *(phys ch)* molecular-beam method (technique)
~ **der Molekülorbitale** molecular-orbital method, Hund-Mulliken-Lennard-Jones-Hückel method
~ **der schwebenden Zone** floating-zone method *(zone melting)*
~ **der schwingenden Scheibe** oscillating disk method *(for determining the viscosity of gases)*
~ **der Tiegelverkokung** *(coal)* crucible method
~ **der Valenzstrukturen** valence-bond method, VB method, method of valence-bond structures
~ **der wandernden Grenzflächen** *(anal)* moving-boundary method, Tiselius method, free electrophoresis
~ **des inneren Standards** *(spectr)* internal standard method
~ **des quasistationären Zustands** *(phys ch)* steady-state [approximation] method
~ **des selbstkonsistenten Feldes** self-consistent-field method
~ **des verlorenen Wachsmodells** *(met)* lost-wax process
~**/differentielle** differential method *(for obtaining kinetic data)*
~**/dynamische** dynamic method *(for determining vapour pressures)*
~**/dynamische volumetrische** dynamic volumetric method *(for preparing gas mixtures)*
~**/erprobte** well-tested method
~**/gasvolumetrische** gasometric method *(of gas analysis)*
~**/gravimetrische** gravimetric method
~**/Heumannsche** Heumann method *(for synthesizing indigo)*
~**/isopiestische** isopiestic method *(for determining molecular weights)*
~**/kolorimetrische** *(anal)* colorimetric method
~**/konduktometrische** *(anal)* conductometric (conductance) method
~**/lichtelektrische kolorimetrische** *(anal)* photocolorimetric method
~**/magnetische** *(petrol)* magnetic method
~**/potentiometrische** *(anal)* potentiometric method
~**/pulvermetallurgische** powder-metallurgical method, powder-metallurgy (powdered-metal) technique
~**/röntgenographische** *(anal)* X-ray method
~**/seismische** *(petrol)* seismic method
~**/selbstkonsistente** *(phys ch)* self-consistent method
~**/standardisierte** standard method (procedure, technique)
~**/statische** static method *(for measuring vapour pressures)*
~**/statische volumetrische** static volumetric method *(for preparing gas mixtures)*
~**/Stelznersche** *(nomencl)* Stelzner method
~**/titrimetrische** *(anal)* titrimetric method
~**/turbidimetrische** *(anal)* turbidimetric method
~**/Volhardsche** Volhard titration (method) *(for determining chlorine, bromine, or iodine)*
~ **von Čugaev-Cerevitinov** Chugaev-Zerewitinoff method *(for determining the number of hydroxyl groups)*
~ **von Manning-Shepperd** Manning-Shepperd method *(for determining alkanes)*
~ **von Rabi** *(nucl)* Rabi method
~ **von Roese und Gottlieb** [fat-]Roese-Gottlieb method *(for determining milk-fat content by extraction)*
~ **von Tausky und Shorr** *(bioch)* Taussky-Shorr method *(for determining inorganic phosphate)*
~ **von Tschugajew-Zerewitinow** *s.* ~ von Čugaev-Cerevitinov
Methodik *f* method, *(esp in scientific papers:)* experimental
Methoxid *n* CH_3OM^I methoxide, methylate
Methoxybenzen *n* methoxybenzene, methylphenyl ether, anisole
***p*-Methoxybenzoesäure** *f* *p*-methoxybenzoic acid
Methoxygruppe *f s.* Methoxylgruppe
Methoxylbestimmung *f***/Zeiselsche** Zeisel [methoxyl] determination
Methoxylgruppe *f* CH_3O- methoxyl group (residue), methoxy group
Methoxylierung *f* methoxylation
Methoxylrest *m s.* Methoxylgruppe
Methoxymercurierung *f* methoxymercuration
Methoxymethan *n s.* Dimethylether
Methylacetaldehyd *m s.* Propanal
Methylacetat *n* methyl acetate
Methylacetylen *n* *propyne, methylacetylene
3-Methylacrolein *n* 3-methylacrolein, crotonaldehyde, *but-2-enal
Methylacrylat *n* methyl acrylate
Methylal *n* methylal, *dimethoxymethane, formaldehyde dimethyl acetal
Methylalkohol *m* methyl alcohol, *methanol
methylalkoholisch methanolic
Methylamin *n* methylamine
Methylaminoessigsäure *f* methylaminoacetic acid, sarcosine
***N*-Methylanilin** *n* *N*-methylaniline
Methylat *n* CH_3OM^I methylate, methoxide
Methyläthen *n s.* Propen
Methyläthin *n s.* Propin
Methyläthylcarbinol *n s.* Butan-2-ol
Methylbenzen *n* methylbenzene, toluene
Methylbenzencarbonsäure *f s.* Methylbenzoesäure
Methylbenzoat *n* methyl benzoate
Methylbenzoesäure *f* methylbenzoic acid, toluic acid
Methylbernsteinsäure *f* methylsuccinic acid, *2-methyl-1,4-butanedioic acid

Methylbromid *n* bromomethane, methyl bromide
2-Methylbutan *n* *2-methylbutane, isopentane
3-Methylbutanal *n* *3-methylbutanal, isovaleraldehyde
Methylbutandisäure *f* *2-methyl-1,4-butanedioic acid, methylsuccinic acid
2-Methylbutan-1-ol *n* 2-methylbutan-1-ol
2-Methylbutan-2-ol *n* 2-methylbutan-2-ol
3-Methylbutan-1-ol *n* 3-methylbutan-1-ol
Methylbutinol *n* methylbutynol, MBI
3-Methylbuttersäure *f* 3-methylbutyric acid, isovaleric acid
3-Methylbutyraldehyd *n s.* 3-Methylbutanal
Methylcarboxamidin *n* methyl carboxamidine, acetamidine
Methylcellosolve *n* methylcellosolve, ethylene glycol monomethyl ether
Methylcellulose *f* methyl cellulose
2-Methylchinolin *n* 2-methylquinoline, quinaldine
4-Methylchinolin *n* 4-methylquinoline, lepidine
Methylchlorid *n* chloromethane, methyl chloride
2-Methyl-4-chlorphenoxyessigsäure *f* 2-methyl-2-chlorophenoxyacetic acid, MCPA *(a herbicide)*
Methylchlorsilan *n* methylchlorosilane
Methylcyclohexan *n* *methylcyclohexane, hexahydrotoluene
Methylen *n* 1. $:CR_1R_2$ carbene, *(specif)* $:CH_2$ carbene, methylene; 2. *s.* Methylengruppe
Methylenbernsteinsäure *f* methylenesuccinic acid, itaconic acid, *prop-2-ene-1,2-dicarboxylic acid
Methylenblau *n* methylene blue
Methylenblau[reduktions]probe *f* methylene-blue [reductase] test *(as for determining the bacterial content of milk)*
Methylenbromid *n* *dibromomethane, methylene dibromide
Methylenbrücke *f* methylene bridge
Methylenchlorid *n* *dichloromethane, methylene dichloride
Methylencyanid *n* methylene cyanide, malonitrile
Methylendiphenol *n* methylenediphenol, bisphenol
Methylengruppe *f* $=CH_2$ methylene [group], methanediyl group
Methylenhalogenid *n* methylene halide (halogenide)
Methylenierung *f* methylenation
Methyleniodid *n* *diiodomethane, methylene diiodide
Methylester *m* methyl ester
Methylether *m s.* Dimethylether
Methylethylketon *n* methyl ethyl ketone, MEK, ethyl methyl ketone, butan-2-one
Methylethylsulfid *n* ethyl methyl sulphide, methyl ethyl sulphide
Methylformiat *n* methyl formate
N-**Methylglykokoll** *n* *N*-methylglycine, sarcosine
Methylglyoxal *n* methylglyoxal, pyruvic aldehyde, *2-oxopropanal
Methylgruppe *f* CH_3- methyl group (residue)
~/ringständige ring-methyl group
Methylhalogenid *n* methyl halide (halogenide)
methylieren to methylate
Methylierung *f* methylation
~/erschöpfende exhaustive methylation
Methylierungsmittel *n* methylating agent
Methyliodid *n* iodomethane, methyl iodide
Methylkautschuk *m* methyl rubber
Methyllithium *n* methyllithium
Methylmagnesiumiodid *n* methylmagnesium iodide *(a Grignard reagent)*
Methylmaleinsäure *f* methylmaleic acid, citraconic acid, **cis*-methylbutenedioic acid
Methylmethacrylat *n* methyl methacrylate, MMA, methyl 2-methylacrylate
Methylmethan *n* *ethane, methylmethane
Methylnaphthalen *n* methylnaphthalene
Methylnatrium *n* methylsodium
Methylnitren *n* methyl nitrene
Methylolharnstoff *m* methylolurea, hydroxymethylurea
Methylorange *n* methyl orange, sodium *p*-(*p*-dimethylaminophenylazo) benzenesulphonate
Methylorange-Alkalität *f (hyd)* methyl-orange alkalinity, M alkalinity
Methylorange-Umschlag *m* methyl-orange end-point, M end-point
Methyloxiran *n* 2-methyloxirane, 1,2-epoxypropane, propylene oxide
2-Methylpentan-3-ol *n* 2-methylpentan-3-ol
4-Methylpentansäure *f* 4-methylpentanoic acid, 4-methylvaleric acid
Methylphenol *n* methylphenol, hydroxytoluene, cresol
Methylphenylether *m* methyl phenyl ether, methoxybenzene, anisole
Methylphenylketon *n* methyl phenyl ketone, acetophenone, acetylbenzene
Methylphenylsilicon *n* methyl phenyl silicone
Methylphenylsiliconharz *n* methyl phenyl silicone resin
Methylphenylsiliconöl *n* methyl phenyl silicone fluid
Methylpolysiloxan *n* *polymethylsiloxane, methyl silicone
2-Methylpropan *n* 2-methylpropane, isobutane
2-Methylpropandisäure *f* 2-methylpropanedioic acid, methylmalonic acid, ethane-1,1-dicarboxylic acid
2-Methylpropan-1-ol *n* 2-methylpropan-1-ol
2-Methylpropan-2-ol *n* 2-methylpropan-2-ol
2-Methylpropan-1-thiol *n* 2-methylpropane-1-thiol
2-Methylpropen *n* 2-methylpropene
2-Methylpropionsäure *f* 2-methylpropionic acid, isobutyric acid
Methylpropylacetylen *n* *hex-2-yne, *(deprecated:)* methylpropylacetylene
Methylpropylketon *n* methyl propyl ketone, *pentan-2-one

Methylquecksilberdicyandiamid *n* methylmercuric dicyandiamide
Methylradikal *n* [free] methyl radical
Methylrest *m s.* Methylgruppe
Methylsalicylat *n* methyl salicylate
Methylsilicon *n* methyl silicone, *polymethylsiloxane
Methylsilicongummi *m* methyl silicone rubber
Methylsiliconharz *n* methyl silicone resin
Methylsiliconöl *n* methyl silicone fluid (oil)
Methylsubstituent *m* methyl substituent
Methylsulfat *n s.* Dimethylsulfat
Methylsulfonylgruppe *f* CH_3SO_2- methylsulfonyl group
Methylsulfoxid *n s.* Dimethylsulfoxid
Methylthioethan *n* methylthioethane, methyl ethyl sulphide
Methylthiogruppe *f* CH_3S- methylthio group, methylsulfanyl group
Methylthiophen *n* methylthiophene, thiotolene
Methyltrichlorsilan *n* methyltrichlorosilane
methylverestert esterified with methyl groups
Methylviolett *n* methyl violet
Metol-Hydrochinon-Entwickler *m (phot)* metol-hydroquinone developer, M.Q. developer
Mevalonsäure *f* mevalonic acid, MVA, 3,5-dihydroxy-3-methylvaleric acid
Mezcalin *n s.* Mescalin
MF-Induktionsofen *m* coreless induction furnace
MgH *s.* Magnesiahärte
Mg-KH *s.* Magnesiumkarbonathärte
Mg-NKH *s.* Magnesium-Nichtkarbonathärte
mgl *s.* maschinenglatt
Mgl *s.* Maschinenglätte
MH *s.* Maleinylhydrazin
Miazin *n* pyrimidine, 1,3-diazine, miazine
Michael-Addition *f (org ch)* Michael condensation (reaction)
Michaelis-Arbuzov-Reaktion *f* Michaelis-Arbuzov reaction *(for making a phosphorus-carbon bond)*
Michaelis-Komplex *m (bioch)* enzyme-substrate complex
Michaelis-Konstante *f* Michaelis constant *(enzyme kinetics)*
Michaelis-Menten-Beziehung *f s.* Michaelis-Menten-Gleichung
Michaelis-Menten-Darstellung *f (bioch)* Michaelis-Menten plot
Michaelis-Menten-Gesetzmäßigkeit *f s.* Michaelis-Menten-Schema
Michaelis-Menten-Gleichung *f* Michaelis-Menten expression (relationship) *(enzyme kinetics)*
Michaelis-Menten-Kinetik *f (bioch)* Michaelis-Menten kinetics
Michaelis-Menten-Komplex *m (bioch)* Michaelis-Menten complex
Michaelis-Menten-Konstante *f* Michaelis-Menten constant, substrate saturation constant *(enzyme kinetics)*
Michaelis-Menten-Schema *n* Michaelis-Menten formalism *(enzyme kinetics)*
Mie-Streuung *f (phys ch)* Mie scattering
Migma *n (geol)* migma
Migmabildung *f*, **Migmatisierung** *f (geol)* migmatization
Migränemittel *n* anticephalalgic
Migration *f* migration, *(of ions also)* ion[ic] migration
Migrationsstrom *m* migration current
migrieren to migrate *(as of ions)*
Mikrinit *m (coal)* micrinite *(a maceral)*
mikroaerob *(biot)* microaerobic
Mikroanalyse *f* microanalysis, milligram analysis
mikroanalytisch microanalytic[al]
Mikroarbeitsweise *f s.* Mikromethode
Mikroaufnahme *f* photomicrograph
Mikroben *fpl* microbes, microorganisms *(for compounds s. a. under* Mikroorganismen*)*
Mikrobenaktivität *f* microbial activity
Mikrobenenzym *n* microbial enzyme
Mikrobestandteil *m* microconstituent, microcomponent
Mikrobestimmung *f* microdetermination, microestimation
mikrobiell microbial, microbian, microbic • **mikrobiellen Ursprungs** microbial-derived
Mikrobiologie *f* microbiology
~/industrielle (technische) industrial microbiology
mikrobiologisch microbiologic[al]
mikrobizid microbicidal *(killing microorganisms)*
Mikrobombe *f (lab)* microbomb
Mikrobrenner *m* microburner
Mikrobürette *f* microburette
Mikrochemie *f* microchemistry
mikrochemisch microchemical
Mikrochromatographie *f* microchromatography
Mikrodestillation *f* microdistillation
Mikrodichtemesser *m* microdensitometer
Mikrodosierspritze *f (chromat)* microsyringe
Mikroeinkapselung *f s.* Mikroverkapselung
Mikroelektrode *f* microelectrode
Mikroelektrophorese *f* microelectrophoresis
Mikroelement *n s.* Mikronährstoff
mikroenkapsuliert microencapsulated *(e.g. enzyme)*
mikrofibrillär microfibrillar
Mikrofibrille *f* microfibril
Mikroflocken *fpl (hyd)* microfloc
Mikroflockung *f (hyd)* microflocculation
Mikrofoto *n* photomicrograph
Mikrofotografie *f* 1. photomicrography; 2. photomicrograph
Mikrogasanlage *f* micro gas analysis
Mikrogefüge *n* microstructure
Mikrogel *n (coll)* microgel
Mikrogrammbereich *m (anal)* microgram range *(10^{-6} to 10^{-3} g)*
Mikrogramm-Methode *f (anal)* microgram method
Mikrohärte *f* microhardness

Mikroheterogenität *f* microheterogeneity
Mikrohohlperle *f* microballoon
Mikrohydrierung *f* microhydrogenation
Mikrokalorimeter *n* microcalorimeter
mikrokalorimetrisch microcalorimetric
Mikrokapsel *f* microcapsule
Mikroklimatologie *f* microclimatology
Mikroklin *m (min)* microcline *(aluminium potassium silicate)*
Mikrokolorimeter *n* microcolorimeter
Mikrokomponente *f s.* Mikrobestandteil
mikrokristallin microcrystalline
Mikroküvette *f* microcell
Mikroliterspritze *f (chromat)* microsyringe
Mikrolithotype *f (coal)* microlithotype, banded component (constituent)
Mikromanipulator *m* micromanipulator
Mikrometeorologie *f* micrometeorology
Mikrometerschraube *f* [micrometer] caliper
Mikromethode *f* micromethod, milligram (microscale) procedure
~ **von Rast** Rast micromethod, Rast [molecular weight, camphor] method
mikromolekular micromolecular
Mikron *n* micron *(dispersed particle visible in an ordinary microscope)*
Mikronährstoff *m (agric)* micronutrient, microelement, minor [nutrient] element, [nutritional] trace element
Mikroorganismen *mpl* microorganisms, microbes
• **von ~ erzeugt** microbial-derived
~/abbauende decomposers, reducers, microconsumers
~/antibiotikabildende antibiotic-producing microorganisms
~/autotrophe autotrophs
~/Belebtschlamm bildende *(hyd)* activated-sludge organisms
~/cellulolytische (celluloseabbauende) cellulolytic microorganisms
~/enzymbildende enzyme-producing microorganisms
~/genetisch (gentechnologisch) veränderte *(biot)* genetically engineered microorganisms
~/heterotrophe heterotrophs
~/industrielle (industriell genutzte) industrial microorganisms
~/mesophile mesophilic microorganisms, mesophiles *(growth optimum 20 to 45 °C)*
~/nitrifizierende nitrifiers
~/psychrophile psychrophilic microorganisms, psychrophiles *(growth optimum 5 to 20 °C)*
~/SCP-bildende SCP-producing microorganisms
~/thermophile thermophilic microorganisms, thermophiles *(growth optimum 45 to 55 °C)*
~/zersetzende (zerstörende) *s.* ~/abbauende
Mikroorganismeneiweiß *n* microbial protein
Mikroorganismenfermentation *f (biot)* microbial fermentation
Mikroorganismenfilm *m s.* Rasen/biologischer
Mikroorganismenflocken *fpl (hyd)* microbial floc
Mikroorganismengenetik *f* microbial genetics
Mikroorganismenkonzentration *f* microbial (biomass) concentration, concentration of microorganisms (suspended biomass)
Mikroorganismenkultur *f* microbial culture (population), culture of microorganisms
Mikroorganismenmasse *f (hyd)* microbial mass, biomass
Mikroorganismenmischkultur *f (biot)* mixed microbial population
Mikroorganismenoberfläche *f (biot)* microbial surface
Mikroorganismensammlung *f (biot)* collection [of cultures] of microorganisms, culture collection
Mikroorganismenstamm *m* microbial strain
~/„maßgeschneiderter" *(biot)* custom-tailored (laboratory-tailored) microbial strain
Mikroorganismensuspension *f (biot)* microbial suspension
Mikroorganismenzahl *f* microbial (microorganism) count
Mikroorganismenzucht *f*, **Mikroorganismenzüchtung** *f (biot)* microbe cultivation, cultivation of microorganisms
Mikropacksäule *f* microbore column *(gas chromatography)*
Mikroparaffin *n* micro[crystalline] wax
Mikrophorese *f (anal)* microelectrophoresis
Mikrophysik *f* microphysics
Mikropipette *f* micropipette
Mikropore *f* micropore
mikroporös microporous
Mikroprobe *f* micro sample *(< 0.01 g)*
Mikropyrometer *n* micropyrometer
Mikroradiometer *n* microradiometer
Mikroreagenzglas *n* micro test tube
Mikrosäule *f (chromat)* packed capillary column
Mikrosieb *n (hyd)* microsieve
Mikrosiebanlage *f s.* Mikrosiebfilter
Mikrosiebfilter *n (hyd)* microstrainer, microstraining filter
Mikrosiebfiltertrommel *f (hyd)* microstrainer drum
Mikrosiebfiltration *f (hyd)* microstraining
Mikrosiebgewebe *n (hyd)* microfabric
mikroskopisch microscopic
mikrosomal *(bioch)* microsomal
Mikrosonde *f* microprobe
Mikrospatel *m* micro-spatula
Mikrospur *f (anal)* micro-trace *(* 10^{-4} to 10^{-7} ppm)*
Mikro-Spuren-Analyse *f* micro-trace analysis *(* sample weight 10^{-2} to 10^{-3} g)*
Mikrostruktur *f* microstructure
Mikrosublimation *f* microsublimation
Mikrotechnik *f* 1. microtechnique, microtechnic, microscopic technique, micrology; 2. *s.* Mikromethode
Mikrotitration *f* microtitration, microanalytic[al] titration
Mikroträger *m (biot)* microcarrier *(for cell cultures)*

Mikrotröpfchen *n* microdroplet
Mikrotubulus *m (bioch)* microtubule
Mikrountersuchung *f* microexamination
Mikroverkapselung *f* [micro]encapsulation
Mikrovermischung *f* micromixing, local mixing
Mikroverunreinigung *f* micropollutant
Mikroverunreinigungen *fpl***/organische** *(hyd)* trace organics
Mikrovitrain *m*, **Mikrovitrit** *m (coal)* microvitrain
Mikrowaage *f* microchemical balance
Mikrowachs *n s.* Mikroparaffin
Mikrowellenbereich *m (spectr)* microwave region
Mikrowellendetektor *m (spectr)* microwave detector
Mikrowellen-Hohlraumresonator *m (spectr)* cavity resonator
Mikrowellenplasma *n***/kapazitiv gekoppeltes** capacitively coupled microwave plasma, CMP
Mikrowellen-Plasmadetektor *m* microwave-induced plasma detector, MPD
Mikrowellensender *m (anal)* microwave source
Mikrowellenspektroskop *n* microwave spectroscope
Mikrowellenspektroskopie *f* microwave spectroscopy
Mikrowellenspektrum *n* microwave spectrum
Mikrowellentechnik *f (anal)* microwave technique
Mikrozustand *m (phys ch)* microstate, microscopic state
Milbenbekämpfungsmittel *n*, **Milbengift** *n* acaricide, miticide
milbentötend acaricidal, miticidal
Milch *f* milk
~/dickgelegte soured milk, fermented (cultured) milk
~/eingedampfte (eingedickte) *s.* ~/kondensierte
~/entrahmte skim[med] milk, separated milk
~/evaporierte *s.* ~/kondensierte
~/fettreiche rich milk
~/gereifte ripened (acidified) milk
~/geronnene curd[s]
~/gesäuerte *s.* ~/gereifte
~/kondensierte condensed milk, evaporated (concentrated) milk
~/mit Säureweckern gesäuerte (versetzte) *s.* ~/dickgelegte
~/rekonstituierte reconstituted milk *(redissolved milk powder)*
~/saure sour milk
~/spontan gesäuerte spontaneously (naturally) soured milk
~/sterilisierte sterilized milk
~/UHT-erhitzte (ultrahocherhitzte) UHT [processed] milk
~/walzengetrocknete roller[-dried] milk powder
~/weichgerinnende soft-curd milk
Milchabsonderung *f* milk secretion
Milchalbumin *n* lactalbumin, milk albumin
milchartig milk-like, milky
Milchbehandlung *f* milk treatment
Milchbestandteile *mpl* milk constituents
Milchbutyrometer *n* lactobutyrometer
Milchchemie *f* dairy chemistry
Milchdauerwaren *fpl* milk preserves
Milcheiweiß *n* milk protein
Milchenzym *n* milk enzyme
Milcherhitzer *m*, **Milcherhitzungsapparat** *m* [milk] pasteurizer
Milcherzeugnis *n* milk product
Milcherzeugung *f* milk production
Milchfehler *m* milk defect
Milchferment *n s.* Milchenzym
Milchfett *n* milk fat
Milchfettsynthese *f* milk fat synthesis
Milchgefäß *n (bot)* laticiferous (latex) vessel
Milchgerinnungsenzym *n* milk-clotting (milk-coagulating) enzyme
Milchglas *n* milk glass
Milchglobulin *n* milk globulin
milchhaltig lactiferous, *(bot also)* laticiferous
milchig milky, *(as opposed to translucent also)* opaque
Milchindustrie *f* dairy industry
Milchkühler *m* milk cooler
Milchmargarine *f* milk margarine
Milchopal *m (min)* milk opal *(silicon(IV) oxide)*
Milchphase *f* milk phase *(in margarine making)*
Milchprodukt *n* dairy (milk) product
Milchprotein *n* milk protein
Milchpulver *n* milk powder, dry (dried) milk
Milchpulvermilch *f* reconstituted milk
Milchquarz *m* milky quartz
Milchreifung *f* milk ripening
Milchröhre *f (bot)* laticiferous (latex) tube
Milchsaft *m (bot)* latex, milky sap (juice), milk
milchsaftführend *(bot)* laticiferous, lactiferous, latex-bearing
Milchsalz *n* milk salt
Milchsäuerung *f* souring of milk
Milchsäure *f* lactic acid, hydroxypropionic acid, *(specif)* $CH_3CH(OH)COOH$ lactic acid, *2-hydroxypropionic acid
~/gewöhnliche *s. DL*-Milchsäure
~/linksdrehende *s. D*(–)-Milchsäure
(±)-Milchsäure *f s. DL*-Milchsäure
D(–)-**Milchsäure** *f* D(–)-lactic acid, laevolactic acid
d-**Milchsäure** *f s. L*(+)-Milchsäure
dl-**Milchsäure** *f s. DL*-Milchsäure
DL-**Milchsäure** *f* DL-lactic acid, ordinary lactic acid, *i*-lactic acid, lactic acid of fermentation
l-**Milchsäure** *f s. D*(–)-Milchsäure
L(+)-**Milchsäure** *f* L(+)-lactic acid, sarcolactic acid
RS-**Milchsäure** *f s. DL*-Milchsäure
S(+)-**Milchsäure** *f s. L*(+)-Milchsäure
Milchsäureanhydrid *n* lactic anhydride
Milchsäurebakterien *npl* lactic-acid[-producing] bacteria
Milchsäurebildner *mpl* lactic-acid[-producing] microorganisms, lactic-acid producers

Milchsäuredehydrase *f s.* Milchsäuredehydrogenase
Milchsäuredehydrogenase *f* lactic dehydrogenase
Milchsäureerzeuger *mpl s.* Milchsäurebildner
Milchsäureethylester *m* ethyl lactate
Milchsäuregärung *f* lactic[-acid] fermentation
Milchsäuremikroben *fpl s.* Milchsäurebildner
Milchsäurenitril *n s.* Lactonitril
Milchschleuder *f s.* Milchzentrifuge
Milchsekretion *f* milk secretion
Milchseparator *m s.* Milchzentrifuge
Milchserum *n* milk serum, whey
Milchserumprotein *n* whey (milk serum) protein
Milchspindel *f* lactodensimeter
Milchstein *f* milk stone
Milchsteinentferner *m* milk stone remover
Mlichtrockenmasse *f* milk solids
Milchverarbeitung *f* milk processing
Milchvorratstank *m* milk storage vessel
Milchwirtschaft *f* dairying
Milchzentrifuge *f* milk centrifuge, milk (cream) separator
Milchzucker *m* lactose, lactobiose, milk sugar
Milchzuckergärung *f* lactose fermentation
mild 1. mild, bland *(e.g. taste or remedy)*; 2. mild *(reaction conditions)*
Milieu *n* environment
Miller-Indizes *mpl* Miller [crystal] indices
Milliäquivalent *n s.* Milligrammäquivalent
Milligrammäquivalent *n* milliequivalent, mequiv, meq
Milligrammbereich *m (anal)* milligram range *(10^{-3} to 10^{-2} g)*
Milligramm-Methode *f (anal)* milligram method
Millimeter *mpl* **Quecksilbersäule** millimetres of mercury *(unit of pressure of fluids, 1 mm Hg = 1 Torr = 133.3 Pa)*
Millival *n s.* Milligrammäquivalent
Mills-Packard-Kammer *f* Mills-Packard chamber *(for producing sulphuric acid)*
Miloriblau *n* Milori blue *(variety of iron blue)*
Mimeographenfarbe *f* mimeograph ink
Mimosengummi *n s.* Akaziengummi
Minderheitsträger *m* minority carrier *(in a semiconductor)*
mindern to lower, to reduce, to decrease, to diminish
~/im Wert to deteriorate
Minderung *f* lowering, reduction, decrease, diminution
minderwertig of inferior quality, *(esp of raw materials:)* low-grade
Mindestaufenthaltszeit *f* minimum residence time, *(hyd also)* washout residence time *(activated-sludge process)*
Mindestbodenzahl *f (distil)* minimum number of plates (trays)
Mindestdosis *f* minimum dose (dosage)
Mindestenergie *f* minimum energy
Mindestfettgehalt *m* minimum fat content
Mindestrücklaufverhältnis *n* minimum reflux ratio
Mindesttemperatur *f* minimum temperature
Mindesttrennstufenzahl *f s.* Mindestbodenzahl
Mine *f* mine
Mineral *n* mineral
~/akzessorisches accessory mineral (component, constituent)
~/allothigenes allogenic (allothigenic) mineral, allogene, allothigene, allothogene *(transported to the site of deposition)*
~/authigenes authigenic mineral, authigene *(found at the site of formation)*
~/beigemengtes *s.* ~/akzessorisches
~/gesteinsbildendes rock-forming mineral
~/kritisches critical mineral
~/nichtmetallisches non-metallic mineral
~/primäres primary mineral
~/schweres heavy mineral
~/sekundäres secondary mineral
Mineralaggregat *n* mineral aggregate
Mineralassoziation *f* mineral association
Mineralaufbereitung *f* mineral dressing
Mineralaustauscher *m***/künstlicher** *s.* Zeolith/künstlicher
Mineralchemie *f* mineral (mineralogical) chemistry
Mineralcorticoid *n* mineralocorticoid *(a hormone)*
Mineraldüngemittel *n*, **Mineraldünger** *m* mineral (inorganic) fertilizer
Mineralfarbe *f s.* Mineralpigment
Mineralfaser *f* mineral fibre
Mineralfaserstoff *m* mineral fibre
Mineralfazies *f* mineral facies
mineralfrei mineral-matter-free, mmf
Mineralgang *m (geol)* mineral vein, mineralized lode
Mineralgehalt *n s.* Mineralstoffgehalt
Mineralgerbung *f* mineral tanning
Mineralhefe *f* mineral yeast
Mineralisation *f (geol, soil, hyd)* mineralization
Mineralisator *m (geol, ceram)* mineralizer
mineralisch mineral
mineralisieren *(geol, soil, hyd)* to mineralize
Mineralisierung *f (geol, soil, hyd)* mineralization
Mineralkermes *m* kermes mineral *(a double compound of antimony trisulphide and antimony trioxide)*
Mineralkohle *f* mineral coal, natural (fossil) coal
Mineralkombination *f (geol)* mineral association
Mineralkunde *f* mineralogy
Minerallaugung *f* mineral leaching
Mineralmörser *m* diamond (percussion) mortar
Mineralneubildung *f* neomineralization
Mineralog[e] *m* mineralogist
Mineralogie *f* mineralogy
Mineralöl *n* mineral oil
Mineralöltechnologie *f* mineral-oil technology
Mineralphosphat *n* rock (mineral) phosphate
Mineralpigment *n* manufactured mineral pigment, synthetic inorganic pigment

Mineralprovinz *f (geol)* mineral province
Mineralquelle *f* mineral spring
Mineralsalz *n* mineral salt
Mineralsalzernährung *f (agric)* mineral nutrition
Mineralsalzgehalt *m* mineral content
Mineralsäure *f* mineral acid
Mineralschwarz *n* slate black, black chalk *(a natural pigment)*
Mineralstoff *m* mineral matter (substance)
Mineralstoffdüngung *f* mineral (inorganic) fertilization
mineralstofffrei mineral-matter-free, mmf
Mineralstoffgehalt *m* mineral-matter content
Mineralstoffwechsel *m* mineral metabolism
Mineralvergesellschaftung *f (geol)* mineral association
Mineralverwitterung *f* mineral weathering
Mineralwasser *n* mineral water
Mineralwolle *f* mineral wool (cotton), rock wool
Minimaltemperatur *f* minimum temperature
Mini-Massmann-Graphitrohrküvette *f (spectr)* carbon-rod atomizer
Minimum *n* minimum
Minimumazeotrop *n* minimum-boiling azeotrope, low-boiling azeotrope
Minimum-Siedepunkt *m* minimum boiling point
Minoritäts[ladungs]träger *m* minority carrier *(in a semiconductor)*
Minton-Ofen *m (ceram)* Minton oven
minus-Stamm *m (biot)* (–) strain
15-Minuten-Entspannungstemperatur *f (glass)* annealing point
Miotikum *n (pharm)* miotic, myotic
miotisch miotic, myotic
MIR *s.* Infrarotgebiet/mittleres
Mirbanessenz *f*, **Mirbanöl** *n (cosmet)* mirbane (myrbane) oil, essence of mirbane (myrbane) *(nitrobenzene)*
Mischabwasser *n (hyd)* combined waste water
Mischanilinpunkt *m* mixed aniline point
Mischanlage *f* mixing (blending) plant
Mischapparat *m s.* Mischmaschine
Mischausrüstung *f* mixing equipment
mischbar miscible
~/begrenzt incompletely (partially) miscible
~/beliebig (in jedem Verhältnis) miscible in all proportions
~/leicht freely miscible
~/mit Wasser water-miscible
~/nicht immiscible, non-miscible
~/nicht mit Wasser water-immiscible
~/teilweise partially (incompletely) miscible
~/unbegrenzt fully miscible
Mischbarkeit *f* miscibility
~/begrenzte (teilweise) incomplete (partial) miscibility
Mischbecken *n (hyd)* mixing basin
~/vollständiges *(hyd)* well-mixed [flow] reactor, completely mixed reactor (tank)
Mischbehälter *m* mixing tank (vessel), blending tank; mixer bowl *(of a kneader)*
Mischbett *n* mixed bed, *(hyd also)* mixed ion exchange bed
Mischbett[ionen]austauscher *m* mixed-bed [ion] exchanger
Mischbettsäule *f (hyd, chromat)* mixed-bed column
Mischbett-Vollentsalzungsanlage *f (hyd)* mixed-bed demineralizer (deionizer)
Mischblende *f* orifice mixer
Mischbottich *m* mixing chest (vat)
Mischbunker *m* mixing (mixer) bin
Mischbütte *f s.* Mischbottich
Mischdünger *m* 1. mixed (dry-blended) fertilizer; 2. *s.* Mehrnährstoffdünger
Mischdüngerwerk *n* mixed-fertilizer plant, bulk mixing plant
Mischdüse *f* mixing nozzle
Mischelement *n* polyisotopic element
mischen to mix, *(esp if so that the constituents cannot be distinguished:)* to blend; *(in accordance with a recipe:)* to compound; *(esp of solids with a liquid to obtain a desired consistency:)* to temper
~/auf dem Walzwerk *(rubber)* to mill[-mix]
~ im Bleichholländer *(pap)* to potch, to poach
~/innig to mix intimately, to blend
~/mit Masterbatches (Vormischungen) *(rubber)* to masterbatch
~/sich to mix, to blend
~/wieder to re-mix
Mischen *n* **im Fertigtank** *(petrol)* batch blending
~ in der Pumpleitung *(petrol)* in-line blending
~ mit Masterbatches (Vormischungen) *(rubber)* masterbatch method of mixing, masterbatching
~ von Feststoffkomponenten dry (solid-solid) mixing (blending)
Mischer *m* 1. mixer, blender; 2. *s.* Mischbehälter
~/geschlossener closed mixer
~/kontinuierlich arbeitender continuous mixer
~/liegender horizontal mixer
~ mit Wechselbehälter change-can mixer
~/pneumatischer air-agitated mixer
~/satzweise arbeitender batch mixer
Mischer-Abscheider *m s.* Mischer-Scheider-Extrakteur
Mischerbehälter *m s.* Mischbehälter
Mischerschaufel *f* mixing blade
Mischer-Scheider-Extrakteur *m* mixer-settler *(for solvent extraction)*
Mischerz *n* complex ore
Mischfarbe *f* 1. mixed colour *(phenomenon)*; 2. *s.* Mischfarbstoff
Mischfarbstoff *m* mixed colouring matter, *(if soluble:)* mixed dye
Mischfaserfarbstoff *m* union dye
Mischflügel *m* mixing blade, agitator (stirrer) blade, agitator
Mischfolge *f (rubber)* order of adding materials (compounding ingredients)

mischfunktionell *(bioch)* mixed-function
Mischgalvanispannung *f s.* Mischpotential
Mischgarn *n* mixture yarn
Mischgas *n* mixed gas
Mischgefäß *n s.* Mischbehälter
Mischgeschwindigkeit *f* rate of mixing
Mischgestein *n* hybrid rock, migmatite
Mischgewebe *n* union fabric
Mischgewebefärben *n* union dyeing
Mischgut *n* material being *or* to be mixed (blended)
Mischholländer *m (pap)* [mixing] potcher, poacher, potching (poaching) engine
Mischindikator *m* mixed indicator
Mischkalk *m* compound lime fertilizer
Mischkammer *f* 1. mixing chamber *(as of a condenser)*; 2. *(rubber)* compounding room
Mischkatalysator *m* mixed catalyst
Mischkeramik *f* cermet, ceramal, ceramel, ceramet
Mischkessel *m* mixing vessel
Mischklebstoff *m* mixed adhesive
Mischkneter *m* kneader-mixer
Mischkollergang *m* muller mixer
Mischkomplex *m* mixed complex *(coordination chemistry)*
Mischkomponente *f* blend component
Mischkondensation *f (plast)* co-condensation
Mischkondensator *m* [direct-]contact condenser
~/barometrischer barometric condenser
~/nasser wet (jet) condenser
Mischkristall *m* mixed crystal, mix-crystal, solid solution
Mischkultur *f (biot)* mixed culture
Mischleiter *m* mixed conductor
Mischmaschine *f* mixing machine, mixer, blender
Mischmetall *n* misch metal *(an alloy consisting of rare-earth metals)*
Mischoctanzahl *f* blending octane number, blending value
Mischöl *n* mixed oil; mixed-base petroleum (crude oil, crude)
Mischoxid *n* mixed oxide
Misch-OZ *f s.* Mischoctanzahl
Mischphase *f* mixed phase
~/labile *(bioch)* metabolic pool, central area of metabolism
Mischpolymerisation *f s.* Copolymerisation
Mischpotential *n* mixed (mixture) potential
Mischreaktor *m* [stirred-]tank reactor, stirred tank, well-mixed [flow] reactor, completely mixed reactor
Mischreaktorkaskade *f* series of stirred-tank reactors, series of perfect mixers, stirred-tank reactors in series
Mischrührphase *f (hyd)* rapid mix period, rapid mixing step *(flocculation)*
Mischsalz *n* mixed salt
Mischsalzkatalysator *m*, **Mischsalzkontakt** *m* mixed-salt catalyst
Mischsäure *f (tech)* mixed acid, nitrating acid *(consisting of concentrated nitric acid and sulphuric acid)*
Mischschmelzpunkt *m* mixed melting point
Mischspannung *f* mixed (mixture) potential
Mischstrom *m* mixed feed *(combination of cocurrent and countercurrent flow)*
Mischstromführung *f* mixed-feed operation *(as in a multiple-effect evaporator)*
Mischsystem *n (hyd)* combined system [of sewerage], combined sewer system
Mischtank *m* mixing (blending) tank
Misch-Trenn-Behälter *m* mixer-settler *(for solvent extraction)*
Mischtrommel *f s.* Trommelmischer
Misch- und Reaktionszone *f (hyd)* mixing and reaction zone *(of a solids contact clarifier)*
~/primäre primary mixing and reaction zone
~/sekundäre secondary mixing and reaction zone
Mischung *f* 1. mixing, blending; 2. mixture, mix, blend; *(rubber)* compound, stock, composition
~/azeotrope azeotropic mixture, azeotrope
~/eutektische eutectic [mixture]
~ für die Schlauchseele *(rubber)* inner-tube compound
~ für Kordgummierung *(rubber)* cord-rubberizing compound
~ für Walzen *(rubber)* roll compound
~/konjugierte *(phys ch)* conjugate solution
~/rußgefüllte (rußhaltige) *(rubber)* [carbon-]black compound
~/schwach gefüllte *(rubber)* low-load compound
~/ungefüllte *(rubber)* pure gum compound
~/unvulkanisierte *(rubber)* green compound
Mischungsbestandteil *m* blend component, ingredient; *(rubber)* compounding ingredient
Mischungsenthalpie *f* enthalpy of mixing
Mischungsentropie *f* entropy of mixing, mixing entropy
Mischungsentwickler *m*, **Mischungsfachmann** *m* *(rubber)* compound designer, compounder
Mischungsgrad *m* degree of mixing
Mischungsherstellung *f (rubber)* compounding
Mischungshöhe *f* mixing height *(of pollutants in the atmosphere)*
Mischungskalorimeter *n* water calorimeter
Mischungskoeffizient *m* mixing coefficient *(bonding theory)*
Mischungslücke *f* miscibility gap
Mischungspunkt *m* **bei gleichbleibender Temperatur/kritischer** plait (isothermal critical) point *(of a two-component system)*
~/kritischer 1. consolute (critical solution) point *(regarding the composition of a two-component system)*; 2. *s.* Mischungstemperatur/kritische
Mischungsrezept *n*, **Mischungsrezeptur** *f (rubber)* compound[ing] formula, mix[ing] formula, compounding recipe, recipe of mix
Mischungsspektrum *n* mixture spectrum

Mischungstemperatur f/kritische consolute (critical solution) temperature *(of a two-component system)*
~**/obere kritische** upper consolute temperature
~**/untere kritische** lower consolute temperature
Mischungsverhältnis *n* 1. mixing (blending) ratio, formula; 2. abundance ratio *(of isotopes)*
Mischungswärme *f* heat of mixing
Mischungszustand *m* mixing state
Mischverfahren *n* 1. mixing process; 2. *s.* Mischsystem
Mischvorgang *m* mixing process
Mischvorrichtung *f* mixing device
Mischvorschrift *f* mixing instruction, *(rubber also)* order of milling
Mischwalze *f* mixing (homogenizing) roll
Mischwalzwerk *n* mixing mill (rolls)
Mischwasserkanal *m (hyd)* combined storm and sanitary sewer
Mischwasserkanalisation *f*, **Mischwasserkanalnetz** *n (hyd)* combined storm and sanitary sewerage
Mischwerk *n* mixer
Mischzeit *f* blending time
Mischzone *f* mixing section (zone)
Mißbildung *f* malformation
Mißfärbung *f (glass)* discoloration
Mißpickel *m (min)* mispickel, arsenic[al] iron, arsenopyrite, arsenical pyrite *(iron sulpharsenide)*
Miszella *f* miscella *(an extractant containing an extracted oil or grease)*
mitabscheiden to co-deposit
Mitabscheidung *f* co-deposition
Mitchell-Hypothese *f (bioch)* chemiosmotic[-coupling] hypothesis *(of phosphorylation)*
mitfallen to coprecipitate
mitfällen to coprecipitate
Mitfallen *n* coprecipitation
Mitfällung *f*[**/induzierte**] coprecipitation
mitführen to entrain, to carry over (off) *(as in a gas stream)*
Mitführen *n* entrainment, carry-over *(as in a gas stream)*
Mitführungsmethode *f* gas saturation method *(for measuring vapour pressures)*
Mitisgrün *n s.* Grün/Schweinfurter
mitlaufen *(anal)* to co-chromatograph
~ **lassen** to co-chromatograph
Mitläufer *m (rubber)* wrapper, leader; *(text)* back [grey] cloth
Mitläufergewebe *n*, **Mitläuferstoff** *m (rubber)* lining, liner
Mitnehmer *m* 1. *(distil)* entrainer, entraining (azeotroping, separating) agent, azeotrope-former; 2. flight *(of a conveyor)*; lifter *(as in a rotary dryer)*
Mitnehmerblech *n* lifting flight (plate) *(as in a rotary dryer)*
Mitnehmerleiste *f* lifting (lifter) bar *(as in a rotary dryer)*
Mitnehmerstange *f (petrol)* kelly
mitochondrial *(biol)* mitochondrial
Mitochondrien-DNA *f (bioch)* mitochondrial deoxyribonucleic acid, mtRNA
Mitochondrion *n* mitochondrion *(cytochemistry)*
mitogen *(bioch)* mitogenic, mitogenetic, inducing mitosis
Mitogen *n (bioch)* mitogen *(a substance which induces mitosis)*
mitogenetisch *s.* mitogen
Mitose *f (bioch)* mitosis • ~ **auslösend** *s.* mitogen
Mitosegift *n (bioch)* mitotic poison
Mitosehemmer *m (bioch)* mitotic inhibitor
mitreißen to entrain, to carry over (off) *(as in a gas stream)*; to carry down *(in a precipitate)*
Mitreißen *n* entrainment, carry-over *(as in a gas stream)*; carrying down *(in a precipitate)*
Mittel *n* 1. agent; *(pharm)* preparation, remedy; 2. *s.* Mittelwert
~**/absetzverhinderndes** antisettling (suspending) agent
~**/absorptionsbeschleunigendes (absorptionsförderndes)** absorbefacient
~**/adstringierendes** astringent, styptic
~**/aktivierendes** 1. activator *(floatation)*; 2. *(met)* energizer *(for promoting carburization)*
~**/alkylierendes** alkylating agent
~**/analgetisches** analgesic, pain-reliever
~**/anregendes** analeptic, central nervous system stimulant
~**/antikonzeptionelles** contraceptive
~**/antiperspirierendes** *s.* ~/schweißhemmendes
~**/antiseptisches** antiseptic [agent]
~**/antistatisches** antistatic [agent]
~**/appetitanregendes** stomachic
~**/arithmetisches** arithmetic mean *(statistics)*
~**/aufkohlendes** *(met)* carburizing agent, [case-hardening] carburizer
~**/auswurfförderndes** expectorant
~**/bakteriostatisches** bacteriostat[ic]
~**/belebendes** activator *(floatation)*
~**/blähungstreibendes** carminative
~**/blasenziehendes** vesicant, blister agent
~**/blutdruckerhöhendes** hypertensor
~**/blutdrucksenkendes** antihypertensive (hypotensive) drug, blood pressure depressant
~**/blutstillendes** haemostatic, styptic
~**/chemotherapeutisches** chemotherapeutic agent
~**/depilierendes** depilator, depilatory [agent], depilitant, hair remover
~**/desinfizierendes** disinfectant
~**/desodor[is]ierendes** deodorizer, deodorant
~**/die Milchsekretion förderndes** milk-ejecting agent, galactagogue
~**/dispergierendes** dispersing agent, dispersant
~**/diuretisches** diuretic
~**/drückendes** depressant *(floatation)*
~**/empfängnisverhütendes** contraceptive
~**/endometatoxisches** *(agric)* systemic poison

~/entzündungshemmendes antiphlogistic
~/erweichendes *(tech)* softener, softening agent; *(cosmet)* emollient, softener
~/feuerhemmendes fire-retardant agent, fire retardant
~/fiebersenkendes antipyretic
~/galenisches *(pharm)* galenical
~/galle[n]treibendes cholagogue
~/gefäßerweiterndes vasodilator, vasodepressor
~/gefäßkontrahierendes (gefäßverengendes) vasoconstrictor, vasoexcitor
~ gegen Beschlagen antidim
~ gegen Bluthochdruck *s.* ~/blutdrucksenkendes
~ gegen depressive Verstimmung antidepressant
~ gegen Durchfall antidiarrhoeic, styptic
~ gegen Epilepsie antiepileptic
~ gegen Erbrechen antiemetic
~ gegen Festfressen *(plast)* antiseize agent
~ gegen Gicht antiarthritic
~ gegen Kesselstein descaling agent, descaler
~ gegen Krätze scabicide, scabieticide
~ gegen Malaria antimalarial
~ gegen Nervenschmerzen antineuralgic
~ gegen Rheuma[tismus] antirheumatic
~ gegen Rückvergrauung *(text)* antiredeposition agent
~ gegen Schaumbildung antifoam[ing] agent, antifrothing (froth-preventing) agent, foam inhibitor
~ gegen Schnecken molluscacide, molluscide
~ gegen Wasserschnecken aquatic molluscacide
~ gegen Zuckerkrankheit antidiabetic
~/geometrisches geometric mean *(statistics)*
~/gerinnungshemmendes (gerinnungsverzögerndes) anticoagulant
~/geruchsbeseitigendes (geruchszerstörendes) deodorizer, deodorant
~/gewogenes weighted mean *(statistics)*
~/harntreibendes diuretic
~/hauterweichendes skin softener
~/hydrophobierendes hydrophobing agent, water repellent
~/innertherapeutisches *s.* ~/systemisches
~/indifferentes *(pharm)* placebo
~/insektenabschreckendes (insektenvertreibendes) insect repellent, insectifuge
~/keimbildendes *(cryst)* nucleation (nucleating) agent, nucleator
~/keimfreimachendes (keimtötendes) germicidal agent, germicide, disinfectant
~/koagulierendes coagulating agent, coagulant, coagulator
~/kohlendes *s.* ~/aufkohlendes
~/Konvulsionen auslösendes (erregendes) convulsant
~/korrodierendes (korrosives) corrosive (agent], corrodent
~/kräftigendes roborant, tonic
~/krampflösendes antispasmodic, spasmolytic
~/maskierendes *s.* Maskierungsmittel
~/menstruationsförderndes emmenagogue
~/mikrobizides microbicide
~/oberflächenaktives surface-active agent, surfactant
~/örtlich schmerzstillendes local analgesic
~/oxidierendes oxidizing agent, oxidant, oxidizer
~/oxytozisches uterotonic, oxytocic [agent]
~/passivierendes 1. depressant *(floatation)*; 2. passivator *(for metals)*
~/pharmazeutisches pharmaceutic[al]
~/pilztötendes fungicide
~/protektives (protektiv wirkendes) protective
~/pupillenerweiterndes mydriatic
~/pupillenverengendes miotic, myotic
~/reduzierendes reducing agent, reductant, reducer
~/regelndes modifying agent, modifier *(floatation)*
~/schaumerzeugendes foaming agent, frothing (froth-forming) agent, foamer, frother
~/schleierdämpfendes (schleierverhütendes) *(phot)* antifog[ging] agent, antifoggant
~/schmerzlinderndes (schmerzstillendes) analgesic, pain-reliever
~/Schüttelkrämpfe auslösendes (erregendes) convulsant
~/schwangerschaftsverhütendes contraceptive
~/schweißhemmendes (schweißlinderndes) antiperspirant, antihidrotic, perspiration check
~/schweißtreibendes sudorific, diaphoretic
~/spermienabtötendes (spermizides) spermatocide, spermicide
~/stärkendes roborant, tonic
~/sulfonierendes sulphonating agent
~/systemisches systemic [chemical, poison, insecticide]
~/taubes gangue [mineral], matrix
~/tonisierendes *s.* ~/stärkendes
~/unwirksames *(pharm)* placebo
~/verdauungsförderndes digestive stimulant, digester
~/virentötendes (viruzides) virucide, viricide, viricidal agent
~/vorbeugendes (vorbeugend wirkendes) prophylactic, protective
~/wasserabspaltendes dehydrating agent, dehydrator
~/wasserabstoßendes (wasserabweisendes) water repellent
~/wasserdichtmachendes waterproofing agent
~/wasserentziehendes dehydrating agent, dehydrator
~/wehenerregendes *s.* ~/oxytozisches
~/wurmabtreibendes helminthagogue, vermifuge
~/wurmtötendes vermicide
~/wurmwidriges anthelmint[h]ic
~ zur Erhöhung der Viskosität viscosity enhancer
~ zur Herabsetzung der Viskosität viscosity depressant (decreaser)
~ zur *p*H-Regelung *p*H regulator *(floatation)*

~ zur Verhinderung von Ablagerungen *(hyd)* deposit control agent (chemical)
~/zusammenziehendes *(pharm)* astringent, styptic
mittelaktiv *(nucl)* medium-level active
Mittelbenzin *n* medium[-heavy] gasoline
Mittelbrechen *n* intermediate crushing
Mitteldestillat *n* middle distillate
Mitteldrucksynthese *f* medium-pressure synthesis
mittelfein moderately fine
mittelfeinkörnig medium-grained
Mittelfrequenzinduktionsofen *m* high-frequency induction furnace, coreless induction furnace
mittelgekohlt medium-carbon *(e.g. steel)*
mittelgrob moderately coarse
Mittelgut *n* middlings product, intermediate material *(classifying)*
mittelhart medium-hard *(material to be crushed)*; half-hard *(cold-rolled metal)*
Mittelhartzerkleinerung *f* size reduction of medium-hard materials
Mittelkammer *f s.* Mittelraum
mittelkörnig medium-grained
Mittelöl *n* middle oil
Mittelpech *n* medium-hard (medium-soft) pitch
Mittelprodukt *n s.* Mittelgut
Mittelproduktfüllmasse *f (sugar)* intermediate fillmass, second-grade massecuite, B massecuite
Mittelproduktzucker *m* intermediate sugar, B sugar
Mittelraum *m* middle chamber (compartment) *(as of an electrolytic cell)*
Mittelsand *m* medium-grained sand
Mittelschneide *f* principal (central) knife-edge *(of a balance)*
Mittelschwerbenzin *n s.* Mittelbenzin
Mittelsieder *m* medium boiler *(e.g. a solvent)*
mittelständig centrally located
mittelstark moderately strong *(e.g. acid)*
Mittelstellung *f* intermediate position
Mitteltemperaturentgasung *f s.* Mitteltemperaturverkokung
Mitteltemperaturkoks *m* medium-temperature coke
Mitteltemperaturverkokung *f* medium-temperature carbonization
Mitteltöne *mpl (phot)* middle tones
mittelviskos moderately viscous, medium-viscosity
Mittelwand *f (pap)* midfeather, midwall, midriff, centre division *(of a Hollander beater)*
Mittelwert *m* average, av., mean [value]; expected value, expectation *(statistics)*; expectation value *(quantum mechanics)*
Mittelzuckerfüllmasse *f s.* Mittelproduktfüllmasse
mitten to centre
mittig on-centre
Mixer *m* mixer
Mixer-Settler-Extraktor *m s.* Mischer-Scheider-Extrakteur
Mixtur *f (pharm)* mixture

Mizell *n s.* Mizelle
mizellar micellar
Mizellarstrang *m* micellar string
Mizellarstruktur *f* micellar structure
Mizellartheorie *f* micellar theory (hypothesis)
Mizellbildungskonzentration *f***/kritische** *(coll)* critical micelle concentration, c.m.e.
Mizelle *f* micelle, micell[a], *(in fibrous material also)* crystallite
~/inverse inverted (inverse) micelle, reversed (reverse) micelle
Mizellgerüst *n* micellar framework
Mizellkolloid *n* micellar (association) colloid
Mizellkonzentration *f***/kritische** *s.* Mizellbildungskonzentration/kritische
Mizelloberfläche *f* micellar surface
MKR-... *(magnetische* ***Kernresonanz****)* *s.* NMR-...
m-Lösung *f* molar solution
MMK *s.* Kraft/magnetomotorische
MO *s.* Molekülorbital
Möbelpolitur *f* furniture polish
mobil mobile
mobilisieren to mobilize
Mobilisierung *f* mobilization
Mobilzeit *f s.* Durchflußzeit
Möbius-System *n* Möbius system *(a cyclic conjugated hydrocarbon)*
Modacrylfaser *f* modacrylic (modified acrylic) fibre
Modacrylfaserstoff *m* modacrylic (modified acrylic) fibre
Modacrylnitrilfaser *f* modacrylonitrile fibre
Modacrylnitrilfaserstoff *m* modacrylonitrile fibre
Mode *f (spectr)* [transmission] mode, mode of vibration *(propagation of guided waves)*
Modeldruck *m (text)* block printing
Modell *n* model
~/ausschmelzbares *s.* ~/verlorenes
~ der dichtesten statistischen Packung *(phys ch)* dense random packing model
~ der harten Kugeln *(phys ch)* hard-sphere model
~/globuläres globular (subunit) model *(of cell membranes)*
~/räumliches three-dimensional model
~/strukturelles structural model
~/verlorenes investment (fusible alloy) pattern *(foundry)*
Modellexperiment *n* model experiment
Modellfermentation *f (biot)* model fermentation
Modellreaktion *f* model reaction
Modellverbindung *f* model compound
Modellversuch *m* model experiment
Modenkopplung *f (spectr)* mode locking
Moder *m (soil)* duff *(one form of humus)*
Moderator *m*, **Moderatorsubstanz** *f (nucl)* moderator, slowing-down agent
moderieren *(nucl)* to moderate, to slow down
Modifikation *f* modification
~/allotrope allotropic modification (form), allotrope *(of an element)*

~/geometrisch isomere geometric[al] isomer
~/posttranslationelle *(bioch)* posttranslational modification
Modifikationsmittel *n* modifying agent, modifier
Modifikator *m (text)* modifier, modifying agent
modifizieren to modify
Modifizierer *m (glass)* network modifier
Modifizierung *f* modification
Modul *m* modulus
~/Youngscher Young's modulus [of elasticity], elastic modulus
Modul *n* module *(as of an analyser)*
Modulationsfrequenz *f (spectr)* modulation frequency
Modulationspolarographie *f (anal)* modulation polarography
Modulator *m (bioch)* modulator
~/fördernder stimulatory (positive) modulator
~/hemmender inhibitory (negative) modulator
~/negativer *s.* ~/hemmender
~/positiver *s.* ~/fördernder
Moellon *n* moellon, degras *(a fatty substance used in dressing leather)*
Mohnalkaloid *n* opium alkaloid
Mohnöl *n* poppy[-seed] oil
Mohnsäure *f s.* Mekonsäure
Mohs-Skala *f* Mohs' [hardness] scale
Moiré-Effekt *m (text)* moiré effect
moirieren *(text)* to cloud
moiriert *(text)* cloudy
Mojonnier-Test *m (food)* Mojonnier [solids] test; Mojonnier [fat] test
Mokkastein *m (min)* Mocha stone *(chalcedony containing dendritic inclusions)*
Mol *n* mole, mol
molal molal
Molalität *f* molality, molal concentration
molar molar
Molardispersion *f s.* Molekulardispersion
Molarität *f* molarity, molar concentration
Molarkonzentration *f s.* Molarität
Molch *m (petrol)* go-devil
Molekel *f s.* Molekül
Molekül *n* molecule
~/aktives (aktiviertes) active molecule, activated (energized) molecule
~/angeregtes excited molecule
~ aus gleichen Atomen *s.* ~/homonukleares
~ aus verschiedenartigen Atomen *s.* ~/heteronukleares
~/elektronisch angeregtes electronically excited molecule
~/energiereicheres *s.* ~/aktives
~/geknäueltes coiled molecule
~/gelöstes solute molecule
~/heteronukleares heteronuclear molecule
~/heteronukleares zweiatomiges heteronuclear diatomic molecule
~/homonukleares homonuclear molecule
~/homonukleares zweiatomiges homonuclear diatomic molecule
~/homöopolares (homöopolar gebundenes) homopolar molecule
~/langgestrecktes long molecule
~/lineares linear molecule
~/mehratomiges polyatomic molecule
~ mit angeregten Elektronen electronically excited molecule
~ mit fluktuierenden Bindungen fluxional molecule
~/nichtpolares non-polar molecule
~/polares polar molecule
~/scheibenförmiges disk-like molecule
~/stäbchenförmiges rod-like molecule
~/stabförmiges rod-like molecule
~/trigonal ebenes trigonal planar molecule
~/unpolares non-polar molecule
~/van-der-Waalssches van der Waals molecule
~/vernetztes cross-linked molecule
~/verzweigtes branched molecule
~/vielatomiges polyatomic molecule
~/zweiatomiges diatomic molecule
Molekül... *s. a.* Molekular...
Molekülaggregat *n* molecular (molecule) aggregate, aggregate of molecules
Molekülaggregation *f* molecular aggregation, aggregation of molecules
Molekülaktivierung *f* molecular activation
Molekülanziehung *f* molecular attraction
molekular molecular
Molekular... *s. a.* Molekül...
Molekularattraktion *f* molecular attraction
Molekularbewegung *f* molecular motion (movement)
~/Brownsche Brownian motion (movement)
Molekularbiologie *f* molecular biology
Molekulardestillation *f* molecular distillation
Molekulardestillierapparat *m* molecular still
molekulardispers molecularly disperse
Molekulardispersion *f* molecular (molar) dispersion (dispersivity) *(difference in molar refraction)*
Molekulardrehung *f* molecular rotation
Molekulargewicht *n* molecular weight • **mit (von) geringem ~** low-molecular-weight • **mit (von) hohem ~** high-molecular-weight
Molekulargewichtsbestimmung *f* molecular-weight determination
~ mit der Ultrazentrifuge sedimentation-equilibrium method *(of determining molecular weights)*
Molekulargewichtsmittelwert *m* molecular-weight average
Molekulargewichtsverteilung *f* molecular-weight distribution, MWD
Molekularität *f* **[der Reaktion]** molecularity [of reaction], reaction molecularity
Molekularkraft *f* [inter]molecular force
Molekularmasse *f s.* Molekülmasse
Molekularorbital *n s.* Molekülorbital
Molekularpolarisation *f s.* Molpolarisation

Molekularrefraktion *f s.* Molrefraktion
Molekularrotation *f* molecular rotation
Molekularsieb *n* molecular sieve
Molekularsiebchromatographie *f* molecular sieve (exclusion) chromatography
Molekularsiebkatalysator *m* sieve catalyst
Molekularsiebsäule *f (chromat)* molecular sieve column
Molekularstrahl *m* molecular beam
Molekularstrahlapparatur *f* molecular-beam apparatus
Molekularstrahlen *mpl***/gekreuzte** crossed molecular beams
Molekularstrahlmessung *f* molecular-beam measurement
Molekularstrahlmethode *f* molecular-beam method (technique)
Molekularstrahlspektroskopie *f* molecular-beam spectroscopy
Molekularstrahlversuch *m* molecular-beam experiment
Molekülassoziation *f* molecular association
Molekülasymmetrie *f* molecular asymmetry (dissymmetry)
Molekülbahn... *s.* Molekülorbital...
Molekülbande *f (spectr)* molecular band
Molekülbandenspektrum *n* molecular band spectrum
Molekülbildung *f* molecule formation
Molekülbruchstück *n* molecular fragment
Moleküldissoziation *f* molecular dissociation
Moleküldurchmesser *m* molecular diameter
Moleküleigenfunktion *f* molecular eigenfunction
Moleküleinheit *f* molecular unit
Moleküleinschlußverbindung *f* molecular inclusion compound
Molekülelektronenspektrum *n* molecular electronic spectrum
Molekülformel *f* molecular formula
~/empirische empirical molecular formula
Molekülfragment *n* molecular fragment
Molekülgeometrie *f* molecular geometry
Molekülgeschwindigkeit *f* molecular speed (velocity)
Molekülgitter *n* molecular lattice
Molekülion *n* molecular ion, *(as opposed to fragment ions also)* parent ion
Molekülkette *f* molecular chain
Molekülkolloid *n* molecular colloid
Molekülkomplex *m* molecular complex
Molekülkonformation *f* molecular conformation
Molekülkristall *m* molecular crystal
Molekülmasse *f* molecular mass
~/mittlere relative average relative molecular mass, average RMM
~/relative relative molecular mass, RMM
Molekülmodell *n* molecular model
Molekülorbital *n* molecular orbital, MO
~/antibindendes antibonding molecular orbital
~/bindendes bonding molecular orbital, molecular bonding orbital
~/delokalisiertes delocalized molecular orbital
~/höchstes besetztes highest[-energy] occupied molecular orbital, HOMO
~/Hückelsches Hückel molecular orbital, HMO
~/lokalisiertes localized molecular orbital
~/lockerndes antibonding molecular orbital
~/niedrigstes unbesetztes lowest[-energy] unoccupied molecular orbital, LUMO
π-Molekülorbital *n* π molecular orbital, pi-orbital, π-orbital
σ-Molekülorbital *n* σ molecular orbital, sigma-orbital, σ-orbital
Molekülorbitalmethode *f* molecular-orbital method, Hund-Mulliken-[Lennard-Jones-]Hückel method
Molekülorbitalnäherung *f* molecular-orbital approach (approximation)
Molekülorbitalrechnung *f* molecular-orbital calculation
Molekülorbitaltheorie *f* molecular-orbital theory, Hund-Mulliken-[Lennard-Jones-]Hückel theory
Molekülorientierung *f* molecular orientation
Molekülpeak *m (spectr)* molecular peak, parent [mass] peak
Molekülphosphoreszenz *f* molecular phosphorescence
Molekülpolarisierbarkeit *f* molecular polarizability
Molekülsäure *f* molecular acid
Molekülschicht *f* molecular layer
Molekülschwarm *m* swarm (bundle) of molecules
Molekülschwingung *f* molecular vibration
Molekülsieb *n s.* Molekularsieb
Molekülspektroskopie *f* molecular spectroscopy
Molekülspektroskopiker *m* molecular spectroscopist
molekülspektroskopisch by molecular spectroscopy
Molekülspektrum *n* molecular spectrum, band[ed] spectrum
Molekülspinorbital *n* molecular spin orbital
Molekülstrahl *m s.* Molekularstrahl
Molekülstruktur *f* molecular structure
Molekülverband *m* union of molecules, cluster
Molekülverbindung *f* molecular (addition) compound
Molekülwellenfunktion *f* molecular wave function
Molekülzusammenstoß *m* molecular collision
Molenbruch *m* mole (molar) fraction
Moler *m*, **Molererde** *f* moler *(a kind of diatomaceous earth)*
Molettewasserzeichen *n (pap)* impressed (rubber-stamp) mark, *(Am)* press mark
Molgewicht *n s.* Molekulargewicht
Molisch-Reagens *n* Molisch reagent *(alcoholic α-naphthol)*
Molisch-Reaktion *f* Molisch reaction *(for detecting carbohydrates)*

Molke *f* whey, milk serum
~/**süße** sweet whey
Molken *m s.* Molke
Molkeneiweiß *n s.* Molkenprotein
Molkenmargarine *f* whey margarine
Molkenprotein *n* whey (milk serum) protein
Molkenpulver *n* whey powder, powdered (dried, dry) whey
Molkerei *f* dairy, *(Am also)* creamery
Molkereiabwasser *n* dairy waste water, milk waste
Molkereibutter *f* dairy butter
Molkereierzeugnisse *npl*, **Molkereiprodukte** *npl* dairy products (foods)
Molkonzentration *f* molar concentration, molarity
Molleharz *n* American mastic *(a gum from Schinus molle L.)*
Möller *m (met)* burden
möllern *(met)* to burden
Möllersonde *f* stock level indicator *(of a blast furnace)*
Möllerwagen *m* scale car *(for charging blast furnaces)*
Mollier-Diagramm *n* Mollier (enthalpy-entropy) chart (diagram)
Molluskizid *n (agric)* molluscacide, molluscide
Molmasse *f* molar mass • **von geringer** ~ low-molar-mass
Molmassenmittelwert *m* molar-mass average
Molmassenverteilung *f* molar-mass distribution
Molozonid *n* molozonide, 1,2,3-trioxolane
Molpolarisation *f* molar (molecular) polarization
Molprozent *n* **Ungesättigtheit** *(rubber)* mole per cent unsaturation
Molrefraktion *f* molar (molecular) refraction (refractivity), MR
Molsieb *n s.* Molekularsieb
Molsuszeptibilität *f* molar susceptibility
Molverhältnis *n* molar (mole) ratio
Molvolumen *n* molar volume, [gram-]molecular volume
~/**kritisches** critical molar volume
~/**partielles** partial molar volume
Molwärme *f s.* Wärmekapazität/molare
Molybdän *n* Mo molybdenum
Molybdänblau *n* molybdenum blue *(molybdenum(V,VI) oxide)*
Molybdäncarbid *n* molybdenum carbide
Molybdän(III)-chlorid *n* molybdenum trichloride
Molybdän(IV)-chlorid *n* molybdenum tetrachloride
Molybdän(II)-dihydroxidtetrabromid *n* molybdenum tetrabromide dihydroxide
Molybdän(II)-dihydroxidtetrachlorid *n* molybdenum tetrachloride dihydroxide
Molybdändioxiddibromid *n* molybdenum dibromide dioxide
Molybdändioxiddichlorid *n* molybdenum dichloride dioxide
Molybdändisulfid *n s.* Molybdän(IV)-sulfid
Molybdän-Eisen-Protein *n (bioch)* molybdoiron protein
Molybdänerz *n* molybdenum ore
Molybdänglanz *m s.* Molybdänit
molybdänhaltig containing molybdenum, *(esp relating to ores:)* molybdeniferous
Molybdänit *m (min)* molybdenite *(molybdenum(IV) sulphide)*
Molybdänocker *m (min)* 1. molybdic ochre, molybdite *(molybdenum(VI) oxide)*; 2. ferromolybdite *(iron(III) molybdate(V))*
Molybdän(III)-oxid *n* molybdenum(III) oxide, dimolybdenum trioxide
Molybdän(V)-oxid *n* molybdenum(V) oxide, dimolybdenum pentoxide
Molybdän(VI)-oxid *n* molybdenum(VI) oxide, molybdenum trioxide
Molybdänoxidtetrachlorid *n* molybdenum tetrachloride oxide
Molybdänoxidtetrafluorid *n* molybdenum tetrafluoride oxide
Molybdänpentoxid *n s.* Molybdän(V)-oxid
Molybdänpulver *n* molybdenum powder
Molybdänsäure *f* molybdic acid
Molybdänstahl *m* molybdenum steel
Molybdän(III)-sulfid *n* molybdenum(III) sulphide, dimolybdenum trisulphide
Molybdän(IV)-sulfid *n* molybdenum(IV) sulphide, molybdenum disulphide
Molybdäntetrachlorid *n* molybdenum tetrachloride
Molybdäntrichlorid *n* molybdenum trichloride
Molybdäntrioxid *n s.* Molybdän(VI)-oxid
Molybdäntrioxidhexachlorid *n* molybdenum hexachloride trioxide
Molybdäntrioxidpentachlorid *n* molybdenum pentachloride trioxide
Molybdat(VI) *n* $M^{I}_{2}MoO_4$ molybdate(VI)
Molybdatophosphat *n* molybdophosphate, *(specif)* $M^{I}_{3}[PMo_{12}O_{40}]$ dodecamolybdophosphate
Molybdatophosphorsäure *f* molybdophosphoric acid, *(specif)* $H_3[PMo_{12}O_{40}]$ dodecamolybdophosphoric acid
Molzahl *f* number of moles
Moment *n* moment
~/**atomares magnetisches** atomic magnetic moment
~/**bahnmagnetisches** orbital magnetic moment
~/**kernmagnetisches** nuclear magnetic moment
~/**magnetisches** magnetic [dipole] moment
~/**orbitalmagnetisches** *s.* ~/bahnmagnetisches
~/**spinmagnetisches** electron spin magnetic moment
Momentanpasteurisation *f*, **Momenterhitzung** *f* *(food)* flash pasteurization, flashing
MO-Methode *f s.* Molekülorbitalmethode
MO-Näherung *f* molecular-orbital approximation (approach)
monAk *s.* Antikörper/monoklonaler
Monamid *n* monoamide

Monamin *n* monoamine
Monammingallium(III)-chlorid *n* monoammine-gallium(III) chloride
Monardaöl *n* monarda (horsemint) oil *(essential oil from Monarda specc.)*
Monazit *m (min)* monazite *(cerium phosphate)*
Monazitsand *m* monazite sand
Mönchspergament *n* vellum [paper]
Mond-Gas *n* Mond gas *(a producer gas)*
Mond-Gasgenerator *m* Mond [gas] producer
Mond-Gasverfahren *n* Mond process
Mond-Generator *m s.* Mond-Gasgenerator
Mondgestein *n* lunar rock
Mondglas *n* crown glass
Mondmineral *n* lunar mineral
Mond-Niederdruckcarbonylverfahren *n (met)* Mond [carbonyl] process
Mondstaub *m* lunar dust
Mondstein *m (min)* moonstone *(a feldspar)*
Mond-Verfahren *n s.* 1. Mond-Gasverfahren; 2. Mond-Niederdruckcarbonylverfahren
Mongolismus *m (med)* mongolism, Down's syndrome, trisomy 21
Mong Yu *n* stillingia (tallow-seed) oil *(from Sapium sebiferum (L.) Roxb.)*
Monnier-Ofen *m (ceram)* Monnier kiln
Monoacetin *n* monoacetin, glycerol, monoacetate
Monoalkylbenzen *n*, **Monoalkylbenzol** *n* monoalkylbenzene
monoalkylieren to monoalkylate
Monoalkylierung *f* monoalkylation
Monoamid *n* monoamide
Monoamin *n* monoamine
Monoarsan *n* monoarsane, arsane, arsine
Monoarsin *n s.* Monoarsan
Monoäth... *s.* Monoeth...
monoatomar mon[o]atomic
Monoazofarbstoff *m* monoazo dye
Monobasizität *f* monobasicity *(of acids)*
Monoboran *n* monoborane(3), borane(3)
Monoborid *n* monoboride
Monoborin *n s.* Monoboran
Monoborsäure *f* orthoboric acid, boric acid, trioxoboric acid
Monobrombenzen *n*, **Monobrombenzol** *n* bromobenzene
Monobromcampher *m* bromocamphor, brominated (monobrominated) camphor
Monobromid *n* monobromide
monobromieren to monobrominate
Monobromierung *f* monobromination
Monobrommethan *n* monobromomethane, bromomethane
Monocarbonsäure *f* monocarboxylic acid
Monochloralkan *n* monochloroalkane, chloroalkane
Monochlorderivat *n* monochloro derivative
Monochlorethan *n* monochloroethane, chloroethane
Monochlorid *n* monochloride
monochlorieren to monochlorinate
Monochlorierung *f* monochlorination
Monochlorsilan *n* monochlorosilane, chlorosilane
Monochromasie *f* monochromatism, monochromasy
monochromatisch monochromatic, monochrome
monochromatisieren to monochromatize *(light)*
Monochromator *m* monochromator, monochromatic illuminator
Monochromiumarsenid *n* monochromium arsenide
Monochromiumborid *n* monochromium boride
Monochromsäure *f* chromic acid
monocistronisch *(bioch)* monocistronic *(1. expressed or controlled by only one gene; 2. bearing only one gene)*
monocyclisch monocyclic
Monocyclus *m* monocyclic compound
Monoderivat *n* mono derivative
monodispers monodisperse
Monod-[Wyman-Changeux-]Modell *n* MWC (Monod-Wyman-Changeux) model, symmetry model, concerted (all-or-none) model *(enzyme kinetics)*
Monoester *m* monoester
Monoethanolamin *n* *2-aminoethanol, monoethanolamine, MEA, colamine
Monoethylamin *n* ethylamine
Monofil[garn] *n* monofil, monofilament [yarn]
Monofluorid *n* monofluoride
monofunktionell monofunctional
Monogerman *n* monogermane, germane, germanium tetrahydride
Monoglycerid *n* monoglyceride
Monoglyceridlipase *f* intestinal lipase
Monohalogenalkan *n* monohalogen alkane, alkyl monohalide
Monohalogenderivat *n* monohalogen derivative
Monohalogenid *n* monohalogenide, monohalide
monohalogenieren to monohalogenate
Monohalogenierung *f* monohalogenation
Monohydrat *n* monohydrate
Monohydrid *n* monohydride
Monohydrogenphosphat *n* $M^{I}_{2}HPO_4$ monohydrogenphosphate
Monohydrogensalz *n* monohydrogen salt
Monohydroxyverbindung *f* monohydroxy compound
Monoiodid *n* monoiodide
monoisotop monoisotopic
Monokaliumoxalat *n* potassium hydrogen oxalate
Monoketon *n* monoketone
Monoketonimid *n* monoketone imide
monokl. *s.* monoklin
monoklin *(cryst)* monoclinic, mon., mn.
monoklin-prismatisch *(cryst)* monoclinic-prismatic
Monokultur *f (biot)* monoculture
monomer monomeric
Monomer[e] *n* monomer, *(relating to copolymerization:)* comonomer
Monomereinheit *f* monomer unit

Monomereinschub *m* monomer insertion
Monomerenverhältnis *n* monomer ratio
Monomergemisch *n*, **Monomermischung** *f* monomer mixture
Monomermolekül *n* monomer molecule
monomineralisch monomineral[ic]
monomolekular monomolecular, unimolecular
Monomolekularfilm *m s.* Monoschicht
Mononatriumglutamat *n* monosodium glutamate
mononitrieren to mononitrate
Mononitrierung *f* mononitration
Mononitrokörper *m* mononitro body
Mononitroverbindung *f* mononitro compound
Mononucleotid *n* mononucleotide
Monoolefin *n* monoolefin, alkene, ethylenic hydrocarbon
Monoperoxyphthalsäure *f* monoperoxyphthalic acid
Monophosphan *n* monophosphane, phosphane, phosphine
Monophosphat *n* $M^{I}_{3}O_4$ monophosphate, orthophosphate
Monophosphid *n* monophosphide
Monophosphin *n s.* Monophosphan
Monophosphorsäure *f* monophosphoric acid, orthophosphoric acid, phosphoric acid
Monosaccharid *n* monosaccharide
Monosauerstoff *m* monooxygen, atomic oxygen
Monoschicht *f* monolayer, monomolecular (unimolecular) layer (film)
Monoschichtadsorption *f* monomolecular adsorption
Monoschwefelwasserstoff *m* hydrogen sulphide, monosulphane
Monose *f s.* Monosaccharid
Monosilan *n* monosilane
Monosolverfahren *n (petrol)* single-solvent process
Monospiro-Verbindung *f* monospiro compound (hydrocarbon)
Monostearin *n* monostearin, glycerol monostearate, GMS, glycerol octadecanoate
Monostiban *n* monostibane, stibane, stibine
monosubstituieren to monosubstitute
Monosubstitution *f* monosubstitution
Monosubstitutionsprodukt *n* monosubstitution product
Monosulfan *n* monosulphane, hydrogen sulphide
Monosulfid *n* monosulphide
Monosutfidbrücke *f* monosulphide bridge (crosslink)
Monosulfitaufschluß *m (pap)* pulping with sodium sulphite
Monosulfonsäure *f* monosulphonic acid
Monoterpen *n* monoterpene
~/acyclisches acyclic monoterpene
~/bicyclisches bicyclic monoterpene
~/monocyclisches monocyclic monoterpene
Monoterpenalkaloid *n* monoterpenoid alkaloid
Monoterpenoid *n* monoterpenoid
Monothioacetal *n* monothioacetal
Monothioketal *n* monothioketal
Monotreibstoff *m* monofuel; monopropellant
monotrop monotropic
Monotropie *f* monotropy
monovalent monovalent, univalent
monovariant monovariant, univariant
Monowasserstoff *m* monohydrogen, atomic hydrogen
Monoxid *n* monooxide, monoxide
Montage *f* setting-up, erection, assembling *(of an apparatus)*
Montagegitter *n (lab)* assembly
Montansäure *f* montanic acid, *octacosanoic acid
Montanwachs *n* montan[in] wax
~/doppelt gebleichtes double-bleached (double-refined) montan wax
~/gebleichtes (raffiniertes) bleached (refined) montan wax
~/rohes crude montan wax
Montanwachsleim *m (pap)* montan-wax size
Montanwachsleimung *f (pap)* sizing with montan wax
Montanwachspech *n* montan-wax pitch
Mont-Cenis-Verfahren *n* Mont Cenis process *(for producing ammonia)*
Montejus *n* montejus, acid egg, blowcase *(an apparatus for lifting liquids)*
montieren to set up, to erect, to assemble, to mount *(an apparatus)*
Monuron *n* monuron, 3-(*p*-chlorophenyl)-1,1-dimethylurea *(a herbicide)*
Mooney-Anvulkanisationszeit *f* Mooney scorch [time]
Mooney-Grad *m (rubber)* Mooney unit
Mooney-Plastizität *f (rubber)* Mooney plasticity
Mooney-Plastometer *n s.* Mooney-Viskosimeter
Mooney-Viskosimeter *n (rubber)* Mooney viscometer (plastometer, instrument)
Mooney-Viskosität *f (rubber)* Mooney viscosity
Mooney-Wert *m*, **Mooney-Zahl** *f (rubber)* Mooney [value]
Moore-Campbell-Ofen *m* Moore-Campbell kiln *(an electric tunnel kiln)*
Moore-Filter *n* Moore filter
Moortorf *m* bog peat
Moos *n*/**Irländisches** *s.* Karrag[h]een
Moosachat *m (min)* moss agate
Moosgummi *m* microcellular rubber
Moostorf *m* moss peat
MORD *s.* Rotationsdispersion/magnetooptische
MO-Rechnung *f* molecular-orbital calculation
Morgan-Gaserzeuger *m*, **Morgan-Generator** *m* Morgan [gas] producer
Morin *n* morin, 2',3,4',5,7-pentahydroxyflavone
morphinähnlich morphine-like
Morphinalkaloid *n* morphine alkaloid
Morphinhydrochlorid *n* morphine hydrochloride
Morphinsulfat *n* morphine sulphate

Morphol *n* morphol, 3,4-dihydroxyphenanthrene
Morpholin *n* morpholine, tetrahydroxy-1,4-oxazine
Morphologie *f* morphology *(1. of a crystal; 2. branch of science)*
morphologisch *(cryst)* morphologic[al]
morsch werden *(text)* to tender
Morse-Funktion *f (anal)* Morse function (equation)
Mörser *m* mortar
Mörserkeule *f s.* Pistill
mörsern to grind (triturate) in a mortar
Mörtel *m* mortar
~/an der Luft erhärtender non-hydraulic mortar
~/fetter rich mortar
~/feuerfester refractory mortar
~/hydraulischer hydraulic mortar
Mörtelstruktur *f (geol)* mortar structure
Mosaikbau *m s.* Mosaikstruktur
Mosaikblock *m,* **Mosaikblöckchen** *n s.* Domäne
Mosaikgold *n* mosaic gold, ormolu *(1. tin(IV) sulphide; 2. a sort of brass)*
Mosaikkristall *m* mosaic crystal
Mosaikstruktur *f,* **Mosaiktextur** *f (cryst)* mosaic structure (texture)
Moschus *m* musk
~ **Ambrette** musk ambrette, 2,6-dinitro-3-methoxy-4-*tert*-butyltoluene
~ **Baur** Baur musk *(a synthetic musk)*
~ **C** *s.* ~ Keton
~/echter natural musk
~ **Keton** musk ketone, ketone musk, musk C *(an acetophenone derivative)*
~/künstlicher *s.* ~/synthetischer
~/natürlicher natural musk
~/synthetischer synthetic (artificial) musk *(common name of several organic compounds)*
~ **Xylol** musk xylol (xylene), 1,3-dimethyl-5-*tert*-butyl-2,4,6-dinitrobenzene
moschusartig musk-like
Moschusketon *n s.* Moschus Keton
Moschuskörneröl *n* ambrette (amber seed) oil *(from Hibiscus abelmoschus L.)*
Moschusöl *n* sumbul oil *(from Ferula sumbul Hook.)*
Moseley-Diagramm *n (spectr)* Moseley diagram
Mößbauer-Effekt *m (phys ch)* Mössbauer effect
Mößbauer-Spektroskopie *f* Mössbauer[-effect] spectroscopy
Mößbauer-Spektrum *n* Mössbauer spectrum
Most *m* must, stum
Mostrich *m* [table] mustard
MO-Theorie *f s.* Molekülorbitaltheorie
Motor[en]benzin *n* motor gasoline (spirit)
Motorenbenzol *n* motor benzole, benzole mixture (motor spirit)
Motorenkraftstoff *m* motor fuel
Motorenöl *n* motor oil
Motorenpetroleum *n* power kerosine (vaporizing oil)
Motorkraftstoff *m* motor fuel
Motormethode *f* motor method, F2 method *(for octane rating)*
Motor-Octanzahl *f* motor[-method] octane number, MON, F2 octane
Motorverfahren *n s.* Motormethode
Motorverstäuber *m (agric)* power duster
mottenbeständig *s.* mottenecht
mottenecht mothproof • ~ **machen** to mothproof
Mottenechtappretur *f* mothproof finish
Mottenechtausrüstung *f* 1. mothproofing; 2. mothproof finish
Mottenechtheit *f* resistance to moth
mottenfest *s.* mottenecht
Mottenkugel *f* moth ball
Mottenpapier *n* mothproof paper
Mottenschutz *m* mothproofing
Mottenschutzmittel *n* mothproofing agent, mothproofer, moth repellent
mottensicher *s.* mottenecht
motzen *(glass)* to marver *(a gather in an ovoid mould)*
moussieren to effervesce, to sparkle
Moussieren *n* effervescence
moussierend effervescent
Mova *(Monovinylacetylen) s.* Vinylacetylen
Mowra[h]butter *f,* **Mowra[h]öl** *n* mowra butter (fat, oil), mowrah (moura) butter *(from Madhuca specc.)*
Moyno-Pumpe *f* Moyno pump *(a single-rotor screw pump)*
MPC-Ruß *m* medium processing channel black, MPC black
MPD *s.* Multiphotonendissoziation
MPI *s.* Multiphotonenionisation
MRH *(**M**elanotropin-**R**eleasing**h**ormon) s.* Melanoliberin
Ms *s.* Messing
M-Schale *f* M-shell *(of an atom)*
MSH *s.* Hormon/melanozytenstimulierendes
MT *s.* Metallfaserstoff
mtRNA *s.* RNA/mitochondriale
MT-Ruß *m* medium thermal black, MT black
Mucinsäure *f* mucic acid, galactosaccharic acid
Mücken[schutz]mittel *n* mosquito repellent
Mucobromsäure *f* mucobromic acid, dibromoaldehydoacrylic acid
Mucochlorsäure *f* mucochloric acid, dichloraldehydoacrylic acid
Mucoid *n* mucoid *(a glycoprotein)*
Mucoitinschwefelsäure *f* mucoitinsulphuric acid, mucoitin sulphate *(an acidic polysaccharide)*
Muconsäure *f* muconic acid, hexa-2,4-dienedioic acid
Mucopeptid *n* mucopeptide
Mucopolysaccharid *n* mucopolysaccharide
Mucoproteid *n,* **Mucoprotein** *n* mucoprotein
Mud *m* 1. *(petrol)* mud; 2. *(tann)* bloom, exudation
Muffe *f* socket, boss
Muffeldrehrohrofen *m* rotary muffle kiln *(as for calcining)*

Muffelofen *m (lab)* muffle furnace; *(ceram)* muffle kiln
Muffeltunnelofen *m (ceram)* muffle tunnel kiln
Muffenrohr *n* socket[ed] pipe
Muffenschweißverbindung *f* socket-weld joint *(a pipe connection)*
Muffenverbinder *m*, **Muffenverbindungsstück** *n* socket fitting
Mühle *f* 1. mill *(works)*; 2. [grinding] mill, grinder *(apparatus)*
~/autogen arbeitende autogenous mill
~/chilenische Chilean (Chile) mill, pan[-type roller] mill, edge[-runner] mill, edgerunner
Mühlenfeuerung *f* mill firing
Mühlengehäuse *n* mill shell
Mühlenzusatz *m (ceram)* mill addition
Mühlstein *m* grindstone, millstone, bur[r]stone, buhr[stone]
mukos, mukös slimy
Mulde *f* trough, pan
Muldenmischer *m* trough mixer
Muldenrolle *f* troughing idler
Muldenrost *m* trough grate
Muldentrockner *m* trough conveyor dryer
Müll *m* waste [material, product], solid waste, refuse, rubbish, *(Am also)* garbage
~/häuslicher domestic (household) refuse, domestic (private) rubbish
~/industrieller industrial solid waste
~/kommunaler municipal solid waste, municipal refuse
Müllaufbereitungsanlage *f* waste-treatment plant
Müllbeseitigung *f* waste (refuse) disposal
Müllerei *f (food)* [flour] milling
Müller-Rochow-Synthese *f*, **Müller-Rochow-Verfahren** *n* Müller-Rochow synthesis (process) *(for producing chlorosilanes)*
Mullit *m (min)* mullite *(aluminium silicate)*
Mullitporzellan *n* mullite porcelain
Müllkippe *f* refuse (waste) tip, *(Am also)* garbage dump
Müllveraschung *f s.* Müllverbrennung
Müllverbrennung *f* refuse incineration
Müllverbrennungsanlage *f* incineration (incinerating) plant
Müllverbrennungsofen *m* [refuse, garbage] incinerator, [refuse] destructor
Multiaerozyklon *m* multitube cyclone separator
Multi-copy-Plasmid *n (bioch)* multi-copy plasmid
Multienzymkomplex *m* multienzyme complex
Multienzymsystem *n* multienzyme system
Multifil[garn] *n* multifil, multifilament [yarn]
Multiflash-Verdampfung *f* multiflash (multistage flash) evaporation, MSF evaporation (distillation)
Multiflash-Verdampfungsanlage *f* multistage flash evaporator, MSF evaporator
Multiklon *m s.* Multiaerozyklon
Multiphotonenabsorption *f* multiphoton absorption
Multiphotonendissoziation *f* multiphoton dissociation, MPD
Multiphotonenionisation *f* multiphoton ionization, MPI
Multiplett *n (spectr)* multiplet
~/normales (regelrechtes) normal (regular) multiplet
~/verkehrtes inverted multiplet
Multiplettaufspaltung *f* multiplet splitting
Multiplettniveau *n* multiplet level
Multiplettstruktur *f* multiplet structure
Multiplett-Term *m* multiplet level
Multiplexanlage *f* multiplex-roll plant *(a system with more than two pairs of rolls)*
Multiplexvorteil *m (spectr)* multiplex (Fellgett) advantage
Multiplexwalze *f* multiplex [roll]
Multiplikationsfaktor *m (nucl)* multiplication constant
Multiplikativzahl *f* multiplying prefix, multiplicative numer[ic]al prefix
Multiplizität *f* multiplicity *(of an electronic state)*
~/maximale maximum multiplicity
Multiplizitätsprinzip *n*/**Hundsches** Hund maximum-multiplicity principle (rule), Hund's first rule
Multirotation *f s.* Mutarotation
Multi-sweep-Polarographie *f (anal)* multisweep polarography
Mu-Meson *n s.* Myon
Mundblaseglas *n* hand-blown (hand-made) glass
Mundblasverfahren *n (glass)* hand-blown process
mundgeblasen *(glass)* hand-blown
Mundstück *n* mouthpiece; *(ceram)* die *(of an extruder)*
Mündung *f* orifice
~/versetzte *(glass)* offset finish *(a defect)*
Mündungsbär *m (met)* skull *(in a converter)*
Mundwasser *n* mouthwash
Munkettinußöl *n* Manketti nut oil *(from Ricinodendron rautaneni Schinz)*
Muntz-Metall *n* muntz metal *(60 % Cu, 40 % Zn, up to 0.8 % Pb added)*
Münzbronze *f* coinage bronze
Münzgold *n* coin gold
Münzlegierung *f* coinage alloy
Münzmetall *n* coinage metal
Muon *n*, **Müon** *n s.* Myon
Murakami-Reagens *n* Murakami's reagent *(for etching metals)*
Muraminsäure *f* muramic acid, 3-*O*-α-carboxyethyl-D-glucosamine
Murein *n* murein, peptidoglycan *n (a polysaccharide-peptide complex in bacterial cell membranes)*
Murexid *n* murexide *(ammonium salt of purpuric acid)*
Murexidprobe *f* murexide test *(for detecting uric acid)*
Muropeptid *n* muropeptide *(of bacterial cell membranes)*

Muschelgold *n*[**/unechtes**] artificial gold
muschelig *(min)* conchoidal *(surface produced by fracture)*
Muschelkalk *m* shell lime, coquina
Muschelkalkstein *m* shell (coquinoid) limestone
Muscon *n* muscone, *3-methylcyclopentadecanone
Musivgold *n* mosaic gold, ormolu *(1. tin(IV) sulphide; 2. a sort of brass)*
Muskatbalsam *m s.* Muskatnußbutter
Muskatblüte *f* mace *(from Myristica fragrans Houtt.)*
Muskatnußbutter *f* nutmeg butter (oil) *(from Myristica fragrans Houtt.)*
Muskatnußöl *n s.* 1. Muskatnußbutter; 2. Muskatöl/ätherisches
Muskatöl *n*/**ätherisches** nutmeg (myristica) oil *(from Myristica fragrans Houtt.)*
Muskeladenylsäure *f* [muscle] adenylic acid, adenosine 5'-phosphate
Muskelinosinsäure *f s.* Inosinsäure
Muskelöl *n (cosmet)* muscle oil
Muskelspritzverfahren *n (food)* stitch-pump method *(for curing meat)*
Muskovit *m (min)* muscovite, potassium (potash) mica *(a phyllosilicate)*
Muster *n* 1. sample; 2. pattern • **nach ~ färben** *(text)* to match
~/chromatographisches *(anal)* fingerprint
Musterfärbejigger *m* sample-dye[ing] jig
Musterfärbung *f* sample dyeing
Musterspektren *npl* library [reference] spectra
mutagen *(bioch)* mutagenic
Mutagen *n (bioch)* mutagen, mutagenic agent
Mutagenbehandlung *f (biot)* mutagen treatment
Mutagenese *f (bioch)* mutagenesis
Mutagenität *f (bioch)* mutagenicity
Mutante *f*/**auxotrophe** *(bioch)* auxotrophic mutant
Mutantenstamm *m (biot)* mutant strain *(of microorganisms)*
Mutarotation *f* mutarotation, multirotation *(changed optical rotation of sugars)* • **~ zeigen** to mutarotate
Mutasynthese *f (biot)* mutasynthesis, mutational biosynthesis
Mutation *f*/**spontane** *(biol)*spontaneous mutation
mutationsauslösend mutagenic, mutation-inducing
Mutations-Biosynthese *f s.* Mutasynthese
Mutationshäufigkeit *f (biol)* mutation frequency
Mutationssynthese *f s.* Mutasynthese
Mutterboden *m* topsoil, surface soil
Mutterelement *n* parent element
Mutterform *f (ceram)* master mould
Muttergestein *n* 1. *(geol)* parent (mother, source) rock *(as of sediments)*; matrix, groundmass *(in which larger crystals are embedded)*; 2. *(soil)* bedrock
Mutterhefe *f* inoculating (seed) yeast
Mutterkornalkaloid *n* ergot alkaloid
Mutterkornvergiftung *f* ergotism
Mutterkultur *f* mother culture (starter), original starter culture *(margarine making)*
Mutterlauge *f* mother liquor
Muttermilch *f* breast (human) milk
Mutterpause *f* transparent (translucent) master *(reprography)*
Muttersaft *m (food)* natural juice
Muttersäurekultur *f s.* Mutterkultur
Muttersubstanz *f* mother (parent) substance
Mutungsbohrung *f (petrol)* exploration drilling, wildcat
MVA *s.* Müllverbrennungsanlage
MW-... *s.* Mikrowellen...
MWC-Modell *n s.* Monod-Wyman-Changeux-Modell
m-Wert *m (hyd)* methyl-orange alkalinity, M alkalinity
MWG *s.* Massenwirkungsgesetz
Mycolipensäure *f* mycolipenic acid, *trans-2,4,6-trimethyltetracos-2-enoic acid
Mycolsäure *f* mycolic acid *(any of a group of acids occurring in tubercle bacilli)*
Mycophenolsäure *f* mycophenolic acid *(antibiotic)*
Mycosterin *n*, **Mycosterol** *n* mycosterol
Mydriatikum *n (pharm)* mydriatic
mydriatisch mydriatic
Myogen *n* myogen *(a mixture of albumins found in muscle)*
Myoglobin *n*, **Myohämoglobin** *n (bioch)* myoglobin
Myon *n (nucl)* muon, mu meson, μ-meson *(an elementary particle)*
Myonchemie *f* muon chemistry
Myoniumchemie *f* muonium chemistry
Myonspinrotation *f (nucl)* muon spin rotation, μSR
Myrcen *n* myrcene, *7-methyl-3-methylene-octa-1,6-diene
Myricylalkohol *m* myricyl alcohol *(1. $C_{30}H_{61}OH$ triacontanol; 2. $C_{31}H_{63}OH$ hentriacontanol)*
Myricylpalmitat *n* myricyl palmitate *(palmitic acid ester of either triacontanol or hentriacontanol)*
Myrikatalg *m*, **Myrikawachs** *n* myrica (bayberry) tallow *(from Myrica specc.)*
Myristaldehyd *m* myristaldehyde, *tetradecanal
Myristat *n* myristate *(a salt or ester of myristic acid)*
Myristicinaldehyd *m* myristicinaldehyde, 3-methoxy-4,5-methylenedioxybenzaldehyde
Myristicinsäure *f* myristicic acid, 3-methoxy-4,5-methylenedioxybenzoic acid
Myristinaldehyd *m s.* Myristaldehyd
Myristinalkohol *m s.* Myristylalkohol
Myristinsäure *f* myristic acid, *tetradecanoic acid
Myristinsäureglycerylester *m* glycerol trimyristate, trimyristin
Myristoleinsäure *f* myristoleic acid, *tetradec-9-enoic acid
Myriston *n* myristone, heptacosan-14-one
Myristylaldehyd *m s.* Myristaldehyd
Myristylalkohol *m* myristyl alcohol, 1-tetradecanol

Myronsäure *f* myronic acid
Myrosin *n* myrosin *(an enzyme occurring in various brassicaceous plants)*
Myrrhe *f*, **Myrrhenharz** *n* myrrh gum *(a gum resin from Commiphora specc.)*
Myrrhenöl *n* myrrh oil *(from Commiphora specc.)*
Myrtenal *n* myrtenal, 2-formyl-6,6-dimethyl-2-nor-pinene
Myrtenöl *n* myrtle oil *(from Myrtus communis L.)*
Myrtensäure *f* myrtenic acid, 6,6-dimethyl-2-nor-pinene-2-carboxylic acid
Myrtenwachs *n s.* Myrikatalg
Myrtol *n* myrtol *(a fraction of myrtle oil distilling between 160 and 180 °C)*
Myzel *n (biol)* mycelium
Myzeldecke *f (biot)* mycelium layer
Myzelfilter *n (biot)* mycelium filter
myzelgebunden *(biot)* mycelium-bound
Myzelkugeln *fpl s.* Myzelpellets
Myzelmasse *f (biot)* mycelial weight
Myzelpellets *npl (biot)* mycelial (mycelium) pellets
Myzelschicht *f (biot)* mycelium cake
Myzelsuspension *f (biot)* mycelial suspension
Myzeltrockenmasse *f*, **Myzeltrockensubstanz** *f (biot)* mycelial dry weight
Myzelwäsche *f (biot)* mycelial wash

N

N_0 *s.* Avogadro-Zahl
N_A *s.* Avogadro-Konstante
NAA *s.* Neutronenaktivierungsanalyse
Na-Austauscher *m s.* Natriumaustauscher
nachappretieren *(text)* to resize
Nachappretur *f (text)* additional finish, resizing
Nachäscher *m (tann)* fresh lime
Nachauflaufbehandlung *f (agric)* post-emergence treatment
Nachauflaufherbizid *n (agric)* post-emergence herbicide
Nachbaratom *n* neighbouring (adjacent) atom
Nachbareffekt *m (phot)* adjacency effect
Nachbargruppenbeteiligung *f* neighbouring group participation
Nachbargruppeneffekt *m* neighbouring effect
Nachbarmolekül *n* neighbouring (adjacent) molecule
Nachbarschaftshäufigkeit *f (bioch)* frequency of neighbouring, nearest-neighbour [sequence] frequency *(of purine and pyrimidine bases)*
Nachbarschaftshäufigkeitsbestimmung *f* nearest-neighbour base sequencing, nearest-neighbour base-frequency analysis
nachbarständig vicinal, adjacent, neighbouring
Nachbarstellung *f* vicinal (adjacent, neighbouring) position
nachbearbeiten *(tech)* to finish
Nachbearbeitung *f (tech)* finish[ing]
nachbehandeln to aftertreat, to re-treat
Nachbehandlung *f* aftertreatment, re-treatment, secondary treatment, post-treatment, curing, cure
~ **mit Dampf** steam-curing *(of concrete)*
~ **mit Doktorlauge (Doktorlösung)** *(petrol)* doctor treatment (sweetening)
~/reduktive *(text)* reduction clearing
Nachbehandlungsfarbstoff *m* aftertreated dye
nachbelüften *(hyd)* to post-aerate
Nachbelüftung *f (hyd)* post-aeration
nachbessern *(tann)* to mend *(the lime liquor)*; to feed [in] *(tanning agents)*
nachbilden/sich to recover *(as of isotopes)*
Nachbildung *f* recovery *(as of isotopes)*
nachblasen *(met)* to after-blow
Nachblasen *n (met)* after-blow
Nachbleiche *f* final bleaching
Nachblütenspritzung *f (agric)* post-blossom spray
Nachbrand *m (ceram)* refiring
Nachbrecher *m* secondary crusher
nachbrennen *(ceram)* to refire
nachchloren *(hyd)* to post-chlorinate
nachchlorieren *(org ch, pap, text)* to post-chlorinate, to after-chlorinate
Nachchlorierung *f (org ch, pap, text)* post-chlorinating, post-chlorination, after-chlorination
Nachchlorung *f (hyd)* post-chlorination, final chlorination
nachchromieren *(text)* to after-chrome
Nachchromierfarbstoff *m (text)* after-chrome dye, top chrome dye, chrome-developed dye
nachchromiert *(text)* after-chromed, chrome-topped
Nachchromierung *f (text)* after-chroming, top-chroming
Nachchromierungsfarbstoff *m s.* Nachchromierfarbstoff
Nachchromier[ungs]verfahren *n* after-chrome dyeing process, top chrome dyeing process
nachdecken *(text)* to fill up, to top
nachdiazotieren to rediazotize
nachdosieren to make up
Nachdosierung *f* make-up
nachdunkeln to darken
Nachenthärtung *f (hyd)* final softening
~ **mit Trinatriumphosphat** two-stage hot lime-soda phosphate treatment
nachentwickeln *(phot)* to redevelop
Nachentwicklung *f (phot)* redevelopment
Nachfällung *f* post-precipitation, after-precipitation, delayed precipitation
nachfärben to redye, to top *(one component in textile-fibre mixtures)*
Nachfärbung *f* redyeing, topping, cross dyeing *(of one component in textile-fibre mixtures)*
Nachfaulbecken *n*, **Nachfaulbehälter** *m (hyd)* secondary digestion tank
Nachfiltration *f* post-filtration
Nachflotation *f* second-stage floatation

Nachfüllbahn *f (bioch)* anaplerotic sequence
nachfüllen to replenish, to fill up, to refill
Nachfüllösung *f (phot)* replenisher [solution]
Nachfülltechnik *f (chromat)* refill technique
Nachfüllung *f* replenishment, filling-up, refill[ing]
Nachgärung *f* secondary fermentation
nachgeben 1. to relax, to yield *(as by an applied stress)*; 2. to supply, to add
nachgefällt post-precipitated
nachgerben to retan, to fill
Nachgerbung *f* retannage, filling
Nachgeschmack *m* aftertaste
Nachgiebigkeit *f* give; *(text)* compliance; *(tann)* run *(of leather)*
~/elastische *(text)* elastic compliance; *(rubber)* [elastic] resilience
Nachgiebigkeitsverhältnis *n (text)* compliance ratio
Nachglimmen *n*, **Nachglühen** *n* afterglow
Nachguß *m (ferm)* sparge liquor
nachhärten *(plast)* to after-bake
Nachhärtung *f (plast)* after-bake, post-cure
Nachheizung *f s.* Nachvulkanisation
Nachklärbecken *n (hyd)* secondary clarifier (tank), secondary sedimentation (settling) tank, final clarifier (settling tank)
~ einer Belebtschlammanlage activated-sludge final settling tank
~ einer Tropfkörperanlage humus tank
Nachklärbeckenablauf *m*, **Nachklärbeckenabfluß** *m (hyd)* secondary [clarifier] effluent
Nachklärbeckenschlamm *m (hyd)* secondary [sedimentation] sludge, sludge from the final clarifier
Nachklärer *m s.* Nachklärbecken
Nachklärschlamm *m s.* Nachklärbeckenschlamm
Nachklärung *f (hyd)* secondary settling, final clarification
Nachkristallisation *f* after-crystallization, post-crystallization, secondary crystallization
Nachkühlung *f* aftercooling, secondary cooling
nachkupfern to aftercopper
Nachkupferung *f* aftercoppering, copper after-treatment
nachlassen to die down (away), to quieten down, to subside *(of a reaction)*
Nachlauf *m* 1. *(distil)* tailing[s], tail[s], foots, back end, *(esp petrol)* heavy ends; 2. *(sugar)* wash syrup
Nachlaufdelle *f* wake *(rheology)*
Nachleuchten *n* afterglow
~ im abklingenden strömenden Plasma flowing afterglow, FAG
Nachmehl *n (food)* middlings
Nachozon[is]ierung *f (hyd)* post-ozonation
Nachperiode *f* final period, post-period *(in calorimetric measurements)*
Nachpolymerisation *f* post-polymerization
Nachprodukt *n (sugar)* after-product
Nachproduktfüllmasse *f (sugar)* final (third-grade) massecuite, C massecuite
Nachproduktzucker *m* C sugar
nachprüfen to recheck
Nachprüfung *f* recheck
nachreifen to cure *(as of superphosphate)*
Nachreifen *n* curing, cure *(as of superphosphate)*
Nachreinigung *f (hyd)* advanced (tertiary) waste treatment, third-stage treatment
nachsalzen *(tann)* to resalt
Nachsaturation *f (sugar)* final saturation
Nachsäulenderivatisierung *f (chromat)* post-column derivatization
nachschäumen *(glass)* to reboil
Nachscheidung *f (sugar)* redefecation
Nachschwaden *m (mine)* after-damp *(after explosions of firedamp)*
Nachschwinden *n (ceram)* aftershrinkage, after-contraction; *(plast)* aftershrinkage, postmoulding deformation
Nachschwingung *f (spectr)* wiggle
Nachseifen *n (text)* soaping aftertreatment
nachsetzen to slip *(a Söderberg electrode)*
Nachsetzvorrichtung *f* slipping device *(for Söderberg electrodes)*
nachsintern to resinter
nachsortieren to rescreen
Nachsortierer *m* secondary (second, fine) screen
Nachsortierung *f* secondary (fine) screening, rescreening
Nachspülbad *n (text)* clearing bath
nachspülen to [re]rinse, to rewash
Nachspülen *n* [re]rinsing, [re]rinse, rewashing
Nachspülmittel *n* rinsing agent, rinse
Nachtcreme *f* night cream
nachtönen to tint, to tone
Nachtrockenzylinder *m*, **Nachtrockner** *m* after-dryer
Nachturm *m (pap)* weak[-acid] tower *(of a two-tower system)*
nachverarbeiten to reprocess
Nachverbrennung *f* afterburning *(of pollutants in waste gas)*
Nachverbrennungskammer *f (pap)* combustion chamber
nachverdichten 1. to further consolidate; 2. to seal *(in anodic oxidation)*
Nachverformung *f s.* Nachschwinden
Nachverstrecken *n (text)* after-stretching, post-stretching
Nachvulkanisation *f (rubber)* aftercure, aftervulcanization, post-vulcanization, post-cure
~ im Ofen post-oven cure
nachvulkanisch postvolcanic
Nachwachsen *n (ceram)* afterexpansion
nachwaschen to rewash
nachwässern *(phot)* to rewash
Nachweis *m* detection, identification, [confirmatory, reaffirming] test
~ selektierter Ionen multiple ion detection, MID

nachweisbar detectable
Nachweisbarkeit *f* detectability
Nachweisempfindlichkeit *f* *sensitivity, detection sensitivity
nachweisen to detect, to identify, to reaffirm the presence *(of a substance)*
Nachweisgerät *n* detection device
Nachweisgrenze *f* detection (identification) limit, minimum detection (detectable) limit (level), MDL, lower detection limit
~/absolute absolute detection limit
~/relative relative detection limit
~/untere *s.* Nachweisgrenze
Nachweislinien *fpl (spectr)* persistent (ultimate) lines, raies ultimes
Nachweismethode *f* detection method, method of detection
~/elektrochemische electrochemical method of detection
Nachweismittel *n***[/chemisches]** *s.* Nachweisreagens
Nachweisreagens *n* analytical reagent, A. R., detection agent
Nachweisreaktion *f* detection (test) reaction
Nachweisschwelle *f* detection threshold
Nachweisverfahren *n* detection technique
Nachweisvermögen *n* power of detection *(of an analytical procedure)*
Nachwirkung *f* residual action; residual effect, aftereffect
~/elastische elastic aftereffect, delayed elasticity, memory effect
Nachwürze *f (food)* afterwort, last wort
Nachzuckerfüllmasse *f s.* Nachproduktfüllmasse
NAD *s.* Nicotinsäureamid-adenin-dinucleotid
Nadel *f s.* Nadelkristall
Nadelausreißfestigkeit *f (rubber)* stitch-tear strength, needle-tear resistance
Nadelausreißprüfung *f (rubber)* stitch-tear test
Nadelausreißwiderstand *m s.* Nadelausreißfestigkeit
Nadeleisenerz *n (min)* goethite, göthite *(iron hydroxide oxide)*
nadelförmig needle-like, needle-shaped, acicular
Nadelholz *n* softwood, coniferous wood
Nadelholzzellstoff *m* softwood pulp
nadelig *s.* nadelförmig
Nadelkristall *m* needle, [crystal] whisker
Nadelpunktanguß *m (plast)* pinpoint (pinhole) gate
Nadelstich *m (ceram, coat)* pinhole *(a defect)*
Nadelventil *n* needle valve
Nadelverfahren *n (cosmet)* ecuelle method *(for expressing lemon oil)*
Nadelwärmeaustauscher *m*, **Nadelwärmeübertrager** *m* bayonet-tube heat exchanger
Na-D-Linie *f* sodium D line
NADP *s.* Nicotinsäureamid-adenin-dinucleotidphosphat
Nagelfang *m (pap)* button trap (catcher)
Nagelhautentferner *m (cosmet)* cuticle remover
Nagellack *m (cosmet)* nail lacquer
Nagellackentferner *m (cosmet)* nail lacquer remover
Nageln *n* diesel knock
Nagelpflegemittel *n (cosmet)* manicure preparation
Nagelpoliermittel *n*, **Nagelpolitur** *f (cosmet)* nail polish
Nagetiergift *n* rodenticide
Näherung *f* approximation
~/Bornsche Born approximation *(for computing wave functions)*
~/quasistationäre *(phys ch)* steady-state approximation
Näherungsformel *f* approximate formula
Näherungsverfahren *n* approximation method, approximate procedure
~/empirisches trial-and-error procedure
Näherungswert *m* approximate value
Nahordnung *f*, **Nahordnungsgrad** *m* short-range [crystalline] order
Nähragar *m(n)* nutrient agar
Nährboden *m***[/fester]** *(biot)* [solid] nutrient medium
Nährbouillon *f* nutrient broth
Nährcreme *f (cosmet)* nourishing cream, skin food
Nährelement *n s.* Nährstoffelement
nähren to nourish
Nährflüssigkeit *f* nutrient broth
Nährhefe *f* nutritional (food) yeast
Nährhumus *m* friable (nutritive) humus
Nährlösung *f* nutrient solution *(for higher plants)*; *(biot)* liquid nutrient medium, nutrient broth • **in ~ kultiviert** solution-grown
~/komplexe complex nutrient solution
~ nach Hoagland Hoagland solution
~ nach Johnson Johnson solution
~ nach Knop Knop solution
~/verbrauchte spent medium (broth)
Nährmedium *n (biot)* nutrient medium, nutritive (culture, growth) medium, substrate
~/festes *s.* Nährboden
~/flüssiges *s.* Nährlösung
~/komplexes complex [nutrient] medium
~/künstliches (synthetisches) synthetic medium
Nährsalz *n* nutrient salt
Nährstoff *m* nutrient [substance], nutritive, foodstuff
~/akzessorischer *(food)* minor nutrient
~/entbehrlicher *(agric)* non-essential element
~/limitierender limiting nutrient
~/unentbehrlicher *(agric)* essential element
Nährstoffanreicherung *f* nutrient enrichment
Nährstoffansprüche *mpl s.* Nährstoffbedarf
nährstoffarm poor in nutrients, *(soil also)* infertile
Nährstoffarmut *f* nutrient deficiency (lack), *(soil also)* infertility
Nährstoffaufnahme *f* nutrient uptake (adsorption)
Nährstoffausnutzung *f* nutrient utilization

Nährstoffauswaschung *f* nutrient elution (leaching)
Nährstoffbedarf *m* nutrient demand, nutritional requirements
Nährstoffbilanz *f* nutrient balance
Nährstoffelement *n (agric)* nutrient (food) element
Nährstoffeliminierung *f*, **Nährstoffentfernung** *f (hyd)* nutrient removal *(from waste water)*
Nährstoffentzug *m* nutrient withdrawal
Nährstofffluß *m (biot)* nutrient flow, feed stream
Nährstoffgehalt *m* nutrient content, *(if expressed in percentage* $N-P_2O_5-K_2O$*:)* fertilizer analysis, grade; *(hyd)* nutrient level *(in waste water)*
Nährstoffkreislauf *m* nutrient cycle
Nährstofflinie *f* nutrient line *(in the periodic table)*
Nährstoffmangel *m* nutrient deficiency (lack), *(agric also)* starvation
Nährstoffmangelerscheinung *f (agric)* nutrient deficiency symptom
Nährstoffnachlieferung *f* nutrient supply
nährstoffreich nutritious, rich in nutrients, *(soil also)* fertile
Nährstoffreichtum *m* nutritiousness, *(soil also)* fertility
Nährstoffreserve *f* nutrient reserve
Nährstoffrückwanderung *f* nutrient remigration
Nährstoffspeicher *m (bioch)* nutritional reservoir
Nährstoffträger *m* nutrient carrier *(in fertilizers)*
Nährstoffverhältnis *n* nutrient ratio
Nährstoffverlust *m* nutrient loss
Nährstoffverlagerung *f (bot)* nutrient displacement (translocation)
Nährstoffversorgung *f* nutrient supply
Nährstoffvorrat *m* nutrient reserve
Nährstoffzufuhr *f* nutrient supply
Nährstoffzugabe *f (hyd)* nutrient addition *(biological sewage treatment)*
Nährsubstrat *n s.* Nährmedium
Nahrung *f* food, diet, nourishment
Nahrungseiweiß *n* food protein
Nahrungsfett *n* dietary fat, edible (food) fat
Nahrungskette *f* food chain
Nahrungslipid *n* dietary lipid
Nahrungslockstoff *m* food lure *(as for insect control)*
Nahrungsmittel *n* food[stuff], nourishment
Nahrungsmittelchemie *f* food chemistry
Nahrungsmittelindustrie *f* food[-processing] industry, foodstuff (provisions) industry
Nahrungsmittelvergiftung *f* food poisoning
Nahrungsprotein *n* food protein
Nährwert *m* nutritional quality (value), nutrient (food) value
Naht *f* seam
~/geschweißte weld
Nahtstelle *f* **der Form** *(plast)* mould-parting line
Nahwirkungskraft *f (phys ch)* short-range force
Nakrit *m (min)* nacrite *(a phyllosilicate)*
Nalixidinsäure *f (bioch)* nalixidic acid
N-Alkylierung *f* N-alkylation, nitrogen alkylation
Name *m (nomencl)* name, term
~/additiver additive name
~/allgemeiner generic (non-proprietary) name
~/falscher misnomer
~/funktioneller functional name
~/generischer *s.* ~/allgemeiner
~/Genfer Geneva name
~/geschützter proprietary name
~/halbsystematischer (halbtrivialer) semisystematic (semitrivial) name
~/kommerzieller trade (commercial) name
~/konjunktiver conjunctive name
~/nach dem Ring-Index gebildeter Ring Index name
~/nach den IUPAC-Regeln gebildeter IUPAC name
~ nach Patterson Patterson name
~/nicht geschützter *s.* ~/allgemeiner
~/nichtsystematischer *s.* ~/trivialer
~/offizieller official (approved) name
~/radikofunktioneller radicofunctional name
~/rationeller (systematischer) systematic name
~/trivialer (unsystematischer) trivial (unsystematic) name
~/zusammengesetzter conjunctive name
Namengebung *f (nomencl)* naming
Namenreaktion *f* name reaction
Nametkin-Umlagerung *f* Nametkin rearrangement *(of a carbenium ion by migration of a methyl group)*
NANA = *N*-Acetylneuraminsäure
Nanogrammbereich *m (anal)* nanogram range *(*10^{-9} *to* 10^{-6} *g)*
Nanomol *n* nanomole
Napalm *n* napalm
Napfmanschette *f* cup [ring]
Naphtha *n(f)* 1. [heavy] naphtha *(boiling range 150 to 210 °C)*; 2. *s.* Erdöl
~/leichtes light gasoline (naphtha)
Naphthacen *n* naphthacene, 2,3-benzanthracene
Naphthalen *n* naphthalene
~/durch Abpressen gereinigtes hot-pressed naphthalene
~/durch Zentrifugieren gereinigtes whizzed naphthalene
~/hochgereinigtes pure flake naphthalene
Naphthalencarbonsäure *f* naphthalenecarboxylic acid, naphthoic acid
Naphthalendampf *m* naphthalene vapour
Naphthalendicarbonsäure *f* naphthalenedicarboxylic acid
Naphthalendisulfonsäure *f* naphthalenedisulphonic acid
Naphthalenöl *n* naphthalene oil
Naphthalenpfanne *f* naphthalene tray
Naphthalenreihe *f* naphthalene series
Naphthalensulfochlorid *n* naphthalene sulphonyl chloride
Naphthalensulfonsäure *f* naphthalenesulphonic acid

Naphthalensulfonylchlorid *n s.* Naphthalensulfochlorid
Naphthalen-2-thiol *n* naphthalene-2-thiol
Naphthalin *n s.* Naphthalen
Naphthalin[indol]indigo *m(n) (dye)* naphthindigo
Naphthalol *n* naphthalol, betol, 2-naphthyl salicylate
Naphthalsäure *f* naphthalic acid, naphthalene-1,8-dicarboxylic acid
Naphthan *n s.* Decahydronaphthalen
Naphthen *n* naphthene, cycloalkane, cyclane, cycloparaffin
naphthenartig naphthenic
Naphthenat *n* naphthenate
Naphthenbasis *f* naphthene base *(of a crude oil)*
• **auf** ~ naphthene-based
Naphthenbasisöl *n,* **Naphthenerdöl** *n* naphthene-base petroleum (crude oil), naphthenic petroleum
naphthenisch naphthenic
Naphthenöl *n s.* Naphthenbasisöl
Naphtensäure *f* naphthenic acid
Naphth[indol]indigo *m(n) (dye)* naphthindigo
Naphthionsäure *f* naphthionic acid, 1-naphthylamine-4-sulphonic acid
α-**Naphthochinolin** *n s.* 7,8-Benzochinolin
β-**Naphthochinolin** *n s.* 5,6-Benzochinolin
Naphthochinon *n* naphthoquinone
Naphthoesäure *f* naphthoic acid, naphthalenecarboxylic acid
Naphth-1-ol *n,* **1-Naphthol** *n* naphth-1-ol, 1-hydroxynaphthalene
α-**Naphthol** *n s.* Naphth-1-ol
Naphtholblauschwarz *n* **B** naphthol blue black B
Naphtholdisulfonsäure *f* naphtholdisulphonic acid
Naphtholgelb *n* **S** naphthol (sulphur) yellow S, acid yellow 1
Naphtholkomponente *f* naphthol component
α-**Naphtholorange** *n* α-naphthol orange, orange I, sodium-azo-α-naphthol sulphanilate
Naphtholpech *n* naphthol pitch
Naphtholsulfonsäure *f* naphtholsulphonic acid
β-**Naphtholsulfonsäure** *f s.* Naphth-2-ol-7-sulfonsäure
Naphth-1-ol-4-sulfonsäure *f* naphth-1-ol-4-sulphonic acid, *4-hydroxynaphthalenesulphonic acid, Nevile-Winther acid, NW acid
Naphth-2-ol-6-sulfonsäure *f* naphth-2-ol-6-sulphonic acid, *6-hydroxynaphthalene-2-sulphonic acid, Schäffer acid
Naphth-2-ol-7-sulfonsäure *f* naphth-2-ol-7-sulphonic acid, *7-hydroxynaphthalene-2-sulphonic acid
Naphthylamin *n* naphthylamine
Naphthylamindisulfonsäure *f* naphthylaminedisulphonic acid
~ **S** naphth-1-ylamine-4,8-disulphonic acid, *8-aminonaphthalene-1,5-disulphonic acid
Naphthylaminsulfat *n* naphthylamine sulphate
Naphthylaminsulfonsäure *f* naphthylaminesulphonic acid
Naphthylessigsäure *f* naphthylacetic acid
Naphthylgruppe *f,* **Naphthylrest** *m* $C_{10}H_7$– naphthyl group (residue)
α-**Naphthylthioharnstoff** *m* 1-naphthylthiourea *(a rodenticide)*
Narbenfestigkeit *f (tann)* grain crack resistance
Narbenpressen *n (tann)* embossing
narbenrein *(tann)* clean-grained
Narbenschicht *f (tann)* grain layer
Narbenspalt *m (tann)* grain [split]
Narkoseether *m* anaesthesia ether
Narkosemittel *n* narcotic
Narkotikum *n* narcotic
narkotisch narcotic
narrensicher fool-proof
Nasen-Rachen-Reizstoff *m (tox)* sternutator, nose irritant, sneeze gas, irritant smoke
Nasenstein *m* tuckstone *(in a glass furnace)*
naß wet, moist
Naßablagerung *f* wet deposition *(of acids from the atmosphere)*
Naßabscheider *m* wet collector, [gas] scrubber, gas washer
Naßabscheidung *f* wet collecting (collection), wet scrubbing
Naßanalyse *f* wet analysis
naßaufbereiten *(min tech)* to wet-clean, to wash
Naßaufbereitung *f (min tech)* wet cleaning, washing; *(ceram)* wet preparation (mixing)
Naß-auf-Naß-Druckverfahren *n (text)* wet-on-wet printing method
Naßausschuß *m (pap)* wet broke
Naßaustrag *m* wet discharge
Naßbehandlung *f* wet treatment
Naßbeize *f (agric)* wet treatment *(of seed)*
Naßbetrieb *m* steaming *(in making water gas)*
Naßdampf *m* wet steam
Naßdekatur *f (text)* wet decatizing, roll boiling
Nässe *f* wetness, moisture
naßecht *(text)* fast to wetting
Naßechtheit *f (text)* wet fastness, fastness to wetting
Naßelektroabscheider *m,* **Naßelektrofilter** *n* wet (film) precipitator *(for electrical gas cleaning)*
Naßentrindungsanlage *f (pap)* waterous barker
Naßentstauber *m s.* Naßabscheider
naßfest 1. wet-strength *(paper)*; 2. *s.* naßecht
Naßfestigkeit *f* 1. wet strength *(of paper)*; 2. *s.* Naßechtheit
Naßfestleim *m (pap)* wet-strength resin
Naßfilz *m (pap)* wet felt
~**/wollener** wool (woollen) felt
Naßfilzleitwalze *f (pap)* wet-felt roll
Naßgas *n* wet gas
Naßgasreinigung *f* wet gas cleaning
Naßguß *m* green-sand casting
Naßgußform *f* green-sand mould
Naßgußformen *n* green-sand moulding

Naßguß[form]sand *m* green [moulding] sand, greensand
Naßgut *n* wet product, *(material to be processed also)* wet feed
Naßgutaufgabe *f* wet feeding
Naßgutaufgabevorrichtung *f* wet feeder
Naßherd *m (min tech)* wet table
Naß-in-Naß-Druckverfahren *n (text)* wet-on-wet printing method
Naßkarbonisation *f (text)* wet carbonizing *(of wool)*
Naßklassieren *n* wet classifying, water sizing
Naßklassierer *m* wet classifier
Naßklebrigkeit *f* wet tack
Naßknitterarm-Ausrüstung *f (text)* no-iron (smooth-drying) finish
Naßkoller[gang] *m* wet pan
Naßkollodiumplatte *f (phot)* wet collodion plate
Naßkollodiumverfahren *n (phot)* wet collodion process
Naßlöschen *n* wet quenching *(of coke)*
Naß-Luft-Oxidation *f (hyd)* wet [air] oxidation, wet combustion *(of sludge)*
Naßmagnetscheider *m* wet magnetic separator
Naßmahlung *f* wet milling (grinding)
Naßmetallurgie *f* hydrometallurgy, wet metallurgy
naßmetallurgisch hydrometallurgical
Naßoxidation *f* wet [air] oxidation *(as a natural process)*
Naßpartie *f (pap)* wet part (end)
Naßphosphorsäure *f* wet-process phosphoric acid, green acid
Naßplatte *f (phot)* wet collodion plate
naßpökeln *(food)* to brine, to pickle
Naßpökelung *f (food)* brining, brine curing (cure, salting), pickling, pickle curing (cure)
Naßprallabscheider *m* inertia scrubber *(gas cleaning)*
Naßpressen *n (ceram)* wet (plastic) pressing
Naßpressenpartie *f (pap)* press part (section)
Naßprobe *f (met)* wet assay
naßreinigen to wet-clean
Naßreiniger *m* wet cleaner
Naßreinigung *f* wet cleaning
~ eines Gases wet gas cleaning
Naßrühren *n (ceram)* blunging
naßsalzen *(food)* to brine
Naßscheidung *f (sugar)* wet liming, defecation with milk of lime
Naßschlamm *m* wet sludge
Naßschmelze *f (food)* wet rendering
~ auf Dampf steam rendering
Naßschnitzel *npl (sugar)* wet pulp
Naßsetzmaschine *f (min tech)* wet jig, jig washer
Naßsieben *n* wet screening
Naßspinnen *n* wet spinning
Naßstaubabscheider *m s.* Naßabscheider
Naßverbrennung *f* 1. wet combustion *(of waste products)*, *(hyd also)* Zimmermann process, Zimpro [process], wet [air] oxidation; 2. burning of wet fuels
Naßverfahren *n* wet process, wet-processing method; *(ceram)* slip process; ice-water (wet-cooling) method *(margarine making)*
Naß-Verfahren-Phosphorsäure *f s.* Naßphosphorsäure
Naßverfestigungsmittel *n (pap)* wet-strength agent
Naßvermahlung *f* wet milling (grinding)
Naßwäsche *f* wet cleaning (washing)
Naßzyklon *m* liquid cyclone [separator], wet-cyclone classifier, hydraulic cyclone separator, hydrocyclone [separator], hydroclone
naszierend nascent
nativ native
Nativdextran *n* native dextran
Nativpolysaccharid *n s.* Polysaccharid/pflanzliches
Nativserum *n* native serum
Natrit *m (min)* natrite, natron, soda *(sodium carbonate 10-water)*
Natrium *n* Na sodium
~ in Bandform sodium ribbon
~/radioaktives radioactive sodium, radiosodium, *(specif)* ^{24}Na sodium-24
Natrium-24 *n* ^{24}Na sodium-24
Natriumabietat *n* sodium abietate
Natriumacetat *n* sodium acetate
Natriumacetessigester *m* sodioacetoacetic ester
Natriumacetylid *n* sodium acetylide (carbide)
Natriumalaun *m* sodium (soda) alum, aluminium sodium sulphate 12-water
Natriumalginat *n* sodium alginate, sodium polymannuronate
Natriumalkoholat *n* sodium alkoxide
Natriumaluminat *n* sodium aluminate
Natriumaluminiumchlorid *n* aluminium sodium chloride
Natriumaluminiumfluorid *n s.* Natriumhexafluoroaluminat
Natriumaluminiumsulfat *n* aluminium sodium sulphate
Natriumalumosilicat *n* sodium aluminosilicate
Natriumamalgam *n* sodium amalgam
Natriumamid *n* sodium amide
Natrium-*p*-aminobenzoat *n* sodium *para*-aminobenzoate, PABA sodium
Natriumammoniumhydrogenphosphat-4-Wasser *n* ammonium sodium hydrogenphosphate 4-water, phosphorus salt
Natriumammoniumsulfat *n* ammonium sodium sulphate
Natriumanilid *n* sodium anilide
Natriumanthrachinon-2-sulfonat *n* sodium anthraquinone-2-sulphonate, silver salt
Natriumarsenat(III) *n* sodium arsenite
Natriumarsenat(V) *n* sodium arsenate
Natriumarsenit *n* sodium arsenite
Natriumascorbat *n* sodium ascorbate
Natriumäthoxid *n*, **Natriumäthylat** *n s.* Natriumethylat

Natriumaustauscher *m* sodium[-cycle cation] exchanger, Na-form exchanger
Natriumazid *n* sodium azide
Natriumbenzensulfonat *n* sodium benzene sulphonate
Natriumbenzoat *n* sodium benzoate
Natriumberylliumfluorid *n s.* Natriumtetrafluoroberyllat
Natriumbisulfitbleiche *f (pap)* sodium bisulphite bleaching
Natriumbisulfitkochsäure *f (pap)* sodium bisulphite cooking liquor, sodium-base [sulphite] liquor, sodium-base acid
Natriumbisulfitlösung *f (pap)* sodium bisulphite liquor
Natrium-Blei-Legierung *f* sodium-lead alloy
Natriumboranat *n* sodium tetrahydridoborate, sodium hydridoborate
Natriumborhydrid *n,* **Natriumborwasserstoff** *m s.* Natriumboranat
Natriumbromat *n* sodium bromate
Natriumbromid *n* sodium bromide
Natrium-Butadienkautschuk *m* sodium-butadiene rubber
Natriumbutyrat *n* sodium butyrate
Natriumcarbid *n* sodium carbide (acetylide)
Natriumcarbonat *n* sodium carbonate, soda
~/wasserfreies anhydrous sodium carbonate, *(tech also)* calcined soda, [soda] ash
Natriumcarbonat-Wasserstoffperoxid *n* sodium carbonate peroxide
Natriumcarboxymethylcellulose *f* sodium carboxymethyl cellulose
Natriumcaseinat *n* sodium caseinate, casein sodium
Natriumcelluloseglykolat *n s.* Natriumcarboxymethylcellulose
Natriumcellulosexanthogenat *n* sodium cellulose xanthate
Natriumchloracetat *n* sodium chloroacetate
Natriumchlorat *n* sodium chlorate
Natriumchlorid *n* sodium chloride
Natriumchloridgitter *n* sodium chloride lattice
Natriumchloridlösung *f* **zum Regenerieren** *(hyd)* regenerant brine, brine regenerant, water-softener [regeneration] brine *(ion exchange)*
Natriumchlorit *n* sodium chlorite
Natriumchloritbleiche *f (pap)* sodium chlorite bleaching
Natriumchloritbleichlauge *f (pap)* sodium chlorite bleaching liquor
Natriumchromat *n* sodium chromate
Natriumcitrat *n* sodium citrate
Natriumcyanat *n* sodium cyanate
Natriumcyanid *n* sodium cyanide
Natriumcyclamat *n* sodium cyclamate, sodium cyclohexylsulphamate
Natriumdampflampe *f* sodium-vapour [discharge] lamp, sodium lamp
Natriumderivat *n (org ch)* sodio derivative
Natriumdiacetat *n* sodium diacetate *(commercially for sodium acetate containing additional acetic acid)*
Natriumdichromat *n* sodium dichromate
Natriumdicyanoaurat(I) *n* sodium cyanoaurate(I), sodium gold cyanide
Natrium-*N,N*-diethyldithiocarbamat *n* sodium diethyldithiocarbamate
Natriumdihydrogenarsenat *n* sodium dihydrogenarsenate
Natriumdihydrogendiphosphat *n* sodium dihydrogendiphosphate, sodium dihydrogenpyrophosphate
Natriumdihydrogenphosphat *n* sodium dihydrogenphosphate
Natriumdihydrogenpyrophosphat *n s.* Natriumdihydrogendiphosphat
Natriumdinitrophenolat *n* sodium dinitrophenate
Natriumdiphosphat *n* sodium diphosphate, sodium pyrophosphate
Natriumdisilicat *n* sodium disilicate
Natriumdisulfat *n* sodium disulphate
Natriumdisulfit *n* sodium disulphite
Natriumdithionat *n* sodium dithionate
Natriumdithionit *n* sodium dithionite
Natriumdithiosulfatoaurat(I) *n* sodium dithiosulphatoaurate(I)
Natriumdiuranat *n* sodium diuranate
Natriumdivanadat(V) *n* sodium divanadate(V)
Natrium-D-Linie *f (anal)* sodium D line
Natriumdodecamolybdatophosphat *n* sodium dodecamolybdophosphate, sodium 12-molybdophosphate
Natriumdodecawolframatophosphat *n* sodium dodecatungstophosphate, *sodium dodecawolframophosphate, *sodium 12-wolframophosphate
Natriumdodecylsulfat *n s.* Natriumlaurylsulfat
Natriumdraht *m* sodium wire
Natriumeisen(III)-oxalat *n* sodium trioxalatoferrate(III)
Natriumethylat *n* sodium ethoxide
Natriumethylxanthogenat *n* sodium ethylxanthate, sodium xanthate, sodium xanthogenate
Natriumferrat(III) *n* sodium ferrate(III)
Natriumflamme *f* sodium flame
Natriumfluorid *n* sodium fluoride
Natriumfluoracetat *n* sodium fluoroacetate
Natriumfluoroborat *n* sodium fluoroborate
Natriumfolat *n* sodium folate, sodium pteroylglutamate
Natriumformaldehydsulfoxylat *n* sodium formaldehydesulphoxylate, SFS, sodium sulphoxylate formaldehyde
Natriumformiat *n* sodium formate
Natriumgluconat *n* sodium gluconate
Natriumglutamat *n* sodium glutamate
Natriumgold(III)-chlorid *n s.* Natriumtetrachloroaurat(III)
Natriumgold(I)-cyanid *n s.* Natriumdicyanoaurat(I)

Natriumgold(I)-sulfid *n* gold sodium sulphide
Natrium-Graphit-Reaktor *m (nucl)* sodium graphite reactor
Natriumheptoxodivanadat(V) *n s.* Natriumdivanadat(V)
Natriumhexachloroiridat(III) *n* sodium hexachloroiridate(III)
Natriumhexachloroosmat(IV) *n* sodium hexachloroosmate(IV)
Natriumhexachloroplatinat(IV) *n* sodium hexachloroplatinate(IV)
Natriumhexachlororhodat(III) *n* sodium hexachlororhodate(III)
Natriumhexacyanoferrat(III) *n* sodium hexacyanoferrate(III)
Natriumhexafluoroaluminat *n* sodium hexafluoroaluminate
Natriumhexafluoroantimonat(V) *n* sodium hexafluoroantimonate
Natriumhexafluorosilicat *n* sodium hexafluorosilicate
Natriumhexahydroxostannat(IV) *n* sodium hexahydroxostannate(IV), preparing salt
Natriumhexaiodoplatinat(IV) *n* sodium hexaiodoplatinate(IV)
Natriumhexametaphosphat *n* sodium hexametaphosphate
Natriumhexanitrocobaltat(III) *n* sodium hexanitrocobaltate(III)
Natriumhydrid *n* sodium hydride
Natriumhydrogencarbonat *n* sodium hydrogencarbonate
Natriumhydrogenfluorid *n* sodium hydrogenfluoride
Natriumhydrogenperoxid *n* sodium hydrogenperoxide
Natriumhydrogenphosphat *n* sodium hydrogenphosphate
Natriumhydrogensulfat *n* sodium hydrogensulphate
Natriumhydrogensulfid *n* sodium hydrogensulphide
Natriumhydrogensulfit *n* sodium hydrogensulphite
Natriumhydrogentartrat *n* sodium hydrogentartrate
Natriumhydrosulfit *n s.* Natriumdithionit
Natriumhydroxid *n* sodium hydroxide
Natriumhypochlorit *n* sodium hypochlorite
Natriumhypochloritbleiche *f* sodium hypochlorite bleaching
Natriumhypochloritbleichlauge *f* sodium hypochlorite bleaching liquor, liquid bleach
Natriumhyponitrit *n* sodium hyponitrite
Natriumhypophosphat *n* sodium hypophosphate
Natriumhypophosphit *n* sodium hypophosphite, *sodium phosphinate
Natriumiodat *n* sodium iodate
Natriumiodid *n* sodium iodide
Natriumionendurchbruch *m* sodium leakage *(ion exchange)*
Natriumionenschlupf *m* sodium slippage *(ion exchange)*
natriumkatalysiert sodium-catalyzed
Natriumkondensation *f (org ch)* sodium condensation
Natriumkuchen *m* nitre cake *(consisting of sodium sulphate and sodium hydrogensulphate)*
Natriumlactat *n* sodium lactate
Natriumlampe *f s.* Natriumdampflampe
Natriumlaurylsulfat *n* sodium lauryl sulphate
Natriumlicht *n* sodium light
Natriumlöffel *m* sodium spoon
Natriummanganat(VI) *n* sodium manganate(VI)
Natriummanganat(VII) *n s.* Natriumpermanganat
Natriummetaarsenat(III) *n* sodium dioxoarsenate(III)
Natriummetaarsenat(V) *n* sodium trioxoarsenate(V)
Natriummetaborat *n* sodium metaborate
Natriummetaperiodat *n s.* Natriumtetroxoiodat(VII)
Natriummetaphosphat *n* sodium metaphosphate
Natriummetaphosphatperle *f* sodium phosphate bead
Natriummetasilicat *n* sodium metasilicate
Natriummetavanadat *n s.* Natriumtrioxovanadat(V)
Natriummethoxid *n s.* Natriummethylat
Natriummethyl *n s.* Methylnatrium
Natriummethylat *n* sodium methylate, sodium methoxide
Natriummethylsiliconat *n* sodium methylsiliconate
Natriummineral *n* sodium mineral
Natriummolybdat *n* sodium molybdate
Natriummolybdat-2-Wasser *n* sodium molybdate 2-water, sodium molybdate crystals
Natriummyristat *n* sodium myristate
Natriumnaphthionat *n* sodium naphthionate, sodium α-naphthylamine sulphonate
Natrium-α-naphthochinonsulfonat *n* sodium β-naphthoquinone-4-sulphonate
Natriumnitrat *n* sodium nitrate
Natriumnitrid *n* sodium nitride
Natriumnitrit *n* sodium nitrite
Natriumnitroprussiat *n*, **Natriumnitroprussid** *n s.* Nitroprussidnatrium
Natriumoleat *n* sodium oleate
Natriumorthophosphat *n* sodium orthophosphate
Natriumorthosilicat *n* sodium orthosilicate, sodium tetraoxosilicate
Natriumorthovanadat *n s.* Natriumtetroxovanadat(V)
Natriumoxalat *n* sodium oxalate
Natriumoxid *n* sodium oxide
Natriumpalmitat *n* sodium palmitate
Natriumpentachlorphenolat *n* sodium pentachlorophenate
Natriumperchlorat *n* sodium perchlorate
Natriumpermanganat *n* sodium permanganate
Natriumperoxid *n* sodium peroxide
Natriumperoxoborat *n* sodium peroxoborate
Natriumperoxochromat *n* sodium peroxochromate
Natriumperoxodisulfat *n* sodium peroxodisulphate

Natriumperrhenat *n* sodium perrhenate, *sodium tetraoxorhenate(VII)
Natriumphenolat *n* sodium phenate
Natriumphosphat *n* sodium phosphate, *(specif)* sodium orthophosphate
Natriumphosphid *n* sodium phosphide
Natriumphosphit *n* sodium phosphite, *sodium phosphonate
Natriumpolybutadien *n* sodium polybutadien
Natriumpolymerisation *f* sodium[-catalyzed] polymerization
Natriumpolysulfid *n* sodium polysulphide
Natriumpresse *f* sodium [wire] press
Natriumpteroylglutamat *n s.* Natriumfolat
Natriumpyrophosphat *n s.* Natriumdiphosphat
Natriumpyrosulfit *n s.* Natriumdisulfit
Natriumpyrovanadat(V) *n s.* Natriumdivanadat(V)
Natriumrhodanid *n s.* Natriumthiocyanat
Natriumsalicylat *n* sodium salicylate
Natriumschlupf *m* sodium slippage *(ion exchange)*
Natriumseife *f* sodium (soda) soap, hard soap
Natriumselenat *n* sodium selenate
Natriumselenid *n* sodium selenide
Natriumselenit *n* sodium selenite
Natriumsesquisilicat *n* sodium sesquisilicate
Natriumsilicat *n* sodium silicate
Natriumsilicatglas *n* soda-silica glass
Natriumstearat *n* sodium stearate
Natriumsuccinat *n* sodium succinate
Natriumsulfat *n* sodium sulphate
Natriumsulfat-10-Wasser *n* sodium sulphate 10-water, Glauber salt
Natriumsulfhydrat *n (tann)* sodium hydrogensulphide, sodium sulphydrate
Natriumsulfid *n* sodium sulphide
Natriumsulfit *n* sodium sulphite
Natriumsulfonat *n* sodium sulphonate
Natriumsulfoxylat *n* sodium sulphoxylate
Natriumtartrat *n* sodium tartrate
Natriumtetraborat *n***/wasserfreies** sodium tetraborate, *(tech also)* calcined (burnt, anhydrous, dehydrated) borax
Natriumtetraborat-5-Wasser *n* sodium tetraborate 5-water, octahedral borax
Natriumtetraborat-10-Wasser *n* sodium tetraborate 10-water, borax
Natriumtetrachloroaurat(III) *n* sodium tetrachloroaurate(III)
Natriumtetrachloropalladat(II) *n* sodium tetrachloropalladate(II)
Natriumtetrachloroplatinat(II) *n* sodium tetrachloroplatinate(II)
Natriumtetrafluoroberyllat *n* sodium tetrafluoroberyllate
Natriumtetrafluoroborat *n* sodium tetrafluoroborate
Natriumtetrahydridoborat *n s.* Natriumboranat
Natriumtetraphenylborat *n* sodium tetraphenylborate, tetraphenylboron sodium
Natriumtetrasulfid *n* sodium tetrasulphide
Natriumtetrathionat *n* sodium tetrathionate
Natriumtetroxoiodat(VII) *n* sodium tetraoxoiodate(VII), sodium periodate, sodium metaperiodate
Natriumtetroxorhenat(VII) *n s.* Natriumperrhenat
Natriumtetroxosilicat *n s.* Natriumorthosilicat
Natriumtetroxovanadat(V) *n* sodium tetraoxovanadate(V)
Natriumthioantimonat(V) *n* sodium thioantimonate
Natriumthiocarbonat *n* sodium thiocarbonate, sodium trithiocarbonate
Natriumthiocyanat *n* sodium thiocyanate
Natriumthioglycolat *n* sodium thioglycolate, sodium mercaptoacetate
Natriumthiosulfat *n* sodium thiosulphate, *(phot also)* hyposulphite
Natriumtrichloracetat *n* sodium trichloroacetate, sodium TCA
Natriumtrioxobismutat(V) *n* sodium trioxobismuthate(V)
Natriumtrioxovanadat(V) *n* sodium trioxovanadate(V)
Natriumtriphosphat *n* sodium triphosphate
Natriumuranat *n s.* Natriumdiuranat
Natriumuranylacetat *n* sodium uranyl acetate
Natriumwolframat *n* sodium,wolframate, sodium tungstate
Natriumzange *f* sodium tongs
Natriumzyklus *m* sodium cycle *(ion exchange)*
Natrolith *m (min)* natrolite, needle zeolite *(a hydrous aluminium sodium silicate)*
Natron *n* 1. *(min)* soda, natron, natrite *(sodium carbonate 10-water)*; 2. *s.* Natriumhydrogencarbonat
Natronalaun *m s.* Natriumalaun
Natronaufschluß *m (pap)* soda pulping
Natronbleichlauge *f* Labarraque's solution, eau de Labarraque *(aqueous solution containing sodium hypochlorite)*
Natroncellulose *f* natron cellulose, *(Am)* soda cellulose
Natronglas *n* soda (soft) glass
Natronglimmer *m (min)* soda mica, paragonite *(a phyllosilicate)*
Natronkalk *m* soda lime *(a mixture of caustic soda with caustic lime)*
Natronkalkglas *n* soda-lime glass
Natron-Kalk-Kieselsäureglas *n* soda-lime-silica glass
Natronkalkrohr *n* soda lime tube
Natronkochlauge *f (pap)* soda cooking (digestion) liquor, soda liquor (lye)
Natronkochung *f (pap)* soda cook
Natronlauge *f* sodium hydroxide solution, caustic-soda solution, caustic lye of soda
Natronlauge-Aluminatlösung *f* sodium aluminate solution, aluminate liquor *(used in the Bayer process)*
Natronsalpeter *m* soda nitre, Chile saltpetre (nitre, nitrate), Chilean (Chilian) nitrate *(sodium nitrate)*

Natronseife *f* soda (sodium) soap, hard soap
Natronstoff *m s.* Natronzellstoff
Natronverfahren *n (pap)* soda process, soda [wood-]pulp process
Natronwasserglas *n* [soda] water glass, sodium silicate • **mit ~ geleimt** *(pap)* silicate-sized
Natronweinstein *m* Rochelle salt, potassium sodium tartrate 4-water
Natronzellstoff *m* soda pulp
Natronzellstoffabrik *f* soda mill
Natronzellstoffkocher *m* soda digester
Naturambra *f* ambergris, ambergrease
Naturasphalt *m* rock (native, natural) asphalt
Naturauslagerung *f* natural (field) exposure
Naturbenzin *n s.* Naturgasbenzin
Naturbewitterung *f* outdoor weathering
Naturbewitterungsversuch *m* outdoor weathering test
Naturbleicherde *f* natural (naturally occurring) clay
Naturfarbstoff *m* natural colouring matter, *(esp text)* natural dyestuff; *(bioch)* biochrome
Naturfaser *f* natural fibre
Naturfaserstoff *m* natural fibre
Naturfett *n* natural fat
Naturformsand *m* natural [moulding] sand, naturally bonded sand
Naturgas *n* natural gas
~/feuchtes (nasses) wet natural gas
~/trockenes dry natural gas
Naturgasbenzin *n* natural gasoline, casing-head gasoline (spirit)
~/durch Absorption gewonnenes absorption gasoline
Naturgasflüssigkeit *f (petrol)* natural gas liquid, NGL *(mixture of natural gasoline and liquid gas)*
Naturgebilde *n s.* Naturobjekt
Naturglas *n* natural glass
Naturgummi *n* natural gum
Naturharz *n* natural resin
Naturindigo *m(n)* natural indigo
Naturkautschuk *m* natural rubber, NR
Naturkautschuklatex *m* natural-rubber latex
Naturkautschukmischung *f* natural-rubber compound (mix, stock)
Naturkautschukvulkanisat *n* natural-rubber vulcanizate
Naturkohle *f* natural (mineral, fossil) coal
Naturkohlenwasserstoff *m* natural hydrocarbon
Naturkork *m* bark cork
Naturkunstdruckpapier *n* imitation art paper
Naturlatex *m s.* Naturkautschuklatex
Naturlegierung *f* natural alloy
natürlich [vorkommend] naturally occurring, found in nature, from natural sources, native
Naturmoschus *m* natural musk
Naturobjekt *n* natural entity (object)
Naturprodukt *n* natural product
Naturriechstoff *m* natural perfume
Natursand *m s.* Naturformsand
Naturseide *f* natural silk
Naturstoff *m* natural product (material); *(bioch)* natural compound
~/insektizider botanical
~ mikrobiellen Ursprungs microbial product
~/organischer natural organic product
~/plastischer natural plastic
Naturstoffchemie *f* chemistry of natural products
Naturton *m* natural (naturally occurring) clay
Naturumlauf *m* natural circulation, gravity return
Naturumlaufsystem *n* natural-circulation (gravity-return) system
Naturversuch *m* field test (trial)
Naturzement *m* natural cement
NBS *s. N*-Brombernsteinsäureimid
Nc-Lack *m*, **N.C.-Lack** *m s.* Cellulosenitratlack
Neapelgelb *n* Naples (antimony) yellow
Nebel *m* fog, mist, liquid aerosol
~/saurer acid fog
Nebelabscheider *m* mist eliminator
Nebelblaser *m*, **Nebelgerät** *n (agric)* fog generator (appliance), fogging machine, fogger, nebulizer, aero-mist sprayer
Nebelhorizont *m* fog horizon
Nebelkammer *f*[/**Wilsonsche]** [Wilson] cloud chamber, [Wilson] cloud-track apparatus
Nebelkammeraufnahme *f*, **Nebelkammerbild** *n* cloud-chamber photograph
Nebeln *n (agric)* fogging
Nebelspur *f (phys ch)* cloud (fog) track
Nebeltröpfchen *n* fog droplet
Nebenalkaloid *n* companion alkaloid (base)
Nebenbande *f (spectr)* side (subsidiary) band
Nebenbase *f s.* Nebenalkaloid
Nebenbestandteil *m* minor constituent *(* 1 to 0.01 %)*
Nebenbild *n (phot)* ghost image
Nebenbindungsstelle *f (bioch)* accessory binding site
Nebenerzeugnis *n s.* Nebenprodukt
Nebengemengteile *mpl* accessory minerals (components, constituents)
Nebengewinnungsofen *m s.* Nebenproduktenofen
Nebengruppe *f* subgroup, B group *(of the periodic table)*
Nebenkolonne *f* side-stream column
Nebenkomponente *f s.* Nebenbestandteil
Nebenmineral *n* minor mineral
Nebennierenrindenhormon *n* adrenocortical (adrenalcortical) hormone, corticoid (adrenal cortex) hormone
Nebenpigment *n* auxiliary (accessory) pigment *(in photosynthesis)*
Nebenprodukt *n* by-product, secondary product *(of a chemical process)*; side product *(of a chemical reaction)*
Nebenproduktenanlage *f* by-product [recovery] plant
Nebenproduktengewinnung *f* by-product recovery

Nebenproduktenofen *m* by-product [recovery] oven
Nebenquantenzahl *f* azimuthal (subsidiary) quantum number, orbital [angular momentum] quantum number
Nebenreaktion *f* side (secondary) reaction
Nebenserie *f*/**diffuse** *s.* ~/erste
~/erste *(spectr)* diffuse series
~/scharfe *s.* ~/zweite
~/zweite *(spectr)* sharp series
Nebenstoffwechsel *m* secondary metabolism
Nebenturm *m (petrol)* side[stream] stripper, stripper [column]
Nebenvalenz *f* secondary valency
Nebenvalenzbindung *f* secondary [valency] bond
Nebenvalenzkraft *f* secondary valency force
Nebenwirkung *f (pharm)* side effect
Neber-Umlagerung *f* Neber rearrangement *(of sulphonic acid esters of ketoximes into aminoketones)*
Nebligwerden *n* blooming *(of oil varnishes)*
Necinsäure *f* necic acid *(acid component of senecio alkaloids)*
Neel-Temperatur *f (cryst)* Neel temperature (point)
Nef-Reaktion *f* Nef reaction *(for obtaining aldehydes and ketones)*
negativ/dreifach trinegative
~/einfach uninegative
~/fünffach pentanegative, quinque-negative
~ geladen negatively charged, negative
~/sechsfach hexanegative
~/vierfach tetranegative
~/zweifach dinegative, binegative
Negativ *n (phot)* negative
Negativbild *n (phot)* negative image
Negativemulsion *f (phot)* negative emulsion
Negativentwickler *m (phot)* negative developer
Negativentwicklung *f (phot)* negative development
Negativfilm *m (phot)* negative film
Negativität *f* negativity
Negativkopie *f (phot)* negative copy
Negativladung *f* negative charge
Negativmaterial *n (phot)* negative material
Negativpapier *n (phot)* negative paper
~/abziehbares stripping paper
Negatron *n* negatron, [negative] electron
Neigung *f* 1. inclination, *(quantitatively:)* gradient, slope; 2. tendency, propensity *(as to chemical reaction)*
Neigungswinkel *m* angle of inclination (incline)
nektarführend melliferous
NE-Legierung *f* non-ferrous alloy
Nelkenöl *n* caryophyllus (clove) oil, oil of cloves *(from Syzygium aromaticum (L.) Merr. et L. M. Perry)*
Nelkenpfeffer *m* allspice *(from Pimenta dioica (L.) Merr.)*
Nelkenrinde *f*, **Nelkenzimt** *m* clove bark *(from Dicypellum caryophyllatum Nees)*
Nelson-Zelle *f (el ch)* Nelson cell
nematizid nematocidal, nema[ti]cidal
Nematizid *n* nematocide, nema[ti]cide
nematoblastisch *(geol)* nematoblastic
Nematozid *n s.* Nematizid
NE-Metall *n* non-ferrous metal
N-endständig N-terminal
Neodym *n* Nd neodymium
Neodymacetat *n* neodymium acetate
Neodymbromat *n* neodymium bromate
Neodymbromid *n* neodymium bromide
Neodymchlorid *n* neodymium chloride
Neodymglas *n* neodymium glass
Neodymiodid *n* neodymium iodide
Neodymlaser *m* neodymium laser
Neodymmolybdat(VI) *n* neodymium molybdate(VI)
Neodymnitrat *n* neodymium nitrate
Neodymnitrid *n* neodymium nitride
Neodymoxid *n* neodymium oxide
Neodymsulfat *n* neodymium sulphate
Neodymsulfid *n* neodymium sulphide
Neon *n* Ne neon
Neonröhre *f* neon discharge tube
Neopentan *n* neopentane, *2,2-dimethylpropane
Nepalkardamom *m(n)* Nepal (Bengal) cardamom *(from Amomum aromaticum Roxb. and A. subulatum Roxb.)*
Nephelin *m (min)* nepheline, nephelite *(a tectosilicate)*
Nephelometer *n* nephelometer
Nephelometrie *f* nephelometry
nephelometrisch nephelometric
nephrotoxisch nephrotoxic *(poisonous to the kidney)*
Neptunium *n* Np neptunium
Neral *n* neral, citral b, **cis*-3,7-dimethylocta-2,6-dienal
Nernst-Beziehung *f s.* Nernst-Gleichung
Nernst-Brenner *m s.* Nernst-Lampe
Nernst-Gleichung *f* Nernst equation
Nernst-Lampe *f (spectr)* Nernst lamp (glower)
Nernst-Potential *n s.* Gleichgewichtspotential
Nernst-Stift *m (spectr)* Nernst glower
Nerol *n* nerol, *3,7-dimethylocta-2,6-dien-1-ol
Neroliöl *n* neroli oil *(from Citrus aurantium L. ssp. aurantium)*
Nerv *m (rubber)* nerve, snap
Nervengas *n* nerve gas
Nervengift *n* nerve poison (agent), neurotoxin
nervenschädigend neurotoxic
Nervenwachstumsfaktor *m* nerve growth factor, NGF
nervig *(rubber)* nervy, snappy
Nervonsäure *f* nervonic acid, *cis*-tetracos-15-enoic acid
Nesmejanow-Reaktion *f* Nesmejanov reaction *(for obtaining arylmercury chlorides)*
Nesosilicat *n* nesosilicate *(a silicate containing independent SiO_4 tetrahedra)*

Neßler-Zylinder *m* Nessler cylinder (glass, tube) *(colorimetry)*
Nestdüngung *f (agric)* nest fertilization
Nesterbehandlung *f (agric)* spot treatment *(as with herbicides)*
Nettogewinn *m* net gain *(as in energy)*
Nettoladung *f* net charge
Nettoreaktion *f* net reaction
Nettoretentionsvolumen *n (chromat)* net retention volume
Nettosynthese *f (bioch)* net synthesis
Nettovertikalfluß *m* net vertical flux
netzbar wettable
Netzbarkeit *f* wettability
Netzbildung *f* 1. *(phot)* reticulation; 2. *(coat)* stringing
Netzbottich *m (text)* steeping pan
Netzebene *f (cryst)* lattice plane, net (atomic) plane
Netzebenenabstand *m (cryst)* lattice distance (spacing), spacing of the planes
Netzeigenschaften *fpl* wetting properties (characteristics)
Netzelektrode *f* gauze electrode
netzen to wet, *(text also)* to dew, to damp[en]
Netzer *m s.* Netzmittel
Netzfähigkeit *f* wetting ability
Netzkatode *f* gauze cathode
Netzkontakt *m* screen (gauze) catalyst
Netzkraft *f* wetting power (strength)
Netzmittel *n* wetting agent (aid), wetter, spreading agent, spreader, humectant
Netzpulver *n* wettable powder *(pest control)*
Netzschwefel *m* wettable sulphur *(pest control)*
Netzspannung *f* mains voltage
Netzspirale *f* gauze plug *(in a combustion tube)*
Netzvermögen *n* wetting ability
Netzwärme *f* heat of wetting
Netzwerk *n* network
~/dreidimensionales three-dimensional network
~/interpenetrierendes interpenetrating network, IPN
~/räumliches *s.* ~/dreidimensionales
Netzwerkbildner *m (glass)* network former, network-forming ion
Netzwerkbildner *m* **und -wandler** *m* network coformer
Netzwerkhypothese *f* **von W. H. Zachariasen** *(glass)* Zachariasen's theory
Netzwerkwandler *m (glass)* network modifier, network-modifying ion
Netzwerkzwitter *m (glass)* net intermediate
Netzwirkung *f* wetting action
Neuappretur *f (text)* resizing, additional finish
Neubauer-Tiegel *m* Monroe (Neubauer) crucible
Neubekohlung *f* anode renewal *(electrolysis)*
Neubestimmung *f* redetermination
Neubildungsdauer *f (bioch)* turnover time
Neublau *n* new blue *(any of several blue dyes and pigments)*
~ **R** new blue R, Meldola's blue, basic blue 6
Neubohrung *f (petrol)* wildcat
Neufuchsin *n* new fuchsine, basic violet 2 *(a triphenylmethane dye)*
Neufüllung *f (filtr)* rebedding
Neugewürz *n* allspice *(from Pimenta dioica (L.) Merr.)*
Neugrün *n* 1. malachite (fast) green, basic green 4 *(a triphenylmethane dye)*; 2. new green *(copper(II) acetate arsenite)*
Neuraminsäure *f* neuraminic acid *(an amino sugar)*
Neurin *n* neurine, trimethylvinylammonium hydroxide
Neuroleptikum *n (pharm)* neuroleptic [drug], antipsychotic, major tranquilizer, CNS-depressant, central nervous system depressant
neuroleptisch neuroleptic
Neurot *n* scarlet red, Biebrich [scarlet] red
Neurotoxin *n* neurotoxin, nerve poison (agent)
neurotoxisch neurotoxic
Neurotoxizität *f* neurotoxicity
Neusilber *n* nickel silver, *(Am)* nickel brass
neutral neutral • ~ **reagieren** to react neutral
~/elektrisch uncharged
Neutralaustausch *m (hyd)* Na-form (sodium cycle) exchange, ion exchange in (on) the sodium cycle
Neutralaustauscher *m (hyd)* Na-form exchanger, sodium exchanger
Neutralbereich *m* neutral range
Neutralfett *n* neutral fat
Neutralglycerid *n* triglyceride
Neutralisation *f* neutralization
~ **mittels Ionenaustauschs** *(hyd)* ion-exchange neutralization
Neutralisationsanalyse *f* [volumetric] neutralization titration
Neutralisationsanlage *f* neutralizing plant
Neutralisationsbehälter *m* neutralizer
Neutralisationsindikator *m* neutralization indicator
Neutralisationskurve *f* neutralization curve
Neutralisationsmittel *n* neutralizing agent, neutralizer
Neutralisationsmittellösung *f (hyd)* neutralizing solution
Neutralisationsreaktion *f* neutralization reaction, acid-base neutralization [reaction]
Neutralisationstitration *f* neutralization titration, acid-base titration
Neutralisationswärme *f* heat of neutralization
Neutralisationszahl *f* neutralization value, acid value (number), A.V.
Neutralisator *m s.* Neutralisationsmittel
neutralisieren to neutralize
Neutralisierungs... *s.* Neutralisations...
Neutralität *f* neutrality
Neutrallard *n (food)* neutral lard
Neutralligand *m* neutral ligand
Neutralmolekül *n* zero-charge molecule *(as opposed to cations and anions)*
Neutralöl *n* neutral oil

Neutralpunkt *m* point of neutrality, neutralization point • **um den** ~ around (near) neutrality
Neutralrot *n* neutral red *(an oxidation-reduction indicator)*
Neutralsalz *n* neutral (normal) salt
Neutralsalzeffekt *m s.* Neutralsalzwirkung
Neutralsalzfehler *m* [neutral-]salt error *(in pH determinations)*
Neutralsalzquellung *f (tann)* osmotic swelling
Neutralsalzverfahren *n (rubber)* neutral [reclaiming] process
Neutralsalzwirkung *f* neutral-salt effect
Neutralsäure *f (phys ch)* molecular acid
Neutralschmalz *n* neutral lard
Neutralsulfitablauge *f (pap)* neutral sodium sulphite waste liquor, neutral sulphite semichemical spent liquor
Neutralsulfit-Halbzellstoff *m* neutral sulphite semichemical pulp, NSSC pulp
Neutralsulfit-Halbzellstoffaufschluß *m* neutral sulphite semichemical pulping, NSSC pulping
Neutralsulfitkochlauge *f (pap)* neutral sulphite semichemical liquor, NSSC liquor, neutral sodium sulphite cooking liquor, semichemical pulping liquor
Neutralsulfitstoff *m s.* Neutralsulfit-Halbzellstoff
Neutralsulfitverfahren *n (pap)* neutral sulphite [semichemical] process, NSSC process, neutral sodium sulphite process
Neutralverfahren *n (rubber)* neutral [reclaiming] process
Neutretto *n* neutretto, neutral meson
Neutrino *n* neutrino
Neutron *n* neutron
~/energiereiches high-energy neutron
~/gestreutes scattered neutron
~/kaltes cold neutron
~/langsames slow neutron
~/schnelles fast (high-speed) neutron
~/thermisches thermal neutron
~/unterthermisches *s.* ~/kaltes
~/unverzögertes *s.* ~/schnelles
~/verzögertes delayed neutron
Neutronenabsorber *m* neutron absorber
Neutronenaktivierung *f* neutron activation
Neutronenaktivierungsanalyse *f* neutron-activation analysis, NAA
Neutronenbeschuß *m* neutron bombardment
neutronenbestrahlt neutron-irradiated
Neutronenbestrahlung *f* neutron irradiation
Neutronenbeugung *f* neutron diffraction
Neutronenbindungsenergie *f* neutron-binding energy
Neutronenbremsung *f* neutron moderation
Neutronendichte *f* neutron density
Neutroneneinfang *m* neutron capture
~/parasitärer parasitic neutron capture
Neutroneneinfangquerschnitt *m* neutron-capture cross section
Neutronenemission *f* neutron emission
~/verzögerte delayed neutron emission
Neutronenfänger *m* neutron absorber, curtain
Neutronenfluß *m* neutron flux
Neutronenmasse *f* neutron [rest] mass
Neutronennachweis *m* neutron detection
Neutronenquelle *f* neutron source
Neutronenruh[e]masse *f* neutron [rest] mass
Neutronenspektrum *n* neutron spectrum
Neutronenstrahl *m* neutron ray, *(if bundled:)* neutron beam
Neutronenstrahlenquelle *f* neutron source
Neutronenstrahlung *f* neutron radiation
Neutronenstreuung *f* neutron scattering
~/unelastische *(anal)* inelastic neutron scattering, INS
Neutronenüberschuß *m* neutron excess
Neutronenzerfall *m* neutron decay
Neuverteilung *f* redistribution
Nevile-Winther-Säure *f* Nevile-Winther-acid, NW acid, naphth-1-ol-4-sulphonic acid, *4-hydroxynaphthalenesulphonic acid
Newcastle-Ofen *m (ceram)* Newcastle kiln *(a horizontal-draught kiln)*
New-Jersey-Zinkverfahren *n* New Jersey zinc[-recovery] process
Newton-Anordnung *f*, **Newton-Aufstellung** *f (spectr)* Newtonian mounting
Newton-Zahl *f* Newton's number
NF-Ofen *m s.* Nichols-Freeman-Ofen
Ngaicampher *m* ngai camphor *(chemically nearly pure L-borneol)*
NGF *(**n**erve **g**rowth **f**actor) s.* Nervenwachstumsfaktor
NH_3-... *s. a.* Ammoniak...
NH_3-Abtrieb *m (hyd)* ammonia stripping
NH_3-Entfernung *f (hyd)* ammonia removal
NH_3-Reaktor *m* ammonia synthesis reactor, synthetic ammonia apparatus
NHI-Protein *n s.* Nichthämeisenprotein
Niacin *n s.* Nicotinsäure
Niacinamid *n s.* Nicotinamid
Niccolit *m (min)* niccolite, arsenical nickel *(nickel arsenide)*
Nichols-Freeman-Ofen *m* Nichols-Freeman flash roaster
Nicholson-Blau *n* Nicholson blue
nichtabsetzbar non-settleable *(e.g. floc)*
nichtaggressiv non-corrosive
nichtaktiviert non-activated
nichtalkoholisch non-alcoholic
nichtangreifbar unattackable, stable, resistant
~/chemisch stable (resistant) to chemical attack, chemically stable (resistant)
Nichtangreifbarkeit *f* unattackability, stability, resistance
~/chemische stability (resistance) to chemical attack, chemical stability (resistance)
nichtaromatisch non-aromatic

nichtaustauschbar non-exchangeable
nichtbelastet unpolluted, uncontaminated, non-contaminated *(water, air)*
nichtbenzoid non-benzenoid
Nichtcellulosebestandteile *mpl (pap)* non-cellulosic constituents
nichtchinoid non-quinonoid
nichtcyclisch non-cyclic[al], acyclic
Nichtedelmetall *n* base (non-noble) metal
Nichtedelmetallkatalysator *m* base-metal catalyst
nichteinheitlich non-uniform
Nichteinheitlichkeit *f* non-uniformity
nichteinlaufend *s.* nichtkrumpfend
Nichteisenlegierung *f* non-ferrous alloy
Nichteisenmetall *n* non-ferrous metal
Nichteisenmetallurgie *f* non-ferrous metallurgy
Nichteiweißanteil *m* non-protein moiety (fraction) *(as of enzymes)*
Nichteiweißstickstoff *m* non-protein nitrogen
Nichteiweißstoff *m* non-protein substance
Nichtelektrolyt *m* non-electrolyte
Nichtelektrolytchelat *n* non-electrolyte chelate
nichtentflammbar non-[in]flammable, uninflammable, flameproof
Nichtentflammbarkeit *f* non-[in]flammability, uninflammability, flameproofness
nichtenzymatisch non-enzymatic
Nichterz *n* gangue [mineral], gang, waste rock, matrix
nichtessentiell *(bioch)* non-essential
Nichtexistenz *f* non-existence
nichtfettig non-greasy
nichtflüchtig non-volatile
Nichtflüchtiges *n* non-volatile matter
Nichtflüchtigkeit *f* non-volatility
Nichtgerbstoff *m* non-tan[nin]
nichtgilbend *(pap)* non-fading, non-yellowing
Nichtgleichgewichtsvorgang *m* non-equilibrium process
Nichthämeisen *n* non-haem iron, Fe_{NH}, *(Am)* nonheme iron
Nichthämeisenprotein *n* non-haem iron protein, NHI protein
Nicht-Hämineisen *n s.* Nichthämeisen
nichthelikal, nichthelixartig *(bioch)* non-helical
Nicht-Helix-Region *f (bioch)* non-helical region (section)
nichthybridisiert unhybridized
nichthydratisiert non-hydrated
nichthygroskopisch non-hygroscopic
nichtideal non-ideal
nichtidentisch non-identical
nichtionisch non-ionic
nichtionisierend *s.* nichtionogen
nichtionisiert unionized
nichtionogen non-ionogenic, non-ionizing
Nichtkarbonathärte *f (hyd)* non-carbonate hardness, permanent hardness
Nichtkarbonathärtebildner *mpl (hyd)* non-carbonate-hardness constituents
nichtkatalysiert uncatalyzed
Nichtkautschukbestandteil *m* non-rubber constituent
Nichtkautschuksubstanz *f* non-rubber substance (material)
nichtklebend non-stick
nichtklopfend knock-free, knockless, non-knocking *(carburetting fuel)*
nichtkondensierbar non-condensable
Nichtkondensierbarkeit *f* non-condensability
nichtkonjugiert non-conjugated *(double bond)*
nichtkorrosiv non-corrosive
nichtkristallin[isch] non-crystalline
nichtkrumpfend *(text)* shrink-resistant, non-shrinking, shrinkproof, unshrinkable
nichtkumuliert non-cumulative *(double bond)*
nichtleitend non-conducting
Nichtleiter *m* non-conductor, dielectric [material], electrical insulator
nichtleuchtend non-luminous
nichtlinear non-linear
Nichtlinearität *f* non-linearity
nichtlokalisiert delocalized, non-localized
Nichtlokalisierung *f* delocalization
Nichtlöser *m* non-solvent
nichtlöslich insoluble, i.s., non-soluble, indissoluble
Nichtlöslichkeit *f* insolubility, insolubleness
Nichtlösungsmittel *n* non-solvent
nichtmagnetisch non-magnetic
Nichtmetall *n* non-metal
nichtmetallisch non-metallic
nichtmikrobiell non-microbial
Nichtmischbarkeit *f* immiscibility
nichtmodifiziert unmodified
Nichtnetzer *m* non-wetter
nichtoxidierend non-oxidizing
nichtphenolisch non-phenolic
nichtpigmentiert unpigmented
nichtplastisch non-plastic
nichtpolar non-polar, apolar
nichtpolarisierbar non-polarizable
Nichtproteinanteil *m* non-protein moiety (fraction) *(as of enzymes)*
Nichtproteinstickstoff *m* non-protein nitrogen
nichtradioaktiv non-radioactive
nichtreaktionsfähig non-reactive, unreactive, inactive
nichtreduzierend non-reducing
nichtregenerativ non-regenerative
nichtregenerierbar non-regenerable
nichtrelativistisch non-relativistic
nichtreplizierend *(biot)* non-replicating
nichtrostend stainless, rustless, rust-resistant, resistant to rusting
Nichts *n*/**weißes** nihilum album, nix alba *(white woolly zinc oxide)*
Nichtsättigung *f* unsaturation
nichtschäumend foamless; *(cosmet)* non-lathering

nichtschrumpfend *s.* nichtkrumpfend
nichtspaltbar non-fissile, non-fissionable
nichtstarr non-rigid
nichtstaubend dustless, dust-free
Nichtstöchiometrie *f* non-stoichiometry
nichtstöchiometrisch non-stoichiometric
nichtsubstituiert unsubstituted
nichtsulfoniert unsulphonated
nichttoxisch non-toxic, non-poisonous
nichttrocknend non-drying
nichtumgesetzt, nichtumgewandelt unreacted, unconverted
nichtverfestigt unconsolidated
nichtvergilbend *(pap)* non-fading, non-yellowing
nichtvernetzt uncross-linked, uncured, *(rubber also)* unvulcanized
nichtverschmutzt unpolluted, free from polluting substances, uncontaminated, non-contaminated *(water, air)*
nichtverseifend non-saponifying
nichtwandernd non-migrating
nichtwasserlöslich water-insoluble, insoluble in water
nichtwäßrig non-aqueous
Nichtzuckeranteil *m* non-sugar portion, aglycon
Nichtzuckerstoff *m* non-sugar [substance]
nichtzyklisch *s.* nichtcyclisch
Nickel *n* Ni nickel
Nickelacetat *n* nickel acetate
Nickelarsenat *n* nickel arsenate
Nickelblüte *f (min)* nickel bloom, annabergite *(nickel arsenate)*
Nickel(II)-bromid *n* nickel(II) bromide, nickel dibromide
Nickel-Cadmium-Akkumulator *m* nicad (nickel-cadmium) battery, cadmium-nickel storage cell
Nickelcarbid *n* nickel carbide
Nickelcarbonat *n* nickel carbonate
Nickelchelat *n* nickel chelate
Nickel(II)-chlorid *n* nickel(II) chloride, nickel dichloride
Nickelcyanid *n* nickel cyanide
Nickeldi... *s. a.* Nickel(II)-...
Nickeldiacetyldioxim *n s.* Nickeldimethylglyoxim
Nickeldimethylglyoxim *n* nickel dimethylglyoxime
Nickeldithionat *n* nickel dithionate
Nickel-Eisen-Akkumulator *m* nickel-iron accumulator (battery, cell), Edison accumulator
Nickeleisenkern *m (geoch)* nickel-iron core *(obsolete theory; better:)* centrosphere, barysphere
Nickelelektrode *f* nickel electrode
Nickel(II)-fluorid *n* nickel(II) fluoride, nickel difluoride
Nickelformiat *n* nickel formate
nickelhaltig containing nickel, nickel-bearing, *(esp relating to ores:)* nickeliferous
Nickel(II)-hexacyanoferrat(II) *n* nickel(II) hexacyanoferrate(II)
Nickelhexafluorosilicat *n* nickel hexafluorosilicate
Nickel(II)-hydroxid *n* nickel(II) hydroxide
Nickelin *m s.* Niccolit
Nickel(II)-iodid *n* nickel(II) iodide, nickel diiodide
Nickelkatalysator *m* nickel catalyst
Nickelkugeln *fpl (met)* nickel pellets *(as produced by the Mond carbonyl process)*
Nickellegierung *f* nickel alloy
Nickelmonosulfid *n s.* Nickel(II)-sulfid
Nickelmonoxid *n s.* Nickel(II)-oxid
Nickelnitrat *n* nickel nitrate
Nickelorthophosphat *n* nickel orthophosphate
Nickel(II)-oxid *n* nickel(II) oxide, nickel monooxide
Nickel(II,III)-oxid *n* nickel(II,III) oxide, trinickel tetraoxide
Nickel(III)-oxid *n* nickel(III) oxide, dinickel trioxide
Nickelperchlorat *n* nickel perchlorate
Nickelphthalocyanin *n* nickel phthalocyanine
Nickelrückgewinnung *f* nickel recovery
Nickel[schutz]schicht *f* nickel coating
~/elektrochemisch (galvanisch) hergestellte nickel plate
Nickelschwamm *m* spongy nickel
Nickelschwammkatalysator *m* spongy-nickel catalyst
Nickelskutterudit *m (min)* nickel-skutterudite, white nickel, chloanthite *(nickel arsenide)*
Nickelstahl *m* nickel [alloy] steel
Nickelstein *m (met)* nickel matte
Nickelsulfat *n* nickel sulphate
Nickel(II)-sulfid *n* nickel(II) sulphide, nickel monosulphide
Nickel(II,III)-sulfid *n* nickel(II,III) sulphide, trinickel tetrasulphide
Nickeltetracarbonyl *n* nickel tetracarbonyl
Nickeltiegel *m* nickel crucible
Nickelvitriol *m (min)* nickel vitriol, morenosite *(nickel sulphate 7-water)*
Nickschwingung *f (spectr)* wagging vibration
Nicol-Prisma *n* Nicol prism
Nicol-Prismen *npl***/gekreuzte** crossed Nicol prisms
Nicotin *n* nicotine
Nicotinamid *n s.* Nicotinsäureamid
Nicotinsäure *f* nicotinic acid, niacin, pyridine-3-carboxylic acid
Nicotinsäureamid *n* nicotinamide, nicotinic acid amide, niacin amide, pyridine-3-carboxamide
Nicotinsäureamid-adenin-dinucleotid *n* nicotinamide-adenine dinucleotide, NAD
Nicotinsäureamid-adenin-dinucleotidphosphat *n* nicotinamide adenine dinucleotide phosphate, NADP
Nicotinsäurebenzylester *m* benzyl nicotinate
Nicotinvergiftung *f* nicotine poisoning
niederblasen *(glass)* to blow down
Niederblasen *n (glass)* settle blow
niederbringen *(mine)* to sink *(a shaft)*
~/eine Bohrung *(petrol)* to sink a bore
Niederdruck *m* low pressure
Niederdruckdampf *m* low-pressure steam, LP steam, ordinary-pressure steam

Niederdruckharz *n* low-pressure resin
Niederdruckkessel *m* low-pressure boiler
Niederdrucklaminieren *n* low-pressure laminating
Niederdruckleitung *f* low-pressure line
Niederdruckpolyethylen *n* low-pressure (high-density, linear) polyethylene, HDPE, H.D. polythene
Niederdruckpressen *n (plast)* low-pressure moulding
Niederdruckschicht[preß]stoff *m* low-pressure laminate
Niederdrucksprühgerät *n (agric)* low-pressure sprayer
Niederdruckverfahren *n* **nach Ziegler** Ziegler process *(for polymerizing alkenes)*
niederfrequent low-frequency
Niederfrequenzinduktionsofen *m* low-frequency induction furnace
niederinkohlt low-rank
Niederkräusen *pl (ferm)* low krausen, *(Am)* low curls
niedermolekular low-molecular
Niedermoortorf *m* fen peat
Niederschachtofen *m* low-shaft furnace
Niederschlag *m* precipitate, ppt., sediment, [bottom] settlings, B.S. , bottoms, deposit, foots, *(esp ferm)* lees; condensate *(from vapour)*
• einen ~ bilden *s.* niederschlagen/sich
~/atmosphärischer atmospheric precipitation
~/flockiger flocculate, flocculation
~/galvanischer electrodeposit
~/käsiger curdy precipitate
niederschlagbar precipitable, settleable; condensable *(vapour)*
Niederschlagbarkeit *f* precipitability, settleability; condensability *(of vapour)*
niederschlagen to precipitate, to sediment[ate], to deposit, to throw (lay) down; to condense *(vapour)*
~/elektrochemisch (elektrolytisch, galvanisch) to electrodeposit
~/sich to precipitate, to sediment, to set, to settle [down, out], to deposit, to subside; to condense *(of vapour)*
~/sich elektrochemisch (elektrolytisch, galvanisch) to plate out
Niederschlagsarbeit *f s.* Niederschlagsverfahren
Niederschlagselektrode *f* precipitating electrode, collecting (receiving) electrode
Niederschlagsmenge *f* quantity (amount) of precipitate
Niederschlagsmittel *n* precipitant, precipitating agent, precipitator
Niederschlagsplatte *f* collecting plate
Niederschlagsverfahren *n (met)* precipitation process
Niederschlagswasser *n* condensed water, condensate [water]; *(hyd)* atmospheric (precipitated, meteoric) water
niederschmelzen to melt down
Niederschmelzen *n* melting-down
Niederspannungselektrophorese *f* low-voltage electrophoresis
Niederspannungs[elektro]porzellan *n* low-tension [electrical] porcelain
Niederstruktur-Ruß *m (rubber)* low-structure [carbon] black
Niedertemperaturofen *m (ceram)* low-temperature kiln
Niedertemperaturveraschung *f (anal)* low-temperature ashing
niederwertig 1. of lower valency, lower-valent, lower-valency *(chemical-bond theory)*; 2. *s.* minderwertig
niedrigaktiv *(nucl)* low-level active
niedrigerfrequent lower-frequency
Niedrigfeuer *n (ceram)* slow fire
niedriggekohlt low-carbon *(e.g. steel)*
niedriginkohlt low-rank
niedrigmolekular low-molecular
niedrignitriert low-nitrated *(cotton)*
niedrigoctan[zahl]ig low-octane
niedrigphosphorhaltig low-phosphorus
niedrigschmelzend low-melting[-point], low-fusion
niedrigsiedend low-boiling, light
Niedrigsieder *m* low boiler *(as of solvents)*
niedrigviskos of low viscosity, low viscosity
Niemann-Pick-Syndrom *n (med)* Niemann-Pick disease *(accumulation of sphingomyelin caused by sphingomyelinase deficiency)*
nierenschädigend nephrotoxic
Niesmittel *n (pharm)* sternutator
Nife *n s.* Nickeleisenkern
NiFe-Akkumulator *m* nickel-iron accumulator (cell, battery), Edison accumulator
Nife-Kern *m s.* Nickeleisenkern
Nigeröl *n* niger-seed oil, Ramtilla oil *(from Guizotia abyssinica (L.f.)Cass.)*
Nigrotinsäure *f* nigrotic acid, 3,5-dihydroxy-7-sulpho-2-naphthoic acid
Nihilum *n* **album** *s.* Nichts/weißes
Nilgummi *n* Somali gum *(from several Acacia specc.)*
Ninhydrinreaktion *f* ninhydrin reaction (test) *(for detecting proteins and amino acids)*
Niob *n* Nb niobium
Niobat *n* niobate
Niob(V)-bromid *n* niobium(V) bromide, niobium pentabromide
Niobcarbid *n* niobium carbide
Niob(V)-chlorid *n* niobium(V) chloride, niobium pentachloride
Niobdioxid *n s.* Niob(IV)-oxid
Niobeöl *n* niobe oil, methyl benzoate
Niob(V)-fluorid *n* niobium(V) fluoride, niobium pentafluoride
Niobhydrid *n* niobium hydride
Niobit *m* niobite *(a mineral containing niobium and tantalum)*

Niobmonoxid *n s.* Niob(II)-oxid
Niob(II)-oxid *n* niobium(II) oxide, niobium monoxide
Niob(IV)-oxid *n* niobium(IV) oxide, niobium dioxide
Niob(V)-oxid *n* niobium(V) oxide, niobium pentaoxide
Niob(V)-oxid-Hydrat *n s.* Niobsäure
Niobpenta... *s.* Niob(V)-...
Niobpentoxid *n s.* Niob(V)-oxid
Niobsäure *f*, **Niob(V)-säure** *f* niobic acid
Nioxim *n* nioxime, 1,2-cyclohexanedionedioxime
NIR *s.* Infrarotgebiet/nahes
Nisinsäure *f* nisinic acid *(a tetracosahexaenoic acid)*
Niton *n s.* Radon
Nitramid *n* nitramide
Nitramin *n* nitramine *(general formula $RHN{-}NO_2$ or $R_1R_2N{-}NO_2$)*
Nitranilin *n* nitroaniline
Nitranilinrot *n* paranitraniline red, para red
Nitranilsäure *f* nitranilic acid
Nitrat *n* nitrate
Nitratbakterien *npl*, **Nitratbildner** *mpl* nitrate (nitric) bacteria, nitrobacteria *(genus Nitrobacter)*
Nitratcellulose *f s.* Cellulosenitrat
Nitrateliminierung *f*, **Nitratentfernung** *f (hyd)* nitrate removal
Nitratgehalt *m (hyd)* nitrate level
Nitrator *m s.* Nitrierapparat
Nitratstickstoff *m* nitrate nitrogen
Nitren *n* :NR nitrene, aminylene, aminediyl, imidogen, azene
Nitrid *n* nitride
Nitridhärtung *f s.* Nitrierhärtung
Nitrierabteilung *f* nitrating department
Nitrieranlage *f* nitration plant, nitrating unit
Nitrierapparat *m* nitrator
~ **nach Kubierschky** Kubierschky's nitrator
~ **nach Weller ter Meer** ter Meer's nitrator
Nitrierbad *n (met)* nitriding bath
nitrieren to nitrate; *(met)* to nitride
Nitriergefäß *n* nitrating pan
Nitriergemisch *n* nitration mixture
nitrierhärten to nitride *(steel)*
Nitrierhärtung *f* nitride hardening, nitriding, nitridation, nitrogen [case-]hardening *(of steel)*
Nitrierkasten *m* nitriding box *(for treating steel)*
Nitrierkessel *m* nitrating pan
Nitrierkrepp *m* nitrated (nitrate, nitrating) paper
Nitriermittel *n* nitrating agent
Nitrierofen *m* nitriding furnace *(for treating steel)*
Nitrierprodukt *n* nitration product
Nitrierreagens *n* nitrating agent
Nitriersalzbad *n* nitriding bath *(for treating steel)*
Nitriersäure *f* nitrating acid, mixed acid *(a mixture of concentrated nitric and sulphuric acid)*
Nitrierschicht *f* nitride (nitrided) case (layer) *(on steel)*
Nitrierstahl *m* nitriding steel
Nitriertiefe *f* nitriding depth *(in steel)*
Nitrierung *f* 1. nitration; 2. *s.* Nitrierhärtung
~/direkte direct nitration
~/diskontinuierliche batch nitration
~/elektrophile electrophilic nitration
~/kontinuierliche continuous nitration
~/oxidative oxidative nitration, oxynitration
Nitrierungs... *s.* Nitrier...
Nitrierverfahren *n* 1. nitration process; 2. nitriding process, nitrogen case-hardening process *(for treating steel)*
Nitrifikanten *mpl s.* Nitrifikationsbakterien
Nitrifikation *f (agric)* nitrification
Nitrifikationsbakterien *npl* nitrifying bacteria, nitrobacteria *(collectively for nitrite and nitrate bacteria)*
Nitrifizierung *f (agric)* nitrification
Nitril *n* R–C≡N nitrile
Nitril-Chloroprenkautschuk *m* nitrile-chloroprene rubber, NCR
Nitrilgruppe *f* –C≡N nitrile group (residue)
Nitrilium-Ion *n* nitrilium ion
Nitrilkautschuk *m* [acrylo]nitrile-butadiene rubber, NBR, nitrile rubber
~/carboxylgruppenhaltiger (carboxylierter) carboxynitrile rubber, carboxy-modified nitrile rubber
Nitriloxid *n* nitrile oxide
Nitrilotriessigsäure *f* nitrilotriacetic acid, NTA, tri(carboxymethyl)amine
Nitrilsilicongummi *m s.* Nitrilsiliconkautschuk
Nitrilsiliconkautschuk *m* nitrilesilicone rubber, NSR, cyano silicone rubber
Nitrilsynthese *f* nitrile synthesis
Nitrit *n* nitrite
Nitritbakterien *npl*, **Nitritbildner** *mpl* nitrite-forming bacteria, nitrosobacteria, nitrous bacteria, ammonia oxidizers
nitrithaltig nitrite-containing
Nitritstickstoff *m* nitrite nitrogen
3-Nitroalizarin *n* 3-nitroalizarin, alizarin orange, 1,2-dihydroxynitroanthraquinone
Nitroalkan *n* nitroalkane, nitroparaffin
Nitroanilin *n* nitroaniline
Nitroanthrachinon *n* nitroanthraquinone
Nitrobakterien *npl s.* Nitrifikationsbakterien
Nitrobenzaldehyd *m* nitrobenzaldehyde
Nitrobenzen *n* nitrobenzene
Nitrobenzencarbonsäure *f s.* Nitrobenzoesäure
p-**Nitrobenzensulfochlorid** *n*, *p*-**Nitrobenzensulfonylchlorid** *n p*-nitrobenzenesulphonyl chloride
Nitrobenzoesäure *f* nitrobenzoic acid
Nitrobenzol *n s.* Nitrobenzen
Nitrocellulose *f s.* Cellulosenitrat
Nitrochlorbenzen *n*, **Nitrochlorbenzol** *n s.* Chlornitrobenzen
Nitrochloroform *n* nitrochloroform, chloropicrin, *trichloronitromethane
Nitrocobaltat *n* nitrocobaltate
Nitroderivat *n* nitro derivative

Nitroechtfarbstoff *m* fast nitro dye
Nitroessigsäure *f* nitroacetic acid
Nitroethan *n* nitroethane
Nitroethylierung *f* nitroethylation
Nitrofarbstoff *m* nitro dye
Nitrofluorierung *f* nitrofluorination
Nitrogen *n* N nitrogen
Nitrogenbakterien *npl* nitrogen-fixing bacteria
Nitroglyzerin *n s.* Glyceroltrinitrat
Nitrogruppe *f* $-NO_2$ nitro group
Nitrojektion *f (agric)* nitrojection
Nitrokörper *m* nitro body
Nitrolack *m* cellulose nitrate lacquer
Nitrolsäure *f* nitrolic acid *(any of a class of compounds* $RC(=NOH)NO_2$*)*
Nitrolyse *f* nitrolysis
Nitrometer *n* nitrometer, acetometer
Nitromethan *n* nitromethane
Nitromoschus *m* nitro musk
Nitron *n* nitrone, azomethine oxide
Nitronaphthalen *n* nitronaphthalene
Nitroniumion *n s.* Nitrylion
Nitroniumperchlorat *n s.* Nitrylperchlorat
Nitronsäure *f* $R=NO(OH)$ nitronic acid, alkylideneazinic acid, *aci*-nitro compound
Nitroparaffin *n* nitroparaffin, nitroalkane
Nitroperbenzoesäure *f* nitroperbenzoic acid
p-**Nitrophenol** *n p*-nitrophenol, PNP
Nitrophosphat *n* nitrophosphate *(any of a group of nitrogenphosphorus fertilizers)*
Nitroprussiat *n s.* Nitroprussid
Nitroprussid *n* $M^I_2[Fe(CN)_5(NO)]$ nitroprusside, *pentacyanonitrosylferrate
Nitroprussidnatrium *n* sodium nitroprusside, *disodium pentacyanonitrosylferrate
Nitroprussidnatriumpapier *n* sodium nitroprusside paper
nitros nitrous *(containing nitrogen oxides)*
Nitrosamid *n* nitrosamide *(1. any of the amides of nitrous acid; 2. any of the N-nitroso derivatives of amides)*
Nitrosamin *n* nitrosamine *(any of a class of compounds* R_1R_2N-NO*)*
Nitrosaminrot *n* nitrosamine red
Nitrosat *n (org ch)* nitrosate
Nitrose *f* nitrous vitriol *(an intermediate in manufacturing sulphuric acid)*
Nitrosebakterien *npl s.* Nitritbakterien
nitrosieren to nitrosate
Nitrosiermittel *n* nitrosating agent
Nitrosierung *f* nitrosation
~/oxidative oxidative nitrosation
Nitrosit *n (org ch)* nitrosite
p-**Nitrosoanilin** *n p*-nitrosoaniline
Nitrosobenzen *n*, **Nitrosobenzol** *n* nitrosobenzene
Nitrosochlorierung *f* nitrosochlorination
Nitrosocresol *n* nitrosocresol
Nitrosofarbstoff *m* nitroso dye
Nitrosogruppe *f* $-N=O$ nitroso group
Nitrosokautschuk *m* nitroso rubber
Nitrosonaphthol *n* nitrosonaphthol
Nitrosoverbindung *f* nitroso compound
Nitrostärke *f s.* Stärkenitrat
Nitrosylchlorid *n* nitrosyl chloride
Nitrosylfluorid *n* nitrosyl fluoride
Nitrosylhydrogensulfat *n* nitrosyl hydrogensulphate
Nitrosylion *n* NO^+ nitrosyl ion
Nitrotoluidin *n* nitrotoluidine
Nitroverbindung *f* nitro compound
aci-**Nitroverbindung** *f s.* Nitronsäure
Nitrovinylierung *f* nitrovinylation
Nitroxylen *n*, **Nitroxylol** *n* nitroxylene
Nitrylchlorid *n* nitryl chloride
Nitrylperchlorat *n* nitryl perchlorate
Niveau *n (phys ch, tech)* level
~/angeregtes excited (excitation) level
~ der Fermentationslösung *(biot)* fermenter (working) level
~/hängendes suspended level *(as in viscometers)*
Niveaubirne *f* [gas] levelling bulb
Niveaufläche *f* equipotential (potential energy) surface
Niveauflasche *f*, **Niveaugefäß** *n (lab)* levelling bottle
Niveaukonstanthalter *m* constant-level device; *(petrol)* constant-level tank
Niveaukugel *f* [gas] levelling bulb (gas analysis)
Niveauliniendarstellung *f* **der Potentialfläche** potential-energy contour map
Niveaumessung *f* level measurement
Niveauregler *m* level controller
Niveaurohr *n* levelling (compensation) tube *(gas analysis)*
Niveauschema *n (spectr)* level diagram
nivellieren to level *(titration)*
Nivellierung *f* 1. levelling *(titration)*; 2. *(phys ch)* levelling effect
NK *s.* Naturkautschuk
NKH *s.* Nichtkarbonathärte
nl *s.* nichtlöslich
N_2-**Laser** *m* nitrogen laser
n-leitend n-type [semi]conducting, excess [semi-] conducting
N-Lost *m s.* Stickstoffyperit
n-Lösung *f* N solution, normal solution
NMR *(**n**uclear **m**agnetic **r**esonance) s.* Resonanz/ kernmagnetische
NMR-Spektrometer *n* NMR spectrometer
NMR-Spektroskopie *f* NMR spectroscopy
~/dynamische dynamic NMR spectroscopy, DNMR
~/hochauflösende high-resolution NMR spectroscopy
~/zweidimensionale two-dimensional NMR spectroscopy, 2D-NMR
NMR-Spektrum *n* NMR spectrum
NNR-Hormon *n s.* Nebennierenrindenhormon
Nobelium *n* No nobelium

No-iron-Ausrüstung *f (text)* no-iron finish
Nomenklatur *f* nomenclature
~/chemische chemical nomenclature
~/Genfer Geneva nomenclature
~/Stocksche Stock nomenclature
Nomenklaturkommission *f* commission on nomenclature, nomenclature commission
Nomenklaturregel *f* nomenclature rule
Nomenklatursystem *n* nomenclature system
~/Genfer Geneva system of nomenclature (naming)
Nonacosan *n (org ch)* nonacosane
Nonactinsäure *f* nonactinic acid *(a furan derivative)*
Nonandisäure *f* *nonanedioic acid, azelaic acid
Nonan-1-ol *n*, **1-Nonanol** *n* nonan-1-ol
Nonansäure *f* *nonanoic acid, pelargonic acid
Non-1-in *n*, **Nonin-(1)** *n* non-1-yne
Nonsens-Codon *n*, **Nonsens-Triplett** *n s.* Terminationscodon
nonvariant non-variant, invariant
n-**Nonylaldehyd** *m* *nonanal, *(deprecated:)* *n*-nonylic aldehyde
n-**Nonylalkohol** *m* nonan-1-ol, *(deprecated:)* *n*-nonyl alcohol
Nonylcarbinol *n* *decan-1-ol, *(deprecated:)* nonyl carbinol
Nonylon *n* *heptadecan-1-one, nonylone
n-**Nonylsäure** *f s.* Nonansäure
Nootkaten *n* nootkatene *(a sesquiterpene)*
Nootkatin *n* nootkatin *(a tropolone)*
Noppenfärben *n (text)* burl dyeing
2-Norbornen *n* norbornene, *bicyclo[2,2,1]-hept-2-ene
Norgesalpeter *m* Norway (Norwegian) saltpetre, Norge nitre *(calcium nitrate)*
Norm... *s. a.* Normal...
normal normal
~ anfärbend regular-dyeing
Normal *n* standard
Normal... *s. a.* Norm...
Normalalkohol *m* proof spirit
Normalatmosphäre *f* standard atmosphere
Normalausrüstung *f* standard equipment
Normalbedingungen *fpl s.* Normzustand
Normalblende *f* **mit Durchflußmengenmesser** orifice [flow]meter
Normalbutan *n* *butane, *(deprecated:)* *n*-butane
Normaldosis *f* normal dose
Normaldruck *m* normal (standard) pressure
Normaldrucksynthese *f* normal-pressure synthesis
Normaldrucktrockner *m* atmospheric dryer
Normalelektrode *f* normal electrode
Normalelement *n* standard cell
~/Westonsches Weston [normal] cell, standard Weston cell
Normalentwickler *m (phot)* normal developer
normalglühen to normalize *(steel)*
Normalglühen *n* normalizing, normalization *(of steel)*
Normalglühofen *m* normalizing furnace *(for treating steel)*
Normalheptan *n* *heptane, *(deprecated:)* *n*-heptane
Normalhexan *n* *hexane, *(deprecated:)* *n*-hexane
normalisieren *s.* normalglühen
Normalisierofen *m s.* Normalglühofen
Normalisierungsglühen *n s.* Normalglühen
Normalität *f* normality *(of solutions)*
Normalitätsfaktor *m (anal)* normality factor, volumetric (titrimetric) factor
Normalkalomelelektrode *f* normal calomel electrode
Normalklima *n (text)* standard[ized] conditions
Normalkomplex *m* outer (high-spin, spin-free) complex
Normallösung *f* standard (normal) solution, *(specif)* N solution, normal solution *(containing one gram equivalent per litre)*
1/10-**Normallösung** *f* decinormal solution
1/100-**Normallösung** *f* centinormal solution
1/1000-**Normallösung** *f* millinormal solution
Normalluftdruck *m* standard (normal) pressure
Normal-Nitritlösung *f (dye)* standard solution of sodium nitrite
Normaloctan *n* *octane, *(deprecated:)* *n*-octane
Normalpentan *n* *pentane, *(deprecated:)* *n*-pentane
Normalpotential *n* normal potential
Normalprobe *f* standard sample
Normalschwingung *f (phys ch)* normal (fundamental) vibration, normal mode of vibration
Normalsieb *n* standard sieve (screen)
Normalsiebreihe *f*, **Normalsiebskala** *f* standard sieve scale (series)
Normal-Silber-Silberchloridelektrode *f* normal silver-silver chloride electrode
Normalsintern *n* pressureless sintering
Normalspannung *f* 1. normal voltage; 2. normal stress *(mechanically)*
Normalspektrum *n* normal spectrum
normalstark proof *(of liquids containing alcohol)*
Normalstärke *f* proof *(of liquids containing alcohol)*
Normaltemperatur *f* normal temperature
Normalthermometer *n* standard thermometer
Normalton *m (dye)* standard shade
Normaltontiefe *f (dye)* standard depth [of shade]
Normalverbindung *f* normal compound
Normalverdampfer *m* standard evaporator
Normalverkokung *f* normal (high-temperature) carbonization (coking)
Normalverteilung *f* normal distribution
~/logarithmische log-normal distribution, logarithmic normal distribution
Normalvolumen *n* standard (normal) volume
Normalwasserstoffelektrode *f* normal hydrogen electrode, N.H.E.
Normalweingeist *m* proof spirit

Normalwert *m* standard value *(alcoholometry)*
Normalwiderstand *m* standard resistance
Normalwiderstandsthermometer *n* standard resistance thermometer
Normalzustand *m* 1. normal (ground) state, atomic ground (unexcited) state, ground term; 2. *s.* Normzustand
Normbedingungen *fpl s.* Normzustand
Normblende *f* standard orifice *(flow measurement)*
Normdichte *f* normal density
Normdüse *f* standard nozzle *(flow measurement)*
Normprüfsieb *n* standard (normal) test sieve (screen)
Normschliff *m (lab)* standard ground glass joint
Normzustand *m* normal (standard) conditions, normal (standard) temperature and pressure, NTP, STP *(0 °C and 101.325 kPa)*
~/technischer atmospheric temperature and pressure, ATP *(20 °C and 98.0665 kPa)*
Norrish-Typ-I-Reaktion *f* Norrish type I photoreaction *(alpha-cleavage of a carbonyl compound)*
Norrish-Typ-II-Reaktion *f* Norrish type II photoreaction *(abstraction of a gamma-hydrogen from a carbonyl compound)*
Nosean *m (min)* nosean, noselite *(a feldspar)*
Notation *f (nomencl)* notation
Notationssystem *n (nomencl)* notation system
~ von Wiswesser Wiswesser [notation] system
Notbrause *f* safety (emergency, drench) shower
Novolack *m s.* Novolak
Novolak *m*, **Novolakharz** *n* novolak [resin], two-stage resin
N-Oxid *n s.* Aminoxid
N-Schale *f* N-shell *(of an atom)*
NSSC-Stoff *m (pap)* neutral sodium sulphite semichemical pulp, NSSC pulp
NSSC-Verfahren *n (pap)* neutral sulphite [semichemical] process, NSSC process, neutral sodium sulphite process
n-stufig N-effect *(evaporator)*
NST-Wert *m (plast)* no-strength temperature
NTE *s.* Nitrilotriessigsäure
N-terminal N-terminal
Nuance *f* shade, tint, tone, hue, *(text also)* cast
nuancieren to shade, to tint, to tone, *(text also)* to cast
Nuancierung *f* 1. shading, tinting, toning, *(text also)* casting; 2. *s.* Nuance
Nuclealreaktion *f*/**Feulgensche** Feulgen reaction *(for detecting DNA)*
Nuclein *n* 1. nuclein; 2. *s.* Nucleinsäure
Nucleinsäure *f (bioch)* nucleic acid
Nucleinsäurebaustein *m*/**seltener** *(bioch)* rare (minor) base *(a purine or pyrimidine derivative)*
Nucleinstoff *m* nuclein
Nucleohiston *n (bioch)* nucleohistone
nucleophil nucleophilic
Nucleophil *n* nucleophile
Nucleophilie *f* nucleophilicity *(quantitatively also)* nucleophilic power
Nucleoplasma *n (bioch)* nuclear sap
Nucleoproteid *n* nucleoprotein
Nucleosid *n* nucleoside
Nucleosid-Antibiotikum *n* nucleoside antibiotic
Nucleosidphosphat *n*, **Nucleotid** *n* nucleotide
Nucleotid-Excisionsreparatur *f (biot)* nucleotide-excision repair
Nucleotidsequenz *f (bioch)* nucleotide sequence
Nugget *n* gold nugget
Nujol *n* nujol *(refined paraffin oil)*
Nujol-Technik *f* nujol technique *(wetting of finely ground sample with nujol for IR spectroscopy)*
nuklear nuclear
Nuklein *n s.* Nuclein
Nukleon *n* nucleon, nuclear particle (constituent)
Nukleonenkomponente *f* nucleonic component
Nukleonenzahl *f* nucleon number
Nukleonik *f* nucleonics
Nuklid *n* nuclide
~/radioaktives radioactive nuclide, radionuclide
Nuklid[en]masse *f* nuclidic (nuclide) mass
~/relative relative nuclidic mass
Nullabgleich *m (spectr)* optical null system
Nulladung *f* zero charge
Nulladungspunkt *m (phys ch)* point of zero charge, PZC
Nullage *f* rest point *(of a balance)*
Nulleffekt *m (nucl)* background
Nullelektrode *f* null electrode
Nullfeld *n (spectr)* zero field
Nullfeldaufspaltung *f (spectr)* zero-field splitting
Nullfläche *f (agric)* check plot, nil *(as in testing fertilizer effects)*
Nullinie *f (spectr)* zero line, band origin
Nullinstrument *n* null[-point] instrument, null-balance instrument
Nullmethode *f* null method [of measurement], [null-]balance method, zero method
Nullparzelle *f s.* Nullfläche
Nullporosität *f* zero porosity
Nullpunkt *m* zero [point] *(of a scale)*; null point *(of an instrument)* • **auf den ~ einstellen** to zero
~/absoluter absolute zero
Nullpunkteinstellung *f* zero adjustment, zeroing
~/automatische autozero
Nullpunktsenergie *f* zero-point energy
Nullpunktsentropie *f* zero-point entropy, entropy at absolute zero
Nullpunktskonfiguration *f* zero-point configuration
Nullpunktskorrektur *f*/**automatische** auto zero
Nullpunktsschwingung *f* residual (zero-point) vibration
Nullrate *f (nucl)* background
Nullschwingung *f s.* Nullpunktsschwingung
Nullstelle *f s.* Nullinie
Nullstellung *f* zero position
Nulltoleranz *f (tox)* zero tolerance

Nulluft *f* zero air
Nullvariante *f (agric)* nil *(as in testing fertilizer effects)*
Nullversuch *m* 1. blank, blank experiment (test, trial); 2. *s.* Nullvariante
Nullviskosität *f* zero shear-rate viscosity
nullwertig zero-valent
Nullwertigkeit *f* zero valence
Nullzweig *m* Q-branch *(of a band spectrum)*
numerieren *(nomencl)* to number
Numerierung *f (nomencl)* numbering
~ im Uhrzeigersinn clockwise numbering
Numerierungssystem *n (nomencl)* numbering system
Nummer *f (text)* number, count
~ der EC-Nomenklatur *(bioch)* EC number, enzyme classification number
Nur-Glas-Papier *n* glass paper *(an insulating material)*
Nusselt-Kennzahl *f*, **Nusselt-Zahl** *f* Nusselt number *(of heat transfer)*
Nußöl *n* nut oil
Nutringdichtung *f* U-seal
Nutsche *f* nutsch[e], nutsch filter
nutschen to filter [off] by suction, to filter under suction
Nutzarbeit *f (phys ch)* useful (net) work
~/maximale useful maximum work
nutzbar usable, available *(e.g. resource)*
nutzerfreundlich user-friendly
Nutzleistung *f* efficiency
Nutzraum *m (ceram)* setting space *(of a kiln)*
Nutzungsdauer *f* service life, operating (working, useful) life; *(hyd)* bed life *(of activated carbon in the filter bed)*
~/normative service life expectancy
Nutzwasser *n s.* Brauchwasser
Nu-Zahl *f s.* Nusselt-Kennzahl
n-Verbindung *f* normal compound *(as opposed to iso compound)*
NVK *s.* Volumenkapazität/nutzbare
Nylonfarbstoff *m* nylon dye
Nylonfilz *m (pap)* nylon felt
Nylonmembran *f (hyd)* nylon membrane *(reverse osmosis)*
N-Yperit *n s.* Stickstoffyperit

O

Oakes-Maschine *f (rubber)* Oakes frother
O-Alkylierung *f O*-alkylation, oxygen alkylation
OAS = optische Atomspektroskopie
OA-Spektroskopie *f s.* Optoakustik-Spektroskopie
O_2-Aufblaskonverter *m s.* Oberwindkonverter
O_2-Aufblasverfahren *n s.* Oberwindfrischverfahren
Obenaufgabe *f (tech)* top feed
Oberbainit *m (met)* upper bainite
Oberbauseitenwand *f* casement (casing) wall, jamb (breast) wall *(of a glass-melting furnace)*
Oberboden *m (soil)* topsoil, eluvial horizon, A-horizon
Oberdruckpresse *f s.* Oberkolbenpresse
Oberfilz *m (pap)* top felt, overfelt *(of a cylinder board machine)*
Oberfläche *f* surface, *(quantitatively:)* surface area • **die ~ behandeln** to surface, to finish • **mit glatter ~** smooth-surfaced
~/äußere external (outer) surface
~ der Makroporen macroporous area *(as in activated carbon)*
~ der Mikroporen microporous area *(as in activated carbon)*
~ des Filtermaterials *(hyd)* bed size
~/gehämmerte batter *(a defect in glass)*
~/innere internal surface, inner (inside) surface
~/rauhe rough surface; pulled surface *(a defect in plastics)*
~/spezifische specific surface
~/wirksame effective area
Oberflächenabfluß *m (hyd)* surface runoff
oberflächenaktiv surface-active
Oberflächenaktivität *f* surface activity
~/spezifische specific surface activity
Oberflächenanästhetikum *n* surface anaesthetic
Oberflächenantigen *n* [cell] surface antigen
Oberflächenarbeit *f* free surface energy
Oberflächenatom *n* surface atom
Oberflächenbedeckung *f* surface coverage
oberflächenbehandeln to surface
Oberflächenbehandlung *f* surface treatment, surfacing
Oberflächenbelastung *f (hyd)* surface loading [rate], loading rate per unit area *(sedimentation tanks, trickling filters: $m^3/m^2 \cdot h$)*; *(filtr)* filtration rate *($m^3/m^2 \cdot h$)*
~/hydraulische *(hyd)* hydraulic loading per unit area
Oberflächenbelüfter *m (hyd)* surface aerator
~/ortsfester fixed-position surface aerator
Oberflächenbelüftung *f (hyd)* surface (mechanical) aeration
Oberflächenbelüftungsanlage *f (hyd)* surface (mechanical) aeration unit
Oberflächenbeschaffenheit *f* surface condition (appearance), *(of treated surfaces also:)* finish
Oberflächenbeschickung *f s.* Oberflächenbelastung
Oberflächenbild *n (phot)* surface image
~/latentes surface latent image
Oberflächenblase *f* skin blister *(a defect in glass)*
Oberflächenchemie *f* surface chemistry
Oberflächendenaturierung *f (bioch)* surface denaturation
Oberflächendiffusion *f* surface diffusion
Oberflächendiffusionskoeffizient *m* surface diffusivity
Oberflächendruck *m* surface pressure
Oberflächeneffekt *m* surface effect
Oberflächeneigenschaften *fpl* surface properties

Oberflächenenergie *f* surface energy
~/freie free surface energy
~/spezifische specific surface work (free energy), surface tension *(of solids)*
Oberflächenenthalpie *f* surface enthalpy
Oberflächenentropie *f* surface entropy
Oberflächenentwickler *m (phot)* surface developer
Oberflächenentwicklung *f (phot)* surface development
Oberflächenerneuerungstheorie *f* surface renewal theory *(of mass transfer)*
Oberflächenerscheinung *f* surface phenomenon
Oberflächenfärbung *f (pap)* surface colouring (staining), tub colouring, dipping
~ im Kalander calender colouring (staining), padding, stuffing
Oberflächenfermentation *f (biot)* surface fermentation
Oberflächenfilm *m* surface (overlying) film, surface skin
~/kondensierter condensed film
~/monomolekularer monomolecular (unimolecular) surface film
Oberflächenfilter *n* surface (edge) filter
Oberflächenfiltration *f* surface (edge) filtration
oberflächengefärbt *(pap)* surface-coloured
oberflächengeleimt *(pap)* surface-sized, top-sized
~/im Leimbadtauchverfahren surface-sized with size tub, tub-sized, T.S., vat-sized
~/in der Leimpresse surface-sized with size press
~/mit Gelatine *s.* ~/mit Tierleim
~/mit Stärke surface-sized with starch
~/mit Tierleim surface-sized with animal glue, animal-sized, gelatin-sized
Oberflächenglanz *m* surface lustre, gloss, glaze
Oberflächengröße *f* surface area
Oberflächengüte *f* [surface] finish
Oberflächenhärte *f* surface hardness
oberflächenhärten to surface-harden *(metals)*
~/durch Diffusion to cement
Oberflächenhärten *n* surface hardening *(of metals)*
~ durch Diffusion cementation
Oberflächenhaut *f s.* Oberflächenfilm
Oberflächenheterogenität *f* surface heterogeneity
oberflächeninaktiv surface-inactive
Oberflächenionisation *f (anal)* surface-induced dissociation, SID
Oberflächenkatalysator *m* heterogeneous catalyst
Oberflächenkatalyse *f* heterogeneous catalysis, surface (contact) catalysis
Oberflächenkondensator *m* surface condenser
Oberflächenkonzentration *f* surface concentration
Oberflächenkraft *f* surface force
Oberflächenkultur *f (biot)* surface culture
Oberflächenladung *f (phys ch)* surface charge
Oberflächenleim *m (pap)* surface-sizing agent, tub size
Oberflächenleimmaschine *f (pap)* surface-sizing (tub-sizing) machine
Oberflächenleimung *f (pap)* surface (top) sizing
~ im Leimbadtauchverfahren surface sizing with size tub, tub (vat) sizing, T.S., size-tub treatment
~ in der Leimpresse surface sizing with size press
~ mit Gelatine *s.* ~ mit Tierleim
~ mit Stärke surface sizing with starch
~ mit Tierleim surface sizing with animal glue, animal tub sizing, A.T.S., gelatin sizing
Oberflächenlüftung *f* surface aeration
Oberflächenmatte *f (plast)* surfacing mat, overlay sheet
Oberflächenoxidation *f* surface oxidation
oberflächenporös *(chromat)* superficially porous
Oberflächenpotential *n* surface potential
Oberflächenrauhigkeit *f* surface roughness
Oberflächenreaktion *f* surface reaction
Oberflächenreaktor *m (biot)* surface film reactor
Oberflächenriß *m* surface crack; *(glass)* check, vent, *(in the neck of a bottle)* smear
Oberflächenrückstand *m* extrasurface residue *(of pesticides)*
Oberflächenrüttler *m* surface vibrator
Oberflächenrüttlung *f* surface vibration
Oberflächenschicht *f* surface layer
~/aufgekohlte (eingesetzte, zementierte) carburized case *(on steel)*
Oberflächenschliere *f* surface cord *(a defect in glass)*
Oberflächenschutz *m* surface protection
Oberflächensieden *n* subcooled boiling
Oberflächenspannung *f* surface tension
oberflächenspannungsvermindernd lowering the surface tension
Oberflächentemperatur *f* surface temperature
Oberflächentextur *f* surface texture
Oberflächentrockner *m (coat)* surface drier
Oberflächenverbindung *f* surface compound
Oberflächenverbrennung *f* surface combustion *(of gas-air or vapour-air mixtures at the surface of incandescent solids)*
Oberflächenverdichter *m* surface condenser
Oberflächenverdichtung *f (build)* surface compaction
Oberflächenverdunstung *f* surface evaporation, *(quantitatively:)* evaporation loss
Oberflächenverfahren *n (biot)* surface[-culture] process
Oberflächenverwitterung *f* surface weathering
Oberflächenwachstum *n* surface growth
Oberflächenwasser *n (hyd)* surface water
Oberflächenwasserbeschaffenheit *f s.* Oberflächenwassergüte
Oberflächenwasserentnahme *f* surface water withdrawal
Oberflächenwassergüte *f* surface water quality
Oberflächenwasservorkommen *n* surface water source
Oberflächenwiderstand *m* surface resistance
~/spezifischer surface resistivity

oberflächenwirksam surface-active
Oberflächenwirkung *f* surface effect
Oberflächenzone *f s.* Oberflächenschicht
Oberflächenzustand *m s.* Oberflächenbeschaffenheit
obergärig top-fermenting, top-fermented
Obergärung *f* top fermentation
Oberhefe *f* top[-fermentation] yeast
Oberkolben *m (plast)* top ram (force) *(of a press)*
Oberkolbenpresse *f (plast)* down-stroke press, top ram press
Oberleder *n* upper (dressing) leather
Obermesser *n (pap)* revolving (fly) knife *(of a cross-cutter)*
Oberphase *f (chromat)* upper phase
Oberphos-Verfahren *n* Oberphos process *(for manufacturing superphosphate)*
Obersäule *f (distil)* enriching (rectifying) section
Oberschale *f* **der Petrischale** *(lab)* Petri-dish top
Oberschicht *f* top layer
Oberschwingung *f (spectr)* overtone
Oberschwingungsbande *f (spectr)* overtone band
Oberschwingungsfrequenz *f (spectr)* overtone frequency
Oberseite *f (pap)* top (felt) side
Oberstempel *m (plast)* top ram (force) *(of a press)*; *(ceram)* top punch; *(met)* upper plunger *(of a die)*
Oberton *m*, **Obertonschwingung** *f s.* Oberschwingung
Obertrum *m(n)* top strand, carrying side, *(relating to belt conveyors also)* drive belt
Obertuch *n (pap)* top felt, overfelt
Oberwalze *f* top roll
~ **der Leimpresse** *(pap)* top size press roll
Oberwellenwechselstrompolarographie *f (anal)* higher-harmonic alternating current polarography
Oberwindfrischkonverter *m* basic (top-blown) oxygen converter (furnace)
Oberwindfrischverfahren *n (met)* basic (top-blown) oxygen converter process, basic oxygen [steel] process
Objekt *n* object; *(phys ch)* entity, object
~/diskretes discrete entity
~/elementares elementary entity
~/individuelles individual entity
~/natürliches natural entity
~/komplexes complex entity
~/molekulares molecular entity
~/physikalisches physical entity
~/strukturelles structural entity
Objektträger *m* [microscope] slide
Objektträgerzellentechnik *f*/**Wrightsche** Wright slide-cell technique *(for testing antibiotics)*
Obstbaumspritzmittel *n* fruit tree spray
~/fungizides fruit-fungicide spray
Obstessig *m* fruit vinegar
Obstsaft *m* [fruit] juice
Obstwein *m* fruit wine
Ocimen *n* ocimene, *3,7-dimethylocta-1,3,6-triene
Ocker *m (min)* ochre
~/Gelber yellow ochre *(a mixture of limonite with clay and silica used as a pigment)*
~/Italienischer Italian red *(a pigment consisting of iron(III) oxide)*
~/Roter red ochre (rudd), stone red *(a red haematite used as a pigment)*
ockerhaltig ochreous
OC/load-Wert *m s.* Sauerstoffzufuhrwert
Octacosansäure *f* *octacosanoic acid, montanic acid
Octacyanowolframat(IV) *n* $M^{I}_{4}[W(CN)_8]$ octacyanowolframate(IV), octacyanotungstate(IV)
Octadeca-9,12-diensäure *f* *octadeca-9,12-dienoic acid, linoleic acid
Octadecan *n* octadecane
Octadecanal *n* *octadecanal, stearaldehyde
Octadecanamid *n* *octadecanoamide, stearamide, stearic acid amide
Octadecananilid *n* octadecanoanilide, stearanilide
Octadecannitril *n* *octadecanonitrile, stearonitrile
Octadecan-1-ol *n* *octadecan-1-ol, octadecyl alcohol
Octadecansäure *f* *octadecanoic acid, stearic acid
Octadecatriensäure *f* octadecatrienoic acid
Octadec-11-en-9-insäure *f* *octadec-11-en-9-ynoic acid, santalbic acid
Octadecensäure *f* octadecenoic acid
Octadec-9-insäure *f* *octadec-9-ynoic acid, stearolic acid
Octadecylamin *n* octadecylamine, stearylamine
Octaeder *n (cryst)* octahedron
octaedrisch *(cryst)* octahedral, oct.
Octafluorid *n* octafluoride
Octahydrat *n* octahydrate
Octahydrid *n* octahydride
Octamer[e] *n* octamer
Octamolybdat *n* $M^{I}_{4}Mo_8O_{26}$ octamolybdate
Octan *n* octane
Octanal *n* octanal
Octan-1,8-dicarbonsäure *f* *octane-1,8-dicarboxylic acid, *decanedioic acid, sebacic acid
Octandisäure *f* *octanedioic acid, *hexane-1,5-dicarboxylic acid, suberic acid
Octan-1-ol *n* *octan-1-ol, octyl alcohol
Octansäure *f* octanoic acid
Octanzahl *f* octane number (rating, value) • **mit hoher** ~ high-octane • **mit niedriger** ~ low-octane
Octanzahlbestimmung *f* octane rating
octasubstituiert octasubstituted
octavalent octavalent
Octavalenz *f* octavalency
Octawolframat *n* *octawolframate, octatungstate
Oct-1-in *n* oct-1-yne
Octose *f* octose *(any of a class of monosaccharides)*
Octoxid *n* octaoxide
Octylacetylen *n* *dec-1-yne, *(deprecated:)* octylacetylene

***n*-Octylalkohol** *m s.* Octan-1-ol
***n*-Octylaldehyd** *m s.* Octanal
***n*-Octylsäure** *f s.* Octansäure
Oderberg-Mühle *f* Oderberg [colloid] mill
Odorans *n* odorant
odorieren to odorize *(toxic gases)*
Odoriermittel *n* odorant
Odorierung *f* odorization *(of toxic gases)*
Odorierungsmittel *n* odorant
Odorimetrie *f* 1. odorimetry *(measurement of the intensity of odours)*; 2. *s.* Olfaktometrie
odorisieren *s.* odorieren
O_2-Elektrode *f (biot)* pO_2 electrode
OES *s.* Emissionsspektroskopie/optische
Ofen *m (tech)* furnace, *(esp ceram)* kiln, *(esp for lower temperatures)* oven • **im ~ trocknen** to kiln-dry, to oven-dry
~/außenbeheizter externally heated furnace
~/Belgischer *(ceram)* Belgian kiln
~/brennstoffbeheizter fuel-heated furnace
~/deckenbeheizter *s.* ~/von oben beheizter
~/direkt beheizter direct-fired furnace, direct[-heat] furnace
~/elektrischer (elektrisch beheizter, elektrothermischer) electric furnace
~ für durchlaufenden (kontinuierlichen) Betrieb continuous furnace
~/gemuffelter muffle furnace; *(ceram)* muffle kiln
~/halbgemuffelter *(ceram)* semimuffle kiln
~/holzgefeuerter wood-fired furnace; *(ceram)* wood-fired kiln
~/holzkohlengefeuerter charcoal-fired furnace
~/indirekt beheizter indirect-fired furnace, indirect[-heat] furnace
~/induktionsbeheizter induction (inductance) furnace
~/intermittierender *s.* ~/periodischer
~/Kasseler *(ceram)* Kassel[er] kiln
~/Kingscher King furnace *(for thermal photolysis)*
~/kontinuierlicher (kontinuierlich arbeitender) continuous furnace
~/Mannheimer Mannheim furnace *(for producing hydrochloric acid)*
~/mehretagiger (mehrherdiger) multihearth (multiple-hearth) furnace
~ mit aufsteigender Flamme *(ceram)* updraught kiln
~ mit Außenbeheizung *s.* ~/außenbeheizter
~ mit elektrischer Beheizung *s.* ~/elektrischer
~ mit horizontaler Flammenführung *(ceram)* horizontal-draught kiln
~ mit indirekter Beheizung *s.* ~/indirekt beheizter
~ mit Längsgewölbe *(ceram)* longitudinal arch kiln
~ mit rascher Brandfolge *(ceram)* short-cycle kiln
~ mit Sohlebeheizung sole-flue oven
~ mit überschlagender Flamme *(ceram)* down-draught kiln
~ mit U-Flammenführung *(glass)* end-fired (end-port) furnace
~ mit waagerechter Flammenführung *(ceram)* horizontal-draught kiln
~ mit wanderndem Feuer *(ceram)* moving-fire kiln
~ mit Widerstandserhitzung (Widerstandsheizung) resistance (resistor) furnace, resistance-heated furnace
~/periodischer (periodisch arbeitender) batch-type furnace; *(ceram)* periodic kiln
~/rotierender rotary furnace; *(for sintering or calcining:)* rotary kiln
~/von oben beheizter top-fired furnace, over-fired furnace; *(ceram)* top-fired kiln
~/widerstandsbeheizter *s.* ~ mit Widerstandserhitzung
~/zweietagiger *(ceram)* two-tier kiln
Öfen *mpl***/gekoppelte** *(ceram)* linked kilns
Ofenabwärme *f* furnace waste heat
Ofenalterung *f (rubber)* [air] oven ageing
Ofenatmosphäre *f* furnace atmosphere
Ofenauskleidung *f*, **Ofenausmauerung** *f* furnace lining
Ofenausschuß *m (ceram)* kiln loss
Ofenbeschickung *f* furnace charge
Ofenbetrieb *m* furnace operation
Ofenboden *m s.* Ofensohle
Ofencharge *f* furnace charge
Ofendrehwerk *n* furnace-rotating mechanism
Ofeneinsatz *m* furnace charge
Ofenfutter *n* furnace lining
~/basisches *(met)* basic lining
~/saures *(met)* acid lining
Ofengas *n* furnace gas
Ofengestell *n* furnace hearth
ofengetrocknet kiln-dried, oven-dried
Ofenkammer *f* furnace chamber
Ofenlack *m* stoving lacquer; *(if unpigmented:)* stoving varnish
Ofenladung *f* furnace charge
Ofenmantel *m* furnace shell
Ofenraum *m* furnace chamber
Ofenruß *m (rubber)* furnace [combustion] black
Ofenschacht *m* furnace shaft
Ofenschlacke *f* furnace slag (clinker)
Ofenschwarz *n s.* Ofenruß
Ofensohle *f* furnace bottom; *(ceram)* kiln floor; *(glass)* bench, siege *(of a pot furnace)*
Ofenstützmaterial *n (ceram)* kiln furniture
Ofentransformator *m* furnace transformer
ofentrocken kiln-dried, oven-dried
Ofentrocknung *f* kiln (oven) drying
Ofentür *f***/gemauerte** *(ceram)* [kiln] wicket
Ofenverfahren *n (rubber)* furnace [combustion] process, continuous-furnace method *(for producing carbon black)*
Ofenvorlage *f* gas collecting main *(of a coke-oven battery)*
Ofenwagen *m (ceram)* kiln car
Ofenwanne *f* crucible *(of an arc furnace)*
Ofenzug *m* flue

Ofenzustellung *f (met)* furnace lining
offenkettig *(org ch)* open-chain
offenzellig open-cell *(foamed plastics)*
offizinell *(pharm)* official, pharmacopoeial
öffnen to open; to dismantle *(a filter press)*
Öffnung *f* opening, *(esp of a nozzle:)* orifice, *(esp of a bottle:)* mouth, *(esp for intake or exhaust of fluids:)* port, *(esp for charging or discharging solids:)* door, *(esp for the passage of radiation:)* aperture
Öffnungsdruck *m* opening pressure *(of a valve)*
Öffnungsweite *f* **[des Siebs]** screen (sieve) size, [screen] aperture
Öffnungswinkel *m* aperture angle *(of a cone of radiation)*
Off-resonance-Entkopplung *f (spectr)* off-resonance decoupling
Offsetdruck *m* offset printing
Offsetdruckfarbe *f* offset [printing] ink
Offsetdruckpapier *n* offset [printing] paper
Offsetdruckverfahren *n* offset [printing] process
Offsetpapier *n* offset [printing] paper
Offsetpresse *f (pap)* offset (smoothing) press
OFHC-Kupfer *n* oxygen-free high-conductivity copper, O.F.H.C. copper
Ogia-Kopal *m* Accra copal *(from Daniella ogea Rolfe)*
OH-Austauscher *m (hyd)* OH-form (hydroxyl-form) exchanger, anion exchanger
OH-Gruppe *f* OH group, hydroxyl (hydroxy) group (residue)
OH-Ionenaustauscher *m s.* OH-Austauscher
OH-Radikal *n* OH radical, *(specif)* free OH radical
OH-Rest *m s.* OH-Gruppe
OHZ *s.* Hydroxylzahl
Oiazin *n s.* Pyridazin
Oiticicaöl *n* oiticica oil *(from Licania rigida Benth.)*
Okasaki-Fragment *n*, **Okasaki-Stück** *n (bioch)* Okasaki fragment *(of the DNA)*
okkludieren to occlude
Okklusion *f* occlusion
Ökosphäre *f* ecosphere, biosphere
Ökotoxikologie *f* ecotoxicology, environmental toxicology
ökotoxikologisch ecotoxicological
Ökotoxizität *f* ecotoxicity, environmental toxicity
Okt... *s. a.* Oct...
n-**Oktadezylalkohol** *m s.* Octadecan-1-ol
Oktett *n* octet
Oktettaufweitung *f* octet expansion
Oktettprinzip *n*, **Oktettregel** *f* octet rule
Okular *n* eyepiece, ocular *(of a microscope)*
Öl *n* oil • **in ~ ablöschen (abschrecken)** to oil-quench • **in ~ härten** to oil-harden *(steel)* • **mit ~ beheizt** oil-heated • **mit ~ getränkt** oil-impregnated
~/abgepreßtes *(petrol)* pressed distillate, blue oil
~/abgetopptes *s.* ~/getopptes
~/absolutes *(cosmet)* absolute essence, absolute [from concrete]
~/ätherisches essential (volatile) oil
~/auf Erdölbasis petroleum oil
~/aufgeschwommenes *(hyd)* scum oil
~ aus Rückstandsaufarbeitung recovered oil *(in coal hydrogenation)*
~/compoundiertes compounded oil
~/destilliertes distilled oil
~/Dippelsches Dippel's (bone) oil
~/doktor-negatives *(petrol)* sweet oil
~/doktor-positives *(petrol)* sour oil
~/eingedicktes thickened oil; *(coat)* bodied (polymerized) oil
~/emulgierbares emulsifiable oil, soluble (miscible) oil
~/entbastes *(coal)* base-free oil
~/entphenoltes *(coal)* dephenolated (phenol-free) oil
~/fettes 1. fat[ty] oil, fixed oil *(as opposed to essential oil)*; 2. *(petrol)* rich oil *(an absorption oil for light hydrocarbons)*
~/geblasenes blown oil
~/gebranntes distilled oil
~/gefettetes compounded oil
~/gehärtetes hardened (hydrogenated) oil
~/gesäuertes *s.* ~/saures
~/geschwefeltes sulphurized (sulphurated) oil
~/getopptes topped crude [petroleum], reduced crude [oil], reduced oil
~/halbtrocknendes semidrying oil
~/„harzfreies“ non-sludging oil
~/helles pale oil *(a lubricating-oil distillate)*
~/hydriertes *s.* ~/gehärtetes
~/kaltgepreßtes (kaltgeschlagenes) cold-drawn oil
~/konkretes *(cosmet)* concrete [oil]
~/leichtes light oil
~/lösliches soluble oil
~/medizinisches medicinal oil
~/mineralisches mineral oil
~/mischbares 1. *(agric)* emulsifiable concentrate *(used as a pesticide)*; 2. *s.* ~/emulgierbares
~ mit negativem Doktortest *(petrol)* sweet oil
~ mit positivem Doktortest *(petrol)* sour oil
~/naphthenhaltiges (naphthenisches) naphthenic oil
~/neutrales neutral oil
~/„nicht verharzendes“ non-sludging oil
~/nichtflüchtiges fixed oil
~/nichttrocknendes non-drying oil, permanent oil
~/oxidiertes *(coat)* blown oil
~/Paalsgardsches Paalsgard emulsion oil, P.E.O.
~/pflanzliches vegetable oil
~/reduziertes *s.* ~/getopptes
~/rohes *(petrol)* crude [oil]
~/rostschützendes rust-inhibiting oil
~/saures *(petrol)* sour oil *(acid-treated oil before neutralization)*
~/schwach trocknendes *s.* ~/halbtrocknendes
~/schwefelbehandeltes *s.* ~/geschwefeltes
~/schweres heavy oil

~/staubbindendes dust-laying oil
~/sulfatiertes (sulfiertes) sulphated oil
~/sulfoniertes (sulfuriertes) sulphonated oil
~/tierisches animal oil
~/trocknendes drying oil
~/vegetabilisches vegetable oil
~/wasserlösliches *s.* ~/emulgierbares
~/zurückgewonnenes recovered oil
Ölablöschung *f* oil quenching
Ölabscheider *m* oil separator
Ölabscheidung *f* separation of oil, oil removal
Ölabschreckung *f* oil quenching
Ölabsorption *f* oil absorption
Ölabtrennung *f s.* Ölabscheidung
ölabweisend oil-repellent, oleophobic
Ölabweisungsvermögen *n* oil repellency
Ölanreicherung *f*, **Ölansammlung** *f* 1. oil accumulation; 2. oil pool (reservoir, accumulation)
ölartig oily, oleaginous
Ölausbruch *m (petrol)* blow-out
Ölbad *n* oil bath
Ölbatch *m (rubber)* oil masterbatch
Ölbehälter *m* oil tank (container); oil cup *(of a viscometer)*
ölbeheizt oil-heated
Ölbeheizung *f* oil[-fired] heating
Ölbeize *f (coat)* oil stain
ölbeladen *(hyd)* oil-coated, oil-wet *(solids)*
ölbeständig resistant to oil, oil-resistant, oil-resisting
Ölbeständigkeit *f* resistance to oil, oil resistance
ölbildend oil-forming
Ölbitumen *n* oily bitumen
Ölbohrloch *n*, **Ölbohrung** *f* oil (petroleum) well
Ölbrenner *m* oil burner (gun)
Olbrücke *f* ol (olation) bridge *(between metal atoms and OH groups)*
Ölbrunnen *m* oil (petroleum) well
~/pumpender pumping well
öldicht oiltight *(joint)*; oilproof *(paper)*
Öldichtigkeit *f* oiltightness *(of a joint)*; oilproofness *(of paper)*
Oleat *n* oleate
Olefin *n* olefin, *alkene
Olefinierung *f* olefination
Olefinierungsmittel *n*, **Olefinierungsreagens** *n* olefin-forming reagent
olefinisch olefinic
Olefinpolymerisation *f* olefin polymerization
Olefinreihe *f* olefin series, alkene family
Olein *n* 1. olein, glycerol oleate; 2. olein, commercial oleic acid
Öleinsatz *m* oil feed
~/dampfförmiger vapour feed *(in Thermofor catalytic cracking)*
~/flüssiger liquid feed *(in Thermofor catalytic cracking)*
Oleinsäure *f s.* Ölsäure
ölen to oil
Oleo[margarin] *n* oleomargarin[e] *(a certain kind of beef fat)*
oleophob *s.* ölabweisend
Oleoresin *n* oleoresin *(a mixture of an essential oil and a resin)*
Oleostearin *n*, **Oleostock** *n (food)* oleostearin
Oleum *n* oleum, fuming sulphuric acid
Oleylalkohol *m* oleyl alcohol, **cis*-octadec-9-en-1-ol
1-Oleylglycerylether *m* glycerol 1-oleyl ether, selachyl alcohol
Olfaktometrie *f (med)* olfactometry
Ölfalle *f* oil trap
Ölfänger *m* oil separator
Ölfarbe *f* oil paint, oil-base[d] paint, *(esp in art:)* oil colour
Ölfeld *n* oil field (pool)
Ölfeldentwicklung *f* oil-field development
Ölfeldwasser *n (petrol)* edge water
ölfest *s.* ölbeständig
Ölfeuerung *f* oil firing
Ölfilter *n* oil filter
Ölfirnis *m* boiled oil; oil varnish *(for printing)*
Ölfleck *m* oil spot
ölfrei free from oil, oil-free
Ölfrucht *f* oil plant
ölführend oil-bearing, petroleum-bearing, petroliferous
Öl-Furnace-Anlage *f (rubber)* oil-furnace plant
Öl-Furnace-Ruß *m (rubber)* oil-furnace black
Öl-Furnace-Verfahren *n (rubber)* oil-furnace process
Ölgas *n* oil (fatty) gas
ölgefeuert oil-fired
Ölgehalt *m* oil content; *(coat)* oil length *(related to resin)*
Ölgemisch *n* oil mixture
ölgestreckt *(rubber)* oil-extended, oil-filled
ölgetränkt oil-impregnated
Ölgrün *n* 1. oil green *(chromium(III) oxide)*; 2. chrome green *(consisting of iron blue and chrome yellow)*
ölhaltig 1. oil-containing, oily, oleaginous; 2. *(rubber)* oil-extended, oil-filled; 3. *s.* ölführend
ölhärten to oil-harden *(steel)*
Ölhärter *m*, **Ölhärtestahl** *m* oil-hardening steel
Ölhärtung *f* 1. oil hardening *(of steel)*; 2. *(food)* hydrogenation of oil
Ölharz *n* oleoresin
Ölharzfarbe *f* oleoresinous paint
Ölharzlack *m* oleoresinous varnish
Öl-Harz-Verhältnis *n* oil/resin ratio, oil-to-resin ratio
Ölhavarie *f* oil spill
Ölheizung *f* oil[-fired] heating
Ölhorizont *m (geol)* oil layer (horizon)
Olibanum *n* [frank]incense, olibanum *(from Boswellia specc.)*
Olibanumöl *n (pharm)* frankincense (olibanum) oil *(from Boswellia specc.)*

ölig oily, oleaginous, *(esp of crystals:)* unctuous
Öligkeit *f* oiliness, *(esp of crystals:)* unctuousness
oligofunktionell oligofunctional
Oligomer[e] *n* oligomer *(molecule having up to 10 repeating units)*
Oligomerisation *f* oligomerization
Oligonucleotid *n* oligonucleotide
Oligopeptid *n* oligopeptide *(containing up to 10 amino acids)*
Oligosaccharid *n* oligosaccharide
oligotroph oligotrophic *(deficient in dissolved plant nutrients)*
Ölindustrie *f* oil industry
Öl-in-Wasser-Emulsion *f* oil[-in]-water emulsion, O/W emulsion
Öl-in-Wasser-Typ *m* oil-in-water type, O/W type *(of emulsions)*
Olive *f (lab)* hose coupling (connection, connector)
Olivenit *m (min)* olivenite *(copper(II) hydroxide tetraoxoarsenate)*
Olivenöl *n* olive oil *(from Olea europaea L.)*
Oliver-Filter *n* Oliver filter
Olivin *m (min)* olivine *(a nesosilicate)*
Olivinerzeugnis *n (ceram)* olivine refractory
Ölkautschuk *m s.* Faktis
Ölkern *m s.* Ölsandkern
Ölkracken *n* oil cracking
Ölkuchen *m* oil (mill) cake
Ölkuchenbrecher *m* cake mill
Ölkuchenmehl *n* oil meal
Öllack *m* oil varnish
~/fetter long-oil varnish
~/halbfetter medium-oil varnish
~/magerer short-oil varnish
~/mittelfetter medium-oil varnish
~/überfetter extra long-oil varnish
Öllos-Lager *n (tech)* oilless bearing
öllöslich oil-soluble
Öllöslichkeit *f* oil solubility, solubility in oil
Ölmischung *f* oil mixture
ölmodifiziert oil-modified
Ölmühle *f* oil mill
Öl-Naturharz-Farbe *f* oleoresinous paint
Öl-Naturharz-Lack *m* oleoresinous varnish
Ölniveau *n* oil level
Öl[pack]papier *n* oiled paper
Ölpflanze *f* oil plant
ölplastiziert *s.* ölgestreckt
Ölpumpe *f* oil pump
OLP-Verfahren *n (met)* O.L.P. process *(an oxygen-lance process)*
Ölquelle *f* oil (petroleum) well
Ölraffination *f* oil refining
Ölräumschild *m (hyd)* oil skimmer
ölreaktiv *(coat)* oil-reactive
Ölrückgewinnung *f* oil recovery
Öl-Ruß-Batch *m (rubber)* oil/carbon black masterbatch
Ölsaat *f* oil-bearing seed
Ölsand *m (geol, met)* oil sand
Ölsandkern *m* oil-sand core *(foundry)*
Ölsäure *f* oleic acid, *cis*-octadec-9-enoic acid
~/rohe (technische) olein, commercial oleic acid
Ölscheidung *f* oil liberation *(in emulsions)*
Ölschicht *f* 1. oil layer, *(if thin)* oil film; 2. *(geol)* oil layer (horizon)
Ölschiefer *m (geol)* oil shale
Ölschlamm *m (petrol)* oil sludge; engine sludge *(in an internal combustion engine)*; *(hyd)* oily sludge
Ölschwarz *n* black chalk, slate black *(a natural pigment)*
Ölspachtel *m(f) (coat)* oil filler
Ölspaltung *f (petrol)* oil cracking
Ölspiegel *m* oil level
Ölspülung *f (petrol)* oil-base mud
Ölstand *m* oil level
Ölstreckung *f (rubber)* oil extension
Ölsüß *n s.* Glycerol
Ölteer *m* oil tar
Ölträger *m (petrol)* producing formation
Öltränkung *f* oil impregnation
Öltröpfchen *n* oil droplet
Öltropfenmethode *f* oil-drop method *(as for determining the charge of electrons)*
Ölturbinen[ultra]zentrifuge *f* oil-turbine ultracentrifuge
Ölumlauf *m* oil circulation
ölundurchlässig oilproof *(paper)*
Ölundurchlässigkeit *f* oilproofness *(of paper)*
Ölvergasung *f* oil gasification
Ölvormischung *f (rubber)* oil masterbatch
Ölwäsche *f* oil washing (scrubbing) *(of gases)*
Ölwäscher *m* oil washer (scrubber) *(for gases)*
Ommatin *n* ommatine *(an eye pigment)*
Ommin *n* ommine *(an eye pigment)*
Ommochrom *n* ommochrome *(any of a class of eye pigments)*
OMP = Orotidin-5'-monophosphat
Omunketenußöl *n* Manketti nut oil *(from Ricinodendron rautaneni Schinz)*
Önanthaldehyd *m* *heptanal, *(deprecated:)* oenanthic aldehyde
Önanthalkohol *m* *heptan-1-ol, *(deprecated:)* oenanthic alcohol
Önanthat *n* *heptanoate, *(deprecated:)* oenanthate *(salt or ester of heptanoic acid)*
Önanthol *n s.* Önanthaldehyd
Önanthsäure *f* *heptanoic acid, *(deprecated:)* oenanthic acid
Önanthyliden *n s.* Hept-1-in
Onia-Gegi-Verfahren *n (petrol)* Onia-Gegi process
oniumartig onium-like
Oniumverbindung *f* onium compound
onkogen oncogenic, oncogenous, tumorigenic, tumor-causing
Önologie *f (food)* oenology
önologisch *(food)* oenological
Önometer *n* oenometer

Onsäure *f* aldonic acid *(any of a class of acids derived from aldoses)*
Onyx *m (min)* onyx *(silicon(IV) oxide)*
Oolith *m (geol)* oolite *(chiefly calcium carbonate)*
oolithisch *(geol)* oolitic
OPA *s. o*-Phthalaldehyd
opak opaque
Opakglas *n* opaque glass
Opakglasur *f (ceram)* opaque glaze
Opaksubstanz *f (coal)* opaque matter
Opal *m (min)* opal *(silicon(IV) oxide)*
Opaleszenz *f* opalescence
Opaleszenzfarbe *f* opalescence colour
opaleszieren to opalesce
opaleszierend opalescent
Opalglas *n* opal glass
opalisieren to opalesce
opalisierend opalescent
Opazität *f* opacity
Operation *f***/grundlegende** basic (fundamental) operation
Operator *m (bioch)* operator, o locus
Operment *n* orpiment [yellow], yellow arsenic [sulphide], arsenic (royal) yellow, king's yellow (gold) *(technically pure arsenic(III) sulphide)*
Operon *n (bioch)* operon *(a group of genes which act cooperatively)*
Operonmodell *n (bioch)* operon hypothesis
Opferanode *f* sacrificial (galvanic, expendable) anode
Opium *n* opium
Opiumalkaloid *n* opium alkaloid
Opiumpulver *n* powdered opium
~/eingestelltes standardized powdered opium
Opiumsäure *f s.* Mekonsäure
Opiumtinktur *f* tincture of opium
~/benzoesäurehaltige benzoated tincture of opium
OP-Kautschuk *m* oil-extended styrene-butadiene rubber, OE-SBR, oil-extended (oil-masterbatched) polymer, OEP
Oppenauer-Reaktion *f* Oppenauer oxidation (reaction) *(for dehydrogenating secondary alcohols)*
Oppenheimer-Phillips-Prozeß *m (nucl)* Oppenheimer-Phillips process
optisch aktiv optically active
~ **einachsig** [optically] uniaxial
~ **inaktiv** optically inactive
~ **isomer** enantiomeric, enantiomorphic, enantiomorphous
~ **isotrop** optically isotropic
~ **zweiachsig** [optically] biaxial
Optoakustik-Spektroskopie *f* photoacoustic spectroscopy, PAS, optoacoustic spectroscopy
Orange *n* **I** orange I, α-naphthol orange, sodium-azo-α-naphthol sulphanilate, acid orange 20
~ **II** orange II, sodium-azo-β-naphthol sulphanilate, acid orange 7
~ **III** orange III, methyl orange, sodium *p*-(*p*-dimethylaminophenylazo)benzenesulphonate, acid orange 52
~ **IV** orange IV, tropaeolin 00, sodium *p*-diphenylamine-azobenzenesulphonate, acid orange 5
~ **N** *s.* ~ IV
Orangemennige *f* orange lead (mineral)
Orangenschaleneffekt *m (coat)* orange peel
Orangenschalenöl *n* orange-peel oil
Orangenschellack *m* orange shellac (lac)
Orbital *n* orbital
~/antibindendes antibonding orbital
~/atomares *s.* Atomorbital
~/bindendes bonding orbital
~/elektronisches electron orbital
~/*sp*-hybridisiertes hybrid *sp* orbital
~/lockerndes antibonding orbital
~/lokalisiertes localized orbital
~/molekulares *s.* Molekülorbital
~/nichtbindendes non-bonding orbital
***p*-Orbital** *n p* orbital
***s*-Orbital** *n s* orbital
***sp*-Orbital** *n sp* orbital
π-Orbital *n* pi-orbital, π-orbital, π molecular orbital
σ-Orbital *n* sigma-orbital, σ-orbital, σ molecular orbital
Orbitalausrichtung *f* orbital steering
Orbitalbewegung *f* orbital motion
Orbitaldrehimpuls *m* orbital [angular] momentum
Orbitaldrehimpulsquantenzahl *f* azimuthal (subsidiary) quantum number, orbital [angular momentum] quantum number
Orbitalelektron *n* orbital electron
Orbitalmoment *n* orbital [magnetic] moment
Orbitalsymmetrie *f* orbital symmetry
Orbitaltheorie *f* orbital theory
Orcein *n (dye)* orcein
Orcin *n* orcinol, 3,5-dihydroxytoluene
O.R.D. *s.* Rotationsdispersion/optische
Ordnung *f* order
~/gebrochene fractional order *(reaction kinetics)*
~/laterale [molekulare] lateral order *(of polymers)*
~/pseudo-erste pseudo-first order *(reaction kinetics)* • **pseudo-erster** ~ pseudo-unimolecular
~/weitreichende *s.* Fernordnung
Ordnungsgrad *m* degree of order (orientation) *(as of polymers)*
Ordnungsparameter *m* order parameter
Ordnungsumwandlung *f s.* Ordnung-Unordnung-Übergang
Ordnungszahl *f* atomic (ordinal) number, A.N., *(symbol:)* Z
~/effektive effective atomic number, E.A.N.
~/ungerade odd atomic number
Ordnung-Unordnung-Übergang *m*, **Ordnung-Unordnung-Umwandlung** *f (cryst)* order-disorder transition (transformation)
Orford-Verfahren *n (met)* Orford process, top-and-bottom smelting process
Organiker *m* organic chemist
organisch organic
~-chemisch organic-chemical

Organismengift *n* biocide
Organkultur *f (biot)* organ culture
Organoberylliumverbindung *f* organoberyllium compound
Organoboran *n* organoborane
Organoborverbindung *f* organoboron compound
Organocadmiumverbindung *f* organocadmium compound
Organochemikalie *f* organic chemical
Organochemiker *m* organic chemist
Organochlorsilan *n* organochlorosilane
Organoderivat *n* organoderivative
organofunktionell organofunctional, carbon-functional
Organogel *n* organogel
organogen organogenic
Organogen *n* organogen *(any of the elements characteristic of organic compounds)*
Organogruppe *f* organic group
Organohalogensilan *n* organosilicon halide, organohalogenosilane, organohalosilane
Organohalogenverbindungen *fpl* haloorganic (halogenated organic) compounds, HOC, haloorganics, organic halides, organohalides
~/austreibbare *(hyd)* purgeable organic halides, POX
~/nichtaustreibbare *(hyd)* non-purgeable organic halides, NPOX
Organoleptik *f* organoleptic (sensory) testing
organoleptisch organoleptic
Organolithiumverbindung *f* organolithium compound
Organomagnesiumhalogenid *n* organomagnesium halide
Organometallverbindung *f* organometallic (metallo-organic) compound
Organopalladiumverbindung *f* organopalladium compound
Organophosphorverbindung *f* organophosphorus compound
Organopolysiloxan *n* organopolysiloxane, polyorganosiloxane, polymeric organosiloxane
Organoquecksilberbeize *f (agric)* organomercury dressing
Organoquecksilberton *m* organomercury clay
Organoquecksilberverbindung *f* organomercury compound, organomercurial
Organosilan *n* organosilane, organic silane
Organosilazan *n* organosilazane
Organosiliciumchemie *f* organosilicon chemistry
Organosiliciumhalogenid *n s.* Organohalogensilan
Organosiliciumoxid *n s.* Organosiloxan
Organosiliciumpolymer[e] *n* organosilicon polymer
Organosiliciumverbindung *f* organosilicon compound
Organosilicon *n* organosilicone
Organosiloxan *n* organosiloxane, organic siloxane, organosilicon oxide
~/polymeres *s.* Organosiloxanpolymer
Organosiloxanpolymer[e] *n* organosiloxane polymer, organopolysiloxane, polyorganosiloxane
Organosol *n* organosol
Organozinkverbindung *f* organozinc compound
Organozinnstabilisator *m* organotin stabilizer
Organozinnverbindung *f* organotin compound
orientieren to orient[ate], *(in linear direction also)* to align
orientiert/nach oben up-oriented *(atomic group)*
~/nach unten down-oriented
Orientierung *f* orientation, *(in linear direction also)* alignment
~/axiale monoaxial orientation
~/biaxiale biaxial orientation
~/einachsige monoaxial orientation
~/molekulare molecular orientation
~/nichtbevorzugte (regellose) random orientation
Orientierungsbeziehung *f* epitaxy
Orientierungseffekt *m* orientation effect *(as with molecules)*
Orientierungserscheinung *f (rubber)* grain effect *(in sheets)*
Orientierungsgrad *m* degree of order (orientation)
Orientierungskraft *f* permanent dipole-dipole force
Orientierungspolarisation *f* orientation polarization
Orientierungsquantenzahl *f* magnetic quantum number
O-Ring *m* O-ring *(seal)*
Orlean *m* annatto, annotta, arnatto, arnotta *(a colouring matter from Bixa orellana L.)*
Ornamentglas *n* patterned (figured) glass
Ornithin *n* ornithine, *2,5-diaminopentanoic acid
Ornithinzyklus *m (bioch)* ornithine (urea) cycle, Krebs-Henseleit cycle
Orotidin-5'-phosphorsäure *f* orotidine 5'-phosphoric acid, orotidylic acid
Orotsäure *f* orotic acid, uracil-4-carboxylic acid
Orotsäureurie *f (med)* orotic aciduria
Orsat *m s.* Orsat-Apparat
Orsat-Analyse *f* Orsat analysis *(of gases)*
Orsat-Apparat *m*, **Orsat-Gerät** *n* Orsat apparatus, Orsat gas [analysis] apparatus
Orseille *f* orchil, archil *(a lichen dye)*
Orsellinsäure *f* orsellic (orsellinic) acid, 4,6-dihydroxy-*o*-toluic acid
Ort *m* site *(of reaction)*; position *(of an elementary particle)* • **an ~ und Stelle, vor ~** in situ *(investigation, sampling)*
Ortbeton *m* in-situ concrete
Orthanilsäure *f* orthanilic acid, aniline-*o*-sulphonic acid
Orthit *m s.* Allanit
Orthoameisensäureethylester *m* ethyl orthoformate
orthoanelliert *(org ch)* ortho-fused
Orthoanellierung *f (org ch)* ortho fusion
Orthoarsenat(III) *n* $M^I_3AsO_3$ *trioxoarsenate(III), arsenite, *(deprecated:)* orthoarsenite

Orthoarsenat(V) *n* $M^I_3AsO_4$ *tetraoxoarsenate(V), arsenate, *(deprecated:)* orthoarsenate
Orthoborat *n* $M^I_3BO_3$ orthoborate, borate, *trioxoborate
Orthoborsäure *f* orthoboric acid, boric acid, *trioxoboric acid
Orthocarbonat *n* $M^I_4CO_4$ orthocarbonate
Orthocarbonsäure *n* ortho acid
Orthocarbonsäureester *m* ortho ester
orthochromatisch *(phot)* orthochromatic
ortho-dirigierend ortho-directing
Orthoester *m* ortho ester
Orthoflow-Verfahren *n (petrol)* Orthoflow [catalytic cracking] process
Orthogestein *n* ortho rock
ortho-Isomer[e] *n* ortho isomer, *o*-isomer
Orthokieselsäure *f* orthosilicic acid, silicic acid, *tetraoxosilicic acid
Orthoklas *m (min)* orthoclase *(a feldspar)*
Orthokohlensäure *f* orthocarbonic acid
Orthokondensation *f* ortho fusion
orthokondensiert ortho-fused
ortho-Molekül *n* ortho molecule
Ortho-Öl *n* ortho oil
ortho-Orientierung *f* ortho orientation
ortho-para-dirigierend ortho-para-directing
ortho-peri-anelliert, ortho-peri-kondensiert ortho[-and]-peri-fused
Orthoperiodat *n* $M^I_5[IO_6]$ orthoperiodate, *hexaoxoiodate(VII)
Orthoperiodsäure *f* orthoperiodic acid, *hexaoxoiodic(VII) acid
Orthophosphat *n* $M^I_3PO_4$ orthophosphate, phosphate
~/neutrales $M^I_3PO_4$ neutral (normal) orthophosphate (phosphate)
~/primäres *s.* Dihydrogenphosphat
~/sekundäres *s.* Hydrogenphosphat
~/tertiäres *s.* ~/neutrales
Orthophosphit *n* $M^I_2PHO_3$ orthophosphite, phosphite, *phosphonate
Orthophosphorsäure *f* orthophosphoric acid, phosphoric acid
Orthoplumbat *n* $M^I_4PbO_4$ *tetraoxoplumbate(IV), *(deprecated:)* orthoplumbate
Ortho-Positronium *n (nucl)* orthopositronium
orthorhombisch *(cryst)* orthorhombic, o-rh.
Orthosilicat *n* $M^I_4SiO_4$ orthosilicate, silicate, *tetraoxosilicate
ortho-ständig ortho, in ortho position • **~ sein** to be [located, situated] ortho
Orthostannat *n* $M^I_4SnO_4$ *tetraoxostannate(IV), *(deprecated:)* orthostannate
ortho-Stellung *f* ortho position • **in ~** in ortho position, ortho • **nach der ~ dirigierend** ortho-directing
ortho-Substituent *m* ortho substituent
ortho-substituiert ortho-substituted, *o*-substituted
ortho-Substitution *f* ortho-substitution
Orthotellurat *n* $M^I_6TeO_6$ orthotellurate, tellurate, *hexaoxotellurate
Orthotellursäure *f* orthotelluric acid, telluric acid, *hexaoxotelluric acid
Orthotitanat *n* $M^I_4TiO_4$ *tetraoxotitanate(IV), *(deprecated:)* orthotitanate
Orthotitaniumsäure *f* *tetraoxotitanic acid, *(deprecated:)* orthotitanic acid
ortho-Umlagerung *f* 1,2-shift
Orthovanadat *n* $M^I_3VO_4$ *tetraoxovanadate(V), *(deprecated:)* orthovanadate
ortho-Verbindung *f* ortho compound
Orthowasserstoff *m* ortho hydrogen
Orthozinnsäure *f* *tetraoxostannic acid, *(deprecated:)* orthostannic acid
ortho-Zustand *m* ortho state
Orton-Kegel *m (ceram)* Orton cone *(a pyrometric cone used in the USA)*
Orton-Umlagerung *f* Orton rearrangement (reaction) *(of N-halogenated arylamines into 1,2-halogenated and 1,4-halogenated arylamines)*
Ortsbestimmung *f* localization [of position], location
ortsbeweglich movable, mobile
ortseigen *(geol)* autochthonous
ortsfremd *(geol)* allochthonous
Ortshöhe *f* potential head
Ortsisomerie *f s.* Stellungsisomerie
Ortsschäumen *n (plast)* foaming in place (situ)
Ortstein *m (soil)* ironpan, hardpan, ortstein
O_2-Sättigungswert *m (hyd)* oxygen saturation concentration (value, level), oxygen concentration at saturation
Osazon *n (org ch)* osazone
Osazonbildung *f (org ch)* osazone formation
Osazonierung *f (org ch)* osazonation
Osmat(VI) *n* $M^I_2OsO_4$ osmate(VI), tetraoxoosmate(VI)
Osmium *n* Os osmium
Osmium(II)-chlorid *n* osmium(II) chloride, osmium dichloride
Osmium(III)-chlorid *n* osmium(III) chloride, osmium trichloride
Osmium(IV)-chlorid *n* osmium(IV) chloride, osmium tetrachloride
Osmiumdichlorid *n s.* Osmium(II)-chlorid
Osmiumdioxid *n s.* Osmium(IV)-oxid
Osmiumdisulfid *n s.* Osmium(IV)-sulfid
Osmium(IV)-fluorid *n* osmium(IV) fluoride, osmium tetrafluoride
Osmium(VI)-fluorid *n* osmium(VI) fluoride, osmium hexafluoride
Osmium(VIII)-fluorid *n* osmium(VIII) fluoride, osmium octafluoride
Osmiumhexafluorid *n* s. Osmium(VI)-fluorid
Osmiummonoxid *n s.* Osmium(II)-oxid
Osmiumoctafluorid *n s.* Osmium(VIII)-fluorid
Osmium(II)-oxid *n* osmium(II) oxide, osmium monooxide

Osmium(III)-oxid *n* osmium(III) oxide, diosmium trioxide
Osmium(IV)-oxid *n* osmium(IV) oxide, osmium dioxide
Osmium(VIII)-oxid *n* osmium(VIII) oxide, osmium tetraoxide
Osmiumsäure *f* osmic acid
Osmium(IV)-sulfid *n* osmium(IV) sulphide, osmium disulphide
Osmium(VIII)-sulfid *n* osmium(VIII) sulphide, osmium tetrasulphide
Osmiumtetrachlorid *n s.* Osmium(IV)-chlorid
Osmiumtetrafluorid *n s.* Osmium(IV)-fluorid
Osmiumtetrasulfid *n s.* Osmium(VIII)-sulfid
Osmiumtetroxid *n s.* Osmium(VIII)-oxid
Osmiumtrichlorid *n s.* Osmium(III)-chlorid
Osmol *n* osmole *(1 osmol = 1 mol dissolved material per kg of solvent or per l of solution)*
Osmolalität *f* osmolality *(total molar concentration of dissolved material per kg of solvent)*
Osmolarität *f* osmolarity *(total molar concentration of dissolved material per l of solution)*
Osmometer *n* osmometer
Osmometrie *f* osmometry
Osmose *f* osmosis
~/umgekehrte reverse osmosis, RO
Osmotierung *f* diffusion treatment *(wood preservation)*
osmotisch osmotic
Oson *n (org ch)* osone
Osteolith *m (min)* osteolite *(a massive earthy apatite)*
Östradiol *n* oestradiol *(a sex hormone)*
östrogen oestrogenic, oestrus-producing
Östrogen *n* oestrogen *(any of a class of sex hormones)*
Ostwald-de Waele-Reibungsgesetz *n* Ostwald-de-Waele equation
Ostwald-Reifung *f (cryst)* Ostwald ripening
Ostwald-Verfahren *n* Ostwald process *(for obtaining nitric acid)*
Ostwald-Viskosimeter *n* Ostwald viscometer (viscosity pipette)
Oszillation *f* oscillation, vibration
Oszillationsenergie *f* vibrational energy
Oszillationsviskosimeter *n* oscillating viscometer
Oszillator *m* oscillator
~/anharmonischer anharmonic oscillator
~/harmonischer harmonic oscillator
Oszillatorenstärke *f (spectr)* oscillator strength, *f* number
oszillatorisch oscillatory, vibratory
oszillieren to oscillate, to vibrate
Oszillometrie *f* oscillometry
Oszillopolarogramm *n* oscillographic polarogram
Oszillopolarographie *f* oscillographic polarography
oszillopolarographisch oscillo-polarographic
o. T. *s.* Tiegel/offener
Otto-Hoffmann-Koksofen *m* Otto-Hoffmann coke oven
Ouabain *n* ouabain, *g*-strophanthin *(glycoside)*
Ouricury-Wachs *n* ouricury wax *(from Cocos coronata Mart.)*
Ovalbumin *n* egg albumin
Overhauser-Effekt *m (spectr)* Overhauser effect
ovizid ovicidal
Ovizid *n* ovicide *(pest control)*
Ovomukoid *n* ovomucoid *(a protein)*
Ovovitellin *n* ovovitellin, egg vitellin *(a phosphoprotein)*
Ovulationshemmer *m* ovulation inhibitor, antifertility agent
Ö/W *s.* Öl-in-Wasser-Emulsion
Owens-Maschine *f (glass)* Owens (bottle) machine
Owens-Verfahren *n* Owens process *(for making bottles)*
Oxacyclobutan *n s.* Oxetan
Oxalacetatweg *m (bioch)* oxaloacetate pathway
Oxalaldehyd *m* oxalaldehyde, glyoxal, *ethanedial
Oxalaldehydsäure *f s.* Oxoethansäure
Oxalat *n* oxalate • **mit Oxalaten behandeln** to oxalate *(e.g. blood)*
~/saures *s.* Hydrogenoxalat
Oxalatoaluminat *n* oxalatoaluminate
Oxalatochromat(III) *n* $M^I_3[Cr(C_2O_4)_3]$ oxalatochromate(III), trioxalatochromate(III)
Oxalatocobaltat(III) *n* $M^I_3[Co(C_2O_4)_3]$ oxalatocobaltate(III), trioxalatocobaltate(III)
Oxalatokomplex *m* oxalate complex
Oxalbernsteinsäure *f* oxalosuccinic acid
Oxalbernsteinsäurecarboxylase *f* oxalosuccinic carboxylase
Oxalessigester *m s.* Oxalessigsäurediethylester
Oxalessigsäure *f* oxalacetic acid, oxosuccinic acid
Oxalessigsäurecarboxylase *f* oxalacetic carboxylase
Oxalessigsäurediethylester *m* diethyl oxalacetate
Oxalsäure *f* oxalic acid, *ethanedioic acid
Oxalsäuredialdehyd *m s.* Oxalaldehyd
Oxalsäurediethylester *m* diethyl oxalate, oxalic acid diethyl ester, oxalic ester
Oxalsäuremonoureid *n s.* Oxalursäure
Oxalsäurenitril *n* oxalonitrile, cyanogen
Oxalurie *f (med)* oxaluria
Oxalursäure *f* oxaluric acid, mono-oxalylurea
Oxalylharnstoff *m* oxalylurea, parabanic acid, imidazolidine-2,4,5-trione
Oxalylierung *f* oxalylation
Oxamid *n* oxamide, oxalic acid diamide
Oxamidsäure *f* oxamic acid, oxalic acid monoamide
Oxazinfarbstoff *m* oxazine dye
Oxazol *n* oxazole
Oxazolinon *n*, **Oxazolon** *n* oxazolone, azlactone
Oxetan *n* oxetane, trimethylene oxide, 1,3-epoxypropane
Oxford-Methode *f* Oxford (cup) method *(for evaluating penicillin)*

Oxid *n* oxide
~/basisches basic oxide
~/saures acidic oxide
~/siliciumorganisches organosilicon oxide, organosiloxane, organic siloxane
oxidabel oxidizable, capable of oxidation
Oxidans *n* oxidant, oxidizing agent
Oxidase *f* oxidase
~/kupferhaltige copper oxidase
~/mischfunktionelle mixed-function oxidase
Oxidation *f* oxidation, de-electronation
~/aerobe aerobic oxidation
~/anodische anodic oxidation, *(met also)* anodizing, anodization, anodic coating (treatment)
~/biologische biological oxidation, bio-oxidation
~ durch Luftsauerstoff air oxidation, atmospheric (aerial) oxidation, oxidation by air (atmospheric oxygen)
~/elektrochemische (elektrolytische) electrochemical (electrolytic) oxidation
~/enzymatische enzymatic oxidation
~ im Wirbelbett fluidized oxidation
~/induzierte induced oxidation
~/katalytische catalytic oxidation
~ mit Luft *s.* ~ durch Luftsauerstoff
~/oberflächliche surface oxidation
~/Oppenauersche Oppenauer oxidation *(for dehydrogenating secondary alcohols)*
~/partielle partial oxidation
~/photochemische photochemical oxidation, photooxidation
~/radiochemische radiochemical oxidation
~/schonende mild oxidation
~/selektive selective (preferential) oxidation *(as in fire refining)*
~/spontane spontaneous oxidation
~/subterminale subterminal oxidation
~/teilweise *s.* ~/partielle
~/terminale terminal oxidation
~/vorhergehende (vorherige) pre-oxidation
β-Oxidation *f (bioch)* beta oxidation *(as of fatty acids)*
~/Knoop-Dakinsche Knoop's beta oxidation *(scheme of fatty acid catabolism)*
oxidationsanfällig prone to oxidation
Oxidationsanfälligkeit *f* proneness to oxidation
Oxidationsätze *f (text)* oxidation discharge
Oxidationsbad *n* oxidizing bath
oxidationsbeständig resistant (stable) to oxidation, oxidation-resistant, oxidatively stable
Oxidationsbeständigkeit *f* resistance (stability) to oxidation, oxidation resistance
Oxidationsbleiche *f* oxidation bleaching, oxidizing bleach
oxidationsempfindlich oxidation-sensitive, oxidation-susceptible, sensitive (susceptible) to oxidation
Oxidationsempfindlichkeit *f* sensitivity (susceptibility) to oxidation
Oxidationsenzym *n* oxydative enzyme; *(specif) s.* ~/gelbes
~/gelbes yellow enzyme, flavin[e] enzyme *(any of a class of redoxases)*
Oxidationsferment *n s.* Oxidationsenzym
Oxidationsflamme *f* oxidizing flame
Oxidationsgeschmack *m* oxidized flavour
Oxidationsgeschwindigkeit *f* rate of oxidation
Oxidationsgraben *m (hyd)* oxidation ditch
Oxidationsgrad *m* degree of oxidation
Oxidationsinhibitor *m* oxidation inhibitor, antioxidant, antioxidizing agent, antioxygen, *(petrol also)* gum inhibitor
Oxidationsintensität *f* oxidation intensity
Oxidationskatalysator *m* oxidation (oxidizing) catalyst
Oxidationskraft *f* oxidizing power
Oxidationsmittel *n* oxidizing agent, oxidant
Oxidationsmittelbedarf *m* oxidant demand
Oxidationsneigung *f* tendency to oxidize
Oxidationspotential *n* oxidation potential
Oxidationsprodukt *n* oxidation product
Oxidationsraum *m* oxidizing zone *(of a burner flame)*
Oxidationsreaktion *f* oxidation reaction
Oxidations-Reduktions-... *s.* Redox...
Oxidationsschicht *f s.* Oxidschicht
Oxidationsschritt *m* oxidation step
Oxidationsstabilität *f s.* Oxidationsbeständigkeit
Oxidationsstufe *f* level of oxidation, oxidation state, *(quantitatively:)* oxidation (Stock) number
Oxidationsteich *m (hyd)* [bio-]oxidation pond
Oxidationstrübung *f (ferm)* oxidative haze
Oxidationsverfahren *n* oxidation process
~/anodisches *(met)* anodizing process
Oxidationsverhinderer *m s.* Oxidationsinhibitor
Oxidationsvermögen *n* oxidizing capacity
Oxidationsvorgang *m* oxidation process
Oxidationsweg *m***/direkter** *(bioch)* pentose shunt (phosphate pathway)
Oxidationswirkung *f* oxidizing action; oxidizing effect
Oxidationszahl *f* oxidation (Stock) number
Oxidationszone *f* oxidation (oxidizing) zone; combustion zone *(of a blast furnace)*
Oxidationszustand *m* oxidation state
oxidativ oxidative
oxidbedeckt oxide-coated
Oxidbelag *m* oxide layer, *(if thin:)* oxide film
Oxidchlorid *n* chloride oxide
Oxidelektrode *f* oxide electrode
Oxidfilm *m*, **Oxidhaut** *f* oxide film (skin)
Oxidhydrat *n* hydrated oxide
Oxidhydratsol *n* sol of hydrated oxide
oxidierbar oxidizable, capable of oxidation
~/leicht readily oxidizable
Oxidierbarkeit *f* oxidizability, capability of oxidation
oxidieren to oxidize *(something)*; to oxidize, to undergo oxidation

~/anodisch *(met)* to anodize
~/elektrochemisch (elektrolytisch) to oxidize electrochemically (electrolytically)
~/vorher to pre-oxidize
oxidierend oxidizing, oxidative
oxidiert werden to undergo oxidation
Oxidimetrie *f* oxidimetry
oxidimetrisch oxidimetric
oxidisch oxidic
Oxidkeramik *f* oxide ceramics, oxide-ceramic products
Oxidoreductase *f* oxido-reductase, oxidation-reduction enzyme, redoxase
Oxidoreduktion *f* oxidoreduction, oxidation-reduction, redox reaction
Oxidphosphor *m* oxide phosphor *(any of a class of compounds which exhibit phosphorescence)*
Oxidrot *n (coat)* red oxide
Oxidsalz *n* oxide salt
Oxidschicht *f* oxide layer, *(if thin:)* oxide film
Oxidschutzschicht *f (met)* oxide coating
Oxidsinterung *f (ceram)* oxide sintering
Oxim *n* oxime *(any of a class of compounds containing the group >C=NOH)*
Oximierung *f* oximation
Oxin *n* oxine, 8-hydroxyquinoline
Oxinat *n* oxinate *(any of the complex compounds of 8-hydroxyquinoline)*
Oxindol *n* oxindole, 2-hydroxyindole
Oxiran *n* oxiran, epoxide, ethylene oxide, epoxyethane
2-Oxoadipinsäure *f* 2-oxoadipic acid, *2-oxohexanedioic acid
Oxoanion *n* oxo anion
Oxobrücke *f* oxo bridge
Oxo-Claisen-Umlagerung *f* Claisen rearrangement
Oxo-Cyclo-Tautomerie *f* oxo-cyclo tautomerism
Oxoessigsäure *f s.* Oxoethansäure
Oxoethansäure *f* oxoethanoic acid, glyoxylic acid
Oxoform *f* oxo form
Oxofunktion *f* oxo function
Oxoglutaramidsäure *f* oxoglutaramic acid
Oxoglutarsäure *f* oxoglutaric acid, *(specif)* 2-oxoglutaric acid, *2-oxopentanedioic acid
Oxogruppe *f* >C=O oxo (carbonyl) group
Oxokation *n* oxo cation
Oxokomplex *m* oxo complex
Oxolinsäure *f (bioch)* oxolinic acid
Oxomalonsäure *f* oxomalonic acid, mesoxalic acid, *oxopropanedioic acid
Oxomethan *n s.* Methanal
Oxoniumion *n s.* Hydroniumion
Oxoniumsalz *n* oxonium salt
Oxoniumverbindung *f* oxonium compound
Oxopentandisäure *f* *oxopentanedioic acid, oxoglutaric acid
4-Oxopentansäure *f* *4-oxopentanoic acid, 4-oxovaleric acid, laevulinic acid
Oxophosphoran *n* phosphine oxide
2-Oxopropanal *n* *2-oxopropanal, pyruvic aldehyde
Oxopropandisäure *f* *oxopropanedioic acid, oxomalonic acid
2-Oxopropansäure *f* *2-oxopropanoic acid, pyruvic acid
Oxoreaktion *f s.* Oxosynthesereaktion
Oxosalz *n* oxo salt *(salt of an oxo acid)*
Oxosäure *f* oxo acid, oxoacid, oxyacid, oxiacid, oxacid *(any of the acids having oxygen in the acidic group)*
Oxosynthese *f* oxo synthesis, hydroformylation
Oxosynthesereaktion *f* oxo (hydroformylation) reaction, Roelen reaction
Oxoverbindung *f* oxo compound
Oxovinylierung *f* ketovinylation
9-Oxoxanthen *n* 9-oxoxanthene, xanthone
Oxy... *s. a.* Hydroxy...
oxybiontisch *(biol)* oxybiotic, aerobiotic *(living in the presence of air oxygen)*
Oxybiose *f (biol)* oxybiosis, aerobiosis *(life in the presence of air oxygen)*
Oxycellulose *f* oxycellulose
Oxychlorierung *f* oxychlorination
Oxydiessigsäure *f s.* 2,2'-Oxy-diethansäure
2,2'-Oxy-diethansäure *f* *2,2'-oxydiethanoic acid, diglycolic (diglycollic) acid
Oxygen *n* O oxygen
Oxygenase *f* oxygenase
~/mischfunktionelle mixed-function oxygenase, monooxygenase, hydroxylase
Oxyhämocyanin *n* oxyhaemocyanin *(a copper-containing blood pigment)*
Oxyhämoglobin *n* oxyhaemoglobin
Oxyhydroxid-Kation *m* oxyhydroxide cation
Oxyliquit *n* oxyliquit *(an explosive)*
Oxyl-Synthese *f* oxyl process *(for synthesizing alcohols from CO und H_2)*
Oxymetallierung *f* oxymetalation
Oxyn *n* oxyn *(any of the solid oxidation products of drying oils)*
Oxyneurin *n* oxyneurine, betaine, *NNN*-trimethylammonioacetate, lycine
Oxynitrierung *f* oxynitration, oxidative nitration
α-Oxypropionsäure *f s.* 2-Oxopropansäure
Oxytocin *n* oxytocin *(a polypeptide hormone)*
Oxytozikum *n (pharm)* oxytocic [agent], uterotonic
OZ *s.* 1. Ordnungszahl; 2. Octanzahl
OZ-Bestimmung *f* octane rating
Ozokerit *m (min)* ozokerite, earth (ader) wax, native paraffin
Ozon *n* ozone, trioxygen • **in ~ verwandeln** to ozonize, to convert into ozone • **sich in ~ verwandeln** to ozonize, to ozonify
Ozonabbau *m s.* Ozonspaltung
Ozonalterung *f (rubber, plast)* ozone [exposure] test
ozonartig ozone-like, ozonic, ozonous

Ozonbehandlung *f (hyd)* ozon[iz]ation
ozonbeständig ozone-resistant, ozone-resisting, resistant to ozone
Ozonbeständigkeit *f* ozone resistance, resistance to ozone
ozonfest *s.* ozonbeständig
Ozongenerator *m s.* Ozonisator
ozonhaltig containing ozone, ozoniferous, ozonic, ozonous
Ozonid *n* ozonide
Ozonidspaltung *f s.* Ozonspaltung
ozonieren *s.* ozonisieren
Ozonisation *f s.* Ozonisierung
Ozonisator *m* ozonizer, ozonator, ozone generator
ozonisieren 1. to ozonize, to ozonate, to ozonify *(to treat, impregnate, or combine with ozone)*; 2. to ozonize, to convert into ozone
Ozonisierung *f* ozon[iz]ation, ozonification
Ozonloch *n* ozone hole
Ozonolyse *f s.* Ozonspaltung
Ozonosphäre *f* ozonosphere, ozone layer
Ozonpapier *n* ozone [test] paper, potassium-iodide-starch paper
Ozonprüfung *f (rubber, plast)* ozone [exposure] test
ozonresistent *s.* ozonbeständig
Ozonriß *m (rubber)* ozone crack (cut)
Ozonrißbildung *f (rubber)* ozone cracking
Ozonschicht *f s.* Ozonosphäre
Ozonschild *m* ozone shield
Ozonschutzmittel *n* antiozidant, antiozonant, sunproofing agent
Ozonspaltung *f* ozonolysis, cleavage by ozone
Ozonung *f (hyd)* ozon[iz]ation
ozonzerstörend ozone-destroying
Ozonzerstörung *f* ozone destruction
O_2-Zuführung *f*/**abgestufte** *(hyd)* tapered aeration *(activated-sludge process)*
O-Zweig *m* O-branch *(in Raman spectra)*

P

p *s.* Proton
$\bar{p}$ *s.* Antiproton
P *s.* Parachor
p.a. *(**p**ro **a**nalysi) s.* analysenrein
PA *s.* 1. Polyamid; 2. Polyamidfaserstoff
Paal-Knorr-Synthese *f* Paal-Knorr synthesis *(of pyrroles or furans from 1,4-diketones)*
Paalsgard-Emulsionsöl *n* Paalsgard emulsion oil, P.E.O.
Paarbildung *f* pairing *(of electrons, nucleons)*
Paarerzeugung *f* pair production *(as of electron-positron pairs)*
Paarung *f s.* Paarbildung
Paarungsenergie *f (nucl)* pairing energy
Paarvernichtung *f* annihilation, energy pooling *(esp of an electron and a positron)*
Pachuca-Tank *m* Pachuca tank *(air-agitated vessel)*
Pack *m (text)* package
packen to pack[age]
Packen *n* packing, package, packaging
Packer *m (petrol)* packer *(as for sealing part of a borehole)*
Packfärbeapparat *m (text)* package dyeing machine
Packfärben *n*, **Packfärberei** *f (text)* pack[age] dyeing
packgefärbt *(text)* package-dyed
Packgewebe *n* reinforced paper, papyrolin *(cloth-faced or cloth-centred paper)*
Packkrepp *m* crêpe wrapping paper
Packleinen *n* burlap, gunny, hessian
Packpapier *n* wrapping (package) paper
~ für Papierrollen mill wrapper (wrapping)
Packpresse *f* platen press
Packseidenpapier *n* wrapping (commercial) tissue, tissue wrapper (wrapping)
Packstoff *m* adherend *(a body to be attached to another one by an adhesive)*
Packung *f* 1. packing *(of a column)*, *(specif)* stacked packing; chromatographic packing; 2. *(cryst)* packing; 3. seal *(as in a valve)*; 4. pack[age] *(a packed quantity)*
~/dichteste *(cryst)* closest (close) packing
~/halbmetallische semimetallic packing *(as in a valve)*
~/hexagonal dichteste *(cryst)* hexagonal closest (close) packing
~ mit radioaktivem Heilschlamm radium pack
Packungsanteil *m (nucl)* packing fraction
Packungsdichte *f* packing density
~ der Hackschnitzel *(pap)* chip capacity
Packungseffekt *m (nucl)* packing effect
Packungsmaterial *n* 1. packing *(for a column)*; chromatographic packing; 2. packing material *(as for valves)*
Packungsring *m* packing (seal, sealing) ring
Packungssuspension *f (chromat)* packing slurry
Paddel *n* paddle *(as of a mixer)*
Paddelfärbemaschine *f (text)* paddle [wheel] dyeing machine
Paddelrad *n* paddle wheel
Paddelrührer *m* paddle agitator (mixer), blade mixer
PAK *s.* Kohlenwasserstoff/polycyclischer aromatischer
paketieren to pack[age]
Paketstahl *m* refined steel (iron, bar), shear steel, merchant bar
Paläobiochemie *f* palaeobiochemistry
Palette *f (tech)* pallet
Palingenese *f*, **Palingenesis** *f (geol, biol)* palingenesis
palisadenartig *(cryst)* columnar
Palladat *n* palladate *(any of a class of complex salts having Pd as a central atom)*
Palladium *n* Pd palladium

Palladiumasbest *m* palladinized asbestos
Palladium(II)-chlorid *n* palladium (II) chloride, palladium dichloride
Palladiumchloridpapier *n* palladium-chloride paper
Palladiumdi... *s. a.* Palladium(II)-...
Palladiumdioxid *n s.* Palladium(IV)-oxid
Palladium(II)-fluorid *n* palladium(II) fluoride, palladium difluoride
Palladium(III)-fluorid *n* palladium(III) fluoride, palladium trifluoride
Palladiumgold *n (min)* palladium gold, porpezite *(a natural alloy)*
Palladium(II)-iodid *n* palladium(II) iodide, palladium diiodide
Palladiummohr *n* palladium black
Palladiummonoxid *n s.* Palladium(II)-oxid
Palladium(II)-oxid *n* palladium(II) oxide, palladium monooxide
Palladium(IV)-oxid *n* palladium(IV) oxide, palladium dioxide
Palladiumrohr *n* palladium tube *(for separating hydrogen)*
Palladiumschwarz *n* palladium black
Palladiumtrifluorid *n s.* Palladium(III)-fluorid
Palladiumverbindung *f*/**organische** organopalladium compound
Pallasit *m* pallasite, pallas iron *(a meteorite consisting of iron, nickel, and olivine)*
Palliativum *n (pharm)* palliative
Pall-Ring *m (distil)* Pall ring *(a kind of packing)*
Palmarosaöl *n* palmarosa oil, Indian geranium (grass) oil *(from Cymbopogon martini [Roxb.] Stapf)*
Palmensago *m*, **Palmenstärke** *f* palm starch, sago *(from Metroxylon specc.)*
Palmer-Verfahren *n (rubber)* Palmer (high-pressure) process *(a reclaiming process)*
Palmfett *n s.* Palmöl
Palmitat *n* palmitate *(salt or ester of palmitic acid)*
Palmitinsäure *f* palmitic acid, *hexadecanoic acid
Palmitinsäurecetylester *m* hexadecyl palmitate, cetin *(deprecated:)* cetyl palmitate
Palmitinsäurechlorid *n s.* Palmitoylchlorid
Palmitoleinsäure *f* palmitoleic acid, zoomaric acid, *hexadec-9-enoic acid
Palmitoylchlorid *n* palmitoyl chloride, *hexadecanoyl chloride
Palmkernfett *n* palm kernel (nut) oil *(refined)*
Palmkernhartfett *n* hydrogenated palm kernel oil
Palmkernöl *n* palm kernel oil *(from Elaeis guineensis Jacq.)*
Palmöl *n* palm oil (butter) *(from Elaeis guineensis Jacq.)*
Palmwein *m* palm wine
Palmzucker *m* palm sugar
Palygorskit *m* palygorskite *(a phyllosilicate)*
Pamaquin *n* pamaquin[e] *(a quinoline derivative)*
PAN *s.* 1. Polyacrylnitril; 2. Peroxyacetylnitrat
Panazee *f (pharm)* panacea, cure-all
panchromatisch *(phot)* panchromatic • ~ **machen (sensibilisieren)** to panchromatize
Pandermit *m (min)* pandermite *(a soroborate)*
Pankreasbeize *f (tann)* pancreatic bate
Pankreaslipase *f (bioch)* pancreatic lipase
Pankreassaft *m (bioch)* pancreatic juice
pantoffeln *(tann)* to grain
Pantoinsäure *f (bioch)* pantoic acid
Pantothensäure *f* pantothenic acid
Pan-Verfahren *n (rubber)* pan [reclaiming] process, pan devulcanization
Papageiengrün *n* parrot (Paris, emerald) green *(copper acetoarsenite)*
Papier *n* paper • **auf (zu)** ~ **verarbeiten** to make into paper
~/acetyliertes *(chromat)* acetylated paper
~/bituminiertes asphalt (tar, pitch) paper, tarred [brown] paper
~/Chinesisches China (Chinese) paper, India (Indian) paper
~/chromatographisches chromatographic paper
~/doppelt logarithmisch geteiltes loglog paper
~/farbig gestrichenes coloured coated paper
~/farbiges coloured paper
~/feuerfestes (feuersicheres) fireproof paper, fire-resistant (fire-resisting) paper
~/flammsicheres (flammsicher imprägniertes) flameproof paper
~/fotografisches photographic (photo) paper
~/gegautschtes duplex paper
~/gekrepptes crêpe paper
~/gestrichenes coated (surfaced) paper
~/getränktes impregnated paper
~/gummiertes gummed (adhesive) paper
~/hadernhaltiges rag content paper
~/halblogarithmisches semilog[arithmic] paper
~/handgeschöpftes [genuine] hand-made paper, vat paper
~/holzfreies wood-free paper
~/holzhaltiges wood-containing paper, groundwood (woody) paper
~/imprägniertes impregnated paper
~/konservierendes preservative (preserving) paper
~/korrosionsschützendes corrosion-protective paper, anti-corrosion (anti-tarnish) paper
~/leinengeprägtes linen[-embossed] paper, linen-finished (linen-faced) paper
~/logarithmisches logarithmic paper
~/mit Wasserzeichen versehenes watermarked paper
~/naßfestes wet-strength paper
~/paraffiniertes paraffin[ed] paper, wax[ed] paper
~/satiniertes [super]calendered paper, glazed paper
~/säurefreies acid-free paper
~/schwachgeleimtes weakly sized paper, slack-sized (soft-sized) paper
~/technisches technical paper, paper for technical purposes

~/textilverstärktes reinforced paper
~/ungeleimtes waterleaf paper
~/veredeltes processed paper
~/wasserfestes wet-strength paper
Papierabfälle *mpl* waste (old) paper
Papierabzug *m (phot)* paper print
Papieraufrolltrommel *f* reel (reeling) drum (cylinder)
Papieraufrollung *f*, **Papieraufwicklung** *f* winding, reeling
Papierausrüstung *f* paper finishing
Papierausschuß *m* broken [material, paper], [mill, machine] broke, brokes, waste stuff
Papierbahn *f* [paper] web, mat
Papierbahn[ab]riß *m* break in the web
Papierbild *n (phot)* paper print
Papierbrei *m* paper[making] stock
Papierchromatographie *f* paper chromatography, PC
~/absteigende descending paper chromatography
~/aufsteigende ascending paper chromatography
~/eindimensionale one-dimensional (one-way) paper chromatography
~/zweidimensionale two-dimensional (two-way) paper chromatography
papierchromatographisch paper-chromatographic
Papierchromatogramm *n* paper chromatogram, papergram
~/zweidimensionales two-dimensional paper chromatogram
Papierebene *f* plane of the page *(stereochemistry)*
Papierelektrophorese *f* paper electrophoresis
Papierentwickler *m (phot)* paper developer
Papierentwicklung *f (phot)* paper development
Papierfabrik *f* paper mill (factory)
Papierfabrikabwasser *n* paper mill waste
Papierfärben *n*, **Papierfärberei** *f* paper dyeing, *(Am also)* paper coloring
Papierfaser *f* papermaking fibre
Papierfaserstoff *m* [paper, raw] stock, raw papermaking material
Papierfehler *m* defect in [the] paper
Papierfilter *n* paper filter
Papierformat *n* paper size
Papierfüllstoff *m* [paper] filler, loader
Papiergarn *n* paper yarn
Papiergewicht *n* paper weight, weight of paper
Papiergradation *f*, **Papierhärtegrad** *m (phot)* paper grade
Papierherstellung *f* papermaking
Papierholz *n* pulpwood
Papierindustrie *f* paper industry
Papierkalander *m (pap)* calender [machine], machine calender stack
Papierkalanderwalze *f* paper bowl
Papierklebstoff *m* paper[-bonding] adhesive
Papierkohle *f* paper coal
Papierleimung *f* paper sizing
Papierleitwalze *f* fly roll
Papiermacher *m* papermaker
Papiermacheralaun *m* papermaker's alum *(technical aluminium sulphate)*
Papiermacherei *f* papermaking
Papiermaschine *f* paper[making] machine
~/langsamlaufende slow-speed paper machine
~ mit zwei Langsieben twin-wire paper machine
~ mittlerer Geschwindigkeit moderate-speed paper machine
~/schnellaufende high-speed paper machine
Papiermaschinenfilz *m* paper machine felt, papermaker's felt
Papiermaschinensieb *n* [paper] machine wire, travelling wire
Papiermasse *f* 1. paper[making] stock; 2. paper weight, weight of paper
Papiermühle *f* paper mill
Papierrohstoff *m* [paper, raw] stock, raw papermaking material
Papierrolle *f* roll [of paper], reel [of paper]
~/von der Maschine kommende machine (mill, jumbo) roll
Papierrollstange *f* winder (rewind) shaft
Papiersack *m* paper bag (sack)
~/mehrlagiger multiwall paper bag
Papierschnitzel *npl(mpl)* chopped paper, shavings
Papiersorte *f* grade of paper
Papierstoff *m*[**/fertiger**] paper[making] stock, [finished] stuff
Papierstoffleimung *f* sizing
Papiertambour *m s.* Papierrolle
Papiertrockenzylinder *m* paper dryer
Papiertrocknung *f* paper drying
Papierunterlage *f (phot)* paper base
Papiervlies *n s.* Papierbahn
Papierwalze *f s.* 1. ~/elastische; 2. Papierkalanderwalze
~/elastische paper (resilient, filled) roll *(of a supercalender)*
Papierwolle *f* paper wool
Papierzellstoff *m* paper[making] pulp
Papierzuschnitt *m (chromat)* paper geometry
Pappe *f* [paper]board, cardboard
~/beklebte lined board
~/gedeckte (gegautschte) couched board, [vat]-lined board, *(Am)* nonpasted board
~/gehärtete hardboard, panel board
~/im Format geklebte (kaschierte) sheet-lined board
~/in der Rolle geklebte (kaschierte) mill-lined board
~/kaschierte lined board
Pappebogen *m* sheet of board
Pappenfabrik *f* paperboard mill
Pappenmaschine *f* board[-making] machine
Pappenrundsiebmaschine *f* cylinder board machine
Para *m s.* Parakautschuk
Paraacetaldehyd *m s.* Paraldehyd
Paraaminophenolentwickler *m (phot)* paraminophenol (paraaminophenol) developer

Parabansäure *f* parabanic acid, imidazolidine-2,4,5-trione
Paracasein *n* paracasein *(insoluble casein)*
Paracetaldehyd *m s.* Paraldehyd
Parachor *m (phys ch)* parachor
Paradichlorbenzen *n* paradichlorobenzene, *p*-dichlorobenzene
Paradieskörner *npl* grains of paradise *(from Aframomum melegueta Schum.)*
para-dirigierend para-directing
Paraffin *n* 1. paraffin [wax], hydrocarbon wax; 2. *s.* Alkan
~/amorphes *s.* ~/mikrokristallines
~/festes solid paraffin
~/flüssiges liquid (medicinal) paraffin, liquid petrolatum, paraffin oil
~ für Sprühzwecke spray (light liquid) paraffin
~/hartes hard paraffin
~/mikrokristallines microparaffin, micro wax
~/weiches soft paraffin
Paraffinanteil *m* paraffinicity *(percentage of alkanes as in insecticidal oils)*
Paraffinbasis *f* paraffin base *(of crude petroleum)*
Paraffinbasisöl *n (petrol)* paraffin-base petroleum, paraffinic petroleum, paraffin-base crude [oil]
Paraffindestillat *n* paraffin distillate
Paraffinemulsion *f (pap)* wax emulsion
Paraffineur *m (text)* waxing device
Paraffingatsch *m* [paraffin] slack wax
paraffinhaltig containing paraffin, paraffinic
paraffinieren to paraffin *(to treat or coat with paraffin)*
paraffinisch paraffinic
Paraffinität *f s.* Paraffinanteil
Paraffinkohlenwasserstoff *m* paraffin [hydrocarbon], saturated hydrocarbon, *alkane
~/monochlorierter monochloroparaffin
Paraffinkuchen *m* [paraffin] wax cake
Paraffinleim *m (pap)* [paraffin] wax size
Paraffinleimung *f (pap)* paraffin wax sizing, sizing with wax emulsions
Paraffinöl *n* 1. paraffin[ic] oil, liquid paraffin (petrolatum); 2. *s.* Paraffinbasisöl
Paraffinpapier *n* paraffin[ed] paper, wax[ed] paper
Paraffinreihe *f s.* Alkanreihe
Paraffinschuppen *fpl* paraffin scale, scale wax
Paraffinwachs *n* paraffin wax
~ aus Erdöl petroleum wax
~/mikrokristallines *s.* Paraffin/mikrokristallines
Paraform *n s.* Paraformaldehyd
Paraformaldehyd *m* paraformaldehyde, polyoxymethylene
Parafuchsin *n* parafuchsine
Paragummi *m s.* Parakautschuk
Parahelium *n* parahelium, parhelium
Para-Isomer[e] *n* para isomer, *p*-isomer
Parakautschuk *m* Para rubber *(from Hevea brasiliensis (H.B.K.) Muell. Arg.)*
parakristallin paracrystalline
Paraldehyd *m* paraldehyde, paraacetaldehyde, *2,4,6-trimethyl-1,3,5-trioxane
Paraleukorosanilin *n* leucopararosaniline
Parallaxenfehler *m* parallax error *(as in reading burettes)*
Parallelplattendruckgerät *n*, **Parallelplattenplastometer** *n (rubber)* parallel plate plastometer
Parallelreaktion *f* parallel (simultaneous) reaction, competitive (competing, concurrent) reaction
Parallelschieber *m* parallel-seat gate valve
Parallelstrom *m* parallel flow, concurrent (co-current) flow • **im ~ [geführt]** co-current
Parallelverschiebung *f (cryst)* translation
Paramagnetikum *n* paramagnetic [material, substance]
paramagnetisch paramagnetic
Paramagnetismus *m* paramagnetism
Parameter *m* parameter, *(cryst also)* intercept
Paramilchsäure *f* paralactic acid, L(+)-lactic acid, dextrorotatory lactic acid
Paraminophenolentwickler *m s.* Paraaminophenolentwickler
Paramolybdat *n* paramolybdate
Paranitranilin *n* paranitroaniline, *p*-nitroaniline
Paranitranilinrot *n* paranitraniline red, para red *(a pigment dye)*
Paraperiodsäure *f* paraperiodic acid
Paraplasma *n (biol)* paraplasm, ergastoplasm *(collectively for the reserve and waste inclusions of protoplasm)*
Para-Positronium *n* parapositronium
Pararosanilin *n* parafuchsine, pararosaniline
Pararosolsäure *f* pararosolic acid, rosolic acid
Pararot *n s.* Paranitranilinrot
Parasorbinsäure *f* parasorbic acid
para-ständig para, in para position • **~ sein** to be [located, situated] para
para-Stellung *f* para position • **in ~** in para position, para • **nach der ~ dirigierend** para-directing
para-Substituent *m* para substituent
para-substituiert para-substituted, *p*-substituted
para-Substitution *f* para substitution
Parasympathikomimetikum *n (pharm)* parasympathomimetic agent
parasympathikomimetisch parasympathomimetic
Parathion *n* parathion, diethyl-*p*-nitrophenylphosphorothionate *(an insecticide)*
Parathormon *n (bioch)* parathyroid hormone, *parathyrin
para-Verbindung *f* para compound
Parawasserstoff *m* para hydrogen
Paraweinsäure *f* (±)-tartaric acid, racemic (inactive) tartaric acid
Parawolframat *n* *parawolframate, paratungstate
para-Zustand *m* para state
Parfüm *n* perfume, essence
parfümieren to perfume, *(relating to tobacco also)* to flavour
Parfümpapier *n* perfumed paper

Parfümranzigkeit *f (food)* ketonic rancidity
Parhelium *n s.* Parahelium
Pariangips *m* Parian cement *(a hard plaster made from calcined gypsum and borax)*
Parität *f (phys ch)* parity
Parker-Verfahren *n (coal)* Parker process *(low-temperature carbonization)*
Parkes-Reagens *n* Parkes reagent *(for detecting artificial colourants in fats)*
Parkes-Verfahren *n* Parkes process *(for removing noble metals from lead)*
Parr-Bombe *f* Parr bomb *(for digesting substances in organic analysis)*
Partialdampfdruck *m* partial vapour pressure
Partialdruck *m* partial pressure
~ **Eins** unit partial pressure
Partialdruckgesetz *n*/**Daltonsches** Dalton's law of partial pressures
Partialdruckkurve *f* partial pressure curve
Partialhydrolysat *n* partial hydrolyzate
Partialhydrolyse *f* partial (restricted) hydrolysis
Partialladung *f* partial (fractional) charge
Partialoxidation *f* partial oxidation
Partialvalenz *f* partial valency (valence)
Partialvalenztheorie *f* theory of partial valencies
Partie *f (dye)* batch
partiell partial
Partikel *n* particle
Partikeldichte *f* number density *(number of particles per unit reactor volume)*
Partikelgröße *f* particle size
Partikelgrößenverteilung *f* particle-size distribution
Partikelgrößen-Verteilungschromatographie *f* hydrodynamic chromatography, HDC
Partikel *npl*/**suspendierte** suspended particles, particulates, particulate matter
partikulär particulate
Partner *m* participant *(of a reaction)*, reactant
PAS *s.* Photo-Akustik-Spektroskopie
Paschen-Back-Effekt *m* Paschen-Back effect *(splitting-up of spectral lines in a strong magnetic field)*
Paschen-Runge-Anordnung *f*, **Paschen-Runge-Aufstellung** *f (spectr)* Paschen-Runge mounting
Paschen-Serie *f* Paschen series *(of the hydrogen spectrum)*
PA-Signal *n* photoacoustic signal
PA-Spektroskopie *f s.* Photo-Akustik-Spektroskopie
Passage *f* pass *(in zone melting)*
Passageofen *m (ceram)* multipassage kiln
Paßburg-Trockenschrank *m* Passburg dryer
Passerini-Reaktion *f* Passerini reaction *(for obtaining α-acyloxy amides)*
passieren to pass, to penetrate
passiv passive
Passivator *m* passivator, passivating agent *(for metals)*; inhibitor, negative catalyst, anticatalyst, retarder *(of a chemical reaction)*
Passivgut *n s.* Siebfeines
passivieren 1. *(phys ch)* to passivate *(metals)*; to inhibit, to retard *(a chemical reaction)*; 2. *(min tech)* to depress
Passivierung *f* 1. *(phys ch)* passivation *(of metals)*; inhibition, retardation *(of a chemical reaction)*; 2. *(min tech)* depressing
Passivierungsmittel *n* passivating agent, passivator *(for metals)*
Passivität *f (phys ch)* passivity
~/anodische anodic passivity
~/chemische chemical passivity
Passivsammler *m* passive sampler *(for trace components from gases)*
Paßstück *n* adapter
Paste *f* paste
~/dünne light paste
~/steife (zähe) heavy paste
Pastellkreide *f* crayon
Pastellstift *m* crayon
pastenartig paste-like, pasty
Pastengießen *n (plast)* slush moulding
Pastenharz *n* paste resin
Pasteur-Effekt *m* Pasteur effect *(the inhibition of anaerobic fermentation by oxygen)*
Pasteurisation *f s.* Pasteurisierung
Pasteuriseur *m*, **Pasteurisierapparat** *m* pasteurizer
pasteurisieren to pasteurize
~/wiederholt to repasteurize
Pasteurisierung *f* pasteurization, pasteurizing
~/kontinuierliche continuous pasteurization
Pasteur-Kolben *m* Pasteur flask
pastieren to paste *(lead-acid accumulators)*
pastig *s.* pastös
Pastille *f (pharm)* pastille
Pastillenpech *n* pastillated pitch
Pastillenpresse *f* briquetting (briquette) press *(for calorimetric tests)*
Pasting-Verfahren *n (tann)* pasting process
pastös pasty, paste-like
Patentanmeldung *f* application for a patent
Patenterteilung *f* patent grant[ing]
Patentgrün *n s.* Grün/Schweinfurter
patentieren to patent *(1. an invention; 2. wire by heat)*
Patentierofen *m* patenting furnace *(for heat treatment of wire)*
Patentpapier *n* machine[-made] paper
Paterno-Büchi-Reaktion *f* Paterno-Büchi reaction *(photocycloaddition yielding an oxetane)*
pathogen pathogenic
Pathogen *n* pathogen
Patina *f* patina
Patrize *f (plast)* patrix, moulding (force) plug, male form (mould)
Patrone *f* cartridge
Patronenfilter *n* cartridge filter
Patronenheizkörper *m* cartridge heater
patschen *(glass)* to paddle

Patschoulialkohol *m* patchouli alcohol
Patschouliöl *n* patchouli oil *(from Pogostemon cablin (Blanco) Benth.)*
Pattinson-Bleiweiß *n* Pattinson's white lead
Pattinson-Verfahren *n* Pattinson process *(for separating silver from lead)*
paucidispers *(coll)* paucidisperse
Pauli-Prinzip *n* [Pauli] exclusion principle
Pauschalanalyse *f* proximate analysis *(determination of main constituents only)*
Pauschanalyse *f s.* Pauschalanalyse
pauschen *(met)* to liquate
Pauschen *n (met)* liquating, liquation
Pausleinen *n* [translucent] tracing cloth
Pauspapier *n* tracing paper
PbS-Zelle *f (spectr)* lead sulphide cell
PC *s.* 1. Papierchromatographie; 2. Polycarbonat
PCDD *s.* Dibenzo-*p*-dioxin/polychloriertes
PCDF *s.* Dibenzofuran/polychloriertes
PCE *(**p**yrometric-**c**one **e**quivalent) s.* Schmelzkegeläquivalent
PCP *s.* Pentachlorphenol
PCTFE *s.* Polychlortrifluorethylen
PCV *s.* Polyvinylcarbazol
PE *s.* 1. Polyethylen; 2. Polyesterfaserstoff
Peachy-Verfahren *n* Peachy process *(of curing rubber with SO_2 and H_2S)*
Peak *m (anal)* peak
~/chromatographischer chromatographic peak
Peakasymmetrie *f* peak asymmetry
Peakaufweitung *f* peak broadening
Peakbasis *f* peak base
Peakbreite *f* peak width
~ in halber Höhe peak width at half height
Peakdetektor *m* peak finder (separator, picker)
Peakelutionsvolumen *n (chromat)* peak elution volume
Peakerkennung *f* peak identification
Peakfläche *f* peak area
Peakflächenauswertung *f* peak-size analysis
Peakform *f* peak shape
Peakhöhe *f* peak height
Peakintegration *f* peak [area] integration
Peakintensität *f* peak intensity
Peaklage *f* peak position
Peakmaximum *n* peak apex
Peakpotential *n* peak potential
Peakprofil *n s.* Peakform
Peaksignal *n* peak
Peakstrom *m* peak current
Peaküberlagerung *f*, **Peaküberlappung** *f* superposition of peaks
Peakvergleich *m* peak matching
Peakverschärfung *f (chromat)* peak focussing
Pebble-Heater-Pyrolyse *f (petrol)* pebble-heater pyrolysis
Pech *n* pitch
~/Kanadisches Canada (hemlock) pitch *(usually from Tsuga canadensis (L.) Carr.)*
pechartig pitchy, pitch-like
Pechblende *f (min)* pitchblende *(uranium(IV) oxide)*
Pechkohle *f* pitch coal, bright brown coal, bituminous (black) lignite
Pechkoks *m* pitch coke
Pechmann-Acetylen-Addition *f*, **Pechmann-Reaktion** *f* Pechmann-type addition, Pechmann reaction
Pechpolitur *f (glass)* pitch polishing
Pechsee *m (geol)* pitch (asphalt) lake
Peclét-Zahl *f* Peclét number *(as for scaling-up pilot-plant results)*
Pedersen-Verfahren *n* Pedersen process *(for obtaining aluminium)*
Pedologie *f* pedology, soil science
pedologisch pedologic[al]
PEG *s.* Polyethylenglykol
Pegel *m* 1. *(tech)* level *(as of a liquid)*; 2. *(glass)* tip
Pegelpotential *n s.* Normalpotential
Pegukatechu *n* Pegu catechu (cutch), black (dark) catechu *(from Acacia catechu Willd.)*
Pehameter *n s.* *p*H-Meßgerät
Peierls-Phasenübergang *m*, **Peierls-Übergang** *m* Peierls transition *(a metal-insulator transition)*
peilen to dip *(to measure the liquid level in a tank)*
Peilen *n* dip *(measuring of the liquid level in a tank)*
Peilstab *m* dip (gauge) stick
Peirce-Smith-Konverter *m (met)* Peirce-Smith converter
Pektat *n* pectate *(a salt or ester of a pectic acid)*
Pektin *n* 1. pectin; 2. *s.* Pektinstoff
~/eigentliches pectin proper
~ H *s.* ~/hochverestertes
~/hochverestertes high-ester pectin
~ L *s.* ~/niederverestertes
~/leichtverestertes (methoxylarmes) *s.* ~/niederverestertes
~/niederverestertes (niedrig verestertes) low-ester (low-methoxyl) pectin
pektinabbauend pect[in]olytic
Pektinat *n* pectinate *(a salt or ester of a pectinic acid)*
Pektinchemie *f* pectin chemistry
Pektingel *n*, **Pektingelee** *n* pectin jelly
pektinolytisch pect[in]olytic
Pektinpräparat *n* pectin preparation
Pektinpulver *n* dry pectin, powdered (solid) pectin
Pektinsäure *f* pectic acid *(a high-molecular-weight polymer of D-galacturonic acid)*
pektinspaltend pect[in]olytic
Pektinstoff *m* pectic (pectinous) substance, pectin
Pektinzucker *m* pectin sugar, pectinose
Pektisation *f (coll)* pectization, flocculation
pektisieren *(coll)* to pectize, to flocculate
pektolytisch pect[in]olytic
Pektose *f s.* Protopektin
Pelargon *n* *heptadecan-9-one, pelargone, dioctyl ketone
Pelargonaldehyd *m* *nonanal, pelargonic aldehyde

Pelargonsäure *f* *nonanoic acid, pelargonic acid
Pellagrapräventivvitamin *n* pellagra-preventive factor, PP factor *(either nicotinic acid or nicotinamide)*
Pellet *n* pellet
Pellet[aus]bildung *f* pellet formation
Pelletier... *s.* Pelletisier...
pelletieren *s.* pelletisieren
Pelletisieranlage *f* pelletizing plant
Pelletisiereinrichtung *f* pelletizing (balling) device
pelletisieren to pellet[ize], to ball
Pelletisierkonus *m* pelletizing (balling) cone
Pelletisiermaschine *f* pellet[izing] machine, pelletizer
Pelletisierteller *m* pelletizing (balling) disk
Pelletisiertrommel *f* pelletizing (balling) drum
Pelletisierungsanlage *f* pelletizing plant
Pelletisier[ungs]verfahren *n* pelletizing process
Pelzfarbstoff *m* fur dye
Penaldin-F-Säure *f* penaldic-F acid, pent-2-enylpenaldic acid
Penaldin-G-Säure *f* penaldic-G acid, benzylpenaldic acid
Penaldin-K-Säure *f* penaldic-K acid, heptylpenaldic acid
Penaldinsäure *f* penaldic acid *(any of a group of acids RCONHCH(CHO)COOH)*
Penaldin-X-Säure *f* penaldic-X acid, *p*-hydroxybenzylpenaldic acid
Penaldsäure *f s.* Penaldinsäure
Penam *n* penam *(any of a group of antibiotics)*
Pendelbecherwerk *n* pivoted-bucket conveyor
Pendelfallmethode *f* pendulum method *(for testing rubber)*
Pendelmühle *f s.* Pendelrollenmühle
Pendelrollenmühle *f* pendulum roller mill, ring-roll mill *(with horizontal grinding ring)*
Pendelschlagwerk *n* impact pendulum machine
Pendelzentrifuge *f* link-suspended centrifuge
Penem *n* penem *(any of a group of antibiotics)*
Penetration *f* 1. penetration; 2. *(cryst)* intergrowth
Penetrationstheorie *f* penetration theory *(of mass transfer)*
Penetrationszwillinge *mpl (cryst)* penetration twins
penetrieren 1. to penetrate; 2. *(cryst)* to intergrow
Penetrometerverfahren *n (coal)* penetrometer method
Penicillamin *n* penicillamine
Penicillaminsäure *f* penicillaminic acid
Penicillansäure *f* penicillanic acid *(a building brick of penicillins)*
Penicillin *n* penicillin
~/natürliches natural penicillin
penicillinresistent penicillin-resistant
Penicillinsäure *f s.* Penicillsäure
Penicillinwirksamkeit *f* penicillin activity
Penicilloat *n* penicilloate
Penicilloinsäure *f s.* Penicillosäure
Penicillosäure *f* penicilloic acid *(any of a group of amidodicarboxylic acids $RCONH(C_6H_{10}NS)(COOH)_2$)*
Penicillsäure *f* penicillic acid, 3-methoxy-5-methyl-4-oxohexa-2,5-dienoic acid
Penill-F-Säure *f* penillic-F acid, pent-2-enylpenillic acid
Penill-G-Säure *f* penillic-G acid, benzylpenillic acid
Penill-K-Säure *f* penillic-K acid, heptylpenillic acid
Penilloaldehyd *m* penilloaldehyde
Penillo-G-Säure *f* penilloic-G acid, benzylpenilloic acid
Penillo-K-Säure *f* penilloic-K acid, heptylpenilloic acid
Penillosäure *f* penilloic acid *(any of a group of acids produced by Penicillium specc.)*
Penillo-X-Säure *f* penilloic-X acid, *p*-hydroxybenzylpenilloic acid
Penillsäure *f* penillic acid *(any of a group of inactivation products of penicillins)*
Penill-X-Säure *f* penillic-X acid, *p*-hydroxybenzylpenillic acid
Pennin *m (min)* penninite, pennine *(a phyllosilicate)*
Penning-Vakuummeter *n* Penning (Philips) gauge, cold-cathode ionization gauge
Pensky-Martens-Gerät *n* Pensky-Martens [flashpoint] apparatus
Pentaboran *n* pentaborane
Pentaborat *n* pentaborate
Pentabromid *n* pentabromide
Pentacen *n* pentacene, dibenz[b,i]anthracene
Pentachlorid *n* pentachloride
Pentachlorphenol *n* pentachlorophenol
Pentacontan *n* pentacontane
Pentacosan *n* pentacosane
pentacyclisch pentacyclic
Pentadecan *n* pentadecane
Pentadecanol *n* pentadecanol, *(specif)* $CH_3[CH_2]_{13}CH_2OH$ pentadecan-1-ol
Pentadecansäure *f* pentadecanoic acid
Pentadecylalkohol *m* pentadecyl alcohol, *pentadecan-1-ol
Pentadecylsäure *f s.* Pentadecansäure
Pentadien *n* pentadiene, *(specif)* $CH_2=CH-CH=CHCH_3$ *penta-1,3-diene, piperylene
Penta-2,4-diensäure *f* *penta-2,4-dienoic acid, 3-vinylacrylic acid
Pentaerythritol *n* pentaerythritol, PE, tetrahydroxytetramethylmethane
Pentaerythrit-tetranitrat *n* pentaerythritol tetranitrate, PETN, penthrite
Pentahydrat *n* pentahydrate
Pentahydroxychinon *n* pentahydroxyquinone
Pentaiodid *n* pentaiodide
pentakoordiniert pentacoordinate, five-coordinate
Pentamethonium *n* pentamethonium
Pentamethylbenzoesäure *f* pentamethylbenzoic acid
Pentamethylen *n s.* Cyclopentan

Pentamethylendiamin *n* pentamethylenediamine, cadaverine
Pentammin *n* pentammine
Pentan *n* pentane
Pentanal *n* *pentanal, valeraldehyde
Pentancarbonsäure *f* pentanecarboxylic acid
Pentandial *n* *pentanedial, glutaraldehyde
Pentandicarbonsäure *f* pentanedicarboxylic acid
Pentandiol *n* pentanediol
Pentandisäure *f* pentanedioic acid
Pentanitroosmat(III) *n* $M^I_2[Os(NO_2)_5]$ pentanitroosmate(III), nitroosmate(III)
Pentan-1-ol *n*, **Pentanol-(1)** *n* pentan-1-ol
Pentaquin *n* pentaquin *(a quinoline derivative)*
Pentaquo... pentaaqua..., pentaaquo...
Pentaschwefelwasserstoff *m s.* Pentasulfan
Pentaselenid *n* pentaselenide
Pentasilan *n* pentasilane
pentasubstituiert pentasubstituted
Pentasulfan *n* pentasulphane, hydrogen pentasulphide
Pentasulfid *n* pentasulphide
Pentathionat *n* $M^I_2S_5O_6$ pentathionate
Pentathionsäure *f* pentathionic acid
Pentatriacontan *n* pentatriacontane
pentavalent pentavalent, quinquevalent
Pentavalenz *f* pentavalency, quinquevalency
Pentawolframat *n* *pentawolframate, pentatungstate
Pentazolyl *n* pentazolyl *(a heterocyclic group of atoms)*
Pent-1-en *n* pent-1-ene
Pent-2-enylpenicilloinsäure *f* pent-2-enylpenicilloic acid, penicilloic-F acid
Pent-2-enylpenillsäure *f* pent-2-enylpenillic acid, penillic-F acid
Pent-1-in *n*, **Pentin-(1)** *n* pent-1-yne
Pent-2-in *n*, **Pentin-(2)** *n* pent-2-yne
Pentlandit *m (min)* pentlandite *(an iron nickel sulphide)*
Pentosan *n* pentosan *(any of a class of polysaccharides)*
Pentose *f* pentose, five-carbon sugar
Pentosephosphat-Weg *m (bioch)* pentose phosphate pathway, pentose-*P* pathway, phosphogluconate pathway, pentose cycle (shunt)
Pentosephosphatzyklus *m*/**oxidativer** *s.* Pentosephosphat-Weg
~/reduktiver ribulose diphosphate cycle, Calvin[-Bassham] cycle, Calvin pathway, C_3 pentose phosphate cycle, C_3 pathway *(of CO_2 assimilation)*
Pentoseweg *m*/**oxidativer** *s.* Pentosephosphat-Weg
Pentoxid *n* pentaoxide
Pentoxoiodat(VII) *n* $M^I_3[IO_5]$ pentaoxoiodate(VII), mesoperiodate
Pentoxorhenat(VII) *n* $M^I_3[ReO_5]$ pentaoxorhenate(VII)
Pentylalkohol *m s.* Pentan-1-ol
Pepsinogen *n* pepsinogen *(inactive precursor of pepsin)*
Pepsinverdauung *f* peptic digestion
Peptid *n* peptide
~/cyclisches cyclic peptide
Peptidalkaloid *n* peptide alkaloid
Peptidanteil *m* peptide moiety (portion)
Peptidantibiotikum *n* peptide antibiotic
Peptidbindung *f* peptide bond
Peptidbindungsort *m (bioch)* peptidyl-tRNA site, P site, donor (condensing) site
Peptidgruppe *f* peptide group
Peptidkarte *f (bioch)* peptide map
Peptidkartierung *f (bioch)* peptide mapping
Peptidkette *f* peptide chain
Peptidknüpfung *f* interpeptide linkage
Peptidkomponente *f s.* Peptidanteil
Peptidoglykan *n (bioch)* peptidoglycan, murein *(a polysaccharide-peptide complex of bacterial cell walls)*
Peptidteil *m s.* Peptidanteil
Peptidverknüpfung *f* interpeptide linkage
Peptidylort *m s.* Peptidbindungsort
Peptisation *f s.* Peptisierung
Peptisationsmittel *n s.* Peptisator
Peptisator *m* peptizer, peptizing agent, *(coll also)* deflocculating agent, deflocculant, deflocculator, *(rubber also)* [chemical] plasticizer, [chemical] plasticizing agent
peptisieren to peptize, *(coll also)* to deflocculate, *(rubber also)* to plasticize
Peptisiermittel *n s.* Peptisator
Peptisierung *f* peptization, *(coll also)* deflocculation, *(rubber also)* plasticization
Peptisierungsmittel *n s.* Peptisator
Peptolyse *f* peptolysis
peptolytisch peptolytic
Pepton *n* peptone *(any of various high-molecular protein derivatives)*
peptonisieren to peptonize
Peptonisierung *f* peptonization
Perameisensäure *f* performic acid, peroxyformic acid
Peräthansäure *f s.* Peressigsäure
Perbenzoesäure *f* perbenzoic acid, peroxybenzoic acid
Perbenzolcarbonsäure *f s.* Perbenzoesäure
Perchlorat *n* M^IClO_4 perchlorate
Perchlorethan *n* perchloroethane, *hexachloroethane
Perchlormethan *n* perchloromethane, *tetrachloromethane, carbon tetrachloride
Perchlormethylmercaptan *n s.* Trichlormethansulfenylchlorid
Perchlorsäure *f* perchloric acid
Peressigsäure *f* peracetic acid, peroxyacetic acid
Perester *m* peroxy ester
Perezon *n* perezone, pipitzahoic acid *(a benzoquinone derivative)*

Perfektkautschuk *m* superior processing rubber, S.P. rubber
Perfluoralkylierung *f* perfluoroalkylation
Perfluorethen *n*, **Perfluorethylen** *n* perfluoroethylene, tetrafluoroethylene, T.F.E.
perfluorieren to perfluorinate
Perfluorierung *f* perfluorination
Perfluorvinylchlorid *n s.* Chlortrifluorethylen
Perforation *f* 1. *(tech)* perforation; 2. *(lab)* continuous extraction of a liquid
Perforator *m (lab)* apparatus for continuous extraction of a liquid
perforieren 1. *(tech)* to perforate *(to make holes in)*; 2. *(lab)* to extract continuously *(a liquid by another one)*
Pergament *n* parchment
~/animalisches (tierisches) animal parchment, skin (natural, writing) parchment
~/vegetabilisches vegetable parchment, parchment paper
Pergamentersatz *m*, **Pergamentersatzpapier** *n* artificial (imitation) parchment
pergamentieren *(pap)* to parchmentize
Pergamentierung *f (pap)* parchmentization
Pergamentierungsmittel *n (pap)* parchmentizing agent
Pergamentpapier *n***[/echtes]** parchment paper, vegetable parchment
Pergamentrohstoff *m* paper for parchmentizing
Pergamin[papier] *n*, **Pergamyn** *n* pergamyn, glassine [paper]
perhydrieren to perhydrogenate, to perhydrogenize
Perhydrierung *f* perhydrogenation
perianelliert peri-fused
Perianellierung *f* peri fusion
Peridot *m (min)* peridot[e] *(a variety of olivine)*
Periklas *m (min)* periclase, periclasite *(magnesium oxide)*
Periklin *m (min)* pericline *(a tectosilicate)*
Perikondensation *f* peri fusion
perikondensiert peri-fused
Perillaalkohol *m* perilla (perillic, perillyl) alcohol, *1-hydroxymethyl-4-isopropenylcyclohexene
Perillaldehyd *m* perillaldehyde, perillic (perillyl) aldehyde, *4-isopropenyl-cyclohex-1-ene-1-aldehyde
Perillaöl *n* perilla oil *(from Perilla specc.)*
Perillasäure *f* perillic acid, *4-isopropenylcyclohex-1-ene-1-carboxylic acid
Periodat *n* periodate; *(specif) s.* Metaperiodat
Periode *f* period *(as of the periodic table)*
~/große *s.* ~/lange
~/kleine *s.* ~/kurze
~/kurze short period
~/lange long period
Periodenfrequenz *f* linear frequency
Periodengesetz *n* periodic law
Periodensystem *n* **[der Elemente]** periodic table (system)
~/Mendelejewsches Mendeléeff periodic table, Mendeleev periodic table
periodisch periodic, *(relating to operations preferably:)* batch[wise], intermittent
Periodizität *f* periodicity
Periodsäure *f* periodic acid; *(specif) s.* Metaperiodsäure
Periodsäure/Schiff-Reagens *n (bioch)* periodic acid Schiff stain
periplasmatisch *(bioch)* periplasmic
Perisäure *f* peri acid, naphth-1-ylamine-8-sulphonic acid
peri-Stellung *f* peri position
Peritektikum *n (phys ch)* peritectic (transition-type) system
peritektisch *(phys ch)* peritectic
Perkin-Kondensation *f*, **Perkin-Reaktion** *f* Perkin condensation (reaction)
Perkinviolett *n* Perkin's mauve (purple, violet), aniline purple
Perkolat *n* percolate, leachate
Perkolation *f* percolation; *(min tech)* percolation leaching; *(petrol)* percolation filtration
~/kontinuierliche continuous percolation
~ unter Druck diacolation
Perkolationsverfahren *n* percolation process
Perkolator *m* percolator, percolation extractor
perkolieren to percolate
Perlanlage *f (rubber)* pelletizing equipment
Perlasche *f* pearl ash *(potassium carbonate)*
Perle *f* bead
perlen 1. to bubble, *(of wine also)* to sparkle; 2. to pelletize *(soot)*
Perlen *fpl* shot, slug *(a defect in fibre-glass products)*
perlend bubbling, *(of beverages also)* sparkling, brisk
Perlenessenz *f (coat, cosmet)* [natural] pearl essence
perlenförmig beaded
Perlenprobe *f*, **Perlenreaktion** *f (anal)* bead test
Perlessenz *f s.* Perlenessenz
Perlglimmer *m (min)* pearl-mica, margarite *(a phyllosilicate)*
Perlit *m* 1. *(met)* pearlite *(a microconstituent of steel)*; 2. *(geol)* perlite *(a natural glass)*
perlitisch 1. *(met)* pearlitic; 2. *(geol)* perlitic
Perlkontakt *m* bead catalyst
Perlkontaktmasse *f* beaded material *(in catalytic cracking)*
Perlmutt *n s.* Perlmutter
Perlmutt... *s. a.* Perlmutter...
Perlmutteffekt *m* nacreous (mother-of-pearl) effect
Perlmutter *f* nacre, mother of pearl • **aus ~ [bestehend]** nacr[e]ous
perlmutterähnlich, perlmutterartig nacr[e]ous, pearly
Perlmutterglanz *f* pearly lustre

perlmutterglänzend nacr[e]ous, pearly
Perlmutterpapier *n* mother-of-pearl paper, iridescent [paper]
Perlpolymerisat *n* bead polymerizate
Perlpolymerisation *f* bead (pearl) polymerization, suspension polymerization
Perlruß *m* beaded (pelletized) black
Perlspat *m (min)* pearl spar *(loosely for dolomite and aragonite)*
Perlstein *m (geol)* perlite *(a natural glass)*
Perlwein *m* carbonated wine
Perlweiß *n* pearl (bismuth, Spanish) white, cosmetic bismuth *(consisting of bismuth chloride oxide or bismuth nitrate oxide)*
Permanentappretur *f*, **Permanentausrüstung** *f (text)* durable finish
Permanentblau *n* permanent (French) blue *(an artificially prepared pigment)*
Permanentgrün *n* permanent green *(a pigment consisting of barium sulphate and Guignet green)*
Permanenthärte *f (hyd)* permanent hardness
Permanentrot *n* permanent red *(an azo dye)*
Permanentweiß *n* permanent (fixed) white, blanc fixe *(precipitated barium sulphate)*
Permanganat *n* M^IMnO_4 permanganate
Permanganatoxidation *f* permanganate oxidation
Permanganatprobe *f* Baeyer (permanganate) test *(for detecting alkenes)*
Permanganatverbrauch *m* 1. *(hyd)* permanganate consumption; 2. *s.* Permanganatzahl
Permanganatzahl *f (hyd)* permanganate number (value), PV
Permanganometrie *f* permanganometry
Permangansäure *f* permanganic acid
permeabel permeable
Permeabilität *f* permeability
Permeat *n* permeate
Permeation *f* permeation
Permeationschromatographie *f s.* Gelfiltration
Permeationstechnik *f*, **Permeationsverfahren** *n* permeation method *(for preparing calibration gas mixtures)*
permeieren to permeate
Permeiervermögen *n* permeativity
Permethansäure *f s.* Perameisensäure
Permittivität *f* [absolute] permittivity
~/relative *s.* Permittivitätszahl
Permittivitätszahl *f* relative permittivity (dielectric constant), specific inductive capacity, SIC
Pernambukholz *n (dye)* brazilwood *(from Caesalpinia specc., specif from C. echinata Lam.)*
Pernambukokautschuk *m s.* Mangabeirakautschuk
Perowskit *m (min)* perovskite, perofskite *(a calcium titanate)*
Peroxid *n* peroxide
Peroxidbildung *f* peroxide formation
Peroxidbindung *f* peroxide bond
Peroxidbleiche *f (pap, text)* peroxide bleaching
~ bei hoher Stoffdichte *(pap)* high-density peroxide bleaching
Peroxidbleichlösung *f* peroxide bleaching solution
Peroxideffekt *m* peroxide effect *(directive influence of peroxides in the addition of HBr to alkanes)*
Peroxidhydrat *n s.* Peroxyhydrat
Peroxidigkeit *f s.* Peroxidranzigkeit
peroxidisch peroxidic
Peroxidranzigkeit *f* peroxide (oxidative) rancidity, peroxydation rancidity, oiliness, tallowiness
Peroxidvernetzung *f* peroxide cross-linking
Peroxidvulkanisation *f (rubber)* peroxide cure (vulcanization)
Peroxidwert *m*, **Peroxidzahl** *f* peroxide number (value) *(measure of rancidity)*
Peroxisom *n* peroxisome, microbody *(cytochemistry)*
Peroxoborat *n* peroxoborate
Peroxoborsäure *f* peroxoboric acid
Peroxocarbonat *n* $M^I_2C_2O_6$ peroxocarbonate
Peroxocarbonat-Peroxyhydrat *n* peroxyhydrated peroxocarbonate
Peroxochromat *n* peroxochromate
Peroxochromsäure *f* peroxochromic acid
Peroxoderivat *n* peroxo derivative
Peroxodischwefelsäure *f* peroxodisulphuric acid
Peroxodisulfat *n* $M^I_2S_2O_8$ peroxodisulphate
Peroxogruppe *f* –O–O– peroxo group *(–O–O– with inorganic compounds)*
Peroxohydrat *n* peroxohydrate, hydroperoxidate
Peroxokohlensäure *f* peroxocarbonic acid
Peroxomonophosphat *n* $M^I_3PO_5$ peroxomonophosphate
Peroxomonophosphorsäure *f* peroxomonophosphoric acid
Peroxomonoschwefelsäure *f* peroxomonosulphuric acid, Caro's acid
Peroxomonosulfat *n* $M^I_2SO_5$ peroxomonosulphate
Peroxonitrat *n* M^INO_4 peroxonitrate
Peroxonitrit *n* $M^I[OON=O]$ peroxonitrite
Peroxophosphat *n* peroxophosphate, *(specif)* $M^I_3PO_5$ peroxomonophosphate
Peroxophosphorsäure *f* peroxophosphoric acid, *(specif)* peroxomonophosphoric acid
Peroxosalpetersäure *f* peroxonitric acid
Peroxosalz *n* peroxo salt
Peroxosäure *f* peroxo acid
Peroxoschwefelsäure *f* peroxosulphuric acid, *(specif)* peroxodisulphuric acid
Peroxosulfat *n* peroxosulphate, *(specif)* $M^I_2S_2O_8$ peroxodisulphate
Peroxouranat *n* $M^I_2UO_6$ peroxouranate
Peroxovanadat *n* peroxovanadate
Peroxovanadiumsäure *f* peroxovanadic acid
Peroxoverbindung *f* peroxo compound
Peroxy... *s. a.* Peroxo... *for inorganic compounds*
Peroxyacetylnitrat *n* peroxyacetyl nitrate
Peroxyameisensäure *f s.* Perameisensäure
Peroxybenzoesäure *f s.*Perbenzoesäure
Peroxycarbonsäure *f* peroxycarboxylic acid

Peroxidaseprobe *f*, **Peroxidasetest** *m* peroxidase test *(liberation of iodine from potassium iodide by peroxidases in the presence of* H_2O_2*)*
Peroxidation *f* peroxidation
peroxidatisch peroxidatic *(of or relating to peroxidase)*
peroxidieren to peroxidize, to peroxidate
Peroxidierung *f* peroxidation
Peroxyessigsäure *f s.* Peressigsäure
Peroxyester *m* peroxy ester
Peroxygenierung *f s.* Peroxidierung
Peroxygruppe *f (org ch)* –O–O– peroxy group *(s. a.* Peroxogruppe*)*
Peroxyhydrat *n* peroxyhydrate
Peroxyradikal *n* peroxy radical
Peroxysäure *f* 1. *(org ch)* RC(=O)OOH peroxy acid; 2. *s.* Peroxosäure
Peroxyverbindung *f* 1. *(org ch)* peroxy compound; 2. *s.* Peroxoverbindung
Perpetuum *n* **mobile erster Art** *(phys ch)* perpetual motion machine of the first kind
~ **mobile zweiter Art** perpetual motion machine of the second kind
Perrhenat *n* M^IReO_4 perrhenate, tetraoxorhenate(VII)
Perrheniumsäure *f* perrhenic acid, tetraoxorhenic(VII) acid
Perrin-Verfahren *n* Perrin process *(for producing ingot steel)*
Perruthenat *n* perruthenate
Persalz *n* per-salt
Persäure *f* 1. per-acid, *(Am)* peracid; 2. *(org ch)* RC(=O)OOH peroxy acid
Persio *m* persis, persio, cudbear *(dried paste of archil, a lichen dye)*
Persischrot *n* Persian red, chromate (chrome) red, Austrian cinnabar *(a basic lead chromate)*
persistent persistent • ~ **sein** to persist
~/in der Umwelt environmentally persistent
Persistenz *f* persistence
~ **in der Umwelt** environmental persistence
Persoz-Reagens *n (text)* Persoz's reagent *(for detecting silk in the presence of wool)*
Persubstitution *f* per substitution
Persulfatoxidation *f*/**Elbssche** Elbs persulphate oxidation *(of phenols)*
Pertechnetat *n* M^ITcO_4 pertechnate
Pertechnetiumsäure *f* pertechnetic acid
Perthiocarbonat *n* $M^I_2CS_4$ perthiocarbonate
Perthiokohlensäure *f* perthiocarbonic acid
Perubalsam *m* Peru (Peruvian) balsam, Indian (black) balsam, China oil *(from Myroxylon balsamum (L.) Harms var. pereirae)*
Perverbindung *f* per compound
Perylen *n* perylene *(a polycyclic hydrocarbon)*
Perylencarbonsäure *f* perylenecarboxylic acid
Perylenchinon *n* perylenequinone
Perylenringsystem *n* perylene ring system
PES *s.* Photoelektronenspektroskopie
Pestizid *n* pesticide, [pest] control agent, biocide
Pestizidrückstand *m* pesticide residue
Petalit *m (min)* petalite *(a lithium aluminium silicate)*
Petersen-Verfahren *n* Petersen process *(for manufacturing sulphuric acid)*
Petersiliencampher *m* parsley camphor, apiol, 2,5-dimethoxy-3,4-methylenedioxy-1-allylbenzene
Petersilienöl *n* parsley oil *(from Petroselinum crispum (Mill.) Nym.)*
PETN *s.* Pentaerythrittetranitrat
PETP *s.* Polyethylenterephthalat
Petrifikation *f (geol)* petrifaction
petrifizieren *(geol)* to petrify
Petri-Oberschale *f* Petri dish top
Petrischale *f* Petri [culture] dish
Petrischalenbüchse *f* Petri dish box
Petri-Unterschale *f* Petri dish bottom
Petrochemie *f* 1. petrochemistry, chemistry of rocks; 2. *s.* Petrolchemie
Petrochemikalie *f s.* Petrolchemikalie
petrochemisch 1. petrochemical *(relating to the chemistry of rocks)*; 2. *s.* petrolchemisch
petrogen petrogenic, rock-forming
Petrogenese *f*, **Petrogenesis** *f (geol)* petrogenesis
petrogenetisch petrogen[et]ic *(relating to the formation of rocks)*
Petrographie *f* petrography
petrographisch petrographic[al]
Petrol *n s.* Petroleum
Petrolasphalt *m s.* Petroleumasphalt
Petrolat *n s.* Petrolatum
Petroläther *m* petroleum ether, ligroin[e], light petroleum (ligroin), benzin[e] *(with a boiling-point range of 40 to 70 °C)*
Petrolatum *n* petrolatum, petroleum (mineral) jelly, mineral fat
Petrolchemie *f* petrochemistry
Petrolchemikalie *f* petrochemical
petrolchemisch petrochemical, petroleum-chemical
Petroleum *n* kerosene, kerosine, paraffin oil
Petroleumasphalt *m* petroleum asphalt
Petroleumäther *m s.* Petroläther
Petroleumbenzin *n* petroleum benzine
Petroleumemulsion *f* white-oil spray *(for pest control)*
Petroleumfraktion *f* kerosene fraction
Petroleumgefäß *n* oil cup *(of a flash-point tester)*
Petrolfraktion *f* kerosene fraction
Petrolharz *n* petroleum resin
Petrolkoks *m* petroleum (still) coke
Petrolnaphtha *n(f)* petroleum naphtha
Petrologie *f* petrology
petrologisch petrologic[al]
Petrolpech *n* petroleum pitch
Petroselinsäure *f* petroselic (petroselinic) acid, **cis*-octadec-6-enoic acid
Pe-tun-tse *m (ceram)* petun[t]se, petun[t]ze, china stone

Pe-Zahl *f s.* Peclét-Zahl
Pfanne *f* pan; ladle *(as for conveying molten metal)*; plate *(of a balance)*
Pfannenamalgamation *f*, **Pfannenamalgamierung** *f* pan amalgamation *(of noble metals)*
Pfannenbär *m (met)* skull
Pfannenfutter *n (met)* ladle lining
Pfannenkristallisator *m* tank crystallizer
Pfaundler-Hurler-Syndrom *n s.* Gargoylismus
PFC *s.* Polychlortrifluorethen
Pfefferöl *n* [black] pepper oil *(from Piper nigrum L.)*
Pfeife *f (glass)* blowpipe, blow[ing] iron, *(in the tube-drawing* process *also)* mandrel
Pfeifenende *n*, **Pfeifenkopf** *m (glass)* nose-piece, nose
Pfeifenton *m* pipeclay
Pfeilgift *n* arrow poison
Pfeilwurzelmehl *n* arrowroot *(from Maranta specc.)*
PF-Harz *n s.* Phenolformaldehydharz
Pfirsichkernöl *n* peach-kernel oil
PFK = Phosphofructokinase
Pflanze f/gerbstoffhaltige tanniferous plant
~/honigende nectariferous plant
~/kautschukführende (kautschukhaltige) rubber-bearing (rubber-producing) plant, rubber plant
~/kautschukliefernde rubber-yielding plant
~/stärkeliefernde starch-yielding plant
Pflanzenaustrockner *m (agric)* plant desiccant
Pflanzenauszug *m* plant extract
Pflanzenbiochemie *f* plant biochemistry
Pflanzenblindwert *m (tox)* plant blank value
Pflanzenbutter *f* vegetable butter
Pflanzenernährung *f* plant (crop) nutrition
Pflanzenextrakt *m* plant extract
Pflanzenfarbstoff *m* plant pigment
Pflanzenfaser *f* vegetable fibre
Pflanzenfett *n* vegetable (plant) fat
Pflanzengift *n* plant poison
Pflanzengummi *n* gum, plant (tree) gum
Pflanzenhormon *n* plant hormone, phytohormone
Pflanzenindican *n* indican of plants, indoxyl-β-glucoside
Pflanzenindigo *m(n)* natural indigo
Pflanzenlecithin *n* vegetable lecithin
Pflanzenleim *m* vegetable glue (adhesive)
Pflanzenmargarine *f* vegetable margarine
Pflanzennährstoff *m* plant nutrient
Pflanzenöl *n* vegetable oil
Pflanzenpolysaccharid *n* plant polysaccharide
Pflanzenprotein *n* plant (vegetable) protein
~/texturiertes *(biot)* texture vegetable protein, TVP
Pflanzenresistenz *f* plant resistance
Pflanzensaft *m* [plant] juice; *(bot)* sap; *(pharm)* succus
pflanzenschädigend phytotoxic
Pflanzenschädigung *f* plant damage
Pflanzenschleim *m* mucilage
Pflanzenschutz *m* crop protection
Pflanzenschutzantibiotikum *n (biot)* antibiotic used in plant pathology
Pflanzenschutzgerät *n (agric)* crop protection apparatus, applicator, application apparatus
Pflanzenschutzmittel *n* agricultural pesticide (control chemical), economic poison, crop protection chemical, plant protection product
~/flüssiges plant spray
~/nicht persistentes non-persistent pesticide
~/protektives (vorbeugend wirkendes) plant protective, protective toxicant, protectant
Pflanzenschutzpräparat *n s.* Pflanzenschutzmittel
Pflanzensterin *n*, **Pflanzensterol** *n* phytosterol, plant sterol
Pflanzentalg *m* vegetable tallow
pflanzentötend phytocidal
pflanzenverfügbar *(agric)* available *(nutrients)*
Pflanzenverfügbarkeit *f (agric)* availability *(of nutrients)*
pflanzenverträglich non-phytotoxic
Pflanzenzellkultur *f (biot)* plant cell culture
pflanzlich vegetable
Pflanzungskautschuk *m* plantation (estate) rubber
Pflatschen *n (text)* slop-padding
pflegeleicht *(text)* easy-care, minicare
Pflegeleicht-Ausrüstung *f (text)* easy-care finish
Pflegeleichtigkeit *f (text)* ease of care, easy care
Pflugschararm *m* plough bar *(of a dryer)*
Pfropf *m s.* Pfropfen
Pfropfcopolymer[e] *n*, **Pfropfcopolymerisat** *n* graft copolymer
Pfropfelastomer[e] *n* graft elastomer
pfropfen *(plast)* to graft
Pfropfen *m* stopper, plug, cork
~/kalter *(plast)* cold slug
Pfropfenbildung *f (plast)* plug-up *(a defect in injection moulding)*
Pfropfenströmung *f* plug flow, piston (rodlike) flow
Pfropfenströmungsreaktor *m* plug-flow reactor, ideal tubular-flow reactor
Pfropfpolymer[e] *n* graft polymer
~ von Naturkautschuk natural-rubber graft [polymer]
Pfropfpolymerisat *n s.* Pfropfpolymer[e]
Pfropfpolymerisation *f* graft polymerization
Pfropfreaktion *f (plast)* grafting reaction
Pfropfströmung *f s.* Pfropfenströmung
Pfropfung *f (plast)* grafting
PFT *s.* Polytetrafluorethylenfaserstoff
Pfund-Serie *f (spectr)* Pfund series
PH *s.* Polyharnstoffaserstoff
PhA = Phosphoreszenzanregung
***p*H-Abfall** *m* *p*H decrease (drop, decline)
***p*H-abhängig** *p*H-dependent, depending (dependent) on *p*H
***p*H-Abhängigkeit** *f* *p*H dependence
***p*H-Abnahme** *f s.* *p*H-Abfall
Phage *m* [bacterio]phage
Phageninfektion *f (biot)* phage infection, contamination with phages
phagenresistent *(biot)* phage-resistant

***p*H-Änderung** *f* *p*H change
phanerokristallin phanerocrystalline
Phänomen *n* phenomenon
~/Purkinjesches *(phot)* Purkinje effect *(shifting in the spectral sensitivity of emulsions)*
***p*H-Anstieg** *m* *p*H increase
Phantastikum *n (pharm)* psychodysleptic, psychotomimetic [drug], hallucinogen, psychedelic drug
Phantombild *n (phot)* ghost image
***p*H-Anzeigegerät** *n* *p*H indicator
Pharmakochemie *f* pharmaceutic[al] chemistry, medicinal chemistry
Pharmakochemiker *m* pharmaceutic[al] chemist, medicinal chemist
Pharmakodynamie *f*, **Pharmakodynamik** *f* pharmacodynamics
pharmakodynamisch pharmacodynamic
Pharmakognosie *f* pharmacognosy, pharmacognosia
pharmakognostisch pharmacognostic
Pharmakokinetik *f* pharmacokinetics
Pharmakologie *f* pharmacology, pharmacologia
pharmakologisch pharmacologic[al]
Pharmakon *n* pharmacon
~/psychotropes psychopharmacologic drug (agent), psychotropic agent
Pharmakopöe *f* pharmacopoeia
pharmakotherapeutisch pharmacotherapeutic[al]
Pharmakotherapie *f* pharmacotherapy
Pharmazeut *m* pharmacist
Pharmazeutik *f* pharmaceutics
Pharmazeutikum *n* pharmaceutic[al]
pharmazeutisch pharmaceutic[al]
Pharmazie *f* pharmacy
Phase *f* phase, stage; *(phys ch)* phase • **in homogener** ~ homogeneously
~/amorphe amorphous phase
~/bewegliche *s.* ~/mobile
~/chemisch gebundene *(chromat)* bonded phase
~/cholester[in]ische cholesteric phase
~/dampfförmige vapour phase
~ der Flockenbildung (Flockung) *(hyd)* flocculation (floc-building) stage
~ der Flockung/orthokinetische orthokinetic flocculation
~ der Flockung/perikinetische perikinetic flocculation
~ der Transportvorgänge *s.* ~ der Flockenbildung
~ des aktiven Wachstums *(biot)* trophophase
~/disperse disperse phase, dispersed (discontinuous, internal) phase
~/feste solid phase; solid *(in zone melting)*
~/fluide fluid phase
~/flüssige liquid phase; liquid *(in zone melting)*
~/gasförmige gas phase
~/gemischte mixed phase
~/geochemische (geologische) geochemical stage *(of coalification)*
~ geringerer Dichte V phase *(as with extraction, distillation)*
~/geschlossene continuous (external) phase
~/glasige glassy (vitreous) phase
~ höherer Dichte L phase *(as with extraction, distillation)*
~/Hume-Rotherysche *(cryst)* Hume-Rothery phase
~/in den Poren stehende mobile *(chromat)* stagnant mobile phase
~/innere *s.* ~/disperse
~/intermetallische intermetallic (electron, metal) compound, intermediate constituent (phase), intermetallic
~/kristalline crystalline phase
~/letale *(biot, hyd)* death (endogenous growth) phase
~/milde *(chromat)* subtle phase
~/mobile *(chromat)* mobile (moving) phase, developer (carrier) phase
~/nematische *(coll)* nematic phase
~/offene *s.* ~/disperse
~/smektische *(coll)* smectic phase
~/stagnierende mobile *(chromat)* stagnant mobile phase
~/stationäre 1. *(chromat)* stationary (immobile, non-mobile) phase, partitioner [phase]; 2. *(biot)* stationary (resting) phase *(in the growth of microorganisms)*
~/unbewegliche *s.* ~/stationäre 1.
~/wäßrige aqueous (water) phase
~/zunehmend absterbende *s.* ~/letale
~/zusammenhängende *s.* ~/geschlossene
Phasen *fpl***/koexistierende** coexisting phases
~/umgekehrte reversed phases
Phasenänderung *f* phase change (transition)
Phasenbeziehung *f* phase relation
Phasendiagramm *n* phase (equilibrium) diagram, constitution[al] diagram
Phasendifferenz *f* phase difference
Phasendrehung *f* phase shift
phasenempfindlich *(spectr)* phase-sensitive
Phasengeschwindigkeit *f* phase velocity
Phasengesetz *n s.* Phasenregel
Phasengleichgewicht *n* phase equilibrium
Phasengrenze *f* phase boundary
~ fest-flüssig solid-liquid boundary
Phasengrenzfläche *f* [phase] interface, boundary (bounding) surface, junction
~ flüssig-flüssig liquid-liquid interface, liquid junction
Phasengrenzpotential *n* phase-boundary potential
Phasengrenzreaktion *f* boundary reaction
Phasenkolloid *n* dispersion colloid, dispersoid
Phasenkontrastmikroskop *n* phase-contrast microscope
Phasenkopplung *f* mode locking *(with lasers)*
Phasenregel *f* **[von Gibbs]** [Gibbs] phase rule, Gibbs rule
Phasenschiebung *f s.* Phasenverschiebung
Phasenstabilität *f* phase stability
Phasentransferkatalysator *m* phase-transfer catalyst

Phasentransferkatalyse *f* phase-transfer catalysis, PTC
Phasentransformation *f s.* Phasenumwandlung
Phasentrennung *f* phase separation
Phasenübergang *m s.* Phasenumwandlung
Phasenumkehr *f* phase inversion, reversal of phases
Phasenumwandlung *f* phase transition (change)
~/antiferroelektrische antiferroelectric transition
~/antiferromagnetische antiferromagnetic transition
~/diskontinuierliche *s.* ~ erster Art (Ordnung)
~/displazive displacive transition
~/enantiotrope enantiotropic transition
~ erster Art (Ordnung) first-order [phase] transition, discontinuous transition
~/ferrimagnetische ferrimagnetic transition
~/ferroelastische ferroelastic transition
~/ferroelektrische ferroelectric transition
~/ferromagnetische ferromagnetic transition
~ höherer Ordnung higher-order transition, smooth transition
~/irreversible irreversible transition
~/kongruente congruent transition
~/kontinuierliche *s.* ~ zweiter Art (Ordnung)
~ normal-supraleitende superconducting transition
~/polymorphe polymorphic transition
~/rekonstruktive reconstructive transition
~/reversible reversible transition
~/strukturelle structural transition
~ zweiter Art (Ordnung) second-order [phase] transition, continuous transition
Phasenumwandlungsenthalpie *f* enthalpy of phase transition
Phasenumwandlungsentropie *f* entropy of phase transition
Phasenunterschied *m* phase difference
Phasenverhältnis *n (chromat)* phase ratio
Phasenverschiebung *f* phase shift
Phasenverteilungschromatographie *f* partition chromatography
Phasenwinkel *m* phase angle
PHB = *p*-Hydroxybenzoesäure
***p*H-Bereich** *m pH* range
***p*H-Bestimmung** *f pH* determination
***p*H-Einheit** *f pH* unit
***p*H-Elektrode** *f pH* electrode
Phellandren *n* phellandrene *(a monocyclic terpene)*
Phellonsäure *f* phellonic acid, *22-hydroxydocosanoic acid
Phenacetaminoessigsäure *f s.* Phenacetursäure
Phenacetin *n* phenacetin, acetophenetidine, acet-*p*-phenetidide
Phenacetursäure *f* phenaceturic acid, phenylacetylglycine
Phenacetylglycin *n*, **Phenacetylglykokoll** *n s.* Phenacetursäure
Phenacetylharnstoff *m* phenacetylurea
Phenacylalkohol *m* phenacyl alcohol, α-hydroxyacetophenone
Phenacylchlorid *n* phenacyl chloride, α-chloroacetophenone
Phenacylgruppe *f* C_6H_5–CO–CH_2– phenacyl group
Phenacylidengruppe *f* C_6H_5–CO–CH= phenacylidene group
Phenakit *m (min)* phenakite, phenacite *(beryllium orthosilicate)*
Phenanthren *n* phenanthrene
Phenanthrenchinon *n* phenanthraquinone, *(specif)* 9,10-phenanthraquinone
Phenanthrenringsystem *n* phenanthrene ring system
Phenanthridin *n* phenanthridine, bezo[*c*]quinoline
Phenanthrochinolizidin-Alkaloid *n* phenanthroquinolizidine alkaloid
Phenanthroindolizidin-Alkaloid *n* phenanthroindolizidine alkaloid
Phenanthrol *n* phenanthrol, hydroxyphenanthrene
Phenanthrolin *n* phenanthroline
Phenarsazinchlorid *n (tox)* *10-chloro-5,10-dihydrophenarsazine, phenarsazine chloride
Phenarsazinsäure *f* phenarsazinic acid
Phenat *n* phenate, phenolate, phenoxide
Phenazarsinsäure *f s.* Phenarsazinsäure
Phenazin *n* phenazine, azophenylene
Phenazinfarbstoff *m* azine (phenazine-based) dye
Phenazon *n* phenazone, antipyrine
Phenethylalkohol *m* phenethyl alcohol, 2-phenylethanol
Phenethylamin *n* phenethylamine, *phenylethylamine, aminoethylbenzene
Phenethylgruppe *f* $C_6H_5CH_2CH_2$– phenethyl group
Phenetidin *n* phenetidine, aminophenol ethyl ether
Phenetol *n* phenetol, ethoxybenzene, *ethylphenyl ether
Phenindion *n* phenindione, 2-phenyl-1,3-indanedione
Phenol *n* phenol, arenol, *(specif)* C_6H_5OH phenol, benzophenol, hydroxybenzene
~/einwertiges monohydric phenol
~/dreiwertiges trihydric phenol
~/mehrwertiges polyhydric phenol
~/verflüssigtes *(pharm)* liquefied phenol
~/zweiwertiges dihydric phenol
Phenolabwasser *n* phenol[ic] waste
Phenolaldehyd *m* phenolic aldehyde
Phenolalkohol *m* phenol alcohol
Phenolat *n* phenolate, phenate, phenoxide, aryloxide
Phenoläther *m* s. Diphenylether
Phenolatverfahren *n* phenolate process *(for removing H_2S from gas)*
Phenolcarbonsäure *f* phenolic benzoic acid, phenolic acid *(any of a group of aromatic hydroxycarboxylic acids)*

Phenolester *m* phenolic ester
Phenolformaldehyd *m (plast)* phenolformaldehyde, PF
Phenolformaldehydharz *n* phenolformaldehyde resin
Phenolformaldehydkondensation *f* phenolformaldehyde condensation
phenolfrei free from phenol
Phenolfurfuralharz *n* phenol-furfural resin
Phenolgeschmack *m* phenolic taste
phenolhaltig containing phenol, phenolic
Phenolharz *n* phenolic resin
~ **im A-Zustand** A-stage resin, resol
~ **im B-Zustand** B-stage resin, resitol
~ **im C-Zustand** C-stage resin, resite
Phenolharzkitt *m* phenolic cement
Phenolharzklebstoff *m* phenolic adhesive
Phenolharzkunststoff *m* phenoplast, phenolic plastic
Phenolharzlack *m* phenolic varnish
Phenolharzlaminat *n* phenolic laminate
Phenolharzpreßmasse *f* phenolic moulding compound
Phenolharzschaum[stoff] *m* phenolic[-resin] foam
Phenolhydroxyl *n* phenolic hydroxyl
phenolisch phenolic
phenolisieren to phenolate, to phenolize
Phenolkalium *n s.* Kaliumphenolat
Phenolkern *m* phenol nucleus
Phenolkitt *m s.* Phenolharzkitt
Phenolkleber *m s.* Phenolharzklebstoff
Phenolkoeffizient *m* phenol coefficient *(of disinfectants)*
2-Phenolmethylal *n s.* Salicylaldehyd
Phenolnatrium *n s.* Natriumphenolat
Phenoloxidase *f* phenol oxidase, phenolase, tyrosinase
Phenolphthalein *n* phenolphthalein
Phenolphthalein-Alkalität *f (hyd)* phenolphthalein alkalinity, P alkalinity
Phenolphthaleinumschlagpunkt *m* phenolphthalein end-point, *(hyd also)* P end-point
Phenolreaktion *f*/**Liebermannsche** Liebermann reaction [for phenols]
Phenolring *m* phenol ring
Phenolrot *n* phenol red *(phenolsulphonephthalein)*
Phenolschaum *m s.* Phenolharzschaum
Phenolsulfonphthalein *n* phenolsulphonephthalein
Phenolsulfonsäure *f* phenolsulphonic acid
Phenolwasser *n* phenol water
Phenolyse *f* phenolysis
Phenonium-Ion *n* phenonium ion
Phenoplast *m* phenoplast, phenolic plastic
Phenothiazin *n* phenothiazine, dibenzothiazine, thiophenylamine
Phenoxid *n* phenoxide, phenolate, phenate
Phenoxyalkylierung *f* phenoxyalkylation
Phenoxyessigsäure *f* phenoxyacetic acid
Phenoxygruppe *f* C_6H_5O- phenoxy group (residue)
Phenoxyharz *n* phenoxy resin
Phenoxyrest *m s.* Phenoxygruppe
***N*-Phenylacetamid** *n N*-phenylacetamide, acetanilide
Phenylacetat *n* phenyl acetate
Phenylacetonitril *n* phenylacetonitrile, benzyl cyanide
***N*-Phenylacetursäure** *f N*-phenylaceturic acid, *N*-acetylphenylglycine
Phenylacetylen *n* ethynylbenzene, *(deprecated:)* phenylacetylene
Phenylacetylharnstoff *m* phenacetylurea
Phenylacrylsäure *f* phenylacrylic acid
α-Phenylacrylsäure *f* α-phenylacrylic acid, 2-phenylacrylic acid, atropic acid
β-Phenylacrylsäure *f*, *trans*-**β-Phenylacrylsäure** *f* β-phenylacrylic acid, *trans*-cinnamic acid
2-Phenylacrylsäure *f s.* α-Phenylacrylsäure
α-Phenylalanin *n* α-phenylalanine, *2-amino-2-phenylpropionic acid
β-Phenylalanin *n* β-phenylalanine, *1-amino-2-phenylpropionic acid
Phenylalkan *n* phenylalkane
1-Phenylallylalkohol *m* 1-phenylallyl alcohol
***N*-Phenylamid** *n N*-phenyl amide, anilide
Phenylamin *n* *phenylamine, aminobenzene, aniline
Phenyläth... *s.* Phenyleth...
Phenyläther *m s.* Diphenylether
α-Phenyläthylalkohol *m s.* 1-Phenylethanol
β-Phenyläthylalkohol *m s.* 2-Phenylethanol
Phenylbenzen *n* phenylbenzene, biphenyl
Phenylbenzoat *n* phenyl benzoate
Phenylbenzol *n s.* Phenylbenzen
Phenylbenzylcarbinol *n s.* 1,2-Diphenylethanol
Phenylbernsteinsäure *f* phenylsuccinic acid
Phenylborierung *f* phenylboration
Phenylboronsäure *f s.* Phenylborsäure
Phenylborsäure *f* benzeneboronic acid, phenylboric acid
Phenylbrenztraubensäure *f* phenylpyruvic acid
Phenylbromid *n* bromobenzene, phenyl bromide
Phenylbutansäure *f*, **Phenylbuttersäure** *f* phenylbutyric acid
Phenylcarbamid *n* phenylcarbamide, phenylurea
Phenylcarbamidsäure *f* phenylcarbamic acid, carbanilic acid
Phenylcarbinol *n s.* Benzylalkohol
Phenylcarbylamin *n* phenylcarbylamine, phenyl isocyanide
Phenylchlorid *n* chlorobenzene, phenyl chloride
Phenylchloroform *n* α,α,α-trichlorotoluene, phenylchloroform
Phenylchlorsilan *n* phenylchlorosilane
2-Phenylchromenyliumsalz *n*, **2-Phenylchromyliumsalz** *n* 2-phenylchromenylium salt, flavylium salt
Phenyldisulfid *n s.* Diphenyldisulfid
Phenyldithiobenzol *n s.* Diphenyldisulfid

Phenylenblau *n* phenylene blue *(an indamine dye)*
Phenylendiamin *n* phenylenediamine, diaminobenzene
Phenylendimethylen *n* phenylene dimethylene, xylylene
Phenylengruppe *f*, **Phenylenrest** *m* $-C_6H_4-$ phenylene group (residue)
Phenylessigsäure *f* phenylacetic acid, α-toluic acid
Phenylessigsäureethylester *m* ethyl phenylacetate
Phenylessigsäurenitril *n s.* Phenylacetonitril
Phenylester *m* phenyl ester
Phenylethan *n* phenylethane, ethylbenzene
1-Phenylethanol *n* 1-phenylethanol
2-Phenylethanol *n* 2-phenylethanol, phenethyl alcohol
Phenylethen *n* phenylethene, vinylbenzene, styrene
Phenylethylamin *n* aminoethylbenzene, phenylethylamine
Phenylethylierung *f* phenethylation
Phenylglycin *n*, **Phenylglykokoll** *n* phenylglycine, *(specif)* $C_6H_5NHCH_2COOH$ *N*-phenylglycine, anilinoacetic acid
Phenylglykolsäure *f* phenylglycollic acid, mandelic acid, 2-hydroxy-2-phenylacetic acid
O-**Phenylglykolsäure** *f* glycollic acid phenyl ether, phenoxyacetic acid
Phenylglyoxylsäure *f* phenylglyoxylic acid, benzoylformic acid
Phenylgruppe *f* C_6H_5- phenyl group (residue)
Phenylharnstoff *m* phenylurea, phenylcarbamide
2-Phenylhydracrylsäure *f* 2-phenylhydracrylic acid, tropic acid, *3-hydroxy-2-phenylpropanoic acid
Phenylhydrazin *n* phenylhydrazine
Phenylhydrazon *n* phenylhydrazone *(any of several phenylhydrazine derivatives* $C_6H_5NHN{=}CR^1R^2$*)*
phenylieren to phenylate
Phenylierung *f* phenylation
Phenyliodid *n* iodobenzene, phenyl iodide
Phenyl-I-Säure *f s.* Phenyl-J-Säure
Phenylisocyanid *n* phenylisocyanide, phenylcarbylamine
Phenyl-J-Säure *f* phenyl-J acid, 7-anilino-4-hydroxynaphthalene-2-sulphonic acid
Phenylkation *n* phenyl kation, phenylium
Phenylketon *n s.* Diphenylketon
Phenylketonurie *f (med)* phenylketonuria, PKU
Phenylmagnesiumbromid *n* phenylmagnesium bromide
Phenylmethan *n* methylbenzene, phenylmethane, toluene
2-Phenylmilchsäure *f* 2-phenyl-lactic acid, *2-hydroxy-2-phenylpropanoic acid
Phenylperisäure *f* phenyl-peri acid, *N*-phenylnaphth-1-ylamine-8-sulphonic acid
Phenylphenazoniumsalz *n* phenylphenazonium salt
Phenylphosphinsäure *f* phenylphosphinic acid, benzenephosphinic acid
Phenylphosphonsäure *f* *phenylphosphonic acid, benzenephosphonic acid
2-Phenylpropan-2-ol *n* 2-phenyl-2-propanol, dimethylphenyl carbinol, DMPC
2-Phenylpropansäure *f s.* 2-Phenylpropionsäure
trans-**3-Phenylpropensäure** *f s.* β-phenylacrylic acid
Phenylpropinsäure *f s.* Phenylpropiolsäure
Phenylpropiolsäure *f* phenylpropiolic acid, 3-phenylprop-2-ynoic acid
2-Phenylpropionsäure *f* 2-phenylpropionic acid, hydratropic acid
Phenylquecksilberacetat *n* phenylmercuric acetate, PMA *(a pesticide)*
Phenylquecksilberharnstoff *m* phenylmercury urea
Phenylradikal *n* phenyl [free] radical
Phenylrest *m s.* Phenylgruppe
Phenylsalicylat *n* phenyl salicylate, salol
Phenyl-γ-Säure *f* phenyl-gamma acid, 6-anilino-4-hydroxynaphthalene-2-sulphonic acid
Phenylschwefelsäure *f* phenylsulphuric acid
Phenylsilicon *n* phenyl siloxane
Phenylsulfamidsäure *f*, **Phenylsulfaminsäure** *f* phenylsulphamic acid
Phenylsulfonsäure *f s.* Benzensulfonsäure
Pheromon *n (bioch)* pheromone
Pheron *n* pheron *(colloid carrier of an enzyme)*
*p***H-Gebiet** *n p*H range
PHI = Phosphohexoisomerase
Philips-Vakuummeter *n* Philips (Penning) gauge, cold-cathode ionization gauge
Phillips-Verfahren *n* Phillips process *(for producing high-density polyethylene)*
philodien *(org ch)* dienophilic
Philodien *n (org ch)* dienophile
Philosophenwolle *f s.* Zinkblumen
*p***H-Indikator** *m p*H indicator
*p***H-Intervall** *n p*H interval
Phiole *f* [glass] vial
*p***H-Kontrolle** *f p*H control
*p***H-Korrektur** *f s. p*H-Wert-Korrektur
Phlegma *n (distil)* less volatile component
phlegmatisieren to desensitize *(an explosive)*
Phlegmatisierung *f* desensitization *(of an explosive)*
Phlobaphen *n* phlobaphene, tanner's red
Phlogistontheorie *f* phlogiston theory *(historically)*
Phloridzin *n* phlori[d]zin *(β-glucoside)*
Phloroglucin *n* phloroglucinol, 1,3,5-trihydroxybenzene
Phloroglucincarbonsäure *f* phloroglucinol-carboxylic acid, 2,4,6-trihydroxybenzoic acid
Phlorrhizin *n s.* Phloridzin
*p***H-Meßgerät** *n p*H meter (instrument)

***p*H-Meßsystem** *n* *p*H-measuring system
***p*H-Messung** *f* *p*H measurement
***p*H-Meter** *n s.* *p*H-Meßgerät
Phonon *n* phonon
Phoron *n* phorone, *2,6-dimethylhepta-2,5-dien-4-one
Phosgen *n* phosgene, carbonyl chloride, carbon dichloride oxide
phosgenieren to phosgenate
Phosgenierung *f* phosgenation
Phosphan *n* P_nH_{n+2} phosphane, *(specif)* PH_3 phosphane, phosphine
λ^5-Phosphan *n s.* Phosphoran
Phosphanoxid *n* phosphine oxide
Phosphat *n* phosphate, *(specif)* orthophosphate
~/neutrales neutral (normal) phosphate
~/primäres *s.* Dihydrogenphosphat
~/sekundäres *s.* Hydrogenphosphat
~/tertiäres *s.* Orthophosphat/neutrales
Phosphatase f/saure *(bioch)* acid phosphatase
Phosphataseprobe *f (food)* phosphatase test
Phosphatbindungsenergie *f (bioch)* phosphate-bond energy
Phosphatdosierung *f (hyd)* addition of phosphates
Phosphatdüngemittel *n* phosphate fertilizer
~/stickstoffhaltiges nitrogen-phosphorus fertilizer
Phosphateliminierung *f*, **Phosphatentfernung** *f (hyd)* phosphate removal
Phosphatenthärtung *f (hyd)* phosphate (threshold) treatment
Phosphatentschwefelungsverfahren *n (petrol)* phosphate process *(esp for desulphurizing natural gas)*
Phosphaterz *n* phosphate ore (rock)
Phosphatgehalt *m* phosphate content; phosphorus nutrient level *(in waste water)*
phosphatgepuffert phosphate-buffered
Phosphatglas *n* phosphate glass
Phosphatid *n (bioch)* phosphatide, phosphoglyceride, glycerophospholipid
Phosphatidsäure *f (bioch)* phosphatidic acid
Phosphatid-Thesaurismose *f s.* Niemann-Pick-Syndrom
Phosphatidylethanolamin *n* 3-phosphatidyl ethanolamine
Phosphatidylserin *n* 3-phosphatidyl serine
phosphatieren to phosphate, to phosphatize *(for preventing corrosion)*
Phosphatieren *n* phosphating [treatment], phosphation, phosphatizing *(for preventing corrosion)*
Phosphatimpfung *f s.* Phosphatenthärtung
Phosphatlöslichkeit *f (agric)* phosphate solubility
Phosphatpuffer *m* phosphate buffer
Phosphatquelle *f (agric)* phosphate source
Phosphatregulation *f (biot)* phosphate regulation
Phosphatreinigung *f (hyd)* phosphate treatment
Phosphatträger *m (agric)* phosphate carrier
Phosphatverfahren *n s.* Phosphatentschwefelungsverfahren
Phosphatweichmacher *m* phosphate plasticizer
Phosphensäure *f* 1. $HOPO_2$ phosphenic acid; 2. *(org ch)* $R^1R^2P(OH)$ phosphinous acid
Phosphid *n* phosphide
Phosphin *n* phosphine *(PH_3 and its derivatives)*
Phosphinalkylen *n s.* Phosphoniumylid
Phosphinigsäure *f* 1. $RPH{-}OH \rightleftarrows RPH_2{=}O$ phosphinous acid *(IUPAC-nomenclature)*; 2. $RPH{=}O(OH)$ phosphinic acid *(Beilstein nomenclature)*, *(specif)* HPH_2O_2 phosphinic acid, hypophosphorous acid
Phosphinoxid *n* phosphine oxide
Phosphit *n* 1. phosphite, *(specif)* $M^I_2PHO_3$ orthophosphite, *phosphonate; 2. phosphite *(an ester of the hypothetical acid $P(OH)_3$)*
Phosphodiester *m (bioch)* phosphodiester
6-Phosphogluconat *n (bioch)* 6-phosphogluconate
6-Phosphogluconsäure *f (bioch)* 6-phosphogluconic acid
Phosphogluconat-Weg *m (bioch)* phosphogluconate (pentose phosphate) pathway, pentose cycle (shunt)
Phosphoglycerid *n (bioch)* phosphoglyceride, glycerophospholipide, phosphatide
Phosphoglycerinsäure *f s.* Phosphoglycersäure
Phosphoglycersäure *f (bioch)* phosphoglyceric acid
Phosphohexoketolaseweg *m s.* Phosphoketolaseweg
Phosphoketolaseweg *m (bioch)* phosphoketolase pathway
Phospholipase *f* phospholipase, lecithinase
Phospholipid *n*, **Phospholipoid** *n* phospholipid[e]
Phosphonat *n* phosphonate
Phosphonigsäure *f* $RP(OH)_2$ phosphonous acid
Phosphoniumbase *f* phosphonium base
Phosphoniumbromid *n* phosphonium bromide
Phosphoniumchlorid *n* phosphonium chloride
Phosphoniumiodid *n* phosphonium iodide
Phosphoniumsulfat *n* phosphonium sulphate
Phosphoniumverbindung *f* phosphonium compound
Phosphoniumylid *n* phosphonium ylide, phosphorus ylide, Wittig reagent
Phosphonoethylierung *f* phosphonoethylation
Phosphonovinylierung *f* phosphonovinylation
Phosphonsäure *f* $RP{=}O(OH)_2$ phosphonic acid, *(specif)* H_2PHO_3 phosphonic acid
Phosphonsäureester *m* phosphonate
Phosphonylierung *f* phosphonylation
Phosphoproteid *n*, **Phosphoprotein** *n* phosphoprotein
Phosphor *m* 1. P phosphorus; 2. phosphor *(phosphorescent substance)*
~/amorpher amorphous phosphorus
~/farbloser (gelber) *s.* ~/weißer
~/hellroter scarlet amorphous phosphorus
~/hexagonal kristallisierter weißer β-white phosphorus

~/Hittorfscher *s.* ~/violetter
~/kubisch kristallisierter weißer α-white phosphorus
~/radioaktiver radioactive phosphorus, radiophosphorus, *(specif)* ^{32}P phosphorus-32
~/roter 1. red phosphorus *(commercial product)*; 2. *s.* ~/hellroter
~/schwarzer black (β-metallic) phosphorus, phosphorus IV
~/violetter violet (α-metallic) phosphorus, phosphorus III
~/weißer white (yellow) phosphorus
Phosphor-32 *m* ^{32}P phosphorus-32
Phosphoran *n* phosphorane, λ^5-phosphane
Phosphorandisäure *f* phosphoranedioic acid
Phosphoranpentasäure *f* phosphoranepentoic acid
Phosphoransäure *f* phosphoranoic acid
Phosphorantetrasäure *f* phosphoranetetroic acid
Phosphorantrisäure *f* phosphoranetrioic acid
phosphorarm poor in phosphorus, low-phosphorus
Phosphorbedarf *m (agric)* phosphorus needs
Phosphor(III)-bromid *n* phosphorus(III) bromide, phosphorus tribromide
Phosphor(V)-bromid *n* phosphorus(V) bromide, phosphorus pentabromide
Phosphorbronze *f* phosphor bronze
Phosphor(III)-chlorid *n* phosphorus(III) chloride, phosphorus trichloride
Phosphor(V)-chlorid *n* phosphorus(V) chloride, phosphorus pentachloride
Phosphor(V)-dibromidtrichlorid *n* phosphorus dibromide trichloride
Phosphor(V)-dibromidtrifluorid *n* phosphorus dibromide trifluoride
Phosphordichlorid *n* phosphorus dichloride
Phosphor(V)-dichloridtrifluorid *n* phosphorus dichloride trifluoride
Phosphorentfernung *f (hyd)* phosphorus (phosphate) removal
Phosphoreszenz *f* phosphorescence
Phosphoreszenzfarbe *f* phosphorescent paint
Phosphoreszenzspektroskopie *f* phosphorescence spectroscopy
Phosphoreszenzspektrum *n* phosphorescence spectrum
phosphoreszieren to phosphoresce
phosphoreszierend phosphorescent, phosphoric, phosphorous
Phosphorfestlegung *f (agric)* phosphorus fixation
Phosphor(III)-fluorid *n* phosphorus(III) fluoride, phosphorus trifluoride
Phosphor(V)-fluorid *n* phosphorus(V) fluoride, phosphorus pentafluoride
phosphorfrei free from phosphorus, phosphorus-free
Phosphorgehalt *m* phosphorus content; *(hyd)* phosphorus nutrient level *(of waste water)* • **mit hohem** ~ rich in phosphorus, high-phosphorus • **mit niedrigem** ~ poor in phosphorus, low-phosphorus
Phosphorhalogenid *n* phosphorus halide
phosphorhaltig containing phosphorus, phosphorus-bearing
Phosphorheptasulfid *n* phosphorus heptasulphide, tetraphosphorus heptasulphide
Phosphor(III)-hydrid *n* phosphorus trihydride, monophosphine, phosphine
Phosphorigsäure-alkylester-alkylimid *n* (RO)P = NR alkoxyalkyliminophosphine, alkyl *N*-alkylphosphenimidite, *(Kosolapoffs' nomenclature:)* alkyl- alkylimidophosphite
Phosphorigsäureester *m* phosphite
Phosphorinsektizid *n*/**organisches** O–P insecticide
Phosphor(III)-iodid *n* phosphorus(III) iodide, phosphorus triiodide
Phosphorit *m* phosphorite, phosphate rock
Phosphormonoselenid *n* phosphorus monoselenide
Phosphornährstoffe *mpl* phosphorus nutrients
Phosphornekrose *f (med)* phossy jaw
Phosphornitrid *n* phosphorus nitride, triphosphorus pentanitride
Phosphornitriddibromid *n* phosphorus dibromide nitride
Phosphornitriddichlorid *n* phosphorus dichloride nitride
Phosphorofen *m* phosphorus (phosphate) furnace *(for manufacturing phosphoric acid)*
Phosphorogen *n* phosphorogen *(a substance which produces or induces phosphorescence)*
phosphoroklastisch phosphoroclastic *(cleavage of pyruvate)*
Phosphorolyse *f* phosphorolysis
phosphorolytisch phosphorolytic
Phosphororganikum *n*/**toxisches** *(agric)* O-P toxicant
Phosphor(III)-oxid *n* phosphorus(III) oxide, phosphorus trioxide, diphosphorus trioxide
Phosphor(V)-oxid *n* phosphorus(V) oxide, phosphorus pentaoxide, diphosphorus pentaoxide
Phosphor(V)-oxidchlorid *n s.* Phosphorylchlorid
Phosphoroxidtriamid *n s.* Phosphoryltriamid
Phosphorpent..., Phosphorpenta... *s.* Phosphor(V)-...
Phosphorproteid *n s.* Phosphoproteid
phosphorreich rich in phosphorus, high-phosphorus
Phosphor(III)-rhodanid *n s.* Phosphor(III)-thiocyanat
Phosphorsalz *n* phosphorus salt, microcosmic salt, ammonium sodium hydrogenphosphate 4-water
Phosphorsalzperle *f* [sodium] phosphate bead, microcosmic [salt] bead
Phosphorsäure *f* phosphoric acid, *(specif)* H_3PO_4 orthophosphoric acid, phosphoric acid
~/auf trockenem Wege hergestellte *s.* ~/thermische
~ aus Naßaufschluß (dem Naßverfahren) wet-process phosphoric acid, green acid

~/glasige *s.* Metaphosphorsäure
~/thermische (thermisch erzeugte) electric-furnace phosphoric acid, furnace acid
Phosphorsäurepolymerisationsverfahren *n* phosphoric-acid polymerization process
Phosphorsäuretriamid *n s.* Phosphoryltriamid
Phosphorsäuretricresylester *m* tritolyl phosphate, tricresyl phosphate, TCP
Phosphorsäuretriethylester *m* triethyl phosphate
Phosphorsäuretriphenylester *m* triphenyl phosphate
Phosphorsäureverfahren *n* phosphoric-acid process *(catalytic polymerization)*
Phosphorstickstoff *m s.* Phosphornitrid
Phosphorstoffwechsel *m (bioch)* phosphorus metabolism
Phosphor(III)-sulfid *n* phosphorus(III) sulphide, diphosphorus trisulphide
Phosphor(V)-sulfid *n* phosphorus(V) sulphide, diphosphorus pentasulphide
Phosphor(V)-tetrabromidtrichlorid *n* phosphorus tetrabromide trichloride
Phosphortetroxid *n* phosphorus tetraoxide, diphosphorus tetraoxide
Phosphor(III)-thiocyanat *n* phosphorus(III) thiocyanate, phosphorus(III) rhodanide
Phosphortri... *s.* Phosphor(III)-...
Phosphorwasserstoff *m* phosphorus hydride, phosphane
Phosphorylbromid *n* phosphoryl bromide, phosphorus tribromide oxide
Phosphorylchlorid *n* phosphoryl chloride, phosphorus trichloride oxide
Phosphorylfluorid *n* phosphoryl fluoride, phosphorus trifluoride oxide
Phosphorylgruppe *f* ≡PO phosphoryl group
Phosphorylid *n* phosphorus ylide, phosphonium ylide, Wittig reagent
phosphorylieren *(bioch)* to phosphorylate
phosphorylierend *(bioch)* phosphorylative
Phosphorylierung *f* phosphorylation
~/oxidative *(bioch)* oxidative (respiratory-chain) phosphorylation
Phosphorylierungsmittel *n (bioch)* phosphorylating agent
Phosphoryltriamid *n* phosphoryl triamide, phosphoric triamide
Phosphosphingolipid *n (bioch)* phosphosphingolipid, sphingophospholipid
Photo... *s. a.* Foto...
Photoaddition *f* photoaddition
photoaktiv photoactive
Photoaktivierung *f* photoactivation
Photoaktivität *f* photoactivity
Photoakustikspektroskopie *f* photoacoustic (optoacoustic) spectroscopy, PAS
Photoakustikspektrum *n* photoacoustic spectrum
Photobromierung *f* photochemical bromination, photobromination
Photochemie *f* photochemistry
photochemisch photochemical
Photochlorierung *f* photochemical chlorination, photochlorination
photochrom[atisch] photochromic, phototropic *(reversibly changing colour when exposed to radiant energy)*
Photochromie *f* photochromism, phototropism
Photodiode *f* photodiode
Photodissoziation *f* photodissociation
Photoeffekt *m* photoelectric effect
photoelektrisch photoelectric
Photoelektrizität *f* photoelectricity
Photoelektron *n* photoelectron
Photoelektronenspektroskopie *f* photoelectron spectroscopy
~ innerer Elektronen photoelectron spectroscopy of inner-shell electrons
~/röntgenstrahlangeregte X-ray[-induced] photo electron spectroscopy, XPS, electron spectroscopy for chemical analysis, ESCA
Photoelektronenvervielfacher *m* photomultiplier [tube], PMT, multiplier phototube, secondary-emission electron multiplier
Photoelement *n* photovoltaic cell, photochemical (photobarrier, photoelectrolytic, barrier-layer) cell
Photoeliminierung *f* photoelimination
Photoemission *f* photoemission
Photoemissionszelle *f* photoelectric cell, photocell, phototube, photovalve
Photo-Fries-Umlagerung *f* photo-Fries rearrangement *(of esters)*
Photogravüre *f* photogravure
Photohalogenid *n* photohalide
Photoinaktivierung *f* photoinactivation
Photoinitiierung *f* photoinitiation *(as of polymerization)*
Photoionisation *f* photoionization
Photoionisationsdetektor *m* photoionization detector, PID
Photoionisierung *f* photoionization
Photokatalysator *m* photocatalyst
Photokatalyse *f* photocatalysis
photokatalysiert light-catalysed
photokatalytisch photocatalytic
Photokatode *f* photocathode
Photoleitfähigkeit *f* photoconductivity
Photoleitungseffekt *m* photoconductive effect
Photolumineszenz *f* photoluminescence
Photolyse *f* photolysis, photodecomposition, photodegradation • **durch ~ zerlegbar** photolysable
~ von Ozon ozone photolysis
Photolyseblitz *m* photolysis flash, photoflash *(kinetics)*
photolytisch photolytic
Photometer *n* photometer
Photometerbank *f* photometer bench, bench photometer
Photometerkopf *m* photometer head

Photometrie *f* photometry
~/lichtelektrische (objektive) photoelectric photometry
photometrisch photometric
Photon *n* photon
~/virtuelles virtual photon
Photonenflußdichte *f* photon flux density
Photonenzählung *f (spectr)* [single] photon counting
Photoneutron *n* photoneutron
photoorganotroph *(bioch)* photoorganotrophic
Photooxidation *f* photooxidation
Photooxygenierung *f* photooxygenation
Photophorese *f* photophoresis
photophosphorylieren to photophosphorylate
Photophosphorylierung *f* photosynthetic phosphorylation, photophosphorylation
Photopolymer[e] *n* photopolymer
Photopolymerisation *f* photopolymerization
Photoproton *n* photoproton
Photoreaktion *f* photochemical reaction, photoreaction
~/adiabatische adiabatic photoreaction
~/diabatische (nichtadiabatische) diabatic (nonadiabatic) photoreaction
Photoreaktivierung *f (biot)* photoreactivation
Photoreaktor *m* photochemical reactor
Photoresist *m* photoresist *(photolithography)*
Photosekundärelektronenvervielfacher *m s.* Photoelektronenvervielfacher
photosensibel photosensitive
Photosensibilisation *f* photosensitization
Photosensibilisator *m* photosensitizer
photosensibilisieren to photosensitize
Photosensibilisierung *f* photosensitization
Photosensibilität *f* photosensitivity
photosensitiv photosensitive
Photostrom *m* photocurrent
Photosubstitution *f* photosubstitution
Photosynthese *f* photosynthesis
Photosynthesezyklus *m (bioch)* Calvin[-Bassham] cycle, ribulose diphosphate cycle *(of CO_2 assimilation)*
photosynthetisch photosynthetic
Photosystem *n (bot, bioch)* photosystem
phototrop *s.* photochrom[atisch]
phototroph *(bioch)* phototrophic
Phototropie *f s.* Photochromie
Photovervielfacher *m s.* Photoelektronenvervielfacher
Photo-Volta-Effekt *m*, **Photovolteffekt** *m* photovoltaic effect
Photowiderstand *m*, **Photowiderstandszelle** *f* photoresistor, photoconductive cell
Photozelle *f* photoelectric cell, photocell, phototube, photovalve
Photozersetzung *f* photodecomposition, photolysis
***p*H-Papier** *n p*H paper
***p*H-Regelgerät** *n p*H controller
***p*H-Regelsystem** *n p*H-control system
***p*H-Regelung** *f p*H control
***p*H-Regler** *m* 1. *p*H controller *(apparatus)*; 2. *p*H regulator *(floatation agent)*
***p*H-Skala** *f p*H scale
***p*H-Standard** *m p*H standard
***o*-Phthalaldehyd** *m o*-phthalic aldehyde, OPA, phthalaldehyde
Phthalamid *n* phthalamide, phthalic acid diamide
Phthalamidsäure *f* phthalamic acid, phthalic acid monoamide
Phthalaminsäure *f s.* Phthalamidsäure
Phthalat *n* phthalate
Phthalatweichmacher *m* phthalate plasticizer
Phthalazin *n* phthalazine
***o*-Phthaldialdehyd** *m s. o*-Phthalaldehyd
Phthalein *n* phthalein
Phthalid *n* phthalide
Phthalimid *n* phthalimide
Phthalocyaninfarbstoff *m* phthalocyanine dye
Phthalocyaninpigment *n* phthalocyanine pigment
Phthalocyaninreihe *f* phthalocyanine series
Phthalodinitril *n* phthalonitrile, phthalic acid dinitrile
Phthalogenbrillantblau *n (dye)* phthalogen brilliant blue
Phthalomonopersäure *f s.* Monoperoxyphthalsäure
Phthalophenon *n* phthalophenon
Phthaloylchlorid *n* phthaloyl chloride
Phthalsäure *f* phthalic acid, *(specif) o*-phthalic acid
***m*-Phthalsäure** *f m*-phthalic acid, isophthalic acid, benzene-*m*-dicarboxylic acid
***o*-Phthalsäure** *f* o-phthalic acid, phthalic acid *(proper)*, benzene-*o*-dicarboxylic acid
***p*-Phthalsäure** *f p*-phthalic acid, terephthalic acid, benzene-*p*-dicarboxylic acid
Phthalsäureanhydrid *n* phthalic anhydride, PA
Phthalsäurediamid *n s.* Phthalamid
Phthalsäurediethylester *m* diethyl phthalate, D.E.P.
Phthalsäuredimethylester *m* dimethyl phthalate, D.M.P.
Phthalsäuredinitril *n s.* Phthalodinitril
Phthalsäure-di-*n*-octylester *m* dioctyl phthalate
Phthalsäureimid *n s.* Phthalimid
Phthalsäuremonoamid *n s.* Phthalamidsäure
Phthiokol *n* phthiocol, 2-hydroxy-3-methyl-1,4-naphthoquinone
***p*H-unabhängig** *p*H-independent, independent of *p*H
***p*H-Unabhängigkeit** *f p*H independence
***p*H-Wert** *m p*H value (number, level), hydrogen ion exponent • **von gleichem ~** isohydric
***p*H-Wert-abhängig** *p*H-dependent, depending (dependent) on *p*H
***p*H-Wert-Abhängigkeit** *f p*H dependence
***p*H-Wert-Bestimmung** *f p*H determination
***p*H-Wert-Heraufsetzung** *f p*H elevation

***p*H-Wert-Korrektur** *f* adjustment of the *p*H value, adjustment of *p*H, *p*H correction
***p*H-Wert-Messer** *m*, ***p*H-Wert-Meßgerät** *n* *p*H meter (instrument)
***p*H-Wert-Meßsystem** *n* *p*H-measuring system
***p*H-Wert-Messung** *f* *p*H measurement
***p*H-Wert-Regelsystem** *n* *p*H-control system
***p*H-Wert-Regelung** *f* *p*H control
***p*H-Wert-Regler** *m s.* *p*H-Regler
***p*H-Wert-unabhängig** *p*H-independent, independent of *p*H
***p*H-Wert-Unabhängigkeit** *f* *p*H independence
Phycocyan *n* phycocyan[in] *(a protein pigment of the blue-green algae)*
Phycokolloid *n* phycocolloid *(a polysaccharide of brown and red algae)*
Phyllochinon *n* phylloquinone, coagulation (antihaemorrhagic) vitamin
Phyllosilicat *n (min)* phyllosilicate, sheet silicate *(any of a class of polymeric silicates)*
Physetölsäure *f s.* Zoomarinsäure
Physik f/chemische chemical physics
physikalisch-chemisch physicochemical, physical-chemical
Physikochemiker *m* physical chemist
physikochemisch *s.* physikalisch-chemisch
physiologisch physiologic[al]
Physisorption *f* physisorption, physical (van der Waals) adsorption
Phyteral *n* phyteral *(a vegetable structural element of coal)*
Phytinsäure *f* phytic acid
Phytochemie *f* phytochemistry
phytogen phytogenic, of plant origin, plant-produced
Phytohormon *n* phytohormone, plant hormone
Phytosterin *n*, **Phytosterol** *n* phytosterol, plant sterol
phytotoxisch phytotoxic
Phytotoxizität *f* phytotoxicity
***p*H-Zahl** *f* *p*H-Wert
Piazin *n s.* Pyrazin
PIB *s.* Polyisobuten
Pi-Bindung *f* pi bond, π bond
Picein *n* picein, piceoside, *p*-hydroxyacetophenone-β-glucoside
Picen *n* picene, 1,2,7,8-dibenzphenanthrene
pichen to pitch
Pickel *m* 1. *(tann)* pickle [liquor, solution], pickling solution; 2. *(plast)* pimple *(a moulding defect)*
pickeln *(tann)* to pickle, to sour
Pick-up-Walze *f (pap)* pickup roll
Picogrammbereich *m (anal)* picogram range *(10^{-12} to 10^{-9} g)*
Picolinsäure *f* picolinic acid, pyridine-2-carboxylic acid
Picomenge *f*, **Picospur** *f (anal)* picotrace *(* 10^{-10} to 10^{-13} ppm)*
PICS-Methode *f (chromat)* pulse-induced critical scattering method
Pictet-Gams-Reaktion *f*, **Pictet-Gams-Synthese** *f* Pictet-Gams synthesis (reaction) *(of isoquinolines)*
Pidgeon-Verfahren *n* Pidgeon [vacuum] process *(for producing metallic magnesium)*
Piezochemie *f* piezochemistry
Piezochromie *f* piezochromism
Piezodruckmesser *m* piezometer
Piezoeffekt *m* piezo[electric] effect
piezoelektrisch piezoelectric
Piezoelektrizität *f* piezoelectricity
Piezokristall *m* piezoelectric crystal
Piezokristallisation *f* piezocrystallization
Piezometer *n* piezometer
Pigment *n* pigment
~/geflushtes flushed pigment, *(Am also)* flushed color
~/künstliches anorganisches synthetic inorganic pigment
~/metallisches metal[lic] pigment
~/mikronisiertes micronized pigment
~/natürliches natural pigment
~/natürliches anorganisches earth (mineral) pigment
~/respiratorisches *(bioch)* respiratory pigment
Pigmentanreibung *f* pigment grinding
Pigmentation *f* pigmentation
Pigment-Bindemittel-Verhältnis *n* pigment-binder ratio
Pigmentdispergierung *f*, **Pigmentdispersion** *f* pigment dispersion
Pigmentdruck *m* pigment printing
Pigmentfarbstoff *m* pigment [dyestuff, dye], *(Am also)* pigment color; pigment colour *(for artists)*; *(biol)* pigment
pigmentieren to pigment
Pigmentklotzung *f (text)* pigment padding
Pigmentkollektiv *n (bioch)* pigment assembly, photosynthetic unit
Pigmentrot *n* pigment (para) red, paranitraniline red
Pigmentvolumenkonzentration *f* pigment volume concentration, p.v.c., PVC
Pigmentwanderung *f* pigment migration
Pik *m s.* Peak
pikant brisk
Pikraminsäure *f* picramic acid, 2-amino-4,6-dinitrophenol
Pikrat *n* picrate
Pikrinsäure *f* picric acid, 2,4,6-trinitrophenol
Pile *m* pile, [nuclear] reactor
Pile *f* [amalgam] decomposer *(electrolysis)*
Pilinußöl *n* pili nut oil *(from Canarium specc.)*
Pilkington-Verfahren *n* Pilkington process *(plate-glass manufacture)*
Pille *f* pellet *(as of a catalyst)*; *(pharm)* pill
pillieren to pill
Pilocarpinnitrat *n* pilocarpine nitrate

Pilotanlage *f* pilot plant, semiworks
Pilzamylase *f* fungal amylase
Pilzdecke *f (biot)* mycelium layer
Pilzdiastase *f s.* Pilzamylase
Pilze *mpl***/technisch wichtige** *(biot)* industrial fungi
Pilzenzym *n* fungal enzyme
Pilzfarbstoff *m* fungus (fungal) pigment
Pilzfermentation *f (biot)* fungal fermentation
pilzfest fungus-proof
pilzlich fungal
Pilzlipase *f (biot)* fungal lipase
Pilzmaischverfahren *n* amylo fermentation process *(use of fungal amylases for fermenting starchy materials)*
Pilzmyzel *n (biot)* fungal mycelium
Pilzprotease *f (biot)* fungal protease
Pilzstamm *m (biot)* fungal strain
pilztötend fungicidal
Pilzventil *n* mushroom-seated valve
pilzwidrig, pilzwirksam antifungal
Pilzzüchtung *f (biot)* cultivation of fungi
(+)-Pimarsäure *f* (+)-pimaric acid, dextropimaric acid
(–)-Pimarsäure *f* (–)-pimaric acid, laevopimaric acid, *(proposed name:)* (–)-sapietic acid
Pimelinsäure *f* pimelic acid, heptanedioic acid
Piment *n* allspice *(from Pimenta dioica (L.) Merr.)*
Pinakoid *n (cryst)* pinacoid
pinakoidal *(cryst)* pinacoidal
Pinakol *n* pinacol, *2,3-dimethylbutane-2,3-diol
Pinakolin *n s.* Pinakolon
Pinakolinumlagerung *f s.* Pinakol-Pinakolon-Umlagerung
Pinakolon *n* pinacolone, *3,3-dimethylbutan-2-one, 1,1,1-trimethylacetone
Pinakol-Pinakolon-Umlagerung *f* pinacol rearrangement
Pinakon *n s.* Pinakol
Pinakryptolgelb *n* pinacryptol yellow *(an isocyanine)*
Pinakryptolgrün *n* pinacryptol green *(an isocyanine)*
Pincheffekt *m (phys ch)* pinch effect
Pinen *n* pinene *(a bicyclic monoterpene)*
Pineyharz *n* piney resin, piney (white) damar, Indium copal *(from Vateria indica L.)*
Pineytalg *m* piney tallow, Dhupa fat *(from Vateria indica L.)*
Ping-pong-Mechanismus *m* ping-pong mechanism *(enzyme kinetics)*
Ping-pong-Reaktion *f* ping-pong reaction, double displacement reaction
Pinit *m* 1. *(min)* pinite *(any of several pseudomorphs of mica-like minerals)*; 2. *s.* Pinitol
Pinitol *n* pinitol, inositol 3-monomethyl ether
Pinksalz *n* pink salt, ammonium hexachlorostannate(IV)
Pinne *f (ceram)* pin
Pinolin *n* pinolin[e], pinolene, rosin (resin) spirit
Pinonen *n* pinonene, (–)-4-carene, *3,7,7-trimethylbicyclo[2,2,1]hept-2-ene
Pintsch-Gas *n* Pintsch gas *(an oil gas)*
Pinzette *f* pincers, tweezers
Pion *n (nucl)* pion, pi meson, π-meson *(an elementary particle)*
Pipecolinsäure *f* pipecolic acid, piperidine-2-carboxylic acid
Pipeline *f* **für Fertigerzeugnisse** *(petrol)* refined-product pipeline
Pipeline-Gas *n* pipeline [quality] gas
Piperazin *n (org ch)* piperazine
Piperidin *n* piperidine
Piperidinalkaloid *n* piperidine alkaloid
Piperinsäure *f* piperic acid, *5-(3,4-methylenedioxyphenyl)penta-2,4-dienoic acid
Piperonal *n* piperonal, 3,4-methylenedioxybenzaldehyde
Piperonylsäure *f* piperonylic acid, 3,4-methylenedioxybenzoic acid
Piperylen *n* piperylene, *penta-1,3-diene
Pipestill-Anlage *f (petrol)* pipe-still plant (unit), pipe (tube) still
Pipette *f* pipette, *(if small also)* dropper
~ **mit Farbmarkierung** colour-code pipette
Pipettenbürste *f* pipette brush
Pipettenetagere *f*, **Pipettengestell** *n s.* Pipettenständer
Pipettenhütchen *n* dropper teat
Pipettenspitze *f* pipette tip
Pipettenständer *m* pipette rack (stand, support)
pipettieren to pipette
Pipettmethode *f* pipetting method
Pipitzahoinsäure *f* pipitzahoic acid, perezone *(a benzoquinone derivative)*
Pirani-Manometer *n*, **Pirani-Vakuummeter** *n* Pirani gauge
Pisolith *m (min)* pisolite *(calcium carbonate)*
Pistill *n (lab)* pestle
Pitot-Rohr *n* Pitot tube *(for measuring the velocity of a flowing medium)*
Pittsburgh-Verfahren *n* Pittsburgh [sheet] process, Pennvernon process *(for the vertical drawing of sheet glass)*
Pitzer-Spannung *f* torsional strain *(in molecules)*
Piuri *n (dye)* piuri, Indian yellow *(from Mangifera indica L.)*
Pivalaldehyd *m* pivalic aldehyde, pivalaldehyde, 2,2-dimethylpropanal
Pivalinsäure *f* pivalic acid, *2,2-dimethylpropanoic acid
Pi-Yu *n s.* Chinatalg
PK *s.* Polycarbonatfaserstoff
Plachenherd *m*, **Plachentisch** *m (min tech)* vanner
Placierung *f* placement *(of fertilizers or pesticides)*
Plagioklas *m (min)* plagioclase, sodium-calcium feldspar *(any of a series of tectosilicates)*
Plakatfarbe *f* poster paint (colour)
Plakatpapier *n* poster paper

Planck-Konstante *f* Planck (action) constant, [Planck] quantum of action

Planetenrührapparat *m* planetary-type mixer

Planfilm *m (phot)* sheet film

Planfilter *n* table filter

Plangitter *n* plane grating *(of a grating spectrograph)*

Plangitterspektrograph *m s.* Gitterspektrograph

planieren to level

Planierstange *f* levelling (coal leveller) bar *(in a coke chamber)*

Planiervorrichtung *f* levelling device

Planknotenfänger *m (pap)* flat strainer (screen)

Planlager *n* plane bearing *(of a balance)*

Planrätter *m* gyratory riddle

Planschleifen *n (ceram, glass)* planar grinding

Planschliffverbindung *f* plane (flat-flange) joint

Planschwingsiebmaschine *f* oscillating (flat) screen *(oscillating parallel to the screen)*; gyratory (gyrating) screen, gyratory sifter *(having a series of screens)*

Plansichter *m*, **Plansieb** *n*, **Plansortierer** *m s.* Planschwingsiebmaschine

Plantagenkautschuk *m* plantation (estate) rubber

Plantagenlatex *m* plantation latex

Plasma *n* 1. *(phys ch)* plasma; 2. *(biol)* plasma; 3. *(min)* plasma *(variety of chalcedony)*

~/durch Gleichstrombogen erzeugtes direct-current plasma, DCP

~/induktiv gekoppeltes inductively coupled plasma, ICP

~/mikrowelleninduziertes microwave-induced plasma, MIP

Plasmaätzen *n* plasma etching

Plasmabrenner *m* plasma burner

Plasmachemie *f* plasma chemistry

~/nichtthermische non-thermal plasma chemistry

~/thermische thermal plasma chemistry

Plasmaexpander *m (biot, med)* blood plasma extender

Plasmalipoprotein *n* plasma lipoprotein

Plasmalogen *n* plasmalogen *(any of a group of glycerophospholipids)*

Plasmapolymerisation *f* plasma polymerization

Plasmaprotein *n* plasma protein

Plasmazustand *m (phys ch)* plasma state

Plasmid *n (biot)* plasmid

Plast *n* plastic [material] *(for compounds s.* Kunststoff*)*

Plastifikation *f (plast, rubber)* plasticization

Plastifikationsmittel *n*, **Plastifikator** *m s.* Plastifiziermittel

Plastifiziermittel *n (plast, rubber)* plasticizer, plasticizing agent

plastifizieren *(plast, rubber)* to plasticize

Plastigel *n* plastigel

Plastik *n* plastic [material] *(for compunds s.* Kunststoff*)*

Plastikator *m* 1. plasticator *(a machine for plasticizing rubber or plastics)*; 2. *s.* Plastifiziermittel

plastisch plastic

Plastisol *n* plastisol

plastizieren *(plast, rubber)* to plasticize, to plasticate, to plastify, to soften, *(rubber also)* to break down

~/mit Peptisiermitteln to peptize

~/thermisch to heat-soften

Plastizierleistung *f* plasticizing capacity

Plastiziermaschine *f* plasticator

Plastizierung *f (plast, rubber)* plasticization, plasti[fi]cation, softening, *(rubber also)* breakdown

~/chemische chemical plasticization

~/mechanische *(rubber)* mechanical (mill) breakdown

~ mit Peptisiermitteln peptization

~/thermische thermal plasticization, thermal (heat) softening

Plastizierungsmittel *n* plasticizer, plasticizing agent

~/chemisches chemical plasticizer, *(rubber also)* peptizer, peptizing agent

Plastizität *f* plasticity

Plastizitätsbereich *m* plastic range

Plastizitätsmessung *f* plasticity measurement

Plastizitätsprüfgerät *n s.* Plastometer

Plastizitätsprüfung *f* plasticity test

Plastizitätswasser *n (ceram)* water of plasticity

Plastochinon *n (bioch)* plastoquinone

Plastograph *m* plastograph *(for determining plasticity)*

Plastographie *f* resinography *(science of resins, high polymers, and their products)*

Plastomer[e] *n* plastomer

Plastometer *n* plastometer, plastimeter

~/Gieselersches Gieseler plastometer

~ von Williams Williams plastometer

Plateau *n (rubber)* cure plateau • **mit breitem ~** flat-curing *(having a wide optimum range of vulcanization)* • **mit kurzem ~** peaky[-curing] *(having a narrow optimum range of vulcanization)*

Plateaueffekt *m (rubber)* plateau (flat-curing) effect

Platformat *n (petrol)* platformate

Platformer *m s.* Platforming-Anlage

Platformerprodukt *n s.* Platformat

Platformieren *n (petrol)* platforming, platinum reforming

Platforming-Anlage *f (petrol)* platforming unit, platformer

Platforming-Produkt *n s.* Platformat

Platforming-Verfahren *n (petrol)* platforming process

Platiak *n* platinum ammine, platinammine

Platin *n* Pt platinum

Platinasbest *m* platinized asbestos

Platin(II)-chlorid *n* platinum(II) chloride, platinum dichloride

Platin(III)-chlorid *n* platinum(III) chloride, platinum trichloride

Platin(IV)-chlorid *n* platinum(IV) chloride, platinum tetrachloride

Platinchlorwasserstoffsäure *f s.* Hexachloroplatin(IV)-säure
Platin(II)-cyanid *n* platinum(II) cyanide
Platindichlorid *n s.* Platin(II)-chlorid
Platindioxid *n s.* Platin(IV)-oxid
Platindiphosphat *n* platinum diphosphate, platinum pyrophosphate
Platindisulfid *n s.* Platin(IV)-sulfid
Platindraht *m* platinum wire
Platindruck *m* platinotype *(reprography)*
Platinelektrode *f* platinum electrode
~/platinierte *(el ch)* platinized platinum electrode
platinhaltig platinum-bearing, platiniferous
platinieren to platinize, to platinate
Platinieren *n* platinizing, platinization, *(el ch also)* platinum plating
platiniert platinized, platinated, platinum-coated
Platinkatalysator *m*, **Platinkontakt** *m* platinum catalyst
Platinmohr *n* platinum black, platina mohr
Platinmonosulfid *n s.* Platin(II)-sulfid
Platinmonoxid *n s.* Platin(II)-oxid
Platin(II)-oxid *n* platinum(II) oxide, platinum monoxide
Platin(IV)-oxid *n* platinum(IV) oxide, platinum dioxide
Platin(VI)-oxid *n* platinum(VI) oxide, platinum trioxide
Platinpapier *n (phot)* platinotype paper
Platinpyrophosphat *n s.* Platindiphosphat
Platinschale *f* platinum dish
Platinschiffchen *n* platinum boat
Platinschwamm *m* platinum sponge, spongy platinum
Platinschwarz *n s.* Platinmohr
Platinsol *n* platinum sol
Platin(IV)-sulfat *n* platinum(IV) sulphate
Platin(II)-sulfid *n* platinum(II) sulphide, platinum monosulphide
Platin(III)-sulfid *n* platinum(III) sulphide, platinum trisulphide, diplatinum trisulphide
Platin(IV)-sulfid *n* platinum(IV) sulphide, platinum disulphide
Platintetrachlorid *n s.* Platin(IV)-chlorid
Platintiegel *m* platinum crucible
Platintonung *f (phot)* platinum toning
Platintrichlorid *n s.* Platin(III)-chlorid
Platintrioxid *n s.* Platin(VI)-oxid
Platinwiderstandsthermometer *n* platinum resistance thermometer
Platte *f* plate, *(if thick:)* slab, *(if thin:)* sheet; tile *(as of fired clay or concrete)*; board *(as of wood pulp)*; *(filtr)* disk; *(rubber)* sheet, slab
~/amalgamierte amalgamated plate
~/bewegliche *(plast)* floating plate *(of a press)*
~/fotografische photographic plate
~/stranggepreßte *(plast)* extruded sheet
~/xerographische xerographic plate
Plattenabscheider *m* 1. plate precipitator *(gas cleaning)*; 2. *(hyd)* lamellar separator
Plattenabsetzanlage *f (hyd)* lamellar settler
Plattenbandförderer *m* apron conveyor
Plattenelektroabscheider *m*, **Plattenelektrofilter** *n* plate precipitator *(gas cleaning)*
Plattenerhitzer *m (food)* plate pasteurizer
Plattenfilter *n* plate filter
Plattenförderer *m* apron conveyor
plattenförmig plate-like; *(cryst)* lamellar, flat
Plattenformung *f (plast)* sheet forming
Plattengel *n* [horizontal] slab gel *(electrophoresis)*
Plattengrenzschicht *f* laminar boundary layer
Plattenpresse *f* platen press
Plattenschieber *m* parallel-seat gate valve
Plattensedimentation *f (hyd)* lamella sedimentation
Plattentrockner *m* shelf dryer
Plattenwärmeaustauscher *m* plate-type [heat] exchanger, parallel-plate heat exchanger
~/berippter plate-fin heat exchanger
Plattenwärmeübertrager *m s.* Plattenwärmeaustauscher
Plattenziehen *n (rubber)* sheet calendering, sheeting[-out]
plattieren to plate *(metal)*, *(by bonding or welding:)* to clad; *(tann)* to strike (set) out; *(text)* to plate
Plattierungswerkstoff *m* plating (cladding) material
plattstengelig *(cryst)* bladed
Platzbedarf *m* land (space) requirements *(of an industrial plant)*
Plätzchen *n* pellet *(as of potassium hydroxide)*
platzen to burst, to break, to explode *(by the force of internal pressure)*; to crack *(as of a glass plate)*
Platzscheibe *f* bursting (rupture) disk
Plauson-Mühle *f* Plauson [colloid] mill
Plazebo *n (med)* placebo *(pharmacologically inactive substance)*
Plazentagonadotropin *n* human chorionic gonadotropin, hCG
Plazentalactogen *n (bioch)* human lactogen
PLB-Teilchen *n (chromat)* porous layer bead, PLB
p-leitend p-type [semi]conducting, defect [semi-]conducting
Pleochroismus *m (cryst)* pleochro[mat]ism, polychroism
pleochroitisch *(cryst)* pleochro[mat]ic, polychroic
Pleonast *m (min)* pleonaste, ceylonite, ceylanite *(a spinel containing divalent iron)*
pl-Phase *f (coll)* nematic phase
Plumban *n* plumbane, lead hydride
Plumbat *n* $M^{I}_{2}Pb(OH)_{6}$ *or* $M^{I}_{4}PbO_{4}$ plumbate
Plumbitverfahren *n (petrol)* plumbite [sweetening] process
Plunger *m* plunger; *(glass)* plunger, needle *(of a feeder)*
Plungerkolben *m* plunger
Plungerpumpe *f* plunger (ram) pump
Plüschpapier *n* velour (flock) paper
Plusplatte *f (el ch)* positive plate

plus-Stamm *m (biot)* (+) strain
Plutonium *n* Pu plutonium
PMA, PMAS *s.* Phenylquecksilberacetat
PMMA *s.* Polymethylmethacrylat
PMP *s.* Poly-4-methylpent-1-en
Pneumatikreifen *m* pneumatic [tyre]
Pneumatikventil *n* pneumatic (air) valve
pneumatisch pneumatic
pn-Übergang *m* p-n junction *(in semiconductors)*
PO *s.* 1. Polyolefin; 2. Polyolefinfaserstoff
Pochwerk *n (min tech)* stamp battery, stamp[ing] mill
Podbielniak-Extraktor *m,* **Podbielniak-Kontaktor** *m s.* Podbielniak-Zentrifugalextraktor
Podbielniak-Zentrifugalextraktor *m,* **Podbielniak-Zentrifuge** *f* Podbielniak [centrifugal] extractor, Podbielniak [centrifugal] contactor
Podocarpren *n* podocarprene *(a diterpene)*
Podsol[boden] *m* podzol [soil], podsol [soil], podzolic soil
Podsolierung *f (soil)* podzolization
pO_2-Elektrode *f (biot)* pO_2 electrode
Poiseuille-Gesetz *n s.* Hagen-Poiseuille-Strömungsgesetz
Poisson-Verteilung *f* Poisson distribution
Pökelfaß *n (food)* curing vat
Pökelfleisch *n* cured meat
Pökelflüssigkeit *f,* **Pökellake** *f (food)* curing (pickling) solution, curing pickle, pickle [liquor, solution], souse
pökeln *(food)* to cure
Pökeln *n (food)* curing, cure
Pökelsalzlösung *f s.* Pökelflüssigkeit
polar polar
Polarimeter *n* polarimeter, polariscope
Polarimetrie *f* polarimetry
Polarisation *f* polarization
~ des Lichts light polarization
~ des Vakuums vacuum polarization
~/dielektrische dielectric polarization
~/elektrolytische electrolytic polarization
~/elliptische elliptical polarization
~/galvanische electrolytic polarization
~/lineare linear (plane) polarization
~/zirkulare circular polarization
Polarisationsebene *f* polarization plane
Polarisationseffekt *m* polarization (polarizing) effect
Polarisationsellipsoid *n* polarization ellipsoid
Polarisationsgrad *m* degree of polarization
Polarisationsmikroskop *n* polarizing microscope
Polarisationsrohr *n* sample tube *(of a polarimeter)*
Polarisationssättigung *f* polarization saturation
Polarisationsspannung *f* polarization voltage (potential)
Polarisationsstrom *m* polarization (polarizing) current
Polarisationsstromtitration *f* dead-stop titration
Polarisationswiderstand *m* polarization resistance
Polarisationswinkel *m* angle of polarization, polarizing (Brewster) angle
Polarisationswirkung *f s.* Polarisationseffekt
Polarisator *m* polarizer
polarisierbar polarizable
Polarisierbarkeit *f* polarizability
~ des Moleküls molecular polarizability
~/mittlere mean polarizability
~/molekulare *s.* ~ des Moleküls
Polarisierbarkeitsellipsoid *n* polarization ellipsoid
polarisieren to polarize
polarisiert/elliptisch elliptically polarized
~/linear linearly polarized, plane-polarized
~/linkszirkular left-circularly polarized, left-hand circularly polarized
~/rechtszirkular right-circularly polarized, right-hand circularly polarized
~/zirkular circularly polarized
Polarisierung *f* polarization
Polarität *f* polarity
Polarogramm *n* polarogram
Polarograph *m* polarograph
Polarographie *f* polarography
~ mit Wechselstrom/oszillographische multisweep polarography
~/oszillographische oscillographic polarography
~/semiintegrale semiintegral polarography
polarographisch polarographic
Poleiöl *n* European pennyroyal oil *(essential oil from Mentha pulegium L.)*
polen *(met)* to pole
~/zu weit to overpole
Polenske-Zahl *f* Polenske number (value) *(indicating the content of volatile water-insoluble acids in fat)*
Polgewebe *n (text)* polo fabric
Polierblech *n* polishing plate
polieren to polish
~/elektrolytisch to electropolish
Polierfilter *n* polishing (clarifying) filter
Polierfiltration *f* polishing [filtration], clarification
polierfiltrieren to polish
Poliergold *n (ceram)* burnish[ed] gold, best gold
Poliermasse *f* polishing compound
Poliermittel *n* polishing agent (material)
Polieröl *n* polishing oil
Polierpech *n* polishing pitch
Polierrot *n* polishing rouge *(iron(III) oxide)*
Polierstein *m,* **Poliertisch** *m (glass)* polisher block
Politur *f* 1. polish[ing agent]; 2. lustre, gloss, polish
Polizeikampfmittel *n* riot control agent
Polonium *n* Po polonium
Polpapier *n* pole-finding paper, pole reagent paper, *(Am)* polarity paper
Polprüfer *m* polarity tester
Polreagenzpapier *n s.* Polpapier
Polstermischung *f (rubber)* cushion stock
Polyacetal *n s.* Polyoxymethylen
Polyacetylen *n* polyacetylene, *polyyne

Polyacrylamid *n* polyacrylamide
Polyacrylamidgel-Elektrophorese *f* polyacrylamide gel electrophoresis, PAGE
Polyacrylat *n s.* Polyacrylharz
Polyacrylat-Elastomer[e] *n* polyacrylate elastomer, acrylate (acrylic) elastomer
Polyacrylharz *n* polyacrylate, acrylate resin, acrylic[-acid] resin
Polyacrylnitril *n* polyacrylonitrile, PAN, *poly(1-cyanoethylene)
Polyacrylnitrilfaser *f* polyacrylonitrile (acrylic) fibre
Polyacrylnitrilfaserstoff *m* polyacrylonitrile (acrylic) fibre
Polyacrylsäure *f* polyacrylic acid
Polyacrylsäureamid *n* polyacrylamide
Polyacrylsäureester *m* polyacrylate
Polyaddition *f* polyaddition, addition polymerization
Polyaddukt *n* addition polymer
Polyadenylierung *f (bioch)* polyadenylation
Polyaffinität *f* polyaffinity
Polyaffinitätstheorie *f* polyaffinity theory
Polyalkohol *m* polyalcohol, polyol, polyfunctional (polyhydric, polyhydroxy) alcohol
Polyalkylenoxid *n* polyalkylene oxide, polyether
Polyalkylierung *f* polyalkylation
Polyalkylsiloxan *n* alkyl polysiloxane
Polyallomer[e] *n* polyallomer
Polyamid *n* polyamide, PA
Polyamidfaser *f* polyamide fibre
Polyamidfaserstoff *m* polyamide fibre
Polyampholyt *m* polyampholyte *(a polymer reacting with acids as well as with bases)*
Polyanion *n* polyanion
Polyarylether *m* polyaryl ether
Polyäther *m s.* Polyether
Polyäthylen *n s.* Polyethylen
polyatomar polyatomic
Polybenzimidazen *n*, **Polybenzimidazol** *n* polybenzimidazole, PBI
Polybenzothiazol *n* polybenzothiazole, PBT
Polyblend *n* polyblend, polymer blend *(a mixture of several thermoplastics)*
Polybrombiphenyl *n* polybrominated biphenyl, PBB
Polybutadien *n* polybutadiene, butadiene polymer, *poly(1-butenylene)
Polybuten *n*, **Polybutylen** *n* polybutylene, *polybutene
Polycaprolactam *n* polycaprolactam, poly(ε-caprolactam), *poly[imino(1-oxohexamethylene)]
Polycarbamid *n s.* Polyharnstoff
Polycarbodiimid *n* polycarbodiimide
Polycarbonat *n* polycarbonate, PC
Polycarbonatfaser *f* polycarbonate fibre
Polycarbonatfaserstoff *m* polycarbonate fibre
Polycarbonatharz *n* polycarbonate resin
Polycarbonsäure *f* polycarboxylic acid
Polychloräthan *n s.* Polychlorethan
Polychlorbiphenyl *n* polychlorinated biphenyl
Polychlorcamphen *n* toxaphene, technical chlorinated camphene *(insecticide)*
Polychlordibenzo-1,4-dioxin *n* polychlorinated dibenzo-1,4-dioxin, PCDD
Polychlorethan *n* polychloroethane
Polychloropren *n* polychloroprene, PCP
Polychlorstyren *n*, **Polychlorstyrol** *n* polychlorostyrene
Polychlortrifluorethen *n*, **Polychlortrifluorethylen** *n* polychlorotrifluoroethylene, PCTFE
Polychromasie *f* polychromasia *(of a radiation)*
polycistronisch *(bioch)* polycistronic
polycyclisch polycyclic
Polycyclisierung *f* polycyclization, polycyclocondensation
Polycyclochinon *n* polycyclic quinone
Polycyclokondensation *f s.* Polycyclisierung
Polycyclotrimerisierung *f* polycyclotrimerization
Polycyclus *m* polycyclic compound (ring system)
polydispers polydisperse
Polydispersität *f* polydispersity
Polyeder *n (cryst)* polyhedron
polyedrisch *(cryst)* polyhedral
Polyelektrolyt *m* polyelectrolyte
Polyen *n (org ch)* polyene
Polyen-Antibiotikum *n* polyene antibiotic
Polyen-Makrolid *n (bioch)* polyene macrolide
Polyepoxid *n* polyepoxide
Polyester *m* polyester
~/ungesättigter unsaturated polyester
Polyesterbildung *f* polyesterification
Polyesterfaser *f* polyester fibre
Polyesterfaserstoff *m* polyester fibre
Polyesterharz *n* polyester resin
Polyesterkautschuk *m* polyester rubber
Polyethen *n s.* Polyethylen
Polyether *m* polyether, polyalkylene oxide
Polyether-Antibiotikum *n* polyether antibiotic
Polyetherpolyol *n* polyether polyol, polyoxyalkylene glycol
Polyethylen *n* polyethylene, polythene, polyethene, PE
~/chlorsulfoniertes chlorosulphonated polyethylene
~ hoher Dichte high-density polyethylene, H.D. polythene
~ mittlerer Dichte medium-density polyethylene
~ niedriger Dichte low-density polyethylene, L.D. polythene
~/sulfochloriertes sulphochlorinated polyethylene
~/unverzweigtes unbranched polyethylene, linear (low-pressure) polyethylene
~/verzweigtes branched (high-pressure) polyethylene
Polyethylenadipat *n* polyethylene adipate
Polyethylenfaser *f* polyethylene fibre
Polyethylenfaserstoff *m* polyethylene fibre
Polyethylenglykol *n* polyethylene glycol, PEG
Polyethylenimin *n* polyethylene imine

Polyethylenoxid *n* polyethylene oxide, PEO, *poly(oxyethylene)
Polyethylenschaum[stoff] *m* polyethylene foam
Polyethylenterephthalat *n* polyethylene terephthalate, PETP, PET, *poly(oxyethyleneoxyterephthaloyl)
Polyformaldehyd *m s.* Polyoxymethylen
Polyformen *n (petrol)* polyforming
Polyform[ing]-Verfahren *n (petrol)* polyform[ing] process
polyfunktionell polyfunctional, multifunctional, multiple-function
Polygalacturonase *f* polygalacturonase
Polygalacturonsäure *f* polygalacturonic acid
Polyglycerin *n*, **Polyglycerol** *n* polyglycerol
Polyglykol *n* polyglycol
polygonal polygonal
Polyhalogenid *n* polyhalide, *polyhalogenide
Polyharnstoff *m* polyurea
Polyharnstoffaser *f* polyurea fibre
Polyharnstoffaserstoff *m* polyurea fibre
Polyhydrat *n* polyhydrate
Polyhydroxyaldehyd *m* polyhydroxy aldehyde
Polyhydroxyanthrachinon *n* polyhydroxyanthraquinone
Polyhydroxydicarbonsäure *f* polyhydroxy dicarboxylic acid
Polyhydroxyketon *n* polyhydroxy ketone
Polyhydroxysäure *f* polyhydroxy acid
Polyhydroxyverbindung *f* polyhydroxy compound
Polyimid *n* polyimide, PI
Polyimidazopyrrolon *n* polyimidazopyrrolone, pyrrone
Polyin *n (org ch)* polyyne, polyacetylene
Polyinsertion *f* insertion polymerization
Polyiodid *n* polyiodide
Polyion *n* polyion
Polyisobuten *n*, **Polyisobutylen** *n* polyisobutylene, PIB, *poly(1,1-dimethylethylene)
Polyisocyanat *n s.* Polyurethan
Polyisopren *n* polyisoprene, *poly(1-methyl-1-butenylene)
polyisotop polyisotopic
Polykation *n* polycation
Polyketid *n* polyketide, ketide, acetogenin
Polyketon *n* polyketone
Polykieselsäure *f* polysilicic acid
Polykondensat *n* polycondensate, condensation polymer
Polykondensation *f* polycondensation, condensation polymerization
~ **in der Schmelze** melt condensation
~ **in Lösung** solution polycondensation
Polykras *m* polycrase *(an oxidic rare-earth mineral)*
Polykristall *m* polycrystal
polykristallin polycrystalline
polymer polymeric
Polymer *n* polymer, *(tech also)* polymerizate
~/amorphes amorphous polymer
~/anorganisches inorganic polymer
~/ataktisches atactic polymer
~/eindimensionales linear polymer
~/einsträngiges single-strand polymer
~/elementarfadenbildendes *s.* ~/fadenbildendes
~/eutaktisches eutactic (stereoregular) polymer
~/fadenbildendes fibrous polymer
~/flüssiges *(rubber)* [polysulphide] liquid polymer
~/hochstyrenhaltiges (hochstyrolhaltiges) *(rubber)* high-styrene polymer (copolymer, resin), self-reinforced elastomer
~/isomeres isomeric polymer
~/isotaktisches isotactic polymer
~/langkettiges long-chain polymer
~/lebendes living polymer
~/lineares linear polymer
~/metallorganisches organometallic polymer
~/organisches organic polymer
~/räumlich vernetztes three-dimensional polymeric network
~/siliciumorganisches organosilicon polymer
~/stereoreguläres stereoregular (eutactic) polymer
~/stereospezifisches stereospecific polymer
~/sterisch regelmäßiges stereoregular (eutactic) polymer
~/syndiotaktisches syndiotactic polymer
~/totes dead polymer
~/vernetztes cross-linked polymer
~/verzweigtes branched polymer
Polymerbenzin *n* polymer gasoline
Polymerchemie *f* polymer chemistry
Polymerdosis *f (hyd)* flocculant dosage
polymereinheitlich polymer-homologous
Polymereinkristall *m* polymer single crystal
Polymere *n s.* Polymer
Polymerflockungsmittel *n (hyd)* polymer flocculant
polymerhomolog polymer-homologous
Polymerhomolog[e] *n* polymer homologue
Polymerisat *n* polymerizate, polymer *(for compounds s. under* Polymer*)*
Polymerisatbinder *m* polymer binder
Polymerisation *f* polymerization
~ **an Ort und Stelle** in situ polymerization
~/anionische anionic polymerization
~/cyclisierende cyclopolymerization
~/durch freie Radikale ausgelöste [free-]radical polymerization
~ **in der Gasphase** gas (gaseous) polymerization
~ **in einer Druckschnecke/kontinuierliche** continuous screw-feed process of polymerization
~ **in Emulsion** emulsion polymerization
~ **in Masse (Substanz)** bulk (mass) polymerization
~/ionische ionic polymerization
~/katalytische catalytic polymerization
~/kationische cationic polymerization
~/koordinative coordination polymerization
~/photoaktivierte photoinduced polymerization
~/radikalische [free-]radical polymerization

~/ringöffnende ring-opening (ring-scission) polymerization
~/stereoselektive stereoselective polymerization
~/stereospezifische stereospecific polymerization
~/strahlenchemische (strahleninduzierte) radiation[-induced] polymerization
~/thermische *(petrol)* thermal polymerization
Polymerisationsabstoppmittel *n (rubber, plast)* shortstopping agent, shortstop, stopper
Polymerisationsaktivator *m* activator of polymerization
Polymerisationsansatz *m* polymerization recipe
Polymerisationsbenzin *n* polymer gasoline
Polymerisationserreger *m* polymerization initiator
polymerisationsfähig polymerizable
Polymerisationsfähigkeit *f* polymerizability
Polymerisationsgerbung *f* polymerization (polymeric) tannage
Polymerisationsgeschwindigkeit *f* rate of polymerization
Polymerisationsgrad *m* degree of polymerization, DP
Polymerisationsinitiator *m* polymerization initiator
Polymerisationskessel *m* polymerization kettle
Polymerisationsprodukt *n* polymerization product
Polymerisationsreaktion *f* polymerization reaction
Polymerisationsreaktor *m* polymerization reactor
Polymerisationsstopper *m s.* Polymerisationsabstoppmittel
polymerisierbar polymerizable
Polymerisierbarkeit *f* polymerizability
polymerisieren to polymerize *(something)*; to polymerize, to undergo polymerization
Polymerisierung *f s.* Polymerisation
Polymerkette *f* polymer chain
Polymermischung *f* polyblend, polymer blend *(a mixture of several thermoplastics)*
Polymer-Ruß-Batch *m (rubber)* carbon black [master]batch, black batch
Polymerweichmacher *m* polymeric (resinous) plasticizer
Polymerzugabe *f*, **Polymerzusatz** *m (hyd)* flocculant addition
Polymethacrylat *n* polymethacrylate, polymethyl acrylate, methacrylate resin, *poly[1-(methoxycarbonyl)ethylene]
Polymethacrylsäure *f* polymethacrylic acid
Polymethacrylsäureester *m s.* Polymethacrylat
Polymethacrylsäuremethylester *m s.* Polymethylmethacrylat
Polymetamorphose *f (geol)* polymetamorphism
Polymethinfarbstoff *m* polymethine dye
Polymethylen *n* polymethylene
Polymethylmethacrylat *n* polymethyl methacrylate, PMMA, *poly[1-(methoxycarbonyl)-1-methylethylene]
Poly-4-methylpent-1-en *n* poly-4-methylpent-1-ene
polymolekular polymolecular
Polymolekularität *f* polymolecularity
polymorph polymorphic, polymorphous
Polymorphie *f*, **Polymorphismus** *m* polymorphism
Polynitroderivat *n* polynitro derivative
Polynosefaser *f* polynosic fibre
Polynosefaserstoff *m* polynosic fibre
polynuklear polynuclear
Polyol *n s.* Polyalkohol
Polyolefin *n* polyolefin
Polyolefinfaser *f* polyolefin fibre
Polyolefinfaserstoff *m* polyolefin fibre
Polyolefinkautschuk *m* polyolefin rubber
Polyorganosiloxan *n* polyorganosiloxane, organopolysiloxane, polymeric organosiloxane
Polyose *f s.* Polysaccharid
Polyoxacyclobutan *n* polyoxacyclobutane
Polyoxymethylen *n* *poly(oxymethylene), POM, polyformaldehyde, polyacetal
Polyparabansäure *f* polyparabanic acid, 2,4,5-triketoimidazolidine polymer
Polypeptid *n* polypeptide
Polypeptidantibiotikum *n* polypeptide antibiotic
Polypeptidkette *f* polypeptide chain
Polyphenylen *n* polyphenylene
Polyphenylenoxid *n* polyphenylene oxide, PPO, *poly(oxy-1,4-phenylene)
Polyphenylensulfid *n* polyphenylene sulphide, PPS, polythio-1,4-phenylene
Polyphenylensulfon *n s.* Polysulfon
Polyphenylethylen *n s.* Polystyren
Polyphenylsulfid *n* polyphenyl sulphide
Polyphosphat *n* polyphosphate
Polyphosphazen *n* polyphosphazene
Polyphosphorsäure *f* polyphosphoric acid *(any of the phosphoric acids* $H_{n+2}[P_nO_{3n+1}]$*)*
Polyporsäure *f* polyporic acid, 3,6-dihydroxy-2,5-diphenyl-*p*-benzoquinone
Polyprolin-Helix *f (bioch)* polyproline helix
Polypropen *n s.* Polypropylen
Polypropylen *n* polypropylene, polypropene, PP
~ mit vorgebildeter Faserstruktur fibrillated polypropylene
Polypropylenfaser *f* polypropylene fibre
Polypropylenfaserstoff *m* polypropylene fibre
Polypropylenschaum[stoff] *m* polypropylene foam
Polyquinan *n* polyquinane *(polycyclic hydrocarbon)*
Polyquinen *n* polyquinene *(unsaturated polycyclic hydrocarbon)*
Polyreaktion *f* polyreaction *(polymerization, polycondensation, or polyaddition)*
Polysaccharid *n* polysaccharide
~/mikrobielles *(biot)* microbial polysaccharide
~/pflanzliches plant polysaccharide
Polysaccharidbildner *mpl* polysaccharide-producing microorganisms
Polyschwefelwasserstoff *m* hydrogen polysulphide
Polysiloxan *n* polysiloxane, polymeric siloxane, *(specif)* polyorganosiloxan
~/organisches *s.* Polyorganosiloxan

Polyspiroverbindung *f* polyspiro compound
Polystyren *n* polystyrene, PS, *poly(1-phenylethylene)
~/aufschäumbares expandable polystyrene
~/geschäumtes foamed (expanded) polystyrene
~/hochschlagfestes high-impact polystyrene
~/schlagfestes toughened (impact) polystyrene
Polystyrenfaser *f* polystyrene fibre
Polystyrenfaserstoff *m* polystyrene fibre
Polystyrenperle *f***/aufschäumbare** expandable polystyrene bead
Polystyrenschaum[stoff] *m* polystyrene foam
Polystyrenspritzgußmasse *f* injection-moulding polystyrene
Polystyrol *n s.* Polystyren
polysubstituiert polysubstituted
Polysubstitution *f* polysubstitution
Polysulfan *n* hydrogen polysulphide
Polysulfid *n* polysulphide
Polysulfidbrücke *f (rubber)* polysulphide bridge (cross-link, link)
polysulfidisch polysulphidic
Polysulfidkautschuk *m* polysulphide rubber
~/flüssiger [polysulphide] liquid polymer
Polysulfon *n* polysulphone, polyphenylene sulphone
Polysulfonharz *n* polysulphone resin
Polyterpen *n* polyterpene
Polytetrafluorethen *n s.* Polytetrafluorethylen
Polytetrafluorethylen *n* polytetrafluoroethylene, PTFE, *poly(difluoromethylene) • **mit ~ beschichtet** PTFE-walled
Polytetrafluorethylenfaser *f* polytetrafluoroethylene fibre
Polytetrafluorethylenfaserstoff *m* polytetrafluoroethylene fibre
Polythiocarbamid *n* polythiourea
Polythionat *n* $M^{I}_{2}[S_{x}O_{6}]$ polythionate
Polythionsäure *f* polythionic acid
Polythio-1,4-phenylen *n s.* Polyphenylensulfid
Polytriazin *n* polytriazine, triazine polymer
Polytriazol *n* polytriazole
Polytrifluorchloräthylen *n s.* Polychlortrifluorethen
polytropisch *(phys ch)* polytropic
Polyumesterung *f* polytransesterification
Polyurethan *n* polyurethan[e]
Polyurethanelastomer[e] *n* polyurethane elastomer
~/walzbares millable polyurethane elastomer
Polyurethanfaser *f* polyurethane fibre
Polyurethanfaserstoff *m* polyurethane fibre
Polyurethanharz *n* polyurethane (isocyanate) resin
Polyurethankautschuk *m* polyurethane (isocyanate) rubber
Polyurethanschaum[stoff] *m* polyurethane foam
Polyuronid *n* polyuronid[e]
Polyuronsäure *f* polyuronic acid
polyvalent *(agric)* broad-scale, broad-spectrum *(insecticide)*
Polyvinylacetal *n* polyvinyl acetal
Polyvinylacetat *n* polyvinyl acetate, PVAC, *poly(1-acetoxyethylene)
Polyvinylalkohol *m* polyvinyl alcohol, PVAL, *poly(1-hydroxyethylene)
Polyvinylalkoholfaser *f* polyvinyl alcohol fibre
Polyvinylalkoholfaserstoff *m* polyvinyl alcohol fibre
Polyvinyläther *m s.* Polyvinylether
Polyvinylbenzolfaser *f s.* Polystyrenfaser
Polyvinylbutyral *n* polyvinyl butyral, PVB, *poly[(2-propyl-1,3-dioxane-4,6-diyl)methylene]
Polyvinylcarbazen *n*, **Polyvinylcarbazol** *n* polyvinylcarbazole
Polyvinylchlorid *n* polyvinyl chloride, PVC, *poly(1-chloroethylene)
~/hochschlagfestes high-impact polyvinyl chloride
~/unplastifiziertes (weichmacherfreies) unplasticized (rigid) polyvinyl chloride
Polyvinylchloridacetat *n* polyvinyl chloride acetate
Polyvinylchloridfaser *f* polyvinyl chloride fibre
Polyvinylchloridfaserstoff *m* polyvinyl chloride fibre
Polyvinylcyclohexan *n* polyvinyl cyclohexane
Polyvinylester *m* polyvinyl ester
Polyvinylether *m* polyvinyl ether
Polyvinylethylether *m* polyvinyl ethyl ether
Polyvinylfaser *f* polyvinyl fibre
Polyvinylfaserstoff *m* polyvinyl fibre
Polyvinylfluorid *n* polyvinyl fluoride, PVF
Polyvinylformal *n* polyvinyl formal
Polyvinyl-Formaldehydacetal *n s.* Polyvinylformal
Polyvinylidenchlorid *n* polyvinylidene chloride
Polyvinylidenchloridfaser *f* polyvinylidene chloride fibre
Polyvinylidenchloridfaserstoff *m* polyvinylidene chloride fibre
Polyvinylidenchloridharz *n* polyvinylidene chloride resin
Polyvinylidencyanidfaser *f* polyvinylidene cyanide fibre
Polyvinylidencyanidfaserstoff *m* polyvinylidene cyanide fibre
Polyvinylidendinitrilfaser *f* polyvinylidene dinitrile fibre
Polyvinylidendinitrilfaserstoff *m* polyvinylidene dinitrile fibre
Polyvinylidenfluorid *n* polyvinylidene fluoride
Polyvinylmethylether *m* polyvinyl methyl ether
Polyvinylpropionat *n* polyvinyl propionate
Polyvinylpropionatharz *n* polyvinyl propionate resin
Polyvinylpyrrolidin *n* polyvinylpyrrolidine, PVP
Polyvinylpyrrolidon *n* polyvinylpyrrolidone, PVP
Polyvinyltoluen *n*, **Polyvinyltoluol** *n* polyvinyl toluene
Poly-*p*-xylylen *n* poly-*p*-xylylene, poly-*p*-xylene
polyzentrisch polycentric, multicentre
POM *s.* Polyoxymethylen
Pomade *f (cosmet)* pomade, pomatum

Pomeranzenblütenöl *n* orange-flower oil, neroli oil *(from Citrus aurantium L. ssp. aurantium)*
Pomeranzenschalenöl *n* orange-peel oil
~/bitteres bitter orange-peel oil *(from Citrus aurantium L. ssp. aurantium)*
~/süßes sweet orange-peel oil *(from Citrus sinensis [L.] Osbeck)*
Pomeranz-Fritsch-Reaktion *f*, **Pomeranz-Fritsch-Synthese** *f* Pomeranz-Fritsch synthesis (reaction) *(of isoquinolines)*
Pomilio-Verfahren *n (pap)* Pomilio process *(pulping with chlorine)*
Pompejanischrot *n* Pompeian red *(iron trioxide)*
Pontianak *m s.* Djelutung
Poort *m* bort, boort, boart *(collectively for diamonds of inferior quality)*
P/O-Quotient *m (bioch)* P/O ratio, phosphate/oxygen ratio
Pore *f* 1. pore, void; *(coat)* pinhole; 2. *(rubber)* cell
Porenbeton *m* aerated concrete, gas (gassy) concrete
porenbildend pore-forming
Porenbildung *f* pore formation; *(build)* air entrainment *(for improving the properties of concrete)*; *(coat)* pinholing *(a defect)*
Porendiffusion *f* pore diffusion
Porendurchmesser *m* pore diameter
porenfrei non-porous
Porenfüller *m*, **Porenfüllmittel** *n* pore filler; *(coat)* sealer, sealing paint
Porengeometrie *f (chromat)* pore geometry
Porengröße *f* pore size
Porengrößenverteilung *f* pore-size distribution
Porengummi *m* microcellular rubber
Porenraum *m* pore space
~/relativer *(filtr)* porosity, voidage
Porensaugwasser *n (build)* water of capillarity
Porenschließer *m (coat)* sealer, sealing paint
Porensinter *m* [lightweight] expanded clay aggregate; expanded shale
Porenstruktur *f* pore structure
Porenvolumen *n* pore (void) volume *(as of a catalyst)*; *(soil)* volume of pore space
~/relatives *(filtr)* porosity, voidage
Porenvolumenverteilung *f* pore-volume distribution
Porenwasser *n (ceram, build)* pore water
Porenweite *f* pore size
porig pored
porös 1. porous, porose, poriferous; 2. *s.* porig
Porosimeter *n* porosimeter
Porosität *f* 1. porosity; 2. *(quantitatively:)* void fraction *(of a catalyst)*; 3. *s.* Porenvolumen/relatives
~/scheinbare *(ceram)* apparent porosity
~/wahre *(ceram)* true porosity
Porphin *n* porphin[e] *(a pyrrole pigment)*
Porphinskelett *n* porphin[e] ring
Porphyr *m* porphyry
Porphyrglattwalze *f* smooth porphyry roll
Porphyrie *f (med)* porphyria
Porphyrin *n* porphyrin *(substituted porphin)*
~/mit Griff versehenes korbförmiges basket handle porphyrin
~/mit Kappe und Brücke versehenes capped strapped porphyrin
~/mit Kappe versehenes capped porphyrin
~/mit Zaun versehenes fenced porphyrin
~/verkapptes capped porphyrin
~/verkrontes crowned porphyrin
porphyrisch porphyritic
Porphyrwalze *f* porphyry roll
P-Ort *m s.* Peptidbindungsort
Porteus-Verfahren *n (hyd)* Porteus process *(for conditioning sludge by heat)*
portionsweise in portions
Portlandzement *m* portland cement
Portlandzementklinker *m* portland cement clinker
Portugalöl *n s.* Pomeranzenschalenöl/süßes
Porzellan *n* 1. porcelain, *(for non-technical use also)* china; 2. *s.* Porzellanware • **aus ~** *s.* porzellanen
~/chemisches chemical porcelain
~/chemisch-technisches heavy (large-size) chemical porcelain
~/elektrotechnisches electrical porcelain
~ für hohe Temperaturen high-temperature porcelain
~/lithiumoxidhaltiges lithia porcelain
~ mit hohem Aluminiumoxidgehalt (Tonerdegehalt) high-alumina porcelain
~/nichttechnisches china
Porzellanabdampfschale *f* porcelain evaporating basin (dish)
Porzellanbehälter *m* porcelain tank
Porzellandreieck *n (lab)* porcelain triangle
porzellanen porcelan[e]ous, porcelainous
Porzellanerde *f* porcelain (china) clay, kaolin[e], bolus alba, white bole
~/geschlämmte [china] clay, kaolin[e]
Porzellanfilter *n* porcelain filter
Porzellanfiltertiegel *m* porous porcelain crucible, porcelain filtering-crucible
Porzellanfliese *f* porcelain tile
Porzellangut *n* vitreous china
Porzellanherstellung *f* porcelain manufacture
Porzellanisolator *m* porcelain insulator
Porzellanjaspis *m (min)* porcelain jasper
Porzellankasserole *f* porcelain casserole
Porzellankitt *m* porcelain cement
Porzellanrohr *n* porcelain pipe
Porzellanschale *f* porcelain basin (dish)
Porzellanscharffeuerglasur *f* high-firing porcelain glaze
Porzellanscherben *m (ceram)* porcelain body
Porzellanschiffchen *n (lab)* porcelain boat
Porzellantiegel *m (lab)* porcelain crucible
Porzellanware *f* porcelain [ware], *(for non-technical use also)* china[ware]

Position *f s.* Stellung
positiv/dreifach tripositive
~/einfach unipositive
~/fünffach pentapositive, quinque-positive
~ geladen positively charged
~/sechsfach hexapositive
~/vierfach tetrapositive
~/zweifach dipositive, bipositive
Positiv *n (phot)* positive
Positivabzug *m (phot)* positive print
Positivbild *n (phot)* positive image
Positivemulsion *f (phot)* positive emulsion
Positiventwickler *m (phot)* positive developer
Positiventwicklung *f* positive development
Positivfilm *m (phot)* positive film
Positivform *f (plast)* positive mould, *(in drape and vacuum forming:)* male mould
positivieren to increase the positive nature
Positivität *f* positivity, positiveness
Positivkopie *f s.* Positivabzug
Positivladung *f* positive charge
Positiv-Lichtpausverfahren *n* autopositive photocopying process
Positivmaterial *n (phot)* positive material
Positron *n* positron, positive electron
Positronchemie *f* positron chemistry
Positron-Elektron-Paar *n* positron-electron pair, positive-negative electron pair
Positronenbildung *f* positron formation
Positronenemission *f* positron emission
Positronenstrahler *m* positron radiator
Positronenstrahlung *f* positron radiation
Positronenzerfall *m* positron (positive beta) decay
Positronenzerstrahlung *f* destruction of positrons
Positronium *n* positronium *(a system consisting of a positron and an electron)*
Positroniumchemie *f* positronium chemistry
Posten *m (tech)* batch; *(glass)* [glass] gob, gather [of glass]
Postenform *f (glass)* gob shape
Postengewicht *n (glass)* gob weight
Postenspeiser *m (glass)* gob feeder
Postenspeisung *f (glass)* gob feeding
postenweise *(tech)* batchwise
Postpapier *n* letter (note) paper, *(Am)* correspondence paper
postvulkanisch postvolcanic
Potential *n* potential
~/äußeres elektrisches outer (Volta) potential
~/chemisches chemical potential
~/elektrisches electric[al] potential
~/elektrochemisches electrochemical potential
~/elektrokinetisches electrokinetic potential, zeta (double-layer) potential, ZP
~/Gibbssches Gibbs energy, G
~/inneres elektrisches inner (Galvani) potential
~/retardiertes retarded potential
~/thermodynamisches thermodynamic potential
ζ-Potential *n s.* Potential/elektrokinetisches
Potentialabfall *m* potential drop, fall of potential
potentialabhängig potential-dependent
Potentialabhängigkeit *f* potential dependency
Potentialänderung *f* potential change (shift)
Potentialbarriere *f s.* Potentialwall
potentialbedingt potential-dependent
Potentialberg *m s.* Potentialwall
potentialbestimmend potential-determining
potentialbildend potential-forming
Potentialdifferenz *f* potential difference, p.d.
Potentialeinstellung *f* potential control
Potentialenergie *f* potential energy
Potentialenergiefläche *f s.* Potentialfläche
Potentialenergiekurve *f* potential-energy curve
Potentialfeld *n* potential field
Potentialfläche *f* potential-energy [reaction] surface, equipotential surface
Potentialflächendiagramm *n* potential-energy contour map
Potentialfunktion *f* potential function
Potentialgefälle *n* potential gradient
potentialgeregelt potential-controlled
potentialgesteuert potential-dependent
Potentialgleichung *f* potential[-energy] equation
Potentialgradient *m* potential gradient
Potentialinversion *f s.* Potentialumkehr
Potentialkasten *m s.* Potentialtopf
Potentialkorrektur *f* potential control
Potentialkurve *f* potential-energy curve
Potentialmessung *f* potential measurement
Potentialmulde *f s.* Potentialtopf
Potentialregelung *f* potential control
Potentialrückgang *m* potential drop, drop of potential
Potentialschwelle *f s.* Potentialwall
Potentialsprung *m* potential jump
Potentialstreuung *f* potential scattering
Potentialströmung *f* potential flow *(fluid mechanics)*
Potentialstufen-Chronocoulometrie *f s.* Chronocoulometrie
Potentialtopf *m* potential well (hole, basin)
Potentialumkehr *f* potential swing
Potentialunterschied *m* potential difference, p.d.
Potentialverlauf *m* potential run
Potentialvermittler *m* potential mediator
Potentialverschiebung *f s.* Potentialänderung
Potentialwall *m* potential[-energy] barrier, potential hill
potentiell potential
Potentiometer *n* potentiometer
Potentiometerverfahren *n* potentiometric method
Potentiometrie *f* potentiometry
potentiometrisch potentiometric
Potenz *f*/**nucleophile** nucleophilicity, nucleophilic power
Pottasche *f* potash, potassa, carbonate of potash, potassium carbonate
Pottasche-Verfahren *n* potassium carbonate process *(for removing acid constituents from gases)*
Pott-Broche-Verfahren *n* Pott-Broche process *(coal extraction)*

Potten *n (text)* potting
Pouchon-Savarit-Methode *f (distil)* Pouchon-Savarit method *(for determining the plate number)*
Pourbaix-Diagramm *n (phys ch)* Pourbaix (predominance-region, potential-*p*H) diagram
Pourpoint *m* pour point *(as of a lubricating oil)*
Pourpoint-Depressor *m* pour-point depressant
Po-Z *s.* Polenske-Zahl
Pozz[u]olanerde *f s.* Puzzolanerde
PP *s.* 1. Polypropylen; 2. Polypropylenfaserstoff
PP-Faktor *m s.* Pellagrapräventivvitamin
PPO *s.* Polyphenylenoxid
PPP-Methode *f (spectr)* PPP method, Pariser-Parr-Pople method
PPS *s.* Polyphenylensulfid
PP-Weg *m s.* Pentosephosphat-Weg
Prädioxin *n (tox)* predioxin
Prädissoziation *f* predissociation
Prädissoziationsspektrum *n* predissociation spectrum
Präexponentialfaktor *m* [Arrhenius] pre-exponential factor, Arrhenius factor, A factor, frequency factor *(kinetics)*
Präfix *n (nomencl)* prefix
~/multiplizierendes *s.* ~/vervielfachendes
~/numerisches numer[ic]al prefix
~/vervielfachendes multiplying prefix, multiplicative numeral
Prägleichgewicht *n* near-equilibrium
Präionisation *f* preionization, autoionization
Praktikum *n***[/chemisches]** laboratory course
Praktikumsassistent *m* lab[oratory] instructor
Präkursor *m* precursor, progenitor
präkursorfrei precursor-free
Präkursorverfütterung *f (biot)* precursor feeding
Prallabscheiden *n* inertial (impingement) separation
Prallabscheider *m* inertial separator, impingement (momentum) separator, impingement collector
Prallblech *n s.* Prallfläche
Prallbrecher *m* impact crusher
Pralldüse *f* impact (deflector) nozzle
Prallfläche *f* baffle, baffle (impingement, deflector) plate • **mit Prallflächen ausstatten** to baffle • **ohne Prallflächen** unbaffled
~ aus feuerfestem Ton fireclay baffle
Prallmühle *f* impact mill
Prallplatte *f s.* Prallfläche
Prallscheider *m s.* Prallabscheider
Prallwand *f s.* Prallfläche
Prallzerkleinerung *f* impact crushing
Präparat *n* preparation
~/galenisches *(pharm)* galenical
~/humanmedizinisches human-health product
~/kosmetisches cosmetic [preparation]
~/pharmazeutisches pharmaceutic[al] preparation
~/tiermedizinisches (veterinärmedizinisches) animal-health product
~/virentötendes (viruzides) virucide, viricide, viricidal agent
Präparatenchemie *f* preparative chemistry
Präparatenglas *n* specimen jar, preservation (museum) jar, show (inverted) bottle
Präparationsgalette *f (text)* sizing pad
präparativ preparative • **in präparativem Maßstab** on a preparative scale
präparieren to prepare
Präpariermikroskop *n* dissecting microscope
Präpariernadel *f* dissecting needle
~/lanzettenförmige lancet-point dissecting needle
Präparierpinzette *f* pinning forceps
Präpariersalz *n* preparing salt, sodium hexahydroxostannate(IV)
Präresonanz... *(spectr)* pre-resonance ...
Prasem *m (min)* prase *(a variety of chalcedony)*
Praseodym *n* Pr praseodymium
Praseodymcarbonat *n* praseodymium carbonate
Praseodymchlorid *n* praseodymium chloride
Praseodymdioxid *n s.* Praseodym(IV)-oxid
Praseodym(III)-oxid *n* praseodymium(III) oxide, praseodymium trioxide
Praseodym(IV)-oxid *n* praseodymium(IV) oxide, praseodymium dioxide
Praseodymsulfat *n* praseodymium sulphate
Praseodymsulfid *n* praseodymium sulphide
Praseodymtrioxid *n s.* Praseodym(III)-oxid
Präserve *f* partly preserved food
Prästationärenzymkinetik *f* pre-steady-state kinetics
Prayon-Filter *n* Prayon [continuous] filter, tilting-pan filter
Präzipitat *n* 1. precipitate *(any of several mercury compounds)*; 2. *s.* Niederschlag
~/gelbes yellow precipitate, yellow mercuric oxide *(modification of mercury(II) oxide)*
~/rotes red precipitate, red mercuric oxide *(modification of mercury(II) oxide)*
~/schmelzbares weißes fusible white precipitate, diamminemercury(II) chloride
~/unschmelzbares weißes infusible white precipitate, aminomercury(II) chloride, *(pharm also)* ammoniated mercury
Präzipitation *f* precipitation
präzipitieren to precipitate
präzipitierend precipitative
Präzision *f (anal)* precision
Präzisionsapothekerwaage *f* prescription balance
Präzisionsguß *m (met)* precision casting
~ nach dem Ausschmelzverfahren precision investment casting
Präzisionsphotometrie *f* precision photometry
Präzisionspolarimeter *n* precision polarimeter
Präzisionswaage *f* precision balance
Precoatfilter *n* precoat[ed] filter, precoat pressure filter
Precoatschicht *f* filter precoat, precoat [layer, bed, filter cake]
Prehnit *m (min)* prehnite *(a sorosilicate)*
Prehnitol *n* 1,2,3,4-tetramethylbenzene, *vic*-tetramethylbenzene, *(deprecated:)* prehnitene, prehnitol

Prehnitsäure *f* prehnitic acid *(a term confusingly used for benzene-1,2,3,4-tetracarboxylic acid and benzene-1,2,3,5-tetracarboxylic acid respectively)*
Prehnitylsäure *f* prehnitylic acid, 2,3,4-trimethylbenzoic acid
Premier jus *m* premier jus *(fine edible tallow)*
Premier-Kolloidmühle *f* Premier [colloid] mill
Premium-Benzin *n*, **Premium-Kraftstoff** *m* premium gasoline (motor fuel, spirit)
Premium-Öl *n* premium motor oil
Premix-Masse *f (plast)* premix, premixed moulding compound
Prepaktbeton *m* prepacked (grouted) concrete
Prephensäure *f* prephenic acid *(a cyclohexadiene derivative)*
Prepolymer-Verfahren *n (plast)* prepolymer process *(foaming)*
Prepreg *n (plast)* prepreg *(preimpregnated glass-fibre material)*
Preßband *n* compacted strip *(in powder rolling)*
Preßblasmaschine *f (glass)* press-and-blow machine
Preßblasverfahren *n (glass)* press-and-blow process
Preßdauer *f (plast)* moulding cycle
preßdicht compact
Preßdruck *m* pressing pressure, *(relating to solid particles also)* compacting pressure; *(plast)* moulding pressure; *(coal)* briquetting pressure
~ **beim Formpressen** *(plast)* compression-moulding pressure
~ **beim Preßspritzen (Spritzpressen)** *(plast)* transfer-moulding pressure
Presse *f* press; *(food)* press, squeezer; *(plast)* moulding press
~/**beheizbare** hot press
~/**einhüftige** open-side press, open-gap (gap-type, jaw-type, C-frame) press
~/**filzlose (glättende)** *(pap)* smoothing (offset) press
~ **mit Einzelantrieb** self-contained press
pressen 1. to press *(e.g. pellets)*; to press, to compress, to compact *(e.g. powders)*; 2. to mould *(e.g. plastics)*; 3. *(food)* to press, to express, to squeeze [out]
~/**heiß** to hot-press, *(relating to powders also)* to sinter under pressure
~/**nochmals** to re-press
~/**zu Briketts** to briquette
Pressen *n* **in halbtrockenem Zustand** *(ceram)* semidry pressing
~ **mit Gummisack** *(plast)* [rubber-]bag moulding
~/**plastisches** *(ceram)* plastic (wet) pressing
Pressenanordnung *f* press arrangement
Pressenheizung *f (rubber)* press cure (curing, vulcanization)
Pressenpartie *f (pap)* press part (section)
Pressenschleifer *m (pap)* pocket grinder
3-Pressen-Schleifer *m (pap)* three-pocket grinder
Pressentisch *m (plast)* press table, table press, ram, *(Am)* [press] platen
Preßfett *n* expressed fat
Preßfilz *m (pap)* press[ing] felt
Preßfläche *f (plast)* projected area
Preßform *f* mould; die *(of an extruder)*
Preßglanzdekatur *f (text)* pressure decatizing
Preßglas *n* pressed glass
Preßgrat *m (plast)* fin
Preßguß *m s.* Kaltkammerdruckgießen
Preßgut *n* 1. material being *or* to be compacted; 2. material being *or* to be pressed (expressed)
Preßharz *n* [compression-]moulding resin
Preßhefe *f* compressed yeast
Preßkasten *m (pap)* pocket *(of a pulpwood grinder)*
Preßkohle *f* briquetted coal
Preßkorb *m* curb *(of a wine press)*
Preßkörper *m* 1. *s.* Preßling 1.; 2. compressed cartridge *(technology of explosives)*
Preßkuchen *m (tech)* press[ed] cake; *(food)* oil (mill) cake; *(plast)* biscuit *(for pressing disk records)*
Preßlauge *f* press liquor
Preßling *m* 1. *(plast, ceram, glass)* moulding; compact *(powder metallurgy)*; 2. *(coal)* briquet[te]; 3. *(spectr)* pellet, *(for IR-spectroscopy:)* pressed disk
~/**gesinterter** sintered[-powder metal] compact
Preßlingsfläche *f (plast)* projected area
Preßluft *f* compressed (compression) air
Preßluftleitung *f* compressed-air line
Preßlufttrüttler *m* pneumatic (air-driven) vibrator
Preßluftventil *n* pneumatic (air) valve
Preßmasse *f* 1. *(ceram)* press body (mix); press[-ing] dust *(in dry pressing)*; 2. *(plast)* compression-moulding material
~/**pulvrige** *(plast)* moulding powder
Preßmassenfilter *n* pad filter
Preßöl *n (food)* expressed oil; *(petrol)* pressed distillate, blue oil *(obtained by dewaxing)*
pressorisch *(pharm)* pressor, raising blood pressure
Preßplatte *f (pap)* pressure foot *(of a pocket grinder)*
Preßpumpe *f* high-pressure (high-head) pump
Preßring *m* clamp ring *(as on a Söderberg electrode)*
Preßrückstand *m* expressed residue
Preßrunzel *f (glass)* flow line *(a surface defect)*
Preßsaft *m* press-juice
Preßschichtholz *n* compreg, compressed resin-impregnated wood
Preßsintern *n* sintering under pressure, hot pressing *(of metal powder)*
Preßspan *m* pressboard, pressing board, press[s]pahn
~ **für Elektrotechnik** electrical pressboard
Preßspanersatz *m* imitation pressboard
Preßspritzen *n (plast)* transfer (flow) moulding, *(Am also)* plunger molding
Preßspritzwerkzeug *n (plast)* transfer mould

Preßstaub *m (ceram)* press[ing] dust
Preßstempel *m (plast)* male form (mould), moulding (force) plug, patrix, plunger
Preßstück *n s.* Preßling
Preßtalg *m (food)* pressed tallow, oleostearin[e]
Preßtasche *f (pap)* pocket *(of a pulpwood grinder)*
Preßtechnik *f (spectr)* pressed disk technique
Preßteil *n (plast)* moulding
~ **aus Schichtstoff** moulded laminate
~/**ausgehärtetes** cured moulding
~ **mit Schnitzelfüllstoff** macerate moulding
Preßtuch *n* press cloth
Preßtuchmatte *f* filter mat
preßverdichten to compact
Preßverdichtung *f* compaction
Preßvulkanisation *f* press cure (curing, vulcanization)
Preßwalze *f* press roll, pressure (compression, squeeze) roll; *(coal)* briquetting roll
Preßwasserreaktor *m* pressurized-water reactor, PWR
Preßwerkzeug *n* pressing tool; *(plast)* mould
~ **mit vertieft liegendem Abquetschrand** *(plast)* semipositive mould
~/**zusammengesetztes** *(plast)* composite mould
Preßwindsinterapparat *m* updraught sinter machine
Preßzyklus *m (plast)* moulding cycle
Preußischblau *n* Prussian blue *(a complex iron cyanide)*
Preventer *m (petrol)* blow-out preventer
PRH *(**P**rolactin-**R**eleasing**h**ormon) s.* Prolactoliberin
Pribnow-Box *f (bioch)* Pribnow box *(portion of the DNA having similar sequences of amino acids)*
Prileschajew-Reaktion *f* Prileshajew reaction *(for obtaining epoxides)*
prillen to prill *(to convert a solution or suspension into pellets)*
Prillturm *m* prilling tower
Primaquin *n* primaquine *(a quinoline derivative)*
Primäracetat *n (text)* primary [cellulose] acetate
Primäraggregat *n (coll, soil)* primary aggregate
Primärbatterie *f* primary battery
Primärbeschleuniger *m (rubber)* primary accelerator
Primärbezugskraftstoff *m* primary reference fuel
Primärcharge *f*/**zusätzlich verdünnte** *(petrol)* primary dilute charge *(in dewaxing)*
Primärdestillation *f* primary distillation
Primärelektron *n* primary (initiating) electron
Primärelement *n (el ch)* primary cell *(not capable of being regenerated)*
Primärenergie *f* primary energy
Primärfaden *m (glass)* basic fibre
Primärgraphit *m (met)* kish, keesh
Primärionisation *f* initial ionization
Primärkeimbildung *f (cryst)* primary nucleation
Primärlagerstätte *f* primary deposit
Primärluft *f* primary air
Primärlunker *m*[/**offener**] *(met)* primary pipe *(in an ingot)*
Primärmetabolismus *m (bioch)* primary metabolism
Primärmetabolit *m (bioch)* primary metabolite, primary product of metabolism
Primärprodukt *n* primary product
Primärproduzent *m (biol)* primary producer
Primärreaktion *f* primary (initiating) reaction
~/**photochemische** primary photoreaction (photochemical reaction)
Primärreaktionszone *f* primary reaction zone
Primärschadstoff *m* primary pollutant, precursor
Primärschlamm *m (hyd)* primary [sedimentation] sludge
Primärschritt *m* initiating step *(of a reaction)*
Primärsprengstoff *m* initial detonating agent
Primärstandard *m* primary standard *(pH measurement)*
Primärstoffwechsel *m (bioch)* primary metabolism
Primärstruktur *f (bioch)* primary structure
Primärstufe *f* initiating step
Primärteer *m* primary (low-temperature) tar
Primärton *m* primary (residual) clay
Primärwand *f* primary wall, outside (outer) wall *(of a vegetable fibre)*
Primärweichmacher *m* primary plasticizer
Primärzentrifuge *f* primary centrifuge
Primulinbase *f* primuline base
Primulingelb *n* primuline yellow
Primulinrot *n* primuline red
Prins-Reaktion *f* Prins reaction *(addition of formaldehyde to an olefin or arene)*
Prinzip *n* 1. principle, rule, law; 2. principle, fundamental constituent, base
~/**aktives** *s.* ~/wirksames
~/**Babinetsches** *(cryst)* Babinet absorption rule
~/**Berthelot-Thomsensches** Thomsen-Berthelot principle
~/**Carnotsches** Carnot theorem
~ **der Erhaltung der Energie** law of conservation of energy, energy principle
~ **der geringsten Strukturänderung** *(org ch)* principle of minimum structural change
~ **der größten Multiplizität** maximum-multiplicity principle (rule), Hund's first rule
~ **der harten und weichen Säuren und Basen** HSAB principle
~ **der korrespondierenden Zustände** *(phys ch)* principle of corresponding states
~ **der mikroskopischen Reversibilität** *(phys ch)* principle of microscopic reversibility
~ **des beweglichen Gleichgewichts** *s.* ~ des kleinsten Zwanges
~ **des detaillierten Gleichgewichts** *(org ch)* principle of detailed balancing
~ **des kleinsten Zwanges** Le Chatelier's principle, Le Chatelier-Braun principle, principle of mobile equilibrium
~ **des quasistationären Zustands** steady-state [approximation] method
~/**färbendes (färberisches)** colouring principle

~/fluoreszierendes fluorophore, fluorogen *(a group of atoms which give a molecule fluorescent properties)*
~/Franck-Condonsches *(phys ch)* Franck-Condon principle
~/Hundsches *s.* ~ der größten Multiplizität
~/Le Chatelier-Braunsches *s.* ~ des kleinsten Zwanges
~/Paulisches [Pauli] exclusion principle
~/toxisches toxic principle
~/wirksames active principle (ingredient, agent, substance)
Priorität *f* [nomenclature] priority, precedence, seniority
Prioritätenfolge *f*, **Prioritätsfolge** *f (nomencl)* order of priority (precedence, seniority)
Prisma *n*/**Nicolsches** Nicol prims
~ zur Vorzerlegung *(spectr)* fore-prism
prismatisch *(cryst)* prismatic
Prismenspektralapparat *m s.* 1. Prismenspektrograph; 2. Prismenspektroskop
Prismenspektrograph *m* prism spectrograph
Prismenspektroskop *n* prism spectroscope
Prismenteller *m (spectr)* prism table
Pro *s.* Prolin
pro mille parts per thousand, ppt
Probe *f* 1. sample; *(chromat)* probe *(a macromolecular compound having well-defined properties)*; 2. test, *(esp met)* assay *(for compounds s. a. under* Prüfung*)*; 3. *s.* Probekörper • **eine ~ entnehmen** to sample, to take (draw, withdraw) a sample
~/Baeyersche Baeyer (permanganate) test *(for detecting alkenes)*
~/Baudouinsche Baudouin test *(for detecting sesame oil)*
~/Bettendorfsche Bettendorf's test [for arsenic]
~/Gutzeitsche Gutzeit test *(for detecting arsenic)*
~/Hellersche Heller's ring test *(for proteins)*
~/Lassaignesche Lassaigne['s] test *(for detecting nitrogen in organic substances)*
~/Marshsche Marsh's arsenic test, Marsh's test [for arsenic]
~/nasse *(met)* wet assay
~/Reinschsche Reinsch test [for arsenic]
~/repräsentative representative sample
~/trockene *(met)* dry assay
~/zu untersuchende test sample
Probeabzug[s]papier *n* proof[ing] paper
Probeentnahme *f* sampling
Probefärbung *f* trial dyeing
probehaltig proof *(of standard alcoholic content)*
Probekörper *m* test piece, specimen
~/bogenförmiger *(rubber)* crescent test piece
~/Delfter *(rubber)* Delft test piece
~/ringförmiger *(rubber)* ring test piece, ring sample
~/stabförmiger test rod; *(rubber)* dumb-bell test piece, dumb-bell strip, dumb bell
Probelauf *m* experimental run, trial (test, dry) run
Probelösung *f* solution to be tested; solution under examination
Probematerial *n* test material
Probemischung *f* trial mix[ture]
Probenahme *f* sampling, sample collection, withdrawal of samples
~/diskontinuierliche discontinous sampling
~/geschichtete stratified sampling
~/isokinetische isokinetic sampling
~/kontinuierliche continuous sampling
~ mittels Probenstechers thief sampling
Probenahmeanordnung *f* sampling train
Probenahmefehler *m* sampling error
Probenahmegerät *n s.* Probenehmer
Probenahmemethode *f* sampling technique (procedure)
Probenahmemodell *n* sampling model (schedule)
Probenahmeort *m* sampling location
Probenahmeschaufel *f* hand scoop sampler, sampling scoop
Probenahmestelle *f* sampling point (site), point of sampling
Probenahmetechnik *f* sampling technique (procedure)
Probenahmevorrichtung *f* sampling device, sampler
Probenahmevorschrift *f* sampling specification
Probenaufbereitung *f (anal)* sample preparation
Probenaufbewahrung *f* sample storage
Probenaufgabe *f* sample application
~ in die Speicherschleife *(chromat)* sample loop loading
~ mit Gasstromteilung (Strömungsteilung) *(chromat)* split sampling
~ ohne Gasstromteilung (Strömungsteilung) *(chromat)* splitless sampling
Probenaufgabeteil *n (chromat)* sample injection unit, sample injector system
Probenbecher *m (spectr)* sampling cup
Probenbehälter *m* sample container
Probenbohrer *m* auger sampler
Probendiskriminierung *f (anal)* sample discrimination
Probendosierung *f (spectr)* sample introduction
Probendurchsatz *m (anal)* sample throughput
Probenehmen *n s.* Probenahme
Probenehmer *m* sampling device (tool), sampler, sample collector (collection unit), collector, *(esp for bulk material:)* trier
Probenehmerhahn *m* sampling cock
Probeneinlaß *m* sample inlet (pickup)
Probeneinlaßsystem *n* [sample] inlet system
Probenentnahme *f s.* Probenahme
Probenfehler *m s.* Probenahmefehler
Probenflasche *f* sample bottle
Probengabe *f s.* Probenaufgabe
Probengeber *m* [sample] dispenser, sample loader; *(chromat)* sample injector
~/automatisch arbeitender autosampler
~ für Kapillarsäulen *(chromat)* capillary injector

Probengefäß *n* sample container
Probengröße *f* sample size
Probengut *n* test material
Probenhalterung *f* sample holder
Probeninjektion *f* sample injection
~ **direkt auf die Säulenpackung** *(chromat)* on-column injection
Probenkonservierung *f* sample preservation
Probenküvette *f (spectr)* sample cell
Probenmatrix *f (spectr)* sample matrix
Probenmenge *f* sample amount (quantity)
Probennahme *f s.* Probenahme
Probenort *m s.* Probenahmeort
Probenpräparation *f* sample preparation
Probenraum *m (spectr)* sample chamber (compartment)
Probenrohr *n* sample tube
Probenschleife *f (chromat)* sample loop
Probenschleifeninjektion *f (chromat)* loop flushing
Probenschleifenventil *n (chromat)* loop valve
Probenschöpfer *m (hyd)* water sampler
Probenspeicher *m (spectr)* sampler carousel
Probenstecher *m* sampling thief, trier
~ **mit längsgeteiltem Rohr** split-tube thief
~/**pneumatisch arbeitender** power-driven thief, pneumatic sampler
~/**rohrförmiger** tubular thief
Probenstrom *m* sample stream
Probenteiler *m* sample divider (reducer)
~/**mechanischer** mechanical sample divider (reducer)
Probenteilung *f* sample division
Probenträger *m* sample holder
Probentransfer *m*, **Probenüberführung** *f* sample transfer
Probenumfang *m* 1. sample size *(statistically)*; 2. sample amount (size) *(sample weight, volume, or dimensions)*
Probenverarbeitung *f* sample reduction *(in a larger sense, relating to volume and grain size)*
Probenverjüngung *f* sample reduction (division)
Probenwechsel *m* sample changing
Probenwechselvorrichtung *f*, **Probenwechsler** *m* sample changer
Probenzerkleinerung *f* sample reduction
Probenzuführung *f* sample introduction
Probeschleife *f s.* Probenschleife
Probespektrum *n* sample spectrum
Probestab *m* test rod
Probestück *n* sample, *(in metallography also)* coupon *(for preparing test specimens)*
Probesubstanz *f* test (experimental) substance, substance under investigation, substance being *or* to be investigated
Probeversorgung *f* sample introduction
probieren 1. *(food)* to taste; 2. *(met)* to assay; 3. *s.* prüfen
Probierglas *n s.* Reagenzglas
Probiergläschen *n* taster *(as for wine)*
Probierhahn *m* sampling cock
Probierstein *m* touchstone *(streak plate for gold)*
Probitmortalität *f (tox)* probit mortality
Problemlabor *n* pioneering research laboratory
prochiral prochiral *(stereochemistry)*
Prochiralität *f* prochirality *(stereochemistry)*
Proctor-Trockner *m (ceram)* Proctor dryer *(a tunnel dryer)*
Produkt *n (ch, tech)* product; make *(of a specified factory)*; *(agric)* produce *(as of a specified country)*
~/**disubstituiertes** disubstitution product
~/**feuerfestes** refractory [product]
~/**geringveredeltes** low-added-value product
~/**Habersches** *(tox)* ct product
~/**handelsfähiges** commercial product
~/**helles** *(petrol)* white product
~/**monosubstituiertes** monosubstitution product
~/**primäres** primary product
~/**reformiertes** *(petrol)* reformate
~/**schadstoffbekämpfendes** pollution-control product
~/**verperltes** shot
~/**vulkanisiertes** vulcanized product
~/**weißes** *(petrol)* white product
Produktabtrennung *f* product separation
Produktaufarbeitung *f* product recovery
Produktausbeute *f (biot)* product yield, process (conversion) yield
Produktbildner *mpl (biot)* producers, producing microorganisms
Produktbildung *f (biot)* [biochemical] product formation
Produktbildungsphase *f (biot)* product formation phase, production phase, idiophase
Produktbildungsrate *f (biot)* rate of product formation, fermentation (conversion) rate
Produktbildungsvermögen *n (biot)* capability of product formation
Produktenhemmung *f* feedback (product) inhibition, end-product repression *(enzyme kinetics)*
Produktenleitung *f (petrol)* refined-product pipeline
Produktengas *n* product gas
Produkthemmung *f s.* Produktenhemmung
Produktion *f* 1. *(know-how:)* manufacture; 2. *(in a specified period or scale:)* production; 3. *(of a specified plant:)* make
~ **in großtechnischem Maßstab** large-scale production
~ **in halbtechnischem Maßstab** pilot[-plant-scale] production
Produktionsabwasser *n* factory (works, trade) effluent, process (industrial) waste-water
Produktionsanlage *f* production plant, *(as opposed to pilot plant:)* full-scale plant, commercial[-scale] plant
Produktionsausbeute *f s.* Produktausbeute
Produktionsbetrieb *m* production plant, *(as opposed to pilot plant:)* full-scale plant, commercial[-scale] plant

Produktionsbohrung *f (petrol)* exploitation (development) well
Produktionsfermentation *f (biot)* production (trade) fermentation
Produktionsfermenter *m (biot)* production (main) fermenter
Produktionskraft *f (agric)* productive capacity *(of soils)*
Produktionskultur *f (biot)* production (main) culture
Produktionsleistung *f* production output
Produktionsmedium *n (biot)* production medium
Produktionsmenge *f s.* Produktionsleistung
Produktionsphase *f* make (run) part *(of a production cycle)*
Produktionsprogramm *n* production pattern
Produktionsreaktor *m* commercial[-scale] reactor
Produktionsreife *f* production-line status
Produktionsstamm *m (biot)* production strain, producing (working) strain *(of microorganisms)*
Produktionsverfahren *n* manufacturing (production) process
~/mikrobiologisch-industrielles (mikrobiologisch-technisches) industrial microbiological process
Produktionsvermögen *n* capacity
Produktionswasser *n* process[ing] water, water for manufacturing use
Produktisolierung *f (biot)* product isolation
Produktkonzentration *f (biot)* product concentration
Produktkühler *m (distil)* product cooler
Produktmasse *f*, **Produktmenge** *f (biot)* product weight
Produktphase *f* product phase
Produktregel *f* **von Teller und Redlich** *(anal)* Teller-Redlich product rule
Produktreinigung *f* product purification
Produktsynthese *f (biot)* product synthesis
Produktverteilung *f* product distribution
Produzent *m* manufacturer; *(biot)* producer, producing microorganism
Produzentenstamm *m s.* Produktionsstamm
Proenzym *n*, **Proferment** *n* zymogen, proenzyme, pre-enzyme
Profil *n* profile, shape; *(plast)* section
~/lorentzförmiges *(spectr)* Lorentzian profile (band shape, line shape)
profilieren to profile, to shape
Profilkalander *m (rubber)* profiling calender
Progesteron *n* progesterone *(a hormone)*
Projektionsformel *f* projection formula
~/Fischersche Fischer projection formula
~ von Haworth/sterische Haworth formula *(for sugars)*
Projektionsgalvanometer *n* projection galvanometer
Pro-Kopf-Verbrauch *m* per capita consumption (use, usage)
Pro-Kopf-Wasserverbrauch *m* water consumption per capita, per capita use of water
Prolactin *n* prolactin, lactogenic (luteotrophic) hormone
Prolactoliberin *n* prolactin-releasing hormone, PRH
Prolactostatin *n (bioch)* prolactin release-inhibiting factor
Prolamin *n* prolamine *(a simple vegetable protein)*
Prolin *n* proline, Pro, pyrrolidine-2-carboxylic acid
Promethium *n* Pm promethium
Promotion *f (phys ch)* promotion
Promotionsenergie *f (phys ch)* promotion energy
Promotor *m* promoter, promoting agent, activator, activating substance
~/struktureller structural promoter
Promotorwirkung *f* promoter action
Promovierung *f (phys ch)* promotion
Prooxidans *n* prooxidant [agent]
Prooxygen *n s.* Prooxidans
Propadien *n* propadiene, allene
Propagierung *f (biot)* multiplication, propagation *(of microorganisms)*
Propan *n* propane
Propanal *n* *propanal, propionaldehyde
Propan-1,2-diamin *n*, **1,2-Propandiamin** *n* propane-1,2-diamine, propylenediamine
Propan-1,2-diol *n*, **Propandiol-(1,2)** *n* *propane-1,2-diol, 1,2-dihydroxypropane
Propandisäure *f* *propanedioic acid, malonic acid
Propanentasphaltierung *f* propane deasphalting (deasphaltation), PDA
Propanentasphaltierungsanlage *f* propane-deasphalting plant
Propanentparaffinierung *f* propane dewaxing
Propanentparaffinierungsanlage *f* propane-dewaxing plant
Propanextraktion *f* **von Asphalt** *s.* Propanentasphaltierung
Propannitril *n s.* Propionitril
Propan-1-ol *n*, **Propanol-(1)** *n* propan-1-ol
Propan-2-ol *n*, **Propanol-(2)** *n* propan-2-ol
Propanolyse *f* propanolysis
Propanon *n* *propanone, acetone, dimethylketone
Propansäure *f s.* Propionsäure
Propan-1-thiol *n* propane-1-thiol
Propan-1,2,3-tricarbonsäure *f* propane-1,2,3-tricarboxylic acid
Propargylalkohol *m* propargyl alcohol, *prop-2-yn-1-ol
Propargylierung *f* propargylation
Propargylsäure *f s.* Propiolsäure
Propektin *n s.* Protopektin
Propellan *n (org ch)* propellane
Propellermischer *m* propeller mixer (agitator), *(esp lab)* propeller stirrer
Propellerpumpe *f* propeller (axial-flow) pump
Propellerrührer *m*, **Propellerrührwerk** *n s.* Propellermischer

Propellerventilator *m* propeller (axial-flow) fan
Propen *n* propene
Propenal *n* *propenal, acraldehyde, acrolein
Propenamid *n* *propenamide, acrylamide
Propennitril *n* *propenenitrile, acrylonitrile, vinyl cyanide
Prop-2-en-1-ol *n*, **Propen-(2)-ol-(1)** *n* *prop-2-en-1-ol, allyl alcohol
Propenol-(3) *n s.* Prop-2-en-1-ol
Propensäure *f* *propenoic acid, acrylic acid
Propenylbromid *n* *1-bromopropene, propenyl bromide
Propenylgruppe *f*, **Propenylrest** *m* $CH_3CH=CH-$ propenyl group (residue)
Propepsin *n s.* Pepsinogen
Prophylaktikum *n (pharm)* prophylactic
prophylaktisch prophylactic
Propin *n* propyne
Prop-2-in-1-ol *n*, **Propin(2)-ol-(1)** *n* *prop-2-yn-1-ol, propargyl alcohol
Propio-1,3-lacton *n*, **β-Propiolacton** *n* *propio-1,3-lactone, β-propiolactone, BPL
Propiolalkohol *m s.* Prop-2-in-1-ol
Propiolsäure *f* propiolic acid, propargylic acid, *propynoic acid
Propionaldehyd *m* propionaldehyde, *propanal
Propionat *n* propionate *(salt or ester of propionic acid)*
Propionitril *n* propionitrile, ethyl cyanide
Propionsäure *f* propionic acid, *propanoic acid
Propionsäurebenzylester *m* benzyl propionate
Propionsäureethylester *m* ethyl propionate
Propionsäurenitril *n s.* Propionitril
Propionylbenzen *n*, **Propionylbenzol** *n* propionylbenzene, propiophenone
Propionylgruppe *f*, **Propionylrest** *m* C_2H_5CO- propionyl group (residue)
Propiophenon *n* propiophenone, *ethyl phenyl ketone
Propolis *f* propolis, bee glue
Proportion *f* proportion
Proportionalitätsbereich *m* proportional region
Proportionalitätsfaktor *m* proportionality constant
Proportionalitätsgrenze *f* proportional limit; *(plast)* offset yield strength (stress)
Proportional[itäts]wägung *f* direct weighing
Proportionalzähler *m*, **Proportionalzählrohr** *n* proportional counter *(for charged particles)*
Propylacetat *n* propyl acetate
n-**Propylacetylen** *n s.* Pent-1-in
Propylalkohol *m* *propanol, propyl alcohol, *(specif)* *propan-1-ol
sec-**Propylalkohol** *m s.* Propan-2-ol
Propylamin *n* propylamine
n-**Propyläthylen** *n s.* Pent-1-en
Propylcarbinol *n s.* Butan-1-ol
Propylchlorid *n* *1-chloropropane, propyl chloride
Propylen *n s.* Propen
Propylenaldehyd *m s.* Crotonaldehyd
Propylenbromid *n s.* Propylendibromid
Propylendiamin *n* *propane-1,2-diamine, propylenediamine
Propylendibromid *n* *1,2-dibromopropane, propylene dibromide
Propylendicarbonsäure *f* *prop-2-ene-1,2-dicarboxylic acid, itaconic acid
Propylenglykol *n* *propane-1,2-diol, propylene glycol
Propylenoxid *n* propylene oxide, 1,2-epoxypropane, 2-methyloxiran
Propylessigsäure *f* *pentanoic acid, *(deprecated:)* propyl acetic acid
Propylgallat *n* propyl gallate, PG
Propylierung *f* propylation
Propylmercaptan *n*/**primäres** *s.* Propan-1-thiol
prospektieren *(petrol, mine)* to prospect
Prospektierung *f (petrol, mine)* prospecting
Prostaglandin *n* prostaglandin *(any of a group of animal hormones)*
Prostansäure *f (bioch)* prostanoic acid
prosthetisch prosthetic *(enzymology)*
Protaktinium *n* Pa protactinium
Protamin *n* protamine *(any of a class of simple proteins)*
Protease *f* protease, proteolytic (protein-digesting) enzyme
~/bakterielle *(biot)* bacterial protease
~/mikrobielle *(biot)* microbial protease
Proteaseinhibitor *m (biot)* protease inhibitor
Proteid *n* conjugated protein, proteid[e]
Protein *n* protein
~/acylübertragendes acyl-carrier protein
~/bakterielles bacterial protein
~ der M-Linie M-line protein *(within the muscle)*
~/einfaches simple protein
~/faserartiges (faserförmiges) *s.* ~/fibrilläres
~/fibrilläres fibrillar protein, fibrous (skeletal) protein, scleroprotein
~/fremdes foreign protein
~ für die menschliche Ernährung human feed protein
~/globuläres globular protein
~/helixdestabilisierendes SSB protein, single-stranded [DNA] binding protein
~/konjugiertes *s.* Proteid
~/kugelförmiges globular protein
~/mikrobielles microbial protein
~/natives native protein
~/pflanzliches plant (vegetable) protein
~/reines *s.* ~/einfaches
~/tierisches animal protein
~/zusammengesetztes *s.* Proteid
Proteinabbau *m* protein degradation (breakdown), proteolysis
proteinabbauend proteolytic, proteoclastic, protein-digesting
Proteinabtrennung *f* protein separation
Proteinanteil *m* protein moiety (component)

proteinarm low-protein
proteinartig protein-like, proteinaceous
Proteinaseinhibitor *m* proteinase inhibitor
Proteinbestimmung *f* protein determination
Proteinbestimmungsmethode *f* **nach Lowry** Lowry method [for protein determination]
Proteinbiosynthese *f* protein biosynthesis translation *(in a larger sense)*
Proteinchemie *f* protein chemistry
Proteinchemiker *m* protein chemist
Proteindenaturierung *f* protein denaturation
Proteinfaktor *m* protein factor *(for estimating the protein content from nitrogen determination)*
Proteinfaser *f* protein[aceous] fibre
Proteinfaserstoff *m* protein[aceous] fibre
Proteinfilament *n* protein filament
proteinfrei protein-free
Proteinfreisetzung *f* protein release
proteingebunden protein-bound
proteinhaltig protein-containing, containing protein
Proteinhydrolysat *n* protein hydrolyzate
proteinisch proteinaceous
Proteinisolat *n* protein isolate
Proteinkomponente *f s.* Proteinanteil
Proteinkonzentrat *n* protein concentrate
Proteinkunststoff *m* protein plastic
Proteinlösung *f* protein solution
proteinreich protein-rich
Proteinsequenator *m (anal)* sequenator
Proteinsilber *n (pharm)* silver protein[ate]
Proteinsol *n* protein sol
proteinspaltend *s.* proteolytisch
Proteinstoffwechsel *m* protein metabolism
Proteinsynthese *f* protein synthesis
Proteinurie *f* proteinuria *(excretion of proteins via the kidneys)*
Proteinveränderung *f* protein change
Protektor *m (rubber)* tread, wearing surface
Protektorgummi *m* tread rubber
Protektorspritzkopf *m (rubber)* tread head
Protektorspritzmaschine *f (rubber)* tread extruder
Proteohormon *n* proteohormone, protein hormone
Proteolipid *n (bioch)* proteolipid
Proteolyse *f* proteolysis, protein cleavage
proteolytisch proteolytic, proteoclastic, protein-digesting
Proteosynthese *f* protein synthesis
Protid *n* $^{1}H^{-}$ protide
protisch *s.* protonisch
Protium *n* ^{1}H protium, light hydrogen
Protocatechualdehyd *m* protocatechuic aldehyde, 3,4-dihydroxybenzaldehyde
Protocatechusäure *f* protocatechuic acid, 3,4-dihydroxybenzoic acid
Protofibrille *f* protofibril
Protohämin *n* protohaemin, haemin chloride
Protolyse *f* protolysis
Protolysetitration *f* neutralization (acid-base) titration
Protolyt *m* protolyte
protolytisch protolytic
Protomer[e] *n* protomer, protomeric unit *(protein chemistry)*
Protomerie *f s.* Prototropie
Proton *n* proton
Protonenabgabe *f* proton donation
protonenabspaltend protogenic
Protonenaffinität *f* proton affinity
Protonenakzeptor *m* proton acceptor, Brønsted-Lowry base
Protonenaufnahme *f* proton acceptance
Protonenbindungsenergie *f* proton binding energy
Protonen-Breitlinienresonanzspektroskopie *f* broad-line proton spin resonance spectroscopy
Protonendonator *m* proton donor, proton[ic] acid, Brønsted-Lowry acid
Protonenfänger *m* proton catcher
protonenfrei proton-free
Protonengeber *m s.* Protonendonator
Protonen-Kernresonanz *f* proton [magnetic] resonance, pmr, PMR
Protonenmasse *f* proton [rest] mass
Protonennehmer *m s.* Protonenakzeptor
Protonenpumpe *f (bioch)* proton pump
Protonenresonanz *f s.* Protonen-Kernresonanz
Protonenresonanzspektrum *n* proton spectrum
Protonenruh[e]masse *f* proton [rest] mass
Protonensäure *f s.* Protonendonator
Protonentranslokation *f*, **Protonentransport** *m (bioch)* proton translocation
Protonenübertragung *f* proton transfer
Protonenübertragungsreaktion *f* proton transfer reaction
Protonenverschiebung *f* proton shift
protonieren to protonate
Protonierung *f* protonation
protonisch protic
protonogen protogenic
protonophil protophilic
Protonsäure *f s.* Protonendonator
Protopektin *n* protopectin, pectinogen *(any of a group of water-insoluble pectic substances)*
Protoplasma *n* protoplasm
Protoplastenfusion *f (biot)* protoplast fusion
Protoplastentransformation *f (biot)* protoplast transformation
Protoplastenverschmelzung *f (biot)* protoplast fusion
prototrop prototropic
Prototropie *f* prototropy, prototropic rearrangement *(one form of tautomerism)*
Proustit *m (min)* proustite, light red silver ore *(arsenic(III) silver sulphide)*
Provitamin *n* provitamin, vitamin precursor
Prozentgehalt *m* percentage
Prozeß *m* process *(for compounds s. a.* Verfahren*)*
~/photophysikalischer photophysical process
Prozeßabwasser *n* process waste water

Prozeßanalyse *f* on-line analysis
Prozeßausrüstung *f* process equipment
Prozeßchemikalie *f* process chemical
Prozeßdampf *m* process steam
Prozeßgas *n* process gas
Prozeßgestaltung *f* process design
Prozeßgröße *f* process quantity
Prozeßpumpe *f* process pump
Prozeßschritt *m* process[ing] step, treatment step
Prozeßstufe *f* process[ing] stage, treatment stage
Prozeßvariable *f* process variable
Prozeßwärme *f* process heat
Prozeßwasser *n* process[ing] water, water for manufacturing use
Prozeßziel *n* process goal
PRPP = 5'-Phosphoribosyl-1-pyrophosphat
Prüfbecher *m (plast)* flow cup
Prüfbogen *m (pap)* test (hand, pulp) sheet
Prüfdauer *f* testing time (period)
prüfen to examine, *(thoroughly:)* to scrutinize; to test *(esp for a specified substance or for purity)*; *(met)* to assay *(ores)*; to test *(materials)*; to check *(esp the correctness or completeness)*
~/auf Gehalt *(pharm, met)* to assay
~/auf Geschmack to taste
Prüfer *m* 1. tester; *(food)* taster; 2. *s.* Prüfgerät
Prüfgasgemisch *n*, **Prüfgasmischung** *f* calibration gas mixture
Prüfgerät *n* testing apparatus, tester
Prüfglas *n* test glass
Prüfgut *n* entire (parent) lot, entire mass
Prüfkörper *m*, **Prüfling** *m s.* Probekörper
Prüflösung *f* test[ing] solution
Prüfmaterial *n* test material, material being *or* to be tested
Prüfmethode *f* test[ing] method
~/standardisierte standard test[ing] method
Prüfmischung *f (rubber)* test compound
Prüfmittel *n* testing agent
Prüfmuster *n s.* Probekörper
Prüfpapier *n* test (indicator) paper, *(Am)* reaction paper
Prüfprotokoll *n* testing protocol
Prüfsieb *n* test (testing) sieve (screen)
~/standardisiertes standard (normal) test sieve
Prüfsiebreihe *f*, **Prüfsiebsatz** *m* test sieve series, screen scale
Prüfstab *m* test rod
Prüftiegel *m* test cup *(of a flash-point tester)*
Prüfung *f* 1. examination, testing, *(thorough:)* scrutiny, testing *(of materials)*; 2. test *(esp for a specified substance or for purity)*; *(met)* assay; check *(esp for ensuring correctness or completeness)*
~ auf Ameisensäure formic-acid test
~ auf Biegefestigkeit cross-bend[ing] test
~ auf Biegerißfestigkeit flex-cracking test
~ auf Formaldehyd formaldehyde test
~ auf Formaldehyd nach Arnold und Mentzel Arnold-Mentzel formaldehyde test
~ auf Fuselöl fusel-oil test
~ auf Kohlendioxid test for carbon dioxide
~ auf Lichtbeständigkeit (Lichtechtheit) light test
~ auf Löslichkeit solubility test
~ auf Phenol phenol test
~ auf Sterilität sterility test
~/beschleunigte accelerated testing
~ durch Außenbewitterung outdoor weathering test
~/dynamische 1. dynamic testing; 2. dynamic test
~ im Labormaßstab 1. lab[oratory]-scale testing; 2. lab[oratory]-scale test
~ mit dem ballistischen Pendel ballistic pendulum test *(of explosives)*
~ mit Röntgenstrahlen 1. X-ray testing; 2. X-ray test
~/organoleptische 1. organoleptic (sensory) testing (examination); 2. organoleptic (sensory) test
~/orientierende preliminary (basic) test *(as of pesticides)*
~/sinnesphysiologische *s.* ~/organoleptische
~/statische 1. static testing; 2. static test
~/zerstörungsfreie 1. non-destructive testing, NDT, non-destructive examination (inspection); 2. non-destructive test
Prüfungsvorschrift *f* specification
Prüfverfahren *n* test[ing] method
Prüfvorrichtung *f s.* Prüfgerät
Prüfzeit *f s.* Prüfdauer
Prussiat *n*, **Prussid** *n* *pentacyanoferrate, prussiate, prussate
PS *s.* Polystyren
PSC = präparative Schichtchromatographie
Pschorr-Synthese *f* Pschorr reaction (synthesis) *(for obtaining phenanthrene derivatives)*
PSE *s.* Periodensystem [der Elemente]
p-Serie *f (spectr)* principal series
Pseudoanthrazit *m (carb)* pseudo-anthracite
Pseudoaromaten *pl* pseudo-aromatics
Pseudoasymmetrie *f* pseudo-asymmetry
pseudoasymmetrisch pseudo-asymmetric[al]
Pseudobase *f* pseudo base
Pseudobenzol *n* inorganic benzene, borazole, triborine triamine
Pseudocumen *n*, **Pseudocumol** *n* ψ-cumene, pseudo-cumene, 1,2,4-trimethylbenzene
pseudodimolekular pseudo-dimolecular
Pseudoecgonin *n* ψ-ecgonine, pseudo-ecgonine
Pseudohalogen *n* pseudo-halogen
Pseudohalogenid *n* pseudo-halide
Pseudokannelkohle *f* pseudocannel [coal]
Pseudokatalyse *f* pseudo-catalysis
Pseudokontaktverschiebung *f (spectr)* pseudo-contact (neighbour anisotropy) shift
pseudokristallin pseudo-crystalline
Pseudolösung *f* pseudo-solution
pseudomonomolekular pseudo-first-order, *(deprecated:)* pseudo-unimolecular

pseudomorph *(cryst)* pseudomorphic, pseudomorphous
Pseudomorphie *f (cryst)* pseudomorphism
Pseudomorphose *f (cryst)* 1. pseudomorphosis *(process)*; 2. pseudomorph *(substance)*
Pseudomorphosierung *f s.* Pseudomorphose 1.
pseudoplastisch pseudo-plastic
Pseudoplastizität *f* pseudo-plasticity
pseudoracemisch pseudo-racemic
Pseudorotation *f* pseudo-rotation
Pseudosalz *n* pseudo salt
Pseudosäure *f* pseudo acid
pseudostabil pseudo-stable
Pseudosymmetrie *f* pseudo-symmetry
pseudosymmetrisch pseudo-symmetric[al]
Pseudouridylsäure *f (bioch)* pseudouridylic acid
Psilomelan *m (min)* psilomelane *(manganese(IV) oxide)*
PSM *s.* Pflanzenschutzmittel
Psychochemikalie *f* psychochemical
Psychodysleptikum *n s.* Psychotomimetikum
Psychogift *n* psychochemical
Psycholeptikum *n (pharm)* neuroleptic [drug], antipsychotic, major tranquil[l]izer
Psychomimetikum *n s.* Psychotomimetikum
Psychopharmakon *n (pharm)* psychopharmacologic drug (agent), psychotropic agent
Psychosedativum *n (pharm)* [minor] tranquil[l]izer, tranquillizing drug, anxiolytic [sedative]
Psychosomimetikum *n s.* Psychotomimetikum
Psychostimulans *n (pharm)* psychostimulant
Psychotikum *n s.* Psychotomimetikum
Psychotomimetikum *n (pharm)* psychotomimetic [drug], psychodysleptic, hallucinogen, psychedelic drug
psychotomimetisch psychotomimetic, hallucinogenic
Psychotonikum *n (pharm)* psychostimulant
Psychotropikon *n s.* Psychopharmakon
Psychrometer *n* psychrometer, wet-and-dry-bulb hygrometer (thermometer), psychrometric hygrometer
PT *s.* Polyethylenfaserstoff
PTC *s.* Phasentransferkatalyse
Pteridin *n* pteridine, pyrimido-[4,5-*b*]-pyrazine
Pterin *n* pterin *(any of the pteridine derivatives)*
Pteroinsäure *f* pteroic acid
Pteroylglutamat *n* pteroylglutamate, folate
Pteroylglutaminsäure *f* pteroylglutamic acid, PGA, folic acid
PTFE *s.* Polytetrafluorethylen
Ptomain *n* ptomaine
Ptyalin *n* ptyalin *(salivary amylase)*
PU *s.* Polyurethanfaserstoff
Puddeleisen *n s.* Schweißstahl
puddeln *(met)* to puddle
Puddelofen *m (met)* puddling furnace
Puddelroheisen *n* forge pig iron
Puddelstahl *m s.* Schweißstahl
Puddelverfahren *n (met)* puddling process
Puder *m* powder
~/desodor[is]ierender deodorant powder
~/flüssiger liquid powder
~/gepreßter compressed powder
~/kompakter compact powder
Pudermittel *n* dusting powder, dusting (powdering) agent, *(rubber also)* chalk; coating substance *(as for conditioning fertilizers)*
pudern to dust, to powder, *(rubber also)* to chalk; to coat *(fertilizers)*
~/mit Talkum *(rubber)* to soapstone
Puderpapier *n (cosmet)* powder paper
Puderstoff *m* coating substance *(as for conditioning fertilizers)*
Puderzucker *m* powdered (castor, icing) sugar, *(Am)* confectioners' sugar
Puffbildung *f (bioch)* puffing *(of chromosomes)*
Puffer *m* 1. *(ch)* buffer; 2. *(petrol)* surge tank *(clay contacting process)*
Pufferbase *f* buffer base
Pufferbereich *m* buffer region
Puffergefäß *n* buffer vessel
Puffergemisch *n* buffer[ing] mixture
Pufferion *n* buffer ion
Pufferkapazität *f* buffering capacity (power)
Pufferlösung *f* buffer solution
~/standardisierte standard buffer [solution]
Puffermischung *f* buffer[ing] mixture
puffern to buffer
Pufferreservoir *n* buffer reservoir (chamber) *(electrophoresis)*
Puffersäure *f* buffer acid
Puffersubstanz *f* buffering agent (substance), buffer [re]agent
Puffersystem *n* buffer system
Pufferung *f* buffering
Puffer[ungs]vermögen *n* buffering capacity (power)
Pufferwert *m* buffer value (index), BI
Pufferwirkung *f* buffer[ing] action; buffer[ing] effect
Pufferzone *f* buffer region
Pulegon *n* pulegone *(a monocyclic ketone)*
Pulfrich-Refraktometer *n* Pulfrich refractometer
Pullulan *n (bioch)* pullulan *(a polysaccharide)*
Pulpe *f*, **Pülpe** *f (food)* [fruit] pulp, pomace, pumace
Pülpefänger *m (sugar)* beet pulp catcher
Pulper *m (pap)* pulper, pulping engine, hydrapulper
~ mit vier Auflösescheiben quatropulper
~ mit zwei Auflösescheiben duopulper
Pulsation *f* pulsation
Pulsationsdämpfer *m* pulse dampener, pulsation dampener (snubber)
Pulsationsdämpfung *f* pulse dampening
pulsationsfrei non-pulsating, pulseless, pulse-free
Pulsationskolonne *f* pulsed column (tower)
Pulsationschwingung *f* [symmetrical] breathing vibration
Pulsator *m* pulser, pulsing device
Pulse-Polarographie *f s.* Pulspolarographie
Puls-Experiment *n (bioch)* pulse experiment

Puls-Fourier-Transformation *f* pulse Fourier transform, PFT
pulsfrei *s.* pulsationsfrei
pulsieren to pulse, to pulsate
Pulsometer *n* pulsometer [pump], acid egg, blow case
Pulspolarographie *f (anal)* pulse polarography
~/derivative derivative pulse polarography
Pulsradiolyse *f* pulse[d] radiolysis *(for investigating fast reactions)*
Pulswinkel *m (spectr)* pulse angle
Pulver *n* powder • **zu ~ zerfallen** to fall to powder
~/einbasiges single-base powder *(technology of explosives)*
~/elektrolytisches (katodisches) electrolytic powder
~/metallisches metal powder, powder[ed] metal
~/oberflächenaktives wettable powder *(crop protection)*
~/rauchloses (rauchschwaches) smokeless powder
~/zweibasiges double-base powder *(technology of explosives)*
Pulveraktivkohle *f* powdered activated carbon
pulverartig powdery, pulverulent
pulveraufkohlen *(met)* to pack-carburize
Pulveraufkohlen *n (met)* pack carburizing, solid[-pack] carburizing
Pulveraufnahme *f s.* Pulverdiagramm
Pulverband *n***/dichtgepreßtes** compacted strip *(in powder rolling)*
Pulverdiagramm *n (cryst)* powder diagram, [X-ray] powder pattern, [X-ray] powder photograph
Pulverdiffraktometer *n* X-ray powder diffractometer, powder [diffraction] camera
pulvereinsetzen *s.* pulveraufkohlen
Pulverflasche *f* wide-neck (wide-mouth) bottle
pulverförmig, pulverig powdery, pulverulent, powder-form
pulverisieren to pulverize, to reduce to powder, to powder, to triturate
Pulverisiermühle *f* pulverizing mill, pulverizer
Pulverisolierung *f* powder insulation *(cryogenics)*
Pulverkaffee *m* instant (soluble) coffee
Pulverkohle *f* powdered [activated] carbon
Pulverkohlereaktivierung *f* powdered carbon reactivation
~ im Fließbett (Wirbelbett) fluidized-bed powdered carbon reactivation
Pulverkörper *m* propellant grain
Pulverlöscher *m* powder extinguisher, dry chemical [fire] extinguisher
Pulvermetallurgie *f* powder metallurgy, metal ceramics
pulvermetallurgisch powder-metallurgical, metal-ceramic
Pulvermethode *f (cryst)* [X-ray] powder method
pulvern *s.* pulverisieren
Pulverpreßkörper *m*, **Pulverpreßling** *m* [powder metal] compact
Pulverseele *f* [powder] core *(of a blasting fuse)*
Pulversintern *n* powder moulding (sintering)
Pulversprengstoff *m* powder (low) explosive, deflagrating powder, propellant [explosive]
Pulvertrichter *m* powder funnel, filling (wide-stemmed) funnel
Pulververfahren *n s.* Pulvermethode
Pulververstäuber *m (agric)* dusting machine, duster
Pulverwalzen *n* powder (direct) rolling *(of powder metal)*
pulverzementieren *s.* pulveraufkohlen
pulvrig *s.* pulverförmig
Pummerer-Umlagerung *f* Pummerer rearrangement *(of sulphoxides into α-acyloxysulphides)*
Pumpbeton *m* pumping (pumped) concrete
Pumpe *f* pump
~/dreistufige three-stage pump
~/einseitig saugende single-suction pump
~/einstufige single-stage pump
~/elektromagnetische electromagnetic pump
~ für Gase gas pump
~ für heiße Medien hot-charge pump
~/halbaxiale mixed-flow pump, turbine pump
~ in diagonaler Bauart *s.* ~/halbaxiale
~/mehrstufige multistage pump
~ mit einseitigem Flüssigkeitseintritt single-suction pump
~ mit gleichbleibendem Druck constant-pressure pump
~ mit Leitrad diffuser (turbine) pump
~ mit zweiseitigem Flüssigkeitseintritt double-suction pump
~/peristaltische peristaltic pump
~/rotierende rotary pump
~/vierstufige four-stage pump
~/zweiseitig saugende double-suction pump
~/zweistufige two-stage pump
pumpen to pump
Pumpengehäuse *n*, **Pumpenkörper** *m* pump casing
Pumpenwirkungsgrad *m* pump efficiency
pumpfähig pumpable, capable of being pumped
Pumpgrenze *f* pumping limit (point) *(of a compressor)*
Pumpsystem *n***/durchflußgeregeltes** *(chromat)* flow-feedback solvent-metering system
Punkt *m***/azeotrop[isch]er** azeotropic point
~/dunkler *(plast)* dark speck, hull *(as in laminated fibres)*
~/elektrisch neutraler *s.* ~/isoelektrischer
~/eutektischer eutectic [point]
~/isoelektrischer isoelectric point, zero point of charge, ZPC
~/isoionischer isoionic point
~/isosbestischer isosbestic point
~/kritischer critical point *(as in three-component systems)*; critical moisture point *(in drying processes)*
~/kryohydratischer cryohydric point
~/peritektischer peritectic (transition) point

Punktbeschichten *n (plast)* spot coating
Punktcodon *n (bioch)* terminator codon, termination (chain-terminating) codon
Punktdefekt *m (cryst)* point defect
Punktfehlstelle *f (cryst)* point defect
Punktgruppe *f* 1. *(spectr)* point group; 2. *s.* Punktsymmetriegruppe
Punktladung *f (phys ch)* point charge
Punktlagensymmetrie *f* site symmetry
Punktmutation *f (biol)* point mutation
Punktquelle *f* point source [of emission]
Punktstörung *f* point defect
Punktsymmetriegruppe *f (cryst)* point (symmetry) group, crystal (symmetry) class
pupillenerweiternd mydriatic
pupillenverengend miotic
Puppe *f (rubber, plast)* puppel, billet
PUR *s.* Polyurethan
Purgans *n*, **Purgativum** *n (pharm)* purgative
Purge-and-trap-Verfahren *n* purge-and-trap technique *(gas chromatography)*
Purifikation *f* purification *(of emulsions)*
Purinalkaloid *n* purine alkaloid
Purinbase *f* purine base
Purinlücke *f (biot)* purine gap
6-Purinon *n* 6(1H)-purinone, hypoxanthine, 6-hydroxypurine
Purinstoffwechsel *m* purine metabolism
Purkinje-Phänomen *n (phot)* Purkinje effect
Purpur *m* purple
~/Antiker (Byzantinischer) Phoenician (Tyrian) purple, purple of the ancients *(6,6'-dibromoindigo)*
~ der Alten *s.* ~/Antiker
~/Französischer archil, orchil *(a lichen dye)*
~/Tyrischer *s.* ~/Antiker
Purpurerz *n* purple ore, blue billy *(leached residue of roasted pyrites containing copper)*
Purpursäure *f* purpuric acid
Purpursäurechelat *n* purpureate chelate
putzen 1. to fettle, to trim *(metal castings, plastics mouldings, or excess body in pottery-ware)*; 2. *(build)* to plaster
Putzen *n* **von Hand** hand fettling
Putzmaschine *f* fettling machine
Putzmittel *n* scouring agent
Putzmörtel *m* plaster [mortar]
Putztrommel *f* tumbling barrel
Puzzolanerde *f (build)* pozzolana, puzzolan[a]
Puzzolanzement *m* pozzolanic (puzzolanic) cement
PV *s.* Polyvinylfaserstoff
PVA *s.* 1. Polyvinylalkohol; 2. Polyvinylalkoholfaserstoff
PVAC *s.* Polyvinylacetat
PVAL *s.* Polyvinylalkohol
PVB *s.* Polyvinylbutyral
PVC *s.* 1. Polyvinylchlorid; 2. Polyvinylchloridfaserstoff
PVCA *s.* Polyvinylchloridacetat
PVC-H, PVC-hart *n* unplasticized (rigid) PVC
PVC-Schaumstoff *m* cellular PVC, PVC foam
PVC-W, PVC-weich *n* plasticized (flexible) PVC
PVD *s.* Polyvinylidenchloridfaserstoff
PVDC *s.* Polyvinylidenchlorid
PVDF *s.* Polyvinylidenfluorid
PVF *s.* Polyvinylfluorid
PVK *s.* 1. Pigmentvolumenkonzentration; 2. Polyvinylcarbazen
PVP *s.* 1. Polyvinylpyrrolidon; 2. Polyvinylpyrrolidin
PVY *s.* Polyacrylnitrilfaserstoff
p-Wert *m (hyd)* phenolphthalein alkalinity, P alkalinity
Pyknometer *n* pycnometer, density (specific-gravity) bottle (flask)
pyknometrisch pycnometric
Pyran *n (org ch)* pyran
Pyranose *f* pyranose *(a cyclic monosaccharide)*
Pyranoseform *f* pyranose form *(of sugars)*
Pyranosering *m* pyranose ring
Pyranosestruktur *f* pyranose structure
Pyranosid *n* pyranoside
Pyranylierung *f* pyranylation
Pyrargyrit *m* pyrargyrite, dark red silver [ore], red silver ore, silver ruby *(antimony(III) silver sulphide)*
Pyrazin *n* pyrazine, 1,4-diazine
Pyrazol *n* pyrazole, 1,2-diazole
Pyrazolon *n* pyrazolone
Pyrazolon-Azofarbstoff *m*, **Pyrazolonfarbstoff** *m* [azo-]pyrazolone dye
Pyren *n* pyrene *(a tetracyclic compound)*
Pyrethrineinwirkung *f (tox)* pyrethrinization
Pyrethroid *n* pyrethroid *(any of a series of insecticidal compounds)*
Pyridazin *n* pyridazine, 1,2-diazine
Pyridin *n* pyridine
Pyridinalkaloid *n* pyridine[-type] alkaloid
Pyridinbase *f* pyridine base
Pyridin-Butadien-Kautschuk *m* pyridine-butadiene rubber, PBR
Pyridin-3-carbonsäure *f* pyridine-3-carboxylic acid, nicotinic acid
Pyridindicarbonsäure *f* pyridinedicarboxylic acid
Pyridinextraktion *f* pyridine extraction
Pyridinring *m* pyridine ring
Pyridinsynthese *f*/**Hantzschsche** Hantzsch pyridine synthesis
Pyridin-2,3,5-tricarbonsäure *f* pyridine-2,3,5-tricarboxylic acid, carbodinicotinic acid
Pyridin-2,4,5-tricarbonsäure *f* pyridine-2,4,5-tricarboxylic acid, berberonic acid
Pyridon *n* pyridone, hydroxypyridine
Pyridoxalphosphat *n* pyridoxal phosphate *(coenzyme of decarboxylase)*
Pyridoxin *n* pyridoxin, adermin, 3-hydroxy-4,5-di(hydroxymethyl)-2-methylpyridine *(vitamin B_6)*
Pyridylethylierung *f* pyridylethylation
Pyrimidin *n* pyrimidine, 1,3-diazine
Pyrimidinbase *f (bioch)* pyrimidine base

Pyrit *m (min)* [iron] pyrite[s], mundic *(iron disulphide)*
Pyritkonzentrat *n* pyrite[s] concentrate
Pyritröstung *f (met)* roasting of pyrite[s]
Pyritschmelzen *n (met)* pyritic smelting
Pyritschwefel *m* pyritic sulphur
Pyroantimonat(V) *n s.* Diantimonat(V)
Pyroantimonsäure *f s.* Diantimon(V)-säure
Pyroarsenat(III) *n s.* Diarsenat(III)
Pyroarsenat(V) *n s.* Diarsenat(V)
Pyroarsensäure *f s.* Diarsen(V)-säure
Pyroborat *n s.* Tetraborat
Pyroborax *m* dehydrated borax, calcined (burnt, anhydrous) borax *(sodium tetraborate)*
Pyroborsäure *f s.* Tetraborsäure
Pyrocatechol *n s.* Brenzcatechin
Pyrochlor *m (min)* pyrochlore
Pyrogallol *n* pyrogallol, pyrogallic acid, 1,2,3-trihydroxybenzene
Pyrogallolgerbstoff *m* pyrogallol tan
Pyrogallussäure *f s.* Pyrogallol
pyrogen pyrogenic
Pyrohyporhenat *n* $M^{I}_{4}Re_2O_7$ heptaoxodirhenate, *(deprecated:)* pyrohyporhenate
Pyroligninsäure *f* pyroligneous acid *(crude acetic acid obtained by wood distillation)*
Pyrolyse *f* pyrolysis
~/gelenkte controlled pyrolysis
~ mit Pebbles pebble-heater pyrolysis
~/schnelle fast pyrolysis
Pyrolyse-Feldionisations-Massenspektrometrie *f* pyrolysis field ionization mass spectrometry
Pyrolysegas *n* pyrolysis gas
Pyrolyse-Gaschromatographie *f* pyrolysis gas chromatography, PGC
Pyrolyseprodukt *n* pyrolyzate
Pyrolysereaktion *f* pyrolysis (pyrolytic) reaction
pyrolysieren to pyrolyze
pyrolytisch pyrolytic
Pyromellithsäure *f* pyromellitic acid, benzene-1,2,4,5-tetracarboxylic acid
Pyromellithsäuredianhydrid *n* pyromellitic dianhydride, PMDA
Pyrometallurgie *f* pyrometallurgy
pyrometallurgisch pyrometallurgical
Pyrometer *n* pyrometer
~/optisches optical pyrometer
~/photoelektrisches photoelectric pyrometer
~/thermoelektrisches thermoelectric pyrometer
Pyrometrie *f* pyrometry
pyrometrisch pyrometric
Pyromorphit *m (min)* pyromorphite, green (brown) lead ore *(lead chloride phosphate)*
Pyron *n* pyrone *(any of a class of heterocyclic compounds containing the oxo group)*
Pyrop *m (min)* pyrope *(a nesosilicate)*
pyrophor pyrophoric, pyrophorous
Pyrophosphat *n s.* Diphosphat
Pyrophosphatspaltung *f (bioch)* pyrophosphate cleavage
Pyrophosphit *n s.* Diphosphit
Pyrophosphorsäure *f s.* Diphosphorsäure
Pyrophosphorylierung *f (bioch)* pyrophosphorylation
Pyrosäure *f* pyroacid
Pyroschleimsäure *f s.* Brenzschleimsäure
Pyroskop *n (ceram)* pyroscope
Pyrosol *n (coll)* pyrosol *(a type of solid sols)*
Pyrosulfit *n s.* Disulfit
Pyrosulfurylchlorid *n s.* Disulfurylchlorid
Pyrotechnik *f* pyrotechnics
Pyrotechniker *m* pyrotechnist, pyrotechnician
pyrotechnisch pyrotechnic[al]
Pyrotritarsäure *f* pyrotritaric acid, 2,5-dimethylfuran-3-carboxylic acid
Pyrovanadat *n s.* Divanadat
Pyroweinsäure *f* pyrotartaric acid, methylsuccinic acid, 2-methylbutane-1,4-dioic acid
Pyroxen *m (min)* pyroxene *(a member of a group of inosilicates)*
Pyroxenfamilie *f (min)* pyroxene group
Pyrrhotin *m (min)* pyrrhotite, pyrrhotine, magnetic pyrites *(iron(II) sulphide)*
Pyrrol *n* pyrrole
Pyrrolfarbstoff *m* pyrrole pigment
Pyrrolidin *n* pyrrolidine, tetrahydropyrrole
Pyrrolidinalkaloid *n* pyrrolidine alkaloid
Pyrrolidin-2-carbonsäure *f* pyrrolidine-2-carboxylic acid, proline
Pyrrolizidinalkaloid *n* pyrrolizidine (senecio) alkaloid
Pyrrolring *m* pyrrole ring
Pyrrolsynthese *f*/**Knorrsche** Knorr pyrrole synthesis
Pyrrolylen *n s.* Buta-1,3-dien
Pyrron *n* pyrrone, polyimidazopyrrolone
Pyruvat *n* pyruvate *(salt or ester of pyruvic acid)*
Pyruvinaldehyd *m s.* Methylglyoxal
Pyruvinsäure *f s.* Brenztraubensäure
PZ *s.* Portlandzement
P-Zweig *m* P-branch *(of a band spectrum)*

Q

Q-Einheit *f* Q unit, tetrafunctional unit *(a structural unit)*
Q-Enzym *n* Q enzyme, branching (branch-point) enzyme
***Q-e*-Schema** *n* *Q-e* scheme *(copolymerization)*
Quaderkalk *m* ashlar lime
Quadranteneinbau *m* quadrant flights *(of a rotary dryer)*
Quadratbecken *n* square basin (tank)
Quadratmetergewicht *n s.* Masse je Flächeneinheit
Quadrupeleffektverdampfer *m* quadruple-effect evaporator
Quadrupelpunkt *m (phys ch)* quadruple point
Quadrupol *m (phys ch)* quadrupole

Quadrupolkopplung *f*[**/elektrische**] *(nucl)* quadrupole coupling
Quadrupolkräfte *fpl* quadrupole forces
Quadrupolmassenspektrometer *n* quadrupole mass spectrometer
Quadrupolmoment *n* quadrupole moment
~ **des Kerns** nuclear quadrupole moment
Quadrupolrelaxation *f (spectr)* quadrupole relaxation
Quadrupolstrahlung *f* quadrupole radiation
Qualität *f* grade, quality • **von minderer** ~ low-grade
~/handelsübliche commercial grade
Qualitätsanforderungen *fpl* quality demands
Qualitätsdüngung *f* quality fertilization
Qualitätsgröße *f (phys ch)* intensive property (quantity)
Qualitätskontrolle *f* quality control
Qualitätsminderung *f* deterioration in quality
Qualitätsprüfung *f* quality test
Qualitätssicherung *f* quality assurance
Qualitätsverbesserung *f* improvement in quality, upgrading
Quant *n (phys ch)* quant[um]
quanteln to quantize
Quantelung *f* quantization
~ **der Energie** quantization of energy
~/räumliche space quantization, quantization of direction
Quantenäquivalenz *f* quantum equivalence
Quantenäquivalenzgesetz *n* Einstein photochemical equivalence law, Einstein law of photochemical equivalence, Einstein-Stark law
Quantenausbeute *f* quantum yield (efficiency)
~/differentielle differential quantum yield
~/integrale integral quantum yield
Quantenbedingung *f* quantum condition
Quantenchemie *f* quantum chemistry
Quantenelektrodynamik *f* quantum electrodynamics
Quantenempfänger *m (anal)* quantum effect detector
Quantenenergie *f* quantum energy
Quantenflüssigkeit *f* quantum liquid
Quantenhypothese *f*/**Plancksche** Planck's hypothesis *(of quantized energy)*
Quantenmechanik *f* quantum (matrix) mechanics
quantenmechanisch quantum-mechanical
Quantensprung *m* quantum jump (transition)
Quantenstatistik *f* quantum statistics
Quantentheorie *f* quantum theory
Quantenzahl *f* quantum number
~/azimutale azimuthal (subsidiary) quantum number, orbital [angular momentum] quantum number
~/bahnmagnetische *s.* ~/magnetische
~/innere inner quantum number
~/magnetische magnetic quantum number
~/radiale radial quantum number
~/räumliche *s.* ~/magnetische
~/sekundäre *s.* ~/azimutale
Quantenzähler *m* quantum counter
Quantenzustand *m* quantum state
quantisieren *s.* quanteln
Quantitätsgröße *f (phys ch)* extensive property (quantity)
Quantum *n* quantum, quantity, amount; portion
Quark *n* quark *(a hypothetical particle)*
quartär quaternary
Quartärsalz *n* quaternary salt
Quartärstruktur *f* quaternary structure *(of proteins)*
Quartation *f* quartation *(separating gold and silver by hot nitric acid)*
Quartettaufspaltung *f (phys ch)* quartett splitting
quartieren *(anal)* to quarter
Quarz *m* quartz • **aus** ~ quartzose, quartzous, quartzy
~/linker left-handed quartz
~/rechter right-handed quartz
Quarzboot *n* quartz boat
quarzführend quartz-bearing, quartziferous *(rock)*
Quarzgefäß *n* quartz vessel
Quarzglas *n* quartz glass, transparent [vitreous] silica, fused quartz
Quarzgut *n* translucent vitreous silica, fused silica
quarzhaltig containing quartz, quartzic, quartzose, *(esp relating to rocks:)* quartz-bearing, quartziferous
quarzig quartzose, quartzous, quartzy
Quarzit *m (min)* quartzite
quarzitisch quartzitic
Quarzkapillare *f (chromat)* fused-silica [open tubular] capillary, FSOT capillary
Quarzkeil *m* quartz wedge
Quarzkorn *n* quartz grain
Quarzkristall *m* quartz crystal
Quarzlampe *f* quartz lamp
Quarzporphyr *m* quartz porphyry
Quarzsand *m* quartz (silica) sand
Quarzschale *f* quartz dish
Quarzschiffchen *n* quartz boat
Quarzspektrograph *m* quartz spectrograph
Quarztiegel *m* quartz crucible
Quarz-UV *n*, **Quarz-UV-Bereich** *m* near ultraviolet
Quasi-Fermi-Niveau *n* quasi-Fermi level
Quasifließen *n* pseudo-plastic flow
Quasigleichgewicht *n* quasi-equilibrium
quasikristallin quasi-crystalline
quasiplastisch pseudo-plastic
Quasiracemat *n* quasi-racemate
quasistabil quasi-stable
quasistationär quasi-stationary
Quasistationaritätsprinzip *n* steady-state [approximation] method
quasistatisch quasi-static
quasiviskos quasi-viscous
quaternär quaternary
quaternisieren to quaternize *(e.g. amines)*
Quaternisierung *f* quaternization *(as of amines)*
Quaternisierungsmittel *n* quaternizing agent

Quayle-Zyklus *m (bioch)* Quayle cycle, ribulose monophosphate cycle
Quebrachoextrakt *m (tann)* quebracho extract
Quecksilber *n* Hg mercury
~/gediegenes native mercury
Quecksilber(I)-acetat *n* mercury(I) acetate, mercurous acetate
Quecksilber(II)-acetat *n* mercury(II) acetate, mercuric acetate
Quecksilber(II)-acetylid *n* mercury(II) acetylide, mercuric acetylide
Quecksilberalkyl *n* alkylmercury [compound]
Quecksilber(II)-amidochlorid *n* amidomercury(II) chloride, infusible white precipitate
Quecksilberauffangwanne *f* mercury tray
Quecksilber(I)-azid *n* mercury(I) azide, mercurous azide
Quecksilber(I)-bromat *n* mercury(I) bromate, mercurous bromate
Quecksilber(II)-bromat *n* mercury(II) bromate, mercuric bromate
Quecksilber(I)-bromid *n* mercury(I) bromide, mercurous bromide
Quecksilber(II)-bromid *n* mercury(II) bromide, mercuric bromide
Quecksilber(II)-bromidiodid *n* mercury(II) bromide iodide, mercuric bromide iodide
Quecksilber(I)-carbonat *n* mercury(I) carbonate, mercurous carbonate
Quecksilber(I)-chlorat *n* mercury(I) chlorate, mercurous chlorate
Quecksilber(II)-chlorat *n* mercury(II) chlorate, mercuric chlorate
Quecksilber(I)-chlorid *n* mercury(I) chloride, mercurous chloride, calomel
Quecksilber(II)-chlorid *n* mercury(II) chloride, mercuric chloride, sublimate
Quecksilber(II)-chloridiodid *n* mercury(II) chloride iodide, mercuric chloride iodide
Quecksilber(I)-chromat *n* mercury(I) chromate, mercurous chromate
Quecksilber(II)-chromat *n* mercury(II) chromate, mercuric chromate
Quecksilber(II)-cyanid *n* mercury(II) cyanide, mercuric cyanide
Quecksilberdampf *m* mercury vapour
Quecksilberdampflampe *f* mercury[-vapour] lamp, mercury arc (discharge) lamp
Quecksilberdestillationsapparat *m* mercury still
Quecksilberdi... *s.* Quecksilber(II)-...
Quecksilberdichtung *f* mercury seal *(as on a stirrer)*
Quecksilberdiffusionspumpe *f* mercury diffusion pump, mercury[-vapour] pump
Quecksilberelektrode *f* mercury electrode
~/gerührte großflächige stirred mercury-pool electrode
~/strömende venous mercury electrode
Quecksilbererz *n* mercury ore
Quecksilberfaden *m* mercury thread *(in thermometers)*
Quecksilberfahlerz *n (min)* schwazite *(a tetrahedrite containing mercury)*
Quecksilberfalle *f* mercury trap
Quecksilber(I)-fluorid *n* mercury(I) fluoride, mercurous fluoride
Quecksilber(II)-fluorid *n* mercury(II) fluoride, mercuric fluoride
Quecksilber(II)-fulminat *n* mercury fulminate, fulminating mercury, mercuric fulminate
quecksilberhaltig containing mercury, mercurial
Quecksilber(I)-hexafluorosilicat *n* mercury(I) hexafluorosilicate, mercurous fluorosilicate
Quecksilber(II)-hexafluorosilicat *n* mercury(II) hexafluorosilicate, mercuric fluorosilicate
Quecksilber(II)-hexoxotellurat(VI) *n* mercury(II) hexaoxotellurate(VI), mercury(II) orthotellurate, mercuric orthotellurate
Quecksilber-Hochdrucklampe *f* high-pressure mercury arc lamp
Quecksilber(II)-hydrogenarsenat(V) *n* mercury(II) hydrogenarsenate, mercuric hydrogenarsenate
Quecksilber(I)-iodat *n* mercury(I) iodate, mercurous iodate
Quecksilber(II)-iodat *n* mercury(II) iodate, mercuric iodate
Quecksilber(I)-iodid *n* mercury(I) iodide, mercurous iodide
Quecksilber(II)-iodid *n* mercury(II) iodide, mercuric iodide
~/gelbes yellow mercuric iodide
~/rotes red mercuric iodide
Quecksilber-Kaltdampftechnik *f (spectr)* cold-vapour technique
Quecksilberkatode *f* mercury cathode
Quecksilberlampe *f s.* Quecksilberdampflampe
Quecksilberlichtbogen *m* mercury arc
Quecksilbermanometer *n* mercury (mercurial) manometer, mercury gauge
Quecksilbermikroelektrode *f* mercury microelectrode
Quecksilberniederdrucklampe *f* low-pressure mercury vapour lamp
Quecksilber(I)-nitrat *n* mercury(I) nitrate, mercurous nitrate
Quecksilber(II)-nitrat *n* mercury(II) nitrate, mercuric nitrate
Quecksilber(II)-nitrid *n* mercury(II) nitride, mercuric nitride
Quecksilber(I)-nitrit *n* mercury(I) nitrite, mercurous nitrite
Quecksilber(I)-orthoarsenat(V) *n* mercury(I) tetraoxoarsenate, *(deprecated:)* mercurous orthoarsenate
Quecksilber(II)-orthoarsenat(V) *n* mercury(II) tetraoxoarsenate, *(deprecated:)* mercuric orthoarsenate
Quecksilber(I)-orthophosphat *n* mercury(I) orthophosphate, mercurous orthophosphate

Quecksilber(II)-orthophosphat *n* mercury(II) orthophosphate, mercuric orthophosphate
Quecksilber(I)-oxid *n* mercury(I) oxide, mercurous oxide
Quecksilber(II)-oxid *n* mercury(II) oxide, mercuric oxide
~/gefälltes (gelbes) yellow mercuric oxide, yellow precipitate
~/rotes red mercuric oxide, red precipitate
Quecksilberpumpe *f s.* Quecksilberdiffusionspumpe
Quecksilber(I)-rhodanid *n s.* Quecksilber(I)-thiocyanat
Quecksilber(II)-rhodanid *n s.* Quecksilber(II)-thiocyanat
Quecksilbersalbe *f* mercurial ointment
Quecksilber(I)-salz *n* mercury(I) salt, mercurous salt
Quecksilber(II)-salz *n* mercury(II) salt, mercuric salt
Quecksilbersäule *f* mercury column
Quecksilber(II)-selenid *n* mercury(II) selenide, mercuric selenide
Quecksilberstand *m* mercury level
Quecksilber(I)-sulfat *n* mercury(I) sulphate, mercurous sulphate
Quecksilber(II)-sulfat *n* mercury(II) sulphate, mercuric sulphate
Quecksilber(I)-sulfid *n* mercury(I) sulphide, mercurous sulphide
Quecksilber(II)-sulfid *n* mercury(II) sulphide, mercuric sulphide
~/rotes red mercuric sulphide
Quecksilbertauchlampe *f* mercury immersion lamp
Quecksilber(II)-tetroxotellurat(VI) *n* mercury(II) tetraoxotellurate(VI), mercury(II) metatellurate, mercuric metatellurate
Quecksilberthermometer *n* mercury-in-glass thermometer
Quecksilber(I)-thiocyanat *n* mercury(I) thiocyanate, mercurous thiocyanate
Quecksilber(II)-thiocyanat *n* mercury(II) thiocyanate, mercuric thiocyanate
Quecksilbertropfelektrode *f* dropping mercury electrode, DME
Quecksilbertropfkatode *f* dropping mercury cathode
Quecksilberverbindung *f* mercury compound, mercurial
Quecksilberverfahren *n* mercury-cell process, [intermediate] mercury electrode process *(electrolysis)*
Quecksilbervergiftung *f* mercury poisoning, mercurialism, hydrargyrism
Quecksilberverstärker *m (phot)* mercury intensifier
Quecksilberverstärkung *f (phot)* mercury intensification
Quecksilber(I)-wolframat *n* *mercury(I) wolframate, mercury(I) tungstate, mercurous tungstate
Quecksilber(II)-wolframat *n* *mercury(II) wolframate, mercury(II) tungstate, mercuric tungstate
Quecksilberzange *f* mercury tongs
Quecksilberzelle *f* mercury [cathode] cell *(electrolysis)*
quellbar capable of swelling, swellable
~/in Wasser water-swellable
Quellbarkeit *f* capability of swelling, swelling capacity, swellability
quellbeständig resistant to swelling, swell-resistant, non-swelling
Quellbeständigkeit *f* resistance to swelling
Quellbottich *m (ferm)* steep tank, steeping vat, steeper
Quelle *f* 1. source; 2. spring
~/mobile mobile source [of emission]
~/muriatische brine spring
quellen to swell; to steep, to [cause to] swell
quellfähig capable of swelling
Quellfähigkeit *f* 1. capability of swelling, swelling capacity; 2. swelling power
Quellfassung *f s.* Quellwasserfassung
quellfest resistant to swelling, swell resistant, non-swelling
Quellfestmittel *n* non-swelling agent
Quellgrad *m s.* Quellungsgrad
Quellprüfung *f* swelling test
Quellpunkt *m (glass)* hot spot
Quellschweißen *n* solvent welding
Quellstock *m s.* Quellbottich
Quellungsbetrag *m s.* Quellungsgrad
Quellungsdruck *m* swelling pressure
Quellungsgeschwindigkeit *f* rate of swelling
Quellungsgrad *m* degree (extent, amount) of swelling
Quellungsmittel *n* swelling agent
Quellungsprüfung *f*, **Quellungsversuch** *m* swelling test
Quellungswärme *f* heat of swelling
Quellverhalten *n* swelling behaviour (properties)
Quellvermögen *n s.* Quellfähigkeit
Quellwasser *n* spring water
Quellwasserfassung *f* spring protection
Quellwirkung *f* swelling effect
Quellzement *m* expanding (expansive) cement
quenchen to quench *(to slow down rapidly esp a reaction)*
Quencher *m* quenching agent *(photochemistry)*
Quenchöl *n (met)* quench[ing] oil
Querbruchfestigkeit *f* transverse strength
Querdiffusion *f (chromat)* lateral diffusion
Querflammenwanne *f (glass)* side-fired (side-port) furnace
Querlauf *m s.* Querrichtung
Quermischung *f* radial mixing
Querrichtung *f (pap)* cross direction (way)
Querschlag *m* cross-gallery *(underground gasification)*

querschleifen *(pap)* to grind across the grain
Querschleifen *n (pap)* cross-grinding
Querschleifer *m (pap)*cross-grinder
querschneiden *(pap)* to cross-cut, to cut across, to sheet
Querschneiden *n (pap)* cross-cutting, sheeting
~ **mit rotierenden Messern** rotary cutting
Querschneider *m (pap)* cross-cutter, sheet cutter, sheeter
~ **mit rotierenden Messern** rotary [knife] cutter, revolving-knife cutting machine
Querschnitt *m*/**effektiver** effective cross section
~ **im Augenblick des Bruchs** *s.* ~/wirklicher
~/**ursprünglicher** original cross section
~/**wirklicher** *(rubber)* cross section at break
Querschnittsfläche *f* cross-sectional area
Querschnittsverminderung *f (text)* necking *(on stretching filaments)*
Querspritzkopf *m (plast)* cross (transversal) extruder head, crosshead
Querstrom *m* cross flow; cross current
Querstromkühlturm *m* cross-flow cooling tower
Querströmung *f* cross flow
Quervermischung *f* radial mixing
quervernetzen to cross-link
quervernetzend cross-linking
Quervernetzung *f* cross-linkage, *(result also:)* cross-link
Querzahl *f* Poisson's ratio *(of transverse to longitudinal strain in a material under tension)*
Quetsche *f* press, squeezer
quetschen to press, to squeeze
Quetschfalten *fpl (pap)* calender cuts *(a defect)*
Quetschhahn *m* pinchcock, hose cock, pinch clamp
~ **nach Day** Day pinchcock
~ **nach Hoffmann** Hoffmann clamp, Bunsen screw clip
~ **nach Mohr** Mohr pinchcock (clip)
Quetschklemme *f s.* Quetschhahn
Quetschkolben *m* compressor *(of a diaphragm valve)*
Quetschwalze *f* press (pressure, compression) roll, squeeze (squeezing) roll, squeegee
Quirl *m s.* Massequirl
quirlen *(ceram)* to blunge
Quotient *m*/**respiratorischer** *(bioch)* respiratory quotient (ratio)
QUV *s.* Quarz-UV
Q-Wert *m* Q-value *(of a nuclear reaction)*
Q-Zweig *m* Q-branch *(in Raman spectra)*

R

R *s.* Röntgen-Einheit
Rabi-Methode *f (nucl)* Rabi method
Racemat *n* racemate *(1. optically inactive compound; 2. salt or ester of DL-tartaric acid)*
~/**partielles** partial racemate
Racematspaltung *f*, **Racemattrennung** *f* resolution of racemates, splitting (separation) of racemic mixtures
Racematverbindung *f* racemic compound
Racemform *f* racemic form
racemisch racemic
racemisieren to racemize
Racemisierung *f* racemization
~/**partielle** partial racemization
Rad *n*, **Rad-Einheit** *f* rad *(a unit of absorbed dose of ionizing radiation)*
Radialbeschleunigung *f* angular acceleration
Radialkolbenpumpe *f* radial-piston pump
Radialschaufel *f* radial blade
radialstengelig, radialstrahlig *(cryst)* radiating, divergent
Radialstromreaktor *m* radial-flow [catalytic] reactor, radial fixed-bed reactor
Radialventilator *m* centrifugal fan
Radierbarkeit *f*, **Radierfestigkeit** *f (pap)* erasability
Radikal *n* [free] radical
~/**langlebiges (persistentes)** persistent (long-lived) radical
Radikalanion *n* radical anion, anion radical
radikalartig radical-like
Radikalausbeutefaktor *m* efficiency factor, initiator efficiency *(radical polymerization)*
Radikalbildner *m* radical former
Radikalbildung *f* radical formation
Radikalfalle *f* free-radical trap
Radikalfänger *m* free-radical scavenger
Radikalion *n* radical ion, ion radical
radikalisch radical
Radikalkation *n* radical cation, cation radical
Radikalkettenpolymerisation *f* [free-]radical polymerization
Radikalkettenreaktion *f* free-radical chain reaction, radical-chain reaction
Radikallieferant *m s.* Radikalbildner
radikalliefernd radical-producing
Radikalmechanismus *m* free-radical mechanism
Radikalname *m* radical name
Radikalpolymerisation *f s.* Radikalkettenpolymerisation
Radikalreaktion *f* [free-]radical reaction
Radikalrekombination *f* radical recombination
Radikalübertragung *f* radical transfer
Radikalzentrum *n* radical centre
Radioactinium *n* ^{227}Th, RdAc, thorium-227, radioactinium
radioaktiv radioactive • ~ **machen** to radioactivate • ~ **markiert** radio-labelled
~/**hochgradig** *s.* ~/stark
~/**nicht** non-radioactive, cold
~/**schwach** feebly radioactive
~/**stark** highly radioactive, hot
Radioaktivität *f* radioactivity
~/**induzierte (künstliche)** induced radioactivity
Radioautographie *f* autoradiography, radioautography

Radiocarbonmethode *f* radiocarbon method, ^{14}C method
Radiochemie *f* radiochemistry
Radiochemiker *m* radiochemist
radiochemisch radiochemical
Radiochromatographie *f* radiochromatography
Radiocobalt *n* radiocobalt, radioactive cobalt, *(specif)* ^{60}Co cobalt-60
Radioelement *n* radioelement, radioactive element
radiogen radiogenic
Radiographie *f* radiography *(materials testing)*
radiographisch radiographic
Radioindikator *m* radiotracer, radioactive indicator (tracer)
Radioindikatormethode *f* radiotracer method
radioindiziert radio-labelled
Radioiod *n* radioiodine, radioactive iodine, *(specif)* ^{131}I iodine-131
Radioisotop *n s.* Radionuklid
Radiokohlenstoff *m* radiocarbon, radioactive carbon, *(specif)* ^{14}C carbon-14
Radiokohlenstoffmethode *f s.* Radiocarbonmethode
Radiokolloid *n* radiocolloid
Radiologie *f* radiology
Radiolumineszenz *f* radioluminescence
Radiolyse *f* radiolysis
Radiometer *n* radiometer
Radiometrie *f* radiometry
radiometrisch radiometric
Radiomimetikum *n (biol)* radiomimetic
radiomimetisch *(biol)* radiomimetic
Radionatrium *n* radiosodium, radioactive sodium, *(specif)* ^{24}Na sodium-24
Radionuklid *n* radionuclide, radioactive nuclide
Radiophosphor *m* radiophosphorus, radioactive phosphorus, *(specif)* ^{32}P phosphorus-32
Radioschwefel *m* radiosulphur, radioactive sulphur, *(specif)* ^{35}S sulphur-35
Radiosonde *f* radiosonde
Radiostrahlung *f* radio radiation
Radiostrontium *n* radiostrontium, radioactive strontium, *(specif)* ^{90}Sr strontium-90
Radiothorium *n* ^{228}Th, RdTh thorium-228, radiothorium
Radiotoxizität *f* radiotoxicity
Radiotracer *m* radiotracer, radioactive tracer (indicator)
Radiotracertechnik *f* radiotracer method
Radium *n* Ra radium
Radiumbehandlung *f (med)* radium therapy
Radium-Beryllium-Neutronenquelle *f* radium-beryllium neutron source
Radiumbromid *n* radium bromide
Radiumcarbonat *n* radium carbonate
Radiumchlorid *n* radium chloride
Radiumeinlage *f (med)* radium pack
Radium-Emanation *f s.* Radon-222
Radiumgehalt *m* radium content
Radiumiodat *n* radium iodate
Radiumisotop *n* radium isotope
Radiummoulage *f (med)* radium mould
Radiumpräparat *n* radium preparation
Radiumreihe *f* radium series
Radiumsulfat *n* radium sulphate
Radiumtherapie *f* radium therapy
Radius *m***/Bohrscher** Bohr radius *(of the hydrogen atom)*
~/Goldschmidtscher Goldschmidt radius *(of ions)*
~/van-der-Waalsscher van der Waals radius *(of atoms)*
Radon *n* Rn radon
Radon-218 *n* ^{218}Rn radon-218
Radon-219 *n* ^{219}Rn radon-219
Radon-220 *n* ^{220}Rn radon-220
Radon-222 *n* ^{222}Rn radon-222
Radonfluorid *n* radon fluoride
Raffinade *f* refined sugar
Raffinadekläre *f (sugar)* refined liquor
Raffinadezucker *m* refined sugar
Raffinat *n* raffinate *(solvent extraction)*
Raffinatblei *n* refined lead
Raffinatende *n* raffinate end *(solvent extraction)*
Raffination *f* refining, refinement, purification *(as of metals, oils, sugar)*; refining, [refining] treatment *(of petroleum and its products)*
~ im Schmelzfluß fire refining
~/elektrolytische electrolytic refining, electrorefining
~/hydrierende hydrorefining
Raffinationsanlage *f* refinery, refining plant
Raffinationsrückstand *m* refinery residue
Raffinatkupfer *n* refined (casting) copper
Raffinatphase *f* raffinate phase *(solvent extraction)*
Raffinatseite *f* raffinate end *(solvent extraction)*
Raffinatstripper *m* raffinate stripper *(solvent extraction)*
Raffinatverdampfer *m* raffinate evaporator *(solvent extraction)*
Raffinerie *f* refinery, refining plant
~/carbochemische (kohlechemische) coal refinery
Raffinerieabwasser *n* waste from refineries (petrochemical plants, petroleum refining), petroleum refinery waste water, refinery waste
Raffineriegas *n (petrol)* refinery gas
Raffineriemelasse *f (sugar)* refinery molasses
raffinieren to refine, to purify *(e.g. metals, oils, sugar)*; to refine, to treat *(petroleum and its products)*
~/im Schmelzfluß to fire-refine
Raffiniergas *n (petrol)* refinery gas
Raffinierstahl *m* refined steel (iron, bar), shear steel, merchant bar
raffiniert/mit Lösungsmitteln solvent-refined
Ragmischung *f (rubber)* rag mix (stock)
Rahm *m* cream
~/geschlagener whipped cream
~/saurer cultured cream
Rahmeis *n* ice cream, cream ice

Rahmen *n* creaming *(of emulsions)*
Rahmenfilter *n* 1. screen (envelope) filter *(for gases)*; 2. plate-end-frame filter *(for liquids)*
Rahmen[filter]presse *f* plate-and-frame press (filter press, filter), flush-plate [filter] press
Rahmkelle *f* skimmer
Rahmkühlwanne *f* cream chilling (cooling) vat
Rahmlöffel *m* skimmer
Rahmplasma *n* cream plasma
Rahmreifer *m* cream (milk) ripener, cream ripening tank (vat)
Rahmreifung *f* cream ripening
Rahmseparator *m* cream separator, skimming machine
Rahnwerden *n* darkening *(of wine)*
Rainfarnöl *n* tansy oil *(from Chrysanthemum vulgare (L.) Bernh.)*
Rainout *m* rain-out *(the pollutants scavenged by raindrops)*
Rainout *n* rain-out, in-cloud scavenging *(of pollutants by raindrops)*
Rakel *f (text, pap)* doctor blade (knife) *(in printing)*; squeegee *(for screen printing)*
Rakelappretur *f (text)* doctor finish
Rakelauftragmaschine *f s.* Rakelstreichmaschine
Rakelmesser *n (plast, rubber)* doctor blade (knife)
Rakelstreichmaschine *f* doctor [kiss] coater, knife coater
Rakelstreifen *m* doctor streak
Raketentreibstoff *m* rocket propellant (fuel)
~/fester solid [rocket] propellant, solid [rocket] fuel
~/flüssiger liquid [rocket] propellant, liquid [rocket] fuel
~/hypergoler hypergolic [rocket] propellant, hypergolic [rocket] fuel, hypergol *(self-igniting upon contact of components)*
Ramachandran-Diagramm *n (bioch)* Ramachandran plot *(of conformations of polypeptides)*
ramanaktiv Raman-active
Raman-Bande *f* Raman band
Raman-Effekt *m* Raman effec;
~/stimulierter stimulated Raman scattering
Raman-Frequenz *f* Raman frequency
ramaninaktiv Raman-inactive
Raman-Intensität *f* Raman intensity
Raman-Linie *f* Raman line
Raman-Spektroskopie *f* Raman spectroscopy
~/inverse inverse Raman spectroscopy, IRS
~ mit Laser-Mikrosonde molecular optics laser examination, MOLE
~/photoakustische photoacoustic Raman spectroscopy, PARS
ramanspektroskopisch by Raman spectroscopy
Raman-Spektrum *n* Raman spectrum
~/stimuliertes stimulated Raman spectrum
Raman-Streustrahlung *f* Raman scattered radiation
Raman-Streuung *f* Raman scatter[ing]
Raman-Untersuchung *f* Raman study (approach)
Raman-Verschiebung *f* Raman shift (displacement)
Raman-Zirkular-Intensitätsdifferenz *f* Raman circular intensity difference, RCID
Ramiedichtung *f*, **Ramiepackung** *f* ramie packing
Rammbrunnen *m (hyd)* driven well
Rammelkamp-Methode *f* Rammelkamp method *(for testing penicillin)*
Rampe *f* platform
~/schräge ramp, slope
Rampenbildung *f* casing (outer layer) effect *(a defect in glass)*
Ramsbottom-Carbon-Wert *m s.* Ramsbottom-Verkokungswert
Ramsbottom-Methode *f* Ramsbottom [coking] method, Ramsbottom carbon residue method
Ramsbottom-Test *m* Ramsbottom test *(for determining the carbon residue of oils)*
Ramsbottom-Verkokungswert *m*, **Ramsbottom-Verkokungszahl** *f* Ramsbottom value (coke number)
Rand *m* 1. edge, border, brim; 2. *s.* Randschicht
randaufkohlen *(met)* to case-carburize
Randaufkohlung *f (met)* case carburization
Randbedingung *f* boundary condition
Randblase *f* subcutaneous blowhole *(foundry)*
Randeffekt *m (phys ch)* edge effect; *(phot)* border effect
Rändern *n (ceram)* banding
randkohlen *s.* randaufkohlen
Randschicht *f (met)* case, surface layer
~/aufgekohlte carburized case
~/eingesetzte *s.* ~/aufgekohlte
~/gehärtete hardened case
~/nitrierte nitride[d] case
~/zementierte *s.* ~/aufgekohlte
Randspritzstoff *m (pap)* squirt-trimmed stock, squirt trim
Randwalzen *fpl* edge rolls *(sheet-glass manufacture)*
Randwasser *n (petrol)* edge water
Randwassergrenze *f (petrol)* water table
Randwasserzeichen *n (pap)* edge (marginal) watermark
Randwinkel *m* contact (wetting) angle
Randzone *f s.* Randschicht
Raney-Katalysator *m* Raney catalyst, [alloy] skeleton catalyst
Raney-Nickel *n* Raney nickel [catalyst]
Rang *m (coal)* rank
Rangfolge *f (nomencl)* order of priority (precedence, seniority)
Rangklassifikation *f* **der Kohlen** rank classification of coals
Rangordnung *f s.* Rangfolge
Rangstufe *f (coal)* rank
Rankine-Skale *f* Rankine [temperature] scale
Ranzidität *f s.* Ranzigkeit
Ranziditätsprüfung *f (food)* rancidity test

ranzig *(food)* rancid • ~ **werden** to rancidify
Ranzigkeit *f (food)* rancidity, rancidness
~/hydrolytische hydrolytic rancidity
Ranzigwerden *n (food)* rancidification
Raoult-Gesetz *n* Raoult's law
Rapid-Equilibrium-Random-Mechanismus *m* rapid-equilibrium random[-order] mechanism *(enzyme kinetics)*
Rapidnetzer *m* rapid wetting agent
Rapshartfett *n* hydrogenated rape-seed oil
Rapsöl *n* rape[-seed] oil *(from Brassica napus L. em. Metzg.)*
Rasamalaharz *n* Rasamala resin (wood oil) *(from Altingia excelsa Noron.)*
Raschig-Ring *m* Raschig ring *(a piece of packing)*
Raschig-Synthese *f* Raschig [hydrazine] synthesis
Raschig-Verfahren *n* Raschig process (method) *(catalytic conversion of benzene to phenol)*
raschwirkend quick-acting, short-action
Rasen *m***/biologischer** *(hyd)* biological film (layer, growth, gel, slime), biofilm, biomass film (layer), microbial (fixed) film, bacteria bed, filter slime *(trickling filter process)*
Rasendicke *f (hyd)* [biological] film thickness *(trickling filter process)*
Raseneisenerz *n (min)* bog iron [ore], bog ore
Rasenröste *f (text)* dewret[ting]
Rasiercreme *f (cosmet)* shaving cream
~/schäumende lather shaving cream
Rasier[hilfs]mittel *n (cosmet)* shaving preparation
Rasiersahne *f (cosmet)* brushless shaving cream
Rasierstein *m* styptic pencil
Rasierwasser *n (cosmet)* shaving lotion
~/nachbehandelndes after-shave [lotion]
~/vorbehandelndes pre-shave [lotion]
Rast *f* bosh *(of a blast furnace)*
Rasterelektronenmikroskop *n* scanning electron microscope, SEM
Rasterelektronenmikroskopie *f* scanning electron microscopy, SEM
Rastermutation *f (biot)* frameshift mutation
Rast-Methode *f* Rast method, Rast's molecular weight determination
Ratiometer *n (spectr)* ratio-recording spectrometer
Rationalitätsgesetz *n (cryst)* rational index law, law of rational indices, Haüy law
Rattenbekämpfungsmittel *n*, **Rattengift** *n* rat poison, raticide
Rätter *m* gyratory riddle
Rauch *m* smoke *(as of a stack)*; fume *(as of concentrated acids)*
rauchen to smoke *(as of a stack)*; to fume *(as of concentrated acids)*
rauchend fuming *(e.g. acids)*
Räucherapparat *m* fumigator *(pest control)*
Räucherei *f (food)* 1. smoke curing (drying), smoking; 2. smokery, smokehouse
Räucherkautschuk *m* smoked sheet [rubber]
Räucherkerze *f* fumigating candle
Räuchermittel *n* [dry] fumigant *(pest control)*
räuchern *(food)* to smoke; to fume *(timber)*; to fumigate *(e.g. rooms or plants for pest control)*
~/mit Schwefel to sulphur
Räuchern *n (food)* smoking, smoke preservation; fuming *(of timber)*; fumigation *(for pest control)*
Räucherofen *m* smoking kiln
Räucherpapier *n* fumigating paper *(for destroying insects)*
Räucherpulver *n (agric)* fumigating (combustible) powder
Räucherung *f s.* Räuchern
Rauchfahne *f* [gas] plume
~/fächerförmige fanning plume
~/kegelförmige (konische) coning plume
~/schleifenförmige looping plume
Rauchfangdach *n* fume (canopy) hood
Rauchfeuer *n* soft fire
Rauchgas *n* flue gas
Rauchgasanalysator *m* flue-gas analyser
Rauchgasanalyse *f* flue-gas analysis
Rauchgasechtheit *f (text)* gas-fume fastness, fastness to gas fading
Rauchgasentschwefelung *f* flue-gas desulphurization, FGD
Rauchgasentschwefelungsverfahren *n* flue-gas desulphurization process
Rauchgasentstauber *m* fly-ash precipitator
Rauchgaskanal *m* breeching
Rauchgasprobenahme *f* stack sampling
Rauchgasprüfer *m* flue gas analyser
Rauchgassammelkanal *m* flue
Rauchgasuntersuchungsapparat *m* flue gas analyser
~ **nach Orsat-Lunge** Orsat-Lunge apparatus
Rauchgasverlust *m* stack loss
Rauchgasvorwärmer *m* flue-gas preheater, economizer
Rauchgaswäscher *m* flue-gas scrubber
Rauchgenerator *m* smoke generator
~/pyrotechnischer pyrotechnic smoke generator
Rauchmeldeanlage *f* smoke (flue dust) monitor
Rauchnebel *m* smaze *(one type of air pollution)*
Rauchopium *n* chandoo
Rauchpunkt *m (food)* smoke point
Rauchquarz *m (min)* smoky qartz, cairngorm [stone]
Rauchrohr *n* fire tube
Rauchrohrkessel *m* fire-tube boiler
Rauchsäule *f* column of smoke
Rauchsignal *n* smoke signal
Rauchwacke *f* cellular dolomite
rauh rough
Rauhbrand *m (ceram)* biscuit firing, biscuitting
Rauheit *f* roughness
Rauhigkeit *f* roughness; *(plast)* pulled surface *(a defect)*
Rauhigkeitsgrad *m* degree of roughness
Rauhschliff *m (glass)* grey cutting

Rauhwacke *f* cellular dolomite
Raum *m* 1. space; 2. room, chamber, cabinet
~/feldfreier field-free region *(as in spectrographs)*
~/luftleerer absolute vacuum
~/luftverdünnter partial vacuum
~/reiner *s.* Reinraum
~/schädlicher 1. clearance volume *(of a pump)*; 2. *s.* ~/toter
~/toter *(chromat)* dead volume (space)
Raumausdehnungskoeffizient *m* isobaric coefficient of thermal expansion, isobaric thermal expansivity
Raumbeanspruchung *f s.* Raumerfüllung
Raumbegasungsmittel *n* space fumigant
Raumbelastung *f (hyd)* loading rate per unit volume *(expressed as kg/m^3 · d)*
~/hydraulische hydraulic loading per unit volume
raumbeständig volume-stable
Raumbeständigkeit *f* volume stability
Raumchemie *f* stereochemistry
Raumelement *n* volume element
räumen to unload *(e.g. a sludge drying bed)*
Raumerfüllung *f* space-filling properties *(of a substituent)*
Raumformel *f* space (configurational) formula
Räumgerät *n* **für Rundbecken** *(hyd)* circular sludge collector
Raumgeschwindigkeit *f* space velocity
Raumgewicht *n s.* Raummasse
Raumgitter *n (cryst)* space lattice
Raumgruppe *f (cryst)* space group
Raumhundertstel *n s.* Volumenprozent
Rauminhalt *m* volume
raumisomer stereoisomeric
Raumisomer[e] *n* stereo[iso]mer, space isomer
Raumisomerie *f* stereoisomerism, space isomerism
Raumladung *f* space charge
räumlich spatial, steric
Raummasse *f* bulk density, B.D.
Raummodell *n* space model
Raumquantelung *f* space quantization, quantization of direction
Räumschild *m (hyd)* sludge collection flight
Raumspray *m* space (household) spray *(for insect control)*; household air refresher
Raumsymmetriegruppe *f (cryst)* space group
Raumteil *m* part by volume
Raumtemperatur *f* room (ordinary) temperature
raumtemperaturhärtend *(plast)* room-temperature curing
Raumtemperaturhärtung *f (plast)* room-temperature cure
Raumtemperaturvernetzung *f (rubber)* room[-temperature] cure, room-temperature vulcanization
Räumung *f* unloading *(e.g. of a sludge drying bed)*
Raumverhältnis *n* proportion by volume
raumvernetzt enmeshed *(e.g. starch molecules)*
Raum-Zeit-Ausbeute *f* space-time yield
raumzentriert *(cryst)* space-centred, body-centred
rauscharm *(anal)* low-noise
Rauschen *n (anal)* [analytical] noise
~/thermisches thermal (Johnson) noise
~/weißes white noise
Rauschentkopplung *f (spectr)* broad-band decoupling
Rauschgelb *n* yellow arsenic [sulphide], arsenic yellow, king's yellow (gold), royal yellow, orpiment [yellow] *(technically pure arsenic(III) sulphide)*
Rauschgift *n* narcotic, drug
Rauschleistung *f (anal)* noise power
Rauschpegel *m (anal)* noise level
Rauschrot *n* ruby arsenic, red orpiment *(tetraarsenic tetrasulphide)*
Rauwolfiaalkaloid *n* rauvolfia alkaloid
Rayleigh-Interferometer *n* Rayleigh refractometer
Rayleigh-Streustrahlung *f* Rayleigh radiation
Rayleigh-Streuung *f* Rayleigh scattering
Raymond-Pendel[rollen]mühle *f* Raymond [roller] mill, Raymond ring-roll[er] mill
Raymond-Schüsselmühle *f* Raymond bowl mill
RaZ *s.* Rhodanzahl
RBW *s.* Wirksamkeit/relative biologische
R_B-Wert *m (chromat)* R_B value
R.D. *s.* Rotationsdispersion
Reagens *n* reagent
~/Abels Abel reagent *(for etching metals)*
~/anionisches *s.* ~/nucleophiles
~/Barfoeds Barfoed reagent *(for determining monosaccharides)*
~/Barnardsches Barnard reagent *(for detecting aldehydes)*
~/Bealesches Beale reagent *(a biological stain)*
~/Benedictsches Benedict's reagent (solution) *(for detecting reducing sugars)*
~/Bials Bial reagent *(for detecting pentoses)*
~/Brückesches Brücke reagent [for proteins]
~/Cerevitinovs Zerewitinoff reagent *(methyl magnesium chloride in butyl ether)*
~/chelatbildendes chelating agent
~/chemisches reagent chemical
~/Coopersches Cooper reagent *(for detecting trivalent iron ions)*
~/Dragendorffs Dragendorff [alkaloid] reagent
~/drückendes *(min tech)* depressant
~/elektrophiles electrophilic reagent, electrophile
~/Fleigsches Fleig reagent [for blood]
~/Folins Folin's reagent *(β-naphthoquinone plus sulphuric acid for detecting amino acids)*
~/Fröhdes Fröhde reagent *(for detecting alkaloids)*
~/Frysches Fry reagent *(for etching steel)*
~/Gibbs' Gibbs reagent *(for detecting hydroxyflavones)*
~/Giemsasches Giemsa reagent *(for detecting quinine)*
~/Grignardsches Grignard reagent *(for synthesizing various organic compounds)*
~/Mandelins Mandelin reagent *(for detecting alkaloids)*

~/Marmes Marme reagent (solution) *(for detecting alkaloids)*
~/Marquis' Marquis solution *(for detecting alkaloids)*
~/Mayers Mayer reagent *(for detecting alkaloids)*
~/Meckes Mecke solution *(for detecting alkaloids)*
~/Millons Millon's reagent *(for detecting proteins)*
~/Mohlers Mohler solution *(for detecting tartaric acid)*
~ nach Bey Bey reagent *(for detecting cadmium and tin)*
~ nach Bezssonow Bezssonov reagent *(for detecting polyphenols)*
~ nach Florence Florence reagent *(for detecting blood and bile pigments in urine)*
~ nach Molisch Molisch reagent *(for detecting albumin and peptone)*
~ nach Nadi Nadi reagent *(for detecting indophenol oxidase)*
~/Neßlers Nessler reagent (solution) *(for detecting ammonia and various amines)* • **mit Neßlers ~ versetzen** to nesslerize
~/nucleophiles nucleophilic reagent, nucleophile
~/Nylanders Nylander solution *(for detecting glucose in urine)*
~/passivierendes *(min tech)* depressant
~/regelndes *(min tech)* modifying agent, modifier
~/Rieglers *(med, food)* Riegler reagent
~/Sangersches Sanger reagent *(for detecting amino acids and proteins)*
~/Scheiblers Scheibler reagent *(for detecting alkaloids)*
~/Schiffsches Schiff reagent *(for detecting aldehydes)*
~/Schweizers Schweizer reagent, cuprammonium [hydroxide] solution, cuprammonia *(for dissolving or detecting cellulose)*
~/spezifisches special reagent
~/Steadsches Stead reagent *(for detecting phosphorus segregation in steel)*
~/Vervens Verven solution *(for detecting alkaloids)*
~/Wagners Wagner's reagent (solution) *(for detecting alkaloids)*
Reagenserzeugung *f* **außerhalb der Titrierzelle** external generation *(coulometry)*
~ innerhalb der Titrierzelle internal generation
Reagenslösung *f* reagent solution
Reagensüberschuß *m* excess reagent
Reagenz *f* reagency
Reagenzglas *n* test tube, proof
Reagenzglasbürste *f* test-tube brush
Reagenzglasgestell *n* test-tube rack (stand)
~ für Wasserbäder water-bath rack
Reagenzglashalter *m*, **Reagenzglasklemme** *f* test-tube holder
Reagenzglasversuch *m* test-tube experiment, t.t. experiment
Reagenzienblindwert *m* reagent blank
Reagenzienbord *n* reagent shelf
Reagenzienflasche *f* reagent bottle
Reagenziengestell *n* reagent rack
Reagenzienraum *n* reagent room
Reagenziensatz *m* reagent set
Reagenzpapier *n* test (indicator) paper, *(Am)* reaction paper
reagieren to react, to undergo reaction
~/alkalisch to react alkaline
~/auf Düngung *(agric)* to respond to fertilizing
~/heftig to react vigorously (violently)
~/neutral to react neutral
~/sauer to react (be) acid
~/stürmisch to react stormily
~/träge to react sluggishly
Reaktant *m* reactant
Reaktantgas *n* reactant gas *(mass spectrometry)*
Reaktantharz *n* reactant-type resin
Reaktion *f* reaction • **die ~ in Gang halten** to keep the reaction in progress • **in ~ treten** to enter into reaction • **zur ~ bringen** to cause to react
~/abbauende degradation (degradative) reaction, decomposition (breakdown) reaction
~/alkalische alkaline reaction
~/anionoide *s.* ~/nucleophile
~/anodische anode reaction
~/aufbauende build-up reaction
~/autokatalytische autocatalytic reaction
~/Bartsche Bart reaction *(for preparing aromatic arsonic acids)*
~/basische alkaline reaction
~/Bialsche Bial's test *(for detecting pentoses)*
~/bimolekulare bimolecular reaction
~/Blancsche Blanc [chloromethylation] reaction
~/Bouveault-Blancsche Bouveault-Blanc reaction *(for reducing esters to alcohols)*
~/Buchererersche Bucherer reaction *(the conversion of a naphthylamine to a naphthol or vice versa)*
~/Cannizzarosche Cannizzaro reaction *(aldehyde dismutation)*
~/cheletrope *(org ch)* chelotropic (cheletropic) reaction
~/chemische chemical reaction
~/Čugaevsche Chugaev reaction *(for preparing olefins from alcohols)*
~/dimolekulare bimolecular reaction
~/Doebnersche Doebner synthesis *(of substituted cinchoninic acids)*
~/dreistufige three-step reaction
~ dritter Ordnung third-order reaction
~/einfache simple reaction
~/einstufige one-step reaction
~/elektrocyclische *(org ch)* electrocyclic reaction
~/elektrophile electrophilic reaction
~/endotherme endothermic reaction
~/enzymatische (enzymkatalysierte) enzymatic (enzyme-catalyzed) reaction
~/epithermische epithermal reaction
~ erster Ordnung first-order reaction
~ erster Ordnung/umkehrbare reversible first-order reaction

~/Étardsche Étard reaction *(for preparing aromatic aldehydes)*
~/eutektische eutectic reaction
~/eutektoide eutectoid reaction
~/exotherme exothermic reaction
~/Feiglsche Feigl microreaction
~/Feulgensche Feulgen reaction *(for detecting deoxyribonucleic acid)*
~/Friedel-Craftssche Friedel-Crafts reaction *(for synthesizing aromatic hydrocarbon derivatives)*
~/fundamentale *s.* ~/grundlegende
~/gegenläufige opposing (opposed) reaction, oppositely directed reaction
~/gegenseitige interreaction
~/gekoppelte coupled reaction
~/gequantelte *(tox)* quantal response
~/grundlegende basic (fundamental) reaction
~/Hehnersche Hehner formaldehyde test
~/heiße hot-state reaction
~/heterogene heterogeneous reaction
~/heterogen-katalytische heterogeneous catalytic reaction
~/heterogen-nichtkatalytische heterogeneous non-catalytic reaction
~/heterolytische heterolytic reaction
~/Hillsche *(bioch)* Hill reaction
~/Hinsbergsche Hinsberg [amine] test
~ höherer Ordnung higher-order reaction
~/homogene homogeneous reaction
~/homolytische homolytic reaction
~/im Neutralbereich liegende circumneutral reaction
~ im Phasensystem fest-flüssig liquid-solid[-phase heterogeneous] reaction
~ in [homogener] flüssiger Phase liquid-phase reaction, liquid-liquid reaction
~ in Lösung solution reaction, reaction in solution
~/induzierte induced (sympathetic) reaction
~/ionische ionic (ion-ion) reaction
~/irreversible irreversible (one-way) reaction
~/isolierte isolated reaction
~/katalysierte (katalytische) catalyzed (catalytic) reaction
~/kationoide *s.* ~/elektrophile
~/katodische cathode reaction
~/Kolbesche Kolbe reaction *(for synthesizing aromatic hydroxy acids)*
~/Kolbe-Schmittsche Kolbe-Schmitt reaction *(for synthesizing aromatic hydroxy acids)*
~/komplexe composite (complex) reaction
~/Landoltsche Landolt reaction *(liberation of iodine by oxidizing sulphurous acid with iodates)*
~/Liebermannsche Liebermann reaction [for phenols]
~/mechanochemische mechanochemical reaction
~/Millonsche Millon reaction *(for detecting proteins)*
~/Molischsche Molisch reaction *(for detecting carbohydrates)*
~/monomolekulare monomolecular (unimolecular) reaction
~/monotektische monotectic reaction
~/monotektoide monotectoid reaction
~ nach Arnold und Mentzel Arnold-Mentzel formaldehyde test
~ nach Claisen-Tišcenko Claisen-Tishchenko reaction *(for converting aldehydes into esters)*
~ nach Zimmermann Zimmermann reaction *(for determining ketonic steroids)*
~/nichtkatalysierte (nichtkatalytische) non-catalyzed reaction, non-catalytic reaction
~/nichtumkehrbare s. ~/irreversible
~/nucleophile nucleophilic reaction
~ nullter Ordnung zero-order reaction
~/oszillierende oscillating (periodic) reaction
~/Paulysche Pauly [protein] reaction
~/pericyclische *(org ch)* pericyclic reaction
~/periodische *s.* ~/oszillierende
~/peritektische peritectic (incongruent) reaction
~/peritektoide peritectoid reaction
~/Perkinsche Perkin [condensation] reaction *(for synthesizing unsaturated carboxylic acids)*
~/Pfitzingersche Pfitzinger reaction *(for preparing quinoline)*
~/photochemische photochemical reaction, photoreaction
~/physikochemische physicochemical reaction
~/Pictet-Spenglersche Pictet-Spengler reaction *(isoquinoline ring closure)*
~/protolytische protolytic reaction
~ pseudo-erster Ordnung pseudo-first-order reaction
~/pseudomonomolekulare pseudomonomolecular (pseudounimolecular) reaction
~ pseudo-nullter Ordnung pseudo-zero-order reaction
~/radikalische free-radical reaction
~/radiochemische radiochemical reaction
~/Reedsche Reed reaction *(photocatalytic sulphochlorination of hydrocarbons)*
~/Reformatskysche Reformatsky reaction *(of 3-hydroxycarboxylic-acid esters)*
~/reversible reversible (balanced) reaction
~/rhythmische *s.* ~/oszillierende
~/Sabatier-Senderenssche Sabatier-Senderens reaction *(for reducing organic compounds by hydrogen)*
~/Sandmeyersche Sandmeyer [diazo] reaction
~/Schiffsche Schiff's test *(for detecting aldehydes)*
~/Schmidtsche Schmidt reaction *(between hydrazoic acid and carbonyl compounds)*
~/schnelle fast [chemical] reaction, rapid reaction
~/Schotten-Baumannsche Schotten-Baumann reaction *(acylation)*
~/Schwarzsche Schwarz reaction *(for detecting naphthalene or chloroform)*
~/Selivanovsche Seliwanoff test *(for detecting hexoses)*
~/sich selbst unterhaltende self-sustaining reaction
~/stereoselektive stereoselective reaction

~/stereospezifische stereospecific reaction
~/stoßinduzierte collision-induced reaction
~/synchrone synchronous reaction
~/termolekulare *s.* ~/trimolekulare
~/thermonukleare thermonuclear reaction
~/Tollenssche Tollens' test *(for furfurol, for detecting pentoses)*
~/topochemische topochemical reaction
~/topotaktische *(cryst)* topotactic (insertion) reaction
~/trimolekulare trimolecular (termolecular) reaction
~/Tschugajewsche *s.* ~/Čugaevsche
~/Ullmannsche Ullmann reaction *(for synthesizing diaryls)*
~/umkehrbare *s.* ~/reversible
~/unimolekulare *s.* ~/monomolekulare
~/unkatalysierte *s.* ~/nichtkatalysierte
~/wechselseitige interreaction
~/Wurtzsche Wurtz reaction *(for synthesizing alkanes)*
~/Zeiselsche Zeisel reaction *(demethylation)*
~/zusammengesetzte *s.* ~/komplexe
~/zweistufige two-step reaction
~ zweiter Ordnung second-order reaction
Reaktionsabbruch *m* termination of the reaction
Reaktionsablauf *m* course (progress) of reaction
Reaktionsablaufdiagramm *n* progress-of-reaction diagram
Reaktionsaffinität *f (phys ch)* affinity, driving force (potential)
Reaktionsapparat *m* reactor
~/chemischer chemical reactor
Reaktionsarbeit *f (phys ch)* maximum [useful, net] work
Reaktionsbedingungen *fpl* reaction conditions
Reaktionsbehälter *m* reaction vessel
reaktionsbereit reactive
Reaktionsbestreben *n* tendency to react
Reaktionsdrehofen *m* rotary kiln, *(esp met)* rotary furnace
Reaktionsenergie *f* reaction energy
Reaktionsenthalpie *f* reaction enthalpy
~/freie reaction Gibbs function, [Gibbs] free energy change, change in free energy
Reaktionsentropie *f* reaction entropy
reaktionsfähig reactive
Reaktionsfähigkeit *f* reactivity
~ gegen[über] Sauerstoff reactivity to (with) oxygen
Reaktionsfähigkeitsindex *m* reactivity index
Reaktionsfolge *f* reaction sequence, sequence of reactions
reaktionsfreudig reactive
Reaktionsfreudigkeit *f* reactivity
Reaktionsgas *n* reaction gas
Reaktions-Gaschromatographie *f* destructive gas chromatography
Reaktionsgebiet *n* reaction region
Reaktionsgefäß *n* reaction vessel
Reaktionsgemisch *n* reaction mixture
Reaktionsgeschehen *n* reaction processes
Reaktionsgeschwindigkeit *f* reaction rate
~ der Elementarreaktion elementary reaction rate
~/spezifische *s.* Reaktionsgeschwindigkeitskonstante
Reaktionsgeschwindigkeitsgleichung *f* rate equation (law), empirical differential rate equation
Reaktionsgeschwindigkeitskonstante *f* rate coefficient, *(relating to elementary reactions:)* [reaction-]rate constant, specific reaction rate, unitary rate constant
Reaktionsgleichung *f***[/chemische]** [chemical-] reaction equation, chemical equation
~/vereinfachte simplified equation
Reaktionsgrundiermittel *n*, **Reaktionsgrundierung** *f s.* Reaktionsprimer
Reaktionshemmung *f* reaction inhibition
Reaktionsisobare *f***[/van't-Hoffsche]** van't Hoff [reaction] isobar
Reaktionsisochore *f***[/van't-Hoffsche]** van't Hoff [reaction] isochore
Reaktionsisotherme *f***[/van't-Hoffsche]** van't Hoff [reaction] isotherm
Reaktionskammer *f* reaction chamber; *(petrol)* soaking chamber (drum), soaker *(in the tube-and-tank process)*
Reaktionskessel *m* reaction vessel
Reaktionskette *f* reaction chain
Reaktionskinetik *f***[/chemische]** reaction (chemical) kinetics
Reaktionskinetiker *m* kineticist
Reaktionskleber *m*, **Reaktionsklebstoff** *m* chemically reactive adhesive, mixed adhesive
Reaktionskonstante *f* reaction constant
Reaktionskoordinate *f* reaction coordinate
Reaktionskurve *f* reaction curve
Reaktionslaufzahl *f* extent (advancement) of reaction
Reaktionslenkung *f* reaction control
reaktionslos non-reactive, reactionless
Reaktionslosigkeit *f* non-reactivity, lack (absence) of reaction
Reaktionsmasse *f* reaction mass
Reaktionsmechanismus *m* reaction mechanism
Reaktionsmolekularität *f* molecularity [of reaction], reaction molecularity
Reaktionsofen *m* reactor, converter
~ für Flammenreaktionen flame reactor
Reaktionsordnung *f* reaction order
~ bezüglich eines Reaktanten partial order [of reaction]
~/gebrochene fractional order
~/nicht determinierte random mechanism *(enzyme kinetics)*
Reaktionsort *m* reaction site
Reaktionspartner *m* reaction partner, [co]reactant, participant in a reaction
Reaktionsprimer *m* wash primer, etch (etching, self-etch, pre-treatment) primer, wash coat [primer]

Reaktionsprodukt *n* reaction product
Reaktionsquerschnitt *m* reaction (reactive) cross section
Reaktionsraum *m* reaction chamber
Reaktionsrichtung *f* direction of reaction, reaction direction
Reaktionsschema *n* reaction scheme
Reaktionsschicht *f (el ch)* reaction layer
Reaktionsschichtdicke *f (el ch)* thickness of the reaction layer
Reaktionsschritt *m* reaction step
Reaktionsserie *f* reaction series
reaktionsspezifisch *(biot)* reaction-specific
Reaktionspezifität *f* reaction specificity *(of an enzyme)*
Reaktionsstelle *f* reaction site
Reaktionssystem *n* reaction (reacting) system
Reaktionstank *m***/biochemischer (biologischer)** *s.* Bioreaktor
Reaktionstechnik *f***/chemische** chemical reaction engineering
Reaktionsteilnehmer *m s.* Reaktionspartner
Reaktionstemperatur *f* reaction temperature
reaktionsträge [chemically] inert, chemically indifferent, inactive
Reaktionsträgheit *f***[/chemische]** [chemical] inertness
Reaktionsturm *m* reaction (reacting) tower; *(pap)* retention tower
Reaktionstyp *m* reaction type, type of reaction
reaktionsunfähig unreactive, non-reactive
Reaktionsunfähigkeit *f* non-reactivity
Reaktionsverfahren *n* reaction process
Reaktionsverhalten *n* reaction behaviour
Reaktionsverlauf *m* course (progress) of reaction
Reaktionsvermögen *n* reactivity
Reaktionsverschiebung *f s. p*H-Änderung
Reaktionsvolumen *n* reaction volume
Reaktionsvorgang *m* reaction process
Reaktionswärme *f* reaction heat, heat of reaction
Reaktionsweg *m* reaction path[way]
Reaktionsweise *f* mode of reaction
Reaktionswiderstand *m* reaction resistance, resistance to reaction
Reaktionszeit *f* contact time
Reaktionszentrum *n* reaction centre
Reaktionszone *f* reaction zone
Reaktionszwischenstufe *f* reaction intermediate
reaktiv reactive
Reaktivfarbstoff *m* reactive dye
Reaktivgruppe *f* reactive group
reaktivieren to reactivate, *(activated carbon also)* to revivify, to regenerate
Reaktivierung *f* reactivation, *(of activated carbon also)* revivification, regeneration
Reaktivierungsanlage *f* reactivation plant
Reaktivierungsofen *m* reactivation furnace
Reaktivität *f* reactivity
~/elektrophile electrophilicity, electrophilic power

Reaktor *m* 1. reactor, converter; 2. [nuclear] reactor, pile
~/adiabat[isch]er adiabatic reactor
~/biologischer *s.* Bioreaktor
~/chemischer chemical reactor
~/diskontinuierlicher batch reactor
~/festbettkatalytischer fixed-bed catalytic reactor, catalytic fixed-bed reactor
~ für aerobe Mikroorganismen ohne Belüftung *(biot)* anoxic reactor
~ für aerobe Verfahren *(biot)* aerobic reactor
~ für anaerobe Verfahren *(biot)* anaerobic reactor
~ für Fluid-Feststoff-Reaktionen fluid-solid reactor
~ für Gas-Feststoff-Reaktionen gas-solid reactor
~ für Gas-Flüssig-Reaktionen gas-liquid reactor
~ für heterogene Reaktionssysteme heterogeneous reactor
~ für homogene Flüssigphasenreaktionen homogeneous liquid-phase reactor
~ für homogene Reaktionssysteme homogeneous reactor
~ für homogene Reaktionssysteme/strömungstechnisch idealer diskontinuierlicher perfect homogeneous batch reactor
~ für katalytische Reaktionen catalytic reactor
~ für nichtkatalytische Reaktionen non-catalytic reactor
~ für Oberflächenverfahren *(biot)* surface film reactor
~ für Submersverfahren *(biot)* submerged fermenter
~/graphitmoderierter *(nucl)* graphite-moderated reactor
~/halbkontinuierlicher (halbkontinuierlich arbeitender) semi-batch reactor
~/heterogener *(nucl)* heterogeneous reactor
~/homogener *(nucl)* homogeneous reactor
~/homogenphasiger *(ch)* homogeneous reactor
~/idealer ideal reactor
~/isothermer isothermal reactor
~/katalytischer catalytic reactor
~/kontinuierlicher (kontinuierlich durchflossener) continuous-[flow] reactor, flow reactor
~ mit Flüssigmetallbrennstoff *(nucl)* liquid-metal-fuelled reactor, LMFR
~ mit Sauerstoffeintrag *(biot)* oxygenic reactor
~ mit suspendiertem Katalysator [catalyst-]slurry reactor
~/natriumgekühlter *(nucl)* sodium[-cooled] reactor
~/nichtadiabat[isch]er non-adiabatic reactor
~/nichtisothermer non-isothermal reactor
~/nichtstationär arbeitender non-steady-state reactor, non-steady-flow reactor
~/photochemischer photochemical reactor
~/schneller *(nucl)* fast [neutron] reactor
~/stationär arbeitender steady-state [flow-type] reactor, flowstream reactor
~/strömungstechnisch idealer *s.* ~/idealer

~/technischer commercial[-scale] reactor
~/thermischer thermal reactor
~/thermonuklearer thermonuclear reactor
~/überkritischer *(nucl)* supercritical reactor
~/unterkritischer *(nucl)* subcritical reactor
~/vollständig gemischter well mixed [flow] reactor
~/wassermoderierter *(nucl)* water-moderated reactor
Reaktorabschirmung *f (nucl)* reactor shielding
Reaktorart *f* reactor type
Reaktorgift *n (nucl)* fission (neutron) poison
Reaktorgröße *f* reactor size
Reaktorinhalt *m* reactor contents
Reaktorkaskade *f* reactors in series, series of reactors
Reaktorkonstruktion *f* [chemical] reactor design
Reaktormodell *n* reactor model
Reaktorprodukt *n* reactor product
Reaktortechnik *f (nucl)* reactor engineering
Reaktortyp *m* reactor type
Reaktorvolumen *n* reactor volume
real real *(e.g. gas)*; actual *(as opposed to theoretical)*
Realgar *m (min)* realgar *(tetraarsenic tetrasulphide)*
Realkristall *m* real (imperfect) crystal
Realpotential *n (phys ch)* formal potential
Rebromierung *f (phot)* rebromination
Rechen *m* 1. rake; 2. *s.* Rechenanlage
Rechenanlage *f (hyd)* [bar] rack, trash removal facility
Rechenarm *m* rake (raking) arm
Rechenbrett *n (spectr)* calculating board
Rechengut *n (hyd)* rakings, screenings
Rechengutbeseitigung *f (hyd)* disposal of rakings
Rechengutentfernung *f*, **Rechengutrückhalt** *m (hyd)* removal of rakings, coarse solids removal
Rechengutzerkleinerer *m (hyd)* comminutor, screenings disintegrator
Rechengutzerkleinerung *f (hyd)* grinding-up of rakings
Rechenklassierer *m* rake classifier
Rechenstab *m (hyd)* bar *(of a rack)*
Rechteckbecken *n (hyd)* rectangular clarifier, rectangular [settling, sedimentation] basin
Rechteckofen *m* rectangular kiln
Rechteckwellenpolarographie *f* square-wave polarography
Rechtsdraht *m (text)* Z twist
rechtsdrehend dextrorota[to]ry, dextro, *(esp cryst)* right-handed
Rechtsdrehung dextrorotation, *(esp cryst)* right-handed rotation
Rechtsform *f* dextro[rotatory] form, (+)-form *(of an optically active compound)*
Rechtsgängigkeit *f* right-handed sense *(of a helix)*
Rechtskristall *m* right-handed crystal
Rechtsmilchsäure *f* L(+)-lactic acid, dextrolactic acid
Rechtsquarz *m* right-handed quartz
Rechtssäure *f* dextro[rotatory] acid
Rechtsweinsäure *f s.* *L*(+)-Weinsäure
rechtszirkular polarisiert right-circularly polarized, right-hand circularly polarized
recken *(text, plast)* to stretch, to draw
Recken *n (text, plast)* stretching, drawing
~/biaxiales (zweiachsiges) biaxial stretching
Reckfestigkeit *f (text)* stretch resistance
Reckgrad *m* degree of stretching
Reckung *f s.* Recken
Reckverhältnis *n* **beim Extrudieren** extrusion ratio
Reclamator-Verfahren *n (rubber)* reclamator process *(a reclaiming process)*
Rectisol-Anlage *f* Rectisol wash unit
Rectisol-Gasreinigung *f* Rectisol gas purification
Rectisol-Verfahren *n* Rectisol process *(for cleaning gases)*
Rectisol-Wäsche *f* Rectisol wash
Redestillat *n (petrol)* rerun oil
Redestillation *f* redistillation, rerunning
Redestillationskolonne *f (petrol)* rerun tower
redestillieren to redistil, to rerun
Redler *m*, **Redler-Band** *n s.* Redler-Förderer
Redler-Förderer *m*, **Redler-Kettenförderer** *m* Redler conveyor, skeleton-flight conveyor
Redoxanalyse *f* redox analysis
Redoxase *f* redoxase, oxido-reductase, oxidation-reduction enzyme
Redoxelektrode *f* redox electrode
Redoxgleichgewicht *n* redox equilibrium
Redoxharz *n* redox resin
Redoxindikator *m* redox indicator
Redoxkatalysator *m* redox catalyst
Redoxkatalyse *f* redox catalysis
Redoxpaar *n* redox couple
Redoxpolymerisat *n* redox polymer
Redoxpotential *n* redox (oxidation-reduction) potential, ORP
Redoxreaktion *f* redox (oxidation-reduction) reaction, oxidoreduction
Redoxskala *f* redox scale
Redoxspezies *f* redox species
Redoxsystem *n* redox system
Redoxtitration *f* redox titration
Reductaseprobe *f s.* Reduktionsprobe
Reduktion *f* reduction, electronation • **der ~ unterliegen** to undergo reduction
~/Bouveault-Blancsche Bouveault-Blanc reduction *(of esters to alcohols)*
~/direkte direct reduction
~/elektrochemische (elektrolytische) electrochemical (electrolytic) reduction
~ mit Wasserstoff hydrogen reduction
~ nach Wolff-Kižner Wolff-Kishner reduction *(for converting aldehydes and ketones into their corresponding hydrocarbons)*
~/radiochemische radiochemical reduction
~/Sabatier-Senderenssche Sabatier-Senderens reduction *(of organic compounds by hydrogen)*
~/schonende mild reduction
~/thermische thermal reduction

Reduktionsaffinität *f* reduction affinity
Reduktionsanlage *f* reduction plant
Reduktionsapparatur *f* reduction unit
Reduktionsbad *n* reducing bath
Reduktionsbleiche *f* reduction bleaching
Reduktionsbrühe *f (dye)* reduction liquor *(Béchamp reduction)*
Reduktionsflamme *f* reducing flame
Reduktionsflüssigkeit *f* reduction liquor
Reduktionsgas *n* reducing gas
Reduktionsgemisch *n* reduction mixture
Reduktionsintensität *f* reduction intensity
Reduktionskolben *m* reduction flask
Reduktionskraft *f* reducing power
Reduktionslauge *f* s Reduktionsbrühe
Reduktionsmethode *f* reduction method
Reduktionsmischung *f* reduction mixture
Reduktionsmittel *n* reducing agent, reductant, reducer
Reduktions-Oxidations-... *s.* Redox...
Reduktionspotential *n* reduction potential
Reduktionsprobe *f* reductase (dye reduction) test *(for determining the bacterial content of milk)*
~ **mit Methylenblau** methylene-blue [reductase] test
Reduktionsraum *m* reducing zone *(of a burner flame)*
Reduktionsverfahren *n* reduction process, *(lab preferably)* reduction technique
Reduktionsvermögen *n* reductive capacity
Reduktionsvorgang *m* reduction process
Reduktionswirkung *f* reducing action; reducing effect
Reduktionszone *f* reduction (reducing) zone
reduktiv reductive
Redukton *n* RC(OH) = C(OH)COR reductone, enediol, *(esp)* dihydroxyacrolein, reductone
Reduktor *m* 1. reduction pan; 2. *s.* Reduktionsmittel
Redundanz *f (bioch)* redundancy, redundance
Reduplikation *f s.* Replikation
Reduzent *m (biol)* reducer, decomposer
reduzierbar reducible
Reduzierbarkeit *f* reducibility
reduzieren 1. *(ch)* to reduce; 2. to reduce, to lower, to decrease *(e.g. pressure or temperature)*
~/auf ein Mindestmaß to minimize
~ **lassen/sich** to reduce
reduzierend reductive
reduziert werden to undergo reduction
Reduzierstück *n* reducer, reducing fitting *(for pipes)*; *(lab)* reducing (reduction) adapter *(small socket to large cone)*
Reduzierung *f* reduction, lowering, decrease *(as of pressure or temperature)*
Reduzierventil *n* reducing valve
Redwood-Viskosimeter *n* Redwood viscometer
Reesterifizierung *f s.* Umesterung
Referateorgan *n*, **Referatezeitschrift** *f* abstract[ing] journal
Referenzmaterial *n (anal)* reference material
Referenzstrahl *m (anal)* reference beam
Refiner *m* 1. *(rubber)* refiner, refining mill; 2. *(pap)* refiner, refining machine (engine), perfecting engine
refinern *(rubber)* to refine
Refinern *n (rubber)* refining [treatment], refinement
Refinerscheibe *f (pap)* refiner disk
Refiner-Walzwerk *n (rubber)* refining mill, refiner
reflektieren to reflect [back]
Reflexbild *n (phot)* ghost image
Reflexion *f* reflection
~/diffuse *(spectr)* diffuse reflectance
~/mehrfache multiple reflection
~ **von Röntgenstrahlen** X-ray reflection
Reflexionsbeugung *f* **schneller Elektronen** *(anal)* reflection high-energy electron diffraction, RHEED
Reflexionsfähigkeit *f* reflectivity, reflecting power
Reflexionsgesetz *n*/**Braggsches** *(cryst)* Bragg law
Reflexionsgitter *n (spectr)* reflection grating
Reflexionsgleichung *f*/**Braggsche** *(cryst)* Bragg equation
Reflexionsgoniometer *n (cryst)* reflection goniometer
Reflexionsgrad *m*, **Reflexionskoeffizient** *m* reflectance, reflection coefficient (factor) *(optics)*
Reflexionskraft *f s.* Reflexionsfähigkeit
Reflexionslage *f* reflecting position
Reflexionsspektroskopie *f* reflectance spectroscopy
~/diffuse diffuse reflectance spectroscopy
~/innere internal reflectance spectroscopy, IRS
Reflexionsspektrum *n* reflectance spectrum
Reflexionsvermögen *n* reflectivity, reflecting power; *(quantitatively:)* reflectance, reflection coefficient (factor)
Reflexionswinkel *m* reflection angle
Reflexionszahl *f* 1. reflectivity *(radiation of heat)*; 2. *s.* Reflexionsgrad
Reflexkopierverfahren *n (phot)* reflex copying
Reflux *m (distil)* reflux [stream]
Reformanlage *f s.* Reformieranlage
Reformat *n (petrol)* reformate
Reformatsky-Reaktion *f* Reformatsky reaction *(of 3-hydroxycarboxylic-acid esters)*
Reformbenzin *n s.* Reformierbenzin
Reformen *n s.* Reformieren
Reformer *m s.* Reformieranlage
Reformieranlage *f (petrol)* reforming plant, reformer
Reformierbenzin *n* reformed gasoline
reformieren *(petrol)* to reform
Reformieren *n* **an Platinkatalysatoren (Platinkontakten)** *(petrol)* platinum reforming, platforming
~/katalytisches catalytic reforming, cat-forming
~/thermisches thermal reforming

reformiert/katalytisch *(petrol)* cat-reformed
Reformierung *f (petrol)* reforming
Reformierungsanlage *f s.* Reformieranlage
Reformierungsreaktion *f (petrol)* reforming reaction
Reformier[ungs]verfahren *n (petrol)* reforming process
Reforming-Anlage *f s.* Reformieranlage
Reforming-Benzin *n* reformed gasoline
Reformingkatalysator *m* [petroleum-]reforming catalyst
Reformingstock *m s.* Reformstock
Reformreaktion *f s.* Reformierungsreaktion
Reformstock *m (petrol)* reformer feedstock
Refraktion *f* refraction
~/spezifische specific refraction (refractive index, refractivity)
Refraktionsmethode *f* refraction method
Refraktionsvermögen *n* refractivity
Refraktometer *n* refractometer
Refraktometrie *f* refractometry
refraktometrisch refractometric
Regel *f* rule, principle
~/Abeggsche Abegg rule *(of positive and negative valences of a chemical element)*
~/Antonovsche Antonoff rule *(of interfacial tension)*
~/Astonsche Aston whole number rule *(of the atomic weights of isotopes)*
~/Auwers-Skitasche Auwers-Skita rule *(of catalytic hydrogenation)*
~/Avogadrosche Avogadro hypothesis (law) *(of the number of molecules in gases)*
~/Babinetsche *(cryst)* Babinet absorption rule
~/Blancsche Blanc rule *(of the dehydration of dicarboxylic acids)*
~/Braggsche *(nucl)* Bragg rule
~/Bredtsche Bredt rule *(of double bonds within bridged polycyclic systems)*
~ der größten Multiplizität[/Hundsche] *s.* ~/1. Hundsche
~ der IUC IUC rule
~ der IUPAC IUPAC rule
~/Drapersche Draper law *(of chemically effective radiation)*
~/Dühringsche Dühring's rule *(for vapour pressures of related liquids)*
~/Dulong-Petitsche Dulong and Petit's law *(of atomic heats)*
~/Eötvössche Eötvös rule *(of molar surface energy)*
~/Friessche Fries rule *(of the bond structure of polynuclear compounds)*
~/Geiger-Nuttallsche *(nucl)* Geiger-Nuttall rule
~/Hildebrandsche Hildebrand rule *(of constant entropy of vaporization)*
~/Hiltsche *(coal)* Hilt's law (rule)
~/Hofmannsche Hofmann rule *(of orientation in β-eliminations)*
~/Hume-Rotherysche Hume-Rothery rule *(of alloy systems)*
~/Hundsche Hund's rule (principle) *(of the energy of atomic states)*
~/1. Hundsche *(spectr)* Hund's first rule, [Hund] maximum multiplicity rule
~/2. Hundsche *(spectr)* Hund's second rule, angular momentum rule
~/3. Hundsche *(spectr)* Hund's third rule, fine-structure rule
~/Konovalovsche *(phys ch)* Konowaloff rule
~/Koppsche Kopp law *(of molar heats)*
~/Markovnikovsche Markovnikov's rule *(of the addition of compounds to olefins)*
~/Mattauchsche *(nucl)* Mattauch rule
~/Matthiessensche Matthiessen rule *(of the resistivity of metals)*
~/Ramsay-Youngsche Ramsay-Young rule *(of temperatures for equal vapour pressures)*
~/Schürmannsche *(coal)* Schürmann's rule
~/Stokessche Stokes rule *(of luminescence)*
~/Traubesche Traube rule *(of the surface tension of water)*
~/Troutonsche Trouton's rule (law) *(of the heat of evaporation)*
~/Vegardsche *(cryst)* Vegard's rule (law)
~/Waldensche *(phys ch)* Walden rule (law)
Regelanlage *f*, **Regeleinrichtung** *f* controlling device, controller
Regelkreis *m* feedback (closed-loop) control system
regellos random
regelmäßig regular
~/sterisch stereoregular
Regelmäßigkeit *f* regularity
~ der Struktur structural regularity
~/sterische stereoregularity
Regelmechanismus *m* control mechanism, regulatory (regulation) mechanism
regeln to control, *(esp manually:)* to adjust
Regelstab *m (nucl)* control rod
Regelung *f* control, *(esp manually:)* adjustment; *s.* ~/automatische
~/automatische automatic (feedback) control
~/nichtselbsttätige manual control
~/selbsttätige *s.* ~/automatische
Regelungsrechner *m* control computer
Regelungssystem *n* control system
Regelventil *n* control valve
Regelvorgang *m* control process
regelwidrig anomalous, abnormal
Regelwidrigkeit *f* anomaly, abnormality
Regen *m***/ saurer** acid rain
Regenbett *n* raining bed *(fluid-bed system consisting of falling particles in upstream fluid)*
regendicht rainproof, rain-tight, shower-proof
Regenerat *n (rubber)* reclaim, reclaimed rubber, shoddy; *(plast)* reclaim, reground material
Regeneratcellulose *f* regenerated cellulose
Regeneratcellulosefaser *f* regenerated cellulose fibre

Regeneratcellulosefaserstoff *m* regenerated cellulose fibre
Regeneratdispersion *f* reclaim [rubber] dispersion, dispersed reclaimed rubber
Regeneratfaser *f* regenerated fibre, semisynthetic (manufactured) fibre
Regeneratfaserstoff *m* regenerated fibre, semisynthetic (manufactured) fibre
Regenerathersteller *m (rubber, plast)* reclaimer
Regeneration *f s.* Regenerierung
Regenerationsmittel *n s.* Regeneriermittel
regenerativ regenerative
Regenerativfeuerung *f* regenerative firing
Regenerativgummi *m* reclaimed rubber, reclaim, shoddy
Regenerativkammer *f* regenerator chamber
Regenerativofen *m* regenerative furnace
Regenerativprinzip *n* regenerative principle
Regenerativschmelzofen *m* regenerative melting furnace
Regenerativsystem *n* regenerative system
Regenerativ-Verbund[koks]ofen *m* **nach Still** Still oven
Regeneratmischung *f (rubber)* reclaim compound (mix)
Regeneratmischwalzwerk *n (rubber)* reclaim mixing mill
Regenerator *m* 1. regenerator, *(in catalytic cracking also)* kiln; revivifier *(of catalysts)*; 2. *s.* Regeneratorlösung
Regeneratorkammer *f* regenerator chamber
Regeneratorlösung *f (phot)* replenisher [solution]
Regeneratorraum *m* regenerator chamber
Regeneratpulver *n (rubber)* powdered reclaim
Regeneratwolle *f* reclaimed (recovered) wool
Regenerierabwasser *n (hyd)* spent regenerant waste, regeneration waste, recharge waste effluent, waste from regeneration
~ **der Vollentsalzung** spent demineralizer regenerant
~ **der Wasserenthärtung** water-softener waste water, water-softener recharge effluent
regenerierbar regenerable, capable of being regenerated
~/nicht non-regenerable
Regenerierbarkeit *f* capability of being regenerated
Regenerierchemikalie *f* regenerating (regenerant) chemical, chemical regenerant *(as for ion exchange)*
Regenerierdauer *f* regeneration period, regenerant contact time
regenerieren to regenerate, *(activated carbon also)* to reactivate, *(catalysts also)* to revivify, *(ion exchangers also)* to recharge; *(rubber, plast)* to reclaim, to recover; *(pap)* to remanufacture
Regenerierkolonne *f* regeneration column *(ion exchange)*
Regenerierlauge *f* regenerant caustic, caustic used for regeneration *(ion exchange)*
Regenerierlösung *f s.* Regeneriermittellösung
Regeneriermittel *n* regenerant *(as for ion exchange)*; *(rubber)* reclaiming agent
Regeneriermittellösung *f* regenerant (regenerating) solution, *(if containing sodium chloride:)* brine regenerant *(ion exchange)*
~/verbrauchte used regenerant, spent regenerant (regeneration solution), *(if sodium chloride solution has been used:)* spent brine
Regeneriermittelmenge *f* regenerant dosage (level, volume)
Regeneriermittelüberschuß *m* excess regenerant
Regeneriermittelverbrauch *m* regenerant consumption
Regeneriermittelvolumen *n s.* Regeneriermittelmenge
Regenerierofen *m* regenerator, kiln *(in catalytic cracking)*
Regeneriersalz *n* regeneration (recharge) salt *(ion exchange)*
Regeneriersalzmenge *f* regeneration (recharge) salt dosage, amount of salt [for regeneration]
Regeneriersäure *f* acid regenerant, regenerant acid *(ion exchange)*
regeneriert/mit Kochsalzlösung (Kochsalzsole, Natriumchloridlösung) salt-regenerated, brine-regenerated, regenerated with sodium chloride brine *(ion exchange)*
~/mit Säure acid-regenerated
Regenerierung *f* regeneration, *(of activated carbon also)* reactivation, *(of catalysts also)* revivification, *(of ion exchangers also)* recharge; *(rubber, plast)* reclaiming, reclamation, recovery; *(pap)* remanufacture
~/biologische biological regeneration *(of activated carbon)*
~/externe external regeneration *(of ion-exchange resins)*
~ **im Gegenstrom** countercurrent (counterflow) regeneration
~ **im Gleichstrom** co-current regeneration
~ **mit Kochsalzlösung (Kochsalzsole)** salting, brining *(of ion exchange resins)*
~ **mit Lauge** caustic regeneration
~ **mit Natriumchloridlösung** *s.* ~ mit Kochsalzlösung
~ **mit Natronlauge** *s.* ~ mit Lauge
~ **mit Säure** acid regeneration (wash)
~/thermische thermal regeneration *(of activated carbon)*
~ **von Aktivkohle** carbon regeneration (reactivation)
Regenerierungsbecken *n (hyd)* stabilization tank *(contact stabilization of activated sludge)*
Regenerierungsmittel *n s.* Regeneriermittel
Regenerierverfahren *n* regeneration process; *(rubber, plast)* reclaiming process
Regeneriervorgang *m* regeneration process; regeneration (recharge) cycle (step) *(ion exchange)*
Regenwasser *n* rain water, storm water
~/saures acidic rain water

Regenwasserablauf *m (hyd)* storm-water runoff
Regenwasseranfall *m (hyd)* storm-water [in]flow
Regenwasserrückhaltebecken *n (hyd)* storm-water retention (holding) basin, catch basin for rainwater, rainwater collection tank
regioselektiv *(org ch)* regioselective
Regioselektivität *f (org ch)* regioselectivity
regiospezifisch *(org ch)* regiospecific, site-specific
Regiospezifität *f (org ch)* regiospecificity, site specificity
Registerpartie *f (pap)* table-roll section
Registerschienen *fpl (pap)* shake rails
Registerteil *m (pap)* table-roll section
Registerwalze *f (pap)* table (tube, wire-cloth) roll
registrieren 1. to index; 2. to record *(measuring values)*
Registriergerät *n* recording instrument
Registriername *m (nomencl)* index name
Registrierung *f* 1. indexing; 2. recording *(of measuring values)*
Registrierungssystem *n (nomencl)* indexing system
Regler *m* 1. [automatic] controller, control[ling] unit; 2. chain transfer agent *(polymerization)*; modifier, modifying agent *(floatation)*
Reglermembran *f* governor diaphragm
Reglersubstanz *f* chain-transfer agent *(polymerization)*
Regner *m* sprinkler
regulär regular
Regularität *f* regularity
Regulation *f* **der Transkription** *(bioch)* transcriptional control
~ der Translation translational control
~ durch Isoenzyme isoenzyme control
~/koordinierte coordinate control
Regulationsmechanismus *m* control mechanism, regulatory (regulation) mechanism
Regulationsmutante *f (biot)* regulatory mutant
Regulationsprotein *n (bioch)* regulatory protein
Regulatorgen *n (bioch)* regulator gene
Regulatorprotein *n (bioch)* regulatory protein
regulieren to control, to adjust
Regulus *m (lab)* regulus
Regulusmetall *n* regulus metal *(an alloy containing 90 % Pb, 8 % Sb, and 2 % Sn)*
Rehalogen[is]ierung *f (phot)* rehalogenation
Reib... *s. a.* Reibungs...
Reibechtheit *f (text)* fastness to rubbing, rub[bing] fastness, *(relating to dyes also)* crock fastness
reiben to rub; to grind, to triturate *(to a fine powder)*
Reiberwalze *f* triturating roll *(as for preparing oil paints)*
Reibfläche *f* abrasive surface *(for safety matches)*
Reibmittel *n (text)* abradant
Reibmühle *f* attrition mill
Reibschale *f* mortar
Reibung *f* friction [force]
~/innere internal friction, viscous force
Reibungseffekt *m***/richtungsabhängiger** directional frictional effect
Reibungsempfindlichkeit *f* sensitiveness to friction
Reibungsentrinder *m* **nach Thorne** *(pap)* Thorne (waterous) barker
Reibungsfaktor *m s.* Reibungskoeffizient
reibungsfrei frictionless
Reibungsgesetz *n* **nach Ostwald und de Waele** Ostwald-de Waele equation
~/Newtonsches Newton's law of friction
Reibungshöhe *f* friction head *(in pumps)*
Reibungskalander *m (pap, rubber)* friction[ing] calender
Reibungskoeffizient *m* coefficient of friction, frictional constant
Reibungskraft *f s.* Reibung
reibungslos frictionless
Reibungslumineszenz *f* triboluminescence
Reibungsverhältnis *n* friction ratio
Reibungsverlust *m* friction loss; pressure loss from friction *(rheology)*
Reibungsverschleiß *m* abrasive wear, abrasion, attrition
Reibungswärme *f* friction heat
Reibungswiderstand *m* resistance to friction, friction resistance; drag *(acting on a body immersed in a moving fluid)*
Reibwert *m s.* Reibungskoeffizient
Reichert-Meissl-Zahl *f* Reichert-Meissl number (value), R-M number *(for evaluating oils and fats)*
Reichgas *n* rich gas
Reichölerhitzer *m* rich-oil heater
Reichweite-Energie-Beziehung *f* range-energy relation
Reid-Dampfdruck *m* Reid vapour pressure, R.V.P.
reif ripe, mature
Reif *m (food)* bloom *(as on fruit or chocolate)*
Reife *f* 1. ripeness, maturity; 2. *s.* Reifung
Reifebeschleuniger *m (food)* ripening agent
Reifegrad *m (text)* maturity level, degree of ripeness
Reifegradbestimmung *f (text)* maturity test
reifen to ripen, to mature; to age *(viscose)*
Reifen *m (rubber)* tyre
~/schlauchloser tubeless tyre
Reifenaufbaumaschine *f (rubber)* tyre-building machine (drum), lay-up machine
Reifeneinzelheizer *m (rubber)* single tyre press, unit vulcanizer for tyres
Reifenform *f (rubber)* tyre mould
Reifenheizung *f (rubber)* tyre curing
Reifenkord *m (rubber)* tyre cord
Reifenmischung *f (rubber)* tyre compound
Reifenrohling *m (rubber)* green tyre
Reifenwickelmaschine *f s.* Reifenaufbaumaschine
Reifenwickeltrommel *f (rubber)* tyre-building drum, building (case-making) drum
Reifenwulst *m (rubber)* tyre bead
Reifezahl *f s.* Reifegrad

Reifung *f* 1. ripening, maturing, maturation; ageing *(of viscose)*; processing *(of ribonucleic acid)*; 2. *(phot)* digestion *(of an emulsion)*; 3. *(filtr)* ripening
Reifungsbeschleuniger *m (food)* ripening agent
Reifungsgrad *m (food)* degree of ripening
Reifungsvorgang *m* ripening process
Reifwerden *n* ripening, maturing, maturation
Reihe *f* series; family *(as of hydrocarbons)*
~/eluotrope *(chromat)* eluotropic series
~/Hofmeistersche Hofmeister series, lyotropic order (series)
~/homologe homologous series
~/idioblastische *(min)* crystalloblastic series
~/isologe isologous series
~/kristalloblastische *(min)* crystalloblastic series
~/lyotrope *s.* ~/Hofmeistersche
~/radioaktive radioactive [decay] series
Reihendüngung *f* row dressing
Reihenrührer *m*, **Reihenrührwerk** *n (hyd)* gang-stirrer
Reihenverdünnung *f* serial dilution
Reihenverdünnungsmethode *f* serial-dilution method *(as for evaluating antibiotics)*
Reimer-Tiemann-Synthese *f* Reimer-Tiemann synthesis *(of phenolic aldehydes)*
rein 1. pure, *(of noble metals also)* fine, *(of chemical elements also)* elemental; plain, unalloyed *(steel)*; absolute *(alcohol)*; neat *(wine)*; 2. clean *(surface)* • ~ **darstellen** to prepare in pure form, to prepare in a pure condition (state), to isolate *(natural products)* • ~ **erhalten** to obtain pure (in pure form), to obtain in a pure condition (state)
~/chemisch chemically pure, C.P.
~/chromatographisch chromatographically pure
~/extrem ultrapure
~/nicht impure
~/technisch technical
Reinaluminium *n* pure aluminium
Reinargon *n* very-high-purity argon
Reinblau *n* celestial (ethereal) blue *(any of several iron-blue pigments)*
Reinchemikalie *f* pure chemical
Reindarstellung *f* isolation *(of natural products)*
Reineck[e]at *n* reineckate *(a salt of Reinecke acid)*
Reinecke-Salz *n* Reinecke salt, ammonium tetrathiocyanatodiamminechromate(III)
Reinecke-Säure *f* Reinecke acid
Reinelement *n* monoisotopic element
Reinerzeugnis *n* pure product
Reingas *n* clean[ed] gas
Reinhardt-Zimmermann-Lösung *f (anal)* Zimmermann-Reinhardt [preventive] solution, Z-R reagent
Reinheit *f* purity *(as of chemicals)*; clean[li]ness *(as of surface)* • **von höchster** ~ superpure
Reinheitsanforderung *f* purity specification
Reinheitsgrad *m* degree (level) of purity, purity level, *(esp of reagents:)* grade
Reinheitsprüfung *f* purity test
Reinheitsquotient *m (sugar)* purity quotient (coefficient)
reinigen 1.to clean[se] *(surfaces)*; 2. to clean up *(gases esp for removing particulate matter)*; to purify *(chemicals, or gases esp for removing gaseous components)*; to refine *(metals)*; to treat, to purify, to clean [up] *(water, waste water)*
~/chemisch to dry-clean *(clothing)*
~/durch Zonenschmelzen to zone-refine, to zone-purify
~/mit einem Schaber to doctor *(e.g. a roll)*
~/mit einer Bürste to scrub
~/trocken to dry-clean *(e.g. gas or clothing)*
~/vorher to preclean
reinigend detergent
Reiniger *m s.* 1. Reinigungsanlage; 2. Reinigungsmittel
Reinigung *f* 1. clean[s]ing *(of surfaces)*; 2. cleaning, clean-up *(of gases esp for removing particulate matter)*; purification *(of chemicals, or of gases esp for removing gaseous compounds)*; refining *(of metals)*; treatment, purification, cleaning, clean-up *(of water, waste water)*
~/elektrische (elektrostatische) electrical (electrostatic) precipitation
~/extreme superrefining, ultrapurification *(as of metals)*
~ im Aufwärtsstrom *(hyd)* upflow cleaning
~/mechanische *(hyd)* primary (first) waste treatment, primary treatment
~/nasse wet cleaning *(as of gas)*
~/trockene dry cleaning *(as of gas)*
~/vollbiologische *(hyd)* complete biological treatment
Reinigungsanlage *f* purification plant, purifying unit; *(coal, pap)* cleaning plant; *(hyd)* treatment plant (unit)
Reinigungsapparat *m* purifier
Reinigungsbad *n (text)* clearing (scouring) bath
Reinigungsbenzin *n* cleaner's naphtha (solvent)
Reinigungscreme *f (cosmet)* cleansing cream
Reinigungseffekt *m* 1. *(text)* cleaning (detergent) effect; 2. *(filtr)* clarification efficiency *(per cent)*; *(hyd)* clarification effect
Reinigungsflüssigkeit *f (filtr)* washing liquid (liquor), wash [solvent]
Reinigungsgrad *m* degree of purification; *(hyd)* degree of clarification *(of municipal or industrial water)*; degree of [particle] removal *(from waste water)*; degree of treatment (purification) *(of waste water before its discharge)*
Reinigungsheizer *m (chromat)* clean-up heater *(of an HPLC-MS coupling interface)*
Reinigungshilfsmittel *n* cleaning aid
Reinigungskraft *f s.* Reinigungsvermögen
Reinigungsleistung *f (text)* cleaning efficiency, detergent performance; *(hyd)* [contaminant] removal efficiency, removal performance
Reinigungslotion *f (cosmet)* cleansing lotion

Reinigungsmittel *n* cleaning (cleansing) agent, clean[s]er, detergent; purifier *(as for chemicals)*
~/synthetisches [synthetic] detergent, syndet, soapless soap
Reinigungsstufe *f (hyd)* treatment stage
~/biologische *s.* ~/zweite
~/dritte tertiary waste treatment stage
~/erste primary (first) waste treatment stage
~/zweite secondary waste treatment stage
Reinigungstechnologie *f* **für Abwässer** waste-water technology
Reinigungsturm *m* tower purifier
Reinigungsverfahren *n* **mittels hochbelasteter Tropfkörper** *(hyd)* high-rate biological filtration
Reinigungsvermögen *n (text)* detergent (cleansing) power, detergent properties, detergency
Reinigungsverstärker *m (text)* cleaning promoter (intensifier)
Reinigungswirkung *f* 1. *(text)* cleaning action; 2. *(hyd)* clarifying action; 3. *s.* Reinigungseffekt
Reinigungszusatz *m* detergent additive
Reinkali *n* potassium oxide, [soluble] potash *(in fertilizer analyses)*
Reinkohle *f* pure (clean) coal *(a coal of minimum ash content)*
Reinkohlensubstanz *f* pure coal material (substance)
Reinkultur *f* pure culture, monoculture *(of microorganisms)*
Reinkupfer *n* pure copper
Reinlecithin *n* pure lecithin
reinmachen *(tann)* to scud *(to remove remaining hairs or lime from hides or skins)*
Reinmetall *n* pure metal
Reinprodukt *n* pure [product]
Reinprotein *n* pure protein
Reinraum *m (anal)* clean room *(provided with filtered air)*
Reinsauerstoff *m* pure oxygen
Reinsauerstoff-Verfahren *n (hyd)* aeration with pure oxygen
Reinsole *f* pure brine
reinst of highest purity, ultrapure, ultrahigh-purity, superpure, super-purity
Reinstaluminium *n* super-pure (super-purity) aluminium
Reinstoff *m* pure substance (material)
Reinststoff *m* ultrapure substance (material)
Reinstwasser *n* ultrapure (ultrahigh-purity) water
Reinsubstanz *f* pure substance (material)
Reintransmissionsgrad *m* internal transmittance
Reinverbindung *f* pure compound
Reinvulkanisat *n (rubber)* [pure] gum vulcanizate
Reinwasser *n (hyd)* clean water; *(as a product of water treatment:)* treated water, finished [drinking] water; *(obtained by filtration:)* filtered water, filtrate; *(obtained by reverse osmosis:)* permeate
~/durch Entsalzung hergestelltes manufactured (man-made, product) fresh water
Reinwasserabfluß *m*, **Reinwasserabführung** *f s.* Reinwasserablauf
Reinwasserablauf *m (hyd)* treated-water outlet, *(from filters:)* filtered-water outlet
Reinwasseranalyse *f (hyd)* treated-water analysis
Reinwassergüte *f (hyd)* treated-water quality, *(relating to filter efficiency:)* filtrate quality
Reinwasserherstellung *f (hyd)* fresh-water production *(by desalination of sea water)*
Reinwasserqualität *f s.* Reinwassergüte
Reinwassersammelrinne *f (hyd)* effluent collector flume
Reinzucht *f (biot)* pure culture (growth)
Reinzuchthefe *f* pure-culture yeast
Reisbier *n* rice beer
Reiswein *m* sake, rice wine
Reisglas *n* alabaster glass
Reismehl *n* rice flour
Reispapier *n*[**/Chinesisches**] rice paper *(from the pith of Tetrapanax papyriferum (Hook.) K. Koch)*
Reispuder *m* rice powder
Reisschleifmehl *n* rice polish (dust) *(removed from rice in polishing)*
Reißdehnung *f s.* Bruchdehnung
reißen to crack *(of surface coatings)*, to craze *(of glazes)*; to break, to tear, to rupture *(as of paper webs)*; to macerate, to tear *(fibrous material)*
/Elementarfäden auf Stapel *(text)* to staple
Reissert-Verbindung *f (org ch)* Reissert compound *(obtained by adding cyanide ions to N-benzoylquinoline hydrochloride)*
Reißfestigkeit *f* tear resistance (strength), resistance to tearing, breaking strength (tenacity)
Reißkonverterverfahren *n (text)* tow-to-top breaking system
Reißlänge *f (text)* breaking length, strength-to-weight ratio
Reißscheibe *f* rupture (bursting) disk
Reisstärke *f* rice starch
Reißverschlußreaktion *f (plast)* chain unzipping reaction
Reißwerk *n* macerator *(as for peat)*
Reißwolle *f* reclaimed (recovered) wool, *(if recovered from heavily felted wool goods or wastes:)* mungo
Reiter *m* [balance] rider, rider weight *(of an analytical balance)*
Reiterlineal *n* rider bar (carrier) *(of an analytical balance)*
Reiterwägestück *n s.* Reiter
reizen/zu Tränen to prompt tears, to make the eyes produce tears, to cause the flow of tears
~/zum Husten to provoke cough
~/zur Blasenbildung to vesicate, to blister
reizend *(med)* irritant, irritating
~/zu Tränen lachrymatory, lacrimatory
~/zum Husten cough-provoking
~/zur Blasenbildung vesicant, vesicatory
Reizkampfstoff *m* irritant

reizlos *(cosmet)* non-irritant
~/physiologisch physiologically inert
Reizlosigkeit *f (cosmet)* non-irritance, freedom from irritation
~/physiologische physiological inertness
Reizmittel *n (pharm)* stimulant, stimulatory drug, *(esp if used externally:)* irritant
Reizschwellenwert *m (tox)* activation threshold
Reizstoff *m s.* Reizmittel
Reizwirkung *f* irritant action; irritant effect
Rekaleszenz *f (cryst)* recalescence
rekarbonisieren *(hyd)* to recarbonate
Rekarbonisierung *f (hyd)* recarbonation
Rekombination *f* recombination
~/illegitime *(biot)* illegitimate recombination
~/intraspezifische *(biot)* intraspecific recombination
Rekombinationsabbruch *m* coupling termination, [chain] termination by coupling
Rekombinationsgeschwindigkeit *f* rate of recombination
Rekombinationskoeffizient *m* coefficient of recombination
Rekombinationsreaktion *f* recombination reaction
Rekombinationsreparatur *f (bioch)* recombination repair *(of deoxyribonucleic acid)*
~/postreplikative postreplicative recombination repair
Rekombinationstechnik *f (bioch)* recombinant DNA technique
Rekombinationswärme *f* heat of recombination
rekombinieren to recombine
~/sich to recombine
rekonstruieren to reconstruct, to remodel
Rekonstruktion *f* reconstruction
Rekristallisation *f* recrystallization
~/primäre *(met)* [primary] recrystallization
~/sekundäre *(met)* secondary recrystallisation, grain growth
~/verformungsbedingte *s.* ~/primäre
Rekristallisationsglühen *n* recrystallization annealing
rekristallisieren to recrystallize
Rektifikation *f* rectification
~/diskontinuierliche batch rectification
~/kontinuierliche (stetige) continuous rectification
~/unstetige *s.* ~/diskontinuierliche
Rektifikations... *s. a.* Rektifizier...
Rektifikationsanlage *f* rectifying plant
Rektifikationsapparat *m* rectifying apparatus, rectification still
Rektifikationskolonne *f* rectifying (rectification) column
Rektifikationssäule *f s.* Rektifikationskolonne
Rektifikationsteil *m*, **Rektifikationszone** *f* rectifying (enriching) section, rectifier
Rektifizier... *s. a.* Rektifikations...
Rektifizierboden *m* plate, tray
rektifizieren to rectify
Rektifizierstrecke *f s.* Rektifikationsteil
rektifiziert/doppelt (zweimal) twice-rectified
Rektifizierung *f* rectification
rekuperativ recuperative
Rekuperativfeuerung *f* recuperative firing
Rekuperativofen *m* recuperative furnace
Rekuperativsystem *n* continuous-recuperative system
Rekuperator *m* recuperator
Relativgeschwindigkeit *f* relative velocity
relativistisch relativistic
Relativphotometrie *f* relative photometry
Relaxation *f* relaxation
Relaxationseffekt *m* relaxation (asymmetry) effect
Relaxationsgeschwindigkeit *f* relaxation rate
Relaxationsmechanismus *m (phys ch)* relaxation mechanism
Relaxationsmethode *f* relaxation method (technique) *(for investigating fast reactions)*
Relaxationsperiode *f* relaxation time
Relaxationstechnik *f*, **Relaxationsverfahren** *n s.* Relaxationsmethode
Relaxationszeit *f s.* Relaxationsperiode
Releasinghormon *n* releasing hormone, release factor
Reliktmineral *n* relict mineral
REM *s.* Rasterelektronenmikroskopie
renaturieren to renature *(e.g. denatured proteins)*
Renaturierung *f* renaturation *(as of denatured proteins)*
Rendzina *f (soil)* rendzina
Rennkraftstoff *m* racing fuel
Reoxidation *f* reoxidation
Reparatur *f*/**adaptive** *(biot)* adaptive repair
Reparaturenzym *n (bioch)* repair enzyme
Reparaturlack *m* repair enamel, touch-up paint
Repellent *n (agric)* repellent
~ gegen Heuschrecken grasshopper repellent
~ gegen Nagetiere rodent repellent
Repellentstoff *m s.* Repellent
Repetiereinheit *f* repeating unit *(as of macromolecules)*
Replastizieren *n* premilling *(of silicone rubber mixtures)*
Replikase *f*/**umgekehrte** *s.* Revertase
Replikation *f (bioch)* replication *(of deoxyribonucleic acid)*
~/semikonservative semiconservative replication
Replikationsgabel *f (bioch)* replication fork
Replikationsursprung *m (bioch)* origin of replication
replikativ *(bioch)* replicative
replizieren *(bioch)* to replicate *(deoxyribonucleic acid)*
Reppe-Chemie *f* Reppe chemistry *(industrial chemistry of acetylene)*
Reppe-Synthese *f* Reppe synthesis *(of various compounds from acetylene)*
Reppe-Verfahren *n* Reppe process *(for synthesizing various compounds from acetylene)*

Repression *f (bioch)* [feedback] repression *(feedback inhibition of enzyme formation)*
~/koordinierte coordinate repression
Repressor *m (bioch)* repressor
Repressor-Induktor-Komplex *m (bioch)* repressor-inducer complex
reprimieren to repress *(a reaction)*
Reproduktion *f* reproduction
Reproduktionsfaktor *m (nucl)* multiplication constant
reproduzierbar reproducible
~/schlecht (schwer) poorly reproducible
Reproduzierbarkeit *f* reproducibility
Reprographie *f* reprography
Repulsion *f (phys ch)* repulsion
RER *s.* Reticulum/rauhes endoplasmatisches
Resazurinprobe *f* resazurin [reduction] test *(for testing the keeping quality of milk)*
Research-Methode *f* research method, F1 method *(for determining the octane number)*
Research-Octanzahl *f* research octane number, research-method rating, RON
Reserpinsäure *f*, **Reserpsäure** *f* reserpic acid
Reservagedruck *m s.* Reservedruck
Reserve *f* 1. reserve, store, stock; 2. *s.* Reservierungsmittel
Reserve-Antibiotikum *n* reserve antibiotic
Reservecellulose *f* moss starch, lichenin
Reservedruck *m (text)* reserve (resist) printing
Reserveeiweiß *n (bot)* reserve protein
Reservekohlenhydrat *n (bot)* reserve carbohydrate
Reservelipid *n (bioch)* storage (depot) lipid
Reservemittel *n s.* Reservierungsmittel
reservieren *(text)* to reserve, to resist
Reservierung *f (text)* reservation, resisting
Reservierungsmittel *n (text)* reserve, resist[ing agent]
Reservierungspaste *f (text)* resist paste
Reservoir *n* reservoir, tank
Residualaffinität *f* residual affinity
Residualfungizid *n* protective fungicide
Residualöl *n (petrol)* residual oil (stock)
Residualton *m (geoch)* residual (primary) clay
Residualwirkung *f* residual action; residual effect
Residuum *n* residue, *(petrol also)* resid[uum]
Resiliometer *n* resiliometer, resilience meter
Resinat *n* resinate *(resin soap or resin ester)*
Resinit *m* resinite *(coal maceral)*
Resinoid *n (cosmet)* resinoid *(alcoholic extract from aromatic resins and other odoriferous drugs)*
Resinosäure *f* resin acid
Resist *m* resist *(photolithography)*
resistent resistant, resisting, stable
Resistenz *f* resistance, stability
~/chemische chemical resistance (stability), resistance (stability) to chemical attack
~ gegen Chemikalien resistance to chemicals
~/mikrobiologische microbiological resistance
~/pflanzliche plant resistance *(as to pesticides)*
Resistenzentwicklung *f (biot)* development of [antibiotic] resistance, build-up of resistance
Resit *n* resite, C-stage resin
Resitol *n* resitol, B-stage resin
Resol *n* resol, A-stage (one-stage) resin
Resolsäure *f* resolic acid *(a methyl derivative of aurine)*
Resonanz *f* 1. *(org ch)* resonance, mesomerism; 2. resonance *(physics)*
~/elektronenparamagnetische *s.* ~/paramagnetische
~/kernmagnetische nuclear magnetic resonance, n.m.r., NMR *(for compounds s. under* NMR*)*
~/laserelektrische laser-electric resonance, LER
~/lasermagnetische laser-magnetic resonance, LMR
~/quantenmechanische quantum-mechanical resonance
~/paramagnetische paramagnetic [electronic] resonance, p.m.r., electron spin resonance, e.s.r., ESR, electron paramagnetic resonance, e.p.r., EPR
Resonanzabsorption *f (nucl)* resonance absorption
resonanzaktiv *(spectr)* resonant
Resonanzbegriff *m* concept of resonance
Resonanzbereich *m (nucl)* resonance region
Resonanzeffekt *m* resonance effect
Resonanzeinfang *m (nucl)* resonance capture
Resonanzenergie *f s.* 1. Delokalisierungsenergie; 2. Stabilisierungsenergie
~/Dewarsche *s.* Stabilisierungsenergie
Resonanzentkommwahrscheinlichkeit *f (nucl)* resonance escape probability
Resonanzerscheinung *f* resonance phenomenon
Resonanzfluoreszenz *f (anal)* resonance fluorescence
Resonanzformel *f* resonance formula
resonanzfrei non-resonant, resonance-free
Resonanzfrequenz *f* resonance (resonant) frequency
Resonanzhybrid *n (org ch)* resonance hybrid
Resonanzintegral *n* resonance integral *(quantum chemistry)*
Resonanzlinie *f* resonance [spectral] line
Resonanzmethode *f* resonance method
Resonanzneutron *n* resonance neutron
Resonanzniveau *n* resonance level (state)
Resonanzpfeil *m* double-headed arrow
Resonanzphänomen *n* resonance phenomenon
Resonanzpotential *n (phys ch)* resonance potential
Resonanz-Raman-Effekt *m* resonance Raman effect, RRE
~/rigoroser rigorous resonance Raman effect
Resonanz-Raman-Spektroskopie *f* resonance Raman spectroscopy
Resonanz-Raman-Streuung *f* resonance Raman scattering, RRS
Resonanzsignal *n (spectr)* resonance signal, *(in a graph also)* resonance peak

Resonanzspektroskopie *f* resonance spectroscopy
~/kernmagnetische nuclear magnetic resonance spectroscopy, NMR spectroscopy
~/magnetische magnetic resonance spectroscopy
~/paramagnetische electron paramagnetic (spin) resonance spectroscopy, EPR (ESR) spectroscopy
Resonanzspektrum *n* resonance spectrum
~/kernmagnetisches nuclear magnetic resonance spectrum, NMR spectrum
~/paramagnetisches electron paramagnetic (spin) resonance spectrum, EPR (ESR) spectrum
resonanzstabilisiert *(org ch)* resonance-stabilized
Resonanzstabilisierung *f (org ch)* resonance stabilization, stabilization through resonance
Resonanzstrahlung *f* resonance radiation
Resonanzstreuung *f* resonance scattering
Resonanzstruktur *f (org ch)* resonance (resonating) structure
Resonanztheorie *f (org ch)* resonance theory
Resonanztransfer *m* resonance transfer
~/zufälliger accidental resonance transfer
Resonanzübergang *m (spectr)* resonance transition
Resonanzvalenzbindungssystem *n* resonating valence bond system
Resonanzvorstellung *f (org ch)* concept of resonance
Resonanzwechselwirkung *f* resonance interaction *(stereochemistry)*
Resonanzzustand *m (org ch)* resonance state
resorbieren to resorb
resorbiert werden to resorb, to undergo resorption
Resorcin *n s.* Resorcinol
Resorcinblau *n* resorcinol blue, lac[k]moid
Resorcingelb *n* resorcinol yellow, tropaeolin O *(sodium azoresorcinol-sulphanilate)*
Resorcinharz *n* resorcinol[-formaldehyde] resin
Resorcinmonoethylether *m* resorcinol monoethyl ether, *m*-ethoxyphenol
Resorcinol *n* resorcinol, *m*-dihydroxybenzene
Resorcinolphthalein *n*, **Resorcinphthalein** *n* resorcinolphthalein, fluorescein
Resorption *f* resorption
~ über die Haut skin absorption
Respiration *f* respiration
Respirationsquotient *m (bioch)* respiratory quotient, RQ
Respirator *m* breathing mask
respiratorisch respiratory
Responsefaktor *m (chromat)* response factor
~/relativer (substanzspezifischer) relative response factor
Rest *m* 1. remnant, remainder *(as of material)*; 2. residue, group *(of a molecule)*; 3. balance *(in analyses)*
~/C-terminaler C-terminal residue (group) *(in proteins)*
Restabilisierung *f (hyd)* restabilization
Restaffinität *f* residual affinity
Restaktivität *f (biot)* remaining activity *(of an enzyme)*
Restalkaligehalt *m*, **Restalkalität** *f (hyd, pap)* residual alkalinity
Restbrühe *f (tann)* tailing[s], tails
Rest-BSB *m (hyd)* residual (final) BOD (biochemical oxygen demand)
Restchlor *n (hyd)* 1. residual chlorine; 2. *s.* Restchlorgehalt
~/freies wirksames *s.* Restchlorgehalt
~/gebundenes combined residual chlorine
Restchlorgehalt *m (hyd)* [amount of] chlorine residual, [free] residual chlorine, free [available] chlorine residual, excess [of] chlorine
Restchlorkonzentration *f (hyd)* residual-chlorine concentration
Restdextrin *s.* Grenzdextrin
Restenthärtung *f (hyd)* final softening
~ mit Trinatriumphosphat two-stage hot lime-soda phosphate treatment
Restfeuchte *f* residual moisture
Restfeuchtebeladung *f* residual moisture content
Restfeuchtegehalt *m* residual moisture content
Restfeuchtigkeit *f* residual moisture
Restflüssigkeit *f* residual liquid (liquor)
Restgas *n* residual (residue) gas
Restgehalt *m* residual (final) content
~ an freiem [wirksamem] Chlor *s.* Restchlorgehalt
~ an organischen Inhaltsstoffen *(hyd)* residual organic content
Resthärte *f (hyd)* residual (final) hardness
Restiod *n (hyd)* iodine residual
Restkalkhärte *f (hyd)* residual calcium hardness
Restkarbonathärte *f*, **Rest-KH** *f (hyd)* residual carbonate hardness
Restkohlenwasserstoffe *mpl (hyd)* residual hydrocarbons
Restkoks *m* residual char
Restkonzentration *f* **an Geruchsstoffen** *(hyd)* residual odour
Restkörper *m (bioch)* remnant *(remaining from chylomicrons)*
Restkrumpfung *f (text)* residual shrinkage
Restlast *f (hyd)* residual load
Restlignin *n (pap)* residual lignin, lignin residues
Restlinien *fpl (spectr)* persistent (ultimate) lines, raies ultimes
Restmenge *f***/duldbare (zulässige)** *(tox)* [residue] tolerance
Restöl *n (petrol)* residual oil (stock)
Restparamagnetismus *m* residual paramagnetism
Restriktionsanalyse *f (bioch)* restriction mapping
Restriktions[desoxy]endonuclease *f s.* Restriktionsenzym
Restriktionsenzym *n (bioch)* restriction enzyme (endonuclease)
Restriktionskarte *f (bioch)* restriction map
Restriktionskartierung *f s.* Restriktionsanalyse

Restsauerstoff *m (hyd)* residual dissolved oxygen
Restsauerstoffgehalt *m (hyd)* residual dissolved oxygen content
Restschmutz *m (text)* soil residue
Restschrumpf *m*, **Restschrumpfung** *f (text)* residual shrinkage
Restschwefelgehalt *m* residual sulphur content
Restspannung *f* 1. *(tech)* residual stress; 2. *(el* ch) residual voltage
Reststickstoff *m* residual (non-protein) nitrogen
Reststrahlen *mpl* residual rays, reststrahlen
Reststrahlung *f* residual radiation
Reststrom *m (el ch)* residual current
Restsubstrat *n (biot)* residual substrate (nutrient), feed residues
Restsüße *f (ferm)* residual sugar
Restvalenz *f* residual valency
Restverschmutzung *f***/organische** *(hyd)* residual organic content
Restzucker *m (ferm)* residual sugar
Retardans *n (bioch)* retarder
Retardiermittel *n* retarder, retarding agent, *(text also)* dye retardant
Reten *n* retene, 7-isopropyl-1-methyl-phenanthrene
Retention *f* retention
~ **der Konfiguration** retention of configuration, configuration retention
~**/relative** relative retention *(gas chromatography)*
Retentionsanalyse *f* retention analysis
Retentionsindex *m* **[nach Kováts]** *(chromat)* retention (Kovats) index
Retentionsrate *f*, **Retentionsverhältnis** *n (chromat)* ratio of retention
Retentionsvermögen *n (chromat)* retention power
Retentionsvolumen *n* retention volume
~**/maximales** *(chromat)* peak retention volume
~**/reduziertes** *(chromat)* adjusted retention volume
~**/spezifisches** *(chromat)* specific retention volume
Retentionswert *m (chromat)* retention value
Retentionszeit *f (chromat)* retention (hold-up) time; *(tech)* residence (retention, hold-up, holding) time
Reticulum *n***/agranuläres endoplasmatisches** *s.* ~/glattes endoplasmatisches
~**/glattes endoplasmatisches** *(bioch)* smooth endoplasm[at]ic reticulum, SER
~**/granuläres endoplasmatisches** *s.* ~/rauhes endoplasmatisches
~**/endoplasmatisches** *(bioch)* endoplasm[at]ic reticulum, ER
~**/rauhes endoplasmatisches** *(bioch)* rough endoplasm[at]ic reticulum, RER
Retinoid *n (org ch)* retinoid
Retorte *f* retort • **in der ~ erhitzen** to retort
~**/gemauerte** brick retort
~**/gußeiserne** cast-iron retort
~**/horizontale** horizontal retort
~**/keramische** brick retort
~**/liegende** horizontal retort
~ **mit ruhender Beschickung (Ladung)** static retort
~**/steinerne** brick retort
~**/vertikale** vertical retort
Retortenbatterie *f* retort battery
Retortengas *n* gas-retort gas
Retortengraphit *m* gas carbon
Retortengruppe *f* retort setting
Retortenhals *m* retort neck
Retortenkohle *f* gas carbon
Retortenkoks *m* retort coke
Retortenofen *m* retort furnace (oven)
Retortenschwelen *n* retorting *(of oil shale)*
Retortenverfahren *n (met)* distillation (retort) process
Retro-En-Reaktion *f (org ch)* retro-ene reaction
retrograd retrograde
Retrogradation *f (coll)* retrogradation *(esp of starch solutions)*
Retropinacolin-Umlagerung *f (org ch)* retropinacolin (Wagner-Meerwein) rearrangement
Reversed-phase-Säule *f (chromat)* reversed-phase column
reversibel reversible
Reversibilität *f* reversibility
~**/mikroskopische** microscopic reversibility
~**/thermische** thermal reversibility
Reversierventil *n* reversing valve
Reversion *f (rubber, food)* reversion • **der ~ unterliegen, ~ erleiden** to revert
Reversions-Gaschromatographie *f* reversion gas chromatography
Reversionsgeschmack *m (food)* reversion flavour *(of fats)*
Reversionsneigung *f*, **Reversionstendenz** *f (rubber)* reversion tendency
Reversosmose *f (filtr)* reverse osmosis
Revertase *f (bioch)* reverse transcriptase, RNA-directed DNA polymerase
Revolverpresse *f (ceram)* revolver press
Reynolds-Spannung *f* Reynolds (eddy) stress *(fluid mechanics)*
Reynolds-Zahl *f* Reynolds number
~ **des Rührvorgangs** impeller Reynolds number
Re-Zahl *f s.* Reynolds-Zahl
rezent recent
Rezept *n* recipe, formula
Rezeptaufstellung *f (rubber)* design of compound, compounding
Rezeptorort *m s.* Akzeptorort
Rezeptur *f* recipe, formulation
Rezipient *m (pap)* pressure container (accumulator)
Rezipientenglocke *f (lab)* bell jar
Reziprozitätsbeziehungen *fpl***/Onsagersche** Onsager [reciprocal] relations
Reziprozitätsgesetz *n*, **Reziprozitätsregel** *f (phot)* reciprocity law, Bunsen-Roscoe [reciprocity] law
Rezirkulationsfermenter *m (biot)* fermenter with recycle [loop]
rezirkulieren to recirculate, to recycle, to return to the circuit

RFA *s.* Röntgenfluoreszenzanalyse
R-Faktor *m s.* Releasinghormon
Rf-Wert *m (chromat)* retention (retardation) factor, Rf value
RGK *s.* Reaktionsgeschwindigkeitskonstante
RH *s.* Resthärte
Rhabdophan *m (min)* rhabdophane, rhabdophanite *(a cerium phosphate)*
Rhein *n* rhein, 4,5-dihydroxyanthraquinone-2-carboxylic acid
Rheinpreußen-Koppers-Verfahren *n* Rheinpreussen-Koppers process *(for synthesizing hydrocarbons in a liquid phase)*
Rhenat(IV) *n* $M^I_2ReO_3$ rhenate(IV), trioxorhenate(IV)
Rhenat(VI) *n* $M^I_2ReO_4$ rhenate(VI), rhenate, tetraoxorhenate(VI)
Rhenat(VII) *n* M^IReO_4 perrhenate, tetraoxorhenate(VII)
Rhenium *n* Re rhenium
Rhenium(V)-chlorid *n* rhenium(V) chloride, rhenium pentachloride
Rhenium(VI)-chlorid *n* rhenium(VI) chloride, rhenium hexachloride
Rheniumdioxid *n s.* Rhenium(IV)-oxid
Rheniumheptoxid *n s.* Rhenium(VII)-oxid
Rheniumhexachlorid *n s.* Rhenium(VI)-chlorid
Rhenium(III)-oxid *n* rhenium(III) oxide, dirhenium trioxide
Rhenium(IV)-oxid *n* rhenium(IV) oxide, rhenium dioxide
Rhenium(VI)-oxid *n* rhenium(VI) oxide, rhenium trioxide
Rhenium(VII)-oxid *n* rhenium(VII) oxide, dirhenium heptaoxide
Rheniumpentachlorid *n s.* Rhenium(V)-chlorid
Rheniumperoxid *n* rhenium peroxide
Rheniumsäure *f* rhenic acid, tetraoxorhenic(VI) acid
Rhenium(VII)-säure *f* perrhenic acid, tetraoxorhenic(VII) acid
Rheniumtrioxid *n s.* Rhenium(VI)-oxid
Rheologie *f* rheology
rheologisch rheological
Rheomorphose *f (geoch)* rheomorphism
rheopex *(coll)* rheopectic
Rheopexie *f (coll)* rheopexy
Rheorinne *f* trough washer
Rheotron *n s.* Betatron
Rhesus-Faktor *m*, **Rh-Faktor** *m (med)* rhesus factor (antigen), rh [factor]
Rh-negativ *(med)* rh-negative
Rhodamin *n (dye)* rhodamine *(any of a class of fluorescein derivatives)*
Rhodanese *f* rhodanese *(a transferring enzyme)*
Rhodanid *n s.* Thiocyanat
Rhodanierung *f s.* Thiocyanierung
Rhodano... *s. a.* Thiocyanato...
Rhodanometrie *f* rhodanometry
Rhodanwasserstoffsäure *f s.* Thiocyansäure
Rhodanzahl *f* thiocyanogen number (value) *(a measure of unsaturation of fats)*
Rhodinat *n* $M^I_2RhO_4$ rhodate
rhodinieren to rhodanize *(to plate with rhodium)*
Rhodinieren *n* rhodanizing, rhodium plating
Rhodinsäure *f* rhodinic acid, *3,7-dimethyloct-6-enoic acid
Rhodium *n* Rh rhodium
Rhodium(III)-chlorid *n* rhodium(III) chloride, rhodium trichloride
Rhodiumdioxid *n s.* Rhodium(IV)-oxid
Rhodium(III)-fluorid *n* rhodium(III) fluoride, rhodium trifluoride
Rhodiumholz *n* red gum *(heartwood of Liquidambar styraciflua L.)*
Rhodium(III)-hydrogensulfid *n* rhodium(III) hydrogensulphide
Rhodium(III)-hydroxid *n* rhodium(III) hydroxide, rhodium trihydroxide
Rhodium(IV)-hydroxid *n* rhodium(IV) hydroxide, rhodium tetrahydroxide
Rhodiummohr *n* rhodium black *(finely divided rhodium)*
Rhodiummonosulfid *n s.* Rhodium(II)-sulfid
Rhodiummonoxid *n s.* Rhodium(II)-oxid
Rhodium(III)-nitrat *n* rhodium(III) nitrate
Rhodium(II)-oxid *n* rhodium(II) oxide, rhodium monooxide
Rhodium(III)-oxid *n* rhodium(III) oxide, dirhodium trioxide
Rhodium(IV)-oxid *n* rhodium(IV) oxide, rhodium dioxide
Rhodium(VI)-oxid *n* rhodium(VI) oxide, rhodium trioxide
Rhodiumschwarz *n s.* Rhodiummohr
Rhodium(III)-sulfat *n* rhodium(III) sulphate
Rhodium(II)-sulfid *n* rhodium(II) sulphide, rhodium monosulphide
Rhodium(III)-sulfid *n* rhodium(III) sulphide, dirhodium trisulphide
Rhodiumtri... *s. a.* Rhodium(III)-...
Rhodiumtrioxid *n s.* Rhodium(VI)-oxid
Rhodopsin *n* rhodopsin, visual purple
rhombisch *(cryst)* [ortho]rhombic, o-rh., rhomb.
Rhomboeder *n (cryst)* rhombohedron
rhomboedrisch *(cryst)* rhombohedral
Rh-positiv *(med)* rh-positive
rH-Wert *m* rH [value]
RhZ *s.* Rhodanzahl
Ribbonisation *f* ribbonization *(of glass-fibre reinforced plastics)*
Riboflavin *n* riboflavin[e], lactoflavin[e]
Riboflavinphosphat *n* riboflavin[e] phosphate
Ribonucleat *n* ribonucleate *(a salt of a ribonucleic acid)*
Ribonucleinsäure *f* ribonucleic acid, RNA *(for compounds s. under* RNA*)*
Ribonucleoproteid *n*, **Ribonucleoprotein** *n* ribonucleoprotein

Ribonucleoproteinkern *m (bioch)* core particle *(of ribosomes)*
Ribonucleotid *n* ribonucleotide
Ribose *f* ribose, Rib *(a pentose)*
Ribosom *n (bioch)* ribosome
ribosomal *(bioch)* ribosomal
Ribosylgruppe *f*, **Ribosylrest** *m* ribosyl group
Ribothymidylsäure *f s.* Thymidylsäure
Ribulose-1,5-diphosphatcarboxylase *f (bioch)* ribulose-1,5-diphosphate carboxylase, Rubisco
Ribulose-Diphosphat-Zyklus *m (bioch)* ribulose diphosphate cycle, C_3 pentose phosphate cycle, Calvin[-Bassham] cycle
Ribulose-Monophosphat-Zyklus *m (bioch)* ribulose monophosphate cycle, Quayle cycle
Richardson-Effekt *m* Richardson effect *(emission of electrons from hot metallic surfaces)*
Richtbohren *n (petrol)* directional drilling
Richteffekt *m* orientation effect
Richtigkeit *f* [analytical] accuracy
Richtkeil *m (petrol)* whipstock
Richttyptiefe *f (text)* standard depth [of shade]
Richtung *f* direction
~/bevorzugte preferred direction
Richtungsbevorzugung *f* directional preference
richtungsfokussierend direction-focussing
Richtungsfokussierung *f* direction focussing
Richtungsquantelung *f* space quantization, quantization of direction
Richtungsquantenzahl *f* magnetic quantum number
Richtwert *m* guide value
~/konventioneller *(tox)* working level *(for maximum tolerances)*
Richtwerte *mpl* **für Abwasserinhaltsstoffe** *(hyd)* permitted discharge values
Ricinelaidinsäure *f* ricinelaidic acid, *trans*(+)-12-hydroxyoctadec-9-enoic acid
Ricinoleat *n* ricinoleate *(a salt of ricinoleic acid)*
Ricinoleinsäure *f s.* Ricinolsäure
Ricinolsäure *f* ricinoleic acid, *cis*(+)-12-hydroxyoctadec-9-enoic acid
Ricinusöl *n* castor oil
~/sulfatiertes (sulfoniertes) sulphated castor oil
Ricinusölsäure *f*, **Ricinussäure** *f s.* Ricinolsäure
Ricinuspreßkuchen *m*, **Ricinussaatkuchen** *m* castor pomace (cake, meal)
R.I.-Detektor *m (chromat)* RI detector, refractive-index detector, differential refractometer [detector]
riechen to smell
riechend/angenehm pleasant-smelling
~/aromatisch fragrant
~/stechend pungent[-smelling]
~/süßlich sweet-smelling
~/unangenehm (widerlich) ill-smelling, foul-smelling, obnoxious
Riechsalz *n* smelling salt
Riechstoff *m* 1. odoriferous substance, perfume; 2. *s.* Geruchsstoff
Riegel *m* bar *(as of soap)*
Riemen *m* belt
Ries *n (pap)* ream
Rieseinschlagpapier *n* ream (mill) wrapper (wrapping paper)
Rieselabsorber *m* wetted-wall[-column] absorber
Rieselblech *n* 1. showering flight *(of a rotary dryer)*; 2. *s.* Rieselboden
Rieselblecheinbau *m* showering flights *(of a rotary dryer)*
Rieselboden *m* shower tray
Rieseleinbauten *mpl* film fill (pack) *(as of cooling towers)*
Rieselfähigkeit *f s.* Rieselvermögen
Rieselfeld *n (hyd)* drain[age] field, leach (percolation, seepage) field, sewage farm
Rieselfilmkolonne *f* wetted-wall column
Rieselfilmreaktor *m (biot)* trickling-film reactor, trickle-flow fermenter (reactor)
Rieselkühler *m* trickle (spray, film) cooler
rieseln to trickle, to run; *(relating to bulk material:)* to run
Rieselreaktor *m* trickle-bed reactor
Rieselvermögen *n* flowability *(of bulk material)*
Riesenfeld-Probe *f* Riesenfeld test *(for detecting peroxo acids)*
Riesenimpuls *m (spectr)* giant pulse
Riesenmolekül *n* giant molecule, macromolecule
Riesenpuls *m s.* Riesenimpuls
Riesgewicht *n (pap)* weight per ream
Riffel *f* riffle
Riffelkneter *m* kneading table with fluted roll *(in margarine making)*
riffeln to flute, to corrugate
Riffelteiler *m (anal)* bench-top riffle
Riffelwalze *f* fluted (corrugated) roll
Rille *f* groove, riffle
Rillenwalzentrockner *m* fin drum dryer
Rinde *f* 1. *(bot)* bark, *(esp)* inner bark; *(pharm)* cortex; 2. crust *(of the earth)*
~/ausgelaugte *(tann)* spent bark
Rindenfleck *m* bark speck (spot) *(a defect in paper)*
Rinderfußöl *n* neatsfoot oil
~/geklärtes (gereinigtes) cold-tested neatsfoot oil
Rinderklauenöl *n s.* Rinderfußöl
Rindertalg *m* beef fat (tallow)
Rinderweichfett *n* oleomargarin[e], oleo
Ring *m (org ch)* ring, nucleus; *(tech)* ring, *(esp for tightening:)* washer • **sich zum ~ schließen** *(org ch)* to cyclize
~/anellierter *s.* ~/kondensierter
~/benzoider benzenoid ring
~/einzelner single ring
~/geradzahliger even-membered ring
~/gewöhnlicher common ring *(5 to 7 members)*
~/großer large ring, macroring *(13 or more members)*
~/kleiner small ring *(3 or 4 members)*
~/kondensierter fused (condensed) ring

~/mittelgroßer (mittlerer) medium[-size] ring *(8 to 12 members)*
~/nicht ebener puckered ring
~/normaler *s.* ~/gewöhnlicher
~/sechsgliedriger six-membered ring
~/ungeradzahliger odd-membered ring
Ringaufspaltung *f* ring scission, ring fission (splitting, cleavage, opening)
Ringbildung *f* ring formation
Ringbrenner *m* ring burner
Ringchelat *n* ring chelate
Ringchromatographie *f* radial (circular) chromatography
Ringdichtung *f* ring packing (seal)
Ringdüse *f (plast)* annular die
Ringe *mpl*/**Liesegangsche** Liesegang rings
~/Newtonsche Newton rings
Ringebene *f* ring plane *(stereochemistry)*
Ringelmann-Karte *f* Ringelmann chart *(for evaluating air pollution)*
Ringer-Lösung *f (med)* Ringer's solution, Ringer artificial serum
Ringerweiterung *f* ring enlargement (expansion)
ringförmig ring-shaped, annular, cyclic
Ringgerüst *n* ring skeleton
ringgeschlossen cyclized
Ringglied *n* ring member
Ringgröße *f* ring size
Ring-Index *m (nomencl)* Ring Index
Ring-Index-System *n (nomencl)* Ring Index system
Ringinversion *f* inversion of the ring
Ringkammer *f* annular chamber *(as in gas manufacture)*
Ringketon *n* cyclic ketone
~/großes macrocyclic ketone, macroring (large-ring) ketone
Ring-Ketten-Tautomerie *f* ring-chain tautomerism
Ringkohlenstoffatom *n* ring-carbon atom
Ringkohlenwasserstoff *m* cyclic hydrocarbon
~/anellierter (kondensierter) fused-ring hydrocarbon, condensed-ring hydrocarbon
Ringkomplex *m* ring aggregate
Ringkondensation *f* fusion, anellation, annulization
Ring-Kugel-... *s.* Ring-und-Kugel-...
Ringlüfter *m* tubeaxial (duct) fan
Ringmühle *f s.* Ringrollenmühle
Ringofen *m (ceram)* annular kiln
~/Hoffmannscher Hoffmann kiln
ringoffen non-cyclized
ringöffnend ring-opening *(reaction)*
Ringöffnung *f s.* Ringaufspaltung
Ringöffnungspolymerisation *f* ring-opening (ring-scission) polymerization
Ringöffnungsreaktion *f* ring-opening reaction
Ringpolymer[e] *n* ring polymer
Ringpresse *f* pot press
Ringprobe *f* 1. *(rubber)* ring sample (test piece); 2. brown-ring test *(for detecting nitrate ions)*
~/Hellersche Heller's ring test *(for proteins)*
Ringprüfung *f (ceram)* ring test *(for determining the stress between glaze and body)*
Ringraum *m s.* 1. Ringkammer; 2. ~/freier
~/freier annular space *(as in piston pumps)*
Ringrohr *n* annulus
Ringrollenmühle *f* ring-roll mill (pulverizer), centrifugal grinder (attrition mill), channel-roller pulverizer
Ring-Scheiben-Elektrode *f* ring-disk electrode
Ringschleifer *m (pap)* rotary grinder
Ringschluß *m* ring closure, cyclization
~/doppelter double ring closure
Ringschlußreaktion *f* cyclization (ring closure) reaction
Ringsequenz *f* ring assembly
Ringskelett *n* ring skeleton
Ringspalt-Tellerzentrifuge *f* annular solids-discharge disk centrifuge
Ringspaltung *f s.* Ringaufspaltung
Ringspannung *f* ring (angle) strain *(chemical-bond theory)*
Ringsprengung *f s.* Ringaufspaltung
Ringstruktur *f* ring (annular) structure
Ringsynthese *f* ring synthesis
Ringsystem *n* ring system
~/anelliertes (kondensiertes) fused[-ring] system, anellated (condensed-ring) system
~/kondensiertes aromatisches fused-ring aromatic system
Ring-und-Kugel-Gerät *n (plast)* ring-and-ball apparatus
Ring-und-Kugel-Methode *f (plast)* ring-and-ball method
Ringverbindung *f* ring (cyclic) compound
~/mit großer Gliederzahl large-ring compound
~ mit mehreren Heteroatomen polyheteroatomic-ring compound
Ringvereinigung *f* ring union
Ringvereng[er]ung *f* ring contraction
Ringverformung *f s.* Streckformen mit Ring
Ringversuch *m* interlaboratoy test *(for confirming the accuracy of test methods and results)*
Ringwalzenmühle *f s.* Ringrollenmühle
Ringwalzenpresse *f* ring-roll press
Rinne *f* channel, gutter, trough; *(met)* runner; *(min tech)* launder; chute, trough *(for transporting bulk material)*
~/pneumatische gravity fluidizing conveyor
rinnen to trickle, to run; *(relating to bulk material:)* to run
Rippe *f (tech)* fin
Rippenglas *n* fluted (ribbed) glass
Rippenheizelement *n*, **Rippenheizkörper** *m* finned heater
Rippenrohr *n* fin[ned] tube
Rippenrohrwärmeübertrager *m* fin-tube heat exchanger
Rippentrichter *m* fluted funnel
Rippfilz *m (pap)* ribbed (ribbing) felt

Riß *m* crack, flaw, *(if narrow and deep:)* fissure, crevice
~/interkristalliner intercrystalline (intergranular) crack
~/transkristalliner transcrystalline (transgranular) crack
Rißauslösung *f* crack initiation
rißbeständig cracking-resistant
Rißbeständigkeit *f* 1. cracking resistance; 2. *s.* Reißfestigkeit
Rißbildung *f* crack formation, cracking; *(ceram)* crazing *(a defect in glazes)*
~ infolge Korrosion corrosion cracking
Rißbildungsgrad *m* degree of cracking
rissig cracked, flawy • **~ werden** to crack
Rissigwerden *n* cracking
Rißkeimbildung *f* crack initiation
Rißwachstum *n* crack growth, *(rubber also)* cut growth
Ritter-Reaktion *f* Ritter reaction *(for obtaining primary amines)*
Rittinger-Gesetz *n* Rittinger's law *(of size reduction)*
ritzen to scratch
Ritzfestigkeit *f s.* Ritzhärte
Ritzhärte *f* scratch hardness (resistance), resistance to scratching
Ritzhärteprüfer *m* sclerometer
Ritzprobe *f*, **Ritzprüfung** *f* scratch test
Rizinus... *s.* Ricinus...
RK *s.* Reaktionskoordinate
RKS *s.* Röntgenkleinwinkelstreuung
RL_{50} *(residue-life 50 per cent) s.* Rückstands-Halbwertszeit
RLD *s.* Lineardispersion/reziproke
RMR = relativer molarer Responsewert
RMZ, R-M-Z *s.* Reichert-Meissl-Zahl
RNA *f* RNA, ribonucleic acid
~/aktivierende *s.* ~/lösliche
~ des Kerns/heterogene heterogeneous nuclear RNA
~/lösliche soluble (transfer) ribonucleic acid, sRNA
~/mitochondriale mitochondrial ribonucleic acid, mtRNA
~/ribosomale ribosomal ribonucleic acid, rRNA
RNA-Aufbereitung *f (bioch)* RNA processing
RNA-Polymerase *f***/RNA-abhängige** *s.* RNA-Synthetase
RNA-Synthetase *f* RNA replicase, RNA-directed RNA polymerase
RNS *f (**Ribo**nuclein**säure**) s.* RNA
Robbenöl *n* seal oil
~/mineralisches mineral seal [oil]
Robbentran *m s.* Robbenöl
Roberts-Ringschleifer *m*, **Roberts-Schleifer** *m (pap)* Roberts grinder
Robert-Verdampfer *m* Robert (calandria) evaporator
Robison-[Embden-]Ester *m* Robison-Embden ester *(glucose-6-phosphate)*
Roborans *n (pharm)* roborant
roborierend *(pharm)* roborant
Rochellesalz *n* Rochelle salt, potassium sodium tartrate 4-water
Rockwellhärte *f* Rockwell hardness, R.H.
Rockwell-Härteprüfung *f* Rockwell hardness test
rodentizid rodenticidal
Rodentizid *n* rodenticide
Roelen-Reaktion *f* Roelen reaction, oxo (hydroformylation) reaction
Roelig-Maschine *f* Roelig hysteresis apparatus
Roè-Zahl *f (pap)* Roè chlorine number
Roga-Backzahl *f*, **Roga-Index** *m (coal)* Roga index
Roga-Test *m* Roga test *(for determining the caking properties of coal)*
Rogenstein *m (min) a variety of oolite resembling spawn*
Roggenmehl *n* rye flour, *(if coarse)* rye meal
Roggenstärke *f* rye starch
roh crude *(esp chemicals)*, raw, untreated, unprocessed *(material)*, *(pap also)* uncooked; *(tann)* raw, green; *(ceram)* unfired, green; *(met)* unwrought
Rohabwasser *n (hyd)* raw waste water, untreated sewage
Rohabwasseranfall *m (hyd)* raw waste flow
Rohabwasserzulauf *m (hyd)* 1. raw waste-water influent; 2. incoming (entering) waste water, influent (inlet, feed) waste water, waste-water feed
Rohbase *f (coal)* crude base
Rohbaumwolle *f* raw (grey) cotton
Rohbenzin *n* raw (virgin) gasoline
Rohbenzol *n* crude benzole
Rohbenzolabtreiber *m* crude-benzole still
Rohbenzolanlage *f* crude-benzole plant
Rohbenzoldestillieranlage *f* crude-benzole still
Rohblei *n* crude (pig) lead
Rohblock *m (met)* ingot
Rohbramme *f (met)* slab ingot
Rohbrand *m (ceram)* biscuit firing, biscuitting
Rohbranntwein *m* crude alcohol
Rohbraunkohle *f* raw lignite
Rohbruchfestigkeit *f (ceram)* green strength
Rohdestillat *n* crude distillate
Rohdextran *n (biot)* crude dextran
Rohdichte *f (pap)* bulk; bulk density, B.D. *(of timber)*
Roheisen *n* pig iron
~/graues grey pig iron
~/heißerblasenes hot-blast pig iron
~/kalterblasenes cold-blast pig iron
~/meliertes mottled pig iron
~/weißes white pig iron
Roheisenpfanne *f* hot-metal ladle
Roherde *f* natural earth
Roherdöl *n* crude oil (petroleum), [mineral-oil] crude
~/synthetisches *(coal)* synthetic crude oil, syncrude [oil]

Roherz *n* crude ore, raw (run-of-mine, as-mined) ore
Rohextrakt *m* crude extract
Rohfaser *f (bioch, agric)* crude fibre; *(food)* roughage *(esp cellulose)*
Rohfett *n* crude (raw) fat
Rohfördergut *n (mine)* run-of-mine
Rohförderkohle *f s.* Rohkohle
Rohgas *n* crude (raw) gas, *(in gas cleaning also)* dust-laden gas
Rohgemenge *n (glass)* raw batch
Rohglas *n* rough[-cast] glass
Rohglasplatte *f* rough-cast plate
Rohglasur *f (ceram)* raw glaze
Rohgut *n* crude
Rohharz *n* crude resin
Rohhaut *f (tann)* green hide, rawhide
Rohholz *n* rough wood
Rohholzgeist *m* natural methanol, wood spirit
Rohhumus *m* raw humus, mor
Rohkaolin *m* crude (raw) kaolin
Rohkautschuk *m* crude (raw) rubber
Rohkern *m (food)* suet *(from beef)*
Rohkohle *f* raw (run-of-mine) coal
Rohkonzentrat *n* crude concentrate
Rohkreosot *n* crude creosote
Rohlaufstreifen *m (rubber)* camelback *(for retreading tyres)*
Rohlaufstreifenmischung *f (rubber)* camelback compound
Rohling *m* blank; *(plast)* parison, blank, *(for manufacturing records also)* biscuit, bisque
~/vorgeformter (vorkonfektionierter) *(rubber)* preform
Rohmaterial *n* raw material
Rohmilch *f* raw milk
Rohmischung *f* raw mixture; *(rubber)* green compound
Rohmodell *n* basic model
Rohmontanwachs *n* crude montan wax
Rohmüll *m* crude refuse
Rohöl *n* crude oil; *(petrol)* crude oil (petroleum), [mineral-oil] crude
~/abgetopptes *s.* ~/getopptes
~/asphaltbasisches (asphaltisches) asphalt-base crude, asphaltic petroleum
~/gemischtbasisches mixed-base crude (petroleum)
~/getopptes topped (reduced) crude
~/naphthenbasisches naphthene-base crude, naphthenic petroleum
~/naphthenisch-aromatisches naphthenic-aromatic crude (petroleum)
~/naphthenisches *s.* ~/naphthenbasisches
~/paraffinbasisches (paraffinisches) paraffin-base crude, paraffinic petroleum
~/paraffinisch-naphthenisches paraffinic-naphthenic crude (petroleum)
~/reduziertes *s.* ~/getopptes
~/synthetisches *(coal)* synthetic crude oil, syncrude [oil]
Rohölkühler *m* crude-oil cooler
Rohöllagergefäß *n* crude-oil tank
Rohölleitung *f*, **Rohölpipeline** *f* crude-oil pipeline, crude line
Rohöltank *m* crude-oil tank
Rohöltransport *m (petrol)* crude-oil transportation, dirty service
Rohopium *n* crude (raw) opium
Rohpapier *n* base (raw, body) paper
~/fotografisches photographic base paper
Rohpappe *f* raw (body) board
Rohphosphat *n* rock phosphate
Rohprodukt *n* crude product, *(esp if of vegetable or animal origin:)* raw product
Rohprotein *n* raw (crude) protein
Rohr *n* tube, pipe
~/blindes dummy tube
~/extrudiertes extruded tube
~/gegossenes cast tube
~/geschweißtes welded tube
~/gewickeltes rolled tube
~/glattes bare tube
~/leeres *(chromat)* open tubular [capillary] column
~ mit Klebnaht *(plast)* cemented tube
~/nahtloses seamless tube
~/stranggepreßtes extruded tube
Rohrabsetzbecken *n (hyd)* tube settler
Rohraufhänger *m* tube hanger
Rohrboden *m* tube sheet
~/beweglicher floating head *(of a heat exchanger)*
Rohrbündel *n* tube bundle
Rohrbündelreaktor *m* multitube fixed-bed reactor, multitube-flow reactor
Rohrbündelwärmeübertrager *m* shell-and-tube heat exchanger
~ mit ausziehbarem Rohrbündel pull-through shell-and-tube [heat] exchanger
~ mit festem Rohrbündel non-removable-bundle [heat] exchanger
~ mit Schwimmkopf floating-head shell-and-tube [heat] exchanger
~ mit U-förmig gebogenen Rohren U-tube shell-and-tube [heat] exchanger
Rohrdüker *m* influent (feed) well
Röhre *f* tube, pipe
~/Bourdonsche Bourdon [pressure] gauge
~/Geißlersche Geissler tube, [gas] discharge tube
~/gewendelte offene *(chromat)* coiled open tube
~/Pitotsche Pitot tube
Röhrenabscheider *m* tube (pipe) precipitator
röhrenartig tubular
Röhrenbündel... *s.* Rohrbündel...
Röhrendestillation *f* pipe-still distillation
Röhrendestillationsanlage *f* pipe-still distillation unit
Röhreneis *n* tube ice
Röhrenelektroabscheider *m*, **Röhrenelektrofilter** *n s.* Röhrenabscheider
Röhrenerhitzer *m s.* Röhrenofen

Röhrenfedermanometer *n* Bourdon [pressure] gauge
röhrenförmig tubular
Röhrenglas *n* glass piping
Röhrengutti *n* pipe gamboge *(from Garcinia specc.)*
Röhrenkessel *m* tubular boiler
Röhrenkonverter *m* tubular converter
Röhrenkühler *m* tubular cooler, *(esp lab)* tubular condenser
Röhrenofen *m (distil)* tube (pipe) still, tubular (pipe) furnace (heater), tube[-still] furnace
Röhrenofenanlage *f* tube-still (pipe-still) plant (unit), tube (pipe) still
Röhrenofendestillation *f* tube-still (pipe-still) distillation
Röhrenofendestillationsanlage *f s.* Röhrenofenanlage
Röhrenpresse *f (ceram)* pipe press (machine)
Röhrenreaktor *m s.* 1. Rohrbündelreaktor; 2. Röhrenströmungsreaktor
Röhrensedimentation *f (hyd)* tube sedimentation
Röhrensedimentationsapparat *m (hyd)* tube settler
Röhrenströmungsreaktor *m* tubular flow reactor, *(biot also)* tubular (tube) fermenter
Röhrentrockner *m* tube rotary dryer; *(lab)* drying pistol
~/dampfbeheizter steam-tube rotary dryer, rotary steam-tube dryer
Röhrentrommeltrockner *m* indirect rotary dryer
Röhrenvoltmeter *n* valve voltmeter
Röhrenwachs *n* [sucker-]rod wax
Röhrenwärme[aus]tauscher *m*, **Röhrenwärmeübertrager** *m* tubular heat exchanger
Röhrenzentrifuge *f s.* Rohrzentrifuge
Röhrenziehverfahren *n (glass)* tube-drawing process
Rohrflansch *m* tube (pipe) flange
Rohrgewinde *n* tube (pipe) thread
~/gerades straight tube thread
~/kegliges taper tube thread
Rohrheizelement *n*, **Rohrheizkörper** *m* tubular heater
Rohrkopf *m (petrol)* casing head
Rohrkopfbenzin *n* casing-head gasoline (spirit)
Rohrkorbverdampfer *m* basket evaporator
Rohrkrümmer *m* elbow [fitting]
~ mit rechtwinkliger Ablenkung right-angle elbow, ell
Rohrkühler *m (tech)* tubular cooler
Rohrleitung *f* tubing, piping; *(petrol)* pipeline
~ für Fertigerzeugnisse (Fertigprodukte) refined-product pipeline
Rohrleitungsflansch *m* tube (pipe) flange
Rohrleitungsnetz *n*, **Rohrleitungssystem** *n* piping system (installation), pipe[work] system; distribution network *(as for water)*; transmission grid *(for natural gas)*
Rohrmaterial *n (esp if thin-walled:)* tubing, *(esp if heavy-walled and large in diameter:)* pipe
Rohrmedium *n* tube-side medium (liquid) *(of a heat exchanger)*
Rohrmelasse *f s.* Rohrzuckermelasse
Rohrmischeinrichtung *f* in-line mixer
Rohrmischung *f* in-line mixing
Rohrmühle *f* tube mill
Rohrnetz *n s.* Rohrleitungsnetz
Rohrofen *m (ceram, met)* tube (tubular) furnace
Rohrpresse *f (ceram)* pipe press
Rohrreaktor *m* tubular [flow] reactor, *(biot also)* tubular (tube) fermenter
~/homogenphasiger homogeneous tubular reactor
~/[strömungstechnisch] idealer ideal tubular-flow reactor, plug-flow reactor
Rohrregister *n* tube bank *(of a heat exchanger)*
Rohrregister-Wärmeübertrager *m* air-cooled heat exchanger
Rohrreibung *f* pipe friction
Rohrreihe *f* row of tubes, tube bank
Rohrreiniger *m* tube cleaner
Rohrrohzucker *m* raw cane sugar
Rohrsaft *m* [sugar] cane juice
Rohrsaug[er]filzwäsche *f (pap)* suction pipe felt cleaner
Rohrschelle *f* tube (pipe) clamp
~ für Gasflaschen gas-cylinder support
Rohrschlange *f* pipe coil
~/grätenförmige herringbone coil
Rohrschlangenkondensator *m* multicoil condenser
Rohrschlangenmantel *m* external coil
Rohrschleuder *f* centrifugal cleaner, *(Am)* centrifiner
Rohrspirale *f* pipe coil
Rohrstrang *m* pipeline; *(hyd)* drain
Rohrströmung *f*/**voll ausgebildete** fully developed flow
Rohrstutzen *m* socket
Rohrverbinder *m*, **Rohrverbindung** *f*, **Rohrverbindungsstück** *n* tube (pipe) joint (connection), union
Rohrverdampfer *m* tubular evaporator
Rohrvermischung *f* in-line mixing
Rohrverteiler *m* manifold
Rohrverteilungssystem *n* distribution network
Rohrwand[ung] *f* tube (pipe) wall
Rohrwärmeaustauscher *m*, **Rohrwärmeübertrager** *m* tubular heat exchanger
Rohrzange *f* gas pliers, pipe wrench
Rohrzentrifuge *f* tubular [bowl] centrifuge
Rohrzucker *m* cane sugar *(sucrose, esp from Saccharum officinarum L.)*
Rohrzuckerfabrik *f* cane sugar factory
Rohrzuckerinversion *f* inversion of sucrose
Rohrzuckermelasse *f* cane molasses, cane blackstrap [molasses]
Rohrzunder *m* pipe scale

Rohrzwangsmischer *m* high-energy in-line mixer, pipeline (in-line) agitator, agitated line mixer
Rohsaft *m* raw juice, *(sugar also)* diffusion juice
Rohsaftpumpe *f (sugar)* raw-juice pump
Rohsalz *n* crude (mine-run) salt
Rohsäure *f* crude (raw) acid, *(pap also)* raw sulphite cooking acid, storage (tower) acid
Rohschellack *m* raw lac
Rohschieferöl *n* crude shale oil
Rohschlamm *m (hyd)* raw (feed) sludge
~/eingeleiteter (zugeführter) sludge feed
Rohschlammdichte *f (hyd)* feed sludge density
Rohschlammzulauf *m (hyd)* sludge feed
Rohschlammzulaufgeschwindigkeit *f (hyd)* sludge feed rate
Rohschwefel *m* crude sulphur
Rohseide *f* raw (gum) silk, grege, greige
~/unentbastete hard silk
Rohsoda *f* black ash
Rohspiritus *m*, **Rohsprit** *m* crude alcohol, raw spirit
Rohstahlblock *m* steel ingot
Rohstärke *f* raw starch
Rohstoff *m* raw material
~/chemischer chemical raw material
~ für die Papiererzeugung papermaker's furnish, raw papermaking material, raw stock
~ für die Textilindustrie textile material
~/pflanzlicher plant material
Rohstoffbedarf *m* requirements of raw materials
Rohstoffkosten *pl* raw-material cost[s]
Rohstofflager *n* stock house
Rohstoffquelle *f* source of raw material
~/mineralische mineral source
~/pflanzliche plant source
~/tierische animal source
Rohstück *n* blank
Rohsubstrat *n (biot)* fermentation raw material, industrial fermentation medium, feedstock
Rohsulfat *n* salt cake *(sodium sulphate)*
Rohsulfatzusatz *m (pap)* salt-cake make-up *(for replacing lost alkali)*
Rohsynthesegas *n* raw synthesis gas
Rohtalg *m* raw tallow
Rohteer *m* crude tar
Rohteil *n* blank
Rohton *m* crude (raw) clay
Rohtorf *m* raw peat
Rohvaseline *f* petrolatum, petroleum jelly
Rohvolumen *n (ceram)* bulk volume
Rohwachs *n* crude wax
Rohware *f (text)* grey goods
Rohwasser *n* raw (untreated) water; source water *(from a natural water source)*
Rohwasseranfall *m* raw-water flow
Rohwassereinlauf *m s.* Rohwasserzulauf
Rohwassergüte *f* raw-water quality, influent water quality
Rohwassergütemerkmale *npl* raw-water characteristics
Rohwasserinhaltsstoffe *mpl* raw-water constituents
Rohwasserqualität *f s.* Rohwassergüte
Rohwasserstrom *m* raw-water stream
Rohwasserzulauf *m (hyd)* raw-water influent; hardwater inlet *(ion exchange)*
Rohweinstein *m* wine stone, argol, argal *(potassium hydrogentartrate)*
Rohwolle *f* raw (grease) wool
Rohwollfett *n* crude wool grease, wool wax
Rohzink *n* virgin (primary) zinc, spelter
Rohzucker *m* raw (crude) sugar
~ I first raw sugar
~ II second raw sugar
~/brauner brown (soft) sugar
Rohzuckererstprodukt *n s.* Rohzucker I
Rohzuckerfüllmasse *f* A massecuite
Rohzustand *m* crude (raw) state
Rolle *f* roll[er]; *(rubber)* puppet
Rollenaufwicklung *f (pap)* reeling
Rollenbahn *f* gravity-roller conveyor
Rollenbreite *f (pap)* width of a roll
rollengeglättet *(pap)* web-calendered
Rollenkette *f* roller chain
Rollenkufe *f (text)* back with rollers, roller vat
Rollenkühlofen *m (glass)* roller lehr
Rollenlager *n* roller bearing
Rollenmeißel *m (petrol)* roller bit
Rollenpapier *n* reeled (continuous, roll-finished) paper
Rollenreckmaschine *f (plast)* roller stretching machine
Rollensatinage *f (pap)* web calendering
rollensatiniert *(pap)* web-calendered
Rollensatz *m (pap)* set of rolls
Rollenwälzmühle *f s.* Ringrollenmühle
Roller *m s.* Rollmaschine
Rollfilm *m* roll film
Rollgang *m* roll train *(in a rolling mill)*
Rollgranulieren *n* pelletizing
Rollmaschine *f (pap)* reeling machine, reel, reeler, winder
Rollmühle *f* roll[er] mill
Rollreifenfaß *n* drum *(with rolling hoops)*
Roll-Schicht-Frosten *n* shell freezing *(a freeze-drying process)*
Rollstange *f (pap)* winder (rewind) shaft, reel
Romankalk *m*, **Romanzement** *m* Roman cement (lime), Parker's cement
Römischbraun *n* umber *(an earth pigment)*
rommeln *(tech)* to tumble
röntgen to examine with X-rays, to expose to X-rays, to pass X-rays through, to shoot X-rays at, to X-ray
Röntgen *n* 1. X-ray examination (investigation); 2. *s.* Röntgen-Einheit
Röntgenabsorption *f* X-ray absorption
Röntgenabsorptionsspektrum *n* X-ray absorption spectrum

röntgenamorph X-amorphous
Röntgenanalyse *f* X-ray analysis
röntgenanalytisch X-ray-analytical
Röntgenapparat *m* X-ray apparatus, fluoroscope
Röntgenäquivalent *n* roentgen equivalent, equivalent roentgen
Röntgenaufnahme *f* X-ray photograph (image, picture), radiograph, radiogram
Röntgenbefund *m* X-ray result
Röntgenbestrahlung *f* X-ray irradiation, X-irradiation
Röntgenbeugung *f* X-ray diffraction, XRD
Röntgenbeugungsaufnahme *f*, **Röntgenbeugungsdiagramm** *n* X-ray diffractogram, X-ray diffraction pattern (diagram)
Röntgenbeugungsgerät *n* X-ray diffraction apparatus
Röntgenbeugungsmethode *f* X-ray diffraction method
Röntgenbild *n s.* Röntgenaufnahme
Röntgenbildschirm *m* fluorescent screen
Röntgenbündel *n* X-ray beam
Röntgendaten *pl* X-ray data
Röntgendiagramm *n* X-ray diagram (pattern)
~ eines Einkristalls crystallogram
Röntgendiffraktion *f s.* Röntgenbeugung
Röntgendiffraktometer *n* X-ray diffractometer
Röntgendurchleuchtung *f* fluoroscopy
Röntgen-Einheit *f* roentgen [unit]
Röntgeneinrichtung *f* X-ray equipment
Röntgenemission *f* X-ray emission
~/partikelinduzierte *(anal)* particle-induced X-ray emission
Röntgenemulsion *f* X-ray emulsion
Röntgenfeinstrukturanalyse *f*, **Röntgenfeinstrukturuntersuchung** *f s.* Röntgenstrukturanalyse
Röntgenfilm *m* X-ray film
Röntgenfluoreszenz *f* X-ray fluorescence, XRF
~/energiedispersive energy-dispersive X-ray fluorescence, EDXRF
Röntgenfluoreszenzanalyse *f* X-ray fluorescence analysis
Röntgenfotografie *f s.* Röntgenographie
Röntgenfotogramm *n s.* Röntgenaufnahme
Röntgengebiet *n* X-ray region (range)
Röntgengerät *n s.* Röntgenapparat
Röntgengoniometer *n* X-ray goniometer
Röntgenintensität *f* X-ray intensity
Rönteninterferenz *f* X-ray interference
Röntgenkamera *f* X-ray camera
Röntgenkleinwinkelstreuung *f* X-ray small-angle scattering
Röntgenkontrastmittel *n (med)* contrast medium
~/positives radiopaque contrast medium
Röntgenkristallographie *f* X-ray crystallography
Röntgenkristallstrukturanalyse *f* X-ray crystal-structure analysis, crystal (crystallographic) analysis
Röntgenmessung *f* X-ray measurement
Röntgenmetallographie *f* X-ray metallography
Röntgenmethode *f* X-ray method
Röntgenmikroanalyse *f* X-ray microanalysis
Röntgenmikroskop *n* X-ray microscope
Röntgenmikroskopie *f* X-ray microscopy
Röntgenniveau *n* X-ray level
Röntgenogramm *n s.* Röntgenaufnahme
Röntgenographie *f* X-ray photography, radiography
röntgenographisch X-ray-photographic, radiographic
Röntgenologie *f* roentgenology
röntgenologisch roentgenologic[al]
Röntgenoptik *f* X-ray optics
Röntgenprüfung *f* X-ray test[ing]
Röntgenpulverkamera *f* X-ray powder camera
Röntgenquant *n* X-ray quantum
Röntgenreflexion *f* X-ray reflection
Röntgenröhre *f* X-ray tube
Röntgenschirm *m* fluorescent screen
Röntgenspektralanalyse *f* X-ray spectrometric analysis
Röntgenspektrogramm *n* X-ray spectrogram
Röntgenspektrograph *m* X-ray spectrograph
Röntgenspektrographie *f* X-ray spectrography
Röntgenspektrometer *n* X-ray spectrometer
Röntgenspektrometrie *f* X-ray spectrometry
Röntgenspektroskopie *f* X-ray spectroscopy
~/energiedispersive energy-dispersive X-ray spectroscopy, EDX
~ nach dem Debye-Scherrer-Verfahren (Pulververfahren) Debye-Scherrer X-ray method, X-ray powder spectroscopy
Röntgenspektrum *n* X-ray spectrum, roentgen spectrum
Röntgenstrahl *m* X-ray
Röntgenstrahlanalyse *f* X-ray analysis
Röntgenstrahlbeugung *f s.* Röntgenbeugung
Röntgenstrahlbündel *n* beam of X-rays
Röntgenstrahldiffraktion *f s.* Röntgenbeugung
Röntgenstrahlenabsorption *f* X-ray absorption
Röntgenstrahlenemissionsspektrum *n* X-ray [emission] spectrum
Röntgenstrahlenkunde *f* roentgenology
Röntgenstrahlenmethode *f* X-ray method
Röntgenstrahlenquelle *f* X-ray source
Röntgenstrahlenspektrum *n* X-ray [emission] spectrum
Röntgenstrahlintensität *f* X-ray intensity
Röntgenstrahlinterferenz *f* X-ray interference
Röntgenstrahlmikroanalyse *f* X-ray microanalysis
Röntgenstrahlmikroskop *n* X-ray microscope
Röntgenstrahlstreuung *f* X-ray scattering
Röntgenstrahltechnik *f* X-ray technique
Röntgenstrahlung *f* X-ray radiation, X-radiation
Röntgenstreuung *f* X-ray scattering
Röntgenstruktur *f* X-ray structure
Röntgenstrukturanalyse *f* X-ray [structure, structural] analysis

Röntgentechnik *f* X-ray technique
Röntgenterm *m* X-ray level
Röntgenuntersuchung *f* X-ray investigation (examination, study)
Röntgenverfahren *n* X-ray method
Röntgenwellengebiet *n (anal)* X-ray region
Röntgenwellenlänge *f* X-ray wavelength
Roots-Gebläse *n* Roots (cycloidal) blower, straight-lobe compressor
Rosanilin *n* rosaniline, fuchsin[e], magenta
Rosanilinchlorhydrat *n s.* Rosanilinhydrochlorid
Rosanilinfarbstoff *m* rosaniline dye
Rosanilinhydrochlorid *n* rosaniline hydrochloride
Roscoelith *m (min)* roscoelite, vanadium mica *(a phyllosilicate)*
Roselith *m (min)* roselite *(calcium cobalt(II) tetraoxoarsenate(V))*
Rosendammar *n* rose dammar *(from Vatica rassak Blume)*
Rosenmund-[Zajcev-]Reaktion *f*, **Rosenmund-[Zajcev-]Reduktion** *f* Rosenmund reaction (reduction) *(catalytic hydrogenation of acid chlorides)*
Rosenöl *n* rose oil, oil (otto, attar, essence) of roses
Rosenquarz *m (min)* rose quartz
Rosenwasser *n* rose water
Roseocobaltchlorid *n s.* Aquopentammincobalt(III)-chlorid
Rose-Tiegel *m* Rose crucible
Rosolsäure *f* rosolic acid *(any of several related compounds, esp aurin)*
p-**Rosolsäure** *f p*-rosolic acid, pararosolic acid
Rosolsäurefarbstoff *m* rosolic acid dye[stuff], aurin dyestuff
Ross-Effekt *m (phot)* Ross effect
Rost *m* 1. *(ch)* rust; 2. *(tech)* grid, grate, grating
~/weißer white rust *(consisting of zinc carbonate)*
Röstanlage *f (min tech)* roasting plant
Rostantrieb *m* grate drive
Rostaustrag *m* grating discharge
Röstbakterien *npl* retting bacteria
Röstbassin *n*, **Röstbecken** *n (text)* retting vat
Rostbelag *m* 1. rust layer; 2. sinter cake *(of a sintering machine)*
rostbeständig stainless, rustless, rust-resistant, resistant to rusting
Rostbeständigkeit *f* stainlessness, rust resistance, resistance to rusting
Röstbetriebsdauer *f (min tech)* roasting time
Rostbildung *f* rust formation
Röstdextrin *n* pyrodextrin, torrefaction dextrin
Röste *f (text)* ret[ting]
~/biologische biological retting
~/chemische chemical retting
~ im Wasserbehälter tank retting
~/unvollständige underretting
rosten to rust, to corrode
rösten 1. *(min tech, food)* to roast, to burn, to torrefy, *(relating to ores also)* to calcine; 2. *(text)* to ret, to rot
Rösten *n* 1. *(min tech, food)* roasting, burning, torrefaction, *(of ores also)* calcination; 2. *(text)* ret[-ting], rotting
~/chlorierendes *(min tech)* chloridizing roasting
~ im Mehretagenröstofen *(min tech)* hearth roasting
~/oxidierendes *(min tech)* oxidizing roasting
~/reduzierendes *(min tech)* reducing roasting
~/sulfatisierendes *(min tech)* sulphat[iz]ing roasting
rostentfernend rust-removing
Rostentferner *m*, **Rostentfernungsmittel** *n* rust-removing agent, rust remover
Rostfeuerung *f* grate (fuel-bed) firing
Rostfilm *m* rust film
Rostfleck *m* rust spot, iron stain
rostfrei *s.* rostbeständig
Röstgas *n* roasting (roaster) gas
Rostgelb *n (dye)* iron buff *(hydrated ferric oxide)*
Röstgut *n* material being *or* to be roasted; roasted material, calcine
Röstgutaustrag *m* calcine discharge
Röstherd *m (min tech)* roasting hearth
Rösthorde *f (food)* kiln floor
rostinhibierend *s.* rostschützend
Rostinhibitor *m s.* Rostschutzmittel
Rostkitt *m* rust cement, iron[-rust] cement
Röstofen *m (min tech)* roasting furnace (kiln, oven), roaster, calcining kiln, calciner
~/mechanischer mechanical roaster (burner)
~/mehretagiger (mehrherdiger) multihearth (multiple-hearth) roaster (roasting furnace)
Röstofenanlage *f* roasting plant
Röstprodukt *n* roasted product, product of roasting
Röstprozeß *m* roasting process
Röstreaktion *f (met)* roast reaction
Röstreaktionsverfahren *n* roast-reaction process
Röstreduktionsverfahren *n* roast-reduction process
Röstreife *f (text)* retting maturity
Rostschicht *f* rust layer, *(if thin:)* rust film
Rostschutz *m* rust inhibition (prevention, protection)
Rostschutzadditiv *n* rust-inhibiting (rust-preventing) additive
Rostschutzanstrichstoff *m* rust-protective paint, antirust paint
rostschützend rust-inhibiting, rust-preventing, rust-preventive, rust-protective, antirust
Rostschutzfarbe *f s.* Rostschutzanstrichstoff
Rostschutzfett *n* rust-inhibiting grease
Rostschutzmittel *n* rust inhibitor (preventive), antirust agent
Rostschutzöl *n* rust-inhibiting oil, slushing oil
Rostschutzpapier *n* anticorrosive (antitarnish) paper
rostsicher *s.* rostbeständig
Rostsieb *n* bar (rod) screen
Rostsiebmaschine *f* grizzly [screen]
Roststange *f* grate bar

Röststärke *f* roasted starch
Roststelle *f* rust spot
Rösttrommel *f* roasting cylinder
rostverhindernd, rostverhütend *s.* rostschützend
Rostwärmebelastung *f* grate heat release
Röstwasser *n (text)* retting water
Rot *n***/Pariser** Paris red *(1. minium; 2. iron(III) oxide)*
rotabschattiert degraded to the red *(band spectrum)*
Rotameter *n* rotameter, variable area flowmeter
Rotary[bohr]anlage *f* rotary-drilling installation, rotary rig
Rotarybohren *n* rotary drilling
Rotarybohrtisch *m* rotary table
Rotarybohrverfahren *n* rotary[-drilling] method
Rotarysystem *n* rotary system
Rotation *f* rotation, spinning
~/behinderte restricted rotation
~/freie free rotation
~/optische optical rotation
~ **um den magischen Winkel** magic angle spinning, MAS
Rotationsabsorber *m* rotary absorber
Rotationsachse *f* axis of rotation
rotationsangeregt rotationally excited
Rotationsanregung *f* rotational excitation
Rotationsanteil *m* rotatory contribution
Rotationsbewegung *f* motion of rotation
Rotationsbrenner *m s.* Rotationsölbrenner
Rotationsdispersion *f* rotatory (rotational) dispersion, R.D.
~/anomale anomalous rotatory dispersion
~/magnetooptische magneto-optical rotatory dispersion, MORD
~/normale normal rotatory dispersion
~/optische optical rotatory dispersion, O.R.D.
Rotationsdispersionskurve *f* rotational-dispersion curve
Rotationsdruckfarbe *f* rotary-press ink
Rotationsdruckpapier *n* newsprint [paper]
Rotationsenergie *f* rotational energy, energy of rotation (rotational motion)
Rotationsfeinstruktur *f* rotational fine structure
Rotationsfilter *n* rotary (rotating) filter
Rotationsformen *n (plast)* rotation[al] moulding, rotomoulding
Rotationsfreiheit *f* rotational freedom
Rotationsfreiheitsgrad *m* rotational degree of freedom, degree of rotational freedom
Rotationsfrequenz *f* rotational frequency
Rotationsgebläse *n* rotary blower
Rotationsguß *m (plast)* rotational casting; *(glass)* centrifugal casting
Rotationsisomer[e] *n* rotational isomer
Rotationsisomerie *f* rotational isomerism
Rotationskoaxialzylinderviskosimeter *n* rotating-cylinder viscometer
Rotationskolonne *f* rotary (centrifugal) still (column)
Rotationskompressor *m* rotary compressor
Rotationskonstante *f (spectr)* rotational constant
Rotationslinie *f (spectr)* rotational line
Rotationsnaßabscheider *m* rotary washer
Rotationsniveau *n (spectr)* rotational [energy] level
Rotationsölbrenner *m* rotary-cup [oil] burner, rotary (spinning-cup) burner
Rotationspolarisation *f* rotary polarization, optical activity (rotatory power)
Rotationspressen *n s.* Rotationsformen
Rotationspumpe *f* rotary pump
Rotationsquantenzahl *f* rotation[al] quantum number
Rotationsquerschneider *m (pap)* revolving-knife cutting-machine, rotary [knife] cutter
Rotations-Schwingungs-Bande *f* rotation-vibration band
Rotations-Schwingungs-Spektrum *n* rotation-vibration spectrum
Rotations-Schwingungs-Struktur *f* rotation-vibration structure
Rotationsspektrum *n* rotation[al] spectrum
Rotationsstruktur *f* rotational structure
Rotationsterm *m (spectr)* rotational term
Rotationstiefdruckfarbe *f* rotogravure ink
Rotationsübergang *m (spectr)* rotational transition
Rotationsverdampfer *m* rotary [film] evaporator
Rotationsverdichter *m* rotary compressor
Rotationsversprüher *m* rotary[-cup] atomizer, spinning[-cup] atomizer, rotating atomizer (nozzle)
Rotationsverteilungsfunktion *f* rotational partition function
Rotationsviskosimeter *n* rotational viscometer
~ **mit koaxialen Zylindern** rotating-cylinder viscometer
Rotationsvulkanisation *f* continuous rotary cure
Rotationswalkmaschine *f (text)* rotary milling machine
Rotationswärme *f* rotational heat
Rotationswäscher *m* rotary washer
Rotationswinkel *m* angle of rotation, rotational (torsion) angle
Rotationszerstäuber *m s.* Rotationsversprüher
Rotationszerstäuberbrenner *m s.* Rotationsölbrenner
Rotationszustand *m* rotational state
Rotator *m (spectr)* ro[ta]tor
~/nichtstarrer non-rigid ro[ta]tor
~/starrer rigid ro[ta]tor
Rotätze *f s.* Rotbeize 2.
Rotaxan *n (org ch)* rotaxane
Rotbeize *f* 1. *(text)* red mordant (acetate), red liquor, mordant rouge *(a solution of aluminium acetate in acetic acid)*; 2. *(glass)* red (copper) stain
Rotbleierz *n (min)* red lead ore, crocoite, crocoisite *(lead(II) chromate)*
rotbrüchig *(met)* hot-short
Rotbrüchigkeit *f (met)* hot shortness
Roteisenerz *n*, **Roteisenstein** *m (min)* red iron ore, blood-stone, reddle *(iron(III) oxide)*

Rötel *m (min)* ruddle, reddle, red bole *(iron(III) oxide)*
Rotenoid *n (org ch)* rotenoid
Rotenon *n* rotenone *(an insecticide)*
Roterde *f (soil)* krasnozem; *(ceram)* terra rossa
Rotglas *n* red arsenic glass *(glass-like arsenic sulphide)*
rotglühen to heat to redness, to make red-hot
rotglühend red-hot
Rotglut *f* red heat (glow), R.H., redness • **auf ~ erhitzen** to heat to redness, to make red-hot
~/dunkle dull red heat
~/schwache low redness
Rotgültigerz *n (min)* red silver ore
~/dunkles dark red silver ore, silver ruby, pyrargyrite *(antimony(III) silver sulphide)*
~/lichtes light red silver ore, proustite *(arsenic(III) silver sulphide)*
Rotgummi *n* red (eucalyptus) gum, Australian kino *(from Eucalyptus camaldulensis Dehnh.)*
Rotguß *m* red brass
Rotholz *n* redwood *(collectively for various dyewoods)*
~/Afrikanisches 1. camwood *(from Baphia nitida Afz.)*; 2. barwood *(any of several African dyewoods)*
~/Indisches sappan[wood] *(from Caesalpinia sappan L.)*
rotieren to rotate, to spin
Rotkupfererz *n (min)* red (ruby) copper ore, cuprite *(copper(I) oxide)*
Rotmessing *n*, **Rotmetall** *n* red brass *(zinc content < 18 %)*
Rotnickelkies *m (min)* arsenical nickel, niccolite *(nickel arsenide)*
Rotocker *m s.* Rötel
Rotor *m* rotor; *(pap)* rotor, core, plug, cone, jordan rotor (plug) *(of a perfecting engine)*
~/ausschwingender swinging-bucket rotor, swingout centrifuge head
~ einer Horizontalzentrifuge *s.* ~/ausschwingender
Rotor-Blasstahlverfahren *n* Rotor process
Rotormesser *n* rotor (fly) knife *(of a rotary cutter)*
Rotormesser *npl (pap)* core bars, bars on the rotor, bars in the plug *(of a perfecting engine)*
Rotorscheibe *f* rotor disk *(as of an extraction column)*
Rotorschneidmaschine *f* rotary cutter
Rotorverfahren *n***[/Oberhausener]** *(met)* Rotor process
Rotschlamm *m (met)* red mud *(waste product of bauxite processing being rich in iron(III) oxide)*
Rotspießglanz *m (min)* red antimony, kermesite *(antimony(III) oxide sulphide)*
Rotstein *m s.* Rötel
Rotte *f (text)* ret[ting] *(for compounds s.* Röste*)*
rotten to ret, to rot *(esp flax)*; to ferment *(cocoa beans)*
~/im Haufen to ferment in heaps *(cocoa beans)*
Rottung *f* fermentation *(of cocoa beans)*
~ im Haufen heap fermentation
Rotverschiebung *f* shift to the red, red-shift
~/durch Konjugation bedingte conjugative red-shift
Rotwein *m* red wine
Rotzinkerz *n (min)* red zinc ore, zincite *(zinc oxide)*
Rouge *n (cosmet)* rouge
Rouleauxdruck *m (text)* roller printing
Rouleauxdruckmaschine *f (text)* roller printing machine
Routineanalyse *f* routine analysis
Routinebestimmung *f* routine determination
Roux-Flasche *f*, **Roux-Kolben** *m* Roux bottle
Roving *m* [glass-fibre] roving; *(text)* roving
Rovinggewebe *n (text, glass)* roving fabric, woven roving
Rowland-Anordnung *f*, **Rowland-Aufstellung** *f (spectr)* Rowland grating mount
Rowland-Geister *mpl (spectr)* Rowland ghosts
Rowland-Kreis *m (spectr)* Rowland circle
RQ *s.* Quotient/respiratorischer
rRNA *s.* RNA/ribosomale
RR-Säure *f* RR acid, 2R acid, 2-aminonaphth-8-ol-3,6-disulphonic acid
RS *s.* Geruchsschwellenwert
R-Salz *n* R salt *(disodium salt of naphth-2-ol-3,6-disulphonic acid)*
R-Säure *f* R acid, naphth-2-ol-3,6-disulphonic acid
RSK *s.* Geruchsschwellenkonzentration
R-S-System *n*, **R,S-System** *n* RS system, Cahn-Ingold-Prelog system, CIP system *(for designating absolute configuration)*
Rubeanwasserstoff *m*, **Rubeanwasserstoffsäure** *f* rubeanic acid, *dithiooxamide
Rübenmelasse *f* beet [discard] molasses
Rübenpektin *n* beet pectin
Rübenrohzucker *m* raw beet sugar
Rübensaft *m* beet juice
Rübenschneidmaschine *f* beet slicing machine, beet slicer (cutter)
Rübenschnitzel *npl* beet cossettes (slices), sugar beet chips
~/ausgelaugte [exhausted, sugar] beet pulp, exhausted (leached) cossettes
Rübenschnitzelmaschine *f s.* Rübenschneidmaschine
Rübenzucker *m* beet sugar *(sucrose, esp from Beta vulgaris var. altissima Doell)*
Rübenzuckerfabrik *f* beet sugar factory, sugar beet mill
Rübenzuckerfabrikation *f* beet sugar manufacture
Rübenzuckerindustrie *f* beet sugar industry
Rübenzuckermelasse *f s.* Rübenmelasse
Ruberythrinsäure *f* ruberythric acid, alizarin primveroside
Rubicen *n* rubicene *(an anthrylene derivative)*
Rubidium *n* Rb rubidium
Rubidiumalaun *m* rubidium alum, *(specif)* rubidium aluminium sulphate 12-water

Rubidiumaluminiumalaun *m* rubidium alum, rubidium aluminium sulphate 12-water
Rubidiumcarbonat *n* rubidium carbonate
Rubidiumchlorat *n* rubidium chlorate
Rubidiumchlorid *n* rubidium chloride
Rubidiumchrom(III)-sulfat *n* chromium rubidium sulphate
Rubidiumfluorid *n* rubidium fluoride
Rubidiumhexachloroplatinat(IV) *n* rubidium hexachloroplatinate(IV)
Rubidiumhydrogensulfat *n* rubidium hydrogensulphate
Rubidiumhydroxid *n* rubidium hydroxide
Rubidiumiodat *n* rubidium iodate
Rubidiumiodid *n* rubidium iodide
Rubidiummetaperiodat *n s.* Rubidiumperiodat
Rubidiumnitrat *n* rubidium nitrate
Rubidiumperiodat *n* rubidium periodate, rubidium metaperiodate, rubidium tetraoxoiodate(VII)
Rubidiumpermanganat *n* rubidium permanganate
Rubidiumperoxid *n* rubidium peroxide
Rubidiumsulfat *n* rubidium sulphate
Rubidiumtetroxoiodat(VII) *n s.* Rubidiumperiodat
Rubin *m (min)* [oriental] ruby
Rubinglas *n* ruby glass
Rubinglimmer *m (min)* lepidocrocite *(iron hydroxide oxide)*
Rubinlack *m* garnet lac
Rubinlaser *m* ruby laser
Rubinschellack *m* garnet lac
Rubinschwefel *m* ruby arsenic, red orpiment *(tetraarsenic tetrasulphide)*
Rubinspinell *m (min)* ruby spinel, spinel ruby
Rubinzahl *f* ruby (rubin, rubine) number, Congo rubin number *(a measure for the protective action of a colloid)*
Rüböl *n* colza (rape-seed, rape) oil *(from Brassica rapa L. em. Metzg.)*
~/mineralisches mineral colza [oil]
Rübsenöl *n s.* Rüböl
Rückbildung *f* reformation
Rückbrennen *n (pap)* reburning *(of lime mud)*
Rückdiffusion *f* back-diffusion
Rückdruck *m* back pressure
Rückdrückstift *m (plast)* return pin
Rückenappretur *f (text)* back-sizing, backing
Rückenspritze *f s.* Rückensprüher
Rückensprüher *m*, **Rückensprühgerät** *n* knapsack sprayer *(for pesticides)*
Rückenstäubegerät *n*, **Rücken[ver]stäuber** *m* knapsack duster *(for pesticides)*
rückerwärmen *(glass)* to reheat *(the parison)*
Rückerwärmung *f (glass)* reheat *(of the parison)*
Rückfaltung *f (bioch)* refolding *(of a polypeptide chain)*
rückfedern *(rubber)* to recover, to rebound
Rückfederung *f (rubber)* [elastic] recovery, rebound
Rückfließmethode *f s.* Rücklaufmethode
Rückfluß *m* 1. back (return) flow, *(esp distil)* reflux; 2. *s.* Rücklauf 2. • **unter ~ erhitzen (kochen)** *(distil)* to reflux
~/totaler *(distil)* total reflux
Rückflußabscheider *m (distil)* reflux separator
Rückflußbehälter *m (distil)* reflux tank
Rückflußkühler *m (distil)* reflux condenser
Rückflußrohr *n (distil)* downpipe, downspout, downtake, downcomer
Rückflußsammelbehälter *m*, **Rückflußtank** *m (distil)* reflux tank
Rückflußteiler *m (distil)* reflux divider (splitter)
Rückflußverhältnis *n (distil)* reflux ratio
rückführen to return, to recycle, to feed back
Rückführkondensat *n* process condensate
Rückführöl *n* recycle oil (stock), return oil
Rückführung *f* return, recycle, feedback
~ des Überschußschlamms *(hyd)* sludge recycle (return), solids recycle
~ von Abprodukten recycling
Rückgabebindung *f* back-donation bond
Rückgang *m* reduction, diminution, decrease
~ des Backvermögens *(coal)* reduction of caking power
~ des latenten Bildes *(phot)* latent image regression
rückgewinnen to recover, to reclaim
Rückgewinnung *f* recovery, reclaim
~ von Schwermetallen *(hyd)* heavy-metals recovery
Rückgewinnungsanlage *f* recovery plant
Rückgratkette *f* backbone [chain], skeleton *(of a branched molecule)*
Rückhaltebecken *n (hyd)* detention basin, retention (holding) basin
Rückhaltebehälter *m (hyd)* detention tank (basin)
Rückhaltefaktor *m (chromat)* retention (retardation) factor, Rf value
Rückhalteteich *m (hyd)* detention (holding) pond
Rückhalteträger *m (nucl)* hold-back carrier
Rückhaltevolumen *n (chromat)* retention volume
Rückhaltezeit *f* retention time, residence (hold-up, holding, detention) time
Rückhub *m* return stroke
Rückkondensation *f* retrograde condensation
Rückkopplung *f (bioch)* feedback
~/negative *s.* Rückkopplungshemmung
~/positive positive feedback
Rückkopplungshemmung *f (bioch)* feedback inhibition, retroinhibition, end-product inhibition
Rückkopplungsregulierung *f (bioch)* feedback regulation
Rückkreisöl *n s.* Rücklauföl
Rückkühlzeit *f* cooling-down time
Rücklauf *m* 1. back (return) flow, *(esp distil)* reflux; *(pap)* return journey *(as of the sieve)*; 2. return flowage; *(distil)* reflux [stream, liquid, liquor]
~/totaler *(distil)* total reflux
Rücklaufbehälter *m (pap)* reclaiming tank

Rücklaufflüssigkeit *f (distil)* reflux liquid (liquor)
rückläufig retrograde
Rücklaufkondensator *m (distil)* reflux condenser
Rücklaufmethode *f (chromat)* reverse-flow technique
Rücklauföl *n* recycle oil (stock), return oil
Rücklaufrohr *n s.* Rückflußrohr
Rücklaufschlamm *m (hyd)* return[ed] sludge, recycle[d] sludge, return activated sludge
Rücklaufschlammverhältnis *n (hyd)* recycle ratio
Rücklaufteiler *m (distil)* reflux divider (splitter)
Rücklaufverhältnis *n (distil, hyd)* reflux ratio
Rücklaufwasser *n* return water; *(hyd)* recycle *(trickling filter process)*; *(pap)* white water
Rücklaufzone *f (hyd)* return flow zone *(sludge contact clarifier)*
Rücklauge *f (pap)* relief liquor, release, blow-off
Rückleitung *f* 1. return [pipe, line]; 2. *s.* Rückführung
Rücklösung *f* redissolution
Rückmischung *f s.* Rückvermischung
Rückmutationstest *m* Ames (salmonella) test *(for testing the mutagenicity of chemicals)*
Rückoxidation *f* reoxidation
Rückprall *m* rebound
Rückprallelastizität *f (rubber)* rebound [elasticity, resilience], impact resilience
Rückprallhöhe *f (rubber)* rebound height
Rückprallkitt *m* bouncing putty
Rückprallpendel *n* **nach Lüpke** Lüpke pendulum (resiliometer)
Rückpralltest *m*, **Rückprallversuch** *m (rubber)* rebound (resilience) test
Rückpumpen *n* **von Abwasser (Rücklaufwasser)** *(hyd)* recirculation of effluent *(trickling filter process)*
Rückreaktion *f* reverse reaction, back[ward] reaction
Rückschicht *f (phot)* backing [layer]
Rückschlag *m* blowback
Rückschlagklappe *f* swing check valve
Rückschlagventil *n* check (non-return) valve
rückschwefeln *(met)* to resulphurize
Rückschwefelung *f (met)* resulphurization
Rückseite *f* back side *(as of an atom with rearrangements)*
Rücksprunghärteprüfer *m* scleroscope
rückspülbar *(filtr, hyd)* reversibly washable
Rückspülbarkeit *f (filtr, hyd)* backwash capability
rückspülen *(filtr, hyd)* to backwash, to back-flush, to flush back; *(chromat)* to back-flush *(a column)*
Rückspülgeschwindigkeit *f (hyd)* backwash [flow] rate, backwash velocity, flow rate of backwash water
Rückspülung *f (filtr, hyd)* backwash[ing], back-flushing; *(chromat)* back-flushing *(of a column)*
~ **des Austauscherharzes** *(hyd)* resin backwashing
~ **im Aufwärtsstrom** *(hyd)* up-flow backwash
Rückspülwasser *n (hyd)* backwash [water]
Rückstand *m* residue, *(petrol also)* resid[uum]; *(min tech)* underflow • **Rückstände aufarbeiten** *(petrol)* to run resid
~**/atmosphärischer** *(petrol)* long residue (residuum)
~ **der Vakuumdestillation** vacuum residue
~**/fester** residual solid matter, dry residue
~ **im Boden** soil residue *(of pesticides)*
~**/kutikulärer** cuticular (cuticle) residue *(of pesticides)*
~**/subkutikulärer** subcuticular residue *(of pesticides)*
~**/unlöslicher** insoluble residue
Rückstandsabscheider *m* residue separator
Rückstandsanalytiker *m (tox)* residue chemist
Rückstandsasphalt *m* residual asphalt
Rückstandsbildung *f* residue build-up
Rückstandsbrennstoff *m* residue fuel
Rückstandsfilter *n* cake filter
rückstandsfrei residue-free, non-residue
Rückstandsgas *n* residue (residual) gas
Rückstands-Halbwertszeit *f (tox)* residue-life 50 per cent, RL_{50}, biological half-life
Rückstandsheizöl *n* residual fuel oil
Rückstandskracken *n (petrol)* resid operation
Rückstandskuchen *n (filtr)* filter cake
rückstandslos *s.* rückstandsfrei
Rückstandsmenge *f***/duldbare** residue tolerance *(of a pesticide)*
Rückstandsöl *n (petrol)* residual oil (stock)
Rückstandsschmieröl *n* residual lubricating oil
Rückstandstoxizität *f* residual toxicity *(of pesticides)*
Rückstandswirkung *f* residual action; residual effect
Rückstandszone *f* sludge zone *(of a thickener)*
Rückstoßatom *n* recoil atom
Rückstoßchemie *f* recoil (hot-atom) chemistry
Rückstoßelektron *n* recoil (Compton) electron
Rückstoßkern *m* recoil nucleus
Rückstoßstift *m (plast)* return pin
Rückstoßstrahlung *f* recoil radiation
Rückstoßteilchen *n* recoil particle
Rückstrahl[pulver]diagramm *n (cryst)* back reflection powder diagram (pattern)
Rückstrahltechnik *f* back reflection method *(for investigating crystal structures)*
Rückstrahlung *f* reflection
Rückstrahlungsvermögen *n* reflectivity, reflecting power
Rückstreuung *f (nucl, anal)* backscatter[ing]
β-Rückstreuung *f (nucl, anal)* beta backscatter
Rückstreuverfahren *n (anal)* backscatter method (radiography), radiation backscattering method
β-Rückstreuverfahren *n* beta backscatter method
Rückstrom *m* back flow
Rückstromsperre *f* back-flow valve
Rückstromventil *n* back-flow valve
Rücktitration *f* back titration

rückumwandeln to reconvert, to convert back
~/sich to reconvert, to convert back
Rückumwandlung *f* reconversion
Rückverdampfer *m (petrol)* reboiler [furnace]
Rückverdampfung *f* re-evaporation
Rückverformung *f (rubber)* [elastic] recovery, rebound
Rückvergrauung *f (text)* soil redeposition
Rückvermischung *f* back-mixing
~/axiale axial (longitudinal) mixing
~/partielle (teilweise) partial back-mixing
rück[ver]wandeln *s.* rückumwandeln
Rückwärtsgasung *f* back run *(in producer-gas generation)*
Rückwärtsspülen *n (chromat)* back-flushing *(of a column)*
Rückwasch *m (petrol)* backwash
Rückwäsche *f* backwash[ing]
Rückwasser *n (pap)* white water
~/faser- und füllstoffreiches rich white water
Rückwasserbehälter *m (pap)* white-water chest
Rückwasserpumpe *f (pap)* white-water pump
Rückwassersammelbehälter *m (pap)* white-water chest
Rückzugfeder *f (plast)* return spring
Rückzugkolben *m (plast)* pull-back ram
Rückzugsrandwinkel *m* receding contact angle *(in testing surfactants)*
Ruff-Abbau *m* Ruff degradation *(of sugars)*
Ruheenergie *f* rest energy
Ruheinhalt *m* [liquid] hold-up *(as of a column)*; void volume *(gel chromatography)*
Ruhelage *f* position at rest, resting position, rest point *(as of a balance)*
Ruhemasse *f* rest mass
~ des Elektrons electron [rest] mass
~ des Neutrons neutron [rest] mass
~ des Protons proton [rest] mass
ruhen to rest
Ruheperiode *f* rest[ing] period
Ruherohr *n* resting (recrystallization) tube (cylinder) *(in margarine making)*
Ruhestellung *f s.* Ruhelage
Ruhestoffwechsel *m (bioch)* basal metabolism (metabolic rate)
Ruhewert *m***[/idealer]** equilibrium value *(theory of zone melting)*
Ruhezone *f* calming section *(of an extractor)*
Ruhezustand *m* state of rest
Ruhmasse *f s.* Ruhemasse
Rühranker *m* magnetic (stirring) bar
Rührapparat *m* agitator, *(esp lab)* stirrer, *(esp tech)* mixer *(for compounds s.* Rührwerk*)*
Rührarm *m* agitator (stirring) arm; raking arm *(of a thickener)*; rabble arm *(of a multiple-hearth furnace)*
Rührausrüstung *f* agitation (mixing) equipment
Rührautoklav *m* agitated (stirred) autoclave
rührbar agitable, stirrable
Rührbehälter *m s.* Rührgefäß
Rührblatt *n s.* Rührflügel
Rührdauer *f* duration of agitating (stirring, mixing)
Rühreinrichtung *f s.* Rührwerk
rühren to agitate, *(esp lab)* to stir, *(esp tech) to* mix
Rühren *n* agitation, *(esp lab)* stirring, *(esp tech)* mixing • **unter ~** with agitation
~/kräftiges vigorous agitation
~/pneumatisches air (gas) agitation
Rührenergie *f* mixing energy
Rührer *m* agitator, *(esp lab)* stirrer, *(esp tech)* mixer *(s. a.* Rührwerk*)*
Rührerblatt *n s.* Rührflügel
Rührerdrehzahl *f* stirrer speed
Rührerführung *f* stirrer guide
Rührerschaufel *f s.* Rührflügel
Rührerwelle *f* agitator shaft
Rührfermenter *m (biot)* stirred[-tank] fermenter, stirred bioreactor (tank), mixed (agitated) bioreactor
~/diskontinuierlicher stirred batch fermenter
~/kontinuierlicher continuous stirred-tank fermenter
Rührflügel *m* agitator (stirrer, mixing) blade
Rührgefäß *n* agitated tank (vessel), *(esp lab)* stirrer vessel, *(esp tech)* mixing vat (vessel), mixer bowl
Rührgeschwindigkeit *f* stirring speed (rate), *(esp tech)* mixing velocity
Rührgut *n* material being or to be stirred (mixed)
Rührkessel *m s.* 1. Rührgefäß; 2. Rührkesselreaktor
Rührkesselfermenter *m s.* Rührfermenter
Rührkesselkaskade *f* series of stirred-tank reactors, series of perfect mixers, stirred-tank reactors in series
Rührkesselreaktor *m* stirred-tank reactor
~/diskontinuierlicher batch[-operated] tank reactor, agitated batch reactor
~/idealer (ideal durchmischter) ideal stirred-tank reactor, stirred tank with perfect mixing, completely mixed reactor
~/kontinuierlicher continuous-flow stirred-tank reactor, tank-type flow reactor
~ mit Rückführung well-mixed reactor with recycle
~/strömungstechnisch idealer *s.* ~/idealer
Rührkolonne *f* stirred [pot] still *(as in molecular distillation)*; agitated extraction tower, agitated [tower] extractor
~ nach Scheibel Scheibel column
Rührkristaller *m s.* Rührkristallisator
Rührkristallisator *m* agitated (stirred) crystallizer
Rührlaugung *f (min tech)* agitation leaching
Rührleistung *f* agitator power
Rührmaschine *f* agitator, stirring apparatus, stirrer, *(esp tech)* mixer
~/liegende horizontal mixer
~ mit Planetenrührwerk planetary-type mixer
~/stehende vertical mixer
Rührmotor *m* stirrer motor
Rührorgan *n* agitating (stirring, mixing) element

Rührreaktor *m s.* Rührkesselreaktor
~/mehrstufiger *s.* Rührkesselkaskade
Rührschaufel *f* agitator (mixing) blade
Rührstab *m* stirring pole; *(lab)* stirring rod
~ mit Gummiwischer rubber-tipped policeman
Rührtankreaktor *m s.* 1. Rührfermenter; 2. Rührkesselreaktor
Rührtrockner *m* agitated pan dryer
Rührverschluß *m* stirrer seal
Rührvorrichtung *f s.* Rührwerk
Rührwelle *f* agitator shaft
Rührwerk *n* agitator, *(esp lab)* stirrer, *(esp tech)* mixer; *(hyd)* raking mechanism; *(ceram)* [mixing] blunger
~/gegenläufiges double-motion agitator
~/magnetisches *(lab)* magnetic stirrer
~ mit schräger Rührwelle angular mixer
~/pneumatisches air-agitated mixer
~/zweiachsiges *s.* ~/gegenläufiges
Rührwerkbehälter *m (esp lab)* stirrer vessel, *(esp tech)* mixing vat (vessel), mixer bowl
Rührwerkextrakteur *m* mechanically agitated extractor
Rührwerkkessel *m s.* Rührwerkbehälter
Rührwerkmischextrakteur *m* mechanically agitated extractor
Rührwerksautoklav *m* agitated (stirred) autoclave
RuK *s.* Ring-und-Kugel-Methode
Rummel-Schlackenbadverfahren *n* Otto-Rummel process *(for gasifying coal)*
Rumpeln *n* rumble *(in motors with a compression ratio of more than 10 : 1)*
Rumpf *m* core, kernel, rumpf *(of an atom)*; backbone *(of a molecule)*
Rumpfelektron *n* inner-shell electron
Rundabsetzbecken *n (hyd)* circular clarifier (basin, tank), circular (radial-flow) sedimentation tank
~ mit zentraler Verteilung des Rohwassers centre-feed clarifier
Rundbecken *n* circular tank *(s. a.* Rundabsetzbecken*)*
Rundbrecher *m* gyratory crusher
Runddrahtrost *m* rod deck *(of a grizzly screen)*
runderneuern to retread, to recap *(tyres)*
Rundfilter *n (lab)* filter-paper disk, circle of filter paper, round filter
Rundfilterchromatogramm *n* circular [paper] chromatogram
Rundfilterchromatographie *f* radial-paper chromatography, circular [paper] chromatography
rundführen to recycle
Rundglocke *f (distil)* circular (bell) cap
Rundklärbecken *n*, **Rundklärer** *m s.* Rundabsetzbecken
Rundkolben *m* round-bottom[ed] flask
Rundofen *m (ceram)* round (beehive) kiln
Rundpumpverfahren *n (food)* generator method *(of acetification)*
Rundräumgerät *n (hyd)* circular sludge collector
Rundreibe[maschine] *f (food)* circular conche
Rund[schnur]ring *m* O-Ring *(seal)*
Rundsieb *n* rotary (revolving) screen, drum screen, trommel [screen]
Rundsiebbütte *f* [cylinder] vat *(of the cylinder paper machine)*
Rundsieb-Büttenpapier *n* cylinder-made (machine-made) deckle-edge paper, cylinder machine-made paper, mould-made paper
Rundsiebkartonmaschine *f* cylinder board machine
Rundsiebmaschine *f (pap)* cylinder [vat] machine, vat (mould) machine
Rundsiebpapiermaschine *f* cylinder paper machine
Rundsiebzylinder *m (pap)* cylinder mould
Rundsortierer *m* rotary screen
Rundtischverfahren *n (glass)* round-table system
Runzel *f (glass)* chill mark, flow line *(a surface defect)*; *(coat)* wrinkle
Runzelkorn *n (phot)* reticulation
Runzellack *m* wrinkle varnish (finish)
runzeln *(coat)* to wrinkle
Rupffestigkeit *f (pap)* picking (plucking) resistance
Rupffestigkeitsprüfung *f (pap)* picking-resistance (plucking-resistance) test
Rupfwiderstand *m s.* Rupffestigkeit
Rüping-Sparttränkverfahren *n* Rueping process *(wood preservation)*
Rusagrasöl *n (cosmet)* rusa oil *(from Cymbopogon martini Stapf)*
Ruß *m* soot, *(for technical purposes preferably)* [carbon] black
~/aktiver active (reinforcing) black
~ für kautschuktechnische Zwecke rubber [carbon] black
~/geperlter beaded (pelletized) black
~/halbaktiver (halbverstärkender) *(rubber)* semi-reinforcing black
~/inaktiver *(rubber)* inactive (inert, non-reinforcing) black
~/loser *(rubber)* fluffy black
~/thermatomischer *(rubber)* thermatomic black
Rußbatch *m (rubber)* [carbon-]black batch
Rußdispergierung *f (rubber)* [carbon-]black dispersion
Rußdosierung *f (rubber)* [carbon-]black loading
Russel-Effekt *m (phot)* Russel effect
Russel-Saunders-Kopplung *f (nucl)* Russell-Saunders coupling, LS coupling, electron spin-orbit interaction, spin-orbit coupling
Rußfabrik *f* [carbon-]black plant
Rußflocke *f* smut
rußfrei *(rubber)* non-black
rußgefüllt *(rubber)* [carbon-]black-filled, black-loaded, black-reinforced, black-pigmented
Rußgel *n* [rubber] carbon gel
rußhaltig *s.* rußgefüllt
rußig sooty
Rußpunkt *m (petrol)* smoke point
Rußschwarz *n* carbon black

Rußvormischung *f (rubber)* [carbon] black batch
Rußzusatz *m*, **Rußzuschlag** *m (rubber)* [carbon-] black loading
Ruthenat *n* ruthenate
Ruthenium *n* Ru ruthenium
Ruthenium(II)-chlorid *n* ruthenium(II) chloride, ruthenium dichloride
Ruthenium(IV)-chlorid *n* ruthenium(IV) chloride, ruthenium tetrachloride
Rutheniumdichlorid *n s.* Ruthenium(II)-chlorid
Rutheniumdioxid *n s.* Ruthenium(IV)-oxid
Ruthenium(III)-hydroxid *n* ruthenium(III) hydroxide
Ruthenium(III)-oxid *n* ruthenium(III) oxide, diruthenium trioxide
Ruthenium(IV)-oxid *n* ruthenium(IV) oxide, ruthenium dioxide
Rutheniumrot *n* ruthenium red
Rutheniumtetrachlorid *n s.* Ruthenium(IV)-chlorid
Ruthenrot *n s.* Rutheniumrot
Rutherfordin *m (min)* rutherfordine *(uranyl carbonate)*
Rutherfordium *n* Rf rutherfordium *(element 106)*
Rutil *m (min)* rutile *(titanium(IV) oxide)*
Rutilporzellan *n* rutile porcelain
Rutsche *f* chute
Rutschvermögen *n (pap)* slipperiness
Rutschwinkel *m* angle of slide *(of bulk material)*
Rüttelbeton *m* vibrated concrete
Rüttelformmaschine *f (met)* jolt-ram machine
Rüttelgrobbeton *m* vibrated coarse concrete
rütteln to rap, to vibrate, to shake
Rüttelsieb *n* gyratory riddle
Rüttelvorrichtung *f*, **Rüttler** *m* rapper, vibrator
RWÜ *s.* Rohrbündelwärmeübertrager
Rydberg-Atom *n* Rydberg atom
Rydberg-Bahn *f* Rydberg orbital
Rydberg-Konstante *f* Rydberg constant (number)
Rydberg-Orbital *n* Rydberg orbital
Rydberg-Serie *f (spectr)* Rydberg series
Rydberg-Übergang *m (spectr)* Rydberg transition, R ← N transition
Rydberg-Zahl *f s.* Rydberg-Konstante
Rydberg-Zustand *m (spectr)* Rydberg state
RZ *s.* Regeneratcellulosefaserstoff
R-Zweig *m* R-branch *(of a band spectrum)*

S

s *s.* suprafacial
Saalassistent *m* lab[oratory] instructor
Saatbeize *f* 1. seed protection, brining of seed; 2. *s.* Saatbeizmittel
Saatbeizmittel *n* seed protectant (disinfectant), seed-treatment fungicide
Saatbeizung *f s.* Saatbeize 1.
Saatgutbehandlung *f* seed treatment
Saatgutbeize *f s.* 1. Saatbeize 1.; 2. Saatbeizmittel
Saatkristall *m* seed crystal
Saatschutzmittel *n* seed protectant
~ **gegen Vögel** bird repellent
Sabadillsamen *mpl* sabadilla seeds, cevadilla [seeds] *(from Schoenocaulon officinale (Schl. et Ch.) A. Gray, an insecticide)*
Sabattier-Effekt *m (phot)* Sabattier effect
Säbelkolben *m* **[nach Anschütz]** sausage flask
Sabinen *n* sabinene, 4(10)-thujene *(a bicyclic terpene)*
Sabininsäure *f* sabinic acid, *12-hydroxydodecanoic acid
Saccharase *f* saccharase, sucrase, invertase
Saccharat *n* saccharate, sucrate
Saccharatverfahren *n (sugar)* saccharate process
Saccharid *n* saccharide, carbohydrate
Saccharifikation *f* saccharification, saccharization
saccharifizieren to saccharify, to saccharize
Saccharifizierung *f* saccharification, saccharization
Saccharimeter *n* saccharimeter *(a polarimeter)*
Saccharimetrie *f* saccharimetry
Saccharin *n* saccharin, benzoic sulphimide
Saccharinsäure *f* saccharinic acid *(any of several tetrahydroxycarboxylic acids), (specif)* $HOCH_2{-}CHOH{-}CHOH{-}C(OH)(CH_3)COOH$ saccharinic acid
saccharogen saccharogenic
Saccharogenamylase *f* saccharogenic amylase
Saccharometer *n* saccharometer *(a hydrometer)*
Saccharometrie *f* saccharometry
Saccharose *f* sucrose, saccharose, saccharobiose *(a disaccharide)*
Saccharoseester *m* sucrose ester
Saccharoseether *m* sucrose ether
Saccharoseoctaacetat *n* sucrose octaacetate
Saccharosephosphat *n* sucrose phosphate
Saccharosespaltung *f* sucrose splitting
Sachar... *s.* Sacchar...
Sachse-Mohr-Theorie *f (org ch)* Sachse-Mohr concept *(of strainless rings)*
Sächsischblau *n s.* Smalte
Sackfilter *n* bag filter
Sackleinwand *f* burlap
Sackpapier *n* bag paper
Sadebaumöl *n* savin oil *(from Juniperus sabina L.)*
Saflor *m* 1. zaffre[e], zaffar, zaffer, zaffir *(crude cobalt oxide)*; 2. *(dye)* safflower, safflor *(blossoms from Carthamus tinctorius L.)*
Safloröl *n* safflower (carthamus) oil *(from the seeds of Carthamus tinctorius L.)*
Saflorrot *n* safflor [red], safflower
Safran *m* saffron *(from Crocus sativus L.)*
~/Indischer *(dye)* Indian saffron *(from Curcuma longa L.)*
Safranin *n (dye)* safranin[e], saffranine
SAF-Ruß *m (rubber)* super abrasion furnace black, SAF black
Saft *m* juice, sap; *(pharm)* succus
~/geschiedener *(sugar)* defecated (limed) juice

~/naturreiner natural juice
~/vorgeschiedener *(sugar)* predefecated (predefecation, prelimed) juice
Saftfänger *m (sugar)* juice catcher
Saftpresse *f* squeezer
Saftreinigung *f* juice clarification (purification)
Saftverdrängungsverfahren *n* Boucherie process *(wood preservation)*
Sägemehl *n (anal)* sawdust
Sägespäne *mpl (anal)* sawings
Sägezahnprofil *n (spectr)* sawtooth pattern *(of echelette gratings)*
Sagostärke *f* sago *(from Metroxylon sagu Rottb.)*
Sahne *f* cream
~/saure cultured cream
~/sterilisierte sterilized cream
Sahneeis *n* ice cream, cream ice
Sahnemargarine *f* cream margarine
Saitengalvanometer *n* string galvanometer
~ nach Einthoven Einthoven galvanometer
Saizew-Regel *f* Zaitsev rule *(of orientation in β-eliminations)*
Saké *m* saké, rice wine
Säkulardeterminante *f (phys ch)* secular determinant
Säkulargleichung *f (anal)* secular equation
Sal *n s.* Sial
Saladin-Mälzerei *f (ferm)* Saladin malting (process)
Salammoniak *m s.* Salmiak 2.
Salatöl *n* salad oil
Salbe *f (pharm)* ointment
salbenartig unctuous
Salbenartigkeit *f* unctuousness
Salbengrundlage *f (pharm)* ointment base
Salicylaldehyd *m* salicylaldehyde, *o*-hydroxybenzaldehyde
Salicylalkohol *m* salicyl alcohol, saligenin, α,2-dihydroxytoluene
Salicylamid *n s.* Salicylsäureamid
Salicylanilid *n s.* Salicylsäureanilid
Salicylat *n* salicylate *(salt or ester of salicylic acid)*
Salicyl-β-naphthylester *m s.* Salicylsäurenaphth-2-ylester
***O*-Salicyloylsalicylsäure** *f O*-salicyloylsalicylic acid
Salicylsäure *f* salicylic acid, *o*-hydroxybenzoic acid
Salicylsäureamid *n* salicylamide
Salicylsäureanilid *n* salicylanilide
Salicylsäurebenzylester *m* benzyl salicylate
Salicylsäuremethylester *m* methyl salicylate
Salicylsäurenaphth-2-ylester *m* 2-naphthyl salicylate, naphthalol, betol
Salicylsäurephenylester *m* phenyl salicylate, salol
Salicylsäure-5-sulfonsäure *f* 5-sulphosalicylic acid, 2-hydroxy-5-sulphobenzoic acid
salin[ar] *s.* 1. salzführend; 2. salzig
Saline *f* saltern, salt works
Salmiak *m* 1. salmiac, sal ammoniac, ammonium chloride; 2. *(min)* salmiac *(ammonium chloride)*
~/natürlicher *s.* Salmiak 2.
Salmiakgeist *m* household [aqua] ammonia, ammonia water (solution, spirit)
Salmiaksalz *n s.* Salmiak 1.
Salol *n* salol, phenyl salicylate
Salpeter *m any of several commercially important salts of nitric acid as saltpetre (potassium nitrate) or Chile saltpetre (sodium nitrate)*
~/kubischer *s.* Natronsalpeter
salpeterhaltig containing saltpetre, nitrous
salpetersauer nitric-acid *(solution)*; nitric *(salt) (for specific salts s. ...nitrat)*
Salpetersäure *f* nitric acid
~/konzentrierte concentrated nitric acid
~/rauchende fuming nitric acid, *(esp)* white fuming nitric acid, WFNA *(about 98 % HNO_3)*
~/rote rauchende red fuming nitric acid, RFNA *(containing 86 % HNO_3 and 6 to 15 % nitric oxides)*
Salpetersäureaufschluß *m (pap)* nitric acid pulping
Salpetersäureethylester *m* ethyl nitrate
Salpetersäureherstellung *f* manufacture of nitric acid
Salpetersäureisoamylester *m* isoamyl nitrate
Salpetersäureoxidation *f* nitric acid oxidation
Salpetersäure[zellstoff]verfahren *n (pap)* nitric acid pulping
Salpetersiederei *f* saltpetre refinery
salpetrig nitrous
Salpetrigsäureamylester *m* amyl nitrite, *(specif)* $(CH_3)_2CHCH_2ONO$ [ordinary] amyl nitrite, 3-methyl-1-butyl nitrite
Salpetrigsäureethylester *m* ethyl nitrite
Salvage-Mechanismus *m (bioch)* salvage pathway *(recycling of purine and pyrimidine bases in nucleotide synthesis)*
Salz *n* salt, *(food specif)* common salt *(sodium chloride)* • **in ein ~ überführen** to salify *(an acid or a base)*
~/aus Meer[salz]salinen gewonnenes bay salt
~/basisches oxide *or* hydroxide salt *(containing an O^{2-} or HO^- anion respectively)*, *(deprecated:)* basic salt
~/bromwasserstoffsaures bromide
~/Buntesches Bunte salt *(salts of S-alkylthiosulphuric acid, usually sodium salts)*
~/chlorwasserstoffsaures chloride
~/einfaches simple (single) salt
~/Englisches *s.* Hirschhornsalz
~/fettsaures *carboxylate, fatty-acid salt
~/flüchtiges *s.* Hirschhornsalz
~/Fremysches Fremy's salt *(1. potassium hydrogenfluoride; 2. potassium nitrosodisulphonate)*
~/Grahamsches Graham's salt *(a sodium polyphosphate)*
~/inneres inner salt, internal (intramolecular) salt
~/innerkomplexes inner complex salt
~/intramolekulares *s.* ~/inneres
~/komplexes complex salt

~/Kurrolsches Kurrol salt *(a potassium metaphosphate)*
~/Mohrsches Mohr's salt *(diammonium iron(II) sulphate 6-water)*
~/neutrales (normales) neutral (normal) salt
~/organisches organic salt
~/Peligotsches Peligot's salt *(potassium chlorochromate)*
~/quartäres (quaternäres) quaternary salt
~/salpetersaures nitrate
~/salzsaures chloride
~/saures acid salt
~/Schlippesches Schlippe's salt *(sodium thioantimonate 9-water)*
~/schwefelsaures sulphate
~/zweifachsaures *s.* Dihydrogensalz
Salzablagerung *f* 1. *(geol)* salt deposit; 2. salting *(as on evaporator walls)*
salzähnlich salt-like
Salzanreicherung *f (agric)* salt accumulation
salzarm low-salt, poor in salt
salzartig saline, salt-like
Salzartigkeit *f* salinity
Salzbad *n* salt bath
~/aufkohlendes *(met)* carburizing bath
~/cyan[id]haltiges *(met)* cyanide [salt] bath
Salzbadaufkohlen *n (met)* bath (molten-salt) carburizing, liquid[-salt] carburizing
Salzbadchromieren *n (met)* salt-bath chromizing
Salzbadeinsatzhärten *n (met)* salt-bath [case-] hardening
Salzbadinchromieren *n (met)* salt-bath chromizing
Salzbadzementieren *n s.* Salzbadaufkohlen
Salzbeet *n* salt meadow
salzbildend salt-forming
Salzbildung *f* salt formation
Salzbindung *f s.* Ionenbeziehung
Salzboden *m* saline soil, *(specif)* solonchak
Salzbrücke *f (el ch)* salt bridge
Salzbrückenlösung *f (el ch)* bridge solution
Salzdom *m (geol)* salt dome (plug)
Salzdomfalle *f (geol)* salt-dome trap
Salzeffekt *m (phys ch)* salt effect
~/primärer primary salt effect
~/sekundärer secondary salt effect
salzen to salt
Salzfehler *m* [neutral-]salt error *(in pH determinations)*
Salzfleck *m (tann)* salt stain (spue)
salzfrei salt-free
salzführend saliferous
Salzgarten *m* salt garden (meadow)
Salzgehalt *m* salt content
Salzgehaltmesser *m* salinometer, salinimeter *(a hydrometer for salt solutions)*, *(specif)* salimeter *(for indicating directly the percentage of salt)*
Salzgemisch *n* salt mixture
~/flüssiges (geschmolzenes) molten-salt mixture
Salzgeschmack *m* salt (salty) flavour (taste)
Salzgewicht *n s.* Salzmasse
salzglasieren *(ceram)* to salt-glaze
Salzglasur *f (ceram)* salt glaze, smear
salzhaltig saline, salty, briny *(liquid)*; saliferous, salt-bearing *(rock)*
Salzhaltigkeit *f* salinity
Salzhut *m (geol)* salt dome (plug)
salzig salty, saline, briny
Salzigkeit *f* saltiness, salinity
Salzkristall *m* salt crystal
Salzlager *n* salt deposit, saline
Salzlake *f* brine, pickle • **mit ~ behandeln** *(food, tann)* to brine
Salzlakenbehandlung *f (food, tann)* brining
salzlakenkonserviert *(tann)* brine-cured
Salzlakenkonservierung *f (tann)* brine curing (cure)
Salzlauge *f s.* Salzlake
salzlos *(food)* salt-free
Salzlösebehälter *m*, **Salzlöser** *m (food)* salt dissolver; *(hyd)* wet salt storage basin, salt storage tank, salt-saturating basin, brine tank (saturation basin) *(for ion exchange)*
Salzlösung *f* salt (saline) solution
~ nach Tyrode balanced salt solution, BSS *(a synthetic nutrient solution)*
Salzmasse *f (tann)* cured weight *(of hides)*
Salzmesser *m s.* Salzgehaltmesser
Salzmischung *f s.* Salzgemisch
Salznebelversuch *m s.* Salzsprühversuch
Salzpaar *n* salt pair
Salzpflanze *f* halophyte
salzsauer hydrochloric-acid *(solution)*; hydrochloric *(salt) (for specific salts s. ...chlorid)*
Salzsäure *f* hydrochloric acid
Salzsäureauszug *m* hydrochloric-acid extract
Salzsäuregas *n* hydrochloric-acid gas
Salzsäure-Gruppe *f (anal)* insoluble chloride group
Salzsäureofen *m* hydrochloric-acid furnace
Salzsäureverfahren *n***/Mannheimer** Mannheim furnace process
Salzschmelze *f* molten (fused) salt; *(met)* salt bath
Salzschmelzenreaktor *m (nucl)* molten-salt reactor
Salzschmelzflußextraktion *f (nucl)* molten-salt extraction
Salzsiederei *f s.* Salzwerk
Salzsole *f* [salt] brine, brine solution
Salzsprühversuch *m* salt spray test *(a corrosion test)*
Salztoleranz *f (biol)* salt tolerance
Salzturm *m* salt tower
Salzverbrauch *m* salt consumption *(ion exchange)*
Salzwaage *f s.* Salzgehaltmesser
Salzwasser *n* salt (saline) water
Salzwerk *n* salt works, saline, salina, saltern
Samarium *n* Sm samarium
Samarium(II)-chlorid *n* samarium(II) chloride, samarium dichloride

Samarium(III)-chlorid *n* samarium(III) chloride, samarium trichloride
Samariumdichlorid *n s.* Samarium(II)-chlorid
Samariumerde *f s.* Samarium(III)-oxid
Samarium(III)-hydroxid *n* samarium(III) hydroxide
Samarium(II)-iodid *n* samarium(II) iodide, samarium diiodide
Samarium(III)-iodid *n* samarium(III) iodide, samarium triiodide
Samarium(III)-oxid *n* samarium(III) oxide
Samariumtrichlorid *n s.* Samarium(III)-chlorid
Samenfett *n* seed fat
Samenlack *m* seed (grained) lac
Samenöl *n* seed oil
sämischgar, sämischgegerbt chamois, oil-tanned
Sämischgerber-Degras *m* sod oil *(a by-product from chamois tannage)*
Sämischgerbung *f* chamois (oil) tannage, chamois[ing] process
Sämischleder *n* chamois, chammy, shammy, shamoy
Sammelablaßleitung *f* discharge manifold
Sammelbecher *m (rubber)* collection (tapping) cup
Sammelbecken *n* 1. *(hyd)* collection basin; 2. *(bioch)* pool
~ **des Stoffwechsels** metabolic pool
Sammelbehälter *m* collecting (receiving) tank; *(hyd)* collection basin
Sammelbezeichnung *f s.* Sammelname
Sammelelektrode *f* collecting (receiving) electrode, collector [electrode]
Sammelfalle *f (bioch)* energy sink, trapping centre
Sammelgefäß *n* collection vessel, receiver, receptacle
Sammelkanal *m* 1. *(filtr)* discharge manifold; 2. *s.* Sammelleitung
Sammelleitung *f* collecting main, manifold
~ **für Schwachgas** lean fuel gas main *(of a coke oven)*
~ **für Starkgas** rich fuel gas main *(of a coke oven)*
Sammelmilch *f* bulk milk
sammeln to collect, to accumulate
~/sich to collect, to accumulate
Sammelname *m* generic name (term)
Sammelplatte *f* collecting plate
Sammelprobe *f* cumulative sample
Sammelraum *m (biot)* collection chamber
Sammelrinne *f* gutter; *(pap)* stock sewer (line)
Sammelrohr *n* 1. *(filtr)* discharge manifold; 2. *s.* Sammelleitung
Sammeltrog *m* collecting trough
Sammelvorlage *f* gas collecting main *(of a coke-oven battery)*
Sammler *m* 1. *(min tech)* collecting (promoting) agent, collector, promoter; 2. *(el ch)* [storage] battery, accumulator
~/drückender *(min tech)* depressant
~/kationaktiver (kationischer) *(min tech)* cationic collector
sAMP *s.* Adenylosuccinat
Samtpapier *n* velour (flock) paper
Sand *m* sand
~/bitumenhaltiger (bituminöser) bituminous sand
~/feinster flour (very fine) sand
~ **geringer Gasdurchlässigkeit** close (poor-venting) sand *(foundry)*
~/goldführender auriferous sand
~/grüner green moulding sand, greensand *(foundry)*
~ **guter (hoher) Gasdurchlässigkeit** open (free-venting) sand *(foundry)*
~/nasser *s.* ~/grüner
~/natürlicher (natürlich vorkommender) natural [moulding] sand *(foundry)*
~/ölhaltiger oil sand
~/synthetischer synthetic [moulding] sand *(foundry)*
Sandarach *n* ruby arsenic, red orpiment *(tetraarsenic tetrasulphide)*
Sandarak *m*, **Sandarakharz** *n* gum sandarac (juniper) *(from Tetraclinis articulata (Vahl) Mast.)*
Sandaustrag *m* sand discharge *(of a classifier)*
Sandbad *n* sand bath
Sandbett *n (hyd, filtr)* sand bed
~/wirbelndes *(hyd)* fluidized sand bed
Sandel[holz]öl *n* sandalwood oil *(from Santalum album L.)*
Sanden *n (ceram)* sanding
Sandfang *m*, **Sandfänger** *m* sand trap, *(pap also)* riffler, sand sifter (grate), settling table, bedwasher; *(hyd)* grit chamber
Sandfilter *n* sand filter
Sandflotation *f* sand floatation
Sandform *f* sand mould *(foundry)*
~/getrocknete (trockene) dry-sand mould
Sandguß *m* sand casting *(foundry)* • **im ~ herstellen** to sand-cast
Sandgußstück *n* sand casting *(foundry)*
sandhaltig, sandig sandy, arenaceous, arenarious
Sandigkeit *f* sandiness
Sandkohle *f* sand coal
Sandmeyer-Reaktion *f* Sandmeyer [diazo] reaction
Sandpapier *n* sand paper
Sandrinne *f (met)* runner
Sandrückhalt *m (hyd)* grit (sand) removal
Sandschleudermaschine *f* sandslinger *(foundry)*
Sandschwimmverfahren *n* sand-floatation process
Sandseife *f* sand soap
Sandstein *m* sandstone
sandstrahlen to sandblast
Sandstrahlmattieren *n (glass)* sand carving
Sandstrahlreinigung *f* sandblasting
Sandwichbauweise *f (plast)* sandwich construction
Sandwichbindung *f* sandwich bond *(chemical-bond theory)*
Sandwichkomplex *m* sandwich complex *(chemical-bond theory)*
Sandwichmolekül *n* sandwich molecule, molecular sandwich
Sandwichofen *m (ceram)* sandwich kiln
Sandwichplatte *f (build)* sandwich panel

Sandwichstruktur *f* sandwich structure *(chemical-bond theory)*
Sandwichverbindung *f* sandwich[-bonded] compound *(chemical-bond theory)*
sanforisieren *(text)* to sanforize
Sanidin *m (min)* sanidine *(a feldspar)*
Sanitärabwasser *n* sanitary waste [water]
Sanitärkeramik *f* sanitaryware
Sanitärporzellan *n* vitreous china sanitaryware
Sansibar-Kopal *m* Zanzibar (Madagascar) copal, gum zanzibar *(from Trachylobium specc.)*
Santal *n* santal *(an isoflavone)*
Santalbsäure *f* santalbic acid, *octadec-11-en-9-ynoic acid
Santalen *n* santalene *(a sesquiterpene)*
Santen *n* santene, 2,3-dimethyl-2-norbornene
Santenonalkohol *m* santenone alcohol, 1,7-dimethyl-2-norbornanol
Santensäure *f* santenic acid *(one form of 1,2-dimethylcyclopentane-1,3-dicarboxylic acid)*
Santonin[lacton] *n* santonin, santonic lactone
Santoninsäure *f* santoninic acid
Santonsäure *f* santonic acid
São-Francisco-Kautschuk *m* São Francisco rubber *(from Manihot heptaphylla Ule)*
SAP *s.* Sinteraluminiumpulver
Saphir *m s.* Sapphir
Saponifikation *f s.* Verseifung
Saponin *n* saponin *(any of various plant glucosides)*
Sappanholz *n* sappan[wood], sapanwood *(from Caesalpinia sappan L.)*
Sapphir *m (min)* sapphire *(aluminium oxide)*
Sapphirin *m (min)* sapphirine *(a nesosubsilicate)*
saprogen saprogenic, saprogenous
Sapropel *n(m)* sapropel *(lacustrine or estuarine deposit of organic matter)*
Sapropelgestein *n*, **Sapropelit** *m* sapropelite *(oil shale or coal derived from sapropel)*
Sapropel[it]kohle *f* sapropelic coal
Sapropelwachs *n* sapropel wax
Saprophyt *m* saprophyte *(organism feeding on decaying organic matter)*
saprophytisch saprophytic
Sardonyx *m (min)* sardonyx *(a variety of chalcedony)*
Sarin *n* sarin, isopropyl methylphosphonofluoridate
Sarkin *n s.* Hypoxanthin
Sarkosin *n* sarcosine, methylaminoacetic acid
Sassafrasöl *n* sassafras (saxifrax) oil *(from Sassafras albidum (Nutt.) Nees)*
Sassolin *m (min)* sassolite, sassoline *(orthoboric acid)*
Satelliten-DNA *f (bioch)* satellite (highly repetitive) DNA
Satellitenlinie *f (spectr)* satellite line
Satinage *f (pap)* [super]calendering, glazing
~/scharfe strong glazing
~ von Bogenpapieren sheet calendering
~ von Rollenpapieren web calendering
satinieren *(pap)* to [super]calender, to glaze; *(tann)* to satine
Satinierfalten *fpl* calender cuts *(a defect in paper)*
Satinierflecken *mpl* calender spots *(a defect in paper)*
Satinierkalander *m (pap)* calender [machine], calender section, machine calender stack
Satinierung *f s.* Satinage
Satinier[walz]werk *n s.* Satinierkalander
Satinweiß *n* satin white (spar) *(a pigment)*
Sattdampf *m* saturated vapour, *(water vapour:)* saturated steam
Sattel *m (pap)* backfall crest (crown) *(of a Hollander beater)*
Sattel[füll]körper *m (distil)* saddle
sättigen to saturate
Sättiger *m* saturator
Sättigung *f* saturation
~/progressive progressive saturation
Sättigungsapparat *m* saturator
Sättigungsbeladung *f* saturation capacity
Sättigungsdampfdruck *m* saturation (saturated) vapour pressure
Sättigungsdefizit *n (hyd)* [dissolved] oxygen deficit
Sättigungsdruck *m s.* Sättigungsdampfdruck
Sättigungsfeuchte *f*, **Sättigungsfeuchtigkeit** *f* saturation humidity
Sättigungsgefäß *n* saturator
Sättigungsgrad *m* degree of saturation; *(soil)* base-saturation percentage
Sättigungsgrenze *f* saturation limit
Sättigungsindex *m (hyd)* saturation index
~ nach Langelier Langelier [saturation] index, LSI
Sättigungskinetik *f (bioch)* saturation kinetics
Sättigungskonzentration *f* saturation concentration
Sättigungsmenge *f* amount to produce saturation, amount adsorbed [at saturation]
Sättigungsmethode *f* saturation method *(for preparing calibration gas mixtures)*
Sättigungs-*p*H-Wert *m (hyd)* *p*H of saturation
Sättigungspunkt *m* saturation point
Sättigungsstrom *m (phys ch)* limiting (maximum) diffusion current
Sättigungswassergehalt *m* saturation humidity
Sättigungswert *m* saturation value (level)
Sättigungszone *f (hyd)* zone of saturation
Saturateur *m* saturator
Saturation *f (sugar)* carbon[at]ation *(for removing excess lime)*
~/erste first carbonation
~ mit schwefliger Säure sulphitation
~/zweite second carbonation
Saturationsgefäß *n* **für CO_2** *(sugar)* carbonation (carbonating) tank
Saturationsmethode *f* transpiration (gas-saturation) method *(for measuring vapour pressures)*
Saturationspfanne *f (sugar)* carbonation pan
Saturationssaft *m (sugar)* carbonation juice
~/erster first carbonation juice
~/zweiter second carbonation juice

Saturationsschlamm *m (sugar)* carbonation sludge, *(as a fertilizer also)* sugar-factory lime
Saturator *m* saturator
saturieren *(sugar)* to carbonate *(for removing excess lime)*
~/mit schwefliger Säure to sulphite
saturnin *(med)* saturnine *(relating to lead poisoning)*
Saturnismus *m (med)* saturnism *(lead poisoning)*
Saturnzinnober *m* orange lead (mineral) *(obtained by roasting white lead)*
Satz *m* 1. sediment, subsidence, [bottom] settlings, B.S., dregs, bottoms, *(esp food, ferm)* lees, foots; 2. set, nest *(as of laboratory appliances)*; 3. charge [stock], charging stock, batch, feed[stock]; 4. principle; theorem, law
~/Hessscher Hess's law [of heat summation], law of constant heat summation
~/pyrotechnischer pyrotechnic mixture
~/von der Erhaltung der Energie law of conservation of energy, energy principle
Satzbetrieb *m* batch operation (processing)
satzweise batch[wise], discontinuous
sauber clean *(surface, air)*
~/peinlich scrupulously clean
säubern to clean[se]
Säuberung *f* clean[s]ing
sauer 1. *(ch)* acid; sour *(soil)*; sour *(petroleum distillate)*; 2. acid, sour, hard *(taste)* • **~ ausgekleidet** *(met)* acid-lined • **~ werden** to [become] sour *(relating to milk, beer, wine)* • **~ zugestellt** *(met)* acid-lined
~/schwach weakly (feebly, faintly) acid, subacid
~/sehr stark superacid
~/stark strongly acid
Sauer *m s.* Sauerteig
Sauergas *n* 1. sour gas *(containing acid components such as hydrogen sulphide, carbon dioxide, and hydrogen cyanide)*; 2. acid gas *(e.g. carbon dioxide, hydrogen sulphide)*
Sauerkleesalz *n s.* Kleesalz
Sauerkraut *n s.* Spuckstoff
säuerlich *(food)* sourish, subacid
Sauermilch *f* sour milk
säuern *(food)* to pickle, to souse *(vegetables)*; to sour, to acidulate, to ripen *(milk)*; to leaven *(dough)*; to sour, to ripen *(of milk)*
Saueröl *n (petrol)* sour oil
Sauerrahm *m* sour[ed] cream
Sauerrahmbutter *f* sour[ed] cream butter, ripened cream butter
Sauerstoff *m* O oxygen • **an ~ verarmt** oxygen-depleted • **in Abwesenheit von ~** in the absence of oxygen • **in Anwesenheit von ~** in the presence of oxygen • **mit ~ anreichern** to enrich with oxygen, to oxygenate, to oxygenize • **von ~ befreien** to deoxygenate
~/aktiver active (available) oxygen *(as in bleaching)*
~/atmosphärischer atmospheric oxygen
~/atomarer atomic oxygen
~/flüssiger liquid oxygen
~/gelöster *(hyd)* dissolved oxygen, DO
~/hochreiner high-purity oxygen
~/molekularer O_2 molecular oxygen
Sauerstoffabscheidung *f* oxygen evolution
Sauerstoffabsorption *f* oxygen absorption
Sauerstoffabsorptionsmittel *n* oxygen absorbent
Sauerstoffabsorptionsprüfung *f (rubber)* oxygen absorption test *(an ageing test)*
Sauerstoffaffinität *f* oxygen affinity, affinity for oxygen
sauerstoffähnlich resembling oxygen, oxygenic, oxygenous
Sauerstoffalterung *f (rubber)* oxygen ageing
sauerstoffangereichert oxygen-enriched
Sauerstoffanreicherung *f* oxygen enrichment
Sauerstoffantransport *m* oxygen supply
Sauerstoffanwesenheit *f* presence of oxygen
• **bei ~** in the presence of oxygen
sauerstoffarm poor (low) in oxygen, low-oxygen, oxygen-deficient
Sauerstoffaufblaskonverter *m* top-blown basic oxygen converter (furnace), basic oxygen converter (furnace)
Sauerstoffaufblas[-Konverter]verfahren *n* top-blown oxygen converter process, basic oxygen [converter, furnace, steel] process, oxygen process of steelmaking, oxygen lance process
Sauerstoffaufnahme *f* oxygen uptake (absorption, pick-up)
Sauerstoffaufnahmerate *f (biot)* oxygen uptake (absorption) rate
Sauerstoffausschluß *m* exclusion of oxygen
Sauerstoffbedarf *m* oxygen requirements (demand), *(hyd also)* oxygen uptake requirements
~/biochemischer *(hyd)* biochemical (biological) oxygen demand, BOD *(for compounds s. under* BSB*)*
~/chemischer *s.* Sauerstoffverbrauch/chemischer
~/fünftägiger biochemischer *(hyd)* five days biochemical oxygen demand, five day BOD, BOD_5
Sauerstoffbegasung *f (hyd)* aeration with pure oxygen
sauerstoffbeladen oxygenated *(haemoglobin)*
Sauerstoffbilanz *f* oxygen balance *(as of explosives)*
Sauerstoffbindung *f* oxygen binding
Sauerstoffblaskonverter *m s.* Sauerstoffaufblaskonverter
Sauerstoffblasstahl *m* basic oxygen [furnace] steel
Sauerstoffblasstahlverfahren *n s.* Sauerstoffaufblas[-Konverter]verfahren
Sauerstoffblaswerk *n* [basic] oxygen steel plant
Sauerstoffbombe *f* oxygen bomb
~ nach Bierer und Davis Bierer-Davis oxygen bomb
Sauerstoffbombenalterung *f (rubber)* oxygen bomb ageing, oxygen pressure method

Sauerstoffbrücke *f* oxygen bridge
Sauerstoff-Dampf-Vergasung *f (coal)* oxygen-steam gasification
Sauerstoff(^{1}D)-Atom *n* O(^{1}D) atom, ^{1}D singlet oxygen atom *(formed in ozone photolysis)*
Sauerstoffdefizit *n* oxygen deficiency, *(hyd also)* [dissolved-]oxygen deficit
Sauerstoffdiffusion *f* oxygen diffusion
Sauerstoffdiffusionsgeschwindigkeit *f s.* Sauerstoffübergangsgeschwindigkeit
Sauerstoffdifluorid *n* oxygen difluoride
Sauerstoffdonator *m* oxygen donor
Sauerstoffdruckalterung *f s.* Sauerstoffbombenalterung
Sauerstoffeintrag *m (hyd)* 1. oxygen transfer (transport); 2. *s.* Sauerstoffeintragswert
Sauerstoffeintragsgeschwindigkeit *f s.* Sauerstoffübergangsgeschwindigkeit
Sauerstoffeintragsvermögen *n (hyd)* oxygenation capacity, OC
Sauerstoffeintragswert *m (hyd)* oxygen transfer *(in g $O_2/m^3 \cdot h$)*
Sauerstoffelektrode *f* oxygen electrode
Sauerstoffentwicklung *f* oxygen evolution
Sauerstoffentwicklungsapparat *m* oxygenerator
Sauerstoffertrag *m***[/spezifischer]** *s.* Sauerstoffertragswert
Sauerstoffertragswert *m (hyd)* oxygen transfer rate, rate of oxygen transfer *(in kg O_2/kWh)*
Sauerstofferzeugung *f* oxygen generation
Sauerstofffluorid *n s.* Sauerstoffdifluorid
sauerstofffrei free from oxygen, oxygen-free
Sauerstofffreiheit *f* freedom from oxygen
Sauerstofffrischverfahren *n s.* Sauerstoffaufblas[-Konverter]verfahren
Sauerstoffgegenwart *f s.* Sauerstoffanwesenheit
Sauerstoffgehalt *m* oxygen content (level) • **mit geringem** ~ low-oxygen • **mit hohem** ~ high-oxygen
~/tatsächlicher *s.* Sauerstoffkonzentration/aktuelle
sauerstoffgesättigt oxygen-saturated, *(esp haemoglobin:)* oxygenated
sauerstoffhaltig oxygen-containing, oxygenic, oxygenous
Sauerstoffkonverter *m s.* Sauerstoffaufblaskonverter
Sauerstoffkonzentration *f* oxygen concentration
~/aktuelle *(hyd)* actual (prevailing) oxygen concentration
Sauerstoffkonzentrationszelle *f* oxygen [concentration] cell, [differential] aeration cell *(corrosion)*
Sauerstoffkreislauf *m* oxygen cycle
Sauerstofflanze *f (met)* oxygen lance
Sauerstofflöslichkeit *f* oxygen solubility, solubility of oxygen
Sauerstoffmangel *m* oxygen deficiency
Sauerstoffnachlieferung *f* oxygen replenishment
Sauerstoffpartialdruck *m* oxygen partial pressure
Sauerstoffpunkt *m* oxygen point *(normal boiling point of liquid O_2)*
Sauerstoffquelle *f* oxygen source
Sauerstoffradikal *n* oxygen-centred radical
sauerstoffreich rich in oxygen, oxygen-rich, high-oxygen
Sauerstoffsättigung *f (hyd)* oxygen saturation
Sauerstoffsättigungskonzentration *f*, **Sauerstoffsättigungswert** *m (hyd)* oxygen saturation concentration (value, level), oxygen concentration at saturation
Sauerstoffsäure *f* oxo acid, oxy[gen] acid, ox[i]acid
Sauerstoffschuld *f (med)* oxygen debt
Sauerstoffschwund *m s.* Sauerstoffzehrung
Sauerstoffstrom *m* current (stream) of oxygen
sauerstofftragend oxygen-carrying
Sauerstoffträger *m* oxygen carrier; oxidizer *(for explosives)*
Sauerstofftransferase *f* oxygen transferase, dioxygenase
Sauerstofftransport *m* oxygen transport
Sauerstofftransportpigment *n (bioch)* respiratory pigment
Sauerstoffübergang *m* oxygen transfer
Sauerstoffübergangsgeschwindigkeit *f (hyd)* oxygen transfer rate, OTR, rate of oxygen transfer *(in g $O_2/m^3 \cdot h$)*
Sauerstoffüberspannung *f (el ch)* oxygen overvoltage
Sauerstoffüberträger *m* oxygen transfer agent
Sauerstoffübertragung *f (hyd)* oxygen transfer (transport)
Sauerstoffverarmung *f* oxygen depletion
Sauerstoffverbindung *f* oxygen (oxy) compound
Sauerstoffverbrauch *m* oxygen consumption
~/chemischer *(hyd)* chemical oxygen demand, COD
sauerstoffverbrauchend oxygen-consuming
sauerstoffzehrend *(hyd)* oxygen-depleting, oxygen-consuming
Sauerstoffzehrung *f (hyd)* depletion of dissolved oxygen, dissolved-oxygen sag
Sauerstoffzufuhr *f* 1. oxygen supply; *(hyd)* oxygen transfer (transport); 2. *s.* Sauerstoffzufuhrwert
Sauerstoffzufuhrwert *m (hyd)* OC/load, oxygenation capacity/load
Sauerstoffzutritt *m* access of oxygen • **unter** ~ in the presence of oxygen
Sauerteig *m* sour[dough], leaven, leavening [agent]
Säuerung *f (food)* pickling, pickle cure (curing), vegetable fermentation; souring, acidulation, ripening *(of milk)*; leavening *(of dough)*
Säuerungsbakterien *npl* acid-forming (acid-producing) bacteria, acid-formers, acid-producers
Säuerungsgefäß *n* souring (ripening) tank (vat), [milk] ripener
Säuerungsvorgang *m* souring (ripening) process *(in milk treatment)*
Säuerungswanne *f s.* Säuerungsgefäß

Sauerwerden *n* souring *(as of milk)*
Saug-Absperr-Regulierung *f* closed-suction control *(of a compressor)*
Saugbassin *n*, **Saugbehälter** *m* suction tank
Saugblasmaschine *f (glass)* suck-and-blow machine, suction-type machine
Saugblasverfahren *n (glass)* suck-and-blow (vacuum-and-blow) process, suction process
Saugdruck *m* suction pressure
saugen to suck, to draw
Saugen *n* suction, drawing
Sauger *m s.* Saugerkasten
Säugerhormon *n (biot)* mammalian hormone
Saugerkasten *m (pap)* suction (vacuum, pump) box
Saugerwasser *n (pap)* suction water
saugfähig absorbent, absorptive, *(pap also)* bibulous
Saugfähigkeit *f* absorbing (absorption) capacity, absorbency, *(pap also)* bibulousness
Saugfähigkeitsprüfgerät *n (pap)* bibliometer
Saugfilter *n* suction (vacuum) filter
Saugfiltration *f* suction (vacuum) filtration
Saugflasche *f* suction flask, aspirator bottle, filter[-ing] flask, filtration (Büchner) flask
Saugförderer *m* suction conveyor
Sauggasgenerator *m* suction gas producer, suction generator
Sauggautsche *f (pap)* suction couch [roll], suction roll
Sauggrube *f* suction pit
Saugheber *m* siphon, syphon
Saughöhe *f* suction head
~/größtmögliche net positive suction head, NPSH
Saughöhenprüfgerät *n (pap)* bibliometer
Saughub *m* suction stroke
Saugkammer *f s.* Saugkasten 1.
Saugkasten *m* 1. [suction] wind box, suction box *(of a sintering machine)*; 2. *s.* Saugerkasten
Saugleitung *f* suction line (pipe)
Saugmund *m* suction port
Saugnutsche *f* vacuum nutsche
Saugpapier *n* absorbent paper
Saugpappe *f* absorbent (coaster) board
Saugpresse *f (pap)* suction press
Saugpreßwalze *f (pap)* suction press roll
Saugpumpe *f* suction pump
Saugreibungshöhe *f* suction friction head
Saugrohr *n* suction line (pipe)
Saugseite *f* suction side
Saugspeiser *m (glass)* suction feeder
Saugspeisung *f (glass)* suction feeding
Saugstelle *f* suction point
Saugstrahlgebläse *n*, **Saugstrahlpumpe** *f* ejector, eductor, siphon, syphon
Saugstutzen *m* suction port
Saugtrommeltrockner *m* suction-drum dryer
Saugventil *n* suction valve
Saugvermögen *n s.* Saugfähigkeit
Saugwalze *f (pap)* suction couch [roll], suction roll
Saugwirkung *f* sucking action
~ der Kapillaren capillary suction
Saugzellenfilter *n* rotary-drum vacuum filter, *(pap also)* rotary vacuum drum-type save-all
Saugzone *f* suction area; cake forming (formation) zone *(of a vacuum filter)*
Saugzug *m* induced (forced) draught, down-draught, suction
Saugzuggebläse *n* induced-draught fan
Saugzuglüfter *m* exhauster
Saugzugsinterung *f* downdraught sintering
Säule *f* 1. *(tech)* column, tower; 2. *(cryst)* column, prism; 3. *(chromat)* column
~/chromatographische chromatographic column
~/gepackte *(chromat)* packed column
~ mit rotierenden Scheiben rotary-disk tower, rotating-disk contactor (extractor)
~/positive *(phys ch)* positive column
~/präparative *(chromat)* preparative column
~/schwer beladene *(chromat)* heavily loaded column
Säulenadsorptionschromatographie *f* column adsorption chromatography
säulenartig *(cryst)* columnar
Säulenausgang *m (chromat)* column exit
Säulenbetrieb *m* column operation *(as in the ion-retardation process)*
Säulenbluten *n (chromat)* column bleed, liquid-phase bleeding
Säulenchromatographie *f* column chromatography
säulenchromatographisch by column chromatography
Säuleneffektivität *f (chromat)* column performance
säulenförmig *(cryst)* columnar
Säulenfüllung *f* column packing
Säulenhöhe *f* column height
Säulenkombination *f s.* Säulenverbund
Säulenkopf *m (distil)* column head, top of the column
Säulenlänge *f (chromat)* column length
Säulenofen *m* column oven *(gas chromatography)*
Säulenpacken *n (chromat)* packing of columns
~ mittels Suspendierflüssigkeiten gleicher Dichte balanced-density slurry method
~ mittels Suspendierflüssigkeiten hoher Viskosität high-viscosity method
Säulenpackung *f (chromat)* column packing
Säulenreaktor *m (biot)* column reactor
Säulentrennung *f (chromat)* column separation
Säulenumschalttechnik *f (chromat)* coupled-columns technique
Säulenverbund *m (chromat)* column assembly, assembled column set
Säulenvolumen *n* column volume
Säulenwand *f* column wall
Saumeffekt *m (phot)* fringe effect
Säure *f* 1. *(ch)* acid; 2. sourness, acidity
~/anorganische inorganic (mineral) acid

~/arsenige arsenious acid
~/bromige bromous acid
~/Carosche Caro's acid, peroxomonosulphuric acid
~/Cassellasche Cassella's acid *(naphth-2-ol-7-sulphonic acid or naphth-2-ylamine-4,8-disulphonic acid)*
~/chlorige chlorous acid
~/Clevesche Cleve's acid *(naphth-1-ol-5-sulphonic acid and any of several naphth-1-ylamine sulphonic acids)*
~/diphosphorige diphosphorous acid, *diphosphonic acid
~/dischweflige disulphurous acid
~/dithionige dithionous acid
~/dreibasige (dreiprotonige, dreiwertige) triprotic (tribasic) acid, triacid
~/einbasige *s.* ~/einprotonige
~/eingestellte standard acid
~/einprotonige (einwertige) monoprotic (monobasic) acid, monoacid
~/Freundsche Freund's acid, naphth-1-ylamine-3,6-disulphonic acid
~/frische fresh acid
~/fuchsinschweflige fuchsinesulphurous acid
~/Grahamsche *s.* Metaphosphorsäure
~/harte hard acid *(according to Pearson's classification)*
~/hochkonzentrierte (hochprozentige) high-strength acid
~/hypobromige hypobromous acid
~/hypochlorige hypochlorous acid
~/hypoiodige hypoiodous acid
~/hypophosphorige hypophosphorous acid, *phosphinic acid
~/hyposalpetrige hyponitrous acid
~/isomere iso acid
~/Kochsche Koch's acid, naphth-1-ylamine-3,6,8-trisulphonic acid
~/konzentrierte concentrated (strong) acid
~/korrespondierende conjugate acid
~/Laurentsche Laurent's acid, naphth-1-ylamine-5-sulphonic acid
~/linksdrehende laevo[rotatory] acid
~/magische magic acid *(equimolar mixture of fluorosulphuric acid and antimony pentafluoride)*
~/mehrbasige (mehrprotonige, mehrwertige) polybasic (polyprotic) acid, polyacid
~/metaphosphorige metaphosphorous acid
~/mittelstarke moderately strong acid
~/monophosphorige *s.* ~/phosphorige
~/nitrose nitrous vitriol *(in the chamber process)*
~/normale standard acid
~/organische organic acid
~/orthophosphorige *s.* ~/phosphorige
~/pektinige pectinic acid
~/peroxosalpetrige peroxonitrous acid
~/phosphonige phosphonous acid
~/phosphorige phosphorous acid, *phosphonic acid
~/pyrophosphorige *s.* ~/diphosphorige
~/pyroschweflige *s.* ~/dischweflige
~/racemische racemic acid
~/rechtsdrehende dextro[rotatory] acid
~/salpetrige nitrous acid
~/sauerstofffreie hydracid
~/Schäffersche Schäffer acid, naphth-2-ol-6-sulphonic acid
~/schwache weak acid
~/schweflige sulphurous acid
~/selenige selenious acid
~/standardisierte standard acid
~/starke strong acid
~/ungesättigte unsaturated acid
~/unterbromige *s.* ~/hypobromige
~/unterchlorige *s.* ~/hypochlorige
~/unterhalogenige hypohalous acid
~/unteriodige *s.* ~/hypoiodige
~/verdünnte dilute acid
~/vierbasige (vierprotonige, vierwertige) tetraprotic (tetrabasic) acid, tetraacid
~/Wasserstoffionen abspaltende hydrogen acid
~/weiche soft acid *(according to Pearson's classification)*
~/zweibasige (zweiprotonige, zweiwertige) diprotic (dibasic) acid, diacid
d-**Säure** *f s.* Säure/rechtsdrehende
l-**Säure** *f s.* Säure/linksdrehende
γ-Säure *f* γ-acid *(2-aminonaphth-8-ol-6-sulphonic acid)*
δ-Säure *f* δ-acid *(naphth-1-ol-4,8-disulphonic acid or naphth-1-ylamine-4,8-disulphonic acid)*
ε-Säure *f* ε-acid *(naphth-1-ol-3,8-disulphonic acid or naphth-1-ylamine-3,8-disulphonic acid)*
Säureabscheider *m* acid separator
Säureabsorptionsturm *m* acid-absorption tower
Säureakkumulator *m* lead (lead-acid) accumulator (battery)
Säureamid *n* $RCONH_2$ acid amide
Säureamidabbau *m* degradation of amides
~/Hofmannscher Hofmann degradation of amides, Hofmann reaction
Säureanhydrid *n* acid anhydride
~/cyclisches cyclic [acid] anhydride
Säureanthracenbraun *n* acid anthracene brown
Säureäquivalent *n* acid equivalent
Säureätzung *f* acid etching
Säureaufschluß *m* decomposition (digestion) by acids; acidulation *(of phosphates for manufacturing fertilizer)*; *(pap)* acid pulping
Säureaustausch *m* acid exchange
Säureazid *n* R–CO–N=N=N acid azide
Säurebad *n* acid bath
Säureballon *m* acid carboy
Säure-Base-Definition *f*/**Brönstedsche** Brønsted-Lowry definition
Säure-Base-Dissoziationskurve *f* acid-base dissociation curve *(of proteins)*

Säure-Base-Gleichgewicht *n* acid-base equilibrium (balance)
Säure-Base-Indikator *m* acid-base indicator
Säure-Base-Katalyse *f* acid-base catalysis
~/allgemeine general acid-base catalysis
~/spezifische specific acid-base catalysis
säure-base-katalysiert acid-base catalysed, catalysed by acids and bases
Säure-Base-Paar *n* acid-base pair
~/konjugiertes (korrespondierendes) conjugate acid-base pair
Säure-Base-Reaktion *f* acid-base reaction; acid-base neutralization [reaction]
Säure-Base-Theorie *f* acid-base theory
~/Brönstedsche Brønsted[-Lowry] theory
~ von Lewis Lewis theory of acids and bases
Säure-Base-Titration *f* acid-base titration, neutralization titration
Säure-Base-Verhalten *n* acid-base behaviour
Säurebehälter *m* acid tank
Säurebehandlung *f* acid treatment, *(text also)* acid steeping, grey souring
Säurebereitung *f* acid preparation (making), *(pap also)* cooking-liquor manufacture
säurebeständig resistant to acid[s], acid-resistant, acid-resisting, acid-stable, acid-proof
Säurebeständigkeit *f* resistance (stability) to acid[s], acid resistance (stability)
säurebildend acid-forming
Säurebildner *mpl (food)* acidogens, acid formers, acid-producers, *(esp)* acid-forming bacteria
säurebindend acid-binding
Säureblau *n* acid blue
Säurebraun *n* acid brown
Säurebromid *n* acid bromide
Säurecharakter *m* acidic character
Säurechlorid *n* acid chloride
Säurechlorid-Reduktion *f***/Rosenmund-Zajcevsche** Rosenmund (acid chloride) reduction, Rosenmund reaction
Säuredampf *m* acid vapour (fume)
Säuredämpfen *n (text)* acid ageing
Säuredämpfer *m (text)* acid ager
Säuredenaturierung *f* acid denaturation *(of proteins)*
Säuredissoziation *f* acid[ic] dissociation
Säuredissoziationskonstante *f* acid[ic] dissociation constant
Säuredruckvorlage *f* acid egg
säureecht *(dye)* acid-fast, fast to acids
Säureechtheit *f (dye)* acid fastness, fastness to acids
säureempfindlich acid-sensitive, acid-labile, sensitive to acids
Säureempfindlichkeit *f* sensitivity to acids
Säurefällung *f* acid precipitation
Säurefarbstoff *m* acid[ic] dye
säurefest *s.* säurebeständig
Säureform *f* aci form *(of nitro compounds)*
Säurefraktion *f* acidic fraction
säurefrei acid-free, free from acidity
Säurefuchsin *n* acid fuchsine
Säurefunktion *f* acidic (acidity) function
Säuregärung *f***/gemischte** *(bioch)* mixed (heterolactic) fermentation
säuregefällt acid-precipitated
Säuregehalt *m* acid content
säuregewaschen *(chromat)* acid-washed
Säureglasballon *m* acid carboy
Säuregoudron *m* acid tar
Säuregrad *m* [degree of] acidity
~ nach Soxhlet-Henkel degree Soxhlet-Henkel, degree S/H
Säuregradbestimmung *f* acidity test, test for acidity
Säurehalogenid *n* acid halide
säurehaltig acid-containing, acidic, acidiferous
Säurehaltigkeit *f* acidity
Säurehärtung *f (coat, plast)* acid-catalysed cure, acid hardening
Säureheber *m* acid siphon
Säurehydrolyse *f* acid hydrolysis
Säurekatalysator *m* acid[ic] catalyst
Säurekatalyse *f* acid[ic] catalysis
~/allgemeine general acid catalysis
~/spezifische specific acid catalysis, specific hydrogen-ion catalysis
säurekatalysiert acid-catalysed, catalysed by acid[s]
~/allgemein general-acid-catalysed
~/spezifisch specific-acid-catalysed
Säurekochechtheit *f (text)* fastness to cross-dyeing, fastness to topping
Säurekomponente *f* acid component
Säurekonstante *f* acidity constant
Säurekonzentration *f* acid concentration
säurelabil acid-labile, acid-sensitive, sensitive to acids
Säureleitung *f* acid-proof pipe; *(pap)* liquor-circulating line
säureliebend acidophilic, acidophilous, oxyphil[e], oxyphilic, oxyphilous
säurelöslich acid-soluble, soluble in acids
~/schwer sparingly (difficultly) soluble in acids
Säurelöslichkeit *f* solubility in acids
Säurelösung *f* acid solution
Säure-Maßlösung *f (anal)* standard acid
Säuremattierung *f* acid etching
Säurenebel *m* acid mist
Säureorange *n* acid orange
Säurepergament *n* vegetable parchment, parchment paper
Säurepolieren *n*, **Säurepolitur** *f* acid polishing
Säureprobe *f*, **Säureprüfung** *f* acid test
Säurepumpe *f* acid pump
Säureregenerat *n (rubber)* acid reclaim
Säureregeneration *f (hyd)* regeneration with acid, acid regeneration (wash) *(ion exchange)*

säureresistent *s.* säurebeständig
Säurerest *m* acid residue
Säurescharlach *m* acid scarlet
Säureschicht *f* acid layer
Säureschlamm *m* acid sludge
Säureschutzschürze *f* acid apron
Säureschwarz *n* acid black
Säurespaltung *f* acid[ic] cleavage, cleavage by acids
säurestabil *s.* säurebeständig
Säurestärke *f* acid[ic] strength
Säurestation *f (pap)* acid [preparation] plant, liquor-making plant
Säuretank *m* acid tank
Säureteer *m* acid tar
Säureturm *m (pap)* acid[-making] tower, absorption (reaction, limestone) tower
~ **aus Beton** concrete acid tower
Säureüberschuß *m* excess of acid
säureunbeständig acid-labile
Säure- und Basebegriff *m*/**Brönstedscher** Brønsted[-Lowry] concept of acids and bases
säureunlöslich acid-insoluble, insoluble in acids
Säureunlöslichkeit *f* insolubility in acids
Säureverfahren *n (rubber)* acid [reclaiming] process
Säureverhalten *n* acid behaviour
Säureverhältnis *n (pap)* liquor[-to wood] ratio *(ratio of cooking liquor to wood weight)*
säureverzuckert *(food)* acid-converted
Säurevorratsbehälter *m* acid storage tank
Säurewäsche *f* acid washing *(of crude benzol)*
Säurewasserstoff *m* acid[ic] hydrogen
Säurewecker *m (food)* starter, seeding material
Säureweckerapparat *m (food)* starter heater
Säureweckerdestillat *n (food)* starter distillate
Säureweckerkultur *f (food)* starter culture
säurewidrig antacid
Säurezahl *f* acid value (number), A.V.
Säurezentrum *n* acid site *(in molecules, catalysts)*
säurezersetzlich acid-labile, acid-sensitive, sensitive to acids
Sauter-Durchmesser *m* Sauter (volume-surface) mean diameter
Saybolt-Kolben *m* Saybolt distilling flask
Saybolt-Universalviskosimeter *n (petrol)* Saybolt viscometer
SB *s.* Siedebeginn
S-Benzin *n* liquid-phase gasoline
SBK *s.* Styren-Butadien-Kautschuk
Sbp. *s.* Sublimationspunkt
SBR-Latex *m* SBR latex, styrene-butadiene latex
SBS-Modell *n (bioch)* side-by-side model *(of deoxyribonucleic acid)*
SC *s.* Säulenchromatographie
Scandium *n* Sc scandium
Scandiumbromid *n* scandium bromide
Scandiumcarbonat *n* scandium carbonate
Scandiumchlorid *n* scandium chloride
Scandiumfluorid *n* scandium fluoride
Scandiumhydroxid *n* scandium hydroxide
Scandiumhydroxidnitrat *n* scandium hydroxide nitrate
Scandiumiodid *n* scandium iodide
Scandiumnitrat *n* scandium nitrate
Scandiumoxid *n* scandium oxide
Scandiumsulfid *n* scandium sulphide
scannen *(anal)* to scan
Scanningkalorimeter *n* scanning calorimeter
SCF-LCAO-Rechnung *f* LCAO SCF calculation, LCAO self-consistent-field calculation
SCF-Methode *f* SCF method, self-consistent-field method
SCF-Molekülorbital *n* self-consistent-field molecular orbital
SCF-Rechnung *f* SCF calculation, self-consistent-field calculation
Schabeisen *n (ceram)* scraper
Schabemesser *n* scraper knife (blade); *(for rolls:)* doctor knife (blade)
Schaber *m* scraper; *(for rolls:)* doctor
~ **am Trockenzylinder** *(pap)* dryer doctor
~ **an der Brustwalze** *(pap)* breast roll doctor
~ **an der [oberen] Preßwalze** *(pap)* [top] press roll doctor
~ **an der Siebleitwalze** *(pap)* wire-roll doctor
~/**traversierender** *(pap)* vibrating (oscillating) doctor
Schaberblech *n* raking blade
Schaberklinge *f*, **Schabermesser** *n s.* Schabemesser
Schaberwalze *f* doctor roll
Schablonenätzung *f (glass)* plate etching
Schablonenseide *f* stencil silk
Schabmesser *n s.* Schabemesser
Schacht *m* 1. shaft *(as of a furnace or kiln)*, *(of a blast furnace also)* stack; pocket *(of a pulpwood grinder)*; 2. shaft *(of a mine)*, *(broadly:)* mine
Schachtbrunnen *m (hyd)* dug well
Schachtelpresse *f* pot press
Schacht-Kettenrost *m* shaft-chain grate
~ **von Makar'ev** Makarev shaft-chain grate
Schachtmauerwerk *n* inwall *(of a blast furnace)*
Schachtofen *m (met)* shaft furnace; shaft (vertical, upright) kiln *(esp for sintering and calcining)*
Schachtofenverfahren *n* shaft-furnace process *(for producing iron by direct reduction)*
Schachttrockner *m* tower dryer
Schachtwasser *n* mine water
Schaden *m* damage
Schadensanalyse *f* damage analysis
Schadenserfassung *f* **und -beseitigung** *f* trouble shooting
Schadgas *n* pollutant gas
Schädigung *f* 1. damaging, damage; *(text)* tendering; 2. *s.* Schaden
~ **der Atmosphäre** damage to the atmosphere
Schädigungsfaktor *m* damage factor

schädlich damaging, detrimental, *(esp to health:)* harmful, injurious, deleterious, noxious
Schädlichkeit *f* detrimentalness, *(esp to health:)* harmfulness, injuriousness, deleteriousness, noxiousness
Schädlingsbekämpfung *f* pest control
Schädlingsbekämpfungsmittel *n* pesticide, [pest] control agent, biocide
~/chemisches pesticide (pesticidal) chemical
Schädlingsbekämpfungsmittelrückstand *m* pesticide residue
Schadraum *m* clearance volume *(in a reciprocating engine)*
~/relativer clearance *(ratio of clearance volume to swept volume)*
Schadstoff *m* harmful substance (material), agent of damage, *(esp in air and water:)* pollutant, *(hyd also)* contaminant
Schadstoffadsorption *f* pollutant adsorption
Schadstoffanreicherung *f* pollutant accumulation
schadstoffarm low-polluting, low-pollution
Schadstoffaufnahme *f* pollutant uptake
schadstoffbelastet *f* pollutant-laden, pollutant-bearing
Schadstoffbelastung *f* pollutant load[ing], pollution load[ing]
Schadstoffeinleitung *f* pollutant discharge
Schadstoffeliminierung *f* pollutant removal
Schadstoffemission *f* pollutant (obnoxious) emission
Schadstoffentfernung *f* pollutant removal
schadstofffrei pollutant (pollution) control
Schadstoffimmission *f* air-borne pollution
Schadstoffkontrolle *f s.* Schadstoffbekämpfung
Schadstoffkonzentration *f* pollutant concentration
Schadstoffverminderung *f* pollutant reduction, pollution control
Schadstoffwindrose *f* pollution rose
Schadwirkung *f* damaging (detrimental) effect, *(esp to health:)* harmful (injurious, deleterious) effect
Schäffer-Salz *n* Schäffer salt *(sodium salt of Schäffer acid)*
Schäffer-Säure *f* Schäffer acid, naphth-2-ol-6-sulphonic acid
schal stale, flat • **~ werden** to stale
Schale *f* 1. shell *(of an atom)*; 2. *(lab)* dish; *(tech)* pan, tray; 3. *(bot)* peel, rind, *(if dry:)* husk, hull, *(if hard or fibrous:)* shell
~/abgeschlossene closed shell *(of an atom)*
~/äußere external shell, outer[most] shell *(of an atom)*
~/innere inner shell *(of an atom)*
~/offene open shell
schälen 1. *(pap)* to peel, to [de]bark, *(Am also)* to ross; 2. *(food)* to shell, to hull, to decorticate, to excorticate *(cereals)*; 3. *(tech)* to skim *(as in the knife-discharge centrifuge)*
Schalenaufbau *m* shell structure *(of an atom)*
Schalenentwicklung *f (phot)* dish development
Schalenguß *m* 1. chill casting; 2. chill-cast iron, chilled cast iron, chill casting
Schalengußkern *m* chill[ed] core
Schalengußstück *n s.* Schalenguß 2.
Schalenhartguß *m s.* Schalenguß 1.
Schalenmehl *n (plast)* shell flour *(a filler)*
Schalenmodell *n* shell model *(of atoms)*
Schalenöl *n* peel oil *(from citrus fruits)*
schalenporös *(chromat)* pellicular, superficially porous *(packing)*
Schalenstruktur *f* shell structure *(of an atom)*
Schälfestigkeit *f (plast)* peel strength
Schälfolie *f* sliced sheet, *(if thin:)* sliced film
Schalheit *f* staleness, flatness
Schallabsorption *f* sound absorption
Schallaerozyklon *m* sonic cyclone *(gas cleaning)*
Schalldämmplatte *f* sound-absorbing panel
Schalldämmstoff *m* sound-absorbing material
Schalldruck *m* sound pressure
Schalleistung *f* sound power
Schallenergie *f* sound (sonic) energy
Schallfeld *n* sound field
Schallfrequenz *f* sound frequency
Schallgeschwindigkeit *f* speed of sound, sonic speed (velocity)
Schallintensität *f* sound intensity
Schällöffel *m (food)* skimmer; unloader plough *(of a centrifuge)*
Schallquant *n* phonon
Schallquelle *f* sound source
Schallschwinger *m s.* Ultraschallschwinger
Schallsirene *f s.* Schallaerozyklon
Schallwelle *f* sound wave
Schälmesser *n* unloader knife, skimmer *(as of a centrifuge)*
Schälprüfung *f* peeling test *(for testing the strength of an adhesive-bonded joint)*
Schälrohr *n* skimming tube, skimmer [pipe] *(of a centrifuge)*
Schälschleuder *f s.* Schälzentrifuge
Schalter *m* switch
Schalteröl *n* switch oil
Schäl- und Haftprüfung *f (plast)* peel/bond test
Schälung *f (pap)* peeling, [de]barking, *(Am also)* rossing
Schälzentrifuge *f* skimmer (knife-discharge) centrifuge
Schamotte *f* chamotte
~/zerkleinerte grog
Schamotteerzeugnis *n* fireclay refractory [material]
~/SiO_2-reiches siliceous refractory *(containing 78 to 92 % SiO_2)*; silica refractory *(containing more than 92 % SiO_2)*
Schamottekapsel *f (ceram)* saggar, fireclay box
Schamotteplatte *f* fireclay plate
Schamottestein *m* refractory (fireclay) brick, firebrick
Schamotteton *m* refractory clay, fireclay

Schamotteziegel *m s.* Schamottestein
Schampun *n (cosmet)* shampoo
Schappe[seide] *f* chappe (schappe) silk, [s]chappe
Schardinger-Dextrin *n* Schardinger dextrin, *cyclodextrin
Schardinger-Enzym *n* Schardinger enzyme, xanthine oxidase
scharf 1. severe, rigorous, drastic *(reaction conditions)*; 2. sharp, acrid, pungent *(taste)*; 3. sharp *(melting point)*
Schärfe *f* 1. severity, severeness, rigorousness *(of reaction conditions)*; 2. sharpness, acridity, pungency *(of taste)*; 3. sharpness *(of melting point)*
~ **der Absiebung** cleanliness of cut *(classifying)*
~ **der Küpe** *(text)* sharpness of the vat
schärfen *(text)* to sharpen *(the vat)*
Scharffeuer *n (ceram)* hard (quick) fire
scharfgebrannt *(ceram)* hard-burned, hard-fired
Scharlach *m (dye)* scarlet
~**/Biebricher** Biebrich (scarlet) red
~**/Venezianischer** Venetian scarlet
Scharlachkörner *npl (dye)* scarlet corns, kermes berries (grains), kermes *(dried bodies of the females of various scales, genus Kermes)*
Schatten *mpl (tann)* blasting
Schattenwand *f* shadow (baffle) wall *(of a glass-melting furnace)*
Schattenzeichnung *f (phot)* shadow detail
schattieren *(text)* to shade
Schattierung *f (text)* 1. shade; 2. shading
schätzen to estimate
Schätzung *f* estimation
Schätzwert *m (anal)* estimate
Schaubild *n* chart, graph, diagram, graphical (diagrammatic) representation
Schauer *m (nucl)* shower
Schauerteilchen *n (nucl)* shower particle
Schaufel *f* 1. shovel, scoop; flight *(as in a drying cylinder)*; 2. *s.* Schaufelblatt
Schaufelblatt *n* shovel, blade, paddle, vane
Schaufelelement *n* mixing element *(of an agitator)*
Schaufelkneter *m* kneading machine, kneader, double-arm mixer; paddle kneading table *(margarine making)*
Schaufelmischer *m* blade mixer
Schaufelrad *n* paddle wheel
Schaufelradfärbemaschine *f (text)* paddle[-wheel] dyeing machine
Schaufelradfermenter *m*, **Schaufelradreaktor** *m (biot)* blade-wheel reactor
Schaufelrührer *m* straight-blade[d] turbine
Schaufelwinkel *m* vane angle
Schauglas *n* 1. inspection (sight, gauge) glass, viewing window; 2. show (inverted) bottle, specimen (museum, preservation) jar
Schaukelbecherwerk *n*, **Schaukelförderer** *m* swing-bucket (swing-tray) elevator, pivoted-bucket conveyor
schaukeln to swing, to rock
Schaukelofen *m* rocking furnace
Schaukelrahmen *m (tann)* rocker [frame] *(for moving pelts in suspender pits)*
Schaukelrinne *f* Wulff-Bock crystallizer
Schaukelschwingung *f (spectr)* rocking vibration
Schaukeltrockner *m* tilting (reversing) pan dryer
Schauloch *n* inspection hatch (port), sight (spy) hole, peephole, viewing aperture
Schaum *m* foam, froth, *(if undesired:)* scum, skimmings; *(glass)* scum[ming]; *(met)* dross; *(ferm)* head; *(cosmet)* lather • **sich mit ~ bedecken** to foam, to froth
~**/fester** 1. *(phys ch)* solid foam; 2. *s.* Schaumstoff/fester
~**/zweiphasiger** *(coll)* two-phase foam
Schaumabscheider *m (biot)* foam separator
Schaumabstreifer *m* 1. *(min tech)* froth skimmer; 2. *s.* Schwimmschlammabstreifer
schaumartig foam-like, foamy, frothy
Schaumbekämpfungsöl *n s.* Schaumverhütungsöl
Schaumbeständigkeit *f* foam stability (persistence), lifetime of the foam; *(ferm)* firmness of the head, head retention
Schaumbeton *m* foamed (aerated) concrete, cellular[-expanded] concrete
schaumbildend foam-producing
Schaumbildner *m* foaming agent, frothing (froth-forming) agent, frother; gasifying agent *(for producing foam glass)*
Schaumbildung *f* foam (froth) formation, foaming, frothing; *(ferm)* head formation
Schaumbildungsfähigkeit *f s.* Schaumbildungsvermögen
Schaumbildungsmittel *n s.* Schaumbildner
Schaumbildungsvermögen *n* foaming ability, foaminess, frothiness
Schaumbrecher *m s.* 1. Schaumzerstörer 1.; 2. Schaumzerstörungsmittel
Schaumdämpfer *m*, **Schaumdämpfungsmittel** *n* foam depressant
Schaumdauer *f s.* Schaumbeständigkeit
Schaumdecke *f* foam blanket, foam (froth) layer
Schaumdepressor *m s.* Schaumdämpfer
Schaumeigenschaft *f* foaming property; *(cosmet)* lathering property
schäumen to foam, to expand *(e.g. plastics)*; to foam, to froth, *(by bubbles formed inside a liquid:)* to effervesce; *(cosmet)* to lather
schäumend foaming, frothing, *(by bubbles formed inside a liquid:)* effervescent; *(ferm)* effervescent, brisk
Schaumentwässerung *f* foam draining
Schaumentwicklung *f s.* Schaumbildung
Schäumer *m*, **Schaumerzeuger** *m s.* Schaumbildner
Schaumfaden *m (text)* foam filament
Schaumfleck *m* froth spot (mark) *(a defect in paper)*
Schaumflotation *f* froth floatation
schaumfördernd foam-promoting

Schäumfraktionierung *f* foam fractionation
Schaumglas *n* foam[ed] glass, cellular (sponge) glass
Schaumglasblock *m* foam glass block
Schaumgummi *m* foam (foamed) rubber (latex), latex foam [rubber]
Schaumhaltigkeit *f s.* Schaumstabilität
schaumig foamy, frothy
Schaumigkeit *f* foaminess, frothiness
Schauminhibitor *m s.* Schaumverhütungsmittel
Schaumkonzentrat *n (min tech)* concentrate-laden froth, froth product
Schaumkraft *f* foaming power (potential)
Schaumkrone *f* head *(on beer)*
Schaumkunststoff *m s.* Schaumstoff
Schaumlamelle *f (text)* foam film
Schaumlinie *f (glass)* foam line
Schaumlöscher *m*, **Schaumlöschgerät** *n* foam extinguisher
Schaummaschine *f s.* Schaumschlagmaschine
Schaummittel *n s.* 1. Schaumbildner; 2. Feuerlösch-Schaummittel
Schäummittel *n s.* Schaumbildner
Schaumöl *n s.* Schaumverhütungsöl
Schaumpolystyrol *n* foamed (expanded) polystyrene
Schaumpolyvinylchlorid *n* foamed (expanded) polyvinyl chloride
Schaumprodukt *n (min tech)* froth product
Schaum-PVC *n s.* Schaumpolyvinylchlorid
Schaumraum *m (biot)* foam chamber
Schaumregulator *m*, **Schaumregulierer** *m* foam-control agent
Schaumregulierung *f* foam control
Schaumschicht *f* 1. foam (froth) layer, foam blanket; 2. *s.* Schwimmschicht
Schaumschichttrocknung *f* foam-mat drying
Schaumschlacke *f* foamed slag
Schaumschlagmaschine *f (rubber)* foaming (frothing) machine, beating (whisking) machine, frother
Schaumschwimmaufbereitung *f* froth floatation
Schaumstabilisator *m* foam stabilizer
Schaumstabilität *f s.* Schaumbeständigkeit
Schaumstoff *m* foamed plastic, expanded (cellular) plastic, plastic foam • **mit ~ beschichtet** *(text)* foam-laminated, foam-backed
~/chemisch getriebener chemically foamed plastic
~/fester rigid foam
~/geschlossenzelliger unicellular (closed-cell) foam
~/halbharter semirigid foam
~/harter rigid foam
~/offenzelliger multicellular (open-cell) foam
~/physikalisch getriebener mechanically foamed plastic
~/„schaumloser" foamless foamback *(obtained by melting thin laminates)*
~/weicher (weich-elastischer) flexible foam
Schaumstoffaden *m (text)* foam filament
schaumstoffbeschichtet *s.* schaumstoffkaschiert
Schaumstoffdämmung *f* rigid-foam insulation
Schaumstoffisolierung *f s.* Schaumstoffdämmung
schaumstoffkaschiert *(text)* foam-laminated, foam-backed
Schaumstoffolie *f* expanded sheet
Schaumstofformen *n* foam moulding
Schaumstoffschnittfaden *m (text)* foam filament
Schaumton *m* foamed clay, foamclay
Schaumverhinderungsmittel *n s.* Schaumverhütungsmittel
Schaumverhütung *f* foam prevention, inhibition of foaming
Schaumverhütungsmittel *n* antifoaming (antifrothing) agent, antifoam [agent, compound], foam inhibitor
Schaumverhütungsöl *n* antifoaming oil, [anti]froth oil
Schaumvermögen *n s.* Schaumbildungsvermögen
Schaumvolumen *n* foam volume
Schaumwein *m* sparkling (effervescent) wine
Schaumzahl *f* foam number
Schaumzerstörer *m* 1. foam breaker *(apparatus)*; 2. *s.* Schaumzerstörungsmittel
Schaumzerstörung *f* foam breaking *(mechanically)*; foam destruction *(chemically)*
Schaumzerstörungsmittel *n* defoaming agent, defoamer, foam destructor (breaker, killer)
Schauöffnung *f* inspection hatch (port), viewing aperture
Scheckpapier *n* safety (cheque) paper
Scheibe *f* disk; *(filtr)* leaf, disk; washer *(as for tightening joints)*
~ mit Flügeln (Schaufeln) vaned disk
~/rotierende rotating disk
Scheibel-Kolonne *f* Scheibel column
Scheibenaufschläger *m (pap)* disk refiner
Scheibenbrecher *m* disk crusher
Scheibenelektrode *f* disk electrode
~/rotierende rotating-disk electrode
Scheibenfilter *n* leaf filter; [rotary] disk filter *(a vacuum filter)*
Scheibengasbehälter *m* waterless gas-holder, piston (dry-seal) gas-holder
Scheiben[kolloid]mühle *f* disk [attrition] mill, disk grinder
Scheibenrefiner *m (pap)* disk refiner
Scheibenrührer *m* disk agitator
Scheibensaugfilter *n* disk-type [rotary] vacuum filter, rotary vacuum disk filter
Scheibenseparator *m* disk separator
Scheibentauchtropfkörper *m (hyd)* disk-type trickling filter, rotating biological contactor (disks), RBC unit, rotating-disk biofilter (contactor)
Scheibentrieur *m* disk separator
Scheibenverdampfer *m* disk evaporator
Scheibenversprüher *m* [spinning-]disk atomizer, centrifugal-disk (rotary-disk, spray-disk) atomizer

Scheibenversprühung *f* [spinning-]disk atomization, centrifugal-disk (rotary-disk, spray-disk) atomization
Scheibenzähler *m* disk meter, nutating-piston meter *(flow measurement)*
Scheibenzerstäuber *m s.* Scheibenversprüher
Scheibler-Exsikkator *m* Scheibler desiccator
Scheidebehälter *m s.* Scheidegefäß
Scheidefiltration *f* cake filtration, cake[-filter] operation
Scheideflasche *f* Florentine flask (receiver)
Scheidegefäß *n* separating (separatory) vessel, settler
Scheidegut *n* material being *or* to be separated
Scheidekalk *m* sugar-factory lime
Scheidemittel *n* separating agent
scheiden 1. to separate, to segregate, *(relating to gold or silver:)* to part, *(relating to size:)* to classify, to make a cut; 2. *(sugar)* to defecate, to lime
Scheidepfanne *f (sugar)* defecation tank (pan), defecator
Scheidepresse *f* wringer, press
Scheider *m* separator, *(relating to size:)* classifier; settler, settling (separator) tank *(fluid extraction)*
Scheidesaft *m (sugar)* defecated juice
Scheidesaturation *f (sugar)* defecocarbonation, defecosaturation, lime and carbon dioxide defecation
Scheideschlamm *m (sugar)* carbonation (saturation) sludge, *(as a fertilizer also)* sugar-factory lime
Scheidetrichter *m* separatory (separating) funnel
Scheideverfahren *n***/klassisches** *(sugar)* fractional liming, two stage liming
Scheidewand *f* separating (dividing) wall, partition; *(relating to diffusion:)* diaphragm, membrane, barrier, *(esp osmosis, dialysis:)* membrane, *(esp electrolysis:)* diaphragm; *(pap)* centre division, midfeather, mid-wall, midriff *(of a Hollander beater)*
~/halbdurchlässige *s.* ~/semipermeable
~/poröse porous diaphragm (membrane)
~/semipermeable semipermeable membrane
Scheidewasser *n* aqua fortis *(concentrated nitric acid)*
Scheidung *f* separation, *(relating to gold or silver:)* parting, *(relating to size:)* classification; *(sugar)* defecation, liming
~/elektrostatische electrostatic separation
~/heiße *(sugar)* hot defecation (liming)
~/kalte *(sugar)* cold defecation (liming)
~/nasse *(sugar)* defecation with milk of lime, wet liming
~/trockene *(sugar)* defecation with dry lime, dry liming
~/warme *s.* ~/heiße
Scheinharz *n* mock resin *(affinity chromatography)*
Scheinleitwert *m (anal)* admittance
Scheinmedikament *n* placebo
Scheinporosität *f (ceram)* apparent porosity
Scheinviskosität *f* apparent viscosity
Scheinwiderstand *m (anal)* impedance
Scheitelpunkt *m* peak *(as of a curve)*
Scheitelwert *m* peak
Schellack *m* shellac
~/gebleichter (weißer) bleached (white) shellac
Schellacklack *m* shellac varnish
Schellbach-Bürette *f* Schellbach burette
Schelle *f* clamp, clip
Schellolsäure *f* shellolic acid *(a dicarboxylic acid present in shellac)*
Schema *n* **der Energiezustände** *s.* Energieniveaudiagramm
Q-e-**Schema** *n Q-e* scheme *(copolymerization)*
Schenkel *m* leg *(of a U-tube)*
Schenkelwanderung *f* branch migration *(of portions of the DNA strand)*
Scherbeanspruchung *f* shear stress
Scherben *m (ceram)* [ceramic] body
~/geschrühter (verschrühter) biscuitted body
Scherben *fpl (glass)* cullet; *(ceram)* pitchers
~/fabrikeigene *(glass)* factory (domestic) cullet
~/fremde *(glass)* foreign cullet
Scherbeneis *n* flake ice
Scherbengemenge *n (glass)* raw cullet
Scherbenkobalt *m* native arsenic *(one variety)*
Scherbenoberfläche *f (ceram)* body surface
scheren to shear
Scheren *n* shear[ing]
Scherenbildung *f* chelation, chelate formation *(coordination chemistry)*
Scherenschwingung *f (spectr)* scissor vibration
Scherenverbindung *f* chelate, chelate complex (compound), crab's-claw complex
Scherfestigkeit *f* shear strength
Scherfläche *f* shear plane
Schergeschwindigkeit *f* shear rate, rate of shear
Scherkraft *f* shear force
Schermodul *m* shear modulus [of elasticity], modulus of rigidity (elasticity in shear)
Scherrate *f s.* Schergeschwindigkeit
Scherscheibenviskosimeter *n* shearing-disk viscometer
Scherspannung *f* shear stress
Scherung *f* shear[ing]
Scherungsmodul *m s.* Schermodul
scherzerkleinern to shear
Scherzerkleinerung *f* shear[ing]
scheuerbeständig *(text)* abrasion-resistant, wear-resistant, resistant to abrasion (wear)
Scheuerbeständigkeit *f (text)* abrasion (wear) resistance
scheuerfest *s.* scheuerbeständig
Scheuermittel *n* 1. scouring agent; 2. abrasive, abradant *(for testing textiles)*
scheuern 1. to scour, *(esp by using a brush:)* to scrub; 2. to gall *(as of mating moving parts)*
Scheuerprüfung *f (text)* abrasion test
Scheuerpulver *n* scouring powder

Scheuerseife *f* scouring soap
Schibutter *f* shea (Bambuk, Galam) butter *(from Butyrospermum parkii (Don) Kotschy)*
Schicht *f* layer, *(if thin:)* film *(of a multiphase or multicomponent system)*; layer, stratum *(of bulk material)*; coating, *(if thin:)* film *(for protection)*, *(if generated by electroplating or vacuum metallization also)* deposit; ply *(as of laminated material)*; *(geol)* layer, stratum, bed
~/aufgekohlte *(met)* carburized case
~ des Filterbetts *(hyd)* layer of filtering material *(of a multilayer filter)*
~/eingesetzte *s.* ~/aufgekohlte
~/elektrochemisch (elektrolytisch) aufgebrachte electrodeposit
~/fotografische emulsion, sensitive (photographic) layer
~/galvanisch aufgebrachte electrodeposit
~/gekohlte *s.* ~/aufgekohlte
~/interkalierte intercalated layer
~/lichtempfindliche *s.* ~/fotografische
~/molekulare molecular layer
~/monomolekulare monomolecular (unimolecular) film (layer), monolayer
~/multimolekulare multimolecular layer, multilayer
~/nitrierte *(met)* nitrided case
~/obere top layer
~/ölführende (produzierende) *(petrol)* producing formation
~/reflexmindernde *(phot)* antireflection (antiflare) coating
~/untere bottom layer
~/zementierte *s.* ~/aufgekohlte
Schichtäquilibrierung *f (chromat)* layer equilibration
Schichtbett *n (hyd, filtr)* layered bed
Schichtbettaustauscher *m* layered-bed [ion] exchanger
Schichtdicke *f* 1. *(phys ch)* layer (film) thickness; *(coat)* coating (film) thickness, [film] build; plating thickness *(electroplating)*; *(spectr)* pathlength, length of path; 2. *s.* Schichthöhe
~/durchstrahlte *(spectr)* absorption pathlength
Schichtempfindlichkeit *f (phot)* emulsion sensitivity (speed)
schichten to stratify *(bulk material)*
~/aufeinander to stack [up]
Schichtenbildung *f (geol)* stratification, lamination; *(hyd, filtr)* layering
Schichtenfilter *n s.* Schichtenplattenfilter
Schichtengitter *n (cryst)* layer lattice
Schichtenplattenfilter *n* plate press, sheet filter
Schichtenspaltung *f* delamination
Schichtenströmung *f* laminar (streamline) flow
Schichtentrennung *f* delamination
Schichtfolge *f* layer sequence
Schichtfolie *f* laminated sheet
schichtförmig layered, lamellar
Schichtgestein *n* sedimentary rock, sediment
Schichtgitter *n (cryst)* layer lattice
Schichthöhe *f* bed depth, depth of bed *(as of bulk material)*, *(filtr also)* filter bed height, media depth
~ des Ionenaustauscherbetts *(hyd)* resin bed depth
Schichtlänge *f* **eines theoretischen Bodens** *(chromat)* height equivalent to a theoretical plate, HETP
Schichtlinie *f (cryst)* layer line
Schichtliniendiagramm *n* **der Potentialfläche** potential energy contour map
Schichtoberfläche *f s.* Schichtseite
Schichtpressen *n (plast)* laminating, lamination; laminated moulding
Schichtpreßstoff *m* laminated plastic, [plastic] laminate
Schichtpreßstofferzeugnis *n* laminated product
Schichtpreßstoffplatte *f* laminated sheet
Schichtseite *f (phot)* emulsion surface (side)
Schichtsilicat *n* phyllosilicate, sheet silicate
Schichtspaltung *f* delamination
Schichtstoff *m s.* Schichtpreßstoff
Schichtstoffbauweise *f (plast)* sandwich construction
Schichtstoffpreßteil *n* laminated moulding, moulded laminate
Schichtstoffprofil *n* laminated section
~/[form]gepreßtes moulded laminated section
~/nachgeformtes postformed laminated section
Schichtstoffrohr *n* laminated tube
~/[form]gepreßtes moulded laminated tube
~/gewickeltes rolled laminated tube
Schichtstruktur *f* layer[ed] structure
Schichtträger *m* 1. substrate, adherend *(material on which an adhesive is spread)*; 2. *(phot)* [film] base, [emulsion] support
Schichtung *f* 1. stratification, *(geol also)* striation, lamination; 2. *(plast)* lamination
~/thermische *(hyd)* thermal stratification
schiebefest *(text)* slip-resistant
Schiebefestappretur *f*, **Schiebefestausrüstung** *f (text)* antislip (non-slip) finish
schieben to push *(a reaction)*
Schieber *m* 1. gate, disk *(of a valve)*; 2. *s.* Schieberventil; 3. *(ceram)* damper
Schieberaustrag *m* gate discharge
Schiebersteuerung *f* gate control
Schieberventil *n* gate valve
Schiebestempel *m (plast)* sliding punch
Schiedsanalyse *f* referee check *(forensic chemistry)*
Schiefe *f* skewness *(as of a curve)*
Schiefer *m (geol)* schist *(easily splitting crystalline rock)*; slate *(fine-grained clayey metamorphic rock)*; shale *(fine-grained laminated sedimentary rock)*
~/bituminöser bituminous (oil) shale
~/kristalliner crystalline schist
schieferartig schistose, schistous; slaty; shaly
Schiefergips *m* foliated gypsum
Schieferkohle *f* foliaceous brown coal

Schiefermehl *n* slate flour
Schieferöl *n* shale oil
Schieferpapier *n* slate paper
Schieferplatte *f* slate
Schieferrohöl *n* crude shale oil
Schieferschwarz *n* slate black, black chalk *(a natural pigment)*
Schieferteer *m* shale tar
Schieferton *m* shale [clay]
Schieferweiß *n* flake white *(a lead pigment)*
schiefrig *(geol)* schistose, schistous
Schieler *m s.* Schillerwein
Schiemann-Reaktion *f* Schiemann reaction *(for preparing aryl fluorides)*
Schießbaumwolle *f* gun-cotton, nitrocotton *(cellulose nitrate of high nitrogen content)*
Schießmittel *n* low explosive, propellant [explosive], deflagrating powder
Schießofen *m (lab)* Carius (bomb) furnace
Schießpulver *n* gunpowder
Schießpunkt *m (petrol)* shot point *(in refraction shooting)*
Schießrohr *n* **[nach Carius]** *(lab)* Carius (bomb) tube
Schießstoff *m s.* Schießmittel
Schießwolle *f s.* Schießbaumwolle
Schiffchen *n (lab)* [combustion] boat
Schiff-Reaktion *f* Schiff reaction (test) *(for detecting aldehydes)*
Schiffsbodenfarbe *f* ship-bottom paint
Schiffskesselkohle *f* navigation coal
Schikane *f* flow spoiler
Schilddrüsenhormon *n* thyroid hormone
Schilddrüsenüberfunktion *f (med)* hyperthyroidism, Graves' disease
Schildlausbekämpfungsmittel *n* scalicide
schillern to iridesce
Schillern *n* iridescence
Schillerspat *m (min)* schillerspar, bastite *(an inosilicate)*
Schillerwein *m* rosé wine
Schimmel *m* mould *(as on food)*; mildew *(as on cloth or leather)*
schimmelbeständig mildew-resistant, mildew-proof
Schimmelbeständigkeit *f* mildew resistance
schimmelfest *s.* schimmelbeständig
Schimmelfestappretur *f*, **Schimmelfestausrüstung** *f* mildew-proofing
schimmelgereift *(food)* mould-ripened
schimmeln to mould
Schimmelpilz *m* mould
Schimmelpilzfarbstoff *m* mould pigment
Schipprigfärben *n (text)* tippy dyeing
Schirm *m (tech)* screen
Schirmwand *f* screen wall
Schlacke *f (met)* slag; *(coal)* clinker; *(geol)* scoria
• **~ bilden** to slag; *(coal)* to clinker
~/basische basic slag
~/saure acid slag
schlacken to slag
Schlackenabstich *m* 1. tapping [of slag]; 2. slagging (slag-tap) hole, slag hole (notch)
Schlackenabstichgenerator *m (coal)* slagging[-ash] producer
~ nach Würth Würth producer
Schlackenabstichloch *n s.* Schlackenabstich 2.
Schlackenabstichrinne *f s.* Schlackenrinne
Schlackenangriff *m (met)* slag attack
schlackenartig slaggy, *(esp geol)* scoriaceous
Schlackenbad *n* slag bath
Schlackenbadgenerator *m (coal)* slag-bath gasifier
~ nach Rummel Rummel [slag-bath] gasifier
Schlackenbeständigkeit *f* slag resistance
Schlackenbeton *m* slag concrete
schlackenbildend slag-forming
Schlackenbildung *f (met)* slag formation, slagging; *(coal)* clinkering, clinker formation
Schlackenbrecher *m (coal)* clinker grinder
Schlackendamm *m (met)* skimmer dam (block)
Schlackenebene *f (met)* slag line
Schlackenfaser *f* slag wool
Schlackenmetall *n s.* Schlackenzinn
Schlackenmühle *f (coal)* clinker grinder
Schlackenpfanne *f (met)* slag ladle
Schlackenreaktionsverfahren *n (met)* Perrin process
schlackenreich slaggy
Schlackenrinne *f (met)* slag runner (spout)
Schlackenscherben *m (met)* scorifier
Schlackenstein *m* slag brick
Schlackenstich *m*, **Schlackenstichloch** *n s.* Schlackenabstich 2.
Schlackentiegel *m (met)* scorifier
Schlackenwolle *f* slag wool
Schlackenzement *m* slag cement
Schlackenziegel *m* slag brick (stone)
Schlackenziehen *n (coal)* clinker discharge
Schlackenzinn *n* prill[i]on *(extracted from slag)*
schlackig *s.* schlackenartig
Schlafmittel *n* hypnotic [drug], soporific [drug], sleeping drug, somnifacient, somnificant
Schlagbiegefestigkeit *f* impact bending strength
~ nach Izod *(plast)* Izod impact strength
Schlagbiegezähigkeit *f* impact bending strength
Schlagbohren *n (petrol)* percussion drilling
Schlagbohrverfahren *n (petrol)* percussion drilling method
schlagempfindlich sensitive to impact (shock)
Schlagempfindlichkeit *f* sensitiveness to impact (shock)
Schläger *m* beater *(of a hammer mill)*
Schlägermühle *f* 1. beater mill; 2. *(pap)* chip crusher (breaker), rechipper
schlagfest resistant to impact (shock), impact-resistant, shock-resistant
Schlagfestigkeit *f* resistance to impact (shock), impact (shock) resistance, impact strength
Schlagfestigkeitsprüfung *f* **nach Charpy** Charpy test

Schlaghärte *f* impact hardness
Schlagkorbmühle *f* cage (bar) mill, [squirrel-]cage disintegrator
Schlaglot *n* hard solder
Schlagmühle *f s.* Schlägermühle
Schlagpressen *n (plast)* impact moulding
Schlagprüfung *f* impact testing
Schlagsahne *f* whipped cream
Schlagstiftmühle *f* pinned-disk disintegrator (mill), pin[-type] mill
Schlagversuch *m* impact test
Schlagwetter *pl (mine)* firedamp
Schlagzähigkeit *f s.* Schlagfestigkeit
Schlamm *m* sludge, mud, slime, *(esp if artificially made:)* slurry
~/aktivierter *(hyd)* activated (biological) sludge
~ aus der biochemischen (biologischen) Abwasserreinigung waste biological sludge, biological sewage sludge
~ aus der chemischen Abwasserreinigung waste chemical sludge
~/ausgefaulter *(hyd)* [anaerobic] digested sludge
~/ausgeflockter *(hyd)* flocculated sludge
~/belebter (biologischer) *s.* ~/aktivierter
~ einer hochbelasteten Belebungsanlage *(hyd)* high-rate activated sludge
~/eingedickter 1. *(hyd)* concentrated sludge; 2. *s.* Dickschlamm
~/getrockneter *(hyd)* dried sludge
~/gewerblicher *(hyd)* commercial sludge
~/industrieller *(hyd)* industrial sludge
~/kommunaler *(hyd)* municipal [sewage] sludge
~/überschüssiger *(hyd)* excess [activated] sludge
Schlammablagerung *f (hyd)* sludge layer
Schlammablaß *m (hyd)* sludge blowdown (blow-off)
Schlammablaßleitung *f (hyd)* sludge blowdown (blow-off) line
Schlammablaßrohr *n (hyd)* sludge [drawoff] pipe
Schlammablaßschieber *m (hyd)* desludging valve
Schlammabnahme *f (hyd)* sludge pickup
Schlammabscheider *m* sludge pocket; *(petrol)* slurry settler
Schlammabscheidung *f s.* Schlammabtrennung
Schlammabsetzung *f (hyd)* sludge settling
Schlammabtrennung *f (hyd)* sludge separation
Schlammabzug *m (hyd)* sludge drawoff
Schlammalter *n (hyd)* sludge age
Schlämmanalyse *f* elutriation analysis
Schlammanfall *m (hyd)* amount (quantity) of sludge produced, sludge production [rate], solids generation rate
Schlammanreicherung *f* sludge concentration
Schlämmapparat *m* elutriator
Schlammart *f (hyd)* type of sludge
Schlammaufbereitung *f s.* Schlammkonditionierung
Schlammaufheizung *f (hyd)* sludge heating
Schlammausfaulung *f* sludge digestion
Schlammausräumung *f s.* Schlammberäumung
Schlammaustrag *m* sludge discharge
Schlammbehandlung *f (hyd)* sludge treatment (processing, handling), solids treatment (handling), solid waste handling
Schlammbeize *f (agric)* slurry [method of seed] treatment
Schlammbelastung *f (hyd)* 1. sludge loading; 2. food-to-microbial-mass ratio, food-to-microorganism ratio, F/M ratio, ratio of food to bacterial population
Schlammbelebung *f (hyd)* sludge activation
Schlammbelebungsanlage *f (hyd)* activated-sludge waste-treatment plant, activated-sludge plant (unit)
Schlammbelebungsverfahren *n (hyd)* activated-sludge method
Schlammberäumung *f (hyd)* sludge removal (withdrawal); sludge harvesting *(from sludge-drying beds)*
Schlammbeseitigung *f (hyd)* [waste] sludge disposal, solid waste disposal
Schlämmbeton *m* prepacked (grouted) concrete
Schlammbildung *f (hyd)* sludge formation
Schlammblockierungsmittel *n (min tech)* blinding agent
Schlammdecke *f (hyd)* blanket of sludge, sludge (fluidized) blanket
Schlammdichte *f (hyd)* sludge density
Schlammdurchsatz *m (hyd)* sludge throughput
Schlämme *f* slurry
Schlammeigenschaften *fpl (hyd)* sludge properties
Schlammeindickbecken *n (hyd)* sludge thickening tank
Schlammeindicker *m (hyd)* sludge thickener (concentrator)
~ mit Krählwerk picket-fence slow stirring sludge thickener
Schlammeindickung *f (hyd)* sludge thickening (concentration)
~ durch Druckflotation DAF thickening
Schlammeinleitung *f (hyd)* sludge feed
schlämmen to elutriate, to wash
Schlämmen *n* elutriation, washing
Schlammentnahme *f (hyd)* 1. sludge removal (withdrawal); 2. sludge outlet
Schlammentnahmerohr *n (hyd)* sludge [draw-off] pipe
Schlammentwässerung *f (hyd)* sludge dewatering
~ durch Vakuumfiltration vacuum-filter dewatering
~ durch Zentrifugation centrifuge dewatering *(of sludge)*
~ mittels Trockenbeeten sand-bed dewatering
Schlammentwässerungsbecken *n*, **Schlammentwässerungsteich** *m (hyd)* sludge[-holding] lagoon
Schlammentwicklung *f s.* Schlammbildung
Schlammerwärmung *f (hyd)* sludge heating
Schlammfang *m (hyd)* sludge pocket

Schlammfaulbehälter *m (hyd)* sludge digester (digestion tank)
Schlammfaulraum *m (hyd)* sludge-digester chamber (compartment)
Schlammfaulung *f (hyd)* sludge digestion
~/anaerobe anaerobic sludge digestion
Schlammfeststoffe *mpl (hyd)* sludge solids
Schlammfeststoffgehalt *m (hyd)* [dry] sludge solids
Schlammfilter *n* cake filter
Schlammfiltration *f* cake filtration, cake[-filter] operation
Schlammflocken *fpl (hyd)* sludge floc
Schlammflockung *f (hyd)* sludge flocculation
Schlammfluß *m (hyd)* sludge stream
Schlammfrosten *n (hyd)* freeze-thaw process
Schlammgehalt *m s.* Schlammkonzentration
Schlammgrube *f (petrol)* mud pit *(of a rotary-drilling installation)*
schlammig sludgy, muddy, slimy
Schlammigkeit *f* muddiness, sliminess
Schlammindex *m s.* Schlammvolumenindex
Schlamminhibitor *m* sludge dispersant, detergent
Schlammkaolin *m* washed kaolin, water-washed clay
Schlammkompostierung *f (hyd)* sludge composting, compost treatment of sludge
Schlammkonditionierung *f (hyd)* sludge conditioning
~/thermische sludge conditioning by heat treatment, pressure cooking treatment of sludge
Schlammkontakt *m (hyd)* sludge contact
Schlammkontaktanlage *f (hyd)* solids contact clarifier (unit)
~ mit Schlammwasserkreislauf slurry recirculation clarifier (unit)
Schlammkonzentrat *n* thickener pulp
Schlammkonzentration *f (hyd)* sludge (solids) concentration
~ im Belebungsbecken reactor solids concentration, tank concentration
~ im Rücklaufschlamm recycle sludge (solids) concentration
Schlammkratzer *m (hyd)* sludge scraper
Schlämmkreide *f* prepared (drop) chalk, prepared calcium carbonate, *(for technical purposes:)* whiting
Schlammkreislaufführung *f (hyd)* sludge recycle (return), solids recycle
Schlammkuchen *m (hyd)* sludge cake
Schlammlast *f (hyd)* sludge loading
Schlammöl *n (petrol)* slurry oil
Schlammorganismen *mpl (hyd)* [activated-]sludge organisms
Schlammproduktion *f (hyd)* sludge production (build-up), solids generation; sludge formation *(by microorganisms)*
Schlammpumpe *f* sludge (mud) pump, *(esp for useful suspensions:)* slurry pump; *(sugar)* scum pump
Schlammraum *m* dirt-holding space *(of a bowl centrifuge)*
Schlammräumer *m (hyd)* sludge collector
Schlammräumschild *m (hyd)* sludge-collection flight
Schlammräumung *f (hyd)* sludge removal (withdrawal); sludge harvesting *(from sludge-drying beds)*
Schlammräumvorrichtung *f (hyd)* sludge-removal device (facility)
Schlammrückführung *f (hyd)* sludge return, sludge (solids) recycle
Schlammrücklauf *m s.* Schlammrückführung
Schlammrücklaufverhältnis *n s.* Rücklaufschlammverhältnis
Schlammsaft *m (sugar)* carbonation (saturation) juice
~/erster first carbonation juice, scum juice
~/zweiter second carbonation juice
Schlammsammelschacht *m s.* Schlammsumpf
Schlammschicht *f (hyd)* sludge layer
Schlammschild *m s.* Schlammräumschild
Schlammspiegel *m (hyd)* solids level *(sedimentation)*
Schlammstabilisierung *f (hyd)* sludge stabilization
Schlammstein *m (geol)* mudstone
Schlammsumpf *m (hyd)* sludge storage sump, sludge well
Schlammsuppe *f* pregnant solution, strong liquor *(in thickeners)*
Schlammteich *m s.* Schlammentwässerungsbecken
Schlammteilchen *n (hyd)* sludge particle
Schlammteilchengröße *f (hyd)* sludge particle size
Schlammtrichter *m (hyd)* sludge hopper
Schlammtrockenbeet *n (hyd)* sludge [drying] bed, drying bed; sand [drying] bed; tile field
Schlammtrockensubstanz *f s.* Schlammfeststoffgehalt
Schlammtrocknung *f (hyd)* sludge drying
Schlammtrog *m* sludge trough (vat) *(of a vacuum drum filter)*
Schlammtrübe *f (hyd)* feed (water) slurry, feed sludge
Schlammüberlauf *m (min tech)* slime overflow
Schlammumwälzung *f (hyd)* 1. sludge mixing; 2. *s.* Schlammwasserkreislauf
Schlammveraschung *f*, **Schlammverbrennung** *f (hyd)* sludge incineration, combustion of sludge
Schlammverbrennungsofen *m (hyd)* sludge furnace
Schlammvolumen *n (hyd)* sludge volume, volume of sludge produced
~/sedimentiertes volume of MLSS (mixed-liquor suspended solids)
Schlammvolumenindex *m (hyd)* sludge volume index, SVI, Mohlman index
Schlammvorbehandlung *f s.* Schlammkonditionierung

Schlammwachstum *n (hyd)* sludge growth
Schlammwäsche *f*, **Schlammwaschung** *f (hyd)* sludge washing
Schlammwasser *n (hyd)* 1. supernatant, supernatant liquid (liquor, water), supernate; 2. backwash waste *(filter backwashing)*; 3. *s.* Schlammtrübe; 4. *s.* Faulwasser
Schlammwasserabscheidung *f*, **Schlammwasserabzug** *m (hyd)* supernatant draw-off, separation of supernatant
Schlammwasserkreislauf *m (hyd)* slurry recirculation *(sludge contact clarifier)*
Schlammzone *f (hyd)* sludge zone *(sludge thickening)*
Schlammzufluß *m (hyd)* sludge flow
Schlammzulaufgeschwindigkeit *f (hyd)* sludge feed rate
Schlammzuwachs *m (hyd)* sludge growth
Schlange *f (tech)* coil
Schlangengift *n* snake venom
Schlangenhautglasur *f (ceram)* snakeskin glaze
Schlangenkühler *m* coil (coiled-tube) condenser
Schlangenrohr *n* coiled tube, coil
Schlangenrohrwärmeübertrager *m* coiled tubular [heat] exchanger, coil heat exchanger
Schlangenwärmeaustauscher *m s.* Schlangenrohrwärmeübertrager
Schlappgurt *m* slack belt
Schlauch *m* hose, *(without textile casing:)* tubing; *(filtr)* bag
~/geklöppelter braided hose
~ mit Gewebeeinlage reinforced hose
Schlauchabscheider *m s.* Schlauchfilter
Schlauchbandförderer *m* closed-belt conveyor
Schlaucheinzelheizer *m (rubber)* unit vulcanizer for tubes
Schlaucherdecke *f (ferm)* yeast head
Schlauchfilter *n* bag filter, *(gas cleaning also)* bag (cloth-tube) collector
Schlauchfolie *f (plast)* blown tubing, tubular film, *(if slit:)* blown film
Schlauchkammerfilter *n* bag (cloth-tube) collector *(for gas cleaning)*
Schlauchklemme *f* pinchcock, hose cock, pinch clamp
~ nach Hoffmann Hoffmann clamp, Bunsen screw clip
~ nach Mohr Mohr pinchcock (clip)
Schlauchmaterial *n* **für Gasbrenner** burner tubing
Schlauch[quetsch]pumpe *f* flow inducer
Schlauchschelle *f* hose clamp (clip)
Schlauchseele *f (rubber)* inner tube
Schlauchspritzmaschine *f* tube-extruding (tube-extrusion) press
Schlauchspritzmundstück *n* die for tubing
Schlauchstück *n* piece of tubing
Schlauchtülle *f* hose connector
Schlauchventil *n* pinch valve
Schlauchverbindung *f* hose connection
Schlauchverbindungsstück *n* hose coupling (connection, connector)
Schlaufe *f (bioch)* hairpin loop *(of hydrogen bonds)*
Schlaufenfermenter *m (biot)* loop-type fermenter, tubular loop reactor
Schlaufenreaktor *m* loop (recycle) reactor, tubular loop reactor
schleichend wirkend *(tox)* slow-acting
Schleier *m* 1. *(phot)* fog, haze; 2. *(coat)* bloom
~/dichroitischer dichroic fog
Schleierbildung *f* 1. *(phot)* fogging; 2. *(coat)* blooming
Schleierdichte *f (phot)* fog density
schleierfrei, schleierlos *(phot)* fog-free
schleiern *(phot)* to fog
Schleierschwärzung *f s.* Schleier 1.
Schleierverhinderung *f*, **Schleierverhütung** *f (phot)* fog prevention (inhibition)
Schleifabnutzung *f* abrasive wear
schleifbar grindable
Schleifbarkeit *f* grindability
Schleifdruck *m (pap)* grinding pressure
schleifen to grind, *(finely:)* to polish; to buff *(leather)*
Schleifendosierung *f (chromat)* loop flushing
Schleifer *m (pap)* grinder
~/stetiger continuous grinder
Schleiferei *f (pap)* 1. grinder house (room); 2. *s.* Schleifereibetrieb
Schleifereibetrieb *m (pap)* groundwood mill, [mechanical] pulp mill
Schleiferstein *m (pap)* grindstone, pulpstone, abrasive stone
Schleifertrog *m (pap)* grinder pit
Schleiffläche *f (pap)* grinding surface (area)
Schleifholz *n (pap)* pulp wood
Schleifmaschine *f* grinding machine, grinder; *(tann)* buffing machine
Schleifmasse *f (pap)* mechanical [wood-]pulp, M.W.P., mechanical wood, groundwood [pulp]
Schleifmittel *n* abrasive [material, medium], grinding abrasive
Schleiföl *n* grinding oil
Schleifpapier *n* abrasive paper
Schleifpulver *n* abrasive powder
Schleifrohpapier *n* abrasive body paper
Schleifscheibe *f* grinding (abrasive) wheel
Schleifstein *m* grindstone, pulpstone, abrasive stone
Schleifzone *f s.* Schleiffläche
Schleim *m (tech)* slime; *(bot, pharm)* mucilage
Schleimansammlung *f (pap)* accumulation of slime
Schleimappretur *f (tann)* mucilage dressing
schleimartig *s.* schleimig
Schleimbatzen *m s.* Schleimansammlung
Schleimbekämpfung *f (pap, biot)* slime control
Schleimbildung *f (tech)* slime formation; *(bot)* mucilage formation
Schleimfleck *m* slime spot *(a defect in paper)*
schleimhaltig *(bot, pharm)* mucilaginous

schleimig *(tech)* slimy; *(bot, pharm)* mucilaginous
Schleimigkeit *f (tech)* sliminess
Schleimkontrolle *f s.* Schleimbekämpfung
Schleimsäure *f* mucic acid, galactosaccharic acid
Schleimstoff *m*, **Schleimsubstanz** *f (tech)* slimy substance (material); *(bot, pharm)* mucilaginous substance
Schleimverhütungsmittel *n (pap)* slimicide
Schlempe *f (ceram)* slip; *(ferm)* stillage, [distillery] slop, vinasse, spent wash
schleppend sluggish *(reaction)*
Schlepper *m s.* Schleppmittel
Schleppgas *n* carrier gas *(gas chromatography)*
Schleppkettenförderer *m* chain conveyor
~ **mit Rollen** roller-chain conveyor
Schleppklingenstreichmaschine *f (pap)* trailing blade coater
Schlepplöffelbagger *m* dragline [excavator]
Schleppmittel *n (distil)* entrainer, entraining (azeotroping, separating) agent, azeotrope former
Schlepprakelstreichmaschine *f (pap)* trailing blade coater
Schleppschaufelbagger *m* dragline [excavator]
Schleppströmung *f (plast)* drag flow *(in extruders)*
Schleuder *f* centrifuge, *(tech esp for filtering:)* centrifugal *(for compounds s.* Zentrifuge*)*
Schleuderbeton *m* centrifugally cast concrete, centrifugal (spun) concrete
Schleuderdüngerstreuer *m* centrifugal fertilizer distributor
Schleudereffekt *m s.* Schleuderzahl
Schleuderformmaschine *f (met)* sandslinger
Schleudergießverfahren *n (met)* centrifugal-casting process; *(plast)* centrifugal-moulding process
Schleuderguß *m (met)* centrifugal casting; *(plast)* centrifugal moulding
Schleudergußrohr *n* centrifugally cast pipe
Schleudergußteil *n (met)* centrifugal casting; *(plast)* centrifugal moulding
Schleuderkraftabscheider *m* centrifugal collector (separator)
Schleudermaschine *f (met)* sandslinger
Schleudermühle *f* cage (squirrel-cage) disintegrator (mill), centrifugal (bar) mill; *(pap)* chip crusher (breaker), rechipper
schleudern to centrifuge, to centrifugate; *(for drying:)* to hydroextract, to whiz
Schleudern *n* centrifuging, centrifugation; *(for drying:)* hydroextraction, whizzing
Schleuderscheibe *f* centrifugal disk
Schleudersortierer *m (pap)* centrifugal strainer, erkensator *(for cleaning the stock)*
Schleuderstreuer *m* centrifugal fertilizer distributor
Schleudertrockner *m* hydroextractor, whizzer
Schleuderverfahren *n* 1. gas centrifuge process *(for separating isotopes)*; 2. centrifugal process *(fibre-glass manufacturing)*; 3. *s.* Schleudergießverfahren
Schleuderzahl *f* relative centrifugal force *(of a centrifuge)*
Schleuse *f* 1. sluice; [air] lock; 2. *(bioch)* shuttle [system]
Schleusengas *n* lock gas
Schlichtanlage *f (text)* sizing machine
Schlichtbaum *m (tann)* perch
Schlichte *f (text)* size, sizing [material, substance], dressing
~/haftmittelfreie textile size
~/haftmittelhaltige reinforcement size
~/textile textile size
Schlichteauftragvorrichtung *f (text)* sizing pad
Schlichtebad *n*, **Schlichteflotte** *f (text)* sizing bath
Schlichtekocher *m (text)* size cooker
Schlichtemittel *n s.* Schlichte
schlichten 1. *(text)* to size, to dress, to slash; 2. *(tann)* to perch
Schlichtmaschine *f (text)* sizing machine, slasher
Schlick *m* slime, mud, *(esp geol)* ooze
Schlicker *m* 1. *(ceram)* slip, slop, slurry; 2. *(tann)* slicker
~/flüssiger *(ceram)* liquid slip
~/glasartiger *(ceram)* vitreous slip
Schlickergießen *n (ceram, met)* slip casting
Schlickerglasur *f (ceram)* slip glaze
Schlickerguß *m (ceram, met)* slip casting
Schlickerofen *m (ceram)* slip kiln
Schlickerschicht *f (ceram)* slip coating
Schlickerverfahren *n (ceram)* slip (wet) process
Schliere *f (glass)* stria, vein, cord; *(plast)* stria; *(geol)* streak; schliere *(in a fluid)*
Schlierenaufnahme *f* schlieren photo[graph]
Schlierenbild *n* schlieren picture
Schlierenbildung *f (glass, plast)* striation
Schlierenfotografie *f* schlieren photography
Schlierengerät *n* schlieren apparatus
Schlierenoptik *f* schlieren optics
Schlierenverfahren *n* schlieren method
~/Toeplersches Toepler schlieren method
Schlierigkeit *f* cordiness *(a defect in glass)*
Schließdruck *m (plast)* clamping pressure, [mould-]locking pressure
schließen:
~ **lassen auf** *(anal)* to be suggestive of
~/sich zum Ring to cyclize
schließend/dicht tight-fitting
Schließring *m (plast)* locking ring
Schließweg *m (plast)* closing travel *(of a press)*
Schließzeitbestimmung *f (plast)* cup flow test, flow cup test
Schliff *m* 1. grinding, *(glass also)* cutting; 2. *(result:)* cut *(of glass or gems)*; 3. *(substance:)* grindings; *(pap)* groundwood; section *(of rocks for microscopy)*; 4. *s.* Schliffverbindung
~/chemischer *(pap)* chemigroundwood
Schliffball *m s.* Schliffkugel
Schlifffläche *f* ground surface
Schliffgeräte *npl (lab)* ground-glass equipment

Schliffhahn *m (lab)* ground-in stopcock
Schliffhülse *f (lab)* socket, female tapered joint
Schliffkern *m (lab)* cone, male tapered joint
Schliffkette *f (lab)* chain of joints
Schliffkolben *m (lab)* ground-glass flask
Schliffkugel *f (lab)* ball, male spherical joint
Schliffpfanne *f (lab)* socket, female spherical joint
Schliffschale *f s.* Schliffpfanne
Schliffstopfen *m (lab)* ground[-glass] stopper
• **mit** ~ ground-stoppered
Schliffverbindung *f (lab)* ground[-glass] joint
Schlitz *m* slit, slot
Schlitzaufsatz *m s.* Schlitzbrenneraufsatz
Schlitzbreite *f* slot width
Schlitzbrenner *m* bats-wing (flat-flame, fish-tail) burner
Schlitzbrenneraufsatz *m* burner wing top (tip), flat burner head, [burner] flame spreader
Schlitzbrennerdüse *f* wing tip
Schlitzdüse *f* slot nozzle
Schlitzform *f s.* Breitschlitzdüse
Schlitzglocke *f (distil)* slotted cap
Schlitzsiebnutsche *f (lab)* slit-sieve funnel
Schlot *m* [smoke]stack, chimney
Schluff *m* silt *(grain size 0.02 to 0.002 mm)*
Schlumberger-Methode *f* Schlumberger method *(for measuring oil wells)*
Schlupf *m* slip[page]
Schlüpffaktor *m (biol)* hatching factor *(root excretion causing hatching of nematodes)*
Schluß *m* closure *(as of rings)*
Schlußanstrich *m (coat)* 1. finish[ing] *(act)*; 2. finish[ing] coat, finish, top coat[ing], topcoat, cover coat[ing] *(result)*
Schlußbütte *f (dye)* final vat
Schlüsselatom *n* key atom *(for polarizing a molecule)*
Schlüsselenzym *n (biot)* key enzyme
Schlüsselfrequenz *f (spectr)* group frequency
Schlüsselintermediäre *n (bioch)* key (crucial) intermediate
Schlüsselkomponente *f (distil)* key [component]
~/höhersiedende heavy key
~/niedrigsiedende light key
Schlüsselreaktion *f* key reaction
Schlüssel-Schloß-Beziehung *f (bioch)* lock-and-key relationship
Schlüssel-Schloß-Theorie *f* lock-and-key theory, lock-key hypothesis *(of enzyme action)*
Schlüsselspezies *f* key species
Schlüsselstoff *m* key chemical
Schlüsselsubstanz *f* 1. key substance; 2. *s.* Schlüsselintermediäre
Schlüsselverbindung *f s.* Schlüsselintermediäre
Schlußkupplung *f (dye)* final coupling
Schlußreinigung *f (hyd)* final [effluent] treatment
schmackhaft palatable, tasty
Schmackhaftigkeit *f* palatability, tastiness
Schmalte *f* smalt, powder blue *(cobalt(II) potassium silicate)*
Schmalz *n* melted (rendered) fat, *(esp)* lard, pig fat
Schmälze *f* 1. *(text)* spinning oil, lubricant, lube; 2. *(glass)* binder
schmälzen *(text)* to oil, to lubricate
Schmälzmittel *n s.* Schmälze
Schmälznebel *m (glass)* binder spray
Schmalzöl *n* lard oil
Schmälzöl *n (text)* spinning oil
schmauchen *(ceram)* to water-smoke
Schmauchfeuer *n (ceram)* prefire
Schmauchperiode *f (ceram)* water-smoking period
schmecken to taste
schmeckend/unangenehm ill-tasting
Schmelzaufschluß *m (anal)* opening-up by fusion
Schmelzausdehnung *f* melting dilatation
Schmelzausdehnungskurve *f* melting dilatation curve
Schmelzbad *n* molten bath
schmelzbar fusible, meltable
Schmelzbarkeit *f* fusibility, meltability
Schmelzbarren *m* ingot *(in zone melting)*
Schmelzbereich *m* melting range
Schmelzbeschichten *n (text)* flame lamination
Schmelzbruch *m* melt fracture
Schmelzbutter *f s.* Butterschmalz
Schmelzdiagramm *n* melting[-point] diagram
Schmelzdilatation *f* melting dilatation
Schmelze *f* 1. melt, fusion; *(met)* smelt; molten bath *(for treating or coating)*; *(geol)* fused (molten) rock; liquid *(zone melting)*; 2. *s.* Schmelzen
~/alkalische molten alkali [bath]
Schmelzelektrolyse *f s.* Schmelzflußelektrolyse
schmelzen to melt, to fuse; *(met)* to smelt *(ore)*; *(food)* to render *(fat)*; to thaw *(of ice)*; *(bioch)* to melt out *(of deoxyribonucleic acid)*
~/auf Stein *(met)* to matte-smelt
~/mit Flußmitteln to flux
Schmelzen *n* melting, fusion; *(met)* smelting *(of ore)*; *(food)* rendering *(of fat)*; thawing *(of ice)*; *(bioch)* melting-out *(of DNA)*
~ **auf Stein** *(met)* matte smelting
~/autogenes *(met)* autogenous smelting
~/direktes *(met)* direct smelting
~ **mit Alkali** alkali[ne] fusion
~ **mit alkoholischem Kaliumhydroxid** *(dye)* fusion with alcoholic potassium hydroxide
~ **mit Flußmitteln** fluxing
~/pyritisches *(met)* pyritic smelting
~/unmittelbares *(met)* direct smelting
~ **unter Vakuum** vacuum melting *(of metals for refining or alloying)*
schmelzend/scharf sharp-melting
Schmelzenthalpie *f* enthalpy of fusion (melting)
Schmelzentropie *f* entropy of fusion (melting)
Schmelzer *m (met)* smelter; melter *(foundry)*; *(glass)* teaser, founder, melter
Schmelzextraktor *m (plast)* melt extractor *(of a plunger-type injection machine)*
Schmelzfarbe *f (ceram)* enamel (vitrifiable) colour, overglaze (fused-on) colour

Schmelzfeuerung *f* slag-tap (wet-bottom) furnace *(with separation of slag in a molten condition)*
Schmelzfluß *m* melt fusion; *(met)* smelting flux, smelt; *(geol)* fused (molten) rock
Schmelzflußelektrolyse *f* fused-salt (molten-salt) electrolysis
schmelzflüssig molten
Schmelzformen *n (ceram)* fusion casting
Schmelzgefäß *n s.* Schmelzkessel
Schmelzgießen *n (ceram)* fusion casting
Schmelzgut *n* material being *or* to be melted; molten material; *(met)* material being *or* to be smelted; smelted material
Schmelzharz *n* cast[ing] resin
Schmelzhütte *f (met)* smelting plant
Schmelzindex *m (plast)* melt [flow] index, M.F.I.
Schmelzintervall *n* melting range
Schmelzkäse *m* process[ed] cheese
Schmelzkatalysator *m* fused catalyst
Schmelzkegel *m (ceram)* pyrometric (fusion) cone
~ nach Seger Seger cone
Schmelzkegeläquivalent *n (ceram)* pyrometric-cone equivalent, PCE
Schmelzkessel *m* melting pot (vessel)
Schmelzkleber *m*, **Schmelzklebstoff** *m* hot-melt adhesive
Schmelzkondensation *f* melt condensation
Schmelzkurve *f* melting curve
Schmelzling *m* ingot *(in zone melting)*
Schmelzlöser *m (pap)* [smelt] dissolving tank, dissolving chest, dissolver
Schmelzmargarine *f* rendered margarine, margarine fat
Schmelzmittel *n* fluxing agent, flux
Schmelzofen *m* melting furnace, melter; *(met)* smelting furnace, smelter
~/vollelektrisch beheizter all-electric furnace
~ zur Verbrennung der Schwarzlauge *(pap)* recovery furnace
Schmelzpfanne *f* fusion pan, melt[ing] pan
Schmelzprodukt *n* product of fusion
Schmelzpunkt *m* melting point, m.p. • **mit hohem ~** high-melting[-point], high-fusion • **mit niedrigem ~** low-melting[-point], low-fusion[-point]
Schmelzpunktapparat *m* melting-point apparatus
~ nach Thiele Thiele melting-point tube
Schmelzpunktbad *n* melting-point bath
Schmelzpunktbestimmung *f* melting-point determination
Schmelzpunktbestimmungsapparat *m s.* Schmelzpunktapparat
Schmelzpunktdepression *f* melting-point depression (lowering)
Schmelzpunktkapillare *f*, **Schmelzpunktröhrchen** *n* melting-point capillary (tube)
Schmelzpunktserniedrigung *f s.* Schmelzpunktdepression
Schmelzraum *m (glass)* melting end (chamber), melter
Schmelzsoda *f (pap)* [soda] smelt, black ash
Schmelzspinnanlage *f* melt spinning line
Schmelzspinnen *n* melt spinning (extrusion)
Schmelzspinnverbundstoff *m (text)* spun-bonded product
Schmelztauchaluminieren *n* hot-dip aluminizing
Schmelztauchen *n (coat)* hot-melt coating
Schmelztauchmasse *f (coat)* hot melt (hot-dip) coating
Schmelztauchverzinken *n* hot-dip galvanizing
Schmelzteil *m s.* Schmelzraum
Schmelztemperatur *f* melting temperature, *(glass, plast also)* Tm point
Schmelztiegel *m* melting crucible, *(esp lab)* ignition (fusion) crucible
~ nach Rose Rose crucible
Schmelztiegelzange *f (lab)* crucible tongs
Schmelzvergasung *f (met)* gassing
Schmelzviskosität *f* melting viscosity
Schmelzwanne *f* melting tank, melter, *(glass also)* melting chamber (end)
Schmelzwärme *f* heat of fusion (melting)
Schmelzzone *f* melting zone; *(met)* smelting zone; molten zone *(in zone melting)*
Schmelzzonenbreite *f* zone width *(in zone melting)*
Schmelzzonenlänge *f* zone length *(in zone melting)*
Schmelzzonenrichtung *f* direction of zoning (zone travel) *(in zone melting)*
schmerzlindernd pain-reducing, pain-relieving, analgesic
Schmerzlinderungsmittel *n* pain-reliever, analgesic
schmerzstillend analgesic
Schmidt-Reaktion *f* Schmidt reaction *(between hydrazoic acid and carbonyl compounds)*
schmiedbar *(met)* forgeable
Schmiedbarkeit *f (met)* forgeability
Schmiedekohle *f* fat coal *(proper)*
Schmiedemessing *n* forging brass *(containing 60 % Cu, 38 % Zn, and 2 % Pb)*
schmieden *(met)* to forge
Schmiedeofen *m (met)* forging furnace
Schmiere *f s.* Schmierstoff
Schmiereigenschaften *fpl* lubricating properties (characteristics)
schmieren to lubricate *(e.g. a machine with oil)*; *(tann)* to oil, to stuff, to dub; to smear *(of a substance)*
~/auf der Tafel *(tann)* to dub
Schmierergiebigkeit *f s.* Schmiergüte
Schmierfähigkeit *f* lubricity, lubricating ability
Schmierfähigkeitsverbesserer *m* lubricity additive
Schmierfett *n* lubricating grease
Schmierflüssigkeit *f* lubricating fluid
Schmiergüte *f* oiliness *(of a lubricating oil)*
schmierig greasy, unctuous *(substance)*, *(esp relating to surfaces:)* slippery; *(pap)* wet, slow, soft *(pulp)*
Schmierigkeit *f* greasiness, unctuousness *(of a substance)*, *(esp relating to surfaces:)* slipperiness; *(pap)* wetness, slowness, softness

Schmierigmahlung *f (pap)* wet (slow) beating
Schmiermittel *n s.* Schmierstoff
Schmieröl *n* lubricating (lube) oil
~ **auf Erdölbasis** petroleum lubricating oil
~**/dunkles** black oil
Schmierölausgangsstoff *m* lubricating[-oil] stock
Schmieröldestillat *n* lubricating-oil distillate
Schmierölextrakt *m* lubricating-oil extract
Schmierölfraktion *f* lubricating-oil fraction
Schmierölraffination *f* lubricating-oil refining
Schmierseife *f* soft soap
Schmierstelle *f (plast)* smudge *(on injection-moulded parts)*
Schmierstoff *m* lubricant, lubricating agent, lube
Schmierstoffschicht *f* lubricating film
Schmierung *f* lubrication
Schmierwert *m s.* Schmiergüte
Schmierwirkung *f* lubricating (lubricant) action
Schminkrot *n* rouge
Schminkweiß *n* pearl (bismuth, Spanish) white, cosmetic bismuth *(bismuth chloride oxide)*
Schmirgel *m* emery
Schmirgelleinen *n* emery cloth
Schmirgelpapier *n* emery paper
Schmutz *m* dirt, soil, grime
~**/künstlicher** *(text)* artificial soil
~**/standardisierter** *(text)* standard soil
schmutzabstoßend, schmutzabweisend dirt-repellent, soil-repellent, antisoiling
Schmutzbelag *m (hyd, filtr)* schmutzdecke, deck of turbidity, mat
Schmutzbelastung *f s.* Schmutzstoffbelastung
schmutzen to soil
Schmutzentfernungsvermögen *n (text)* soil removing capacity
Schmutzfang *m*, **Schmutzfänger** *m (pap)* dirt (junk) remover
Schmutzfleck *m* soil, spot, smear, smudge; *(pap)* dirt speck
Schmutzflotte *f (text)* used detergent solution
Schmutzgehalt *m* 1. dirt content *(as of paper)*; 2. *s.* Schmutzstoffgehalt
Schmutzhaftung *f (text)* soil adherence
schmutzig dirty
Schmutzlast *f s.* Schmutzstoffbelastung
Schmutzlösevermögen *n (text)* soil removing capacity
Schmutzmenge *f (hyd)* amount of pollutant
Schmutzraum *m* dirt-holding space *(of a sedimentation centrifuge)*
Schmutzrückhaltevermögen *n* power of holding dirt *(of detergents)*
Schmutzschleuse *f (pap)* dirt (junk) remover
Schmutzstoff *m* contaminant, soil, *(esp in environment:)* pollutant, polluting matter; *(pap)* junk *(for compounds s.* Schmutzstoffe*)*
Schmutzstoffanteil *m s.* Schmutzstoffgehalt
Schmutzstoffbelastung *f (hyd)* contaminant load[-ing], load of contamination, pollutant (polluting) load
~ **des Betriebsabwassers** plant effluent load[ing]
Schmutzstoffe *mpl*:
• **mit Schmutzstoffen belastet** polluted, contaminated *(water, air)*
~**/anthropogene** human[-caused] pollutants
~**/gelöste** dissolved solid pollutants
~**/im Ablauf verbleibende organische** *(hyd)* residual organic content
~ **im Grundwasser** ground-water pollutants
~ **im Oberflächenwasser** surface-water pollutants
~ **im Wasser** water impurities, water pollutants (contaminants)
~ **in der Luft** atmospheric contaminants
~**/organische** organic contaminants (pollutants), organics
~**/restliche organische** *(hyd)* residual organic content
~**/suspendierte** suspended solid pollutants
Schmutzstoffelimination *f*, **Schmutzstoffentfernung** *f* contaminant removal
schmutzstofffrei free from polluting substances *(water, air)*
Schmutzstoffgehalt *m* pollutant level, level of pollutants
~ **des Abwassers** strength of sewage
Schmutzstoffkonzentration *f* contaminant (pollutant) concentration
Schmutzstofflast *f s.* Schmutzstoffbelastung
Schmutztragevermögen *n* dirt-suspending (soil-suspending) power *(of detergents)*
Schmutzwasser *n* sewage, dirty water, slops
Schmutzwasseranfall *m* sewage [in]flow
Schmutzwasserkanal *m* sanitary sewer
Schmutzwasserkanalisation *f* sewerage [system]
Schmutzwasserleitung *f* sewer line
Schmutzwassermenge *f* volume of sewage
Schmutzwasserorganismen *mpl* sewage organisms
Schmutzwasserpumpe *f* sewage pump
Schmutzwolle *f* raw (grease) wool
Schnauze *f* spout *(as of a beaker)*
Schnecke *f (tech)* 1. screw, scroll, worm; 2. *s.* Schneckenförderer
~ **mit Meteringzone** *(plast)* metering screw *(of an extruder)*
~**/tiefgeschnittene** *(plast)* deep-cut screw *(of an extruder)*
Schneckenaufgabegerät *n* screw (worm) feeder
Schneckenaustragzentrifuge *f* helical-conveyor centrifuge
Schneckenbekämpfungsmittel *n* mollus[ca]cide
Schneckendrehzahl *f* screw speed
Schnecken-Filtrierzentrifuge *f* screen-conveyor centrifuge
Schneckenförderer *m* screw (worm) conveyor, spiral (helical) conveyor
Schneckengang *m* screw flight
Schneckengetriebe *n* worm gear
Schneckenkneter *m* screw mixer

Schneckenkompressor *m* screw compressor
Schneckenmischer *m* screw mixer
~/senkrechter vertical screw mixer
Schneckenpresse *f* screw press (extruder); *(ceram)* [extrusion] auger
Schneckenpumpe *f* screw pump
Schneckenrührer *m* screw mixer
Schneckenschleuder *f* helical-conveyor centrifuge
Schnecken-Siebzentrifuge *f* screen-conveyor centrifuge
Schneckenspeiser *m* screw (worm) feeder
Schneckenspritzgießmaschine *f (plast)* screw injection [moulding] machine
Schneckenstrangpresse *f s.* Schneckenpresse
Schneckentrieb *m* worm gear
Schneckentrockner *m* screw-conveyor dryer
Schneckenverdichter *m* screw compressor
Schneckenvertilgungsmittel *n* mollus[ca]cide
Schneckenvorplastizierung *f (plat)* screw pre-plastication
Schneckenwelle *f* worm shaft
Schneckenzentrifuge *f* helical conveyor centrifuge
Schneidapparat *m* cutter
schneidbar cuttable, *(esp min)* sectile
Schneidbarkeit *f* cuttability, *(esp min)* sectility
Schneidbrenner *m* cutting torch, cutting (dissecting) blowpipe
Schneide *f* knife edge *(as of an analytical balance)*
Schneide... *s. a.* Schneid...
Schneidegranulator *m* rotary cutter
schneiden to cut
~/autogen to cut autogenously
~/Elementarfäden auf Stapel *(text)* to staple
~/in Würfel to dice
~/von der Walze to cut (slab) off *(rubber sheet)*
Schneiden *n***/autogenes** autogenous (oxygen) cutting
Schneider *m s.* 1. Schneidvorrichtung; 2. Schneidmaschine
Schneidflüssigkeit *f* cutting fluid
Schneidkeramik *f* cutting ceramics
Schneidkonverterverfahren *n (text)* tow-to-top cutting system
Schneidmahlung *f (pap)* free beating
Schneidmaschine *f* cutting machine, cutter
Schneidmühle *f* cutting mill
Schneidöl *n* cutting oil
~/wasserlösliches soluble cutting oil
Schneidringverbindung *f*, **Schneidringverschraubung** *f* bite-type fitting joint
Schneidvorrichtung *f* cutting device
Schnellanalyse *f* rapid analysis
schnellaufend high-speed
Schnelläufer *m* high-speed (fast-running) machine
Schnellaufschluß *m (pap)* fast pulping
Schnellaufzahl *f* specific speed *(as of a pump)*
Schnellbestimmung *f* rapid determination
schnellbindend rapid-hardening, fast-setting *(e.g. cement)*
Schnellbleiche *f* quick bleach
schnellbleichend quick-bleaching
Schnelldämpfen *n (text)* flash ageing
Schnelldämpfer *m (text)* flash ager
Schnellentwickler *m (phot)* rapid (high-speed) developer
Schnellessigverfahren *n (food)* quick vinegar process, German process
Schnellfilter *n* rapid (fast) filter, high-rate filter, HRF
~/geschlossenes rapid pressure filter, pressure rapid filter
~/offenes rapid gravity filter
Schnellfiltration *f* rapid filtration, fast (high-rate) filtration
Schnellfixierbad *n (phot)* rapid (high-speed) fixing bath, rapid fixer
Schnellfixierung *f (phot)* rapid fixing
Schnellgefrieranlage *f* quick-freezing plant
Schnellgefrierapparat *m* quick-freezer
schnellgefrieren *(food)* to quick-freeze
Schnellgerbung *f* rapid (accelerated) tannage
schnellhärtend *(plast)* quick-curing, fast-curing; quick-hardening *(paint)*; quick-setting *(adhesive)*
Schnellkochung *f (pap)* quick cook
Schnellmethode *f (pharm)* quick-assay method
Schnellmischung *f* rapid mix[ing], high intensity mixing
Schnellpökeln *n*, **Schnellpökelung** *f (food)* quick curing, short (injection) cure
Schnellpreßmasse *f (plast)* quick-curing moulding compound
Schnellpyrolyse *f* fast pyrolysis
schnellrotierend *s.* schnellumlaufend
Schnellrührbehälter *m (hyd)* rapid-mix tank
Schnellrühren *n* rapid mix[ing], high-intensity mixing
Schnellrührphase *f (hyd)* rapid-mix period, rapid mixing step *(flocculation)*
Schnellsandfilter *n* rapid sand filter
Schnellsandfiltration *f* rapid sand filtration
Schnellscan *m (spectr)* rapid scan
Schnellschlußventil *n* quick-operating valve
Schnellschreiber *m* high-speed recorder
Schnellspaltung *f (nucl)* fast (high-energy) fission
Schnellspaltungseffekt *m (nucl)* fast [fission] effect
Schnelltest *m s.* Schnellversuch
schnelltrocknend quick-drying, rapid-drying, fast-drying
Schnelltrocknung *f* quick (rapid) drying, fast (high-speed) drying
schnellumlaufend spinning, high-speed
Schnellverband *m* [sticking] plaster, adhesive bandage
Schnellverdampfer *m* flash evaporator, flasher
Schnellverfahren *n* rapid process
Schnellversuch *m* rapid test; *(pharm)* quick (short-time) assay
schnellvulkanisierend *(rubber)* quick-curing, fast-curing
Schnellwaage *f* fast-weighing balance

schnellwirkend quick-acting
Schnitt *m* 1. cut; [micro]section *(microscopy)*; 2. *(distil)* cut
Schnittbrenner *m s.* Schlitzbrenner
Schnittnarbe *f* shear mark *(a defect in glass)*
Schnittwachstum *n (rubber)* cut growth
Schnitzel *npl s.* 1. Kochschnitzel; 2. Zuckerrübenschnitzel; 3. Schnitzelmaterial
Schnitzelmaterial *n (plast)* macerate *(filler)*
schnitzeln to chop
Schnitzelpreßmasse *f (plast)* macerate moulding compound
Schnitzelpreßwasser *n (sugar)* [beet-]pulp press water
Schnitzelpumpe *f (sugar)* [beet-]pulp pump
Schnitzeltrocknung *f (sugar)* [beet-]pulp drying
Schnupftabak *m* snuff[ing] tobacco
Schnurabnahme *f*, **Schnürenabnahme** *f (filtr)* string discharge
Schnurfang *m (pap)* string catcher
Schockgefrieren *n* rapid (quick) freezing
Schokolade *f* chocolate
Schollenlack *m s.* Schellack
Schöllkopf-Säure *f* Schöllkopf acid *(1. $NH_2C_{10}H_5SO_3H$ naphth-1-ylamine-8-sulphonic acid; 2. $HOC_{10}H_5(SO_3H)_2$ naphth-1-ol-4,8-disulphonic acid)*
Schöne *f s.* Schönungsmittel
schönen *(ferm)* to fine; *(hyd)* to polish *(treated waste water)*
schonend mild *(e.g. oxidation)*
Schönheitsmittel *n* cosmetic, [make-up] preparation
Schönherr-Verfahren *n* Schönherr process *(for fixing atmospheric nitrogen)*
Schönseite *f* top (felt) side *(of paper)*
Schönung *f (ferm)* fining; *(hyd)* polishing *(of treated waste water)*
Schönungsgas *n (chromat)* make-up gas
Schönungsmittel *n (ferm)* fining [agent]
Schönungsteich *m (hyd)* polishing lagoon (pond)
Schöpfbecherwerk *n* scooping bucket elevator
Schöpfbütte *f (pap)* dipping (working) vat
schöpfen *(pap)* to dip out, to mould
Schöpfer *m* 1. *(pap)* dipper, vatman, moulder; 2. *(pap)* dipper *(apparatus)*
Schöpfform *f (pap)* [hand] mould, paper-mould
Schöpfgefäß *n* dipper, scoop
~ **für Chemikalien** chemical dipper
~ **für Probenentnahme** *(hyd)* water sampler
Schöpfkelle *f (glass)* ladle
Schöpfpapier *n* vat (hand-made) paper
Schöpfpapiermuster *n (pap)* pulp (test, hand) sheet
Schöpfprobe *f (glass)* spoon proof
Schöpfrad *n* flighted wheel
Schöpfrahmen *m* deckle, hand-mould, [paper-] mould
Schöpfrand *m (pap)* deckle [edge] • **mit** ~ deckled
Schöpfwerk *n* scooping bucket elevator
Schopper-Dalen-Maschine *f (rubber)* Schopper machine
Schörl *m (min)* schorl, shorl, schorlite *(a cyclosilicate)*
Schornstein *m* chimney, [smoke]stack; *(lab)* burner chimney
~ **zum Anlassen** starting stack *(of a FluoSolids reactor)*
Schornsteinaufsatz *m (lab)* burner chimney
Schornsteinhöhe *f*/**effektive** effective chimney (stack) height
Schornsteinzug *m* draught, chimney pull
Schotten-Baumann-Reaktion *f* Schotten Baumann reaction *(of acid chlorides with alcohols or amines)*
Schotter *m* gravel
Schrägaufzug *m* inclined hoist
Schrägbecherwerk *n* inclined bucket elevator
Schrägbeziehung *f* diagonal relationship (similarity) *(in the periodic system)*
Schrägblattrührer *m* pitched-blade turbine
Schrägbrücke *f* hoist bridge
~ **mit Kippkübel** skip bridge *(of a blast furnace)*
Schrägrinne *f* trough washer
Schrägrohrverdampfer *m* inclined evaporator
Schrägrost *m* sloping grate
Schrägsitzventil *n* inclined-seat valve, Y valve
Schrägspritzkopf *m (plast)* angular extruder head
Schrapper *m* scraper
Schraubenachse *f (cryst)* screw axis
schraubenförmig spiral, helical
Schraubenformstück *n* screwed fitting
Schraubenklassierer *m* spiral classifier
Schraubenkompressor *m* screw compressor
Schraubenkühler *m* Friedrichs [reflux] condenser
Schraubenpumpe *f* screw pump
Schraubenquetschhahn *m (lab)* screw [compressor] clamp, Hoffmann clamp, [Bunsen] screw clip
Schraubenquirl *m (ceram)* propeller blunger
Schraubenrührer *m* propeller agitator (mixer), *(esp lab)* propeller stirrer
Schraubenspindel *f* screw
Schraubenstruktur *f (bioch)* helical structure
Schraubentute *f (petrol)* overshot
Schraubenverbindungsstück *n* screwed fitting
Schraubenverdichter *m* screw compressor
Schraubenversetzung *f (cryst)* screw dislocation
Schraubfitting *m(n)* screwed fitting
Schraubkappe *f (lab)* screw[-on-type] cap, screw-thread cap
Schraubklemme *f* **[nach Hoffmann]** *s.* Schraubenquetschhahn
Schraubverschluß *m s.* Schraubkappe
Schreckplatte *f* chill *(foundry)*
Schreckschicht *f* chilled portion, chill *(foundry)*
Schreiber *m (anal)* [pen] recorder, recording instrument
Schreibgalvanometer *n* galvanometer recorder
Schreibinstrument *n s.* Schreiber
Schreibkreide *f* chalk *(calcium carbonate)*

Schreibmaschinenbänderfarbe *f* typewriter-ribbon ink
Schreibmaschinenpapier *n* typewriting (typewriter) paper, T.W.
Schreibpapier *n* writing paper
Schreibpergament *n* vellum [paper]
Schreibtinte *f* writing ink
Schreibwerk *n* recorder
Schriftmetall *n* type metal
Schritt *m* step, stage
~/geschwindigkeitsbestimmender rate-limiting step, rate-controlling (rate-determining) step *(of a reaction)*
Schrittfolge *f* sequence of steps
Schrittmacher *m (bioch)* pacemaker
Schrittmacherenzym *n* pacemaker enzyme
Schrittmacherreaktion *f* rate-limiting (rate-determining) reaction
Schrödinger-Gleichung *f* Schrödinger [wave] equation
Schrot *n(m)* shot, *(specif)* lead shot
Schrotbeize *f (tann)* bran drench[ing] • **in ~ behandeln** to drench
Schrott *m* scrap [metal]
schrubben to scrub
Schrühbrand *m (ceram)* biscuit firing, biscuitting
Schrühbrandofen *m s.* Schrühofen
Schrühbrandscherben *m (ceram)* biscuitted body
schrühen *(ceram)* to bake
Schrühofen *m (ceram)* biscuit kiln (oven)
Schrühware *f (ceram)* biscuit (biscuit-fired, biscuitted) ware, biscuit earthenware, bisque
schrumpfbeständig *s.* krumpffest
schrumpfen to shrink, to contract
schrumpffest *s.* krumpffest
Schrumpfriß *m* shrinkage crack
Schrumpfung *f* shrinkage, contraction
Schrumpfungsgrad *m* degree of shrinkage
Schrumpfverhältnis *n* shrink ratio
Schrumpfvorrichtung *f (plast)* shrinkage (cooling) jig, shrink (cooling) fixture *(for mouldings)*
Schub *m* 1. pushing force, push; 2. shear[ing]
Schubbeanspruchung *f* shear stress
Schubboden *m* pusher plate (disk)
Schubmodul *m s.* Schermodul
Schubschleuder *f s.* Schubzentrifuge
Schubspannung *f* shear stress
Schubstange *f (min tech)* pitman *(as of a Wilfley table)*
Schubzentrifuge *f* pusher (push-type) centrifuge, reciprocating-pusher (reciprocating-conveyor) centrifuge
Schuhkrem *f* shoe polish
Schuller-Verfahren *n (glass)* Schuller (updraw) process
Schulter *f (phot)* shoulder, knee, region of overexposure *(of the characteristic curve)*; *(spectr)* shoulder
Schulterbande *f (spectr)* shoulder band
Schulterstab *m*/**hantelförmiger** *(rubber)* dumb bell, dumb-bell strip (test piece)
Schumann-Gebiet *n s.* Schumann-UV
Schumann-Platte *f* Schumann plate *(ultraviolet photography)*
Schumann-UV *n* vacuum ultraviolet *(< 2000 Å)*
Schüppchen *n (min)* spangle
Schuppe *f* scale, flake
Schuppenbildung *f* scaling, flaking
schuppenförmig scale-like, scaly
Schuppenglas *n* scaly glass
Schuppenparaffin *n* scale wax, paraffin scale
schuppig scaly, foliated; lepidoblastic *(texture of rocks)*
schüren to stoke
Schüren *n* **von Hand** hand stoking
schürfen *(mine)* to prospect, to explore
Schürfkübelbagger *m* dragline [excavator]
Schürfkübelraupe *f* caterpillar-powered scraper
Schürfkübelwagen *m* dragline [excavator]
Schürfung *f (mine)* prospecting, exploration
Schürloch *n* stoke (fire, fuel) hole
Schurre *f* chute
Schürvorrichtung *f* poker
Schuß *m* shot *(1. yield from one injection-moulding cycle; 2. charge of explosives)*
Schüssel *f* dish, bowl
Schüssel-Kegel-Mühle *f* ring-roll mill *(with horizontal grinding ring)*
Schüsselklassierer *m* bowl classifier
~ mit seitlichem Austrag bowl desiltor
Schüsselmühle *f* [roller-and-]bowl mill, bowl ring-roller mill
~ für Kohlenstaubmahlung bowl-mill coal pulverizer
Schußgewicht *n s.* Schußmasse
Schußmasse *f (plast)* shot size (weight)
~/maximale shot capacity
Schußperforierung *f (petrol)* gun perforating
Schußpunkt *m (petrol)* shot point *(in refraction shooting)*
Schuß[roh]seide *f* tram silk
Schüttdichte *f (ch, mine)* bulk density, B.D., apparent density
~ von Pulver powder density
Schütte *f* chute
Schüttelapparat *m* 1. *(pap)* shake [apparatus]; 2. *s.* Schüttelmaschine
Schüttelautoklav *m* shaker autoclave
Schüttelbock *m (pap)* shake [apparatus]
Schüttelflasche *f* shaking bottle
Schüttelgefäß *n* shaking (shaker) flask
Schüttelgeschwindigkeit *f* shaker speed
Schüttelherd *m (min tech)* shaking table
Schüttelmaschine *f* shaking machine, [mechanical] shaker
schütteln to shake
Schütteln *n* shake, shaking • **unter gelegentlichem ~** with occasional shaking • **unter häufigem ~** with frequent shaking • **unter ständigem ~** with constant shaking

Schüttelrinne *f*, **Schüttelrutsche** *f* shaking chute
Schüttelsieb *n* shaking (shaker) screen (sieve); *(petrol)* vibrating mudscreen *(of a rotary-drilling installation)*
Schüttelsortierer *m* shaking (shaker) screen (sieve)
Schütteltrichter *m* separatory (separating) funnel
Schüttelung *f* shake, shaking
Schüttelzylinder *m* shaking cylinder
schütten to pour
Schüttgewicht *n s.* Schüttdichte
Schüttgut *n* bulk material
Schüttgutbett *n* bed
Schüttgutfilter *n* bed filter
Schüttgutschicht *f* bed
Schüttkegelwinkel *m s.* Schüttwinkel
Schüttschicht *f* bed
Schüttschicht-Staubabscheider *m* granular-bed separator
Schütttrichter *m* [feed, charge] hopper, loading (charging) hopper, feeding funnel; cup *(of a blast furnace)*
Schüttung *f* 1. bed; feed[stock], feed material, charge [stock], charging stock *(as of a blast furnace)*; *(distil)* packing *(of a column)*; 2. pouring *(act)* • **in loser** ~ in bulk
~/bewegte moving bed
~/keramische *(distil)* ceramic packing
~/körnige granular bed
~/ruhende (statische) fixed (static) bed
Schüttungshöhe *f* bed depth; *(distil)* packing depth
Schüttvolumen *n* bulk (dry) volume
Schüttwinkel *m* angle of repose (rest) *(of bulk material)*
Schutz *m* protection; safeguard
~ **durch Fremdstrom/katodischer** impressed current cathodic protection
~ **durch Opferanoden/katodischer** sacrificial protection
~/katodischer cathodic protection
Schütz *n* 1. sluice *(in a liquid stream)*; 2. relay *(in an electric circuit)*
Schutzabdeckung *f***[/isolierende]** resist, stop-off [coating] *(electroplating)*
Schutzanstrich *m* protective [paint] coating
Schutzatmosphäre *f* protective atmosphere
Schutzbekleidung *f s.* Schutzkleidung
Schutzbrett *n (pap)* spatter (baffle) board
Schutzbrille *f* protective (safety) goggles, [pair of] safety glasses
schützend protective
Schutzengobe *f (ceram)* protective engobe
Schutzfilm *m* protective film
Schutzgas *n* protective gas, *(esp welding:)* shielding gas
Schutzgasatmosphäre *f* protective atmosphere
~/kontrollierte controlled atmosphere
Schutzgasglühen *n* protective-gas annealing, bright annealing
Schutzgas-Lichtbogenschweißen *n* inert-gas-shielded arc-welding
Schutzglas *n* safety glass
Schutzgruppe *f* protective (protecting) group
Schutzhandschuhe *mpl* protective gloves
Schutzhaube *f* **für Exsikkatoren** desiccator cage (guard)
Schutzhaut *f* protective skin (film)
Schutzhülle *f* protective sheath (sleeve)
Schutzhülse *f* protective (protecting) tube
Schutzkleidung *f* protective (safety) clothing
Schutzkolloid *n* protective colloid
Schutzkorb *m* **für Exsikkatoren** desiccator cage (guard)
Schutzlack *m* protective lacquer *(physically drying)*; *(if unpigmented:)* protective varnish; *(broadly:)* protective paint
Schutzmagnet *m* tramp-iron magnet (magnetic separator)
Schutzmaßnahme *f* protective measure
Schutzmechanismus *m (bioch)* protection mechanism
Schutzmittel *n* protective (protecting) agent, protective, protectant; *(pharm)* prophylactic, protective
~ **mit abstoßender Wirkung** *(text)* repellent
Schutzrohr *n* protective (protecting) tube
Schutzscheibe *f (lab)* explosion screen *(made from wire glass)*
Schutzschicht *f* 1. [protective] coating, *(if thin:)* protective film (skin); 2. *s.* Schutzabdeckung[/isolierende]
~/abstreifbare (abziehbare) strippable coating
~/anorganische nichtmetallische inorganic coating
~/dekorative decorative coating
~/dünne protective film (skin)
~/elektrochemisch hergestellte electroplated coating (deposit), electrodeposited (galvanic) coating, electroplate, electrodeposit
~/feuerfeste refractory coating
~/galvanische *s.* ~/elektrochemisch hergestellte
~ **gegen Abrieb** antiabrasion layer
~/metallische metal[lic] coating
~/oxidische oxide coating
Schutzschichtbildung *f* formation of a protective coating, coating formation
Schutzschichtmetall *n* coating metal
Schutzschirm *m* explosion screen
Schutzstoff *m s.* Schutzmittel
Schutzüberzug *m* 1. protective cover[ing]; 2. *s.* Schutzschicht
Schutzwirkung *f* protective action
schwach 1. weak *(acid or base, bond)*; 2. faint *(reaction)*; 3. gentle, slight *(heating)*
Schwachbrandstein *m (ceram)* soft[-fired] brick
schwächen 1. to weaken *(e.g. the basicity, a bond)*; 2. *(text)* to tender
schwächer werden to faint *(as of reactions)*
schwachfarbig feebly (weakly) coloured

Schwachfeldscheidung *f (min tech)* low-intensity magnetic separation
Schwachgas *n* poor (lean) gas
schwachgeleimt *(pap)* soft-sized, slack-sized, S.S.
Schwachlasttropfkörper *m s.* Tropfkörper/schwachbelasteter
Schwachlauge *f (pap)* weak liquor
schwachlöslich slightly (sparingly) soluble, low-solubility
schwachsauer weakly (feebly, faintly) acid, sub-acid
Schwachsäure *f (pap)* weak acid
Schwächung *f* 1. weakening *(as of basicity or of a bond)*; 2. *(text)* tendering
Schwaden *m (mine)* choke (black) damp *(low-oxygen air)*
Schwadenhaube *f* hood
schwammartig sponge-like, spongy
Schwammeisen *n* sponge iron
Schwammeisenpulver *n* sponge-iron powder
Schwammgummi *m* sponge rubber
schwammig spongy, porous, porose
Schwammkunststoff *m* sponge plastic
Schwammverfahren *n* sponge process *(for squeezing off essential oil by hand)*
schwangerschaftsverhütend contraceptive
Schwankung *f* variation
~ des Abwasseranfalls (Abwasserzuflusses) variation (fluctuation) in flow, variation in sewage (waste-water) flow, influent waste variation, flow variation
Schwanz *m* 1. *(chromat)* [solvent] tail; 2. *(plast)* tail *(of a monomer)*
Schwanzbildung *f (chromat)* [peak] tailing, non-equilibrium tailing
Schwanzhahn *m* tailkey (tailed) stopcock
Schwanz-Schwanz-Kondensation *f* tail-to-tail condensation
Schwanz-Schwanz-Polymerisation *f* tail-to-tail polymerization
Schwanz-Schwanz-Struktur *f* tail-to-tail structure
Schwarm *m* swarm, bundle *(of molecules)*
Schwarz *n***/Frankfurter** Frankfort black *(usually charred vegetable material)*
~/Kölner bone (animal) black
Schwarzalkaliboden *m (soil)* solonetz
Schwarzbeize *f (dye)* black mordant (liquor), iron [acetate] liquor
Schwarzblech *n* black plate
Schwärze *f* black
Schwärzegrad *m* [thermal] emissivity *(of heat-radiating bodies)*
schwärzen to blacken; to darken, to affect *(the photosensitive layer)*
~/sich to blacken; *(phot)* to darken
Schwarzerde *f (soil)* chernozem, black earth
Schwarzfärbung *f* blackening, black staining
Schwarzglas *n* black glass
schwarzkochen *(pap)* to burn *(the cook)*
Schwarzkochung *f (pap)* 1. burning *(process)*; 2. burned (burnt, black) cook
Schwarzkohle *f* bituminous (black) coal
Schwarzkopie *f (phot)* negative copy
Schwarzkörper *m* black body
Schwarzkupfer *n (met)* black (coarse) copper
Schwarzlack *m* black varnish
Schwarzlauge *f (pap)* black liquor (lye)
~/eingedickte concentrated (evaporated, thick) black liquor
Schwarzlaugenbehälter *m s.* Schwarzlaugenvorratstank
Schwarzlaugenverbrennung *f (pap)* black liquor combustion
Schwarzlaugenvorratstank *m (pap)* black liquor storage [tank]
Schwarzmaterial *n coal or coke in calcium carbide manufacture*
Schwarzmetallurgie *f* ferrous (iron) metallurgy
Schwarzpulver *n* gunpowder, black (blasting) powder
Schwarzschild-Effekt *m (phot)* Schwarzschild effect, reciprocity[-law] failure
Schwarzschmelze *f*, **Schwarzsoda** *f (pap)* black ash
Schwarztorf *m (agric)* black peat
Schwärzung *f* 1. blackening; *(phot)* darkening; fog *(in the unexposed part of an image)*; 2. *s.* Schwärzungsdichte
Schwärzungsabstufung *f (phot)* gradation
Schwärzungsbereich *m (phot)* density range
Schwärzungsdichte *f (phot)* extinction, [optical, photographic] density
Schwärzungshof *m (phot)* halo
Schwärzungskurve *f***[/fotografische]** characteristic curve, Hurter and Driffield curve, H and D curve
Schwärzungsmesser *m (phot)* densitometer
Schwärzungsmessung *f (phot)* densitometry
Schwärzungsring *m (phot)* halo
Schwärzungsschwelle *f (phot)* threshold [point]
Schwarzweißkopie *f* black-and-white print
Schwarz-Weiß-Verhältnis *n* lime-to-coke ratio *(in calcium carbide manufacture)*
Schweb *m* turbidity, suspended matter *(in river water)*
Schwebe *f*:
• **in der ~ halten** to keep (maintain) in suspension
Schwebedichte *f* buoyant density *(density-gradient centrifugation)*
Schwebefilter *n s.* 1. Schwebefilteranlage; 2. Schwebefilterzone
Schwebefilteranlage *f (hyd)* sludge blanket clarifier, blanket-type clarifier
Schwebefilterzone *f (hyd)* sludge (fluidized) blanket, blanket of sludge
Schwebekörper *m* [rotameter] float, plummet *(in flowmeters)*

Schwebekörper-Durchflußmesser *m*, **Schwebekörper-Mengenmesser** *m* rotameter, variable area flowmeter
Schwebemittel *n* antisettling (suspending) agent
Schweberöstung *f s.* 1. Blitzröstung; 2. Suspensionsröstung
Schwebeschmelzen *n*/**autogenes** *(met)* autogenous smelting
Schwebestoff *m s.* Schwebstoff
Schwebeteilchen *n* particulate, suspended particle
Schwebetrockner *m* fluid-bed dryer
Schwebevergasung *f (coal)* suspension (dilute-phase) gasification, entrainment (entrained-bed, pulverized-coal) gasification
Schwebezone *f* floating zone *(in zone melting)*
Schwebezonenapparatur *f* floating-zone apparatus (unit) *(for zone melting)*
Schwebezonenschmelzen *n* floating-zone melting
Schwebezonenverfahren *n* floating-zone method *(of zone melting)*
Schwebstoff *m* suspended material (matter) *(in liquids)*; airborne contaminant
Schwebstoffe *mpl*/**feste** *(hyd)* suspended solids, SS, suspended solid matter *(> $5 \cdot 10^{-4}$ mm)*
schwebstofffrei free from suspended matter
Schwebstoffgehalt *m (hyd)* suspended-solids content (concentration, level)
~ **des Rohwassers** raw-water suspended solids
~ **im Belebtschlamm** mixed-liquor suspended solids [concentration, level], MLSS, solids in aeration (incubation) basin
Schwebstoffilter *n* mechanical filter
Schwebstoffiltergerät *n* mechanical filter respirator
Schwefel *m* S sulphur • **aus ~ bestehend** sulphur[e]ous, sulphuric • **mit ~ behandeln** to [treat with] sulphur • **mit ~ räuchern** to fume with burning sulphur, to sulphur • **mit ~ vernetzbar** *(rubber)* sulphur-curable, sulphur-curing, sulphur-vulcanizable • **mit ~ versetzen** to sulphurize
~/**amorpher** amorphous sulphur
~/**anorganisch gebundener** mineral sulphur
~/**elementarer** elemental sulphur
~/**extrahierbarer** *(rubber)* [total] extractable sulphur
~/**freier** free sulphur, *(rubber also)* true free sulphur
~/**gebundener** bound (combined) sulphur, *(rubber also)* rubber-combined sulphur
~/**gediegener** native (virgin) sulphur
~/**gefällter** precipitated sulphur, milk of sulphur
~/**kolloid[al]er** colloidal sulphur
~/**monokliner** monoclinic sulphur, β-sulphur
~/**natürlicher** *s.* ~/gediegener
~/**organischer (organisch gebundener)** organic sulphur
~/**perlmuttartiger** mother-of-pearl sulphur, nacreous sulphur *(a modification)*
~/**plastischer** plastic sulphur, γ-sulphur
~/**polysulfidisch gebundener** polysulphidic sulphur
~/**radioaktiver** radioactive sulphur, radiosulphur, *(specif)* ^{35}S sulphur-35
~/**rhombischer** rhombic sulphur, α-sulphur
~/**sublimierter** sublimed sulphur, sulphur flowers
~/**totaler** *(rubber)* total sulphur
~/**unlöslicher** insoluble sulphur
Schwefel-35 *m* ^{35}S sulphur-35
α-**Schwefel** *m* α-sulphur, rhombic sulphur
β-**Schwefel** *m* β-sulphur, monoclinic sulphur
γ-**Schwefel** *m* γ-sulphur, plastic sulphur
λ-**Schwefel** *m* λ-sulphur *(an amorphous modification)*
μ-**Schwefel** *m* μ-sulphur *(an amorphous modification)*
Schwefelabdruck *m* sulphur print *(for detecting sulphur)*
Schwefelablagerung *f* sulphur deposit
Schwefelaffinität *f* affinity for sulphur
Schwefelantimon *n s.* Antimon(III)-sulfid
schwefelarm low (poor) in sulphur, low-sulphur
Schwefelarsen *n s.* Arsensulfid
schwefelartig sulphur[e]ous
Schwefelausblühung *f (rubber)* sulphur bloom
Schwefelbakterien *npl* sulphur bacteria
schwefelbeständig resistant to sulphur, sulphur-resistant
Schwefelbeständigkeit *f* resistance to sulphur, sulphur resistance
Schwefelbestimmung *f* determination of sulphur
Schwefelblume *f*, **Schwefelblüte** *f* sulphur flowers, sublimed sulphur
Schwefelbrücke *f (rubber)* sulphur bridge (link, cross-link)
Schwefel(II)-chlorid *n* sulphur(II) chloride, sulphur dichloride
Schwefel(IV)-chlorid *n* sulphur(IV) chloride, sulphur tetrachloride
Schwefeldampf *m* sulphur vapour
Schwefeldichlorid *n s.* Schwefel(II)-chlorid
Schwefeldioxid *n* sulphur dioxide, sulphur(IV) oxide
~/**gebundenes** *(pap)* combined (non-available) sulphur dioxide
Schwefeldonator *m* sulphur donor
Schwefeldosierung *f* sulphur dosage (level)
Schwefelerz *n* sulphide ore
Schwefelfarbstoff *m* sulphur (sulphide) dye (dyestuff), *(Am also)* sulfur color
~/**blauer** sulphur blue
~/**brauner** sulphur brown
~/**gelber** sulphur yellow
~/**schwarzer** sulphur black
schwefelfest *s.* schwefelbeständig
Schwefel(IV)-fluorid *n* sulphur(IV) fluoride, sulphur tetrafluoride
Schwefel(VI)-fluorid *n* sulphur(VI) fluoride, sulphur hexafluoride
schwefelfrei sulphur-free, sulphurless, non-sulphur
schwefelführend sulphur-bearing

Schwefelgehalt *m* sulphur content • **von hohem ~** high-sulphur,rich in sulphur • **von mittlerem ~** medium-sulphur • **von niedrigem ~** low-sulphur, poor in sulphur
Schwefelgewinnung *f* sulphur recovery
schwefelhaltig sulphur-containing, sulphur[e]ous, *(min also)* sulphur-bearing
Schwefelharnstoff *m s.* Thioharnstoff
Schwefelheptoxid *n* sulphur heptaoxide, disulphur heptaoxide
Schwefelhexafluorid *n s.* Schwefel(VI)-fluorid
Schwefelhexaiodid *n s.* Schwefel(VI)-iodid
Schwefel(II)-hydroxid *n* sulphur(II) hydroxide
Schwefelindigoblau *n* sulphur indigo blue
Schwefel(VI)-iodid *n* sulphur(VI) iodide, sulphur hexaiodide
Schwefelkalkbrühe *f* lime sulphur *(a pesticide)*
Schwefelkies *m (min)* iron pyrite[s], pyrite, mundic *(iron disulphide)*
Schwefelkohlenstoff *m* carbon disulphide
Schwefellager *n (geol)* sulphur deposit
Schwefelleber *f* liver of sulphur, hepar sulfuris, sulphurated potash *(technical potassium sulphide)*
Schwefellost *m* mustard gas, sulphur mustard, di-2-chlorodiethyl sulphide
Schwefellösung *f* sulphur solution
Schwefelmehl *n* flour sulphur
Schwefelmilch *f* milk of sulphur, precipitated sulphur
schwefelmodifiziert sulphur-modified
Schwefelmonoxid *n s.* Schwefel(II)-oxid
schwefeln 1. to sulphur[ize], *(esp with sulphurous acid or sulphites:)* to sulphite, *(text also)* to stove; 2. to thionate *(organic compounds for producing dyestuffs)*
Schwefelnachweis *m* detection of sulphur • **zum ~** for detecting sulphur
Schwefelnatrium *n s.* Natriumsulfid
Schwefelnatriumäscher *m (tann)* sulphide lime
Schwefelnitrid *n* tetrasulphur tetranitride
Schwefelofen *m* sulphur burner
~/rotierender rotary sulphur burner
Schwefel(II)-oxid *n* sulphur(II) oxide, sulphur monooxide
Schwefel(IV)-oxid *n* sulphur(IV) oxide, sulphur dioxide
Schwefel(VI)-oxid *n* sulphur(VI) oxide, sulphur trioxide
schwefelreich high-sulphur, rich in sulphur
Schwefelsaturation *f (sugar)* [acid] sulphitation
schwefelsauer sulphuric-acid *(solution)*; sulphuric *(salt) (for specific salts s. ...sulfat)*
Schwefelsäure *f* sulphuric acid • **mit ~ beizen** *(met)* to vitriol
~ aus Rohschwefel sulphur (brimstone) acid
~ des Handels *s.* ~/handelsübliche
~/halbkonzentrierte *s.* ~/mittelkonzentrierte
~/handelsübliche commercial (commercially available) sulphuric acid
~/hochkonzentrierte concentrated sulphuric acid, concentrated (colourless) oil of vitriol *(containing 93 to 98 % of H_2SO_4)*
~/käufliche *s.* ~/handelsübliche
~/konzentrierte 1. concentrated sulphuric acid *(containing a minimum of 65,6 % of H_2SO_4)*; 2. *s.* ~/hochkonzentrierte
~/mäßig konzentrierte fairly concentrated sulphuric acid, sulphuric acid of moderate concentration *(containing 72 to 80 % of H_2SO_4)*
~/mittelkonzentrierte sulphuric acid of medium concentration *(containing about 50 % of H_2SO_4)*
~/nitrose nitrous vitriol *(in the chamber process for manufacturing sulphuric acid)*
~/rauchende fuming sulphuric acid, oleum
Schwefelsäurealkylierung *f (petrol)* sulphuric-acid alkylation
Schwefelsäurebad *n (pap)* bath of sulphuric acid
Schwefelsäurebehandlung *f (petrol)* sulphuric-acid treatment (refining)
Schwefelsäurediethylester *m* diethyl sulphate
Schwefelsäuredimethylester *m* dimethyl sulphate
Schwefelsäureethylester *m s.* Schwefelsäurediethylester
Schwefelsäureherstellung *f* sulphuric acid manufacture
Schwefelsäureindustrie *f* sulphuric-acid industry
Schwefelsäurekontaktverfahren *n* contact process (method)
Schwefelsäuremonoethylester *m* ethyl hydrogensulphate, ethylsulphuric acid
Schwefelsäurepolymerisationsverfahren *n (petrol)* sulphuric-acid polymerization process
Schwefelsäureraffinage *f s.* Schwefelsäurebehandlung
Schwefelsäurewaschprobe *f (dye)* sulphuric-acid test
Schwefelschwarz *n* sulphur black *(any of several sulphur dyes)*
Schwefelschwarzpaste *f* sulphur-black paste
Schwefelschwarzpulver *n* sulphur-black powder
Schwefelsensibilisator *m (phot)* sulphur sensitizer
Schwefelsol *n* sulphur sol
Schwefelspender *m* sulphur donor
Schwefeltetrachlorid *n s.* Schwefel(IV)-chlorid
Schwefeltetrafluorid *n s.* Schwefel(IV)-fluorid
Schwefeltetroxid *n* sulphur tetraoxide
Schwefeltonung *f (phot)* sulphur (sulphite) toning
Schwefeltrioxid *n s.* Schwefel(VI)-oxid
Schwefelung *f* 1. sulphurization, *(esp with sulphurous acid or sulphites:)* sulphitation, *(text also)* stoving; 2. thionation *(of organic compounds for producing dyestuffs)*; 3. *s.* Schwefelsaturation
Schwefelverbindung *f* sulphur compound
Schwefelverbrennungen *fpl (agric)* sulphur scald
Schwefelverbrennungsofen *m* sulphur burner
~/rotierender rotary sulphur burner
Schwefelverlust *m (pap)* loss of sulphur

Schwefelvernetzungsbrücke *f (rubber)* sulphur bridge (link, cross-link)
Schwefelvulkanisat *n* sulphur vulcanizate
Schwefelvulkanisation *f* [elemental] sulphur cure, sulphur vulcanization
Schwefelvulkanisationssystem *n* sulphur curing (vulcanization) system
Schwefelwasserstoff *m* hydrogen sulphide, sulphane, *(specif)* H_2S hydrogen sulphide, monosulphane
Schwefelwasserstoffentfernung *f* hydrogen-sulphide removal
Schwefelwasserstoffgruppe *f (anal)* insoluble sulphide group
Schwefelyperit *n* mustard gas, sulphur mustard, yperite, di-2-chlorodiethyl sulphide
schweflig sulphur[e]ous
Schwefligsäureester *m* sulphite ester
Schweif *m s.* Schwanz 1.
Schweinchen *n (lab)* 1. weighing piggy *(weighing bottle with feet)*; 2. condenser jacket
Schweinefett *n*, **Schweineschmalz** *n* hog (pig) fat, lard
Schweinsgummi *n (pharm)* 1. hog gum *(from Clusia flava L. and other trees confused with it)*; 2. doctor gum *(from Symphonia globulifera L.)*
Schweiß *m* sweat
Schweißacetylen *n* welding-grade acetylene
schweißbar weldable
Schweißbarkeit *f* weldability
Schweißbrenner *m* [welding] torch, blowpipe
schweißecht *(tann, text)* fast to perspiration, perspiration-resistant
Schweißechtheit *f (tann, text)* fastness to perspiration, perspiration resistance
Schweißelektrode *f* welding electrode
schweißen to weld, *(plast also)* to seal
~/autogenes autogeneous (gas) welding
~ durch Anlösen (Anquellen) solvent welding
Schweißflußmittel *n* welding flux
Schweißgerät *n* welding apparatus, *(plast also)* sealing unit
schweißhemmend *(cosmet)* antiperspirant, antihidrotic
Schweißhemmungsmittel *n (cosmet)* antiperspirant, antihidrotic, perspiration check
schweißlindernd *s.* schweißhemmend
Schweißlineal *n (plast)* heated bar
Schweißmittel *n* 1. welding flux; 2. *(pharm)* sudorific; 3. *s.* Schweißhemmungsmittel
Schweißpistole *f* welding gun
Schweißpulver *n* welding powder
Schweißstab *m* welding rod, *(plast also)* filler rod
Schweißstahl *m* wrought iron
schweißtreibend *(pharm)* sudorific
Schweißung *f* weld[ing]
Schweißwolle *f* raw (grease) wool
Schwelanalyse *f*/**Fischersche** Fischer assay *(for determining the tar yield of coal)*
Schwelanlage *f* low-temperature carbonization (carbonizing) plant
Schwelaufbau *m*, **Schwelaufsatz** *m (coal)* superimposed carbonizing chamber
Schwelbrikett *n* carbonized briquette
schwelen to carbonize *(e.g. coal at low temperature)*; to smoulder
~/in der Retorte to retort *(e.g. oil shale)*
Schwelen *n* low-temperature carbonization, *(coal also)* low-temperature coking
Schweler *m* carbonizer
Schwelerei *f s.* Schwelanlage
Schwelgas *n* carbonization (low-temperature) gas; distillation gas *(obtained in a predistillation gas producer)*
Schwelgasleitung *f* distillation gas main *(of a predistillation gas producer)*
Schwelgenerator *m* predistillation [gas] producer, carbonizing (double gas, two-stage) generator, two-zone gasifier
Schwelindustrie *f* carbonizing industry
Schwelkoks *m* low-temperature coke
Schwelläscher *m (tann)* fresh lime
Schwelle *f (phys ch)* threshold; *(phot)* threshold [point] *(with silver density just greater than fog-level)*
schwellen to swell [up], to expand; *(tann)* to plump *(pelts)*
Schwellenenergie *f* threshold energy
Schwellenwert *m* threshold [value]
Schwellenwertbehandlung *f* threshold treatment *(of water)*
Schwellmittel *n (tann)* plumping agent, plumper
Schwellverhalten *n (plast)* jet swelling *(blowing of hollow articles)*
Schwellvorgang *m* swelling, expansion
Schwellzement *m* expanding (expansive) cement
Schwelofen *m* carbonizer
Schwelretorte *f* low-temperature retort
Schwelschacht *m* carbonizing (carbonization) chamber *(of a predistillation gas producer)*
~/aufgesetzter superimposed carbonizing chamber
Schwelteer *m* low-temperature tar
Schwelung *f* low-temperature carbonization, *(coal also)* low-temperature coking
~ im Wirbelbett fluidized carbonization
Schwelverfahren *n* low-temperature carbonization (carbonizing) process
Schwelvorgang *m* low-temperature carbonization (carbonizing) process
Schwelwärme *f* heat of carbonization
Schwelwerk *n* low-temperature carbonization (carbonizing) plant
Schwelzone *f* carbonizing (retorting) zone, [pre]distillation zone *(of a gas producer)*
Schwemmtorf *m* hydro peat
Schwemmwasser *n* flume (fluming) water
schwenkbar turning, turnable, mobile

schwenken to swirl *(e.g. a beaker)*; *(tech)* to turn, to pivot, *(horizontally:)* to swivel, *(to and fro:)* to oscillate
Schwenkmethode *f* oscillating-crystal method *(for investigating crystal structures)*
Schweratomeffekt *m (spectr)* heavy-atom effect *(occurrence of singlet-triplet transitions)*
~/äußerer external heavy atom effect
Schwerbenzin *n* heavy gasoline (benzine, naphtha)
Schwerbenzol *n* heavy benzole
Schwerbeton *m* heavy concrete
Schwerchemikalien *fpl* heavy chemicals *(acids, salts, and alkalies produced on a large scale)*
schwererflüchtig *(distil)* less volatile
schwererschmelzbar higher-melting
schwerersiedend higher-boiling
Schwerersiedende *n* higher-boiling component, less volatile component
Schweretrennung *f* gravity separation
Schweretrübe *f s.* Schwerflüssigkeit
schwerflüchtig difficultly volatile, slow-evaporating, heavy
Schwerflüssigkeit *f (min tech)* heavy (dense) medium, high-gravity medium
Schwerflüssigkeitsanlage *f (min tech)* heavy-medium (dense-medium) separation plant, gravity concentrating (concentration) apparatus
Schwerflüssigkeitsaufbereitung *f (min tech)* heavy-medium (dense-medium) separation (cleaning)
Schwerflüssigkeitsaufbereitungsanlage *f s.* Schwerflüssigkeitsanlage
Schwerflüssigkeitsscheider *m (min tech)* heavy-medium (dense-medium) separator (vessel)
Schwerflüssigkeitssortieren *n s.* Schwerflüssigkeitsaufbereitung
Schwerflüssigkeitsverfahren *n (min tech)* sink-and-float process, sink-float method
Schwergut *n* heavy material
Schwerkraftabscheider *m* gravity (gravitational) separator
Schwerkraftabscheidung *f* gravity (gravitational) separation
Schwerkraftabsetzbehälter *m*, **Schwerkraftabsetzer** *m* gravity settling tank (vessel)
Schwerkraftabsetzung *f s.* Schwerkraftsedimentation
~ in Eindickern *s.* Schwerkrafteindickung
Schwerkraftaufbereitung *f (min tech)* gravity concentration
Schwerkrafteindicker *m (hyd)* gravity thickener
Schwerkrafteindickung *f (hyd)* gravity thickening
Schwerkraftfilter *n* gravity (hydrostatic head) filter
Schwerkraftfiltration *f* gravity (natural) filtration
Schwerkraft-Kornkohlefilter *n (hyd)* gravity carbon contactor
Schwerkraft-Ölabscheider *m (hyd)* gravity-type oil-water separator, oil-water gravity separator
Schwerkraftsedimentation *f (hyd)* gravitational sedimentation, gravity clarification
Schwerkrafttrennung *f s.* Schwerkraftabscheidung
Schwerkraftzuführung *f* gravity feed
schwerkraftzugeführt gravity-fed
Schwerlegierung *f* heavy[-metal] alloy
schwerlöslich poorly soluble, slightly (sparingly, difficultly) soluble • **~ sein** to dissolve slightly, to dissolve with difficulty
Schwermetall *n* heavy metal
Schwermetallegierung *f* heavy[-metal] alloy
Schwermetallgehalt *m* heavy-metals content
schwermetallhaltig heavy-metal-containing
Schwermetallionenkonzentration *f (hyd)* [total] heavy-metal concentration
Schwermetallsalz *n* heavy-metal salt
Schwermetallvorgiftung *f* heavy-metal poisoning
Schwermineral *n* heavy mineral
Schweröl *n* heavy oil
Schwerpunkt *m* **der negativen Ladung** negative charge centre, negative centre of charge, centre of negative charge
~ der positiven Ladung positive charge centre, positive centre of charge, centre of positive charge
Schwerschlamm *m (hyd)* sludge
schwerschmelzbar difficultly fusible, high-melting, high-fusion
schwersiedend high-boiling
Schwersiedende *n* high-boiling component
Schwerspat *m (min)* heavy spar, barite, baryte[s] *(barium sulphate)*
Schwerstange *f* drill collar *(of a rotary-drilling installation)*
Schwerstbeton *m* super-heavy concrete
Schwerstoff *m* high-gravity solid
Schwertkolben *m (lab)* sausage flask
Schwertrübe *f s.* Schwerflüssigkeit
Schwertrübe[wasch]zyklon *m* heavy-medium (dense-medium) cyclone
Schwerwaschmittel *n* heavy-duty [fabric, laundry] detergent
Schwerwasserherstellung *f* heavy-water production
Schwimmanteil *m (min tech)* floating fraction
Schwimmäscher *m (tann)* floating lime
Schwimmaschine *f (min tech)* floatation machine (apparatus)
Schwimmaufbereitung *f* flo[a]tation
Schwimmdecke *f s.* Schwimmschicht
Schwimmdeckenabstreifer *m s.* Schwimmschlammabstreifer
Schwimmdichte *f* buoyant density
Schwimmdüse *f (glass)* debiteuse *(in the Fourcault process)*
Schwimmer *m* float[er]
Schwimmerdruckmesser *m* float-type manometer
Schwimmerkondenstopf *m*, **Schwimmerkondenswasserableiter** *m* ball float trap

Schwimmerkörper *m* float[er]
Schwimmermanometer *n* float-type manometer
Schwimmermesser *m* float gauge *(for liquid-level measurement)*
Schwimmerventil *n* float valve
schwimmfähig floatable
Schwimmfähigkeit *f* floatability
Schwimmgerät *n (min tech)* floatation apparatus (machine)
Schwimmgut *n (min tech)* floating material (matter), floats, floating fraction
Schwimmittel *n (min tech)* floatation agent
~/drückendes depressant
~/regelndes modifying agent, modifier
Schwimmkiesel *m (min)* float stone *(a spongy variety of opal)*
Schwimmkopf *m* floating head *(of a heat exchanger)*
Schwimmkörper *m (hyd)* pontoon
Schwimmkurve *f (min tech)* floats curve
Schwimmschicht *f* scum layer (mat), rag (froth) layer, blanket of froth, floating sludge layer, surface mat, suspended sludge bed
Schwimmschlamm *m (hyd)* [top] scum, rag, skim[mings], float
Schwimmschlammabstreifer *m (hyd)* scum (float) skimmer, scum baffle (board, remover), skimmer blade
Schwimmschlammabzugsrinne *f (hyd)* skimming slot
Schwimmschlammdecke *f s.* Schwimmschicht
Schwimmschlammräumschild *m s.* Schwimmschlammabstreifer
Schwimmschlammrinne *f (hyd)* skimming slot
Schwimmschlammschicht *f s.* Schwimmschicht
Schwimmschlammschild *m s.* Schwimmschlammabstreifer
Schwimmseife *f* floating soap
Schwimm-Sink-Aufbereitung *f (min tech)* sink-float separation, heavy-medium (dense-medium) separation
Schwimm-Sink-Verfahren *n (min tech)* sink-float process
Schwimmstoff *m* 1. *(hyd)* separator skimmings *(oil removal)*; 2. *s.* Schwimmstoffe
~ einer Druckflotationsanlage *(hyd)* DAF skimmings
~ eines API-Abscheiders *(hyd)* API skimmings
Schwimmstoffe *mpl (hyd)* floating matter (material, solids)
Schwimmverfahren *n (min tech)* floatation process
schwinden 1. to shrink, to contract; 2. to evanesce, to fade [away] *(of a tint)*
schwindend 1. shrinking, contracting *(material)*; 2. evanescent, fading [away] *(tint)*
Schwindriß *m (ceram)* shrinkage crack
Schwindung *f* shrinkage, contraction
~/kubische *(ceram)* cubic (volume) shrinkage
~/lineare *(ceram)* linear shrinkage
~/räumliche *s.* ~/kubische
Schwindungshohlraum *m* shrinkage (contraction) cavity
Schwindungskoeffizient *m (ceram)* sintering coefficient
Schwindungsriß *m (ceram)* shrinkage crack
Schwingamplitude *f* vibration amplitude
Schwing[backen]brecher *m* balanced-jaw crusher
schwingen to vibrate, to oscillate
Schwingerbrechbacke *f* moving jaw *(of a jaw crusher)*
Schwingfeuer[nebel]gerät *n* swingfog *(crop protection)*
Schwingfrequenz *f s.* Schwingungsfrequenz
Schwingkreis *m* oscillator circuit *(high-frequency titration)*
Schwingmühle *f* vibratory (vibrating) mill, oscillatory (oscillating) mill
Schwingsieb *n*, **Schwingsiebmaschine** *f* gyratory (gyrating) screen, gyratory sifter *(having a series of screens)*
Schwingsiebschleuder *f*, **Schwingsiebzentrifuge** *f* oscillating-screen (oscillating-basket) centrifuge
Schwingsortierer *m s.* Schwingsiebmaschine
Schwingstabrost-Siebmaschine *f* vibrating [bar, rod] grizzly
Schwingtrockner *m* vibrating conveyor dryer
Schwingung *f* vibration, oscillation
~/anharmonische anharmonic (non-harmonic) vibration
~/antisymmetrische antisymmetric vibration
~/harmonische harmonic vibration, [simple] harmonic motion, SHM
~ in der Molekülebene in-plane vibration
γ-Schwingung *f (spectr)* out-of-plane vibration
δ-Schwingung *f (spectr)* in-plane vibration
ϰ-Schwingung *f (spectr)* wagging vibration
ν-Schwingung *f (spectr)* stretching (valence) vibration
ϱ-Schwingung *f (spectr)* rocking vibration
τ-Schwingung *f (spectr)* twisting vibration
Schwingungsamplitude *f* vibration[al] amplitude
Schwingungsanalyse *f (spectr)* vibrational analysis
Schwingungsbande *f (spectr)* vibration[al] band, vibronic band
Schwingungseinrüttler *m* vibrator
Schwingungs-Elektronenenergieverlust-Spektrometrie *f*/**hochauflösende** very-high-resolution electron-energy-loss spectrometry, VHRELS
Schwingungsenergie *f* vibrational energy, energy of vibrational motion
Schwingungsfeinstruktur *f (spectr)* vibrational (vibronic) fine structure
Schwingungsform *f* [vibrational] mode, mode of vibration, transmission mode *(propagation of guided waves)*
schwingungsfrei vibration-free
Schwingungsfreiheitsgrad *m* degree of vibrational freedom, vibrational degree of freedom

Schwingungsfrequenz *f* vibration[al] frequency, linear frequency
Schwingungsgrundzustand *m* vibrational ground state
Schwingungsklasse *f s.* Schwingungsrasse
Schwingungskorrosion *f* corrosion fatigue
Schwingungsniveau *n* vibrational [energy] level
Schwingungsquantenzahl *f* vibrational quantum number
Schwingungs-Raman-Effekt *m (spectr)* vibrational Raman effect
Schwingungs-Raman-Linie *f (spectr)* vibrational Raman line
Schwingungsrasse *f (spectr)* symmetry species (type)
Schwingungsrelaxation *f* vibrational relaxation
Schwingungsrichtung *f* direction of vibration
Schwingungsrißkorrosion *f* corrosion fatigue
Schwingungsrüttler *m* vibrator
Schwingungsspektroskopie *f* vibrational spectroscopy
Schwingungsspektrum *n* vibration[al] spectrum
Schwingungsstruktur *f s.* Schwingungsfeinstruktur
Schwingungssystem *n* vibrating system
Schwingungsterm *m* vibrational term
Schwingungsübergang *m* vibrational transition
Schwingungsverteilungsfunktion *f* vibrational partition function
Schwingungsviskosimeter *n* oscillating viscometer
Schwingungszahl *f s.* Schwingungsfrequenz
Schwingungszustand *m* vibrational state
Schwingversuch *m* oscillating (oscillatory) experiment, dynamic mechanical experiment
Schwingweg *m*, **Schwingweite** *f* vibration amplitude
Schwitzapparat *m* sweating stove *(for refining paraffin)*
~ von Henderson Henderson stove
Schwitze *f (tann)* sweating *(for removing hairs)*
schwitzen to sweat; *(relating to cement:)* to weep, to bleed; to sweat *(crude paraffin for removing oil)*
Schwitzkammer *f* sweating room (chamber), sweater *(for refining paraffin)*
Schwitzöl *n (petrol)* sweats (foots) oil, sweats
Schwitzpfanne *f s.* Schwitzwanne
Schwitzraum *m s.* Schwitzkammer
Schwitztasse *f s.* Schwitzwanne
Schwitzung *f* sweating, exudation *(for refining paraffin)*
Schwitzverfahren *n* sweating process *(for refining paraffin)*
Schwitzwanne *f* sweating pan (tray), sweat pan *(for refining paraffin)*
Schwitzwasser *n* condensed water, condensate [water]
Schwöde *f (tann)* painting, paint unhairing
Schwödebrei *m (tann)* lime cream (paint)
schwöden *(tann)* to paint
Schwödewolle *f* sulphide-painted wool
Schwund *m* 1. loss, wastage, outage *(a quantity lost in transportation or storage)*; 2. shrinkage, contraction
Schwundriß *m* shrinkage crack
scorchanfällig *(rubber)* scorchy
scorchbeständig *(rubber)* scorch-resistant
Scorchbeständigkeit *f (rubber)* scorch resistance
Scorchcharakteristik *f (rubber)* scorch characteristic
Scorchkurve *f (rubber)* scorch curve
Scorchneigung *f (rubber)* scorch tendency, scorchiness
Scorchperiode *f (rubber)* scorch period
Scorchprüfung *f (rubber)* scorch test
Scorchpunkt *m (rubber)* scorch point
scorchresistent *s.* scorchbeständig
Scorchtendenz *f s.* Scorchneigung
Scorchzeit *f (rubber)* scorch time
SCOT-Säule *f* SCOT column, support-coated open tubular column *(gas chromatography)*
SCP *(single-cell protein) s.* Einzellerprotein
SCP-Anlage *f (biot)* single-cell protein plant
SCP-Bildung *f* single-cell protein production *(by microorganisms)*
SCP-Erzeugung *f*, **SCP-Herstellung** *f (biot)* single-cell protein production, SCP manufacture
SCP-Mikroorganismen *mpl (biot)* SCP-producing microorganisms
SCP-Verfahren *n (biot)* single-cell protein process
screenen *(pharm, biot)* to screen *(e.g. for valuable compounds)*
S-Drehung *f (text)* S twist
SE *s.* 1. Sekundärelektron; 2. Siedeendpunkt
Sebacinsäure *f* sebacic acid, *decanedioic acid
Sebacinsäurediethylester *m* diethyl sebacate
Sebacylsäure *f s.* Sebacinsäure
Secalonsäure *f* secalonic acid *(a fungal pigment from Claviceps purpurea [Fr.] Tul.)*
sechsatomig hexatomic
Sechsblattrührer *m* six-bladed agitator
sechseckig *(cryst)* hexagonal
Sechserring *m s.* Sechsring
sechsfach koordiniert hexacoordinate[d], six-coordinate
sechsfachpositiv hexapositive
sechsgliedrig six-membered
Sechskörperverdampfer *m* sextuple evaporator
Sechsring *m* six-membered ring
sechsschauflig six-bladed *(agitator)*
Sechsstufenbleiche *f (pap)* six-stage bleaching
Sechsstufenverdampfer *m* sextuple evaporator
Sechswegehahn *m (chromat)* six-port valve
sechswertig hexavalent, sexavalent, sexivalent; hexahydric *(alcohol)*
Sechswertigkeit *f* sexivalence, sexavalence
sechszählig 1. *(cryst)* hexad, sixfold; 2. *s.* sechszähnig

sechszähnig hexadentate, sexadentate *(ligand)*
Sedativum *n (pharm)* sedative
Sediment *n* sediment, subsidence, [bottom] settlings, B.S., dregs, bottoms, *(esp food, ferm)* lees, foots; *(geol)* sediment
~/biogenes (organogenes) *(geol)* organic (biogenic) rock, biolith
sedimentär sedimentary
Sedimentation *f* sedimentation, settling
~/freie *(min tech)* free settling
~/gestörte *(min tech)* hindered settling
~ in Absetzbecken *(hyd)* plain sedimentation
Sedimentationsanalyse *f* sedimentation analysis
Sedimentationsdauer *f* settling period (time)
Sedimentationseigenschaften *fpl* settling properties
sedimentationsfähig *(hyd)* settleable *(flocs)*
Sedimentationsfähigkeit *f (hyd)* settleability *(of flocs)*
Sedimentationsgefäß *n* sedimentation (settling) tank, settler
Sedimentationsgeschwindigkeit *f* sedimentation (settling) rate, rate of gravity settling, subsidence rate
Sedimentationsgleichgewicht *n* sedimentation equilibrium
Sedimentationskoeffizient *m*, **Sedimentationskonstante** *f* sedimentation constant (coefficient) *(for determining molar masses)*
Sedimentationskurve *f* settling curve
Sedimentationspotential *n* sedimentation potential
Sedimentationsschlamm *m (hyd)* sedimentation [tank] sludge, clarification (clarifier) sludge
Sedimentationsstoffänger *m (pap)* sedimentation (gravity) save-all
Sedimentationsstrecke *f s.* Sedimentationsweg
Sedimentationstest *m* sedimentation test
Sedimentationswaage *f* sedimentation balance
Sedimentationsweg *m (hyd)* settling path (distance) *(of a particle)*
Sedimentationszeit *f s.* Sedimentationsdauer
Sedimentgestein *n* sedimentary rock, sediment
~/biogenes organic sedimentary rock
sedimentierbar *(hyd)* settleable *(flocs)*
Sedimentierbarkeit *f (hyd)* settleability *(of flocs)*
sedimentieren to sediment[ate], to precipitate, to set *(dispersed particles)*; to deposit, to sediment, to subside, to settle [down, out] *(of a precipitate)*
Sedimentiergefäß *n* sediment cone
Sedimentierzentrifuge *f* sedimentation (sedimenting) centrifuge, centrifugal decanter, solid-bowl (solid-wall, full-bowl) centrifuge
Seehundstran *m* seal oil
Seekreide *f (min)* chalk *(calcium carbonate)*
Seele *f* core *(as of a cable)*
Seelenmischung *f (rubber)* inner tube compound
Seesalz *n* marine (sea) salt, *(if obtained by solar evaporation also)* solar (bay) salt
Seesand *m* sea-shore sand
Seetang *m* [sea]tang
Seetieröl *n* marine [animal] oil
Seewasser *n* 1. lake water; 2. sea water
Segas-Verfahren *n (petrol)* Segas process
Seger-Formel *f (ceram)* Seger formula
Seger-Kegel *m (ceram)* Seger cone *(a pyrometric cone)*
Seger-Porzellan *n* Seger porcelain
Segmentcopolymerisat *n* block copolymer
Segment[ketten]modell *n (plast)* freely orienting chain model
Segregation *f* segregation
Segregationskonstante *f* segregation (partition, distribution) coefficient *(in zone-melting theory)*
Sehfarbstoff *m (bioch)* visual pigment, photopigment
Sehpurpur *m (bioch)* visual purple, rhodopsin
Sehstoff *m s.* Sehfarbstoff
Seide *f* 1. silk; 2. continuous-filament yarn *(manmade fibre)*
~/echte natural silk
~/gereckte drawn yarn
~/gesponnene spun silk
~/halbentbastete souple silk
~/monofile monofil, monofilament [yarn]
~/multifile (polyfile) multifil, multifilament [yarn]
~/reine natural silk
~/souplierte souple silk
~/texturierte bulked yarn
~/wilde wild silk *(e.g. tussah silk)*
seidenartig silk-like, silky
Seidenbast *m s.* Seidenleim
Seidenfibroin *n* silk fibroin
Seidengewebe *n* silk fabric
Seidenglanz *m* silky lustre *(of crystals)*
Seidenkautschuk *m* silk rubber *(from Funtumia elastica Stapf)*
Seidenkokon *m* cocoon
Seidenkreppapier *n* crêpe tissue paper
Seidenleim *m* silk gum (glue), sericin *(a protein occurring in silk)*
Seidenpapier *n* tissue [paper]
Seidenstoff *m* 1. silk fabric; 2. fibroin *(the fibrous component of natural silk)*
seidig silky
Seife *f* 1. soap; 2. *(geol)* placer [deposits]
~/alluviale *(geol)* alluvial placer
~/äolische *(geol)* eolian placer
~/aufgebaute built soap
~/desodorierende deodorant soap
~/feste *s.* ~/harte
~/flüssige liquid soap
~/fluviatile *(geol)* fluviatile placer
~/harte hard soap, soda soap
~ in Riegelform bar soap
~/kastilianische [olive-oil] castile soap, castile
~/marine *(geol)* marine placer
~/Marseiller Marseilles soap
~/medizinische medicated (medicinal) soap

~/neutrale neutral soap
~/scheuernde scouring soap
~/transparente transparent soap
~/überfettete superfatted soap
~/Venezianer (venezianische) Venetian soap
~/weiche soft soap, potash soap
seifecht fast to soaping
Seifechtheit *f* fastness to soaping
Seifenbad *n* soaping bath
Seifenblase *f* soap bubble
Seifenblasen-Durchflußmesser *m* soap film flowmeter
Seifenblätter *npl* shavings
Seifenchromatographie *f* soap chromatography
Seifenflocken *fpl* soap flakes
Seifenfluß *m* soapstock
seifenfrei soapless, non-soapy
Seifengold *n* placer (stream) gold
Seifenherstellung *n* soap manufacture
seifenlos soapless, non-soapy
Seifenmizell *n*, **Seifenmizelle** *f* soap micelle
Seifennachbehandlung *f (text)* soaping aftertreatment
Seifenpapier *n* soap paper (tissue)
Seifenpulver *n* soap powder
Seifenriegel *m* soap bar
Seifenrinde *f* soap (Panama, China) bark *(from Quillaja saponaria Mol.)*
Seifenschaum *m* lather
Seifenschnitzel *npl* soap chippings
Seifenshampoon *n* soap shampoo
Seifenspäne *mpl* shavings
Seifenstange *f* soap bar
Seifenstock *m* soapstock
Seifenstrang *m* log of soap
Seifenstück *n* cake [of soap]
Seifenzinn *n (min)* stream tin
Seifigkeit *f* soapy taste *(of spoiled fats)*
seigern to liquate, to segregate *(metal)*; to liquate [out], to segregate *(said of the metal)*
Seigerraffination *f (met)* liquation refining
Seigerung *f (met)* liquation, segregation
Seignettesalz *n* Rochelle (Seignette) salt, potassium sodium tartrate 4-water
seihen to strain
Seiher *m* 1. strainer; 2. *s.* Seiherkörper
Seiherkörper *m* cage, curb *(of a cage press)*
Seiherpresse *f* cage (curb) press
Seiherverfahren *n (petrol)* percolation process *(for refining bleaching earth)*
Seihfilter *n* bag filter
Seihtuch *n* straining cloth
Seihwasser *n s.* Uferfiltrat
Seilbohranlage *f (petrol)* cable tool installation (rig)
Seilbohren *n***[/pennsylvanisches]** *(petrol)* cable tool drilling
Seilbohrloch *n (petrol)* cable tool well
Seilbohrung *f s.* 1. Seilbohrloch; 2. Seilbohren
Seilbohrwerkzeug *n (petrol)* cable tool
Seilschlag[bohr]verfahren *n (petrol)* cable tool method (system)
Seite *f* side *(as of a molecule)*, *(relating to rings also)* face
~/gemeinsame common face, side of fusion *(in a ring system)*
Seitengruppe *f* side-group, pendant group
Seitenkette *f* side (lateral) chain, branch; spacer *(of a gel in affinity chromatography)*
Seitenkettenabbau *m* breakdown (cleavage) of side chains, side-chain degradation
Seitenkettenchlorierung *f* side-chain chlorination
Seitenkettenhalogenierung *f* side-chain halogenation
Seitenkettensubstitution *f* side-chain substitution
Seitenkolonne *f (petrol)* side[-stream] stripper, stripper [column]
Seitenprodukt *n (distil)* side product
Seitenrohr *n* side tube
Seitenschneide *f* terminal knife edge *(as of an analytical balance)*
Seitenstreifenmischung *f (rubber)* sidewall compound (stock)
Seitenstrom *m* side stream
Seitenturm *m s.* Seitenkolonne
Seitenwand *f* sidewall
Seitenwindkonverter *m* side-blow[n] convertor
Seitenzweig *m s.* Seitenkette
Seitz-Entkeimungsfilter *n*, **Seitz-Filter** *n* Seitz [germ-proofing] filter
Sekretion *f* secretion
Sekretionsvorgang *m* secretory process
sekretorisch secretory
Sekt *m* champagne, sparkling wine
Sektorenverfahren *n* **[der Rundfilterchromatographie]** sector process, sector circular chromatography
Sektorspiegel *m (spectr)* sector mirror
sekundär secondary
Sekundäracetat *n s.* Sekundärcelluloseacetat
Sekundäraggregat *n (coll)* secondary aggregate
Sekundärbatterie *f* secondary (storage) battery
Sekundärbeschleuniger *m (rubber)* secondary accelerator
~/aktivierender activating accelerator, booster
Sekundärbrücke *f (nomencl)* secondary bridge
Sekundärcelluloseacetat *n (text)* secondary [cellulose] acetate, cellulose diacetate
Sekundäreffekt *m* secondary effect
Sekundärelektron *n* secondary electron
Sekundärelektronenvervielfacher *m* photomultiplier [tube], PMT, multiplier phototube, secondary-emission electron multiplier
Sekundärelement *n* secondary (storage) cell
Sekundäremission *f* secondary emission
Sekundärförderung *f (petrol)* secondary recovery
Sekundärionenemission *f (anal)* secondary ion emission

Sekundärionenmassenspektrometer *n* secondary ion mass spectrometer, SIMS
Sekundärionenmassenspektrometrie *f* secondary ion mass spectrometry, SIMS
Sekundärkeimbildung *f (cryst)* secondary (surface) nucleation
Sekundärluft *f* secondary air
Sekundärlunker *m* secondary pipe *(foundry)*
Sekundärmetabolismus *m (biot)* secondary metabolism
Sekundärmetabolit *m (biot)* secondary metabolite, secondary product of metabolism
Sekundärreaktion *f* secondary reaction
~/photochemische secondary photochemical reaction
Sekundärrohstoff *m* waste material
Sekundärschadstoff *m* secondary pollutant
Sekundärstandard *m* secondary standard
Sekundärstoffbildung *f (bioch)* formation of secondary metabolites
Sekundärstoffwechsel *m (biot)* secondary metabolism
Sekundärstruktur *f (bioch)* secondary structure
Sekundärweichmacher *m* secondary plasticizer
Sekundärzelle *f s.* Sekundärelement
Sekundärzentrifuge *f* secondary centrifuge
Selachensäure *f* selacholeic acid, nervonic acid, *cis*-tetracos-15-enoic acid
Selachylalkohol *m* selachyl alcohol, glycerol octadec-1-enyl ether
Selbstabnahmefilz *m (pap)* lick-up overfelt (wet felt, felt)
Selbstabnahmemaschine *f s.* Selbstabnahmepapiermaschine
Selbstabnahmeoberfilz *m*, **Selbstabnahmeobertuch** *n s.* Selbstabnahmefilz
Selbstabnahmepapiermaschine *f* lick-up (single-cylinder) machine, Yankee machine
Selbstabnahmewalze *f (pap)* pick-up roll
Selbstabsorption *f* self-absorption
Selbstacylierung *f* self-acylation
Selbstalkylierung *f* self-alkylation
selbstansaugend self-priming *(pump)*
selbstauflösend *(biol)* autolytic
Selbstauflösung *f (biol)* autolysis, autolytic decomposition
selbstauslöschend self-extinguishing
Selbstbeschleunigung *f* autoacceleration
Selbstdiffusion *f* self-diffusion
Selbstdiffusionskoeffizient *m* self-diffusion coefficient
selbstemulgierend self-emulsifying
selbstentzündlich self-igniting, pyrophoric, pyrophorous
Selbstentzündung *f* self-ignition, autoignition, spontaneous (autogenous) ignition
Selbstentzündungstemperatur *f* self-ignition (spontaneous-ignition) temperature, S.I.T., autogenous ignition temperature
Selbsterhitzung *f*, **Selbsterwärmung** *f* self-heating, spontaneous heating
selbstgängig, selbstgehend self-fluxing *(ore)*
selbsthärtend *(plast)* self-curing
Selbstindizierung *f (anal)* self-diagnosis
Selbstionisation *f* autoionization, preionization
Selbstklebefolie *f* self-adhesive film
selbstklebend self-adherent
Selbstkleber *m* pressure-sensitive adhesive
Selbstkondensation *f* self-condensation, autocondensation
selbstlöschend 1. self-quenching *(photochemistry)*; 2. self-extinguishing
Selbstlöschung *f* self-quenching *(photochemistry)*
Selbstmord *m (bioch)* suicide *(as of macromolecules)*
Selbstorganisation *f (bioch)* self-assembly
Selbstoxidation *f s.* Autoxidation
Selbstreinigung *f (hyd)* self-purification, natural purification, self-cleansing
Selbstreinigungskraft *f*, **Selbstreinigungsvermögen** *n (hyd)* self-purification power
selbstschmierend self-lubricating
Selbstschmierung *f* self-lubrication
Selbstschreiber *m* recording instrument, recorder
selbsttätig automatic
selbsttonend *(phot)* self-toning
Selbstumkehr *f (spectr)* self-reversal
selbstverlöschend self-extinguishing
selbstvulkanisierend *(rubber)* self-curing, self-vulcanizing
Selbstzündpunkt *m*, **Selbstzündtemperatur** *f* spontaneous-ignition temperature, S.I.T.
Selbstzündung *f* self-ignition, autoignition, spontaneous ignition
selektieren to select
Selektion *f* selection
selektiv selective
Selektivaustauscher *m* selective exchanger *(ion exchange)*
Selektivaustauscherharz *n* selective resin *(ion exchange)*
Selektivflotation *f* selective (differential) floatation
Selektivherbizid *n* selective herbicide (weedkiller)
Selektivinsektizid *n* selective insecticide
Selektivität *f* selectivity
~ eines Ionenaustauschers ion selectivity
Selektivitätsfaktor *m* selectivity factor
Selektivitätskoeffizient *m* selectivity coefficient *(ion exchange)*
Selektivitätsreihe *f* order of [ion] selectivity, selectivity list *(ion exchange)*
Selektivkracken *n (petrol)* selective cracking
Selektivlösungsmittel *n* selective solvent
Selektivnährboden *m (biot)* selective medium
Selektivwirkung *f* selectivity
Selen *n* Se selenium
Selenat *n* $M^I_2SeO_4$ selenate
Selen(IV)-bromid *n* selenium(IV) bromide, selenium tetrabromide

Selen(IV)-chlorid *n* selenium(IV) chloride, selenium tetrachloride
Selendioxid *n s.* Selen(IV)-oxid
Selendisulfid *n s.* Selen(IV)-sulfid
Selenfilter *n (phot)* selenium glass
Selen(IV)-fluorid *n* selenium(IV) fluoride, selenium tetrafluoride
Selen(VI)-fluorid *n* selenium(VI) fluoride, selenium hexafluoride
Selengleichrichter *m* selenium rectifier
Selenhalogenid *n* selenium halide (halogenide)
Selenhexafluorid *n s.* Selen(VI)-fluorid
Selenid *n* M^I_2Se selenide
Selenit *m (min)* selenite *(a variety of gypsum)*
Selenit *n* $M^I_2SeO_3$ selenite
Selenmonosulfid *n s.* Selen(II)-sulfid
Selennitrid *n* selenium nitride, tetraselenium tetranitride
Selenon *n (org ch)* selenone
Selenonium-Ion *n* selenonium ion
Selenoniumverbindung *f* selenonium compound
Selen(IV)-oxid *n* selenium(IV) oxide, selenium dioxide
Selen(VI)-oxid *n* selenium(VI) oxide, selenium trioxide
Selenoxidbromid *n* selenium dibromide oxide
Selenoxidchlorid *n* selenium dichloride oxide
Selenoxidfluorid *n* selenium difluoride oxide
Selenrubinglas *n* selenium ruby glass
Selensäure *f* selenic acid
Selenstickstoff *m s.* Selennitrid
Selen(II)-sulfid *n* selenium(II) sulphide, selenium monosulphide
Selen(IV)-sulfid *n* selenium(IV) sulphide, selenium disulphide
Selentetra... *s.* Selen(IV)-...
Selentrioxid *n s.* Selen(VI)-oxid
Selenwasserstoff *m* hydrogen selenide, selenium hydride
Selenwismutglanz *m (min)* guanajuatite *(bismuth selenide)*
Selenzelle *f* selenium cell
Selivanov-Reaktion *f* Seliwanoff reaction *(for detecting hexoses)*
Sellerieöl *n* celery [seed] oil *(from Apium graveolens L.)*
Selleriesalz *n* celery salt
Seltenerden *pl* rare earths
Seltenerdmetall *n* rare-earth element (metal)
Selterswasser *n* seltzer [water], selter, selters water
Seltsamkeit *f (nucl)* strangeness
Semet-Solvay-Ofen *m* Semet-Solvay oven *(a coke oven)*
Semianthrazit *m* semianthracite
Semicarbazid *n (org ch)* semicarbazide
Semicarbazon *n (org ch)* semicarbazone
Semichemical-Zellstoff *m* semichemical pulp
Semichinon *n (org ch)* semiquinone
Semichromgerbung *f* semichrome tannage
semicyclisch semicyclic
Semidinumlagerung *f* semidine rearrangement (transformation)
Semiebonit *n* semiebonite, semihard (half-hard) rubber
Semifusinit *m* semifusinite *(a maceral of coal)*
Semikolloid *n* semicolloid
Semikraft-Verfahren *n (pap)* kraft semichemical process
Semimikroanalyse *f* semimicro (centigram) analysis
semipermeabel semipermeable
Semipermeabilität *f* semipermeability
semipolar semipolar
semiquantitativ semiquantitative
Semi-Reinforcing-Furnace-Ruß *m (rubber)* semi-reinforcing furnace black, SRF black
Semisynthese *f* semisynthesis
semisynthetisch semisynthetical
Semitrivialname *m* semitrivial (semisystematic) name
semizyklisch semicyclic
Senarmontit *m (min)* senarmontite *(antimony(III) oxide)*
Senecioalkaloid *n* senecio (pyrrolizidine) alkaloid
Seneciosäure *f* senecioic acid, 3,3-dimethylacrylic acid
Senf *m (food)* [table] mustard
Senfgas *n* mustard gas, di-2-chloroethyl sulphide, dichlorodiethyl sulphide
Senföl *n* 1. mustard[seed] oil; 2. RNCS isothiocyanate, *(old term:)* mustard oil
Senfölglykosid *n* mustard glycoside
Senfpapier *n (med)* mustard paper
Senkblei *n* plummet, sounding lead
Senkbrunnen *m (hyd)* dug well
Senke *f* sink *(of pollutants, as opposed to a source of pollutants)*
senken to lower, to reduce, to depress
Senkgrube *f (tech)* sump
Senkrechtbecherwerk *n* vertical bucket elevator
Senkrechtförderer *m* vertical elevator
Senkrechtkammer *f* vertical chamber *(as of an oven)*
Senkrechtofen *m* vertical oven *(as for manufacturing gas)*
Senkrechtstellung *f* perpendicular position
Senkrechtziehverfahren *n* **für Tafelglas** vertical sheet drawing process
Senkspindel *f* densi[to]meter, araeometer, hydrometer
Senkung *f* lowering, reduction, depression
Senkwaage *f s.* Senkspindel
Sennaar-Gummi *n* Sennaar gum *(mainly from Acacia senegal (L.) Willd.)*
Sensibilisator *m* sensitizer
~/chemischer chemical sensitizer
~/optischer (spektraler) spectral (optical) sensitizer

sensibilisieren to sensitize
~/panchromatisch to panchromatize
Sensibilisierung *f* sensitization
~/chemische chemical sensitization
~/optische (spektrale) spectral (optical) sensitization
Sensibilisierungsfarbstoff *m* sensitizing dye
Sensibilität *f* sensitivity, sensitiveness
Sensitometer *n (phot)* sensitometer
Sensitometrie *f (phot)* sensitometry
Sensor *m* sensor, sensing element
~/ionenspezifischer ion-selective electrode
Separation *f* separation
Separationsfaktor *m (anal)* separation factor
Separator *m* separator
~/mehrstufiger multistage separator
Separator-Nobel-Verfahren *n* Separator-Nobel process *(for deparaffinizing petroleum)*
Separatstreichen *n*, **Separatstrich** *m (pap)* separate (conversion, off-machine) coating
separieren to separate [out]
Separierung *f* separation
Sepiabraun *n* umber *(an earth pigment)*
Sepialichtpause *f* brown print
Sepia-Lichtpausverfahren *n* sepia negative process, silver-iron process, Vandyke process, brownprint
Sepiatonung *f (phot)* sepia toning
Sepiolith *m (min)* sepiolite, sea foam, meerschaum *(a phyllosilicate)*
Septuminjektion *f* syringe (septum) injection *(gas chromatography)*
Sequenator *m* amino-acid sequenator (sequencer) *(for investigating protein structure)*
Sequenz *f* sequence
~/amphibolische *(bioch)* amphibolic pathway (route), central [metabolic] pathway
~/anaplerotische *(bioch)* anaplerotic sequence
~/codierende *(bioch)* codon sequence
~/katabolische *(bioch)* catabolic pathway (route)
~/redundante (repetitive) *(bioch)* repeating (repeated) sequence *(of deoxyribonucleic acid)*
Sequenzanalyse *f* 1. sequential analysis *(as opposed to simultaneous analysis)*; 2. sequence analysis (determination) *(protein chemistry)*
Sequenzer *m s.* Sequenator
Sequenzermittlung *f s.* Sequenzanalyse 2.
Sequenzhomologie *f (bioch)* sequence homology
Sequenzierung *f s.* Sequenzanalyse 2.
Sequenzwiederholung *f***/direkte** *(bioch)* direct repeat
~/gegenläufige inverted repeat
~/indirekte indirect repeat
~/invertierte inverted repeat
Sequenzzahl *f (plast)* run number
Sequestiermittel *n* sequestering agent, sequestrant
Ser *s.* Serin
Sericin *n* sericin, silk gum (glue) *(a protein occurring in silk)*
Sericit *m (min)* sericite *(a phyllosilicate)*
Serie *f* 1. series; 2. battery, bank *(as of apparatus)*
Serienanalyse *f* routine (repetitive) analysis
Seriengrenze *f (spectr)* series (convergence) limit
Seriengrenzfrequenz *f* convergence frequency *(of a spectral series)*
Serin *n* serine, 2-amino-3-hydroxypropionic acid
Serincephalin *n* 3-phosphatidyl serine
Serinprotease *f (bioch)* serine protease
Serin-Weg *m (biot)* serine pathway *(methanol fermentation)*
Serotonin *n* serotonin, 3-(2-aminoethyl)-5-hydroxyindole
Serpentin *m (min)* serpentine *(any of a group of phyllosilicates)*
Serpentinasbest *m (min)* serpentine asbestos
Serum *n* serum; *(rubber)* skim
~/natives native serum
Serumalbumin *n* [blood] serum albumin
~/menschliches *s.* Humanserumalbumin
Serumglobulin *n* serum globulin
Serumprotein *n* serum protein
Sesamöl *n* sesame oil, benne (gingelly, teel) oil *(from Sesamum indicum L.)*
Sesci-Ofen *m (met)* Sesci furnace
Sesquioxid *n* sesquioxide *(deprecated term for an oxide of the type $M_2^{III}O_3$)*
Sesquiterpen *n* sesquiterpene
Sesquiterpenalkohol *m* sesquiterpene alcohol
Sesquiterpenoid *n* sesquiterpenoid
Sesselform *f* chair [form], staircase form *(stereochemistry)*
Sesselkonformation *f* chair (staircase) conformation
Sesterterpen *n* sesterterpene
Sesterterpenoid *n* sesterterpenoid
Setzapparat *m (min tech)* jig
~/hydraulischer hydraulic (wet) jig
Setzarbeit *f (min tech)* jigging
Setzbett *n (min tech)* jig bed
setzen *(min tech)* to jig; *(ceram)* to place, to set *(material to be burned)*
~/außer Betrieb to put out of operation, to cut out of service, to stop *(a machine)*; to shut [down], to close down *(a factory)*
~/in Betrieb to put (set) in operation, to set in action, to start [up], to prime *(a machine)*
~/in Freiheit to liberate, to release
~/in Gang 1. to initiate, to start up *(a reaction)* 2. *s.* ~/in Betrieb
~/sich to settle [out], to deposit, to sediment, to subside, to set
~/unter Druck to pressurize
Setzfaß *n s.* Setzkasten
Setzgut *n* material being *or* to be separated
Setzherd *m (min tech)* table
Setzkasten *m (min tech)* wash box, hutch *(of a jig washer)*
~/Baumscher Baum wash box

Setzmaschine *f (min tech)* jig [washer]
~/Baumsche Baum jig [washer] *(an air-operated jig)*
~/Harzer Harz [fixed-sieve] jig
~/hydraulische hydraulic (wet) jig
~/luftbewegte (luftgesteuerte) air-operated jig
~ mit bewegtem Sieb movable-sieve jig
~ mit festem Sieb fixed-sieve jig
Setzmilch *f* [naturally, spontaneously] soured milk, sour (set) milk
Setzraum *m (min tech)* jigging compartment, ore box *(of a jig washer)*
Setzsieb *n (min tech)* jig[ging] screen
Setzweise *f***/offene** *(ceram)* open setting *(the arrangement of ware in a kiln without saggars)*
SEV *s.* Sekundärelektronenvervielfacher
Sexagen *n*, **Sexualhormon** *n* sex hormone
Sexuallockstoff *m*, **Sexualpheromon** *n* sex[ual] attractant, sex lure
sezernieren *(biol)* to secrete
S-Finish *n (text)* S finishing, surface saponification
Shampoo[n] *n (cosmet)* shampoo
Sharples-Verfahren *n (petrol)* Sharples [two-stage dewaxing] process
Shatter-Test *m (coal)* shatter test
Sheet *m***/luftgetrockneter** *(rubber)* air-dried sheet, A.D.S.
Sheet-Mangel *f (rubber)* sheeting mill
sherardisieren to sherardize *(to coat with zinc by diffusion coating)*
Shikimisäure *f* shikimic acid, 3,4,5-trihydroxycyclohex-1-ene-1-carboxylic acid
Shikimisäureweg *m (bioch)* shikimic acid pathway
Shine-Delgarno-Sequenz *f (bioch)* Shine-Delgarno sequence *(of the messenger RNA, rich in purines)*
Shoddywolle *f (text)* shoddy
Shonansäure *f* shonanic acid *(a tropolone derivative)*
Shore-Härte *f* Shore hardness
Shore-Härtemesser *m*, **Shore-Härteprüfer** *m* Shore durometer
Showerdeck *n (petrol)* shower deck
SH-Säuregrad *m (food)* degree S/H, degree Soxhlet-Henkel
Shuttle-Vektor *m (bioch)* shuttle vector
SHZ *s.* Sulfathüttenzement
Siaktalg *m* Siak fat (tallow) *(from Palaquium oleiferum Blanco)*
Sial *n* sial, granitic layer *(upper rock layer of the earth's crust)*
Sialinsäure *f* sialic acid *(any of a group of acylated neuraminic acids)*
Sialzone *f s.* Sial
Siambenzoe *f* Siam benzoin *(from Styrax specc.)*
Siamkardamom *m(n)* Siam cardamom *(from Elettaria cardamomum (L.)White et Maton)*
Siaresinolsäure *f* siaresinolic acid *(a polycyclic compound isolated from Siam benzoin)*
Sichelzellenhämoglobin *n (bioch)* sickle-cell haemoglobin, haemoglobin S
Sicherheitsabsperrventil *n* safety cut-off
Sicherheitsbehälter *m (nucl)* containment
Sicherheitsbeiwert *m* safety factor
Sicherheitsbeschleuniger *m (rubber)* delayed-action accelerator
Sicherheitsbestimmung *f* safety regulation
Sicherheitsbrause *f s.* Löschbrause
Sicherheitschlorung *f (hyd)* safety chlorination
Sicherheitsfaktor *m* safety factor
Sicherheitsfarbe *f* safety (sensitive) ink *(printing ink for safety papers)*
Sicherheitsgefäß *n* safety vessel
Sicherheitsglas *n* safety (shatterproof) glass
~/geschichtetes laminated safety [sheet] glass
Sicherheitsglas-Zwischenschicht *f* safety-glass interlayer (interleaver)
Sicherheitsingenieur *m* safety engineer
Sicherheitslicht *n* safelight
Sicherheitsmaßnahme *f* safety measure, precaution
Sicherheitsmaßregel *f* safety rule (principle)
Sicherheitspackung *f* safety package
Sicherheitspapier *n* safety (cheque, security) paper
Sicherheitspipette *f* safety pipette
Sicherheitsrohr *n* guard tube *(as for burettes)*; protective tube *(as on storage bottles)*
Sicherheitssprengstoff *m* safety explosive, *(Am)* permissible [explosive]
Sicherheitsventil *n* safety[-relief] valve, [pressure] relief valve
~/entlastetes balanced relief valve
~/federbelastetes spring-actuated relief valve, spring safety valve
Sicherheitsvorkehrungen *fpl* safety precautions
Sicherheitsvorschrift *f* safety instruction
Sicherheitswaschflasche *f* safety wash-bottle
Sicherheitszündholz *n* safety match
sichern to secure; to establish *(e.g. the structure of a compound)*; to check *(results)*
Sicherung *f* 1. securing; establishing *(of the structure of a compound)*; checking *(of results)*; 2. safeguard, security device
sichtbar visible • **~ machen** to visualize
~/mit unbewaffnetem Auge visible to the naked eye
Sichtbares *n (spectr)* visible region (range)
Sichtbarmachen *n*, **Sichtbarmachung** *f* visualization
sichten to classify pneumatically (by air)
Sichten *n* pneumatic classification, air classifying (sizing), air separation (sweeping, elutriation)
Sichtentwicklung *f (phot)* development by inspection
Sichter *m* pneumatic (air) classifier, air separator
Sichtermühle *f* classifier mill
Sichtfeines *n* undersize [material], minus material *(air classification)*
Sichtfenster *n*, **Sichtglas** *n* inspection (sight) glass, viewing window

Sichtgrobes *n* oversize [material], tailing[s], tails *(air classification)*
Sichtkammer *f* classifying chamber
Sichtmühle *f* classifier mill
Sichtprüfung *f* visual examination
Sichtung *f s.* Sichten
Sichtweite *f* visibility *(in the atmosphere)*
~/meteorologische meteorological range
Sickerlaugung *f (min tech)* percolation leaching
sickern to trickle
~ **lassen** to [allow to] trickle
Sickerverlust *m* leakage, slippage loss, slip
Sickerwasser *n (soil)* percolation (leachate) water; *(hyd)* seep (drainage) water
Siderazot *m (min)* siderazot[e], silvestrite *(an iron nitride)*
Sideringelb *n* siderin yellow *(iron(III) chromate)*
Siderit *m* 1. [holo]siderite, iron meteorite, meteoric iron; 2. *(min)* siderite, spathic iron [ore] *(iron(II) carbonate)*
Siderolith *m* siderolite, sideraerolite *(a kind of iron meteorite)*
Sideroshäre *f s.* Barysphäre
Sieb *n* 1. sieve, *(esp tech)* screen, *(for liquids containing solid particles:)* strainer; *(pap)* wire; 2. *s.* Siebapparat
~/endloses *(pap)* endless wire
~ **mit bewegter Siebfläche** moving screen
~ **mit drei Siebböden (Siebflächen)** triple-decked screen
~ **mit unbewegter Siebfläche** stationary (fixed) screen
~ **mit zwei Siebböden (Siebflächen)** double-decked screen, two-deck sifter
~/standardisiertes standard sieve (screen)
Siebabwasser *n s.* Siebwasser
Siebanalyse *f* sieve (screen) analysis
Siebanlage *f* screening plant
Siebapparat *m* screening machine, screen [classifier], sifter
Siebaustrag *m* screen discharge
Siebblech *n* perforated plate (tray)
Siebboden *m* screen deck *(classification of bulk material)*; perforated bottom *(of a Gooch crucible)*; *(distil)* sieve (perforated) plate (tray); *(ferm)* strainer [bottom]
Siebbodenkolonne *f (distil)* sieve-plate (perforated-plate) column (tower)
~/pulsierte pulsed sieve-plate column, sieve-plate pulse tower *(extraction)*
Siebbodenreaktor *m (biot)* sieve-plate cascade reactor
Siebbreite *f (pap)* width of the wire
Siebdruckfarbe *f* silk-screen (screen-process) ink
Siebdruckverfahren *n* silk-screen process
Siebdurchgang *m*, **Siebdurchlauf** *m* underflow
Siebeinlage *f* strainer
Siebeinsatz *m* strainer; *(plast)* screen pack *(as of an extruder)*
sieben to sieve, *(esp tech)* to screen, to sift
Siebenerring *m s.* Siebenring
siebengliedrig seven-membered
Siebenring *m* seven-membered ring
siebenwertig heptavalent, septivalent
Siebenstufenbleiche *f (pap)* seven-stage bleaching
Sieberei *f* screening station
Siebereianlage *f* screening plant
Sieberfolg *m* screen[ing] efficiency
Siebfeine *f s.* Siebfeines
Siebfeines *n* screen undersize (fines), undersize [material, product], minus material, fines
Siebfeinheit *f* sieve fineness, grade *(quantitatively:)* mesh
Siebfilter *n* screen filter
Siebfläche *f* screen[ing] surface, *(quantitatively:)* screen[ing] area
~/nützliche active screen area
Siebgeschwindigkeit *f (pap)* speed of the wire
Siebgewebe *n* straining cloth, gauze; *(pap)* wire cloth (gauze) • **mit ~ abgedeckt** *(filtr)* screen-covered
Siebgröbe *f s.* Siebgrobes
Siebgrobes *n* screen oversize, plus mesh (material), oversize [material], overflow [product], overs, tailings
Siebgut *n* material being *or* to be screened, screen feed
Siebgütegrad *m* screen[ing] efficiency
Siebkante *f (pap)* wire edge
Siebkasten *m* screen frame
siebklassieren to screen
Siebklassierung *f* screen sizing (classification), screening
Siebkopf *m* screen (straining) head
Siebkopf-Spritzmaschine *f (plast, rubber)* screen head extruder, strainer
Siebkorb *m s.* Siebtrommel
Siebkurve *f* grading curve (limit)
Sieblänge *f (pap)* wire length
Sieblauf *m (pap)* run of the wire
Sieblaufregler *m (pap)* wire guide
Sieblaufregulierwalze *f s.* Siebleitwalze
Siebleder *n (pap)* apron
Siebleistung *f* screening capacity
Siebleitwalze *f (pap)* wire-guide roll
Sieblinie *f s.* Siebkurve
Sieblochung *f* perforation *(of a screen)*, *(relating to diameter also)* orifice, screen aperture (size)
Siebmantel *m (pap)* cylinder cover
siebmarkiert *(pap)* wire-marked
Siebmarkierung *f (pap)* wire mark • **mit** ~ wire-marked
Siebmaschine *f s.* Siebapparat
Siebmühle *f* screen-type mill
Siebnaht *f (pap)* seam of the machine wire
Siebnerring *m s.* Siebenring

Siebnummer *f* mesh *(number of openings per linear inch)*; *(pap)* number

Siebnutzfläche *f* active screen area

Sieboberfläche *f* screen[ing] surface

Sieböffnung *f* screen opening (hole); *(s. a.* Sieböffnungsweite*)*

Sieböffnungsgröße *f s.* Sieböffnungsweite

Sieböffnungsweite *f* screen (sieve) size, [screen] aperture

Siebpartie *f (pap)* wire part (end), Fourdrinier part (section)

~/ausfahrbare removable Fourdrinier [part]

~ der Rundsiebpapiermaschine cylinder part

Siebplättchen *n* perforated plate *(of a Gooch crucible)*

Siebplatte *f* perforated plate; *(plast)* screen pack *(of an extruder)*

Siebpresse *f s.* Siebkopf-Spritzmaschine

Siebrand *m (pap)* wire edge

Siebrandspritzwasser *n (pap)* squirt-trim water

Siebrätter *m* gyratory screen (sifter)

Siebreihe *f* screen (sieve) series (scale)

Siebrost *m* bar (rod) grizzly, grizzly [screen]

Siebrückstand *m s.* Siebgrobes

Siebrüttelmaschine *f* sieve shaker

Siebsatz *m* set of screens (sieves)

Siebsaugwalze *f (pap)* suction [couch] roll

Siebschleuder *f s.* Filtrierzentrifuge

Siebschneckenaustragzentrifuge *f* screen-conveyor centrifuge

Siebschneckenschleuder *f*, **Siebschneckenzentrifuge** *f* screen-conveyor centrifuge

Siebschüttelung *f (pap)* shake of the wire

Siebseite *f* wire side *(of paper)*

Siebskala *f s.* Siebreihe

Siebspannung *f (pap)* wire tension

Siebstation *f* screening station

Siebtisch *m (pap)* wire table (frame), forming table

Siebtrog *m* [cylinder] vat *(of a cylinder paper machine)*

Siebtrommel *f* 1. revolving screen, trommel [screen]; 2. perforated basket (bowl) *(of a centrifugal)*

~/konische conical screen

Siebtrum *m (pap)* wire run

~/rücklaufender (rückläufiger, unterer) return wire run

~/vorlaufender wire run

Siebtuch *n* straining cloth, gauze

Siebtuchpresse *f (pap)* fabric press

Siebübergang *m*, **Siebüberlauf** *m s.* Siebgrobes

Siebüberzug *m (pap)* cylinder cover *(of a cylinder mould)*

Siebunterlauf *m s.* Siebfeines

Siebvorrichtung *f* screen classifier, screening device

~/angebaute (äußere) external screen classifier

~/eingebaute internal screen classifier

Siebwasser *n (pap)* backwater, tray water, pulp (free, loose, save-all) water, [machine] white water

Siebwasserbehälter *m (pap)* backwater tank (box), hog pit, [machine-]wire pit, save-all tray

Siebwasserpumpe *f (pap)* backwater pump

Siebwassersammelbecken *n s.* Siebwasserbehälter

Siebwechsel *m (pap)* wire changing

Siebweite *f s.* Sieböffnungsweite

Siebwirkung *f* screening action; screening effect

Siebwirkungsgrad *m* screen[ing] efficiency

Siebzentrifuge *f s.* Filtrierzentrifuge

~ mit Kegeltrommel (konischer Trommel) *s.* Kegel-Filtrierzentrifuge

~ mit zylindrischer Trommel *s.* Zylinder-Filtrierzentrifuge

Siebzylinder *m (pap)* cylinder mould

Siedeanalyse *f* distillation analysis

Siedebeginn *m* initial boiling point, I.B.P.

Siedebereich *m* boiling[-point] range

Siedediagramm *n* boiling-point diagram

~ mit Maximum maximum boiling-point system

~ mit Minimum minimum boiling-point system

Siedeendpunkt *m* final boiling point, F.B.P, end point, EP

Siedeerleichterer *m* boiling stone; boiling chip

Siedefläche *f* plane of the boiling-point diagram

Siedegrenzen *fpl* boiling range

Siedegrenzenbenzin *n* special boiling-point spirit, SBP spirit

Siedehitze *f* boiling heat

Siedeintervall *n* boiling[-point] range

Siedekapillare *f* capillary air bleed, whipping tube

Siedekonstanz *f* regular boiling

Siedekurve *f s.* 1. Siedelinie; 2. Siedepunktskurve

Siedelinie *f* boiling curve *(of a two-component system)*

sieden to boil

~/nochmals to reboil

Sieden *n* boil[ing] • **am ~ halten** to keep at the boil • **nahe am ~ halten** to keep near the boil

~/konstantes regular boiling

~/örtliches subcooled boiling

siedend boiling

~/höher higher-boiling

~/konstant constant-boiling

~/leichter (niedriger) lower-boiling

~/schwerer higher-boiling

Siedepfanne *f* pan *(for obtaining table salt)*

Siedepunkt *m* boiling point, b.p., bp, boiling temperature

~/mittlerer mid-boiling point

Siedepunktbestimmung *f* boiling-point determination

Siedepunktserhöhung *f* boiling-point elevation, BPE, *(act also)* raising of the boiling point

~/molale (molare) molal boiling-point[-elevation] constant, molal (molar, molecular) elevation constant, ebullioscopic constant

Siedepunktshöchstwert *m* maximum boiling point
Siedepunktskurve *f* boiling point curve *(of a multicomponent system)*
~ **bei geschlossener Verdampfung** [single-]flash curve
Siedepunktsmaximum *n* maximum boiling point
Siedepunktsmaximumazeotrop *n* maximum-boiling azeotrope, high-boiling azeotrope
Siedepunktsminimum *n* minimum boiling point
Siedepunktsminimumazeotrop *n* minimum-boiling azeotrope, low-boiling azeotrope
Siedereaktor *m (nucl)* boiling [water] reactor
Siederohr *n* boiling tube
Siederohrdampferzeuger *m*, **Siederohrkessel** *m* water-tube boiler
Siedesalz *n* evaporated salt
Siedeschaubild *n* boiling-point diagram
Siedeschwanz *m (distil)* heavy ends *(boiling analysis)*
Siedestab *m (lab)* bumping stick
Siedestein *m*, **Siedesteinchen** *n* boiling stone
Siedetemperatur *f* boiling temperature (point)
Siedeverfahren *n* boiling-off process *(for making butter)*
Siedeverzögerung *f s.* Siedeverzug
Siedeverzug *m* delay in boiling
Siedewasserreaktor *m (nucl)* boiling [water] reactor
Siedezone *f* boiling zone
Siegelgerät *n (plast)* sealing unit
Siegellack *m* sealing wax
siegeln *(plast)* to seal
Siegeln *n (plast)* sealing
~ **mit gespritztem Zusatzdraht** extruded-bead sealing
~ **mit Heizstab** heated-bar sealing
~ **mit Schweißlineal** heated-bar sealing
~ **mit stranggepreßtem Zusatzdraht** extruded-bead sealing
Siegler *m (plast)* sealer
Siemens-Martin-Ofen *m* open-hearth furnace, OH-furnace
Siemens-Martin-Schlacke *f* open-hearth slag
Siemens-Martin-Stahl *m* open-hearth steel
Siemens-Martin-Stahlwerk *n* open-hearth steel plant
Siemens-Martin-Verfahren *n* open-hearth process
Sienaerde *f* sienna *(hydrous iron oxide)*
Sigmabindung *f* sigma bond, σ bond
Sigmaelektron *n* sigma electron, σ electron
Sigmaphase *f (met)* sigma phase
Signal *n (anal)* signal
~/spitzes peak
Signalaufspaltung *f (anal)* signal splitting
Signalerkennungspartikel *n (bioch)* signal recognition particle
Signalfläche *f (anal)* peak area
Signalform *f*, **Signalgestalt** *f (anal)* peak shape
Signalhöhe *f (anal)* peak height
Signalintegration *f (anal)* peak area integration
Signalintensität *f (anal)* signal (peak) intensity, signal strength
Signalöl *n* signal (long-time burning) oil
Signal-Rausch-Verhältnis *n (anal)* signal-to-noise ratio, S/N ratio
Signalsequenz *f (bioch)* signal sequence
Signalüberlagerung *f*, **Signalüberlappung** *f (anal)* superposition of peaks
Signal-Untergrund-Verhältnis *n s.* Signal-Rausch-Verhältnis
Signalverbreiterung *f (anal)* peak broadening
Signalverzerrung *f (anal)* peak distortion
Sikkativ *n* liquid drier, *(broadly)* [paint] drier, siccative
Silan *n* silane, *(specif)* SiH_4 monosilane
~/organisches organic silane, organosilane
silanisieren *(chromat)* to silanize
Silanisierung *f (chromat)* silanization
Silanol *n* silanol *(a silicon compound which contains OH groups, specif H_3SiOH)*
Silazan *n* $H_3Si(NHSiH_2)_nNHSiH_3$ silazane
~/organisches organosilazane
Silber *n* Ag silver
~/gediegen[es] native silver
~/knallsaures *s.* Silberfulminat
~/metallisches metallic silver
Silberabscheidung *f* 1. deposition of silver; 2. silver deposit
Silberacetylid *n* silver acetylide (carbide)
Silberarsenat(III) *n* silver arsenite
Silberarsenat(V) *n* silver arsenate
Silberätze *f (glass)* silver stain
Silberazid *n* silver azide, silver nitride
Silberbad *n* 1. *(phot)* silver bath; 2. *s.* Silberelektrolyt
Silberbeize *f (glass)* silver stain
Silberbelag *m* silver deposit
Silberbild *n (phot)* silver image
Silberbromid *n* silver bromide
Silberbromidelektrode *f* silver-bromide electrode
Silberbromidkorn *n (phot)* silver-bromide grain
Silbercarbid *n s.* Silberacetylid
Silberchlorid *n* silver chloride
Silberchloridelektrode *f* silver-chloride electrode
Silberchromat *n* silver chromate
Silbercoulometer *n* silver coulometer (voltameter)
Silberdifluorid *n s.* Silber(II)-fluorid
Silberdiphosphat *n* silver diphosphate, silver pyrophosphate
Silberelektrode *f* silver electrode
Silberelektrolyt *m* silver plating bath (solution)
Silber(I)-fluorid *n* silver(I) fluoride, silver monofluoride
Silber(II)-fluorid *n* silver(II) fluoride, silver difluoride
silberführend *(geoch)* silver-bearing, argentiferous
Silberfulminat *n* silver fulminate
Silbergehalt *m* silver content

Silberglanz *m (min)* silver glance, vitreous silver *(silver sulphide)*
silberglänzend silvery
Silberglätte *f s.* Bleiglätte
Silberhalogenid *n* silver halide (halogenide)
Silberhalogenidemulsion *f (phot)* silver-halide emulsion
Silberhalogenidkorn *n (phot)* silver-halide grain
silberhaltig containing silver, *(esp relating to ores:)* argentiferous, argentian
Silberhexacyanoferrat(II) *n* silver hexacyanoferrate(II)
Silberhexacyanoferrat(III) *n* silver hexacyanoferrate(III)
Silberhexafluorosilicat *n* silver hexafluorosilicate
Silberhydrogenphosphat *n* silver hydrogenphosphate
silberig silvery
Silberiodid *n* silver iodide
Silberkeim *m (phot)* silver nucleus
Silberkorn *n (phot)* silver grain
Silberlot *n* silver solder
Silbermolybdat *n* silver molybdate
Silbermonofluorid *n s.* Silber(I)-fluorid
Silberniederschlag *m* silver deposit
Silbernitrat *n* silver nitrate
Silbernitratpapier *n* silver-nitrate paper
Silbernitroprussiat *n s.* Silbernitroprussid
Silbernitroprussid *n* silver nitroprusside
Silberorthophosphat *n* silver orthophosphate
Silberoxid *n* silver oxide, *(specif)* silver(I) oxide
Silber(I)-oxid *n* silver(I) oxide
Silber(II)-oxid *n* silver(II) oxide
Silber[pack]papier *n* aluminium (silver) paper
silberplattiert silver-clad
Silberpyrophosphat *n s.* Silberdiphosphat
Silberrhodanid *n s.* Silberthiocyanat
Silberrückgewinnung *f* silver recovery
Silbersalz *n* 1. silver salt; 2. *(org ch)* silver salt, sodium anthraquinone-2-sulphonate *(for detecting alkaloids)*
Silbersalzdiffusion *f (phot)* silver-salt diffusion
Silberschicht *f* silver coating
Silber-Silberbromid-Elektrode *f* silver-silver bromide electrode
Silber-Silberchlorid-Elektrode *f* silver-silver chloride electrode
Silberspiegel *m* silver mirror
Silberstrichbildung *f (ceram)* silver (cutlery) marking
Silbersulfat *n* silver sulphate
Silbertetraiodomercurat(II) *n* silver tetraiodomercurate(II)
Silberthiocyanat *n* silver thiocyanate
Silberung *f (hyd)* silver treatment
Silberverstärker *m (phot)* silver intensifier
Silberwolle *f* silver wool
Silicat *n* silicate
~/wasserhaltiges hydrosilicate, hydrous silicate
Silicat... *s. a.* Silikat... *for technical terms*
Silicatbildung *f* silicate formation
Silicatbindung *f* silicate bond
Silicatphosphor *m* silicate phosphor *(any of a class of phosphorescent compounds)*
Silicid *n* silicide
Silicium *n* Si silicon
Siliciumbromoform *n s.* Silicobromoform
Siliciumbronze *f* silicon bronze
Siliciumcarbid *n* silicon carbide
Siliciumchloroform *n s.* Silicochloroform
Siliciumdioxid *n* silicon dioxide
siliciumdioxidhaltig siliceous, silicic, siliciferous
Siliciumdisulfid *n* silicon disulphide, silicon(IV) sulphide
Siliciumeisen *n* silicon iron
Siliciumester *m* silicic-acid ester, silicon ester
Siliciumfluoroform *n s.* Silicofluoroform
Siliciumfluorwasserstoffsäure *f s.* Hexafluorokieselsäure
siliciumfunktionell silicon-functional
Siliciumgleichrichter *m* silicon rectifier
Siliciumguß *m* silicon cast iron
siliciumhaltig 1. containing silicon; 2. *s.* siliciumdioxidhaltig
Siliciumhexabromid *n* *hexabromodisilane, disilicon hexabromide
Siliciumhexachlorid *n* *hexachlorodisilane, disilicon hexachloride
Siliciumhydrid *n s.* Siliciumwasserstoff
Silicium(IV)-iodid *n* silicon(IV) iodide, silicon tetraiodide
Siliciumjodoform *n s.* Silicoiodoform
Silicium-Kohlenstoff-Bindung *f* silicon-carbon bond
Silicium(IV)-oxid *n s.* Siliciumdioxid
Siliciumpolymer[e] *n* silicon polymer
~/organisches organosilicon polymer
Siliciumtetraäthyl *n s.* Tetraethylsilan
Siliciumtetrabromid *n* silicon tetrabromide, silicon(IV) bromide
Siliciumtetrachlorid *n* silicon tetrachloride, silicon(IV) chloride
Siliciumtetrafluorid *n* silicon tetrafluoride, silicon(IV) fluoride
Siliciumtetramethyl *n s.* Tetramethylsilan
Siliciumwasserstoff *m* silicon hydride, silane
Silicoameisensäure *f* silicoformic acid
Silicoameisensäureanhydrid *n* silicoformic anhydride, dioxodisiloxane
Silicobenzoesäure *f* silicobenzoic acid
Silicobromoform *n* *tribromosilane, silicobromoform
Silicochloroform *n* *trichlorosilane, silicochloroform
Silicoessigsäure *f* silicoacetic acid
Silicoethan *n s.* Disilan
Silicofluorid *n s.* Hexafluorosilicat
Silicofluoroform *n* *trifluorosilane, silicofluoroform
Silicoiodoform *n* *triiodosilane, silicoiodoform

Silicomesoxalsäure *f* silicomesoxalic acid
Silicomethan *n s.* Monosilan
Silicomethylether *m s.* Disiloxan
Silicon *n* silicone, *polysiloxane • **mit Siliconen behandeln** to silicone-treat, to siliconize
~/carbofunktionelles carbon-functional silicone
~/elastomeres silicone elastomer
~/organofunktionelles organofunctional silicone
Silicon... *s. a.* Silikon... *for technical terms*
Siliconat *n* siliconate
Siliconchemie *f* silicone chemistry
Siliconelastomer[e] *n* silicone elastomer
Silicononan *n s.* Tetraethylsilan
Siliconpolymer[e] *n* silicone polymer
Silicooxalsäure *f* silicooxalic acid
Silicopropan *n s.* Trisilan
Silicowolframat *n s.* Wolframatosilicat
Silicylengruppe *f s.* Silylengruppe
Silicylgruppe *f s.* Silylgruppe
Silicyloxid *n s.* Disiloxan
silifizieren *(geoch)* to silicify
Silifizierung *f (geoch)* silicification
Silika *f s.* Silikamasse
Silikabaustein *m* silica brick
Silikamasse *f*, **Silikamaterial** *n* silica
Silikamörtel *m* silica cement
Silikasand *m* silica sand
Silikastein *m* silica brick
Silikat... *s. a.* Silicat... *for chemical terms*
Silikatgestein *n* silicate rock
Silikatglas *n* silicate glass
silikatisch siliceous
Silikatschlacke *f* silicate slag
Silikon... *s. a.* Silicon... *for chemical compounds*
Silikonanlage *f* silicone plant
Silikonanstrichfarbe *f* silicone paint
Silikonantischaummittel *n* silicone antifoam
Silikonausrüstung *f* silicone finish
Silikonbasis/auf silicone-base[d]
silikonbehandelt silicone-treated, siliconized
Silikonbehandlung *f* silicone treatment, siliconization
silikonbeschichtet silicone-coated
Silikonemulsion *f* silicone emulsion
Silikonfarbe *f* silicone paint
Silikonfett *n* silicone grease
Silikonfilm *m* silicone film
Silikonfluid *n*, **Silikonflüssigkeit** *f* silicone fluid (liquid, oil)
Silikonform[en]trennmittel *n* silicone mould-release agent
Silikonfüllstoff *m* silicone filler
Silikongrundlage/auf silicone-base[d]
Silikongummi *m* silicone rubber *(vulcanized product)*
Silikongummimischung *f s.* Silikonkautschukmischung
Silikonhahnfett *n* silicone stopcock grease
Silikonharz *n* silicone resin
Silikonhaut *f* silicone film
silikonisieren to siliconize, to silicone-treat
Silikonisierung *f* siliconization, silicone treatment
Silikonkautschuk *m* silicone [rubber] gum
Silikonkautschukmischung *f* silicone rubber compound (mixture, stock)
Silikonkitt *m* silicone putty
Silikonklebstoff *m* silicone adhesive
Silikonkunstharz *n* silicone resin
Silikonlack *m* silicone varnish, *(if pigmented:)* silicone lacquer
silikonmodifiziert silicone-modified
Silikonöl *n* silicone oil (liquid, fluid)
Silikonpaste *f* silicone compound
Silikonrohkautschuk *m* silicone [rubber] gum
Silikonschmiermittel *n* silicone lubricant
Silikonschutzschicht *f* silicone coating
Silikonspringkitt *m* bouncing putty
Silikontrennmittel *n* silicone abherent (release agent)
silikonüberzogen *s.* silikonbeschichtet
Silikonüberzug *m s.* Silikonschutzschicht
Silikose *f (med)* silicosis
Silikospiegel *m* silicospiegel *(an iron-base alloy containing Mn and Si)*
silikothermisch silicothermic
Silitstab *m (spectr)* silicon carbide rod *(as a light source)*
silizieren to siliconize *(metals for protecting them)*
Silizieren *n* siliconization *(of metals)*
Silizierungsgrad *m*, **Silizierungsstufe** *f (met)* silicate degree *(of slag)*
Silizifikation *f*, **Silizifizierung** *f (geoch)* silicification
Silizium *n s.* Silicium
Sillimanit *m (min)* sillimanite *(a nesosubsilicate)*
Sillimaniterzeugnis *n (ceram)* sillimanite refractory
Sillimanitstein *m***[/feuerfester]** sillimanite refractory brick
Silo *n(m)* silo, bin, [storage] hopper
Siloxan *n* $H_3Si(OSiH_2)_nOSiH_3$ siloxane
~/cyclisches cyclic siloxane, cyclosiloxane
~/organisches organic siloxane, organosiloxane
~/polymeres $(H_2SiO)_n$ polymeric siloxane, polysiloxane
~/ringförmiges *s.* ~/cyclisches
Siloxanbindung *f* siloxane bond
Siloxaneinheit *f* siloxane unit
Siloxanpolymer[e] *n* siloxane polymer
Siloxen *n* siloxen[e]
Silt *m (geol)* silt
Silthian *n* $H_3Si(SSiH_2)_nSSiH_3$ silthiane
Silvan *n* silvan, 2-methylfuran
Silvichemikalie *f* silvichemical
Silylengruppe *f* $H_2Si=$ silylene group (residue)
Silylgruppe *f* H_3Si- silyl group (residue)
Silylidingruppe *f* $HSi\equiv$ silylidyne group (residue)
silylieren to silylate
Silylierung *f* silylation
Sima *n* sima, lower crust, LC, intermediate layer *(of the earth's crust)*

SIMA = 1. Sekundärionenmikroanalyse; 2. Sekundärionenmikroanalysator
Simazin *n* simazine *(a herbicidal triazine derivative)*
Simazone *f s.* Sima
Simcar-Kreisel *m (hyd)* Simcar aerator
Simmons-Smith-Reaktion *f* Simmons-Smith reaction *(for obtaining cyclopropanes)*
Simplexpumpe *f* simplex pump
SIMS *s.* 1. Sekundärionenmassenspektrometrie; 2. Sekundärionenmassenspektrometer
Simultanbestimmung *f* simultaneous analysis
Simultanreaktion *f* simultaneous (parallel) reaction, competitive (competing, concurrent) reaction
Sinapinalkohol *m* sinapic alcohol
Sinapinsäure *f* sinapic acid, 3-(4-hydroxy-3,5-dimethoxyphenyl)acrylic acid
Singulett *n* singlet
Singulettbindung *f* one-electron (single-electron) bond, singlet link[age]
Singulettsauerstoff *m* singlet molecular oxygen
Singulett-Singulett-Annihilation *f* singlet-singlet annihilation
Singulett-Singulett-Übergang *m* singlet → singlet transition
Singulett-Term *m (spectr)* singlet energy level
Singulett-Triplett-Übergang *m* singlet → triplet transition
~/strahlungsloser intersystem crossing
Singulettübergang *m* singlet → singlet transition
Singulettzustand *m* singlet [electronic] state
Singulosilikatschlacke *f* monosilicate slag
Sinkanteil *m (min tech)* sinking fraction
sinken 1. to sink, to fall, to subside; *(if bottoms are being formed:)* to sediment, to settle; 2. to drop, to decrease *(of physical data)*
Sinken *n* 1. sinking, fall, subsidence; *(if bottoms are being formed:)* sedimentation, settling; 2. drop, decrease *(of physical data)*
Sinkfraktion *f (min tech)* sinking fraction
Sinkgeschwindigkeit *f* rate (velocity) of fall, subsidence rate; sedimentation (settling) rate (velocity)
~ im Gravitationsfeld rate of fall under gravity; rate of gravity settling
~/stationäre terminal falling velocity; terminal settling velocity
Sinkgut *n* settling (sinking) material; settled material; *(min tech)* underflow, sinks
Sinkkurve *f* sink curve
Sinkscheider *m (min tech)* dense-medium (heavy-medium) separator, dense-medium vessel (washer)
Sinkscheideranlage *f (min tech)* dense-medium (heavy-medium) separation plant, gravity concentration (concentrating) apparatus
Sinkscheideverfahren *n (min tech)* dense-medium (heavy-medium) separation, dense-medium process
Sinkschlamm *m* bottom sludge
Sinkstoffbelastung *f (hyd)* sediment load *(as of a river)*
Sinkstoffe *mpl* settling (sinking) material; deposited matter, settled material, settlings; *(hyd)* settleable solids
Sinkweg *m (hyd)* settling path (distance) *(of a particle)*
Sinnenprüfung *f* sensory (organoleptic) estimation (evaluation)
sinnesphysiologisch organoleptic
Sinter *m (ceram, geol)* sinter; *(met)* scale
Sinteraluminiumpulver *n* sintered aluminium powder, S.A.P.
Sinteranlage *f* sintering plant
Sinterapparat *m* sinter[ing] machine
Sinterband *n* sinter[ing] strand
Sinterberyllerde *f (ceram)* sintered beryllia
Sinterbrand *m (ceram)* sinter firing
Sintercarbid[metall] *n s.* Sinterhartmetall
Sinterdolomit *m (ceram)* sintered (dead-burned) dolomite, refractory lime
Sintereisen *n* sintered iron
Sintererzeugnis *n* sintered product, sinter
Sinterformen *n* powder moulding
Sinterglasplatte *f* sintered (fritted) glass plate; sintered (fritted) glass disk
Sintergut *n* material being *or* to be sintered; sinter, sintered product
Sinterhartmetall *n* [cemented] hard metal, cemented [hard] carbide, sintered carbide
Sinterkörper *m* sintered[-powder metal] compact
Sinterkorund *m (ceram)* sintered alumina
Sintermaschine *f* sinter[ing] machine
Sintermetall *n* sintered[-powder] metal
sintern to sinter, *(esp glass)* to frit
~/dicht *(ceram)* to vitrify
~/drucklos to sinter without pressure
~/glasig *s.* ~/dicht
~/unter Druck to hot-press *(metal powder)*
Sintern *n***/aktiviertes** activated sintering
~/druckloses pressureless sintering
~ unter Druck hot-pressing *(of metal powder)*
Sinterofen *m* sintering furnace
Sinterrösten *n* sinter roasting
Sinterstahl *m* sintered steel
Sinterstoff *m s.* Sintergut
Sintertechnik *f* sintering technique
Sintertonerde *f (ceram)* sintered alumina
Sinterverfahren *n* sintering process
Sintervorgang *m* sintering process
Sinterwanne *f (ceram)* sintering tray
Sinterwerkstoff *m* sintered material
Sinterzone *f* sintering zone
SiO_2-Durchbruch *m (hyd)* silica leakage *(ion exchange)*
Siphon *m (lab)* siphon, syphon *(for handling liquids)*; [siphon] trap *(as of a sink)*; *(tech)* siphon, syphon *(as for condensate removal in gas mains)*
~/feststehender *(tech)* stationary siphon
~/rotierender (umlaufender) *(tech)* revolving siphon

Siphon-Eluatvolumenmesser *m (chromat)* siphon counter
Siphonentleerung *f (chromat)* siphon dump
Siphonrohr *n* siphon pipe
Sirup *m* syrup, sirup; *(sugar)* treacle, *(if dark also)* molasses, *(if bright also)* golden syrup
sirupartig, sirupös syrup-like, syrupy
Si-Stufe *f s.* Silizierungsgrad
Sitz *m* seat *(as of a valve)*
Sitzring *m* seat ring
Sitzventil *n* globe valve
SK *s.* Synthesekautschuk
Skala *f* scale
^{12}C-**Skala** *f* carbon-12 scale *(of atomic weights)*
Skale *f* scale *(on a measuring device)*
Skaleneinteilung *f* scale graduation
Skalenteil *m* scale division (interval)
Skalenteilstrich *m* scale division
Skalenteilung *f* scale graduation
Skalenwert *m* reading
Skammoniumharz *n* scammony [resin], resin of ipomoea *(from Ipomoea orizabensis Ledanois)*
Skarn *m* skarn *(contact metamorphic high-iron hornfels)*
Skatol *n* skatole, 3-methylindole
Skelett *n (org ch)* skeleton, backbone
Skelettisomer[e] *n* skeletal (chain) isomer
Skelettisomerie *f* skeletal (chain) isomerism
Skelettisomerisierung *f* skeletal isomerization
Skelettkatalysator *m*, **Skelettkontakt** *m* skeleton (Raney) catalyst
Skidmore-Eisentiegel *m* Skidmore iron crucible
Skimkautschuk *m* skim rubber
Skimlatex *m (rubber)* skim latex
skimmen 1. *(rubber)* to skim[-coat] *(frictioned fabric)*; 2. to skim *(petroleum)*
Skimmen *n* 1. *(rubber)* skim coating, skimming *(of frictioned fabric)*; 2. skimming *(of petroleum)*
Skim[m]rinne *f (hyd)* skimming slot
Skipgefäß *n* skip [car]
Sklerometer *n* sclerometer
Skleroprotein *n* scleroprotein, structural (skeletal, fibrous) protein
Skleroskop *n* scleroscope
SK-Mischung *f s.* Synthesekautschukmischung
Skorodit *m (min)* scorodite, iron sinter *(iron(III) orthoarsenate)*
Skraup-Synthese *f* Skraup [quinoline] synthesis, Skraup reaction
Skrubber *m* [gas] scrubber, gas washer, wet collector
Skutterudit *m (min)* skutterudite, smaltite, smaltine *(cobalt triarsenide)*
Slack-Merzerisation *f (text)* slack mercerization
Slater-Orbital *n* Slater-type orbital, STO
Slater-Regel *f* Slater's rule *(spectroscopy)*
slö *s.* schwerlöslich
Slop[s]öl *n (petrol)* slop oil
Slop-Wax *n (petrol)* slop wax *(non-pressable wax from heavy cracked distillates)*
S-Lost *m s.* Schwefellost
SM-... *s.* Siemens-Martin-...
Smalte *f* smalt, powder blue *(cobalt(II) potassium silicate)*
Smaltin *m s.* Skutterudit
Smaragd *m (min)* emerald *(a cyclosilicate)*
Smaragdgrün *n* emerald (chrome) green, Guignet's (Mittler's) green *(hydrated chromium oxide)*
smektisch smectic
Smirgel *m s.* Schmirgel
Smithsonit *m (min)* smithsonite, zinc spar, dry-bone ore *(zinc carbonate)*
Smog *m*/**Londoner** London[-type] smog, reducing smog
~/**oxidierender** *s.* ~/photochemischer
~/**photochemischer** photochemical (oxidizing) smog, Los Angeles smog
~/**reduzierender** *s.* Smog/Londoner
Smogalarm *m* smog emergency
Smog-Vorwarnung *f* smog alert
Smogwarnung *f* smog warning
SM-Verfahren *n* open-hearth process
S.M.-Verfahren *n (coal)* Dutch State Mines process
Smythe-Faktor *m* atomic mass conversion factor
S_N**-Reaktion** *f* S_N reaction, nucleophilic substitution
S_N**1-Reaktion** *f* S_N1 reaction, first-order nucleophilic substitution [reaction]
S_N**2-Reaktion** *f* S_N2 reaction, second-order nucleophilic substitution [reaction]
SN-Verfahren *n* Separator-Nobel process *(for deparaffinizing petroleum)*
Soak-Sektion *f (petrol)* soaking section *(of a pipe still)*
Sockel *m* base
Soda *f* 1. soda, sodium carbonate; 2. *(min)* soda, natron, natrite *(sodium carbonate 10-water)*
~/**kalzinierte** calcined soda, [soda] ash, anhydrous sodium carbonate
~/**kaustische** caustic soda, sodium hydroxide *(esp when produced by the lime-soda caustic process)*
~/**kristallwasserfreie** *s.* ~/kalzinierte
~/**modifizierte** modified (neutral) soda *(a mixture of sodium carbonate and sodium hydrogencarbonate used as detergent)*
~/**wasserfreie** *s.* ~/kalzinierte
Sodaablauge *f* spent soda
Sodaalaun *m* soda (sodium) alum *(crystalline aluminium sodium sulphate)*
Sodaaufschluß *m (lab)* fusion with sodium carbonate; *(pap)* soda pulping
Sodaauszug *m (anal)* sodium carbonate extract
Sodakalkglas *n* soda-lime glass
Sodakochung *f (pap)* soda cook
Sodalith *m (min)* sodalite *(a tectosilicate)*
Sodaschmelze *f (pap)* soda smelt, black ash
Sodastein *m* caustic soda
Sodaüberschuß *m (hyd)* excess soda ash

Sodaverfahren *n (pap)* soda process, soda [wood-] pulp process

Sodawäsche *f (petrol)* soda washing

Sodawasser *n* soda [water], carbonated water

Sodazellstoff *m* soda pulp

Söderberg-Elektrode *f* Söderberg [continuous, self-baking] electrode

Söderberg-Elektrodenmasse *f s.* Söderberg-Masse

Söderberg-Masse *f* Söderberg paste

~/grüne green [Söderberg] paste

Sofiaöl *n (cosmet)* ginger-grass oil *(chiefly from Cymbopogon martini (Roxb.) Stapf var. sofia)*

Sohlenkalander *m (rubber)* soling calender

Sohlenmischung *f (rubber)* soling compound

Sojabohnen... *s.* Soja...

Sojaeiweiß *n* soybean protein

Sojaeiweißfaser *f (text)* soybean fibre

Sojaeiweißfaserstoff *m (text)* soybean fibre

Sojaeiweißleim *m* soybean glue (adhesive)

Sojahartfett *n* hydrogenated soybean oil

Sojalecithin *n* soybean lecithin

Sojamehl *n* soy[bean] meal, *(if fine:)* soy[bean] flour

Sojaöl *n* soy[bean] oil, soy, Chinese bean oil

Sojaprotein *n* soybean protein

Sokotra-Aloe *f (pharm)* Socotra (Zanzibar) aloe *(from Aloe perryi Baker)*

Sol *n (coll)* sol

~/festes solid suspension

~/irreversibles irreversible sol

~/lyophiles lyophilic sol

~/lyophobes lyophobic sol

~/reversibles reversible sol

Solanumalkaloid *n* solanum alkaloid

Solarisation *f (phot, glass)* solarization

Solaröl *n* solar oil

Sole *f* [salt] brine, saline water

~/ablaufende spent brine *(chlor-alkali electrolysis)*

~/eutektische eutectic brine

~/verbrauchte *s.* ~/ablaufende

solehaltig briny

Soleil-Doppelplatte *f* biquartz *(polarimetry)*

Solekühler *m* brine cooler (refrigerator)

Solekühlung *f* brine cooling (refrigeration)

Sol-Gel-Transformation *f*, **Sol-Gel-Übergang** *m (coll)* sol-gel transformation (transition, change)

solidensieren to desublimate *(to convert a gas directly into the solid state)*

Solidensieren *n* desublimation *(direct conversion of a gas into the solid state)*

Solidgrün *n s.* Malachitgrün

Solidisieren *n s.* Solidensieren

Soliduskurve *f*, **Soliduslinie** *f* solidus [curve, line] *(of a melting diagram)*

Soliduspunkt *m* solidus point

Sollwert *m* set point

Solonetz *m (soil)* solonetz

Solontschak *m (soil)* solonchak

Solquelle *f* brine spring

Solubilisation *f*, **Solubilisierung** *f* solubilization

Solutizerverfahren *n* solutizer process *(for desulphurizing petroleum distillates)*

Solvat *n* 1. solvate *(solvent and solute or dispersed phase and dispersion medium)*; 2. raffinate *(less soluble residue remaining after solvent extraction)*

Solvatation *f* solvation

Solvatationseffekt *m* solvation effect

Solvatationsenergie *f* solvation energy

Solvatationsenthalpie *f* solvation enthalpy

Solvatationsentropie *f* solvation entropy

Solvatationsgrad *m* degree of solvation

Solvatationskraft *f* solvating power

Solvatationsreaktion *f* solvation reaction

Solvatationssphäre *f* solvation sphere

Solvatationsvermögen *n* solvating power

Solvathülle *f* solvation sheath (layer)

solvatisieren to solvate

solvatisiert/schwach poorly solvated

~/stark highly solvated

Solvatisierung *f s.* Solvatation

Solvatochromie *f* solvatochromism

Solvay-Verfahren *n* Solvay process, [Solvay's] ammonia soda process

Solvay-Zelle *f* Solvay cell *(a mercury cell)*

Solvens *n* solvent, dissolver

~/selektiv wirkendes selective solvent

Solvententölung *f (petrol)* solvent deoiling

Solvententparaffinierung *f*, **Solvententwachsung** *f (petrol)* solvent dewaxing

Solventextraktion *f* solvent extraction, liquid[-liquid] extraction

Solventextraktor *m/***kontinuierlich arbeitender** continuous liquid extraction apparatus

Solventnaphtha *n(f)* solvent naphtha *(a fraction of middle-boiling and high-boiling benzene hydrocarbons)*

Solventraffination *f* solvent refining

Solventtrocknung *f* solvent drying

Solvolyse *f* solvolysis, lyolysis *(decomposition of a solute by a solvent)* • **durch ~ abspalten** to solvolyse off

Solvolysereaktion *f* solvolysis reaction

solvolytisch solvolytic

Solvuskurve *f (phys ch)* solvus [curve, line]

Solzustand *m (coll)* sol state (condition) • **in den ~ übergehen** to solate

Soman *n* soman, methyl-1,2,2-trimethylpropoxyfluorophosphine oxide

Somatomedin *n (bioch)* sulphation factor

Somatotropin *n* somatotropic hormone, somatotropin

SO_2-Meßgerät *n* sulphur dioxide meter

Sommelet-Reaktion *f* Sommelet reaction *(for obtaining aldehydes)*

Sommelet-Umlagerung *f* Sommelet rearrangement *(isomerization of quaternary benzylammonium compounds)*

sommern *(ceram)* to weather
Sommerspritzmittel *n (agric)* summer spray
Sommerspritzung *f (agric)* summer spray[ing]
Sonde *f (petrol)* sonde *(in electrical coring)*; *(anal)* probe
~/chemische chemical probe *(molecule which reacts in a specific manner with parts of another one)*
Sonderabfall *m* special waste
Sonderanteil *m* **der Energie** *s.* Sonderenergie
Sonderenergie *f (phys ch)* resonance energy, mesomeric (delocalization) energy
Sonderkoks *m* special[ty] coke
Sonderlegierung *f* specialty alloy
Sondermüll *m* special solid waste
Sonderpapier *n***/technisches** technical paper
Sonderzement *m* special cement
Sonnenblumenhartfett *n* hydrogenated sunflower oil
Sonnenblumenöl *n* sunflower [seed] oil
Sonnenbräunungsmittel *n (cosmet)* suntan make-up; suntan preparation
Sonnendestillationsanlage *f* solar still (evaporator)
Sonnenenergie *f* solar energy
Sonneneruption *f* solar flare
Sonnenlichtbeständigkeit *f* resistance to sunlight, sunlight resistance (stability)
Sonnenofen *m* solar furnace
Sonnenschutzmittel *n* sunscreen [agent], sun screening agent
Sonnenschutzöl *n* sunscreen oil
Sonnenstein *m (min)* sunstone *(a tectosilicate)*
Sonnenstrahlung *f* solar radiation
Sonnentrocknung *f* solar (sun) drying
Sonolumineszenz *f* sonoluminescence, sonic luminescence
Sophia-Jacoba-Verfahren *n (coal)* Barvoys process
Sorbend *m* material to be sorbed
Sorbens *n* sorbent, sorption agent
~/festes solid sorbent, sorbent solid
sorbieren to sorb
Sorbinsäure *f* sorbic acid, hexa-2,4-dienoic acid
Sorbit *m* 1. *(met)* sorbite; 2. sorbitol, *D-glucitol *(a sugar alcohol)*
sorbitisch *(met)* sorbitic
Sorbitol *n s.* Sorbit 2.
Sorelzement *m* Sorel cement
Sörensen-Titration *f* Sörensen's formol titration
Soret-Bande *f (spectr, bioch)* Soret band
Sorosilicat *n (min)* sorocilicate *(any of a class of polymeric silicates)*
Sorption *f* sorption
Sorptionsisotherme *f* sorption isotherm
Sorptionskapazität *f (soil)* total exchangeable bases
Sorptionskomplex *m (soil)* exchange complex
Sorptionskurve *f* sorption curve
Sorptionsmittel *n* sorbent, sorption agent
Sorptionswaage *f* sorption balance
sorptiv sorptive
Sorptiv *n* sorbate, sorbed material (substance)
Sorte *f* grade *(as of chemicals)*
Sortierblech *n (pap)* screen plate
sortieren to sort, to grade; *(min tech)* to classify, to sort, to separate, *(by hand:)* to pick, *(according to diameter:)* to size
Sortiergut *n* material being *or* to be sorted; *(separation according to diameter:)* material being *or* to be sized
Sortiermaschine *f* grading machine, grader
Sortierplatte *f (pap)* screen plate
Sortiersaal *m (pap)* [rag-]sorting room
Sortierung *f* sorting, grading; *(min tech)* classification, sorting, separation, *(by hand:)* picking, *(according to diameter:)* sizing
~ der Hackschnitzel *(pap)* chip screening
~/statistische *(pap)* sampling
~ von Hand hand sorting, *(min tech also)* picking
SO_2-Rückgewinnung *f (pap)* sulphur dioxide recovery
SOS-Reparatur *f (biot)* SOS repair
Souple *m*, **Soupleseide** *f* souple silk
souplieren *(text)* to souple
SO_2-Verlust *m (pap)* sulphur dioxide loss
Soxhlet[-Apparat] *m*, **Soxhlet-Extraktor** *m* Soxhlet [extractor]
Sozialabwasser *n (hyd)* sanitary waste water *(from industrial plants)*
Spachtel *m(f)*, **Spachtelmasse** *f* filler, surfacer
Spallation *f (nucl)* spallation
Spalt *m* 1. slit, *(between rolls:)* gap; 2. crack, crevice, fissure *(fault)*; 3. *(bioch)* cleft, [catalytic] trough *(in hydrolase molecules)*
Spaltabstand *m s.* Spaltbreite
Spaltanlage *f* 1. *(petrol)* cracking plant; 2. *(agric)* split plot design *(as for fertilizer testing)*
Spaltausbeute *f (nucl)* fission yield
Spaltausbeutekurve *f (nucl)* fission yield curve
spaltbar *(min, cryst)* cleavable, fissile; *(nucl)* fissile, fissionable; divisible, resolvable *(optically active compounds)*
Spaltbarkeit *f (min, cryst)* cleavability, fissility; *(nucl)* fissility, fissionability; divisibility, resolvability *(of optically active compounds)*
~/unvollkommene *(min, cryst)* imperfect cleavage
~/vollkommene *(min, cryst)* perfect cleavage
Spaltbenzin *n* cracked gasoline
Spaltbreite *f (spectr)* slit width
Spalte *f s.* Spalt
Spaltebene *f s.* Spaltfläche
Spalteinfang *m (nucl)* fission capture
Spalteinstellung *f (spectr)* 1. slit setting; 2. slit control *(device)*
spalten to cleave, to crack, to decompose *(chemical compounds)*; to split, to cleave, to open *(a ring)*; to cleave, to break, to crack, to split, to disrupt *(a chemical bond)*; *(nucl)* to fission, to split; to break, to crack, to demulsify *(emulsions)*; to resolve *(a racemate)*; to cut *(a bale of rubber)*
~/katalytisch to cat-crack

~/sich to crack, to decompose, to split up *(chemical compounds)*; *(nucl)* to split, to break up, to [undergo] fission
Spalten *n***/hydrierendes** *(petrol)* hydrogenation cracking, HC
Spaltenergie *f (nucl)* fission energy
Spaltereignis *n (nucl)* fission event
spaltfähig *s.* spaltbar
Spaltfaser *f* split fibre
Spaltfestigkeit *f (plast)* interlaminar strength
Spaltfilter *n* edge filter
Spaltfläche *f (min, cryst)* cleavage plane (face), cleaved face
Spaltgift *n (nucl)* fission poison
Spaltgut *n (petrol)* cracking feed (stock, feedstock)
Spaltkette *f (nucl)* fission [decay] chain
Spaltkorrosion *f* crevice corrosion, gasket (faying-surface) corrosion
Spaltmaschine *f (tann)* splitting machine
Spaltmaterial *n (nucl)* fissionable material
Spaltmethode *f* method of resolution *(stereochemistry)*
Spaltneutron *n* fission neutron
Spaltprodukt *n* cleavage (breakdown) product; *(nucl)* fission product
Spaltproduktausbeute *f (nucl)* fission yield
Spaltproduktausbeutekurve *f (nucl)* fission yield curve
Spaltproduktreihe *f (nucl)* fission [decay] chain
Spaltprozeß *m*, **Spaltreaktion** *f s.* Spaltungsreaktion
Spaltrohrpumpe *f* canned-motor pump
Spaltruß *m***[/thermischer]** thermal [carbon] black, furnace thermal black
Spaltrußverfahren *n* furnace thermal process
Spaltschwelle *f (nucl)* fission threshold
Spaltsieb *n* wedge-wire screen
Spaltstoff *m (nucl)* fissionable material
Spaltstoffelement *n (nucl)* fuel element
Spaltstück *n* fragment, *(nucl also)* fission fragment
Spaltultramikroskop *n* slit ultramicroscope
Spaltung *f* cleavage, cracking, decomposition *(of chemical compounds)*; splitting, cleavage, opening *(of a ring)*; cleavage, breaking, splitting[-up], disruption, scission *(of a chemical bond)*; breaking, cracking, demulsification *(of emulsions)*; *(nucl)* fission; resolution *(of a racemate)* • **[eine] ~ erleiden** to undergo cleavage (scission)
~ durch schnelle Neutronen high-energy fission
~ einer Emulsion emulsion breakdown (breaking), breaking of emulsions
~/enzymatische (fermentative) enzymatic splitting
~/homolytische homolytic cleavage
~/hydrierende *(petrol)* hydrogenation cracking, hydrocracking
~/hydrogenolytische hydrogenolysis
~/hydrolytische hydrolytic cleavage, *(relating to bonds also)* hydrolytic splitting (scission)
~/ionische *s.* ~/katalytische
~/katalytische catalytic (cat, catalyst) cracking
~/radikalische *s.* ~/thermische
~/schnelle *(nucl)* high-energy fission
~/selektive selective cracking
~/thermische thermal decomposition; *(petrol)* thermal cracking
~/thioklastische (thiolytische) thiolytic cleavage *(of fatty acids)*
α-Spaltung *f* alpha-cleavage, α-cleavage *(of a carbonyl compound)*
Spaltungseinfang *m (nucl)* fission capture
Spaltungsenergie *f (nucl)* fission energy
Spaltungskammer *f (nucl)* fission chamber
Spaltungsprodukt *n s.* Spaltprodukt
Spaltungsquerschnitt *m (nucl)* fission cross section
Spaltungsreaktion *f* cleavage (scission) reaction; *(nucl)* fission reaction
Spaltverfahren *n (petrol)* cracking process
~/katalytisches catalytic-cracking process
~ nach Burton Burton [cracking] process
~ nach deFlorez deFlorez [cracking] process
~ nach Holmes und Manley Holmes-Manley [cracking] process
~/selektives selective-cracking process
~/thermisches thermal-cracking process
Spaltvorgang *m (petrol)* cracking process; *(nucl)* fission process
Spaltzone *f (petrol)* cracking zone; *(nucl)* core
Span *m* splinter, chip, shaving, *(esp of wood:)* sliver
Spänehaus *n (pap)* chip loft
Spanholzplatte *f* chipboard
Spanischweiß *n* Spanish (bismuth, pearl) white, cosmetic bismuth *(bismuth nitrate oxide or bismuth chloride oxide)*
Spannbacke *f (lab)* gripping jaw *(of an apparatus clamp)*
Spannbeton *m* prestressed concrete
Spanndruck *m (plast)* [mould-]locking pressure, clamping pressure
Spanneinrichtung *f* tensioning device *(as of a conveyor)*
spannen to strain, to stress, *(esp in length:)* to stretch
Spannrahmentrockner *m* tenter [frame] dryer
Spannring *m* locking ring
Spannrolle *f* tension pulley
Spanntrommel *f* tension pulley
Spannung *f* 1. *(el ch)* voltage, tension; 2. *(mechanically:)* tension; *(if unintended:)* stress, *(loosely also)* strain; 3. strain *(of ring molecules)*
~/eingefrorene *(plast)* frozen-in stress
~/kritische sparking potential *(as in electrical precipitation)*
Spannungsabbau *m* stress relief
Spannungsabfall *m***[/ohmscher]** *(el ch)* drop in voltage, ohmic drop (overpotential, polarization), iR drop, IR drop
spannungsarm low-stress, stress-relieved *(materials science)*; low-strain *(ring molecule)*

Spannungsarmglühen *n (met, glass, ceram)* [stress-relief] annealing
Spannungs-Dehnungs-Diagramm *n* stress-strain diagram
Spannungs-Dehnungs-Linie *f* stress-strain curve
spannungsfrei stress-free, non-stressed, stress-relieved *(materials science)*; strain-free, strainless, free from (of) angle strain *(ring molecule)*
• ~ **machen** *(met, glass, ceram)* to anneal
Spannungskorrosion *f* stress corrosion
spannungslos *(el ch)* dead
spannungsoptisch stress-optical
Spannungsreihe f/elektrochemische electrochemical series, electromotive [force] series, emf series
Spannungsrelaxation *f (rubber)* stress relaxation
Spannungsrelaxationsverfahren *n (rubber)* stress relaxation method
Spannungsrißbildung *f* stress cracking
Spannungsrißkorrosion *f* stress corrosion cracking, SCC
~/katodische hydrogen embrittlement, hydrogen-induced cracking
Spannungsrückgang *m (el ch)* drop in voltage
Spannungsscheibe *f (glass)* strain disk
Spannungstheorie *f (org ch)* strain theory, theory of strain
~/Baeyersche Baeyer [angle] strain theory, Baeyer tension theory
~/Sachse-Mohrsche Sachse-Mohr concept of strainless rings
Spannungsverlust *m* 1. *(el ch)* loss of voltage; 2. loss of tension
Spannungswert *m s.* Dehngrenze
Spannwalze *f (pap)* stretch roll, stenting (tension, hitch) roll, tightener
Spannweite *f* support span
Spanpressen *n (text)* paper pressing
Sparbeton *m* lean (lean-mixed, poor) concrete
Sparflamme *f* small flame
Sparkapsel *f (ceram)* crank *(a type of support in kilns)*
Spartränkverfahren *n* **nach Rüping** Rueping process *(wood preservation)*
Spasmolytikum *n (pharm)* spasmolytic, antispasmodic
spasmolytisch spasmolytic
spatartig *(min)* spathic, spathose
Spatel *m (lab)* spatula
Spatelspitze voll/eine a spatula-tipfull, a spatula-point
Spatenwischer *m (lab)* wing-shape policeman
spatig *s.* spatartig
Specköl *n* grease (lard) oil
Speckstein *m (min)* soapstone, steatite *(a variety of talc)*
Specularit *m (min)* specularite, specular iron [ore] *(a variety of haematite)*
Speerkies *m (min)* spear pyrite *(a variety of marcasite)*
Speichel *m* saliva
Speicher *m* store[house], storage, reservoir; accumulator *(hydraulics)*
~/unterirdischer underground reservoir (storage tank)
Speicherbecken *n (hyd)* storage basin (reservoir)
Speicherbehälter *m* storage tank (vessel), hold[ing] tank, stock tank
Speichergestein *n* reservoir rock, pool *(a sedimentary rock containing petroleum or gas)*
Speichergewebe *n (biol)* storage tissue
Speicherkohlenhydrat *n* reserve carbohydrate
speichern to store [up], to accumulate
Speicherprotein *n (bioch)* storage protein
Speicherschleife *f* sample loop *(gas chromatography)*
Speichertank *m s.* Speicherbehälter
Speicherung *f* storage, accumulation
~/unterirdische underground storage
Speirohr *n* spout
Speise *f* 1. food; 2. *(met)* speiss, speise
Speisebehälter *m* feed tank
Speiseboden *m (distil)* feed tray (plate)
Speiseeis *n* ice cream
Speiseeisbereitung *f* ice-cream making
Speiseessig *m* table vinegar
Speisefett *n* dietary (edible, food) fat
Speisegelatine *f* edible gelatin
Speiseleitung *f* supply line
speisen 1. *(tech)* to feed, to charge; 2. to power *(an electrical circuit)*
Speiseöl *n* edible (food) oil
Speisepumpe *f* feed pump
Speiser *m* feeder
Speiserbecken *n (glass)* feeder bowl (nose), [feeder] spout
Speiserkanal *m (glass)* feeder channel
Speiserkopf *m s.* Speiserbecken
Speisermaschine *f (glass)* gob-fed machine
Speiserring *m (glass)* orifice ring
Speiserrinne *f (glass)* feeder channel
Speiserrohr *n (glass)* feeder sleeve (tube)
Speisertropfen *m* [glass] gob
Speiserverfahren *n (glass)* gob (feeder) process
Speisesalz *n* table salt
Speisesenf *m* [table] mustard
Speisesirup *m* table syrup
Speisetalg *m* edible tallow
Speisewasser *n* feed water
~ **für Dampferzeuger** boiler feed water
Speisewasserverdampfer *m* boiler make-up evaporator
Speisewasservorwärmer *m* boiler feed preheater, feed-water heater, economizer
Speisezone *f (plast)* feed zone (section)
Speisezwecke/für for edible purposes, edible-grade
Speiskobalt *m s.* Skutterudit
Speisung *f* 1. feed, charge; 2. feedstock, charging stock

spektral spectral
Spektralanalyse *f* spectral (spectroscopic) analysis
spektralanalytisch by spectral analysis
Spektralapparat *m*/**optischer** optical spectrum analyser
Spektralbande *f* spectral band
Spektralbereich *m* spectral region (range), spectroscopic region
~/**kurzwelliger** short-wavelength region
~/**langwelliger** long-wavelength region
Spektralfarbe *f* spectral colour
Spektralgebiet *n s.* Spektralbereich
Spektrallinie *f* spectral (spectrum) line
Spektralliniendublett *n* doublet
Spektrallinienintensität *f* line intensity
Spektralphotometer *n* spectrophotometer
~/**Bracesches** Brace-Lemon spectrophotometer
Spektralphotometer-Detektor *m (chromat)* spectrophotometric detector
Spektralphotometrie *f* spectrophotometry
spektralphotometrisch spectrophotometric
spektralrein spectro[-quality] grade
Spektralserie *f* spectral series, series of spectra
Spektralterm *m* spectral (series) term
Spektrenauswertung *f* interpretation of [the] spectra
Spektrendeutung *f*, **Spektreninterpretation** *f s.* Spektrenauswertung
Spektrensammlung *f* collection of spectra, library [reference] spectra
spektrochemisch spectrochemical
Spektrogramm *n* spectrogram
Spektrograph *m* spectrograph
~/**vollautomatisch registrierender** pen-recording spectrograph
spektrographisch spectrographic
Spektrometer *n* spectrometer
~/**Braggsches** Bragg spectrometer
~/**dynamisches** TOF (time-of-flight) mass spectrometer
~/**energiedispersives** energy-dispersion spectrometer
~/**nichtdispersives** non-dispersive spectrometer
Spektrometrie *f* spectrometry
spektrometrisch spectrometric
Spektrophoto... *s.* Spektralphoto...
Spektropolarimeter *n* spectropolarimeter
Spektroskop *n* spectroscope
~/**geradsichtiges** direct-vision spectroscope
Spektroskopie *f* spectroscopy
~/**computergestützte** computer-aided spectroscopy
~/**dreidimensionale** spin mapping
~ **im fernen Infrarot** far-infrared spectroscopy
~ **im sichtbaren Bereich** visible spectroscopy
~ **im Sichtbaren und Ultraviolett (UV-Gebiet)** UV-VIS spectroscopy
~/**optische** optical spectroscopy
~/**photoakustische** photoacoustic (optoacoustic) spectroscopy
~/**zeitaufgelöste (zeitauflösende)** time-resolved spectroscopy
Spektroskopiker *m* spectroscopist
spektroskopisch spectroscopic[al]
Spektrum *n* spectrum
~/**diskretes** discrete spectrum
~/**elektromagnetisches** electromagnetic spectrum
~ **in der Frequenzdomäne** frequency-domain spectrum
~ **in der Zeitdomäne** time-domain spectrum
~/**kontinuierliches** continuous spectrum
~/**optisches** optical spectrum
~/**sichtbares** visible spectrum
α-**Spektrum** *n* alpha-particle spectrum, α spectrum
β-**Spektrum** *n* beta-ray spectrum, β spectrum
spenden to donate *(e.g. electrons)*
Spermazet[i]öl *n s.* Spermöl
spermienabtötend, spermizid spermatocidal, spermicidal
Spermöl *n* sperm [whale] oil
~/**mineralisches** mineral sperm [oil]
Sperreffekt *m (filtr)* blocking effect
sperren to arrest, to lock, to block; *(coat)* to seal
Sperrflüssigkeit *f* sealing liquid (fluid), confining liquid
Sperrflüssigkeitsdichtung *f* liquid-buffered seal
Sperrgrund *m (coat)* sealing paint, sealer
Sperrhahn *m* stopcock
Sperrholz *n* plywood
sperrig bulky
Sperring *m* locking ring
Sperröldichtung *f* oil-buffered seal
Sperrschicht *f* 1. *(el ch)* depletion (space-charge) layer, *(deprecated:)* barrier layer; 2. *(plast)* interlining; 3. barrier layer *(corrosion science)*
Sperrschichteffekt *m* photovoltaic effect
Sperrschichtelement *n* photovoltaic cell, photochemical (photoelectrolytic, barrier-layer) cell
Sperrschichtgleichrichter *m* barrier-layer rectifier
Sperrschichthöhe *f* inversion height *(in the atmosphere)*
Sperrschichtphotoeffekt *m* photovoltaic effect
Sperrschichtphotoelement *n*, **Sperrschicht-[photo]zelle** *f s.* Sperrschichtelement
Sperrstoffe *mpl (hyd)* coarse solids
Sperrvorrichtung *f* arresting mechanism
Spessartin *m (min)* spessartite, spessartine *(aluminium manganese(II) orthosilicate)*
Spezialdünger *m* specialty fertilizer
Spezialfermenter *m (biot)* single-purpose fermenter
Spezialkoks *m* special[ty] coke
Spezialkokskohle *f*/**bituminöse** prime coking coal
Spezialpapier *n* special paper
Spezialwirksamkeit *f* selectivity *(as of pesticides)*
Spezialzement *m* special cement
Spezies *f*/**chemische** chemical species
~/**elektroaktive** electroactive species *(polarography)*
Speziesbestimmung *f (anal)* speciation

spezies-spezifisch *(bioch)* species-specific
Speziesspezifität *f (bioch)* species specificity
Spezifikation *f* specification
Spezifität *f* specificity *(as of an enzyme or a catalyst)*
~/optische optical specificity
~/stereochemische stereospecificity, stereoselectivity
Sphagnumtorf *m* sphagnum peat
Sphalerit *m (min)* sphalerite, zinc blende, *(Am also)* black jack
Sphärizität *f* sphericity
sphäroidal spheroidal
Sphärokolloid *n* spherocolloid, globular colloid
Sphärolith *m (geol)* spherulite
sphärolithisch *(geol)* spherulitic
Sphäroprotein *n* globular protein
Sphen *m (min)* sphene *(a variety of titanite)*
Sphingolipoid *n (bioch)* sphingolipid[e]
Sphingomyelin *n* sphingomyelin *(any of a group of crystalline phosphatides)*
Sphingomyelinose *f s.* Niemann-Pick-Syndrom
Sphingosin *n* sphingosine *(an amino alcohol)*
sp-Hybrid *n* sp hybrid *(chemical-bond theory)*
sp-Hybridisierung *f* sp hybridization *(chemical-bond theory)*
Spiegel *m* level *(of a liquid)*
Spiegelbild *n* mirror image *(stereochemistry)*
spiegelbildisomer enantiomeric
Spiegelbildisomer[e] *n* enantiomer, optical (mirror-image) isomer, optical antipode, antimer
Spiegelbildisomerie *f* enantiomerism, optical (mirror-image) isomerism
Spiegelebene *f (cryst)* plane of symmetry, mirror plane
Spiegeleisen *n* spiegel [iron], spiegeleisen, mirror iron *(a pig iron containing manganese)*
Spiegelfleck *m (phot)* flare *(on a negative)*
Spiegelgalvanometer *n* mirror galvanometer
Spiegelglas *n* [polished] plate glass
Spiegelglaswanne *f* plate-glass furnace
Spiegellackierung *f* mirror varnishing
Spiegelmethode *f* **nach Paneth** Paneth's mirror method, Paneth technique *(for detecting free radicals)*
spiegeln to reflect [back]
Spiegelreflexion *f* mirror reflection
Spiegelung *f* reflection
Spiköl *n* [lavender-]spike oil, aspic (Spanish lavender) oil *(from Lavandula latifolia (L. fil.) Medik.)*
Spin *m* spin, *(of elementary particles also)* [intrinsic] angular momentum
~/nichtkompensierter uncoupled spin
~/nichtverschwindender (von Null verschiedener) non-zero spin
spinabhängig spin-dependent
Spin-Addukt *n* spin adduct
Spinauslöschung *f* quenching of orbital angular momentum
Spin-Bahn-Kopplung *f* spin-orbit coupling, electron spin-orbit interaction, LS coupling, Russell-Saunders coupling
Spin-Bahn-Kopplungskonstante *f* spin-orbit coupling constant
Spin-Bahn-Wechselwirkung *f s.* Spin-Bahn-Kopplung
Spindel *f* 1. araeometer, hydrometer; 2. screw, stem *(as of a valve)*
~ mit Thermometer thermohydrometer
spindelbetätigt screw-operated
Spindelöl *n* spindle oil
Spindelpumpe *f* screw pump
Spindichte *f* spin density
Spindrehimpuls *m* spin angular momentum
Spinecho *n* spin echo
Spinechomethode *f*, **Spinechoverfahren** *n (anal)* spin-echo technique
Spinell *m* spinel *(1. a mineral composed of magnesium aluminate; 2. any of a class of aluminates of the type $M^{II}Al_2O_4$)*
Spin-Gitter-Relaxation *f (spectr)* spin-lattice relaxation (interaction)
Spin-Gitter-Relaxationszeit *f* spin-lattice relaxation time
Spin-Gitter-Wechselwirkung *f s.* Spin-Gitter-Relaxation
Spinglas *n* spin glass
Spinglaszustand *m* spin-glass state
Spin-Hamilton-Operator *m (spectr)* spin Hamiltonian [operator]
Spin-Kopplungsaufspaltung *f* spin decoupling
Spinmarker *m (spectr)* spin label
Spinmarkierung *f (spectr)* spin labelling
Spinmethode *f s.* Valenzbindungsmethode
Spinmoment *n*[**/magnetisches**] electron spin magnetic moment, spin moment
Spinmultiplizität *f* spin multiplicity
Spinnbad *n* spinning bath
Spinnband *n* slubbing
Spinnbrause *f s.* Spinndüse
Spinndüse *f* spinneret, spinning jet (shower)
Spinne *f (distil)* udder, udder-type receiver (changer), pig
spinnen to spin
Spinnen *n* **aus der Schmelze** melt spinning (extrusion)
~ aus Lösungen solution (solvent) spinning
Spinnfaden *m* strand
Spinnfärbung *f* spin (dope) dyeing
Spinnfaser *f* [staple] fibre *(a natural or man-made object of relatively short length)*
spinngefärbt spin-dyed, spun-dyed, dope-dyed
Spinnkabel *n* tow
Spinnkanne *f* spinning can
Spinnkopf *m* spinning head
Spinnkuchen *m* cake *(in manufacturing viscose rayon)*
Spinnlösung *f* spinning solution, [spinning] dope

Spinnmaschine *f* spinning machine
spinnmattiert dull spun
Spinnpapier *n* spinning paper
Spinnpumpe *f* spinning (metering) pump
Spinnroving *m* spun roving
Spinnschacht *m* spinning cabinet (cell, tube)
Spinnstrecken *n* spinning stretch
Spinntisch *m* spinning table
Spinntopf *m* spinning pot (vessel), Topham box
Spinntopfverfahren *n* [centrifugal] pot spinning
Spinnviskosität *f* dope viscosity
Spinnzentrifuge *f s.* Spinntopf
Spinnzwiebel *f* [spinning] bulb
Spinodale *f (phys ch)* spinodal curve
Spinoperator *m* spin operator
Spinorbital *n* spin orbital, SO
~/molekulares *m*olecular spin orbital
Spinpopulation *f* spin population
Spinquantenzahl *f* spin quantum number
~/resultierende spin momentum quantum number
Spins *mpl***/antiparallele (entgegengesetzte)** antiparallel (opposed, opposite) spins
Spin-Spin-Kopplung *f* spin-spin coupling, dipolar coupling (interaction)
Spin-Spin-Kopplungsaufspaltung *f* spin-spin splitting
Spin-Spin-Relaxation *f* spin-spin relaxation
Spin-Spin-Wechselwirkung *f* spin-spin interaction
~/elektronengekoppelte electron-coupled [nuclear] spin-spin interaction
Spinsystem *n* spin system
Spinthariskop *n*, **Spintheriskop** *n* spinthariscope *(a device for investigating alpha rays)*
Spin-tickling *n***/getastetes** *(spectr)* gated spin tickling, GASP
Spin-Trap *m* spin trap
spinverboten spin-forbidden
Spinzustand *m* spin state
Spiralabscheider *m* dust-collecting fan, fan impeller-type collector
Spiraldraht-Vakuumfilter *n (hyd)* coil-type vacuum filter, coil filter
Spirale *f* 1. spiral, coil, helix; 2. *(distil)* beehive *(a device for retaining packing in position)*; spiral tile *(a kind of packing)*; 3. vortex *(of fluid as in a hydrocyclone)*
Spiralgehäuse *n* volute casing *(of pumps)*
Spiralgehäusepumpe *f* volute pump
Spiralklassierer *m* spiral classifier
Spiralkühler *m* **[nach Friedrichs]** Friedrichs condenser
Spiralrohrbündelwärme[aus]tauscher *m*, **Spiralrohrbündelwärmeübertrager** *m* spiral-tube heat exchanger
Spiralrohrschlange *f* spiral coil
Spiralscheider *m s.* Spiralabscheider
Spiralschlauch *m (rubber)* wire-spiral-reinforced hose
Spiraltest *m (plast)* spiral flow test
Spiralwärme[aus]tauscher *m*, **Spiralwärmeübertrager** *m* spiral-plate heat exchanger
Spiran *n s.* Spirokohlenwasserstoff
spirituos, spirituös alcoholic, spirituous
Spirituose *f* spirit
Spiritus *m* spirit[s] *(industrially manufactured ethanol)*
~ absolutus dehydrated alcohol
~ denaturatus *s.* ~/vergällter
~/denaturierter *s.* ~/vergällter
~/vergällter methylated spirit, denatured alcohol
Spiritusbeize *f (coat)* spirit stain
Spiritusbrenner *m (lab)* alcohol burner
Spiritusbrennerei *f* distillery
Spiritusindustrie *f* distilling industry
Spirituslack *m* spirit varnish
Spirituslampe *f (lab)* alcohol lamp
Spiritusumdruckverfahren *n* spirit duplicating
Spiroatom *n (org ch)* spiro atom
Spirobindung *f* spiro union (junction) *(of atoms)*
Spirokohlenwasserstoff *m* spiro hydrocarbon (compound), spiran[e], spirocyclane
Spirometer *n* spirometer
Spiropolymer[e] *n* spiro polymer
Spirostellung *f (org ch)* spiro position
Spirosystem *n (org ch)* spiro-ring system
Spiroverbindung *f s.* Spirokohlenwasserstoff
Spiroverknüpfung *f s.* Spirobindung
Spitze *f* top; vertex *(as of a tetrahedral molecule)*
• **bis zur ~ geteilt** calibrated to jet *(pipette)*
Spitzenanfall *m (hyd)* peak flow, *(specif)* peak sewage flow
Spitzenstrom *m (el ch)* peak (summit, apex) current
Spitzentemperatur *f* peak temperature
Spitzenwert *m* extreme [value], extremum
Spitzigfärben *n* tippy dyeing
Spitzigkeit *f (dye)* tippiness
Spitzkelchglas *n* sediment cone
Spitzkolben *m* pointed flask
Spitztrichter *m* cone classifier
SPK *s.* Strom-Potential-Kurve
SP-Kautschuk *m* superior processing rubber, S.P. rubber
Spleißen *n (bioch)* splicing
~ der RNA RNA splicing
Splint *m*, **Splintholz** *n* sapwood
Splintkohle *f* splint coal
Splitdosierung *f (chromat)* split sampling
Split-Protein *n (bioch)* split protein, SP *(of ribosomes)*
Splitt *m* grit
splitten *(chromat)* to split *(a gas mixture into two unequal streams)*
Splitter *m* splinter, chip, sliver; *(pap)* shim, sliver; wood speck *(a defect in paper)*
Splittereis *n* flake (shaved, chipped) ice
Splitterfänger *m (pap)* shim (sliver, bull) screen
splitterfest, splitterfrei *s.* splittersicher

Splitterkohle *f* splint coal
splittern to shatter, so spall
splittersicher shatterproof *(glass)*
Splittersicherheit *f* shatter resistance (strength) *(of glass)*
Split-Verhältnis *n (chromat)* [flow] split ratio
Spodium *n* spodium, bone char[coal]
Spodumen *m (min)* spodumene *(aluminium lithium silicate)*
Spongiose *f* graphitization *(a type of corrosion)*
Spontangärung *f* spontaneous fermentation
Spontanmutation *f (biol)* spontaneous mutation
Spontansäuerung *f (food)* spontaneous (natural) souring
Spontanzündung *f* spontaneous ignition, autoignition
Sporinit *m* sporinite *(a maceral of coal)*
Sporulationsmedium *n (biot)* sporulation medium
spratzen *(met)* to spit, to spatter
spreitbar spreadable
Spreitbarkeit *f* spreadability
spreiten to spread [out]
Spreitungsdruck *m* spreading pressure
Spreitungskoeffizient *m* spreading coefficient, SC
Spreizschwingung *f* scissor vibration
Sprengel-Pumpe *f* Sprengel pump
sprengen 1. to break, to crack, to rupture, to disrupt *(a chemical bond)*; 2. to blast *(by means of explosives)*
Sprengfähigkeit *f* explosibility, explosiveness, explosivity
Sprenggelatine *f* blasting (explosive) gelatin, gelatin dynamite
Sprengkapsel *f* blasting (detonating) cap, primer, detonator
Sprengkraft *f* explosive power (force), shattering power, brisance
Sprengladung *f* blasting (explosive) charge
Sprengluft *f* oxyliquit *(an explosive)*
Sprengmittel *n* blasting agent
Sprengöl *n* blasting (explosive) oil *(glycerol trinitrate or ethyleneglycol dinitrate or a mixture of both)*
Sprengpulver *n* blasting (black) powder, gunpowder
Sprengsalpeter *m* explosive saltpetre
Sprengschnur *f* detonating fuse
Sprengstoff *m* explosive
~/brisanter high explosive, H.E.
~/initiierender initiating explosive, initiator
Sprengstoffeigenschaften *fpl* explosive properties
Sprengstoffgemisch *n* explosive mixture
Sprengstoffladung *f s.* Sprengladung
Sprengung *f* 1. breaking, cracking, rupture, fission *(of a chemical bond)*; 2. blast[ing], detonation, shot
~ **der C–C-Bindung** C–C [bond] rupture
Sprengwirkung *f* blasting (explosive) action
Sprenkpapier *n* marble[d] paper
springen to burst, to crack, to break
Springkitt *m* bouncing putty
Sprinkler-Feuerlöschanlage *f* sprinkler (fire sprinkling) system
Sprit *m s.* Spiritus
Spritbeize *f (coat)* spirit stain
Spritblau *n* spirit (aniline) blue *(triphenylrosaniline hydrochloride)*
Spritgelb *n* spirit yellow G, solvent yellow 1 *(p-aminoazobenzene)*
spritlöslich spirit-soluble, alcohol-soluble
Spritumdruckverfahren *n s.* Spiritusumdruckverfahren
spritzalitieren, spritzaluminieren to alumetize
Spritzartikel *m (plast)* extruded article; injection-moulded article
Spritzauftrag *m* spray application; splash feed *(in roller dryers)*
spritzbar sprayable; *(plast)* extrudable
Spritzbarkeit *f* sprayability; *(plast)* extrudability
Spritzbelag *m (agric)* spray residue (load)
Spritzbeton *m* gunned concrete, gunite
Spritzbrett *n (pap)* spatter (baffle) board
Spritzbrühe *f (agric)* mixture for spraying, wash
Spritzdorn *m (plast)* extruder core
Spritzdruck *m* spraying pressure; *(plast)* injection pressure
~ **beim Spritzgießen** *(plast)* injection moulding pressure
Spritzdüse *f* spray nozzle; *(plast)* injection nozzle
Spritzeigenschaften *fpl (plast)* extrusion properties; injecting properties *(injection moulding)*
spritzen 1. to spray, to spray-apply *(e.g. coating material)*; to spray, to spray-coat *(surfaces)*; to splash, to spatter, to sputter *(of a liquid)*; 2. *(plast)* to extrude; to inject; 3. *(food)* to pump *(meat with pickle)*
Spritzen *n* 1. spraying, spray application *(as of coating material)*; spraying, spray coating *(of surfaces)*; splashing, spattering, sputtering *(of a liquid)*; 2. *(plast)* extruding, extrusion [moulding]; injection [moulding]; 3. *(food)* pumping *(of meat with pickle)*; 4. *s.* Spritzung
~/druckluftfreies (druckluftloses) *s.* ~/hydraulisches
~ **durch intraarterielle Injektion** artery pumping *(of meat with pickle)*
~ **durch intramuskuläre Injektion** stitch (spray) pumping *(of meat with pickle)*
~/elektrostatisches *(coat)* electrostatic spraying
~/hydraulisches (luftloses) *(coat)* airless spraying
~/pneumatisches air [atomization] spraying, compressed (conventional) air spraying
Spritzer *m* 1. splash; 2. squirt *(as from a wash bottle)*
Spritzfärbung *f (tann)* spray dyeing
Spritzfehler *m (plast)* injection defect; *(coat)* spraying fault
Spritzflasche *f (lab)* [fine-jet] wash[ing] bottle
~ **aus Weichplast** squeeze bottle

Spritzflüssigkeit *f* spray, *(agric also)* plant spray
Spritzgehäuse *n (plast)* cylinder *(of an extruder)*; barrel *(of an injection moulding machine)*
Spritzgerät *n (agric)* spray machine, sprayer
Spritzgeräte *npl (agric)* spray equipment
Spritzgießen *n (plast)* injection moulding
Spritzgießer *m (plast)* injection moulder
Spritzgießmaschine *f (plast)* injection moulding machine
~ **mit Schneckenkolben** screw injection [moulding] machine
~ **mit Schneckenvorplastizierung** screw preplasticizing machine
Spritzgießteil *n s.* Spritzgußteil
Spritzgießwerkzeug *n (plast)* injection mould
~/angußloses runnerless mould
~ **mit Zentralanguß** centre-gated mould
Spritzgießzylinder *m (plast)* injection cylinder, plasticating (shooting) cylinder
Spritzguß *m (plast)* injection moulding
Spritzgußform *f (plast)* injection mould
Spritzgußmasse *f* injection-moulding material, injection compound
Spritzgußteil *n (plast)* injection moulding, injection-moulded part (article)
Spritzgußwerkzeug *n (plast)* injection mould
Spritzhilfsmittel *n (agric)* auxiliary (supplementary) spray material, spray supplement
Spritzkabine *f* spray booth
Spritzkammer *f* 1. *(coat)* spray chamber; 2. *(plast)* plenum chamber
Spritzkolben *m (plast)* injection plunger (piston, ram) *(injection moulding)*; pot plunger *(transfer moulding)*
Spritzkonzentrat *n (agric)* spray concentrate
Spritzkonzentration *f (agric)* spray strength
Spritzkopf *m (plast)* extruder (extrusion, die) head, die box
spritzlackieren to spray, *(relating to wooden material also)* to varnish by spraying, to spray-varnish
Spritzlackieren *n***/elektrostatisches** electrostatic spraying (spray painting)
Spritzling *m s.* Spritzgußteil
Spritzmaschine *f* 1. *(plast)* extruding (forcing) machine; injection moulding machine; 2. *(ceram)* extrusion auger
Spritzmittel *n* spray, *(agric also)* plant spray
~/fungizides fungicide spray
Spritzmundstück *n (plast)* extruder (extrusion) die
Spritznarben *fpl (coat)* orange peel
Spritznebel *m (coat)* spray mist (fog)
Spritzniederschlag *m (agric)* spray residue (load)
Spritzöl *n (agric)* spray oil
Spritzpfahl *m* injector gun, soil injector *(for applying liquid pesticides)*
Spritzpistole *f (coat)* spray[ing] gun, paint sprayer (spray gun); schooping gun *(for metal spraying)*
~/elektrostatische electrostatic spray gun
Spritzplastometer *n* **nach Dillon-Firestone** *(rubber)* Firestone[-Dillon] plastometer
Spritzpresse *(plast)* transfer moulder
Spritzpressen *n (plast)* transfer (flow) moulding, *(Am also)* plunger moulding
Spritzpreßkolben *m* pot plunger
Spritzpreßmaschine *f s.* Spritzpresse
Spritzpreßteil *n (plast)* transfer moulding
Spritzpreßwerkzeug *n (plast)* transfer mould
Spritzpulver *n (agric)* wettable powder; *(coat)* spray powder
Spritzquellung *f s.* Strangaufweitung
Spritzrad *n* sparger *(of a vinegar generator)*
Spritzrohrfeuchter *m (pap)* spray damper
Spritzrückstand *m (agric)* spray residue (load)
Spritzschaden *m (agric)* spray injury
Spritzschicht *f* spray coat[ing]
Spritzschleier *m (agric)* spray swath[e]
Spritzstreichen *n (pap)* spray coating
Spritzstreichmaschine *f (pap)* spray coater
Spritzteil *n s.* Spritzgußteil
Spritzteller *m* splash plate
Spritztopf *m (plast)* transfer pot
Spritztorf *m* hydro peat
Spritzung *f* high-volume spraying *(application of pesticides with abundant water)*
Spritzvolumen *n (plast)* injection capacity
Spritzwasser *n (pap)* shower (flush) water
Spritzwasserbehälter *m (pap)* shower supply tank
Spritzwasserfalle *f* steam trap *(of an evaporator)*
Spritzwasserpumpe *f (pap)* shower pump
Spritzwechsel *m (agric)* spray rotation *(systematic change of pesticides applied)*
Spritzwinkel *m* spray angle
Spritzzylinder *m (plast)* injection cylinder, plasticating (shooting) cylinder
Sprödbruch *m* brittle fracture (failure)
Sprödbruchtemperatur *f* brittle[-point] temperature, brittleness temperature
spröde brittle • ~ **machen** to embrittle, to make brittle • ~ **werden** to embrittle, to become brittle
Spröde *f* brittleness
Sprödglimmer *m* brittle mica
Sprödigkeit *f* brittleness
Sprödigkeitspunkt *m* brittle point
Sprödwerden *n* embrittlement
S-Protein *n* S protein *(breakdown product of ribonuclease)*
Sprout-Waldron-Mühle *f (pap)* Sprout-Waldron refiner
Sprudel *m* sparkling water
sprudeln to bubble, to effervesce
sprudelnd bubbling, effervescent
Sprudelschicht *f* spouted bed *(fluid-bed technology)*
Sprühabsorber *m* spray absorber
Sprühbeschichten *n (plast)* spray coating
~/elektrostatisches electrostatic spray coating
Sprühblaser *m (agric)* low-volume mist blower, pneumatic (air-blast) sprayer
Sprühdose *f* aerosol bomb, pocket sprayer
Sprühdraht *m* ionizer wire *(as of an electrical precipitator)*

Sprühdüse *f* spray nozzle, atomizing (fog) nozzle
Sprühdüsenkühler *m* spray-type cooler
Sprüheinrichtung *f* sprayer, atomizer
~/rotierende spinning atomizer
Sprühelektrode *f* discharge (ionizing, ionic) electrode
sprühen to spray
Sprühen *n***/elektrostatisches** electrostatic spraying
Sprüher *m* sprayer, atomizer
Sprühflüssigkeit *f* spray
Sprühgefrierverfahren *n (food)* spray freezing process
Sprühgerät *n (agric)* spray machine, [crop] sprayer
Sprühgeräte *npl* spray equipment
Sprühkautschuk *m* [latex-]sprayed rubber
Sprühkegel *m* spray cone
Sprühkegelwinkel *m* spray angle
Sprühkolonne *f* spray column *(gas cleaning)*
Sprühkörper *m (petrol)* shower-deck tray
Sprühkristallisation *f* prilling
sprühkristallisieren to prill
Sprühmilchpulver *n* spray-dried milk [powder]
Sprühmittel *n* spray
~ für den Gartenbau horticultural spray
~ gegen Fliegen fly spray
Sprühnebel *m (agric)* spray mist
Sprühnebler *m s.* Sprühblaser
Sprühparaffin *n* spray (light liquid) paraffin
Sprühpistole *f* spray[ing] gun
Sprühreagens *n* spray reagent
Sprührohr *n* spray pipe
Sprührückstand *m (agric)* spray residue (load)
Sprühsättiger *m* spray-type ammonia absorber
Sprühscheibe *f* 1. spray disk, rotating-disk atomizer; 2. *s.* Versprüher/rotierender
Sprühschleier *m (agric)* spray swath[e]
Sprühstrahl *m (agric)* directed spray
Sprühtank *m* spray tank
Sprühteller *m* splash plate
Sprühtrockner *m* spray dryer
Sprühtrocknung *f* spray drying
Sprühturm *m* spray tower
Sprühwäscher *m* spray scrubber (washer) *(gas cleaning)*
Sprühwasser *n* spray[ing] water
Sprühwinkel *m* spray angle
Sprung *m* 1. crack; *(ceram)* flaw; 2. crack of the grain *(a property of leather relating to its elasticity)*
Sprungpunkt *m*, **Sprungtemperatur** *f* superconductive (transition) temperature *(of a superconductor)*
spucken to prime *(of kettles or distillation columns)*, *(distil also)* to puke
Spuckgrenze *f (distil)* flooding point
Spuckstoff *m (pap)* groundwood (screen) rejects, screen[ing]s, tail[ing]s, coarse (waste) material, waste [product], rejected stock *(classification of mechanical pulp)*
Spülapparat *m* rinser
Spülbad *n* rinsing (scouring) bath
Spülbecken *n* [bench] sink
Spülboden *m (filtr)* scavenger plate
Spüldampf *m (petrol)* stripping (purge) steam
Spüldauer *f (hyd, filtr)* backwash time
Spüldüse *f* scour (sluicing) nozzle
Spule *f (text)* bobbin
~/keglige cone
spulen *(text)* to wind
spülen to rinse, to scour, to wash, to swill, to flush
Spulenspinnverfahren *n* bobbin spinning
Spüler *m* rinser
Spülflüssigkeit *f* rinsing (scouring) liquid, rinsing[s]
Spülflüssigkeitsschieber *m* rinse (scour) valve
Spülgas *n (chromat)* purge (make-up) gas
Spülgas[schwel]verfahren *n* 'Spülgas' process *(gas making)*
Spülgrube *f (petrol)* mud pit
Spülkopf *m (petrol)* swivel
Spülluft *f* scavenging air
Spülmittel *n* rinsing (scouring) agent, rinse, scavenger
Spülmud *m (petrol)* drilling mud
Spülpumpe *f (petrol)* mud pump
Spülsäule *f (petrol)* mud column
Spülschieber *m* scour valve
Spülschlamm *m (petrol)* drilling mud
~ auf Erdölbasis oil-base mud
Spülschlauch *m (petrol)* mud (rotary) hose
Spültropfkörper *m (hyd)* high-rate trickling (biological) filter
Spülung *f* 1. rinse, rinsing, scouring, wash[ing], swilling, flushing; 2. *s.* Spülschlamm
Spülungsbehälter *m (petrol)* mud pit
Spülungssäule *f (petrol)* mud column
Spülungstank *m (petrol)* mud pit
Spülungsumlaufsystem *n (petrol)* drilling fluid circulating system
Spülventil *n* rinse (scour) valve
Spülwasser *n* rinsing water, wash (swill) water; [filter] backwash water
Spülwässer *npl* swills
Spülwasserauffangtrichter *m (hyd)* wash-water hopper *(of a microstrainer)*
Spülwasserbedarf *m (hyd, filtr)* backwash water requirements
Spülwasserbehälter *m (hyd, filtr)* backwash tank
Spülwasserverbrauch *m (hyd, filtr)* backwash water consumption
Spülzyklus *m (hyd, filtr)* backwash cycle
Spund *m* bung, plug
spunden, spünden to bung
Spundloch *n* bunghole
Spur *f* 1. *(anal)* trace [amount, quantity] *(* 10^2 to 10^{-4} ppm)*; remnant *(of an undesired substance)*; 2. trace *(of a recording instrument)*
Spurenanalyse *f* trace analysis

Spurenbestandteil *m* trace constituent (component, species) *(*< 0.01 %)*
~ **der Luft** *m* trace air constituent
Spurenelement *n (biol, agric)* [nutritional] trace element, minor [nutrient] element, microelement
Spurengas *n* trace gas
Spurenmaterial *n* tracer *(for investigating the pathway of reactions or nutrients)*
Spurenmenge *f* trace amount
Spurenmetall *n* trace metal
Spurennährstoff *m* micronutrient
Spurenstoff *m s.* Spurenbestandteil
Spurensucher *m s.* Spurenmaterial
Spürmethode f/magnetische *(petrol)* magnetic method
~/seismische seismic method
Spurstein *m* white metal *(product obtained by removing iron from copper matte)*
sputtern to sputter
S-PVC *s.* Suspensionspolyvinylchlorid
sp^3-Zentrum *n* sp^3 centre *(chemical bond theory)*
Squalen *n* squalene *(an aliphatic triterpene)*
µSR *s.* Myonspinrotation
SR-Benzin *n* straight-run gasoline (benzine, naphtha, spirit), S.R.B.
SRC-Verfahren *n (coal)* SRC process *(for refining coal with solvents)*
SRF-Ruß *m (rubber)* semireinforcing furnace black, SRF black
S-Säure *f* S acid, 1-aminonaphth-8-ol-4-sulphonic acid
2S-Säure *f s.* SS-Säure
S-S-Bindung *f* disulphide bond (cross link, link)
ssb-Protein *n* SSB protein, single-stranded [DNA] binding protein
S-S-Brücke *f* disulphide bridge
ssl. *s.* löslich/sehr schwer
SS-Säure *f* SS acid, 2S acid, Chicago acid, 1-aminonaphth-8-ol-2,4-disulphonic acid
Stababgabe *f (pap)* stick downtake *(in a festoon dryer)*
Stabaufnahme *f (pap)* stick uptake *(in a festoon dryer)*
Stäbchenpech *n* rod (pencil) pitch
Stabchromatographie *f* chromatobar technique
stabil stable, resistant, *(esp relating to pesticides:)* persistent; stable, rigid *(physically)* • ~ **werden** to come into stability
~/biologisch resistant to biological degradation, non-biodegradable, biologically inert, refractory
~/thermisch thermally stable *(e.g. plastics)*
Stabilbenzin *n* stabilized (stable) gasoline
stabilglühen *(met)* to stabilize
Stabilglühen *n (met)* stabilizing [anneal]
Stabilisation *f* stabilization
Stabilisations... *s.* Stabilisier...
Stabilisator *m* 1. stabilizing agent, stabilizer *(relating to suspensions also)* suspending agent; *(rubber)* preserving agent, preservative; *(food)* anticaking agent *(for retaining the flowability)*; 2. *s.* Stabilisierkolonne
Stabilisieranlage *f (petrol)* stabilizer plant
stabilisieren to stabilize
~/sich to stabilize
Stabilisierkolonne *f (petrol)* stabilizer
Stabilisierung *f* stabilization
Stabilisierungsbad *n (phot)* stabilizing bath
Stabilisierungsbecken *n (hyd)* stabilization basin (tank)
Stabilisierungsenergie *f* stabilizing energy
Stabilisierungsglühen *n (met)* stabilizing [anneal]
Stabilisierungsmittel *n s.* Stabilisator 1.
Stabilisierungsteich *m (hyd)* stabilization pond (lagoon)
Stabilität *f* stability, resistance, *(esp relating to pesticides:)* persistence; stability, rigidity *(physically)* • ~ **erlangen** to come into stability
~/thermische thermal stability *(as of plastics)*
Stabilitätsbereich *m* range of stability
Stabilitätskonstante *f s.* Komplexstabilitätskonstante
Stabilitätszone *f (coll)* stability zone
Stabmühle *f* rod mill
Stabrost *m s.* Stabsiebrost
Stabrostsieb *n* bar (rod) screen
Stabrostsiebmaschine *f* grizzly screen
Stabsiebrost *m* [bar, rod] grizzly
Stabspritze *f (agric)* [hand] lance
Stabziehverfahren *n (glass)* drawn-rod method
Stachelwalzenbrecher *m* toothed-roll crusher
Stadium *n* stage
~ **der großtechnischen Erprobung** preproduction stage
~/hydrothermales *(geol)* hydrothermal stage
Stadtentwässerung *f* municipal sewer system, sewerage
Stadtgas *n* town (city) gas
Stadtmüll *m* town refuse, city garbage
Stadtnebel *m* smog *(a type of air pollution)*
Staffelform *f* staggered form *(stereochemistry)*
Staffordshire-Ofen *m (ceram)* Staffordshire kiln
Staffordshire-Seger-Kegel *m (ceram)* Staffordshire [Seger] cone
Stahl *m* steel
~/aufgekohlter *s.* ~/einsatzgehärteter
~/austenitischer austenitic steel
~/basischer basic steel
~/beruhigter (beruhigt vergossener) killed steel
~/einsatzgehärteter case-hardened steel, carburized steel
~/entkohlter decarburized steel
~/ferritischer ferritic steel
~/feuerverzinkter hot-dip galvanized steel
~ **für Einsatzhärtung** case-hardening steel, carburizing steel
~ **für Nitrierhärtung** nitriding steel
~/halbberuhigter semikilled steel
~/herdgefrischter open-hearth steel

~/hitzebeständiger heat-resisting steel
~/hochfester high-strength steel
~/hochlegierter high-alloy steel
~/inchromierter chromized steel
~/kaltgezogener cold-drawn steel
~/knetbarer plastic steel
~/kohlenstoffarmer low-carbon steel
~/korrosionsbeständiger corrosion-resistant steel, *(with high-chromium alloys also)* stainless steel
~/korrosionsträger weathering steel
~/legierter alloy steel
~/lufthärtender air-hardening steel
~/martensitischer martensitic steel
~/nichtrostender stainless steel *(containing more than 12.5 % Cr)*
~/nickellegierter nickel alloy steel
~/niedriglegierter low-alloy steel
~/nitriergehärteter (nitrierter) nitrided steel
~/ölhärtender oil-hardening steel
~/rostfreier *s.* ~/nichtrostender
~/ruhig vergossener killed steel
~/sauerstoffgefrischter basic oxygen [furnace] steel
~/saurer acid steel
~/schwachlegierter low-alloy steel
~/übereutektoider hypereutectoid steel
~/überfrischter overblown steel *(containing ferrous oxide)*
~/unberuhigter (unberuhigt vergossener) rimmed (rimming, wild) steel
~/unlegierter [plain] carbon steel
~/untereutektoider hypoeutectoid steel
~/verzinnter tinned steel
~/wasserhärtender water-hardening steel
~/wasserstoffbeständiger hydrogen-resistant steel
~/weicher mild (soft) steel
~/windgefrischter Bessemer (converter) steel
~/zementierter *s.* ~/einsatzgehärteter
Stahlakkumulator *m* Edison accumulator (cell)
Stahlarmierung *f* 1. steel armouring *(as around a blast furnace)*; 2. *s.* Stahlbewehrung
Stahlband *n* steel strip
Stahlbeton *m* reinforced concrete
Stahlbewehrung *f (build)* steel reinforcement
Stahlblau *n s.* Blau/Berliner
Stahlblech *n* sheet steel *(material)*; steel sheet *(product having definite dimensions)*; steel plate *(thickness > 0.25 inch)*
Stahlblechmantel *m* steel jacket
Stahlblock *m* steel ingot
Stahlbombe *f* steel cylinder
Stahldruckfarbe *f* steel-plate[-engraving] ink
Stahleisen *n* basic (steelmaking) pig iron
Stahlerzeugung *f* steelmaking
Stahlflasche *f* steel cylinder
Stahlformguß *m* cast steel
Stahlgewinnung *f* steelmaking
Stahlguß *m* 1. steel casting; 2. cast steel *(products)*; 3. *s.* Stahlgußstück
Stahlgußstück *n* steel casting
Stahlherstellung *f* steelmaking
Stahlkapillarrohr *n***/glasgefüttertes** *(chromat)* glass-lined metal tubing
Stahlmantel *m* steel jacket
Stahlmörser *m* percussion (diamond) mortar
Stahlpanzer *m* steel shell
Stahlroheisen *n* basic (steelmaking) pig iron
Stahlrohr *n* steel pipe
Stahlschale *f***/druckdichte** *(nucl)* containment
Stahlschmelzofen *m* steelmaking furnace
Stahlschrott *m* steel scrap, scrap steel
Stahlstich[druck]farbe *f* steel-plate[-engraving] ink
stahlummantelt steel-cased, steel-jacketed
Stahlunterbau *m* steel substructure
Stahlwalze *f* steel roll
Stahlwerksofen *m* steelmaking furnace
stalagmitisch *(min)* stalagmitic
Stalagmometer *n* stalagmometer *(for measuring surface tensions)*
Stalagmometrie *f* stalagmometry *(a method for measuring surface tensions)*
stalaktitisch *(min)* stalactitic
Stamm *m* 1. *(nomencl)* parent; 2. strain *(of microorganisms)*
~/mutierter *(biot)* mutant strain
~/produktiver *s.* Produktionsstamm
Stammansatz *m (dye)* stock liquor
Stammbase *f* parent base
Stammbaum *m* 1. family tree *(as of hydrocarbons)*; 2. Stammreihe/radioaktive
Stammemulsion *f* stock emulsion
Stammentwicklung *f (biot)* strain development (improvement)
Stammflotte *f (dye)* stock liquor
Stammhaltung *f (biot)* strain maintenance
Stammkern *m s.* Grundgerüst
Stammkohlenwasserstoff *m* parent hydrocarbon
Stammkonservierung *f (biot)* strain preservation
Stammkörper *m* parent (mother) substance
Stammkultur *f (biot)* stock culture
Stammkulturmedium *n (biot)* stock culture medium
Stammküpe *f (dye)* stock vat
Stammlauge *f* mother liquor
Stammlinie *f (biot)* strain line
Stammlösung *f* stock solution
Stammname *m (nomencl)* parent name
Stammoptimierung *f s.* Stammentwicklung
Stammreihe *f***/radioaktive** radioactive [decay] series
Stammringsystem *n (nomencl)* parent ring system
Stammsäure *f* parent acid
Stammselektion *f (biot)* selection of strains
Stammsubstanz *f s.* Stammverbindung
Stammsubstanzname *m (nomencl)* semisystematic (semitrivial) name

Stammverbindung *f* parent compound
Stammwürze *f (ferm)* 1. original wort; 2. *s.* Stammwürzegehalt
Stammwürzegehalt *m* original extract [content]
stampfen to stamp, to ram, to tamp
Stampfer *m (ceram)* tamp; *(tech)* beater *(of a hammer mill)*
Stampfgemisch *n s.* Stampfmasse 1.
Stampfkalander *m (text)* beetler, beetling machine
Stampfmaschine *f (coal)* stamper
Stampfmasse *f* 1. *(ceram)* ramming mass (material, mix, mixture); 2. electrode material, paste
~/feuerfeste refractory ramming material
Stampfmischung *f s.* Stampfmasse 1.
Stampfmühle *f* stamp mill
Stampfwerk *n (pap)* stamping (hammer) mill, stamper, stamps, stocks
Stand *m* 1. level, height *(as of liquid in a vessel)*; 2. *(tann)* firmness *(a property of leather)*
Standard *m* standard
~/innerer (interner) *(anal)* internal standard
~/radioaktiver *s.* Standardpräparat/radioaktives
~/sekundärer secondary standard
Standardabweichung *f* standard deviation, root-mean-square error, *(in a graph also)* half-peak width *(width at 0.607 h)*
Standard-Aktivierungsenthalpie *f***/freie** standard free energy of activation
Standardausrüstung *f* standard equipment
Standardbedingungen *fpl* standard[ized] conditions
Standardbezugs... *s.* Standard...
Standardbildungsenthalpie *f* standard enthalpy (heat) of formation
~/freie (molare freie) standard free energy of formation, standard Gibbs function of formation
Standardbildungswärme *f s.* Standardbildungsenthalpie
Standarddruck *m* standard (normal) pressure
Standardeinheit *f* standard (normal) unit
Standardelektrode *f* standard electrode (half-cell)
~/sekundäre secondary standard electrode
Standardelektrodenpotential *n* standard [electrode] potential, S.E.P.
Standardelement *n (el ch)* standard cell
Standard-EMK *f* standard electromotive force, standard [reference] emf
Standardenthalpie *f* standard enthalpy
~/freie standard (Gibbs) free energy
~/molare standard molar enthalpy
~/molare freie standard molar Gibbs function
Standardentropie *f* standard entropy
~/molare standard third-law entropy
Standardfarbe *f* standard colour
Standardgold *n* standard gold *(for coinage)*
Standardgoldsol *n* standard gold sol
Standardhalbelement *n*, **Standardhalbzelle** *f s.* Standardelektrode
Standardkatalysator *m* standard catalyst
Standardlinie *f (spectr)* standard line
Standardlösung *f* standard solution
Standardmasse *f* standard mass
Standardmethode *f* standard method (procedure, technique)
Standardmineral *n* standard mineral
Standardnormalpotential *n* standard potential
Standardopaleszenz *f* standard opalescence (turbidity)
Standardoxidationspotential *n* standard oxidation potential
Standardpenicillin *n* standard penicillin
Standardpotential *n* standard (normal) potential
~/chemisches standard chemical potential
~ des Halbelements standard-half-cell potential
~ des Redoxsystems standard redox (oxidation-reduction) potential
Standardpräparat *n* standard preparation
~/radioaktives radioactive (radioactivity) standard
Standardprobe *f* standard sample
Standardprüfsieb *n* standard (normal) test (testing) screen
Standardpuffer *m*, **Standardpufferlösung** *f* standard buffer [solution]
Standardradius *m* standard radius
Standardreagens *n* standard reagent
Standardreaktionsenthalpie *f* standard enthalpy of reaction, standard reaction enthalpy
~/freie (molare freie) standard reaction Gibbs function, standard Gibbs function of reaction
Standardreaktionsentropie *f* standard reaction entropy
Standardredoxpotential *n* standard redox (oxidation-reduction) potential
Standardreduktionspotential *n* standard reduction potential
Standardsaft *m (sugar)* standard liquor
Standardsäure *f* standard acid
Standardschliff *m* standard ground-glass joint
Standardschliffverbindung *f* standard ground-glass joint
Standardsieb *n* standard sieve (screen)
Standardsiebreihe *f* standard sieve scale (series), standard series of screens
Standardsilber *n* standard silver *(for coinage)*
Standardspannung *f* standard [reference] voltage
Standardsubstanz *f* standard [substance]
Standardtemperatur *f* standard temperature
Standardthermometer *n* standard thermometer
Standardthermopaar *n* standard thermocouple
Standardtrübung *f* standard opalescence (turbidity)
Standardverbrennungsenthalpie *f* standard enthalpy of combustion
Standardverfahren *n* standard method (procedure, technique)
Standardversuch *m* standard test
Standardvorschrift *f* standard specification
Standardwasserstoffelektrode *f* standard hydrogen electrode, SHE

Standardwert *m* standard value
Standardwiderstandsthermometer *n* standard resistance thermometer
Standardzelle *f (el ch)* standard cell
Standardzustand *m* standard [reference] state
Standbad *n (text)* standing bath
Standentwicklung *f (phot)* stand development
Ständer *m* pillar *(of a balance)*
Standfast-Färbemaschine *f (text)* Standfast molten metal machine
Standflasche *f* storage (stock) bottle, laboratory bottle
Standglas *n s.* Standzylinder
m-**ständig** in meta position, meta • ~ **sein** to be [located, situated] meta
o-**ständig** in ortho position, ortho
p-**ständig** in para position, para
Standöl *n* stand oil
Standrohr *n* standpipe
Standzeit *f* 1. service (operating) life, working (useful) life *(of a machine)*; *(plast)* pressing time; 2. *s.* Verweilzeit; 3. *s.* Verarbeitungszeit
~/erwartbare service life expectancy
Standzylinder *m* plain cylinder, gas jar; *(hyd)* settling cylinder
Stange *f* 1. *(tech)* rod, bar, pole; 2. roll *(of sulphur)*
Stangenrost *m s.* Stangensiebrost
Stangenrostsieb *n* bar (rod) screen
Stangenschwefel *m* roll sulphur
Stangensiebrost *m* [bar, rod] grizzly
Stangentusche *f* India ink *(in the form of sticks)*
Stannan *n* stannane, tin hydride, stannic hydride
Stannat *n* stannate
Stannin *m (min)* stannite, tin pyrites, bell-metal ore
Stanniol *n*, **Stanniolfolie** *f* tin foil
Stanniolpapier *n* tin-foil paper
Stanton-Zahl *f* Stanton number *(fluid mechanics)*
stanzen to punch, to blank
Stanzform *f* die
Stanzmasse *f (ceram)* dust
Stanzwerkzeug *n* die
Stapel *m* 1. stack; *(ceram)* bung *(as of bricks)*; 2. *(text)* staple [length], fibre staple • **auf ~ reißen (schneiden)** *(text)* to staple
Stapelbecken *n s.* Rückhaltebecken
Stapelfaser *f (text)* staple [fibre]
Stapelfehler *m (cryst)* stacking fault
Stapelglasseide *f* chopped strands
Stapellänge *f (text)* staple [length], fibre staple
stapeln to stack
Stapelplatte *f* pallet
Stapelsalzung *f (tann)* green salting *(of hides)*
Stapeltank *m (hyd)* storage tank
Stapelung *f* stacking
~/hydrophobe *(bioch)* hydrophobic stacking
Stapelungskräfte *fpl***/hydrophobe** *s.* Wechselwirkung/hydrophobe
stark 1. strong *(acid, base, or beverage)*; 2. intense, powerful, vigorous *(reaction)*; 3. intense *(irradiation)*
Stark-Aufspaltung *f (spectr)* Stark splitting
Stärke *f* 1. starch *(a polysaccharide)*; 2. strength *(of an acid, base, or beverage)*; 3. intensity, power *(of a reaction)*; 4. intensity *(of irradiation)*
~ der Röntgenstrahlen X-ray intensity
~ des Abwassers *(hyd)* strength of sewage
~ des Schleiers *(phot)* fog level
~/dünnkochende *s.* ~/lösliche
~/enzymatisch (fermentativ) abgebaute enzyme-converted starch
~/lösliche soluble (thin-boiling) starch
~/modifizierte modified starch
~/native native starch
~/oxidierte oxidized starch
~/tierische animal (liver) starch
Stärkeabbau *m* starch degradation (breakdown)
~/hydrolytischer starch hydrolysis
stärkeartig amyloid[al]
Stärkeblockelektrophorese *f* [starch-]block electrophoresis
Stärkederivat *n* starch derivative
Stark-Effekt *m* Stark effect, electrochromic (electric field) effect *(splitting of spectral lines)*
~/linearer linear Stark effect
~/quadratischer quadratic Stark effect
~ zweiter Ordnung second-order Stark effect
stärkeführend *s.* stärkehaltig
Stärkegehalt *m* starch content
Stärkegelelektrophorese *f* starch-gel electrophoresis
Stärkegranulose *f* amylopectin
Stärkegummi *n* starch gum, artificial (British) gum, dextrin[e] *(a polysaccharide)*
stärkehaltig starch-containing, starchy, amylaceous, amyliferous, farinaceous
Stärkehydrolysat *n* starch hydrolysate
Stärkehydrolyse *f* starch hydrolysis
Stärke-Iodat-Papier *n* starch-iodate paper
Stärkekette *f* starch chain
Stärkekleister *m* starch paste
Stärkekonversion *f s.* Stärkeverzuckerung
Stärkekorn *n* starch granule (grain)
Stärkeleim *m* starch glue (adhesive)
Stärkeleimung *f (pap)* starch sizing
Stärkelieferant *m* starch-yielding (starch-bearing) plant
Stärkemehl *n* starch flour
stärken *(text)* to starch
stärkend *(pharm)* roborant, tonic
Stärkenitrat *n* starch nitrate, nitrostarch
Stärkepapier *n* starch paper
Stärkepflanze *f* starch plant *(a plant which converts excess assimilation products into starch)*
stärkereich rich in starch, starchy, farinaceous
Stärkeretrogradation *f* starch retrogradation
Stärkesirup *m* starch (grain, glucose) syrup
stärkespaltend amylolytic, amyloclastic, starch-splitting
Stärkesuspension *f* starch suspension

Stärketisch *m* starch table
Stärkeumwandlung *f* starch conversion
Stärkeumwandlungsprodukt *n* starch conversion product
stärkeverflüssigend starch-liquefying
Stärkeverflüssigung *f* starch liquefaction
Stärkeverzuckerung *f* starch saccharification (conversion) *(by acids and enzymes)*
Stärkeverzuckerungserzeugnis *n (food)* starch conversion product
Stärkewert *m (agric)* starch equivalent
Stärkezerlegung *f s.* Stärkeabbau
Stärkezucker *m* starch (corn) sugar, dextrose, *D*-glucose *(a monosaccharide)*
Starkfeldscheidung *f (min tech)* high-intensity magnetic separation
Starkgas *n* rich gas
starkgeleimt *(pap)* strongly sized, hard-sized, H. S.
Starkgift *n***/rodentizides** acute (single-dose) rodenticide
Stark-Modulation *f (spectr)* Stark modulation
Starkreiniger *m* heavy-duty detergent
Starksäure *f (pap)* strong acid
Stark-Verbreiterung *f* Stark broadening *(of spectral lines under the influence of electric fields)*
starr rigid *(e.g. molecule, gel)*
Starrheit *f* rigidity *(as of molecules or gels)*
Starrschmiermittel *n* sett grease *(consisting of lime, rosin oil, and mineral oil)*
Start *m* initiation *(as of a reaction)*
Startcodon *n (bioch)* [chain] initiation codon, initiator codon
Startdünger *m* starter [fertilizer]
starten to initiate *(e.g. a reaction)*
Starter *m (plast)* polymerization initiator; *(bioch)* primer
Starterfutter *n (agric)* starter
Starterkultur *f (biot)* starter culture
Startermolekül *n (bioch)* primer
Starter-RNA *f (bioch)* priming RNA
Startfaktor *m (bioch)* initiation factor, IF
Startfleck *m s.* Startpunkt
Startkomplex *m* initiation complex *(protein biosynthesis)*
Startmolekül *n s.* Startermolekül
Startperiode *f (phys ch)* induction period
Startpunkt *m (chromat)* point of application, start, origin
Startreaktion *f* initiation (initiating) reaction
Startreaktionsstadium *n* initiation stage
Startschritt *m (plast)* initiation step; *(bioch)* priming step
Startsignal *n (bioch)* chain-initiating signal
Startstickstoff *m (agric)* starter nitrogen
Startzeichen *n s.* Startsignal
Statik *f***/chemische** chemical statics
~ der Fluide fluid statics
Stationärenzymkinetik *f* steady-state (stationary-state) kinetics
Stationaritätsprinzip *n***[/Bodensteinsches]** Bodenstein [steady-state] approximation, steady-state [approximation] method, stationary-state method
Stationärzustand *m* steady (stationary) state *(kinetics)*
Statistik *f***/Boltzmannsche (klassische)** Boltzmann statistics
Stativ *n (lab)* [retort] stand, support (ring) stand
Stativfuß *m (lab)* retort stand base
Stativhaken *m* **mit Muffe** *(lab)* suspension clamp
Stativharfe *f (lab)* assembly
Stativklemme *f (lab)* apparatus (stand) clamp
~ mit halbrunden Spannbacken condenser clamp
Stativstab *m*, **Stativstange** *f (lab)* retort-stand (ring-stand) rod
Statormesser *n* bed knife *(of a rotary cutter)*
Statorring *m (distil)* stator ring *(of a rotating-disk contactor)*
status-quo-Hormon *n s.* Juvenilhormon
Stau *m (hyd, filtr)* head of water, liquid head *(above a filter medium)*
Staub *m* 1. dust, solid aerosol; *(intentionally made as from stone:)* powder; 2. *(pap)* fines *(in classifying wood flour)*
Staubablagerung *f* 1. dust deposition (fall); 2. dust deposit (residue)
Staubabsaugung *f* dust extraction
Staubabscheider *m* dust collector (separator, catcher)
~/akustischer sonic agglomerator
Staubabscheidezyklon *m* cyclone dust collector
Staubabscheidung *f* dust collection
~/akustische sonic agglomeration
~ durch Ultraschall ultrasonic agglomeration
Staubaufnahme *f* dust absorption
Staubaufnahmevermögen *n* dust-holding capacity
Staubaustrag *m* 1. dust discharge; dust carry-over; 2. dust outlet *(site)*
Staubaustragöffnung *f*, **Staubaustritt** *m* dust outlet
Staubbekämpfung *f* dust control
staubbeladen dust-laden, dust-bearing
Staubbeladung *f* dust loading
Staubbelag *m* dust covering, film of dust
Staubbeseitigung *f* dust removal (elimination)
Staubbildung *f* dust formation
Staubbindeflüssigkeit *f* dust-collecting liquid
Staubbindeöl *n* dust-laying oil
Staubbrenner *m* pulverized-coal burner
Staubbunker *m* dust hopper
Staubcarbid *n* dust carbide
staubdicht dustproof
Staubdruckvergasungsverfahren *n (coal)* high-pressure suspension gasification process
Stäubebelag *m* dust residue *(plant protection)*
Stäubebeutel *m* dust-bag *(plant protection)*
Stäubegerät *n (agric)* dusting appliance, duster
Stäubemaschine *f (agric)* dusting machine

Stäubemittel *n* dusting agent, dust
~/herbizides herbicidal dust
~/insektizides insecticidal dust
~/kombiniertes dust formulation
stauben to dust
stäuben 1. *(agric)* to dust *(with pesticides)*; 2. to dust *(as of heavily filled papers)*
Stäuber *m (pap)* dusting machine, duster *(for cleaning rags)*
Stäubeschwefel *m* dusting sulphur
Staubexplosion *f* dust explosion
Staubfallraum *m* gravity chamber *(gas cleaning)*
Staubfänger *m s.* Staubabscheider
Staubfeuerung *f* pulverized-fuel firing, [solid-fuel] suspension firing
Staubfilter *n* dust[-control] filter, dust collection filter, filter-type dust collector
Staubfließkatalysator *m* fluid[ized] catalyst, fluid-bed catalyst
Staubfließsystem *n* fluid[ized] system
Staubfließtechnik *f* fluidization technique, fluid-bed (fluidized-bed, boiling-bed) technique
Staubfließverfahren *n* fluid[ized] process, fluid-bed process
staubfrei dust-free, dustless
Staubgas *n* dust-laden gas
staubgefeuert pulverized-coal-fired, pulverized-fuel-fired
Staubgehalt *m* dust loading (content)
staubhaltig dust-laden
staubig dusty, dust-laden, pulverulent
Staubkalk *m s.* Kalk/gelöschter
Staubkammer *f* dust chamber, fall-out chamber, settling (settlement, gravity) chamber, drop-out box *(gas cleaning)*
~ mit Prallflächen baffle separator
Staubkohle *f* pulverized (powdered, fluid) coal
Staubkonzentrat *n* dry concentrate *(one kind of pesticide formulation)*
Staubkorn *n* dust particle
Staubluft *f* dust-laden air
Staubmühle *f* pulverizing mill, pulverizer
Staubpartikel *n* dust particle
Staubprobensammler *m* dust impinger (apparatus)
Staubrett *n (pap)* dam *(groundwood pulping)*
Staubrückstand *m* dust residue
Staubsack *m* 1. gravity dust catcher *(of a blast furnace)*; 2. *s.* Staubabscheider
Staubsammelbunker *m* dust hopper
Staubsammler *m s.* Staubabscheider
Staubschutz *m* dust shield
Staubschutzmaske *f* aspirator, mechanical filter respirator
Staubsedimentation *f* dust deposition (fall)
Staubteilchen *n* dust particle
Staubtuff *m (geol)* dust tuff
staubundurchlässig dustproof
Staubvergaser *m (coal)* suspension gasifier, entrained-bed (fully entrained) gasifier
Staubvergasung *f (coal)* pulverized-coal gasification, suspension (dilute-phase, entrained-bed, entrainment) gasification
Staubvergasungsverfahren *n* entrained gasification process
~ nach Koppers[-Totzek] Koppers process [for gasification of pulverized coal]
Staubwolkenverfahren *n* entrained-bed process, fully entrained process *(as for gasifying coal)*
Staubzucker *m* powdered (icing, castor) sugar, *(Am)* confectioners' sugar
Staubzyklon *m* cyclone dust collector
Stauchkammer *f (text)* stuffing (stuffer) tube (box)
Stauchkammertexturieren *n (text)* stuffing-box crimping
Stauchsetzapparat *m (min tech)* moving-sieve-type jig
Staudinger-Einheit *f* base unit, [basic] repeating unit *(of polymers)*
Staudinger-Index *m* intrinsic viscosity, limiting viscosity number
Staudruck *m* stagnation (dynamic) pressure
Stauer *m* expansion trap *(a kind of steam trap)*
Stauhöhe *f (hyd, filtr)* head of water, liquid head; *(pap)* head of stock *(in the headbox)*
Staupunkt *m* 1. *(distil)* loading (phase-inversion) point; 2. stagnation point *(fluid mechanics)*; 3. *(bioch)* crossover point *(with glycolysis)*
Staurand *m* **mit Durchflußmengenmesser** orifice [flow]meter
Staurohr *n* Pitot tube *(flow measurement)*
Stauscheibe *f (plast)* breaker plate
Stearaldehyd *m* stearaldehyde, *octadecanal
Stearamid *n* stearamide, stearic acid amide, *octadecanamide
Stearanilid *n* stearanilide, *octadecananilide
Stearat *n* $CH_3(CH_2)_{16}COOM^I$ stearate
Stearin *n* stearin, *(specif)* tristearin, glyceryl tristearate
Stearinaldehyd *m s.* Stearaldehyd
Stearinöl *n* olein, commercial oleic acid
Stearinpech *n* stearin pitch, candle (fat, fatty-acid) pitch
Stearinsäure *f* stearic acid, *octadecanoic acid
Stearinsäureamid *n s.* Stearamid
Stearinsäurechlorid *n s.* Stearoylchlorid
Stearinsäureethylester *m* ethyl stearate
Stearinseife *f* stearin soap
Stearolsäure *f* stearolic acid, *octadec-9-ynoic acid
Stearon *n* stearone, diheptadecyl ketone, *pentatriacontan-18-one
Stearonitril *n* stearonitrile, *octadecanenitrile
Stearophansäure *f s.* Stearinsäure
Stearoxylsäure *f* stearoxylic acid, *9,10-dioxooctadecanoic acid
Stearoylchlorid *n* stearoyl chloride

Stearylalkohol *m* stearyl alcohol, *octadecan-1-ol
Stearylamin *n* stearylamine, *octadecylamine
Stearylchlorid *n s.* Stearoylchlorid
Steatit *m (min)* steatite, soapstone *(a variety of talc)*
Steatitkeramik *f* steatite ceramics
Steatitporzellan *n* steatite porcelain
Steatitweißware *f* steatite whiteware
stechend pungent *(smell)*
Stechpipette *f* dropping (teat) pipette, medicine dropper
Stedman-Körper *m (distil)* Stedman cone (packing)
Stefan-Boltzmann-Gesetz *n* Stefan-Boltzmann law *(emissive power of black bodies)*
Steffen-Filtrat *n (sugar)* Steffen filtrate, Steffen's waste
Steffen-Melasse *f (sugar)* Steffen molasses
Steffen-Verfahren *n* Steffen process *(for desugarizing molasses)*
Stegkettenförderer *m* scraper[-chain] conveyor, *(specif)* drag (drag-chain, drag-link, slat) conveyor
stehen/äquatorial to be equatorial
~/cis (in *cis*-Stellung) to be cis
~/in Wechselwirkung to interact
~ **lassen** to allow to stand, to let stand, to set aside
~ **lassen/über Nacht** to allow to stand overnight
Stehkocher *m (pap)* upright (vertical) digester
Stehkolben *m* flat-bottom[ed] flask
Stehzeit *f s.* Verweilzeit
Stehzentrifuge *f* underdriven (bottom-driven) centrifuge, base-bearing centrifuge
steif rigid, stiff
Steifheit *f* rigidity, stiffness
Steifwerden *n (coll)* gelation
steigen 1. to increase, to rise *(as of temperature)*; 2. to rise, to pass up[wards] *(as of fluid)*
Steigen *n* 1. increase, rise *(as of temperature)*; 2. rise, passing-up[wards] *(as of fluid)*
steigern to increase *(e.g. number, quantity)*; to raise, to elevate *(e.g. temperature, boiling point)*; to potentiate *(the effect esp of drugs or pesticides by adding another agent)*
~/im Heizwert to enrich *(fuels)*
Steigerohr *n s.* Steigrohr
Steigerung *f* increase *(as of number or quantity)*; raise, elevation *(as of temperature, boiling point)*; potentiation *(of the effect esp of drugs or pesticides by adding another agent)*
Steigerungseffekt *m* enhancement effect *(photosynthesis)*
Steiggefäß *n* ascending chromatography tank, developing chamber
Steiggeschwindigkeit *f (hyd)* rise rate (velocity), rising velocity
Steigleitung *f* rising main
Steigpresse *f (pap)* reverse press
Steigpreßfilz *m (pap)* reverse-press felt
Steigrohr *n* riser [pipe], ascension (lift) pipe, riser tube, upspout
Steigung *f* pitch *(as of the blades of a propeller turbine)*
~ **1.0** square pitch
Steigungswinkel *m* helix angle *(as of an extruder screw)*
Steilförderer *m* elevator
Steilheit *f* steepness *(of a curve or an electrode)*
Steilrohr-Berieselungsverflüssiger *m* vertical shell-and-tube condenser
Steilwurfsieb *n* circle-throw screen
Stein *m* 1. stone; *(ceram)* brick; 2. [glass] stone *(a defect in glass)*; 3. matte *(smelted mixture of metal sulphides)* • **auf ~ [ver]schmelzen** *(met)* to matte-smelt
~/aluminiumoxidreicher *(ceram)* high-alumina [brick], alumina brick
~/feuerfester *(ceram)* refractory (fireclay) brick, firebrick
~/hochfeuerfester *(ceram)* highly refractory brick
~/lithographischer lithographic limestone
~/scharfgebrannter *(ceram)* hard-fired (hard-burned) brick
~/schwachgebrannter *(ceram)* soft[-fired] brick
~/tonerdereicher *s.* ~/aluminiumoxidreicher
Steinabstich *m*, **Steinabstichloch** *n (met)* taphole for matte
Steinbildung *f (hyd)* scaling, scale formation (build-up), formation of hardness scale *(in a vessel)*
~ **durch Calciumcarbonatausfällung** calcium-carbonate scaling
~ **durch Calciumsulfatausbildung** calcium-sulphate scaling
Steinchen *n* [glass] stone *(a defect)*
Steindruck *m* lithographic printing, lithography
Steindruckfarbe *f* lithographic [printing] ink, litho ink
Steindruckpapier *n* lithographic [printing] paper, litho
Steinerhitzer *m* pebble heater (stove)
Steinerhitzerverfahren *n* pebble-heater process
Steinfang *m*, **Steinfänger** *m* stone (rock) catcher
Steingitterwerk *n* chequer brickwork, chequerwork
Steinglätte *f (pap)* flint-glazing machine, flint glazer, stone burnisher
Steingut *n* earthenware
Steingutfilter *n* earthenware filter
Steinguthahn *m* earthenware cock
Steinkohle *f* [hard] coal
~/kurzflammige (kurzflammig brennende) short-flame coal
~/langflammige (langflammig brennende) long-flame coal
Steinkohlenaufbereitung *f* coal preparation (cleaning)
Steinkohlenbildung *f* coal formation (genesis)
Steinkohlenbrikett *n* [hard-]coal briquette
Steinkohlencampher *m s.* Naphthalen
Steinkohlenentgasung *f* coal carbonization
Steinkohlenentstehung *f* coal formation (genesis)

Steinkohlenformation *f*/**produktive** coal measures
Steinkohlengas *n* coal gas
Steinkohlengefügebestandteil *m* coal maceral
Steinkohlenhydrierung *f* coal hydrogenation
Steinkohlenklassifizierung *f* classification of [hard] coals
Steinkohlenklein *n* small[-sized] coal
Steinkohlenkoks *m* coal coke
Steinkohlenkreosot *n* coal-tar creosote, creosote oil
Steinkohlenmazeral *n* coal maceral
Steinkohlenmühle *f* coal[-grinding] mill, coal-dust (coal-pulverizing, pulverized-coal) mill, coal pulverizer
Steinkohlenöl *n* coal[-tar] oil
Steinkohlenpech *n* coal-tar pitch
Steinkohlenrohteer *m* crude coal tar
Steinkohlenschwelteer *m* low-temperature coal tar
Steinkohlenschwelung *f* coal carbonization
Steinkohlenstaub *m* coal dust; pulverized (powdered) coal
Steinkohlenstaubbrenner *m* pulverized-coal burner
Steinkohlenteer *m* coal tar
Steinkohlenteerdestillat *n* coal-tar distillate
Steinkohlenteerkreosot *n* coal-tar creosote, creosote oil
Steinkohlenteeröl *n* coal-tar oil
Steinkohlenteerpech *n* coal-tar pitch
Steinkohlenteerprodukt *n* coal-tar product
Steinkohlen-Tieftemperaturteer *m*, **Steinkohlenurteer** *m* low-temperature coal tar
Steinkohlenverkokung *f* coal carbonization
Steinkohlenverschwelung *f* coal carbonization
Steinkohlenwäsche *f* coal washing (cleaning)
Steinkugel *f* pebble *(as used in a pebble mill or pebble heater)*
Steinmahlgang *m* burstone mill, buhrmill
Steinoberfläche *f (pap)* stone surface
Steinretorte *f* brick retort
Steinsalz *n (min)* rock salt, halite *(sodium chloride)*
Steinsalzgitter *n (cryst)* rock-salt (sodium chloride) lattice
Steinsalzkristall *m* rock-salt (sodium chloride) crystal
Steinsalzprisma *n* rock-salt prism
Steinschicht *f (ceram)* course
Steinschmelzen *n (met)* matte smelting
Steinstich *m*, **Steinstichloch** *n (met)* taphole for matte
Steinumfangsgeschwindigkeit *f (pap)* stone speed
Steinwalze *f* stone roll
Steinwolle *f* rock wool
Steinzeug *n (ceram)* stoneware
~/braunes brown ware
~/chemisches chemical stoneware
~/Delfter delft[ware], delph[ware]
~ für die chemische Industrie *s.* ~/chemisches
~/säurefestes acid-proof stoneware
Steinzeugfüllkörper *m* stoneware packing
Steinzeugrohr *n* stoneware pipe
Steinzeugton *m* stoneware clay
Stelle *f*/**aktive** active site (centre) *(catalysis)*
stellen/alkalisch (basisch) to alkalify, to alkal[in]ize, to make alkaline (basic)
~/größer *(lab)* to turn up *(a burner flame)*
~/typkonform *(dye)* to reduce to standard (type strength)
Stellglied *n* controller *(control engineering)*
~ für Massenstrom (Mengenstrom) flow controller
Stellmotor *m* actuator, operator *(control engineering)*
Stellschraube *f* adjusting (levelling) screw *(of a balance)*
Stellung *f* position
~/äquatoriale equatorial position *(of an electron pair)*
~/axiale axial position *(of an electron pair)*
anti-**Stellung** *f* anti position • **in ~ stehen** to be anti
m-**Stellung** *f* meta position • **sich in ~ befinden** to be [located, situated] meta
o-**Stellung** *f* ortho position
p-**Stellung** *f* para position
syn-**Stellung** *f* syn position • **in ~ stehen** to be syn
1,2-Stellung *f s. o*-Stellung
1,2,3-Stellung *f* vicinal position, neighbouring (adjacent, near-by) position
1,3-Stellung *f s. m*-Stellung
1,4-Stellung *f s. p*-Stellung
Stellungsisomer[e] *n* position[al] isomer
Stellungsisomerie *f* position[al] isomerism, place (substitution) isomerism
Stellungsregler *m* positioner
Stellungssymbol *n (nomencl)* symbol of position
Stellungsziffer *f (nomencl)* position (locator) number
~/akzentuierte (apostrophierte) *s.* ~/gestrichene
~/gestrichene primed number
~/ungestrichene unprimed number
Stellventil *n* control valve
Stelzner-Methode *f (nomencl)* Stelzner method
Stempel *m (tech)* plunger, piston; *(glass)* needle, plunger *(of a feeder)*; plug, *(sometimes also)* plunger *(of a glass-blowing machine for hollow ware)*; *(plast)* force (moulding) plug, male form (mould); *(ceram)* punch
Stempel[kissen]farbe *f* stamping ink
Stempelplatte *f (plast)* force plate (retainer)
Stempelprofil *n (plast)* force (moulding) plug, male form (mould)
Stengel *m (cryst)* column
~/flacher blade
Stengel[bast]faser *f* stem (stalk) fibre
stengelförmig *(cryst)* columnar
Stengelkristall *m* columnar crystal
stengelkristallinisch *(cryst)* columnar

Stengelkristallisation *f* columnar crystallization
Stengel-Verfahren *n* Stengel process *(for making ammonium nitrate fertilizer)*
Stephen-Reaktion *f*, **Stephen-Reduktion** *f* Stephen reduction (reaction) *(for obtaining aldehydes from nitriles)*
Stereoblockpolymer[e] *n* stereoblock polymer
Stereochemie *f* stereochemistry
stereochemisch stereochemical
stereoelektronisch stereoelectronic
Stereoformel *f* stereochemical formula, space (configurational) formula
stereogeordnet stereoregular
stereoisomer stereoisomeric
Stereoisomer[e] *n* stereo[iso]mer, space isomer
Stereoisomerie *f* stereoisomerism, space isomerism
Stereomer[e] *n s.* Stereoisomer[e]
Stereometer *n s.* Volumenometer
stereoregulär stereoregular
Stereoregularität *f* stereoregularity
stereoreguliert stereoregular
stereoselektiv stereoselective
Stereoselektivität *f* stereoselectivity
Stereospektrogramm *n* stereospectrogram
stereospezifisch stereospecific
Stereospezifität *f* stereospecificity, stereochemical specificity
steril 1. sterile, *(if achieved by physical methods also)* aseptic; 2. *(soil)* barren, infertile
Sterilbereich *m (biot)* sterile area
Sterilfermentation *f (biot)* fermentation in a sterile bioreactor
Sterilfiltration *f* sterile filtration, filter sterilization
sterilfiltrieren to sterilize by filtration, to filter aseptically
Sterilhaltung *f* maintenance of asepsis (sterility)
Sterilisation *f* sterilization
~ **der Fermentationsluft** *(biot)* sterilization of fermentation air, air sterilization
~ **in Flaschen** in-bottle sterilization
~/thermische heat sterilization
Sterilisationsapparat *m*, **Sterilisator** *m* sterilizer
Sterilisierbüchse *f* Petri-dish box
Sterilisierdrahtkorb *m* test-tube basket
sterilisieren to sterilize
Sterilisierung *f* sterilization
Sterilität *f* 1. sterility, *(if achieved by physical methods also)* asepsis; 2. *(soil)* barrenness, infertility
Sterilitätsbedingungen *fpl (biot)* aseptic conditions
Sterilleitung *f (biot)* sterile pipe
Sterilmilch *f* sterilized milk
Sterilprozeß *m (biot)* aseptic process
Sterilsahne *f* sterilized cream
Sterin *n s.* Sterol
sterisch steric
~ **gehindert** sterically hindered
~ **geordnet** stereoregular
~ **möglich** sterically feasible
~ **regelmäßig** stereoregular
Sterkuliagummi *n* sterculia gum, karaya [gum], Indian tragacanth *(chiefly from Sterculia urens Roxb.)*
Sternanisöl *n* Japanese anise oil *(from Illicium verum Hook. fil.)*
Sternblende *f (spectr)* star wheel *(an optical attenuator)*
Stern-Gerlach-Versuch *m (phys ch)* Stern-Gerlach experiment
Sternrahmen *m*, **Sternreifen** *m (text)* star frame
Stern-Schicht *f (hyd)* Stern layer *(flocculation)*
Sternutatorium *n (pharm)* sternutator[y], sternutative
Stern-Volmer-Beziehung *f*, **Stern-Volmer-Gleichung** *f* Stern-Volmer kinetic relationship *(of fluorescence quenching)*
Steroid *n* steroid [compound]
Steroidalkaloid *n* steroid[al] alkaloid
Steroid-Antibiotikum *m* steroid[al] antibiotic
Steroidchemie *f* steroid chemistry
Steroidhormon *n* steroid hormone
Steroidumwandlung *f (biot)* steroid conversion (transformation)
~/mikrobielle microbial transformation of steroids
Sterol *n (bioch)* sterol
~/pflanzliches plant sterol, phytosterol
~/tierisches animal sterol, zoosterol
stetig continuous *(operation)*; constant *(e.g. flow)*
Stetigförderer *m* conveyor
Stetigmischer *m* continuous mixer
Stetigschleifer *m (pap)* continuous grinder
steuerbar controllable *(e.g. a chemical reactor)*
Steuerbarkeit *f* controllability *(as of a chemical reactor)*
Steuerdruck *m* control pressure
Steuereinrichtung *f* control equipment
Steuergerät *n* controlling device, controller
Steuermetabolit *m (bioch)* effector
~/heterotroper heterotropic effector
~/homotroper homotropic effector
steuern to control *(a process)*
Steuerung *f* 1. control; 2. *s.* Steuereinrichtung
~/automatische automatic control
~/hormonale *(med)* hormonal control
~/kinetische kinetic control
~/manuelle (nichtselbsttätige) manual control
~/selbsttätige *s.* ~/automatische
~/thermodynamische thermodynamic (equilibrium) control
Steuerungsrechner *m* control computer
Steuerventil *n* control valve
Stevens-Umlagerung *f* Stevens rearrangement *(of a benzyl group in a quaternary ammonium salt)*
STH *s.* Hormon/somatotropes
Stiban *n* Sb_nH_{n+2} stibane, antimony hydride, *(specif) s.* Stibin 1.
Stibin *n* 1. SbH_3 stibine, stibane, antimony trihydride, antimony(III) hydride; 2. SbR_3 stibine *(any of a class of organic antimony compounds)*
~/organisches *s.* Stibin 2.

Stibinsäure *f* RR'SbOOH stibinic acid
Stibnit *m (min)* stibnite, grey (dark) antimony, antimony glance, antimonite *(antimony(III) sulphide)*
Stich *m* 1. *(dye)* hue, shade, tone, tinge, tint; 2. *(met)* tapping; 3. *s.* Stichloch
Stichausreißfestigkeit *f (text)* stitch tear strength
stichfest spadeable *(sludge)*
stichig sour *(wine)* • ~ **werden** to sour *(of wine)*
Stichkultur *f* stab culture *(microbiology)*
Stichloch *n (met)* taphole, tapping hole
Stichprobe *f* random sample
Stickoxid *n* nitrogen oxide, *(specif)* NO nitrogen(II) oxide, nitrogen monooxide
Stickstoff *m* N nitrogen
~/aktiver active nitrogen
~/atmosphärischer atmospheric nitrogen
~/fixierter fixed nitrogen
~/flüssiger liquid nitrogen
~/gebundener fixed nitrogen
~/langsamwirkender *(agric)* slow-release nitrogen
~/verflüssigter liquid nitrogen
stickstoffarm poor in nitrogen, low-nitrogen[-content]
Stickstoffarmut *f (agric)* poverty in nitrogen
Stickstoffatmosphäre *f* nitrogen atmosphere
Stickstoffaufnahme *f* nitrogen uptake
Stickstoffausscheidung *f (bioch)* 1. nitrogen excretion; 2. nitrogen output *(quantity)*
Stickstoffbad *n***/flüssiges** liquid-nitrogen bath
Stickstoffbase *f* nitrogenous base
Stickstoffbestimmung *f* determination (estimation) of nitrogen, nitrogen analysis
~ **nach Dumas** Dumas nitrogen analysis
~ **nach Kjeldahl** Kjeldahl nitrogen analysis, Kjeldahl determination
~ **nach Neßler** Nessler nitrogen analysis, Nessler test
Stickstoffbestimmungsapparat *m* nitrogen analyser
~ **nach Kjeldahl** Kjeldahl digestion apparatus
Stickstoffbilanz *f (bioch)* nitrogen balance
Stickstoffbindung *f* nitrogen fixation *(chemically or biologically)*
~ **durch freilebende Mikroorganismen** *s.* ~/nichtsymbio[n]tische
~/nichtsymbio[n]tische non-symbiotic (non-legume, free) nitrogen fixation, azofication
Stickstoffbrücke *f* nitrogen bridge
Stickstoff(III)-chlorid *n* nitrogen(III) chloride, nitrogen trichloride
Stickstoffdioxid *n* nitrogen dioxide
Stickstoffdon[at]or *m* nitrogen donor
Stickstoffdüngemittel *n* nitrogen (nitrogenous) fertilizer
Stickstoffdüngung *f* nitrogen fertilization
Stickstoff-Fixierung *f s.* Stickstoffbindung
Stickstoff(III)-fluorid *n* nitrogen(III) fluoride, nitrogen trifluoride
stickstofffrei nitrogen-free, non-nitrogenous
Stickstoffgehalt *m* nitrogen content, *(hyd also)* nitrogen nutrient level *(in waste water)*
Stickstoffgruppe *f* nitrogen family *(in the periodic table)*
stickstoffhaltig nitrogen-containing, nitrogenous, *(relating to alloys or minerals also)* nitrogen-bearing
Stickstoffhärtung *f (met)* nitrogen case-hardening, nitride hardening, nitriding, nitridation
Stickstoff(III)-iodid *n* nitrogen(III) iodide, nitrogen triiodide
Stickstoffkreislauf *m* nitrogen cycle
Stickstofflaser *m* nitrogen laser
Stickstofflost *m s.* Stickstoffyperit
Stickstoffmangel *m* nitrogen deficiency
Stickstoffmehrer *m s.* Stickstoffsammler
Stickstoffmodell *n***/Dreidingsches** Dreiding nitrogen model
Stickstoffmonoxid *n s.* Stickstoff(II)-oxid
Stickstoffnachweis *m* detection of nitrogen
• **zum** ~ for detecting nitrogen
Stickstoffnährstoffe *mpl* nitrogen nutrients
Stickstoffoxid *n* nitrogen oxide
Stickstoff(I)-oxid *n* nitrogen(I) oxide, dinitrogen monooxide
Stickstoff(II)-oxid *n* nitrogen(II) oxide, nitrogen monooxide
Stickstoff(III)-oxid *n* nitrogen(III) oxide, dinitrogen trioxide
Stickstoff(IV)-oxid *n* nitrogen(IV) oxide
Stickstoff(V)-oxid *n* nitrogen(V) oxide, dinitrogen pentaoxide
Stickstoffoxidchlorid *n* nitrosyl chloride
Stickstoffoxidfluorid *n* nitrosyl fluoride
Stickstoffpentasulfid *n s.* Stickstoff(V)-sulfid
Stickstoff-Phosphor-Gruppe *f s.* Stickstoffgruppe
Stickstoffprobe *f* **nach Lassaigne** Lassaigne test [for nitrogen]
Stickstoffquelle *f* nitrogen source
Stickstoffradikal *n* nitrogen-centred radical
stickstoffreich rich in nitrogen, high-nitrogen[-content]
Stickstoffreservoir *n (agric)* nitrogen reservoir
Stickstoffsammler *m (agric)* nitrogen-gathering (nitrogen-storing) plant
Stickstoff-Stoffwechsel *m (bioch)* nitrogen metabolism
Stickstoff(V)-sulfid *n* nitrogen(V) sulphide, dinitrogen pentasulphide, nitrogen pentasulphide
Stickstofftetroxid *n* dinitrogen tetraoxide
Stickstoffträger *m (agric)* nitrogen carrier
Stickstofftri... *s.* Stickstoff(III)-...
Stickstoffverarmung *f* nitrogen depletion
Stickstoffversorgung *f (agric)* nitrogen supply
Stickstoffwasserstoffsäure *f* hydrazoic acid, azoimide
Stickstoffwäsche *f* nitrogen wash process *(for purifying synthesis gas)*

Stickstoffyperit *n* nitrogen mustard *(any of several halogen alkylamines)*
Stickstoffzufuhr *f (agric)* nitrogen supply
Stickwetter *pl s.* Wetter/stickende
Stiefel *m* 1. *(glass)* hood, boot, potette; 2. *s.* ~/Freiberger
~/Freiberger *(text)* J box
Stiefelwanne *f (glass)* potette tank
Stiel *m* stem *(of a funnel)*
Stift *m (tech)* pin, tack; *(pap)* sliver, skim; *(cosmet)* stick
~/desodor[is]ierender deodorant stick
Stiftloch *n* pinhole *(a coating defect)*
Stiftlöcherbildung *f* pinholing *(in coatings)*
Stift[scheiben]mühle *f* pinned-disk disintegrator (mill), pin mill
Stilben *n* stilbene, *trans*-1,2-diphenylethylene
Stilbenfarbstoff *m* stilbene dye
stillegen to shut [down]
Stillegung *f* shut[down]
Stillingia-Öl *n* stillingia (tallow-seed) oil *(from Sapium sebiferum (L.) Roxb.)*
Stillingia-Talg *m* Chinese vegetable tallow *(from Sapium sebiferum (L.) Roxb.)*
Still-Koksofen *m*, **Still-Regenerativofen** *m* Still oven
Stillstand *m* standstill *(of a reaction or machine)*; shutdown *(of an industrial plant)* • **zum ~ kommen** *(relating to a reaction:)* to die down, to subside; *(relating to a machine:)* to break down
Stillstandszeit *f* downtime, down period, outage time
Stilpnomelan *m (min)* stilpnomelane *(a phyllosilicate)*
Stimulans *n* stimulant, stimulus, *(pharm also)* stimulatory drug
Stinkasant *m* devil's dung, food of the gods *(gum resin from Ferula specc.)*
Stinkäscher *m (tann)* dead (rotten) lime, mellow lime liquor
Stippen *fpl (rubber)* filler specks; *(text)* specks
Stobbe-Kondensation *f*, **Stobbe-Reaktion** *f* Stobbe condensation (reaction) *(of aldehydes or ketones with esters of succinic acid)*
Stocherloch *n*, **Stocheröffnung** *f* pokehole
Stochervorrichtung *f* poker
Stöchiometrie *f* stoichiometry
Stöchiometriezahl *f* stoichiometric number
stoichiometrisch stoichiometric
Stochloch *n*, **Stochöffnung** *f s.* Stocherloch
Stockblender *m (rubber)* stock blender *(roller system for mixing and cooling sheets)*
Stocklack *m* stick lac
Stockpunkt *m* setting point, s.p., solidification (solidifying, solid) point *(of oils)*
Stockthermometer *n* rod thermometer
Stock-Zahl *f* Stock number *(of valence)*
Stoddard-Solvent *n* Stoddard solvent *(a refined petroleum product for use in dry cleaning)*

Stoff *m* 1. substance, matter, material *(for compounds s. a. under* Stoffe *and* Substanz*)*; 2. *(pap)* [fibrous] pulp, pulp slurry (stock) *(s. a.* Halbstoff *and* Ganzstoff*)*; 3. *(text)* fabric [cloth], cloth, tissue, textile
~/absorbierender absorbing substance (agent), absorbent, absorber
~/absorbierter absorbed substance, absorbate
~/adsorbierender adsorbing substance (agent), adsorbent
~/adsorbierter adsorbed substance, adsorbate, adsorptive
~/aggregierend wirkender *(soil)* aggregating agent
~/aktiver active substance (agent)
~/am schwersten siedender *(distil)* heavier-than-heavy component
~/amphoterer amphoteric (amphiprotic) substance (electrolyte), ampholyte
~/anionaktiver anionic surfactant
~/antibiotischer antibiotic [agent, substance]
~/antimikrobieller microbicide
~/antiseptischer antiseptic [agent]
~/aufgelöster dissolved substance, solute [material]
~/aufgenommener sorbate
~/aufnehmender (aufsaugender) sorbent
~/basischer basic substance
~/bituminöser bituminous substance
~/büttenfertiger *(pap)* accepted (screened) stock, accepts
~/diamagnetischer diamagnetic [substance]
~/einfacher simple substance
~/einheitlicher uniform substance
~/elementarer elementary substance
~/extrahierbarer extractable [matter]
~/färbender (farbgebender) colouring matter (substance), colorant
~/ferroelektrischer ferroelectric [substance]
~/ferromagnetischer ferromagnetic [substance]
~/fester solid [substance]
~/filmbildender film-forming substance, film former, filmogen
~/flüchtiger volatile substance
~/fremder foreign (extraneous) substance
~/gefährlicher hazardous substance
~/gelöster dissolved substance, solute
~/gerbender tanning agent (substance), tan
~/geruchsaktiver (geruchsbildender) odour-causing substance, odour-bearing (odour-producing) substance
~/geschmacksbildender *s.* ~/geschmacksverursachender
~/geschmacksverstärkender flavour enhancer
~/geschmacksverursachender taste-causing substance, taste-bearing (taste-producing) substance
~/glasiger glassy material
~/glaskeramischer glass ceramic, vitroceramic, devitrified (neo-ceramic) glass

~/grenzflächenaktiver surface-active agent, surfactant
~/gummierter rubber-coated fabric, rubberized (rubbered, proofed) fabric, proofing
~/halbleitender semiconducting material
~/halbsynthetisch hergestellter semisynthetic
~/halluzinogen[isierend]er *(pharm)* hallucinogenic substance, hallucinogen
~/hautreizender skin irritant
~/homogener homogeneous substance
~/hygroskopischer hygroscopic substance
~/in mehreren Modifikationen auftretender *s.* ~/polymorpher
~/indifferenter inert substance
~/ionogener grenzflächenaktiver ionic surfactant
~/kanzerogener (karzinogener) carcinogen
~/kationenaktiver cationic surfactant
~/komplexbildender complexing agent, complexer
~/komplexer complex substance
~/kurzröscher *(pap)* short free stock
~/kurzschmieriger *(pap)* short wet stock
~/langröscher *(pap)* long free stock
~/langschmieriger *(pap)* long wet stock
~/maskierender masking (sequestering) agent, sequestrant
~/mineralischer mineral matter (substance)
~/nichteiweißartiger non-protein
~/nichtflüchtiger non-volatile substance
~/nichthygroskopischer non-hygroscopic substance
~/nichtionischer (nichtionogener) grenzflächenaktiver non-ionic [surfactant]
~/nichtsystemischer non-systemic chemical *(crop protection)*
~/oberflächenaktiver surface-active agent (substance), surfactant
~/paramagnetischer paramagnetic [substance]
~/partikulärer particulate matter *(solid or liquid)*
~/pflanzenschädigender phytotoxicant, phytotoxic substance
~/polymorpher polymorph, polymorphic substance
~/protogener *s.* Dysprotid
~/protophiler *s.* Emprotid
~/reagierender reactant
~/reiner pure substance
~/röscher *(pap)* fast stock, free stock (pulp), free-beaten (free-running, free-working) stock
~/schmieriger *(pap)* wet pulp, slow (shiny, soft, greasy) pulp
~/sorbierter sorbate
~/textiler *s.* Stoff 3.
~/therapeutisch wirksamer therapeutic agent
~/thixotroper thixotropic substance
~/Thixotropie erzeugender thixotroping (thixotropic) agent
~/tranquilisierender *(pharm)* tranquillizer, tranquillizing drug
~/wachstumsfördernder growth-promoting substance, growth[-stimulating] substance, growth promotant
~/waschaktiver detergent surfactant
~/wasserlässiger *s.* ~/röscher
~/wiedergewonnener recovered substance; *(pap)* recovered stock
~/zu absorbierender material to be absorbed
~/zu adsorbierender material to be adsorbed
~/zu sublimierender sublimand
~/zurückgewonnener *s.* ~/wiedergewonnener
~/zusammengesetzter compound (complex) substance
Stoffänderung *f* material change
Stoffang *m s.* Stoffänger
Stoffänger *m (pap)* pulp saver, save-all [tray], stuff catcher
~/nach dem Absetzprinzip (Sedimentationsprinzip) arbeitender gravity (sedimentation) save-all
Stoffaufbereitung *f (pap)* stock (fibre) preparation
Stoffauflauf *m* 1. stock flow to (onto) the wire, stock inlet; 2. headbox, stuff (breast, flow) box
~/geschlossener enclosed (closed-type) headbox
~/offener open-type (gravity-type) headbox
~/vakuumgesteuerter vacuum headbox
Stoffauflaufkasten *m s.* Stoffauflauf 2.
Stoffauflöser *m (pap)* [hydra]pulper, pulping engine
Stoffaufschläger *m (pap)* refiner, refining machine (engine), perfecting engine
Stoffaustausch *m* exchange of materials
Stoffaustritt *m (pap)* outgo of pulp
Stoffbahn *f* [paper] web, web of fibre[s], mat
Stoffbehälter *m (pap)* stock tank
stoffbespannt cloth-covered
Stoffbewegung *f (pap)* stock circulation *(in a Hollander beater)*
Stoffbilanz *f* mass (material) balance
Stoffbilanzgleichung *f* mass-balance equation
Stoffbildung *f s.* Stoffproduktion
Stoffbrei *m (pap)* pulp, fibrous pulp (mass), pulp slurry (stock), slush [of] stock
Stoffbütte *f (pap)* pulp chest, stuff (supply, machine) chest, supply tank (vat)
Stoffdichte *f (pap)* stock (pulp) density (consistency)
Stoffdichteregler *m (pap)* consistency regulator
Stoffdruck *m* textile printing
Stoffdurchgang *m* mass transfer between phases
Stoffdurchgangskoeffizient *m* overall mass-transfer coefficient
Stoffe *mpl*:
~/absetzbare settleable solids
~/[echt] gelöste dissolved solids, solubles
~/halbsynthetisch hergestellte semisynthetics
~/refraktäre *s.* Inhaltsstoffe/abbauresistente organische
~/schwimmfähige floatables
~/semisynthetisch hergestellte semisynthetics
~/trübende turbidity-causing solids, turbidity
Stoffeintrag *m (pap)* furnish[ing]
Stoffeintritt *m (pap)* inflow of pulp
Stoffentlüfter *m (pap)* stock deaerator, deculator
Stoffentlüftung *f (pap)* stock deaeration

Stofffluß *m (pap)* stock flow
stoffgeleimt *(pap)* engine-sized, E.S., pulp-sized, beater-sized
Stoffgemisch *n* mixture of substances
Stoffgeschwindigkeit *f (pap)* spouting (stock) velocity, speed of the stock
Stoffgleichung *f* stoichiometric equation
Stoffgrube *f (pap)* blow pit (tank, vat), wash (receiving) tank
Stoffgruppe *f* group of substances
stoffhaltig *(pap)* fibre-bearing *(water)*
Stoffilter *n* cloth (fabric, woven) filter
Stoffkasten *m s.* Stoffgrube
Stoffklasse *f* family of compounds, class of substances
Stoffkonsistenz *f*, **Stoffkonzentration** *f (pap)* stock (pulp) consistency (density)
Stofflauf *m (pap)* stock flow
Stoffleitung *f (pap)* stock line
stofflich material
Stofflöser *m (pap)* [hydra]pulper
~ **mit vier Auflösescheiben** quatropulper
~ **mit zwei Auflösescheiben** duopulper
Stoffmahlung *f (pap)* stock disintegration, beating of the stock
Stoffmasse *f s.* Stoffbrei
Stoffmenge *f* amount (quantity) of substance (material)
Stoffmengeneinheit *f* unit of amount of substance
Stoffmengenregler *m (pap)* stock proportioner, stockmaker
Stoffmühle *f (pap)* beating engine, beater
Stoffproduktion *f* [biochemical] product formation, production of products
~/biotechnologische bioprocess production
~/mikrobielle (mikrobiologische) microbial (microbiological) production
Stoffproduzenten *mpl (biol)* producers, producing microorganisms
Stoffpumpe *f (pap)* stock (stuff) pump
Stoffqualität *f (pap)* stock (pulp) quality
Stoffregulierkasten *m (pap)* regulating box
Stoffreinigung *f (pap)* stock cleaning (clean-up)
Stoffrinne *f (pap)* stock sewer (line) *(groundwood pulping)*
Stoffrückgewinnung *f* recovery, reclaim *(of useful material)*; *(pap)* fibre recovery
Stoffrückgewinnungsanlage *f* 1. recovery plant; 2. *s.* Stoffänger
Stoffsortierung *f (pap)* stock separation
Stoffstrom *m* mass flux; *(pap)* stock flow
Stoffsuspension *f (pap)* pulp suspension (slurry)
Stoffsystem *n*/**einschleusendes** *(bioch)* shuttle [system]
Stoffteilchen *n* particle of matter, material particle
Stofftemperatur *f (pap)* temperature of the stock
Stofftransport *m (phys ch)* mass transport; *(hyd)* transport of material
~ **durch Fließgewässer** *(hyd)* riverine transport of material
Stofftreiber *m (pap)* propeller-type agitator *(of a Hollander beater)*
Stofftrog *m* [cylinder] vat *(of a cylinder paper machine)*
Stofftrübe *f (min tech)* pulp of ore
Stoffturm *m (pap)* retention tower
Stoffübergang *m* mass transfer
Stoffübergangskoeffizient *m* mass-transfer coefficient
Stoffübergangswiderstand *m* mass-transfer resistance
Stoffübergangszahl *f* mass-transfer coefficient
Stoffübertragung *f* mass transfer
Stoffübertragungsapparate *mpl* mass-transfer equipment
Stoffführung *f (pap)* delivery of the stock
Stoffumsatz *m* 1. *(bioch)* turnover; 2. *s.* Stoffumwandlung
Stoffumsetzer *m* [chemical] reactor
Stoffumsetzung *f s.* Stoffumwandlung
Stoffumtrieb *m (pap)* stock circulation *(in a Hollander beater)*
Stoffumwandlung *f* conversion (transformation) of materials, materials conversion
~/enzymatische enzymatic conversion
~/mikrobielle *s.* Biokonversion
Stoffveränderung *f* material change
Stoffverteiler *m (pap)* flow distributor
Stoffwandlung *f s.* Stoffumwandlung
Stoffwandlungsleistung *f (biot)* [substrate] conversion efficiency
Stoffwandlungstechnik *f* materials conversion technology
Stoffwanne *f (pap)* beater tub (vat, tank, pan)
Stoffwechsel *m* metabolism
~/intermediärer intermediary metabolism
~/intrazellulärer *s.* ~/intermediärer
~/mikrobieller microbial metabolism
Stoffwechselablauf *m* metabolic sequence
Stoffwechselbahn *f s.* Stoffwechselweg
Stoffwechselbeziehungen *fpl* metabolic interplay (interrelations)
Stoffwechselblock *m* physiological block
Stoffwechseldefekt *m s.* Stoffwechselstörung
Stoffwechseldynamo *m* metabolic wheel
Stoffwechselenergie *f* metabolic energy
Stoffwechselentgleisung *f s.* Stoffwechselstörung
Stoffwechselkette *f* metabolic chain
stoffwechseln to metabolize
Stoffwechselnetz *n* metabolic network
Stoffwechselpool *m* metabolic pool, central area of metabolism
~/expandierbarer expandable pool
~/interner internal pool
Stoffwechselprodukt *n* metabolic product, metabolite, product of metabolism
~/primäres primary metabolite, primary product of metabolism
~/sekundäres secondary metabolite, secondary product of metabolism

Stoffwechselraum *m (bioch)* compartment *(of a cell)*
Stoffwechselreaktion *f* metabolic reaction
Stoffwechselregulation *f* metabolic control (regulation)
Stoffwechselregulator *m* metabolic regulator
Stoffwechselreservoir *n s.* Stoffwechselpool
Stoffwechselschritt *m* metabolic step
Stoffwechselsequenz *f s.* Stoffwechselweg
Stoffwechselstörung *f* metabolic disturbance (deficiency), error in metabolism
~/angeborene inborn error in (of) metabolism
Stoffwechselvorgang *m* metabolic process
Stoffwechselwärme *f* metabolic heat
Stoffwechselweg *m* metabolic pathway (route), pathway of metabolism
~/katabol[isch]er catabolic pathway (route)
Stoffwechselzusammenhänge *mpl* metabolic interrelations
Stoffweiße *f (pap)* pulp brightness
Stoffwiedergewinnung *f s.* Stoffrückgewinnung
Stoffzuführung *f (pap)* feed (delivery) of the stock
Stoffzuteiler *m s.* Stoffmengenregler
Stohmann-Kolben *m (lab)* Stohmann flask
Stokes-Gesetz *n* Stokes law
Stollmaschine *f (tann)* staking machine, staker
Stomachikum *n (pharm)* stomachic, digestive stimulant
Stopfbuchse *f* stuffing (packing) box, packing (packed) gland
Stopfbuchsverbindung *f* packed-gland joint *(of pipes)*
Stopfen *m* stopper, plug, cork
~/kalter *(plast)* cold slug
stopfend *(pharm)* styptic
Stopfwachs *n* propolis, bee glue
Stoppbad *n (phot)* stop bath
~/saures acid stop bath
Stoppcodon *n (bioch)* terminator codon, termination (chain-terminating) codon
stoppen to terminate, to shortstop *(polymerization)*; to arrest *(a reaction)*
Stopper *m (plast)* chain stopper (terminator)
Stöpsel *m* stopper, plug, cork
störanfällig susceptible to failure
Störanfälligkeit *f* susceptibility to failure
Störanion *n (anal)* interfering anion
Störatom *n* foreign (impurity) atom
Storax *m s.* Styrax
Störelement *n (anal)* interfering element
stören *(anal)* to interfere with
Störgröße *f* disturbance [variable]
Störhalbleiter *m s.* Störstellenhalbleiter
Störion *n (anal)* interfering ion
Stork-Reaktion *f* Stork reaction *(for obtaining α-alkyl or α-acyl carbonyl compounds)*
Störleitung *f s.* Störstellenleitung
Störniveau *n* impurity level
Störpeak *m* ghost (spurious) peak
Störstelle *f* lattice (crystal) defect, lattice imperfection
~/stöchiometrische stoichiometric lattice defect
Störstellenatom *n* impurity (foreign) atom
Störstellenband *n* impurity band
Störstellen[halb]leiter *m* impurity (extrinsic) semiconductor
Störstellenleitung *f* impurity [electric] conduction
Störstellenniveau *n*, **Störstellenterm** *m* impurity level
Störstoff *m*, **Störsubstanz** *f (anal)* interfering substance, interferent, interferant
Störterm *m* impurity level
Störung *f* 1. disturbance, trouble; 2. *(cryst)* imperfection
störungsfrei undisturbed, trouble-free
Störungsmethode *f* perturbation method (technique) *(for investigating fast reactions)*
Stoß *m* push, shock, impact, *(esp relating to particles:)* impingement; *(phys ch)* collision
~/aktivierender (anregender) activating (reactive) collision, collision of the first kind
~/bimolekularer bimolecular collision
~/desaktivierender deactivating collision, collision of the second kind
~/elastischer elastic collision
~ erster Art *s.* ~/aktivierender
~ harter Kugeln hard-sphere collision
~ mit der Gefäßwand wall collision *(with chain reactions)*
~/reaktiver *s.* ~/aktivierender
~/unelastischer inelastic collision
~/wirksamer *s.* ~/aktivierender
~ zweiter Art *s.* ~/desaktivierender
Stoßabscheidekammer *f*, **Stoßabscheider** *m* impingement separator, inertia scrubber *(gas cleaning)*
Stoßaktivierung *f s.* Stoßanregung
stoßangeregt collision-activated
Stoßanregung *f* collision activation, CA, collisional activation (energization)
Stoßappretur *f (tann)* friction finish
Stoßbelastung *f (hyd)* shock load[ing]
Stoßchlorung *f (hyd)* shot chlorination
stoßdämpfend shock-absorbing
Stoßdämpfer *m* dash pot
Stoßdauer *f (phys ch)* duration of collision
Stoßdichte *f (phys ch)* collision density
Stoßdruck *m* impact pressure *(of a moving fluid)*
Stoßdurchmesser *m (phys ch)* collision diameter
Stoßeisen *n (tann)* slicker
Stößel *m (tech)* plunger; *(lab)* pestle *(of a mortar)*; *(glass)* needle, plunger *(of a feeder)*
Stoßelastizität *f* [impact] resilience, rebound [resilience, elasticity]
Stoßelektron *n* impact electron
stoßempfindlich sensitive to impact (shock)
Stoßempfindlichkeit *f* sensitiveness to impact (shock)

stoßen 1. to crush, to chop *(ice)*; 2. to bump *(of boiling liquids)*
Stoßfaktor *m (phys ch)* collision factor
stoßfest impact-resistant, shockproof
Stoßfestigkeit *f* impact resistance (strength), resistance to shock
Stoßfluoreszenz *f* impact fluorescence
Stoßfrequenz *f s.* Stoßzahl
Stoßfront *f* shock front *(kinetics)*
Stoßgalvanometer *n* ballistic galvanometer
Stoßgeschwindigkeit *f s.* Stoßzahl
Stoßgleichung *f* momentum [balance] equation
~/Boltzmannsche Boltzmann [transport] equation
Stoßhäufigkeit *f s.* Stoßzahl
Stoßherd *m (min tech)* shaking table
Stoßintegral *n (phys ch)* collision integral
Stoßkammer *f (spectr)* collision chamber
Stoßkomplex *m (phys ch)* activated (collision) complex
Stoßkraftabscheider *m s.* Stoßabscheider
Stoßmischer *m* batch mixer
Stoßofen *m (ceram)* pusher-type kiln, pusher
Stoßquerschnitt *m (phys ch)* collision cross section
Stoßrohr *n s.* Stoßwellenrohr
Stoßrohrverfahren *n s.* Stoßwellenverfahren
stoßsicher impact-resistant, shockproof
Stoßstange *f (coal)* [coke] pusher ram
Stoßstrahlung *f (phys ch)* collision radiation
Stoßtheorie *f (phys ch)* collision theory
Stoßverbreiterung *f (spectr)* collision broadening
Stoßverdampfung *f* flash (instantaneous) evaporation
Stoßvorgang *m* collision process
Stoßwahrscheinlichkeit *f (phys ch)* probability (likelihood) of collision
Stoßwelle *f* shock wave, *(relating to explosives also)* explosive (detonation) wave
Stoßwellenrohr *n* shock tube *(for investigating fast reactions)*
Stoßwellenverfahren *n* shock-tube technique *(for investigating fast reactions)*
Stoßzahl *f* **[je Zeiteinheit]** *(phys ch)* collision number (rate), collision[al] frequency
Stoßzahldichte *f (phys ch)* collision density
Stoßzündung *f* priming
Strahl *m* 1. ray *(of light or other radiation)*, *(if bundled:)* beam; 2. jet *(of liquid or gas)*
~/außerordentlicher extraordinary ray
~/ordentlicher ordinary ray
~/positiver positive (canal) ray
Strahlenapparatmischer *m* jet mixer
strahlen to radiate, to emit rays
Strahlen *mpl*/**kosmische** cosmic rays
~/weiche soft rays
α-Strahlen *mpl* alpha rays, α-rays
β-Strahlen *mpl* beta rays, β-rays
γ-Strahlen *mpl* gamma rays, γ-rays
Strahlen... *s. a.* Strahlungs...
Strahlenabschirmung *f* radiation shielding
Strahlenabsorption *f* radiation absorption
Strahlenbehandlung *f* radiation treatment (processing)
strahlenbeständig resistant to radiation, radiation-resistant
Strahlenbeständigkeit *f* resistance to radiation, radiation resistance
Strahlenbiologie *f* radiation biology, radiobiology
strahlenbiologisch radiobiologic[al]
Strahlenbündel *n* beam of rays
Strahlenchemie *f* radiation chemistry
strahlenchemisch radiation-chemical
strahlend radiant, radiative
Strahlendetektor *m* radiation detector
Strahlendosimetrie *f* radiation dosimetry
Strahlendosis *f* radiation dosage (dose)
strahlendurchlässig radiolucent
Strahlendurchlässigkeit *f* radiolucency
strahlenempfindlich radiosensitive
Strahlenempfindlichkeit *f* radiosensitivity
Strahlenfilter *n* radiation filter
Strahlengefahr *f* radiation hazard
Strahlengefährdung *f* radiation hazards
strahleninduziert radiation-induced
strahleninitiiert initiated by irradiation *(e.g. polymerization)*
β-Strahlenionisationsdetektor *m* β-ray ionization detector
Strahlenkrankheit *f* radiation sickness (syndrome)
Strahlenkunde *f* radiology
Strahlennachweis *m* detection of radiation
Strahlenpasteurisierung *f* radiation pasteurization, radiopasteurization
Strahlenquelle *f* source of radiation, radiation source, emitter
Strahlenreaktion *f* radiation reaction
strahlenresistent *s.* strahlenbeständig
Strahlenschaden *m* radiation damage
Strahlenschutz *m* radiation protection
Strahlenschutzbeton *m* radiation [shielding] concrete, concrete for [atomic] radiation shielding
Strahlensyndrom *n s.* Strahlenkrankheit
Strahlenüberwachung *f* radiation monitoring (survey)
Strahlenüberwachungsgerät *n* radiation monitor
strahlenundurchlässig radiopaque
Strahlenundurchlässigkeit *f* radiopacity
Strahlenvernetzung *f (plast)* irradiation cross-linking; *(rubber)* vulcanization by high-energy radiation
Strahlenwarngerät *n* radiation monitor
Strahlenwirkung *f* radiation effect
Strahlenzähler *m*, **Strahlenzählrohr** *n* radiation counter
Strahler *m (nucl)* emitter, radiator; *(phys ch)* radiator; radiation (radiating) element *(for heating purposes)*
~/grauer grey body

~/schwarzer black body, black-body radiator
α-Strahler *m (nucl)* alpha emitter, α-emitter
β-Strahler *m (nucl)* beta emitter, β-emitter
Strahlmischer *m* jet mixer
Strahlmühle *f* jet (fluid-energy) mill
Strahlprallmühle *f* flash (nozzle) pulverizer
Strahlpumpe *f* jet pump
Strahlstärke *f* radiation (radiant) intensity
Strahlstein *m (min)* actinolite *(an inosilicate)*
Strahlung *f* radiation
~/durchdringende *s.* ~/energiereiche
~/durchgelassene *(spectr)* transmitted radiation
~/einfallende (eingestrahlte) *(spectr)* incident radiation
~/energiearme soft (low-energy) radiation
~/energiereiche hard (penetrating) radiation, high-energy radiation
~/harte (hochenergetische) *s.* ~/energiereiche
~/infrarote infrared radiation
~/inkohärente incoherent radiation
~/ionisierende ionizing radiation
~/kohärente coherent radiation
~/kosmische cosmic radiation
~/photochemische photochemical radiation
~/photosynthetisch ausnutzbare photosynthetically active radiation, PhAR
~/schwarze black-body radiation
~/solare solar radiation
~/thermische heat (thermal) radiation
~/ultrarote infrared radiation
~/weiche *s.* ~/energiearme
Strahlungs... *s. a.* Strahlen...
strahlungsangeregt radiation-induced
Strahlungsdämpfung *f* radiation damping
Strahlungsdesaktivierung *f* radiative deactivation
Strahlungsdetektor *m* radiation detector
Strahlungsdichte *f* [spectral] radiance
Strahlungsdruck *m* radiation pressure
Strahlungseinfang *m* radiative capture
Strahlungsemission *f* emission of radiation
Strahlungsempfänger *m (anal)* detector
Strahlungsenergie *f* radiant (radiation) energy
Strahlungsenergiedichte *f* radiant-energy density
Strahlungsfeld *n* radiation field
Strahlungsfilter *n (spectr)* monochromator
Strahlungsfluß *m* radiant flux
Strahlungsflußdichte *f* irradiance, radiant-flux density
~/spektrale spectral irradiance
Strahlungsformel *f* radiation formula
~/Plancksche Planck radiation formula
strahlungsfrei radiationless, non-radiative
Strahlungsgesetz *n* radiation law
~/Kirchhoffsches Kirchhoff radiation law
~/Plancksches Planck radiation law
~/Rayleigh-Jeanssches Rayleigh-Jeans radiation law
Strahlungsgleichgewicht *n* radiative equilibrium
Strahlungshaushalt *m* radiation budget
Strahlungsheizung *f* radiation heating
Strahlungsintensität *f* radiant (radiation) intensity, *(quantitatively also)* radiant-flux density
~/spektrale spectral radiant intensity
Strahlungskatalyse *f* radiation catalysis
Strahlungskonstante *f* radiation constant
Strahlungslänge *f* radiation length
Strahlungslebensdauer *f***[/mittlere, natürliche]** radiative lifetime, *(deprecated:)* natural lifetime
Strahlungsleistung *f* radiant power
~/rauschäquivalente noise-equivalent power
strahlungslos radiationless, non-radiative
Strahlungsmeßgerät *n* radiation-measuring device
Strahlungsmessung *f* radiation measurement
Strahlungsofen *m* radiation oven
Strahlungsoszillator *m* radiation (Planck) oscillator
Strahlungspuffer *m* radiation buffer
Strahlungspyrometer *n* radiation pyrometer
Strahlungsquant *n* quantum of radiation, photon
Strahlungsschutz *m* radiation shield
Strahlungsspektrum *n* radiation spectrum
Strahlungsteiler *m (spectr)* beam splitter
Strahlungsthermometer *n* pyrometer
Strahlungstrockner *m* radiation (radiant-heat) dryer
Strahlungstrocknung *f* radiation drying
Strahlungsübergang *m* radiative transition
Strahlungsvereiniger *m (spectr)* beam mixer
Strahlungsverlust *m* radiation loss
Strahlungswärme *f* radiant heat
Strahlungswiderstand *m* radiation resistance
Strahlverlust *m* radiation loss
Strahn *m*, **Strähn** *m*, **Strähne** *f (text)* skein, hank
strähnig *(plast)* nervy *(extrudate)*
Straight-run-Benzin *n* straight-run gasoline (benzine), S.R.B., distillate gasoline
Straight-run-Destillation *f* straight[-run] distillation
Strainer *m (rubber)* strainer, straining machine, screen head extruder
Strainerkopf *m (rubber)* straining (screen) head
strainern *(rubber)* to strain
Straintest *m (rubber)* strain test
Straintester *m (rubber)* strain tester
stramm *(rubber)* stiff
Strammheit *f (rubber)* stiffness
Strang *m* 1. strand *(as of molecules)*; 2. *(met)* billet; 3. *(text)* rope; hank *(coiled or looped bundle of yarn of definite length)*; 4. run *(of an endless belt)*
~/führender *(bioch)* leading strand
~/komplementärer *(bioch)* complementary strand
~/nachhängender (verzögerter) *(bioch)* lagging strand
Strangaufweitung *f* die swell, *(process also)* jet swelling, swelling from the die *(extrusion)*
Strangaufweitungsverhältnis *n* [die] swell ratio *(extrusion)*
Strangfärben *n (text)* hank dyeing *(of yarns)*; rope dyeing *(of cloth)*
Stranggarnfärbemaschine *f (text)* hank-dyeing machine

Stranggarnmerzerisiermaschine *f (text)* hank-mercerizing machine
Stranggarnschlichtmaschine *f (text)* hank-sizing machine
Stranggarnwaschmaschine *f (text)* hank-washing machine, hank washer
Strangmerzerisiermaschine *f (text)* hank-mercerizing machine
Strangpresse *f (plast)* extruder, tuber, tubing (forcing) machine; *(ceram)* extrusion press; plodder *(soap manufacture)*
strangpressen to extrude
Strangpressen *n* extrusion [moulding]
~ **ohne Lösungsmittel** *s.* ~ von Trockenmischung
~ **von Folien** *(plast)* film extrusion
~ **von Trockenmischung** *(plast)* dry[-blend] extrusion
Strangpressenkopf *m* extruder (extrusion, dee) head
Strangpressenmundstück *n* extruder (extrusion) die
Strangpressenzylinder *m* extruder barrel
Strangpreßerzeugnis *n* extrudate
Strangpreßmischung *f* extrusion compound
Strangpreßziegel *m* wire-cut brick
Strangschlichtmaschine *f (text)* hank-sizing machine
Strangwäsche *f (text)* rope scouring
Strangwaschmaschine *f (text)* rope-scouring machine, dolly [washer]; hank-washing machine, hank washer *(for yarn)*
Straß *m* strass *(a glass of high lead content)*
Straßenmarkierungsfarbe *f* road-striping paint
Straßenoctanzahl *f* road octane number
Straßenöl *n* road oil *(for laying dust and for waterproofing)*
Straßenprüfung *f (rubber)* road test
Straßentankwagen *m* road tank wag[g]on, road tanker, tank truck
Straßenteer *m* road tar
Stratopause *f* stratopause
Stratosphäre *f* stratosphere
streckbar stretchable, extensible, extendible, extensile, *(esp relating to metal:)* ductile
Streckbarkeit *f* extensibility, stretchability, *(esp relating to metal:)* ductility
strecken 1. to stretch, to extend *(mechanically)*; *(glass)* to flatten; *(tann)* to break *(after bleaching)*; 2. to extend *(by adding additives)*; to dilute *(liquids)*; 3. *s.* recken
~/mit Wasser to water [down] *(e.g. wine)*
~/sich to expand *(of a filter bed)*
Strecken *n* **auf dem Baum** *(tann)* beaming
Strecker-Abbau *m* Strecker degradation *(of amino acids to aldehydes)*
Strecker-Synthese *f* Strecker synthesis *(of α-amino acids)*
Streckformen *n (plast)* stretch forming; drape forming, draping *(of sheets in vacuo)*
~ **mit pneumatischer Vorstreckung** air-slip forming
~ **mit Ring** plug-and-ring forming
Streckgrenze *f (plast, met)* yield point
~/untere yield value
Streckmetall *n* expanded (protruded) metal
Streckmetallboden *m (distil)* expanded-metal tray
Streckmittel *n* extender, [extending] filler, cheapener, *(relating to liquids also)* diluting agent, diluent
Streckofen *m (glass)* flattening kiln (oven)
Streckschwingung *f* stretching vibration (mode), valence vibration
Streckspannung *f* yield stress
Streckspinnen *n* stretch (reel) spinning
Streckstoff *m s.* Streckmittel
Streckung *f* 1. stretch[ing], extension *(mechanically)*; expansion *(of a filter bed)*; 2. extension *(by adding additives)*; dilution *(of liquids)*; 3. *s.* Recken
Streckungsmittel *n s.* Streckmittel
Streckziehen *n (plast)* drape forming *(of sheets in vacuo)*
Streichanlage *f (pap)* coating plant (mill)
Streichappretur *f (text)* doctor finish
streichen 1. *(plast, pap)* to coat; 2. *(tann)* to scud; 3. *(rubber)* to spread; 4. *(ceram)* to mould *(e.g. tiles)*; 5. *(coat)* to paint; to brush *(the paint onto a surface)*
~/beidseitig *(pap)* to double-coat, to coat on both sides
~/einseitig *(pap)* to coat on one side
~/zweiseitig *s.* ~/beidseitig
Streichen *n* **außerhalb der Maschine** *(pap)* off-machine coating, conversion (separate) coating
~/beidseitiges (doppelseitiges) *(pap)* double[-sided] coating
~/einseitiges *(pap)* one-sided (single-sided) coating
~ **in der Maschine** *(pap)* [on-]machine coating
~ **mit Bürste** *(plast)* brush coating (spreading)
~ **mit Rakel** *(plast, pap)* knife coating
Streicherei *f (pap)* coating plant (mill)
streichfähig *(food)* spreadable
Streichfähigkeit *f (food)* spreadability
Streichfarbe *f* 1. *(coat)* brushing paint; 2. *s.* Streichmasse
Streichgarngewebe *n* wool[l]en fabric
Streichgerät *n (chromat)* spreading device, spreader
Streichgießverfahren *n* cast coating
Streichkarton *m* coated [card]board
Streichlösung *f (rubber)* dough, spreading mix[-ture]
Streichmaschine *f* 1. *(plast, pap)* coating machine, coater; 2. *(rubber)* spreading machine, spreader
~ **für beidseitigen (doppelseitigen) Strich** *(pap)* double (duplex, two-side) coater
~ **für einseitigen Strich** *(pap)* single (one-side) coater

Streichmasse *f (pap)* coating slip (mixture, slurry, substance), coating
Streichmassentrog *m (pap)* coating pan
Streichmesser *n* doctor blade (knife), *(rubber also)* spreading (spreader) knife
Streichmischung *f (rubber)* spreading mix[ture], dough
Streichpapier *n* coated (surfaced) paper
Streichpresse *f (pap)* coating press
Streichrohpapier *n* coated base paper
Streichteig *m s.* Streichmischung
Streichtrog *m (pap)* coating pan
Streichvorrichtung *f (plast, pap)* coating (coater) unit; *(rubber)* spreading unit
Streichwalze *f (plast, rubber)* doctor roll; *(pap)* coating roll
Streifen *m* 1. tape, band; 2. *(phot)* streak *(a defect)*; band *(in a spectrum)*
Streifenart *f (coal)* type of band, microlithotype
Streifenbegiftung *f (agric)* band treatment [with pesticides]
Streifenbehandlung *f (agric)* band treatment
Streifenchromatographie *f* chromatostrip technique
Streifendüngung *f* band placement [of fertilizer], band treatment [with fertilizer]
Streifenkohle *f* banded coal
Streifenschneidemaschine *f*, **Streifenschneider** *m (pap)* slitting machine (device), slitting and [re]winding machine, slitter
Streifenschreiber *m* strip-chart recorder
Streifenstruktur *f (coal)* banded structure
streifig banded
Streifung *f (coal)* banded structure; *(geol)* striation
strengflüssig viscous, thick
Strenglot *n* hard solder
Stretch *m (text)* stretch *(capacity for being stretched)*
Stretchgarn *n (text)* stretch yarn
Streuamplitude *f* scattering amplitude
streubar *(agric)* drillable
Streubarkeit *f (agric)* drillability
Streudiffusion *f* eddy (turbulent) diffusion
Streuelektron *n* scattered electron
streuen 1. to sprinkle *(e.g. powder)*; to drill *(fertilizers or pesticides)*; 2. to scatter *(e.g. rays, electrons)*
streufähig *(agric)* drillable
Streufaktor *m* scattering factor
Streugerät *n (agric)* distributor
Streuintensität *f (spectr)* scattering intensity
Streukoeffizient *m* scattering coefficient
Streulicht *n* scattered (stray) light
Streulichtmessung *f* light-scattering measurement
Streulichtphotometer *n* light-scattering photometer
Streulichtphotometrie *f* light-scattering photometry
Streuneutron *n* scattered neutron
Streupuder *m* dusting powder
Streuquerschnitt *m* scattering cross section
Streusand *m (ceram)* placing sand
Streustrahlung *f* scattered radiation
Streustromkorrosion *f* stray-current corrosion, electrocorrosion
Streuteiler *m* whizzer *(classifying)*
Streuung *f (phys ch)* scatter[ing]
~/anomale elastische resonance scattering
~ der Röntgenstrahlen X-ray scattering
~ des Lichts light scattering
~/elastische elastic scattering
~/unelastische inelastic scattering
Streuungs... *s.* Streu...
Streuvermögen *n* 1. *(phys ch)* scattering power; 2. throwing power *(electroplating)*
Streuwinkel *m* scattering angle
Strich *m* 1. *(pap)* coating *(act)*; coat[ing] *(substance)*; 2. *(min)* streak colour; 3. *(nomencl)* prime *(of a locant)*
~/doppelseitiger *(pap)* double[-sided] coating
~/einseitiger *(pap)* one-sided (single-sided) coating
Strichauftrag *m (pap)* coating application
Strichfarbe *f (min)* streak colour
Strichgitter *n (spectr)* line (ruled) grating
Strichmarke *f* mark *(as of a volumetric flask)*
Strichskale *f* division scale
Strichspektrum *n* stick spectrum
Strichtafel *f (min)* streak plate
Strichteilung *f* division *(of a gauge)*
Strippdampf *m* stripping steam
strippen *(distil)* to strip [off, out]
Strippen *n* **mit Luft** *(distil)* air stripping
~ von Ammoniak ammonia stripping
Stripper *m (distil)* stripper
Stripperkolonne *f s.* Strippkolonne
Strippgas *n* stripping gas
Strippingkolonne *f s.* Strippkolonne
Strippkolonne *f (distil)* stripping (stripper) column
Strippung *f* stripping
Strohaufschluß *m* pulping of cereal straw
Strohhäcksel *m* chopped straw
Strohkochung *f (pap)* cooking of straw
Strohpapier *n* straw paper
Strohpappe *f* straw cardboard, strawboard
Strohstoff *m* 1. straw pulp; 2. *s.* Strohzellstoff
~/gelber coarse (yellow mechanical) straw pulp
~/vollaufgeschlossener *s.* Strohzellstoff
Strohzellstoff *m***[/vollaufgeschlossener]** straw cellulose, fine straw pulp
Strom *m* 1. *(tech)* current, stream *(of a fluid)*; 2. [electric] current; 3. *s.* Strömung
~/abgehender effluent
~/abwärtsgerichteter downward (descending) current
~/aufsteigender upward (ascending) current
~/Faradayscher faradaic current
~/kapazitiver capacity (charging) current, double-layer current

~/katalytischer catalytic current
~/kinetischer kinetic current
~/nichtfaradayscher non-faradaic current
~/photoelektrischer photocurrent
Stromanschluß *m* power connection
Stromapparat *m* hydraulic (countercurrent) classifier, hydrosizer
Stromausbeute *f* current efficiency
Strombedarf *m* current requirements
Strombrecher *m* flow spoiler
Stromdichte *f* current density, C.D.
stromdurchflossen current-carrying
Stromdurchgang *m* current passage
strömen to stream, to flow, to run, to pass, *(if swiftly)* to flush
Strömen *n* **realer Fluide** frictional flow
Stromfaden *m* stream filament *(rheology)*
Stromfluß *m* current flow
stromführend current-carrying
Stromklassieren *n* fluid separation, *(esp)* water sizing, wet classifying
~/nasses water sizing, wet classifying
Stromklassierer *m (min tech)* trough (launder) classifier
Stromleiter *m* conductor of electricity, electric conductor
Stromlinienfilter *n* streamline filter
stromlos electroless, zero-current, dead
Strom-Potential-Kennlinie *f*, **Strom-Potential-Kurve** *f* current-potential curve, current-voltage curve
Stromquelle *f* power (current) source
Stromrichtung *f* 1. current direction; 2. *s.* Strömungsrichtung
Stromrinne *f* trough washer
Stromrohr *n* drying duct *(of a dryer)*
Stromschlüssel *m*[**/elektrolytischer]** salt bridge
Stromsichtermühle *f* air-swept mill
Strom-Spannungs-Kennlinie *f*, **Strom-Spannungs-Kurve** *f s.* Strom-Potential-Kennlinie
Stromstärke *f* current strength (intensity)
Stromstörer *m* flow spoiler
Stromstoßgalvanometer *n* ballistic galvanometer
Stromtrockner *m* pneumatic [conveying] dryer, air-lift dryer
Strom- und Spannungsmeßgerät *n* voltammeter
Strömung *f* flow
~/abwärtsgerichtete downward flow
~/aufwärtsgerichtete upward flow
~/axiale axial flow
~/ideale ideal flow
~/laminare laminar (streamline) flow
~/nichtideale non-ideal flow
~/radiale radial flow
~/reale non-ideal flow
~/reibungsfreie frictionless flow, inviscid (non-viscous) flow
~/stationäre steady[-state] flow, flowstream
~/turbulente turbulent flow

Strömungsapparatur *f* flow system *(for investigating fast reactions)*
Strömungsdoppelbrechung *f (anal)* flow birefringence, double refraction of flow
Strömungsdruck *m (hyd)* head of water
Strömungsform *f* flow pattern *(in a reactor)*
Strömungsgeschwindigkeit *f* flow rate (velocity)
~ des Wassers water flow rate, rate of water flow
~ im Rohr tube velocity
Strömungsgrenzschicht *f***/Prandtlsche** [turbulent, Prandtl] boundary layer
Strömungskalorimeter *n* continuous-flow calorimeter
Strömungskorrosion *f* flow (erosion) corrosion
Strömungsmesser *m* flowmeter, fluid meter
~ für Gase gas flowmeter
Strömungsmethode *f* [continuous-]flow method, [continuous-]flow technique *(kinetics, calorimetry)*
Strömungspotential *n* streaming potential
Strömungsquerschnitt *m* flow area
Strömungsrichtung *f* direction of flow, flow direction
Strömungsrohr *n* 1. flow tube *(for investigating fast reactions)*; 2. [continuous-]tubular-flow reactor, tubular reactor
~/ideales longitudinal reactor
Strömungsrohrreaktor *m s.* Strömungsrohr 2.
Strömungsteiler *m (chromat)* [stream, sample] splitter, stream-splitting device
Strömungsteilung *f (chromat)* [stream] splitting
Strömungsumkehr *f* change of direction of flow
Strömungsverfahren *n* stream method *(underground gasification of coal)*
Strömungswiderstand *m* resistance to fluid flow
Stromversorgung *f* power supply
Strom-Zeit-Kurve *f* current-time curve, i-t curve
Stromzufuhr *f* power supply
Strontian *n*, **Strontianerde** *f s.* Strontiumoxid
Strontianverfahren *n s.* Strontiumsaccharatverfahren
Strontium *n* Sr strontium
~/radioaktives radioactive strontium, radiostrontium, *(specif)* ^{90}Sr strontium-90
Strontium-90 *n* ^{90}Sr strontium-90
Strontiumacetat *n* strontium acetate
Strontiumarsenat(III) *n* strontium arsenite
Strontiumbromid *n* strontium bromide
Strontiumcarbonat *n* strontium carbonate
Strontiumchlorat *n* strontium chlorate
Strontiumchlorid *n* strontium chloride
Strontium-Einheit *f (biol)* strontium unit, S.U. *(activity of 1 picocurie of ^{90}Sr/g Ca)*
Strontiumfluorid *n* strontium fluoride
Strontiumhydrogenphosphat *n* strontium hydrogenphosphate
Strontiumhydroxid *n* strontium hydroxide
Strontiumiodid *n* strontium iodide
Strontiumnitrat *n* strontium nitrate
Strontiumoxid *n* strontium oxide

Strontiumperoxid *n* strontium peroxide
Strontiumsaccharat *n* strontium saccharate, strontium sucrate
Strontiumsaccharatverfahren *n* strontium saccharate process *(for desugaring molasses)*
Strontiumsulfat *n* strontium sulphate
Strophanthin *n* strophanthin *(any of a group of glycosides)*
~ **G** G-strophanthin, g-strophanthin, ouabain
Strudel *m* vortex, eddy
Struktur *f* structure, *(relating to chemical compounds also)* constitution
~/**anisodesmische** *(cryst)* anisodesmic structure
~/**dipolare** dipolar structure
~/**elektronische** electronic structure
~/**geradkettige** straight-chain structure
~/**hochgeordnete** highly-ordered structure
~ **in Haworth-Projektion** Haworth [ring] structure *(of sugars)*
~/**innere** internal structure
~/**isotaktische** isotactic structure
~/**körnige** granularity
~/**makroporöse** macroporous structure
~/**ringförmige** annular structure
~/**syndiotaktische** syndiotactic structure
~/**übermolekulare** supermolecular structure
~/**verzweigte** branched-chain structure
~/**wabenartige (wabenförmige)** honeycomb structure
~/**wahrscheinliche** likely structure
~/**Widmannstättensche** Widmannstätten structure *(metallography)*
~/**zellartige (zellige)** cellular structure
~/**zybotaktische** cybotaxis *(of liquids)*
Strukturamplitude *f (cryst)* structure amplitude
Strukturanalyse *f* structure (structural) analysis
~ **mit Röntgenstrahlen** X-ray structure (structural) analysis
Strukturänderung *f* structural change (modification), change in structure
Strukturaufbau *m* structural make-up
Strukturaufklärung *f*, **Strukturbestimmung** *f* structure (structural) elucidation (determination)
Strukturbeweis *m* proof (evidence) of structure
Strukturbild *n* structural picture
Strukturchemie *f* structure (structural) chemistry
strukturchemisch structure-chemical
Struktureffekt *m* structural effect
Struktureinheit *f* structural unit
~/**sich wiederholende** constitutional repeating unit, CRU *(of polymers)*
Strukturelement *n* structural element
strukturell structural
Strukturermittlung *f s.* Strukturaufklärung
Strukturfaktor *m (cryst)* structure factor
Strukturfarbe *f (biol)* structural colour
Strukturformel *f* [valence] structural formula, line (constitutional, graphic) formula
~/**geometrische** space formula
Strukturgebilde *n* structural entity
Strukturgen *n* structural gene
strukturidentisch structurally identical
strukturiert with structure
~/**wabenartig** honeycombed
Strukturisomer[e] *n* structural isomer
Strukturisomerie *f* structural isomerism
Strukturisomerisierung *f* skeletal isomerization
strukturlos structureless, devoid of structure
Strukturmodell *n* structural model
Strukturparachor *m* structural parachor
Strukturprotein *n* skeletal (fibrous) protein, scleroprotein
Strukturresonanz *f* resonance, mesomerism
Strukturtyp *m (cryst)* lattice (structure) type
Strukturuntersuchung *f* investigation of structure, structural study
Strukturveränderung *f* structural change
~/**prämutative** *(biot)* premutational structural change
strukturviskos pseudoplastic
Strukturviskosität *f* structural viscosity, shear thinning, pseudoplasticity
Strychninhydrochlorid *n* strychnine hydrochloride
Strychnosalkaloid *n* strychnos alkaloid
Stuart-Kalotte *f*, **Stuart-Modell** *n* Stuart model *(for illustrating molecular structures)*
Stückarsenik *m(n) (glass)* glassy (dense) arsenic
Stückbrennstoff *m* lump fuel
Stückbrikett *n* block briquette
Stückenharz *n* crushed resin
Stückerz *n* lump ore
Stückfärbemaschine *f (text)* piece-dyeing machine
Stückfärben *n (text)* piece dyeing
Stuckgips *m* stucco, estrich plaster
Stückgröße *f* particle size; *(rubber)* batch size
stückig lumpy
Stückigkeit *f* lumpiness
Stückigmachen *n* agglomeration
~ **auf einem Rütteltisch** agglomeration tabling
Stückkalk *m* lump lime
Stückkohle *f* lump coal
Stückkoks *m* lump coke
Stückmasse *f (rubber)* batch weight
Stückzucker *m* cut (lump) sugar
Stufe *f* 1. step, stage *(as of a reaction)*; 2. effect *(of an evaporator)*
~/**erste** initiating step *(of a reaction)*
~/**letzte** completing step *(of a reaction)*
~/**polarographische** polarographic wave
Stufenbelastung *f (hyd)* step loading *(activated-sludge process)*
Stufenchromatographie *f* fractional chromatography
Stufeneluierung *f (chromat)* stepwise elution
Stufenfolge *f* gradation, scale
Stufengitter *n* echelon grating *(any of various diffraction gratings)*

Stufenheizung *f (rubber)* step (step-up) cure, vulcanization in stages
Stufenhöhe *f (chromat)* step height; wave height *(polarography)*
~/effektive *(chromat)* height equivalent to an effective theoretical plate, HEETP
Stufenkeil *m (phot)* step wedge
Stufenpolymerisation *f* stepwise polymerization, step-growth (step-reaction) polymerization
Stufenreaktion *f* step[wise] reaction
Stufenregel *f* **/Ostwaldsche** Ostwald rule, law of intermediate reactions (stages), successive reactions law
Stufenrost *m* step grate
Stufenseparator *m (petrol)* multistage separator
Stufenversetzung *f (cryst)* edge dislocation
Stufenwachstumspolymerisation *f s.* Stufenpolymerisation
Stufenwäsche *f* fractional washing
Stufenzahl *f* number of stages
Stuhlzäpfchen *n (pharm)* suppository
Stulpdichtung *f*, **Stulpe** *f* cup [ring]
stumpf matt, dull, lustreless *(surface)*; dead, flat, dull *(colour)* • ~ **werden** to dull
Stumpfheit *f* mattness, dullness *(of a surface)*; flatness, dullness *(of a colour)*
Stumpfwerden *n* dulling *(of a surface or colour)*
15-Stunden-Entspannungstemperatur *f (glass)* strain point (temperature)
Stupp *f* stupp *(a deposit obtained in distilling mercury ores)*
stürmisch vigorous *(reaction)*
Sturtevant-Ring[rollen]mühle *f* Sturtevant mill
stürzen to drop *(e.g. coke)*
~/die Mischung über Kopf *(rubber)* to pass the stock endwise through the mill
Sturzfestigkeit *f* shatter resistance (strength) *(of coke)*
Sturzgießverfahren *n* slush moulding *(for producing hollow articles from polyvinyl chloride plastisols)*
Sturzmühle *f* tumbling mill
~/autogen arbeitende autogenous tumbling mill
Sturzprüfung *f*, **Sturzversuch** *m* [drop] shatter test *(of coke)*
Stutengonadotropin *n (bioch)* pregnant mare serum gonadotropin
Stütze *f (ceram)* post, upright, prop
Stutzen *m* 1. *(tech)* port; fitting, pipe connection; 2. *(lab)* glass cylinder *(broad form)*
Stutzenflasche *f (lab)* aspirator
Stützfaden *m (text)* carrier thread
Stützgewebe *n (text)* back cloth, back grey [cloth]; septum *(of a precoat filter)*
Stützplatte *f* backup plate *(of a filter)*
Stützrolle *f* idler [roller] *(as of a conveyor belt)*
Stützschicht *f* backing layer
Stützschneide *f* central knife edge *(of a balance)*
Stützsieb *n* support screen *(of a filtering centrifuge)*; backup plate *(of a filter)*
Stützweite *f* support span *(in installing piping)*
St.W. *s.* Stärkewert
Styphnat *n* styphnate *(salt or charge-transfer complex of styphnic acid)*
Styphninsäure *f* styphnic acid, 2,4,6-trinitroresorcinol
Styptikum *n (pharm)* styptic
styptisch styptic
Styrax *m* storax, styrax *(a balsam obtained from Liquidambar specc.)*
~/Amerikanischer American storax (styrax), sweet (red) gum *(from Liquidambar styraciflua L.)*
~/Asiatischer *s.* ~/Levantiner
~/Levantiner Levant (oriental) storax, oriental sweet gum *(from Liquidambar orientalis Mill.)*
Styraxöl *n (cosmet)* storax (styrax) oil *(from Liquidambar specc.)*
Styren *n* styrene, vinylbenzene
Styrenalkydharz *n* styrenated alkyd
Styren-Butadien-Kautschuk *m* styrene-butadiene rubber, SBR
Styren-Chloropren-Kautschuk *m* styrene-chloroprene rubber, SCR
Styrendibromid *n* styrene dibromide, α,β-dibromoethylbenzene
Styren-Isopren-Kautschuk *m* styrene-isoprene rubber, SIR
Styrenkautschuk *m s.* Styren-Butadien-Kautschuk
Styrol *n s.* Styren
styrolisieren to styrenate
Styron *n* *cinnamyl alcohol, styryl alcohol, 3-phenylprop-2-en-1-ol
Suakingummi *n* Suakin gum *(from Acacia stenocarpa Hochst.)*
subaquatisch subaqueous, subaquatic
subatomar subatomic
subazid subacid
Subazidität *f* subacidity, *(med also)* hypoacidity *(of gastric juice)*
Subbild *n (phot)* sub-image
subbituminös subbituminous
Subeinheit *f s.* Untereinheit
Suberan *n* suberane, *cycloheptane
Suberin *n (bioch)* suberin
Suberinsäure *f* suberic acid, *octanedioic acid
Suberol *n s.* Suberylalkohol
Suberon *n* suberone, *cycloheptanone
Suberylalkohol *m* suberyl alcohol, suberol, *cycloheptanol
Subkeim *m (cryst)* cluster; *(phot)* sub-image speck
Subklonieren *n (bioch)* subcloning
Sublimand *m* sublimand
Sublimat *n* 1. sublimate *(a product obtained by sublimation)*; 2. $HgCl_2$ sublimate, mercury(II) chloride, mercury dichloride
Sublimation *f* sublimation
Sublimationsapparatur *f* sublimator

Sublimationsdruck *m* sublimation [vapour] pressure
Sublimationsenergie *f* sublimation energy
Sublimationsenthalpie *f* enthalpy of sublimation
Sublimationsgut *n* sublimand, material being *or* to be sublimated; sublimate *(product of sublimation)*
Sublimationskurve *f* sublimation curve
Sublimationspunkt *m* sublimation point
Sublimationstrocknung *f s.* Gefriertrocknung
Sublimationsvorlage *f* condenser
Sublimationswärme *f* heat of sublimation
Sublimator *m* sublimator
Sublimatpapier *n* mercury (mercuric) chloride paper *(a test paper)*
Sublimatprobe *f (med)* sublimate test
sublimierbar sublimable
Sublimierblase *f* sublimer
sublimieren to sublimate, to sublime
Sublimiergut *n s.* Sublimationsgut
submers submerged, submersed
Submersfermentation *f (biot)* submerged[-culture] fermentation
Submersfermenter *m (biot)* submerged fermenter
Submerskultur *f (biot)* submerged culture
Submersreaktor *m s.* Submersfermenter
Submerssuspensionskultur *f s.* Submerskultur
Submerstank *m s.* Submersfermenter
Submersverfahren *n (biot)* submerged[-culture] process, submerged-fermentation process
Submerszucht *f (biot)* submerged cultivation
Submikrogefüge *n* submicrostructure
Submikron *n* submicron *(a minute particle visible only with an ultramicroscope)*
Submikroprobe *f* submicro sample *(* 10^{-3} to 10^{-4} g)*
submikroskopisch submicroscopic
Submikrostruktur *f* submicrostructure
Submizelle *f* submicelle
Submolekül *n* submolecule
Suboxid *n* suboxide
Subsilikatschlacke *f (met)* subsilicate slag
Sub-Spuren-Analyse *f* sub-trace analysis *(*sample weight 10^{-3} to 10^{-4} g)*
substantiv *(dye)* substantive, direct
Substantivfarbstoff *m* substantive (direct) dye (dyestuff)
Substantivität *f (dye)* substantivity
Substanz *f* substance, matter, material *(for compounds s. a.* Stoff*)*
~/abgewogene weighed substance
~/abzuwägende substance to be weighed
~/adstringierende astringent, styptic
~/bakterientötende (bakterizide) bactericide
~/ferredoxinreduzierende *(bioch)* ferredoxin-reducing substance, FRS
~/giftige toxic [substance], toxicant
~/individuelle individual substance
~/inkrustierende encrustant, incrustant, encrusting (incrusting) substance
~/ionophore *(bioch)* ionophore
~/methylenblauaktive *(hyd)* methylene blue active substance, MBAS
~/mikrobielle *(biot)* microbial product
~/opake *(coal)* opaque matter
~/pflanzliche vegetable matter
~ S/Reichsteins Reichstein's substance S *(17-hydroxydeoxycorticosterone)*
~/sauerstoffbedürftige *(bioch)* oxygen-demanding substance
~/standardisierte standard substance
~/synthetisch gewonnene synthetic
~/unbekannte unknown [substance]
~/unlösliche insoluble
~/vegetabilische vegetable matter
~/wehenerregende oxytocic [agent]
~/wirksame [active] agent, active substance
Substanzbarren *m* ingot *(in zone melting)*
Substanzbereich *m (chromat)* band
Substanzformel *f* stoichiometric formula, empirical (simplest) formula
Substanzklasse *f* family of compounds, class of substances
Substanzmenge *f* amount (quantity) of substance (material)
Substanznachweis *m* **über Ionenreaktionen** reactant ion monitoring, RIM
Substanzpolymerisation *f* mass (bulk) polymerization
Substanzprobe *f* sample
Substanzschiffchen *n (lab)* boat
~ aus Graphit graphite boat
~ aus Quarz quartz boat
~ aus Tonerde alumina boat
Substanztransport *m* matter transport
Substanzverlust *m* loss of material
Substituent *m* substituent [group]
~/äquatorialer equatorial substituent
~/ausgewechselter substituted group
~/axialer axial substituent
~ erster Ordnung *s.* ~/ortho-para-dirigierender
~ in meta-Stellung (*m*-Stellung) meta substituent
~/meta-dirigierender meta-directing group, meta director
~/meta-ständiger meta substituent
~ mit aktivierender Wirkung activating group
~ mit desaktivierender Wirkung deactivating group
~/ortho-para-dirigierender ortho-para-directing group, ortho-para director
~/verdrängter substituted group
~ zweiter Ordnung *s.* ~/meta-dirigierender
***m*-Substituent** *m* meta substituent
***o*-Substituent** *m* ortho substituent
***p*-Substituent** *m* para substituent
Substituenteneffekt *m* substituent effect
~/mesomerer mesomeric (electromeric) effect
~/polarer polar effect
Substituentenkonstante *f (org ch)* substituent constant, sigma-constant, σ-constant
~/Hammettsche Hammett's substituent constant

substituierbar substitutable, replaceable
Substituierbarkeit *f* substitutability, replaceability
substituieren to substitute, to replace
substituiert:
• ~ **werden** to undergo substitution
~/**dreifach** trisubstituted
~/**einfach** monosubstituted
~/**mehrfach** polysubstituted
~/**vierfach** tetrasubstituted
~/**zweifach** disubstituted, bis-substituted
1,2-substituiert *s.* *o*-substituiert
1,3-substituiert *s.* *m*-substituiert
1,4-substituiert *s.* *p*-substituiert
m-**substituiert** *m*-substituted, meta-substituted
N-**substituiert** *N*-substituted
o-**substituiert** *o*-substituted, ortho-substituted
p-**substituiert** *p*-substituted, para-substituted
Substitution *f* substitution, replacement
~/**anionoide** *s.* ~/nucleophile
~/**bimolekulare nucleophile** second-order nucleophilic substitution [reaction], S_N2 reaction
~/**elektrophile** electrophilic substitution
~/**kationoide** *s.* ~/elektrophile
~/**monomolekulare nucleophile** first-order nucleophilic substitution [reaction], S_N1 reaction
~/**nucleophile** nucleophilic substitution [reaction], S_N reaction • **in nucleophiler ~ ausgetauscht werden** to undergo nucleophilic displacement
Substitutionsbereitschaft *f* susceptibility to substitution
Substitutionsgrad *m* degree of substitution, D.S.
Substitutionsisomerie *f* substitution (place) isomerism, position[al] isomerism
Substitutionslegierung *f* substitutional alloy
Substitutionsmethode *f* **nach Borda** Borda's method [of substitution] *(in weighing)*
Substitutionsmischkristall *m* substitutional solid solution
Substitutionsname *m* substitutive name
Substitutionsprodukt *n* substitution product
Substitutionsreaktion *f* substitution reaction
Substitutionstautomerie *f* substitution tautomerism
Substitutionswägung *f* substitution weighing
Substrat *n* substrate, *(biot also)* medium, *(enzymology also)* reactant
~/**führendes** leading (obligatory) substrate (reactant)
~/**halbfestes** semisolid medium
~/**limitierendes** limiting substrate
~/**obligatorisches** *s.* ~/führendes
~/**technisches** industrial fermentation medium, fermentation raw material, feedstock
Substratabbau *m (biot)* substrate breakdown, degradation of substrate
Substratablaufkonzentration *f (hyd)* effluent substrate concentration
Substratanalogon *n (bioch)* analog of the substrate
Substratbindung *f (bioch)* substrate binding
Substratbindungsmechanismus *m*/**kooperativer** *(bioch)* cooperativity
Substratgehalt *m* substrate level
Substrathemmung *f (bioch)* substrate inhibition
Substratkettenphosphorylierung *f s.* Substratphosphorylierung
Substratkonzentration *f* substrate concentration
~ **im Rücklaufschlamm** *(hyd)* recycle substrate concentration
Substratlimitierung *f (biot)* substrate limitation
Substratlösung *f (biot)* substrate solution
Substratmenge *f* substrate level
Substratphosphorylierung *f (bioch)* substrate-level phosphorylation
Substratsättigung *f* substrate saturation *(enzyme kinetics)*
substratspezifisch *(bioch)* substrate-specific
Substratspezifität *f (bioch)* substrate specificity
Substratstabilisierung *f (biot)* substrate stabilization
Substratüberschußhemmung *f (bioch)* substrate inhibition
Substratverbrauch *m (biot)* 1. substrate consumption (utilization); 2. amount of substrate utilized
substratvermittelt substrate-induced
Substratzulaufkonzentration *f (hyd)* influent substrate concentration, substrate feed concentration
Substratzyklus *m (bioch)* substrate cycle
Subtraktionsmischkristall *m* subtraction solid solution
Subtraktionsname *m*, **Subtraktivname** *m* subtractive name
Succinaldehyd *m s.* Succindialdehyd
Succinamidsäure *f* succinamic acid, succinic acid monoamide
Succinat *n* succinate *(a salt or ester of succinic acid)*
Succinatdehydrogenase *f* succinate dehydrogenase, succinic [acid] dehydrogenase
Succinatoxidase *f* succinoxidase
Succinbromimid *n* *N*-bromosuccinimide, NBS
Succindialdehyd *m* succindialdehyde, *butane-1,4-dial
Succinimid *n* succinimide, 2,5-dioxopyrrolidine
Succinit *m* succinite, amber
Succinsäure *f* succinic acid, *butanedioic acid
Succinylchlorid *n* succinyl chloride
Suchtbildung *f (pharm)* habit formation
suchterzeugend *(pharm)* addictive, habit-forming
Sucrochemie *f* sucrochemistry
Sud *m (ferm)* 1. boiling, brewing *(act)*; 2. brew[ing], gyle *(product)*
Sudangummi *n* gum arabic, Arabian (acacia) gum *(from Acacia specc.)*
Sudhaus *n* brewhouse
Sudhausausbeute *f (ferm)* copper-yield
Sukzin... *s. a.* Succin... *for chemical compounds*
sukzinylieren to succinylate

Sukzinylierung *f* succinylation
Sulfacetamid *n* sulphacetamide *(a sulphonamide)*
Sulfachinoxalin *n* sulphaquinoxaline
Sulfadiazin *n* sulphadiazine, sulphanilamidopyrimidine
Sulfaguanidin *n* sulphanilylguanidine, sulphaguanidine
Sulfalkylierung *f* sulphoalkylation
Sulfamat *n s.* Sulfamidat
Sulfamid *n s.* Sulfonamid
Sulfamidat *n* $NH_2SO_2OM^I$ amidosulphate, sulphamate
Sulfamidsäure *f* sulphamic acid *(a compound H_2NSO_3H or any of its organic derivatives $RNHSO_3H$ or R_2NSO_3H)*
Sulfaminat *n s.* Sulfamidat
Sulfaminierung *f* sulphamation, *N*-sulphonation
Sulfaminsäure *f s.* Sulfonsäureamid
Sulfan *n* sulphane, hydrogen sulphide, *(specif)* H_2S monosulphane, hydrogen sulphide
Sulfanilamid *n* sulphanilamide, *p*-aminobenzenesulphonamide
Sulfanilsäure *f* sulphanilic acid, aniline-*p*-sulphonic acid
Sulfapyridin *n* sulphapyridine, 2-sulphanilamidopyridine
Sulfat *n* $M^I_2SO_4$ sulphate
Sulfatangriff *m (build)* sulphate attack, attack by sulphates
Sulfataufschluß *m (pap)* sulphate pulping
Sulfatbeständigkeit *f* sulphate resistivity
Sulfatblase *f* [sulphate] scab, whitewash *(a defect in glass)*
Sulfathärte *f (hyd)* sulphate hardness
Sulfathiazol *n* sulphathiazole, 2-sulphanilamidothiazole
Sulfathüttenzement *m* super-sulphated cement, slag sulphate cement
sulfatieren to sulphatize, to sulphate *(to esterify alcohols with sulphuric acid)*
Sulfatierung *f* sulphation, sulphatizing *(esterification of alcohols with sulphuric acid)*
Sulfationsfaktor *m (bioch)* sulphation factor, somatomedin
sulfatisieren 1. to sulphatize *(e.g. sulphide ores by roasting)*; 2. to sulphate *(the plates of a lead-acid accumulator)*
Sulfatisierung *f* 1. sulphatizing *(as of sulphide ores by roasting)*; 2. sulphation *(of the plates of a lead-acid accumulator)*
Sulfatkochlauge *f (pap)* sulphate (kraft) cooking liquor, sulphate [digestion] liquor
Sulfatkochung *f (pap)* sulphate cook
~ **für Kraftzellstoff** kraft cook
Sulfatlauge *f s.* Sulfatkochlauge
Sulfatlignin *n (pap)* sulphate lignin
Sulfatpapier *n* sulphate paper
Sulfatstein *m (hyd)* sulphate scale
Sulfatterpentin *n (pap)* sulphate turpentine
Sulfatverfahren *n (pap)* sulphate process
Sulfatzellstoff *m* sulphate pulp
~/**ungewaschener** brown stock (pulp)
Sulfatzellstoffabrik *f* sulphate (kraft) mill
Sulfatzellstoffkocher *m (pap)* sulphate (kraft) digester
Sulfatzellstoffwäsche *f (pap)* brown-stock washing
Sulfen *n (org ch)* sulphene
Sulfenamidbeschleuniger *m (rubber)* sulphenamide accelerator
Sulfensäure *f (org ch)* RSOH sulphenic acid
Sulfenylgruppe *f* sulphenyl (hydrocarbylsulphanyl) group
Sulfenylium-Ion *n* sulphenylium (sulphenium) ion
Sulfenylradikal *n* sulphenyl (hydrocarbylsulphanyl) radical
Sulfethylierung *f* sulphoethylation
Sulfhydrylgruppe *f* –SH sulphydryl (thiol) group, mercapto group
Sulfid *n* M^I_2S sulphide
~/**primäres (saures)** *s.* Hydrogensulfid
Sulfidäscher *m (tann)* sulphide lime
Sulfiderz *n* sulphide ore
Sulfidgehalt *m* sulphide content, *(pap also)* sulphidity
sulfidieren to sulphidize, to sulphide, *(text also)* to xanthate, to churn
Sulfidiertrommel *f (text)* xanthator, [xanthating] churn, baratte
Sulfidierung *f* sulphidizing, *(text also)* xanthation, churning
sulfidisch sulphidic
Sulfidität *f (pap)* sulphidity
Sulfidoxidschale *f*, **Sulfidoxidzone** *f (geoch)* sulphide-oxide shell
Sulfidphosphor *m* sulphide phosphor
Sulfidschwefel *m* sulphide sulphur
Sulfieranlage *f* sulphonation plant (unit)
Sulfierapparat *m* sulphonator
sulfieren to sulphonate *(to treat an organic compound with sulphuric acid or a related agent)*
~ **lassen/sich** to sulphonate
Sulfiergefäß *n*, **Sulfierkessel** *m* sulphonation (sulphonating) pan
Sulfierkolben *m* sulphonation flask
Sulfierung *f* sulphonation *(treatment of an organic compound with sulphuric acid or a related agent)*
Sulfierungs... *s.* Sulfier...
Sulfin *n* sulphine *(S-oxide of a thioaldehyde or of a thioketone)*
Sulfinfarbstoff *m s.* Schwefelfarbstoff
Sulfinsäure *f (org ch)* RSO_2H sulphinic acid
Sulfit *n* $M^I_2SO_3$ sulphite
Sulfitablauge *f (pap)* spent (waste) sulphite liquor, red liquor, sulphite lye
Sulfitation *f (sugar)* [acid] sulphitation
Sulfitaufschluß *m (pap)* sulphite pulping
sulfitieren *(sugar)* to sulphite
Sulfitierung *f (sugar)* [acid] sulphitation

Sulfitkochsäure *f (pap)* sulphite (bisulphite) cooking liquor
Sulfitkochsäureherstellung *f (pap)* cooking-liquor manufacture, acid preparation (making)
Sulfitkochung *(pap)* sulphite cook
Sulfitkraftpapier *n* sulphite kraft paper
Sulfitocobaltat(III) *n* $M^{I}_{3}[Co(SO_3)_3]$ sulphitocobaltate(III)
Sulfitomercurat(II) *n* $M^{I}_{2}[Hg(SO_3)_2]$ sulphitomercurate(II), disulphitomercurate(II)
Sulfitpapier *n* sulphite paper
Sulfitsäure *f s.* Sulfitkochsäure
Sulfitstoff *m s.* Sulfitzellstoff
Sulfitverfahren *n (pap)* sulphite pulping [process]
Sulfitzellstoff *m* sulphite pulp
~ **in Bogenform (Pappenform)** sulphite laps
Sulfitzellstoffabrik *f* sulphite [pulp] mill
Sulfitzellstoffblätter *npl* sulphite laps
Sulfitzellstoffindustrie *f* sulphite pulp industry
Sulfitzellstoffkocher *m* sulphite digester
Sulfitzellstoffwerk *n* sulphite [pulp] mill
Sulfocarbamid *n s.* Thioharnstoff
Sulfochlorid *n* RSO_2Cl sulphonyl chloride
sulfochlorieren to sulphochlorinate
Sulfochlorierung *f* sulphochlorination
Sulfogruppe *f* $-SO_3H$ sulpho group
Sulfomethylierung *f* sulphomethylation
Sulfon *n* sulphone
Sulfonal *n* sulphonal, propane-2,2-diethyldisulphone
Sulfonamid *n s.* Sulfonsäureamid
Sulfonamidpräparat *n* sulpha drug
Sulfonat *n* sulphonate
Sulfonator *m* sulphonator
Sulfongruppe *f s.* Sulfogruppe
Sulfonieranlage *f* sulphonation plant (unit)
sulfonieren to sulphonate
~ **lassen/sich** to sulphonate
Sulfonierer *m* sulphonator
Sulfonierung *f* sulphonation
~**/reduktive (reduzierende)** reductive sulphonation
N-**Sulfonierung** *f N*-sulphonation, sulphamation
Sulfonierungsagens *n* sulphonating [re]agent
Sulfonierungsanlage *f* sulphonation plant (unit)
Sulfonierungsgemisch *n* sulphonation mixture
Sulfonierungsgrad *m* degree of sulphonation
Sulfonierungskessel *m* sulphonation (sulphonating) pan
Sulfonierungsmittel *n* sulphonating [re]agent
Sulfonium-Ion *n* sulphonium ion
Sulfoniumverbindung *f* sulphonium compound
Sulfonphthalein *n* sulphonephthalein
Sulfonsäure *f* sulphonic acid, sulpho acid
Sulfonsäureamid *n* sulphonamide *(any of a class of compounds characterized by the radical* $-SO_2-NHR$*)*
Sulfonsäurechlorid *n s.* Sulfochlorid
Sulfonsäuregruppe *f s.* Sulfogruppe
Sulfonylchlorid *n s.* Sulfochlorid
Sulfonylgruppe *f* $=SO_2$ sulphonyl group
Sulfonylierung *f* sulphonylation
Sulfonyloxygruppe *f* $-OSO_2R$ sulphonyloxy group
Sulforicinoleat *n s.* Ricinusöl/sulfatiertes
Sulfosalicylsäure *f* sulphosalicylic acid *(either of two hydroxy-sulphobenzoic acids)*
Sulfosäure *f s.* Sulfonsäure
Sulfoxid *n* R^1SOR^2 sulphoxide
Sulfoxidation *f* sulphoxidation
Sulfoxylat *n* $M^{I}_{2}SO_2$ sulphoxylate
Sulfoxylsäure *f* sulphoxylic acid
Sulfur *m* S sulphur *(for compounds s. under* Schwefel*)*
Sulfurationsapparat *m* sulphonator
Sulfurationskessel *m* sulphonation (sulphonating) pan
sulfurieren to sulphonate
~ **lassen/sich** to sulphonate
Sulfurierung *f* sulphonation *(broadly, regardless of the nature of the products)*
Sulfurikation *f (soil)* sulphofication *(microbial oxidation of organically bound sulphur to sulphate)*
Sulfuröl *n* sulphur [olive] oil *(olive oil of inferior grade)*
Sulfurylchlorid *n* sulphuryl chloride
Sumatrabenzoe *f* Sumatra benzoin [gum] *(from Styrax benzoin Dryander)*
Sumatracampher *m* Sumatra (Borneo, Malayan, Baros) camphor *(from Dryobalanops aromatica Gaertn. f.)*
Sumbulöl *n* sumbul oil *(from Ferula sumbul Hook.)*
Summenbande *f (spectr)* sum band
Summenformel *f* empirical formula
~**/einfachste** simplest [possible] formula, stoichiometric formula
~**/wahre** true (empirical molecular) formula
Summenregel *f* sum rule
~**/Burger-Dorgelo-Ornsteinsche** Burger-Dorgelo-Ornstein sum rule *(for atomic spectra)*
Sumpf *m (tech)* pond, pit, sump; *(distil)* bottom *(of a column)*; pool *(polarography)*
Sumpfabnahme *f (distil)* withdrawal of bottoms
Sumpfaufgabe *f* top feed *(of a double-drum dryer)*
sumpfen *(ceram)* to soak, to wet
Sumpfgas *n* marsh gas
Sumpfgrube *f (ceram)* soak[ing] pit
Sumpfofen *m s.* Sumpfphasehydrierofen
Sumpfphase *f* liquid phase *(in coal hydrogenation)*
Sumpfphasebenzin *n* liquid-phase gasoline (petrol) *(obtained by coal hydrogenation)*
Sumpfphasehydrierofen *m* liquid-phase converter *(in coal hydrogenation)*
Sumpfphasehydrierung *f* liquid-phase hydrogenation *(of coal)*
Sumpfphasekammer *f* liquid-phase stall *(in coal hydrogenation)*
Sumpfphasekatalysator *m* liquid-phase catalyst *(in coal hydrogenation)*
Sumpfphaseofen *m s.* Sumpfphasehydrierofen
Sumpfprodukt *n (distil)* bottoms, bottom product

Sumpftiefe *f (tech)* pond depth
Super-Abrasion-Furnace-Ruß *m (rubber)* super abrasion furnace black, SAF black
Superadditivität *f (phot)* superadditivity
superazid superacid
Superazidität *f* superacidity, *(med also)* hyperacidity *(of gastric juice)*
Superbenzin *n s.* Superkraftstoff
superfluid superfluid, superliquid
Superfluidität *f* superfluidity, superfluid state
superflüssig *s.* superfluid
superhelikal *(bioch)* superhelical
Superhelix *f (bioch)* superhelix, triple-stranded helix, coiled-coil
Superisolierung *f* superinsulation, multiple-layer insulation *(cryogenic engineering)*
Superkalander *m (pap)* supercalender
Superknäuelung *f (bioch)* supercoiling *(of DNA)*
Superkraftstoff *m* premium fuel (gasoline, spirit), premium motor fuel
Superlegierung *f* superalloy
Supermultiplett *n* supermultiplet
Superphosphat *n* superphosphate
~/einfaches (normales) ordinary (normal) superphosphate
supersauer superacid
Supersäure *f* superacid
Supersekundärstruktur *f (bioch)* supersecondary structure
Superzentrifuge *f* supercentrifuge
Suppositorium *n (pharm)* suppository
Suppression *f* **der Nonsense-Mutation** *(bioch)* nonsense suppression
~ sinnvoller Codons missense suppression
Suppressormutation *f (biot)* suppressor mutation
suprafacial *(org ch)* suprafacial, s
suprafluid superfluid, superliquid
Suprafluidität *f* superfluidity, superfluid state
supraflüssig *s.* suprafluid
Supraflüssigkeit *f* 1. superfluid; 2. *s.* Suprafluidität
supraleitend superconducting, superconductive
Supraleiter *m* superconductor
supraleitfähig *s.* supraleitend
Supraleitfähigkeit *f* superconductivity, supraconductivity, superconduction • **~ zeigen** to exhibit superconductivity, to superconduct
Supraleitung *f s.* Supraleitfähigkeit
Supraleitungselektron *n* superconducting electron
Surrogat *n* substitute
suspendierbar suspensible
Suspendierbarkeit *f* suspensibility
suspendieren to suspend
~/wieder to resuspend
Suspendiermittel *n s.* Suspensionsmittel
Suspendiervermögen *n* suspending capacity
Suspension *f* suspension • **in ~ halten** to keep (maintain) in suspension
~/erneute resuspension
~ mit Ölflockung *(agric)* oil-flocculated suspension
~ mizellare micellar suspension
Suspensionsdichte *f (biot)* cell density *(of a cell suspension)*
Suspensionsgrenze *f* sludge line
Suspensionskolloid *n* suspensoid [colloid]
Suspensionskonzentration *f (hyd)* suspended solids concentration
Suspensionskultur *f (biot)* submerged culture
Suspensionsmittel *n* suspending agent (medium)
Suspensionspartikel *npl* suspended particles, particulates, particulate matter
Suspensionspolymerisation *f* suspension (bead) polymerization
Suspensionspolyvinylchlorid *n* suspension polyvinyl chloride
Suspensionsreaktor *m* [catalyst-]slurry reactor
Suspensionsröstofen *m* suspension roaster
Suspensionsröstung *f* suspension roasting
Suspensionsspritzmittel *n* wettable powder *(crop protection)*
Suspensionstechnik *f* mull technique *(IR spectroscopy)*
Suspensionszulauf *m (filtr)* feed inlet
Suspensoid *n* suspensoid [colloid]
Suspensoid-Kracken *n (petrol)* suspensoid [catalytic] cracking
Suspensoid-Krackverfahren *n (petrol)* suspensoid[-catalytic-cracking] process
süß 1. sweet *(taste)*; 2. sweet[ened] *(petroleum distillate)*
Süße *f* sweetness
süßen 1. *(food)* to sweeten; 2. *(petrol)* to sweeten *(to remove malodorous sulphur compounds)*
Süßerde *f* beryllia, beryllium oxide
Süßholzsaft *m* [pure] licorice, liquorice *(from Glycyrrhiza glabra L.)*
Süßkraft *f* sweetening strength
süßlich sweetish
Süßmaische *f* sweet mash
Süßmittel *n (food)* sweetener, sweetening agent
Süßmolke *f* sweet whey
Süßmolkenpulver *n* sweet-whey powder
Süßmost *m* fruit juice
Süßrahm *m* sweet (unripened) cream
Süßrahmbutter *f* sweet-cream butter
Süßrahmbuttermilch *f* sweet-cream buttermilk
Süßstoff *m* non-caloric sweetener, non-nutritional (non-nutritive, non-sugar) sweetener
Süßung *f* sweetening *(of petroleum distillates)*
Süßungsmittel *n (petrol)* sweetening agent
Süßungsreaktion *f (petrol)* sweetening reaction
Süßungsverfahren *n (petrol)* sweetening process
~/oxidatives oxidation [sweetening] process
Süßwaren *fpl* confectionery
Süßwasser *n* sweet (fresh) water
Süßwassergewinnungsanlage *f* desalination (desalinating) plant
Süßwasservorkommen *n* fresh-water source
Süßwasservorrat *m* fresh-water supply
Süßwein *m* sweet wine

Suszeptibilität *f* susceptibility
~/diamagnetische diamagnetic susceptibility
~/ferromagnetische ferromagnetic susceptibility
~/magnetische magnetic susceptibility
~/molare molar susceptibility, susceptibility per gram mole
~/paramagnetische paramagnetic susceptibility
~/spezifische specific (mass) susceptibility, susceptibility per gram
Svedberg-Einheit *f* Svedberg unit *(determination of molecular weights by sedimentation)*
Swarts-Reaktion *f* Swarts reaction *(for obtaining fluoroalkanes)*
Sweep-Generator *m (spectr)* sweep generator
Sweep-Spule *f (spectr)* sweep coil
Sweetland-Filter *n* Sweetland filter, Sweetland [filter] press
Sweetland-Filterpresse *f*, **Sweetland-Presse** *f s.* Sweetland-Filter
Swellingindex *m (coal)* swelling index (number)
Swenson-Walker-Kristallisator *m* Swenson-Walker crystallizer
S-Wert *m (soil)* S value *(sum of exchangeable bases)*
swf. *s.* löslich/sehr schwer
Sydnon *n* sydnone *(any of a class of mesoionic compounds)*
Sydnonimin *n* sydnone imine
Syenit *m* syenite *(an igneous rock composed essentially of alkali feldspar)*
Sylvan *n* sylvan, 2-methylfuran
Sylvestren *n* sylvestrene *(a cyclic terpene)*
Sylvin *m (min)* sylvite, sylvin[e] *(potassium chloride)*
Symbol *n* symbol, sign, *(for representing chemical elements also)* chemical symbol (sign)
Symbole *npl***/Bravaissche** *(cryst)* Bravais-Miller indices
Symbolik *f* symbolism
sym-, symm- *s.* symmetrisch
Symmetrie *f* symmetry
~/äußere (makroskopische) *(cryst)* external symmetry
Symmetrieachse *f* axis of symmetry, symmetry axis
~/sechszählige sixfold axis of symmetry
~/zweizählige twofold axis of symmetry
Symmetrieebene *f* plane of symmetry, symmetry plane
Symmetrielement *n* element of symmetry, symmetry element
Symmetrieklasse *f* class of crystal symmetry, symmetry (crystal) class, symmetry (point) group
Symmetriemodell *n* **der Ligandenbindung an Proteine** *(bioch)* MWC (Monod-Wyman-Changeux) model
Symmetrieoperation *f* symmetry operation (transformation)
Symmetrierasse *f (spectr)* symmetry species (type)
Symmetrietransformation *f s.* Symmetrieoperation
Symmetriezentrum *n* centre of symmetry, symmetry (inversion) centre
symmetrisch symmetric[al], *(nomencl as a prefix:) sym-*
Symons-Flachkegelbrecher *m* Symons short-head cone crusher
Symons-Kegelbrecher *m* Symons cone crusher
Symons-Scheibenbrecher *m*, **Symons-Tellerbrecher** *m* Symons disk crusher
Sympathikolytikum *n* sympatholytic [agent]
sympathikolytisch sympatholytic
Sympathikomimetikum *n* sympathomimetic [agent]
sympathikomimetisch sympathomimetic
sympatho... *s.* sympathiko...
Symport *m (bioch)* symport *(one form of carrier transport)*
Symproportionierung *f* comproportionation
Synaerese *f s.* Synärese
synantetisch *(geoch)* synante[c]tic *(formed by the reaction of two minerals)*
syn-anti-Isomerie *f* syn-anti isomerism
Synärese *f (coll)* synaeresis • **~ zeigen** to exhibit synaeresis, to synaerize *(of gels)*
Synchrotron *n (nucl)* synchrotron
Synchrotronstrahlung *f (nucl)* synchrotron radiation
Synchrozyklotron *n* synchrocyclotron *(frequency-modulated cyclotron)*
syndiotaktisch syndiotactic, syn[dyo]tactic *(polymers)*
Syndiotaktizität *f* syndiotacticity *(of polymers)*
syndyotaktisch *s.* syndiotaktisch
Synergismus *m* synergism
Synergist *m* synergist
synergistisch synergistic
syn-Form *f* syn form, skew (gauche) form *(stereochemistry)*
syn-Isomer[e] *n* syn isomer
Synovia[flüssigkeit] *f (med)* synovial fluid
±synperiplanar synperiplanar, eclipsed, opposed *(stereochemistry)*
Synproportionierung *f s.* Symproportionierung
syn-Stellung *f* syn position • **in ~ [befindlich]** syn • **in ~ stehen** to be syn
Syntan *n* syntan, synthetic tannin (tanning agent)
Syntangerbung *f* syntan tannage
Synthane-Verfahren *n (coal)* Synthane process *(for gasifying coal in a fluidized bed under high pressure)*
Synthese *f* synthesis
~ an polymeren Trägern solid-phase protein synthesis *(according to Merrifield)*
~/asymmetrische asymmetric synthesis
~/biologische biosynthesis, biogenesis
~/chemische chemical (artificial) synthesis
~/Conrad-Limpachsche Conrad-Limpach synthesis *(of 4-hydroxyquinolines)*

~/Doebnersche Doebner synthesis *(of substituted cinchoninic acids)*
~/enzymatische enzymatic synthesis
~/Erlenmeyersche Erlenmeyer-Plöchl azlactone synthesis *(of α-amino acids)*
~/Fittigsche Fittig synthesis *(of aromatic hydrocarbons)*
~/Friedel-Craftssche Friedel-Crafts synthesis *(of aromatic hydrocarbons or ketones)*
~/Gattermann-Kochsche Gattermann-Koch synthesis *(of phenolic aldehydes)*
~/Heumannsche Heumann indigo synthesis
~/Kilianische Kiliani[-Fischer] synthesis *(for increasing the number of C atoms in the carbon chain of sugars)*
~/Knoevenagelsche Knoevenagel condensation (synthesis) *(of α,β-unsaturated acids or esters)*
~/Kolbesche Kolbe synthesis *(1. of hydrocarbons by electrolysis; 2. of phenolic acids)*
~/Kolbe-Schmittsche Kolbe-Schmitt synthesis *(of aromatic hydroxy acids)*
~ mit umlaufendem Kontaktstaub *(coal)* Kellogg fluidized synthesis *(of hydrocarbons)*
~ nach Müller-Rochow Müller-Rochow synthesis *(of organosilicon compounds)*
~/Perkinsche Perkin condensation (synthesis) *(of unsaturated carboxylic acids)*
~/Reformatskysche Reformatsky synthesis *(of 3-hydroxycarboxylic acid esters)*
~/Reimer-Tiemannsche Reimer-Tiemann synthesis *(of hydroxyaldehydes or hydroxy acids)*
~/Skraupsche Skraup [quinoline] synthesis
~/Streckersche Strecker synthesis *(of α-amino acids)*
~/technische (technisch brauchbare) commercial synthesis
~/Wurtzsche Wurtz synthesis *(of aliphatic hydrocarbons)*
Syntheseammoniak *n* synthetic ammonia
Synthesechemie *f* synthetic chemistry
~/organische synthetic organic chemistry
Synthesechemiker *m* synthetic chemist
Synthesefaser *f* synthetic [polymer] fibre
Synthesefaserstoff *m* synthetic [polymer] fibre
Synthesefett *n* synthetic fat
Synthesegas *n* synthesis gas
~/rohes raw synthesis gas
Synthesekautschuk *m* synthetic rubber, artificial (man-made, chemical) rubber
Synthesekautschukkleber *m* synthetic-rubber adhesive
Synthesekautschuklatex *m* synthetic[-rubber] latex
Synthesekautschukmischung *f* synthetic-rubber mix (stock, compound)
Syntheselatex *m s.* Synthesekautschuklatex
Syntheseleistung *f (biot)* efficiency of synthesis
Syntheseort *m (bioch)* site (locus) of synthesis
Syntheseprodukt *n* synthetic
Syntheseschritt *m* synthesis step
Syntheseweg *m (bioch)* pathway of synthesis, synthesis (synthetic) pathway
Synthesewert *(hyd)* biomass synthesis constant
synthetisch synthetic[al], artificial, man-made, manufactured, non-natural; *(bioch)* anabolic
synthetisieren to synthesize
S-Yperit *n s.* Schwefelyperit
Syringaaldehyd *m*, **Syringaldehyd** *m* syringic aldehyde, syringa-aldehyde, 4-hydroxy-3,5-dimethoxybenzaldehyde
Syringasäure *f* syringic acid, 4-hydroxy-3,5-dimethoxybenzoic acid
System *n***/abgeschlossenes** *(phys ch)* isolated system
~/azeotropes azeotropic system
~/Baeyersches Baeyer system *(of naming bridged hydrocarbons)*
~/binäres binary (two-component) system
~/capto-dativ substituiertes *(bioch)* push-pull system
~ der Chemical Abstracts *(nomencl)* Chemical Abstracts system
~ des Ring-Index *(nomencl)* Ring Index system
~/dispergierendes dispersive system *(of a spectroscope)*
~/disperses disperse system
~/divariantes divariant system
~/einphasiges *s.* ~/homogenes
~/endocyclisches endocyclic (caged ring) system
~/gasförmiges gaseous system
~/geschlossenes *(phys ch)* closed system
~/heteroaromatisches heteroconjugated system
~/heterocyclisches heterocyclic system
~/heterocyclisches konjugiertes heteroconjugated system
~/heterogenes heterogeneous system
~/homogenes homogeneous (one-phase) system
~/inhomogenes *s.* ~/heterogenes
~/isodisperses *(coll)* isodisperse system, isodispersion
~/isoliertes *(phys ch)* isolated system
~/kolloiddisperses (kolloides) colloidal system
~/kondensiertes condensed system
~/konjugiertes conjugated system
~/korrodierendes corrosion system
~/kristallographisches *s.* Kristallsystem
~/mehrphasiges multiphase system
~/metastabiles metastable system
~ mit konjugierten Doppelbindungen conjugated dienoid system
~/monodisperses monodisperse system
~/monovariantes monovariant system
~/offenes *(phys ch)* open system
~/offenkettiges *(org ch)* open-chain system
~/periodisches *s.* Periodensystem [der Elemente]
~/polydisperses *(coll)* polydisperse system, polydispersion
~/polynäres multicomponent system

~/quaternäres quaternary (four-component) system
~/sich selbst organisierendes *(bioch)* self-assembling system
~/spirocyclisches spiro ring system
~/Stocksches Stock system *(of indicating the oxidation state)*
~/ternäres ternary (tertiary, three-component) system
~/ungeordnetes random system
~/unitäres unary (one-component) system
~/zweiphasiges *s.* ~/binäres
Systeminsektizid *n* systemic insecticide
systemisch systemic *(pesticide)*
Systemname *m***/Genfer** *(nomencl)* Geneva name
SZ *s.* Säurezahl
Szent-Györgyi-Krebs-Zyklus *m* Krebs cycle, citric-acid (tricarboxylic-acid) cycle, TCA cycle
Szilard-Chalmers-Detektor *m (nucl)* Szilard-Chalmers detector
Szilard-Chalmers-Effekt *m (nucl)* Szilard-Chalmers effect
Szilard-Chalmers-Methode *f (nucl)* Szilard-Chalmers method
Szilard-Chalmers-Reaktion *f (nucl)* Szilard-Chalmers reaction
Szintillation *f* scintillation
Szintillationslösung *f* scintillation fluid
Szintillationsmethode *f* scintillation method
Szintillationsspektrometer *n* scintillation spectrometer
Szintillationszähler *m* scintillation counter
Szintillator *m* scintillator
szintillieren to scintillate
SZT *s.* Selbstzündtemperatur
S-Zustand *m s.* Singulettzustand
S-Zweig *m* S-branch *(in Raman spectra)*

T

2,4,5-T *s.* 2,4,5-Trichlorphenoxyessigsäure
TA *s.* Triacetatfaserstoff
Tabakalkaloid *n* tobacco alkaloid
Tabaklauge *f* tobacco liquor (water)
Tabakmosaikvirus *n* tobacco mosaic virus, TMV
Tabaksamenöl *n* tobacco[seed] oil
Tablette *f* tablet; *(spectr)* pellet, pressed disk; *(plast)* biscuit, bisque *(for manufacturing disk records)*
Tablettenpresse *f s.* Tablettiermaschine
Tabletten-Rundlaufpresse *f* rotary tablet press
tablettieren to tablet
Tablettiermaschine *f* tabletting (tablet-compressing) machine, tablet press
Tabun *n* tabun *(ethyl ester of dimethylphosphoramidocyanidic acid)*
Tachyhydrit *m (min)* tachyhydrite, tachydrite *(calcium magnesium chloride)*
Tachysterin *n*, **Tachysterol** *n (bioch)* tachysterol
Taenit *m* taenite *(a nickel-iron alloy occurring in iron meteorites)*
Tafel *f* plate, slab, *(if thin:)* sheet; *(cryst)* plate
Tafel-Diagramm *n (el ch)* Tafel diagram (plot)
Tafelessig *m* table vinegar
tafelförmig tabular; *(cryst)* platy
Tafel-Gerade *f (el ch)* Tafel line
Tafelglas *n* sheet glass
Tafelglasziehverfahren *n (glass)* [flat] sheet drawing process
~/Fourcaultsches Fourcault [sheet-drawing] process
Tafel-Gleichung *f (el ch)* Tafel equation
tafelig *s.* tafelförmig
Tafelmargarine *f* table margarine
Tafelöl *n* table oil
Tafelsalz *n* table salt
Tafelschmiere *f (tann)* dubbin[g], stuffing mixture
Tafel-Steigung *f (el ch)* Tafel slope
Tafelwasser *n* mineral water
Taft-Gleichung *f (org ch)* Taft equation *(a linear free enthalpy relation)*
Tagebaubetrieb *m*, **Tagebauförderung** *f* surface (open-cast, open-cut) mining, open pit method, *(esp relating to ores)* [surface] quarrying
Tagesaufnahme *f***/empfohlene** *(food)* recommended daily allowance, RDA *(of nutrients)*
Tagesbedarf *m* daily usage [requirements], daily requirement[s]
Tagescreme *f (cosmet)* vanishing cream
Tagesdosis *f (tox)* daily intake [dose]
~/bedingt duldbare (zulässige) conditional acceptable daily intake
~/duldbare (zulässige) acceptable daily intake, ADI, permissible daily body intake
Tagesgang *m* diurnal variation
Tageslichtbeständigkeit *f* sunlight resistance (stability)
Tageslichtpapier *n (phot)* daylight paper
Tageswanne *f (glass)* day tank
Tagliabue-Prüfer *m* Tag[liabue] closed tester *(for determining the flash point)*
Taigusäure *f* lapachol, taiguic acid *(a naphthoquinone derivative)*
Taktizität *f* tacticity *(of polymers)*
Taktoid *n (coll)* tactoid
Taktosol *n (coll)* tactosol
Talalay-Treibverfahren *n* Talalay process *(for producing foamed rubber)*
Talbotyple *f (phot)* calotype process
Talca-Gummi *n s.* Talha-Gummi
Talg *m* tallow
~/Chinesischer (vegetabilischer) Chinese vegetable tallow *(from Sapium sebiferum (L.) Roxb.)*
talgartig tallowy, sebaceous
Talggeschmack *m* tallowy flavour, tallowiness *(of spoiled fats)*
talgig tallowy, sebaceous

Talgigkeit *f* tallowiness
Talh[a]-Gummi *n* talha (talh, talca, Suakin) gum *(a gum arabic, chiefly from Acacia stenocarpa Hochst.)*
Talk *m* 1. talc[um] *(magnesium dihydrogentetrasilicate as a mineral or synthetic product)*; 2. *s.* Talkum
talkieren *(rubber)* to soapstone
talkig talcose, talcous, talcky
Talkpuder *m s.* Talkum
Talkschiefer *m* talc (talcose) schist (slate)
Talkum *n* talcum [powder], talc
talkumieren *(rubber)* to soapstone
Talkumpuder *m s.* Talkum
Tallöl *n* tall oil, liquid resin (rosin)
Tallölkolophonium *n* tall-oil rosin, sulphate wood rosin
Talonsäure *f* talonic acid
Taloschleimsäure *f* talomucic acid
Talsperrenwasser *n* reservoir water
Tambour *m s.* 1. Tambourrolle; 2. Tambourwalze
Tambourrolle *f (pap)* reel (roll) of paper
Tambourwalze *f (pap)* reel-up drum (cylinder), reeling drum (cylinder)
Tanacetketon *n* tanacetketone, thujaketone, 6-methyl-5-methyleneheptan-2-one
Tanacetöl *n* tansy oil *(from Chrysanthemum vulgare (L.) Bernh.)*
Tanacetylalkohol *m* tanacetyl alcohol, thujyl alcohol, 3-thujanol
Tandemanlage *f (rubber)* tandem calender
Tangentialfeuerung *f* tangential firing
Tangentialkammer *f* **nach Meyer** Meyer tangential chamber *(sulphuric-acid manufacture)*
Tank *m* tank, reservoir
Tank-Absetz-Verfahren *n (petrol)* cold-settling process
Tankanhänger *m* tank trailer *(for lorries)*
Tankauto *n* tank truck, [road] tanker, road tank wag[g]on
Tankboden *m* tank bottom
Tankbodenparaffin *n (petrol)* tank-bottom wax
Tankbodenrückstände *mpl* tank bottoms
Tankbodenwachs *n (petrol)* tank-bottom wax
Tankdialysator *m* tank dialyser
Tankentwickler *m (phot)* tank developer
Tankentwicklung *f (phot)* tank development
Tanker *m s.* Tankschiff
Tankgärverfahren *n* bulk (charmat) process *(for producing sparkling wine)*
Tanklager *n* tank farm
Tankmischmethode *f* tank-mix method *(crop protection)*
Tankrückstandsparaffin *n*, **Tankrückstandswachs** *n (petrol)* tank-bottom wax
Tankschiff *n* tank ship, tanker
Tankschlamm *m* tank sludge
Tankwaage *f* weighing tank
Tankwagen *m* tank truck *(road)*; tank car (wagon) *(railway)*
Tannat *n* tannate *(salt or ester of tannic acid)*
tanniert *(dye)* tannin-mordanted
Tannin *n* tannic acid, gallotannic acid, gallotannin, tannin; *(broadly)* vegetable tannin *(any of a large number of substances used in leather tanning)*
~/eigentliches tannic acid proper
tanningebeizt *(dye)* tannin-mordanted
tanninhaltig tanniferous
Tanninlösung *f* tannic-acid solution, *(broadly)* tannin solution
Tanninreaktiv *n***/Weingärtners** Weingärtner solution *(for precipitating basic coal-tar dyes)*
Tannin-Solutizerverfahren *n* tannin-solutizer process *(for desulphurizing petroleum distillates)*
Tantal *n* Ta tantalum
Tantal(III)-bromid *n* tantalum(III) bromide, tantalum tribromide
Tantal(V)-bromid *n* tantalum(V) bromide, tantalum pentabromide
Tantalcarbid *n* tantalum carbide
Tantal(III)-chlorid *n* tantalum(III) chloride, tantalum trichloride
Tantal(V)-chlorid *n* tantalum(V) chloride, tantalum pentachloride
Tantal(V)-fluorid *n* tantalum(V) fluoride, tantalum pentafluoride
Tantal(V)-hydroxid *n* tantalum(V) hydroxide
Tantal(V)-oxid *n* tantalum(V) oxide, ditantalum pentaoxide, tantalum pentaoxide
Tantalpent[a]... *s.* Tantal(V)-...
Tantalsäure *f* tantalic acid
Tantaltri... *s.* Tantal(III)-...
Tapetenpapier *n* wall paper, hanging [paper]
Tapioka[stärke] *f* tapioca [starch] *(from Manihot utilissima Pohl)*
Tarelaidinsäure *f* petroselidic acid, tarelaidic acid, **trans*-octadec-6-enoic acid
tarieren to tare
Taririnsäure *f* tariric acid, *octadec-6-ynoic acid
Taroxylsäure *f* taroxylic acid, *6,7-dioxo-octadecanoic acid
Tartramid *n* tartramide
Tartramidsäure *f* tartramidic acid, tartaric monoamide
Tartranilsäure *f* tartranilic acid, tartaric monoanilide
Tartrat *n* tartrate *(salt or ester of tartaric acid)*
Tartratkomplex *m* tartrato complex
Tartrazin *n* tartrazine, hydrazine yellow *(a pyrazole derivative)*
Tartronsäure *f* tartronic acid
Tartronylharnstoff *m* tartronylurea, dialuric acid, 5-hydroxybarbituric acid
Tasche *f (pap)* pocket *(of a pulpwood grinder)*
Taschenspektroskop *n* pocket spectroscope
Tassendrehmaschine *f (ceram)* cup jolley
Tassengarniermaschine *f (ceram)* cup-handling machine

Tastpolarographie *f* tast polarography
tato, Tato *(Tagestonnen) s.* Tonnen je Tag
taub *(mine)* barren, dead
tauchaluminieren to dip-aluminize
Tauchanlage *f* dipping plant
Tauchapparat *m* dipping machine (apparatus)
Tauchartikel *mpl* dipped goods (articles)
Tauchbad *n* dipping bath, *(agric also)* dip
Tauchbehälter *m* dip[ping] tank
Tauchbeschichtung *f* dip coating
Tauchbeschichtungseinrichtung *f* dip coater
Tauchblattfilter *n* open-tank leaf filter
Tauchbleiche *f (tann)* dip bleaching
Tauchbottich *m* dip[ping] tank
Tauchbrenner *m* submerged burner, submerged combustion burner (heater)
Tauchbütte *f (pap)* dipping (working) vat, vat of pulp
Tauchdauer *f* dipping time
Tauchelektrode *f* immersion electrode, dipping (dipped) electrode
Tauchemaillieren *n* dip enamelling
tauchen to immerse, to immerge, to plunge, *(for a short time:)* to dip, *(totally:)* to submerge
Tauchen *n* immersion, plunge, *(for a short time:)* dip[ping], *(totally:)* submergence
~ **in Lösungen** *(plast)* solvent moulding
~ **mit heißen Formen** *(rubber)* hot former dipping
~ **mit Koagulationsmitteln** coagulant dipping
~ **von Hand** *(ceram)* hand dipping
Tauchfärbemaschine *f* dip-dyeing machine
tauchfärben to dip-dye
Tauchfilter *n* open-tank leaf filter
Tauchform *f* dipping form, *(rubber also)* former
~/graphit[is]ierte *(glass)* paste mould
Tauchgefäß *n* dip[ping] tank
Tauchgestell *n* dipping rack
Tauchglasieren *n* dip glazing
Tauchglasiermaschine *f* dip-glazing machine
Tauchgummiwaren *fpl* dipped goods (articles)
tauchhärten to dip-harden
Tauchkolben *m* plunger, ram
Tauchkolbenpumpe *f* plunger (ram) pump
Tauchkolorimeter *n* immersion colorimeter
Tauchkühler *m* pond cooler
Tauchlack *m* dipping varnish
Tauchlackieren *n* dip painting (coating), dipping
~/elektrophoretisches electrophoretic coating (painting, dipping), electrocoating, electropainting
Tauchlösung *f* dipping solution
Tauchmischung *f* dipping compound, dip mix
tauchpatentieren to dip-patent *(wire)*
Tauchpresse *f* steeping press
Tauchprüfung *f* total immersion test *(corrosion testing)*
Tauchpumpe *f* wet-pit pump
Tauchrohrkondensator *m*, **Tauchrohrverflüssiger** *m* submerged-coil condenser
Tauchrüttler *m* immersion (poker) vibrator
Tauchschicht *f* dip coat
Tauchsieder *m* immersion heater
Tauchstrahlbegasung *f*, **Tauchstrahlbelüftung** *f (hyd)* bioaeration
Tauchstreichmaschine *f (pap)* dip coater
Tauchtank *m* dip[ping] tank
Tauchtest *m s.* Tauchprüfung
Tauchtiefe *f* submergence
Tauchtränkung *f* steeping
Tauchtropfkörper *m (hyd)* disk-type trickling filter, rotating biological contactor (disks), RBC unit, rotating-disk biofilter (contactor)
Tauchüberzugseinrichtung *f s.* Tauchbeschichtungseinrichtung
tauchveraluminieren to dip-aluminize
tauchverbleien to lead-dip
Tauchverbrennung *f* submerged combustion
Tauchverfahren *n* dipping method (process); *(agric)* immersion (pickling) method
Tauchversuch *m* [total] immersion test, full-immersion test *(corrosion testing)*
Tauchwalze *f* dipping (immersion) roll, *(pap also)* size (fountain) roll
Tauchwalzentrockner *m* dip-feed drum dryer
Tauchwanne *f* dip[ping] tank
Tauchwaren *fpl (rubber)* dipped goods (articles)
Tauchzeit *f s.* Tauchdauer
tauen to thaw
Tauen[pack]papier *n* rope wrapping (brown)
Taukurve *f*, **Taulinie** *f (distil)* dew-point curve, condensation curve
Taumelscheibenzähler *m* disk (nutating-piston) meter
Taupunkt *m* dew point, saturation temperature
Taupunkthygrometer *n* dew point hygrometer
Taupunktsmethode *f (phys ch)* dew-point method
Taurocarbamidsäure *f* taurocarbamic acid, 2-ureidoethane-1-sulphonic acid
Taurocholsäure *f (bioch)* taurocholic acid
Tauröste *f*, **Taurotte** *f (text)* dew-ret[ting]
tautomer tautomeric
Tautomer[e] *n* tautomer[ide], dynamic isomer
Tautomerengleichgewicht *n* tautomeric equilibrium
Tautomerenkonstante *f* tautomerization constant
Tautomerie *f* tautomerism, tautomery, dynamic isomerism
~/cyclisch-offene *s.* Ring-Ketten-Tautomerie
Tautomeriegleichgewicht *n* tautomeric equilibrium
Tautomeriekonstante *f* tautomerization constant
tautomerisieren to tautomerize
Tautomerisierung *f* tautomerization
TBA *s.* 1. Trichlorbenzoesäure; 2. Thiobarbitursäure
TCA *s.* Trichlorethansäure
TCC *s.* Tricarbonsäurezyklus
TCC-Verfahren *n (petrol)* Thermofor [catalytic-cracking] process, TCC process *(with moving catalyst)*

TCDD *n*, **2,3,7,8-TCDD** *n s.* 2,3,7,8-Tetrachlordibenzo-1,4-dioxin
TC-Kautschuk *m* technically classified rubber, T.C. rubber
TCP-Verfahren *n (petrol)* Thermofor continuous-percolation process
Technetat(VII) *n* M^ITcO_4 pertechnetate, pertechnate
Technetium *n* Tc technetium
Technetium(VII)-säure *f* pertechnetic acid
Technik *f* 1. engineering *(branch of science)*; 2. technology *(totality of means employed in the production of material goods)*; 3. technique, procedure, method *(manner of performing technical details, esp in the laboratory)*
~/absteigende *(chromat)* descending technique
~/aufsteigende *(chromat)* ascending technique
~/chemische chemical engineering
~ der Probenahme sampling technique
~/mikroskopische microscopic technique, microtechnique, micrology
Techniker *m* technologist, technician
technisch durchführbar feasible, practicable
~ rein technical
Technologie *f* technology *(1. of the manufacture of specified products; 2. branch of science)*
~/chemische chemical technology
~ der Abwasserbehandlung (Abwasserreinigung) waste-water technology
~ der Kunststoffe (Plaste) plastics technology
~/organisch-chemische organic-chemical technology
~/petrolchemische petrochemical technology
~/pharmazeutische pharmaceutical technology
Teegerbstoff *m* tea tannin
Teelöffel *m*:
• **einen ~ voll** a teaspoonful, tsp, tspn • **einen gestrichenen ~ voll** a level teaspoon
Teeöl *n* tea[seed] oil
~/ätherisches tea oil *(obtained from black tea)*
Teer *m* tar
~/destillierter (präparierter) distilled (prepared) tar
~/schwedischer *s.* ~/Stockholmer
~/Stockholmer Stockholm tar *(a pine tar)*
Teerabscheider *m* tar separator (extractor), detarrer
~/elektrostatischer electrostatic tar filter
Teerabscheidung *f* tar separation
teerartig tarry
Teerausbeute *f* tar yield
Teerbase *f* tar base
Teerbestandteil *m* tar component
Teercresol *n* coal-tar-derived cresylic acid *(a mixture of o-, m-, and p-cresol and other phenolic compounds)*
Teerdachpappe *f* tarred (asphaltic) felt, tar[red] board
Teerdampf *m* tar vapour
Teerdestillation *f* tar distillation
Teer-Elektrofilter *n* electrostatic tar filter
teeren to tar
Teerentfernung *f* detarring, tar separation
Teererzeugnis *n* tar product
Teerfarbe *f s.* Teerfarbstoff
Teerfarbstoff *m* coal-tar dye[stuff], *(Am also)* coal-tar color
Teerfilter *n* tar filter
Teerfraktion *f* tar fraction
teerfrei tarfree
Teerhydrierung *f* tar hydrogenation
teerig tarry
Teerindustrie *f* tar industry
Teerinhaltsstoff *m* tar component
Teerkresol *n s.* Teercresol
Teernebel *m* tar mist
Teeröl *n* tar oil
Teerpapier *n* tarred [brown] paper, tar (asphalt, pitch) paper
Teerpech *n* tar pitch
Teersand *m* tar sand
Teersäure *f* tar acid
Teerscheider *m s.* Teerabscheider
Teerscheidung *f s.* Teerabscheidung
Teerverarbeitung *f* tar processing
Teerwäscher *m* tar scrubber
Teesamenöl *n* teaseed oil
Teich *m s.* Abwasserteich
Teichonsäure *f (bioch)* teichoic acid
Teichreinigung *f (hyd)* pond treatment, ponding, lagooning *(of waste water)*
Teig *m (tech)* dough, paste; *(food)* dough
teigartig dough-like, doughy
teigig dough-like, doughy
Teigkneter *m*, **Teigknetmaschine** *f* dough kneader (mixer), dough kneading (mixing) machine
Teiglockerungsmittel *n s.* Teigtriebmittel
Teigmischer *m*, **Teigmischmaschine** *f s.* Teigkneter
Teigtriebmittel *n (food)* leaven, leavening [agent]
Teigwaren *pl* pasta products
Teil *m* 1. part, portion *(as of bulk material)*, *(esp relating to approximately equal quantities:)* moiety; 2. section *(as of an industrial plant)*
~/aliquoter aliquot [part, portion]
~/durchhängender *(phot)* region of underexposure, toe, foot *(of the characteristic curve)*
~/geradliniger *(phot)* region of correct (normal) exposure, straight[-line] portion, straight line *(of the characteristic curve)*
Teil *n* part
~/grünes green compact *(in powder metallurgy)*
Teilanalyse *f* partial analysis
Teilbande *f (spectr)* sub-band
Teilchen *n* particle
~/energiereiches high-energy particle
~/materielles material particle, particle of matter
~/seltsames *(nucl)* strange particle
α-Teilchen *n* alpha particle, α-particle

β-Teilchen *n* beta particle, β-particle
Teilchen *npl* **/suspendierte** suspended particles, particulates, particulate matter
Teilchenaggregat *n* particle (particulate) aggregate
Teilchenbahn *f s.* Teilchenflugbahn
Teilchenbeschleuniger *m* particle accelerator
~/linearer linear accelerator
Teilchenbeschleunigung *f* particle acceleration
Teilchendichte *f* particle (number) density *(number of particles per unit volume)*
Teilchenenergie *f* particle energy
Teilchenerzeugung *f* particle production
Teilchenfestigkeit *f* particle strength
Teilchenflugbahn *f* particle trajectory, path of the particle
Teilchenfluß *m* flux
Teilchenform *f* particle shape
Teilchengeschwindigkeit *f* particle velocity
Teilchengröße *f* particle size, *(screen classification also)* screen size
Teilchengrößenbereich *m* range of particle sizes, particle-size range, *(screen classification also)* range of screen sizes
Teilchengrößenbestimmung *f* particle size determination
Teilchengrößenverteilung *f* particle-size distribution
Teilchenkollision *f* particle collision
Teilchenladung *f* particle charge
Teilchenstrahlung *f* corpuscular (particle) radiation
Teilchenstruktur *f* particle structure
Teilchenverteilung *f* distribution of particles
Teilchenwachstum *n (hyd)* particle growth
Teilchenzusammenstoß *m* particle collision
Teildampfdruck *m* partial vapour pressure
Teildruck *m* partial pressure
Teile *mpl* **je hundert Millionen Teile** parts per hundred million, pphm
~ je Million Teile parts per million, ppm
~ je tausend Teile parts per thousand, ppt
teilen/in Grade to graduate
Teilenthärtung *f (hyd)* partial lime softening
Teilentsalzung *f* **im Teilstromverfahren** *(hyd)* split-stream dealkalization (dealkalizing)
Teilentsalzungsanlage *f (hyd)* dealkalizer
~ in Teilstromschaltung split-stream dealkalizer
Teilentstaubungsgrad *m* fractional[-weight collection] efficiency *(classifying)*
Teilentwässerung *f* partial dehydration; *(hyd)* partial dewatering
Teilerverhältnis *n* splitter ratio *(gas chromatography)*
Teilfäserchen *n (text)* fibril[la]
Teilfuge *f* [mould-]parting line
Teilkondensation *f* partial condensation, dephlegmation
~/geschlossene (integrale) equilibrium partial condensation
Teilkondensator *m (distil)* [countercurrent] partial condenser, partial-condensation head
Teilkreis *m* divided circle *(as of a refractometer)*
Teilladung *f* partial (fractional) charge
teilnehmen to participate *(as in a reaction)*
Teilordnung *f* partial order [of reaction], individual order
Teilpipette *f* graduated (measuring) pipette
Teilprobe *f (anal)* sub-sample
Teilreaktion *f* partial reaction, half-reaction
Teilreinigung *f* partial purification (treatment) *(of waste water)*
Teilröstung *f (met)* partial roasting
Teilschritt *m* individual step *(of a reaction)*
Teilstrahlungspyrometer *n* [partial-]radiation pyrometer
Teilstrich *m* graduation (division) mark (line), graduation, division
Teilstrichabstand *m* [scale] division
Teilstrom *m* 1. *(el ch)* partial current; 2. *(hyd)* split stream
Teilstromdichte *f (el ch)* partial current density
Teilstrombehandlung *f (hyd)* split treatment
Teilstromprobengeber *m (chromat)* by-pass injector
Teilstromschaltung *f (hyd)* split-stream system *(ion exchange)*
Teilstromverfahren *n s.* Teilstrombehandlung
Teilstromzelle *f (chromat)* two-channel katharometer
Teiltrocknung *f (food)* partial dehydration
Teilungsbild *n* graduation *(as on a measuring vessel)*
Teilungsebene *f (cryst)* cleavage (parting) plane
Teilverbrennung *f* partial combustion
Teilwiderstand *m* partial resistance
Tein *n* caffeine, theine, 1,3,7-trimethylxanthine
T-Einheit *f* trifunctional unit, T unit *(for building up polymers)*
Teinochemie *f* teinochemistry
Tektochinon *n* tectoquinone, 2-methylanthraquinone
Tektosilicat *n (min)* tectosilicate *(any of a class of polymeric silicates)*
tele-Substitution *f (org ch)* tele-substitution
TEL-Fluid *n* ethyl fluid *(an antiknock additive mainly consisting of tetraethyllead)*
Telinit *m* tel[l]inite *(a coal maceral)*
Teller *m (tech)* disk, plate; disk *(of a valve)*; *(lab)* table support *(for stands)*
Telleraufgabegerät *n*, **Telleraufgeber** *m s.* Tellerspeiser
Tellerbrecher *m* disk crusher
Tellerdrehmaschine *f (ceram)* plate-jiggering machine
Tellergaswäscher *m s.* Tellerwäscher
Tellerkneter *m* [rotary] kneading table
Tellermesser *n (pap)* disk knife, slitter
Tellermühle *f* disk [attrition] mill, disk grinder
Teller-Redlich-Regel *f (spectr)* Teller-Redlich product rule

Tellersatz *m* disk stack *(of a centrifuge)*
Tellerschleuder *f s.* Tellerzentrifuge
Teller-Sedimentierzentrifuge *f* disk-bowl solid-wall centrifuge
Tellerseparator *m s.* Tellerzentrifuge
Tellerspeiser *m* [revolving-]disk feeder, rotary-table (rotary-plate) feeder
Tellertrockner *m* disk dryer
Tellertrommel *f* disk [centrifuge] bowl
Tellerventil *n* disk valve
~/pilzförmiges mushroom-seated valve
Tellerwäscher *m* plate scrubber *(gas cleaning)*
~ **nach Theisen** Theisen disintegrator
Tellerzentrifuge *f* disk [bowl] centrifuge, *(food also)* disk separator
~ **mit Düsenaustrag** nozzle-discharge disk centrifuge, disk-nozzle centrifuge
~ **mit Schlitzaustrag** annular solids-discharge disk centrifuge
Tellerzuteiler *m s.* Tellerspeiser
Tellur *n* Te tellurium
Tellurat *n* tellurate
Tellurblei *n (min)* altaite *(lead telluride)*
Tellur(II)-bromid *n* tellurium(II) bromide, tellurium dibromide
Tellur(IV)-bromid *n* tellurium(IV) bromide, tellurium tetrabromide
Tellur(II)-chlorid *n* tellurium(II) chloride, tellurium dichloride
Tellur(IV)-chlorid *n* tellurium(IV) chloride, tellurium tetrachloride
Tellurdibromid *n s.* Tellur(II)-bromid
Tellurdichlorid *n s.* Tellur(II)-chlorid
Tellurdioxid *n s.* Tellur(IV)-oxid
Tellur(VI)-fluorid *n* tellurium(VI) fluoride, tellurium hexafluoride
Tellurhexafluorid *n s.* Tellur(VI)-fluorid
Tellurhydrid *n s.* Tellurwasserstoff
Tellurid *n* M^I_2Te telluride
Tellur(IV)-iodid *n* tellurium(IV) iodide, tellurium tetraiodide
Tellurit *m (min)* tellurite, telluric ochre *(tellurium(IV) oxide)*
Tellurit *n* $M^I_2TeO_3$ tellurite
Tellurmonoxid *n s.* Tellur(II)-oxid
Tellurnickel *n (min)* melonite *(nickel telluride)*
Tellurocker *m s.* Tellurit
Telluronium-Ion *n* telluronium ion
Telluroniumverbindung *f* telluronium compound
Tellur(II)-oxid *n* tellurium(II) oxide, tellurium monoxide
Tellur(IV)-oxid *n* tellurium(IV) oxide, tellurium dioxide
Tellur(VI)-oxid *n* tellurium(VI) oxide, tellurium trioxide
Tellursäure *f* orthotelluric acid, telluric acid, hexaoxotelluric acid
Tellurtetra... *s.* Tellur(IV)-...
Tellurtrioxid *n s.* Tellur(VI)-oxid
Tellurwasserstoff *m* hydrogen telluride, tellurium hydride
Telogen *n* telogen *(agent for controlling the degree of polymerization)*
Telomer[e] *n*, **Telomerisat** *n* telomer
Telomerisation *f (org ch)* telomerization
Telsmith-Kegelbrecher *m* Telsmith cone crusher
Telsmith-Kreiselbrecher *m* Telsmith gyratory crusher, Telsmith breaker
Temperafarbe *f* tempera paint
Temperatur *f*:
~/absolute *s.* ~/thermodynamische
~/charakteristische characteristic (Debye) temperature
~ **der Phasenumwandlung** first-order transition temperature
~/erhöhte elevated temperature
~/eutektische eutectic temperature
~/gewöhnliche normal (ordinary) temperature
~/isokinetische isokinetic temperature
~/kritische critical temperature
~/potentielle potential temperature
~/thermodynamische thermodynamic (absolute) temperature
Θ-Temperatur *f* Flory theta temperature
Temperaturabfall *m* temperature drop
temperaturabhängig temperature-dependent
Temperaturabhängigkeit *f* temperature dependence
Temperaturänderung *f* temperature change, change in temperature
~/schroffe thermal shock
Temperaturanregung *f* thermal excitation
Temperaturanstieg *m* rise (increase) in temperature
Temperaturausgleich *m* temperature equalization (compensation)
Temperaturbeiwert *m* temperature coefficient
Temperaturbereich *m* temperature range, range of temperatures
temperaturbeständig temperature-resistant, temperature-resisting, temperature-stable
Temperaturbeständigkeit *f* temperature resistance (stability)
Temperaturdifferenz *f* temperature difference
~/mittlere logarithmische logarithmic mean temperature difference, LMTD
~/ortsveränderliche overall local temperature difference
temperaturempfindlich temperature-sensitive
Temperaturempfindlichkeit *f* temperature sensitivity
Temperatur-Entropie-Diagramm *n* [temperature-] entropy chart, entropy diagram
Temperaturentwicklung *f s.* Wärmeentwicklung
Temperaturerhöhung *f* temperature raising; rise (increase) in temperature
Temperaturgefälle *n* temperature gradient
Temperaturgleichgewicht *n* temperature equilibrium

Temperaturgrad *m* degree of temperature
Temperaturgradient *m* temperature gradient; [temperature] lapse rate *(in the atmosphere)*
~/adiabatischer vertikaler adiabatic [temperature] lapse rate *(in the atmosphere)*
~/trockenadiabatischer vertikaler dry adiabatic lapse rate *(in the atmosphere)*
~/vertikaler temperature lapse rate *(in the atmosphere)*
Temperaturgrenze *f* temperature limit
Temperaturinversion *f* temperature inversion
~/bodennahe ground level inversion
Temperaturkoeffizient *m* temperature coefficient
~ der Viskosität (Zähigkeit) viscosity-temperature coefficient
Temperaturkompensation *f* temperature compensation
Temperaturleitfähigkeit *f s.* Temperaturleitkoeffizient
Temperaturleitkoeffizient *m*, **Temperaturleitzahl** *f* [thermal] diffusivity, thermometric conductivity
Temperaturmeßfarbe *f* temperature-indicating paint
Temperaturmeßfarbstift *m* temperature crayon
Temperaturmessung *f* temperature measurement, thermometry
Temperaturprofil *n* temperature profile
Temperaturprogrammierung *f* temperature programming
Temperaturregelung *f* temperature control
Temperaturregler *m*, **Temperaturregulator** *m* temperature controller, thermoregulator, thermostat
Temperaturschreiber *m* temperature recorder, thermograph
Temperaturschwankung *f* temperature fluctuation
Temperaturskala *f* temperature scale
~/absolute *s.* ~/thermodynamische
~/ideale gasthermometrische perfect gas temperature scale
~/thermodynamische absolute (thermodynamic) temperature scale
Temperatursprung *m* temperature jump, T-jump
Temperatursprungschicht *f (hyd)* thermocline
temperaturstabil *s.* temperaturbeständig
Temperatursteigerung *f* increase of temperature
Temperaturstift *m* temperature crayon
Temperaturumkehr *f s.* Temperaturinversion
temperaturunabhängig temperature-independent
Temperaturunabhängigkeit *f* temperature independence
Temperaturunterschied *m* temperature difference
Temperaturwechsel *m*[**/schroffer**] thermal shock
temperaturwechselbeständig thermal-shock resistant
Temperaturwechselbeständigkeit *f* thermal-shock resistance, *(ceram also)* [thermal] spalling resistance, thermal stability (endurance)
Temperaturwechsler *m s.* Wärmeübertrager
Temperguß *m* malleable [cast] iron
Temperierbad *n* [constant-]temperature bath
temperieren to temper *(margarine making)*; to bring to *or* to keep at a specified temperature, *(esp)* to thermostat
Temperiergefäß *n*, **Temperierkessel** *m* tempering tank (vat) *(margarine making)*
tempern to malleabl[e]ize, to anneal *(cast iron)*; *(plast)* to anneal, to temper; *(glass)* to anneal
Tenderisierung *f (food)* meat tenderization
Tenderizer *m (food)* meat tenderizer
Tennenmälzerei *f*, **Tennenvermälzung** *f (ferm)* floor malting, flooring
Tensammetrie *f (el ch)* tensammetry
tensammetrisch *(el ch)* tensammetric
Tensid *n* surfactant, surface-active agent
~/amphoteres amphoteric surfactant
~/anionisches anionic surfactant
~/kationisches cationic surfactant
~/nichtionogenes non-ionic [surfactant]
Tensionsthermometer *n* vapour-pressure thermometer
Tensometer *n* extensometer *(materials testing)*
TEPP *s.* Tetraethylpyrophosphat
Teratolith *m (min)* teratolite *(a blue bole)*
Terbinerde *f s.* Terbiumoxid
Terbium *n* Tb terbium
Terbiumchlorid *n* terbium chloride
Terbiumfluorid *n* terbium fluoride
Terbiumnitrat *n* terbium nitrate
Terbiumoxid *n* terbium oxide
Terbiumsulfat *n* terbium sulphate
Terebinsäure *f* terebic acid, 2,2-dimethyl-5-oxo-oxolan-3-carboxylic acid
Terephthalsäure *f* terephthalic acid, TPA, *p*-phthalic acid, benzene-1,4-dicarboxylic acid
Teri *pl (tann)* teri pods *(from Caesalpinia digyna Rottl.)*
Term *m (phys ch)* term [value], energy level
~/fester (konstanter) constant term
~/variabler variable (current) term
Termbezeichnung *f s.* Termsymbol
Termdiagramm *n* energy[-level] diagram, level scheme (diagram)
Termdifferenz *f* term difference
terminal terminal
Terminationscodon *n (bioch)* termination codon, terminator (chain-terminating) codon
termolekular termolecular, trimolecular
Termschema *n s.* Termdiagramm
Termserie *f (spectr)* term series
Termsymbol *n* term symbol
~ eines Atoms atomic term symbol
Termsystem *n* term system
Termwert *m s.* Term
ternär ternary
Ternärkomplex *m* ternary (central) complex *(enzyme kinetics)*
Terpen *n* terpene, *(broadly)* terpenoid

Terpenalkaloid *n* terpenoid alkaloid
Terpenalkohol *m* terpene alcohol
Terpenharz *n* terpene resin
Terpenkohlenwasserstoff *m* terpenoid hydrocarbon, terpene
Terpenoid *n* terpenoid
Terpentin *n* turpentine [oleoresin] *(balsam obtained from coniferous trees)*
~/kanadisches Canada turpentine *(from Abies balsamea (L.) Mill.)*
Terpentinersatz *m* turpentine substitute
Terpentinessenz *f s.* Harzessenz
Terpentingallen *fpl (dye)* turpentine (carob) galls *(from Pistacia terebinthus L.)*
Terpentinharz *n* rosin, colophony, pine resin (rosin)
Terpentinharzöl *n* rosin oil, rosinol *(by fractional distillation of rosin)*
Terpentinöl *n* oil (spirit) of turpentine
Terpentinölersatz *m*, **Terpentinölsurrogat** *n* turpentine substitute
Terpenverbindung *f* terpenoid
Terpenylsäure *f* terpenylic acid, 2,2-dimethyl-5-oxo-oxolan-3-acetic acid
Terphenyl *n* terphenyl, diphenylbenzene, *(specif)* 1,4-diphenylbenzene
Terpin *n* terpin *(a cyclohexanol derivative)*
Terpinen *n (org ch)* terpinene
Terpineol *n* terpineol *(any of three isomeric terpene alcohols)*
Terpinolen *n* terpinolene, 4-isopropylidene-1-methylcyclohexane
Terpolymer[e] *n* terpolymer
Terra rossa *f (ceram)* terra rossa
Terra sigillata *f (ceram)* terra sigillata
Terrakotta *f (ceram)* terra cotta
Terreinsäure *f* terreic acid *(a benzoquinone derivative)*
tertiär tertiary
Tertiärluft *f* tertiary air
Tertiärstruktur *f (bioch)* tertiary structure
Tesla-Funken *m (spectr)* Tesla discharge
Test... *s. a.* Prüf...
testen *s.* prüfen
Testkohle *f* standard coal
Testorganismus *m* test organism
Testosteron *n* testosterone, 17β-hydroxyandrost-4-en-3-one *(a sex hormone)*
Testriol *n* testriol, chimyl alcohol, 2,3-dihydroxypropyl hexadecyl ether
Tetanusserum *n* antitetanus serum
tetartoedrisch *(cryst)* tetartohedral
Tetra *m s.* Tetrachlorkohlenstoff
Tetraacetat *n* tetraacetate
Tetraarsentetrasulfid *n* tetraarsenic tetrasulphide
Tetraäthyl... *s.* Tetraethyl...
Tetrabasizität *f* tetrabasicity *(of acids)*
Tetraboran *n* tetraborane
Tetraborat *n* $M^I_2B_4O_7$ tetraborate, heptaoxotetraborate
Tetraborid *n* tetraboride
Tetraborsäure *f* tetraboric acid, heptaoxotetraboric acid
Tetrabromfluorescein *n* tetrabromofluorescein, eosin
Tetrabromid *n* tetrabromide
Tetrabromindigo *m(n)* tetrabromoindigo
Tetrabromkohlenstoff *m*, **Tetrabrommethan** *n* carbon tetrabromide, *tetrabromomethane, perbromomethane
Tetrabromoborat *n* tetrabromoborate
Tetrabromogold(III)-säure *f* tetrabromoauric(III) acid, bromoauric acid
Tetrabromoplatinat(II) *n* $M^I_2[PtBr_4]$ tetrabromoplatinate(II), bromoplatinate(II)
Tetrabromoplatin(II)-säure *f* tetrabromoplatinic(II) acid, bromoplatinic(II) acid
Tetrabromphenolsulfonphthalein *n* tetrabromophenolsulphonephthalein, bromophenol blue *(a pH indicator)*
Tetrabromphthalsäureanhydrid *n* tetrabromophthalic anhydride
Tetrabromsilan *n* tetrabromosilane
Tetracain *n* *decicaine, tetracaine *(hydrochloride of 2-dimethylaminoethyl p-butylaminobenzoate)*
Tetracarboximidfarbstoff *m* tetracarboxyimide dye
Tetracen *n* naphthacene, 2,3-benzanthracene, *(deprecated:)* tetracene
Tetrachloranthrachinon *n* tetrachloroanthraquinone
Tetrachlor-*p*-benzochinon *n* tetrachloro-*p*-benzoquinone, tetrachloroquinone, chloranil
2,3,7,8-Tetrachlordibenzo-1,4-dioxin *n* 2,3,7,8-tetrachlorodibenzo-1,4-dioxin, 2,3,7,8-tetrachlorodibenzo-*p*-dioxin, 2,3,7,8-TCDD, TCDD, dioxin
1,1,2,2-Tetrachlorethan *n*, ***sym*-Tetrachlorethan** *n* 1,1,2,2-tetrachloroethane
Tetrachlorethen *n*, **Tetrachlorethylen** *n* tetrachloroethylene, perchloroethylene
Tetrachlorid *n* tetrachloride
Tetrachlorkohlenstoff *m*, **Tetrachlormethan** *n* carbon tetrachloride, *tetrachloromethane, perchloromethane
Tetrachloroborat *n* tetrachloroborate
Tetrachlorodiamminplatin(IV) *n* diamminetetrachloroplatinum(IV)
Tetrachlorodioxin *n s.* 2,3,7,8-Tetrachlorodibenzo-1,4-dioxin
Tetrachlorogold(III)-säure *f* tetrachloroauric(III) acid, chloroauric(III) acid
Tetrachloropalladat(II) *n* $M^I_2[PdCl_4]$ tetrachloropalladate(II), chloropalladate(II)
Tetrachloroplatinat(II) *n* $M^I_2[PtCl4]$ tetrachloroplatinate(II), chloroplatinate(II)
Tetrachlorsilan *n* tetrachlorosilane
Tetracosansäure *f* tetracosanoic acid
Tetracyanethylierung *f* tetracyanoethylation

Tetracyanoaurat(III) *n* $M^I[Au(CN)_4]$ tetracyanoaurate(III), cyanoaurate(III)
Tetracyanoplatinat(II) *n* $M^I_2[Pt(CN)_4]$ tetracyanoplatinate(II), cyanoplatinate(II)
Tetradecanal *n* *tetradecanal, tetradecylaldehyde, myristaldehyde
Tetradecan-1-ol *n*, **1-Tetradecanol** *n* *tetradecan-1-ol, myristyl alcohol
Tetradecansäure *f* tetradecanoic acid
Tetradecensäure *f* tetradecenoic acid
Tetraeder *n (cryst)* tetrahedron
Tetraederanordnung *f* tetrahedral arrangement (orientation)
Tetraederorbital *n* tetrahedral orbital
tetraedrisch tetrahedral
Tetraedrit *m (min)* tetrahedrite, grey copper [ore], fahlerz, fahlore *(a sulphide of copper and antimony often containing zinc)*
Tetraen *n (org ch)* tetraene
Tetraethylblei *n* tetraethyl lead, TEL • **mit ~ versetzen** to lead *(motor fuel)*
Tetraethylpyrophosphat *n* tetraethylpyrophosphate, TEPP, *tetraethyldiphosphate
Tetraethylsilan *n* tetraethylsilane
Tetraethylthiuramdisulfid *n* tetraethylthiuram disulphide, disulphiram
Tetrafluorethen *n*, **Tetrafluorethylen** *n* tetrafluoroethylene, TFE, perfluoroethylene
Tetrafluorid *n* tetrafluoride
Tetrafluoroborsäure *f* tetrafluoroboric acid
Tetrafluorsilan *n* tetrafluorosilane
tetrafunktionell tetrafunctional
tetragonal *(cryst)* tetragonal
Tetrahalogenid *n* *tetrahalide, *tetrahalogenide
Tetrahydrat *n* tetrahydrate
Tetrahydrid *n* tetrahydride
Tetrahydridoborat *n* $M^I[BH_4]$ tetrahydridoborate
Tetrahydrobenzen *n*, **Tetrahydrobenzol** *n* tetrahydrobenzene, cyclohexene
Tetrahydrofolsäure *f (bioch)* tetrahydrofolic acid
Tetrahydrofuran *n*, **Tetrahydrofurfuran** *n* tetrahydrofuran, THF
Tetrahydroisochinolin *n* tetrahydroisoquinoline
Tetrahydroisochinolinbase *f* tetrahydroisoquinoline base
Tetrahydronaphthalen *n* tetrahydronaphthalene
Tetrahydrothiophen *n* tetrahydrothiophene
Tetraiodid *n* tetraiodide
Tetraiodoaurat(III) *n* $M^I[AuI_4]$ tetraiodoaurate(III), iodoaurate(III)
Tetraiodomercurat(II) *n* $M^I_2[HgI_4]$ tetraiodomercurate(II), iodomercurate(II)
Tetraiodsilan *n* tetraiodosilane
Tetrakisazofarbstoff *m* tetrakisazo dye
Tetrakistri... *s.* Dodeca...
Tetralacton *n* tetralactone
Tetramer[e] *n* tetramer
Tetramethylarsin *n*, **Tetramethylbiarsyl** *n s.* Tetramethyldiarsin
Tetramethylblei *n* tetramethyl lead, TML
Tetramethyldiarsin *n* tetramethyldiarsine, cacodyl
Tetramethylen *n s.* Cyclobutan
Tetramethylendiamin *n* tetramethylenediamine, putrescine
Tetramethylenimin *n* pyrrolidine, tetramethyleneimine
Tetramethylenoxid *n s.* Tetrahydrofuran
Tetramethylensulfid *n s.* Tetrahydrothiophen
Tetramethylethylenglykol *n* tetramethylethylene glycol, *2,3-dimethylbutane-2,3-diol, pinacol
Tetramethylmethan *n* *2,2-dimethylpropane, neopentane, *(deprecated:)* tetramethylmethane
Tetramethylsilan *n* tetramethylsilane, TMS
Tetrammin *n* tetraammine
Tetramminkupfer(II)-sulfat *n* tetraamminecopper(II) sulphate, cupric tetraammine sulphate
Tetramminnickel(II)-nitrat *n* tetraamminenickel(II) nitrate
Tetramminpalladium(II)-chlorid *n* tetraamminepalladium(II) chloride
Tetramminsalz *n* tetraammine salt
tetramolekular tetramolecular, quadrimolecular
Tetramolybdat *n* tetramolybdate
Tetranatriumsalz *n* tetrasodium salt
Tetranitrid *n* tetranitride
Tetrapeptid *n* tetrapeptide
Tetraphosphor *m* white phosphorus
Tetraphosphorheptasulfid *n* tetraphosphorus heptasulphide, phosphorus heptasulphide
Tetraphosphormonoselenid *n* tetraphosphorus monoselenide
Tetraphosphorpentasulfid *n* tetraphosphorus pentasulphide
Tetraphosphortrisulfid *n* tetraphosphorus trisulphide
Tetrapyrrol *n (org ch)* tetrapyrrole
~/lineares linear tetrapyrrole
~/makrocyclisches macrocyclic tetrapyrrole
Tetraquoeisen(II)-Ion *n* $[Fe(H_2O)_4]^{2+}$ tetraaquairon(II) ion
Tetrarhodanid *n s.* Tetrathiocyanat
Tetrarsentetrasulfid *n* tetraarsenic tetrasulphide
Tetraschwefeltetranitrid *n* tetrasulphur tetranitride
Tetraselentetranitrid *n* tetraselenium tetranitride, selenium nitride
Tetrasilan *n* tetrasilane
Tetrasiloxan *n* tetrasiloxane
tetrasubstituiert tetrasubstituted
Tetrasubstitution *f* tetrasubstitution
Tetrasubstitutionsprodukt *n* tetrasubstitution product
Tetrasulfan *n* tetrasulphane, hydrogen tetrasulphide
Tetrasulfid *n* tetrasulphide
Tetraterpen *n (bioch)* tetraterpene
Tetraterpenoid *n (bioch)* tetraterpenoid
Tetrathiocyanat *n* tetrathiocyanate
Tetrathionat *n* $M^I_2S_4O_6$ tetrathionate

tetravalent tetravalent, quadrivalent, *(relating to molecules also)* tetraatomic
Tetravalenz *f* tetravalence, quadrivalence
Tetrazen *n* 1. tetrazene, 1-(5-tetrazolyl)-4-guanyltetrazene hydrate *(a primary explosive)*; 2. *s.* Tetracen
Tetrazin *n* tetrazine
Tetrazol *n* tetrazole
tetrazotieren *(dye)* to tetraazotize
Tetrazotierung *f (dye)* tetraazotization
Tetrazoverbindung *f* tetraazo compound
Tetrit *m s.* Tetritol
Tetritol *n* tetritol *(a tetrahydroxy alcohol derived from tetrose)*
Tetrose *f* tetrose *(monosaccharide containing four carbon atoms per molecule)*
Tetroxalat *n* tetraoxalate
Tetroxid *n* tetraoxide
Tetroxoiodat(VII) *n* M^IIO_4 tetraoxoiodate(VII), periodate, metaperiodate
Tetroxoiod(VII)-säure *f* tetraoxoiodic(VII) acid, periodic acid, metaperiodic acid
Tetroxokieselsäure *f* tetraoxosilicic acid, orthosilicic acid
Tetroxoosmat(VI) *n* $M^I_2OsO_4$ tetraoxoosmate(VI), osmate(VI)
Tetroxoplumbat(IV) *n* $M^I_4PbO_4$ tetraoxoplumbate(IV)
Tetroxorhenat(VII) *n* M^IReO_4 tetraoxorhenate(VII), perrhenate
Tetroxosilicat *n* $M^I_4SiO_4$ tetraoxosilicate, orthosilicate, silicate
Tetroxostannat(IV) *n* $M^I_4SnO_4$ tetraoxostannate(IV)
Tetroxotellurat(VI) *n* $M^I_2TeO_4$ tetraoxotellurate(VI)
Tetroxovanadat(V) *n* $M^I_3VO_4$ tetraoxovanadate(V)
Tetroxozinnsäure *f* tetraoxostannic acid
Teufelsdreck *m* asaf[o]etida, devil's dung, food of the gods *(gum resin from Ferula specc.)*
Texaco-Vergaser *m (coal)* Texaco [steam-oxygen suspension] gasifier
Textilausrüstung *f* textile finish
Textilchemie *f* textile chemistry
Textilchemiker *m* textile chemist
Textildruck *m* textile printing
Textileinlage *f* textile insertion (casing) *(as in rubber products)*
Textilerzeugnisse *npl* textiles
Textilfaser *f* textile fibre
Textilfaserstoff *m* textile fibre
Textilgewebe *n* fabric [cloth], tissue
Textilhilfsmittel *n* textile auxiliary
Textilien *pl* textiles
~/schaumstoffkaschierte foambacks
~/ungewebte non-woven textiles, non-wovens
Textilkunststoff *m* leathercloth
Textilöl *n* textile oil
Textilreinigungsmittel *n* textile cleanser
Textilschlichte *f* textile size
Textilverbundstoffe *mpl* non-woven textiles, nonwovens
Textilvered[e]lung *f* textile finishing
Textilveredlungsmittel *n* textile auxiliary
Textilzellstoff *m* rayon (dissolving) pulp
Textur *f* 1. texture; 2. *(ceram)* lamination *(a defect)*
texturieren *(text)* to texture, to bulk
Texturseide *f* textured (bulked) yarn
TFFF *s.* Thermo-Feld-Fluß-Fraktionierung
TG *s.* Trockengewicht
Thalenit *m (min)* thalenite *(yttrium disilicate)*
Thallium *m* Tl thallium
Thallium(I)-acetat *n* thallium(I) acetate, thallous acetate
Thallium(III)-acetat *n* thallium(III) acetate, thallic acetate
Thalliumalaun *m* thallium alum
Thallium(I)-chlorid *n* *thallium(I) chloride, thallium monochloride, thallous chloride
Thallium(III)-chlorid *n* *thallium(III) chloride, thallium trichloride, thallic chloride
Thallium(I)-cyanid *n* *thallium(I) cyanide, thallous cyanide
Thalliumhexachloroplatinat(IV) *n* thallium hexachloroplatinate(IV)
Thallium(I)-hydroxid *n* *thallium(I) hydroxide, thallous hydroxide
Thalliummono... *s.* Thallium(I)-...
Thallium(I)-nitrat *n* *thallium(I) nitrate, thallous nitrate
Thallium(III)-nitrat *n* *thallium(III) nitrate, thallic nitrate
Thallium(I)-orthophosphat *n* *thallium(I) orthophosphate, thallium(I) phosphate
Thallium(I)-oxid *n* *thallium(I) oxide, thallium monooxide, thallous oxide
Thallium(III)-oxid *n* *thallium(III) oxide, thallium trioxide, thallic oxide
Thallium(I)-sulfat *n* *thallium(I) sulphate, thallous sulphate
Thallium(III)-sulfat *n* *thallium(III) sulphate, thallic sulphate
Thallium(I)-sulfid *n* *thallium(I) sulphide, thallium monosulphide, thallous sulphide
Thalliumtri... *s.* Thallium(III)-...
Thein *n s.* Tein
Theisen-Desintegrator[wäscher] *m*, **Theisen-Wäscher** *m* Theisen disintegrator *(gas cleaning)*
Thelephorsäure *f* thelephoric acid *(a lichen acid)*
Thenardit *m (min)* thenardite *(sodium sulphate)*
Theobromin *n* theobromine, 2,6-dihydroxy-3,7-dimethylpurine *(alkaloid)*
Theobrominnatriumacetat *n*, **Theobromin-natrium-Natriumacetat** *n* theobromine sodium [and sodium] acetate
Theobrominnatrium-Natriumsalicylat *n*, **Theobrominnatriumsalicylat** *n* theobromine sodium [and sodium] salicylate
Theophyllin *n* theophylline, 2,6-dihydroxy-1,3-dimethylpurine *(alkaloid)*
Theophyllinnatriumacetat *n*, **Theophyllin-natrium-Natriumacetat** *n* theophylline sodium [and sodium] acetate

Theorell-Chance-Mechanismus *m (bioch)* Theorell-Chance enzyme mechanism
Theorem *n*/**Babinetsches** Babinet absorption rule
Theorie *f* theory • **etwas mehr als der ~ entspricht** in slight excess of theory
~ **der absoluten Reaktionsgeschwindigkeit** *s.* ~ des Übergangszustandes
~ **der Böden** plate theory *(as in distillation and chromatography)*
~ **der chemischen Bindung** chemical bond (valence) theory
~ **der Elektronenpaarbindungen** *s.* ~ der Valenzstrukturen
~ **der frei beweglichen Elektronen** free-electron theory
~ **der Molekülorbitale** molecular-orbital theory, Hund-Mulliken-Lennard-Jones-Hückel theory
~ **der Partialvalenzen** theory of partial valencies
~ **der spezifischen Wärme/Debyesche** Debye theory of specific heat
~ **der übereinstimmenden Zustände** *(phys ch)* theory of corresponding states
~ **der Valenzstrukturen** valence-bond (electron-pair) theory, VB theory, Heitler-London-Slater-Pauling theory, HLSP theory
~ **des aktivierten Komplexes** *s.* ~ des Übergangszustandes
~ **des Elektrons[/Diracsche]** Dirac [electron] theory
~ **des radioaktiven Zerfalls** theory of radioactive disintegration (decay)
~ **des Übergangszustandes** transition-state theory, activated-complex theory, absolute-[reaction-]rate theory
~/**dynamische** *(chromat)* kinetic (dynamic, rate) theory *(of band broadening)*
~/**Heitler-Londonsche** Heitler-London theory, HL theory *(of valency)*
~/**instruktive** template theory *(of antibody formation)*
~/**kinetische** 1. *(phys ch)* kinetic theory; 2. *s.* ~/dynamische
~/**molekular-statistische** *s.* ~/stochastische
~/**selektive** clonal theory *(of antibody formation)*
~ **spannungsfreier Ringe[/Sachse-Mohrsche]** Sachse-Mohr concept [of strainless rings]
~/**stochastische** *(chromat)* random-walk model
~/**Wernersche** Werner theory *(of coordination)*
~ **von Danckwerts** surface renewal theory *(of mass transfer)*
Therapeutikum *n* therapeutic agent
therapeutisch therapeutic[al]
Therapie *f*/**medikamentöse** pharmacotherapy
Thermalruß *m* thermal [carbon] black, furnace thermal black
Thermalspaltprozeß *m* [furnace] thermal process *(carbon-black manufacture)*
thermionisch thermionic
Thermisation *f (food)* thermization *(pasteurization at 68 °C to 72 °C for 1 to 40 s)*
thermisch thermal
Thermitverfahren *n* aluminothermic (thermite, Goldschmidt's) process, aluminothermics, aluminothermy
Thermoanalyse *f* thermal analysis, thermoanalysis, TA
Thermochemie *f* thermochemistry
Thermochemiker *m* thermochemist
thermochemisch thermochemical
thermochrom thermochromic
Thermochromie *f* thermochromism
Thermodiffusion *f* thermal diffusion, thermodiffusion
Thermodiffusionsverfahren *n* thermal-diffusion process
Thermodynamik *f* thermodynamics
~/**chemische** chemical thermodynamics
~ **der Nichtgleichgewichtsprozesse** *s.* ~ irreversibler Prozesse
~/**irreversible** *s.* ~ irreversibler Prozesse
~ **irreversibler Prozesse** thermodynamics of irreversible processes, non-equilibrium thermodynamics
~/**statistische** statistical thermodynamics
~/**technische** engineering thermodynamics
thermodynamisch thermodynamic[al]
Thermoelektrizität *f* thermoelectricity
Thermoelement *n* thermocouple
Thermoextraktion *f (anal)* vacuum hot extraction analysis
Thermo-Feld-Fluß-Fraktionierung *f* thermal field flow fractionation, TFFF
thermofixieren to heat-set
Thermofixierung *f* heat setting
Thermofor-Continuous-Percolation-Verfahren *n* Thermofor continuous-percolation process
Thermoformung *f (plast)* thermoforming
Thermofor-Verfahren *n* Thermofor [catalytic-cracking] process, TCC process
Thermogramm *n* thermogram
Thermograph *m* thermograph
Thermographie *f* thermography
thermographisch thermographic
Thermogravimetrie *f* thermogravimetry
~/**derivative** derivative (differential) thermogravimetry, DTG
thermogravimetrisch thermogravimetric
Thermoionisationsdetektor *m (anal)* thermionic detector
Thermokline *f (hyd)* thermocline
Thermokompression *f* thermocompression
Thermokompressor *m* thermocompressor
Thermokonvektion *f s.* Wärmekonvektion
thermolabil thermolabile, heat-labile
Thermolabilität *f* thermolability, thermal lability
Thermolumineszenz *f* thermoluminescence, thermal luminescence
Thermolyse *f* thermolysis
thermolytisch thermolytic

thermomechanisch thermomechanical
Thermometer *n*/**Beckmannsches** Beckmann thermometer
~/**feuchtes** wet-bulb thermometer
~/**trockenes** dry-bulb thermometer
Thermometerfehler *m* thermometer error
Thermometergefäß *n* thermometer bulb
Thermometerglas *n* thermometer glass
Thermometerrohr *n* thermometer tube (pipe)
Thermometerskale *f* thermometer (thermometric) scale
Thermometerstutzen *m* thermometer pocket
Thermometersubstanz *f* thermometric substance
Thermometrie *f* thermometry
thermometrisch thermometric[al]
thermonuklear thermonuclear
thermooxidativ thermal-oxidative
Thermopaar *n* thermocouple
~/**standardisiertes** standard thermocouple
thermophil thermophilic, thermophilous
Thermoplast *m* thermoplastic
~/**verstärkter** reinforced thermoplastic
thermoplastisch thermoplastic
Thermoplastizität *f* thermoplasticity
Thermoregulator *m* thermoregulator
thermoresistent thermoduric, heat-resistant *(microorganisms)*
Thermoresistenz *f* heat resistance *(of microorganisms)*
Thermosäule *m* thermopile *(for detecting photons)*
Thermoskop *n* thermoscope
Thermosol-Klotz-Dämpfverfahren *n (dye)* thermosol pad-steam process
Thermosolverfahren *n (dye)* thermosol method
Thermosphäre *f* thermosphere
thermostabil thermostable, heat-stable *(enzymes, vitamins)*
Thermostabilität *f* thermostability, heat stability *(of enzymes, vitamins)*
Thermostat *m* 1. *s.* Temperaturregler; 2. *(lab)* constant-temperature chamber, thermostat; [constant-]temperature bath
thermostat[is]ieren to thermostat
Thermostat[is]ierung *f* thermostatting
Thermoumformer *m* thermoelement
Thermovulkanisation *f* thermal vulcanization *(of synthetic polymers at temperatures > 190 °C)*
Thermowaage *f* thermobalance
Theta-Lösung *f* pseudoideal solution
Theta-Lösungsmittel *n* theta solvent
Theta-Temperatur *f* theta temperature
Theta-Zustand *m* theta state
Thiamin *n* thiamin[e], aneurin[e] *(vitamin* B_1*)*
Thiaminpyrophosphat *n* thiamine pyrophosphate, TPP, *thiamine diphosphate
Thianaphthen *n* thianaphthene, benzothiofuran
Thiaphen *n s.* Thiophen
Thiazinfarbstoff *m* thiazine dye
Thiazol *n (org ch)* thiazole
Thiazolbeschleuniger *m (rubber)* thiazole accelerator
Thiazolfarbstoff *m* thiazole dye
Thiazolgelb *n* thiazole (titan, Clayton) yellow
Thiazolidin *n* thiazolidine, tetrahydrothiazole
Thiele-Addition *f* Thiele addition *(of acetic anhydride to quinones)*
Thielepape-Aufsatz *m* Thielepape head *(for extracting)*
Thielepape-Extraktor *m* Thielepape extractor
Thioacetal *n (org ch)* thioacetal
Thioacylierung *f* thioacylation
Thioaldehyd *n* thioaldehyde
Thioaldehyd-*S*-oxid *n* thioaldehyde *S*-oxide
Thioalkohol *m* *thiol, thioalcohol, mercaptan
Thioamid *n (org ch)* thio-amide
Thioantimonat(III) *n* $M^I_3SbS_3$ thioantimonite, trithioantimonite
Thioantimonat(V) *n* $M^I_3SbS_4$ thioantimonate, tetrathioantimonate
Thioarsenat(III) *n* $M^I_3AsS_3$ thioarsenite, trithioarsenite
Thioarsenat(V) *n* $M^I_3AsS_4$ thioarsenate, tetrathioarsenate
Thioäthanol *n s.* Ethanthiol
Thioäther *m s.* Thioether
Thiobakterien *npl* sulphur bacteria
Thiobarbitursäure *f* thiobarbituric acid, TBA
Thiocarbamid *n s.* Thioharnstoff
Thiocarbamoylierung *f* thiocarbamylation
Thiocarbanilid *n* thiocarbanilide
Thiocarbonat *n* $M^I_2CS_3$ thiocarbonate, trithiocarbonate
Thiocarbonsäure *f* thiocarboxylic acid
Thiocarbonyldichlorid *n* thiocarbonyl chloride, thiophosgene
Thiocarbonylselenid *n* thiocarbonyl selenide, carbon selenide sulphide
Thiocarbonyltellurid *n* thiocarbonyl telluride, carbon sulphide telluride
Thiocarbonyltetrachlorid *n* trichloromethanesulphenyl chloride, thiocarbonyl tetrachloride
Thioctansäure *f s.* Thioctinsäure
Thioctinsäure *f*, **Thioctsäure** *f* thioctic acid, α-lipoic acid, 3-(4-carboxybutyl)-1,2-dithiolane
Thiocyanat *n* M^ISCN thiocyanate, rhodanide
Thiocyanatoaurat *n* thiocyanatoaurate
Thiocyanatoferrat *n* thiocyanatoferrate
Thiocyanatowolframat *n* *thiocyanatowolframate, thiocyanatotungstate
Thiocyanierung *f* thiocyanation, thiocyanatogenation
Thiocyansäure *f* thiocyanic acid
Thioderivat *n* thio derivative
Thioessigsäure *f* thioacetic acid
Thioether *m* *dialkyl sulphide, *(deprecated:)* thioether
Thioformylierung *f* thioformylation
Thiofuran *n s.* Thiophen

Thioglycerin *n*, **Thioglycerol** *n* thioglycerol
Thioglykolsäure *f* thioglycollic acid
Thioharnstoff *m* thiourea, thiocarbamide
Thioharnstoff-Formaldehydharz *n* thiourea-formaldehyde resin
Thioharnstoffharz *n* thiourea resin, polythiourea
Thiohypophosphat *n* $M^I_4P_2S_6$ thiohypophosphate, hexathiohypophosphate
Thioindigo *m(n)* thioindigo
Thioindoxyl *n* thioindoxyl, 3-hydroxybenzo[*b*]thiophene
Thioketal *n (org ch)* thioketal
Thioketon-*S*-oxid *n (org ch)* thioketone *S*-oxide
thioklastisch *s.* thiolytisch
Thiokohlensäure *f* thiocarbonic acid, trithiocarbonic acid
Thiol *n (org ch)* *thiol, mercaptan
Thiolactonisierung *f* thiolactonization
Thiolgruppe *f* –SH thiol group, sulphanyl (sulphydryl, mercapto) group
Thiolignin *n* thiolignin
Thiolthionkohlensäure *f* thionothiolcarbonic acid, dithiocarbonic acid, xanthic acid
Thiolyse *f (bioch)* thiolysis
thiolytisch *(bioch)* thiolytic
Thiomethylierung *f* thiomethylation
Thiomilchsäure *f* thiolactic acid, 2-mercaptopropionic acid
Thionaphthol *n* *naphthalenethiol, thionaphthol
β-Thionaphthol *n* naphthalene-2-thiol
Thionthiolsäure *f* dithiocarboxylic acid
Thion-Thiol-Umlagerung *f* thion-thiol rearrangement
Thionylbromid *n* thionyl bromide
Thionylchlorid *n* thionyl chloride
Thiooxalat *n* $M^IO–CS–COOM^I$ thiooxalate
Thiophen *n* thiophene
thiophenfrei thiophene-free
Thiophenol *n* thiophenol, phenyl mercaptan
Thiophenprobe *f* thiophene test
Thiophosgen *n s.* Thiocarbonyldichlorid
Thiophosphat *n* thiophosphate
Thiophosphonsäuredichlorid *n* phosphonothioic dichloride
Thiophosphorsäuretriamid *n s.* Thiophosphoryltriamid
Thiophosphorylbromiddichlorid *n* thiophosphoryl bromide dichloride
Thiophosphorylchlorid *n* thiophosphoryl chloride
Thiophosphoryldibromidchlorid *n* thiophosphoryl dibromide chloride
Thiophosphoryltriamid *n* thiophosphoryl amide, thiophosphoric triamide
Thioplast *m* thioplast, polysulphide rubber
Thiopropylalkohol *m* *1-propanethiol, thiopropyl alcohol
Thiosalicylsäure *f* thiosalicylic acid, *o*-mercaptobenzoic acid
Thiosäure *f* thioacid, monothiocarboxylic acid
Thiosemicarbazid *n* thiosemicarbazide, aminothiourea
Thiosulfat *n* $M^I_2S_2O_3$ thiosulphate
Thiosulfatentfernung *f (phot)* hypo elimination
Thiosulfit *n* $M^I_2S_2O_2$ thiosulphite
Thiotolen *n* thiotolene, methylthiophene
Thiozinn(II)-säure *f* thiostannous acid, dithiostannous acid
Thiozinn(IV)-säure *f* thiostannic acid, trithiostannic acid
Thiuramdisulfidvernetzung *f (rubber)* thiuram disulphide cure
Thiuramvernetzung *f*, **Thiuramvulkanisation** *f (rubber)* thiuram cure
thixotrop *(coll)* thixotropic
Thixotropie *f (coll)* thixotropy
Thixotropier[ungs]mittel *n (coll)* thixotroping (thixotropic) agent
Thomas-Birne *f s.* Thomas-Konverter
Thomas-Gasmesser *m* Thomas meter
Thomas-Konverter *m (met)* Thomas (basic Bessemer) converter
Thomas-Konverterstahl *m s.* Thomas-Stahl
Thomas-Konverterverfahren *n s.* Thomas-Verfahren
Thomas-Mehl *n*, **Thomas-Phosphat** *n* Thomas meal (phosphate)
Thomas-Schlacke *f* Thomas (basic, Belgian) slag
Thomas-Stahl *m* Thomas steel, basic [Bessemer, converter] steel
Thomas-Verfahren *n* Thomas[-Gilchrist] process, basic [Bessemer, converter] process
Thomsenolith *m (min)* thomsenolite *(calcium sodium hexafluoroaluminate)*
Thomson-Effekt *m* Thomson [thermoelectric] effect
Thomson-Überfall *m* triangular notch *(flow measurement)*
Thorakalapplikation *f* topical application *(for testing the efficiency of an insecticide)*
Thorerde *f s.* Thoriumoxid
thorieren to thoriate *(e.g. tungsten filaments)*
Thorium *n* Th thorium • **mit ~ beschichten** to thoriate *(e.g. tungsten filaments)*
Thorium-228 *n* ^{228}Th thorium-228, radiothorium
Thoriumbromid *n* thorium bromide
Thoriumchlorid *n* thorium chloride
Thoriumdioxid *n s.* Thoriumoxid
Thorium-Emanation *f s.* Radon-220
Thoriumhydroxid *n* thorium hydroxide
Thoriumnitrat *n* thorium nitrate
Thoriumoxid *n* thorium oxide, thorium dioxide
Thoriumreihe *f (nucl)* thorium [decay] series
Thoriumsulfat *n* thorium sulphate
Thoriumsulfid *n* thorium sulphide
Thoriumzerfallsreihe *f (nucl)* thorium [decay] series
Thorne-Bleichturm *m (pap)* Thorne bleacher
Thoron *n s.* Radon-220

Thorpe-Reaktion *f* Thorpe reaction *(for obtaining cyclic alkanones)*
Thr *s.* Threonin
Threit *m*, **Threitol** *n* threitol, anti-1,2,3,4,-tetrahydroxybutane
Threonin *n* threonine, 2-amino-3-hydroxybutyric acid
Thujaöl *n* thuja (cedar-leaf) oil *(chiefly from Thuja occidentalis L.)*
Thujasäure *f* thujic acid, 4,4-dimethylcycloheptatriene-1-carboxylic acid
Thujopsen *n* thujopsene, widdrene *(a tricyclic sesquiterpene)*
Thujylalkohol *m*, **β-Thujylalkohol** *m* thujyl alcohol, 3-thujanol
Thulium *n* Tm thulium
Thuliumoxid *n* thulium oxide
Thymiancampher *m* thyme camphor, thymol, thymic acid, 1-methyl-3-hydroxy-4-isopropyl benzene
Thymianöl *n* thyme oil *(from Thymus vulgaris L. and Th. zygis L.)*
Thymiansäure *f s.* Thymiancampher
Thymidylsäure *f (bioch)* thymidylic acid, ribothymidylic acid
Thymochinon *n* thymoquinone, 2-isopropyl-5-methyl-1,4-benzoquinone
Thymolblau *n* thymol blue, thymolsulphonephthalein *(a pH indicator)*
Thymolphthalein *n* thymolphthalein *(a pH indicator)*
Thymolsulfophthalein *n s.* Thymolblau
Thymonucleinsäure *f*, **Thymusnucleinsäure** *f s.* Desoxyribonucleinsäure
Thyreoglobulin *n (bioch)* thyroglobuline
thyreotrop thyrotropic
Thyreotropin *n* thyrotropin, thyrotropic hormone, thyroid-stimulating hormone
Thyreotropin-Releasinghormon *n* thyrotropin-releasing hormone (factor), TRH, TRF
Thyssen-Gálocsy-Verfahren *n* Thyssen-Gálocsy process *(of coal gasification)*
Tiefätzung *f (glass)* deep etching
Tiefbau[betrieb] *m*, **Tiefbauförderung** *f* deep (underground) mining, underground work[ing]
Tiefbrunnen *m (hyd)* deep well
Tiefbrunnenwasser *n* deep well water
Tiefdruckfarbe *f* intaglio [printing] ink
Tiefdruckpapier *f* intaglio [printing] paper
Tiefendüngung *f* subsoil fertilization
Tiefenentwickler *m (phot)* depth developer
Tiefenentwicklung *f (phot)* depth development
Tiefenfilter *n (hyd)* depth filter
Tiefenfiltration *f* filter-medium filtration (operation); *(hyd)* deep-bed filtration
Tiefengestein *n* plutonic rock, plutonite, hypogene (deep-seated, irruptive) rock
Tiefenmagma *n (geol)* hypomagma
Tiefenrüttler *m* immersion (poker) vibrator
tieffärbend deep dyeing
Tieffassung *f* low-position shoe *(of an electrode)*
tiefgefrieren to deep-freeze
Tiefkühlanlage *f* deep-cooling plant
Tiefkühltrocknung *f* freeze drying, lyophilization, *(food also)* dehydrofreezing
Tiefkühlung *f* deep cooling
Tiefkühlvorlage *f (distil)* low-temperature receiver
Tiefkultur *f s.* Submerskultur
Tiefkupferglanz *m (min)* low-chalcocite *(copper(I) sulphide)*
tiefmatt *(text)* very dull
Tiefmulden-Gliederbandförderer *m* roller-chain conveyor
Tiefofen *m (met)* soak[ing] pit
Tiefpumpe *f* subsurface pump
Tiefquarz-Modifikation *f* lowquartz modification *(of germanium)*
tiefschmelzend low-melting[-point], low-fusion
tiefsiedend low-boiling, light
Tieftankverfahren *n (biot)* submersion (submerged culture) process
Tieftemperaturabscheidung *f* low-temperature separation
tieftemperaturbeständig low-temperature-resistant, resistant to cold, cold-resistant
Tieftemperaturbeständigkeit *f* low-temperature resistance, resistance to cold
Tieftemperaturchlorierung *f* low-temperature chlorination
Tieftemperaturdestillation *f* low-temperature distillation
Tieftemperatureigenschaften *fpl* low-temperature properties (characteristics)
Tieftemperaturentgasung *f s.* Tieftemperaturverkokung
Tieftemperaturerzeugung *f* production of low temperatures
Tieftemperaturflexibilität *f* low-temperature flexibility
Tieftemperaturform *f* low-temperature form
Tieftemperaturhydrierung *f* low-temperature hydrogenation
Tieftemperaturkautschuk *m* cold[-polymerized] rubber, low-temperature rubber
Tieftemperaturkoks *m* low-temperature coke
Tieftemperaturpolymer[e] *n*, **Tieftemperaturpolymerisat** *n* low-temperature polymer, cold polymer
Tieftemperaturpolymerisation *f* low-temperature polymerization, cold polymerisation
Tieftemperaturtechnik *f* cryogenic (low-temperature) engineering, cryogenics
Tieftemperaturteer *m* low-temperature tar
Tieftemperaturverdampfer *m* low-temperature evaporator
Tieftemperaturverfahren *n* 1. cryogenic process; 2. *(coal)* low-temperature carbonization (carbonizing) process

Tieftemperaturverhalten *n* low-temperature behaviour
Tieftemperaturverkokung *f* low-temperature carbonization
Tieftemperaturwerkstoff *m* low-temperature material
Tieftemperaturzerlegung *f* low-temperature separation
tiefziehen to deep-draw
Tiefziehen *n* deep drawing
~ **mit Gleitvorrichtung** *(plast)* slip forming
~ **mit Ziehring** *(plast)* slip ring forming
Tiefziehteil *n* deep-drawing part
Tiegel *m* 1. crucible; 2. [flash] cup *(of a flash-point tester)*
~/geschlossener closed [flash] cup
~ **nach Cleveland/offener** Cleveland open cup
~/offener open [flash] cup
Tiegel-Blähprobe *f (coal)* crucible swelling test
Tiegeldeckel *m (lab)* crucible lid (cover)
Tiegelkoks *m* crucible coke
Tiegelofen *m (met, lab)* crucible furnace
Tiegelofenverfahren *n (met)* crucible process
Tiegelschmelzverfahren *n s.* Tiegelofenverfahren
Tiegelstahl *m* drill steel, *(obsolete:)* crucible [cast] steel
Tiegel[stahl]verfahren *n s.* Tiegelofenverfahren
Tiegelzange *f* [pair of] crucible tongs
Tierarzneimittel *n* animal health product
Tiereiweiß *n* animal protein
Tiereiweißfaktor *m (bioch)* extrinsic factor, vitamin B_{12}, *(historically:)* animal protein factor
Tierexperiment *n s.* Tierversuch
Tierfaser *f* animal fibre
Tierfett *n* animal fat
tierisch animal
Tierkohle *f* animal char[coal]
Tierkörpermehl *n* [animal, garbage] tankage *(a fertilizer)*
Tierleim *m* animal [protein] glue, animal adhesive; *(pap)* animal size (glue, gelatin)
Tieröl *n* animal oil
~/ätherisches (Dippelsches) hartshorn oil, Dippel's oil
Tierstärke *f* animal starch
Tierversuch *m (pharm, tox)* animal assay (test), test on animals
Tierwachs *n* animal wax
Tiffeneau-Reaktion *f*, **Tiffeneau-Umlagerung** *f* Tiffeneau rearrangement (reaction) *(for converting amino alcohols into carbonyl compounds)*
Tigerauge *n (min)* tiger's eye *(a variety of quartz)*
Tiglinsäure *f* tiglic acid, 2-methylcrotonic acid, trans-2-methylbuten-2-oic acid
Tinkal *m (min)* tincal, borax *(sodium tetraborate 10-water)*
Tinktur *f (pharm)* tincture; *(food)* miscella *(an extractant containing an extracted oil or grease)*
Tinte *f* [writing] ink
~/sympathetische sympathetic (secret) ink
Tintenfarbstoff *m* ink dye
Tintenfestigkeit *f (pap)* ink resistance
Tintenschreiber *m* pen-and-ink recorder
Tintometer *n* tintometer, colorimeter
~ **nach Lovibond** Lovibond tintometer
Tirolit *m (min)* tyrolite, copper froth, froth copper *(an arsenate containing calcium and copper)*
Tischabzug[sschrank] *m (lab)* local exhaust hood, fume closet
Tischrüttler *m* table vibrator
Tischtschenko-Reaktion *f* Tishchenko reaction *(for obtaining esters from aldehydes)*
Tischverfahren *n (glass)* table [casting] process
Tiselius-Elektrophorese *f (anal)* free (moving-boundary) electrophoresis, Tiselius method
Titan *n* Ti titanium
Titanat *n* titanate
Titan(II)-chlorid *n* titanium(II) chloride, titanium dichloride
Titan(III)-chlorid *n* titanium(III) chloride, titanium trichloride
Titan(IV)-chlorid *n* titanium(IV) chloride, titanium tetrachloride
Titanchloridmethode *f* **von Edmund Knecht** titanous-chloride method of E. Knecht *(for identifying azo dyes)*
Titandi... *s. a.* Titan(II)-...
Titandioxid *n s.* Titan(IV)-oxid
Titandiphosphat *n* *titanium diphosphate, titanium pyrophosphate
Titandisulfid *n s.* Titan(IV)-sulfid
Titanerde *f s.* Titan(IV)-oxid
Titan(IV)-fluorid *n* titanium(IV) fluoride, titanium tetrafluoride
titanführend *(geol)* titaniferous
Titangelb *n (dye)* titan (Clayton, thiazole) yellow
titanhaltig titaniferous
Titanhydrid *n* titanium hydride
Titan(IV)-hydroxid *n* titanium(IV) hydroxide
Titan(II)-iodid *n* titanium(II) iodide, titanium diiodide
Titan(IV)-iodid *n* titanium(IV) iodide, titanium tetraiodide
Titanit *m (min)* titanite *(calcium titanium(IV) oxide orthosilicate)*
Titanmonocarbid *n* titanium monocarbide
Titanmonosulfid *n s.* Titan(II)-sulfid
Titanmonoxid *n s.* Titan(II)-oxid
Titannitrid *n* titanium nitride
Titanometrie *f* titanometry
Titan(II)-oxid *n* titanium(II) oxide, titanium monoxide
Titan(III)-oxid *n* titanium(III) oxide, dititanium trioxide
Titan(IV)-oxid *n* titanium(IV) oxide, titanium dioxide
Titanoxidsulfat *n* titanium oxide sulphate
Titanporzellan *n* titania porcelain
Titanpyrophosphat *n s.* Titandiphosphat
Titansäure *f* titanic acid *(any of various hydrates of titanium oxide)*
Titan(IV)-sulfat *n* titanium(IV) sulphate

Titan(II)-sulfid *n* titanium(II) sulphide, titanium monosulphide
Titan(III)-sulfid *n* titanium(III) sulphide, dititanium trisulphide
Titan(IV)-sulfid *n* titanium(IV) sulphide, titanium disulphide
Titantetra... *s.* Titan(IV)-...
Titantri... *s.* Titan(III)-...
Titanweiß *n* titanium white *(a pigment consisting mainly of TiO_2)*
Titanweißware *f (ceram)* titania whiteware
Titer *m* 1. titre, titer *(strength of a solution)*; 2. titre, titer *(for defining the fineness of yarn)*; 3. titre [value] *(the solidifying point of oils)*
Titerlösung *f* standard solution
Titerpumpe *f* spinning (metering) pump
Titersubstanz *f* standard reagent (titrant, titrimetric substance)
Titertest *m* titre test *(for determining the salidifying point of oils)*
Titerwert *m s.* Titer 3.
Titrand *m* solution to be *or* being titrated
Titrandsystem *n s.* Titrand-Titrator-System
Titrand-Titrator-System *n* titration system
Titrans *n*, **Titrant** *m s.* Titrator
Titration *f* titration
~/amperometrische amperometric titration
~/biamperometrische dead-stop titration
~/chelatometrische chelatometric titration
~/coulometrische coulometric titration
~/derivativ-potentiometrische derivative potentiometric titration
~/differenzpotentiometrische differential potentiometric titration
~/direkte direct titration
~/elektrometrische *s.* ~/potentiometrische
~/hochfrequenzkonduktometrische high-frequency conductometric titration
~ in nichtwäßriger Lösung non-aqueous titration
~ in wasserfreiem Medium non-aqueous titration
~/iodometrische iodometric titration
~/komplexometrische complexometric titration
~/konduktometrische conductometric (conductance) titration
~/manganometrische permanganate titration
~ nach Mohr Mohr titration (method) *(argentometry)*
~ nach Volhard Volhard titration (method) *(for determining chlorine, bromine, or iodine)*
~/nephelometrische nephelometric titration
~/oszillometrische high-frequency titration
~/photometrische photometric titration
~/potentiometrische potentiometric (electrometric) titration
~/thermometrische thermometric (thermal) titration
~/turbidimetrische turbidimetric (turbidity) titration
Titrationsapparat *m* titration apparatus
Titrationsazidität *f (soil)* total acidity
Titrationscoulometer *n* titration coulometer
Titrationsfehler *m* titration error
Titrationskurve *f* titration curve
Titrationsmethode *f* titrimetric method
Titrationsmittel *n s.* Titrator
Titrationszelle *f* titration cell
Titrator *m* titrant, titrator
Titrieranalyse *f* titrimetric (volumetric, mensuration) analysis
Titrierapparat *m s.* Titrationsapparat
Titrierautomat *m* automatic titrator, autotitrator
titrierbar titr[at]able
Titrierbecher *m* titration beaker
titrieren to titrate
Titrierfehler *m* titration error
Titriergefäß *n* titration vessel
Titriergerät *n* titrator
Titrierkolben *m* titration flask
Titrierstativ *n* titration stand
Titrierung *f s.* Titration
Titriervorrichtung *f* titrating device
Titrimeter *n* titrimeter, titrator
Titrimetrie *f* titrimetry, volumetry
titrimetrisch titrimetric, volumetric
Tizerahextrakt *m (tann)* tizerah extract *(from Rhus pentaphylla Desf.)*
TMS *s.* Tetramethylsilan
TNT *s.* Trinitrotoluen
TOA *s.* Alttuberkulin
Tobias-Säure *f* Tobias acid, naphth-1-ylamine-1-sulphonic acid
TOC-Bestimmung *f (hyd)* TOC determination
TOC-Gehalt *m (hyd)* TOC content
Tochterdoppelstrang *m (bioch)* daughter double strand *(of DNA)*
Tochterstrang *m (bioch)* daughter strand *(of DNA)*
tödlich deadly poisonous, lethal
Tödlichkeitsdosis *f (tox)* lethal dose, LD, fatal dose
Tödlichkeitsindex *m (tox)* ct product *(product of concentration and survival time)*
Tödlichkeitsprodukt *n*/**Haberscches** *s.* Tödlichkeitsindex
Toilettenpräparat *n* toilet preparation
Toilettenseife *f* toilet soap
Toilettenwasser *n* toilet water
Tokopherol *n (bioch)* tocopherol
Tolan *n* tolan, diphenyl acetylene, *diphenylethyne
Toleranz *f* 1. tolerance, *(relating to dimensions also)* allowance; 2. *s.* Toleranzwert
Toleranzdosis *f s.* Toleranzwert
Toleranzgrenze *f* maximum allowable content, maximum permissible concentration, maximum permitted level *(of one component in a material)*
Toleranzwert *m (tox)* [maximum] tolerance, maximum permissible concentration, maximum permitted level
Tollens-Reagens *n* Tollens' reagent *(for detecting aldehydes)*
Tollens-Reaktion *f* Tollens' reaction *(for detecting monosaccharides)*

Tolubalsam *m* Tolu balsam *(from Myroxylon balsamum (L.) Harms var. balsamum)*
Toluen *n* toluene, methylbenzene
1'-Toluencarbonsäure *f s.* α-Tolylsäure
Toluendiisocyanat *n* toluene diisocyanate, TDI
p-**Toluensulfochlorid** *n p*-toluenesulphonyl chloride, tosyl chloride
p-**Toluensulfonat** *n p*-toluenesulphonate, tosylate
p-**Toluensulfonsäure** *f* toluene-*p*-sulphonic acid
Toluensulfonsäurechloramidnatrium *n* sodium *p*-toluenesulphonchloramine, chloramine-T
p-**Toluensulfonsäurechlorid** *n s. p*-Toluensulfochlorid
p-**Toluensulfonsäureester** *m s. p*-Toluensulfonat
p-**Toluensulfonylchlorid** *n s. p*-Toluensulfochlorid
p-**Toluensulfonylgruppe** *f* $CH_3C_6H_4SO_2$– *p*-toluenesulphonyl group, tosyl group
Toluidin *n* toluidine, aminotoluene
Toluol *n s.* Toluen
Toluylendiamin *n* toluylenediamine, diaminotoluene
Toluylenrot *n* toluylene (neutral) red *(an oxidation-reduction indicator)*
Toluylsäure *f* toluic acid, methylbenzoic acid
Tolylendiamin *n s.* Toluylendiamin
Tolylierung *f* tolylation
α-**Tolylsäure** *f*, **1'-Tolylsäure** *f* α-toluic acid, toluylic acid, phenylacetic acid
Tombak *m* tombac, tombak *(an alloy chiefly consisting of copper and zinc)*
Ton *m* 1. clay, argil[la]; 2. shade, hue *(of colour)* • **einen ~ treffen** *(dye)* to match a shade
~/aktivierter activated clay
~/aluminiumoxidreicher high-alumina clay
~/empfindlicher tender clay
~/fetter plastic clay
~/feuerfester refractory clay, fire-clay
~/gesumpfter soaked clay
~/kieselsäurereicher high-silica clay, siliceous clay
~/natürlicher natural clay, naturally occurring clay, non-activated clay
~/plastischer plastic clay
~/primärer primary (residual) clay
~/reiner *s.* ~/weißer
~/säureaktivierter acid clay *(for refining purposes)*
~/tonerdereicher high-alumina clay
~/weißbrennender white-firing clay
~/weißer white (china, porcelain) clay, kaolin[e], white bole, bolus alba
~/windgesichteter aeroclay
Tonabbau *m* clay mining
tonartig clayey, clayish, argillaceous
Tonaufbereitung *f* clay preparation
Tonaufbereitungsanlage *f* clay preparation plant
Tonboden *m* clay soil
Tondreieck *n* pipeclay triangle
Toneisenstein *m (min)* clay ironstone, ironstone clay, argillaceous haematite
tonen *(phot)* to tone
tönen to tint, to tinge, to tone, to shade
Toner *m (phot)* toning agent
Tonerde *f* alumina *(aluminium oxide)*
~/aktivierte activated alumina *(petroleum refining)*
~/ameisensaure *s.* Aluminiumformiat
~/essigsaure *s.* Aluminiumacetat
~/künstlich aktivierte *s.* ~/aktivierte
~/schwefelsaure 1. *s.* Aluminiumsulfat; 2. *(pap)* papermaker's alum *(crude aluminium sulphate)*
Tonerdegel *n* alumina gel, gelatinous aluminium hydroxide
tonerdehaltig aluminiferous
Tonerdekatalysator *m*, **Tonerdekontakt** *m* alumina catalyst (contact)
Tonerdeporzellan *n* alumina porcelain
Tonerdeschiffchen *n* alumina boat
Tonerdeschmelzzement *m s.* Tonerdezement
Tonerdesilikatglas *n* aluminosilicate glass
Tonerdeweißware *f (ceram)* alumina whiteware
Tonerdezement *m* aluminous (high-alumina) cement
Tonesse *f* burner guard *(for Bunsen burners)*
Tonfraktion *f (soil)* clay fraction
tonfrei free from clay, non-clay
Tongalle *f (geol)* clay gall
tongebunden *(ceram)* clay-bonded
Tongestein *n (geol)* claystone
Tongewinnung *f* clay mining
Tongrube *f* clay pit
Tongut *n* earthenware
tonhaltig containing clay, clayey, *(esp geol)* argilliferous, argillaceous
Tonhobel *m (ceram)* clay cutter
Ton-Humus-Komplex *m (soil)* clay-humus complex, organo-clay (colloidal) complex
tonig clayey, clayish, *(esp geol)* argillaceous
Tonikum *n (pharm)* tonic
Ton-in-Ton-Färbung *f* tone-in-tone dyeing
tonisch *(pharm)* tonic
tonisieren *(pharm)* to tone
tonisierend *(pharm)* tonic
Tonkabohne *f* tonka (tonca, tonga) bean *(from Dipteryx specc.)*
Tonkabohnencampher *m* tonka bean camphor, coumarin
Tonkalk *m (geol)* argillaceous limestone
Tonkneter *m*, **Tonknetmaschine** *f s.* Tonschneider
Tonlager *n*, **Tonlagerstätte** *f* clay deposit
Tonmasse *f (ceram)* clay body
Tonmergel *m (geol)* clay marl
Tonmineral *n* clay mineral
Tonne *f* cask, barrel, *(if large)* tun, *(if small)* keg
Tonnen *fpl* **je Jahr** tons per year (annum), tpy, tpa, metric tons annually, mta
~ je Tag tons per day, tpd
Tonraspler *m (ceram)* clay shredder
Tonrohr *n*, **Tonröhre** *f* clay (earthenware) pipe
Tonschicht *f* clay bank
Tonschiefer *m (geol)* [clay] slate
Tonschiffchen *n (lab)* clay combustion boat

Tonschlempe *f*, **Tonschlicker** *m* clay[-water] slurry
Tonschneider *m (ceram)* pug (clay) mill
Tonsilo *n(m) (ceram)* clay silo
Tonsubstanz *f* clay substance
Tontiegel *m* clay crucible
Tontopf *m* earthenware pot (vessel)
Tonumfang *m (phot)* tone range
Tonung *f (phot)* toning
Tönung *f* 1. tinting, tinging, toning, shading; 2. tint, tinge, tone, shade, cast
Tonvorkommen *n* clay deposit
Tonware *f* clay ware
Ton[wert]wiedergabe *f (phot)* tone rendering (reproduction)
Tonzelle *f*/**poröse** porous pot (cell, cup)
Tonziegel *m* clay [building] brick
Tonzylinder *m*/**poröser** *s.* Tonzelle/poröse
Topas *m (min)* topaz *(an aluminium silicate)*
Topazolith *m (min)* topazolite *(a nesosilicate)*
Topf *m* 1. pot, *(lab also)* jar; 2. *(text)* [spinning] can; pot *(for pot spinning)*
~/Wittscher Witt jar
Topfcurare *n* pot curare *(from Chondrodendron specc.)*
Töpfer *m* potter
Töpferei *f* pottery
Töpferscheibe *f* potter's wheel
Töpferton *m* potter's clay
Töpferware *f* pottery, earthenware
Topffärben *n (text)* potting
topfglühen to pot-anneal
Topfglühofen *m* pot-annealing furnace
Topfglühung *f* pot annealing
Topfmanschette *f* cup [ring]
Topfpresse *f* pot press
Topfspinnverfahren *n* [centrifugal] pot spinning
Topfzeit *f* [liquid] pot life *(as of adhesives and organic coatings)*
Topf-Zentrifugenspinnverfahren *n* [centrifugal] pot spinning
Topochemie *f* topochemistry
topochemisch topochemical
Topomerisierung *f* degenerate rearrangement
topotaktisch *(cryst)* topotactic
Topotaxie *f (cryst)* topotaxy
Toppanlage *f (petrol)* topping (skimming) plant
Toppdestillation *f* topping
toppen *(petrol)* to top, to skim
Toppprodukt *n (petrol)* tops, top (overhead) product, overhead[s]
Topprückstand *m (petrol)* long residue (residuum) • **Topprückstände aufarbeiten** to run resid
Toppung *f (petrol)* topping
Torbernit *m (min)* torbernite, cupro uranite *(a hydrous uranium copper phosphate)*
Torf *m* peat
torfbildend peat-forming
Torfbildung *f* peat formation
Torfbildungsprozeß *m* peat-forming process
Torfboden *m* peat soil
Torfbrikett *n* peat briquette
Torfdolomit *m (geol)* coal ball
Torfentgasung *f* carbonization of peat
Torffräsverfahren *n* milled-peat process
Torfgas *n* peat gas
Torfgewinnung *f* peat winning
Torfhumus *m* peat humus
torfig peaty
Torfkoks *m* peat coke
Torfmaschine *f* peat machine
Torfmasse *f* peat substance
Torfmoor *n* peat bog (moor)
Torfstich *m* peat bank, peatery
Torfteer *m* peat tar
Torkretbeton *m* gunned concrete
torkretieren to gunite
Torontobrenner *m (spectr)* Toronto source
torpedieren *(petrol)* to shoot
Torpedo *m (plast)* torpedo, *(in injection moulding also)* spreader
~/rotierender *(plast)* rotating spreader *(of a plunger-type injection machine)*
Torsion *f* torsion, twist
Torsionsschwingung *f* torsional vibration; *(spectr)* torsional oscillation (mode), twisting vibration
Torsionsschwingungsversuch *m* torsion pendulum experiment *(materials testing)*
Torsionsspannung *f* torsional strain *(in molecules)*
Torsionssteifigkeit *f* stiffness in torsion
Torsionswaage *f* torsion balance
Torsionswinkel *m* torsion (rotational) angle, angle of rotation
Torulahefe *f* torula yeast
Tosylat *n* tosylate, *p*-toluenesulphonate *(salt or ester of p-toluenesulphonic acid)*
Tosylchlorid *n* tosyl chloride, *p*-toluenesulphonyl chloride
Tosylester *m* tosylate, *p*-toluenesulphonate
Tosylgruppe *f* $CH_3C_6H_4SO_2-$ tosyl group, *p*-toluenesulphonyl group
Tosylierung *f* tosylation *(introduction of the p-toluenesulphonyl group)*
tot *(rubber)* lifeless, dead
Totalentsalzung *f s.* Vollentsalzung
Totalherbizid *n* general herbicide, non-selective herbicide (weed-killer), soil sterilant
Totalionenstrom *m* total ion current
Totalkondensation *f (distil)* total condensation
Totalreflexion *f* total reflection
~/abgeschwächte *(anal)* attenuated total reflectance, ATR
Totalsynthese *f* total synthesis
Totalvergasung *f (coal)* complete gasification
Totalvergasungsverfahren *n (coal)* complete gasification process
totbrennen to dead-burn *(e.g. gypsum, dolomite)*
totgerben *(tann)* to case-harden, to overtan
Totgerbung *f (tann)* case-hardening, overtannage

totmahlen to overgrind; *(pap)* to beat dead
totmastizieren *s.* totwalzen
Totraum *m* dead space
totrösten *(met)* to dead-roast
Totrösten *n (met)* dead roasting
Totvolumen *n* dead volume
totvolumenarm low-dead-volume
totvolumenfrei zero-dead-volume
totwalzen *(rubber)* to mill to death, to kill, to overmill, to overmasticate
Totwalzen *n (rubber)* dead milling, killing, overmilling, overmastication
Totweiche *f* oversteeping *(of malt)*
Totzeit *f* 1. dead time *(of a counting tube)*; 2. *(chromat)* [gas] hold-up time, time of passage *(period between injection and detection)*
Totzone *f* dead zone (spot)
Tourill *n* tourill *(one kind of absorption vessel)*
Toxaphen *n* toxaphene, technical chlorinated camphene *(insecticide)*
toxigen *(med)* toxi[co]genic
Toxikologe *m* toxicologist
~/vereidigter official toxicologist
Toxikologie *f* toxicology
toxikologisch toxicologic[al]
Toxikum *n* toxic [substance], toxicant
Toxin *n (bioch)* toxin • **~ erzeugend** toxigenic
toxisch toxic[al], poisonous
~/schwach mildly toxic
~/stark highly toxic
Toxizität *f* toxicity
~/akute acute toxicity
~/chronische chronic toxicity
~ für Säugetiere mammalian toxicity
~/orale oral toxicity
Toxizitätsbewertung *f* toxicity rating
Toxoid *n (med)* toxoid
Tozer-Verfahren *n* Tozer process *(of low-temperature carbonization)*
TPP *s.* Thiaminpyrophosphat
Tracer *m***/radioaktiver** radioactive tracer (indicator), radiotracer
Tracerchemie *f* tracer chemistry
Tracermethode *f* tracer (indicator) method
Tracersubstanz *f* tracer
Tracertechnik *f* tracer technique
Tracerversuch *m* tracer experiment
Trafoöl *n* transformer oil
Tragant *m* tragacanth gum, gum tragacanth *(any of various gums esp from Astragalus specc.)*
~/Afrikanischer African tragacanth *(gum from Sterculia tragacantha Lindl.)*
~/Indischer Indian tragacanth, sterculia gum, karaya [gum], gum karaya *(chiefly from Sterculia urens Roxb.)*
~/Ostindischer *s.* ~/Indischer
~/Persischer Persian tragacanth *(from Astragalus specc.)*
Tragantgummi *n s.* Tragant
Tragantleim *m* tragacanth adhesive
Tragantschleim *m* tragacanth mucilage
Tragasol *n* gum tragasol *(a leather finish from seed shells of Ceratonia siliqua L.)*
träge inert, inactive, passive, indifferent *(chemical)*; sluggish, slow *(reaction)*
tragecht *(text)* resistant to wearing, wear-resistant, wearproof, tough
Tragechtheit *f (text)* resistance to wearing, wear resistance
Trageeigenschaft *f (text)* wearing quality, wearability
Träger *m* 1. carrier, *(esp relating to heat transfer also)* medium; 2. support, supporting material *(for a layer containing active substances, as catalysts or photosensitive compounds)*; 3. substrate *(for pigments)*
~/fester *(chromat)* solid support
~ für adsorptive Bindung *(biot)* adsorption carrier
~/kolloidaler colloid carrier, protector *(corresponding to apoenzyme in recent terminology)*
Trägerbindung *f (biot)* enzyme bonding (binding attachment) to a carrier
~/kovalente covalent bonding to a carrier
Trägerdampfdestillation *f* carrier distillation, codistillation
Trägerelektrode *f* carrier electrode
Trägerelektrophorese *f (anal)* electrochromatography, electropherography
Trägerelement *n (nucl)* carrier
Trägerfaden *m (text)* carrier thread
trägerfixiert *(chromat)* carrier-bound
Trägerflüssigkeit *f* carrier liquid
trägerfrei carrier-free
Trägergasfluß *m (chromat)* carrier gas flow *(in ml/min)*
Trägergasgeschwindigkeit *f* **im Hohlraumbereich/mittlere** *(chromat)* mean interstitial velocity of the carrier gas
Trägergasstrom *m (chromat)* carrier gas stream
Trägergassublimation *f* entrainer (carrier) sublimation
trägergebunden *(biot)* carrier-bound
Trägergitter *n (cryst)* host lattice
Trägerkatalysator *m* supported (high-area) catalyst
trägerlos unsupported *(plastic film)*
Trägerluft *f* transport air
Trägermaterial *n* 1. *(chromat)* partition support; 2. *s.* Träger
~ für Hochdruck-Flüssigkeitschromatographie HPLC support
Trägermatrix *f* 1. *(chromat)* supporting matrix; 2. *(biot)* matrix *(immobilization of enzymes and cells)*
Trägerplatte *f (chromat)* support plate
Trägerstoff *m s.* Träger 1. *und* 2.
Trägerstoffdestillation *f* carrier distillation

Trägerstrom *m* fluid medium *(fluid-bed technology)*
Trägersubstanz *f s.* Träger
Trägerunterlage *f s.* Trägerplatte
Tragfähigkeit *f* [load-]bearing strength, load (bearing) capacity
tragfest *s.* tragecht
Traggestell *n (lab)* carrying frame
Trägheit *f* 1. inertness, inactivity, passivity, indifference *(of a chemical)*; slowness *(of a reaction)*; 2. inertia *(physics)*
Trägheitsachse *f (spectr)* axis of inertia
Trägheitseffekt *m* inertia[l] effect
Trägheitsgesetz *n* law of inertia
Trägheitskraftabscheider *m* inertial separator
Trägheitsmoment *n* moment of inertia
Trägheitsradius *m* radius of gyration
Tragkasten *m (lab)* carrying box
~ **für Flaschen** bottle carrier
Tragkettenförderer *m* rigid arm elevator
Tragkraft *f* lifting capacity *(of cranes)*
Tragplatte *f* bearing plate
Tragrolle *f* idler [roll] *(as of a conveyor belt)*
~ **am Leertrum (Untertrum)** return roll
Tragtrommel *f*, **Tragwalze** *f (pap)* carrying roll, support (supporting) roll, winder drum
Trajektorie *f* trajectory *(in diagrams)*
Traktorenkerosin *n s.* Traktorenpetroleum
Traktorenkraftstoff *m* tractor fuel
Traktorenöl *n s.* Traktorenpetroleum
Traktorenpetrol[eum] *n* tractor [vaporizing] oil
Trame[seide] *f* tram silk
Tran *m* fish (train) oil
Tranausharzung *f (tann)* fish-oil spew (spue)
Träne *f (coat)* tear *(after dipping)*
tränenerregend *s.* tränenreizend
Tränengas *n* tear gas, lachrymator
tränenreizend lachrymatory, lacrimatory, causing (prompting) tears
Tränenreizstoff *m* lachrymator, lacrimator
Tranfettung *f*, **Tranfüllung** *f (tann)* fish-oil stuffing
tränken to impregnate, to saturate, to imbibe, *(using an aqueous solution)* to steep, to soak, to water
~**/mit Harz** *(plast)* to resin
Tränkflüssigkeit *f* impregnation solution; *(dye)* steeping liquor
Tränkharz *n* impregnating resin
Tränklauge *f (pap)* impregnating liquor
Tränkmittel *n*, **Tränkstoff** *m* impregnating (impregnation) material
Tränktrog *m (dye)* steeping pan
Tränkung *f* impregnation, saturation, imbibition, *(using an aqueous solution)* steep[age], soak[age], watering
Tranquilizer *m (pharm)* [minor] tranquil[l]izer, tranquillizing drug, anxiolytic [sedative]
Transacetalisierung *f* transacetalization
Transacylierung *f* transacylation
trans-Addition *f* trans addition
Transalkenylierung *f* transalkenylation
Transalkylierung *f* transalkylation
Transamidierung *f* transamidation
Transaminierung *f* transamination
Transaminoethylierung *f* transaminoethylation
transannular *(org ch)* transannular
Transbromierung *f* transbromination
Transcarbonylierung *f* transcarbonylation
Transcyanethylierung *f* transcyanoethylation
Transduktion *f (bioch)* transduction *(transfer of genetic information by bacteriophages)*
Transferase *f*, **Transferenzym** *n* transferase, transferring enzyme
Transferfaktor *m (bioch)* transfer (elongation, propagation) factor
Transferformung *f (rubber)* transfer moulding
Transferpressen *n (plast)* transfer moulding
Transferpreßwerkzeug *n (plast)* transfer mould
Transfer-Ribonucleinsäure *f*, **Transfer-RNA** *f* transfer (soluble) ribonucleic acid, tRNA, s-RNA
Transfer-Verfahren *n (rubber)* transfer moulding
trans-Form *f* trans form
Transformation *f (phys ch)* transformation
~**/mikrobielle** *s.* Biokonversion
Transformationsintervall *n (phys ch)* transition interval, *(relating to glass:)* transformation range
Transformationstemperatur *f (glass)* glass-transition temperature *(where the viscosity of the glass is 10^{13} dPa · s)*
Transformatorenöl *n* transformer oil
Transfusion *f* diffusion *(of gases through a porous diaphragm)*
Transglykosidierung *f*, **Transglykosylierung** *f (bioch)* transglycosylation
Transhalogenierung *f* transhalogenation
Transhydrogenierung *f* transhydrogenation
Transhydroxymethylierung *f* transhydroxymethylation
Transient *m* [reaction] intermediate
Transiminierung *f* transimination
Transiodierung *f* transiodination
trans-Isomer[e] *n* trans isomer
Transitionszeit *f (el ch)* transition time
trans-Konformation *f* trans conformation, T *(torsion angle 0°)*
Transkript *n***/primäres** *(bioch)* primary transcript
Transkription *f (bioch)* transcription *(enzymatic transfer of genetic information from DNA onto RNA)*
~**/umgekehrte** reverse transcription
transkristallin transcrystalline, transgranular
trans-Lage *f* trans position
Translation *f* 1. *(phys ch)* translation; translation [gliding] *(crystal gliding along a crystal plane)*; 2. *(bioch)* translation *(esp of genetic information into an amino-acid sequence)*
Translationsbewegung *f* translational motion
Translationsebene *f (cryst)* translation plane
Translationsenergie *f* translational [kinetic] energy
~**/molare** molar translational energy

Translationsentropie *f* translational entropy
Translationsfreiheitsgrad *m* translational degree of freedom, degree of translational freedom
Translationsgitter *n (cryst)* space lattice
~/Bravaissches Bravais lattice
Translationsniveau *n* translational [energy] level
Translationsverteilungsfunktion *f* translational partition function
translokal systemic *(pesticide)*
Translokation *f* translocation
Transmembranprotein *n (bioch)* transmembrane protein
Transmercurierung *f* transmercuration
Transmetallierung *f* transmetalation
Transmethylierung *f* transmethylation
Transmissions-Elektronenenergieverlust-Spektroskopie *f* transmission electron energy loss spectrometry, TEELS
Transmissionsgrad *m* transmission ratio, transmittance, transmittancy *(optics)*
Transmissionskoeffizient *m* transmission coefficient *(kinetics)*
Transmutation *f* transmutation
Transnitrosierung *f* transnitrosation
trans-orientiert trans-oriented
transparent transparent
~/unvollkommen translucent, translucid
Transparentglasur *f (ceram)* transparent glaze
Transparentpapier *n* tracing paper
Transparentseife *f* transparent soap
Transparentzeichenpapier *n* tracing paper
Transparenz *f* transparency, light transmittance
~/unvollständige translucence, translucency
Transparenzgitter *n (spectr)* transmission grating
Transphosphorylierung *f* transphosphorylation
transpirationshemmend *(cosmet)* antiperspirant
Transport *m* transport, transfer *(as of electrons or heat)*; *(bioch)* transport
~/aktiver *(bioch)* active transport *(through cell and organelle membranes)*
~/katalysierter *(bioch)* mediated transport
~/passiv katalysierter *(bioch)* facilitated diffusion
~/vermittelter *s.* ~/katalysierter
transportabel [trans]portable
Transportband *n* conveyor (conveying) belt; *(pap)* delivery tape *(of a cross-cutter)*
Transportband-Konfektioniermaschine *f (rubber)* belt building machine
Transportbehälter *m* container
~ für Flaschen *(lab)* bottle carrier
Transportbeton *m* ready-mixed concrete
Transportdetektor *m s.* Flammenionisationsdetektor
Transportfilz *m (pap)* conveyor felt
transportieren to transport, to transfer *(e.g. electrons or heat)*; *(bioch)* to transport
Transportkübel *m* skip [car]
Transportmechanismus *m (phys ch, bioch)* transport mechanism
Transportmetabolit *m (bioch)* co-substrate
Transportprotein *n (bioch)* transport protein
Transportprozeß *m*/**nichtkatalysierter (nichtvermittelter)** *(bioch)* non-mediated process
Transportreaktion *f* transport reaction
Transportreaktor *m* transport (entrained-bed) reactor
Transportschnecke *f* conveyor (conveying) screw (worm)
Transportsystem *n (phys ch, bioch)* transport system, *(bioch also)* carrier, porter, translocase
Transportvorgang *m (phys ch, bioch)* transport process
Transportwalze *f (pap)* support[ing] roll
~/geriffelte fluted roll
Transportwasser *n* carriage (transport) water, water carrier vehicle *(for suspended particles)*
Transportwiderstand *m* transport resistance
Transposon *n (biot)* transposon
trans-Säure *f* trans acid
Transsilylierung *f* transsilylation
trans-ständig trans • **~ [angeordnet] sein** to be trans
trans-Stellung *f* trans position
Transsulfonierung *f* transsulphonation
trans-taktisch transtactic *(polymer)*
trans-Taktizität *f* transtacticity *(of polymers)*
trans-trans-Kohlenwasserstoff *m* trans-trans hydrocarbon
Transuran *n* transuranium element, transuranic (transuranian) element, uranoid
Transvasiermethode *f* transfer system *(for producing sparkling wine)*
Transvinylierung *f* transvinylation
Traß *m (geol)* trass
Traßzement *m* trass cement
Trauben *fpl* clusters *(of fat in creaming milk)*
Traubenbildung *f* clustering, cluster formation *(of fat in creaming milk)*
traubenförmig botryoidal
Traubenkernöl *n* grape-seed (grape-stone) oil
Traubenmost *m*, **Traubensaft** *m* grape juice
Traubensäure *f* racemic acid, racemic (inactive) tartaric acid, (±)-tartaric acid
Traubenwein *m* grape wine
Traubenzucker *m* grape sugar, *D*-glucose, dextrose *(a monosaccharide)*
Traube-Reaktion *f* Traube reaction *(for obtaining purines)*
traubig botryoidal
träufeln to trickle
Traumatinsäure *f* traumatic acid, dodec-2-enedioic acid
Trauzl-Block *m* [Trauzl] lead block *(for testing explosives)*
Trauzl-Blockausweitung *f* [Trauzl] lead-block expansion *(in testing explosives)*
Trauzl-Mörser *m s.* Trauzl-Block
Treber *pl* [brewer's] grains, spent grains

Treffplatte *f* target *(as of an X-ray tube)*
Treibarbeit *f (met)* cupellation
Treibdampf *m* operating (motive) steam *(as in injector-type jet pumps)*
Treibdampfbrenner *m* steam-atomizing burner
Treibdampfpumpe *f* vapour jet pump
Treibdruck *m* swelling pressure *(of coal)*
treiben 1. *(met)* to cupel *(to extract gold and silver from lead)*; 2. *(tann)* to paddle; 3. to expand *(of cement)*
~/an die Oberfläche to buoy up
Treiben *n* 1. *(met)* cupellation *(extraction of gold and silver from lead)*; 2. *(tann)* paddling; 3. expansion *(of cement)*
Treiber *m (glass)* needle, plunger *(of a feeder)*
Treibgas *n* 1. fuel gas; 2. propellant [gas], propellent *(for liquids)*
~ für Aerosole aerosol propellant
Treibhauseffekt *m* greenhouse effect
Treibhausgas *n* greenhouse gas
Treibladung *f* propellant charge
Treibladungskörper *m* propellant grain
Treibladungspulver *n* propellant powder
~/einbasiges single-base powder
~/zweibasiges double-base powder
Treibmittel *n* 1. expanding agent, *(plast, rubber also)* blowing agent; gasifying agent *(for producing foam glass)*; *(food)* leavening [agent], leaven; 2. pumping (motivating) fluid *(of a jet pump)*; 3. aerosol propellant; 4. *s.* Treibstoff 2.
Treibmittelpumpe *f* jet pump
Treibneigung *f* expansion *(of cement)*
Treibrolle *f* driving pulley
Treibspiritus *m* power (fuel) alcohol
Treibstoff *m* 1. fuel, *(esp for rockets:)* propellant; 2. propellant [explosive], propellent, low explosive, deflagrating powder
~/fester solid fuel, *(esp for rockets:)* solid propellant
~/homogener monofuel
~/hypergoler hypergolic fuel (rocket propellant), hypergol
Treibtrommel *f* driving pulley
Treibverfahren *n (met)* cupellation *(for extracting gold and silver from lead)*
Treibversuch *m (coal)* swelling-pressure test
Trennaufgabe *f* separation task
trennbar separable
Trennbarkeit *f* separability
Trennbereich *m (anal)* separation range
Trenneffekt *m* separation effect; *(plast)* release effect
Trenneffizienz *f s.* Trennwirksamkeit
Trenneigenschaften *fpl* separation characteristics
Trenneinrichtung *f* separating device, separator
trennen 1. *(ch)* to separate; to break, to crack, to demulsify *(emulsions)*; to resolve *(racemates)*; 2. *(tech)* to disconnect *(e.g. the joints of an apparatus)*; to release *(mouldings from the mould)*
~/in Schichten to delaminate
~/nach Korn[größen]klassen to size[-separate], to grade
~/sich to separate
~/sich nach Korn[größen]klassen to size-fractionate
Trennentwässerung *f* separate [sewerage] system
Trennerfolg *m* separation efficiency
Trennfähigkeit *f s.* Trennvermögen
Trennfaktor *m (anal)* separation factor; relative centrifugal force *(of a centrifuge)*
Trennfiltration *f* solids recovery filtration
Trennfläche *f (cryst)* cleavage (parting) plane
Trennflüssigkeit *f s.* Trennmedium
Trennfuge *f* 1. parting line *(of a mould)*; 2. joint (parting) line, match (mould) mark, mould seam *(on a moulding)*
Trenngrad *m* degree of separation, separation efficiency
Trenngüte *f*, **Trenngütegrad** *m (min tech)* efficiency of cut
Trennkammer *f* chromatography chamber, chromatographic cabinet
Trennkanalisation *f s.* Trennsystem
Trennkapillare *f* open tubular [capillary] column *(gas chromatography)*
Trennkolonne *f (distil)* rectifying (rectification) column
Trennkorngröße *f* size (mesh) of separation, critical diameter, cut size (point)
Trennkörper *m*/**schalenporöser** *(chromat)* porous layer bead, pellicular packing (support), solid core support
Trennleistung *f* separation efficiency
~ der Säule *(chromat)* column performance
Trennlinie *f* 1. interface line *(between two components)*; 2. *s.* Trennfuge
Trennmechanismus *m (anal)* separation mechanism
Trennmedium *n (min tech)* separating fluid
Trennmethode *f* separation method
Trennmittel *n* 1. release agent, parting (separating, antitack) agent, abherent *(for mouldings)*; 2. *(distil)* separating agent; *(min tech)* separating fluid; 3. *(chromat)* mobile solvent
~/äußeres *(plast)* external lubricant
Trennoperation *f* separative operation
Trennplatte *f (ceram)* parting dish
Trennproblem *n* separation task
Trennrohr *n* thermal-diffusion column *(for separating isotopes)*
Trennrohrverfahren *n*[**/Clusiussches**] thermal-diffusion method *(for separating isotopes)*
Trennsäule *f (chromat)* analytical (separation) column; *(distil)* rectifying (rectification) column
~/dünne narrow-bore column (tube) *(for high-performance liquid chromatography)*
Trennschärfe *f* sharpness (degree) of separation, separation efficiency, selectivity
Trennschicht *f* interlayer, interlining

Trennschleuder *f* centrifuge
Trennschnitt *m (distil)* cut
Trennstrecke *f (chromat)* separation path
Trennstufe *f* separation stage, *(distil also)* distillation stage
~/praktische *(distil)* actual plate (tray)
~/theoretische *(distil)* theoretical plate (tray), ideal (perfect) plate
Trennstufenhöhe *f (anal, distil)* plate height, *(distil also)* height equivalent to a theoretical plate, HETP
Trennstufenzahl *f***/theoretische** number of theoretical plates (trays)
Trennsystem *n* separate system *(of transporting rain water and sewage)*
Trenntank *m (petrol)* separator
Trenntechnik *f* separation technique
~/absteigende *(chromat)* descending technique
~/aufsteigende *(chromat)* ascending technique
Trenntrichter *m* separatory (separating) funnel
Trennung *f* 1. *(ch)* separation; breaking, cracking, demulsification *(of emulsions)*; resolution *(of racemates)*; 2. *(tech)* disconnection *(as of the joints of an apparatus)*; release *(of mouldings from the mould)*
~/elektrolytische electrolytic separation
~/flotative *(min tech)* floatation separation
~ flüssig-fest solids-liquid separation, S/L separation
~ in Gruppen *(anal)* group separation, separation into groups
~ in Schweretrüben *(min tech)* heavy-medium (dense-medium) separation (cleaning)
~ mit Umkehrphasen *(chromat)* reversed-phase separation
~ mittels semipermeabler Membranen *(hyd)* membrane separation
~ nach der Dichte density separation (cut)
~ nach der Korngröße particle sizing
~ nach Gleichfälligkeit wet classification
~ nach Korn[größen]klassen grading [into size], size classification (grading, separation), sizing
~/saubere clean separation
~/säulenchromatographische column separation
6σ-Trennung *f (chromat)* 6σ separation
Trennungs... *s. a.* Trenn...
Trennungsenergie *f* **[der Bindung]** bond dissociation energy
Trennungsgang *m* qualitative analysis scheme, separation scheme
Trennungsleuchten *n* triboluminescence
Trennverfahren *n* separation process, *(esp lab)* separation procedure
Trennvermögen *n* separation (separating) power, *(relating to release agents for mouldings also)* abhesiveness
Trennvorgang *m* separation process
Trennwand *f* separating (dividing) wall, partition; *(relating to diffusion:)* diaphragm, membrane, barrier, *(esp osmosis, dialysis:)* membrane, *(esp electrolysis:)* diaphragm; *(min tech)* centre board *(of a plunger jig)*
~/halbdurchlässige (semipermeable) semipermeable membrane
Trennwirksamkeit *f* separation efficiency
Trennwirkung *f s.* Trenneffekt
Trennzentrifuge *f* separator
Treppenrost *m* step (cascade) grate
Treppenrostgenerator *m* step-grate producer
Treppenstufenpolarographie *f (anal)* staircase polarography
Trester *pl (ferm)* marc, rape, [grape] pomace, pummace
treten:
~/in Reaktion to enter into reaction
~/in Wechselwirkung to interact
~/zutage *(geol)* to crop out, to outcrop
TRH *s.* Thyreotropin-Releasinghormon
Triacetat *n* triacetate; *(text)* cellulose triacetate, primary [cellulose] acetate
Triacetatfaser *f* cellulose triacetate fibre
Triacetatfaserstoff *m* cellulose triacetate fibre
Triacontan *n (org ch)* triacontane
Triacontansäure *f* triacontanoic acid
Triade *f* triad *(in the periodic table)*
~/Döbereinersche Döbereiner's triad
Triadenregel *f***/Döbereinersche** Döbereiner's law of triads
Trialkylaluminium *n* trialkylaluminium
Triallylcyanurat *n* triallyl cyanurate
Triamidophosphorsäure *f s.* Phosphoryltriamid
Triaminchelat *n* triamine chelate
Triarylmethanfarbstoff *m* triarylmethane dye
Triäthyl... *s.* Triethyl...
Triäthylborin *n s.* Triethylboran
Triäthylolamin *n s.* Triethanolamin
Triazin *n (org ch)* triazine
Triazinpolymer[e] *n* triazine polymer, polytriazine
Triazol *n (org ch)* triazole
Tribasizität *f* tribasicity *(of acids)*
Tribochemie *f* tribochemistry
Tribolumineszenz *f* triboluminescence
tribolumineszierend triboluminescent
Triborid *n* triboride
Tribromacetaldehyd *m s.* Tribromethanal
Tribromanilin *n* tribromoaniline
Tribromethanal *n* *tribromoethanal, tribromoacetaldehyde, bromal *s.* Tribromacetaldehyd
Tribromethanol *n*, **Tribromethylalkohol** *m* tribromoethanol, tribromoethyl alcohol
Tribromgerman *n* tribromogermane, germanium bromoform
Tribromid *n* tribromide
Tribrommethan *n* tribromomethane, bromoform
Tribromsilan *n* tribromosilane
Tributylzinnverbindung *f* tributyl tin [compound], TBT [compound]

Tricalciumorthophosphat *n*, **Tricalciumphosphat** *n* tricalcium orthophosphate, calcium phosphate
Tricarballylsäure *f* tricarballylic acid, *propane-1,2,3-tricarboxylic acid
Tricarbonsäure *f* tricarboxylic acid
Tricarbonsäurezyklus *m (bioch)* tricarboxylic-acid cycle, TCA cycle, citric-acid cycle, Krebs cycle
Trichloracetaldehyd *m s.* Trichloroethanal
Trichloracetaldehydhydrat *n* trichloroacetaldehyde hydrate, chloral hydrate
1,1,1-Trichloraceton *n* 1,1,1-trichloroacetone
Trichloracetylierung *f* trichloroacetylation
Trichloraldehyd *m s.* Trichloracetaldehyd
Trichlorbenzen *n* trichlorobenzene, TCB
Trichlorbenzoesäure *f* trichlorobenzoic acid
Trichlorbutylalkohol *m* trichloro-*tert*-butyl alcohol, chloretone, *1,1,1-trichloro-2-methylpropan-2-ol
Trichlorderivat *n* trichloro derivative
Trichloressigsäure *f* trichloroacetic acid, TCA
Trichlorethan *n* trichloroethane, TCE
1,1,1-Trichlorethan *n* *1,1,1-trichloroethane, methylchloroform
1,1,2-Trichlorethan *n* 1,1,2-trichloroethane
Trichlorethanal *n* *trichloroethanal, trichloroacetaldehyde, chloral
Trichlorethannitril *n* trichloroacetonitrile
Trichlorethansäure *f* trichloroacetic acid, TCA
Trichlorethen *n*, **Trichlorethylen** *n* trichloroethene
Trichlorethylidenglykol *n s.* Trichloracetaldehydhydrat
Trichlorgerman *n* trichlorogermane, germanium chloroform
Trichlorid *n* trichloride
Trichlormethan *n* *trichloromethane, chloroform
Trichlormethansulfenylchlorid *n* trichloromethanesulphenyl chloride, perchloromethanethiol
α-**Trichlormethylbenzen** *n s.* α-Trichlortoluen
Trichlormethylierung *f* trichloromethylation
Trichlornitromethan *n* trichloronitromethane, chloropicrin
2,4,5-Trichlorphenoxyessigsäure *f* 2,4,5-trichlorophenoxyacetic acid, 2,4,5-T *(a herbicide)*
2-(2,4,5-Trichlorphenoxy)propionsäure *f* 2-(2,4,5-trichlorophenoxy)propionic acid, fenoprop, 2,4,5-TP *(a herbicide)*
2,3,6-Trichlorphenylessigsäure *f* 2,3,6-trichlorophenylacetic acid, fenac *(a herbicide)*
Trichlorsilan *n* trichlorosilane
α-**Trichlortoluen** *n*, α-**Trichlortoluol** α,α,α-trichlorotoluene, benzotrichloride
Trichlor-*sym*-triazin *n* 2,4,6-trichloro-1,3,5-triazine, cyanuric chloride
Trichroismus *m (cryst)* trichroism
Trichromat *n* $M^I_2Cr_3O_{10}$ trichromate
Trichromdicarbid *n* trichromium dicarbide
Trichromtetrasulfid *n* trichromium tetrasulphide
Trichter *m* funnel; *(tech)* hopper; cup *(of a blast furnace)*
~ **mit glatter Wandung** plain glass funnel
~ **mit kurzem Rohr (Stiel)** short-stem[med] funnel
~ **mit langem Rohr (Stiel)** long-stem[med] funnel, Bunsen funnel
~ **nach Hirsch** Hirsch funnel
Trichterbecken *n (hyd)* hopper bottom sedimentation tank
Trichtereinlage *f* **zum Filtrieren** filter cone
Trichterhalter *m* funnel holder
Trichterrohr *n (lab)* thistle funnel (tube), funnel tube
~ **mit Schleife und Kugel** thistle funnel with safety bulb
Trichterröhre *f s.* Trichterrohr
Trichterstiel *m* funnel stem
Trichterstoffänger *m (pap)* cone save-all, settling cone
Trichtertrockner *m* hopper dryer
Trickle-[Phase-]Verfahren *n (petrol)* trickle [flow] process *(hydrodesulphurization)*
Tricobalttetroxid *n* tricobalt tetraoxide, cobalt(II, III) oxide
Tricosan *n (org ch)* tricosane
Tricresylphosphat *n* tritolyl phosphate, tricresyl phosphate, TCP
Tridecan *n* tridecane
Tridecandisäure *f* *tridecanedioic acid, brassylic acid
Tridecansäure *f* tridecanoic acid
Tridepsid *n* tridepside *(ester consisting of three phenolic benzoic acids)*
Tridymit *m* tridymite *(one form of silicon dioxide)*
Tridyne-Verfahren *n (plast)* Tridyne process *(transfer moulding)*
Triebkraft *f* 1. driving force (potential), [chemical] affinity *(of a reaction)*; 2. dough raising power *(as of yeast)*; 3. *(tech)* momentum
Triebmittel *n (food)* leaven, leavening [agent]
Trien *n* triene *(any of a class of hydrocarbons containing three carbon double bonds)*
Triester *m (org ch)* triester
Triethanolamin *n* triethanolamine, TEA, tri(2-hydroxyethyl)amine
Triethylaluminium *n* triethylaluminium
Triethylamin *n* triethylamine
Triethylboran *n* triethylborane
Triethylcellulose *f* ethylcellulose
Triethylcitrat *n* triethyl citrate
Triethylenglykol *n* triethylene glycol, TEG
Triethylphosphat *n* triethyl phosphate
Trifluorchloräthylen *n s.* Chlortrifluorethylen
Trifluoressigsäure *f* trifluoroacetic acid
Trifluorethansäure *f s.* Trifluoressigsäure
Trifluorid *n* trifluoride
Trifluormethan *n* *trifluoromethane, fluoroform
Trifluormethansulfonsäure *f* trifluoromethane sulphonic acid, triflic acid
Trifluorsilan *n* trifluorosilane
Triftröhre *f (anal)* klystron valve

trifunktionell trifunctional
trig. *s.* trigonal
Trigerman *n* trigermane, germanium octahydride
Trigermaniumdinitrid *n* trigermanium dinitride
Trigermaniumtetranitrid *n* trigermanium tetranitride
Triglycerid *n* triglyceride
~/einsäuriges simple triglyceride
~/gemischtes (gemischtsäuriges) mixed triglyceride
~/gleichsäuriges *s.* ~/einsäuriges
~/heterogenes *s.* ~/gemischtes
~/homogenes *s.* ~/einsäuriges
Triglykol *n s.* Triethylenglykol
trigonal *(cryst)* trigonal, trig.
Trihalogenid *n* trihalide, trihalogenide
Trihalogenmethan *n* trihalomethane, *(hyd also)* THM
~/bromhaltiges *(hyd)* bromine-containing trihalomethane, BTHM
Trihalomethan *n s.* Trihalogenmethan
Trihydrat *n* trihydrate
Trihydroxid *n* trihydroxide
Trihydroxyanthrachinon *n* trihydroxyanthraquinone
Trihydroxybenzen *n* trihydroxybenzene
Trihydroxybenzoesäure *f* trihydroxybenzoic acid
Trihydroxybenzol *n* trihydroxybenzene
Triiodid *n* triiodide
Triiodmethan *n* triiodomethane, iodoform
Triiodsilan *n* triiodosilane
Trikaliumorthophosphat *n*, **Trikaliumphosphat** *n* tripotassium orthophosphate, potassium phosphate
trikl. *s.* triklin
triklin *(cryst)* triclinic, tric., anorthic
Trikohlenstoffdioxid *n* tricarbon dioxide
Trikohlenstoffdisulfid *n* tricarbon disulphide
Trikupferphosphid *n* tricopper monophosphide, copper(I) phosphide, cuprous phosphide
Trillo *m (tann)* drillo *(from the cupulae of several oriental Quercus specc.)*
Trimellithsäure *f* trimellitic acid, *benzene-1,2,4-tricarboxylic acid
trimer trimeric
Trimer[e] *n* trimer
Trimerisation *f* trimerization
trimerisieren to trimerize; to trimerize, to undergo trimerization
Trimesinsäure *f* trimesic acid, *benzene-1,3,5-tricarboxylic acid
Trimethoxybenzoesäure *f* trimethoxybenzoic acid
Trimethylaluminium *n* trimethylaluminium
Trimethylamin *n* trimethylamine
Trimethylammonioacetat *n NNN*-trimethylammonioacetate, betaine, oxyneurine, lycine
Trimethylbenzen *n* trimethylbenzene
Trimethylbenzoesäure *f* trimethylbenzoic acid, isodurylic acid
Trimethylbenzol *n* trimethylbenzene
Trimethylbor *n s.* Trimethylboran
Trimethylboran *n* trimethylborane
Trimethylbrommethan *n s.* 2-Brom-2-methylpropan
2,2,3-Trimethylbutan *n* *2,2,3-trimethylbutane, triptane
Trimethylcarbinol *n s.* 2-Methylpropan-2-ol
Trimethylchinolin *n* trimethylquinoline
Trimethylen *n s.* Cyclopropan
Trimethylessigsäure *f s.* 2,2-Dimethylpropionsäure
Trimethylglycin *n*, **Trimethylglykokoll** *n* trimethylglycine, lycine, oxyneurine, betaine *(proper)*
Trimethylmethan *n s.* 2-Methylpropan
1,1,1-Trimethylolethan *n* 1,1,1-trimethylolethane, pentaglycerol, *2-hydroxymethyl-2-methylpropane-1,3-diol
Trimethylsilylgruppe *f* $-Si(CH_3)_3$ trimethylsilyl group
Trimethylsilylierung *f* trimethylsilylation
trimolekular trimolecular
Trimolybdat *n* $M^I_2Mo_3O_{10}$ trimolybdate
Trimyristin *n* trimyristin, glycerol trimyristate
Trinatriumarsenat *n* trisodium orthoarsenate, sodium arsenate
Trinatriumorthophosphat *n*, **Trinatriumphosphat** *n* trisodium orthophosphate, sodium phosphate
Trinatriumphosphatverfahren *n (hyd)* phosphate treatment
~ **mit Vorenthärtung** two-stage hot lime-soda phosphate treatment
Trinatriumsalz *n* trisodium salt
Trinickeltetrasulfid *n* trinickel tetrasulphide, nickel(II, III) sulphide
Trinitrat *n* trinitrate
Trinitrid *n* trinitride
trinitriert trinitrated
Trinitrierung *f* trinitration
2,4,6-Trinitrophenol *n* 2,4,6-trinitrophenol, picric acid
2,4,6-Trinitroresorcin *n* 2,4,6-trinitroresorcinol, styphnic acid
Trinitrotoluen *n*, **Trinitrotoluol** *n* trinitrotoluene, TNT
trinkbar potable
Trinkbarkeit *f* potability
Trinkbranntwein *m* potable spirit, [distilled] beverage spirit, beverage alcohol
trinkfertig ready-to-drink
Trinkmilch *f* beverage milk
Trinkwasser *n* drinking (potable) water, *(specif)* municipal [drinking] water, city water
~/aufbereitetes finished drinking water
Trinkwasseraufbereitung *f* drinking-water treatment
Trinkwasserenthärtung *f* drinking-water softening
Trinkwasserentkeimung *f* drinking-water disinfection
~ **durch Iodierung** iodination disinfection

Trinkwasser-Pasteurisieranlage *f* water pasteurizer
Trinkwasserqualität *f* drinking-water quality
Trinkwasserschutzzone *f* aquifer protection zone
Trinkwasser-Standard *m* drinking-water standards (regulations)
Trinkwasserversorgung *f* drinking-water supply
Trinkwasserwerk *n* drinking-water treatment plant
Triol *n* triol, trihydric alcohol
Triolein *n* triolein, glycerol trioleate, olein
Triose *f* triose *(monosaccharide containing three carbon atoms per molecule)*
Triosephosphatdehydr[ogen]ase *f* triose-phospho-dehydrogenase
Trioxalatochromat(III) *n* $M^{I}_{3}[Cr(C_2O_4)_3]$ trioxalatochromate(III), oxalatochromate(III)
Trioxalatocobaltat(III) *n* $M^{I}_{3}[Co(C_2O_4)_3]$ trioxalatocobaltate(III), oxalatocobaltate(III)
1,3,5-Trioxan *n* 1,3,5-trioxan, trioxymethylene, metaformaldehyde
Trioxid *n* trioxide
Trioxoborat *n* $M^{I}_{3}BO_3$ trioxoborate, orthoborate, borate
Trioxoborsäure *f* trioxoboric acid, orthoboric acid, boric acid
Trioxokieselsäure *f* trioxosilicic acid, metasilicic acid
Trioxoplumbat(IV) *n* $M^{I}_{2}PbO_3$ trioxoplumbate(IV), metaplumbate(IV)
Trioxosilicat *n* $M^{I}_{2}SiO$ trioxosilicate, metasilicate
Trioxotitanat(IV) *n* $M^{I}_{2}TiO_3$ trioxotitanate(IV), metatitanate(IV)
Trioxovanadat(V) *n* $M^{I}VO_3$ trioxovanadate(V), metavanadate
Trioxozirconat(IV) *n* $M^{I}_{2}ZrO_3$ trioxozirconate(IV), metazirconate(IV)
Trioxymethylen *n s.* 1,3,5-Trioxan
Tripalmitin *n* tripalmitin, glycerol tripalmitate
Tripel *m (min)* tripoli *(schistose deposits of silica)*
Tripeleffekt *m s.* Tripeleffektverdampfer
Tripeleffektverdampfer *m* triple-effect evaporator (evaporating unit)
Tripelhelix *f (bioch)* triple[-stranded] helix, superhelix
Tripelion *n* triple ion
Tripelpunkt *m* triple point
Tripelsalz *n* triple salt
Tripeptid *n* tripeptide
Triphenylamin *n* triphenylamine
Triphenylaminfarbstoff *m* triphenylamine dye
Triphenylbor *n s.* Triphenylboran
Triphenylboran *n* triphenylborane
Triphenylcarbinol *n s.* Triphenylmethanol
Triphenylen *n* triphenylene, 1,2,3,4-dibenznaphthalene
Triphenylmethan *n* triphenylmethane
Triphenylmethanfarbstoff *m* triphenylmethane dye
Triphenylmethanol *n* triphenylmethanol
Triphenylmethylierung *f* triphenylmethylation, tritylation
Triphenylphosphat *n* triphenyl phosphate
Triphenylphosphin *n* triphenylphosphine
Triphenylstibin *n* triphenylstibine
Triphenylzinnchlorid *n* triphenyltin chloride
Triphosphat *n* $M^{I}_{5}P_3O_{10}$ triphosphate
Triphosphopyridinnucleotid *n s.* Nicotinamid-adenin-dinucleotidphosphat
Triphosphorpentanitrid *n* triphosphorus pentanitride, phosphorus nitride
Triphylin *m (min)* triphylite, triphyline *(a phosphate of lithium, iron, and manganese)*
Triplett *n* 1. *(phys ch, spectr)* triplet; 2. *(bioch)* triplet [codon]
Triplettaufspaltung *f (phys ch)* triplet splitting
Triplettcode *m (bioch)* triplet code
Triplett-Singulett-Übergang *m (phys ch)* triplet → singlet transition
Triplettspektrallinie *f s.* Triplett 1.
Triplettsystem *n (phys ch)* triplet system
Triplett-Term *m (spectr)* triplet energy level
Triplett-Triplett-Annihilation *f* triplet-triplet annihilation
Triplett-Triplett-Übergang *m (phys ch)* triplet → triplet transition
Triplett-Triplett-Übertragung *f* triplet-triplet energy transfer
Triplettzustand *m* triplet [electronic] state
Triplexkarton *m* triplex board
Triplexpappe *f* triplex board
Triplexpumpe *f* triplex (three-throw) pump
Triptan *n s.* 2,2,3-Trimethylbutan
Trisaccharid *n* trisaccharide
Trisauerstoff *m s.* Ozon
Trisazofarbstoff *m* trisazo dye
Trischwefelwasserstoff *m s.* Trisulfan
Trisilan *n* trisilane
Trisilicat *n* trisilicate
Trisilicatschlacke *f* trisilicate slag
Trisiloxan *n* trisiloxane
Trisilthian *n* trisilthiane
Trisomie *f* **21** *(med)* trisomy 21, Down's syndrome, mongolism
Trispiro-Verbindung *f* trispiro compound (hydrocarbon)
Trispuffer *m (bioch)* tris buffer
Tristearin *n* tristearin, glyceryl tristearate
trisubstituiert trisubstituted
Trisubstitutionsprodukt *n* trisubstitution product
Trisulfan *n* trisulphane, hydrogen trisulphide
Trisulfat *n* $M^{I}_{2}S_3O_{10}$ trisulphate
Trisulfid *n* trisulphide
Trisulfonsäure *f* trisulphonic acid
Tritan *n* tritane, triphenylmethane
Triterpen *n (org ch)* triterpene
Triterpenoid *n (org ch)* triterpenoid
Trithioarsenat(V) *n* $M^{I}AsS_3$ trithioarsenate, metathioarsenate

Trithiocarbonat *n* $M^I_2CS_3$ trithiocarbonate, thiocarbonate
Trithiokohlensäure *f* trithiocarbonic acid, thiocarbonic acid
Trithionat *n* $M^I_2S_3O_6$ trithionate
Trithiostannat(IV) *n* $M^I_2SnS_3$ trithiostannate(IV), metathiostannate(IV)
tritiieren to tritiate
Tritiierung *f* tritiation
Tritium *n* T, ^3_1H, tritium • **mit ~ markiert** tritium-labelled
tritiumhaltig tritium-containing
Tritol *n s.* Trinitrotoluen
Triton *n (nucl)* triton
Tritriacontan *n (org ch)* tritriacontane
Trituration *f (pharm)* trituration
Tritylchlorid *n* trityl chloride, α-chlorotriphenylmethane
Tritylfarbstoff *m* triarylmethane dye
Tritylierung *f* tritylation, triphenylmethylation
Triuranoctoxid *n* triuranium octaoxide, uranium(IV) uranate
trivalent trivalent, tervalent
Trivalenz *f* trivalency, tervalency
trivariant trivariant
Trivialname *m* trivial (common, unsystematic) name
~/verbotener abandoned trivial name
~/zugelassener (zulässiger) recognized trivial name
t-RNA *s.* Transfer-Ribonucleinsäure
trocken dry
~/absolut bone-dry, oven-dry, oven-dried, OD
~ und mineral[stoff]frei dry and mineral-matter-free, d.m.m.f., D.M.F.
Trockenablagerung *f* dry deposition *(of pollutants from the atmosphere)*
Trockenabschnitt *m* beach section *(of a helical-conveyor centrifuge)*
Trockenanlage *f* drying plant
Trockenapparat *m* dryer, *(lab also)* drying apparatus
Trockenaufbereitung *f* 1. *(min tech)* dry (pneumatic) cleaning; 2. *(ceram)* dry preparation (mixing, mix)
Trockenausschuß *m (pap)* dry broke
Trockenbatterie *f* dry battery
Trockenbeet *n (hyd)* sludge [drying] bed, sand [drying] bed, drying bed, tile field
Trockenbeize *f (agric)* dry [seed] treatment, dust treatment
Trockenbestandteil *m* solid constituent
Trockenbiomasse *f (biot)* dry weight of biomass
trockenblasen/mit Druckluft *(filtr)* to air-blow
Trockenblech *n* [drying] tray
Trockenboden *m (ceram)* hot floor; *(pap)* drying loft • **auf dem ~ getrocknet** *(pap)* loft-dried
Trockenbrett *n (lab)* draining board
~/aufhängbares wall-mounting draining board
trockencyanieren to dry-cyanide, to gas-cyanide, to carbonitride *(steel)*
Trockencyanieren *n* dry (gas) cyaniding (cyanization), carbonitriding, nicarbing, nitrocementation *(of steel)*
Trockendampf *m* dry [saturated] steam
Trockendämpfen *n*, **Trockendekatieren** *n*, **Trokkendekatur** *f (text)* dry steaming (decatizing)
Trockendestillation *f* dry (destructive) distillation
Trockendosiereinrichtung *f*, **Trockendosierer** *m* dry feeder
Trockendosierung *f* dry feeding
Trockeneinfärben *n (plast)* dry colouring *(of moulding compounds)*
Trockeneis *n* dry ice, carbon dioxide ice (snow), solid carbon dioxide
Trockenelektroabscheider *m*, **Trockenelektrofilter** *n* dry precipitator
Trockenelement *n* dry cell
Trockenemulsion *f (phot)* dry emulsion
Trockenentschwefelung *f* dry desulphurization *(of gas)*
Trockenextrakt *m* dry extract
Trockenfeld *n* drying ground *(winning of peat)*
Trockenfestigkeit *f* dry strength; *(ceram)* green strength
Trockenfilter *n* dry filter
Trockenfilz *m (pap)* dry[er] felt
Trockenfilzleitwalze *f (pap)* dry-felt roll
Trockenfläche *f* drying area (surface)
Trockenflecken *mpl (phot)* drying marks
Trockenfließpapier *n* dry blotting paper
Trockenfurfural *n* dry furfural
Trockenfutterhefe *f* mineral yeast
Trockengas *n* 1. dry [natural] gas *(main constituent methane)*; 2. *s.* Trocknungsgas
Trockengasreinigung *f* dry gas cleaning
Trockengehalt *m (pap)* solid[s] content *(of sulphite waste liquor)*
Trockengel *n* xerogel
trockengepreßt *(ceram)* dry-pressed
Trockengerbung *f* dry tannage
Trockengeschwindigkeit *f* drying rate
Trockengestell *n (ceram)* drying rack
Trockengewicht *n* dry weight
Trockenglatt-Ausrüstung *f (text)* smooth-drying finish
Trockenglättwerk *n (pap)* calender, calender machine (section)
Trockengruppe *f (pap)* dryer group (section)
Trockenguß *m* dry-sand casting *(foundry)*
Trockengußform *f* dry-sand mould *(foundry)*
Trockengußformen *n* dry[-sand] moulding *(foundry)*
Trockenguß[form]sand *m* dry sand *(foundry)*
Trockengut *n* material being *or* to be dried; dry product
Trockenhänge *f (text)* festoon dryer
Trockenhaspel *f (text)* drying reel
Trockenhefe *f* dried (dry) yeast, yeast powder

Trockenherd *m* dryer (drying) hearth *(of a roasting furnace)*
Trockenheit *f* dryness
Trockenhitzebehandlung *f* baking
Trockenhorde *f* [drying] tray
Trockenkammer *f* drying room (chamber), *(if small:)* drying cabinet (box)
Trockenkarbonisation *f (text)* dry carbonizing
Trockenkautschukgehalt *m* dry rubber content, DRC
Trockenköder *m (agric)* dry bait
Trockenkollergang *m* dry pan
Trockenkonzentrat *n (agric)* dry concentrate
Trockenkugeltemperatur *f* dry-bulb temperature
Trockenlöscher *m* dry chemical [fire] extinguisher, powder extinguisher
Trockenmagermilch *f* non-fat dry milk, dry skim milk, skim-milk powder
Trockenmahlung *f* dry milling (grinding)
Trockenmaschine *f (text, phot)* drying machine, dryer
Trockenmasse *f* 1. solids; 2. [bone-]dry weight, moisture-free weight
~ **der Mikroorganismenzellen** *(biot)* microbial dry weight
~ **des Holzes** *(pap)* dry wood weight
~**/fettfreie** *(food)* non-fat[ty] solids, solids-non-fat, S.N.F.
Trockenmedium *n s.* Trockenmittel
Trockenmilch *f* dried (dry) milk, milk powder
~ **auf Milchkonzentration verdünnte** reconstituted milk
Trockenmischer *m* dry blender (mixer)
Trockenmischung *f* dry blend (mix)
Trockenmittel *n* desiccant, desiccating agent, drying (dehydrating) agent (medium), dehydrator, dehumidifier
Trockenmittelkolben *m* desiccant chamber *(of a drying pistol)*
Trockenmolke *f* dried (dry) whey, whey powder
Trockenofen *m* drying oven, *(esp ceram)* drying kiln; *(coat)* stoving (baking) oven
Trockenpacken *n (chromat)* dry-packing technique
Trockenpartie *f* drying (dryer) part (section), dry part (end) *(of a papermaking machine)*
Trockenpektin *n* dry pectin, powdered (solid) pectin
Trockenpistole *f* [vacuum] drying pistol
Trockenplatte *f (phot)* dry plate
Trockenplatz *m* drying ground *(winning of peat)*
trockenpökeln to dry-cure, to dry-salt
Trockenpökelung *f* dry curing (salting), dry-salt cure
Trockenpräparat *n* dry preparation
Trockenpressen *n (ceram)* dry pressing, *(relating to tiles also)* dust pressing
Trockenpreßmasse *f (ceram)* dry pressing mix (body)
Trockenprobe *f (met)* dry assay
Trockenraum *m* drying room (chamber)
Trockenreiniger *m* dry cleaner (purifier)
Trockenreinigung *f* dry cleaning *(1. of gases; 2. of clothes)*
Trockenreinigungsechtheit *f (text)* fastness to dry cleaning
Trockenriß *m (ceram)* drying crack
Trockenrohr *n s.* Trockenpistole
trockensalzen to dry-cure, to dry-salt
Trockensalzen *n* dry curing (cure, salting)
Trockensand *m* dry sand
Trockensandform *f* dry-sand mould *(foundry)*
Trockensandformen *n* dry[-sand] moulding *(foundry)*
Trockensäule *f (chromat)* dry column
Trockenschacht *m* drying shaft
Trockenschale *f* drying tray
Trockenscheidung *f (sugar)* dry liming, defecation with dry lime
Trockenschlamm *m (hyd)* dry (dried) sludge
Trockenschlammentfernung *f (hyd)* dry sludge removal
Trockenschleuder *f* hydroextractor
Trockenschmelze *f*, **Trockenschmelzen** *n (food)* dry rendering
Trockenschnecke *f* screw-conveyor dryer
Trockenschrank *m (lab)* drying oven, [air] oven
• **im ~ getrocknet** oven-dry, oven-dried, OD • **im ~ trocknen** to oven-dry
~**/elektrischer** electric drying oven
Trockenschrank-Heißluftsterilisator *m* hot-air sterilizer
Trockenschuppen *m* drying shed
Trockenschwindung *f (ceram)* drying shrinkage (contraction), air shrinkage
Trockenshampoo[n] *n (cosmet)* dry shampoo
Trockensieben *n* dry screening (sieving)
Trockenspeicher *m* drying loft
Trockenspiegel *m* plane of evaporation
Trockenspinnen *n* dry spinning
Trockenspritzen *n (coat)* dry spray
Trockenstärke *f (food)* dry starch
Trockenstoff *m s.* Trockenmittel
Trockenstoffmasse *f* [bone-]dry weight, moisture-free weight
Trockensubstanz *f* dry (solid) matter, solids, dry residue (substance)
~ **der Schwarzlauge** *(pap)* black-liquor solids
~ **im Abwasser-Belebtschlamm-Gemisch/organische** *(hyd)* mixed-liquor volatile suspended solids, MLVSS, volatile portion of the mixed-liquor suspended solids
Trockensubstanzgehalt *m* solids [content, concentration]
~ **des Kuchens** cake solids [content, concentration]
Trockensubstanzmasse *f s.* Trockenstoffmasse
Trockentemperatur *f* drying temperature
Trockenthermometer *n* dry-bulb thermometer
Trockentorf *m* dry peat

Trockentrommel *f* 1. drying (dryer) cylinder (drum); 2. *s.* Trommeltrockner
Trockentunnel *m* drying tunnel
Trockenturm *m* 1. drying tower; 2. *(lab)* [gas] drying jar
Trockenverarbeitung *f* dry processing
Trockenverfahren *n* dry process
Trockenverlust *m* drying loss
Trockenvermahlung *f* dry milling (grinding)
Trockenverschluß *m* dry seal
Trockenvollmilch *f* dry whole milk, whole milk powder
Trockenwalze *f* 1. drying (dryer) drum; 2. *s.* Walzentrockner
Trockenware *f (food)* dry product
Trockenwaschverfahren *n (text)* solvent scouring process *(for treating raw wool)*
Trockenwetterabfluß *m (hyd)* dry-weather flow, D.W.F.
trockenwischen to wipe dry
Trockenzeit *f* drying period (time)
Trockenzentrifuge *f* centrifugal dryer, whizzer, hydroextractor
Trockenzone *f* drying zone *(of a multiple-hearth incinerator)*; drying (liquid extraction) zone, *(of a vacuum filter:)* dewatering part
trockenzyanieren *s.* trockencyanieren
Trockenzylinder *m* 1. drying (dryer) cylinder (roll); 2. *s.* Zylindertrockner
Trockne *f* dryness • **zur ~ eindampfen** to evaporate to dryness
~/beginnende incipient (moist) dryness
trocknen to dry, to dehydrate, to desiccate, *(esp relating to gases:)* to dehumidify; to season *(wood)*
~/an der Luft to air-dry
~/an der Sonne to sun-dry
~ bis zur Gewichtskonstanz (Massekonstanz) to dry to constant weight
~/durch Abtropfenlassen to drain-dry, to drip-dry
~/im Ofen *(coat)* to stove
~/im Sprühverfahren to spray-dry
~/im Trockenschrank to oven-dry
~/im Vakuum to vacuum-dry
~/im Zerstäubungsverfahren to spray-dry
~/lederhart *(ceram)* to dry to leather-hard
~/lyophil to lyophilize, to freeze-dry
~/nochmals to redry
~/schwach to dry soft
~/stark to dry hard
~/thermisch to stove, to bake
~/unter Vakuum to vacuum-dry
~/unvollständig (unzureichend) to underdry
~/wieder to redry
trocknend/chemisch (durch chemische Reaktion) convertible *(organic coating)*
~/langsam slow-drying
~/physikalisch non-convertible *(organic coating)*
~/schnell quick-drying
Trockner *m* 1. dryer, *(text, phot also)* drying machine, *(lab also)* drying apparatus; 2. *s.* Trockenmittel
~/atmosphärischer atmospheric (air) dryer
~/begehbarer walk-in dryer
~/diskontinuierlich arbeitender batch dryer
~/kontinuierlich arbeitender continuous dryer
~ mit Durchbelüftung air-through circulation dryer
~/pneumatischer pneumatic [conveying] dryer
Trockneraufgabegut *n* material to be dried
Trocknerkammer *f (ceram)* dryer corridor
Trocknertrommel *f* dryer drum
Trocknerwalze *f* dryer roll
Trocknerzylinder *m* dryer cylinder
Trocknung *f* drying, dehydration, desiccation, *(esp relating to gases:)* dehumidification; seasoning *(of wood)*
~ an der Luft air drying
~ an der Sonne solar (sun) drying
~/atmosphärische air drying
~ bis zur Gewichtskonstanz (Massekonstanz) drying to constant weight
~/dielektrische dielectric (radio-frequency) drying
~/künstliche artificial drying
~/lyophile lyophilic (freeze) drying, lyophilization
~ mit festem Trocknungsmittel dry-desiccant dehydration
~ mittels Lösungsmitteln solvent drying
~/natürliche air drying
~/pneumatische pneumatic conveying drying
~/thermische thermal drying, stoving
~/übermäßige excessive drying
~/ungleichmäßige uneven drying
~/unvollständige (unzureichende) underdrying
Trocknungs... *s. a.* Trocken...
Trocknungsabschnitt *m* period of drying
Trocknungsdauer *f* drying period (time)
Trocknungsgas *n* drying gas
Trocknungsgrad *m* **des Filterkuchens** degree of cake dryness
Trocknungsgruppe *f (pap)* dryer group (section)
Trocknungsgut *n* material being *or* to be dried
Trocknungskurve *f* drying curve
Trocknungsluft *f* drying air
Trocknungspotential *n* drying potential
Trocknungsrohr *n* heating chamber *(of a drying pistol)*
Trocknungstriebkraft *f* drying potential
Trocknungsverfahren *n* drying process
Trocknungsverlust *m* loss on drying
Trocknungsvorgang *m* drying process
Trog *m* trough, vat, tank, tub
Trogboden *m (pap)* floor of the tub *(of a Hollander beater)*
Trogkammer *f s.* Trennkammer
Trogkettenförderer *m* skeleton-flight (continuous-flow) conveyor, continuous (Redler, en masse) conveyor

Trogkneter *m*, **Trogmischer** *m* trough (open-pan) mixer
Trogpresse *f* pot press
Trogsohle *f s.* Trogboden
Trogtränkung *f* steeping *(of timber)*
~ **mit Wärmestandsänderung** hot-and-cold open tank treatment
Trombe *f* vortex
Trombenbildung *f* vortex formation
Trommel *f* drum, cylinder; bowl, basket *(of a centrifuge)* • **in der ~ färben** *(text)* to drum-dye
~/**konische** conical bowl *(of a centrifuge)*
Trommelausstoßmaschine *f (tann)* drum setting machine
Trommelentrindung *f (pap)* drum barking
Trommelentrindungsmaschine *f (pap)* drum barker
Trommelerhitzer *m (food)* cylindrical batch pasteurizer
Trommelfallmühle *f* autogenous tumbling mill
Trommelfärbemaschine *f (text)* drum-dyeing machine
Trommelfärbung *f (text)* drum dyeing
Trommelfilter *n* [rotary-]drum filter
~ **mit ablaufendem Filtertuch** rotary-drum belt-type vacuum filter
~/**zellenloses** single-compartment (single-cell) drum filter
Trommelhülse *f (text)* winding head
Trommelinnenfilter *n* inside drum filter, internal [rotary-]drum filter
Trommelkonverter *m* **nach Peirce-Smith** *(met)* Peirce-Smith converter
Trommelkühlung *f* drum cooling
Trommellackieren *n (coat)* barrel painting (coating)
Trommelmälzerei *f (ferm)* drum malting
Trommelmischer *m* drum mixer, barrel blender (mixer)
Trommelmühle *f* drum mill
trommeln *(plast, coal)* to tumble *(mass-production parts)*
Trommelnaßmühle *f* wet-cylinder mill
Trommelneigung *f* drum slope
Trommelpolieren *n (plast)* barrel polishing (burnishing)
Trommelprüfung *f (coal)* tumbler (trommel) test
~ **nach Cochrane** Cochrane test
Trommelreifen *m (rubber)* drum-built tyre
Trommelsaugfilter *n* rotary-drum vacuum filter, [rotary] vacuum drum filter
Trommelscheider *m* drum separator
Trommelschieber *m* coal inlet valve *(of a gas retort)*
Trommelschlichtmaschine *f (text)* cylinder sizing machine
Trommelschneidmaschine *f (sugar)* rotating-drum slicer
Trommelschreiber *m* drum[-chart] recorder
Trommelsieb *n* drum (trommel, revolving) screen
Trommeltest *m s.* Trommelprüfung
Trommeltrockner *m* 1. rotary [drum] dryer, rotatory dryer; 2. *(sugar)* granulator • **im ~ trocknen** to drum-dry
~ **mit Kontaktheizung** indirect rotary dryer
Trommelverfahren *n* dry [drum-]cooling method, chill-roll method *(of margarine making)*
Trommelversuch *m s.* Trommelprüfung
Trommelzellenfilter *n* multicompartment drum filter
Trommelzentrifuge *f* bowl (basket) centrifuge
~ **mit Einsatztellern** disk [bowl] centrifuge, disk separator
Trommsdorff-[Norrish-]Effekt *m (plast)* Trommsdorff effect, gel effect
Trona *m(f) (min)* trona *(a hydrous acid sodium carbonate)*
Trona-Verfahren *n* Trona process *(potash industry)*
Troostit *m (min)* troostite *(a nesosilicate)*
Tropaalkaloid *n* tropane alkaloid
Tropan *n (org ch)* tropane
Tropanalkaloid *n* tropane alkaloid
Tropasäure *f* tropic acid, 3-hydroxy-2-phenylpropionic acid
Tropenas-Konverter *m (met)* Tropenas [side-blown] converter
tropenbeständig *s.* tropenfest
tropenfest resistant to tropical conditions, stable under tropical conditions
Tropenfestigkeit *f* resistance to tropical conditions, stability under tropical conditions
Tropenfestmachen *n* tropicalization
Tropfbenzoltank *m* drains tank *(of a benzole plant)*
Tröpfchen *n* droplet
Tröpfchenbildung *f* formation of droplets
Tröpfchengröße *f* droplet size
Tropfelektrode *f* drop[ping] electrode
tröpfeln to trickle
tropfen to drop, to drip
Tropfen *m* 1. drop; 2. *(coat)* tear, drip; 3. *(glass)* gob
Tropfenabgabe *f (glass)* gob delivery
Tropfenabziehen *n (coat)* detearing
~/**elektrostatisches** electrostatic detearing
Tropfenbildung *f* drop formation
Tropfenfänger *m (lab)* Kjeldahl connecting bulb
Tropfenform *f (glass)* gob shape
tropfenförmig drop-shaped
Tropfen-Gegenstromchromatographie *f* droplet counter-current chromatography, DCCC
Tropfengewicht *n (glass)* gob weight
Tropfengewichtsmethode *f (phys ch)* drop-weight method
Tropfengröße *f* drop size
Tropfengrößenverteilung *f* drop-size distribution
Tropfenkondensation *f* dropwise condensation
Tropfenspeiser *m (glass)* gob feeder
tropfenweise dropwise, drop by drop
Tropfenzähler *m (lab)* 1. drop counter; 2. *s.* Tropfflasche; 3. *s.* Tropfpipette

Tropfer *m s.* Tropfpipette
Tropfflasche *f*, **Tropfglas** *n (lab)* dropping bottle
Tropfkatode *f* dropping cathode
Tropfkörper *m (hyd)* trickling (percolating) filter, biological filter, biofilter, fixed-film reactor, packed-bed biological film reactor
~/hochbelasteter high-rate trickling filter
~/höchstbelasteter super-rate trickling filter
~ **mit klassischem Füllstoff** mineral-packed biological filter, stone-filled biological filter
~ **mit Kunststoff-Füllstoff** plastic-packed biological filter
~/schwachbelasteter low-rate trickling filter
Tropfkörperablauf *m (hyd)* trickling-filter effluent
Tropfkörperanlage *f (hyd)* trickling-filter plant
Tropfkörperboden *m (hyd)* underdrain of a trickling filter
Tropfkörperfüllmaterial *n*, **Tropfkörperfüllstoff** *m (hyd)* filter (packing) medium of a trickling filter
Tropfkörperleistung *f (hyd)* trickling-filter performance, trickling filtration performance
Tropfkörperoberfläche *f (hyd)* trickling-filter surface
Tropfkörperreaktor *m (biot)* trickling film reactor, trickle-flow fermenter (reactor)
Tropfkörperverfahren *n (hyd)* trickling filter process, trickling filtration
Tropfpipette *f (lab)* dropping (teat) pipette, [medicine] dropper
Tropfpunkt *m* drop[ping] point
~ **nach Ubbelohde** Ubbelohde drop[ping] point
Tropfrohr *n (lab)* drip tube (pipe)
Tropfspeisung *f (glass)* gob feeding
Tropftrichter *m (lab)* dropping (tap) funnel
tropfwassergeschützt drip-proof
Trophophase *f (biot)* trophophase *(growth of microorganisms)*
Tropilidon *n* tropilidene, cyclohepta-1,3,5-triene
Tropinalkaloid *n* tropane alkaloid
Tropinmandelsäureester *m* mandelyltropine, homatropine, phenylglycollyltropine
Tropinsäure *f* tropinic acid *(a degradation product of atropine)*
Tropon *n* tropone, cyclohepta-2,4,6-trienone
Tropolon *n (org ch)* tropolone
Tropopause *f* tropopause
Troposphäre *f* troposphere
Tropylium-Ion *n* tropylium ion, cycloheptatrienylium ion
Trotyl *n s.* Trinitrotoluen
Trp *s.* Tryptophan
Trub *m (ferm)* sediment, settling[s], *(relating to wine also)* lees, *(brewing also)* trub
trüb[e] opaque, *(esp relating to liquids:)* turbid, hazy, cloudy, feculent; dull, dusky *(shade)*
Trübe *f* 1. slurry, pulp; *(filtr)* prefilt, prefilt slurry (feed), material being *or* to be filtered; fluid pulp *(classifying)*; *(min tech)* pulp [of ore]; 2. *s.* Schlammtrübe; 3. *s.* Trub; 4. *s.* Trübheit
~/schwere *(min tech)* heavy (dense) medium, high-gravity medium
~/zulaufende feed slurry (pulp)
Trübeaufgaberinne *f (min tech)* feed launder
Trübefeststoff *m* medium solid *(dense-medium separation)*
Trübefeststoffgehalt *m (hyd)* inlet (influent) solids concentration
Trübehöhe *f (hyd)* fluid depth *(sedimentation)*
~ **im Filtertrog** vat level
Trübekreislauf *m* medium circuit *(dense-medium separation)*
trüben/sich to opacify, *(esp of liquids)* to become turbid
Trübeniveau *n* surface level of the medium *(dense-medium separation)*
Trübeteilchen *npl (hyd)* particles of turbidity, suspended particles
Trübeumlauf *m s.* Trübekreislauf
Trübezulauf *m*, **Trübezuleitung** *f* feed inlet, *(min tech also)* pulp inlet
Trübglas *n* opaque (opal) glass
Trübglasur *f (ceram)* opaque glaze
Trübheit *f* opacity, *(esp of liquids:)* turbidity, haziness, cloudiness, feculence; dullness, duskiness *(of a colour)*
Trüblauf *m (filtr)* bleeding
Trübstoffdurchbruch *m (hyd)* turbidity breakthrough
Trübstoffe *mpl (hyd)* turbidity-causing solids, turbidity, turbidities
~/im Rohwasser befindliche raw-water turbidities
Trübstoffelimination *f*, **Trübstoffentfernung** *f (hyd)* removal of turbidity, turbidity removal
trübstofffrei *(hyd)* turbidity-free
Trübstoffgehalt *m (hyd)* level of turbidity
~ **im Ablauf** effluent turbidity
~ **im Zulauf** influent turbidity
trübstoffhaltig *(hyd)* containing turbidity
Trübstoffteilchen *n (hyd)* particles of turbidity, suspended particles
Trübung *f* 1. *s.* Trübheit; 2. haze *(in beer)*, casse *(in wine)*; 3. opacifying, *(esp of liquids:)* clouding
~ **durch Reflexion** *(coll)* reflection turbidity
~/milchige milkiness
Trübungsanalyse *f* 1. turbidimetric analysis; 2. *s.* Turbidimetrie
Trübungsgrad *m* degree of turbidity
Trübungsmesser *m* turbidimeter, turbidometer, nephelometer
Trübungsmessung *f* turbidimetric (turbidity) measurement
Trübungsmittel *n* opacifier *(as for glass and plastics)*
Trübungspunkt *m* turbidity (cloud) point *(of solutions or oils)*; *(petrol)* cloud point; titre *(of a soap)*
Trübungsstoffe *mpl s.* Trübstoffe
Trübungstemperatur *f*/**maximale** precipitation threshold *(of solutions)*

Trübungstitration *f* turbidimetric (turbidity) titration
Trübwasser *n* turbid water
True-Vapour-Phase-Verfahren *n (petrol)* true vapour-phase [cracking] process, TVP process
Trum *m(n)* strand *(of a conveyor)*
Truxillo-Koka *f* Truxillo coca *(from Erythroxylum novogranatense (Morris) Hieron.)*
Trypanblau *n* trypan blue, direct blue 14
trypanozid [wirkend] *(pharm)* trypanocidal *(tending or used to destroy trypanosomes)*
Trypanrot *n* trypan red *(a biological stain)*
Trypsin *n* trypsin *(a proteolytic enzyme or a preparation containing proteolytic enzymes)*
Trypsin-Verfahren *n (rubber)* trypsin method *(heat sensitization of latex)*
Tryptophan *n* tryptophane, 2-amino-3,3'-indolylpropionic acid
Tryptophanreaktion *f* **nach Adamkiewicz** Adamkiewicz reaction *(for detecting tryptophane)*
TS *s.* Trockensubstanz
Tschandu *n* chandu, chandoo *(a kind of prepared opium)*
Tscherenkow-Strahlung *f (nucl)* Cherenkov radiation
Tschernosjom *m(n) (soil)* chernozem, black earth
Tschitschibabin-Kohlenwasserstoff *m* Chichibabin hydrocarbon
Tschitschibabin-Reaktion *f* Chichibabin reaction *(for preparing amino derivatives of heterocyclic bases)*
Tschugajew-Reaktion *f* Chugaev (Tschugaeff) reaction *(for obtaining alkenes)*
T-s-Diagramm *n* temperature-entropy chart, entropy chart (diagram)
TSH *s.* Hormon/thyreotropes
T-Stück *n* T-shape connecting tube, T-piece, T-type connector, tee [connector] • **mit einem ~ verbinden** to tee
~ mit Reduzierung reducer tee
tt *s.* transtaktisch
T-50-Test *m* T-50 test *(for determining the stage of vulcanization)*
TTT *s.* Tieftemperaturteer
Tubasäure *f* tubaic acid *(a benzofuran derivative)*
Tube-and-Tank-Verfahren *n (petrol)* tube-and-tank [cracking] process
Tuberkulin *n (med)* tuberculin
~ Koch old tuberculin
Tuberkulosemittel *n*, **Tuberkulostatikum** *n* antitubercular (antituberculosis) drug
Tubocurare *n* tubocurare, tube (pot) curare
Tubularreaktor *m s.* Rohrreaktor
Tubus *m* beak *(of a retort)*
Tuch *n* [woven] fabric, *(if of definite size:)* cloth
tuchbespannt cloth-covered
Tuchfilter *n* cloth (fabric) filter, woven[-fabric] filter
Tuchherd *m (min tech)* blanket table
Tuchpapier *n* velour (flock) paper
Tuff *m* tufa, *(of volcanic origin also)* tuff
Tüllenbürste *f* test-tube brush
Tully-Anlage *f* Tully plant *(for making water gas)*
Tully-Verfahren *n* Tully process *(for making water gas)*
Tulpe *f (lab)* crucible adapter
tumorerzeugend tumour-causing, tumorigenic, oncogenic, oncogenous
tumorhemmend antitumour
tumorinduzierend *s.* tumorerzeugend
Tünche *f* limewash, whitewash, distemper
Tungöl *n* tung oil *(from seeds of Aleurites fordii Hemsl.)*
~/Japanisches Japanese tung oil *(from seeds of Aleurites cordata (Thunb.) R.Br. ex Steud.)*
Tungstit *m (min)* tungstite, tungstic ochre *(a hydrous tungsten trioxide)*
Tunkbad *n (tann)* dipping bath
Tunkfärbung *f (tann)* dip dyeing
Tunneleffekt *m (phys ch)* tunnel effect
Tunnelglocke *f (distil)* tunnel cap
Tunnelofen *m* tunnel furnace, *(esp ceram also)* tunnel kiln
Tunneltrockner *m* tunnel dryer (drying machine)
Tunnelung *f (phys ch)* tunnel[l]ing *(penetration of the energy barrier)*
Tüpfelanalyse *f* spot-test analysis, drop analysis
tüpfeln to spot, to test by spotting
Tüpfelpapier *n (anal)* drop-reaction paper
Tüpfelplatte *f* spot (spotting, cavity) plate
Tüpfelprobe *f* spot [plate] test, drop test
Tüpfelreaktion *f* spot (drop) reaction
tupfen to tip, to spot, to dot
Tupfen *m* spot
Türabheber *m*, **Türabhebevorrichtung** *f* door extractor
Turbidimeter *n* turbidimeter, turbidometer, nephelometer
Turbidimetrie *f* turbidimetry, turbidimetric analysis
turbidimetrisch turbidimetric
Turbidostat *m (biot)* turbidostat
Turbine *f*/**spülungsbetriebene** *(petrol)* mud turbine
Turbinenbelüfter *m (hyd)* turbine aerator
Turbinenblatt *n* turbine blade
Turbinen[dreh]bohren *n (petrol)* turbine drilling, turbodrill[ing]
Turbinenöl *n* turbine oil
Turbinenpumpe *f* turbine (diffuser) pump
Turbinenrührer *m* turbine mixer (agitator, impeller)
Turbinen-Tellertrockner *m* turbo[-shelf] dryer, turbo-tray dryer, rotating-shelf turbo dryer
Turbinentreibstoff *m* turbine fuel
~ für Flugturbinen aviation (aircraft) turbine fuel
Turbinentrockner *m s.* Turbinen-Tellertrockner
Turbobohren *n s.* Turbinendrehbohren
Turbogebläse *n* turboblower, turbine blower
~/dampfgetriebenes steam-driven turboblower
Turbogridboden *m* turbogrid tray
Turbokompressor *m* turbocompressor
Turbolöser *m* turbodissolver

Turbomischer *m*, **Turborührer** *m* turbine mixer (agitator, stirrer)
turbulent turbulent
Turbulenz *f* turbulence
~/freie free turbulence
~/isotrope isotropic turbulence *(fluid mechanics)*
Türheber *m* door extractor
Turille *f* tourill *(an absorption vessel)*
Türkis *m (min)* turquois[e], kalaite *(a hydrous basic aluminium copper phosphate)*
Türkischrot *n* Turkey red *(an alizarin lake)*
Türkischrotfärberei *f* Turkey-red dyeing
Türkischrotöl *n* Turkey-red oil, sulphated castor oil
Türkischrotölseife *f* Turkey-red oil soap
Turm *m* tower
Turmalin *m (min)* tourmaline *(a cyclosilicate)*
~/blauer indicolite, indigolite
Turmalinisierung *f (geoch)* tourmalinization
Turmbiologie-Verfahren *n (hyd)* biotower process
Turmbleiche *f (pap)* tower bleaching
Turmdämpfer *m (text)* tower steamer
Turmextraktor *m* tower extractor
Turmfermentation *f (biot)* tower fermentation
Turmfermenter *m (biot)* tower reactor (fermenter)
~ **zur Essigherstellung** tower acetifier, vinegar tower
Turmfertigbleiche *f (pap)* final tower bleaching
Turmkammer *f* **von Gaillard** Gaillard tower *(for concentrating sulphuric acid)*
Turmkühler *m* cooling tower
Turmreaktor *m s.* Turmfermenter
Turmreiniger *m* tower purifier *(for gases)*
Turmrollenblock *m* crown block *(of a rotary-drilling installation)*
Turmsäure *f* 1. *(pap)* tower (storage, raw) acid, raw sulphite cooking acid; 2. Glover [tower] acid *(chamber process)*
Turmsäureherstellung *f (pap)* manufacture of raw acid, *(per unit time:)* raw-acid production
Turmsystem *n (pap)* tower system
Turmtrockner *m* drying tower
Turmwäscher *m* tower scrubber, scrubbing (gas-washing) tower, [gas] scrubber
Turnover *n (bioch)* molar (molecular) activity, [metabolic] turnover
Tusche *f* **[/chinesische]** India (China, Chinese) ink
~/lithographische lithographic tusche
Tussaseide *f* tussah (tussur) silk
Tütenpapier *n* bag paper
TVP-Verfahren *n (petrol)* TVP process, true vapour-phase [cracking] process
Twaddell-Grad *m* degree Twaddell
T-Wert *m (soil)* total exchangeable bases
T-50-Wert *m (rubber)* T-50 value
Twistbootkonformation *f* twist conformation
Twistingpapier *n* twisting paper
Twisting-Schwingung *f (spectr)* twisting vibration, torsional oscillation (mode)
Twitchell-Reagens *n* Twitchell reagent *(a sulphonated addition product of naphthalene and oleic acid)*
Twitchell-Verfahren *n* Twitchell process *(for hydrolyzing glycerides)*
Tyler-Normalsiebskala *f*, **Tyler-Siebreihe** *f* Tyler standard screen (sieve) scale, Tyler scale (series)
Tyndall-Effekt *m (coll)* Tyndall effect (phenomenon)
Tyndall-Kegel *m (coll)* [Faraday-]Tyndall cone
Tyndall[o]meter *n (coll)* tyndallimeter, tyndallometer, Tyndall meter
Tyndallometrie *f (coll)* tyndallimetry, tyndallometry
Tyndall-Phänomen *n s.* Tyndall-Effekt
Typfärbung *f (text)* standard dyeing
typkonform *(dye)* equal to type • ~ **stellen** to reduce to standard (type strength)
Tyr *s.* Tyrosin
Tyramin *n* tyramine, 2-(*p*-hydroxyphenyl)ethylamine
Tyrosin *n* tyrosine, 2-amino-3-(*p*-hydroxyphenyl)-propionic acid
T-Zustand *m s.* Triplettzustand

U

Ubbelohde-Viskosimeter *n* Ubbelohde viscometer
übel disgusting, disagreeable, objectionable *(smell)*
übelriechend malodorous, ill-smelling, foul-smelling, noxious-smelling, obnoxious
Überallzünder *m* strike-anywhere match
Überäscherung *f (tann)* excessive liming
überbelasten to overload
überbelichten *(phot)* to overexpose
Überbelichtung *f (phot)* overexposure
Überbelüftung *f* cross [air] circulation *(in drying processes)*
Überbleiche *f* overbleaching
überbleichen to overbleach
überbrennen to overburn *(e.g. cement clinker)*; *(ceram)* to overfire; *(coat)* to overstove
überbrücken to bridge
Überchlorierung *f s.* Überschußchlorung
Überchlorsäure *f s.* Perchlorsäure
Überchlorung *f s.* Überschußchlorung
überdecken 1. to cover; 2. to mask *(a reaction)*
überdestillieren to distil over *(of human agent)*; to distil [over], to pass (come) over *(of a distillate)*
überdimensionieren to oversize *(a plant)*
überdosieren to overdose, to overfeed
Überdosierung *f* overdosage, overfeed[ing]
Überdosis *f* overdose
Überdruck *m* 1. excess[ive] pressure, overpressure; 2. *(text) s.* Überdrucken
Überdrucken *n (text)* top printing, cross-printing
Überdruckfilter *n* pressure filter
Überdrucksicherung *f* pressure relief device
Überdruckventil *n* pressure relief valve
überdüngen to fertilize excessively, to overfertilize
Überdüngung *f* excessive fertilization, overfertilization
übereinanderlagern to superimpose *(stereochemistry)*

überempfindlich *(med, phot)* hypersensitive, supersensitive
Überempfindlichkeit *f (med, phot)* hypersensitivity, hypersensitiveness, supersensitivity
überentwickeln *(phot)* to overdevelop
Überentwicklung *f (phot)* overdevelopment
übereutektisch hypereutectic
übereutektoid[isch] hypereutectoid
Überfall *m* notch *(flow measurement)*
~/dreieckiger triangular notch
~/rechteckiger rectangular notch
Überfallwehr *n (distil)* overflow weir (lip)
überfangen *(glass)* to flash
Überfangglas *n* flashed glass
überfärbeecht fast to cross-dyeing
Überfärbeechtheit *f* fastness to cross-dyeing
überfärben *(text)* 1. to overdye *(unintentionally)*; 2. to dye over, to overdye; to cross-dye *(a second component in fibre mixtures)*; 3. to top *(by applying further dye to achieve a desired final shade)*
Überfettung *f (tann)* excessive stuffing
Überfeuerung *f (ceram)* overfiring *(a defect)*
überfließen to overflow
überflüssig *s.* superfluid
überfluten to flood *(a column unintentionally)*
Überflutung *f* flooding *(of a column by unintentional build-up of liquid)*
Überflutungsgrenze *f (distil)* flooding point
überformen *(ceram)* to jigger
überfrischen *(met)* to overblow
überführen 1. *(chemically:)* to convert; 2. *(mechanically:)* to transfer
~/in Dampf to vaporize
~/in den Fließbettzustand to fluidize
~/in den industriellen Maßstab to scale up to industrial use
~/in Dextrin to dextrinate, to dextrinize
~/in ein Carbonat to carbonate
~/in ein Salz to salify *(an acid or a base)*
~/in einen Komplex to complex
~/in Gelee to gelatinize, to gelatinate, to jellify, to jelly
~/ineinander to interconvert
Überführfilz *m (pap)* conveyor felt
Überführung *f* 1. *(chemically:)* conversion; *(el ch)* transference; 2. *(mechanically:)* transfer; 3. *s.* Überführungskanal
Überführungskanal *m* crossover flue *(of a coke oven)*
Überführungsspannung *f s.* Diffusionsspannung
Überführungsventil *n* by-pass valve
Überführungszahl *f (el ch)* transference (transport) number
~/anomale abnormal transference number
~/Hittorfsche Hittorf number
~/wahre true transference number
Übergang *m* 1. transition, conversion, change *(into another state or modification)*; *(el ch)* transference; change *(of colour)*; 2. junction *(in semiconductors)*
~/antiferroelektrischer antiferroelectric transition
~ 1. Art *s.* ~ 1. Ordnung
~/erlaubter allowed transition *(of electrons)*
~/ferroelektrischer ferroelectric transition
~ höherer Ordnung higher-order transition, smooth transition
~ in den Glaszustand glass transition
~ in den Spinglaszustand spin-glass transition
~/kongruenter congruent transition
~/kontinuierlicher continuous (second-order) transition
~/konzertierter *(bioch)* concerted transition (transfer)
~/magnetischer magnetic transition
~ Normalleitung-Supraleitung superconducting transition
~ 1. Ordnung *m* first-order transition, discontinuous transition
~/spinverbotener spin-forbidden transition
~/strahlender radiative transition
~/strahlungsfreier (strahlungsloser) radiationless transition
~/verbotener forbidden transition *(of electrons)*
~ vom flüssigen in den festen Zustand fluid-solid transition
pn-**Übergang** *m* p-n junction *(in semiconductors)*
$\pi \rightarrow \pi^*$-**Übergang** *m (phys ch)* $\pi \rightarrow \pi^*$ transition
$\pi \rightarrow \sigma^*$-**Übergang** *m (phys ch)* $\pi \rightarrow \sigma^*$ transition
$\sigma \rightarrow \sigma^*$-**Übergang** *m (phys ch)* $\sigma \rightarrow \sigma^*$ transition
Übergangsbereich *m* transition region; transition interval *(of a colour indicator)*
Übergangsdipolmoment *n* transition [dipole] moment
Übergangseinheit *f (phys ch)* transfer unit
~ in der Dampfphase vapour-phase transfer unit
~ in der flüssigen Phase liquid-phase transfer unit
Übergangselement *n* transition element, transition[al] metal
Übergangsfließen *n* transient flow
Übergangsform *f* intermediate form
Übergangsfraktion *f (distil)* intermediate fraction (cut)
Übergangsgebiet *n* transition region, *(fluid mechanics also)* dip region
Übergangsintervall *n* transition interval *(of a double salt)*
Übergangskriechen *n (cryst)* transient (primary) creep
Übergangsmetall *n* transition[al] metal, transition element
Übergangsmetallhydrid *n* transition-metal hydride
~/binäres transition-metal binary hydride
Übergangsmoment *n* transition moment *(for electrons)*
Übergangsphase *f (bioch)* transient state
Übergangsreaktion *f*/**eutektische** eutectic reaction
~/eutektoide eutectoid reaction
~/monotektische monotectic reaction

~/monotektoide monotectoid reaction
~/peritektische peritectic (incongruent) reaction
~/peritektoide peritectoid reaction
Übergangsreihe *f* transition series *(in the periodic table)*
Übergangsschicht *f* buffer zone (layer) *(of a boundary layer with turbulent flow)*
Übergangsstück *n (distil)* adapter
~ [Form] A reducing (reduction) adapter *(with small socket on larger cone)*
~ [Form] B enlarging (expanding, expansion) adapter *(with large socket on smaller cone)*
~ von Kegelschliff auf Kugelschliff conical-spherical adapter
~ von Kugelschliff auf Kegelschliff (Normschliff) spherical-conical adapter
Übergangstemperatur *f* transition temperature
Übergangswahrscheinlichkeit *f (nucl)* transition[al] probability
~/Einsteinsche Einstein transition probability
Übergangswiderstand *m* transfer resistance, resistance to transfer
Übergangszeit *f (el ch)* transition time
Übergangszone *f* transition region
Übergangszustand *m* transition state, *(reaction theory also)* activated complex
übergehen to pass, to be converted; to change *(into another state or modification)*; *(distil)* to come (pass) over, to distil [over]; *(el ch)* to transfer; to change *(in colour)*
~/gemeinsam to distil together
~/in den Fließbettzustand to fluidize
~/in den Gelzustand *(coll)* to gel
~/in den Solzustand *(coll)* to solate
Übergemengteile *mpl* accessory components (constituents, minerals) *(in a rock)*
Übergerbung *f* overtannage
Übergitter *n (cryst)* superlattice, superstructure
überhärten *(plast)* to overcure
Überhärtung *f (plast)* overcure, overcuring
überheizen to overheat
überhitzen to superheat, to overheat
Überhitzer *m* superheater
Überhitzung *f* superheating, overheating
~/lokale (örtliche) local superheating
Überhitzungswärme *f* superheat
Überiodsäure *f s.* Metaperiodsäure
überkalken *(sugar, agric)* to overlime
Überkalkung *f (sugar, agric)* overliming
überkochen 1. to boil over; 2. *(pap)* to overcook
Überkochen *n* boilover
Überkochung *f (pap)* overcooking
überkohlen to supercarburize, to overcarburize *(steel)*
Überkohlung *f* supercarburization, overcarburization *(of steel)*
Überkopfprodukt *n (distil)* overhead (top) product, overhead[s]
Überkorn *n* oversize [material, product], tailings, tails, plus material *(classifying)*, *(screening also)* screen oversize, plus mesh
überkritisch *(nucl)* supercritical
überkrusten to encrust, to incrust
Überkrustung *f* encrustation, incrustation
Überlademethode *f* F4 method *(for octane rating)*
überlagern to superpose, to superimpose
Überlagerung *f* superposition, *(act also)* superimposition; spectral overlap
Überlagerungsmethode *f* heterodyne beat method *(for measuring dielectric constants)*
Überlagerungspeak *m (anal)* superposition peak
überlappen to overlap *(1. orbital; 2. genetic code)*
~/sich to overlap
überlappend/nicht *(bioch)* non-overlapping *(code)*
Überlappung *f* overlap[ping] *(1. of orbitals; 2. of genetic code)*
~ der Orbitale orbital overlap
Überlappungsbereich *m* overlap region *(of orbitals)*
Überlappungsintegral *n* overlap integral *(chemical-bond theory)*
Überlappungsraum *m s.* Überlappungsbereich
überlasten to overload
Überlastungsmelder *m* overload alarm
Überlauf *m* 1. overflow [weir, lip, port], weir; *(met)* skimmer *(for separating the slag)*; 2. overflow [fraction, product], overs, tailings, tails *(classifying)*; 3. overflow rate
Überlaufdamm *m s.* Überlauf 1.
überlaufen to run over, to overflow; *(with heat:)* to boil over
Überlaufen *n* overflow; *(with heat:)* boiling over
Überlauffraktion *f* overflow fraction
Überlaufgut *n s.* Überlauf 2.
Überlaufgüte *f* centrifugate quality (clarity) *(centrifugation)*
Überlaufkasten *m* overflow box *(as of a thickener)*; *(pap)* weir box
Überlaufklasse *f* overflow fraction *(classifying)*
Überlauföffnung *f* overflow port
Überlaufprodukt *n s.* Überlauf 2.
Überlaufrinne *f* overflow launder
Überlaufrohr *n*, **Überlaufstutzen** *m* overflow pipe (tube)
Überlaufvorrichtung *f* overflow
Überlaufwehr *n* overflow weir (lip)
Überlebensdauer *f (tox)* survival time
Überlebensfaktor *m (biot)* survival factor
überleiten to pass (carry) over *(e.g. vapour)*
übermahlen to overgrind
Übermangansäure *f s.* Permangansäure
Übermaß *n* excess, surplus
übermastizieren *(rubber)* to overmasticate, to overmill, to kill
Übermastizieren *n (rubber)* overmastication, overmilling, killing, dead milling
Übermolekül *n s.* Molekülaggregat

Übermöllerung *f (met)* overburdening
überpolen to overpole *(copper)*
Überproduktion *f* over-production, excess production
Überproduzenten *mpl (biot)* high-yielding microorganisms
überprüfen to recheck
Überrest *m* remainder, remains, residue
Überrheniumsäure *f s.* Perrheniumsäure
Überröste *f (text)* excess retting
übersättigen to supersaturate
übersättigt *(geoch)* oversaturated, [per]silicic
Übersättigung *f* supersaturation, supersolubility
Übersättigungsgrad *m* degree of supersaturation
Übersättigungskurve *f* supersaturation (supersolubility) curve
Übersäure *f* peracid
überschäumen to froth (foam) over
überschichten to cover with a layer *(of another liquid)*
Überschönung *f* overfining *(of wine)*
überschreiten to exceed, to overrun, to overshoot *(a specified value)*
Überschuß *m* excess, surplus • **mit einem geringen ~ an** in slight excess of
Überschußbelebtschlamm *m (hyd)* excess (surplus) activated sludge
Überschußchlor[ier]ung *f* excess chlorination, superchlorination *(of water)*
Überschußelektron *n* excess electron
Überschußenergie *f* excess energy
Überschußgas *n* excess (surplus) gas
Überschußhalbleiter *m* n-type semiconductor
überschüssig excess[ive]
Überschußladung *f* excess charge
Überschußladungsträger *m (phys ch)* excess carrier
überschußleitend n-type [semi]conducting
Überschußluft *f* excess air
Überschußschlammabzug *m (hyd)* discharge of excess sludge
Überschußwasser *n* excess water
Überschußwasserstoff *m* excess hydrogen
überschwänzen *(ferm)* to sparge
Überschwänzwasser *n (ferm)* sparge water
Übersensibilisator *m (phot)* supersensitizer
übersensibilisieren *(phot)* to hypersensitize, to supersensitize
Übersensibilisierung *f (phot)* hypersensitization, supersensitization
übersetzen to top *(leather previously dyed in acid medium with basic dyestuff)*
Überspannung *f* **[/elektrochemische, elektrolytische]** overvoltage, overpotential, excess potential
~/katodische cathodic overvoltage
übersprühen to spray
Überstand *m* supernatant [liquid, liquor]; *(biot)* culture supernatant
Überstau *m (hyd, filtr)* head of water, liquid head
überstehend supernatant *(liquid)*
übersteigen to exceed, to overrun, to overshoot *(a specified value)*
überstöchiometrisch hyperstoichiometric
überströmen to overflow
Überströmkanal *m* crossover flue *(as of a coke oven)*
Überströmrohr *n* overflow pipe (tube)
Überstruktur *f (cryst)* superstructure, superlattice
übertitrieren to overtitrate, to overrun (overshoot) the end point
übertragen to transfer
Überträger *m* carrier; chain-transfer agent *(polymerization)*
Überträgerstoff *m (bioch)* transfer agent
Übertragung *f* transfer[ence]
Übertragungsfunktion *f* transfer function
Übertragungskonstante *f* transfer constant *(polymerization)*
Übertragungsreaktion *f* transfer reaction *(polymerization)*
Übertragungsregler *m* chain-transfer agent *(polymerization)*
übertreiben *(distil)* to carry (distil, pass) over
~/langsam to sweat off
Übertrieb *m s.* Übertriebsäure
Übertriebgas *n (pap)* [digester] relief gas, release, blow-off
Übertriebsäure *f (pap)* relief liquor, release, blow-off
übertrocknen to overdry
Übertrocknung *f* overdrying, excessive drying
übervernetzen *s.* übervulkanisieren
Übervulkanisation *f* overcure, overcuring, overvulcanization
übervulkanisieren to overcure, to over-vulcanize
überwachen to monitor *(e.g. an experiment)*; to supervise *(by an authority)*
Überwachsung *f (cryst)* overgrowth
Überwachung *f* monitoring *(as of an experiment)*; supervision *(by an authority)*
Überwachungseinrichtung *f* 1. monitor; 2. *(tox)* regulatory agency
Überwachungssystem *n* monitoring system
Überweiche *f* oversteeping *(of malt)*
überziehen 1. to cover *(with prefabricated sheet)*, *(esp with sheet metal:)* to clad; *(ceram)* to engobe *(with slip)*; 2. *s.* beschichten
~/mit einer Kruste to encrust
~/mit Filz to cover with felt, to felt
~/mit Gummi to rubber-cover
~/sich to become covered
Überzug *m* 1. cover[ing] *(consisting of prefabricated sheet)*, *(esp consisting of sheet metal:)* cladding; *(phot)* supercoat *(for protecting the emulsion)*; 2. *s.* Schutzschicht
Überzugsharz *n s.* Lackharz

Überzugsmetall *n* 1. cladding metal, veneer of metal; 2. *s.* Schutzschichtmetall
Überzugspapier *n* lining paper, pasting [paper], liners
Überzugswerkstoff *m* covering material, *(esp relating to metals:)* cladding material
ubiquitär ubiquitous, ubiquitously distributed
Ubiquität *f* ubiquity
UDP *s.* Uridindiphosphat
UDPG, UDPGlc, UDP-Glucose *f s.* Uridindiphosphoglucose
U-Eisen *n* channel iron *(for producing channel black)*
Uferfiltrat *n (hyd)* riverbank filtrate
Uferfiltration *f (hyd)* riverbank filtration
Uferfiltratwasser *n s.* Uferfiltrat
U-Feuerung *f* fantail firing *(a suspension firing)*
U-Flammen-Wanne *f (glass)* end-fired (end-port) furnace
U-förmig U-shaped
U-Gas-Verfahren *n (coal)* U-gas process *(for gasifying coal in a fluidized bed)*
Ugi-Reaktion *f* Ugi reaction *(for obtaining α-amino acids or peptides)*
ug-Kern *m s.* Ungerade-gerade-Kern
Uhde-Zelle *f* Uhde cell *(a mercury cell)*
Uhrenöl *n* watch oil
Uhrglas *n*, **Uhrglasschale** *f (lab)* watch (clock) glass
Uhrzeigersinn/entgegen dem counterclockwise
~/im clockwise
UHT-Erhitzung *f s.* Ultrahocherhitzung
UHT-Milch *f* UHT [processed] milk
U-I-Kennlinie *f* current-voltage curve
U-Korrektur *f (spectr)* background correction
UKS = Ultrakurzzeitspektroskopie
Ullmann-Reaktion *f* Ullmann reaction *(for synthesizing diaryls)*
Ulmin *n (soil)* ulmin
Ulminstoff *m (soil)* ulmin material
Ultrabeschallung *f* ultrasonic treatment
Ultrabeschleuniger *m (rubber)* ultra-accelerator, superaccelerator, ultrafast (ultrarapid) accelerator
Ultrafilter *n* ultrafilter
Ultrafiltrat *n* ultrafiltrate
Ultrafiltration *f* ultrafiltration, UF
ultrafiltrieren to ultrafilter
Ultrafiltriermembran *f* ultrafiltration membrane
Ultraformen *n* ultraforming *(a variety of catalytic reforming)*
Ultrahocherhitzung *f (food)* ultra-high temperature processing
Ultrahocherhitzungsverfahren *n (food)* ultra-high temperature process
Ultramarin *n* ultramarine blue
~/gelbes 1. yellow ultramarine *(a mixture of zinc and calcium chromate)*; 2. *s.* Ultramaringelb
Ultramarinblau *n* ultramarine blue
Ultramaringelb *n* yellow ultramarine, lemon chrome, Steinbühl yellow, ultramarine (barium, baryta) yellow *(barium chromate)*
Ultramikroanalyse *f* ultramicroanalysis
Ultramikrobestimmung *f* ultramicrodetermination
Ultramikrochemie *f* ultramicrochemistry
Ultramikroprobe *f* ultramicro sample *(*< 10^{-4} g)*
Ultramikroskop *n* ultramicroscope
ultramikroskopisch ultramicroscopic
Ultramikrowaage *f* ultramicrobalance
Ultrapasteurisation *f (food)* uperization
ultrarein ultrapure, extremely pure
Ultrarot *n s.* Infrarot
Ultraschallabsorption *f* ultrasonic absorption
Ultraschallaufschluß *m (bioch)* cell breakage by sonication
Ultraschallbehandlung *f* ultrasonic treatment
Ultraschallbestrahlung *f* ultrasonic irradiation
Ultraschallenergie *f* ultrasonic energy
Ultraschallerzeuger *m*, **Ultraschallgenerator** *m* ultrasonic generator
Ultraschallkoagulation *f* ultrasonic coagulation
Ultraschallprüfung *f* ultrasonic (supersonic) testing
Ultraschallreiniger *m* ultrasonic cleaner (cleaning plant)
Ultraschallreinigung *f* ultrasonic cleaning
Ultraschallreinigungsanlage *f s.* Ultraschallreiniger
Ultraschallschweißen *n (plast)* ultrasonic welding
Ultraschallschwinger *m* ultrasonic transducer
Ultraschallsirene *f* ultrasonic agglomerator *(gas cleaning)*
Ultraschallversprüher *m* ultrasonic atomizer
Ultraschallwaschanlage *f* ultrasonic cleaner (cleaning plant)
Ultraschallwellen *fpl* ultrasonic waves
Ultra-Spuren-Analyse *f* ultra-trace analysis *(*sample weight ≤ 10^{-4} g)*
Ultraviolett *n* ultraviolet [radiation], uv
~/nahes near ultraviolet
Ultraviolett... *s.* UV-...
Ultrazentrifuge *f* ultracentrifuge, high-speed centrifuge
Ultrazentrifugation *f s.* Ultrazentrifugieren
Ultrazentrifugieren *n* ultracentrifugation, high-speed centrifugation
ULV-Verfahren *n* ultralow (very low) volume method (spraying) *(spraying of pesticides without water in amounts of only 1 to 5 gallons liquid/acre)*
Umacylierung *f* transacylation
Umbelliferon *n* umbelliferone, 7-hydroxy-2*H*-chromen-2-one
Umber *m s.* Umbra
Umbra *f*, **Umbraun** *n* umber *(an earth pigment)*
umdestillieren to redistil, to rerun
Umdrehungsgeschwindigkeit *f* speed of rotation
~ der Trommel drum speed *(as of a rotary vacuum filter)*

Umdruckpapier *n* transfer paper
umestern to interesterify, to transesterify, to re-esterify
Umesterung *f* interesterification, transesterification, re-esterification, interchange esterification, ester interchange
~/gelenkte (gerichtete) directed interesterification *(of fats)*
~/ungelenkte (ungerichtete) random interesterification *(of fats)*
umfällen to reprecipitate
Umfällung *f* reprecipitation
Umfangsgeschwindigkeit *f* peripheral speed
umfärben *(text)* to redye
umformen to form *(materials)*; to change *(a structure)*; to convert, to transform *(substances)*
~/sich to change *(of a structure)*
Umformung *f* forming *(of materials)*; change *(of a structure)*; conversion, transformation *(of substances)*
umfüllen to transfer *(substances into another vessel)*
Umfüllen *n* transfer *(of substances)*
Umgang *m* handling *(as of dangerous materials)*
umgeben to pack, to invest
umgebend ambient
Umgebung *f* environment; vicinity
~/korrodierend wirkende corrosive environment
Umgebungsdruck *m* ambient pressure
Umgebungsfeuchtigkeit *f* ambient humidity
Umgebungsluft *f* ambient air
Umgebungsluftqualität *f* ambient-air quality
Umgebungstemperatur *f* ambient temperature
umgehen to by-pass
umgesetzt/nicht unreacted, unconverted
~ werden to undergo conversion
umgewandelt/nicht *s.* umgesetzt/nicht
Umgriff *m* throwing power *(electrophoretic painting)*
umgruppieren to rearrange
~/sich to rearrange
Umgruppierung *f* rearrangement
umhausen to house *(a treatment unit)*
umhüllen to jacket, to sheathe
Umhüllung *f* jacket, sheath[ing]
Umkehr *f* reversal
umkehrbar reversible, invertible
~/nicht non-reversible, irreversible
Umkehrbarkeit *f* reversibility, invertibility
Umkehremulsion *f (phot)* reversal emulsion
umkehren to reverse, to invert *(a process)*
Umkehrentwickler *m (phot)* reversal developer
Umkehrentwicklung *f (phot)* reversal development (processing)
Umkehrfilm *m* reversal film
Umkehrkammer *f***/frei bewegliche** floating head *(of a heat exchanger)*
Umkehrmaterial *n (phot)* reversal material
Umkehrosmose *f* reverse osmosis, RO
Umkehrosmoseanlage *f* reverse osmosis plant, RO plant
~ zur Meerwasserentsalzung sea water RO plant
Umkehrosmosemodul *m* reverse osmosis unit
Umkehrosmosezelle *f* reverse osmosis unit
Umkehrphasen *fpl* reversed phases
Umkehrphasenchromatographie *f* reversed-phase chromatography, RPC
Umkehrphasen-Flüssig[keits]chromatographie *f* reversed-phase liquid chromatography, RPLC
Umkehrtranskriptase *f s.* Revertase
Umkehrung *f* reversion, reversal, inversion
~/Waldensche *(org ch)* Walden inversion
Umkehrverfahren *n (phot)* reversal process
Umklappen *n* turnover, flipping-over, flip *(of bonds as in the Walden inversion)*
~ des Ringes ring flip
Umklappprozeß *m (nucl)* umklapp process
umkleiden *s.* umhüllen
Umklonieren *n (bioch)* subcloning
Umkristallisation *f* recrystallization
~/postkinematische (posttektonische) *(geoch)* posttectonic recrystallization
umkristallisieren to recrystallize
umladen to change the sign of the charge
Umladung *f* reversal of the sign [of the charge]
umlagern to rearrange
~/sich to rearrange
Umlagerung *f* [molecular] rearrangement
~ am Aromaten aromatic rearrangement
~/Beckmannsche Beckmann rearrangement (molecular transformation) *(of a ketoxime into an amide derivative)*
~/entartete degenerate rearrangement
~/Friessche Fries rearrangement (migration) *(as for synthesizing phenolic ketones)*
~/innermolekulare (intramolekulare) intramolecular rearrangement
~/Lossensche Lossen rearrangement *(of aromatic hydroxamic acids into isocyanates)*
~/sigmatrope *(org ch)* sigmatropic rearrangement
~/Stevenssche Stevens rearrangement *(of a benzyl group in quaternary ammonium salts)*
~/Wolffsche Wolff rearrangement *(of diazoketones)*
1,2-Umlagerung *f* 1,2-shift
Umlagerungsgeschwindigkeit *f* velocity of rearrangement
Umlagerungspolymerisation *f* rearrangement polymerization
Umlagerungsreaktion *f* rearrangement reaction
Umlauf *m* [re]circulation
~/natürlicher natural circulation
~/sauberer *(petrol)* clean circulation *(in thermal cracking)*
Umlaufbahn *f* orbit
~/kreisförmige circular orbit
Umlaufbeladung *f* circulating load
umlaufen to circulate *(in a closed cycle)*; to rotate, to revolve, *(if rapidly:)* to spin
Umlauffilter *n* band filter, [linear] belt filter
Umlaufgas *n* recycle gas

Umlaufgut *n* circulating load
Umlaufkolbengebläse *n* positive-displacement blower, [positive] rotary blower
Umlaufkolbenpumpe *f* rotary pump
Umlauföl *n* recycle oil
Umlaufpumpe *f* circulating pump, recirculation (recycle) pump, circulator
Umlaufspannung *f* magnetomotive force
Umlaufsystem *n* circulation system
Umlaufverdampfer *m* circulation evaporator; *(distil)* forced-circulation reboiler
Umlaufwasser *n* circulating water
umlegen to reverse *(e.g. the direction of flow)*
Umlenkblech *n* baffle [plate] • **mit Umlenkblechen [versehen]** baffled • **ohne Umlenkbleche** unbaffled
Umlenkplatte *f s.* Umlenkblech
Umlenkrinne *f (glass)* deflector
ummanteln to jacket, to sheathe
Ummantelung *f* jacket, sheath[ing]
Ummetallierung *f* transmetalation
Umnetzung *f* umnetzung *(displacement of one liquid by another as on a fibre)*
Umordnung *f* rearrangement
Umorientierung *f* reorientation
UMP = Uridin-5-monophosphat
Umpherston-Holländer *m (pap)* Umpherston beater
Umpump *m* forced circulation
umpumpen to recirculate, to recycle
umrechnen to convert
Umrechnung *f* conversion
Umrechnungsfaktor *m* conversion factor
~/Smythescher atomic-mass conversion factor
~ zwischen physikalischer und chemischer Atommassenskala *s.* ~/Smythescher
Umrechnungstabelle *f* conversion (converting) table
umrollen *(pap)* to rereel, to rewind
Umroller *m (pap)* reel-slitting (roll-slitting) machine, rereeling (rewinding, slitting) machine, rewinder, slitter
umrühren to agitate, *(esp relating to molten metal:)* to puddle
Umrühren *n* agitation, *(esp relating to molten metal:)* puddling
Umrüstung *f* retrofitting
Umsatz *m* conversion
~/doppelter *s.* Umsetzung/doppelte
Umsatzgeschwindigkeit *f* conversion rate
Umsatzgleichung *f*[**/chemische**] chemical equation, [chemical-]reaction equation
Umsatzkurve *f* conversion curve
Umsatzrate *f (biot)* conversion (fermentation) rate, rate of product formation
Umsatzreaktion *f***/doppelte** double-decomposition reaction, metathesis (metathetical) reaction
umschalten to reverse
umschichten/sich to overturn *(water in a lake)*
Umschichtung *f* overturn *(of water in a lake)*
Umschlag *m* break *(as in titration)*; change[over], transition *(of an indicator)*
umschlagen 1. to change *(of colours or reactions)*; 2. to reverse *(of emulsions)*
Umschlagen *n* 1. change *(of colours or reactions)*; 2. reversion *(of emulsions)*
Umschlagpapier *n* cover paper
Umschlagsbereich *m*, **Umschlagsgebiet** *n s.* Umschlagsintervall
Umschlagsintervall *n* transition (colour-change) interval *(of a pH indicator)*
Umschlagspunkt *m* point of change *(titration)*
umschmelzen to remelt, *(met also)* to refuse
Umschreibung *f (bioch)* transcription *(of genetic informations by enzymes)*
umschwenken to swirl
umsetzen to convert, *(bioch also)* to metabolize
~/sich to react, to convert, *(bioch also)* to metabolize
Umsetzer *m* reactor
Umsetzung *f* conversion • **[eine] ~ erleiden** to undergo conversion
~/doppelte double (mutual) decomposition, metathesis
~/einfache simple decomposition
~/enzymatische enzym[at]ic conversion
~/gegenseitige interconversion [reaction]
~/mikrobielle *s.* Biokonversion
~/photochemische photochemical reaction, photoreaction
~/stoffliche conversion of materials, materials conversion
~/wechselseitige interconversion [reaction]
Umsetzungsgeschwindigkeit *f* conversion rate (velocity)
Umsetzungsgrad *m* degree of conversion
Umsetzungsprodukt *n* conversion product, *(biot also)* fermentation product
Umsetzungsreaktion *f* conversion reaction
umsieden to distil
Umsieden *n* distillation
umspülen to flow round
umstellen 1. to rearrange; 2. to reverse *(e.g. the direction of flow)*
Umstellung *f* 1. rearrangement; 2. reversal *(as of the direction of flow)*
Umstellventil *n* reversing valve
Umtauschkapazität *f* exchange capacity; *(soil quantitatively:)* total exchangeable bases
Umtriebpropeller *m (pap)* propeller-type agitator, revolving paddles *(of a Hollander beater)*
umwälzen to circulate
Umwälzgeschwindigkeit *f* circulation rate
Umwälzheizeinrichtung *f* circulation heater
Umwälzpumpe *f* circulating pump, recirculation (recycle) pump, circulator
Umwälzschlamm *m (hyd)* recirculated sludge
Umwälzung *f* circulation

Umwälzverdampfer *m* forced-circulation evaporator
umwandelbar convertible, transformable
~/ineinander (wechselseitig) [mutually] interconvertible, reversibly convertible; enantiotropic *(modifications)*
Umwandelbarkeit *f* convertibility, transformability
~/wechselseitige interconvertibility; enantiotropy *(of modifications)*
umwandeln to transform, to convert, to change; to reform *(hydrocarbons)*; *(nucl)* to transform, to transmute; *(cryst)* to invert
~/gegenseitig to interconvert
~/in Dextrin to dextrinate, to dextrinize
~/in ein Carbonat to carbonatize, to carbonate
~/in Kohlenstoff to carbonize
~/in Zucker to saccharify, to saccharize
~/ineinander to interconvert
~/sich to convert, to transform, to revert, to undergo change, to be (become) converted; *(nucl)* to transform, to transmute, to undergo transformation (transmutation); *(cryst)* to invert
~/sich gegenseitig to interconvert
~/sich in die metallische Form (Modifikation) to metallize
~/sich ineinander (wechselseitig) to interconvert
~/wechselseitig to interconvert
Umwandlung *f* transformation, conversion, change; reforming *(of hydrocarbons)*; *(nucl)* transformation, transmutation, *(by decay also)* devolution; transition *(into another phase)*; *(cryst)* transition, inversion • **[eine] ~ erleiden** to undergo conversion
~/allosterische *(bioch)* allosteric effect
~/allotrope allotropic (allotriomorphic) transition *(of a pure element)*
~ 1. Art *s.* ~ 1. Ordnung
~/äußere external conversion *(of an electronic state)*
~ bei gleichbleibender Temperatur isothermal (constant-temperature) transformation
~ bei kontinuierlicher stetiger Abkühlung continuous-cooling transformation
~/biochemische biochemical transformation
~/diffusionslose diffusionless transition
~/diskontinuierliche *s.* ~ 1. Ordnung
~/displazive displacive transition
~/druckinduzierte pressure-induced transition
~/enantiotrope enantiotropic transition
~/enzymatische enzym[at]ic conversion
~ erster Ordnung *s.* ~ 1. Ordnung
~/ferrimagnetische ferrimagnetic transition
~/ferroelastische ferroelastic transition
~/gegenseitige interconversion [reaction]
~ höherer Ordnung higher-order transition, smooth transition
~ in ein Carbonat carbonatization, carbonation
~ in Kohlenstoff carbonization
~/innere internal conversion *(of an electronic state)*
~/irreversible irreversible transition
~/isotherme isothermal (constant-temperature) transformation
~/kontinuierliche *s.* ~ 2. Ordnung
~/martensitische martensitic transition
~/metamagnetische metamagnetic transition
~/monotrope monotropic transition
~ normal-supraleitend superconducting transition
~ 1. Ordnung first-order transition, discontinuous transition
~ 2. Ordnung second-order transition, continuous transition
~/polymorphe polymorphic transition
~/radioaktive radioactive transformation (transmutation)
~/rekonstruktive reconstructive transition
~/reversible reversible transition
~/stoffliche conversion (transformation) of materials, materials conversion
~/strukturelle structural transition
~/topotaktische topotactic transition
~/wechselseitige interconversion [reaction]
~ zweiter Ordnung *s.* ~ 2. Ordnung
Umwandlungsbeginn *m* start of transformation
Umwandlungsende *n* finish of transformation
Umwandlungsgeschwindigkeit *f* rate of transformation, conversion rate, rate of change
Umwandlungsgrad *m* degree of conversion
Umwandlungsintervall *n* transition interval *(of a double salt)*
Umwandlungsprodukt *n* transformation (conversion) product
Umwandlungspunkt *m* transition point (temperature), *(cryst also)* inversion point (temperature)
~ erster Ordnung first-order transition point (temperature)
~ zweiter Ordnung second-order transition point (temperature), *(plast, rubber also)* glass transition point, Tg [point]
Umwandlungsrate *f* disintegration rate, activity *(of a radioactive substance)*
Umwandlungsreaktion *f* conversion reaction
Umwandlungsschaubild *n* transformation diagram
~ für gleichbleibende Temperatur isothermal transformation diagram
~ für kontinuierliche Abkühlung continuous-cooling transformation diagram
Umwandlungstemperatur *f s.* Umwandlungspunkt
Umwandlungswärme *f* heat of transition, latent heat *(of phases or crystals)*
Umwandlungszone *f* transition zone *(in an extruder)*
Umweltanalyse *f* environmental analysis
Umweltanalytik *f* environmental analytical chemistry, environmental analysis
Umweltbedingungen *fpl* environmental conditions (factors)
Umweltbelastung *f* environmental load[ing], environmental burden
Umweltbiochemie *f* environmental biochemistry

Umweltblei *n* environmental lead
Umweltchemie *f* environmental chemistry
Umweltchemikalie *f* environmental chemical
Umweltchemiker *m* environmental chemist
Umwelteinfluß *m* environmental influence
Umweltentgiftung *f* environmental detoxification
Umweltfaktor *m* environmental factor
umweltfreundlich environmentally acceptable (beneficial, friendly, compatible)
Umweltgefahr *f* environmental hazard (danger)
umweltgefährdend, umweltgefährlich environmentally hazardous (dangerous)
Umweltgift *n* environmental toxicant
umweltgünstig *s.* umweltfreundlich
Umweltkatastrophe *f* environmental disaster
umweltkompatibel *s.* umweltfreundlich
Umweltkontaminant *m* environmental contaminant
Umweltkontaminierung *f* environmental contamination
Umweltkontrolle *f* environmental control
Umweltkonzentration *f* environmental concentration
Umweltmedium *n* environmental medium
~ **Boden** soil environment
~ **Luft** air environment
~ **Wasser** water environment
Umweltprobe *f* environmental sample
Umweltquecksilber *n* environmental mercury
Umweltradioaktivität *f* environmental radioactivity
Umweltschaden *m* enviromental damage (harm)
umweltschädigend enviromentally damaging (harmful)
Umweltschädigung *f* environmental degradation
Umweltschadstoff *m* environmental pollutant
Umweltschmutzstoff *m* environmental contaminant
Umweltschutz *m* environmental protection
Umweltschutzbestimmung *f* environmental protection regulation
Umweltschutztechnik *f* environmental technology
umweltsicher environmentally safe
Umweltsicherheit *f* environmental safety
Umweltstoff *m* environmental substance
~/toxischer environmental toxicant
Umweltsubstanz *f s.* Umweltstoff
Umweltsystem *n* environmental system
Umwelttoxikologie *f* environmental toxicology
Umwelttoxizität *f* environmental toxicity
Umweltverschmutzung *f* environmental contamination
~ **durch Schadstoffe** environmental pollution
umweltverträglich environmentally compatible (acceptable)
Umweltverträglichkeit *f* environmental compatibility (acceptability)
umwickeln *s.* umrollen
Umxanthogenierung *f (text)* rexanthation
unabgesättigt unsaturated
Unabhängigkeitsverbundwirkung *f (tox)* independent joint action *(without reciprocal influence of the components)*
unabsorbierbar non-absorbable
unabtrennbar inseparable
unangegriffen unchanged, unattacked, unaffected
unangenehm disagreeable, disgusting, unpleasant, objectionable *(e.g. smell)*
~ **riechend** ill-smelling, foul-smelling, obnoxious
~ **schmeckend** ill-tasting
unangreifbar unattackable, stable, resistant
~/chemisch stable (resistant) to chemical attack, chemically stable (resistant)
Unangreifbarkeit *f* unattackability, stability, resistance
~/chemische stability (resistance) to chemical attack, chemical stability (resistance)
unaufgeschlossen undigested
unbehandelt untreated, unprocessed, unfinished, raw, virgin
unbeimpft *(biot)* uninoculated *(nutrient medium)*
unbelichtet *(phot)* unexposed, raw
unbenetzbar non-wettable
unbesetzt vacant *(lattice position)*; unoccupied *(subshell)*
unbeständig unstable, instable, labile, transient, *(relating to isotopes also)* evanescent
~/thermisch thermolabile, heat-labile
Unbeständigkeit *f* instability, lability, transience
~/thermische thermolability, thermal lability
Unbestimmtheitsbeziehung *f s.* Unbestimmtheitsrelation
Unbestimmtheitsrelation *f* **[/Heisenbergsche]** [Heisenberg] uncertainty relation
unbeweglich immobile, non-mobile
unbrennbar incombustible, non-combustible, fireproof • ~ **machen** to fireproof
Unbrennbarkeit *f* incombustibility
Unbrennbarmachen *n* fireproofing
Undecan *n* undecane
Undecanal *n* undecanal, undecyl aldehyde
Undecandisäure *f* undecanedioic acid
Undecanon *n* undecanone *(any of several isomeric ketones $C_{11}H_{22}O$)*
Undecansäure *f* undecanoic acid
Undecen *n* undecene *(any of several isomeric alkenes $C_{11}H_{22}$)*
Undecensäure *f* undecenoic acid *(any of several isomeric alkenoic acids $C_{11}H_{20}O_2$)*
Undec-9-ensäure *f* undec-9-enoic acid
Undecin *n* undecyne *(any of several isomeric alkynes $C_{11}H_{20}$)*
Undecinsäure *f* undecynoic acid *(any of several isomeric alkynoic acids $C_{11}H_{18}O_2$)*
Undecylaldehyd *m s.* Undecanal
Undecylalkohol *m* undecyl alcohol, *undecan-1-ol
Undecylamin *n* undecylamine *(any of several isomeric amines $C_{11}H_{25}N$)*
Undecylen *n s.* Undecen

Undecylensäure *f s.* Undecensäure
Undecylsäure *f s.* Undecansäure
undicht leaky, pervious, porous, porose • ~ **sein** to leak, to run • ~ **werden** to spring a leak
Undichtheit *f*, **Undichtigkeit** *f* leakiness
undissoziiert undissociated
undurchdringlich *s.* undurchlässig
undurchlässig impermeable, impenetrable, impervious, [leak]tight, [leak]proof; *(optically:)* opaque • ~ **machen** to make impervious
~ **für Röntgenstrahlen** radiopaque
Undurchlässigkeit *f* impermeability, impenetrability, imperviousness, tightness, proofness; *(optically:)* opacity
~ **für Röntgenstrahlen** radiopacity
Undurchlässigmachen *n* proofing
undurchsichtig opaque, non-transparent
Undurchsichtigkeit *f* opacity, non-transparency
unecht 1. artificial, factitious; 2. *(dye)* not fast, fugitive
unedel base, non-noble, [re]active *(metal)*
Unedelmetall *n* base (non-noble) metal
uneinheitlich non-uniform
~**/innerlich** inhomogeneous
Uneinheitlichkeit *f* non-uniformity
~**/innerliche** inhomogeneity
unelastisch inelastic
unempfindlich insensitive • ~ **machen** *(phot)* to desensitize
Unempfindlichkeit *f* insensitivity, insensitiveness
unentbehrlich *(bioch, agric)* essential
Unentbehrlichkeit *f (bioch, agric)* essentiality
unentflammbar non-[in]flammable, uninflammable, flameproof
Unentflammbarkeit *f* non-flammability, uninflammability, flameproofness
Unentflammbarmachen *n* flameproofing
unersetzlich *s.* unentbehrlich
Unfallverhütung *f* accident prevention
unfruchtbar *(soil)* infertile, barren
Unfruchtbarkeit *f (soil)* infertility, barrenness
ungealtert *(rubber)* unaged
ungebeizt unmordanted
ungebleicht unbleached
ungebleit unleaded *(motor fuel)*
ungebrannt *(ceram)* unfired, unburned, green, raw
ungebunden unbonded, unbound, uncombined *(atoms, ions)*
ungechlort *(hyd)* unchlorinated, non-chlorinated
ungefährlich harmless
Ungefährlichkeit *f* harmlessness
ungefüllt filler-free, unfilled, unloaded, *(rubber also)* non-pigmented
ungeglättet *(pap)* unfinished, unglazed
ungekocht uncooked, raw
ungeladen uncharged
ungeleimt *(pap)* unsized
ungelöst undissolved
ungemahlen unground; *(pap)* unbeaten
Ungenauigkeitsbeziehung *f*, **Ungenauigkeitsrelation** *f s.* Unbestimmtheitsrelation
ungenießbar inedible
Ungenießbarkeit *f* inedibility
ungeordnet unordered, disordered, random
ungepaart unpaired *(e.g. electron)*
ungepreßt un[com]pressed
ungepuffert unbuffered
Ungerade-gerade-Kern *m* odd-even nucleus
Ungerade-ungerade-Kern *m* odd-odd nucleus
ungeradzahlig odd-number[ed]
ungereckt *(text)* undrawn *(man-made fibres)*
ungesalzen unsalted, *(tann also)* fresh
ungesättigt unsaturated *(solution or compound)*
~**/doppelt** *s.* ~/zweifach
~**/dreifach** triply unsaturated
~**/einfach** monounsaturated, monoenoic
~**/mehrfach** polyunsaturated, polyenoic
~**/stark** *s.* ~/mehrfach
~**/zweifach** diunsaturated, dienoic, doubly unsaturated
Ungesättigte *npl (petrol)* unsaturate[d]s
Ungesättigtheit *f* unsaturation
~**/geringe** low unsaturation
Ungesättigtheitsgrad *m* degree of unsaturation
ungesäuert unsoured
ungeschlichtet *(text)* unsized
ungesintert unsintered
ungespannt unstrained
ungiftig non-toxic, non-poisonous
Ungiftigkeit *f* non-toxicity, freedom from toxicity
unglasiert unglazed
ungleich[artig] dissimilar
Ungleichartigkeit *f* dissimilarity; *(relating to composition:)* heterogeneity
Ungleichgewicht *n* imbalance, unbalance, non-equilibrium
unhaltig *(mine)* barren
unharmonisch anharmonic
unhybridisiert unhybridized
unhydrierbar unhydrogenable
Unifarbe *f* self-colour
Unifärben *n* union dyeing
Unifining-Verfahren *n (petrol)* unifining process
unimolekular unimolecular, monomolecular
Union *f* **für reine und angewandte Chemie/Internationale** International Union of Pure and Applied Chemistry, IUPAC
unionisiert unionized
Unipolarzelle *f* monopolar cell
Unipolymer[e] *n* homopolymer
unitär unary *(system)*
unitarisch homopolar, non-polar, covalent *(chemical bond)*
univariant univariant, monovariant
Universaldoppelmuffe *f (lab)* swivel clamp holder
Universalechtheit *f (text)* all-round fastness
Universalemulsion *f (phot)* universal emulsion
Universalentwickler *m (phot)* universal developer

Universalfermenter *m (biot)* multi-purpose fermenter
Universalindikator *m* universal indicator
Universalindikatorpapier *n* universal indicator paper
Universalinsektizid *n* general-purpose insecticide
Universalmittel *n (pharm)* panacea, cure-all
Universalstativ *n (lab)* assembly
Universal-Stativklemme *f (lab)* universal stand-clamp
Universalwaschmittel *n* all-purpose washing agent
unkatalysiert uncatalyzed
unkoordiniert uncoordinated
Unkrautbekämpfung *f* weed control (eradication), weeding
Unkrautbekämpfungsmittel *n* herbicide, weed-killer, weed-control agent
~ **auf Wuchsstoffbasis** hormone weed-killer
Unkrautvernichter *m*, **Unkrautvertilgungsmittel** *n s.* Unkrautbekämpfungsmittel
unl. *s.* unlöslich
unlegiert unalloyed
unlöslich insoluble, i.s., non-soluble, indissoluble
• ~ **machen** to insolubilize
~ **in Alkali** insoluble in alkali
~ **in Alkohol** insoluble in alcohol
~**/in der Kälte** cold-insoluble
~ **in Wasser** water-insoluble
Unlösliches *n* insoluble, i., *(in tar:)* free carbon
Unlöslichkeit *f* insolubility, insolubleness
~**/gegenseitige** mutual insolubility
unmagnetisch non-magnetic
unmischbar immiscible
Unmischbarkeit *f* immiscibility
unmodifiziert unmodified
unnatürlich unnatural
Unnilquadium *n* Db dubnium *(element 104)*
Unordnung *f* disorder, randomness
~**/positionelle** *(cryst)* positional disordering
unpaar[ig] unpaired
unpigmentiert unpigmented
unplastifiziert unplasticized
unplastisch non-plastic
unplastiziert unplasticized
unpolar non-polar, apolar; non-polar, homopolar, covalent *(chemical bond)*
unpolarisierbar non-polarizable
unraffiniert unrefined
unregelmäßig anomalous
Unregelmäßigkeit *f* anomaly
unrein impure
Unreinheit *f* impurity, *(if localized also)* speck, spot
uns. *s.* unsymmetrisch
unsauber impure
unschädlich harmless, innocuous, benign
Unschädlichkeit *f* harmlessness, innocuousness, innocuity, benignity
Unschärfebeziehung *f s.* Unschärferelation
Unschärferelation *f*[**/Heisenbergsche**] [Heisenberg] uncertainty relation
unschmackhaft unpalatable, distasteful
unschmelzbar infusible
Unschmelzbarkeit *f* infusibility
unspezifisch non-specific
unstabil unstable, instable
unstabilisiert unstabilized
unstetig discontinuous, batch[wise], intermittent
~ **arbeitend** batch *(apparatus)*
unstöchiometrisch non-stoichiometric
Unstöchiometrie *f* non-stoichiometry
unstrukturiert structureless, devoid of structure
Unsymmetrie *f* asymmetry, dissymmetry
unsymmetrisch asymmetric[al], dissymmetric[al], unsymmetric[al]
Untenaustrag *m*, **Untenentleerung** *f* bottom discharge
Unteranstrich *m* undercoat
Unterbainit *m (met)* lower bainite
Unterbau *m* 1. *(tech)* substructure; 2. *(rubber)* case, casing, carcass, carcase *(of a pneumatic tyre)*
unterbelasten to underload
unterbelichten *(phot)* to underexpose
Unterbelichtung *f (phot)* underexposure
Unterbezugskraftstoff *m* secondary reference fuel
Unterbleiche *f (pap)* underbleaching
unterbleichen *(pap)* to underbleach
Unterboden *m (agric)* subsoil
unterbrechen to discontinue *(e.g. heating)*
Unterbrecherbad *n (phot)* stop bath
Unterbrenner *m* underjet
Unterbrennerkoksofen *m* underjet coke oven
Unterbrennerleitungen *fpl* underjet piping *(of a coke oven)*
unterbringen to locate *(e.g. atoms in interstitial lattice sites)*
Unterbringung *f* location *(as of atoms in interstitial lattice sites)*
unterdosieren to underdose, to underfeed
Unterdosierung *f* underdosage, underfeed[ing]
Unterdosis *f* underdose
Unterdruckdestillation *f* distillation under vacuum (reduced pressure)
unterdrücken to suppress, to repress *(e.g. a reaction)*
Unterdruckentgaser *m (hyd)* vacuum deaerator (degasifier)
Unterdruckfilter *n* vacuum (suction) filter
Unterdruckfiltration *f* vacuum filtration
Unterdruckkokillenguß *m* vacuum diecasting
Unterdruckpresse *f (plast)* bottom ram press
Unterdruckventil *n* vacuum relief valve, vacuum breaker
Untereinheit *f* subunit *(protein chemistry)*
~**/katalytische** catalytic subunit *(of enzymes)*
~**/regulatorische** regulatory subunit *(of enzymes)*
Untereinheitenmodell *n (bioch)* subunit model *(of cell and organelle membranes)*

unterentwickeln *(phot)* to underdevelop
Unterentwicklung *f (phot)* underdevelopment
untereutektisch hypoeutectic
untereutektoid[isch] hypoeutectoid
Unterfilz *m (pap)* bottom (lower, mould) felt *(of a cylinder board machine)*
Unterflottenjigger *m (text)* immersion jigger
untergärig bottom-fermenting, bottom-fermented
Untergärung *f* bottom fermentation
untergetaucht submerged, submersed
Unterglasurdekor *m (ceram)* underglaze decoration
Unterglasurfarbe *f (ceram)* underglaze colour
Unterglasurmalerei *f (ceram)* underglaze painting
Untergrund *m* 1. *(coat)* ground, undersurface; 2. *(agric)* C-horizon, bedrock; 3. *(anal, nucl)* background
Untergrundanstrich *m* priming [coat], primer (ground) coat
Untergrunddüngung *f* fertilization of subsoil
Untergrundemission *f (spectr)* background emission
Untergrundintensität *f (anal)* background intensity
Untergrundkompensation *f (anal)* background correction
~ **unter Ausnutzung des Zeeman-Effekts** Zeeman-effect background correction
Untergrundkorrektur *f s.* Untergrundkompensation
Untergrundmessung *f (anal)* background scan
Untergrundrauschen *n (anal)* background (baseline) noise
Untergrundspektrum *n* background (residual) spectrum
Untergrundstörung *f (spectr)* background interference
Untergrundstrahlung *f* background radiation
Untergrundversickerung *f (hyd)* infiltration into the ground (soil), soil percolation, ground infiltration
Untergruppe *f* subgroup; sub-subclass
Untergruppennummer *f*, **Untergruppenziffer** *f* subgroup number *(of the international coal classification system)*
unterhalten 1. *(tech)* to maintain; 2. to support, to sustain *(e.g. combustion)*
unterhaltend/sich selbst self-supporting, self-sustaining, self-sustained *(reaction)*
Unterhaltung *f* 1. *(tech)* maintenance, upkeep; 2. support, sustainment *(as of combustion)*
Unterhaltungskosten *pl* maintenance cost[s], cost of upkeep
Unterhärtung *f (plast)* undercure
Unterhefe *f* bottom[-fermentation] yeast
Unterkeim *m (cryst)* cluster
Unterklasse *f* subclass
unterkochen *(pap)* to undercook
Unterkochung *f (pap)* undercooking
Unterkolben *m (plast)* bottom ram (force) *(of a press)*
Unterkolbenpresse *f (plast)* up-stroke press, bottom ram press
Unterkorn *n* undersize [material, product], fines, minus material *(classifying)*, *(screening also)* screen undersize (fines)
unterkritisch *(nucl, cryst)* subcritical
unterkühlen to supercool, to subcool, *(glass also)* to overcool
Unterlage *f* base, pad, *(esp phot)* support
Unterlagspapier *n* carpet felt
Unterlagspappe *f* carpet felt
Unterlagsplatte *f* bed plate
Unterlauf *m* underflow *(classifying)*
Unterlaufprodukt *n* underflow *(classifying)*
Unterluftzelle *f (min tech)* subaeration floatation cell
Untermesser *n (pap)* bed knife *(of a cross-cutter)*
Unterniveau *n* sublevel *(of electrons)*
Unterphase *f (chromat)* lower phase
Unterpulverschweißen *n* submerged-arc welding
untersättigt subsaturated, undersaturated
Untersättigung *f* subsaturation, undersaturation
Untersatzschale *f* **für Säureflaschen** *(lab)* bottle tray, acid dish
Untersäule *f (distil)* exhausting (stripping) section
Unterschale *f* 1. [electronic] subshell; 2. *(lab)* dish bottom *(as of a Petri dish)*
Unterschicht *f*/**laminare** viscous sublayer *(of a boundary layer with turbulent flow)*
unterschichten to add to form a lower layer
Unterschubfeuerung *f* underfeed firing, underfiring
Unterschubrost *m* underfeed stoker
Unterseite *f (pap)* wire side
untersinken to sink
Unterstempel *m (plast)* bottom ram (force) *(of a press)*; *(ceram)* bottom punch; *(met)* lower plunger *(of a die)*
unterstöchiometrisch hypostoichiometric
Unterstruktur *f (cryst)* substructure
Unterstützung *f*/**anchimere** anchimeric assistance *(of neighbouring groups in accelerating the reaction rate)*
untersuchen to investigate, to examine, to assay, to analyse
untersucht werden to undergo examination
Untersuchung *f* investigation, research, examination, assay, analysis
~/**mikroskopische** microexamination
~/**organoleptische** organoleptic (sensory) examination
~/**röntgenographische** X-ray investigation
~/**sinnesphysiologische** *s.* ~/organoleptische
Untersuchungsbohrung *f (petrol)* exploration drilling, wildcat
Untersuchungsflüssigkeit *f* liquid for *or* under investigation (examination)
Untersuchungslösung *f* solution for *or* under investigation (examination), solution being *or* to be tested, test solution
Untersuchungsmaterial *n* material for *or* under investigation (examination), experimental (test) material

Untersuchungsmethode *f* investigational method, test[ing] method
~/standardisierte standard test[ing] method
Untersuchungsprobe *f* test sample *(product of sample reduction)*
Untersuchungssubstanz *f s.* Untersuchungsmaterial
Untertagebau *m* underground mining (working), deep mining
Untertagespeicher *m* underground reservoir (storage tank)
Untertagespeicherung *f* underground storage
Untertagevergasung *f* underground gasification
untertauchen to submerge, to immerse
Untertauchen *n* submersion, immersion
unterteilen to classify; to graduate
Unterteilung *f* classification; graduation
Untertrum *m(n)* return side *(conveying)*
Unter-Unterklasse *f* sub-subclass
untervernetzen *s.* untervulkanisieren
Untervulkanisation *f* undercure, undercuring, undervulcanization
untervulkanisieren to undercure, to undervulcanize
Unterwalze *f* bottom roll
~ der Leimpresse *(pap)* bottom size press roll
Unterwasseranstrichfarbe *f* underwater paint
~/anwuchsverhindernde antifouling paint
Unterwasserbohrung *f (petrol)* marine drilling
Unterwasserjigger *m (text)* immersion jigger
Unterwasserkorrosion *f* underwater corrosion
Unterwasserpumpe *f* submersible (submerged) pump
Unterwerkzeug *n (plast)* die
Unterwind *m* downdraught
Unterwindfeuerung *f* overfeed firing
Unterwindfrischkonverter *m (met)* bottom-blown converter
Unterwindfrischverfahren *n (met)* bottom-blown-converter process
Unterwindgebläse *n* forced-draught fan (blower)
untoxisch non-toxic, non-poisonous
untrennbar inseparable
unumgesetzt unreacted, unconverted
ununterbrochen continuous *(operation)* • **~ arbeitend** continuous *(apparatus)*
unveränderlich invariable
unverändert unchanged, unaltered
unverbleit unleaded *(motor fuel)*
unverbrannt unburned, unburnt
Unverbranntes *n* unburned combustible [matter]
unverbraucht unspent *(chemicals)*; unreacted *(reactant)*
unverbrennbar incombustible, non-combustible
Unverbrennbare *n*, **Unverbrennliche** *n* incombustible [matter], non-combustible [matter]
unverdampft unevaporated
unverdaulich indigestible
Unverdaulichkeit *f* indigestibility
unverdichtet uncompressed
unverdickt *(coat)* unbodied
unverdünnt undiluted
unverfestigt unconsolidated
unvergärbar unfermentable
unvergast ungasified
unvermischbar immiscible
Unvermischbarkeit *f* immiscibility
unvermischt unmixed
unvernetzt uncross-linked, uncured, *(rubber also)* unvulcanized
unverpackt unpacked
unverrohrt *(petrol)* uncased
unverschmutzt uncontaminated, non-contaminated, unpolluted, free from polluting substances *(water, air)*
unverseifbar unsaponifiable, non-saponifiable
Unverseifbares *n* unsaponifiable matter (residue)
unverseift unsaponified
unverstärkt unreinforced *(e.g. plastic material)*
unverstreckt undrawn *(man-made fibres)*
unverträglich incompatible
Unverträglichkeit *f* incompatibility
unverwitterbar unweatherable
unverzweigt unbranched[-chain]
unvollkommen *s.* unvollständig
unvollständig non-quantitative *(e.g. precipitation)*
Unvollständigkeit *f* non-quantitativeness *(as of a precipitation)*
unvulkanisiert *(rubber)* uncured, unvulcanized
unwirksam ineffective • **~ machen** to deactivate, to inactivate, to block
Unwirksammachen *n* deactivation, inactivation, blocking
unzerbrechlich unbreakable
unzersetzt undecomposed
unzerstörbar non-destructible
unzugänglich *(agric)* unavailable *(nutrients)*
UP *s.* Polyester/ungesättigter
Upas[gift] *n* upas, Malay poison *(any of several arrow poisons)*
Uperisation *f (food)* uperization
uperisieren *(food)* to uperize
UP-Schweißen *n s.* Unterpulverschweißen
Uracil *n* uracil, pyrimidine-2,4-dione
Uracil-4-carbonsäure *f* uracil-4-carboxylic acid, orotic acid
uralitisieren *(min)* to uralitize
Uralitisierung *f (min)* uralitization *(development of amphiboles from pyroxenes)*
Uramil *n* uramil, 5-aminobarbituric acid
Uran *n* U uranium • **an ~ verarmt** uranium-barren
Uran-Actinium-Reihe *f*, **Uran-Actinium-Zerfallsreihe** *f* actinium [decay] series, uranium-actinium [disintegration] series
Uranat *n* uranate *(salt or ester of uranic acid)*
Uranblüte *f (min)* zippeite *(a uranyl sulphate)*
Urandioxid *n s.* Uran(IV)-oxid
Uranerz *n* uranium ore

Uran(IV)-fluorid *n* uranium(IV) fluoride, uranium tetrafluoride
Uran(VI)-fluorid *n* uranium(VI) fluoride, uranium hexafluoride
Urangelb *n* uranium yellow *(sodium diuranate 6-water)*
Uranglas *n* uranium glass
uranhaltig uranium-containing, *(esp relating to ores:)* uraniferous, uranium-bearing
Uranhexafluorid *n s.* Uran(VI)-fluorid
Uranhydrid *n* uranium hydride
Uranid *n s.* Transuran
Uranin *n* uranin[e], sodium fluorescein
Uranmineral *n* uranium mineral
Uranocker *m s.* Uranopilit
Uranoid *n s.* Transuran
Uranophan *m (min)* uranophane, uranotil *(a hydrous calcium uranium silicate)*
Uranopilit *m (min)* uranopilite, uranic ochre *(a uranyl sulphate)*
Uran(IV)-oxid *n* uranium(IV) oxide, uranium dioxide
Uran(IV,VI)-oxid *n* triuranium octaoxide, uranium(IV) uranate
Uran(VI)-oxid *n* uranium(VI) oxide, uranium trioxide
Uranpechblende *f*, **Uranpecherz** *n (min)* pitchblende, uraninite *(uranium(IV) oxide)*
Uranperoxid *n s.* Urantetroxid
Uranpyrochlor *m (min)* uranpyrochlore
Uran-Radium-Reihe *f*, **Uran-Radium-Zerfallsreihe** *f* uranium [decay] series, uranium-radium [disintegration] series
Uransäure *f* uranic acid
Uranspaltung *f* uranium fission
Uran(III)-sulfid *n* uranium(III) sulphide, diuranium trisulphide
Urantetrafluorid *n s.* Uran(IV)-fluorid
Urantetroxid *n* uranium tetraoxide
Urantrioxid *n s.* Uran(VI)-oxid
Uran(IV)-uranat *n* uranium(IV) uranate, triuranium octaoxide
Uranvitriol *m (min)* uranvitriol, johannite *(a uranyl sulphate)*
Uranylacetat *n* uranyl acetate
Uranylbromid *n* uranyl bromide
Uranylchlorid *n* uranyl chloride
Uranylhexacyanoferrat(II) *n* uranyl hexacyanoferrate(II)
Uranylhydroxid *n* uranyl hydroxide
Uranylnitrat *n* uranyl nitrate
Uranylsalz *n* uranyl salt
Uranylverbindung *f* uranyl compound
Uranzerfallsreihe *f s.* Uran-Radium-Reihe
Urat *n* urate *(a salt of uric acid)*
Uratoxidase *f* uricase
p-**Urazin** *n* *p*-urazine, hexahydro-*s*-tetrazine-3,6-dione
Urbarmachungskrankheit *f (agric)* reclamation disease *(caused by Cu shortage)*
Urbezugskraftstoff *m* primary reference fuel
Ureid *n* ureide *(an acyl derivative of urea)*
~/cyclisches cyclic ureide
~/offenes acyclic ureide
Ureidoessigsäure *f* ureidoacetic acid, hydantoic acid
2-Ureidoethan-1-sulfonsäure *f* 2-ureidoethane-1-sulphonic acid, taurocarbamic acid
Ureidosäure *f* ureido acid
Ureometer *n* ureometer, ureameter *(for determining the amount of urea)*
ureotel ureotelic *(excreting nitrogen as urea)*
Ureotelie *f* ureotelism *(excretion of nitrogen as urea)*
Ureotelier *m* ureotelic animal
Urethan *n* urethane
~/polymeres polyurethane
Urethanelastomer[e] *n* [poly]urethane elastomer
~/auf Polyesteramidbasis aufgebautes polyesteramide urethane
~/auf Polyesterbasis aufgebautes polyester urethane
~/auf Polyetherbasis aufgebautes polyether urethane
Urethankautschuk *m* [poly]urethane rubber, isocyanate rubber
Urethanöl *n* urethane oil
Urethanschaumstoff *m* urethane foam
Uricolyse *f* uricolysis *(the conversion of uric acid to urea)*
uricolytisch uricolytic
Uridin *n (org ch)* uridine
Uridindiphosphat *n* uridine diphosphate, UDP
Uridindiphosphatglucose *f*, **Uridindiphosphoglucose** *f* uridinediphosphateglucose, uridinediphosphoglucose, UDPG
Uridinphosphat *n* uridine phosphate, *(esp)* uridine monophosphate, uridine phosphoric acid, UMP
Uridinphosphorsäure *f* uridine phosphoric acid
Uridintriphosphat *n*, **Uridintriphosphorsäure** *f* uridine triphosphate, UTP
Uridylsäure *f (bioch)* uridylic acid, uridine 5'-monophosphate, UMP
urikotel uricotelic *(excreting nitrogen as uric acid)*
Urikotelie *f* uricotelism *(excretion of nitrogen as uric acid)*
Urikotelier *m* uricotelic animal
Urlauge *f* mother liquid (liquor); *(pap)* red (spent sulphite) liquor, sulphite lye (waste liquor)
Urobilin *n* urobilin *(a pigment of urine)*
Urocaninsäure *f*, **Urocansäure** *f* urocanic acid, urocaninic acid, 4-imidazoleacrylic acid
Urochrom *n* urochrome *(a pigment of urine)*
Urochromogen *n* urochromogen *(the colourless precursor of urochrome)*
U-Rohr *n* U-tube
U-Rohr-Manometer *n* U-tube manometer
U-Rohr-Wärmeaustauscher *m*, **U-Rohr-Wärmeübertrager** *m* U-tube heat exchanger
Uronsäure *f* $OHC[CHOH]_nCOOH$ uronic acid *(any of a series of aldehyde acids)*

Urreaktion *f* elementary reaction
Ursäure *f* ur-acid *(any of a class of hydrolytic products of ureides)*
Urspannung *f***[/elektrische]** electromotive force, emf
Urspannungsnormal *n* standard of emf
Ursprung *m* origin, source • **pflanzlichen Ursprungs** of vegetable (plant) origin, plant-derived • **tierischen Ursprungs** of animal origin • **vulkanischen Ursprungs** of volcanic origin, *(esp of gases)* plume-borne
Ursprungsgestein *n* parent (mother, source) rock
Ursprungssubstanz *f* parent substance
Ursubstanz *f s.* Urtitersubstanz
Urteer *m* primary (low-temperature) tar
Urtitersubstanz *f* primary-standard chemical, primary standard *(in titrimetric analysis)*
Urundayextrakt *m (tann)* urunday extract *(from Astronium balansae Engl.)*
USC-Verfahren *n (petrol)* USC process, ultraselective conversion process
Usnetininsäure *f* usnetinic acid *(a lichen acid)*
Usnetinsäure *f* lobaric acid, usnetic acid *(a lichen acid)*
Usnidinsäure *f s.* Usnetinsäure
Usninsäure *f* usnic acid *(a lichen acid)*
Uterotonikum *n*, **Uterustonikum** *n (pharm)* uterotonic, oxytocic [agent]
uu-Kern *m s.* Ungerade-ungerade-Kern
UV UV, ultraviolet
UV-Abbau *m* UV degradation
UV-Absorber *m* UV absorber
UV-Absorption *f* UV absorption
UV-Bereich *m* UV region, ultraviolet [spectral] region
UV-Beständigkeit *f* UV resistance
UV-Bestrahlung *f* UV irradiation
UV-Bestrahlungsanlage *f* **zur Wasserentkeimung** *(hyd)* UV water-disinfection unit
UV-Detektor *m* UV detector
UV-Fotografie *f* UV photography
UV-Gebiet *n s.* UV-Bereich
UV-Lampe *f* UV lamp
UV-Läsion *f (biot)* UV-induced lesion
UVS... *s. a.* UV-VIS-...
UVS-Bereich *m*, **UVS-Gebiet** *n* UV-VIS range (region), ultraviolet-visible (UV-visible) region
UV-Spektroskopie *f* UV spectroscopy
UV-Spektrum *n* UV spectrum
UV-Stabilisator *m* UV stabilizer
UV-Strahlung *f* UV radiation
UV-VIS-Absorptionsspektroskopie *f* UV-VIS absorption spectroscopy
UV-VIS-Spektralphotometrie *f* UV-VIS spectrophotometry
UV-VIS-Spektroskopie *f* UV-VIS spectroscopy
UV-VIS-spektroskopisch by UV-VIS spectroscopy
Uvinsäure *f* uvinic acid, 2,5-dimethylfuran-3-carboxylic acid

V

Vacanceine-Rot *n* Vacanceine red *(obtained by coupling β-naphthol with β-naphthylamine)*
Vaccensäure *f* vaccenic acid, *octadec-11-enoic acid *(specif trans form)*
vakant vacant
Vakuum *n* vacuum • **~ herstellen** to create a vacuum • **unter ~ arbeiten** to operate under a vacuum
~/Torricellisches Torricellian vacuum
Vakuumanschluß *m* vacuum connection (intake, port)
Vakuumapparat *m* vacuum pan *(for producing sugar or salt)*
~ mit Heizschlangen *(sugar)* strike pan
Vakuumarbeitsraum *m* vacuum chamber
Vakuumaufdampfung *f* vacuum deposition
Vakuumbandfilter *n* rotary-drum belt-type vacuum filter
Vakuumbegasung *f* vacuum fumigation
Vakuumbrennen *n (ceram)* vacuum firing
Vakuumdestillat *n* vacuum distillate, VD
Vakuumdestillation *f* vacuum distillation
Vakuumdestillationsanlage *f* vacuum-distillation plant
Vakuumdestillierapparat *m* vacuum still
vakuumdestilliert vacuum-distilled, distilled in vacuo
vakuumdicht vacuum-tight
Vakuumdrehfilter *n* rotary vacuum filter
Vakuumdruckguß *m* vacuum diecasting
Vakuumeindampfung *f* vacuum concentration
Vakuumentgaser *m (hyd)* vacuum deaerator (degasifier)
Vakuumentgasung *f (hyd)* vacuum deaeration (degasification)
Vakuumentzinkung *f* vacuum dezincing
Vakuumexsikkator *m* vacuum desiccator
Vakuumfett *n* vacuum grease
Vakuumfilter *n* vacuum (suction) filter
Vakuumfilternutsche *f* vacuum nutsche
Vakuumfiltration *f* vacuum (suction) filtration
~ mit Precoatschicht precoat vacuum filtration
Vakuumflotation *f (hyd)* vacuum floatation
Vakuumformbarkeit *f* vacuum formability
Vakuumformen *n* vacuum forming
~ mit [mechanischer] Vorstreckung *(plast)* plug-assist [vacuum] forming
Vakuumformmaschine *f* vacuum-forming machine
Vakuumformung *f s.* Vakuumformen
Vakuumfülltrichter *m* vacuum hopper
Vakuumgasöl *n* vacuum gas oil, VGO
Vakuumgefäß *n* vacuum vessel
Vakuumgummisackverfahren *n (plast)* vacuum-bag moulding
Vakuumheißextraktion *f (anal)* vacuum hot extraction analysis
Vakuumheizplattentrockenschrank *m* vacuum shelf dryer

Vakuuminnenzellenfilter *n* inside drum filter, internal [rotary-]drum filter
Vakuumisolierung *f* vacuum insulation
Vakuumkitt *m (plast)* vacuum cement
Vakuumkneter *m* vacuum kneader (blender)
Vakuumkochapparat *m (sugar)* vacuum pan
Vakuumkolben *m* vacuum flask
Vakuumkolonne *f (distil)* vacuum column (still)
Vakuumkristallisation *f* vacuum crystallization
Vakuumkristallisator *m* vacuum crystallizer
Vakuumkühlanlage *f*, **Vakuumkühler** *m* vacuum cooler
Vakuumkühlung *f* vacuum cooling
Vakuum-Lecksuchgerät *n* vacuum tester
Vakuumleitung *f* vacuum line
Vakuummantel *m* vacuum jacket
Vakuummeßgerät *n* vacuum gauge, vacuometer
Vakuummetallisierung *f* vacuum metallizing, vapour (gas) plating
Vakuummeter *n* vacuum gauge, vacuometer
Vakuumnutsche *f* vacuum nutsche
Vakuumpfanne *f* vacuum pan
Vakuumplattentrockner *m* vacuum shelf dryer
Vakuumpolarisation *f* vacuum polarization
Vakuumpulverisolierung *f* evacuated powder insulation *(cryogenics)*
Vakuumpumpe *f* vacuum pump
Vakuumpumpenanschluß *m* vacuum-pump connection
Vakuumraum *m* vacuum vessel *(of a dryer)*
Vakuumrotationsfilter *n* rotary vacuum filter
Vakuumrückstand *m (petrol)* vacuum residue, VR, short residue (residuum)
Vakuumsack *m (plast)* vacuum bag
Vakuumsaugverfahren *n (plast)* straight vacuum forming
Vakuumschaufeltrockner *m* vacuum rotary dryer, rotary vacuum dryer
Vakuumscheibenfilter *n* disk-type vacuum filter
Vakuum-Scheibenzellenfilter *n* disk-type rotary vacuum filter, rotary [vacuum] disk filter
Vakuumschlauch *m* vacuum tubing *(material)*; vacuum hose
Vakuumschmelzen *n* vacuum melting
Vakuumspektrograph *m* vacuum spectrograph
Vakuumspektroskopie *f* vacuum spectroscopy
Vakuumstoffauflauf *m (pap)* vacuum headbox
Vakuumstrangpresse *f (ceram)* vacuum extrusion press, de-airing auger (pug mill)
Vakuumsublimation *f* vacuum sublimation
Vakuumtaumeltrockner *m* rotating vacuum dryer
Vakuumtechnik *f* vacuum technology
Vakuumtiefziehen *n (plast)* straight vacuum forming
Vakuumtonschneider *m s.* Vakuumstrangpresse
Vakuumtrockenanlage *f* vacuum-drying plant
Vakuumtrockenapparat *m* vacuum dryer
Vakuumtrockenpartie *f (pap)* vacuum dryer
Vakuumtrockenschrank *m* vacuum drying cabinet, vacuum [drying] oven
~ **nach Paßburg** Passburg dryer
Vakuumtrockner *m* vacuum dryer
Vakuumtrocknung *f* vacuum drying (dehydration)
Vakuumtrommelfilter *n* [rotary] vacuum drum filter, rotary-drum vacuum filter
Vakuumtrommelzellenfilter *n* multicompartment drum filter
Vakuum-UV *n* vacuum ultraviolet
Vakuum-UV-Spektroskopie *f* vacuum UV spectroscopy
Vakuumverdampfapparat *m*, **Vakuumverdampfer** *m* vacuum evaporator
Vakuumverdampfung *f* vacuum evaporation
Vakuumverformung *f s.* Vakuumformen
Vakuum-Vielschichtisolierung *f* multiple-layer insulation, superinsulation *(cryogenic engineering)*
Vakuumvorlage *f (lab)* vacuum receiver
Vakuumwalzentrockner *m* vacuum drum dryer
Vakuumwäscher *m* vacuum washer
Vakuumzellenfilter *n (pap)* rotary vacuum drum-type save-all
Vakuumzerstäuben *n* sputtering
Vakuumziehen *n (plast)* vacuum forming
~ **mit Vorstreckung** plug-assist vacuum forming
Vakzensäure *f s.* Vaccensäure
Vakzine *f* vaccine
Val *n* gram equivalent, g. equiv.
Valenz *f* 1. valence, valency *(unit of combining power)*; 2. *s.* Wertigkeit; 3. *s.* Bindungskraft 1.
~/gerichtete directed valence
Valenzabsättigung *f* valence saturation
Valenzband *n* valence band
Valenzbindung *f* valence bond
Valenzbindungsmethode *f* valence-bond method, VB method, electron-pair method, HLSP (Heitler-London-Slater-Pauling) method
Valenzbindungsresonanz *f* valence-bond resonance
Valenzbindungstheorie *f* valence-bond theory, VB theory, electron-pair theory, HLSP (Heitler-London-Slater-Pauling) theory
Valenzbindungswinkel *m* valence angle, bond (interbonding) angle
Valenzelektron *n* valence electron, outermost (valence shell, optical) electron
Valenzelektronenpaar *n* valence (outer-shell) electron pair, valence-shell [electron] pair
Valenzfrequenz *f* stretching frequency
Valenzisomerisierung *f* valence isomerization
~/reversible valence tautomerism
Valenzkraft *f* valence (stretching) force
Valenzkraftkonstante *f* stretching-force constant
Valenzlehre *f* theory of valence, valence theory
Valenzorbital *n* valence (bond) orbital, outer-shell orbital
Valenzschale *f* valence shell

Valenzschwingung *f* valence (stretching) vibration, stretching mode
Valenzstrichformel *f* [valence] structural formula, line (constitutional, graphic) formula
Valenzstruktur *f* valence-bond structure
Valenzstrukturmethode *f s.* Valenzbindungsmethode
Valenzstrukturtheorie *f s.* Valenzbindungstheorie
Valenzstufe *f* valence state
Valenztautomerie *f* valence tautomerism
Valenztheorie *f* theory of valence, valence theory
Valenzwechsel *m* valence change
Valenzwinkel *m* valence angle, bond (interbonding) angle
Valenzzahl *f* valence number
Valeraldehyd *m* valeraldehyde, *pentanal
Valerat *n* valerate *(salt or ester of a valeric acid)*
Valerianat *n s.* Valerat
Valeriansäure *f* valeric acid, *(specif)* $CH_3[CH_2]_3COOH$ *pentanoic acid
Valeriansäureanhydrid *n* valeric anhydride
Valeriansäureethylester *m* ethyl valerate
Valeriansäureisoamylester *m* isoamyl valerate
Valerolactam *n* valerolactam, α-piperidone
Valerylen *n s.* Pent-2-in
Valin *n* valine, *2-amino-3-methylbutanoic acid
Vallez-Filter *n* Vallez filter, horizontal-tank sluicing filter
Valoneasäure *f* valoneaic acid *(a depside)*
Vanadat *n* vanadate
Vanadin *n s.* Vanadium
Vanadinglimmer *m (min)* roscoelite, *(deprecated:)* vanadium mica *(a phyllosilicate)*
Vanadium *n* V vanadium
Vanadium(III)-bromid *n* vanadium(III) bromide, vanadium tribromide
Vanadium(II)-chlorid *n* vanadium(II) chloride, vanadium dichloride
Vanadium(III)-chlorid *n* vanadium(III) chloride, vanadium trichloride
Vanadiumdichlorid *n s.* Vanadium(II)-chlorid
Vanadiumdiiodid *n s.* Vanadium(II)-iodid
Vanadiumdioxid *n s.* Vanadium(IV)-oxid
Vanadium(III)-fluorid *n* vanadium(III) fluoride, vanadium trifluoride
Vanadium(V)-fluorid *n* vanadium(V) fluoride, vanadium pentafluoride
vanadiumhaltig vanadium-containing, *(esp relating to ores:)* vanadiferous
Vanadium(II)-iodid *n* vanadium(II) iodide, vanadium diiodide
Vanadiummonosulfid *n s.* Vanadium(II)-sulfid
Vanadiummonoxid *n s.* Vanadium(II)-oxid
Vanadium(II)-oxid *n* vanadium(II) oxide, vanadium monooxide
Vanadium(III)-oxid *n* vanadium(III) oxide, vanadium trioxide, divanadium trioxide
Vanadium(IV)-oxid *n* vanadium(IV) oxide, vanadium dioxide
Vanadium(V)-oxid *n* vanadium(V) oxide, vanadium pentaoxide, divanadium pentaoxide
Vanadium(III)-oxidchlorid *n* vanadium(III) monochloride oxide
Vanadium(V)-oxidchlorid *n* vanadium(V) trichloride oxide
Vanadiumoxiddichlorid *n* vanadium(IV) dichloride oxide
Vanadiumoxidmonochlorid *n s.* Vanadium(III)-oxidchlorid
Vanadium(IV)-oxidsulfat *n* vanadium(IV) oxide sulphate
Vanadiumoxidtrichlorid *n s.* Vanadium(V)-oxidchlorid
Vanadiumpentafluorid *n s.* Vanadium(V)-fluorid
Vanadiumpentasulfid *n s.* Vanadium(V)-sulfid
Vanadiumpentoxid *n s.* Vanadium(V)-oxid
Vanadiumsäure *f* vanadic acid
Vanadium(II)-sulfat *n* vanadium(II) sulphate
Vanadium(II)-sulfid *n* vanadium(II) sulphide, vanadium monosulphide
Vanadium(III)-sulfid *n* vanadium(III) sulphide, vanadium trisulphide, divanadium trisulphide
Vanadium(V)-sulfid *n* vanadium(V) sulphide, vanadium pentasulphide, divanadium pentasulphide
Vanadiumtri... *s.* Vanadium(III)-...
Vanadyl... *s.* Vanadiumoxid...
Van-de-Graaff-Bandgenerator *m*, **Van-de-Graaff-Beschleuniger** *m s.* Van-de-Graaff-Generator
Van-de-Graaff-Generator *m* van de Graaff generator (accelerator) *(an electrostatic machine)*
Van-Deemter-Gleichung *f (chromat)* van Deemter equation (expression, formulation)
Van-der-Waals-Anziehung *f*, **Van-der-Waals-Attraktion** *f* van der Waals attraction
Van-der-Waals-Bindung *f* van der Waals bond
Van-der-Waals-Kräfte *fpl* van der Waals forces [of attraction]
Van-der-Waals-Kristall *m* van der Waals crystal
Van-der-Waals-Molekül *n* van der Waals molecule
Van-der-Waals-Radius *m* van der Waals radius
Van-Dyck-Braun *n* Vandyke brown *(a natural pigment)*
Van-Dyck-Rot *n* Vandyke red *(copper(II) hexacyanoferrate(II))*
Vanillal *n* vanillal, bourbonal, 3-ethoxy-4-hydroxybenzaldehyde
Vanillaldehyd *m*, **Vanillin** *n* vanillin, 4-hydroxy-3-methoxybenzaldehyde
Vanillinsäure *f* vanillic acid, 4-hydroxy-3-methoxybenzoic acid
Van-Slyke-Methode *f* Van Slyke method *(for determining free amino groups)*
Van't-Hoff-Gleichung *f* van't Hoff equation *(osmosis)*
Variabilitätskoeffizient *m* coefficient of variation *(statistics)*
Varianz *f* variance *(statistics)*

Varietät *f (min)* variety
Variole *f (geol)* variole *(a spherule of a variolite)*
Vasodilatans *n*, **Vasodilat[at]or** *m (pharm)* vasodilator
vasodilatatorisch vasodilating
Vasokonstriktor *m (pharm)* vasoconstrictor
vasokonstriktorisch vasoconstrictive
Vateriafett *n* Dhupa fat, piney tallow *(from Vateria indica L.)*
VB-Methode *f s.* Valenzbindungsmethode
VB-Näherung *f* valence-bond approximation (approach), VB approximation
VB-Theorie *f s.* Valenzbindungstheorie
vegetabilisch vegetable
Vektor *m*/**bifunktioneller** *(bioch)* shuttle vector
vektoriell *(bioch)* vectorial *(transport mechanism)*
Velinglasur *f (ceram)* vellum glaze, satin[-vellum] glaze
Velinpapier *n* wove paper
Vello-Verfahren *n (glass)* Vello process
Velourleder *n* suede leather
Velourpapier *n* velour (flock) paper
Venetianischrot *n* Venetian red *(iron(III) oxide)*
Ventil *n* valve
~/doppelsitziges double-seat[ed] valve
~/einsitziges single-seat[ed] valve
~/membranbetätigtes diaphragm motor valve
~ mit geteiltem Gehäuse split-body valve
~ mit Hilfssteuerung pilot-controlled valve
~ mit kugeligem Gehäuse globe valve
~/vorgesteuertes pilot-controlled valve
Ventilator *m* blower, fan
~ mit geraden Schaufeln straight-blade fan
~ mit rückwärtsgekrümmten Schaufeln backward-curved-blade fan
~ mit vorwärtsgekrümmten Schaufeln forward-curved-blade fan
Ventilatorkühlturm *m* forced-draught cooling tower, induced-draught (mechanical-draught) cooling tower
Ventilatorschwefel *m* winnowed (wind-blown) sulphur
Ventilauskleidung *f* valve trim
Ventilboden *m* valve tray
Ventilgehäuse *n* valve body
Ventilhaube *f* valve bonnet
Ventilkörper *m* valve body
Ventilspindel *f* valve stem
Ventiltellerzentrifuge *f* nozzle discharge disk centrifuge
Venturi-Abscheider *m s.* Venturi-Wascher
Venturi-Düse *f* Venturi tube
Venturi-Kanal *m* Venturi flume *(for flow measurement)*
Venturi-Messer *m* Venturi meter
Venturi-Naßabscheider *m s.* Venturi-Wascher
Venturi-Rohr *n* Venturi tube
Venturi-Skrubber *m*, **Venturi-Staubabscheider** *n s.* Venturi-Wascher
Venturi-Wascher *m* Venturi scrubber (washer), Venturi-type water jet scrubber
Venushaar *n (min)* love arrows, flèche d'amour, cupid's darts *(a fibrous variety of rutile, chemically titanium dioxide)*
verabreichen to apply, *(pharm also)* to administer
Verabreichung *f* application, *(pharm also)* administration
veraluminieren *s.* aluminieren
verändern/sich to undergo change
~/sich chemisch to undergo chemical change
Veränderung *f* change • **eine chemische ~ erfahren (erleiden)** to undergo chemical change
~/enzymatische enzymatic change
~/nukleare nuclear change
~/stoffliche change of material, material change
verarbeitbar processable, processible, workable, *(pap)* runnable
Verarbeitbarkeit *f* processability, processibility, workability; *(pap)* runnability
verarbeiten to process, to work
~/auf Papier to make (convert) into paper
~/bis zur Fellbildung *(rubber)* to sheet [out]
~/zu Krümeln *(rubber)* to pellet[ize]
~/zu Pellets to pellet[ize]
Verarbeitung *f* processing, working; *(petrol)* refining
~ von Polymeren polymer processing
Verarbeitungsanlage *f* processing plant
Verarbeitungsbereich *m* working range
Verarbeitungseigenschaften *fpl* processing characteristics (properties)
verarbeitungsfähig *s.* verarbeitbar
Verarbeitungshilfsmittel *n* processing agent (aid)
Verarbeitungsindustrie *f* processing industry
Verarbeitungsprozeß *m* manufacturing process
Verarbeitungsrichtlinie *f* [processing] specification
verarbeitungssicher safe for [factory] processing
Verarbeitungssicherheit *f* processing safety
Verarbeitungstechnik *f* processing technology *(branch of science or its application)*
Verarbeitungstechnologie *f* processing technology *(sequence of processing steps)*
Verarbeitungsverfahren *n* manufacturing process
Verarbeitungsvorschrift *f* [processing] specification
Verarbeitungszeit *f* [liquid] pot life *(of reaction coatings)*
verarmen to become poor (depleted, impoverished)
~ lassen to deplete, to impoverish
verarmt/an Sauerstoff oxygen-depleted
Verarmung *f* depletion, impoverishment
~ an Sauerstoff oxygen depletion
Verarmungsschicht *f* depletion (barrier) layer *(with semiconductors)*
veraschen to ash, to reduce to ashes, to incinerate, *(filtr also)* to burn off
Veraschen *n* ashing, incineration
~ auf nassem Wege *s.* ~/nasses

~ auf trockenem Wege *s.* ~/trockenes
~/nasses wet ashing
~/trockenes dry ashing
Verascher *m (pap)* incinerator
verascht/naß wet-ashed
~/trocken dry-ashed
Veraschung *f s.* Veraschen
Veraschungsschälchen *n* incinerating dish
verästelt *(cryst)* dendritic[al]
veräthern *s.* verethern
Veratraldehyd *m s.* Veratrumaldehyd
Veratrumaldehyd *m* veratric aldehyde, 3,4-dimethoxybenzaldehyde
Veratrumsäure *f* veratric acid, dimethoxybenzoic acid, *(specif)* 3,4-dimethoxybenzoic acid
verätzen to burn, *(agric also)* to scorch; *(med)* to cauterize, to burn *(e.g. a wound)*
Verätzung *f* 1. *(act:)* burning, *(agric also)* scorching; *(med)* cauterization, cautery *(as of wounds)*; 2. *(result:)* burn, *(agric also)* scorch, *(med also)* chemical burn
verbacken to bake *(amines for sulphonation)*; to set up *(as of hygroscopic material)*
Verband *m* union *(of atoms, molecules)*
Verbandwatte *f* sanitary cotton
Verbenaöl *n*/**echtes** *(cosmet)* verbena oil *(from Lippia triphylla (L'Hérit.) O. Kuntze)*
~/Indisches East Indian verbena oil, lemon-grass oil *(from Cymbopogon specc.)*
verbessern to improve; to upgrade *(the quality of a material)*
~/die Oberflächenbeschaffenheit (Oberflächengüte) to finish
Verbesserung *f* improvement; upgrading *(of the quality of a material)*
Verbesserungsmittel *n (food)* improver
verbinden 1. to combine *(elements, compounds)*; to bond [together], to link [together] *(atoms)*; 2. to connect, to join, to link [together], *(esp by means of an adhesive:)* to bond
~/durch eine Rohrleitung to pipe
~/mit einem T-Stück to tee
~/miteinander *s.* verbinden
~/sich [miteinander] to combine *(of elements, compounds)*; to bond, to link [together] *(of atoms)*
Verbindung *f* 1. *(act or process:)* combination *(of elements or compounds)*; bonding, linking, linkage *(of atoms)*; *(mechanically:)* connection, joining, linkage; 2. *(substance:)* compound; 3. *(piece:)* connection, joint, link, union, *(esp for pipes and hoses:)* fitting; 4. *(state:)* connection, *(esp by an adhesive:)* bond • **eine [chemische] ~ eingehen** to enter into [chemical] combination (union), to combine
~/abbauresistente persistent (refractory) compound
~/acyclische acyclic compound
~/additive additive (addition) compound
~/alicyclische alicyclic compound
~/aliphatische aliphatic compound
~/analoge analogue
~/anorganische inorganic [compound]
~/antiaromatische antiaromatic compound
~/aromatische aromatic compound
~/asymmetrische unsymmetrical compound
~/ausgegossene poured joint *(of tubes)*
~/berthollide berthollide compound, non-stoichiometric (non-Daltonian, non-daltonide) compound
~/berylliumorganische organoberyllium compound
~/binäre binary compound
~/biologisch nicht abbaubare non-biodegradable compound, biorefractory compound
~/bleiorganische organolead compound
~/bororganische organoboron compound
~/cadmiumorganische organocadmium compound
~/carbocyclische *s.* ~/isocyclische
~/chemische chemical compound
~/chlororganische organochlorine compound
~/cyclische cyclic (ring) compound
~/cycloaliphatische alicyclic compound
~/daltonide Daltonian (daltonide) compound
~/diastereomere diastereo[iso]mer
~/1,2-dipolare 1,2-dipolar compound
~/flüchtige organische volatile organic compound, VOC
~/geometrisch isomere geometric[al] isomer
~/halbleitende semiconducting compound
~/Herzsche *(dye)* Herz compound
~/heterocyclische heterocycle, heterocyclic [compound]
~/heteropolare heteropolar (polar, ionic) compound
~/homocyclische *s.* ~/isocyclische
~/homologe homolog[ue]
~/homöopolare homopolar (non-polar, non-ionic) compound
~/hydroaromatische hydroaromatic compound
~/innerkomplexe inner complex salt
~/intermediäre intermediate [compound]
~/intermetallische intermetallic (metal) compound, intermetallic, electron compound, intermediate constituent (phase)
~/interstitielle interstitial compound
~/isocyclische isocyclic compound, homocyclic (carbocyclic) compound, homocycle
~/isomere isomeric compound
~/isostere isosteric compound, isostere
~/kettenförmige chain compound
~/komplexe complex compound
~/lamellare lamellar compound, intercalation (intercalate) compound
~/lithiumorganische organolithium compound
~/makrocyclische macrocyclic compound, macroring (large-ring) compound
~/markierte [isotopically-]labelled compound, tagged compound
~/mehrkernige *(org ch)* polynuclear compound
~/mesoionische mesoionic compound
~/mesomere resonance hybrid

~/metallische intermediäre *s.* ~/intermetallische
~/metallorganische organometallic (metallo-organic) compound, organometal
~ mit großem Ring large-ring compound, macrocyclic (macroring) compound
~ mit kleinem Ring small-ring compound
~ mit mittelgroßem (mittlerem) Ring medium-ring (medium-size ring) compound
~ mit Überwurfmutter union joint *(of tubes)*
~ mit verdecktem Maximum *(cryst)* hidden maximum system
~/natriumorganische organosodium compound
~/nichtdaltonide (nichtdaltonische) *s.* ~/berthollide
~/nichtradioaktive non-radioactive compound, inactive compound
~/nichtsteroide non-steroid compound
~/oberflächenaktive surface-active compound, surfactant
~/offenkettige open-chain compound
~/optisch isomere optical isomer (antipode), antimer
~/organische organic [compound]
~/organometallische *s.* ~/metallorganische
~/paramagnetische paramagnetic compound
~/persistente persistent (refractory) compound
~/phosphororganische organophosphorus compound
~/polare *s.* ~/heteropolare
~/polycyclische polycyclic compound
~/quecksilberorganische organomercury compound, organomercurial
~/racemische racemic compound
~/ringförmige cyclic (ring) compound
~/selbstdichtende pressure-seal joint *(for pipes)*
~/siliciumorganische organosilicon compound
~/spirocyclische spiro hydrocarbon (compound), spiran[e], spirocyclane
~/stabile stable compound
~/stöchiometrisch zusammengesetzte *s.* ~/daltonide
~/ternäre ternary compound
~/trimere trimer
~/unpolare non-polar compound
~/unsymmetrische unsymmetrical compound
~ von nichtkonstanter Zusammensetzung *s.* ~/berthollide
~/zinnorganische organotin compound
m-**Verbindung** *f* meta compound
o-**Verbindung** *f* ortho compound
p-**Verbindung** *f* para compound
Verbindungsbildung *f* compound formation
Verbindungsfähigkeit *f* combining ability (capacity)
Verbindungsgewicht *n s.* Äquivalentmasse
Verbindungsklasse *f* family, class of compounds
Verbindungskraft *f* combining force (power)
Verbindungsneigung *f* combining tendency, tendency to combine
Verbindungspeptid *n (bioch)* connecting peptide
Verbindungsrohr *n* connecting tube
Verbindungsschlicker *m (ceram)* joining slip
Verbindungsstamm *m* backbone [chain], skeleton *(of a chain molecule)*; parent ring system
Verbindungsstück *n* connection, connector; *(for pipes and hoses:)* fitting
~/Y-förmiges Y-shape connecting tube
Verbindungstendenz *f s.* Verbindungsneigung
Verbindungsverhältnis *n***/atomares** *(anal)* atomic [combining] ratio, atomic proportion, proportion by atoms
Verbindungswärme *f* heat of combination
Verbindungsweise *f* mode of combination
verblasen *(glass, met)* to blow
~/im Konverter *(met)* to convert, to bessemerize
Verblaseofen *m (met)* fuming furnace
Verblaserösten *n (met)* blast roasting
Verblaseverfahren *n (met)* slag-fuming process
verblassen to fade, to discolour
Verblassen *n* fading, discoloration
verblassend/nicht *(dye)* fadeless
verbleichen *s.* verblassen
verbleien 1. to lead *(motor fuel)*; 2. to lead[-coat] *(surfaces for protection)*, *(relating to the inside also)* to lead-line; *(using prefabricated material:)* to lead-clad
verbleit 1. lead-lined *(surface)*; 2. leaded *(gasoline)*
~/schwach low-leaded
~/stark high-leaded
verbrannt werden to undergo combustion
Verbrauch *m* consumption
verbrauchen to consume; to spend, to exhaust *(e.g. dye liquor)* • **zu ~ bis ...** use by ...
Verbrauchsgeschwindigkeit *f* rate of consumption (disappearance) *(of a reactant)*
Verbrauchszucker *m* consumption (white) sugar *(as opposed to raw sugar)*
~/direkt hergestellter direct-consumption sugar *(without intermediate raw sugar stage)*
verbraucht spent, exhausted *(e.g. solution)*; *(tech)* worn out
verbrennbar combustible
Verbrennbarkeit *f* combustibility
verbrennen to burn;to incinerate *(garbage, sludge)*; *(agric)* to burn, to scorch *(e.g. leaves by excess fertilization)*; to burn, to undergo combustion; *(agric)* to be burnt (scorched)
verbrennlich combustible
Verbrennliche *n* combustible
Verbrennlichkeit *f* combustibility
Verbrennung *f* combustion, burning; incineration *(of garbage, sludge)*; *(agric)* burn, scorch *(as of leaves by excess fertilization)* • **die ~ unterhalten** to sustain combustion
~/direkte direct combustion
~/partielle partial combustion
~/stille slow combustion
~/unmittelbare direct combustion
~ unter vermindertem Sauerstoffzutritt restricted combustion

~/unvollkommene (unvollständige) incomplete combustion
Verbrennungsabgas *n* burner gas; furnace gas
Verbrennungsanalyse *f* combustion analysis
Verbrennungsapparat *m* combustion train *(for elementary organic analysis)*
Verbrennungsbombe *f* calorimeter (calorimetric, explosion) bomb, [oxygen] bomb calorimeter
Verbrennungseigenschaften *fpl* combustion characteristics
Verbrennungsenthalpie *f* enthalpy of combustion *(heat of combustion at constant pressure)*
Verbrennungsgas *n* combustion gas *(s. a.* Verbrennungsabgas*)*
Verbrennungsgeschwindigkeit *f* rate of combustion, burning rate
Verbrennungskammer *f* combustion (furnace) chamber
Verbrennungslöffel *m* combustion (deflagration) spoon
Verbrennungsluft *f* combustion air
Verbrennungsmarkierung *f (plast)* burned spot *(an injection defect)*
Verbrennungsofen *m* combustion furnace, burner
~/rotierender rotary burner
Verbrennungsprodukt *n* product of combustion
Verbrennungsprozeß *m* combustion process
Verbrennungsraum *m* combustion space; incineration chamber *(for refuse)*
Verbrennungsreaktion *f* combustion reaction
Verbrennungsrechnung *f* combustion calculation
Verbrennungsrohr *n*, **Verbrennungsröhre** *f* combustion tube
Verbrennungsrückstand *m* residue of combustion
Verbrennungsschaden *m (agric)* burn, scorch *(as by excess fertilization)*
~ durch Schwefel *(agric)* sulphur scald
Verbrennungsschale *f* combustion barge
Verbrennungsschiffchen *n* combustion boat
~ aus Ton clay combustion boat
Verbrennungsverfahren *n* combustion method (technique) *(for separating components to be analysed)*
Verbrennungsvorgang *m* combustion process
Verbrennungswärme *f* 1. heat of combustion; 2. *s.* Brennwert/spezifischer
~/molare *s.* Brennwert/stoffmengenbezogener
Verbrennungszone *f* combustion (oxidation) zone
Verbrühen *(tann)* to scald *(pelts in the bate)*
Verbundbauweise *f (plast)* sandwich construction
verbunden/über Wasserstoff hydrogen-bonded
Verbundfolie *f* laminated (composite) film
Verbundglas *n* laminated glass
Verbundkoksofen *m* combination oven
~ mit Unterbrennern combination underjet coke oven
Verbundmühle *f* compound mill, [multi]compartment mill
Verbundname *m (nomencl)* conjunctive name
Verbundofen *m* combination oven
~ nach Still Still oven
Verbundplatte *f* sandwich panel
Verbundplattenbauweise *f* sandwich construction
Verbundrohrmühle *f s.* Verbundmühle
Verbundsicherheitsglas *n* laminated safety [sheet] glass
Verbundtrommeltrockner *m* direct-indirect rotary dryer
Verbund-Unterbrennerofen *m* combination underjet coke oven
Verbundwerkstoff *m* composite
~ mit Wabenkern honeycomb sandwich material
Verbundwirkung *f* joint action
verbuttern to churn [to butter]
verchromen *(el ch)* to plate with chromium, to chrome; to chromize *(by thermal diffusion)*
verd. *s.* verdünnt
Verdampfanlage *f (sugar)* evaporating (evaporator) station
Verdampfapparat *m* evaporator *(for compounds s.* Verdampfer*)*
verdampfbar [e]vaporable, vaporizable
~/leicht volatile, volatilizable
Verdampfbarkeit *f* [e]vaporability
verdampfen *(of human agent:)* to vaporize, to boil away (down), to evaporate, to volat[il]ize, *(suddenly as by expansion:)* to flash; *(of a liquid:)* to evaporate, to vaporize, to volat[il]ize, *(suddenly as by expansion:)* to flash
Verdampfer *m* evaporator, vaporizer; expander *(cryogenics)*
~ für Extraktlösung *(petrol)* extract solvent evaporator
~/mehrstufiger multistage evaporator
~ mit Brüdenverdichtung thermocompression evaporator
~ mit eingehängtem Rohrkorb basket evaporator
~ mit Heizschlange coiled-tube evaporator
~ mit natürlichem Flüssigkeitsumlauf (Umlauf) natural-circulation evaporator
~ mit Plattenheizkörpern flat-plate evaporator
~ mit Thermokompression thermocompression (vapour-compression) evaporator
Verdampferanlage *f* **zur Meerwasserentsalzung** *(hyd)* evaporative desalination plant
Verdampferapparat *m s.* Verdampfer
Verdampferdruck *m* evaporator pressure
Verdampfereinheit *f* evaporator unit *(s. a.* Verdampferkörper*)*
Verdampferfläche *f* evaporator area
Verdampferkörper *m* body, *(in a series of evaporators preferably)* effect
Verdampferreaktor *m s.* Siedewasserreaktor
Verdampferschlange *f* evaporator (evaporation) coil; expansion coil *(in cryogenic processes)*
Verdampferstufe *f* effect
Verdampfkristallisator *m* evaporative (evaporator) crystallizer

Verdampfstation *f (sugar)* evaporating (evaporator) station
Verdampfung *f (esp process:)* evaporation, *(esp act:)* vaporization, *(esp if readily:)* volatilization; *(rapidly as by expansion:)* flash
~ **durch Sonnenbestrahlung** *(hyd)* solar evaporation (distillation)
~**/geschlossene** *(distil)* equilibrium [flash] vaporization
~ **im Übergangsgebiet** transition boiling
Verdampfungsbecken *n* evaporator pan *(desalination of sea water)*
Verdampfungseinrichtung *f* evaporator
Verdampfungsenthalpie *f* enthalpy of vaporization
Verdampfungsentropie *f* entropy of vaporization
verdampfungsfähig *s.* verdampfbar
Verdampfungsfläche *f* evaporative (evaporating) surface, *(quantitatively:)* evaporative (evaporating) area
Verdampfungsgeschwindigkeit *f* evaporation rate, rate of vaporization
Verdampfungsgut *n* evaporant
Verdampfungskammer *f* flash chamber, flash vessel (trap) *(of a flash evaporator)*
Verdampfungskristallisation *f* evaporative crystallization
Verdampfungskristallisator *m* evaporative crystallizer, crystallizing (salting-out) evaporator
Verdampfungskühlung *f* 1. vaporization (evaporative) cooling *(using low-boiling organic solvents)*; 2. *s.* Sieden/örtliches
Verdampfungsleistung *f* evaporating efficiency
Verdampfungsofen *m (distil)* still pot (body), reboiler
Verdampfungspfanne *f* evaporating (boiling-down) pan
Verdampfungsrückstand *m* residue on evaporation
Verdampfungstrocknung *f* drying by evaporation, evaporation drying
~ **im Vakuum** drying by vacuum evaporation, puff drying
Verdampfungsverlust *m* evaporation (evaporative) loss, volatile loss
Verdampfungswärme *f* heat of evaporation (vaporization)
verdauen to digest
verdaulich digestible
Verdaulichkeit *f* digestibility
Verdauung *f* digestion
Verdauungsenzym *n*, **Verdauungsferment** *n (biot)* digestive enzyme
verdauungsfördernd stomachic[al]
Verdauungskoeffizient *m*, **Verdauungsquotient** *m* digestibility (digestion) coefficient
Verdauungssaft *m* digestive juice
Verdauungswert *m s.* Verdauungskoeffizient
verdeckt opposed, eclipsed *(stereochemistry)*
Verderb *m (food)* decay, deterioration, spoilage
~**/enzymatischer** enzymatic deterioration
~**/mikrobieller** microbial spoilage
~**/oxidativer** oxidative deterioration
verderben to decay, to deteriorate, to spoil, to perish
verderblich perishable
Verderblichkeit *f* perishability
Verderbnis *f s.* Verderb
Verderbniserreger *mpl*/**mikrobielle** spoilage microorganisms
Verdet-Konstante *f* Verdet constant *(of the magnetic rotatory power)*
verdichtbar compressible; condensable *(vapour)*
Verdichtbarkeit *f* compressibility; condensability *(of vapour)*
verdichten to densify, to compress, *(esp relating to bulk material:)* to compact, to consolidate; to condense *(vapours)*; to thicken *(paper pulp)*
~**/sich** to condense *(of vapours)*
Verdichten *n* **von Hand** hand compaction *(as of concrete)*
Verdichter *m* compressor, *(relating to refrigerating machines also)* vapour compressor
~**/einstufiger** single-stage compressor
~**/mehrstufiger** multistage compressor
~**/ölfreier** non-lubricated compressor
~**/rotierender** rotary compressor
Verdichtung *f* densification, compression, *(esp relating to bulk material:)* compacting, consolidation; condensation *(of vapours)*; thickening *(of paper pulp)*
~**/beidseitige (doppelseitige)** double-action compacting *(powder metallurgy)*
~**/einseitige** single-action compacting *(powder metallurgy)*
~**/zweiseitige** *s.* ~/beidseitige
Verdichtungsarbeit *f* work of compression *(as of a pump)*
Verdichtungsdruck *m* compression pressure, *(esp relating to bulk material:)* compacting pressure
Verdichtungsfähigkeit *f s.* Verdichtbarkeit
Verdichtungsgrad *m (plast)* bulk factor, *(Am)* compression ratio
Verdichtungsverhältnis *n* compression ratio *(in an internal-combustion engine)*
Verdichtungszone *f* compression zone
verdicken *s.* eindicken
Verdickungsmasse *f*, **Verdickungspaste** *f (text)* thickening paste
Verdopplungszeit *f (biot)* [cell] doubling time *(growth of microorganisms)*
verdrängbar *(ch)* displaceable
verdrängen *(ch, tech)* to displace; to expel, to push (sweep) out, to eject *(e.g. gases)*
Verdränger *m (chromat)* displacer
Verdrängermaschine *f* positive-displacement unit (compressor)
Verdrängerpumpe *f* positive-displacement pump

Verdrängung *f (ch, tech)* displacement; expulsion, ejection *(as of gases)*
Verdrängungsanalyse *f*, **Verdrängungschromatographie** *f* displacement analysis (chromatography)
Verdrängungsentwicklung *f (chromat)* displacement development
Verdrängungshemmung *f (bioch)* competitive inhibition
Verdrängungskörper *m* 1. displacer *(of a liquid-level gauge)*; 2. *(plast)* torpedo, spreader
Verdrängungsmethode *f (chromat)* displacement method, [positive] displacement technique
Verdrängungsmittel *n (chromat)* displacer
Verdrängungsname *m* replacement name
Verdrängungspumpe *f s.* Verdrängerpumpe
Verdrängungsreaktion *f* displacement reaction
~/doppelte double displacement reaction, ping-pong reaction *(enzyme kinetics)*
Verdrängungstechnik *f s.* Verdrängungsmethode
Verdrängungstitration *f* displacement (replacement) titration
Verdrängungsvolumenzähler *m* positive-displacement flowmeter, displacement meter
Verdrängungswaschung *f* displacement wash[ing]
Verdrehungsschwingung *f s.* Torsionsschwingung
Verdrehungssteifigkeit *f* stiffness in torsion
verdrillt twisted, interwound, intertwined *(macromolecules)*
Verdunklung *f (phot)* blackout
verdünnbar dilutable *(liquid)*
~/mit Wasser water-dilutable
Verdünnbarkeit *f* dilutability
verdünnen to dilute, to thin, to attenuate, *(esp relating to gases:)* to rarefy; to potentiate *(homoeopathy)*
Verdünnen *n* dilution, thinning, attenuation, *(esp relating to gases:)* rarefaction; potentiation *(homoeopathy)*
~ in der Stoffgrube *(pap)* blow-pit (blow-tank) dilution
Verdünner *m s.* Verdünnungsmittel
verdünnt dilute
~/unendlich infinitely dilute
Verdünnung *f* 1. dilution *(diluted liquid)*; potency *(homoeopathy)*; 2. *s.* Verdünnungsmittel; 3. *s.* Verdünnen
~/magnetische magnetic dilution [technique]
~/unendliche infinite dilution
Verdünnungsanalyse *f (spectr)* dilution analysis
Verdünnungsenthalpie *f* enthalpy of dilution
Verdünnungsfaktor *m* dilution factor
Verdünnungsgas *n* diluent (complementary) gas
Verdünnungsgesetz *n***/Ostwaldsches** Ostwald dilution law
Verdünnungsgrad *m* degree of dilution
Verdünnungsmittel *n* diluting agent, diluent; *(coat)* thinner, thinning agent
Verdünnungsprinzip *n***/Ruggli-Zieglersches** Ruggli high-dilution principle
Verdünnungsrate *f (biot)* dilution rate
Verdünnungsreihe *f* dilution series
Verdünnungsverhältnis *n* dilution ratio
Verdünnungswärme *f* heat of dilution
~/differentiale (differentielle) differential (partial) heat of dilution
~/integrale integral heat of dilution
Verdünnungswasser *n* dilution water, water of dilution
verdunsten to evaporate, to vaporize, to volat[il]ize *(below normal boiling point)*
Verdunstung *f* evaporation, vaporization, volatilization *(below normal boiling point)*
~/solare solar evaporation
Verdunstungsfläche *f* evaporative (evaporating) surface, *(quantitatively:)* evaporative (evaporating) area
Verdunstungsgeschwindigkeit *f* rate of evaporation
Verdunstungshaube *f* hood
Verdunstungskühlung *f* evaporative (evaporation) cooling
Verdunstungsmesser *m*, **Verdunstungsmeßgerät** *n* atmometer, evaporimeter
Verdunstungstrocknung *f* drying by evaporation
Verdunstungsverlust *m* evaporation loss
Verdunstungswärme *f* heat of evaporation
Verdunstungszahl *f* relative evaporation rate
verdüsen to atomize, to spray
Verdüsung *f* [nozzle] atomization, spraying
veredeln to refine, to improve; to finish *(a surface)*; *(text)* to finish, to process; *(pap)* to refine *(pulp)*
Vered[e]lung *f* refining [treatment], refinement, improvement; finish[ing] *(of a surface)*; *(text)* finish[ing], processing; *(pap)* [alkali] refining *(of pulp)*
vereinigen 1. to combine *(elements)*; 2. to assemble *(parts of an apparatus)*
~/sich to combine *(of elements)*; to coalesce *(as of gas bubbles)*
~/sich paarweise to pair *(as of electrons)*
Vereinigung *f* 1. combination, union *(of elements or chemical compounds)*; 2. mixing *(of filtrates)*; coalescence *(as of gas bubbles)*; 3. assembly *(of parts of an apparatus)*
~/chemische chemical union (combination) *(process)*
Vereinigungsbestreben *n* tendency to combine
Vereinigungsreaktion *f* combination reaction
Vereinigungsweise *f* mode of union
vereisen to ice
Vereisung *f* icing
Vereisungsverhinderer *m* anti-icing additive (agent)
Verengung *f* throat, restriction *(as of a nozzle)*
~ am Venturi-Rohr Venturi throat
Vererzung *f (geoch)* metallization
verestern to esterify

Veresterung *f* esterification
~/**extraktive** extractive esterification
Veresterungsgrad *m* degree of esterification
Veresterungskatalysator *m* esterification catalyst
verethern to etherify
Veretherung *f* etherification
verfahren to proceed
Verfahren *n* process, method; *(manner of performing technical details, esp lab:)* method, technique, procedure
~/**abgekürztes** short-cut method
~/**aluminothermisches** aluminothermic process
~/**basisches** basic process *(of steelmaking)*
~/**Béchampsches** Béchamp method *(of reducing aromatic nitro compounds to amines)*
~/**bodenblasendes** *(met)* bottom-blown-converter process
~ **der Dampfdichtebestimmung** vapour-density method *(for determining molecular weights)*
~/**direktes** direct process *(as for producing ammonia or chlorosilanes)*
~/**diskontinuierliches** batch process
~/**dynamisches volumetrisches** dynamic volumetric method *(for preparing gas mixtures)*
~/**ebullioskopisches** ebullioscopic method *(for determining molecular weights)*
~/**elektrostatisches** electrostatic method (process)
~/**elektrothermisches** electrothermic method (process)
~/**großtechnisches** large-scale process
~/**halbdirektes** semidirect process *(as for producing ammonia)*
~/**halbkontinuierliches** semi-batch process
~/**Heumannsches** Heumann method *(for synthesizing indigo)*
~/**holländisches** Dutch (stack) process *(for manufacturing lead white)*
~/**indirektes** indirect process *(as for producing ammonia)*
~/**intensivbiologisches** *(hyd)* high-rate activated sludge process
~/**Kassnersches** Kassner process *(for producing oxygen)*
~/**konduktometrisches** conductometric (conductance) method
~/**kontinuierliches** continuous process
~/**Linz-Donawitzer** Linz-Donawitz process *(of steelmaking)*
~/**manometrisches** manometric method *(gas analysis)*
~/**maschinelles** machine process
~/**mechanisch-thermisches** *(rubber)* thermomechanical process
~ **mit bewegtem Katalysatorbett** moving-bed process *(as for catalytic cracking)*
~ **mit flüssigem Schlackenabzug** *(coal)* slagging process
~ **mit immobilisierten Enzymen** *(biot)* immobilized enzyme process
~ **mit umlaufender Beschickung** moving-burden process *(for the complete gasification of coal)*
~/**Mondsches** Mond process *(1. for producing town gas; 2. for producing nickel)*
~/**Münchner** *(pap)* Kesting electrolytic process *(for producing chlorine-dioxide bleaching liquor)*
~ **nach Thiele und McCabe/graphisches** *(distil)* McCabe-Thiele method (construction) *(for estimating the number of plates)*
~/**nasses** wet process
~/**periodisches** batch process (operation)
~/**plastisches** wire-cut process *(for producing bricks)*
~/**potentiometrisches** potentiometric method *(titration)*
~/**pulvermetallurgisches** powder-metallurgical (powder-metallurgy) process (technique)
~/**röntgenographisches** X-ray method *(as in crystallography)*
~/**rotationsviskosimetrisches** rotating-cylinder method *(viscometry)*
~/**saures** acid process *(of steelmaking)*
~/**seismisches** seismic method *(of prospecting for petroleum)*
~/**sekundäres** *(petrol)* secondary recovery method
~/**selbstkonsistentes** *(phys ch)* self-consistent method
~/**silikothermisches** *(met)* silicothermic process
~/**standardisiertes** standard method
~/**statisches volumetrisches** static volumetric method *(for preparing gas mixtures)*
~/**technisches** commercial process *(as opposed to lab-scale techniques or pilot-plant-scale processes)*
~/**thermisches** thermal process
~/**thermomechanisches** *(rubber)* thermomechanical process
~/**trockenes** dry process
~/**turbidimetrisches** turbidimetric method
~ **von Pott-Broche** Pott-Broche process *(for extracting coal)*
~/**weichplastisches** *(ceram)* soft-mud process
~ **zur SCP-Bildung** *(biot)* single-cell protein process
~/**zweistufiges** two-stage (two-step) process
Verfahrenschemie *f* process chemistry
~ **der Wasseraufbereitung** water treatment chemistry
Verfahrenschemiker *m* process chemist
Verfahrensentwicklung *f* process development
Verfahrensfehler *m* error of method
Verfahrensindustrie *f* process industry
Verfahrensingenieur *m* process engineer
Verfahrensregelung *f* process control
Verfahrensschritt *m* process[ing] step, treatment step
Verfahrenssteuerung *f* process control
Verfahrensstufe *f* process[ing] stage, treatment stage
Verfahrenstechnik *f* process engineering
~/**biochemische** biochemical engineering

~/biotechnologische bioprocess engineering
~/chemische chemical engineering
Verfahrenstechniker *m* process engineer
Verfahrensweise *f* processing mode
Verfahrensziel *n* process goal
Verfahrenszug *m* process[ing] train, treatment train, process sequence (line)
Verfall *m* decay *(as of organic matter)*
verfallen 1. to decay *(as of organic matter)*; 2. *(tann)* to fall *(of pelts)* • ~ **machen** *(tann)* to bring down, to deplete, to fall *(pelts)*
Verfallen *n (tann)* falling, depletion *(of pelts)*
verfälschen to adulterate
Verfälschung *f* adulteration
Verfälschungsmittel *n* adulterant
Verfaltung *f* fold, lap *(a defect in glass)*
verfärben to discolour, *(esp if locally:)* to stain
~/sich to discolour, *(esp if locally:)* to stain; to fade *(to lose intensity of colour)*
Verfärbung *f* 1. *(process:)* discoloration, *(esp if locally:)* staining; fading *(loss of colour intensity)*; 2. *(state:)* discoloration, stain
verfaulen to putrefy
verfeinern to improve, to sophisticate *(e.g. an analytical method)*
Verfeinerung *f* improvement *(e.g. of an analytical method)*
verfestigen 1. to compact, to consolidate *(bulk material)*; to solidify *(a fluid)*; 2. *(met)* to work-harden *(by cold forming)*; *(glass)* to strengthen
~/chemisch *(glass)* to strengthen chemically
~/sich 1. to compact, to consolidate *(as of bulk material)*; *(relating to a fluid)* to solidify, to set; 2. *(met)* to harden *(as by cold forming)*
Verfestigen *n (met)* [work-]hardening *(as by cold forming)*; *(glass)* strengthening
Verfestigung *f* 1. compaction, consolidation *(of bulk material)*; solidification, set[ting] *(of a fluid)*; 2. *s.* Verfestigen
Verfestigungsmittel *n* solidifying agent
verfilzen/sich to felt [together], to mat [together] *(as of fibres)*
Verfilzungsvermögen *n* felting power *(of fibres)*
Verflocker *m (hyd)* flocculation tank, flocculator
verflüchtigen to volat[il]ize
~/sich to volat[il]ize
verflüchtigend/leicht zu volatilizable
Verflüchtigung *f* volatilization
verflüssigbar liquefiable
verflüssigen 1. to liquefy *(a solid or gas)*; 2. *(ceram)* to deflocculate *(a glaze slip)*
~/sich to liquefy *(of a solid or gas)*; to run *(of metal)*
Verflüssiger *m* 1. liquefier *(in gas liquefaction)*; 2. condenser *(of a refrigerating machine)*
Verflüssigerdruck *m* condenser pressure *(refrigeration)*
Verflüssigung *f* 1. liquefaction *(of a solid or gas)*; 2. *(ceram)* deflocculation *(of a glaze slip)*
Verflüssigungsdruck *m* condensation (condensing) pressure *(refrigeration)*
Verflüssigungsmittel *n (ceram)* deflocculant, deflocculent, deflocculating agent
verformbar *s.* formbar
verformen 1. to deform, *(relating to elastic material also)* to strain; 2. *s.* umformen
~/sich to deform
Verformung *f* 1. deformation, *(relating to elastic material also)* strain; 2. *s.* Umformung
~/bleibende permanent (residual, plastic) deformation, permanent set
~/elastische elastic deformation
~/irreversible *s.* ~/bleibende
~ nach Druckeinwirkung/bleibende [permanent] compression set
~/nichteleastische (plastische) *s.* ~/bleibende
Verformungsarbeit *f* resilience, resiliency
Verformungsrest *m s.* Verformung/bleibende
verfügbar available
~/nicht unavailable
Verfügbarkeit *f* availability
verfüttern *(biot)* to feed *(nutrients to microorganisms)*
vergällen to denature, to denaturize, *(ferm also)* to methylate
Vergällung *f* denaturation, denaturing, *(ferm also)* methylation
Vergällungsmittel *n* denaturant, denaturing agent
vergänglich evanescent *(e.g. tint)*
vergärbar fermentable
Vergärbarkeit *f* fermentability
vergären to ferment
vergasen 1. to gasify *(e.g. coal)*; 2. to carburet *(motor fuel)*; to volat[il]ize *(pesticides)*; *(met)* to gas *(a melt)*
~/hydrierend *(coal)* to hydrogasify
Vergaser *m* 1. *(coal)* gasifier; 2. carburet[t]or, carburetter *(of an internal-combustion engine)*
~ mit flüssigem Schlackenabzug *(coal)* slagging gasifier
~/mit Luft betriebener *(coal)* air-blown gasifier
~/mit Sauerstoff betriebener *(coal)* oxygen-blown gasifier
~/zweistufiger *(coal)* two-stage gasifier
Vergaserkraftstoff *m* carburetting fuel, carburant
Vergasung *f* 1. gasification *(as of coal)*; 2. carburetting *(of motor fuel)*; volatilization *(of pesticides)*; *(met)* gassing *(of a melt)*
~/atmosphärische *(coal)* atmospheric-pressure gasification
~/autotherme *(coal)* autothermic gasification
~/drucklose *s.* ~/atmosphärische
~/hydrierende *(coal)* hydrogasification
~ im Flöz *(coal)* underground gasification
~ in der Flugstaubwolke (Staubwolke) *(coal)* suspension gasification, dilute-phase (entrained-bed, entrainment) gasification, pulverized-coal gasification

~ **mit flüssigem Schlackenabzug** *(coal)* slagging gasification
~ **mit Wasserdampf und Sauerstoff** *(coal)* steam-oxygen gasification
~/restlose (rückstandslose) *s.* ~/vollständige
~ **unter atmosphärischem Druck** *s.* ~/atmosphärische
~ **unter Normaldruck** *s.* ~/atmosphärische
~/unterirdische *(coal)* underground gasification
~/vollständige *(coal)* complete (total) gasification
Vergasungsanlage *f (coal)* gasification plant
Vergasungsapparat *m (coal)* gasifier
Vergasungsdampf *m (coal)* gasification steam
Vergasungsdruck *m (coal)* gasification pressure
Vergasungskammer *f (coal)* gasification chamber
Vergasungsmedium *n* gasifying (gasification) medium *(for pulverized coal)*
Vergasungsmittel *n* 1. fumigant, fumigator *(crop protection)*; 2. *s.* Vergasungsmedium
Vergasungsraum *m (coal)* 1. gasification chamber; 2. gasification space
Vergasungsreaktion *f (coal)* gasification reaction
Vergasungsreaktor *m (coal)* gasification reactor
Vergasungsschacht *m (coal)* gasification shaft
Vergasungsstoff *m (coal)* material being gasified
Vergasungsstufe *f (coal)* gasification step
Vergasungstechnik *f (coal)* gasification technology
Vergasungstechnologie *f (coal)* gasification technology
Vergasungsverfahren *n (coal)* gasification process
Vergasungswirkungsgrad *m (coal)* gasification efficiency
Vergasungszone *f (coal)* gasification zone (section)
Vergépapier *n* laid paper
vergesellschaften/sich *(min)* to associate
Vergesellschaftung *f (min)* association
vergießbar castable, pourable
Vergießbarkeit *f* castability, pourability
vergießen to cast, to pour *(molten material into a mould)*
~/durch Druck to [pressure-]diecast
~/in der Kokille to diecast
~/in metallischen Dauerformen to gravity-diecast
vergiften to poison, to toxify
~/mit Gas to gas
Vergiftung *f* poisoning, toxification
~/absichtliche deliberate poisoning *(of a catalyst)*
~/akute acute poisoning
~/chronische chronic poisoning
~/tödliche fatal poisoning
Vergiftungsgefahr *f* poisoning hazard
vergilben to [go] yellow, *(pap also)* to discolour, to age
Vergilbung *f* yellowing, *(pap also)* discoloration, ag[e]ing
vergilbungsbeständig non-yellowing
vergipsen to plaster
verglasen *(ceram, geoch)* to vitrify
Verglasung *f (ceram, geoch)* vitrification
Verglasungsbereich *m (ceram)* vitrification range
vergleichmäßigen to homogenize
Vergleichmäßigung *f* **der Konzentration** smoothing-out of concentration
Vergleichselektrode *f* reference electrode (element)
Vergleichsküvette *f* reference cell
Vergleichslösung *f* standard (reference) solution
Vergleichsmassenschale *f* right-hand pan
Vergleichsmassestück *n* balance weight
Vergleichsprobe *f* 1. standard (blank) sample, control, reference [sample, material]; 2. *s.* Vergleichstest
Vergleichsprojektor *m (anal)* spectrum comparator
Vergleichsspannung *f* reference voltage
Vergleichsspektrum *n* reference (comparison) spectrum
Vergleichsstandard *m* reference standard
Vergleichsstrahl *m (spectr)* reference beam
Vergleichssubstanz *f* reference substance
Vergleichstest *m* blank test
Vergleichsverbindung *f* reference (comparison) compound
Vergleichsverfahren *n* comparison method
Verglühbrand *m (ceram)* biscuit firing, biscuitting; hardening-on *(of the decoration before glazing)*
verglühen *(ceram)* to biscuit-fire; to harden on *(the decoration before glazing)*; to cease glowing
vergolden to gild
~/elektrochemisch (galvanisch) to gold-plate
Vergraben *n* burial *(as of industrial wastes)*
vergrauen *(text)* to grey
vergrößern[/im Maßstab] to scale up *(a plant)*
Vergrößerung *f* **[im Maßstab]** scale-up *(of a plant)*
Vergrößerungspapier *n (phot)* enlarging paper
Vergußharz *n* cast[ing] resin
vergüten *(met)* to heat-treat, to quench and temper; *(glass)* to coat
Vergüten *n (met)* heat-treatment, quenching and tempering; *(glass)* antireflection (antiflare) coating
Verhakung *f* entanglement *(of polymer chains)*
verhalten/sich to behave *(of material)*
~/sich ideal to behave perfectly
Verhalten *n* behaviour, performance *(of material)*
~ **bei hohen Temperaturen** high-temperature behaviour
~ **bei Kälte** low-temperature behaviour
~/chemisches chemical behaviour
~/entropieelastisches *s.* ~/gummielastisches
~/fettabweisendes grease repellency
~/gummielastisches rubber-elasticity behaviour
~/Hookesches Hookean behaviour *(of elastic material)*
~/kautschukelastisches *s.* ~/gummielastisches
~/Newtonsches Newtonian behaviour *(of viscous fluids)*
~/nicht-Newtonsches non-Newtonian behaviour *(of viscous fluids)*
~/ölabweisendes oil repellency
~/rheologisches rheological behaviour

~/rheopexes rheopectic behaviour, antithixotrophy
~/strukturviskoses shear thinning, pseudoplasticity
~/wasserabweisendes water repellency
Verhaltensresistenz *f (biol)* behaviouristic resistance *(as to pesticides)*
Verhältnis *n* relation; *(quantitatively:)* ratio, proportion • **in jedem ~ mischbar** miscible in all proportions • **in molekularem ~** in molecular proportions
~/atomares *(anal)* atomic [combining] ratio, atomic proportion, proportion by atoms
~ Deckgebirge zu Kohle *(mine)* ratio of overburden to coal
~/gyromagnetisches [nuclear] gyromagnetic ratio
~ von Harz zu Öl *(coat)* resin/oil ratio, resin-to-oil ratio
~ Katalysator (Kontakt) zu Öl catalyst/oil ratio, catalyst-to-oil ratio
~ Öl zu Harz *(coat)* oil length, oil/resin ratio, oil-to-resin ratio
Verhältnisformel *f* stoichiometric formula, simplest [possible] formula
verhältnisregistrierend *(anal)* ratio-recording
Verhältnisse *npl* **/aerobe** aerobic conditions
~/anaerobe anaerobic conditions
verhängen *(text)* to expose to [the] air
Verhängen *n (text)* exposure to [the] air
verhärten to harden, to solidify
Verhärtung *f* hardening, solidification
verharzbar resinifiable
verharzen to resinify, *(specif petrol)* to gum
Verharzung *f* resinification, *(esp petrol)* gum formation, gumming
Verharzungsprodukte *npl* **/aktuelle** *(petrol)* existent (preformed) gum
~/potentielle potential gum
Verhieb *m (mine)* working
verhindern to prevent, to hinder, to inhibit, to control
Verhinderung *f* **von Ablagerungen** *(hyd)* deposit control
verholzen to lignify
Verholzung *f* lignification
verhornen *(biol)* to keratinize
Verhornung *f (biol)* keratinization
verhüten *s.* verhindern
verhütten to smelt *(ores)*
verjagen to expel, to dispel, to drive off (out) *(volatile matter)*
Verjagung *f* expulsion *(of volatile matter)*
verjüngen/sich to taper *(as of a pipe)*
verjüngend/sich taper[ing]
Verjüngung *f* taper *(as of a pipe)*
verkapseln to encapsulate
Verkapselung *f* encapsulation
Verkaufsausbeute *f (biot)* commercial fermentation yield
verketten to link *(molecules)*
Verkettung *f* linking, linkage *(of molecules)*; concatenation *(of reactions)*
verkieseln *(geoch)* to silicify
Verkieselung *f (geoch)* silicification
verkippen to dump, to dispose of to tip, to dispose of by tipping, to deposit (place) on a tip *(waste products)*
~/ins Meer to dump at sea, to dispose of to sea, to dispose of in the ocean
Verkippen *n* dumping, disposal to tip, tipping *(of waste products)*
~ auf hoher See *s.* ~ ins Meer
~ ins Meer dumping at sea, sea (ocean) dumping, sea burial
verkirnen to churn *(margarine)*
verkitten to putty, to lute, to cement, to seal *(e.g. joints of tubes)*
verklappen *s.* verkippen/ins Meer
verkleben to cement, to glue, to bond, to agglutinate; to stick together, to agglutinate
Verklebung *f* cementation, gluing, bond, bonding, agglutination *(act)*; agglutination *(process)*
verkleiden to cover, to case, to jacket, to sheathe, *(esp relating to metal:)* to clad
Verkleidung *f* cover[ing], casing, jacket, sheathing, *(esp relating to metal:)* cladding
verkleistern to gelatinize *(starch)*
Verkleisterung *f* gelatinization *(of starch)*
verklumpen to agglomerate, to clog, to clot, to lump, to agglutinate, to curd[le]
Verklumpung *f* agglomeration, clogging, clotting, lumping, agglutination, curd[l]ing
verknappen to squeeze *(of resources)*
Verknappung *f* squeeze *(of resources)*
verknüpfen[/miteinander] to link [together], to bond [together], to couple *(atoms)*
Verknüpfung *f* 1. linking, linkage, bonding, coupling *(of atoms) (for compounds s.* Bindung*)*; 2. concatenation *(of reactions)*
Verknüpfungsstelle *f* binding site, point of linkage, position of attachment *(of atoms)*
verkochen to boil down, to concentrate; to boil away
~/auf Korn *(sugar)* to boil to grain, *(Am also)* to sugar off *(esp maple sap)*
Verkochen *n* boildown, boiling-down, concentration; boiling-away
verkohlen to char, to carbonize
Verkohlung *f* charring, carbonization
verkoken to coke, to carbonize
Verkokung *f* coking, carbonization, *(specif)* high-temperature coking (carbonization)
~/kontinuierliche katalytische *(petrol)* continuous contact coking
~/verzögerte *(petrol)* delayed coking
Verkokungsanlage *f* coking plant, carbonizing (coke) plant
Verkokungsbatterie *f* retort (coke-oven) battery, carbonizing bench
Verkokungsblase *f* coking still

Verkokungseigenschaften *fpl* coking properties
Verkokungsfähigkeit *f* coking power
Verkokungsgas *n* coke-oven gas, carbonization gas
Verkokungsgefäß *n (petrol)* coking furnace
~ für den Ramsbottom-Test Ramsbottom coking furnace
Verkokungskammer *f (petrol, coal)* coking (coke) chamber
Verkokungskohle *f* coking coal
Verkokungskrackverfahren *n* non-residue method *(of cracking)*
Verkokungsofen *m* coke (coking) oven
Verkokungsprobe *f s.* Verkokungstest
Verkokungsrückstand *m* carbon (coke) residue
~ nach Conradson Conradson carbon (coke) residue
~ nach Ramsbottom Ramsbottom carbon (coke) residue
Verkokungstest *m* carbon-residue test, coking test
~ nach Conradson Conradson [carbon-residue] test
~ nach Ramsbottom Ramsbottom [carbon-residue] test
Verkokungsverfahren *n* 1. carbonization (coking) process; 2. non-residue method *(of cracking)*
Verkokungsverhalten *n* coking properties
Verkokungsvermögen *n* coking power
Verkokungsvorgang *m* coking process
Verkokungswärme *f* coking heat, heat of carbonization
~/obere gross coking heat
~/untere net coking heat
Verkokungswert *m*, **Verkokungszahl** *f* carbon-residue value, coke value (number)
verkorken 1. to cork; 2. *(bot)* to suberize
Verkorkung *f* 1. corking; 2. *(bot)* suberization, suberification
Verkoster *m (food)* taster
verkrusten to encrust, to incrust, to scale
Verkrustung *f* encrustation, incrustation, scaling
Verkrustungsfaktor *m* fouling factor *(with evaporators)*
verküpbar *(dye)* vattable
verküpen *(dye)* to vat
verkupfern to copper
~/galvanisch (elektrochemisch) to plate with copper, to copper-plate
Verkupferungsbad *n s.* Verkupferungselektrolyt
Verkupferungselektrolyt *m* copper plating bath (solution)
Verküpung *f (dye)* vatting
Verküpungsverfahren *n (dye)* vat process
verlaben to rennet *(milk)*
verlagern to displace; to shift *(e.g. an equilibrium)*; to translocate *(e.g. nutrients in plants)*
~/sich to shift *(as of an equilibrium)*
Verlagerung *f* displacement; shift *(as of an equilibrium)*; translocation *(as of nutrients in plants)*
verlängern to lengthen *(a chain)*
verlangsamen to slow down, to decelerate, to retard; *(nucl)* to moderate
~/sich to slow down, to decelerate
Verlangsamung *f* slowing-down, deceleration, retardation; *(nucl)* moderation
Verlauf *m* 1. course, progress *(as of a reaction)*; 2. *(coat)* flow
~/schlechter *(coat)* bad flow
~/zeitlicher time course
verlaufen 1. to proceed, to go, to run *(as of reactions)*; 2. *(coat)* to flow
~/glatt to proceed smoothly
~/schleppend to proceed poorly (sluggishly)
~/stürmisch to proceed vigorously
~/träge *s.* ~/schleppend
~/über eine Zwischenstufe to go via an intermediate
Verlaufmittel *n (coat)* flow-control agent
verlegen to plug *(pores, orifices)*
Verlegen *n* pluggage, plugging *(of pores, orifices)*
verleimen to cement, to glue
verlieren to lose *(e.g. hydrate water)*
verlöschen to go out, *(gradually:)* to die out
Verlöschen *n* going-out, *(gradually:)* dying-out
Verlust *m* loss
~/dielektrischer dielectric loss
~ durch Mitreißen entrainment loss
~ durch Schäumen foaming loss
~ durch Unverbranntes unburned combustible (fuel) loss
Verlustbeiwert *m* **der Düse** nozzle coefficient
Verlustfaktor *m***[/dielektrischer]** loss tangent, dissipation factor
Verlustmutante *f (biot)* auxotrophic mutant
Verlustwinkel *m* loss angle
Verlustziffer *f***[/dielektrische]** [dielectric] loss factor
vermahlbar grindable
Vermahlbarkeit *f* grindability
vermahlen to grind, to mill, *(relating to soft material also)* to disintegrate, *(relating to hard material also)* to pulverize
Vermahlen *n* grinding, milling, *(relating to soft material also)* disintegration, *(relating to hard material also)* pulverization
vermälzen to malt
vermehren *(nucl)* to breed *(fissionable material)*; to multiply *(neutrons)*; *(biot)* to propagate, to multiply
~/sich *(nucl)* to multiply *(of neutrons)*; *(biot)* to propagate, to multiply
Vermehrung *f (nucl)* breeding *(of fissionable material)*; multiplication *(of neutrons)*; *(biot)* propagation, multiplication
Vermehrungsfaktor *m (nucl)* multiplication factor (constant)
vermengen to mingle, to mix *(solids)*
Vermiculit *m (min)* vermiculite *(a group of phyllosilicates)*

Vermillo[-Zinnober] *m* vermil[l]ion, Victoria red *(precipitated red mercury(II) sulphide)*
vermischen to mix, *(esp relating to solids:)* to mingle, *(specif if so that the components cannot be distinguished:)* to blend
~/innig to mix intimately, to blend
~/sich to [inter]mix, to blend
Vermischen *n* mix[ing], mixture, *(esp relating to solids:)* mingling, *(specif if so that the components cannot be distinguished:)* blending
~ im Fertigtank *(petrol)* batch blending
~ in der Pumpleitung *(petrol)* inline blending
~/vollständiges complete mixing
~ von Feststoffkomponenten dry mixing (blending)
Vermizid *n* vermicide
Vermoderungshorizont *m (soil)* fermentation layer, F-layer
vernachlässigbar negligible
vernachlässigen[d]/zu negligible
vernebeln to nebulize, to aerosolize
Verneb[e]lung *f* nebulization, aerosolization
vernetzbar cross-linkable, curable, *(rubber also)* vulcanizable
~/mit Schwefel *(rubber)* sulphur-curable, sulphur-vulcanizable
~/nicht non-curing, *(rubber also)* non-vulcanizable
vernetzen to cross-link, to cure, *(rubber also)* to vulcanize
~/räumlich to enmesh *(e.g. starch molecules)*
Vernetzer *m s.* Vernetzungsmittel
Vernetzerkombination *f s.* Vernetzungssystem
Vernetzung *f* cross-linking, cross-linkage, cure, *(rubber also)* vulcanization
~ durch Bestrahlung *(rubber)* radiation vulcanization
~ durch energiereiche Strahlen (Strahlung) *(rubber)* vulcanization by high-energy radiation
~/kovalente covalent cross-linking *(as of an enzyme)*
~ mit Metalloxiden *(rubber)* metallic-oxide vulcanization
~ mit Schwefel *(rubber)* [elemental-]sulphur vulcanization
~/peroxidische peroxide cross-linking
~/photochemische photocrosslinking
~/räumliche enmeshing *(as of starch molecules)*
~/schwefelfreie *(rubber)* sulphurless (non-sulphur) vulcanization
~ über C–C-Verknüpfung carbon-carbon cross-linking
Vernetzungsdichte *f* cross-link density, degree of cross-linking
vernetzungsfähig *s.* vernetzbar
Vernetzungsgrad *m s.* Vernetzungsdichte
Vernetzungsmittel *n* cross-linking agent, curing agent, *(rubber also)* vulcanizing agent
Vernetzungsreaktion *f* cross-linking reaction
Vernetzungsstelle *f* cross-link[age]
Vernetzungssystem *n* cross-linking system, curing (curative) system, *(rubber also)* vulcanizing (vulcanization) system
vernichten *(phys ch)* to annihilate
Vernichtung *f (phys ch)* annihilation
~/strahlungslose radiationless annihilation
Vernichtungsrate *f (phys ch)* annihilation rate
Vernichtungsspektrum *n (phys ch)* annihilation spectrum
Vernichtungsstrahlung *f (phys ch)* annihilation radiation
vernickeln to nickel[ize]
~/elektrochemisch (galvanisch) to plate with nickel, to nickel-plate
Vernickeln *n* nickelization
~/elektrochemisches (galvanisches) nickel plating
Vernickelung *f s.* 1. Vernickeln; 2. Nickelschutzschicht
Vernickelungsbad *n*, **Vernickelungselektrolyt** *m* nickel plating bath (solution)
verolen to olate *(of hydroxo compounds)*
Verolung *f* olation *(of hydroxo compounds)*
verpacken 1. to pack[age]; 2. *(met)* to pack *(with a carburizing powder)*
~/in Dosen to tin, to can
Verpacken *n* 1. pack[ag]ing, package; 2. *(met)* packing *(in a carburizing powder)*
Verpackung *f* 1. packing, package, pack[ag]ing material; 2. *s.* Verpacken 1.
Verpackungsfolie *f* packaging film; packaging foil *(of metal)*
Verpackungsglas *n* container glass
Verpackungsmaterial *n* pack[ag]ing material, package, packing, *(relating to paper, plastic film or cloth also)* wrapping
Verpackungspapier *n* packing (wrapping, package) paper
verperlen to prill
verpreßbar *(plast)* mouldable
Verpreßbarkeit *f (plast)* mouldability
verpressen *(plast)* to mould
~/heiß to hot-press, *(relating to powders also)* to sinter under pressure
~/zu Briketts to briquette
Verpressen *n* **von Schnitzelpreßmasse** *(plast)* macerate moulding
verprillen 1. *(biot)* to prill, to microencapsulate *(an enzyme)*; 2. *s.* verperlen
Verprillung *f (biot)* prilling, [micro]encapsulation *(of an enzyme)*
verpuffen to deflagrate
Verpuffung *f* deflagration
verputzen to trim, to fettle, *(plast also)* to deburr, to deflash
Verrauchung *f* fumigation, downwash *(of stack gases)*
Verrauchungsfahne *f* fumigating plume

verreiben to grind, to powder, to pulverize, *(esp pharm)* to triturate
~/gemeinsam to powder together
Verreiben *n* grinding, powdering, pulverization, *(esp pharm)* trituration
Verreibung *f* trituration *(medicament)*
verrohren to pipe, to furnish (equip) with pipes; *(petrol)* to case
Verrohrung *f* piping, tubing; *(petrol)* casing *(act or material)*
verrosten to rust, to corrode
verrotten to rot
verrottungsbeständig *s.* verrottungsfest
verrottungsfest rot-resistant, rotproof
Verrottungsfestappretur *f* rot-resistant finish
Verrottungsfestigkeit *f* rot resistance, rotproofness
Verrottungsschutzmittel *n* rotproofing agent
verrühren *(esp lab)* to stir up, *(esp tech)* to mix up
versagen to fail, to break down
Versagen *n* failure, breakdown
~ durch Ermüdung fatigue failure
versalzen *(soil)* to salinize
Versalzung *f (soil)* salinization
Versand *m* shipment
Versandgefäß *n* shipping container
Versandvorschrift *f* shipping regulation
Versatz *m* 1. *(ceram)* batch [composition]; 2. *(tann)* layers, dusters, layer pits; 3. *(mine)* waste material; 4. blinding *(as of screens, filter cloth)*
Versatzformel *f (ceram)* batch formula
Versatzgut *n*, **Versatzmaterial** *n (mine)* waste material
versauern *(agric)* to acidify *(a soil, as of fertilizers)*; to sour, to become acid *(of soils)*
Versauerung *f (agric)* souring *(of soils)*
verschäumbar *(plast)* foamable, expandable, expandible
verschäumen *(plast)* to foam, to expand, to froth
Verschäumen *n* **am Anwendungsort** *(plast)* foaming in place (situ)
Verschäumungstrocknung *f* foam-mat drying
verschiebbar shiftable, *(relating to atoms or radicals also)* displaceable
verschieben to shift, *(relating to atoms or radicals also)* to displace
~/sich to shift *(frequency, electron, equilibrium)*
Verschiebestempel *m (plast)* sliding punch
Verschiebung *f* shift, *(relating to atoms or radicals also)* displacement
~/bathochrome bathochromic shift
~/chemische *(spectr)* chemical shift, nmr shift
~/Friessche Fries migraton (rearrangement) *(of phenyl esters or phenyl ethers)*
~/hypsochrome hypsochromic shift, blue-shift
~ nach Rot *(spectr)* shift to the red
Verschiebungsgesetz *n*/**Wiensches** Wien displacement law *(a radiation law)*
Verschiebungspolarisation *f* induced (distortion) polarization
Verschiebungssatz *m (nucl)* [radioactive-]displacement law, group displacement law
~/Sommerfeld-Kosselscher *s.* ~/spektroskopischer
~/spektroskopischer spectroscopic displacement law [of Kossel and Sommerfeld]
verschießen *(text)* to fade
Verschießen *n* **in Abgasatmosphäre** *(text)* gas fading
verschießend/nicht *(text)* fadeless
verschimmeln to mould
verschlacken to slag, to scorify *(impurities)*; to slag *(of impurities)*; to clinker *(of ashes)*
Verschlackung *f* slagging, scorification; clinkering *(of ashes)*
Verschlackungsbeständigkeit *f* resistance to slagging
verschlammen to clog with mud
verschlechtern to deteriorate
~/sich to deteriorate
Verschlechterung *f* deterioration
verschleiern *(phot)* to fog
verschleifen to grind
~/zu Holzschliff *(pap)* to make into pulp, to reduce to pulp, to pulp
Verschleiß *m* wear
~/reibender abrasive wear, abrasion
verschleißbeständig *s.* verschleißfest
verschleißen to wear [out]
Verschleißfaktor *m* wear factor
verschleißfest wear-resistant, resistant to wear, *(tech also)* abrasion-resistant, resistant to abrasion
Verschleißfestigkeit *f* wear resistance, resistance to wear, *(tech also)* abrasion resistance, resistance to abrasion
Verschleißschutzschicht *f* antiabrasion layer
Verschleißwiderstand *m s.* Verschleißfestigkeit
verschleppen to carry over (through)
Verschleppen *n* carry-over
Verschleppungsverluste *mpl* carry-over losses
verschließen to close; to stopper, to plug *(e.g. a flask)*; *(if gas-tight or water-tight:)* to seal
verschlucken to absorb *(rays)*
Verschluß *m* 1. *(appurtenance:)* closure, *(if gas-tight or water-tight:)* seal; 2. *(act:)* closure; sealing
~/hydraulischer water seal
Verschlußdüse *f (plast)* shut-off nozzle
Verschlußglocke *f* bell *(of a blast furnace)*
verschmelzen to fuse, to melt [together]; to seal *(as in working glass)*; to coalesce *(as of gas bubbles)*; *(nucl)* to fuse, to merge
~/auf Stein *(met)* to matte-smelt
Verschmelzung *f* coalescence *(as of gas bubbles)*
Verschmelzungsname *m (nomencl)* fusion name
verschmieren to lute *(e.g. a pipe joint)*; *(unintentionally:)* to choke [up] *(e.g. screen apertures)*
verschmutzen to soil, *(esp relating to the environment:)* to pollute, *(esp with poisonous matter:)* to contaminate; to be soiled

verschmutzt/durch Abwässer sewage-contaminated
~/organisch *(hyd)* organic-laden, organic-containing
Verschmutzung *f* 1. *(act or process:)* soiling, contamination, *(esp relating to the environment:)* pollution; 2. *(state:)* pollution, contamination, dirtiness; 3. contaminant, soil,*(esp in the environment:)* pollutant, polluting matter
~/anthropogene human[-induced] pollution
~ des Grundwassers ground-water pollution
~ durch Abwässer *(hyd)* sewage pollution (contamination)
~ durch Fett *(hyd)* grease contamination
~ durch Produktaustritt *(hyd)* process contamination
~ durch Schadstoffe pollution
~ durch Spurenstoffe *(hyd)* trace contamination
Verschmutzungsgefahr *f* danger of pollution
Verschmutzungsgrad *m* degree of soiling; degree of pollution *(of air or water)*, *(hyd also)* contaminant (pollutant) concentration
Verschmutzungsstoff *m s.* Verschmutzung 3.
verschneidbar *(coat)* dilutable
Verschneidbarkeit *f (coat)* dilutability, *(quantitatively.)* hydrocarbon tolerance
verschneiden *(food, rubber)* to blend; *(coat)* to dilute *(solvents)*; *(coat)* to extend *(pigments)*; to cut back, to flux *(high-boiling petroleum fractions)*
Verschneidmittel *n (coat)* diluent, diluting agent, indirect (latent) solvent; [paint] extender, [extending] filler *(for pigments)*
Verschneidwert *m (coat)* dilution value
Verschnitt *m (food, rubber)* 1. blending *(process)*; 2. blend *(product)*
Verschnittbitumen *n* cutback [bitumen], bitumen cutback
verschnittfähig *s.* verschneidbar
Verschnittmittel *n s.* Verschneidmittel
Verschnittöl *n (petrol)* flux [oil]
Verschnittpigment *n* extender pigment, extending filler
Verschnittprodukt *n (petrol)* cutback product
verschoben/nach tieferen Feldern *(spectr)* downfield
Verschönerungsmittel *n (cosmet)* make-up [preparation]
verschreiben to prescribe *(a medicine)*
verschrühen *(ceram)* to biscuit-fire; to harden on *(for fixing the decoration before firing)*
verschütten to spill
verschwefeln to thionate *(organic compounds for producing dyestuffs)*
Verschwefelung *f* thionation *(of organic compounds for producing dyestuffs)*
verschweißen to weld, *(plast also)* to seal
Verschweißen *n* **durch Wärme** *(plast)* heat welding, *(esp relating to films:)* thermal (heat) sealing
verschwelen to carbonize *(e.g. coal at low temperatures)*; to char *(organic matter by heat)*; to char *(of organic matter under the influence of heat)*
Verschwelung *f (coal)* [low-temperature] carbonization, low-temperature coking
verschwenden to waste
Verschwendung *f* wastage, wasteful spending
verschwinden to fade away *(coloration)*
versehen/mit einem Deckanstrich (Schlußanstrich) *(coat)* to finish
~/mit Rohren to pipe
verseifbar saponifiable
~/nicht unsaponifiable, non-saponifiable
Verseifbares *n* saponifiable matter
verseifen to saponify
verseift/partiell partly saponified
Verseifung *f* saponification
~/alkalische alkaline saponification
~/oberflächliche *(text)* surface saponification, S finishing
Verseifungsgeschwindigkeit *f* rate of saponification
Verseifungskolben *m* saponification flask
Verseifungsverfahren *n***/diskontinuierliches** batch saponification procedure
Verseifungszahl *f* saponification value (number), sap. value, S.V., Koettstorfer number (value)
versengen to scorch
Versenk *m(n) (tann)* handlers, lay-away pits (vats), floaters
versenken to sink, to submerge, *(relating to industrial wastes:)* to bury
Versenken *n* sinking, submergence, submersion, *(relating to industrial wastes:)* burial
~ ins Meer sea disposal (burial)
versetzen 1. *(filtr)* to clog, to blind; 2. to lace *(with a minor quantity of something)*, to add
~/in Schwingungen to vibrate
~/mit Borverbindungen to boronate *(fertilizers)*
~/mit Citrat to citrate
~/mit Hefe to yeast
~/mit Hopfen to hop *(the wort)*
~/mit Lab to rennet *(milk)*
~/mit Luft to aerate
~/mit Malz to malt
~/mit Neßlers Reagens to nesslerize
~/mit Tetraethylblei to lead *(motor fuel)*
versetzt/gegeneinander *(cryst)* dislocated; staggered *(stereochemistry)*
Versetzung *f (cryst)* dislocation
Versetzungsätzgrube *f (cryst)* dislocation etch pit
Versetzungsdipol *m s.* Versetzungsschleife
Versetzungsenergie *f (cryst)* energy of dislocation
Versetzungsring *m (cryst)* dislocation ring
Versetzungsschleife *f (cryst)* dislocation loop (dipole)
verseuchen[/radioaktiv] to contaminate
Verseuchung *f***[/radioaktive]** [radioactive] contamination
versickern to seep [away], to soak [away], to percolate, *(esp if slowly:)* to ooze [away]
Versickerung *f* seepage, soaking, percolation, *(esp if slowly:)* oozing; floor drain *(waste-water treatment)*

Versickerungsverlust *m (hyd)* seepage [loss], water loss due to seepage
versiegeln to seal
versilbern to silver
~/elektrochemisch (galvanisch) to silver-plate
Versilbern *n* silvering
~/elektrochemisches (galvanisches) silver plating
Versilberung *f s.* 1. Versilbern; 2. Silberschicht
Versilberungsbad *n*, **Versilberungselektrolyt** *m* silver-plating bath (solution)
verspannen *(glass)* to temper
versperren to choke [up] *(e.g. filter pores)*
verspinnbar spinnable
Verspinnbarkeit *f* spinnability
verspinnen to spin *(a dope)*
verspritzen to splash, to spatter, to spill
verspröden to embrittle
Versprödung *f* embrittlement
Versprödungstemperatur *f* brittle[ness] temperature, brittle-point temperature
versprühen to atomize *(liquids)*, to spray
Versprüher *m* [liquid] atomizer, sprayer
~ mit Beschleunigungsschaufeln/rotierender vaned-disk atomizer, rotary-vane atomizer
~/rotierender rotating (rotary) atomizer
Versprühung *f* atomization, spraying
~ durch Düsen nozzle atomization
~ mit Hilfsstoff auxiliary-fluid atomization
~ ohne Hilfsstoff single-fluid atomization
verspunden to bung [up]
verstärken 1. to fortify *(e.g. a construction)*; to reinforce *(e.g. plastics)*; *(text)* to splice; 2. to intensify, to potentiate *(an action)*; 3. to fortify, to strengthen *(solutions)*, *(esp by evaporation:)* to graduate; 4. *(phot)* to intensify
Verstärker *m* 1. *(phot)* intensifier; 2. *(met)* energizer; 3. *s.* ~/synergetischer; 4. *s.* Verstärkerfüllstoff
~/proportionaler *(phot)* proportional intensifier
~/superproportionaler *(phot)* superproportional intensifier
~/synergetischer activator, [catalyst] promoter, activating (promoting) agent
~/überproportionaler *s.* ~/superproportionaler
Verstärkerfüllstoff *m (rubber)* reinforcing filler (ingredient, pigment), active filler
~/heller white (non-black) reinforcing filler
Verstärkerwirkung *f* reinforcing (strengthening) action
Verstärkung *f* 1. fortification *(as of a construction)*; reinforcement *(as of plastics)*; 2. intensification, potentiation *(as of an action)*; 3. fortification, strengthening *(of solutions)*, *(esp by evaporation:)* graduation; 4. *(phot)* intensification
~/chemische *(phot)* chemical intensification
~ des latenten Bildes *(phot)* latent-image intensification, latensification
Verstärkungsfaktor *m (spectr)* enhancement factor
Verstärkungsgerade *f*, **Verstärkungslinie** *f (distil)* enrichment (rectifying operating) line
Verstärkungsmaterial *n* reinforcing agent (material) *(as for plastics)*
Verstärkungsteil *m (distil)* enriching section, rectifying section
Verstärkungsverhältnis *n***/mittleres** *(distil)* overall column (plate) efficiency *(ratio of number of theoretical plates to number of actual plates)*
verstäubbar dustable
Verstäubbarkeit *f* dustability
verstäuben to dust *(e.g. pesticides)*
Verstäuber *m (agric)* duster, dusting machine (appliance)
~/tragbarer rotary hand duster
Verstäubungsgerät *n s.* Verstäuber
Verstaubungsverlust *m* dust loss *(e.g. with granulating)*
versteifen to stiffen
versteinern *(geol)* to lithify, to petrify
Versteinerung *f (geol)* lithification, petrifaction
Verstellpumpe *f* variable-displacement pump
versticken 1. *(met)* to nitride *(undesirably)*; 2. *s.* aufsticken
Verstickung *f (met)* 1. nitriding, nitridation *(undesired process)*; 2. *s.* Aufsticken
verstopfen to clog [up], to choke [up], to blind, to plug *(e.g. screen openings)*
~/sich to clog, to choke, to plug *(as screen openings)*
Verstopfungsfiltration *f s.* Klärfiltration
verstöpseln to stopper, to cork
verstrammen *(rubber)* to stiffen
verstrecken *s.* recken
Verstreckwiderstand *m s.* Reckfestigkeit
Versuch *m* experiment, trial, assay, *(if conducted under specified conditions:)* test • **einen ~ durchführen** to run (carry out) an experiment, to perform (conduct) an experiment • **Versuche anstellen** to experiment[alize], to run (carry out) experiments
~/halbtechnischer semicommercial-scale test
~ mit Leitisotopen *(bioch)* tracer experiment, atom tagging experiment
~ mit Molekularstrahlen molecular-beam experiment
~/statischer *(rubber)* static test
~/Stern-Gerlachscher *(phys ch)* Stern-Gerlach experiment
Versuchsanlage *f* experimental plant
~/halbtechnische pilot plant, semiworks
Versuchsanordnung *f* experimental (test) arrangement
Versuchsbetrieb *m* 1. test run; 2. *s.* Versuchsanlage
Versuchsdaten *pl* experimental data
Versuchsdauer *f* duration of the experiment, test duration (period)
Versuchsdurchführung *f* performance of the experiment; experimental procedure, test practice *(know-how)*

Versuchselektrode *f* working electrode *(as opposed to the reference electrode)*
Versuchsergebnis *n* experimental (test) result
Versuchsfärbung *f* trial dyeing
Versuchsfehler *m* experimental error
Versuchskammer *f* test chamber; model oven *(for determining the swelling pressure of coal)*
Versuchskochung *f (pap)* experiment boil
Versuchslösung *f* experimental solution
Versuchsperson *f*/**freiwillige** *(tox)* volunteer
Versuchsreaktor *m* experimental reactor
Versuchsstadium *n* experimental stage
Versuchsstation *f* experiment[al] station
Versuchssubstanz *f* experimental (test) substance (material), substance for *or* under investigation
Versuchstier *n* experimental (test) animal
Versuchswert *m* experimental value
Vertauschungswägung *f* **[nach Gauß]** [Gauss's method of] double weighing
verteilen to distribute, to partition; to spread [out] *(over a surface)*; to disperse *(e.g. solid particles in a liquid)*; to homogenize *(e.g. for forming an emulsion)*
Verteiler *m* 1. distributor, distributing device; 2. *s.* Verteilerplatte
Verteilerbürste *f (distil)* wiper
Verteilereinrichtung *f (hyd)* [air] diffuser, sparger
~ **aus porösem Filtermaterial** porous diffuser
Verteilerplatte *f* deflector [plate], distributor plate
Verteilerring *m (hyd)* diffuser (sparge) ring *(of an aerator)*
Verteilerrohr *n* distributing pipe
Verteilerwirksamkeit *f* spreading efficiency *(of surfactants)*
Verteilplatte *f s.* Verteilerplatte
verteilt/fein finely divided, disperse
~**/regellos (statistisch, zufällig)** randomly distributed
Verteilung *f* distribution, partition; spreading *(over a surface)*; dispersion *(as of solid particles in a liquid)*; homogenization *(as for forming an emulsion)* • **in feiner** ~ finely divided, disperse
~**/bimodale** bimodal (double-peaked) distribution *(the occurrence of two maxima in a frequency distribution)*
~**/Bose-Einsteinsche** Bose-Einstein distribution *(of gas particles or photons)*
~ **der relativen Molekülmassen** *s.* Molmassenverteilung
~**/fraktionierte** countercurrent extraction (separation)
~**/klassische** *(phys ch)* classical distribution
~**/Maxwell-Boltzmannsche** Maxwell-Boltzmann distribution
~**/Maxwellsche** Maxwell distribution
~ **mit Phasenumkehr** *(chromat)* reversed-phase partition
~**/räumliche** spatial distribution *(of electrons)*
~**/regellose (statistische, zufällige)** random distribution
~**/zweigipflige** *s.* ~/bimodale
verteilungsanalytisch by distribution analysis
Verteilungschromatographie *f* partition (extraction) chromatography
~ **mit Phasenumkehr** reversed-phase partition chromatography
verteilungschromatographisch by partition chromatography, partition-chromatographic
Verteilungseigenschaften *fpl* spreading properties *(of surfactants)*
Verteilungsfunktion *f* distribution function; *(phys ch)* partition function
~ **der Rotationsenergie** rotational partition function
~ **der Schwingungsenergie** vibrational partition function
~ **der Translationsenergie** translational partition function
~**/elektronische** electronic partition function
~**/Gaußsche (normale)** Gaussian (normal) distribution function
~**/radiale** radial distribution (probability) function *(for electrons)*
~**/vollständige** complete partition function *(for energy)*
Verteilungs-Gaschromatographie *f* gas-liquid partition chromatography
Verteilungsgasleitung *f* distribution gas main
Verteilungs-GC *f s.* Verteilungs-Gaschromatographie
Verteilungsgefäß *n* partition vessel
Verteilungsgesetz *n* distribution (partition) law
~**/Boltzmannsches** Boltzmann distribution law *(of energy)*
~**/klassisches (Maxwell-Boltzmannsches)** Maxwell-Boltzmann [velocity-]distribution law, classical distribution law
~**/Nernstsches** *s.* Verteilungssatz/Nernstscher
~**/Rosin-Rammlersches** Rosin-Rammler exponential law *(relating to particle size in grinding)*
Verteilungsgleichgewicht *n* distribution equilibrium
Verteilungskoeffizient *m* distribution (partition) coefficient (ratio), *(in zone refining also)* segregation coefficient
~**/effektiver** effective distribution (segregation) coefficient *(in zone refining)*
~**/idealer** equilibrium distribution (segregation) coefficient *(in zone refining)*
Verteilungskonstante *f s.* Verteilungskoeffizient
Verteilungskurve *f* distribution curve
~**/Gaußsche** Gaussian curve *(statistics)*
Verteilungsleitung *f* distribution line
Verteilungsnetz *n (hyd)* distribution network
Verteilungsrohr *n* distributing pipe
Verteilungssatz *m*/**Nernstscher** Nernst distribution (partition) law
Verteilungstrennsäule *f (chromat)* partition column
Verteilungsverfahren *n* dispersion method *(of preparing colloidal solutions)*

Verteilungsverhältnis *n* [mass] distribution ratio, partition ratio, capacity factor
Verteil[ungs]vorrichtung *f* distributing device
vertiefen to intensify *(a colour)*
Vertiefung *f* intensification *(of a colour)*
Vertikalbeziehung *f* family relationship *(in the periodic system)*
Vertikalelektrofilter *n* vertical-flow electrical precipitator
Vertikalkammer *f* vertical chamber
Vertikalofen *m* vertical oven *(as for gas production)*
Vertikalreihe *f s.* Vertikalspalte
Vertikalretorte *f* vertical retort
~ **mit kontinuierlicher Beschickung** continuous vertical retort
~**/stetig betriebene** continuous vertical retort
Vertikalrohrheizkammer *f* vertical-tube calandria *(of an evaporator)*
Vertikalrohrverdampfer *m* vertical [tube] evaporator
~ **mit Innenheizkammer** standard (calandria, Robert) evaporator
Vertikalspalte *f* vertical column *(in the periodic system)*
Vertikalzentrifuge *f* vertical centrifuge
Vertikalziehverfahren *n (glass)* vertical sheet drawing process
Vertikalzug *m* vertical flue *(of an oven)*
Vertorfung *f* peat formation
verträglich compatible
Verträglichkeit *f* compatibility
Vertrauensbereich *m* confidence interval *(statistics)*
Vertrauensgrenze *f* confidence limit *(statistics)*
Vertrauensintervall *n s.* Vertrauensbereich
vertreiben to drive off (out), to expel, to dispel *(volatile matter)*; to repel *(e.g. insects by repellents)*
Vertreibung *f* expulsion *(of volatile matter)*; repulsion *(as of insects by repellents)*
verunreinigen to soil, *(esp relating to the environment:)* to pollute, *(esp with poisonous matter:)* to contaminate
Verunreinigung *f* 1. soiling, contamination, *(esp relating to the environment:)* pollution; 2. impurity, foreign matter *(in materials)*; contaminant, soil, *(esp in environment:)* pollutant, polluting matter, *(esp in zone melting:)* solute
~**/zufällige** chance contaminant
Verunreinigungen *fpl*/**gelöste** dissolved solid pollutants
~**/suspendierte** suspended [solid] pollutants
Verunreinigungsniveau *n* impurity level *(of insulators and semiconductors)*
Verunreinigungsstoff *m*, **Verunreinigungssubstanz** *f s.*Verunreinigung 2.
Vervielfacherphotozelle *f s.* Sekundärelektronenvervielfacher
Vervielfältigungspapier *n* duplicating (duplicator) paper
verwachsen *(cryst, coal)* to intergrow
Verwachsenes *n (coal)* intergrown material
Verwachsung *f (cryst, coal)* intergrowth
Verwachsungszwillinge *mpl (cryst)* penetration twins
verwandeln *s.* umwandeln
verwandt related, allied *(chemical substances)*
Verwandtschaftsgruppe *f* family *(in the periodic system)*
Verwehung *f* **des Sprühmittels** *(agric)* spray drift
Verweilbehälter *m (hyd)* detention tank (basin)
Verweilgefäß *n (hyd)* detention vessel
Verweilzeit *f* residence time, retention (hold-up, holding, detention) time, *(bioch also)* turnover time
~ **im Reaktor** reactor residence time
~**/mittlere** average (mean) residence time
verweilzeitabhängig depending on residence time
Verweilzeitverteilung *f* residence-time distribution, RTD
verwendbar applicable
~**/allgemein (universell)** generally applicable, general-purpose
Verwendbarkeit *f* applicability
verwenden to apply, to use
Verwendungsmöglichkeit *f* applicability
verwerfen *(lab)* to discard, to reject
verwesen to decay, to decompose, to undergo decomposition
Verwesung *f* decay, decomposition
verwirbeln to vortex *(material in a cyclone)*
Verwirbelung *f* vortexing *(of material in a cyclone)*
verwitterbar weatherable
Verwitterbarkeit *f* weatherability
verwittern to weather
~**/unter Kristallwasserverlust** *(cryst)* to effloresce
Verwitterung *f* weathering, decay, disintegration
~**/chemische** chemical weathering
~**/mechanische (physikalische)** physical (mechanical) weathering
~ **unter Kristallwasserverlust** *(cryst)* efflorescence
Verwitterungsprodukt *n* weathered (weathering) product
Verwitterungston *m* residual (primary) clay
Verwitterungsvorgang *m* weathering process
verzerren to distort *(e.g. an electron cloud)*
Verzerrung *f* distortion *(as of an electron cloud)*
verziehen/sich to be distorted (deformed), *(esp of metal)* to buckle, *(of ceramics or wood also)* to warp
verzinken to zinc, *(esp by hot-dipping:)* to galvanize
~**/elektrochemisch (galvanisch)** to electrogalvanize, to zinc-plate
~**/im Pulver** to sherardize
Verzinken *n* zinc[k]ing, *(esp by hot-dipping:)* galvanizing, galvanization
~**/elektrochemisches (galvanisches)** electrogalvanizing, zinc plating, wet (cold) galvanizing
~ **im Pulver** sherardizing
Verzinkung *f s.* 1. Verzinken; 2. Zink[schutz]schicht

Verzinkungsbad *n*, **Verzinkungselektrolyt** *m* zinc plating bath (solution)
verzinnen to tin
~/elektrochemisch (galvanisch) to tin-plate, to electrotin
Verzinnen *n* tinning
~/elektrochemisches (galvanisches) tin plating, electrotinning
Verzinnung *f s.* 1. Verzinnen; 2. Zinn[schutz]-schicht
Verzinnungsbad *n*, **Verzinnungselektrolyt** *m* tin plating bath (solution)
Verzinsungsgabe *f (agric)* interest dosage *(of fertilizers)*
Verzögerer *m* retarder, retarding agent, inhibitor, anticatalyst, negative catalyst; *(rubber)* retarder, antiscorcher, antiscorching agent; *(phot)* restrainer, restraining agent
verzögern to retard, to inhibit, to delay
~/sich to retard
verzögernd retardant, inhibitory, inhibitive
Verzögerung *f* retardation, inhibition, delay
~/sterische *(org ch)* steric retardation, F strain effect
Verzögerungsfaktor *m (chromat)* retardation (retention) factor, Rf value
Verzögerungskolonne *f s.* Verzögerungssäule
Verzögerungsmittel *n s.* Verzögerer
Verzögerungsphase *f* lag phase (time)
Verzögerungssäule *f (chromat)* retardation column
verzuckern to saccharify
Verzuckerung *f* saccharification
~/enzymatische *(food)* enzymatic (enzyme) conversion
~ mit Säure *(food)* acid conversion
~ und Vergärung *f***/einstufige** *(biot)* simultaneous saccharification/fermentation, SSF
Verzuckerungsrast *f*, **Verzuckerungszeit** *f (ferm)* saccharification period (rest, time)
Verzug *m s.* Verzögerung
verzundern *(met)* to scale
Verzunderung *f (met)* scaling
verzweigen/sich to branch *(molecules and reaction chains)*
verzweigt branched; *(cryst)* dendritic[al]
~/schwach lightly branched
~/stark highly branched
verzweigtkettig branched-chain
Verzweigung *f* 1. branching *(process)*; branch *(state)*; 2. *s.* ~/radioaktive
~/radioaktive *(nucl)* branched (multiple) disintegration (decay)
Verzweigungsanteil *m (nucl)* branching fraction
Verzweigungsenzym *n (bioch)* branching enzyme
Verzweigungsgrad *m* degree of branching
Verzweigungskoeffizient *m* branching probability
Verzweigungspunkt *m s.* Verzweigungsstelle
Verzweigungsreaktion *f* branched-chain reaction
Verzweigungsstelle *f* branch point *(of a molecule or of a metabolic pathway)*
Verzweigungsverhältnis *n* branching ratio
Verzwillingung *f (cryst)* twinning
~/polysynthetische polysynthetic twinning
Vesuvian *m (min)* vesuvian[ite] *(a sorosilicate)*
Vesuvin *n (dye)* vesuvine brown, vesuvin
Vetiverol *n (cosmet)* vetiverol, vetivol *(a mixture of alcohols from Vetiveria zizanioides (L.) Nash)*
Vetiveröl *n* vetiver (cuscus) oil, vetivert *(from Vetiveria zizanioides (L.) Nash)*
Vetiverylacetat *n (cosmet)* vetivert acetate *(a mixture of esters)*
VFA-Zahl *f (rubber)* VFA number
VI *s.* 1. Viskositätsindex; 2. Viskosefaserstoff
Vibration *f* vibration, oscillation
Vibrationsbandtrockner *m* vibrating conveyor dryer
Vibrationsbeanspruchung *f* vibrating stress
Vibrationsbeton *m* vibrated concrete
Vibrationsdüse *f* vibrating nozzle
Vibrationsfilter *n* vibration filter
Vibrationsknotenfänger *m (pap)* vibrating screen
Vibrationsmischer *m* reciprocating-impeller agitator
Vibrationsplattentrockner *m* vibrating tray dryer
Vibrationsquantenzahl *f* vibrational quantum number
Vibrationsrührer *m* reciprocating-impeller agitator
Vibrationsschaber *m (pap)* vibrating (oscillating) doctor
Vibrationsschüttelsieb *n (petrol)* vibrating mud-screen *(of a rotary-drilling installation)*
Vibrationssieb *n*, **Vibrationssortierer** *m* vibrating (reciprocating) screen
Vibrationsverdichtung *f* vibrational compaction
Vibrator *m* vibrator
Vibratorsieb *n s.* Vibrationssieb
vibrieren to vibrate, to oscillate
~/lassen to vibrate, to oscillate
Vibrieren *n* vibration, oscillation
Vibromischer *m* reciprocating impeller agitator
Vibrosieb *n s.* Vibrationssieb
vic. *s.* vicinal
Vicat-Apparat *m*, **Vicat-Nadel** *f* Vicat apparatus (needle) *(materials testing)*
Vicat-Zahl *f (plast)* Vicat softening point (temperature), V.S.P., Vicat needle point
vicinal vicinal, in 1,2,3 position *or* 1,2,3,4 position
Vicinalfunktion *f* vicinal function *(optical activity)*
Vickers-Härte *f* Vickers hardness, diamond pyramid hardness, DPH
Vickers-Härteprüfer *m* Vickers tester
Vickery-Filzinstandhalter *m (pap)* Vickery felt conditioner
Vidal-Schwarz *n (dye)* Vidal black
Viehbademittel *n* stock dip *(for insect control)*
Viehbesprühung *f* cattle spraying *(for insect control)*
Viehsalz *n* cattle salt (lick)
vielatomig polyatomic

Vielfachanregungsgerät *n (spectr)* multisource unit
Vielfachapparat *m* multiple [unit]
Vielfach-ATR *f (anal)* multiple attenuated total reflectance, MATR
Vielfacheffektanlage *f* multiple-effect evaporator
Vielfachstreuung *f* multiple scattering
Vielfachzyklon *m* multiple[-unit] cyclone
Vielfarbeneffekt *m (text)* multicolour[ed] effect
vielflächig *(cryst)* polyhedral
Vielflächner *m (cryst)* polyhedron
vielgestaltig polymorphic, polymorphous
Vielgestaltigkeit *f* polymorphism
vielgliedrig multimembered, many-membered *(ring)*
Vielkanal-Analysator *m***/optischer** *(spectr)* optical multichannel analyser
Vielkomponentenanalyse *f* multicomponent analysis
Vielkristall *m* polycrystal
Vielmesserhackmaschine *f (pap)* multiknife chipper
Vielstoffgemisch *n* multicomponent mixture
Vielstufenbleiche *f (pap)* multistage bleaching
vielstufig multistep *(process)*
vielwertig multivalent, polyvalent, polyad
vielzähnig multidentate, polydentate *(ligand)*
Vielzellenabscheider *m*, **Vielzellenentstauber** *m* multicell dust collector (extractor)
Vielzellenverdichter *m* [sliding-]vane compressor
Vielzentrenbindung *f* multicentre bond
Vielzentrenmolekülorbital *n* multicentre molecular orbital
Vielzweckkalander *m* universal calender
Vielzweckkleber *m* all-purpose (general-purpose) adhesive
vieratomig tetra-atomic
vierbasig tetrabasic, tetraprotic *(acid)*; tetrabasic, tetra-acid *(base)*
vierbindig tetracovalent, quadricovalent
Vierblattrührer *m* four-bladed agitator
Vierelektronensystem *n* four-electron system
Viererring *m s.* Vierring
vierfachpositiv [geladen] tetrapositive
vierflächig *(cryst)* tetrahedral
Vierflächner *m (cryst)* tetrahedron
viergliedrig four-membered
Vierhalskolben *m* four-neck[ed] flask
Vierhalsrundkolben *m* round-bottom four-neck flask
Vierkohlenstoffverbindung *f (bioch)* four-carbon compound
Vierkomponentensystem *n* four-component system, quaternary system
Vierkörperverdampfer *m* quadruple-effect [evaporator]
vierprotonig tetraprotic, tetrabasic *(acid)*
Vierring *m* four-membered ring
viersäurig tetra-acid, tetrabasic *(base)*
vierschauflig four-bladed *(agitator)*
Vierstoffsystem *n s.* Vierkomponentensystem
Vierstufenreaktion *f* four-step reaction
Vierstufenverdampfer *m* quadruple-effect [evaporator]
Vierstufenverfahren *n* four-step process
viertelgeleimt *(pap)* quarter-sized, 1/4 sized
vierteln *(anal)* to [cone and] quarter
Viertelstufenpotential *n (el ch)* quarter-transition-time potential
Viertelung *f (anal)* [coning and] quartering
Vierwalzenbrustkalander *m* inverted L type of calender
Vierwalzenkalander *m* four-bowl (four-roll) calender
~ mit oberer Brustwalze inverted L type of calender
~ mit übereinanderliegenden Walzen four-bowl stack type of calender
~ mit unten vorliegender Walze L type of calender
~ mit Z-Anordnung Z type of calender
Vierwegehahn *m*, **Vierwegeventil** *n* four-way valve
vierwertig tetravalent, quadrivalent *(element)*; tetrabasic, tetraprotic *(acid)*; tetrabasic, tetra-acid *(base)*; tetrahydric *(alcohol)*
~/koordinativ tetracovalent
Vierwertigkeit *f* tetravalence, tetravalency, quadrivalence, quadrivalency *(of an element)*; tetrabasicity *(of an acid or base)*
vierzählig 1. *(cryst)* tetrad; 2. *s.* vierzähnig
vierzähnig tetradentate, quadridentate *(ligand)*
Vigoureuxdruck *m (text)* vigoureux (top) printing
Vigreux-Kolonne *f (distil)* Vigreux column
Viktoriagrün *n* Victoria (malachite) green *(a triphenylmethane dye)*
Viktoriarot *n s.* Chromrot
Villard-Effekt *m (phot)* Villard effect
Vilsmeier-Haack-Reaktion *f*, **Vilsmeier-Haack-Synthese** *f* Vilsmeier-Haack synthesis (reaction) *(for obtaining aldehydes by formylation)*
Vinaconsäure *f* vinaconic acid, *cyclopropane-1,1-dicarboxylic acid
Vinylacetat *n* vinyl acetate
Vinylacetylen *n* *but-1-en-3-yne, *(deprecated:)* vinylacetylene
3-Vinylacrylsäure *f* 3-vinylacrylic acid, *penta-2,4-dienoic acid
Vinylalfaser *f s.* Polyvinylalkoholfaser
Vinylalkohol *m* vinyl alcohol, *ethenol
Vinyläther *m s.* Divinylether
Vinyläthylen *n* *buta-1,3-diene, *(deprecated:)* vinylethylene
Vinylbenzen *n*, **Vinylbenzol** *n* vinylbenzene, phenylethylene, styrene
Vinylbromid *n* vinyl bromide, *bromoethene
Vinylcarbinol *n s.* Prop-2-en-1-ol
Vinylcarbonsäure *f s.* Propensäure
Vinylchlorid *n* vinyl chloride, *chloroethene

Vinylcyanid *n* vinyl cyanide, *cyanoethene, acrylonitrile
Vinylengruppe *f* –HC = CH– vinylene group
Vinylester *m* vinyl ester
Vinylgruppe *f* CH_2=CH– vinyl (vinylic) group (residue)
Vinylhalogenid *n* vinyl halide, vinyl halogenide
Vinylharz *n* vinyl (ethenoic) resin
Vinylharzkunststoff *m* vinyl plastic
Vinylharzlack *m* vinyl lacquer
Vinylharzschaum *m* vinyl foam
vinylhomolog *s.* vinylog
Vinylhomolog[e] *n s.* Vinyloge
Vinylhomologie *f s.* Vinylogie
Vinylidenchlorid *n* 1,1-dichloroethylene, vinylidene chloride
Vinylidencyanid *n s.* 1,1-Dicyanethen
Vinylierung *f* vinylation
Vinylkation *n* vinyl[ic] cation
Vinylkunststoff *m* vinyl plastic
vinylog vinylogous
Vinyloge *n* vinylog[ue], vinyl homologue
Vinylogie *f* vinylogy
Vinylpolymerisation *f* vinyl polymorization
Vinylradikal *n* vinyl radical, *(specif)* ·CH = CH_2 free vinyl radical
Vinylrest *m s.* Vinylgruppe
Vinylsilicon *n* vinyl silicone
Vinylsulfonfarbstoff *m* vinyl sulphone dye
Vinylsulfongruppe *f* vinyl sulphone group
Vinyltrichlorid *n s.* 1,1,2-Trichlorethan
Vinylverbindung *f* vinyl compound
Violarit *m (min)* violarite *(iron nickel sulphide)*
Violett *n***/Döbners** Döbner's violet *(a triphenylmethane dye)*
~/Hofmanns Hofmann's violet *(an aniline dye)*
violettabschattiert degraded to[wards] the violet *(band spectrum)*
Violursäure *f* violuric acid, 5-isonitrosobarbituric acid
virentötend *s.* virustötend
Virialgleichung *f (phys ch)* virial equation [of state]
Virialkoeffizient *m (phys ch)* virial coefficient
Virialsatz *m (phys ch)* virial equation
Viridian *n s.* Smaragdgrün
Virologe *m* virologist
Viruseiweiß *n* viral protein
Virushüllprotein *n* [viral] coat protein, capsid protein
Virus-Nucleinsäure *f (bioch)* viral nucleic acid
Virusprotein *n* viral protein
virustötend, viruzid virucidal, viricidal, antiviral
viskoelastisch viscoelastic
Viskoelastizität *f* viscoelasticity, viscous elasticity
viskos viscous
Viskose *f* viscose
Viskoseerspinnlösung *f* viscose [spinning] solution, viscose dope
Viskosefaser *f* viscose [staple] fibre
Viskosefaserstoff *m* viscose fibre
Viskosefolie *f* viscose film
Viskosemodifikator *m*, **Viskosemodifizierungsmittel** *n* viscose modifier
Viskosereifung *f* viscose ripening
Viskoseschwamm *m* cellulose sponge
Viskoseseide *f* viscose rayon
Viskosespinnlösung *f s.* Viskoseerspinnlösung
Viskoseverfahren *n (text)* viscose [rayon] process
Viskosimeter *n* viscometer, viscosimeter
~/Sayboltsches *(petrol)* Saybolt viscometer
Viskosimetrie *f* viscometry, viscosimetry
viskosimetrisch viscometric, viscosimetric
Viskosität *f* viscosity
~/absolute *s.* ~/dynamische
~/dynamische dynamic (absolute) viscosity; *(quantitatively:)* viscosity coefficient
~/kinematische kinematic viscosity, viscosity/density ratio
~/reduzierte reduced viscosity
~/relative relative viscosity
~/scheinbare apparent viscosity
~/spezifische specific viscosity
Viskositätsbeständigkeit *f* viscosity stability
Viskositätsbrechen *n (petrol)* viscosity breaking, visbreaking
Viskositäts-Dichte-Verhältnis *n* viscosity/density ratio, kinematic viscosity
Viskositätsindex *m* viscosity index, V.I. *(of lubricating oils)*
Viskositätsindexerhöher *m*, **Viskositätsindexverbesserer** *m* viscosity index improver
Viskositätskoeffizient *m*, **Viskositätskonstante** *f* viscosity coefficient
Viskositätskonstanz *f* viscosity stability
Viskositätsmessung *f* viscometry, viscosimetry
Viskositätsmethode *f (chromat)* high-viscosity method *(for preparing stable suspensions)*
Viskositätsmittel *n* viscosity average *(of relative molecular mass)*
Viskositätsstabilisator *m* viscosity stabilizer
Viskositätsstabilität *f* viscosity stability
Viskositäts-Temperatur-Koeffizient *m* viscosity-temperature coefficient, temperature coefficient of viscosity
Viskositäts-Temperatur-Kurve *f* viscosity-temperature curve (slope)
Viskositätszahl *f* viscosity number
Vitalfarbstoff *m (biol)* vital stain
Vitalfärbung *f (biol)* vital staining
Vitamere *n* vitamer
Vitamin *n* vitamin • **mit Vitaminen anreichern** *s.* vitaminisieren
~/antihämorrhagisches antihaemorrhagic vitamin, phylloquinone, vitamin K
~/antirachitisches antirachitic vitamin, vitamin D
~/antiskorbutisches antiscorbutic vitamin, vitamin C
~/antixerophthalmisches antixerophthalmic vitamin, vitamin A
~/fettlösliches lipovitamin

Vitaminanaloge *n* vitamer
Vitaminantagonist *m* antivitamin
vitaminarm poor in vitamins
Vitaminaufnahme *f* vitamin intake
Vitaminbedarf *m* vitamin requirements (needs)
Vitamin-B-Komplex *m* vitamin B complex
vitaminfrei vitamin-free
Vitamingehalt *m* vitamin content
vitaminhaltig vitamin-containing
vitaminisieren to vitaminize, to fortify (enrich) by vitamins
Vitaminisierung *f* vitaminization
Vitaminkonzentrat *n* vitamin concentrate
Vitaminmangel *m* vitamin deficiency
Vitaminpräparat *n* vitamin preparation
vitaminreich rich in vitamins, vitamined
Vitaminverlust *m* loss of vitamin, vitamin loss
Vitaminwirksamkeit *f* vitamin potency
Vitaminwirkung *f* vitamin activity
Vitellin *n* egg vitellin, ovovitellin *(a phosphoprotein)*
Vitellus *m* vitellus, [egg] yolk
Vitrain *m (coal)* vitrain
Vitrinertit *m (coal)* vitrinertite
Vitrinit *m (coal)* vitrinite
vitrinitisch *(coal)* vitrinitic
Vitriol *n* vitriol *(a hydrated sulphate of a divalent metal)*
Vitriolschiefer *m* alum shale
Vitriolstein *m* vitriol stone *(main component iron(III) sulphate)*
Vitrit *m (coal)* vitrain
vitritähnlich *(coal)* vitrain-like
Vitritlinse *f (coal)* vitrain lens
Vitrokeram *n*, **Vitrokeramik** *f* vitroceramic, glass ceramic, devitrified (neo-ceramic) glass
vitro[por]phyrisch *(geol)* vitrophyric
Vivianit *m (min)* vivianite *(iron(II) orthophosphate)*
VK *s.* 1. Vergaserkraftstoff; 2. Vulkanisationskoeffizient
Vlies *n (text)* fleece; *(glass)* mat
Vliesfolie *f* non-woven fabric
Vlieswolle *f* fleece wool
V-Lunker *m (met)* secondary pipe
V-Mischer *m* vee-type (twin-shell) blender (mixer)
Vogelabschreckmittel *n* bird repellent
Vogelbekämpfungsmittel *n* avicide
Vogelfraß-Abwehrmittel *n* bird repellent
Vogelguano *m* bird guano
Vol.% *s.* Volumenprozent
volatil volatile
Vollanalyse *f* complete analysis
Vollcasein *n* whole casein
Volldünger *m* complete fertilizer
Volldüngung *f* complete fertilization
vollenthärten *(hyd)* to soften completely
Vollenthärtung *f (hyd)* complete softening, softening to zero hardness
~ **mittels Kalk-Soda-Verfahrens** complete lime softening
~ **mittels Neutralaustauschs** sodium cycle softening
vollentsalzen *(hyd)* to demineralize, *(by ion exchange)*, to deionize [completely]
Vollentsalzung *f (hyd)* demineralization *(by ion exchange)*, [complete] deionization, DI
~ **mittels Mischbettaustauschers** mixed-bed demineralization
Vollentsalzungsanlage *f (hyd)* demineralizing system, demineralizer, deionization unit
Vollfeuer *n (ceram)* full fire
vollflächig *(cryst)* holohedral
Vollflächnerkristall *m* holohedral crystal
Vollflußventil *n* inclined-seat valve
vollgeleimt *(pap)* hard-sized, H.S., strongly sized
Vollgerbstoffsyntan *n* replacement [syn]tan
Vollgummireifen *m* solid[-rubber] tyre, band tyre
Vollguß *m (ceram)* solid casting
Vollkegeldüse *f* solid-cone nozzle
Vollkornmehl *n* whole meal
vollkristallin[isch] holocrystalline
Vollküken *n* solid stopper *(of a glass stopcock)*
Vollmantelschleuder *f*, **Vollmantelzentrifuge** *f s.* Sedimentierzentrifuge
Vollmilch *f* whole (full) milk
~/eingedickte (kondensierte) condensed whole milk
Vollmilchpulver *n* whole-milk powder, dry whole milk
vollmundig palateful, rich in flavour *(e.g. beer)*
Vollmundigkeit *f* palatefulness, ful[l]ness *(as of beer)*
Vollpipette *f* transfer pipette, volumetric (bulb) pipette
~ **mit einer Marke** one-mark pipette
vollpumpen to charge by pumping
Vollrahmmargarine *f* whipped margarine
Vollreinigung *f (hyd)* complete purification (treatment), complete (overall) removal
Vollrohrmodell *n* full-scale model *(as of a pipe system)*
vollsaugen/sich to soak
Vollsprühkegel *m* solid spray cone
Vollsprühkegeldüse *f* solid-cone nozzle
Vollständigglühen *n (met)* full (true) annealing
Vollstromwechselofen *m* **nach Collin** Collin oven *(a coke oven)*
Volltränkverfahren *n* full-cell process *(wood preservation)*
Volltrum *m(n)* carrying side, top strand, *(relating to belt conveyors also)* drive belt
Vollverkokung *f* normal (high-temperature) carbonization (coking)
vollverseift completely saponified
Vollwaschmittel *n* heavy-duty detergent
Vollwelle *f* solid shaft
Vollzellstoff *m* chemical pulp
Voltameter *n* voltameter, coulo[mb]meter
Voltammetrie *f (anal)* voltammetry

~/inverse anodic-stripping analysis (voltammetry)
~ mit anodischer Auflösung *s.* ~/inverse
~/spannungsgeregelte voltage-scan voltammetry
~/stromgeregelte current-scan voltammetry
~/zyklische cyclic voltammetry
voltammetrisch voltammetric
Volta-Potential *n* Volta (outer) potential
Voltzin *m* voltzine *(a sulphidic zinc mineral containing arsenic)*
Volum... *s.* Volumen...
Volumen *n* volume • **mit konstantem ~** constant-volume
~/ausgeschlossenes excluded volume *(of a coiled macromolecule)*
~ der Zwischenräume void volume
~/kritisches critical volume
~/partielles molares partial molar (molal) volume
~/spezifisches specific volume
~/stoffmengenbezogenes molar volume
Volumenabnahme *f* decrease (diminution) in volume, volume decrease
Volumenänderung *f* change in volume, volume change
Volumenänderungsarbeit *f s.* Volumenarbeit
Volumenarbeit *f* work of expansion, expansion work, p,V-work
~/reversible reversible work of expansion, work of reversible expansion
~/reversible isotherme (technische) reversible isothermal work of expansion
Volumenausdehnung *f* cubic[al] expansion, volume expansion
Volumenausdehnungskoeffizient *m* coefficient of cubic[al] expansion, coefficient of volume expansion
~/thermischer isobaric coefficient of thermal expansion, isobaric thermal expansivity
volumenbeständig volume-stable
Volumenbeständigkeit *f* volume stability
Volumencoulometer *n* volumetric coulometer
Volumendosiervorrichtung *f* volumetric feeder (feeding device)
Volumendurchsatz *m* volume flux
Volumeneinheit *f* unit of volume • **je ~** per unit volume
Volumenfluß *m (chromat)* volumetric flow rate
Volumengetterung *f* dispersal gettering *(vacuum technology)*
Volumenkapazität *f***/nutzbare** *(hyd)* effective (operating) capacity *(of an ion exchanger)*
Volumenkonzentration *f***/molare** molar concentration, molarity
Volumenmischungsverhältnis *n* volume mixing ratio
volumenmolar molar
Volumenmolarität *f* molarity, molar concentration
Volumenometer *n* volumenometer, stereometer
Volumenprozent *n* percentage (per cent) by volume
Volumenschwindung *f* volume (cubic) shrinkage *(materials science)*
Volumenstrom *m* volumetric flow rate
Volumensuszeptibilität *f* volume susceptibility *(magnetochemistry)*
Volumenteil *m* part by volume
Volumenveränderung *f s.* Volumenänderung
Volumenvergrößerung *f s.* Volumenzunahme
Volumenverhältnis *n* proportion by volume, volume ratio
Volumenverminderung *f s.* Volumenabnahme
Volumenzunahme *f* increase in volume, volume increase
Volumetrie *f* volumetric analysis, *(using solutions also)* titrimetry, titrimetric analysis
volumetrisch volumetric, *(using solutions also)* titrimetric
voluminös voluminous
Volumometer *n* volumenometer, stereometer
Vorabscheider *m* precleaner *(air cleaning)*
Voranstrichstoff *m* undercoat paint
Vorappretur *f (text)* grey finish
Voraufbereitung *f* pretreatment, preconditioning *(of water)*
Vorauflaufbehandlung *f (agric)* pre-emergence treatment
Vorauflaufherbizid *n* pre-emergence herbicide (weed-killer)
Vorausrüstung *f (text)* grey finish
Voraussaat... *s.* Vorsaat...
voraussagen to predict
Vorauswahl *f* screening *(as of newly developed preparations)*
Vorbad *n (phot)* forebath
vorbehandeln to pretreat, to prepare, to [pre]condition
Vorbehandlung *f* pretreatment, preparation, [pre]conditioning, preparatory (preliminary) treatment
~ der Trübe *(filtr)* slurry preparation
Vorbehandlungsabschnitt *m* pretreatment section (zone)
Vorbehandlungsanlage *f* pretreatment unit
Vorbehandlungsstufe *f* pretreatment step
Vorbehandlungszone *f* pretreatment zone (section)
vorbeharzen *(plast)* to pre-impregnate, to precompound
vorbeiführen to by-pass
vorbelichten *(phot)* to pre-expose
Vorbelichtung *f (phot)* pre-exposure
vorbelüften *(hyd)* to pre-aerate
Vorbelüftung *f (hyd)* pre-aeration
vorbereiten to prepare, to prime
Vorbereitung *f* preparation, priming
Vorbereitungsabschnitt *m (glass)* conditioning section (zone) *(of the feeder channel)*
vorbestrahlen *(plast)* to pre-irradiate
Vorbestrahlung *f (plast)* pre-irradiation

Vorbleiche *f (pap)* prechlorination
vorbleichen *(pap)* to prechlorinate
Vorblütenspritzung *f (agric)* pre-bloom spray
Vorbrecher *m* prebreaker, precrusher, primary crusher
vorbrennen *(ceram)* to prefire
Vorce-Zelle *f* Vorce cell *(dialysis)*
vorchloren *(hyd)* to prechlorinate
vorchlorieren *(pap)* to prechlorinate
Vorchlorierung *f (pap)* prechlorination
Vorchlorung *f (hyd)* prechlorination
vorchromieren to prechrome
vordämpfen *(pap)* to presteam *(chips)*; *(text)* to preset
Vorderflanke *f*, **Vorderfront** *f (anal)* front *(of a peak)*
Vorderwürze *f (ferm)* first (original) wort
Vordestillationskolonne *f* primary column
Vordetachiermittel *n* pre-spotter
Vordruckwalze *f (pap)* watermarking dandy [roll], dandy [roll]
Voreindickung *f* initial thickening, preliminary concentration
Vorelektrolyse *f* pre-electrolysis
Voremulsion *f* preliminary emulsion
Vorentgasung *f* preliminary degassing
Vorenthärtung *f (hyd)* prior softening
vorerhitzen to preheat
Vorerhitzer *m* preheater
Vorerhitzung *f* preheating
Vorfermentation *f (biot)* prefermentation
Vorfermenter *m (biot)* prefermenter
vorfertigen to prefabricate; to precast *(e.g. concrete slabs)*
Vorfeuer *n (ceram)* prefire
Vorfilter *n* prefilter, roughing filter
vorfixieren *(text)* to preset; *(cosmet)* to prefix
Vorfluter *m (hyd)* receiving [body of] water, *(specif)* receiving stream
vorflutergerecht, vorfluterwürdig *(hyd)* acceptable for discharge to a receiving stream
vorflutgerecht, vorflutwürdig *s.* vorflutergerecht
Vorform *f (glass)* blank [mould], parison mould
Vorformboden *m (glass)* baffle
Vorformbodennaht *f*, **Vorformbodennarbe** *f (glass)* baffle mark
vorformen to preform
Vorformkammer *f (plast)* plenum chamber
Vorformling *m (plast)* preform, *(if hollow:)* parison, *(if massive:)* pill
~/extrudierter extruded parison *(in extrusion blowing)*
~/geschichteter laminated preform
~/schlauchförmiger [tubular] parison
~/spritzgegossener injection-moulded parison
Vorformmaschine *f* preform machine, preformer
Vorformpresse *f* preforming press
Vorformschirm *m* preform screen *(for glass-fibre reinforced plastics)*
Vorformverfahren *n* preform moulding (process)
Vorformwerkzeug *n* preforming tool
vorfraktionieren *(petrol, chromat)* to prefractionate
Vorfraktionierturm *m (petrol)* prefractionator
Vorfraktionierung *f (petrol, chromat)* prefractionation
vorfüllen to prime *(a pump)*
Vorgang *m* process
~/irreversibler (nicht umkehrbarer) irreversible process
~/reversibler (umkehrbarer) reversible process
Vorgarn *n* 1. roving; 2. *(glass)* sliver
Vorgärung *f* prefermentation
vorgerben to pretan
Vorgerbung *f* pretannage
vorgeschrumpft *(text)* preshrunk
vorgesteuert pilot-controlled, pilot-operated *(hydraulic and pneumatic valves)*
Vorhaltwirkung *f* derivative (rate) action *(process control)*
Vorhang *m (coat)* curtain, sag *(coating fault)*
Vorhangbildung *f (coat)* curtaining, sagging
vorhärten *(plast)* to precure
Vorhärtung *f (plast)* precure, precuring
vorheizen to preheat; *(rubber)* to prevulcanize, to precure
Vorheizer *m*, **Vorheizofen** *m* preheater
Vorheizung *f* preheating; *(rubber)* prevulcanization, precure, set cure, semicure
Vorheizzone *f* preheating zone (compartment)
Vorherd *m (met, glass)* forehearth
vorhersagen to predict
Vorhydrolyse *f* prehydrolysis; *(pap)* pre-impregnation, preliminary impregnation (penetration), presoaking, steeping, steepage *(of chips)*
vorimprägnieren to pre-impregnate, *(plast also)* to precompound, *(pap also)* to presoak, to steep
Vorimprägnierung *f* 1. pre-impregnation, preliminary impregnation (penetration), *(plast also)* precompounding; 2. *s.* Vorhydrolyse
Vorkalkung *f (sugar)* preliming, predefecation
Vorkammeranguß *m (plast)* tab gate
Vorkehrung *f* provision
Vorklärbecken *n (hyd)* primary clarifier (tank), primary settling (sedimentation) tank, presedimentation (primary sedimentation) basin
Vorklärbeckenabfluß *m s.* Vorklärbeckenablauf
Vorklärbeckenablauf *m (hyd)* primary [clarifier] effluent
Vorklärbeckenschlamm *m (hyd)* primary [sedimentation] sludge
vorklären *(hyd, filtr)* to preclarify
Vorklärschlamm *m (hyd)* primary [sedimentation] sludge
Vorklärung *f (hyd, filtr)* preclarification, *(hyd also)* primary sedimentation, presedimentation
Vorklassierung *f* preliminary screening (sizing)
vorkochen *(pap)* to predigest
Vorkochung *f (pap)* predigestion

vorkommen to occur, to be found
Vorkommen *n* 1. occurrence; 2. *(geol)* deposit
~/natürliches occurrence in nature, *(esp of a chemical element:)* natural abundance
vorkommend/natürlich naturally occurring, found in nature, from natural sources, native
Vorkondensat *n (plast)* precondensate
Vorkondensation *f (plast)* precondensation, precure, precuring
Vorkondensationsprodukt *n (plast)* precondensate
Vorkonzentration *f* 1. *(anal)* preconcentration technique; 2. *s.* Vorkonzentrierung
vorkonzentrieren to preconcentrate
Vorkonzentrierung *f* preliminary concentration, preconcentration
Vorkristaller *m* precrystallizer
Vorkristallisation *f* precrystallization
Vorkristallisator *m* precrystallizer
vorkühlen to precool, to prechill
Vorkühler *m* precooler, primary cooler
Vorkühlung *f* precooling, preliminary cooling, prechill
vorkultivieren *(biot)* to precultivate
Vorkultur *f (biot)* preculture, preliminary culture
Vorlage *f* [distillate, distillation, still] receiver, *(lab also)* receiving flask
~ nach Bredt udder[-type receiver changer]
Vorlauf *m (distil)* first runnings, forerun[s], forerunning[s], *(esp in distilling alcohol:)* heads, foreshot[s]; *(sugar)* green syrup
~/aldehydhaltiger *(ferm)* heads alcohol
Vorläufer *m* precursor, progenitor
Vorläufersubstanz *f* precursor, progenitor
Vorlaufherbizid *n s.* Vorauflaufherbizid
Vorleitschaufel *f* inlet vane
Vormastikation *f (rubber)* premastication
vormastizieren *(rubber)* to premasticate
vormetallisieren to premetallize
vormischen to premix, to preblend
Vormischgefäß *n* premixer
Vormischgerät *n* premixer
Vormischung *f* premix, preblend, initial mixture; *(rubber)* masterbatch, mother stock • **Vormischungen herstellen** *(rubber)* to masterbatch, to mix into a masterbatch • **mit Vormischungen mischen** *(rubber)* to masterbatch
~ aus Polymer und Ruß *(rubber)* [carbon] black masterbatch
Vorneutralisation *f* preneutralization, preliminary neutralization
vorneutralisieren to preneutralize
Vor-Ort-Analyse *f* on-site analysis
Vorozon[is]ierung *f (hyd)* pre-ozonation
Vorperiode *f* pre-period, initial period *(as of calorimetric measurement)*
vorplastifizieren *s.* vorplastizieren
vorplastizieren *(plast)* to preplasticate, to preplasticize
Vorplastiziersystem *n (plast)* preplasticating system
Vorplastizierung *f (plast)* preplastication, preplasticating, preplasticizing
Vorplastizierzylinder *m (plast)* preplasticator cylinder
Vorpolymer[e] *n*, **Vorpolymerisat** *n* prepolymer
Vorpresse *f (pap)* baby (pony) press
Vorpreßling *m (plast)* preform
Vorpreßwalze *f (pap)* 1. baby press roll, pony roll; 2. watermarking dandy [roll], [water]marking roll, dandy roll
Vorprobe *f* preliminary test
Vorprodukt *n* intermediate [product]
vorprogrammiert *(bioch)* preprogrammed
Vorprüfung *f* preliminary examination
~/trockene dry analysis
Vorpumpe *f* forepump, backing pump *(vacuum technology)*
Vorrang *m* [nomenclature] priority, seniority, precedence
vorrangig *(nomencl)* senior
Vorrat *m* stock, store
Vorratsbehälter *m* storage vessel, *(tech also)* storage tank (bin), hold[ing] tank, stock bin; *(pap)* storage chest
~ für Aufschlußchemikalien *(pap)* chemical storage tank
~ für Hackschnitzel *(pap)* chip [storage] bin, chip silo
Vorratsbunker *m* storage (stock) bin
Vorratsbürette *f* dispensing burette
Vorratsbütte *f (pap)* storage chest
Vorratsflasche *f* storage bottle, stock (dispensing) bottle
Vorratsgefäß *n* storage jar
Vorratshaltung *f* stockpiling, storing
Vorratskasten *m (pap)* storage cell
Vorratslösung *f* stock solution
Vorratsraum *m* store (stock) room, storage, store
Vorratsschutz *m* protection of stored products
Vorratssilo *n(m)* storage (stock) bin
Vorratstank *m* storage (store) tank; *(pap)* storage chest
vorreduziert *(met)* prereduced *(ore)*
vorreinigen to preclean; *(hyd)* to pretreat, to precondition *(water)*; to preclarify *(waste water)*
Vorreiniger *m* precleaner
Vorreinigung *f* precleaning, preliminary cleaning (purification); *(hyd)* pretreatment, preconditioning *(of water)*; pretreatment, primary treatment, primary (first) waste treatment stage, presedimentation, preclarification *(of waste water)*
Vorrichtung *f* contrivance, device
vorrösten *(met)* to preroast
Vorröstung *f (met)* preroast
Vorsaatanwendung *f* pre-sowing application *(of pesticides)*

Vorsaatbehandlung *f* pre-sowing treatment *(of soils with pesticides)*
Vorsaatherbizid *n* pre-sowing herbicide *(weed-killer)*
Vorsatzkuchen *m (glass)* shear cake
Vorsatzpapier *n* [book] end paper, book-lining paper
Vorsäule *f (chromat)* precolumn, guard column
Vorsäulenderivatisierung *f (chromat)* precolumn derivatization
vorschärfen *(text)* to sharpen
vorschäumen *(plast)* to pre-expand, to prefoam
Vorschäumer *m (plast)* pre-expander
Vorscheidesaft *m (sugar)* predefecation (predefecated, prelimed) juice
Vorscheideschlamm *m (sugar)* predefecation sludge
Vorscheidung *f (sugar)* predefecation, preliming
~/heiße hot predefecation
~/kalte cold predefecation
~/warme *s.* ~/heiße
vorschmelzen to premelt, to prefuse
Vorschmelzkammer *f (pap)* sulphur melter *(of a sulphur burner)*
vorschreiben to order, to prescribe; to specify *(the qualities of a product)*; to formulate *(e.g. the mixture of a batch)*
Vorschrift *f* instruction, direction; specification *(relating to the qualities of a product)*; formula *(as for mixing a batch)*; *(pharm)* prescription • **den Vorschriften entsprechen** to meet the specifications
vorschrumpfen *(text)* to preshrink
Vorschrumpfung *f (text)* preshrinking
Vorschub *m* feed[ing]
Vorschubgeschwindigkeit *f* rate of feed[ing]
vorschwelen to precarbonize
Vorschwelung *f* precarbonization, *(in producing gas also)* predistillation
vorsichtig gentle, slight *(heating)*
Vorsichtsmaßnahme *f* [safety] precaution • **Vorsichtsmaßnahmen treffen** to take precautions
Vorsichtsmaßregel *f* safety rule (principle)
Vorsieb *n* preconditioning screen
Vorsilbe *f***/vervielfachende** *(nomencl)* multiplying prefix, multiplicative numeral (numerical prefix)
vorsintern to presinter
Vorsinterung *f* presintering
vorsortieren *(pap)* to prescreen
Vorsortierer *m (pap)* preknotter
Vorsortierung *f (pap)* prescreening, [pre]knotting
vorspannen to prestress; *(glass)* to temper
vorspinnen *(text)* to rove
Vorspinnmaschine *f (text)* flyer
vorstabilisieren *(text)* to preset
Vorstabilisierung *f (text)* presetting
Vorsteuerleitung *f* pilot-supply line *(hydraulics and pneumatics)*
Vorsteuerventil *n* pilot valve *(hydraulics and pneumatics)*

Vorstoß *m* adapter; *(distil)* [condenser] adapter, receiver adapter (tube), delivery tube
~ für Frittentiegel *(lab)* crucible adapter
Vorstoßpapier *n s.* Vorsatzpapier
Vorstreichfarbe *f* undercoat paint
Vorstufe *f* precursor, progenitor
vorstufenfrei precursor-free
Vortex *m* vortex
Vortrennung *f (chromat)* preliminary separation
Vortrockenzone *f* drying zone *(of a multiple-hearth incinerator)*
Vortrockenzylinder *m (pap)* predryer, baby (receiving) dryer
vortrocknen to predry
Vortrockner *m* 1. predryer; *(ceram)* preheating dryer; 2. *s.* Vortrockenzylinder
Vortrocknung *f* predrying, preliminary drying
Vorturm *m (pap)* strong[-acid] tower *(of a two-tower system)*
Voruntersuchung *f* preliminary examination (investigation)
Vorvakuum *n* forevacuum
Vorvakuumpumpe *f* forepump, backing pump
Vorverdampfer *m* pre-evaporator
Vorverflüssigung *f (biot)* preliquefaction *(of starch)*
Vorversilbern *n* silver striking (strike)
Vorversilberungsbad *n s.* Vorversilberungselektrolyt
Vorversilberungselektrolyt *m* silver strike, strike solution for silver plating
Vorversilberungsschicht *f* silver strike
Vorverstärker *m (anal)* pre-amplifier
Vorversuch *m* preliminary test
~ mit kleinen Substanzmengen small-scale [preliminary] test
Vorverzuckerung *f (biot)* presaccharification
Vorvulkanisation *f (rubber)* prevulcanization, precure, semicure, set cure
vorvulkanisieren *(rubber)* to prevulcanize, to precure
Vorwachs *n* propolis, bee glue
vorwärmen to preheat, to warm [up]; *(glass)* to warm in
Vorwärmer *m* preheater, feed heater
~/regenerativer [heat] regenerator
~/rekuperativer recuperator
Vorwärmgerät *n* preheater
Vorwärmkammer *f* regenerator chamber
Vorwärmung *f* preheating, forewarming, warming[-up]; *(glass)* warming-in
~/dielektrische dielectric preheating
Vorwärmwalze *f (rubber)* preheater
Vorwärmwalzwerk *n (rubber)* preheating mill, warming (warm-up) mill
Vorwärmzone *f* preheating zone (compartment); non-boiling zone *(of an evaporator)*
Vorwärtskontrolle *f (bioch)* feed-forward regulation
Vorwäsche *f* prewashing; *(text)* bottoming *(before bleaching)*

vorwaschen to prewash; *(text)* to bottom *(before bleaching)*
Vorweiche *f (tann)* presoaking
vorweichen *(tann)* to presoak; *(pap)* to pre-impregnate, to presoak, to steep
Vorweichen *n (pap)* pre-impregnation, preliminary impregnation (penetration), presoaking, steeping, steepage
Vorzeichen/mit umgekehrtem opposite in sign
Vorzugsbenennung *f (nomencl)* preferred name
Vorzugsmilch *f* certified milk
Vorzugsorientierung *f* preferred orientation
Vorzugsretention *f (bioch)* preferential retention
Vorzugsrichtung *f* preferred direction, directional preference
Vorzugswellenlänge *f (spectr)* blaze wavelength
Votator *m*, **Votatoranlage** *f* votator [chilling unit], votator margarine plant, margarine votator
Votatormargarine *f* votator margarine
Votatorverfahren *n* votator process *(for continuous margarine manufacture)*
VPI *s.* VPI-Stoff
VPI-Korrosionsschutzpapier *n*, **VPI-Papier** *n* vapour-phase inhibitor paper
VPI-Stoff *m* vapour-phase inhibitor, V.P.I.
VTC *s.* Viskositäts-Temperatur-Koeffizient
VT-Kurve *f* viscosity-temperature curve (slope)
Vulkanfiber *f* vulcanized fibre
Vulkanfiberersatz *m* semivulcanized board
Vulkanglas *n* volcanic glass
Vulkanisat *n (rubber)* vulcanizate, vulcanized product
γ-Vulkanisat *n* gamma vulcanizate
Vulkanisatabfälle *mpl* [vulcanized] rubber scrap, [vulcanized] waste rubber
Vulkanisateigenschaften *fpl* vulcanizate properties
Vulkanisation *f (rubber)* vulcanization, *(in compounds usually)* cure, curing
~/absatzweise length-by-length cure
~ bei Raumtemperatur room-temperature cure
~ durch Bestrahlung (energiereiche Strahlung) radiation cure, cure by high-energy radiation
~ im Dampfrohr/kontinuierliche continuous steam cure
~ in Dampf steam cure
~ in der Presse (Preßform) press cure
~ in Formen mould cure, moulding
~ in Heißluft hot-air cure (vulcanization), HAV, [dry-]air cure, heat cure
~ in offenem Dampf open steam cure
~ in Wasser hydraulic cure
~ in zwei Stufen two-step cure
~/kontinuierliche continuous cure (vulcanization), CV
~ mit Epoxidharzen epoxy cure
~ mit Peroxid peroxide cure
~ mit Schwefelspendern sulphur-donor cure, non-elemental sulphur cure, NES cure
~ mit Thiuramdisulfiden thiuram disulphide cure
~ nach dem Trocknen von Latex postcure, post-vulcanization
~ nach Peachey Peachey cure
~ ohne freien Schwefel *s.* ~ mit Schwefelspendern
~/optimale optimum cure
~/schwefelfreie sulphurless (non-sulphur) cure
~/stückweise *s.* ~/absatzweise
~ unter Blei lead-press cure
Vulkanisations... *s. a.* Vulkanisier...
Vulkanisationsagens *n s.* Vulkanisationsmittel
Vulkanisationsbeschleuniger *m* vulcanization (cure) accelerator
Vulkanisationseigenschaften *fpl* vulcanization (curing) characteristics
Vulkanisationseinsatz *m* starting of vulcanization (cure), beginning (onset) of vulcanization
~/später (verzögerter) scorch delay
vulkanisationsfreudig susceptible to vulcanization (cure)
Vulkanisationsfreudigkeit *f* susceptibility to vulcanization (cure)
Vulkanisationsgrad *m s.* Vulkanisationskoeffizient
Vulkanisationshilfsmittel *n* vulcanization assistant
Vulkanisationskoeffizient *m* vulcanization coefficient, degree of vulcanization (cure)
Vulkanisationskurve *f* vulcanization (curing) curve
Vulkanisationsmittel *n* vulcanizing (curing) agent
Vulkanisationsmittel *npl* vulcanizing (curing) ingredients, curatives
Vulkanisationsoptimum *n* optimum of vulcanization (cure)
Vulkanisationsplateau *n* cure plateau, plateau effect • **mit breitem ~** flat-curing • **mit kurzem ~** peaky-curing
Vulkanisationsreaktion *f* vulcanization (curing) reaction
Vulkanisationssystem *n* vulcanization (vulcanizing) system, curing (curative) system
Vulkanisationsverfahren *n* vulcanization (curing) process
Vulkanisationsverhalten *n* vulcanization (curing) characteristics
Vulkanisationsverlauf *m* course of vulcanization (cure)
Vulkanisationsverzögerer *m* antiscorcher, antiscorching agent, retarder
Vulkanisationsverzögerung *f* retardation of vulcanization (cure)
Vulkanisationszustand *m* state of vulcanization (cure)
Vulkanisator *m s.* Vulkanisierapparat
vulkanisch volcanic, vulcanic, igneous
Vulkanisierapparat *m* vulcanizer, vulcanizing apparatus, heater
vulkanisierbar vulcanizable, curable
~/mit Schwefel sulphur-vulcanizable, sulphur-curable, sulphur-curing
~/nicht non-vulcanizable, non-vulcanizing, non-curing

vulkanisieren to vulcanize, to cure
~/bei Raumtemperatur to vulcanize (cure) at room temperature
~/in der Kälte *s.* ~/bei Raumtemperatur
~/in Formen to mould
vulkanisierend/bei Raumtemperatur room-temperature-vulcanizing, RTV
~/langsam slow-curing
~/rasch (schnell) fast-curing, quick-curing
Vulkanisierform *f* vulcanizing (curing) mould
Vulkanisiergerät *n s.* Vulkanisierapparat
Vulkanisierkessel *m* vulcanizing autoclave (boiler), open-steam vulcanizer
~/liegender horizontal vulcanizer
Vulkanisiermaschine *f* continuous vulcanizer (vulcanizing machine)
Vulkanisier... *s. a.* Vulkanisations...
Vulkanisierofen *m* vulcanizing (curing) oven
Vulkanisierpresse *f* vulcanizing press, curing (moulding) press
~/hydraulische hydraulic vulcanizing press
vulkanisiert/mit Peroxid peroxide-cured
~/mit Schwefel sulphur-cured
Vulkanisiertrommel *f* vulcanizing (curing) drum, cylinder
Vulkanisierung *f* vulcanization, cure
Vulkanit *m* volcanic rock, effusive (extrusive) rock
VUV *s.* Vakuum-UV
VZ *s.* Verseifungszahl
V-Zentrum *n* V-centre *(a colour centre in spectroscopy)*

W

Waage *f* balance, *(of simple construction also)* scales
~/analytische analytical balance
~/chemische chemical (assay) balance
~/gleicharmige equal-arm balance
~/kurzarmige short-arm balance
~ mit Dämpfung[seinrichtung] damped balance
~ mit Luftdämpfung air-damped balance
~ mit magnetischer Dämpfung magnetically damped balance
~/Mohrsche Mohr balance
~/Mohr-Westphalsche Mohr-Westphal balance
~/Westphalsche Westphal balance
Waagebalken *m* balance beam
Waagengehäuse *n*, **Waagenkasten** *m* balance case
Waagenraum *m* balance room
Waagensäule *f* balance column
Waagenzimmer *n* balance room
Waagerechtziehverfahren *n* **für Tafelglas** horizontal sheet-drawing process
Waagschale *f* balance pan
~/linke left-hand pan *(of an analytical balance)*
~/rechte right-hand pan *(of an analytical balance)*
Wabe *f* honeycomb
wabenartig strukturiert honeycombed
Wabenhonig *m* comb honey
Wabenkern *m (plast)* honeycomb core *(of a sandwich construction)*
Wabenmittellage *f (plast)* honeycomb sandwich
Wabenstruktur *f* honeycomb structure • **mit ~** honeycombed
Wacholder[beer]öl *n* juniper (Jupiter) oil, oil of juniper *(from Juniperus communis L.)*
Wacholderteer *m* gum juniper *(from Juniperus specc.)*
Wachs *n* wax
~/amorphes *s.* ~/mikrokristallines
~/Chinesisches Chinese [tree] wax, insect wax, vegetable spermaceti *(secreted by scale lice)*
~/gebleichtes bleached wax
~/gelbes yellow wax *(unbleached beeswax)*
~/grünes *s.* Myrikatalg
~/Japanisches *s.* ~/vegetabilisches
~/mikrokristallines micro[crystalline] wax, microparaffin
~/mineralisches mineral (fossil) wax
~/rohes crude wax
~/tierisches animal wax
~/vegetabilisches vegetable wax, *(specif)* sumac wax, Japan tallow (wax) *(from Rhus succedanea L.)*
~/weißes white wax, bleached beeswax
Wachsappretur *f* wax finish
wachsartig wax-like, waxy
Wachsausschmelzmodell *n (met)* lost-wax investment pattern, wax pattern
Wachsausschmelzverfahren *n (met)* lost-wax (cire-perdue) process
Wachsbraunkohle *f* waxy coal
wachsen 1. to wax; 2. to grow *(as of crystals, microorganisms)*; to grow, to propagate *(of polymer chains)*; to increase *(of physical parameters)*
wächsern waxy
wachsfrei wax-free
Wachsglanz *m (min)* waxy lustre
wachshaltig wax-containing, wax-bearing
Wachskerze *f* wax candle
Wachskohle *f* waxy coal
Wachsleim *m (pap)* wax size
Wachsmodell *n***[/verlorenes]** *(met)* lost-wax investment pattern, wax pattern
Wachspapier *n* wax[ed] paper
Wachsstärke *f* waxy starch
Wachstuch *n* oilcloth
Wachstum *n* growth *(as of crystals or microorganisms)*; growth, propagation *(of polymer chains)*; increase *(of physical parameters)*
~/diauxisches diauxic growth *(of microorganisms)*
Wachstumsbedingungen *fpl* growth conditions
Wachstumsfaktor *m* growth factor
wachstumsfördernd growth-promoting
Wachstumsgeschwindigkeit *f* growth rate, rate of growth, *(relating to polymer chains also)* rate of propagation
~ der Mikroorganismen *(hyd)* biomass growth rate, rate of biomass formation (production)
~/maximale maximum growth rate

wachstumshemmend growth-inhibiting, growth-inhibitory
Wachstumshemmung *f* growth inhibition
Wachstumshormon *n* growth hormone, GH, somatotropin
~/menschliches human growth hormone, HGH
Wachstumsinhibitor *m* growth inhibitor
Wachstumskinetik *f (biot)* growth kinetics
Wachstumskurve *f (biot)* growth curve
Wachstumsmechanismus *m* growth mechanism *(polymerization)*
Wachstumsmedium *n (biot)* growth medium
Wachstumsperiode *f* period of growth; period of chain growth (propagation) *(polymerization)*
Wachstumsphase *f (biot, hyd)* growth phase
~/abnehmende declining (declined) growth phase
~/endogene death (endogenous growth) phase
~/exponentielle *s.* ~/logarithmische
~/logarithmische logarithmic growth phase, log phase
Wachstumsrate *f* growth rate, rate of growth
Wachstumsreaktion *f* growth (propagation) reaction *(polymerization)*
Wachstumsregulator *m* growth-regulating substance, growth regulator (modifier)
Wachstumsschritt *m* growth (propagation) step *(polymerization)*
Wachstumsstadium *n* growth (propagation) stage *(of polymers)*
wachstumsstimulierend growth-promoting
Wächter *m (tech)* safeguard
Wackelsitz *m (bioch)* wobble position *(of the third base of a base triplet)*
Wad *n(m) (min)* wad, bog manganese, black ochre *(manganese(IV) oxide)*
Wadsworth-Anordnung *f*, **Wadsworth-Aufstellung** *f (spectr)* Wadsworth mounting
waf *s.* wasser- und aschefrei
wägbar weighable
Wägebehälter *m* weighing tank
Wägebürette *f* weighing (weight) burette
Wägefehler *m* weighing error, error in weighing
Wägefläschchen *n* **[für Dichtemessungen]** density (specific gravity) bottle (flask), pycnometer
Wägeform *f* weighing form *(gravimetric analysis)*
Wägegefäß *n* weighing tank
Wägeglas *n*, **Wägegläschen** *n* weighing bottle
Wägegut *n* material being *or* to be weighed
Wägekasten *m* weight box
wägen to weigh
~/auf ein Milligramm genau to weigh to the nearest milligram, to weigh to 1 mg accuracy
~/nochmals to reweigh
~/vorher to preweigh
Wägepipette *f* weighing pipette
Wägeraum *m* weighing (balance) room
Wägeröhrchen *n* weighing piggy
Wägesatz *m* set of weights
Wägeschiffchen *n* weighing scoop, balance dish
Wägeschweinchen *n s.* Wägeröhrchen
Wägestück *n* balance weight
Wägestückkasten *m* weight box
Wägetisch *m* balance table
Wägezimmer *n* weighing (balance) room
Wagging-Schwingung *f (spectr)* wagging vibration
Wagner-Meerwein-Umlagerung *f (org ch)* Wagner-Meerwein rearrangement
Wägung *f* weighing
~/Bordasche Borda's method of weighing
~/direkte (einfache) direct weighing
~/Gaußsche Gauss's method of double weighing
Wägungs... *s.* Wäge...
wahrnehmbar/geruchlich detectable by odour
~/geschmacklich detectable by taste
Wahrscheinlichkeit *f*/**thermodynamische** thermodynamic probability
Wahrscheinlichkeitsdichte *f* probability density
~ der Elektronen electron probability density
Wahrscheinlichkeitsfaktor *m* probability (steric) factor *(reaction kinetics)*
Wahrscheinlichkeitsverteilung *f* probability distribution, distribution of a random variable
Waid *m* woad *(natural dye from Isatis tinctoria L.)*
Waldboden *m*/**brauner** brown forest soil, brown earth
Walden-Umkehr *f* Walden inversion, inversion of configuration
Waldtorf *m* forest peat
Walke *f* 1. *(text)* milling, fulling; 2. *s.* Walkmaschine
~/alkalische alkali[ne] milling
~/saure acid milling
Walkechtheit *f (text)* fastness to milling
walken 1. *(text, tann)* to mill, to full; 2. *(ceram)* to wedge
Walk[er]erde *f* fuller's earth
Walkfett *n (tann)* dressing grease
Walkmaschine *f* milling (fulling) machine, mill, beater
Wallace-Härtemesser *m (rubber)* Wallace pocket meter
Wallach-Umlagerung *f* Wallach rearrangement *(of azoxybenzene into 4-hydroxyazobenzene)*
Wallebertran *m* whale-liver oil
wallen to bubble, to boil up
Wallner-Linien *fpl (glass)* Wallner lines
Walnußöl *n* walnut oil *(from Juglans regia L.)*
Walöl *n* 1. whale (train) oil; 2. *s.* Walratöl
Walrat *m(n)* spermaceti [wax]
Walratöl *n* sperm [whale] oil
~/mineralisches mineral sperm [oil]
Waltran *m* whale (train, blubber) oil
Waltranhartfett *n* hydrogenated whale oil
Walzblech *n* rolled plate
Walzblock *m (met)* billet
Walzdruck *m* roll pressure
Walze *f* roll[er], *(if hollow:)* cylinder, drum • **mit mehreren Walzen [versehen]** multiroll[er], multiple-roll

~ **der Greiferpresse (Transportpresse, Zugpresse)** *(pap)* tag roll, squeeze (squeezing, drawing-in) roll
~/**elastische** *(pap)* filled (resilient) roll *(of a supercalender)*
~/**geriffelte** corrugated (fluted) roll
~/**gummierte** rubber-covered roll
~/**parallel geführte** parallel roll
~/**schwimmende** *(text)* swimming roll
walzen to roll, to mill
Walzen *fpl*/**gegenläufige** contrarotating rolls
wälzen *(glass)* to marver *(a gather on a flat plate)*
Walzenabnahme *f* roll discharge
Walzenanpreßdruck *m* nip pressure
Walzenauftragmaschine *f* roll coater
Walzenaushebeverfahren *n (glass)* machine cylinder method
Walzenbelastung *f* roll loading
Walzenbelüfter *m*/**mit Platten bestückter** *(hyd)* plate aerator
Walzenblasverfahren *n (glass)* hand cylinder method
Walzenbombage *f* roll crown
Walzenbrecher *m* roll[er] crusher
~ **mit geriffelten Walzen** corrugated-roll crusher
~ **mit glatten Walzen** smooth-roll crusher
Walzenbrikett[ier]presse *f* roll-type briquette (briquetting) machine, Belgium roll machine
Walzendruck *m* 1. roll[er] pressure; 2. *(text)* roll[er] printing
Walzendünnschichttrockner *m* drum film dryer
Walzenglättwerk *n* calender [machine]
Walzenkoronascheider *m* high-tension separator
Walzenlager *n* roll[er] bearing
Walzenmesser *npl (pap)* [beater] roll bars, fly bars, roll blades *(of a Hollander beater)*
Walzenmilch *f s.* Walzenmilchpulver
Walzenmilchpulver *n* roller-dried milk powder
Walzenmischer *m* mixing mill (rolls)
Walzenmischung *f (rubber)* roll compound
Walzenmühle *f* roll[er] mill, roller-milling system
Walzenoberfläche *f* roll surface
Walzenpaar *n* roll[er] pair
Walzenpresse *f* 1. roll[er] press; 2. *(lab)* cork roller
Walzenpulver *n s.* Walzenmilchpulver
Walzenringmühle *f* ring-roll mill *(with vertical grinding ring)*
Walzensatz *m* set (stack) of rolls
Walzenscheider *m* rotor separator, induced-roll [magnetic] separator, magnetic drum [separator]
Walzenschiff *n (rubber)* mill pan *(in a mixing mill)*
Walzenschränkung *f* skew (cross-axis) mounting
Walzenschüsselmühle *f* [roller-and-]bowl mill
Walzensinter *m s.* Walzzunder
Walzenspalt *m* roll nip, nip of the rolls, bite *(clearance between the rolls)*
Walzenstreichmaschine *f* roll coater
Walzenstuhl *m* roll[er] mill, roller-milling system
Walzentrockner *m* drum dryer
Walzentrocknung *f* drum drying
Walzfell *n (plast)* rolled sheet
Walzgerüst *n* rolling-mill stand
Walzglas *n* rolled glass
Walzhaut *f s.* Walzzunder
Wälzkolbengebläse *n* Roots (cycloidal) blower
Wälzkolbenverdichter *m* straight-lobe compressor
Wälzlagerfett *n* antifriction bearing grease
Walzmaschine *f (glass)* rolling (casting) machine
Wälzmühle *f* roll[er] mill
Wälzofen *m (met)* Waelz kiln
Wälzplatte *f (glass)* marver [plate]
Walzpuppe *f (plast)* billet
Wälzsieb *n* revolving (drum) screen, trommel [screen]
Walzsinter *m s.* Walzzunder
Walzwerk *n* rolling mill; *(rubber)* open roll mill • **auf dem ~ mischen** *(rubber)* to mill-mix
~/**enggestelltes** *(rubber)* tight mill
~ **zum Mastizieren** *(rubber)* masticating mill
Walzzunder *m (met)* roll[ing] scale, mill scale
Wand *f*/**Blochsche** *(cryst)* Bloch (domain) wall
~/**halbdurchlässige (semipermeable)** semipermeable membrane
Wanddicke *f* wall thickness
Wandeinfluß *m* wall effect *(on the course of a reaction)*
Wanderbett *n* moving bed
Wanderbettreaktor *m* moving-bed reactor
Wanderbettverfahren *n* moving-bed process
Wanderfläche *f (nucl)* migration area
Wanderlänge *f (nucl)* migration length
wandern to travel *(as of bulk material being processed)*; to migrate *(as of ions, groups, or pigments)*; to move *(as in a chromatogram)*; *(petrol)* to migrate; to drift *(as of zero point)*
Wandern *n* **der Schmelzzone** zone travel[ling] *(in zone melting)*
Wandernutsche *f* travelling-pan filter, TP filter
Wanderrost *m* travelling (chain) grate
Wanderrostfeuerung *f* chain-grate stoker
Wanderung *f* travel *(as of bulk material being processed)*; migration *(as of ions, groups, or pigments)*; movement *(as in a chromatogram)*; *(petrol)* migration; drift *(as of zero point)*
wanderungsbeständig non-migrating *(e.g. pigments)*
Wanderungsgeschwindigkeit *f* travel rate *(as of bulk material being processed)*; migration rate (velocity) *(as of ions)*
~ **der Schmelzzone** rate of zone travel, zone (zoning) speed *(in zone melting)*
~ **der Teilchen** velocity of particle motion
Wanderungsrichtung *f* **der Schmelzzone** direction of zoning (zone travel) *(in zone melting)*
Wanderungsstrom *m (el ch)* migration current
Wandfarbe *f* wall paint
~/**geleimte** distemper *(in a larger sense, white or tinted)*

~/weiße geleimte calcimine *(powder)*; [white] distemper, whitewash *(paste, jelly, or suspension)*
Wandfläche *f* **der Makroporen** macroporous area *(in activated carbon)*
~ der Mikroporen microporous area *(in activated carbon)*
Wandfliese *f* wall tile
Wandkatalyse *f* wall catalysis
Wandpappe *f* wall board
Wandreaktion *f* wall reaction
Wandreibung *f* wall friction
Wandturbulenz *f* wall turbulence
Wandung *f* wall
Wanne *f* 1. *(tech)* trough, vat; back *(brewing, dyeing, soap manufacture)*; *(glass)* tank; crucible *(of an arc furnace)*; 2. *s.* Wannenform
~/kontinuierliche *(glass)* continuous tank
~/periodische *(glass)* day tank
~/pneumatische pneumatic trough
Wannenform *f* boat [form] *(stereochemistry)*
Wannenglas *n* tank glass
Wannenkonformation *f* boat (tub) conformation *(stereochemistry)*
Wannenofen *m (glass)* tank furnace
~ mit Längsfeuerung end-fired (end-port) furnace
~ mit Querbrennern (Querfeuerung, querziehender Flamme) *s.* ~/querbeheizter
~/querbeheizter side-fired (side-port) furnace
Wannenstein *m (glass)* tank block
Warburg-Dickens-Horecker-Schema *n s.* Pentosephosphat-Weg
Ward-Feuerung *f* Ward bagasse furnace
Ware *f (ceram)* ware
~/Delfter delft[ware], delph[ware]
~/einmal gebrannte once-fired ware
~/geschrühte biscuit, bisque, biscuitted (biscuit-fired) ware
Warendichte *f (text)* gauge, gg.
Warenname *m***/freier** non-proprietary name
Warenprobe *f* sample
Warenspeicher *m (text)* J box *(as for bleaching)*
Warenzeichen *n* trademark
~/eingetragenes (registriertes) registered trademark
Warenzeicheninhaber *m* registrant
warmbehandeln *(met)* to heat-treat
Warmbehandlung *f (met)* heat treatment
Warmbehandlungsofen *m* heat-treatment furnace
warmblasen to blast, to blow *(in producing water gas)*
Warmblasen *n* blasting, blow[ing] *(in producing water gas)*
Warmblaseperiode *f* blow period *(in producing water gas)*
Warmbleiche *f (pap)* warm bleach[ing]
warmbrüchig *(met)* hot-short
Warmbrüchigkeit *f (met)* hot shortness
Wärme *f (phys ch, tech)* heat; *(sensation:)* warmness, warmth
~/differentielle differential heat
~/fühlbare sensible heat
~/gebundene latent heat
~/integrale integral heat
~/intermediäre *s.* ~/differentielle
~/latente latent heat
~/mäßige moderate heat
~/radiogene radiogenic (radioactive) heat
~/spezifische *s.* Wärmekapazität/spezifische
Wärmeabbau *m* thermal degradation, degradation by heat
wärmeabgebend exothermic, heat-giving
Wärmeableitung *f* dissipation of heat, thermal dissipation • **mit geringer ~** low-thermal-dissipation
Wärmealterung *f* heat ageing, thermosenescence
Wärmeänderung *f* heat change
Wärmeanstieg *m* heat rise
Wärmeanwendung *f* application of heat
Wärmeäquivalent *n* equivalent of heat
~/elektrisches electrical equivalent of heat
~/mechanisches mechanical equivalent of heat
wärmeaufnehmend endothermic
Wärmeausdehnung *f* thermal expansion
Wärmeausdehnungskoeffizient *m*, **Wärmeausdehnungszahl** *f* coefficient of thermal expansion
Wärmeausgleichgrube *f (met)* soak[ing] pit
Wärmeausstrahlung *f* heat radiation, thermal (calorific, caloric) radiation
Wärmeaustausch *m* heat exchange (interchange), thermal transfer
Wärmeaustauschabteilung *f***/regenerative** regeneration section *(of a plate pasteurizer)*
Wärmeaustauschapparat *m s.* Wärmeübertrager
Wärmeaustauscher *m s.* Wärmeübertrager
Wärmeaustauschfläche *f* heat-exchanging (heat-exchange) surface
Wärmebearbeitung *f (ch)* heat processing
Wärmebedarf *m* heat requirement[s], *(quantitatively also)* amount of heat required
Wärmebehälter *m* heat reservoir
wärmebehandeln to heat-treat
Wärmebehandlung *f* heat treatment (processing)
Wärmebehandlungsofen *m* heat-treatment furnace
Wärmebelastung *f* heat load
wärmebeständig heat-resistant, thermally stable *(e.g. plastics)*
Wärmebeständigkeit *f* heat resistance, thermal stability *(as of plastics)*
Wärmebewegung *f* thermal motion (agitation)
Wärmebilanz *f* heat balance
Wärmebildung *f* heat production
Wärmebildungskoeffizient *m (biot)* heat production coefficient
Wärmebildungsrate *f (biot)* heat production rate
wärmebindend endothermic
wärmedämmend heat-insulating
Wärmedämmstoff *m* heat-insulating material, thermal (heat) insulator

Wärmedämmung *f* thermal (heat) insulation • **mit ~** heat-insulated
Wärmedehnung *f* thermal expansion
Wärmedehnungsbeiwert *m* coefficient of thermal expansion
Wärmedurchgangskoeffizient *m* overall heat-transfer coefficient
wärmedurchlässig diathermanous, diathermic
Wärmedurchlässigkeit *f* diatherma[n]cy
Wärmeeffekt *m* heat effect
Wärmeeinheit *f* unit of heat, heat unit
Wärmeeintrag *m* heat input (addition)
wärmeempfindlich heat-sensitive
Wärmeempfindlichkeit *f* heat sensitivity
Wärmeenergie *f* thermal (heat) energy
Wärmeentwicklung *f* evolution of heat; *(rubber)* heat (temperature) build-up *(with dynamic stress)*
~/starke large evolution of heat
wärmeerzeugend heat-generating, calorific, calorigenic
Wärmeexplosion *f* thermal explosion
wärmefest *s.* wärmebeständig
Wärmefluß *m* heat flow
Wärmeformbeständigkeit *f* heat deflection temperature *(of plastics)*
Wärmefreisetzung *f* heat release
Wärmefunktion *f***/Gibbssche** Gibbs function (free energy), free energy G, free enthalpy
Wärmegrube *f (met)* soak[ing] pit
wärmehärtbar, wärmehärtend *(plast)* thermosetting, thermoreactive, heat-curable
Wärmehaushalt *m* heat balance
Wärmeinhalt *m* heat content, *(per unit mass also)* enthalpy, heat function at constant pressure
Wärmeinhalts-Konzentrations-Diagramm *n* enthalpy/concentration diagram, heat-content/concentration diagram (chart)
Wärmeinhalts-Temperatur-Diagramm *n* enthalpy/temperature diagram, heat-content/temperature diagram (chart), It diagram
Wärmeisolator *n s.* Wärmedämmstoff
Wärmeisolierung *f s.* Wärmedämmung
Wärmekammer *f* heated chamber
Wärmekapazität *f* heat (thermal) capacity
~ bei konstantem Druck isobaric heat capacity
~ bei konstantem Volumen isochoric (constant volume) heat capacity
~/molare molar heat capacity
~/spezifische specific heat capacity
Wärmekonvektion *f* thermal convection (siphoning)
~ bei erzwungener Strömung forced convection
~ bei freier Strömung natural convection
~/erzwungene forced convection
~/freie natural convection
Wärmeleistung *f* heat flow
Wärmeleiter *m* heat conductor
~/schlechter poor heat conductor
Wärmeleitfähigkeit *f* 1. thermal (heat) conductivity; 2. *s.* Wärmeleitzahl
Wärmeleitfähigkeitsdetektor *m*, **Wärmeleitfähigkeits[meß]zelle** *f* thermal-conductivity detector (cell), katharometer
Wärmeleitung *f* heat (thermal) conduction
Wärmeleitvakuummeter *n* thermal conductivity [vacuum] gauge
Wärmeleitvermögen *n* 1. thermal (heat) conductivity; 2. *s.* Wärmeleitzahl
~/spezifisches *s.* Wärmeleitzahl
Wärmeleitzahl *f* coefficient of thermal conduction, specific thermal conductivity
wärmeliebend thermophilic, thermophilous
wärmeliefernd exothermic, heat-giving
Wärmemenge *f* quantity (amount) of heat
Wärmemitführung *f* thermal convection (siphoning)
wärmen to warm [up]
Wärmenachbehandlung *f* post-heat treatment
Wärmeofen *m* heating furnace
wärmeoxidativ thermal-oxidative
Wärmeplastizität *f* thermoplasticity
Wärmepolymer[e] *n*, **Wärmepolymerisat** *n* *(rubber)* hot (high-temperature) polymer
Wärmepolymerisation *f (rubber)* hot (high-temperature) polymerization; *(petrol)* thermal polymerization
Wärmeproduktion *f* heat production
Wärmepumpe *f* heat pump
Wärmequelle *f* heat source
Wärmeregler *m* temperature controller, thermoregulator, thermostat
Wärmereservoir *n* heat reservoir
Wärmerückgewinnung *f* heat recovery
Wärmesatz *m***/Nernstscher** *s.* Wärmetheorem[/Nernstsches]
Wärmeschutz *m* thermal (heat) insulation
Wärmeschutzglas *n* heat-absorbing glass
Wärmeschutzstoff *m* heat-insulating material, heat insulator
Wärmeschwingung *f (cryst)* thermal vibration
wärmesensibel eingestellt *(rubber)* heat-sensitized
Wärmesensibilisierung *f* heat sensitization
Wärmesensibilisierungsmittel *n* heat sensitizer
Wärmespeicher *m* heat reservoir (accumulator)
Wärmespeicherung *f* heat storage
Wärmespritzen *n (plast)* flame spraying
wärmestabil *s.* wärmebeständig
Wärmestabilisator *m* heat stabilizer
Wärmestabilisierung *f* heat stabilization
Wärmestabilisierungsmittel *n* heat stabilizer
Wärmestein *m* pebble *(of a pebble heater)*
Wärmesteinerhitzer *m* pebble heater (stove)
Wärmesteinschüttung *f* pebble bed *(in a pebble heater)*
Wärmestrahler *m* heat lamp
Wärmestrahlung *f* heat radiation, thermal (calorific, caloric) radiation
Wärmestrom *m* rate of heat flow *(heat conduction)*; rate of heat transfer

Wärmestrombilanz *f* enthalpy balance
Wärmestromdichte *f*, **Wärmestromintensität** *f* heat (thermal) flux
Wärmetauscher *m s.* Wärmeübertrager
Wärmetheorem *n*[/**Nernstsches**] [Nernst] heat theorem, third law of thermodynamics
Wärmetönung *f* heat tonality
Wärmeträger *m* heat carrier, heat-exchanging (heat-transfer) medium, heating medium
~/flüssiger thermal liquid
Wärmetransmissionskoeffizient *m* coefficient of heat transfer
Wärmetransport *m*[/**molekularer**] *s.* Wärmeübertragung
Wärmeübergang *m* heat (thermal) transfer
Wärmeübergangskoeffizient *m*, **Wärmeübergangszahl** *f* heat-transfer coefficient
Wärmeübertrager *m* heat exchanger (interchanger)
~/direkter direct-contact heat exchanger
~ mit rotierenden Einbauten scraped-surface exchanger
~ mit Schwimmkopf floating-head [heat] exchanger
Wärmeüberträger *m s.* 1. Wärmeübertrager; 2. Wärmeträger
Wärmeübertragung *f* heat (thermal) transfer, heat exchange (interchange)
Wärmeübertragungsfläche *f* heat-transfer surface, heat-exchanging (heat-exchange) surface, *(quantitatively:)* heat-transfer area
Wärmeübertragungsmasse *f* heat-transfer cement
Wärmeübertragungsmittel *n s.* Wärmeträger
Wärmeübertragungsöl *n* heat-transfer oil
Wärmeübertragungssalz *n* heat-transfer salt, HTS
wärmeunbeständig thermolabile, heat-labile
wärmeundurchlässig atherm[an]ous
wärmeverbrauchend endothermic
Wärmeverhalten *n* high-temperature behaviour
Wärmeverlust *m* heat loss
Wärmeverteilung *f* heat distribution
wärmevulkanisierbar *(rubber)* heat-curable
wärmevulkanisiert *(rubber)* heat-cured
Wärmewiderstand *m* thermal resistance
Wärmewirkungsgrad *m* thermal efficiency
Wärmezufuhr *f* heat addition (input)
warmfest heat-resistant *(steel up to 600 °C)*
Warmfestigkeit *f* heat resistance *(of steel up to 600 °C)*
Warmfetten *n (tann)* hot[-air] stuffing
Warmformen *n* hot forming (working), *(plast also)* thermoforming
Warmformgebung *f* hot forming (working)
Warmformmaschine *f (plast)* thermoforming machine
warmhalten to stove
Warmhalteofen *m* heating (holding) furnace
Warmhärte *f* hot hardness
Warmkammerdruckgießen *n*, **Warmkammerdruckguß** *m* hot-chamber die (pressure) casting
Warmkammer[druckguß]maschine *f* hot-chamber [die-casting] machine
Warmkleber *m* hot-setting adhesive
Warmluft *f* hot air
Warmlufteintritt *m* hot-air inlet
warmpressen to hot-press
Warmpressen *n* hot pressing
Warmpreßgut *n* hot-pressed material
Warmräucherei *f* hot smoking *(at 25 °C)*
warmräuchern to hot-smoke *(at 25 °C)*
Warmspritzen *n (coat)* warm spray[ing]
Warmstreckgrenze *f (plast)* yield point at elevated temperatures
Warmtonentwickler *m (phot)* warm-tone developer
Warmumformen *n* hot forming (working)
warmverarbeiten to hot-work
Warmverarbeitung *f* hot working
Warmverformen *n s.* 1. Warmformgebung; 2. Warmumformen
Warmverpressen *n (coal)* warm briquetting
Warmwasser *n* warm water
Warmwassertrichter *m s.* Heißwassertrichter
Wärmzone *f* heating zone
Warnetikett *n* caution label
Warnstoff *m* warning agent
Warnstufe *f* alert level *(as with smog)*
Warnvorrichtung *f* alarm
Wartefrist *f (agric)* preharvest interval *(after application of pesticides)*
Wartezeit *f* 1. downtime, down period; 2. *s.* Wartefrist
~/geschlossene *(plast)* closed assembly time
~/offene *(plast)* open assembly time
Wartungsaufwand *m* maintenance requirements
Wartungskosten *pl* maintenance cost[s]
WAS *s.* Stoff/waschaktiver
Waschaggregat *n (text)* scouring train
Waschanlage *f* 1. cleaning plant; 2. *(text)* scouring train
Waschbad *n (text)* scouring bath
Waschband *n (filtr)* washing blanket
waschbar *s.* waschecht
Waschbehandlung *f* washing treatment
Waschbenzin *n* cleaner's naphtha (solvent)
waschbeständig *s.* waschecht
Waschblau *n* laundry blue
Waschbrause *f* washing spray
Waschbrett *n (glass)* washboard *(a surface defect)*
Waschdauer *f* washing period
Waschdüse *f (text)* scour nozzle
Wäsche *f* 1. *(tech)* wash[ing], wet cleaning, wash-up; 2. *s.* Waschanlage
~/alkalische *(pap)* alkaline washing stage, alkali [extraction] stage, caustic extraction [stage]
~/mechanische mechanical washing
~ mit flüssigem Stickstoff nitrogen wash process
~ mit Wasser water wash[ing]; *(pap)* water-washing stage
waschecht fast to washing, wash-fast, washable

Waschechtheit *f* fastness to washing, wash[ing] fastness, washability
Wascheffekt *m* cleaning (detergent) effect
Wascheigenschaften *fpl* detergent properties
Wascheindicker *m* washing [tray] thickener *(as in countercurrent decantation)*
waschen to wash, to wet-clean; to scrub *(gases)*; to launder *(textiles)*
~/durch Rückspülung to backwash
~/im Gegenstrom to wash countercurrently
~/in der [Naß-]Setzmaschine *(min tech)* to jig-wash
Waschen *n* wash[ing], wet cleaning, [gas] scrubbing, gas washing; laundering *(of textiles)*
~ im Strang *(text)* rope scouring
~ mit Alkalien alkaline wash[ing]
~ mit Säure acid wash[ing]
~ mit Wasser water wash[ing]
Waschentstauber *m* wet collector, scrubber
Wascher *m s.* Wäscher
Wäscher *m* [gas] washer, scrubber, wet collector
~/rotierender (umlaufender) rotary washer
Wascherz *n* placer [deposits]
Wäscheweichspülmittel *n* fabric softener, softening rinse
waschfest *s.* waschecht
Waschflasche *f (lab)* wash[ing] bottle, absorption bottle, bubbler
~ nach Drechsel Drechsel bottle
Waschflaschenbatterie *f* scrubbing train
Waschflotte *f (text)* washing (scouring) liquor, washing bath (liquid), detergent solution
Waschflüssigkeit *f* 1. wash[ing] liquid, washing liquor (solvent), *(if spent also)* washings; scrubbing liquid *(for gases)*; 2. *s.* Waschflotte
Waschflüssigkeitszulauf *m* wash inlet
Waschgold *n* placer (stream) gold
Waschholländer *m (pap)* washer beater, Hollander washer, washing (potching) engine
Waschkasten *m* washing tank
Waschkolonne *f* scrubber (wash) column
Waschkraft *f* detergent power, detergency
Waschkühler *m* washer-cooler
Waschkurve *f (min tech)* washability curve
Waschlauge *f s.* Waschflotte
Waschleistung *f* washing (cleaning) efficiency
Waschmittel *n* detergent, washing agent, *(specif)* laundry (fabric) detergent, laundering formulation, [fabric] laundering composition, washing composition
~/alkalisches alkaline detergent
~/enzymatisches enzyme detergent
~/synthetisches [synthetic] detergent, syndet
Waschmittelherstellung *f* detergent manufacture
Waschmittelindustrie *f* detergent industry
Waschöl *n* wash oil, absorption (scrubbing, stripping) oil
~/armes lean oil *(for an absorption column)*
~/beladenes *s.* ~/reiches
~/frisches (regeneriertes) *s.* ~/armes
~/reiches rich oil *(in an absorption column)*
Waschölabsorption *f* wash-oil absorption
Waschöldestillation *f* wash-oil stripping *(for obtaining benzole)*
Waschölkolonne *f* wash-oil column *(in distilling tar)*
Waschplatte *f (filtr)* washing plate
Waschprobe *f (dye)* wash test
~ nach Barret Barret's [wash] test
Waschpulver *n* washing powder
Waschrinne *f (min tech)* sluice
Waschsieb *n* rinse (drain) screen
Waschsoda *f* washing soda, salt of soda, [sal] soda, natron *(sodium carbonate 10-water)*
Waschtrommel *f* washing cylinder (roll, drum)
Waschturm *m* scrubbing (gas-washing) tower, tower scrubber, [gas] scrubber
Wasch-und-Trage-Erzeugnis *n (text)* wash and wear product
Waschung *f* wash[ing]
Waschwalzwerk *n (rubber)* washing mill (machine)
Waschwasser *n* wash[ing] water, wash [liquid], rinsing (rinse) water, rinse, *(if spent also)* washings
Waschwasserbedarf *m* rinse requirements *(ion exchange)*
Waschwirkung *f* cleaning (detergent) effect
Waschzyklon *m* cyclone washer (scrubber)
Waschzone *f* media washing zone *(of a vacuum filter)*
Washout *m* wash out *(the air pollutants collected by falling raindrops)*
Washout *n* wash out, below-cloud scavenging *(of air pollutants by falling raindrops)*
Wash-Primer *m (coat)* wash primer, pretreatment (self-etch) primer, wash coat [primer]
Wasser *n* 1. H_2O water; 2. *(hyd, tech)* water, *(tech also)* liquor, liquid; *(cosmet)* wash, waters; *(pharm)* waters; 3. *(min)* water *(limpidity and lustre of gems)* • **in ~ quellbar** water-swellable • **mit ~ verdünnbar** water-dilutable
~/ablaufendes *(hyd)* effluent water *(as from a treatment plant)*; underflow *(oil removal)*
~/aufbereitetes *(hyd)* finished (treated) water, treated (plant) effluent
~/chemisch gebundenes combined (chemically bound) water
~/destilliertes distilled water
~/doppelt destilliertes double-distilled water
~/einmal genutztes once-through water
~/entgastes *(hyd)* stripped water
~/enthärtetes softened water
~/entöltes *(hyd)* underflow *(oil removal)*
~/fließendes running water
~/freies free water (moisture), *(coal also)* accidental moisture
~ für Bewässerung irrigation water, water for irrigation [purposes]
~ für den Bevölkerungsbedarf residential water, water for residential use
~ für die gewerbliche Produktion commercial water, water for commercial enterprises (use)

~ **für häusliche Zwecke** domestic water, water for domestic (household) use
~ **für kommunale Zwecke** municipal [drinking] water, water for municipal use
~**/gebundenes** bound water (moisture)
~**/geklärtes** clarified water
~**/Goulardsches** Goulard's extract, vinegar of lead *(aqueous solution of basic lead acetates)*
~**/hartes** hard water
~**/hochreines** ultrapure (ultrahigh-purity) water
~**/hygroskopisches** hygroscopic water, hygroscopic[al] moisture
~**/im Durchlaufbetrieb genutztes** once-through water
~**/in der Natur vorkommendes** *s.* ~/natürliches
~**/inneres** inherent moisture
~**/kohlensäurehaltiges** carbonated water, soda [water]
~**/konstitutiv gebundenes** constitutional water, water of constitution
~**/mäßig verschmutztes** mildly contaminated water
~**/mechanisch gebundenes** mechanically-held water, mechanical water
~ **mit geringem Schwebstoffgehalt** low-turbidity water
~ **mit hohem Schwebstoffgehalt** high-turbidity water
~**/mittels H-Austauschers enthärtetes** *(hyd)* hydrogen-cycle softened water
~**/mittels Neutralaustauschs [voll]enthärtetes** *(hyd)* sodium-cycle softened water
~**/natürliches (natürlich vorkommendes)** natural (environmental) water
~**/salzhaltiges** saline (salt) water
~**/schwebstoffarmes** low-turbidity water
~**/schwebstoffreiches** high-turbidity water
~**/schweres** D_2O heavy water, deuterium oxide
~**/stark belastetes (verschmutztes)** heavily polluted water
~**/trübstoffhaltiges** turbid water
~**/unterirdisches** subsurface (subterranean, underground) water
~**/vollentsalztes** *(hyd)* deionized (demineralized) water
~**/weiches** soft water
~**/zeolithisches (zeolithisch gebundenes)** zeolitic water
Wasserabgabe *f (ch)* liberation of water, *(quantitatively:)* water loss
Wasserablaßhahn *m* pet cock
Wasserablöschung *f (met)* water quenching
Wasserabscheider *m* water separator
Wasserabschluß *m* water seal
Wasserabschreckung *f (met)* water quenching
wasserabsorbierend water-absorbing
Wasserabsorption *f* water absorption
wasserabspaltend dehydrating
Wasserabspaltung *f* elimination of water, dehydration
wasserabstoßend, wasserabweisend water-repellent, hydrophobic, hydrophobe
Wasserabweisung *f* water repellency
Wasserabweisungsvermögen *n* water repellency
Wasseraktivität *f (food)* water activity
Wasseranalyse *f* water[-quality] analysis
Wasseranlagerung *f* water addition, hydrate formation
Wasseranwesenheit *f* presence of water
wasseranziehend water-attracting, hygroscopic[al]
wasserarm water-short *(area)*
Wasserart *f* type of water
wasserartig aqueous
Wasseraufbereitung *f (hyd)* [fresh] water treatment, water conditioning (purification)
Wasseraufbereitungsanlage *f (hyd)* water treatment plant (works), water [purification] plant, waterworks
Wasseraufbereitungstechnologie *f* water [treatment] technology
Wasseraufbereitungsverfahren *n* water treatment process
Wasseraufnahme *f* water absorption, uptake of water
wasseraufnehmend water-absorbing, hydrophilic, hydrophile
Wasseraufsichtsbehörde *f* water pollution control authority
Wasserbad *n* [hot-]water bath
Wasserbakterien *npl (hyd)* water bacteria
Wasserbebrausung *f* water spraying
Wasserbedarf *m* water demand (requirements), demand for water, water[-supply] needs, amount of water required
~ **der Industrie** *s.* ~/industrieller
~**/gewerblicher** commercial water demand
~**/industrieller** industrial water demand
Wasserbedarfsmenge *f* amount of water required
Wasserbehälter *m* water tank
Wasserbehandlung *f s.* 1. Wasseraufbereitung; 2. Abwasserbehandlung
Wasserbeize *f (dye)* water stain
Wasserberegnung *f*, **Wasserberieselung** *f* water spraying
Wasserbeschaffenheit *f* water quality (properties)
wasserbeständig water-resistant
Wasserbeständigkeit *f* water resistance
Wasserbeständigmachen *n* waterproofing
Wasserbestimmungsapparat *m* **nach Dean-Stark** Dean and Stark apparatus
Wasserbewegung *f (hyd)* water movement
Wasserbilanz *f* water balance
Wasserbindefähigkeit *f*, **Wasserbindevermögen** *n s.* Wasserbindungsvermögen
Wasserbindung *f* water binding
Wasserbindungsvermögen *n* water-binding ability (capability)
Wasserblanchierapparat *m (food)* water blancher
Wasserblanchieren *n (food)* water blanching

Wasserchemie *f* water (aquatic) chemistry, hydrochemistry
Wasserchemiker *m* water chemist
Wasserdampf *m* water vapour, *(if generated at boiling point of water:)* steam • **mit ~ behandeln** to steam
~/gesättigter saturated steam
~/überhitzter superheated steam
Wasserdampfaufnahme *f* water vapour absorption
Wasserdampfdestillation *f* steam distillation (stripping)
wasserdampfdicht 1. steam-tight *(e.g. joint)*; 2. *s.* wasserdampfundurchlässig
Wasserdampfdruck *m* water vapour pressure
wasserdampfdurchlässig permeable to water vapour
Wasserdampfdurchlässigkeit *f* water-vapour transmission (permeability), WVT, moisture-vapour transmission (permeability), MVT
wasserdampfflüchtig steam-volatile
Wasserdampfpartialdruck *m* partial pressure of water vapour
wasserdampfundurchlässig impervious to water vapour, moisture-resistant, moistureproof
Wasserdampfundurchlässigkeit *f* imperviousness to water vapour, moisture resistance (proofness)
Wasserdargebot *n (hyd)* available fresh water, available water supply
wasserdicht water-tight, waterproof, impermeable to water • **~ abschließen** to waterproof • **~ machen** *(text)* to waterproof
Wasserdichtausrüstung *f (text)* waterproof finish
Wasserdichtmachen *n (text)* waterproofing
Wasserdichtmacher *m (text)* waterproofing agent
Wasserdruck *m* water pressure; *(tech)* hydraulic pressure; *(petrol)* water drive
Wasserdurchsatz *m* water throughput
wasserecht fast to water
Wasserechtheit *f* fastness to water
Wassereis *n* water ice *(as opposed to dry ice)*
Wasserelektrolyse *f* water electrolysis
wasserenthärtend water-softening
Wasserenthärter *m s.* Wasserenthärtungsmittel
Wasserenthärtung *f* water softening
~ durch Fällverfahren water softening by precipitation
~ nach dem Kalk-Soda-Verfahren lime-soda softening
Wasserenthärtungsanlage *f* water-softening plant
Wasserenthärtungsmittel *n* water-softening agent, water softener
Wasserentkeimung *f* water disinfection
Wasserentnahme *f* 1. water withdrawal (intake) *(from a public water supply)*; water intake *(from a natural resource)*; 2. water sampling
Wasserentsalzung *f* water desalination, demineralization of water
wasserentziehend dehydrating
Wasserentzug *m* water removal, abstraction (removal) of water, dehydration
Wasserfarbe *f* water[-base] paint, *(Am also)* watercolor; water colour *(art)*
Wasserfassungsvermögen *n (soil)* water-holding capacity, WHC
wasserfeindlich hydrophobic, hydrophobe
wasserfest water-resistant
Wasserfestigkeit *f* water resistance
Wasserfestmachen *n s.* Wasserdichtmachen
Wasserfilter *n* water filter
Wasserfiltration *f* water filtration
Wasserfleck *m* water spot; *(phot)* drying mark
Wasserfleckenbildung *f* water spotting
Wasserfluten *n (petrol)* water flooding
Wasserforschung *f* water research, research on water
wasserfrei free from water, *(esp relating to chemical substances:)* anhydrous, anh., *(esp relating to coal:)* moisture-free, mf
Wasserfreiheit *f* freedom from water
wasserführend *(geol, hyd)* water-bearing
Wassergas *n* water gas
~/blaues blue [water] gas
~/karburiertes carburetted (enriched) water gas
Wassergasanlage *f* water-gas plant
Wassergasgenerator *m* water-gas generator
Wassergasgleichgewicht *n* water-gas[-shift] equilibrium
Wasser/Gas-Grenzfläche *f* water/gas interface
Wassergasmaschine *f* water-gas machine
Wassergasreaktion *f* **[/heterogene]** water-gas (steam-carbon) reaction *(reduction of water by means of carbon)*
~/homogene water-gas-shift reaction, carbon-monoxide-shift reaction
Wassergasteer *m* water-gas tar
Wassergasverfahren *n* water-gas process
Wassergebrauch *m s.* Wassernutzung
wassergebremst *(nucl)* water-moderated
Wassergegenwart *f* presence of water
Wassergehalt *m* water content, *(esp of gases and hygroscopic substances:)* moisture content
~ im Filterkuchen filter-cake moisture content
wassergekühlt water-cooled
wassergesättigt water-saturated
wassergeschützt waterproof
Wassergeschwindigkeit *f (hyd)* rate of water flow, water [flow] rate, water velocity
Wassergesetz *n* water pollution regulation
Wasserglas *n* water glass, liquid (soluble) glass *(solution of alkali silicates in water)*
Wassergüte *f* water quality
Wassergütebedingungen *fpl* water-quality standards
Wassergütemerkmale *npl* water[-quality] characteristics, water-quality criteria (parameters)
Wasserhaltevermögen *n (soil)* water-holding capacity, WHC

wasserhaltig hydrous; *(min)* enhydritic, enhydrous
Wasserhärte *f* water hardness
wasserhärten *(met)* to water-harden
Wasserhärter *m*, **Wasserhärtestahl** *m* water-hardening steel
Wasserhärtung *f (met)* water hardening
Wasserhaushalt *m (biol)* water metabolism; hydrologic balance *(of an area)*
wasserhell water-white, water-clear
Wasserhülle *f* water sheath *(as of ions)*
wässerig *s.* wäßrig
Wasser-in-Fett-Emulsion *f* water-in-fat emulsion
Wasserinhaltsstoffe *mpl* water[-quality] constituents, impurities in water
~ **des Kesselwassers** boiler-water constituents
~/**echt gelöste** dissolved solids, solubles
~/**flüchtige organische** volatile organic compounds
~/**grobdisperse** suspended solids, SS, suspended solid matter *(> $5 \cdot 10^{-4}$ mm)*
~/**schädliche** water pollutants (contaminants)
Wasser-in-Öl-Emulsion *f* water-in-oil emulsion, W/O emulsion, *(agric also)* mayonnaise *(as of pesticides)*
Wasser-in-Öl-Typ *m* water-in-oil type, W/O type *(of emulsions)*
Wasserkalander *m (text)* water mangle
Wasserkalk *m hydraulic lime which contains only 10 to 15 % of soluble acid constituents*
Wasserkalorimeter *n* water calorimeter
Wasserkanal *m* water channel
Wasserkapazität *f (soil)* water-holding capacity, WHC
Wasserkesselreaktor *m (nucl)* water-boiler reactor
wasserklar water-clear, water-white
Wasserknappheit *f (hyd)* water shortages, lack of water
Wasserkörper *m (hyd)* water body, body of water
Wasserkreislauf *m* 1. water recycle (cycle, circuit), circulation of water; 2. hydrologic (water) cycle, hydrogeological cycling [of water] *(in nature)*
Wasserkreislaufführung *f* recycling (recirculation) of water, water recirculation
Wasserkühler *m* water-cooled condenser
Wasserkühlung *f* water cooling
Wasserkultur *f (agric)* water (hydroponic) culture, hydroponics
Wasserlabor *n* water laboratory
Wasserlack *m* water varnish; water-base enamel
Wasserleistung *f* capacity of water evaporation *(of a dryer)*
Wasserleitung *f* 1. water main (piping), water-supply line; 2. *(biol)* water transport
Wasserlinien *fpl (pap)* watermarked lines, waterlines
Wasserlinienpapier *n* laid paper
wasserlöslich water-soluble
Wasserlöslichkeit *f* water (aqueous) solubility
Wassermangel *m (hyd)* water shortage, lack of water
Wassermantel *m* water jacket • **mit** ~ water-jacketed
Wassermehrfachnutzung *f* water reuse
Wassermesser *m* water meter
wassermoderiert *(nucl)* water-moderated
Wassermolekül *n* water molecule
Wassermörtel *m* hydraulic mortar
wässern *(of human agent:)* to steep, to soak; *(in running water:)* to rinse; *(phot)* to wash, to rinse, to soak; *(of material:)* to soak
Wassernachweis *m* test for water
Wassernutzer *m (hyd)* user (consumer) of water, water user
Wassernutzung *f (hyd)* water utilization (usage, use)
Wasseroberfläche *f* water surface
Wasserphase *f* aqueous (water) phase
Wasserprobe *f* water sample, sample of water
Wasserqualität *f s.* Wassergüte
Wasserreaktor *m (nucl)* water-boiler reactor
wasserreich rich in water
Wasserreinhaltung *f (hyd)* water pollution control, water protection
Wasserreinigung *f* 1. water purification (clean-up); 2. *s.* Wasseraufbereitung
Wasserreinigungskohle *f* water treatment carbon
Wasserressourcen *fpl* water resources *(in nature)*
Wasserringpumpe *f* water-ring pump
Wasserrohr *n* water tube (pipe)
Wasserrohrdampferzeuger *m*, **Wasserrohrkessel** *m* water-tube boiler
Wasserröste *f (text)* water ret[ting] *(of flax)*
~ **in stehenden Gewässern** dam retting
Wasserrotte *f s.* Wasserröste
Wasserrückgewinnung *f* water recovery
Wasserschadstoff *m* water pollutant
Wasserschicht *f* water layer
Wasserschlag *m* water hammer
Wasserschleier *m* water curtain
Wasserschlepper *m (distil)* water entrainer
Wasserschöpfer *m* water sampler
Wasserschüssel *f* water-sealed trough
Wasserspeicherung *f (hyd)* water storage
Wasserspiegel *m* water level
Wasserspülung *f (petrol)* water-base mud
Wasserstand *m* water level
Wasserstand[s]anzeiger *m* gauge glass
Wasserstand[s]regler *m* water level regulator (controller)
Wasserstein *m* [hardness] scale, mineral scale, hard-water depositions (residue)
Wassersteinbildung *f* formation of hardness scale, scale formation (build-up), scaling
Wasserstoff *m* H hydrogen • **über ~ verbunden** hydrogen-bonded
~/**aktiver** active hydrogen
~/**atomarer (einatomiger)** atomic hydrogen, monohydrogen
~/**indizierter** *(nomencl)* indicated hydrogen

~/leichter ^{1}H protium, light hydrogen
~/schwerer $^{2}_{1}H$, D deuterium, heavy hydrogen
~/überschwerer $^{3}_{1}H$, T tritium
Wasserstoffabscheidung *f* hydrogen evolution (liberation, generation)
wasserstoffabspaltend hydrogen-abstracting
Wasserstoffabspaltung *f* abstraction (elimination) of hydrogen, dehydrogenation
wasserstoffähnlich hydrogen-like
Wasserstoffakzeptor *m* hydrogen acceptor
wasserstoffarm poor in hydrogen
Wasserstoffatmosphäre *f* hydrogen atmosphere
Wasserstoffatom *n* hydrogen atom
~/allylständiges allylic hydrogen atom
~/bewegliches mobile hydrogen atom
~ in γ-Stellung gamma hydrogen, γ-hydrogen
Wasserstoffatomspektrum *n* [atomic] spectrum of hydrogen, hydrogen spectrum
Wasserstoffaustausch *m* hydrogen exchange; *(hyd)* H-form exchange, hydrogen-cycle [cation] exchange, hydrogen-cation exchange
Wasserstoffaustauscher *m s.* Wasserstoffionenaustauscher
Wasserstoffbindung *f* 1. hydrogen bond *(state)*; 2. hydrogen bonding *(process)*
Wasserstoffblasenbildung *f* hydrogen blistering *(of steel)*
Wasserstoffbrüchigkeit *f* acid brittleness
Wasserstoffbrücke *f* hydrogen bridge
~/intermolekulare intermolecular hydrogen bond
~/intramolekulare intramolecular hydrogen bond
Wasserstoffbrückenbindung *f* hydrogen bridge bond
Wasserstoffdisulfid *n* hydrogen disulphide, disulphane
Wasserstoffdon[at]or *m* hydrogen donor
Wasserstoffdruck *m* hydrogen pressure
Wasserstoffelektrode *f* hydrogen [gas] electrode
~/reversible reversible hydrogen electrode, RHE
wasserstoffempfindlich susceptible to hydrogen
Wasserstoffempfindlichkeit *f* susceptibility to hydrogen
Wasserstoffentschwefelung *f* hydrodesulphurization, HDS
Wasserstoffentwicklung *f* hydrogen evolution (liberation, generation)
Wasserstoffentzug *m* abstraction (elimination) of hydrogen, dehydrogenation
Wasserstofferzeugung *f* hydrogen generation
Wasserstoffexponent *m s.* Wasserstoffionenexponent
Wasserstofffluoridlaser *m* hydrogen-fluoride laser, HF laser
Wasserstoffgas *n* hydrogen gas
Wasserstoffhalbelement *n* hydrogen half-cell
wasserstoffhaltig containing hydrogen, hydrogenous
Wasserstoffion *n* hydrogen ion, H^{+} ion
Wasserstoffionenaktivität *f* hydrogen-ion activity
Wasserstoffionenaustauscher *m (hyd)* H-form exchanger, hydrogen[-form] exchanger, hydrogen-cation exchanger
Wasserstoffionenexponent *m* hydrogen-ion exponent, *p*H value (number, level)
Wasserstoffionenkonzentration *f* hydrogen-ion concentration
Wasserstoffkern *m* hydrogen nucleus
wasserstoffliefernd hydrogen-donating
Wasserstoffnachweis *m* detection of hydrogen
Wasserstoffnormalelektrode *f* normal hydrogen electrode, N.H.E.
Wasserstoffoxid *n* hydrogen oxide, water
Wasserstoffpartialdruck *m* hydrogen partial pressure
Wasserstoffpentasulfid *n* hydrogen pentasulphide, pentasulphane
Wasserstoffperoxid *n* hydrogen peroxide, dioxidane
Wasserstoffradius *m*/**Bohrscher** Bohr radius
Wasserstoffreduktion *f* hydrogen reduction
wasserstoffreich rich in hydrogen, hydrogen-rich
Wasserstoff-Sauerstoff-Brennstoffzelle *f* hydrogen-oxygen fuel cell
Wasserstoff-Sauerstoff-Schweißen *n* oxyhydrogen welding
Wasserstoffsäure *f* hydrogen acid, hydracid
Wasserstoffspektrum *n* hydrogen spectrum
Wasserstoffsprödigkeit *f* acid brittleness
Wasserstoffsulfid *n* hydrogen sulphide, monosulphane
Wasserstofftetrasulfid *n* hydrogen tetrasulphide, tetrasulphane
Wasserstofftrisulfid *n* hydrogen trisulphide, trisulphane
Wasserstoffüberspannung *f (el ch)* hydrogen overvoltage
wasserstoffübertragend hydrogen-transferring
Wasserstoffübertragung *f* hydrogen transfer
Wasserstoffverbindung *f* hydrogen compound
Wasserstoffverbrauch *m* hydrogen consumption
Wasserstoffvergaser *m (coal)* hydrogasifier, hydrogasification reactor
Wasserstoffvergasung *f (coal)* hydrogasification
1,5-Wasserstoff-Verschiebung *f* 1,5 sigmatropic shift of hydrogen
Wasserstoffversprödung *f* hydrogen embrittlement
Wasserstoffwechsel *m (biol)* water metabolism
Wasserstrahl *m* water jet
~/scharfer high-pressure water jet
Wasserstrahlentrinder *m (pap)* hydraulic (stream) barker
Wasserstrahlentrindung *f (pap)* hydraulic (stream) barking
Wasserstrahlpumpe *f (lab)* water [suction] pump, water aspirator; *(tech)* water[-operated] ejector
Wasserstrom *m* water stream, current of water
Wassertank *m* water tank

Wassertechnologe *m* water technologist
Wassertechnologie *f* water [treatment] technology
Wassertrieb *m (petrol)* water drive
Wassertrieblagerstätte *f (petrol)* water-drive field (reservoir)
Wassertröpfchen *n* water droplet
Wassertrübung *f* water turbidity
Wasserturbine *f (lab)* water turbine
Wasserturm *m* water tower
Wasserüberlauf *m* clear overflow *(of a thickener)*
Wasserüberschuß *m* excess water
Wasserüberstau *m*, **Wasserüberstauhöhe** *f (hyd, filtr)* head of water, liquid head
Wasserüberwachung *f* water survey
Wasseruhr *f* water meter
Wasserumlauf *m s.* Wasserkreislauf 1.
wasser- und aschefrei moisture-and-ash-free, maf
wasserundurchlässig impermeable to water, water-tight, waterproof • ~ **machen** *(text)* to waterproof
Wässerung *f* steep[ing], steepage, soaking; *(in running water:)* rinse, rinsing; *(phot)* [water] washing, wash, rinse, rinsing, soaking
Wässerungstank *m (phot)* washing tank, print washer
Wässerungszeit *f (phot)* washing period (time)
wasserunlöslich insoluble in water, water-insoluble
Wasserunlöslichkeit *f* water-insolubility
Wasseruntersuchung *f* water examination
Wasserverbrauch *m* water consumption (use, usage)
~ **der Bevölkerung** residential water use
~ **eines Betriebs** plant water use
Wasserverbraucher *m s.* Wassernutzer
wasserverdünnbar water-dilutable
Wasserverlust *m* water loss
~ **durch Oberflächenverdunstung und Transpiration** *(hyd)* evapotranspiration
~ **durch Verdunstung** *(hyd)* evaporation loss, water loss through evaporation
wasservernetzt *(rubber)* water-cross-linked
Wasserverschlechterung *f (hyd)* deterioration of water quality
Wasserverschluß *m* water seal • **mit** ~ water-sealed
Wasserverschmutzung *f* water pollution, *(esp relating to poisons or bacteria:)* water contamination
Wasserversorgung *f* water supply
~**/industrielle** industrial water supply
~**/kommunale** community water supply
~**/öffentliche** public (piped) water supply
~**/städtische** municipal water supply
Wasserversorgungsanlagen *fpl* **/öffentliche** public water utilities
Wasserversorgungsbrunnen *m* water[-supply] well
Wasserversorgungsleitung *f* water-supply line, water conduit
Wasserversorgungspumpe *f* water-supply pump
Wasserverteilung *f* water distribution
Wasserverteilungssystem *n* water distribution system
Wasserverunreinigung *f* 1. water pollutant (contaminant, impurity); 2. *s.* Wasserverschmutzung
Wasserverwendung *f* water utilization (usage, use)
Wasservorhang *m* water curtain
Wasservorkommen *npl* water resources
Wasservorrat *m* water supply
Wasservorwärmer *m* boiler feed preheater
Wasservulkanisation *f* hydraulic cure
Wasserwäsche *f* water wash[ing], *(relating to gases also)* water scrubbing
Wasserwerk *n* waterworks, water-treatment plant (works), water[-purification] plant
Wasserwerksschlamm *m* waterworks sludge, water treatment [plant] sludge
Wasserwerkstatt *f (tann)* beamhouse
Wasserwert *m* water equivalent *(of a calorimeter)*
Wasserwiederverwendung *f* water reuse
Wasserzähler *m* water meter
Wasserzeichen *n (pap)* watermark, w/m. • ~ **einarbeiten** to watermark
~**/echtes** genuine watermark
~ **mit Schattierungen** shaded mark
Wasserzeichenherstellung *f (pap)* watermarking
Wasserzeichenlinien *fpl (pap)* watermarked lines, water-lines
Wasserzeichenpapier *n* watermarked paper
Wasserzeichenwalze *f (pap)* [water]marking roll, dandy roll, watermarking dandy [roll]
Wasserzement *m* hydraulic cement
Wasser-Zement-Faktor *m*, **Wasser-Zement-Wert** *m* water-cement ratio
Wasserzersetzer *m* water electrolyzer
Wasserzersetzung *f* water electrolysis
Wasserzersetzungszelle *f* water electrolyzer
Wasserzusatz *m* water addition
wäßrig aqueous, watery
~**/nicht** non-aqueous
Watkin-Kennkörper *m (ceram)* Watkin [heat] recorder
Watkins-Faktor *m (phot)* Watkins [development] factor
Watson-Crick-Modell *n (bioch)* Watson-Crick model *(of DNA)*
Watte *f* wadding, *(esp med)* cotton wool
~ **in Lagen** batting
Wattebausch *m* wad of cotton [wool]
Wavellit *m (min)* wavellite *(a hydrous basic aluminium phosphate)*
wdfl. *s.* wasserdampfflüchtig
Weber-Zahl *f* Weber number *(fluid mechanics)*
Webkette *f (text)* warp
Wechsel *m* change[over], alteration, *(if periodically:)* alternation
~ **der Strömungsrichtung** change of direction of flow

Wechselbeanspruchung *f* alternating stress
Wechselbeziehung *f* correlation
Wechselbiegeversuch *m (plast)* alternating bending test
wechseln to change, *(if periodically:)* to alternate
Wechselsatz *m*/**spektroskopischer** alternation law of multiplicities
Wechselspannung *f*/**periodische** periodic voltage
~/**sinusförmige** alternating voltage
Wechselstrom *m* alternating current, a.c.
~/**periodischer** periodic current
Wechselstrom[licht]bogen *m* a.c. arc
Wechselstrompolarographie *f* a.c. polarography
Wechselstromwiderstand *m* impedance
Wechseltauchversuch *m* alternate immersion test *(a corrosion test)*
Wechselumsetzung *f* metathesis, double (mutual) decomposition
Wechselventil *n* reversing valve
Wechselvorlage *f (distil)* receiver changer
wechselwirken to interact
Wechselwirkung *f* interaction • **in ~ stehen** to interact • **in ~ treten** to interact
~/**chemische** chemical interaction
~ **durch Stapelkräfte** *(bioch)* stacking interaction
~/**gegenseitige** mutual interaction
~/**hydrophobe** hydrophobic interaction
~/**interionische** ionic (ion-ion) interaction, interionic action
~/**intermolekulare** [inter]molecular interaction
~/**intramolekulare** intramolecular interaction
~/**zwischenmolekulare** *s.* ~/intermolekulare
Wechselwirkungskraft *f* interaction force
~/**interionische** interionic force
Wechselwirkungspotential *n* interaction potential
Wechselzahl *f (bioch)* turnover number
Wechselzersetzung *f s.* Wechselumsetzung
Wedge-Ofen *m* Wedge [roasting] furnace, Wedge roaster (burner)
Weg *m* 1. path[way] *(of a reaction)*; 2. trajectory, path *(of a particle)*
wegabhängig dependent on the path
Wegabhängigkeit *f* path dependence
wegbrennen to burn off
wegdiffundieren to diffuse away
Wegdiffusion *f* diffusing-away
wegkochen to boil away
Weglänge *f (phys ch)* length of path
~/**freie** free path
~/**mittlere freie** mean free path
~/**optische** *(spectr)* optical pathlength, light path
weglösen to dissolve away; to disperse *(printing-ink adhesive from paper fibres)*
wegspülen to rinse away (off)
wegunabhängig independent of the path
Wegunabhängigkeit *f* path independence
wegwandern to migrate out *(as of ions)*
wegwaschen to wash away
Wegwerfpatrone *f (filtr)* throw-away cartridge
wehenerregend oxytocic
Wehenmittel *n (pharm)* uterotonic [agent], oxytocic [agent]
Wehr *n* weir
Wehrhöhe *f* weir level *(of a bubble-cap plate)*
weich soft • **~ machen** to soften *(e.g. water, plastics)*
Weichasphalt *m* soft asphalt
Weichblei *n* pure lead *(> 99,9 % Pb)*
Weichbraunkohle *f* soft brown coal
~/**schieferige** foliaceous brown coal
Weichdichtung *f* soft packing
Weiche *f* 1. *(tann)* soaking; 2. *(ferm)* steep tank, steeper
weichen to steep, to soak; to soak *(of material)*
Weichen *n* steep[ing], steepage, soaking *(act)*; soaking *(process)*
Weichferrit *m (ceram)* soft ferrite
Weichglas *n* soft [sealing] glass
weichglühen to soft-anneal, to spheroidize
Weichglühen *n* soft annealing, softening anneal, spheroidizing [anneal], spheroidization
Weichgriffigkeit *f (text)* soft handle
Weichgummi *m* soft rubber
Weichgummiwalze *f* soft rubber-covered roll
Weichharz *n* soft resin
Weichheitsgrad *m* degree of softness
Weichheitsprüfgerät *n* hardness tester (meter)
Weichheitszahl *f (plast)* softness index (number)
Weichholz *n* soft wood
weichkochen to cook soft *(cellulose)*
Weichkohle *f* soft coal
Weichlot *n* soft solder [alloy]
weichlöten to soft-solder
Weichlöten *n* soft soldering
weichmachen to soften, *(esp plast)* to plasticize, to flexibilize; *(tann)* to dress *(chamois leather)*
Weichmachen *n* softening, *(esp plast)* plasticization, flexibilization; *(tann)* dressing *(of chamois leather)*
~/**äußeres** external plasticization
~/**inneres** internal plasticization
Weichmacher *m* softener, softening agent, *(esp plast)* plasticizer, plasticizing agent, flexibilizer
~/**äußerer** external plasticizer
~/**innerer** internal plasticizer
~/**lösender** primary plasticizer
~/**nichtlösender** secondary plasticizer
~/**polymerer** polymeric (resinous) plasticizer
~/**polymerisierbarer** polymerizable plasticizer
~/**primärer** primary plasticizer
~/**sekundärer** secondary plasticizer
weichmacherfrei unplasticized
Weichmacheröl *n* plasticizing oil
Weichmacherwanderung *f* migration of plasticizer
Weichmacherwirksamkeit *f* plasticizer efficiency
Weichmachung *f s.* Weichmachen
Weichmasse *f (ceram)* soft paste, pâte tendre
Weichmüllerei *f* size reduction of soft materials

Weichpackung *f* s. Weichdichtung
Weichparaffin *n* soft paraffin [wax]
Weichpech *n* soft pitch
Weichporzellan *n* soft[-paste] porcelain
Weich-PVC *n* flexible (plasticized) PVC
Weichschaum[stoff] *m* flexible foam
Weichseide *f* souple silk
Weichspüler *m*, **Weichspülmittel** *n* *(text)* softening rinse, fabric softener
Weichstahl *m* soft (mild) steel
Weichstock *m* *(ferm)* steep tank, steeper
Weichwachs *n* soft wax
Weichwasser *n* 1. *(ferm)* steep[ing] water; *(tann)* soak liquor; 2. *(hyd)* soft[ened] water
Weichwasseraustritt *m* effluent water outlet *(ion exchange)*
Weichwassergüte *f* effluent [water] quality *(ion exchange)*
Weichwerden *n* softening
Weichzerkleinerung *f* size reduction of soft materials
Weihnachtsbaum *m* *(petrol)* Christmas tree *(at the well head for controlling oil and gas production)*
Weihrauch *m* [frank]incense, olibanum *(a gum resin from Boswellia specc.)*
Weihrauchöl *n* *(pharm)* frankincense (olibanum) oil
Wein *m* wine
~/alkoholisierter (gespriteter) fortified wine
~/trockener dry wine
Weinbrand *m* brandy
Weinbrandverschnitt *m* blended brandy
Weinessig *m* grape (wine) vinegar
Weinfachkunde *f* oenology
weinfachkundlich oenological
Weinfehler *m* *(ferm)* wine disorder
Weingeist *m* spirit[s] of wine *(aqueous ethyl alcohol)*
Weinhefe *f* wine yeast
Weinhold-Gefäß *n* Dewar [flask, vessel] *(for holding liquid gases)*
Weinkunde *f* oenology
weinkundlich oenological
Weinsäure *f* tartaric acid
~/gewöhnliche s. *(2R,3R)*-(+)-Weinsäure
~/linksdrehende s. *(2S,3S)*-(–)-Weinsäure
~/racemische s. *DL*-Weinsäure
~/rechtsdrehende s. *(2R,3R)*-(+)-Weinsäure
anti-**Weinsäure** *f* s. *(2R,3S)*-Weinsäure
d-**Weinsäure** *f* s. *(2R,3R)*-(+)-Weinsäure
D(–)-**Weinsäure** *f* s. *(2S,3S)*-(–)-Weinsäure
dl-**Weinsäure** *f* s. *DL*-Weinsäure
DL-**Weinsäure** *f* (±)-tartaric acid, racemic (inactive) tartaric acid
l-**Weinsäure** *f* s. *(2S,3S)*-(–)-Weinsäure
L(+)-**Weinsäure** *f* s. *(2R,3R)*-(+)-Weinsäure
meso-**Weinsäure** *f* s. *(2R,3S)*-Weinsäure
para-**Weinsäure** *f* s. *DL*-Weinsäure
(2R,3R)-**(+)-Weinsäure** *f* *(2R,3R)*-(+)-tartaric acid, L-tartaric acid, dextrotartaric acid, dextrorotatory tartaric acid
(2R,3S)-**Weinsäure** *f* *(2R,3S)*-tartaric acid, mesotartaric acid
(2S,3S)-**(–)-Weinsäure** *f* *(2S,3S)*-(–)-tartaric acid, D-tartaric acid, laevotartaric acid, laevorotatory tartaric acid
Weinsäurediamid *n* tartramide, diamide of tartaric acid
Weinsäuremonoamid *n* tartaric monoamide, tartramidic acid
Weinsäuremonoanilid *n* tartaric monoanilide, tartranilic acid
Weinschönungsmittel *n* wine-fining agent
Weinspiritus *m* s. Weingeist
Weinstein *m* tartar
~/gereinigter cream of tartar, potassium monotartrate
~/roher wine stone, crude cream of tartar, argol, argal
Weinsteinrahm *m* s. Weinstein/gereinigter
Weinsteinsalz *n* salt of tartar, potassium carbonate
Weinsteinsäure *f* s. *(2R,3R)*-(+)-Weinsäure
Weintraubenkernöl *n* grape-seed (raisin-seed) oil, grape-stone (wine-stones) oil
Weinwaage *f* oenometer
Weisel[zellen]futtersaft *m* *(pharm)* royal jelly, queen-bee's nutrient jelly
Weiß *n* white *(sensation or substance)*
~/Pariser Paris white *(finely ground calcium carbonate)*
Weißablauf *m* *(sugar)* wash syrup, second molasses
Weißanlaufen *n* blushing *(esp of nitrocellulose lacquer)*
Weißarsenik *n* white arsenic, arsenic trioxide
Weißätze *f* *(text)* white discharge
Weißätzung *f* *(text)* white discharge
Weiß-Bezirk *m* *(cryst)* Weiss [molecular magnetic] field, ferromagnetic domain
Weißbier *n* weiss beer
Weißblech *n* tinplate, tinned sheet iron
Weißblechbüchse *f*, **Weißblechdose** *f* tin [can], tinplate (tin-plated) can
Weißbleierz *n* *(min)* cerussite *(lead carbonate)*
weißbrennend white-burning
Weiße *f* s. Weißgehalt
Weißei *n* egg white, [egg] albumen
Weißenberg-Böhm-Verfahren *n* s. Weißenberg-Verfahren
Weissenberg-Effekt *m* Weissenberg effect *(with viscoelastic liquids)*
Weißenberg-Verfahren *n* *(cryst)* Weissenberg method (technique)
weißgar alum-tanned, alum-dressed, alumed
Weißgehalt *m* degree of white[ness], *(pap also)* brightness [level]
~ des Zellstoffs pulp brightness
~ vor der Bleiche initial brightness
Weißgehaltserhöhung *f* *(pap)* increase in brightness

weißgerben to taw
Weißgerber-Degras *m (tann)* sod oil *(a by-product of the chamois tannage)*
Weißgerberei *f*, **Weißgerbung** *f* tawing, alum tannage
Weißglas *n* white flint
weißglühen to incandesce
weißglühend incandescent, white-hot
Weißglut *f* incandescence, incandescency, white heat, W.H. • **auf (bis zur)** ~ erhitzen to incandesce
Weißgrad *m s.* Weißgehalt
Weißguß *m* white cast iron
Weißkalk *m (build)* white lime, fat (rich) lime *(with CaO content of about 90 %)*; *(dye)* pyrolignite of lime
Weißkalkäscher *m (tann)* straight lime liquor, fresh lime
Weißlauge *f (pap)* white (fresh cooking) liquor
Weißlaugenbehälter *m (pap)* white-liquor storage tank
Weißleder *n* white leather
Weißmacher *m* [detergent] brightener, whitening agent
Weißmaterial *n* limestone *(in the manufacture of calcium carbide)*
Weißmetall *n* white metal *(1. any of several bearing metals; 2. copper matte having its iron removed)*
Weißnickelkies *m (min)* white nickel, chloanthite, nickel skutterudite *(nickel arsenide)*
Weißöl *n* [petroleum] white oil, white mineral (petroleum) oil
~/technisches technical white oil
Weißprodukt *n (petrol)* white product
Weißruß *m* white carbon [black]
Weißsirup *m (sugar)* wash syrup, second molasses
Weißtöner *m* optical brightener (bleach), fluorescent brightener, optical brigthening (whitening, bleaching) agent
Weißtünche *f* whitewash
Weißware *f (ceram)* whiteware
Weißwein *m* white wine
Weißwerden *n* whitening, *(esp of nitrocellulose lacquer:)* blushing
Weißzucker *m* white sugar
Weißzuckervakuumapparat *m* white pan
weiten to stretch
Weitenverteilung *f* size distribution *(as of pores)*
Weiternitrierung *f* further nitration
weiterreagieren to react further, to undergo further reaction
Weiterreaktion *f* further reaction
Weiterreißen *n (pap)* further tearing
Weiterreißfestigkeit *f s.* Weiterreißwiderstand
Weiterreißfestigkeitsprüfung *f s.* Weiterreißversuch
Weiterreißversuch *m* tear[ing] test
Weiterreißwiderstand *m* tear resistance (strength), resistance to further tearing, *(tann also)* tongue tear strength
weitertragen to propagate *(e.g. a reaction)*
Weitertragen *n* propagation *(as of a reaction)*
Weiterverarbeitung *f* further processing
Weithalsartikel *mpl (glass)* wide-mouth ware
Weithalsflasche *f* wide-mouth (wide-neck) bottle
weithalsig wide-mouth[ed], wide-neck[ed]
Weithalskolben *m* wide-mouth (wide-neck) flask
Weithalsrundkolben *m* round-bottom wide-mouth flask
weitlumig coarse-grained *(wood)*
weitmaschig coarse-mesh[ed]
Weitwegkopplung *f (phys ch)* long-range coupling (interaction)
Weitwinkelaufnahme *f (cryst)* wide-angle X-ray pattern
Weizenkeimöl *n* wheat germ oil
Weizenmehl *n* wheat flour, *(if coarse:)* wheat meal
Weizenstärke *f* wheat starch
Weldon-Verfahren *n* Weldon [chlorine] process
Wellasbest *m* corrugated asbestos
Welle *f* 1. wave; 2. *(tech)* shaft
~/polarographische polarographic wave
~/zentrale *(tech)* central shaft
Wellenausbreitung *f* wave propagation
Wellenberg *m* wave crest
Wellenbewegung *f* wave motion
Wellenbildung *f* casing (outer layer) effect *(a defect in glass)*
Wellenbrecher *m* flow spoiler
Wellendichtring *m* oil seal ring
Welleneigenschaft *f* wave property
Wellenfunktion *f* wave function
~/atomare atomic wave function
~ des Elektrons electronic wave function
~/molekulare molecular wave function
~/molekulare elektronische molecular electronic wave function
~/selbstkonsistente self-consistent wave function
Wellengleichung *f* wave equation
~/Schrödingersche Schrödinger [wave] equation
Wellengruppe *f* wave packet
Wellenkatode *f* angular cathode *(in a Billiter cell)*
Wellenlänge *f* wavelength
Wellenlängenbereich *m* wavelength range
Wellenlängenskale *f* wavelength scale
Wellenmechanik *f* wave mechanics
Wellennatur *f* wave nature
Wellenpaket *n* wave packet
Wellental *n* wave trough; *(spectr)* valley
Wellentheorie *f* wave theory
Wellenvektor *m* wave vector
Wellenzahl *f* wave number
Wellenzahlvektor *m* wave vector
Wellkarton *m* corrugated cardboard
Wellman-Galusha-Generator *m (coal)* Wellman-Galusha producer
Wellmittel *n***/chemisches** *(cosmet)* cold-permanent-waving preparation, cold-permanent-wave preparation

Wellpapier *n s.* Wellpappenpapier
Wellpappe *f* corrugated (corrugating) board, cellular board
Wellpappenpapier *n* corrugated (corrugating) paper
Wellplatte *f (plast)* corrugated sheet
Wellrohr *n* corrugated tube (pipe)
Wellrohr[dehnungs]ausgleicher *m*, **Wellrohrkompensator** *m* corrugated (bellows-type) expansion joint
Wemco-Trommel[sink]scheider *m* Wemco separator
Wendefilz *m (pap)* reverse press felt
Wendel *f (distil)* helix
Wendelrutsche *f* spiral chute
Wendelscheider *m* spiral separator
Wendepflug *m* turnover plough *(in margarine making)*
Wendepresse *f (pap)* reverse press
Wendepunkt *m* inflection point *(of a curve)*
Wendewalze *f (pap)* hitch roll
werfen/sich to warp
Werfen *n* warpage, warping
Werg *n* tow, oakum
Werkblei *n* crude (pig) lead
Werkdruckpapier *n* book[-printing] paper, *(Am also)* text paper
Werksabwasser *n* plant waste water, plant (works, factory) effluent
Werkschemiker *m* industrial chemist
Werkskanalisation *f (hyd)* plant sewer
Werkstatt *f*/**galvanische** [electro]plating shop
Werkstoff *m* material, matter
~/**ablativer** ablative material
~/**abrasiver** abrasive
~ **auf Hartmetallbasis** cemented carbide material
~ **aus Kohlenstoff** carbon material
~ **für die Tieftemperaturtechnik** low-temperature material
~/**geschichteter** laminated material (plastic), laminate
~/**glasiger** glassy material
~/**halbleitender** semiconducting material
~/**hochtemperaturbeständiger** high-temperature material
~/**keramischer** ceramic material
~/**keramometallischer** *s.* ~/metallkeramischer
~/**metallischer** metallic material
~/**metallkeramischer (mischkeramischer)** cermet, ceramal, ceramel, ceramet
~/**nichtmetallischer** non-metallic material
~/**poriger (poröser)** porous material
~/**warmfester** high-temperature material
Werkstoffkunde *f* materials science
Werkstoffkundler *m* materials scientist
Werkstoffprüfung *f* materials testing
Werkstofftechnik *f* materials technology
Werkstoffwissenschaft *f* materials science
Werkstrom *m* working (operating) current
Werkzeug *n* 1. *(plast)* mould, form; 2. tool
~/**geschlossenes** closed mould
~ **mit Heizkanälen** cored mould
~/**offenes** open mould
~/**zusammengesetztes** composite (split) mould
Werkzeugaufnahmegestell *n (plast)* spider *(in centrifugal casting)*
Werkzeughälfte *f (plast)* mould half
~/**bewegliche** moving mould half
~/**feststehende** stationary mould half
Werkzeugharz *n (plast)* tooling resin
Werkzeughohlraum *m (plast)* mould cavity
Werkzeugkonstruktion *f (plast)* mould design
Werkzeugschließdruck *m (plast)* mould-locking pressure
Werkzeugschließsystem *n (plast)* [mould-]clamping mechanism
Werkzeugschließzeit *f (plast)* mould-closing time
Werkzeugschluß *m (plast)* mould closing
Werkzeugschwindmaß *n (plast)* mould shrinkage
Werkzeugstahl *m* tool steel
Werkzeugtrennmittel *n (plast)* release agent
Werkzeugzuhaltekraft *f (plast)* mould-clamping force
Wermutöl *n* absinth, wormwood oil
Werner-Komplex *m* Werner complex *(chemical-bond theory)*
Werner-Pfleiderer-Kneter *m* Werner-Pfleiderer mixer
Wert *m* value • **einen konstanten ~ aufweisen** to show a constant reading • **etwas über dem theoretischen ~** in slight excess of theory, slightly over the theoretical • **etwas unter dem theoretischen ~** slightly short of theory
~/**absoluter** absolute value
~/**abweichender** *(anal)* outlier, maverick
~/**experimenteller** experimental value
~/**kalorischer** *(food)* calorific value, c.v.
~/**quasistationärer** steady-state value
~/**vorgegebener** preset value
ν-Wert *m* Abbe number (value), ν-value, constringence *(reciprocal relative dispersion)*
wertarm low-grade
Wertbestimmung *f*/**biologische** biological assay, bioassay
Wertigkeit *f* valence, valency
~/**elektrochemische** electrochemical valence, electrovalence
~/**koordinative** coordination (covalence) number, coordination, ligancy
~/**kovalente** covalence, covalency
~/**maximale** maximum valence
~/**stöchiometrische** stoichiometric valence
Wertigkeitsänderung *f* valence change
Wertigkeitsbezeichnung *f* valence state symbol
~/**Stocksche** Stock notation
Wertigkeitsstufe *f* valence state
Wertigkeitstheorie *f* theory of valence, valence theory

Wertigkeitswechsel *m* valence change
Wertminderung *f* deterioration
Wertpapierdruck *m* bond printing
Wertpapierdruckfarbe *f* bond ink
Wertsteigerung *f* upgrading
Wertstoff *m* valuable product, product of value, useful material
Wertstoffe *mpl* values
Wertstoffrückgewinnung *f* recovery (reclaim) of values (useful material)
wesentlich essential
West-Kühler *m (distil)* West-type condenser
Weston-Element *n* Weston cell, Weston normal (standard) cell, Weston saturated cadmium cell
~/ungesättigtes unsaturated Weston cell
Weston-Normalelement *n s.* Weston-Element
Weston-Standardelement *n* unsaturated Weston cell
Weston-Zahl *f (phot)* Weston figure
Wetherill-Ofen *m (met)* Wetherill furnace
Wetter *pl***/böse** *(mine)* damp[s] *(noxious gas)*
~/matte choke damp, dead air *(stifling gas), (esp if consisting of carbon dioxide also)* black damp
~/schlagende firedamp
~/stickende *s.* ~/matte
wetterbeständig weather-resistant; *(text)* weatherproof
Wetterbeständigkeit *f* weather[ing] resistance, resistance to weathering, weatherability; *(text)* weatherproofness
Wetterbeständigkeitsprüfgerät *n* weatherometer
wetterfest *s.* wetterbeständig
wettergeschützt weather-protected, weatherproof *(apparatus)*
wettersicher *s.* 1. wetterbeständig; 2. wettergeschützt
Wettersprengstoff *m (mine)* safety explosive
wf *s.* wasserfrei
Wheatstone-Brücke *f* Wheatstone bridge
Wheeler-Mühle *f* Wheeler mill *(a jet mill)*
Wheland-Intermediat *n (org ch)* Wheland intermediate, arenium σ-adduct
Whirlpool *m (biot)* whirlpool separator
Whisker *m* [crystal] whisker
Whisky *m* whisky, whiskey
White-Desaminierung *f*, **White-Reaktion** *f* White deamination (reaction)
Wichte *f* specific weight *(the weight of a substance per unit volume)*
Wickel *m (text)* lap
Wickelhülse *f (pap)* core, centre
Wickelkörper *m (text)* package
Wickeltrommel *f (rubber)* casemaking drum, [tyre-]building drum
Widdren *n* widdrene, thujopsene *(a tricyclic sesquiterpene)*
Widdrol *n* widdrol *(a sesquiterpene alcohol)*
widerlich disagreeable, obnoxious, repulsive, vile *(odour)*
Widerstand *m* 1. resistance; 2. resistor
~/aerodynamischer drag [force]
~/elektrischer 1. electrical resistance; 2. resistor
~ gegen die Trägheitskräfte form drag *(fluid mechanics)*
~ gegen Einreißen tear-initiation strength
~ gegen Rißwachstum resistance to crack growth
~ gegen Schnittwachstum resistance to cut growth
~ gegen Temperaturwechsel thermal-shock resistance
~/hydrodynamischer fluid friction, drag [force]
~/komplexer *(anal)* impedance
~/photoelektrischer photoconductive cell, photoresistor
~/spezifischer specific resistance, resistivity
~/thermischer thermal resistance
Widerstandsabschwächer *m* antiresistant *(pest control)*
Widerstandsbeheizung *f***[/elektrische]** resistance heating
Widerstandsbeiwert *m* power number *(on agitating)*
Widerstandsbrücke *f***[/elektrische]** resistance bridge
Widerstandserhitzung *f***[/elektrische]** resistance heating
widerstandsfähig resistant, stable, fast
Widerstandsfähigkeit *f* resistance, stability, fastness, *(for compounds s. a. under* Beständigkeit*)*
~ bei hohen Temperaturen stability at high temperatures
~ gegen Bruch resistance to breakage
~ gegen Ritzen resistance to scratching
~ gegen Schimmel mildew resistance
~ gegen Verschlackung resistance to slagging
Widerstandsheizelement *n*, **Widerstandsheizkörper** *m* resistance (resistive) heater
Widerstandsheizung *f***[/elektrische]** resistance heating
Widerstandskapazität *f* cell constant *(of a conductance cell)*
Widerstandskurve *f* resistivity curve
Widerstandsmaterial *n* resistor material
Widerstandsofen *m***[/elektrischer]** resistance (resistance-heated, resistor) furnace
Widerstandsphotozelle *f* photoconductive cell, photoresistor
Widerstandspolarisation *f* ohmic polarization (overpotential, drop), iR drop
Widerstandsschweißen *n* resistance welding
Widerstandsthermometer *n* resistance thermometer
Widerstandsüberspannung *f s.* Widerstandspolarisation
Widerstandswerkstoff *m* resistor material
Widerstandswert *m* resistance
Widerstandswicklung *f* resistance coil

Widerstandszahl *f* drag coefficient *(fluid mechanics)*
Widerstandszelle *f s.* Widerstandsphotozelle
Widmer-Kolonne *f (distil)* Widmer spiral column
wiederanreichern to re-enrich
wiederaufarbeiten to reprocess, to rework, to reclaim
wiederaufbereiten to reprocess *(e.g. nuclear fuel)*; to remanufacture *(e.g. waste paper)*
Wiederaufbereitung *f* reprocessing *(as of nuclear fuel)*; remanufacture *(as of waste paper)*
~/chemische *(nucl)* chemical reprocessing
Wiederaufbereitungsanlage *f* reprocessing plant, *(nucl also)* fuel-reprocessing plant
wiederaufkohlen *(met)* to recarburize
Wiederaufkohlung *f (met)* recarburization
Wiederaufkohlungsmittel *n (met)* recarburizing agent, recarburizer
wiederauflösen to redissolve
Wiederauflösung *f* redissolution
wiederaufschwemmen to repulp, to reslurry
Wiederaufziehen *n (text)* redeposition *(of soil)*
wiederausstrahlen to reradiate, to re-emit
Wiederausstrahlung *f* reradiation, re-emission
wiederbeleben to revivify, to regenerate *(a sorbent or a catalyst)*
Wiederbelebung *f* revivification, regeneration *(of a sorbent or a catalyst)*
Wiederbelebungsmittel *n* regenerant *(for sorbents)*
Wiederbelüftung *f (hyd)* reaeration
wiederbenutzbar reusable
Wiederbenutzung *f* reuse
Wiedereinfangen *n* recapture *(as of ions)*
Wiedereintauchen *n* resubmergence *(of the filter drum)*
Wiederfindungsrate *f (anal)* percentage recovery
Wiedergabetreue *f* fidelity *(degree to which a system accurately reproduces impressed characteristics)*
wiedergeben to reproduce, to represent, *(phot also)* to render
Wiedergebrauch *m* reuse
wiedergewinnbar recoverable, reclaimable
wiedergewinnen to recover, to reclaim
Wiedergewinnung *f* recovery, reclaim[ing]
Wiedergewinnungsanlage *f* recovery plant
wiederherstellen to re-establish, to restore
~/das Gleichgewicht to re-establish equilibrium
Wiederherstellung *f* re-establishment, restoration
~ des Gleichgewichts re-equilibration
wiederholbar repeatable *(experiment)*
Wiederholbarkeit *f* repeatability *(of an experiment)*
Wiederholstreubereich *m* repeatability *(statistics)*
Wiederholung *f* replicate, replication *(statistics)*
Wiederholungseinheit *f* repeat[ing] unit *(as in a macromolecule)*
Wiederholungslänge *f (cryst)* repeat distance
wiederverarbeiten to reprocess
Wiederverarbeitung *f* reprocessing
wiedervereinigen *(ch)* to recombine
~/sich to recombine
Wiedervereinigung *f (ch)* recombination
Wiedervereinigungsgeschwindigkeit *f* recombination rate (velocity)
Wiederverfestigung *f* resolidification
Wiederverkeimung *f (hyd)* [bacterial] aftergrowth
wiederverwendbar reusable
wiederverwenden to reuse
Wiederverwendung *f* reuse
wiegen to weigh
Wieland-Gumlich-Aldehyd *m* Wieland-Gumlich aldehyde, caracurine-VII
Wien-Effekt *m (el ch)* Wien effect
Wien-Verschiebungsgesetz *n* Wien displacement law
Wiesenkalk *m*, **Wiesenmergel** *m (soil)* bog lime
WIG-Schweißen *n s.* Wolframinertgasschweißen
Wijs-Lösung *f* Wijs [iodine monochloride] solution *(for determining the iodine number of fats)*
Wildcat-Bohrung *f (petrol)* wildcat, exploration drilling
Wildhefe *f* wild yeast
Wildkautschuk *m* wild rubber
Wildleder *n* suede leather
Wildseide *f* wild silk *(e.g. tussah silk)*
Wildstamm *m (biot)* wild strain *(of microorganisms)*
Wildverbißschutzmittel *n* game deterrent
Wilfley-Herd *m (min tech)* Wilfley table
Williams-Abriebprüfer *m (rubber)* Williams abrader, DuPont-Grasselli-Williams machine
Williams-Einheit *f (text)* Williams unit *(a roller vat)*
Williams-Landel-Ferry-Gleichung *f (plast)* Williams-Landel-Ferry equation, WLF equation
Williamson-Ofen *m* Williamson kiln *(a tunnel kiln)*
Williamson-Synthese *f* Williamson [ether] synthesis
Williams-Plastometer *n (rubber)* Williams plastometer
Williams-Prüfer *m s.* Williams-Abriebprüfer
Willstätter-Nagel *m* Willstätter nail *(filter aid)*
Wilson-Aufnahme *f (nucl)* cloud-chamber photograph
Wilson-Kammer *f (nucl)* cloud (Wilson) chamber, [Wilson] cloud-track apparatus
Wind *m* 1. wind; 2. *(met)* [air] blast
~/elektrischer electric (ionic) wind
~/heißer *(met)* hot[-air] blast
~/kalter *(met)* cold[-air] blast
Winddüse *f s.* Windform
winden *(text)* to reel [up]
Winderhitzer *m (met)* hot-blast stove, air-blast (blast-furnace) stove, air heater
Windform *f (met)* air-blast tuyère
Windformebene *f (met)* tuyère level
Windformenzone *f (met)* tuyère zone
Windformkühlkasten *m (met)* tuyère cooler
windfrischen *(met)* to bessemerize, to air-refine, to convert

Windfrischen *n (met)* bessemerizing, air refining
Windfrischkonverter *m (met)* Bessemer converter
Windfrischstahl *m (met)* Bessemer (converter) steel
Windfrischverfahren *n (met)* Bessemer (converter) process
~/basisches basic Bessemer (converter) process, Thomas[-Gilchrist] process
~/saures acid Bessemer (converter) process
Windgebläse *n* air blower
windgesichtet air-floated
Windkasten *m* wind box
Windkessel *m* air vessel (receiver, chamber), surge chamber
Windleitung *f (met)* [air-]blast main
Windmantel *m (met)* wind belt *(of a cupola)*
Windmesser *m* anemometer
Windröstverfahren *n* **[nach Huntington und Heberlein]** *(met)* Huntington-Heberlein process
Windsichten *n s.* Sichten
Windsichter *m s.* Sichter
Windtemperatur *f (met)* [air-]blast temperature
Windung *f (tech, bioch)* turn *(of a screw or an alpha helix)*
Windzufuhr *f* air supply
Winkel *m***/Braggscher** *(cryst)* Bragg angle
~/Brewsterscher Brewster (polarizing) angle
~ zwischen benachbarten Elektronenpaaren interpair angle
Winkelbeschleunigung *f* angular acceleration
Winkeldispersion *f (spectr)* angular dispersion
Winkelfrequenz *f* angular frequency
Winkelgeschwindigkeit *f* angular velocity
Winkelkopf *m* [fixed-]angle head, [fixed-]angle rotor, angular rotor *(of a centrifuge)*
Winkelmesser *m (cryst)* goniometer
Winkelpresse *f* angle press
Winkelrohr *n s.* Winkelstück
Winkelrotor *m s.* Winkelkopf
Winkelspannung *f* angle strain
Winkelstück *n (tech)* elbow [fitting]; *(lab)* angle connector, bent-tube connection, bent tube, elbow
Winkelthermometer *n* angle thermometer
Winkelverteilung *f* angular distribution
Winkler-Gaserzeuger *m s.* Winkler-Generator
Winkler-Gaserzeugung *f* fluidized-bed gasification
Winkler-Generator *m* Winkler generator *(a fluidized-bed gasifier)*
Winkler-Generatorverfahren *n s.* Winkler-Vergasungsverfahren
Winkler-Koch-Spaltverfahren *n (petrol)* Winkler-Koch process
Winkler-Vergasungsverfahren *n* Winkler process *(for gasifying lignite in a fluidized bed)*
Wintergrünöl *n* oil of wintergreen *(from Gaultheria procumbens L.)*
~/künstliches artificial oil of wintergreen, methyl salicylate
Winterisation *f s.* Winterung
wintern 1. to winterize, to demargarinate, to destearinate, to destearinize *(oils)*; 2. *(ceram)* to winter, to weather
Winterspritzmittel *n (agric)* dormant spray, winter wash
~/öliges dormant oil [spray]
Winterspritzung *f (agric)* dormant spray[ing], dormant winter spray[ing]
Winterung *f* winterization, demargarination, destearinization *(of oils)*
Wipprahmen *m (tann)* rocker [frame] *(for moving pelts in suspender pits)*
Wirbel *m* eddy, whirl, swirl, *(if large:)* vortex
Wirbelabscheider *m* cyclone collector (separator), cyclone
Wirbelbett *n* fluid[ized] bed *(for compounds s. a. under* Wirbelschicht*)*
~ aus Quarzsand *(hyd)* fluidized sand bed
Wirbelbett... *s. a.* Wirbelschicht...
Wirbelbettkatalysator *m* fluid[ized] catalyst, fluid-bed catalyst
Wirbelbett-Reaktivierungsanlage *f (hyd)* fluid-bed reactivation plant
Wirbelbewegung *f* vortex motion
Wirbelbildung *f* eddy formation
Wirbelbrenner *m* vortex burner
Wirbeldiffusion *f* eddy (turbulent) diffusion
Wirbeldiffusionskoeffizient *m* eddy diffusivity
Wirbeldispersion *f* eddy dispersion
Wirbelfeuerung *f* cyclone firing
Wirbelfließverfahren *n* disperse-phase (lean-phase) fluidization
Wirbelgas *n* fluidizing (fluidization) gas
Wirbelgeschwindigkeit *f* fluidization (fluidizing) velocity *(in a fluidized bed)*
~/minimale *s.* Wirbelpunktgeschwindigkeit
wirbelig turbulent
Wirbelkammer *f* vortex (cyclone) chamber *(of a suspension gasifier)*
Wirbelkammervergaser *m (coal)* vortex (cyclone) gasifier
Wirbelpumpe *f* regenerative pump
Wirbelpunkt *m* incipient fluidization point
Wirbelpunktgeschwindigkeit *f* minimum fluidization velocity, velocity at incipient fluidization
Wirbelreiniger *m s.* Wirbelsichter
Wirbelscheider *m s.* Wirbelabscheider
Wirbelschicht *f* fluid[ized] bed
~/brodelnde bubbling bed
~/kochende boiling bed
~/stoßende slugging bed
Wirbelschichtadsorber *m* fluid[ized]-bed adsorber
Wirbelschichtadsorption *f* fluidized adsorption
Wirbelschichtgenerator *m (coal)* fluid[ized]-bed gasifier
Wirbelschichtkracken *n***/katalytisches** fluid catalytic cracking, FCC
Wirbelschichtofen *m (hyd)* fluid[ized-bed] incinerator

Wirbelschichtreaktor *m* fluid[ized]-bed reactor; *(biot)* fluid[ized]-bed fermenter (bioreactor)
~/[heterogen-]katalytischer fluid[ized]-bed catalytic reactor
Wirbelschichtröstofen *m* fluid-bed roaster (roasting furnace), fluidized[-bed] roaster
Wirbelschichttechnik *f* fluid[ized]-bed technology, fluid[ized]-bed technique, fluidized[-solid] technique
Wirbelschichttrockner *m* fluid[ized]-bed combustion, fluid-bed burning
Wirbelschichtverfahren *n* fluid[-bed] process, fluidized process
Wirbelschichtvergaser *m (coal)* fluid[ized]-bed gasifier
Wirbelschichtvergasung *f (coal)* fluid[ized]-bed gasification
Wirbelschleuder *f s.* Wirbelsichter
Wirbelsichter *m* centrifugal cleaner, *(Am)* centrifiner
Wirbelsinterbeschichten *n*, **Wirbelsintern** *n (plast)* fluid[ized]-bed coating
Wirbelstraße *f* vortex street
Wirbelstrombrenner *m* vortex burner
Wirbelstromheizung *f* eddy current heating
Wirbelströmung *f* eddy current, turbulent (sinuous) flow
Wirbelsucher *m* vortex finder
Wirbeltrockner *m* vortex dryer
Wirbelzellenwärmeaustauscher *m* plate-fin heat exchanger
Wirkdosis *f s.* Wirkungsdosis
Wirkdruck *m* differential pressure (head)
Wirkdruck-Durchfluß[mengen]messer *m*, **Wirkdruck-Mengenstrommesser** *m* head flowmeter
Wirkdruckmesser *m* differential-pressure meter
wirken to act
~/als Kristallisationskeim to form a nucleus, to nucleate
~/antifungal to have antifungal activity
~/füllend *(coat)* to body
~/fungizid *s.* -/antifungal
wirkend/langsam slow-acting
~/rasch quick-acting
~/schleichend *(tox)* slow-acting
~/schnell quick-acting
~/trypynozid *(pharm)* trypanocidal *(tending or used to destroy trypanosomes)*
Wirkgruppe *f* active group, coenzyme, prosthetic group, agon
Wirkkraft *f (pharm)* potency
Wirkprinzip *n* mode of action
Wirkquerschnitt *m s.* Wirkungsquerschnitt
wirksam active *(substance, component)*; efficient, effective *(method)*; *(with emphasis:)* potent *(agent, method)*
~/anodisch galvanic, sacrificial *(coating)*
Wirksamkeit *f* activity *(of a substance, component)*; efficiency *(of a method)*
~/antibakterielle antibacterial activity
~/antibiotische antibiotic activity
~/biologische biological activity
~/fungizide fungicidal activity, fungitoxicity
~/herbizide herbicidal activity
~/insektizide insecticidal activity
~/katalytische catalytic activity
~/relative biologische relative biological effectiveness, RBE *(radiation biology)*
~/systemische systemic activity *(of a pesticide)*
~/therapeutische therapeutical activity
Wirksamkeitsverlust *m* loss of activity
Wirkstoff *m* [active] agent, active substance (material), *(biol also)* ergone, *(if part of a mixture:)* active ingredient (component, constituent)
~/antibakterieller bactericide
~/antibiotischer antibiotic
~/antimikrobieller antimicrobial agent
~/chemischer chemical agent
~/giftiger toxicant, toxic [substance]
~/therapeutischer therapeutic agent
Wirkstoffgehalt *m* content of active ingredient (component)
Wirkstoffkonzentration *f* concentration of active ingredient (component)
Wirkstoffnebel *m* aerosol
Wirkstoffproduktion *f s.* Stoffproduktion
Wirkstoffzubereitung *f* formulation [of the active ingredient]
~ mit aktivierendem Zusatz activated formulation *(crop protection)*
Wirksubstanz *f s.* Wirkstoff
Wirkung *f* 1. action; 2. effect *(result)*
~/adstringierende *(pharm)* stypticity
~/anästhe[ti]sierende anaesthetic action
~/antagonistische antagonistic action
~/aussalzende salting-out action
~/betäubende anaesthetic action
~/desinfizierende germicidal action
~/dirigierende directive influence *(as on substituents)*
~/dispergierende dispersing (dispersant) action
~/dominierende overriding influence
~/erweichende *(rubber)* peptizing action
~/farberhöhende hypsochromic action
~ fremdioniger Zusätze diverse ion effect
~/fungizide fungicidal action
~/geschwulsterregende tumorigenicity
~ gleichioniger Zusätze common-ion effect
~/heilende curative action
~/herbizide herbicidal action
~/insektizide insecticidal action
~/katalytische catalytic action
~/keimtötende germicidal action
~/klopfhemmende antiknock (antidetonating) action
~/konservierende preservative action
~/korrodierende corrosiveness, corrosivity
~/krebserregende carcinogenicity

~/kumulative cumulative action
~/lösungsvermittelnde solubilizing action
~/netzende wetting action
~/nitrierende *(met)* nitriding action
~/oxidierende oxidizing action
~/reduzierende reducing action
~/reinigende detergent action
~/selektive selectivity
~/synergistische synergistic action
~/toxische toxic action
~/verstärkende strengthening action, *(rubber also)* reinforcing action
~/zementierende *(met)* carburizing action
Wirkungsbreite *f* spectrum of activity *(as of pesticides)* • **mit großer** ~ broad-spectrum, broad-scale
~/umfassende all-round efficiency
Wirkungsdauer *f* period (duration) of action
Wirkungsdosis *f (tox, pharm)* effective dose
~/minimale *(tox)* activation threshold
Wirkungsgrad *m* 1. *(ch)* strength *(of a reagent)*; 2. *(tech)* efficiency [factor], efficiency of action • **mit hohem** ~ *(tech)* efficient
~ **bei Stoß-Druck-Beanspruchung/elastischer** *(rubber)* rebound [elasticity], rebound (impact) resilience
~/Carnotscher *(phys ch)* Carnot efficiency
~ **des biologischen Abbaus** *(hyd)* biological efficiency
~ **einer Abwasserbehandlungsanlage** *(hyd)* plant efficiency
~/elastischer *(rubber)* resilience, resiliency
~/hydraulischer hydraulic efficiency
~/katalytischer catalytic efficiency
~/maximaler maximum efficiency
~/thermischer thermal efficiency
~/thermodynamischer thermodynamic efficiency
~/volumetrischer volumetric efficiency *(of pumps)*
wirkungslos ineffective
Wirkungsmechanismus *m* mechanism of action
Wirkungsprodukt *n***/Habersches** *(tox)* ct product *(product of concentration and survival time)*
Wirkungsquantum *n***/Plancksches** Planck [action] constant, [Planck] quantum of action
Wirkungsquerschnitt *m (anal)* activation cross section; *(nucl)* cross-section target area, [nuclear] cross section
Wirkungsspektrum *n* spectrum of activity *(as of pesticides)* • **mit breitem** ~ broad-spectrum, broad-scale
~/antimikrobielles antimicrobial spectrum *(of an antibiotic)*
wirkungsspezifisch reaction-specific *(enzyme)*
Wirkungsspezifität *f* reaction specificity *(of an enzyme)*
Wirkungsstärke *f (pharm)* strength, potency
Wirkungssteigerung *f* fortification
Wirkungsweise *f* mode (mechanism) of action
Wirt *m* host [component, compound] *(of an inclusion compound)*
Wirtschaftsabwasser *n (hyd)* sanitary waste water *(from industrial plants)*
Wirtselement *n (min, geoch)* host element
Wirtsgestein *n* host rock
Wirtsgitter *n* host [crystal] lattice
Wirtskomponente *f* host [component] *(of an inclusion compound)*
Wirtsmolekül *n* host molecule
Wirtsorganismus *m (biot)* host [micro]organism
Wirtsverbindung *f* host compound
Wirtszelle *f (bioch)* host cell
Wismut *n s.* Bismut
Wismut... *s.* Bismut... *for chemical compounds*
Wismutbronze *f* bismuth bronze
Wismuterz *n* bismuth ore
Wismutglanz *m (min)* bismuth glance, bismuthin[it]e *(bismuth(III) sulphide)*
Wismutgold *n (min)* bismuth gold, maldonite *(a natural alloy)*
Wismutocker *m (min)* bismuth ochre
Wismutspat *m (min)* bismutite, *(deprecated:)* bismuth spar *(bismuth carbonate oxide)*
Wismutweiß *n* bismuth (pearl, Spanish) white, cosmetic bismuth *(consisting of bismuth nitrate oxide or bismuth chloride oxide)*
Wiswesser-Notation *f (nomencl)* Wiswesser [line] notation
Wiswesser-Notationssystem *n (nomencl)* Wiswesser [notation] system
Witherit *m (min)* witherite *(barium carbonate)*
witterungsbeständig *s.* wetterbeständig
Wittig-Reaktion *f* Wittig reaction *(between alkylidene phosphoranes and carbonyl compounds)*
Wittig-Umlagerung *f* Wittig [ether] rearrangement
W.K. *s.* Wasserkapazität
WLD *s.* Wärmeleitfähigkeitsdetektor
WLF-Gleichung *f s.* Williams-Landel-Ferry-Gleichung
Wobblebase *f (bioch)* wobble base
Wobblehypothese *f (bioch)* wobble hypothesis
Wohl-Abbau *m* Wohl degradation *(of sugars)*
wohldefiniert well-defined *(compound)*
wohlgeordnet well-ordered *(structure)*
Wohlgeruch *m* fragrance, aroma, scent, odour
Wohlgeschmack *m* tastiness, palatability
wohlriechend fragrant, aromatic, flavourful
wohlschmeckend tasty, palatable, aromatic, flavourful
Wohl-Ziegler-Reaktion *f* Wohl-Ziegler reaction *(for brominating alkenes)*
Wolff-Kishner-Reaktion *f (org ch)* Wolff-Kishner reaction (reduction)
Wolff-Umlagerung *f* Wolff rearrangement *(of diazoketones into ketenes)*
Wolfram *n* W tungsten, wolfram
Wolframat *n* *wolframate, tungstate
~/normales $M^I_2WO_4$ *normal wolframate, normal tungstate
Wolframatoarsenat *n* *wolframoarsenate, tungstoarsenate

Wolframatoborat *n* *wolframoborate, tungstoborate
Wolframatoborsäure *f* *wolframoboric acid, tungstoboric acid
Wolframatokieselsäure *f* *wolframosilicic acid, tungstosilicic acid
Wolframatophosphat *n* *wolframophosphate, tungstophosphate
Wolframatophosphorsäure *f* *wolframophosphoric acid, tungstophosphoric acid
Wolframatosilicat *n* *wolframosilicate, tungstosilicate
Wolframbandlampe *f (spectr)* tungsten source
Wolframbronze *f* tungsten bronze
Wolframcarbid *n* tungsten carbide
~/gesintertes cemented tungsten carbide
Wolframcarbidhartmetall *n* cemented tungsten carbide
Wolfram(II)-chlorid *n* tungsten(II) chloride, tungsten dichloride, wolfram(II) chloride
Wolfram(IV)-chlorid *n* tungsten(IV) chloride, tungsten tetrachloride, wolfram(IV) chloride
Wolfram(V)-chlorid *n* tungsten(V) chloride, tungsten pentachloride, wolfram(V) chloride
Wolfram(VI)-chlorid *n* tungsten(VI) chloride, tungsten hexachloride, wolfram(VI) chloride
Wolframdi... *s. a.* Wolfram(II)-...
Wolframdioxid *n s.* Wolfram(IV)-oxid
Wolframdioxiddichlorid *n* tungsten dichloride dioxide, wolfram dichloride dioxide
Wolframdisulfid *n s.* Wolfram(IV)-sulfid
Wolfram(VI)-fluorid *n* tungsten(VI) fluoride, tungsten hexafluoride, wolfram(VI) fluoride
Wolframglühfaden *m* tungsten filament
Wolframhexa... *s.* Wolfram(VI)-...
Wolframinertgasschweißen *n* tungsten-inert gas welding, TIG welding, gas tungsten-arc welding
Wolfram(II)-iodid *n* tungsten(II) iodide, tungsten diiodide, wolfram(II) iodide
Wolfram(IV)-iodid *n* tungsten(IV) iodide, tungsten tetraiodide, wolfram(IV) iodide
Wolframit *m (min)* wolframite *(iron manganese wolframate)*
Wolframocker *m (min)* tungstite, tungstic ochre
Wolfram(IV)-oxid *n* tungsten(IV) oxide, tungsten dioxide, wolfram(IV) oxide
Wolfram(VI)-oxid *n* tungsten(VI) oxide, tungsten trioxide, wolfram(VI) oxide
Wolframoxidtetrachlorid *n* tungsten tetrachloride oxide, wolfram tetrachloride oxide
Wolframpenta... *s.* Wolfram(V)-...
Wolframpulver *n* tungsten powder
Wolframsäure *f* *wolframic acid, tungstic acid
Wolframsintercarbid *n* cemented tungsten carbide
Wolframstahl *m* tungsten steel
Wolfram(IV)-sulfid *n* tungsten(IV) sulphide, tungsten disulphide, wolfram(IV) sulphide
Wolfram(VI)-sulfid *n* tungsten(VI) sulphide, tungsten trisulphide, wolfram(VI) sulphide
Wolframtetra... *s.* Wolfram(IV)-...
Wolframtrioxid *n s.* Wolfram(VI)-oxid
Wolframtrisulfid *n s.* Wolfram(VI)-sulfid
Wolke *f* cloud
π-Wolke *f* π cloud *(chemical-bond theory)*
wolkig cloudy
Wolkigkeit *f (pap)* cloud effect
Wollastonit *m (min)* wollastonite *(calcium metasilicate)*
Wolle *f (from sheep:)* wool; *(from other animals:)* hair fibre
wollen wool[l]en
Wollfarbstoff *m* wool dye
Wollfett *n* wool grease, *(text also)* yolk, suint
~/gereinigtes lanolin, wool fat
~/rohes crude wool grease, wool wax
Wollfettalkohol *m* wool alcohol
Wollfilz *m (pap)* wool[len] felt
Wollfilzpappe *f* wool-felt board, rag felt
Wollgewebe *n* wool[len] fabric
Wollkeratin *n* wool keratin
Wollschweiß *m s.* Wollfett
Wollstoff *m* wool[len] fabric
Wolltrockenfilz *m (pap)* woollen dry felt, wool dryer felt
Wollwachs *n* wool wax, crude wool grease
Wollwäsche *f* wool scouring
Wollwaschmittel *n* wool detergent
Woodall-Duckham-Ofensystem *n (coal)* Woodall-Duckham system
Woodall-Duckham-Retorte *f (coal)* Woodall-Duckham continuous vertical retort
Wood-Glas *n* Wood's glass
Woodward-Regel *f (spectr)* Woodward's rule
WRK *s.* Wasserreinigungskohle
WSE *s.* Struktureinheit/sich wiederholende
wss., wssr. *s.* wäßrig
Wuchshormon *n (bot)* growth hormone
Wuchsstoff *m* growth substance, *(specif)* growth-promoting (growth-stimulating) substance, growth promotant
Wuchsstoffherbizid *n* hormone weed-killer, [plant-]growth regulator
Wuchsstoffmittel *n* growth-regulating substance, growth regulator (modifier)
Wuchsstoffpräparat *n s.* 1. Wuchsstoffmittel; 2. Wuchsstoffherbizid
wulchern *(glass)* to marver *(a gather in an ovoid mould)*
Wulff-Bock-Kristallisator *m* Wulff-Bock crystallizer
Wulff-Verfahren *n* Wulff process *(for manufacturing acetylene)*
Wulst *m(f)* bead, boss; *(rubber)* bead, *(in the roll nip:)* bank
Wulstmischung *f (rubber)* bead compound
Wulstschneidemaschine *f (rubber)* bead cutter, debeader, debeading machine
Wulstschutzstreifen *m (rubber)* chafer [strip]
Wundererde *f*/**Sächsische** *(min)* teratolite *(a blue bole)*

Wunderkerze *f* sparkler
Wundverband *m* wound dressing *(crop protection)*
Würfelbruch *m (glass)* dice
Würfelfestigkeit *f* cube strength *(testing of concrete)*
würfelförmig cubic[al]
Würfelgitter *n (cryst)* cubic lattice (system, pattern, structure)
~/flächenzentriertes face-centred cubic lattice
~/raumzentriertes body-centred cubic lattice
Würfelmischer *m* cubical blender, cube mixer
würfeln *(plast)* to dice
Würfelschneider *m (plast)* dicing cutter (machine), dicer
Würfelzucker *m* cube sugar
Wurfförderer *m*, **Wurfförderrinne** *f* directional-throw conveyor
Wurfherd *m (min tech)* shaking table
Wurmmittel *n (pharm)* vermifuge, anthelmint[h]ic, helminthagogue
Wurmsamenöl *n (pharm)* chenopodium oil *(from Chenopodium ambrosioides L. var. anthelminthicum)*
wurmvertreibend, wurmwidrig anthelmint[h]ic
Würth-Abstichgaserzeuger *m*, **Würth-Generator** *m (coal)* Würth producer
Wurtz-Fittig-Synthese *f* Wurtz-Fittig synthesis *(of hydrocarbons)*
Wurtzit *m (min)* wurtzite *(zinc sulphide)*
Wurtz-Synthese *f* Wurtz reaction, Wurtz synthesis *(of hydrocarbons)*
Würze *f* 1. *(ferm)* [beer] wort; 2. aroma, flavour *(of wine)*; 3. *s.* Gewürz
~/gehopfte *(ferm)* hopped wort
Würze[koch]kessel *m s.* Würzepfanne
Würzekühler *m (ferm)* wort cooler
Wurzelausscheidung *f* root excretion (exudate, diffusate)
Wurzelharz *n*, **Wurzelkolophonium** *n* wood rosin
Würzepfanne *f (ferm)* wort (brew) kettle, [wort] copper
würzig aromatic, spicy
Würzigkeit *f* aromaticity, spiciness
Würzmittel *n* condiment, seasoning
Wüstenkruste *f*, **Wüstenlack** *m*, **Wüstenrinde** *f (geol)* desert varnish
WW *s.* Wasserwerk
Wz. *s.* Warenzeichen
WZ-Faktor *m*, **WZ-Wert** *m* water-cement ratio

X

Xanthan *n* 1. *(biot)* xanthan gum *(a microbial polysaccharide)*; 2. *s.* Xanthen
Xanthansäure *f s.* Xanthen-9-carbonsäure
Xanthanwasserstoff *m* xanthan hydride, isoperthiocyanic acid
Xanthat *n s.* Xanthogenat
Xanthatkneter *m (text)* xanthator, xanthating churn, baratte
Xanthen *n* xanthene, *(specif)* dibenzo[a,e]pyran
Xanthen-9-carbonsäure *f* xanthene-9-carboxylic acid
Xanthenfarbstoff *m* xanthene dye[stuff]
Xanthenringsystem *n* xanthene ring system
Xanthenthion *n s.* Xanthion
xanthieren *s.* xanthogenieren
Xanthin *n* xanthine, *(specif)* 2,6-dihydroxypurine
Xanthinbase *f* xanthine base
Xanthinoxidase *f* xanthine oxidase
Xanthion *n* xanthion, xanthene-9-thione
Xanthogenat *n* xanthate, xanthogenate *(salt or ester of a xanthic acid)*
xanthogenieren *(text)* to xanthate, to sulphidize, to sulphide
Xanthogenierung *f (text)* xanthation, sulphidizing
Xanthogensäure *f* 1. RO–CS–SH xanthic acid, xanthogenic acid, *O*-ester of dithiocarbonic acid, *(specif)* C_2H_5O–CS–SH dithiocarbonic *O*-ethyl ester, ethylxanthogenic acid; 2. HO–CS–SH dithiocarbonic acid
Xanthogensäureester *m* 1. RO–CS–SR xanthic-acid ester; 2. RO–CS–SH *O*-ester of dithiocarbonic acid
Xanthomatose *f (med)* xanthomatosis *(deposition of lipids in the skin)*
Xanthon *n* xanthone, xanthen-9-one, dibenzopyrone
Xanthophyll *n* xanthophyll *(any of a group of carotenoid pigments)*
Xanthoprotein *n* xanthoprotein
Xanthoproteinreaktion *f* xanthoproteic (xanthoprotein) reaction
Xanthoproteinsäure *f* xanthoproteic acid
Xanthosin *n* xanthosine, xanthine 9-ribofuranoside *(a nucleoside)*
Xanthurensäure *f* xanthurenic acid, 4,8-dihydroxyquinoline-2-carboxylic acid
Xanthyliumsalz *n* xanthylium salt
Xanthylsäure *f (bioch)* xanthylic acid, xanthosine 5'-monophosphate, XMP
XE *s.* X-Einheit
X-Einheit *f* X unit
Xenat *n* xenate *(salt or ester of xenic acid)*
Xenoblast *m (geol)* xenoblast *(a mineral of foreign crystal structure in metamorphic rock)*
xenoblastisch *(geol)* xenoblastic
Xenolith *m (geol)* xenolith *(exogenous enclosure)*
xenomorph *(cryst)* xenomorphic, allotriomorphic, anhedral
Xenon *n* Xe xenon
Xenonlampe *f* xenon [arc] lamp
Xenonsäure *f* xenic acid
Xenotim *m (min)* xenotime *(yttrium phosphate)*
Xenylamin *n* xenylamine, *p*-aminobiphenyl
Xerogel *n (coll)* xerogel
Xerographie *f* xerography

xerographisch xerographic
Xeroradiographie *f* xeroradiography
Ximeninsäure *f* ximenynic acid, santalbic acid, *octadec-11-en-9-ynoic acid
Xylan *n* xylan *(a polysaccharide)*
Xylarsäure *f* xylaric acid, *xylo*-trihydroxyglutaric acid
Xylen *n* xylene, dimethylbenzene, *(esp commercially for impure products:)* xylol
Xylenol *n* xylenol, hydroxyxylene, dimethylphenol
Xylenolharz *n* xylenol resin
Xylidin *n* xylidine, aminodimethylbenzene
Xylit *m* 1. xylite, woody lignite *(brown coal)*; 2. *s.* Xylitol
Xylitol *n* xylitol *(a pentanepentol)*
Xylochinon *n* xyloquinone, dimethylbenzoquinone
Xylodesose *f* deoxyxylose, xylodesose *(a monosaccharide)*
Xyloketose *f s.* Xylulose
Xylol *n s.* Xylen
Xylollichtgelb *n* xylene light yellow
Xylolmoschus *m* musk xylol, musk xylene, xylene musk, *2,4,6-trinitro-1,3-dimethyl-5-*tert*-butylbenzene
Xylolsulfonsäure *f* xylenesulphonic acid
Xylonsäure *f* xylonic acid *(a tetrahydroxypentanoic acid)*
Xylorcin *n*, **Xylorcinol** *n* xylorcinol, dihydroxyxylene
Xylose *f* xylose, wood sugar *(a monosaccharide)*
Xylotrihydroxyglutarsäure *f s.* Xylarsäure
Xyloylgruppe *f* $(CH_3)_2C_6H_3CO-$ xyloyl group
Xylulose *f* xylulose, xyloketose
Xylylbromid *n* α-bromoxylene, xylyl bromide
Xylylchlorid *n* α-chloroxylene, xylyl chloride
Xylylenbromid *n* α,α'-dibromoxylene, xylylene dibromide
Xylylenchlorid *n* α,α'-dichloroxylene, xylylene dichloride
Xylylsäure *f* xylylic acid, dimethylbenzoic acid
x-y-Schreiber *m* X-Y recorder, function plotter

Y

Yankee-Maschine *f (pap)* Yankee (single-cylinder, lick-up) machine
Ylang-Ylang-Öl *n* ilang-ilang (ylang-ylang) oil *(from Cananga odorata (Lam.) Hook. fil. et Thomson)*
Ylid *n* ylide *(any of a class of internal salts)*
P-**Ylid** *n* phosphonium (phosphorus) ylide, Wittig reagent
Ylidreaktion *f* ylide reaction
Yohimbealkaloid *n* yohimbé alkaloid
Yohimbinsäure *f* yohimbic acid
Yperit *n* yperite, *di-2-chloroethylsulphide
Yphantis-Verfahren *n* zero-meniscus concentration technique *(high-speed centrifugation with low liquid level)*
Ypsilonstück *n* Y-shape connecting tube, Y-piece, Y-type connector
Ysopöl *n* hyssop oil *(from Hyssopus officinalis L.)*
Y-Stück *n s.* Ypsilonstück
Ytterbinerde *f s.* Ytterbiumoxid
Ytterbium *n* Yb ytterbium
Ytterbium(II)-chlorid *n* ytterbium(II) chloride, ytterbium dichloride
Ytterbium(III)-chlorid *n* ytterbium(III) chloride, ytterbium trichloride
Ytterbiumdichlorid *n s.* Ytterbium(II)-chlorid
Ytterbiumoxid *n* ytterbium oxide
Ytterbium(III)-sulfat *n* ytterbium(III) sulphate
Ytterbiumtrichlorid *n s.* Ytterbium(III)-chlorid
Yttererde *f* 1. yttrium earth *(class name)*; 2. *s.* Yttriumoxid
Yttrialith *m (min)* yttrialite *(a sorosilicate containing yttrium and thorium)*
Yttrium *n* Y yttrium
Yttriumacetat *n* yttrium acetate
Yttrium-Aluminium-Granat *m* yttrium-aluminium garnet, YAG
Yttriumbromid *n* yttrium bromide
Yttriumcarbid *n* yttrium dicarbide
Yttriumcarbonat *n* yttrium carbonate
Yttriumchlorid *n* yttrium chloride
Yttriumhydroxid *n* yttrium hydroxide
Yttriumnitrat *n* yttrium nitrate
Yttriumoxid *n* yttrium oxide
Yttriumsulfat *n* yttrium sulphate

Z

Z *s.* Ordnungszahl
Zacke *f*, **Zacken** *m* peak *(as of a chromatogram)*
Zaffer *m* zaffre, zaffar, zaffir *(a roasted mixture of cobalt ore and sand)*
zäh[e] 1. tough, tenacious *(material)*; *(soil)* tenacious; 2. *s.* zähflüssig
zähflüssig high-viscosity, viscid, viscous, semiliquid, ropy • ~ **machen** to thicken • ~ **werden** to thicken, to inspissate
Zähflüssigkeit *f* viscosity, ropiness, thickness
Zähigkeit *f* 1. toughness, tenacity; 2. *s.* Viskosität
Zähigkeitskraft *f s.* Reibung/innere
Zahl *f* 1. number, value *(for characterizing a property)*; 2. *s.* Zahlenindex
~/Avogadrosche *s.* Avogadro-Konstante
~ der theoretischen Böden number of theoretical plates, *(chromat also)* plate count
~/Loschmidtsche *s.* Avogadro-Konstante
~/Pecletsche Peclet number *(as for scaling-up pilot-plant results)*
~/Poissonsche Poisson's ratio *(the ratio of transverse to longitudinal strain in a material under tension)*
~/Reichert-Meisslsche Reichert-Meissl number (value), R-M number *(for fats)*

~/Reynoldssche Reynolds number, Re. *(rheology)*
~/Stocksche Stock number *(of valence)*
Zählapparat *m s.* Zählwerk
zählen to enumerate *(e.g. the atoms of a ring system)*
Zahlenbuna *m* numbered buna rubber
Zahlenindex *m (nomencl)* numeral
~/hochgestellter superscript [numeral], numeric superscript, upper index
~/tiefgestellter subscript [numeral], numeric subscript, lower index
Zahlenpräfix *n*, **Zahlenvorsatz** *m (nomencl)* numerical prefix
Zähler *m* 1. meter *(for fluids)*; 2. *(nucl)* counter, counting tube; 3. *s.* Zählwerk
Zählgerät *n s.* Zählwerk
Zähligkeit *f* ligancy, coordination, coordination (covalence, covalency) number
Zählmarke *f (chromat)* count, dump
Zählrohr *n (nucl)* counting tube, counter
~/selbstlöschendes self-quenched (self-quenching) counter
Zählung *f* numbering, enumeration *(as of the atoms of a ring system)*
Zählvorrichtung *f s.* Zählwerk
Zählwalze *f (pap)* counting roll
Zählweise *f (nomencl)* numbering (enumeration) system
Zählwerk *n* counting apparatus (device), counter
Zahlwort *n*/**multiplikatives** *(nomencl)* multiplying prefix, multiplicative numeral
Zahlwortpräfix *n (nomencl)* numerical prefix
Zahnbein *n* dentine
Zahnfüllung *f* dental filling
Zahngold *n* dental gold [alloy]
Zahnpaste *f* tooth-paste
Zahnpflegemittel *n* dentifrice, dental cleanser (composition)
Zahnporzellan *n* dental porcelain
Zahnputzmittel *n s.* Zahnpflegemittel
Zahnradpumpe *f* gear pump
Zahnradspinnpumpe *f* gear-type metering (spinning) pump
Zahnscheibenmühle *f* toothed-disk mill
Zahnschmelz *m* [dental] enamel
Zahnstein *m* scale
Zahnwalzenbrecher *m* toothed-roll crusher
Zahnzement *m* dental cement, cementum
zähpolen *(met)* to toughen by poling, to pole
Zajcev-Regel *f* Zaitsev rule *(of orientation in β-eliminations)*
Zak-Reaktion *f* Zak reaction *(for detecting cholesterol)*
Zange *f* [pair of] tongs, forceps, *(if small)* pincers
zapfen *(rubber)* to tap
Zapfen *m* 1. trunnion, pivot, journal, neck *(as of a shaft or cylinder)*; 2. bung, spigot, plug, plug cock (bib) *(on a cask)*; 3. tit *(a defect in glass)*
Zapfenlager *n* journal bearing
Zapfloch *n* bunghole
Zapfmesser *n (rubber)* tapping knife
Zapfschnitt *m (rubber)* tapping cut
Zapfung *f (rubber)* tapping
Zartmachersalz *n (food)* meat tenderizer
Zäsium *n s.* Caesium
Zaun-Porphyrin *n (org ch)* fenced porphyrin
Z-Drehung *f (rubber)* Z twist
Zedernblätteröl *n* cedar-leaf oil, thuja oil *(chiefly from Thuja occidentalis L.)*
Zederncampher *m* cedar[wood] camphor, cedrol
Zedernholzöl *n* cedarwood oil *(from Cedrus atlantica Manetti or Juniperus specc.)*
Zeeman-Atomabsorptionsspektrophotometrie *f* Zeeman atomic absorption spectrophotometry, ZAAS
Zeeman-Aufspaltung *f* **[der Energieniveaus]** *s.* Zeeman-Effekt
Zeeman-Effekt *m* Zeeman effect
~/anomaler anomalous Zeeman effect
~/normaler normal Zeeman effect
Zeeman-Niveau *n*, **Zeeman-Term** *m* Zeeman term (energy level)
Zeeman-Verbreiterung *f* Zeeman broadening *(of spectral lines under the influence of magnetic fields)*
Zehntelnormallösung *f* decinormal solution
zehnzählig, zehnzähnig decadentate *(coordination chemistry)*
Zeichen *n*/**chemisches** chemical symbol (sign)
Zeichenkarton *m* drawing [card]board, painters' (artists') cardboard
Zeichenkreide *f* crayon
Zeichenpapier *n* drawing paper
Zeichensprache *f*/**chemische** chemical shorthand
Zeiger *m* 1. pointer, indicator, index *(of an apparatus)*; 2. *(biol)* indicator *(of soil conditions)*
Zein *n* zein *(a prolamin obtained from maize)*
Zeinfaser *f* zein staple [fibre], maize protein staple
Zeinkunststoff *m* zein plastic
Zeisel-Bestimmung *f* Zeisel determination *(of alkoxy groups)*
Zeiß-Abbe-Refraktometer *n* Abbe refractometer
Zeit *f*/**mittlere freie** *(phys ch)* mean free time *(between two collisions)*
Zeitdomäne *f (spectr)* time domain
Zeiteinheit *f* unit of time • **in der** ~ per unit time
Zeitentwicklung *f (phot)* development by time
Zeit-Gamma-Kurve *f (phot)* time-gamma curve
Zeitgeber *m* constant-time device
Zeitgesetz *n s.* Geschwindigkeitsgleichung
Zeitkonstante *f* time constant
Zeitpunkt *m* **des Ionendurchbruchs** *(hyd)* exhaustion point *(ion exchange)*
zeitraubend time-consuming
Zeitreaktion *f* clock (time) reaction
Zeitschaltgerät *n*, **Zeitschaltuhr** *f* timer, timing device
Zeitschrift *f*/**referierende** abstract[ing] journal

Zeitschriftenpapier *n* magazine paper
Zeitstandfestigkeit *f* creep strength (resistance)
Zeitstandversuch *m* creep test (experiment)
Zeit-Temperatur-Umwandlungsdiagramm *n* time-temperature-transformation diagram, T.T.T. diagram
~ für kontinuierliche Abkühlung continuous-cooling transformation diagram
~/isothermes isothermal transformation diagram
Zeitungsdruckfarbe *f* newsprint (news) ink
Zeitungsdruckpapier *n* newsprint paper, news[-print]
Zeitvariable *f* time variable
Zellagglomerat *n*, **Zellaggregat** *n* *(biot)* cell agglomerate
Zellatmung *f* cellular respiration
Zellausbeute *f* *(biot)* cell yield
Zellbestandteil *m* *(biol)* cellular constituent
Zellbildungsrate *f* *(biot)* cell formation rate
Zelldichte *f* *(biot)* cell (culture, microbial) density
Zelle *f* cell, *(tech also)* compartment, chamber
~/antikörperproduzierende *(biot)* antibody-producing cell
~/bipolare *(el ch)* bipolar cell
~/elektrochemische *s.* ~/galvanische
~/elektrolytische electrolytic (electrolysis) cell
~/galvanische voltaic cell, galvanic (electrical, chemical) cell
~/immobilisierte *(biot)* immobilized cell
~/lichtelektrische (photoelektrische) photoelectric cell, photocell, phototube, photovalve
~/photogalvanische photogalvanic cell
~/unipolare *(el ch)* monopolar cell
Zellenaggregat *n* *(el ch)* cell assembly
zellenartig cellular
Zellenbeton *m* cellular concrete
Zellendolomit *m* cellular dolomite
Zellenenzym *n* *s.* Enzym/intrazelluläres
Zellenfilter *n* cellular filter
Zellenflüssigkeit *f* *(el ch)* cell liquor
Zellengefüge *n* *s.* Zellenstruktur
Zellenkalk *m* *(geol)* cellular lime
Zellenofen *m* cell-type oven
Zellenrad *n* star wheel (valve)
Zellenradaufgeber *m* star (rotary-vane) feeder
Zellenreaktion *f* *(phys ch)* cell reaction
Zellensaal *m* *(el ch)* cell room
Zellenschleuse *f* *s.* Zellenrad
Zellenspannung *f* *(phys ch)* cell voltage
Zellenspeicher *m* bin, silo
Zellenstruktur *f* *(biol, coal)* cellular structure
Zellenverdichter *m* [sliding-]vane compressor
Zellenzym *n* *s.* Enzym/intrazelluläres
Zellflocke *f* *s.* Zellagglomerat
Zellflüssigkeit *f* *(biol)* cell sap, cytosol
Zellfusion *f* *(biot)* cell fusion
zellgebunden *(biol)* cell-bound
Zellgefüge *n* *s.* Zellenstruktur
Zellgewebe *n* *(text)* cellular tissue
Zellgewinnung *f* *(biot)* cell production
Zellgift *n* cytotoxin
Zellglas *n* cellophane, cellulose film
Zellgummi *m* cellular (expanded) rubber
Zellhaltung *f* *(biot)* cell maintenance
Zellhämin *n* *s.* Cytochrom
Zellhartgummi *m* cellular ebonite
Zellhaufen *m* *(biot)* cell clump
Zellhaut *f* *s.* Zellglas
Zellhorn *n* celluloid
zellig cellular
Zellimmobilisierung *f* *(biot)* cell immobilization
Zellkern *m* *(biol)* nucleus
Zellklumpen *m* *(biot)* cell clump
Zellkonzentration *f* *(biot)* cell concentration
Zellkonzentrierung *f* *(biot)* cell collection *(e.g. by sedimentation)*
Zellkultivierung *f* *(biot)* cell cultivation, cultivation of cells
Zellkultur *f* *(biot)* cell culture
Zell-Linie *f* *(biot)* cell line
Zellmasse *f* *(biot)* cell mass (weight)
Zellmaterial *n* *(biot)* cell material (matter)
Zellmembran *f* *(biol)* cell membrane
Zellprotein *n* cell[ular] protein
Zellrad *n*, **Zellradschleuse** *f* *s.* Zellenrad
Zellreaktion *f* *(phys ch)* cell reaction
Zellreste *mpl* *(biot)* cell residue
Zellsaft *m* *(biol)* cell sap, cytosol
zellschädigend cytotoxic
Zellspannung *f* *(el ch)* cell voltage
Zellstoff *m* 1. *(tech)* [chemical] pulp, *(specif)* [chemical] wood pulp, CWP; 2. *s.* Cellulose
~/alkalisch aufgeschlossener (erkochter, gekochter) alkaline-cooked pulp, alkali pulp
~/bleichbarer bleaching pulp
~ für die Chemiefaserindustrie rayon (dissolving) pulp
~ für die Papierindustrie paper[making] pulp
~/harter (hartgekochter) hard (strong, low-boiled) pulp
~ in Bogenform (Pappenform) wood-pulp board, lap[ped] pulp, sheets (laps) of chemical wood pulp
~/klassischer chemical pulp
~/leicht bleichbarer easy-bleaching pulp
~ mit hohem Weißgehalt high-brightness pulp
~/schwer bleichbarer hard-bleaching pulp
~/sehr harter (roher) *s.* ~/unaufgeschlossener
~/unaufgeschlossener high-strength pulp, prime strong pulp
~/weicher (weichgekochter) soft (well-cooked, high-boiled) pulp
~/weit heruntergekochter *s.* ~/weicher
~/wenig aufgeschlossener *s.* ~/harter
Zellstoffabrik *f* pulp mill
Zellstoffabrikabwasser *n* pulp-mill waste water, pulping waste
Zellstoffaufschluß *m* chemical pulping

Zellstoffausbeute *f* pulp yield
Zellstoffbahn *f* web of pulp
Zellstoffblätter *npl s.* Zellstoff in Bogenform
Zellstoffbleiche *f* pulp bleaching
Zellstoffbogen *m* pulp sheet
Zellstoffbrei *m* pulp
Zellstoffentwässerungsmaschine *f* pulp[-drying] machine, wet machine (press), half-stuff machine, presse-pâte
Zellstofferzeugung *f* pulp making (manufacture)
Zellstoffestigkeit *f* pulp strength
Zellstoffhersteller *m* pulpmaker
Zellstoffindustrie *f* pulp industry
Zellstoffkarton *m* pulp cardboard
Zellstoffkocher *m* digester
Zellstoffpapier *n* wood-free paper
Zellstoffpappe *f s.* Zellstoff in Bogenform
Zellstoffproduzent *m* pulpmaker
Zellstoffreinigung *f* pulp purification
Zellstoffsuspension *f (pap)* fibre suspension, fibrous pulp, pulp slurry (stock)
Zellstofftrocknung *f* pulp drying
Zellstoff- und Papierfabrik *f* integrated mill
Zellstoff- und Papierfabrikabwasser *n* pulp/paper-mill waste water
Zellstoffveredelung *f* pulp refining (purification), [alkaline] refining of pulp
Zellstoffveredelungslauge *f*/**alkalische** alkali refining liquor
Zellstoffwäsche *f* pulp washing
Zellstoffwäscher *m* pulp washer
Zellstoffwatte *f* artificial cotton, *(Am)* cellulose (pulp) wadding
Zellstoffwechsel *m (biol)* cell metabolism
Zellstoffwerk *n* pulp mill
Zellstruktur *f* cellular structure
Zellsuspension *f (biot)* cell suspension (slurry)
~/autolysierte autolyzed cell suspension
Zelltrockenmasse *f*, **Zelltrockensubstanz** *f (biot)* cell dry weight, dry weight of cells
Zell-TS *f s.* Zelltrockenmasse
zellulär cellular
Zelluloid *n* celluloid
Zellulose *f s.* Cellulose
Zellverlust *m (biot)* cell loss
Zellverschmelzung *f (biot)* cell fusion
Zellwand *f (biol)* cell wall
Zellwolle *f* [viscose] staple fibre
Zellzucht *f s.* Zellkultivierung
Zeltbegasung *f (agric)* tent fumigation
Zement *m* 1. *(build, rubber)* cement; 2. *(geoch)* cement, cementing agent, binder, agglutinant
~/hydraulischer hydraulic cement
~/loser bulk cement
~/sulfatbeständiger sulphate-resisting cement
~/treibender expanding (expansive) cement
~/wasserabweisender hydrophobe (water-repellent) cement
~/wasserbindender hydraulic cement
~/weißer white cement
zementartig cementitious
Zementation *f* 1. *(met, geol)* cementation *(precipitation of a metal from salt solutions by the action of a less noble one)*; 2. *(met)* carburization
Zementationsbad *n (met)* carburizing bath
Zementationsgas *n (met)* carburizing gas
Zementationsgemisch *n (met)* carburizing mixture
Zementationshärten *n (met)* case-hardening *(carburizing and subsequent hardening)*
Zementationskasten *m (met)* carburizing box
Zementationsmittel *n (met)* carburizing medium (agent), [case-hardening] carburizer
Zementationspulver *n (met)* carburizing powder
Zementationsschicht *f (met)* carburized case
Zementationstiefe *f (met)* carburizing (carburization) depth, depth of case
Zementationszone *f (geoch)* zone of cementation
Zementbrennen *n* cement burning
Zementbrennofen *m* cement kiln
Zementchemie *f* cement chemistry
Zementdreh[rohr]ofen *m* rotary cement kiln
Zementformsand *m* cement-bonded sand
Zementherstellung *f* manufacture of cement
Zementier... *s. a.* Zementations...
zementieren 1. *(build)* to cement; 2. *(met, geoch)* to cement *(to precipitate a metal from salt solutions by the action of a less noble one)*; 3. *(met)* to carburize
~/im Salzbad *(met)* to liquid-carburize, to bath-carburize
~/in der Randschicht (Randzone) *s.* zementieren 3.
~ in festem Einsatz, ~ in festen Mitteln *(met)* to pack-carburize
~/in flüssigen Mitteln *(met)* to liquid-carburize, to bath-carburize
~/in gasförmigen Mitteln *(met)* to gas-carburize
Zementieren *n* 1. *(build)* cementing; 2. *(met)* cementing *(precipitating a metal from salt solutions by the action of a less noble one)*; 3. *(met)* carburizing
~ im Salzbad *(met)* liquid[-salt] carburizing, bath carburizing
~ in festem Einsatz, ~ in festen Mitteln *(met)* pack carburizing, solid[-pack] carburizing
~ in flüssigen Mitteln *(met)* liquid[-salt] carburizing, bath carburizing
~ in gasförmigen Mitteln *(met)* gas carburizing
Zementierofen *m (met)* carburizing oven
Zementierung *f s.* Zementation
Zementit *m (met)* cementite, iron carbide
Zementkalk *m s.* Kalk/hydraulischer
Zementklinker *m (build)* [cement] clinker
Zementkuchen *m (build)* cement pat
Zementkupfer *n* cement (precipitated) copper
Zementleim *m* cement paste
Zementmilch *f* laitance
Zementmörtel *m* cement mortar
Zementofen *m s.* Zementschachtofen
Zementsand *m* cement-bonded sand

Zementschachtofen *m* cement kiln
Zementschlamm *m*, **Zementschlempe** *f* laitance
Zementschwarz *n* manganese black *(manganese dioxide)*
Zentigrammbereich *m (anal)* centigram range
Zentigramm-Methode *f (anal)* centigram method
Zentralanguß *m (plast)* centre gate
Zentralatom *n* central atom
Zentralbahn *f (bioch)* central [metabolic] pathway, amphibolic pathway
Zentralgenerator *m* independent producer *(gas making)*
Zentralion *n* central ion
Zentralkohlenstoffatom *n* central carbon atom
Zentralmetall *n* central metal *(of a complex compound)*
Zentralrohr *n* central pipe (tube)
zentralsymmetrisch centrosymmetric
Zentralwelle *f* central shaft
Zentrifugalabscheider *m* centrifugal collector (separator)
Zentrifugalabsorber *m* centrifugal [gas] absorber
Zentrifugalbecherwerk *n* centrifugal-discharge bucket elevator
Zentrifugalbeschleunigung *f* centrifugal acceleration
Zentrifugalchromatographie *f* centrifugal chromatography
Zentrifugaldehnung *f s.* Zentrifugalverzerrung
Zentrifugalextraktor *m* centrifugal extractor
Zentrifugalfeld *n* centrifugal field
Zentrifugalfilter *n* centrifugal filter, filtering centrifuge, [filtering] centrifugal, screen (perforate-bowl) centrifuge
Zentrifugalgasabsorber *m* centrifugal gas absorber
Zentrifugalgaswäscher *m* disintegrator [washer]
Zentrifugal-Gebläse *n* centrifugal compressor
Zentrifugalgießen *n*, **Zentrifugalguß** *m* centrifugal casting
Zentrifugalklassierer *m* centrifugal classifier
Zentrifugalkraft *f* centrifugal force
Zentrifugalkraftfilter *n s.* Zentrifugalfilter
Zentrifugalkraftklassierer *m*, **Zentrifugalkraftsichter** *m* centrifugal classifier
Zentrifugalpumpe *f* centrifugal pump
Zentrifugalreiniger *m* centrifugal cleaner; *(pap)* centrifugal strainer, erkensator *(for cleaning wood pulp)*
Zentrifugalscheibe *f* centrifugal disk
Zentrifugalscheider *m* centrifugal collector (separator)
Zentrifugalsichter *m* centrifugal classifier; *(pap)* centrifugal-type screen *(for cleaning mechanical wood pulp)*
Zentrifugalsortierer *m* centrifugal classifier; *(pap)* centrifugal strainer, erkensator *(for cleaning wood pulp)*
Zentrifugaltrockenmaschine *f* whizzer
Zentrifugalversprüher *m* centrifugal atomizer
Zentrifugalversprühung *f* centrifugal atomization
Zentrifugalverzerrung *f (spectr)* centrifugal distortion (stretching)
Zentrifugalwäscher *m* disintegrator washer
Zentrifugalzerstäuber *m* centrifugal atomizer
Zentrifugalzerstäubung *f* centrifugal atomization
Zentrifugat *n* centrifugate
Zentrifugatgüte *f* centrifugate quality (clarity)
Zentrifuge *f* centrifuge, *(tech esp for filtering:)* centrifugal
~ **mit kontinuierlichem Schlammaustrag** continuous solids-discharge centrifuge
~ **mit seitlicher Entleerung** *s.* ~ mit Umfangsaustrag
~ **mit Umfangsaustrag** peripheral discharge centrifuge
~ **mit Untenaustrag** bottom discharge centrifuge
~/stehende underdriven (bottom-driven) centrifuge, base-bearing centrifuge
~/unten entleerende *s.* ~ mit Untenaustrag
~/von unten angetriebene *s.* ~/stehende
Zentrifugenablauf *m* centrifugate
Zentrifugenaustrag *m s.* Zentrifugenkuchen
Zentrifugenglas *n* centrifuge tube
Zentrifugenkuchen *m* [solids] cake, filter cake *(of a centrifuge)*
Zentrifugenleistung *f* centrifuge performance
Zentrifugenmittel *n* z average *(of relative molecular mass)*
Zentrifugenrotor *m* centrifuge rotor (head)
Zentrifugenspinnen *n* [centrifugal] pot spinning
Zentrifugentrommel *f* bowl, centrifuge basket
Zentrifugentrommeldrehzahl *f* rotational speed of the bowl, bowl speed
Zentrifugenüberlauf *m* centrifugate
Zentrifugenverfahren *n* gas centrifuge process *(for separating isotopes)*
Zentrifugenwickel *m* cake
Zentrifugenwirkungsgrad *m* centrifuge efficiency
Zentrifugenzahl *f* relative centrifugal force
zentrifugieren to centrifugate, to centrifuge
Zentrifugierung *f* centrifugation
~/isopyknische isopycnic centrifugation
Zentripetalkraft *f* centripetal force
Zentrireiniger *m (pap)* centricleaner
zentrisch centric, central, on-centre
Zentrosphäre *f (geoch)* centrosphere *(core of the earth)*
zentrosymmetrisch centrosymmetric
Zentrum *n***/aktives** active site *(in molecules, catalysts)*
~/allosterisches *(bioch)* allosteric site
~/reaktives reactive site *(in molecules)*
~/saures acid site *(in molecules, catalysts)*
sp^3**-Zentrum** *n* sp^3 centre *(chemical bond theory)*
Zentrumsaktivität *f***/katalytische** *(bioch)* turnover number
Zeolith *m (min)* zeolite
~/künstlicher artificial (synthetic) zeolite, zeolite exchange resin *(ion exchange)*

Zeolithisation *f* zeolitization
zeolithisch zeolitic
Zeolithisierung *f* zeolitization
Zeolithwasser *n* zeolitic water
Zer *n s.* Cer
zerbrechen to break
zerbrechlich breakable, fragile, brittle
Zerbrechlichkeit *f* fragility, brittleness
zerbröckeln to crumble; to crumble [away], to slake *(of material)*
zerdrücken to crush, to mill
Zerewitinow-Bestimmung *f* Zerewitinoff determination *(of active H atoms)*
Zerfall *m (ch)* decomposition, *(into ions:)* dissociation; *(nucl)* disintegration, fission, decay; *(biol)* decomposition, decay; *(tech)* disintegration, breakdown of size • **durch radioaktiven ~ entstanden** radiogenic • **zum ~ bringen** to disintegrate
~/dualer *(nucl)* branched (multiple) disintegration (decay), branching
~/monomolekularer monomolecular (unimolecular) decomposition
~/radioaktiver radioactive disintegration (decay)
~/stoßinduzierter *(anal)* collision-induced dissociation, CID
~/thermischer thermal decomposition (degradation)
~/verzweigter *s.* ~/dualer
β-**Zerfall** *m (nucl)* beta (β-ray) disintegration (decay)
β^+-**Zerfall** *m (nucl)* positive beta decay, positron decay
β^--**Zerfall** *m (nucl)* negative beta decay
zerfallen *(ch)* to decompose, to undergo decomposition, *(of molecules:)* to fragment, *(into ions:)* to dissociate; *(nucl)* to disintegrate, to decay; *(biol)* to decompose, to decay; *(tech)* to disintegrate, to break down, to crumble [away], *(esp of coal)* to slake
~/in Schichten to delaminate
~/in Stücke to crumble to pieces
~/zu Pulver to fall to powder
Zerfallsart *f (nucl)* decay mode
Zerfallselektron *n (nucl)* disintegration (decay) electron
Zerfallsenergie *f (nucl)* disintegration (decay) energy
Zerfallsgeschwindigkeit *f (ch)* decomposition rate; *(nucl)* rate of disintegration (decay)
Zerfallsgesetz *n (nucl)* [radioactive-]decay law
Zerfallskonstante *f (nucl)* disintegration constant, decay (transformation) constant, decay coefficient (factor)
Zerfallskurve *f (nucl)* disintegration (decay) curve
Zerfallsleuchten *n (nucl)* decay luminescence
Zerfallsprodukt *n (ch)* decomposition product; *(nucl)* disintegration (decay) product
Zerfallsrate *f (nucl)* rate of disintegration (decay)
Zerfallsreaktion *f (ch)* decomposition reaction
Zerfallsreihe *f*[**/radioaktive**] radioactive [decay] series
Zerfallsteilchen *n (nucl)* disintegration (decay) particle
Zerfallswahrscheinlichkeit *f (nucl)* probability of disintegration (decay)
Zerfallswärme *f (nucl)* decay heat
Zerfallsweg *m* fragmentation path *(of molecules in mass spectrometry)*
Zerfallszeit *f (nucl)* disintegration (decay) period (time)
Zerfaserer *m (pap)* shredding (kneading) machine, shredder, kneader *(recovery of waste paper)*
zerfasern *(pap)* to defibre, to defibrate, to reduce to fibres, to shred, *(Am also)* to [de]fiberize
Zerfasern *n (pap)* defib[e]ring, defibration, shredding, *(Am also)* [de]fiberization
Zerfaserungsmaschine *f s.* Zerfaserer
zerfließen to deliquesce, to liquefy
Zerfließen *n* deliquescence
zerfließlich deliquescent
Zerfließlichkeit *f* deliquescence
zerfressen to corrode, to eat
Zerfressen *n* corrosion
zergehen to deliquesce, to liquefy; to dissolve
zerhacken to chop, to chip *(mechanically)*; *(spectr)* to chop
Zerhacker *m (spectr)* chopper
zerkleinern to comminute, to reduce [in size]; to mill, to grind; to chip, to chop; to crush *(brittle material)*; to shred *(garbage)*
Zerkleinerung *f* comminution, [size] reduction; milling, grinding; chipping, chopping; crushing *(of brittle material)*; shredding *(of garbage)*
~ mit gegenseitiger Teilchenbehinderung choke crushing
~ ohne gegenseitige Teilchenbehinderung free crushing
Zerkleinerungsanlage *f* comminution plant
Zerkleinerungsgesetz *n* **nach Bond** Bond's law
~ nach Kick Kick's law
Zerkleinerungsgrad *m* degree of reduction, [size-] reduction ratio
Zerkleinerungsmaschine *f* comminuting machine
Zerkleinerungsvorrichtung *f* agglomerate (lump) breaker *(in a mixer)*
zerknallen to explode *(of vessels)*
zerkrümeln to crumble; to crumble [away], to slake *(of material)*
zerlegbar decomposable
~/durch Photolyse photolysable
zerlegen *(ch)* to decompose, to split [up], to break down, *(bioch also)* to catabolize; *(physically:)* to fractionate, to split [up], to break down, to separate
~/elektrolytisch to electrolyze
~/in Schichten to delaminate
~/nach Korn[größen]klassen to size, to fractionate

Zerlegung *f (ch)* decomposition, breakdown, splitting[-up]; *(physically:)* fractionation, splitting[-up], breakdown, separation
~/elektrolytische electrolysis
~/hydrolytische hydrolytic decomposition (breakdown)
~/oxidative oxidative decomposition (breakdown)
Zerlegungsprodukt *n* decomposition (breakdown) product
zermahlen to grind, to mill, to triturate
zermalmen to bruise, to crush
zerplatzen to crack, *(violently:)* to explode, to blow up
zerpulvern to pulverize, to powder, to triturate
zerquetschen to crush, to mash
zerreiben to triturate, to grind, to mill
zerreiblich friable, triturable
Zerreiblichkeit *f* friability
Zerreißdehnung *f* strain at break
zerreißen to tear, to rupture, to break; to macerate, to tear *(fibrous material)*; to break, to crack *(of material)*
Zerreißfestigkeit *f* resistance to tear[ing], tearing (tensile, bursting) strength
Zerreißgrenze *f* ultimate [tensile] strength, bursting strength
Zerreißmaschine *f* 1. tensile-strength tester (testing machine); 2. macerator *(for fibrous material)*
Zerreißprüfung *f* ultimate tensile-strength test
Zerreißpunkt *m (rubber)* breaking point
Zerreißwerk *n* macerator *(for fibrous material)*
zerrieseln 1. to disintegrate *(of granulated fertilizers)*; 2. *(ceram)* to dust *(of materials with a high content of calcium orthosilicate)*
Zerrieseln *n* 1. disintegration *(of granulated fertilizers)*; 2. *(ceram)* dusting *(of materials with a high content of calcium orthosilicate)*
zerschlagen to crush, to smash
zerschleifen to grind *(wood)*
zerschmelzen to melt
Zerschmelzen *n* melting
zersetzbar *s.* zersetzlich
zersetzen *(ch, biol)* to decompose
~/durch Solvolyse to solvolyze
~/elektrolytisch to electrolyze
~/sich *(ch)* to undergo decomposition, to decompose, *(biol also)* to decay
zersetzend destructive
Zersetzer *m*, **Zersetzerzelle** *f* decomposer *(electrolysis)*
zersetzlich decomposable
~/leicht readily (easily) decomposing
Zersetzlichkeit *f* decomposability
Zersetzung *f (ch)* decomposition; *(biol)* decay, decomposition • **~ erleiden** to undergo decomposition
~/durch Licht photolysis, photodecomposition
~/elektrolytische electrolysis, electrolytic dissociation
~/hydrolytische hydrolytic decomposition
~/strahlenchemische radiolysis
~/thermische thermal decomposition (degradation)
Zersetzungsdestillation *f* destructive distillation
Zersetzungserscheinung *f* decomposition phenomenon
zersetzungsfähig *s.* zersetzlich
Zersetzungsgeschwindigkeit *f* decomposition rate
Zersetzungskatalysator *m* decomposition catalyst
Zersetzungspotential *n* decomposition potential
Zersetzungsprodukt *n* decomposition product
Zersetzungspunkt *m* decomposition point
Zersetzungsreaktion *f* decomposition reaction
Zersetzungsspannung *f* decomposition voltage
Zersetzungswärme *f* heat of decomposition
Zersetzungszelle *f* decomposer
Zersetzungszone *f (hyd)* decomposition zone
zerspalten *s.* spalten
zersplittern to spall, to shatter; *(min)* to delaminate
zerspringen to crack, to shatter
zersprühen to atomize
Zersprühen *n* atomizing, atomization
zerstäuben to atomize
Zerstäuber *m* atomizer; *(spectr)* nebulizer
~ mit Hilfsstoff auxiliary-fluid atomizer
Zerstäuberbrenner *m s.* Zerstäubungsbrenner
Zerstäuber-Brenner-Kombination *f (spectr)* direct-injection burner
Zerstäuberdüse *f* atomizing nozzle
Zerstäuberscheibe *f s.* Sprühscheibe
Zerstäubung *f* atomization
~ durch Düsen nozzle atomization
~/elektrische electrical dispersion, electrodispersion
~ ohne Hilfsstoff single-fluid atomization
Zerstäubungsbrenner *m* atomizing (spray) burner *(for liquid fuel)*
Zerstäubungsmilchpulver *n* spray-dried milk [powder], spray powder milk
Zerstäubungsschwefelverbrennungsofen *m (pap)* spray-type sulphur burner
Zerstäubungstrockner *m* spray dryer
Zerstäubungstrocknung *f* spray drying
zerstören to destroy; *(bioch)* to decompose; to break, to crack, to demulsify *(emulsions)*
~/oberflächlich to corrode
Zerstörer *m (bioch)* decomposer, reducer, microconsumer
zerstört werden to break down *(of emulsions)*
Zerstörung *f* destruction; *(bioch)* decomposition; *(el ch)* breakdown *(of passivity or a passive film)*; breaking, cracking *(of emulsions)*
~/biologische biodeterioration *(of materials)*
zerstörungsfrei non-destructive
zerstoßen to crush, to triturate
Zerstoßen *n* crush[ing], trituration
zerstrahlen to undergo annihilation
Zerstrahlung *f* annihilation, energy pooling
Zerstrahlungsspektrum *n* annihilation spectrum

zerteilen to disperse; *(coll)* to deflocculate; *(relating to solids:)* to comminute, to reduce, *(relating to droplets:)* to reduce in size, to subdivide, to atomize
Zerteilung *f* dispersion, dispersal; *(coll)* deflocculation; *(relating to solids:)* comminution, [size] reduction, *(relating to droplets:)* size reduction, subdivision, atomization
Zerteilungsgrad *m* degree of dispersion
zertrümmern to shatter, to destroy; *(esp for further processing:)* to break up *(e.g. ore)*
Zertrümmerung *f* shatter[ing], destruction; *(esp for further processing as of ore:)* breaking-up
Zerwellen *n* wavy sheet disintegration *(in atomizing liquids)*
Zetameter *n (hyd)* zeta meter
Zeta-Potential *n* zeta potential, ZP, electrokinetic (double-layer) potential
Zeugmatographie *f (spectr)* spin mapping
Zibet *m (cosmet)* civet
Zickzackanordnung *f* zigzag arrangement
Zickzackkette *f* zigzag chain
Zickzackofen *m (ceram)* zigzag kiln
Zickzackschema *n* Z scheme *(of photosynthesis)*
Zider *m* cider, *(Am)* hard (fermented) cider
Zideressig *m* cider vinegar
Ziegel *m* brick
~/gebrannter fired brick
~/geschnittener wire-cut brick
~/glasierter glazed brick
~/hochfeuerfester highly refractory brick
Ziegelauskleidung *f* brick lining
Ziegelei *f* brickworks
Ziegeleierzeugnis *n* brickware
Ziegelerde *f* brick earth
Ziegelformmaschine *f (ceram)* brick machine
Ziegelmehl *n* brick dust
Ziegelofen *m* brick kiln
Ziegelpresse *f (ceram)* brick machine
Ziegelsplitt *m* broken brick
Ziegelstein *m s.* Ziegel
Ziegeltee *m* brick tea
Ziegelton *m* brick[-making] clay
Ziegenleder *n* goatskin leather
Ziegler-Katalysator *m s.* Ziegler-Natta-Katalysator
Ziegler-Methode *f* Ziegler method *(for obtaining cyclic ketones)*
Ziegler-Natta-Katalysator *m* Ziegler-Natta catalyst
Ziegler-Natta-Katalyse *f* Ziegler-Natta catalysis
Ziegler-Verfahren *n* Ziegler process *(for polymerizing alkenes)*
Ziehbalken *m (glass)* draw bar
ziehbar ductile *(metal)*
Ziehbarkeit *f* ductility
Ziehdüse *f (glass)* debiteuse *(in the Fourcault sheet-drawing process)*
ziehen 1. to draw, to pull *(e.g. glas or plastics)*; 2. to pull *(a reaction)*; 3. *(of viscous material:)* to slide *(e.g. to the discharge point)*
~/auf Flaschen to bottle (in, up)
~/direkt auf Baumwolle *(dye)* to be direct to cotton
~/Elektronen to withdraw electrons
~/auf Platten *(rubber)* to sheet [out] *(on the calender)*
Ziehen *n* **aus der Schmelze** crystal pulling *(of single crystals)*
~ von Bohrkernen *(geol)* coring
~ von Platten *(rubber)* sheet calendering, sheeting[-out]
~ von Seitenkernen *(petrol)* sidewall coring
Ziehfett *n* pastry fat
Ziehglas *n* drawn glass
Ziehherd *m (glass)* drawing pot
Ziehkammer *f (glass)* drawing chamber
Ziehmargarine *f* puff (flaky) pastry margarine
Ziehmaschine *f (glass)* drawing machine
Ziehschacht *m (glass)* drawing shaft
Ziehstreifen *m (glass)* drawing mark *(a defect)*
Ziehverfahren *n (glass)* drawing process
Ziehvermögen *n (dye)* absorptive (absorbing) capacity (power)
Ziehwalze *f (glass)* forming roll *(in the sheet-drawing process)*
Ziehzwiebel *f* bulb *(for producing glass silk)*
Zierfliese *f* decorative tile
Ziervogel-Verfahren *n* Ziervogel process *(for extracting silver from sulphide ores)*
Ziffer *f***/akzentuierte (apostrophierte)** *s.* ~/gestrichene
~/gestrichene *(nomencl)* primed number
~/ungestrichene *(nomencl)* unprimed number
Ziffernfolge *f (nomencl)* series of locants
Zigarettenpapier *n* cigarette paper, *(Am)* cigarette tissue
Zigarrendeckblattpapier *n* cigar wrapping paper
Zimm-Diagramm *n* Zimm plot *(for determining the molecular weights of polymers)*
Zimmermann-Reaktion *f* Zimmermann reaction *(for determining ketonic steroids)*
Zimmermann-Verfahren *n (hyd)* Zimmermann process, Zimpro process *(wet air oxidation)*
Zimmertemperatur *f* room temperature, normal (ordinary) temperature
Zimt *m* cinnamon
~/Chinesischer Chinese cinnamon *(from Cinnamomum aromaticum Nees)*
~/Echter Ceylon cinnamon *(from Cinnamomum zeylanicum Bl.)*
Zimtaldehyd *m* cinnamaldehyde, cinnamic aldehyde, *3-phenylpropenal
Zimtalkohol *m* cinnamyl alcohol, *3-phenyl-2-propen-1-ol
Zimtblätteröl *n* cinnamon leaf oil *(from Cinnamomum zeylanicum Bl.)*
Zimtkassia *f s.* Zimt/Chinesischer
Zimtöl *n* cinnamon oil
~/Chinesisches cassia oil *(from Cinnamomum aromaticum Nees)*

Zimtrinde *f* cinnamon bark
Zimtsäure *f* cinnamic acid, 3-phenylacrylic acid
~/gewöhnliche *s. trans*-Zimtsäure
trans-**Zimtsäure** *f trans*-cinnamic acid, ordinary cinnamic acid
Zimtsäurebenzylester *m* benzyl cinnamate, cinnamein
Zimtsäureethylester *m* ethyl cinnamate
Zimtsäure-4-hydroxylase *f* cinnamic acid hydroxylase
Zineb *n* zineb, zinc ethylenebisdithiocarbamate
Zingeron *n* zingerone, 4-hydroxy-3-methoxybenzylacetone
Zingiberen *n* zingiberene *(a monocyclic sesquiterpene)*
Zingiberol *n* zingiberol *(a monocyclic sesquiterpene alcohol)*
Zink *n* Zn zinc
~/granuliertes mossy zinc
Zinkalkyl *n s.* Dialkylzink
Zinkamalgam *n* zinc amalgam
zinkarm low-zinc, poor in zinc
Zinkat *n* zincate
Zinkäthid *n*, **Zinkäthyl** *n s.* Diethylzink
Zinkblende *f (min)* zinc blende, sphalerite *(zinc sulphide)*
Zinkblendegitter *n (cryst)* zinc-blende lattice
Zinkblumen *fpl* flowers of zinc *(white woolly zinc oxide)*
Zinkblüte *f (min)* hydrozincite *(a basic zinc carbonate)*
Zinkbutter *f* butter of zinc *(zinc chloride)*
Zinkchlorid *n* zinc chloride
Zinkchromat *n* 1. zinc chromate; 2. *s.* Zinkgelb
Zinkchromgelb *n s.* Zinkgelb
Zinkdampf *m* zinc vapour
Zinkdialkyl *n s.* Dialkylzink
Zinkdiäthyl *n s.* Diethylzink
Zinkdichromat *n* zinc dichromate
Zinkdimethyl *n s.* Dimethylzink
Zinkdithionit *n* zinc dithionite
Zinkelektrode *f* zinc electrode
Zinkgelb *n* zinc yellow, zinc[-potassium] chromate
Zinkgranalien *fpl* mossy zinc
Zinkgrau *n* zinc grey *(any of several preparations containing zinc dust or zinc oxide)*
Zinkhexacyanoferrat(II) *n* zinc hexacyanoferrate(II)
Zinkhexafluorosilicat *n* zinc hexafluorosilicate
Zinkhydrid *n* zinc hydride
Zinkhydrosulfitbleiche *f (pap)* zinc-hydrosulphite bleaching
Zinkit *m (min)* zincite, red zinc ore *(zinc oxide)*
Zinkkaliumchromat *n s.* Zinkgelb
Zink-Kalk-Küpe *f (text)* zinc-lime vat
Zinkkronglas *n* zinc crown glass
Zinkmanganat(VII) *n s.* Zinkpermanganat
Zinkmetasilicat *n* zinc metasilicate, zinc trioxosilicate
Zinkmethid *n*, **Zinkmethyl** *n s.* Dimethylzink
Zinkmonochromat *n s.* Zinkchromat 1.
Zinkorthophosphat *n* zinc orthophosphate
Zinkorthosilicat *n* zinc orthosilicate, zinc tetraoxosilicate
Zinkoxid *n* zinc oxide
Zinkoxidkatalysator *m* zinc-oxide catalyst
Zinkpermanganat *n* zinc permanganate
zinkreich zinc-rich, high-zinc, rich in zinc
Zinkrost *m* white rust
Zink[schutz]schicht *f* zinc coating
Zinkspat *m (min)* zinc spar, smithsonite, dry-bone ore *(zinc carbonate)*
Zinkspinell *m (min)* zinc spinel, gahnite *(zinc aluminate)*
Zinkstaub *m* zinc dust
Zinkstaubdestillation *f* zinc-dust distillation
Zinktetroxosilicat *n s.* Zinkorthosilicat
Zinktrioxosilicat *n s.* Zinkmetasilicat
Zinkverbindung *f*/**organische** organozinc compound
Zinkvitriol *m (min)* goslarite, zinc vitriol, white vitriol (copperas) *(zinc sulphate 7-water)*
Zinkvitriol *n* zinc vitriol, zinc sulphate 7-water
Zinkwasserstoff *m* zinc hydride
Zinkweiß *n* zinc white *(crude zinc oxide)*
Zinn *n* Sn tin
~/graues *s.* α-Zinn
α-**Zinn** *n* alpha (grey) tin, α tin
β-**Zinn** *n* beta (white) tin, β tin
γ-**Zinn** *n* gamma (brittle) tin, γ tin
Zinn(II)-acetat *n* tin(II) acetate, tin diacetate, stannous acetate
Zinnasche *f* flowers of tin, tin ash[es] *(tin(IV) oxide)*
Zinnbad *n* tin bath
Zinn-Blei-Lot *n* tinman's solder
Zinn(II)-bromid *n* tin(II) bromide, tin dibromide, stannous bromide
Zinn(IV)-bromid *n* tin(IV) bromide, tin tetrabromide, stannic bromide
Zinnbronze *f* tin bronze
Zinnbutter *f* butter of tin *(tin(IV) chloride 5-water)*
Zinn(II)-chlorid *n* tin(II) chloride, tin dichloride, stannous chloride
Zinn(IV)-chlorid *n* tin(IV) chloride, tin tetrachloride, stannic chloride
Zinndi... *s. a.* Zinn(II)-...
Zinn(II)-dihydrogenphosphat *n* tin(II) dihydrogenphosphate, stannous dihydrogenphosphate
Zinndioxid *n s.* Zinn(IV)-oxid
Zinn(II)-diphosphat *n* tin(II) diphosphate, stannous diphosphate
Zinndisulfid *n s.* Zinn(IV)-sulfid
Zinnelektrolyt *m* tin plating bath (solution)
Zinnerz *n* tin ore
Zinnfolie *f* tinfoil
Zinnfolienpapier *n* tinfoil paper
Zinngeschrei *n* tin cry
Zinnglasur *f (ceram)* tin glaze
zinnhaltig tin-bearing

Zinnhydrid *n* tin hydride, stannic hydride, *stannane
Zinn(II)-hydrogenphosphat *n* tin(II) hydrogenphosphate, stannous hydrogenphosphate
Zinn(II)-hydroxid *n* tin(II) hydroxide, stannous hydroxide
Zinnkies *m (min)* tin pyrites, stannite
Zinnlegierung *f* tin alloy
Zinnmonosulfid *n s.* Zinn(II)-sulfid
Zinn(II)-nitrat *n* tin(II) nitrate, stannous nitrate
Zinn(IV)-nitrat *n* tin(IV) nitrate, stannic nitrate
Zinnober *m* cinnabar, red mercuric sulphide, *(min also)* liver ore *(mercury(II) sulphide)*
~/Chinesischer Chinese vermilion *(red mercury(II) sulphide with small amounts of antimony sulphide)*
~/Grüner green cinnabar, chrome [oxide] green, oil green *(chromium(III) oxide)*
Zinnöl *n (ceram)* tin oil *(a mixture of stannic and stannous chlorides and oils)*
Zinn(II)-orthophosphat *n* tin(II) orthophosphate, tin(II) phosphate, stannous orthophosphate
Zinn(II)-oxalat *n* tin(II) oxalate, stannous oxalate
Zinn(IV)-oxid *n* tin (IV) oxide, tin dioxide, stannic oxide
Zinnpest *f* tin pest (plague, disease)
Zinn(II)-pyrophosphat *n s.* Zinn(II)-diphosphat
zinnreich tin-rich, rich in tin
Zinnsalz *n* tin salt, *(specif)* $SnCl_2 \cdot 2H_2O$ tin(II) chloride 2-water, tin salt
Zinnsäure *f* stannic acid
~/gewöhnliche *s.* α-Zinnsäure
a-**Zinnsäure** *f s.* α-Zinnsäure
b-**Zinnsäure** *f s.* β-Zinnsäure
α-**Zinnsäure** *f* metastannic α acid
β-**Zinnsäure** *f* metastannic β acid
Zinnschrei *m* tin cry
Zinnschutzschicht *f* tin coating
Zinnstanniol *n* tin foil
Zinnstein *m (min)* tin stone, cassiterite *(tin(IV) oxide)*
Zinn(II)-sulfat *n* tin(II) sulphate, stannous sulphate
Zinn(IV)-sulfat *n* tin(IV) sulphate, stannic sulphate
Zinn(II)-sulfid *n* tin(II) sulphide, tin monosulphide, stannous sulphide
Zinn(IV)-sulfid *n* tin(IV) sulphide, tin disulphide, stannic sulphide
Zinntetra ... *s.* Zinn(IV)- ...
Zinnwasserstoff *m s.* Zinnhydrid
Zipfel *m* tit *(a defect in glass)*
Ziram *n* ziram, zinc dimethyldithiocarbamate
Zirconat *n* zirconate *(salt of zirconic acid)*
Zirconium *n* Zr zirconium
Zirconium(II)-bromid *n* zirconium(II) bromide, zirconium dibromide
Zirconiumcarbid *n* zirconium carbide
Zirconium(II)-chlorid *n* zirconium(II) chloride, zirconium dichloride
Zirconium(III)-chlorid *n* zirconium(III) chloride, zirconium trichloride
Zirconium(IV)-chlorid *n* zirconium(IV) chloride, zirconium tetrachloride
Zirconiumdibromid *n s.* Zirconium(II)-bromid
Zirconiumdichlorid *n s.* Zirconium(II)-chlorid
Zirconiumdioxid *n s.* Zirconium(IV)-oxid
Zirconiumdioxidhydrat *n s.* Zirconsäure
Zirconiumhydrid *n* zirconium hydride
Zirconium(IV)-oxid *n* zirconium(IV) oxide, zirconium dioxide
Zirconiumoxidbromid *n* zirconium dibromide oxide
Zirconiumoxidchlorid *n* zirconium dichloride oxide
Zirconiumoxidhydroxid *n* zirconium dihydroxide oxide
Zirconiumsilicat *n* zirconium silicate, *(specif)* zirconium orthosilicate
Zirconium(IV)-sulfat *n* zirconium(IV) sulphate
Zirconium(IV)-sulfid *n* zirconium(IV) sulphide
Zirconiumtetra ... *s.* Zirconium(IV)- ...
Zirconiumtrichlorid *n s.* Zirconium(III)-chlorid
Zirconsäure *f* zirconic acid
Zirconylbromid *n s.* Zirconiumoxidbromid
Zirconylchlorid *n s.* Zirconiumoxidchlorid
Zirconylhydroxid *n s.* Zirconiumoxidhydroxid
Zirkon *m (min)* zircon *(zirconium orthosilicate)*
Zirkonerde *f s.* Zirconium(IV)-oxid
Zirkongerbung *f* zirconium tannage
Zirkonmasse *f (ceram)* zircon body
Zirkonporzellan *n* zircon porcelain
Zirkonsand *m* zircon sand
Zirkularchromatographie *f* radial (circular) chromatography
Zirkulardichroismus *m* circular dichroism, CD
Zirkularkomponente *f* circular component *(of polarized light)*
Zirkularpolarisation *f* circular polarization
zirkularpolarisiert circularly polarized
Zirkulation *f* [re]circulation
Zirkulationsfärbeapparat *m* circulating-liquor dyeing machine
Zirkulationsgas *n* recycle gas
Zirkulationspumpe *f* circulating pump, circulator
Zirkulationssystem *n* circulation system
Zirkulationstechnik *f (chromat)* recycle technique
zirkulieren to circulate
~/lassen to circulate
Zisterne *f (hyd)* cistern
Zitronengelb *n* 1. lemon chrome, chrome yellow *(lead chromate)*; 2. *s.* Zinkgelb
Zitronengrasöl *n (cosmet)* lemon-grass oil, East Indian verbena oil *(from Cymbopogon specc.)*
Zitronenöl *n* citrus oil
Zittersieb *n* vibrating (reciprocating) screen
Z-Kalander *m* Z type of calender
z-Mittel *n* z average *(of relative molecular mass)*
ZMP = Zahl möglicher Peaks
Zoisit *m (min)* zoisite *(a basic aluminium calcium silicate)*

Zone *f* zone, region

~/aufgeschmolzene molten zone *(in zone melting)*

~ freien Absetzens free-settling zone

~/freischwebende floating zone *(in zone melting)*

~/glühende incandescent zone

~/luftbeeinflußte *(hyd, geol)* zone of aeration

~/schwebende floating zone *(in zone melting)*

~/stagnierende stagnant zone, dead space *(in a reactor)*

~/verbotene *(phys ch)* forbidden (unallowed) band, forbidden region, energy gap

Zonenabsetzgeschwindigkeit *f (hyd)* zone settling velocity, ZSV

Zonenachse *f (cryst)* zone axis

Zonenbreite *f* zone width *(in zone melting)*

Zonendurchgang *m* zone pass

Zonendurchgangszahl *f* number of zone passes *(in zone melting)*

Zonenebnen *n* zone levelling *(in zone melting)*

Zonenelektrophorese *f* zone electrophoresis

Zonengeschwindigkeit *f* rate of zone travel, zone (zoning) speed *(in zone melting)*

Zonenlänge *f* zone length *(in zone melting)*

Zonenlegieren *n s.* Zonennivellieren

Zonennivellieren *n* zone levelling *(in zone melting)*

Zonenplanieren *n s.* Zonennivellieren

zonenreinigen to zone-refine, to zone-purify

Zonenreinigung *f* zone refining (purification)

~ nach dem Schwebezonenverfahren *s.* ~/tiegelfreie

~/tiegelfreie (tiegellose) floating-zone refining

Zonenreinigungsanlage *f* zone-refining apparatus (unit), zone refiner

Zonenrichtung *f* direction of zoning (zone travel) *(in zone melting)*

Zonenschmelzanlage *f* zone-melting apparatus (unit)

Zonenschmelzdurchgang *m* zone pass

zonenschmelzen to zone melt

Zonenschmelzen *n* zone melting

~ nach dem Schwebezonenverfahren *s.* ~/tiegelfreies

~/tiegelfreies (tiegelloses) floating-zone melting

Zonenschmelzgerät *n* zone-melting apparatus (unit)

Zonenschmelzofen *m* zone-melting furnace

Zonenschmelzverfahren *n* zone-melting process

Zonensedimentation *f (hyd)* zone settling

Zonenverbreiterung *f (chromat)* band broadening

Zonenwanderung *f* zone travel[ling] *(in zone melting)*

Zonenzahl *f* number of zone passes *(in zone melting)*

Zonenzentrifugation *f (anal)* zonal centrifugation

Zoomarinsäure *f* zoomaric acid, palmitoleic acid, *hexadec-9-enoic acid

Zoosterin *n*, **Zoosterol** *n (bioch)* zoosterol, animal sterol

Zopfwinde *f (pap)* rag catcher, [de]ragger

Zschocke-Desintegrator *m* Zschocke disintegrator

ZT *s.* Zimmertemperatur

ZTU-Diagramm *n* time-temperature-transformation diagram, T.T.T. diagram

~ für kontinuierliche Abkühlung continuous-cooling transformation diagram

~/isothermes isothermal transformation diagram

Zuber *m* tub, vat

zubereiten to prepare, to make up

zubereitet/frisch freshly prepared

Zubereitung *f* preparation, formulation *(act or substance)*

~/galenische *(pharm)* galenical

~/kosmetische cosmetic preparation

zubessern *(tann)* to mend *(the lime liquor)*

Zubringevorrichtung *f* feed mechanism

Zubringewagen *m* transfer car

Zucht *f s.* Züchtung

Zuchtbedingungen *fpl (bioch)* culture (cultural) conditions

züchten *(cryst)* to grow; *(biot)* to culture, to grow

Zuchthefe *f (biot)* culture[d] yeast, industrial yeast, barm

Züchtung *f (cryst)* growth; *(biot)* cultivation, growth

~ im Submersverfahren *(biot)* submerged cultivation

Züchtungsbedingungen *fpl (bioch)* culture (cultural) conditions

Zucker *m* sugar • **in ~ umwandeln** to saccharify, to saccharize

~/affinierter affinated (affination) sugar

~/brauner brown (soft) sugar

~/einfacher simple sugar, monosaccharide

~/flüssiger liquid sugar

~/geblauter blued sugar

~/gebrannter (karamelisierter) caramelized sugar, caramel

~/reduzierender reducing sugar

~/seltener unusual sugar

Zuckerabbaurate *f (biot)* rate of sugar breakdown

Zuckerabkömmling *m* sugar derivative

Zuckeralkohol *m* sugar alcohol

Zuckeranhydrid *n* sugar anhydride

Zuckeranteil *m* sugar moiety *(as of a glycoside)*

zuckerartig sugar-like, saccharine, saccharoid

Zuckeraufbau *m* 1. building-up of sugars; 2. structure (constitution) of sugars

Zuckerbruchstück *n* sugar fragment

Zuckercouleur *f* sugar colouring (dye)

Zuckerderivat *n* sugar derivative

Zuckerdicarbonsäure *f* aldaric acid

Zuckerersatzstoff *m* sugar substitute

Zuckerester *m* sugar ester

Zuckerether *m* sugar ether

Zuckerfabrik *f* sugar refinery (factory)

Zuckerfabrikabwasser *n* sugar-factory waste

Zuckerfarbe *f* sugar colouring (dye)

zuckerfremd non-sugar *(e.g. portion of a glycoside)*

Zuckergehalt *m* sugar content
zuckerhaltig sacchariferous, sugary, sugar-bearing, sugar-containing
Zuckerhaus *n* sugar house
Zuckerhut *m* sugar loaf
Zuckerindustrie *f* sugar industry
Zuckerkand[is] *m* candy [sugar], sugar candy, rock candy
Zuckerkohle *f* sugar charcoal
Zuckerkomponente *f* sugar moiety *(as of a glycoside)*
Zuckerkristall *m* sugar crystal
zuckerliefernd 1. *(bioch)* glycogenic *(e.g. amino acid)*; 2. *s.* zuckerhaltig
Zuckerpflanze *f* sugar plant *(a plant not converting its assimilation products into starch)*
Zuckerraffination *f* sugar refining
Zuckerraffinerie *f* sugar refinery
Zuckerraffineur *m* sugar refiner
zuckerreich high-sugar, rich in sugar
Zuckerreif *m* sugar bloom *(on chocolate)*
Zuckerreihe *f* sugar series
Zuckerrohrbagasse *f* [sugar-cane] bagasse, begass[e], megass[e]
Zuckerrohrmelasse *f* [sugar-]cane molasses, cane blackstrap [molasses]
Zuckerrohrsaft *m* sugar-cane juice
Zuckerrohrwachs *n* [sugar-]cane wax
Zuckerrübenanbau *m* beet growing
Zuckerrübenmelasse *f* [sugar-]beet molasses, beet discard molasses
Zuckerrübenschnitzel *npl* [beet] cossettes, beet slices
Zuckersaft *m* sugar juice
Zuckersäure *f* sugar acid, *(specif)* $HOOC[CHOH]_4COOH$ saccharic acid, glucosaccharic acid *(one form of 2,3,4,5-tetrahydroxyhexanedioic acid)*
Zuckertechnologie *f* sugar technology
Zuckerumwandlung *f* sugar conversion
Zuckerwerk *n* confectionery, sweetmeats, *(Am)* candy
Zuckerzerfall *m* sugar fragmentation
Zuckerzerfallsprodukt *n* sugar fragment
zudosieren to charge, to apportion
Zufallsauslese *f (biot)* random screening
Zufallsbeobachtung *f* chance observation
Zufallsfehler *m* random (accidental) error
Zufallsknäuel *n* random coil *(chemistry of macromolecules)*
Zufallsknäuelung *f* random coil conformation *(of macromolecules)*
Zufallsorientierung *f (cryst)* random orientation
Zufallsprobe *f* random sample
Zufallsprobe[nent]nahme *f* random sampling
Zufallsstichprobe *f* random sample
Zufallsvariable *f* variate *(statistics)*
zufließen to flow in, to run in
~ lassen to run in
Zufließen *n* inflow, afflux
Zufluß *m* 1. *s.* Zulauf; 2. *(bioch)* influx
Zuflußschwankung *f (hyd)* variation in sewage (waste-water) flow, influent waste variation, flow variation
zufügen *s.* zugeben
Zufuhr *f* feed[ing]
zuführen to feed *(a material)*
~/wieder to return
Zuführung *f* 1. feed[ing]; 2. [feed] inlet
Zuführungsleitung *f* supply (lead) line
Zuführungsrohr *n* feed pipe
Zuführungstrichter *m* [feed] hopper; cup *(of a blast furnace)*
zufüttern *(biot)* to feed *(nutrients to microorganisms)*
Zug *m* 1. flue *(passageway as of an oven)*; 2. draught, pull, suction *(as caused by a stack or fan)*; 3. *(tann)* stretch
~/künstlicher forced draught
~/natürlicher natural draught
~/senkrechter vertical flue
~/waagerechter horizontal flue
Zugabe *f* addition, supplementation
Zugabemenge *f* dosage
Zugabeort *m*, **Zugabestelle** *f* dosing point, point of addition (application) *(of chemicals)*
zugänglich *(agric)* available *(nutrients)*
Zugänglichkeit *f (agric)* availability *(of nutrients)*
Zugbruch *m* tensile failure
Zugdehnung *f* strain
Zug-Dehnungs-Diagramm *n s.* Spannungs-Dehnungs-Diagramm
Zugdehnungseigenschaften *fpl* tensile [stress-strain] characteristics
Zugdehnungsprüfgerät *n (rubber)* tensile-strength tester (testing machine), tensile tester
~/Bauart Schopper Schopper machine
Zugdehnungsverhalten *n s.* Zugdehnungseigenschaften
zugeben to add
~/chargenweise (portionsweise) to charge
~/tropfenweise to add dropwise
Zugeben *n* addition
~/chargenweises (portionsweises) charging
~/tropfenweises dropwise addition
zügeln to control *(e.g. a reaction)*
zugestellt/basisch *(met)* basic-lined
~/sauer acid-lined
zugfest tenacious
Zugfestigkeit *f* tensile strength, tenacity; *(pap)* breaking strength
~ in trockenem Zustand *(text)* dry tensile strength
Zugfestigkeitsprüfgerät *n* tensile-strength tester (testing machine), tensile tester
zügig 1. tacky *(printing ink)*; 2. *(tann)* stretchy
Zügigkeit *f* 1. tack[iness] *(of printing ink)*; 2. *(tann)* stretch
Zugkraft *f* tensile force
Zugmesser *m* draught gauge *(as for chimneys)*

Zugspannung *f* tensile stress
Zugstange *f* pitman *(of a jaw crusher)*
Zugverformungseigenschaften *fpl s.* Zugdehnungseigenschaften
Zugverformungsrest *m* permanent [set at] elongation, permanent (tensile) set, residual elongation
Zugversuch *m* tensile (tension) test, stress-strain experiment
zukorken to cork
Zulassung *f* permit, registration *(permission for manufacturing a pesticide)*
Zulauf *m* 1. *(liquid:)* influent, affluent, afflux, inflow, *(esp distil)* feed [stream]; 2. *(site:)* feed [liquor] inlet; 3. *(process:)* inflow, afflux
Zulaufbehälter *m* feed tank
Zulaufbereich *m (hyd)* inlet section (zone) *(of a sedimentation tank)*
Zulaufboden *m (distil)* feed tray (plate)
zulaufen to run in, to flow in
~/konisch to taper
~ lassen to run in
zulaufend/konisch taper[ing], tapered
Zulaufgefäß *n* feed box
Zulaufkonzentration *f* influent concentration
Zulaufrohr *n* feed pipe (tube), charging (influent) pipe
Zulaufschieber *m* feed gate
Zulaufseite *f* feed end
Zulaufstutzen *m* charging pipe
Zulauftauchrohr *n* feed (influent) well
Zulaufventil *n* feed valve
Zulaufwehr *n (distil)* inlet weir
Zulaufzusammensetzung *f (distil)* feed composition
Zuleitung *f* 1. feed[ing]; 2. feed pipe (line)
Zuluft *f* incoming (inlet) air
Zuluftfilter *n (biot)* incoming air filter
zumessen to meter, to dose, to proportion
Zumeßpumpe *f* metering pump, dosing (proportioning, controlled-volume) pump
Zumessung *f* metering, dosing, dosage, proportioning
zumischen to admix
Zumischung *f* admixture
Zunahme *f* increase, growth, rise
Zündanlage *f* ignition system
Zündbeschleuniger *m* pro-ignition dope, cetane improver
Zünddraht *m* ignition (firing) wire
Zündeigenschaften *fpl* ignition performance (quality)
zünden to ignite, to fire
Zunder *m* 1. [oxide, oxidation] scale; 2. *s.* Walzzunder
Zünder *m* igniter, primer
zunderbeständig non-scaling
Zunderbildung *f* scale formation (build-up)
zunderfrei non-scaling
zundern to scale
Zunderschicht *f* scale (oxide) layer
Zündhaube *f (met)* igniter *(of a sintering machine)*
Zündholzparaffin *n* match wax
Zündhütchen *n* ignition cap, primer
Zündmittel *n* igniting agent, igniter, priming medium
Zündofen *m (met)* ignition furnace, igniter *(of a sintering machine)*
Zündpol *m* firing terminal *(as of a calorimetric bomb)*
Zündpunkt *m* spontaneous-ignition temperature, S.I.T.
Zündquelle *f* ignition source
Zündsatz *m* priming composition
Zündschicht *f* ignition layer
Zündschnur *f* [blasting] fuse
~/detonierende detonating fuse
Zündspannung *f* sparking potential *(as in electrical precipitation)*
Zündsprengstoff *m* initiating (primary) explosive, initiator, primer, detonator
Zündstein *m* lighter flint [tip]
Zündstoff *m s.* 1. Zündmittel; 2. Zündsprengstoff
Zündsystem *n* ignition system
Zündtemperatur *f* ignition temperature
Zündung *f* 1. ignition, inflammation, *(relating to explosives also)* firing; 2. *(bioch)* sparking *(of fatty-acid oxidation)*
Zündverhalten *n* ignition performance (quality)
Zündverzögerung *f*, **Zündverzug** *m* ignition delay
Zündverzugszeit *f* ignition delay period
Zündvorrichtung *f* ignition device, igniter
Zündwilligkeit *f* ignition performance (quality)
Zündzeit *f* ignition time
zunehmen to increase, to grow, to rise
Zunge *f* pointer, index *(as of a measuring device)*
Zungenreißfestigkeit *f (tann)* tongue tear strength
zupfropfen to stopper, to cork
zurichten *(tann)* to dress, to finish, to curry
Zuricht[hilfs]mittel *n (tann)* dressing (finishing) auxiliary (agent)
zurückbilden to re-form
~/sich to re-form
zurückfließen to flow back, to return
zurückführen to return
~/in den Kreislauf to return to the circuit, to recirculate, to recycle
zurückgehen to revert *(of soluble into insoluble phosphate fertilizers)*
Zurückgehen *n* reversion *(of soluble into insoluble phosphate fertilizers)*
zurückgewinnen to recover, to reclaim
zurückhalten to retain, to trap
Zurückhaltung *f* retention
zurücklaufen to run back
zurückoxidieren to reoxidize, to oxidize back
Zurückoxidieren *n* reoxidation
zurückprallen to rebound; *(coat)* to bounce back
Zurückprallen *n* rebound; *(coat)* bounce-back
zurücksaugen to suck back

zurückschlagen to strike (flash) back *(of flame in a burner)*; to suck back *(of liquid in a pipe)*
Zurückschlagen *n* striking-back, flashback, flare-back *(of flame in a burner)*; sucking-back *(of liquid in a pipe)*
zurückspringen to rebound, to spring back, *(rubber also)* to recover; to drop, to return, to fall *(of electrons to a lower energy level)*
Zurückspringen *n* rebound, springing-back, recoil, resilience, *(rubber also)* [elastic] recovery; dropping, return, falling *(of electrons to a lower energy level)*
zurückstrahlen to reflect [back]
zurücktitrieren to back-titrate
Zurücktitrieren *n* back-titration
zurückverwandeln to reconvert, to convert back
~/sich to reconvert, to convert back
zurückwandern to shift back *(as of a pointer)*; to migrate back *(as of ions)*
zurückwerfen to reflect [back]
zusammenbacken to agglomerate, to set up, to stick together, *(esp under the influence of heat:)* to cake
Zusammenbacken *n* agglomeration, setting-up, *(esp under the influence of heat:)* caking
zusammenballen to agglomerate, to agglutinate, to ball [up]
~/sich to agglomerate, to aggregate, to agglutinate, to ball [up], to clog, to clot, to lump
Zusammenballen *n* 1. *(of human agent:)* agglomeration; 2. *(of material:)* agglomeration, aggregation, agglutination, balling, clogging, clotting, lumping
Zusammenbau *m* 1. assembly; 2. *(rubber)* assembly, building
zusammenbauen 1. to assemble; 2. *(rubber)* to assemble, to build
zusammenbrechen to collapse, to break down *(as of foam)*; *(el ch)* to break down
Zusammenbruch *m* collapse, breakage *(as of foam)*; *(el ch)* breakdown *(of passivity, a passive film, or potential)*
zusammendrückbar compressible
Zusammendrückbarkeit *f* compressibility
zusammendrücken to compress, to squeeze
Zusammendrücken *n* compression, compressing, squeezing
Zusammendrückungsrest *m* [permanent] compression set *(materials science)*
zusammenfließen to flow together, to coalesce
Zusammenfließen *n* coalescence
zusammenfrieren to freeze *(as of coal)*
zusammenfritten to agglomerate, to cake *(under the influence of heat)*
Zusammenfritten *n* agglomeration *(under the influence of heat)*
zusammengautschen *(pap)* to couch together, to laminate, to line
zusammengesetzt/gleichartig homogeneous
~/ungleichartig heterogeneous
Zusammenhalt *m* coherence, coherency
zusammenhalten to cohere, to hold together
zusammenhaltend coherent, cohesive
zusammenkitten to cement together
zusammenkleben to stick together
zusammenlagern/sich to congregate
zusammenlaufen to coalesce
zusammenmischen to mix, *(esp relating to bulk material)* to blend
Zusammenprall *m* collision, impact, impingement
zusammenprallen to collide, to impact, to impinge
zusammenpressen to compact, to compress, to squeeze
Zusammenpressen *n* compaction, compression, squeezing
zusammenquetschen *s.* zusammenpressen
zusammenrühren to stir together
zusammenschmelzen to melt (fuse) together; to melt down
zusammensetzen to arrange, to set up *(mechanically)*
~ **aus/sich** to be made up of, to consist of
Zusammensetzung *f* composition, make-up, analysis *(nature of a chemical compound or mixture)*
• **von unklarer** ~ ill-defined, of ill-defined composition
~/chemische chemical composition
~ **der Atmosphäre** atmosphere's composition, composition of the atmosphere
~/durchschnittliche average analysis
~/eutektische eutectic composition
~/mittlere average analysis
~/prozentuale percent[age] composition
Zusammensetzungsänderung *f* compositional change
zusammensinken to break, to collapse *(of foam)*
Zusammensinken *n* breakage, collapse *(of foam)*
zusammenstellen to arrange; to compound, to prepare, to put up *(e.g. a prescription)*
Zusammenstellung *f* arrangement; compounding, composition, preparation *(as of a prescription)*
Zusammenstoß *m* collision, impact, impingement
~ **harter Kugeln** *(phys ch)* hard-sphere collision
zusammenstoßen to collide, to impact, to impinge
zusammentreffen to encounter *(of molecules in solutions)*
Zusammentreffen *n* encounter *(of molecules in solutions)*
zusammentreten/paarweise to pair *(as of electrons)*
zusammenwachsen *(cryst)* to coalesce, to grow together, to intergrow
Zusammenwachsen *n (cryst)* coalescence, intergrowth
zusammenziehen/sich to contract
zusammenziehend astringent, styptic
Zusatz *m* 1. addition, admixture *(act)*; 2. additive [substance], admixture *(s. a.* Zusatzstoff*)*
~/aktivierender (belebender) *(min tech)* activator
~/drückender *(min tech)* depressant

~/geschmacksverbessernder *(pharm)* corrigent, corrective
~/keimbildender *(cryst)* nucleation (nucleating) agent, nucleator
~/passivierender *(min tech)* depressant
~/pH-regelnder *p*H regulator
~/reinigender detergent additive
~/staubverhindernder dust-preventing additive, anti-dust
~/weichmachender plasticizer, plasticizing agent
~/zündbeschleunigender pro-ignition dope *(for motor fuel)*
Zusatzbeschleuniger *m (rubber)* secondary accelerator
~/aktivierender activating accelerator, booster
Zusatzchemikalie *f* make-up [chemical] *(for compensating losses)*
Zusatzdünger *m* supplemental fertilizer
Zusatzdüngung *f* supplemental fertilizing
Zusatzelektrolyt *m* support[ing] electrolyte, base (indifferent) electrolyte *(polarography)*
zusatzfrei plain
Zusatzfunktion *f (phys ch)* excess function
Zusatzgas *n (chromat)* make-up gas
Zusatzkesselspeisewasser *n* make-up boiler [feed] water, boiler make-up [water], feed-water make-up
Zusatzkomponente *f (distil)* codistillant
Zusatzmittel *n s.* Zusatzstoff
Zusatzspeisewasser *n s.* Zusatzkesselspeisewasser
Zusatzstoff *m* additive [substance], accessory agent, *(esp for cheapening or weighting:)* loading material, load; conditioner *(for improving physical properties)*; *(distil)* codistillant, separating agent; *(food)* intentional food additive; blending agent *(for improving the octane number of motor fuel)*
~/luftporenbildender *(build)* air-entraining additive (admixture)
Zusatzwasser *n* make-up water, *(specif)* make-up boiler water, boiler make-up
Zuschlag *m* 1. loading *(as of filling materials)*; 2. *s.* Zuschlagstoff
Zuschlagstoff *m (met)* flux; *(build)* aggregate; loading material *(as for filling rubber)*
~/feinkörniger *(build)* fine aggregate
~/grober *(build)* coarse aggregate
~/künstlicher *(build)* manufactured aggregate
~/leichter *(build)* lightweight aggregate
zuschmelzen to seal [up]
Zuschußwasser *n s.* Zusatzwasser
zusetzen 1. to add, to admix; 2. to clog [up], to blind *(e.g. screen openings)*
~/sich to clog, to plug *(as of screen openings)*
Zusetzen *n* clogging, pluggage, plugging *(as of screen openings)*
zuspeisen to feed
Zuspeisen *n* feed[ing]
zuspunden to bung [up]
Zustand *m* state, condition • **in fein verteiltem ~** in a fine state • **in freiem ~** in the free state • **in gebundenem ~** in the combined state • **in reinem ~ darstellen** to prepare in pure form, to prepare in a pure condition (state), to isolate *(natural products)* • **in reinem ~ gewinnen** to obtain pure (in pure form), to obtain in a pure condition (state)
~/aktivierter energized state
~/angeregter excited state
~/antibindender antibonding state
~/atomarer atomic state
~/bindender bonding state
~/fester solid state
~/flüssiger liquid state
~/flüssig-kristalliner *s.* ~/mesomorpher
~/freier free state
~/gasförmiger gaseous state
~/gebundener combined state
~/glasartiger (glasiger) vitreous (glass-like, glassy) state
~/grüner *(ceram)* green state
~/hochangeregter superexcited state
~/kristallin-flüssiger *s.* ~/mesomorpher
~/liquokristalliner *s.* ~/mesomorpher
~/lockernder *s.* ~/antibindender
~/mesomerer *(org ch)* resonance state
~/mesomorpher mesomorphic (liquid crystalline) state, mesomorphism
~/metallischer metallic state
~/metastabiler metastable state
~/nichtbindender non-bonding state
~/plastischer plastic state; *(coal)* stage of plasticity
~/quasistationärer steady (stationary) state *(kinetics)*
~/stabiler (stationärer) steady (stationary) state
~/superangeregter superexcited state
~/superfluider (superflüssiger) superfluid state, superfluidity
~/suprafluider (supraflüssiger) *s.* ~/superfluider
~/supraleitender superconducting state
~/überflüssiger *s.* ~/superfluider
~/zähgepolter *(met)* tough-pitch condition
Zustände *mpl*/**übereinstimmende** *(phys ch)* corresponding states
Zustandsänderung *f* change of state
~/adiabatische adiabatic change
Zustandsbereich *m*/**metastabiler** region of metastability
Zustandsdiagramm *n* constitution[al] diagram, equilibrium (phase) diagram
Zustandsenergie *f* potential energy
Zustandsfunktion *f* state function
Zustandsgleichung *f* equation of state
~/Beattie- und Bridgemansche Beattie and Bridgeman equation [of state]
~/Berthelotsche Berthelot equation
~/Clausiussche Clausius equation
~ idealer Gase[/thermische] ideal gas equation, ideal (perfect) gas law

~/reduzierte reduced equation of state
~/thermodynamische thermodynamic equation of state
~/van-der-Waalssche van der Waals equation [of state]
Zustandsgröße *f* property of state
~/reduzierte reduced property
Zustandsschaubild *n s.* Zustandsdiagramm
Zustandssumme *f s.* Verteilungsfunktion
Zustandsvariable *f* state variable, variable of state
~/reduzierte reduced variable
zustellen *(met)* to line
Zustellung *f (met)* lining *(act or material)*
~/basische basic lining
~/saure acid lining
zustöpseln to stopper, to cork, to plug
zustreben/dem Gleichgewicht to go toward equilibrium
Zutageliegen *n*, **Zutagetreten** *n (geol)* out-crop[-ping]
Zuteileinrichtung *f* dosing (proportioning) apparatus, feeder
~ für Chemikalien chemical feeder
~ für Flüssigkeiten liquid feeder
zuteilen to dose, to proportion, to charge, to batch
Zuteiler *m*, **Zuteilvorrichtung** *f s.* Zuteileinrichtung
zutropfen to add dropwise, to add drops of
Zutropfen *n* dropwise addition
Zuwachs *m* increase
zuwandern to migrate in *(as of ions)*
Z-Walzenkalander *m* Z type of calender
Zwangdurchlaufdampferzeuger *m*, **Zwangdurchlaufkessel** *m* once-through[-flow] boiler
Zwanglauf *m* 1. once-through flow; 2. *s.* Zwangumlauf
Zwangsumlauf *m*, **Zwangszirkulation** *f s.* Zwangumlauf
Zwangumlauf *m* forced circulation
Zwangumlaufverdampfer *m* forced-circulation evaporator
~ mit Brüdenverdichtung forced-circulation vapour compression plant
zweiachsig *(cryst)* biaxial
~/optisch optically biaxial
zweiatomig diatomic
Zweibadchromgerbung *f* two-bath chrome tannage (tanning)
Zweibadentwicklung *f (phot)* two-bath development
Zweibadfixierung *f (phot)* two-bath fixation
Zweibadverfahren *n (text)* two-bath method
zweibasig dibasic, diprotic *(acid)*; dibasic, diacid *(base)*
zweibindig divalent, bivalent *(relating to homopolar bonds)*
Zweidecker *m*, **Zweidecker-Siebmaschine** *f* double-decked screen, two-deck sifter
zweidimensional two-dimensional
Zweieinhalb-Acetat *n (text)* secondary cellulose acetate
Zweielektronenbindung *f* two-electron bond
Zweielektronenkonfiguration *f* two-electron configuration
Zweielektronenreduktion *f* two-electron reduction
Zweielektronensystem *n* two-electron system
Zweierkombination *f* binary ionic recombination, ion-ion mutual neutralization
Zweierstoß *m (phys ch)* bimolecular collision, dual (binary, two-body) collision
Zweietagenofen *m (ceram)* double-deckle (two-tier) kiln
Zweifachbindung *f* double bond (link, linkage)
Zweifachfilter *n* dual media filter
zweifachfrei divariant, bivariant
zweifachnegativ [geladen] dinegative
zweifachpositiv [geladen] dipositive
Zweifachzucker *m* disaccharide
Zweifarbeneffekt *m (text)* bicolour effect
Zweifarbenspritzgießen *n (plast)* double-shot moulding
zweifarbig dichromatic
Zweifarbigkeit *f* dichromatism
Zweifilmtheorie *f* two-film theory *(of mass transfer)*
Zweiflächner *m (cryst)* pinacoid
Zweig *m* 1. *(spectr)* branch; 2. bridge *(of a bridge-ring compound)*
~/negativer P-branch *(of a band spectrum)*
~/positiver R-branch *(of a band spectrum)*
zweigängig two-pass *(e.g. heat exchanger)*
zweigliedrig binary
Zweigutapparat *m* two-product unit
zweihalsig two-neck[ed]
Zweihalskolben *m* two-neck[ed] flask
Zweihalsrundkolben *m* round-bottom two-neck flask
Zweihordendarre *f* two-floor (double-floor) kiln
Zweikanalofen *m (ceram)* twin-tunnel kiln
Zweikanalverstärker *m***/frequenzselektiver** *(spectr)* lock-in amplifier
zweikernig binuclear, binucleate
Zweikomponentenfarbe *f* two-component paint, two-can (two-pack) paint
Zweikomponentenkleber *m* two-component adhesive, mixed adhesive
Zweikomponentensystem *n (phys ch)* two-component system, binary system; *(coat)* two-can (two-pack) system
Zweikörperverdampfer *m* double-effect evaporator
zweiladig *s.* zweiwertig
Zweilösungsmittelverfahren *n (petrol)* two-solvent process
zweimolar two-molar
Zweiphasengleichgewicht *n* two-phase equilibrium
Zweiphasenofen *m* two-phase furnace
Zweiphasenschaum *m* two-phase foam
Zweiphasensystem *n* two-phase system
zweiphasig two-phase
Zweiphotonenabsorption *f* two-photon absorption, TPA

Zweiphotonenanregung *f* two-photon excitation, biphotonic excitation

Zweiphotonenprozeß *m* two-photon process, biphotonic process

Zweiplattenschieber *m* double-disk gate valve

Zweipressenschleifer *m (pap)* two-pocket grinder

Zweiproduktenapparat *m* two-product unit

zweiprotonig diprotic, dibasic *(acid)*

Zweipunktregelung *f* two-position (on-off) control

Zweisäulenanordnung *f (chromat)* dual-column configuration

Zweisäulen-Apparat *m* double-column arrangement *(air separation)*

zweisäurig diacid, dibasic *(base)*

Zweischachtgenerator *m (coal)* double-shaft (twin-shaft) gasifier

Zweischalenentwicklung *f (phot)* two-bath development

Zweischicht[en]film *m* double-coated film

Zweischichtenfilter *n* dual-media filter

Zweischichtenfilterbett *n* dual-media bed

Zweischneckenextruder *m* double-screw (twin-screw) extruder

zweiseitig *(pap)* two-sided

Zweiseitigkeit *f (pap)* two-sidedness

~ in der Färbung colour two-sidedness

Zweisiebpapiermaschine *f* twin-wire paper machine

Zwei-Solvent-Extraktion *f* two-solvent extraction

Zweistoffdüse *f* two fluid (gas atomizing) nozzle

Zweistoffgemisch *n* binary mixture

Zweistofflegierung *f* binary alloy

Zweistoffsystem *n* two-component system, binary system

Zweistoffversprüher *m* two-fluid (auxiliary-fluid) atomizer

Zweistoffversprühung *f* two-fluid [nozzle] atomization, pneumatic nozzle atomization

Zweistoffzerstäuber *m s.* Zweistoffversprüher

Zweistrahlgerät *n s.* Zweistrahlspektralphotometer

Zweistrahlspektralphotometer *n*, **Zweistrahlspektrometer** *n* double-beam spectro[photo]meter

zweisträngig double-strand *(e.g. conveyor)*

Zweistrangkette *f* double-strand chain *(conveying)*

Zweistrom-Apparat *m* double-pipe (concentric-tube) exchanger *(heat exchange)*

Zweistufenbleiche *f (pap)* two-stage bleaching

Zweistufenmechanismus *m* two-step reaction mechanism

Zweistufenreaktion *f* two-step reaction

Zweistufenspritzgießen *n (plast)* double-shot moulding

Zweistufenverdampfer *m* double-effect evaporator

Zweistufenverfahren *n* two-stage (two-step) process; *(met)* duplex process

zweistufig two-stage, two-step, double-stage

Zwei-Substrat-Reaktion *f* bisubstrate (two-substrate) reaction *(enzyme kinetics)*

Zweitbeschleuniger *m (rubber)* secondary accelerator

~/aktivierender activating accelerator, booster

Zweitdestillation *f* redistillation, rerun[ning]

Zweitemperaturverfahren *n (nucl)* dual-temperature process

Zweitischmaschine *f (glass)* two-table machine

Zweitkomponente *f (dye)* secondary component

Zweitluft *f* secondary air

Zweitsubstituent *m* second substituent

Zweiturmsystem *n (pap)* two-tower [acid] system, Jensen two-tower (acid-making) system

Zweiwalzen[feucht]kalander *m (pap)* two-roll calender, nip (intermediate) rolls

Zweiwalzenmühle *f* two-roll mill

Zweiwalzentrockner *m* double-drum dryer

Zweiwalzen-Walzwerk *n* two-roll mill

Zweiweghahn *m* two-way stopcock

zweiwertig divalent *(element)*; dibasic, diprotic *(acid)*; dibasic, diacid *(base)*; dihydric *(alcohol)*

Zweiwertigkeit *f* divalency, bivalency *(of an element)*; dibasicity *(of an acid or base)*

zweizählig 1. *(cryst)* diadic; 2. *s.* zweizähnig

zweizähnig bidentate *(ligand)*

Zweizentrenbindung *f* two-centre bond *(chemical-bond theory)*

Zweizentren[molekül]orbital *n* two-centre [molecular] orbital

~/bindendes two-centre bonding orbital

Z-Wert *m* [Kossower] Z-value *(for characterizing the polarity of solvents)*

Zwiebel *f* 1. *(tech)* bulb; 2. *(glass)* onion, meniscus *(in vertical sheet drawing)*

Zwiebelhautpapier *n*, **Zwiebelschalenpapier** *n* onion skin

Zwilling *m s.* Zwillingskristall

Zwillingsachse *f (cryst)* twin axis

Zwillingsbildung *f (cryst)* twinning, twin formation

~/polysynthetische polysynthetic twinning

Zwillingsebene *f (cryst)* twin[ning] plane

Zwillingsgesetz *n (cryst)* twin law

Zwillingskalorimeter *n* differential calorimeter

Zwillingskristall *m* twin [crystal], crystal twin

Zwillingspumpe *f* duplex pump

Zwillingstunnelofen *m (ceram)* twin-tunnel kiln

Zwillingstunneltrockner *m (ceram)* twin-tunnel dryer

Zwillingsverbundofen *m* **nach Otto** *(coal)* Otto oven

Zwinge *f* clamp, clip

Zwischenabzweigstück *n*/**T-förmiges** T-shape connecting tube, T-type connector, T-piece, tee [connector]

~/Y-förmiges Y-shape connecting tube, Y-piece, Y-type connector

Zwischenanstrich *m* undercoat

Zwischenanstrichstoff *m* undercoat [paint], undercoater

Zwischenbehälter *m (petrol)* intermediate container; engaging chamber *(in the pebble-heater process)*

Zwischenbehandlung *f* intermediate treatment
~/alkalische *(pap)* in-between alkali stage *(bleaching step)*
Zwischenboden *m* false bottom
Zwischenchelat *n* intermediate chelate
Zwischenchelatform *f* intermediate chelate form
Zwischenerhitzer *m* intermediate heater
Zwischenerzeugnis *n* intermediate [product]
Zwischenfaserbindung *f (pap)* interfibre bonding
Zwischenferment *n* glucose-6-phosphate dehydrogenase
Zwischenform *f* intermediate form
Zwischenfraktion *f* 1. *(distil)* intermediate fraction (cut); 2. intermediate material, middlings product *(classifying)*
zwischengelagert intercalary
Zwischengitteratom *n* interstitial atom, [lattice] interstitial
Zwischengitterion *n* interstitial ion
Zwischengitterpaar *n* interstitial pair
Zwischengitterplatz *m* interstitial [lattice] site, interstitial position
Zwischengitterplatzdiffusion *f* interstitial diffusion
Zwischenglasurdekor *n (ceram)* inter-glaze (in-glaze) decoration
Zwischenglied *n (tech)* link; *(nucl)* intermediate element *(of a radioactive series)*
Zwischenglühen *n* process (commercial) annealing *(of steel)*
Zwischengut *m* intermediate [product]
Zwischenkern *n* intermediate nucleus
Zwischenkomplex *m* intermediate complex
Zwischenkornvolumen *n* intergranular (void) volume
zwischenkristallin intercrystalline
Zwischenkühler *m (tech)* intercooler
Zwischenlage *f* intermediate layer, interlayer, interlining, ply
Zwischenlagebogen *m (pap)* set-off sheet
Zwischenlagepapier *n* set-off paper, tympan paper, *(Am)* slip-sheet paper
Zwischenlauf *m (distil)* intermediate cut (fraction)
Zwischenläufer *m (rubber)* wrapper, leader
Zwischenlegepapier *n s.* Zwischenlagepapier
Zwischenleinen *n (rubber)* wrapper, leader
zwischenmolekular intermolecular
Zwischenphase *f* intermediate phase
Zwischenplatte *f (plast)* backing plate
~/bewegliche floating plate
Zwischenprodukt *n* 1. intermediate [product]; 2. *s.* Zwischenstoff
~/chemisches intermediate chemical
Zwischenraum *m* interstice, spacing
Zwischenschicht *f* intermediate layer, interlayer, interlining, ply
Zwischenschichtraum *m* interlayer space
Zwischenstadium *n* intermediate stage
Zwischenstoff *m* [reaction] intermediate, intermediate substance (product)
~/Arrheniusscher Arrhenius intermediate
~/reaktiver reactive intermediate
~/van't Hoffscher van't Hoff intermediate
Zwischenstoffwechsel *m (bioch)* intermediary metabolism
Zwischenstück *n* spacer; adapter, connector, *(if tubular:)* connecting tube
Zwischenstufe *f* intermediate stage
Zwischenstufengefüge *n (met)* bainite [structure], bainitic structure
Zwischensystemübergang *m* intersystem cross[-ing], ISC *(between terms of different multiplicity)*
Zwischenverbindung *f* intermediate [compound]
~/Herzsche *(dye)* [intermediate] Herz compound *(a benzodithiazole)*
Zwischenwand *f* partition [wall], *(if thin:)* diaphragm; *(pap)* midfeather, midwall, midriff, centre division *(of a Hollander beater)*
Zwischenzahl *f s.* Dehngrenze
Zwischenzustand *m* intermediate (transitory) state (condition)
Zwitterion *n* zwitterion, zwitterionic compound, inner (internal, intramolecular) salt, amphion, dipolar ion
zwitterionisch zwitterionic
Zwölfflächner *m (cryst)* dodecahedron
Zyan... *s. a.* Cyan...
Zyanose *f (med)* cyanosis *(due to deficient oxygenation of the blood)*
Zyanotypie *f* 1. blue-printing, blueprint, ferroprussiate process; 2. cyanotype, blue print *(product)*
• **Zyanotypien herstellen** to blueprint
zybotaktisch *(phys ch)* cybotactic
zyklisch cyclic
Zyklo... *s. a.* Cyclo...
Zyklon[abscheider] *m* [centrifugal] cyclone separator, centrifugal (cyclonic) separator (collector), cyclone
Zyklonbatterie *f* multiple[-unit] cyclone
Zyklonbrenner *m* cyclone burner
Zyklonentstauber *m* cyclone dust collector
Zyklonfeuerung *f* cyclone firing
Zyklonieren *n* cyclonic (cyclone) separation
Zyklon-Oberflächenverdampfer *m* cyclone evaporator
Zyklonscheider *m s.* Zyklonabscheider
Zyklonskrubber *m*, **Zyklonwäscher** *m* cyclonic (cyclone) scrubber (washer)
Zyklotron *n* cyclotron
~/frequenzmoduliertes frequency-modulated cyclotron, synchrocyclotron
Zyklus *m* cycle
~ **Beladen** service (loading) cycle (step), service (operating) run, exhaustion cycle (reaction) *(ion exchange)*
~ **Beladen und Regenerieren** exhaust-regenerate cycle *(ion exchange)*
~ **Regenerieren** regeneration cycle (step), recharge cycle *(ion exchange)*
~/sinnloser *(bioch)* futile cycle
Zylinder-Filtrierzentrifuge *f* cylindrical-screen centrifuge

zylinderförmig cylindrical
Zylindergruppe *f (pap)* dryer group (section)
Zylindermantel *m (pap)* dryer shell
Zylindermethode *f s.* Zylinderplattenmethode
Zylinderöl *n* cylinder [lubricating] oil
Zylinderölstock *m* cylinder stock
Zylinderplattenmethode *f* Oxford (cup) method *(for evaluating penicillin)*
Zylinder[rohr]schlange *f* helical coil
Zylinderschlichtmaschine *f (text)* cylinder sizing machine
Zylindertrockner *m (pap, text)* cylinder (can) dryer
~ **einer Selbstabnahmemaschine** *(pap)* Yankee dryer
Zylinderverfahren *n (glass)* cylinder process
Zylinderwalke *f (text)* rotary milling machine
Zylinderzelle *f* round cell *(electrolysis)*
Zylinderzellenapparat *m (petrol)* vertical tube sweating stove
~ **von Henderson** Henderson stove
zylindrisch cylindrical
Zymase *f* zymase *(a complex of enzymes isolated from yeast)*
zymogen zymogenic, zymogenous
Zymogen *n (bioch)* zymogen, pre-enzyme
Zymologie *f* zymology
Zymotechnik *f* zymotechnics
zymotechnisch zymotechnic[al]
zymotisch *s.* zymogen
Zypressencampher *m s.* Zederncampher
zytostatisch cytostatic
Zytostatikum *n (pharm)* cytostatic agent